MW01094053

ArtScroll Mesorah Series®

Rabbi Nosson Scherman / Rabbi Meir Zlotowitz
General Editors

חול / שבת / שלש רגלים

NUSACH ASHKENAZ — נוסח אשכנז

Published by

Mesorah Publications, ltd

THE RABBINICAL COUNCIL OF AMERICA
EDITION OF

The ArtScroll SIDDUR

WEEKDAY / SABBATH / FESTIVAL

A new translation and anthologized commentary
by Rabbi Nosson Scherman

Overview by
Rabbi Saul J. Berman

Co-edited by
Rabbi Meir Zlotowitz

Designed by
Rabbi Sheah Brander

FIRST EDITION
First Impression . . . January 1987
Second Impression . . . November 1988
Third Impression . . . June 1989

SECOND EDITION
Thirteen Impressions: July 1990 - March 1999
Fourteenth Impression . . . July 1999
Fifteenth Impression . . . May 2000
Sixteenth Impression . . December 2000

Published and Distributed by
MESORAH PUBLICATIONS, Ltd.
4401 Second Avenue
Brooklyn, New York 11232

Distributed in Europe by
LEHMANNS
Unit E, Viking Industrial Park
Rolling Mill Road
Jarrow, Tyne & Wear NE32 3DP
England

Distributed in Australia & Zew Zealand by
GOLDS WORLD OF JUDAICA
3-13 William Street
Balaclava, Melbourne 3183
Victoria Australia

Distributed in Israel by
SIFRIATI / A. GITLER — BOOKS
6 Hayarkon Street
Bnei Brak 51127

Distributed in South Africa by
KOLLEL BOOKSHOP
Shop 8A Norwood Hypermarket
Norwood 2196, Johannesburg, South Africa

THE ARTSCROLL MESORAH SERIES ®
THE RABBINICAL COUNCIL OF AMERICA EDITION OF
"SIDDUR KOL YAAKOV / THE COMPLETE ARTSCROLL SIDDUR" — Nusach Ashkenaz

4401 Second Avenue / Brooklyn, N.Y. 11232 / (718) 921-9000 / www.artscroll.com

---

ISBN: 0-89906-662-3

Typography by CompuScribe at ArtScroll Studios, Ltd., *Brooklyn, NY*

Bound by Sefercraft, Inc. Brooklyn, NY

This Siddur is lovingly dedicated by

חיים יוסף ולאה בערלינר ומשפחתם שיחיו

Joseph H. and Lea Berliner

and their family

to his parents, of blessed memory,
whose lives embodied
devotion to Torah and faith in the One
Who mercifully hears the prayers
of his people Israel —

ר׳ יעקב בן ר׳ מנחם מאנעס ע״ה

כ״ה טבת תשכ״ג

מרת אסתר הינדא בת ר׳ משה אליהו ע״ה

י״ג סיון ת״ש

With their children they fled the Holocaust
to keep alive the flame of faith.
A mother's body could not survive Siberia
but her soul lived on to inspire her family.
A father and children came to America
and planted anew the eternal seed.
It grew and flourished and nourished the flame
that overcame adversity and torment —
With faith in their hearts and a siddur in hand
their family remains a bastion of Torah.

ת נ צ ב ה

ולעילוי נשמות זקנינו וזקנותינו
שזכרונם נשאר נר תמיד לכל צאצאיהם

ר׳ משה אליהו ב״ר חיים   ר׳ אשר ב״ר יוסף מרדכי
חנה פיגא בת ר׳ לייבל   שיינדל בת ר׳ יעקב קאפפעל
למשפחת מרגנשטרן   למשפחת מארק

ר׳ מנחם מאנעס ב״ר בצלאל   נתן דוב ב״ר משה מנחם
חיה בת ר׳ שלום   אסתר בת ר׳ אברהם
למשפחת ברלינר   למשפחת שווארץ

ת נ צ ב ה

TABLE OF CONTENTS

◈§ Publisher's Preface

Since the ArtScroll Series came into existence, more requests have come for an ArtScroll Siddur than for any other work. From rabbis and laymen, teachers and students, men and women, scholars and strivers for knowledge, came an insistence that the times demand a complete yet functional Siddur, with clear and accurate laws and instructions. The Rabbinical Council of America, too, has recognized this need and we are gratified it has selected the ArtScroll Siddur in this special edition for its congregational use. It features:

◈§ **Translation** *The translation seeks to balance the lofty beauty of the heavily nuanced text with an easily understood English. Where a choice had to be made, we generally preferred fidelity to the text over inaccurate simplicity, but occasionally, we had to stray a bit from the literal translation in order to capture the essence of a phrase in an accessible English idiom.*

◈§ **Commentary** *The commentary has two goals: to explain difficult passages and to involve the reader in the emotional, spiritual and inspirational experience of prayer. We have eliminated purely technical comments. Unattributed comments are sometimes the author's own, but usually distill the general trend of several authorities.*

◈§ **Laws and Instructions** *Clear instructions are provided throughout. More complex or lengthy halachos are discussed in the 'Laws' section at the end of the Siddur, which the reader will find to be a very helpful guide. It includes such relevant laws as women's obligation to pray, an omitted* Ya'aleh V'Yavo *or* Mashiv HaRuach, *and the order of priorities for calling people to the Torah. Where relevant, we refer to it by paragraph number (§).*

◈§ **Layout and Typography** *This Siddur is not a maze, but a convenient, functional book for practical use. The first and last phrases of the translation on each page parallel the first and last phrases of the Hebrew text. Paragraphs begin with bold type words to facilitate finding individual* tefillos; *each paragraph in the translation is introduced with the parallel Hebrew word to ease cross checking; portions said aloud by the* chazzan *are indicated by the symbol ∵ in the Hebrew text and by the word* chazzan *in the English. Almost always, each full* tefillah, *such as* Minchah *or* Maariv, *is given in its entirety, including every* Kaddish. *An asterisk* after a word indicates that that word or phrase is treated in the commentary. Numbered footnotes give the Scriptural sources of the countless verses that have been melded into the prayers. A footnote beginning "Cf." indicates that the Scriptural source is paraphrased.*

◈§ **Hebrew Grammar** *As a general rule in the Hebrew language, the accent is on the last syllable. Where the accent is on an earlier syllable, it is indicated with a* messeg, *a vertical line below the accented letter:* שֽׁ֫ירוּ. *A* שְׁוָא נָע [sh'va na] *is indicated by a hyphen mark above the letter:* בָּרְ֫כוּ, *except above the first letter of a word, which is always a* sh'va na. *In identifying a* sh'va na, *we have followed the rules of the* Vilna Gaon *and* Rabbi Yaakov Emden.

We are grateful to the many distinguished gedolim, *patrons, friends, and colleagues whose help and cooperation made this work possible. They are acknowledged in the Preface to the regular edition of the Siddur.*

We conclude with gratitude to Hashem Yisborach for His infinite blessings and for the opportunity to have been the quill that records His word. May He guide our work in the future for the benefit of His people.

Kislev 5747 — Rabbi Meir Zlotowitz / Rabbi Nosson Scherman
Brooklyn, NY

Acknowledgments

Only through the generous support of many people was it possible to produce the work and keep it within reach of the average family and congregation. Among those to whom we are grateful are:

MR. *and* MRS. JOSEPH H. BERLINER *and family, who dedicated this full-size Ashkenaz Siddur in memory of his parents; it has been named* KOL YAAKOV *in memory of his father. This noble gesture perpetuates the memory of those who would not give up hope of Jewish rebirth despite suffering, starvation, and Holocaust;*

MR. *and* MRS. AARON L. HEIMOWITZ *and* FAMILY, *who dedicated the pocket-sized Ashkenaz Siddur, Mr. Heimowitz has been a true friend of Mesorah Publications and numerous Torah institutions;*

MR. *and* MRS. HIRSCH WOLF, *who, with his brothers, dedicated the full-size Sefard Siddur in memory of his father, R' Chaim,* ז״ל. *An internationally respected patron of Torah, he is a long-time friend;*

MR. *and* MRS. BEREL TENNENBAUM *and family, who dedicated the pocket-sized Sefard Siddur in memory of his beloved parents, Holocaust survivors who built lives of Judaism and Torah support after the war;*

MRS. MALA WASSNER *and family who dedicated the large-type Ashkenaz Siddur in memory of her late husband, Reb David* ז״ל, *a man of legendary kindness and service to all in need;*

MR. *and* MRS. ZALMAN MARGULIES *of London, whose dedication of the* Kabbalas Shabbos Siddur *provided the impetus that made this work possible;*

MR. *and* MRS. DAN SUKENIK *and* MR. *and* MOSHE SUKENIK *who are living legends — for what they do and for the way they do it;*

MR. *and* MRS. SHELDON BEREN; "EZRA," *an anonymous friend;* RABBI *and* MRS. YITZCHAK FELDMAN; MR. *and* MRS. ABRAHAM FRUCHTHANDLER; MR. *and* MRS. LOUIS GLICK; MR. *and* MRS. MANNY HABER; MR. *and* MRS. NACHMAN HERMAN; RABBI CHAIM LEIBEL; RABBI *and* MRS. JOSEPH MARCUS; MR. *and* MRS. MOSES MARX; THE MESIVTA *of* LONG BEACH; MR. *and* MRS. SHLOMO PERL; MR. *and* MRS. ALBERT REICHMAN; MR. JEROME STERN; MR *and* MRS. IRVING I. STONE *in honor of* MR. JACOB SAPIRSTEIN'S *99th birthday;* MR. *and* MRS. LAURENCE A. TISCH; *and* MR. *and* MRS. WILLY WIESNER.

This author translated and commented, but others shaped his material into 'a Siddur.' My colleagues' goal was to produce an instructive, beautiful, and easy to use volume. I cannot praise them enough. I am everlastingly indebted to: RABBI MEIR ZLOTOWITZ *and* REB SHEAH BRANDER, *whose genius and dedication are responsible for the ArtScroll series;* RABBI HERSH GOLDWURM, RABBI AVIE GOLD; SHMUEL BLITZ *and his successors* SHIMON GOLDING *and* SHMUEL KLAVER; *and the entire ArtScroll staff.*

The author concludes with gratitude to Hashem Yisborach for His infinite blessings and for the opportunity to have been the quill that records His word. May He guide our work in the future for the benefit of His people.

Tammuz 5747
Brooklyn, NY

Nosson Scherman

◆§ Preface to the Rabbinical Council of America Edition

Almost three decades ago the Rabbinical Council of America issued its first authorized Siddur. It was not a dearth of prayer books that motivated its publication but rather a plethora of Siddurim. Most of them had been reprinted from Eastern European editions and had inaccuracies in the Hebrew text, inelegant translations and inadequate rubrics if at all, and were not very pleasing to the eye. Such Siddurim may have been acceptable to the immigrant generation but not to the emerging generation of American-born Jews.

To meet the needs of increasing numbers of members of their own congregations, the Rabbinical Council of America undertook a Siddur project. From its inception to its completion took a number of years and spanned several administrations. The work involved some of the most respected names in the American Orthodox rabbinate. Finally there appeared THE TRADITIONAL PRAYER BOOK FOR SABBATHS AND FESTIVALS, *translated and edited by Rabbi David de Sola Pool and published by Behrman House, Inc.*

The Siddur was well received and became the standard Sabbath and Festival prayer book in most congregations served by members of the Rabbinical Council of America. Its accurate Hebrew text and poetic translation conformed to Halakhah. Its aesthetic appearance won it the acclaim of non-Orthodox Jews as well. The pulpit-size edition was selected as an offering by a major American-Jewish book club.

THE TRADITIONAL PRAYER BOOK FOR SABBATHS AND FESTIVALS *has been reprinted many times since its original publication and continues in use in most large Orthodox congregations. It will continue to be available for those congregations which want it.*

Today a new generation of American-born Orthodox Jews has different needs in a Siddur. A growing number attend services every day and therefore require a Siddur that is not limited to Sabbaths and Festivals. While insisting on the traditional Hebrew text, many of today's worshipers want a more literal translation as well as words of commentary and inspirational direction.

This Siddur differs from others in the ArtScroll Series in several ways. The text of the Prayer for the Welfare of the State reflects the fact that this Siddur was intended for Jews who reside in democratic countries where they enjoy constitutionally guaranteed political equality and civil rights and are not ruled by despots. Moreover, it recognizes the importance of the the State of Israel within contemporary Jewish history. Included, therefore, are the Prayer for the Welfare of the State of Israel and memorial prayers for the fallen members of the Israel Defense Forces.

These were some of the considerations that stimulated the publication of this RABBINICAL COUNCIL OF AMERICA EDITION OF THE ARTSCROLL SIDDUR. *Once again the decision was not taken in haste. The initial discussions took place during the administration of Rabbi Sol Roth. His successors, Rabbi Gilbert Klaperman, who was involved in shaping the first Siddur, and Rabbi Louis Bernstein moved the project along. Rabbi Emanuel Holzer served as the indefatigable chairman of the Publication Committee, and our energetic Executive Vice President Rabbi Binyamin Walfish guided the work. It is my privilege* לברך על המוגמר.

Rabbi Milton H. Polin, President
Rabbinical Council of America

An Overview / The "Approach" In Prayer

◆§ An Overview — The "Approach" In Prayer

HaGaon Rav Joseph B. Soloveitchik states a fundamental Jewish truth:

> ... the very essence of prayer is the covenantal experience of being together with and talking to God and that the concrete performance such as the recitation of texts represents the technique of implementation of prayer and not prayer itself ("The Lonely Man of Faith," *Tradition* 7:2, Summer 1965, p. 35).

The text of the Siddur which lies before us is then no more than a vehicle to facilitate what is truly the essence of prayer — *avodah she'balev* — service of the heart, dialogue between person and God.

But overwhelming questions spring to mind. Firstly, how can the human being, a minuscule element of the universe which God created, presume to engage his Creator in conversation? By what right do we stand before Him to beseech or even to praise? Secondly, on whose behalf do we rightfully pray? What is the nature of the interplay between the petitioner as an individual and the broader society-community of which he is part; is there really such a thing as totally private prayer or do we always represent a constituency beyond ourselves? Thirdly, to what qualities in God do we appeal? As we attempt to evoke responses from the Deity, can we identify with greater clarity which of the relational qualities of God we desire to see exercised?

Surely these are not all the essential questions about prayer, but the answers will help us frame the nature of the experience of prayer of the heart.

A simple *minhag* may help answer these questions. Before we recite the *Amidah* — prayer par excellence — we take three steps forward to symbolize our awe in approaching the King of Kings. Rabbi Eleazar ben Judah (c. 1165 - c. 1230), author of the *Sefer Rokeach,* relates those three steps to the fact that — as an introduction to a petition — the word וַיִּגַּשׁ, "and he approached," appears three times in *Tanach.* Analysis of those three Biblical narratives will uncover the most fundamental elements of Jewish prayer.

I. The Petition of Avraham

When told by God that Sodom and Amorah were to be destroyed, Avraham responds with shocking audacity: "... וַיִּגַּשׁ אַבְרָהָם, Avraham approached and said: 'Will You indeed destroy the righteous with the wicked?' " *(Genesis* 18:23).

A. *By What Right?*

By what right did Avraham speak so familiarly with God? Had he not just before this (*Gen.* 17:1-27) entered into a covenant with God of which his circumcision was the symbol! Consequently he can turn to God as if to say, "I have consented to serve You and to teach the world of Your existence, Your greatness and Your justice; how can I do so if Your behavior appears unjust?" Thus, Avraham's right to petition God, to challenge His conduct of the world, emerges from the partnership generated by the Covenant. It is as a *"ben brit,"* a "member of the covenant" that Avraham petitions God.

B. *On Behalf of Whom?*

It is both astonishing and instructive that the first formal petition by the first circumcized Jew was not on his own behalf, nor on behalf of a member of his family, the nuclear Jewish people, — it was on behalf of strangers, human beings whose lives were apparently of ultimate value to Avraham. Indeed, according to many commentators, Avraham's initial petition of *Gen.* 18:23 was an attempt not only to save the few righteous citizens of Sodom, but to rescue even the evildoers in the merit of the righteous (see *Rashi* to *Gen.* 18:25). Avraham already recognized that his covenantal duty was to risk offending God Himself, to speak valiantly on behalf of the endangered humans — even though their own evil deeds had created the threat of Divine retribution.

C. *For What Quality?*

"Will the Judge of all the universe not act justly?!" (*Gen.* 18:25), Avraham cries out. He is not casting about in the darkness to elicit G-d's positive response. He has targeted a specific quality which inheres in God — the quality of justice. Avraham felt what every one of his descendants was destined to recognize: the fundamental expectation that God will act justly. It is precisely for that reason that the single philosophical problem which has most plagued men of faith throughout the ages has been the problem of Theodicy — attempting to understand God's justice in the face of the reality of suffering by the righteous. Indeed, God Himself concedes that Avraham is correct — that the final fate of Sodom must be just, that His own quality of justice could not be compromised.

To recapitulate then the central issues in this narrative:

A. By what right does Avraham petition God? As a *"ben brit"* — one who stands in a convenantal relationship with God.

B. For whom does he pray? For fellow human beings.

C. For what Divine quality does Avraham petition? For Justice.

II. The petition of Judah

The second time the word וַיִּגַּשׁ, "and he approached," is used in the context of petition is in the story of Joseph and his brothers in *Genesis* Chapter 44. Benjamin is accused of theft and is arrested by Joseph. Judah, who had assumed responsibility (*Arvut*) for Benjamin's well-being (*Genesis* 43:9), now pleads for Benjamin's release. This petition is different from Avraham's in every essential element.

A. *By What Right?*

By what right did Judah petition the viceroy of Egypt? Certainly not as one with a modicum of equality with Joseph. On the contrary, Judah emphasizes the disparity of their positions: Joseph is "like unto Pharaoh," while he himself is merely a "servant" pleading to be heard (*Genesis* 44:18). Still, וַיִּגַּשׁ אֵלָיו יְהוּדָה, "Judah approached him." Judah was not intimidated, did not simply abandon his duty, his responsibility to his brother and his father, his quest to successfully complete his mission. Despite his lowly position, he pursues his petition with force and passion.

B. *On Behalf of Whom?*

Here too, the contrast between the petitions of Avraham and Judah could not be sharper. Avraham's was universalistic, without a shred of self-interest. Judah's is the paradigm of particularism — it responded to his own need to execute his own responsibility, and its beneficiaries would be his father and brother. Indeed only his petition's success could avoid the bitter dissolution of the household of Israel (*Beit Yisrael*). No wonder then at the force and passion of Judah's representation. But his petition was not made petty by its particularism. Instead, it was based on the same principle which infused the prayer of Avraham — the ultimate worth of a single life. In fact, this petition is a perfect example of how the destiny of an entire nation, perhaps even of the entire world, could be determined by the fate of a single individual.

C. *For What Quality?*

Judah does not seek justice from Joseph. To the best of his knowledge, Benjamin is guilty of the theft; Joseph's desire to imprison only the guilty party, freeing the others to return to their father (*Gen.* 44:17), is fair and just. In this situation justice will yield tragedy. Judah's petition therefore is for mercy. He recalls Jacob's prior bereavement and his reluctance to let Benjamin go to Egypt. He describes movingly the special attachment between Jacob and Benjamin and suggests how totally broken Jacob would be if Benjamin too were lost to him. Judah casts aside all considerations of justice; he offers no defense of Benjamin, no ameliorating circumstances which might cause a tempering of pure justice — that would be counterproductive. Judah's prayer is a singleminded pursuit of a different quality — of mercy. And he succeeds.

As we recapitulate the central issues in Judah's prayer we will see how strikingly different its elements are from those in the petition of Avraham.

A. By what right does Judah petition Joseph? As an "*eved,*" a servant — one in a distictly inferior position.

B. For whom does Judah pray? For himself, his family, the Jewish people.

C. For what quality does Judah petition? For the quality of mercy.

III. The Petition of Eliyahu

The third and final instance of the use of the word וַיִּגַּשׁ, "and he approached," in a Biblical narrative of petition, is in the confrontation between the prophet Eliyahu and the false prophets (*I Kings*, chapter 18). Tragically the Jewish People were deeply engaged in the idolatrous worship of Baal. Even the King of Israel, Ahab, and his murderous wife, Queen Jezebel, suppressed the Jewish faith. Against that backdrop, Eliyahu conceived of a risk-laden, last stab at regaining the allegiance of the Jewish people to God and His Torah. He challenged the false prophets to a direct, public competition on Mount Carmel. After the dismal failure of the idolatrous prophets to gain any response from their deity, Eliyahu "approaches," וַיִּגַּשׁ אֵלִיָּהוּ הַנָּבִיא:

> Elijah the prophet stepped near and said: Eternal God of Abraham, Isaac and of Israel, let it be known this day that You are God in Israel and that I am Your servant, and that I have done all these things at Your word. Hear me O Eternal, hear me; that this people may know that You are the Eternal God and that You have turned their heart back (*I Kings*, 18:36-37).

God responded. Fire descended to consume the offering of Eliyahu, and the faith of the Jewish people in their God was restored.

A. *By What Right?*

If Judah's petition was impassioned, if Avraham's petition was audacious, how can one describe the confrontational quality of Eliyahu's? By what right did he attempt to "coerce" God to comply with his prayer? As a prophet — an "*Ish Elokim ...,*" "a man of God in whose mouth is the true word of God" (*I Kings* 17:24), Eliyahu had a relationship with God in which sometimes the prophet and sometimes God took the initiative to assure that the Divine message would reach the Jewish people. It was precisely due to the constancy and intimacy of his relationship to God that Eliyahu had the right to make an otherwise unconscionable demand.

B. *On Behalf of Whom?*

It is true that there was an element of self-interest in Eliyahu's prayer — that his own role of prophet be affirmed (see *Metzudat David* to *I Kings* 18:36). It is equally true that the entire Jewish people would benefit from being turned back to faith in God. However, in Eliyahu's prayer there is a new beneficiary — God Himself. Eliyahu's plea for a miracle was based in part on his awareness that God desires the worship of the Jewish people and that this was the propitious moment for God to regain that commitment.

Can one truly say that God has desires which mere mortals can satisfy, so that we can plead with Him to act in His own interest? We can't, and yet we do! It is a central paradox of prayer, but Eliyahu charted a path which we have extensively trodden since. As we shall see, our prayers are laden with petitions on behalf of God. Like all the elements of petitional prayer, this element as well has come to form part of the essential structure of our fixed prayer.

C. *For What Quality?*

Avraham did not tell God how to resolve the problem of Sodom; he only asked for a resolution in which justice would be manifest. Judah did not tell Joseph how to balance the diverse needs of justice and mercy; he asked only for a resolution in which mercy would dominate. Similarly, while Eliyahu had created a framework for the restoration of the relationship between God and the Jewish people, he did not insist on a specific act. His petition was that in that moment of opportunity a particular quality of God be revealed — the quality of Divine presence, of "*Gilui Shechinah.*" Whatever circumstances had previously caused the presence of God to be hidden from the Jewish people, whether the sinfulness of the people or the withdrawal of God, now was the time for those obscuring clouds to be banished and for the full glory of God's involvement and concern for His people to be revealed.

Let us now recapitulate Eliyahu's petition and note how different its elements are from those present in the petitions of Avraham and Judah.

A. By what right does Eliyahu petition God? As a prophet — one engaged in a continuous and intimate relationship with God.

B. For whom does Eliyahu pray? For God Himself.

C. For what Divine quality does Eliyahu petition? For the quality of Divine presence — "*Gilui Shechinah.*"

A schematic outline of the elements we have seen thus far may help place the processes of petitional prayer in clear perspective.

	BY WHAT RIGHT	FOR WHOM	FOR WHAT QUALITY
AVRAHAM	As "*ben brit*" — party to a covenant	Mankind	Justice
JUDAH	As servant	Self and Family — the Jewish People	Mercy
ELIYAHU	As prophet — party to a continuous and intimate relationship with God	God Himself	Presence — Revelation

Let us return now to the remarkable insight of Rabbi Eleazar ben Judah, author of the *Sefer Rokeach*, who sees a special connection between the *minhag* of taking three steps forward at the outset of the *Amidah*, and the three petitional prayers where we find the word וַיִּגַּשׁ, "and he approached." That simple suggestion may hold infinite riches. For the three prayers of Avraham, Judah and Eliyahu are paradigms for us. Throughout our prayers, and particularly in our quintessential prayer, the *Amidah Lifnei Hashem*, our "standing before God," we constantly address the same three questions which have occupied our attention heretofore.

How do we explain our right to appear before God to speak our personal petitions? At the very beginning of the *Amidah* we identify ourselves as *b'nei brit*, parties to a covenant with God. As HaGaon Rav Soloveitchik asserts:

> The fact that we commence the recital of the "Eighteen Benedictions" by addressing ourselves to the God of Abraham, Isaac and Jacob, is indicative of the covenantal relationship which, in the opinion of our sages, lies at the very root of prayer. ("The Lonely Man of Faith," p. 35)

But, if that first blessing of *Avot* presents us as partners with God, the second, the blessing of *Gevurot*, presents us as God's subjects and servants, needful of His kindness and mercy, of His support and His healing. The constant prayerful affirmation of God as King in the *Amidah* and elsewhere is our reminder to ourselves that we address Him as subjects and servants.

It is obvious that we could not, as Eliyahu did, petition God based on our being prophets, but we come as close to that as truthfulness and integrity allow. We engage in a constant and intimate relationship with God — one analogous to that of the angels who daily praise God. This is the key to the third blessing of the *Amidah*, and explains why we appropriate the *Kedushah*, with which the universe itself declares the holiness of God.

The paradigmatic character of the petitions of Avraham, Judah and Eliyahu extends as well to the question of for whom we pray. That our prayer fluctuates in broad swings between the universalistic and the particularistic is clear. One need only compare the ninth blessing of the *Amidah*, with its plea for God's blessing for the entire earth, to the tenth with its particularistic pleading for the ingathering of the exiled Jewish people into the land of Israel. But beyond any human benefit, we, like Eliyahu, audaciously base our petitions on benefit to God Himself. In the very first blessing of the *Amidah* we remind God of His promise to send a redeemer, not for our sake, but לְמַעַן שְׁמוֹ, "for the sake of His Own Name." Likewise in the seventh blessing of the *Amidah* we directly petition God to redeem us only לְמַעַן שְׁמֶךָ, "for the sake of Your name." In our prayers, we repeatedly note that the fate of the Jewish people is a reflection on God's greatness and holiness, and that, therefore, God's attentiveness to our well being, even when we do not deserve it, is necessary, in order, so to speak, to protect His reputation in the world.

It is worth noting further that while the petitions of Judah and Eliyahu involved personal benefit to them, such personal welfare was not central in their prayer, but was rather subsumed within their outward perspective. Likewise, the entire Amidah, and the bulk of all of our prayer, is in the plural, not in the singular. As HaGaon Rav Soloveitchik forcefully contends:

> Man should avoid praying for himself alone. The plural form of prayer is of central Halachic significance. When disaster strikes, one must not be

> immersed completely in his own passional destiny, thinking exclusively of himself, being concerned only with himself, and petitioning God merely for himself. The foundation of efficacious and noble prayer is human solidarity and sympathy or the convenantal awareness of existential togetherness, of sharing and experiencing the travail and suffering of [others] ("The Lonely Man of Faith," pp. 37-38).

In a third and final way, these three models of petitional prayer infuse our own praying. Like Avraham, Judah and Eliyahu, we do not attempt to bind the hands of God to do our will through specific acts. We present a problem to God, a concern, a worry; we tell Him that we are suffering, that our exile has been too long, that illness afflicts us, that we need wisdom and wise leaders. We then ask Him to help us, but in ways that would manifest Divine qualities. Which qualities do we seek? That of justice, as explicitly found in the eleventh blessing of the *Amidah;* and obviously that of mercy which runs as an undercurrent in almost all of the petitions and bursts into words in the first, the fourth, the sixth, the eighth, the eleventh, the fourteenth, the sixteenth, the seventeenth, the eighteenth and the nineteenth blessings.

But, we are not satisfied even with Divine mercy. We urgently desire one further quality, the Divine presence. As we cry out in the seventeenth blessing of the *Amidah,* "May our eyes behold Your return to Zion in compassion." We have tired of *"hester panim,"* of the hiddeness of the *Shechinah.* We can no longer bear the precariousness of our physical and spiritual existence without the *Beit HaMikdash* and without God's manifest hand in the governance of human history. We therefore plead for *Gilui Shechinah* — for a revelation of God's presence.

It is interesting that these three qualities for which we plead, form the pinnacle of our prayerful expression as the central three blessings of the *Mussaf Amidah* of Rosh Hashanah. *Malchiyot* — Divine Kingship, *Zichronot* — Remembrance, and *Shofrot* — the call for God's self-revelation, are simply alternate ways of describing the qualities of justice, mercy and Divine presence.

Before we begin the *Amidah,* we recite a verbal meditation asking God to give power to our lips and our mouths to speak in words that which is contained in our hearts. But even before we do that, we engage in a behavioral meditation, to prepare both body and mind to speak with God. We take three steps forward to remember the three paradigms of prayer, to define our agenda with God in the spirit of Avraham, Judah and Eliyahu Hanavi. With each step we remind ourselves of by what right we appear before God, for whom we are about to pray and for what Divine qualities we pray.

May the steps of our feet, the meditations of our hearts and the words of our mouths be adequate to approach God and to find favor in His presence.

Rabbi Saul Berman

Tammuz 5746
New York, NY

תְּפִלַּת שַׁחֲרִית

Shacharis/Morning Service

The Names of God

The Four-Letter Name of God [י־ה־ו־ה] indicates that God is timeless and infinite, since the letters of this Name are those of the words הָיָה הֹוֶה וְיִהְיֶה, *He was, He is, and He will be.* This Name is *never* pronounced as it is spelled.

During prayer, or when a blessing is recited, or when Torah verses are read, the Four-Letter Name should be pronounced as if it were spelled אֲדֹנָי, *Adonai,* the Name that identifies God as the Master of All. At other times, it should be pronounced הַשֵּׁם, *Hashem,* literally, "the Name."

According to the *Shulchan Aruch,* one should have both meanings – the Master of All and the Timeless, Infinite One – in mind when reciting the Four-Letter Name during prayer (*Orach Chaim,* 5). According to the Gaon of Vilna, however, one need have in mind only the meaning of the Name as it is pronounced – the Master of All (*ibid.*).

When the Name is spelled אֲדֹנָי in the prayer or verse, all agree that one should have in mind that God is the Master of All.

The Name אֱלֹהִים, *God,* refers to Him as the One Who is all-powerful and Who is in direct overlordship of the universe (*ibid.*). It is also used as a generic name for the angels, a court, rulers, and even idols. However, when the term אֱלֹהִים is used for the God of Israel, it means the One Omniscient God, Who is uniquely identified with His Chosen People.

In this work, the Four Letter Name of God is translated *"Hashem,"* the pronunciation traditionally used for the Name to avoid pronouncing it unnecessarily. This pronunciation should be used when studying the meanings of the prayers. However, if one prays in English, he should say "God"or "Lord" or he should pronounce the Name in the proper Hebrew way – *Adonai* – in accord with the ruling of most halachic authorities.

השכמת הבוקר

A Jew should wake up with gratitude to God for having restored his faculties and with a lionlike resolve to serve his Creator. Before getting off the bed or commencing any other conversation or activity, he declares his gratitude:

מוֹדֶה אֲנִי לְפָנֶיךָ,* מֶלֶךְ חַי וְקַיָּם, שֶׁהֶחֱזַרְתָּ בִּי נִשְׁמָתִי בְּחֶמְלָה — רַבָּה אֱמוּנָתֶךָ.

Wash the hands according to the ritual procedure: pick up the vessel of water with the right hand, pass it to the left, and pour water over the right. Then with the right hand pour over the left. Follow this procedure until water has been poured over each hand three times. Then, recite:

רֵאשִׁית חָכְמָה יִרְאַת יהוה, שֵׂכֶל טוֹב לְכָל עֹשֵׂיהֶם, תְּהִלָּתוֹ עֹמֶדֶת לָעַד.[1] בָּרוּךְ שֵׁם כְּבוֹד מַלְכוּתוֹ לְעוֹלָם וָעֶד.

לבישת ציצית

Hold the *tallis kattan* in readiness to put on, inspect the *tzitzis* (see commentary) and recite the following blessing. Then, don the *tallis kattan* and kiss the *tzitzis*. One who wears a *tallis* for *Shacharis* does not recite this blessing (see commentary).

בָּרוּךְ אַתָּה יהוה אֱלֹהֵינוּ מֶלֶךְ הָעוֹלָם, אֲשֶׁר קִדְּשָׁנוּ בְּמִצְוֹתָיו, וְצִוָּנוּ עַל מִצְוַת צִיצִת.

יְהִי רָצוֹן מִלְּפָנֶיךָ, יהוה אֱלֹהַי וֵאלֹהֵי אֲבוֹתַי, שֶׁתְּהֵא חֲשׁוּבָה מִצְוַת צִיצִת לְפָנֶיךָ, כְּאִלּוּ קִיַּמְתִּיהָ בְּכָל פְּרָטֶיהָ וְדִקְדּוּקֶיהָ וְכַוָּנוֹתֶיהָ, וְתַרְיַ״ג מִצְוֹת הַתְּלוּיִם בָּהּ. אָמֵן סֶלָה.

עטיפת טלית

Before donning the *tallis,* inspect the *tzitzis* (see commentary) while reciting these verses:

בָּרְכִי נַפְשִׁי* אֶת יהוה, יהוה אֱלֹהַי גָּדַלְתָּ מְּאֹד, הוֹד וְהָדָר לָבָשְׁתָּ. עֹטֶה אוֹר כַּשַּׂלְמָה, נוֹטֶה שָׁמַיִם כַּיְרִיעָה.[2]

הַשְׁכָּמַת הַבּוֹקֶר / UPON ARISING

מוֹדֶה אֲנִי לְפָנֶיךָ — *I gratefully thank You.* A Jew opens his eyes and thanks God for restoring his faculties to him in the morning. Then, he acknowledges that God did so in the expectation that he will serve Him, and that He is abundantly faithful to reward those who do.

לְבִישַׁת צִיצִית / DONNING THE TZITZIS

Since *tzitzis* need not be worn at night, the commandment of *tzitzis* [*Numbers* 15:38] is classified as a time-related commandment, and as such, is not required of women. It may be fulfilled in two ways: by means of the *tallis kattan* (lit. small garment), popularly known simply as 'the *tzitzis,*' which is worn all day, usually under the shirt; and by means of the familiar large *tallis,* commonly known simply as 'the *tallis,*' which is worn during *Shacharis.* Among Sephardic and German Jews, the *tallis* is worn even by children, but in most Ashkenazic congregations it is worn during prayer only by one who is or has been married. Although,

UPON ARISING

A Jew should wake up with gratitude to God for having restored his faculties and with a lionlike resolve to serve his Creator. Before getting off the bed or commencing any other conversation or activity, he declares his gratitude:

מוֹדֶה אֲנִי *I gratefully thank You,* O living and eternal King, for You have returned my soul within me with compassion — abundant is Your faithfulness!*

Wash the hands according to the ritual procedure: pick up the vessel of water with the right hand, pass it to the left, and pour water over the right. Then with the right hand pour over the left. Follow this procedure until water has been poured over each hand three times. Then, recite:

רֵאשִׁית חָכְמָה *The beginning of wisdom is the fear of* HASHEM *— good understanding to all their practitioners; His praise endures forever.*[1] *Blessed is the Name of His glorious kingdom for all eternity.*

DONNING THE TZITZIS

Hold the *tallis kattan* in readiness to put on, inspect the *tzitzis* (see commentary) and recite the following blessing. Then don the *tallis kattan* and kiss the *tzitzis.* One who wears a *tallis* for *Shacharis* does not recite this blessing (see commentary).

בָּרוּךְ *Blessed are You,* HASHEM, *our God, King of the universe, Who has sanctified us with His commandments, and has commanded us regarding the commandment of tzitzis.*

יְהִי רָצוֹן *May it be Your will,* HASHEM, *my God and the God of my forefathers, that the commandment of tzitzis be as worthy before You as if I had fulfilled it in all its details, implications, and intentions, as well as the six hundred thirteen commandments that are dependent upon it. Amen, Selah!*

DONNING THE TALLIS

Before donning the *tallis,* inspect the *tzitzis* (see commentary) while reciting these verses:

בָּרְכִי נַפְשִׁי *Bless* HASHEM, *O my soul;** HASHEM, *my God, You are very great; You have donned majesty and splendor; cloaked in light as with a garment, stretching out the heavens like a curtain.*[2]

(1) *Psalms* 111:10. (2) 104:1-2.

strictly speaking, one should recite the appropriate blessings over each garment upon donning it, the custom is that one who wears a *tallis* at *Shacharis* does not recite the blessing עַל מִצְוַת צִיצִת, *regarding the commandment of tzitzis,* when donning the *tallis kattan.* Instead before donning the large *tallis* he has in mind that the blessing לְהִתְעַטֵּף בְּצִיצִת, *to wrap ourselves in tzitzis,* should apply to both garments.

Before donning his *tallis* or *tallis kattan,* one must untangle the fringes and examine them carefully to be sure that none of the strings have torn. It is especially important to check the places where the strings are looped through the holes in the corners of the garment, for if one of the strings is torn there, the *tzitzis* are invalid and the garment may not be worn.

עֲטִיפַת טַלִּית / DONNING THE TALLIS

בָּרְכִי נַפְשִׁי — *Bless ... O my soul.* These two verses describe God figuratively as donning garments of majesty and light. Because the *tallis* symbolizes the splendor of God's command-

Many recite the following declaration of intent before donning the *tallis:*

לְשֵׁם יִחוּד* קֻדְשָׁא בְּרִיךְ הוּא וּשְׁכִינְתֵּהּ, בִּדְחִילוּ וּרְחִימוּ לְיַחֵד שֵׁם* י״ה בְּו״ה בְּיִחוּדָא שְׁלִים, בְּשֵׁם כָּל יִשְׂרָאֵל.

הֲרֵינִי* מִתְעַטֵּף גּוּפִי בַּצִּיצִת, כֵּן תִּתְעַטֵּף נִשְׁמָתִי וּרְמַ״ח אֵבָרַי וּשְׁסָ״ה גִידַי* בְּאוֹר הַצִּיצִת הָעוֹלֶה תַרְיַ״ג. וּכְשֵׁם שֶׁאֲנִי מִתְכַּסֶּה בְּטַלִּית בָּעוֹלָם הַזֶּה, כַּךְ אֶזְכֶּה לַחֲלוּקָא דְרַבָּנָן וּלְטַלִּית נָאֶה לָעוֹלָם הַבָּא בְּגַן עֵדֶן. וְעַל יְדֵי מִצְוַת צִיצִת תִּנָּצֵל נַפְשִׁי וְרוּחִי וְנִשְׁמָתִי וּתְפִלָּתִי מִן הַחִיצוֹנִים. וְהַטַּלִּית יִפְרוֹשׂ כְּנָפָיו עֲלֵיהֶם וְיַצִּילֵם כְּנֶשֶׁר יָעִיר קִנּוֹ, עַל גּוֹזָלָיו יְרַחֵף.[1] וּתְהֵא חֲשׁוּבָה מִצְוַת צִיצִת לִפְנֵי הַקָּדוֹשׁ בָּרוּךְ הוּא כְּאִלּוּ קִיַּמְתִּיהָ בְּכָל פְּרָטֶיהָ וְדִקְדּוּקֶיהָ וְכַוָּנוֹתֶיהָ וְתַרְיַ״ג מִצְוֹת הַתְּלוּיִם בָּהּ. אָמֵן סֶלָה.

Unfold the *tallis*, hold it in readiness to wrap around yourself, and recite the following blessing:

בָּרוּךְ אַתָּה יהוה אֱלֹהֵינוּ מֶלֶךְ הָעוֹלָם, אֲשֶׁר קִדְּשָׁנוּ בְּמִצְוֹתָיו, וְצִוָּנוּ לְהִתְעַטֵּף בַּצִּיצִת.

Wrap the *tallis* around your head and body, then recite:

מַה יָּקָר חַסְדְּךָ אֱלֹהִים, וּבְנֵי אָדָם בְּצֵל כְּנָפֶיךָ יֶחֱסָיוּן. יִרְוְיֻן מִדֶּשֶׁן בֵּיתֶךָ, וְנַחַל עֲדָנֶיךָ תַשְׁקֵם. כִּי עִמְּךָ מְקוֹר חַיִּים, בְּאוֹרְךָ נִרְאֶה אוֹר. מְשֹׁךְ חַסְדְּךָ לְיֹדְעֶיךָ, וְצִדְקָתְךָ לְיִשְׁרֵי לֵב.[2]

סדר הנחת תפילין

Many recite the following declaration of intent before putting on *tefillin:*

לְשֵׁם יִחוּד* קֻדְשָׁא בְּרִיךְ הוּא וּשְׁכִינְתֵּהּ, בִּדְחִילוּ וּרְחִימוּ לְיַחֵד שֵׁם י״ה בְּו״ה בְּיִחוּדָא שְׁלִים, בְּשֵׁם כָּל יִשְׂרָאֵל.

---

ments, we liken our wearing of it to wrapping ourselves in God's glory and brilliance. Similarly, the Kabbalistic references in the following לְשֵׁם יִחוּד prayer associate the *tallis* with protection, elevation, and illumination.

⁂ לְשֵׁם יִחוּד ... הֲרֵינִי — *For the sake of the unification ... I am ready.* This preliminary formulation serves two purposes. It is a statement of intent that the act about to be performed is to fulfill the Torah's commandment. The second purpose, indicated by the mystical references, is a prayer that the Kabbalistic spiritual qualities of the commandment be realized. Some authorities omit the sentence beginning לְשֵׁם יִחוּד and start the supplication from הֲרֵינִי. Others omit the entire prayer, but all agree that one should have intent to fulfill the *mitzvah.*

לְיַחֵד שֵׁם ... — *To unify the Name ...* The first half of the Divine Name, formed of the letters *yud* and *hei*, symbolizes the Attribute of Judgment, while the second half, formed of the letters *vav* and *hei*, symbolizes the Attribute of Mercy. The blend of both attributes leads to His desired goal for Creation. Since these letters form the sacred Four-Letter Name that is not to be uttered as it is spelled, and since many commentators maintain that this prohibition extends even to uttering the four letters of the Name, the commonly used pronunciation of these letters in the לְשֵׁם יִחוּד prayer is *yud-kei b'vav kei.*

רְמַ״ח אֵבָרַי וּשְׁסָ״ה גִידַי — *My two hundred forty-*

Many recite the following declaration of intent before donning the *tallis:*

לְשֵׁם יִחוּד *For the sake of the unification* of the Holy One, Blessed is He, and His Presence, in fear and love to unify the Name* — yud-kei with vav-kei — in perfect unity, in the name of all Israel.*

הֲרֵינִי *I am ready* to wrap my body in tzitzis, so may my soul, my two hundred forty-eight organs and my three hundred sixty-five sinews* be wrapped in the illumination of tzitzis which has the numerical value of six hundred thirteen. Just as I cover myself with a tallis in This World, so may I merit the rabbinical garb and a beautiful cloak in the World to Come in the Garden of Eden. Through the commandment of tzitzis may my life-force, spirit, soul, and prayer be rescued from the external forces. May the tallis spread its wings over them and rescue them like an eagle rousing his nest, fluttering over his eaglets.*[1] *May the commandment of tzitzis be worthy before the Holy One, Blessed is He, as if I had fulfilled it in all its details, implications, and intentions, as well as the six hundred thirteen commandments that are dependent upon it. Amen, Selah!*

Unfold the *tallis*, hold it in readiness to wrap around yourself, and recite the following blessing:

בָּרוּךְ *Blessed are You, HASHEM, our God, King of the universe, Who has sanctified us with His commandments and has commanded us to wrap ourselves in tzitzis.*

Wrap the *tallis* around your head and body, then recite:

מַה יָּקָר *How precious is Your kindness, O God! The sons of man take refuge in the shadow of Your wings. May they be sated from the abundance of Your house; and may You give them to drink from the stream of Your delights. For with You is the source of life — by Your light we shall see light. Extend Your kindness to those who know You, and Your charity to the upright of heart.*[2]

ORDER OF PUTTING ON TEFILLIN

Many recite the following declaration of intent before putting on *tefillin:*

לְשֵׁם יִחוּד *For the sake of the unification* of the Holy One, Blessed is He, and His Presence, in fear and love, to unify the Name — yud-kei with vav-kei — in perfect unity, in the name of all Israel.*

(1) *Deuteronomy* 32:11 (2) *Psalms* 36:8-11.

eight organs and my three hundred sixty-five sinews. The Sages' computation of the important organs, two hundred forty-eight, is equal to the number of positive commandments, while the three hundred sixty-five sinews equal the number of negative commandments. This symbolizes the principle that man was created to perform God's will. The total number of sinews and organs in man, and the total of Divine commandments, are each six hundred thirteen, a number symbolized by the commandment of צִיצִית, *tzitzis* [צ=90; י=10; צ=90; י=10; ת=400, totaling 600; the 5 knots and 8 threads of each fringe make up the other 13]. Thus, by wrapping our bodies in the *tallis,* we dedicate ourselves totally to the task of serving God.

Additionally, as mentioned later in this prayer, the *tallis* represents the concept that God protects those who serve Him.

הַנָּחַת תְּפִלִּין / PUTTING ON TEFILLIN

לְשֵׁם יִחוּד — *For the sake of the unification.* In its broad outline, this introductory supplication serves the same dual purpose as the לְשֵׁם יִחוּד for

הִנְנִי מְכַוֵּן בְּהַנָּחַת תְּפִלִּין לְקַיֵּם מִצְוַת בּוֹרְאִי, שֶׁצִּוָּנוּ לְהָנִיחַ תְּפִלִּין, כַּכָּתוּב בְּתוֹרָתוֹ: וּקְשַׁרְתָּם לְאוֹת עַל יָדֶךָ, וְהָיוּ לְטֹטָפֹת בֵּין עֵינֶיךָ.[1] וְהֵם אַרְבַּע פַּרְשִׁיּוֹת אֵלּוּ — שְׁמַע, וְהָיָה אִם שָׁמֹעַ, קַדֶּשׁ, וְהָיָה כִּי יְבִאֲךָ — שֶׁיֵּשׁ בָּהֶם יִחוּדוֹ וְאַחְדוּתוֹ יִתְבָּרַךְ שְׁמוֹ בָּעוֹלָם; וְשֶׁנִּזְכּוֹר נִסִּים וְנִפְלָאוֹת שֶׁעָשָׂה עִמָּנוּ בְּהוֹצִיאָנוּ מִמִּצְרָיִם; וַאֲשֶׁר לוֹ הַכֹּחַ וְהַמֶּמְשָׁלָה בָּעֶלְיוֹנִים וּבַתַּחְתּוֹנִים לַעֲשׂוֹת בָּהֶם כִּרְצוֹנוֹ. וְצִוָּנוּ לְהָנִיחַ עַל הַיָּד, לְזִכְרוֹן זְרוֹעַ הַנְּטוּיָה, וְשֶׁהִיא נֶגֶד הַלֵּב, לְשַׁעְבֵּד בָּזֶה תַּאֲוַת וּמַחְשְׁבוֹת לִבֵּנוּ לַעֲבוֹדָתוֹ, יִתְבָּרַךְ שְׁמוֹ. וְעַל הָרֹאשׁ נֶגֶד הַמּוֹחַ, שֶׁהַנְּשָׁמָה שֶׁבְּמוֹחִי, עִם שְׁאָר חוּשַׁי וְכֹחוֹתַי, כֻּלָּם יִהְיוּ מְשֻׁעְבָּדִים לַעֲבוֹדָתוֹ, יִתְבָּרַךְ שְׁמוֹ. וּמִשֶּׁפַע מִצְוַת תְּפִלִּין יִתְמַשֵּׁךְ עָלַי לִהְיוֹת לִי חַיִּים אֲרוּכִים, וְשֶׁפַע קֹדֶשׁ, וּמַחֲשָׁבוֹת קְדוֹשׁוֹת בְּלִי הִרְהוּר חֵטְא וְעָוֹן כְּלָל; וְשֶׁלֹּא יְפַתֵּנוּ וְלֹא יִתְגָּרֶה בָּנוּ יֵצֶר הָרָע, וְיַנִּיחֵנוּ לַעֲבֹד אֶת יהוה כַּאֲשֶׁר עִם לְבָבֵנוּ. וִיהִי רָצוֹן מִלְּפָנֶיךָ, יהוה אֱלֹהֵינוּ וֵאלֹהֵי אֲבוֹתֵינוּ, שֶׁתְּהֵא חֲשׁוּבָה מִצְוַת הֲנָחַת תְּפִלִּין לִפְנֵי הַקָּדוֹשׁ בָּרוּךְ הוּא כְּאִלּוּ קִיַּמְתִּיהָ בְּכָל פְּרָטֶיהָ וְדִקְדּוּקֶיהָ וְכַוָּנוֹתֶיהָ, וְתַרְיַ״ג מִצְוֹת הַתְּלוּיִם בָּהּ. אָמֵן סֶלָה.

Stand while putting on *tefillin*. Place the arm-*tefillin* upon the left biceps (or the right biceps of one who writes left-handed), hold it in place ready for tightening, then recite the following blessing:

בָּרוּךְ אַתָּה יהוה אֱלֹהֵינוּ מֶלֶךְ הָעוֹלָם, אֲשֶׁר קִדְּשָׁנוּ בְּמִצְוֹתָיו, וְצִוָּנוּ לְהָנִיחַ תְּפִלִּין.

Tighten the arm-*tefillin* and wrap the strap seven times around the arm. Without any interruption whatsoever, put the head-*tefillin* in place, above the hairline and opposite the space between the eyes. Before tightening the head-*tefillin* recite the following blessing:

בָּרוּךְ אַתָּה יהוה אֱלֹהֵינוּ מֶלֶךְ הָעוֹלָם, אֲשֶׁר קִדְּשָׁנוּ בְּמִצְוֹתָיו, וְצִוָּנוּ עַל מִצְוַת תְּפִלִּין.

Tighten the head-*tefillin* and recite:

בָּרוּךְ שֵׁם* כְּבוֹד מַלְכוּתוֹ לְעוֹלָם וָעֶד.

---

tzitzis. Four separate Scriptural passages command Israel to put on *tefillin;* all four are mentioned here and, incidentally, the parchments inserted into the *tefillin* contain these passages. Much of the language of this prayer is drawn from *Ramban* to *Exodus* 13:16, who explains that the arm-*tefillin* represents God's strength and our resolve to submit our hearts and power to Him. The head-*tefillin* represents our resolve to dedicate the seat of our intellect to Him.

Tefillin are described as an אות, *a sign,* of the covenant between God and Israel *(Exodus* 13:9,16; *Deuteronomy* 4:8, 11:18) — a measure of their profound significance.

Since *tefillin* are not worn on the Sabbath, festivals, or in the evening, it is a time-related commandment and therefore is not incumbent upon women.

Nowhere does the Scriptural *mitzvah* of *tefillin* specify that it should be worn only during prayer. Indeed, through the generations, righteous people made it a practice to wear *tefillin* all day, except when they were engaged in activities unbecoming to the sanctity of *tefillin.* However, the halachah requires that one maintain intellectual and bodily purity while wearing *tefillin,* a task that is by no means easy. Consequently, the custom was adopted that

הִנְנִי מְכַוֵּן *Behold, in putting on tefillin I intend to fulfill the commandment of my Creator, Who has commanded us to put on tefillin, as is written in His Torah: 'Bind them as a sign upon your arm and let them be tefillin between your eyes.'*[1] *These four portions [contained in the tefillin] — [1] 'Shema' (Deuteronomy 6:4-9); [2] 'And it will come to pass, if you will hearken' (Deuteronomy 11:13-21); [3] 'Sanctify' (Exodus 13:1-10); and [4] 'And it will come to pass when He shall bring you' (Exodus 13:11-16) — contain His Oneness and Unity, may His Name be blessed, in the universe; so that we will recall the miracles and wonders that He did with us when He removed us from Egypt; and that He has the strength and dominion over those above and those below to do with them as He wishes. He has commanded us to put [tefillin] upon the arm to recall the 'outstretched arm' [of the Exodus] and that it be opposite the heart thereby to subjugate the desires and thoughts of our heart to His service, may His Name be blessed; and upon the head opposite the brain, so that the soul that is in my brain, together with my other senses and potentials, may all be subjugated to His service, may His Name be blessed. May some of the spiritual influence of the commandment of tefillin be extended upon me so that I have a long life, a flow of holiness, and holy thoughts, without even an inkling of sin or iniquity; and that the Evil Inclination will not seduce us nor incite against us, and that it permit us to serve HASHEM as is our hearts' desire. May it be Your will, HASHEM, our God and the God of our forefathers, that the commandment of putting on tefillin be considered as worthy before the Holy One, Blessed is He, as if I had fulfilled it in all its details, implications, and intentions, as well as the six hundred thirteen commandments that are dependent upon it. Amen, Selah.*

Stand while putting on *tefillin.* Place the arm-*tefillin* upon the left biceps (or the right biceps of one who writes left-handed), hold it in place ready for tightening, then recite the following blessing:

בָּרוּךְ *Blessed are You, HASHEM, our God, King of the universe, Who has sanctified us with His commandments and has commanded us to put on tefillin.*

Tighten the arm-*tefillin* and wrap the strap seven times around the arm. Without any interruption whatsoever, put the head-*tefillin* in place, above the hairline and opposite the space between the eyes. Before tightening the head-*tefillin* recite the following blessing:

בָּרוּךְ *Blessed are You, HASHEM, our God, King of the universe, Who has sanctified us with His commandments and has commanded us regarding the commandment of tefillin.*

Tighten the head-*tefillin* and recite:

Blessed is the Name of His glorious kingdom for all eternity.*

(1) *Deuteronomy* 6:8.

tefillin be worn only during *Shacharis.* The Sages teach that a man who recites the *Shema* and *Shemoneh Esrei* but does not wear *tefillin* is like one who bears false witness against himself (*Berachos* 14b). This is because *tefillin* and those two prayers are all symbolic of man's total submission to God. Thus, to utter the prayers without *tefillin* subtly implies a lack of sufficient submission (*R' Yonah,* ibid.).

בָּרוּךְ שֵׁם — *Blessed is the Name.* See commentary on page 91.

After the head-*tefillin* is securely in place, recite:

וּמֵחָכְמָתְךָ אֵל עֶלְיוֹן, תַּאֲצִיל עָלַי; וּמִבִּינָתְךָ תְּבִינֵנִי; וּבְחַסְדְּךָ תַּגְדִּיל עָלַי; וּבִגְבוּרָתְךָ תַּצְמִית אֹיְבַי וְקָמַי. וְשֶׁמֶן הַטּוֹב תָּרִיק עַל שִׁבְעָה קְנֵי הַמְּנוֹרָה, לְהַשְׁפִּיעַ טוּבְךָ לִבְרִיּוֹתֶיךָ. פּוֹתֵחַ אֶת יָדֶךָ, וּמַשְׂבִּיעַ לְכָל חַי רָצוֹן.[1]

Wrap the strap around the middle finger and hand according to your custom.
While doing this, recite:

וְאֵרַשְׂתִּיךְ לִי* לְעוֹלָם, וְאֵרַשְׂתִּיךְ לִי בְּצֶדֶק וּבְמִשְׁפָּט וּבְחֶסֶד וּבְרַחֲמִים. וְאֵרַשְׂתִּיךְ לִי בֶּאֱמוּנָה, וְיָדַעַתְּ אֶת יהוה.[2]

It is proper, while wearing *tefillin,* to recite the four Scriptural passages that are contained in the *tefillin.* Two of them — שְׁמַע and וְהָיָה אִם שָׁמֹעַ — will be recited later as part of *Krias Shema* (p. 90). The other two passages, given below, are recited either after putting on the *tefillin,* or before removing them.

שמות יג: א־י

וַיְדַבֵּר יהוה* אֶל מֹשֶׁה לֵּאמֹר: קַדֶּשׁ לִי כָל בְּכוֹר,* פֶּטֶר כָּל רֶחֶם בִּבְנֵי יִשְׂרָאֵל בָּאָדָם וּבַבְּהֵמָה,* לִי הוּא. וַיֹּאמֶר מֹשֶׁה אֶל הָעָם: זָכוֹר אֶת הַיּוֹם הַזֶּה אֲשֶׁר יְצָאתֶם מִמִּצְרַיִם, מִבֵּית עֲבָדִים, כִּי בְּחֹזֶק יָד הוֹצִיא יהוה אֶתְכֶם מִזֶּה, וְלֹא יֵאָכֵל חָמֵץ. הַיּוֹם אַתֶּם יֹצְאִים, בְּחֹדֶשׁ הָאָבִיב.* וְהָיָה כִי יְבִיאֲךָ יהוה אֶל אֶרֶץ הַכְּנַעֲנִי וְהַחִתִּי וְהָאֱמֹרִי וְהַחִוִּי וְהַיְבוּסִי אֲשֶׁר נִשְׁבַּע לַאֲבֹתֶיךָ לָתֶת לָךְ, אֶרֶץ זָבַת חָלָב וּדְבָשׁ, וְעָבַדְתָּ אֶת הָעֲבֹדָה הַזֹּאת בַּחֹדֶשׁ הַזֶּה. שִׁבְעַת יָמִים תֹּאכַל מַצֹּת,* וּבַיּוֹם הַשְּׁבִיעִי חַג* לַיהוה. מַצּוֹת יֵאָכֵל אֵת

⚜ **וְאֵרַשְׂתִּיךְ לִי** — *I will betroth you to Me.* God declares that Israel eternally remains His betrothed. This is symbolized by the wrapping of the *tefillin* strap around the fingers in the manner of a groom putting the betrothal ring on his bride's finger.

⚜ **וַיְדַבֵּר ה׳** — *HASHEM spoke.* God spoke these words to Moses immediately after the death of the Egyptian firstborns and the Exodus of the Jewish people from Egypt. The portion commands Israel forever to commemorate the Exodus in the form of specific commandments.

קַדֶּשׁ לִי כָל בְּכוֹר — *Sanctify to Me every firstborn.* In the most obvious sense, the sanctification of firstborn Jews is in commemoration of the fact that when God slew the Egyptian firstborn, He spared those of Israel. Although these firstborn are redeemed at the age of thirty days *(Numbers* 18:16), this commandment always keeps fresh in the Jewish mind that God has first claim, as it were, on its firstborn. In another sense, this unique sanctity of the first involves not only people, but firstborn domestic animals, first fruits, first crops and the various tithes. All of them are dedicated in one way or another to God's service. This particular chapter discusses human and animal firstborn; the others are discussed elsewhere in the Torah.

וּבַבְּהֵמָה — *And of beast.* Firstborn male cattle, sheep and goats are given to the *Kohen* to be offered on the Altar. But if the firstborn animal

After the head-*tefillin* is securely in place, recite:

וּמֵחָכְמָתְךָ *From Your wisdom, O supreme God, may You imbue me; from Your understanding give me understanding; with Your kindness do greatly with me; with Your power cut down my foes and rebels. [May] You pour goodly oil upon the seven arms of the menorah, to cause Your good to flow to Your creatures. [May] You open Your hand and satisfy the desire of every living thing.*[1]

Wrap the strap around the middle finger and hand according to your custom. While doing this, recite:

וְאֵרַשְׂתִּיךְ *I will betroth you to Me* forever, and I will betroth you to Me with righteousness, justice, kindness, and mercy. I will betroth you to Me with fidelity, and you shall know* HASHEM.[2]

It is proper, while wearing *tefillin,* to recite the four Scriptural passages that are contained in the *tefillin.* Two of them — שְׁמַע, *Shema,* and וְהָיָה אִם שָׁמֹעַ, *It will come to pass, if you will hearken* — will be recited later as part of *Krias Shema* (p. 90). The other two passages, given below, are recited either after putting on the *tefillin*, or before removing them.

Exodus 13:1-10

וַיְדַבֵּר HASHEM *spoke* to Moses, saying: Sanctify to Me every firstborn,* the first issue of every womb among the Children of Israel, both of man and of beast,* is Mine. Moses said to the people: Remember this day on which you departed from Egypt, from the house of bondage, for with a strong hand* HASHEM *removed you from here, and therefore no chametz may be eaten. Today you are leaving in the month of springtime.* And it will come to pass, when* HASHEM *shall bring you to the land of the Canaanites, Hittites, Emorites, Hivvites, and Jebusites, which He swore to your forefathers to give you — a land flowing with milk and honey — you shall perform this service in this month. Seven days you shall eat matzos,* and on the seventh day there shall be a festival* to* HASHEM. *Matzos shall be eaten throughout the*

(1) *Psalms* 145:16. (2) *Hoshea* 2:21-22.

has a physical blemish that renders it invalid as an offering, it becomes the personal property of the *Kohen* to use as he wishes.

בְּחֹדֶשׁ הָאָבִיב — *In the month of springtime.* This phrase is a key element in the Hebrew calendar because it ordains that Pesach, the festival of the Exodus, always occur in springtime. Since twelve ordinary lunar months have only 354 days, a thirteenth month is added to the Hebrew calendar seven times every nineteen years in order that Pesach will indeed fall in the spring. [The workings of the calendar are discussed at length in ArtScroll *Bircas HaChammah* and *Mishnah Rosh Hashanah.*] The relationship between spring and the Exodus symbolizes the idea that the Jewish people always remain fresh and filled with the potential for growth.

שִׁבְעַת יָמִים תֹּאכַל מַצֹּת — *Seven days you shall eat matzos.* The absolute requirement that one eat *matzah* applies only to the *Seder* night. This verse means that if one wishes to eat 'bread' at any time during Pesach, it must be *matzah.* The prohibition of *chametz,* however, applies throughout the festival.

וּבַיּוֹם הַשְּׁבִיעִי חַג — *And on the seventh day there shall be a festival.* The seventh day is a *Yom Tov* on which labor is forbidden. Outside of *Eretz Yisrael,* an eighth day is added to Pesach.

שִׁבְעַת הַיָּמִים, וְלֹא יֵרָאֶה לְךָ חָמֵץ,* וְלֹא יֵרָאֶה לְךָ שְׂאֹר בְּכָל גְּבֻלֶךָ. וְהִגַּדְתָּ לְבִנְךָ בַּיּוֹם הַהוּא לֵאמֹר: בַּעֲבוּר זֶה* עָשָׂה יהוה לִי בְּצֵאתִי מִמִּצְרָיִם. וְהָיָה לְךָ לְאוֹת עַל יָדְךָ,* וּלְזִכָּרוֹן בֵּין עֵינֶיךָ, לְמַעַן תִּהְיֶה תּוֹרַת יהוה בְּפִיךָ, כִּי בְּיָד חֲזָקָה הוֹצִאֲךָ יהוה מִמִּצְרָיִם. וְשָׁמַרְתָּ אֶת הַחֻקָּה הַזֹּאת לְמוֹעֲדָהּ, מִיָּמִים יָמִימָה.

שמות יג:יא־טז

וְהָיָה כִּי יְבִאֲךָ יהוה* אֶל אֶרֶץ הַכְּנַעֲנִי כַּאֲשֶׁר נִשְׁבַּע לְךָ וְלַאֲבֹתֶיךָ, וּנְתָנָהּ לָךְ. וְהַעֲבַרְתָּ כָל פֶּטֶר רֶחֶם לַיהוה, וְכָל פֶּטֶר שֶׁגֶר בְּהֵמָה אֲשֶׁר יִהְיֶה לְךָ, הַזְּכָרִים לַיהוה. וְכָל פֶּטֶר חֲמֹר תִּפְדֶּה בְשֶׂה,* וְאִם לֹא תִפְדֶּה וַעֲרַפְתּוֹ, וְכֹל בְּכוֹר אָדָם בְּבָנֶיךָ תִּפְדֶּה. וְהָיָה כִּי יִשְׁאָלְךָ בִנְךָ מָחָר לֵאמֹר, מַה זֹּאת,* וְאָמַרְתָּ אֵלָיו, בְּחֹזֶק יָד הוֹצִיאָנוּ יהוה מִמִּצְרַיִם מִבֵּית עֲבָדִים. וַיְהִי כִּי הִקְשָׁה פַרְעֹה לְשַׁלְּחֵנוּ, וַיַּהֲרֹג יהוה כָּל בְּכוֹר בְּאֶרֶץ מִצְרַיִם, מִבְּכֹר אָדָם וְעַד בְּכוֹר בְּהֵמָה, עַל כֵּן אֲנִי זֹבֵחַ לַיהוה כָּל פֶּטֶר רֶחֶם הַזְּכָרִים, וְכָל בְּכוֹר בָּנַי אֶפְדֶּה. וְהָיָה לְאוֹת עַל יָדְכָה וּלְטוֹטָפֹת* בֵּין עֵינֶיךָ, כִּי בְּחֹזֶק יָד הוֹצִיאָנוּ יהוה מִמִּצְרָיִם.

לֹא יֵרָאֶה לְךָ חָמֵץ — *No chametz may be seen in your possession.* This verse is the basis for the prohibition against keeping or owning *chametz* during Pesach. Among the familiar observances resulting from this commandment is the search for *chametz* the night before Pesach and the selling of *chametz* to a non-Jew.

בַּעֲבוּר זֶה — *It is because of this.* Tell your children that we were redeemed from Egypt because we were ready to observe God's commandments. In the Haggadah this verse is the answer to the wicked son who questions the purpose of fulfilling the commandments. He is told, *'It is because of this that HASHEM acted on* **my** *behalf* ... i.e., He acted to remove me from Egypt, but had you, the wicked son, been there, you would not have been redeemed.'

לְאוֹת עַל יָדְךָ — *As a sign on your arm.* As expressed in the לְשֵׁם יִחוּד prayer, the placement of *tefillin* symbolizes that we subjugate our physical strength, the arm, and our soul and intellect, the head, to the service of God.

וְהָיָה כִּי יְבִאֲךָ ה׳ — *And it shall come to pass, when HASHEM will bring you.* The Talmud (*Bechoros* 4b-5a) offers two versions: either the consecration of the firstborn would affect only those born after the Jewish nation was brought into *Eretz Yisrael;* or the nation would earn its right to the Holy Land in the merit of sanctifying the firstborn.

וְכָל פֶּטֶר חֲמֹר תִּפְדֶּה בְשֶׂה — *Every first issue donkey you shall redeem with a lamb or kid.* In Hebrew, the word שֶׂה refers to the young of both sheep

seven days; no chametz may be seen in your possession, nor may leaven be seen in your possession in all your borders. And you shall tell your son on that day, saying: 'It is because of this* that HASHEM acted on my behalf when I left Egypt.' And it shall serve you as a sign on your arm* and as a reminder between your eyes — so that HASHEM's Torah may be in your mouth; for with a strong hand HASHEM removed you from Egypt. And you shall observe this ordinance at its designated time from year to year.*

Exodus 13:11-16

וְהָיָה *And it shall come to pass, when HASHEM will bring you* to the land of the Canaanites as He swore to you and your forefathers, and will have given it to you. Then you shall set apart every first issue of the womb to HASHEM, and every first issue that is dropped by cattle that belong to you, the males shall belong to HASHEM. Every first issue donkey you shall redeem with a lamb or kid;* if you do not redeem it, then you must axe the back of its neck. And you must redeem every human firstborn among your sons. And it shall be when your son asks you at some future time, 'What is this?'* you shall answer him, 'With a strong hand HASHEM removed us from Egypt, from the house of bondage. And it happened, when Pharaoh stubbornly refused to let us go, that HASHEM killed all the firstborn in the land of Egypt, from the firstborn of man to the firstborn of beast. Therefore, I sacrifice to HASHEM all first male issue of the womb, and redeem all the firstborn of my sons.' And it shall be a sign upon your arm and totafos* between your eyes, for with a strong hand HASHEM removed us from Egypt.*

---

and goats (as, for example, in *Genesis* 30:32, *Numbers* 15:11, and *Deuteronomy* 14:4). There is no equivalent word in English, therefore we are forced to translate שֶׂה as *lamb or kid.*

The donkey is the only non-kosher animal that has the privileged status of the firstborn. Although the Talmud *(Bechoros* 5b) refers to this as a decree, it also offers the reason that this commandment is a memorial of the Exodus when the Jews left Egypt with countless donkeys laden with the riches of the land. *Rashi* suggests also that the donkey recalls the plague on the Egyptians who were likened to donkeys *(Ezekiel* 23:20).

Since a donkey cannot be consecrated as an offering, it is redeemed with a lamb or kid, which becomes the private property of a *Kohen* while the donkey may be used unrestrictedly by its owner. Should the Israelite owner refuse to redeem his donkey, he is denied its use: he must put it to death instantly by administering a blow with an axe to the back of the neck.

מַה זֹּאת — *What is this?* In the Haggadah, this question is ascribed to the simple child, who wishes to learn but cannot analyze the Seder service very well.

טוֹטָפֹת — *Totafos.* Many interpretations are given for this untranslatable word; all agree, however, that it refers to the *tefillin* on the head.

ברכות השחר

Recite the following collection of verses upon entering the synagogue:

מַה טֹּבוּ אֹהָלֶיךָ* יַעֲקֹב, מִשְׁכְּנֹתֶיךָ יִשְׂרָאֵל.[1] וַאֲנִי בְּרֹב
חַסְדְּךָ אָבוֹא בֵיתֶךָ, אֶשְׁתַּחֲוֶה אֶל הֵיכַל קָדְשְׁךָ
בְּיִרְאָתֶךָ.[2] יהוה אָהַבְתִּי מְעוֹן בֵּיתֶךָ, וּמְקוֹם מִשְׁכַּן כְּבוֹדֶךָ.[3]
וַאֲנִי אֶשְׁתַּחֲוֶה וְאֶכְרָעָה, אֶבְרְכָה לִפְנֵי יהוה עֹשִׂי.[4] וַאֲנִי,
תְפִלָּתִי לְךָ יהוה, עֵת רָצוֹן, אֱלֹהִים בְּרָב חַסְדֶּךָ, עֲנֵנִי בֶּאֱמֶת
יִשְׁעֶךָ.[5]

אֲדוֹן עוֹלָם* אֲשֶׁר מָלַךְ, בְּטֶרֶם כָּל יְצִיר נִבְרָא.
לְעֵת נַעֲשָׂה בְחֶפְצוֹ כֹּל, אֲזַי מֶלֶךְ שְׁמוֹ נִקְרָא.
וְאַחֲרֵי כִּכְלוֹת הַכֹּל, לְבַדּוֹ יִמְלוֹךְ נוֹרָא.
וְהוּא הָיָה וְהוּא הֹוֶה, וְהוּא יִהְיֶה בְּתִפְאָרָה.
וְהוּא אֶחָד וְאֵין שֵׁנִי, לְהַמְשִׁיל לוֹ לְהַחְבִּירָה.
בְּלִי רֵאשִׁית בְּלִי תַכְלִית, וְלוֹ הָעֹז וְהַמִּשְׂרָה.
וְהוּא אֵלִי וְחַי גֹּאֲלִי, וְצוּר חֶבְלִי בְּעֵת צָרָה.
וְהוּא נִסִּי וּמָנוֹס לִי, מְנָת כּוֹסִי בְּיוֹם אֶקְרָא.
בְּיָדוֹ אַפְקִיד רוּחִי, בְּעֵת אִישַׁן וְאָעִירָה.
וְעִם רוּחִי גְּוִיָּתִי, יהוה לִי וְלֹא אִירָא.

יִגְדַּל אֱלֹהִים חַי* וְיִשְׁתַּבַּח, נִמְצָא וְאֵין עֵת אֶל מְצִיאוּתוֹ.*
אֶחָד וְאֵין יָחִיד כְּיִחוּדוֹ, נֶעְלָם וְגַם אֵין סוֹף לְאַחְדּוּתוֹ.

בִּרְכוֹת הַשַּׁחַר / MORNING BLESSINGS

מַה טֹּבוּ אֹהָלֶיךָ — *How goodly are your tents.* The Sages interpret this praise of Israel as a reference to its 'tents of learning and prayer. In a deeper sense, the Jewish home achieves its highest level when it incorporates the values of the synagogue and study hall. This collection of verses expresses love and reverence for the synagogue that, in the absence of the Holy Temple, is *the place where God's glory resides* among Israel.

אֲדוֹן עוֹלָם — *Master of the universe.* This inspiring song of praise is attributed to R' Shlomo ibn Gabirol, one of the greatest early *paytanim* [liturgical poets], who flourished in the eleventh century. The daily prayer service is inaugurated with the Name אֲדוֹן to recall the merit of Abraham, the first one to address God with this title [*Genesis* 15:2] *(Etz Yosef)*, and the one who instituted the morning prayers [*Berachos* 26b] *(Vilna Gaon)*.

The song emphasizes that God is timeless, infinite and omnipotent. Mankind can offer Him only one thing: to proclaim Him as King, by doing His will and praising Him. Despite God's greatness, however, He involves Himself with man's personal needs in time of pain and distress. The prayer concludes on the inspiring note that, lofty though He is, *HASHEM is with me, I shall not fear.*

יִגְדַּל אֱלֹהִים חַי — *Exalted be the Living God.* This song of uncertain authorship summarizes the 'Thirteen Principles of Faith' expounded by *Rambam* [Maimonides] in his *Commentary to Mishnah, Sanhedrin,* ch. 10, and stated succinctly in the famous *Ani Maamin* prayer (p. 178, see commentary there). They comprise the

MORNING BLESSINGS

Recite the following collection of verses upon entering the synagogue:

מַה טֹּבוּ *How goodly are your tents,* O Jacob, your dwelling places, O Israel.*[1] *As for me, through Your abundant kindness I will enter Your House; I will prostrate myself toward Your Holy Sanctuary in awe of You.*[2] *O* HASHEM, *I love the House where You dwell, and the place where Your glory resides.*[3] *I shall prostrate myself and bow, I shall kneel before* HASHEM *my Maker.*[4] *As for me, may my prayer to You,* HASHEM, *be at an opportune time; O God, in Your abundant kindness, answer me with the truth of Your salvation.*[5]

אֲדוֹן עוֹלָם *Master of the universe,* Who reigned*
before any form was created,
At the time when His will brought all into being —
then as 'King' was His Name proclaimed.
After all has ceased to be,
He, the Awesome One, will reign alone.
It is He Who was, He Who is,
and He Who shall remain, in splendor.
He is One — there is no second
to compare to Him, to declare as His equal.
Without beginning, without conclusion —
His is the power and dominion.
He is my God, my living Redeemer,
Rock of my pain in time of distress.
He is my banner, a refuge for me,
the portion in my cup on the day I call.
Into His hand I shall entrust my spirit
when I go to sleep — and I shall awaken!
With my spirit shall my body remain.
HASHEM *is with me, I shall not fear.*

יִגְדַּל *Exalted be the Living God* and praised,*
*He exists — unbounded by time is His existence.**
He is One — and there is no unity like His Oneness.
Inscrutable and infinite is His Oneness.

(1) *Numbers* 24:5. (2) *Psalms* 5:8. (3) 26:8. (4) Cf. 95:6. (5) 69:14.

basic principles that every Jew is required to believe. In *Rambam's* view to deny any of them constitutes heresy.

וְאֵין עֵת אֶל מְצִיאוּתוֹ — *Unbounded by time is His existence.* If God's existence were timebound, it would be no different in kind from that of any living, but not eternal, being. *Rambam* comments that the principle of God's timelessness, with neither beginning nor end, implies that He cannot be dependent in any way on any other being: the timebound is inherently inferior to the timeless. Nothing can exist without God, but He depends on no one and on nothing.

אֵין לוֹ דְּמוּת הַגּוּף וְאֵינוֹ גוּף,* לֹא נַעֲרוֹךְ אֵלָיו קְדֻשָּׁתוֹ.
קַדְמוֹן לְכָל דָּבָר אֲשֶׁר נִבְרָא, רִאשׁוֹן וְאֵין רֵאשִׁית לְרֵאשִׁיתוֹ.
הִנּוֹ אֲדוֹן עוֹלָם* לְכָל נוֹצָר, יוֹרֶה גְדֻלָּתוֹ וּמַלְכוּתוֹ.
שֶׁפַע נְבוּאָתוֹ* נְתָנוֹ, אֶל אַנְשֵׁי סְגֻלָּתוֹ וְתִפְאַרְתּוֹ.
לֹא קָם בְּיִשְׂרָאֵל כְּמֹשֶׁה* עוֹד, נָבִיא וּמַבִּיט אֶת תְּמוּנָתוֹ.
תּוֹרַת אֱמֶת* נָתַן לְעַמּוֹ אֵל, עַל יַד נְבִיאוֹ נֶאֱמַן בֵּיתוֹ.
לֹא יַחֲלִיף הָאֵל וְלֹא יָמִיר דָּתוֹ, לְעוֹלָמִים לְזוּלָתוֹ.
צוֹפֶה וְיוֹדֵעַ סְתָרֵינוּ, מַבִּיט לְסוֹף דָּבָר בְּקַדְמָתוֹ.
גּוֹמֵל לְאִישׁ חֶסֶד כְּמִפְעָלוֹ, נוֹתֵן לְרָשָׁע רָע כְּרִשְׁעָתוֹ.
יִשְׁלַח לְקֵץ הַיָּמִין מְשִׁיחֵנוּ, לִפְדּוֹת מְחַכֵּי קֵץ יְשׁוּעָתוֹ.
מֵתִים יְחַיֶּה אֵל בְּרֹב חַסְדּוֹ, בָּרוּךְ עֲדֵי עַד שֵׁם תְּהִלָּתוֹ.

Although many hold that the blessing עַל נְטִילַת יָדָיִם should be recited immediately after the ritual washing of the hands upon arising, others customarily recite it at this point. Similarly, some recite אֲשֶׁר יָצַר immediately after relieving themselves in the morning, while others recite it here.

בָּרוּךְ אַתָּה יהוה אֱלֹהֵינוּ מֶלֶךְ הָעוֹלָם, אֲשֶׁר קִדְּשָׁנוּ בְּמִצְוֹתָיו, וְצִוָּנוּ עַל נְטִילַת יָדָיִם.*

בָּרוּךְ אַתָּה יהוה אֱלֹהֵינוּ מֶלֶךְ הָעוֹלָם, אֲשֶׁר יָצַר אֶת הָאָדָם בְּחָכְמָה,* וּבָרָא בוֹ נְקָבִים נְקָבִים, חֲלוּלִים* חֲלוּלִים. גָּלוּי וְיָדוּעַ לִפְנֵי כִסֵּא כְבוֹדֶךָ, שֶׁאִם יִפָּתֵחַ אֶחָד מֵהֶם, אוֹ יִסָּתֵם אֶחָד מֵהֶם, אִי אֶפְשַׁר לְהִתְקַיֵּם וְלַעֲמוֹד לְפָנֶיךָ. בָּרוּךְ אַתָּה יהוה, רוֹפֵא כָל בָּשָׂר וּמַפְלִיא לַעֲשׂוֹת.*

At this point, some recite אֱלֹהַי נְשָׁמָה, (p. 18).

וְאֵינוֹ גוּף — *Nor is He corporeal.* God has no physicality, not even that of invisible, intangible angels.

הִנּוֹ אֲדוֹן עוֹלָם — *Behold! He is Master of the universe.* Because He is absolute Master, there is nothing else to which prayers may be directed.

שֶׁפַע נְבוּאָתוֹ — *His flow of prophecy.* Judaism depends on the principle that God, through His prophets, revealed His will to Israel.

כְּמֹשֶׁה — *Like Moses.* It is necessary to acknowledge that Moses' prophecy is unparalleled; otherwise another 'prophet' could conceivably challenge or amend it, thus challenging the authenticity of the Torah.

תּוֹרַת אֱמֶת — *A Torah of truth.* God gave Moses not only the Written Law, but the Oral Law as well. Neither is complete without the other, and *Torah of truth* is a term that includes both.

⊶ **עַל נְטִילַת יָדָיִם** — *Regarding washing the hands.* In the case of blessings, the general rule is that they should be recited in conjunction with the acts to which they apply. Nevertheless, some postpone the blessings עַל נְטִילַת יָדָיִם for washing the hands and אֲשֶׁר יָצַר for relieving oneself so that they will be recited as part of *Shacharis* (see *Mishnah Berurah* 4:4 and 6:9).

⊶ **אֲשֶׁר יָצַר אֶת הָאָדָם בְּחָכְמָה** — *Who fashioned man with wisdom.* This phrase has two meanings: (a) When God created man, He gave him the gift of wisdom; and (b) God used wisdom when He created man, as is

*He has no semblance of a body nor is He corporeal;**
nor has His holiness any comparison.
He preceded every being that was created —
the First, and nothing precedes His precedence.
Behold! He is Master of the universe to every creature,*
He demonstrates His greatness and His sovereignty.
*He granted His flow of prophecy**
to His treasured splendrous people.
In Israel none like Moses arose again —*
a prophet who perceived His vision clearly.
*God gave His people a Torah of truth,**
by means of His prophet, the most trusted of His household.
God will never amend nor exchange His law
for any other one, for all eternity.
He scrutinizes and knows our hiddenmost secrets;
He perceives a matter's outcome at its inception.
He recompenses man with kindness according to his deed;
He places evil on the wicked according to his wickedness.
By the End of Days He will send our Messiah,
to redeem those longing for His final salvation.
God will revive the dead in His abundant kindness —
Blessed forever is His praised Name.

Although many hold that the blessing עַל נְטִילַת יָדָיִם, *'... regarding washing of the hands,'* should be recited immediately after the ritual washing of the hands upon arising, others customarily recite it at this point. Similarly, some recite אֲשֶׁר יָצַר, *'Who fashioned ...,'* immediately after relieving themselves in the morning, while others recite it here.

בָּרוּךְ *Blessed are You, HASHEM, our God, King of the universe, Who has sanctified us with His commandments and has commanded us regarding washing the hands.**

בָּרוּךְ *Blessed are You, HASHEM, our God, King of the universe, Who fashioned man with wisdom* and created within him many openings and many cavities.* It is obvious and known before Your Throne of Glory that if but one of them were to be ruptured or but one of them were to be blocked it would be impossible to survive and to stand before You. Blessed are You, HASHEM, Who heals all flesh and acts wondrously.**

At this point, some recite אֱלֹהַי נְשָׁמָה, *'My God, the soul ...,'* (p. 18).

---

demonstrated in the precise balance of his organs and functions.

נְקָבִים, חֲלוּלִים — *Openings and cavities.* The mouth, nostrils, and other orifices are the *openings* that lead in and out of the body. The *cavities* are the inner hollows that contain such organs as the lungs, heart, stomach, and brain.

וּמַפְלִיא לַעֲשׂוֹת — *And acts wondrously.* The delicate balance of the organs is a wonder of wonders *(Beis Yosef);* alternatively, it is wondrous that the spiritual soul fuses with the physical body to create a human being *(Rama).*

ברכות התורה

It is forbidden to study or recite Torah passages before reciting the following blessings. Since the commandment to study Torah is in effect all day long, these blessings need not be repeated if one studies at various times of the day. Although many *siddurim* begin a new paragraph at וְהַעֲרֶב נָא, according to the vast majority of commentators the first blessing does not end until לְעַמּוֹ יִשְׂרָאֵל.

בָּרוּךְ אַתָּה יהוה אֱלֹהֵינוּ מֶלֶךְ הָעוֹלָם, אֲשֶׁר קִדְּשָׁנוּ בְּמִצְוֹתָיו, וְצִוָּנוּ לַעֲסוֹק בְּדִבְרֵי תוֹרָה. וְהַעֲרֶב נָא יהוה אֱלֹהֵינוּ אֶת דִּבְרֵי תוֹרָתְךָ בְּפִינוּ וּבְפִי עַמְּךָ בֵּית יִשְׂרָאֵל. וְנִהְיֶה אֲנַחְנוּ וְצֶאֱצָאֵינוּ וְצֶאֱצָאֵי עַמְּךָ בֵּית יִשְׂרָאֵל, כֻּלָּנוּ יוֹדְעֵי שְׁמֶךָ וְלוֹמְדֵי תוֹרָתֶךָ לִשְׁמָהּ.* בָּרוּךְ אַתָּה יהוה, הַמְלַמֵּד תּוֹרָה לְעַמּוֹ יִשְׂרָאֵל.

בָּרוּךְ אַתָּה יהוה אֱלֹהֵינוּ מֶלֶךְ הָעוֹלָם, אֲשֶׁר בָּחַר בָּנוּ מִכָּל הָעַמִּים וְנָתַן לָנוּ אֶת תּוֹרָתוֹ. בָּרוּךְ אַתָּה יהוה, נוֹתֵן הַתּוֹרָה.

במדבר ו:כד־כו

יְבָרֶכְךָ יהוה וְיִשְׁמְרֶךָ. יָאֵר יהוה פָּנָיו אֵלֶיךָ וִיחֻנֶּךָּ. יִשָּׂא יהוה פָּנָיו אֵלֶיךָ, וְיָשֵׂם לְךָ שָׁלוֹם.

משנה, פאה א:א

אֵלּוּ דְבָרִים שֶׁאֵין לָהֶם שִׁעוּר:* הַפֵּאָה וְהַבִּכּוּרִים וְהָרַאְיוֹן* וּגְמִילוּת חֲסָדִים וְתַלְמוּד תּוֹרָה.

שבת קכז.

אֵלּוּ דְבָרִים שֶׁאָדָם אוֹכֵל פֵּרוֹתֵיהֶם בָּעוֹלָם הַזֶּה וְהַקֶּרֶן קַיֶּמֶת לוֹ* לָעוֹלָם הַבָּא. וְאֵלּוּ הֵן: כִּבּוּד אָב וָאֵם, וּגְמִילוּת חֲסָדִים, וְהַשְׁכָּמַת בֵּית הַמִּדְרָשׁ שַׁחֲרִית וְעַרְבִית, וְהַכְנָסַת אוֹרְחִים, וּבִקּוּר חוֹלִים, וְהַכְנָסַת כַּלָּה, וּלְוָיַת הַמֵּת, וְעִיּוּן תְּפִלָּה, וַהֲבָאַת שָׁלוֹם בֵּין אָדָם לַחֲבֵרוֹ — וְתַלְמוּד תּוֹרָה כְּנֶגֶד כֻּלָּם.

בִּרְכוֹת הַתּוֹרָה / Blessings of the Torah

As stated explicitly in the Talmudic selection [אֵלּוּ דְבָרִים] at the conclusion of these blessings, the study of Torah is the paramount commandment. Without it, man cannot know God's will; with it he can penetrate the wisdom of the Creator Himself. Each part of the blessings expresses a different idea. The first, אֲשֶׁר קִדְּשָׁנוּ, *Who has sanctified us*, applies to the commandments; the second, וְהַעֲרֶב נָא, *Sweeten the words*, is a prayer; the third, אֲשֶׁר בָּחַר בָּנוּ, *Who selected us*, is an expression of thanks for the gift of the Torah.

לִשְׁמָהּ — *For its own sake.* May we study Torah for no other reason than to know it and become imbued with its wisdom.

Selections from the Written and Oral Torah

Whenever a blessing is recited for a *mitzvah*, the *mitzvah* must be performed immediately. Having recited the blessings for the study of

BLESSINGS OF THE TORAH

It is forbidden to study or recite Torah passages before reciting the following blessings. Since the commandment to study Torah is in effect all day long, these blessings need not be repeated if one studies at various times of the day. Although many *siddurim* begin a new paragraph at וְהַעֲרֶב נָא, *'Please, HASHEM,'* according to the vast majority of commentators the first blessing does not end until לְעַמּוֹ יִשְׂרָאֵל, *'... His people Israel.'*

בָּרוּךְ *Blessed are You, HASHEM, our God, King of the universe, Who has sanctified us with His commandments and has commanded us to engross ourselves in the words of Torah. Please, HASHEM, our God, sweeten the words of Your Torah in our mouth and in the mouth of Your people, the family of Israel. May we and our offspring and the offspring of Your people, the House of Israel — all of us — know Your Name and study Your Torah for its own sake.* Blessed are You, HASHEM, Who teaches Torah to His people Israel.*

בָּרוּךְ *Blessed are You, HASHEM, our God, King of the universe, Who selected us from all the peoples and gave us His Torah. Blessed are You, HASHEM, Giver of the Torah.*

Numbers 6:24-26

יְבָרֶכְךָ *May HASHEM bless you and safeguard you. May HASHEM illuminate His countenance for you and be gracious to you. May HASHEM turn His countenance to you and establish peace for you.*

Mishnah, *Peah* 1:1

אֵלּוּ דְבָרִים *These are the precepts that have no prescribed measure:* the corner of a field [which must be left for the poor], the first-fruit offering, the pilgrimage,* acts of kindness, and Torah study.*

Talmud, *Shabbos* 127a

אֵלּוּ דְבָרִים *These are the precepts whose fruits a person enjoys in This World but whose principal remains intact for him* in the World to Come. They are: the honor due to father and mother, acts of kindness, early attendance at the house of study morning and evening, hospitality to guests, visiting the sick, providing for a bride, escorting the dead, absorption in prayer, bringing peace between man and his fellow — and the study of Torah is equivalent to them all.*

Torah, we immediately recite selections from both the Written and Oral Torah. First we recite the Scriptural verses of the Priestly Blessings (for commentary, see p. 116), then a Talmudic selection from the *Mishnah* [אֵלּוּ דְבָרִים שֶׁאֵין] *(Peah* 1:1) and *Gemara* [אֵלּוּ דְבָרִים שֶׁאָדָם] *(Shabbos* 127a). The Talmudic selection discusses the reward for various commandments and concludes with the declaration that Torah study is equivalent to them all, an appropriate addendum to the Blessings of the Torah.

☙ **אֵלּוּ דְבָרִים שֶׁאֵין לָהֶם שִׁעוּר** — *These are the precepts that have no prescribed measure.* The Torah does not prescribe how much is involved in the performance of the following commandments *(Rav).*

וְהָרֵאָיוֹן — *The pilgrimage.* Though the Torah ordains that a Jew visit the Temple on each of the three festivals (Pesach, Shavuos, and Succos), one may visit as often as he wishes. Alternatively, there is no set amount for the value of the elevation-offering [עוֹלַת רְאִיָּה] that one must bring at such times.

וְהַקֶּרֶן קַיֶּמֶת לוֹ — *But whose principal remains intact for him.* Though one is rewarded for these *mitzvos* in This World, his reward in the World to Come is not diminished.

אֱלֹהַי, נְשָׁמָה* שֶׁנָּתַתָּ בִּי טְהוֹרָה הִיא. אַתָּה בְרָאתָהּ אַתָּה יְצַרְתָּהּ, אַתָּה נְפַחְתָּהּ בִּי, וְאַתָּה מְשַׁמְּרָהּ בְּקִרְבִּי, וְאַתָּה עָתִיד לִטְּלָהּ מִמֶּנִּי, וּלְהַחֲזִירָהּ בִּי לֶעָתִיד לָבֹא. כָּל זְמַן שֶׁהַנְּשָׁמָה בְקִרְבִּי, מוֹדֶה אֲנִי לְפָנֶיךָ, יהוה אֱלֹהַי וֵאלֹהֵי אֲבוֹתַי, רִבּוֹן כָּל הַמַּעֲשִׂים, אֲדוֹן כָּל הַנְּשָׁמוֹת. בָּרוּךְ אַתָּה יהוה, הַמַּחֲזִיר נְשָׁמוֹת לִפְגָרִים מֵתִים.

The *chazzan* recites the following blessings aloud, and the congregation responds אָמֵן to each blessing. Nevertheless, each person must recite these blessings for himself. Some people recite the blessings aloud for one another so that each one can have the merit of responding אָמֵן many times (see commentary).

בָּרוּךְ* אַתָּה יהוה אֱלֹהֵינוּ מֶלֶךְ הָעוֹלָם, אֲשֶׁר נָתַן לַשֶּׂכְוִי בִינָה*[1] לְהַבְחִין בֵּין יוֹם וּבֵין לָיְלָה.

בָּרוּךְ אַתָּה יהוה אֱלֹהֵינוּ מֶלֶךְ הָעוֹלָם, שֶׁלֹּא עָשַׂנִי גּוֹי.*

בָּרוּךְ אַתָּה יהוה אֱלֹהֵינוּ מֶלֶךְ הָעוֹלָם, שֶׁלֹּא עָשַׂנִי עָבֶד.*

Men say:

בָּרוּךְ אַתָּה יהוה אֱלֹהֵינוּ מֶלֶךְ הָעוֹלָם, שֶׁלֹּא עָשַׂנִי אִשָּׁה.*

Women say:

בָּרוּךְ אַתָּה יהוה אֱלֹהֵינוּ מֶלֶךְ הָעוֹלָם, שֶׁעָשַׂנִי כִּרְצוֹנוֹ.

בָּרוּךְ אַתָּה יהוה אֱלֹהֵינוּ מֶלֶךְ הָעוֹלָם, פּוֹקֵחַ עִוְרִים.[2]

בָּרוּךְ אַתָּה יהוה אֱלֹהֵינוּ מֶלֶךְ הָעוֹלָם, מַלְבִּישׁ עֲרֻמִּים.

בָּרוּךְ אַתָּה יהוה אֱלֹהֵינוּ מֶלֶךְ הָעוֹלָם, מַתִּיר אֲסוּרִים.[3]

בָּרוּךְ אַתָּה יהוה אֱלֹהֵינוּ מֶלֶךְ הָעוֹלָם, זוֹקֵף כְּפוּפִים.[2]

⁂ **אֱלֹהַי, נְשָׁמָה** — *My God, the soul ...* This prayerful blessing is an expression of gratitude to God for restoring our vitality in the morning with a soul of pure, celestial origin, and for maintaining us in life and health.

⁂ **בָּרוּךְ** — *Blessed.* This series of fifteen blessings is based on *Berachos* 60b, where the Sages teach that as one experiences the phenomena of the new day, he should bless God for providing them. For example, one thanks God for giving man the crucial ability to make distinctions in life, such as that between day and night; when he rubs his eyes and sees; when he gets dressed, and so on. Some of these phenomena are not so obvious from the text of the blessing. Among them are: sitting up and stretching [*releases the bound*]; getting out of bed [*straightens the bent*]; standing on the floor [*spreads out the earth ...*]; donning shoes which symbolizes man's ability to go on his way comfortably [*provided me my every need*]; setting out on one's destination [*firms ... footsteps*]; fastening one's clothing [*girds Israel ...*]; putting on a hat, which symbolizes the Jew's reminder that Someone is above him [*crowns Israel ...*]; feeling the passing of nighttime exhaustion [*gives strength ...* and *removes sleep ...*].

Arizal teaches that each day a righteous person should endeavor to respond to a minimum of ninety blessings, four times *Kedushah* (i.e., the verse קָדוֹשׁ קָדוֹשׁ קָדוֹשׁ, *Holy, Holy, Holy ...*), ten times *Kaddish*, and to recite no less than one hundred blessings. These figures are alluded to by the letters of the word צַדִּיק, *righteous one*, which have the numerical equivalents of 90, 4, 10, and 100 respectively. To assure ninety *Amen* responses, some people recite these fifteen blessings aloud for one another.

אֲשֶׁר נָתַן לַשֶּׂכְוִי בִינָה — *Who gave the heart understanding.* The word שֶׂכְוִי means both *heart* and *rooster.* In the context of this blessing, both meanings are implied: the rooster crows, but man's heart reacts and understands how to deal with new situations *(Rosh).*

אֱלֹהַי *My God, the soul* You placed within me is pure. You created it, You fashioned it, You breathed it into me, You safeguard it within me, and eventually You will take it from me, and restore it to me in Time to Come. As long as the soul is within me, I gratefully thank You,* HASHEM, *my God and the God of my forefathers, Master of all works, Lord of all souls. Blessed are You,* HASHEM, *Who restores souls to dead bodies.*

The *chazzan* recites the following blessings aloud, and the congregation responds *'Amen'* to each blessing. Nevertheless, each person must recite these blessings for himself. Some people recite the blessings aloud for one another so that each one can have the merit of responding *Amen* many times (see commentary).

בָּרוּךְ *Blessed* are You,* HASHEM, *our God, King of the universe, Who gave the heart understanding**[1] *to distinguish between day and night.*

Blessed are You, HASHEM, *our God, King of the universe, for not having made me a gentile.**

Blessed are You, HASHEM, *our God, King of the universe, for not having made me a slave.**

Men say:	Women say:
Blessed are You, HASHEM, *our God, King of the universe, for not having made me a woman.**	*Blessed are You,* HASHEM, *our God, King of the universe, for having made me according to His will.*

Blessed are You, HASHEM, *our God, King of the universe, Who gives sight to the blind.*[2]

Blessed are You, HASHEM, *our God, King of the universe, Who clothes the naked.*

Blessed are You, HASHEM, *our God, King of the universe, Who releases the bound.*[3]

Blessed are You, HASHEM, *our God, King of the universe, Who straightens the bent.*[2]

(1) Cf. *Job* 38:36. (2) *Psalms* 146:8. (3) v. 7.

שֶׁלֹּא עָשַׂנִי גּוֹי ... עָבֶד ... אִשָּׁה — *For not having made me a gentile ... a slave ... a woman.* The Torah assigns missions to respective groups of people. Within Israel, for example, the Davidic family, *Kohanim,* and Levites are set apart by virtue of their particular callings, in addition to their shared mission as Jews. All such missions carry extra responsibilities and call for the performance of the *mitzvos* associated with them. We thank God, therefore, for the challenge of improving His universe in accordance with His will. Male, free Jews have responsibilities and duties not shared by others. For this, they express gratitude that, unlike women, they were *not* freed from the obligation to perform the time-related commandments. This follows the Talmudic dictum that an obligatory performance of a commandment is superior to a voluntary one, because it is human nature to resist obligations [גָּדוֹל הַמְצֻוֶּה וְעוֹשֶׂה מִמִּי שֶׁאֵינוֹ מְצֻוֶּה וְעוֹשֶׂה]. Women, on the other hand, both historically and because of their nature, are the guardians of tradition, the molders of character, children, and family. Furthermore, women have often been the protectors of Judaism when the impetuosity and aggressiveness of the male nature led the men astray. The classic precedent was in the Wilderness when the men — not the women — worshiped the Golden Calf. Thus, though women were not given the privilege of the challenge assigned to men, they are created closer to God's ideal of satisfaction. They express

בָּרוּךְ אַתָּה יהוה אֱלֹהֵינוּ מֶלֶךְ הָעוֹלָם, רוֹקַע הָאָרֶץ עַל הַמָּיִם.*[1]

בָּרוּךְ אַתָּה יהוה אֱלֹהֵינוּ מֶלֶךְ הָעוֹלָם, שֶׁעָשָׂה לִי כָּל צָרְכִּי.

בָּרוּךְ אַתָּה יהוה אֱלֹהֵינוּ מֶלֶךְ הָעוֹלָם, הַמֵּכִין מִצְעֲדֵי גָבֶר.[2]

בָּרוּךְ אַתָּה יהוה אֱלֹהֵינוּ מֶלֶךְ הָעוֹלָם, אוֹזֵר יִשְׂרָאֵל בִּגְבוּרָה.

בָּרוּךְ אַתָּה יהוה אֱלֹהֵינוּ מֶלֶךְ הָעוֹלָם, עוֹטֵר יִשְׂרָאֵל בְּתִפְאָרָה.

בָּרוּךְ אַתָּה יהוה אֱלֹהֵינוּ מֶלֶךְ הָעוֹלָם, הַנּוֹתֵן לַיָּעֵף כֹּחַ.[3]

Although many *siddurim* begin a new paragraph at וִיהִי רָצוֹן, the following is one long blessing that ends at לְעַמּוֹ יִשְׂרָאֵל.

בָּרוּךְ אַתָּה יהוה אֱלֹהֵינוּ מֶלֶךְ הָעוֹלָם, הַמַּעֲבִיר שֵׁנָה מֵעֵינָי וּתְנוּמָה מֵעַפְעַפָּי. וִיהִי רָצוֹן* מִלְּפָנֶיךָ, יהוה אֱלֹהֵינוּ וֵאלֹהֵי אֲבוֹתֵינוּ, שֶׁתַּרְגִּילֵנוּ בְּתוֹרָתֶךָ וְדַבְּקֵנוּ בְּמִצְוֹתֶיךָ, וְאַל תְּבִיאֵנוּ לֹא לִידֵי חֵטְא,* וְלֹא לִידֵי עֲבֵרָה וְעָוֹן, וְלֹא לִידֵי נִסָּיוֹן, וְלֹא לִידֵי בִזָּיוֹן, וְאַל תַּשְׁלֶט בָּנוּ יֵצֶר הָרָע. וְהַרְחִיקֵנוּ מֵאָדָם רָע וּמֵחָבֵר רָע. וְדַבְּקֵנוּ בְּיֵצֶר הַטּוֹב וּבְמַעֲשִׂים טוֹבִים, וְכוֹף אֶת יִצְרֵנוּ לְהִשְׁתַּעְבֶּד לָךְ. וּתְנֵנוּ הַיּוֹם וּבְכָל יוֹם לְחֵן וּלְחֶסֶד וּלְרַחֲמִים בְּעֵינֶיךָ, וּבְעֵינֵי כָל רוֹאֵינוּ, וְתִגְמְלֵנוּ חֲסָדִים טוֹבִים. בָּרוּךְ אַתָּה יהוה, גּוֹמֵל חֲסָדִים טוֹבִים לְעַמּוֹ יִשְׂרָאֵל.

יְהִי רָצוֹן* מִלְּפָנֶיךָ, יהוה אֱלֹהַי וֵאלֹהֵי אֲבוֹתַי, שֶׁתַּצִּילֵנִי הַיּוֹם וּבְכָל יוֹם מֵעַזֵּי פָנִים וּמֵעַזּוּת פָּנִים, מֵאָדָם רָע, וּמֵחָבֵר רָע, וּמִשָּׁכֵן רָע, וּמִפֶּגַע רָע, וּמִשָּׂטָן הַמַּשְׁחִית, מִדִּין קָשֶׁה וּמִבַּעַל דִּין קָשֶׁה, בֵּין שֶׁהוּא בֶן בְּרִית,* וּבֵין שֶׁאֵינוֹ בֶּן בְּרִית.

---

their gratitude in the blessing שֶׁעָשַׂנִי כִּרְצוֹנוֹ, *for having made me according to His will (R' Munk).*

רוֹקַע הָאָרֶץ עַל הַמָּיִם — *Who spreads out the earth upon the water.* By nature, water spreads and floods everything in its path, while earth tends to sink beneath the surface of the water. God formed the earth so that it remains always in place *(Radak).*

וִיהִי רָצוֹן — *And may it be Your will.* As is common in prayers, we call upon God as *the God of our forefathers,* because we wish to identify with the merit of our righteous forebears *(Etz Yosef).*

When a person starts off well, his chances for future success are enhanced immeasurably. Having thanked God for giving us new life, health, and vigor at the start of a new day, we pray that He provide us the conditions to serve Him and that He remove impediments to His service *(Siach Yitzchak).*

Blessed are You, HASHEM, our God, King of the universe, Who spreads out the earth upon the waters.[*1]

Blessed are You, HASHEM, our God, King of the universe, Who has provided me my every need.

Blessed are You, HASHEM, our God, King of the universe, Who firms man's footsteps.[2]

Blessed are You, HASHEM, our God, King of the universe, Who girds Israel with strength.

Blessed are you, HASHEM, our God, King of the universe, Who crowns Israel with splendor.

Blessed are You, HASHEM, our God, King of the universe, Who gives strength to the weary.[3]

Although many *siddurim* begin a new paragraph at וִיהִי רָצוֹן, *'And may it be Your will,'* the following is one long blessing that ends at לְעַמּוֹ יִשְׂרָאֵל, *'... His people Israel.'*

בָּרוּךְ *Blessed are You, HASHEM, our God, King of the universe, Who removes sleep from my eyes and slumber from my eyelids. And may it be Your will,* HASHEM, our God, and the God of our forefathers, that You accustom us to [study] Your Torah and attach us to Your commandments. Do not bring us into the power of error,* nor into the power of transgression and sin, nor into the power of challenge, nor into the power of scorn. Let not the Evil Inclination dominate us. Distance us from an evil person and an evil companion. Attach us to the Good Inclination and to good deeds and compel our Evil Inclination to be subservient to You. Grant us today and every day grace, kindness, and mercy in Your eyes and in the eyes of all who see us, and bestow beneficent kindnesses upon us. Blessed are You, HASHEM, Who bestows beneficent kindnesses upon His people Israel.*

יְהִי רָצוֹן *May it be Your will,* HASHEM, my God, and the God of my forefathers, that You rescue me today and every day from brazen men and from brazenness, from an evil man, an evil companion, an evil neighbor, an evil mishap, the destructive spiritual impediment, a harsh trial and a harsh opponent, whether he is a member of the covenant* or whether he is not a member of the covenant.*

(1) Cf. *Psalms* 136:6. (2) Cf. 37:23. (3) *Isaiah* 40:29.

לִידֵי חֵטְא — *Into the power of error.* Literally, the term לִידֵי means *into the hands of,* a synonym for power.

יְהִי רָצוֹן — *May it be Your will.* This personal prayer was recited by Rabbi Yehudah HaNassi every day after *Shacharis (Berachos* 16b). It is a prayer for protection in day-to-day dealings with one's fellow men. During the recitation, one may add his personal requests for God's help during the day *(Tur).*

בֶּן בְּרִית — *A member of the covenant,* i.e., Abraham's covenant of circumcision, the emblem of Israel's bond with God.

❧ עקדה ☙

The following supplicatory paragraph is omitted on the Sabbath and Festivals.

אֱלֹהֵינוּ* וֵאלֹהֵי אֲבוֹתֵינוּ, זָכְרֵנוּ בְּזִכָּרוֹן טוֹב לְפָנֶיךָ, וּפָקְדֵנוּ בִּפְקֻדַּת יְשׁוּעָה וְרַחֲמִים מִשְּׁמֵי שְׁמֵי קֶדֶם. וּזְכָר לָנוּ יהוה אֱלֹהֵינוּ אַהֲבַת הַקַּדְמוֹנִים אַבְרָהָם יִצְחָק וְיִשְׂרָאֵל עֲבָדֶיךָ, אֶת הַבְּרִית וְאֶת הַחֶסֶד וְאֶת הַשְּׁבוּעָה שֶׁנִּשְׁבַּעְתָּ לְאַבְרָהָם אָבִינוּ בְּהַר הַמּוֹרִיָּה, וְאֶת הָעֲקֵדָה שֶׁעָקַד אֶת יִצְחָק בְּנוֹ עַל גַּבֵּי הַמִּזְבֵּחַ, כַּכָּתוּב בְּתוֹרָתֶךָ:

בראשית כב:א־יט

וַיְהִי אַחַר הַדְּבָרִים הָאֵלֶּה, וְהָאֱלֹהִים נִסָּה אֶת אַבְרָהָם, וַיֹּאמֶר אֵלָיו, אַבְרָהָם; וַיֹּאמֶר, הִנֵּנִי. וַיֹּאמֶר, קַח נָא אֶת בִּנְךָ, אֶת יְחִידְךָ, אֲשֶׁר אָהַבְתָּ, אֶת יִצְחָק, וְלֶךְ לְךָ אֶל אֶרֶץ הַמֹּרִיָּה, וְהַעֲלֵהוּ שָׁם לְעֹלָה עַל אַחַד הֶהָרִים אֲשֶׁר אֹמַר אֵלֶיךָ. וַיַּשְׁכֵּם אַבְרָהָם בַּבֹּקֶר,* וַיַּחֲבֹשׁ אֶת חֲמֹרוֹ, וַיִּקַּח אֶת שְׁנֵי נְעָרָיו* אִתּוֹ, וְאֵת יִצְחָק בְּנוֹ, וַיְבַקַּע עֲצֵי עֹלָה, וַיָּקָם וַיֵּלֶךְ אֶל הַמָּקוֹם אֲשֶׁר אָמַר לוֹ הָאֱלֹהִים. בַּיּוֹם הַשְּׁלִישִׁי, וַיִּשָּׂא אַבְרָהָם אֶת עֵינָיו, וַיַּרְא אֶת הַמָּקוֹם מֵרָחֹק. וַיֹּאמֶר אַבְרָהָם אֶל נְעָרָיו, שְׁבוּ לָכֶם פֹּה עִם הַחֲמוֹר, וַאֲנִי וְהַנַּעַר נֵלְכָה עַד כֹּה, וְנִשְׁתַּחֲוֶה וְנָשׁוּבָה אֲלֵיכֶם.* וַיִּקַּח אַבְרָהָם אֶת עֲצֵי הָעֹלָה, וַיָּשֶׂם עַל יִצְחָק בְּנוֹ, וַיִּקַּח בְּיָדוֹ אֶת הָאֵשׁ וְאֶת הַמַּאֲכֶלֶת, וַיֵּלְכוּ שְׁנֵיהֶם יַחְדָּו. וַיֹּאמֶר יִצְחָק אֶל אַבְרָהָם אָבִיו, וַיֹּאמֶר, אָבִי; וַיֹּאמֶר, הִנֶּנִּי בְנִי; וַיֹּאמֶר, הִנֵּה הָאֵשׁ וְהָעֵצִים, וְאַיֵּה הַשֶּׂה לְעֹלָה. וַיֹּאמֶר אַבְרָהָם, אֱלֹהִים יִרְאֶה לּוֹ הַשֶּׂה* לְעֹלָה, בְּנִי; וַיֵּלְכוּ שְׁנֵיהֶם יַחְדָּו. וַיָּבֹאוּ אֶל הַמָּקוֹם אֲשֶׁר אָמַר לוֹ הָאֱלֹהִים,

---

❧ עֲקֵדָה / THE AKEIDAH ☙

The *Akeidah* is the story of the most difficult challenge to Abraham's faith in God: he was commanded to sacrifice Isaac, his beloved son and sole heir, to God. Father and son jointly demonstrated their total devotion, upon which God ordered Abraham to release Isaac. The Kabbalistic masters, from *Zohar* to *Arizal,* have stressed the great importance of the daily recitation of the *Akeidah.* In response to their writings, the *Akeidah* has been incorporated into the great majority of *Siddurim,* although it is not recited in all congregations. In some congregations, it is recited individually rather than as part of the public morning service. The *Zohar* records that this recitation of Abraham and Isaac's readiness to put love of God ahead of life itself is a source of heavenly mercy whenever Jewish lives are threatened. *Avodas HaKodesh* comments that the *Akeidah* should inspire us toward greater love of God, by following the example of Abraham and Isaac. *Arizal* teaches that the recitation brings atonement to someone who repents sincerely, for he identifies himself with the two Patriarchs who placed loyalty to God above all other considerations.

❧ **אֱלֹהֵינוּ** — *Our God.* This preliminary supplication is one of the highlights of the Rosh

THE AKEIDAH

The following supplicatory paragraph is omitted on the Sabbath and Festivals.

אֱלֹהֵינוּ *Our God* and the God of our forefathers, remember us with a favorable memory before You, and recall us with a recollection of salvation and mercy from the primeval loftiest heavens. Remember on our behalf — O HASHEM, our God — the love of the Patriarchs, Abraham, Isaac and Israel, Your servants; the covenant, the kindness, and the oath that You swore to our father Abraham at Mount Moriah, and the Akeidah, when he bound his son Isaac atop the altar, as it is written in Your Torah:*

Genesis 22:1-19

וַיְהִי *And it happened after these things that God tested Abraham and said to him, 'Abraham.'*

And he replied, 'Here I am.'

And He said, 'Please take your son, your only one, whom you love — Isaac — and get yourself to the Land of Moriah; bring him up there as an offering, upon one of the mountains which I shall indicate to you.'

So Abraham awoke early in the morning and he saddled his donkey; he took his two young men* with him, and Isaac, his son. He split the wood for the offering, and rose and went toward the place which God had indicated to him.*

*On the third day, Abraham looked up, and perceived the place from afar. And Abraham said to his young men, 'Stay here by yourselves with the donkey, while I and the lad will go yonder; we will prostrate ourselves and we will return to you.'**

And Abraham took the wood for the offering, and placed it on Isaac, his son. He took in his hand the fire and the knife, and the two of them went together. Then Isaac spoke to Abraham his father and said, 'Father — '

And he said 'Here I am, my son.'

And he said, 'Here are the fire and the wood, but where is the lamb for the offering?'

And Abraham said, 'God will seek out for Himself the lamb for the offering, my son.' And the two of them went together.*

They arrived at the place which God indicated to him.

Hashanah *Mussaf.*

וַיַּשְׁכֵּם אַבְרָהָם בַּבֹּקֶר — *So Abraham awoke early in the morning.* He began early, with alacrity, to do God's will, even though he had been commanded to slaughter his beloved Isaac. From this verse the Sages derive that one should perform his religious obligations (e.g., circumcision) as early in the day as possible *(Pesachim* 4a).

שְׁנֵי נְעָרָיו — *His two young men.* Ishmael, his older son, and Eliezer, his trusted servant.

וְנִשְׁתַּחֲוֶה וְנָשׁוּבָה — *We will prostrate ourselves and we will return.* An unintended prophecy came from Abraham's lips. Instead of saying 'I will return,' — without Isaac — he said 'we,' for such, indeed was God's intention.

אֱלֹהִים יִרְאֶה לּוֹ הַשֶּׂה — *God will seek out for Himself the lamb.* The Midrash teaches that Isaac understood from this reply that he would

וַיִּבֶן שָׁם אַבְרָהָם אֶת הַמִּזְבֵּחַ, וַיַּעֲרֹךְ אֶת הָעֵצִים, וַיַּעֲקֹד אֶת יִצְחָק בְּנוֹ, וַיָּשֶׂם אֹתוֹ עַל הַמִּזְבֵּחַ מִמַּעַל לָעֵצִים. וַיִּשְׁלַח אַבְרָהָם אֶת יָדוֹ, וַיִּקַּח אֶת הַמַּאֲכֶלֶת לִשְׁחֹט אֶת בְּנוֹ. וַיִּקְרָא אֵלָיו מַלְאַךְ יהוה מִן הַשָּׁמַיִם, וַיֹּאמֶר, אַבְרָהָם, אַבְרָהָם; וַיֹּאמֶר, הִנֵּנִי. וַיֹּאמֶר, אַל תִּשְׁלַח יָדְךָ אֶל הַנַּעַר, וְאַל תַּעַשׂ לוֹ מְאוּמָה, כִּי עַתָּה יָדַעְתִּי כִּי יְרֵא אֱלֹהִים אַתָּה, וְלֹא חָשַׂכְתָּ אֶת בִּנְךָ אֶת יְחִידְךָ מִמֶּנִּי. וַיִּשָּׂא אַבְרָהָם אֶת עֵינָיו וַיַּרְא, וְהִנֵּה אַיִל, אַחַר, נֶאֱחַז בַּסְּבַךְ בְּקַרְנָיו, וַיֵּלֶךְ אַבְרָהָם וַיִּקַּח אֶת הָאַיִל, וַיַּעֲלֵהוּ לְעֹלָה תַּחַת בְּנוֹ. וַיִּקְרָא אַבְרָהָם שֵׁם הַמָּקוֹם הַהוּא יהוה יִרְאֶה,* אֲשֶׁר יֵאָמֵר הַיּוֹם, בְּהַר יהוה יֵרָאֶה. וַיִּקְרָא מַלְאַךְ יהוה אֶל אַבְרָהָם, שֵׁנִית מִן הַשָּׁמָיִם. וַיֹּאמֶר, בִּי נִשְׁבַּעְתִּי נְאֻם יהוה, כִּי יַעַן אֲשֶׁר עָשִׂיתָ אֶת הַדָּבָר הַזֶּה, וְלֹא חָשַׂכְתָּ אֶת בִּנְךָ אֶת יְחִידֶךָ. כִּי בָרֵךְ אֲבָרֶכְךָ, וְהַרְבָּה אַרְבֶּה אֶת זַרְעֲךָ כְּכוֹכְבֵי הַשָּׁמַיִם, וְכַחוֹל אֲשֶׁר עַל שְׂפַת הַיָּם, וְיִרַשׁ זַרְעֲךָ אֵת שַׁעַר אֹיְבָיו. וְהִתְבָּרְכוּ בְזַרְעֲךָ כֹּל גּוֹיֵי הָאָרֶץ, עֵקֶב אֲשֶׁר שָׁמַעְתָּ בְּקֹלִי. וַיָּשָׁב אַבְרָהָם אֶל נְעָרָיו, וַיָּקֻמוּ וַיֵּלְכוּ יַחְדָּו אֶל בְּאֵר שָׁבַע, וַיֵּשֶׁב אַבְרָהָם בִּבְאֵר שָׁבַע.

The following supplicatory paragraph is omitted on the Sabbath and Festivals.

רִבּוֹנוֹ שֶׁל עוֹלָם, יְהִי רָצוֹן מִלְּפָנֶיךָ, יהוה אֱלֹהֵינוּ וֵאלֹהֵי אֲבוֹתֵינוּ, שֶׁתִּזְכָּר לָנוּ בְּרִית אֲבוֹתֵינוּ. כְּמוֹ שֶׁכָּבַשׁ אַבְרָהָם אָבִינוּ אֶת רַחֲמָיו מִבֶּן יְחִידוֹ, וְרָצָה לִשְׁחוֹט אוֹתוֹ כְּדֵי לַעֲשׂוֹת רְצוֹנֶךָ, כֵּן יִכְבְּשׁוּ רַחֲמֶיךָ אֶת כַּעַסְךָ מֵעָלֵינוּ, וְיָגֹלּוּ רַחֲמֶיךָ עַל מִדּוֹתֶיךָ, וְתִכָּנֵס אִתָּנוּ לִפְנִים מִשּׁוּרַת דִּינֶךָ, וְתִתְנַהֵג עִמָּנוּ, יהוה אֱלֹהֵינוּ, בְּמִדַּת הַחֶסֶד וּבְמִדַּת הָרַחֲמִים. וּבְטוּבְךָ הַגָּדוֹל, יָשׁוּב חֲרוֹן אַפְּךָ מֵעַמְּךָ וּמֵעִירְךָ וּמֵאַרְצְךָ וּמִנַּחֲלָתֶךָ. וְקַיֶּם לָנוּ, יהוה אֱלֹהֵינוּ, אֶת הַדָּבָר שֶׁהִבְטַחְתָּנוּ עַל יְדֵי מֹשֶׁה עַבְדֶּךָ, כָּאָמוּר: וְזָכַרְתִּי אֶת בְּרִיתִי יַעֲקוֹב, וְאַף אֶת בְּרִיתִי יִצְחָק, וְאַף אֶת בְּרִיתִי אַבְרָהָם אֶזְכֹּר, וְהָאָרֶץ אֶזְכֹּר.[1]

---

be the sacrificial 'lamb.' Nevertheless, though Isaac was in the prime of life at the age of 37 and Abraham was a century his senior, *the two of them went together,* united in their dedication.

ה׳ יִרְאֶה — HASHEM *Yireh,* literally, HASHEM *will see,* i.e., God will see the mountain where the *Akeidah* took place as the appropriate site for His Temple. Indeed, the *Akeidah* took place on

Abraham built the altar there, and arranged the wood; he bound Isaac, his son, and he placed him on the altar atop the wood. Abraham stretched out his hand, and took the knife to slaughter his son.

And an angel of HASHEM, *called to him from heaven, and said, 'Abraham! Abraham!'*

And he said, 'Here I am.'

And he said, 'Do not stretch out your hand against the lad nor do anything to him, for now I know that you are a God-fearing man, since you have not withheld your son, your only one, from Me.'

*And Abraham looked up and saw — behold a ram! — after it had been caught in the thicket by its horns. So Abraham went and took the ram and brought it as an offering instead of his son. And Abraham named that site '*HASHEM *Yireh,'* as it is said this day: On the mountain* HASHEM *is seen.*

The angel of HASHEM *called to Abraham, a second time from heaven, and said, '' 'By Myself I swear,' declared* HASHEM, *'that since you have done this thing, and have not withheld your son, your only one, I shall surely bless you and greatly increase your offspring like the stars of the heavens and like the sand on the seashore; and your offspring shall inherit the gate of its enemy; and all the nations of the earth shall bless themselves by your offspring, because you have listened to My voice.' ''*

Abraham returned to his young men, and they rose and went together to Beer Sheba, and Abraham stayed at Beer Sheba.

The following supplicatory paragraph is omitted on the Sabbath and Festivals.

רִבּוֹנוֹ שֶׁל עוֹלָם *Master of the universe! May it be Your will,* HASHEM, *our God, and the God of our forefathers, that You remember for our sake the covenant of our forefathers. Just as Abraham our forefather suppressed his mercy for his only son and wished to slaughter him in order to do Your will, so may Your mercy suppress Your anger from upon us and may Your mercy overwhelm Your attributes. May You overstep with us the line of Your law and deal with us — O* HASHEM, *our God — with the attribute of kindness and the attribute of mercy. In Your great goodness may You turn aside Your burning wrath from Your people, Your city, Your land, and Your heritage. Fulfill for us,* HASHEM, *our God, the word You pledged through Moses, Your servant, as it is said: 'I shall remember My covenant with Jacob; also My covenant with Isaac, and also My covenant with Abraham shall I remember; and the land shall I remember.'*[1]

(1) *Leviticus* 26:42.

the future Temple Mount *(Onkelos)*. Alternatively, God will eternally 'see' the *Akeidah* as a source of merit for the offspring of Abraham and Isaac *(R' Bachya)*.

לְעוֹלָם* יְהֵא אָדָם יְרֵא שָׁמַיִם בְּסֵתֶר וּבַגָּלוּי,* וּמוֹדֶה עַל הָאֱמֶת,* וְדוֹבֵר אֱמֶת בִּלְבָבוֹ,* וְיַשְׁכֵּם וְיֹאמַר:

רִבּוֹן כָּל הָעוֹלָמִים,* לֹא עַל צִדְקוֹתֵינוּ אֲנַחְנוּ מַפִּילִים תַּחֲנוּנֵינוּ לְפָנֶיךָ, כִּי עַל רַחֲמֶיךָ הָרַבִּים. מָה אֲנַחְנוּ, מֶה חַיֵּינוּ, מֶה חַסְדֵּנוּ, מַה צִּדְקוֹתֵינוּ, מַה יְּשׁוּעָתֵנוּ, מַה כֹּחֵנוּ, מַה גְּבוּרָתֵנוּ. מַה נֹּאמַר לְפָנֶיךָ, יהוה אֱלֹהֵינוּ וֵאלֹהֵי אֲבוֹתֵינוּ, הֲלֹא כָּל הַגִּבּוֹרִים כְּאַיִן לְפָנֶיךָ, וְאַנְשֵׁי הַשֵּׁם כְּלֹא הָיוּ, וַחֲכָמִים כִּבְלִי מַדָּע, וּנְבוֹנִים כִּבְלִי הַשְׂכֵּל. כִּי רוֹב מַעֲשֵׂיהֶם תֹּהוּ, וִימֵי חַיֵּיהֶם הֶבֶל לְפָנֶיךָ, וּמוֹתַר הָאָדָם מִן הַבְּהֵמָה אָיִן, כִּי הַכֹּל הָבֶל.[1]

אֲבָל אֲנַחְנוּ* עַמְּךָ, בְּנֵי בְרִיתֶךָ, בְּנֵי אַבְרָהָם אֹהַבְךָ שֶׁנִּשְׁבַּעְתָּ לּוֹ בְּהַר הַמּוֹרִיָּה, זֶרַע יִצְחָק יְחִידוֹ שֶׁנֶּעֱקַד עַל גַּב הַמִּזְבֵּחַ, עֲדַת יַעֲקֹב בִּנְךָ בְּכוֹרֶךָ, שֶׁמֵּאַהֲבָתְךָ שֶׁאָהַבְתָּ אוֹתוֹ וּמִשִּׂמְחָתְךָ שֶׁשָּׂמַחְתָּ בּוֹ, קָרָאתָ אֶת שְׁמוֹ יִשְׂרָאֵל וִישֻׁרוּן.*

לְפִיכָךְ אֲנַחְנוּ חַיָּבִים לְהוֹדוֹת לְךָ, וּלְשַׁבֵּחֲךָ, וּלְפָאֶרְךָ, וּלְבָרֵךְ וּלְקַדֵּשׁ וְלָתֵת שֶׁבַח וְהוֹדָיָה לִשְׁמֶךָ. אַשְׁרֵינוּ,* מַה טּוֹב חֶלְקֵנוּ, וּמַה נָּעִים גּוֹרָלֵנוּ, וּמַה יָּפָה יְרֻשָּׁתֵנוּ. ❖ אַשְׁרֵינוּ, שֶׁאֲנַחְנוּ מַשְׁכִּימִים וּמַעֲרִיבִים, עֶרֶב וָבֹקֶר וְאוֹמְרִים פַּעֲמַיִם בְּכָל יוֹם:

☙ **לְעוֹלָם** — *Always.* The section beginning with לְעוֹלָם and extending until קָרְבָּנוֹת/*Offerings,* is in its totality a profound and succinct summation of basic Jewish faith and loyalty to God. What is more, it is a ringing declaration of joyous pride in our Jewishness, a pride that overcomes all persecutions and that moves us to pray for the time when all will recognize the truth of the Torah's message, and we will proudly proclaim the message that the anti-Semites of the world attempt to still.

Furthermore, the declarations contained in this section represent the manner in which a Jew should conduct himself *always,* not merely on ceremonial occasions.

יְרֵא שָׁמַיִם בְּסֵתֶר וּבַגָּלוּי — *God-fearing privately and publicly.* Some people behave piously when in the view of others, but not when their behavior goes unseen. Others are God-fearing in private but are ashamed to do so in public for fear of being labeled as non-conformists. But the Jew must strive to be consistently God-fearing, whatever his surroundings.

וּמוֹדֶה עַל הָאֱמֶת — [*Let him*] *acknowledge the truth.* One who seeks the truth is not ashamed to concede his errors. But if he cares more about his reputation than the truth, he will stubbornly persist in falsehood and sin.

וְדוֹבֵר אֱמֶת בִּלְבָבוֹ — [*Let him*] *speak the truth within his heart.* The Sages cite Rav Safra as the prototype of inner honesty (*Chullin* 94b and *Rashi* to *Makkos* 24a). Once, while he was praying and therefore not permitted to speak, Rav Safra was offered a satisfactory price for something he wished to sell. The buyer did not realize why Rav Safra did not respond, so he kept raising his bid. When Rav Safra finished his prayers, he insisted on accepting no more than the first offer, because in his heart he had intended to sell for that price.

לְעוֹלָם *Always* let a person be God-fearing privately and publicly,* acknowledge the truth,* speak the truth within his heart,* and arise early and proclaim:*

Master of all worlds! Not in the merit of our righteousness do we cast our supplications before You, but in the merit of Your abundant mercy. What are we? What is our life? What is our kindness? What is our righteousness? What is our salvation? What is our strength? What is our might? What can we say before You,* HASHEM, *our God, and the God of our forefathers — are not all the heroes like nothing before You, the famous as if they had never existed, the wise as if devoid of wisdom and the perceptive as if devoid of intelligence? For most of their deeds are desolate and the days of their lives are empty before You. The preeminence of man over beast is non-existent for all is vain.*[1]

But we are Your people, members of Your covenant, children of Abraham, Your beloved, to whom You took an oath at Mount Moriah; the offspring of Isaac, his only son, who was bound atop the altar; the community of Jacob , Your firstborn son, whom — because of the love with which You adored him and the joy with which You delighted in him — You named Israel and Jeshurun.**

לְפִיכָךְ *Therefore, we are obliged to thank You, praise You, glorify You, bless, sanctify, and offer praise and thanks to Your Name. We are fortunate* — how good is our portion, how pleasant our lot, and how beautiful our heritage!* Chazzan— *We are fortunate for we come early and stay late, evening and morning, and proclaim twice each day:*

(1) *Ecclesiastes* 3:19.

רִבּוֹן כָּל הָעוֹלָמִים — *Master of all worlds!* We now begin leading up to *Shema*, the affirmation of the Oneness of God and acknowledgment of His absolute mastery. We declare that, given the inherent powerlessness and inadequacy of man, Israel is enormously privileged in having been selected as God's Chosen People. Therefore, we dedicate ourselves to proclaim His Oneness through the *Shema*. After the blessing that follows the *Shema* we pray for Israel's salvation so that we may be able to sanctify His Name without hindrance. This prayer was composed by the Talmudic sage Rabbi Yochanan *(Yoma* 87b) for use in the Yom Kippur *vidui* (confession) service.

אֲבָל אֲנַחְנוּ — *But we are.* In contrast to the above-described futility of man, we Jews are privileged to carry on the legacy and mission of our forefathers. Abraham is described as God's beloved, which, our Sages explain, means that he sought always to make God beloved in the eyes of his fellow human beings. God made an oath to him at Mount Moriah where the *Akeidah* took place and where Isaac demonstrated his own devotion to God. Jacob is called God's firstborn because the Jewish nation, which bears his name, was given that title by God Himself *(Exodus* 4:22) and to ratify the fact that God considered Jacob, not Esau, to be the legitimate firstborn.

יִשְׂרָאֵל וִישֻׁרוּן — *Israel and Jeshurun.* These two names are descriptive of Jacob's stature. The name יִשְׂרָאֵל (from שְׂרָרָה, *mastery)* means that Jacob *triumphed* over an angel (see *Genesis* 35:10) and יְשֻׁרוּן (from יָשָׁר, *upright, fair)* refers to *dedication to justice* in accordance with God's will.

אַשְׁרֵינוּ — *We are fortunate.* Although, as noted in *Tikkun Tefillah*, this section of the service was compiled during a period of intense persecution, we do not feel downtrodden. To the contrary, we are fortunate to be God's Chosen People and proud to proclaim His Oneness.

שְׁמַע יִשְׂרָאֵל,* יהוה אֱלֹהֵינוּ, יהוה אֶחָד.[1]

In an undertone— בָּרוּךְ שֵׁם כְּבוֹד מַלְכוּתוֹ לְעוֹלָם וָעֶד.

Some congregations complete the first chapter of *Shema* (following paragraph) at this point, although most omit it. However if you fear that you will not recite the full *Shema* later in *Shacharis* before the prescribed time has elapsed, (see *Laws* §17) recite all three chapters of *Shema* (p. 90) here.

דברים ו:ה־ט

וְאָהַבְתָּ אֵת יהוה אֱלֹהֶיךָ, בְּכָל לְבָבְךָ, וּבְכָל נַפְשְׁךָ, וּבְכָל מְאֹדֶךָ. וְהָיוּ הַדְּבָרִים הָאֵלֶּה, אֲשֶׁר אָנֹכִי מְצַוְּךָ הַיּוֹם, עַל לְבָבֶךָ. וְשִׁנַּנְתָּם לְבָנֶיךָ, וְדִבַּרְתָּ בָּם, בְּשִׁבְתְּךָ בְּבֵיתֶךָ, וּבְלֶכְתְּךָ בַדֶּרֶךְ, וּבְשָׁכְבְּךָ וּבְקוּמֶךָ. וּקְשַׁרְתָּם לְאוֹת עַל יָדֶךָ, וְהָיוּ לְטֹטָפֹת בֵּין עֵינֶיךָ. וּכְתַבְתָּם עַל מְזֻזוֹת בֵּיתֶךָ וּבִשְׁעָרֶיךָ.

אַתָּה הוּא* עַד שֶׁלֹּא נִבְרָא הָעוֹלָם, אַתָּה הוּא מִשֶּׁנִּבְרָא הָעוֹלָם, אַתָּה הוּא בָּעוֹלָם הַזֶּה, וְאַתָּה הוּא לָעוֹלָם הַבָּא. ❖ קַדֵּשׁ אֶת שִׁמְךָ עַל מַקְדִּישֵׁי שְׁמֶךָ,* וְקַדֵּשׁ אֶת שִׁמְךָ בְּעוֹלָמֶךָ. וּבִישׁוּעָתְךָ תָּרִים וְתַגְבִּיהַּ קַרְנֵנוּ. בָּרוּךְ אַתָּה יהוה, מְקַדֵּשׁ אֶת שִׁמְךָ בָּרַבִּים.* (Cong.— אָמֵן.)

אַתָּה הוּא יהוה אֱלֹהֵינוּ, בַּשָּׁמַיִם וּבָאָרֶץ וּבִשְׁמֵי הַשָּׁמַיִם הָעֶלְיוֹנִים. אֱמֶת, אַתָּה הוּא רִאשׁוֹן, וְאַתָּה הוּא אַחֲרוֹן,* וּמִבַּלְעָדֶיךָ אֵין אֱלֹהִים.[2] קַבֵּץ קוֶֹיךָ מֵאַרְבַּע כַּנְפוֹת הָאָרֶץ. יַכִּירוּ וְיֵדְעוּ כָּל בָּאֵי עוֹלָם כִּי אַתָּה הוּא הָאֱלֹהִים לְבַדְּךָ לְכֹל מַמְלְכוֹת הָאָרֶץ. אַתָּה עָשִׂיתָ אֶת הַשָּׁמַיִם וְאֶת הָאָרֶץ,[3] אֶת הַיָּם, וְאֶת כָּל אֲשֶׁר בָּם. וּמִי בְּכָל מַעֲשֵׂה יָדֶיךָ בָּעֶלְיוֹנִים אוֹ בַתַּחְתּוֹנִים שֶׁיֹּאמַר לְךָ, מַה תַּעֲשֶׂה. אָבִינוּ שֶׁבַּשָּׁמַיִם, עֲשֵׂה עִמָּנוּ חֶסֶד בַּעֲבוּר שִׁמְךָ הַגָּדוֹל שֶׁנִּקְרָא עָלֵינוּ, וְקַיֶּם לָנוּ יהוה אֱלֹהֵינוּ מַה שֶּׁכָּתוּב: בָּעֵת הַהִיא אָבִיא אֶתְכֶם, וּבָעֵת קַבְּצִי אֶתְכֶם, כִּי אֶתֵּן אֶתְכֶם לְשֵׁם וְלִתְהִלָּה בְּכֹל עַמֵּי הָאָרֶץ, בְּשׁוּבִי אֶת שְׁבוּתֵיכֶם לְעֵינֵיכֶם, אָמַר יהוה.[4]

❧ **שְׁמַע יִשְׂרָאֵל** — *Hear, O Israel.* During the middle of the fifth century the Persian king, Yezdegerd II, forbade the Jews to observe the Sabbath and to recite the *Shema*. His purpose was to eradicate belief in Hashem as the Creator (which is symbolized by the Sabbath) and in His Oneness, as it is proclaimed in the *Shema*. To insure that the *Shema* would not be read in defiance of his decree, the king stationed guards in the synagogue for the first quarter of the day, when the *Shema* must be read. To counteract his design, the Sages instituted two recitations of the first verse of *Shema:* the one here, which was to be recited at home, and another one as part of the Sabbath *Kedushah* of *Mussaf* (see p. 464). Although these services contain only the first verse of the *Shema*, this is sufficient to fulfill the *Shema* obligation in cases of extreme emergency (*Berachos* 13b). Even when Yezdegerd was killed in response to the prayers of the Sages and his

Hear, O Israel:* HASHEM is our God, HASHEM, the One and Only.[1]

In an undertone— *Blessed is the Name of His glorious kingdom for all eternity.*

Some congregations complete the first chapter of the *Shema* (following paragraph) at this point, although most omit it. However if you fear that you will not recite the full *Shema* later in *Shacharis* before the prescribed time has elapsed (see *Laws* §17), recite all three chapters of *Shema* (p. 90) here.

Deuteronomy 6:5-9

וְאָהַבְתָּ *You shall love HASHEM, your God, with all your heart, with all your soul and with all your resources. Let these matters, which I command you today, be upon your heart. Teach them thoroughly to your children and speak of them while you sit in your home, while you walk on the way, when you retire and when you arise. Bind them as a sign upon your arm and let them be tefillin between your eyes. And write them on the doorposts of your house and upon your gates.*

אַתָּה *It was You* before the world was created, it is You since the world was created, it is You in This World, and it is You in the World to Come.* Chazzan— *Sanctify Your Name through those who sanctify Your Name,* and sanctify Your Name in Your universe. Through Your salvation may You exalt and raise our pride. Blessed are You, HASHEM, Who sanctifies Your Name among the multitudes.**

(Cong.— *Amen.*)

אַתָּה *It is You Who are HASHEM, our God, in heaven and on earth and in the loftiest heavens. True — You are the First and You are the Last,* and other than You there is no God.[2] Gather in those who yearn for You, from the four corners of the earth. Let all who walk the earth recognize and know that You alone are the God over all the kingdoms of the earth. You have made the heavens, the earth,[3] the sea, and all that is in them. Who among all Your handiwork, those above and those below, can say to You, 'What are You doing?' Our Father in Heaven, treat us with kindness for the sake of Your great Name that has been proclaimed upon us. Fulfill for us HASHEM, our God, what is written: " 'At that time I will bring you and at that time I will gather you in, for I will set you up for renown and praise among all the peoples of the earth, when I bring back your captivity, before your own eyes,' said HASHEM."[4]*

(1) *Deuteronomy* 6:4. (2) Cf. *Isaiah* 44:6. (3) *II Kings* 19:15. (4) *Zephaniah* 3:20.

decree was lifted, the two *Shema* recitations remained part of the regular ritual, and the one that had been recited at home was moved to this part of the synagogue service.

⸎ אַתָּה הוּא — *It was You.* The first four phrases of this prayer express the idea that God is eternal and unchanging, unaffected by time or place.

קַדֵּשׁ אֶת שִׁמְךָ עַל מַקְדִּישֵׁי שְׁמֶךָ — *Sanctify Your Name through those who sanctify Your Name.* When originally composed, this referred to the Jewish martyrs who had sanctified the Name through unyielding loyalty. In later times, it came to refer also to those who cling to the commandments despite hardship and temptation.

מְקַדֵּשׁ אֶת שִׁמְךָ בָּרַבִּים — *Who sanctifies Your Name* [some versions read שְׁמוֹ, *His Name*] *among the multitudes.* May the time come when no Jew need ever fear to express his Jewishness openly.

רִאשׁוֹן ... אַחֲרוֹן — *The First ... the Last.* We mean

קרבנות

הכיור

שמות ל:יז־כא

וַיְדַבֵּר יהוה אֶל מֹשֶׁה לֵּאמֹר. וְעָשִׂיתָ כִּיּוֹר נְחֹשֶׁת, וְכַנּוֹ נְחֹשֶׁת, לְרָחְצָה, וְנָתַתָּ אֹתוֹ בֵּין אֹהֶל מוֹעֵד וּבֵין הַמִּזְבֵּחַ, וְנָתַתָּ שָׁמָּה מָיִם. וְרָחֲצוּ אַהֲרֹן וּבָנָיו מִמֶּנּוּ, אֶת יְדֵיהֶם וְאֶת רַגְלֵיהֶם. בְּבֹאָם אֶל אֹהֶל מוֹעֵד יִרְחֲצוּ מַיִם וְלֹא יָמֻתוּ,* אוֹ בְגִשְׁתָּם אֶל הַמִּזְבֵּחַ לְשָׁרֵת לְהַקְטִיר אִשֶּׁה לַיהוה. וְרָחֲצוּ יְדֵיהֶם וְרַגְלֵיהֶם וְלֹא יָמֻתוּ, וְהָיְתָה לָהֶם חָק עוֹלָם, לוֹ וּלְזַרְעוֹ לְדֹרֹתָם.

תרומת הדשן

ויקרא ו:א־ו

וַיְדַבֵּר יהוה אֶל מֹשֶׁה לֵּאמֹר. צַו אֶת אַהֲרֹן וְאֶת בָּנָיו לֵאמֹר, זֹאת תּוֹרַת הָעֹלָה, הִוא הָעֹלָה עַל מוֹקְדָה עַל הַמִּזְבֵּחַ כָּל הַלַּיְלָה* עַד הַבֹּקֶר, וְאֵשׁ הַמִּזְבֵּחַ תּוּקַד בּוֹ. וְלָבַשׁ הַכֹּהֵן מִדּוֹ בַד,* וּמִכְנְסֵי בַד יִלְבַּשׁ עַל בְּשָׂרוֹ, וְהֵרִים אֶת הַדֶּשֶׁן* אֲשֶׁר תֹּאכַל הָאֵשׁ אֶת הָעֹלָה עַל הַמִּזְבֵּחַ, וְשָׂמוֹ אֵצֶל הַמִּזְבֵּחַ. וּפָשַׁט אֶת בְּגָדָיו,* וְלָבַשׁ בְּגָדִים אֲחֵרִים, וְהוֹצִיא אֶת הַדֶּשֶׁן אֶל מִחוּץ

---

only to say that God pre-existed everything and will survive everything — not that He had a beginning or will have an end, for God is infinite and timeless.

קָרְבָּנוֹת / OFFERINGS

From the beginning of its existence as a nation, Israel *saw* — whether or not it understood why or how — that the sacrificial service brought it a closeness to God and the manifestation of His Presence. The offerings represented the Jew's submission to God of his self and his resources.

Abraham asked God how Israel would achieve forgiveness when the Temple would lie in ruins and they could no longer offer sacrifices.

God replied, 'When Israel recites the Scriptural order of the offerings, I will consider it as if they had brought the sacrifices and I will forgive their sins' *(Megillah* 31a; *Taanis* 27b).

Rav Yitzchak said: The Torah writes זֹאת תּוֹרַת הַחַטָּאת, *this is the Torah* [i.e., teaching] *of the sin-offering (Leviticus* 6:18) to imply that whoever involves himself in the study of the sin-offering is regarded as if he had actually brought a sin-offering *(Menachos* 110a).

In the inspiring words of *R' Hirsch (Horeb* §624): 'The Temple has fallen, the Altar has disappeared, the harps of the singers are heard no more, but their spirit has become the heritage of Israel; it still infuses the word which alone survives as an expression of the inward Divine service.'

The section dealing with the קָרְבָּנוֹת, *offerings,* logically follows the previous prayer, אַתָּה הוּא, which longs for Israel's redemption. Given the fact that the offerings require the existence of the Holy Temple as the spiritual center of the nation, we pray that God gather us in from our dispersion. Then, our message will become a truly universal one, for God will have set us up *'for renown and praise among all the peoples of the earth.'*

The offerings whose laws are about to be recited are all communal ones; the Sages chose them because they illustrate our wish that Israel become united as a single nation in God's service.

הַכִּיּוֹר / The Laver

Before the *Kohanim* could begin the Temple service, they had to take sanctified water and pour it over their hands and feet. This water was drawn from the כִּיּוֹר, *laver,* a large copper basin

OFFERINGS

THE LAVER

Exodus 30:17-21

וַיְדַבֵּר *HASHEM spoke to Moses, saying: Make a laver of copper, and its base of copper, for washing; and place it between the Tent of Appointment and the Altar and put water there. Aaron and his sons are to wash their hands and feet from it. When they arrive at the Tent of Appointment they are to wash with water so that they not die,* or when they approach the Altar to serve, to burn a fire-offering to HASHEM. They are to wash their hands and feet so that they not die; and this shall be an eternal decree for them — for him and for his offspring — throughout their generations.*

THE TAKING OF ASHES

Leviticus 6:1-6

וַיְדַבֵּר *HASHEM spoke to Moses saying: Instruct Aaron and his sons saying: This is the teaching of the elevation-offering, it is the elevation-offering that stays on the pyre on the Altar all night* until morning, and the fire of the Altar should be kept burning on it. The Kohen should don his linen garment,* and he is to don linen breeches upon his flesh; he is to pick up the ashes* of what the fire consumed of the elevation-offering upon the Altar and place it next to the Altar. Then he should remove his garments* and don other garments; then he should remove the ashes to the outside of*

---

in the Temple Courtyard. In preparation for our 'verbal sacrificial service' therefore, we 'wash' ourselves with water from the laver, as it were.

וְלֹא יָמֻתוּ — *So that they not die.* The offense of performing the service without washing did *not* incur a court-imposed death penalty, but the violator makes himself liable to a Heavenly punishment for his display of contempt.

תְּרוּמַת הַדֶּשֶׁן / The Taking of Ashes

These verses are recited here because they concern the first service of the day: to remove a small portion of the ashes from the previous day's offerings. It was done first thing in the morning, before the *tamid,* daily continual offering, was brought. In addition, the passage contains three references to fire on the Altar: (a) עַל מוֹקְדָה, *on the pyre;* (b) וְאֵשׁ הַמִּזְבֵּחַ, *the fire of the Altar;* (c) וְהָאֵשׁ עַל הַמִּזְבֵּחַ, *the fire on the Altar.* This teaches that three fires were kept burning on the Altar *(Yoma* 45a). They were: מַעֲרָכָה גְדוֹלָה, *the large pyre,* upon which the offerings were burned; מַעֲרָכָה שְׁנִיָּה שֶׁל קְטֹרֶת, *the second pyre for the incense,* from which burning coals were taken and brought into the Sanctuary for the morning and afternoon incense service; and מַעֲרָכָה לְקִיּוּם הָאֵשׁ, *the pyre for perpetuation of the flame,* which was kept burning at all times in case either of the other fires became extinguished.

הוּא הָעֹלָה ... כָּל הַלַּיְלָה — *It is the elevation-offering ... all night.* Although it was preferable to burn a day's offerings during the day, it was permitted to place them on the fires all night, provided the service of the blood was completed during the day.

מִדּוֹ בַד — *His linen garment.* The *Kohen* must wear his full priestly raiment; like all Temple services, this one may not be performed if the *Kohen* is lacking even one of the prescribed garments (described in *Exodus* 28).

וְהֵרִים אֶת הַדֶּשֶׁן — *He is to pick up the ashes.* He is to take glowing ashes from the burnt flesh of offerings, not from wood ashes. The portion taken for this service need be no larger than a handful and it is placed on the floor of the Courtyard, to the east of the ramp leading up to the Altar (the ramp is on the south side of the Altar). This removal of ashes is a required part of the daily morning service, whether or not the Altar had to be cleaned of excess ashes.

וּפָשַׁט אֶת בְּגָדָיו — *Then he should remove his garments.* Unlike the previous verse that

לַמַּחֲנֶה, אֶל מָקוֹם טָהוֹר. וְהָאֵשׁ עַל הַמִּזְבֵּחַ תּוּקַד בּוֹ, לֹא תִכְבֶּה, וּבִעֵר עָלֶיהָ הַכֹּהֵן עֵצִים בַּבֹּקֶר בַּבֹּקֶר,* וְעָרַךְ עָלֶיהָ הָעֹלָה, וְהִקְטִיר עָלֶיהָ חֶלְבֵי הַשְּׁלָמִים.* אֵשׁ תָּמִיד תּוּקַד עַל הַמִּזְבֵּחַ, לֹא תִכְבֶּה.

קרבן התמיד

Some authorities hold that the following (until קְטֹרֶת) should be recited standing.
In some congregations, the following supplication is omitted on the Sabbath and Festivals.

יְהִי רָצוֹן מִלְּפָנֶיךָ,* יהוה אֱלֹהֵינוּ וֵאלֹהֵי אֲבוֹתֵינוּ, שֶׁתְּרַחֵם עָלֵינוּ וְתִמְחַל לָנוּ עַל כָּל חַטֹּאתֵינוּ, וּתְכַפֶּר לָנוּ אֶת כָּל עֲוֹנוֹתֵינוּ, וְתִסְלַח לְכָל פְּשָׁעֵינוּ, וְתִבְנֶה בֵּית הַמִּקְדָּשׁ בִּמְהֵרָה בְיָמֵינוּ, וְנַקְרִיב לְפָנֶיךָ קָרְבַּן הַתָּמִיד שֶׁיְּכַפֵּר בַּעֲדֵנוּ, כְּמוֹ שֶׁכָּתַבְתָּ עָלֵינוּ בְּתוֹרָתֶךָ עַל יְדֵי מֹשֶׁה עַבְדֶּךָ, מִפִּי כְבוֹדֶךָ, כָּאָמוּר:

במדבר כח:א־ח

וַיְדַבֵּר יהוה אֶל מֹשֶׁה לֵּאמֹר. צַו אֶת בְּנֵי יִשְׂרָאֵל וְאָמַרְתָּ אֲלֵהֶם, אֶת קָרְבָּנִי לַחְמִי* לְאִשַּׁי, רֵיחַ נִיחֹחִי, תִּשְׁמְרוּ לְהַקְרִיב לִי בְּמוֹעֲדוֹ. וְאָמַרְתָּ לָהֶם, זֶה הָאִשֶּׁה אֲשֶׁר תַּקְרִיבוּ לַיהוה, כְּבָשִׂים בְּנֵי שָׁנָה תְמִימִם, שְׁנַיִם לַיּוֹם, עֹלָה תָמִיד. אֶת הַכֶּבֶשׂ אֶחָד תַּעֲשֶׂה בַבֹּקֶר, וְאֵת הַכֶּבֶשׂ הַשֵּׁנִי תַּעֲשֶׂה בֵּין הָעַרְבָּיִם. וַעֲשִׂירִית הָאֵיפָה סֹלֶת לְמִנְחָה,* בְּלוּלָה בְּשֶׁמֶן כָּתִית רְבִיעִת הַהִין. עֹלַת תָּמִיד, הָעֲשֻׂיָה בְּהַר סִינַי, לְרֵיחַ נִיחֹחַ, אִשֶּׁה לַיהוה. וְנִסְכּוֹ רְבִיעִת הַהִין לַכֶּבֶשׂ הָאֶחָד, בַּקֹּדֶשׁ הַסֵּךְ נֶסֶךְ שֵׁכָר לַיהוה. וְאֵת הַכֶּבֶשׂ הַשֵּׁנִי תַּעֲשֶׂה בֵּין הָעַרְבָּיִם, כְּמִנְחַת הַבֹּקֶר וּכְנִסְכּוֹ תַּעֲשֶׂה, אִשֵּׁה רֵיחַ נִיחֹחַ לַיהוה.

---

discusses a daily *mitzvah*, this verse discusses the cleaning of the Altar, which was done whenever the accumulation of ashes atop the Altar interfered with the service, but need not be done daily. The ashes were removed and taken to a designated place outside of Jerusalem; in the Wilderness, they were taken to a place outside of the Israelite camp. In speaking of 'removal' of the priestly garments the verse advises that the *Kohen* should wear less expensive or well-worn priestly garments when performing this service because the ashes would tend to soil his clothing: 'The outfit one wears while cooking his master's meal, one should not wear while filling his master's goblet' (*Yoma* 23a).

עֵצִים בַּבֹּקֶר בַּבֹּקֶר — *Wood ... every morning.* Wood must be placed on the Altar fire every morning.

הָעֹלָה ... הַשְּׁלָמִים — *The elevation-offering ... the peace-offerings.* The morning continual elevation-offering had to go on the Altar before any other offerings; similarly, the last offering of the day was the afternoon continual offering.

⊱ הַתָּמִיד / The Tamid (Continual) Offering

⊱ **יְהִי רָצוֹן מִלְּפָנֶיךָ** — *May it be Your will.* We are about to begin 'offering' our communal sacrifices, as it were. Before doing so, we recite a brief prayer that God end the exile and make it possible for us to offer the true offerings, not just the recitations that take their place.

the camp to a pure place. The fire on the Altar shall be kept burning on it, it may not be extinguished, and the Kohen shall burn wood upon it every morning. He is to prepare the elevation-offering upon it and burn upon it the fats of the peace-offerings.* A permanent fire should remain burning on the Altar; it may not be extinguished.*

THE TAMID OFFERING

Some authorities hold that the following (until קְטֹרֶת/Incense) should be recited standing. In some congregations, the following supplication is omitted on the Sabbath and Festivals.

יְהִי רָצוֹן *May it be Your will,* HASHEM, our God, and the God of our forefathers, that You have mercy on us and pardon us for all our errors, atone for us all our iniquities, forgive all our willful sins; and that You rebuild the Holy Temple speedily, in our days, so that we may offer to You the continual offering that it may atone for us, as You have prescribed for us in Your Torah through Moses, Your servant, from Your glorious mouth, as it is said:*

Numbers 28:1-8

וַיְדַבֵּר *HASHEM spoke to Moses, saying: Command the Children of Israel and tell them: My offering, My food* for My fires, My* ***satisfying aroma, you are to be scrupulous to offer Me in its appointed time. And you are to tell them: 'This is the fire-offering that you are to bring to HASHEM: [male] first-year lambs, unblemished, two a day, as a continual elevation-offering. One lamb-service you are to perform in the morning and the second lamb-service you are to perform in the afternoon; with a tenth-ephah of fine flour for a meal-offering,* mixed with a quarter-hin of crushed olive oil. It is the continual elevation-offering that was done at Mount Sinai, for a satisfying aroma, a fire-offering to HASHEM. And its libation is a quarter-hin for each lamb, to be poured on the Holy [Altar], a fermented libation to HASHEM. And the second lamb-service you are to perform in the afternoon, like the meal-offering of the morning and its libation are you to make, a fire-offering for a satisfying aroma to HASHEM.***

וַיְדַבֵּר ה' ... קָרְבָּנִי לַחְמִי — *HASHEM spoke ... My offering, My food.* The offering referred to here is the עֹלַת תָּמִיד, *continual elevation-offering* or *tamid.* The offering is called תָּמִיד, *continual,* because it is brought regularly, day in and day out; it is a communal offering purchased with the annual half-*shekel* contributions, collected especially for this purpose. The offering is called *food* in the figurative sense, referring to the parts that are burned on the Altar. The *satisfying odor* does not refer to the odor *per se,* for just as God does not require our 'food', He does not benefit from the aroma of burning flesh. Rather, the aroma of the burning offering is pleasing to God because it represents the culmination of our performance of His will. In the words of the Sages, God is pleased, שֶׁאָמַרְתִּי וְנַעֲשָׂה רְצוֹנִי, *for I have spoken, and My will has been done.*

סֹלֶת לְמִנְחָה — *Fine flour for a meal-offering.* Every elevation- and peace-offering, whether communal or private, is accompanied by a meal-offering, which is burned completely on the Altar, and a libation of wine, which is poured onto the Altar. The wine is called נְסָכִים and the meal-offering, which consists of fine flour mixed with olive oil, is called מִנְחַת נְסָכִים. The amount of flour, oil and wine depends on the species of the animal. For sheep — the animal used for the *tamid* — the amounts are a tenth-*ephah*

וְשָׁחַט אֹתוֹ עַל יֶרֶךְ הַמִּזְבֵּחַ צָפֹנָה לִפְנֵי יהוה, וְזָרְקוּ בְּנֵי אַהֲרֹן הַכֹּהֲנִים אֶת דָּמוֹ עַל הַמִּזְבֵּחַ סָבִיב.*[1]

In some congregations, the following supplication is omitted on the Sabbath and Festivals.

יְהִי רָצוֹן מִלְּפָנֶיךָ, יהוה אֱלֹהֵינוּ וֵאלֹהֵי אֲבוֹתֵינוּ, שֶׁתְּהֵא אֲמִירָה זוּ חֲשׁוּבָה וּמְקֻבֶּלֶת וּמְרֻצָּה לְפָנֶיךָ כְּאִלּוּ הִקְרַבְנוּ קָרְבַּן הַתָּמִיד בְּמוֹעֲדוֹ וּבִמְקוֹמוֹ וּכְהִלְכָתוֹ.

קטרת

אַתָּה הוּא יהוה אֱלֹהֵינוּ שֶׁהִקְטִירוּ אֲבוֹתֵינוּ לְפָנֶיךָ אֶת קְטֹרֶת הַסַּמִּים בִּזְמַן שֶׁבֵּית הַמִּקְדָּשׁ קַיָּם, כַּאֲשֶׁר צִוִּיתָ אוֹתָם עַל יְדֵי מֹשֶׁה נְבִיאֶךָ, כַּכָּתוּב בְּתוֹרָתֶךָ:

שמות ל:לד־לו, ז־ח

וַיֹּאמֶר יהוה אֶל מֹשֶׁה, קַח לְךָ סַמִּים,* נָטָף וּשְׁחֵלֶת וְחֶלְבְּנָה, סַמִּים וּלְבֹנָה זַכָּה, בַּד בְּבַד יִהְיֶה.* וְעָשִׂיתָ אֹתָהּ קְטֹרֶת, רֹקַח, מַעֲשֵׂה רוֹקֵחַ, מְמֻלָּח, טָהוֹר, קֹדֶשׁ. וְשָׁחַקְתָּ* מִמֶּנָּה הָדֵק, וְנָתַתָּה מִמֶּנָּה* לִפְנֵי הָעֵדֻת בְּאֹהֶל מוֹעֵד אֲשֶׁר אִוָּעֵד לְךָ שָׁמָּה, קֹדֶשׁ קָדָשִׁים תִּהְיֶה לָכֶם.

וְנֶאֱמַר: וְהִקְטִיר עָלָיו אַהֲרֹן קְטֹרֶת סַמִּים, בַּבֹּקֶר בַּבֹּקֶר, בְּהֵיטִיבוֹ אֶת הַנֵּרֹת* יַקְטִירֶנָּה. וּבְהַעֲלֹת אַהֲרֹן אֶת הַנֵּרֹת בֵּין הָעַרְבַּיִם, יַקְטִירֶנָּה, קְטֹרֶת תָּמִיד לִפְנֵי יהוה לְדֹרֹתֵיכֶם.

(approximately 4½ lbs.) of flour, and a quarter-*hin* (approx. 30 fl. oz.) each of oil and wine. A table of the amounts needed for other species may be found on p. 42.

סָבִיב — *All around.* Immediately after slaughter, the blood of the *tamid* was caught by a *Kohen* in a sacred utensil and dashed on the northeast and southwest corners of the Altar. This is called 'all around' because blood thrown at a corner would spread out to the two adjacent sides, so there would be some blood on each of the Altar's four sides.

קְטֹרֶת / INCENSE

Incense, blended according to a strictly prescribed formula, was burned in the Temple on the Golden Altar, morning and evening. The Golden Altar was located inside the Temple building. It was much smaller than the Altar used for offerings, which was covered with copper plates and was located in the Courtyard. *Arizal* writes that the careful recitation of this section helps bring one to repentance. *R' Hirsch* comments that the incense symbolized Israel's duty to make all its actions pleasing to God.

According to *Zohar*, the chapter and laws of קְטֹרֶת should be recited here 'in order to remove impurity from the world prior to the prayers [i.e., the complete *Shacharis* service] that take the place of offerings.' In response to the *Zohar's* dictum, it has become customary to include קְטֹרֶת in this part of the service. Interestingly, the Halachah also called for the recitation of קְטֹרֶת after *Shacharis* every day, following the Psalm of the Day, a practice still followed in *Nusach Sefard. Rama,* however, notes that since it is important to pronounce each of the ingredients and measurements carefully and clearly, because the recitation takes the place of the actual mixture which, as we shall see below, had to be exact; and since working people, under the stress of hurrying to earn their livelihood, often tend to slur or omit words in the last part of *Shacharis*, *Nusach Ashkenaz* omits the קְטֹרֶת at the end of *Shacharis*. Nevertheless, it is retained here

*He is to slaughter it on the north side of the Altar before HASHEM, and Aaron's sons the Kohanim are to dash its blood upon the Altar, all around.**[1]

In some congregations, the following supplication is omitted on the Sabbath and Festivals.

יְהִי רָצוֹן *May it be Your will, HASHEM, our God and the God of our forefathers, that this recital be worthy and acceptable, and favorable before You as if we had offered the continual offering in its set time, in its place, and according to its requirement.*

INCENSE

אַתָּה *It is You, HASHEM, our God, before Whom our forefathers burned the incense-spices in the time when the Holy Temple stood, as You commanded them through Moses Your prophet, as is written in Your Torah:*

Exodus 30:34-36, 7-8

וַיֹּאמֶר *HASHEM said to Moses: Take yourself spices* — stacte, onycha, and galbanum — spices and pure frankincense; they are all to be of equal weight.* You are to make it into incense, a spice-compound, the handiwork of an expert spice-compounder, thoroughly mixed, pure and holy. You are to grind* some of it finely and place some of it* before the Testimony in the Tent of Appointment, where I shall designate a time to meet you; it shall be a holy of holies for you.*

It is also written: Aaron shall burn upon it the incense-spices every morning; when he cleans the lamps he is to burn it. And when Aaron ignites the lamps in the afternoon, he is to burn it, as continual incense before HASHEM throughout your generations.*

(1) *Leviticus* 1:11.

---

because people who come to the synagogue early enough will recite it properly. On the Sabbath and festivals, however, קְטֹרֶת is indeed recited after *Mussaf* because on those days people have the time and peace of mind to recite the passages carefully *(Orach Chaim* 132:2).

וַיֹּאמֶר ה׳ ... קַח לְךָ סַמִּים — *HASHEM said to Moses: Take yourself spices.* As enumerated below in the Talmudic passage beginning תָּנוּ רַבָּנָן, *the Rabbis taught,* eleven different spices were used in the incense mixture, but only four of them — stacte, onycha, galbanum, and frankincense — are named in the Scriptural verse. The identity of the other spices is part of the Oral Law. That there are a total of eleven spices is derived from this verse in the following manner: סַמִּים, *spices,* is plural, yielding two kinds; then three spices are named, for a total of five; the word סַמִּים appears again implying the addition of another group of five (equivalent to the five given above). Finally *frankincense* is added, for a total of eleven.

It should be noted tnat the exact translations of the spices are not known with absolute certainty.

בַּד בְּבַד יִהְיֶה — *They are all to be of equal weight.* The four spices given by name are of equal weight. The other seven, however, were different from these four, as will be seen from the Talmudic passage that follows.

וְשָׁחַקְתָּ — *You are to grind.* The incense must be pulverized into a fine powder.

מִמֶּנָּה ... מִמֶּנָּה — *Some of it ... some of it.* The repetition alludes to the special Yom Kippur incense service, when the incense is reground and the *Kohen Gadol* [High Priest] takes it into the Holy of Holies, the only time of the year when a human being enters that most sacred place. On all other days, incense is burned twice a day in the Sanctuary.

בְּהֵיטִיבוֹ אֶת הַנֵּרֹת — *When he cleans the lamps.* The *Kohen* cleans the lamps of the Menorah every morning, after which the incense is burned.

כריתות ו., ירושלמי יומא ד:ה

תָּנוּ רַבָּנָן, פִּטּוּם הַקְּטֹרֶת כֵּיצַד.* שְׁלֹשׁ מֵאוֹת וְשִׁשִּׁים וּשְׁמוֹנָה מָנִים* הָיוּ בָהּ. שְׁלֹשׁ מֵאוֹת וְשִׁשִּׁים וַחֲמִשָּׁה כְּמִנְיַן יְמוֹת הַחַמָּה — מָנֶה לְכָל יוֹם, פְּרַס בְּשַׁחֲרִית וּפְרַס בֵּין הָעַרְבָּיִם; וּשְׁלֹשָׁה מָנִים יְתֵרִים,* שֶׁמֵּהֶם מַכְנִיס כֹּהֵן גָּדוֹל מְלֹא חָפְנָיו בְּיוֹם הַכִּפֻּרִים. וּמַחֲזִירָם לְמַכְתֶּשֶׁת בְּעֶרֶב יוֹם הַכִּפֻּרִים, וְשׁוֹחֲקָן יָפֶה יָפֶה כְּדֵי שֶׁתְּהֵא דַקָּה מִן הַדַּקָּה. וְאַחַד עָשָׂר סַמָּנִים הָיוּ בָהּ, וְאֵלּוּ הֵן: (א) הַצֳּרִי, (ב) וְהַצִּפֹּרֶן, (ג) הַחֶלְבְּנָה, (ד) וְהַלְּבוֹנָה, מִשְׁקַל שִׁבְעִים שִׁבְעִים מָנֶה; (ה) מוֹר, (ו) וּקְצִיעָה, (ז) שִׁבֹּלֶת נֵרְדְּ, (ח) וְכַרְכֹּם, מִשְׁקַל שִׁשָּׁה עָשָׂר שִׁשָּׁה עָשָׂר מָנֶה; (ט) הַקֹּשְׁטְ שְׁנֵים עָשָׂר, (י) וְקִלּוּפָה שְׁלֹשָׁה, (יא) וְקִנָּמוֹן תִּשְׁעָה. בֹּרִית כַּרְשִׁינָה תִּשְׁעָה קַבִּין, יֵין קַפְרִיסִין סְאִין* תְּלָתָא וְקַבִּין תְּלָתָא, וְאִם אֵין לוֹ יֵין קַפְרִיסִין, מֵבִיא חֲמַר חִוַּרְיָן עַתִּיק, מֶלַח סְדוֹמִית רֹבַע הַקָּב; מַעֲלֶה עָשָׁן* כָּל שֶׁהוּא. רַבִּי נָתָן הַבַּבְלִי אוֹמֵר: אַף כִּפַּת הַיַּרְדֵּן כָּל שֶׁהוּא. וְאִם נָתַן בָּהּ דְּבַשׁ, פְּסָלָהּ. וְאִם חִסַּר* אַחַת מִכָּל סַמָּנֶיהָ, חַיָּב מִיתָה.

רַבָּן שִׁמְעוֹן בֶּן גַּמְלִיאֵל אוֹמֵר: הַצֳּרִי אֵינוֹ אֶלָּא שְׂרָף הַנּוֹטֵף מֵעֲצֵי הַקְּטָף. בֹּרִית כַּרְשִׁינָה לָמָּה הִיא בָאָה, כְּדֵי לְיַפּוֹת בָּהּ אֶת הַצִּפֹּרֶן, כְּדֵי שֶׁתְּהֵא נָאָה. יֵין קַפְרִיסִין לָמָּה הוּא בָא, כְּדֵי לִשְׁרוֹת בּוֹ אֶת הַצִּפֹּרֶן, כְּדֵי שֶׁתְּהֵא עַזָּה. וַהֲלֹא מֵי רַגְלַיִם יָפִין לָהּ, אֶלָּא שֶׁאֵין מַכְנִיסִין מֵי רַגְלַיִם בַּמִּקְדָּשׁ מִפְּנֵי הַכָּבוֹד.

תַּנְיָא, רַבִּי נָתָן אוֹמֵר: כְּשֶׁהוּא שׁוֹחֵק, אוֹמֵר הָדֵק הֵיטֵב, הֵיטֵב הָדֵק, מִפְּנֵי שֶׁהַקּוֹל יָפֶה לַבְּשָׂמִים. פִּטְּמָהּ לַחֲצָאִין,* כְּשֵׁרָה; לִשְׁלִישׁ וְלִרְבִיעַ, לֹא שָׁמָעְנוּ. אָמַר רַבִּי יְהוּדָה: זֶה הַכְּלָל — אִם כְּמִדָּתָהּ, כְּשֵׁרָה לַחֲצָאִין; וְאִם

תָּנוּ רַבָּנָן פִּטּוּם הַקְּטֹרֶת כֵּיצַד — *The Rabbis taught: How is the incense mixture formulated?* This passage explains how the incense mixture was prepared and it gives the names and amounts that are not specified in Scriptures.

מָנִים — *Maneh.* A *maneh* is equal to approximately twenty ounces.

וּשְׁלֹשָׁה מָנִים יְתֵרִים — *And three extra maneh.* In addition to the regular incense service on Yom Kippur, there was a special service that was performed in the Holy of Holies. Three *maneh* were taken before Yom Kippur and ground again

Talmud, *Kereisos* 6a, *Yerushalmi Yoma* 4:5

תָּנוּ רַבָּנָן *The Rabbis taught: How is the incense mixture formulated?* Three hundred sixty-eight maneh* were in it: three hundred sixty-five corresponding to the days of the solar year — a maneh for each day, half in the morning and half in the afternoon; and three extra maneh,* from which the Kohen Gadol would bring both his handfuls [into the Holy of Holies] on Yom Kippur. He would return them to the mortar on the day before Yom Kippur, and grind them very thoroughly so that it would be exceptionally fine. Eleven kinds of spices were in it, as follows: (1) stacte, (2) onycha, (3) galbanum, (4) frankincense — each weighing seventy maneh; (5) myrrh, (6) cassia, (7) spikenard, (8) saffron — each weighing sixteen maneh; (9) costus — twelve maneh; (10) aromatic bark — three; and (11) cinnamon — nine. [Additionally] Carshina lye, nine kab; Cyprus wine, three se'ah* and three kab — if he has no Cyprus wine, he brings old white wine; Sodom salt, a quarter-kab; and a minute amount of maaleh ashan.* Rabbi Nassan the Babylonian says: Also a minute amount of Jordan amber. If he placed the fruit-honey into it, he invalidated it. But if he left out* any of its spices, he is liable to the death penalty.*

רַבָּן שִׁמְעוֹן *Rabban Shimon ben Gamliel says: The stacte is simply the sap that drips from balsam trees. Why is Carshina lye used? To bleach the onycha, to make it pleasing. Why is Cyprus wine used? So that the onycha could be soaked in it, to make it pungent. Even though urine is more suitable for that, nevertheless they do not bring urine into the Temple out of respect.*

תַּנְיָא *It is taught, Rabbi Nassan says: As one would grind [the incense] another would say, 'Grind thoroughly, thoroughly grind,' because the sound is beneficial for the spices. If one mixed it in half-quantities,* it was fit for use, but as to a third or a quarter — we have not heard the law. Rabbi Yehudah said: This is the general rule — In its proper proportion, it is fit for use in half the full amount; but if*

---

to make them extra fine. From that incense, the *Kohen Gadol* filled both hands, which he used for the special Yom Kippur service.

קַבִּין ... סְאִין — *Kab ... se'ah.* A *kab* contains a volume of approximately forty fluid ounces (but see p. 43). A *se'ah* is equal to six *kab.*

מַעֲלֶה עָשָׁן — *Maaleh ashan* [lit. *a smoke-raising herb*]. As implied by its name, the addition of this herb caused the smoke of the incense to ascend straight as a pillar.

וְאִם חִסַּר — *But if he left out,* i.e., if he used either more or less than the prescribed amount of any ingredient, he is liable to the heavenly death penalty *(Etz Yosef).* According to *Rashi* (*Kereisos* 6b) this liability applies only to the annual Yom Kippur service performed in the Holy of Holies, because the *Kohen Gadol* is considered to have made a בִּיאָה רֵיקָנִית, *an empty-handed coming,* since he did not have the proper mixture. *Rambam,* however, applies this ruling to the whole year *(Hil. Klei HaMikdash* 2:8) because it is regarded as קְטֹרֶת זָרָה, *strange* [i.e., unauthorized] *incense.*

פִּטְּמָהּ לַחֲצָאִין — *If one mixed it in half-quantities.* Instead of mixing 368 *maneh* as was customarily

חִסַּר אַחַת מִכָּל סַמָּנֶיהָ, חַיָּב מִיתָה.

תַּנְיָא, בַּר קַפָּרָא אוֹמֵר: אַחַת לְשִׁשִּׁים אוֹ לְשִׁבְעִים שָׁנָה* הָיְתָה בָאָה שֶׁל שִׁירַיִם לַחֲצָאִין. וְעוֹד תָּנֵי בַּר קַפָּרָא: אִלּוּ הָיָה נוֹתֵן בָּהּ קוֹרְטוֹב שֶׁל דְּבַשׁ,* אֵין אָדָם יָכוֹל לַעֲמֹד מִפְּנֵי רֵיחָהּ. וְלָמָּה אֵין מְעָרְבִין בָּהּ דְּבַשׁ, מִפְּנֵי שֶׁהַתּוֹרָה אָמְרָה: כִּי כָל שְׂאֹר וְכָל דְּבַשׁ לֹא תַקְטִירוּ מִמֶּנּוּ אִשֶּׁה לַיהוה.[1]

The next three verses, each beginning 'ה, are recited three times each.

יהוה צְבָאוֹת עִמָּנוּ,* מִשְׂגָּב לָנוּ אֱלֹהֵי יַעֲקֹב, סֶלָה.[2]

יהוה צְבָאוֹת, אַשְׁרֵי אָדָם בֹּטֵחַ בָּךְ.[3]

יהוה הוֹשִׁיעָה, הַמֶּלֶךְ יַעֲנֵנוּ בְיוֹם קָרְאֵנוּ.[4]

אַתָּה סֵתֶר לִי, מִצַּר תִּצְּרֵנִי, רָנֵּי פַלֵּט, תְּסוֹבְבֵנִי, סֶלָה.[5] וְעָרְבָה לַיהוה מִנְחַת יְהוּדָה וִירוּשָׁלָיִם, כִּימֵי עוֹלָם וּכְשָׁנִים קַדְמֹנִיּוֹת.[6]

יומא לג.

אַבַּיֵי הֲוָה מְסַדֵּר* סֵדֶר הַמַּעֲרָכָה מִשְּׁמָא דִגְמָרָא וְאַלִּבָּא דְאַבָּא שָׁאוּל: מַעֲרָכָה גְדוֹלָה* קוֹדֶמֶת לְמַעֲרָכָה שְׁנִיָּה* שֶׁל קְטֹרֶת; וּמַעֲרָכָה שְׁנִיָּה שֶׁל קְטֹרֶת קוֹדֶמֶת לְסִדּוּר

---

done, someone mixed only 184 *maneh.* Since the manner of compounding was transmitted orally, the question arose whether it was forbidden to prepare spice-mixtures totaling *less* than the usual 368 *maneh.* Rabbi Nassan stated that he had learned that it *was* permitted to make mixtures containing exactly half the normal amount, but he did not know whether smaller mixtures, too, were permitted. To this Rabbi Yehudah replied that any amount, even a one-day supply, was acceptable, provided the ingredients were in the correct proportion.

אַחַת לְשִׁשִּׁים אוֹ לְשִׁבְעִים שָׁנָה — *Once every sixty or seventy years.* We learned earlier that three *maneh* were set aside from which the *Kohen Gadol* filled his hands on Yom Kippur. A quantity (depending on the size of the *Kohen Gadol's* hands) of this mixture was unused, and was set aside. Over many years, enough of this leftover incense had accumulated to provide 184 *maneh,* or a half-year supply of incense. When that happened, only half the normal mixture had to be made for the coming year.

קוֹרְטוֹב שֶׁל דְּבַשׁ — *A kortov of fruit-honey.* Honey or any other fruit juice or product would have made the scent irresistible, but the Torah forbids the use of fruit products in the incense *(Rashi* to *Leviticus* 2:11; see *Mishnah L'Melech* to *Hil. Issurei Mizbe'ach* 5:1).

A *kortov* equals 1/256 of a *kab,* or approximately one-twentieth of a fluid ounce. Here it is used to mean a minimal amount, a touch.

☙ **ה׳ צְבָאוֹת עִמָּנוּ** — *HASHEM, Master of Legions, is with us. Yerushalmi Berachos* 5:1 cites Rabbi Yochanan who says of the first two verses, 'One should never let them depart from his mouth.' Therefore, they have been introduced into the daily prayers at several points. *Arizal* teaches that they should be repeated three times after each mention of קְטֹרֶת, *incense,* which is why they are inserted here and (in *Nusach Sefard)* when קְטֹרֶת is again recited after the morning prayers.

The first verse proclaims the principle of הַשְׁגָּחָה פְּרָטִית, *individual Providence,* while the second declares the praise of one who trusts in God. *Iyun Tefillah* points to two events that show how הַשְׁגָּחָה פְּרָטִית and total trust in God played important roles in shaping Rabbi Yochanan's life and lifestyle:

he left out any one of its spices, he is liable to the death penalty.

תַּנְיָא *It is taught, Bar Kappara says: Once every sixty or seventy years,* the accumulated leftovers reached half the yearly quantity. Bar Kappara taught further: Had one put a kortov of fruit-honey* into it, no person could have resisted its scent. Why did they not mix fruit-honey into it? — because the Torah says: 'For any leaven or any fruit-honey, you are not to burn from them a fire-offering to* H*ASHEM.'*[1]

The next three verses, each beginning, *'HASHEM,'* are recited three times each.

*HASHEM, Master of Legions, is with us,**
a stronghold for us is the God of Jacob, Selah![2]
HASHEM, Master of Legions,
praiseworthy is the person who trusts in You.[3]
HASHEM, save! May the King answer us on the day we call![4]

You are a shelter for me; from distress You preserve me; with glad song of rescue, You envelop me, Selah![5] *May the offering of Judah and Jerusalem be pleasing to HASHEM, as in days of old and in former years.*[6]

Talmud, *Yoma* 33a

אַבַּיֵי *Abaye listed* the order of the Altar service based on the tradition and according to Abba Shaul: The arrangement of the large pyre* precedes that of the secondary pyre* for the incense-offering; the secondary pyre for the incense-offering precedes the placement of*

(1) *Leviticus* 2:11. (2) *Psalms* 46:8. (3) 84:13. (4) 20:10. (5) 32:7. (6) *Malachi* 3:4.

Once, Rabbi Yochanan and his colleague Ilfa were so poverty stricken that they had no choice but to leave the study hall to seek their fortune. On the way, Rabbi Yochanan — but not Ilfa — heard one angel say to another that the two former students deserve to die because 'they forsake the eternal life and go to engage in a temporary life.' Since Ilfa did not hear the message, Rabbi Yochanan understood that it was directed not at Ilfa but at himself. He returned to the yeshivah and became the outstanding sage of his time (*Taanis* 21a). Thus, Rabbi Yochanan's life was changed by a particular incident of individual Providence.

As an elderly man, Rabbi Yochanan, who had become wealthy despite his Torah study, pointed out to Rabbi Chiya bar Abba many valuable properties that he had sold in order to enable him not to interrupt his Torah study. Rabbi Chiya wept at the thought that Rabbi Yochanan had left nothing for his own old age. Rabbi Yochanan replied, 'Chiya my son, do you think so little of what I have done? I have sold a material thing, that was presented after six days, as it says (*Exodus* 20:11): *For in six days HASHEM made heaven and earth.* But the Torah was given after forty days [of God's instruction to Moses] as it says (ibid. 34:28): *And* [Moses] *was there with HASHEM for forty days.'* It was because of such commitment that Rabbi Yochanan was regarded by his generation as the very symbol of dedication to Torah study and faith that God would provide for his material needs *(Shir HaShirim Rabbah* to 8:7). As a man of such faith, Rabbi Yochanan personifies the verse ... *praiseworthy is the person who trusts in You.*

אַבַּיֵי הֲוָה מְסַדֵּר — *Abaye listed.* **To conclude the description of the daily Temple service, we recite its full order as transmitted by Abaye. Although he lived several generations after the Destruction, he taught the order, as it had been transmitted orally, in the name of Abba Shaul, a Mishnaic sage *(tanna)* who lived in the time of Rabbi Meir. For the convenience of the reader we will define the less familiar terms:**

מַעֲרָכָה גְדוֹלָה — *The large pyre.* At the center of the Altar, a large pyre was arranged upon which the offerings were burned.

מַעֲרָכָה שְׁנִיָּה — *The secondary pyre.* Near the southwest corner of the Altar, a smaller pyre was

שְׁנֵי גִזְרֵי עֵצִים;* וְסִדּוּר שְׁנֵי גִזְרֵי עֵצִים קוֹדֵם לְדִשּׁוּן מִזְבֵּחַ הַפְּנִימִי;* וְדִשּׁוּן מִזְבֵּחַ הַפְּנִימִי קוֹדֵם לַהֲטָבַת חָמֵשׁ נֵרוֹת;* וַהֲטָבַת חָמֵשׁ נֵרוֹת קוֹדֶמֶת לְדַם הַתָּמִיד;* וְדַם הַתָּמִיד קוֹדֵם לַהֲטָבַת שְׁתֵּי נֵרוֹת; וַהֲטָבַת שְׁתֵּי נֵרוֹת קוֹדֶמֶת לִקְטֹרֶת; וּקְטֹרֶת קוֹדֶמֶת לְאֵבָרִים;* וְאֵבָרִים לְמִנְחָה;* וּמִנְחָה לַחֲבִתִּין;* וַחֲבִתִּין לִנְסָכִין;* וּנְסָכִין לְמוּסָפִין;* וּמוּסָפִין לְבָזִיכִין;* וּבָזִיכִין קוֹדְמִין לְתָמִיד שֶׁל בֵּין הָעַרְבָּיִם, שֶׁנֶּאֱמַר: וְעָרַךְ עָלֶיהָ הָעֹלָה, וְהִקְטִיר עָלֶיהָ חֶלְבֵי הַשְּׁלָמִים.[1] עָלֶיהָ הַשְׁלֵם* כָּל הַקָּרְבָּנוֹת כֻּלָּם.

אָנָּא בְּכֹחַ* גְּדֻלַּת יְמִינְךָ תַּתִּיר צְרוּרָה. אב״ג ית״ץ
קַבֵּל רִנַּת עַמְּךָ שַׂגְּבֵנוּ טַהֲרֵנוּ נוֹרָא. קר״ע שט״ן
נָא גִבּוֹר דּוֹרְשֵׁי יִחוּדְךָ כְּבָבַת שָׁמְרֵם. נג״ד יכ״ש
בָּרְכֵם טַהֲרֵם רַחֲמֵם צִדְקָתְךָ תָּמִיד גָּמְלֵם. בט״ר צת״ג
חֲסִין קָדוֹשׁ בְּרוֹב טוּבְךָ נַהֵל עֲדָתֶךָ. חק״ב טנ״ע
יָחִיד גֵּאֶה לְעַמְּךָ פְּנֵה זוֹכְרֵי קְדֻשָּׁתֶךָ. יג״ל פז״ק
שַׁוְעָתֵנוּ קַבֵּל וּשְׁמַע צַעֲקָתֵנוּ יוֹדֵעַ תַּעֲלֻמוֹת. שק״ו צי״ת
בָּרוּךְ שֵׁם כְּבוֹד מַלְכוּתוֹ לְעוֹלָם וָעֶד.

In some congregations, the following paragraph is omitted on the Sabbath and Festivals.

רִבּוֹן הָעוֹלָמִים,* אַתָּה צִוִּיתָנוּ לְהַקְרִיב קָרְבַּן הַתָּמִיד בְּמוֹעֲדוֹ, וְלִהְיוֹת כֹּהֲנִים בַּעֲבוֹדָתָם, וּלְוִיִּם בְּדוּכָנָם, וְיִשְׂרָאֵל בְּמַעֲמָדָם. וְעַתָּה בַּעֲוֹנוֹתֵינוּ חָרַב בֵּית הַמִּקְדָּשׁ וּבָטֵל

---

maintained, from which glowing coals were taken into the Sanctuary for the burning of the daily incense.

סִדּוּר שְׁנֵי גִזְרֵי עֵצִים — *The placement of two logs.* Two large sections of wood were placed on the large pyre every morning. More wood could be added during the day, as needed.

מִזְבֵּחַ הַפְּנִימִי — *The Inner Altar.* Made of wood plated with gold and much smaller than the Outer Altar (one cubit across versus thirty-two), the Inner Altar was used on a daily basis and only for incense.

הֲטָבַת חָמֵשׁ נֵרוֹת — *The cleaning of five lamps* [*of the Menorah*]. The Temple Menorah had seven lamps. Scriptural exegesis teaches that the lamps, which had burned all night, are cleaned in two steps, first five and then the remaining two.

דַּם הַתָּמִיד — *The* [dashing of the] *blood of the continual offering.* The slaughter had taken place before the cleaning of the lamps.

אֵבָרִים — *The* [burning of the] *limbs,* of the *tamid,* continual offering.

מִנְחָה — *The meal-offering,* that accompanied the *tamid.*

חֲבִתִּין — *The pancakes.* The *Kohen Gadol* was required to bring a meal-offering every day, half in the morning and half in the afternoon. It was baked in a low, flat pan called a מַחֲבַת, hence the name מִנְחַת חֲבִתִּין [the Hebrew **חֲבִתִּין** is related to **מַחֲבַת**].

נְסָכִין — *The wine-libations,* that accompanied the *tamid.*

מוּסָפִין — *The mussaf-offering,* on the Sabbath,

two logs; the placement of two logs precedes the removal of ashes from the Inner Altar;* the removal of ashes from the Inner Altar precedes the cleaning of five lamps [of the Menorah];* the cleaning of the five lamps precedes the [dashing of the] blood of the continual offering; the blood of the continual offering* precedes the cleaning of the [other] two lamps; the cleaning of the two lamps precedes the incense; the incense precedes the [burning of the] limbs;* the [burning of the] limbs [precedes] the meal-offering;* the meal-offering [precedes] the pancakes;* the pancakes [precede] the wine-libations;* the wine-libations [precede] the mussaf-offering;* the mussaf-offering [precedes] the bowls [of frankincense];* the bowls [precede] the afternoon continual offering, for it is said: 'And he is to arrange the elevation-offering upon it and burn the fats of the peace-offerings upon it,'[1] — 'upon it' [the elevation-offering] you are to complete* all the [day's] offerings.*

אָנָּא בְּכֹחַ *We beg You! With the strength* of Your right hand's greatness, untie the bundled sins. Accept the prayer of Your nation; strengthen us, purify us, O Awesome One. Please, O Strong One — those who foster Your Oneness, guard them like the pupil of an eye. Bless them, purify them, show them pity, may Your righteousness always recompense them. Powerful Holy One, with Your abundant goodness guide Your congregation. One and only Exalted One, turn to Your nation, which proclaims Your holiness. Accept our entreaty and hear our cry, O Knower of mysteries.*

Blessed is the Name of His glorious Kingdom for all eternity.

In some congregations, the following paragraph is omitted on the Sabbath and Festivals.

רִבּוֹן הָעוֹלָמִים *Master of the worlds,* You commanded us to bring the continual offering at its set time, and that the Kohanim be at their assigned service, the Levites on their platform, and the Israelites at their station. But now, through our sins, the Holy Temple is destroyed, the*

(1) *Leviticus* 6:5.

festivals, and Rosh Chodesh.

בָּזִיכִין — *The bowls* [*of frankincense*]. Two bowls of לְבוֹנָה, *frankincense,* were placed with the showbread every week. The bread was eaten by the *Kohanim* and the incense was burned on the Altar after the showbread was removed from the Table.

הַשְּׁלָמִים עָלֶיהָ הַשְׁלֵם — *Of the peace-offerings ... upon it you are to complete.* The Sages expound the word הַשְּׁלָמִים, *the peace-offering.* It is interpreted as if pronounced הַשְׁלָמִים, *the completions,* meaning that all the services of the day should be completed after the morning *tamid,* and before the afternoon *tamid.*

⇐§ **אָנָּא בְּכֹחַ** — *We beg You! With the strength ...* This prayer — ascribed to the *tanna* Rabbi Nechunia ben Hakanah — has profound mystical significance. It is inserted at this point because it is an eloquent prayer that God save Israel from exile. After having recited the order of the Temple service, it is a most fitting time for us to pray for the redemption *(Seder HaYom).* A commentary can be found on p. 315.

⇐§ **רִבּוֹן הָעוֹלָמִים** — *Master of the worlds.* We pray that our recitation of the morning service be accepted in place of the Temple service that we cannot perform. As we say later in this prayer, *'Let our lips compensate for the bulls,'* meaning

הַתָּמִיד, וְאֵין לָנוּ לֹא כֹהֵן בַּעֲבוֹדָתוֹ, וְלֹא לֵוִי בְּדוּכָנוֹ, וְלֹא יִשְׂרָאֵל בְּמַעֲמָדוֹ.* וְאַתָּה אָמַרְתָּ: וּנְשַׁלְּמָה פָרִים שְׂפָתֵינוּ.[1] לָכֵן יְהִי רָצוֹן מִלְּפָנֶיךָ, יהוה אֱלֹהֵינוּ וֵאלֹהֵי אֲבוֹתֵינוּ, שֶׁיְּהֵא שִׂיחַ שִׂפְתוֹתֵינוּ חָשׁוּב וּמְקֻבָּל וּמְרֻצֶּה לְפָנֶיךָ, כְּאִלּוּ הִקְרַבְנוּ קָרְבַּן הַתָּמִיד בְּמוֹעֲדוֹ, וְעָמַדְנוּ עַל מַעֲמָדוֹ.

On the Sabbath add (במדבר כח:ט-י):

וּבְיוֹם הַשַּׁבָּת שְׁנֵי כְבָשִׂים בְּנֵי שָׁנָה תְּמִימִם, וּשְׁנֵי עֶשְׂרֹנִים סֹלֶת מִנְחָה בְּלוּלָה בַשֶּׁמֶן, וְנִסְכּוֹ. עֹלַת שַׁבַּת בְּשַׁבַּתּוֹ, עַל עֹלַת הַתָּמִיד וְנִסְכָּהּ.

On Rosh Chodesh add (במדבר כח:יא-טו):

וּבְרָאשֵׁי חָדְשֵׁיכֶם תַּקְרִיבוּ עֹלָה לַיהוה, פָּרִים בְּנֵי בָקָר שְׁנַיִם, וְאַיִל אֶחָד, כְּבָשִׂים בְּנֵי שָׁנָה שִׁבְעָה, תְּמִימִם. וּשְׁלֹשָׁה עֶשְׂרֹנִים סֹלֶת מִנְחָה בְּלוּלָה בַשֶּׁמֶן לַפָּר הָאֶחָד, וּשְׁנֵי עֶשְׂרֹנִים סֹלֶת מִנְחָה בְּלוּלָה בַשֶּׁמֶן לָאַיִל הָאֶחָד. וְעִשָּׂרֹן עִשָּׂרוֹן, סֹלֶת מִנְחָה בְּלוּלָה בַשֶּׁמֶן, לַכֶּבֶשׂ הָאֶחָד, עֹלָה רֵיחַ נִיחֹחַ, אִשֶּׁה לַיהוה. וְנִסְכֵּיהֶם — חֲצִי הַהִין יִהְיֶה לַפָּר, וּשְׁלִישִׁת הַהִין לָאַיִל, וּרְבִיעִת הַהִין לַכֶּבֶשׂ — יָיִן; זֹאת עֹלַת חֹדֶשׁ בְּחָדְשׁוֹ לְחָדְשֵׁי הַשָּׁנָה. וּשְׂעִיר עִזִּים אֶחָד לְחַטָּאת לַיהוה, עַל עֹלַת הַתָּמִיד יֵעָשֶׂה, וְנִסְכּוֹ.

משנה, זבחים פרק ה

[א] **אֵיזֶהוּ** מְקוֹמָן* שֶׁל זְבָחִים. קָדְשֵׁי קָדָשִׁים* שְׁחִיטָתָן בַּצָּפוֹן.* פַּר וְשָׂעִיר שֶׁל יוֹם הַכִּפּוּרִים שְׁחִיטָתָן

that our recitation must take the place of the actual offerings.

לֹא כֹהֵן בַּעֲבוֹדָתוֹ, וְלֹא לֵוִי בְּדוּכָנוֹ, וְלֹא יִשְׂרָאֵל בְּמַעֲמָדוֹ — *Neither Kohen at his service, nor Levite on his platform, nor Israelite at his station.* All three categories of Jews were represented in the daily communal service. The *Kohanim* performed the service, Levites stood on a platform to sing the psalm of the day (see p. 162), and the rest of the nation had delegates who recited special prayers and Scriptural passages.

☙ Mussaf / Additional Offerings

On the Sabbath, festivals, and Rosh Chodesh, the *mussaf* — literally *additional* — offerings are brought in addition to the regular *tamid* offering. Therefore, we recite the verses that detail the particular offering, just as we recite the passages regarding the other communal offerings. As noted above, all elevation- and peace-offerings are accompanied by meal-offerings [consisting of meal mixed with olive oil] and wine-libations. The amounts of these offerings vary according to the kind of animal they accompany; the larger the species, the more meal and wine. For the convenience of the reader, we offer the following conversions into ounces. The amount of oil used for each meal-offering is the same as the amount of wine used for the libation.

It should be noted that the Talmud gives the various measurements in terms of the volume of

Animal Offering	Volume of Meal			Volume of Wine-Libation		
	Biblical	eggs	fluid oz.	Biblical	eggs	fluid oz.
פַּר, *Bull*	3 tenth-*ephah*	129.6	220	½ *hin*	36	61.2
אַיִל, *Ram*	2 tenth-*ephah*	86.4	147	⅓ *hin*	24	40.8
כֶּבֶשׂ, *Yearling Lamb*	1 tenth-*ephah*	43.2	73	¼ *hin*	18	30.6

continual offering is discontinued, and we have neither Kohen at his service, nor Levite on his platform, nor Israelite at his station. But You said: 'Let our lips compensate for the bulls'*[1] *— therefore may it be Your will,* HASHEM, *our God and the God of our forefathers, that the prayer of our lips be worthy, acceptable and favorable before You, as if we had brought the continual offering at its set time and we had stood at its station.*

On the Sabbath add (*Numbers* 28:9-10):

וּבְיוֹם *On the Sabbath day [the mussaf-offering is]: two [male] first-year lambs, unblemished; two tenth-ephah of fine flour for a meal-offering, mixed with olive oil, and its wine-libation. The elevation-offering of the Sabbath must be on its particular Sabbath, in addition to the continual elevation-offering and its wine-libation.*

On Rosh Chodesh add (*Numbers* 28:11-15):

וּבְרָאשֵׁי *On the first days of your months you are to bring an elevation-offering to* HASHEM, *two young bulls, one ram, seven [male] first-year lambs, unblemished. And three tenth-ephah of fine flour for a meal-offering mixed with olive oil for each bull, and two tenth-ephah of fine flour for a meal-offering mixed with olive oil for each ram. And a tenth-ephah of fine flour for a meal-offering mixed with olive oil for each lamb — an elevation-offering, a satisfying aroma, a fire-offering to* HASHEM. *And their libations — there is to be a half-hin for a bull, a third-hin for a ram, a quarter-hin for a lamb — of wine. This is the elevation-offering of the month upon its renewal, for the months of the year. And one he-goat for a sin-offering to* HASHEM, *in addition to the continual elevation-offering, should it be made — and its wine libation.*

Mishnah, *Zevachim* Chapter 5

[1] **אֵיזֶהוּ** *What is the location* of the offerings? [Regarding] the most holy offerings,* their slaughter is in the north.* The slaughter of the bull and the he-goat of Yom Kippur is in the*

(1) *Hoshea* 14:3.

an average egg. We base our conversions on the minimal authoritative opinion, which estimates the volume of the Talmudic 'egg' at 1.7 fluid ounces. Other authoritative estimates range to as much as twice this figure.

אֵיזֶהוּ מְקוֹמָן / What is the Location

The Talmud *(Kiddushin* 30a) teaches that one should study Scripture, Mishnah [i.e., the compilation of laws], and Gemara [i.e., the explanation of the laws] every day. In fulfillment of that injunction, the Sages instituted that appropriate passages from each of these three categories be included in this section of *Shacharis.* Since Scriptural passages regarding the Temple offerings are part of the service in any case, the Sages chose a chapter of the Mishnah on the same subject. Chapter 5 of *Zevachim,* which begins אֵיזֶהוּ מְקוֹמָן, *What is the location,* was chosen for three reasons: (a) It discusses all the sacrifices; (b) it is the only chapter in the Mishnah in which there is no halachic dispute; and (c) its text is of very ancient origin, possibly even from the days of Moses.

1. אֵיזֶהוּ מְקוֹמָן — *What is the location?* In discussing the various categories of animal offerings, this chapter focuses on the location in the Courtyard where they were slaughtered and the part of the Altar upon which their blood was placed.

קָדְשֵׁי קָדָשִׁים — *The most holy offerings.* Sin- [חַטָּאוֹת], guilt- [אֲשָׁמוֹת], elevation- [עוֹלוֹת], and communal peace- [זִבְחֵי שַׁלְמֵי צִבּוּר] offerings are called 'most holy offerings' because they have stricter laws than individual peace- [שְׁלָמִים] and

בְּצָפוֹן, וְקִבּוּל דָּמָן בִּכְלִי שָׁרֵת* בְּצָפוֹן. וְדָמָן טָעוּן הַזָּיָה עַל בֵּין הַבַּדִּים,* וְעַל הַפָּרֹכֶת,* וְעַל מִזְבַּח הַזָּהָב.* מַתָּנָה אַחַת מֵהֶן מְעַכֶּבֶת.* שְׁיָרֵי הַדָּם הָיָה שׁוֹפֵךְ עַל יְסוֹד מַעֲרָבִי שֶׁל מִזְבֵּחַ הַחִיצוֹן; אִם לֹא נָתַן, לֹא עִכֵּב.

[ב] **פָּרִים** הַנִּשְׂרָפִים* וּשְׂעִירִים הַנִּשְׂרָפִים* שְׁחִיטָתָן בְּצָפוֹן, וְקִבּוּל דָּמָן בִּכְלִי שָׁרֵת בְּצָפוֹן. וְדָמָן טָעוּן הַזָּיָה עַל הַפָּרֹכֶת וְעַל מִזְבַּח הַזָּהָב. מַתָּנָה אַחַת מֵהֶן מְעַכֶּבֶת. שְׁיָרֵי הַדָּם הָיָה שׁוֹפֵךְ עַל יְסוֹד מַעֲרָבִי שֶׁל מִזְבֵּחַ הַחִיצוֹן; אִם לֹא נָתַן, לֹא עִכֵּב. אֵלּוּ וָאֵלּוּ נִשְׂרָפִין בְּבֵית הַדֶּשֶׁן.*

[ג] **חַטֹּאת** הַצִּבּוּר וְהַיָּחִיד* — אֵלּוּ הֵן חַטֹּאת הַצִּבּוּר, שְׂעִירֵי רָאשֵׁי חֳדָשִׁים וְשֶׁל מוֹעֲדוֹת — שְׁחִיטָתָן בְּצָפוֹן, וְקִבּוּל דָּמָן בִּכְלִי שָׁרֵת בְּצָפוֹן. וְדָמָן טָעוּן אַרְבַּע מַתָּנוֹת עַל אַרְבַּע קְרָנוֹת. כֵּיצַד, עָלָה בַכֶּבֶשׁ, וּפָנָה לַסּוֹבֵב* וּבָא לוֹ לְקֶרֶן דְּרוֹמִית מִזְרָחִית, מִזְרָחִית צְפוֹנִית, צְפוֹנִית מַעֲרָבִית, מַעֲרָבִית דְּרוֹמִית. שְׁיָרֵי הַדָּם הָיָה שׁוֹפֵךְ עַל

---

thanksgiving- [תּוֹדָה] offerings [see below, 6-8], which are called 'offerings of lesser holiness' [קָדָשִׁים קַלִּים]. Among the stricter laws that typify the most-holy offerings are that they must be eaten in, and may not be removed from, the Temple Courtyard; and that anyone who makes personal use of them, even before their blood is sprinkled [מוֹעֵל בְּהֶקְדֵּשׁ], must undergo a procedure of atonement. Offerings of lesser holiness, on the other hand, may be eaten and taken anywhere within the walls of Jerusalem, and one who makes personal use of them requires atonement only if he does so after the blood has been sprinkled.

בְּצָפוֹן — *In the north,* i.e., in the Courtyard to the north of the Altar.

בִּכְלִי שָׁרֵת — *In a service-vessel.* Special vessels were set aside in the Sanctuary for the purpose of receiving blood from the animal's neck after slaughter.

עַל בֵּין הַבַּדִּים — *Between the poles* [*of the Holy Ark*]. On Yom Kippur, the *Kohen Gadol* brought blood into the Holy of Holies and sprinkled part of it toward the Holy Ark, between the two poles of the Ark that extended from either side of it toward the Sanctuary.

וְעַל הַפָּרֹכֶת — *And toward the Curtain,* that separated the Holy of Holies from the Sanctuary. Toward this Curtain, too, the *Kohen Gadol* sprinkled blood.

מִזְבַּח הַזָּהָב — *The Golden Altar,* upon which the incense was burned every day. See above p. 34.

מַתָּנָה אַחַת מֵהֶן מְעַכֶּבֶת — *Every one of these applications* [*of blood*] *is essential* [lit. *prevents*], i.e., atonement has not been achieved if even one of the above blood applications was omitted.

2. פָּרִים הַנִּשְׂרָפִים — *The bulls that are completely burned.* Certain parts (see *Leviticus* 4:8-12) of the animal are placed upon the Altar-pyre to be consumed by the fire. The remainder of the animal is burned outside of Jerusalem (see below).

With the exception of the Yom Kippur sacrifices, only two kinds of bull offerings are completely burned, no part of them being eaten by the *Kohanim.* They are (a) פַּר הֶעְלֵם דָּבָר שֶׁל צִבּוּר, the bull brought if the Sanhedrin erred in a halachic ruling, and, as a result of following that ruling, most of the people violated a commandment for which, if the sin had been committed intentionally, the penalty would be כָּרֵת, *spiritual excision;* (b) פַּר כֹּהֵן מָשִׁיחַ, the bull brought by the *Kohen Gadol* if he made an erroneous halachic decision regarding the above

north and the reception of their blood in a service-vessel is in the north. Their blood requires sprinkling between the poles [of the Holy Ark],* and toward the Curtain* [of the Holy of Holies] and upon the Golden Altar.* Every one of these applications [of blood] is essential.* The leftover blood he would pour onto the western base of the Outer Altar; but if he failed to apply it [the leftover blood on the base], he has not prevented [atonement].*

[2] **פָּרִים** *[Regarding] the bulls that are completely burned* and he-goats that are completely burned,* their slaughter is in the north, and the reception of their blood in a service-vessel is in the north. Their blood requires sprinkling toward the Curtain and upon the Golden Altar. Every one of these applications is essential. The leftover blood he would pour onto the western base of the Outer Altar; but if he failed to apply it [the leftover blood on the base] he has not prevented [atonement]. Both these and those [the Yom Kippur offerings] are burned in the place where the [Altar] ashes are deposited.**

[3] **חַטֹּאת** *[Regarding] sin-offerings of the community and of the individual* — the communal sin-offerings are the following: the he-goats of Rosh Chodesh and festivals — their slaughter [of all sin-offerings] is in the north and the reception of their blood in a service-vessel is in the north. Their blood requires four applications, [one] on [each of] the four corners [of the Altar]. How is it done? He [the Kohen] ascended the [Altar] ramp, turned to the surrounding ledge* and arrived at the southeast [corner], the northeast, the northwest, and the southwest. The leftover blood he would pour out*

---

type of sin and himself acted on this ruling.

שְׂעִירִים הַנִּשְׂרָפִים — *He-goats that are completely burned.* If the Sanhedrin (highest court) erroneously permitted an act that was a violation of the laws against idol worship, and a majority of the community followed their ruling, their atonement consists of a communal sin-offering — a he-goat that is completely burned.

נִשְׂרָפִין בְּבֵית הַדָּשֶׁן — *Are burned in the place where the [Altar] ashes are deposited.* The excess ashes from the Altar were removed whenever necessary to a ritually clean place outside of Jerusalem. The offerings mentioned in this mishnah and also the offerings of Yom Kippur were burned in that place.

3. חַטֹּאת הַצִּבּוּר וְהַיָּחִיד — *Sin-offerings of the community and of the individual.* Before giving the laws of sin-offerings, the mishnah lists the kinds of communal sin-offerings that fall under this category. The listing is necessary, because the earlier mishnayos, too, have discussed communal sin-offerings, but they fell under the special category of offerings that were completely burned.

וּפָנָה לַסּוֹבֵב — *Turned to the surrounding ledge.* The Altar was ten cubits high. Six cubits above the ground, a one-cubit wide ledge went completely around the Altar. The walls ascended another three cubits to the Altar top upon which the pyres (see p. 31) burned. In the square cubit located at each corner of the Altar top, the walls rose an additional cubit. These four protrusions were called קַרְנוֹת הַמִּזְבֵּחַ, *the 'corners' of the Altar,* and it was on these 'corners' that the blood of the sin-offerings was placed. In order to reach these ten-cubit high 'corners,' the *Kohen* walked around the Altar on the surrounding ledge, with the utensil containing the blood. He stopped at each 'corner' of the Altar, dipped his right index finger into the utensil containing the blood, and

יְסוֹד דְּרוֹמִי. וְנֶאֱכָלִין לִפְנִים מִן הַקְּלָעִים,* לְזִכְרֵי כְהֻנָּה, בְּכָל מַאֲכָל, לְיוֹם וָלַיְלָה, עַד חֲצוֹת.*

[ד] **הָעוֹלָה** קֹדֶשׁ קָדָשִׁים. שְׁחִיטָתָהּ בַּצָּפוֹן, וְקִבּוּל דָּמָהּ בִּכְלִי שָׁרֵת בַּצָּפוֹן. וְדָמָהּ טָעוּן שְׁתֵּי מַתָּנוֹת שֶׁהֵן אַרְבַּע;* וּטְעוּנָה הֶפְשֵׁט* וְנִתּוּחַ,* וְכָלִיל לָאִשִּׁים.

[ה] **זִבְחֵי** שַׁלְמֵי צִבּוּר* וַאֲשָׁמוֹת,* אֵלּוּ הֵן אֲשָׁמוֹת: אֲשַׁם גְּזֵלוֹת,* אֲשַׁם מְעִילוֹת,* אֲשַׁם שִׁפְחָה חֲרוּפָה,* אֲשַׁם נָזִיר,* אֲשַׁם מְצוֹרָע,* אָשָׁם תָּלוּי.* שְׁחִיטָתָן בַּצָּפוֹן, וְקִבּוּל דָּמָן בִּכְלִי שָׁרֵת בַּצָּפוֹן, וְדָמָן טָעוּן שְׁתֵּי מַתָּנוֹת שֶׁהֵן אַרְבַּע. וְנֶאֱכָלִין לִפְנִים מִן הַקְּלָעִים לְזִכְרֵי כְהֻנָּה, בְּכָל מַאֲכָל, לְיוֹם וָלַיְלָה, עַד חֲצוֹת.

[ו] **הַתּוֹדָה*** וְאֵיל נָזִיר* קָדָשִׁים קַלִּים.* שְׁחִיטָתָן בְּכָל מָקוֹם בָּעֲזָרָה, וְדָמָן טָעוּן שְׁתֵּי מַתָּנוֹת שֶׁהֵן אַרְבַּע. וְנֶאֱכָלִין בְּכָל הָעִיר, לְכָל אָדָם, בְּכָל מַאֲכָל, לְיוֹם

---

deposited the blood upon the 'corner.' Then he would go on to the next 'corner.'

וְנֶאֱכָלִין לִפְנִים מִן הַקְּלָעִים — *They are eaten within the [Courtyard] curtains.* After the specified fats are removed to be burned on the Altar, the flesh of the sin-offerings is distributed to be eaten by male *Kohanim.* It could be prepared and eaten only within the Temple Courtyard. The term 'curtains' is borrowed from the period in the Wilderness, when the Tabernacle Courtyard was enclosed not by walls, but by curtains.

עַד חֲצוֹת — *Until midnight.* A sin-offering could be eaten for the remainder of the day on which it was sacrificed and for the following evening. Under Scriptural law it could be eaten until dawn, but the Sages imposed a deadline of midnight to prevent mishaps.

4. שְׁתֵּי מַתָּנוֹת שֶׁהֵן אַרְבַּע — *Two applications that are equivalent to four.* As explained above in the chapter of the *tamid,* p. 34, blood was thrown from the service-vessel at two corners of the Altar walls: the northeast and the southwest. The blood would spread out to the two adjacent walls. Thus, the two applications of blood would put blood on all four walls of the Altar.

הֶפְשֵׁט — *Flaying.* The hide of all offerings of greater holiness (other than those discussed in mishnah 2) was removed and given to the *Kohanim.*

וְנִתּוּחַ — *And dismemberment.* The elevation offering was cut up in a prescribed way; only then was it completely burned.

5. זִבְחֵי שַׁלְמֵי צִבּוּר — *Communal peace-offerings.* The only such offerings are the two sheep that are brought in addition to the Shavuos *mussaf*-offering [*Leviticus* 23:19]. The other communal offerings are either sin- or elevation-offerings.

אֲשָׁמוֹת — *Guilt-offerings.* There are six kinds of guilt-offerings, all of which are listed in this mishnah. They are:

(a) אֲשַׁם גְּזֵלוֹת — ... *for thefts.* If someone owed money — whether a loan, a theft, an article held in safekeeping, or whatever — and intentionally swore falsely that he did not owe it, he is required to bring a guilt-offering as an atonement. See *Leviticus* 5:20-26.

(b) אֲשַׁם מְעִילוֹת — ... *for misuse of sacred objects.* If someone unintentionally used objects belonging to the Sanctuary for his personal benefit he must atone by bringing a guilt-offering. See ibid. 5:14-16.

(c) אֲשַׁם שִׁפְחָה חֲרוּפָה — ... [*for violating*] *a betrothed maidservant.* The woman involved

on the southern base. They are eaten within the [Courtyard] curtains, by males of the priesthood, prepared in any manner, on the same day and that night until midnight.**

[4] **הָעוֹלָה** *The elevation-offering is among the most holy offerings. Its slaughter is in the north and the reception of its blood in a service-vessel is in the north. Its blood requires two applications that are equivalent to four.* It requires flaying* and dismemberment,* and it is entirely consumed by the fire.*

[5] **זִבְחֵי** *[Regarding] communal peace-offerings* and [personal] guilt-offerings* — the guilt-offerings are as follows: the guilt-offering for thefts,* the guilt-offering for misuse of sacred objects,* the guilt-offering [for violating] a betrothed maidservant,* the guilt-offering of a Nazirite,* the guilt-offering of a metzora,* and a guilt-offering in case of doubt* — their slaughter is in the north and the reception of their blood in a service-vessel is in the north. Their blood requires two applications that are equivalent to four. They are eaten within the [Courtyard] curtains, by males of the priesthood, prepared in any manner, on the same day and that night until midnight.*

[6] **הַתּוֹדָה** *The thanksgiving-offering* and the ram of a Nazirite* are offerings of lesser holiness.* Their slaughter is anywhere in the Courtyard, and their blood requires two applications that are equivalent to four. They are eaten throughout the City [of Jerusalem] by anyone, prepared in any manner, on the same day*

---

was a non-Jewish slave who had been owned by two Jewish partners. One of the partners freed her, thus making her half free and half slave. But since a freed non-Jewish slave has the same status as a proselyte, this half free maidservant is half Jewish and half non-Jewish and is forbidden to marry either a non-Jew or a Jew. She is, however, permitted to a Jewish indentured servant [עֶבֶד עִבְרִי], who is permitted to both a Jewish woman and a non-Jewish maidservant. If she became betrothed to a Jewish indentured servant and subsequently had relations with another man, the adulterer must bring a guilt-offering in atonement.

(d) אֲשַׁם נָזִיר — ... *of a Nazirite,* who became טָמֵא, *ritually contaminated,* through contact with a corpse. See *Numbers* 6:9-12.

(e) אֲשַׁם מְצוֹרָע — ... *of a metzora.* One afflicted by the leprous disease described in *Leviticus* (ch. 13) regains his complete ritual purity upon bringing a series of offerings after he is cured. The guilt-offering is brought on the eighth day after he is pronounced cured. See *Leviticus* 14:10-12.

(f) אָשָׁם תָּלוּי — ... *in case of doubt.* This is the only guilt-offering not prescribed for a specific offense or phenomenon. It is required whenever there is a question of whether one has become liable to bring a חַטָּאת, *sin-offering.* As long as such a doubt exists, the possible transgressor can protect himself from punishment through a guilt-offering. However, if and when it becomes established that the offense was indeed committed, the person must bring his sin-offering. See *Leviticus* 5:17-19.

6. הַתּוֹדָה — *The thanksgiving-offering.* This offering is brought by someone who survives serious danger or illness. See ibid. 7:12.

אֵיל נָזִיר — *Ram of a Nazirite,* which is brought when a Nazirite completes the period of abstinence he has accepted upon himself. See *Numbers* 6:13-21.

קָדָשִׁים קַלִּים — *Offerings of lesser holiness.* Their greater leniency is obvious from a comparison of the laws in this mishnah with those above.

וְלַיְלָה, עַד חֲצוֹת. הַמּוּרָם מֵהֶם* כַּיּוֹצֵא בָהֶם, אֶלָּא שֶׁהַמּוּרָם נֶאֱכָל לַכֹּהֲנִים, לִנְשֵׁיהֶם וְלִבְנֵיהֶם וּלְעַבְדֵיהֶם.

[ז] **שְׁלָמִים*** קָדָשִׁים קַלִּים. שְׁחִיטָתָן בְּכָל מָקוֹם בָּעֲזָרָה, וְדָמָן טָעוּן שְׁתֵּי מַתָּנוֹת שֶׁהֵן אַרְבַּע. וְנֶאֱכָלִין בְּכָל הָעִיר, לְכָל אָדָם, בְּכָל מַאֲכָל, לִשְׁנֵי יָמִים וְלַיְלָה אֶחָד. הַמּוּרָם מֵהֶם כַּיּוֹצֵא בָהֶם, אֶלָּא שֶׁהַמּוּרָם נֶאֱכָל לַכֹּהֲנִים, לִנְשֵׁיהֶם וְלִבְנֵיהֶם וּלְעַבְדֵיהֶם.

[ח] **הַבְּכוֹר** וְהַמַּעֲשֵׂר וְהַפֶּסַח קָדָשִׁים קַלִּים. שְׁחִיטָתָן בְּכָל מָקוֹם בָּעֲזָרָה, וְדָמָן טָעוּן מַתָּנָה אֶחָת,* וּבִלְבָד שֶׁיִּתֵּן כְּנֶגֶד הַיְסוֹד. שִׁנָּה בַאֲכִילָתָן: הַבְּכוֹר נֶאֱכָל לַכֹּהֲנִים, וְהַמַּעֲשֵׂר לְכָל אָדָם. וְנֶאֱכָלִין בְּכָל הָעִיר, בְּכָל מַאֲכָל, לִשְׁנֵי יָמִים וְלַיְלָה אֶחָד. הַפֶּסַח אֵינוֹ נֶאֱכָל אֶלָּא בַלַּיְלָה, וְאֵינוֹ נֶאֱכָל אֶלָּא עַד חֲצוֹת, וְאֵינוֹ נֶאֱכָל אֶלָּא לִמְנוּיָו,* וְאֵינוֹ נֶאֱכָל אֶלָּא צָלִי.

ברייתא דר' ישמעאל — ספרא, פתיחה

רַבִּי יִשְׁמָעֵאל אוֹמֵר: בִּשְׁלֹשׁ עֶשְׂרֵה מִדּוֹת הַתּוֹרָה נִדְרֶשֶׁת בָּהֵן. (א) מִקַּל וָחֹמֶר; (ב) וּמִגְּזֵרָה

הַמּוּרָם מֵהֶם — *The [priestly] portion separated from them.* In the case of most 'offerings of lesser holiness,' the *Kohen's* portion consists of the breast and right thigh before they are cooked. In the case of the Nazirite's ram, he also receives the cooked right foreleg.

7. שְׁלָמִים — *Peace-offerings.* The peace-offerings may be eaten for *two* days and the night between them, while thanksgiving-offerings (mishnah 6) are eaten for only *one* day and a night.

8. וְדָמָן טָעוּן מַתָּנָה אֶחָת — *Their blood requires a single application.* Unlike all the offerings mentioned above, the offerings mentioned in this mishnah do not require multiple applications of blood. The יְסוֹד, *base*, is a part of the Altar, one cubit high and one cubit wide, that juts out along the entire lengths of the west and north walls, but only one cubit along the south and east walls. The blood may be applied only to a part of the Altar wall that is directly above the base.

הַפֶּסַח ... לִמְנוּיָו — *The Pesach-offering ... by those registered for it.* Those who eat from a particular Pesach-offering must reserve their share in it before the slaughter. [See *Exodus* 12:4.] In the case of all other offerings, any qualified person may partake of the flesh.

רַבִּי יִשְׁמָעֵאל / Rabbi Yishmael

As noted above, the Sages prefaced *Shacharis* with selections from Scripture, Mishnah, and Gemara. As used in the Talmud, Mishnah means a listing of laws and Gemara means the logic behind and the application of the laws. As a selection from Gemara, the Sages chose one that gives the thirteen methods used in Scriptural interpretation. This passage is a *baraisa* [literally *outside*], meaning that it is one of the countless Talmudic teachings that was 'left out' of the Mishnah when that basic compendium of laws was formulated. Though not part of the Mishnah, the *baraisos* are authoritative and are cited by the Gemara constantly. Unlike most *baraisos* which are statements of law, this one is a basic introduction to an understanding of the derivation of the laws. It shows us how the very brief statements of the Torah can be 'mined' to reveal a host of principles and teachings. This is

and that night until midnight. The [priestly] portion separated from them is treated like them, except that that portion may be eaten only by the Kohanim, their wives, children and slaves.*

[7] **שְׁלָמִים** *The peace-offerings* are offerings of lesser holiness. Their slaughter is anywhere in the Courtyard, and their blood requires two applications that are equivalent to four. They are eaten throughout the City [of Jerusalem] by anyone, prepared in any manner, for two days and one night. The [priestly] portion separated from them is treated like them, except that that portion may be eaten only by the Kohanim, their wives, children and slaves.*

[8] **הַבְּכוֹר** *The firstborn and tithe of animals and the Pesach-offering are offerings of lesser holiness. Their slaughter is anywhere in the Courtyard, and their blood requires a single application,* provided he applies it above the base. They differ in their consumption: The firstborn is eaten by Kohanim, and the tithe by anyone. They are eaten throughout the City [of Jerusalem], prepared in any manner, for two days and one night. The Pesach-offering is eaten only at night and it may be eaten only until midnight; it may be eaten only by those registered for it;* and it may be eaten only if roasted.*

Introduction to *Sifra*

רַבִּי יִשְׁמָעֵאל *Rabbi Yishmael says: Through thirteen rules is the Torah elucidated: (1) Through a conclusion inferred from a lenient law to a strict one, and vice versa; (2) through tradition*

---

why such use of these thirteen rules is called דְּרַשׁ, which implies *investigation* and *seeking out;* we seek to elicit principles and laws from the sometimes cryptic words of the Torah.

This particular *baraisa* is the introduction to *Sifra,* a midrashic work that exhaustively interprets the Book of *Leviticus.* Since most of *Sifra* is of a halachic nature, it was natural that it be introduced with a listing of the principles of halachic interpretation. And since *Sifra* deals mainly with the Temple service, this *baraisa* is particularly apt for this section of *Shacharis.*

☙ The Oral Law

The Torah was composed by God according to the rules of logic and textual analysis contained in Rabbi Yishmael's *baraisa.* (These rules are also known as hermeneutic principles.) The oral tradition governs the way in which these rules are applied and we have no authority to use them in a manner that contradicts or is not sanctioned by the Oral Law. Thus, when we speak of Rabbinic exegesis, or the way in which the Torah is expounded, we do not speak of the invention of new laws, but of the means by which the Oral Law was implied in the Torah itself. It should also be noted that the great majority of the laws were handed down for many centuries from teacher to student, and they were well known without a need to search for their Scriptural sources. Consequently, in the Talmud era when the Sages attempted to set forth the Scriptural derivation of such well-known laws as the use of an esrog or the law that an eye-for-an-eye refers to monetary compensation, there were disputes concerning the exact Scriptural interpretations although the laws were familiar.

☙ The Thirteen Rules

The following is a brief explanation with illustrations of the Thirteen Rules by means of which the Torah is expounded:

(1) קַל וָחֹמֶר. Logic dictates that if a lenient case has a stringency, the same stringency applies to a stricter case. Another way of putting it is that laws can be derived from less obvious situations and applied to more obvious ones. For example, if it is forbidden to pluck an apple from a tree on *festivals* (when food may be prepared by cooking and other means that may be prohibited on the Sabbath) surely plucking is forbidden on the *Sabbath.* Conversely, if it is permitted to slice vegetables on the Sabbath, it is surely permitted on festivals.

שָׁוָה; (ג) מִבִּנְיַן אָב מִכָּתוּב אֶחָד, וּמִבִּנְיַן אָב מִשְּׁנֵי כְתוּבִים; (ד) מִכְּלָל וּפְרָט; (ה) וּמִפְּרָט וּכְלָל; (ו) כְּלָל וּפְרָט וּכְלָל, אִי אַתָּה דָן אֶלָּא כְּעֵין הַפְּרָט; (ז) מִכְּלָל שֶׁהוּא צָרִיךְ לִפְרָט, וּמִפְּרָט שֶׁהוּא צָרִיךְ לִכְלָל; (ח) כָּל דָּבָר שֶׁהָיָה בִּכְלָל וְיָצָא מִן הַכְּלָל לְלַמֵּד, לֹא לְלַמֵּד עַל עַצְמוֹ יָצָא, אֶלָּא לְלַמֵּד עַל הַכְּלָל כֻּלּוֹ יָצָא; (ט) כָּל דָּבָר שֶׁהָיָה בִּכְלָל וְיָצָא לִטְעוֹן טוֹעַן אֶחָד שֶׁהוּא כְעִנְיָנוֹ, יָצָא לְהָקֵל וְלֹא לְהַחֲמִיר; (י) כָּל דָּבָר שֶׁהָיָה בִּכְלָל וְיָצָא לִטְעוֹן טֹעַן אַחֵר שֶׁלֹּא כְעִנְיָנוֹ, יָצָא לְהָקֵל וּלְהַחֲמִיר; (יא) כָּל דָּבָר שֶׁהָיָה בִכְלָל וְיָצָא לִדּוֹן בַּדָּבָר הֶחָדָשׁ, אִי אַתָּה יָכוֹל לְהַחֲזִירוֹ לִכְלָלוֹ, עַד שֶׁיַּחֲזִירֶנּוּ הַכָּתוּב

---

(2) גְּזֵרָה שָׁוָה. In strictly limited cases, the Sinaitic tradition teaches that two independent laws or cases are meant to shed light upon one another. The indication that the two laws are complementary can be seen in two ways: (a) The same or similar words appear in both cases, e.g., the word בְּמוֹעֲדוֹ, *in its proper time (Numbers* 28:2), is understood to indicate that the daily offering must be brought even on the Sabbath. Similarly, the same word in the context of the Pesach-offering *(Numbers* 9:2) should be interpreted to mean that it is offered even if its appointed day, too, falls on the Sabbath *(Pesachim* 66a); (b) When two different topics are placed next to one another (this is also called הֶיקֵּשׁ, *comparison),* e.g., many laws regarding the technical processes of divorce and betrothal are derived from one another because Scripture *(Deuteronomy* 24:2) mentions divorce and betrothal in the same phrase by saying ... וְיָצְאָה וְהָיְתָה לְאִישׁ אַחֵר, *she shall depart* [through divorce] ... *and become betrothed to another man.* This juxtaposition implies that the two changes of marital status are accomplished through similar legal processes *(Kiddushin* 5a).

(3) בִּנְיַן אָב... A general principle derived from one verse is applied to all cases that logically appear to be similar. This rule is also known as a מָה מָצִינוּ, lit. *'what do we find?'* For example, since the Torah specifies that one may not marry even his maternal half sister, this בִּנְיַן אָב dictates that the prohibition against marrying one's father's sister applies equally to his father's maternal half sister (*Yevamos* 54b). The same rule applies when two different verses shed light on one another. Similar situations may be derived from the combination of the two verses.

(4) כְּלָל וּפְרָט. When a generality is followed by a specific, the law is applied only to the specific. For example, in listing the animals from which sacrificial offerings may be brought, the Torah says: *From the* [*domestic*] *animals, from the cattle and sheep/goats (Leviticus* 1:2). This rule teaches that no animals but cattle and sheep/goats may be used. In such cases the generality [i.e., domestic animals] is mentioned only to teach that no part of the species is included in the law except for the specified items.

(5) פְּרָט וּכְלָל. This is the reverse of the above case. In describing the obligation to return lost objects, the Torah says that one should return: *His donkey ... his garment ... any lost object (Deuteronomy* 22:3). The concluding generality teaches that there are *no* exceptions to this rule.

(6) כְּלָל וּפְרָט וּכְלָל... The difference between this rule and כְּלָל וּפְרָט (rule 4), is that here the Scriptural phrase is concluded by a general statement. The two general statements imply that everything is included while the specific items in the middle imply that only they are meant. The apparent contradiction is resolved this way: Everything *is* included, provided it is essentially similar to the items specified. For example, in the verse imposing a fine on a thief, there are two general terms — *for any matter of dishonesty* and *for any lost item* — implying that the thief is liable no matter what he has taken. However, sandwiched between these general terms, a number of specific items are mentioned: *an ox ... or a garment (Exodus* 22:8). This teaches that the fine applies to any movable object that has intrinsic value, but *not* to real estate, which is not movable, or to contracts, which testify to a debt, but have no intrinsic value *(Bava Metzia* 57b).

(7) כְּלָל שֶׁהוּא צָרִיךְ לִפְרָט ... This rule tells us that the principles of כְּלָל וּפְרָט and פְּרָט וּכְלָל (numbers 4 and 5 above) do not apply in cases where the introductory general statement or specification requires further clarification for its meaning to be clear. For example, the Torah commands that after slaughtering fowl or non-domesticated kosher animals, וְכִסָּהוּ בֶּעָפָר, *he is to cover* [*its blood*] *with dirt (Leviticus* 17:13). The generalization *to cover* requires clarification

that similar words in different contexts are meant to clarify one another; (3) through a general principle derived from one verse, and a general principle derived from two verses; (4) through a general statement limited by a specification; (5) through a specification broadened by a general statement; (6) through a general statement followed by a specification followed, in turn, by another general statement — you may only infer whatever is similar to the specification; (7) when a general statement requires a specification or a specification requires a general statement to clarify its meaning; (8) anything that was included in a general statement, but was then singled out from the general statement in order to teach something, was not singled out to teach only about itself, but to apply its teaching to the entire generality; (9) anything that was included in a general statement, but was then singled out to discuss a provision similar to the general category, has been singled out to be more lenient rather than more severe; (10) anything that was included in a general statement, but was then singled out to discuss a provision not similar to the general category, has been singled out both to be more lenient and more severe; (11) anything that was included in a general statement, but was then singled out to be treated as a new case, cannot be returned to its general statement unless Scripture returns it

---

because it could be taken to mean that it can be poured into an enclosed pot or covered with wood or some other solid. Therefore, *with dirt* is needed to indicate that the covering must be a soft substance that can easily mix with the blood. Accordingly, it is not a 'specification' in the sense of principle 4, but a clarification *(Chullin* 88b).

(8) ... כָּל דָּבָר שֶׁהָיָה בִּכְלָל וְיָצָא ... לְלַמֵּד. This principle is best explained by an example. The Torah *(Leviticus* 7:19) forbids the eating of sacrificial meat by anyone who is טָמֵא, *ritually contaminated.* The very next verse singles out the שְׁלָמִים, *peace-offering,* and states that a contaminated person who eats of it is liable to כָּרֵת, *spiritual excision.* This principle teaches that the peace-offering is not an exception to the general rule; rather that the punishment specified for the peace-offering applies to all offerings.

(9) ... כְּעִנְיָנוֹ ... וְיָצָא לִטְעוֹן ... Again, this principle requires an example. In imposing the death penalty on a murderer *(Leviticus* 24:21), the Torah does not differentiate between premeditated and careless murders. Then the Torah describes a person who chops wood carelessly with the result that someone is killed by a flying piece of wood. Although this case would seem to require the death penalty discussed earlier, the Torah requires such a murderer to go into exile. This principle teaches that he has been singled out for *lenient* treatment, meaning that his exile is *instead* of the death penalty, not in *addition* to it.

(10) ... כְּעִנְיָנוֹ שֶׁלֹּא ... וְיָצָא לִטְעוֹן ... After describing the laws regulating a Jewish indentured servant (עֶבֶד עִבְרִי) who goes free after six years of service *(Exodus* 21:1-6), the Torah turns to a Jewish indentured maidservant — who should have been included with her male counterpart. Instead, the Torah says of her that her avenues of going free are entirely unlike those of the male. This has lenient applications, for she may go free even before six years of service (upon the onset of puberty or the death of her master) and it also has a stringent application, for her master can betroth her against her will to himself or to his son (see *Exodus* 21:7-11).

(11) ... וְיָצָא לִדּוֹן ... A *Kohen's* entire family is permitted to eat *terumah* [the priestly tithe], but if his daughter marries a non-*Kohen,* she is no longer permitted to eat *terumah (Leviticus* 22:11,12). What if she is widowed or divorced and returns to her father's household? Since marriage had removed her from the permitted status of the rest of the family, she would not have been permitted to eat *terumah* again unless the Torah had specifically returned her to the family group (which it did, ibid. 22:13).

לִכְלָלוֹ בִּפֵרוּשׁ; (יב) דָּבָר הַלָּמֵד מֵעִנְיָנוֹ, וְדָבָר הַלָּמֵד מִסּוֹפוֹ; (יג) וְכֵן שְׁנֵי כְתוּבִים הַמַּכְחִישִׁים זֶה אֶת זֶה, עַד שֶׁיָּבוֹא הַכָּתוּב הַשְּׁלִישִׁי וְיַכְרִיעַ בֵּינֵיהֶם.

יְהִי רָצוֹן מִלְּפָנֶיךָ, יהוה אֱלֹהֵינוּ וֵאלֹהֵי אֲבוֹתֵינוּ, שֶׁיִּבָּנֶה בֵּית הַמִּקְדָּשׁ בִּמְהֵרָה בְיָמֵינוּ, וְתֵן חֶלְקֵנוּ בְּתוֹרָתֶךָ. וְשָׁם נַעֲבָדְךָ בְּיִרְאָה כִּימֵי עוֹלָם וּכְשָׁנִים קַדְמוֹנִיּוֹת.

קדיש דרבנן

In the presence of a *minyan,* mourners recite קַדִּישׁ דְּרַבָּנָן. See *Laws* §120-121.

יִתְגַּדַּל וְיִתְקַדַּשׁ שְׁמֵהּ רַבָּא.* (.Cong— אָמֵן.*) בְּעָלְמָא דִּי בְרָא כִרְעוּתֵהּ.* וְיַמְלִיךְ מַלְכוּתֵהּ, בְּחַיֵּיכוֹן* וּבְיוֹמֵיכוֹן וּבְחַיֵּי דְכָל בֵּית יִשְׂרָאֵל, בַּעֲגָלָא וּבִזְמַן קָרִיב.* וְאִמְרוּ: אָמֵן.

(.Cong— אָמֵן. יְהֵא שְׁמֵהּ רַבָּא מְבָרַךְ לְעָלַם וּלְעָלְמֵי עָלְמַיָּא.)

יְהֵא שְׁמֵהּ רַבָּא* מְבָרַךְ לְעָלַם וּלְעָלְמֵי עָלְמַיָּא.

יִתְבָּרַךְ* וְיִשְׁתַּבַּח וְיִתְפָּאַר וְיִתְרוֹמַם וְיִתְנַשֵּׂא וְיִתְהַדָּר וְיִתְעַלֶּה וְיִתְהַלָּל שְׁמֵהּ דְּקֻדְשָׁא בְּרִיךְ הוּא (.Cong— בְּרִיךְ הוּא)

---

(12) דָּבָר הַלָּמֵד מֵעִנְיָנוֹ. In the Ten Commandments, the Torah commands, *'You shall not steal.'* The Sages derive from the context that the theft in question must be a capital offense since the injunction against stealing is preceded by the commandments not to kill and not to commit adultery with a married woman which are both capital offenses. The only theft for which someone can receive the death penalty is kidnaping a fellow Jew and treating him as a slave. Thus, *You shall not steal* refers to kidnaping.

דָּבָר הַלָּמֵד מִסּוֹפוֹ. Another form of contextual clarification is that which is found in *Leviticus* 14:34,35. First the Torah teaches that a house with a 'leprous' spot must be torn down. From the end of the passage — which describes the cleansing of the stone, wood and mortar of the house — we derive that this law applies only to houses made of stone, wood, and mortar.

(13) ... שְׁנֵי כְתוּבִים. Two verses may seem to be contradictory, until a third verse explains that each of the two has its own application. After being commanded to remove Isaac from the altar, Abraham asked God to explain two contradictory verses. First God said that Isaac would be the forefather of Israel *(Genesis* 21:12) and then He commanded that Abraham slaughter him (ibid. 22:2). God explained that the wording of the command was to *place Isaac on the altar,* but not to *slaughter* him on it *(Midrash* to *Genesis* 22:12). Thus, there is no contradiction.

יְהִי רָצוֹן ... שֶׁיִּבָּנֶה בֵּית הַמִּקְדָּשׁ — *May it be Your will ... that the Holy Temple be rebuilt.* Having substituted the laws of the offerings for the actual Temple service, we pray that we may soon be able to offer them in the rebuilt Temple.

קַדִּישׁ דְּרַבָּנָן / The Rabbis' Kaddish

'Whenever ten or more Israelites engage in the study of the Oral Law — for example, Mishnah, Halachah, and even Midrash or Aggadah — one of them recites the Rabbis' *Kaddish* [upon conclusion of the study]' *(Rambam, Nusach HaKaddish).* Many commentators maintain that it is recited only after Midrashic material or Scriptural exegesis. *Magen Avraham,* therefore, rules that unless Scriptural verses have been expounded upon, as in the above section of *Shacharis,* a brief Aggadic passage should be taught after halachic study in order that this *Kaddish* may be recited. It has become customary in most communities for this *Kaddish* to be recited by mourners.

[A full commentary and Overview appear in the ArtScroll *Kaddish.*]

explicitly to its general statement; (12) a matter elucidated from its context, or from the following passage; (13) similarly, two passages that contradict one another — until a third passage comes to reconcile them.

יְהִי רָצוֹן *May it be Your will, HASHEM, our God and the God of our forefathers, that the Holy Temple be rebuilt, speedily in our days, and grant us our share in Your Torah, and may we serve You there with reverence as in days of old and in former years.*

THE RABBIS' KADDISH

In the presence of a *minyan,* mourners recite the Rabbis' *Kaddish* (see *Laws* §120-121).

[A transliteration of this *Kaddish* appears on page 1042.]

יִתְגַּדַּל *May His great Name grow exalted and sanctified** (Cong.— *Amen.**) *in the world that He created as He willed.* May He give reign to His kingship in your lifetimes* and in your days, and in the lifetimes of the entire Family of Israel, swiftly and soon.* Now respond: Amen.*

(Cong.— *Amen. May His great Name be blessed forever and ever.*)

May His great Name be blessed forever and ever.*

Blessed, praised, glorified, exalted, extolled, mighty, upraised, and lauded be the Name of the Holy One, Blessed is He* (Cong.— *Blessed is*

יִתְגַּדַּל וְיִתְקַדַּשׁ שְׁמֵהּ רַבָּא — *May His great Name grow exalted and sanctified.* The ultimate sanctification of God's Name will come when Israel is redeemed; in this sense *Kaddish* is a plea for the final Redemption. It is also an expression of Israel's mission to bring recognition of His sovereignty to all people on earth. This mission is incumbent primarily upon the community as a whole, and *Kaddish* is therefore recited only in the presence of a *minyan* [a quorum of ten males over *bar mitzvah*] *(R' Munk).*

אָמֵן — *Amen.* The word אָמֵן, *Amen,* is the listener's acknowledgment that he believes in what the reader has just said. It is derived from the same root as אֱמוּנָה, *faithfulness (Tur, Orach Chaim* 124). Additionally, it stands for אֵל מֶלֶךְ נֶאֱמָן, *God, the trustworthy King (Shabbos* 119b).

בְּעָלְמָא דִּי בְרָא כִרְעוּתֵהּ — *In the world that He created as He willed.* God had His concept of a perfect world before He began creation. Then He began to create in accordance with His prior will *(Ran).* Or it refers to the *future.* Only then will mankind function in accordance with God's original intention *(R' Yehudah ben Yakar).*

בְּחַיֵּיכוֹן — *In your lifetimes.* The one reciting the *Kaddish* expresses the hope that his fellow congregants may all live to witness the Redemption of Israel and the sanctification of God's Name *(Abudraham).*

בַּעֲגָלָא וּבִזְמַן קָרִיב — *Swiftly and soon.* May the travail preceding the Messianic epoch be over *swiftly* and not be drawn out; and may it begin very soon *(Aruch HaShulchan).*

יְהֵא שְׁמֵהּ רַבָּא — *May His great Name* ... The Talmud stresses in several places that the response, יְהֵא שְׁמֵהּ רַבָּא, *May His great Name...,* has an enormous cosmic effect. Indeed, the *halachah* states that an opportunity to respond to *Kaddish* takes precedence over an opportunity to respond to any other prayer, even *Kedushah* and *Borchu.* Consequently, if *Kaddish* is about to be recited in one room and *Kedushah* in another, one should go to hear *Kaddish (Mishnah Berurah* 56:6).

The Talmud *(Shabbos* 19b) teaches that one must respond יְהֵא שְׁמֵהּ רַבָּא 'with all his power,' meaning his total concentration *(Rashi, Tosafos).* Though it is preferable to raise one's voice when saying it, one should not say it so loudly that he will invite ridicule *(R' Yonah).* And it must be enunciated clearly *(Maharal).*

יִתְבָּרַךְ — *Blessed.* This begins a series of praises that continue the central theme of *Kaddish:* namely that in time to come God's greatness will be acknowledged by all of mankind *(Emek Berachah).*

— °לְעֵלָּא מִן כָּל (—From Rosh Hashanah to Yom Kippur substitute °לְעֵלָּא וּלְעֵלָּא* מִכָּל) בִּרְכָתָא* וְשִׁירָתָא תֻּשְׁבְּחָתָא וְנֶחֱמָתָא, דַּאֲמִירָן בְּעָלְמָא. וְאִמְרוּ: אָמֵן. (.Cong— אָמֵן.)

עַל יִשְׂרָאֵל וְעַל רַבָּנָן,* וְעַל תַּלְמִידֵיהוֹן וְעַל כָּל תַּלְמִידֵי תַלְמִידֵיהוֹן, וְעַל כָּל מָאן דְּעָסְקִין בְּאוֹרַיְתָא, דִּי בְאַתְרָא הָדֵין וְדִי בְכָל אֲתַר וַאֲתַר.* יְהֵא לְהוֹן וּלְכוֹן* שְׁלָמָא רַבָּא, חִנָּא וְחִסְדָּא וְרַחֲמִין,* וְחַיִּין אֲרִיכִין, וּמְזוֹנֵי רְוִיחֵי, וּפֻרְקָנָא מִן קֳדָם אֲבוּהוֹן דִּי בִשְׁמַיָּא* (וְאַרְעָא). וְאִמְרוּ: אָמֵן. (.Cong— אָמֵן.)

יְהֵא שְׁלָמָא רַבָּא מִן שְׁמַיָּא, וְחַיִּים (טוֹבִים) עָלֵינוּ וְעַל כָּל יִשְׂרָאֵל. וְאִמְרוּ: אָמֵן. (.Cong— אָמֵן.)

Take three steps back. Bow left and say ... עֹשֶׂה; bow right and say ... הוּא; bow forward and say וְעַל כָּל ... אָמֵן. Remain standing in place for a few moments, then take three steps forward.

עֹשֶׂה שָׁלוֹם בִּמְרוֹמָיו, הוּא בְּרַחֲמָיו יַעֲשֶׂה שָׁלוֹם עָלֵינוּ, וְעַל כָּל יִשְׂרָאֵל. וְאִמְרוּ: אָמֵן. (.Cong— אָמֵן.)

ON THE SABBATH AND FESTIVALS CONTINUE ON PAGE 368.

INTRODUCTORY PSALM TO PESUKEI D'ZIMRAH

תהלים ל

מִזְמוֹר שִׁיר חֲנֻכַּת הַבַּיִת* לְדָוִד. אֲרוֹמִמְךָ יהוה כִּי דִלִּיתָנִי, וְלֹא שִׂמַּחְתָּ אֹיְבַי לִי. יהוה אֱלֹהָי, שִׁוַּעְתִּי אֵלֶיךָ וַתִּרְפָּאֵנִי. יהוה הֶעֱלִיתָ מִן שְׁאוֹל נַפְשִׁי,* חִיִּיתַנִי מִיָּרְדִי בוֹר.

לְעֵלָּא מִן כָּל בִּרְכָתָא — *Beyond any blessing.* No words or ideas can praise God adequately.

לְעֵלָּא וּלְעֵלָּא — *Exceedingly beyond* [lit. *beyond and beyond*]. During עֲשֶׂרֶת יְמֵי תְשׁוּבָה, *the Ten Days of Repentance* [from Rosh Hashanah to Yom Kippur], the word לְעֵלָּא is repeated to stress that God's majesty is even more pronounced during this period of judgment than it is all year around. The two words מִן כָּל are contracted into the single word מִכָּל. This is done to keep the total number of words in this section of *Kaddish* at twenty-eight, the number of human experiences listed in *Ecclesiastes* 3:2-8: *A time to be born and a time to die ... a time for war and a time for peace.* The underlying theme is that in every stage of life and every form of existence, man must search for the way to utilize it to serve God.

[In some congregations the conjunctive ו, *and*, is omitted and the phrase reads לְעֵלָּא לְעֵלָּא.]

עַל יִשְׂרָאֵל וְעַל רַבָּנָן — *Upon Israel, (and) upon the teachers.* It is because of this section that this *Kaddish* is called the Rabbis' *Kaddish.* Though this is a prayer for the benefit of the Torah community, it begins with mention of Israel. Any prayer for Torah scholars is a prayer for the nation, because Israel's welfare depends on Torah study *(R' Hirsch).*

דִּי בְאַתְרָא הָדֵין וְדִי בְכָל אֲתַר וַאֲתַר — *Who are here or anywhere else.* The references to all the various places are meant to imply that every town and neighborhood, individually, benefits from those who study Torah within it.

יְהֵא לְהוֹן וּלְכוֹן — *May they and you have.* The blessing is extended not only to the Torah teachers and their students, but to all the people present in the congregation.

חִנָּא וְחִסְדָּא וְרַחֲמִין — *Grace, kindness, and mercy.* [These terms are often used synonymously, but when they are used together we must assume that they have distinct meanings. Some interpretations are as follows:]

— These characteristics refer to how God views us: The most deserving people are nourished through God's חִנָּא, *grace,* while at the other extreme, even the least worthy are recipients of רַחֲמִין, *mercy,* because He displays compassion to every living thing. Those in

He) — (From Rosh Hashanah to Yom Kippur add: *exceedingly*) *beyond* any blessing* and song, praise and consolation that are uttered in the world. Now respond: Amen.* (Cong.— *Amen.*)

Upon Israel, upon the teachers, their disciples and all of their disciples and upon all those who engage in the study of Torah, who are here or anywhere else;* may they and you have* abundant peace, grace, kindness, and mercy,* long life, ample nourishment, and salvation from before their Father Who is in Heaven* (and on earth). Now respond: Amen.* (Cong.— *Amen.*)

May there be abundant peace from Heaven, and (good) life, upon us and upon all Israel. Now respond: Amen. (Cong.— *Amen.*)

Take three steps back. Bow left and say, *'He Who makes peace ...'*; bow right and say, *'may He ...'*; bow forward and say, *'and upon all Israel ...'* Remain standing in place for a few moments, then take three steps forward.

He Who makes peace in His heights, may He, in His compassion, make peace upon us, and upon all Israel. Now respond: Amen. (Cong.— *Amen.*)

ON THE SABBATH AND FESTIVALS CONTINUE ON PAGE 368.

INTRODUCTORY PSALM TO PESUKEI D'ZIMRAH

Psalm 30

מִזְמוֹר *A psalm — a song for the inauguration of the Temple*— by David. I will exalt You, Hashem, for You have drawn me up and not let my foes rejoice over me. Hashem, my God, I cried out to You and You healed me. Hashem, You have raised my soul from the lower world,* You have preserved me from my descent to the Pit.*

---

between are provided for through חִסְדָּא, *kindness (R' Hirsch).*

— Or, these are characteristics that *we* hope to have: חִנָּא, *grace,* is the quality that makes a person beloved by others; חִסְדָּא, *kindness,* refers to a generous, considerate human being who is kind to others, even the undeserving; רַחֲמִין, *mercy,* is the quality of compassion by which one withholds punishment even when a wrongdoer has earned it *(Siach Yitzchak).*

אֲבוּהוֹן דִּי בִשְׁמַיָּא — *Their Father Who is in Heaven.* Some *siddurim* add the word וְאַרְעָא, *and on earth,* an addition which, although rejected by some commentators, is used in many congregations.

מִזְמוֹר שִׁיר / Psalm 30

This psalm is not part of *Pesukei D'zimrah* (see below) and it did not become customary to include it in the morning prayers until the seventeenth century. Apparently, it was decided to include it in *Shacharis* because it was sung to inaugurate the morning Temple service, and thus is an appropriate prelude to the prayers that take the place of that service *(Tikun Tefillah).* It is also a fitting conclusion to the Scriptural and Talmudical passages regarding the offerings. Additionally, מִזְמוֹר שִׁיר is an appropriate introduction to the morning psalms of praise because of its emphasis in the faith that God rescues from even the most hopeless situations *(R' Munk).*

חֲנֻכַּת הַבַּיִת — *The inauguration of the Temple.* How is this psalm, which deals only with David's illness, related to the dedication of the Temple? *Radak* explains that Solomon's eventual inauguration of the Temple represented David's vindication against the taunts and charges of his enemies. His offspring could not have gained the privilege of building the Temple if David had been a sinner.

Another explanation is that the Temple's purpose is best achieved when each individual Jew recognizes God's presence and help in his personal life. Accordingly, by never losing his faith in God, and by finally being vindicated through God's deliverance, David is the perfect embodiment of the Temple's role in the life of the nation *(R' Hirsch).*

ה׳ הֶעֱלִיתָ מִן שְׁאוֹל נַפְשִׁי — *Hashem You have raised my soul from the lower world. R' Yerucham Levovitz* notes that David speaks as if he had

זַמְּרוּ לַיהוה חֲסִידָיו, וְהוֹדוּ לְזֵכֶר קָדְשׁוֹ. כִּי רֶגַע בְּאַפּוֹ, חַיִּים בִּרְצוֹנוֹ, בָּעֶרֶב יָלִין בֶּכִי וְלַבֹּקֶר רִנָּה. וַאֲנִי אָמַרְתִּי בְשַׁלְוִי, בַּל אֶמּוֹט לְעוֹלָם. יהוה בִּרְצוֹנְךָ הֶעֱמַדְתָּה לְהַרְרִי עֹז, הִסְתַּרְתָּ פָנֶיךָ הָיִיתִי נִבְהָל. אֵלֶיךָ יהוה אֶקְרָא, וְאֶל אֲדֹנָי אֶתְחַנָּן. מַה בֶּצַע בְּדָמִי, בְּרִדְתִּי אֶל שָׁחַת, הֲיוֹדְךָ עָפָר, הֲיַגִּיד אֲמִתֶּךָ. שְׁמַע יהוה וְחָנֵּנִי, יהוה הֱיֵה עֹזֵר לִי. ❖ הָפַכְתָּ מִסְפְּדִי לְמָחוֹל לִי, פִּתַּחְתָּ שַׂקִּי, וַתְּאַזְּרֵנִי שִׂמְחָה. לְמַעַן יְזַמֶּרְךָ כָבוֹד וְלֹא יִדֹּם, יהוה אֱלֹהַי לְעוֹלָם אוֹדֶךָּ.

קדיש יתום

In the presence of a *minyan,* mourners recite קַדִּישׁ יָתוֹם:

יִתְגַּדַּל וְיִתְקַדַּשׁ שְׁמֵהּ רַבָּא. (.Cong — אָמֵן.) בְּעָלְמָא דִּי בְרָא כִרְעוּתֵהּ. וְיַמְלִיךְ מַלְכוּתֵהּ, בְּחַיֵּיכוֹן וּבְיוֹמֵיכוֹן וּבְחַיֵּי דְכָל בֵּית יִשְׂרָאֵל, בַּעֲגָלָא וּבִזְמַן קָרִיב. וְאִמְרוּ: אָמֵן.

(.Cong — אָמֵן. יְהֵא שְׁמֵהּ רַבָּא מְבָרַךְ לְעָלַם וּלְעָלְמֵי עָלְמַיָּא.)

יְהֵא שְׁמֵהּ רַבָּא מְבָרַךְ לְעָלַם וּלְעָלְמֵי עָלְמַיָּא.

יִתְבָּרַךְ וְיִשְׁתַּבַּח וְיִתְפָּאַר וְיִתְרוֹמַם וְיִתְנַשֵּׂא וְיִתְהַדָּר וְיִתְעַלֶּה וְיִתְהַלָּל שְׁמֵהּ דְּקֻדְשָׁא בְּרִיךְ הוּא (.Cong — בְּרִיךְ הוּא) — °לְעֵלָּא מִן כָּל (From Rosh Hashanah to Yom Kippur substitute — °לְעֵלָּא וּלְעֵלָּא מִכָּל) בִּרְכָתָא וְשִׁירָתָא תֻּשְׁבְּחָתָא וְנֶחֱמָתָא, דַּאֲמִירָן בְּעָלְמָא. וְאִמְרוּ: אָמֵן. (.Cong — אָמֵן.)

יְהֵא שְׁלָמָא רַבָּא מִן שְׁמַיָּא, וְחַיִּים עָלֵינוּ וְעַל כָּל יִשְׂרָאֵל. וְאִמְרוּ: אָמֵן. (.Cong — אָמֵן.)

Take three steps back. Bow left and say ... עֹשֶׂה; bow right and say ... הוּא; bow forward and say וְעַל כָּל ... אָמֵן. Remain standing in place for a few moments, then take three steps forward.

עֹשֶׂה שָׁלוֹם בִּמְרוֹמָיו, הוּא יַעֲשֶׂה שָׁלוֹם עָלֵינוּ, וְעַל כָּל יִשְׂרָאֵל. וְאִמְרוּ: אָמֵן. (.Cong — אָמֵן.)

---

already died and descended to the 'lower world,' where sinners are punished after death. From this we learn that one can suffer the anguish of purgatory even while alive! As the Talmud (*Nedarim* 22a) teaches: 'Whoever becomes angry is subjected to all types of *Gehinnom.*' The flames of frustration, anguish, and melancholy are the equivalent of the fires of *Gehinnom.*

Make music to HASHEM, His devout ones, and give thanks to His Holy Name. For His anger endures but a moment; life results from His favor. In the evening one lies down weeping, but with dawn — a cry of joy! I had said in my serenity, 'I will never falter.' But, HASHEM, all is through Your favor — You supported my greatness with might; should You but conceal Your face, I would be confounded. To You, HASHEM, I would call and to my Lord I would appeal. What gain is there in my death, when I descend to the Pit? Will the dust acknowledge You? Will it declare Your truth? Hear, HASHEM, and favor me; HASHEM, be my Helper! Chazzan— *You have changed for me my lament into dancing; You undid my sackcloth and girded me with gladness. So that my soul might make music to You and not be stilled, HASHEM my God, forever will I thank You.*

THE MOURNER'S KADDISH

In the presence of a *minyan,* mourners recite קַדִּישׁ יָתוֹם, the Mourner's *Kaddish* (see *Laws* §119):

[A transliteration of this *Kaddish* appears on page 1043.]

יִתְגַּדַּל *May His great Name grow exalted and sanctified* (Cong.— *Amen.*) *in the world that He created as He willed. May He give reign to His kingship in your lifetimes and in your days, and in the lifetimes of the entire Family of Israel, swiftly and soon. Now respond: Amen.*

(Cong.— *Amen. May His great Name be blessed forever and ever.*)

May His great Name be blessed forever and ever.

Blessed, praised, glorified, exalted, extolled, mighty, upraised, and lauded be the Name of the Holy One, Blessed is He (Cong.— *Blessed is He*) — (From Rosh Hashanah to Yom Kippur add: *exceedingly*) *beyond any blessing and song, praise and consolation that are uttered in the world. Now respond: Amen.* (Cong.— *Amen.*)

May there be abundant peace from Heaven, and life, upon us and upon all Israel. Now respond: Amen. (Cong.— *Amen.*)

Take three steps back. Bow left and say, *'He Who makes peace ...';* bow right and say, *'may He ...';* bow forward and say, *'and upon all Israel ...'* Remain standing in place for a few moments, then take three steps forward.

He Who makes peace in His heights, may He make peace upon us, and upon all Israel. Now respond: Amen. (Cong.— *Amen.*)

Throughout the Book of *Psalms,* most references to 'falling into the lower world' refer to this type of emotional inferno.

קַדִּישׁ יָתוֹם / MOURNERS' KADDISH

For the eleven months following the death of a parent and on the *yahrzeit,* or anniversary of the death, a son is obligated to recite *Kaddish* as a source of merit for the soul of the departed. For commentary see 'The Rabbis' *Kaddish,*' p. 53. A discussion of the concept and bases underlying the recitation of the Mourner's *Kaddish* appears in the ArtScroll *Kaddish.*

פסוקי דזמרה

Some recite this short Kabbalistic declaration of intent before beginning *Pesukei D'zimrah:*

הֲרֵינִי מְזַמֵּן אֶת פִּי לְהוֹדוֹת וּלְהַלֵּל וּלְשַׁבֵּחַ אֶת בּוֹרְאִי. לְשֵׁם יִחוּד קֻדְשָׁא בְּרִיךְ הוּא וּשְׁכִינְתֵּיהּ עַל יְדֵי הַהוּא טָמִיר וְנֶעְלָם, בְּשֵׁם כָּל יִשְׂרָאֵל.

Pesukei D'zimrah begins with the recital of בָּרוּךְ שֶׁאָמַר.
Stand while reciting בָּרוּךְ שֶׁאָמַר. During its recitation, hold the two front *tzitzis* of the *tallis* (or *tallis kattan)* in the right hand, and at its conclusion kiss the *tzitzis* and release them.
Conversation is forbidden from this point until after *Shemoneh Esrei,* except for certain prayer responses (see commentary, p. 59 and *Laws* §33-38).

בָּרוּךְ שֶׁאָמַר וְהָיָה הָעוֹלָם,* בָּרוּךְ הוּא. בָּרוּךְ עֹשֶׂה בְרֵאשִׁית, בָּרוּךְ אוֹמֵר וְעֹשֶׂה,* בָּרוּךְ גּוֹזֵר וּמְקַיֵּם, בָּרוּךְ מְרַחֵם עַל הָאָרֶץ,* בָּרוּךְ מְרַחֵם עַל הַבְּרִיּוֹת, בָּרוּךְ מְשַׁלֵּם שָׂכָר טוֹב לִירֵאָיו,* בָּרוּךְ חַי לָעַד וְקַיָּם לָנֶצַח,* בָּרוּךְ פּוֹדֶה וּמַצִּיל,* בָּרוּךְ שְׁמוֹ.* בָּרוּךְ אַתָּה יהוה אֱלֹהֵינוּ מֶלֶךְ הָעוֹלָם, הָאֵל הָאָב הָרַחֲמָן* הַמְּהֻלָּל בְּפֶה

פְּסוּקֵי דְזִמְרָה / PESUKEI D'ZIMRAH

The Sages taught that one should set forth the praises of God before making requests of Him *(Berachos* 32a). In this section of *Shacharis,* we concentrate on God's revelation in nature and history — on how His glory can be seen in creation and in the unfolding of events. Accordingly פְּסוּקֵי דְזִמְרָה means *Verses of Praise.* However, many commentators relate the word דְזִמְרָה to the verb תִזְמֹר, *prune (Leviticus* 25:4). In this view, we now recite 'Verses of Pruning,' which are designed to cut away' the mental and spiritual hindrances to proper prayer. Thus, by focusing on God's glory all around us, we prepare ourselves for the *Shema* and *Shemoneh Esrei,* when we accept Him as our King and pray for the needs of the Jewish people.

Because it is a separate section of *Shacharis* with a purpose all its own, *Pesukei D'zimrah* is introduced with a blessing [בָּרוּךְ שֶׁאָמַר] and concluded with a blessing [יִשְׁתַּבַּח]. In this way, it is similar to *Hallel,* which is a complete unit and is therefore introduced by, and concluded with, a blessing.

בָּרוּךְ שֶׁאָמַר / Baruch She'amar

The commentators record an ancient tradition that this prayer was transcribed by the Men of the Great Assembly approximately 2400 years ago from a script that fell from heaven. The prayer contains 87 words, equal to the numerical value of פָּז, *finest gold.* This alludes to the verse *(Song of Songs* 5:11): רֹאשׁוֹ כֶּתֶם פָּז, *His opening words* [i.e., the introductory words of *Pesukei D'zimrah*] *were finest gold.*

In recognition of its lofty status, one must stand when reciting *Baruch She'amar.* Kabbalists teach that one should hold his two front *tzitzis* during *Baruch She'amar* and kiss them upon concluding the prayer. Mystically, this signifies that *Baruch She'amar* has an effect on 'the higher regions.'

Baruch She'amar begins with a series of phrases in which we bless seven aspects of God. *Rabbi David Hoffmann,* cited and explained in *World of Prayer,* asserts that these seven ideas are all implied by the Four-Letter Name, י־ה־ו־ה. That Name contains the letters of הָיָה הֹוֶה יִהְיֶה, *He was, He is, He will be.* It is the Name that symbolizes God's eternity, mastery of all conditions, and the fact that He brought everything into being and will carry out His will and word. The seven ideas expressed by this Name are:

(1) שֶׁאָמַר וְהָיָה הָעוֹלָם — *Who spoke and the world came into being.* God is the Creator Who brought all of creation into being and maintains it [עוֹשֶׂה בְרֵאשִׁית] with no more than His word.

(2) אוֹמֵר וְעֹשֶׂה — *Who speaks and does.* God brings His promise into being even when people no longer seem to deserve His generosity. Conversely, גּוֹזֵר וּמְקַיֵּם, He *decrees and fulfills;* when He warns of punishment, the sinner cannot escape unless he repents sincerely.

(3) מְרַחֵם עַל הָאָרֶץ — *Who has mercy on the earth.* The Four-Letter Name also refers to Him as the merciful God, Who has compassion on the *earth* and all its בְּרִיּוֹת, *creatures,* human or otherwise.

(4) מְשַׁלֵּם שָׂכָר טוֹב לִירֵאָיו — *Who gives goodly reward to those who fear Him.* His reward may not be dispensed in This World, but it will surely be dispensed in the World to Come. Whatever the case, no good deed goes unrewarded.

(5) חַי לָעַד וְקַיָּם לָנֶצַח — *Who lives forever and*

PESUKEI D'ZIMRAH

Some recite this short Kabbalistic declaration of intent before beginning *Pesukei D'zimrah:*

I now prepare my mouth to thank, laud, and praise my Creator. For the sake of the unification of the Holy One, Blessed is He, and His Presence, through Him Who is hidden and inscrutable — [I pray] in the name of all Israel.

Pesukei D'zimrah begins with the recital of בָּרוּךְ שֶׁאָמַר, *'Blessed is He Who spoke...'* Stand while reciting בָּרוּךְ שֶׁאָמַר. During its recitation, hold the two front *tzitzis* of the *tallis* (or the *tallis kattan)* in the right hand, and at its conclusion kiss the *tzitzis* and release them. Conversation is forbidden from this point until after *Shemoneh Esrei,* except for certain prayer responses (see commentary, p. 59 and *Laws* §33-38).

בָּרוּךְ שֶׁאָמַר *Blessed is He Who spoke, and the world came into being* — blessed is He. Blessed is He Who maintains creation; blessed is He Who speaks and does;* blessed is He Who decrees and fulfills; blessed is He Who has mercy on the earth;* blessed is He Who has mercy on the creatures; blessed is He Who gives goodly reward to those who fear Him; *blessed is He Who lives forever and endures to eternity;* blessed is He Who redeems and rescues* — blessed is His Name!* Blessed are You, HASHEM, our God, King of the universe, the God, the merciful Father,* Who is lauded by the mouth*

---

endures to eternity. Not only is God's existence infinite and eternal, He *endures forever,* in the sense that He continues to involve Himself in the affairs of the universe.

(6) פּוֹדֶה וּמַצִּיל — *Who redeems* people from moral decline *and rescues* them from physical danger. The classic example of this is the Redemption from Egypt, when God took a degraded, powerless rabble and made it a great nation.

(7) בָּרוּךְ שְׁמוֹ — *Blessed is His Name!* The Name by which we call God can in no way express His true essence. Nevertheless, in His kindness to man, He allows us to glimpse some of His properties and express them in a Name.

הָאֵל הָאָב הָרַחֲמָן — *The God, the merciful Father.* We bless God with awareness that He is both all-powerful [אֵל] and filled with mercy, like a father whose behavior is a constant expression of

Permitted responses during Pesukei D'zimrah

From this point until after *Shemoneh Esrei* conversation is forbidden. During *Pesukei D'zimrah* [from בָּרוּךְ שֶׁאָמַר until יִשְׁתַּבַּח, p. 82] certain congregational and individual responses [e.g., בָּרוּךְ הוּא וּבָרוּךְ שְׁמוֹ] are omitted. The following responses, however, should be made: אָמֵן, *Amen,* after any blessing; *Kaddish; Borchu; Kedushah;* and the Rabbi's *Modim.* Additionally, one should join the congregation in reciting the first verse of the *Shema,* and may recite the אֲשֶׁר יָצַר blessing if he had to relieve himself during *Pesukei D'zimrah.*

If one is in the middle of *Pesukei D'zimrah* and the congregation has already reached the Torah reading, it is preferable that he not be called to the Torah. However, if (a) one is the only *Kohen* or Levite present, or (b) the *gabbai* inadvertently called him to the Torah, then he may recite the blessings and even read the portion softly along with the Torah reader.

If after beginning *Pesukei D'zimrah* one realizes that he has forgotten to recite the morning Blessings of the Torah (p. 16), he should pause to recite them, and the accompanying verses. Likewise, if he fears that he will not reach the *Shema* before the prescribed time (see *Laws* §17), he should recite all three paragraphs of *Shema.*

On days that *Hallel* (p. 632) is recited in its abridged form, if one is reciting *Pesukei D'zimrah* when the congregation begins *Hallel,* he should pause, recite the verses of *Hallel* (but not the blessings that precede and follow it), then return to where he left off.

In all cases of permitted responses it is preferable to respond between psalms wherever possible. Thus, for example, if one realizes that the congregation is approaching *Kedushah,* he should not begin a new psalm, but should wait for the congregation to recite *Kedushah,* then continue his prayers.

The responses permitted above do not apply during the 'final blessing' portions of בָּרוּךְ שֶׁאָמַר [i.e., בָּרוּךְ אַתָּה ה׳ מֶלֶךְ מְהֻלָּל בַּתִּשְׁבָּחוֹת], and יִשְׁתַּבַּח [i.e., from the words בָּרוּךְ אַתָּה ה׳, until the blessing's conclusion] where no interruptions are permitted.

עַמּוֹ,* מְשַׁבֵּחַ וּמְפָאֵר בִּלְשׁוֹן חֲסִידָיו וַעֲבָדָיו,* וּבְשִׁירֵי דָוִד
עַבְדֶּךָ. נְהַלֶּלְךָ יהוה אֱלֹהֵינוּ, בִּשְׁבָחוֹת וּבִזְמִרוֹת. נְגַדֶּלְךָ
וּנְשַׁבֵּחֲךָ וּנְפָאֶרְךָ וְנַזְכִּיר שִׁמְךָ וְנַמְלִיכְךָ, מַלְכֵּנוּ אֱלֹהֵינוּ.
❖ יָחִיד, חֵי הָעוֹלָמִים, מֶלֶךְ מְשֻׁבָּח וּמְפֹאָר עֲדֵי עַד שְׁמוֹ
הַגָּדוֹל. בָּרוּךְ אַתָּה יהוה, מֶלֶךְ מְהֻלָּל בַּתִּשְׁבָּחוֹת. (.Cong—אָמֵן)

דברי הימים א טז:ח-לו

הוֹדוּ לַיהוה* קִרְאוּ בִשְׁמוֹ,* הוֹדִיעוּ בָעַמִּים עֲלִילֹתָיו. שִׁירוּ
לוֹ, זַמְּרוּ לוֹ, שִׂיחוּ בְּכָל נִפְלְאֹתָיו. הִתְהַלְלוּ בְּשֵׁם
קָדְשׁוֹ, יִשְׂמַח לֵב מְבַקְשֵׁי יהוה. דִּרְשׁוּ יהוה וְעֻזּוֹ, בַּקְּשׁוּ פָנָיו
תָּמִיד. זִכְרוּ נִפְלְאֹתָיו אֲשֶׁר עָשָׂה, מֹפְתָיו וּמִשְׁפְּטֵי פִיהוּ. זֶרַע
יִשְׂרָאֵל עַבְדּוֹ, בְּנֵי יַעֲקֹב בְּחִירָיו. הוּא יהוה אֱלֹהֵינוּ, בְּכָל
הָאָרֶץ מִשְׁפָּטָיו. זִכְרוּ לְעוֹלָם בְּרִיתוֹ, דָּבָר צִוָּה לְאֶלֶף דּוֹר.*
אֲשֶׁר כָּרַת אֶת אַבְרָהָם, וּשְׁבוּעָתוֹ לְיִצְחָק. וַיַּעֲמִידֶהָ לְיַעֲקֹב
לְחֹק, לְיִשְׂרָאֵל בְּרִית עוֹלָם. לֵאמֹר, לְךָ אֶתֵּן אֶרֶץ כְּנָעַן, חֶבֶל
נַחֲלַתְכֶם. בִּהְיוֹתְכֶם מְתֵי מִסְפָּר, כִּמְעַט וְגָרִים בָּהּ. וַיִּתְהַלְּכוּ
מִגּוֹי אֶל גּוֹי, וּמִמַּמְלָכָה אֶל עַם אַחֵר. לֹא הִנִּיחַ לְאִישׁ
לְעָשְׁקָם, וַיּוֹכַח עֲלֵיהֶם מְלָכִים. אַל תִּגְּעוּ בִּמְשִׁיחָי, וּבִנְבִיאַי
אַל תָּרֵעוּ. שִׁירוּ לַיהוה* כָּל הָאָרֶץ, בַּשְּׂרוּ מִיּוֹם אֶל יוֹם
יְשׁוּעָתוֹ. סַפְּרוּ בַגּוֹיִם אֶת כְּבוֹדוֹ, בְּכָל הָעַמִּים נִפְלְאוֹתָיו.

---

mercy, even when he must be harsh (*Siach Yitzchak*).

בְּפֶה עַמּוֹ — *By the mouth of His people.* The Kabbalists comment that בְּפֶה has the numerical value of 87, and alludes to the number of words in this prayer. *Magen Avraham* and *Mishnah Berurah* (51:1) favor the usage of this word. Nevertheless, some commentators feel that the word בְּפִי, which has the same meaning, is the preferred grammatical form.

חֲסִידָיו וַעֲבָדָיו — *His devout ones and His servants.* We would not dare to compose praises on our own, for we are totally inadequate to evaluate God. We praise Him with the words of the great and holy people of the past and with the psalms of David, which are the backbone of *Pesukei D'zimrah* (*Etz Yosef*).

⧫§ הוֹדוּ / **Give Thanks**

הוֹדוּ לַה׳ — *Give thanks to HASHEM.* The first twenty-nine verses of this lengthy prayer form a jubilant song that David taught Assaf and his colleagues. Assaf and his family were musicians

and psalmists whose own compositions are included in the *Book of Psalms*. This song was intended by David to be sung when the Holy Ark was brought to Jerusalem.

According to *Seder Olam*, during the last forty-three years before Solomon inaugurated the Temple, the first fifteen of these verses were sung in the Tabernacle every day during the morning *tamid*-offering service, and the last fourteen were sung during the afternoon *tamid* service. With very minor changes, these verses are also found in *Psalms 105:1-15, 96:2-13,* and 106:47-48. [Incidentally, it is because these verses were recited during the sacrificial service that the *Nusach Sephard* ritual places הוֹדוּ before *Pesukei D'zimrah.* Given the fact that these verses relate to the offerings, they should be recited immediately after the *Korbanos* section of *Shacharis.* *Nusach Ashkenaz*, however, does not make this change, because the verses are in general praise, and thus similar to the rest of *Pesukei D'zimrah*].

In its entirety this song calls upon Israel to maintain its faith in God and its confidence that

of His people, praised and glorified by the tongue of His devout ones and His servants* and through the psalms of David Your servant. We shall laud You, HASHEM, our God, with praises and songs. We shall exalt You, praise You, glorify You, mention Your Name and proclaim Your reign, our King, our God.* Chazzan— *O Unique One, Life-giver of the worlds, King Whose great Name is eternally praised and glorified. Blessed are You, HASHEM, the King Who is lauded with praises.*

(Cong.—*Amen.*)

I Chronicles 16:8-36

הוֹדוּ *Give thanks to HASHEM,* declare His Name,* make His acts known among the peoples. Sing to Him, make music to Him, speak of all His wonders. Glory in His holy Name, be glad of heart, you who seek HASHEM. Search out HASHEM and His might, seek His Presence always. Remember His wonders that He wrought, His marvels and the judgments of His mouth. O seed of Israel, His servant, O children of Jacob, His chosen ones — He is HASHEM, our God, over all the earth are His judgments. Remember His covenant forever — the word He commanded for a thousand generations* — that He made with Abraham and His vow to Isaac. Then He established it for Jacob as a statute, for Israel as an everlasting covenant; saying, 'To you I shall give the Land of Canaan, the lot of your heritage.' When you were but few in number, hardly dwelling there, and they wandered from nation to nation, from one kingdom to another people. He let no man rob them, and He rebuked kings for their sake: 'Dare not touch My anointed ones, and to My prophets do no harm.' Sing to HASHEM,* everyone on earth, announce His salvation daily. Relate His glory among the nations, among all the peoples His wonders.*

He will bring it salvation from exile and persecution. The first fifteen verses refer to the miracles of past salvations and how our Patriarchs had complete faith in God even though they had nothing to go by but His covenant and oath. The second group of fourteen verses begins שִׁירוּ לַה׳ כָּל הָאָרֶץ, *Sing to HASHEM, everyone on earth.* It refers to the song of gratitude that everyone will sing in Messianic times. Thus, this section parallels the theme of the morning *Shema* blessings (p. 84) in which we emphasize the redemption of the past, while the second section parallels the evening *Shema* blessings (p. 237) in which we stress the redemption of the future.

The third section of this prayer continues with a collection of verses. It is discussed on the next page, s.v. רוֹמְמוּ.

קִרְאוּ בִשְׁמוֹ — *Declare His Name.* Whatever you accomplish, ascribe it to God's help, and let even the gentile nations know that God's guiding hand is everywhere *(Vilna Gaon).*

לְאֶלֶף דּוֹר — *For a thousand generations.* God's *word,* i.e., His covenant with Israel lasts for a *thousand generations,* a poetic expression meaning forever. He sealed His covenant with Abraham, designated Isaac as Abraham's successor, and then chose Jacob over Esau, thus making Israel His chosen people everlastingly *(Tzilosa D'Avraham).*

שִׁירוּ לַה׳ — *Sing to HASHEM.* As we find repeatedly in the Prophets, in Messianic times all nations will follow Israel's lead in recognizing and serving God. The fourteen verses beginning here allude to those days. However, David also referred to a salvation that occurred in his own lifetime. The Philistines had captured the Holy Ark and destroyed the Tabernacle at Shiloh. But the presence of the Ark in the Philistine cities brought plagues upon them. Recognizing the hand of God in their suffering, the Philistines returned the Ark with a gift of tribute to God. The same will happen in future times when Israel's oppressors will recognize God's mastery.

כִּי גָדוֹל יהוה וּמְהֻלָּל מְאֹד, וְנוֹרָא הוּא עַל כָּל אֱלֹהִים. ❖ כִּי כָּל אֱלֹהֵי הָעַמִּים אֱלִילִים, (pause) וַיהוה שָׁמַיִם עָשָׂה.*

הוֹד וְהָדָר לְפָנָיו, עֹז וְחֶדְוָה בִּמְקֹמוֹ. הָבוּ לַיהוה מִשְׁפְּחוֹת עַמִּים, הָבוּ לַיהוה כָּבוֹד וָעֹז. הָבוּ לַיהוה כְּבוֹד שְׁמוֹ, שְׂאוּ מִנְחָה וּבֹאוּ לְפָנָיו, הִשְׁתַּחֲווּ לַיהוה בְּהַדְרַת קֹדֶשׁ. חִילוּ מִלְּפָנָיו כָּל הָאָרֶץ, אַף תִּכּוֹן תֵּבֵל בַּל תִּמּוֹט.* יִשְׂמְחוּ הַשָּׁמַיִם וְתָגֵל הָאָרֶץ, וְיֹאמְרוּ בַגּוֹיִם, יהוה מָלָךְ. יִרְעַם הַיָּם וּמְלוֹאוֹ, יַעֲלֹץ הַשָּׂדֶה וְכָל אֲשֶׁר בּוֹ. אָז יְרַנְּנוּ עֲצֵי הַיָּעַר, מִלִּפְנֵי יהוה, כִּי בָא לִשְׁפּוֹט אֶת הָאָרֶץ. הוֹדוּ לַיהוה כִּי טוֹב, כִּי לְעוֹלָם חַסְדּוֹ. וְאִמְרוּ הוֹשִׁיעֵנוּ אֱלֹהֵי יִשְׁעֵנוּ, וְקַבְּצֵנוּ וְהַצִּילֵנוּ מִן הַגּוֹיִם, לְהֹדוֹת לְשֵׁם קָדְשֶׁךָ, לְהִשְׁתַּבֵּחַ בִּתְהִלָּתֶךָ. בָּרוּךְ יהוה אֱלֹהֵי יִשְׂרָאֵל מִן הָעוֹלָם וְעַד הָעֹלָם, וַיֹּאמְרוּ כָל הָעָם, אָמֵן, וְהַלֵּל לַיהוה.

❖ רוֹמְמוּ יהוה אֱלֹהֵינוּ* וְהִשְׁתַּחֲווּ לַהֲדֹם רַגְלָיו, קָדוֹשׁ הוּא.[1] רוֹמְמוּ יהוה אֱלֹהֵינוּ וְהִשְׁתַּחֲווּ לְהַר קָדְשׁוֹ, כִּי קָדוֹשׁ יהוה אֱלֹהֵינוּ.[2]

וְהוּא רַחוּם יְכַפֵּר עָוֹן וְלֹא יַשְׁחִית, וְהִרְבָּה לְהָשִׁיב אַפּוֹ, וְלֹא יָעִיר כָּל חֲמָתוֹ.[3] אַתָּה יהוה, לֹא תִכְלָא רַחֲמֶיךָ מִמֶּנִּי, חַסְדְּךָ וַאֲמִתְּךָ תָּמִיד יִצְּרוּנִי.[4] זְכֹר רַחֲמֶיךָ יהוה וַחֲסָדֶיךָ, כִּי מֵעוֹלָם הֵמָּה.[5] תְּנוּ עֹז לֵאלֹהִים, עַל יִשְׂרָאֵל גַּאֲוָתוֹ, וְעֻזּוֹ בַּשְּׁחָקִים. נוֹרָא אֱלֹהִים מִמִּקְדָּשֶׁיךָ, אֵל יִשְׂרָאֵל הוּא נֹתֵן עֹז וְתַעֲצֻמוֹת לָעָם, בָּרוּךְ אֱלֹהִים.[6] אֵל נְקָמוֹת יהוה, אֵל נְקָמוֹת הוֹפִיעַ. הִנָּשֵׂא שֹׁפֵט הָאָרֶץ, הָשֵׁב גְּמוּל עַל גֵּאִים.[7] לַיהוה הַיְשׁוּעָה, עַל עַמְּךָ בִרְכָתֶךָ סֶּלָה.[8] ❖ יהוה צְבָאוֹת עִמָּנוּ, מִשְׂגָּב לָנוּ אֱלֹהֵי יַעֲקֹב סֶלָה.[9] יהוה צְבָאוֹת, אַשְׁרֵי אָדָם בֹּטֵחַ בָּךְ.[10] יהוה הוֹשִׁיעָה, הַמֶּלֶךְ יַעֲנֵנוּ בְיוֹם קָרְאֵנוּ.[11]

וַה׳ שָׁמַיִם עָשָׂה — *But HASHEM made heaven.* After having proclaimed that the gods of the nations are vain and useless *nothings,* David made this logical argument: the most prominent and seemingly powerful idols were the heavenly bodies — but since *HASHEM made heaven,* how can anyone justify worshiping His creatures in preference to Him? *(Radak).*

It is important to pause between אֱלִילִים, *nothings* [i.e., the idols] and וַה׳, *but* [lit. *and*] *HASHEM.* If the two words are read together, it could be understood to mean ח״ו: *all of the gods … are nothings and HASHEM,* as if to say that He is like them.

תֵּבֵל בַּל תִּמּוֹט — *The world … it cannot falter.* Though the turbulent history of war and conflict often makes it seem as though man will destroy his planet, the climax of history will be the peace

That HASHEM *is great and exceedingly lauded, and awesome is He above all heavenly powers.* Chazzan— *For all the gods of the peoples are nothings — but* HASHEM *made heaven!**

Glory and majesty are before Him, might and delight are in His place. Render to HASHEM, *O families of the peoples, render to* HASHEM *honor and might. Render to* HASHEM *honor worthy of His Name, take an offering and come before Him, prostrate yourselves before* HASHEM *in His intensely holy place. Tremble before Him, everyone on earth, indeed, the world is fixed so that it cannot falter.* The heavens will be glad and the earth will rejoice and say among the nations, '*HASHEM has reigned!' The sea and its fullness will roar, the field and everything in it will exult. Then the trees of the forest will sing with joy before* HASHEM, *for He will have arrived to judge the earth. Give thanks to* HASHEM, *for He is good, for His kindness endures forever. And say, 'Save us, O God of our salvation, gather us and rescue us from the nations, to thank Your Holy Name and to glory in Your praise!' Blessed is* HASHEM, *the God of Israel, from This World to the World to Come — and let the entire people say, 'Amen and praise to* HASHEM!'

Chazzan— *Exalt* HASHEM, *our God,* and bow at His footstool; He is holy!*[1] *Exalt* HASHEM, *our God, and bow at His holy mountain; for holy is* HASHEM, *our God.*[2]

He, the Merciful One, is forgiving of iniquity and does not destroy; frequently, He withdraws His anger, not arousing His entire rage.[3] *You,* HASHEM *— withhold not Your mercy from me; may Your kindness and Your truth always protect me.*[4] *Remember Your mercies,* HASHEM, *and Your kindnesses, for they are from the beginning of the world.*[5] *Render might to God, Whose majesty hovers over Israel and Whose might is in the clouds. You are awesome, O God, from Your sanctuaries, O God of Israel — it is He Who grants might and power to the people, blessed is God.*[6] *O God of vengeance,* HASHEM, *O God of vengeance, appear! Arise, O Judge of the earth, render recompense to the haughty.*[7] *Salvation is* HASHEM'*s, upon Your people is Your blessing, Selah.*[8] Chazzan— HASHEM, *Master of Legions, is with us, a stronghold for us is the God of Jacob, Selah.*[9] HASHEM, *Master of Legions, praiseworthy is the person who trusts in You.*[10] HASHEM, *save! May the King answer us on the day we call.*[11]

(1) *Psalms* 99:5. (2) 99:9. (3) 78:38. (4) 40:12. (5) 25:6.
(6) 68:35-36. (7) 94:1-2. (8) 3:9. (9) 46:8. (10) 84:13. (11) 20:10.

and fulfillment of Messianic times. God has ordained that the world will survive (*Radak*).

רוֹמְמוּ ה׳ אֱלֹהֵינוּ — *Exalt* HASHEM, *our God* ... From this point until its end, the prayer contains a collection of verses from throughout *Psalms,* which Rabbi Profiat Duran, a refugee from the Spanish massacres of 1391, describes as פְּסוּקֵי דְרַחְמֵי, *Verses of Mercy,* because they are effective in pleading for God's mercy. Accordingly, they were adopted in the prayers for an end to exile and dispersion.

From *Etz Yosef, World of Prayer* and others, the following progression of thought emerges from these verses. Even if הֲדֹם רַגְלָיו, *His footstool,* i.e., the Temple, has been destroyed, God heeds our prayers at הַר קָדְשׁוֹ, *His holy*

הוֹשִׁיעָה אֶת עַמֶּךָ, וּבָרֵךְ אֶת נַחֲלָתֶךָ, וּרְעֵם וְנַשְּׂאֵם עַד הָעוֹלָם.1 נַפְשֵׁנוּ חִכְּתָה לַיהוה, עֶזְרֵנוּ וּמָגִנֵּנוּ הוּא. כִּי בוֹ יִשְׂמַח לִבֵּנוּ, כִּי בְשֵׁם קָדְשׁוֹ בָטָחְנוּ. יְהִי חַסְדְּךָ יהוה עָלֵינוּ, כַּאֲשֶׁר יִחַלְנוּ לָךְ.2 הַרְאֵנוּ יהוה חַסְדֶּךָ, וְיֶשְׁעֲךָ תִּתֶּן לָנוּ.3 קוּמָה עֶזְרָתָה לָּנוּ, וּפְדֵנוּ לְמַעַן חַסְדֶּךָ.4 אָנֹכִי יהוה אֱלֹהֶיךָ הַמַּעַלְךָ מֵאֶרֶץ מִצְרָיִם, הַרְחֶב פִּיךָ וַאֲמַלְאֵהוּ.5 אַשְׁרֵי הָעָם שֶׁכָּכָה לּוֹ, אַשְׁרֵי הָעָם שֶׁיהוה אֱלֹהָיו.6 ❖ וַאֲנִי בְּחַסְדְּךָ בָטַחְתִּי, יָגֵל לִבִּי בִּישׁוּעָתֶךָ, אָשִׁירָה לַיהוה, כִּי גָמַל עָלָי.7

מִזְמוֹר לְתוֹדָה (*Psalm* 100) is recited while standing.

THIS PRAYER IS OMITTED ON EREV YOM KIPPUR, EREV PESACH AND CHOL HAMOED PESACH.

מִזְמוֹר לְתוֹדָה,* הָרִיעוּ לַיהוה כָּל הָאָרֶץ. עִבְדוּ אֶת יהוה בְּשִׂמְחָה,* בֹּאוּ לְפָנָיו בִּרְנָנָה. דְּעוּ כִּי יהוה הוּא אֱלֹהִים, הוּא עָשָׂנוּ, וְלוֹ אֲנַחְנוּ, עַמּוֹ וְצֹאן מַרְעִיתוֹ. בֹּאוּ שְׁעָרָיו בְּתוֹדָה, חֲצֵרֹתָיו בִּתְהִלָּה, הוֹדוּ לוֹ, בָּרְכוּ שְׁמוֹ. ❖ כִּי טוֹב יהוה, לְעוֹלָם חַסְדּוֹ, וְעַד דֹּר וָדֹר אֱמוּנָתוֹ.

ON HOSHANAH RABBAH CONTINUE WITH לַמְנַצֵּחַ (PAGE 374) AND THE SABBATH *PESUKEI D'ZIMRAH* UNTIL PAGE 388, THEN CONTINUE HERE.

The following prayer should be recited with special intensity.

יְהִי כְבוֹד* יהוה לְעוֹלָם, יִשְׂמַח יהוה בְּמַעֲשָׂיו.8 יְהִי שֵׁם יהוה מְבֹרָךְ, מֵעַתָּה וְעַד עוֹלָם. מִמִּזְרַח שֶׁמֶשׁ עַד מְבוֹאוֹ, מְהֻלָּל שֵׁם יהוה. רָם עַל כָּל גּוֹיִם יהוה, עַל הַשָּׁמַיִם כְּבוֹדוֹ.9 יהוה שִׁמְךָ לְעוֹלָם, יהוה זִכְרְךָ* לְדֹר וָדֹר.10 יהוה

---

mountain. But the millions of Jews who cannot come to the Temple Mount need not fear that their prayers are in vain because God is always merciful and ready to withdraw His anger in the face of sincere prayer. Though Israel may have suffered grievously in the many places of its dispersion, God avenges it and helps those who call upon Him.

The term God's 'footstool' refers to the place on earth where He rests His glory, as we find in *Isaiah* 66:1: *So says* HASHEM, *'The heaven is My throne and the earth is My footstool.'*

☙ **מִזְמוֹר לְתוֹדָה** — *A psalm of thanksgiving.* During Temple times, a person would bring a תּוֹדָה, *thanksgiving-offering,* whenever he survived a life-threatening situation, such as a serious illness, a sea voyage, a desert journey, or captivity. This psalm was chanted during the service. However, every human being goes through any number of potential dangers in the course of his life, dangers of which he most often is not even aware. As a daily reminder of this, the psalm of thanksgiving was inserted into the morning service.

The thanksgiving-offering was not offered on the Sabbath and Festivals, when only communal offerings could be brought. Therefore the psalm is omitted on those days. Also, the offering, which includes *chametz,* i.e., leavened loaves, may be consumed only until the midnight after it was offered. Consequently, it was not offered on the day before Pesach nor during that festival, since the *chametz* loaves could not be eaten. Similarly, it was not offered on the day before Yom Kippur because it could not be eaten that night. Therefore, the psalm is not recited on those days.

Given the theme of the psalm, its contents take on special meaning. We are joyous in our gratitude and express the conviction that God is our Maker, Shepherd, and Protector.

עִבְדוּ אֶת ה׳ בְּשִׂמְחָה — *Serve* HASHEM *with*

Save Your people and bless Your heritage, tend them and elevate them forever.[1] *Our soul longed for HASHEM — our help and our shield is He. For in Him will our hearts be glad, for in His Holy Name we trusted. May Your kindness, HASHEM, be upon us, just as we awaited You.*[2] *Show us Your kindness, HASHEM, and grant us Your salvation.*[3] *Arise — assist us, and redeem us by virtue of Your kindness.*[4] *I am HASHEM, your God, Who raised you from the land of Egypt, open wide your mouth and I will fill it.*[5] *Praiseworthy is the people for whom this is so, praiseworthy is the people whose God is HASHEM.*[6] Chazzan— *As for me, I trust in Your kindness; my heart will rejoice in Your salvation. I will sing to HASHEM, for He dealt kindly with me.*[7]

מִזְמוֹר לְתוֹדָה, *'A Psalm of thanksgiving'* (*Psalm* 100) is recited while standing.
THIS PRAYER IS OMITTED ON EREV YOM KIPPUR, EREV PESACH AND CHOL HAMOED PESACH.

מִזְמוֹר לְתוֹדָה *A psalm of thanksgiving,* call out to HASHEM, everyone on earth. Serve HASHEM with gladness,* come before Him with joyous song. Know that HASHEM, He is God, it is He Who made us and we are His, His people and the sheep of His pasture. Enter His gates with thanksgiving, His courts with praise, give thanks to Him, bless His Name.* Chazzan— *For HASHEM is good, His kindness endures forever, and from generation to generation is His faithfulness.*

ON HOSHANAH RABBAH CONTINUE WITH לַמְנַצֵּחַ, *'FOR THE CONDUCTOR . . .'* (PAGE 375)
AND THE SABBATH *PESUKEI D'ZIMRAH* UNTIL PAGE 388, THEN CONTINUE HERE.

The following prayer should be recited with special intensity.

יְהִי כְבוֹד *May the glory of HASHEM* endure forever, let HASHEM rejoice in His works.*[8] *Blessed be the Name of HASHEM, from this time and forever. From the rising of the sun to its setting, HASHEM's Name is praised. High above all nations is HASHEM, above the heavens is His glory.*[9] *'HASHEM' is Your Name forever, 'HASHEM' is Your memorial* throughout the generations.*[10] *HASHEM*

(1) *Psalms* 28:9. (2) 33:20-22. (3) 85:8. (4) 44:27. (5) 81:11. (6) 144:15. (7) 13:6.
(8) 104:31. (9) 113:2-4. (10) 135:13.

gladness. But in *Psalms* 2:11 we are told to *serve HASHEM with awe* — how can we reconcile gladness with awe? To feel fear, respect, and awe for God is essential to spiritual growth. Once a person realizes that his fear is the beginning of a process that leads to personal greatness and bliss, even the difficulties along the way can be accepted gladly *(Ikkarim).*

☙ **יְהִי כְבוֹד ה׳** — *May the glory of HASHEM.* This is a collection of verses, primarily from *Psalms,* that revolves around two themes: the sovereignty of God and the role of Israel. Central to *tefillah* and to the purpose of creation is מַלְכוּת שָׁמַיִם, *the Kingship of Heaven,* which means that every being exists as part of God's plan and is dedicated to His service. This idea is found in nature itself, for, as David says lyrically, man attains awareness of God when he contemplates the beauty and perfection of the universe. The Sages chose *Psalms* 104:31 to begin this prayer because it was the praise proclaimed by an angel when the newly created plant world developed according to God's wishes *(Chullin* 60a). In other words, the 'glory' of God is revealed on earth when His will is done. Most of this prayer deals with this idea of God's glory and Kingship. The last five verses speak of God's selection of the Jewish people and pleads for His mercy and attentiveness to their prayers (see *World of Prayer).*

ה׳ שִׁמְךָ ... זִכְרְךָ — *'HASHEM' is Your Name ... Your memorial.* The *Name* of God represents what He

בַּשָּׁמַיִם הֵכִין כִּסְאוֹ, וּמַלְכוּתוֹ בַּכֹּל מָשָׁלָה.[1] יִשְׂמְחוּ הַשָּׁמַיִם
וְתָגֵל הָאָרֶץ,* וְיֹאמְרוּ בַגּוֹיִם יהוה מָלָךְ.[2] יהוה מֶלֶךְ,*[3] יהוה
מָלָךְ,[4] יהוה יִמְלֹךְ לְעֹלָם וָעֶד.[5] יהוה מֶלֶךְ עוֹלָם וָעֶד, אָבְדוּ
גוֹיִם* מֵאַרְצוֹ.[6] יהוה הֵפִיר עֲצַת גּוֹיִם, הֵנִיא מַחְשְׁבוֹת עַמִּים.[7]
רַבּוֹת מַחֲשָׁבוֹת בְּלֶב אִישׁ, וַעֲצַת יהוה הִיא תָקוּם.[8] עֲצַת יהוה
לְעוֹלָם תַּעֲמֹד, מַחְשְׁבוֹת לִבּוֹ לְדֹר וָדֹר.[9] כִּי הוּא אָמַר וַיֶּהִי,
הוּא צִוָּה וַיַּעֲמֹד.[10] כִּי בָחַר יהוה בְּצִיּוֹן, אִוָּהּ לְמוֹשָׁב לוֹ.[11] כִּי
יַעֲקֹב בָּחַר לוֹ יָהּ, יִשְׂרָאֵל לִסְגֻלָּתוֹ.[12] כִּי לֹא יִטֹּשׁ יהוה עַמּוֹ,
וְנַחֲלָתוֹ לֹא יַעֲזֹב.[13] ❖ וְהוּא רַחוּם יְכַפֵּר עָוֹן וְלֹא יַשְׁחִית,
וְהִרְבָּה לְהָשִׁיב אַפּוֹ, וְלֹא יָעִיר כָּל חֲמָתוֹ.[14] יהוה הוֹשִׁיעָה,
הַמֶּלֶךְ יַעֲנֵנוּ בְיוֹם קָרְאֵנוּ.[15]

אַשְׁרֵי יוֹשְׁבֵי בֵיתֶךָ, עוֹד יְהַלְלוּךָ סֶּלָה.[16] אַשְׁרֵי הָעָם שֶׁכָּכָה
לּוֹ, אַשְׁרֵי הָעָם שֶׁיהוה אֱלֹהָיו.[17]

תהלים קמה

תְּהִלָּה לְדָוִד,

אֲרוֹמִמְךָ* אֱלוֹהַי הַמֶּלֶךְ, וַאֲבָרְכָה שִׁמְךָ לְעוֹלָם וָעֶד.
בְּכָל יוֹם אֲבָרְכֶךָּ,* וַאֲהַלְלָה שִׁמְךָ לְעוֹלָם וָעֶד.
גָּדוֹל יהוה וּמְהֻלָּל מְאֹד, וְלִגְדֻלָּתוֹ אֵין חֵקֶר.*

---

truly is and implies a thorough understanding of His actions and the reasons for them. But because man's limited intelligence cannot reach this level of understanding, we do not pronounce the Name יה־ו־ה as it is spelled; thereby we symbolize our inability to know God as He truly is. In this sense, the pronunciation HASHEM is God's *memorial* (see *Pesachim* 50a).

יִשְׂמְחוּ הַשָּׁמַיִם וְתָגֵל הָאָרֶץ — *The heavens will be glad and the earth will rejoice.* The celestial and terrestrial parts of creation serve God. They will truly rejoice when all nations, too, acknowledge that *HASHEM has reigned.*

ה׳ מֶלֶךְ ... — *HASHEM reigns ...* — This is one of the most familiar verses in the entire liturgy, but, surprisingly enough, it is not found in Scripture. Rather, each phrase comes from a different part of Scripture. In combination, the three phrases express the eternity of God's reign.

אָבְדוּ גוֹיִם — *Even when the nations will have perished.* The verse refers only to the *evil* people among the nations, for their deeds prevent others from acknowledging God *(Rashi, Radak).*

אַשְׁרֵי ❧ / Ashrei

Rambam writes: The Sages praised anyone who recites hymns from the Book of Psalms every day, from תְּהִלָּה לְדָוִד, *A psalm of praise by David* [145:1; the third verse of *Ashrei*] to the end of the Book [*i.e.,* the six psalms including *Ashrei,* and the five familiarly known as the *Halleluyahs*]. It has become customary to recite other verses before and after these, and [the Sages] instituted a blessing, *Baruch She'amar,* before these psalms and a blessing, *Yishtabach,* after them (*Hil. Tefillah* 7:12).

From *Rambam's* formulation, it is clear that the six psalms beginning with *Ashrei* are the very essence of *Pesukei D'zimrah.* This is based on the Talmud *(Shabbos* 118b) which cites Rabbi Yose: 'May my share be with those who complete *Hallel* every day.' The Talmud explains that, in Rabbi Yose's context, *Hallel* means the six concluding chapters of *Psalms* that we are about to recite. [However, see *Rashi.*]

Ashrei has a special significance of its own, because the Talmud *(Berachos* 4b) teaches that the Sages assured a share in the World to Come to anyone who recites it properly three times a day. It has this special status because no other psalm possesses both of its two virtues: (a) Beginning with the word אֲרוֹמִמְךָ (the first substantive word of the psalm), the initials of the

has established His throne in the heavens, and His kingdom reigns over all.[1] *The heavens will be glad and the earth will rejoice,* they will proclaim among the nations, 'HASHEM has reigned!'*[2] *HASHEM reigns,**[3] *HASHEM has reigned,*[4] *HASHEM shall reign for all eternity.*[5] *HASHEM reigns forever and ever, even when the nations will have perished* from His earth.*[6] *HASHEM annuls the counsel of nations, He balks the designs of peoples.*[7] *Many designs are in man's heart, but the counsel of HASHEM — only it will prevail.*[8] *The counsel of HASHEM will endure forever, the designs of His heart throughout the generations.*[9] *For He spoke and it came to be; He commanded and it stood firm.*[10] *For HASHEM selected Zion, He desired it for His dwelling place.*[11] *For God selected Jacob as His own, Israel as His treasure.*[12] *For HASHEM will not cast off His people, nor will He forsake His heritage.*[13] Chazzan— *He, the Merciful One, is forgiving of iniquity and does not destroy; frequently He withdraws His anger, not arousing His entire rage.*[14] *HASHEM, save! May the King answer us on the day we call.*[15]

אַשְׁרֵי *Praiseworthy are those who dwell in Your house; may they always praise You, Selah!*[16] *Praiseworthy is the people for whom this is so, praiseworthy is the people whose God is HASHEM.*[17]

Psalm 145 *A psalm of praise by David:*

א *I will exalt You,* my God the King,*
and I will bless Your Name forever and ever.

ב *Every day I will bless You,**
and I will laud Your Name forever and ever.

ג *HASHEM is great and exceedingly lauded,*
*and His greatness is beyond investigation.**

(1) *Psalms* 103:19. (2) *I Chronicles* 16:31. (3) *Psalms* 10:16. (4) 93:1 et al. (5) *Exodus* 15:18. (6) *Psalms* 10:16. (7) 33:10. (8) *Proverbs* 19:21. (9) *Psalms* 33:11. (10) 33:9. (11) 132:13. (12) 135:4. (13) 94:14. (14) 78:38. (15) 20:10. (16) 84:5. (17) 144:15.

psalm's respective verses follow the order of the *Aleph-Beis;* and (b) it contains the inspiring and reassuring testimony to God's mercy, פּוֹתֵחַ אֶת ... יָדֶךָ, *You open Your hand* ... As *Zohar* teaches, the recitation of this verse in *Pesukei D'zimrah* is not considered a *request* that God open His hand for us; rather it is purely a recitation of praise. Similarly, the five psalms that follow are expressions of sublime ecstatic praise.

As noted above, psalm 145 begins with the verse תְּהִלָּה לְדָוִד; the two preliminary verses, each beginning with the word אַשְׁרֵי, are affixed to תְּהִלָּה לְדָוִד for two reasons: (a) By expressing the idea that those who can dwell in God's house of prayer and service are praiseworthy, these verses set the stage for the succeeding psalms of praise, for we, the praiseworthy ones, are about to laud the God in Whose house we dwell; and (b) the word אַשְׁרֵי is found three times in these verses. This alludes to the Talmudic dictum that one who recites psalm 145 three times a day is assured of a share in the World to Come; thus, those who do so are indeed אַשְׁרֵי, *praiseworthy.*

תְּהִלָּה ... אֲרוֹמִמְךָ — *A psalm ... I will exalt You.* Beginning with the word אֲרוֹמִמְךָ, the initials of the respective verses follow the order of the *Aleph-Beis.* According to *Abudraham* the *Aleph-Beis* structure symbolizes that we praise God with every sound available to the organs of speech. *Midrash Tadshei* records that the Psalmists and Sages used the *Aleph-Beis* formula in chapters that they wanted people to follow more easily or memorize.

בְּכָל יוֹם אֲבָרְכֶךָּ — *Every day I will bless You.* True, no mortal can pretend to know God's essence, but each of us *is* equipped to appreciate life, health, sustenance, sunshine, rainfall, and so on. For them and their daily renewal, we give daily blessings *(Siach Yitzchak).*

וְלִגְדֻלָּתוֹ אֵין חֵקֶר — *And His greatness is beyond investigation.* Much though we may try, we can

דּוֹר לְדוֹר יְשַׁבַּח מַעֲשֶׂיךָ, וּגְבוּרֹתֶיךָ יַגִּידוּ.
הֲדַר כְּבוֹד הוֹדֶךָ, וְדִבְרֵי נִפְלְאוֹתֶיךָ אָשִׂיחָה.
וֶעֱזוּז נוֹרְאוֹתֶיךָ יֹאמֵרוּ, וּגְדוּלָּתְךָ אֲסַפְּרֶנָּה.
זֵכֶר רַב טוּבְךָ יַבִּיעוּ, וְצִדְקָתְךָ יְרַנֵּנוּ.
חַנּוּן וְרַחוּם* יהוה, אֶרֶךְ אַפַּיִם וּגְדָל חָסֶד.
טוֹב יהוה לַכֹּל, וְרַחֲמָיו עַל כָּל מַעֲשָׂיו.
יוֹדוּךָ יהוה כָּל מַעֲשֶׂיךָ, וַחֲסִידֶיךָ יְבָרְכוּכָה.
כְּבוֹד מַלְכוּתְךָ יֹאמֵרוּ, וּגְבוּרָתְךָ יְדַבֵּרוּ.
לְהוֹדִיעַ לִבְנֵי הָאָדָם גְּבוּרֹתָיו, וּכְבוֹד הֲדַר מַלְכוּתוֹ.
מַלְכוּתְךָ מַלְכוּת כָּל עֹלָמִים, וּמֶמְשַׁלְתְּךָ בְּכָל דּוֹר וָדֹר.
סוֹמֵךְ יהוה* לְכָל הַנֹּפְלִים, וְזוֹקֵף לְכָל הַכְּפוּפִים.
עֵינֵי כֹל אֵלֶיךָ יְשַׂבֵּרוּ,* וְאַתָּה נוֹתֵן לָהֶם אֶת אָכְלָם בְּעִתּוֹ.

Concentrate while reciting the verse פּוֹתֵחַ. It is customary to touch the arm-*tefillin* while saying the first half of the verse, and the head-*tefillin* while saying the second.

פּוֹתֵחַ* אֶת יָדֶךָ,
וּמַשְׂבִּיעַ לְכָל חַי רָצוֹן.

צַדִּיק יהוה בְּכָל דְּרָכָיו, וְחָסִיד* בְּכָל מַעֲשָׂיו.
קָרוֹב יהוה לְכָל קֹרְאָיו, לְכֹל אֲשֶׁר יִקְרָאֻהוּ בֶאֱמֶת.
רְצוֹן יְרֵאָיו יַעֲשֶׂה, וְאֶת שַׁוְעָתָם יִשְׁמַע וְיוֹשִׁיעֵם.
שׁוֹמֵר יהוה אֶת כָּל אֹהֲבָיו, וְאֵת כָּל הָרְשָׁעִים יַשְׁמִיד.
❖ תְּהִלַּת יהוה יְדַבֶּר פִּי, וִיבָרֵךְ כָּל בָּשָׂר שֵׁם קָדְשׁוֹ לְעוֹלָם וָעֶד. וַאֲנַחְנוּ נְבָרֵךְ* יָהּ, מֵעַתָּה וְעַד עוֹלָם, הַלְלוּיָהּ.*[1]

---

understand neither God's essence nor His ways through human analysis, for He is infinite. We *must* rely on the traditions that have come to us from earlier generations, as the next verse suggests *(Rama).*

חַנּוּן וְרַחוּם — *Gracious and merciful.* Because God is *merciful,* He is אֶרֶךְ אַפַּיִם, *slow to anger,* so that punishment, although deserved, is delayed as long as possible to allow time for repentance. And because He is *gracious* He is גְּדָל חָסֶד, *great in bestowing kindness (Siach Yitzchak).*

סוֹמֵךְ ה' — *HASHEM supports.* No verse in *Ashrei* begins with a נ, because in the context of this verse that speaks of God supporting the fallen, the letter נ can be taken as an allusion to נְפִילָה, Israel's future *downfall,* ח"ו, and the Psalmist refused to use a letter that could suggest such tragedy. Nevertheless, knowing that downfalls would take place, the Psalmist comforted Israel by saying *God supports all the fallen ones.* This is an implied guarantee that even when a dreaded downfall happens, the people can look forward to His support *(Berachos* 4b). *Maharsha* comments that by omitting a direct mention of downfall, the Psalmist implies that even when Israel *does* suffer reverses, those reverses will never be complete. Rather, as the next verse declares, God will support the fallen.

עֵינֵי כֹל אֵלֶיךָ יְשַׂבֵּרוּ — *The eyes of all look to You with hope.* Even animals instinctively rely upon God for their sustenance [how much more so should man recognize the beneficence of his Maker!] *(Radak).*

פּוֹתֵחַ — [*You*] *open.* When reciting this verse, one must have in mind the translation of the words because this declaration of God's universal goodness is one of the two reasons the Sages required the thrice-daily recitation of this psalm. One who forgot to concentrate on the translation, must recite the verse again *(Tur* and

ד *Each generation will praise Your deeds to the next*
and of Your mighty deeds they will tell;
ה *The splendrous glory of Your power*
and Your wondrous deeds I shall discuss.
ו *And of Your awesome power they will speak,*
and Your greatness I shall relate.
ז *A recollection of Your abundant goodness they will utter*
and of Your righteousness they will sing exultantly.
ח *Gracious and merciful* is* HASHEM,
slow to anger, and great in [bestowing] kindness.
ט HASHEM *is good to all; His mercies are on all His works.*
י *All Your works shall thank You,* HASHEM,
and Your devout ones will bless You.
כ *Of the glory of Your kingdom they will speak,*
and of Your power they will tell;
ל *To inform human beings of His mighty deeds,*
and the glorious splendor of His kingdom.
מ *Your kingdom is a kingdom spanning all eternities,*
and Your dominion is throughout every generation.
ס HASHEM *supports* all the fallen ones and straightens all the bent.*
ע *The eyes of all look to You with hope**
and You give them their food in its proper time;
פ *You open* Your hand,*
and satisfy the desire
of every living thing.

Concentrate while reciting the verse, *'You open ....* It is customary to touch the arm-*tefillin* while saying the first half of the verse, and the head-*tefillin* while saying the second.

צ *Righteous is* HASHEM *in all His ways*
and magnanimous in all His deeds.*
ק HASHEM *is close to all who call upon Him —*
to all who call upon Him sincerely.
ר *The will of those who fear Him He will do;*
and their cry He will hear, and save them.
ש HASHEM *protects all who love Him;*
but all the wicked He will destroy.
ת Chazzan— *May my mouth declare the praise of* HASHEM
and may all flesh bless His Holy Name forever and ever.
We will bless God from this time and forever, Halleluyah!**[1]

(1) *Psalms* 115:18.

Shulchan Aruch 51:7). This verse should be recited with great joy at the knowledge that God cares for every creature *(Yesod V'Shoresh HaAvodah).*

צַדִּיק ... וְחָסִיד — *Righteous ... and magnanimous.* God's ways are just and *righteous* means that He judges people only according to their deeds. Nevertheless, even when justice calls for grievous punishment He is *magnanimous* in softening the blow, for He is merciful *(Vilna Gaon).*

וַאֲנַחְנוּ נְבָרֵךְ — *We will bless.* This verse is appended to *Ashrei* for two reasons: (a) To lead naturally into the next five psalms, all of which begin and end with the word *Halleluyah;* and (b) Having recited *Ashrei* which holds an

תהלים קמו

הַלְלוּיָהּ, הַלְלִי נַפְשִׁי אֶת יהוה.* אֲהַלְלָה יהוה בְּחַיָּי, אֲזַמְּרָה לֵאלֹהַי בְּעוֹדִי. אַל תִּבְטְחוּ בִנְדִיבִים, בְּבֶן אָדָם* שֶׁאֵין לוֹ תְשׁוּעָה. תֵּצֵא רוּחוֹ, יָשֻׁב לְאַדְמָתוֹ, בַּיּוֹם הַהוּא אָבְדוּ עֶשְׁתֹּנֹתָיו. אַשְׁרֵי שֶׁאֵל יַעֲקֹב בְּעֶזְרוֹ, שִׂבְרוֹ עַל יהוה אֱלֹהָיו. עֹשֶׂה שָׁמַיִם וָאָרֶץ,* אֶת הַיָּם וְאֶת כָּל אֲשֶׁר בָּם, הַשֹּׁמֵר אֱמֶת לְעוֹלָם. עֹשֶׂה מִשְׁפָּט לָעֲשׁוּקִים, נֹתֵן לֶחֶם לָרְעֵבִים, יהוה מַתִּיר אֲסוּרִים. יהוה פֹּקֵחַ עִוְרִים, יהוה זֹקֵף כְּפוּפִים, יהוה אֹהֵב צַדִּיקִים. יהוה שֹׁמֵר אֶת גֵּרִים,* יָתוֹם וְאַלְמָנָה יְעוֹדֵד, וְדֶרֶךְ רְשָׁעִים יְעַוֵּת. ❖ יִמְלֹךְ יהוה לְעוֹלָם, אֱלֹהַיִךְ צִיּוֹן, לְדֹר וָדֹר, הַלְלוּיָהּ.

תהלים קמז

הַלְלוּיָהּ, כִּי טוֹב* זַמְּרָה אֱלֹהֵינוּ, כִּי נָעִים נָאוָה תְהִלָּה. בּוֹנֵה יְרוּשָׁלַיִם יהוה, נִדְחֵי יִשְׂרָאֵל יְכַנֵּס. הָרוֹפֵא לִשְׁבוּרֵי לֵב, וּמְחַבֵּשׁ לְעַצְּבוֹתָם. מוֹנֶה מִסְפָּר לַכּוֹכָבִים,* לְכֻלָּם שֵׁמוֹת יִקְרָא. גָּדוֹל אֲדוֹנֵינוּ וְרַב כֹּחַ, לִתְבוּנָתוֹ אֵין מִסְפָּר. מְעוֹדֵד עֲנָוִים יהוה, מַשְׁפִּיל רְשָׁעִים עֲדֵי אָרֶץ. עֱנוּ לַיהוה בְּתוֹדָה, זַמְּרוּ לֵאלֹהֵינוּ בְכִנּוֹר. הַמְּכַסֶּה שָׁמַיִם בְּעָבִים, הַמֵּכִין לָאָרֶץ מָטָר, הַמַּצְמִיחַ הָרִים חָצִיר. נוֹתֵן לִבְהֵמָה לַחְמָהּ, לִבְנֵי עֹרֵב אֲשֶׁר יִקְרָאוּ. לֹא בִגְבוּרַת הַסּוּס יֶחְפָּץ, לֹא בְשׁוֹקֵי הָאִישׁ* יִרְצֶה. רוֹצֶה יהוה אֶת יְרֵאָיו, אֶת הַמְיַחֲלִים לְחַסְדּוֹ. שַׁבְּחִי יְרוּשָׁלַיִם אֶת יהוה, הַלְלִי אֱלֹהַיִךְ צִיּוֹן. כִּי חִזַּק בְּרִיחֵי* שְׁעָרָיִךְ,

---

assurance of the World to Come, we express the hope that we will bless God *forever* — that is, in both worlds *(Levush)*.

הַלְלוּיָהּ — *Halleluyah.* This familiar word is a contraction of two words: הַלְלוּ יָהּ, *praise God.* The term הַלְלוּ denotes crying out in happy excitement, while the unique meaning implied by the Name יָהּ means 'the One Who is forever.' The Psalmist addresses everyone, saying: Use your energy to be *excited* over God and nothing else *(R' Avigdor Miller)*.

☙ **הַלְלוּיָהּ הַלְלִי נַפְשִׁי אֶת ה׳** — *Halleluyah! Praise* HASHEM, *O my soul! Radak* interprets this psalm as a hymn of encouragement for Jews in exile. It begins with the Psalmist insisting that he will praise God as long as he lives and warning his fellow Jews not to rely on human beings. After praising God as the One Who cares for the underprivileged and oppressed, the Psalmist concludes that God will reign forever — despite the current ascendancy of our enemies.

בְּבֶן אָדָם — *Nor on a human being.* Even when rulers help Israel, it is because God has influenced them to do so. So it will be when the nations seem to have a hand in the Messianic redemption *(Radak)*.

עֹשֶׂה שָׁמַיִם וָאָרֶץ — *Maker of heaven and earth.* Unlike kings and rulers whose powers are limited in both time and space, God is everywhere and all-powerful *(Yerushalmi Berachos 9:1)*.

Psalm 146

הַלְלוּיָהּ *Halleluyah! Praise* HASHEM, *O my Soul!* I will praise* HASHEM *while I live, I will make music to my God while I exist. Do not rely on nobles, nor on a human being* for he holds no salvation. When his spirit departs he returns to his earth, on that day his plans all perish. Praiseworthy is one whose help is Jacob's God, whose hope is in* HASHEM, *his God. He is the Maker of heaven and earth,* the sea and all that is in them, Who safeguards truth forever. He does justice for the exploited; He gives bread to the hungry;* HASHEM *releases the bound.* HASHEM *gives sight to the blind;* HASHEM *straightens the bent;* HASHEM *loves the righteous.* HASHEM *protects strangers;* orphan and widow He encourages; but the way of the wicked He contorts.* Chazzan— HASHEM *shall reign forever — your God, O Zion — from generation to generation. Halleluyah!*

Psalm 147

הַלְלוּיָהּ *Halleluyah! For it is good* to make music to our God, for praise is pleasant and befitting. The Builder of Jerusalem is* HASHEM, *the outcast of Israel He will gather in. He is the Healer of the broken-hearted, and the One Who binds up their sorrows. He counts the number of the stars,* to all of them He assigns names. Great is our Lord and abundant in strength, His understanding is beyond calculation.* HASHEM *encourages the humble, He lowers the wicked down to the ground. Call out to* HASHEM *with thanks, with the harp sing to our God — Who covers the heavens with clouds, Who prepares rain for the earth, Who makes mountains sprout with grass. He gives to an animal its food, to young ravens that cry out. Not in the strength of the horse does He desire, and not in the legs of man* does He favor.* HASHEM *favors those who fear Him, those who hope for His kindness. Praise* HASHEM, *O Jerusalem, laud your God, O Zion. For He has strengthened the bars* of your gates,*

ה׳ שֹׁמֵר אֶת גֵּרִים — *HASHEM protects strangers.* God is the Protector of all weak and defenseless strangers, whether uprooted Jews or gentile converts *(Radak).*

⁂ הַלְלוּיָהּ כִּי טוֹב — *Halleluyah! For it is good ...* Continuing the theme of redemption, this psalm places its primary focus on Jerusalem, the center from which holiness, redemption, and Torah will emanate. In this sense, Jerusalem cannot be considered rebuilt until the Redemption, because the city's spiritual grandeur cannot be recaptured by mere architecture and growing numbers of people.

מוֹנֶה מִסְפָּר לַכּוֹכָבִים — *He counts the number of the stars.* Having given the assurance that God will rebuild Jerusalem and gather in Israel in joy, the Psalmist goes on to illustrate God's ability to do so. The next series of verses catalogue His might, compassion and attention to individual needs.

The stars number in the billions, but God is aware of each one and gives it a 'name' that denotes its purpose in the universe. Thus, nothing goes unnoticed or unprovided for.

בִּגְבוּרַת הַסּוּס ... בְשׁוֹקֵי הָאִישׁ — *The strength of the horse ... the legs of man.* The earlier verses spoke of God's compassion for helpless creatures. Now the Psalmist says in contrast, God is unimpressed with powerful battle horses or with the skill of the rider who controls the horse with his legs *(Radak; Ibn Ezra).*

כִּי חִזַּק בְּרִיחֵי — *For He has strengthened the bars.* The verse is figurative. The Jerusalem of the future will need no bars on its gates. The people will feel secure because God will protect their city *(Radak).*

הַשָּׂם גְּבוּלֵךְ שָׁלוֹם, חֵלֶב חִטִּים* יַשְׂבִּיעֵךְ. בֵּרַךְ בָּנַיִךְ בְּקִרְבֵּךְ. הַשֹּׁלֵחַ אִמְרָתוֹ אָרֶץ, עַד מְהֵרָה יָרוּץ דְּבָרוֹ. הַנֹּתֵן שֶׁלֶג כַּצָּמֶר, כְּפוֹר כָּאֵפֶר יְפַזֵּר. מַשְׁלִיךְ קַרְחוֹ כְפִתִּים, לִפְנֵי קָרָתוֹ מִי יַעֲמֹד. יִשְׁלַח דְּבָרוֹ וְיַמְסֵם,* יַשֵּׁב רוּחוֹ יִזְּלוּ מָיִם. ❖ מַגִּיד דְּבָרָיו לְיַעֲקֹב,* חֻקָּיו וּמִשְׁפָּטָיו לְיִשְׂרָאֵל. לֹא עָשָׂה כֵן לְכָל גּוֹי, וּמִשְׁפָּטִים בַּל יְדָעוּם, הַלְלוּיָהּ.

תהלים קמח

הַלְלוּיָהּ, הַלְלוּ אֶת יהוה* מִן הַשָּׁמַיִם,* הַלְלוּהוּ בַּמְּרוֹמִים. הַלְלוּהוּ כָל מַלְאָכָיו, הַלְלוּהוּ כָּל צְבָאָיו.* הַלְלוּהוּ שֶׁמֶשׁ וְיָרֵחַ, הַלְלוּהוּ כָּל כּוֹכְבֵי אוֹר. הַלְלוּהוּ שְׁמֵי הַשָּׁמָיִם, וְהַמַּיִם אֲשֶׁר מֵעַל הַשָּׁמָיִם. יְהַלְלוּ אֶת שֵׁם יהוה, כִּי הוּא צִוָּה וְנִבְרָאוּ. וַיַּעֲמִידֵם לָעַד לְעוֹלָם, חָק נָתַן* וְלֹא יַעֲבוֹר. הַלְלוּ אֶת יהוה מִן הָאָרֶץ, תַּנִּינִים וְכָל תְּהֹמוֹת. אֵשׁ וּבָרָד, שֶׁלֶג וְקִיטוֹר, רוּחַ סְעָרָה עֹשָׂה דְבָרוֹ. הֶהָרִים וְכָל גְּבָעוֹת, עֵץ פְּרִי וְכָל אֲרָזִים. הַחַיָּה וְכָל בְּהֵמָה, רֶמֶשׂ וְצִפּוֹר כָּנָף. מַלְכֵי אֶרֶץ וְכָל לְאֻמִּים, שָׂרִים וְכָל שֹׁפְטֵי אָרֶץ. בַּחוּרִים וְגַם בְּתוּלוֹת,* זְקֵנִים עִם נְעָרִים. ❖ יְהַלְלוּ אֶת שֵׁם יהוה, כִּי נִשְׂגָּב שְׁמוֹ לְבַדּוֹ, הוֹדוֹ עַל אֶרֶץ וְשָׁמָיִם. וַיָּרֶם קֶרֶן לְעַמּוֹ, תְּהִלָּה לְכָל חֲסִידָיו, לִבְנֵי יִשְׂרָאֵל עַם קְרֹבוֹ, הַלְלוּיָהּ.

תהלים קמט

הַלְלוּיָהּ, שִׁירוּ לַיהוה* שִׁיר חָדָשׁ, תְּהִלָּתוֹ בִּקְהַל חֲסִידִים. יִשְׂמַח יִשְׂרָאֵל בְּעֹשָׂיו,* בְּנֵי צִיּוֹן* יָגִילוּ בְמַלְכָּם.

חֵלֶב חִטִּים — *The cream of the wheat.* Wheat is a symbol of prosperity and, therefore, it is an omen of peace, because prosperous people are less contentious *(Berachos* 57a).

יִשְׁלַח דְּבָרוֹ וְיַמְסֵם — *He issues His command and it melts them.* The Psalmist had spoken of the many solid forms of moisture: snow, frost, ice — but at God's command, everything melts and flows like water. The Jew should emulate nature by conforming to the will of God *(R' Hirsch).*

מַגִּיד דְּבָרָיו לְיַעֲקֹב — *He relates His Word to Jacob.* God gave *His word,* the Torah, to *Jacob,* i.e., the entire Jewish nation, even those who are not capable of understanding its intricacies and mysteries. But to *Israel,* i.e., the greatest members of the nation, He made known the many variations and shadings of wisdom to be found within His statutes and judgments *(Zohar).*

Lest you wonder at the many centuries that have gone by without the redemption of Jerusalem and Israel, do not forget that the Torah itself — the very purpose of creation — was not given to man until 2448 years after creation. That God sees fit to delay is no cause for despair *(Siach Yitzchak).*

❧ הַלְלוּיָהּ הַלְלוּ אֶת ה׳ — *Halleluyah! Praise* HASHEM. Only after the Temple and Jerusalem are rebuilt will all the universe join in joyous songs of praise to God. Zion is the meeting point of heaven and earth, as it were, because it is from there that God's heavenly blessings emanate to the rest of the universe.

הַלְלוּ ... מִן הַשָּׁמַיִם — *Praise ... from the heavens.* The Psalmist begins by calling upon the heavenly beings to praise God, and then he directs his call to earthly beings. God's praises echo from the heavens and descend to earth, where the devout echo the heavenly songs with

and blessed your children in your midst; He Who makes your borders peaceful, and with the cream of the wheat He sates you; He Who dispatches His utterance earthward; how swiftly His commandment runs! He Who gives snow like fleece, He scatters frost like ashes. He hurls His ice like crumbs — before His cold, who can stand? He issues His command and it melts them,* He blows His wind — the waters flow.* Chazzan— *He relates His Word to Jacob,* His statutes and judgments to Israel. He did not do so for any other nation, such judgments — they know them not. Halleluyah!*

Psalm 148

הַלְלוּיָהּ *Halleluyah! Praise* HASHEM** from the heavens;* praise Him in the heights. Praise Him, all His angels; praise Him, all His legions.* Praise Him, sun and moon; praise Him, all bright stars. Praise Him, the most exalted of the heavens and the waters that are above the heavens. Let them praise the Name of* HASHEM, *for He commanded and they were created. And He established them forever and ever, He issued a decree* that will not change. Praise* HASHEM *from the earth, sea giants and all watery depths. Fire and hail, snow and vapor, stormy wind fulfilling His word. Mountains and all hills, fruitful trees and all cedars. Beasts and all cattle, crawling things and winged fowl. Kings of the earth and all governments, princes and all judges on earth. Young men and also maidens,* old men together with youths.* Chazzan— *Let them praise the Name of* HASHEM, *for His Name alone will have been exalted; His glory is above earth and heaven. And He will have exalted the pride of His nation, causing praise for all His devout ones, for the Children of Israel, His intimate people. Halleluyah!*

Psalm 149

הַלְלוּיָהּ *Halleluyah! Sing to* HASHEM** a new song, let His praise be in the congregation of the devout. Let Israel exult in its Maker,* let the Children of Zion* rejoice in their King. Let*

---

their own praises *(Sforno).*

מַלְאָכָיו ... צְבָאָיו — *His angels ... His legions.* The *angels* are spiritual beings without physical form while the *legions* are the heavenly bodies, which are so numerous that they are likened to legions *(Radak).*

חָק נָתַן — *He issued a decree.* God ordained that the sun shine by day and the moon by night, and this *decree* can never be violated *(Rashi).*

בַּחוּרִים וְגַם בְּתוּלוֹת — *Young men and also maidens.* The use here of the word וְגַם, *and also,* is noteworthy. The Psalmist does not say that young men *and* women will be together, because such mingling would be immodest. Only later, when he speaks of old men and youths does the Psalmist say עִם, *with* — that they will be *together (Sefer Chassidim).*

הַלְלוּיָהּ שִׁירוּ לַה׳ — *Halleluyah! Sing to* HASHEM. In every generation, God confronts us with new challenges and problems, yet He provides us with the opportunity to solve them. For this, our songs of praise never grow stale, because they are always infused with new meaning. But the greatest, newest song of all will spring from Israel's lips when history reaches its climax with the coming of Messiah.

בְּעֹשָׂיו — *In its Maker.* Although God made *all* nations, only Israel is His Chosen People *(Sforno).*

בְּנֵי צִיּוֹן — *The Children of Zion.* The future holiness of Zion — the place from which the Torah's teachings will emanate — will be of a higher order than anything we now know. The Jews who benefit from this spiritual aura will be called *the Children of Zion.*

יְהַלְּלוּ שְׁמוֹ בְמָחוֹל, בְּתֹף וְכִנּוֹר יְזַמְּרוּ לוֹ. כִּי רוֹצֶה יהוה בְּעַמּוֹ,* יְפָאֵר עֲנָוִים בִּישׁוּעָה. יַעְלְזוּ חֲסִידִים בְּכָבוֹד, יְרַנְּנוּ עַל מִשְׁכְּבוֹתָם.* רוֹמְמוֹת אֵל בִּגְרוֹנָם,* וְחֶרֶב פִּיפִיּוֹת בְּיָדָם. לַעֲשׂוֹת נְקָמָה בַּגּוֹיִם, תּוֹכֵחוֹת* בַּלְאֻמִּים. ❖ לֶאְסֹר מַלְכֵיהֶם בְּזִקִּים, וְנִכְבְּדֵיהֶם בְּכַבְלֵי בַרְזֶל. לַעֲשׂוֹת בָּהֶם מִשְׁפָּט כָּתוּב,* הָדָר הוּא לְכָל חֲסִידָיו, הַלְּלוּיָהּ.

תהלים קנ

הַלְּלוּיָהּ, הַלְּלוּ אֵל* בְּקָדְשׁוֹ, הַלְּלוּהוּ בִּרְקִיעַ עֻזּוֹ. הַלְּלוּהוּ בִּגְבוּרֹתָיו, הַלְּלוּהוּ כְּרֹב גֻּדְלוֹ. הַלְּלוּהוּ בְּתֵקַע שׁוֹפָר, הַלְּלוּהוּ בְּנֵבֶל וְכִנּוֹר. הַלְּלוּהוּ בְּתֹף וּמָחוֹל, הַלְּלוּהוּ בְּמִנִּים וְעוּגָב. הַלְּלוּהוּ בְצִלְצְלֵי שָׁמַע, הַלְּלוּהוּ בְּצִלְצְלֵי תְרוּעָה. ❖ כֹּל הַנְּשָׁמָה תְּהַלֵּל* יָהּ, הַלְּלוּיָהּ.* כֹּל הַנְּשָׁמָה תְּהַלֵּל יָהּ, הַלְּלוּיָהּ.

בָּרוּךְ יהוה לְעוֹלָם,* אָמֵן וְאָמֵן.*[1] בָּרוּךְ יהוה מִצִּיּוֹן, שֹׁכֵן יְרוּשָׁלָיִם, הַלְּלוּיָהּ.[2] בָּרוּךְ יהוה אֱלֹהִים אֱלֹהֵי יִשְׂרָאֵל, עֹשֵׂה נִפְלָאוֹת לְבַדּוֹ. ❖ וּבָרוּךְ שֵׁם כְּבוֹדוֹ לְעוֹלָם, וְיִמָּלֵא כְבוֹדוֹ אֶת כָּל הָאָרֶץ, אָמֵן וְאָמֵן.[3]

One must stand from וַיְבָרֶךְ דָּוִיד, until after the phrase אַתָּה הוּא ה' הָאֱלֹהִים, however, there is a generally accepted custom to remain standing until after בָּרְכוּ (p. 84).

דברי הימים א כט:י-יג

וַיְבָרֶךְ דָּוִיד* אֶת יהוה לְעֵינֵי כָּל הַקָּהָל, וַיֹּאמֶר דָּוִיד: בָּרוּךְ אַתָּה יהוה, אֱלֹהֵי יִשְׂרָאֵל אָבִינוּ,* מֵעוֹלָם וְעַד עוֹלָם.

כִּי רוֹצֶה ה' בְּעַמּוֹ — *For HASHEM favors His nation.* God looks forward to Israel's praises *(Radak).*

עַל מִשְׁכְּבוֹתָם — *Upon their beds.* The righteous will thank God for allowing them to go to bed without fear of danger and attack *(Etz Yosef).*

רוֹמְמוֹת אֵל בִּגְרוֹנָם — *The lofty praises of God are in their throats.* Though Israel goes into battle holding its *double-edged sword,* it knows that its victory depends on the help of God to Whom it sings praises *(Rashi; Radak).* The expression *in their throats* symbolizes that the prayers are not merely mouthed, but are deeply felt internally *(Radak).*

תּוֹכֵחוֹת — *Rebukes.* Though Israel is forced to wage battle against its enemies, its primary goal is that they accept moral rebuke and mend their ways.

לַעֲשׂוֹת בָּהֶם מִשְׁפָּט כָּתוּב — *To execute upon them written judgment.* The future judgment upon the nations has been written in the Prophets. The execution of that judgment will bring the reign of justice to earth, and that will be the *splendor* — the pride and vindication — of the righteous who have always lived that way.

❧ **הַלְלוּיָהּ הַלְלוּ אֵל** — *Halleluyah! Praise God.* In this, the final psalm in the *Book of Psalms,* the Psalmist sums up his task by saying that man must enrich his spiritual self by recognizing God's greatness and kindness and by praising Him. The Psalmist's long list of musical instruments reflects the full spectrum of human emotions and spiritual potential, all of which can be aroused by music.

[A series of musical instruments is mentioned here. In many cases, we do not know the exact translations; those given here are based on the interpretations of various major commentators. A full exposition can be found in the ArtScroll *Tehillim/Psalms.*]

כֹּל הַנְּשָׁמָה תְּהַלֵּל — *Let all souls praise.* Far greater

them praise His Name with dancing, with drums and harp let them make music to Him. For HASHEM favors His nation, He adorns the humble with salvation. Let the devout exult in glory, let them sing joyously upon their beds.* The lofty praises of God are in their throats,* and a double-edged sword is in their hand — to execute vengeance among the nations, rebukes* among the governments.* Chazzan— *To bind their kings with chains, and their nobles with fetters of iron. To execute upon them written judgment* — that will be the splendor of all His devout ones. Halleluyah!*

Psalm 150

הַלְלוּיָהּ *Halleluyah! Praise God* in His Sanctuary; praise Him in the firmament of His power. Praise Him for His mighty acts; praise Him as befits His abundant greatness. Praise Him with the blast of the shofar; praise Him with lyre and harp. Praise Him with drum and dance; praise Him with organ and flute. Praise Him with clanging cymbals; praise Him with resonant trumpets.* Chazzan— *Let all souls praise* God, Halleluyah!* Let all souls praise God, Halleluyah!*

בָּרוּךְ *Blessed is HASHEM forever,* Amen and Amen.*[1] Blessed is HASHEM from Zion, Who dwells in Jerusalem, Halleluyah.[2] Blessed is HASHEM, God, the God of Israel, Who alone does wonders.* Chazzan— *Blessed is His glorious Name forever, and may all the earth be filled with His glory, Amen and Amen.[3]*

One must stand from *'And David Blessed ...,'* until after the phrase *'It is You, HASHEM the God,'* however, there is a generally accepted custom to remain standing until after בָּרְכוּ, *Borchu* (p. 84).

I Chronicles 29:10-13

וַיְבָרֶךְ *And David blessed* HASHEM in the presence of the entire congregation; David said, 'Blessed are You, HASHEM, the God of Israel our forefather* from This World to the World to Come.*

(1) *Psalms* 89:53. (2) 135:21. (3) 72:18-19.

than the most sublime instrumental songs of praise is the song of the human soul. God's greatest praise is the soul that utilizes its full potential in His service *(Radak).*

Having now concluded the six psalms that are the main part of *Pesukei D'zimrah,* we repeat the last verse to signify that this section has come to an end *(Avudraham).*

הַלְלוּיָהּ — *Halleluyah.* The root הלל, *praise,* appears thirteen times in this psalm, an allusion to God's Thirteen Attributes of Mercy. [In counting the thirteen times, the repetition of the last verse is not included, since it appears only one time in *Psalms.*] *(Radak)*

בָּרוּךְ ה׳ לְעוֹלָם ◆ — *Blessed is HASHEM forever.* This collection of verses, each of which begins with the word בָּרוּךְ, is in the nature of a blessing after the six psalms that, as noted above, are the very essence of *Pesukei D'zimrah (Etz Yosef). The term* בָּרוּךְ, which refers to God as the Source of all blessing, is particularly relevant to the just concluded psalms, since they describe God's kindness, power, and future redemption *(R' Munk).*

אָמֵן וְאָמֵן — *Amen and Amen.* The repetition is meant to re-emphasize the statement. A listener's *Amen* can have three connotations *(Shavuos* 29b): (a) to accept a vow upon oneself, (b) to acknowledge the truth of a statement, and (c) to express the hope that a statement come true. In our prayers, any or all are expressed by *Amen,* depending on the context *(Iyun Tefillah).*

וַיְבָרֶךְ דָּוִיד ◆ — *And David blessed.* The following selections from the praises of David, Nehemiah, and Moses, in that order, were appended to *Pesukei D'zimrah* because the fifteen terms of praise used in *Yishtabach* are based on these selections *(Avudraham).*

The first four verses of this prayer were uttered by David at one of the supreme moments of his life: although he had been denied Divine permission to build the Holy Temple, he had

לְךָ יהוה הַגְּדֻלָּה* וְהַגְּבוּרָה וְהַתִּפְאֶרֶת וְהַנֵּצַח וְהַהוֹד, כִּי כֹל בַּשָּׁמַיִם וּבָאָרֶץ; לְךָ יהוה הַמַּמְלָכָה וְהַמִּתְנַשֵּׂא לְכֹל לְרֹאשׁ. וְהָעֹשֶׁר וְהַכָּבוֹד מִלְּפָנֶיךָ, וְאַתָּה מוֹשֵׁל בַּכֹּל, וּבְיָדְךָ כֹּחַ וּגְבוּרָה, וּבְיָדְךָ לְגַדֵּל וּלְחַזֵּק לַכֹּל. וְעַתָּה אֱלֹהֵינוּ מוֹדִים אֲנַחְנוּ לָךְ, וּמְהַלְּלִים לְשֵׁם תִּפְאַרְתֶּךָ.

It is customary to set aside something for charity at this point (see commentary).

נחמיה ט:ו-יא

אַתָּה הוּא יהוה* לְבַדֶּךָ, אַתָּה עָשִׂיתָ אֶת הַשָּׁמַיִם, שְׁמֵי הַשָּׁמַיִם* וְכָל צְבָאָם, הָאָרֶץ וְכָל אֲשֶׁר עָלֶיהָ, הַיַּמִּים וְכָל אֲשֶׁר בָּהֶם, וְאַתָּה מְחַיֶּה אֶת כֻּלָּם,* וּצְבָא הַשָּׁמַיִם לְךָ מִשְׁתַּחֲוִים.* ❖ אַתָּה הוּא יהוה הָאֱלֹהִים אֲשֶׁר בָּחַרְתָּ בְּאַבְרָם,* וְהוֹצֵאתוֹ מֵאוּר כַּשְׂדִּים, וְשַׂמְתָּ שְׁמוֹ אַבְרָהָם.* וּמָצָאתָ אֶת לְבָבוֹ נֶאֱמָן לְפָנֶיךָ —

— וְכָרוֹת* עִמּוֹ הַבְּרִית לָתֵת אֶת אֶרֶץ הַכְּנַעֲנִי הַחִתִּי הָאֱמֹרִי וְהַפְּרִזִּי וְהַיְבוּסִי וְהַגִּרְגָּשִׁי, לָתֵת* לְזַרְעוֹ, וַתָּקֶם אֶת דְּבָרֶיךָ, כִּי צַדִּיק אָתָּה.* וַתֵּרֶא אֶת עֳנִי אֲבֹתֵינוּ בְּמִצְרָיִם, וְאֶת זַעֲקָתָם שָׁמַעְתָּ עַל יַם סוּף. וַתִּתֵּן אֹתֹת וּמֹפְתִים* בְּפַרְעֹה וּבְכָל עֲבָדָיו וּבְכָל עַם אַרְצוֹ, כִּי יָדַעְתָּ כִּי הֵזִידוּ* עֲלֵיהֶם, וַתַּעַשׂ לְךָ שֵׁם כְּהַיּוֹם הַזֶּה.* ❖ וְהַיָּם בָּקַעְתָּ לִפְנֵיהֶם, וַיַּעַבְרוּ

---

assembled the necessary contributions and materials so that his heir, Solomon, could be ready to build upon assuming the throne. In the presence of the assembled congregation, he thanked and blessed God for having allowed him to set aside resources for the Divine service (*I Chronicles* 29:10-13). For this reason, many adopted the custom of setting aside something for charity at this point.

יִשְׂרָאֵל אָבִינוּ — *Israel our forefather.* David mentioned only Israel/Jacob, because he was the first to make a vow to contribute tithes for a holy cause as a source of merit in a time of distress (*Genesis* 28:20), an example followed by David (*Bereishis Rabbah* 70:1); and also because it was Jacob who first spoke of the Holy Temple (*Radak*) and designated Mount Moriah as its site [see ArtScroll *Bereishis* 28:16-19].

לְךָ ה׳ הַגְּדֻלָּה — *Yours, HASHEM, is the greatness.* In his moment of public glory, David scrupulously made clear that his every achievement was made possible by God and that it was meant to be utilized in His service. Lest anyone think that his attainments are to his *own* credit, David proclaims that God is Master of everything in heaven and earth and — because He has *sovereignty over every leader* — He decrees who shall gain high positions and who shall be toppled.

אַתָּה הוּא ה׳ — *It is You alone, HASHEM.* The next six verses were recited by the people, led by Ezra, Nechemiah, and the most distinguished Levites the day after Shemini Atzeres, when the newly returned Jews had completed their first festival season in Jerusalem after returning from their Babylonian exile. They gathered in devotion and repentance and echoed the resolve voiced by David nearly five hundred years earlier.

שְׁמֵי הַשָּׁמַיִם — *The most exalted heaven.* This refers either to the highest spiritual spheres or to the furthest reaches of space.

וְאַתָּה מְחַיֶּה אֶת כֻּלָּם — *And You give them all life.* Even inanimate objects have 'life' in the sense that they have whatever conditions are necessary for their continued existence (*Iyun Tefillah*).

לְךָ מִשְׁתַּחֲוִים — *Bow to You.* Despite their awesome size and power over other parts of the universe, the heavenly bodies *bow* in the sense that they exist totally to serve God (*Iyun Tefillah*).

אֲשֶׁר בָּחַרְתָּ בְּאַבְרָם — *Who selected Abram.* After cataloguing the endless array of creation and its

Yours, HASHEM, is the greatness, the strength, the splendor, the triumph, and the glory, even everything in heaven and earth; Yours, HASHEM, is the kingdom, and the sovereignty over every leader.* It is customary to set aside something for charity at this point (see commentary). *Wealth and honor come from You and You rule everything — in Your hand is power and strength and it is in Your hand to make anyone great or strong. So now, our God, we thank You and praise Your splendrous Name.'*

Nechemiah 9:6-11

It is You alone, HASHEM, You have made the heaven, the most exalted heaven* and all their legions, the earth and everything upon it, the seas and everything in them and You give them all life;* the heavenly legions bow to You.** Chazzan— *It is You, HASHEM the God, Who selected Abram,* brought him out of Ur Kasdim and made his name Abraham.* You found his heart faithful before You —*

— and You established the covenant with him to give the land of the Canaanite, Hittite, Emorite, Perizzite, Jebusite, and Girgashite, to give* it to his offspring; and You affirmed Your word, for You are righteous.* You observed the suffering of our forefathers in Egypt and their outcry You heard at the Sea of Reeds. You imposed signs and wonders* upon Pharaoh and upon all his servants, and upon all the people of his land. For You knew that they sinned flagrantly* against them, and You brought Yourself renown as clear as this very day.** Chazzan— *You split the Sea before them and they crossed*

---

components, we acknowledge that from them all, God chose Abraham and his offspring as His chosen ones — an astonishing testimony to the Patriarch and the nation he founded *(Siach Yitzchak).*

וְשַׂמְתָּ שְּׁמוֹ אַבְרָהָם — *And made his name Abraham.* The change of name signified that Abram's mission had been changed and elevated. His original name was a contracted version of אַב אֲרָם, *father of Aram,* because he had been a spiritual father of his native Aram. The additional ה implies that he had become אַב הֲמוֹן גּוֹיִם, *father of a multitude of nations,* marking him as the spiritual mentor of all mankind (see *Genesis* 17:4-5).

וְכָרוֹת — *And You established* ... We have followed the virtually universal practice that *siddurim* begin a paragraph with וְכָרוֹת, however in the Book of *Nechemiah,* this is not the beginning of a new verse, but a continuation of the above; namely, that in reward for Abraham's faithfulness, God made a covenant with him.

In many congregations, the section beginning with וְכָרוֹת is chanted aloud when a circumcision is to be performed in the synagogue, because the circumcision sealed the covenant of which Abraham's new name was part. There are varying customs regarding reciting this section at a circumcision. In most of these congregations it is said by the *mohel,* in some by the rabbi. In some, all the verses from וְכָרוֹת until (but not including) יִשְׁתַּבַּח are recited responsively, with the *mohel* reciting the first aloud, the congregation the next, and so on. However, no verses are actually *omitted* by anyone; those not said aloud are said quietly. In some congregations, the *mohel* recites aloud only the verses from וְכָרוֹת until בְּמַיִם עַזִּים.

לָתֵת ... לָתֵת — *To give ... to give.* In effect, the Land was given twice: once it was pledged to Abraham, and centuries later it was ceded to his offspring *(Iyun Tefillah).*

כִּי צַדִּיק אָתָּה — *For You are righteous.* God keeps His word even when Israel, on its own merits, would have been unworthy of the gift *(Iyun Tefillah).*

אֹתֹת וּמֹפְתִים — *Signs and wonders. Signs* are miracles that were foretold by a prophet; *wonders* take place without prior announcement *(Rambam).*

כִּי הֵזִידוּ — *That they sinned flagrantly* [lit. *willfully*]. The Egyptians sinned against the Jews by mistreating and enslaving them. Had the servitude not been so harsh and hatefully cruel, the Egyptians would not have suffered such devastation.

כְּהַיּוֹם הַזֶּה — *As [clear as] this very day.* The

בְּתוֹךְ הַיָּם בַּיַּבָּשָׁה, וְאֶת רֹדְפֵיהֶם הִשְׁלַכְתָּ בִמְצוֹלֹת, כְּמוֹ אֶבֶן בְּמַיִם עַזִּים.

שירת הים

שמות יד:ל־טו:יט

וַיּוֹשַׁע יהוה בַּיּוֹם הַהוּא אֶת־יִשְׂרָאֵל מִיַּד מִצְרָיִם, וַיַּרְא יִשְׂרָאֵל אֶת־מִצְרַיִם מֵת עַל־שְׂפַת הַיָּם: ❖ וַיַּרְא יִשְׂרָאֵל אֶת־הַיָּד הַגְּדֹלָה אֲשֶׁר עָשָׂה יהוה בְּמִצְרַיִם, וַיִּירְאוּ הָעָם אֶת־יהוה, וַיַּאֲמִינוּ בַּיהוה וּבְמֹשֶׁה עַבְדּוֹ:

אָז יָשִׁיר־מֹשֶׁה וּבְנֵי יִשְׂרָאֵל אֶת־הַשִּׁירָה הַזֹּאת לַיהוה, וַיֹּאמְרוּ
לֵאמֹר, אָשִׁירָה לַיהוה כִּי־גָאֹה גָּאָה, סוּס
וְרֹכְבוֹ רָמָה בַיָּם: עָזִּי וְזִמְרָת יָהּ* וַיְהִי־לִי
לִישׁוּעָה, זֶה אֵלִי* וְאַנְוֵהוּ,* אֱלֹהֵי
אָבִי וַאֲרֹמְמֶנְהוּ: יהוה אִישׁ מִלְחָמָה, יהוה
שְׁמוֹ:* מַרְכְּבֹת פַּרְעֹה וְחֵילוֹ יָרָה בַיָּם, וּמִבְחַר
שָׁלִשָׁיו טֻבְּעוּ בְיַם־סוּף: תְּהֹמֹת יְכַסְיֻמוּ, יָרְדוּ בִמְצוֹלֹת כְּמוֹ־
אָבֶן: יְמִינְךָ* יהוה נֶאְדָּרִי בַּכֹּחַ, יְמִינְךָ
יהוה תִּרְעַץ אוֹיֵב: וּבְרֹב גְּאוֹנְךָ תַּהֲרֹס
קָמֶיךָ, תְּשַׁלַּח חֲרֹנְךָ יֹאכְלֵמוֹ כַּקַּשׁ: וּבְרוּחַ
אַפֶּיךָ נֶעֶרְמוּ מַיִם, נִצְּבוּ כְמוֹ־נֵד
נֹזְלִים, קָפְאוּ תְהֹמֹת בְּלֶב־יָם: אָמַר

---

miracles of the Exodus were public and indisputable *(Etz Yosef).*

שִׁירַת הַיָּם / The Song at the Sea

The early commentators note that the miracles of the Exodus, beginning with the Ten Plagues, illustrated that God controls every facet of nature at will. Thus, they remained the testimony to God as the all-powerful Creator: no human being saw the creation of the universe, but millions of Jews witnessed the Exodus. The climax of those miraculous events was the splitting of the sea; as the *Passover Haggadah* relates, the miracles at the sea were five times as great as those that took place in Egypt itself. That event was celebrated by Moses and the entire nation in the glorious Song of the Sea, a combination of praise and faith that fits in with the theme of *Pesukei D'zimrah.*

We have included the cantillation symbols [*trop*] for the convenience of those who recite the Song in the manner it is read from the Torah. Nevertheless, we have inserted commas for those unfamiliar with this notation. The basis for reciting the Song with this cantillation is found in Kabbalistic literature which attaches great importance to the joyful, musical recitation of the Song, as if one were standing at the seashore witnessing the miracle. The *Zohar* states that one who recites the Song with the proper intent will merit to sing the praises of future miracles.

וַיּוֹשַׁע ה׳ — *HASHEM saved.* The Torah sums up the miracle at the sea as a prelude to Moses' song.

וַיִּירְאוּ ... וַיַּאֲמִינוּ — *(They) feared ... and they had faith.* The fact that God has the power to perform miracles is unimportant; the Creator of the universe has no difficulty in stopping the flow of a sea. What *did* matter was the effect the miracle had on Israel. The people felt a new and higher degree of *fear,* in the sense of awe and reverence. And their *faith* increased immeasurably, for they had seen that, through His prophet, God promised salvation from danger and had indeed saved them.

אָז יָשִׁיר — *Then ... chose to sing.* Rather than שָׁר, *sang,* the Torah uses the verb יָשִׁיר, literally

in the midst of the Sea on dry land; but their pursuers You hurled into the depths, like a stone into turbulent waters.

THE SONG AT THE SEA

Exodus 14:30-15:19

ויושע *HASHEM saved* — on that day — Israel from the hand of Egypt, and Israel saw the Egyptians dead on the seashore.* Chazzan— *Israel saw the great hand that HASHEM inflicted upon Egypt and the people feared HASHEM, and they had faith* in HASHEM and in Moses, His servant.*

Then Moses and the Children of Israel chose to sing this song to HASHEM, and they said the following:*

I shall sing to HASHEM for He is exalted above the arrogant, having hurled horse with its rider into the sea.

God is my might and my praise, and He was a salvation for me. This is my God,* and I will build Him a Sanctuary;* the God of my father, and I will exalt Him.*

*HASHEM is Master of war, through His Name HASHEM.**

Pharaoh's chariots and army He threw into the sea; and the pick of his officers were mired in the Sea of Reeds.

Deep waters covered them; they descended in the depths like stone.

Your right hand, HASHEM, is adorned with strength; Your right hand, HASHEM, smashes the enemy.*

In Your abundant grandeur You shatter Your opponents; You dispatch Your wrath, it consumes them like straw.

At a blast from Your nostrils the waters were heaped up; straight as a wall stood the running water, the deep waters congealed in the heart of the sea.

---

will sing. In the simple sense, the verse means that upon seeing the miracle the people decided that they *would* sing. Midrashically, the verb implies the principle that God will bring the dead back to life in Messianic times — and then they *will* sing God's praises once again *(Rashi).*

עָזִּי וְזִמְרָת יָהּ — *God is my might and my praise.* The translation follows *Targum Onkelos.* According to *Rashi* the phrase is translated: *God's might and His cutting away [of the enemy] was a salvation for me.*

זֶה אֵלִי — *This is my God.* So obvious was God's Presence, that the Jews could point to it, as it were, and say 'This is my God.' As the Sages put it: 'A maidservant at the sea saw more than the prophet Yechezkel [saw in his heavenly prophecy]' *(Rashi).*

וְאַנְוֵהוּ — *And I will build Him a Sanctuary.* The root of the word is נָוֶה, *abode.* An alternative interpretation based on the same root: I will make myself into a Godly sanctuary *(Rashi)* — to remake oneself in God's image is to build the greatest of all sanctuaries.

Another translation is *I will beautify* or *glorify Him* [based on the root נאה, *fitting, beautiful*]. The Sages teach that this should be done by performing the commandments in a beautiful manner, by having beautiful *tefillin,* a beautiful *succah,* a beautiful *esrog* and so on *(Shabbos* 133b).

ה׳ שְׁמוֹ — *Through His Name HASHEM.* Mortal kings require legions and armaments, but God overcomes His enemies with nothing more than His Name. Moreover, this Name of mercy applies to Him even when He is forced to vanquish the wicked *(Rashi).*

יְמִינְךָ — *Your right hand.* Of course God has no 'hand' or any other physical characteristic. All the many Scriptural references to physicality are allegorical. The *right hand* symbolizes power. Similarly, below God's *wrath* is described as a blast from His nostrils, because angry people tend to snort.

אוֹיֵב,* אֶרְדֹּף אַשִּׂיג אֲחַלֵּק שָׁלָל, תִּמְלָאֵמוֹ
נַפְשִׁי, אָרִיק חַרְבִּי, תּוֹרִישֵׁמוֹ יָדִי: נָשַׁפְתָּ
בְרוּחֲךָ כִּסָּמוֹ יָם, צָלֲלוּ כַּעוֹפֶרֶת בְּמַיִם,
אַדִּירִים: מִי־כָמֹכָה בָּאֵלִם יהוה, מִי
כָּמֹכָה נֶאְדָּר בַּקֹּדֶשׁ, נוֹרָא תְהִלֹּת עֹשֵׂה
פֶלֶא: נָטִיתָ יְמִינְךָ, תִּבְלָעֵמוֹ אָרֶץ: נָחִיתָ
בְחַסְדְּךָ עַם־זוּ גָּאָלְתָּ, נֵהַלְתָּ בְעָזְּךָ אֶל־נְוֵה
קָדְשֶׁךָ:* שָׁמְעוּ עַמִּים יִרְגָּזוּן, חִיל
אָחַז יֹשְׁבֵי פְּלָשֶׁת: אָז נִבְהֲלוּ אַלּוּפֵי
אֱדוֹם,* אֵילֵי מוֹאָב יֹאחֲזֵמוֹ רָעַד, נָמֹגוּ
כֹּל יֹשְׁבֵי כְנָעַן: תִּפֹּל עֲלֵיהֶם אֵימָתָה
וָפַחַד, בִּגְדֹל זְרוֹעֲךָ יִדְּמוּ כָּאָבֶן, עַד־
יַעֲבֹר עַמְּךָ יהוה,* עַד־יַעֲבֹר עַם־זוּ
קָנִיתָ: תְּבִאֵמוֹ* וְתִטָּעֵמוֹ בְּהַר נַחֲלָתְךָ, מָכוֹן
לְשִׁבְתְּךָ פָּעַלְתָּ יהוה, מִקְּדָשׁ אֲדֹנָי כּוֹנְנוּ
יָדֶיךָ: יהוה | יִמְלֹךְ* לְעֹלָם וָעֶד:

יהוה יִמְלֹךְ לְעֹלָם וָעֶד. (יהוה מַלְכוּתֵהּ קָאֵם, לְעָלַם וּלְעָלְמֵי עָלְמַיָּא.) כִּי בָא סוּס פַּרְעֹה בְּרִכְבּוֹ וּבְפָרָשָׁיו בַּיָּם, וַיָּשֶׁב יהוה עֲלֵהֶם אֶת מֵי הַיָּם, וּבְנֵי יִשְׂרָאֵל הָלְכוּ בַיַּבָּשָׁה בְּתוֹךְ הַיָּם. ❖ כִּי לַיהוה הַמְּלוּכָה,* וּמֹשֵׁל בַּגּוֹיִם.[1] וְעָלוּ מוֹשִׁעִים* בְּהַר צִיּוֹן, לִשְׁפֹּט אֶת הַר עֵשָׂו, וְהָיְתָה לַיהוה הַמְּלוּכָה.[2] וְהָיָה יהוה לְמֶלֶךְ* עַל כָּל הָאָרֶץ, בַּיּוֹם הַהוּא יִהְיֶה יהוה אֶחָד וּשְׁמוֹ אֶחָד.*[3] (וּבְתוֹרָתְךָ כָּתוּב לֵאמֹר: שְׁמַע יִשְׂרָאֵל יהוה אֱלֹהֵינוּ יהוה אֶחָד.[4])

אָמַר אוֹיֵב — *The enemy declared.* In order to coax his people to join him in pursuit of the Jews, Pharaoh *(the enemy)* spoke confidently of his ability to overtake and plunder them.

אֶל נְוֵה קָדְשֶׁךָ — *To Your holy abode,* i.e., the Holy Temple. Although the Temple would not be built for over four hundred years, it is typical for prophetic song to combine the past with the future, because in the Divine perception they are interrelated.

פְּלָשֶׁת ... אֱדוֹם ... — *Philistia ... Edom ...* Not all the nations were of equal status. Philistia and Canaan rightly feared conquest because their lands comprised *Eretz Yisrael.* Edom and Moab, on the other hand, would not be attacked by Israel. They did not fear losing their land, but they feared retribution because they did not and would not show compassion for Jewish suffering *(Rashi).*

עַד יַעֲבֹר עַמְּךָ — *Until Your people passes through.* This phrase continues the previous thought; the terror of the nations would continue until Israel crossed into *Eretz Yisrael.* The term *passes through* is used twice: once in reference to the crossing of the Jordan and once in reference to the waters of the Arnon, on the border of Israel and Moab [see *Numbers* 21:13-20] *(Rashi).*

תְּבִאֵמוֹ — *You shall bring them.* Moses unconsciously prophesied that he would not enter into the Land, for he said, 'You shall bring *them,*' and not 'You shall bring *us*' *(Rashi).*

ה׳ יִמְלֹךְ — *HASHEM shall reign.* This verse is

The enemy declared: 'I will pursue, I will overtake, I will divide plunder; I will satisfy my lust with them; I will unsheathe my sword, my hand will impoverish them.'*

You blew with Your wind — the sea enshrouded them; the mighty ones sank like lead in the waters.

Who is like You among the heavenly powers, HASHEM! Who is like You, mighty in holiness, too awesome for praise, doing wonders!

You stretched out Your right hand — the earth swallowed them.

*You guided in Your kindness this people that You redeemed; You led with Your might to Your holy abode.**

Peoples heard — they were agitated; convulsive terror gripped the dwellers of Philistia.

Then the chieftains of Edom were confounded, trembling gripped the powers of Moab, all the dwellers of Canaan dissolved.*

May fear and terror befall them, at the greatness of Your arm may they be still as stone; until Your people passes through, HASHEM, until this people You have acquired passes through.*

You shall bring them and implant them on the mount of Your heritage, the foundation of Your dwelling-place, which You, HASHEM, have made: the Sanctuary, my Lord, that Your hands established.*

HASHEM shall reign for all eternity.*

HASHEM shall reign for all eternity. (HASHEM — His kingdom is established forever and ever.) When Pharaoh's cavalry came — with his chariots and horsemen — into the sea and HASHEM turned back the waters of the sea upon them, the Children of Israel walked on the dry bed amid the sea. Chazzan— *For the sovereignty is HASHEM's* and He rules over nations.*[1] *The saviors* will ascend Mount Zion to judge Esau's mountain, and the kingdom will be HASHEM's.*[2] *Then HASHEM will be King* over all the world, on that day HASHEM will be One and His Name will be One.**[3] *(And in Your Torah it is written: Hear O Israel: HASHEM is our God, HASHEM, the One and Only.*[4]*)*

(1) *Psalms* 22:29. (2) *Ovadiah* 1:21. (3) *Zechariah* 14:9. (4) *Deuteronomy* 6:4.

repeated to signify that it is the climax of the Song — that God's sovereignty shall be recognized forever. Because of the importance of this idea, most congregations follow the *Arizal*, who taught that the Aramaic Targum of this verse also be recited.

כִּי לַה׳ הַמְּלוּכָה — *For the sovereignty is HASHEM's.* The collected verses attached to the Song are appropriate to the climactic verse that God will reign forever.

מוֹשִׁעִים — *The saviors.* Those who will in the future lead Israel out of exile will come to Mount Zion from which they will complete the conquest of the archenemy, Esau, whose descendants were responsible for the current exile *(Rashi).*

וּמשֵׁל ... לְמֶלֶךְ — *He rules ... be King.* The term מוֹשֵׁל, *ruler,* refers to one who forces his subjects to obey him, while מֶלֶךְ, *king,* is one who is willingly accepted. Now God is *King* over Israel alone because only Israel acknowledges His sovereignty with love, but He *rules* the nations despite their unwillingness to accept Him as their God. In the future, however, all nations will proclaim Him as their King *(Vilna Gaon).*

ה׳ אֶחָד וּשְׁמוֹ אֶחָד — *HASHEM will be One and His Name will be One.* But does He not have One Name today? Rabbi Nachman bar Yitzchak taught: The world of the future will be unlike the world of today. In the world of today God's Name is spelled one way and pronounced differently, whereas in the world of the future all will be One — the spelling and pronunciation will both be י־ה־ו־ה *(Pesachim* 50a). This means that since we fail to perceive God's nature as it is expressed in the true pronunciation of His Name,

ישתבח

Stand while reciting יִשְׁתַּבַּח. The fifteen expressions of praise — שִׁיר ... וְהוֹדָאוֹת — should be recited without undue pause, preferably in one breath.

יִשְׁתַּבַּח שִׁמְךָ לָעַד מַלְכֵּנוּ, הָאֵל הַמֶּלֶךְ הַגָּדוֹל וְהַקָּדוֹשׁ, בַּשָּׁמַיִם וּבָאָרֶץ. כִּי לְךָ נָאֶה יהוה אֱלֹהֵינוּ וֵאלֹהֵי אֲבוֹתֵינוּ, שִׁיר וּשְׁבָחָה, הַלֵּל וְזִמְרָה, עֹז וּמֶמְשָׁלָה, נֶצַח* גְּדֻלָּה וּגְבוּרָה, תְּהִלָּה וְתִפְאֶרֶת, קְדֻשָּׁה וּמַלְכוּת, בְּרָכוֹת וְהוֹדָאוֹת מֵעַתָּה וְעַד עוֹלָם. ❖ בָּרוּךְ אַתָּה יהוה, אֵל מֶלֶךְ גָּדוֹל בַּתִּשְׁבָּחוֹת,* אֵל הַהוֹדָאוֹת, אֲדוֹן הַנִּפְלָאוֹת, הַבּוֹחֵר בְּשִׁירֵי זִמְרָה,* מֶלֶךְ אֵל חֵי הָעוֹלָמִים.* (Cong.— אָמֵן.)

From Rosh Hashanah to Yom Kippur and on Hoshana Rabbah many congregations recite שִׁיר הַמַּעֲלוֹת. The ark is opened and each verse is recited by the *chazzan*, then by the congregation.

שִׁיר הַמַּעֲלוֹת, מִמַּעֲמַקִּים קְרָאתִיךָ יהוה. אֲדֹנָי שִׁמְעָה בְקוֹלִי, תִּהְיֶינָה אָזְנֶיךָ קַשֻּׁבוֹת, לְקוֹל תַּחֲנוּנָי. אִם עֲוֹנוֹת תִּשְׁמָר יָהּ, אֲדֹנָי מִי יַעֲמֹד. כִּי עִמְּךָ הַסְּלִיחָה, לְמַעַן תִּוָּרֵא. קִוִּיתִי יהוה קִוְּתָה נַפְשִׁי, וְלִדְבָרוֹ הוֹחָלְתִּי. נַפְשִׁי לַאדֹנָי, מִשֹּׁמְרִים לַבֹּקֶר, שֹׁמְרִים לַבֹּקֶר. יַחֵל יִשְׂרָאֵל אֶל יהוה, כִּי עִם יהוה הַחֶסֶד, וְהַרְבֵּה עִמּוֹ פְדוּת. וְהוּא יִפְדֶּה אֶת יִשְׂרָאֵל, מִכֹּל עֲוֹנוֹתָיו.

If a *minyan* is present, the *chazzan* recites חֲצִי קַדִּישׁ and בָּרְכוּ.

יִתְגַּדַּל וְיִתְקַדַּשׁ שְׁמֵהּ רַבָּא. (Cong.— אָמֵן.) בְּעָלְמָא דִּי בְרָא כִרְעוּתֵהּ. וְיַמְלִיךְ מַלְכוּתֵהּ, בְּחַיֵּיכוֹן וּבְיוֹמֵיכוֹן וּבְחַיֵּי דְכָל בֵּית יִשְׂרָאֵל, בַּעֲגָלָא וּבִזְמַן קָרִיב. וְאִמְרוּ: אָמֵן.

(Cong.— אָמֵן. יְהֵא שְׁמֵהּ רַבָּא מְבָרַךְ לְעָלַם וּלְעָלְמֵי עָלְמַיָּא.)

יְהֵא שְׁמֵהּ רַבָּא מְבָרַךְ לְעָלַם וּלְעָלְמֵי עָלְמַיָּא.

יִתְבָּרַךְ וְיִשְׁתַּבַּח וְיִתְפָּאַר וְיִתְרוֹמַם וְיִתְנַשֵּׂא וְיִתְהַדָּר וְיִתְעַלֶּה וְיִתְהַלָּל שְׁמֵהּ דְּקֻדְשָׁא בְּרִיךְ הוּא (Cong.— בְּרִיךְ הוּא) — °לְעֵלָּא מִן כָּל (From Rosh Hashanah to Yom Kippur substitute— °לְעֵלָּא וּלְעֵלָּא מִכָּל) בִּרְכָתָא וְשִׁירָתָא תֻּשְׁבְּחָתָא וְנֶחֱמָתָא, דַּאֲמִירָן בְּעָלְמָא. וְאִמְרוּ: אָמֵן. (Cong.— אָמֵן.)

---

we may not utter it. But in time to come, there will be no contradiction between perception and reality.

ישתבח / Yishtabach

As noted in the commentary to בָּרוּךְ שֶׁאָמַר, (p. 58), the יִשְׁתַּבַּח prayer ends the *Pesukei D'zimrah* section of *Shacharis*. The theme of fifteen is repeated twice in this prayer: there are fifteen expressions of praise in the first half of the paragraph, and after בָּרוּךְ אַתָּה ה׳, there are fifteen words. This number alludes to the fifteen שִׁיר הַמַּעֲלוֹת, *Songs of Ascents* [*Psalms* 120-134], composed by David. Also, fifteen is the numerical value of the Divine Name יָהּ, the letters of which were used by God to create heaven and earth, therefore, it alludes to the idea that everything is God's and He is its Creator.

עֹז וּמֶמְשָׁלָה נֶצַח ... — *Power and dominion, triumph* ... Although these qualities are attributed to God, we find them in people as

YISHTABACH

Stand while reciting *'May Your Name be praised ...'* The fifteen expressions of praise — *'song and praise ... blessing and thanksgivings'* — should be recited without undue pause.

יִשְׁתַּבַּח *May your Name be praised forever — our King, the God, the great and holy King — in heaven and on earth. Because for You is fitting — O HASHEM, our God, and the God of our forefathers — song and praise, lauding and hymns, power and dominion, triumph,* greatness and strength, praise and splendor, holiness and sovereignty, blessings and thanksgivings from this time and forever.* Chazzan— *Blessed are You, HASHEM, God, King exalted through praises,* God of thanksgivings, Master of wonders, Who chooses musical songs* of praise — King, God, Life-giver of the world.** (Cong.—*Amen.*)

From Rosh Hashanah until Yom Kippur and on Hoshana Rabbah many congregations recite *Psalm* 130. The Ark is opened and each verse is recited by the *chazzan*, then by the congregation.

שִׁיר הַמַּעֲלוֹת *A song of ascents: From the depths I called You, HASHEM. My Lord, hear my voice, may Your ears be attentive to the sound of my pleas. If You preserve iniquities, O God, my Lord, who could survive? For with You is forgiveness, that You may be feared. I put confidence in HASHEM, my soul put confidence, and I hoped for His word. I yearn for my Lord, among those longing for the dawn, those longing for the dawn. Let Israel hope for HASHEM, for with HASHEM is kindness, and with Him is abundant redemption. And He shall redeem Israel from all its iniquities.*

If a *minyan* is present, the *chazzan* recites Half-*Kaddish* and *Borchu*.

יִתְגַּדַּל *May His great Name grow exalted and sanctified* (Cong.—*Amen.*) *in the world that He created as He willed. May He give reign to His kingship in your lifetimes and in your days, and in the lifetimes of the entire Family of Israel, swiftly and soon. Now respond: Amen.*

(Cong.—*Amen. May His great Name be blessed forever and ever.*)

May His great Name be blessed forever and ever.

Blessed, praised, glorified, exalted, extolled, mighty, upraised, and lauded be the Name of the Holy One, Blessed is He (Cong.— *Blessed is He*) — (From Rosh Hashanah to Yom Kippur add: *exceedingly*) *beyond any blessing and song, praise and consolation that are uttered in the world. Now respond: Amen.* (Cong.—*Amen.*)

---

well. When man uses them to further God's goals, they are praiseworthy. But if people seek power and pursue triumph for their own selfish ends, they bring destruction upon the world *(R' Gedaliah Schorr).*

גָּדוֹל בַּתִּשְׁבָּחוֹת — *Exalted through praises.* The implication is not that God requires our praises in order to become exalted; for His infinite greatness is beyond our capacity to comprehend, much less express. Rather, it is His will that we have the privilege of exalting Him, despite our inability to do so adequately. This is the implication of *Who chooses musical songs,* i.e., we praise Him because He wishes us to.

הַבּוֹחֵר בְּשִׁירֵי זִמְרָה — *Who chooses musical songs.* *Rabbi Bunam of P'shis'cha* interpreted homiletically that the word שִׁירֵי can be translated *remnants* (from שִׁירַיִים, *leftovers).* God wishes to see how much of the lofty sentiments of our prayers remain with us after we close our *siddur*. Thus, He *chooses what is left over* after the Songs of Praise have been uttered.

חֵי הָעוֹלָמִים — *Life-giver of the world.* This essential principle of Jewish belief reiterates that creation is an ongoing process — God created and continues to create. Because He gives life constantly, our thanks and praise are likewise constant *(R' Munk).*

⊲§ שִׁיר הַמַּעֲלוֹת — *A song of ascents.* Although most congregations recite שִׁיר הַמַּעֲלוֹת at this

ברכו

In some congregations the *chazzan* chants a melody during his recitation of בָּרְכוּ so that the congregation can then recite יִתְבָּרַךְ.

Chazzan bows at בָּרְכוּ and straightens up at 'ה.

בָּרְכוּ אֶת יהוה* הַמְּבֹרָךְ.

Congregation, followed by *chazzan*, responds, bowing at בָּרוּךְ and straightening up at 'ה.

בָּרוּךְ יהוה הַמְּבֹרָךְ* לְעוֹלָם וָעֶד.

יִתְבָּרַךְ* וְיִשְׁתַּבַּח וְיִתְפָּאַר וְיִתְרוֹמַם וְיִתְנַשֵּׂא שְׁמוֹ שֶׁל מֶלֶךְ מַלְכֵי הַמְּלָכִים, הַקָּדוֹשׁ בָּרוּךְ הוּא. שֶׁהוּא רִאשׁוֹן וְהוּא אַחֲרוֹן, וּמִבַּלְעָדָיו אֵין אֱלֹהִים.[1] סֹלּוּ, לָרֹכֵב בָּעֲרָבוֹת, בְּיָהּ שְׁמוֹ, וְעִלְזוּ לְפָנָיו.[2] וּשְׁמוֹ מְרוֹמָם עַל כָּל בְּרָכָה וּתְהִלָּה.[3] בָּרוּךְ שֵׁם כְּבוֹד מַלְכוּתוֹ לְעוֹלָם וָעֶד. יְהִי שֵׁם יהוה מְבֹרָךְ, מֵעַתָּה וְעַד עוֹלָם.[4]

ברכות קריאת שמע

It is preferable that one sit while reciting the following series of prayers — particularly the *Kedushah* verses, קָדוֹשׁ קָדוֹשׁ קָדוֹשׁ and בָּרוּךְ כְּבוֹד — until *Shemoneh Esrei.*

Touch arm-*tefillin* at יוֹצֵר אוֹר, and head-tefillin at וּבוֹרֵא חֹשֶׁךְ.

בָּרוּךְ אַתָּה יהוה אֱלֹהֵינוּ מֶלֶךְ הָעוֹלָם, יוֹצֵר אוֹר וּבוֹרֵא חֹשֶׁךְ,* עֹשֶׂה שָׁלוֹם וּבוֹרֵא אֶת הַכֹּל.[5]

הַמֵּאִיר לָאָרֶץ וְלַדָּרִים* עָלֶיהָ בְּרַחֲמִים, וּבְטוּבוֹ מְחַדֵּשׁ בְּכָל יוֹם תָּמִיד מַעֲשֵׂה בְרֵאשִׁית. מָה רַבּוּ מַעֲשֶׂיךָ*

---

point only in the Rosh Hashanah and Yom Kippur services, many others recite it here throughout the Ten Days of Repentance. The contents of the psalm are clearly suited to this period, since it speaks of supplications for forgiveness and of reliance on God as the only Source of kindness and redemption. It is one of the fifteen Songs of Ascents that symbolize the fifteen steps leading up to the Sanctuary and also the rungs of man's spiritual ladder of fulfillment. This fifteen-psalm unit with a commentary may be found on page 532.

בָּרְכוּ / BORCHU

בָּרְכוּ אֶת ה' — *Bless HASHEM.* בָּרְכוּ is recited only in the presence of a *minyan,* a quorum of ten adult males. The *chazzan* calls upon the congregation to proclaim their blessing of God. This call is in the nature of a summons to the assembled people to join in the forthcoming prayers known as בִּרְכוֹת קְרִיאַת שְׁמַע, *Blessings of the Shema.* As the *Zohar* puts it: All sacred acts require summoning.

With relation to God, the term *bless* cannot mean that we add anything to His powers or possessions. Rather it constitutes our declaration that He is the *source* of all blessing *(Kad HaKemach).* Furthermore, it represents our dedication to allow His will to be fulfilled by our obedience to His commandments. Thus, in a sense we *do* confer something upon Him, for it is in our power to accomplish His goals for man *(R' Hirsch).* [See Overview for a discussion of these concepts.]

בָּרוּךְ ה' הַמְּבֹרָךְ ... — *Blessed is HASHEM, the blessed One.* With or without our *human* acknowledgment, God is constantly 'blessed' by all aspects of Creation — from the spiritual beings above to the humblest pebble — through the fact that they function in accordance with His will *(Kad HaKemach; Kol Bo).*

Having called upon the congregation to bless God, the *chazzan* must not let it appear as though he excludes himself from the obligation to bless Him. Therefore, when the congregation has concluded its response, he repeats it after them, lest he seem not to concur with their sentiment *(Tur).*

יִתְבָּרַךְ — *Blessed.* This short prayer is discussed in *Orach Chaim* 57:1.

בִּרְכוֹת קְרִיאַת שְׁמַע/BLESSINGS OF THE SHEMA

The third section of *Shacharis* is about to begin. Its central feature is the *Shema,* whose recitation is required by the Torah and which is the basic acknowledgment of God's sovereignty and Oneness. The *Shema* is accompanied by three blessings (two before it and one after it), which express God's mastery over nature, pray for intellectual and moral attainment through the study of Torah, and describe God's role in the flow of history *(R' Munk).*

BORCHU

In some congregations the *chazzan* chants a melody during his recitation of *Borchu,* so that the congregation can then recite *'Blessed, praised ...'*

Chazzan bows at *'Bless,'* and straightens up at *'HASHEM.'*

Bless HASHEM,* the blessed One.

Congregation, followed by *chazzan,* responds, bowing at *'Blessed'* and straightening up at *'HASHEM.'*

Blessed is HASHEM, the blessed One,* for all eternity.

Blessed, praised, glorified, exalted and upraised is the Name of the King Who rules over kings — the Holy One, Blessed is He. For He is the First and He is the Last and aside from Him there is no god.*[1] *Extol Him — Who rides the highest heavens — with His Name, YAH, and exult before Him.*[2] *His Name is exalted beyond every blessing and praise.*[3] *Blessed is the Name of His glorious kingdom for all eternity. Blessed be the Name of HASHEM from this time and forever.*[4]

BLESSINGS OF THE SHEMA

It is preferable that one sit while reciting the following series of prayers — particularly the *Kedushah* verses, *'Holy, holy, holy ...'* and *'Blessed is the glory ...'* — until *Shemoneh Esrei.*

Touch arm-*tefillin* at *'Who forms light,'* and head-*tefillin* at *'and creates darkness.'*

בָּרוּךְ *Blessed are You, HASHEM, our God, King of the Universe, Who forms light and creates darkness,* makes peace and creates all.*[5]

הַמֵּאִיר *He Who illuminates the earth and those who dwell* upon it, with compassion; and in His goodness renews daily, perpetually, the work of creation. How great are Your works,**

(1) Cf. *Isaiah* 44:6. (2) *Psalms* 68:5. (3) Cf. *Nechemiah* 9:5. (4) *Psalms* 113:2. (5) Cf. *Isaiah* 45:7.

יוֹצֵר אוֹר וּבוֹרֵא חֹשֶׁךְ — *Who forms light and creates darkness.* Since the beginning of time, the term 'light' has symbolized new life, wisdom, happiness — all the things associated with goodness. 'Darkness,' however, is associated with suffering, failure and death. The philosophers of idolatry claimed that the 'good' god who creates light cannot be the 'bad' one who creates darkness. Therefore, they reasoned, there must be at least two gods. In modern times, the same argument is presented in different terms: how can there be a God if He allows bad things to happen? This blessing refutes the argument that anything people find unpleasant either is not an act of God or proves that He lacks power. To the contrary, we believe unequivocally that God is One; what appears to our limited human intelligence to be contradictory or evil is really part of the plan of the One Merciful God, despite our failure to understand it.

The 'light' of this blessing refers not merely to the newly dawned day, but to the physical forces of creation itself. Light is the energy-giving, life-giving force of the universe, and, in the words of the Psalmist (19:2): *The heavens declare the glory of God,* by functioning harmoniously and efficiently in accordance with His will *(R' Munk).*

הַמֵּאִיר לָאָרֶץ וְלַדָּרִים — *He Who illuminates the earth and those who dwell.* The earth's dwellers enjoy the light, but so does the earth itself, because sunlight makes vegetation possible.

מָה רַבּוּ מַעֲשֶׂיךָ — *How great are Your works.* This

Interruptions During Blessings of the Shema

As a general rule, no אָמֵן or other prayer response may be recited between בָּרְכוּ and *Shemoneh Esrei,* but there are exceptions. The main exception is 'between chapters' [בֵּין הַפְּרָקִים] of the *Shema Blessings* — i.e., after יוֹצֵר הַמְּאוֹרוֹת and בְּאַהֲבָה ... הַבּוֹחֵר, and between the three chapters of *Shema.* At those points, אָמֵן (but not בָּרוּךְ הוּא וּבָרוּךְ שְׁמוֹ) may be responded to every blessing. Some responses, however, are so important that they are permitted at any point in the *Shema* blessings. They are:

(a) In *Kaddish,* אָמֵן יְהֵא שְׁמֵהּ רַבָּה ... עָלְמַיָּא and the אָמֵן after דַּאֲמִירָן בְּעָלְמָא; (b) the response to בָּרְכוּ (even of one called to the Torah); and (c) during the *chazzan's* repetition of *Shemoneh Esrei* — 1) in *Kedushah,* the verses קָדוֹשׁ, קָדוֹשׁ קָדוֹשׁ ... כְּבוֹדוֹ and בָּרוּךְ כְּבוֹד ה' מִמְּקוֹמוֹ; 2) the אָמֵן after הָאֵל הַקָּדוֹשׁ and after שׁוֹמֵעַ תְּפִלָּה; 3) the three words מוֹדִים אֲנַחְנוּ לָךְ.

During the recital of the two verses שְׁמַע and בָּרוּךְ שֵׁם, absolutely no interruptions are permitted.

יהוה, כֻּלָּם בְּחָכְמָה עָשִׂיתָ, מָלְאָה הָאָרֶץ קִנְיָנֶךָ.[1] הַמֶּלֶךְ הַמְּרוֹמָם לְבַדּוֹ* מֵאָז, הַמְּשֻׁבָּח וְהַמְּפֹאָר וְהַמִּתְנַשֵּׂא מִימוֹת עוֹלָם. אֱלֹהֵי עוֹלָם, בְּרַחֲמֶיךָ הָרַבִּים רַחֵם עָלֵינוּ, אֲדוֹן עֻזֵּנוּ, צוּר מִשְׂגַּבֵּנוּ, מָגֵן יִשְׁעֵנוּ, מִשְׂגָּב בַּעֲדֵנוּ. אֵל בָּרוּךְ* גְּדוֹל דֵּעָה, הֵכִין וּפָעַל זָהֳרֵי חַמָּה, טוֹב יָצַר כָּבוֹד לִשְׁמוֹ, מְאוֹרוֹת נָתַן סְבִיבוֹת עֻזּוֹ, פִּנּוֹת צְבָאָיו קְדוֹשִׁים רוֹמְמֵי שַׁדַּי, תָּמִיד מְסַפְּרִים כְּבוֹד אֵל וּקְדֻשָּׁתוֹ. תִּתְבָּרַךְ יהוה אֱלֹהֵינוּ עַל שֶׁבַח מַעֲשֵׂה יָדֶיךָ, וְעַל מְאוֹרֵי אוֹר שֶׁעָשִׂיתָ, יְפָאֲרוּךָ, סֶּלָה.

תִּתְבָּרַךְ צוּרֵנוּ* מַלְכֵּנוּ וְגוֹאֲלֵנוּ, בּוֹרֵא קְדוֹשִׁים. יִשְׁתַּבַּח שִׁמְךָ לָעַד מַלְכֵּנוּ, יוֹצֵר מְשָׁרְתִים, וַאֲשֶׁר מְשָׁרְתָיו כֻּלָּם עוֹמְדִים בְּרוּם עוֹלָם, וּמַשְׁמִיעִים בְּיִרְאָה יַחַד בְּקוֹל דִּבְרֵי אֱלֹהִים חַיִּים וּמֶלֶךְ עוֹלָם.[2] כֻּלָּם אֲהוּבִים, כֻּלָּם בְּרוּרִים, כֻּלָּם גִּבּוֹרִים, וְכֻלָּם עֹשִׂים בְּאֵימָה וּבְיִרְאָה רְצוֹן קוֹנָם. ❖ וְכֻלָּם פּוֹתְחִים אֶת פִּיהֶם בִּקְדֻשָּׁה וּבְטָהֳרָה, בְּשִׁירָה וּבְזִמְרָה, וּמְבָרְכִים וּמְשַׁבְּחִים וּמְפָאֲרִים וּמַעֲרִיצִים וּמַקְדִּישִׁים וּמַמְלִיכִים —

אֶת שֵׁם הָאֵל הַמֶּלֶךְ הַגָּדוֹל הַגִּבּוֹר וְהַנּוֹרָא קָדוֹשׁ הוּא.[3] ❖ וְכֻלָּם מְקַבְּלִים עֲלֵיהֶם עֹל מַלְכוּת שָׁמַיִם זֶה מִזֶּה,* וְנוֹתְנִים רְשׁוּת זֶה לָזֶה, לְהַקְדִּישׁ לְיוֹצְרָם, בְּנַחַת רוּחַ בְּשָׂפָה בְרוּרָה וּבִנְעִימָה. קְדֻשָּׁה כֻּלָּם כְּאֶחָד עוֹנִים וְאוֹמְרִים בְּיִרְאָה:

— Congregation recites aloud.

קָדוֹשׁ קָדוֹשׁ קָדוֹשׁ* יהוה צְבָאוֹת,* מְלֹא כָל הָאָרֶץ כְּבוֹדוֹ.[4]

---

refers to the heavenly bodies and other major forces in creation. Homiletically, the Talmud (*Chullin* 127a) interprets, *how diverse are Your works;* some can live only on land, others only in the sea, and so on.

הַמֶּלֶךְ הַמְּרוֹמָם לְבַדּוֹ — *The King Who was exalted in solitude.* Before Creation God was *exalted in solitude,* because there were no creatures to praise Him (*Etz Yosef*).

אֵל בָּרוּךְ — *The blessed God.* From here until תָּמִיד, the words follow the order of the *Aleph-Beis.* This use of the *Aleph-Beis* acrostic conveys the idea that we praise God with every available sound and that His greatness is absolutely complete and harmonious.

☙ תִּתְבָּרַךְ צוּרֵנוּ — *May You be blessed, our Rock.* The previous paragraph expressed man's praise of God. Now we turn to the angels' praise of Him. Since there have been people who worshiped the heavenly bodies as independent gods, we now cite the prayers of the heavenly legions, for they know that the sun and the moon are but God's creatures and servants.

וְכֻלָּם מְקַבְּלִים ... זֶה מִזֶּה — *Then they all accept ...*

HASHEM, You make them all with wisdom, the world is full of Your possessions.[1] *The King Who was exalted in solitude* before creation, Who is praised, glorified, and upraised since days of old. Eternal God, with Your abundant compassion be compassionate to us — O Master of our power, our rocklike stronghold, O Shield of our salvation, be a stronghold for us. The blessed God,* Who is great in knowledge, prepared and worked on the rays of the sun; the Beneficent One fashioned honor for His Name, emplaced luminaries all around His power; the leaders of His legions, holy ones, exalt the Almighty, constantly relate the honor of God and His sanctity. May You be blessed, HASHEM, our God, beyond the praises of Your handiwork and beyond the bright luminaries that You have made — may they glorify You — Selah!*

תִּתְבָּרַךְ *May You be blessed, our Rock,* our King and Redeemer, Creator of holy ones; may Your Name be praised forever, our King, O Fashioner of ministering angels; all of Whose ministering angels stand at the summit of the universe and proclaim — with awe, together, loudly — the words of the living God and King of the universe.*[2] *They are all beloved; they are all flawless; they are all mighty, they all do the will of their Maker with dread and reverence.* Chazzan— *And they all open their mouth in holiness and purity, in song and hymn — and bless, praise, glorify, revere, sanctify and declare the kingship of —*

אֶת שֵׁם *The Name of God, the great, mighty, and awesome King; holy is He.*[3] Chazzan— *Then they all accept upon themselves the yoke of heavenly sovereignty from one another,* and grant permission to one another to sanctify the One Who formed them, with tranquillity, with clear articulation, and with sweetness. All of them as one proclaim His holiness and say with awe:*

Congregation recites aloud: **'Holy, holy, holy* is HASHEM, Master of Legions,* the whole world is filled with His glory.'**[4]

(1) *Psalms* 104:24. (2) Cf. *Jeremiah* 10:10. (3) Cf. *Deuteronomy* 10:17; *Psalms* 99:3. (4) *Isaiah* 6:3.

from one another. Tanna d'Bei Eliyahu contrasts the behavior of the angels with that of human beings. Unlike people whose competitive jealousies cause them to thwart and outdo one another, the angels urge one another to take the initiative in serving and praising God. Conflict is the foe of perfection, harmony is its ally.

☙ קָדוֹשׁ קָדוֹשׁ קָדוֹשׁ — *Holy, holy, holy. Targum Yonasan (Isaiah* 6:3) renders: *Holy* in the most exalted heaven, the abode of His Presence; *holy* on earth, product of His strength; *holy* forever and ever is HASHEM, Master of Legions ...

כָּבוֹד refers to the glory of God that is present *within* the material world; it is the degree of Godliness that man is capable of perceiving even within creation. קָדוֹשׁ, on the other hand, refers to God's essence, which is beyond all comprehension.

צְבָאוֹת — *Master of Legions.* Although it is commonly translated simply as *hosts* or *legions,* the word צְבָאוֹת is a Name of God (see *Shavuos* 35a), which means that He is the *Master* of all the heavenly hosts. The word צָבָא is used to refer to an organized, disciplined group. Thus, an army is commonly called צָבָא. In the context of this Divine Name, it refers to the idea that the infinite

❖ וְהָאוֹפַנִּים* וְחַיּוֹת הַקֹּֽדֶשׁ בְּרַֽעַשׁ גָּדוֹל מִתְנַשְּׂאִים לְעֻמַּת שְׂרָפִים. לְעֻמָּתָם מְשַׁבְּחִים וְאוֹמְרִים:

Congregation recites aloud— **בָּרוּךְ כְּבוֹד יהוה מִמְּקוֹמוֹ.***[1]

לְאֵל בָּרוּךְ* נְעִימוֹת יִתֵּֽנוּ. לְמֶֽלֶךְ* אֵל חַי וְקַיָּם, זְמִרוֹת יֹאמֵֽרוּ, וְתִשְׁבָּחוֹת יַשְׁמִֽיעוּ. כִּי הוּא לְבַדּוֹ פּוֹעֵל גְּבוּרוֹת, עֹשֶׂה חֲדָשׁוֹת, בַּֽעַל מִלְחָמוֹת, זוֹרֵֽעַ צְדָקוֹת,* מַצְמִֽיחַ יְשׁוּעוֹת, בּוֹרֵא רְפוּאוֹת, נוֹרָא תְהִלּוֹת, אֲדוֹן הַנִּפְלָאוֹת. הַמְּחַדֵּשׁ בְּטוּבוֹ בְּכָל יוֹם תָּמִיד מַעֲשֵׂה בְרֵאשִׁית. כָּאָמוּר: לְעֹשֵׂה אוֹרִים גְּדֹלִים, כִּי לְעוֹלָם חַסְדּוֹ.[2] ❖ אוֹר חָדָשׁ* עַל צִיּוֹן תָּאִיר, וְנִזְכֶּה כֻלָּֽנוּ מְהֵרָה לְאוֹרוֹ. בָּרוּךְ אַתָּה יהוה, יוֹצֵר הַמְּאוֹרוֹת. (Cong.—אָמֵן.)

אַהֲבָה רַבָּה* אֲהַבְתָּֽנוּ יהוה אֱלֹהֵֽינוּ, חֶמְלָה גְדוֹלָה וִיתֵרָה חָמַֽלְתָּ עָלֵֽינוּ. אָבִֽינוּ מַלְכֵּֽנוּ, בַּעֲבוּר אֲבוֹתֵֽינוּ שֶׁבָּֽטְחוּ בְךָ, וַתְּלַמְּדֵם חֻקֵּי חַיִּים, כֵּן תְּחָנֵּֽנוּ וּתְלַמְּדֵֽנוּ. אָבִֽינוּ הָאָב הָרַחֲמָן הַמְּרַחֵם, רַחֵם עָלֵֽינוּ, וְתֵן בְּלִבֵּֽנוּ לְהָבִין וּלְהַשְׂכִּיל, לִשְׁמֹֽעַ לִלְמוֹד וּלְלַמֵּד, לִשְׁמֹר וְלַעֲשׂוֹת וּלְקַיֵּם אֶת כָּל דִּבְרֵי תַלְמוּד תּוֹרָתֶֽךָ בְּאַהֲבָה. וְהָאֵר עֵינֵֽינוּ* בְּתוֹרָתֶֽךָ,* וְדַבֵּק לִבֵּֽנוּ בְּמִצְוֹתֶֽיךָ, וְיַחֵד לְבָבֵֽנוּ* לְאַהֲבָה וּלְיִרְאָה אֶת שְׁמֶֽךָ,[3] וְלֹא נֵבוֹשׁ לְעוֹלָם וָעֶד.* כִּי בְשֵׁם קָדְשְׁךָ הַגָּדוֹל וְהַנּוֹרָא בָּטָֽחְנוּ, נָגִֽילָה וְנִשְׂמְחָה בִּישׁוּעָתֶֽךָ. וַהֲבִיאֵֽנוּ

---

heavenly bodies are organized according to God's will to do His service.

וְהָאוֹפַנִּים — *Then the Ofanim.* The varieties of angels are not translated since we lack the vocabulary to define them. *Rambam (Yesodei HaTorah* 2:7) notes that there are ten levels of angels. Their names are *Chayos, Ofanim, Er'elim, Chashmalim, Seraphim, Malachim, Elohim, B'nai Elohim, Cherubim,* and *Ishim.*

בָּרוּךְ ... מִמְּקוֹמוֹ — *Blessed ... from His place.* 'Place' refers to a particular position or level of eminence. For example, we say that a person 'takes his father's place.' But in the case of God — all we can do is bless His eminence as *we* perceive it coming to us *from* His place. In other words, we see Him acting as Sustainer, Healer, Judge, Life-giver and so on, but we don't know what He really is. Though the angels have a better knowledge of God than people, they too have no comprehension of His true essence *(Nefesh HaChaim).*

לְאֵל בָּרוּךְ — *To the blessed God.* Earlier in this *Shema* blessing (p. 86), we recited a twenty-two word *Aleph-Beis* acrostic that began with this same expression: אֵל בָּרוּךְ, *the blessed God.* Now, in keeping with the general principle regarding a long blessing, we conclude it by returning to the theme with which the blessing began. Thus, we return to the theme of *the blessed God,* Whom we gratefully praise for His works of creation in general and the heavenly luminaries in particular — upon which we will conclude by blessing Him as יוֹצֵר הַמְּאוֹרוֹת, [God] *Who fashions the luminaries.*

Chazzan— *Then the Ofanim* and the holy Chayos with great noise raise themselves towards the Seraphim. Facing them they give praise saying:*

Cong. recites aloud: **'Blessed is the glory of HASHEM from His place.'***[1]

לְאֵל *To the blessed God* they shall offer sweet melodies; to the King,* the living and enduring God, they shall sing hymns and proclaim praises. For He alone effects mighty deeds, makes new things, is Master of wars, sows kindnesses,* makes salvations flourish, creates cures, is too awesome for praise, is Lord of wonders. In His goodness He renews daily, perpetually, the work of creation. As it is said: '[Give thanks] to Him Who makes the great luminaries, for His kindness endures forever.'*[2] Chazzan— *May You shine a new light* on Zion, and may we all speedily merit its light. Blessed are You, HASHEM, Who fashions the luminaries.* (Cong.— *Amen*)

אַהֲבָה *With an abundant love* have You loved us, HASHEM, our God; with exceedingly great pity have You pitied us. Our Father, our King, for the sake of our forefathers who trusted in You and whom You taught the decrees of life, may You be equally gracious to us and teach us. Our Father, the merciful Father, Who acts mercifully, have mercy upon us, instill in our hearts to understand and elucidate, to listen, learn, teach, safeguard, perform, and fulfill all the words of Your Torah's teaching with love. Enlighten our eyes* in Your Torah,* attach our hearts to Your commandments, and unify our hearts* to love and fear Your Name,*[3] *and may we not feel inner shame for all eternity.* Because we have trusted in Your great and awesome holy Name, may we exult and rejoice in Your salvation. Bring us*

(1) *Ezekiel* 3:12. (2) *Psalms* 136:7. (3) Cf. 86:11.

לְאֵל ... לְמֶלֶךְ — *To the ... God ... to the King.* The commentators differ regarding the vocalization of these two words. Many hold that they are read לָאֵל and לַמֶּלֶךְ. We have followed the version of most *siddurim,* but every congregation should maintain its custom.

זוֹרֵעַ צְדָקוֹת — *Sows kindnesses.* God does not merely reward man for his good deeds; He rewards him even for the chain reaction that results from human kindness. Thus, an act of kindness is like a seed that can produce luxuriant vegetation *(Etz Yosef).*

אוֹר חָדָשׁ — *A new light.* The *new* light is actually a return of the original brilliance of creation. That light was concealed for the enjoyment of the righteous in the Messianic era. May it soon shine upon Zion *(Yaavetz).*

אַהֲבָה רַבָּה ◆§ — *With an abundant love.* Up to now, we have blessed God for having created the luminaries, but there is a light even greater than that of the brightest stars and the sun — the light of the Torah. Now, in this second blessing before *Shema,* we thank God for the Torah and pray that He grant us the wisdom to understand it properly *(Yaavetz; R' Munk).*

וְהָאֵר עֵינֵינוּ — *Enlighten our eyes.* This begins a series of brief supplications with one general purpose: A Jew's involvement with Torah study and observance must saturate all his activities, even his business, leisure, and social life.

בְּתוֹרָתֶךָ — *In Your Torah.* Enlighten us so that we may understand all aspects of Your Torah.

וְיַחֵד לְבָבֵנוּ — *And unify our hearts.* Man's likes and needs propel him in many directions. We ask God to unify our emotions and wishes to serve Him in love and fear.

וְלֹא נֵבוֹשׁ לְעוֹלָם וָעֶד — *And may we not feel inner shame for all eternity.* Inner shame is the

At this point, gather the four *tzitzis* between the fourth and fifth fingers of the left hand. Hold *tzitzis* in this manner throughout שְׁמַע.

לְשָׁלוֹם מֵאַרְבַּע כַּנְפוֹת הָאָרֶץ, וְתוֹלִיכֵנוּ קוֹמְמִיּוּת לְאַרְצֵנוּ. כִּי אֵל פּוֹעֵל יְשׁוּעוֹת אָתָּה, וּבָנוּ בָחַרְתָּ מִכָּל עַם וְלָשׁוֹן. ❖ וְקֵרַבְתָּנוּ לְשִׁמְךָ הַגָּדוֹל סֶלָה בֶּאֱמֶת, לְהוֹדוֹת לְךָ וּלְיַחֶדְךָ בְּאַהֲבָה. בָּרוּךְ אַתָּה יהוה, הַבּוֹחֵר בְּעַמּוֹ יִשְׂרָאֵל בְּאַהֲבָה. (Cong. — אָמֵן.)

שמע

Immediately before reciting the *Shema* concentrate on fulfilling the positive commandment of reciting the *Shema* every morning. It is important to enunciate each word clearly and not to run words together. See *Laws* §46-60.

When praying without a *minyan*, begin with the following three-word formula:

אֵל מֶלֶךְ נֶאֱמָן.*

Recite the first verse aloud, with the right hand covering the eyes, and concentrate intensely upon accepting God's absolute sovereignty.

שְׁמַע | יִשְׂרָאֵל,* יהוה | אֱלֹהֵינוּ, יהוה | אֶחָד:*[1]

In an undertone — בָּרוּךְ שֵׁם* כְּבוֹד מַלְכוּתוֹ לְעוֹלָם וָעֶד.

Psalm 72:19

---

humiliation one feels deep within himself when he knows he has done wrong — even though the people around him may sing his praises. The cost of such shame is borne primarily in the World to Come, where it can diminish one's eternal bliss or even destroy it entirely. Therefore we pray that our eternity not be marred by inner shame.

שְׁמַע / THE SHEMA

The recitation of the three paragraphs of *Shema* is required by the Torah, and one must have in mind that he is about to fulfill this commandment. Although one should try to concentrate on the meaning of all three paragraphs, one must concentrate at least on the meaning of the first verse (שְׁמַע) and the second verse (בָּרוּךְ שֵׁם) because the recitation of *Shema* represents fulfillment of the paramount commandment of acceptance of God's absolute sovereignty (קַבָּלַת עוֹל מַלְכוּת שָׁמַיִם). By declaring that God is One, Unique, and Indivisible, we subordinate every facet of our personalities, possessions — our very lives — to His will.

A summary of the laws of the *Shema* appears on pp. 982-983. For a full commentary and Overview, see ArtScroll *Shema Yisrael*. In the שְׁמַע we have included the cantillation symbols *(trop)* for the convenience of those who recite שְׁמַע in the manner it is read from the Torah. Nevertheless, to enable those unfamiliar with this notation to group the words properly, commas have been inserted. Additionally, vertical lines have been placed between any two words that are prone to be slurred into one and are not separated by a comma.

אֵל מֶלֶךְ נֶאֱמָן — *God, trustworthy King.* The Sages teach that there are both 248 organs in the human body and 248 positive commandments. This parallel number symbolizes that the purpose of physical existence is to obey the precepts of the Torah. The total number of words in the three paragraphs of *Shema* is 245. The Sages wished to convey the above symbolism in the recitation of the *Shema*, so they added three words to it. If a *minyan* is present, the congregation listens to the *chazzan's* repetition aloud of the three words ה׳ אֱלֹהֵיכֶם אֱמֶת. If there is no *minyan* the three words אֵל מֶלֶךְ נֶאֱמָן are recited before *Shema* is begun. These words were chosen because their initials spell אָמֵן [literally, *it is true*], thus testifying to our faith in the truths we are about to recite.

The three words of the verse mean: He is אֵל, *God*, the All-Powerful source of all mercy; He is the מֶלֶךְ, *King*, Who rules, leads, and exercises supervision over all; and He is נֶאֱמָן, *trustworthy*, i.e., fair, apportioning no more suffering nor less good than one deserves *(Anaf Yosef)*.

שְׁמַע יִשְׂרָאֵל — *Hear, O Israel.* Although the commentators find many layers of profound meaning in this seminal verse, one should have at least the following points in mind during its recitation:

□ At this point in history, HASHEM is only

At this point, gather the four *tzitzis* between the fourth and fifth fingers of the left hand. Hold *tzitzis* in this manner throughout the *Shema.*

in peacefulness from the four corners of the earth and lead us with upright pride to our land. For You effect salvations, O God; You have chosen us from among every people and tongue. Chazzan— *And You have brought us close to Your great Name forever in truth, to offer praiseful thanks to You, and proclaim Your Oneness with love. Blessed are You, HASHEM, Who chooses His people Israel with love.* (Cong.— *Amen.)*

THE SHEMA

Immediately before reciting the *Shema* concentrate on fulfilling the positive commandment of reciting the *Shema* every morning. It is important to enunciate each word clearly and not to run words together. See *Laws,* §46-60.

When praying without a *minyan,* begin with the following three-word formula:

*God, trustworthy King.**

Recite the first verse aloud, with the right hand covering the eyes, and concentrate intensely upon accepting God's absolute sovereignty.

Hear, O Israel:* HASHEM is our God, HASHEM, the One and Only.*[1]

In an undertone— *Blessed is the Name* of His glorious kingdom for all eternity.*

(1) *Deuteronomy* 6:4.

אֱלֹהֵינוּ, *our God,* for He is not acknowledged universally. Ultimately, however, all will recognize Him as ה׳ אֶחָד, *the One and Only God (Rashi; Aruch Hashulchan* 61:4).

□ ה׳ — *HASHEM.* God is the Eternal One, Who was, is, and always will be [הָיָה הֹוֶה וְיִהְיֶה], and He is אָדוֹן, *Master,* of all.

□ אֱלֹהֵינוּ — *Our God.* He is all-Powerful (*Orach Chaim* 5).

אֶחָד — *The One [and only].* The word has two connotations: (a) There is no God other than HASHEM (*Rashbam*); and, (b) though we perceive God in many roles — kind, angry, merciful, wise, judging, and so on — these different attitudes are not contradictory, even though human intelligence does not comprehend their harmony. *Harav Gedaliah Schorr* likened this concept to a ray of light seen through a prism. Though one sees a myriad of different colors, they are all a single ray of light. So, too, God's many manifestations are truly one.

In saying the word אֶחָד, *the One and Only,* draw out the second syllable (חָ) a bit and emphasize the final consonant (ד). While drawing out the ח — a letter with the numerical value of eight — bear in mind that God is Master of the earth and the seven heavens. While clearly enunciating the final ד — which has the numerical value of four — bear in mind that God is Master in all four directions, meaning everywhere.

The enlarged ע and ד

In Torah scrolls, the letters ע of שְׁמַע and ד of אֶחָד are written large. Together they form the word עֵד, *witness.* The enlarged letters allude to the thought that every Jew, by pronouncing the *Shema,* bears witness to HASHEM's unity and declares it to all the world *(Rokeach; Kol Bo; Abudraham).*

בָּרוּךְ שֵׁם — *Blessed is the Name.* Having proclaimed God as our King, we are grateful for the privilege of serving the One Whose kingdom is eternal and unbounded *(Etz Yosef).*

The Sages give two reasons for saying this verse silently:

(a) At Jacob's deathbed his children affirmed their loyalty to God by proclaiming the verse *Shema* [the word 'Israel' in that context refers to Jacob]. Jacob responded with the words *'Blessed is the Name ...'* The Sages taught: Should we say these words in our prayers because Jacob said them? Yes. But, on the other hand, Moses did not transmit them to us, for they are not found in the Torah. Therefore, let us say them silently *(Pesachim* 56a).

(b) Moses heard this beautiful prayer from the angels, and taught it to Israel. We dare not say it aloud, because we are sinful and therefore unworthy of using an angelic formula. On Yom Kippur, however, when Israel elevates itself to the sin-free level of angels, we may proclaim it loudly *(Devarim Rabbah* 2:36).

While reciting the first paragraph (דברים ו:ה־ט), concentrate on accepting the commandment to love God.

וְאָהַבְתָּ* אֵת יהוה | אֱלֹהֶיךָ, בְּכָל־לְבָבְךָ, וּבְכָל־נַפְשְׁךָ, וּבְכָל־מְאֹדֶךָ: וְהָיוּ הַדְּבָרִים הָאֵלֶּה, אֲשֶׁר | אָנֹכִי מְצַוְּךָ הַיּוֹם,* עַל־לְבָבֶךָ:* וְשִׁנַּנְתָּם לְבָנֶיךָ, וְדִבַּרְתָּ בָּם, בְּשִׁבְתְּךָ בְּבֵיתֶךָ, וּבְלֶכְתְּךָ בַדֶּרֶךְ, וּבְשָׁכְבְּךָ וּבְקוּמֶךָ: וּקְשַׁרְתָּם* לְאוֹת | עַל־יָדֶךָ, וְהָיוּ לְטֹטָפֹת בֵּין | עֵינֶיךָ: וּכְתַבְתָּם | עַל־מְזֻזוֹת בֵּיתֶךָ, וּבִשְׁעָרֶיךָ:

Touch the arm-*tefillin* at ... וּקְשַׁרְתָּם, and the head-*tefillin* at ... וְהָיוּ לְטֹטָפֹת; then kiss your fingertips.

While reciting the second paragraph (דברים יא:יג־כא), concentrate on accepting all the commandments and the concept of reward and punishment.

וְהָיָה,* אִם־שָׁמֹעַ תִּשְׁמְעוּ אֶל־מִצְוֹתַי, אֲשֶׁר | אָנֹכִי מְצַוֶּה | אֶתְכֶם הַיּוֹם, לְאַהֲבָה אֶת־יהוה | אֱלֹהֵיכֶם וּלְעָבְדוֹ, בְּכָל־לְבַבְכֶם, וּבְכָל־נַפְשְׁכֶם: וְנָתַתִּי מְטַר־אַרְצְכֶם בְּעִתּוֹ, יוֹרֶה וּמַלְקוֹשׁ, וְאָסַפְתָּ דְגָנֶךָ וְתִירֹשְׁךָ וְיִצְהָרֶךָ: וְנָתַתִּי | עֵשֶׂב | בְּשָׂדְךָ לִבְהֶמְתֶּךָ, וְאָכַלְתָּ וְשָׂבָעְתָּ: הִשָּׁמְרוּ* לָכֶם, פֶּן־יִפְתֶּה לְבַבְכֶם, וְסַרְתֶּם וַעֲבַדְתֶּם | אֱלֹהִים | אֲחֵרִים, וְהִשְׁתַּחֲוִיתֶם לָהֶם:* וְחָרָה | אַף־יהוה בָּכֶם, וְעָצַר | אֶת־הַשָּׁמַיִם, וְלֹא־יִהְיֶה מָטָר, וְהָאֲדָמָה לֹא תִתֵּן אֶת־יְבוּלָהּ, וַאֲבַדְתֶּם* | מְהֵרָה מֵעַל הָאָרֶץ הַטֹּבָה | אֲשֶׁר יהוה נֹתֵן לָכֶם: וְשַׂמְתֶּם | אֶת־דְּבָרַי | אֵלֶּה, עַל־לְבַבְכֶם וְעַל־נַפְשְׁכֶם, וּקְשַׁרְתֶּם | אֹתָם לְאוֹת | עַל־יֶדְכֶם, וְהָיוּ לְטוֹטָפֹת בֵּין | עֵינֵיכֶם: וְלִמַּדְתֶּם | אֹתָם | אֶת־בְּנֵיכֶם, לְדַבֵּר בָּם, בְּשִׁבְתְּךָ בְּבֵיתֶךָ,* וּבְלֶכְתְּךָ בַדֶּרֶךְ, וּבְשָׁכְבְּךָ וּבְקוּמֶךָ: וּכְתַבְתָּם | עַל־מְזוּזוֹת בֵּיתֶךָ, וּבִשְׁעָרֶיךָ: לְמַעַן | יִרְבּוּ | יְמֵיכֶם* וִימֵי בְנֵיכֶם, עַל הָאֲדָמָה | אֲשֶׁר נִשְׁבַּע | יהוה לַאֲבֹתֵיכֶם לָתֵת לָהֶם, כִּימֵי הַשָּׁמַיִם | עַל־הָאָרֶץ:*

Touch the arm-*tefillin* at ... וּקְשַׁרְתֶּם, and the head-*tefillin* at ... וְהָיוּ לְטוֹטָפֹת; then kiss your fingertips.

וְאָהַבְתָּ — *You shall love.* One should learn to fulfill the commandments out of love, rather than fear — and certainly not out of habit. The Mishnah (*Berachos* 9:5) explains that one should serve God with all his emotions and desires (*with all your heart*), even to the point of giving up his life for God (*with all your soul*), and even at the cost of his wealth (*with all your resources*).

אֲשֶׁר אָנֹכִי מְצַוְּךָ הַיּוֹם — *That I command you today.* But have they all been commanded today? — This teaches that although the Torah was given thousands of years ago, we are not to regard the commandments as an ancient rite that we follow out of loyalty and habit. Rather, we are to regard them with as much freshness and enthusiasm as if God had given them this very day (*Sifre*).

עַל לְבָבֶךָ — *Upon your heart.* Always be conscious of the demands of God and His Torah. Then, you will convey them to your children and *speak of them,* i.e., try to study, concentrate, and review wherever you are.

וּקְשַׁרְתָּם — *Bind them. Tefillin* on the arm, next to the heart, and on the head consecrate one's physical, emotional, and intellectual capacities to God's service (*Ramban*). The *mezuzah* on the doorpost consecrates one's home to Him.

וְהָיָה — *And it will come to pass.* Unlike the first paragraph of *Shema,* this one specifies the duty to perform מִצְוֹתַי, *My commandments,* and teaches that when the nation is righteous, it will

While reciting the first paragraph (*Deuteronomy* 6:5-9), concentrate on accepting the commandment to love God.

וְאָהַבְתָּ *You shall love* HASHEM, your God, with all your heart, with all your soul and with all your resources. Let these matters that I command you today* be upon your heart.* Teach them thoroughly to your children and speak of them while you sit in your home, while you walk on the way, when you retire and when you arise.*

Touch the arm-*tefillin* at *'Bind them...'* and the head-*tefillin* at *'and let them be tefillin ...'*; then kiss your fingertips.

Bind them as a sign upon your arm and let them be tefillin between your eyes. And write them on the doorposts of your house and upon your gates.*

While reciting the second paragraph (*Deuteronomy* 11:13-21), concentrate on accepting all the commandments and the concept of reward and punishment.

וְהָיָה *And it will come to pass* that if you continually hearken to My commandments that I command you today, to love HASHEM, your God, and to serve Him, with all your heart and with all your soul — then I will provide rain for your land in its proper time, the early and late rains, that you may gather in your grain, your wine, and your oil. I will provide grass in your field for your cattle and you will eat and be satisfied. Beware* lest your heart be seduced and you turn astray and serve gods of others and bow to them.* Then the wrath of HASHEM will blaze against you. He will restrain the heaven so there will be no rain and the ground will not yield its produce. And you will swiftly be banished* from the goodly land which HASHEM gives you. Place these words of Mine upon your heart and upon your soul;*

Touch the arm-*tefillin* at *'Bind them...'*, and the head-*tefillin* at *'and let them be tefillin ...'*; then kiss your fingertips.

bind them for a sign upon your arm and let them be tefillin between your eyes. Teach them to your children, to discuss them, while you sit in your home, while you walk on the way, when you retire and when you arise. And write them on the doorposts of your house and upon your gates. In order to prolong your days* and the days of your children upon the ground that HASHEM has sworn to your ancestors to give them, like the days of the heaven on the earth.**

---

be rewarded with success and prosperity. When it sins, it must expect poverty and exile.

וְאָכַלְתָּ וְשָׂבָעְתָּ הִשָּׁמְרוּ — *And you will eat and be satisfied. Beware* ... Prosperity is often the greatest challenge to religious devotion. People who are rich in wealth but poor in sophistication often succumb to temptation *(Rashi).*

יִפְתֶּה ... וְהִשְׁתַּחֲוִיתֶם לָהֶם — *Be seduced ... and bow to them,* i.e., to strange gods. An imperceptible, seemingly innocent surrender to temptation can be the beginning of a course that will end in idolatry *(Rashi).*

וְלֹא יִהְיֶה מָטָר ... וַאֲבַדְתֶּם — *So there will be no rain ... and you will ... be banished.* First will come famine. If that does not bring repentance, exile will follow *(Vilna Gaon).*

וְלִמַּדְתֶּם ... בְּשִׁבְתְּךָ — *Teach them ... while you sit.* In giving the command to educate children in the Torah, the verse speaks in the plural (וְלִמַּדְתֶּם), while the other words in the verse (בְּשִׁבְתְּךָ and so on) are in singular. This alludes to a *communal* responsibility to arrange for the Torah education of children *(Iyun Tefillah).*

לְמַעַן יִרְבּוּ יְמֵיכֶם — *In order to prolong your days.* [Although many *siddurim* set this verse as a new paragraph, leading some to believe that there are *four* paragraphs in the *Shema,* the verse is part of the paragraph which begins וְהָיָה.]

כִּימֵי הַשָּׁמַיִם עַל הָאָרֶץ — *Like the days of the heaven on the earth. Eretz Yisrael* is the eternal heritage

Before reciting the third paragraph (במדבר טו:לז־מא) the *tzitzis,* which have been held in the left hand, are taken in the right hand also. The *tzitzis* are kissed at each mention of the word צִיצִת, and at the end of the paragraph, and are passed before the eyes at וּרְאִיתֶם אֹתוֹ.

וַיֹּאמֶר | יהוה* | אֶל־מֹשֶׁה לֵּאמֹר: דַּבֵּר | אֶל־בְּנֵי | יִשְׂרָאֵל, וְאָמַרְתָּ אֲלֵהֶם, וְעָשׂוּ לָהֶם צִיצִת, עַל־כַּנְפֵי בִגְדֵיהֶם לְדֹרֹתָם, וְנָתְנוּ | עַל־צִיצִת הַכָּנָף, פְּתִיל תְּכֵלֶת:* וְהָיָה לָכֶם לְצִיצִת, וּרְאִיתֶם | אֹתוֹ, וּזְכַרְתֶּם | אֶת־כָּל־מִצְוֹת | יהוה, וַעֲשִׂיתֶם | אֹתָם, וְלֹא תָתוּרוּ* אַחֲרֵי לְבַבְכֶם וְאַחֲרֵי | עֵינֵיכֶם, אֲשֶׁר־אַתֶּם זֹנִים | אַחֲרֵיהֶם: לְמַעַן תִּזְכְּרוּ, וַעֲשִׂיתֶם | אֶת־כָּל־מִצְוֹתָי, וִהְיִיתֶם קְדֹשִׁים לֵאלֹהֵיכֶם: אֲנִי יהוה | אֱלֹהֵיכֶם, אֲשֶׁר הוֹצֵאתִי | אֶתְכֶם | מֵאֶרֶץ מִצְרַיִם, לִהְיוֹת לָכֶם לֵאלֹהִים, אֲנִי | יהוה | אֱלֹהֵיכֶם: אֱמֶת —

Concentrate on fulfilling the commandment of remembering the Exodus from Egypt.

Although the word אֱמֶת belongs to the next paragraph, it is appended to the conclusion of the previous one, as explained in the commentary.

—*Chazzan* repeats **יהוה אֱלֹהֵיכֶם אֱמֶת.**

וְיַצִּיב* וְנָכוֹן וְקַיָּם וְיָשָׁר וְנֶאֱמָן וְאָהוּב וְחָבִיב וְנֶחְמָד וְנָעִים וְנוֹרָא וְאַדִּיר וּמְתֻקָּן וּמְקֻבָּל וְטוֹב וְיָפֶה הַדָּבָר הַזֶּה עָלֵינוּ לְעוֹלָם וָעֶד. אֱמֶת אֱלֹהֵי עוֹלָם מַלְכֵּנוּ צוּר יַעֲקֹב, מָגֵן יִשְׁעֵנוּ, לְדֹר וָדֹר הוּא קַיָּם, וּשְׁמוֹ קַיָּם, וְכִסְאוֹ נָכוֹן, וּמַלְכוּתוֹ וֶאֱמוּנָתוֹ לָעַד קַיֶּמֶת. וּדְבָרָיו חָיִים וְקַיָּמִים, נֶאֱמָנִים וְנֶחֱמָדִים לָעַד (kiss the *tzitzis* and release them) וּלְעוֹלְמֵי עוֹלָמִים. ❖ עַל אֲבוֹתֵינוּ וְעָלֵינוּ, עַל בָּנֵינוּ וְעַל דּוֹרוֹתֵינוּ, וְעַל כָּל דּוֹרוֹת זֶרַע יִשְׂרָאֵל עֲבָדֶיךָ.

עַל הָרִאשׁוֹנִים וְעַל הָאַחֲרוֹנִים, דָּבָר טוֹב וְקַיָּם לְעוֹלָם וָעֶד, אֱמֶת וֶאֱמוּנָה חֹק וְלֹא יַעֲבֹר. אֱמֶת שָׁאַתָּה הוּא יהוה אֱלֹהֵינוּ וֵאלֹהֵי אֲבוֹתֵינוּ, ❖ מַלְכֵּנוּ מֶלֶךְ אֲבוֹתֵינוּ, גֹּאֲלֵנוּ גֹּאֵל אֲבוֹתֵינוּ, יוֹצְרֵנוּ צוּר יְשׁוּעָתֵנוּ, פּוֹדֵנוּ וּמַצִּילֵנוּ מֵעוֹלָם שְׁמֶךָ, אֵין אֱלֹהִים זוּלָתֶךָ.

---

of the Jewish people, just as heaven will always remain above the earth. Alternatively, just as heaven always showers blessings upon the earth in the form of life-giving rain, so too Israel will be blessed in the land God has sworn to it.

☙ **ויאמר ה׳** — *And HASHEM said.* The third paragraph of *Shema* is recited to fulfill the commandment to recall the Exodus every day. By freeing Israel from Egypt, God laid claim to the nation's eternal allegiance. No Jew is free to absolve himself of that obligation *(Rashi).*

פְּתִיל תְּכֵלֶת — *A thread of techeiles. Techeiles* is sky-blue wool dyed with the secretion of an amphibian called *chilazon.* For many centuries the identity of the animal has been unknown. Even in the absence of the *techeiles* thread, however, the commandment of *tzitzis* remains binding *(Menachos* 38a).

Before reciting the third paragraph *(Numbers* 15:37-41) the *tzitzis,* which have been held in the left hand, are taken in the right hand also. The *tzitzis* are kissed at each mention of the word *tzitzis* and at the end of the paragraph, and are passed before the eyes at *'that you may see it.'*

וַיֹּאמֶר *And HASHEM said* to Moses saying: Speak to the Children of Israel and say to them that they are to make themselves tzitzis on the corners of their garments, throughout their generations. And they are to place upon the tzitzis of each corner a thread of techeiles.* And it shall constitute tzitzis for you, that you may see it and remember all the commandments of HASHEM and perform them; and not explore* after your heart and after your eyes after which you stray. So that you may remember and perform all My commandments; and be holy to your God. I am HASHEM, your God, Who has removed you from the land of Egypt to be a God to you. I am HASHEM your God — it is true —*

Concentrate on fulfilling the commandment of remembering the Exodus from Egypt.

Although the word אֱמֶת, *'it is true,'* belongs to the next paragraph, it is appended to the conclusion of the previous one, as explained in the commentary.

Chazzan repeats: **HASHEM, your God, is true.***

וְיַצִּיב *And certain,* established and enduring,. fair and faithful, beloved and cherished, delightful and pleasant, awesome and powerful, correct and accepted, good and beautiful is this affirmation to us forever and ever. True — the God of the universe is our King; the Rock of Jacob is the Shield of our salvation. From generation to generation He endures and His Name endures and His throne is well established; His sovereignty and faithfulness endure forever. His words are living and enduring, faithful and delightful forever* (kiss the *tzitzis* and release them) *and to all eternity;* Chazzan— *for our forefathers and for us, for our children and for our generations, and for all the generations of Your servant Israel's offspring.*

עַל הָרִאשׁוֹנִים *Upon the earlier and upon later generations, this affirmation is good and enduring forever. True and faithful, it is an unbreachable decree. It is true that You are HASHEM, our God and the God of our forefathers,* Chazzan— *our King and the King of our forefathers, our Redeemer, the Redeemer of our forefathers; our Molder, the Rock of our salvation; our Liberator and our Rescuer — this has ever been Your Name. There is no God but You.*

וְלֹא תָתוּרוּ — *And not explore.* The eye sees, then the heart covets, then the body sins *(Rashi).*

אֱמֶת ◆§ — *True.* The law that one may not interrupt between the last words of the *Shema* and אֱמֶת is of ancient origin. The reason for it is so that we may declare as did the prophet [*Jeremiah* 10:10] וַה׳ אֱלֹהִים אֱמֶת, *HASHEM, God, is true (Berachos* 14a).

אֱמֶת ... וְיַצִּיב — *True ... and certain.* This paragraph begins the third and final blessing of the *Shema,* which ends with גָּאַל יִשְׂרָאֵל, *Who redeemed Israel.* Like אֱמֶת וֶאֱמוּנָה, *True and faithful,* its counterpart in the Evening Service, this blessing continues our fulfillment of the requirement to recall the Exodus, morning and evening.

As the Sages teach *(Berachos* 12a), whoever omits either the morning or evening blessing has not properly discharged his obligation of reciting the *Shema* and its attendant prayers. Although both the morning and evening blessings of redemption refer to the Exodus, there is a basic difference between them. The Talmud (ibid.)

עֶזְרַת אֲבוֹתֵינוּ* אַתָּה הוּא מֵעוֹלָם, מָגֵן וּמוֹשִׁיעַ לִבְנֵיהֶם אַחֲרֵיהֶם בְּכָל דּוֹר וָדוֹר. בְּרוּם עוֹלָם מוֹשָׁבֶךָ, וּמִשְׁפָּטֶיךָ וְצִדְקָתְךָ עַד אַפְסֵי אָרֶץ. אַשְׁרֵי אִישׁ שֶׁיִּשְׁמַע לְמִצְוֹתֶיךָ, וְתוֹרָתְךָ וּדְבָרְךָ יָשִׂים עַל לִבּוֹ. אֱמֶת אַתָּה הוּא אָדוֹן לְעַמֶּךָ וּמֶלֶךְ גִּבּוֹר לָרִיב רִיבָם. אֱמֶת אַתָּה הוּא רִאשׁוֹן וְאַתָּה הוּא אַחֲרוֹן, וּמִבַּלְעָדֶיךָ אֵין לָנוּ מֶלֶךְ[1] גּוֹאֵל וּמוֹשִׁיעַ. מִמִּצְרַיִם גְּאַלְתָּנוּ יהוה אֱלֹהֵינוּ, וּמִבֵּית עֲבָדִים פְּדִיתָנוּ. כָּל בְּכוֹרֵיהֶם הָרָגְתָּ, וּבְכוֹרְךָ גָּאָלְתָּ, וְיַם סוּף בָּקַעְתָּ, וְזֵדִים טִבַּעְתָּ, וִידִידִים הֶעֱבַרְתָּ, וַיְכַסּוּ מַיִם צָרֵיהֶם, אֶחָד מֵהֶם לֹא נוֹתָר.[2] עַל זֹאת שִׁבְּחוּ אֲהוּבִים וְרוֹמְמוּ אֵל, וְנָתְנוּ יְדִידִים זְמִרוֹת שִׁירוֹת וְתִשְׁבָּחוֹת, בְּרָכוֹת וְהוֹדָאוֹת, לְמֶלֶךְ אֵל חַי וְקַיָּם, רָם וְנִשָּׂא, גָּדוֹל וְנוֹרָא, מַשְׁפִּיל גֵּאִים, וּמַגְבִּיהַּ שְׁפָלִים, מוֹצִיא אֲסִירִים, וּפוֹדֶה עֲנָוִים, וְעוֹזֵר דַּלִּים, וְעוֹנֶה לְעַמּוֹ בְּעֵת שַׁוְּעָם אֵלָיו.

Rise for *Shemoneh Esrei.* Some take three steps backward at this point; others do so before צוּר יִשְׂרָאֵל.

❖ תְּהִלּוֹת לְאֵל עֶלְיוֹן, בָּרוּךְ הוּא וּמְבֹרָךְ. מֹשֶׁה וּבְנֵי יִשְׂרָאֵל לְךָ עָנוּ שִׁירָה בְּשִׂמְחָה רַבָּה וְאָמְרוּ כֻלָּם:

מִי כָמֹכָה בָּאֵלִם יהוה, מִי כָּמֹכָה נֶאְדָּר בַּקֹּדֶשׁ, נוֹרָא תְהִלֹּת עֹשֵׂה פֶלֶא.[3] ❖ שִׁירָה חֲדָשָׁה שִׁבְּחוּ גְאוּלִים לְשִׁמְךָ עַל שְׂפַת הַיָּם, יַחַד כֻּלָּם הוֹדוּ וְהִמְלִיכוּ וְאָמְרוּ:

יהוה יִמְלֹךְ לְעֹלָם וָעֶד.[4]

It is forbidden to interrupt or pause between גָּאַל יִשְׂרָאֵל and *Shemoneh Esrei,* even for *Kaddish, Kedushah* or *Amen.*

❖ **צוּר יִשְׂרָאֵל,*** קוּמָה בְּעֶזְרַת יִשְׂרָאֵל, וּפְדֵה כִנְאֻמֶךָ יְהוּדָה וְיִשְׂרָאֵל. גֹּאֲלֵנוּ יהוה צְבָאוֹת שְׁמוֹ, קְדוֹשׁ יִשְׂרָאֵל.[5] בָּרוּךְ אַתָּה יהוה, גָּאַל יִשְׂרָאֵל.*

---

teaches that the formulation of these blessings is based on the verse לְהַגִּיד בַּבֹּקֶר חַסְדֶּךָ וֶאֱמוּנָתְךָ בַּלֵּילוֹת, *to relate Your kindness in the dawn and Your faithfulness in the nights (Psalms* 92:3). This implies that in the morning we express gratitude for already existing *kindness,* while in the evening we express our *faith* in something that has not yet taken place.

As *Rashi* and *Tosafos* explain, the morning blessing of אֱמֶת וְיַצִּיב, which is recited after *dawn,* concentrates on God's *kindness* in having redeemed us from Egypt, while אֱמֶת וֶאֱמוּנָה, which is recited at *night,* is based on the theme of our *faith* that God will redeem us in the future, just as He did at the time of Exodus.

Including the word אֱמֶת, *true,* there are sixteen adjectives describing הַדָּבָר הַזֶּה, *this affirmation* [lit. *this thing*]. What is this 'thing'? It is the total message contained in the sixteen verses of the first two paragraphs of the *Shema* (including בָּרוּךְ שֵׁם). Thus, it is as if we affirm each verse with an adjective acknowledging its truth. *Etz Yosef* and others show how each adjective is suited to the verse it affirms.

עֶזְרַת *The Helper of our forefathers* are You alone, forever, Shield and Savior for their children after them in every generation. At the zenith of the universe is Your dwelling, and Your justice and Your righteousness extend to the ends of the earth. Praiseworthy is the person who obeys Your commandments and takes to his heart Your teaching and Your word. True — You are the Master for Your people and a mighty King to take up their grievance. True — You are the First and You are the Last, and other than You we have no king,*[1] *redeemer, or savior. From Egypt You redeemed us, HASHEM, our God, and from the house of slavery You liberated us. All their firstborn You slew, but Your firstborn You redeemed; the Sea of Reeds You split; the wanton sinners You drowned; the dear ones You brought across; and the water covered their foes — not one of them was left.*[2] *For this, the beloved praised and exalted God; the dear ones offered hymns, songs, praises, blessings, and thanksgivings to the King, the living and enduring God — exalted and uplifted, great and awesome, Who humbles the haughty and lifts the lowly; withdraws the captive, liberates the humble, and helps the poor; Who responds to His people upon their outcry to Him.*

Rise for *Shemoneh Esrei*. Some take three steps backward at this point; others do so before צוּר יִשְׂרָאֵל, *'Rock of Israel.'*

Chazzan— *Praises to the Supreme God, the blessed One Who is blessed. Moses and the children of Israel exclaimed a song to You with great joy and they all said:*

'Who is like You among the heavenly powers, HASHEM! Who is like You, mighty in holiness, too awesome for praise, doing wonders.'[3]

Chazzan— *With a new song the redeemed ones praised Your Name at the seashore, all of them in unison gave thanks, acknowledged [Your] sovereignty, and said:*

'HASHEM shall reign for all eternity.'[4]

It is forbidden to interrupt or pause between *'Who redeemed Israel'* and *Shemoneh Esrei*, even for *Kaddish, Kedushah* or *Amen*.

צוּר יִשְׂרָאֵל Chazzan— *Rock of Israel,* arise to the aid of Israel and liberate, as You pledged, Judah and Israel. Our Redeemer — HASHEM, Master of Legions, is His Name — the Holy One of Israel.*[5] *Blessed are You, HASHEM, Who redeemed Israel.**

(1) Cf. *Isaiah* 44:6. (2) *Psalms* 106:11. (3) *Exodus* 15:11. (4) 15:18. (5) *Isaiah* 47:4.

☙ **עֶזְרַת אֲבוֹתֵינוּ** — *The Helper of our forefathers.* This passage elaborates upon the Exodus within the context of God's eternal supervision of Israel and mastery over its destiny.

☙ **צוּר יִשְׂרָאֵל** — *Rock of Israel.* Since the end of *Shema,* we have concentrated on an elaboration of the miracles of the Exodus. We do not lose sight, however, of our faith that there is another, greater redemption yet to come. Thus we conclude with a plea that God rise up again to redeem Israel from this exile as He did in ancient Egypt.

גָּאַל יִשְׂרָאֵל — *Who redeemed Israel.* The text of the blessing is in keeping with the Talmudic dictum that prayer, i.e., *Shemoneh Esrei,* should follow mention of God's redemption of Israel. Only after we have set forth our faith in God as our Redeemer may we begin *Shemoneh Esrei,* in which we pray to Him for our personal and national needs *(R' Hirsch).*

שמונה עשרה — עמידה

Moses advanced through three levels of holiness when he went up to Sinai. Therefore we take three steps forward as we 'approach' God in the *Shemoneh Esrei* prayer.

Remain standing with the feet together while reciting *Shemoneh Esrei.* Recite it with quiet devotion and without any interruption, verbal or otherwise. Although it should not be audible to others, one must pray loudly enough to hear himself. See *Laws* §61-90 for a brief summary of its laws, including how to rectify the omission of phrases or paragraphs that are added at particular times of the year.

אֲדֹנָי שְׂפָתַי תִּפְתָּח,* וּפִי יַגִּיד תְּהִלָּתֶךָ.[1]

אבות

Bend the knees at בָּרוּךְ; bow at אַתָּה; straighten up at ה׳.

בָּרוּךְ אַתָּה* יהוה אֱלֹהֵינוּ וֵאלֹהֵי אֲבוֹתֵינוּ,* אֱלֹהֵי אַבְרָהָם, אֱלֹהֵי יִצְחָק, וֵאלֹהֵי יַעֲקֹב, הָאֵל הַגָּדוֹל הַגִּבּוֹר וְהַנּוֹרָא, אֵל עֶלְיוֹן, גּוֹמֵל חֲסָדִים טוֹבִים וְקוֹנֵה הַכֹּל,* וְזוֹכֵר חַסְדֵי אָבוֹת, וּמֵבִיא גוֹאֵל* לִבְנֵי בְנֵיהֶם, לְמַעַן שְׁמוֹ בְּאַהֲבָה.

From Rosh Hashanah to Yom Kippur add:

זָכְרֵנוּ לְחַיִּים,* מֶלֶךְ חָפֵץ בַּחַיִּים, וְכָתְבֵנוּ בְּסֵפֶר הַחַיִּים, לְמַעַנְךָ אֱלֹהִים חַיִּים.

[If forgotten, do not repeat *Shemoneh Esrei.* See *Laws* §61.]

Bend the knees at בָּרוּךְ; bow at אַתָּה; straighten up at ה׳.

מֶלֶךְ עוֹזֵר וּמוֹשִׁיעַ וּמָגֵן.* בָּרוּךְ אַתָּה יהוה, מָגֵן אַבְרָהָם.*

גבורות

אַתָּה גִּבּוֹר לְעוֹלָם אֲדֹנָי, מְחַיֵּה מֵתִים* אַתָּה, רַב לְהוֹשִׁיעַ.

שמונה עשרה / SHEMONEH ESREI

The Talmud refers to *Shemoneh Esrei* simply as תְּפִלָּה, *The Prayer,* for it is only in *Shemoneh Esrei* that we formulate our needs and ask God to fulfill them. The three *Shemoneh Esrei* prayers of the day were instituted by the Patriarchs and they are in place of the daily Temple offerings (*Berachos* 26b).

The term *Shemoneh Esrei* means eighteen, and, indeed, the original *Shemoneh Esrei* consisted of eighteen blessings. The requirement that there be precisely eighteen is based on various Scriptural supports (*Megillah* 17b). The text of the individual blessings was composed by the Men of the Great Assembly at the beginning of the Second Temple period and it was put into its final form under Rabban Gamliel II after the Destruction; over four centuries later (ibid.). A nineteenth blessing was added later (see commentary to וְלַמַּלְשִׁינִים, p. 106), but the name *Shemoneh Esrei* was left unchanged. The *Zohar* refers to the *Shemoneh Esrei* as the *Amidah* ['standing prayer'], and the two names are used interchangeably.

Shemoneh Esrei has three sections: (a) In the first three blessings, the supplicant pays homage to God, like a slave praising his master before he dares make a request; (b) the middle section of thirteen (originally, twelve) blessings contains the supplicant's requests; (c) in the last three blessings, he takes leave, expressing gratitude and confidence in his Master's graciousness (*Berachos* 34a).

Even the middle section is not merely a catalogue of selfish requests. In each blessing, we first acknowledge God's mastery, and only then make the request. Thus, each blessing is an affirmation of God's power (*Vilna Gaon*).

אֲדֹנָי שְׂפָתַי תִּפְתָּח — *My Lord, open my lips ...* Man's mind and heart may be ready for prayer, but he needs God's help to express himself properly (*Abudraham*). Alternatively, שְׂפָתַי, *my lips,* can mean *my boundaries.* Thus we ask God to free us from our limitations so that we can praise Him properly (*Ramban*).

אָבוֹת / Patriarchs

The first blessing of *Shemoneh Esrei* is known as אָבוֹת, *Patriarchs,* because it recalls the greatness of our forefathers in whose merit God pledged to help Israel throughout history, even if we are unworthy.

בָּרוּךְ אַתָּה — *Blessed are You.* [Since God is perfect by definition, what benefit can man's blessing confer upon Him?]

— This is a declaration of fact: God *is* blessed in the sense that He is perfect and complete (*Sefer HaChinuch* 430).

— God is the *Source* of inexhaustible blessing, and He has created the world in order to do good

SHEMONEH ESREI — AMIDAH

Moses advanced through three levels of holiness when he went up to Sinai. Therefore we take three steps forward as we 'approach' God in the *Shemoneh Esrei* prayer.

Remain standing with the feet together while reciting *Shemoneh Esrei.* Recite it with quiet devotion and without any interruption, verbal or otherwise. Although it should not be audible to others, one must pray loudly enough to hear himself. See *Laws* §61-90 for a brief summary of its laws, including how • rectify the omission of phrases or paragraphs that are added at particular times of the year.

My Lord, open my lips, that my mouth may declare Your praise.*[1]

PATRIARCHS

Bend the knees at *'Blessed'*; bow at *'You'*; straighten up at *'HASHEM'*.

בָּרוּךְ *Blessed are You,* HASHEM, our God and the God of our forefathers,* God of Abraham, God of Isaac, and God of Jacob; the great, mighty, and awesome God, the supreme God,* Who bestows beneficial kindnesses and creates everything,* Who recalls the kindnesses of the Patriarchs and brings a Redeemer* to their children's children, for His Name's sake, with love.*

From Rosh Hashanah to Yom Kippur add the following.

Remember us for life, O King Who desires life,*
and inscribe us in the Book of Life — for Your sake, O Living God.

[If forgotten, do not repeat *Shemoneh Esrei.* See *Laws* §61.]

Bend the knees at *'Blessed'*; bow at *'You'*; straighten up at *'HASHEM'*.

O King, Helper, Savior, and Shield. Blessed are You, HASHEM, Shield of Abraham.**

GOD'S MIGHT

אַתָּה *You are eternally mighty, my Lord, the Resuscitator of the dead* are You; abundantly able to save,*

(1) *Psalms* 51:17.

to His creatures. Since this is His will, we pray for the Redemption, when man will be worthy of His utmost blessing *(Rashba; R' Bachya).*

אֱלֹהֵינוּ וֵאלֹהֵי אֲבוֹתֵינוּ — *Our God and the God of our forefathers.* First we call Him *our God* because we are obligated to serve Him and know Him to the limit of *our* capacity. But there is much about His ways that we cannot understand. In response to such doubts we proclaim that He is *the God of our forefathers,* and we have faith in the tradition they transmitted *(Dover Shalom).*

אֵל עֶלְיוֹן — *The supreme God.* The word עֶלְיוֹן, *supreme,* means that God is so exalted that He is far beyond the comprehension of even the holiest angels. We can understand Him only superficially, by studying His deeds, i.e., that He *bestows beneficial kindnesses (Siach Yitzchak).*

וְקוֹנֵה הַכֹּל — *And creates everything.* The translation is based on the consensus of commentators, both here and to *Genesis* 14:19. Some translate *the Owner of everything.* Either way, the sense of the phrase is that God is Master of all creation.

וּמֵבִיא גוֹאֵל — *And brings a Redeemer.* The phrase is in present tense. Every event, no matter how terrible it may seem, is a step toward the ultimate redemption by the Messiah *(Siach Yitzchak).*

זָכְרֵנוּ לְחַיִּים — *Remember us for life.* During the Ten Days of Repentance, our prayers stress our pleas for life. But we want it to be the sort of life that God considers useful — לְמַעַנְךָ, *for Your sake (Sefer HaChaim).*

עוֹזֵר וּמוֹשִׁיעַ וּמָגֵן — *Helper, Savior, and Shield.* God 'helps' [עוֹזֵר] those who try to help themselves; He 'saves' [מוֹשִׁיעַ] even without the victim's participation; and 'shields' [מָגֵן] to prevent danger from approaching *(Iyun Tefillah).* In a different interpretation, *B'nai Yisas'char* comments that עוֹזֵר refers to the help that God gives without any prayer on the part of the victim, while מוֹשִׁיעַ refers to God's response to a prayer.

מָגֵן אַבְרָהָם — *Shield of Abraham.* God preserves the spark of Abraham within every Jew, no matter how far he may have strayed *(Chiddushei HaRim).*

גְּבוּרוֹת / God's Might

מְחַיֵּה מֵתִים — *The Resuscitator of the dead.* The concept that God restores life is found three times in this section, alluding to the three kinds

Between Shemini Atzeres and Pesach add:

מַשִּׁיב הָרְוּחַ וּמוֹרִיד °הַגֶּשֶׁם [some say – °הַגֶּשֶׁם].

[If forgotten, see *Laws* §70-75.]

מְכַלְכֵּל חַיִּים בְּחֶסֶד, מְחַיֵּה מֵתִים בְּרַחֲמִים רַבִּים, סוֹמֵךְ נוֹפְלִים, וְרוֹפֵא חוֹלִים, וּמַתִּיר אֲסוּרִים, וּמְקַיֵּם אֱמוּנָתוֹ לִישֵׁנֵי עָפָר. מִי כָמְוֹךָ בַּעַל גְּבוּרוֹת, וּמִי דּוֹמֶה לָּךְ, מֶלֶךְ מֵמִית וּמְחַיֶּה וּמַצְמִיחַ יְשׁוּעָה.*

From Rosh Hashanah to Yom Kippur add:

מִי כָמְוֹךָ אַב הָרַחֲמִים, זוֹכֵר יְצוּרָיו לְחַיִּים בְּרַחֲמִים.

[If forgotten, do not repeat *Shemoneh Esrei*. See *Laws* §61.]

וְנֶאֱמָן אַתָּה לְהַחֲיוֹת מֵתִים. בָּרוּךְ אַתָּה יהוה, מְחַיֵּה הַמֵּתִים.

During the silent *Shemoneh Esrei* continue with אַתָּה קָדוֹשׁ, p. 102.
During the *chazzan's* repetition, *Kedushah* is recited at this point.

קדושה

When reciting *Kedushah,* one must stand with his feet together, and avoid any interruptions. One should rise to his toes when saying the words קָדוֹשׁ, קָדוֹשׁ, קָדוֹשׁ; בָּרוּךְ (of בָּרוּךְ כְּבוֹד); and יִמְלֹךְ.

—Cong. then *Chazzan* נְקַדֵּשׁ אֶת שִׁמְךָ בָּעוֹלָם, כְּשֵׁם שֶׁמַּקְדִּישִׁים אוֹתוֹ בִּשְׁמֵי מָרוֹם, כַּכָּתוּב עַל יַד נְבִיאֶךָ, וְקָרָא זֶה אֶל זֶה וְאָמַר:

—All קָדוֹשׁ קָדוֹשׁ קָדוֹשׁ* יהוה צְבָאוֹת, מְלֹא כָל הָאָרֶץ כְּבוֹדוֹ.*[1]

—*Chazzan* לְעֻמָּתָם בָּרוּךְ יֹאמֵרוּ:*

—All בָּרוּךְ כְּבוֹד יהוה, מִמְּקוֹמוֹ.*[2]

—*Chazzan* וּבְדִבְרֵי קָדְשְׁךָ כָּתוּב לֵאמֹר:

—All יִמְלֹךְ יהוה* לְעוֹלָם, אֱלֹהַיִךְ צִיּוֹן לְדֹר וָדֹר, הַלְּלוּיָהּ.[3]

—*Chazzan* only concludes לְדוֹר וָדוֹר נַגִּיד גָּדְלֶךָ וּלְנֵצַח נְצָחִים קְדֻשָּׁתְךָ נַקְדִּישׁ, וְשִׁבְחֲךָ אֱלֹהֵינוּ מִפִּינוּ לֹא יָמוּשׁ לְעוֹלָם וָעֶד, כִּי אֵל מֶלֶךְ גָּדוֹל וְקָדוֹשׁ אָתָּה. בָּרוּךְ אַתָּה יהוה, °הָאֵל הַקָּדוֹשׁ.

—From Rosh Hashanah to Yom Kippur substitute °הַמֶּלֶךְ הַקָּדוֹשׁ.

Chazzan continues ... אַתָּה חוֹנֵן.

---

of resuscitation: man's awakening every morning after deathlike slumber; the rain that has the life-sustaining quality of making vegetation grow; and the literal resuscitation of the dead, that will take place in the Messianic age *(Abudraham).*

וּמַצְמִיחַ יְשׁוּעָה — *And makes salvation sprout.* Good deeds are like seeds that are planted and produce crops. People can earn resuscitation because of the good their children do or because of beneficial results of undertakings they initiated in their lifetimes *(Siach Yitzchak).*

קְדוּשָּׁה / Kedushah

Kedushah, Sanctification, expresses the concept that God is exalted above and separated from the limitations of material existence. When a *minyan* (quorum of ten) is present, it becomes the representative of the nation and echoes the angels who sing God's praise by proclaiming His holiness and glory. We do this by reciting *Kedushah,* a prayer based on that of the angels themselves, and with feet together, in the manner of the angels *(Ezekiel* 1:7). When reciting the words — קָדוֹשׁ, קָדוֹשׁ, קָדוֹשׁ; בָּרוּךְ (of בָּרוּךְ כְּבוֹד); and יִמְלֹךְ — we rise up on our toes to symbolize that we seek to break loose from the bonds of earth and unite our service with that of the angels.

Based on the teachings of *Arizal,* everyone

Between Shemini Atzeres and Pesach add the following.

Who makes the wind blow and makes the rain descend;

[If forgotten, see *Laws* §70-75.]

*Who sustains the living with kindness, resuscitates the dead with abundant mercy, supports the fallen, heals the sick, releases the confined, and maintains His faith to those asleep in the dust. Who is like You, O Master of mighty deeds, and who is comparable to You, O King Who causes death and restores life and makes salvation sprout!**

From Rosh Hashanah to Yom Kippur add the following.

Who is like You, Merciful Father, Who recalls His creatures mercifully for life!

[If forgotten, do not repeat *Shemoneh Esrei*. See *Laws*, §61.]

And You are faithful to resuscitate the dead. Blessed are You, HASHEM, *Who resuscitates the dead.*

During the silent *Shemoneh Esrei* continue with *'You are holy'* p. 102.
During the chazzan's repetition, *Kedushah* is recited at this point.

KEDUSHAH

When reciting *Kedushah*, one must stand with his feet together and avoid any interruptions. One should rise to his toes when saying the words *Holy, Holy, Holy; Blessed is;* and HASHEM *shall reign.*

Cong. then Chazzan— **נְקַדֵּשׁ** *We shall sanctify Your Name in this world, just as they sanctify it in heaven above, as it is written by Your prophet, "And one [angel] will call another and say:*

All— *'Holy, holy, holy* is* HASHEM, *Master of Legions, the whole world is filled with His glory.' "**[1]

Chazzan— *Those facing them say 'Blessed':**

All— *'Blessed is the glory of* HASHEM *from His place.'**[2]

Chazzan— *And in Your holy Writings the following is written:*

All— *'*HASHEM *shall reign* forever — your God, O Zion — from generation to generation, Halleluyah!'*[3]

Chazzan only concludes— *From generation to generation we shall relate Your greatness and for infinite eternities we shall proclaim Your holiness. Your praise, our God, shall not leave our mouth forever and ever, for You O God, are a great and holy King. Blessed are You* HASHEM, *°the holy God.*

°From Rosh Hashanah to Yom Kippur substitute: *the holy King.*

Chazzan continues אַתָּה חוֹנֵן, *You graciously endow ...*

---

(1) *Isaiah* 6:3. (2) *Ezekiel* 3:12. (3) *Psalms* 146:10.

---

recites the entire *Kedushah* (from נְקַדֵּשׁ until הַלְלוּיָהּ), even the parts labeled *'Chazzan.'* Many congregations, however, follow the custom recorded in *Shulchan Aruch* (ch. 125) that only the verses labeled 'Cong.' or 'All' are recited by everyone. Each congregation, of course, should maintain its own custom.

קָדוֹשׁ קָדוֹשׁ קָדוֹשׁ — *Holy, holy, holy.* God is *holy* with relation to the physical world, *holy* with relation to the spiritual world and *holy* with relation to the World to Come *(Targum Yonasan).*

מְלֹא כָל הָאָרֶץ כְּבוֹדוֹ — *The whole world is filled with His glory.* Man can bring God's holiness — awesome though it is — to earth, by fulfilling the Torah's commandments *(Zohar).*

לְעֻמָּתָם בָּרוּךְ יֹאמֵרוּ — *Those facing them say 'Blessed'.* They respond to קָדוֹשׁ, *Holy ...,* with the verse ... בָּרוּךְ כְּבוֹד, *Blessed is the glory,* which the congregation will now recite in full.

מִמְּקוֹמוֹ — *From His place.* See comm. on p. 88.

יִמְלֹךְ ה׳ — HASHEM *shall reign.* The Sages inserted this verse into *Kedushah* because they wanted all prayers to include an implied or direct plea for the rebuilding of Jerusalem [Zion] *(Abudraham).*

קדושת השם

אַתָּה קָדוֹשׁ וְשִׁמְךָ קָדוֹשׁ,* וּקְדוֹשִׁים* בְּכָל יוֹם יְהַלְּלוּךָ סֶּלָה. בָּרוּךְ אַתָּה יהוה, °הָאֵל הַקָּדוֹשׁ.*

°הַמֶּלֶךְ הַקָּדוֹשׁ.* —From Rosh Hashanah to Yom Kippur substitute
[If forgotten, repeat *Shemoneh Esrei.* See *Laws,* §62-63.]

בינה

אַתָּה חוֹנֵן לְאָדָם דַּעַת,* וּמְלַמֵּד לֶאֱנוֹשׁ בִּינָה. חָנֵּנוּ מֵאִתְּךָ דֵּעָה בִּינָה וְהַשְׂכֵּל. בָּרוּךְ אַתָּה יהוה, חוֹנֵן הַדָּעַת.

תשובה

הֲשִׁיבֵנוּ אָבִינוּ* לְתוֹרָתֶךָ, וְקָרְבֵנוּ מַלְכֵּנוּ לַעֲבוֹדָתֶךָ, וְהַחֲזִירֵנוּ* בִּתְשׁוּבָה שְׁלֵמָה לְפָנֶיךָ. בָּרוּךְ אַתָּה יהוה, הָרוֹצֶה בִּתְשׁוּבָה.

סליחה

Strike the left side of the chest with the right fist while reciting the words חָטָאנוּ and פָּשָׁעְנוּ.

סְלַח לָנוּ אָבִינוּ כִּי חָטָאנוּ, מְחַל* לָנוּ מַלְכֵּנוּ כִּי פָשָׁעְנוּ, כִּי מוֹחֵל וְסוֹלֵחַ אָתָּה. בָּרוּךְ אַתָּה יהוה, חַנּוּן הַמַּרְבֶּה לִסְלוֹחַ.

גאולה

רְאֵה בְעָנְיֵנוּ,* וְרִיבָה רִיבֵנוּ, וּגְאָלֵנוּ*[1] מְהֵרָה לְמַעַן שְׁמֶךָ,* כִּי גּוֹאֵל חָזָק אָתָּה. בָּרוּךְ אַתָּה יהוה, גּוֹאֵל יִשְׂרָאֵל.

קדושות / God's Holiness

See prefatory comment to *Kedushah.*

אַתָּה קָדוֹשׁ וְשִׁמְךָ קָדוֹשׁ — *You are holy and Your Name is holy.* The 'Name' of God refers to the manner in which we perceive His actions. The person who enjoys good health and prosperity perceives God as the 'Merciful One,' whereas the person who suffers pain and poverty sees Him as the God of Judgment.

וּקְדוֹשִׁים — *And holy ones.* The term may refer to the angels *(Iyun Tefillah)* or, as most commentators agree, to Israel *(Abudraham).* As *Ramban (Leviticus* 18:2) defines it, human holiness is measured by how well a person controls his permissible desires. Someone who seeks ways to indulge his lusts and passions without directly violating the law, is described as a נָבָל בִּרְשׁוּת הַתּוֹרָה, *degenerate with the Torah's permission.*

הָאֵל/הַמֶּלֶךְ הַקָּדוֹשׁ. — *The holy God/King.* The Name אֵל, *God,* has the connotation of mercy. During the Ten Days of Repentance when God sits on His Throne of Judgment, as it were, the term *King,* with its connotation of strict judgment, is more appropriate. Thus, although we plead for mercy, we recognize His majesty.

בִּינָה / Insight

אַתָּה חוֹנֵן לְאָדָם דַּעַת — *You graciously endow man with wisdom.* [This blessing begins the middle section of the *Shemoneh Esrei,* in which man makes his requests of God. The first plea is for wisdom and understanding — because man's intelligence is his primary characteristic, the one that sets him apart from animals.] We ask for *wisdom* and for *insight,* so that we can draw proper conclusions and achieve intellectual discernment *(Vilna Gaon).*

HOLINESS OF GOD'S NAME

אַתָּה *You are holy and Your Name is holy,* and holy ones* praise You every day, forever. Blessed are You, HASHEM, °the holy God.**

°From Rosh Hashanah to Yom Kippur substitute: *the holy King.**
[If forgotten, repeat *Shemoneh Esrei.* See *Laws,* §62-63.]

INSIGHT

אַתָּה *You graciously endow man with wisdom* and teach insight to a frail mortal. Endow us graciously from Yourself with wisdom, insight, and discernment. Blessed are You, HASHEM, gracious Giver of wisdom.*

REPENTANCE

הֲשִׁיבֵנוּ *Bring us back, our Father,* to Your Torah, and bring us near, our King, to Your service, and influence us to return* in perfect repentance before You. Blessed are You, HASHEM, Who desires repentance.*

FORGIVENESS

Strike the left side of the chest with the right fist while reciting the words *'erred'* and *'sinned'.*

סְלַח *Forgive us, our Father, for we have erred; pardon* us, our King, for we have willfully sinned; for You pardon and forgive. Blessed are You, HASHEM, the gracious One Who pardons abundantly.*

REDEMPTION

רְאֵה *Behold our affliction,* take up our grievance, and redeem us*[1] speedily for Your Name's sake,* for You are a powerful Redeemer. Blessed are You, HASHEM, Redeemer of Israel.*

(1) Cf. *Psalms* 119:153-154.

⁂ תְּשׁוּבָה / Repentance

אָבִינוּ — *Our Father.* Only in this prayer for repentance, and in the next one, for forgiveness, do we refer to God as *our Father.* A father has the responsibility to teach his son the proper way to live — but even if a son has rebelled and become estranged, the father's compassion will assert itself if his son repents and seeks forgiveness *(Etz Yosef).*

וְהַחֲזִירֵנוּ — *And influence us to return.* God never *compels* anyone to repent, but if a person makes a sincere beginning, God will make his way easier.

⁂ סְלִיחָה / Forgiveness

סְלַח ... מְחַל — *Forgive ... pardon.* סְלִיחָה, *forgiveness,* means not even harboring resentment or ill-will, but מְחִילָה, *pardon,* means giving up the right to punish for a wrong (*Abudraham*).

⁂ גְּאוּלָּה / Redemption

רְאֵה בְעָנְיֵנוּ — *Behold our affliction.* Though Israel suffers because of its own sins, our enemies have no right to claim that they are merely doing God's work, because they cause Israel to suffer much more than necessary. Similarly, many commentators explain that the Egyptians were punished for oppressing and enslaving the Jews, even though God had decreed suffering and slavery, because the Egyptians, in their wickedness, went far beyond God's decree *(Etz Yosef).*

וּגְאָלֵנוּ — *And redeem us* from the trials and agonies of everyday life *(Rashi; Megillah* 17b).

לְמַעַן שְׁמֶךָ — *For Your Name's sake.* Israel's suffering is a reflection on our God, and, therefore, a desecration of His Name *(Etz Yosef).*

On a fast day, the *chazzan* recites עֲנֵנוּ at this point. See commentary.

עֲנֵנוּ* יהוה עֲנֵנוּ, בְּיוֹם צוֹם תַּעֲנִיתֵנוּ, כִּי בְצָרָה גְדוֹלָה אֲנָחְנוּ. אַל תֵּפֶן אֶל רִשְׁעֵנוּ, וְאַל תַּסְתֵּר פָּנֶיךָ מִמֶּנּוּ,* וְאַל תִּתְעַלַּם מִתְּחִנָּתֵנוּ. הֱיֵה נָא קָרוֹב לְשַׁוְעָתֵנוּ, יְהִי נָא חַסְדְּךָ לְנַחֲמֵנוּ, טֶרֶם נִקְרָא אֵלֶיךָ עֲנֵנוּ, כַּדָּבָר שֶׁנֶּאֱמַר: וְהָיָה טֶרֶם יִקְרָאוּ וַאֲנִי אֶעֱנֶה, עוֹד הֵם מְדַבְּרִים וַאֲנִי אֶשְׁמָע.[1] כִּי אַתָּה יהוה הָעוֹנֶה בְּעֵת צָרָה, פּוֹדֶה וּמַצִּיל בְּכָל עֵת צָרָה וְצוּקָה. בָּרוּךְ אַתָּה יהוה, הָעוֹנֶה בְּעֵת צָרָה.

רפואה

רְפָאֵנוּ יהוה וְנֵרָפֵא,* הוֹשִׁיעֵנוּ וְנִוָּשֵׁעָה, כִּי תְהִלָּתֵנוּ אָתָּה,[2] וְהַעֲלֵה רְפוּאָה שְׁלֵמָה לְכָל מַכּוֹתֵינוּ,°° כִּי אֵל מֶלֶךְ רוֹפֵא נֶאֱמָן וְרַחֲמָן אָתָּה. בָּרוּךְ אַתָּה יהוה, רוֹפֵא חוֹלֵי עַמּוֹ יִשְׂרָאֵל.

ברכת השנים

In the following blessing וְתֵן בְּרָכָה is recited Chol HaMoed Pesach through *Minchah* of December 4th (or 5th in the year before a civil leap year). וְתֵן טַל וּמָטָר לִבְרָכָה is recited from *Maariv* of December 4th (or 5th) until Pesach. [If the wrong phrase is recited, see *Laws*, §79-83.]

בָּרֵךְ עָלֵינוּ* יהוה אֱלֹהֵינוּ אֶת הַשָּׁנָה הַזֹּאת וְאֶת כָּל מִינֵי תְבוּאָתָהּ לְטוֹבָה, (וְתֵן בְּרָכָה) (וְתֵן טַל וּמָטָר לִבְרָכָה) עַל פְּנֵי הָאֲדָמָה, וְשַׂבְּעֵנוּ מִטּוּבֶךָ,* וּבָרֵךְ שְׁנָתֵנוּ כַּשָּׁנִים הַטּוֹבוֹת. בָּרוּךְ אַתָּה יהוה, מְבָרֵךְ הַשָּׁנִים.

°°At this point one may interject a prayer for one who is ill:

יְהִי רָצוֹן מִלְּפָנֶיךָ יהוה אֱלֹהַי וֵאלֹהֵי אֲבוֹתַי, שֶׁתִּשְׁלַח מְהֵרָה רְפוּאָה שְׁלֵמָה מִן הַשָּׁמַיִם, רְפוּאַת הַנֶּפֶשׁ וּרְפוּאַת הַגּוּף

—for a male לַחוֹלֶה (patient's name) בֶּן (mother's name) בְּתוֹךְ שְׁאָר חוֹלֵי יִשְׂרָאֵל.

—for a female לַחוֹלָה (patient's name) בַּת (mother's name) בְּתוֹךְ שְׁאָר חוֹלֵי יִשְׂרָאֵל.

continue—כִּי אֵל ...

עֲנֵנוּ / Fast Day Prayer

On fast days, the prayer עֲנֵנוּ, *Answer us,* is recited during *Shemoneh Esrei.* In the *chazzan's* repetition of *Shacharis* and *Minchah,* עֲנֵנוּ is a separate blessing following the blessing of גְּאוּלָה, *Redemption* (but see below). The individual, however, recites עֲנֵנוּ only during *Minchah,* and then not as a separate blessing, but incorporated into the blessing of קַבָּלַת תְּפִלָּה, *Acceptance of Prayer.* He does not recite עֲנֵנוּ at *Shacharis* lest he become ill and not complete the fast.

The *chazzan* recites this prayer as a separate blessing only if a full *minyan* of ten expects to complete the fast (some authorities require only seven, see *Laws* §85). If less members of the *minyan* are fasting, or if the *chazzan* forgot עֲנֵנוּ, he incorporates it into the 'Acceptance of Prayer' blessing (p. 114), and omits the concluding blessing of עֲנֵנוּ (see *Laws* §87).

וְאַל תַּסְתֵּר פָּנֶיךָ מִמֶּנּוּ — *Do not hide Your Face from us,* i.e., permit us to understand the reasons for Your behavior toward us.

רְפוּאָה / Health and Healing

רְפָאֵנוּ ה׳ וְנֵרָפֵא — *Heal us,* HASHEM *— then we will be healed.* Sometimes human beings or angels are God's agents to heal illness, but in that case, the cure may be only partial or temporary. [Or the pain or other symptoms may be relieved, while

On a fast day, the *chazzan* recites עֲנֵנוּ, *'Answer us,'* at this point. See commentary.

עֲנֵנוּ *Answer us,* HASHEM, answer us, on this day of our fast, for we are in great distress. Do not pay attention to our wickedness; do not hide Your Face from us;* and do not ignore our supplication. Please be near to our outcry; please let Your kindness comfort us — before we call to You answer us, as it is said: 'And it will be that before they call, I will answer; while they yet speak, I will hear.'[1] For You, HASHEM, are the One Who responds in time of distress, Who redeems and rescues in every time of distress and woe. Blessed are You, HASHEM, Who responds in time of distress.*

HEALTH AND HEALING

רְפָאֵנוּ ***Heal us, HASHEM — then we will be healed;* save us — then we will be saved, for You are our praise.[2] Bring complete recovery for all our ailments, °for You are God, King, the faithful and compassionate Healer. Blessed are You, HASHEM, Who heals the sick of His people Israel.***

YEAR OF PROSPERITY

In the following blessing *'give a blessing,'* is recited from Chol Hamoed Pesach through *Minchah* of December 4th (or 5th in the year before a civil leap year); *'give dew and rain,'* is recited from *Maariv* of December 4th (or 5th) until Pesach. [If the wrong phrase is recited, see *Laws,* §79-83.]

בָּרֵךְ *Bless on our behalf* — O HASHEM, our God — this year and all its kinds of crops for the best, and give (dew and rain for) a blessing on the face of the earth, and satisfy us from Your bounty,* and bless our year like the best years. Blessed are You, HASHEM, Who blesses the years.*

°At this point one may interject a prayer for one who is ill:

May it be Your will, HASHEM, my God, and the God of my forefathers, that You quickly send a complete recovery from heaven, spiritual healing and physical healing to the patient (name) son/daughter of (mother's name) among the other patients of Israel.

Continue: ***For You are God ...***

(1) *Isaiah* 65:24. (2) Cf. *Jeremiah* 17:14.

the illness itself remains uncured *(Siach Yitzchak).*] But if God *Himself* undertakes to cure the patient, we are confident that it will not be a temporary nor a partial measure: *then we will be healed (Etz Yosef* from *Zohar).*

⊰ בִּרְכַּת הַשָּׁנִים / Year of Prosperity

בָּרֵךְ עָלֵינוּ — *Bless on our behalf.* We request a blessing on our general business activities and then go on to ask for abundant crops. Even in bad times some people prosper, and even in good times some farms and businesses fail. We ask not only for general prosperity, but that we be enabled to share in it *(R' S.R. Hirsch).*

טַל וּמָטָר — *Dew and rain.* The mention of rain (מוֹרִיד הַגָּשֶׁם) in the second blessing of *Shemoneh Esrei* is an expression of *praise* only. There we praise God the Lifegiver, Who controls the elements and provides wind and moisture as needed in the seasons when they generally occur. Here we make the *request* that He give us rain; therefore it is made only when rain is actually needed in the agricultural cycle. Since rain is needed in early fall in *Eretz Yisrael,* the recitation is begun there on 7 Cheshvan, much earlier than elsewhere.

מִטּוּבֶךָ — *From Your bounty.* Food acquired in a tainted manner lacks the holiness to nourish the soul. Therefore, we ask that God satisfy us from *His* bounty, not from earnings to which we are not entitled *(Yaaros D'vash).*

קיבוץ גליות

תְּקַע בְּשׁוֹפָר גָּדוֹל* לְחֵרוּתֵנוּ, וְשָׂא נֵס לְקַבֵּץ גָּלֻיּוֹתֵינוּ, וְקַבְּצֵנוּ יַחַד מֵאַרְבַּע כַּנְפוֹת הָאָרֶץ.[1] בָּרוּךְ אַתָּה יהוה, מְקַבֵּץ נִדְחֵי עַמּוֹ יִשְׂרָאֵל.

דין

הָשִׁיבָה שׁוֹפְטֵינוּ כְּבָרִאשׁוֹנָה,* וְיוֹעֲצֵינוּ* כְּבַתְּחִלָּה,[2] וְהָסֵר מִמֶּנּוּ יָגוֹן וַאֲנָחָה,* וּמְלוֹךְ עָלֵינוּ אַתָּה יהוה לְבַדְּךָ בְּחֶסֶד וּבְרַחֲמִים, וְצַדְּקֵנוּ בַּמִּשְׁפָּט. בָּרוּךְ אַתָּה יהוה, °מֶלֶךְ אוֹהֵב צְדָקָה וּמִשְׁפָּט.

°הַמֶּלֶךְ הַמִּשְׁפָּט. —From Rosh Hashanah to Yom Kippur substitute
[If forgotten, do not repeat *Shemoneh Esrei*. See *Laws* §64.]

ברכת המינים

וְלַמַּלְשִׁינִים* אַל תְּהִי תִקְוָה, וְכָל הָרִשְׁעָה כְּרֶגַע תֹּאבֵד, וְכָל אֹיְבֶיךָ* מְהֵרָה יִכָּרֵתוּ, וְהַזֵּדִים מְהֵרָה תְעַקֵּר וּתְשַׁבֵּר וּתְמַגֵּר וְתַכְנִיעַ בִּמְהֵרָה בְיָמֵינוּ. בָּרוּךְ אַתָּה יהוה, שׁוֹבֵר אֹיְבִים וּמַכְנִיעַ זֵדִים.

צדיקים

עַל הַצַּדִּיקִים וְעַל הַחֲסִידִים, וְעַל זִקְנֵי עַמְּךָ בֵּית יִשְׂרָאֵל, וְעַל פְּלֵיטַת סוֹפְרֵיהֶם,* וְעַל גֵּרֵי הַצֶּדֶק וְעָלֵינוּ, יֶהֱמוּ רַחֲמֶיךָ יהוה אֱלֹהֵינוּ, וְתֵן שָׂכָר טוֹב לְכָל הַבּוֹטְחִים בְּשִׁמְךָ בֶּאֱמֶת, וְשִׂים חֶלְקֵנוּ עִמָּהֶם לְעוֹלָם, וְלֹא נֵבוֹשׁ* כִּי בְךָ בָּטָחְנוּ. בָּרוּךְ אַתָּה יהוה, מִשְׁעָן וּמִבְטָח לַצַּדִּיקִים.

קִיבּוּץ גָּלֻיּוֹת / Ingathering of Exiles

תְּקַע בְּשׁוֹפָר גָּדוֹל — *Sound the great shofar.* There are three differences between this prayer for redemption and the earlier one of גְּאוּלָה, *Redemption:* (a) The earlier blessing refers to God's *daily* help in all sorts of crises and suffering, while this one refers to the *future* Redemption from exile; (b) the earlier blessing refers only to *physical* salvation, while this one is a plea for *spiritual* deliverance; (c) this one specifies not only freedom from oppression, but the ingathering of all exiles to *Eretz Yisrael.*

דִּין / Restoration of Justice

הָשִׁיבָה שׁוֹפְטֵינוּ כְּבָרִאשׁוֹנָה — *Restore our judges as in earliest times.* When Elijah heralds Messiah's coming, he will first reestablish the Sanhedrin, and then the Redemption will begin. A secondary theme of this prayer is the wish that God help all Jewish judges rule wisely and justly *(Yaaros D'vash).*

וְיוֹעֲצֵינוּ — *And our counselors,* i.e., the prophets who gave wise advice in both spiritual and temporal affairs *(Olas Tamid).*

יָגוֹן וַאֲנָחָה — *Sorrow and groan.* יָגוֹן, *sorrow,* results from actual want or pain, such as hunger or destruction. אֲנָחָה, *groan,* refers to inner turmoil, such as worry, depression, or fear *(Vilna Gaon).*

בִּרְכַּת הַמִּינִים / Against Heretics

וְלַמַּלְשִׁינִים — *And for slanderers.* Chrono-

INGATHERING OF EXILES

תְּקַע *Sound the great shofar* for our freedom, raise the banner to gather our exiles and gather us together from the four corners of the earth.*[1] *Blessed are You, HASHEM, Who gathers in the dispersed of His people Israel.*

RESTORATION OF JUSTICE

הָשִׁיבָה *Restore our judges as in earliest times* and our counselors* as at first;*[2] *remove from us sorrow and groan;* and reign over us — You, HASHEM, alone — with kindness and compassion, and justify us through judgment. Blessed are You, HASHEM, the °King Who loves righteousness and judgment.*

°From Rosh Hashanah to Yom Kippur substitute: *the King of judgment.*
[If forgotten, do not repeat *Shemoneh Esrei.* See *Laws* §64.]

AGAINST HERETICS

וְלַמַּלְשִׁינִים *And for slanderers* let there be no hope; and may all wickedness perish in an instant; and may all Your enemies* be cut down speedily. May You speedily uproot, smash, cast down, and humble the wanton sinners — speedily in our days. Blessed are You, HASHEM, Who breaks enemies and humbles wanton sinners.*

THE RIGHTEOUS

עַל הַצַּדִּיקִים *On the righteous, on the devout, on the elders of Your people the Family of Israel, on the remnant of their scholars,* on the righteous converts and on ourselves — may Your compassion be aroused, HASHEM, our God, and give goodly reward to all who sincerely believe in Your Name. Put our lot with them forever, and we will not feel ashamed,* for we trust in You. Blessed are You, HASHEM, Mainstay and Assurance of the righteous.*

(1) Cf. *Isaiah* 11:12. (2) Cf. 1:26.

---

logically, this is the *nineteenth* blessing of *Shemoneh Esrei;* it was instituted in Yavneh, during the tenure of Rabban Gamliel II as *Nassi* of Israel, some time after the destruction of the Second Temple. The blessing was composed in response to the threats of such heretical Jewish sects as the Sadducees, Boethusians, Essenes, and the early Christians. They tried to lead Jews astray through example and persuasion, and they used their political power to oppress observant Jews and to slander them to the anti-Semitic Roman government.

In this atmosphere, Rabban Gamliel felt the need to compose a prayer against the heretics and slanderers, and to incorporate it in the *Shemoneh Esrei* so that the populace would be aware of the danger.

Despite the disappearance from within Israel of the particular sects against whom it was directed, it is always relevant, because there are still non-believers and heretics who endanger the spiritual continuity of Israel *(Yaaros D'vash).*

וְכָל אֹיְבֶיךָ — *And may all Your enemies.* Any enemy of Israel is an enemy of God *(Tikun Tefillah).*

צַדִּיקִים / The Righteous

פְּלֵיטַת סוֹפְרֵיהֶם — *The remnant of their scholars.* The term סוֹפֵר refers to those who transmit the Oral Torah from generation to generation *(Avodas Yisrael).* These four categories of people — righteous, devout, elders, scholars — are the leaders of the nation. Because the nation needs them, the Sages instituted a special prayer for their welfare *(R' Yehudah ben Yakar).*

וְלֹא נֵבוֹשׁ — *And we will not feel ashamed.* One who puts his faith in people feels shamed — because he has been shown to be helpless on his own. But he is not ashamed to have trusted in God, because no one can succeed without His help *(Dover Shalom).*

בנין ירושלים

וְלִירוּשָׁלַיִם* עִירְךָ בְּרַחֲמִים תָּשׁוּב, וְתִשְׁכּוֹן בְּתוֹכָהּ כַּאֲשֶׁר דִּבַּרְתָּ, וּבְנֵה אוֹתָהּ בְּקָרוֹב בְּיָמֵינוּ בִּנְיַן עוֹלָם, וְכִסֵּא דָוִד* מְהֵרָה לְתוֹכָהּ תָּכִין. בָּרוּךְ אַתָּה יהוה, בּוֹנֵה יְרוּשָׁלָיִם.

מלכות בית דוד

אֶת צֶמַח דָּוִד* עַבְדְּךָ מְהֵרָה תַצְמִיחַ, וְקַרְנוֹ תָּרוּם בִּישׁוּעָתֶךָ, כִּי לִישׁוּעָתְךָ קִוִּינוּ כָּל הַיּוֹם. בָּרוּךְ אַתָּה יהוה, מַצְמִיחַ קֶרֶן יְשׁוּעָה.

קבלת תפלה

שְׁמַע קוֹלֵנוּ יהוה אֱלֹהֵינוּ, חוּס וְרַחֵם* עָלֵינוּ, וְקַבֵּל בְּרַחֲמִים וּבְרָצוֹן אֶת תְּפִלָּתֵנוּ, כִּי אֵל שׁוֹמֵעַ תְּפִלּוֹת וְתַחֲנוּנִים* אָתָּה. וּמִלְּפָנֶיךָ מַלְכֵּנוּ רֵיקָם אַל תְּשִׁיבֵנוּ,°

°On a fast day if the *chazzan* has not said עֲנֵנוּ (p. 104) earlier, he should insert it here.

During the silent *Shemoneh Esrei* one may insert either or both of these personal prayers.

For forgiveness:

אָנָּא יהוה, חָטָאתִי עָוִיתִי וּפָשַׁעְתִּי לְפָנֶיךָ, מִיּוֹם הֱיוֹתִי עַל הָאֲדָמָה עַד הַיּוֹם הַזֶּה (וּבִפְרַט בַּחֵטְא ....). אָנָּא יהוה, עֲשֵׂה לְמַעַן שִׁמְךָ הַגָּדוֹל, וּתְכַפֶּר לִי עַל עֲוֹנַי וַחֲטָאַי וּפְשָׁעַי שֶׁחָטָאתִי וְשֶׁעָוִיתִי וְשֶׁפָּשַׁעְתִּי לְפָנֶיךָ, מִנְּעוּרַי עַד הַיּוֹם הַזֶּה. וּתְמַלֵּא כָּל הַשֵּׁמוֹת שֶׁפָּגַמְתִּי* בְּשִׁמְךָ הַגָּדוֹל.

For livelihood:

אַתָּה הוּא יהוה הָאֱלֹהִים, הַזָּן וּמְפַרְנֵס וּמְכַלְכֵּל מִקַּרְנֵי רְאֵמִים עַד בֵּיצֵי כִנִּים.* הַטְרִיפֵנִי לֶחֶם חֻקִּי, וְהַמְצֵא לִי וּלְכָל בְּנֵי בֵיתִי מְזוֹנוֹתַי קוֹדֶם שֶׁאֶצְטָרֵךְ לָהֶם, בְּנַחַת וְלֹא בְצַעַר, בְּהֶתֵּר וְלֹא בְאִסּוּר, בְּכָבוֹד וְלֹא בְבִזָּיוֹן, לְחַיִּים וּלְשָׁלוֹם, מִשֶּׁפַע בְּרָכָה וְהַצְלָחָה, וּמִשֶּׁפַע בְּרֵכָה עֶלְיוֹנָה, כְּדֵי שֶׁאוּכַל לַעֲשׂוֹת רְצוֹנֶךָ וְלַעֲסוֹק בְּתוֹרָתֶךָ וּלְקַיֵּם מִצְוֹתֶיךָ. וְאַל תַּצְרִיכֵנִי לִידֵי מַתְּנַת בָּשָׂר וָדָם. וִיקֻיַּם בִּי מִקְרָא שֶׁכָּתוּב: פּוֹתֵחַ אֶת יָדֶךָ, וּמַשְׂבִּיעַ לְכָל חַי רָצוֹן.[1] וְכָתוּב: הַשְׁלֵךְ עַל יהוה יְהָבְךָ וְהוּא יְכַלְכְּלֶךָ.[2]

Continue— כִּי אַתָּה ...

⊰ בִּנְיַן יְרוּשָׁלַיִם / Rebuilding Jerusalem

וְלִירוּשָׁלַיִם — *And to Jerusalem.* After having sought God's blessing on Israel's leaders and righteous people, we seek His blessing for the Holy City. No blessing is complete until the seat of holiness, Jerusalem, is rebuilt in all its grandeur *(Iyun Tefillah).*

וְכִסֵּא דָוִד — *The throne of David.* Jerusalem cannot be considered rebuilt unless an heir of David sits on the throne *(R' Yitzchak Zev Soloveitchik).*

⊰ מַלְכוּת בֵּית דָּוִד / Davidic Reign

אֶת צֶמַח דָּוִד — *The offspring ... of David. Zechariah* (6:12) teaches that Messiah's name will be צֶמַח, *Tzemach,* literally, the *sprouting* or *flourishing* of a plant. This indicates that the normal process of redemption is like the barely noticeable daily growth of a plant *(Iyun Tefillah).*

David has been mentioned in the previous blessing as well. There, it indicates that the fulfillment of Jerusalem depends on the Davidic heir. Here we are taught that the ultimate salvation of the Jewish people is possible only through the Davidic Messiah.

⊰ תְּפִלָּה / Acceptance of Prayer

[In the middle section of *Shemoneh Esrei* we have asked God to grant our specific needs. We now close the section with a general plea that He

REBUILDING JERUSALEM

וְלִירוּשָׁלַיִם *And to Jerusalem,* Your city, may You return in compassion, and may You rest within it, as You have spoken. May You rebuild it soon in our days as an eternal structure, and may You speedily establish the throne of David* within it. Blessed are You, HASHEM, the Builder of Jerusalem.*

DAVIDIC REIGN

אֶת צֶמַח *The offspring of Your servant David* may You speedily cause to flourish, and enhance his pride through Your salvation, for we hope for Your salvation all day long. Blessed are You, HASHEM, Who causes the pride of salvation to flourish.*

ACCEPTANCE OF PRAYER

שְׁמַע קוֹלֵנוּ *Hear our voice, HASHEM our God, pity and be compassionate* to us, and accept — with compassion and favor — our prayer, for God Who hears prayers and supplications* are You. From before Yourself, our King, turn us not away empty-handed,°*

°On a fast day if the chazzan has not said עֲנֵנוּ (p. 104) earlier, he should insert it here.

During the silent *Shemoneh Esrei* one may insert either or both of these personal prayers.

For forgiveness:

אָנָּא *Please, O HASHEM, I have erred, been iniquitous, and willfully sinned before You, from the day I have existed on earth until this very day (and especially with the sin of ...). Please, HASHEM, act for the sake of Your Great Name and grant me atonement for my iniquities, my errors, and my willful sins through which I have erred, been iniquitous, and willfully sinned before You, from my youth until this day. And make whole all the Names that I have blemished* in Your Great Name.*

For livelihood:

אַתָּה *It is You, HASHEM the God, Who nourishes, sustains, and supports, from the horns of re'eimim to the eggs of lice.* Provide me with my allotment of bread; and bring forth for me and all members of my household, my food, before I have need for it; in contentment but not in pain, in a permissible but not a forbidden manner, in honor but not in disgrace, for life and for peace; from the flow of blessing and success and from the flow of the Heavenly spring, so that I be enabled to do Your will and engage in Your Torah and fulfill Your commandments. Make me not needful of people's largesse; and may there be fulfilled in me the verse that states, 'You open Your hand and satisfy the desire of every living thing'[1] and that states, 'Cast Your burden upon HASHEM and He will support you.'[2]*

Continue: *for You hear the prayer ...*

(1) *Psalms* 145:16. (2) 55:23.

take note of our call and grant our requests.]

חוּס וְרַחֵם — *Pity and be compassionate.* The term חוּס, *pity,* refers to an artisan's special regard for the product of his hands; while רַחֲמִים, *compassion,* describes the emotion aroused upon seeing someone who is pathetically helpless. O God — *pity* us because we are Your handiwork, and *be compassionate* because we are nothing without You! *(Vilna Gaon).*

תְּפִלּוֹת וְתַחֲנוּנִים — *Prayers and supplications. Rashi (Deut.* 3:23) explains that תַּחֲנוּן is a request for מַתְּנַת חִנָּם, *an unearned gift.* This expression is used by the most righteous people, because they are aware that no human being can claim that God 'owes' him something. *Gur Aryeh* explains that the righteous use the term תַּחֲנוּן only when praying for themselves, but when praying for the community they use תְּפִלָּה, because Israel as a *community* deserves God's help.

אָנָּא ... אַתָּה הוּא / Personal Prayers for Forgiveness and Prosperity

In the blessing שְׁמַע קוֹלֵנוּ, one may add specific, personal requests for any private or general need. *Yaaros D'vash* emphasizes that such prayers may be in any language or style, for the feelings and devotion of the supplicant are more important than the form of the prayer.

הַשֵּׁמוֹת שֶׁפָּגַמְתִּי — *The Names that I have blemished.* This Kabbalistic concept refers to the various Divine manifestations [i.e., ways in which He reveals His conduct] in the universe. These manifestations are known as God's 'Names'. By sinning, we interfere with the fulfillment of His will and thus 'blemish His

כִּי אַתָּה שׁוֹמֵעַ תְּפִלַּת עַמְּךָ יִשְׂרָאֵל בְּרַחֲמִים. בָּרוּךְ אַתָּה יהוה, שׁוֹמֵעַ תְּפִלָּה.

עבודה

רְצֵה* יהוה אֱלֹהֵינוּ בְּעַמְּךָ יִשְׂרָאֵל וּבִתְפִלָּתָם, וְהָשֵׁב אֶת הָעֲבוֹדָה* לִדְבִיר בֵּיתֶךָ. וְאִשֵּׁי יִשְׂרָאֵל* וּתְפִלָּתָם בְּאַהֲבָה תְקַבֵּל בְּרָצוֹן, וּתְהִי לְרָצוֹן תָּמִיד עֲבוֹדַת יִשְׂרָאֵל עַמֶּךָ.

On Rosh Chodesh and Chol HaMoed add the following paragraph:
(During the *chazzan's* repetition, the congregation responds אָמֵן as indicated).

אֱלֹהֵינוּ וֵאלֹהֵי אֲבוֹתֵינוּ, יַעֲלֶה, וְיָבֹא, וְיַגִּיעַ, וְיֵרָאֶה, וְיֵרָצֶה, וְיִשָּׁמַע, וְיִפָּקֵד, וְיִזָּכֵר זִכְרוֹנֵנוּ וּפִקְדוֹנֵנוּ, וְזִכְרוֹן אֲבוֹתֵינוּ, וְזִכְרוֹן מָשִׁיחַ בֶּן דָּוִד עַבְדֶּךָ, וְזִכְרוֹן יְרוּשָׁלַיִם עִיר קָדְשֶׁךָ, וְזִכְרוֹן כָּל עַמְּךָ בֵּית יִשְׂרָאֵל לְפָנֶיךָ, לִפְלֵיטָה לְטוֹבָה, לְחֵן וּלְחֶסֶד וּלְרַחֲמִים, לְחַיִּים וּלְשָׁלוֹם בְּיוֹם

on Rosh Chodesh	on Pesach	on Succos
רֹאשׁ הַחֹדֶשׁ	חַג הַמַּצּוֹת	חַג הַסֻּכּוֹת

הַזֶּה. זָכְרֵנוּ יהוה אֱלֹהֵינוּ בּוֹ לְטוֹבָה (.Cong — אָמֵן), וּפָקְדֵנוּ בוֹ לִבְרָכָה (.Cong — אָמֵן), וְהוֹשִׁיעֵנוּ בוֹ לְחַיִּים (.Cong — אָמֵן). וּבִדְבַר יְשׁוּעָה וְרַחֲמִים, חוּס וְחָנֵּנוּ וְרַחֵם עָלֵינוּ וְהוֹשִׁיעֵנוּ, כִּי אֵלֶיךָ עֵינֵינוּ, כִּי אֵל מֶלֶךְ חַנּוּן וְרַחוּם אָתָּה.[1]

[If forgotten, repeat *Shemoneh Esrei*. See *Laws* §89.]

וְתֶחֱזֶינָה עֵינֵינוּ* בְּשׁוּבְךָ לְצִיּוֹן בְּרַחֲמִים. בָּרוּךְ אַתָּה יהוה, הַמַּחֲזִיר שְׁכִינָתוֹ לְצִיּוֹן.

Names.' However, *His Great Name*, i.e., God's essence, can never be blemished, and we pray that He will rectify the effect of our sins.

מִקַּרְנֵי רְאֵמִים עַד בֵּיצֵי כִנִּים — *From the horns of re'eimim to the eggs of lice.* The expression is a Talmudic figure of speech *(Shabbos* 107b), signifying from the greatest to the smallest. Whatever the size of a living thing and whatever its needs, God supplies them. The exact translation of *re'eim* is unknown. It is variously translated as unicorn, rhinoceros, buffalo, antelope, and others. Its use in Scripture, however, indicates that it has a long and powerful horn.

עֲבוֹדָה / Temple Service

רְצֵה — *Be favorable.* This begins the final section of *Shemoneh Esrei.* Like a servant who is grateful for having had the opportunity to express himself before his master, we thank God for hearing us out.

הָעֲבוֹדָה — *The service.* As we conclude *Shemoneh Esrei,* which is our substitute for the Temple's sacrificial service, we ask that the *true* service be restored to the Temple *(Etz Yosef).*

וְאִשֵּׁי יִשְׂרָאֵל — *The fire-offerings of Israel.* Since the Temple is not standing this phrase is taken in an allegorical sense. It refers to: the souls and the deeds of the righteous, which are as pleasing as sacrifices; Jewish prayers that are like offerings; or the altar fires and sacrifices of Messianic times. Some repunctuate the blessing to read: ... *and restore the service ... and the fire-offerings of Israel. Their prayer accept with love ...*

for You hear the prayer of Your people Israel with compassion. Blessed are You, HASHEM, Who hears prayer.

TEMPLE SERVICE

רְצֵה *Be favorable,* HASHEM, our God, toward Your people Israel and their prayer and restore the service* to the Holy of Holies of Your Temple. The fire-offerings of Israel* and their prayer accept with love and favor, and may the service of Your people Israel always be favorable to You.*

On Rosh Chodesh and Chol HaMoed add the following paragraph:
(During the *chazzan's* repetition, the congregation responds *Amen* as indicated.)

אֱלֹהֵינוּ *Our God and God of our forefathers, may there rise, come, reach, be noted, be favored, be heard, be considered, and be remembered — the remembrance and consideration of ourselves; the remembrance of our forefathers; the remembrance of Messiah, son of David, Your servant; the remembrance of Jerusalem, the City of Your Holiness, the remembrance of Your entire people the Family of Israel — before You, for deliverance, for goodness, for grace, for kindness, and for compassion, for life, and for peace on this day of*

on Rosh Chodesh	on Passover	on Succos
Rosh Chodesh.	*the Festival of Matzos.*	*the Succos Festival.*

Remember us on it, HASHEM, our God, for goodness (Cong.— *Amen); consider us on it for blessing* (Cong.— *Amen); and help us on it for life* (Cong.— *Amen). In the matter of salvation and compassion, pity, be gracious and compassionate with us and help us, for our eyes are turned to You; because You are God, the gracious and compassionate King.*[1]

[If forgotten, repeat *Shemoneh Esrei*. See *Laws*, §89.]

וְתֶחֱזֶינָה *May our eyes behold* Your return to Zion in compassion. Blessed are You, HASHEM, Who restores His Presence to Zion.*

(1) Cf. *Nechemiah* 9:31.

יַעֲלֶה וְיָבֹא / Festival Prayer

On Rosh Chodesh and festivals, we add this prayer that God remember us for good and blessing. The logical place for this prayer is the רְצֵה blessing, which asks for a return of the service to the Temple, where Rosh Chodesh and festivals will be marked by special offerings. This call for a remembrance on just these days is based on *Numbers* 10:10 *(Levush, Orach Chaim* 487).

This prayer contains eight words [יַעֲלֶה ... וְיִזָּכֵר] expressing the same general idea — that our remembrance rise before God and be favorably received. *Rabbi S.R. Hirsch* offers the following interpretations of the eight expressions: May our personal behavior and fortune *rise* [יַעֲלֶה] above ordinary human existence; and *come* [וְיָבֹא] before God to merit His interest; may nothing prevent them from *reaching* [וְיַגִּיעַ] God and gaining His acceptance; may they be *noted* [וְיֵרָאֶה] in the best possible light; may they be worthy of God's *favor* [וְיֵרָצֶה]; may God *hear* [וְיִשָּׁמַע] the impact these remembrances have on our lives; may God *consider* [וְיִפָּקֵד] our needs; and may He *remember* [וְיִזָּכֵר] us and our relationship to Him.

וְתֶחֱזֶינָה עֵינֵינוּ — *May our eyes behold.* One does not see the splendor of the miracles bringing about his salvation unless he is personally worthy. Therefore, we pray that *we* may be worthy to witness the return to Zion with our own eyes *(Yaaros D'vash).*

הודאה

Bow at מוֹדִים; straighten up at 'ה. In his repetition the *chazzan* should recite the entire מוֹדִים aloud, while the congregation recites מוֹדִים דְּרַבָּנָן softly.

מוֹדִים אֲנַחְנוּ לָךְ שָׁאַתָּה הוּא יהוה אֱלֹהֵינוּ וֵאלֹהֵי אֲבוֹתֵינוּ לְעוֹלָם וָעֶד. צוּר חַיֵּינוּ,* מָגֵן יִשְׁעֵנוּ אַתָּה הוּא לְדוֹר וָדוֹר. נוֹדֶה לְּךָ* וּנְסַפֵּר תְּהִלָּתֶךָ[1] עַל חַיֵּינוּ* הַמְּסוּרִים בְּיָדֶךָ, וְעַל נִשְׁמוֹתֵינוּ הַפְּקוּדוֹת לָךְ,* וְעַל נִסֶּיךָ שֶׁבְּכָל יוֹם עִמָּנוּ, וְעַל נִפְלְאוֹתֶיךָ* וְטוֹבוֹתֶיךָ שֶׁבְּכָל עֵת, עֶרֶב וָבֹקֶר וְצָהֳרָיִם. הַטּוֹב כִּי לֹא כָלוּ רַחֲמֶיךָ, וְהַמְּרַחֵם כִּי לֹא תַמּוּ חֲסָדֶיךָ,[2] מֵעוֹלָם קִוִּינוּ לָךְ.

מוֹדִים דְּרַבָּנָן

מוֹדִים אֲנַחְנוּ לָךְ, שָׁאַתָּה הוּא יהוה אֱלֹהֵינוּ וֵאלֹהֵי אֲבוֹתֵינוּ, אֱלֹהֵי כָל בָּשָׂר, יוֹצְרֵנוּ, יוֹצֵר בְּרֵאשִׁית.* בְּרָכוֹת וְהוֹדָאוֹת לְשִׁמְךָ הַגָּדוֹל וְהַקָּדוֹשׁ, עַל שֶׁהֶחֱיִיתָנוּ וְקִיַּמְתָּנוּ. כֵּן תְּחַיֵּנוּ וּתְקַיְּמֵנוּ, וְתֶאֱסוֹף גָּלֻיּוֹתֵינוּ לְחַצְרוֹת קָדְשֶׁךָ, לִשְׁמוֹר חֻקֶּיךָ וְלַעֲשׂוֹת רְצוֹנֶךָ, וּלְעָבְדְּךָ בְּלֵבָב שָׁלֵם, עַל שֶׁאֲנַחְנוּ מוֹדִים לָךְ. בָּרוּךְ אֵל הַהוֹדָאוֹת.

On Chanukah and Purim add the following.
If forgotten, do not repeat *Shemoneh Esrei.*

(וְ)עַל הַנִּסִּים,* וְעַל הַפֻּרְקָן, וְעַל הַגְּבוּרוֹת, וְעַל הַתְּשׁוּעוֹת, וְעַל הַמִּלְחָמוֹת, שֶׁעָשִׂיתָ לַאֲבוֹתֵינוּ בַּיָּמִים הָהֵם בַּזְּמַן הַזֶּה.*

Continue ... בִּימֵי (p. 114).

הוֹדָאָה / Thanksgiving [Modim]

צוּר חַיֵּינוּ — *Rock of our lives.* Our parents are the 'rocks' from whom our bodies are hewn, but from You we receive life itself *(Etz Yosef).*

נוֹדֶה לְּךָ — *We shall thank You.* Having begun the blessing by describing God's greatness and our relationship to Him, we now specify what we thank Him for.

עַל חַיֵּינוּ — *For our lives.* Lest anyone think that he is master over his own life, we acknowledge that every breath and heartbeat is a direct result of God's mercy *(Olas Tamid).*

נִשְׁמוֹתֵינוּ הַפְּקוּדוֹת לָךְ — *Our souls that are entrusted to You.* The word נְשָׁמָה, *neshamah,* refers to the higher soul that gives man his holiness, as opposed to the lower soul that merely keeps him alive. During slumber, the *neshamah* leaves the body and is, so to speak, entrusted to God's safekeeping, to be returned to man in the morning *(Derech Hashem).*

נִסֶּיךָ ... נִפְלְאוֹתֶיךָ — *Your miracles ... Your wonders. Miracles* are the extraordinary events that everyone recognizes as the results of God's intervention. *Wonders* are the familiar things that we do not regard as miracles because we have grown accustomed to them, such as breathing, raining, and growing. We thank God for both *miracles* and *wonders,* because we know that He is their Creator *(Etz Yosef).*

מוֹדִים דְּרַבָּנָן / Modim of the Rabbis

When the *chazzan* bows and recites *Modim* in the manner of a slave accepting the total authority of his master, the congregation must join him in accepting God's sovereignty. Therefore each member of the congregation must make his own declaration of submission *(Abudraham).* The Talmud *(Sotah* 40a and *Yerushalmi* 1:8) cites the personal declarations used by a number of rabbis, and concludes that the proper custom is to recite them all. This collection of prayers was thus given the name *Modim of the Rabbis.*

THANKSGIVING [MODIM]

Bow at *'We gratefully thank You'*; straighten up at *'HASHEM'*. In his repetition the *chazzan* should recite the entire *Modim* aloud, while the congregation recites *Modim of the Rabbis* softly.

מוֹדִים *We gratefully thank You, for it is You Who are HASHEM, our God and the God of our forefathers for all eternity; Rock of our lives,* Shield of our salvation are You from generation to generation. We shall thank You* and relate Your praise[1] — for our lives,* which are committed to Your power and for our souls that are entrusted to You; *for Your miracles that are with us every day; and for Your wonders* and favors in every season — evening, morning, and afternoon. The Beneficent One, for Your compassions were never exhausted, and the Compassionate One, for Your kindnesses never ended[2] — always have we put our hope in You.*

MODIM OF THE RABBIS

מוֹדִים *We gratefully thank You, for it is You Who are HASHEM, our God and the God of our forefathers, the God of all flesh, our Molder, the Molder of the universe.* Blessings and thanks are due Your great and holy Name for You have given us life and sustained us. So may You continue to give us life and sustain us and gather our exiles to the Courtyards of Your Sanctuary, to observe Your decrees, to do Your will and to serve You wholeheartedly. [We thank You] for inspiring us to thank You. Blessed is the God of thanksgivings.*

On Chanukah and Purim add the following. If forgotten, do not repeat *Shemoneh Esrei.*

(וְ)עַל ***(And) for the miracles,* and for the salvation, and for the mighty deeds, and for the victories, and for the battles which You performed for our forefathers in those days, at this time.****

Continue *'In the days of ...'* (p. 115).

(1) Cf. *Psalms* 79:13. (2) Cf. *Lamentations* 3:22.

יוֹצֵר בְּרֵאשִׁית — *The Molder of the universe.* Although the literal meaning of בְּרֵאשִׁית is *the beginning*, it is used to mean the entire universe that was set in motion when God made the first statement of creation at the beginning of *Genesis* *(Iyun Tefillah).*

◆§ עַל הַנִּסִּים/Chanukah — Purim

This is a declaration of thanks for the miracles of Chanukah and Purim. Therefore, it is inserted in this section of *Shemoneh Esrei* that is likewise devoted to expressions of gratitude.

(וְ)עַל הַנִּסִּים — *(And) for the miracles.* Most of the early sources omit the conjunctive prefix וְ, *and*. Nevertheless, since this declaration continues the recitation of God's beneficence for which we give thanks, *Mishnah Berurah* 682 maintains that it should be said.

בַּיָּמִים הָהֵם בַּזְּמַן הַזֶּה — *In those days, at this time.* The miracles occurred in days of yore during this season — Chanukah during Kislev, and Purim during Adar. According to this view, we praise God in this prayer only for the miracles He performed for our ancestors *(Etz Yosef).*

Levush, however, holds that this phrase contains a double measure of praise: for the miracles performed in ancient days *(in those days)* and also for the countless hidden miracles that are constantly performed every day *(at this time)* to preserve life and health, both for the individual and for the nation.

There is a particular significance in the date of a miracle, because God visits the holy emanations of each miracle upon Israel annually on the date it occurred. (See *Overview*, ArtScroll edition of *Lamentations.*)

On Chanukah:

בִּימֵי מַתִּתְיָהוּ בֶּן יוֹחָנָן כֹּהֵן גָּדוֹל חַשְׁמוֹנָאִי וּבָנָיו, כְּשֶׁעָמְדָה מַלְכוּת יָוָן הָרְשָׁעָה עַל עַמְּךָ יִשְׂרָאֵל, לְהַשְׁכִּיחָם תּוֹרָתֶךָ, וּלְהַעֲבִירָם מֵחֻקֵּי רְצוֹנֶךָ.* וְאַתָּה בְּרַחֲמֶיךָ הָרַבִּים, עָמַדְתָּ לָהֶם בְּעֵת צָרָתָם, רַבְתָּ אֶת רִיבָם, דַּנְתָּ אֶת דִּינָם, נָקַמְתָּ אֶת נִקְמָתָם.[1] מָסַרְתָּ גִבּוֹרִים בְּיַד חַלָּשִׁים, וְרַבִּים בְּיַד מְעַטִּים, וּטְמֵאִים בְּיַד טְהוֹרִים, וּרְשָׁעִים בְּיַד צַדִּיקִים, וְזֵדִים* בְּיַד עוֹסְקֵי תוֹרָתֶךָ. וּלְךָ עָשִׂיתָ שֵׁם גָּדוֹל וְקָדוֹשׁ בְּעוֹלָמֶךָ, וּלְעַמְּךָ יִשְׂרָאֵל עָשִׂיתָ תְּשׁוּעָה גְדוֹלָה[2] וּפֻרְקָן כְּהַיּוֹם הַזֶּה.* וְאַחַר כֵּן* בָּאוּ בָנֶיךָ לִדְבִיר בֵּיתֶךָ, וּפִנּוּ אֶת הֵיכָלֶךָ, וְטִהֲרוּ אֶת מִקְדָּשֶׁךָ, וְהִדְלִיקוּ נֵרוֹת בְּחַצְרוֹת קָדְשֶׁךָ, וְקָבְעוּ שְׁמוֹנַת יְמֵי חֲנֻכָּה אֵלּוּ, לְהוֹדוֹת וּלְהַלֵּל לְשִׁמְךָ הַגָּדוֹל.

On Purim:

בִּימֵי מָרְדְּכַי וְאֶסְתֵּר בְּשׁוּשַׁן הַבִּירָה, כְּשֶׁעָמַד עֲלֵיהֶם* הָמָן הָרָשָׁע, בִּקֵּשׁ לְהַשְׁמִיד לַהֲרֹג וּלְאַבֵּד אֶת כָּל הַיְּהוּדִים, מִנַּעַר וְעַד זָקֵן, טַף וְנָשִׁים בְּיוֹם אֶחָד, בִּשְׁלוֹשָׁה עָשָׂר לְחֹדֶשׁ שְׁנֵים עָשָׂר, הוּא חֹדֶשׁ אֲדָר, וּשְׁלָלָם לָבוֹז.[3] וְאַתָּה בְּרַחֲמֶיךָ הָרַבִּים הֵפַרְתָּ אֶת עֲצָתוֹ, וְקִלְקַלְתָּ אֶת מַחֲשַׁבְתּוֹ, וַהֲשֵׁבוֹתָ לּוֹ גְּמוּלוֹ בְּרֹאשׁוֹ,* וְתָלוּ אוֹתוֹ וְאֶת בָּנָיו עַל הָעֵץ.

וְעַל כֻּלָּם יִתְבָּרַךְ וְיִתְרוֹמַם שִׁמְךָ מַלְכֵּנוּ תָּמִיד לְעוֹלָם וָעֶד.

From Rosh Hashanah to Yom Kippur add:

וּכְתוֹב לְחַיִּים טוֹבִים* כָּל בְּנֵי בְרִיתֶךָ.

[If forgotten, do not repeat *Shemoneh Esrei*. See *Laws* §61.]

Bend the knees at בָּרוּךְ; bow at אַתָּה; straighten up at ה'.

וְכֹל הַחַיִּים* יוֹדוּךָ סֶּלָה, וִיהַלְלוּ אֶת שִׁמְךָ בֶּאֱמֶת, הָאֵל יְשׁוּעָתֵנוּ וְעֶזְרָתֵנוּ סֶלָה. בָּרוּךְ אַתָּה יהוה, הַטּוֹב שִׁמְךָ וּלְךָ נָאֶה לְהוֹדוֹת.

חֲנוּכָּה / Chanukah ❧

לְהַשְׁכִּיחָם תּוֹרָתֶךָ וּלְהַעֲבִירָם מֵחֻקֵּי רְצוֹנֶךָ — *To make them forget Your Torah and compel them to stray from the statutes of Your Will.* The Syrian-Greeks knew that the key to the Jewish religion is the study of Torah; if Torah study were neglected, then the decline of ritual observance would be inevitable and swift. Therefore they concentrated first on causing Torah to be forgotten, knowing that the deterioration of observance would soon follow *(R' Hirsch).*

טְמֵאִים ... רְשָׁעִים ... זֵדִים — *Impure ... wicked ... wanton.* The wicked people in this passage were not the Syrian-Greeks, but their Jewish collaborators. They were טְמֵאִים, *impure,* preferring Grecian immorality to Jewish moral purity; רְשָׁעִים, *wicked,* in their lowly lack of restraint in contrast to the Jewish requirement that one stop to consider every act in the light of the Law; and זֵדִים, *wanton,* in their drive to eradicate the study of the Torah *(R' Hirsch).*

כְּהַיּוֹם הַזֶּה — *As this very day.* This is an expression used in Scripture to indicate unquestionable clarity: the miracle was as great and as obvious as this very day. [Cf. *Genesis* 25:31, 50:20; *Nechemiah* 9:10.]

וְאַחַר כֵּן — *Thereafter.* By their actions after the success of their revolt, the Jews proved that they were interested not in military victory, nor in political power, but in undisturbed service of God *(Chofetz Chaim).*

On Chanukah:

בִּימֵי *In the days of Mattisyahu, the son of Yochanan, the High Priest, the Hasmonean, and his sons — when the wicked Greek kingdom rose up against Your people Israel to make them forget Your Torah and compel them to stray from the statutes of Your Will* — You in Your great mercy stood up for them in the time of their distress. You took up their grievance, judged their claim, and avenged their wrong.[1] You delivered the strong into the hands of the weak, the many into the hands of the few, the impure into the hands of the pure, the wicked into the hands of the righteous, and the wanton* into the hands of the diligent students of Your Torah. For Yourself You made a great and holy Name in Your world, and for Your people Israel you worked a great victory[2] and salvation as this very day.* Thereafter,* Your children came to the Holy of Holies of Your House, cleansed Your Temple, purified the site of Your Holiness and kindled lights in the Courtyards of Your Sanctuary; and they established these eight days of Chanukah to express thanks and praise to Your great Name.*

On Purim:

בִּימֵי *In the days of Mordechai and Esther, in Shushan, the capital, when Haman, the wicked, rose up against them* and sought to destroy, to slay, and to exterminate all the Jews, young and old, infants and women, on the same day, on the thirteenth of the twelfth month which is the month of Adar, and to plunder their possessions.[3] But You, in Your abundant mercy, nullified his counsel and frustrated his intention and caused his design to return upon his own head* and they hanged him and his sons on the gallows.*

For all these, may Your Name be blessed and exalted, our King, continually forever and ever.

From Rosh Hashanah to Yom Kippur add the following.

*And inscribe all the children of Your covenant for a good life.**

If forgotten, do not repeat *Shemoneh Esrei.* See *Laws* §61.]

Bend the knees at *'Blessed'*; bow at *'You'*; straighten up at *'HASHEM'.*

Everything alive will gratefully acknowledge You, Selah! and praise Your Name sincerely, O God of our salvation and help, Selah! Blessed are You, HASHEM, Your Name is 'The Beneficent One' and to You it is fitting to give thanks.*

(1) Cf. *Jeremiah* 51:36. (2) Cf. *I Samuel* 19:5. (3) *Esther* 3:13.

פּוּרִים / Purim

כְּשֶׁעָמַד עֲלֵיהֶם — *When ... rose up against them.* The paragraph describing the miracle of Purim is far briefer than that describing Chanukah. The danger of Purim was straightforward — the extermination of the nation — and requires no elaboration. The peril of Chanukah was more subtle. It involved assimilation and impurity. The unaware do not perceive danger unless it is starkly physical in nature. Therefore, it requires a more elaborate explanation *(R' Hirsch).*

וַהֲשֵׁבוֹתָ לוֹ גְּמוּלוֹ בְּרֹאשׁוֹ — *And caused his design to return upon his own head.* All Haman's plans boomeranged! The gallows he prepared for Mordechai was used for him; the day he designated for the murder of the Jews became the day on which they rose up against their enemies. His primary anger was against the Jewish children, but his own children hung from the gallows he built for Mordechai *(Etz Yosef).*

וּכְתוֹב לְחַיִּים טוֹבִים — *And inscribe ... for a good life.* As we thank God for life and protection, in the period of repentance and judgment we ask God to inscribe us for a good life — *good* meaning a life dedicated to His will.

וְכֹל הַחַיִּים — *Everything alive.* As long as there is life, people can express their thanks to God. This prayer refers specifically to the universal praise that will come with the restoration of the Divine service in the rebuilt Temple.

ברכת כהנים

The *chazzan* recites בִּרְכַּת כֹּהֲנִים during his repetition, except in a house of mourning. *Chazzan* faces to the right at וְיִשְׁמְרֶךָ and to the left at פָּנָיו אֵלֶיךָ וִיחֻנֶּךָּ.

אֱלֹהֵינוּ, וֵאלֹהֵי אֲבוֹתֵינוּ, בָּרְכֵנוּ* בַבְּרָכָה הַמְשֻׁלֶּשֶׁת,* בַּתּוֹרָה הַכְּתוּבָה עַל יְדֵי מֹשֶׁה עַבְדֶּךָ, הָאֲמוּרָה מִפִּי אַהֲרֹן וּבָנָיו, כֹּהֲנִים עַם קְדוֹשֶׁךָ,* כָּאָמוּר:

יְבָרֶכְךָ יהוה,* וְיִשְׁמְרֶךָ.* (Cong.— כֵּן יְהִי רָצוֹן.)

יָאֵר יהוה פָּנָיו אֵלֶיךָ* וִיחֻנֶּךָּ.* (Cong.— כֵּן יְהִי רָצוֹן.)

יִשָּׂא יהוה פָּנָיו אֵלֶיךָ* וְיָשֵׂם לְךָ שָׁלוֹם.*[1] (Cong.— כֵּן יְהִי רָצוֹן.)

שלום

שִׂים שָׁלוֹם,* טוֹבָה, וּבְרָכָה, חֵן, וָחֶסֶד וְרַחֲמִים* עָלֵינוּ וְעַל כָּל יִשְׂרָאֵל עַמֶּךָ. בָּרְכֵנוּ אָבִינוּ, כֻּלָּנוּ כְּאֶחָד בְּאוֹר פָּנֶיךָ, כִּי בְאוֹר פָּנֶיךָ נָתַתָּ לָּנוּ, יהוה אֱלֹהֵינוּ, תּוֹרַת חַיִּים וְאַהֲבַת חֶסֶד,* וּצְדָקָה, וּבְרָכָה, וְרַחֲמִים, וְחַיִּים, וְשָׁלוֹם. וְטוֹב בְּעֵינֶיךָ לְבָרֵךְ אֶת עַמְּךָ יִשְׂרָאֵל, בְּכָל עֵת וּבְכָל שָׁעָה בִּשְׁלוֹמֶךָ.

°בָּרוּךְ אַתָּה יהוה, הַמְבָרֵךְ אֶת עַמּוֹ יִשְׂרָאֵל בַּשָּׁלוֹם.

°From Rosh Hashanah to Yom Kippur substitute the following [see *Laws* §65]:

בְּסֵפֶר חַיִּים בְּרָכָה וְשָׁלוֹם, וּפַרְנָסָה טוֹבָה, נִזָּכֵר וְנִכָּתֵב לְפָנֶיךָ, אֲנַחְנוּ וְכָל עַמְּךָ בֵּית יִשְׂרָאֵל, לְחַיִּים טוֹבִים וּלְשָׁלוֹם. בָּרוּךְ אַתָּה יהוה, עֹשֵׂה הַשָּׁלוֹם.

[If forgotten, do not repeat *Shemoneh Esrei.* See *Laws* §61.]

The *Chazzan's* repetition of *Shemoneh Esrei* ends here. Individuals continue until next page. Many hold that this verse should be recited here by individuals and the *chazzan:*

יִהְיוּ לְרָצוֹן* אִמְרֵי פִי וְהֶגְיוֹן לִבִּי לְפָנֶיךָ, יהוה צוּרִי וְגֹאֲלִי.[2]

בִּרְכַּת כֹּהֲנִים / The Priestly Blessing

God commanded Aaron and his descendants to bless the Jewish people by pronouncing the blessings listed in the Torah (*Numbers* 6:22-27). Although in earlier times the *Kohanim* pronounced these blessings every day, a centuries-old custom has developed that they do so only on Festivals when the Jewish people still feel the joy that should accompany these blessings. Only in parts of *Eretz Yisrael* and in some Sephardic communities has the original practice of daily recitation been retained. Where the *Kohanim* do not bless the nation every day, the following prayer is recited by the *chazzan* at *Shacharis, Mussaf,* and at the *Minchah* of fast days. It contains the text of the Priestly Blessing and the prayer that God fulfill it upon us.

אֱלֹהֵינוּ ... בָּרְכֵנוּ — *Our God ... bless us.* Although the blessing is pronounced by the *Kohanim,* it is God who actually gives the blessing. This is made clear in the Scriptural commandment, which ends with God's pledge וַאֲנִי אֲבָרְכֵם, *and I will bless them* (*Numbers* 2:27).

בַּבְּרָכָה הַמְשֻׁלֶּשֶׁת — *With the three-verse blessing.* The Priestly Blessing contains three verses, and it is found ... בַּתּוֹרָה הַכְּתוּבָה, *in the Torah that was written by the hand of Moses.*

עַם קְדוֹשֶׁךָ — *Your holy people.* The *Kohanim* are described as a holy people (*I Chronicles* 23:13) because they were designated to serve God and bless Israel.

יְבָרֶכְךָ ה׳ — *May* HASHEM *bless you,* with increasing wealth (*Rashi*) and long lives (*Ibn Ezra*).

וְיִשְׁמְרֶךָ — *And safeguard you.* May the above blessings be preserved against loss or attack. Only God can guarantee that no one or nothing can tamper with the gifts He confers upon His loved ones (*Midrash Rabbah*).

יָאֵר ה׳ פָּנָיו אֵלֶיךָ — *May* HASHEM *illuminate His countenance for you.* This is the blessing of spiritual growth, the light of Torah, which is symbolized by God's 'countenance' (*Sifre*).

וִיחֻנֶּךָּ — *And be gracious to you.* May you find favor in God's eyes (*Ramban*); or, may you find

THE PRIESTLY BLESSING

The *chazzan* recites the Priestly Blessing during his repetition, except in a house of mourning.

אֱלֹהֵינוּ *Our God and the God of our forefathers, bless us* with the three-verse blessing* in the Torah that was written by the hand of Moses, Your servant, that was said by Aaron and his sons, the Kohanim, Your holy people,* as it is said:*

May HASHEM bless you and safeguard you.** (Cong.— *So may it be.*)

May HASHEM illuminate His countenance for you and be gracious to you.** (Cong.— *So may it be.*)

May HASHEM turn His countenance to you and establish peace for you.**[1] (Cong.— *So may it be.*)

PEACE

שִׂים *Establish peace,* goodness, blessing, graciousness, kindness, and compassion* upon us and upon all of Your people Israel. Bless us, our Father, all of us as one, with the light of Your countenance, for with the light of Your countenance You gave us, HASHEM, our God, the Torah of life and a love of kindness,* righteousness, blessing, compassion, life, and peace. And may it be good in Your eyes to bless Your people Israel, in every season and in every hour with Your peace. °Blessed are You, HASHEM, Who blesses His people Israel with peace.*

°From Rosh Hashanah to Yom Kippur substitute the following [see *Laws* §65]:

In the book of life, blessing, and peace, good livelihood, may we be remembered and inscribed before You — we and Your entire people the Family of Israel for a good life and for peace. Blessed are You, HASHEM, Who makes peace.

[If forgotten, do not repeat *Shemoneh Esrei*. See *Laws* §61.]

The *chazzan's* repetition of *Shemoneh Esrei* ends here. Individuals continue until next page. Many hold that this verse should be recited here by individuals and the *chazzan:*

May the expressions of my mouth and the thoughts of my heart find favor before You, HASHEM, my Rock and my Redeemer.*[2]

(1) *Numbers* 6:24-26. (2) *Psalms* 19:15.

favor in the eyes of others, for all a person's talents and qualities will avail him little if others dislike him *(Ohr HaChaim).*

יִשָּׂא ה׳ פָּנָיו אֵלֶיךָ — *May HASHEM turn His countenance to you.* May He suppress His anger against you, even if you are sinful and deserve to be punished *(Rashi).* One's face is indicative of his attitude toward someone else. If he is angry, he will turn away from the one he dislikes. God 'turns His face' *toward* Israel to show that He loves them *(Maharzu).*

וְיָשֵׂם לְךָ שָׁלוֹם — *And establish peace for you.* Peace is the seal of all blessings, because without peace — prosperity, health, food, and drink are worthless *(Sifre).*

שָׁלוֹם / Peace

שִׂים שָׁלוֹם, *Establish peace,* is recited only at times when *Bircas Kohanim,* the Priestly Blessing, is pronounced *(Orach Chaim* 127:2). At other times, שָׁלוֹם רָב, *Abundant peace* is recited instead. The text of שִׂים שָׁלוֹם contains allusions to the Priestly Blessing, and the six forms of goodness listed here — peace, goodness, blessing, graciousness, kindness, and compassion — allude to the six blessings of *Bircas Kohanim (Etz Yosef).*

חֵן וָחֶסֶד וְרַחֲמִים — *Graciousness, kindness, and compassion.* Man goes through stages of development in life. When he is growing and improving, he is the recipient of God's חֵן, *graciousness.* In his period of maturity, when an individual may not improve, but continues the accomplishments of his more fruitful period, then God grants him חֶסֶד, *kindness.* Sometimes he declines or does not deserve God's help — but even then God shows רַחֲמִים, *compassion (Ikkarim).*

וְאַהֲבַת חֶסֶד — *And a love of kindness.* God is not content if we merely act kindly toward others. He wants us to *love* kindness. What someone loves to do is never a chore *(Chofetz Chaim).*

יִהְיוּ לְרָצוֹן — *May ... find favor.* We conclude *Shemoneh Esrei* with this brief prayer that our prayers find favor before God. Kabbalistic literature attaches great sanctity to this verse and stresses that it be recited slowly and fervently.

See commentary for permissible responses while reciting this final paragraph of *Shemoneh Esrei.*

אֱלֹהַי, נְצוֹר לְשׁוֹנִי מֵרָע,* וּשְׂפָתַי מִדַּבֵּר מִרְמָה,[1] וְלִמְקַלְלַי נַפְשִׁי תִדּוֹם, וְנַפְשִׁי כֶּעָפָר* לַכֹּל תִּהְיֶה. פְּתַח לִבִּי בְּתוֹרָתֶךָ,* וּבְמִצְוֹתֶיךָ תִּרְדּוֹף נַפְשִׁי. וְכֹל הַחוֹשְׁבִים עָלַי רָעָה, מְהֵרָה הָפֵר עֲצָתָם וְקַלְקֵל מַחֲשַׁבְתָּם. עֲשֵׂה לְמַעַן שְׁמֶךָ, עֲשֵׂה לְמַעַן יְמִינֶךָ, עֲשֵׂה לְמַעַן קְדֻשָּׁתֶךָ, עֲשֵׂה לְמַעַן תּוֹרָתֶךָ. לְמַעַן יֵחָלְצוּן יְדִידֶיךָ, הוֹשִׁיעָה יְמִינְךָ וַעֲנֵנִי.[2]

Some recite verses pertaining to their names at this point. See page 924.

יִהְיוּ לְרָצוֹן אִמְרֵי פִי וְהֶגְיוֹן לִבִּי לְפָנֶיךָ, יהוה צוּרִי וְגֹאֲלִי.[3]

Bow and take three steps back. Bow left and say ... עֹשֶׂה; bow right and say ... הוּא יַעֲשֶׂה; bow forward and say וְעַל כָּל ... אָמֵן.

עֹשֶׂה שָׁלוֹם בִּמְרוֹמָיו, הוּא יַעֲשֶׂה שָׁלוֹם עָלֵינוּ, וְעַל כָּל יִשְׂרָאֵל. וְאִמְרוּ: אָמֵן.

יְהִי רָצוֹן מִלְּפָנֶיךָ* יהוה אֱלֹהֵינוּ וֵאלֹהֵי אֲבוֹתֵינוּ, שֶׁיִּבָּנֶה בֵּית הַמִּקְדָּשׁ בִּמְהֵרָה בְיָמֵינוּ, וְתֵן חֶלְקֵנוּ בְּתוֹרָתֶךָ. וְשָׁם נַעֲבָדְךָ בְּיִרְאָה, כִּימֵי עוֹלָם וּכְשָׁנִים קַדְמוֹנִיּוֹת. וְעָרְבָה לַיהוה מִנְחַת יְהוּדָה וִירוּשָׁלָיִם, כִּימֵי עוֹלָם וּכְשָׁנִים קַדְמוֹנִיּוֹת.[4]

THE INDIVIDUAL'S RECITATION OF *SHEMONEH ESREI* ENDS HERE.

The individual remains standing in place until the *chazzan* reaches *Kedushah* — or at least until the *chazzan* begins his repetition — then he takes three steps forward. The *chazzan* himself, or one praying alone, should remain in place for a few moments before taking three steps forward.

On most weekdays Shacharis continues with *Tachanun.* On Mondays and Thursdays, begin *Tachanun* on p. 124; on other days, begin p. 132.

From Rosh Hashanah to Yom Kippur continue with אָבִינוּ מַלְכֵּנוּ (p. 120).

On fast days (with the exception of Tishah B'Av) *Selichos* are recited (p. 816).

On Rosh Chodesh, Chanukah, Chol HaMoed and Hoshana Rabbah continue with הַלֵּל (p. 632-542).

On other days when *Tachanun* is omitted (see p. 125 for listing) the *chazzan* recites חֲצִי קַדִּישׁ (p. 138), individuals go on to אַשְׁרֵי (p. 150).

Some authorities maintain that since יִהְיוּ לְרָצוֹן closes the *Shemoneh Esrei* prayer, it should be recited before אֱלֹהַי נְצוֹר, which is not an integral part of *Shemoneh Esrei* (see below). Others hold that since the Sages have appended אֱלֹהַי נְצוֹר, *Shemoneh Esrei* is not over until the end of אֱלֹהַי נְצוֹר, at which point יִהְיוּ לְרָצוֹן should be said. To accommodate both views, some authorities hold that יִהְיוּ לְרָצוֹן should be said both before and after אֱלֹהַי נְצוֹר.

אֱלֹהַי נְצוֹר / Concluding Prayers

Many of the Talmudic Sages composed individual supplications that they would recite at the conclusion of the prayer. Some of these supplications are cited in Berachos 16b-17a. The prayer now in universal use is based on that of Mar, son of Rabina (ibid. 18a).

While one is reciting אֱלֹהַי נְצוֹר, he may not respond to blessings and the like except for the exceptions given below. In the case of those exceptions, it is preferable to recite יִהְיוּ לְרָצוֹן before responding, but if there is not enough time to do so, the responses should be said anyway. The responses are: *Borchu,* the *amen* after הָאֵל הַקָּדוֹשׁ and שׁוֹמֵעַ תְּפִלָּה; אָמֵן יְהֵא שְׁמֵהּ רַבָּה and the last *amen* of the Half *Kaddish;* and in *Kedushah* the two verses קָדוֹשׁ and בָּרוּךְ כְּבוֹד; and the three words מוֹדִים אֲנַחְנוּ לָךְ. (See *Orach Chaim* ch. 122.)

אֱלֹהַי נְצוֹר לְשׁוֹנִי מֵרָע — *My God, guard my tongue from evil.* We pray that God protect us from situations that would tempt us to speak ill of others *(Abudraham).*

The Midrash [*Vayikra Rabbah* 33:1] relates that Rabban Shimon ben Gamliel once sent his servant, Tavi, to buy 'good food.' Tavi, who was famous for his wisdom, brought back a tongue. Thereupon Rabban Shimon sent him to buy

See commentary for permissible responses while reciting this final paragraph of *Shemoneh Esrei.*

אֱלֹהַי *My God, guard my tongue from evil* and my lips from speaking deceitfully.*[1] *To those who curse me, let my soul be silent; and let my soul be like dust* to everyone. Open my heart to Your Torah,* then my soul will pursue Your commandments. As for all those who design evil against me, speedily nullify their counsel and disrupt their design. Act for Your Name's sake; act for Your right hand's sake; act for Your sanctity's sake; act for Your Torah's sake. That Your beloved ones may be given rest; let You. right hand save, and respond to me.*[2]

Some recite verses pertaining to their names at this point. See commentary.

May the expressions of my mouth and the thoughts of my heart find favor before You, HASHEM, my Rock and my Redeemer.[3]

Bow and take three steps back. Bow left and say, *'He Who makes peace ...';* bow right and say *'may He make peace ...';* bow forward and say, *'and upon all Israel ... Amen.'*

He Who makes peace in His heights, may He make peace upon us, and upon all Israel. Now respond: Amen.

יְהִי רָצוֹן *May it be Your will,* HASHEM our God and the God of our forefathers, that the Holy Temple be rebuilt, speedily in our days. Grant us our share in Your Torah, and may we serve You there with reverence, as in days of old and in former years. Then the offering of Judah and Jerusalem will be pleasing to HASHEM, as in days of old and in former years.*[4]

THE INDIVIDUAL'S RECITATION OF *SHEMONEH ESREI* ENDS HERE.

The individual remains standing in place until the *chazzan* reaches *Kedushah* — or at least until the *chazzan* begins his repetition — then he takes three steps forward. The *chazzan* himself, or one praying alone, should remain in place for a few moments before taking three steps forward.

On most weekdays Shacharis continues with *Tachanun.* On Mondays and Thursdays, begin *Tachanun* on p. 124; on other days, begin p. 132.

From Rosh Hashanah to Yom Kippur continue with *Avinu Malkeinu* (p. 120).

On fast days (with the exception of Tishah B'Av) *Selichos* are recited (p. 816).

On Rosh Chodesh, Chanukah, Chol HaMoed and Hoshana Rabbah continue with הַלֵּל (p. 632-542).

On other days when *Tachanun* is omitted (see p. 125 for listing) the *chazzan* recites חֲצִי קַדִּישׁ (p. 138), individuals go on to אַשְׁרֵי (p. 150).

(1) Cf. *Psalms* 34:14. (2) 60:7; 108:7. (3) 19:15. (4) *Malachi* 3:4.

some bad food.' Again, he returned with a tongue. Rabban Shimon asked him to explain how the same food could be both good and bad. Tavi said, 'From a tongue can come good or bad. When a tongue speaks *good,* there is nothing better, but when a tongue speaks *ill,* there is nothing worse.'

נַפְשִׁי תִדּוֹם ... כֶּעָפָר — *Let my soul be silent ... like dust.* We should ignore barbs and insults, because the less a person cares about his prestige, the less he will let selfishness interfere with his service of God and his efforts at self-improvement *(Ruach Chaim).*

פְּתַח לִבִּי בְּתוֹרָתֶךָ — *Open my heart to Your Torah.* Our goal is to serve God in a positive manner by studying Torah and fulfilling its commandments *(Abudraham).*

◆§ Verses for People's Names

Kitzur Sh'lah teaches that it is a source of merit to recite a Torah verse that symbolizes one's name before reciting the verse יִהְיוּ לְרָצוֹן. The verse should either contain the person's name or else begin and end with the first and last letters of his name. A list of such verses may be found on page 924.

◆§ יְהִי רָצוֹן מִלְּפָנֶיךָ — *May it be Your will.* As noted above, the *Shemoneh Esrei,* as the primary prayer, takes the place of the Temple Service. Thus it is appropriate to conclude with this plea (from *Avos* 5:23) that God permit the rebuilding

ודוי

Some congregations recite the *vidui*/confessional before *Tachanun*. It is recited while standing, and is omitted on days that *Tachanun* is omitted (see p. 125).

אֱלֹהֵינוּ וֵאלֹהֵי אֲבוֹתֵינוּ, תָּבֹא לְפָנֶיךָ תְּפִלָּתֵנוּ,[1] וְאַל תִּתְעַלַּם מִתְּחִנָּתֵנוּ,[2] שֶׁאֵין אָנוּ עַזֵּי פָנִים וּקְשֵׁי עֹרֶף, לוֹמַר לְפָנֶיךָ יהוה אֱלֹהֵינוּ וֵאלֹהֵי אֲבוֹתֵינוּ, צַדִּיקִים אֲנַחְנוּ וְלֹא חָטָאנוּ, אֲבָל אֲנַחְנוּ וַאֲבוֹתֵינוּ חָטָאנוּ.[3]

Strike the left side of the chest with the right fist while reciting each of the sins of the following confessional litany:

אָשַׁמְנוּ, בָּגַדְנוּ, גָּזַלְנוּ, דִּבַּרְנוּ דֹפִי. הֶעֱוִינוּ, וְהִרְשַׁעְנוּ, זַדְנוּ, חָמַסְנוּ, טָפַלְנוּ שֶׁקֶר. יָעַצְנוּ רָע, כִּזַּבְנוּ, לַצְנוּ, מָרַדְנוּ, נִאַצְנוּ, סָרַרְנוּ, עָוִינוּ, פָּשַׁעְנוּ, צָרַרְנוּ, קִשִּׁינוּ עֹרֶף. רָשַׁעְנוּ, שִׁחַתְנוּ, תִּעַבְנוּ, תָּעִינוּ, תִּעְתָּעְנוּ.

סַרְנוּ מִמִּצְוֹתֶיךָ וּמִמִּשְׁפָּטֶיךָ הַטּוֹבִים, וְלֹא שָׁוָה לָנוּ.[4] וְאַתָּה צַדִּיק עַל כָּל הַבָּא עָלֵינוּ, כִּי אֱמֶת עָשִׂיתָ וַאֲנַחְנוּ הִרְשָׁעְנוּ.[5]

One praying without a *minyan* omits from here until לְכָל קֹרְאֶיךָ.

אֵל אֶרֶךְ אַפַּיִם אַתָּה, וּבַעַל הָרַחֲמִים נִקְרֵאתָ, וְדֶרֶךְ תְּשׁוּבָה הוֹרֵיתָ. גְּדֻלַּת רַחֲמֶיךָ וַחֲסָדֶיךָ, תִּזְכּוֹר הַיּוֹם וּבְכָל יוֹם לְזֶרַע יְדִידֶיךָ. תֵּפֶן אֵלֵינוּ בְּרַחֲמִים, כִּי אַתָּה הוּא בַּעַל הָרַחֲמִים. בְּתַחֲנוּן וּבִתְפִלָּה פָּנֶיךָ נְקַדֵּם, כְּהוֹדַעְתָּ לֶעָנָיו מִקֶּדֶם. מֵחֲרוֹן אַפְּךָ שׁוּב, כְּמוֹ בְּתוֹרָתְךָ כָּתוּב. וּבְצֵל כְּנָפֶיךָ נֶחֱסֶה וְנִתְלוֹנָן, כְּיוֹם וַיֵּרֶד יהוה בֶּעָנָן. ❖ תַּעֲבוֹר עַל פֶּשַׁע וְתִמְחֶה אָשָׁם, כְּיוֹם וַיִּתְיַצֵּב עִמּוֹ שָׁם. תַּאֲזִין שַׁוְעָתֵנוּ וְתַקְשִׁיב מֶנּוּ מַאֲמַר, כְּיוֹם וַיִּקְרָא בְשֵׁם יהוה,[6] וְשָׁם נֶאֱמַר:

Congregation and *chazzan* recite loudly and in unison:

וַיַּעֲבֹר יהוה עַל פָּנָיו וַיִּקְרָא:

יהוה, יהוה, אֵל, רַחוּם, וְחַנּוּן, אֶרֶךְ אַפַּיִם, וְרַב חֶסֶד, וֶאֱמֶת, נֹצֵר חֶסֶד לָאֲלָפִים, נֹשֵׂא עָוֹן, וָפֶשַׁע, וְחַטָּאָה, וְנַקֵּה.[7] וְסָלַחְתָּ לַעֲוֹנֵנוּ וּלְחַטָּאתֵנוּ וּנְחַלְתָּנוּ.[8] סְלַח לָנוּ אָבִינוּ כִּי חָטָאנוּ, מְחַל לָנוּ מַלְכֵּנוּ כִּי פָשָׁעְנוּ. כִּי אַתָּה אֲדֹנָי טוֹב וְסַלָּח, וְרַב חֶסֶד לְכָל קֹרְאֶיךָ.[9]

---

of the Temple so that we can perform the Service in actuality. We ask further that God give us our share in the Torah, both because of the extreme importance of Torah study and because, as noted above (p. 30), the study of the laws of the offerings takes the place of the offerings themselves.

✤ ודוי / Confession

The custom of confessing as a prelude to *Tachanun* is based on the *Zohar*. The confession, beginning with the last phrase of the opening paragraph (אֲנַחְנוּ וַאֲבוֹתֵינוּ חָטָאנוּ, *rather we and our forefathers have erred*), should be said while one stands with head and body slightly bowed to symbolize contrition and submission. It is customary to strike oneself lightly opposite the heart with the right fist while saying each individual expression of sin. This act symbolizes that sin is caused by the desires of the heart and that the beginning of repentance is the resolve to curb ones passions (*Matanos Kehunah* to *Koheles Rabbah*, ch. 7).

The confession is formulated in the plural because the Jewish people are like a single body and each of us is like one of its organs. We are responsible for one another, for the good or evil of every Jew affects us all.

The confession follows the order of the *aleph-beis* because God created the universe with the

VIDUI/CONFESSION

Some congregations recite the *vidui*/confessional before *Tachanun*.
It is recited while standing, and is omitted on days that *Tachanun* is omitted (see p. 125).

אֱלֹהֵינוּ *Our God and the God of our forefathers, may our prayer come before You,*[1] *and do not ignore our supplication*[2] *for we are not so brazen and obstinate as to say before You, HASHEM, our God, and the God of our forefathers, that we are righteous and have not sinned — rather, we and our forefathers have sinned.*[3]

Strike the left side of the chest with the right fist while reciting each of the sins of the following confessional litany:

אָשַׁמְנוּ *We have become guilty, we have betrayed, we have robbed, we have spoken slander. We have caused perversion, we have caused wickedness, we have sinned willfully, we have extorted, we have accused falsely. We have given evil counsel, we have been deceitful, we have scorned, we have rebelled, we have provoked, we have turned away, we have been perverse, we have acted wantonly, we have persecuted, we have been obstinate. We have been wicked, we have corrupted, we have been abominable, we have strayed, You have let us go astray.*

סַרְנוּ *We have turned away from Your commandments and from Your good laws but to no avail.*[4] *But You are righteous in all that has come upon us, for You have acted truthfully while we have caused wickedness.*[5]

One praying without a *minyan* omits from here until *'who call upon You.'*

אֵל *O God — You are slow to anger, You are called the Master of Mercy, and You have taught the way of repentance. May You remember this day and every day the greatness of Your mercy and Your kindness to the offspring of Your beloved Ones. Turn to us in mercy for You are the Master of Mercy. With supplication and prayer we approach Your Presence in the manner that You made known to the humble one [Moses] in ancient times. Turn back from Your fierce anger as it is written in Your Torah. In the shadow of Your wings may we find shelter and lodging as on the day 'HASHEM descended in a cloud' [to appear to Moses on Sinai].* Chazzan—*Overlook sin and erase guilt as on the day 'He [God] stood there with him [Moses].' Give heed to our cry and hearken to our declaration as on day of 'He called out with the Name HASHEM,'*[6] *and there it was said:*

Congregation and *chazzan* recite loudly and in unison:

And HASHEM passed before him [Moses] and proclaimed:

יהוה *HASHEM, HASHEM, God, Compassionate and Gracious, Slow to anger, and Abundant in Kindness and Truth. Preserver of kindness for thousands of generations, Forgiver of iniquity, willful sin, and error, and Who cleanses.*[7] *May You forgive our iniquities and our errors and make us Your heritage.*[8] *Forgive us, our Father, for we have erred; pardon us, our King, for we have willfully sinned; for You, my Lord, are good and forgiving and abundantly kind to all who call upon You.*[9]

(1) Cf. *Psalms* 88:3. (2) Cf. 55:2. (3) Cf. 106:6. (4) Cf. *Job* 33:27.
(5) *Nechemiah* 9:33. (6) *Exodus* 34:5. (7) 34:6-7. (8) 34:9. (9) *Psalms* 86:5.

---

sacred letters (see Overview to ArtScroll *Wisdom of the Hebrew Alphabet*), and our sins have damaged that Creation. By expressing our repentance through the very letters whose accomplishments we have tainted, we help repair the damage our sins have caused.

⋄§ אֵל אֶרֶךְ אַפַּיִם וי״ג מדּוֹת הָרַחֲמִים / O God — You Are Slow to Anger
The Thirteen Attributes of Mercy

The *Zohar* teaches that the Thirteen Attributes of Mercy should always be recited with *Tachanun*. The paragraph אֵל אֶרֶךְ אַפַּיִם

אבינו מלכנו

From Rosh Hashanah to Yom Kippur and on fast days, most congregations recite אָבִינוּ מַלְכֵּנוּ after *Shemoneh Esrei* of both *Shacharis* and *Minchah* [except on those days on which *Tachanun* is omitted (see box, p. 125); when Erev Yom Kippur falls on a Friday, however, אָבִינוּ מַלְכֵּנוּ is recited during *Shacharis,* even though *Tachanun* is omitted.]

On public fast days, *Selichos* (p. 820) are recited at *Shacharis* before אָבִינוּ מַלְכֵּנוּ.

The doors of the Ark are kept open while אָבִינוּ מַלְכֵּנוּ is recited. [As the Ark is opened, some say the words: 'פְּתַח שַׁעֲרֵי שָׁמַיִם לִתְפִלָּתֵנוּ, *Open the gates of heaven to our prayer.*']

אָבִינוּ מַלְכֵּנוּ, חָטָאנוּ לְפָנֶיךָ.

אָבִינוּ מַלְכֵּנוּ, אֵין לָנוּ מֶלֶךְ אֶלָּא אָתָּה.

אָבִינוּ מַלְכֵּנוּ, עֲשֵׂה עִמָּנוּ לְמַעַן שְׁמֶךָ.

אָבִינוּ מַלְכֵּנוּ, (חַדֵּשׁ —from Rosh Hashanah to Yom Kippur)(בָּרֵךְ —on fast days)
עָלֵינוּ שָׁנָה טוֹבָה.

אָבִינוּ מַלְכֵּנוּ, בַּטֵּל מֵעָלֵינוּ כָּל גְּזֵרוֹת קָשׁוֹת.

אָבִינוּ מַלְכֵּנוּ, בַּטֵּל מַחְשְׁבוֹת שׂוֹנְאֵינוּ.

אָבִינוּ מַלְכֵּנוּ, הָפֵר עֲצַת אוֹיְבֵינוּ.

אָבִינוּ מַלְכֵּנוּ, כַּלֵּה כָּל צַר וּמַשְׂטִין מֵעָלֵינוּ.

אָבִינוּ מַלְכֵּנוּ, סְתוֹם פִּיּוֹת מַשְׂטִינֵנוּ וּמְקַטְרִיגֵנוּ.

אָבִינוּ מַלְכֵּנוּ, כַּלֵּה דֶּבֶר וְחֶרֶב וְרָעָב וּשְׁבִי וּמַשְׁחִית וְעָוֺן וּשְׁמַד מִבְּנֵי בְרִיתֶךָ.

אָבִינוּ מַלְכֵּנוּ, מְנַע מַגֵּפָה מִנַּחֲלָתֶךָ.

אָבִינוּ מַלְכֵּנוּ, סְלַח וּמְחַל לְכָל עֲוֹנוֹתֵינוּ.

אָבִינוּ מַלְכֵּנוּ, מְחֵה וְהַעֲבֵר פְּשָׁעֵינוּ וְחַטֹּאתֵינוּ מִנֶּגֶד עֵינֶיךָ.

אָבִינוּ מַלְכֵּנוּ, מְחוֹק בְּרַחֲמֶיךָ הָרַבִּים כָּל שִׁטְרֵי חוֹבוֹתֵינוּ.

The next nine verses are recited responsively, first by the *chazzan* and then by the congregation.

אָבִינוּ מַלְכֵּנוּ, הַחֲזִירֵנוּ בִּתְשׁוּבָה שְׁלֵמָה לְפָנֶיךָ.

אָבִינוּ מַלְכֵּנוּ, שְׁלַח רְפוּאָה שְׁלֵמָה לְחוֹלֵי עַמֶּךָ.

אָבִינוּ מַלְכֵּנוּ, קְרַע רוֹעַ גְּזַר דִּינֵנוּ.

אָבִינוּ מַלְכֵּנוּ, זָכְרֵנוּ בְּזִכָּרוֹן טוֹב לְפָנֶיךָ.

On fast days:

אָבִינוּ מַלְכֵּנוּ, זָכְרֵנוּ לְחַיִּים טוֹבִים.

אָבִינוּ מַלְכֵּנוּ, זָכְרֵנוּ לִגְאֻלָּה וִישׁוּעָה.

From Rosh Hashanah to Yom Kippur:

אָבִינוּ מַלְכֵּנוּ, כָּתְבֵנוּ בְּסֵפֶר חַיִּים טוֹבִים.

אָבִינוּ מַלְכֵּנוּ, כָּתְבֵנוּ בְּסֵפֶר גְּאֻלָּה וִישׁוּעָה.

---

introduces the Thirteen Attributes.

The verse of the Thirteen Attributes may be said only in the presence of a *minyan.* If there is no *minyan,* it may be recited not in the form of a

AVINU MALKEINU

From Rosh Hashanah to Yom Kippur and on fast days, most congregations recite אָבִינוּ מַלְכֵּנוּ, *Avinu Malkeinu,* after *Shemoneh Esrei* of both *Shacharis* and *Minchah* [except on those days on which *Tachanun* is omitted (see box, p. 125); when Erev Yom Kippur falls on a Friday, however, *Avinu Malkeinu* is recited during *Shacharis,* even though *Tachanun* is omitted].

On public fast days, *Selichos* (p. 820) are recited at *Shacharis* before אָבִינוּ מַלְכֵּנוּ, *Avinu Malkeinu.*

The doors of the Ark are kept open while *Avinu Malkeinu* is recited. [As the Ark is opened, some say the words: *'Open the gates of heaven to our prayer.'*]

אָבִינוּ מַלְכֵּנוּ *Our Father, our King, we have sinned before You.*

Our Father, our King, we have no King but You.

Our Father, our King, deal [kindly] with us for Your Name's sake.

Our Father, our King, (on fast days: *bless us with a good year).*

(from Rosh Hashanah to Yom Kippur: *inaugurate upon us a good year).*

Our Father, our King, nullify all harsh decrees upon us.

Our Father, our King, nullify the designs of those who hate us.

Our Father, our King, thwart the counsel of our enemies.

Our Father, our King, exterminate every foe and adversary from upon us.

Our Father, our King, seal the mouths of our adversaries and accusers.

Our Father, our King, exterminate pestilence, sword, famine, captivity, destruction, iniquity and eradication from the members of Your covenant.

Our Father, our King, withhold the plague from Your heritage.

Our Father, our King, forgive and pardon all our iniquities.

Our Father, our King, wipe away and remove our willful sins and errors from Your sight.

Our Father, our King, erase through Your abundant compassion all records of our guilt.

The next nine verses are recited responsively, first by the *chazzan* and then by the congregation.

Our Father, our King, return us to You in perfect repentance.

Our Father, our King, send complete recovery to the sick of Your people.

Our Father, our King, tear up the evil decree of our verdict.

Our Father, our King, recall us with a favorable memory before You.

On fast days:

Our Father, our King, remember us for a good life.

Our Father, our King, remember us for redemption and salvation.

From Rosh Hashanah to Yom Kippur:

Our Father, our King, inscribe us in the book of good life.

Our Father, our King, inscribe us in the book of redemption and salvation.

---

prayer, but in the manner of reading from the Torah, that is, with the musical cantillation *(trop)* of the Torah reading *(Orach Chaim* 565:5).

אָבִינוּ מַלְכֵּנוּ / AVINU MALKEINU

Avinu Malkeinu, which is recited on fast days and during the Ten Days of Repentance between Rosh Hashanah and Yom Kippur, combines pleas for our personal and national needs with expressions of repentance. The prayer is based on an incident in the life of Rabbi Akiva as related in the Talmud *(Taanis* 25b). During a

On fast days:

אָבִינוּ מַלְכֵּנוּ, זָכְרֵנוּ לְפַרְנָסָה וְכַלְכָּלָה.
אָבִינוּ מַלְכֵּנוּ, זָכְרֵנוּ לִזְכֻיּוֹת.
אָבִינוּ מַלְכֵּנוּ, זָכְרֵנוּ לִסְלִיחָה וּמְחִילָה.

From Rosh Hashanah to Yom Kippur:

אָבִינוּ מַלְכֵּנוּ, כָּתְבֵנוּ בְּסֵפֶר פַּרְנָסָה וְכַלְכָּלָה.
אָבִינוּ מַלְכֵּנוּ, כָּתְבֵנוּ בְּסֵפֶר זְכֻיּוֹת.
אָבִינוּ מַלְכֵּנוּ, כָּתְבֵנוּ בְּסֵפֶר סְלִיחָה וּמְחִילָה.

End of responsive reading.

אָבִינוּ מַלְכֵּנוּ, הַצְמַח לָנוּ יְשׁוּעָה בְּקָרוֹב.
אָבִינוּ מַלְכֵּנוּ, הָרֵם קֶרֶן יִשְׂרָאֵל עַמֶּךָ.
אָבִינוּ מַלְכֵּנוּ, הָרֵם קֶרֶן מְשִׁיחֶךָ.
אָבִינוּ מַלְכֵּנוּ, מַלֵּא יָדֵינוּ מִבִּרְכוֹתֶיךָ.
אָבִינוּ מַלְכֵּנוּ, מַלֵּא אֲסָמֵינוּ שָׂבָע.
אָבִינוּ מַלְכֵּנוּ, שְׁמַע קוֹלֵנוּ, חוּס וְרַחֵם עָלֵינוּ.
אָבִינוּ מַלְכֵּנוּ, קַבֵּל בְּרַחֲמִים וּבְרָצוֹן אֶת תְּפִלָּתֵנוּ.
אָבִינוּ מַלְכֵּנוּ, פְּתַח שַׁעֲרֵי שָׁמַיִם לִתְפִלָּתֵנוּ.
אָבִינוּ מַלְכֵּנוּ, זָכוֹר כִּי עָפָר אֲנָחְנוּ.
אָבִינוּ מַלְכֵּנוּ, נָא אַל תְּשִׁיבֵנוּ רֵיקָם מִלְּפָנֶיךָ.
אָבִינוּ מַלְכֵּנוּ, תְּהֵא הַשָּׁעָה הַזֹּאת שְׁעַת רַחֲמִים וְעֵת רָצוֹן מִלְּפָנֶיךָ.
אָבִינוּ מַלְכֵּנוּ, חֲמוֹל עָלֵינוּ וְעַל עוֹלָלֵינוּ וְטַפֵּנוּ.
אָבִינוּ מַלְכֵּנוּ, עֲשֵׂה לְמַעַן הֲרוּגִים עַל שֵׁם קָדְשֶׁךָ.
אָבִינוּ מַלְכֵּנוּ, עֲשֵׂה לְמַעַן טְבוּחִים עַל יִחוּדֶךָ.
אָבִינוּ מַלְכֵּנוּ, עֲשֵׂה לְמַעַן בָּאֵי בָאֵשׁ וּבַמַּיִם עַל קִדּוּשׁ שְׁמֶךָ.
אָבִינוּ מַלְכֵּנוּ, נְקוֹם לְעֵינֵינוּ נִקְמַת דַּם עֲבָדֶיךָ הַשָּׁפוּךְ.
אָבִינוּ מַלְכֵּנוּ, עֲשֵׂה לְמַעַנְךָ אִם לֹא לְמַעֲנֵנוּ.
אָבִינוּ מַלְכֵּנוּ, עֲשֵׂה לְמַעַנְךָ וְהוֹשִׁיעֵנוּ.
אָבִינוּ מַלְכֵּנוּ, עֲשֵׂה לְמַעַן רַחֲמֶיךָ הָרַבִּים.
אָבִינוּ מַלְכֵּנוּ, עֲשֵׂה לְמַעַן שִׁמְךָ הַגָּדוֹל הַגִּבּוֹר וְהַנּוֹרָא, שֶׁנִּקְרָא עָלֵינוּ.

❖ אָבִינוּ מַלְכֵּנוּ, חָנֵּנוּ וַעֲנֵנוּ, כִּי אֵין בָּנוּ מַעֲשִׂים, עֲשֵׂה עִמָּנוּ צְדָקָה וָחֶסֶד וְהוֹשִׁיעֵנוּ.

On fast days:

Our Father, our King, remember us for sustenance and support.
Our Father, our King, remember us for merits.
Our Father, our King, remember us for forgiveness and pardon.

From Rosh Hashanah to Yom Kippur:

Our Father, our King, inscribe us in the book of sustenance and support.
Our Father, our King, inscribe us in the book of merits.
Our Father, our King, inscribe us in the book of forgiveness and pardon.

End of responsive reading.

Our Father, our King, make salvation sprout for us soon.
Our Father, our King, raise high the pride of Israel, Your people.
Our Father, our King, raise high the pride of Your anointed.
Our Father, our King, fill our hands from Your blessings.
Our Father, our King, fill our storehouses with abundance.
Our Father, our King, hear our voice, pity and be compassionate to us.
Our Father, our King, accept — with compassion and favor — our prayer.
Our Father, our King, open the gates of heaven to our prayer.
Our Father, our King, remember that we are but dust.
Our Father, our King, please do not turn us from You empty-handed.
Our Father, our King, may this moment be a moment of compassion and a time of favor before You.
Our Father, our King, take pity upon us, and upon our children and our infants.
Our Father, our King, act for the sake of those who were murdered for Your Holy Name.
Our Father, our King, act for the sake of those who were slaughtered for Your Oneness.
Our Father, our King, act for the sake of those who went into fire and water for the sanctification of Your Name.
Our Father, our King, avenge before our eyes the spilled blood of Your servants.
Our Father, our King, act for Your sake if not for our sake.
Our Father, our King, act for Your sake and save us.
Our Father, our King, act for the sake of Your abundant compassion.
Our Father, our King, act for the sake of Your great, mighty, and awesome Name that is proclaimed upon us.

Chazzan— *Our Father, our King, be gracious with us and answer us, though we have no worthy deeds; treat us with charity and kindness, and save us.*

---

drought, the Sages proclaimed a day of public fast and prayer, but no rain fell. Thereupon Rabbi Akiva said five brief supplications, each beginning *Our Father, our King,* and it began to

❀{ תחנון }❀

On Monday and Thursday mornings, the longer form of *Tachanun,* beginning וְהוּא רַחוּם (below) is recited. On other weekday mornings, *Tachanun* begins with וַיֹּאמֶר דָּוִד, (p. 132). However, *Tachanun* is not recited on all days. The exceptions are listed below (see box).
Remain standing from the beginning of וְהוּא רַחוּם until וַיֹּאמֶר דָּוִד, p. 132.

וְהוּא רַחוּם* יְכַפֵּר עָוֹן וְלֹא יַשְׁחִית, וְהִרְבָּה לְהָשִׁיב אַפּוֹ
וְלֹא יָעִיר כָּל חֲמָתוֹ.[1] אַתָּה יהוה, לֹא תִכְלָא
רַחֲמֶיךָ מִמֶּנּוּ, חַסְדְּךָ וַאֲמִתְּךָ תָּמִיד יִצְּרוּנוּ.[2] הוֹשִׁיעֵנוּ יהוה
אֱלֹהֵינוּ וְקַבְּצֵנוּ מִן הַגּוֹיִם, לְהוֹדוֹת לְשֵׁם קָדְשֶׁךָ, לְהִשְׁתַּבֵּחַ
בִּתְהִלָּתֶךָ.[3] אִם עֲוֹנוֹת תִּשְׁמָר* יָהּ, אֲדֹנָי מִי יַעֲמֹד. כִּי עִמְּךָ
הַסְּלִיחָה, לְמַעַן תִּוָּרֵא.[4] לֹא כַחֲטָאֵינוּ תַּעֲשֶׂה לָנוּ, וְלֹא
כַעֲוֹנוֹתֵינוּ תִּגְמֹל עָלֵינוּ.[5] אִם עֲוֹנֵינוּ עָנוּ בָנוּ, יהוה עֲשֵׂה לְמַעַן
שְׁמֶךָ.[6]* זְכֹר רַחֲמֶיךָ יהוה וַחֲסָדֶיךָ, כִּי מֵעוֹלָם הֵמָּה.[7] יַעֲנֵנוּ
יהוה בְּיוֹם צָרָה, יְשַׂגְּבֵנוּ שֵׁם אֱלֹהֵי יַעֲקֹב.[8] יהוה הוֹשִׁיעָה,
הַמֶּלֶךְ יַעֲנֵנוּ בְיוֹם קָרְאֵנוּ.[9] אָבִינוּ מַלְכֵּנוּ חָנֵּנוּ וַעֲנֵנוּ, כִּי

---

rain.

Over the course of the generations, various communities added brief prayers with this beginning. This explains why Rabbi Akiva's five supplications have grown to over forty, and, in the Sephardic rite, over fifty. The introductory formula expresses our dual relationship to God: because He created and loves us, He is our merciful *Father;* because it is our duty to serve Him, He is our *King.*

The Sabbath and festivals are days of joy and contentment when it is not proper to pray for specific needs or to recall sad thoughts. *Avinu Malkeinu* is inappropriate on these days because: (a) many of its verses parallel specific requests of the weekday *Shemoneh Esrei,* such as those for health, prosperity, forgiveness, etc., which are omitted on festive days; and (b) it was composed originally for times of distress.

❀{ תַּחֲנוּן / TACHANUN }❀

The Talmud *(Bava Metzia* 59a) teaches that if one submissively places his head upon his arm in fervent, intense prayer immediately after *Shemoneh Esrei,* his prayer is warmly accepted by God and can achieve great results. Therefore, there must be no significant interruption between *Shemoneh Esrei* and this prayer, which is known as תַּחֲנוּן, *Tachanun,* lit. *supplication,* a term that implies an especially heartfelt plea for God's gracious compassion. The essential part of *Tachanun* is נְפִילַת אַפַּיִם, lit. *falling on the face,* which begins with וַיֹּאמֶר דָּוִד, *And David said, (p. 132).*

On Mondays and Thursdays, the *Tachanun* service is augmented with additional supplications prior to and following the 'falling on the face.' The choice of these two days for special prayers is based on one of the earliest events in Israel's national history. According to the Midrashic tradition, Moses ascended Mount Sinai to receive the Second Tablets on Thursday, the first day of Elul, and descended forty days later on Monday, Yom Kippur. Since those were days when God accepted Israel's repentance for the sin of the Golden Calf, and demonstrated His love for Israel with the greatest of all gifts — the Torah, in the form of the Second Tablets — Monday and Thursday remain days of Divine mercy (see *Bava Kamma* 82a; *Tos. s.v.* כדי). Ezra instituted that rabbinical courts should convene on Monday and Thursday, and Kabbalistic literature teaches that on these days the Heavenly Court judges man. Consequently, extra supplications were introduced into the *Tachanun* recited each Monday and Thursday. These supplications must be said while standing and, because of their nature, with great feeling.

Kol Bo and others record a tradition regarding the authorship of these prayers. Three elders, Rabbi Shmuel, Rabbi Binyamin, and Rabbi Yosef, were set adrift on rudderless boats by the Romans after the destruction of Jerusalem. They landed on a distant shore where they were persecuted by the local ruler. Each of the three composed a prayer requesting the easing of their plight. God heeded their supplications: the ruler died and was succeeded by a benevolent king who treated the three with respect and kindness. Seeing that their prayers had been pleasing to God, they distributed copies of the text to other Jewish communities, which added them to the

TACHANUN

On Monday and Thursday mornings, the longer form of *Tachanun,* beginning with *'He, the Merciful One'* (below), is recited. On other weekday mornings, *Tachanun* begins with, *'And David said ...'* (p. 133). However, *Tachanun* is not recited on all days. The exceptions are listed below (see box).

Remain standing from *'He the Merciful One ...',* until *'And David said ...'* (p. 133).

וְהוּא רַחוּם *He, the Merciful One,* is forgiving of iniquity and does not destroy, frequently withdrawing His anger, not arousing His entire rage.*[1] *You, HASHEM — withhold not Your mercy from us; may Your kindness and Your truth always protect us.*[2] *Save us, HASHEM, our God, and gather us from among the peoples, to give thanks to Your Holy Name and to glory in Your praise.*[3] *If You preserve iniquities,* O God, my Lord, who could survive? For with You is forgiveness, that You may be feared.*[4] *Do not treat us according to our sins, do not repay us according to our iniquities.*[5] *Though our iniquities testify against us, O HASHEM, act for Your Name's sake.**[6] *Remember Your mercies, HASHEM, and Your kindnesses, for they are from the beginning of the world.*[7] *May HASHEM answer us on the day of distress, may the Name of Jacob's God make us impregnable.*[8] *HASHEM, save — the King will answer us on the day we call.*[9] *Our Father, our King, be gracious with us and answer us though*

(1) *Psalms* 78:38. (2) Cf. 40:12. (3) 106:47. (4) 130:3-4. (5) Cf. 103:10.
(6) *Jeremiah* 14:7. (7) *Psalms* 25:6. (8) Cf. 20:2. (9) 20:10.

Tachanun of Monday and Thursday.

וְהוּא רַחוּם — *He, the Merciful One.* In a mystical comment on this verse, *Zohar* teaches that God, in His mercy, does not allow the forces of impurity to prevent our prayers from reaching Him. Were they to succeed, we could never hope to achieve forgiveness.

אִם עֲוֹנוֹת תִּשְׁמָר — *If You preserve iniquities.* By virtue of man's human frailties he cannot survive unless God is willing to overlook his sins to some degree. The next verse continues that since we are fully aware that only God — not an angel or any other power — can forgive, we stand in awe of Him *(Iyun Tefillah).*

לְמַעַן שְׁמֶךָ — *For Your Name's sake.* In a theme repeated often in *Tachanun* and elsewhere, we make the point that if Israel is permitted to suffer excessively, God's *Own* Name is desecrated because it appears as though He is powerless to help His chosen ones. In pleading for Israel after the sins of the Golden Calf and the spies, Moses also argued that if Israel were to perish, the Egyptians would claim that it was because God did not intend, or was unable, to bring them into the Land of Israel *(Exodus* 32:12, *Numbers* 14:16).

Occasions and Days on which Tachanun Is Omitted

(a) In a house of mourning during the *shivah* period;
(b) In the presence of a bridegroom, from the day of his wedding until after the *Sheva Berachos* week (if both bride and groom have been previously married, their period of celebration extends for only three days);
(c) In the synagogue where a circumcision will take place later that day, or in the presence of a primary participant (i.e., the father, the *mohel* or the *sandak)* in a circumcision that will take place later that day;
(d) On the Sabbath; festivals (including Chol Hamoed); Rosh Chodesh; the entire month of Nissan; Lag B'Omer; from Rosh Chodesh Sivan until the day after Shavuos (some congregations do not resume *Tachanun* until 14 Sivan); Tishah B'Av; 15 Av; between Yom Kippur and the day after Succos (some congregations do not resume until 2 Cheshvan); Chanukah; Tu B'Shevat; Purim and Shushan Purim (in a leap year this applies also to 14-15 Adar I); or at *Minchah* of the day preceding any of the days listed above;
(e) On Erev Rosh Hashanah and Erev Yom Kippur;
(f) In some congregations, it is omitted on Pesach Sheni (14 Iyar).

אֵין בָּֽנוּ מַעֲשִׂים, צְדָקָה עֲשֵׂה עִמָּֽנוּ לְמַֽעַן שְׁמֶֽךָ. אֲדוֹנֵֽינוּ אֱלֹהֵֽינוּ,
שְׁמַע קוֹל תַּחֲנוּנֵֽינוּ, וּזְכָר־לָֽנוּ אֶת בְּרִית אֲבוֹתֵֽינוּ וְהוֹשִׁיעֵֽנוּ לְמַֽעַן
שְׁמֶֽךָ.

וְעַתָּה אֲדֹנָי אֱלֹהֵֽינוּ,* אֲשֶׁר הוֹצֵֽאתָ אֶת עַמְּךָ מֵאֶֽרֶץ
מִצְרַֽיִם בְּיָד חֲזָקָה וַתַּֽעַשׂ לְךָ שֵׁם כַּיּוֹם הַזֶּה, חָטָֽאנוּ רָשָֽׁעְנוּ.
אֲדֹנָי, כְּכָל צִדְקֹתֶֽיךָ יָֽשָׁב נָא אַפְּךָ וַחֲמָתְךָ מֵעִירְךָ יְרוּשָׁלַֽיִם הַר
קָדְשֶֽׁךָ, כִּי בַחֲטָאֵֽינוּ וּבַעֲוֹנוֹת אֲבֹתֵֽינוּ, יְרוּשָׁלַֽיִם וְעַמְּךָ לְחֶרְפָּה
לְכָל סְבִיבֹתֵֽינוּ. וְעַתָּה שְׁמַע אֱלֹהֵֽינוּ אֶל תְּפִלַּת עַבְדְּךָ וְאֶל
תַּחֲנוּנָיו, וְהָאֵר פָּנֶֽיךָ עַל מִקְדָּשְׁךָ הַשָּׁמֵם, לְמַֽעַן אֲדֹנָי.*[1]

הַטֵּה אֱלֹהַי אָזְנְךָ* וּשֲׁמָע, פְּקַח עֵינֶֽיךָ וּרְאֵה שֹׁמְמֹתֵֽינוּ, וְהָעִיר
אֲשֶׁר נִקְרָא שִׁמְךָ עָלֶֽיהָ, כִּי לֹא עַל צִדְקֹתֵֽינוּ אֲנַֽחְנוּ
מַפִּילִים תַּחֲנוּנֵֽינוּ לְפָנֶֽיךָ, כִּי עַל רַחֲמֶֽיךָ הָרַבִּים. אֲדֹנָי שְׁמָֽעָה,
אֲדֹנָי סְלָֽחָה, אֲדֹנָי הַקְשִֽׁיבָה וַעֲשֵׂה, אַל תְּאַחַר, לְמַעַנְךָ אֱלֹהַי,
כִּי שִׁמְךָ נִקְרָא* עַל עִירְךָ וְעַל עַמֶּֽךָ.[2] אָבִֽינוּ הָאָב הָרַחֲמָן,*
הַרְאֵֽנוּ אוֹת לְטוֹבָה וְקַבֵּץ נְפוּצֹתֵֽינוּ מֵאַרְבַּע כַּנְפוֹת הָאָֽרֶץ, יַכִּֽירוּ
וְיֵדְעוּ כָּל הַגּוֹיִם, כִּי אַתָּה יהוה אֱלֹהֵֽינוּ. וְעַתָּה יהוה אָבִֽינוּ אָֽתָּה,
אֲנַֽחְנוּ הַחֹֽמֶר וְאַתָּה יֹצְרֵֽנוּ, וּמַעֲשֵׂה יָדְךָ כֻּלָּֽנוּ.[3] הוֹשִׁיעֵֽנוּ לְמַֽעַן
שְׁמֶֽךָ, צוּרֵֽנוּ מַלְכֵּֽנוּ וְגֹאֲלֵֽנוּ. חֽוּסָה* יהוה עַל עַמֶּֽךָ וְאַל תִּתֵּן
נַחֲלָתְךָ לְחֶרְפָּה לִמְשָׁל בָּם גּוֹיִם. לָֽמָּה יֹאמְרוּ בָעַמִּים, אַיֵּה
אֱלֹהֵיהֶם.[4] יָדַֽעְנוּ כִּי חָטָֽאנוּ וְאֵין מִי יַעֲמֹד בַּעֲדֵֽנוּ, שִׁמְךָ הַגָּדוֹל
יַעֲמָד־לָֽנוּ בְּעֵת צָרָה. יָדַֽעְנוּ כִּי אֵין בָּֽנוּ מַעֲשִׂים, צְדָקָה עֲשֵׂה
עִמָּֽנוּ לְמַֽעַן שְׁמֶֽךָ. כְּרַחֵם אָב עַל בָּנִים, כֵּן תְּרַחֵם יהוה עָלֵֽינוּ,[5]
וְהוֹשִׁיעֵֽנוּ לְמַֽעַן שְׁמֶֽךָ. חֲמֹל עַל עַמֶּֽךָ, רַחֵם עַל נַחֲלָתֶֽךָ, חֽוּסָה
נָא כְּרֹב רַחֲמֶֽיךָ. חָנֵּֽנוּ וַעֲנֵֽנוּ, כִּי לְךָ יהוה הַצְּדָקָה, עֹשֵׂה נִפְלָאוֹת
בְּכָל עֵת.

וְעַתָּה ה' אֱלֹהֵֽינוּ — *And now, My Lord our God.* The next five verses are the end of a long, sixteen-verse prayer recited by Daniel (9:4-19). When Daniel came to fear that the Babylonian exile might never end, he pleaded for God's guidance and help. The prayer had three components that are familiar parts of Jewish supplications: praise of God, confession, and the prayer itself. This paragraph of *Tachanun* is concluded with the last three verses of Daniel's confession. The next paragraph begins with his

two verses of prayer.

לְמַֽעַן אֲדֹנָי — *For my Lord's sake.* In a homiletical interpretation the Sages say that this refers to Abraham, who preached to an unknowing world that only Hashem is the true Lord [אֲדֹנָי]. Thus: 'Help us for the sake of the one who proclaimed You as the Lord' (*Berachos* 7b).

הַטֵּה אֱלֹהַי אָזְנְךָ — *Incline Your ear, my God.* Despite the sins we have just confessed, we plead with God to heed our call. Even if we are not

we have no worthy deeds; treat us with charity for Your Name's sake. Our Master, our God, hear the sound of our supplications; recall for us the covenant of our forefathers and save us for Your Name's sake.

And now, My Lord our God, Who has taken Your people out of the land of Egypt with a strong hand and gained Yourself renown as of this day — we have sinned and acted wickedly. My Lord, in keeping with all Your righteousness, please let Your anger and Your fury turn away from Your city Jerusalem, Your holy mountain; for because of our sins and the iniquities of our ancestors, Jerusalem and Your people have become the scorn of all those around us. And now, pay heed, our God, to the prayer of Your servant and to his supplications, and let Your countenance shine upon Your desolate Sanctuary for my Lord's sake.*[1]*

הַטֵּה *Incline Your ear, my God,* and listen, open Your eyes and see our desolation and that of the city upon which Your Name is proclaimed; for not because of our righteousness do we cast down our supplications before You, rather because of Your abundant compassion. O my Lord, heed; O my Lord, forgive; O my Lord, be attentive and act, do not delay; for Your sake, my God, for Your Name is proclaimed* upon Your city and upon Your people.[2] Our Father, the merciful Father* — show us an omen for good and gather in our dispersed from the four corners of the world; let all the nations recognize and realize that You are* HASHEM, *our God. And now,* HASHEM, *You are our Father; we are the clay and You are our Molder and Your handiwork are we all.[3] Save us for Your Name's sake, our Rock, our King, and our Redeemer. Pity* Your people,* HASHEM; *let not Your heritage be an object of scorn, for nations to dominate. Why should they say among the peoples, 'Where is their God?'[4] We know that we have sinned and there is no one to stand up for us — let Your great Name stand up for us in time of distress. We know that there are no worthy deeds in us — treat us with charity for Your Name's sake. As a father has mercy on his children, so may You have mercy on us, O* HASHEM,[5] *and save us for Your Name's sake. Have compassion on Your people, have mercy on Your heritage; have pity, we beg You, according to Your abundant mercy. Be gracious with us and answer us, for Yours,* HASHEM, *is the righteousness, He Who does wonders always.*

(1) *Daniel* 9:15-17. (2) 9:18-19. (3) *Isaiah* 64:7. (4) *Joel* 2:17. (5) Cf. *Psalms* 103:13.

deserving, at least let Him help us for the sake of His Name that is desecrated by the destruction of His city and the persecution of His people.

כִּי שִׁמְךָ נִקְרָא — *For Your Name is proclaimed.* Each nation has an angel appointed to oversee its fortunes, but God Himself maintains personal dominion over Israel and Jerusalem (*Tikunei Zohar*).

הָאָב הָרַחֲמָן — *The merciful Father.* We do not claim to be worthy, but a father loves his children even when they stray.

חוּסָה — *Pity.* This term expresses the idea that a craftsman always has special regard for the object he has created. Since we are God's handiwork — as the previous verse puts it, we are the clay and He is our Molder — He should not permit His Own product to be demolished.

הַבֶּט נָא* רַחֶם נָא עַל עַמְּךָ מְהֵרָה לְמַעַן שְׁמֶךָ. בְּרַחֲמֶיךָ הָרַבִּים, יהוה אֱלֹהֵינוּ, חוּס וְרַחֵם וְהוֹשִׁיעָה צֹאן מַרְעִיתֶךָ, וְאַל יִמְשָׁל בָּנוּ קֶצֶף, כִּי לְךָ עֵינֵינוּ תְלוּיוֹת. הוֹשִׁיעֵנוּ לְמַעַן שְׁמֶךָ, רַחֵם עָלֵינוּ לְמַעַן בְּרִיתֶךָ.* הַבִּיטָה וַעֲנֵנוּ בְּעֵת צָרָה, כִּי לְךָ יהוה הַיְשׁוּעָה. בְּךָ תוֹחַלְתֵּנוּ, אֱלוֹהַּ סְלִיחוֹת, אָנָּא סְלַח נָא אֵל טוֹב וְסַלָּח, כִּי אֵל מֶלֶךְ חַנּוּן וְרַחוּם אָתָּה.[1]

אָנָּא* מֶלֶךְ חַנּוּן וְרַחוּם, זְכֹר וְהַבֵּט לִבְרִית בֵּין הַבְּתָרִים, וְתֵרָאֶה לְפָנֶיךָ עֲקֵדַת יָחִיד* לְמַעַן יִשְׂרָאֵל. אָבִינוּ מַלְכֵּנוּ חָנֵּנוּ וַעֲנֵנוּ, כִּי שִׁמְךָ הַגָּדוֹל נִקְרָא עָלֵינוּ. עֹשֵׂה נִפְלָאוֹת בְּכָל עֵת, עֲשֵׂה עִמָּנוּ כְּחַסְדֶּךָ. חַנּוּן וְרַחוּם, הַבִּיטָה וַעֲנֵנוּ בְּעֵת צָרָה, כִּי לְךָ יהוה הַיְשׁוּעָה. אָבִינוּ מַלְכֵּנוּ, מַחֲסֵנוּ, אַל תַּעַשׂ עִמָּנוּ כְּרֹעַ מַעֲלָלֵינוּ. זְכֹר רַחֲמֶיךָ יהוה וַחֲסָדֶיךָ, וּכְרֹב טוּבְךָ הוֹשִׁיעֵנוּ וַחֲמָל נָא עָלֵינוּ, כִּי אֵין לָנוּ אֱלוֹהַּ אַחֵר מִבַּלְעָדֶיךָ צוּרֵנוּ. אַל תַּעַזְבֵנוּ יהוה אֱלֹהֵינוּ, אַל תִּרְחַק מִמֶּנּוּ,[2] כִּי נַפְשֵׁנוּ קְצָרָה* מֵחֶרֶב וּמִשְּׁבִי וּמִדֶּבֶר וּמִמַּגֵּפָה וּמִכָּל צָרָה וְיָגוֹן. הַצִּילֵנוּ, כִּי לְךָ קִוִּינוּ, וְאַל תַּכְלִימֵנוּ יהוה אֱלֹהֵינוּ. וְהָאֵר פָּנֶיךָ בָּנוּ, וּזְכָר לָנוּ אֶת בְּרִית אֲבוֹתֵינוּ, וְהוֹשִׁיעֵנוּ לְמַעַן שְׁמֶךָ. רְאֵה בְצָרוֹתֵינוּ וּשְׁמַע קוֹל תְּפִלָּתֵנוּ, כִּי אַתָּה שׁוֹמֵעַ תְּפִלַּת כָּל פֶּה.

אֵל רַחוּם וְחַנּוּן,* רַחֵם עָלֵינוּ וְעַל כָּל מַעֲשֶׂיךָ,* כִּי אֵין כָּמוֹךָ. יהוה אֱלֹהֵינוּ, אָנָּא שָׂא נָא פְשָׁעֵינוּ. אָבִינוּ מַלְכֵּנוּ צוּרֵנוּ וְגוֹאֲלֵנוּ, אֵל חַי וְקַיָּם הַחֲסִין בַּכֹּחַ, חָסִיד וָטוֹב עַל כָּל מַעֲשֶׂיךָ, כִּי אַתָּה הוּא יהוה אֱלֹהֵינוּ. אֵל אֶרֶךְ אַפַּיִם וּמָלֵא רַחֲמִים, עֲשֵׂה עִמָּנוּ כְּרֹב רַחֲמֶיךָ, וְהוֹשִׁיעֵנוּ לְמַעַן שְׁמֶךָ. שְׁמַע

הַבֵּט נָא — *Look, we beg You.* This prayer for compassion stresses our helplessness and total dependence on Him. It introduces the concept that we are the 'sheep of God's pasture.' Like sheep we depend totally on the guidance and protection of our Shepherd.

לְמַעַן בְּרִיתֶךָ — *For the sake of Your covenant.* This introduces a new concept. Even if repentance is insincere and pleadings unavailing, there remains the unbreakable covenant that God struck with Abraham, Isaac, and Jacob. Even if the merit of the Patriarchs has been used up, the *covenant* with them remains in force (*Shabbos* 55a, *Tos.* s.v. שמואל).

אָנָּא — *Please.* This supplication emphasizes the experiences of the Patriarchs, Abraham and Isaac. It singles out the בְּרִית בֵּין הַבְּתָרִים, *Covenant Between the Parts* (*Genesis* ch. 15), and the *Akeidah* of Isaac (*Genesis* ch. 22; see commentary above, p. 22). In the Covenant, God sealed a treaty with Abraham that his descendants would inherit *Eretz Yisrael* and always be God's nation. The covenant was made in response to Abraham's wish to know how he could be sure that sinfulness or changing conditions would not prevent his offspring from inheriting the Land. Thus, it remains an eternal assurance to Israel, despite exile and oppression.

עֲקֵדַת יָחִיד — *The binding of the only son.* In commanding Abraham to bind Isaac on the

הַבֵּט נָא *Look, we beg You,* and have mercy on Your people speedily for Your Name's sake. In Your abundant mercy, HASHEM, our God, pity, have mercy upon, and save the sheep of Your pasture; let not anger dominate us, for on You do our eyes depend. Save us for Your Name's sake; have mercy on us for the sake of Your covenant.* Look and answer us in time of distress, for salvation is Yours, HASHEM. Upon You is our hope, O God of forgiveness; please forgive now, O good and forgiving God, for You are God, the gracious and compassionate King.*[1]

אָנָּא *Please,* O gracious and compassionate King, remember and look to the Covenant between the Parts; may there appear before You the binding of the only son* — for Israel's sake. Our Father, our King — be gracious with us and answer us, for Your great Name has been proclaimed upon us. O Maker of miracles at all times, treat us according to Your kindness. Gracious and Compassionate One, look and answer us in time of distress, for Yours, HASHEM, is the salvation. Our Father, our King, our Protector, do not treat us according to the evil of our deeds. Recall Your mercies, HASHEM, and Your kindnesses; according to Your abundant goodness save us and have pity on us, we beg You, for we have no god other than You, our Rock. Do not forsake us, HASHEM, our God, be not distant from us,*[2] *for our soul is diminished* by sword and captivity, pestilence and plague, and every distress and woe. Rescue us, for we hope to You; do not humiliate us, HASHEM, our God. Illuminate Your countenance within us, recall for us the covenant of our forefathers, and save us for Your Name's sake. Observe our troubles and hear the voice of our prayer, for You hear the prayer of every mouth.*

אֵל רַחוּם *O compassionate and gracious God,* have mercy on us and on all Your works,* for there is none like You. Please HASHEM, our God — forgive our willful sins. Our Father, our King, our Rock and Redeemer, living and enduring God, Who is mighty in strength, generous and good to all Your works; for You are HASHEM, our God. O God Who is slow to anger and full of mercy, treat us according to Your abundant mercy and save us for Your Name's sake. Hear*

(1) Cf. *Nechemiah* 9:31. (2) Cf. *Psalms* 38:22.

altar, God referred to Isaac as אֶת בִּנְךָ אֶת יְחִידְךָ, *your only son.* The Sages teach that the memory of the *Akeidah* always remains before God as a source of merit for Isaac's offspring. Thus, the two events mentioned here — the Covenant and the *Akeidah* — have spiritual effects that transcend time and distance. [For a full commentary and Overviews explaining these events, see ArtScroll *Genesis,* vol. II.]

נַפְשֵׁנוּ קָצְרָה — *Our soul is diminished.* This part of the prayer has a dual significance. We ask for deliverance from our troubles because they *diminish* our spiritual capacity. And we plead that many of our shortcomings are due to the many distresses and woes inflicted upon us.

אֵל רַחוּם וְחַנּוּן — *O compassionate and gracious God.* In this supplication, we refer to God not only as the Master of Israel, but as the God of all creatures and as the All-Powerful. He is the Master of history and, as such, has given us our role in it. Only if He shows us mercy and forgives our shortcomings can we serve Him. Therefore we beg Him not to cast us aside and abandon us.

וְעַל כָּל מַעֲשֶׂיךָ — *And on all Your works.* Despite our own needs, we pray for all God's creatures, as well as ourselves.

מַלְכֵּנוּ תְּפִלָּתֵנוּ, וּמִיַּד אוֹיְבֵינוּ הַצִּילֵנוּ. שְׁמַע מַלְכֵּנוּ תְּפִלָּתֵנוּ וּמִכָּל צָרָה וְיָגוֹן הַצִּילֵנוּ. אָבִינוּ מַלְכֵּנוּ אָתָּה, וְשִׁמְךָ עָלֵינוּ נִקְרָא, אַל תַּנִּחֵנוּ.[1] אַל תַּעַזְבֵנוּ אָבִינוּ, וְאַל תִּטְּשֵׁנוּ בּוֹרְאֵנוּ, וְאַל תִּשְׁכָּחֵנוּ יוֹצְרֵנוּ, כִּי אֵל מֶלֶךְ חַנּוּן וְרַחוּם אָתָּה.[2]

אֵין כָּמוֹךָ* חַנּוּן וְרַחוּם יהוה אֱלֹהֵינוּ, אֵין כָּמוֹךָ אֵל אֶרֶךְ אַפַּיִם וְרַב חֶסֶד וֶאֱמֶת. הוֹשִׁיעֵנוּ בְּרַחֲמֶיךָ הָרַבִּים, מֵרַעַשׁ וּמֵרֹגֶז הַצִּילֵנוּ. זְכֹר לַעֲבָדֶיךָ לְאַבְרָהָם לְיִצְחָק וּלְיַעֲקֹב, אַל תֵּפֶן אֶל קְשְׁיֵנוּ וְאֶל רִשְׁעֵנוּ וְאֶל חַטָּאתֵנוּ.[3] שׁוּב מֵחֲרוֹן אַפֶּךָ וְהִנָּחֵם עַל הָרָעָה לְעַמֶּךָ.[4] וְהָסֵר מִמֶּנּוּ מַכַּת הַמָּוֶת כִּי רַחוּם אָתָּה, כִּי כֵן דַּרְכֶּךָ, עוֹשֶׂה חֶסֶד חִנָּם בְּכָל דּוֹר וָדוֹר. חוּסָה יהוה עַל עַמֶּךָ וְהַצִּילֵנוּ מִזַּעְמֶךָ, וְהָסֵר מִמֶּנּוּ מַכַּת הַמַּגֵּפָה וּגְזֵרָה קָשָׁה, כִּי אַתָּה שׁוֹמֵר יִשְׂרָאֵל. לְךָ אֲדֹנָי הַצְּדָקָה וְלָנוּ בֹּשֶׁת הַפָּנִים.[5] מַה נִּתְאוֹנֵן, מַה נֹּאמַר, מַה נְּדַבֵּר, וּמַה נִּצְטַדָּק. נַחְפְּשָׂה דְרָכֵינוּ וְנַחְקֹרָה, וְנָשׁוּבָה אֵלֶיךָ,[6] כִּי יְמִינְךָ פְשׁוּטָה לְקַבֵּל שָׁבִים. אָנָּא יהוה הוֹשִׁיעָה נָּא, אָנָּא יהוה הַצְלִיחָה נָא.[7] אָנָּא יהוה עֲנֵנוּ בְיוֹם קָרְאֵנוּ.[8] לְךָ יהוה חִכִּינוּ, לְךָ יהוה קִוִּינוּ, לְךָ יהוה נְיַחֵל. אַל תֶּחֱשֶׁה וּתְעַנֵּנוּ, כִּי נָאֲמוּ גוֹיִם, אָבְדָה תִקְוָתָם. כָּל בֶּרֶךְ וְכָל קוֹמָה לְךָ לְבַד תִּשְׁתַּחֲוֶה.

הַפּוֹתֵחַ יָד* בִּתְשׁוּבָה לְקַבֵּל פּוֹשְׁעִים וְחַטָּאִים, נִבְהֲלָה נַפְשֵׁנוּ מֵרֹב עִצְּבוֹנֵנוּ, אַל תִּשְׁכָּחֵנוּ נֶצַח. קוּמָה וְהוֹשִׁיעֵנוּ, כִּי חָסִינוּ בָךְ. אָבִינוּ מַלְכֵּנוּ, אִם אֵין בָּנוּ צְדָקָה וּמַעֲשִׂים טוֹבִים, זְכָר לָנוּ אֶת בְּרִית אֲבוֹתֵינוּ וְעֵדוּתֵינוּ בְּכָל יוֹם, יהוה אֶחָד. הַבִּיטָה בְעָנְיֵנוּ כִּי רַבּוּ מַכְאוֹבֵינוּ וְצָרוֹת לְבָבֵנוּ. חוּסָה יהוה עָלֵינוּ בְּאֶרֶץ שִׁבְיֵנוּ וְאַל תִּשְׁפֹּךְ חֲרוֹנְךָ עָלֵינוּ, כִּי אֲנַחְנוּ עַמְּךָ בְּנֵי בְרִיתֶךָ. אֵל, הַבִּיטָה דַּל כְּבוֹדֵנוּ בַּגּוֹיִם, וְשִׁקְּצוּנוּ כְּטֻמְאַת הַנִּדָּה. עַד מָתַי עֻזְּךָ בַּשְּׁבִי,* וְתִפְאַרְתְּךָ בְּיַד צָר.[9] עוֹרְרָה

אֵין כָּמוֹךָ — *There is none like You.* This supplication consists mainly of verses from various parts of Scripture. Their unifying theme is an acknowledgment that we cannot justify our deeds. Nevertheless we have confidence that — against all odds and against our enemies' confident predictions of our doom — God's mercy is constant and He will help us find the way to repentance and forgiveness.

הַפּוֹתֵחַ יָד — *You Who opens a hand.* Sometimes a person has become so sinful that there is no reason to think that he can still repent. Even then, however, there is hope. As the Sages put it, God opens a place for the penitent beneath His Own Heavenly Throne, as it were. The point is

our prayer, our King, and rescue us from our foes; hear our prayer, our King, and rescue us from every distress and woe. You are our Father, our King, and Your Name is proclaimed upon us — do not set us aside.[1] *Do not abandon us, our Father, do not cast us away, our Creator; do not forget us, our Molder; for You are God, the gracious and compassionate King.*[2]

אֵין כָּמְוֹךָ *There is none like You,* gracious and compassionate,* HASHEM, *our God. There is none like You, God Who is slow to anger and is abundant in kindness and truth. Save us with Your abundant mercy; from storm and anger save us. Remember Your servants Abraham, Isaac, and Jacob; regard not our stubbornness, our wickedness, and our sinfulness.*[3] *Turn back from Your flaring anger and relent from the evil meant for Your people.*[4] *Remove from us the scourge of death for You are compassionate, for such is Your manner: doing undeserved kindness in every generation. Have pity upon Your people,* HASHEM, *rescue us from Your wrath; remove from us the scourge of plague and harsh decree, for You are the Guardian of Israel. Yours, my Lord, is the righteousness and ours is the shamefacedness.*[5] *What complaint can we make? What can we say? What can we declare? What justification can we offer? Let us examine our ways and analyze — and return to You,*[6] *for Your right hand is extended to accept penitents. Please* HASHEM, *save now; please* HASHEM, *bring success now!*[7] *Please* HASHEM, *answer us on the day we call.*[8] *For You,* HASHEM, *we have waited; for you,* HASHEM, *we have hoped; for You,* HASHEM, *we long. Do not be silent while letting us suffer, for the nations have declared, 'Their hope is lost.' Let every knee and every erect being bow to You alone.*

הַפּוֹתֵחַ יָד *You Who opens a hand* for repentance, to welcome rebels and sinners: our soul is confounded by the abundance of our depression — forget us not eternally. Arise and save us for we take refuge in You. Our Father, our King, if we lack righteousness and good deeds, recall for us the covenant of our forefathers and our daily testimonies that '*HASHEM *is the One and Only.' Look upon our affliction, for many are our sufferings and the distresses of our hearts. Have pity upon us,* HASHEM, *in the land of our captivity and do not pour Your wrath upon us — for we are Your people, the members of Your covenant. O God, look upon the impoverishment of our honor among the nations and how they abhor us like menstrual impurity. How long will Your strength be in bondage* and Your splendor in the enemy's power?*[9] *Arouse*

(1) *Jeremiah* 14:9. (2) Cf. *Nechemiah* 9:31. (3) Cf. *Deuteronomy* 9:27. (4) *Exodus* 32:12. (5) *Daniel* 9:7. (6) Cf. *Lamentations* 3:40. (7) *Psalms* 118:25. (8) Cf. 20:10. ((9) Cf. 78:61.

that God's mercy exceeds all imaginable boundaries (*Etz Yosef*).

עַד מָתַי עֻזְּךָ בַּשְּׁבִי — *How long will Your strength be in bondage.* This is based on *Psalms* 78:61, which describes the Philistine capture of the Holy Ark in the time of Eli and Samuel. In our context, it refers to the holy places and spiritual power that seem to have lost their ability to protect Israel.

גְבוּרָתְךָ וְקִנְאָתְךָ עַל אוֹיְבֶיךָ. הֵם יֵבוֹשׁוּ וְיֵחַתּוּ מִגְּבוּרָתָם, וְאַל יְמַעֲטוּ לְפָנֶיךָ תְּלָאוֹתֵינוּ. מַהֵר יְקַדְּמוּנוּ רַחֲמֶיךָ בְּיוֹם צָרָתֵנוּ, וְאִם לֹא לְמַעֲנֵנוּ, לְמַעַנְךָ פְעַל, וְאַל תַּשְׁחִית זֵכֶר שְׁאֵרִיתֵנוּ. וְחֹן אֹם הַמְיַחֲדִים שִׁמְךָ פַּעֲמַיִם בְּכָל יוֹם תָּמִיד בְּאַהֲבָה וְאוֹמְרִים: שְׁמַע יִשְׂרָאֵל יהוה אֱלֹהֵינוּ יהוה אֶחָד.[1]

נפילת אפים

Tachanun begins here, except on Monday and Thursday mornings when the longer version (beginning p. 124) is said. See p. 125 for days on which *Tachanun* is omitted.

In the presence of a Torah Scroll, the following (until יֵבֹשׁוּ רָגַע) is recited with the head resting on the arm, preferably while seated. Elsewhere, it is recited with the head held erect.

וַיֹּאמֶר דָּוִד* אֶל גָּד, צַר לִי מְאֹד, נִפְּלָה נָּא בְיַד יהוה, כִּי רַבִּים רַחֲמָיו, וּבְיַד אָדָם אַל אֶפֹּלָה.[2]

רַחוּם וְחַנּוּן* חָטָאתִי לְפָנֶיךָ. יהוה מָלֵא רַחֲמִים, רַחֵם עָלַי וְקַבֵּל תַּחֲנוּנָי.

תהלים ו:ב-יא

יהוה אַל בְּאַפְּךָ* תוֹכִיחֵנִי, וְאַל בַּחֲמָתְךָ תְיַסְּרֵנִי. חָנֵּנִי יהוה, כִּי אֻמְלַל אָנִי, רְפָאֵנִי יהוה, כִּי נִבְהֲלוּ עֲצָמָי. וְנַפְשִׁי נִבְהֲלָה מְאֹד, וְאַתָּה יהוה, עַד מָתָי.* שׁוּבָה יהוה, חַלְּצָה נַפְשִׁי, הוֹשִׁיעֵנִי לְמַעַן חַסְדֶּךָ. כִּי אֵין בַּמָּוֶת זִכְרֶךָ, בִּשְׁאוֹל מִי יוֹדֶה לָּךְ. יָגַעְתִּי בְּאַנְחָתִי, אַשְׂחֶה בְכָל לַיְלָה מִטָּתִי, בְּדִמְעָתִי עַרְשִׂי אַמְסֶה. עָשְׁשָׁה מִכַּעַס עֵינִי, עָתְקָה בְּכָל צוֹרְרָי. סוּרוּ מִמֶּנִּי כָּל פֹּעֲלֵי אָוֶן, כִּי שָׁמַע יהוה קוֹל בִּכְיִי. שָׁמַע יהוה תְּחִנָּתִי, יהוה תְּפִלָּתִי יִקָּח. יֵבֹשׁוּ וְיִבָּהֲלוּ מְאֹד כָּל אֹיְבָי, יָשֻׁבוּ יֵבֹשׁוּ רָגַע.

נְפִילַת אַפַּיִם / PUTTING DOWN THE HEAD

Tachanun consists mainly of *Psalms* 6:2-11, which begins ה׳ אַל בְּאַפְּךָ. However, two verses, both of which reflect the theme of *Tachanun*, are inserted to introduce the primary psalm.

The act of נְפִילַת אַפַּיִם, *putting down the head*, i.e., 'burying' one's face in submissive supplication, is based on the behavior of Moses, Aaron and Joshua. These three cast themselves down before God in times of stress and tragedy (*Numbers* 16:22; *Joshua* 7:6).

This portion of *Tachanun* is recited with the head down and resting on the left arm, and preferably in a sitting position. One wearing *tefillin* on the left arm rests his head on his right arm out of respect for the *tefillin*. The head should not rest on the bare arm; rather the arm should be covered with a sleeve, *tallis*, or even a cloth. This posture is an indication of the feelings of despair and guilt that combine with the undying hope that God's mercy will rescue the supplicant no matter how hopeless his plight. Since Joshua cast himself down in the presence of the Holy Ark, the act of falling on the face is done only in the presence of a Torah scroll, i.e., an Ark containing a Torah scroll. If a Torah is not present, *Tachanun* is recited with the head held erect.

וַיֹּאמֶר דָּוִד — *And David said.* King David had sinned by taking a census of the Jews in a manner contrary to that prescribed in the Torah (see *Exodus* 30:12). God, through the

Your strength and Your zeal against Your enemies. Let them be shamed and broken of their strength; and may our travails not seem petty to You. May Your mercies meet us swiftly in our time of distress; and if not for our sake, act for Your own sake and do not destroy our remnant's remembrance. Be gracious to the nation that ascribes Oneness to Your Name twice daily, constantly with love, saying: 'Hear, O Israel, HASHEM is our God, HASHEM, the One and Only.'[1]

PUTTING DOWN THE HEAD

Tachanun begins here, except on Monday and Thursday mornings when the longer version (beginning p. 124) is said. See p. 125 for days on which *Tachanun* is omitted.

In the presence of a Torah Scroll, the following (until *'instantly shamed'*) is recited with the head resting on the arm, preferably while seated. Elsewhere, it is recited with the head held erect.

וַיֹּאמֶר דָּוִד *And David said* to Gad, 'I am exceedingly distressed. Let us fall into HASHEM's hand for His mercies are abundant, but let me not fall into human hands.'*[2]

O compassionate and gracious One, I have sinned before You. HASHEM, Who is full of mercy, have mercy on me and accept my supplications.*

Psalms 6:2-11

יהוה *HASHEM, do not rebuke me in Your anger,* nor chastise me in Your rage. Favor me, HASHEM, for I am feeble; heal me, HASHEM, for my bones shudder. My soul is utterly confounded, and You, HASHEM, how long?* Desist, HASHEM, release my soul; save me as befits Your kindness. For there is no mention of You in death; in the Lower World who will thank You? I am wearied with my sigh, every night I drench my bed, with my tears I soak my couch. My eye is dimmed because of anger, aged by my tormentors. Depart from me, all evildoers, for HASHEM has heard the sound of my weeping. HASHEM has heard my plea, HASHEM will accept my prayer. Let all my foes be shamed and utterly confounded, they will regret and be instantly shamed.*

(1) *Deuteronomy* 6:4. (2) *II Samuel* 24:14.

agency of the prophet Gad, gave King David a choice of three calamities, one of which he and his people would have to suffer in atonement for his sin: seven years of hunger; three months of defeat in battle; or a three-day death plague. David chose the last because that one would be inflicted directly by God, Whose mercy is everpresent, even when His wrath is aroused. His choice proved the correct one when God mercifully halted the plague after a duration of only half a day. Similarly, in *Tachanun*, we cast ourselves upon God's compassion.

רַחוּם וְחַנּוּן — *O compassionate and gracious One.* This verse is not of Scriptural origin. It is based on the dictum that God tempers the judgment of someone who confesses that he has sinned *(Etz Yosef).*

ה׳ אַל בְּאַפְּךָ — *HASHEM, do not . . . in Your anger.* David composed this psalm when he was sick and in pain. He intended his prayer for every person in distress, and particularly for Israel when it suffered oppression and deprivation.

Even if he must be punished for his deeds, David pleaded, let God do so gradually, but not *in anger*, for then it would be beyond human endurance *(Radak).*

עַד מָתָי — *How long?* How long will You watch my suffering and not cure me?

On Sunday, Tuesday, Wednesday and Friday, *Tachanun* continues with שׁוֹמֵר יִשְׂרָאֵל (p. 136).
On Monday and Thursday, *Tachanun* continues with ה' אֱלֹהֵי יִשְׂרָאֵל (below).

יהוה אֱלֹהֵי יִשְׂרָאֵל,* שׁוּב מֵחֲרוֹן אַפֶּךָ וְהִנָּחֵם עַל הָרָעָה לְעַמֶּךָ.[1]

הַבֵּט מִשָּׁמַיִם וּרְאֵה כִּי הָיִינוּ לַעַג וָקֶלֶס בַּגּוֹיִם, נֶחְשַׁבְנוּ כְּצֹאן לַטֶּבַח יוּבָל, לַהֲרֹג וּלְאַבֵּד וּלְמַכָּה וּלְחֶרְפָּה.[2] וּבְכָל זֹאת* שִׁמְךָ לֹא שָׁכָחְנוּ, נָא אַל תִּשְׁכָּחֵנוּ.

יהוה אֱלֹהֵי יִשְׂרָאֵל, שׁוּב מֵחֲרוֹן אַפֶּךָ וְהִנָּחֵם עַל הָרָעָה לְעַמֶּךָ.

זָרִים אוֹמְרִים אֵין תּוֹחֶלֶת וְתִקְוָה, חֹן אֹם לְשִׁמְךָ מְקַוָּה, טָהוֹר יְשׁוּעָתֵנוּ קָרְבָה, יָגַעְנוּ וְלֹא הוּנַח לָנוּ,[3] רַחֲמֶיךָ יִכְבְּשׁוּ אֶת כַּעַסְךָ מֵעָלֵינוּ. אָנָּא שׁוּב מֵחֲרוֹנְךָ, וְרַחֵם סְגֻלָּה אֲשֶׁר בָּחָרְתָּ.[4]

יהוה אֱלֹהֵי יִשְׂרָאֵל, שׁוּב מֵחֲרוֹן אַפֶּךָ וְהִנָּחֵם עַל הָרָעָה לְעַמֶּךָ.

חוּסָה יהוה עָלֵינוּ בְּרַחֲמֶיךָ, וְאַל תִּתְּנֵנוּ בִּידֵי אַכְזָרִים. לָמָּה יֹאמְרוּ הַגּוֹיִם אַיֵּה נָא אֱלֹהֵיהֶם,[5] לְמַעַנְךָ עֲשֵׂה עִמָּנוּ חֶסֶד וְאַל תְּאַחַר.[6] אָנָּא שׁוּב מֵחֲרוֹנְךָ, וְרַחֵם סְגֻלָּה אֲשֶׁר בָּחָרְתָּ.

יהוה אֱלֹהֵי יִשְׂרָאֵל, שׁוּב מֵחֲרוֹן אַפֶּךָ וְהִנָּחֵם עַל הָרָעָה לְעַמֶּךָ.

קוֹלֵנוּ תִשְׁמַע וְתָחֹן, וְאַל תִּטְּשֵׁנוּ בְּיַד אוֹיְבֵינוּ לִמְחוֹת אֶת שְׁמֵנוּ. זְכֹר אֲשֶׁר נִשְׁבַּעְתָּ לַאֲבוֹתֵינוּ כְּכוֹכְבֵי הַשָּׁמַיִם אַרְבֶּה אֶת זַרְעֲכֶם,[7] וְעַתָּה נִשְׁאַרְנוּ מְעַט מֵהַרְבֵּה.[8] וּבְכָל זֹאת שִׁמְךָ לֹא שָׁכָחְנוּ, נָא אַל תִּשְׁכָּחֵנוּ.

יהוה אֱלֹהֵי יִשְׂרָאֵל, שׁוּב מֵחֲרוֹן אַפֶּךָ וְהִנָּחֵם עַל הָרָעָה לְעַמֶּךָ.

ה' אֱלֹהֵי יִשְׂרָאֵל — *HASHEM, God of Israel.* According to tradition, this section of *Tachanun* was composed by King Hezekiah. When Jerusalem was besieged by Sennacherib and the situation seemed hopeless, the righteous king went to the Temple and poured out his heart in this supplication. As its stanzas show clearly, it is an eloquent plea for God's intervention in the face of impending disaster, and thus expresses our hope that God will help Israel today as He did in Hezekiah's time. The commentators note that Hezekiah spelled his name in the initials of the stanzas [י׳, הַבֵּט, זָרִים, חוּסָה, קוֹלֵנוּ], but with the modesty for which he was famous, he put the letters out of order so that it would not be obvious that he was the supplication's author.

Or Hayashar notes that the numerical value

On Sunday, Tuesday, Wednesday and Friday, *Tachanun* continues with *'O Guardian of Israel'* (p. 137). On Monday and Thursday, *Tachanun* continues with *'HASHEM, God of Israel'* (below).

יהוה *HASHEM, God of Israel,* turn back from Your flaring anger and relent from the evil meant for Your people.*[1]

הַבֵּט *Look from heaven and perceive that we have become an object of scorn and derision among the nations; we are regarded as the sheep led to slaughter, to be killed, destroyed, beaten, and humiliated.*[2] *But despite all this* we have not forgotten Your Name — we beg You not to forget us.*

HASHEM, God of Israel, turn back from Your flaring anger and relent from the evil meant for Your people.

זָרִים *Foreigners say, 'There is no expectation nor hope!' Be gracious to the nation whose hope is in Your Name. O Pure One, bring near Your salvation! We are exhausted but are allowed no rest.*[3] *May Your mercies conquer Your anger against us. We beg You, turn back from Your anger and have mercy on the treasured nation that You have chosen.*[4]

HASHEM, God of Israel, turn back from Your flaring anger and relent from the evil meant for Your people.

חוּסָה *HASHEM, pity us in Your mercy and do not turn us over to sadists. Why should the nations say, 'Where is their God now?'*[5] *For Your sake, treat us with kindness and do not delay.*[6] *We beg You, turn back from Your anger and have mercy on the treasured nation that You have chosen.*

HASHEM, God of Israel, turn back from Your flaring anger and relent from the evil meant for Your people.

קוֹלֵנוּ *Listen to our voice and be gracious — do not cast us off into the hand of our enemies to blot out our name. Remember what You swore to our forefathers: 'Like the stars of the heaven will I multiply your offspring'*[7] *— but now we are few left from many.*[8] *But despite all this, we have not forgotten Your Name — we beg You not to forget us.*

HASHEM, God of Israel, turn back from Your flaring anger and relent from the evil meant for Your people.

(1) *Exodus* 32:12. (2) Cf. *Psalms* 44:14,23; *Isaiah* 53:7. (3) *Lamentations* 5:5. (4) Cf. *Deuteronomy* 7:6. (5) *Psalms* 115:2. (6) Cf. *Daniel* 9:19. (7) Cf. *Exodus* 32:13. (8) Cf. *Jeremiah* 42:2.

of ה' אֱלֹהֵי יִשְׂרָאֵל, *HASHEM, God of Israel,* is 613. Hezekiah used this particular salutation because the reminder that Israel observes the 613 commandments is sure to evoke God's compassion.

וּבְכָל זֹאת — *But despite all this.* In a major sense, this is the crux of our plea: No matter what befalls us, we refuse to give up our faith in You — we beg You to reciprocate by remembering us as well.

עָזְרֵנוּ אֱלֹהֵי יִשְׁעֵנוּ עַל דְּבַר כְּבוֹד שְׁמֶךָ, וְהַצִּילֵנוּ וְכַפֵּר עַל חַטֹּאתֵינוּ לְמַעַן שְׁמֶךָ.[1]

יהוה אֱלֹהֵי יִשְׂרָאֵל, שׁוּב מֵחֲרוֹן אַפֶּךָ וְהִנָּחֵם עַל הָרָעָה לְעַמֶּךָ.

On all days, *Tachanun* continues with שׁוֹמֵר יִשְׂרָאֵל. [On Sunday, Tuesday, Wednesday and Friday remain seated until after the three words וַאֲנַחְנוּ לֹא נֵדַע, then stand until the conclusion of *Tachanun*.]

שׁוֹמֵר יִשְׂרָאֵל,* שְׁמוֹר שְׁאֵרִית יִשְׂרָאֵל, וְאַל יֹאבַד יִשְׂרָאֵל, הָאֹמְרִים, שְׁמַע יִשְׂרָאֵל.

שׁוֹמֵר גּוֹי אֶחָד, שְׁמוֹר שְׁאֵרִית עַם אֶחָד, וְאַל יֹאבַד גּוֹי אֶחָד, הַמְּיַחֲדִים שִׁמְךָ, יהוה אֱלֹהֵינוּ יהוה אֶחָד.

שׁוֹמֵר גּוֹי קָדוֹשׁ, שְׁמוֹר שְׁאֵרִית עַם קָדוֹשׁ, וְאַל יֹאבַד גּוֹי קָדוֹשׁ, הַמְּשַׁלְּשִׁים בְּשָׁלֹשׁ קְדֻשּׁוֹת לְקָדוֹשׁ.

מִתְרַצֶּה* בְּרַחֲמִים וּמִתְפַּיֵּס בְּתַחֲנוּנִים, הִתְרַצֵּה וְהִתְפַּיֵּס לְדוֹר עָנִי, כִּי אֵין עוֹזֵר. אָבִינוּ מַלְכֵּנוּ, חָנֵּנוּ וַעֲנֵנוּ, כִּי אֵין בָּנוּ מַעֲשִׂים, עֲשֵׂה עִמָּנוּ צְדָקָה וָחֶסֶד וְהוֹשִׁיעֵנוּ.

וַאֲנַחְנוּ לֹא נֵדַע מַה נַּעֲשֶׂה,* כִּי עָלֶיךָ עֵינֵינוּ.[2] זְכֹר רַחֲמֶיךָ יהוה וַחֲסָדֶיךָ, כִּי מֵעוֹלָם הֵמָּה.[3] יְהִי חַסְדְּךָ יהוה עָלֵינוּ, כַּאֲשֶׁר יִחַלְנוּ לָךְ.*[4] אַל תִּזְכָּר לָנוּ עֲוֹנוֹת רִאשׁוֹנִים, מַהֵר יְקַדְּמוּנוּ רַחֲמֶיךָ, כִּי דַלּוֹנוּ מְאֹד.*[5] חָנֵּנוּ יהוה חָנֵּנוּ, כִּי רַב שָׂבַעְנוּ בוּז.[6] בְּרֹגֶז רַחֵם תִּזְכּוֹר.[7] כִּי הוּא יָדַע יִצְרֵנוּ, זָכוּר כִּי עָפָר אֲנָחְנוּ.[8] ❖ עָזְרֵנוּ אֱלֹהֵי יִשְׁעֵנוּ עַל דְּבַר כְּבוֹד שְׁמֶךָ, וְהַצִּילֵנוּ וְכַפֵּר עַל חַטֹּאתֵינוּ לְמַעַן שְׁמֶךָ.[9]

☙ שׁוֹמֵר יִשְׂרָאֵל — *O Guardian of Israel.* As noted above, this plea to God as our Guardian enforces the theme that we are helpless and totally dependent on His mercy. However, we do not come to God with nothing in our favor; each of the paragraphs beginning שׁוֹמֵר, *O Guardian,* stresses an aspect of Israel's importance to God. Israel deserves God's mercy because: (a) It continues to proclaim its allegiance to God by proclaiming the *Shema;* (b) Israel is unique in that it demonstrates to the world that God is One and Unique; and (c) like the angels, Israel praises and exalts God with the trebled proclamation of His holiness, i.e., *Kedushah* (see p. 100).

מִתְרַצֶּה — *You Who are favorable.* May we have succeeded through our pleadings in arousing God's mercy.

☙ וַאֲנַחְנוּ לֹא נֵדַע מַה נַּעֲשֶׂה — *We know not what to do.* We have prayed in every possible manner — sitting, standing, and casting ourselves down in supplication. Moses, too, prayed in these three postures. Now, we beg of God to help, for 'we know not what else we can do.' To allude to this thought it is customary to sit while reciting the first three words of this prayer and then to stand (*Abudraham*).

We are like orphaned children who depend

Assist us, O God of our salvation, for the sake of Your Name's glory; rescue us, and atone for our sins for Your Name's sake.[1]

HASHEM, God of Israel, turn back from Your flaring anger and relent from the evil meant for Your people.

On all days, *Tachanun* continues with *'O Guardian of Israel.'* [On Sunday, Tuesday, Wednesday and Friday remain seated until after the three words *'We know not,'* then stand until the conclusion of *Tachanun.*]

שׁוֹמֵר יִשְׂרָאֵל *O Guardian of Israel,* protect the remnant of Israel; let not Israel be destroyed — those who proclaim, 'Hear O Israel.'*

O Guardian of the unique nation, protect the remnant of the unique people; let not the unique nation be destroyed — those who proclaim the Oneness of Your Name, 'HASHEM is our God, HASHEM — the One and Only!'

O Guardian of the holy nation, protect the remnant of the holy people; let not the holy nation be destroyed — those who proclaim three-fold sanctifications to the Holy One.

You Who are favorable through compassion and appeased through supplications. Become favorable and appeased to the poor generation for there is no helper. Our Father, our King, be gracious with us and answer us, though we have no worthy deeds; treat us with charity and kindnesses, and save us.*

וַאֲנַחְנוּ *We know not what to do* — but our eyes are upon You.*[2] *Remember Your mercies, HASHEM, and Your kindnesses, for they are from the beginning of the world.*[3] *May Your kindness be upon us, HASHEM, just as we awaited You.**[4] *Recall not against us the sins of the ancients; may Your mercies meet us swiftly, for we have become exceedingly impoverished.**[5] *Be gracious to us, HASHEM, be gracious to us, for we are abundantly sated with scorn.*[6] *Amid rage — remember to be merciful!*[7] *For He knew our nature, He remembers that we are dust.*[8] Chazzan– *Assist us, O God of our salvation, for the sake of Your Name's glory; rescue us and atone for our sins for Your Name's sake.*[9]

(1) *Psalms* 79:9. (2) *II Chronicles* 20:12. (3) *Psalms* 25:6. (4) 33:22. (5) 79:8. (6) *Psalms* 123:3. (7) *Habakkuk* 3:2. (8) *Psalms* 103:14. (9) 79:9.

totally on their guardian. Similarly, we look to God for His help and mercy, recognizing that only He can rescue us from our plight (*Etz Yosef*). Appropriately, this verse is from the prayer of King Yehoshafat, who prayed for help against an overwhelming invasion.

כַּאֲשֶׁר יִחַלְנוּ לָךְ — *Just as we awaited You.* If we are undeserving, O God, then help us because You will thereby sanctify Your Name (*Alshich*).

כִּי דַלּוֹנוּ מְאֹד — *For we have become exceedingly impoverished.* The prayer concludes with the plea that we have already suffered mightily and that God in His mercy knows that we are helpless without Him.

Chazzan recites חֲצִי קַדִּישׁ.

יִתְגַּדַּל וְיִתְקַדַּשׁ שְׁמֵהּ רַבָּא. (Cong. – אָמֵן.) בְּעָלְמָא דִּי בְרָא כִרְעוּתֵהּ, וְיַמְלִיךְ מַלְכוּתֵהּ, בְּחַיֵּיכוֹן וּבְיוֹמֵיכוֹן וּבְחַיֵּי דְכָל בֵּית יִשְׂרָאֵל, בַּעֲגָלָא וּבִזְמַן קָרִיב. וְאִמְרוּ: אָמֵן.

(Cong. – אָמֵן. יְהֵא שְׁמֵהּ רַבָּא מְבָרַךְ לְעָלַם וּלְעָלְמֵי עָלְמַיָּא.)

יְהֵא שְׁמֵהּ רַבָּא מְבָרַךְ לְעָלַם וּלְעָלְמֵי עָלְמַיָּא.

יִתְבָּרַךְ וְיִשְׁתַּבַּח וְיִתְפָּאַר וְיִתְרוֹמַם וְיִתְנַשֵּׂא וְיִתְהַדָּר וְיִתְעַלֶּה וְיִתְהַלָּל שְׁמֵהּ דְּקֻדְשָׁא בְּרִיךְ הוּא (Cong. – בְּרִיךְ הוּא) – °לְעֵלָּא מִן כָּל (From Rosh Hashanah to Yom Kippur substitute – °לְעֵלָּא וּלְעֵלָּא מִכָּל) בִּרְכָתָא וְשִׁירָתָא תֻּשְׁבְּחָתָא וְנֶחֱמָתָא, דַּאֲמִירָן בְּעָלְמָא. וְאִמְרוּ: אָמֵן. (Cong. – אָמֵן.)

הוצאת ספר תורה

The following short supplication is recited, while standing erect, before the Torah reading on Monday and Thursday. It is omitted on Festivals (including Chol HaMoed), Rosh Chodesh, Erev Pesach, Tishah B'Av, (in some congregations, 15 Av), Erev Yom Kippur, Chanukah, Purim and Shushan Purim, the 14th and 15th of Adar I (Purim Kattan), and in a house of mourning.

In most *siddurim* this prayer appears in two versions: version A, ascribed to the communities of Germany, Bohemia and Lesser Poland (Western Galicia); and version B, to the communities of Greater Poland (Poland and Lithuania). In some congregations both versions are recited.

VERSION A

אֵל אֶרֶךְ אַפַּיִם* וְרַב חֶסֶד וֶאֱמֶת,[1] אַל בְּאַפְּךָ תוֹכִיחֵנוּ.[2] חוּסָה יהוה עַל עַמֶּךָ,[3] וְהוֹשִׁיעֵנוּ מִכָּל רָע. חָטָאנוּ לְךָ אָדוֹן, סְלַח נָא כְּרֹב רַחֲמֶיךָ אֵל.

VERSION B

אֵל אֶרֶךְ אַפַּיִם* וְרַב חֶסֶד וֶאֱמֶת,[1] אַל תַּסְתֵּר פָּנֶיךָ מִמֶּנּוּ.[4] חוּסָה יהוה עַל יִשְׂרָאֵל עַמֶּךָ,[5] וְהַצִּילֵנוּ מִכָּל רָע. חָטָאנוּ לְךָ אָדוֹן, סְלַח נָא כְּרֹב רַחֲמֶיךָ אֵל.

From the moment the Ark is opened until the Torah is returned to it, one must conduct himself with the utmost respect, and avoid unnecessary conversation. It is commendable to kiss the Torah as it is carried to the *bimah* [reading table] and back to the Ark.

All rise and remain standing until the Torah is placed on the *bimah*.
The Ark is opened; before the Torah is removed the congregation recites:

וַיְהִי בִּנְסֹעַ הָאָרֹן, וַיֹּאמֶר מֹשֶׁה, קוּמָה יהוה וְיָפֻצוּ אֹיְבֶיךָ, וְיָנֻסוּ מְשַׂנְאֶיךָ מִפָּנֶיךָ.[6] כִּי מִצִּיּוֹן תֵּצֵא תוֹרָה, וּדְבַר יהוה מִירוּשָׁלָיִם.[7] בָּרוּךְ שֶׁנָּתַן תּוֹרָה לְעַמּוֹ יִשְׂרָאֵל בִּקְדֻשָּׁתוֹ.

Between Rosh Hashanah and Yom Kippur and on Hoshana Rabbah some congregations recite additional prayers at this point. See page 434.

Chazzan recites Half-*Kaddish*.

יִתְגַּדַּל *May His great Name grow exalted and sanctified* (Cong.– *Amen.*) *in the world that He created as He willed. May He give reign to His kingship in your lifetimes and in your days, and in the lifetimes of the entire Family of Israel, swiftly and soon. Now respond: Amen.*

(Cong.– *Amen. May His great Name be blessed forever and ever.*)

May His great Name be blessed forever and ever.

Blessed, praised, glorified, exalted, extolled, mighty, upraised, and lauded be the Name of the Holy One, Blessed is He (Cong.– *Blessed is He*) — (From Rosh Hashanah to Yom Kippur add: *exceedingly*) *beyond any blessing and song, praise and consolation that are uttered in the world. Now respond: Amen.* (Cong.– *Amen.*)

REMOVAL OF THE TORAH FROM THE ARK

The following short supplication is recited, while standing erect, before the Torah reading on Monday and Thursday. It is omitted on Festivals (including Chol HaMoed), Rosh Chodesh, Erev Pesach, Tishah B'Av, Erev Yom Kippur, Chanukah, Purim and Shushan Purim, the 14th and 15th of Adar I (Purim Kattan), and in a house of mourning.

In most *siddurim* this prayer appears in two versions: version A, ascribed to the communities of Germany, Bohemia and Lesser Poland (Western Galicia); and version B, ascribed to the communities of Greater Poland (Poland and Lithuania). In some congregations both versions are recited.

VERSION A

אֵל *O God, slow to anger* and abundant in kindness and truth,*[1] *do not chastise us in Your anger.*[2] *Pity,* HASHEM, *Your people*[3] *and save us from any evil. We have sinned against You, Master; forgive us, we beg You, in accordance with Your abundant mercy, O God.*

VERSION B

אֵל *O God, slow to anger* and abundant in kindness and truth,*[1] *do not conceal Your face from us.*[4] *Pity,* HASHEM, *Israel, Your people,*[5] *and rescue us from all evil. We have sinned against You, Master; forgive us, we beg You, in accordance with Your abundant mercy, O God.*

From the moment the Ark is opened until the Torah is returned to it, one must conduct himself with the utmost respect, and avoid unnecessary conversation. It is commendable to kiss the Torah as it is carried to the *bimah* [reading table] and back to the Ark.

All rise and remain standing until the Torah is placed on the *bimah*.
The Ark is opened; before the Torah is removed the congregation recites:

וַיְהִי בִּנְסֹעַ *When the Ark would travel, Moses would say, 'Arise,* HASHEM, *and let Your foes be scattered, let those who hate You flee from You.'*[6] *For from Zion will the Torah come forth and the word of* HASHEM *from Jerusalem.*[7] *Blessed is He Who gave the Torah to His people Israel in His holiness.*

Between Rosh Hashanah and Yom Kippur, and on Hoshana Rabbah, some congregations recite additional prayers at this point. See page 434.

(1) Cf. *Exodus* 34:6. (2) *Psalms* 6:2. (3) *Joel* 2:17. (4) Cf. *Psalms* 27:9.
(5) Cf. *Joel* 2:17. (6) *Numbers* 10:35. (7) *Isaiah* 2:3.

אֵל אֶרֶךְ אַפַּיִם — *O God, Slow to Anger.* As we prepare for the Torah to be removed from the Ark, we recognize that we have fallen far short of the standards it sets for us. Realizing how unworthy we are to take the Torah into our hands, we recite the brief prayer אֵל אֶרֶךְ אַפַּיִם, *O God, slow to anger,* which is both a confession and a plea for mercy *(R' Hirsch).*

זוהר ויקהל שסט:א

בְּרִיךְ שְׁמֵהּ דְּמָרֵא עָלְמָא, בְּרִיךְ כִּתְרָךְ וְאַתְרָךְ. יְהֵא רְעוּתָךְ עִם עַמָּךְ יִשְׂרָאֵל לְעָלַם, וּפֻרְקַן יְמִינָךְ אַחֲזֵי לְעַמָּךְ בְּבֵית מַקְדְּשָׁךְ, וּלְאַמְטְוּיֵי לָנָא מִטּוּב נְהוֹרָךְ, וּלְקַבֵּל צְלוֹתָנָא בְּרַחֲמִין. יְהֵא רַעֲוָא קֳדָמָךְ, דְּתוֹרִיךְ לָן חַיִּין בְּטִיבוּתָא, וְלֶהֱוֵי אֲנָא פְקִידָא בְּגוֹ צַדִּיקַיָּא, לְמִרְחַם עָלַי וּלְמִנְטַר יָתִי וְיַת כָּל דִּי לִי וְדִי לְעַמָּךְ יִשְׂרָאֵל. אַנְתְּ הוּא זָן לְכֹלָּא, וּמְפַרְנֵס לְכֹלָּא, אַנְתְּ הוּא שַׁלִּיט עַל כֹּלָּא. אַנְתְּ הוּא דְּשַׁלִּיט עַל מַלְכַיָּא, וּמַלְכוּתָא דִּילָךְ הִיא. אֲנָא עַבְדָּא דְקֻדְשָׁא בְּרִיךְ הוּא, דְּסָגִידְנָא קַמֵּהּ וּמִקַּמָּא דִּיקַר אוֹרַיְתֵהּ בְּכָל עִדָּן וְעִדָּן. לָא עַל אֱנָשׁ רָחִיצְנָא, וְלָא עַל בַּר אֱלָהִין סָמִיכְנָא, אֶלָּא בֶּאֱלָהָא דִשְׁמַיָּא, דְּהוּא אֱלָהָא קְשׁוֹט, וְאוֹרַיְתֵהּ קְשׁוֹט, וּנְבִיאוֹהִי קְשׁוֹט, וּמַסְגֵּא לְמֶעְבַּד טַבְוָן וּקְשׁוֹט. בֵּהּ אֲנָא רָחִיץ, וְלִשְׁמֵהּ קַדִּישָׁא יַקִּירָא אֲנָא אֵמַר תֻּשְׁבְּחָן. יְהֵא רַעֲוָא קֳדָמָךְ, דְּתִפְתַּח לִבָּאִי בְּאוֹרַיְתָא, וְתַשְׁלִים מִשְׁאֲלִין דְּלִבָּאִי, וְלִבָּא דְכָל עַמָּךְ יִשְׂרָאֵל, לְטַב וּלְחַיִּין וְלִשְׁלָם. (אָמֵן.)

The Torah is removed from the Ark and presented to the *chazzan,* who accepts it in his right arm. He then turns to the Ark and raises the Torah slightly as he bows and recites:

גַּדְּלוּ לַיהוה אִתִּי, וּנְרוֹמְמָה שְׁמוֹ יַחְדָּו.[1]

The *chazzan* turns to his right and carries the Torah to the *bimah,* as the congregation responds:

לְךָ יהוה הַגְּדֻלָּה וְהַגְּבוּרָה וְהַתִּפְאֶרֶת וְהַנֵּצַח וְהַהוֹד, כִּי כֹל בַּשָּׁמַיִם וּבָאָרֶץ, לְךָ יהוה הַמַּמְלָכָה וְהַמִּתְנַשֵּׂא לְכֹל לְרֹאשׁ.[2] רוֹמְמוּ יהוה אֱלֹהֵינוּ וְהִשְׁתַּחֲווּ לַהֲדֹם רַגְלָיו, קָדוֹשׁ הוּא. רוֹמְמוּ יהוה אֱלֹהֵינוּ וְהִשְׁתַּחֲווּ לְהַר קָדְשׁוֹ, כִּי קָדוֹשׁ יהוה אֱלֹהֵינוּ.[3]

אַב הָרַחֲמִים הוּא יְרַחֵם עַם עֲמוּסִים, וְיִזְכֹּר בְּרִית אֵיתָנִים, וְיַצִּיל נַפְשׁוֹתֵינוּ מִן הַשָּׁעוֹת הָרָעוֹת, וְיִגְעַר בְּיֵצֶר הָרַע מִן הַנְּשׂוּאִים, וְיָחֹן אוֹתָנוּ לִפְלֵיטַת עוֹלָמִים, וִימַלֵּא מִשְׁאֲלוֹתֵינוּ בְּמִדָּה טוֹבָה יְשׁוּעָה וְרַחֲמִים.

The Torah is placed on the *bimah* and prepared for reading.
The appropriate portions for the weekday readings may be found beginning on p. 927.
The laws of the Torah reading are found on pp. 987-989.

The two versions of the prayer differ only slightly from one another. Version A asks that we not be chastised as a result of God's anger at our shortcomings; while version B asks that God

Zohar, Vayakhel 369a

בְּרִיךְ שְׁמֵהּ *Blessed is the Name of the Master of the universe, blessed is Your crown and Your place. May Your favor remain with Your people Israel forever; may You display the salvation of Your right hand to Your people in Your Holy Temple, to benefit us with the goodness of Your luminescence and to accept our prayers with mercy. May it be Your will that You extend our lives with goodness and that I be numbered among the righteous; that You have mercy on me and protect me, all that is mine and that is Your people Israel's. It is You Who nourishes all and sustains all, You control everything. It is You Who control kings, and kingship is Yours. I am a servant of the Holy One, Blessed is He, and I prostrate myself before Him and before the glory of His Torah at all times. Not in any man do I put trust, nor on any angel do I rely — only on the God of heaven Who is the God of truth, Whose Torah is truth and Whose prophets are true and Who acts liberally with kindness and truth. In Him do I trust, and to His glorious and holy Name do I declare praises. May it be Your will that You open my heart to the Torah and that You fulfill the wishes of my heart and the heart of Your entire people Israel for good, for life, and for peace. (Amen.)*

The Torah is removed from the Ark and presented to the *chazzan,* who accepts it in his right arm. He then turns to the Ark and raises the Torah slightly as he bows and recites:

Declare the greatness of HASHEM with me, and let us exalt His Name together.[1]

The *chazzan* turns to his right and carries the Torah to the *bimah,* as the congregation responds:

לְךָ *Yours, HASHEM, is the greatness, the strength, the splendor, the triumph, and the glory; even everything in heaven and earth; Yours, HASHEM, is the kingdom, and the sovereignty over every leader.*[2] *Exalt HASHEM, our God, and bow at His footstool; He is Holy! Exalt HASHEM, our God, and bow at His holy mountain; for holy is HASHEM, our God.*[3]

אַב הָרַחֲמִים *May the Father of mercy have mercy on the nation that is borne by Him, and may He remember the covenant of the spiritually mighty. May He rescue our souls from the bad times, and upbraid the Evil Inclination to leave those borne by Him, graciously make us an eternal remnant, and fulfill our requests in good measure, for salvation and mercy.*

The Torah is placed on the *bimah* and prepared for reading.
The appropriate portions for the weekday readings may be found beginning on p. 927.
The laws of the Torah reading are found on pp. 987-989.

(1) *Psalms* 34:4. (2) *I Chronicles* 29:11. (3) *Psalms* 99:5,9.

not conceal His face from us, i.e., that He not make it impossible for us to perceive His Presence and gain some understanding of His ways. Some early authorities such as *Kol Bo,*

The *gabbai* uses the following formula to call a *Kohen* to the Torah:

וְתִגָּלֶה וְתֵרָאֶה מַלְכוּתוֹ עָלֵינוּ בִּזְמַן קָרוֹב, וְיָחֹן פְּלֵיטָתֵנוּ וּפְלֵיטַת עַמּוֹ בֵּית יִשְׂרָאֵל לְחֵן וּלְחֶסֶד וּלְרַחֲמִים וּלְרָצוֹן. וְנֹאמַר אָמֵן. הַכֹּל הָבוּ גֹדֶל לֵאלֹהֵינוּ וּתְנוּ כָבוֹד לַתּוֹרָה. כֹּהֵן° קְרָב, יַעֲמֹד (insert name) הַכֹּהֵן.

°If no *Kohen* is present, the *gabbai* says:
"אֵין כַּאן כֹּהֵן, יַעֲמֹד (insert name) יִשְׂרָאֵל (לֵוִי) בִּמְקוֹם כֹּהֵן."

בָּרוּךְ שֶׁנָּתַן תּוֹרָה לְעַמּוֹ יִשְׂרָאֵל בִּקְדֻשָּׁתוֹ. (תּוֹרַת יהוה תְּמִימָה מְשִׁיבַת נָפֶשׁ, עֵדוּת יהוה נֶאֱמָנָה מַחְכִּימַת פֶּתִי. פִּקּוּדֵי יהוה יְשָׁרִים מְשַׂמְּחֵי לֵב, מִצְוַת יהוה בָּרָה מְאִירַת עֵינָיִם.[1] יהוה עֹז לְעַמּוֹ יִתֵּן, יהוה יְבָרֵךְ אֶת עַמּוֹ בַשָּׁלוֹם.[2] הָאֵל תָּמִים דַּרְכּוֹ, אִמְרַת יהוה צְרוּפָה, מָגֵן הוּא לְכֹל הַחֹסִים בּוֹ.[3])

Congregation, then *gabbai:*

וְאַתֶּם הַדְּבֵקִים בַּיהוה אֱלֹהֵיכֶם, חַיִּים כֻּלְּכֶם הַיּוֹם:[4]

קריאת התורה

[See *Laws* §97-114.] The reader shows the *oleh* (person called to the Torah) the place in the Torah. The *oleh* touches the Torah with a corner of his *tallis,* the strap of his *tefillin,* or the belt or mantle of the Torah, and kisses it. He then begins the blessing, bowing at בָּרְכוּ, and straightening up at ה'.

בָּרְכוּ אֶת יהוה הַמְּבֹרָךְ.

Congregation, followed by *oleh,* responds, bowing at בָּרוּךְ, and straightening up at ה'.

בָּרוּךְ יהוה הַמְּבֹרָךְ לְעוֹלָם וָעֶד.

Oleh continues:

בָּרוּךְ אַתָּה יהוה אֱלֹהֵינוּ מֶלֶךְ הָעוֹלָם, אֲשֶׁר בָּחַר בָּנוּ מִכָּל הָעַמִּים, וְנָתַן לָנוּ אֶת תּוֹרָתוֹ. בָּרוּךְ אַתָּה יהוה, נוֹתֵן הַתּוֹרָה. (Cong.— אָמֵן.)

After his Torah portion has been read, the *oleh* recites:

בָּרוּךְ אַתָּה יהוה אֱלֹהֵינוּ מֶלֶךְ הָעוֹלָם, אֲשֶׁר נָתַן לָנוּ תּוֹרַת אֱמֶת, וְחַיֵּי עוֹלָם נָטַע בְּתוֹכֵנוּ. בָּרוּךְ אַתָּה יהוה, נוֹתֵן הַתּוֹרָה. (Cong.— אָמֵן.)

ברכת הגומל*

The following is recited by one who has survived a dangerous situation.

בָּרוּךְ אַתָּה יהוה אֱלֹהֵינוּ מֶלֶךְ הָעוֹלָם, הַגּוֹמֵל לְחַיָּבִים טוֹבוֹת, שֶׁגְּמָלַנִי כָּל טוֹב.

Congregation responds:

אָמֵן. מִי שֶׁגְּמָלְךָ כָּל טוֹב, הוּא יִגְמָלְךָ כָּל טוֹב, סֶלָה.

בִּרְכַּת הַגּוֹמֵל / Thanksgiving Blessing

When the Temple stood, a person who had been spared from a life-threatening situation

Abudraham, and *Levush* hold that both versions should be recited, but only a few congregations follow this practice.

The *gabbai* uses the following formula to call a *Kohen* to the Torah:

וְתִגָּלֶה *And may His kingship over us be revealed and become visible soon, and may He be gracious to our remnant and the remnant of His people the Family of Israel, for graciousness, kindness, mercy, and favor. And let us respond, Amen. All of you ascribe greatness to our God and give honor to the Torah. Kohen,*° *approach. Arise* (name) *son of* (father's name) *the Kohen.*

°If no *Kohen* is present, the *gabbai* says: *'There is no Kohen present, stand* (name) *son of* (father's name) *an Israelite (Levite) in place of the Kohen.'*

Blessed is He Who gave the Torah to His people Israel in His holiness. (The Torah of HASHEM is perfect, restoring the soul; the testimony of HASHEM is trustworthy, making the simple one wise. The orders of HASHEM are upright, gladdening the heart; the command of HASHEM is clear, enlightening the eyes.[1] *HASHEM will give might to His people; HASHEM will bless His people with peace.*[2] *The God Whose way is perfect, the promise of HASHEM is flawless, He is a shield for all who take refuge in Him.*[3]*)*

Congregation, then *gabbai:*

You who cling to HASHEM, your God — you are all alive today.[4]

READING OF THE TORAH

[See *Laws* §97-114.] The reader shows the *oleh* (person called to the Torah) the place in the Torah. The *oleh* touches the Torah with a corner of his *tallis,* the strap of his *tefillin,* or the belt or mantle of the Torah, and kisses it. He then begins the blessing, bowing at *'Bless',* and straightening up at 'HASHEM.'

Bless HASHEM, the blessed One.

Congregation, followed by *oleh,* responds, bowing at 'Blessed,' and straightening up at 'HASHEM'.

Blessed is HASHEM, the blessed One, for all eternity.

Oleh continues:

בָּרוּךְ *Blessed are You, HASHEM, our God, King of the universe, Who selected us from all the peoples and gave us His Torah. Blessed are You, HASHEM, Giver of the Torah.* (Cong.— *Amen.)*

After his Torah portion has been read, the *oleh* recites:

בָּרוּךְ *Blessed are You, HASHEM, our God, King of the universe, Who gave us the Torah of truth and implanted eternal life within us. Blessed are You, HASHEM, Giver of the Torah.* (Cong.— *Amen.)*

THANKSGIVING BLESSING*

The following is recited by one who has survived a dangerous situation.

בָּרוּךְ *Blessed are You HASHEM, King of the universe, Who bestows good things upon the guilty, Who has bestowed every goodness upon me.*

Congregation responds:

Amen. May He Who has bestowed goodness upon you continue to bestow every goodness upon you forever.

(1) *Psalms* 19:8-9. (2) 29:11. (3) 18:31. (4) *Deuteronomy* 4:4.

would bring a thanksgiving offering. Now, the obligation to thank God is discharged by reciting the thanksgiving blessing during the Torah reading, within three days of the event, if

ברוך שפטרני

After a *bar mitzvah* boy completes his first *aliyah*, his father recites the following.

בָּרוּךְ (אַתָּה יהוה אֱלֹהֵינוּ מֶלֶךְ הָעוֹלָם), שֶׁפְּטָרַנִי מֵעָנְשׁוֹ שֶׁלָּזֶה.

PRAYER FOR A SICK PERSON

מִי שֶׁבֵּרַךְ אֲבוֹתֵינוּ אַבְרָהָם יִצְחָק וְיַעֲקֹב, מֹשֶׁה אַהֲרֹן דָּוִד וּשְׁלֹמֹה,

for a man

הוּא יְבָרֵךְ וִירַפֵּא אֶת הַחוֹלֶה (patient's name) בֶּן (mother's name) בַּעֲבוּר שֶׁ(name of supplicant) יִתֵּן לִצְדָקָה בַּעֲבוּרוֹ. בִּשְׂכַר זֶה, הַקָּדוֹשׁ בָּרוּךְ הוּא יִמָּלֵא רַחֲמִים עָלָיו, לְהַחֲלִימוֹ וּלְרַפְּאתוֹ וּלְהַחֲזִיקוֹ וּלְהַחֲיוֹתוֹ, וְיִשְׁלַח לוֹ מְהֵרָה רְפוּאָה שְׁלֵמָה מִן הַשָּׁמַיִם, לִרְמַ״ח אֵבָרָיו, וּשְׁסָ״ה גִּידָיו, בְּתוֹךְ שְׁאָר חוֹלֵי יִשְׂרָאֵל,

for a woman

הוּא יְבָרֵךְ וִירַפֵּא אֶת הַחוֹלָה (patient's name) בַּת (mother's name) בַּעֲבוּר שֶׁ(name of supplicant) יִתֵּן לִצְדָקָה בַּעֲבוּרָהּ. בִּשְׂכַר זֶה, הַקָּדוֹשׁ בָּרוּךְ הוּא יִמָּלֵא רַחֲמִים עָלֶיהָ, לְהַחֲלִימָהּ וּלְרַפְּאתָהּ וּלְהַחֲזִיקָהּ וּלְהַחֲיוֹתָהּ, וְיִשְׁלַח לָהּ מְהֵרָה רְפוּאָה שְׁלֵמָה מִן הַשָּׁמַיִם, לְכָל אֵבָרֶיהָ, וּלְכָל גִּידֶיהָ, בְּתוֹךְ שְׁאָר חוֹלֵי יִשְׂרָאֵל,

רְפוּאַת הַנֶּפֶשׁ, וּרְפוּאַת הַגּוּף, הַשְׁתָּא, בַּעֲגָלָא וּבִזְמַן קָרִיב. וְנֹאמַר: אָמֵן. (Cong.— אָמֵן.)

The מִי שֶׁבֵּרַךְ for the *oleh* and for a mother and her newborn child is found on p. 442.

In many congregations the *gabbai* recites אֵל מָלֵא רַחֲמִים, *O God, full of mercy,* in memory of the deceased, either on or prior to the day of a *Yahrzeit.*

אֵל מָלֵא רַחֲמִים, שׁוֹכֵן בַּמְּרוֹמִים, הַמְצֵא מְנוּחָה נְכוֹנָה עַל כַּנְפֵי הַשְּׁכִינָה, בְּמַעֲלוֹת קְדוֹשִׁים וּטְהוֹרִים כְּזֹהַר הָרָקִיעַ מַזְהִירִים,

for a man

אֶת נִשְׁמַת (name of deceased) בֶּן (his father's name) שֶׁהָלַךְ לְעוֹלָמוֹ, בַּעֲבוּר שֶׁ(name of supplicant) יִתֵּן צְדָקָה בְּעַד הַזְכָּרַת נִשְׁמָתוֹ, בְּגַן עֵדֶן תְּהֵא מְנוּחָתוֹ, לָכֵן בַּעַל הָרַחֲמִים יַסְתִּירֵהוּ בְּסֵתֶר כְּנָפָיו לְעוֹלָמִים, וְיִצְרוֹר בִּצְרוֹר הַחַיִּים אֶת נִשְׁמָתוֹ, יהוה הוּא נַחֲלָתוֹ, וְיָנוּחַ בְּשָׁלוֹם עַל מִשְׁכָּבוֹ, וְנֹאמַר: אָמֵן. (Cong.— אָמֵן.)

for a woman

אֶת נִשְׁמַת (name of deceased) בַּת (her father's name) שֶׁהָלְכָה לְעוֹלָמָהּ, בַּעֲבוּר שֶׁ(name of supplicant) יִתֵּן צְדָקָה בְּעַד הַזְכָּרַת נִשְׁמָתָהּ, בְּגַן עֵדֶן תְּהֵא מְנוּחָתָהּ, לָכֵן בַּעַל הָרַחֲמִים יַסְתִּירֶהָ בְּסֵתֶר כְּנָפָיו לְעוֹלָמִים, וְיִצְרוֹר בִּצְרוֹר הַחַיִּים אֶת נִשְׁמָתָהּ, יהוה הוּא נַחֲלָתָהּ, וְתָנוּחַ בְּשָׁלוֹם עַל מִשְׁכָּבָהּ, וְנֹאמַר: אָמֵן. (Cong.— אָמֵן.)

---

possible. It is customary, but not required, that the person reciting the blessing be called for an *aliyah*. The types of events that require one to recite the blessing are derived from *Psalm* 107. They are: (a) completion of a sea journey; (b) completion of a hazardous land journey; (c) recovery from a major illness; (d) release from captivity. By extension, however, the blessing

BAR MITZVAH BLESSING*

After a *bar mitzvah* boy completes his first *aliyah,* his father recites the following.

בָּרוּךְ *Blessed is the One (are You,* HASHEM, *our God, King of the universe), Who has freed me from the punishment due this boy.*

PRAYER FOR A SICK PERSON

מִי שֶׁבֵּרַךְ *He Who blessed our forefathers Abraham, Isaac and Jacob, Moses and Aaron, David and Solomon — may He bless and heal the sick person (*patient's Hebrew name*) son/daughter of (*patient's mother's Hebrew name*) because (*name of supplicant*) will contribute to charity on*

for a man

his behalf. In reward for this, may the Holy One, Blessed is He, be filled with compassion for him to restore his health, to heal him, to strengthen him, and to revivify him. And may He send him speedily a complete recovery from heaven for his two hundred forty-eight organs and three hundred sixty-five blood vessels,

for a woman

her behalf. In reward for this, may the Holy One, Blessed is He, be filled with compassion for her to restore her health, to heal her, to strengthen her, and to revivify her. And may He send her speedily a complete recovery from heaven for all her organs and all her blood vessels,

among the other sick people of Israel, a recovery of the body and a recovery of the spirit, swiftly and soon. Now let us respond: Amen. (Cong.— *Amen.)*

In many congregations the *gabbai* recites אֵל מָלֵא רַחֲמִים, *O God, full of mercy,* in memory of the deceased, either on or prior to the day of a *Yahrzeit.*

אֵל *O God, full of mercy, Who dwells on high, grant proper rest on the wings of the Divine Presence — in the lofty levels of the holy and the pure ones, who shine like the glow of the firmament — for the soul of*

for a man

(name of deceased) *son of* (name of his father)*, who went on to his world, for* (name of supplicant) *will contribute to charity in remembrance of his soul. May his resting place be in the Garden of Eden — therefore may the Master of mercy shelter him in the shelter of His wings for eternity; and may He bind his soul in the Bond of Life.* HASHEM *is his heritage, and may he repose in peace on his resting place. Now let us respond: Amen.* (Cong.— *Amen.)*

for a woman

(name of deceased) *daughter of* (name of her father)*, who went on to her world, for* (name of supplicant) *will contribute to charity in remembrance of her soul. May her resting place be in the Garden of Eden — therefore may the Master of mercy shelter her in the shelter of His wings for eternity; and may He bind her soul in the Bond of Life.* HASHEM *is her heritage, and may she repose in peace on her resting place. Now let us respond: Amen.* (Cong.— *Amen.)*

---

should be recited whenever someone has been spared from a life-threatening situation (*Orach Chaim* 219:9).

בָּרוּךְ שֶׁפְּטָרַנִי / Bar Mitzvah Blessing

The *Midrash Rabbah* to *Genesis* 25:27 teaches that this blessing is to be said by a father when his son becomes a *bar mitzvah.* Since the calling to the Torah is symbolic of religious adulthood, the father recites the blessing after his son has said the blessing following his *aliyah.* Although in most congregations the blessing is recited in

When the Torah reading has been completed the reader recites Half-*Kaddish* (p. 138), then the Torah is raised for all to see. Each person looks at the Torah and recites aloud:

וְזֹאת הַתּוֹרָה אֲשֶׁר שָׂם מֹשֶׁה לִפְנֵי בְּנֵי יִשְׂרָאֵל,[1] עַל פִּי יהוה בְּיַד מֹשֶׁה.[2]

Some add the following verses:

עֵץ חַיִּים הִיא לַמַּחֲזִיקִים בָּהּ, וְתֹמְכֶיהָ מְאֻשָּׁר.[3] דְּרָכֶיהָ דַרְכֵי נֹעַם, וְכָל נְתִיבוֹתֶיהָ שָׁלוֹם.[4] אֹרֶךְ יָמִים בִּימִינָהּ, בִּשְׂמֹאלָהּ עֹשֶׁר וְכָבוֹד.[5] יהוה חָפֵץ לְמַעַן צִדְקוֹ, יַגְדִּיל תּוֹרָה וְיַאְדִּיר.[6]

Before the Torah is returned to the Ark on Monday and Thursday, the *chazzan* recites the following prayer. It is omitted on days when *Tachanun* is not recited.

יְהִי רָצוֹן* מִלִּפְנֵי אָבִינוּ שֶׁבַּשָּׁמַיִם, לְכוֹנֵן אֶת בֵּית חַיֵּינוּ,* וּלְהָשִׁיב אֶת שְׁכִינָתוֹ בְּתוֹכֵנוּ, בִּמְהֵרָה בְיָמֵינוּ. וְנֹאמַר: אָמֵן.

(Cong.— אָמֵן.)

יְהִי רָצוֹן מִלִּפְנֵי אָבִינוּ שֶׁבַּשָּׁמַיִם, לְרַחֵם עָלֵינוּ וְעַל פְּלֵיטָתֵנוּ,* וְלִמְנֹעַ מַשְׁחִית וּמַגֵּפָה מֵעָלֵינוּ וּמֵעַל כָּל עַמּוֹ בֵּית יִשְׂרָאֵל. וְנֹאמַר: אָמֵן.

(Cong.— אָמֵן.)

יְהִי רָצוֹן מִלִּפְנֵי אָבִינוּ שֶׁבַּשָּׁמַיִם, לְקַיֶּם בָּנוּ חַכְמֵי יִשְׂרָאֵל,* הֵם וּנְשֵׁיהֶם וּבְנֵיהֶם וּבְנוֹתֵיהֶם וְתַלְמִידֵיהֶם וְתַלְמִידֵי תַלְמִידֵיהֶם, בְּכָל מְקוֹמוֹת מוֹשְׁבוֹתֵיהֶם. וְנֹאמַר: אָמֵן.

(Cong.— אָמֵן.)

יְהִי רָצוֹן מִלִּפְנֵי אָבִינוּ שֶׁבַּשָּׁמַיִם, שֶׁנִּשְׁמַע וְנִתְבַּשֵּׂר בְּשׂוֹרוֹת טוֹבוֹת, יְשׁוּעוֹת וְנֶחָמוֹת, וִיקַבֵּץ נִדָּחֵינוּ מֵאַרְבַּע כַּנְפוֹת הָאָרֶץ. וְנֹאמַר: אָמֵן.

(Cong.— אָמֵן.)

The entire congregation, followed by the *chazzan,* recites the next stanza aloud:

אַחֵינוּ* כָּל בֵּית יִשְׂרָאֵל, הַנְּתוּנִים בְּצָרָה וּבְשִׁבְיָה, הָעוֹמְדִים בֵּין בַּיָּם וּבֵין בַּיַּבָּשָׁה, הַמָּקוֹם יְרַחֵם עֲלֵיהֶם וְיוֹצִיאֵם מִצָּרָה לִרְוָחָה, וּמֵאֲפֵלָה לְאוֹרָה, וּמִשִּׁעְבּוּד לִגְאֻלָּה, הַשְׁתָּא בַּעֲגָלָא וּבִזְמַן קָרִיב. וְנֹאמַר: אָמֵן.

(Cong.— אָמֵן.)

---

abbreviated form (omitting the parenthesized phrase), many major Rabbinic authorities, with the concurrence of *Vilna Gaon,* rule that the blessing should be recited in its full form.

יְהִי רָצוֹן — *May it be the Will.* This very ancient series of prayers dates from the days of Rav Amram Gaon (9th century), whose *siddur* prescribed that it be recited after the Torah reading on Monday and Thursday. Apparently, the merit of communal Torah reading makes the time most fitting to beseech God for the fulfillment of His people's yearnings.

בֵּית חַיֵּינוּ — *The House of our lives.* The Temple is a primary factor in Jewish life because it is there that the Presence of God will rest. Consequently, it will give strength and meaning to Jewish spiritual life.

When the Torah reading has been completed the reader recites Half-*Kaddish* (p. 138), then the Torah is raised for all to see. Each person looks at the Torah and recites aloud:

This is the Torah that Moses placed before the Children of Israel,[1] upon the command of HASHEM, through Moses' hand.[2]

Some add the following verses:

It is a tree of life for those who grasp it, and its supporters are praiseworthy.[3] Its ways are ways of pleasantness and all its paths are peace.[4] Lengthy days are at its right; at its left are wealth and honor.[5] HASHEM desired, for the sake of its [Israel's] righteousness, that the Torah be made great and glorious.[6]

Before the Torah is returned to the Ark on Monday and Thursday, the *chazzan* recites the following prayer. It is omitted on days when *Tachanun* is not recited.

יְהִי רָצוֹן *May it be the will* of our Father Who is in heaven to establish the House of our lives* and to settle His Presence within us, speedily in our days — and let us say: Amen.* (Cong.— *Amen.*)

יְהִי רָצוֹן *May it be the will of our Father Who is in heaven to have mercy upon us and upon our remnant* and to keep destruction and plague away from us and from all of His people the Family of Israel — and let us say: Amen.* (Cong.— *Amen.*)

יְהִי רָצוֹן *May it be the will of our Father Who is in heaven to preserve among us the sages of Israel,* them, their wives, their sons, their daughters, their disciples and the students of their disciples in all their dwelling places — and let us say: Amen.* (Cong.— *Amen.*)

יְהִי רָצוֹן *May it be the will of our Father Who is in heaven that we may hear and be informed of good tidings, salvations, and consolations, and that our dispersed be gathered from the four corners of the earth — and let us say: Amen.* (Cong.— *Amen.*)

The entire congregation, followed by the *chazzan*, recites the next stanza aloud:

אַחֵינוּ *Our brothers,* the entire family of Israel, who are delivered into distress and captivity, whether they are on sea or dry land — may the Omnipresent One have mercy on them and remove them from distress to relief, from darkness to light, from subjugation to redemption, now, speedily, and soon — and let us say: Amen.* (Cong.— *Amen.*)

---

(1) *Deuteronomy* 4:44. (2) *Numbers* 9:23. (3) *Proverbs* 3:18. (4) 3:17. (5) 3:16. (6) *Isaiah* 42:21.

וְעַל פְּלֵיטָתֵנוּ — *And upon our remnant.* In the literal sense, this phrase refers to the many remnants of our people that escaped the countless pogroms, persecutions, expulsions, and slaughters of Jewish history. In the broader sense, it refers to the exiled nation that still survives the Destruction of the Temple and the dispersion of its people.

חַכְמֵי יִשְׂרָאֵל — *The sages of Israel.* Singled out are the Torah sages, for Israel was, is, and will be a nation only by virtue of the Torah.

⁂ אַחֵינוּ — *Our brothers.* This brief plea for God's mercy on all suffering Jews is often recited communally when prayers are offered for Jews who are in danger.

The *chazzan* takes the Torah in his right arm and recites:

יְהַלְלוּ אֶת שֵׁם יהוה, כִּי נִשְׂגָּב שְׁמוֹ לְבַדּוֹ —

Congregation responds:

— הוֹדוֹ עַל אֶרֶץ וְשָׁמָיִם. וַיָּרֶם קֶרֶן לְעַמּוֹ, תְּהִלָּה לְכָל חֲסִידָיו, לִבְנֵי יִשְׂרָאֵל עַם קְרֹבוֹ, הַלְלוּיָהּ.[1]

As the Torah is carried to the Ark, congregation recites Psalm 24, לְדָוִד מִזְמוֹר.

לְדָוִד מִזְמוֹר,* לַיהוה הָאָרֶץ וּמְלוֹאָהּ, תֵּבֵל וְיֹשְׁבֵי בָהּ. כִּי הוּא עַל יַמִּים יְסָדָהּ, וְעַל נְהָרוֹת יְכוֹנְנֶהָ. מִי יַעֲלֶה בְהַר יהוה, וּמִי יָקוּם בִּמְקוֹם קָדְשׁוֹ. נְקִי כַפַּיִם וּבַר לֵבָב, אֲשֶׁר לֹא נָשָׂא לַשָּׁוְא נַפְשִׁי וְלֹא נִשְׁבַּע לְמִרְמָה. יִשָּׂא בְרָכָה מֵאֵת יהוה, וּצְדָקָה מֵאֱלֹהֵי יִשְׁעוֹ. זֶה דּוֹר דֹּרְשָׁיו, מְבַקְשֵׁי פָנֶיךָ, יַעֲקֹב, סֶלָה. שְׂאוּ שְׁעָרִים רָאשֵׁיכֶם, וְהִנָּשְׂאוּ פִּתְחֵי עוֹלָם, וְיָבוֹא מֶלֶךְ הַכָּבוֹד. מִי זֶה מֶלֶךְ הַכָּבוֹד, יהוה עִזּוּז וְגִבּוֹר, יהוה גִּבּוֹר מִלְחָמָה. שְׂאוּ שְׁעָרִים רָאשֵׁיכֶם, וּשְׂאוּ פִּתְחֵי עוֹלָם, וְיָבֹא מֶלֶךְ הַכָּבוֹד. מִי הוּא זֶה מֶלֶךְ הַכָּבוֹד, יהוה צְבָאוֹת הוּא מֶלֶךְ הַכָּבוֹד, סֶלָה.

As the Torah is placed into the Ark, congregation recites the following verses:

וּבְנֻחֹה יֹאמַר,* שׁוּבָה יהוה רִבְבוֹת אַלְפֵי יִשְׂרָאֵל.[2] קוּמָה יהוה* לִמְנוּחָתֶךָ, אַתָּה וַאֲרוֹן עֻזֶּךָ. כֹּהֲנֶיךָ יִלְבְּשׁוּ צֶדֶק, וַחֲסִידֶיךָ יְרַנֵּנוּ. בַּעֲבוּר דָּוִד עַבְדֶּךָ אַל תָּשֵׁב פְּנֵי מְשִׁיחֶךָ.[3] כִּי לֶקַח טוֹב* נָתַתִּי לָכֶם, תּוֹרָתִי אַל תַּעֲזֹבוּ.[4] ❖ עֵץ חַיִּים הִיא לַמַּחֲזִיקִים בָּהּ, וְתֹמְכֶיהָ מְאֻשָּׁר.[5] דְּרָכֶיהָ דַרְכֵי נֹעַם, וְכָל נְתִיבֹתֶיהָ שָׁלוֹם.[6] הֲשִׁיבֵנוּ* יהוה אֵלֶיךָ וְנָשׁוּבָה, חַדֵּשׁ יָמֵינוּ כְּקֶדֶם.[7]

ON TISHAH B'AV, *KINNOS* ARE RECITED. ON PURIM THE *MEGILLAH* IS READ (SEE P. 786).

⊷§ **לְדָוִד מִזְמוֹר** — *Of David a psalm.* This psalm is recited when the Torah is brought back to the Ark because its final verses: *Raise up your heads, O gates ...* were recited when King Solomon brought the Ark into the newly built Temple. The commentary to this psalm appears with the Songs of the Day (p. 162).

⊷§ **וּבְנֻחֹה יֹאמַר** — *And when it rested he would say.* This is the companion verse to וַיְהִי בִּנְסֹעַ הָאָרֹן, *When the Ark would travel,* above (p. 138), which Moses said when the Ark began to journey. When it came to rest, he expressed this hope that God's Presence would find comfortable repose among the multitudes of the Jewish people. In other words, that Israel should be worthy of being host to God's holiness.

The rest of this paragraph is a selection of verses from Scripture on the themes of a resting place for God's Law, the greatness of the Torah, and the hope that God will see fit to draw us closer to His service.

קוּמָה ה׳ — *Arise, HASHEM.* These three verses (*Psalms* 132:8-10) were recited by Solomon, with minor changes, when he dedicated the Temple (*II Chronicles* 6:41-42). The first verse asks that God establish His resting place among Israel. The

The *chazzan* takes the Torah in his right arm and recites:

Let them praise the Name of HASHEM, for His Name alone will have been exalted —

Congregation responds:

— His glory is above earth and heaven. And He will have exalted the pride of His people, causing praise for all His devout ones, for the Children of Israel, His intimate nation. Halleluyah![1]

As the Torah is carried to the Ark, congregation recites Psalm 24, *'Of David a psalm.'*

לְדָוִד *Of David a psalm.* HASHEM's is the earth and its fullness, the inhabited land and those who dwell in it. For He founded it upon seas, and established it upon rivers. Who may ascend the mountain of HASHEM, and who may stand in the place of His sanctity? One with clean hands and pure heart, who has not sworn in vain by My soul and has not sworn deceitfully. He will receive a blessing from HASHEM and just kindness from the God of his salvation. This is the generation of those who seek Him, those who strive for Your Presence — Jacob, Selah. Raise up your heads, O gates, and be uplifted, you everlasting entrances, so that the King of Glory may enter. Who is this King of Glory? — HASHEM, the mighty and strong, HASHEM, the strong in battle. Raise up your heads, O gates, and raise up, you everlasting entrances, so that the King of Glory may enter. Who then is the King of Glory? HASHEM, Master of Legions, He is the King of Glory. Selah!*

As the Torah is placed into the Ark, congregation recites the following verses:

וּבְנֻחֹה *And when it rested he would say,* 'Return HASHEM to the myriad thousands of Israel.'*[2] *Arise, HASHEM,* to Your resting place, You and the Ark of Your strength. Let Your priests be clothed in righteousness, and Your devout ones will sing joyously. For the sake of David, Your servant, turn not away the face of Your anointed.*[3] *For I have given you a good teaching,* do not forsake My Torah.*[4] Chazzan— *It is a tree of life for those who grasp it, and its supporters are praiseworthy.*[5] *Its ways are ways of pleasantness and all its paths are peace.*[6] *Bring us back* to You, HASHEM, and we shall return, renew our days as of old.*[7]

ON TISHAH B'AV, *KINNOS* ARE RECITED. ON PURIM THE *MEGILLAH* IS READ (SEE P. 786).

(1) *Psalms* 148:13-14. (2) *Numbers* 10:36. (3) *Psalms* 132:8-10. (4) *Proverbs* 4:2. (5) 3:18. (6) 3:17. (7) *Lamentations* 5:21.

next verse refers to the *priests* who dedicate themselves to God's service, and the Levites whose song accompanies the Temple ritual. Finally, David prayed that the site chosen for the Temple — a choice that was made by David and the prophet Nathan — not be spurned, but that it remain eternally holy *(Radak; Ibn Ezra).*

כִּי לֶקַח טוֹב — *For ... a good teaching.* The next three verses, all from *Proverbs,* are a call to Israel: The Torah is God's most precious gift. It benefits those who are loyal to it; and it results in pleasantness and peace.

הֲשִׁיבֵנוּ — *Bring us back.* Finally, the Jewish soul cries out that it wants to find its way back to the spiritual greatness of yore. If only God will help us begin, we will continue with alacrity.

אשרי — ובא לציון

This concluding section of *Shacharis* is recited every weekday.

אַשְׁרֵי* יוֹשְׁבֵי בֵיתֶךָ, עוֹד יְהַלְּלְוּךָ סֶּלָה.[1] אַשְׁרֵי הָעָם שֶׁכָּכָה לּוֹ, אַשְׁרֵי הָעָם שֶׁיהוה אֱלֹהָיו.[2]

תהלים קמה

תְּהִלָּה לְדָוִד,

אֲרוֹמִמְךָ אֱלוֹהַי הַמֶּלֶךְ, וַאֲבָרְכָה שִׁמְךָ לְעוֹלָם וָעֶד.

בְּכָל יוֹם אֲבָרְכֶךָּ, וַאֲהַלְלָה שִׁמְךָ לְעוֹלָם וָעֶד.

גָּדוֹל יהוה וּמְהֻלָּל מְאֹד, וְלִגְדֻלָּתוֹ אֵין חֵקֶר.

דּוֹר לְדוֹר יְשַׁבַּח מַעֲשֶׂיךָ, וּגְבוּרֹתֶיךָ יַגִּידוּ.

הֲדַר כְּבוֹד הוֹדֶךָ, וְדִבְרֵי נִפְלְאֹתֶיךָ אָשִׂיחָה.

וֶעֱזוּז נוֹרְאוֹתֶיךָ יֹאמֵרוּ, וּגְדוּלָּתְךָ אֲסַפְּרֶנָּה.

זֵכֶר רַב טוּבְךָ יַבִּיעוּ, וְצִדְקָתְךָ יְרַנֵּנוּ.

חַנּוּן וְרַחוּם יהוה, אֶרֶךְ אַפַּיִם וּגְדָל חָסֶד.

טוֹב יהוה לַכֹּל, וְרַחֲמָיו עַל כָּל מַעֲשָׂיו.

יוֹדְוּךָ יהוה כָּל מַעֲשֶׂיךָ, וַחֲסִידֶיךָ יְבָרְכוּכָה.

כְּבוֹד מַלְכוּתְךָ יֹאמֵרוּ, וּגְבוּרָתְךָ יְדַבֵּרוּ.

לְהוֹדִיעַ לִבְנֵי הָאָדָם גְּבוּרֹתָיו, וּכְבוֹד הֲדַר מַלְכוּתוֹ.

מַלְכוּתְךָ מַלְכוּת כָּל עֹלָמִים, וּמֶמְשַׁלְתְּךָ בְּכָל דּוֹר וָדֹר.

סוֹמֵךְ יהוה לְכָל הַנֹּפְלִים, וְזוֹקֵף לְכָל הַכְּפוּפִים.

עֵינֵי כֹל אֵלֶיךָ יְשַׂבֵּרוּ, וְאַתָּה נוֹתֵן לָהֶם אֶת אָכְלָם בְּעִתּוֹ.

Concentrate while reciting the verse פּוֹתֵחַ. It is customary to touch the arm-*tefillin* while saying the first half of the verse, and the head-*tefillin* while saying the second.

פּוֹתֵחַ אֶת יָדֶךָ,
וּמַשְׂבִּיעַ לְכָל חַי רָצוֹן.

צַדִּיק יהוה בְּכָל דְּרָכָיו, וְחָסִיד בְּכָל מַעֲשָׂיו.

קָרוֹב יהוה לְכָל קֹרְאָיו, לְכֹל אֲשֶׁר יִקְרָאֻהוּ בֶאֱמֶת.

אַשְׁרֵי — וּבָא לְצִיּוֹן / ASHREI — UVA L'TZION

אַשְׁרֵי — *Praiseworthy.* With *Shemoneh Esrei* and *Tachanun*, both the *Shacharis* service and we who have recited it reached the climax of spiritual elevation. Now, we return to the everyday life with which we will grapple for the rest of the day. *Ashrei* is the perfect symbol of this transition, because it praises not only God's omnipotence, but also His closeness to and compassion for all creatures. Most importantly, it contains the critical verse, *You open Your hand, and satisfy the desire of every living thing,* which, the Sages teach, is the reason *Ashrei* is recited three times daily. The *Zohar* teaches that the *Ashrei* of *Pesukei D'zimrah* is meant as praise of God rather than a plea for mercy and sustenance. The *Ashrei* we are about to recite now, however, is our plea that God provide our needs, coming as it does after the prayers of *Shemoneh Esrei*. Only now, after the praise and exaltation of *Shemoneh Esrei* may we pray for ourselves *(World of Prayer)*. [A commentary to *Ashrei* appears on pages 66-70.]

ASHREI — UVA L'TZION

This concluding section of *Shacharis* is recited every weekday.

אַשְׁרֵי *Praiseworthy* are those who dwell in Your house; may they always praise You, Selah!*[1] *Praiseworthy is the people for whom this is so, praiseworthy is the people whose God is* HASHEM.[2]

Psalm 145 *A psalm of praise by David:*

א *I will exalt You, my God the King,*
and I will bless Your Name forever and ever.
ב *Every day I will bless You,*
and I will laud Your Name forever and ever.
ג HASHEM *is great and exceedingly lauded,*
and His greatness is beyond investigation.
ד *Each generation will praise Your deeds to the next*
and of Your mighty deeds they will tell;
ה *The splendrous glory of Your power*
and Your wondrous deeds I shall discuss.
ו *And of Your awesome power they will speak,*
and Your greatness I shall relate.
ז *A recollection of Your abundant goodness they will utter*
and of Your righteousness they will sing exultantly.
ח *Gracious and merciful is* HASHEM,
slow to anger, and great in [bestowing] kindness.
ט HASHEM *is good to all; His mercies are on all His works.*
י *All Your works shall thank You,* HASHEM,
and Your devout ones will bless You.
כ *Of the glory of Your kingdom they will speak,*
and of Your power they will tell.
ל *To inform human beings of His mighty deeds,*
and the glorious splendor of His kingdom.
מ *Your kingdom is a kingdom spanning all eternities,*
and Your dominion is throughout every generation.
ס HASHEM *supports all the fallen ones and straightens all the bent.*
ע *The eyes of all look to You with hope*
and You give them their food in its proper time;
פ *You open Your hand,*
and satisfy the desire
of every living thing.

Concentrate while reciting the verse, *'You open ...'.* It is customary to touch the arm-*tefillin* while saying the first half of the verse, and the head-*tefillin* while saying the second.

צ *Righteous is* HASHEM *in all His ways*
and magnanimous in all His deeds.
ק HASHEM *is close to all who call upon Him —*
to all who call upon Him sincerely.

---

(1) *Psalms* 84:5. (2) 144:15.

רְצוֹן יְרֵאָיו יַעֲשֶׂה, וְאֶת שַׁוְעָתָם יִשְׁמַע וְיוֹשִׁיעֵם. שׁוֹמֵר יהוה אֶת כָּל אֹהֲבָיו, וְאֵת כָּל הָרְשָׁעִים יַשְׁמִיד. ❖ תְּהִלַּת יהוה יְדַבֶּר פִּי, וִיבָרֵךְ כָּל בָּשָׂר שֵׁם קָדְשׁוֹ לְעוֹלָם וָעֶד. וַאֲנַחְנוּ נְבָרֵךְ יָהּ, מֵעַתָּה וְעַד עוֹלָם, הַלְלוּיָהּ.[1]

Psalm 20, לַמְנַצֵּחַ, is recited each weekday morning except: Rosh Chodesh, Erev Pesach, Chol HaMoed, Tishah B'Av, Erev Yom Kippur, Chanukah, Purim and Shushan Purim, the 14th and 15th of Adar I (Purim Kattan), and in a house of mourning.

לַמְנַצֵּחַ* מִזְמוֹר לְדָוִד. יַעַנְךָ יהוה בְּיוֹם צָרָה,* יְשַׂגֶּבְךָ שֵׁם אֱלֹהֵי יַעֲקֹב.* יִשְׁלַח עֶזְרְךָ מִקֹּדֶשׁ,* וּמִצִּיּוֹן יִסְעָדֶךָּ. יִזְכֹּר כָּל מִנְחֹתֶיךָ,* וְעוֹלָתְךָ יְדַשְּׁנֶה סֶלָה. יִתֶּן לְךָ כִלְבָבֶךָ וְכָל עֲצָתְךָ יְמַלֵּא. נְרַנְּנָה בִּישׁוּעָתֶךָ, וּבְשֵׁם אֱלֹהֵינוּ נִדְגֹּל, יְמַלֵּא יהוה כָּל מִשְׁאֲלוֹתֶיךָ. עַתָּה יָדַעְתִּי* כִּי הוֹשִׁיעַ יהוה מְשִׁיחוֹ, יַעֲנֵהוּ מִשְּׁמֵי קָדְשׁוֹ, בִּגְבוּרוֹת יֵשַׁע יְמִינוֹ. אֵלֶּה בָרֶכֶב,* וְאֵלֶּה בַסּוּסִים, וַאֲנַחְנוּ בְּשֵׁם יהוה אֱלֹהֵינוּ נַזְכִּיר. הֵמָּה כָּרְעוּ וְנָפָלוּ וַאֲנַחְנוּ* קַמְנוּ וַנִּתְעוֹדָד. ❖ יהוה הוֹשִׁיעָה, הַמֶּלֶךְ יַעֲנֵנוּ בְיוֹם קָרְאֵנוּ.

As noted in the commentary, the primary part of וּבָא לְצִיּוֹן is the reference to the *Kedushah* recited by the angels. These verses are presented in bold type and it is preferable that the congregation recite them aloud and in unison. However, the interpretive translation in Aramaic (which follows the verses in bold type) should be recited softly.

לַמְנַצֵּחַ — *For the Conductor. Vilna Gaon* comments that this psalm has seventy words, alluding to the seventy-year exile before the construction of the Second Temple. Since this psalm alludes to the period before the construction of an earlier Temple, it was inserted into the daily prayers to symbolize the period before the building of the Third and final Temple. This period is called by the Sages חֶבְלֵי מָשִׁיחַ, the *birthpangs of the Messiah.* Just as labor pains are immeasurably more severe than the discomfort of childbirth, and just as the time of greatest suffering precedes the intense joy of giving birth, so the trials of the exile will intensify before the coming of Messiah. Therefore, this psalm was inserted into the daily prayers to beseech God for help in time of distress. Because of its somber nature, the psalm is omitted on festive days.

בְּיוֹם צָרָה — *On the day of distress;* before it is too late *(Malbim).*

אֱלֹהֵי יַעֲקֹב — *Jacob's God.* Of all the Patriarchs, Jacob had the hardest life — the threats from Esau, exile under Laban and Pharaoh, the death of Rachel, the kidnaping of Dinah, the loss of Joseph — but God protected him. Therefore, in time of distress we call upon Jacob's God *(Kad HaKemach).*

יִשְׁלַח עֶזְרְךָ מִקֹּדֶשׁ — *May He dispatch your help from the Sanctuary,* i.e., from the Holy of Holies inside the Temple where the Holy Ark rests and where God's spirit dwells. From there will go forth divine aid in battle *(Radak).* We pray that our aid come from the Sanctuary, based in holiness, and not from unholy sources such as the hands of gentile kings and armies which may fight on our side. It is the holiness of the Jewish people themselves, their sacred deeds and words, that is their main ally in battle.

מִנְחֹתֶיךָ — *Your offerings,* i.e., Israel's offerings in the Temple *(Ibn Ezra);* or the prayers offered in time of danger *(Rashi).*

עַתָּה יָדַעְתִּי — *Now I know.* After God grants the salvation discussed in the previous verses, I will know that He is the Source of help and triumph *(Radak).*

אֵלֶּה בָרֶכֶב — *Some with chariots.* Some of our foes rely on chariots and others on cavalry, but we trust in God *(Rashi).*

הֵמָּה ... וַאֲנַחְנוּ — *They ... but we.* Our seemingly

ר *The will of those who fear Him He will do; and their cry He will hear, and save them.*

ש *HASHEM protects all who love Him; but all the wicked He will destroy.*

ת Chazzan— *May my mouth declare the praise of HASHEM and may all flesh bless His Holy Name forever and ever. We will bless God from this time and forever, Halleluyah!*[1]

Psalm 20, *'For the Conductor,'* is recited each weekday morning except: Rosh Chodesh, Erev Pesach, Chol Hamoed, Tishah B'Av, Erev Yom Kippur, Chanukah, Purim and Shushan Purim, the 14th and 15th of Adar I (Purim Kattan), and in a house of mourning.

לַמְנַצֵּחַ *For the Conductor;* a psalm of David. May HASHEM answer you on the day of distress,* may the Name of Jacob's God* make you impregnable. May He dispatch your help from the Sanctuary,* and support you from Zion. May He remember all your offerings,* and consider your burnt sacrifices generous, Selah. May He grant you your heart's desire, and fulfill your every plan. May we sing for joy at your salvation, and raise our banner in the name of our God, may HASHEM fulfill all your requests. Now I know* that HASHEM has saved His anointed one; He will answer him from His sacred heaven, with the omnipotent salvations of His right arm. Some with chariots,* and some with horses, but we — in the Name of HASHEM, our God, we call out. They slumped and fell, but we* arose and were invigorated.* Chazzan— *HASHEM save! May the King answer us on the day we call.*

As noted in the commentary, the primary part of וּבָא לְצִיּוֹן, *'A redeemer shall come ...,'* is the reference to the *Kedushah* recited by the angels. These verses are presented in bold type and it is preferable that the congregation recite them aloud and in unison. However, the interpretive translation in Aramaic (which follows the verses in bold type) should be recited softly.

(1) *Psalms* 115:18.

invincible enemies were the ones who slumped in defeat, but we, who had been losing, arose and overwhelmed them when we called out in God's Name *(Radak).*

וּבָא לְצִיּוֹן / Uva L'tzion

The most important part of the וּבָא לְצִיּוֹן prayer is the recitation in unison of the angel's praises of God. The Talmud refers to this part of the prayer as קְדוּשָּׁה דְסִדְרָא, *the Order of Kedushah.*

The Talmud *(Sotah* 49a) declares that since the destruction of the Temple, even the physical beauty and pleasures of the world began deteriorating. If so, by what merit does the world endure? Rava teaches, because of *The Order of Kedushah* that is contained in the prayer *Uva L'tzion,* and the recitation of *Kaddish* following the public study of Torah. *Rashi* explains that after the Destruction, the primary focus of holiness in the universe is Torah study. In *Uva L'tzion,* the Talmudic Sages combined the Scriptural verses containing the angel's praise of God with the interpretive translation of *Yonasan ben Uziel.* Thus, this prayer constitutes Torah study and, because it is placed toward the end of the service, when even latecomers are present in the synagogue, it involves the entire congregation in Torah study. This emphasis on Torah study is further stressed by the latter part of *Uva L'tzion* which lauds the study and observance of the Torah. The *Kaddish* recited after public Torah study is a further affirmation of the Torah's central role in Jewish existence.

R' Yaakov Emden explains the significance of *Uva L'tzion* differently. Since the Destruction, we lack the Temple service as a means to assure acceptance of Israel's prayers. But God does not spurn the prayers of those who repent, nor is the merit of Torah study diminished. Thus, at the conclusion of *Shacharis,* the Sages inserted *Uva L'tzion,* which begins with a prophetic assurance to penitents and contains Torah study revolving around the sublime angelic praise: *Holy, Holy, Holy.*

In a mourner's home, and on Tishah B'Av, omit the verse וַאֲנִי זֹאת and continue וְאַתָּה קָדוֹשׁ

וּבָא לְצִיּוֹן גּוֹאֵל,* וּלְשָׁבֵי פֶשַׁע בְּיַעֲקֹב, נְאֻם יהוה. וַאֲנִי,
זֹאת בְּרִיתִי* אוֹתָם, אָמַר יהוה, רוּחִי אֲשֶׁר
עָלֶיךָ, וּדְבָרַי אֲשֶׁר שַׂמְתִּי בְּפִיךָ, לֹא יָמְוּשׁוּ מִפִּיךָ וּמִפִּי זַרְעֲךָ*
וּמִפִּי זֶרַע זַרְעֲךָ, אָמַר יהוה, מֵעַתָּה וְעַד עוֹלָם:[1] ❖ וְאַתָּה קָדוֹשׁ
יוֹשֵׁב תְּהִלּוֹת יִשְׂרָאֵל.*[2] וְקָרָא זֶה אֶל זֶה וְאָמַר:

קָדוֹשׁ, קָדוֹשׁ, קָדוֹשׁ יהוה צְבָאוֹת, מְלֹא כָל הָאָרֶץ כְּבוֹדוֹ.[3]
וּמְקַבְּלִין דֵּין מִן דֵּין וְאָמְרִין:
קַדִּישׁ בִּשְׁמֵי מְרוֹמָא עִלָּאָה בֵּית שְׁכִינְתֵּהּ,
קַדִּישׁ עַל אַרְעָא עוֹבַד גְּבוּרְתֵּהּ,
קַדִּישׁ לְעָלַם וּלְעָלְמֵי עָלְמַיָּא, יהוה צְבָאוֹת,
מַלְיָא כָל אַרְעָא זִיו יְקָרֵהּ.[4]

❖ וַתִּשָּׂאֵנִי רוּחַ,* וָאֶשְׁמַע אַחֲרַי קוֹל רַעַשׁ גָּדוֹל:
בָּרוּךְ כְּבוֹד יהוה מִמְּקוֹמוֹ.[5]
וּנְטָלַתְנִי רוּחָא, וְשִׁמְעֵת בַּתְרַי קָל זִיעַ סַגִּיא
דִּמְשַׁבְּחִין וְאָמְרִין:
בְּרִיךְ יְקָרָא דַיהוה מֵאֲתַר בֵּית שְׁכִינְתֵּהּ.[6]
יהוה יִמְלֹךְ לְעֹלָם וָעֶד.[7]
יהוה מַלְכוּתֵהּ קָאֵם לְעָלַם וּלְעָלְמֵי עָלְמַיָּא.[8]

יהוה אֱלֹהֵי אַבְרָהָם יִצְחָק וְיִשְׂרָאֵל אֲבֹתֵינוּ, שָׁמְרָה זֹּאת*
לְעוֹלָם, לְיֵצֶר מַחְשְׁבוֹת לְבַב עַמֶּךָ, וְהָכֵן לְבָבָם אֵלֶיךָ.[9] וְהוּא
רַחוּם, יְכַפֵּר עָוֹן וְלֹא יַשְׁחִית, וְהִרְבָּה לְהָשִׁיב אַפּוֹ, וְלֹא יָעִיר
כָּל חֲמָתוֹ.[10] כִּי אַתָּה אֲדֹנָי טוֹב וְסַלָּח, וְרַב חֶסֶד לְכָל

וּבָא לְצִיּוֹן גּוֹאֵל — *A redeemer shall come to Zion.* God pledges that Messiah will come to redeem the city Zion and the people of Israel. Not only those who remained righteous throughout the ordeal of exile will be saved, but even those who had been sinners will join in the glorious future, provided they return to the ways of God *(Etz Yosef).*

זֹאת בְּרִיתִי — *This is My covenant.* God affirms that His covenant with Israel will always remain in force: that His *spirit* [of prophecy] and the *words* [of His Torah] will remain with Israel forever *(Metzudos).*

מִפִּיךָ וּמִפִּי זַרְעֲךָ ... — *From your mouth nor from the mouth of your offspring ...* — Three generations are mentioned here. This is a Divine assurance that if a family produces three consecutive generations of profound Torah scholars, the blessing of Torah knowledge *will not be withdrawn* from its posterity *(Bava Metzia* 85a). In a broader sense, we see the fulfillment of this blessing in the miracle that Torah greatness has remained with Israel throughout centuries of exile and flight from

In a mourner's home, and on Tishah B'Av, omit the verse *'And as for Me ...'* and continue *'You are the Holy One ...'*

ובא לציון *'A redeemer shall come to Zion* and to those of Jacob who repent from willful sin,' the words of* HASHEM. *'And as for Me, this is My covenant* with them,' said* HASHEM, *'My spirit that is upon you and My words that I have placed in your mouth shall not be withdrawn from your mouth, nor from the mouth of your offspring,* nor from the mouth of your offspring's offspring,' said* HASHEM, *'from this moment and forever.'*[1] Chazzan— *You are the Holy One, enthroned upon the praises of Israel.**[2] *And one [angel] will call another and say:*

'Holy, holy, holy is HASHEM, Master of Legions, the whole world is filled with His glory.'[3]

And they receive permission from one another and say:
'Holy in the most exalted heaven, the abode of His Presence;
holy on earth, product of His strength;
holy forever and ever is HASHEM, *Master of Legions —*
the entire world is filled with the radiance of His glory.'[4]

Chazzan— *And a wind lifted me;* and I heard behind me the sound of a great noise:*

'Blessed is the glory of HASHEM from His place.'[5]

And a wind lifted me and I heard behind me the sound of the powerful movement of those who praised saying:
'Blessed is the honor of HASHEM
from the place of the abode of His Presence.'[6]

HASHEM shall reign for all eternity.[7]

HASHEM *— His kingdom is established forever and ever.*[8]

HASHEM, *God of Abraham, Isaac, and Israel, our forefathers, may You preserve this* forever as the realization of the thoughts in Your people's heart, and may You direct their heart to You.*[9] *He, the Merciful One, is forgiving of iniquity and does not destroy; frequently He withdraws His anger, not arousing His entire rage.*[10] *For You, my Lord, are good and forgiving, and abundantly kind to all*

(1) *Isaiah* 59:20-21. (2) *Psalms* 22:4. (3) *Isaiah* 6:3. (4) *Targum Yonasan* to *Isaiah* 6:3.
(5) *Ezekiel* 3:12. (6) *Targum Yonasan* to *Ezekiel* 3:12. (7) *Exodus* 15:18.
(8) *Targum Onkelos* to *Exodus* 15:18. (9) *I Chronicles* 29:18. (10) *Psalms* 78:38.

country to country and from continent to continent *(Siach Yitzchak).*

יוֹשֵׁב תְּהִלּוֹת יִשְׂרָאֵל — *Enthroned upon the praises of Israel.* Although God is praised by myriad angels, He values the praises of Israel above all; as the Sages teach *(Chullin* 90b), the angels are not permitted to sing their praises above until the Jews sing theirs below *(Abudraham).*

קָדוֹשׁ — *Holy.* The commentary to the song of the angels appears on pp. 86-88.

וַתִּשָּׂאֵנִי רוּחַ — *And a wind lifted me.* These words were uttered by the prophet Yechezkel, who had just been commanded to undertake a difficult mission on behalf of the exiled Jews. God sent a wind to lift him and transport him to Babylon, and as he was lifted, Yechezkel heard the song of the angels. This suggests that the person who ignores his own convenience in order to serve God can expect to climb spiritual heights beyond his normal capacity.

שָׁמְרָה זֹּאת — *May You preserve this.* May God help us remain permanently with the above fervent declaration of His holiness and kingship *(Abudraham).*

קְרָאֶיךָ.[1] צִדְקָתְךָ צֶדֶק לְעוֹלָם,* וְתוֹרָתְךָ אֱמֶת.[2] תִּתֵּן אֱמֶת לְיַעֲקֹב, חֶסֶד לְאַבְרָהָם,* אֲשֶׁר נִשְׁבַּעְתָּ לַאֲבֹתֵינוּ מִימֵי קֶדֶם.[3] בָּרוּךְ אֲדֹנָי יוֹם יוֹם יַעֲמָס לָנוּ,* הָאֵל יְשׁוּעָתֵנוּ סֶלָה.[4] יהוה צְבָאוֹת עִמָּנוּ, מִשְׂגָּב לָנוּ אֱלֹהֵי יַעֲקֹב סֶלָה.[5] יהוה צְבָאוֹת, אַשְׁרֵי אָדָם בֹּטֵחַ בָּךְ.[6] יהוה הוֹשִׁיעָה, הַמֶּלֶךְ יַעֲנֵנוּ בְיוֹם קָרְאֵנוּ.[7]

בָּרוּךְ הוּא אֱלֹהֵינוּ שֶׁבְּרָאָנוּ לִכְבוֹדוֹ, וְהִבְדִּילָנוּ מִן הַתּוֹעִים, וְנָתַן לָנוּ תּוֹרַת אֱמֶת, וְחַיֵּי עוֹלָם נָטַע בְּתוֹכֵנוּ. הוּא יִפְתַּח לִבֵּנוּ* בְּתוֹרָתוֹ, וְיָשֵׂם בְּלִבֵּנוּ אַהֲבָתוֹ וְיִרְאָתוֹ וְלַעֲשׂוֹת רְצוֹנוֹ וּלְעָבְדוֹ בְּלֵבָב שָׁלֵם, לְמַעַן לֹא נִיגַע לָרִיק, וְלֹא נֵלֵד לַבֶּהָלָה.[8]

יְהִי רָצוֹן מִלְּפָנֶיךָ יהוה אֱלֹהֵינוּ וֵאלֹהֵי אֲבוֹתֵינוּ, שֶׁנִּשְׁמֹר חֻקֶּיךָ בָּעוֹלָם הַזֶּה, וְנִזְכֶּה וְנִחְיֶה וְנִרְאֶה וְנִירַשׁ טוֹבָה וּבְרָכָה לִשְׁנֵי יְמוֹת הַמָּשִׁיחַ וּלְחַיֵּי הָעוֹלָם הַבָּא. לְמַעַן יְזַמֶּרְךָ כָבוֹד וְלֹא יִדֹּם, יהוה אֱלֹהַי לְעוֹלָם אוֹדֶךָּ.[9] בָּרוּךְ הַגֶּבֶר אֲשֶׁר יִבְטַח בַּיהוה,* וְהָיָה יהוה מִבְטַחוֹ.[10] בִּטְחוּ בַיהוה עֲדֵי עַד, כִּי בְּיָהּ יהוה צוּר עוֹלָמִים.[11] ❖ וְיִבְטְחוּ בְךָ יוֹדְעֵי שְׁמֶךָ, כִּי לֹא עָזַבְתָּ דֹרְשֶׁיךָ, יהוה.[12] יהוה חָפֵץ לְמַעַן צִדְקוֹ, יַגְדִּיל תּוֹרָה וְיַאְדִּיר.[13]

The regular weekday *Shacharis* continues with the Full *Kaddish* (below).
On Rosh Chodesh and Chol Hamoed the *chazzan* recites Half-*Kaddish;* then the congregation recites the *Mussaf Shemoneh Esrei* (for Rosh Chodesh, p. 644; for Chol Hamoed, p. 674).

קדיש שלם

יִתְגַּדַּל וְיִתְקַדַּשׁ שְׁמֵהּ רַבָּא. (Cong.— אָמֵן.) בְּעָלְמָא דִּי בְרָא כִרְעוּתֵהּ. וְיַמְלִיךְ מַלְכוּתֵהּ, בְּחַיֵּיכוֹן וּבְיוֹמֵיכוֹן וּבְחַיֵּי דְכָל בֵּית יִשְׂרָאֵל, בַּעֲגָלָא וּבִזְמַן קָרִיב. וְאִמְרוּ: אָמֵן.

(Cong.— אָמֵן. יְהֵא שְׁמֵהּ רַבָּא מְבָרַךְ לְעָלַם וּלְעָלְמֵי עָלְמַיָּא.)

יְהֵא שְׁמֵהּ רַבָּא מְבָרַךְ לְעָלַם וּלְעָלְמֵי עָלְמַיָּא.

יִתְבָּרַךְ וְיִשְׁתַּבַּח וְיִתְפָּאַר וְיִתְרוֹמַם וְיִתְנַשֵּׂא וְיִתְהַדָּר וְיִתְעַלֶּה וְיִתְהַלָּל שְׁמֵהּ דְּקֻדְשָׁא בְּרִיךְ הוּא (Cong.— בְּרִיךְ הוּא) — °לְעֵלָּא מִן כָּל (From Rosh Hashanah to Yom Kippur substitute— °לְעֵלָּא וּלְעֵלָּא מִכָּל) בִּרְכָתָא וְשִׁירָתָא תֻּשְׁבְּחָתָא וְנֶחֱמָתָא, דַּאֲמִירָן בְּעָלְמָא. וְאִמְרוּ: אָמֵן. (Cong.— אָמֵן.)

צִדְקָתְךָ צֶדֶק לְעוֹלָם — *Your righteousness remains righteous forever.* People question the ways of God because they do not see the righteous rewarded nor the wicked punished. But this question is a product of shortsightedness. God's justice is not measured in months or years. His reward lasts forever, so it does not matter if it is delayed during the temporary stay of our bodies

who call upon You.[1] Your righteousness remains righteous forever, and Your Torah is truth.[2] Grant truth to Jacob, kindness to Abraham,* as You swore to our forefathers from ancient times.[3] Blessed is my Lord for every single day, He burdens us with blessings,* the God of our salvation, Selah.[4] HASHEM, Master of Legions, is with us, a stronghold for us is the God of Jacob, Selah.[5] HASHEM, Master of Legions, praiseworthy is the man who trusts in You.[6] HASHEM, save! May the King answer us on the day we call.[7]*

Blessed is He, our God, Who created us for His glory, separated us from those who stray, gave us the Torah of truth and implanted eternal life within us. May He open our heart through His Torah and imbue our heart with love and awe of Him and that we may do His will and serve Him wholeheartedly, so that we do not struggle in vain nor produce for futility.[8]*

May it be Your will, HASHEM, our God and the God of our forefathers, that we observe Your decrees in This World, and merit that we live and see and inherit goodness and blessing in the years of Messianic times and for the life of the World to Come. So that my soul might sing to You and not be stilled, HASHEM, my God, forever will I thank You.[9] Blessed is the man who trusts in HASHEM, then HASHEM will be his security.[10] Trust in HASHEM forever, for in God, HASHEM, is the strength of the worlds.[11]* Chazzan— *Those knowing Your Name will trust in You, and You forsake not those Who seek You, HASHEM.[12] HASHEM desired, for the sake of its [Israel's] righteousness, that the Torah be made great and glorious.[13]*

The regular weekday *Shacharis* continues with the Full *Kaddish* (below).
On Rosh Chodesh and Chol Hamoed the *chazzan* recites Half-*Kaddish;* the congregation recites the *Mussaf Shemoneh Esrei* (for Rosh Chodesh, p. 644; for Chol Hamoed, p. 674).

FULL KADDISH

יִתְגַּדַּל *May His great Name grow exalted and sanctified* (Cong.— *Amen.*) *in the world that He created as He willed. May He give reign to His kingship in your lifetimes and in your days, and in the lifetimes of the entire Family of Israel, swiftly and soon. Now respond: Amen.*

(Cong.— *Amen. May His great Name be blessed forever and ever.*)

May His great Name be blessed forever and ever.

Blessed, praised, glorified, exalted, extolled, mighty, upraised, and lauded be the Name of the Holy One, Blessed is He (Cong.— *Blessed is He*) — (From Rosh Hashanah to Yom Kippur add: *exceedingly*) *beyond any blessing and song, praise and consolation that are uttered in the world. Now respond: Amen.* (Cong.— *Amen.*)

(1) *Psalms* 86:5. (2) 119:142. (3) *Micah* 7:20. (4) *Psalms* 68:20.
(5) 46:8. (6) 84:13. (7) 20:10. (8) Cf. *Isaiah* 65:23. (9) *Psalms* 30:13.
(10) *Jeremiah* 17:7. (11) *Isaiah* 26:4. (12) *Psalms* 9:11. (13) *Isaiah* 42:21.

---

on earth *(Siach Yitzchak).*

תִּתֵּן אֱמֶת לְיַעֲקֹב — *Grant truth to Jacob.* Even if we are undeserving of Your salvation, nevertheless, fulfill Your promise to the Patriarchs that You will help their offspring. Thus, You will establish Your attribute of truth, the attribute symbolized by Jacob *(Etz Yosef).*

יַעֲמָס לָנוּ — *He burdens us* [*with blessings*]. God gives us the daily responsibility to perform countless commandments *(Targum)* because He

On Tisha B'Av continue יְהֵא שְׁלָמָא.

(.Cong—קַבֵּל בְּרַחֲמִים וּבְרָצוֹן אֶת תְּפִלָּתֵנוּ.)

תִּתְקַבַּל צְלוֹתְהוֹן וּבָעוּתְהוֹן דְּכָל בֵּית יִשְׂרָאֵל קֳדָם אֲבוּהוֹן דִּי בִשְׁמַיָּא. וְאִמְרוּ: אָמֵן. (.Cong— אָמֵן.)

(.Cong—יְהִי שֵׁם יהוה מְבֹרָךְ, מֵעַתָּה וְעַד עוֹלָם.[1])

יְהֵא שְׁלָמָא רַבָּא מִן שְׁמַיָּא, וְחַיִּים עָלֵינוּ וְעַל כָּל יִשְׂרָאֵל. וְאִמְרוּ: אָמֵן. (.Cong— אָמֵן.)

(.Cong—עֶזְרִי מֵעִם יהוה, עֹשֵׂה שָׁמַיִם וָאָרֶץ.[2])

Take three steps back. Bow left and say ... עֹשֶׂה; bow right and say ... הוּא; bow forward and say וְעַל כָּל ... אָמֵן. Remain standing in place for a few moments, then take three steps forward.

עֹשֶׂה שָׁלוֹם בִּמְרוֹמָיו, הוּא יַעֲשֶׂה שָׁלוֹם עָלֵינוּ, וְעַל כָּל יִשְׂרָאֵל. וְאִמְרוּ: אָמֵן. (.Cong— אָמֵן.)

Stand while reciting עָלֵינוּ.

עָלֵינוּ לְשַׁבֵּחַ לַאֲדוֹן הַכֹּל, לָתֵת גְּדֻלָּה לְיוֹצֵר בְּרֵאשִׁית, שֶׁלֹּא עָשָׂנוּ כְּגוֹיֵי הָאֲרָצוֹת, וְלֹא שָׂמָנוּ כְּמִשְׁפְּחוֹת הָאֲדָמָה. שֶׁלֹּא שָׂם חֶלְקֵנוּ כָּהֶם, וְגוֹרָלֵנוּ* כְּכָל הֲמוֹנָם. (שֶׁהֵם מִשְׁתַּחֲוִים* לְהֶבֶל וָרִיק, וּמִתְפַּלְּלִים אֶל אֵל לֹא יוֹשִׁיעַ.[3]) וַאֲנַחְנוּ כּוֹרְעִים וּמִשְׁתַּחֲוִים וּמוֹדִים, לִפְנֵי מֶלֶךְ מַלְכֵי הַמְּלָכִים הַקָּדוֹשׁ בָּרוּךְ הוּא. שֶׁהוּא נוֹטֶה שָׁמַיִם וְיֹסֵד אָרֶץ,[4] וּמוֹשַׁב יְקָרוֹ בַּשָּׁמַיִם מִמַּעַל, וּשְׁכִינַת עֻזּוֹ בְּגָבְהֵי מְרוֹמִים. הוּא אֱלֹהֵינוּ, אֵין עוֹד. אֱמֶת מַלְכֵּנוּ, אֶפֶס זוּלָתוֹ, כַּכָּתוּב בְּתוֹרָתוֹ: וְיָדַעְתָּ הַיּוֹם וַהֲשֵׁבֹתָ אֶל לְבָבֶךָ,* כִּי יהוה הוּא הָאֱלֹהִים בַּשָּׁמַיִם מִמַּעַל וְעַל הָאָרֶץ מִתָּחַת, אֵין עוֹד.[5]

Bow while reciting וַאֲנַחְנוּ כּוֹרְעִים וּמִשְׁתַּחֲוִים.

---

desires to load us with blessings *(Radak)*.

הוּא יִפְתַּח לִבֵּנוּ — *May He open our heart.* This verse contains a major principle of the nature of Torah study. Though it is a rigorous and demanding intellectual pursuit, it cannot be mastered without pure motives, faith and love of God, and Divine help. If someone studies Torah only for the sake of the prestige it will give him to outwit less accomplished scholars, he will not succeed: his struggle for knowledge *will be in vain.* Or if someone has attained Torah knowledge in a commendable way, but later discards his faith, he will have lost the merit of his study — and will have *produced for futility (Vilna Gaon).*

אֲשֶׁר יִבְטַח בַּה׳ — *Who trusts in* HASHEM. In direct proportion to the extent that someone trusts in God, God *will be his security (Chiddushei HaRim).*

עָלֵינוּ / Aleinu

According to many early sources, among them a Gaonic responsum attributed to *Rabbi Hai Gaon, Rokeach* and *Kol Bo,* this declaration of faith and dedication was composed by Joshua after he led Israel across the Jordan. During the Talmudic era it was part of the Rosh Hashanah *Mussaf* service, and at some point during medieval times it began to find its way into the daily service.

Bach (Orach Chaim 133) explains that *Aleinu* was added to the daily prayers to implant faith in the Oneness of God's kingship, and the conviction that He will one day *remove detestable idolatry from the earth ...,* thus preventing Jews from being tempted to follow the beliefs and lifestyles of the nations among whom they dwell (see *Iyun Tefillah* and *Emek Brachah).*

As we can surmise from its authorship and its placement at the conclusion of every service, its significance is profound. Its first paragraph [עָלֵינוּ] proclaims the difference between Israel's concept of God and that of the other nations. The second paragraph [עַל כֵּן] expresses our

(Cong.— *Accept our prayers with mercy and favor.*)

May the prayers and supplications of the entire Family of Israel be accepted before their Father Who is in Heaven. Now respond: Amen. (Cong.— *Amen.*)

(Cong.— *Blessed be the Name of* HASHEM, *from this time and forever.*[1])

May there be abundant peace from Heaven, and life, upon us and upon all Israel. Now respond: Amen. (Cong.— *Amen.*)

(Cong.— *My help is from* HASHEM, *Maker of heaven and earth.*[2])

Take three steps back. Bow left and say, *'He Who makes peace ...,* bow right and say, *'may He ...';* bow forward and say, *'and upon all Israel ...'* Remain standing in place for a few moments, then take three steps forward.

He Who makes peace in His heights, may He make peace upon us, and upon all Israel. Now respond: Amen. (Cong.— *Amen.*)

Stand while reciting עָלֵינוּ, *'It is our duty ...'*

עָלֵינוּ ***It is our duty to praise the Master of all, to ascribe greatness to the Molder of primeval creation, for He has not made us like the nations of the lands and has not emplaced us like the families of the earth; for He has not assigned our portion like theirs nor our lot* like all their multitudes. (For they bow* to vanity and emptiness and pray to a god which helps not.[3]) But we bend our knees, bow, and acknowledge our thanks before the King Who reigns over kings, the Holy One, Blessed is He. He stretches out heaven and establishes earth's foundation,[4] the seat of His homage is in the heavens above and His powerful Presence is in the loftiest heights. He is our God and there is none other. True is our King, there is nothing beside Him, as it is written in His Torah: 'You are to know this day and take to your heart* that HASHEM is the only God — in heaven above and on the earth below — there is none other.'[5]***

Bow while reciting *'But we bend our knees.'*

(1) *Psalm* 113:2. (2) 121:2. (3) *Isaiah* 45:20. (4) 51:13. (5) *Deuteronomy* 4:39.

confidence that all humanity will eventually recognize His sovereignty and declare its obedience to His commandments. It should be clear, however, that this does not imply a belief or even a hope that they will convert to Judaism. Rather, they will accept Him as *the only God* and obey the universal Noachide laws that are incumbent upon all nations *(R' Hirsch).*

חֶלְקֵנוּ ... וְגוֹרָלֵנוּ — *Our portion ... our lot.* God does not punish gentile nations until they have reached the full quota of sin, beyond which He no longer extends mercy. Then He brings retribution upon them, often wiping them out. Such powerful ancient empires as Egypt, Persia, Greece, Rome, and Carthage have disappeared or become inconsequential. God does not act this way with regard to Israel, however. The world survives whether or not there is a Roman Empire, but the world could not survive without Israel. Therefore, God punishes Israel piecemeal, so that it may never be destroyed *(Siach Yitzchak).*

שֶׁהֵם מִשְׁתַּחֲוִים ... — *For they bow ...* The inclusion of this verse follows the original version of *Aleinu.* In the year 1400, a baptized Jew, no doubt seeking to prove his loyalty to the Church, spread the slander that this passage was meant to slur Christianity. He 'proved' his contention by the coincidence that the numerical value of וָרִיק, *emptiness,* is 316, the same as יֵשׁוּ, the Hebrew name of their messiah. The charge was refuted time and again, particularly by Manasseh ben Israel, the seventeenth century scholar, but repeated persecutions and Church insistence, backed by governmental enforcement, caused the line to be dropped from most Ashkenazic *siddurim.* While most congregations have not returned it to the *Aleinu* prayer, some prominent authorities, among them Rabbi Yehoshua Leib Diskin, insist that *Aleinu* be recited in its original form *(World of Prayer; Siach Yitzchak).*

וְיָדַעְתָּ הַיּוֹם וַהֲשֵׁבֹתָ אֶל לְבָבֶךָ — *You are to know this day and take to your heart.* The masters of *Mussar* explain that an abstract belief in God is

עַל כֵּן נְקַוֶּה לְּךָ* יהוה אֱלֹהֵינוּ לִרְאוֹת מְהֵרָה בְּתִפְאֶרֶת עֻזֶּךָ, לְהַעֲבִיר גִּלּוּלִים מִן הָאָרֶץ, וְהָאֱלִילִים כָּרוֹת יִכָּרֵתוּן, לְתַקֵּן עוֹלָם בְּמַלְכוּת שַׁדַּי. וְכָל בְּנֵי בָשָׂר יִקְרְאוּ בִשְׁמֶךָ, לְהַפְנוֹת אֵלֶיךָ כָּל רִשְׁעֵי אָרֶץ. יַכִּירוּ וְיֵדְעוּ כָּל יוֹשְׁבֵי תֵבֵל, כִּי לְךָ תִּכְרַע כָּל בֶּרֶךְ, תִּשָּׁבַע כָּל לָשׁוֹן.[1] לְפָנֶיךָ יהוה אֱלֹהֵינוּ יִכְרְעוּ וְיִפֹּלוּ, וְלִכְבוֹד שִׁמְךָ יְקָר יִתֵּנוּ. וִיקַבְּלוּ כֻלָּם אֶת עוֹל מַלְכוּתֶךָ, וְתִמְלֹךְ עֲלֵיהֶם מְהֵרָה לְעוֹלָם וָעֶד. כִּי הַמַּלְכוּת שֶׁלְּךָ הִיא וּלְעוֹלְמֵי עַד תִּמְלוֹךְ בְּכָבוֹד, כַּכָּתוּב בְּתוֹרָתֶךָ: יהוה יִמְלֹךְ לְעֹלָם וָעֶד.[2] ❖ וְנֶאֱמַר: וְהָיָה יהוה לְמֶלֶךְ עַל כָּל הָאָרֶץ, בַּיּוֹם הַהוּא יִהְיֶה יהוה אֶחָד וּשְׁמוֹ אֶחָד.[3]

Some congregations recite the following after עָלֵינוּ:

אַל תִּירָא* מִפַּחַד פִּתְאֹם, וּמִשֹּׁאַת רְשָׁעִים כִּי תָבֹא.[4] עֻצוּ עֵצָה וְתֻפָר, דַּבְּרוּ דָבָר וְלֹא יָקוּם, כִּי עִמָּנוּ אֵל.[5] וְעַד זִקְנָה אֲנִי הוּא, וְעַד שֵׂיבָה אֲנִי אֶסְבֹּל, אֲנִי עָשִׂיתִי וַאֲנִי אֶשָּׂא, וַאֲנִי אֶסְבֹּל וַאֲמַלֵּט.[6]

קדיש יתום

In the presence of a *minyan,* mourners recite קַדִּישׁ יָתוֹם, the Mourner's *Kaddish* (see *Laws* §119).

יִתְגַּדַּל וְיִתְקַדַּשׁ שְׁמֵהּ רַבָּא. (.Cong.— אָמֵן.) בְּעָלְמָא דִּי בְרָא כִרְעוּתֵהּ. וְיַמְלִיךְ מַלְכוּתֵהּ, בְּחַיֵּיכוֹן וּבְיוֹמֵיכוֹן וּבְחַיֵּי דְכָל בֵּית יִשְׂרָאֵל, בַּעֲגָלָא וּבִזְמַן קָרִיב. וְאִמְרוּ: אָמֵן.

(.Cong.— אָמֵן. יְהֵא שְׁמֵהּ רַבָּא מְבָרַךְ לְעָלַם וּלְעָלְמֵי עָלְמַיָּא.)

יְהֵא שְׁמֵהּ רַבָּא מְבָרַךְ לְעָלַם וּלְעָלְמֵי עָלְמַיָּא.

יִתְבָּרַךְ וְיִשְׁתַּבַּח וְיִתְפָּאַר וְיִתְרוֹמַם וְיִתְנַשֵּׂא וְיִתְהַדָּר וְיִתְעַלֶּה וְיִתְהַלָּל שְׁמֵהּ דְּקֻדְשָׁא בְּרִיךְ הוּא (.Cong.— בְּרִיךְ הוּא) — °לְעֵלָּא מִן כָּל (—From Rosh Hashanah to Yom Kippur substitute °לְעֵלָּא וּלְעֵלָּא מִכָּל) בִּרְכָתָא וְשִׁירָתָא תֻּשְׁבְּחָתָא וְנֶחֱמָתָא, דַּאֲמִירָן בְּעָלְמָא. וְאִמְרוּ: אָמֵן. (.Cong.— אָמֵן.)

יְהֵא שְׁלָמָא רַבָּא מִן שְׁמַיָּא, וְחַיִּים עָלֵינוּ וְעַל כָּל יִשְׂרָאֵל. וְאִמְרוּ: אָמֵן. (.Cong.— אָמֵן.)

Take three steps back. Bow left and say ... עֹשֶׂה; bow right and say ... הוּא; bow forward and say וְעַל כָּל ... אָמֵן. Remain standing in place for a few moments, then take three steps forward.

עֹשֶׂה שָׁלוֹם בִּמְרוֹמָיו, הוּא יַעֲשֶׂה שָׁלוֹם עָלֵינוּ, וְעַל כָּל יִשְׂרָאֵל. וְאִמְרוּ: אָמֵן. (.Cong.— אָמֵן.)

---

not sufficient to make people observe the *mitzvos* as they should. After obtaining knowledge we must take it to heart; that is, develop an emotional commitment to act upon the knowledge.

עַל כֵּן נְקַוֶּה לְּךָ ⁂ — *Therefore we put our hope in You.* Having stated that God chose us from among all the nations to serve Him, we are entitled to hope that He will speedily reveal his greatness and rid the earth of spiritual

עַל כֵּן *Therefore we put our hope in You,* HASHEM our God, that we may soon see Your mighty splendor, to remove detestable idolatry from the earth, and false gods will be utterly cut off, to perfect the universe through the Almighty's sovereignty. Then all humanity will call upon Your Name, to turn all the earth's wicked toward You. All the world's inhabitants will recognize and know that to You every knee should bend, every tongue should swear.*[1] *Before You, HASHEM, our God, they will bend every knee and cast themselves down and to the glory of Your Name they will render homage, and they will all accept upon themselves the yoke of Your kingship that You may reign over them soon and eternally. For the kingdom is Yours and You will reign for all eternity in glory as it is written in Your Torah: HASHEM shall reign for all eternity.*[2] Chazzan— *And it is said: HASHEM will be King over all the world — on that day HASHEM will be One and His Name will be One.*[3]

Some congregations recite the following after *Aleinu:*

אַל תִּירָא *Do not fear* sudden terror, or the holocaust of the wicked when it comes.*[4] *Plan a conspiracy and it will be annulled; speak your piece and it shall not stand, for God is with us.*[5] *Even till your seniority, I remain unchanged; and even till your ripe old age, I shall endure. I created you and I shall bear you; I shall endure and rescue.*[6]

MOURNER'S KADDISH

In the presence of a *minyan,* mourners recite קַדִּישׁ יָתוֹם, the Mourner's *Kaddish* (see *Laws* §119).

[A transliteration of this *Kaddish* appears on page 1043.]

יִתְגַּדַּל *May His great Name grow exalted and sanctified* (Cong.— *Amen.*) *in the world that He created as He willed. May He give reign to His kingship in your lifetimes and in your days, and in the lifetimes of the entire Family of Israel, swiftly and soon. Now respond: Amen.*

(Cong.—*Amen. May His great Name be blessed forever and ever.*)

May His great Name be blessed forever and ever

Blessed, praised, glorified, exalted, extolled, mighty, upraised, and lauded be the Name of the Holy One, Blessed is He (Cong.— *Blessed is He*) — (From Rosh Hashanah to Yom Kippur add: *exceedingly*) *beyond any blessing and song, praise and consolation that are uttered in the world. Now respond: Amen.* (Cong.— *Amen*).

May there be abundant peace from Heaven, and life, upon us and upon all Israel. Now respond: Amen. (Cong.— *Amen.*)

Take three steps back. Bow left and say, *'He Who makes peace ...';* bow right and say, *'may He ...';* bow forward and say, *'and upon all Israel ...'* Remain standing in place for a few moments, then take three steps forward.

He Who makes peace in His heights, may He make peace upon us, and upon all Israel. Now respond: Amen. (Cong.— *Amen.*)

(1) Cf. *Isaiah* 45:23. (2) *Exodus* 15:18. (3) *Zechariah* 14:9. (4) *Proverbs* 3:25. (5) *Isaiah* 8:10. (6) 46:4.

abomination *(Abudraham).*

אַל תִּירָא — *Do not fear. Zichron Zion* cites the custom of reciting these three verses after *Aleinu.* They express confidence in God's protection and are regarded as auguries of deliverance: (a) Do not fear an evildoer's intention, no matter how dangerous it seems; (b)

❦ שיר של יום ❦

The last part of *Shacharis* is שִׁיר שֶׁל יוֹם, *the Song of the Day,* a different psalm for each day of the week. On special occasions, additional psalms are recited after the Song of the Day. They are:
From Rosh Chodesh Elul to Shemini Atzeres, Psalm 27; לְדָוִד ה׳ אוֹרִי (p. 170);
on Rosh Chodesh, Psalm 104, בָּרְכִי נַפְשִׁי (p. 172); on Chanukah, Psalm 30, מִזְמוֹר שִׁיר (p. 54);
in a house of mourning, Psalm 49, לַמְנַצֵּחַ לִבְנֵי קֹרַח (p. 174).
After *Shacharis,* many people recite additional verses and prayers. See pp. 176ff.

SUNDAY

הַיּוֹם יוֹם רִאשׁוֹן בַּשַּׁבָּת, שֶׁבּוֹ הָיוּ הַלְוִיִּם אוֹמְרִים בְּבֵית הַמִּקְדָּשׁ:

תהלים כד

לְדָוִד מִזְמוֹר, לַיהוה הָאָרֶץ* וּמְלוֹאָהּ, תֵּבֵל וְיֹשְׁבֵי בָהּ. כִּי הוּא עַל יַמִּים יְסָדָהּ,* וְעַל נְהָרוֹת יְכוֹנְנֶהָ. מִי יַעֲלֶה* בְהַר יהוה, וּמִי יָקוּם בִּמְקוֹם קָדְשׁוֹ. נְקִי כַפַּיִם* וּבַר לֵבָב, אֲשֶׁר לֹא נָשָׂא לַשָּׁוְא נַפְשִׁי,* וְלֹא נִשְׁבַּע לְמִרְמָה. יִשָּׂא בְרָכָה* מֵאֵת יהוה, וּצְדָקָה מֵאֱלֹהֵי יִשְׁעוֹ. זֶה דּוֹר דֹּרְשָׁיו, מְבַקְשֵׁי פָנֶיךָ יַעֲקֹב סֶלָה. שְׂאוּ שְׁעָרִים* רָאשֵׁיכֶם, וְהִנָּשְׂאוּ פִּתְחֵי עוֹלָם,* וְיָבוֹא מֶלֶךְ הַכָּבוֹד. מִי זֶה מֶלֶךְ הַכָּבוֹד,* יהוה עִזּוּז וְגִבּוֹר, יהוה גִּבּוֹר מִלְחָמָה. ❖ שְׂאוּ שְׁעָרִים רָאשֵׁיכֶם, וּשְׂאוּ פִּתְחֵי עוֹלָם, וְיָבֹא מֶלֶךְ הַכָּבוֹד. מִי הוּא זֶה מֶלֶךְ הַכָּבוֹד, יהוה צְבָאוֹת, הוּא מֶלֶךְ הַכָּבוֹד סֶלָה.

In the presence of a *minyan,* mourners recite קַדִּישׁ יָתוֹם, the Mourner's *Kaddish* (p. 160).

MONDAY

הַיּוֹם יוֹם שֵׁנִי בַּשַּׁבָּת, שֶׁבּוֹ הָיוּ הַלְוִיִּם אוֹמְרִים בְּבֵית הַמִּקְדָּשׁ:

תהלים מח

שִׁיר מִזְמוֹר לִבְנֵי קֹרַח. גָּדוֹל יהוה וּמְהֻלָּל מְאֹד, בְּעִיר אֱלֹהֵינוּ, הַר קָדְשׁוֹ. יְפֵה נוֹף, מְשׂוֹשׂ כָּל הָאָרֶץ*, הַר צִיּוֹן* יַרְכְּתֵי צָפוֹן,* קִרְיַת מֶלֶךְ רָב. אֱלֹהִים בְּאַרְמְנוֹתֶיהָ נוֹדַע לְמִשְׂגָּב. כִּי הִנֵּה

---

let the enemies of Israel conspire and plan — they will fail; (c) God remains the eternal protector of Israel, even though it has sinned.

❦ שִׁיר שֶׁל יוֹם / SONG OF THE DAY ❦

As part of the morning Temple service, the Levites chanted a psalm that was suited to the significance of that particular day of the week *(Tamid* 7:4). As a memorial to the Temple, these psalms have been incorporated into *Shacharis.* The Talmud *(Rosh Hashanah* 31a) explains how each psalm was appropriate to its respective day; we will note the reasons in the commentary. The introductory sentence, *'Today is the first day of the Sabbath ...'* helps fulfill the Torah's command to remember the Sabbath always. By counting the days of the week with reference to the forthcoming Sabbath we tie our existence to the Sabbath. This is in sharp contrast to the non-Jewish custom of assigning names to the days in commemoration of events or gods, such as Sunday for the sun, Monday for the moon and so on *(Ramban, Exodus* 20:8).

❦ יוֹם רִאשׁוֹן / The First Day

The first day's psalm teaches that everything belongs to God, because on the first day of creation, God was the sole Power — even the angels had not yet been created. He took possession of His newly created world with the intention of ceding it to man *(Rosh Hashanah* 31a).

לַה׳ הָאָרֶץ — *HASHEM's is the earth.* Since the world belongs to God, anyone who derives pleasure from His world without reciting the proper blessing expressing thanks to the Owner is regarded as a thief *(Berachos* 35a).

כִּי הוּא עַל יַמִּים יְסָדָהּ — *For He founded it upon seas.* The entire planet was covered with water until God commanded it to gather in seas and rivers and to expose the dry land *(Ibn Ezra).*

מִי יַעֲלֶה ... — *Who may ascend ...?* God's most intense Presence is in the Temple, so those who wish to draw near and to perceive His splendor must be especially worthy *(Rashi).* By extension, one who wishes to enjoy spiritual elevation must refine his behavior.

נְקִי כַפַּיִם — *One with clean hands.* This verse answers the previous questions. To 'ascend,' one

SONG OF THE DAY

The last part of *Shacharis* is the Song of the Day, a different psalm for each day of the week. On special occasions, additional psalms are recited after the Song of the Day. They are:
From Rosh Chodesh Elul to Shemini Atzeres, Psalm 27, *'Of David: HASHEM is my light,'* (p. 170); on Rosh Chodesh, Psalm 104, *'Bless HASHEM,'* (p. 172); on Chanukah, Psalm 30, *'A Psalm'* (p. 54); in a house of mourning, Psalm 49, *'For the conductor, by the sons of Korach'* (p. 174).
After *Shacharis*, many people recite additional verses and prayers. See pp. 176ff.

SUNDAY

Today is the first day of the Sabbath, on which the Levites would recite in the Holy Temple:

Psalm 24

לְדָוִד *Of David a psalm.* HASHEM*'s is the earth* and its fullness, the inhabited land and those who dwell in it. For He founded it upon seas,* and established it upon rivers. Who may ascend* the mountain of* HASHEM*, and who may stand in the place of His sanctity? One with clean hands* and pure heart, who has not sworn in vain by My soul* and has not sworn deceitfully. He will receive a blessing* from* HASHEM *and just kindness from the God of his salvation. This is the generation of those who seek Him, those who strive for Your Presence — Jacob, Selah.* ***Raise up your heads, O gates,* and be uplifted, you everlasting entrances,* so that the King of Glory* may enter. Who is this King of Glory? —*** **HASHEM*****, the mighty and strong,*** **HASHEM*****, the strong in battle.*** Chazzan— ***Raise up your heads, O gates, and raise up, you everlasting entrances, so that the King of Glory may enter. Who then is the King of Glory?*** **HASHEM*****, Master of Legions, He is the King of Glory. Selah!***

In the presence of a *minyan,* mourners recite קַדִּישׁ יָתוֹם, the Mourner's *Kaddish* (p. 160).

MONDAY

Today is the second day of the Sabbath, on which the Levites would recite in the Holy Temple:

Psalm 48

שִׁיר מִזְמוֹר *A song, a psalm, by the sons of Korach. Great is* HASHEM *and much praised, in the city of our God, Mount of His Holiness. Fairest of sites, joy of all the earth* is Mount Zion,* by the northern sides* of the great king's city. In her palaces God is known as the Stronghold. For behold*

---

must have hands clean from dishonest gain, he must be honest in his dealings with man, and reverent in his attitude toward God.

נַפְשִׁי — *My soul.* God is the 'speaker.' He refers to one who swears falsely as having treated God's soul,' as it were, with disrespect.

יִשָּׂא בְרָכָה ... — *He will receive a blessing.* Because he honors God's Name in heart and behavior, such a person earns God's *blessing, kindness,* and *salvation (R' Hirsch).*

שְׂאוּ שְׁעָרִים — *Raise up ... O gates.* When Solomon sought to bring the Ark into the Temple, the gates remained shut despite all his pleas, until he prayed that God open the gates in the merit of David, who made all the preparations to build the Temple. Thus, this verse alludes to Solomon's future prayer *(Shabbos* 30a). The plea to the gates is repeated later to allude to the Ark's re-entry when the Third Temple will be built *(Ibn Ezra).*

פִּתְחֵי עוֹלָם — *Everlasting entrances,* i.e. the holiness of the Temple gates is eternal.

מֶלֶךְ הַכָּבוֹד — *The King of Glory.* God is given this title because He gives glory to those who revere Him *(Midrash).*

יוֹם שֵׁנִי / The Second Day

On this day, God separated between the heavenly and earthly components of the universe and ruled over both. Nevertheless, the psalm specifies Jerusalem because the seat of His holiness is Jerusalem *(Rosh Hashanah* 31a). *Resisei Laylah* comments that this day's separation between heaven and earth initiated the eternal strife between the spiritual and the physical. This is why the Levites chose a psalm composed by the sons of Korach, the man who instigated a quarrel against Moses.

מְשׂוֹשׂ כָּל הָאָרֶץ — *Joy of all the earth.* This title was given to Jerusalem because the Holy City gave joy to the troubled who gained atonement

הַמְּלָכִים נוֹעֲדוּ,* עָבְרוּ יַחְדָּו. הֵמָּה רָאוּ כֵּן תָּמָהוּ, נִבְהֲלוּ נֶחְפָּזוּ. רְעָדָה אֲחָזָתַם שָׁם, חִיל כַּיּוֹלֵדָה. בְּרוּחַ קָדִים תְּשַׁבֵּר אֳנִיּוֹת תַּרְשִׁישׁ.* כַּאֲשֶׁר שָׁמַעְנוּ* כֵּן רָאִינוּ בְּעִיר יהוה צְבָאוֹת, בְּעִיר אֱלֹהֵינוּ, אֱלֹהִים יְכוֹנְנֶהָ עַד עוֹלָם סֶלָה. דִּמִּינוּ אֱלֹהִים חַסְדֶּךָ, בְּקֶרֶב הֵיכָלֶךָ. כְּשִׁמְךָ אֱלֹהִים* כֵּן תְּהִלָּתְךָ, עַל קַצְוֵי אֶרֶץ, צֶדֶק מָלְאָה יְמִינֶךָ. יִשְׂמַח הַר צִיּוֹן, תָּגֵלְנָה בְּנוֹת יְהוּדָה, לְמַעַן מִשְׁפָּטֶיךָ. סֹבּוּ צִיּוֹן וְהַקִּיפוּהָ, סִפְרוּ מִגְדָּלֶיהָ. ❖ שִׁיתוּ לִבְּכֶם לְחֵילָה, פַּסְּגוּ אַרְמְנוֹתֶיהָ, לְמַעַן תְּסַפְּרוּ לְדוֹר אַחֲרוֹן. כִּי זֶה אֱלֹהִים אֱלֹהֵינוּ עוֹלָם וָעֶד, הוּא יְנַהֲגֵנוּ עַל־מוּת.*

In the presence of a *minyan,* mourners recite קַדִּישׁ יָתוֹם, the Mourner's *Kaddish* (p. 160).

TUESDAY

הַיּוֹם יוֹם שְׁלִישִׁי בַּשַּׁבָּת, שֶׁבּוֹ הָיוּ הַלְוִיִּם אוֹמְרִים בְּבֵית הַמִּקְדָּשׁ:

תהלים פב

מִזְמוֹר לְאָסָף,* אֱלֹהִים נִצָּב בַּעֲדַת אֵל,* בְּקֶרֶב אֱלֹהִים יִשְׁפֹּט. עַד מָתַי* תִּשְׁפְּטוּ עָוֶל, וּפְנֵי רְשָׁעִים תִּשְׂאוּ סֶלָה. שִׁפְטוּ דָל וְיָתוֹם, עָנִי וָרָשׁ הַצְדִּיקוּ. פַּלְּטוּ דַל וְאֶבְיוֹן, מִיַּד רְשָׁעִים הַצִּילוּ. לֹא יָדְעוּ* וְלֹא יָבִינוּ, בַּחֲשֵׁכָה יִתְהַלָּכוּ, יִמּוֹטוּ כָּל מוֹסְדֵי אָרֶץ. אֲנִי אָמַרְתִּי אֱלֹהִים אַתֶּם, וּבְנֵי עֶלְיוֹן כֻּלְּכֶם. אָכֵן כְּאָדָם תְּמוּתוּן, וּכְאַחַד הַשָּׂרִים תִּפֹּלוּ. ❖ קוּמָה אֱלֹהִים שָׁפְטָה הָאָרֶץ, כִּי אַתָּה תִנְחַל* בְּכָל הַגּוֹיִם.

In the presence of a *minyan,* mourners recite קַדִּישׁ יָתוֹם, the Mourner's *Kaddish* (p. 160).

WEDNESDAY

הַיּוֹם יוֹם רְבִיעִי בַּשַּׁבָּת, שֶׁבּוֹ הָיוּ הַלְוִיִּם אוֹמְרִים בְּבֵית הַמִּקְדָּשׁ:

תהלים צד:א־צה:ג

אֵל נְקָמוֹת יהוה, אֵל נְקָמוֹת הוֹפִיעַ. הִנָּשֵׂא שֹׁפֵט הָאָרֶץ, הָשֵׁב גְּמוּל עַל גֵּאִים. עַד מָתַי רְשָׁעִים, יהוה, עַד מָתַי רְשָׁעִים יַעֲלֹזוּ.

---

through the Temple service, and because the spiritual uplift of its holiness eased troubles *(Rashi).*

הַר צִיּוֹן — *Mount Zion.* The word Zion comes from צִיּוּן, a *monument.* The site of God's Sanctuary remains an eternal memorial to truth and sanctity *(R' Hirsch).*

יַרְכְּתֵי צָפוֹן — *The northern sides.* Mount Zion was north of the City of David, the *great king (Radak).* The source of joy was the northern part of the Temple Courtyard, because atonement offerings were slaughtered there *(Rashi).*

הַמְּלָכִים נוֹעֲדוּ — *The kings assembled.* When kings assembled at various times to attack Jerusalem, they saw that God was its *stronghold.* Seeing His miracles (next verse) they were astounded and fled *(Radak).*

אֳנִיּוֹת תַּרְשִׁישׁ — *The ships of Tarshish.* A sea near Africa, Tarshish represents invading fleets that were dispatched against *Eretz Yisrael.*

כַּאֲשֶׁר שָׁמַעְנוּ — *As we heard.* From our ancestors we heard of God's miraculous salvations — but we will see similar wonders as well *(Rashi).*

כְּשִׁמְךָ אֱלֹהִים — *Like Your Name, O God.* The prophets gave You exalted Names, but we can testify that *Your praise,* given You for actual deeds, justifies those glorious titles *(Radak).*

עַל־מוּת — *Like children.* The two words are rendered as one: עַלְמוּת, *youth.* God will guide us like a father caring for his young *(Targum; Rashi);* or He will preserve the enthusiasm and vigor of our youth *(Meiri).* According to the Masoretic tradition that these are two words, they mean that God will continue to guide us *beyond death,* i.e., in the World to Come.

⁂ יוֹם שְׁלִישִׁי / The Third Day

On the third day, God caused the dry land to become visible and fit for habitation. He did so in order that man follow the Torah's laws and deal justly with other people. Therefore the psalm speaks of justice *(Rosh Hashanah* 31a). *Maharsha* explains that the theme of this psalm

— the kings assembled, they came together. They saw and they were astounded, they were confounded and hastily fled. Trembling gripped them there, convulsions like a woman in birth travail. With an east wind You smashed the ships of Tarshish.* As we heard,* so we saw in the city of* HASHEM, *Master of Legions, in the city of our God — may God establish it to eternity, Selah! We hoped, O God, for Your kindness, in the midst of Your Sanctuary. Like Your Name, O God,* so is Your praise — to the ends of the earth; righteousness fills Your right hand. May Mount Zion be glad, may the daughters of Judah rejoice, because of Your judgments. Walk about Zion and encircle her, count her towers.* Chazzan— *Mark well in your hearts her ramparts, raise up her palaces, that you may recount it to the succeeding generation: that this is God, our God, forever and ever, He will guide us like children.**

In the presence of a *minyan*, mourners recite קַדִּישׁ יָתוֹם, the Mourner's *Kaddish* (p. 160).

TUESDAY

Today is the third day of the Sabbath,
on which the Levites would recite in the Holy Temple:

Psalm 82

מִזְמוֹר *A psalm of Assaf:* God stands in the Divine assembly,* in the midst of judges shall He judge. Until when* will you judge lawlessly and favor the presence of the wicked, Selah? Judge the needy and the orphan, vindicate the poor and impoverished. Rescue the needy and destitute, from the hand of the wicked deliver them. They do not know* nor do they understand, in darkness they walk; all foundations of the earth collapse. I said, 'You are angelic, sons of the Most High are you all.' But like men you shall die, and like one of the princes you shall fall.* Chazzan— *Arise, O God, judge the earth, for You allot the heritage* among all the nations.*

In the presence of a *minyan*, mourners recite קַדִּישׁ יָתוֹם, the Mourner's *Kaddish* (p. 160).

WEDNESDAY

Today is the fourth day of the Sabbath,
on which the Levites would recite in the Holy Temple:

Psalm 94:1-95:3

אֵל נְקָמוֹת *O God of vengeance,* HASHEM; *O God of vengeance, appear! Arise, O Judge of the earth, render recompense to the haughty. How long shall the wicked — O* HASHEM *— how long shall the wicked exult?*

— the maintenance of equity and justice — is a prerequisite for the continued existence of the world that was revealed on the third day. But this message is not limited only to courts. In his own personal life, every Jew is a judge, for his opinions and decisions about people can affect their lives in a thousand different ways.

לְאָסָף — *Of Assaf.* A descendant of Korach, Assaf was one of the psalmists whose compositions David incorporated into the Book of Psalms.

בַּעֲדַת אֵל — *In the Divine assembly.* Judges who seek truth and justice are the *Divine assembly,* because they represent God's justice on earth. As a result of their sincerity, God Himself penetrates into their hearts — בְּקֶרֶב אֱלֹהִים, *in the midst of judges* — to assure them of reaching a just verdict *(Alshich).*

עַד מָתַי — *Until when ...?* The next three verses are addressed directly to judges who fail to carry out their responsibilities. Included in this exhortation is the clear message that judges should take the initiative in seeking out and correcting injustice.

לֹא יָדְעוּ — *They do not know.* The Psalmist exclaims that many judges are unaware of their awesome responsibility; they walk in darkness, blinded by prejudice and selfishness.

כִּי אַתָּה תִנְחַל — *For You allot the heritage.* Assaf, the Psalmist, addresses God: You sought to avoid strife by allotting a fair share to all nations. Now step in to *judge the earth* and undo man's destructiveness.

יוֹם רְבִיעִי / The Fourth Day

On the fourth day, God created the sun, moon,

יַבִּיעוּ יְדַבְּרוּ עָתָק, יִתְאַמְּרוּ כָּל פֹּעֲלֵי אָוֶן. עַמְּךָ יהוה יְדַכְּאוּ, וְנַחֲלָתְךָ יְעַנּוּ. אַלְמָנָה וְגֵר יַהֲרֹגוּ, וִיתוֹמִים יְרַצֵּחוּ. וַיֹּאמְרוּ לֹא יִרְאֶה יָּהּ,* וְלֹא יָבִין אֱלֹהֵי יַעֲקֹב. בִּינוּ* בֹּעֲרִים בָּעָם, וּכְסִילִים מָתַי תַּשְׂכִּילוּ. הֲנֹטַע אֹזֶן הֲלֹא יִשְׁמָע, אִם יֹצֵר עַיִן הֲלֹא יַבִּיט. הֲיֹסֵר גּוֹיִם הֲלֹא יוֹכִיחַ, הַמְלַמֵּד אָדָם דָּעַת. יהוה יֹדֵעַ מַחְשְׁבוֹת אָדָם, כִּי הֵמָּה הָבֶל. אַשְׁרֵי הַגֶּבֶר* אֲשֶׁר תְּיַסְּרֶנּוּ יָּהּ, וּמִתּוֹרָתְךָ תְלַמְּדֶנּוּ. לְהַשְׁקִיט לוֹ* מִימֵי רָע, עַד יִכָּרֶה לָרָשָׁע שָׁחַת. כִּי לֹא יִטֹּשׁ יהוה עַמּוֹ, וְנַחֲלָתוֹ* לֹא יַעֲזֹב. כִּי עַד צֶדֶק יָשׁוּב מִשְׁפָּט,* וְאַחֲרָיו כָּל יִשְׁרֵי לֵב. מִי יָקוּם לִי עִם מְרֵעִים, מִי יִתְיַצֵּב לִי עִם פֹּעֲלֵי אָוֶן. לוּלֵי יהוה עֶזְרָתָה לִּי, כִּמְעַט שָׁכְנָה דוּמָה נַפְשִׁי. אִם אָמַרְתִּי מָטָה רַגְלִי,* חַסְדְּךָ יהוה יִסְעָדֵנִי. בְּרֹב שַׂרְעַפַּי בְּקִרְבִּי, תַּנְחוּמֶיךָ יְשַׁעַשְׁעוּ נַפְשִׁי. הַיְחָבְרְךָ כִּסֵּא הַוּוֹת, יֹצֵר עָמָל* עֲלֵי חֹק. יָגוֹדּוּ עַל נֶפֶשׁ צַדִּיק, וְדָם נָקִי יַרְשִׁיעוּ. וַיְהִי יהוה לִי לְמִשְׂגָּב, וֵאלֹהַי לְצוּר מַחְסִי. וַיָּשֶׁב עֲלֵיהֶם אֶת אוֹנָם, וּבְרָעָתָם יַצְמִיתֵם, יַצְמִיתֵם יהוה אֱלֹהֵינוּ.

❖ לְכוּ נְרַנְּנָה* לַיהוה, נָרִיעָה לְצוּר יִשְׁעֵנוּ. נְקַדְּמָה פָנָיו בְּתוֹדָה, בִּזְמִרוֹת נָרִיעַ לוֹ. כִּי אֵל גָּדוֹל יהוה, וּמֶלֶךְ גָּדוֹל עַל כָּל אֱלֹהִים.

In the presence of a *minyan,* mourners recite קַדִּישׁ יָתוֹם, the Mourner's *Kaddish* (p. 160).

THURSDAY

הַיּוֹם יוֹם חֲמִישִׁי בַּשַּׁבָּת, שֶׁבּוֹ הָיוּ הַלְוִיִּם אוֹמְרִים בְּבֵית הַמִּקְדָּשׁ:

תהלים פא

לַמְנַצֵּחַ עַל הַגִּתִּית* לְאָסָף. הַרְנִינוּ לֵאלֹהִים עוּזֵּנוּ, הָרִיעוּ לֵאלֹהֵי יַעֲקֹב. שְׂאוּ זִמְרָה וּתְנוּ תֹף, כִּנּוֹר נָעִים עִם נָבֶל. תִּקְעוּ בַחֹדֶשׁ שׁוֹפָר,* בַּכֶּסֶה לְיוֹם חַגֵּנוּ. כִּי חֹק לְיִשְׂרָאֵל הוּא, מִשְׁפָּט* לֵאלֹהֵי יַעֲקֹב. עֵדוּת בִּיהוֹסֵף שָׂמוֹ,* בְּצֵאתוֹ עַל אֶרֶץ מִצְרָיִם, שְׂפַת לֹא יָדַעְתִּי אֶשְׁמָע.

---

and stars, but instead of recognizing them as God's servants, man eventually came to regard the luminaries as independent gods that should be worshiped. Because of this idolatry, God showed Himself to be, as this psalm describes Him, the *God of vengeance,* for despite His almost endless patience and mercy, He does not tolerate evil forever.

וַיֹּאמְרוּ לֹא יִרְאֶה יָּהּ — *And they say, 'God will not see ...'* When the Temple was destroyed, it was as if God's power had been diminished and His Four-letter Name abbreviated to the two letters of יָהּ *(Eruvin* 18b). This gives evildoers the pretext to claim that God was detached from the world and unable to see the wickedness being done on earth *(Zera Yaakov).*

בִּינוּ — *Understand.* If only the boors would realize that God cannot be fooled or ignored! *(Radak).*

אַשְׁרֵי הַגֶּבֶר — *Praiseworthy is the man.* The wicked ask why the righteous suffer, if God truly controls everything. The Psalmist answers that God afflicts the righteous only when it is to their benefit, to correct them, to make them realize the futility of physical pleasures, or to atone for their sins *(Radak; Meiri).*

לְהַשְׁקִיט לוֹ — *To give him rest.* The suffering of good people on earth spares them from the far worse *days of evil* in *Gehinnom,* but they will not suffer forever — only until evil is purged from the world and *a pit is dug for the wicked (Rashi).*

וְנַחֲלָתוֹ — *His heritage.* Even in exile, Israel knows it will survive, because it is God's *heritage (Radak).*

יָשׁוּב מִשְׁפָּט — *Shall revert to righteousness.* For the good person who has sinned, God's punishment will cause him to repent *(Rashi).*

מָטָה רַגְלִי — *'My foot falters.'* When Israel fears it will falter, God's goodness supports it *(Radak).*

יֹצֵר עָמָל ... — *Those who fashion evil ...* Would God associate with those who legitimize their evil by turning it into a code of law? *(Radak).*

לְכוּ נְרַנְּנָה — *Come — let us sing.* The next three verses are not part of the psalm of the day, and

They speak freely, they utter malicious falsehood, they glorify themselves, all workers of iniquity. Your nation, HASHEM, they crush, and they afflict Your heritage. The widow and the stranger they slay, and the orphans they murder. And they say, 'God will not see, nor will the God of Jacob understand.' Understand,* you boors among the people; and you fools, when will you gain wisdom? He Who implants the ear, shall He not hear? He Who fashions the eye, shall He not see? He Who chastises nations, shall He not rebuke? — He Who teaches man knowledge. HASHEM knows the thoughts of man, that they are futile. Praiseworthy is the man* whom God disciplines, and whom You teach from Your Torah. To give him rest* from the days of evil, until a pit is dug for the wicked. For HASHEM will not cast off His people, nor will He forsake His heritage.* For justice shall revert to righteousness,* and following it will be all of upright heart. Who will rise up for me against evildoers? Who will stand up for me against the workers of iniquity? Had HASHEM not been a help to me, my soul would soon have dwelt in silence. If I said, 'My foot falters,'* Your kindness, HASHEM, supported me. When my forebodings were abundant within me, Your comforts cheered my soul. Can the throne of destruction be associated with You? — those who fashion evil* into a way of life. They join together against the soul of the righteous, and the blood of the innocent they condemn. Then HASHEM became a stronghold for me, and my God, the Rock of my refuge. He turned upon them their own violence, and with their own evil He will cut them off, HASHEM, our God, will cut them off.*

Chazzan— *Come — let us sing* to HASHEM, let us call out to the Rock of our salvation. Let us greet Him with thanksgiving, with praiseful songs let us call out to Him. For a great God is HASHEM, and a great King above all heavenly powers.*

In the presence of a *minyan*, mourners recite קַדִּישׁ יָתוֹם, the Mourner's *Kaddish* (p. 160).

THURSDAY

Today is the fifth day of the Sabbath,
on which the Levites would recite in the Holy Temple:

Psalm 81

לַמְנַצֵּחַ *For the Conductor, upon the gittis,* by Assaf. Sing joyously to the God of our might, call out to the God of Jacob. Raise a song and sound the drum, the sweet harp with the lyre. Blow the shofar at the moon's renewal,* at the time appointed for our festive day. Because it is a decree for Israel, a judgment day* for the God of Jacob. He imposed it as a testimony for Joseph* when he went forth over the land of Egypt — 'I understood a language I never*

---

are not recited in all congregations. They are the beginning of the next psalm and are recited because of their inspiring message that is an apt climax to the song of the day.

יוֹם חֲמִישִׁי / The Fifth Day

On the fifth day of creation, God made the birds and the fish, which bring joy to the world. When people observe the vast variety of colorful birds and fish, they are awed by the tremendous scope of God's creative ability, and they are stirred to praise Him with song *(Rosh Hashanah* 31a).

הַגִּתִּית — *The gittis.* A musical instrument named after the town of Gath, where it was made *(Rashi).*

תִּקְעוּ בַחֹדֶשׁ שׁוֹפָר — *Blow the shofar at the moon's renewal.* The *moon's renewal* is a poetic term for the first day of the lunar month, when the moon becomes visible again. This verse refers to Rosh Hashanah, which occurs on the first day of Tishrei and when the shofar is blown.

חֹק ... מִשְׁפָּט — *Decree ... judgment* [*day*]. It is a Divine decree that Israel blow the shofar on Rosh Hashanah, the day when God sits in judgment *(Rashi).*

עֵדוּת בִּיהוֹסֵף שָׂמוֹ — *He imposed it as a testimony for Joseph.* This entire verse is based on the life

הֲסִירוֹתִי* מִסֵּבֶל שִׁכְמוֹ, כַּפָּיו מִדּוּד תַּעֲבֹרְנָה. בַּצָּרָה קָרָאתָ, וָאֲחַלְּצֶךָּ, אֶעֶנְךָ בְּסֵתֶר רַעַם, אֶבְחָנְךָ עַל מֵי מְרִיבָה,* סֶלָה. שְׁמַע עַמִּי וְאָעִידָה בָּךְ, יִשְׂרָאֵל אִם תִּשְׁמַע לִי. לֹא יִהְיֶה בְךָ אֵל זָר, וְלֹא תִשְׁתַּחֲוֶה לְאֵל נֵכָר. אָנֹכִי יהוה אֱלֹהֶיךָ, הַמַּעַלְךָ מֵאֶרֶץ מִצְרָיִם, הַרְחֶב פִּיךָ* וַאֲמַלְאֵהוּ. וְלֹא שָׁמַע עַמִּי לְקוֹלִי, וְיִשְׂרָאֵל לֹא אָבָה לִי. וָאֲשַׁלְּחֵהוּ בִּשְׁרִירוּת לִבָּם, יֵלְכוּ בְּמוֹעֲצוֹתֵיהֶם. לוּ עַמִּי שֹׁמֵעַ לִי, יִשְׂרָאֵל בִּדְרָכַי יְהַלֵּכוּ. כִּמְעַט אוֹיְבֵיהֶם אַכְנִיעַ, וְעַל צָרֵיהֶם אָשִׁיב יָדִי. מְשַׂנְאֵי יהוה יְכַחֲשׁוּ לוֹ,* וִיהִי עִתָּם לְעוֹלָם.* ❖ וַיַּאֲכִילֵהוּ* מֵחֵלֶב חִטָּה, וּמִצּוּר דְּבַשׁ אַשְׂבִּיעֶךָ.

In the presence of a *minyan,* mourners recite קַדִּישׁ יָתוֹם, the Mourner's *Kaddish* (p. 160).

FRIDAY

הַיּוֹם יוֹם שִׁשִּׁי בַּשַּׁבָּת, שֶׁבּוֹ הָיוּ הַלְוִיִּם אוֹמְרִים בְּבֵית הַמִּקְדָּשׁ:

תהלים צג

יהוה מָלָךְ, גֵּאוּת לָבֵשׁ,* לָבֵשׁ יהוה עֹז* הִתְאַזָּר, אַף תִּכּוֹן תֵּבֵל בַּל תִּמּוֹט. נָכוֹן כִּסְאֲךָ מֵאָז,* מֵעוֹלָם אָתָּה. נָשְׂאוּ נְהָרוֹת יהוה, נָשְׂאוּ נְהָרוֹת קוֹלָם,* יִשְׂאוּ נְהָרוֹת דָּכְיָם. מִקֹּלוֹת מַיִם רַבִּים, אַדִּירִים מִשְׁבְּרֵי יָם, אַדִּיר בַּמָּרוֹם יהוה. ❖ עֵדֹתֶיךָ* נֶאֶמְנוּ מְאֹד לְבֵיתְךָ נַאֲוָה קֹדֶשׁ, יהוה לְאֹרֶךְ יָמִים.*

In the presence of a *minyan,* mourners recite קַדִּישׁ יָתוֹם, the Mourner's *Kaddish* (p. 160).

---

of Joseph. The Talmud *(Rosh Hashanah* 10b) teaches that Joseph was released from prison and appointed viceroy of Egypt on Rosh Hashanah. In honor of that event, God ordained the *mitzvah* of shofar on Rosh Hashanah as a *testimony,* i.e., a reminder of Joseph's freedom. In order to qualify as a ruler under Egyptian law, Joseph had to know all the languages — a requirement that was fulfilled when the angel Gabriel taught them to him. Thus Joseph exclaimed, *'I understood a language I never knew' (Rashi).*

Joseph's name, usually spelled יוֹסֵף, appears here with an extra letter, יְהוֹסֵף. The Talmud explains that because Joseph sanctified God's Name by refusing the temptation of his master's wife, God inserted a letter of His own Name — i.e., the letter ה — into Joseph's *(Sotah* 12a).

הֲסִירוֹתִי — *I removed.* On the same day, God freed Joseph from his menial prison chores of carrying burdens and cooking with kettles *(Rashi).*

מֵי מְרִיבָה — *The Waters of Strife.* When Israel had no water and engaged in 'strife' against Moses. See *Numbers* 20:1-13.

הַרְחֶב פִּיךָ — *Open wide your mouth,* with requests, and I will fulfill them. God urges Israel to ask all that its heart desires *(Ibn Ezra).* By asking God for *everything* that he needs, a person demonstrates his faith that God's power and generosity know no bounds *(Taanis* 3:6).

מְשַׂנְאֵי ה' יְכַחֲשׁוּ לוֹ — *Those who hate* HASHEM [i.e., because Israel's enemies are God's as well] *lie to Him.* They deny that they ever harmed Israel *(Rashi).*

וִיהִי עִתָּם לְעוֹלָם — *So their destiny is eternal.* Israel's tormentors will be condemned to eternal suffering. In contrast, concerning Israel, God promises that:

וַיַּאֲכִילֵהוּ — *He would feed him.* In the Wilderness, God provided Israel with manna that was finer than *the cream of the wheat* and provided them with honey-sweet water from a rock *(Ibn Ezra).*

◆§ יוֹם שִׁשִּׁי / The Sixth Day

Because it describes God in His full grandeur and power as He was when He completed the six days of Creation, and because it describes Him as 'donning' grandeur and 'girding' Himself like one dressing in his Sabbath finery, this psalm

knew!' I removed his shoulder from the burden, his hands let go of the kettle. In distress you called out, and I released you, I answered you with thunder when you hid, I tested you at the Waters of Strife,* Selah. Listen, My nation, and I will attest to you; O Israel, if you would but listen to Me. There shall be no strange god within you, nor shall you bow before an alien god. I am HASHEM, your God, who elevated you from the land of Egypt, open wide your mouth* and I will fill it. But My people did not heed My voice and Israel did not desire Me. So I let them follow their heart's fantasies, they follow their own counsels. If only My people would heed Me, if Israel would walk in My ways. In an instant I would subdue their foes, and against their tormentors turn My hand. Those who hate HASHEM lie to Him* — so their destiny is eternal.** Chazzan— *But He would feed him* with the cream of the wheat, and with honey from a rock sate you.*

In the presence of a *minyan,* mourners recite קַדִּישׁ יָתוֹם, the Mourner's *Kaddish* (p. 160).

FRIDAY

Today is the sixth day of the Sabbath,
on which the Levites would recite in the Holy Temple:

Psalm 93

יהוה *HASHEM will have reigned, HASHEM will have donned grandeur;* HASHEM will have donned might* and girded Himself; He even made the world firm so that it should not falter. Your throne was established from of old,* eternal are You. Like rivers they raised, O HASHEM, like rivers they raised their voice;* like rivers they shall raise their destructiveness. More than the roars of many waters, mightier than the waves of the sea — You are mighty on high, HASHEM.* Chazzan— *Your testimonies* are exceedingly trustworthy about Your House, the Sacred Dwelling — O HASHEM, may it be for long days.**

In the presence of a *minyan,* mourners recite קַדִּישׁ יָתוֹם, the Mourner's *Kaddish* (p. 160).

---

was designated as the song of Friday, when the footsteps of the Sabbath begin to be heard *(Rosh Hashanah* 31a; *R' Yaakov Emden).*

גֵּאוּת לָבֵשׁ — *He will have donned grandeur.* The concept of *grandeur* represents God's revelation as mightier than any force in nature. In man, grandeur — or arrogance — is a contemptible trait, because man's power is limited at best. But to God, *grandeur* is becoming because all forces owe their existence to Him while He is dependent on nothing *(Midrash Shocher Tov).*

God dons grandeur — It is similar to a person donning a garment; our comprehension of Him is guided by the contours and quality of the garment, but the garment is hardly His essence. No matter how much of God's greatness we think we understand, our puny intellect grasps but the minutest fraction of His infinite greatness. He does us the favor of allowing mankind this degree of perception so that we can aspire to the privilege of praising Him.

עֹז — *Might.* While *grandeur* represents God's supernatural manifestation, *might* represents His imperceptible guidance of creation through nature *(Malbim).*

מֵאָז — *From of old.* Even before the creation of the universe, God's throne as the Infinite and Eternal was secure *(Radak).*

נָשְׂאוּ נְהָרוֹת קוֹלָם — *Like rivers they raised their voice.* The enemies of Israel will roar against Israel like raging rivers at flood stage *(Radak).*

The repetition of the phrase represents the destruction of the two Temples *(Etz Yosef).*

עֵדֹתֶיךָ — *Your testimonies.* The assurances of Your prophets regarding the eventual rebuilding of the Temple *(Rashi).*

ה' לְאֹרֶךְ יָמִים — *O HASHEM, may it be for long days.* The psalm closes with a plea that when the *trustworthy* prophecies about the Third Temple are finally fulfilled, may it stand for *long days,* a Scriptural idiom meaning forever *(Radak).*

From Rosh Chodesh Elul through Shemini Atzeres, *Psalm 27*, לְדָוִד, is recited.
During the month of Elul (except on Erev Rosh Hashanah) the *shofar* is sounded at this point.
In some congregations it is sounded after this psalm.

לְדָוִד, יהוה אוֹרִי* וְיִשְׁעִי, מִמִּי אִירָא, יהוה מָעוֹז חַיַּי, מִמִּי אֶפְחָד.
בִּקְרֹב עָלַי מְרֵעִים לֶאֱכֹל אֶת בְּשָׂרִי, צָרַי וְאֹיְבַי לִי, הֵמָּה
כָשְׁלוּ וְנָפָלוּ. אִם תַּחֲנֶה עָלַי מַחֲנֶה, לֹא יִירָא לִבִּי, אִם תָּקוּם עָלַי
מִלְחָמָה, בְּזֹאת אֲנִי בוֹטֵחַ.* אַחַת שָׁאַלְתִּי מֵאֵת יהוה,* אוֹתָהּ אֲבַקֵּשׁ,
שִׁבְתִּי בְּבֵית יהוה כָּל יְמֵי חַיַּי, לַחֲזוֹת בְּנֹעַם יהוה, וּלְבַקֵּר בְּהֵיכָלוֹ. כִּי
יִצְפְּנֵנִי בְּסֻכֹּה* בְּיוֹם רָעָה, יַסְתִּרֵנִי בְּסֵתֶר אָהֳלוֹ, בְּצוּר יְרוֹמְמֵנִי. וְעַתָּה
יָרוּם רֹאשִׁי עַל אֹיְבַי סְבִיבוֹתַי, וְאֶזְבְּחָה בְאָהֳלוֹ זִבְחֵי תְרוּעָה, אָשִׁירָה
וַאֲזַמְּרָה לַיהוה. שְׁמַע יהוה קוֹלִי אֶקְרָא,* וְחָנֵּנִי וַעֲנֵנִי. לְךָ אָמַר לִבִּי
בַּקְּשׁוּ פָנָי,* אֶת פָּנֶיךָ יהוה אֲבַקֵּשׁ. אַל תַּסְתֵּר פָּנֶיךָ מִמֶּנִּי, אַל תַּט בְּאַף
עַבְדֶּךָ, עֶזְרָתִי הָיִיתָ, אַל תִּטְּשֵׁנִי וְאַל תַּעַזְבֵנִי, אֱלֹהֵי יִשְׁעִי. כִּי אָבִי וְאִמִּי
עֲזָבוּנִי,* וַיהוה יַאַסְפֵנִי. הוֹרֵנִי יהוה דַּרְכֶּךָ, וּנְחֵנִי בְּאֹרַח מִישׁוֹר, לְמַעַן
שׁוֹרְרָי.* אַל תִּתְּנֵנִי בְּנֶפֶשׁ צָרָי, כִּי קָמוּ בִי עֵדֵי שֶׁקֶר, וִיפֵחַ חָמָס.
❖ לוּלֵא הֶאֱמַנְתִּי* לִרְאוֹת בְּטוּב יהוה בְּאֶרֶץ חַיִּים.* קַוֵּה אֶל יהוה,*
חֲזַק וְיַאֲמֵץ לִבֶּךָ,* וְקַוֵּה אֶל יהוה.

In the presence of a *minyan*, mourners recite קַדִּישׁ יָתוֹם, the Mourner's *Kaddish* (p. 160).

◆§ The Shofar

On the first day of Elul, Moses ascended Mount Sinai to begin a sojourn of forty days and nights during which he would receive the second Tablets of the Law. This signified that God had forgiven Israel for the sin of the Golden Calf, which had caused Moses to break the first Tablets. When Moses went up to the mountain, the shofar was sounded in the camp to serve as a warning that the people should maintain their spirit of repentance. We maintain this tradition by sounding the shofar on the second day of Rosh Chodesh Elul, which is the first day of the month. (Some congregations begin on the first day of Rosh Chodesh.) We continue to sound the shofar throughout the month as a call to repentance.

◆§ לְדָוִד ה׳ אוֹרִי / Psalm 27

ה׳ אוֹרִי — *HASHEM is my light.* The custom to recite this psalm during the period of repentance is based on the Midrash. It expounds: *HASHEM is my light,* on Rosh Hashanah; *and my salvation,* on Yom Kippur; *He will hide me in His shelter* (below v. 5), an allusion to Succos. The implication is that on Rosh Hashanah God helps us see the light and repent; on Yom Kippur He provides us *salvation* by forgiving our sins. Once we are forgiven, He shelters us from all foes and dangers, just as He sheltered our ancestors in the Wilderness. Because of this allusion to the preparation for repentance and its aftermath, the custom was adopted to recite this psalm during the entire repentance period from Rosh Chodesh Elul through Shemini Atzeres.

בְּזֹאת אֲנִי בוֹטֵחַ — *In this I trust.* I trust in the motto expressed in the opening verse, *HASHEM is my light and my salvation, whom shall I fear? (Rashi; Radak).*

According to *Ibn Ezra* and *Sforno,* the reason for this trust is expressed in the following verse: I trust in God because I have always requested only spiritual success, and nothing vain and worthless.

אַחַת שָׁאַלְתִּי מֵאֵת ה׳ — *One thing I asked of HASHEM.* Man's desires always change. Each moment breeds new whims and fresh requests, but I have had only one desire ... and what is more: אוֹתָהּ אֲבַקֵּשׁ, *that shall I* [continue to] *seek,* because this request embodies all of my desires: to serve God and understand His ways *(Malbim).*

בְּסֻכֹּה — *In His shelter.* The spelling of this word is בְּסֻכָּה, *in a shelter,* but it is pronounced בְּסֻכּוֹ, *in His shelter.* David declares: 'Often, when I am in danger, *a shelter* seems to appear as if by chance.

From Rosh Chodesh Elul through Shemini Atzeres, *Psalm 27, 'Of David'*, is recited. During the month of Elul (except on Erev Rosh Hashanah) the *shofar* is sounded at this point. In some congregations it is sounded after this psalm.

לְדָוִד *Of David; HASHEM is my light* and my salvation, whom shall I fear? HASHEM is my life's strength, whom shall I dread? When evildoers approach me to devour my flesh, my tormentors and my foes against me — it is they who stumble and fall. Though an army would besiege me, my heart would not fear; though war would arise against me, in this I trust.* One thing I asked of HASHEM,* that shall I seek: That I dwell in the House of HASHEM all the days of my life; to behold the sweetness of HASHEM and to contemplate in His Sanctuary. Indeed, He will hide me in His Shelter* on the day of evil; He will conceal me in the concealment of His Tent, He will lift me upon a rock. Now my head is raised above my enemies around me, and I will slaughter offerings in His Tent accompanied by joyous song; I will sing and make music to HASHEM. HASHEM, hear my voice when I call,* be gracious toward me and answer me. In Your behalf, my heart has said, 'Seek My Presence';* Your Presence, HASHEM, do I seek. Conceal not Your Presence from me, repel not Your servant in anger. You have been my Helper, abandon me not, forsake me not, O God of my salvation. Though my father and mother have forsaken me,* HASHEM will gather me in. Teach me Your way, HASHEM, and lead me on the path of integrity, because of my watchful foes.* Deliver me not to the wishes of my tormentors, for there have arisen against me false witnesses who breathe violence.* Chazzan— *Had I not trusted* that I would see the goodness of HASHEM in the land of life!* Hope to HASHEM,* strengthen yourself and He will give you courage;* and hope to HASHEM.*

In the presence of a *minyan*, mourners recite קַדִּישׁ יָתוֹם, the Mourner's *Kaddish* (p. 160).

I am not misled. I know that God Himself has provided this salvation and that it is *His* shelter' *(R' A. Ch. Feuer).*

שְׁמַע ה' קוֹלִי אֶקְרָא — *HASHEM, hear my voice when I call.* Previously David had discussed his wars against human armies. In such battles, he is confident of Divine salvation. Now he turns his attention to the most difficult struggle of all, the struggle against the Evil Inclination *(Otzar Nechmad).*

לְךָ אָמַר לִבִּי בַּקְּשׁוּ פָנָי — *In Your behalf, my heart has said, 'Seek My Presence'* [lit. *My Face*]. In expressing the desire to seek God's Presence, my own heart spoke as if it were God's emissary. It is He Who implants in the Jew's heart the noble aspiration that he wishes to dwell in the House of God all his life.

כִּי אָבִי וְאִמִּי עֲזָבוּנִי — *Though my father and mother have forsaken me.* After youth and adolescence, they sent me out on my own *(Sforno).*

לְמַעַן שׁוֹרְרָי — *Because of my watchful foes,* i.e., in order to frustrate my enemies who enviously and maliciously seek out my flaws and scrutinize my ways [from שׁוּר, to stare] *(Radak).*

לוּלֵא הֶאֱמַנְתִּי — *Had I not trusted ...!* The meaning of this exclamation is implied: If not for my faith, such false witnesses would have destroyed me long ago. I never stopped believing, so I ignored them and continued to serve God with devotion *(Rashi; Radak).*

בְּאֶרֶץ חַיִּים — *In the land of life.* A reference to the World to Come *(Berachos* 4a).

קַוֵּה אֶל ה' — *Hope to HASHEM.* Because of my boundless faith in HASHEM I hope for His aid at all times and pay no heed to my enemies *(Radak).*

חֲזַק וְיַאֲמֵץ לִבֶּךָ — *Strengthen yourself and He will give you courage.* Just as someone trying to purify himself is given assistance *(Yoma* 38b), so too, someone trying to strengthen his faith is helped by God *(Alshich).*

Malbim observes that hoping for God's help is greatly different from hoping for the aid of man. Heartache and disillusionment are the lot of one who is dependent on people. Not so with God. Placing one's hope in Him is exhilarating, and brings renewed strength.

In many congregations, *Psalm* 104, בָּרְכִי נַפְשִׁי, is recited on Rosh Chodesh:

בָּרְכִי נַפְשִׁי אֶת יהוה, יהוה אֱלֹהַי גָּדַלְתָּ מְּאֹד, הוֹד וְהָדָר לָבָשְׁתָּ. עֹטֶה אוֹר כַּשַּׂלְמָה, נוֹטֶה שָׁמַיִם כַּיְרִיעָה. הַמְּקָרֶה בַמַּיִם עֲלִיּוֹתָיו, הַשָּׂם עָבִים רְכוּבוֹ, הַמְּהַלֵּךְ עַל כַּנְפֵי רוּחַ. עֹשֶׂה מַלְאָכָיו רוּחוֹת, מְשָׁרְתָיו אֵשׁ לֹהֵט. יָסַד אֶרֶץ עַל מְכוֹנֶיהָ, בַּל תִּמּוֹט עוֹלָם וָעֶד.

תְּהוֹם כַּלְּבוּשׁ כִּסִּיתוֹ, עַל הָרִים יַעַמְדוּ מָיִם. מִן גַּעֲרָתְךָ יְנוּסוּן, מִן קוֹל רַעַמְךָ יֵחָפֵזוּן. יַעֲלוּ הָרִים, יֵרְדוּ בְקָעוֹת, אֶל מְקוֹם זֶה יָסַדְתָּ לָהֶם. גְּבוּל שַׂמְתָּ בַּל יַעֲבֹרוּן, בַּל יְשׁוּבוּן לְכַסּוֹת הָאָרֶץ.

הַמְּשַׁלֵּחַ מַעְיָנִים בַּנְּחָלִים, בֵּין הָרִים יְהַלֵּכוּן. יַשְׁקוּ כָּל חַיְתוֹ שָׂדָי, יִשְׁבְּרוּ פְרָאִים צְמָאָם. עֲלֵיהֶם עוֹף הַשָּׁמַיִם יִשְׁכּוֹן, מִבֵּין עֳפָאיִם יִתְּנוּ קוֹל. מַשְׁקֶה הָרִים מֵעֲלִיּוֹתָיו, מִפְּרִי מַעֲשֶׂיךָ תִּשְׂבַּע הָאָרֶץ.

מַצְמִיחַ חָצִיר לַבְּהֵמָה, וְעֵשֶׂב לַעֲבֹדַת הָאָדָם, לְהוֹצִיא לֶחֶם מִן הָאָרֶץ. וְיַיִן יְשַׂמַּח לְבַב אֱנוֹשׁ, לְהַצְהִיל פָּנִים מִשָּׁמֶן, וְלֶחֶם לְבַב אֱנוֹשׁ יִסְעָד. יִשְׂבְּעוּ עֲצֵי יהוה, אַרְזֵי לְבָנוֹן אֲשֶׁר נָטָע. אֲשֶׁר שָׁם צִפֳּרִים יְקַנֵּנוּ, חֲסִידָה בְּרוֹשִׁים בֵּיתָהּ. הָרִים הַגְּבֹהִים לַיְּעֵלִים, סְלָעִים מַחְסֶה לַשְׁפַנִּים.

עָשָׂה יָרֵחַ לְמוֹעֲדִים, שֶׁמֶשׁ יָדַע מְבוֹאוֹ. תָּשֶׁת חֹשֶׁךְ וִיהִי לָיְלָה, בּוֹ תִרְמֹשׂ כָּל חַיְתוֹ יָעַר. הַכְּפִירִים שֹׁאֲגִים לַטָּרֶף, וּלְבַקֵּשׁ מֵאֵל אָכְלָם. תִּזְרַח הַשֶּׁמֶשׁ יֵאָסֵפוּן, וְאֶל מְעוֹנֹתָם יִרְבָּצוּן. יֵצֵא אָדָם לְפָעֳלוֹ, וְלַעֲבֹדָתוֹ עֲדֵי עָרֶב.

מָה רַבּוּ מַעֲשֶׂיךָ יהוה, כֻּלָּם בְּחָכְמָה עָשִׂיתָ, מָלְאָה הָאָרֶץ קִנְיָנֶךָ. זֶה הַיָּם, גָּדוֹל וּרְחַב יָדָיִם, שָׁם רֶמֶשׂ וְאֵין מִסְפָּר, חַיּוֹת קְטַנּוֹת עִם גְּדֹלוֹת. שָׁם אֳנִיּוֹת יְהַלֵּכוּן, לִוְיָתָן זֶה יָצַרְתָּ לְשַׂחֶק בּוֹ. כֻּלָּם אֵלֶיךָ יְשַׂבֵּרוּן, לָתֵת אָכְלָם בְּעִתּוֹ. תִּתֵּן לָהֶם, יִלְקֹטוּן, תִּפְתַּח יָדְךָ, יִשְׂבְּעוּן טוֹב. תַּסְתִּיר פָּנֶיךָ יִבָּהֵלוּן, תֹּסֵף רוּחָם יִגְוָעוּן, וְאֶל עֲפָרָם יְשׁוּבוּן. תְּשַׁלַּח רוּחֲךָ יִבָּרֵאוּן, וּתְחַדֵּשׁ פְּנֵי אֲדָמָה.

יְהִי כְבוֹד יהוה לְעוֹלָם, יִשְׂמַח יהוה בְּמַעֲשָׂיו. הַמַּבִּיט לָאָרֶץ וַתִּרְעָד, יִגַּע בֶּהָרִים וְיֶעֱשָׁנוּ. אָשִׁירָה לַיהוה בְּחַיָּי, אֲזַמְּרָה לֵאלֹהַי בְּעוֹדִי. ❖ יֶעֱרַב עָלָיו שִׂיחִי, אָנֹכִי אֶשְׂמַח בַּיהוה. יִתַּמּוּ חַטָּאִים מִן הָאָרֶץ, וּרְשָׁעִים עוֹד אֵינָם, בָּרְכִי נַפְשִׁי אֶת יהוה, הַלְלוּיָהּ.

In the presence of a *minyan,* mourners recite קַדִּישׁ יָתוֹם, the Mourner's *Kaddish* (p. 160).

⊲§ Rosh Chodesh / Psalm 104

Psalm 104 is recited as the Song of the Day for *Rosh Chodesh*, the New Moon, because the Psalmist alludes to the New Moon in this verse: *He made the moon for festivals (Tur).*

These words are not merely a casual allusion to the new month. Rather, they set the tone of this entire composition, whose main theme is God's complete mastery over every aspect of creation. Throughout the monthly lunar cycle, the size of the moon visibly waxes and wanes, to demonstrate dramatically that God has total

In many congregations, *Psalm* 104, *'Bless* HASHEM, *O my soul'*, is recited on Rosh Chodesh:

בָּרְכִי נַפְשִׁי *Bless* HASHEM, *O my soul.* HASHEM, *my God, You are very great; You have donned majesty and splendor; cloaked in light as with a garment, stretching out the heavens like a curtain. He Who roofs His upper chambers with water; He Who makes clouds His chariot; He Who walks on winged wind; He makes the winds His messengers, the flaming fire His attendants; He established the earth upon its foundations, that it falter not forever and ever.*

The watery deep, as with a garment You covered it; upon the mountains, water would stand. From Your rebuke they flee, from the sound of Your thunder they rush away. They ascend mountains, they descend to valleys, to the special place You founded for them. You set a boundary they cannot overstep, they cannot return to cover the earth.

He sends the springs into the streams, they flow between the mountains. They water every beast of the field, they quench the wild creatures' thirst. Near them dwell the heaven's birds, from among the branches they give forth song. He waters the mountains from His upper chambers, from the fruit of Your works the earth is sated.

He causes vegetation to sprout for the cattle, and plants through man's labor, to bring forth bread from the earth; and wine that gladdens man's heart, to make the face glow from oil, and bread that sustains the heart of man. The trees of HASHEM *are sated, the cedars of Lebanon that He has planted; there where the birds nest, the stork with its home among cypresses; high mountains for the wild goats, rocks as refuge for the gophers.*

He made the moon for festivals, the sun knows its destination. You make darkness and it is night, in which every forest beast stirs. The young lions roar after their prey, and to seek their food from God. The sun rises and they are gathered in, and in their dens they crouch. Man goes forth to his work, and to his labor until evening.

How abundant are Your works, HASHEM; *with wisdom You made them all, the earth is full of Your possessions. Behold this sea — great and of broad measure; there are creeping things without number, small creatures and great ones. There ships travel, this Leviathan You fashioned to sport with. Everything looks to You with hope, to provide their food in its proper time. You give to them, they gather it in; You open Your hand, they are sated with good. When You hide Your face, they are dismayed; when You retrieve their spirit, they perish and to their dust they return. When You send forth Your breath, they are created, and You renew the surface of the earth.*

May the glory of HASHEM *endure forever, let* HASHEM *rejoice in His works. He peers toward the earth and it trembles, He touches the mountains and they smoke. I will sing to* HASHEM *while I live, I will sing praises to my God while I endure.* Chazzan— *May my words be sweet to Him — I will rejoice in* HASHEM. *Sinners will cease from the earth, and the wicked will be no more — Bless* HASHEM, *O my soul. Halleluyah!*

In the presence of a *minyan*, mourners recite קַדִּישׁ יָתוֹם, the Mourner's *Kaddish* (p. 160).

---

mastery over His creations. No other natural phenomenon conveys this message as vividly and forcefully as the moon's cycle. Thus, the theme of the New Moon complements the theme

In a house of mourning, Psalm 49, לַמְנַצֵּחַ, is recited after *Shacharis* and *Maariv*.

לַמְנַצֵּחַ לִבְנֵי קֹרַח מִזְמוֹר. שִׁמְעוּ זֹאת כָּל הָעַמִּים, הַאֲזִינוּ כָּל יֹשְׁבֵי חָלֶד. גַּם בְּנֵי אָדָם, גַּם בְּנֵי אִישׁ,* יַחַד עָשִׁיר וְאֶבְיוֹן.* פִּי יְדַבֵּר חָכְמוֹת, וְהָגוּת לִבִּי תְבוּנוֹת. אַטֶּה לְמָשָׁל אָזְנִי, אֶפְתַּח בְּכִנּוֹר חִידָתִי.* לָמָּה אִירָא בִּימֵי רָע, עֲוֹן עֲקֵבַי* יְסֻבֵּנִי. הַבֹּטְחִים עַל חֵילָם, וּבְרֹב עָשְׁרָם יִתְהַלָּלוּ. אָח לֹא פָדֹה יִפְדֶּה אִישׁ, לֹא יִתֵּן לֵאלֹהִים כָּפְרוֹ.* וְיֵקַר פִּדְיוֹן נַפְשָׁם,* וְחָדַל לְעוֹלָם. וִיחִי עוֹד לָנֶצַח,* לֹא יִרְאֶה הַשָּׁחַת. כִּי יִרְאֶה חֲכָמִים יָמוּתוּ,* יַחַד כְּסִיל וָבַעַר יֹאבֵדוּ, וְעָזְבוּ לַאֲחֵרִים חֵילָם. קִרְבָּם בָּתֵּימוֹ לְעוֹלָם, מִשְׁכְּנֹתָם לְדוֹר וָדֹר, קָרְאוּ בִשְׁמוֹתָם עֲלֵי אֲדָמוֹת. וְאָדָם בִּיקָר בַּל יָלִין,* נִמְשַׁל כַּבְּהֵמוֹת נִדְמוּ. זֶה דַרְכָּם, כֵּסֶל לָמוֹ, וְאַחֲרֵיהֶם בְּפִיהֶם יִרְצוּ, סֶלָה. כַּצֹּאן* לִשְׁאוֹל שַׁתּוּ, מָוֶת יִרְעֵם, וַיִּרְדּוּ בָם יְשָׁרִים לַבֹּקֶר,* וְצוּרָם לְבַלּוֹת* שְׁאוֹל מִזְּבֻל לוֹ.* אַךְ אֱלֹהִים יִפְדֶּה נַפְשִׁי* מִיַּד שְׁאוֹל, כִּי יִקָּחֵנִי סֶלָה. אַל תִּירָא כִּי יַעֲשִׁר אִישׁ, כִּי יִרְבֶּה כְּבוֹד בֵּיתוֹ. כִּי לֹא בְמוֹתוֹ יִקַּח הַכֹּל, לֹא יֵרֵד אַחֲרָיו כְּבוֹדוֹ. כִּי נַפְשׁוֹ בְּחַיָּיו יְבָרֵךְ,* וְיוֹדֻךָ כִּי תֵיטִיב לָךְ. תָּבוֹא* עַד דּוֹר אֲבוֹתָיו, עַד נֵצַח לֹא יִרְאוּ אוֹר. ❖ אָדָם בִּיקָר וְלֹא יָבִין, נִמְשַׁל כַּבְּהֵמוֹת נִדְמוּ.*

In the presence of a *minyan,* mourners recite קַדִּישׁ יָתוֹם, the Mourner's *Kaddish* (p. 160).

---

of this entire hymn of praise to the Master of Creation. [The commentary to this psalm may be found on p. 530.]

◆§ A House of Mourning / Psalm 49

Recognizing their father's greed for wealth as the root of his downfall, the righteous sons of Korach composed this psalm teaching that man should use his sojourn on earth to enhance his spiritual development so that he will be better prepared for the World to Come. This concept is a source of comfort for those who have lost a close relative; therefore it is customary to recite this psalm after *Shacharis* and *Maariv* in the home of someone observing *Shivah,* the seven-day period of mourning.

בְּנֵי אָדָם ... בְּנֵי אִישׁ — *Sons of Adam ... sons of man.* The term *sons of man* refers to people who can trace their ancestry back to men of distinction and thus derive social and financial advantage. *Sons of Adam* includes the vast majority of humans who lack any pedigree except that Adam was their forbear. The message of this psalm is of equal importance of both *(R' Hirsch).*

יַחַד עָשִׁיר וְאֶבְיוֹן — *Together — rich man, poor man.* Both are infatuated by money: the rich man wants more and the poor man thinks it will solve all his problems *(Or Olam).*

אֶפְתַּח בְּכִנּוֹר חִידָתִי — *With a harp I will solve my riddle.* Through spiritually uplifting music, the Psalmist achieves the tranquility to unravel perplexing mysteries *(R' A. Ch. Feuer).*

עֲוֹן עֲקֵבַי — *The sin I trod upon.* Some sins are considered so minor that people seem to crush them underfoot. Because of his cavalier attitude toward such sins, a person may well feel dread as he approaches his time of judgment *(Rashi).* The Psalmist emphasizes that even the minor sins of good people can cause spiritual anguish.

לֹא יִתֵּן ... כָּפְרוֹ — *Nor give ... his personal ransom.* Life and death are in God's hands. No amount of money can ransom a soul God has chosen to take *(Radak).*

וְיֵקַר פִּדְיוֹן נַפְשָׁם — *Too costly is their soul's redemption.* The soul is precious beyond estimation. If man sullies it through his deeds, his money cannot set things aright *(Sifri).*

וִיחִי עוֹד לָנֶצַח — *Can one live eternally.* No one lives forever; no one is spared from the *pit* [i.e., the grave]. Therefore, man should tend to the immortality of the soul *(Radak; Sforno).*

כִּי יִרְאֶה חֲכָמִים יָמוּתוּ — *Though he sees that wise men die.* Sinners are deluded because they see that even good people die. If death grasps everyone equally, then why should the wealthy not indulge his pleasures? *(Rashi; Radak).*

In a house of mourning, *Psalm* 49, *'For the Conductor'*, is recited after *Shacharis* and *Maariv.*

לַמְנַצֵּחַ *For the Conductor, by the sons of Korach, a psalm. Hear this all you peoples, give ear all you dwellers of decaying earth. Sons of Adam and sons of man* alike; together — rich man, poor man.* My mouth shall speak wisdom, and the meditations of my heart are insightful. I will incline my ear to the parable, with a harp I will solve my riddle.* Why should I fear in days of evil? — The sin I trod upon* surrounds me! Those who rely on their possessions, and of their great wealth they are boastful — yet man cannot redeem a brother, nor give to God his personal ransom.* Too costly is their soul's redemption* and unattainable forever. Can one live eternally,* never to see the pit? Though he sees that wise men die;* that the foolish and boorish perish together and leave their possessions for others — in their imagination, their houses are forever, their dwellings for generation after generation; they have proclaimed their names throughout the lands. But as for man — in glory he shall not repose,* he is likened to the silenced animals. This is their way — folly is theirs, yet of their destiny their mouths speak soothingly, Selah! Like sheep,* they are destined for the Lower World, death shall consume them and the upright shall dominate them at daybreak;* their essence is doomed to rot* in the grave, each from his dwelling.* But God will redeem my soul* from the grip of the Lower World, for He will take me, Selah! Fear not when a man grows rich, when he increases the splendor of his house. For upon his death he will not take anything, his splendor will not descend after him. Though he may bless himself in his lifetime,* others will praise you if you improve yourself. It shall come* to the generation of its fathers — to eternity they shall see no light.* Chazzan— *Man is glorious but understands not, he is likened to the silenced animals.**

In the presence of a *minyan*, mourners recite קַדִּישׁ יָתוֹם, the Mourner's *Kaddish* (p. 160).

וְאָדָם בִּיקָר בַּל יָלִין — *But as for man — in glory he shall not repose.* The human condition is precarious indeed. Even Adam, God's own handiwork, sinned and fell from his pinnacle on the very day he was created *(Sanhedrin* 38a).

כַּצֹּאן — *Like sheep.* The wicked are like sheep going contentedly to their doom. Only at the last minute do they become alarmed — but then it is too late *(R' Yonah).*

וַיִּרְדּוּ ... לַבֹּקֶר — *Shall dominate ... at daybreak.* Now, the evil are dominant, but at the *daybreak* of Judgment Day, the righteous will gain the upper hand *(Radak).*

וְצוּרָם לְבַלּוֹת — *Their essence is doomed to rot.* A person's *essence* is his soul, his spiritual content. Evildoers corrupt their souls until they lose the capacity for meaningful growth, therefore, instead of looking forward to an afterlife, they can expect only decay after death *(Radak).*

מִזְּבֻל לוֹ — *Each from his dwelling.* They will leave their luxurious homes to go to the grave *(Radak).*

אַךְ אֱלֹהִים יִפְדֶּה נַפְשִׁי — *But God will redeem my soul.* Having completed his observations regarding the doom facing the wicked, the Psalmist now expresses his confidence that *he* can look forward to the splendor of the World to Come *(Rashi).*

כִּי נַפְשׁוֹ בְּחַיָּיו יְבָרֵךְ — *Though he may bless himself in his lifetime.* In life, the rich preen themselves, confident that they are above criticism, but the way to gain the sincere praise of others is *if you improve yourself (Rashi).*

תָּבוֹא — *It shall come,* i.e., the soul of the evildoer will have the same fate as the souls of its ancestors. None of them will see the light of redemption *(Rashi).*

נִמְשַׁל כַּבְּהֵמוֹת נִדְמוּ — *He is likened to the silenced animals.* Although man is glorious, if he does not understand because he has not studied, he is likened to the animals *(R' Yehudah HaLevi).*

הוספות

שש זכירות

The Torah commands that six events be remembered always. Consequently, some authorities maintain that the verses containing these commandments should be recited daily.

זְכִירַת יְצִיאַת מִצְרָיִם (דברים טז:ג)

לְמַעַן תִּזְכֹּר אֶת יוֹם צֵאתְךָ מֵאֶרֶץ מִצְרַיִם כֹּל יְמֵי חַיֶּיךָ.

זְכִירַת מַעֲמַד הַר סִינָי (דברים ד:ט־י)

רַק הִשָּׁמֶר לְךָ וּשְׁמֹר נַפְשְׁךָ מְאֹד, פֶּן תִּשְׁכַּח אֶת הַדְּבָרִים אֲשֶׁר רָאוּ עֵינֶיךָ, וּפֶן יָסוּרוּ מִלְּבָבְךָ כֹּל יְמֵי חַיֶּיךָ, וְהוֹדַעְתָּם לְבָנֶיךָ וְלִבְנֵי בָנֶיךָ. יוֹם אֲשֶׁר עָמַדְתָּ לִפְנֵי יהוה אֱלֹהֶיךָ בְּחֹרֵב.

זְכִירַת מַעֲשֵׂה עֲמָלֵק (דברים כה:יז־יט)

זָכוֹר אֵת אֲשֶׁר עָשָׂה לְךָ עֲמָלֵק, בַּדֶּרֶךְ בְּצֵאתְכֶם מִמִּצְרָיִם. אֲשֶׁר קָרְךָ בַּדֶּרֶךְ, וַיְזַנֵּב בְּךָ כָּל הַנֶּחֱשָׁלִים אַחֲרֶיךָ, וְאַתָּה עָיֵף וְיָגֵעַ, וְלֹא יָרֵא אֱלֹהִים. וְהָיָה בְּהָנִיחַ יהוה אֱלֹהֶיךָ לְךָ מִכָּל אֹיְבֶיךָ מִסָּבִיב, בָּאָרֶץ אֲשֶׁר יהוה אֱלֹהֶיךָ נֹתֵן לְךָ נַחֲלָה לְרִשְׁתָּהּ, תִּמְחֶה אֶת זֵכֶר עֲמָלֵק מִתַּחַת הַשָּׁמָיִם, לֹא תִּשְׁכָּח.

זְכִירַת מַעֲשֵׂה הָעֵגֶל (דברים ט:ז)

זְכֹר, אַל תִּשְׁכַּח, אֵת אֲשֶׁר הִקְצַפְתָּ אֶת יהוה אֱלֹהֶיךָ, בַּמִּדְבָּר.

זְכִירַת מִרְיָם (דברים כד:ט)

זָכוֹר אֵת אֲשֶׁר עָשָׂה יהוה אֱלֹהֶיךָ לְמִרְיָם, בַּדֶּרֶךְ בְּצֵאתְכֶם מִמִּצְרָיִם.

זְכִירַת הַשַּׁבָּת (שמות כ:ח)

זָכוֹר אֶת יוֹם הַשַּׁבָּת לְקַדְּשׁוֹ.

The Six Remembrances

Kabbalistic literature teaches that it is desirable to recite the six Scriptural passages that command us always to bear in mind specific events. Thus, these major themes in our history are kept alive in our consciousness.

The Exodus. Even though the Exodus is mentioned twice a day, in the *Shema* of *Shacharis* and *Maariv*, it is so essential to Israel's mission that it is recalled yet again. The idea that God once redeemed Israel from degrading slavery should inspire us with confidence in the future redemption.

Receiving the Torah at Sinai. Israel's redemption — its very existence — is based on the mission entrusted to us when God presented us with the Torah, represented by the Ten Commandments, at Sinai. If we are not the nation of Torah, we are nothing.

Amalek's attack. Amalek's ability to attack Israel was a consequence of Israel's failure to study the Torah with sufficient zeal *(Tanchuma, Beshalach).* Thus the episode of Amalek cautions us to hold the Torah precious. Also, the fate of Amalek — total extinction — reminds us that evil has no future.

The Golden Calf. One of the most dismal episodes in Jewish history, the Golden Calf caused Israel to fall from the spiritual pedestal it

READINGS FOLLOWING SHACHARIS

THE SIX REMEMBRANCES

The Torah commands that six events be remembered always. Consequently, some authorities maintain that the verses containing these commandments should be recited daily.

REMEMBRANCE OF THE EXODUS FROM EGYPT (*Deuteronomy* 16:3)

לְמַעַן *That you may remember the day of your departure from the land of Egypt all the days of your life.*

REMEMBRANCE OF RECEIVING THE TORAH AT MOUNT SINAI (*Deuteronomy* 4:9-10)

רַק *Only beware and guard yourself carefully, lest you forget the things your eyes have seen and lest they stray from your heart all the days of your life. And you are to make them known to your children and to your children's children — the day you stood before HASHEM, your God, at Sinai.*

REMEMBRANCE OF AMALEK'S ATTACK (*Deuteronomy* 25:17-19)

זָכוֹר *Remember what Amalek did to you on the way, as you departed from Egypt. How he encountered you on the way and cut down the weaklings trailing behind you, while you were faint and exhausted, and he did not fear God. It shall be that when HASHEM, your God, lets you rest from all your surrounding enemies, in the land that HASHEM, your God, gives you as a heritage to bequeath; you are to erase the memory of Amalek from beneath the heaven. Do not forget.*

REMEMBRANCE OF THE GOLDEN CALF (*Deuteronomy* 9:7)

זְכֹר *Remember, do not forget, how you angered HASHEM, your God, in the Wilderness.*

REMEMBRANCE OF MIRIAM (*Deuteronomy* 24:9)

זָכוֹר *Remember what HASHEM, your God, did to Miriam, on the way when you departed from Egypt.*

REMEMBRANCE OF THE SABBATH (*Exodus* 20:8)

זָכוֹר *Remember the Sabbath day to hallow it.*

---

had ascended, upon receiving the Ten Commandments — and it caused Moses to shatter the Tablets themselves. The lesson that remained was that we must have faith in God's promise and never deviate from His Torah, even if we think that we have found a better way to serve Him.

Miriam. Miriam criticized her brother Moses, on the grounds that he did not live with his wife. She failed to consider that a man of Moses' humility and unselfishness would not have done so unless he had been commanded always to hold himself in readiness for prophecy, a condition that required abstinence. Miriam was punished with *tzara'as,* a disease similar to leprosy, and was healed because of Moses' prayers. This teaches us never to slander another person.

The Sabbath. By refraining from work on the seventh day, the day that God rested upon the completion of Creation, the Jew offers enduring testimony that God created the world. Throughout the week, we remember the Sabbath by directing our purchases and preparations toward its honor.

שלשה עשר עקרים

א **אֲנִי מַאֲמִין** בֶּאֱמוּנָה שְׁלֵמָה, שֶׁהַבּוֹרֵא יִתְבָּרַךְ שְׁמוֹ הוּא בּוֹרֵא וּמַנְהִיג לְכָל הַבְּרוּאִים, וְהוּא לְבַדּוֹ עָשָׂה וְעוֹשֶׂה וְיַעֲשֶׂה לְכָל הַמַּעֲשִׂים.

ב **אֲנִי מַאֲמִין** בֶּאֱמוּנָה שְׁלֵמָה, שֶׁהַבּוֹרֵא יִתְבָּרַךְ שְׁמוֹ הוּא יָחִיד וְאֵין יְחִידוּת כָּמוֹהוּ בְּשׁוּם פָּנִים, וְהוּא לְבַדּוֹ אֱלֹהֵינוּ, הָיָה הֹוֶה וְיִהְיֶה.

ג **אֲנִי מַאֲמִין** בֶּאֱמוּנָה שְׁלֵמָה, שֶׁהַבּוֹרֵא יִתְבָּרַךְ שְׁמוֹ אֵינוֹ גוּף, וְלֹא יַשִּׂיגוּהוּ מַשִּׂיגֵי הַגּוּף, וְאֵין לוֹ שׁוּם דִּמְיוֹן כְּלָל.

ד **אֲנִי מַאֲמִין** בֶּאֱמוּנָה שְׁלֵמָה, שֶׁהַבּוֹרֵא יִתְבָּרַךְ שְׁמוֹ הוּא רִאשׁוֹן וְהוּא אַחֲרוֹן.

ה **אֲנִי מַאֲמִין** בֶּאֱמוּנָה שְׁלֵמָה, שֶׁהַבּוֹרֵא יִתְבָּרַךְ שְׁמוֹ לוֹ לְבַדּוֹ רָאוּי לְהִתְפַּלֵּל, וְאֵין לְזוּלָתוֹ רָאוּי לְהִתְפַּלֵּל.

ו **אֲנִי מַאֲמִין** בֶּאֱמוּנָה שְׁלֵמָה, שֶׁכָּל דִּבְרֵי נְבִיאִים אֱמֶת.

ז **אֲנִי מַאֲמִין** בֶּאֱמוּנָה שְׁלֵמָה, שֶׁנְּבוּאַת מֹשֶׁה רַבֵּנוּ עָלָיו הַשָּׁלוֹם הָיְתָה אֲמִתִּית, וְשֶׁהוּא הָיָה אָב לַנְּבִיאִים, לַקּוֹדְמִים לְפָנָיו וְלַבָּאִים אַחֲרָיו.

ח **אֲנִי מַאֲמִין** בֶּאֱמוּנָה שְׁלֵמָה, שֶׁכָּל הַתּוֹרָה הַמְּצוּיָה עַתָּה בְיָדֵינוּ הִיא הַנְּתוּנָה לְמֹשֶׁה רַבֵּנוּ עָלָיו הַשָּׁלוֹם.

ט **אֲנִי מַאֲמִין** בֶּאֱמוּנָה שְׁלֵמָה, שֶׁזֹּאת הַתּוֹרָה לֹא תְהֵא מֻחְלֶפֶת וְלֹא תְהֵא תּוֹרָה אַחֶרֶת מֵאֵת הַבּוֹרֵא יִתְבָּרַךְ שְׁמוֹ.

י **אֲנִי מַאֲמִין** בֶּאֱמוּנָה שְׁלֵמָה, שֶׁהַבּוֹרֵא יִתְבָּרַךְ שְׁמוֹ יוֹדֵעַ כָּל מַעֲשֵׂה

◆§ שְׁלֹשָׁה עָשָׂר עִקָּרִים / The Thirteen Principles of Faith

Historically, Judaism never separated belief from performance. In the Torah, the commandment to believe in God is not stated differently than the commandment to lend money to a fellow Jew in need, or to refrain from eating non-kosher food. As the centuries rolled by, however, philosophical speculation and dogmas of faith became prevalent among other religions and, in time, began to influence a number of Jews. To counteract this trend, medieval Rabbinical authorities felt the need to respond by defining the principles of Judaism. The 'Thirteen Principles of Faith' are based upon the formulation of *Rambam* [Maimonides] in his *Commentary to Mishnah (Sanhedrin,* ch. 10) and have achieved virtually universal acceptance.

It is a commendable practice to recite the Thirteen Principles every day after *Shacharis.* As *Rambam* himself writes, one does not become imbued with them from a perfunctory reading once or even several times. One must constantly review and study them.

The Thirteen Principles fall into three general categories: (a) the nature of belief in God; (b) the authenticity of the Torah, its validity and immutability; and (c) man's responsibility and ultimate reward.

A) The Nature of Belief in God

1. *God's Existence.* There is no partnership in creation. God is the sole Creator and the universe continues to exist only because He wills it so. He could exist if everything else were to come to an end, but it is inconceivable that there could be any form of existence independent of Him.

2. *God is a complete and total Unity.* He is not a collection of limbs and organs, as are man and animals. He cannot be split as can a rock or divided into component elements as can everything in Creation. This is the concept expressed in the first verse of *Shema.*

3. *God is not physical* nor can His essence be grasped by the human imagination; because we

THE THIRTEEN PRINCIPLES OF FAITH

1. **אֲנִי מַאֲמִין** *I believe with complete faith that the Creator, Blessed is His Name, creates and guides all creatures, and that He alone made, makes, and will make everything.*

2. **אֲנִי מַאֲמִין** *I believe with complete faith that the Creator, Blessed is His Name, is unique, and there is no uniqueness like His in any way, and that He alone is our God, Who was, Who is, and Who always will be.*

3. **אֲנִי מַאֲמִין** *I believe with complete faith that the Creator, Blessed is His Name, is not physical and is not affected by physical phenomena, and that there is no comparison whatsoever to Him.*

4. **אֲנִי מַאֲמִין** *I believe with complete faith that the Creator, Blessed is His Name, is the very first and the very last.*

5. **אֲנִי מַאֲמִין** *I believe with complete faith that the Creator, Blessed is His Name — to Him alone is it proper to pray and it is not proper to pray to any other.*

6. **אֲנִי מַאֲמִין** *I believe with complete faith that all the words of the prophets are true.*

7. **אֲנִי מַאֲמִין** *I believe with complete faith that the prophecy of Moses our teacher, peace upon him, was true, and that he was the father of the prophets — both those who preceded him and those who followed him.*

8. **אֲנִי מַאֲמִין** *I believe with complete faith that the entire Torah now in our hands is the same one that was given to Moses, our teacher, peace be upon him.*

9. **אֲנִי מַאֲמִין** *I believe with complete faith that this Torah will not be exchanged nor will there be another Torah from the Creator, Blessed is His Name.*

10. **אֲנִי מַאֲמִין** *I believe with complete faith that the Creator, Blessed is His Name, knows all the deeds of human beings and their*

---

are physical, we cannot conceive of a Being totally unaffected by material conditions or the laws of nature and physics. The Torah speaks of God's 'eyes,' 'hands,' and so forth only to help man grasp the concepts being conveyed.

4. *God is eternal and the First Source.* Everything in the created universe has a moment when it came into existence; by definition no creature can be infinite. God transcends time, however, because time itself is His creation.

5. *Prayers should be directed to God.* It is tempting to beseech the angels or such mighty forces as the sun and the constellations, because God has entrusted them with carrying out His will. However, this is illusory. None of them have any power independent of what God assigns them. Therefore, prayers should be directed only toward God Himself.

B) Authenticity of the Torah

6. *God communicates with man.* In order for man to carry out his Divinely ordained mission, he must know what it is. Prophecy is the means by which God communicates His wishes to man. It is a gift that man can attain upon reaching heights of self-perfection.

7. *Moses' prophecy is unique.* Moses' prophecy is not only true, but of a quality unapproached by that of any other prophet before or since. It is essential that his prophecy be unrivaled so that no later 'prophet' could ever claim that he had received a 'Torah' that was superior to that of Moses.

8. *The entire Torah is God-given.* Every word in the Torah was dictated to Moses by God. In *Rambam's* classic formulation, all the verses of the Torah have equal sanctity, and 'there is no difference between [the apparently trivial verses:] *and the children of Ham were Cush and Mizrayim,* and *his wife's name was Mehitabel ...* and [the awesomely important verses:] *I am HASHEM, Your God,* and *Hear O Israel.* Moreover, the same applies to the Oral Law that explains the Torah. All was given by God to Moses.

9. *The Torah is unchangeable.* Since both the Written and Oral Law were God-given, they cannot be improved upon in any manner.

בְּנֵי אָדָם וְכָל מַחְשְׁבוֹתָם, שֶׁנֶּאֱמַר: הַיֹּצֵר יַחַד לִבָּם, הַמֵּבִין אֶל כָּל מַעֲשֵׂיהֶם.[1]

יא **אֲנִי מַאֲמִין** בֶּאֱמוּנָה שְׁלֵמָה, שֶׁהַבּוֹרֵא יִתְבָּרַךְ שְׁמוֹ גּוֹמֵל טוֹב לְשׁוֹמְרֵי מִצְוֹתָיו וּמַעֲנִישׁ לְעוֹבְרֵי מִצְוֹתָיו.

יב **אֲנִי מַאֲמִין** בֶּאֱמוּנָה שְׁלֵמָה, בְּבִיאַת הַמָּשִׁיחַ וְאַף עַל פִּי שֶׁיִּתְמַהְמֵהַּ, עִם כָּל זֶה אֲחַכֶּה לּוֹ בְּכָל יוֹם שֶׁיָּבוֹא.

יג **אֲנִי מַאֲמִין** בֶּאֱמוּנָה שְׁלֵמָה, שֶׁתִּהְיֶה תְּחִיַּת הַמֵּתִים בְּעֵת שֶׁיַּעֲלֶה רָצוֹן מֵאֵת הַבּוֹרֵא יִתְבָּרַךְ שְׁמוֹ וְיִתְעַלֶּה זִכְרוֹ לָעַד וּלְנֵצַח נְצָחִים.

לִישׁוּעָתְךָ קִוִּיתִי יהוה.[2] קִוִּיתִי יהוה לִישׁוּעָתְךָ. יהוה לִישׁוּעָתְךָ קִוִּיתִי.
לְפוּרְקָנָךְ סַבַּרִית יהוה. סַבְּרִית יהוה לְפוּרְקָנָךְ. יהוה לְפוּרְקָנָךְ סַבְּרִית.

עשרת הדברות

שמות כ:א־יד

וַיְדַבֵּר אֱלֹהִים אֵת כָּל הַדְּבָרִים הָאֵלֶּה לֵאמֹר. [א] אָנֹכִי יהוה אֱלֹהֶיךָ, אֲשֶׁר הוֹצֵאתִיךָ מֵאֶרֶץ מִצְרַיִם מִבֵּית עֲבָדִים. [ב] לֹא יִהְיֶה לְךָ אֱלֹהִים אֲחֵרִים עַל פָּנָי. לֹא תַעֲשֶׂה לְךָ פֶסֶל וְכָל תְּמוּנָה אֲשֶׁר בַּשָּׁמַיִם מִמַּעַל, וַאֲשֶׁר בָּאָרֶץ מִתָּחַת, וַאֲשֶׁר בַּמַּיִם מִתַּחַת לָאָרֶץ. לֹא תִשְׁתַּחֲוֶה לָהֶם וְלֹא תָעָבְדֵם, כִּי אָנֹכִי יהוה אֱלֹהֶיךָ, אֵל קַנָּא, פֹּקֵד עֲוֹן אָבֹת עַל בָּנִים, עַל שִׁלֵּשִׁים, וְעַל רִבֵּעִים לְשֹׂנְאָי. וְעֹשֶׂה חֶסֶד לַאֲלָפִים, לְאֹהֲבַי, וּלְשֹׁמְרֵי מִצְוֹתָי. [ג] לֹא תִשָּׂא אֶת שֵׁם יהוה אֱלֹהֶיךָ לַשָּׁוְא, כִּי לֹא יְנַקֶּה יהוה, אֵת אֲשֶׁר יִשָּׂא אֶת שְׁמוֹ לַשָּׁוְא. [ד] זָכוֹר אֶת יוֹם הַשַּׁבָּת לְקַדְּשׁוֹ. שֵׁשֶׁת יָמִים תַּעֲבֹד וְעָשִׂיתָ כָּל מְלַאכְתֶּךָ. וְיוֹם הַשְּׁבִיעִי שַׁבָּת לַיהוה אֱלֹהֶיךָ, לֹא תַעֲשֶׂה כָל מְלָאכָה, אַתָּה וּבִנְךָ וּבִתֶּךָ, עַבְדְּךָ וַאֲמָתְךָ וּבְהֶמְתֶּךָ, וְגֵרְךָ אֲשֶׁר בִּשְׁעָרֶיךָ. כִּי שֵׁשֶׁת יָמִים עָשָׂה יהוה אֶת הַשָּׁמַיִם וְאֶת הָאָרֶץ, אֶת הַיָּם וְאֶת כָּל אֲשֶׁר בָּם, וַיָּנַח בַּיּוֹם הַשְּׁבִיעִי, עַל כֵּן בֵּרַךְ יהוה אֶת יוֹם הַשַּׁבָּת וַיְקַדְּשֵׁהוּ. [ה] כַּבֵּד אֶת אָבִיךָ וְאֶת אִמֶּךָ, לְמַעַן יַאֲרִכוּן יָמֶיךָ עַל הָאֲדָמָה אֲשֶׁר יהוה אֱלֹהֶיךָ נֹתֵן לָךְ. [ו] לֹא תִרְצָח [ז] לֹא תִנְאָף [ח] לֹא תִגְנֹב [ט] לֹא תַעֲנֶה בְרֵעֲךָ עֵד שָׁקֶר. [י] לֹא תַחְמֹד בֵּית רֵעֶךָ, לֹא תַחְמֹד אֵשֶׁת רֵעֶךָ, וְעַבְדּוֹ וַאֲמָתוֹ וְשׁוֹרוֹ וַחֲמֹרוֹ, וְכֹל אֲשֶׁר לְרֵעֶךָ.

C) Man's Responsibility and Ultimate Reward

10. *God knows man's thoughts and deeds.* Man's individual deeds are important to God and so are the hopes and thoughts that drive him. God is aware of everything man thinks and does.

11. *Reward and punishment.* No one acts in a vacuum and no deed goes unrewarded or unpunished. This includes the dictum that one cannot cancel out a bad deed with a good one. Each is treated independently.

12. *The Messiah will come.* We are to conduct our lives according to the Torah and remain faithful that the Messiah will come at the time deemed by God to be proper. This faith includes the principle that only the Davidic dynasty will provide the Messianic king.

13. *The dead will live again* in the Messianic era, when the world will attain a new spiritual and physical level of perfection. Those who have not been found too unworthy to enter this exalted state will live again to enjoy it.

thoughts, as it is said, 'He fashions their hearts all together, He comprehends all their deeds.'[1]

11. **אֲנִי מַאֲמִין** *I believe with complete faith that the Creator, Blessed is His Name, rewards with good those who observe His commandments, and punishes those who violate His commandments.*

12. **אֲנִי מַאֲמִין** *I believe with complete faith in the coming of the Messiah, and even though he may delay, nevertheless I anticipate every day that he will come.*

13. **אֲנִי מַאֲמִין** *I believe with complete faith that there will be a resuscitation of the dead whenever the wish emanates from the Creator, Blessed is His Name and exalted is His mention, forever and for all eternity.*

For Your salvation I do long, HASHEM.[2]
I do long, HASHEM, for Your salvation.
HASHEM, for Your salvation I do long.

THE TEN COMMANDMENTS

Exodus 20:1-14

וַיְדַבֵּר *God spoke all these statements, saying:* [1] *I am HASHEM, your God, Who delivered you from the land of Egypt, from the house of slavery.* [2] *You shall not recognize the gods of others before My presence. You shall not make yourself a carved image nor any likeness of that which is in the heavens above, or of that which is on the earth below, or of that which is in the water beneath the earth. You shall not prostrate yourself to them nor shall you worship them; for I am HASHEM, your God — a jealous God, remembering the sins of fathers upon children, to the third and fourth generations of My enemies, but showing kindness for thousands of generations to those who love Me and who keep My commandments.* [3] *You shall not take the Name of HASHEM, your God, in a vain oath; for HASHEM will not absolve anyone who takes His Name in a vain oath.* [4] *Remember the Sabbath day to sanctify it. Six days you are to work and accomplish all your tasks. But the seventh day is Sabbath to HASHEM, your God; you may not do any work — you, your son, your daughter, your manservant, your maidservant, your animal, and the convert within your gates — for in six days HASHEM made the heavens, the earth, the sea and all that is in them, and He rested on the seventh day. Therefore, HASHEM blessed the Sabbath day and sanctified it.* [5] *Honor your father and mother so that your days may be lengthened upon the land which HASHEM, your God, gives you.* [6] *You shall not kill.* [7] *You shall not commit adultery.* [8] *You shall not steal.* [9] *You shall not bear false witness against your neighbor.* [10] *You shall not covet your neighbor's house. You shall not covet your neighbor's wife, nor his manservant, nor his maidservant, nor his bull, nor his donkey, nor anything that is your neighbor's.*

(1) *Psalms* 33:15. (2) *Genesis* 49:18.

עֲשֶׂרֶת הַדִּבְּרוֹת ◆§ / The Ten Commandments

During the Temple era, the Ten Commandments were recited as a part of the *Shema* service each morning. Later, certain heretics denied the validity of the rest of the Torah, but accepted only the Ten Commandments as the word of God. To prove their point, they cited the fact that the Ten Commandments were recited each day, while the rest of the Torah was not. To counteract their claims, the Talmudic Sages (*Berachos* 12a) removed the Ten Commandments from the formal public prayer service and forbade their reinsertion into the service or their recitation in any public forum (except when they appear in the course of the regular Torah readings). Moreover, even an individual may not recite them as a part of the formal service. Nevertheless, an individual may (and, according to some authorities, should) recite them either before or after his regular prayers.

פרשת התשובה

דברים ל:א־י

וְהָיָה כִּי יָבֹאוּ עָלֶיךָ כָּל הַדְּבָרִים הָאֵלֶּה, הַבְּרָכָה וְהַקְּלָלָה אֲשֶׁר נָתַתִּי לְפָנֶיךָ, וַהֲשֵׁבֹתָ אֶל לְבָבֶךָ, בְּכָל הַגּוֹיִם אֲשֶׁר הִדִּיחֲךָ יהוה אֱלֹהֶיךָ שָׁמָּה, וְשַׁבְתָּ עַד יהוה אֱלֹהֶיךָ, וְשָׁמַעְתָּ בְקֹלוֹ, כְּכֹל אֲשֶׁר אָנֹכִי מְצַוְּךָ הַיּוֹם, אַתָּה וּבָנֶיךָ בְּכָל לְבָבְךָ וּבְכָל נַפְשֶׁךָ. וְשָׁב יהוה אֱלֹהֶיךָ אֶת שְׁבוּתְךָ וְרִחֲמֶךָ, וְשָׁב וְקִבֶּצְךָ מִכָּל הָעַמִּים, אֲשֶׁר הֱפִיצְךָ יהוה אֱלֹהֶיךָ שָׁמָּה. אִם יִהְיֶה נִדַּחֲךָ בִּקְצֵה הַשָּׁמָיִם, מִשָּׁם יְקַבֶּצְךָ יהוה אֱלֹהֶיךָ וּמִשָּׁם יִקָּחֶךָ. וֶהֱבִיאֲךָ יהוה אֱלֹהֶיךָ אֶל הָאָרֶץ אֲשֶׁר יָרְשׁוּ אֲבֹתֶיךָ וִירִשְׁתָּהּ, וְהֵיטִבְךָ וְהִרְבְּךָ מֵאֲבֹתֶיךָ. וּמָל יהוה אֱלֹהֶיךָ אֶת לְבָבְךָ וְאֶת לְבַב זַרְעֶךָ, לְאַהֲבָה אֶת יהוה אֱלֹהֶיךָ בְּכָל לְבָבְךָ וּבְכָל נַפְשְׁךָ, לְמַעַן חַיֶּיךָ. וְנָתַן יהוה אֱלֹהֶיךָ אֵת כָּל הָאָלוֹת הָאֵלֶּה, עַל אֹיְבֶיךָ וְעַל שֹׂנְאֶיךָ אֲשֶׁר רְדָפוּךָ. וְאַתָּה תָשׁוּב, וְשָׁמַעְתָּ בְּקוֹל יהוה, וְעָשִׂיתָ אֶת כָּל מִצְוֹתָיו אֲשֶׁר אָנֹכִי מְצַוְּךָ הַיּוֹם. וְהוֹתִירְךָ יהוה אֱלֹהֶיךָ בְּכֹל מַעֲשֵׂה יָדֶךָ, בִּפְרִי בִטְנְךָ וּבִפְרִי בְהֶמְתְּךָ וּבִפְרִי אַדְמָתְךָ לְטֹבָה, כִּי יָשׁוּב יהוה לָשׂוּשׂ עָלֶיךָ לְטוֹב, כַּאֲשֶׁר שָׂשׂ עַל אֲבֹתֶיךָ. כִּי תִשְׁמַע בְּקוֹל יהוה אֱלֹהֶיךָ, לִשְׁמֹר מִצְוֹתָיו וְחֻקֹּתָיו הַכְּתוּבָה בְּסֵפֶר הַתּוֹרָה הַזֶּה, כִּי תָשׁוּב אֶל יהוה אֱלֹהֶיךָ בְּכָל לְבָבְךָ וּבְכָל נַפְשֶׁךָ.

Many recite the following supplicatory paragraph after פָּרָשַׁת הַתְּשׁוּבָה
[it is omitted on the Sabbath and Festivals].

יְהִי רָצוֹן מִלְּפָנֶיךָ יהוה אֱלֹהַי וֵאלֹהֵי אֲבוֹתַי, שֶׁתַּחְתּוֹר חֲתִירָה מִתַּחַת כִּסֵּא כְבוֹדֶךָ, לְהַחֲזִיר בִּתְשׁוּבָה שְׁלֵמָה לְכָל פּוֹשְׁעֵי עַמְּךָ בֵּית יִשְׂרָאֵל. וּבִכְלָלָם תַּחֲזִירֵנִי בִּתְשׁוּבָה שְׁלֵמָה לְפָנֶיךָ, כִּי יְמִינְךָ פְשׁוּטָה לְקַבֵּל שָׁבִים, וְרוֹצֶה אַתָּה בִּתְשׁוּבָה. אָמֵן, סֶלָה.

פרשת היראה

דברים י:יב־יא:ט

וְעַתָּה יִשְׂרָאֵל, מָה יהוה אֱלֹהֶיךָ שֹׁאֵל מֵעִמָּךְ, כִּי אִם לְיִרְאָה אֶת יהוה אֱלֹהֶיךָ, לָלֶכֶת בְּכָל דְּרָכָיו, וּלְאַהֲבָה אֹתוֹ, וְלַעֲבֹד אֶת יהוה אֱלֹהֶיךָ בְּכָל לְבָבְךָ וּבְכָל נַפְשֶׁךָ. לִשְׁמֹר אֶת מִצְוֹת יהוה וְאֶת חֻקֹּתָיו, אֲשֶׁר אָנֹכִי מְצַוְּךָ הַיּוֹם, לְטוֹב לָךְ. הֵן לַיהוה אֱלֹהֶיךָ הַשָּׁמַיִם וּשְׁמֵי הַשָּׁמָיִם, הָאָרֶץ וְכָל אֲשֶׁר בָּהּ. רַק בַּאֲבֹתֶיךָ חָשַׁק יהוה לְאַהֲבָה אוֹתָם, וַיִּבְחַר בְּזַרְעָם אַחֲרֵיהֶם, בָּכֶם, מִכָּל הָעַמִּים כַּיּוֹם הַזֶּה. וּמַלְתֶּם אֵת עָרְלַת לְבַבְכֶם, וְעָרְפְּכֶם לֹא תַקְשׁוּ עוֹד. כִּי יהוה אֱלֹהֵיכֶם הוּא אֱלֹהֵי הָאֱלֹהִים, וַאֲדֹנֵי הָאֲדֹנִים, הָאֵל הַגָּדֹל הַגִּבֹּר וְהַנּוֹרָא, אֲשֶׁר לֹא יִשָּׂא פָנִים, וְלֹא יִקַּח שֹׁחַד. עֹשֶׂה מִשְׁפַּט יָתוֹם וְאַלְמָנָה, וְאֹהֵב גֵּר לָתֶת לוֹ לֶחֶם וְשִׂמְלָה. וַאֲהַבְתֶּם אֶת הַגֵּר, כִּי גֵרִים הֱיִיתֶם בְּאֶרֶץ מִצְרָיִם. אֶת יהוה אֱלֹהֶיךָ תִּירָא, אֹתוֹ תַעֲבֹד, וּבוֹ תִדְבָּק, וּבִשְׁמוֹ תִּשָּׁבֵעַ. הוּא תְהִלָּתְךָ וְהוּא אֱלֹהֶיךָ, אֲשֶׁר עָשָׂה אִתְּךָ אֶת הַגְּדֹלֹת וְאֶת הַנּוֹרָאֹת הָאֵלֶּה, אֲשֶׁר רָאוּ עֵינֶיךָ. בְּשִׁבְעִים נֶפֶשׁ יָרְדוּ אֲבֹתֶיךָ מִצְרָיְמָה, וְעַתָּה שָׂמְךָ יהוה אֱלֹהֶיךָ

THE CHAPTER OF REPENTANCE

Deuteronomy 30:1-10

וְהָיָה *It will be that when all these things come upon you, the blessing and the curse that I have placed before you; and you will take it to your heart among all the nations to which HASHEM, your God, has cast you. Then you will return to HASHEM, your God, and heed His voice according to everything that I command you today; you and your children, with all your heart and with all your soul. Then HASHEM will bring back your captivity and have mercy upon you, and He will again gather you in from all the peoples where HASHEM, your God, has scattered you. If your dispersed will be at the ends of heaven, from there HASHEM, your God, will gather you in and from there He will take you. HASHEM, your God, will bring you to the land that your forefathers inherited and you will possess it; and He will benefit you and increase you beyond your forefathers. HASHEM, your God, will circumcise your heart and the heart of your offspring; to love HASHEM, your God, with all your heart and with all your soul, that you may live. HASHEM, your God, will place all these curses upon your enemies and upon those who hate you, who have pursued you. But you shall repent and listen to the voice of HASHEM; and perform all His commandments in which I instruct you today. HASHEM, your God, will prosper you in all your handiwork, in the fruit of your womb, the fruit of your livestock, and the fruit of your land for good; for HASHEM will return to rejoice over you for good as He had rejoiced over your forefathers. When you heed the voice of HASHEM, your God, to observe His commandments and His decrees that are written in this book of the Torah; when you will return to HASHEM, your God, with all your heart and all your soul.*

Many recite the following supplicatory paragraph after the Chapter of Repentance [it is omitted on the Sabbath and Festivals].

יְהִי רָצוֹן *May it be Your will, HASHEM, my God and the God of my forefathers, that you dig a tunnel beneath your Throne of Glory to bring back in complete repentance all the evildoers of Your people the House of Israel. And among them bring me back in complete repentance before You, for Your right hand is outstretched to accept penitents and You desire repentance. Amen. Selah.*

THE CHAPTER OF REVERENCE FOR GOD

Deuteronomy 10:12 — 11:9

וְעַתָּה *And now, Israel, what does HASHEM, your God, ask of you? — only to revere HASHEM, your God, to go in all His ways and to love Him, and to serve HASHEM, your God, with all your heart and with all your soul. To observe the commandments of HASHEM and His decrees in which I instruct you today; for your benefit. Behold, to HASHEM, your God, belong the heaven and the most exalted heaven, the earth and all that is in it. Yet HASHEM delighted only in your forefathers to love them; and He chose their offspring after them — in you — from among all peoples this day. Cut away the barrier of your heart; and be stubborn no longer. For HASHEM, your God, He is the God of all powers and the Master of all masters; the great, mighty, and awesome God, Who will favor no one and will not accept bribery. Who carries out justice for the orphan and widow; and Who loves the stranger to provide him with food and clothing. You are to love the stranger; for you were strangers in the land of Egypt. Revere HASHEM, your God, serve Him, cling to Him, and swear by His Name. He is Your praise and He is your God, Who did with you all these great and fearsome things that your eyes beheld. With seventy people your forefathers descended to Egypt, and now HASHEM, your God, has made you*

כְּכוֹכְבֵי הַשָּׁמַיִם לָרֹב. וְאָהַבְתָּ אֵת יהוה אֱלֹהֶיךָ, וְשָׁמַרְתָּ מִשְׁמַרְתּוֹ וְחֻקֹּתָיו וּמִשְׁפָּטָיו וּמִצְוֹתָיו כָּל הַיָּמִים. וִידַעְתֶּם הַיּוֹם, כִּי לֹא אֶת בְּנֵיכֶם אֲשֶׁר לֹא יָדְעוּ וַאֲשֶׁר לֹא רָאוּ אֶת מוּסַר יהוה אֱלֹהֵיכֶם, אֶת גָּדְלוֹ, אֶת יָדוֹ הַחֲזָקָה, וּזְרֹעוֹ הַנְּטוּיָה. וְאֶת אֹתֹתָיו, וְאֶת מַעֲשָׂיו אֲשֶׁר עָשָׂה בְּתוֹךְ מִצְרָיִם, לְפַרְעֹה מֶלֶךְ מִצְרַיִם וּלְכָל אַרְצוֹ. וַאֲשֶׁר עָשָׂה לְחֵיל מִצְרַיִם לְסוּסָיו וּלְרִכְבּוֹ, אֲשֶׁר הֵצִיף אֶת מֵי יַם סוּף עַל פְּנֵיהֶם בְּרָדְפָם אַחֲרֵיכֶם, וַיְאַבְּדֵם יהוה עַד הַיּוֹם הַזֶּה. וַאֲשֶׁר עָשָׂה לָכֶם בַּמִּדְבָּר, עַד בֹּאֲכֶם עַד הַמָּקוֹם הַזֶּה. וַאֲשֶׁר עָשָׂה לְדָתָן וְלַאֲבִירָם בְּנֵי אֱלִיאָב בֶּן רְאוּבֵן, אֲשֶׁר פָּצְתָה הָאָרֶץ אֶת פִּיהָ, וַתִּבְלָעֵם וְאֶת בָּתֵּיהֶם וְאֶת אָהֳלֵיהֶם, וְאֵת כָּל הַיְקוּם אֲשֶׁר בְּרַגְלֵיהֶם, בְּקֶרֶב כָּל יִשְׂרָאֵל. כִּי עֵינֵיכֶם הָרֹאֹת אֶת כָּל מַעֲשֵׂה יהוה הַגָּדֹל, אֲשֶׁר עָשָׂה. וּשְׁמַרְתֶּם אֶת כָּל הַמִּצְוָה אֲשֶׁר אָנֹכִי מְצַוְּךָ הַיּוֹם, לְמַעַן תֶּחֶזְקוּ וּבָאתֶם וִירִשְׁתֶּם אֶת הָאָרֶץ אֲשֶׁר אַתֶּם עֹבְרִים שָׁמָּה לְרִשְׁתָּהּ. וּלְמַעַן תַּאֲרִיכוּ יָמִים עַל הָאֲדָמָה אֲשֶׁר נִשְׁבַּע יהוה לַאֲבֹתֵיכֶם לָתֵת לָהֶם וּלְזַרְעָם, אֶרֶץ זָבַת חָלָב וּדְבָשׁ.

Many recite the following supplicatory paragraph after פָּרָשַׁת הַיִּרְאָה
[it is omitted on the Sabbath and Festivals].

יְהִי רָצוֹן מִלְּפָנֶיךָ יהוה אֱלֹהַי וֵאלֹהֵי אֲבוֹתַי, שֶׁתִּטַּע אַהֲבָתְךָ וְיִרְאָתְךָ בְּלִבִּי וּבְלֵב כָּל יִשְׂרָאֵל עַמֶּךָ, לְיִרְאָה אֶת שִׁמְךָ הַגָּדוֹל הַגִּבּוֹר וְהַנּוֹרָא, בְּכָל לְבָבֵנוּ וּבְכָל נַפְשֵׁנוּ, יִרְאַת הָרוֹמְמוּת שֶׁל אֵין סוֹף, בָּרוּךְ וְיִתְעַלֶּה שִׁמְךָ, כִּי גָדוֹל אַתָּה וְנוֹרָא שְׁמֶךָ. אָמֵן, סֶלָה.

פרשת המן

The commentators cite *Yerushalmi* that one who recites this chapter every day is assured that his food will not be lacking. *Levush* explains that this chapter teaches that God provides each day's sustenance — just as He provided the manna each day in the Wilderness.

Many recite the following supplicatory paragraph before פָּרָשַׁת הַמָּן
[it is omitted on the Sabbath and Festivals].

יְהִי רָצוֹן מִלְּפָנֶיךָ, יהוה אֱלֹהֵינוּ וֵאלֹהֵי אֲבוֹתֵינוּ, שֶׁתַּזְמִין פַּרְנָסָה לְכָל עַמְּךָ בֵּית יִשְׂרָאֵל, וּפַרְנָסָתִי וּפַרְנָסַת אַנְשֵׁי בֵיתִי בִּכְלָלָם, בְּנַחַת וְלֹא בְצַעַר, בְּכָבוֹד וְלֹא בְבִזּוּי, בְּהֶתֵּר וְלֹא בְאִסּוּר — כְּדֵי שֶׁנּוּכַל לַעֲבֹד עֲבוֹדָתֶךָ וְלִלְמוֹד תּוֹרָתֶךָ — כְּמוֹ שֶׁזַּנְתָּ לַאֲבוֹתֵינוּ מָן בַּמִּדְבָּר, בְּאֶרֶץ צִיָּה וַעֲרָבָה.

שמות טז:ד-לו

וַיֹּאמֶר יהוה אֶל מֹשֶׁה, הִנְנִי מַמְטִיר לָכֶם לֶחֶם מִן הַשָּׁמָיִם, וְיָצָא הָעָם וְלָקְטוּ דְּבַר יוֹם בְּיוֹמוֹ, לְמַעַן אֲנַסֶּנּוּ הֲיֵלֵךְ בְּתוֹרָתִי אִם לֹא. וְהָיָה בַּיּוֹם הַשִּׁשִּׁי, וְהֵכִינוּ אֵת אֲשֶׁר יָבִיאוּ, וְהָיָה מִשְׁנֶה עַל אֲשֶׁר יִלְקְטוּ יוֹם יוֹם. וַיֹּאמֶר מֹשֶׁה וְאַהֲרֹן אֶל כָּל בְּנֵי יִשְׂרָאֵל, עֶרֶב וִידַעְתֶּם כִּי יהוה הוֹצִיא אֶתְכֶם מֵאֶרֶץ מִצְרָיִם. וּבֹקֶר וּרְאִיתֶם אֶת כְּבוֹד יהוה, בְּשָׁמְעוֹ אֶת תְּלֻנֹּתֵיכֶם עַל יהוה, וְנַחְנוּ מָה, כִּי תַלִּינוּ עָלֵינוּ. וַיֹּאמֶר מֹשֶׁה, בְּתֵת יהוה לָכֶם בָּעֶרֶב בָּשָׂר לֶאֱכֹל וְלֶחֶם בַּבֹּקֶר לִשְׂבֹּעַ, בִּשְׁמֹעַ יהוה אֶת תְּלֻנֹּתֵיכֶם אֲשֶׁר אַתֶּם מַלִּינִם עָלָיו, וְנַחְנוּ מָה, לֹא עָלֵינוּ תְלֻנֹּתֵיכֶם, כִּי

as abundant as the stars of heaven. You shall love HASHEM, your God; you shall observe His charge, His decrees, His ordinances, and His commandments all the days. It is your duty to know this day — for [I speak] not with your children who did not know and who did not see the chastisement of HASHEM, your God, His greatness, His strong hand, and His outstretched arm. His signs and His deeds that He performed amid Egypt, to Pharaoh, the king of Egypt, and to his entire land. And what He did to the army of Egypt, to its horses and to its chariots; Who made the water of the Sea of Reeds inundate them, when they chased after you; and HASHEM destroyed them, to this very day. And what He did for you in the Wilderness, until you arrived at this place. And what He did to Dathan and Abiram, the sons of Eliab, son of Reuben, when the earth opened wide its mouth and swallowed their households, their tents, and all the resources that sustained them, among all Israel. For your own eyes have seen all the great work that He has accomplished. You are to observe the entire commandment in which I instruct you this day; so that you can be strong, and come and possess the land, to which you cross over, to inherit it. And so that you can prolong your days upon the land that HASHEM swore to your forefathers to give to them and to their offspring; a land flowing with milk and honey.

Many recite the following supplicatory paragraph after the Chapter of Reverence [it is omitted on the Sabbath and Festivals].

יְהִי רָצוֹן *May it be Your will, HASHEM, my God and the God of my forefathers that You implant Your reverence and Your love in my heart and in the heart of all Israel, Your people, to revere Your great, mighty, and awesome Name with all our heart and with all our soul, a reverence for the exaltation of the Infinite One, blessed and uplifted be Your Name, for You are great and Your Name is awesome. Amen. Selah.*

THE CHAPTER OF MANNA

The commentators cite *Yerushalmi* that one who recites this chapter every day is assured that his food will not be lacking. *Levush* explains that this chapter teaches that God provides each day's sustenance — just as He provided the manna each day in the Wilderness.

Many recite the following supplicatory paragraph before the Chapter of Manna [it is omitted on the Sabbath and Festivals].

יְהִי רָצוֹן *May it be Your will, HASHEM, our God and the God of our forefathers, that you prepare a livelihood for Your entire people, the House of Israel — and my livelihood and the livelihood of the members of my household among them — with ease and not with pain, with honor and not with disgrace, in a permissible and not in a forbidden manner, so that we will be able to perform Your service, and study Your Torah, as You nourished our forefathers in the Wilderness, in a desolate and arid land.*

Exodus 16:4-36

וַיֹּאמֶר *HASHEM said to Moses: 'Behold I will cause bread to rain down to you from heaven; and the people will go out and gather each day's need in its day, so that I can test whether they will walk according to My teaching or not. And it will be on the sixth day that they will prepare what they will bring; for there will be double what they will gather day by day.' Then Moses and Aaron said to all the Children of Israel: 'This evening you will know that HASHEM removed you from the land of Egypt. And in the morning you will see the glory of HASHEM when He hears your complaints against HASHEM; for what are we, that you complain against us?' Then Moses said: '[This will occur] when HASHEM gives you meat to eat in the evening and bread in the morning to satisfaction, when HASHEM will have heard your complaints that you charge against Him; for what are we? — not against us are your complaints, but*

עַל יהוה. וַיֹּאמֶר מֹשֶׁה אֶל אַהֲרֹן, אֱמֹר אֶל כָּל עֲדַת בְּנֵי יִשְׂרָאֵל, קִרְבוּ לִפְנֵי יהוה, כִּי שָׁמַע אֵת תְּלֻנֹּתֵיכֶם. וַיְהִי כְּדַבֵּר אַהֲרֹן אֶל כָּל עֲדַת בְּנֵי יִשְׂרָאֵל, וַיִּפְנוּ אֶל הַמִּדְבָּר, וְהִנֵּה כְּבוֹד יהוה נִרְאָה בֶּעָנָן.

וַיְדַבֵּר יהוה אֶל מֹשֶׁה לֵּאמֹר. שָׁמַעְתִּי אֶת תְּלוּנֹּת בְּנֵי יִשְׂרָאֵל, דַּבֵּר אֲלֵהֶם לֵאמֹר, בֵּין הָעַרְבַּיִם תֹּאכְלוּ בָשָׂר, וּבַבֹּקֶר תִּשְׂבְּעוּ לָחֶם, וִידַעְתֶּם כִּי אֲנִי יהוה אֱלֹהֵיכֶם. וַיְהִי בָעֶרֶב, וַתַּעַל הַשְּׂלָו וַתְּכַס אֶת הַמַּחֲנֶה, וּבַבֹּקֶר הָיְתָה שִׁכְבַת הַטָּל סָבִיב לַמַּחֲנֶה. וַתַּעַל שִׁכְבַת הַטָּל, וְהִנֵּה עַל פְּנֵי הַמִּדְבָּר דַּק מְחֻסְפָּס, דַּק כַּכְּפֹר עַל הָאָרֶץ. וַיִּרְאוּ בְנֵי יִשְׂרָאֵל, וַיֹּאמְרוּ אִישׁ אֶל אָחִיו, מָן הוּא, כִּי לֹא יָדְעוּ מַה הוּא, וַיֹּאמֶר מֹשֶׁה אֲלֵהֶם, הוּא הַלֶּחֶם אֲשֶׁר נָתַן יהוה לָכֶם לְאָכְלָה. זֶה הַדָּבָר אֲשֶׁר צִוָּה יהוה, לִקְטוּ מִמֶּנּוּ אִישׁ לְפִי אָכְלוֹ, עֹמֶר לַגֻּלְגֹּלֶת, מִסְפַּר נַפְשֹׁתֵיכֶם, אִישׁ לַאֲשֶׁר בְּאָהֳלוֹ תִּקָּחוּ. וַיַּעֲשׂוּ כֵן בְּנֵי יִשְׂרָאֵל, וַיִּלְקְטוּ הַמַּרְבֶּה וְהַמַּמְעִיט. וַיָּמֹדּוּ בָעֹמֶר, וְלֹא הֶעְדִּיף הַמַּרְבֶּה, וְהַמַּמְעִיט לֹא הֶחְסִיר, אִישׁ לְפִי אָכְלוֹ לָקָטוּ. וַיֹּאמֶר מֹשֶׁה אֲלֵהֶם, אִישׁ אַל יוֹתֵר מִמֶּנּוּ עַד בֹּקֶר. וְלֹא שָׁמְעוּ אֶל מֹשֶׁה, וַיּוֹתִרוּ אֲנָשִׁים מִמֶּנּוּ עַד בֹּקֶר וַיָּרֻם תּוֹלָעִים וַיִּבְאַשׁ, וַיִּקְצֹף עֲלֵהֶם מֹשֶׁה. וַיִּלְקְטוּ אֹתוֹ בַּבֹּקֶר בַּבֹּקֶר, אִישׁ כְּפִי אָכְלוֹ, וְחַם הַשֶּׁמֶשׁ וְנָמָס. וַיְהִי בַּיּוֹם הַשִּׁשִּׁי, לָקְטוּ לֶחֶם מִשְׁנֶה, שְׁנֵי הָעֹמֶר לָאֶחָד, וַיָּבֹאוּ כָּל נְשִׂיאֵי הָעֵדָה, וַיַּגִּידוּ לְמֹשֶׁה. וַיֹּאמֶר אֲלֵהֶם, הוּא אֲשֶׁר דִּבֶּר יהוה, שַׁבָּתוֹן שַׁבַּת קֹדֶשׁ לַיהוה מָחָר, אֵת אֲשֶׁר תֹּאפוּ אֵפוּ, וְאֵת אֲשֶׁר תְּבַשְּׁלוּ בַּשֵּׁלוּ, וְאֵת כָּל הָעֹדֵף הַנִּיחוּ לָכֶם לְמִשְׁמֶרֶת עַד הַבֹּקֶר. וַיַּנִּיחוּ אֹתוֹ עַד הַבֹּקֶר כַּאֲשֶׁר צִוָּה מֹשֶׁה, וְלֹא הִבְאִישׁ, וְרִמָּה לֹא הָיְתָה בּוֹ. וַיֹּאמֶר מֹשֶׁה, אִכְלֻהוּ הַיּוֹם, כִּי שַׁבָּת הַיּוֹם לַיהוה, הַיּוֹם לֹא תִמְצָאֻהוּ בַּשָּׂדֶה. שֵׁשֶׁת יָמִים תִּלְקְטֻהוּ, וּבַיּוֹם הַשְּׁבִיעִי שַׁבָּת, לֹא יִהְיֶה בּוֹ. וַיְהִי בַּיּוֹם הַשְּׁבִיעִי, יָצְאוּ מִן הָעָם לִלְקֹט, וְלֹא מָצָאוּ.

וַיֹּאמֶר יהוה אֶל מֹשֶׁה, עַד אָנָה מֵאַנְתֶּם לִשְׁמֹר מִצְוֹתַי וְתוֹרֹתָי. רְאוּ כִּי יהוה נָתַן לָכֶם הַשַּׁבָּת, עַל כֵּן הוּא נֹתֵן לָכֶם בַּיּוֹם הַשִּׁשִּׁי לֶחֶם יוֹמָיִם, שְׁבוּ אִישׁ תַּחְתָּיו, אַל יֵצֵא אִישׁ מִמְּקֹמוֹ בַּיּוֹם הַשְּׁבִיעִי. וַיִּשְׁבְּתוּ הָעָם בַּיּוֹם הַשְּׁבִעִי. וַיִּקְרְאוּ בֵית יִשְׂרָאֵל אֶת שְׁמוֹ מָן, וְהוּא כְּזֶרַע גַּד לָבָן, וְטַעְמוֹ כְּצַפִּיחִת בִּדְבָשׁ. וַיֹּאמֶר מֹשֶׁה, זֶה הַדָּבָר אֲשֶׁר צִוָּה יהוה, מְלֹא הָעֹמֶר מִמֶּנּוּ לְמִשְׁמֶרֶת לְדֹרֹתֵיכֶם, לְמַעַן יִרְאוּ אֶת הַלֶּחֶם אֲשֶׁר הֶאֱכַלְתִּי אֶתְכֶם בַּמִּדְבָּר בְּהוֹצִיאִי אֶתְכֶם מֵאֶרֶץ מִצְרָיִם. וַיֹּאמֶר מֹשֶׁה אֶל אַהֲרֹן, קַח צִנְצֶנֶת אַחַת וְתֶן שָׁמָּה מְלֹא הָעֹמֶר מָן, וְהַנַּח אֹתוֹ לִפְנֵי יהוה, לְמִשְׁמֶרֶת לְדֹרֹתֵיכֶם. כַּאֲשֶׁר צִוָּה יהוה אֶל מֹשֶׁה, וַיַּנִּיחֵהוּ אַהֲרֹן לִפְנֵי הָעֵדֻת לְמִשְׁמָרֶת. וּבְנֵי יִשְׂרָאֵל אָכְלוּ אֶת הַמָּן אַרְבָּעִים שָׁנָה, עַד בֹּאָם אֶל אֶרֶץ נוֹשָׁבֶת אֶת הַמָּן אָכְלוּ עַד בֹּאָם אֶל קְצֵה אֶרֶץ כְּנָעַן. וְהָעֹמֶר עֲשִׂרִית הָאֵיפָה הוּא.

against HASHEM!' Moses said to Aaron: "Say to the entire congregation of the Children of Israel, 'Draw near before HASHEM, for He has heard your complaints.' " And it happened that when Aaron spoke to the entire congregation of the Children of Israel they turned toward the Wilderness and behold! the glory of HASHEM was seen in a cloud.

HASHEM spoke to Moses, saying: "I have heard the complaints of the Children of Israel; speak to them, saying: 'In the afternoon you will eat meat and in the morning you will be sated with bread; and you shall realize that I am HASHEM, your God.' " And it happened in the evening that the quails came up and covered the camp, and in the morning there was a layer of dew surrounding the camp. The layer of dew evaporated; and behold! — upon the surface of the Wilderness was revealed something thin, as thin as frost upon the ground. The Children of Israel saw and said to one another, 'What is this?' — for they did not know what it was; then Moses said to them: "This is the food that HASHEM has given you to eat. This is the thing that HASHEM has commanded, 'Gather from it, everyone according to his consumption; an omer per capita according to the number of your souls, each of you is to take for each person in his tent.' " The Children of Israel did so; they gathered, one more and one less. Then they measured in an omer, and he who took more did not have extra and he who took less was not lacking; each one gathered according to his consumption. Then Moses said to them, 'Let no one leave over from it until morning.' But they did not heed Moses, and some men left part of it over until morning, and it bred worms and became putrid; and Moses became angry at them. They would gather it every morning, everyone according to his consumption; and when the sunlight grew hot, it would melt. It happened on the sixth day that they gathered a double measure of food, two omers for each one; and all the leaders of the congregation came and told Moses. He said to them: 'This is what HASHEM spoke of, tomorrow is a day of rest, a holy Sabbath to HASHEM; what you wish to bake, bake; and what you wish to cook, cook; and whatever is left over, put away for yourselves in safekeeping until morning.' They put it away until morning, as Moses commanded; and it did not become putrid and there were no worms in it. Then Moses said: 'Eat it today for today is the Sabbath to HASHEM; today you will not find it in the field. You are to gather it for six days; but the seventh day is the Sabbath, there will be none on it.' But it happened on the seventh day that some of the people went out to gather; and they did not find.

HASHEM said to Moses: 'How long will you refuse to obey My commandments and My teachings? See — because HASHEM gave you the Sabbath, therefore He provides you on the sixth day with food for two days; let everyone remain in his place, let no one leave his domain on the seventh day.' So the people rested on the seventh day. The House of Israel called it manna, and it tasted like dough kneaded with honey. Moses said: 'This is the matter that HASHEM commanded: an omerful of it is to be a keepsake for your generations, so that they can see the food that I fed you in the Wilderness when I took you out of the land of Egypt.' Moses said to Aaron: 'Take a single earthenware jar and place in it an omerful of manna; and set it down before HASHEM as a keepsake for your generations.' Just as HASHEM commanded Moses, so Aaron set it down before the Testimonial Tablets as a keepsake. The Children of Israel ate the manna for forty years until they arrived at a populated land; they ate the manna until they arrived at the edge of the land of Canaan. The omer is one-tenth of the ephah.

תפלה על הפרנסה

[This prayer is not recited on the Sabbath and Festivals.]

אַתָּה הוּא יהוה לְבַדֶּךָ, אַתָּה עָשִׂיתָ אֶת הַשָּׁמַיִם וּשְׁמֵי הַשָּׁמַיִם, הָאָרֶץ וְכָל אֲשֶׁר עָלֶיהָ, הַיַּמִּים וְכָל אֲשֶׁר בָּהֶם, וְאַתָּה מְחַיֶּה אֶת כֻּלָּם.[1] וְאַתָּה הוּא שֶׁעָשִׂיתָ נִסִּים וְנִפְלָאוֹת גְּדוֹלוֹת תָּמִיד עִם אֲבוֹתֵינוּ. גַּם בַּמִּדְבָּר הִמְטַרְתָּ לָהֶם לֶחֶם מִן הַשָּׁמַיִם,[2] וּמִצּוּר הַחַלָּמִישׁ, הוֹצֵאתָ לָהֶם מָיִם,[3] וְגַם נָתַתָּ לָהֶם כָּל צָרְכֵיהֶם, וְשִׂמְלָתָם לֹא בָלְתָה מֵעֲלֵיהֶם.[4] כֵּן בְּרַחֲמֶיךָ הָרַבִּים וּבַחֲסָדֶיךָ הָעֲצוּמִים, תְּזוּנֵנוּ וּתְפַרְנְסֵנוּ וּתְכַלְכְּלֵנוּ וְתַסְפִּיק כָּל צָרְכֵנוּ, וְצָרְכֵי עַמְּךָ בֵּית יִשְׂרָאֵל הַמְּרֻבִּים, בְּמִלּוּי וּבְרֶוַח, בְּלִי טֹרַח וְעָמָל גָּדוֹל, מִתַּחַת יָדְךָ הַנְּקִיָּה, וְלֹא מִתַּחַת יְדֵי בָשָׂר וָדָם.

יְהִי רָצוֹן מִלְּפָנֶיךָ יהוה אֱלֹהַי וֵאלֹהֵי אֲבוֹתַי, שֶׁתָּכִין לִי וּלְאַנְשֵׁי בֵיתִי, כָּל מַחְסוֹרֵנוּ, וְתַזְמִין לָנוּ כָּל צָרְכֵנוּ. לְכָל יוֹם וָיוֹם מֵחַיֵּינוּ דֵּי מַחְסוֹרֵנוּ, וּלְכָל שָׁעָה וְשָׁעָה מִשְּׁעוֹתֵינוּ, דֵּי סִפּוּקֵנוּ, וּלְכָל עֶצֶם מֵעֲצָמֵינוּ דֵּי מִחְיָתֵנוּ, כְּיָדְךָ הַטּוֹבָה וְהָרְחָבָה, וְלֹא כְּמִעוּט מִפְעָלֵינוּ, וְקֹצֶר חֲסָדֵינוּ, וּמִזְעֵיר גְּמוּלוֹתֵנוּ. וְיִהְיֶה מְזוֹנוֹתַי, וּמְזוֹנוֹת אַנְשֵׁי בֵיתִי, וְזַרְעִי וְזֶרַע זַרְעִי מְסוּרִים בְּיָדְךָ, וְלֹא בְּיַד בָּשָׂר וָדָם.

אחר התפלה — בקר וערב

יְהִי יהוה אֱלֹהֵינוּ עִמָּנוּ, כַּאֲשֶׁר הָיָה עִם אֲבוֹתֵינוּ, אַל יַעַזְבֵנוּ וְאַל יִטְּשֵׁנוּ. לְהַטּוֹת לְבָבֵנוּ אֵלָיו, לָלֶכֶת בְּכָל דְּרָכָיו, וְלִשְׁמֹר מִצְוֹתָיו וְחֻקָּיו וּמִשְׁפָּטָיו, אֲשֶׁר צִוָּה אֶת אֲבֹתֵינוּ. וְיִהְיוּ דְבָרַי אֵלֶּה, אֲשֶׁר הִתְחַנַּנְתִּי לִפְנֵי יהוה, קְרֹבִים אֶל יהוה אֱלֹהֵינוּ יוֹמָם וָלָיְלָה, לַעֲשׂוֹת מִשְׁפַּט עַבְדּוֹ, וּמִשְׁפַּט עַמּוֹ יִשְׂרָאֵל, דְּבַר יוֹם בְּיוֹמוֹ. לְמַעַן דַּעַת כָּל עַמֵּי הָאָרֶץ, כִּי יהוה הוּא הָאֱלֹהִים, אֵין עוֹד.[5] יהוה, נְחֵנִי בְצִדְקָתֶךָ לְמַעַן שׁוֹרְרָי, הַיְשַׁר לְפָנַי דַּרְכֶּךָ.[6] וַאֲנִי בְּתֻמִּי אֵלֵךְ, פְּדֵנִי וְחָנֵּנִי.[7] פְּנֵה אֵלַי וְחָנֵּנִי, כִּי יָחִיד וְעָנִי אָנִי.[8] רַגְלִי עָמְדָה בְמִישׁוֹר, בְּמַקְהֵלִים אֲבָרֵךְ יהוה.[9] יהוה שֹׁמְרִי, יהוה צִלִּי עַל יַד יְמִינִי.[10] עֶזְרִי מֵעִם יהוה, עֹשֵׂה שָׁמַיִם וָאָרֶץ.[11] יהוה יִשְׁמָר צֵאתִי וּבוֹאִי, לְחַיִּים וּלְשָׁלוֹם, מֵעַתָּה וְעַד עוֹלָם.[12] הַשְׁקִיפָה מִמְּעוֹן קָדְשְׁךָ, מִן הַשָּׁמַיִם, וּבָרֵךְ אֶת עַמְּךָ אֶת יִשְׂרָאֵל, וְאֵת הָאֲדָמָה אֲשֶׁר נָתַתָּה לָנוּ, כַּאֲשֶׁר נִשְׁבַּעְתָּ לַאֲבוֹתֵינוּ, אֶרֶץ זָבַת חָלָב וּדְבָשׁ.[13]

אֵל הַכָּבוֹד, אֶתֵּן לְךָ שִׁיר וְהַלֵּל, וְאֶעֱבוֹד לְךָ יוֹם וָלֵיל. בָּרוּךְ יָחִיד וּמְיוּחָד, הָיָה הֹוֶה וְיִהְיֶה, יהוה אֱלֹהִים אֱלֹהֵי יִשְׂרָאֵל, מֶלֶךְ מַלְכֵי הַמְּלָכִים הַקָּדוֹשׁ בָּרוּךְ הוּא. הוּא אֱלֹהִים חַיִּים, מֶלֶךְ חַי וְקַיָּם לָעַד וּלְעוֹלְמֵי עַד. בָּרוּךְ שֵׁם כְּבוֹד מַלְכוּתוֹ לְעוֹלָם וָעֶד. לִישׁוּעָתְךָ קִוִּיתִי יהוה.[14] כִּי, כָּל הָעַמִּים יֵלְכוּ אִישׁ בְּשֵׁם אֱלֹהָיו,

(1) Cf. *Nechemiah* 9:6. (2) Cf. *Exodus* 16:4. (3) Cf. *Deuteronomy* 8:15. (4) Cf. 8:4. (5) *I Kings* 8:57-60. (6) *Psalms* 5:9. (7) 26:11. (8) 25:16. (9) 26:12. (10) Cf. 121:5. (11) 121:2. (12) Cf. 121:8. (13) *Deuteronomy* 26:15. (14) *Genesis* 49:18.

PRAYER FOR LIVELIHOOD

[This prayer is not recited on the Sabbath and Festivals.]

אַתָּה *It is You alone, HASHEM, You have made the heaven, the most exalted heaven, the earth and everything upon it, the seas and everything in them, and You give them all life.[1] It is You who always performed miracles and great wonders with our forefathers. Also in the Wilderness You rained down for them food from heaven,[2] and from the flinty rock You withdrew water for them,[3] and You also provided them all their needs, and their clothing did not wear out upon them.[4] So in Your abundant mercy and powerful kindness, may You nourish us, sustain us, and support us, and supply all our needs and the abundant needs of Your people the House of Israel, with fullness and relief, without travail or great effort, from beneath Your pure hand and not from beneath mortal hands.*

יְהִי רָצוֹן *May it be Your will, HASHEM, my God and the God of my forefathers, that you prepare for me and for the members of my household all our deficiencies and make ready all our needs, every single day of our days according to our needs — every single hour of our hours our adequate supply; and for every bone of our bones sufficient nourishment, in accordance with Your good and generous hand, and not according to the paucity of our accomplishment, the shortness of our kindness, and the diminution of our generosity. May my nourishment and the nourishment of the members of my household, my offspring and the children of my offspring be committed to Your hand and not to the hand of flesh and blood.*

AFTER PRAYER SERVICES — MORNING AND EVENING

יְהִי *May HASHEM, our God, be with us, as He was with our forefathers; may He not forsake us nor cast us off. To turn our hearts to Him, to walk in all His ways and to observe His commandments, decrees, and statutes that He commanded our forefathers. May these words of mine which I have supplicated before HASHEM, be near to HASHEM, our God, by day and by night; that He may bring about justice for His servant and justice for His people Israel, each day's need in its day. That all the peoples of the earth shall know that HASHEM is God — there is no other.[5] HASHEM, guide me in Your righteousness, because of my watchful enemies; make Your way straight before me.[6] As for me, I will walk in my perfect innocence, redeem me and show me favor.[7] Turn to me and show me favor, for I am alone and I am afflicted.[8] My foot is set on the straight path, in assemblies I will bless HASHEM.[9] HASHEM is my Guardian; HASHEM is my Shade at my right hand.[10] My help is from HASHEM, Maker of heaven and earth.[11] HASHEM will guard my departure and my arrival, for life and for peace, from this time and forever.[12] Look down from Your sacred dwelling, from the heavens, and bless Your people Israel and the earth which You have given us — just as you have sworn to our forefathers, a land that flows with milk and honey.[13]*

אֵל *O God of glory, I will present You with song and praise, and I will serve You day and night. Blessed is He Who is unique and Whose uniqueness is proclaimed; Who was, Who is, and Who will be; HASHEM God, the God of Israel, the King Who reigns over kings, the Holy One, Blessed is He. He is the living God, the living and enduring King, forever and for all eternity. Blessed is the Name of His glorious Kingdom for all eternity. For Your salvation do I long, HASHEM.[14] For all the peoples walk, each man in the name of his god;*

וַאֲנִי אֵלֵךְ בְּשֵׁם יהוה אֱלֹהִים חַיִּים וּמֶלֶךְ עוֹלָם.[1] עֶזְרִי מֵעִם יהוה, עֹשֵׂה שָׁמַיִם וָאָרֶץ.[2] יהוה יִמְלֹךְ לְעֹלָם וָעֶד.[3]

תהלים סז

לַמְנַצֵּחַ בִּנְגִינֹת מִזְמוֹר שִׁיר. אֱלֹהִים יְחָנֵּנוּ וִיבָרְכֵנוּ, יָאֵר פָּנָיו אִתָּנוּ סֶלָה. לָדַעַת בָּאָרֶץ דַּרְכֶּךָ, בְּכָל גּוֹיִם יְשׁוּעָתֶךָ. יוֹדְוּךָ עַמִּים, אֱלֹהִים, יוֹדְוּךָ עַמִּים כֻּלָּם. יִשְׂמְחוּ וִירַנְּנוּ לְאֻמִּים, כִּי תִשְׁפֹּט עַמִּים מִישֹׁר, וּלְאֻמִּים בָּאָרֶץ תַּנְחֵם סֶלָה. יוֹדְוּךָ עַמִּים, אֱלֹהִים, יוֹדְוּךָ עַמִּים כֻּלָּם. אֶרֶץ נָתְנָה יְבוּלָהּ, יְבָרְכֵנוּ אֱלֹהִים אֱלֹהֵינוּ. יְבָרְכֵנוּ אֱלֹהִים, וְיִירְאוּ אוֹתוֹ כָּל אַפְסֵי אָרֶץ.

Some recite אֲדוֹן עוֹלָם (p. 12).

תפלה כשיוצא מבית הכנסת

Sit briefly and recite:

אַךְ צַדִּיקִים יוֹדוּ לִשְׁמֶךָ, יֵשְׁבוּ יְשָׁרִים אֶת פָּנֶיךָ.[4]

Stand and say:

כִּי כָּל הָעַמִּים יֵלְכוּ אִישׁ בְּשֵׁם אֱלֹהָיו, וַאֲנִי אֵלֵךְ בְּשֵׁם יהוה אֱלֹהִים חַיִּים וּמֶלֶךְ עוֹלָם.[5] עֶזְרִי מֵעִם יהוה, עֹשֵׂה שָׁמַיִם וָאָרֶץ.[6] יהוה יִמְלֹךְ לְעֹלָם וָעֶד.[7]

Then walk backwards, respectfully, to the exit, as if taking leave of a king. At the door, bow toward the Ark and recite:

יהוה נְחֵנִי בְצִדְקָתֶךָ, לְמַעַן שׁוֹרְרָי, הַיְשַׁר לְפָנַי דַּרְכֶּךָ.[8]

Upon leaving recite:

גָּד גְּדוּד יְגוּדֶנּוּ, וְהוּא יָגֻד עָקֵב.[9] וַיְהִי דָוִד לְכָל דְּרָכָיו מַשְׂכִּיל, וַיהוה עִמּוֹ.[10] וְנֹחַ מָצָא חֵן בְּעֵינֵי יהוה.[11]

One who will engage in commerce recites:

עֶזְרִי מֵעִם יהוה, עֹשֵׂה שָׁמַיִם וָאָרֶץ.[12] הַשְׁלֵךְ עַל יהוה יְהָבְךָ וְהוּא יְכַלְכְּלֶךָ.[13] שְׁמָר תָּם וּרְאֵה יָשָׁר, כִּי אַחֲרִית לְאִישׁ שָׁלוֹם.[14] בְּטַח בַּיהוה וַעֲשֵׂה טוֹב, שְׁכָן אֶרֶץ וּרְעֵה אֱמוּנָה.[15] הִנֵּה אֵל יְשׁוּעָתִי, אֶבְטַח וְלֹא אֶפְחָד, כִּי עָזִּי וְזִמְרָת יָהּ יהוה, וַיְהִי לִי לִישׁוּעָה.[16] אֲנִי רוֹצֶה לֵילֵךְ הַיּוֹם לַעֲשׂוֹת מַשָּׂא וּמַתָּן בִּרְשׁוּת הַשֵּׁם יִתְבָּרֵךְ וּלְמַעַן שְׁמוֹ, וְלִשָּׂא וְלִתֵּן בֶּאֱמוּנָה. רִבּוֹנוֹ שֶׁל עוֹלָם בְּדִבְרֵי קָדְשְׁךָ כָּתוּב לֵאמֹר: וְהַבּוֹטֵחַ בַּיהוה חֶסֶד יְסוֹבְבֶנּוּ.[17] וּכְתִיב: וְאַתָּה מְחַיֶּה אֶת כֻּלָּם.[18] יהוה אֱלֹהִים אֱמֶת,[19] תֵּן בְּרָכָה וְהַצְלָחָה בְּכָל מַעֲשֵׂה יָדַי, כִּי בָטַחְתִּי בְךָ, שֶׁעַל יְדֵי מַשָּׂא וּמַתָּן וַעֲסָקִים שֶׁלִּי, תִּשְׁלַח לִי בְרָכָה, כְּדֵי שֶׁאוּכַל לְפַרְנֵס אֶת עַצְמִי וּבְנֵי בֵיתִי, בְּנַחַת וְלֹא בְצַעַר, בְּהֶתֵּר וְלֹא בְאִסּוּר, לְחַיִּים וּלְשָׁלוֹם. וִיקֻיַּם בִּי מִקְרָא שֶׁכָּתוּב: הַשְׁלֵךְ עַל יהוה יְהָבְךָ, וְהוּא יְכַלְכְּלֶךָ.[20] אָמֵן.

---

(1) Cf. *Micah* 4:5. (2) *Psalms* 121:2. (3) *Exodus* 15:18. (4) *Psalms* 140:14. (5) Cf. *Micah* 4:5. (6) *Psalms* 121:2. (7) *Exodus* 15:18. (8) *Psalms* 5:9. (9) *Genesis* 49:19. (10) *I Samuel* 18:14. (11) *Genesis* 6:8. (12) *Psalms* 121:2. (13) 55:23. (14) 37:37. (15) 37:3. (16) *Isaiah* 12:2. (17) *Psalms* 32:10. (18) *Nehemiah* 9:6. (19) Cf. *Jeremiah* 10:10. (20) *Psalms* 55:23.

but as for me, I will walk in the name of HASHEM, the living God and eternal King.[1] *My help is from HASHEM, Maker of heaven and earth.*[2] *HASHEM shall reign for all eternity.*[3]

Psalm 67

לַמְנַצֵּחַ *For the Conductor, upon Neginos, a psalm, a song. May God favor us and bless us, may He illuminate His countenance with us, Selah. To make known Your way on earth, among all the nations Your salvation. The peoples will acknowledge You, O God, the peoples will acknowledge You, all of them. Nations will be glad and sing for joy, because You will judge the peoples fairly and guide the nations on earth, Selah. Then peoples will acknowledge You, O God, the peoples will acknowledge You, all of them. The earth has yielded its produce, may God, our own God, bless us. May God bless us and may all the ends of the earth fear Him.*

Some recite *Adon Olam* (p. 12).

PRAYER UPON LEAVING THE SYNAGOGUE

Sit briefly and recite:

אַךְ *Only the righteous will thank Your Name; the upright will dwell in Your presence.*[4]

Stand and say:

כִּי *For all the peoples walk, each man in the name of his god; but as for me, I shall walk in the name of HASHEM, the living God and eternal King.*[5] *My help is from HASHEM, Maker of heaven and earth.*[6] *HASHEM shall reign for all eternity.*[7]

Then walk backwards, respectfully, to the exit, as if taking leave of a king.
At the door, bow toward the Ark and recite:

ה' *HASHEM, guide me in Your righteousness, because of my watchful enemies; make Your way straight before me.*[8]

Upon leaving recite:

גָּד *Gad will recruit a regiment and it will retreat in its tracks.*[9] *David was successful in all his ways; and HASHEM was with him.*[10] *And Noah found favor in HASHEM's eyes.*[11]

One who will engage in commerce recites:

עֶזְרִי *My help is from HASHEM, Maker of heaven and earth.*[12] *Cast your burden upon HASHEM and He will support you.*[13] *Safeguard the perfect and watch the upright, for there is a destiny for a man of peace.*[14] *Trust in HASHEM and do good, that you may dwell in the land and be nurtured by faith.*[15] *Behold! God is my salvation, I shall trust and not fear — for God is my might and my praise — HASHEM — and He was a salvation for me.*[16] *Today I wish to go and engage in commerce, with the permission of HASHEM, may He be blessed, and for His Name's sake, and to trade and deal faithfully. O Master of the Universe, in Your holy writings is written: He who trusts in HASHEM, kindness surrounds him;*[17] *and it is written: You give them all life.*[18] *O HASHEM, God of truth,*[19] *grant blessing and success in all my handiwork, for I trust in You that through my commerce and activities, You will send me a blessing so that I can support myself and the members of my household in tranquillity and not in pain, through permissible but not forbidden means, for life and for peace. May there be fulfilled in me the verse that says: Cast your burden upon HASHEM and He will support you.*[20] *Amen.*

﴾ ברכת המזון ﴿

It is customary to recite עַל נַהֲרוֹת בָּבֶל (Psalm 137) in memory of the Temple's destruction, before *Bircas HaMazon* on weekdays. On the Sabbath and Festivals, and on such occasions as the meals celebrating a marriage, *Bris,* or *Pidyon Haben,* it is improper to intrude upon the joy with memories of tragedy. At such times, שִׁיר הַמַּעֲלוֹת (Psalm 126), which describes the joy of redemption, is recited instead.

תהלים קלז

עַל נַהֲרוֹת בָּבֶל,* שָׁם יָשַֽׁבְנוּ גַּם בָּכִֽינוּ, בְּזָכְרֵֽנוּ אֶת צִיּוֹן. עַל עֲרָבִים בְּתוֹכָהּ תָּלִֽינוּ כִּנֹּרוֹתֵֽינוּ. כִּי שָׁם שְׁאֵלֽוּנוּ שׁוֹבֵֽינוּ דִּבְרֵי שִׁיר וְתוֹלָלֵֽינוּ שִׂמְחָה,* שִֽׁירוּ לָֽנוּ מִשִּׁיר צִיּוֹן. אֵיךְ נָשִׁיר אֶת שִׁיר יהוה, עַל אַדְמַת נֵכָר. אִם אֶשְׁכָּחֵךְ יְרוּשָׁלָֽיִם, תִּשְׁכַּח יְמִינִי. תִּדְבַּק לְשׁוֹנִי* לְחִכִּי, אִם לֹא אֶזְכְּרֵֽכִי, אִם לֹא אַעֲלֶה אֶת יְרוּשָׁלַֽיִם עַל רֹאשׁ שִׂמְחָתִי.* זְכֹר יהוה לִבְנֵי אֱדוֹם אֵת יוֹם יְרוּשָׁלָֽיִם, הָאֹמְרִים עָֽרוּ עָֽרוּ, עַד הַיְסוֹד בָּהּ. בַּת בָּבֶל הַשְּׁדוּדָה* אַשְׁרֵי* שֶׁיְּשַׁלֶּם לָךְ אֶת גְּמוּלֵךְ שֶׁגָּמַלְתְּ לָֽנוּ. אַשְׁרֵי שֶׁיֹּאחֵז וְנִפֵּץ אֶת עֹלָלַֽיִךְ אֶל הַסָּֽלַע.

תהלים קכו

שִׁיר הַמַּעֲלוֹת, בְּשׁוּב יהוה אֶת שִׁיבַת צִיּוֹן, הָיִֽינוּ כְּחֹלְמִים. אָז יִמָּלֵא שְׂחוֹק פִּֽינוּ וּלְשׁוֹנֵֽנוּ רִנָּה, אָז יֹאמְרוּ בַגּוֹיִם, הִגְדִּיל יהוה לַעֲשׂוֹת עִם אֵֽלֶּה. הִגְדִּיל יהוה לַעֲשׂוֹת עִמָּֽנוּ, הָיִֽינוּ שְׂמֵחִים. שׁוּבָה יהוה אֶת שְׁבִיתֵֽנוּ, כַּאֲפִיקִים בַּנֶּֽגֶב. הַזֹּרְעִים בְּדִמְעָה בְּרִנָּה יִקְצֹֽרוּ. הָלוֹךְ יֵלֵךְ וּבָכֹה נֹשֵׂא מֶֽשֶׁךְ הַזָּֽרַע, בֹּא יָבֹא בְרִנָּה, נֹשֵׂא אֲלֻמֹּתָיו.

תְּהִלַּת יהוה יְדַבֶּר פִּי, וִיבָרֵךְ כָּל בָּשָׂר שֵׁם קָדְשׁוֹ לְעוֹלָם וָעֶד.[1] וַאֲנַֽחְנוּ נְבָרֵךְ יָהּ, מֵעַתָּה וְעַד עוֹלָם, הַלְּלוּיָהּ.[2] הוֹדוּ לַיהוה כִּי טוֹב, כִּי לְעוֹלָם חַסְדּוֹ.[3] מִי יְמַלֵּל גְּבוּרוֹת יהוה, יַשְׁמִֽיעַ כָּל תְּהִלָּתוֹ.[4]

﴾ בִּרְכַּת הַמָּזוֹן / GRACE AFTER MEALS ﴿

The commandment to thank God after a meal is of Scriptural origin: וְאָכַלְתָּ וְשָׂבָעְתָּ וּבֵרַכְתָּ אֶת ה׳ אֱלֹהֶיךָ עַל הָאָרֶץ הַטֹּבָה אֲשֶׁר נָתַן לָךְ, *And you shall eat and you shall be satisfied and you shall bless* HASHEM, *your God, for the goodly land that He gave you* (*Deuteronomy* 8:10). As the verse indicates, the Scriptural requirement applies only when one has eaten his fill — *you shall eat and you shall be satisfied.* From earliest times, however, the Jewish people has undertaken to express its gratitude to God even after a modest meal, provided one had eaten at least as much bread as the volume of an olive [כְּזַיִת]. There are several opinions regarding the modern equivalent of this Talmudic measurement; they range from one to one and four-fifths fluid ounces.

The first to compose a text for Grace After Meals was Moses, whose text is still recited as the first blessing of the Grace. Although Moses' blessing was composed in gratitude for the manna in the wilderness, it makes no mention of the manna. It is equally noteworthy that the general commandment of Grace After Meals (cited above) was given in the context of a general exhortation to Israel that it remember the heavenly food with which God nourished it in the Wilderness. The message appears rather clear: When we thank God for giving us food, we are recognizing that there is no intrinsic difference between the manna and the livelihood one wrests from the earth through sweat and hard toil; both are gifts from heaven.

⸙ עַל נַהֲרוֹת בָּבֶל / Psalm 137

It is customary to remember the destruction of the Temple at each meal by reciting Psalm 137. It is not said, however, on the Sabbath, festivals, and other days when *Tachanun* is omitted [for it is improper to intrude upon the joy of those festive days with the tragedy of the Destruction *(Eshel Avraham)*]. On those occasions, *A Song of Ascents* (Psalm 126), which describes the joys of redemption, is recited before *Bircas HaMazon (Sh'lah).*

עַל נַהֲרוֹת בָּבֶל — *By the rivers of Babylon.* God endowed King David with a prophetic vision in which he foresaw the destruction of both the First Temple at the hands of Babylon and the

GRACE AFTER MEALS

It is customary to recite *Psalm* 137, in memory of the Temple's destruction, before Grace after Meals on weekdays. On the Sabbath and Festivals, and on such occasions as the meals celebrating a marriage, *Bris*, or *Pidyon Haben*, it is improper to intrude upon the joy with memories of tragedy. At such times, *Psalm* 126, which describes the joy of redemption, is recited instead.

Psalm 137

עַל נַהֲרוֹת *By the rivers of Babylon* — there we sat* and also wept when we remembered Zion. On the willows within it we hung our lyres. There our captors requested words of song from us, with our lyres playing joyous music,* 'Sing for us from Zion's song!' 'How can we sing the song of* HASHEM *upon the alien's soil?' If I forget you, O Jerusalem, let my right hand forget its skill. Let my tongue* adhere to my palate if I fail to recall you, if I fail to elevate Jerusalem above my foremost joy.* Remember,* HASHEM, *for the offspring of Edom, the day of Jerusalem — for those who say 'Destroy! Destroy! to its very foundation.' O violated daughter of Babylon* — praiseworthy* is he who repays you in accordance with the manner that you treated us. Praiseworthy is he who will clutch and dash your infants against the rock.*

Psalm 126

שִׁיר הַמַּעֲלוֹת *A song of ascents. When* HASHEM *will return the captivity of Zion, we will be like dreamers. Then our mouth will be filled with laughter and our tongue with glad song. Then they will declare among the nations, '*HASHEM *has done greatly with these.'* HASHEM *has done greatly with us, we were gladdened. O* HASHEM *— return our captivity like springs in the desert. Those who tearfully sow will reap in glad song. He who bears the measure of seeds walks along weeping, but will return in exultation, a bearer of his sheaves.*

תְּהִלַּת *May my mouth declare the praise of* HASHEM *and may all flesh bless His Holy Name forever.*[1] *We will bless* HASHEM *from this time and forever, Halleluyah!*[2] *Give thanks to God for He is good, His kindness endures forever.*[3] *Who can express the mighty acts of* HASHEM*? Who can declare all His praise.*[4]

(1) *Psalms* 145:21. (2) 115:18. (3) 118:1 (4) 106:2.

Second Temple at the hands of Edom/Rome (*Gittin* 57b).

שָׁם יָשַׁבְנוּ — *There we sat,* i.e., we sat on the river bank on our way into exile.

וְתוֹלָלֵינוּ שִׂמְחָה — *With our lyres* [*playing*] *joyous* [*music*]. תוֹלָלֵנוּ, lit. *our hangings,* refers to the lyres which were hung on the willows (see previous verse; *Radak*). Nebuchadnezzar insisted that the exiles play for him and his court while he ate. The captive Jews hung their instruments on willow trees and said to one another, 'Is it not enough that we caused the destruction of God's Temple — are we to sing and play music for His enemies?'

יְמִינִי ... לְשׁוֹנִי — *My right hand ... my tongue,* i.e., the right hand which strums the strings of instruments and the tongue which speaks and sings praise of God (*Radak*). The phrase *my skill* does not appear in the Hebrew text, but is implied.

אִם לֹא אַעֲלֶה ... עַל רֹאשׁ שִׂמְחָתִי — *If I fail to elevate ... above my foremost joy.* No matter what the occasion of personal joy, the memory of Jerusalem must come first (*Ibn Ezra*). From this verse stems the custom that a bridegroom places ashes on his head [עַל רֹאשׁ, *above ... foremost,* literally *upon the head*] before the marriage ceremony; and the custom that a glass is broken after the ceremony in memory of Jerusalem (*Rama*).

בַּת בָּבֶל הַשְּׁדוּדָה — *O violated daughter of Babylon.* Babylon was soon to be conquered and devastated by Darius the Mede.

אַשְׁרֵי — *Praiseworthy.* Babylon's conqueror will hate and torment her cruelly exactly as she hated and tormented Israel (*Malbim*).

שִׁיר הַמַּעֲלוֹת / Psalm 126

This is one of the fifteen psalms (*Psalms* 120-134) known as the *Songs of Ascents.* They are recited after the Sabbath *Minchah,* from Succos to Pesach. Commentary to this psalm can be **found on p. 537.**

זימון

If three or more males, aged thirteen or older, participate in a meal, a leader is appointed to formally invite the others to join him in the recitation of *Bircas HaMazon.* This formal invitation is called the *zimun.* (On certain occasions a special *zimun* is recited; for a circumcision feast, see p. 216; for *Sheva Berachos,* see p. 204; for a house of mourning, see p. 198.) The regular *zimun* follows:

Leader— רַבּוֹתַי נְבָרֵךְ.

Others— יְהִי שֵׁם יהוה מְבֹרָךְ מֵעַתָּה וְעַד עוֹלָם.[1]

If ten men join in the *zimun* the words in parentheses are added.

Leader— יְהִי שֵׁם יהוה מְבֹרָךְ* מֵעַתָּה וְעַד עוֹלָם.[1] בִּרְשׁוּת* מָרָנָן וְרַבָּנָן וְרַבּוֹתַי, נְבָרֵךְ* (אֱלֹהֵינוּ) שֶׁאָכַלְנוּ מִשֶּׁלוֹ.*

Others°— בָּרוּךְ (אֱלֹהֵינוּ) שֶׁאָכַלְנוּ מִשֶּׁלוֹ וּבְטוּבוֹ חָיִינוּ.

°Those who have not eaten respond:
בָּרוּךְ (אֱלֹהֵינוּ) וּמְבֹרָךְ שְׁמוֹ תָּמִיד לְעוֹלָם וָעֶד.

Leader— בָּרוּךְ (אֱלֹהֵינוּ) שֶׁאָכַלְנוּ מִשֶּׁלוֹ וּבְטוּבוֹ חָיִינוּ.
בָּרוּךְ הוּא וּבָרוּךְ שְׁמוֹ.

The *zimun* leader should recite *Bircas HaMazon* (or, at least, the conclusion of each blessing) aloud thus allowing the others to respond *Amen* to his blessings. Otherwise it is forbidden to interrupt *Bircas HaMazon* for any response other than those permitted during the *Shema.*

ברכת הזן

בָּרוּךְ אַתָּה יהוה אֱלֹהֵינוּ מֶלֶךְ הָעוֹלָם, הַזָּן אֶת הָעוֹלָם כֻּלּוֹ, בְּטוּבוֹ, בְּחֵן בְּחֶסֶד וּבְרַחֲמִים,* הוּא נֹתֵן לֶחֶם לְכָל בָּשָׂר, כִּי לְעוֹלָם חַסְדּוֹ.[2] וּבְטוּבוֹ הַגָּדוֹל, תָּמִיד לֹא חָסַר לָנוּ, וְאַל יֶחְסַר* לָנוּ מָזוֹן לְעוֹלָם וָעֶד. בַּעֲבוּר שְׁמוֹ הַגָּדוֹל, כִּי הוּא אֵל* זָן וּמְפַרְנֵס לַכֹּל, וּמֵטִיב* לַכֹּל, וּמֵכִין מָזוֹן לְכָל בְּרִיּוֹתָיו אֲשֶׁר בָּרָא. ❖ בָּרוּךְ אַתָּה יהוה, הַזָּן אֶת הַכֹּל. (Others— אָמֵן.)

⤛ זימון / Zimun (Invitation)

The word *zimun* has two connotations, *invitation* and *presentation.* When three or more people eat together, one is required to *invite* the others to respond to his praise of God; and all of them jointly are required to *present themselves* as a group to come together in praise of God (based on *Berachos* 49b).

יְהִי שֵׁם ה' מְבוֹרָךְ — *Blessed be the Name ...* The leader, too, repeats the blessings because it would be improper and even sacrilegious for him to ask others to bless God while he, being part of the group, refrains from joining them *(Rashba).*

בִּרְשׁוּת — *With permission.* [Since one of the group assumes the privilege of leading them all in the recitation, he requests their permission.]

נְבָרֵךְ — *Let us bless.* A commandment done by an individual cannot be compared to one performed by a group. When three people recite *Bircas HaMazon* together, they say נְבָרֵךְ, *let us bless;* ten say, נְבָרֵךְ אֱלֹהֵינוּ, *let us bless our God ...* (*Berachos* 49b). A few who perform a commandment are far inferior to a multitude performing a commandment *(Rashi, Lev.* 26:8). When many people unite to do God's will, each individual in the group reaches a far higher level than he would have had he acted alone, no matter how meritoriously *(Chofetz Chaim).*

שֶׁאָכַלְנוּ מִשֶּׁלוֹ — *Of Whose we have eaten.* This text is drawn from Abraham. He would invite wayfarers to his home and serve them lavishly. When they were sated and refreshed and ready to continue on their way, they would thank him. He would insist that their thanks should go not to him, but to God, the One from Whose bounty they had eaten (*Sotah* 10b; *Iyun Tefillah).*

⤛ בִּרְכַּת הַזָּן / First Blessing: For the Nourishment

Bircas HaMazon comprises four blessings, of which the first three are Scripturally ordained

ZIMUN/INVITATION

If three or more males, aged thirteen or older, participate in a meal, a leader is appointed to formally invite the others to join him in the recitation of Grace after Meals. This formal invitation is called *zimun.* (On certain occasions a special *zimun* is recited; for a circumcision feast, see p. 216; for *Sheva Berachos,* see p. 204; for a house of mourning, see p. 198). The regular *zimun* follows:

Leader— *Gentlemen let us bless.*

Others— *Blessed be the Name of* HASHEM *from this time and forever!*[1]

If ten men join in the *zimun* the words in brackets are added.

Leader— *Blessed be the Name of* HASHEM** *from this time and forever!*[1] *With the permission* of the distinguished people present, let us bless* [our God,] He of Whose we have eaten.**

Others°— *Blessed is [our God,] He of Whose we have eaten and through Whose goodness we live.*

°Those who have not eaten respond: *Blessed is He [our God] and blessed is His Name continuously forever.*

Leader— *Blessed is [our God,] He of Whose we have eaten and through Whose goodness we live.*

Blessed is He and Blessed is His Name.

The *zimun* leader should recite Grace after Meals (or, at least, the conclusion of each blessing) aloud thus allowing the others to respond *Amen* to his blessings. Otherwise it is forbidden to interrupt *Bircas HaMazon* for any response other than those permitted during the *Shema.*

FIRST BLESSING: FOR THE NOURISHMENT

בָּרוּךְ *Blessed are You,* HASHEM, *our God, King of the universe, Who nourishes the entire world, in His goodness — with grace, with kindness, and with mercy.* He gives nourishment to all flesh, for His kindness is eternal.*[2] *And through His great goodness, we have never lacked, and may we never lack,* nourishment, for all eternity. For the sake of His Great Name, because He is God Who* nourishes and sustains all, and benefits* all, and He prepares food for all of His creatures which He has created.* Leader— *Blessed are You,* HASHEM, *Who nourishes all.* (Others— *Amen.*)

(1) *Psalms* 113:2. (2) 136:25.

and the fourth was instituted by the Sages. The first blessing was, as noted above, composed by Moses in gratitude for the manna with which God sustained Israel daily in the desert (*Berachos* 48b). For that reason it precedes נוֹדֶה, *the Blessing for the Land,* even though it might seem more logical to thank God first for the land that produces food *(Bayis Chadash).*

בְּטוּבוֹ, בְּחֵן בְּחֶסֶד וּבְרַחֲמִים — *In His goodness — with grace, with kindness, and with mercy.* God's טובו, *goodness,* includes His חֵן *grace,* חֶסֶד, *kindness* and רַחֲמִים *mercy.*

תָּמִיד לֹא חָסַר ... וְאַל יֶחְסַר — *Have never lacked ... and may we never lack.* The subject of the sentence is מָזוֹן, *nourishment,* and the verse expresses the prayer that just as food was never lacking in the desert, may it never be lacking in the future *(Etz Yosef).*

בַּעֲבוּר שְׁמוֹ הַגָּדוֹל כִּי הוּא אֵל — *For the sake of His Great Name, because He is God Who.* We declare that the motive of our request for eternally abundant food is not selfish, but for the sake of *His Great Name* so that we may be better able to serve Him; and we bless Him *because ...*

זָן ... מְפַרְנֵס ... מֵטִיב — *Nourishes ... sustains ... benefits.* זָן, *nourishes,* refers to food; מְפַרְנֵס, *sustains,* refers to clothing; מֵטִיב, *does good,* refers to shelter. In conjunction the three phrases enumerate the basic needs of life, all of which are provided by God *(Etz Yosef).*

ברכת הארץ

נוֹדֶה לְּךָ יהוה אֱלֹהֵינוּ, עַל שֶׁהִנְחַלְתָּ לַאֲבוֹתֵינוּ* אֶרֶץ חֶמְדָּה טוֹבָה וּרְחָבָה.* וְעַל שֶׁהוֹצֵאתָנוּ יהוה אֱלֹהֵינוּ מֵאֶרֶץ מִצְרַיִם, וּפְדִיתָנוּ מִבֵּית עֲבָדִים, וְעַל בְּרִיתְךָ שֶׁחָתַמְתָּ בִּבְשָׂרֵנוּ,* וְעַל תּוֹרָתְךָ שֶׁלִּמַּדְתָּנוּ, וְעַל חֻקֶּיךָ שֶׁהוֹדַעְתָּנוּ, וְעַל חַיִּים חֵן וָחֶסֶד שֶׁחוֹנַנְתָּנוּ, וְעַל אֲכִילַת מָזוֹן שָׁאַתָּה זָן וּמְפַרְנֵס אוֹתָנוּ תָּמִיד, בְּכָל יוֹם וּבְכָל עֵת וּבְכָל שָׁעָה.

On Chanukah and Purim add:

(וְ)עַל הַנִּסִּים וְעַל הַפֻּרְקָן וְעַל הַגְּבוּרוֹת וְעַל הַתְּשׁוּעוֹת וְעַל הַמִּלְחָמוֹת שֶׁעָשִׂיתָ לַאֲבוֹתֵינוּ בַּיָּמִים הָהֵם בַּזְּמַן הַזֶּה.

On Chanukah:

בִּימֵי מַתִּתְיָהוּ בֶּן יוֹחָנָן כֹּהֵן גָּדוֹל חַשְׁמוֹנָאִי וּבָנָיו, כְּשֶׁעָמְדָה מַלְכוּת יָוָן הָרְשָׁעָה עַל עַמְּךָ יִשְׂרָאֵל, לְהַשְׁכִּיחָם תּוֹרָתֶךָ, וּלְהַעֲבִירָם מֵחֻקֵּי רְצוֹנֶךָ. וְאַתָּה בְּרַחֲמֶיךָ הָרַבִּים, עָמַדְתָּ לָהֶם בְּעֵת צָרָתָם, רַבְתָּ אֶת רִיבָם, דַּנְתָּ אֶת דִּינָם, נָקַמְתָּ אֶת נִקְמָתָם.[1] מָסַרְתָּ גִבּוֹרִים בְּיַד חַלָּשִׁים, וְרַבִּים בְּיַד מְעַטִּים, וּטְמֵאִים בְּיַד טְהוֹרִים, וּרְשָׁעִים בְּיַד צַדִּיקִים, וְזֵדִים בְּיַד עוֹסְקֵי תוֹרָתֶךָ. וּלְךָ עָשִׂיתָ שֵׁם גָּדוֹל וְקָדוֹשׁ בְּעוֹלָמֶךָ, וּלְעַמְּךָ יִשְׂרָאֵל עָשִׂיתָ תְּשׁוּעָה גְדוֹלָה[2] וּפֻרְקָן כְּהַיּוֹם הַזֶּה. וְאַחַר כֵּן בָּאוּ בָנֶיךָ לִדְבִיר בֵּיתֶךָ, וּפִנּוּ אֶת הֵיכָלֶךָ, וְטִהֲרוּ אֶת מִקְדָּשֶׁךָ, וְהִדְלִיקוּ נֵרוֹת בְּחַצְרוֹת קָדְשֶׁךָ, וְקָבְעוּ שְׁמוֹנַת יְמֵי חֲנֻכָּה אֵלּוּ, לְהוֹדוֹת וּלְהַלֵּל לְשִׁמְךָ הַגָּדוֹל.

On Purim:

בִּימֵי מָרְדְּכַי וְאֶסְתֵּר בְּשׁוּשַׁן הַבִּירָה, כְּשֶׁעָמַד עֲלֵיהֶם הָמָן הָרָשָׁע, בִּקֵּשׁ לְהַשְׁמִיד לַהֲרֹג וּלְאַבֵּד אֶת כָּל הַיְּהוּדִים, מִנַּעַר וְעַד זָקֵן, טַף וְנָשִׁים בְּיוֹם אֶחָד, בִּשְׁלוֹשָׁה עָשָׂר לְחֹדֶשׁ שְׁנֵים עָשָׂר, הוּא חֹדֶשׁ אֲדָר, וּשְׁלָלָם לָבוֹז.[3] וְאַתָּה בְּרַחֲמֶיךָ הָרַבִּים הֵפַרְתָּ אֶת עֲצָתוֹ, וְקִלְקַלְתָּ אֶת מַחֲשַׁבְתּוֹ, וַהֲשֵׁבוֹתָ לּוֹ גְּמוּלוֹ בְּרֹאשׁוֹ, וְתָלוּ אוֹתוֹ וְאֶת בָּנָיו עַל הָעֵץ.

בִּרְכַּת הָאָרֶץ ◆§ / Second Blessing: For the Land

The second blessing was also ordained by the Torah [*Deut.* 8:10, see *Overview* to ArtScroll *Bircas HaMazon*] and formulated by Joshua (*Berachos* 48a). He saw how much Moses wanted to enter *Eretz Yisrael,* and how anxious the Patriarchs were to be buried in it. Therefore, when Joshua was privileged to enter it, he composed this blessing in its honor *(Shibolei Haleket).*

The blessing begins and ends with thanks. The expression of gratitude refers to each of the enumerated items: the Land, the Exodus, the covenant, the Torah, the statutes, life, grace, kindness, and food.

עַל שֶׁהִנְחַלְתָּ לַאֲבוֹתֵינוּ — *Because You have given to our forefathers as a heritage. Eretz Yisrael* is referred to as נַחֲלָה, *a heritage,* implying that it remains eternally the inheritance of Israel. Thus, the long exile means only that God denied us access to it in punishment for our sins, not that it ceased to be ours.

טוֹבָה וּרְחָבָה — *Good and spacious.* Whoever does not say that the Land is *desirable, good, and spacious* has not properly fulfilled his obligation [of *Bircas HaMazon*] (*Berachos* 48b); because, once the Torah required that the Land be mentioned, the Sages decreed that its praises, too, should be enumerated *(Talmidei R' Yonah).*

וְעַל בְּרִיתְךָ שֶׁחָתַמְתָּ בִּבְשָׂרֵנוּ — *(And) for Your covenant which You sealed in our flesh.* The reference is to circumcision, mention of which the Sages required in the blessing of the Land (*Berachos* 48b) because the Land was promised to Abraham in the merit of circumcision (*Genesis* 17:7-8).

Women are not subject to the commandments

SECOND BLESSING: FOR THE LAND

נוֹדֶה *We thank You,* HASHEM, *our God, because You have given to our forefathers as a heritage* a desirable, good and spacious* land; because You removed us,* HASHEM, *our God, from the land of Egypt and You redeemed us from the house of bondage; for Your covenant which You sealed in our flesh;* for Your Torah which You taught us and for Your statutes which You made known to us; for life, grace, and lovingkindness which You granted us; and for the provision of food with which You nourish and sustain us constantly, in every day, in every season, and in every hour.*

On Chanukah and Purim add:

(וְ)עַל *(And) for the miracles, and for the salvation, and for the mighty deeds, and for the victories, and for the battles which You performed for our forefathers in those days, at this time.*

On Chanukah :

בִּימֵי *In the days of Mattisyahu, the son of Yochanan, the High Priest, the Hasmonean, and his sons — when the wicked Greek kingdom rose up against Your people Israel to make them forget Your Torah and compel them to stray from the statutes of Your Will — You in Your great mercy stood up for them in the time of their distress. You took up their grievance, judged their claim, and avenged their wrong.[1] You delivered the strong into the hands of the weak, the many into the hands of the few, the impure into the hands of the pure, the wicked into the hands of the righteous, and the wanton into the hands of the diligent students of Your Torah. For Yourself You made a great and holy Name in Your world, and for Your people Israel you worked a great victory[2] and salvation as this very day. Thereafter, Your children came to the Holy of Holies of Your House, cleansed Your Temple, purified the site of Your Holiness and kindled lights in the Courtyards of Your Sanctuary; and they established these eight days of Chanukah to express thanks and praise to Your great Name.*

On Purim:

בִּימֵי *In the days of Mordechai and Esther, in Shushan, the capital, when Haman, the wicked, rose up against them and sought to destroy, to slay, and to exterminate all the Jews, young and old, infants and women, on the same day, on the thirteenth of the twelfth month which is the month of Adar, and to plunder their possessions.[3] But You, in Your abundant mercy, nullified his counsel and frustrated his intention and caused his design to return upon his own head and they hanged him and his sons on the gallows.*

(1) Cf. *Jeremiah* 51:36. (2) Cf. *I Samuel* 19:5. (3) *Esther* 3:13.

of circumcision and Torah study. Nevertheless, women do say, *For Your covenant which You sealed in our flesh; for Your Torah which You taught us. Magen Avraham* explains that since women do not require circumcision, they are considered as equivalent to circumcised men in this regard; and since women must study the laws of whatever commandments are applicable to them they have a share in the study of Torah.

(וְ)עַל הַנִּסִּים / Al HaNissim: On Chanukah and Purim

This prayer is a declaration of thanks for the miracles of Chanukah and Purim. Therefore, it is inserted in this section of *Bircas HaMazon* which likewise is devoted to expressions of gratitude.

If One Forgot to Recite עַל הַנִּסִּים

If one omitted עַל הַנִּסִּים and realized his error before reaching the name *HASHEM* of the next blessing (בָּרוּךְ אַתָּה ה׳, *Blessed are You, HASHEM* [p. 188]) he should go back to עַל הַנִּסִּים and continue from there.

If he has already recited the phrase בָּרוּךְ אַתָּה ה׳, *Blessed are You, HASHEM,* then he should continue reciting *Bircas HaMazon* until reaching the series of seasonal prayers which begin הָרַחֲמָן, *The compassionate One,* (p. 194), and rectify the omission as indicated there. If the omission is not discovered until after that point, nothing need be done.

וְעַל הַכֹּל יהוה אֱלֹהֵינוּ אֲנַחְנוּ מוֹדִים לָךְ, וּמְבָרְכִים אוֹתָךְ, יִתְבָּרַךְ שִׁמְךָ בְּפִי כָּל חַי תָּמִיד לְעוֹלָם וָעֶד. כַּכָּתוּב, וְאָכַלְתָּ וְשָׂבָעְתָּ, וּבֵרַכְתָּ אֶת יהוה אֱלֹהֶיךָ, עַל הָאָרֶץ הַטֹּבָה אֲשֶׁר נָתַן לָךְ.[1] ❖ בָּרוּךְ אַתָּה יהוה, עַל הָאָרֶץ וְעַל הַמָּזוֹן. (Others— אָמֵן.)

בנין ירושלים

רַחֵם יהוה אֱלֹהֵינוּ עַל יִשְׂרָאֵל עַמֶּךָ, וְעַל יְרוּשָׁלַיִם עִירֶךָ, וְעַל צִיּוֹן מִשְׁכַּן כְּבוֹדֶךָ, וְעַל מַלְכוּת בֵּית דָּוִד מְשִׁיחֶךָ,* וְעַל הַבַּיִת הַגָּדוֹל וְהַקָּדוֹשׁ שֶׁנִּקְרָא שִׁמְךָ עָלָיו. אֱלֹהֵינוּ אָבִינוּ רְעֵנוּ זוּנֵנוּ פַּרְנְסֵנוּ וְכַלְכְּלֵנוּ וְהַרְוִיחֵנוּ,* וְהַרְוַח לָנוּ יהוה אֱלֹהֵינוּ מְהֵרָה מִכָּל צָרוֹתֵינוּ. וְנָא אַל תַּצְרִיכֵנוּ יהוה אֱלֹהֵינוּ, לֹא לִידֵי מַתְּנַת בָּשָׂר וָדָם,* וְלֹא לִידֵי הַלְוָאָתָם, כִּי אִם לְיָדְךָ הַמְּלֵאָה הַפְּתוּחָה הַקְּדוֹשָׁה וְהָרְחָבָה, שֶׁלֹּא נֵבוֹשׁ וְלֹא נִכָּלֵם לְעוֹלָם וָעֶד.

On the Sabbath add:

רְצֵה וְהַחֲלִיצֵנוּ יהוה אֱלֹהֵינוּ בְּמִצְוֹתֶיךָ, וּבְמִצְוַת יוֹם הַשְּׁבִיעִי הַשַּׁבָּת הַגָּדוֹל וְהַקָּדוֹשׁ הַזֶּה, כִּי יוֹם זֶה גָּדוֹל וְקָדוֹשׁ הוּא לְפָנֶיךָ, לִשְׁבָּת בּוֹ וְלָנוּחַ בּוֹ בְּאַהֲבָה כְּמִצְוַת רְצוֹנֶךָ, וּבִרְצוֹנְךָ הָנִיחַ לָנוּ יהוה אֱלֹהֵינוּ, שֶׁלֹּא תְהֵא צָרָה וְיָגוֹן וַאֲנָחָה בְּיוֹם מְנוּחָתֵנוּ, וְהַרְאֵנוּ יהוה אֱלֹהֵינוּ בְּנֶחָמַת צִיּוֹן עִירֶךָ, וּבְבִנְיַן יְרוּשָׁלַיִם עִיר קָדְשֶׁךָ, כִּי אַתָּה הוּא בַּעַל הַיְשׁוּעוֹת וּבַעַל הַנֶּחָמוֹת.

However, רְצֵה and יַעֲלֶה וְיָבֹא, the prayers for Sabbath, Rosh Chodesh, and Festivals, contain requests for God's assistance in the rebuilding of Jerusalem; hence they are recited later, in the blessing where similar requests are made. [For commentary on *Al HaNissim*, see p. 113.]

❧ בּוֹנֵה יְרוּשָׁלָיִם / Third Blessing: For Jerusalem

The third blessing is the final one required by the Torah. It was composed in stages by David and Solomon. David, who occupied Jerusalem, made reference to *Israel, Your people,* and *Jerusalem, Your city.* Solomon, following his construction of the Temple, added, *the great and holy House (Berachos* 48b*).*

Their blessing was a prayer that God continue the tranquillity of the Land. Following the destruction and exile, the blessing was changed to embody a prayer for the return of the Land, the Temple, and the Davidic dynasty. Before Joshua's conquest of the Land, the blessing took yet another form *(Tur),* a request for God's mercy upon the nation *(Aruch Hashulchan).*

וְעַל מַלְכוּת בֵּית דָּוִד מְשִׁיחֶךָ — *(And) on the monarchy of the house of David, Your anointed.* It is required that the monarchy of David's dynasty be mentioned in this blessing; whoever has not mentioned it has not fulfilled his obligation (*Berachos* 49a), because it was David who sanctified Jerusalem *(Rashi);* and because the consolation for the exile will not be complete until David's kingdom is restored *(Rambam).*

רְעֵנוּ זוּנֵנוּ פַּרְנְסֵנוּ וְכַלְכְּלֵנוּ וְהַרְוִיחֵנוּ — *Tend us, nourish us, sustain us, support us, relieve us. Etz Yosef* explains each of the apparently redundant phrases. *Tend us* means provide us with the absolute necessities of life, i.e., bread and water; *nourish us* is a request for additional food such as fruits and vegetables — foods that are important but not indispensable; *sustain us* with clothing and shelter; *support us* by providing our needs steadily and securely rather than sporadically and in a worrisome manner; and *relieve us* of the need to scrimp and budget by providing our needs generously and abundantly.

וְנָא אַל תַּצְרִיכֵנוּ ... לֹא לִידֵי מַתְּנַת בָּשָׂר וָדָם — *Please ... make us not needful of the gifts of human hands,*

וְעַל הַכֹּל *For all, HASHEM, our God, we thank You and bless You. May Your Name be blessed by the mouth of all the living, continuously for all eternity. As it is written: 'And you shall eat and you shall be satisfied and you shall bless HASHEM, your God, for the good land which He gave you.'*[1] Leader— *Blessed are You, HASHEM, for the land and for the nourishment.* (Others—*Amen.*)

THIRD BLESSING: FOR JERUSALEM

רַחֵם *Have mercy HASHEM, our God, on Israel Your people; on Jerusalem, Your city, on Zion, the resting place of Your Glory; on the monarchy of the house of David, Your anointed;* and on the great and holy House upon which Your Name is called. Our God, our Father — tend us, nourish us, sustain us, support us, relieve us;* HASHEM, our God, grant us speedy relief from all our troubles. Please, make us not needful — HASHEM, our God — of the gifts of human hands* nor of their loans, but only of Your Hand that is full, open, holy, and generous, that we not feel inner shame nor be humiliated for ever and ever.*

On the Sabbath add:

רְצֵה *May it please You, HASHEM, our God — give us rest through Your commandments and through the commandment of the seventh day, this great and holy Sabbath. For this day is great and holy before You to rest on it and be content on it in love, as ordained by Your will. May it be Your will, HASHEM, our God, that there be no distress, grief, or lament on this day of our contentment. And show us, HASHEM, our God, the consolation of Zion, Your city, and the rebuilding of Jerusalem, City of Your holiness, for You are the Master of salvations and Master of consolations.*

(1) *Deuteronomy* 8:10.

i.e., do not make us dependent upon others. The firm believer knows that God's blessing will come inevitably without requiring him to beg for favors. However, if one feels compelled by need to seek the help of others, his faith can become eroded. Thus we pray that God not put us to such a test (*Olas Tamid*).

רְצֵה / Retzei: On the Sabbath

The word הַחֲלִיצֵנוּ has multiple connotations. It

If One Omitted רְצֵה or יַעֲלֶה וְיָבֹא.

(a) If he realizes his omission after reciting the blessing of בּוֹנֵה, *Who rebuilds,* he makes up for the omission by reciting the appropriate Compensatory Blessing (p. 196).

(b) If he realizes his omission after having recited the first six words of the fourth blessing, he may still switch immediately into the compensatory blessing since the words בָּרוּךְ אַתָּה... הָעוֹלָם are identical in both blessings. (However, the Compensatory Blessing need not be recited after the third Sabbath meal if *Bircas HaMazon* is recited after sunset.)

(c) If the omission is discovered after having recited the word הָאֵל, *the Almighty,* of the fourth blessing, it is too late for the Compensatory Blessing to be recited. In that case:

(i) On the Sabbath and on a Festival day, at the first two meals, *Bircas HaMazon* must be repeated in its entirety; at the third meal, nothing need be done.

(ii) On Rosh Chodesh and Chol HaMoed nothing need be done except if the day fell on the Sabbath and רְצֵה, *Retzei,* was omitted. In that case, at the first two meals, *Bircas HaMazon* must be repeated. But if רְצֵה, *Retzei,* was recited and יַעֲלֶה וְיָבֹא, *Yaaleh VeYavo,* was omitted, nothing need be done.

On Rosh Chodesh and Festivals add the following paragraph:

אֱלֹהֵינוּ וֵאלֹהֵי אֲבוֹתֵינוּ, יַעֲלֶה, וְיָבֹא, וְיַגִּיעַ, וְיֵרָאֶה, וְיֵרָצֶה, וְיִשָּׁמַע, וְיִפָּקֵד, וְיִזָּכֵר זִכְרוֹנֵנוּ וּפִקְדּוֹנֵנוּ, וְזִכְרוֹן אֲבוֹתֵינוּ, וְזִכְרוֹן מָשִׁיחַ בֶּן דָּוִד עַבְדֶּךָ, וְזִכְרוֹן יְרוּשָׁלַיִם עִיר קָדְשֶׁךָ, וְזִכְרוֹן כָּל עַמְּךָ בֵּית יִשְׂרָאֵל לְפָנֶיךָ, לִפְלֵיטָה לְטוֹבָה לְחֵן וּלְחֶסֶד וּלְרַחֲמִים, לְחַיִּים וּלְשָׁלוֹם בְּיוֹם

On Rosh Chodesh	On Pesach	On Shavuos	On Rosh Hashanah
רֹאשׁ הַחֹדֶשׁ	חַג הַמַּצּוֹת	חַג הַשָּׁבֻעוֹת	הַזִּכָּרוֹן

On Succos	On Shemini Atzeres and Simchas Torah
חַג הַסֻּכּוֹת	הַשְּׁמִינִי חַג הָעֲצֶרֶת

הַזֶּה. זָכְרֵנוּ יהוה אֱלֹהֵינוּ בּוֹ לְטוֹבָה, וּפָקְדֵנוּ בוֹ לִבְרָכָה, וְהוֹשִׁיעֵנוּ בוֹ לְחַיִּים. וּבִדְבַר יְשׁוּעָה וְרַחֲמִים, חוּס וְחָנֵּנוּ וְרַחֵם עָלֵינוּ וְהוֹשִׁיעֵנוּ, כִּי אֵלֶיךָ עֵינֵינוּ, כִּי אֵל (On Rosh Hashanah add— מֶלֶךְ) חַנּוּן וְרַחוּם אָתָּה.[1]

[If forgotten, see page 189.]

In a house of mourning, נַחֵם, p. 198, is substituted for the next two paragraphs. If it was omitted, *Bircas HaMazon* need not be repeated.

❖ **וּבְנֵה** יְרוּשָׁלַיִם* עִיר הַקֹּדֶשׁ בִּמְהֵרָה בְיָמֵינוּ. בָּרוּךְ אַתָּה יהוה, בּוֹנֵה (בְּרַחֲמָיו)* יְרוּשָׁלָיִם. אָמֵן.* (Others—אָמֵן.)

הטוב והמטיב

בָּרוּךְ אַתָּה יהוה אֱלֹהֵינוּ מֶלֶךְ הָעוֹלָם, הָאֵל אָבִינוּ מַלְכֵּנוּ אַדִּירֵנוּ בּוֹרְאֵנוּ גּוֹאֲלֵנוּ יוֹצְרֵנוּ קְדוֹשֵׁנוּ קְדוֹשׁ יַעֲקֹב, רוֹעֵנוּ רוֹעֵה יִשְׂרָאֵל, הַמֶּלֶךְ הַטּוֹב וְהַמֵּטִיב לַכֹּל, שֶׁבְּכָל יוֹם וָיוֹם* הוּא הֵטִיב, הוּא מֵטִיב, הוּא יֵיטִיב לָנוּ. הוּא גְמָלָנוּ הוּא גוֹמְלֵנוּ הוּא יִגְמְלֵנוּ לָעַד, לְחֵן וּלְחֶסֶד וּלְרַחֲמִים וּלְרֶוַח הַצָּלָה וְהַצְלָחָה, בְּרָכָה וִישׁוּעָה נֶחָמָה פַּרְנָסָה וְכַלְכָּלָה ❖ וְרַחֲמִים וְחַיִּים וְשָׁלוֹם וְכָל טוֹב, וּמִכָּל טוּב לְעוֹלָם אַל יְחַסְּרֵנוּ.* (Others—אָמֵן.)

---

can be translated as *help us avoid* [all suffering]; *strengthen or fortify us; save us* [from troubles that have engulfed us]; and, finally, *allow us to rest* [from the travail of seeking a livelihood] (*Vayikra Rabbah* 34:15).

❧ יַעֲלֶה וְיָבֹא / Yaaleh V'yavo: On Rosh Chodesh and Festivals

For commentary, see p. 110.

❧ וּבְנֵה יְרוּשָׁלַיִם — *Rebuild Jerusalem.* This is the conclusion of the third blessing, and thus returns to the theme with which the blessings began — a plea for God's mercy on Jerusalem (*Pesachim* 104a).

בְּרַחֲמָיו — *In His mercy.* Based on the prophecy of *Zechariah* (1:16): שַׁבְתִּי לִירוּשָׁלַיִם בְּרַחֲמִים, *I have returned to Jerusalem with mercy (Mordechai; Rama);* and because it is in consonance with the introductory phrase to this blessing, רַחֵם, *have mercy (Levush),* many authorities include the word בְּרַחֲמָיו, *in His Mercy,* in this blessing. Others, however cite the verse צִיּוֹן בְּמִשְׁפָּט תִּפָּדֶה, *Zion shall be redeemed with judgment* (*Isaiah* 1:27), which implies that the redemption of Jerusalem will be through *judgment* rather than *mercy,* and thus omit the word בְּרַחֲמָיו from the blessing *(Orchos Chaim; Kol Bo).*

אָמֵן — *Amen.* This blessing is unique in that one responds *Amen* after his own blessing. The purpose of this unusual formula is to serve as a demarcation between the first three blessings which are ordained by the Torah and the next

On Rosh Chodesh and Festivals add the following paragraph:

אֱלֹהֵינוּ *Our God and God of our forefathers, may there rise, come, reach, be noted, be favored, be heard, be considered, and be remembered — the remembrance and consideration of ourselves; the remembrance of our forefathers; the remembrance of Messiah, son of David, Your servant; the remembrance of Jerusalem, the City of Your Holiness; the remembrance of Your entire people the Family of Israel — before You for deliverance, for goodness, for grace, for kindness, and for compassion, for life, and for peace on this day of*

On Rosh Chodesh	On Passover	On Shavuos
Rosh Chodesh.	*the Festival of Matzos.*	*the Shavuos Festival.*
On Rosh Hashanah	On Succos	On Shemini Atzeres
Remembrance.	*the Succos Festival.*	*the Shemini Atzeres Festival.*

Remember us on it, HASHEM, our God, for goodness; consider us on it for blessing; and help us on it for life. In the matter of salvation and compassion, pity, be gracious and compassionate with us and help us, for our eyes are turned to You, because You are God, the gracious, and compassionate[1] (On Rosh Hashanah add:— *King).*

[If forgotten, see page 189.]

In a house of mourning, *'Comfort, O HASHEM...,'* p. 198, is substituted for the next two paragraphs. If it was omitted, Grace After Meals need not be repeated.

וּבְנֵה *Rebuild Jerusalem,* the Holy City, soon in our days. Blessed are You, HASHEM, Who rebuilds Jerusalem (in His mercy).* Amen.**

(Others—*Amen.)*

FOURTH BLESSING: GOD'S GOODNESS

בָּרוּךְ *Blessed are You, HASHEM, our God, King of the universe, the Almighty, our Father, our King, our Sovereign, our Creator, our Redeemer, our Maker, our Holy One, Holy One of Jacob, our Shepherd, the Shepherd of Israel, the King Who is good and Who does good for all. For every single day* He did good, He does good, and He will do good to us. He was bountiful with us, He is bountiful with us, and He will forever be bountiful with us — with grace and with kindness and with mercy, with relief, salvation, success, blessing, help, consolation, sustenance, support,* Leader— *mercy, life, peace, and all good; and of all good things may He never deprive us.** (Others—*Amen.)*

(1) Cf. *Nechemiah* 9:31.

blessing which is Rabbinic in origin *(Berachos* 45b; *Rambam; Tur).* Since the word *Amen* is not part of the actual blessing, there should be a slight pause before it is said.

הַטּוֹב וְהַמֵּטִיב / Fourth Blessing: For God's Goodness.

The essence of this blessing is the two-word phrase הַטּוֹב וְהַמֵּטִיב, *Who is good and Who does good.* The blessing was composed by the court of Rabban Gamliel the Elder in Yavneh in gratitude to God for preserving the bodies of the victims of the Roman massacre at Betar, and for eventually allowing them to be brought to burial (*Berachos* 48b).

שֶׁבְּכָל יוֹם וָיוֹם — *For every single day.* It is not nearly sufficient to thank God for His graciousness to *past* generations of Jews. We must be conscious of the fact that His goodness and bounty are daily, constant occurrences.

אַל יְחַסְּרֵנוּ — *May He never deprive us.* This is the end of the blessing, and the listeners should respond *Amen.* Unlike the other parts of *Bircas HaMazon,* this one does not conclude with a brief blessing summing up the theme of the section. As noted above, the essential text of the blessing consists of only two words — הַטּוֹב וְהַמֵּטִיב, *Who is Good and Who does good* — and it is therefore no different from the short blessings recited before performing a commandment or partaking of food. The addition to the text of considerable outpourings of gratitude does not alter the fact that the brief text does not call for a double blessing *(Rashi* to *Berachos* 49a).

הָרַחֲמָן* הוּא יִמְלוֹךְ עָלֵינוּ לְעוֹלָם וָעֶד. הָרַחֲמָן הוּא יִתְבָּרַךְ בַּשָּׁמַיִם וּבָאָרֶץ. הָרַחֲמָן הוּא יִשְׁתַּבַּח לְדוֹר דּוֹרִים, וְיִתְפָּאַר בָּנוּ לָעַד וּלְנֵצַח נְצָחִים, וְיִתְהַדַּר בָּנוּ לָעַד וּלְעוֹלְמֵי עוֹלָמִים.* הָרַחֲמָן הוּא יְפַרְנְסֵנוּ בְּכָבוֹד. הָרַחֲמָן הוּא יִשְׁבּוֹר עֻלֵּנוּ מֵעַל צַוָּארֵנוּ, וְהוּא יוֹלִיכֵנוּ קוֹמְמִיּוּת לְאַרְצֵנוּ. הָרַחֲמָן הוּא יִשְׁלַח לָנוּ בְּרָכָה מְרֻבָּה בַּבַּיִת הַזֶּה, וְעַל שֻׁלְחָן זֶה שֶׁאָכַלְנוּ עָלָיו. הָרַחֲמָן הוּא יִשְׁלַח לָנוּ אֶת אֵלִיָּהוּ הַנָּבִיא זָכוּר לַטּוֹב,* וִיבַשֶּׂר לָנוּ בְּשׂוֹרוֹת טוֹבוֹת יְשׁוּעוֹת וְנֶחָמוֹת.

The Talmud (*Berachos* 46a) gives a rather lengthy text of the blessing that a guest inserts here for the host. It is quoted with minor variations in *Shulchan Aruch* (*Orach Chaim* 201) and many authorities are at a loss to explain why the prescribed text has fallen into disuse in favor of the briefer version commonly used. The text found in *Shulchan Aruch* is:

יְהִי רָצוֹן שֶׁלֹּא יֵבוֹשׁ וְלֹא יִכָּלֵם בַּעַל הַבַּיִת הַזֶּה, לֹא בָעוֹלָם הַזֶּה וְלֹא בָעוֹלָם הַבָּא, וְיַצְלִיחַ בְּכָל נְכָסָיו, וְיִהְיוּ נְכָסָיו מוּצְלָחִים וּקְרוֹבִים לָעִיר, וְאַל יִשְׁלוֹט שָׂטָן בְּמַעֲשֵׂה יָדָיו, וְאַל יִזְדַּקֵּק לְפָנָיו שׁוּם דְּבַר חֵטְא וְהִרְהוּר עָוֹן, מֵעַתָּה וְעַד עוֹלָם.

Those eating at their own table recite (including the words in parentheses that apply):

הָרַחֲמָן הוּא יְבָרֵךְ אוֹתִי (וְאֶת אִשְׁתִּי/ בַּעְלִי. וְאֶת זַרְעִי) וְאֶת כָּל אֲשֶׁר לִי.

Guests recite the following (children at their parents' table include the words in parentheses):

הָרַחֲמָן הוּא יְבָרֵךְ אֶת (אָבִי מוֹרִי) בַּעַל הַבַּיִת הַזֶּה, וְאֶת (אִמִּי מוֹרָתִי) בַּעֲלַת הַבַּיִת הַזֶּה, אוֹתָם וְאֶת בֵּיתָם וְאֶת זַרְעָם וְאֶת כָּל אֲשֶׁר לָהֶם.

אוֹתָנוּ וְאֶת כָּל אֲשֶׁר לָנוּ, כְּמוֹ שֶׁנִּתְבָּרְכוּ אֲבוֹתֵינוּ אַבְרָהָם יִצְחָק וְיַעֲקֹב בַּכֹּל מִכֹּל כֹּל,*[1] כֵּן יְבָרֵךְ אוֹתָנוּ כֻּלָּנוּ יַחַד בִּבְרָכָה שְׁלֵמָה, וְנֹאמַר, אָמֵן.

בַּמָּרוֹם יְלַמְּדוּ עֲלֵיהֶם* וְעָלֵינוּ* זְכוּת, שֶׁתְּהֵא לְמִשְׁמֶרֶת שָׁלוֹם.* וְנִשָּׂא בְרָכָה מֵאֵת יהוה, וּצְדָקָה מֵאֱלֹהֵי יִשְׁעֵנוּ, וְנִמְצָא חֵן וְשֵׂכֶל טוֹב בְּעֵינֵי אֱלֹהִים וְאָדָם.[2]

At a circumcision feast, continue with הָרַחֲמָן, p. 216.

⊲§ הָרַחֲמָן — *The compassionate One!* The four blessings of *Bircas HaMazon* end with לְעוֹלָם אַל יְחַסְּרֵנוּ, *may He never deprive us.* The remainder of *Bircas HaMazon* is a collection of brief prayers for God's compassion *(Aruch HaShulchan).*

לָנֶצַח נְצָחִים ... לְעוֹלְמֵי עוֹלָמִים — *To the ultimate ends ... for all eternity.* These expressions mean 'forever' and are essentially synonymous. Our translation is based on *R' Hirsch* who renders נצח from נצחון, *triumph,* for God's plan for the future will ultimately overcome all the barriers that stand in the way. The word עולם is related to נֶעְלָם, *hidden,* implying that the hand of God is present in all occurrences, even though it seems to be hidden.

זָכוּר לַטּוֹב — *He is remembered for good.* The Sages use this generic term to refer to people who have rendered great and unforgettable service to the entire Jewish nation (see *Berachos* 3a, *Shabbos* 13b, *Bava Basra* 21a, *Avodah Zarah* 8b). In addition to the great service he rendered the nation during his years on earth, Elijah will bring the news of the arrival of Messiah [*Malachi* 3:23] *(Iyun Tefillah).*

בַּכֹּל מִכֹּל כֹּל — *In everything, from everything,*

הָרַחֲמָן *The compassionate One!* May He reign over us forever. The compassionate One! May He be blessed in heaven and on earth. The compassionate One! May He be praised throughout all generations, may He be glorified through us forever to the ultimate ends, and be honored through us forever and for all eternity.* The compassionate One! May He sustain us in honor. The compassionate One! May He break the yoke of oppression from our necks and guide us erect to our Land. The compassionate One! May He send us abundant blessing to this house and upon this table at which we have eaten. The compassionate One! May He send us Elijah, the Prophet — he is remembered for good* — to proclaim to us good tidings, salvations, and consolations.*

The Talmud (*Berachos* 46a) gives a rather lengthy text of the blessing that a guest inserts here for the host. It is quoted with minor variations in *Shulchan Aruch* (*Orach Chaim* 201) and many authorities are at a loss to explain why the prescribed text has fallen into disuse in favor of the briefer version commonly used. The text found in *Shulchan Aruch* is:

יְהִי רָצוֹן *May it be God's will that this host not be shamed nor humiliated in This World or in the World to Come. May he be successful in all his dealings. May his dealings be successful and conveniently close at hand. May no evil impediment reign over his handiwork, and may no semblance of sin or iniquitous thought attach itself to him from this time and forever.*

Those eating at their own table recite (including the words in parentheses that apply):

The compassionate One! May He bless me (my wife/husband and my children) and all that is mine.

Guests recite the following (children at their parents' table include the words in parentheses):

The compassionate One! May He bless (my father, my teacher) the master of this house, and (my mother, my teacher) lady of this house, them, their house, their family, and all that is theirs.

*Ours and all that is ours — just as our forefathers Abraham, Isaac, and Jacob were blessed in everything, from everything, with everything.**[1] *So may He bless us all together with a perfect blessing. And let us say: Amen!*

בַּמָּרוֹם *On high, may merit be pleaded upon them* and upon us,* for a safeguard of peace.* May we receive a blessing from* HASHEM *and just kindness from the God of our salvation, and find favor and good understanding in the eyes of God and man.*[2]

At a circumcision feast, continue with *'The Compassionate One ...'*, p. 216.

(1) Cf. *Genesis* 24:1; 27:33; 33:11. (2) Cf. *Proverbs* 3:4.

with everything. The three expressions, each indicating that no necessary measure of goodness was lacking, are used respectively by the Torah referring to the Patriarchs: Abraham, Isaac, and Jacob. The Talmud (*Bava Basra* 16b-17a) derives from these verses that the Patriarchs were granted an inkling of the World to Come, and that the Evil Inclination had no dominion over them, for the word כֹּל, *everything,* implies perfection, a total unflawed blessing.

עֲלֵיהֶם — *Upon them,* i.e., the master and mistress of the home, or any others who were mentioned in the preceding prayer.

וְעָלֵינוּ — *And upon us,* i.e., the others gathered around the table. [This term is included even when one eats alone. In that case, it refers to whatever people were previously specified and to the Jewish people in general.]

לְמִשְׁמֶרֶת שָׁלוֹם — *For a safeguard of peace,* i.e., to

If any of the following seasonal verses were omitted, *Bircas HaMazon* need not be repeated.

On the Sabbath add:

הָרַחֲמָן הוּא יַנְחִילֵנוּ יוֹם שֶׁכֻּלּוֹ שַׁבָּת* וּמְנוּחָה לְחַיֵּי הָעוֹלָמִים.

On Rosh Chodesh add:

הָרַחֲמָן הוּא יְחַדֵּשׁ עָלֵינוּ אֶת הַחֹדֶשׁ הַזֶּה לְטוֹבָה וְלִבְרָכָה.

On Festivals add:

הָרַחֲמָן הוּא יַנְחִילֵנוּ יוֹם שֶׁכֻּלּוֹ טוֹב.

On Rosh Hashanah add:

הָרַחֲמָן הוּא יְחַדֵּשׁ עָלֵינוּ אֶת הַשָּׁנָה הַזֹּאת לְטוֹבָה וְלִבְרָכָה.

On Succos add:

הָרַחֲמָן הוּא יָקִים לָנוּ אֶת סֻכַּת דָּוִיד הַנֹּפֶלֶת.*[1]

On Chanukah or Purim, if עַל הַנִּסִּים was not recited in its proper place, add:

הָרַחֲמָן הוּא יַעֲשֶׂה לָנוּ נִסִּים וְנִפְלָאוֹת
כַּאֲשֶׁר עָשָׂה לַאֲבוֹתֵינוּ בַּיָּמִים הָהֵם בַּזְּמַן הַזֶּה.

Continue with בִּימֵי מָרְדְּכַי or בִּימֵי מַתִּתְיָהוּ, p. 186. Then go on from this point.

הָרַחֲמָן הוּא יְזַכֵּנוּ לִימוֹת הַמָּשִׁיחַ וּלְחַיֵּי הָעוֹלָם הַבָּא.
מַגְדִּל* —On weekdays   מִגְדּוֹל* —On the Sabbath, Festivals and Rosh Chodesh
יְשׁוּעוֹת מַלְכּוֹ וְעֹשֶׂה חֶסֶד לִמְשִׁיחוֹ לְדָוִד וּלְזַרְעוֹ עַד עוֹלָם.[2]
עֹשֶׂה שָׁלוֹם בִּמְרוֹמָיו,* הוּא יַעֲשֶׂה שָׁלוֹם עָלֵינוּ וְעַל כָּל
יִשְׂרָאֵל. וְאִמְרוּ, אָמֵן.

יְראוּ אֶת יהוה קְדֹשָׁיו, כִּי אֵין מַחְסוֹר לִירֵאָיו.* כְּפִירִים רָשׁוּ
וְרָעֵבוּ, וְדֹרְשֵׁי יהוה לֹא יַחְסְרוּ כָל טוֹב.[3] הוֹדוּ לַיהוה כִּי
טוֹב, כִּי לְעוֹלָם חַסְדּוֹ.[4] פּוֹתֵחַ אֶת יָדֶךָ, וּמַשְׂבִּיעַ לְכָל חַי רָצוֹן.[5]
בָּרוּךְ הַגֶּבֶר אֲשֶׁר יִבְטַח בַּיהוה, וְהָיָה יהוה מִבְטַחוֹ.[6]* נַעַר
הָיִיתִי גַּם זָקַנְתִּי, וְלֹא רָאִיתִי צַדִּיק נֶעֱזָב, וְזַרְעוֹ מְבַקֶּשׁ לָחֶם.[7]*
יהוה עֹז לְעַמּוֹ יִתֵּן, יהוה יְבָרֵךְ אֶת עַמּוֹ בַשָּׁלוֹם.[8]*

---

assure that the home will be contented and peaceful.

☙ **יוֹם שֶׁכֻּלּוֹ שַׁבָּת** — *The day which will be completely a Sabbath,* an allusion to the World to Come after the final redemption.

☙ **סֻכַּת דָּוִיד הַנֹּפֶלֶת** — *David's fallen booth.* This phrase was used by God when He promised to restore the kingship of the Davidic dynasty which is figuratively called סֻכָּה [*succah*], *booth.* The word *succah* is derived from סָכַךְ, *protection,* and refers to the king's protection of his people. By extension, this also refers to the Temple, which is called David's because he longed to build it and prepared for its construction. As the abode of God's Presence, it, too, protects Israel.

☙ **מַגְדִּל/מִגְדּוֹל** — *He Who makes great/A tower.* It is customary to recite the phrase מַגְדִּל יְשׁוּעוֹת מַלְכּוֹ, *He Who makes great the salvations of His king* (*Psalms* 18:51), on weekdays; and to substitute מִגְדּוֹל יְשׁוּעוֹת מַלְכּוֹ, *He Who is a tower of salvations to His king* (*II Samuel* 22:51), on Sabbaths, festivals and Rosh Chodesh. Both verses were written by King David and, in the context of *Bircas HaMazon,* the word *king* refers to King Messiah. *Etz Yosef* explains that the phrase from *Psalms* [מַגְדִּל] was chosen for the less holy weekdays because it was written before David became king. The phrase from *Samuel* [מִגְדּוֹל] was composed when David was at the peak of his greatness, and it is therefore more suited to the Sabbath and festivals.

עֹשֶׂה שָׁלוֹם בִּמְרוֹמָיו — *He Who makes peace in His heights.* Even the heavenly beings require God to

If any of the following seasonal verses were omitted, Grace after Meals need not be repeated.

On the Sabbath add:

The compassionate One! May He cause us to inherit the day which will be completely a Sabbath and rest day for eternal life.*

On Rosh Chodesh add:

The compassionate One! May He inaugurate this month upon us for goodness and for blessing.

On Festivals add:

The compassionate One! May He cause us to inherit the day which is completely good.

On Rosh Hashanah add:

The compassionate One! May He inaugurate this year upon us for goodness and for blessing.

On Succos add:

*The compassionate One! May He erect for us David's fallen booth.**[1]

On Chanukah or Purim, if *'For the miracles ...'* was not recited in its proper place, add:

The compassionate One! May He perform for us miracles and wonders as He performed for our forefathers in those days, at this time.

Continue with *'In the days of Mattisyahu/Mordechai ...'*, p. 187. Then go on from this point.

הָרַחֲמָן *The compassionate One! May He make us worthy of the days of Messiah and the life of the World to Come.*

On weekdays:	On the Sabbath, Festivals and Rosh Chodesh:
He Who makes great the salvations of His king*	*He Who is a tower* of salvations to His king*

and does kindness for His anointed, to David and to his descendants forever.[2] *He Who makes peace in His heights,* may He make peace upon us and upon all Israel. Now respond: Amen!*

יִראוּ *Fear* HASHEM, *you — His holy ones — for there is no deprivation for His reverent ones.* Young lions may want and hunger, but those who seek* HASHEM *will not lack any good.*[3] *Give thanks to God for He is good; His kindness endures forever.*[4] *You open Your hand and satisfy the desire of every living thing.*[5] *Blessed is the man who trusts in* HASHEM, *then* HASHEM *will be his security.**[6] *I was a youth and also have aged, and I have not seen a righteous man forsaken, with his children begging for bread.**[7] HASHEM *will give might to His people;* HASHEM *will bless His people with peace.**[8]

(1) Cf. *Amos* 9:11.(2) *Psalms* 18:51; *II Samuel* 22:51. (3) *Psalms* 34:10-11. (4) 136:1 et al. (5) 145:16. (6) *Jeremiah* 17:7. (7) *Psalms* 37:25. (8) 29:11.

make peace among them, how much more so fractious man! *(Etz Yosef).*

⊰ יִראוּ ... כִּי אֵין מַחְסוֹר לִירֵאָיו — *Fear ... for there is no deprivation for His reverent ones.* Those who fear God are content, even if they are lacking in material possessions. But the wicked are never satisfied; whatever they have only whets their appetite for more *(Anaf Yosef).*

אֲשֶׁר יִבְטַח בַּה׳ וְהָיָה ה׳ מִבְטַחוֹ — *Who trusts in* HASHEM, *then* HASHEM *will be his security.* God will be a fortress of trust to a man in direct proportion to the amount of trust he places in God *(Chidushei HaRim).*

צַדִּיק נֶעֱזָב וְזַרְעוֹ מְבַקֶּשׁ לָחֶם — *A righteous man forsaken, with his children begging for bread.* A righteous man may suffer misfortune, but God will surely have mercy on His children *(Radak; Malbim).* I have never seen a righteous man consider himself forsaken even if his children must beg for bread. Whatever his lot in life, he

ברכות למי ששכח

If one forgot to recite either רְצֵה (p. 188) on the Sabbath or יַעֲלֶה וְיָבֹא (p. 190) on a Festival or Rosh Chodesh, he should insert the appropriate blessing below before the fourth blessing of *Bircas HaMazon.* See page 189 for guidelines.

After the appropriate blessing below, continue with the fourth blessing, p. 190.

If one forgot רְצֵה on the Sabbath:

בָּרוּךְ אַתָּה יהוה אֱלֹהֵינוּ מֶלֶךְ הָעוֹלָם, אֲשֶׁר נָתַן שַׁבָּתוֹת לִמְנוּחָה לְעַמּוֹ יִשְׂרָאֵל בְּאַהֲבָה, לְאוֹת וְלִבְרִית. בָּרוּךְ אַתָּה יהוה, מְקַדֵּשׁ הַשַּׁבָּת.

If one forgot יַעֲלֶה וְיָבֹא on Rosh Chodesh:

בָּרוּךְ אַתָּה יהוה אֱלֹהֵינוּ מֶלֶךְ הָעוֹלָם, אֲשֶׁר נָתַן רָאשֵׁי חֳדָשִׁים לְעַמּוֹ יִשְׂרָאֵל לְזִכָּרוֹן.

If one forgot רְצֵה and יַעֲלֶה וְיָבֹא on a Rosh Chodesh that falls on the Sabbath:

בָּרוּךְ אַתָּה יהוה אֱלֹהֵינוּ מֶלֶךְ הָעוֹלָם, אֲשֶׁר נָתַן שַׁבָּתוֹת לִמְנוּחָה לְעַמּוֹ יִשְׂרָאֵל בְּאַהֲבָה, לְאוֹת וְלִבְרִית, וְרָאשֵׁי חֳדָשִׁים לְזִכָּרוֹן. בָּרוּךְ אַתָּה יהוה, מְקַדֵּשׁ הַשַּׁבָּת וְיִשְׂרָאֵל וְרָאשֵׁי חֳדָשִׁים.

If one forgot יַעֲלֶה וְיָבֹא on a Festival:

בָּרוּךְ אַתָּה יהוה אֱלֹהֵינוּ מֶלֶךְ הָעוֹלָם, אֲשֶׁר נָתַן יָמִים טוֹבִים לְעַמּוֹ יִשְׂרָאֵל לְשָׂשׂוֹן וּלְשִׂמְחָה, אֶת יוֹם

On Pesach:	On Shavuos:	On Succos:	On Shemini Atzeres/Simchas Torah:
חַג הַמַּצּוֹת	חַג הַשָּׁבֻעוֹת	חַג הַסֻּכּוֹת	הַשְּׁמִינִי חַג הָעֲצֶרֶת

הַזֶּה. בָּרוּךְ אַתָּה יהוה, מְקַדֵּשׁ יִשְׂרָאֵל וְהַזְּמַנִּים.

If one forgot רְצֵה and יַעֲלֶה וְיָבֹא on a Festival that falls on the Sabbath:

בָּרוּךְ אַתָּה יהוה אֱלֹהֵינוּ מֶלֶךְ הָעוֹלָם, אֲשֶׁר נָתַן שַׁבָּתוֹת לִמְנוּחָה לְעַמּוֹ יִשְׂרָאֵל בְּאַהֲבָה, לְאוֹת וְלִבְרִית, וְיָמִים טוֹבִים לְשָׂשׂוֹן וּלְשִׂמְחָה, אֶת יוֹם

On Pesach:	On Shavuos:	On Succos:	On Shemini Atzeres/Simchas Torah:
חַג הַמַּצּוֹת	חַג הַשָּׁבֻעוֹת	חַג הַסֻּכּוֹת	הַשְּׁמִינִי חַג הָעֲצֶרֶת

הַזֶּה. בָּרוּךְ אַתָּה יהוה, מְקַדֵּשׁ הַשַּׁבָּת וְיִשְׂרָאֵל וְהַזְּמַנִּים.

If one forgot יַעֲלֶה וְיָבֹא on Rosh Hashanah:

בָּרוּךְ אַתָּה יהוה אֱלֹהֵינוּ מֶלֶךְ הָעוֹלָם, אֲשֶׁר נָתַן יָמִים טוֹבִים לְעַמּוֹ יִשְׂרָאֵל אֶת יוֹם הַזִּכָּרוֹן הַזֶּה. בָּרוּךְ אַתָּה יהוה, מְקַדֵּשׁ יִשְׂרָאֵל וְיוֹם הַזִּכָּרוֹן.

If one forgot רְצֵה and יַעֲלֶה וְיָבֹא on Rosh Hashanah that falls on the Sabbath:

בָּרוּךְ אַתָּה יהוה אֱלֹהֵינוּ מֶלֶךְ הָעוֹלָם, אֲשֶׁר נָתַן שַׁבָּתוֹת לִמְנוּחָה לְעַמּוֹ יִשְׂרָאֵל בְּאַהֲבָה לְאוֹת וְלִבְרִית, וְיָמִים טוֹבִים לְיִשְׂרָאֵל אֶת יוֹם הַזִּכָּרוֹן הַזֶּה. בָּרוּךְ אַתָּה יהוה, מְקַדֵּשׁ הַשַּׁבָּת וְיִשְׂרָאֵל וְיוֹם הַזִּכָּרוֹן.

COMPENSATORY BLESSINGS

If one forgot to recite either *Retzei* [*May it please You,* p. 188] on the Sabbath or *Yaaleh V'yavo* [*Our God,* p. 190] on a Festival or Rosh Chodesh, he should insert the appropriate blessing below before the fourth blessing of *Bircas HaMazon.* See page 189 for guidelines.

After the appropriate blessing below, continue with the fourth blessing, p. 190.

If one forgot *Retzei* on the Sabbath:

בָּרוּךְ *Blessed are You* HASHEM, *our God, King of the universe, Who gave Sabbaths for contentment to His people Israel with love, for a sign and a covenant. Blessed are You* HASHEM, *Who sanctifies the Sabbath.*

If one forgot *Yaaleh V'yavo* on Rosh Chodesh:

בָּרוּךְ *Blessed are You* HASHEM, *our God, King of the universe, Who gave New Moons to His people Israel as a remembrance.*

If one forgot *Retzei* and *Yaaleh V'yavo* on a Rosh Chodesh that falls on the Sabbath:

בָּרוּךְ *Blessed are You* HASHEM, *our God, King of the universe, Who gave Sabbaths for contentment to His people Israel with love, for a sign and a covenant; and New Moons for a remembrance. Blessed are You* HASHEM, *Who sanctifies the Sabbath, Israel, and New Moons.*

If one forgot *Yaaleh V'yavo* on a Festival:

בָּרוּךְ *Blessed are You* HASHEM, *our God, King of the universe, Who gave festivals to His people Israel for happiness and gladness, this festival day of Matzos | Shavuos | Succos | Shemini Atzeres Blessed are You* HASHEM, *Who sanctifies Israel and the seasons.*

If one forgot *Retzei* and *Yaaleh V'yavo* on a Festival that falls on the Sabbath:

בָּרוּךְ *Blessed are You* HASHEM, *our God, King of the universe, Who gave Sabbaths for contentment to His people Israel with love for a sign and a covenant, and festivals for happiness and gladness, this festival day of Matzos | Shavuos | Succos | Shemini Atzeres Blessed are You* HASHEM, *Who sanctifies the Sabbath, Israel, and the seasons.*

If one forgot *Yaaleh V'yavo* on Rosh Hashanah:

בָּרוּךְ *Blessed are You* HASHEM, *our God, King of the universe, Who gave festivals to His people Israel, this Day of Remembrance. Blessed are You* HASHEM, *Who sanctifies Israel and the Day of Remembrance.*

If one forgot *Retzei* and *Yaaleh V'yavo* on a Rosh Hashanah that falls on the Sabbath:

בָּרוּךְ *Blessed are You* HASHEM, *our God, King of the universe, Who gave Sabbaths for contentment to His people Israel with love for a sign and a covenant, and festivals to Israel, this Day of Remembrance. Blessed are You* HASHEM, *Who sanctifies the Sabbath, Israel, and the Day of Remembrance.*

---

trusts that God brings it upon him for a constructive and merciful purpose *(Anaf Yosef).*

The verse does not say that no righteous man would ever be reduced to poverty; were that the case, it would equate poverty with wickedness — a patent falsehood. Rather the verse says that no righteous person will be completely forsaken even if he must beg alms for his sustenance. Since Jews are obligated to help one another, it is no disgrace for one to require the help of another *(R' Hirsch).*

בְּשָׁלוֹם — *With peace.* Rabbi Shimon ben Chalafta said: 'The Holy One, Blessed is He, could find no container which would hold Israel's blessings as well as peace, as it says: *'*HASHEM *will give might to His people,* HASHEM *will bless His people with peace'* (*Uktzin* 3:12). The blessing of peace is so vital and precious that the word שָׁלוֹם, *peace,* is used to conclude the Oral Law (ibid.), the final blessing of *Shemoneh Esrei,* the *Priestly Blessings,* and *Bircas HaMazon.* It is also the essential word in our greetings to one another.

ברכת המזון בבית האבל

The following special version of *Bircas HaMazon* for a house of mourning is rooted in the Talmud and *Shulchan Aruch.* However, it has not always been practiced universally (see *Be'er HaGolah* 379:6).

Leader— רַבּוֹתַי נְבָרֵךְ.

Others— יְהִי שֵׁם יהוה מְבֹרָךְ מֵעַתָּה וְעַד עוֹלָם.[1]

Leader— יְהִי שֵׁם יהוה מְבֹרָךְ מֵעַתָּה וְעַד עוֹלָם.[1] בִּרְשׁוּת מָרָנָן וְרַבָּנָן וְרַבּוֹתַי, נְבָרֵךְ מְנַחֵם אֲבֵלִים שֶׁאָכַלְנוּ מִשֶּׁלּוֹ.

Others— בָּרוּךְ מְנַחֵם אֲבֵלִים שֶׁאָכַלְנוּ מִשֶּׁלּוֹ וּבְטוּבוֹ חָיִינוּ.

Leader— בָּרוּךְ מְנַחֵם אֲבֵלִים שֶׁאָכַלְנוּ מִשֶּׁלּוֹ וּבְטוּבוֹ חָיִינוּ. בָּרוּךְ הוּא וּבָרוּךְ שְׁמוֹ.

Continue with *Bircas Hamazon,* p. 184, until וּבְנֵה יְרוּשָׁלַיִם, p. 190.
Then substitute the following blessings for וּבְנֵה יְרוּשָׁלַיִם and the fourth blessing:

נַחֵם יהוה אֱלֹהֵינוּ אֶת אֲבֵלֵי יְרוּשָׁלַיִם* וְאֶת הָאֲבֵלִים הַמִּתְאַבְּלִים בָּאֵבֶל הַזֶּה. נַחֲמֵם מֵאֶבְלָם וְשַׂמְּחֵם מִיגוֹנָם, כָּאָמוּר: כְּאִישׁ אֲשֶׁר אִמּוֹ תְּנַחֲמֶנּוּ, כֵּן אָנֹכִי אֲנַחֶמְכֶם וּבִירוּשָׁלַיִם תְּנֻחָמוּ.[2] בָּרוּךְ אַתָּה יהוה, מְנַחֵם צִיּוֹן בְּבִנְיַן יְרוּשָׁלָיִם. אָמֵן.

בָּרוּךְ אַתָּה יהוה אֱלֹהֵינוּ מֶלֶךְ הָעוֹלָם, הָאֵל אָבִינוּ מַלְכֵּנוּ אַדִּירֵנוּ בּוֹרְאֵנוּ גֹּאֲלֵנוּ יוֹצְרֵנוּ קְדוֹשֵׁנוּ קְדוֹשׁ יַעֲקֹב, רוֹעֵנוּ רוֹעֵה יִשְׂרָאֵל, הַמֶּלֶךְ הַטּוֹב וְהַמֵּטִיב לַכֹּל, שֶׁבְּכָל יוֹם וָיוֹם הוּא הֵטִיב, הוּא מֵטִיב, הוּא יֵיטִיב לָנוּ. הַמֶּלֶךְ הַחַי, הַטּוֹב וְהַמֵּטִיב, אֵל אֱמֶת, דַּיַּן אֱמֶת, שׁוֹפֵט בְּצֶדֶק, לוֹקֵחַ נְפָשׁוֹת בְּמִשְׁפָּט, וְשַׁלִּיט בְּעוֹלָמוֹ לַעֲשׂוֹת בּוֹ כִּרְצוֹנוֹ. כִּי כָל דְּרָכָיו בְּמִשְׁפָּט, וַאֲנַחְנוּ עַמּוֹ וַעֲבָדָיו. וְעַל הַכֹּל אֲנַחְנוּ חַיָּבִים לְהוֹדוֹת לוֹ וּלְבָרְכוֹ. גּוֹדֵר פִּרְצוֹת יִשְׂרָאֵל, הוּא יִגְדּוֹר אֶת הַפִּרְצָה הַזֹּאת, מֵעָלֵינוּ וּמֵעַל הָאָבֵל הַזֶּה, לְחַיִּים וּלְשָׁלוֹם וְכָל טוֹב, וּמִכָּל טוּב לְעוֹלָם אַל יְחַסְּרֵנוּ.

Continue ... הָרַחֲמָן הוּא יִמְלוֹךְ, p. 192.

נַחֵם ... אֶת אֲבֵלֵי יְרוּשָׁלַיִם — *O comfort ... the mourners of Jerusalem.* Just as personal prayers are always mingled with national prayers, so, too, the grief of an individual is always submerged in the national grief over the loss of the Temple and the destruction of Jerusalem. Since the coming of Messiah will bring with it the resuscitation of the dead, the prayer for comfort of those who mourn for close relatives goes together with the plea that the national mourning over Jerusalem be ended by Divine consolation.

GRACE AFTER MEALS IN A HOUSE OF MOURNING

The following special version of Grace After Meals for a house of mourning is rooted in the Talmud and *Shulchan Aruch*. However, it has not always been practiced universally (see *Be'er HaGolah* 379:6).

Leader— *Gentlemen, let us bless.*

Others— *Blessed is the Name of HASHEM from this time and forever.*[1]

Leader— *Blessed is the Name of HASHEM from this time and forever.*[1] *With the permission of the distinguished people present let us bless the One Who comforts mourners, of Whose we have eaten.*

Others— *Blessed is He Who comforts mourners of Whose we have eaten and through Whose goodness we live.*

Leader— *Blessed is He Who comforts mourners of Whose we have eaten and through Whose goodness we live.*
Blessed is He and Blessed is His Name.

Continue with Grace after Meals, p. 184 until וּבְנֵה יְרוּשָׁלַיִם, *'Rebuild Jerusalem,'* p. 190.

Then substitute the following blessings for וּבְנֵה יְרוּשָׁלַיִם, *'Rebuild Jerusalem,'* and the fourth blessing:

נַחֵם *O comfort, HASHEM, our God, the mourners of Jerusalem* and those who mourn this sad event. Console them from their mourning and gladden them from their grief, as it is said, 'Like a man whose mother consoles him, so I will console you, and in Jerusalem you will be consoled.'*[2] *Blessed are You, HASHEM, Comforter of Zion through the rebuilding of Jerusalem. Amen.*

בָּרוּךְ *Blessed are You, HASHEM our God, King of the universe, the Almighty, our Father, our King, our Sovereign, our Creator, our Redeemer, our Maker, our Holy One, Holy One of Jacob, our Shepherd, the Shepherd of Israel, the good and beneficent King, for every single day He did good, does good, and will do good to us. He is the living King Who is good and Who does good for all, God of truth, Judge of truth,* Who judges with righteousness, Who takes souls with justice, Who rules His universe to do with it as He wishes, for all His ways are with justice and we are His nation and His servants. For everything, we are obliged to thank Him and to bless Him.* He Who repairs the breaches of Israel, may He repair this breach from us and from this sad event for life, for peace, and for all good; and of all good things may He never deprive us.*

Continue with *'The Compassionate One, may He reign ...'*, p. 192.

(1) *Psalms* 113:2. (2) *Isaiah* 66:13.

אֵל אֱמֶת דַּיַּן אֱמֶת — *God of truth, Judge of truth.* The mourners and their guests declare that the bereavement was not capricious; it was an act of truth and justice.

אֲנַחְנוּ חַיָּבִים לְהוֹדוֹת לוֹ וּלְבָרְכוֹ — *We are obliged to thank Him and to bless Him.* What is more, we, the aggrieved, acknowledge that we should thank and bless Him even in time of sadness, for it is only our lack of understanding that does not permit us to realize that His every act is for the good.

ברכות אחרונות

מעין שלש

The following blessing is recited after partaking of (a) grain products (other than bread or matzah) made from wheat, barley, rye, oats, or spelt; (b) grape wine or grape juice; (c) grapes, figs, pomegranates, olives, or dates. (If foods from two or three of these groups were consumed, then the insertions for each group are connected with the conjunctive וְ, thus וְעַל. The order of insertion in such a case is grain, wine, fruit.)

בָּרוּךְ אַתָּה יהוה אֱלֹהֵינוּ מֶלֶךְ הָעוֹלָם,

After grain products:	After wine:	After fruits:
עַל הַמִּחְיָה*	עַל הַגֶּפֶן	עַל הָעֵץ
וְעַל הַכַּלְכָּלָה,*	וְעַל פְּרִי הַגֶּפֶן,	וְעַל פְּרִי הָעֵץ,

וְעַל תְּנוּבַת הַשָּׂדֶה, וְעַל אֶרֶץ חֶמְדָּה* טוֹבָה וּרְחָבָה, שֶׁרָצִיתָ וְהִנְחַלְתָּ לַאֲבוֹתֵינוּ, לֶאֱכוֹל מִפִּרְיָהּ וְלִשְׂבּוֹעַ מִטּוּבָהּ.* רַחֵם יהוה אֱלֹהֵינוּ עַל יִשְׂרָאֵל עַמֶּךָ, וְעַל יְרוּשָׁלַיִם עִירֶךָ, וְעַל צִיּוֹן מִשְׁכַּן כְּבוֹדֶךָ, וְעַל מִזְבְּחֶךָ וְעַל הֵיכָלֶךָ. וּבְנֵה יְרוּשָׁלַיִם עִיר הַקֹּדֶשׁ בִּמְהֵרָה בְיָמֵינוּ, וְהַעֲלֵנוּ לְתוֹכָהּ, וְשַׂמְּחֵנוּ בְּבִנְיָנָהּ, וְנֹאכַל מִפִּרְיָהּ, וְנִשְׂבַּע מִטּוּבָהּ, וּנְבָרֶכְךָ עָלֶיהָ בִּקְדֻשָּׁה וּבְטָהֳרָה.

On the Sabbath— וּרְצֵה וְהַחֲלִיצֵנוּ בְּיוֹם הַשַּׁבָּת הַזֶּה.
On Rosh Chodesh— וְזָכְרֵנוּ לְטוֹבָה בְּיוֹם רֹאשׁ הַחֹדֶשׁ הַזֶּה.
On Pesach— וְשַׂמְּחֵנוּ בְּיוֹם חַג הַמַּצּוֹת הַזֶּה.
On Shavuos— וְשַׂמְּחֵנוּ בְּיוֹם חַג הַשָּׁבֻעוֹת הַזֶּה.
On Succos— וְשַׂמְּחֵנוּ בְּיוֹם חַג הַסֻּכּוֹת הַזֶּה.
On Shemini Atzeres/Simchas Torah— וְשַׂמְּחֵנוּ בְּיוֹם הַשְּׁמִינִי חַג הָעֲצֶרֶת הַזֶּה.
On Rosh Hashanah— וְזָכְרֵנוּ לְטוֹבָה בְּיוֹם הַזִּכָּרוֹן הַזֶּה.

כִּי אַתָּה יהוה טוֹב וּמֵטִיב לַכֹּל,* וְנוֹדֶה לְּךָ עַל הָאָרֶץ

After grain products:	After wine:	After fruit:
וְעַל הַמִּחְיָה.	וְעַל פְּרִי הַגָּפֶן.	וְעַל הַפֵּרוֹת.°
בָּרוּךְ אַתָּה יהוה, עַל הָאָרֶץ וְעַל הַמִּחְיָה.	בָּרוּךְ אַתָּה יהוה, עַל הָאָרֶץ וְעַל פְּרִי הַגָּפֶן.	בָּרוּךְ אַתָּה יהוה, עַל הָאָרֶץ וְעַל הַפֵּרוֹת.°

°If the fruit grew in *Eretz Yisrael,* substitute פֵּרוֹתֶיהָ for הַפֵּרוֹת.

מֵעֵין שָׁלֹשׁ / The Three-Faceted Blessing

The Sages instituted a special blessing of thanks to be recited after partaking of the Seven Species for which the Torah praises Eretz Yisrael (*Deut.* 8:8). This blessing is known as בְּרָכָה אַחַת מֵעֵין שָׁלֹשׁ, — literally, a single blessing that is an abridgment of three — because it summarizes the three Scripturally ordained blessings of *Bircas HaMazon.* Actually, the fourth blessing, too, is included (see *comm.* further), but the title does not allude to it because the fourth blessing is Rabbinic in origin.

הַמִּחְיָה — *Nourishment.* This is a generic term referring to all foods made from the five species of grain: wheat, barley, rye, oats, and spelt. The word מָזוֹן is a synonym for מִחְיָה, but the Sages preferred not to use the more familiar מָזוֹן because, had they done so, the concluding blessing would have been עַל הָאָרֶץ וְעַל הַמָּזוֹן, *for the Land and the nourishment* — exactly the same

BLESSINGS AFTER OTHER FOODS

THE THREE-FACETED BLESSING

The following blessing is recited after partaking of (a) grain products (other than bread or matzah) made from wheat, barley, rye, oats or spelt; (b) grape wine or grape juice; (c) grapes, figs, pomegranates, olives, or dates. (If foods from two or three of these groups were consumed, then the insertions for each group are connected with the conjunctive וְ, thus וְעַל. The order of insertion in such a case is grain, wine, fruit.)

בָּרוּךְ *Blessed are You, HASHEM, our God, King of the universe, for the*

After grain products:	After wine:	After fruits:
nourishment and the sustenance,**	*vine and the fruit of the vine,**	*tree and the fruit of the tree,*

and for the produce of the field; for the desirable, good and spacious Land that You were pleased to give our forefathers as a heritage, to eat of its fruit and to be satisfied with its goodness. Have mercy,* HASHEM, our God, on Israel, Your people; on Jerusalem, your city; and on Zion, the resting place of Your glory; upon Your altar, and upon Your Temple. Rebuild Jerusalem, the city of holiness, speedily in our days. Bring us up into it and gladden us in its rebuilding and let us eat from its fruit and be satisfied with its goodness and bless You upon it in holiness and purity.*

On the Sabbath—*And be pleased to let us rest on this Sabbath day.*

On Rosh Chodesh—*And remember us (for goodness) on this Rosh Chodesh.*

On Pesach—*And gladden us on this festival of Matzos.*

On Shavuos—*And gladden us on this festival of Shavuos.*

On Succos—*And gladden us on this festival of Succos.*

On Shemini Atzeres/Simchas Torah—*And gladden us on this festival of Shemini Atzeres.*

On Rosh Hashanah—*And remember us for goodness on this day of rememberance.*

For You, HASHEM, are good and do good to all and we thank you for the land and for the*

After grain products:	After wine:	After fruit:
nourishment.	*fruit of the vine.*	*fruit.°*

Blessed are You, HASHEM, for the land and for the

nourishment.	*fruit of the vine.*	*fruit.°*

°If the fruit grew in *Eretz Yisrael,* substitute *'its fruit.'*

---

as the second blessing of *Bircas HaMazon.* Instead they preferred to make this blessing distinct from any other *(Vayaas Abraham).*

כַּלְכָּלָה — *Support.* This concludes the first section of the Three-Part Blessing. It is parallel to the first blessing of *Bircas HaMazon* which thanks God for the blessing of food *(Talmidei R' Yonah).*

עַל הַגֶּפֶן וְעַל פְּרִי הַגֶּפֶן — *For the vine and the fruit of the vine.* Wine has its own particular blessing, both before partaking of it — i.e., בּוֹרֵא פְּרִי הַגָּפֶן, *Who creates the fruit of the vine* — and after, as in our blessing. The uniqueness of wine is due to its special qualities: it gladdens and satiates and is used in the performance of such commandments as *Kiddush* and *Havdalah* (*Berachos* 35b).

וְעַל אֶרֶץ חֶמְדָּה — *And for the desirable ... Land.* This begins the second section of the blessing. It parallels the second blessing of *Bircas HaMazon* in thanking God for *Eretz Yisrael.*

רַחֵם — *Have mercy.* This begins the third section of the blessing, paralleling the third blessing of *Bircas HaMazon.*

אַתָּה ... טוֹב וּמֵטִיב לַכֹּל — *You are good and do good to all.* This section of the blessing parallels the fourth and Rabbinically instituted blessing of *Bircas HaMazon.*

בורא נפשות

After eating or drinking any food for which neither *Bircas Hamazon* nor the Three-Faceted Blessing applies, such as fruits other than the above, vegetables or beverages other than wine, recite:

בָּרוּךְ אַתָּה יהוה אֱלֹהֵינוּ מֶלֶךְ הָעוֹלָם, בּוֹרֵא נְפָשׁוֹת רַבּוֹת* וְחֶסְרוֹנָן, עַל כָּל מַה שֶּׁבָּרָא(תָ)* לְהַחֲיוֹת בָּהֶם נֶפֶשׁ כָּל חָי. בָּרוּךְ חֵי הָעוֹלָמִים.

סדר ברכות ארוסין ונשואין

When the groom reaches the *chupah*, the *chazzan* sings:

בָּרוּךְ הַבָּא. מִי אַדִּיר עַל הַכֹּל, מִי בָּרוּךְ עַל הַכֹּל, מִי גָּדוֹל עַל הַכֹּל, מִי דָּגוּל עַל הַכֹּל, הוּא יְבָרֵךְ אֶת הֶחָתָן וְאֶת הַכַּלָּה.

As the bride approaches the *chupah*, the groom should take a step or two forward in greeting. She then circles the groom, according to the custom, and the *chazzan* sings:

בְּרוּכָה הַבָּאָה. מִי בָּן* שִׂיחַ שׁוֹשַׁן חוֹחִים,* אַהֲבַת כַּלָּה מְשׂוֹשׂ דּוֹדִים. הוּא יְבָרֵךְ אֶת הֶחָתָן וְאֶת הַכַּלָּה.

The *mesader kiddushin* holds a cup of wine and recites:

בָּרוּךְ אַתָּה יהוה אֱלֹהֵינוּ מֶלֶךְ הָעוֹלָם, בּוֹרֵא פְּרִי הַגָּפֶן. (All— אָמֵן.)

בָּרוּךְ אַתָּה יהוה אֱלֹהֵינוּ מֶלֶךְ הָעוֹלָם, אֲשֶׁר קִדְּשָׁנוּ בְּמִצְוֹתָיו, וְצִוָּנוּ עַל הָעֲרָיוֹת,* וְאָסַר לָנוּ אֶת הָאֲרוּסוֹת, וְהִתִּיר לָנוּ אֶת הַנְּשׂוּאוֹת לָנוּ עַל יְדֵי חֻפָּה וְקִדּוּשִׁין. בָּרוּךְ אַתָּה יהוה, מְקַדֵּשׁ עַמּוֹ יִשְׂרָאֵל עַל יְדֵי חֻפָּה וְקִדּוּשִׁין. (All— אָמֵן.)

בּוֹרֵא נְפָשׁוֹת / Borei Nefashos

בּוֹרֵא נְפָשׁוֹת רַבּוֹת — *Who creates numerous living things.* This blessing, like *Bircas HaMazon,* thanks God not only for His grace to humans, but to all נְפָשׁוֹת, *living things (Iyun Tefillah).*

שֶׁבָּרָא(תָ) — *That You have created.* Authorities differ regarding the reading of this word. Some read שֶׁבָּרָאתָ, *that 'You' have created* (in second person). Others read שֶׁבָּרָא, *that 'He' has created* (in third person). Either version is halachically acceptable.

חֵי הָעוֹלָמִים — *The Life of the worlds.* The phrase is based on Daniel 12:7 where God is described as the One Who gives life to the entire universe. Daniel used the singular חֵי הָעוֹלָם, referring to God as the *Provider of Life to This World.* The plural form of our blessing describes Him as the Life Giver of both this world and the World to Come *(Abudraham).* [See ArtScroll *Daniel,* p. 325.]

אֵרוּסִין וְנִשּׂוּאִין / THE MARRIAGE SERVICE

From the beginning of time, it was made a condition of creation that man and woman join together as a single unit in loyalty and devotion to one another (see *Genesis* 2:24). The Talmud sees the relationship between man and wife as the habitat for God's Own Presence, as it were. The name for man, אִישׁ, contains the letter י, while the name for woman, אִשָּׁה, contains the letter ה. These two letters spell one of God's Names, thus, when man and wife come together in harmony and purity, when they are devoted to one another in the shared responsibility of carrying out the duties prescribed for them by God and his Torah, they jointly become a resting place on earth for God's majesty *(Sotah* 17a).

Indeed, one of the Talmud's most frequently used terms for the betrothal ceremony קִדּוּשִׁין, *kiddushin,* is indicative of this sanctity. The literal translation of *kiddushin* is consecration, for when a Jewish groom places a ring on his bride's finger and recites the familiar הֲרֵי אַתְּ מְקֻדֶּשֶׁת לִי, *behold you are consecrated to me ...,* his words put their future relationship on a higher plane, one that aspires to holiness and achievement in the service of God Himself (see *Kiddushin* 2b).

The wedding ceremony consists of two separate and technically unrelated parts. The first is *kiddushin,* also known as *erusin.* It takes effect when the bride accepts the ring from her groom. When *kiddushin/erusin* is accomplished, the couple is considered to be married to the

BOREI NEFASHOS

After eating or drinking any food for which neither *Bircas HaMazon* nor the Three-Faceted blessing applies, such as fruits other than the above, vegetables or beverages other than wine, recite:

בָּרוּךְ *Blessed are You, HASHEM, our God, King of the universe, Who creates numerous living things* with their deficiencies; for all that You have created* with which to maintain the life of every being. Blessed is He, the life of the worlds.*

THE MARRIAGE SERVICE

When the groom reaches the *chupah,* the *chazzan* sings:

בָּרוּךְ הַבָּא *Blessed is he who has come! He Who is powerful above all, He Who is blessed above all, He Who is great above all, He Who is supreme above all — may He bless the groom and bride.*

As the bride approaches the *chupah,* the groom should take a step or two forward in greeting. She then circles the groom, according to the custom, and the *chazzan* sings:

בְּרוּכָה הַבָּאָה *Blessed is she who has come! He Who understands* the speech of the rose among the thorns,* the love of a bride, who is the joy of the beloved ones — may He bless the groom and bride.*

The *mesader kiddushin* holds a cup of wine and recites:

בָּרוּךְ *Blessed are You, HASHEM, our God, King of the universe, Who creates the fruit of the vine.* (All— *Amen.*)

בָּרוּךְ *Blessed are You, HASHEM, our God, King of the universe, Who has sanctified us with His commandments, and has commanded us regarding forbidden unions;* Who forbade betrothed women to us, and permitted women who are married to us through canopy and consecration. Blessed are You, HASHEM, Who sanctifies His people Israel through canopy and consecration.* (All— *Amen.*)

---

extent that their relationship can be severed only by means of divorce or death. [It should be noted that the English language does not contain a term for this status since it is unique to Torah law.] However, the couple may not live together nor do they have the halachic marital obligations to one another until the next ceremony takes place. That ceremony is נִשּׂוּאִין, *nisu'in,* or marriage, also known as *chupah* or canopy, because it commonly takes place under a canopy held aloft on four posts.

The canopy signifies the new household being formed by the union of the new couple, and the recitation of the blessings under the canopy consecrates the new relationship.

Before the *chupah* part of the service takes place, the *kesubah* is read aloud. The *kesubah* is the standard, halachically required marriage contract that spells out the obligations of a man to his wife during the marriage and provides for the wife's support if the marriage comes to an end. After the reading, this document is handed to the bride and she must maintain custody of it in a safe place.

מִי בָּן — *He Who understands.* God understands the idealism and purity upon which a new Jewish home is built, as is expressed further.

שִׂיחַ שׁוֹשַׁן חוֹחִים — *The speech of the rose among the thorns.* The allusion to Israel as a rose among thorns appears in *Shir Hashirim* (2:2). The Midrash interprets the 'rose' as an allusion to the Jewish bride and wife who scrupulously observes the laws of family purity. Also, it refers to the *mesader kiddushin,* the rare person who is thoroughly conversant with the laws and procedures of the marriage ceremony. Thus, this brief song that is chanted just as the marriage ceremony is about to begin is in praise of two of the participants: the bride whose idealism and loyalty to Halachah will maintain the purity of the family, and the *mesader kiddushin* whose knowledge of the law assures that the ceremony will be performed properly.

וְצִוָּנוּ עַל הָעֲרָיוֹת — *And commanded us regarding forbidden unions.* Although this blessing begins with the formula usually reserved for blessings

Groom and bride each drink from the wine. The groom then holds his ring ready to place on the bride's right index finger and says to her:

הֲרֵי אַתְּ מְקֻדֶּשֶׁת לִי, בְּטַבַּעַת זוּ,* כְּדַת מֹשֶׁה וְיִשְׂרָאֵל.

After the ring is placed on the bride's finger, the *kesubah* (marriage contract) is read aloud and handed to the groom who presents it to the bride. Then a second cup of wine is poured and seven blessings (שֶׁבַע בְּרָכוֹת) are recited aloud. First the blessing over wine is recited and then blessings 1-6 on p. 206. The honor of reciting these seven blessings may be divided among several people, but the first two should be recited by the same person. After the blessings both groom and bride drink from the wine. The groom then smashes a glass with his right foot to symbolize that until the Temple is rebuilt our joy cannot be complete. This act concludes the public marriage service. Then the groom and bride must spend some time together in a completely private room.

שבע ברכות

When the *Sheva Berachos* are recited, the following *zimun*, recited by the leader with a cup of wine in hand, is used:

זימון

Leader— רַבּוֹתַי נְבָרֵךְ.

Others— יְהִי שֵׁם יהוה מְבֹרָךְ מֵעַתָּה וְעַד עוֹלָם.[1]

Leader— יְהִי שֵׁם יהוה מְבֹרָךְ מֵעַתָּה וְעַד עוֹלָם.[1] דְּוַי הָסֵר* וְגַם חָרוֹן, וְאָז אִלֵּם בְּשִׁיר יָרוֹן,* נְחֵנוּ בְּמַעְגְּלֵי צֶדֶק,[2] שְׁעֵה בִּרְכַּת בְּנֵי אַהֲרֹן.* בִּרְשׁוּת מָרָנָן וְרַבָּנָן וְרַבּוֹתַי, נְבָרֵךְ אֱלֹהֵינוּ שֶׁהַשִּׂמְחָה בִמְעוֹנוֹ,* וְשֶׁאָכַלְנוּ מִשֶּׁלּוֹ.

Others— בָּרוּךְ אֱלֹהֵינוּ שֶׁהַשִּׂמְחָה בִמְעוֹנוֹ, וְשֶׁאָכַלְנוּ מִשֶּׁלּוֹ, וּבְטוּבוֹ חָיִינוּ.

Leader— בָּרוּךְ אֱלֹהֵינוּ שֶׁהַשִּׂמְחָה בִמְעוֹנוֹ, וְשֶׁאָכַלְנוּ מִשֶּׁלּוֹ, וּבְטוּבוֹ חָיִינוּ. בָּרוּךְ הוּא וּבָרוּךְ שְׁמוֹ.

Continue with *Bircas HaMazon*, p. 184.

---

over *Mitzvos* [אֲשֶׁר קִדְּשָׁנוּ בְּמִצְוֹתָיו ..., *Who has sanctified us with His commandments* ...] *Rosh (Kesubos* §12) explains that this blessing is totally unrelated to the commandment of פְּרוּ וּרְבוּ, *be fruitful and multiply*. Rather it falls under the category of blessings of praise, i.e., we thank and praise God for elevating the Jewish people by giving us a unique moral standard that specifies with whom we may and may not live.

בְּטַבַּעַת זוּ — *By means of this ring*. The groom's presentation of a ring which has a minimum value of a *perutah* conforms with the law that *Kiddushin* can be effected by means of money or something of value. Why was a ring chosen for this purpose?

— So that a Jewish woman can always wear something that recalls the moment when she and her husband consecrated, and embarked on, their new life together *(Chinuch)*.

— Just as a ring is round and therefore without end, so may the blessings and joy of the new couple be endless *(Dover Shalom)*.

— Just as a ring resembles a link in a chain, so may this new family become a link in the eternal chain of the Jewish heritage.

שֶׁבַע בְּרָכוֹת / SHEVA BERACHOS

The number seven in Jewish thought denotes completion — seven days in the week, seven years in the Sabbatical Year cycle, seven days to inaugurate the Tabernacle and so on. Thus we find that both Jacob and Samson celebrated their marriages for seven days *(Genesis* 29:27, *Rashi; Judges* 14:17). Accordingly, if either the bride or groom has never been married, their joy is complete and they celebrate it for seven full days (one day if each had been married previously).

The seven days (one day if both groom and bride were previously married) beginning with the wedding day are known as the week of שֶׁבַע בְּרָכוֹת, *Sheva Berachos* [lit. *Seven Blessings*]. During this period, the seven blessings recited under the marriage canopy are repeated after each meal attended by the newly married couple,

Groom and bride each drink from the wine. The groom holds his ring ready to place upon the bride's right index finger and says to her:

Behold, you are consecrated to me by means of this ring,* according to the ritual of Moses and Israel.

After the ring is placed on the bride's finger, the *kesubah* (marriage contract) is read aloud and handed to the groom who presents it to the bride. Then a second cup of wine is poured and seven blessings are recited aloud. First the blessing over wine is recited and then blessings 1-6 on p. 206. The honor of reciting these seven blessings may be divided among several people, but the first two should be recited by the same person. After the blessings both groom and bride drink from the wine. The groom then smashes a glass with his right foot to symbolize that until the Temple is rebuilt our joy cannot be complete. This act concludes the public marriage service. Then the groom and bride must spend some time together in a completely private room.

SHEVA BERACHOS

When the *Sheva Berachos* are recited the following *zimun*, recited by the leader with a cup of wine in hand, is used:

ZIMUN

Leader— *Gentlemen let us bless.*

Others— *Blessed is the Name of* HASHEM *from this time and forever!*[1]

Leader— *Blessed is the Name of* HASHEM *from this time and forever!*[1] *Banish pain* and also wrath, and then the mute will exult in song.* Guide us in paths of righteousness;*[2] *heed the blessing of the children of Aaron.* With the permission of the distinguished people present let us bless our God in Whose abode is this celebration,* of Whose we have eaten.*

Others— *Blessed is our God in Whose abode is this celebration, of Whose we have eaten, and through Whose goodness we live.*

Leader— *Blessed is our God in Whose abode is this celebration, of Whose we have eaten, and through Whose goodness we live. Blessed is He and Blessed is His Name.*

Continue with Grace after Meals, p. 184.

(1) *Psalms* 113:2. (2) Cf. 23:3.

if certain other conditions are met: (a) a *minyan* is present at the meal; (b) at least one person is present who did not participate in any of the couple's earlier meals. However, a newcomer is not required on the Sabbath or on a festival.

Zimun for Sheva Berachos

דְּוַי הָסֵר — *Banish pain.* The initials of the stanzas spell דוּנָשׁ, *Donash* ben Labrat, composer of this brief poem. He was also the author of the Sabbath hymn, דְּרוֹר יִקְרָא, *Dror Yikra,* and a pioneer Hebrew grammarian. He lived during the tenth century and is frequently cited by *Rashi.*

אִלֵּם בְּשִׁיר יָרֹן — *The mute will exult with song.* This is based on the prophecy of Isaiah (35:6) that all handicaps will be healed in the World to Come.

בִּרְכַּת בְּנֵי אַהֲרֹן — *The blessing of the children of Aaron.* Most commentators *(Shaarei Tefillah, Anaf Yosef, Avodas Yisrael, Iyun Tefillah)* agree that this was the original text composed by Donash. The blessing referred to is *Bircas Kohanim,* the Priestly Blessing (*Numbers* 6:24-26).

However, later commentators changed the text to בְּנֵי יְשׁוּרוּן, *the children of Jeshurun* (a synonym for Israel, as in *Deut.* 33:5), meaning that the 'blessing' refers to *Bircas HaMazon,* which is recited by all Jews (see *Taz, Even Ha'ezer* 62, and *Sheirusa Ditzlosa*).

Some say both: בִּרְכַּת בְּנֵי יְשׁוּרוּן בְּנֵי אַהֲרֹן, the blessing of the *children of Jeshurun the children of Aaron.* Still another version, that of *Eshel Avraham,* the *Rav of Butchatch,* reads בִּרְכַּת יְשׁוּרוּן כְּבִרְכַּת בְּנֵי אַהֲרֹן, *[Turn to] the blessing of Jeshurun as if it were the blessing of the children of Aaron.*

שֶׁהַשִּׂמְחָה בִּמְעוֹנוֹ — *In Whose abode is this celebration.* The unmixed joy with which we celebrate the marriage is a gift of God, because there is no sadness before Him; only joy *(Etz Yosef).*

After *Bircas HaMazon,* a second cup is poured and the following seven blessings are recited. They may be recited by one person or divided among several people. Whoever recites a blessing should hold the cup as he does so.

1. **בָּרוּךְ** אַתָּה יהוה אֱלֹהֵינוּ מֶלֶךְ הָעוֹלָם, שֶׁהַכֹּל בָּרָא לִכְבוֹדוֹ.* (All— אָמֵן.)

2. **בָּרוּךְ** אַתָּה יהוה אֱלֹהֵינוּ מֶלֶךְ הָעוֹלָם, יוֹצֵר הָאָדָם.* (All— אָמֵן.)

3. **בָּרוּךְ** אַתָּה יהוה אֱלֹהֵינוּ מֶלֶךְ הָעוֹלָם, אֲשֶׁר יָצַר אֶת הָאָדָם בְּצַלְמוֹ,* בְּצֶלֶם דְּמוּת תַּבְנִיתוֹ,* וְהִתְקִין לוֹ מִמֶּנּוּ* בִּנְיַן עֲדֵי עַד.* בָּרוּךְ אַתָּה יהוה, יוֹצֵר הָאָדָם. (All— אָמֵן.)

4. **שׂוֹשׂ** תָּשִׂישׂ* וְתָגֵל הָעֲקָרָה,* בְּקִבּוּץ בָּנֶיהָ לְתוֹכָהּ בְּשִׂמְחָה. בָּרוּךְ אַתָּה יהוה, מְשַׂמֵּחַ צִיּוֹן בְּבָנֶיהָ.* (All— אָמֵן.)

5. **שַׂמֵּחַ** תְּשַׂמַּח* רֵעִים הָאֲהוּבִים,* כְּשַׂמֵּחֲךָ יְצִירְךָ* בְּגַן עֵדֶן מִקֶּדֶם.* בָּרוּךְ אַתָּה יהוה, מְשַׂמֵּחַ חָתָן וְכַלָּה.* (All— אָמֵן.)

6. **בָּרוּךְ** אַתָּה יהוה אֱלֹהֵינוּ מֶלֶךְ הָעוֹלָם, אֲשֶׁר בָּרָא שָׂשׂוֹן וְשִׂמְחָה, חָתָן וְכַלָּה, גִּילָה רִנָּה, דִּיצָה וְחֶדְוָה, אַהֲבָה וְאַחֲוָה, וְשָׁלוֹם וְרֵעוּת. מְהֵרָה יהוה אֱלֹהֵינוּ יִשָּׁמַע בְּעָרֵי יְהוּדָה וּבְחֻצוֹת יְרוּשָׁלָיִם, קוֹל שָׂשׂוֹן וְקוֹל שִׂמְחָה, קוֹל חָתָן וְקוֹל כַּלָּה,[1] קוֹל מִצְהֲלוֹת חֲתָנִים מֵחֻפָּתָם, וּנְעָרִים מִמִּשְׁתֵּה נְגִינָתָם. בָּרוּךְ אַתָּה יהוה, מְשַׂמֵּחַ חָתָן עִם הַכַּלָּה. (All— אָמֵן.)

The leader of *Bircas Hamazon* recites the seventh blessing:

7. **בָּרוּךְ** אַתָּה יהוה אֱלֹהֵינוּ מֶלֶךְ הָעוֹלָם, בּוֹרֵא פְּרִי הַגָּפֶן. (All— אָמֵן.)

The leader drinks some of the wine from his cup; then wine from the two cups is mixed together and one cup is given to the groom and the other to the bride. It is laudable for those present to drink a bit of wine from the כּוֹס שֶׁל בְּרָכָה, *Cup of Blessing,* since it was used in the performance of a *mitzvah.*

---

1. שֶׁהַכֹּל בָּרָא לִכְבוֹדוֹ — *Who has created everything for His glory.* This blessing does not deal directly with marriage. It was instituted in honor of the guests who gathered to celebrate the marriage, for they emulate God Himself, Who served as a member of the wedding party in the Garden of Eden when Adam married Eve (*Rashi, Kesuvos* 8a).

2. יוֹצֵר הָאָדָם — *Who fashioned the Man.* This blessing refers to the creation of Adam, the first human being, and constitutes an introduction to the next blessing which thanks God for the creation of males and females *(Rashi).*

3. בְּצַלְמוֹ — *In His image.* The commentators generally agree that the Divine *image* refers to wisdom, intelligence, and free will (see ArtScroll *Genesis* 1:26).

בְּצֶלֶם דְּמוּת תַּבְנִיתוֹ — *In the image of his likeness.* The translation spells the word *his* with a lower-case 'h' following *Abudraham* who interprets the phrase as referring to the human body. Thus, we are thanking God for providing man with a body that serves as host to the soul and as a tool for the performance of commandments.

וְהִתְקִין לוֹ מִמֶּנּוּ — *And prepared for him — from himself.* Eve was created *from Adam himself,* i.e., from a part of Adam's body.

בִּנְיַן עֲדֵי עַד — *A building for eternity.* Eve is called a *building* following the verse (*Genesis* 2:22) that narrates her creation *(Rashi).* The resultant human couple was to reproduce and populate the earth forever *(Avodas Yisrael).*

4. שׂוֹשׂ תָּשִׂישׂ — *Bring intense joy.* The repetition of the Hebrew verb form indicates intensity and continuity. The same is true of the next blessing. Thus we pray that the joy and gladness of both Jerusalem and the new couple will be intense and never-ending.

הָעֲקָרָה — *The barren one,* i.e., Jerusalem, whose

After *Bircas HaMazon* a second cup is poured and the following seven blessings are recited. They may be recited by one person or divided among several people. Whoever recites a blessing should hold the cup as he does so.

1. **בָּרוּךְ** *Blessed are You,* HASHEM, *our God, King of the universe, Who has created everything for His glory.** (All— *Amen.*)

2. **בָּרוּךְ** *Blessed are You,* HASHEM, *our God, King of the universe, Who fashioned the Man.** (All— *Amen.*)

3. **בָּרוּךְ** *Blessed are You,* HASHEM, *our God, King of the universe, Who fashioned the Man in His image,* in the image of his likeness* and prepared for him — from himself* — a building for eternity.* Blessed are You,* HASHEM, *Who fashioned the Man.* (All— *Amen.*)

4. **שׂוֹשׂ** *Bring intense joy* and exultation to the barren one* through the ingathering of her children amidst her in gladness. Blessed are You,* HASHEM, *Who gladdens Zion through her children.** (All— *Amen.*)

5. **שַׂמֵּחַ** *Gladden* the beloved companions* as You gladdened Your creature* in the Garden of Eden from aforetime.* Blessed are You,* HASHEM, *Who gladdens groom and bride.** (All— *Amen.*)

6. **בָּרוּךְ** *Blessed are You,* HASHEM, *our God, King of the universe, Who created joy and gladness, groom and bride, mirth, glad song, pleasure, delight, love, brotherhood, peace, and companionship.* HASHEM, *our God, let there soon be heard in the cities of Judah and the streets of Jerusalem the sound of joy and the sound of gladness, the voice of the groom and the voice of the bride,*[1] *the sound of the grooms' jubilance from their canopies and of youths from their song-filled feasts. Blessed are You, Who gladdens the groom with the bride.* (All— *Amen.*)

The leader of *Bircas Hamazon* recites the seventh blessing:

7. **בָּרוּךְ** *Blessed are You* HASHEM, *our God, King of the universe, Who creates the fruit of the vine.* (All— *Amen.*)

The leader drinks some of the wine from his cup; then wine from the two cups is mixed together and one cup is given to the groom and the other to the bride. It is laudable for those present to drink a bit of wine from the כּוֹס שֶׁל בְּרָכָה, *Cup of Blessing,* since it was used in the performance of a *mitzvah.*

(1) Cf. *Jeremiah* 33:10-11.

---

future joy is likened by the prophets to the joy of bride and groom (see *Isaiah* 62:5).

מְשַׂמֵּחַ צִיּוֹן בְּבָנֶיהָ — *Who gladdens Zion through her children.* How will God comfort Jerusalem? — By gathering her children to her in happiness *(Tanchuma; Abudraham).*

5. שַׂמֵּחַ תְּשַׂמַּח — *Gladden.* May God bring joy to the newly joined lives of the bride and groom *(Etz Yosef).*

רֵעִים הָאֲהוּבִים — *The beloved companions,* i.e., the bride and groom who, through marriage, become loving companions to one another *(Avodas Yisrael).*

יְצִירְךָ — *Your creature,* i.e., Adam whose lonely life was gladdened when Eve was fashioned and brought to him *(Avodas Yisrael).*

מִקֶּדֶם — *From aforetime.* This follows the theme of this blessing, which asks that the newlyweds be granted the bliss of Adam and Eve.

מְשַׂמֵּחַ חָתָן וְכַלָּה — *Who gladdens groom and bride,* individually, i.e., each must be the recipient of God's blessing. The following blessing reads חָתָן עִם הַכַּלָּה, *the groom 'with' the bride,* an expression of thanks for the joy of the couple.

6. שָׂשׂוֹן ... וְרֵעוּת — *Joy ... and companionship.* There are ten expressions of joy in this blessing, all of them linked to חָתָן וְכַלָּה, *groom and bride.* They allude to the ten canopies which, according to the Talmud *(Bava Basra* 75a), God erected for Adam and Eve in the Garden of Eden.

ברית מילה

When the infant is brought in, the entire assemblage greets him:

בָּרוּךְ הַבָּא!*

The *mohel* (in some congregation, all those present) then recites:

וַיְדַבֵּר יהוה אֶל מֹשֶׁה לֵּאמֹר. פִּינְחָס* בֶּן אֶלְעָזָר בֶּן אַהֲרֹן הַכֹּהֵן הֵשִׁיב אֶת חֲמָתִי מֵעַל בְּנֵי יִשְׂרָאֵל, בְּקַנְאוֹ אֶת קִנְאָתִי בְּתוֹכָם, וְלֹא כִלִּיתִי אֶת בְּנֵי יִשְׂרָאֵל בְּקִנְאָתִי. לָכֵן אֱמֹר, הִנְנִי נֹתֵן לוֹ אֶת בְּרִיתִי שָׁלוֹם.[1]

Two seats are prepared, one upon which the *sandak* will sit as he holds the baby during the circumcision. The second is prepared for אֵלִיָּהוּ הַנָּבִיא, *Eliyahu the prophet*. The baby is first placed upon the כִּסֵּא שֶׁל אֵלִיָּהוּ, *Throne of Eliyahu,* by the father or one of the prominent guests, whereupon the *mohel* says:

זֶה הַכִּסֵּא שֶׁל אֵלִיָּהוּ* הַנָּבִיא, זָכוּר לַטּוֹב.*

The *mohel* then says:

לִישׁוּעָתְךָ* קִוִּיתִי יהוה.[2] שִׂבַּרְתִּי לִישׁוּעָתְךָ יהוה, וּמִצְוֹתֶיךָ עָשִׂיתִי.[3] אֵלִיָּהוּ מַלְאַךְ הַבְּרִית,* הִנֵּה שֶׁלְּךָ לְפָנֶיךָ, עֲמוֹד עַל יְמִינִי וְסָמְכֵנִי.* שִׂבַּרְתִּי לִישׁוּעָתְךָ יהוה. שָׂשׂ אָנֹכִי עַל אִמְרָתֶךָ, כְּמוֹצֵא שָׁלָל רָב.[4] שָׁלוֹם רָב לְאֹהֲבֵי תוֹרָתֶךָ, וְאֵין לָמוֹ מִכְשׁוֹל.[5] אַשְׁרֵי, תִּבְחַר* וּתְקָרֵב, יִשְׁכֹּן חֲצֵרֶיךָ —

All present respond:

— נִשְׂבְּעָה, בְּטוּב בֵּיתֶךָ, קְדֹשׁ הֵיכָלֶךָ.[6]

⁂ בְּרִית מִילָה / CIRCUMCISION

The commandment of מִילָה *(milah), circumcision*, was given to Abraham when he was ninety-nine years old. As indicated by the Torah *(Genesis*, ch. 17) and expounded by the Sages and commentators, circumcision signifies perfection, the indelible mark of the Jew as God's servant, and the covenant between God and the Jewish people. Only after Abraham's circumcision could he and Sarah have a son and begin the building of the Jewish nation. In later centuries, the entire nation circumcised itself prior to the Exodus from Egypt, and those born during the forty-year sojourn in the Wilderness were circumcised upon entering *Eretz Yisrael* under Joshua's leadership. Clearly, circumcision is crucial to Israel's very existence as a nation.

The Talmud *(Shabbos* 130a) teaches that every commandment originally accepted with joy is still performed with joy — and *milah* is the prime example of such a commandment. The joy with which parents bring their newborn sons into the 'Covenant of Abraham' remains a universal expression of devotion to their Jewish heritage. Although parents ordinarily would never dream of inflicting pain on and drawing blood from their child, they celebrate his *milah* with a festive air because they are conferring upon him the seal of Jewish eternity as God's chosen people.

בָּרוּךְ הַבָּא — *Blessed is he who arrives!* In addition to its simple meaning as a greeting to the baby, this is an allusion to the circumcision itself, since the numerical value of the word הַבָּא is eight, the day when circumcision is performed *(Abudraham).*

פִּינְחָס — *Phineas.* Circumcision is associated with the prophet Elijah. As we shall see below, Elijah complained to God that the Jewish people were not sufficiently zealous in observing the *mitzvah* of *milah.* Since there is an opinion that Elijah and Phineas are one and the same (see *Bava Metzia* 114b, *Rashi* s.v. לאו), it is customary to recite this passage which: (a) states the Divine assurance that the zealousness of Phineas/Elijah was for the benefit of Israel; and (b) contains God's pledge that Phineas would be given the *covenant* (an allusion to the circumcision covenant) of peace.

זֶה הַכִּסֵּא שֶׁל אֵלִיָּהוּ — *This is the Throne of Elijah.* The custom of setting aside a chair — preferably a handsome one — as the 'Throne of

⁂ CIRCUMCISION ⁂

When the infant is brought in, the entire assemblage greets him:

Blessed is he who arrives!*

The *mohel* (in some congregations, all those present) then recites:

וַיְדַבֵּר *HASHEM spoke to Moses, saying: Phineas,* son of Elazar the son of Aaron the Kohen, withdrew My wrath from upon the Children of Israel when he zealously took up My jealousy among them, so that I did not annihilate the Children of Israel in My jealousy. Therefore say, 'Behold! I give him My covenant of peace.'*[1]

Two seats are prepared, one upon which the *sandak* will sit as he holds the baby during the circumcision. The second is prepared for Eliyahu (Elijah) the prophet. The baby is first placed upon the 'Throne of Eliyahu' by the father or one of the prominent guests, whereupon the *mohel* says:

זֶה *This is the Throne of Elijah* the prophet, who is remembered for the good.**

The *mohel* then says:

לִישׁוּעָתְךָ *For Your salvation* do I long, HASHEM.*[2] *I hoped for Your salvation, HASHEM, and I performed Your commandments.*[3] *O Elijah, messenger of the covenant,* behold yours is now before you; stand at my right and be near me.* I hoped for Your salvation, HASHEM. I rejoice over Your word, like one who finds abundant spoils.*[4] *There is abundant peace for the lovers of Your Torah, and there is no stumbling block for them.*[5] *Praiseworthy is the one You choose* and draw near to dwell in Your courts —*

All present respond:

— may we be satisfied by the goodness of Your House — Your Holy Temple.[6]

(1) *Numbers* 25:10-12. (2) *Genesis* 49:18. (3) *Psalms* 119:166. (4) 119:162. (5) 119:165. (6) 65:5.

Elijah' is based on a passage in *Pirkei deR' Eliezer* (ch. 29). After fleeing from the wrath of King Ahab, Elijah declared to God that he had zealously defended the Divine honor against sinners who neglected His בְּרִית, *covenant*, a reference to Israel's neglect of circumcision (*I Kings* 19:10). God replied, 'By your life, henceforth Jews will perform circumcision only when you see it with your own eyes.' Some commentators see this pledge as a reward for Elijah's zeal, while others see it as a rebuke that implied he was wrong in blaming the whole nation for the neglect of some sinners (*Drishah, Yoreh De'ah* 265). Whatever the interpretation, the Sages instituted the ritual of placing the infant on the Throne of Elijah, who, as מַלְאַךְ הַבְּרִית, *messenger of the covenant* (see below), attends every circumcision.

זָכוּר לַטּוֹב — *Who is remembered for the good.* This Talmudic expression of respect and blessing is used sparingly and only for people whose service to the Jewish people is of eternal benefit.

⁂ לִישׁוּעָתְךָ — *For Your salvation.* This collection of verses, all but one of Scriptural origin, expresses our total reliance on God for our needs and salvation, and our joy in serving Him through the performance of His commandments.

אֵלִיָּהוּ מַלְאַךְ הַבְּרִית — *O Elijah, messenger of the covenant.* The term מַלְאַךְ הַבְּרִית, *messenger of the covenant*, is found in *Malachi* 3:1, where *Radak* refers it to Elijah, who will come to herald the Redemption. It can also be translated *angel of the covenant*, because Elijah has the status of an angel.

וְסָמְכֵנִי — *And be near me.* As the one with responsibility to oversee the performance of circumcision, Elijah is asked to stand close to the *mohel*. Immediately after this declaration, the *mohel* repeats his hope for God's salvation, to stress that he prays only to God, not to Elijah (*Iyun Tefillah*).

אַשְׁרֵי תִּבְחַר — *Praiseworthy is the one You choose.* God picked Israel to be His chosen people, and the choice is expressed by sealing Israel's flesh with the mark of the covenant (*Iyun Tefillah*).

When the *mohel* is ready to perform the circumcision, the baby's father says:

הִנְנִי מוּכָן וּמְזֻמָּן לְקַיֵּם מִצְוַת עֲשֵׂה שֶׁצִּוַּנִי הַבּוֹרֵא יִתְבָּרֵךְ, לָמוּל אֶת בְּנִי.

In some congregations at this point the father verbally appoints the *mohel* as his agent to perform circumcision on his son. The *mohel* then takes the infant and proclaims joyously:

אָמַר הַקָּדוֹשׁ בָּרוּךְ הוּא* לְאַבְרָהָם אָבִינוּ, הִתְהַלֵּךְ לְפָנַי וֶהְיֵה תָמִים.[1]
הִנְנִי מוּכָן וּמְזֻמָּן לְקַיֵּם מִצְוַת עֲשֵׂה שֶׁצִּוָּנוּ הַבּוֹרֵא יִתְבָּרֵךְ לָמוּל.

The baby is placed on the *sandak's* knees. Just before performing the circumcision, the *mohel* recites:

בָּרוּךְ* אַתָּה יהוה אֱלֹהֵינוּ מֶלֶךְ הָעוֹלָם, אֲשֶׁר קִדְּשָׁנוּ בְּמִצְוֹתָיו, וְצִוָּנוּ עַל הַמִּילָה. (All— אָמֵן.)

As the *mohel* performs the circumcision, the father (or, if the father is not present, the *sandak*) recites:

בָּרוּךְ אַתָּה יהוה אֱלֹהֵינוּ מֶלֶךְ הָעוֹלָם, אֲשֶׁר קִדְּשָׁנוּ בְּמִצְוֹתָיו, וְצִוָּנוּ לְהַכְנִיסוֹ בִּבְרִיתוֹ שֶׁל אַבְרָהָם אָבִינוּ.

All respond, loudly and joyfully:

אָמֵן. כְּשֵׁם שֶׁנִּכְנַס לַבְּרִית,* כֵּן יִכָּנֵס לְתוֹרָה וּלְחֻפָּה וּלְמַעֲשִׂים טוֹבִים.

When the circumcision is complete, the baby is given to one of the prominent guests to hold, while the following prayers (including the giving of the name) are recited. The honor of reciting them may be given to one person, or they may be divided between two people. If so, the first person recites the two blessings and the second person recites the prayer during which the baby is given his name.

בָּרוּךְ אַתָּה יהוה אֱלֹהֵינוּ מֶלֶךְ הָעוֹלָם, בּוֹרֵא פְּרִי הַגָּפֶן. (All— אָמֵן.)

בָּרוּךְ אַתָּה יהוה אֱלֹהֵינוּ מֶלֶךְ הָעוֹלָם, אֲשֶׁר קִדֵּשׁ יְדִיד מִבֶּטֶן,* וְחֹק בִּשְׁאֵרוֹ שָׂם, וְצֶאֱצָאָיו חָתַם בְּאוֹת בְּרִית קֹדֶשׁ. עַל כֵּן בִּשְׂכַר זֹאת,* אֵל חַי, חֶלְקֵנוּ צוּרֵנוּ, צַוֵּה* לְהַצִּיל יְדִידוּת שְׁאֵרֵנוּ מִשַּׁחַת.* לְמַעַן בְּרִיתוֹ אֲשֶׁר שָׂם בִּבְשָׂרֵנוּ. בָּרוּךְ אַתָּה יהוה, כּוֹרֵת הַבְּרִית. (All— אָמֵן.)

אָמַר הַקָּדוֹשׁ בָּרוּךְ הוּא — *The Holy One ... said.* God said this to Abraham just before giving him the commandment of *milah,* implying that only through this *mitzvah* can a Jew attain perfection.

בָּרוּךְ ◆ — *Blessed.* The two blessings signify two aspects of the *mitzvah:* that the organ of desire be controlled and that the child become worthy to enter the spiritual realm represented by the covenant made between God and Abraham *(Dover Shalom).*

As noted in *Yoreh Deah* 265:7, the authorities differ on the question of whether the father should recite שֶׁהֶחֱיָנוּ, *Who has kept us alive ...* The prevailing custom in most communities is not to recite it since the joy of the occasion is dulled because of the pain inflicted upon the infant.

כְּשֵׁם שֶׁנִּכְנַס לַבְּרִית — *Just as he has entered into the covenant.* The assembled guests proclaim their joy that a new member has been added to the covenant of Abraham. Simultaneously they offer their blessing that he may live a life of happiness and spiritual fulfillment. *Abudraham* notes that this blessing involves the father's responsibilities to his son: just as he has carried out his duty to circumcise, so may he carry out his duties to teach him Torah, arrange his marriage, and train him in the performance of good deeds.

Why are these three blessings listed in this order?

— *Abudraham* notes that the order is chronological. First, he studies Torah. Then, as the Mishnah *(Avos* 5:25) prescribes, comes marriage at eighteen; finally, since the Heavenly Court withholds punishment until age twenty, comes the time when a failure to do good deeds is no longer tolerated.

— Torah study begins in early childhood. Even when one is so burdened with family responsibility that time for study is lacking, he must still perform good deeds (cf. *Dover Shalom).*

◆ The Blessings following the Bris

אֲשֶׁר קִדֵּשׁ יְדִיד מִבֶּטֶן — *Who sanctified the beloved*

When the *mohel* is ready to perform the circumcision, the baby's father says:

הִנְנִי *Behold, I am prepared and ready to perform the positive commandment that the Creator, blessed is He, has commanded me, to circumcise my son.*

In some congregations at this point the father verbally appoints the *mohel* as his agent to perform circumcision on his son. The *mohel* then takes the infant and proclaims joyously:

אָמַר *The Holy One, Blessed is He, said* to Abraham, our forefather, 'Walk before me and be perfect.'*[1] *Behold I am prepared and ready to perform the positive commandment that the Creator, blessed is He, has commanded us, to circumcise.*

The baby is placed on the *sandak's* knees. Just before performing the circumcision, the *mohel* recites:

בָּרוּךְ *Blessed* are You, HASHEM, our God, King of the universe, Who has sanctified us with His commandments, and has commanded us regarding circumcision.* (All— *Amen.*)

As the *mohel* performs the circumcision, the father (or, if the father is not present, the *sandak*) recites:

בָּרוּךְ *Blessed are You, HASHEM, our God, King of the universe, Who has sanctified us with His commandments, and has commanded us to bring him into the covenant of Abraham, our forefather.*

All respond, loudly and joyfully:

Amen. Just as he has entered into the covenant,* so may he enter into the Torah, the marriage canopy, and good deeds.

When the circumcision is complete, the baby is given to one of the prominent guests to hold, while the following prayers (including the giving of the name) are recited. The honor of reciting them may be given to one person, or they may be divided between two people. If so, the first person recites the two blessings and the second person recites the prayer during which the baby is given his name.

בָּרוּךְ *Blessed are You, HASHEM, our God, King of the universe, Who creates the fruit of the vine.* (All— *Amen.*)

בָּרוּךְ *Blessed are You, HASHEM, our God, King of the universe, Who sanctified the beloved one from the womb* and placed the mark of the decree in his flesh, and sealed his offspring with the sign of the holy covenant. Therefore, as reward for this,* O Living God, our Portion, our Rock, may You issue the command* to rescue the beloved soul within our flesh from destruction,* for the sake of His covenant that He has placed in our flesh. Blessed are You HASHEM, Who establishes the covenant.* (All— *Amen.*)

(1) Genesis 17:1.

---

one from the womb. There are several interpretations of this phrase. Primary among them are:

— The *beloved one* is Isaac, the first person to be sanctified from the womb, in the sense that he was conceived after the commandment of circumcision was given. He and *his offspring* throughout the generations have in their flesh the *mark of the decree,* which is the sign of the holy covenant *(Rashi, Shabbos* 137b).

— The blessing tells how God put His seal, i.e., circumcision, in all the generations of the Jewish people. It started with Abraham, God's *beloved,* for whose righteousness God longed when he was still in the womb; continued with Isaac, in whose flesh *the mark of the decree was placed;* and then went on to Isaac's offspring, i.e., Jacob and his descendants *(Rabbeinu Tam* ibid., and *Menachos* 53a).

בִּשְׂכַר זֹאת — *As reward for this,* i.e., for circumcising ourselves.

צַוֵּה — *May You issue the command.* This is a prayer that God preserve the souls of the circumcised, as noted below. Some *siddurim* read in the past tense: צִוָּה, *You commanded.*

יְדִידוּת שְׁאֵרֵנוּ מִשַּׁחַת — *The beloved soul within our flesh from destruction.* In the merit of circumcising our flesh, may our soul be spared the destructive suffering of *Gehinnom.* As the Sages teach *(Eruvin* 19a), Abraham saves his circumcised offspring from *Gehinnom.*

קריאת השם

Upon reaching the words in bold type, the reader pauses while all present recite them aloud; he then repeats them and continues:

אֱלֹהֵינוּ וֵאלֹהֵי אֲבוֹתֵינוּ, קַיֵּם אֶת הַיֶּלֶד הַזֶּה לְאָבִיו וּלְאִמּוֹ, וְיִקָּרֵא שְׁמוֹ, בְּיִשְׂרָאֵל (baby's Hebrew name) בֶּן (baby's father's Hebrew name).
יִשְׂמַח הָאָב בְּיוֹצֵא חֲלָצָיו, וְתָגֵל אִמּוֹ בִּפְרִי בִטְנָהּ. כַּכָּתוּב: יִשְׂמַח אָבִיךָ וְאִמֶּךָ, וְתָגֵל יוֹלַדְתֶּךָ.[1] וְנֶאֱמַר: וָאֶעֱבֹר עָלַיִךְ וָאֶרְאֵךְ מִתְבּוֹסֶסֶת בְּדָמָיִךְ, **וָאֹמַר לָךְ בְּדָמַיִךְ חֲיִי, וָאֹמַר לָךְ בְּדָמַיִךְ חֲיִי.***[2] וְנֶאֱמַר: זָכַר לְעוֹלָם בְּרִיתוֹ, דָּבָר צִוָּה לְאֶלֶף דּוֹר. אֲשֶׁר כָּרַת אֶת אַבְרָהָם, וּשְׁבוּעָתוֹ לְיִשְׂחָק. וַיַּעֲמִידֶהָ לְיַעֲקֹב לְחֹק, לְיִשְׂרָאֵל בְּרִית עוֹלָם.[3] וְנֶאֱמַר. וַיָּמָל אַבְרָהָם אֶת יִצְחָק בְּנוֹ, בֶּן שְׁמֹנַת יָמִים, כַּאֲשֶׁר צִוָּה אֹתוֹ אֱלֹהִים.[4] **הוֹדוּ לַיהוה כִּי טוֹב,* כִּי לְעוֹלָם חַסְדּוֹ. הוֹדוּ לַיהוה כִּי טוֹב, כִּי לְעוֹלָם חַסְדּוֹ.**[5]
(baby's Hebrew name) בֶּן (father's Hebrew name) זֶה הַקָּטָן גָּדוֹל יִהְיֶה.

כְּשֵׁם שֶׁנִּכְנַס לַבְּרִית, כֵּן יִכָּנֵס לְתוֹרָה, וּלְחֻפָּה, וּלְמַעֲשִׂים טוֹבִים.

The one who recited the blessings drinks some wine. The *mohel* blesses the child:

מִי שֶׁבֵּרַךְ אֲבוֹתֵינוּ אַבְרָהָם יִצְחָק וְיַעֲקֹב, הוּא יְבָרֵךְ אֶת הַיֶּלֶד רַךְ הַנִּמּוֹל (baby's Hebrew name) בֶּן (father's Hebrew name), וְיִשְׁלַח לוֹ רְפוּאָה שְׁלֵמָה, בַּעֲבוּר שֶׁנִּכְנַס לַבְּרִית. וּכְשֵׁם שֶׁנִּכְנַס לַבְּרִית כֵּן יִכָּנֵס לְתוֹרָה, וּלְחֻפָּה, וּלְמַעֲשִׂים טוֹבִים. וְנֹאמַר: אָמֵן.

The *mohel* and father then recite the following prayer:

רִבּוֹנוֹ שֶׁל עוֹלָם, יְהִי רָצוֹן מִלְּפָנֶיךָ, שֶׁיְּהֵא חָשׁוּב וּמְרֻצֶּה וּמְקֻבָּל לְפָנֶיךָ, כְּאִלּוּ הִקְרַבְתִּיהוּ לִפְנֵי כִּסֵּא כְבוֹדֶךָ. וְאַתָּה, בְּרַחֲמֶיךָ הָרַבִּים, שְׁלַח עַל יְדֵי מַלְאָכֶיךָ הַקְּדוֹשִׁים נְשָׁמָה קְדוֹשָׁה וּטְהוֹרָה

Mohel says:	Father says:
לְ(baby's Hebrew name) בֶּן (fathers' Hebrew name)	לִבְנִי (baby's Hebrew name)

הַנִּמּוֹל עַתָּה לִשְׁמְךָ הַגָּדוֹל, וְשֶׁיִּהְיֶה לִבּוֹ פָּתוּחַ כְּפִתְחוֹ שֶׁל אוּלָם, בְּתוֹרָתְךָ הַקְּדוֹשָׁה, לִלְמֹד וּלְלַמֵּד, לִשְׁמֹר וְלַעֲשׂוֹת. וְתֶן לוֹ אֲרִיכוּת יָמִים

קְרִיאַת הַשֵּׁם / Giving the Name

The custom of naming a boy at his circumcision is based on the fact that God gave Abram the name Abraham in conjunction with the *mitzvah* commandment of *milah,* and that Moses' parents gave him the Hebrew name Yekusiel at the time of his *milah (Pirkei D'R' Eliezer).* At the time of the *bris,* the infant enters the covenant of Israel, and it is then appropriate to give him the name that expresses his sanctity because the spiritual destiny of a person is contained in his name.

Among Ashkenazic Jews, it is customary to name a child after a deceased forebear or spiritual leader to whom the family has had ties. Thereby it is hoped that the infant will benefit from the merit of the deceased and also carry on his good works *(Dover Shalom).* [This subject is discussed in detail in the ArtScroll *Bris Milah.*]

וָאֹמַר לָךְ בְּדָמַיִךְ חֲיִי — *And I said to you, 'In your blood, live!'* This verse is an allusion to the time in Egypt just before the Exodus when Israel was commanded to circumcise its males and to bring the Pesach offering. In the merit of these two commandments, both involving blood, the nation would earn redemption and eternal life as God's chosen people *(Sifre; Targum* to *Ezekiel* 16:6). *Milah* on the Jew's body marks him as

GIVING THE NAME

Upon reaching the words in bold type, the reader pauses while all present recite them aloud; he then repeats them and continues:

אֱלֹהֵינוּ *Our God and the God of our forefathers, preserve this child for his father and mother, and may his name be called in Israel* (baby's Hebrew name) *son of* (father's Hebrew name). *May his father rejoice in the issue of his loins and may his mother exult in the fruit of her womb, as it is written: 'May your father and mother rejoice and may she who gave birth to you exult.'*[1] *And it is said: "Then I passed by you and saw you downtrodden in your blood,* **and I said to you: 'In your blood, live!' and I said to you: 'In your blood, live!' "***[2] *And it is said: 'He remembered His covenant forever; the word of His command for a thousand generations — that He made with Abraham and His vow to Isaac. Then He established it for Jacob as a statute, for Israel as an everlasting statute.'*[3] *And it is said: 'Abraham circumcised his son Isaac at the age of eight days as God had commanded him.'*[4] **Give thanks to HASHEM for He is good;* His kindness endures forever!**[5] **Give thanks to HASHEM for He is good; His kindness endures forever!** *May this little one* (baby's Hebrew name) *son of* (father's Hebrew name) *become great.* **Just as he has entered the covenant so may he enter into the Torah, the marriage canopy, and good deeds.**

The one who recited the blessings drinks some wine. The *mohel* blesses the child:

מִי שֶׁבֵּרַךְ *He Who blessed our forefathers Abraham, Isaac, and Jacob, may He bless the tender, circumcised child* (baby's Hebrew name) *son of* (father's Hebrew name) *and send him a complete recovery, because he has entered the covenant. Just as he has entered the covenant, so may he enter into the Torah, the marriage canopy, and good deeds. And let us say, Amen.*

The *mohel* and father then recite the following prayer:

רִבּוֹנוֹ *Master of the universe, may it be your will that he be worthy, favored, and acceptable before You as if I had offered him before the throne of Your glory, and may You, in Your abundant mercy, send through Your holy angels a holy and pure soul to*

Father says:	*Mohel* says:
my son, (baby's Hebrew name)	(baby's Hebrew name) *son of* (father's Hebrew name)

who has now been circumcised for the sake of Your Great Name, and may his heart be as open to Your holy Torah as the entrance of the Temple, to learn and to teach, to observe and to perform. Give him long days and

(1) *Proverbs* 23:25. (2) *Ezekiel* 16:6. (3) *Psalms* 105:8-10. (4) *Genesis* 21:4. (5) *Psalms* 118:1, et al.

God's servant, while the *Pesach* offering symbolizes that he is ready actively to carry out God's will *(Gur Aryeh, Exodus* 12:6). [See ArtScroll *Ezekiel* for a further discussion of the subject.]

The congregation recites this statement aloud two times, symbolizing life in both worlds. Each time, the *mohel* dips his finger into the wine and puts a drop into the infant's mouth, symbolizing the commandments of *milah* and *Pesach* that bring life to the Jewish people *(Tur, Yoreh Deah* 265).

הודו לה' — *Give praise to HASHEM.* When Yocheved gave birth to Moses, she saw that he was טוב, *good (Exodus* 2:2), which the Talmud *(Sotah* 12a) understands to mean that he was born circumcised. Thus, we praise God for being *good,* meaning that He has now enabled the newborn infant to attain the degree of goodness

וְשָׁנִים, חַיִּים שֶׁל יִרְאַת חֵטְא, חַיִּים שֶׁל עֹשֶׁר וְכָבוֹד, חַיִּים שֶׁתְּמַלֵּא מִשְׁאֲלוֹת לִבּוֹ לְטוֹבָה. אָמֵן, וְכֵן יְהִי רָצוֹן.

Congregation recites עָלֵינוּ (p. 158), followed by the Mourner's Kaddish.

סעודת הברית

This liturgical poem, composed by the 12th century *paytan* Rabbi Yehudah HaLevi, is customarily sung at the circumcision feast. The initial letters of the stanzas form the author's name.

יוֹם לְיַבָּשָׁה נֶהֶפְכוּ מְצוּלִים,* שִׁירָה חֲדָשָׁה שִׁבְּחוּ גְאוּלִים.

הִטְבַּעְתָּ בְּתַרְמִית רַגְלֵי בַּת עֲנָמִית,* וּפַעֲמֵי שׁוּלַמִּית* יָפוּ בַּנְּעָלִים.
שִׁירָה חֲדָשָׁה שִׁבְּחוּ גְאוּלִים.

וְכָל רוֹאֵי יְשׁוּרוּן,* בְּבֵית הוֹדִי יְשׁוֹרְרוּן, אֵין כָּאֵל יְשׁוּרוּן, וְאוֹיְבֵינוּ פְּלִילִים.
שִׁירָה חֲדָשָׁה שִׁבְּחוּ גְאוּלִים.

דְּגָלַי כֵּן תָּרִים,* עַל הַנִּשְׁאָרִים, וּתְלַקֵּט נִפְזָרִים, כִּמְלַקֵּט שִׁבֳּלִים.
שִׁירָה חֲדָשָׁה שִׁבְּחוּ גְאוּלִים.

הַבָּאִים עִמְּךָ,* בִּבְרִית חוֹתָמְךָ, וּמִבֶּטֶן לִשְׁמֶךָ, הֵמָּה נִמּוֹלִים.
שִׁירָה חֲדָשָׁה שִׁבְּחוּ גְאוּלִים.

הַרְאֵה אוֹתוֹתָם,* לְכָל רוֹאֵי אוֹתָם, וְעַל כַּנְפֵי כְסוּתָם, יַעֲשׂוּ גְּדִילִים.*
שִׁירָה חֲדָשָׁה שִׁבְּחוּ גְאוּלִים.

לְמִי זֹאת* נִרְשֶׁמֶת, הַכֵּר נָא דְּבַר אֱמֶת, לְמִי הַחוֹתֶמֶת, וּלְמִי הַפְּתִילִים.
שִׁירָה חֲדָשָׁה שִׁבְּחוּ גְאוּלִים.

וְשׁוּב שֵׁנִית לְקַדְּשָׁהּ,* וְאַל תּוֹסִיף לְגָרְשָׁהּ, וְהַעֲלֵה אוֹר שִׁמְשָׁהּ, וְנָסוּ הַצְּלָלִים.
שִׁירָה חֲדָשָׁה שִׁבְּחוּ גְאוּלִים.

יְדִידִים רוֹמְמוּךָ, בְּשִׁירָה קִדְּמוּךָ, מִי כָמֹכָה, יהוה בָּאֵלִים.
שִׁירָה חֲדָשָׁה שִׁבְּחוּ גְאוּלִים.

בִּגְלַל אָבוֹת תּוֹשִׁיעַ בָּנִים, וְתָבִיא גְאֻלָּה לִבְנֵי בְנֵיהֶם.

---

symbolized by *milah (Hamanhig).*

☙ יוֹם לְיַבָּשָׁה נֶהֶפְכוּ מְצוּלִים — *The day the depths turned to dry land.* The reference is to the seventh day of Pesach, when the sea split for the benefit of the Jewish people. Not only the Sea of Reeds, but all concentrations of water split; therefore, the *zemer* uses the plural מְצוּלִים, *depths.*

עֲנָמִית — *Anamite.* Egypt is entitled Anamite because Anamim was a son of Mitzraim, the progenitor of Egypt *(Genesis* 10:13).

וּפַעֲמֵי שׁוּלַמִּית — *But the footsteps of the wholesome one,* i.e., Israel. The beautifully shod footsteps of Israel refers to the loyalty of the Jewish people in going to Jerusalem three times a year for the pilgrimage festivals *(Sotah* 49b).

יְשׁוּרוּן — *Jeshurun.* A title representing Israel in its state of righteousness and spiritual exaltation, from יָשָׁר, *upright.*

דְּגָלַי כֵּן תָּרִים — *May You raise my banners.* A prayer that God gather up the scattered survivors of our people wherever they are and bring them together as a farmer collects stalks during the harvest.

הַבָּאִים עִמְּךָ — *Those who come with You.* The Jewish people approach God with the mark of

years, a life of fear of sin, a life of wealth and honor, a life in which You fulfill all the wishes of his heart for good. Amen — may such be Your will.

Congregation recites *Aleinu* (p. 158), followed by the Mourner's *Kaddish*.

THE CIRCUMCISION FEAST

This liturgical poem, composed by the 12th century *paytan* Rabbi Yehudah HaLevi, is customarily sung at the circumcision feast. The initial letters of the stanzas form the author's name.

יוֹם לְיַבָּשָׁה *The day the depths turned to dry land,* the redeemed ones sang a new song.*

ה *Because of her deceitfulness, You caused the Anamite* daughter's feet to sink; but the footsteps of the wholesome one* were beautiful in shoes — the redeemed ones sang a new song.*

ו *All who see Jeshurun* will sing in My Majestic Home: 'There is none like the God of Jeshurun', and our enemies are judged — the redeemed ones sang a new song.*

ד *May You raise my banners* over the survivors; and may You gather the scattered ones as one gathers sheaves — the redeemed ones sang a new song.*

ה *Those who come with You* into the covenant of Your seal, and from the womb they are circumcised for Your Name's sake — the redeemed ones sang a new song.*

ה *Display their signs* to all who see them, and on the corners of their garments they will make fringes* — the redeemed ones sang a new song.*

ל *Whose is this Torah,* inscribed with commandments? — Please recognize the truth! Whose is the signet and whose are the threads? — the redeemed ones sang a new song.*

ו *Betroth her again* and drive her out no more; let her sunlight rise and let the shadows flee — the redeemed ones sang a new song.*

י *The beloved ones exalt You, with song they come and greet You; who is like You, HASHEM, among the mighty ones — the redeemed ones sang a new song.*

For the sake of the forefathers may You save the offspring and bring redemption to their children's children.

---

the covenant sealed into their flesh. From early infancy, almost as soon he emerges from his mother's womb, a Jewish boy is circumcised. This stanza, which calls for God's mercy in the merit of *milah*, is the reason this *zemer* is sung at the circumcision feast.

הַרְאֵה אוֹתוֹתָם — *Display their signs.* The Divine Presence resting upon the Jewish people is the *sign* that they are God's people (see *Deuteronomy* 28:10).

יַעֲשׂוּ גְּדִילִים — *They will make fringes. Tzitzis* are like the insignia of a royal servant.

לְמִי זֹאת — *Whose is this* [*Torah*]. This stanza proclaims that Israel's loyalty to God is plain to *all.* What other nation observes the Torah's commandments? What other nation has the signet, i.e., the seal of circumcision, and the threads of *tzitzis?*

וְשׁוּב שֵׁנִית לְקַדְּשָׁהּ — *Betroth her again.* May God renew His ties to Israel by bringing her back into His 'home' and never again exiling her. May He show her the bright sun of redemption and banish the shadows of exile.

זימון לסעודת הברית

If a *minyan* is present, the *zimun* is recited by the leader with a cup of wine in hand:

Leader—רַבּוֹתַי נְבָרֵךְ.

Others—יְהִי שֵׁם יהוה מְבֹרָךְ מֵעַתָּה וְעַד עוֹלָם.[1]

Leader—יְהִי שֵׁם יהוה מְבֹרָךְ מֵעַתָּה וְעַד עוֹלָם.[1]
נוֹדֶה לְשִׁמְךָ* בְּתוֹךְ אֱמוּנַי,* בְּרוּכִים אַתֶּם לַיהוה.

Others—נוֹדֶה לְשִׁמְךָ בְּתוֹךְ אֱמוּנַי, בְּרוּכִים אַתֶּם לַיהוה.

Leader—בִּרְשׁוּת אֵל אָיוֹם וְנוֹרָא, מִשְׂגָּב לְעִתּוֹת בַּצָּרָה,
אֵל נֶאְזָר בִּגְבוּרָה, אַדִּיר בַּמָּרוֹם יהוה.

Others—נוֹדֶה לְשִׁמְךָ בְּתוֹךְ אֱמוּנַי, בְּרוּכִים אַתֶּם לַיהוה.

Leader—בִּרְשׁוּת הַתּוֹרָה הַקְּדוֹשָׁה, טְהוֹרָה הִיא וְגַם פְּרוּשָׁה,
צִוָּה לָנוּ מוֹרָשָׁה,* מֹשֶׁה עֶבֶד יהוה.*

Others—נוֹדֶה לְשִׁמְךָ בְּתוֹךְ אֱמוּנַי, בְּרוּכִים אַתֶּם לַיהוה.

Leader—בִּרְשׁוּת הַכֹּהֲנִים הַלְוִיִּם אֶקְרָא לֵאלֹהֵי הָעִבְרִיִּים,
אֲהוֹדֶנּוּ בְּכָל אִיִּים,* אֲבָרְכָה אֶת יהוה.

Others—נוֹדֶה לְשִׁמְךָ בְּתוֹךְ אֱמוּנַי; בְּרוּכִים אַתֶּם לַיהוה.

Leader—בִּרְשׁוּת מָרָנָן וְרַבָּנָן וְרַבּוֹתַי, אֶפְתְּחָה בְּשִׁיר פִּי וּשְׂפָתַי,
וְתֹאמַרְנָה עַצְמוֹתַי, בָּרוּךְ הַבָּא בְּשֵׁם יהוה.

Others—נוֹדֶה לְשִׁמְךָ בְּתוֹךְ אֱמוּנַי, בְּרוּכִים אַתֶּם לַיהוה.

Leader—בִּרְשׁוּת מָרָנָן וְרַבָּנָן וְרַבּוֹתַי, נְבָרֵךְ אֱלֹהֵינוּ שֶׁאָכַלְנוּ מִשֶּׁלּוֹ.

Others—בָּרוּךְ אֱלֹהֵינוּ שֶׁאָכַלְנוּ מִשֶּׁלּוֹ, וּבְטוּבוֹ חָיִינוּ.

Leader—בָּרוּךְ אֱלֹהֵינוּ שֶׁאָכַלְנוּ מִשֶּׁלּוֹ, וּבְטוּבוֹ חָיִינוּ.
בָּרוּךְ הוּא וּבָרוּךְ שְׁמוֹ.

Continue with *Bircas HaMazon* (p. 184), until בְּעֵינֵי אֱלֹהִים וְאָדָם (p. 192). Then a designated person (or persons) recites the following prayers aloud.

Someone other than the father should recite the following stanza.

הָרַחֲמָן הוּא יְבָרֵךְ אֲבִי הַיֶּלֶד וְאִמּוֹ, וְיִזְכּוּ לְגַדְּלוֹ וּלְחַנְּכוֹ וּלְחַכְּמוֹ,* מִיּוֹם הַשְּׁמִינִי וָהָלְאָה יֵרָצֶה דָמוֹ,* וִיהִי יהוה אֱלֹהָיו עִמּוֹ.

(All—אָמֵן.)

◄§ Bircas HaMazon for Bris Milah

נוֹדֶה לְשִׁמְךָ — *We give thanks to Your Name.* There are indications that this song was recited following *all* festive meals by Polish Jews. With the passage of time, it was discontinued except at circumcisions [possibly because circumcisions, as the Sages teach *(Shabbos* 130a), have always been celebrated with particular joy].

אֱמוּנַי — *My faithful.* The one who leads the group in *Bircas HaMazon* refers to his companions as *faithful,* i.e., people whose faith is in God.

מוֹרָשָׁה — *Heritage.* The Torah is the *heritage* of Israel. As such we are not free to neglect it or cede it to any other nation.

עֶבֶד ה׳ — *Servant* [lit. *slave*] *of* HASHEM. A slave is totally the property of his master. He has no personality or initiative of his own. Moses is honored with this title because he was completely devoted to the will of God.

אִיִּים — *Islands.* The expression *islands* is used to indicate that the praise of God will be so universal that even the isolated inhabitants of far-flung islands will praise Him (see *Isaiah* 42:10 and *Malbim* there).

ZIMUN FOR THE CIRCUMCISION FEAST

If a *minyan* is present, this *zimun* is recited by the leader with a cup of wine in hand:

Leader— *Gentlemen let us bless.*

Others— *Blessed be the Name of HASHEM from this time and forever!*[1]

Leader— *Blessed be the Name of HASHEM from this time and forever!*[1]
We give thanks to Your Name among my faithful;* blessed are you to HASHEM.*

Others— *We give thanks to Your Name among my faithful; blessed are you to HASHEM.*

Leader— *With permission of the Almighty — fearful and awesome, the Refuge in times of trouble, the Almighty girded with strength, the Mighty on high — HASHEM.*

Others— *We give thanks to Your Name among my faithful; blessed are you to HASHEM.*

Leader— *With permission of the holy Torah, it is pure and explicit, commanded to us as a heritage,* by Moses, servant of HASHEM.**

Others— *We give thanks to Your Name among my faithful; blessed are you to HASHEM.*

Leader— *With permission of the Kohanim (from) the tribe of Levi, I call upon the God of the Hebrews, I will thank Him unto all islands,* I will give blessing to HASHEM.*

Others— *We give thanks to Your Name among my faithful; blessed are you to HASHEM.*

Leader— *With permission of the distinguished people present, I open in song my mouth and lips, and my bones shall proclaim, 'Blessed is he who comes in the Name of HASHEM.'*

Others— *We give thanks to Your Name among my faithful; blessed are you to HASHEM.*

Leader— *With the permission of the distinguished people present let us bless our God of Whose we have eaten.*

Others— *Blessed be our God of Whose we have eaten and through Whose goodness we live.*

Leader— *Blessed be our God of Whose we have eaten and through Whose goodness we live.*
Blessed is He and Blessed is His Name.

Continue with Grace after Meals (p. 184) until '... *in the eyes of God and of man*' (p. 192). Then a designated person (or persons) recites the following prayers aloud.

Someone other than the father should recite the following stanza.

הָרַחֲמָן ***The compassionate One! May He bless the father and mother of the child; and may they merit to raise him, to educate him, and to make him wise,* from the eighth day onward may his blood be pleasing,* and may HASHEM, his God, be with him.*** (All— *Amen.*)

(1) *Psalms* 113:2.

הָרַחֲמָן / The compassionate One!

At the end of every *Bircas Hamazon*, it is customary to insert prayers calling upon הָרַחֲמָן, *the Compassionate One*, to bless the nation, participants in a meal, or the particular festive day. The following brief and poetic prayers are recited in honor of the *Bris Milah* celebration.

לְגַדְּלוֹ וּלְחַנְּכוֹ וּלְחַכְּמוֹ — *To raise him, to educate him, and to make him wise.* 'To raise him' physically by providing for his needs; 'to rear him,' by teaching him proper behavior and his obligations to God and people; 'to make him wise,' by teaching him the Torah.

מִיּוֹם הַשְּׁמִינִי וָהָלְאָה יֵרָצֶה דָמוֹ — *From the eighth day*

Someone other than the *sandak* should recite the following stanza:

הָרַחֲמָן הוּא יְבָרֵךְ בַּעַל בְּרִית הַמִּילָה,* אֲשֶׁר שָׂשׂ לַעֲשׂוֹת צֶדֶק בְּגִילָה, וִישַׁלֵּם פָּעֳלוֹ וּמַשְׂכֻּרְתּוֹ כְּפוּלָה,* וְיִתְּנֵהוּ לְמַעְלָה לְמָעְלָה. (All— אָמֵן.)

הָרַחֲמָן הוּא יְבָרֵךְ רַךְ הַנִּמּוֹל לִשְׁמוֹנָה, וְיִהְיוּ יָדָיו וְלִבּוֹ* לָאֵל אֱמוּנָה, וְיִזְכֶּה לִרְאוֹת פְּנֵי הַשְּׁכִינָה,* שָׁלֹשׁ פְּעָמִים בַּשָּׁנָה.* (All— אָמֵן.)

Someone other than the *mohel* should recite the following stanza:

הָרַחֲמָן הוּא יְבָרֵךְ הַמָּל בְּשַׂר הָעָרְלָה, וּפָרַע וּמָצַץ דְּמֵי הַמִּילָה, אִישׁ הַיָּרֵא וְרַךְ הַלֵּבָב עֲבוֹדָתוֹ פְּסוּלָה, וְאִם שְׁלָשׁ אֵלֶּה* לֹא יַעֲשֶׂה לָהּ. (All— אָמֵן.)

הָרַחֲמָן הוּא יִשְׁלַח לָנוּ מְשִׁיחוֹ הוֹלֵךְ תָּמִים, בִּזְכוּת חֲתַן* לַמּוּלוֹת דָּמִים, לְבַשֵּׂר בְּשׂוֹרוֹת טוֹבוֹת וְנִחוּמִים, לְעַם אֶחָד מְפֻזָּר וּמְפֹרָד בֵּין הָעַמִּים. (All— אָמֵן.)

הָרַחֲמָן הוּא יִשְׁלַח לָנוּ כֹּהֵן צֶדֶק* אֲשֶׁר לֻקַּח לְעֵילוֹם,* עַד הוּכַן כִּסְאוֹ כַּשֶּׁמֶשׁ וְיָהֲלוֹם, וַיָּלֶט פָּנָיו בְּאַדַּרְתּוֹ* וַיִּגְלוֹם, בְּרִיתִי הָיְתָה אִתּוֹ הַחַיִּים וְהַשָּׁלוֹם. (All— אָמֵן.)

On weekdays continue ... הָרַחֲמָן הוּא יְזַכֵּנוּ, p. 212.
(On the Sabbath and Festivals, continue with the appropriate הָרַחֲמָן, p. 212.)

פדיון הבן

The father stands holding his child, and declares to the *Kohen*:

זֶה, בְּנִי בְכוֹרִי,* הוּא פֶּטֶר רֶחֶם לְאִמּוֹ. וְהַקָּדוֹשׁ בָּרוּךְ הוּא צִוָּה לִפְדּוֹתוֹ.

---

onward may his blood be pleasing. Animals are acceptable for Temple offerings from the eighth day after birth. Thus, the blessing is that the eight-day-old infant be beloved to God from this eighth day of his life as if he were a holy offering.

בַּעַל בְּרִית הַמִּילָה — *The master of the circumcision covenant.* This phrase refers to the *sandak,* the one who held the infant while the circumcision was performed *(Maharil).*

וּמַשְׂכֻּרְתּוֹ כְּפוּלָה — *And may his recompense be doubled.* He has performed the physical act of circumcision, and he has done it joyfully. For each — the precept and the joy — he earns recompense *(Dover Shalom).*

יָדָיו וְלִבּוֹ — *His strength* [lit. *his hands*] *and (his) heart,* i.e., may he devote all his physical and intellectual abilities to God's service.

לִרְאוֹת פְּנֵי הַשְּׁכִינָה — *To perceive the Divine Presence.* The juxtaposition of circumcision with God's Presence is based on an account in the *Zohar* which tells that God's Presence once departed from the Jews because an uncircumcised person mingled with them *(R' Reuven Margulies).*

שָׁלֹשׁ פְּעָמִים בַּשָּׁנָה — *Three times a year,* i.e., during the festivals of Pesach, Shavuos, and Succos when Jews are required to go to the Temple where they perceive the Presence of God (*Deut.* 16:16).

וְאִם שְׁלָשׁ אֵלֶּה — *If ... these three.* The three essential parts of the precept: מִילָה, *circumcision;* פְּרִיעָה, *uncovering;* and מְצִיצָה, *drawing.*

חֲתַן — *Groom.* The word חָתָן, *groom,* in Hebrew is used to refer to any honored person, whether it is a bridegroom or the infant being circumcised.

כֹּהֵן צֶדֶק — *The righteous Kohen,* i.e., the Prophet Elijah who was a *Kohen,* and who will herald the Messiah *(Dover Shalom).*

לְעֵילוֹם — *Into hiding.* Elijah was swept up to

Someone other than the *sandak* should recite the following stanza:

הָרַחֲמָן *The compassionate One! May He bless the master of the circumcision covenant,* who rejoiced to do justice with glee, and may his deed be rewarded, his recompense be doubled,* and may He place him ever higher.* (All— *Amen.*)

הָרַחֲמָן *The compassionate One! May He bless the tender circumcised eight-day old and may his strength and heart* be a trust to God, and may he merit to perceive the Divine Presence,* three times a year.** (All— *Amen.*)

Someone other than the *mohel* should recite the following stanza:

הָרַחֲמָן *The compassionate One! May He bless him who circumcised the uncut flesh, and revealed and drew the bloods of the circumcision, the service of the coward and the faint-hearted is unfit — and if he does not perform upon it these three* acts.* (All— *Amen.*)

הָרַחֲמָן *The compassionate One! May He send us His anointed who goes with wholesomeness, in the merit of the groom* bloodied for the sake of circumcision, to proclaim good tidings and consolations, to the one nation dispersed and splintered among the nations.* (All— *Amen.*)

הָרַחֲמָן *The compassionate One! May He send us the righteous Kohen* who was taken into hiding,* until His throne is established bright as sun and diamond, he who covered his face with his cloak* and enwrapped himself, My covenant was with him for life and peace.* (All— *Amen.*)

On weekdays continue, *'The compassionate One! May He make us worthy ...'*, p. 212.
(On the Sabbath and Festivals, continue with the appropriate prayer, p. 212.)

PIDYON HABEN/REDEMPTION OF THE FIRSTBORN

The father stands holding his child, and declares to the *Kohen*:

זֶה *This is my firstborn son;* he is the first issue of his mother's womb and the Holy One, Blessed is He, has commanded to redeem him, as it is said:*

---

heaven while still alive (see *II Kings* 2:1), to remain concealed until the coming of Messiah. Then Elijah will be revealed as if on a throne.

וַיָּלֶט פָּנָיו בְּאַדַּרְתּוֹ — *He who covered his face with his cloak.* When Elijah fled from the death threat of Ahab and Jezebel and hid in a cave, God came to him. Upon hearing the 'small, still voice' of God, Elijah *covered his face with his cloak* (*I Kings* 19:13).

פִּדְיוֹן הַבֵּן / REDEMPTION OF THE FIRSTBORN

When a male baby who was his mother's first conception becomes a month old, his father must redeem him by giving five silver *shekels* to a *Kohen*. It is commonly accepted that five silver dollars are adequate for the performance of this *mitzvah* although some authorities hold that the silver dollar is less than the *shekel* and so seven silver dollars should be used. Like the marriage and circumcision ceremonies, the redemption is celebrated with a festive meal. The ceremony is customarily performed as soon as the guests are seated and have made the *Hamotzi* blessing over bread. Thereupon the baby is brought to the place where the father and the *Kohen* are seated. To show love for the *mitzvah*, the baby is usually brought on a silver tray and bedecked in jewelry.

In declaring that firstborn males must be redeemed, the Torah teaches that God laid claim to all firstborn Jews at the time that He slew all the firstborn Egyptians in the last of the Ten Plagues. *Sefer HaChinuch (Mitzvah* 18) explains that this *mitzvah* teaches man to dedicate his very first achievements to God. Although firstborn children, like first fruits, are the culmination of much yearning, labor, and sacrifice, and it is human nature to want them for oneself, the Torah wants us to recognize that they are a gift from God and should be dedicated to His service. Thus, man *redeems* his firstborn.

זה בני בכורי — *This is my firstborn son.* The dialogue between the father and the *Kohen* is not an integral part of the *mitzvah* and indeed, the

שֶׁנֶּאֱמַר: וּפְדוּיָו מִבֶּן חֹדֶשׁ תִּפְדֶּה, בְּעֶרְכְּךָ, כֶּסֶף חֲמֵשֶׁת שְׁקָלִים, בְּשֶׁקֶל הַקֹּדֶשׁ עֶשְׂרִים גֵּרָה הוּא.[1] וְנֶאֱמַר: קַדֶּשׁ לִי כָל בְּכוֹר, פֶּטֶר כָּל רֶחֶם בִּבְנֵי יִשְׂרָאֵל, בָּאָדָם וּבַבְּהֵמָה לִי הוּא.[2]

The *Kohen* asks:

מַאי בָּעִית טְפֵי,* לִיתֵּן לִי בִּנְךָ בְּכוֹרְךָ שֶׁהוּא פֶּטֶר רֶחֶם לְאִמּוֹ, אוֹ בָּעִית לִפְדּוֹתוֹ בְּעַד חָמֵשׁ סְלָעִים כִּדְמִחֻיַּבְתָּא מִדְּאוֹרַיְתָא?

The father replies:

חָפֵץ אֲנִי לִפְדּוֹת אֶת בְּנִי, וְהֵילָךְ דְּמֵי פִדְיוֹנוֹ כִּדְמִחֻיַּבְנָא מִדְּאוֹרַיְתָא.

With the redemption money in hand, the father recites the following blessings:

בָּרוּךְ אַתָּה יהוה אֱלֹהֵינוּ מֶלֶךְ הָעוֹלָם, אֲשֶׁר קִדְּשָׁנוּ בְּמִצְוֹתָיו, וְצִוָּנוּ עַל פִּדְיוֹן הַבֵּן. (All— אָמֵן.)

בָּרוּךְ אַתָּה יהוה אֱלֹהֵינוּ מֶלֶךְ הָעוֹלָם, שֶׁהֶחֱיָנוּ וְקִיְּמָנוּ וְהִגִּיעָנוּ לַזְּמַן הַזֶּה. (All— אָמֵן.)

The *Kohen* accepts the money, and, swinging it in a circular motion over the infant's head, he says:

זֶה תַּחַת זֶה.* זֶה חִלּוּף זֶה. זֶה מָחוּל עַל זֶה. וְיִכָּנֵס זֶה הַבֵּן לְחַיִּים, לְתוֹרָה וּלְיִרְאַת שָׁמָיִם. יְהִי רָצוֹן שֶׁכְּשֵׁם שֶׁנִּכְנַס לְפִדְיוֹן כֵּן יִכָּנֵס לְתוֹרָה וּלְחֻפָּה וּלְמַעֲשִׂים טוֹבִים. אָמֵן.

The *Kohen* stands, places his right hand on the infant's head and blesses him:

יְשִׂמְךָ אֱלֹהִים כְּאֶפְרַיִם וְכִמְנַשֶּׁה.[3] יְבָרֶכְךָ יהוה וְיִשְׁמְרֶךָ. יָאֵר יהוה פָּנָיו אֵלֶיךָ וִיחֻנֶּךָּ. יִשָּׂא יהוה פָּנָיו אֵלֶיךָ, וְיָשֵׂם לְךָ שָׁלוֹם.[4] כִּי אֹרֶךְ יָמִים וּשְׁנוֹת חַיִּים וְשָׁלוֹם יוֹסִיפוּ לָךְ.[5] יהוה יִשְׁמָרְךָ מִכָּל רָע, יִשְׁמֹר אֶת נַפְשֶׁךָ.[6]

The *Kohen* hands the infant to the father; then the *Kohen* takes a cup of wine and recites:

בָּרוּךְ אַתָּה יהוה אֱלֹהֵינוּ מֶלֶךְ הָעוֹלָם, בּוֹרֵא פְּרִי הַגָּפֶן. (All— אָמֵן.)

The festive meal in celebration of the *mitzvah* continues, followed by *Bircas HaMazon*, p. 200.

---

text varies from community to community. The purpose of the conversation is simply to establish that the infant is a firstborn and that the father and *Kohen* are empowered to carry out the redemption.

מַאי בָּעִית טְפֵי — *Which do you prefer.* Despite the implication that the father has the choice of leaving his son with the *Kohen* if he prefers not to part with five shekels, this is not so. Firstly, the Torah *requires* the father to redeem his son; secondly, the child is not the property of the *Kohen* and is not taken from his parents even if the father refuses to redeem him. Rather this question is so framed in order to increase the father's love for his son and the *mitzvah* of redeeming him. One must also recognize that during many periods, five silver shekels was an enormous sum for most people *(Chut Hashani).*

זֶה תַּחַת זֶה — *This is instead of that.* The *Kohen*

'And those who must be redeemed, from the age of a month are you to redeem, according to your estimate, five silver shekels in the shekel of the Sanctuary, which is twenty gerah.'[1] *And it is said: 'Sanctify for Me every firstborn, the first issue of every womb among the Children of Israel, both of man and of beast, is Mine.'*[2]

The *Kohen* asks:

מַאי *Which do you prefer:* to give away your firstborn son, who is the first issue of his mother's womb, or do you prefer to redeem him for five shekels as you are required to do by the Torah?*

The father replies:

חָפֵץ *I wish to redeem my son. I present you with the cost of his redemption as I am required to do by the Torah.*

With the redemption money in hand, the father recites the following blessings:

בָּרוּךְ *Blessed are You,* H*ASHEM, our God, King of the universe, Who has sanctified us with His commandments and has commanded us regarding the redemption of a son.* (All— *Amen.*)

בָּרוּךְ *Blessed are You,* H*ASHEM, our God, King of the universe, Who has kept us alive, sustained us, and brought us to this season.* (All— *Amen.*)

The *Kohen* accepts the money and, while swinging it in a circular motion over the infant's head, says:

זֶה *This is instead of that;* this is in exchange for that; this is pardoned because of that. May this son enter into life, into Torah and into fear of Heaven. May it be Your will that just as he has entered into this redemption, so may he enter into the Torah, the marriage canopy, and good deeds, Amen.*

The *Kohen* places his right hand on the infant's head and blesses him:

יְשִׂמְךָ *May God make you like Ephraim and like Menashe.*[3] *May* H*ASHEM bless you and safeguard you. May* H*ASHEM illuminate His countenance for you and be gracious to you. May* H*ASHEM turn His countenance to you and establish peace for you.*[4] *For lengthy days, and years of life, and peace shall He increase for you.*[5] H*ASHEM will protect you from every evil; He will guard your soul.*[6]

The *Kohen* hands the infant to his father; then the *Kohen* takes a cup of wine and recites:

בָּרוּךְ *Blessed are You,* H*ASHEM, our God, King of the universe, Who creates the fruit of the vine.* (All— *Amen.*)

The festive meal in celebration of the *mitzvah* continues, followed by Grace after Meals, p. 182.

(1) *Numbers* 18:16. (2) *Exodus* 13:2. (3) *Genesis* 48:20. (4) *Numbers* 6:24-26. (5) *Proverbs* 3:2. (6) *Psalms* 121:7.

signifies his acceptance of the redemption, which frees the infant of all future obligations regarding this *mitzvah.* The reference to *pardon* is not to suggest that the infant has sinned; rather it means that he need not suffer because of the shortcomings of his father and that he will not be required to redeem himself when he becomes *bar mitzvah.*

תפלת הדרך

One who sets out on a journey should recite the following prayer once he leaves the city limits. See commentary for details.

יְהִי רָצוֹן מִלְּפָנֶיךָ יהוה אֱלֹהֵינוּ וֵאלֹהֵי אֲבוֹתֵינוּ שֶׁתּוֹלִיכֵנוּ לְשָׁלוֹם,* וְתַצְעִידֵנוּ לְשָׁלוֹם, וְתַדְרִיכֵנוּ לְשָׁלוֹם. וְתַגִּיעֵנוּ לִמְחוֹז חֶפְצֵנוּ לְחַיִּים וּלְשִׂמְחָה וּלְשָׁלוֹם,* [one who is planning to return on the same day adds – וְתַחֲזִירֵנוּ לְבֵיתֵנוּ לְשָׁלוֹם,] וְתַצִּילֵנוּ מִכַּף כָּל אוֹיֵב וְאוֹרֵב (וְלִסְטִים וְחַיּוֹת רָעוֹת) בַּדֶּרֶךְ,* וּמִכָּל מִינֵי פֻּרְעָנִיּוֹת הַמִּתְרַגְּשׁוֹת לָבוֹא לָעוֹלָם, וְתִשְׁלַח בְּרָכָה בְּ(כָל) מַעֲשֵׂה יָדֵינוּ, וְתִתְּנֵנוּ לְחֵן וּלְחֶסֶד וּלְרַחֲמִים בְּעֵינֶיךָ וּבְעֵינֵי כָל רוֹאֵינוּ, וְתִשְׁמַע קוֹל תַּחֲנוּנֵינוּ, כִּי אֵל שׁוֹמֵעַ תְּפִלָּה וְתַחֲנוּן אָתָּה. בָּרוּךְ אַתָּה יהוה, שׁוֹמֵעַ תְּפִלָּה.

Recite three times— וַיַּעֲקֹב הָלַךְ לְדַרְכּוֹ,* וַיִּפְגְּעוּ בוֹ מַלְאֲכֵי אֱלֹהִים. וַיֹּאמֶר יַעֲקֹב כַּאֲשֶׁר רָאָם, מַחֲנֵה אֱלֹהִים זֶה, וַיִּקְרָא שֵׁם הַמָּקוֹם הַהוּא מַחֲנָיִם.[1]*

Recite three times— לִישׁוּעָתְךָ* קִוִּיתִי יהוה.[2] קִוִּיתִי יהוה לִישׁוּעָתְךָ. יהוה לִישׁוּעָתְךָ קִוִּיתִי.

Recite three times— הִנֵּה אָנֹכִי שֹׁלֵחַ מַלְאָךְ* לְפָנֶיךָ לִשְׁמָרְךָ בַּדָּרֶךְ, וְלַהֲבִיאֲךָ אֶל הַמָּקוֹם אֲשֶׁר הֲכִנֹתִי.[3]

Recite three times— יהוה עֹז לְעַמּוֹ יִתֵּן, יהוה יְבָרֵךְ אֶת עַמּוֹ בַשָּׁלוֹם.[4]*

תְּפִלַּת הַדֶּרֶךְ / WAYFARER'S PRAYER

Someone who sets out on a journey must pray that he complete it safely *(Berachos* 29b). This applies even if there is no reason to expect danger, provided that the trip will be at least one *parsah* (approx. 3 miles). The prayer should be recited as soon as one has gone about 140 feet past the last house of his town. In the event the entire journey will be less than one *parsah,* the prayer may be recited, but the final blessing (בָּרוּךְ אַתָּה ה׳ שׁוֹמֵעַ תְּפִלָּה, *Blessed are You, HASHEM, Who hears prayer)* should be omitted. The prayer is recited once each day, even though the journey will be interrupted by rest, work, sightseeing and so on. However, if one's journey has ended, and he subsequently decides to embark on another journey on the same day, the Wayfarer's Prayer should be recited a second time. On a journey that will last for many days, the prayer is recited once each day.

It is preferable to recite a blessing before the beginning of the prayer so that it will be preceded as well as concluded by blessings. Customarily this is done by eating something before beginning the prayer. It is also customary for one member of a group to recite it aloud and for the others to fulfill their obligation by listening and responding אָמֵן, *Amen.*

Although it is preferable to interrupt one's travel and to stand while reciting the prayer, this need not be done if it is difficult.

שֶׁתּוֹלִיכֵנוּ לְשָׁלוֹם — *That You lead us toward peace.* In connection with this prayer, the Talmud *(Berachos* 30a) stresses that it be said in the plural. Whenever one unites himself with the needs of others, he increases the chance that his prayer will be heard.

לְחַיִּים וּלְשִׂמְחָה וּלְשָׁלוֹם — *For life, gladness, and peace.* Though we have prayed that we reach our destination, that is hardly enough. We re-emphasize that whatever our goals in life, they are worthwhile only if reaching them does not come at the cost of life, gladness, and peace.

וְחַיּוֹת רָעוֹת בַּדֶּרֶךְ — *And evil animals along the way.* Even in societies where bandits and wild animals do not exist, these terms are relevant because they refer figuratively to all the problems and perils that are associated with travel. The Sages teach that a person's sins are

WAYFARER'S PRAYER

One who sets out on a journey should recite the following prayer once he leaves the city limits. See commentary for details.

יְהִי *May it be Your will, HASHEM, our God and the God of our forefathers, that You lead us toward peace,* emplace our footsteps toward peace, guide us toward peace, and make us reach our desired destination for life, gladness, and peace** [one who is planning to return on the same day adds: *and return us to our homes in peace*]. *May You rescue us from the hand of every foe, ambush, (bandits, and evil animals) along the way,* and from all manner of punishments that assemble to come to earth. May You send blessing in our (every) handiwork, and grant us grace, kindness, and mercy in Your eyes and in the eyes of all who see us. May You hear the sound of our supplication, because You are God Who hears prayer and supplication. Blessed are You, HASHEM, Who hears prayer.*

Recite three times:

Jacob went on his way and angels of God encountered him. Jacob said when he saw them, 'This is a Godly camp.' So he named the place Machanayim.*[1]*

Recite three times:

For Your salvation I do long, HASHEM.*[2] *I do long, HASHEM, for Your salvation. HASHEM, for Your salvation I do long.*

Recite three times:

Behold I send an angel before you to protect you on the way and to bring you to the place that I have prepared.*[3]

Recite three times:

*HASHEM will give might to His nation, HASHEM will bless His nation with peace.**[4]

(1) *Genesis* 32:2-3. (2) 49:18. (3) *Exodus* 23:20. (4) *Psalms* 29:11.

more likely to be recalled against him when he is traveling.

וַיַּעֲקֹב הָלַךְ לְדַרְכּוֹ — *Jacob went on his way.* At this point it is customary to add various Scriptural selections that embody either prayers or assurances that God will assist wayfarers. The first two verses tell of Jacob traveling from the house of Laban back to *Eretz Yisrael.* As he entered the Land, he was met by angels who were sent to assist and protect him.

מַחֲנָיִם — *Machanayim.* The name Machanayim, literally 'two camps,' refers to Jacob's own entourage and that of the angels. *Ramban* explains that Jacob intended to equate the two camps, the human one and the angelic one. Since both were composed of dedicated servants of God, they were of comparable caliber. This is fitting for the Wayfarer's Prayer because, as many commentators teach, one should repent before setting out on a journey. If this is done, then the traveler may indeed be likened to an angel.

לִישׁוּעָתְךָ — *For Your salvation.* In Jacob's deathbed blessing to his children, he prophetically quoted this brief prayer that Samson would later utter when he was a blinded, degraded captive of the Philistines *(Rashi).* The Kabbalists find in these three words mystical combinations of letters that provide salvation against enemies *(R' Bachya).* Thus, this prayer applies to the perils of the way as well.

הִנֵּה אָנֹכִי שֹׁלֵחַ מַלְאָךְ — *Behold I send an angel.* God gave this assurance to Moses as the Jewish people were about to embark from Mount Sinai to *Eretz Yisrael.*

ה' יְבָרֵךְ אֶת עַמּוֹ בַשָּׁלוֹם — *HASHEM will bless His nation with peace.* The Wayfarer's Prayer makes constant reference to peace, which the Sages describe as the only vessel that can contain blessings *(Uktzin* 3:12).

❧ ברכות הנהנין ☙

ברכות קודם האכילה והשתיה

Upon washing the hands before eating bread:

בָּרוּךְ אַתָּה יהוה אֱלֹהֵינוּ מֶלֶךְ הָעוֹלָם, אֲשֶׁר קִדְּשָׁנוּ בְּמִצְוֹתָיו, וְצִוָּנוּ עַל נְטִילַת יָדָיִם.

Before eating bread:

בָּרוּךְ אַתָּה יהוה אֱלֹהֵינוּ מֶלֶךְ הָעוֹלָם, הַמּוֹצִיא לֶחֶם מִן הָאָרֶץ.

Before eating products of wheat, barley, rye, oats, or spelt (and rice, according to many opinions):

בָּרוּךְ אַתָּה יהוה אֱלֹהֵינוּ מֶלֶךְ הָעוֹלָם, בּוֹרֵא מִינֵי מְזוֹנוֹת.

Before drinking grape wine or grape juice:

בָּרוּךְ אַתָּה יהוה אֱלֹהֵינוּ מֶלֶךְ הָעוֹלָם, בּוֹרֵא פְּרִי הַגָּפֶן.

Before eating tree-grown fruit:

בָּרוּךְ אַתָּה יהוה אֱלֹהֵינוּ מֶלֶךְ הָעוֹלָם, בּוֹרֵא פְּרִי הָעֵץ.

Before eating produce that grew directly from the earth:

בָּרוּךְ אַתָּה יהוה אֱלֹהֵינוּ מֶלֶךְ הָעוֹלָם, בּוֹרֵא פְּרִי הָאֲדָמָה.

Before eating or drinking any other foods:

בָּרוּךְ אַתָּה יהוה אֱלֹהֵינוּ מֶלֶךְ הָעוֹלָם, שֶׁהַכֹּל נִהְיֶה בִּדְבָרוֹ.

ברכות הריח

Upon entering a perfumery or upon smelling fragrances of (a) non-vegetable origin (e.g., musk); (b) undetermined origin; or (c) a blend of spices of different origins:

בָּרוּךְ אַתָּה יהוה אֱלֹהֵינוּ מֶלֶךְ הָעוֹלָם, בּוֹרֵא מִינֵי בְשָׂמִים.

Upon smelling fragrant shrubs and trees, or their flowers (e.g., roses):

בָּרוּךְ אַתָּה יהוה אֱלֹהֵינוּ מֶלֶךְ הָעוֹלָם, בּוֹרֵא עֲצֵי בְשָׂמִים.

Upon smelling fragrant herbs, grasses or flowers:

בָּרוּךְ אַתָּה יהוה אֱלֹהֵינוּ מֶלֶךְ הָעוֹלָם, בּוֹרֵא עִשְׂבֵי בְשָׂמִים.

Upon smelling fragrant edible fruit or nuts:

בָּרוּךְ אַתָּה יהוה אֱלֹהֵינוּ מֶלֶךְ הָעוֹלָם, הַנּוֹתֵן רֵיחַ טוֹב בַּפֵּרוֹת.

⧼ Blessings

Ideally, every act and pleasure should be undertaken with an awareness that it is God Who is being served and He Who dispenses to us our needs and desires. In order to help inculcate this awareness in the Jewish people, the Sages, from the time of Ezra and his court, composed the various blessings and ordained the occasions upon which they must be recited. The very fact that the day is filled with events that require blessings provides constant inspiration. The thinking person finds himself drawn ever closer to the loving God by the awareness that every delicious morsel and soothing drink affords him a fresh opportunity to recognize and thank the Giver of all. In the words of the Talmud, whoever enjoys this world's pleasures without reciting a blessing is tantamount to one who steals from God (*Berachos* 35a).

BLESSINGS OVER FOOD, DRINK AND FRAGRANCE

BLESSINGS BEFORE FOOD OR DRINK

Upon washing the hands before eating bread:

Blessed are You, HASHEM, our God, King of the universe, Who has sanctified us with His commandments, and commanded us regarding washing the hands.

Before eating bread:

Blessed are You, HASHEM, our God, King of the universe, Who brings forth bread from the earth.

Before eating products of wheat, barley, rye, oats or spelt (and rice, according to many opinions):

Blessed are You, HASHEM, our God, King of the universe, Who creates species of nourishment.

Before drinking grape wine or grape juice:

Blessed are You, HASHEM, our God, King of the universe, Who creates the fruit of the vine.

Before eating tree-grown fruit:

Blessed are You, HASHEM, our God, King of the universe, Who creates the fruit of the tree.

Before eating produce that grew directly from the earth:

Blessed are You, HASHEM, our God, King of the universe, Who creates the fruit of the ground.

Before eating or drinking any other foods:

Blessed are You, HASHEM, our God, King of the universe, through Whose word everything came to be.

BLESSINGS OVER FRAGRANCES

Upon entering a perfumery or upon smelling fragrances of (a) non-vegetable origin (e.g., musk); (b) undetermined origin; or (c) a blend of spices of different origins:

Blessed are You, HASHEM, our God, King of the universe, Who creates species of fragrance.

Upon smelling fragrant shrubs and trees or their flowers (e.g., roses):

Blessed are You, HASHEM, our God, King of the universe, Who creates fragrant trees.

Upon smelling fragrant herbs, grasses or flowers:

Blessed are You, HASHEM, our God, King of the universe, Who creates fragrant herbage.

Upon smelling fragrant edible fruit or nuts:

Blessed are You, HASHEM, our God, King of the universe, Who places a good aroma into fruits.

There are three categories of blessings:

1. בִּרְכּוֹת הַנֶּהֱנִין, *blessings for enjoyment,* which apply when one has physical pleasure such as eating and drinking;

2. בִּרְכּוֹת הַמִּצְוֹות, *blessings for the performance of the commandments,* such as those recited upon putting on *tefillin* or lighting the Sabbath candles; and

3. בִּרְכּוֹת הוֹדָאָה, *blessings of praise and gratitude,* like those recited upon witnessing natural

ברכות המצות

Upon affixing a *mezuzah* to the doorpost:

בָּרוּךְ אַתָּה יהוה אֱלֹהֵינוּ מֶלֶךְ הָעוֹלָם, אֲשֶׁר קִדְּשָׁנוּ בְּמִצְוֹתָיו, וְצִוָּנוּ לִקְבֹּעַ מְזוּזָה.

Upon building a protective railing around one's roof.

בָּרוּךְ אַתָּה יהוה אֱלֹהֵינוּ מֶלֶךְ הָעוֹלָם, אֲשֶׁר קִדְּשָׁנוּ בְּמִצְוֹתָיו, וְצִוָּנוּ לַעֲשׂוֹת מַעֲקֶה.

Upon immersing in a *mikveh* metal or glass utensils (used for the preparation or serving of food or drink) that have been made by or purchased from a gentile:

בָּרוּךְ אַתָּה יהוה אֱלֹהֵינוּ מֶלֶךְ הָעוֹלָם, אֲשֶׁר קִדְּשָׁנוּ בְּמִצְוֹתָיו, וְצִוָּנוּ עַל טְבִילַת כֵּלִים (If only one utensil is immersed conclude— כֶּלִי).

An olive-size piece of dough must be separated and burned from each batch of dough that is at least 2 pounds 10 ounces. Regarding the amount of dough required for the recitation of the blessing, opinions vary from 3 lbs. 10.7 oz. — 4 lbs. 15.2 oz.

בָּרוּךְ אַתָּה יהוה אֱלֹהֵינוּ מֶלֶךְ הָעוֹלָם, אֲשֶׁר קִדְּשָׁנוּ בְּמִצְוֹתָיו, וְצִוָּנוּ לְהַפְרִישׁ חַלָּה מִן הָעִסָּה.

הפרשת תרומות ומעשרות

See commentary for a brief introduction to this requirement. One puts a bit more than one percent of the food aside. Then, if the food is *tevel* (see commentary), he recites the following blessing and declaration. If the food is *demai*, the blessing is omitted, but the declaration is recited.

בָּרוּךְ אַתָּה יהוה אֱלֹהֵינוּ מֶלֶךְ הָעוֹלָם, אֲשֶׁר קִדְּשָׁנוּ בְּמִצְוֹתָיו, וְצִוָּנוּ לְהַפְרִישׁ תְּרוּמוֹת וּמַעַשְׂרוֹת.

מַה שֶּׁהוּא יוֹתֵר מֵאֶחָד מִמֵּאָה מִן הַכֹּל שֶׁיֵּשׁ כָּאן, הֲרֵי הוּא תְּרוּמָה גְדוֹלָה בִּצְפוֹנוֹ, וְהָאֶחָד מִמֵּאָה שֶׁנִּשְׁאַר כָּאן עִם תִּשְׁעָה חֲלָקִים כָּמוֹהוּ, בְּצַד הָעֶלְיוֹן שֶׁל הַפֵּרוֹת הַלָּלוּ, הֲרֵי הֵם מַעֲשֵׂר רִאשׁוֹן. אוֹתוֹ הָאֶחָד מִמֵּאָה שֶׁעֲשִׂיתִיו מַעֲשֵׂר רִאשׁוֹן הֲרֵי הוּא תְּרוּמַת מַעֲשֵׂר. עוֹד תִּשְׁעָה חֲלָקִים כָּאֵלֶּה בְּצַד הַתַּחְתּוֹן שֶׁל הַפֵּרוֹת הֲרֵי הֵם מַעֲשֵׂר שֵׁנִי, וְאִם הֵם חַיָּבִים בְּמַעֲשַׂר עָנִי — הֲרֵי הֵם מַעֲשַׂר עָנִי.

If the second tithe had definitely not been separated as yet, it must be redeemed and the following blessing and declaration are recited. If there is doubt as to whether the second tithe has been redeemed, the blessing is omitted, but the declaration is recited.

בָּרוּךְ אַתָּה יהוה אֱלֹהֵינוּ מֶלֶךְ הָעוֹלָם, אֲשֶׁר קִדְּשָׁנוּ בְּמִצְוֹתָיו וְצִוָּנוּ לִפְדּוֹת מַעֲשֵׂר שֵׁנִי.

מַעֲשֵׂר שֵׁנִי זֶה, הוּא וְחֻמְשׁוֹ, הֲרֵי הוּא מְחֻלָּל עַל פְּרוּטָה אַחַת מִן הַמַּטְבֵּעַ שֶׁיִּחַדְתִּי לְפִדְיוֹן מַעֲשֵׂר שֵׁנִי.

---

phenomena (p. 228), the blessings in *Shemoneh Esrei* and other prayers, and the blessings for heavenly benefits that do not involve physical pleasure (p. 230), such as the שֶׁהֶחֱיָנוּ blessing that is recited upon various occasions when one feels great joy at having lived to see a particular event (*Rambam, Hil. Berachos* 1:2-4).

הַפְרָשַׁת תְּרוּמוֹת וּמַעַשְׂרוֹת / Separation of Terumah and Maaser

Grains, fruits, and vegetables that grew in the halachic boundaries of *Eretz Yisrael* may not be eaten (in any form) until תְּרוּמָה *(terumah), the Priestly tithe*, and the various forms of מַעֲשֵׂר

BLESSINGS OVER MITZVOS

Upon affixing a *mezuzah* to the doorpost:

Blessed are You, HASHEM, *our God, King of the universe,*
Who has sanctified us with His commandments,
and has commanded us to affix a mezuzah.

Upon building a protective railing around one's roof.

Blessed are You, HASHEM, *our God, King of the universe,*
Who has sanctified us with His commandments,
and has commanded us to construct a parapet.

Upon immersing in a *mikveh* metal or glass utensils (used for the preparation or serving of food or drink) that have been made by or purchased from a gentile:

Blessed are You, HASHEM, *our God, King of the universe,*
Who has sanctified us with His commandments,
and has commanded us regarding the immersion of vessels
(if only one utensil is immersed, conclude— *of a vessel).*

An olive-size piece of dough must be separated and burned from each batch of dough that is at least 2 pounds 10 ounces. Regarding the amount of dough required for the recitation of the blessing, opinions vary from 3 lbs. 10.7 oz. — 4 lbs. 15.2 oz.

Blessed are You, HASHEM, *our God, King of the universe,*
Who has sanctified us with His commandments,
and has commanded us to separate challah from the dough.

SEPARATION OF TERUMAH AND TITHES FROM FOODS GROWN IN ERETZ YISRAEL

See commentary for a brief introduction to this requirement. One puts a bit more than one percent of the food aside. Then, if the food is *tevel* (see commentary), he recites the following blessing and declaration. If the food is *demai*, the blessing is omitted, but the declaration is recited.

בָּרוּךְ *Blessed are you* HASHEM, *our God, King of the universe, Who has sanctified us with His commandments and has commanded us to separate terumos and tithes.*

Whatever [of the portion set aside] is more than one per cent of everything here is hereby declared to be the priestly tithe and is the northerly portion. The one per cent remaining here, together with nine equal portions at the upper side of this produce, are declared to be the first [Levite] tithe. The one out of a hundred that I have made the first tithe is hereby declared to be the terumah portion of the tithe. Nine more equal portions at the lower side of the produce are declared to be the second tithe, but if this produce must have the tithe of the poor separated from it — let [the lower nine portions] be the tithe of the poor.

If the second tithe had definitely not been separated as yet, it must be redeemed and the following blessing and declaration are recited. If there is doubt as to whether the second tithe has been redeemed, the blessing is omitted, but the declaration is recited.

בָּרוּךְ *Blessed are You,* HASHEM, *our God, King of the universe, Who has sanctified us with His commandments and has commanded us to redeem the second tithe.*

This second tithe — it and its extra fifth — is redeemed by one perutah out of the coin that I have set aside for the redemption of the second tithe.

(maaser), tithes [for the Levites, the poor, and the portion that was to be eaten in Jerusalem in Temple times], are separated from them. If the tithes have definitely not been taken as yet, the food is known as *tevel* and a blessing is made when they are separated. If their status is doubtful, they are known as *demai* and tithes are separated, but without a blessing. In either case

ברכות הודאה

ברכות הראיה והשמיעה

The first three blessings of this section may be recited only once each day, unless the skies have cleared completely and then the clouds returned. Except as otherwise indicated, the remaining blessings are recited only if thirty days have elapsed since the phenomenon was last seen.

If unsure whether to recite one of the blessings in this section on a particular occasion, recite the blessing, but omit the phrase 'אַתָּה ... הָעוֹלָם.'

Upon seeing lightning:

בָּרוּךְ אַתָּה יהוה אֱלֹהֵינוּ מֶלֶךְ הָעוֹלָם, עֹשֶׂה מַעֲשֵׂה בְרֵאשִׁית.

Upon hearing thunder:

בָּרוּךְ אַתָּה יהוה אֱלֹהֵינוּ מֶלֶךְ הָעוֹלָם, שֶׁכֹּחוֹ וּגְבוּרָתוֹ מָלֵא עוֹלָם.

Upon seeing a rainbow in the sky:

בָּרוּךְ אַתָּה יהוה אֱלֹהֵינוּ מֶלֶךְ הָעוֹלָם,
זוֹכֵר הַבְּרִית, וְנֶאֱמָן בִּבְרִיתוֹ, וְקַיָּם בְּמַאֲמָרוֹ.

Upon experiencing an earthquake, or seeing a comet, exceptionally lofty mountains, or exceptionally large rivers (in their natural course):

בָּרוּךְ אַתָּה יהוה אֱלֹהֵינוּ מֶלֶךְ הָעוֹלָם, עֹשֶׂה מַעֲשֵׂה בְרֵאשִׁית.

Upon seeing the ocean (some authorities include the Mediterranean Sea in this category):

בָּרוּךְ אַתָּה יהוה אֱלֹהֵינוּ מֶלֶךְ הָעוֹלָם, שֶׁעָשָׂה אֶת הַיָּם הַגָּדוֹל.

Upon seeing exceptionally beautiful people, trees or fields:

בָּרוּךְ אַתָּה יהוה אֱלֹהֵינוּ מֶלֶךְ הָעוֹלָם, שֶׁכָּכָה לּוֹ בְּעוֹלָמוֹ.

Upon seeing exceptionally strange-looking people or animals:

בָּרוּךְ אַתָּה יהוה אֱלֹהֵינוּ מֶלֶךְ הָעוֹלָם, מְשַׁנֶּה הַבְּרִיּוֹת.

Upon seeing fruit trees in bloom during the spring (this blessing may be recited only once each year):

בָּרוּךְ אַתָּה יהוה אֱלֹהֵינוּ מֶלֶךְ הָעוֹלָם, שֶׁלֹּא חִסַּר בְּעוֹלָמוֹ דָּבָר, וּבָרָא בוֹ בְּרִיּוֹת טוֹבוֹת וְאִילָנוֹת טוֹבִים, לְהַנּוֹת בָּהֶם בְּנֵי אָדָם.

Upon seeing an outstanding Torah scholar:

בָּרוּךְ אַתָּה יהוה אֱלֹהֵינוּ מֶלֶךְ הָעוֹלָם, שֶׁחָלַק מֵחָכְמָתוֹ לִירֵאָיו.

Upon seeing an outstanding secular scholar:

בָּרוּךְ אַתָּה יהוה אֱלֹהֵינוּ מֶלֶךְ הָעוֹלָם, שֶׁנָּתַן מֵחָכְמָתוֹ לְבָשָׂר וָדָם.

Upon seeing a gentile king who rules lawfully, but who cannot be overruled, and who has the power of life and death, the following is recited. Regarding modern-day elected rulers, opinions differ. Most authorities suggest that the blessing be recited with the phrase אַתָּה ... הָעוֹלָם omitted.

בָּרוּךְ אַתָּה יהוה אֱלֹהֵינוּ מֶלֶךְ הָעוֹלָם, שֶׁנָּתַן מִכְּבוֹדוֹ לְבָשָׂר וָדָם.

---

the declaration beginning מַה שֶּׁהוּא, *Whatever is,* should be recited. Moreover, this declaration must be understood by the person separating the *terumah* and tithes, and should therefore be recited in a language that he understands.

The laws regarding these matters are varied and one going to *Eretz Yisrael* or eating produce that grew there should become familiar with

BLESSINGS OF PRAISE AND GRATITUDE

BLESSINGS OVER PHENOMENA AND EVENTS

The first three blessings of this section may be recited only once each day, unless the skies have cleared completely and then the clouds returned. Except as otherwise indicated, the remaining blessings are recited only if thirty days have elapsed since the phenomenon was last seen.

If unsure whether to recite one of the blessings in this section on a particular occasion, recite the blessing but omit the opening clause, *'Blessed ... universe,'* and substitute, *'Blessed is He.'*

Upon seeing lightning:

Blessed are You, HASHEM, our God, King of the universe, Who makes the work of Creation.

Upon hearing thunder:

Blessed are You, HASHEM, our God, King of the universe, for His strength and His power fill the universe.

Upon seeing a rainbow in the sky:

Blessed are You, HASHEM, our God, King of the universe, Who remembers the covenant, is trustworthy in His covenant, and fulfills His word.

Upon experiencing an earthquake, or seeing a comet, exceptionally lofty mountains, or exceptionally large rivers (in their natural course):

Blessed are You, HASHEM, our God, King of the universe, Who makes the work of Creation.

Upon seeing the ocean (some authorities include the Mediterranean Sea in this category):

Blessed are You, HASHEM, our God, King of the universe, Who made the great sea.

Upon seeing exceptionally beautiful people, trees or fields:

Blessed are You, HASHEM, our God, King of the universe, Who has such in His universe.

Upon seeing exceptionally strange-looking people or animals:

Blessed are You, HASHEM, our God, King of the universe, Who makes the creatures different.

Upon seeing fruit trees in bloom during the spring (this blessing may be recited only once each year):

Blessed are You, HASHEM, our God, King of the universe, for nothing is lacking in His universe, and He created in it good creatures and good trees, to cause mankind pleasure with them.

Upon seeing an outstanding Torah scholar:

Blessed are You, HASHEM, our God, King of the universe, Who has apportioned of His knowledge to those who fear Him.

Upon seeing an outstanding secular scholar:

Blessed are You, HASHEM, our God, King of the universe, Who has given of His knowledge to human beings.

Upon seeing a gentile king who rules lawfully, but who cannot be overruled, and who has the power of life and death, the following is recited. Regarding modern-day elected rulers, opinions differ. Most authorities suggest that the blessing be recited with the phrase *'are You ... universe'* omitted.

Blessed are You, HASHEM, our God, King of the universe, Who has given of His glory to human beings.

Upon seeing 600,000 or more Jews together:

בָּרוּךְ אַתָּה יהוה אֱלֹהֵינוּ מֶלֶךְ הָעוֹלָם, חֲכַם הָרָזִים.

Upon one's first meeting with a friend who has recovered from a life-threatening illness:

בְּרִיךְ רַחֲמָנָא מַלְכָּא דְעָלְמָא, דִּי יַהֲבָךְ לָן, וְלָא יַהֲבָךְ לְעַפְרָא.

Upon seeing a destroyed synagogue:

בָּרוּךְ אַתָּה יהוה אֱלֹהֵינוּ מֶלֶךְ הָעוֹלָם, דַּיַּן הָאֱמֶת.

Upon seeing a destroyed synagogue that has been restored to its previous grandeur (many omit the words in parentheses):

בָּרוּךְ (אַתָּה יהוה אֱלֹהֵינוּ מֶלֶךְ הָעוֹלָם) מַצִּיב גְּבוּל אַלְמָנָה.

Upon seeing a place where one had earlier experienced a miracle that saved him from imminent danger (one who experienced such salvation in more than one place during his lifetime must append a roster of the other places to the end of the blessing):

בָּרוּךְ אַתָּה יהוה אֱלֹהֵינוּ מֶלֶךְ הָעוֹלָם, שֶׁעָשָׂה לִי נֵס בַּמָּקוֹם הַזֶּה (וּבְ...).

Upon seeing a place where one's parents, forebears, Torah teacher, or the nation as a whole was miraculously saved from imminent danger:

בָּרוּךְ אַתָּה יהוה אֱלֹהֵינוּ מֶלֶךְ הָעוֹלָם, שֶׁעָשָׂה

parent	forebears	teacher	the nation
לְאָבִי / לְאִמִּי	לַאֲבוֹתַי	לְרַבִּי	לַאֲבוֹתֵינוּ

נֵס בַּמָּקוֹם הַזֶּה.

ברכות שונות

Upon (a) eating seasonal fruits of a new season for the first time;
(b) purchasing a new garment of significant value to the wearer (e.g., a new suit or dress);
(c) performance of a seasonal *mitzvah;* or (d) deriving significant benefit from an event
(if others also benefit, the blessing הַטּוֹב וְהַמֵּטִיב — see below — is substituted):

בָּרוּךְ אַתָּה יהוה אֱלֹהֵינוּ מֶלֶךְ הָעוֹלָם,
שֶׁהֶחֱיָנוּ וְקִיְּמָנוּ וְהִגִּיעָנוּ לַזְּמַן הַזֶּה.

Upon hearing unusually good news which benefits both oneself and others:

בָּרוּךְ אַתָּה יהוה אֱלֹהֵינוּ מֶלֶךְ הָעוֹלָם, הַטּוֹב וְהַמֵּטִיב.

Upon hearing unusually bad news:

בָּרוּךְ אַתָּה יהוה אֱלֹהֵינוּ מֶלֶךְ הָעוֹלָם, דַּיַּן הָאֱמֶת.

Upon donning a new garment of significant value to the wearer (e.g., a new suit or dress):

בָּרוּךְ אַתָּה יהוה אֱלֹהֵינוּ מֶלֶךְ הָעוֹלָם, מַלְבִּישׁ עֲרֻמִּים.

For the blessings recited ...
at a *bris milah* (circumcision), see p. 210.
at a *pidyon haben* (redemption of the firstborn), see p. 220.
at a wedding ceremony and a *sheva berachos,* see pp. 202-206.
when kindling the Sabbath and Yom Tov candles, see. p. 296.
when kindling the Chanukah menorah, see p. 782
when reading the *Megillah,* see p. 786.
when donning a *tallis,* see p. 2.
when donning *tefillin,* see p. 6.
at the public Torah reading, see p. 440.
upon setting an *eruv,* see p. 656.
upon entering a *succah* for a meal, see p. 720.
upon visiting a cemetery, see p. 796.
upon taking the Lulav and Esrog, see p. 630.

Upon seeing 600,000 or more Jews together:

Blessed are You, HASHEM, our God, King of the universe,
Knower of secrets.

Upon one's first meeting with a friend who has recovered from a life-threatening illness:

Blessed is the Merciful One, King of the universe,
Who has given you to us, and has not given you to the dust.

Upon seeing a destroyed synagogue:

Blessed are You, HASHEM, our God, King of the universe,
the true Judge.

Upon seeing a destroyed synagogue that has been restored to its previous grandeur (many omit the words in parentheses):

Blessed (are You, HASHEM, our God, King of the universe),
Who sets a limit for a widow.

Upon seeing a place where one had earlier experienced a miracle that saved him from imminent danger (one who experienced such salvation in more than one place during his lifetime must append a roster of the other places to the end of the blessing):

Blessed are You, HASHEM, our God, King of the universe,
Who performed a miracle for me at this place (and at ...).

Upon seeing a place where one's parents, forebears, Torah teacher, or the nation as a whole was miraculously saved from imminent danger:

Blessed are You, HASHEM, our God, King of the universe,
Who performed a miracle for
my father/my mother/my forebears/my teacher/our ancestors
at this place.

VARIOUS BLESSINGS

Upon (a) eating seasonal fruits of a new season for the first time; (b) purchasing a new garment of significant value to the wearer (e.g., a new suit or dress); (c) performance of a seasonal *mitzvah;* or (d) deriving significant benefit from an event (if others also benefit, the blessing *'Who is good and does good'* — see below — is substituted):

Blessed are You, HASHEM, our God, King of the universe,
Who has kept us alive, sustained us, and brought us to this season.

Upon hearing unusually good news that benefits both oneself and others:

Blessed are You, HASHEM, our God, King of the universe,
Who is good and does good.

Upon hearing unusually bad news:

Blessed are You, HASHEM, our God, King of the universe,
the true Judge.

Upon donning a new garment of significant value to the wearer (e.g., a new suit or dress):

Blessed are You, HASHEM, our God, King of the universe,
Who clothes the naked.

---

them. Here, we offer only the texts that must be recited when the tithes are separated.

The bit of food that was set aside may not be eaten nor may it be thrown away. It should be wrapped up and buried or put aside to decompose naturally.

תְּפִלַּת מִנְחָה וּמַעֲרִיב

Weekday Minchah/Afternoon and Maariv/Evening Services

מנחה לחול

For the Sabbath and Festival *Minchah*, see page 502.

אַשְׁרֵי יוֹשְׁבֵי בֵיתֶךָ, עוֹד יְהַלְלְוּךָ סֶּלָה.[1] אַשְׁרֵי הָעָם שֶׁכָּכָה לּוֹ, אַשְׁרֵי הָעָם שֶׁיהוה אֱלֹהָיו.[2]

תהלים קמה

תְּהִלָּה לְדָוִד,

אֲרוֹמִמְךָ אֱלוֹהַי הַמֶּלֶךְ, וַאֲבָרְכָה שִׁמְךָ לְעוֹלָם וָעֶד.
בְּכָל יוֹם אֲבָרְכֶךָּ, וַאֲהַלְלָה שִׁמְךָ לְעוֹלָם וָעֶד.
גָּדוֹל יהוה וּמְהֻלָּל מְאֹד, וְלִגְדֻלָּתוֹ אֵין חֵקֶר.
דּוֹר לְדוֹר יְשַׁבַּח מַעֲשֶׂיךָ, וּגְבוּרֹתֶיךָ יַגִּידוּ.
הֲדַר כְּבוֹד הוֹדֶךָ, וְדִבְרֵי נִפְלְאֹתֶיךָ אָשִׂיחָה.
וֶעֱזוּז נוֹרְאוֹתֶיךָ יֹאמֵרוּ, וּגְדוּלָּתְךָ אֲסַפְּרֶנָּה.
זֵכֶר רַב טוּבְךָ יַבִּיעוּ, וְצִדְקָתְךָ יְרַנֵּנוּ.
חַנּוּן וְרַחוּם יהוה, אֶרֶךְ אַפַּיִם וּגְדָל חָסֶד.
טוֹב יהוה לַכֹּל, וְרַחֲמָיו עַל כָּל מַעֲשָׂיו.
יוֹדְוּךָ יהוה כָּל מַעֲשֶׂיךָ, וַחֲסִידֶיךָ יְבָרְכוּכָה.
כְּבוֹד מַלְכוּתְךָ יֹאמֵרוּ, וּגְבוּרָתְךָ יְדַבֵּרוּ.
לְהוֹדִיעַ לִבְנֵי הָאָדָם גְּבוּרֹתָיו, וּכְבוֹד הֲדַר מַלְכוּתוֹ.
מַלְכוּתְךָ מַלְכוּת כָּל עֹלָמִים, וּמֶמְשַׁלְתְּךָ בְּכָל דּוֹר וָדֹר.
סוֹמֵךְ יהוה לְכָל הַנֹּפְלִים, וְזוֹקֵף לְכָל הַכְּפוּפִים.
עֵינֵי כֹל אֵלֶיךָ יְשַׂבֵּרוּ, וְאַתָּה נוֹתֵן לָהֶם אֶת אָכְלָם בְּעִתּוֹ.

Concentrate intently while reciting the verse, פּוֹתֵחַ.

פּוֹתֵחַ אֶת יָדֶךָ, וּמַשְׂבִּיעַ לְכָל חַי רָצוֹן.
צַדִּיק יהוה בְּכָל דְּרָכָיו, וְחָסִיד בְּכָל מַעֲשָׂיו.
קָרוֹב יהוה לְכָל קֹרְאָיו, לְכֹל אֲשֶׁר יִקְרָאֻהוּ בֶאֱמֶת.
רְצוֹן יְרֵאָיו יַעֲשֶׂה, וְאֶת שַׁוְעָתָם יִשְׁמַע וְיוֹשִׁיעֵם.
שׁוֹמֵר יהוה אֶת כָּל אֹהֲבָיו, וְאֵת כָּל הָרְשָׁעִים יַשְׁמִיד.
❖ תְּהִלַּת יהוה יְדַבֶּר פִּי, וִיבָרֵךְ כָּל בָּשָׂר שֵׁם קָדְשׁוֹ לְעוֹלָם וָעֶד. וַאֲנַחְנוּ נְבָרֵךְ יָהּ, מֵעַתָּה וְעַד עוֹלָם, הַלְלוּיָהּ.[1]

Public fast days: *Ashrei* and Half-*Kaddish* are recited. If seven members of the *minyan* are fasting, the Torah, and *Haftarah*, are read (see p. 138). The readings are on p. 952. On *Tishah B'Av, tallis* and *tefillin* are worn, and passages omitted from *Shacharis* are recited.

WEEKDAY MINCHAH / מִנְחָה לִימוֹת הַחוֹל

Minchah corresponds to the *tamid*, the daily afternoon offering in the Temple *(Berachos* 26b), so it is recited only when it was permissible to offer the *tamid:* from half an hour after midday until evening. The preferable time, however, is not before three and a half variable hours after midday *(Orach Chaim* 233:1). A variable hour is one-twelfth of the time from sunrise to sunset.

WEEKDAY MINCHAH

For the Sabbath and Festival *Minchah,* see p. 502.

אַשְׁרֵי *Praiseworthy are those who dwell in Your house; may they always praise You, Selah![1] Praiseworthy is the people for whom this is so, praiseworthy is the people whose God is HASHEM.[2]*

Psalm 145 *A psalm of praise by David:*

א *I will exalt You, my God the King,*
and I will bless Your Name forever and ever.
ב *Every day I will bless You,*
and I will laud Your Name forever and ever.
ג *HASHEM is great and exceedingly lauded,*
and His greatness is beyond investigation.
ד *Each generation will praise Your deeds to the next*
and of Your mighty deeds they will tell.
ה *The splendrous glory of Your power*
and Your wondrous deeds I shall discuss.
ו *And of Your awesome power they will speak,*
and Your greatness I shall relate.
ז *A recollection of Your abundant goodness they will utter*
and of Your righteousness they will sing exultantly.
ח *Gracious and merciful is HASHEM,*
slow to anger, and great in [bestowing] kindness.
ט *HASHEM is good to all; His mercies are on all His works.*
י *All Your works shall thank You, HASHEM,*
and Your devout ones will bless You.
כ *Of the glory of Your kingdom they will speak,*
and of Your power they will tell;
ל *To inform human beings of His mighty deeds,*
and the glorious splendor of His kingdom.
מ *Your kingdom is a kingdom spanning all eternities,*
and Your dominion is throughout every generation.
ס *HASHEM supports all the fallen ones and straightens all the bent.*
ע *The eyes of all look to You with hope*
and You give them their food in its proper time;
פ *You open Your hand,* Concentrate intently while reciting the verse, *'You open...'*
and satisfy the desire of every living thing.
צ *Righteous is HASHEM in all His ways and magnanimous in all His deeds.*
ק *HASHEM is close to all who call upon Him —*
to all who call upon Him sincerely.
ר *The will of those who fear Him He will do;*
and their cry He will hear, and save them.
ש *HASHEM protects all who love Him;*
but all the wicked He will destroy.
ת Chazzan— *May my mouth declare the praise of HASHEM*
and may all flesh bless His Holy Name forever and ever.
We will bless God from this time and forever, Halleluyah![3]

(1) *Psalms* 84:5. (2) 144:15. (3) 115:18.

In the presence of a *minyan,* the *chazzan* recites חֲצִי קַדִּישׁ:

יִתְגַּדַּל וְיִתְקַדַּשׁ שְׁמֵהּ רַבָּא. (—Cong. אָמֵן.) בְּעָלְמָא דִּי בְרָא כִרְעוּתֵהּ. וְיַמְלִיךְ מַלְכוּתֵהּ, בְּחַיֵּיכוֹן וּבְיוֹמֵיכוֹן וּבְחַיֵּי דְכָל בֵּית יִשְׂרָאֵל, בַּעֲגָלָא וּבִזְמַן קָרִיב. וְאִמְרוּ: אָמֵן.

(—Cong. אָמֵן. יְהֵא שְׁמֵהּ רַבָּא מְבָרַךְ לְעָלַם וּלְעָלְמֵי עָלְמַיָּא.)

יְהֵא שְׁמֵהּ רַבָּא מְבָרַךְ לְעָלַם וּלְעָלְמֵי עָלְמַיָּא.

יִתְבָּרַךְ וְיִשְׁתַּבַּח וְיִתְפָּאַר וְיִתְרוֹמַם וְיִתְנַשֵּׂא וְיִתְהַדָּר וְיִתְעַלֶּה וְיִתְהַלָּל שְׁמֵהּ דְּקֻדְשָׁא בְּרִיךְ הוּא (—Cong. בְּרִיךְ הוּא) — °לְעֵלָּא מִן כָּל (—From Rosh Hashanah to Yom Kippur substitute °לְעֵלָּא וּלְעֵלָּא מִכָּל) בִּרְכָתָא וְשִׁירָתָא תֻּשְׁבְּחָתָא וְנֶחֱמָתָא, דַּאֲמִירָן בְּעָלְמָא. וְאִמְרוּ: אָמֵן. (—Cong. אָמֵן.)

שמונה עשרה — עמידה

Take three steps backward, then three steps forward. Remain standing with the feet together while reciting *Shemoneh Esrei.* It should be recited with quiet devotion and without any interruption, verbal or otherwise. Although its recitation should not be audible to others, one must pray loudly enough to hear himself. See *Laws* §61-96 for a brief summary of its laws, including how to rectify the omission of phrases that are added at particular times of the year. For commentary, see pages 98-118.

כִּי שֵׁם יהוה אֶקְרָא, הָבוּ גֹדֶל לֵאלֹהֵינוּ.[1]

אֲדֹנָי שְׂפָתַי תִּפְתָּח, וּפִי יַגִּיד תְּהִלָּתֶךָ.[2]

אבות

Bend the knees at בָּרוּךְ; bow at אַתָּה; straighten up at ה׳.

בָּרוּךְ אַתָּה יהוה אֱלֹהֵינוּ וֵאלֹהֵי אֲבוֹתֵינוּ, אֱלֹהֵי אַבְרָהָם, אֱלֹהֵי יִצְחָק, וֵאלֹהֵי יַעֲקֹב, הָאֵל הַגָּדוֹל הַגִּבּוֹר וְהַנּוֹרָא, אֵל עֶלְיוֹן, גּוֹמֵל חֲסָדִים טוֹבִים וְקוֹנֵה הַכֹּל, וְזוֹכֵר חַסְדֵי אָבוֹת, וּמֵבִיא גּוֹאֵל לִבְנֵי בְנֵיהֶם, לְמַעַן שְׁמוֹ בְּאַהֲבָה.

From Rosh Hashanah to Yom Kippur add:

זָכְרֵנוּ לְחַיִּים, מֶלֶךְ חָפֵץ בַּחַיִּים, וְכָתְבֵנוּ בְּסֵפֶר הַחַיִּים, לְמַעַנְךָ אֱלֹהִים חַיִּים.

[If forgotten, do not repeat *Shemoneh Esrei.* See *Laws* §61.]

Bend the knees at בָּרוּךְ; bow at אַתָּה; straighten up at ה׳.

מֶלֶךְ עוֹזֵר וּמוֹשִׁיעַ וּמָגֵן. בָּרוּךְ אַתָּה יהוה, מָגֵן אַבְרָהָם.

גבורות

אַתָּה גִּבּוֹר לְעוֹלָם אֲדֹנָי, מְחַיֵּה מֵתִים אַתָּה, רַב לְהוֹשִׁיעַ.

Between Shemini Atzeres and Pesach add:

מַשִּׁיב הָרוּחַ וּמוֹרִיד °הַגֶּשֶׁם [some say – °הַגָּשֶׁם].

[If forgotten, see *Laws* §70-75.]

מְכַלְכֵּל חַיִּים בְּחֶסֶד, מְחַיֵּה מֵתִים בְּרַחֲמִים רַבִּים, סוֹמֵךְ נוֹפְלִים, וְרוֹפֵא חוֹלִים, וּמַתִּיר אֲסוּרִים, וּמְקַיֵּם אֱמוּנָתוֹ לִישֵׁנֵי עָפָר. מִי כָמוֹךָ בַּעַל גְּבוּרוֹת, וּמִי דּוֹמֶה לָּךְ, מֶלֶךְ מֵמִית וּמְחַיֶּה וּמַצְמִיחַ יְשׁוּעָה.

In the presence of a *minyan*, the *chazzan* recites Half-*Kaddish*.

יִתְגַּדַּל *May His great Name grow exalted and sanctified* (Cong.— *Amen.*) *in the world that He created as He willed. May He give reign to His kingship in your lifetimes and in your days, and in the lifetimes of the entire Family of Israel, swiftly and soon. Now respond: Amen.*

(Cong.— *Amen. May His great Name be blessed forever and ever.*)

May His great Name be blessed forever and ever.

Blessed, praised, glorified, exalted, extolled, mighty, upraised, and lauded be the Name of the Holy One, Blessed is He (Cong.— *Blessed is He*) — (From Rosh Hashanah to Yom Kippur add: *exceedingly*) *beyond any blessing and song, praise and consolation that are uttered in the world. Now respond: Amen.* (Cong.— *Amen.*)

SHEMONEH ESREI — AMIDAH

Take three steps backward, then three steps forward. Remain standing with the feet together while reciting *Shemoneh Esrei*. It should be recited with quiet devotion and without any interruption, verbal or otherwise. Although its recitation should not be audible to others, one must pray loudly enough to hear himself. See *Laws* §61-96 for a brief summary of its laws, including how to rectify the omission of phrases that are added at particular times of the year. For commentary, see pages **98-118**.

When I call out the Name of Hashem, *ascribe greatness to our God.*[1]

My Lord, open my lips, that my mouth may declare Your praise.[2]

PATRIARCHS

Bend the knees at *'Blessed'*; bow at *'You'*; straighten up at *'*Hashem*.'*

בָּרוּךְ *Blessed are You,* Hashem, *our God and the God of our forefathers, God of Abraham, God of Isaac, and God of Jacob; the great, mighty, and awesome God, the supreme God, Who bestows beneficial kindnesses and creates everything, Who recalls the kindnesses of the Patriarchs and brings a Redeemer to their children's children, for His Name's sake, with love.*

From Rosh Hashanah to Yom Kippur add:

Remember us for life, O King Who desires life,

and inscribe us in the Book of Life — for Your sake, O Living God.

[If forgotten, do not repeat *Shemoneh Esrei*. See *Laws* §61.]

Bend the knees at *'Blessed'*; bow at *'You'*; straighten up at 'Hashem'.

O King, Helper, Savior, and Shield. Blessed are You, Hashem, *Shield of Abraham.*

GOD'S MIGHT

אַתָּה *You are eternally mighty, my Lord, the Resuscitator of the dead are You; abundantly able to* ***save,***

Between Shemini Atzeres and Pesach add:

Who makes the wind blow and makes the rain descend;

[If forgotten, see *Laws* §70-75.]

Who sustains the living with kindness, resuscitates the dead with abundant mercy, supports the fallen, heals the sick, releases the confined, and maintains His faith to those asleep in the dust. Who is like You, O Master of mighty deeds, and who is comparable to You, O King Who causes death and restores life and makes salvation sprout!

(1) *Deuteronomy* 32:3. (2) *Psalms* 51:17.

From Rosh Hashanah to Yom Kippur add:

מִי כָמְוֹךָ אַב הָרַחֲמִים, זוֹכֵר יְצוּרָיו לְחַיִּים בְּרַחֲמִים.

[If forgotten, do not repeat *Shemoneh Esrei.* See *Laws* §61.]

וְנֶאֱמָן אַתָּה לְהַחֲיוֹת מֵתִים. בָּרוּךְ אַתָּה יהוה, מְחַיֵּה הַמֵּתִים.

During the *chazzan's* repetition, *Kedushah* (below) is recited at this point.

קדושת השם

אַתָּה קָדוֹשׁ וְשִׁמְךָ קָדוֹשׁ, וּקְדוֹשִׁים בְּכָל יוֹם יְהַלְּלְוּךָ סֶּלָה. בָּרוּךְ אַתָּה יהוה, °הָאֵל הַקָּדוֹשׁ.

°הַמֶּלֶךְ הַקָּדוֹשׁ. —From Rosh Hashanah to Yom Kippur substitute
[If forgotten, repeat *Shemoneh Esrei.* See *Laws* §62-63.]

בינה

אַתָּה חוֹנֵן לְאָדָם דַּעַת, וּמְלַמֵּד לֶאֱנוֹשׁ בִּינָה. חָנֵּנוּ מֵאִתְּךָ דֵּעָה בִּינָה וְהַשְׂכֵּל. בָּרוּךְ אַתָּה יהוה, חוֹנֵן הַדָּעַת.

תשובה

הֲשִׁיבֵנוּ אָבִינוּ לְתוֹרָתֶךָ, וְקָרְבֵנוּ מַלְכֵּנוּ לַעֲבוֹדָתֶךָ, וְהַחֲזִירֵנוּ בִּתְשׁוּבָה שְׁלֵמָה לְפָנֶיךָ. בָּרוּךְ אַתָּה יהוה, הָרוֹצֶה בִּתְשׁוּבָה.

סליחה

Strike the left side of the chest with the right fist while reciting the words חָטָאנוּ and פָּשָׁעְנוּ.

סְלַח לָנוּ אָבִינוּ כִּי חָטָאנוּ, מְחַל לָנוּ מַלְכֵּנוּ כִּי פָשָׁעְנוּ, כִּי מוֹחֵל וְסוֹלֵחַ אָתָּה. בָּרוּךְ אַתָּה יהוה, חַנּוּן הַמַּרְבֶּה לִסְלוֹחַ.

קדושה

When reciting *Kedushah,* one must stand with his feet together, and avoid any interruptions. One should rise to his toes when saying the words קָדוֹשׁ, קָדוֹשׁ, קָדוֹשׁ; בָּרוּךְ (of בָּרוּךְ כְּבוֹד); and יִמְלֹךְ.

—Cong. then *Chazzan* **נְקַדֵּשׁ** אֶת שִׁמְךָ בָּעוֹלָם, כְּשֵׁם שֶׁמַּקְדִּישִׁים אוֹתוֹ בִּשְׁמֵי מָרוֹם, כַּכָּתוּב עַל יַד נְבִיאֶךָ, וְקָרָא זֶה אֶל זֶה וְאָמַר:

—All קָדוֹשׁ קָדוֹשׁ קָדוֹשׁ יהוה צְבָאוֹת, מְלֹא כָל הָאָרֶץ כְּבוֹדוֹ.[1]

—*Chazzan* לְעֻמָּתָם בָּרוּךְ יֹאמֵרוּ:

—All בָּרוּךְ כְּבוֹד יהוה, מִמְּקוֹמוֹ.[2]

—*Chazzan* וּבְדִבְרֵי קָדְשְׁךָ כָּתוּב לֵאמֹר:

—All יִמְלֹךְ יהוה לְעוֹלָם, אֱלֹהַיִךְ צִיּוֹן לְדֹר וָדֹר, הַלְלוּיָהּ.[3]

—*Chazzan* only concludes לְדוֹר וָדוֹר נַגִּיד גָּדְלֶךָ וּלְנֵצַח נְצָחִים קְדֻשָּׁתְךָ נַקְדִּישׁ, וְשִׁבְחֲךָ אֱלֹהֵינוּ מִפִּינוּ לֹא יָמוּשׁ לְעוֹלָם וָעֶד, כִּי אֵל מֶלֶךְ גָּדוֹל וְקָדוֹשׁ אָתָּה. בָּרוּךְ אַתָּה יהוה, °הָאֵל הַקָּדוֹשׁ.

°הַמֶּלֶךְ הַקָּדוֹשׁ. —From Rosh Hashanah to Yom Kippur substitute

Chazzan continues ... אַתָּה חוֹנֵן.

From Rosh Hashanah to Yom Kippur add:
Who is like You, Merciful Father, Who recalls His creatures mercifully for life!
[If forgotten, do not repeat *Shemoneh Esrei.* See *Laws* §61.]

And You are faithful to resuscitate the dead. Blessed are You, HASHEM, Who resuscitates the dead.

During the *chazzan's* repetition, *Kedushah* (below) is recited at this point.

HOLINESS OF GOD'S NAME

אַתָּה *You are holy and Your Name is holy, and holy ones praise You every day, forever. Blessed are You, HASHEM, °the holy God.*

°From Rosh Hashanah to Yom Kippur substitute: *the holy King.*
[If forgotten, repeat *Shemoneh Esrei.* See *Laws* §62-63.]

INSIGHT

אַתָּה *You graciously endow man with wisdom and teach insight to a frail mortal. Endow us graciously from Yourself with wisdom, insight, and discernment. Blessed are You, HASHEM, gracious Giver of wisdom.*

REPENTANCE

הֲשִׁיבֵנוּ *Bring us back, our Father, to Your Torah, and bring us near, our King, to Your service, and influence us to return in perfect repentance before You. Blessed are You, HASHEM, Who desires repentance.*

FORGIVENESS

Strike the left side of the chest with the right fist while reciting the words *'erred'* and *'sinned'.*

סְלַח *Forgive us, our Father, for we have erred; pardon us, our King, for we have willfully sinned; for You pardon and forgive. Blessed are You, HASHEM, the gracious One Who pardons abundantly.*

KEDUSHAH

When reciting *Kedushah,* one must stand with his feet together and avoid any interruptions. One should rise to his toes when saying the words *Holy, holy, holy; Blessed is;* and *HASHEM shall reign.*
(A commentary to *Kedushah* may be found on page 100.)

Cong. then Chazzan— **נְקַדֵּשׁ** *We shall sanctify Your Name in this world, just as they sanctify it in heaven above, as it is written by Your prophet, "And one [angel] will call another and say:*

All— *'Holy, holy, holy is HASHEM, Master of Legions, the whole world is filled with His glory.'"*[1]

Chazzan— *Those facing them say 'Blessed':*

All— *'Blessed is the glory of HASHEM from His place.'*[2]

Chazzan— *And in Your holy Writings the following is written:*

All— *'HASHEM shall reign forever — your God, O Zion — from generation to generation, Halleluyah!'*[3]

Chazzan only concludes— *From generation to generation we shall relate Your greatness and for infinite eternities we shall proclaim Your holiness. Your praise, our God, shall not leave our mouth forever and ever, for You O God, are a great and holy King. Blessed are You HASHEM, °the holy God.*

°From Rosh Hashanah to Yom Kippur substitute: *the holy King.*

Chazzan continues אַתָּה חוֹנֵן, *You graciously endow ...*

---

(1) *Isaiah* 6:3. (2) *Ezekiel* 3:12. (3) *Psalms* 146:10.

גאולה

רְאֵה בְעָנְיֵנוּ, וְרִיבָה רִיבֵנוּ, וּגְאָלֵנוּ[1] מְהֵרָה לְמַעַן שְׁמֶךָ, כִּי גוֹאֵל חָזָק אָתָּה. בָּרוּךְ אַתָּה יהוה, גּוֹאֵל יִשְׂרָאֵל.

On a fast day, the *chazzan* recites עֲנֵנוּ at this point. See *Laws* §85-87.
[If he forgot to recite it at this point, he may insert it in שְׁמַע קוֹלֵנוּ, p. 242.]

עֲנֵנוּ יהוה עֲנֵנוּ, בְּיוֹם צוֹם תַּעֲנִיתֵנוּ, כִּי בְצָרָה גְדוֹלָה אֲנָחְנוּ. אַל תֵּפֶן אֶל רִשְׁעֵנוּ, וְאַל תַּסְתֵּר פָּנֶיךָ מִמֶּנּוּ, וְאַל תִּתְעַלַּם מִתְּחִנָּתֵנוּ. הֱיֵה נָא קָרוֹב לְשַׁוְעָתֵנוּ, יְהִי נָא חַסְדְּךָ לְנַחֲמֵנוּ, טֶרֶם נִקְרָא אֵלֶיךָ עֲנֵנוּ, כַּדָּבָר שֶׁנֶּאֱמַר: וְהָיָה טֶרֶם יִקְרָאוּ וַאֲנִי אֶעֱנֶה, עוֹד הֵם מְדַבְּרִים וַאֲנִי אֶשְׁמָע.[2] כִּי אַתָּה יהוה הָעוֹנֶה בְּעֵת צָרָה, פּוֹדֶה וּמַצִּיל בְּכָל עֵת צָרָה וְצוּקָה. בָּרוּךְ אַתָּה יהוה, הָעוֹנֶה בְּעֵת צָרָה.

רפואה

רְפָאֵנוּ יהוה וְנֵרָפֵא, הוֹשִׁיעֵנוּ וְנִוָּשֵׁעָה, כִּי תְהִלָּתֵנוּ אָתָּה,[3] וְהַעֲלֵה רְפוּאָה שְׁלֵמָה לְכָל מַכּוֹתֵינוּ,°° כִּי אֵל מֶלֶךְ רוֹפֵא נֶאֱמָן וְרַחֲמָן אָתָּה. בָּרוּךְ אַתָּה יהוה, רוֹפֵא חוֹלֵי עַמּוֹ יִשְׂרָאֵל.

ברכת השנים

In the following blessing וְתֵן בְּרָכָה is recited from the beginning of Pesach through *Minchah* of December 4th (or 5th in the year before a civil leap year). וְתֵן טַל וּמָטָר לִבְרָכָה is recited from *Maariv* of December 4th (or 5th) until Pesach. [If the wrong phrase is recited, see *Laws*, §79-83.]

בָּרֵךְ עָלֵינוּ יהוה אֱלֹהֵינוּ אֶת הַשָּׁנָה הַזֹּאת וְאֶת כָּל מִינֵי תְבוּאָתָהּ לְטוֹבָה, (וְתֵן בְּרָכָה) (וְתֵן טַל וּמָטָר לִבְרָכָה) עַל פְּנֵי הָאֲדָמָה, וְשַׂבְּעֵנוּ מִטּוּבֶךָ, וּבָרֵךְ שְׁנָתֵנוּ כַּשָּׁנִים הַטּוֹבוֹת. בָּרוּךְ אַתָּה יהוה, מְבָרֵךְ הַשָּׁנִים.

קיבוץ גליות

תְּקַע בְּשׁוֹפָר גָּדוֹל לְחֵרוּתֵנוּ, וְשָׂא נֵס לְקַבֵּץ גָּלֻיּוֹתֵינוּ, וְקַבְּצֵנוּ יַחַד מֵאַרְבַּע כַּנְפוֹת הָאָרֶץ.[4] בָּרוּךְ אַתָּה יהוה, מְקַבֵּץ נִדְחֵי עַמּוֹ יִשְׂרָאֵל.

°°At this point one may interject a prayer for one who is ill:

יְהִי רָצוֹן מִלְּפָנֶיךָ יהוה אֱלֹהַי וֵאלֹהֵי אֲבוֹתַי, שֶׁתִּשְׁלַח מְהֵרָה רְפוּאָה שְׁלֵמָה מִן הַשָּׁמַיִם, רְפוּאַת הַנֶּפֶשׁ וּרְפוּאַת הַגּוּף

לַחוֹלֶה (patient's name) בֶּן (mother's name) בְּתוֹךְ שְׁאָר חוֹלֵי יִשְׂרָאֵל. —for a male

לַחוֹלָה (patient's name) בַּת (mother's name) בְּתוֹךְ שְׁאָר חוֹלֵי יִשְׂרָאֵל. —for a female

continue—כִּי אֵל ...

REDEMPTION

רְאֵה *Behold our affliction, take up our grievance, and redeem us*[1] *speedily for Your Name's sake, for You are a powerful Redeemer. Blessed are You, HASHEM, Redeemer of Israel.*

On a fast day, the chazzan recites עֲנֵנוּ, *'Answer us,'* at this point. See *Laws* §85-87. [If he forgot to recite it at this point, he may insert it in שְׁמַע קוֹלֵנוּ, 'Hear our voice' (p. 242).]

עֲנֵנוּ *Answer us, HASHEM, answer us, on this day of our fast, for we are in great distress. Do not pay attention to our wickedness; do not hide Your Face from us; and do not ignore our supplication. Please be near to our outcry; please let Your kindness comfort us — before we call to You answer us, as it is said: 'And it will be that before they call, I will answer; while they yet speak, I will hear.'*[2] *For You, HASHEM, are the One Who responds in time of distress, Who redeems and rescues in every time of distress and woe. Blessed are You, HASHEM, Who responds in time of distress.*

HEALTH AND HEALING

רְפָאֵנוּ *Heal us, HASHEM — then we will be healed; save us — then we will be saved, for You are our praise.*[3] *Bring complete recovery for all our ailments, °°for You are God, King, the faithful and compassionate Healer. Blessed are You, HASHEM, Who heals the sick of His people Israel.*

YEAR OF PROSPERITY

In the following blessing, *'give a blessing'* is recited from the beginning of Pesach through *Minchah* of December 4th (or 5th in the year before a civil leap year); *'give dew and rain for a blessing'* is recited from *Maariv* of December 4th (or 5th) until Pesach. [If the wrong phrase is recited, see *Laws*, §79-83.]

בָּרֵךְ *Bless on our behalf — O HASHEM, our God — this year and all its kinds of crops for the best, and give (dew and rain for) a blessing on the face of the earth, and satisfy us from Your bounty, and bless our year like the best years. Blessed are You, HASHEM, Who blesses the years.*

INGATHERING OF EXILES

תְּקַע *Sound the great shofar for our freedom, raise the banner to gather our exiles and gather us together from the four corners of the earth.*[4] *Blessed are You, HASHEM, Who gathers in the dispersed of His people Israel.*

°°At this point one may interject a prayer for one who is ill:

May it be Your will, HASHEM, my God, and the God of my forefathers, that You quickly send a complete recovery from heaven, spiritual healing and physical healing to the patient (name) son/daughter of (mother's name) among the other patients of Israel. Continue: *For You are God ...*

(1) Cf. *Psalms* 119:153-154. (2) *Isaiah* 65:24. (3) Cf. *Jeremiah* 17:14. (4) Cf. *Isaiah* 11:12.

דין

הָשִׁיבָה שׁוֹפְטֵינוּ כְּבָרִאשׁוֹנָה, וְיוֹעֲצֵינוּ כְּבַתְּחִלָּה,[1] וְהָסֵר מִמֶּנּוּ יָגוֹן וַאֲנָחָה, וּמְלוֹךְ עָלֵינוּ אַתָּה יהוה לְבַדְּךָ בְּחֶסֶד וּבְרַחֲמִים, וְצַדְּקֵנוּ בַּמִּשְׁפָּט. בָּרוּךְ אַתָּה יהוה, °מֶלֶךְ אוֹהֵב צְדָקָה וּמִשְׁפָּט.

°הַמֶּלֶךְ הַמִּשְׁפָּט. —From Rosh Hashanah to Yom Kippur substitute
[If forgotten, do not repeat *Shemoneh Esrei*. See *Laws* §64.]

ברכת המינים

וְלַמַּלְשִׁינִים אַל תְּהִי תִקְוָה, וְכָל הָרִשְׁעָה כְּרֶגַע תֹּאבֵד, וְכָל אֹיְבֶיךָ מְהֵרָה יִכָּרֵתוּ, וְהַזֵּדִים מְהֵרָה תְעַקֵּר וּתְשַׁבֵּר וּתְמַגֵּר וְתַכְנִיעַ בִּמְהֵרָה בְיָמֵינוּ. בָּרוּךְ אַתָּה יהוה, שׁוֹבֵר אֹיְבִים וּמַכְנִיעַ זֵדִים.

צדיקים

עַל הַצַּדִּיקִים וְעַל הַחֲסִידִים, וְעַל זִקְנֵי עַמְּךָ בֵּית יִשְׂרָאֵל, וְעַל פְּלֵיטַת סוֹפְרֵיהֶם, וְעַל גֵּרֵי הַצֶּדֶק וְעָלֵינוּ, יֶהֱמוּ רַחֲמֶיךָ יהוה אֱלֹהֵינוּ, וְתֵן שָׂכָר טוֹב לְכָל הַבּוֹטְחִים בְּשִׁמְךָ בֶּאֱמֶת, וְשִׂים חֶלְקֵנוּ עִמָּהֶם לְעוֹלָם, וְלֹא נֵבוֹשׁ כִּי בְךָ בָּטָחְנוּ. בָּרוּךְ אַתָּה יהוה, מִשְׁעָן וּמִבְטָח לַצַּדִּיקִים.

בנין ירושלים

וְלִירוּשָׁלַיִם עִירְךָ בְּרַחֲמִים תָּשׁוּב, וְתִשְׁכּוֹן בְּתוֹכָהּ כַּאֲשֶׁר דִּבַּרְתָּ, וּבְנֵה אוֹתָהּ בְּקָרוֹב בְּיָמֵינוּ בִּנְיַן עוֹלָם, וְכִסֵּא דָוִד מְהֵרָה לְתוֹכָהּ תָּכִין. °בָּרוּךְ אַתָּה יהוה, בּוֹנֵה יְרוּשָׁלָיִם.

°During *Minchah* of Tishah B'Av substitute the following conclusion.
[If forgotten, do not repeat *Shemoneh Esrei*.]

נַחֵם יהוה אֱלֹהֵינוּ אֶת אֲבֵלֵי צִיּוֹן, וְאֶת אֲבֵלֵי יְרוּשָׁלָיִם, וְאֶת הָעִיר הָאֲבֵלָה וְהַחֲרֵבָה וְהַבְּזוּיָה וְהַשּׁוֹמֵמָה. הָאֲבֵלָה מִבְּלִי בָנֶיהָ, וְהַחֲרֵבָה מִמְּעוֹנוֹתֶיהָ, וְהַבְּזוּיָה מִכְּבוֹדָהּ, וְהַשּׁוֹמֵמָה מֵאֵין יוֹשֵׁב. וְהִיא יוֹשֶׁבֶת וְרֹאשָׁהּ חָפוּי כְּאִשָּׁה עֲקָרָה שֶׁלֹּא יָלָדָה. וַיְבַלְּעוּהָ לִגְיוֹנוֹת, וַיִּירָשׁוּהָ עוֹבְדֵי זָרִים, וַיָּטִילוּ אֶת עַמְּךָ יִשְׂרָאֵל לֶחָרֶב, וַיַּהַרְגוּ בְזָדוֹן חֲסִידֵי עֶלְיוֹן. עַל כֵּן צִיּוֹן בְּמַר תִּבְכֶּה, וִירוּשָׁלַיִם תִּתֵּן קוֹלָהּ. לִבִּי לִבִּי עַל חַלְלֵיהֶם, מֵעַי מֵעַי עַל חַלְלֵיהֶם, כִּי אַתָּה יהוה בָּאֵשׁ הִצַּתָּהּ, וּבָאֵשׁ אַתָּה עָתִיד לִבְנוֹתָהּ, כָּאָמוּר: וַאֲנִי אֶהְיֶה לָּהּ, נְאֻם יהוה, חוֹמַת אֵשׁ סָבִיב וּלְכָבוֹד אֶהְיֶה בְתוֹכָהּ.[2] בָּרוּךְ אַתָּה יהוה, מְנַחֵם צִיּוֹן וּבוֹנֵה יְרוּשָׁלָיִם.

continue—...אֶת צֶמַח

RESTORATION OF JUSTICE

הָשִׁיבָה *Restore our judges as in earliest times and our counselors as at first;*[1] *remove from us sorrow and groan; and reign over us — You,* Hashem*, alone — with kindness and compassion, and justify us through judgment. Blessed are You,* Hashem*, the °King Who loves righteousness and judgment.*

°From Rosh Hashanah to Yom Kippur substitute: *the King of judgment.*
[If forgotten, do not repeat *Shemoneh Esrei.* See *Laws* §64.]

AGAINST HERETICS

וְלַמַּלְשִׁינִים *And for slanderers let there be no hope; and may all wickedness perish in an instant; and may all Your enemies be cut down speedily. May You speedily uproot, smash, cast down, and humble the wanton sinners — speedily in our days. Blessed are You,* Hashem*, Who breaks enemies and humbles wanton sinners.*

THE RIGHTEOUS

עַל הַצַּדִּיקִים *On the righteous, on the devout, on the elders of Your people the Family of Israel, on the remnant of their scholars, on the righteous converts and on ourselves — may Your compassion be aroused,* Hashem*, our God, and give goodly reward to all who sincerely believe in Your Name. Put our lot with them forever, and we will not feel ashamed, for we trust in You. Blessed are You,* Hashem*, Mainstay and Assurance of the righteous.*

REBUILDING JERUSALEM

וְלִירוּשָׁלַיִם *And to Jerusalem, Your city, may You return in compassion, and may You rest within it, as You have spoken. May You rebuild it soon in our days as an eternal structure, and may you speedily establish the throne of David within it. °°Blessed are You,* Hashem*, the Builder of Jerusalem.*

°During *Minchah* of Tishah B'Av substitute the following conclusion.
[If forgotten, do not repeat *Shemoneh Esrei.*]

נַחֵם O *Hashem, our God, console the mourners of Zion and the mourners of Jerusalem, and the city that is mournful, ruined, scorned, and desolate: mournful without her children, ruined without her abodes, scorned without her glory, and desolate without inhabitant. She sits with covered head like a barren woman who never gave birth. Legions have devoured her, and idolaters have conquered her; they have cast Your people Israel to the sword and wantonly murdered the devout servants of the Supreme One. Therefore, Zion weeps bitterly and Jerusalem raises her voice. My heart, my heart — [it aches] for their slain! My innards, my innards — [they ache] for their slain! For You* Hashem*, with fire You consumed her and with fire You will rebuild her, as it is said: 'I will be for her, the words of* Hashem*, a wall of fire around and I will be glorious in her midst.'*[2] *Blessed are You,* Hashem*, Who consoles Zion and rebuilds Jerusalem.*

Continue: *The offspring ...*

(1) Cf. *Isaiah* 1:26. (2) *Zechariah* 2:9.

נַחֵם — *Console.* On Tishah B'Av, the anniversary of both Temple's destructions, the prayer for Jerusalem is concluded with this poignant insertion. In the prophetic manner, it uses Jerusalem as the metaphor for the entire Jewish exile experience. It depicts Jerusalem as a lonely, bereaved mother and closes with confidence in God's pledge of future redemption.

מלכות בית דוד

אֶת צֶמַח דָּוִד עַבְדְּךָ מְהֵרָה תַצְמִיחַ, וְקַרְנוֹ תָּרוּם בִּישׁוּעָתֶךָ, כִּי לִישׁוּעָתְךָ קִוִּינוּ כָּל הַיּוֹם. בָּרוּךְ אַתָּה יהוה, מַצְמִיחַ קֶרֶן יְשׁוּעָה.

קבלת תפלה

שְׁמַע קוֹלֵנוּ יהוה אֱלֹהֵינוּ, חוּס וְרַחֵם עָלֵינוּ, וְקַבֵּל בְּרַחֲמִים וּבְרָצוֹן אֶת תְּפִלָּתֵנוּ, כִּי אֵל שׁוֹמֵעַ תְּפִלּוֹת וְתַחֲנוּנִים אָתָּה. וּמִלְּפָנֶיךָ מַלְכֵּנוּ רֵיקָם אַל תְּשִׁיבֵנוּ.°° כִּי אַתָּה שׁוֹמֵעַ תְּפִלַּת עַמְּךָ יִשְׂרָאֵל בְּרַחֲמִים. בָּרוּךְ אַתָּה יהוה, שׁוֹמֵעַ תְּפִלָּה.

עבודה

רְצֵה יהוה אֱלֹהֵינוּ בְּעַמְּךָ יִשְׂרָאֵל וּבִתְפִלָּתָם, וְהָשֵׁב אֶת הָעֲבוֹדָה לִדְבִיר בֵּיתֶךָ. וְאִשֵּׁי יִשְׂרָאֵל וּתְפִלָּתָם בְּאַהֲבָה תְקַבֵּל בְּרָצוֹן, וּתְהִי לְרָצוֹן תָּמִיד עֲבוֹדַת יִשְׂרָאֵל עַמֶּךָ.

°°On fast days, including *Tishah B'Av,* one who is fasting adds the following. [If forgotten, do not repeat *Shemoneh Esrei.*]

עֲנֵנוּ יהוה עֲנֵנוּ, בְּיוֹם צוֹם תַּעֲנִיתֵנוּ, כִּי בְצָרָה גְדוֹלָה אֲנָחְנוּ. אַל תֵּפֶן אֶל רִשְׁעֵנוּ, וְאַל תַּסְתֵּר פָּנֶיךָ מִמֶּנּוּ, וְאַל תִּתְעַלַּם מִתְּחִנָּתֵנוּ. הֱיֵה נָא קָרוֹב לְשַׁוְעָתֵנוּ, יְהִי נָא חַסְדְּךָ לְנַחֲמֵנוּ, טֶרֶם נִקְרָא אֵלֶיךָ עֲנֵנוּ, כַּדָּבָר שֶׁנֶּאֱמַר: וְהָיָה טֶרֶם יִקְרָאוּ וַאֲנִי אֶעֱנֶה, עוֹד הֵם מְדַבְּרִים וַאֲנִי אֶשְׁמָע.[1] כִּי אַתָּה יהוה הָעוֹנֶה בְּעֵת צָרָה, פּוֹדֶה וּמַצִּיל בְּכָל עֵת צָרָה וְצוּקָה.

Continue —כִּי אַתָּה ...

°°During the silent *Shemoneh Esrei* one may insert either or both of these personal prayers.

For forgiveness:

אָנָּא יהוה, חָטָאתִי עָוִיתִי וּפָשַׁעְתִּי לְפָנֶיךָ, מִיּוֹם הֱיוֹתִי עַל הָאֲדָמָה עַד הַיּוֹם הַזֶּה (וּבִפְרַט בַּחֵטְא ....). אָנָּא יהוה, עֲשֵׂה לְמַעַן שִׁמְךָ הַגָּדוֹל, וּתְכַפֶּר לִי עַל עֲוֹנַי וַחֲטָאַי וּפְשָׁעַי שֶׁחָטָאתִי וְשֶׁעָוִיתִי וְשֶׁפָּשַׁעְתִּי לְפָנֶיךָ, מִנְּעוּרַי עַד הַיּוֹם הַזֶּה. וּתְמַלֵּא כָּל הַשֵּׁמוֹת שֶׁפָּגַמְתִּי בְּשִׁמְךָ הַגָּדוֹל.

For livelihood:

אַתָּה הוּא יהוה הָאֱלֹהִים, הַזָּן וּמְפַרְנֵס וּמְכַלְכֵּל מִקַּרְנֵי רְאֵמִים עַד בֵּיצֵי כִנִּים. הַטְרִיפֵנִי לֶחֶם חֻקִּי, וְהַמְצֵא לִי וּלְכָל בְּנֵי בֵיתִי מְזוֹנוֹתַי קוֹדֶם שֶׁאֶצְטָרֵךְ לָהֶם, בְּנַחַת וְלֹא בְצַעַר, בְּהֶתֵּר וְלֹא בְאִסּוּר, בְּכָבוֹד וְלֹא בְבִזָּיוֹן, לְחַיִּים וּלְשָׁלוֹם, מִשֶּׁפַע בְּרָכָה וְהַצְלָחָה, וּמִשֶּׁפַע בְּרֵכָה עֶלְיוֹנָה, כְּדֵי שֶׁאוּכַל לַעֲשׂוֹת רְצוֹנֶךָ וְלַעֲסוֹק בְּתוֹרָתֶךָ וּלְקַיֵּם מִצְוֹתֶיךָ. וְאַל תַּצְרִיכֵנִי לִידֵי מַתְּנַת בָּשָׂר וָדָם. וִיקֻיַּם בִּי מִקְרָא שֶׁכָּתוּב: פּוֹתֵחַ אֶת יָדֶךָ, וּמַשְׂבִּיעַ לְכָל חַי רָצוֹן.[2] וְכָתוּב: הַשְׁלֵךְ עַל יהוה יְהָבְךָ וְהוּא יְכַלְכְּלֶךָ.[3]

Continue —כִּי אַתָּה ...

DAVIDIC REIGN

אֶת צֶמַח *The offspring of Your servant David may You speedily cause to flourish, and enhance his pride through Your salvation, for we hope for Your salvation all day long. Blessed are You, HASHEM, Who causes the pride of salvation to flourish.*

ACCEPTANCE OF PRAYER

שְׁמַע קוֹלֵנוּ *Hear our voice, HASHEM our God, pity and be compassionate to us, and accept — with compassion and favor — our prayer, for God Who hears prayers and supplications are You. From before Yourself, our King, turn us not away empty-handed.°° For You hear the prayer of Your people Israel with compassion. Blessed are You, HASHEM, Who hears prayer.*

TEMPLE SERVICE

רְצֵה *Be favorable, HASHEM, our God, toward Your people Israel and their prayer and restore the service to the Holy of Holies of Your Temple. The fire-offerings of Israel and their prayer accept with love and favor, and may the service of Your people Israel always be favorable to You.*

°°On fast days, including Tishah B'Av, one who is fasting adds the following. [If forgotten, do not repeat *Shemoneh Esrei*.]

עֲנֵנוּ *Answer us, HASHEM, answer us, on this day of our fast, for we are in great distress. Do not pay attention to our wickedness; do not hide Your Face from us; and do not ignore our supplication. Please be near to our outcry; please let Your kindness comfort us — before we call to You answer us, as it is said: 'And it will be that before they call, I will answer; while they yet speak, I will hear.'[1] For You, HASHEM, are the One Who responds in time of distress, Who redeems and rescues in every time of distress and woe.* Continue: *For You hear the prayer...*

°°During the silent *Shemoneh Esrei* one may insert either or both of these personal prayers.

For forgiveness:

אָנָּא *Please, O HASHEM, I have erred, been iniquitous, and willfully sinned before You, from the day I have existed on earth until this very day (and especially with the sin of ...). Please, HASHEM, act for the sake of Your Great Name and grant me atonement for my iniquities, my errors, and my willful sins through which I have erred, been iniquitous, and willfully sinned before You, from my youth until this day. And make whole all the Names that I have blemished in Your Great Name.*

For livelihood:

אַתָּה *It is You, HASHEM the God, Who nourishes, sustains, and supports, from the horns of re'eimim to the eggs of lice. Provide me with my allotment of bread; and bring forth for me and all members of my household, my food, before I have need for it; in contentment but not in pain, in a permissible but not a forbidden manner, in honor but not in disgrace, for life and for peace; from the flow of blessing and success and from the flow of the Heavenly spring, so that I be enabled to do Your will and engage in Your Torah and fulfill Your commandments. Make me not needful of people's largesse; and may there be fulfilled in me the verse that states, 'You open Your hand and satisfy the desire of every living thing'[2] and that states, 'Cast Your burden upon HASHEM and He will support you.'[3]*

Continue: *For You hear the prayer ...*

(1) *Isaiah* 65:24. (2) *Psalms* 145:16. (3) 55:23.

On Rosh Chodesh and Chol HaMoed add the following paragraph:
(During the *chazzan's* repetition, the congregation responds אָמֵן as indicated).

אֱלֹהֵינוּ וֵאלֹהֵי אֲבוֹתֵינוּ, יַעֲלֶה, וְיָבֹא, וְיַגִּיעַ, וְיֵרָאֶה, וְיֵרָצֶה, וְיִשָּׁמַע, וְיִפָּקֵד, וְיִזָּכֵר זִכְרוֹנֵנוּ וּפִקְדוֹנֵנוּ, וְזִכְרוֹן אֲבוֹתֵינוּ, וְזִכְרוֹן מָשִׁיחַ בֶּן דָּוִד עַבְדֶּךָ, וְזִכְרוֹן יְרוּשָׁלַיִם עִיר קָדְשֶׁךָ, וְזִכְרוֹן כָּל עַמְּךָ בֵּית יִשְׂרָאֵל לְפָנֶיךָ, לִפְלֵיטָה לְטוֹבָה, לְחֵן וּלְחֶסֶד וּלְרַחֲמִים, לְחַיִּים וּלְשָׁלוֹם בְּיוֹם

on Rosh Chodesh: רֹאשׁ הַחֹדֶשׁ | on Pesach: חַג הַמַּצּוֹת | on Succos: חַג הַסֻּכּוֹת

הַזֶּה. זָכְרֵנוּ יהוה אֱלֹהֵינוּ בּוֹ לְטוֹבָה (Cong. — אָמֵן), וּפָקְדֵנוּ בוֹ לִבְרָכָה (Cong. — אָמֵן), וְהוֹשִׁיעֵנוּ בוֹ לְחַיִּים (Cong. — אָמֵן). וּבִדְבַר יְשׁוּעָה וְרַחֲמִים, חוּס וְחָנֵּנוּ וְרַחֵם עָלֵינוּ וְהוֹשִׁיעֵנוּ, כִּי אֵלֶיךָ עֵינֵינוּ, כִּי אֵל מֶלֶךְ חַנּוּן וְרַחוּם אָתָּה.[1]

[If forgotten, repeat *Shemoneh Esrei*. See *Laws* §89.]

וְתֶחֱזֶינָה עֵינֵינוּ בְּשׁוּבְךָ לְצִיּוֹן בְּרַחֲמִים. בָּרוּךְ אַתָּה יהוה, הַמַּחֲזִיר שְׁכִינָתוֹ לְצִיּוֹן.

הודאה

Bow at מוֹדִים; straighten up at ה׳. In his repetition the *chazzan* should recite the entire מוֹדִים aloud, while the congregation recites מוֹדִים דְּרַבָּנָן softly.

מוֹדִים אֲנַחְנוּ לָךְ שָׁאַתָּה הוּא יהוה אֱלֹהֵינוּ וֵאלֹהֵי אֲבוֹתֵינוּ לְעוֹלָם וָעֶד. צוּר חַיֵּינוּ, מָגֵן יִשְׁעֵנוּ אַתָּה הוּא לְדוֹר וָדוֹר. נוֹדֶה לְּךָ וּנְסַפֵּר תְּהִלָּתֶךָ[2] עַל חַיֵּינוּ הַמְּסוּרִים בְּיָדֶךָ, וְעַל נִשְׁמוֹתֵינוּ הַפְּקוּדוֹת לָךְ, וְעַל נִסֶּיךָ שֶׁבְּכָל יוֹם עִמָּנוּ, וְעַל נִפְלְאוֹתֶיךָ וְטוֹבוֹתֶיךָ שֶׁבְּכָל עֵת, עֶרֶב וָבֹקֶר וְצָהֳרָיִם. הַטּוֹב כִּי לֹא כָלוּ רַחֲמֶיךָ, וְהַמְּרַחֵם כִּי לֹא תַמּוּ חֲסָדֶיךָ,[3] מֵעוֹלָם קִוִּינוּ לָךְ.

מודים דרבנן

מוֹדִים אֲנַחְנוּ לָךְ, שָׁאַתָּה הוּא יהוה אֱלֹהֵינוּ וֵאלֹהֵי אֲבוֹתֵינוּ, אֱלֹהֵי כָל בָּשָׂר, יוֹצְרֵנוּ, יוֹצֵר בְּרֵאשִׁית. בְּרָכוֹת וְהוֹדָאוֹת לְשִׁמְךָ הַגָּדוֹל וְהַקָּדוֹשׁ, עַל שֶׁהֶחֱיִיתָנוּ וְקִיַּמְתָּנוּ. כֵּן תְּחַיֵּנוּ וּתְקַיְּמֵנוּ, וְתֶאֱסוֹף גָּלֻיּוֹתֵינוּ לְחַצְרוֹת קָדְשֶׁךָ, לִשְׁמוֹר חֻקֶּיךָ וְלַעֲשׂוֹת רְצוֹנֶךָ, וּלְעָבְדְּךָ בְּלֵבָב שָׁלֵם, עַל שֶׁאֲנַחְנוּ מוֹדִים לָךְ. בָּרוּךְ אֵל הַהוֹדָאוֹת.

On Chanukah and Purim add:

(וְ)עַל הַנִּסִּים, וְעַל הַפֻּרְקָן, וְעַל הַגְּבוּרוֹת, וְעַל הַתְּשׁוּעוֹת, וְעַל הַמִּלְחָמוֹת, שֶׁעָשִׂיתָ לַאֲבוֹתֵינוּ בַּיָּמִים הָהֵם בַּזְּמַן הַזֶּה.

On Chanukah:

בִּימֵי מַתִּתְיָהוּ בֶּן יוֹחָנָן כֹּהֵן גָּדוֹל חַשְׁמוֹנַאי וּבָנָיו, כְּשֶׁעָמְדָה מַלְכוּת יָוָן הָרְשָׁעָה עַל עַמְּךָ יִשְׂרָאֵל, לְהַשְׁכִּיחָם תּוֹרָתֶךָ, וּלְהַעֲבִירָם מֵחֻקֵּי רְצוֹנֶךָ. וְאַתָּה

On Purim:

בִּימֵי מָרְדְּכַי וְאֶסְתֵּר בְּשׁוּשַׁן הַבִּירָה, כְּשֶׁעָמַד עֲלֵיהֶם הָמָן הָרָשָׁע, בִּקֵּשׁ לְהַשְׁמִיד

(1) Cf. *Nechemiah* 9:31. (2) Cf. *Psalms* 79:13. (3) Cf. *Lamentations* 3:22.

On Rosh Chodesh and Chol HaMoed add the following paragraph:
(During the *chazzan's* repetition, the congregation responds *Amen* as indicated.)

אֱלֹהֵינוּ *Our God and God of our forefathers, may there rise, come, reach, be noted, be favored, be heard, be considered, and be remembered — the remembrance and consideration of ourselves; the remembrance of our forefathers; the remembrance of Messiah, son of David, Your servant; the remembrance of Jerusalem, the City of Your Holiness, the remembrance of Your entire people the Family of Israel — before You, for deliverance, for goodness, for grace, for kindness, and for compassion, for life, and for peace on this day of*

on Rosh Chodesh	on Passover	on Succos
Rosh Chodesh	*the Festival of Matzos*	*the Festival of Succos.*

Remember us on it, HASHEM, our God, for goodness (Cong.— *Amen); consider us on it for blessing* (Cong.— *Amen); and help us on it for life* (Cong.— *Amen). In the matter of salvation and compassion, pity, be gracious and compassionate with us and help us, for our eyes are turned to You, because You are God, the gracious, and compassionate King.*[1] [If forgotten, repeat *Shemoneh Esrei.* See Laws, §89.]

וְתֶחֱזֶינָה *May our eyes behold Your return to Zion in compassion. Blessed are You, HASHEM, Who restores His Presence to Zion.*

THANKSGIVING [MODIM]

Bow at *'We gratefully thank You';* straighten up at *'HASHEM'.* In his repetition the *chazzan* should recite the entire *Modim* aloud, while the congregation recites *Modim of the Rabbis* softly.

מוֹדִים *We gratefully thank You, for it is You Who are HASHEM, our God and the God of our forefathers for all eternity; Rock of our lives, Shield of our salvation are You from generation to generation. We shall thank You and relate Your praise*[2] *— for our lives, which are committed to Your power and for our souls that are entrusted to You; for Your miracles that are with us every day; and for Your wonders and favors in every season — evening, morning, and afternoon. The Beneficent One, for Your compassions were never exhausted, and the Compassionate One, for Your kindnesses never ended*[3] *— always have we put our hope in You.*

MODIM OF THE RABBIS

מוֹדִים *We gratefully thank You, for it is You Who are HASHEM, our God and the God of our forefathers, the God of all flesh, our Molder, the Molder of the universe. Blessings and thanks are due Your great and holy Name for You have given us life and sustained us. So may You continue to give us life and sustain us and gather our exiles to the Courtyards of Your Sanctuary, to observe Your decrees, to do Your will and to serve You wholeheartedly. [We thank You] for inspiring us to thank You. Blessed is the God of thanksgivings.*

On Chanukah and Purim add:

(וְ)עַל *(And) for the miracles, and for the salvation, and for the mighty deeds, and for the victories, and for the battles which You performed for our forefathers in those days, at this time.*

On Chanukah:

בִּימֵי *In the days of Mattisyahu, the son of Yochanan, the High Priest, the Hasmonean, and his sons — when the wicked Greek kingdom rose up against Your people Israel to make them forget Your Torah and compel them to stray from the statutes of Your Will — You in Your great mercy stood up for them in the time*

On Purim:

בִּימֵי *In the days of Mordechai and Esther, in Shushan, the capital, when Haman, the wicked, rose up against them and sought to destroy, to slay,*

On Chanukah:

בְּרַחֲמֶיךָ הָרַבִּים, עָמַדְתָּ לָהֶם בְּעֵת צָרָתָם, רַבְתָּ אֶת רִיבָם, דַּנְתָּ אֶת דִּינָם, נָקַמְתָּ אֶת נִקְמָתָם.[1] מָסַרְתָּ גִּבּוֹרִים בְּיַד חַלָּשִׁים, וְרַבִּים בְּיַד מְעַטִּים, וּטְמֵאִים בְּיַד טְהוֹרִים, וּרְשָׁעִים בְּיַד צַדִּיקִים, וְזֵדִים בְּיַד עוֹסְקֵי תוֹרָתֶךָ. וּלְךָ עָשִׂיתָ שֵׁם גָּדוֹל וְקָדוֹשׁ בְּעוֹלָמֶךָ, וּלְעַמְּךָ יִשְׂרָאֵל עָשִׂיתָ תְּשׁוּעָה גְדוֹלָה[2] וּפֻרְקָן כְּהַיּוֹם הַזֶּה. וְאַחַר כֵּן בָּאוּ בָנֶיךָ לִדְבִיר בֵּיתֶךָ, וּפִנּוּ אֶת הֵיכָלֶךָ, וְטִהֲרוּ אֶת מִקְדָּשֶׁךָ, וְהִדְלִיקוּ נֵרוֹת בְּחַצְרוֹת קָדְשֶׁךָ, וְקָבְעוּ שְׁמוֹנַת יְמֵי חֲנֻכָּה אֵלּוּ, לְהוֹדוֹת וּלְהַלֵּל לְשִׁמְךָ הַגָּדוֹל.

On Purim:

לַהֲרֹג וּלְאַבֵּד אֶת כָּל הַיְּהוּדִים, מִנַּעַר וְעַד זָקֵן, טַף וְנָשִׁים בְּיוֹם אֶחָד, בִּשְׁלוֹשָׁה עָשָׂר לְחֹדֶשׁ שְׁנֵים עָשָׂר, הוּא חֹדֶשׁ אֲדָר, וּשְׁלָלָם לָבוֹז.[3] וְאַתָּה בְּרַחֲמֶיךָ הָרַבִּים הֵפַרְתָּ אֶת עֲצָתוֹ, וְקִלְקַלְתָּ אֶת מַחֲשַׁבְתּוֹ, וַהֲשֵׁבוֹתָ לּוֹ גְּמוּלוֹ בְּרֹאשׁוֹ, וְתָלוּ אוֹתוֹ וְאֶת בָּנָיו עַל הָעֵץ.

[If forgotten, do not repeat *Shemoneh Esrei*. See *Laws* §90.]

וְעַל כֻּלָּם יִתְבָּרַךְ וְיִתְרוֹמַם שִׁמְךָ מַלְכֵּנוּ תָּמִיד לְעוֹלָם וָעֶד.

From Rosh Hashanah to Yom Kippur add:

וּכְתוֹב לְחַיִּים טוֹבִים כָּל בְּנֵי בְרִיתֶךָ.

[If forgotten, do not repeat *Shemoneh Esrei*. See *Laws* §61.]

Bend the knees at בָּרוּךְ; bow at אַתָּה; straighten up at 'ה.

וְכֹל הַחַיִּים יוֹדוּךָ סֶּלָה, וִיהַלְלוּ אֶת שִׁמְךָ בֶּאֱמֶת, הָאֵל יְשׁוּעָתֵנוּ וְעֶזְרָתֵנוּ סֶלָה. בָּרוּךְ אַתָּה יהוה, הַטּוֹב שִׁמְךָ וּלְךָ נָאֶה לְהוֹדוֹת.

ברכת כהנים

On public fast days only, the *chazzan's* repetition includes the Priestly Blessing, except in a house of mourning. *Chazzan* faces to the right at וְיִשְׁמְרֶךָ and to the left at פָּנָיו אֵלֶיךָ וִיחֻנֶּךָּ.

אֱלֹהֵינוּ, וֵאלֹהֵי אֲבוֹתֵינוּ, בָּרְכֵנוּ בַבְּרָכָה הַמְּשֻׁלֶּשֶׁת, בַּתּוֹרָה הַכְּתוּבָה עַל יְדֵי מֹשֶׁה עַבְדֶּךָ, הָאֲמוּרָה מִפִּי אַהֲרֹן וּבָנָיו, כֹּהֲנִים עַם קְדוֹשֶׁךָ, כָּאָמוּר:

יְבָרֶכְךָ יהוה, וְיִשְׁמְרֶךָ. (Cong.— כֵּן יְהִי רָצוֹן.)

יָאֵר יהוה פָּנָיו אֵלֶיךָ וִיחֻנֶּךָּ. (Cong.— כֵּן יְהִי רָצוֹן.)

יִשָּׂא יהוה פָּנָיו אֵלֶיךָ וְיָשֵׂם לְךָ שָׁלוֹם.[4] (Cong.— כֵּן יְהִי רָצוֹן.)

שלום

שָׁלוֹם רָב עַל יִשְׂרָאֵל עַמְּךָ תָּשִׂים* לְעוֹלָם, כִּי אַתָּה הוּא מֶלֶךְ אָדוֹן לְכָל הַשָּׁלוֹם. וְטוֹב בְּעֵינֶיךָ* לְבָרֵךְ אֶת עַמְּךָ יִשְׂרָאֵל בְּכָל עֵת וּבְכָל שָׁעָה בִּשְׁלוֹמֶךָ.

On public fast days substitute:

שִׂים שָׁלוֹם, טוֹבָה, וּבְרָכָה, חֵן, וָחֶסֶד וְרַחֲמִים עָלֵינוּ וְעַל כָּל יִשְׂרָאֵל עַמֶּךָ. בָּרְכֵנוּ אָבִינוּ, כֻּלָּנוּ כְּאֶחָד בְּאוֹר פָּנֶיךָ, כִּי בְאוֹר פָּנֶיךָ נָתַתָּ לָּנוּ, יהוה אֱלֹהֵינוּ, תּוֹרַת חַיִּים וְאַהֲבַת חֶסֶד, וּצְדָקָה, וּבְרָכָה, וְרַחֲמִים, וְחַיִּים, וְשָׁלוֹם. וְטוֹב בְּעֵינֶיךָ לְבָרֵךְ אֶת עַמְּךָ יִשְׂרָאֵל, בְּכָל עֵת וּבְכָל שָׁעָה בִּשְׁלוֹמֶךָ.

On Chanukah:

of their distress. You took up their grievance, judged their claim, and avenged their wrong.[1] You delivered the strong into the hands of the weak, the many into the hands of the few, the impure into the hands of the pure, the wicked into the hands of the righteous, and the wanton into the hands of the diligent students of Your Torah. For Yourself You made a great and holy Name in Your world, and for Your people Israel you worked a great victory[2] and salvation as this very day. Thereafter, Your children came to the Holy of Holies of Your House, cleansed Your Temple, purified the site of Your Holiness and kindled lights in the Courtyards of Your Sanctuary; and they established these eight days of Chanukah to express thanks and praise to Your great Name.

On Purim:

and to exterminate all the Jews, young and old, infants and women, on the same day, on the thirteenth of the twelfth month which is the month of Adar, and to plunder their possessions.[3] But You, in Your abundant mercy, nullified his counsel and frustrated his intention and caused his design to return upon his own head and they hanged him and his sons on the gallows.

[If forgotten, do not repeat *Shemoneh Esrei.* See *Laws* §90.]

For all these, may Your Name be blessed and exalted, our King, continually forever and ever.

From Rosh Hashanah to Yom Kippur add the following.

And inscribe all the children of Your covenant for a good life.

If forgotten, do not repeat *Shemoneh Esrei.* See *Laws* §61.]

Bend the knees at *'Blessed'*; bow at *'You'*; straighten up at *'HASHEM'*.

Everything alive will gratefully acknowledge You, Selah! and praise Your Name sincerely, O God of our salvation and help, Selah! Blessed are You, HASHEM, Your Name is 'The Beneficent One' and to You it is fitting to give thanks.

THE PRIESTLY BLESSING

On public fast days only, the *chazzan's* repetition includes the Priestly Blessings, except in a house of mourning.

אֱלֹהֵינוּ *Our God and the God of our forefathers, bless us with the three-verse blessing in the Torah that was written by the hand of Moses, Your servant, that was said by Aaron and his sons, the Kohanim, Your holy people, as it is said:*

May HASHEM bless you and safeguard you. (Cong.— *So may it be.*)

May HASHEM illuminate His countenance for you and be gracious to you. (Cong.— *So may it be.*)

May HASHEM turn His countenance to you and establish peace for you.[4] (Cong.— *So may it be.*)

PEACE

שָׁלוֹם רָב *Establish abundant peace* upon Your people Israel forever, for You are King, Master of all peace. May it be good in Your eyes* to bless Your people Israel at every time and every hour with Your peace.*

On public fast days substitute:

שִׂים *Establish peace, goodness, blessing, graciousness, kindness, and compassion upon us and upon all of Your people Israel. Bless us, our Father, all of us equally with the light of Your Face, for with the light of Your Face You gave us, HASHEM, our God, the Torah of life and a love of kindness, righteousness, blessing, compassion, life, and peace. And may it be good in Your eyes to bless your people Israel, in every season and in every hour with Your Peace.*

(1) Cf. *Jeremiah* 51:36. (2) Cf. *I Samuel* 19:5. (3) *Esther* 3:13. (4) *Numbers* 6:24-26.

°בָּרוּךְ אַתָּה יהוה, הַמְּבָרֵךְ אֶת עַמּוֹ יִשְׂרָאֵל בַּשָּׁלוֹם.

°From Rosh Hashanah to Yom Kippur substitute the following [see *Laws* §65]:

בְּסֵפֶר חַיִּים בְּרָכָה וְשָׁלוֹם, וּפַרְנָסָה טוֹבָה, נִזָּכֵר וְנִכָּתֵב לְפָנֶיךָ, אֲנַחְנוּ וְכָל עַמְּךָ בֵּית יִשְׂרָאֵל, לְחַיִּים טוֹבִים וּלְשָׁלוֹם. בָּרוּךְ אַתָּה יהוה, עוֹשֵׂה הַשָּׁלוֹם.

[If forgotten, do not repeat *Shemoneh Esrei*. See *Laws* §61.]

The *chazzan's* repetition of *Shemoneh Esrei* ends here. Individuals continue to bottom of page.

יִהְיוּ לְרָצוֹן אִמְרֵי פִי וְהֶגְיוֹן לִבִּי לְפָנֶיךָ, יהוה צוּרִי וְגֹאֲלִי.[1]

On Erev Yom Kippur the וִדּוּי, *Confessional* (page 776), is recited by individuals.

אֱלֹהַי, נְצוֹר לְשׁוֹנִי מֵרָע, וּשְׂפָתַי מִדַּבֵּר מִרְמָה,[2] וְלִמְקַלְלַי נַפְשִׁי תִדּוֹם, וְנַפְשִׁי כֶּעָפָר לַכֹּל תִּהְיֶה. פְּתַח לִבִּי בְּתוֹרָתֶךָ, וּבְמִצְוֹתֶיךָ תִּרְדּוֹף נַפְשִׁי. וְכֹל הַחוֹשְׁבִים עָלַי רָעָה, מְהֵרָה הָפֵר עֲצָתָם וְקַלְקֵל מַחֲשַׁבְתָּם. עֲשֵׂה לְמַעַן שְׁמֶךָ, עֲשֵׂה לְמַעַן יְמִינֶךָ, עֲשֵׂה לְמַעַן קְדֻשָּׁתֶךָ, עֲשֵׂה לְמַעַן תּוֹרָתֶךָ. לְמַעַן יֵחָלְצוּן יְדִידֶיךָ, הוֹשִׁיעָה יְמִינְךָ וַעֲנֵנִי.[3]

Some recite verses pertaining to their names at this point. See page 924.

°°יִהְיוּ לְרָצוֹן אִמְרֵי פִי וְהֶגְיוֹן לִבִּי לְפָנֶיךָ, יהוה צוּרִי וְגֹאֲלִי.[1] עֹשֶׂה שָׁלוֹם בִּמְרוֹמָיו, הוּא יַעֲשֶׂה שָׁלוֹם עָלֵינוּ, וְעַל כָּל יִשְׂרָאֵל. וְאִמְרוּ: אָמֵן.

יְהִי רָצוֹן מִלְּפָנֶיךָ יהוה אֱלֹהֵינוּ וֵאלֹהֵי אֲבוֹתֵינוּ, שֶׁיִּבָּנֶה בֵּית הַמִּקְדָּשׁ בִּמְהֵרָה בְיָמֵינוּ, וְתֵן חֶלְקֵנוּ בְּתוֹרָתֶךָ. וְשָׁם נַעֲבָדְךָ בְּיִרְאָה, כִּימֵי עוֹלָם וּכְשָׁנִים קַדְמוֹנִיּוֹת. וְעָרְבָה לַיהוה מִנְחַת יְהוּדָה וִירוּשָׁלָיִם, כִּימֵי עוֹלָם וּכְשָׁנִים קַדְמוֹנִיּוֹת.[4]

THE INDIVIDUAL'S RECITATION OF שְׁמוֹנֶה עֶשְׂרֵה ENDS HERE.

°°An individual who wishes to accept a fast upon himself recites the following declaration at this point during *Minchah* (or afterwards while it is still daytime) of the day before his fast:

רִבּוֹן כָּל הָעוֹלָמִים, הֲרֵי אֲנִי לְפָנֶיךָ בְּתַעֲנִית נְדָבָה לְמָחָר. יְהִי רָצוֹן מִלְּפָנֶיךָ יהוה אֱלֹהַי וֵאלֹהֵי אֲבוֹתַי, שֶׁתְּקַבְּלֵנִי בְּאַהֲבָה וּבְרָצוֹן, וְתָבֹא לְפָנֶיךָ תְּפִלָּתִי, וְתַעֲנֶה עֲתִירָתִי בְּרַחֲמֶיךָ הָרַבִּים. כִּי אַתָּה שׁוֹמֵעַ תְּפִלַּת כָּל פֶּה.

At *Minchah* on the afternoon of the fast, the following is recited:

רִבּוֹן כָּל הָעוֹלָמִים, גָּלוּי וְיָדוּעַ לְפָנֶיךָ, בִּזְמַן שֶׁבֵּית הַמִּקְדָּשׁ קַיָּם אָדָם חוֹטֵא וּמֵבִיא קָרְבָּן, וְאֵין מַקְרִיבִים מִמֶּנּוּ אֶלָּא חֶלְבּוֹ וְדָמוֹ, וְאַתָּה בְּרַחֲמֶיךָ הָרַבִּים מְכַפֵּר. וְעַכְשָׁו יָשַׁבְתִּי בְתַעֲנִית, וְנִתְמַעֵט חֶלְבִּי וְדָמִי. יְהִי רָצוֹן מִלְּפָנֶיךָ שֶׁיְּהֵא מִעוּט חֶלְבִּי וְדָמִי שֶׁנִּתְמַעֵט הַיּוֹם, כְּאִלּוּ הִקְרַבְתִּיו לְפָנֶיךָ עַל גַּב הַמִּזְבֵּחַ, וְתִרְצֵנִי.

⁂ שָׁלוֹם רָב ... תָּשִׂים — *Establish abundant peace.* The consensus of commentators is that שָׁלוֹם רָב, *abundant peace,* is the standard text of this blessing during *Minchah,* and that שִׂים שָׁלוֹם, *Establish peace,* is recited only at times when the Priestly Blessings are recited, because it alludes to those blessings. See p. 117.

אֲדוֹן לְכָל הַשָּׁלוֹם ... וְטוֹב בְּעֵינֶיךָ — *Master of all peace. May it be good in Your eyes.* For a blessing to come true, there must be two

°*Blessed are You, HASHEM, Who blesses His people Israel with peace.*

°From Rosh Hashanah to Yom Kippur substitute the following [see *Laws* §65]:

In the book of life, blessing, and peace, good livelihood, may we be remembered and inscribed before You — we and Your entire people the Family of Israel for a good life and for peace. Blessed are You, HASHEM, Who makes peace.

[If forgotten, do not repeat *Shemoneh Esrei*. See *Laws* §61.]

The *chazzan's* repetition of *Shemoneh Esrei* ends here. Individuals continue to bottom of page.

May the expressions of my mouth and the thoughts of my heart find favor before You, HASHEM, my Rock and my Redeemer.[1]

On Erev Yom Kippur the וִדּוּי, *Confessional* (page 776), is recited by individuals.

אֱלֹהַי *My God, guard my tongue from evil and my lips from speaking deceitfully.*[2] *To those who curse me, let my soul be silent; and let my soul be like dust to everyone. Open my heart to Your Torah, then my soul will pursue Your commandments. As for all those who design evil against me, speedily nullify their counsel and disrupt their design. Act for Your Name's sake; act for Your right hand's sake; act for Your sanctity's sake; act for Your Torah's sake. That Your beloved ones may be given rest; let Your right hand save, and respond to me.*[3]

Some recite verses pertaining to their names at this point. See page 924.

°°*May the expressions of my mouth and the thoughts of my heart find favor before You, HASHEM, my Rock and my Redeemer.*[1] *He Who makes peace in His heights, may He make peace upon us, and upon all Israel. Now respond: Amen.*

יְהִי רָצוֹן *May it be Your will, HASHEM our God and the God of our forefathers, that the Holy Temple be rebuilt, speedily in our days. Grant us our share in Your Torah, and may we serve You there with reverence, as in days of old and in former years. Then the offering of Judah and Jerusalem will be pleasing to HASHEM, as in days of old and in former years.*[4]

THE INDIVIDUAL'S RECITATION OF *SHEMONEH ESREI* ENDS HERE.

°°An individual who wishes to accept a fast upon himself recites the following declaration at this point during *Minchah* (or afterwards while it is still daytime) of the day before his fast:

רִבּוֹן *Master of all the worlds, I come before You [to accept] a voluntary fast for tomorrow. May it be Your will, HASHEM, my God and the God of my forefathers, that You accept me with love and favor, that my prayer come before You, and that You answer my entreaty in Your abundant mercy, for You hear the prayer of every mouth.*

At *Minchah* on the afternoon of the fast, the following is recited:

רִבּוֹן *Master of all the worlds, it is revealed and known before You that in the time when the Holy Temple existed, if someone sinned, he brought an offering — yet nothing of it was offered [on the Altar] except for its fat and blood, yet You in Your abundant mercy would atone. Now I have engaged in a fast and my own fat and blood have been diminished. May it be Your will that the diminution of my fat and blood that was diminished today should be as if I had offered it upon the Altar and may You show me favor.*

(1) *Psalms* 19:15. (2) Cf. 34:14. (3) 60:7; 108:7. (4) *Malachi* 3:4.

conditions: (a) the one from whom the blessing is sought must have the power to confer it, and (b) he must be willing to do so. Therefore, we declare that God is the *Master of all peace* and we pray that *it be good in* [His] *eyes* to bestow it upon us *(Acharis Shalom).*

The individual remains standing in place until the *chazzan* reaches *Kedushah* — or at least until the *chazzan* begins his repetition — then he takes three steps forward. The *chazzan* himself, or one praying alone, should remain in place for a few moments before taking three steps forward.

On most weekdays *Minchah* continues with *Tachanun,* whether or not a *minyan* is present. However, *Tachanun* is omitted in the evening in the event that *Minchah* begins late (see p. 132 for laws of *Tachanun*). On most fast days and from Rosh Hashanah to Yom Kippur insert אָבִינוּ מַלְכֵּנוּ (p. 120) before *Tachanun.* See page 125 for days when *Tachanun* is omitted. On those days, the *chazzan* goes directly to קַדִּישׁ שָׁלֵם (p. 252); individuals go on to עָלֵינוּ.

תחנון/נפילת אפים

In the presence of a Torah Scroll the following (until יֵבֹשׁוּ רָגַע) is recited with the head resting on the left arm, preferably while seated. Elsewhere, it is recited with the head erect. [Commentary on p. 132.]

וַיֹּאמֶר דָּוִד אֶל גָּד, צַר לִי מְאֹד, נִפְּלָה נָּא בְיַד יהוה, כִּי רַבִּים רַחֲמָיו, וּבְיַד אָדָם אַל אֶפְּלָה.[1]

רַחוּם וְחַנּוּן חָטָאתִי לְפָנֶיךָ. יהוה מָלֵא רַחֲמִים, רַחֵם עָלַי וְקַבֵּל תַּחֲנוּנָי.

תהלים ו:ב-יא

יהוה אַל בְּאַפְּךָ תוֹכִיחֵנִי, וְאַל בַּחֲמָתְךָ תְיַסְּרֵנִי. חָנֵּנִי יהוה, כִּי אֻמְלַל אָנִי, רְפָאֵנִי יהוה, כִּי נִבְהֲלוּ עֲצָמָי. וְנַפְשִׁי נִבְהֲלָה מְאֹד, וְאַתָּה יהוה, עַד מָתָי. שׁוּבָה יהוה, חַלְּצָה נַפְשִׁי, הוֹשִׁיעֵנִי לְמַעַן חַסְדֶּךָ. כִּי אֵין בַּמָּוֶת זִכְרֶךָ, בִּשְׁאוֹל מִי יוֹדֶה לָּךְ. יָגַעְתִּי בְּאַנְחָתִי, אַשְׂחֶה בְכָל לַיְלָה מִטָּתִי, בְּדִמְעָתִי עַרְשִׂי אַמְסֶה. עָשְׁשָׁה מִכַּעַס עֵינִי, עָתְקָה בְּכָל צוֹרְרָי. סוּרוּ מִמֶּנִּי כָּל פֹּעֲלֵי אָוֶן, כִּי שָׁמַע יהוה קוֹל בִּכְיִי. שָׁמַע יהוה תְּחִנָּתִי, יהוה תְּפִלָּתִי יִקָּח. יֵבֹשׁוּ וְיִבָּהֲלוּ מְאֹד כָּל אֹיְבָי, יָשֻׁבוּ יֵבֹשׁוּ רָגַע.

Sit up erect and recite:

שׁוֹמֵר יִשְׂרָאֵל, שְׁמוֹר שְׁאֵרִית יִשְׂרָאֵל, וְאַל יֹאבַד יִשְׂרָאֵל, הָאֹמְרִים, שְׁמַע יִשְׂרָאֵל.

שׁוֹמֵר גּוֹי אֶחָד, שְׁמוֹר שְׁאֵרִית עַם אֶחָד, וְאַל יֹאבַד גּוֹי אֶחָד, הַמְּיַחֲדִים שִׁמְךָ, יהוה אֱלֹהֵינוּ יהוה אֶחָד.

שׁוֹמֵר גּוֹי קָדוֹשׁ, שְׁמוֹר שְׁאֵרִית עַם קָדוֹשׁ, וְאַל יֹאבַד גּוֹי קָדוֹשׁ, הַמְשַׁלְּשִׁים בְּשָׁלֹשׁ קְדֻשּׁוֹת לְקָדוֹשׁ.

מִתְרַצֶּה בְרַחֲמִים וּמִתְפַּיֵּס בְּתַחֲנוּנִים, הִתְרַצֶּה וְהִתְפַּיֵּס לְדוֹר עָנִי, כִּי אֵין עוֹזֵר. אָבִינוּ מַלְכֵּנוּ, חָנֵּנוּ וַעֲנֵנוּ, כִּי אֵין בָּנוּ מַעֲשִׂים, עֲשֵׂה עִמָּנוּ צְדָקָה וָחֶסֶד וְהוֹשִׁיעֵנוּ.

Stand up after the words וַאֲנַחְנוּ לֹא נֵדַע, until the conclusion of the paragraph.

וַאֲנַחְנוּ לֹא נֵדַע מַה נַּעֲשֶׂה, כִּי עָלֶיךָ עֵינֵינוּ.[2] זְכֹר רַחֲמֶיךָ יהוה וַחֲסָדֶיךָ, כִּי מֵעוֹלָם הֵמָּה.[3] יְהִי חַסְדְּךָ

The individual remains standing in place until the *chazzan* reaches *Kedushah* — or at least until the *chazzan* begins his repetition — then he takes three steps forward. The *chazzan* himself, or one praying alone, should remain in place for a few moments before taking three steps forward.

On most weekdays *Minchah* continues with *Tachanun,* whether or not a *minyan* is present. However, *Tachanun* is omitted in the evening in the event that *Minchah* begins late (see p. 132 for laws of *Tachanun*). On most fast days and from Rosh Hashanah to Yom Kippur insert אָבִינוּ מַלְכֵּנוּ (p. 120) before *Tachanun.* See page 125 for days when *Tachanun* is omitted. On those days, the *chazzan* goes directly to Full-*Kaddish* (p. 252); individuals go on to עָלֵינוּ.

TACHANUN/PUTTING DOWN THE HEAD

Recite until *'instantly shamed'* with the head resting on the left arm, preferably while seated.

וַיֹּאמֶר דָּוִד *And David said to Gad, 'I am exceedingly distressed. Let us fall into* HASHEM*'s hand for His mercies are abundant, but let me not fall into human hands.'*[1]

O compassionate and gracious One, I have sinned before You. HASHEM, *Who is full of mercy, have mercy on me and accept my supplications.*

Psalms 6:2-11

יהוה HASHEM, *do not rebuke me in Your anger, nor chastise me in Your rage. Favor me,* HASHEM, *for I am feeble; heal me,* HASHEM, *for my bones shudder. My soul is utterly confounded, and You,* HASHEM, *how long? Desist,* HASHEM, *release my soul; save me as befits Your kindness. For there is no mention of You in death; in the Lower World who will thank You? I am wearied with my sigh, every night I drench my bed, with my tears I soak my couch. My eye is dimmed because of anger, aged by my tormentors. Depart from me, all evildoers, for* HASHEM *has heard the sound of my weeping.* HASHEM *has heard my plea,* HASHEM *will accept my prayer. Let all my foes be shamed and utterly confounded, they will regret and be instantly shamed.*

Sit up erect and recite:

שׁוֹמֵר יִשְׂרָאֵל *O Guardian of Israel, protect the remnant of Israel; let not Israel be destroyed — those who proclaim, 'Hear O Israel.'*

*O Guardian of the unique nation, protect the remnant of the unique people; let not the unique nation be destroyed — those who proclaim the Oneness of Your Name, '*HASHEM *is our God,* HASHEM *— the One and Only!'*

O Guardian of the holy nation, protect the remnant of the holy people; let not the holy nation be destroyed — those who proclaim three-fold sanctifications to the Holy One.

Become favorable through compassion and become appeased through supplications. Become favorable and appeased to the poor generation for there is no helper. Our Father, our King — be gracious with us and answer us, though we have no worthy deeds; treat us with charity and kindness, and save us.

Stand up after the words *'We know not,* until the conclusion of the paragraph.

וַאֲנַחְנוּ *We know not what to do — but our eyes are upon You.*[2] *Remember Your mercies,* HASHEM, *and Your kindness, for they are from the beginning of the world.*[3] *May Your kindness be*

(1) *II Samuel* 24:14. (2) *II Chronicles* 20:12. (3) *Psalms* 25:6.

יהוה עָלֵינוּ, כַּאֲשֶׁר יִחַלְנוּ לָךְ.[1] אַל תִּזְכָּר לָנוּ עֲוֹנוֹת רִאשׁוֹנִים, מַהֵר יְקַדְּמוּנוּ רַחֲמֶיךָ, כִּי דַלּוֹנוּ מְאֹד.[2] חָנֵּנוּ יהוה חָנֵּנוּ, כִּי רַב שָׂבַעְנוּ בוּז.[3] בְּרֹגֶז רַחֵם תִּזְכּוֹר.[4] כִּי הוּא יָדַע יִצְרֵנוּ, זָכוּר כִּי עָפָר אֲנָחְנוּ.[5] עָזְרֵנוּ אֱלֹהֵי יִשְׁעֵנוּ עַל דְּבַר כְּבוֹד שְׁמֶךָ, וְהַצִּילֵנוּ וְכַפֵּר עַל חַטֹּאתֵינוּ לְמַעַן שְׁמֶךָ.[6]

The *chazzan* recites קַדִּישׁ שָׁלֵם:

יִתְגַּדַּל וְיִתְקַדַּשׁ שְׁמֵהּ רַבָּא. (.Cong —אָמֵן.) בְּעָלְמָא דִּי בְרָא כִרְעוּתֵהּ. וְיַמְלִיךְ מַלְכוּתֵהּ, בְּחַיֵּיכוֹן וּבְיוֹמֵיכוֹן וּבְחַיֵּי דְכָל בֵּית יִשְׂרָאֵל, בַּעֲגָלָא וּבִזְמַן קָרִיב. וְאִמְרוּ: אָמֵן.

(.Cong— אָמֵן. יְהֵא שְׁמֵהּ רַבָּא מְבָרַךְ לְעָלַם וּלְעָלְמֵי עָלְמַיָּא.)

יְהֵא שְׁמֵהּ רַבָּא מְבָרַךְ לְעָלַם וּלְעָלְמֵי עָלְמַיָּא.

יִתְבָּרַךְ וְיִשְׁתַּבַּח וְיִתְפָּאַר וְיִתְרוֹמַם וְיִתְנַשֵּׂא וְיִתְהַדָּר וְיִתְעַלֶּה וְיִתְהַלָּל שְׁמֵהּ דְּקֻדְשָׁא בְּרִיךְ הוּא (.Cong— בְּרִיךְ הוּא) — °לְעֵלָּא מִן כָּל (From Rosh Hashanah to Yom Kippur substitute— °לְעֵלָּא וּלְעֵלָּא מִכָּל) בִּרְכָתָא וְשִׁירָתָא תֻּשְׁבְּחָתָא וְנֶחֱמָתָא, דַּאֲמִירָן בְּעָלְמָא. וְאִמְרוּ: אָמֵן. (.Cong— אָמֵן.)

(.Cong—קַבֵּל בְּרַחֲמִים וּבְרָצוֹן אֶת תְּפִלָּתֵנוּ.)

תִּתְקַבֵּל צְלוֹתְהוֹן וּבָעוּתְהוֹן דְּכָל בֵּית יִשְׂרָאֵל קֳדָם אֲבוּהוֹן דִּי בִשְׁמַיָּא. וְאִמְרוּ: אָמֵן. (.Cong— אָמֵן.)

(.Cong—יְהִי שֵׁם יהוה מְבֹרָךְ, מֵעַתָּה וְעַד עוֹלָם.[7])

יְהֵא שְׁלָמָא רַבָּא מִן שְׁמַיָּא, וְחַיִּים עָלֵינוּ וְעַל כָּל יִשְׂרָאֵל. וְאִמְרוּ: אָמֵן. (.Cong— אָמֵן.)

(.Cong—עֶזְרִי מֵעִם יהוה, עֹשֵׂה שָׁמַיִם וָאָרֶץ.[8])

Take three steps back. Bow left and say ... עֹשֶׂה; bow right and say ... הוּא; bow forward and say וְעַל כָּל ... אָמֵן. Remain standing in place for a few moments, then take three steps forward.

עֹשֶׂה שָׁלוֹם בִּמְרוֹמָיו, הוּא יַעֲשֶׂה שָׁלוֹם עָלֵינוּ, וְעַל כָּל יִשְׂרָאֵל. וְאִמְרוּ: אָמֵן. (.Cong— אָמֵן.)

Stand while reciting עָלֵינוּ.

עָלֵינוּ לְשַׁבֵּחַ לַאֲדוֹן הַכֹּל, לָתֵת גְּדֻלָּה לְיוֹצֵר בְּרֵאשִׁית, שֶׁלֹּא עָשָׂנוּ כְּגוֹיֵי הָאֲרָצוֹת, וְלֹא שָׂמָנוּ כְּמִשְׁפְּחוֹת הָאֲדָמָה. שֶׁלֹּא שָׂם חֶלְקֵנוּ כָּהֶם, וְגוֹרָלֵנוּ כְּכָל הֲמוֹנָם. (שֶׁהֵם מִשְׁתַּחֲוִים לְהֶבֶל וָרִיק, וּמִתְפַּלְלִים אֶל אֵל לֹא יוֹשִׁיעַ.[9]) וַאֲנַחְנוּ כּוֹרְעִים וּמִשְׁתַּחֲוִים וּמוֹדִים, לִפְנֵי מֶלֶךְ מַלְכֵי הַמְּלָכִים הַקָּדוֹשׁ בָּרוּךְ הוּא. שֶׁהוּא נוֹטֶה שָׁמַיִם וְיֹסֵד אָרֶץ,[10] וּמוֹשַׁב יְקָרוֹ בַּשָּׁמַיִם מִמַּעַל, וּשְׁכִינַת עֻזּוֹ בְּגָבְהֵי מְרוֹמִים. הוּא אֱלֹהֵינוּ, אֵין עוֹד. אֱמֶת מַלְכֵּנוּ, אֶפֶס זוּלָתוֹ,

Bow while reciting וַאֲנַחְנוּ כּוֹרְעִים וּמִשְׁתַּחֲוִים.

upon us, Hashem, just as we awaited you.[1] *Recall not against us the sins of the ancients; may Your mercies meet us swiftly, for we have become exceedingly impoverished.*[2] *Be gracious to us, Hashem, be gracious to us, for we are abundantly sated with scorn.*[3] *Amid rage — remember to be merciful!*[4] *For He knew our nature, He remembers that we are dust.*[5] *Assist us, O God of our salvation, for the sake of Your Name's glory; rescue us and atone for our sins for Your Name's sake.*[6]

FULL KADDISH

The *chazzan* recites the Full *Kaddish:*

יִתְגַּדַּל *May His great Name grow exalted and sanctified* (Cong.— *Amen.*) *in the world that He created as He willed. May He give reign to His kingship in your lifetimes and in your days, and in the lifetimes of the entire Family of Israel, swiftly and soon. Now respond: Amen.*

(Cong.— *Amen. May His great Name be blessed forever and ever.*)

May His great Name be blessed forever and ever.

Blessed, praised, glorified, exalted, extolled, mighty, upraised, and lauded be the Name of the Holy One, Blessed is He (Cong.— *Blessed is He*) — (From Rosh Hashanah to Yom Kippur add: *exceedingly*) *beyond any blessing and song, praise and consolation that are uttered in the world. Now respond: Amen.* (Cong.— *Amen*).

(Cong.— *Accept our prayers with mercy and favor.*)

May the prayers and supplications of the entire Family of Israel be accepted before their Father Who is in Heaven. Now respond: Amen. (Cong.— *Amen.*)

(Cong.— *Blessed be the Name of Hashem from this time and forever.*[7])

May there be abundant peace from Heaven, and life, upon us and upon all Israel. Now respond: Amen. (Cong.— *Amen.*)

(Cong.— *My help is from Hashem, Maker of heaven and earth.*[8])

Take three steps back. Bow left and say, *'He Who makes peace ...';* bow right and say, *'may He ...';* bow forward and say, *'and upon all Israel ...'* Remain standing in place for a few moments, then take three steps forward.

He Who makes peace in His heights, may He make peace upon us, and upon all Israel. Now respond: Amen. (Cong.—*Amen.*)

Stand while reciting עָלֵינוּ, *'It is our duty...'*

עָלֵינוּ ***It is our duty to praise the Master of all, to ascribe greatness to the Molder of primeval creation, for He has not made us like the nations of the lands and has not emplaced us like the families of the earth; for He has not assigned our portion like theirs nor our lot like all their multitudes. (For they bow to vanity and emptiness and pray to a god which helps not.***[9]***) But we bend our knees, bow, and acknowledge our thanks before the King Who reigns over kings, the Holy One, Blessed is He. He stretches out heaven and establishes earth's foundation,***[10] ***the seat of His homage is in the heavens above and His powerful Presence is in the loftiest heights. He is our God and there is none other. True is our King, there is***

Bow while reciting *'But we bend our knees.'*

(1) *Psalms* 33:22. (2) 79:8. (3) 123:3. (4) *Habakkuk* 3:2. (5) *Psalms* 103:14. (6) 79:9. (7) 113:2. (8) 121:2. (9) *Isaiah* 45:20. (10) 51:13.

כַּכָּתוּב בְּתוֹרָתוֹ: וְיָדַעְתָּ הַיּוֹם וַהֲשֵׁבֹתָ אֶל לְבָבֶךָ, כִּי יהוה הוּא הָאֱלֹהִים בַּשָּׁמַיִם מִמַּעַל וְעַל הָאָרֶץ מִתָּחַת, אֵין עוֹד.[1]

עַל כֵּן נְקַוֶּה לְךָ* יהוה אֱלֹהֵינוּ לִרְאוֹת מְהֵרָה בְּתִפְאֶרֶת עֻזֶּךָ, לְהַעֲבִיר גִּלּוּלִים מִן הָאָרֶץ, וְהָאֱלִילִים כָּרוֹת יִכָּרֵתוּן, לְתַקֵּן עוֹלָם בְּמַלְכוּת שַׁדַּי. וְכָל בְּנֵי בָשָׂר יִקְרְאוּ בִשְׁמֶךָ, לְהַפְנוֹת אֵלֶיךָ כָּל רִשְׁעֵי אָרֶץ. יַכִּירוּ וְיֵדְעוּ כָּל יוֹשְׁבֵי תֵבֵל, כִּי לְךָ תִּכְרַע כָּל בֶּרֶךְ, תִּשָּׁבַע כָּל לָשׁוֹן.[4] לְפָנֶיךָ יהוה אֱלֹהֵינוּ יִכְרְעוּ וְיִפֹּלוּ, וְלִכְבוֹד שִׁמְךָ יְקָר יִתֵּנוּ. וִיקַבְּלוּ כֻלָּם אֶת עוֹל מַלְכוּתֶךָ, וְתִמְלֹךְ עֲלֵיהֶם מְהֵרָה לְעוֹלָם וָעֶד. כִּי הַמַּלְכוּת שֶׁלְּךָ הִיא וּלְעוֹלְמֵי עַד תִּמְלוֹךְ בְּכָבוֹד, כַּכָּתוּב בְּתוֹרָתֶךָ: יהוה יִמְלֹךְ לְעֹלָם וָעֶד.[5] ❖ וְנֶאֱמַר: וְהָיָה יהוה לְמֶלֶךְ עַל כָּל הָאָרֶץ, בַּיּוֹם הַהוּא יִהְיֶה יהוה אֶחָד וּשְׁמוֹ אֶחָד.[6]

In some congregations the following is recited after עָלֵינוּ:

אַל תִּירָא מִפַּחַד פִּתְאֹם, וּמִשֹּׁאַת רְשָׁעִים כִּי תָבֹא.[5] עֻצוּ עֵצָה וְתֻפָר, דַּבְּרוּ דָבָר וְלֹא יָקוּם, כִּי עִמָּנוּ אֵל.[6] וְעַד זִקְנָה אֲנִי הוּא, וְעַד שֵׂיבָה אֲנִי אֶסְבֹּל, אֲנִי עָשִׂיתִי וַאֲנִי אֶשָּׂא, וַאֲנִי אֶסְבֹּל וַאֲמַלֵּט.[7]

קדיש יתום

In the presence of a *minyan,* mourners recite קַדִּישׁ יָתוֹם, the Mourner's *Kaddish* (see *Laws* §119):

יִתְגַּדַּל וְיִתְקַדַּשׁ שְׁמֵהּ רַבָּא. (.Cong— אָמֵן.) בְּעָלְמָא דִּי בְרָא כִרְעוּתֵהּ. וְיַמְלִיךְ מַלְכוּתֵהּ, בְּחַיֵּיכוֹן וּבְיוֹמֵיכוֹן וּבְחַיֵּי דְכָל בֵּית יִשְׂרָאֵל, בַּעֲגָלָא וּבִזְמַן קָרִיב. וְאִמְרוּ: אָמֵן.

(.Cong— אָמֵן. יְהֵא שְׁמֵהּ רַבָּא מְבָרַךְ לְעָלַם וּלְעָלְמֵי עָלְמַיָּא.)

יְהֵא שְׁמֵהּ רַבָּא מְבָרַךְ לְעָלַם וּלְעָלְמֵי עָלְמַיָּא.

יִתְבָּרַךְ וְיִשְׁתַּבַּח וְיִתְפָּאַר וְיִתְרוֹמַם וְיִתְנַשֵּׂא וְיִתְהַדָּר וְיִתְעַלֶּה וְיִתְהַלָּל שְׁמֵהּ דְּקֻדְשָׁא בְּרִיךְ הוּא (.Cong— בְּרִיךְ הוּא) — °לְעֵלָּא מִן כָּל (From Rosh Hashanah to Yom Kippur substitute— °לְעֵלָּא וּלְעֵלָּא מִכָּל) בִּרְכָתָא וְשִׁירָתָא תֻּשְׁבְּחָתָא וְנֶחֱמָתָא, דַּאֲמִירָן בְּעָלְמָא. וְאִמְרוּ: אָמֵן. (.Cong— אָמֵן.)

יְהֵא שְׁלָמָא רַבָּא מִן שְׁמַיָּא, וְחַיִּים עָלֵינוּ וְעַל כָּל יִשְׂרָאֵל. וְאִמְרוּ: אָמֵן. (.Cong— אָמֵן.)

Take three steps back. Bow left and say ... עֹשֶׂה; bow right and say ... הוּא; bow forward and say וְעַל כָּל ... אָמֵן. Remain standing in place for a few moments, then take three steps forward.

עֹשֶׂה שָׁלוֹם בִּמְרוֹמָיו, הוּא יַעֲשֶׂה שָׁלוֹם עָלֵינוּ, וְעַל כָּל יִשְׂרָאֵל. וְאִמְרוּ: אָמֵן. (.Cong— אָמֵן.)

In the synagogue, Chanukah lights are kindled between *Minchah* and *Maariv.* See p. 782.

nothing beside Him, as it is written in His Torah: 'You are to know this day and take to your heart that HASHEM is the only God — in heaven above and on the earth below — there is none other.'[1]

עַל כֵּן *Therefore we put our hope in You, HASHEM our God, that we may soon see Your mighty splendor, to remove detestable idolatry from the earth, and false gods will be utterly cut off, to perfect the universe through the Almighty's sovereignty. Then all humanity will call upon Your Name, to turn all the earth's wicked toward You. All the world's inhabitants will recognize and know that to You every knee should bend, every tongue should swear.*[2] *Before You, HASHEM, our God, they will bend every knee and cast themselves down and to the glory of Your Name they will render homage, and they will all accept upon themselves the yoke of Your kingship that You may reign over them soon and eternally. For the kingdom is Yours and You will reign for all eternity in glory as it is written in Your Torah: HASHEM shall reign for all eternity.*[3] Chazzan — *And it is said: HASHEM will be King over all the world — on that day HASHEM will be One and His Name will be One.*[4]

Some congregations recite the following after *Aleinu.*

אַל תִּירָא *Do not fear sudden terror, or the holocaust of the wicked when it comes.*[5] *Plan a conspiracy and it will be annulled; speak your piece and it shall not stand, for God is with us.*[6] *Even till your seniority, I remain unchanged; and even till your ripe old age, I shall endure. I created you and I shall bear you; I shall endure and rescue.*[7]

MOURNER'S KADDISH

In the presence of a *minyan,* mourners recite קַדִּישׁ יָתוֹם, the Mourner's *Kaddish* (see *Laws* §119):

[A transliteration of this *Kaddish* appears on page 1043, and commentary on p. 57.]

יִתְגַּדַּל *May His great Name grow exalted and sanctified* (Cong.— *Amen.*) *in the world that He created as He willed. May He give reign to His kingship in your lifetimes and in your days, and in the lifetimes of the entire Family of Israel, swiftly and soon. Now respond: Amen.*

(Cong.— *Amen. May His great Name be blessed forever and ever.*)

May His great Name be blessed forever and ever.

Blessed, praised, glorified, exalted, extolled, mighty, upraised, and lauded be the Name of the Holy One, Blessed is He (Cong.— *Blessed is He*) — (From Rosh Hashanah to Yom Kippur add: *exceedingly*) *beyond any blessing and song, praise and consolation that are uttered in the world. Now respond: Amen.* (Cong.— *Amen.*)

May there be abundant peace from Heaven, and life, upon us and upon all Israel. Now respond: Amen. (Cong.— *Amen.*)

Take three steps back. Bow left and say, *'He Who makes peace ...';* bow right and say, *'may He ...';* bow forward and say, *'and upon all Israel ...'* Remain standing in place for a few moments, then take three steps forward.

He Who makes peace in His heights, may He make peace upon us, and upon all Israel. Now respond: Amen. (Cong.— *Amen.*)

In the synagogue, Chanukah lights are kindled between *Minchah* and *Maariv.* See p. 782.

(1) *Deuteronomy* 4:39. (2) Cf. *Isaiah* 45:23. (3) *Exodus* 15:18. (4) *Zechariah* 14:9.
(5) *Proverbs* 3:25. (6) *Isaiah* 8:10. (7) 46:4.

מעריב לחול ולמוצאי שבת

Congregation, then *chazzan:*

וְהוּא רַחוּם יְכַפֵּר עָוֹן וְלֹא יַשְׁחִית, וְהִרְבָּה לְהָשִׁיב אַפּוֹ, וְלֹא יָעִיר כָּל חֲמָתוֹ.[1] יהוה הוֹשִׁיעָה, הַמֶּלֶךְ יַעֲנֵנוּ בְיוֹם קָרְאֵנוּ.[2]

In some congregations the *chazzan* chants a melody during his recitation of בָּרְכוּ so that the congregation can then recite יִתְבָּרַךְ.

Chazzan bows at בָּרְכוּ and straightens up at ה׳.

בָּרְכוּ אֶת יהוה הַמְּבֹרָךְ.

Congregation, followed by *chazzan,* responds, bowing at בָּרוּךְ and straightening up at ה׳.

בָּרוּךְ יהוה הַמְּבֹרָךְ לְעוֹלָם וָעֶד.

יִתְבָּרַךְ וְיִשְׁתַּבַּח וְיִתְפָּאַר וְיִתְרוֹמַם וְיִתְנַשֵּׂא שְׁמוֹ שֶׁל מֶלֶךְ מַלְכֵי הַמְּלָכִים, הַקָּדוֹשׁ בָּרוּךְ הוּא. שֶׁהוּא רִאשׁוֹן וְהוּא אַחֲרוֹן, וּמִבַּלְעָדָיו אֵין אֱלֹהִים.[3] סֹלּוּ, לָרֹכֵב בָּעֲרָבוֹת, בְּיָהּ שְׁמוֹ, וְעִלְזוּ לְפָנָיו.[4] וּשְׁמוֹ מְרוֹמָם עַל כָּל בְּרָכָה וּתְהִלָּה.[5] בָּרוּךְ שֵׁם כְּבוֹד מַלְכוּתוֹ לְעוֹלָם וָעֶד. יְהִי שֵׁם יהוה מְבֹרָךְ, מֵעַתָּה וְעַד עוֹלָם.[6]

ברכות קריאת שמע

בָּרוּךְ אַתָּה יהוה אֱלֹהֵינוּ מֶלֶךְ הָעוֹלָם, אֲשֶׁר בִּדְבָרוֹ* מַעֲרִיב עֲרָבִים, בְּחָכְמָה פּוֹתֵחַ שְׁעָרִים,* וּבִתְבוּנָה מְשַׁנֶּה עִתִּים,* וּמַחֲלִיף אֶת הַזְּמַנִּים, וּמְסַדֵּר אֶת הַכּוֹכָבִים בְּמִשְׁמְרוֹתֵיהֶם בָּרָקִיעַ כִּרְצוֹנוֹ. בּוֹרֵא יוֹם וָלָיְלָה, גּוֹלֵל אוֹר מִפְּנֵי חֹשֶׁךְ וְחֹשֶׁךְ מִפְּנֵי אוֹר. וּמַעֲבִיר יוֹם וּמֵבִיא לָיְלָה, וּמַבְדִּיל

מַעֲרִיב / THE EVENING SERVICE

Like *Shacharis* and *Minchah, Maariv* has its basis in the Temple service. In the Temple, no sacrifices were offered in the evening, but any sacrificial parts that had not been burned during the day could be placed on the Altar and burned at night. Thus, although no sacrificial service was *required* during the night, it was uncommon for the Altar not to be in use. This explains why *Maariv* began as a voluntary service; unlike *Shacharis* and *Minchah* that took the place of the required *Tamid* offerings, the evening service on the Altar was optional in the sense that it was unnecessary if all the parts could be burned during the day. During Talmudic times, the universal consensus of Jewry adopted *Maariv* as an obligatory service, so it now has the status of *Shacharis* and *Minchah.* (It should be noted that the original optional status of *Maariv* applied only to *Shemoneh Esrei;* the *Shema* reading, however, is required by Scriptural law.)

Laws of Maariv

As a general rule, no אָמֵן, *Amen,* or other prayer response may be recited between *Borchu* and *Shemoneh Esrei,* but there are exceptions. The main exception is 'between chapters' [בֵּין הַפְּרָקִים] of the *Shema Blessings* — i.e., after each of the blessings, and between the three chapters of *Shema.* At those points, every אָמֵן (but not בָּרוּךְ הוּא וּבָרוּךְ שְׁמוֹ) may be said.

Some responses, however, are so important that they are permitted at any point in the *Shema* blessings. They are: (a) In *Kaddish,* אָמֵן יְהֵא שְׁמֵהּ רַבָּא ... עָלְמַיָּא and the אָמֵן after דַּאֲמִירָן בְּעָלְמָא; and (b) the response to בָּרְכוּ. Additionally, if one has already begun *Maariv* while a different *minyan* has not yet completed *Minchah,* one may respond: (a) in *Kedushah,* the verses קָדוֹשׁ קָדוֹשׁ קָדוֹשׁ ... כְּבוֹדוֹ and בָּרוּךְ כְּבוֹד ה׳ מִמְּקוֹמוֹ; (b) the אָמֵן after הָאֵל הַקָּדוֹשׁ and after שׁוֹמֵעַ תְּפִלָּה; and (c) the three words מוֹדִים אֲנַחְנוּ לָךְ (of the *Modim* of the Rabbis, during the *chazzan's* repetition of *Shemoneh Esrei*).

No interruptions whatever are permitted during the two verses of שְׁמַע and בָּרוּךְ שֵׁם.

The ideal time for *Maariv* is after dark. However, if one will not have a *minyan* later, he may recite *Maariv* as much as one and a quarter variable hours (see commentary p. 232; *Laws* §25) before sunset, in which case he must repeat the three chapters of *Shema* after dark.

MAARIV FOR WEEKDAYS AND CONCLUSION OF SABBATH

Congregation, then *chazzan:*

וְהוּא רַחוּם *He, the Merciful One,* is forgiving of iniquity and does not destroy. Frequently He withdraws His anger, not arousing His entire rage.[1] HASHEM, save! May the King answer us on the day we call.[2]*

In some congregations the *chazzan* chants a melody during his recitation of *Borchu,* so that the congregation can then recite *'Blessed, praised ...'*

Chazzan bows at *'Bless,'* and straightens up at *'HASHEM.'*

Bless HASHEM, the blessed One.

Congregation, followed by *chazzan,* responds, bowing at *'Blessed'* and straightening up at *'HASHEM.'*

Blessed is HASHEM, the blessed One, for all eternity.

Blessed, praised, glorified, exalted and upraised is the Name of the King Who rules over kings — the Holy One, Blessed is He. For He is the First and He is the Last and aside from Him there is no god.[3] Extol Him — Who rides the highest heavens — with His Name, YAH, and exult before Him.[4] His Name is exalted beyond every blessing and praise.[5] Blessed is the Name of His glorious kingdom for all eternity. Blessed be the Name of HASHEM from this time and forever.[6]

BLESSINGS OF THE SHEMA

בָּרוּךְ *Blessed are You, HASHEM, our God, King of the universe, Who by His word* brings on evenings, with wisdom opens gates,* with understanding alters periods,* changes the seasons, and orders the stars in their heavenly constellations as He wills. He creates day and night, removing light before darkness and darkness before light. He causes day to pass and brings night, and separates*

(1) *Psalms* 78:38. (2) 20:10. (3) Cf. *Isaiah* 44:6. (4) *Psalms* 68:5. (5) Cf. *Nechemiah* 9:5. (6) *Psalms* 113:2.

וְהוּא רַחוּם — *He, the Merciful One.* The night represents darkness, judgment, suffering. Therefore the custom developed to recite this verse that calls upon God's mercy. This particular verse is especially apt because it has thirteen words, alluding to God's Thirteen Attributes of Mercy *(Tola'as Yaakov).*

בָּרְכוּ / Borchu

Borchu is recited only in the presence of a *minyan,* a quorum of ten adult males. The *chazzan* calls upon the congregation to proclaim their blessing of God. This call is in the nature of summons to the assembled people to join in the forthcoming prayers known as בִּרְכוֹת קְרִיאַת שְׁמַע, *Blessings of the Shema.* For commentary to *Borchu,* see page 84.

בִּרְכוֹת קְרִיאַת שְׁמַע / Blessings of the Shema

The nighttime Blessings of the Shema are similar in theme to those of the morning, except that there are three in the morning and four in the evening. The total of seven is based on the verse *(Psalms* 119:164): *Seven times a day I praise You (Berachos* 11a, *Rashi).* Of the evening blessings, the first describes God's control over nature, seasons, and the cycles of light. The second blessing speaks of God's gift of the Torah, the very essence of Israel's survival. The third refers to the Exodus, but with emphasis on the future redemption. The fourth, which the Talmud describes as an extension of the theme of redemption, stresses God's protection of His people from the terrors and dangers of night and slumber. In post-Talmudic times, a fifth blessing was added [בָּרוּךְ ה׳ לְעוֹלָם]. Not an integral part of *Maariv,* its origin and purpose are discussed below (p. 265).

בָּרוּךְ אַתָּה ... אֲשֶׁר בִּדְבָרוֹ — *Blessed are You ... Who by His word.* The command of God created day just as it created night, for every moment of the day and night has a purpose in God's plan. This recognition of God's everpresent will is especially important at night, which represents the period of fear, failure, and exile *(R' Hirsch).*

פּוֹתֵחַ שְׁעָרִים — *Opens gates.* A figurative reference to the 'gates' which 'open' to release the light of the morning sun and 'close' upon it in the evening — as if the sun were brought out at dawn and put to rest at dusk *(Iyun Tefillah).*

וּבִתְבוּנָה מְשַׁנֶּה עִתִּים — *With understanding alters periods.* With deep understanding of the needs of a particular time segment, God varies weather conditions from day to day and from hour to hour *(Siach Yitzchak).*

בֵּין יוֹם וּבֵין לָיְלָה, יהוה צְבָאוֹת* שְׁמוֹ. ❖ אֵל חַי וְקַיָּם, תָּמִיד יִמְלוֹךְ עָלֵינוּ, לְעוֹלָם וָעֶד. בָּרוּךְ אַתָּה יהוה, הַמַּעֲרִיב עֲרָבִים. (.Cong.— אָמֵן)

אַהֲבַת עוֹלָם* בֵּית יִשְׂרָאֵל עַמְּךָ אָהָבְתָּ. תּוֹרָה וּמִצְוֹת, חֻקִּים וּמִשְׁפָּטִים, אוֹתָנוּ לִמַּדְתָּ. עַל כֵּן יהוה אֱלֹהֵינוּ, בְּשָׁכְבֵנוּ וּבְקוּמֵנוּ נָשִׂיחַ בְּחֻקֶּיךָ, וְנִשְׂמַח* בְּדִבְרֵי תוֹרָתֶךָ, וּבְמִצְוֹתֶיךָ לְעוֹלָם וָעֶד. ❖ כִּי הֵם חַיֵּינוּ, וְאֹרֶךְ יָמֵינוּ,* וּבָהֶם נֶהְגֶּה יוֹמָם וָלָיְלָה. וְאַהֲבָתְךָ, אַל תָּסִיר מִמֶּנּוּ לְעוֹלָמִים. בָּרוּךְ אַתָּה יהוה, אוֹהֵב עַמּוֹ יִשְׂרָאֵל. (.Cong.— אָמֵן)

שמע

Immediately before reciting the *Shema* concentrate on fulfilling the positive commandment of reciting the *Shema* twice daily. It is important to enunciate each word clearly and not to run words together. For this reason, vertical lines have been placed between two words that are prone to be slurred into one and are not separated by a comma or a hyphen. See laws of *Shema* on p. 982.

When praying without a *minyan,* begin with the following three-word formula:

אֵל מֶלֶךְ נֶאֱמָן.

Recite the first verse aloud, with the right hand covering the eyes, and concentrate intensely upon accepting God's absolute sovereignty.

שְׁמַע | יִשְׂרָאֵל, יהוה | אֱלֹהֵינוּ, יהוה | אֶחָד:[1]

In an undertone— בָּרוּךְ שֵׁם כְּבוֹד מַלְכוּתוֹ לְעוֹלָם וָעֶד.

While reciting the first paragraph (דברים ו:ה־ט), concentrate on accepting the commandment to love God.

וְאָהַבְתָּ אֵת | יהוה | אֱלֹהֶיךָ, בְּכָל־לְבָבְךָ, וּבְכָל־נַפְשְׁךָ, וּבְכָל־מְאֹדֶךָ: וְהָיוּ הַדְּבָרִים הָאֵלֶּה, אֲשֶׁר | אָנֹכִי מְצַוְּךָ הַיּוֹם, עַל־לְבָבֶךָ: וְשִׁנַּנְתָּם לְבָנֶיךָ, וְדִבַּרְתָּ בָּם, בְּשִׁבְתְּךָ בְּבֵיתֶךָ, וּבְלֶכְתְּךָ בַדֶּרֶךְ, וּבְשָׁכְבְּךָ וּבְקוּמֶךָ: וּקְשַׁרְתָּם לְאוֹת | עַל־יָדֶךָ, וְהָיוּ לְטֹטָפֹת בֵּין | עֵינֶיךָ: וּכְתַבְתָּם | עַל־מְזֻזוֹת בֵּיתֶךָ, וּבִשְׁעָרֶיךָ:

ה׳ צְבָאוֹת — *HASHEM, Master of Legions.* He takes the infinite number of forces and conditions that form the universe and harmonizes them to perform His will *(R' Hirsch).*

אַהֲבַת עוֹלָם ◆§ — *[With] an eternal love.* Like the blessing immediately before the morning *Shema,* this blessing is an ecstatic expression of gratitude to God for the gift of Torah. Only after acknowledging our dependence on, and love for, the Torah, can we go on to express our undivided loyalty and dedication to ה׳ אֶחָד, *HASHEM, the One and Only God,* Who gave us this most precious gift.

The blessing begins with an expression of an axiom of Jewish existence: God loves us. The fact that He chose to give us His Torah proves that it is the vehicle for our national fulfillment. Therefore we dedicate ourselves to study it — constantly, joyously, and devotedly *(Siach Yitzchak).*

וְנִשְׂמַח — *And we will rejoice.* Torah study must be seen not as a chore, but as a source of joy. A mourner, for example, is forbidden to study Torah except for tragic passages or relevant laws, because normal study would gladden him at a time when he is required to feel grief over his loss.

כִּי הֵם חַיֵּינוּ וְאֹרֶךְ יָמֵינוּ — *For they are our life and the length of our days.* The word life means

between day and night — HASHEM, Master of Legions, is His Name.* Chazzan— *May the living and enduring God continuously reign over us, for all eternity. Blessed are You, HASHEM, Who brings on evenings.* (Cong.— *Amen.*)

אַהֲבַת *With an eternal love* have You loved the House of Israel, Your nation. Torah and commandments, decrees and ordinances have You taught us. Therefore HASHEM, our God, upon our retiring and arising, we will discuss Your decrees and we will rejoice* with the words of Your Torah and with Your commandments for all eternity.* Chazzan— *For they are our life and the length of our days* and about them we will meditate day and night. May You not remove Your love from us forever. Blessed are You, HASHEM, Who loves His nation Israel.* (Cong.— *Amen.*)

THE SHEMA

Immediately before reciting the *Shema* concentrate on fulfilling the positive commandment of reciting the *Shema* twice daily. It is important to enunciate each word clearly and not to run words together. See laws of *Shema* on p. 982.

When praying without a *minyan,* begin with the following three-word formula:

God, trustworthy King.

Recite the first verse aloud, with the right hand covering the eyes, and concentrate intensely upon accepting God's absolute sovereignty.

Hear, O Israel: HASHEM is our God, HASHEM, the One and Only.[1]

In an undertone— *Blessed is the Name of His glorious kingdom for all eternity.*

While reciting the first paragraph (*Deuteronomy* 6:5-9), concentrate on accepting the commandment to love God.

וְאָהַבְתָּ *You shall love HASHEM, your God, with all your heart, with all your soul and with all your resources. Let these matters that I command you today be upon your heart. Teach them thoroughly to your children and speak of them while you sit in your home, while you walk on the way, when you retire and when you arise. Bind them as a sign upon your arm and let them be tefillin between your eyes. And write them on the doorposts of your house and upon your gates.*

(1) *Deuteronomy* 6:4.

different things to different people. The Torah teaches us that the only *true* life is one in the service of God, one that is dedicated to the study of Torah and the performance of *mitzvos.* When a person lives such a life on earth, he is assured that a natural consequence of his efforts is אֹרֶךְ יָמִים, *lengthy days,* of blessing and joy in the eternal World to Come *(Or HaChaim).*

שְׁמַע / The Shema

The recitation of the three paragraphs of *Shema* is required by the Torah, and one must have in mind that he is about to fulfill this commandment. Although one should try to concentrate on the meaning of all three paragraphs, one must concentrate at least on the meaning of the first (שְׁמַע, *Hear* ...) and the second verses (בָּרוּךְ שֵׁם, *Blessed* ...) because the recitation of *Shema* represents fulfillment of the paramount commandment of acceptance of God's absolute sovereignty [קַבָּלַת עוֹל מַלְכוּת שָׁמַיִם]. By declaring that God is One, Unique, and Indivisible, we subordinate every facet of our personalities, possessions — our very lives — to His will.

For a summary of the laws of *Shema,* see *Laws* §46-60; for a commentary, see pages 90-94. In the שְׁמַע we have included the cantillation symbols *(trop)* for the convenience of those who recite שְׁמַע in the manner it is read from the

While reciting the second paragraph (דברים יא:יג־כא), concentrate on accepting all the commandments and the concept of reward and punishment.

וְהָיָה, אִם־שָׁמֹעַ תִּשְׁמְעוּ אֶל־מִצְוֹתַי, אֲשֶׁר | אָנֹכִי מְצַוֶּה |
אֶתְכֶם הַיּוֹם, לְאַהֲבָה אֶת־יהוה | אֱלֹהֵיכֶם וּלְעָבְדוֹ,
בְּכָל־לְבַבְכֶם, וּבְכָל־נַפְשְׁכֶם: וְנָתַתִּי מְטַר־אַרְצְכֶם בְּעִתּוֹ, יוֹרֶה
וּמַלְקוֹשׁ, וְאָסַפְתָּ דְגָנֶךָ וְתִירֹשְׁךָ וְיִצְהָרֶךָ: וְנָתַתִּי | עֵשֶׂב | בְּשָׂדְךָ
לִבְהֶמְתֶּךָ, וְאָכַלְתָּ וְשָׂבָעְתָּ: הִשָּׁמְרוּ לָכֶם, פֶּן־יִפְתֶּה לְבַבְכֶם,
וְסַרְתֶּם וַעֲבַדְתֶּם | אֱלֹהִים | אֲחֵרִים, וְהִשְׁתַּחֲוִיתֶם לָהֶם: וְחָרָה |
אַף־יהוה בָּכֶם, וְעָצַר אֶת־הַשָּׁמַיִם, וְלֹא־יִהְיֶה מָטָר, וְהָאֲדָמָה
לֹא תִתֵּן אֶת־יְבוּלָהּ, וַאֲבַדְתֶּם | מְהֵרָה מֵעַל הָאָרֶץ הַטֹּבָה |
אֲשֶׁר | יהוה נֹתֵן לָכֶם: וְשַׂמְתֶּם | אֶת־דְּבָרַי | אֵלֶּה, עַל־לְבַבְכֶם
וְעַל־נַפְשְׁכֶם, וּקְשַׁרְתֶּם | אֹתָם לְאוֹת | עַל־יֶדְכֶם, וְהָיוּ לְטוֹטָפֹת
בֵּין | עֵינֵיכֶם: וְלִמַּדְתֶּם | אֹתָם | אֶת־בְּנֵיכֶם, לְדַבֵּר בָּם, בְּשִׁבְתְּךָ
בְּבֵיתֶךָ, וּבְלֶכְתְּךָ בַדֶּרֶךְ, וּבְשָׁכְבְּךָ וּבְקוּמֶךָ: וּכְתַבְתָּם | עַל־
מְזוּזוֹת בֵּיתֶךָ, וּבִשְׁעָרֶיךָ: לְמַעַן | יִרְבּוּ | יְמֵיכֶם וִימֵי בְנֵיכֶם, עַל
הָאֲדָמָה | אֲשֶׁר נִשְׁבַּע | יהוה לַאֲבֹתֵיכֶם לָתֵת לָהֶם, כִּימֵי
הַשָּׁמַיִם | עַל־הָאָרֶץ:

במדבר טו:לז־מא

וַיֹּאמֶר | יהוה | אֶל־מֹשֶׁה לֵּאמֹר: דַּבֵּר | אֶל־בְּנֵי | יִשְׂרָאֵל,
וְאָמַרְתָּ אֲלֵהֶם, וְעָשׂוּ לָהֶם צִיצִת, עַל־כַּנְפֵי בִגְדֵיהֶם
לְדֹרֹתָם, וְנָתְנוּ | עַל־צִיצִת הַכָּנָף, פְּתִיל תְּכֵלֶת: וְהָיָה לָכֶם
לְצִיצִת, וּרְאִיתֶם | אֹתוֹ, וּזְכַרְתֶּם | אֶת־כָּל־מִצְוֹת | יהוה,
וַעֲשִׂיתֶם | אֹתָם, וְלֹא תָתֻרוּ | אַחֲרֵי לְבַבְכֶם וְאַחֲרֵי | עֵינֵיכֶם,
אֲשֶׁר־אַתֶּם זֹנִים | אַחֲרֵיהֶם: לְמַעַן תִּזְכְּרוּ, וַעֲשִׂיתֶם | אֶת־כָּל־
מִצְוֹתָי, וִהְיִיתֶם קְדֹשִׁים לֵאלֹהֵיכֶם: אֲנִי יהוה |
אֱלֹהֵיכֶם, אֲשֶׁר הוֹצֵאתִי | אֶתְכֶם | מֵאֶרֶץ
מִצְרַיִם, לִהְיוֹת לָכֶם לֵאלֹהִים, אֲנִי | יהוה | אֱלֹהֵיכֶם: אֱמֶת —

Concentrate on fulfilling the commandment of remembering the Exodus from Egypt.

Although the word אֱמֶת belongs to the next paragraph, it is appended to the conclusion of the previous one, as explained in the commentary, p. 95.

—*Chazzan* repeats **יהוה אֱלֹהֵיכֶם אֱמֶת.**

וֶאֱמוּנָה* כָּל זֹאת, וְקַיָּם עָלֵינוּ, כִּי הוּא יהוה אֱלֹהֵינוּ וְאֵין
זוּלָתוֹ, וַאֲנַחְנוּ יִשְׂרָאֵל עַמּוֹ. הַפּוֹדֵנוּ מִיַּד מְלָכִים,

While reciting the second paragraph (*Deuteronomy* 11:13-21), concentrate on accepting all the commandments and the concept of reward and punishment.

וְהָיָה *And it will come to pass that if you continually hearken to My commandments that I command you today, to love* HASHEM, *your God, and to serve Him, with all your heart and with all your soul — then I will provide rain for your land in its proper time, the early and late rains, that you may gather in your grain, your wine, and your oil. I will provide grass in your field for your cattle and you will eat and be satisfied. Beware lest your heart be seduced and you turn astray and serve gods of others and bow to them. Then the wrath of* HASHEM *will blaze against you. He will restrain the heaven so there will be no rain and the ground will not yield its produce. And you will swiftly be banished from the goodly land which* HASHEM *gives you. Place these words of Mine upon your heart and upon your soul; bind them for a sign upon your arm and let them be tefillin between your eyes. Teach them to your children, to discuss them, while you sit in your home, while you walk on the way, when you retire and when you arise. And write them on the doorposts of your house and upon your gates. In order to prolong your days and the days of your children upon the ground that* HASHEM *has sworn to your ancestors to give them, like the days of the heaven on the earth.*

Numbers 15:37-41

וַיֹּאמֶר *And* HASHEM *said to Moses saying: Speak to the Children of Israel and say to them that they are to make themselves tzitzis on the corners of their garments, throughout their generations. And they are to place upon the tzitzis of each corner a thread of techeiles. And it shall constitute tzitzis for you, that you may see it and remember all the commandments of* HASHEM *and perform them; and not explore after your heart and after your eyes after which you stray. So that you may remember and perform all My commandments; and be holy to your God. I am* HASHEM, *your God, Who has removed you from the land of Egypt to be a God to you; I am* HASHEM *your God — it is true —*

Concentrate on fulfiling the commandment of remembering the Exodus from Egypt.

Although the word אֱמֶת, *'true,'* belongs to the next paragraph, it is appended to the conclusion of the previous one, as explained in the commentary, p. 95.

Chazzan repeats: **HASHEM, your God, is true.**

וֶאֱמוּנָה ***And faithful* is all this, and it is firmly established for us that He is*** **HASHEM** ***our God, and there is none but Him, and we are Israel, His nation. He redeems us from the power of kings, our***

Torah. Nevertheless, to enable those unfamiliar with this notation to group the words properly, commas have been inserted. Additionally, vertical lines have been placed between two words that are prone to be slurred into one and are not separated by a comma.

☙ אֱמֶת וֶאֱמוּנָה — *True and faithful.* This paragraph continues our fulfillment of the obligation to recall the Exodus in the evening. The morning blessing of אֱמֶת וְיַצִּיב, *True and certain,* concentrates on God's kindness in having redeemed us from Egypt, while אֱמֶת וֶאֱמוּנָה, *True and faithful,* recited at night, symbolizes exile and stresses our faith that God will redeem us from this exile just as He did at the time of the Exodus *(Berachos* 12a; *Rashi* and *Tosafos).*

מַלְכֵּנוּ הַגּוֹאֲלֵנוּ מִכַּף כָּל הֶעָרִיצִים. הָאֵל הַנִּפְרָע לָנוּ מִצָּרֵינוּ, וְהַמְּשַׁלֵּם גְּמוּל לְכָל אֹיְבֵי נַפְשֵׁנוּ.* הָעֹשֶׂה גְדֹלוֹת עַד אֵין חֵקֶר,* וְנִפְלָאוֹת עַד אֵין מִסְפָּר.[1] הַשָּׂם נַפְשֵׁנוּ בַּחַיִּים,* וְלֹא נָתַן לַמּוֹט רַגְלֵנוּ.[2] הַמַּדְרִיכֵנוּ עַל בָּמוֹת אוֹיְבֵינוּ, וַיָּרֶם קַרְנֵנוּ עַל כָּל שׂנְאֵינוּ. הָעֹשֶׂה לָּנוּ נִסִּים וּנְקָמָה בְּפַרְעֹה, אוֹתוֹת וּמוֹפְתִים בְּאַדְמַת בְּנֵי חָם.* הַמַּכֶּה בְעֶבְרָתוֹ כָּל בְּכוֹרֵי מִצְרָיִם, וַיּוֹצֵא אֶת עַמּוֹ יִשְׂרָאֵל מִתּוֹכָם לְחֵרוּת עוֹלָם. הַמַּעֲבִיר בָּנָיו בֵּין גִּזְרֵי יַם סוּף, אֶת רוֹדְפֵיהֶם וְאֶת שׂוֹנְאֵיהֶם בִּתְהוֹמוֹת טִבַּע. וְרָאוּ בָנָיו גְּבוּרָתוֹ, שִׁבְּחוּ וְהוֹדוּ לִשְׁמוֹ. ❖ וּמַלְכוּתוֹ בְּרָצוֹן קִבְּלוּ עֲלֵיהֶם. מֹשֶׁה וּבְנֵי יִשְׂרָאֵל לְךָ עָנוּ שִׁירָה, בְּשִׂמְחָה רַבָּה, וְאָמְרוּ כֻלָּם:

מִי כָמֹכָה בָּאֵלִם יהוה, מִי כָּמֹכָה נֶאְדָּר בַּקֹּדֶשׁ, נוֹרָא תְהִלֹּת,* עֹשֵׂה פֶלֶא.[3] ❖ מַלְכוּתְךָ רָאוּ בָנֶיךָ* בּוֹקֵעַ יָם לִפְנֵי מֹשֶׁה, זֶה אֵלִי[4] עָנוּ וְאָמְרוּ:

יהוה יִמְלֹךְ לְעֹלָם וָעֶד.[5] ❖ וְנֶאֱמַר: כִּי פָדָה יהוה אֶת יַעֲקֹב,* וּגְאָלוֹ מִיַּד חָזָק מִמֶּנּוּ.[6] בָּרוּךְ אַתָּה יהוה, גָּאַל יִשְׂרָאֵל.

(Cong. — אָמֵן.)

הַשְׁכִּיבֵנוּ* יהוה אֱלֹהֵינוּ לְשָׁלוֹם,* וְהַעֲמִידֵנוּ מַלְכֵּנוּ לְחַיִּים, וּפְרוֹשׂ עָלֵינוּ סֻכַּת שְׁלוֹמֶךָ, וְתַקְּנֵנוּ בְּעֵצָה טוֹבָה* מִלְּפָנֶיךָ, וְהוֹשִׁיעֵנוּ לְמַעַן שְׁמֶךָ. וְהָגֵן בַּעֲדֵנוּ, וְהָסֵר

Alternatively, the faithfulness of the nights refers to man's confidence that God will return his soul in the morning refreshed and rested after a night of sleep *(Talmidei R' Yonah; Tos., Berachos* 12a; *Rashi* in *Pardes).*

Chiddushei HaRim explains that אֱמֶת, *truth,* refers to something that we know to be true, either because our senses tell us so or because we have conclusive evidence. אֱמוּנָה, *faith,* refers to something that we *believe,* even though we have seen neither it nor proof that it happened. We know the Exodus to be *true,* because it was witnessed by millions of people, but the future redemption is not yet an accomplished fact. Nevertheless we have a perfect *faith* that God will bring it about, as He promised through the prophets. This is just as real for us as our *faith* in another phenomenon that has not yet taken place — that we will wake up from our sleep tomorrow morning.

מִצָּרֵינוּ ... אֹיְבֵי נַפְשֵׁנוּ — *From our foes ... enemies of our soul.* The term *foe* [צָר] refers to one who actually causes harm, while *enemy* [אוֹיֵב] is one who hates and encourages harm, even though he has not done anything actively *(Malbim* to *Isaiah* 59:18). Later a third kind of enemy is mentioned: שׂוֹנֵא, *one who hates.* A שׂוֹנֵא does nothing against the object of his hate; he merely rejoices at his suffering and downfall *(Siach Yitzchak).*

The expression *enemies of our soul* implies that their enmity is directed against Israel's spiritual essence. They do not desire the physical destruction of the Jewish people, but they cannot abide Israel's loyalty to the Torah *(Siach Yitzchak).*

גְּדֹלוֹת עַד אֵין חֵקֶר — *Great deeds that are beyond comprehension.* If our entire solar system were to disappear, the loss would not even be noticed in the vastness of space *(Malbim, Job* 9:10).

הַשָּׂם נַפְשֵׁנוּ בַּחַיִּים — *Who set our soul in life.* A reference to the night in Egypt when all non-Jewish firstborn died, but Jewish souls were preserved *(Abudraham).* This also implies God's protection from the murderous designs of our enemies in all generations *(Siach Yitzchak).*

King Who delivers us from the hand of all the cruel tyrants. He is the God Who exacts vengeance for us from our foes and Who brings just retribution upon all enemies of our soul; Who performs great deeds that are beyond comprehension,* and wonders beyond number.*[1] *Who set our soul in life* and did not allow our foot to falter.*[2] *Who led us upon the heights of our enemies and raised our pride above all who hate us; Who wrought for us miracles and vengeance upon Pharaoh; signs and wonders on the land of the offspring of Ham;* Who struck with His anger all the firstborn of Egypt and removed His nation Israel from their midst to eternal freedom; Who brought His children through the split parts of the Sea of Reeds while those who pursued them and hated them He caused to sink into the depths. When His children perceived His power, they lauded and gave grateful praise to His Name.* Chazzan– *And His Kingship they accepted upon themselves willingly. Moses and the Children of Israel raised their voices to You in song with abundant gladness — and said unanimously:*

מִי כָמֹכָה *Who is like You among the heavenly powers, HASHEM! Who is like You, mighty in holiness, too awesome for praise,* doing wonders!*[3] Chazzan– *Your children beheld Your majesty,* as You split the sea before Moses: 'This is my God!'*[4] *they exclaimed, then they said:*

יהוה *'HASHEM shall reign for all eternity!'*[5] Chazzan– *And it is further said: 'For HASHEM has redeemed Jacob* and delivered him from a power mightier than he.'*[6] *Blessed are You HASHEM, Who redeemed Israel.* (Cong.—*Amen.)*

הַשְׁכִּיבֵנוּ *Lay us down* to sleep, HASHEM our God, in peace,* raise us erect, our King, to life; and spread over us the shelter of Your peace. Set us aright with good counsel* from before Your Presence, and save us for Your Name's sake. Shield us, remove*

(1) *Job* 9:10. (2) *Psalms* 66:9. (3) *Exodus* 15:11. (4) 15:2. (5) 15:18. (6) *Jeremiah* 31:10.

בְּנֵי חָם — *The offspring of Ham.* Mitzrayim, forerunner of the Egyptian nation, was a son of Ham [*Genesis* 10:6].

נוֹרָא תְהִלֹּת — *Too awesome for praise.* We are too terrified to attempt a complete assessment of His greatness, because whatever we say is insufficient *(Rashi).*

Ramban comments that it is impossible for people to praise God adequately; the only way to laud Him is by simply recounting His awe-inspiring deeds. Thus he would render this phrase: [God's] *awesomeness constitutes His praises.*

מַלְכוּתְךָ רָאוּ בָנֶיךָ — *Your children beheld Your majesty* [lit. *Your kingship*]. As the Sages taught: A maidservant saw more [of God's majesty and holiness] at the Sea than did even Ezekiel in his prophecies! *(Etz Yosef).*

כִּי פָדָה ה׳ אֶת יַעֲקֹב — *For HASHEM has redeemed Jacob.* Jacob/Israel was the Patriarch who solidified the Jewish destiny. It was he who faced more dangerous, hostile situations than either Abraham or Isaac *(Acharis Shalom).*

This blessing should be said with intense joy in the confident knowledge that God is our past and future Redeemer *(Yesod V'Shoresh HaAvodah).*

הַשְׁכִּיבֵנוּ — *Lay us down.* The Talmud *(Berachos* 4a) describes this blessing as an extension of the previous blessing of redemption [גְּאוּלָה אֲרִיכְתָּא]. Whereas the theme of the earlier blessing was God's redemption of Israel from Egypt [and the allusion to the future redemption], this one describes Him as our Savior from the dangers and afflictions associated with the terrors of night, literally and figuratively *(Seder HaYom).*

הַשְׁכִּיבֵנוּ ... לְשָׁלוֹם — *Lay us down to sleep ... in*

מֵעָלֵינוּ אוֹיֵב, דֶּבֶר, וְחֶרֶב, וְרָעָב, וְיָגוֹן, וְהָסֵר שָׂטָן מִלְּפָנֵינוּ
וּמֵאַחֲרֵינוּ,* וּבְצֵל כְּנָפֶיךָ* תַּסְתִּירֵנוּ,[1] כִּי אֵל שׁוֹמְרֵנוּ וּמַצִּילֵנוּ
אָתָּה, כִּי אֵל מֶלֶךְ חַנּוּן וְרַחוּם אָתָּה.[2] ❖ וּשְׁמוֹר צֵאתֵנוּ וּבוֹאֵנוּ,
לְחַיִּים וּלְשָׁלוֹם מֵעַתָּה וְעַד עוֹלָם.[3] בָּרוּךְ אַתָּה יהוה, שׁוֹמֵר
עַמּוֹ יִשְׂרָאֵל לָעַד. (Cong. — אָמֵן.)

For instances when the following prayer (until Half-*Kaddish*) is omitted, see commentary.

בָּרוּךְ יהוה לְעוֹלָם, אָמֵן וְאָמֵן.[4] בָּרוּךְ יהוה מִצִּיּוֹן, שֹׁכֵן
יְרוּשָׁלָיִם, הַלְלוּיָהּ.[5] בָּרוּךְ יהוה אֱלֹהִים אֱלֹהֵי יִשְׂרָאֵל,
עֹשֵׂה נִפְלָאוֹת לְבַדּוֹ. וּבָרוּךְ שֵׁם כְּבוֹדוֹ לְעוֹלָם, וְיִמָּלֵא כְבוֹדוֹ
אֶת כָּל הָאָרֶץ, אָמֵן וְאָמֵן.[6] יְהִי כְבוֹד יהוה לְעוֹלָם, יִשְׂמַח יהוה
בְּמַעֲשָׂיו.[7] יְהִי שֵׁם יהוה מְבֹרָךְ, מֵעַתָּה וְעַד עוֹלָם.[8] כִּי לֹא יִטֹּשׁ
יהוה אֶת עַמּוֹ בַּעֲבוּר שְׁמוֹ הַגָּדוֹל, כִּי הוֹאִיל יהוה לַעֲשׂוֹת
אֶתְכֶם לוֹ לְעָם.[9] וַיַּרְא כָּל הָעָם וַיִּפְּלוּ עַל פְּנֵיהֶם, וַיֹּאמְרוּ, יהוה
הוּא הָאֱלֹהִים, יהוה הוּא הָאֱלֹהִים.[10] וְהָיָה יהוה לְמֶלֶךְ עַל כָּל
הָאָרֶץ, בַּיּוֹם הַהוּא יִהְיֶה יהוה אֶחָד וּשְׁמוֹ אֶחָד.[11] יְהִי חַסְדְּךָ
יהוה עָלֵינוּ, כַּאֲשֶׁר יִחַלְנוּ לָךְ.[12] הוֹשִׁיעֵנוּ יהוה אֱלֹהֵינוּ, וְקַבְּצֵנוּ
מִן הַגּוֹיִם, לְהוֹדוֹת לְשֵׁם קָדְשֶׁךָ, לְהִשְׁתַּבֵּחַ בִּתְהִלָּתֶךָ.[13] כָּל
גּוֹיִם אֲשֶׁר עָשִׂיתָ יָבוֹאוּ וְיִשְׁתַּחֲווּ לְפָנֶיךָ אֲדֹנָי, וִיכַבְּדוּ לִשְׁמֶךָ.
כִּי גָדוֹל אַתָּה וְעֹשֵׂה נִפְלָאוֹת, אַתָּה אֱלֹהִים לְבַדֶּךָ.[14] וַאֲנַחְנוּ
עַמְּךָ וְצֹאן מַרְעִיתֶךָ, נוֹדֶה לְּךָ לְעוֹלָם, לְדוֹר וָדֹר נְסַפֵּר
תְּהִלָּתֶךָ.[15] בָּרוּךְ יהוה בַּיּוֹם. בָּרוּךְ יהוה בַּלָּיְלָה. בָּרוּךְ יהוה
בְּשָׁכְבֵנוּ. בָּרוּךְ יהוה בְּקוּמֵנוּ. כִּי בְיָדְךָ נַפְשׁוֹת הַחַיִּים וְהַמֵּתִים.
אֲשֶׁר בְּיָדוֹ נֶפֶשׁ כָּל חָי, וְרוּחַ כָּל בְּשַׂר אִישׁ.[16] בְּיָדְךָ אַפְקִיד
רוּחִי, פָּדִיתָה אוֹתִי, יהוה אֵל אֱמֶת.[17] אֱלֹהֵינוּ שֶׁבַּשָּׁמַיִם יַחֵד
שִׁמְךָ, וְקַיֵּם מַלְכוּתְךָ תָּמִיד, וּמְלוֹךְ עָלֵינוּ לְעוֹלָם וָעֶד.

---

peace. The purpose of sleep is to allow the body to rejuvenate itself, the better to serve God the next day *(R' Hirsch).*

וְתַקְּנֵנוּ בְּעֵצָה טוֹבָה — *Set us aright with good counsel.* Help us plan well at night for the activity of the next day, and let the relaxation of the night give us a clearer perspective for the deliberations of the day *(R' Hirsch).*

מִלְּפָנֵינוּ וּמֵאַחֲרֵינוּ — *From before us and behind us.* Protect us from spiritual harm in the future [*before us*] and from the consequences of what has already occurred [*behind us*] *(R' Hirsch).*

וּבְצֵל כְּנָפֶיךָ — *(And) in the shadow of Your wings. Psalms* 91:4 likens God's protection to the wings of a mother bird sheltering her young.

☙ בָּרוּךְ ה׳ לְעוֹלָם — *Blessed is HASHEM forever.* The following collection of Scriptural verses was introduced during the Gaonic era. At that time most people gathered in the fields for prayers (apparently on the way from their farms to their homes). In order to shorten the service so that it could be completed before dark, this collection of verses was substituted for *Shemoneh Esrei,* which would be recited later by each individual in the safety of his home. Another version has it that these verses were added in order to allow

from us foe, plague, sword, famine, and woe; and remove spiritual impediment from before us and behind us and in the shadow of Your wings* shelter us*[1] *— for God Who protects and rescues us are You; for God, the gracious and compassionate King, are You.*[2] Chazzan— *Safeguard our going and coming — for life and for peace from now to eternity.*[3] *Blessed are You,* HASHEM, *Who protects His people Israel forever.* (Cong.—*Amen.)*

For instances when the following prayer (until Half-*Kaddish)* is omitted, see commentary.

בָּרוּךְ *Blessed is* HASHEM *forever, Amen and Amen.*[4] *Blessed is* HASHEM *from Zion, Who dwells in Jerusalem, Halleluyah!*[5] *Blessed is* HASHEM, *God, the God of Israel, Who alone does wondrous things. Blessed is His glorious Name forever, and may all the earth be filled with His glory, Amen and Amen.*[6] *May the glory of* HASHEM *endure forever, let* HASHEM *rejoice in His works.*[7] *Blessed be the Name of* HASHEM *from this time and forever.*[8] *For* HASHEM *will not cast off His nation for the sake of His Great Name, for* HASHEM *has vowed to make you His own people.*[9] *Then the entire nation saw and fell on their faces and said, '*HASHEM *— only He is God!* HASHEM *— only He is God!'*[10] *Then* HASHEM *will be King over all the world, on that day* HASHEM *will be One and His Name will be One.*[11] *May Your kindness,* HASHEM, *be upon us, just as we awaited You.*[12] *Save us,* HASHEM, *our God, gather us from the nations, to thank Your Holy Name and to glory in Your praise!*[13] *All the nations that You made will come and bow before You, My Lord, and shall glorify Your Name. For You are great and work wonders; You alone, O God.*[14] *Then we, Your nation and the sheep of Your pasture, shall thank You forever; for generation after generation we will relate Your praise.*[15] *Blessed is* HASHEM *by day; Blessed is* HASHEM *by night; Blessed is* HASHEM *when we retire; Blessed is* HASHEM *when we arise. For in Your hand are the souls of the living and the dead. He in Whose hand is the soul of all the living and the spirit of every human being.*[16] *In Your hand I shall entrust my spirit, You redeemed me,* HASHEM, *God of truth.*[17] *Our God, Who is in heaven, bring unity to Your Name; establish Your kingdom forever and reign over us for all eternity.*

(1) Cf. *Psalms* 17:8. (2) Cf. *Nechemiah* 9:31. (3) Cf. *Psalms* 121:8. (4) 89:53. (5) 135:21. (6) 72:18-19. (7) 104:31. (8) 113:2. (9) *I Samuel* 12:22. (10) *I Kings* 18:39. (11) *Zechariah* 14:9. (12) *Psalms* 33:22. (13) 106:47. (14) 86:9-10. (15) 79:13. (16) *Job* 12:10. (17) *Psalms* 31:6.

latecomers more time to catch up to the congregation. Whichever the reason, it was retained even after the practice of praying in the fields was discontinued.

Since they took the place of *Shemoneh Esrei* in the communal service, the verses of בָּרוּךְ ה׳ were selected so as to contain the name HASHEM nineteen times, paralleling the blessings of *Shemoneh Esrei.* The theme of this prayer is redemption, because it follows the *Shema* blessings of redemption.

Since בָּרוּךְ ה׳ was instituted originally for the benefit of working people, it was never recited on days when work is forbidden. Therefore it is always omitted from the *Maariv* of the Sabbath and Festivals. While most congregations recite these verses on all other evenings, there are some that also omit it from the *Maariv* immediately after the Sabbath and Festivals and during Chol HaMoed [Intermediate Days of Pesach and Succos]. According to some customs, it is omitted entirely nowadays.

יִרְאוּ עֵינֵינוּ וְיִשְׂמַח לִבֵּנוּ וְתָגֵל נַפְשֵׁנוּ בִּישׁוּעָתְךָ בֶּאֱמֶת, בֶּאֱמֹר לְצִיּוֹן מָלַךְ אֱלֹהָיִךְ.[1] יהוה מֶלֶךְ,[2] יהוה מָלָךְ,[3] יהוה יִמְלֹךְ לְעֹלָם וָעֶד.[4] ❖ כִּי הַמַּלְכוּת שֶׁלְּךָ הִיא, וּלְעוֹלְמֵי עַד תִּמְלוֹךְ בְּכָבוֹד, כִּי אֵין לָנוּ מֶלֶךְ אֶלָּא אָתָּה. בָּרוּךְ אַתָּה יהוה, הַמֶּלֶךְ בִּכְבוֹדוֹ תָּמִיד יִמְלוֹךְ עָלֵינוּ לְעוֹלָם וָעֶד, וְעַל כָּל מַעֲשָׂיו. (.Cong— אָמֵן.)

חצי קדיש

If a *minyan* is present, the *chazzan* recites חֲצִי קַדִּישׁ:

יִתְגַּדַּל וְיִתְקַדַּשׁ שְׁמֵהּ רַבָּא. (.Cong— אָמֵן.) בְּעָלְמָא דִּי בְרָא כִרְעוּתֵהּ, וְיַמְלִיךְ מַלְכוּתֵהּ, בְּחַיֵּיכוֹן וּבְיוֹמֵיכוֹן וּבְחַיֵּי דְכָל בֵּית יִשְׂרָאֵל, בַּעֲגָלָא וּבִזְמַן קָרִיב. וְאִמְרוּ: אָמֵן.

(.Cong— אָמֵן. יְהֵא שְׁמֵהּ רַבָּא מְבָרַךְ לְעָלַם וּלְעָלְמֵי עָלְמַיָּא.)

יְהֵא שְׁמֵהּ רַבָּא מְבָרַךְ לְעָלַם וּלְעָלְמֵי עָלְמַיָּא.

יִתְבָּרַךְ וְיִשְׁתַּבַּח וְיִתְפָּאַר וְיִתְרוֹמַם וְיִתְנַשֵּׂא וְיִתְהַדָּר וְיִתְעַלֶּה וְיִתְהַלָּל שְׁמֵהּ דְּקֻדְשָׁא בְּרִיךְ הוּא (.Cong— בְּרִיךְ הוּא) — °לְעֵלָּא מִן כָּל (From Rosh Hashanah to Yom Kippur substitute— °לְעֵלָּא וּלְעֵלָּא מִכָּל) בִּרְכָתָא וְשִׁירָתָא תֻּשְׁבְּחָתָא וְנֶחֱמָתָא, דַּאֲמִירָן בְּעָלְמָא. וְאִמְרוּ: אָמֵן. (.Cong— אָמֵן.)

שמונה עשרה — עמידה

Take three steps backward, then three steps forward. Remain standing with the feet together while reciting *Shemoneh Esrei.* It should be recited with quiet devotion and without any interruption, verbal or otherwise. Although its recitation should not be audible to others, one must pray loudly enough to hear himself. See *Laws* §61-96 for a brief summary of its laws including how to rectify the omission of phrases that are added at particular times of the year.

אֲדֹנָי שְׂפָתַי תִּפְתָּח, וּפִי יַגִּיד תְּהִלָּתֶךָ.[5]

אבות

Bend the knees at בָּרוּךְ; bow at אַתָּה; straighten up at 'ה.

בָּרוּךְ אַתָּה יהוה אֱלֹהֵינוּ וֵאלֹהֵי אֲבוֹתֵינוּ, אֱלֹהֵי אַבְרָהָם, אֱלֹהֵי יִצְחָק, וֵאלֹהֵי יַעֲקֹב, הָאֵל הַגָּדוֹל הַגִּבּוֹר וְהַנּוֹרָא, אֵל עֶלְיוֹן, גּוֹמֵל חֲסָדִים טוֹבִים וְקוֹנֵה הַכֹּל, וְזוֹכֵר חַסְדֵי אָבוֹת, וּמֵבִיא גוֹאֵל לִבְנֵי בְנֵיהֶם, לְמַעַן שְׁמוֹ בְּאַהֲבָה.

From Rosh Hashanah to Yom Kippur add:

זָכְרֵנוּ לְחַיִּים, מֶלֶךְ חָפֵץ בַּחַיִּים, וְכָתְבֵנוּ בְּסֵפֶר הַחַיִּים, לְמַעַנְךָ אֱלֹהִים חַיִּים.

[If forgotten, do not repeat *Shemoneh Esrei.* See *Laws* §61.]

Bend the knees at בָּרוּךְ; bow at אַתָּה; straighten up at 'ה.

מֶלֶךְ עוֹזֵר וּמוֹשִׁיעַ וּמָגֵן. בָּרוּךְ אַתָּה יהוה, מָגֵן אַבְרָהָם.

גבורות

אַתָּה גִּבּוֹר לְעוֹלָם אֲדֹנָי, מְחַיֵּה מֵתִים אַתָּה, רַב לְהוֹשִׁיעַ.

יִרְאוּ *May our eyes see, our heart rejoice and our soul exult in Your salvation in truth, when Zion is told, 'Your God has reigned!'*[1] *HASHEM reigns,*[2] *HASHEM has reigned,*[3] *HASHEM will reign for all eternity.*[4] Chazzan— *For the kingdom is Yours and You will reign for all eternity in glory, for we have no King but You. Blessed are You, HASHEM, the King in His glory — He shall constantly reign over us forever and ever, and over all His creatures.* (Cong.— *Amen.)*

HALF KADDISH

If a *minyan* is present, the *chazzan* recites Half-*Kaddish:*

יִתְגַּדַּל *May His great Name grow exalted and sanctified* (Cong.— *Amen.) in the world that He created as He willed. May He give reign to His kingship in your lifetimes and in your days, and in the lifetimes of the entire Family of Israel, swiftly and soon. Now respond: Amen.*

(Cong.— *Amen. May His great Name be blessed forever and ever.)*

May His great Name be blessed forever and ever.

Blessed, praised, glorified, exalted, extolled, mighty, upraised, and lauded be the Name of the Holy One, Blessed is He (Cong.— *Blessed is He*) — (From Rosh Hashanah to Yom Kippur add: *exceedingly) beyond any blessing and song, praise and consolation that are uttered in the world. Now respond: Amen.* (Cong.— *Amen*).

SHEMONEH ESREI — AMIDAH

Take three steps backward, then three steps forward. Remain standing with the feet together while reciting *Shemoneh Esrei.* It should be recited with quiet devotion and without any interruption, verbal or otherwise. Although its recitation should not be audible to others, one must pray loudly enough to hear himself. See *Laws* §61-96 for a brief summary of its laws including how to rectify the omission of phrases that are added at particular times of the year.

My Lord, open my lips, that my mouth may declare Your praise.[5]

PATRIARCHS

Bend the knees at *'Blessed'*; bow at *'You'*; straighten up at *'HASHEM.'*

בָּרוּךְ *Blessed are You, HASHEM, our God and the God of our forefathers, God of Abraham, God of Isaac, and God of Jacob; the great, mighty, and awesome God, the supreme God, Who bestows beneficial kindnesses and creates everything, Who recalls the kindnesses of the Patriarchs and brings a Redeemer to their children's children, for His Name's sake, with love.*

From Rosh Hashanah to Yom Kippur add the following.
Remember us for life, O King Who desires life,
and inscribe us in the Book of Life — for Your sake, O Living God.
[If forgotten, do not repeat *Shemoneh Esrei.* See *Laws* §61.]

Bend the knees at *'Blessed'*; bow at *'You'*; straighten up at *'HASHEM'*.

O King, Helper, Savior, and Shield. Blessed are You, HASHEM, Shield of Abraham.

GOD'S MIGHT

אַתָּה *You are eternally mighty, my Lord, the Resuscitator of the dead are You; abundantly able to save,*

(1) Cf. *Isaiah* 52:7. (2) *Psalms* 10:16. (3) 93:1 et al. (4) *Exodus* 15:18. (5) *Psalms* 51:17.

Between Shemini Atzeres and Pesach add:

מַשִּׁיב הָרְוּחַ וּמוֹרִיד °הַגֶּשֶׁם [some say – °הַגֶּשֶׁם].

[If forgotten, see *Laws* §70-75.]

מְכַלְכֵּל חַיִּים בְּחֶסֶד, מְחַיֵּה מֵתִים בְּרַחֲמִים רַבִּים, סוֹמֵךְ נוֹפְלִים, וְרוֹפֵא חוֹלִים, וּמַתִּיר אֲסוּרִים, וּמְקַיֵּם אֱמוּנָתוֹ לִישֵׁנֵי עָפָר. מִי כָמְוֹךָ בַּעַל גְּבוּרוֹת, וּמִי דְּוֹמֶה לָּךְ, מֶלֶךְ מֵמִית וּמְחַיֶּה וּמַצְמִיחַ יְשׁוּעָה.

From Rosh Hashanah to Yom Kippur add:

מִי כָמְוֹךָ אַב הָרַחֲמִים, זוֹכֵר יְצוּרָיו לְחַיִּים בְּרַחֲמִים.

[If forgotten, do not repeat *Shemoneh Esrei*. See *Laws* §61.]

וְנֶאֱמָן אַתָּה לְהַחֲיוֹת מֵתִים. בָּרוּךְ אַתָּה יהוה, מְחַיֵּה הַמֵּתִים.

קדושת השם

אַתָּה קָדוֹשׁ וְשִׁמְךָ קָדוֹשׁ, וּקְדוֹשִׁים בְּכָל יוֹם יְהַלְלְוּךָ סֶּלָה. בָּרוּךְ אַתָּה יהוה, °הָאֵל הַקָּדוֹשׁ.

°הַמֶּלֶךְ הַקָּדוֹשׁ. —From Rosh Hashanah to Yom Kippur substitute

[If forgotten, repeat *Shemoneh Esrei*. See *Laws* §62-63.]

בינה

אַתָּה חוֹנֵן לְאָדָם דַּעַת, וּמְלַמֵּד לֶאֱנוֹשׁ בִּינָה.

After the Sabbath or a Festival, add [if forgotten do not repeat *Shemoneh Esrei; see Laws* §66]:

אַתָּה חוֹנַנְתָּנוּ* לְמַדַּע תּוֹרָתֶךָ, וַתְּלַמְּדֵנוּ לַעֲשׂוֹת חֻקֵּי רְצוֹנֶךָ וַתַּבְדֵּל יהוה אֱלֹהֵינוּ בֵּין קֹדֶשׁ לְחוֹל בֵּין אוֹר לְחוֹשֶׁךְ, בֵּין יִשְׂרָאֵל לָעַמִּים, בֵּין יוֹם הַשְּׁבִיעִי לְשֵׁשֶׁת יְמֵי הַמַּעֲשֶׂה. אָבִינוּ מַלְכֵּנוּ הָחֵל עָלֵינוּ הַיָּמִים הַבָּאִים לִקְרָאתֵנוּ לְשָׁלוֹם חֲשׂוּכִים מִכָּל חֵטְא וּמְנֻקִּים מִכָּל עָוֹן וּמְדֻבָּקִים בְּיִרְאָתֶךָ. וְ...

חָנֵּנוּ מֵאִתְּךָ דֵּעָה בִּינָה וְהַשְׂכֵּל. בָּרוּךְ אַתָּה יהוה, חוֹנֵן הַדָּעַת.

תשובה

הֲשִׁיבֵנוּ אָבִינוּ לְתוֹרָתֶךָ, וְקָרְבֵנוּ מַלְכֵּנוּ לַעֲבוֹדָתֶךָ, וְהַחֲזִירֵנוּ בִּתְשׁוּבָה שְׁלֵמָה לְפָנֶיךָ. בָּרוּךְ אַתָּה יהוה, הָרוֹצֶה בִּתְשׁוּבָה.

סליחה

Strike the left side of the chest with the right fist while reciting the words חָטָאנוּ and פָּשָׁעְנוּ.

סְלַח לָנוּ אָבִינוּ כִּי חָטָאנוּ, מְחַל לָנוּ מַלְכֵּנוּ כִּי פָשָׁעְנוּ, כִּי מוֹחֵל וְסוֹלֵחַ אָתָּה. בָּרוּךְ אַתָּה יהוה, חַנּוּן הַמַּרְבֶּה לִסְלוֹחַ.

אַתָּה חוֹנַנְתָּנוּ — *You have graced us.* The *Havdalah* blessing that differentiates between the Sabbath and the weekdays is quite properly inserted in the blessing of wisdom because of the well known dictum of the Sages: אִם אֵין דֵּעָה הַבְדָּלָה מִנַּיִן, *if there is no wisdom, how can there be differentiation? (Yerushalmi, Berachos 5:2). Seder Hayom* offers a novel reason for its

Between Shemini Atzeres and Pesach add the following.

Who makes the wind blow and makes the rain descend;

[If forgotten, see *Laws* §70-75.]

Who sustains the living with kindness, resuscitates the dead with abundant mercy, supports the fallen, heals the sick, releases the confined, and maintains His faith to those asleep in the dust. Who is like You, O Master of mighty deeds, and who is comparable to You, O King Who causes death and restores life and makes salvation sprout!

From Rosh Hashanah to Yom Kippur add the following.

Who is like You, Merciful Father, Who recalls His creatures mercifully for life!

[If forgotten, do not repeat *Shemoneh Esrei.* See *Laws* §61.]

And You are faithful to resuscitate the dead. Blessed are You, HASHEM, Who resuscitates the dead.

HOLINESS OF GOD'S NAME

אַתָּה *You are holy and Your Name is holy, and holy ones praise You every day, forever. Blessed are You, HASHEM, °the holy God.*

°From Rosh Hashanah to Yom Kippur substitute: *the holy King.*

[If forgotten, repeat *Shemoneh Esrei.* See *Laws* §62-63.]

INSIGHT

אַתָּה. *You graciously endow man with wisdom and teach insight to a frail mortal.*

After the Sabbath or Festival, add [if forgotten do not repeat *Shemoneh Esrei;* see *Laws* §66]:

אַתָּה *You have graced* us with intelligence to study Your Torah and You have taught us to perform the decrees You have willed. HASHEM, our God, You have distinguished between the sacred and the secular,* between light and darkness, between Israel and the peoples, between the seventh day and the six days of labor. Our Father, our King, begin for us the days approaching us for peace, free from all sin, cleansed from all iniquity and attached to fear of You. And ...*

Endow us graciously from Yourself with wisdom, insight, and discernment. Blessed are You, HASHEM, gracious Giver of wisdom.

REPENTANCE

הֲשִׁיבֵנוּ *Bring us back, our Father, to Your Torah, and bring us near, our King, to Your service, and influence us to return in perfect repentance before You. Blessed are You, HASHEM, Who desires repentance.*

FORGIVENESS

Strike the left side of the chest with the right fist while reciting the words *'erred'* and *'sinned'.*

סְלַח *Forgive us, our Father, for we have erred; pardon us, our King, for we have willfully sinned; for You pardon and forgive. Blessed are You, HASHEM, the gracious One Who pardons abundantly.*

---

placement: the word בִּינָה, *insight,* contains the initials of the four blessings of the *Havdalah* service: בְּשָׂמִים, יַיִן, נֵר, הַבְדָּלָה, *spices, wine, flame, Havdalah.*

If one forgets to recite אַתָּה חוֹנַנְתָּנוּ, *You have graced us,* he need not rectify his omission for he will recite or hear *Havdalah* after *Maariv.*

וַתַּבְדֵּל ... בֵּין קֹדֶשׁ לְחוֹל – *You have distinguished between the sacred and the secular.* Four

גאולה

רְאֵה בְעָנְיֵנוּ, וְרִיבָה רִיבֵנוּ, וּגְאָלֵנוּ[1] מְהֵרָה לְמַעַן שְׁמֶךָ, כִּי גוֹאֵל חָזָק אָתָּה. בָּרוּךְ אַתָּה יהוה, גּוֹאֵל יִשְׂרָאֵל.

רפואה

רְפָאֵנוּ יהוה וְנֵרָפֵא, הוֹשִׁיעֵנוּ וְנִוָּשֵׁעָה, כִּי תְהִלָּתֵנוּ אָתָּה,[2] וְהַעֲלֵה רְפוּאָה שְׁלֵמָה לְכָל מַכּוֹתֵינוּ,°° כִּי אֵל מֶלֶךְ רוֹפֵא נֶאֱמָן וְרַחֲמָן אָתָּה. בָּרוּךְ אַתָּה יהוה, רוֹפֵא חוֹלֵי עַמּוֹ יִשְׂרָאֵל.

ברכת השנים

In the following blessing וְתֵן בְּרָכָה is recited from the beginning of Pesach through *Minchah* of December 4th (or 5th in the year before a civil leap year). וְתֵן טַל וּמָטָר לִבְרָכָה is recited from *Maariv* of December 4th (or 5th) until Pesach. [If the wrong phrase is recited, see *Laws,* §79-83.]

בָּרֵךְ עָלֵינוּ יהוה אֱלֹהֵינוּ אֶת הַשָּׁנָה הַזֹּאת וְאֶת כָּל מִינֵי תְבוּאָתָהּ לְטוֹבָה, (וְתֵן בְּרָכָה) (וְתֵן טַל וּמָטָר לִבְרָכָה) עַל פְּנֵי הָאֲדָמָה, וְשַׂבְּעֵנוּ מִטּוּבֶךָ, וּבָרֵךְ שְׁנָתֵנוּ כַּשָּׁנִים הַטּוֹבוֹת. בָּרוּךְ אַתָּה יהוה, מְבָרֵךְ הַשָּׁנִים.

קיבוץ גליות

תְּקַע בְּשׁוֹפָר גָּדוֹל לְחֵרוּתֵנוּ, וְשָׂא נֵס לְקַבֵּץ גָּלֻיּוֹתֵינוּ, וְקַבְּצֵנוּ יַחַד מֵאַרְבַּע כַּנְפוֹת הָאָרֶץ.[3] בָּרוּךְ אַתָּה יהוה, מְקַבֵּץ נִדְחֵי עַמּוֹ יִשְׂרָאֵל.

דין

הָשִׁיבָה שׁוֹפְטֵינוּ כְּבָרִאשׁוֹנָה, וְיוֹעֲצֵינוּ כְּבַתְּחִלָּה,[4] וְהָסֵר מִמֶּנּוּ יָגוֹן וַאֲנָחָה, וּמְלוֹךְ עָלֵינוּ אַתָּה יהוה לְבַדְּךָ בְּחֶסֶד וּבְרַחֲמִים, וְצַדְּקֵנוּ בַּמִּשְׁפָּט. בָּרוּךְ אַתָּה יהוה, °מֶלֶךְ אוֹהֵב צְדָקָה וּמִשְׁפָּט.

°הַמֶּלֶךְ הַמִּשְׁפָּט. —From Rosh Hashanah to Yom Kippur substitute
[If forgotten, do not repeat *Shemoneh Esrei.* See *Laws* §61.]

ברכת המינים

וְלַמַּלְשִׁינִים אַל תְּהִי תִקְוָה, וְכָל הָרִשְׁעָה כְּרֶגַע תֹּאבֵד, וְכָל אֹיְבֶיךָ מְהֵרָה יִכָּרֵתוּ, וְהַזֵּדִים מְהֵרָה

°°At this point one may interject a prayer for one who is ill:
יְהִי רָצוֹן מִלְּפָנֶיךָ יהוה אֱלֹהַי וֵאלֹהֵי אֲבוֹתַי, שֶׁתִּשְׁלַח מְהֵרָה רְפוּאָה שְׁלֵמָה מִן הַשָּׁמַיִם, רְפוּאַת הַנֶּפֶשׁ וּרְפוּאַת הַגּוּף
לַחוֹלֶה (patient's name) בֶּן (mother's name) בְּתוֹךְ שְׁאָר חוֹלֵי יִשְׂרָאֵל. —for a male
לַחוֹלָה (patient's name) בַּת (mother's name) בְּתוֹךְ שְׁאָר חוֹלֵי יִשְׂרָאֵל. —for a female
כִּי אֵל ...—continue

REDEMPTION

רְאֵה *Behold our affliction, take up our grievance, and redeem us*[1] *speedily for Your Name's sake, for You are a powerful Redeemer. Blessed are You, HASHEM, Redeemer of Israel.*

HEALTH AND HEALING

רְפָאֵנוּ *Heal us, HASHEM — then we will be healed; save us — then we will be saved, for You are our praise.*[2] *Bring complete recovery for all our ailments,* °°*for You are God, King, the faithful and compassionate Healer. Blessed are You, HASHEM, Who heals the sick of His people Israel.*

YEAR OF PROSPERITY

In the following blessing, *'give a blessing'* is recited from the beginning of Pesach through *Minchah* of December 4th (or 5th in the year before a civil leap year); *'give dew and rain for a blessing'* is recited from *Maariv* of December 4th (or 5th) until Pesach. [If the wrong phrase is recited, see *Laws,* §79-83.]

בָּרֵךְ *Bless on our behalf — O HASHEM, our God — this year and all its kinds of crops for the best, and give (dew and rain for) a blessing on the face of the earth, and satisfy us from Your bounty, and bless our year like the best years. Blessed are You, HASHEM, Who blesses the years.*

INGATHERING OF EXILES

תְּקַע *Sound the great shofar for our freedom, raise the banner to gather our exiles and gather us together from the four corners of the earth.*[3] *Blessed are You, HASHEM, Who gathers in the dispersed of His people Israel.*

RESTORATION OF JUSTICE

הָשִׁיבָה *Restore our judges as in earliest times and our counselors as at first;*[4] *remove from us sorrow and groan; and reign over us — You, HASHEM, alone — with kindness and compassion, and justify us through judgment. Blessed are You, HASHEM, the* °*King Who loves righteousness and judgment.*

°From Rosh Hashanah to Yom Kippur substitute: *the King of judgment.*
[If forgotten, do not repeat *Shemoneh Esrei.* See *Laws* §64.]

AGAINST HERETICS

וְלַמַּלְשִׁינִים *And for slanderers let there be no hope; and may all wickedness perish in an instant; and may all Your enemies be cut down speedily. May You speedily*

°°At this point one may interject a prayer for one who is ill:

May it be Your will, HASHEM, my God, and the God of my forefathers, that You quickly send a complete recovery from heaven, spiritual healing and physical healing to the patient (name) son/daughter of (mother's name) among the other patients of Israel. Continue: ***For You are God ...***

(1) Cf. *Psalms* 119:153-154. (2) Cf. *Jeremiah* 17:14. (3) Cf. *Isaiah* 11:12. (4) Cf. 1:26.

distinctions are enumerated here: (1) Between the holy and the secular — not the profane, but the mundane factors in life that prevent us from recognizing and achieving holiness; (2) between light and darkness, which also symbolizes the distinction between good and evil; (3) the fact that God took Israel to be His chosen people from among all the nations; and (4) between the day that testifies to God as the Creator and the days when His Presence is less apparent.

תְעַקֵּר וּתְשַׁבֵּר וּתְמַגֵּר וְתַכְנִיעַ בִּמְהֵרָה בְיָמֵינוּ. בָּרוּךְ אַתָּה יהוה, שׁוֹבֵר אֹיְבִים וּמַכְנִיעַ זֵדִים.

צדיקים

עַל הַצַּדִּיקִים וְעַל הַחֲסִידִים, וְעַל זִקְנֵי עַמְּךָ בֵּית יִשְׂרָאֵל, וְעַל פְּלֵיטַת סוֹפְרֵיהֶם, וְעַל גֵּרֵי הַצֶּדֶק וְעָלֵינוּ, יֶהֱמוּ רַחֲמֶיךָ יהוה אֱלֹהֵינוּ, וְתֵן שָׂכָר טוֹב לְכָל הַבּוֹטְחִים בְּשִׁמְךָ בֶּאֱמֶת, וְשִׂים חֶלְקֵנוּ עִמָּהֶם לְעוֹלָם, וְלֹא נֵבוֹשׁ כִּי בְךָ בָּטָחְנוּ. בָּרוּךְ אַתָּה יהוה, מִשְׁעָן וּמִבְטָח לַצַּדִּיקִים.

בנין ירושלים

וְלִירוּשָׁלַיִם עִירְךָ בְּרַחֲמִים תָּשׁוּב, וְתִשְׁכּוֹן בְּתוֹכָהּ כַּאֲשֶׁר דִּבַּרְתָּ, וּבְנֵה אוֹתָהּ בְּקָרוֹב בְּיָמֵינוּ בִּנְיַן עוֹלָם, וְכִסֵּא דָוִד מְהֵרָה לְתוֹכָהּ תָּכִין. בָּרוּךְ אַתָּה יהוה, בּוֹנֵה יְרוּשָׁלָיִם.

מלכות בית דוד

אֶת צֶמַח דָּוִד עַבְדְּךָ מְהֵרָה תַצְמִיחַ, וְקַרְנוֹ תָּרוּם בִּישׁוּעָתֶךָ, כִּי לִישׁוּעָתְךָ קִוִּינוּ כָּל הַיּוֹם. בָּרוּךְ אַתָּה יהוה, מַצְמִיחַ קֶרֶן יְשׁוּעָה.

קבלת תפלה

שְׁמַע קוֹלֵנוּ יהוה אֱלֹהֵינוּ, חוּס וְרַחֵם עָלֵינוּ, וְקַבֵּל בְּרַחֲמִים וּבְרָצוֹן אֶת תְּפִלָּתֵנוּ, כִּי אֵל שׁוֹמֵעַ תְּפִלּוֹת וְתַחֲנוּנִים אָתָּה. וּמִלְּפָנֶיךָ מַלְכֵּנוּ רֵיקָם אַל תְּשִׁיבֵנוּ,°

°During the silent *Shemoneh Esrei* one may insert either or both of these personal prayers.

For forgiveness:

אָנָּא יהוה, חָטָאתִי עָוִיתִי וּפָשַׁעְתִּי לְפָנֶיךָ, מִיּוֹם הֱיוֹתִי עַל הָאֲדָמָה עַד הַיּוֹם הַזֶּה (וּבִפְרַט בַּחֵטְא ....). אָנָּא יהוה, עֲשֵׂה לְמַעַן שִׁמְךָ הַגָּדוֹל, וּתְכַפֶּר לִי עַל עֲוֹנַי וַחֲטָאַי וּפְשָׁעַי שֶׁחָטָאתִי וְשֶׁעָוִיתִי וְשֶׁפָּשַׁעְתִּי לְפָנֶיךָ, מִנְּעוּרַי עַד הַיּוֹם הַזֶּה. וּתְמַלֵּא כָּל הַשֵּׁמוֹת שֶׁפָּגַמְתִּי בְּשִׁמְךָ הַגָּדוֹל.

For livelihood:

אַתָּה הוּא יהוה הָאֱלֹהִים, הַזָּן וּמְפַרְנֵס וּמְכַלְכֵּל מִקַּרְנֵי רְאֵמִים עַד בֵּיצֵי כִנִּים. הַטְרִיפֵנִי לֶחֶם חֻקִּי, וְהַמְצֵא לִי וּלְכָל בְּנֵי בֵיתִי מְזוֹנוֹתַי קוֹדֶם שֶׁאֶצְטָרֵךְ לָהֶם, בְּנַחַת וְלֹא בְצַעַר, בְּהֶתֵּר וְלֹא בְאִסּוּר, בְּכָבוֹד וְלֹא בְּבִזָּיוֹן, לְחַיִּים וּלְשָׁלוֹם, מִשֶּׁפַע בְּרָכָה וְהַצְלָחָה, וּמִשֶּׁפַע בְּרֵכָה עֶלְיוֹנָה, כְּדֵי שֶׁאוּכַל לַעֲשׂוֹת רְצוֹנֶךָ וְלַעֲסוֹק בְּתוֹרָתֶךָ וּלְקַיֵּם מִצְוֹתֶיךָ. וְאַל תַּצְרִיכֵנִי לִידֵי מַתְּנַת בָּשָׂר וָדָם. וִיקֻיַּם בִּי מִקְרָא שֶׁכָּתוּב: פּוֹתֵחַ אֶת יָדֶךָ וּמַשְׂבִּיעַ לְכָל חַי רָצוֹן.[1] וְכָתוּב: הַשְׁלֵךְ עַל יהוה יְהָבְךָ וְהוּא יְכַלְכְּלֶךָ.[2]

Continue—כִּי אַתָּה ...

uproot, smash, cast down, and humble the wanton sinners — speedily in our days. Blessed are You, HASHEM, *Who breaks enemies and humbles wanton sinners.*

THE RIGHTEOUS

עַל הַצַּדִּיקִים *On the righteous, on the devout, on the elders of Your people the Family of Israel, on the remnant of their scholars, on the righteous converts and on ourselves — may Your compassion be aroused,* HASHEM, *our God, and give goodly reward to all who sincerely believe in Your Name. Put our lot with them forever, and we will not feel ashamed, for we trust in You. Blessed are You,* HASHEM, *Mainstay and Assurance of the righteous.*

REBUILDING JERUSALEM

וְלִירוּשָׁלַיִם *And to Jerusalem, Your city, may You return in compassion, and may You rest within it, as You have spoken. May You rebuild it soon in our days as an eternal structure, and may you speedily establish the throne of David within it. Blessed are You,* HASHEM, *the Builder of Jerusalem.*

DAVIDIC REIGN

אֶת צֶמַח *The offspring of Your servant David may You speedily cause to flourish, and enhance his pride through Your salvation, for we hope for Your salvation all day long. Blessed are You,* HASHEM, *Who causes the pride of salvation to flourish.*

ACCEPTANCE OF PRAYER

שְׁמַע קוֹלֵנוּ *Hear our voice,* HASHEM *our God, pity and be compassionate to us, and accept — with compassion and favor — our prayer, for God Who hears prayers and supplications are You. From before Yourself, our King, turn us not away empty-handed.*°

°During the silent *Shemoneh Esrei* one may insert either or both of these personal prayers.

For forgiveness:

אָנָּא *Please, O* HASHEM, *I have erred, been iniquitous, and willfully sinned before You, from the day I have existed on earth until this very day (and especially with the sin of ...). Please,* HASHEM, *act for the sake of Your Great Name and grant me atonement for my iniquities, my errors, and my willful sins through which I have erred, been iniquitous, and willfully sinned before You, from my youth until this day. And make whole all the Names that I have blemished in Your Great Name.*

For livelihood:

אַתָּה *It is You,* HASHEM *the God, Who nourishes, sustains, and supports, from the horns of re'eimim to the eggs of lice. Provide me with my allotment of bread; and bring forth for me and all members of my household, my food, before I have need for it; in contentment but not in pain, in a permissible but not a forbidden manner, in honor but not in disgrace, for life and for peace; from the flow of blessing and success and from the flow of the Heavenly spring, so that I be enabled to do Your will and engage in Your Torah and fulfill Your commandments. Make me not needful of people's largesse; and may there be fulfilled in me the verse that states, 'You open Your hand and satisfy the desire of every living thing'*[1] *and that states, 'Cast Your burden upon* HASHEM *and He will support you.'*[2]

Continue: *For You hear the prayer ...*

(1) *Psalms* 145:16. (2) 55:23.

כִּי אַתָּה שׁוֹמֵעַ תְּפִלַּת עַמְּךָ יִשְׂרָאֵל בְּרַחֲמִים. בָּרוּךְ אַתָּה יהוה, שׁוֹמֵעַ תְּפִלָּה.

עבודה

רְצֵה יהוה אֱלֹהֵינוּ בְּעַמְּךָ יִשְׂרָאֵל וּבִתְפִלָּתָם, וְהָשֵׁב אֶת הָעֲבוֹדָה לִדְבִיר בֵּיתֶךָ. וְאִשֵּׁי יִשְׂרָאֵל וּתְפִלָּתָם בְּאַהֲבָה תְקַבֵּל בְּרָצוֹן, וּתְהִי לְרָצוֹן תָּמִיד עֲבוֹדַת יִשְׂרָאֵל עַמֶּךָ.

On Rosh Chodesh and Chol HaMoed add the following.

אֱלֹהֵינוּ וֵאלֹהֵי אֲבוֹתֵינוּ, יַעֲלֶה, וְיָבֹא, וְיַגִּיעַ, וְיֵרָאֶה, וְיֵרָצֶה, וְיִשָּׁמַע, וְיִפָּקֵד, וְיִזָּכֵר זִכְרוֹנֵנוּ וּפִקְדוֹנֵנוּ, וְזִכְרוֹן אֲבוֹתֵינוּ, וְזִכְרוֹן מָשִׁיחַ בֶּן דָּוִד עַבְדֶּךָ, וְזִכְרוֹן יְרוּשָׁלַיִם עִיר קָדְשֶׁךָ, וְזִכְרוֹן כָּל עַמְּךָ בֵּית יִשְׂרָאֵל לְפָנֶיךָ, לִפְלֵיטָה לְטוֹבָה, לְחֵן וּלְחֶסֶד וּלְרַחֲמִים, לְחַיִּים וּלְשָׁלוֹם בְּיוֹם

on Rosh Chodesh	on Pesach	on Succos
רֹאשׁ הַחֹדֶשׁ	חַג הַמַּצּוֹת	חַג הַסֻּכּוֹת

הַזֶּה. זָכְרֵנוּ יהוה אֱלֹהֵינוּ בּוֹ לְטוֹבָה, וּפָקְדֵנוּ בוֹ לִבְרָכָה, וְהוֹשִׁיעֵנוּ בוֹ לְחַיִּים. וּבִדְבַר יְשׁוּעָה וְרַחֲמִים, חוּס וְחָנֵּנוּ וְרַחֵם עָלֵינוּ וְהוֹשִׁיעֵנוּ, כִּי אֵלֶיךָ עֵינֵינוּ, כִּי אֵל מֶלֶךְ חַנּוּן וְרַחוּם אָתָּה.[1]

[If forgotten, repeat *Shemoneh Esrei* (except at *Maariv* of Rosh Chodesh). See *Laws* §89.]

וְתֶחֱזֶינָה עֵינֵינוּ בְּשׁוּבְךָ לְצִיּוֹן בְּרַחֲמִים. בָּרוּךְ אַתָּה יהוה, הַמַּחֲזִיר שְׁכִינָתוֹ לְצִיּוֹן.

הודאה

Bow at מוֹדִים; straighten up at ה׳.

מוֹדִים אֲנַחְנוּ לָךְ שָׁאַתָּה הוּא יהוה אֱלֹהֵינוּ וֵאלֹהֵי אֲבוֹתֵינוּ לְעוֹלָם וָעֶד. צוּר חַיֵּינוּ, מָגֵן יִשְׁעֵנוּ אַתָּה הוּא לְדוֹר וָדוֹר. נוֹדֶה לְּךָ וּנְסַפֵּר תְּהִלָּתֶךָ[2] עַל חַיֵּינוּ הַמְּסוּרִים בְּיָדֶךָ, וְעַל נִשְׁמוֹתֵינוּ הַפְּקוּדוֹת לָךְ, וְעַל נִסֶּיךָ שֶׁבְּכָל יוֹם עִמָּנוּ, וְעַל נִפְלְאוֹתֶיךָ וְטוֹבוֹתֶיךָ שֶׁבְּכָל עֵת, עֶרֶב וָבֹקֶר וְצָהֳרָיִם. הַטּוֹב כִּי לֹא כָלוּ רַחֲמֶיךָ, וְהַמְרַחֵם כִּי לֹא תַמּוּ חֲסָדֶיךָ,[3] מֵעוֹלָם קִוִּינוּ לָךְ:

On Chanukah and Purim add the following.
[If forgotten do not repeat *Shemoneh Esrei*. See *Laws* §90.]

(וְ)עַל הַנִּסִּים, וְעַל הַפֻּרְקָן, וְעַל הַגְּבוּרוֹת, וְעַל הַתְּשׁוּעוֹת, וְעַל הַמִּלְחָמוֹת, שֶׁעָשִׂיתָ לַאֲבוֹתֵינוּ בַּיָּמִים הָהֵם בַּזְּמַן הַזֶּה.

For You hear the prayer of Your people Israel with compassion. Blessed are You, HASHEM, Who hears prayer.

TEMPLE SERVICE

רְצֵה *Be favorable, HASHEM, our God, toward Your people Israel and their prayer and restore the service to the Holy of Holies of Your Temple. The fire-offerings of Israel and their prayer accept with love and favor, and may the service of Your people Israel always be favorable to You.*

On Rosh Chodesh and Chol HaMoed add the following.

אֱלֹהֵינוּ *Our God and God of our forefathers, may there rise, come, reach, be noted, be favored, be heard, be considered, and be remembered — the remembrance and consideration of ourselves; the remembrance of our forefathers; the remembrance of Messiah, son of David, Your servant; the remembrance of Jerusalem, the City of Your Holiness, the remembrance of Your entire people the Family of Israel — before You, for deliverance, for goodness, for grace, for kindness, and for compassion, for life, and for peace on this day of*

on Rosh Chodesh	on Passover	on Succos
Rosh Chodesh.	*the Festival of Matzos.*	*the Succos Festival.*

Remember us on it, HASHEM, our God, for goodness; consider us on it for blessing; and help us on it for life. In the matter of salvation and compassion, pity, be gracious and compassionate with us and help us, for our eyes are turned to You, because You are God, the gracious, and compassionate King.[1]

[If forgotten, repeat *Shemoneh Esrei* (except at *Maariv* of Rosh Chodesh). See *Laws* §89.]

וְתֶחֱזֶינָה *May our eyes behold Your return to Zion in compassion. Blessed are You, HASHEM, Who restores His Presence to Zion.*

THANKSGIVING [MODIM]

Bow at *'We gratefully thank You'*; straighten up at *'HASHEM.'*

מוֹדִים *We gratefully thank You, for it is You Who are HASHEM, our God and the God of our forefathers for all eternity; Rock of our lives, Shield of our salvation are You from generation to generation. We shall thank You and relate Your praise*[2] *— for our lives, which are committed to Your power and for our souls that are entrusted to You; for Your miracles that are with us every day; and for Your wonders and favors in every season — evening, morning, and afternoon. The Beneficent One, for Your compassions were never exhausted, and the Compassionate One, for Your kindnesses never ended*[3] *— always have we put our hope in You.*

On Chanukah and Purim add the following.
[If forgotten do not repeat *Shemoneh Esrei.* See *Laws* §90.]

(וְ)עַל *(And) for the miracles, and for the salvation, and for the mighty deeds, and for the victories, and for the battles which You performed for our forefathers in those days, at this time.*

(1) Cf. *Nechemiah* 9:31. (2) Cf. *Psalms* 79:13. (3) Cf. *Lamentations* 3:22.

On Chanukah:

בִּימֵי מַתִּתְיָהוּ בֶּן יוֹחָנָן כֹּהֵן גָּדוֹל חַשְׁמוֹנַאי וּבָנָיו, כְּשֶׁעָמְדָה מַלְכוּת יָוָן הָרְשָׁעָה עַל עַמְּךָ יִשְׂרָאֵל, לְהַשְׁכִּיחָם תּוֹרָתֶךָ, וּלְהַעֲבִירָם מֵחֻקֵּי רְצוֹנֶךָ. וְאַתָּה בְּרַחֲמֶיךָ הָרַבִּים, עָמַדְתָּ לָהֶם בְּעֵת צָרָתָם, רַבְתָּ אֶת רִיבָם, דַּנְתָּ אֶת דִּינָם, נָקַמְתָּ אֶת נִקְמָתָם.[1] מָסַרְתָּ גִבּוֹרִים בְּיַד חַלָּשִׁים, וְרַבִּים בְּיַד מְעַטִּים, וּטְמֵאִים בְּיַד טְהוֹרִים, וּרְשָׁעִים בְּיַד צַדִּיקִים, וְזֵדִים בְּיַד עוֹסְקֵי תוֹרָתֶךָ. וּלְךָ עָשִׂיתָ שֵׁם גָּדוֹל וְקָדוֹשׁ בְּעוֹלָמֶךָ, וּלְעַמְּךָ יִשְׂרָאֵל עָשִׂיתָ תְּשׁוּעָה גְדוֹלָה[2] וּפֻרְקָן כְּהַיּוֹם הַזֶּה. וְאַחַר כֵּן בָּאוּ בָנֶיךָ לִדְבִיר בֵּיתֶךָ, וּפִנּוּ אֶת הֵיכָלֶךָ, וְטִהֲרוּ אֶת מִקְדָּשֶׁךָ, וְהִדְלִיקוּ נֵרוֹת בְּחַצְרוֹת קָדְשֶׁךָ, וְקָבְעוּ שְׁמוֹנַת יְמֵי חֲנֻכָּה אֵלּוּ, לְהוֹדוֹת וּלְהַלֵּל לְשִׁמְךָ הַגָּדוֹל.

On Purim:

בִּימֵי מָרְדְּכַי וְאֶסְתֵּר בְּשׁוּשַׁן הַבִּירָה, כְּשֶׁעָמַד עֲלֵיהֶם הָמָן הָרָשָׁע, בִּקֵּשׁ לְהַשְׁמִיד לַהֲרֹג וּלְאַבֵּד אֶת כָּל הַיְּהוּדִים, מִנַּעַר וְעַד זָקֵן, טַף וְנָשִׁים בְּיוֹם אֶחָד, בִּשְׁלוֹשָׁה עָשָׂר לְחֹדֶשׁ שְׁנֵים עָשָׂר, הוּא חֹדֶשׁ אֲדָר, וּשְׁלָלָם לָבוֹז.[3] וְאַתָּה בְּרַחֲמֶיךָ הָרַבִּים הֵפַרְתָּ אֶת עֲצָתוֹ, וְקִלְקַלְתָּ אֶת מַחֲשַׁבְתּוֹ, וַהֲשֵׁבוֹתָ לּוֹ גְּמוּלוֹ בְּרֹאשׁוֹ, וְתָלוּ אוֹתוֹ וְאֶת בָּנָיו עַל הָעֵץ.

וְעַל כֻּלָּם יִתְבָּרַךְ וְיִתְרוֹמַם שִׁמְךָ מַלְכֵּנוּ תָּמִיד לְעוֹלָם וָעֶד.

From Rosh Hashanah to Yom Kippur add the following.

וּכְתוֹב לְחַיִּים טוֹבִים כָּל בְּנֵי בְרִיתֶךָ.

[If forgotten, do not repeat *Shemoneh Esrei*. See *Laws* §61.]

Bend the knees at בָּרוּךְ; bow at אַתָּה; straighten up at ה'.

וְכֹל הַחַיִּים יוֹדוּךָ סֶּלָה, וִיהַלְלוּ אֶת שִׁמְךָ בֶּאֱמֶת, הָאֵל יְשׁוּעָתֵנוּ וְעֶזְרָתֵנוּ סֶלָה. בָּרוּךְ אַתָּה יהוה, הַטּוֹב שִׁמְךָ וּלְךָ נָאֶה לְהוֹדוֹת.

שלום

שָׁלוֹם רָב עַל יִשְׂרָאֵל עַמְּךָ תָּשִׂים לְעוֹלָם, כִּי אַתָּה הוּא מֶלֶךְ אָדוֹן לְכָל הַשָּׁלוֹם. וְטוֹב בְּעֵינֶיךָ לְבָרֵךְ אֶת עַמְּךָ יִשְׂרָאֵל בְּכָל עֵת וּבְכָל שָׁעָה בִּשְׁלוֹמֶךָ. °בָּרוּךְ אַתָּה יהוה, הַמְּבָרֵךְ אֶת עַמּוֹ יִשְׂרָאֵל בַּשָּׁלוֹם.

°From Rosh Hashanah to Yom Kippur substitute the following [see *Laws* §65].

בְּסֵפֶר חַיִּים בְּרָכָה וְשָׁלוֹם, וּפַרְנָסָה טוֹבָה, נִזָּכֵר וְנִכָּתֵב לְפָנֶיךָ, אֲנַחְנוּ וְכָל עַמְּךָ בֵּית יִשְׂרָאֵל, לְחַיִּים טוֹבִים וּלְשָׁלוֹם. בָּרוּךְ אַתָּה יהוה, עֹשֵׂה הַשָּׁלוֹם.

[If forgotten, do not repeat *Shemoneh Esrei*. See *Laws* §61.]

יִהְיוּ לְרָצוֹן אִמְרֵי פִי וְהֶגְיוֹן לִבִּי לְפָנֶיךָ, יהוה צוּרִי וְגֹאֲלִי.[4]

אֱלֹהַי, נְצוֹר לְשׁוֹנִי מֵרָע, וּשְׂפָתַי מִדַּבֵּר מִרְמָה,[5] וְלִמְקַלְלַי נַפְשִׁי תִדּוֹם, וְנַפְשִׁי כֶּעָפָר לַכֹּל תִּהְיֶה. פְּתַח לִבִּי

On Chanukah:

בִּימֵי *In the days of Mattisyahu, the son of Yochanan, the High Priest, the Hasmonean, and his sons — when the wicked Greek kingdom rose up against Your people Israel to make them forget Your Torah and compel them to stray from the statutes of Your Will — You in Your great mercy stood up for them in the time of their distress. You took up their grievance, judged their claim, and avenged their wrong.[1] You delivered the strong into the hands of the weak, the many into the hands of the few, the impure into the hands of the pure, the wicked into the hands of the righteous, and the wanton into the hands of the diligent students of Your Torah. For Yourself You made a great and holy Name in Your world, and for Your people Israel you worked a great victory[2] and salvation as this very day. Thereafter, Your children came to the Holy of Holies of Your House, cleansed Your Temple, purified the site of Your Holiness and kindled lights in the Courtyards of Your Sanctuary; and they established these eight days of Chanukah to express thanks and praise to Your great Name.*

On Purim:

בִּימֵי *In the days of Mordechai and Esther, in Shushan, the capital, when Haman, the wicked, rose up against them and sought to destroy, to slay, and to exterminate all the Jews, young and old, infants and women, on the same day, on the thirteenth of the twelfth month which is the month of Adar, and to plunder their possessions.[3] But You, in Your abundant mercy, nullified his counsel and frustrated his intention and caused his design to return upon his own head and they hanged him and his sons on the gallows.*

For all these, may Your Name be blessed and exalted, our King, continually forever and ever.

From Rosh Hashanah to Yom Kippur add the following.
And inscribe all the children of Your covenant for a good life.
[If forgotten, do not repeat *Shemoneh Esrei.* See *Laws* §61.]

Bend the knees at *'Blessed'*; bow at *'You'*; straighten up at *'HASHEM'*.

Everything alive will gratefully acknowledge You, Selah! and praise Your Name sincerely, O God of our salvation and help, Selah! Blessed are You, HASHEM, Your Name is 'The Beneficent One' and to You it is fitting to give thanks.

PEACE

שָׁלוֹם רָב *Establish abundant peace upon Your people Israel forever, for You are King, Master of all peace. May it be good in Your eyes to bless Your people Israel at every time and every hour with Your peace. °Blessed are You, HASHEM, Who blesses His people Israel with peace.*

°From Rosh Hashanah to Yom Kippur substitute the following [see *Laws* §65].
In the book of life, blessing, and peace, good livelihood, may we be remembered and inscribed before You — we and Your entire people the Family of Israel for a good life and for peace. Blessed are You, HASHEM, Who makes peace.
[If forgotten, do not repeat *Shemoneh Esrei.* See *Laws* §61.]

May the expressions of my mouth and the thoughts of my heart find favor before You, HASHEM, my Rock and my Redeemer.[4]

אֱלֹהַי *My God, guard my tongue from evil and my lips from speaking deceitfully.[5] To those who curse me, let my soul be silent; and let my soul be like dust to everyone. Open my heart*

(1) Cf. *Jeremiah* 51:36. (2) Cf. *I Samuel* 19:5. (3) *Esther* 3:13. (4) *Psalms* 19:15. (5) Cf. 34:14

בְּתוֹרָתֶךָ, וּבְמִצְוֹתֶיךָ תִּרְדּוֹף נַפְשִׁי. וְכֹל הַחוֹשְׁבִים עָלַי רָעָה, מְהֵרָה הָפֵר עֲצָתָם וְקַלְקֵל מַחֲשַׁבְתָּם. עֲשֵׂה לְמַעַן שְׁמֶךָ, עֲשֵׂה לְמַעַן יְמִינֶךָ, עֲשֵׂה לְמַעַן קְדֻשָּׁתֶךָ, עֲשֵׂה לְמַעַן תּוֹרָתֶךָ. לְמַעַן יֵחָלְצוּן יְדִידֶיךָ, הוֹשִׁיעָה יְמִינְךָ וַעֲנֵנִי.[1]

Some recite verses pertaining to their names at this point. See page 924.

יִהְיוּ לְרָצוֹן אִמְרֵי פִי וְהֶגְיוֹן לִבִּי לְפָנֶיךָ, יהוה צוּרִי וְגֹאֲלִי.[2] עֹשֶׂה שָׁלוֹם בִּמְרוֹמָיו, הוּא יַעֲשֶׂה שָׁלוֹם עָלֵינוּ, וְעַל כָּל יִשְׂרָאֵל. וְאִמְרוּ: אָמֵן.

יְהִי רָצוֹן מִלְּפָנֶיךָ יהוה אֱלֹהֵינוּ וֵאלֹהֵי אֲבוֹתֵינוּ, שֶׁיִּבָּנֶה בֵּית הַמִּקְדָּשׁ בִּמְהֵרָה בְיָמֵינוּ, וְתֵן חֶלְקֵנוּ בְּתוֹרָתֶךָ. וְשָׁם נַעֲבָדְךָ בְּיִרְאָה, כִּימֵי עוֹלָם וּכְשָׁנִים קַדְמוֹנִיּוֹת. וְעָרְבָה לַיהוה מִנְחַת יְהוּדָה וִירוּשָׁלָיִם, כִּימֵי עוֹלָם וּכְשָׁנִים קַדְמוֹנִיּוֹת.[3]

Shemoneh Esrei ends here. *Chazzan* does not repeat *Shemoneh Esrei* at *Maariv.*

קדיש שלם

The *Chazzan* recites קַדִּישׁ שָׁלֵם.
At the conclusion of the Sabbath (except on Tishah B'Av and Purim when the Full-*Kaddish* is recited), *chazzan* recites Half *Kaddish* (until תִּתְקַבֵּל); then congregation continues וִיהִי נֹעַם, p. 594.

יִתְגַּדַּל וְיִתְקַדַּשׁ שְׁמֵהּ רַבָּא. (Cong.— אָמֵן.) בְּעָלְמָא דִּי בְרָא כִרְעוּתֵהּ. וְיַמְלִיךְ מַלְכוּתֵהּ, בְּחַיֵּיכוֹן וּבְיוֹמֵיכוֹן וּבְחַיֵּי דְכָל בֵּית יִשְׂרָאֵל, בַּעֲגָלָא וּבִזְמַן קָרִיב. וְאִמְרוּ: אָמֵן.

(Cong.— אָמֵן. יְהֵא שְׁמֵהּ רַבָּא מְבָרַךְ לְעָלַם וּלְעָלְמֵי עָלְמַיָּא.)

יְהֵא שְׁמֵהּ רַבָּא מְבָרַךְ לְעָלַם וּלְעָלְמֵי עָלְמַיָּא.

יִתְבָּרַךְ וְיִשְׁתַּבַּח וְיִתְפָּאַר וְיִתְרוֹמַם וְיִתְנַשֵּׂא וְיִתְהַדָּר וְיִתְעַלֶּה וְיִתְהַלָּל שְׁמֵהּ דְּקֻדְשָׁא בְּרִיךְ הוּא (Cong.— בְּרִיךְ הוּא) — °לְעֵלָּא מִן כָּל (From Rosh Hashanah to Yom Kippur substitute— °לְעֵלָּא וּלְעֵלָּא מִכָּל) בִּרְכָתָא וְשִׁירָתָא תֻּשְׁבְּחָתָא וְנֶחֱמָתָא, דַּאֲמִירָן בְּעָלְמָא. וְאִמְרוּ: אָמֵן. (Cong.— אָמֵן.)

(Cong.— קַבֵּל בְּרַחֲמִים וּבְרָצוֹן אֶת תְּפִלָּתֵנוּ.)

תִּתְקַבֵּל צְלוֹתְהוֹן וּבָעוּתְהוֹן דְּכָל בֵּית יִשְׂרָאֵל קֳדָם אֲבוּהוֹן דִּי בִשְׁמַיָּא. וְאִמְרוּ: אָמֵן. (Cong.— אָמֵן.)

(Cong.— יְהִי שֵׁם יהוה מְבֹרָךְ, מֵעַתָּה וְעַד עוֹלָם.[4])

יְהֵא שְׁלָמָא רַבָּא מִן שְׁמַיָּא, וְחַיִּים עָלֵינוּ וְעַל כָּל יִשְׂרָאֵל. וְאִמְרוּ: אָמֵן. (Cong.— אָמֵן.)

(Cong.— עֶזְרִי מֵעִם יהוה, עֹשֵׂה שָׁמַיִם וָאָרֶץ.[5])

Take three steps back. Bow left and say ... עֹשֶׂה; bow right and say ... הוּא; bow forward and say וְעַל כָּל ... אָמֵן. Remain standing in place for a few moments, then take three steps forward.

עֹשֶׂה שָׁלוֹם בִּמְרוֹמָיו, הוּא יַעֲשֶׂה שָׁלוֹם עָלֵינוּ, וְעַל כָּל יִשְׂרָאֵל. וְאִמְרוּ: אָמֵן. (Cong.— אָמֵן.)

to Your Torah, then my soul will pursue Your commandments. As for all those who design evil against me, speedily nullify their counsel and disrupt their design. Act for Your Name's sake; act for Your right hand's sake; act for Your sanctity's sake; act for Your Torah's sake. That Your beloved ones may be given rest; let Your right hand save, and respond to me.[1]

Some recite verses pertaining to their names at this point. See page 924.

May the expressions of my mouth and the thoughts of my heart find favor before You, HASHEM, my Rock and my Redeemer.[2]

He Who makes peace in His heights, may He make peace upon us, and upon all Israel. Now respond: Amen.

יְהִי רָצוֹן *May it be Your will, HASHEM our God and the God of our forefathers, that the Holy Temple be rebuilt, speedily in our days. Grant us our share in Your Torah, and may we serve You there with reverence, as in days of old and in former years. Then the offering of Judah and Jerusalem will be pleasing to HASHEM, as in days of old and in former years.*[3]

Shemoneh Esrei ends here. *Chazzan* does not repeat *Shemoneh Esrei* at Maariv.

FULL KADDISH

The *chazzan* recites the Full *Kaddish:*

At the conclusion of the Sabbath, the *chazzan* recites Half-Kaddish (except Tishah B'Av and Purim when the Full *Kaddish* is recited) then the congregation continues ויהי, *May the* ... (p. 594).

יִתְגַּדַּל *May His great Name grow exalted and sanctified* (Cong.— *Amen.*) *in the world that He created as He willed. May He give reign to His kingship in your lifetimes and in your days, and in the lifetimes of the entire Family of Israel, swiftly and soon. Now respond: Amen.*

(Cong.— *Amen. May His great Name be blessed forever and ever.*)

May His great Name be blessed forever and ever.

Blessed, praised, glorified, exalted, extolled, mighty, upraised, and lauded be the Name of the Holy One, Blessed is He (Cong.— *Blessed is He*) — (From Rosh Hashanah to Yom Kippur add: *exceedingly*) *beyond any blessing and song, praise and consolation that are uttered in the world. Now respond: Amen.* (Cong.— *Amen.*)

(Cong.— *Accept our prayers with mercy and favor.*)

May the prayers and supplications of the entire Family of Israel be accepted before their Father Who is in Heaven. Now respond: Amen. (Cong.— *Amen.*)

(Cong.— *Blessed be the Name of HASHEM, from this time and forever.*[4])

May there be abundant peace from Heaven, and life, upon us and upon all Israel. Now respond: Amen. (Cong.— *Amen.*)

(Cong.— *My help is from HASHEM, Maker of heaven and earth.*[5])

Take three steps back. Bow left and say, *'He Who makes peace ...';* bow right and say, *'may He ...';* bow forward and say, *'and upon all Israel ...'* Remain standing in place for a few moments, then take three steps forward.

He Who makes peace in His heights, may He make peace upon us, and upon all Israel. Now respond: Amen. (Cong.— *Amen.*)

---

(1) *Psalms* 60:7; 108:7. (2) 19:15 (3) *Malachi* 3:4. (4) *Psalms* 113:2. (5) 121:2.

BETWEEN PESACH AND SHAVUOS THE OMER IS COUNTED (P. 282). ON TISHAH B'AV, *EICHAH* AND *KINNOS* ARE RECITED. ON PURIM, THE *MEGILLAH* (P. 786) IS READ.

Stand while reciting עָלֵינוּ (commentary on p. 158).

עָלֵינוּ לְשַׁבֵּחַ לַאֲדוֹן הַכֹּל, לָתֵת גְּדֻלָּה לְיוֹצֵר בְּרֵאשִׁית, שֶׁלֹּא עָשָׂנוּ כְּגוֹיֵי הָאֲרָצוֹת, וְלֹא שָׂמָנוּ כְּמִשְׁפְּחוֹת הָאֲדָמָה. שֶׁלֹּא שָׂם חֶלְקֵנוּ כָּהֶם, וְגוֹרָלֵנוּ כְּכָל הֲמוֹנָם. (שֶׁהֵם מִשְׁתַּחֲוִים לְהֶבֶל וָרִיק, וּמִתְפַּלְּלִים אֶל אֵל לֹא יוֹשִׁיעַ.[1]) וַאֲנַחְנוּ כּוֹרְעִים וּמִשְׁתַּחֲוִים וּמוֹדִים, לִפְנֵי מֶלֶךְ מַלְכֵי הַמְּלָכִים הַקָּדוֹשׁ בָּרוּךְ הוּא. שֶׁהוּא נוֹטֶה שָׁמַיִם וְיֹסֵד אָרֶץ,[2] וּמוֹשַׁב יְקָרוֹ בַּשָּׁמַיִם מִמַּעַל, וּשְׁכִינַת עֻזּוֹ בְּגָבְהֵי מְרוֹמִים. הוּא אֱלֹהֵינוּ, אֵין עוֹד. אֱמֶת מַלְכֵּנוּ, אֶפֶס זוּלָתוֹ, כַּכָּתוּב בְּתוֹרָתוֹ: וְיָדַעְתָּ הַיּוֹם וַהֲשֵׁבֹתָ אֶל לְבָבֶךָ, כִּי יהוה הוּא הָאֱלֹהִים בַּשָּׁמַיִם מִמַּעַל וְעַל הָאָרֶץ מִתָּחַת, אֵין עוֹד.[3]

Bow while reciting וַאֲנַחְנוּ כּוֹרְעִים וּמִשְׁתַּחֲוִים.

עַל כֵּן נְקַוֶּה לְּךָ* יהוה אֱלֹהֵינוּ לִרְאוֹת מְהֵרָה בְּתִפְאֶרֶת עֻזֶּךָ, לְהַעֲבִיר גִּלּוּלִים מִן הָאָרֶץ, וְהָאֱלִילִים כָּרוֹת יִכָּרֵתוּן, לְתַקֵּן עוֹלָם בְּמַלְכוּת שַׁדַּי. וְכָל בְּנֵי בָשָׂר יִקְרְאוּ בִשְׁמֶךָ, לְהַפְנוֹת אֵלֶיךָ כָּל רִשְׁעֵי אָרֶץ. יַכִּירוּ וְיֵדְעוּ כָּל יוֹשְׁבֵי תֵבֵל, כִּי לְךָ תִּכְרַע כָּל בֶּרֶךְ, תִּשָּׁבַע כָּל לָשׁוֹן.[4] לְפָנֶיךָ יהוה אֱלֹהֵינוּ יִכְרְעוּ וְיִפֹּלוּ, וְלִכְבוֹד שִׁמְךָ יְקָר יִתֵּנוּ. וִיקַבְּלוּ כֻלָּם אֶת עוֹל מַלְכוּתֶךָ, וְתִמְלֹךְ עֲלֵיהֶם מְהֵרָה לְעוֹלָם וָעֶד. כִּי הַמַּלְכוּת שֶׁלְּךָ הִיא וּלְעוֹלְמֵי עַד תִּמְלוֹךְ בְּכָבוֹד, כַּכָּתוּב בְּתוֹרָתֶךָ: יהוה יִמְלֹךְ לְעֹלָם וָעֶד.[5] ❖ וְנֶאֱמַר: וְהָיָה יהוה לְמֶלֶךְ עַל כָּל הָאָרֶץ, בַּיּוֹם הַהוּא יִהְיֶה יהוה אֶחָד וּשְׁמוֹ אֶחָד.[6]

Some congregations recite the following after עָלֵינוּ:

אַל תִּירָא* מִפַּחַד פִּתְאֹם, וּמִשֹּׁאַת רְשָׁעִים כִּי תָבֹא.[7] עֻצוּ עֵצָה וְתֻפָר, דַּבְּרוּ דָבָר וְלֹא יָקוּם, כִּי עִמָּנוּ אֵל.[8] וְעַד זִקְנָה אֲנִי הוּא, וְעַד שֵׂיבָה אֲנִי אֶסְבֹּל, אֲנִי עָשִׂיתִי וַאֲנִי אֶשָּׂא, וַאֲנִי אֶסְבֹּל וַאֲמַלֵּט.[9]

קדיש יתום

In the presence of a *minyan,* mourners recite קַדִּישׁ יָתוֹם, the Mourner's *Kaddish* (see *Laws* §119):

יִתְגַּדַּל וְיִתְקַדַּשׁ שְׁמֵהּ רַבָּא. (Cong.— אָמֵן.) בְּעָלְמָא דִּי בְרָא כִרְעוּתֵהּ. וְיַמְלִיךְ מַלְכוּתֵהּ, בְּחַיֵּיכוֹן וּבְיוֹמֵיכוֹן וּבְחַיֵּי דְכָל בֵּית יִשְׂרָאֵל, בַּעֲגָלָא וּבִזְמַן קָרִיב. וְאִמְרוּ: אָמֵן.

(1) *Isaiah* 45:20. (2) 51:13. (3) *Deuteronomy* 4:39. (4) Cf. *Isaiah* 45:23. (5) *Exodus* 15:18. (6) *Zechariah* 14:9. (7) *Proverbs* 3:25. (8) *Isaiah* 8:10. (9) 46:4.

BETWEEN PESACH AND SHAVUOS THE OMER IS COUNTED (P. 282). ON TISHAH B'AV, *EICHAH* AND *KINNOS* ARE RECITED. ON PURIM, THE *MEGILLAH* (P. 786) IS READ.

Stand while reciting עָלֵינוּ, *'It is our duty ...' (commentary on p. 158).*

עָלֵינוּ *It is our duty to praise the Master of all, to ascribe greatness to the Molder of primeval creation, for He has not made us like the nations of the lands and has not emplaced us like the families of the earth; for He has not assigned our portion like theirs nor our lot like all their multitudes. (For they bow to vanity and emptiness and pray to a god which helps not.[1]) But we bend our knees, bow, and acknowledge our thanks before the King Who reigns over kings, the Holy One, Blessed is He. He stretches out heaven and establishes earth's foundation,[2] the seat of His homage is in the heavens above and His powerful Presence is in the loftiest heights. He is our God and there is none other. True is our King, there is nothing beside Him, as it is written in His Torah: 'You are to know this day and take to your heart that* HASHEM *is the only God — in heaven above and on the earth below — there is none other.'[3]*

Bow while reciting *'But we bend our knees.'*

עַל כֵּן *Therefore we put our hope in You,* HASHEM *our God, that we may soon see Your mighty splendor, to remove detestable idolatry from the earth, and false gods will be utterly cut off, to perfect the universe through the Almighty's sovereignty. Then all humanity will call upon Your Name, to turn all the earth's wicked toward You. All the world's inhabitants will recognize and know that to You every knee should bend, every tongue should swear.[4] Before You,* HASHEM, *our God, they will bend every knee and cast themselves down and to the glory of Your Name they will render homage, and they will all accept upon themselves the yoke of Your kingship that You may reign over them soon and eternally. For the kingdom is Yours and You will reign for all eternity in glory as it is written in Your Torah:* HASHEM *shall reign for all eternity.[5]* Chazzan — *And it is said:* HASHEM *will be King over all the world — on that day* HASHEM *will be One and His Name will be One.[6]*

In some congregations the following is recited after *Aleinu:*

אַל תִּירָא *Do not fear sudden terror, or the holocaust of the wicked when it comes.[7] Plan a conspiracy and it will be annulled; speak your piece and it shall not stand, for God is with us.[8] Even till your seniority, I remain unchanged; and even till your ripe old age, I shall endure. I created you and I shall bear you; I shall endure and rescue.[9]*

THE MOURNER'S KADDISH

In the presence of a *minyan,* mourners recite the Mourner's *Kaddish* (see *Laws* §119):

[A transliteration of this *Kaddish* appears on page 1043, commentary on p. 57.]

יִתְגַּדַּל *May His great Name grow exalted and sanctified* (Cong.— *Amen.*) *in the world that He created as He willed. May He give reign to His kingship in your lifetimes and in your days, and in the lifetimes of the entire Family of Israel, swiftly and soon. Now respond: Amen.*

(.Cong— אָמֵן. יְהֵא שְׁמֵהּ רַבָּא מְבָרַךְ לְעָלַם וּלְעָלְמֵי עָלְמַיָּא.)
יְהֵא שְׁמֵהּ רַבָּא מְבָרַךְ לְעָלַם וּלְעָלְמֵי עָלְמַיָּא.

יִתְבָּרַךְ וְיִשְׁתַּבַּח וְיִתְפָּאַר וְיִתְרוֹמַם וְיִתְנַשֵּׂא וְיִתְהַדָּר וְיִתְעַלֶּה וְיִתְהַלָּל שְׁמֵהּ דְּקֻדְשָׁא בְּרִיךְ הוּא (.Cong— בְּרִיךְ הוּא) — °לְעֵֽלָּא מִן כָּל (From Rosh Hashanah to Yom Kippur substitute— °לְעֵֽלָּא וּלְעֵֽלָּא מִכָּל) בִּרְכָתָא וְשִׁירָתָא תֻּשְׁבְּחָתָא וְנֶחֱמָתָא, דַּאֲמִירָן בְּעָלְמָא. וְאִמְרוּ: אָמֵן. (.Cong— אָמֵן.)

יְהֵא שְׁלָמָא רַבָּא מִן שְׁמַיָּא, וְחַיִּים עָלֵינוּ וְעַל כָּל יִשְׂרָאֵל. וְאִמְרוּ: אָמֵן. (.Cong— אָמֵן.)

עֹשֶׂה שָׁלוֹם בִּמְרוֹמָיו, הוּא יַעֲשֶׂה שָׁלוֹם עָלֵינוּ, וְעַל כָּל יִשְׂרָאֵל. וְאִמְרוּ: אָמֵן. (.Cong— אָמֵן.)

From Rosh Chodesh Elul through Shemini Atzeres, *Psalm 27*, לְדָוִד, is recited; comm. p. 170.

לְדָוִד, יהוה אוֹרִי וְיִשְׁעִי, מִמִּי אִירָא, יהוה מָעוֹז חַיַּי, מִמִּי אֶפְחָד. בִּקְרֹב עָלַי מְרֵעִים לֶאֱכֹל אֶת בְּשָׂרִי, צָרַי וְאֹיְבַי לִי, הֵמָּה כָשְׁלוּ וְנָפָלוּ. אִם תַּחֲנֶה עָלַי מַחֲנֶה, לֹא יִירָא לִבִּי, אִם תָּקוּם עָלַי מִלְחָמָה, בְּזֹאת אֲנִי בוֹטֵחַ. אַחַת שָׁאַלְתִּי מֵאֵת יהוה, אוֹתָהּ אֲבַקֵּשׁ, שִׁבְתִּי בְּבֵית יהוה כָּל יְמֵי חַיַּי, לַחֲזוֹת בְּנֹעַם יהוה, וּלְבַקֵּר בְּהֵיכָלוֹ. כִּי יִצְפְּנֵנִי בְּסֻכֹּה בְּיוֹם רָעָה, יַסְתִּרֵנִי בְּסֵתֶר אָהֳלוֹ, בְּצוּר יְרוֹמְמֵנִי. וְעַתָּה יָרוּם רֹאשִׁי עַל אֹיְבַי סְבִיבוֹתַי, וְאֶזְבְּחָה בְאָהֳלוֹ זִבְחֵי תְרוּעָה, אָשִׁירָה וַאֲזַמְּרָה לַיהוה. שְׁמַע יהוה קוֹלִי אֶקְרָא, וְחָנֵּנִי וַעֲנֵנִי. לְךָ אָמַר לִבִּי בַּקְּשׁוּ פָנָי, אֶת פָּנֶיךָ יהוה אֲבַקֵּשׁ. אַל תַּסְתֵּר פָּנֶיךָ מִמֶּנִּי, אַל תַּט בְּאַף עַבְדֶּךָ, עֶזְרָתִי הָיִיתָ, אַל תִּטְּשֵׁנִי וְאַל תַּעַזְבֵנִי, אֱלֹהֵי יִשְׁעִי. כִּי אָבִי וְאִמִּי עֲזָבוּנִי, וַיהוה יַאַסְפֵנִי. הוֹרֵנִי יהוה דַּרְכֶּךָ, וּנְחֵנִי בְּאֹרַח מִישׁוֹר, לְמַעַן שׁוֹרְרָי. אַל תִּתְּנֵנִי בְּנֶפֶשׁ צָרָי, כִּי קָמוּ בִי עֵדֵי שֶׁקֶר, וִיפֵחַ חָמָס. ❖ לוּלֵא הֶאֱמַנְתִּי לִרְאוֹת בְּטוּב יהוה בְּאֶרֶץ חַיִּים. קַוֵּה אֶל יהוה, חֲזַק וְיַאֲמֵץ לִבֶּךָ, וְקַוֵּה אֶל יהוה.

In the presence of a *minyan,* mourners recite קַדִּישׁ יָתוֹם (p. 280).

In a house of mourning, Psalm 49, לַמְנַצֵּחַ, *For the conductor* (p. 174), is recited after *Maariv.*

ספירת העומר

The Omer is counted from the second night of Pesach until the night before Shavuos. See commentary for pertinent laws.

In some congregations the following Kabbalistic prayer precedes the Counting of the Omer.

לְשֵׁם יִחוּד קוּדְשָׁא בְּרִיךְ הוּא וּשְׁכִינְתֵּיהּ, בִּדְחִילוּ וּרְחִימוּ לְיַחֵד שֵׁם יו״ד הֵ״א בְּוָא״ו הֵ״א בְּיִחוּדָא שְׁלִים, בְּשֵׁם כָּל יִשְׂרָאֵל. הִנְנִי מוּכָן וּמְזוּמָן לְקַיֵּם מִצְוַת עֲשֵׂה שֶׁל סְפִירַת הָעוֹמֶר, כְּמוֹ שֶׁכָּתוּב בַּתּוֹרָה: וּסְפַרְתֶּם לָכֶם מִמָּחֳרַת הַשַּׁבָּת, מִיּוֹם הֲבִיאֲכֶם אֶת עֹמֶר הַתְּנוּפָה, שֶׁבַע שַׁבָּתוֹת תְּמִימֹת תִּהְיֶינָה. עַד מִמָּחֳרַת הַשַּׁבָּת הַשְּׁבִיעִת תִּסְפְּרוּ חֲמִשִּׁים יוֹם, וְהִקְרַבְתֶּם מִנְחָה חֲדָשָׁה לַיהוה. וִיהִי נֹעַם אֲדֹנָי אֱלֹהֵינוּ עָלֵינוּ, וּמַעֲשֵׂה יָדֵינוּ כּוֹנְנָה עָלֵינוּ, וּמַעֲשֵׂה יָדֵינוּ כּוֹנְנֵהוּ.

(Cong.— *Amen. May His great Name be blessed forever and ever.*)

May His great Name be blessed forever and ever.

Blessed, praised, glorified, exalted, extolled, mighty, upraised, and lauded be the Name of the Holy One, Blessed is He (Cong.— *Blessed is He*) — (From Rosh Hashanah to Yom Kippur add: *exceedingly*) *beyond any blessing and song, praise and consolation that are uttered in the world. Now respond: Amen.* (Cong.— *Amen.*)

May there be abundant peace from Heaven, and life, upon us and upon all Israel. Now respond: Amen. (Cong.— *Amen.*)

He Who makes peace in His heights, may He make peace upon us, and upon all Israel. Now respond: Amen. (Cong.— *Amen.*)

From Rosh Chodesh Elul through Shemini Atzeres, *Psalm 27, 'Of David'*, is recited; comm. p. 170.

לְדָוִד *Of David; HASHEM is my light and my salvation, whom shall I fear? HASHEM is my life's strength, whom shall I dread? When evildoers approach me to devour my flesh, my tormentors and my foes against me — it is they who stumble and fall. Though an army would besiege me, my heart would not fear; though war would arise against me, in this I trust. One thing I asked of HASHEM, that shall I seek: That I dwell in the House of HASHEM all the days of my life; to behold the sweetness of HASHEM and to contemplate in His Sanctuary. Indeed, He will hide me in His Shelter on the day of evil; He will conceal me in the concealment of His Tent, He will lift me upon a rock. Now my head is raised above my enemies around me, and I will slaughter offerings in His Tent accompanied by joyous song; I will sing and make music to HASHEM. HASHEM, hear my voice when I call, be gracious toward me and answer me. In Your behalf, my heart has said, 'Seek My Presence'; Your Presence, HASHEM, do I seek. Conceal not Your Presence from me, repel not Your servant in anger. You have been my Helper, abandon me not, forsake me not, O God of my salvation. Though my father and mother have forsaken me, HASHEM will gather me in. Teach me Your way, HASHEM, and lead me on the path of integrity, because of my watchful foes. Deliver me not to the wishes of my tormentors, for there have arisen against me false witnesses who breathe violence.* Chazzan— *Had I not trusted that I would see the goodness of HASHEM in the land of life! Hope to HASHEM, strengthen yourself and He will give you courage; and hope to HASHEM.*

In the presence of a *minyan*, mourners recite the Mourner's *Kaddish* (p. 280).

In a house of mourning, Psalm 49, לַמְנַצֵּחַ, *For the conductor* (p. 174), is recited after *Maariv*.

COUNTING THE OMER

The Omer is counted from the second night of Pesach until the night before Shavuos, See commentary for pertinent laws.

In some congregations the following Kabbalistic prayer precedes the Counting of the Omer.

לְשֵׁם *For the sake of the unification of the Holy One, Blessed is He, and His Presence, in fear and love to unify the Name Yud-Kei with Vav-Kei in perfect unity, in the name of all Israel. Behold I am prepared and ready to perform the commandment of counting the Omer, as is written in the Torah: 'You are to count from the morrow of the rest day, from the day you brought the Omer-offering that is waved — they are to be seven complete weeks — until the morrow of the seventh week you are to count fifty days, and then offer a new meal-offering to HASHEM.'*[1] *May the pleasantness of my Lord, our God, be upon us — may He establish our handiwork for us; our handiwork, may He establish.*

(1) *Leviticus* 23:15.

סְפִירַת הָעוֹמֶר / Counting the Omer

The Torah commands that from the second day of Pesach — the day the *Omer* offering of new barley is brought in the Temple — forty-nine days are to be counted; and the festival of Shavuos celebrated on the fiftieth day. This period is called *Sefiras HaOmer*, the Counting of the Omer. The *Sefirah* count also recalls an earlier event. During the seven weeks following the Exodus, our ancestors prepared themselves for receiving the Torah at Mount Sinai. This responsibility to prepare oneself to receive the

Chazzan, followed by congregation, recites the blessing and counts.
One praying without a *minyan* should, nevertheless, recite the entire Omer service.

בָּרוּךְ אַתָּה יהוה אֱלֹהֵינוּ מֶלֶךְ הָעוֹלָם, אֲשֶׁר קִדְּשָׁנוּ בְּמִצְוֹתָיו וְצִוָּנוּ עַל סְפִירַת הָעְוֹמֶר.

INSERT THE APPROPRIATE DAY'S COUNT. SEE CHART P. 286.

הָרַחֲמָן הוּא יַחֲזִיר לָנוּ עֲבוֹדַת בֵּית הַמִּקְדָּשׁ לִמְקוֹמָהּ, בִּמְהֵרָה בְיָמֵינוּ. אָמֵן סֶלָה.

תהלים סז (commentary on p. 595)

לַמְנַצֵּחַ בִּנְגִינֹת מִזְמוֹר שִׁיר. אֱלֹהִים יְחָנֵּנוּ וִיבָרְכֵנוּ, יָאֵר פָּנָיו אִתָּנוּ סֶלָה. לָדַעַת בָּאָרֶץ דַּרְכֶּךָ, בְּכָל גּוֹיִם יְשׁוּעָתֶךָ. יוֹדוּךָ עַמִּים אֱלֹהִים, יוֹדוּךָ עַמִּים כֻּלָּם. יִשְׂמְחוּ וִירַנְּנוּ לְאֻמִּים, כִּי תִשְׁפֹּט עַמִּים מִישֹׁר, וּלְאֻמִּים בָּאָרֶץ תַּנְחֵם סֶלָה. יוֹדוּךָ עַמִּים, אֱלֹהִים, יוֹדוּךָ עַמִּים כֻּלָּם. אֶרֶץ נָתְנָה יְבוּלָהּ, יְבָרְכֵנוּ אֱלֹהִים אֱלֹהֵינוּ. יְבָרְכֵנוּ אֱלֹהִים, וְיִירְאוּ אוֹתוֹ כָּל אַפְסֵי אָרֶץ.

For commentary to the following paragraph, see p. 315.

אָנָּא בְּכֹחַ גְּדֻלַּת יְמִינְךָ תַּתִּיר צְרוּרָה. אב״ג ית״ץ
קַבֵּל רִנַּת עַמְּךָ שַׂגְּבֵנוּ טַהֲרֵנוּ נוֹרָא. קר״ע שט״ן
נָא גִבּוֹר דּוֹרְשֵׁי יִחוּדְךָ כְּבָבַת שָׁמְרֵם. נג״ד יכ״ש
בָּרְכֵם טַהֲרֵם רַחֲמֵם צִדְקָתְךָ תָּמִיד גָּמְלֵם. בט״ר צת״ג
חֲסִין קָדוֹשׁ בְּרוֹב טוּבְךָ נַהֵל עֲדָתֶךָ. חק״ב טנ״ע
יָחִיד גֵּאֶה לְעַמְּךָ פְּנֵה זוֹכְרֵי קְדֻשָּׁתֶךָ. יג״ל פז״ק
שַׁוְעָתֵנוּ קַבֵּל וּשְׁמַע צַעֲקָתֵנוּ יוֹדֵעַ תַּעֲלֻמוֹת. שק״ו צי״ת
בָּרוּךְ שֵׁם כְּבוֹד מַלְכוּתוֹ לְעוֹלָם וָעֶד.

רִבּוֹנוֹ שֶׁל עוֹלָם, אַתָּה צִוִּיתָנוּ עַל יְדֵי מֹשֶׁה עַבְדֶּךָ לִסְפּוֹר סְפִירַת הָעְוֹמֶר, כְּדֵי לְטַהֲרֵנוּ מִקְּלִפּוֹתֵינוּ וּמִטֻּמְאוֹתֵינוּ, כְּמוֹ שֶׁכָּתַבְתָּ בְּתוֹרָתֶךָ: וּסְפַרְתֶּם לָכֶם מִמָּחֳרַת הַשַּׁבָּת מִיּוֹם הֲבִיאֲכֶם אֶת עֹמֶר הַתְּנוּפָה, שֶׁבַע שַׁבָּתוֹת תְּמִימֹת תִּהְיֶינָה. עַד מִמָּחֳרַת הַשַּׁבָּת הַשְּׁבִיעִית תִּסְפְּרוּ חֲמִשִּׁים יוֹם.[1] כְּדֵי שֶׁיִּטָּהֲרוּ נַפְשׁוֹת עַמְּךָ יִשְׂרָאֵל מִזֻּהֲמָתָם. וּבְכֵן יְהִי רָצוֹן מִלְּפָנֶיךָ יהוה אֱלֹהֵינוּ וֵאלֹהֵי אֲבוֹתֵינוּ, שֶׁבִּזְכוּת סְפִירַת הָעוֹמֶר שֶׁסָּפַרְתִּי הַיּוֹם, (Insert the appropriate *sefirah;* see chart p. 286.) יְתֻקַּן מַה שֶּׁפָּגַמְתִּי בִּסְפִירָה וְאֶטָּהֵר וְאֶתְקַדֵּשׁ בִּקְדֻשָּׁה שֶׁל מַעְלָה, וְעַל יְדֵי זֶה יֻשְׁפַּע שֶׁפַע רַב בְּכָל הָעוֹלָמוֹת. וּלְתַקֵּן אֶת נַפְשׁוֹתֵינוּ, וְרוּחוֹתֵינוּ, וְנִשְׁמוֹתֵינוּ, מִכָּל סִיג וּפְגַם, וּלְטַהֲרֵנוּ וּלְקַדְּשֵׁנוּ בִּקְדֻשָּׁתְךָ הָעֶלְיוֹנָה. אָמֵן סֶלָה.

In some congregations, if a mourner is present קַדִּישׁ יָתוֹם (p. 280) is recited, followed by עָלֵינוּ. In others, עָלֵינוּ is recited immediately.

(1) *Leviticus* 23:15-16.

Torah is present every year, as we relive the Exodus from bondage and materialism, and strive to be worthy of the gift of Torah. In ancient times, the *Sefirah* period was a time of rejoicing, but it is now observed as a time of semi-mourning because of several reasons: the absence of the Temple; the death of R' Akiva's 24,000 students during thirty-three days of the *Sefirah;* and a string of bloody massacres of Jewish communities during the Crusades.

Chazzan, followed by congregation, recites the blessing and counts.
One praying without a *minyan* should, nevertheless, recite the entire Omer service.

בָּרוּךְ *Blessed are You, HASHEM, our God, King of the universe, Who has sanctified us with His commandments and has commanded us regarding the counting of the Omer.*

INSERT THE APPROPRIATE DAY'S COUNT. SEE CHART, P. 287.

הָרַחֲמָן *The Compassionate One! May He return for us the service of the Temple to its place, speedily in our days. Amen, selah!*

Psalm 67 (Commentary on p. 595.)

לַמְנַצֵּחַ *For the Conductor, upon Neginos, a psalm, a song. May God favor us and bless us, may He illuminate His countenance with us, Selah. To make known Your way on earth, among all the nations Your salvation. The peoples will acknowledge You, O God, the peoples will acknowledge You, all of them. Nations will be glad and sing for joy, because You will judge the peoples fairly and guide the nations on earth, Selah. The peoples will acknowledge You, O God, the peoples will acknowledge You, all of them. The earth has yielded its produce, may God, our own God, bless us. May God bless us and may all the ends of the earth fear Him.*

For commentary to the following paragraph, see p. 315.

אָנָּא *We beg You! With the strength of Your right hand's greatness, untie the bundled sins. Accept the prayer of Your nation; strengthen us, purify us, O Awesome One. Please, O Strong One — those who foster Your Oneness, guard them like the apple of an eye. Bless them, purify them, show them pity, may Your righteousness always recompense them. Powerful Holy One, with Your abundant goodness guide Your congregation. One and only Exalted One, turn to Your nation, which proclaims Your holiness. Accept our entreaty and hear our cry, O Knower of mysteries.*

Blessed is the Name of His glorious Kingdom for all eternity.

רִבּוֹנוֹ שֶׁל עוֹלָם *Master of the universe, You commanded us through Moses, Your servant, to count the Omer Count in order to cleanse us from our encrustations of evil and from our contaminations, as You have written in Your Torah: You are to count from the morrow of the rest day, from the day you brought the Omer-offering that is waved — they are to be seven complete weeks. Until the morrow of the seventh week you are to count fifty days,*[1] *so that the souls of Your people Israel be cleansed of their contamination. Therefore, may it be Your will, HASHEM, our God and the God of our forefathers, that in the merit of the Omer Count that I have counted today, may there be corrected whatever blemish I have caused in the sefirah* (insert the appropriate *sefirah;* see chart p. 286). *May I be cleansed and sanctified with the holiness of Above, and through this may abundant bounty flow in all the worlds. And may it correct our lives, spirits, and souls from all sediment and blemish; may it cleanse us and sanctify us with Your exalted holiness. Amen, Selah!*

In some congregations, if a mourner is present, the Mourner's *Kaddish* (p. 280) is recited, followed by *Aleinu.* In others, *Aleinu* is recited immediately.

☙ A Summary of Laws of Sefirah

The *Omer* is counted, standing, after nightfall. Before reciting the blessing, one should be careful *not* to say 'Today is the ____th day.' If he did so, for example, in response to someone who asked which day it is, he may not recite the blessing, since he has already counted that day. Where there are days and weeks, this does not apply unless he also mentioned the week. In both cases, he may recite the blessing on succeeding nights.

If one forgets to count at night, he counts during the day *without* a blessing, but may recite the blessing on succeeding nights. But if one forgot to count all day, he counts without a blessing on succeeding nights.

[In many congregations the word בָּעוֹמֶר is substituted for לָעוֹמֶר.]

SEFIRAH	COUNT	DAY
חֶסֶד שֶׁבְּחֶסֶד	הַיּוֹם יוֹם אֶחָד לָעוֹמֶר	1
גְבוּרָה שֶׁבְּחֶסֶד	הַיּוֹם שְׁנֵי יָמִים לָעוֹמֶר	2
תִּפְאֶרֶת שֶׁבְּחֶסֶד	הַיּוֹם שְׁלֹשָׁה יָמִים לָעוֹמֶר	3
נֶצַח שֶׁבְּחֶסֶד	הַיּוֹם אַרְבָּעָה יָמִים לָעוֹמֶר	4
הוֹד שֶׁבְּחֶסֶד	הַיּוֹם חֲמִשָּׁה יָמִים לָעוֹמֶר	5
יְסוֹד שֶׁבְּחֶסֶד	הַיּוֹם שִׁשָּׁה יָמִים לָעוֹמֶר	6
מַלְכוּת שֶׁבְּחֶסֶד	הַיּוֹם שִׁבְעָה יָמִים, שֶׁהֵם שָׁבוּעַ אֶחָד, לָעוֹמֶר	7
חֶסֶד שֶׁבִּגְבוּרָה	הַיּוֹם שְׁמוֹנָה יָמִים, שֶׁהֵם שָׁבוּעַ אֶחָד וְיוֹם אֶחָד, לָעוֹמֶר	8
גְבוּרָה שֶׁבִּגְבוּרָה	הַיּוֹם תִּשְׁעָה יָמִים, שֶׁהֵם שָׁבוּעַ אֶחָד וּשְׁנֵי יָמִים, לָעוֹמֶר	9
תִּפְאֶרֶת שֶׁבִּגְבוּרָה	הַיּוֹם עֲשָׂרָה יָמִים, שֶׁהֵם שָׁבוּעַ אֶחָד וּשְׁלֹשָׁה יָמִים, לָעוֹמֶר	10
נֶצַח שֶׁבִּגְבוּרָה	הַיּוֹם אַחַד עָשָׂר יוֹם, שֶׁהֵם שָׁבוּעַ אֶחָד וְאַרְבָּעָה יָמִים, לָעוֹמֶר	11
הוֹד שֶׁבִּגְבוּרָה	הַיּוֹם שְׁנֵים עָשָׂר יוֹם, שֶׁהֵם שָׁבוּעַ אֶחָד וַחֲמִשָּׁה יָמִים, לָעוֹמֶר	12
יְסוֹד שֶׁבִּגְבוּרָה	הַיּוֹם שְׁלֹשָׁה עָשָׂר יוֹם, שֶׁהֵם שָׁבוּעַ אֶחָד וְשִׁשָּׁה יָמִים, לָעוֹמֶר	13
מַלְכוּת שֶׁבִּגְבוּרָה	הַיּוֹם אַרְבָּעָה עָשָׂר יוֹם, שֶׁהֵם שְׁנֵי שָׁבוּעוֹת, לָעוֹמֶר	14
חֶסֶד שֶׁבְּתִפְאֶרֶת	הַיּוֹם חֲמִשָּׁה עָשָׂר יוֹם, שֶׁהֵם שְׁנֵי שָׁבוּעוֹת וְיוֹם אֶחָד, לָעוֹמֶר	15
גְבוּרָה שֶׁבְּתִפְאֶרֶת	הַיּוֹם שִׁשָּׁה עָשָׂר יוֹם, שֶׁהֵם שְׁנֵי שָׁבוּעוֹת וּשְׁנֵי יָמִים, לָעוֹמֶר	16
תִּפְאֶרֶת שֶׁבְּתִפְאֶרֶת	הַיּוֹם שִׁבְעָה עָשָׂר יוֹם, שֶׁהֵם שְׁנֵי שָׁבוּעוֹת וּשְׁלֹשָׁה יָמִים, לָעוֹמֶר	17
נֶצַח שֶׁבְּתִפְאֶרֶת	הַיּוֹם שְׁמוֹנָה עָשָׂר יוֹם, שֶׁהֵם שְׁנֵי שָׁבוּעוֹת וְאַרְבָּעָה יָמִים, לָעוֹמֶר	18
הוֹד שֶׁבְּתִפְאֶרֶת	הַיּוֹם תִּשְׁעָה עָשָׂר יוֹם, שֶׁהֵם שְׁנֵי שָׁבוּעוֹת וַחֲמִשָּׁה יָמִים, לָעוֹמֶר	19
יְסוֹד שֶׁבְּתִפְאֶרֶת	הַיּוֹם עֶשְׂרִים יוֹם, שֶׁהֵם שְׁנֵי שָׁבוּעוֹת וְשִׁשָּׁה יָמִים, לָעוֹמֶר	20
מַלְכוּת שֶׁבְּתִפְאֶרֶת	הַיּוֹם אֶחָד וְעֶשְׂרִים יוֹם, שֶׁהֵם שְׁלֹשָׁה שָׁבוּעוֹת, לָעוֹמֶר	21
חֶסֶד שֶׁבְּנֶצַח	הַיּוֹם שְׁנַיִם וְעֶשְׂרִים יוֹם, שֶׁהֵם שְׁלֹשָׁה שָׁבוּעוֹת וְיוֹם אֶחָד, לָעוֹמֶר	22
גְבוּרָה שֶׁבְּנֶצַח	הַיּוֹם שְׁלֹשָׁה וְעֶשְׂרִים יוֹם, שֶׁהֵם שְׁלֹשָׁה שָׁבוּעוֹת וּשְׁנֵי יָמִים, לָעוֹמֶר	23
תִּפְאֶרֶת שֶׁבְּנֶצַח	הַיּוֹם אַרְבָּעָה וְעֶשְׂרִים יוֹם, שֶׁהֵם שְׁלֹשָׁה שָׁבוּעוֹת וּשְׁלֹשָׁה יָמִים, לָעוֹמֶר	24
נֶצַח שֶׁבְּנֶצַח	הַיּוֹם חֲמִשָּׁה וְעֶשְׂרִים יוֹם, שֶׁהֵם שְׁלֹשָׁה שָׁבוּעוֹת וְאַרְבָּעָה יָמִים, לָעוֹמֶר	25
הוֹד שֶׁבְּנֶצַח	הַיּוֹם שִׁשָּׁה וְעֶשְׂרִים יוֹם, שֶׁהֵם שְׁלֹשָׁה שָׁבוּעוֹת וַחֲמִשָּׁה יָמִים, לָעוֹמֶר	26
יְסוֹד שֶׁבְּנֶצַח	הַיּוֹם שִׁבְעָה וְעֶשְׂרִים יוֹם, שֶׁהֵם שְׁלֹשָׁה שָׁבוּעוֹת וְשִׁשָּׁה יָמִים, לָעוֹמֶר	27
מַלְכוּת שֶׁבְּנֶצַח	הַיּוֹם שְׁמוֹנָה וְעֶשְׂרִים יוֹם, שֶׁהֵם אַרְבָּעָה שָׁבוּעוֹת, לָעוֹמֶר	28
חֶסֶד שֶׁבְּהוֹד	הַיּוֹם תִּשְׁעָה וְעֶשְׂרִים יוֹם, שֶׁהֵם אַרְבָּעָה שָׁבוּעוֹת וְיוֹם אֶחָד, לָעוֹמֶר	29
גְבוּרָה שֶׁבְּהוֹד	הַיּוֹם שְׁלֹשִׁים יוֹם, שֶׁהֵם אַרְבָּעָה שָׁבוּעוֹת וּשְׁנֵי יָמִים, לָעוֹמֶר	30
תִּפְאֶרֶת שֶׁבְּהוֹד	הַיּוֹם אֶחָד וּשְׁלֹשִׁים יוֹם, שֶׁהֵם אַרְבָּעָה שָׁבוּעוֹת וּשְׁלֹשָׁה יָמִים, לָעוֹמֶר	31
נֶצַח שֶׁבְּהוֹד	הַיּוֹם שְׁנַיִם וּשְׁלֹשִׁים יוֹם, שֶׁהֵם אַרְבָּעָה שָׁבוּעוֹת וְאַרְבָּעָה יָמִים, לָעוֹמֶר	32
הוֹד שֶׁבְּהוֹד	הַיּוֹם שְׁלֹשָׁה וּשְׁלֹשִׁים יוֹם, שֶׁהֵם אַרְבָּעָה שָׁבוּעוֹת וַחֲמִשָּׁה יָמִים, לָעוֹמֶר	33
יְסוֹד שֶׁבְּהוֹד	הַיּוֹם אַרְבָּעָה וּשְׁלֹשִׁים יוֹם, שֶׁהֵם אַרְבָּעָה שָׁבוּעוֹת וְשִׁשָּׁה יָמִים, לָעוֹמֶר	34
מַלְכוּת שֶׁבְּהוֹד	הַיּוֹם חֲמִשָּׁה וּשְׁלֹשִׁים יוֹם, שֶׁהֵם חֲמִשָּׁה שָׁבוּעוֹת, לָעוֹמֶר	35
חֶסֶד שֶׁבִּיסוֹד	הַיּוֹם שִׁשָּׁה וּשְׁלֹשִׁים יוֹם, שֶׁהֵם חֲמִשָּׁה שָׁבוּעוֹת וְיוֹם אֶחָד, לָעוֹמֶר	36
גְבוּרָה שֶׁבִּיסוֹד	הַיּוֹם שִׁבְעָה וּשְׁלֹשִׁים יוֹם, שֶׁהֵם חֲמִשָּׁה שָׁבוּעוֹת וּשְׁנֵי יָמִים, לָעוֹמֶר	37
תִּפְאֶרֶת שֶׁבִּיסוֹד	הַיּוֹם שְׁמוֹנָה וּשְׁלֹשִׁים יוֹם, שֶׁהֵם חֲמִשָּׁה שָׁבוּעוֹת וּשְׁלֹשָׁה יָמִים, לָעוֹמֶר	38
נֶצַח שֶׁבִּיסוֹד	הַיּוֹם תִּשְׁעָה וּשְׁלֹשִׁים יוֹם, שֶׁהֵם חֲמִשָּׁה שָׁבוּעוֹת וְאַרְבָּעָה יָמִים, לָעוֹמֶר	39
הוֹד שֶׁבִּיסוֹד	הַיּוֹם אַרְבָּעִים יוֹם, שֶׁהֵם חֲמִשָּׁה שָׁבוּעוֹת וַחֲמִשָּׁה יָמִים, לָעוֹמֶר	40
יְסוֹד שֶׁבִּיסוֹד	הַיּוֹם אֶחָד וְאַרְבָּעִים יוֹם, שֶׁהֵם חֲמִשָּׁה שָׁבוּעוֹת וְשִׁשָּׁה יָמִים, לָעוֹמֶר	41
מַלְכוּת שֶׁבִּיסוֹד	הַיּוֹם שְׁנַיִם וְאַרְבָּעִים יוֹם, שֶׁהֵם שִׁשָּׁה שָׁבוּעוֹת, לָעוֹמֶר	42
חֶסֶד שֶׁבְּמַלְכוּת	הַיּוֹם שְׁלֹשָׁה וְאַרְבָּעִים יוֹם, שֶׁהֵם שִׁשָּׁה שָׁבוּעוֹת וְיוֹם אֶחָד, לָעוֹמֶר	43
גְבוּרָה שֶׁבְּמַלְכוּת	הַיּוֹם אַרְבָּעָה וְאַרְבָּעִים יוֹם, שֶׁהֵם שִׁשָּׁה שָׁבוּעוֹת וּשְׁנֵי יָמִים, לָעוֹמֶר	44
תִּפְאֶרֶת שֶׁבְּמַלְכוּת	הַיּוֹם חֲמִשָּׁה וְאַרְבָּעִים יוֹם, שֶׁהֵם שִׁשָּׁה שָׁבוּעוֹת וּשְׁלֹשָׁה יָמִים, לָעוֹמֶר	45
נֶצַח שֶׁבְּמַלְכוּת	הַיּוֹם שִׁשָּׁה וְאַרְבָּעִים יוֹם, שֶׁהֵם שִׁשָּׁה שָׁבוּעוֹת וְאַרְבָּעָה יָמִים, לָעוֹמֶר	46
הוֹד שֶׁבְּמַלְכוּת	הַיּוֹם שִׁבְעָה וְאַרְבָּעִים יוֹם, שֶׁהֵם שִׁשָּׁה שָׁבוּעוֹת וַחֲמִשָּׁה יָמִים, לָעוֹמֶר	47
יְסוֹד שֶׁבְּמַלְכוּת	הַיּוֹם שְׁמוֹנָה וְאַרְבָּעִים יוֹם, שֶׁהֵם שִׁשָּׁה שָׁבוּעוֹת וְשִׁשָּׁה יָמִים, לָעוֹמֶר	48
מַלְכוּת שֶׁבְּמַלְכוּת	הַיּוֹם תִּשְׁעָה וְאַרְבָּעִים יוֹם, שֶׁהֵם שִׁבְעָה שָׁבוּעוֹת, לָעוֹמֶר.	49

DAY	COUNT
1	*Today is one day of the Omer.*
2	*Today is two days of the Omer.*
3	*Today is three days of the Omer.*
4	*Today is four days of the Omer.*
5	*Today is five days of the Omer.*
6	*Today is six days of the Omer.*
7	*Today is seven days, which are one week, of the Omer.*
8	*Today is eight days, which are one week and one day, of the Omer.*
9	*Today is nine days, which are one week and two days, of the Omer.*
10	*Today is ten days, which are one week and three days, of the Omer.*
11	*Today is eleven days, which are one week and four days, of the Omer.*
12	*Today is twelve days, which are one week and five days, of the Omer.*
13	*Today is thirteen days, which are one week and six days, of the Omer.*
14	*Today is fourteen days, which are two weeks, of the Omer.*
15	*Today is fifteen days, which are two weeks and one day of the Omer.*
16	*Today is sixteen days, which are two weeks and two days, of the Omer.*
17	*Today is seventeen days, which are two weeks and three days, of the Omer.*
18	*Today is eighteen days, which are two weeks and four days, of the Omer.*
19	*Today is nineteen days, which are two weeks and five days, of the Omer.*
20	*Today is twenty days, which are two weeks and six days, of the Omer.*
21	*Today is twenty-one days, which are three weeks, of the Omer.*
22	*Today is twenty-two days, which are three weeks and one day, of the Omer.*
23	*Today is twenty-three days, which are three weeks and two days, of the Omer.*
24	*Today is twenty-four days, which are three weeks and three days, of the Omer.*
25	*Today is twenty-five days, which are three weeks and four days, of the Omer.*
26	*Today is twenty-six days, which are three weeks and five days, of the Omer.*
27	*Today is twenty-seven days, which are three weeks and six days, of the Omer.*
28	*Today is twenty-eight days, which are four weeks, of the Omer.*
29	*Today is twenty-nine days, which are four weeks and one day, of the Omer.*
30	*Today is thirty days, which are four weeks and two days, of the Omer.*
31	*Today is thirty-one days, which are four weeks and three days, of the Omer.*
32	*Today is thirty-two days, which are four weeks and four days, of the Omer.*
33	*Today is thirty-three days, which are four weeks and five days, of the Omer.*
34	*Today is thirty-four days, which are four weeks and six days, of the Omer.*
35	*Today is thirty-five days, which are five weeks of the Omer.*
36	*Today is thirty-six days, which are five weeks and one day, of the Omer.*
37	*Today is thirty-seven days, which are five weeks and two days, of the Omer.*
38	*Today is thirty-eight days, which are five weeks and three days, of the Omer.*
39	*Today is thirty-nine days, which are five weeks and four days, of the Omer.*
40	*Today is forty days, which are five weeks and five days, of the Omer.*
41	*Today is forty-one days, which are five weeks and six days, of the Omer.*
42	*Today is forty-two days, which are six weeks, of the Omer.*
43	*Today is forty-three days, which are six weeks and one day, of the Omer.*
44	*Today is forty-four days, which are six weeks and two days, of the Omer.*
45	*Today is forty-five days, which are six weeks and three days, of the Omer.*
46	*Today is forty-six days, which are six weeks and four days, of the Omer.*
47	*Today is forty-seven days, which are six weeks and five days, of the Omer.*
48	*Today is forty-eight days, which are six weeks and six days, of the Omer.*
49	*Today is forty-nine days, which are seven weeks, of the Omer.*

קריאת שמע על המטה

רִבּוֹנוֹ שֶׁל עוֹלָם הֲרֵינִי מוֹחֵל לְכָל מִי שֶׁהִכְעִיס וְהִקְנִיט אוֹתִי, אוֹ שֶׁחָטָא כְּנֶגְדִּי – בֵּין בְּגוּפִי, בֵּין בְּמָמוֹנִי, בֵּין בִּכְבוֹדִי, בֵּין בְּכָל אֲשֶׁר לִי; בֵּין בְּאֹנֶס, בֵּין בְּרָצוֹן, בֵּין בְּשׁוֹגֵג, בֵּין בְּמֵזִיד; בֵּין בְּדִבּוּר, בֵּין בְּמַעֲשֶׂה, בֵּין בְּמַחֲשָׁבָה, בֵּין בְּהִרְהוּר; בֵּין בְּגִלְגּוּל זֶה, בֵּין בְּגִלְגּוּל אַחֵר* – לְכָל בַּר יִשְׂרָאֵל, וְלֹא יֵעָנֵשׁ שׁוּם אָדָם בְּסִבָּתִי. יְהִי רָצוֹן מִלְּפָנֶיךָ יהוה אֱלֹהַי וֵאלֹהֵי אֲבוֹתַי, שֶׁלֹּא אֶחֱטָא עוֹד. וּמַה שֶּׁחָטָאתִי לְפָנֶיךָ מְחוֹק בְּרַחֲמֶיךָ הָרַבִּים, אֲבָל לֹא עַל יְדֵי יִסּוּרִים וָחֳלָיִים רָעִים. יִהְיוּ לְרָצוֹן אִמְרֵי פִי וְהֶגְיוֹן לִבִּי לְפָנֶיךָ, יהוה צוּרִי וְגֹאֲלִי.[1]

המפיל

בָּרוּךְ אַתָּה יהוה אֱלֹהֵינוּ מֶלֶךְ הָעוֹלָם, הַמַּפִּיל חֶבְלֵי שֵׁנָה עַל עֵינָי, וּתְנוּמָה עַל עַפְעַפָּי.* וִיהִי רָצוֹן מִלְּפָנֶיךָ יהוה אֱלֹהַי וֵאלֹהֵי אֲבוֹתַי, שֶׁתַּשְׁכִּיבֵנִי לְשָׁלוֹם וְתַעֲמִידֵנִי לְשָׁלוֹם. וְאַל יְבַהֲלוּנִי רַעְיוֹנַי,* וַחֲלוֹמוֹת רָעִים, וְהַרְהוֹרִים רָעִים. וּתְהֵא מִטָּתִי שְׁלֵמָה לְפָנֶיךָ. וְהָאֵר עֵינַי פֶּן אִישַׁן הַמָּוֶת.[2]* כִּי אַתָּה הַמֵּאִיר לְאִישׁוֹן בַּת עָיִן.* בָּרוּךְ אַתָּה יהוה, הַמֵּאִיר לָעוֹלָם כֻּלּוֹ בִּכְבוֹדוֹ.

אֵל מֶלֶךְ נֶאֱמָן.

Recite the first verse aloud, with the right hand covering the eyes, and concentrate upon accepting God's absolute sovereignty.

שְׁמַע | יִשְׂרָאֵל, יהוָה | אֱלֹהֵינוּ, יהוָה | אֶחָד:

In an undertone— בָּרוּךְ שֵׁם כְּבוֹד מַלְכוּתוֹ לְעוֹלָם וָעֶד.

THE BEDTIME SHEMA / קְרִיאַת שְׁמַע עַל הַמִּטָּה

The recital of the *Shema* immediately before retiring is perceived as a protection against the dangers of the night *(Berachos* 5a).

The essence of this *Shema* is the *HaMapil* benediction and the first section of *Shema.* The recital of the other psalms and verses are of ancient origin – many of the sources can be traced to the Talmud and earliest halachic treatises such as *Kol Bo (Eliyah Rabbah).*

A full treatment of the Bedtime *Shema* appears in the ArtScroll edition of *Shema.*

רִבּוֹנוֹ שֶׁל עוֹלָם / Master of the Universe

Before retiring for the evening it is proper for one to examine his deeds of that day; should one discover an ill deed he should pray for forgiveness and undertake to correct his ways. It is also proper for one to forgive those who have wronged him. In merit of this one will attain long life *(Mishnah Berurah* 239:1:9). Accordingly, many recite this prayer before beginning the *Shema.*

בֵּין בְּגִלְגּוּל זֶה בֵּין בְּגִלְגּוּל אַחֵר – *Whether in this transmigration or another transmigration.* This term *gilgul* refers to the doctrine of גִּלְגּוּל נְשָׁמוֹת, *transmigration of souls,* one of the most mystical doctrines in Kabbalistic literature. In very simple terms it refers to the reincarnation of certain souls for a second period of physical life on earth.

הַמַּפִּיל / HaMapil

There is a difference of opinion regarding the sequence of the prayers. The printed versions in most prayerbooks – which we follow in this volume – has the *HaMapil* benediction first and then the *Shema.* This follows the order recorded by *Rambam (Hilchos Tefillah* 7:1). According to *Shulchan Aruch,* however, since *HaMapil* refers directly to the onset of slumber it should be recited as close as possible to the moment of sleep, i.e., at the very end of the *Shema* service *(Orach Chaim* 239:1, apparently following the Talmud, *Berachos* 60b).

It is not proper to eat, drink, or talk after

THE BEDTIME SHEMA

רִבּוֹנוֹ שֶׁל עוֹלָם *Master of the universe, I hereby forgive anyone who angered or antagonized me or who sinned against me — whether against my body, my property, my honor or against anything of mine; whether he did so accidentally, willfully, carelessly, or purposely; whether through speech, deed, thought, or notion; whether in this transmigration or another transmigration* — I forgive every Jew. May no man be punished because of me. May it be Your will, HASHEM, my God and the God of my forefathers, that I may sin no more. Whatever sins I have done before You, may You blot out in Your abundant mercies, but not through suffering or bad illnesses. May the expressions of my mouth and the thoughts of my heart find favor before You, HASHEM, my Rock and my Redeemer.*[1]

HAMAPIL

בָּרוּךְ *Blessed are You, HASHEM, our God, King of the universe, Who casts the bonds of sleep upon my eyes and slumber upon my eyelids.* May it be Your will, HASHEM, my God and the God of my forefathers, that You lay me down to sleep in peace and raise me erect in peace. May my ideas, bad dreams, and bad notions not confound me;* may my offspring be perfect before You, and may You illuminate my eyes lest I die in sleep,**[2] *for it is You Who illuminates the pupil of the eye.* Blessed are You, HASHEM, Who illuminates the entire world with His glory.*

God, trustworthy King.

Recite the first verse aloud, with the right hand covering the eyes, and concentrate upon accepting God's absolute sovereignty.

Hear, O Israel: HASHEM is our God, HASHEM, the One and Only.

In an undertone— *Blessed is the Name of His glorious kingdom for all eternity.*

(1) *Psalms* 19:15. (2) Cf. 13:4.

---

reciting the הַמַּפִּיל benediction; one should go to sleep immediately thereafter. One who cannot fall asleep should repeat the passages of the *Shema* and Psalms until sleep overtakes him *(Derech HaChaim; Aruch HaShulchan).*

הַמַּפִּיל חֶבְלֵי שֵׁנָה עַל עֵינַי וּתְנוּמָה עַל עַפְעַפָּי — *Who casts the bonds of sleep upon my eyes and slumber upon my eyelids.* This directly corresponds to the benediction recited in the morning: הַמַּעֲבִיר שֵׁנָה מֵעֵינָי וּתְנוּמָה מֵעַפְעַפָּי, *Who removes sleep from my eyes, and slumber from my eyelids.* There we thank God for returning us to active living; here we thank Him for the gift of sleep *(World of Prayer).*

The expression *bonds of sleep* figuratively depicts the whole body as being securely chained in sleep. Others render חֶבְלֵי שֵׁנָה as 'portion' of sleep [see *Deut.* 32:9: *Chizkuni; Abudraham*].

וְאַל יְבַהֲלוּנִי רַעְיוֹנַי — *May my ideas ... not confound me.* May the ideas and fantasies that we nurse in our wakeful hours not produce disturbing nightmares or immoral dreams. Such dreams menace the purity of our thoughts and feelings even during our waking hours *(World of Prayer).*

וְהָאֵר עֵינַי פֶּן אִישַׁן הַמָּוֶת — *And may You illuminate my eyes lest I die in sleep.* When asleep we are in a state related to death and utter darkness, but God guards our souls, as it were. We now beseech Him to return us to a state of vigorous and sparkling light on the morrow lest our slumber becomes the sleep of death.

הַמֵּאִיר לְאִישׁוֹן בַּת עָיִן — *Who illuminates the pupil of the eye.* When one craves sleep the pupils of his eyes are figuratively darkened; when one has slept and is fully rested, his eyes are 'brightened' *(Abudraham).*

שְׁמַע / Shema

The first paragraph of *Shema* is recited at bedtime. However, one who recited *Maariv* before the stars were out should recite all three paragraphs now *(Aruch HaShulchan). Magen Avraham* notes that it is desirable to recite all three paragraphs in any case. When reciting all three paragraphs, recite the words אֵל מֶלֶךְ נֶאֱמָן as well *(Machatzis HaShekel),* otherwise omit them.

דברים ו:ה־ט (Commentary on p. 92)

וְאָהַבְתָּ אֵת | יהוה | אֱלֹהֶיךָ, בְּכָל־לְבָבְךָ, וּבְכָל־נַפְשְׁךָ, וּבְכָל־מְאֹדֶךָ: וְהָיוּ הַדְּבָרִים הָאֵלֶּה, אֲשֶׁר | אָנֹכִי מְצַוְּךָ הַיּוֹם, עַל־לְבָבֶךָ: וְשִׁנַּנְתָּם לְבָנֶיךָ, וְדִבַּרְתָּ בָּם, בְּשִׁבְתְּךָ בְּבֵיתֶךָ, וּבְלֶכְתְּךָ בַדֶּרֶךְ, וּבְשָׁכְבְּךָ וּבְקוּמֶךָ: וּקְשַׁרְתָּם לְאוֹת | עַל־יָדֶךָ, וְהָיוּ לְטֹטָפֹת בֵּין | עֵינֶיךָ: וּכְתַבְתָּם | עַל־מְזֻזוֹת בֵּיתֶךָ, וּבִשְׁעָרֶיךָ:

וִיהִי נֹעַם אֲדֹנָי אֱלֹהֵינוּ עָלֵינוּ, וּמַעֲשֵׂה יָדֵינוּ כּוֹנְנָה עָלֵינוּ, וּמַעֲשֵׂה יָדֵינוּ כּוֹנְנֵהוּ.[1]

תהלים צא (Commentary on p. 380)

יֹשֵׁב בְּסֵתֶר עֶלְיוֹן, בְּצֵל שַׁדַּי יִתְלוֹנָן. אֹמַר לַיהוה, מַחְסִי וּמְצוּדָתִי, אֱלֹהַי אֶבְטַח בּוֹ. כִּי הוּא יַצִּילְךָ מִפַּח יָקוּשׁ, מִדֶּבֶר הַוּוֹת. בְּאֶבְרָתוֹ יָסֶךְ לָךְ, וְתַחַת כְּנָפָיו תֶּחְסֶה, צִנָּה וְסֹחֵרָה אֲמִתּוֹ. לֹא תִירָא מִפַּחַד לָיְלָה, מֵחֵץ יָעוּף יוֹמָם. מִדֶּבֶר בָּאֹפֶל יַהֲלֹךְ, מִקֶּטֶב יָשׁוּד צָהֳרָיִם. יִפֹּל מִצִּדְּךָ אֶלֶף, וּרְבָבָה מִימִינֶךָ, אֵלֶיךָ לֹא יִגָּשׁ. רַק בְּעֵינֶיךָ תַבִּיט, וְשִׁלֻּמַת רְשָׁעִים תִּרְאֶה. כִּי אַתָּה יהוה מַחְסִי, עֶלְיוֹן שַׂמְתָּ מְעוֹנֶךָ. לֹא תְאֻנֶּה אֵלֶיךָ רָעָה, וְנֶגַע לֹא יִקְרַב בְּאָהֳלֶךָ. כִּי מַלְאָכָיו יְצַוֶּה לָּךְ, לִשְׁמָרְךָ בְּכָל דְּרָכֶיךָ. עַל כַּפַּיִם יִשָּׂאוּנְךָ, פֶּן תִּגֹּף בָּאֶבֶן רַגְלֶךָ. עַל שַׁחַל וָפֶתֶן תִּדְרֹךְ, תִּרְמֹס כְּפִיר וְתַנִּין. כִּי בִי חָשַׁק וַאֲפַלְּטֵהוּ, אֲשַׂגְּבֵהוּ, כִּי יָדַע שְׁמִי. יִקְרָאֵנִי וְאֶעֱנֵהוּ, עִמּוֹ אָנֹכִי בְצָרָה, אֲחַלְּצֵהוּ וַאֲכַבְּדֵהוּ. אֹרֶךְ יָמִים אַשְׂבִּיעֵהוּ, וְאַרְאֵהוּ בִּישׁוּעָתִי. אֹרֶךְ יָמִים אַשְׂבִּיעֵהוּ, וְאַרְאֵהוּ בִּישׁוּעָתִי.

תהלים ג:ב־ט

יהוה מָה רַבּוּ צָרָי, רַבִּים קָמִים עָלָי. רַבִּים אֹמְרִים לְנַפְשִׁי, אֵין יְשׁוּעָתָה לּוֹ בֵאלֹהִים סֶלָה. וְאַתָּה יהוה מָגֵן בַּעֲדִי, כְּבוֹדִי וּמֵרִים רֹאשִׁי. קוֹלִי אֶל יהוה אֶקְרָא, וַיַּעֲנֵנִי* מֵהַר קָדְשׁוֹ סֶלָה. אֲנִי שָׁכַבְתִּי וָאִישָׁנָה, הֱקִיצוֹתִי,* כִּי יהוה יִסְמְכֵנִי. לֹא אִירָא מֵרִבְבוֹת עָם, אֲשֶׁר סָבִיב שָׁתוּ עָלָי. קוּמָה יהוה, הוֹשִׁיעֵנִי אֱלֹהַי, כִּי הִכִּיתָ אֶת כָּל אֹיְבַי לֶחִי, שִׁנֵּי רְשָׁעִים שִׁבַּרְתָּ. לַיהוה הַיְשׁוּעָה, עַל עַמְּךָ בִרְכָתֶךָ* סֶלָה.

ה׳ מָה רַבּוּ צָרָי / Psalm 3

This psalm was composed by David when he perceived through Divine inspiration that his salvation was forthcoming. Verse 6 — *I lay down*

Deuteronomy 6:5-9 (Commentary on p. 92.)

וְאָהַבְתָּ *You shall love* HASHEM, *your God, with all your heart, with all your soul and with all your resources. Let these matters that I command you today be upon your heart. Teach them thoroughly to your children and speak of them while you sit in your home, while you walk on the way, when you retire and when you arise. Bind them as a sign upon your arm and let them be tefillin between your eyes. And write them on the doorposts of your house and upon your gates.*

וִיהִי נֹעַם *May the pleasantness of my Lord, our God, be upon us — may He establish our handiwork for us; our handiwork may He establish.*[1]

Psalm 91 (Commentary on p. 380)

יֹשֵׁב *Whoever sits in the refuge of the Most High, he shall dwell in the shadow of the Almighty. I will say of* HASHEM, *'He is my refuge and my fortress, my God, I will trust in Him.' That He will deliver you from the ensnaring trap and from devastating pestilence. With His pinion He will cover you, and beneath His wings you will be protected; shield and armor is His truth. You shall not be afraid of the terror of night, nor of the arrow that flies by day; nor the pestilence that walks in gloom, nor the destroyer who lays waste at noon. Let a thousand encamp at your side and a myriad at your right hand, but to you they shall not approach. You will merely peer with your eyes and you will see the retribution of the wicked. Because [you said], 'You,* HASHEM, *are my refuge'; you have made the Most High your dwelling place. No evil will befall you, nor will any plague come near your tent. He will charge His angels for you, to protect you in all your ways. On your palms they will carry you, lest you strike your foot against a stone. Upon the lion and the viper you will tread; you will trample the young lion and the serpent. For he has yearned for Me and I will deliver him; I will elevate him because he knows My Name. He will call upon Me and I will answer him, I am with him in distress, I will release him and I will honor him. With long life will I satisfy him, and I will show him My salvation. With long life will I satisfy him, and I will show him My salvation.*

Psalms 3:2-9

יהוה HASHEM, *how many are my tormentors! The great rise up against me! The great say of my soul, 'There is no salvation for him from God.' Selah! But You* HASHEM *are a shield for me — for my soul, and to raise up my pride. With my voice I call out to* HASHEM, *and He answers me* from His holy mountain, Selah. I lay down and slept; yet I awoke,* for* HASHEM *supports me. I fear not the myriad people deployed against me from every side. Rise up,* HASHEM, *save me, my God! For You struck all of my enemies on the cheek, You broke the teeth of the wicked. Salvation is* HASHEM*'s, upon Your people is Your blessing,* Selah.*

(1) *Psalms* 90:17

and slept; yet I awoke, for HASHEM *supports me* — makes this psalm especially appropriate for the night.

וַיַּעֲנֵנִי — *And He answers me* [lit. *'He did answer me'*]. The word literally is in past tense. David had so much confidence in God's response that whenever he prayed he was sure that his wish would be fulfilled. It was as if God had *already* answered his request *(Radak).*

הֱקִיצוֹתִי — *Yet I awoke.* From my worries I awoke triumphantly, filled with confidence that God would support me *(Rashi).*

עַל עַמְּךָ בִרְכָתֶךָ — *Upon Your people is* [i.e. their duty is] *Your blessing.* Your people are obliged

הַשְׁכִּיבֵנוּ* יהוה אֱלֹהֵינוּ לְשָׁלוֹם, וְהַעֲמִידֵנוּ מַלְכֵּנוּ לְחַיִּים. וּפְרוֹשׂ עָלֵינוּ סֻכַּת שְׁלוֹמֶךָ. וְתַקְּנֵנוּ בְּעֵצָה טוֹבָה מִלְּפָנֶיךָ. וְהוֹשִׁיעֵנוּ לְמַעַן שְׁמֶךָ. וְהָגֵן בַּעֲדֵנוּ, וְהָסֵר מֵעָלֵינוּ אוֹיֵב דֶּבֶר וְחֶרֶב וְרָעָב וְיָגוֹן. וְהָסֵר שָׂטָן מִלְּפָנֵינוּ וּמֵאַחֲרֵינוּ. וּבְצֵל כְּנָפֶיךָ תַּסְתִּירֵנוּ.[1] כִּי אֵל שׁוֹמְרֵנוּ וּמַצִּילֵנוּ אָתָּה, כִּי אֵל מֶלֶךְ חַנּוּן וְרַחוּם אָתָּה.[2] וּשְׁמוֹר צֵאתֵנוּ וּבוֹאֵנוּ לְחַיִּים וּלְשָׁלוֹם, מֵעַתָּה וְעַד עוֹלָם.[3]

בָּרוּךְ יהוה בַּיּוֹם, בָּרוּךְ יהוה בַּלָּיְלָה, בָּרוּךְ יהוה בְּשָׁכְבֵנוּ, בָּרוּךְ יהוה בְּקוּמֵנוּ. כִּי בְיָדְךָ נַפְשׁוֹת הַחַיִּים וְהַמֵּתִים. אֲשֶׁר בְּיָדוֹ נֶפֶשׁ כָּל חָי, וְרוּחַ כָּל בְּשַׂר אִישׁ.[4] בְּיָדְךָ אַפְקִיד רוּחִי, פָּדִיתָה אוֹתִי, יהוה אֵל אֱמֶת.[5] אֱלֹהֵינוּ שֶׁבַּשָּׁמַיִם, יַחֵד שִׁמְךָ וְקַיֵּם מַלְכוּתְךָ תָּמִיד, וּמְלוֹךְ עָלֵינוּ לְעוֹלָם וָעֶד.

יִרְאוּ עֵינֵינוּ, וְיִשְׂמַח לִבֵּנוּ, וְתָגֵל נַפְשֵׁנוּ בִּישׁוּעָתְךָ בֶּאֱמֶת, בֶּאֱמֹר לְצִיּוֹן מָלַךְ אֱלֹהָיִךְ.[6] יהוה מֶלֶךְ,[7] יהוה מָלָךְ,[8] יהוה יִמְלֹךְ לְעֹלָם וָעֶד.[9] כִּי הַמַּלְכוּת שֶׁלְּךָ הִיא, וּלְעוֹלְמֵי עַד תִּמְלוֹךְ בְּכָבוֹד, כִּי אֵין לָנוּ מֶלֶךְ אֶלָּא אָתָּה.

הַמַּלְאָךְ* הַגֹּאֵל אֹתִי מִכָּל רָע יְבָרֵךְ אֶת הַנְּעָרִים, וְיִקָּרֵא בָהֶם שְׁמִי,* וְשֵׁם אֲבֹתַי אַבְרָהָם וְיִצְחָק, וְיִדְגּוּ לָרֹב* בְּקֶרֶב הָאָרֶץ.[10]

וַיֹּאמֶר, אִם שָׁמוֹעַ תִּשְׁמַע* לְקוֹל יהוה אֱלֹהֶיךָ, וְהַיָּשָׁר בְּעֵינָיו תַּעֲשֶׂה, וְהַאֲזַנְתָּ לְמִצְוֹתָיו, וְשָׁמַרְתָּ כָּל חֻקָּיו, כָּל הַמַּחֲלָה אֲשֶׁר שַׂמְתִּי בְמִצְרַיִם* לֹא אָשִׂים עָלֶיךָ, כִּי אֲנִי יהוה רֹפְאֶךָ.[11]

וַיֹּאמֶר יהוה אֶל הַשָּׂטָן,* יִגְעַר יהוה בְּךָ הַשָּׂטָן, וְיִגְעַר יהוה בְּךָ הַבֹּחֵר בִּירוּשָׁלָיִם, הֲלוֹא זֶה אוּד מֻצָּל מֵאֵשׁ.[12]

הִנֵּה מִטָּתוֹ* שֶׁלִּשְׁלֹמֹה, שִׁשִּׁים גִּבֹּרִים סָבִיב לָהּ,

---

to bless You and to offer thanks for Your salvation *(Rashi).* [God derives strength, so to speak, from the blessings and prayers of man. Man's appreciation of God's control of human events influences His guidance of the universe.]

הַשְׁכִּיבֵנוּ — *Lay us down to sleep.* The following three prayers are essentially repeated from the *Maariv* service. Commentary begins on page 262.

הַמַּלְאָךְ — *May the angel.* The following passages are a collection of Scriptural verses discussing God's 'mercy.' This first verse, *May the angel who redeems,* etc. was Jacob's blessing to his grandsons Ephraim and Menashe *(Genesis* 48:16). The prayer is directed not to the angel, who has no power except as an agent of God, but to God Who dispatched the angel.

וְיִקָּרֵא בָהֶם שְׁמִי — *And may my name be declared*

הַשְׁכִּיבֵנוּ *Lay us down to sleep* in peace, HASHEM, our God; raise us erect, our King, to life, and spread over us the shelter of Your peace. Set us aright with good counsel from before Your Presence, and save us for Your Name's sake. Shield us, remove from us foe, plague, sword, famine, and woe; and remove spiritual impediment from before us and behind us and in the shadow of Your wings shelter us*[1] *— for God Who protects us and rescues us are You, for God, the Gracious and Compassionate King, are You.*[2] *Safeguard our going and coming — for life and peace from now to eternity.*[3]

Blessed is HASHEM by day; Blessed is HASHEM by night; Blessed is HASHEM when we retire; Blessed is HASHEM when we arise. For in Your hand are the souls of the living and the dead. He in Whose hand is the soul of all the living and the spirit of every human being.[4] *In Your hand I shall entrust my spirit, You redeemed me, HASHEM, God of truth.*[5] *Our God Who is in heaven, bring unity to Your Name; establish Your kingdom forever, and reign over us for all eternity.*

May our eyes see, our heart rejoice, and our soul exult in Your salvation in truth, when Zion is told, 'Your God has reigned!'[6] *HASHEM reigns,*[7] *HASHEM has reigned,*[8] *HASHEM will reign for all eternity.*[9] *For the kingdom is Yours and You will reign for all eternity in glory, for we have no king but You!*

הַמַּלְאָךְ *May the angel* who redeems me from all evil bless the lads, and may my name be declared upon them* — and the names of my forefathers Abraham and Isaac — and may they proliferate abundantly like fish* within the land.*[10]

He said: 'If you diligently heed the voice of HASHEM, your God, and do what is proper in His eyes, and you listen closely to His commandments and observe His decrees — the entire malady that I inflicted upon Egypt* I will not inflict upon you, for I am HASHEM your Healer.'*[11]

HASHEM said to the Satan, 'HASHEM shall denounce you, O Satan, and HASHEM, Who selects Jerusalem, shall denounce you again. This is indeed a firebrand rescued from flames.'*[12]

Behold! The couch of Shlomo! Sixty mighty ones round about it,*

(1) Cf. *Psalms* 17:8. (2) Cf. *Nechemiah* 9:31. (3) Cf. *Psalms* 121:8. (4) *Job* 12:10. (5) *Psalms* 31:6. (6) Cf. *Isaiah* 52:7. (7) *Psalms* 10:16. (8) 93:1 et al. (9) *Exodus* 15:18. (10) *Genesis* 48:16. (11) *Exodus* 15:26. (12) *Zechariah* 3:2.

---

upon them. May they constantly strive to such heights that they will be worthy to have their names coupled with those of the Patriarchs *(R' Avraham ben HaRambam).*

וְיִדְגּוּ לָרֹב — *And may they proliferate abundantly like fish. R' Hirsch* explains that just as fish enjoy contentment hidden from the gaze of human beings, so Jews who live in the sphere assigned them by God will have a degree of serenity and happiness far beyond the comprehension of those around them.

וַיֹּאמֶר אִם שָׁמוֹעַ תִּשְׁמַע — *He said, 'If you diligently heed.'* This passage forms the basis for the Talmudic statement [*Berachos* 5a] that Torah study, no less than the reading of the *Shema,* wards off danger *(World of Prayer).*

כָּל הַמַּחֲלָה אֲשֶׁר שַׂמְתִּי בְמִצְרַיִם — *The entire malady* [i.e., the plagues] *that I inflicted upon Egypt.* If the Jews remain loyal, they will be spared physical affliction *(Ramban).*

וַיֹּאמֶר ה׳ אֶל הַשָּׂטָן — *HASHEM said to the Satan.* Satan had accused the high priest Joshua of being too permissive with his sinful children and of hindering the rebuilding of the Temple. Thereupon God — Who chose Jerusalem — rebuked Satan, reminding him that Joshua had been Divinely vindicated inasmuch as he had been miraculously spared from the fires of Nebuchadnezzar. This metaphor also applies to the Jewish nation as a whole. It, too, is like *a firebrand plucked from fire,* for it had suffered from the fires of exile and endured it.

הִנֵּה מִטָּתוֹ — *Behold! The couch.* This passage refers allegorically to the Jewish people symbol-

מִגִּבֹּרֵי יִשְׂרָאֵל. כֻּלָּם אֲחֻזֵי חֶרֶב, מְלֻמְּדֵי מִלְחָמָה, אִישׁ חַרְבּוֹ עַל יְרֵכוֹ מִפַּחַד בַּלֵּילוֹת.[1]

—Recite three times יְבָרֶכְךָ יהוה* וְיִשְׁמְרֶךָ. יָאֵר יהוה פָּנָיו אֵלֶיךָ, וִיחֻנֶּךָּ. יִשָּׂא יהוה פָּנָיו אֵלֶיךָ, וְיָשֵׂם לְךָ שָׁלוֹם.[2]

—Recite three times הִנֵּה לֹא יָנוּם* וְלֹא יִישָׁן, שׁוֹמֵר יִשְׂרָאֵל.[3]

—Recite three times לִישׁוּעָתְךָ קִוִּיתִי יהוה.*[4] קִוִּיתִי יהוה לִישׁוּעָתְךָ. יהוה לִישׁוּעָתְךָ קִוִּיתִי.

—Recite three times בְּשֵׁם יהוה* אֱלֹהֵי יִשְׂרָאֵל, מִימִינִי מִיכָאֵל, וּמִשְּׂמֹאלִי גַּבְרִיאֵל, וּמִלְּפָנַי אוּרִיאֵל, וּמֵאֲחוֹרַי רְפָאֵל, וְעַל רֹאשִׁי שְׁכִינַת אֵל.

תהלים קכח (Commentary on page 538)

שִׁיר הַמַּעֲלוֹת, אַשְׁרֵי כָּל יְרֵא יהוה, הַהֹלֵךְ בִּדְרָכָיו. יְגִיעַ כַּפֶּיךָ כִּי תֹאכֵל, אַשְׁרֶיךָ וְטוֹב לָךְ. אֶשְׁתְּךָ כְּגֶפֶן פֹּרִיָּה בְּיַרְכְּתֵי בֵיתֶךָ, בָּנֶיךָ כִּשְׁתִלֵי זֵיתִים, סָבִיב לְשֻׁלְחָנֶךָ. הִנֵּה כִי כֵן יְבֹרַךְ גָּבֶר, יְרֵא יהוה. יְבָרֶכְךָ יהוה מִצִּיּוֹן, וּרְאֵה בְּטוּב יְרוּשָׁלָיִם כֹּל יְמֵי חַיֶּיךָ. וּרְאֵה בָנִים לְבָנֶיךָ, שָׁלוֹם עַל יִשְׂרָאֵל.

—Recite three times רִגְזוּ וְאַל תֶּחֱטָאוּ,* אִמְרוּ בִלְבַבְכֶם עַל מִשְׁכַּבְכֶם, וְדֹמּוּ סֶלָה.[5]

אֲדוֹן עוֹלָם* אֲשֶׁר מָלַךְ, בְּטֶרֶם כָּל יְצִיר נִבְרָא. לְעֵת נַעֲשָׂה בְחֶפְצוֹ כֹּל, אֲזַי מֶלֶךְ שְׁמוֹ נִקְרָא. וְאַחֲרֵי כִּכְלוֹת הַכֹּל, לְבַדּוֹ יִמְלוֹךְ נוֹרָא. וְהוּא הָיָה וְהוּא הֹוֶה, וְהוּא יִהְיֶה בְּתִפְאָרָה. וְהוּא אֶחָד וְאֵין שֵׁנִי, לְהַמְשִׁיל לוֹ לְהַחְבִּירָה. בְּלִי רֵאשִׁית בְּלִי תַכְלִית, וְלוֹ הָעֹז וְהַמִּשְׂרָה. וְהוּא אֵלִי וְחַי גֹּאֲלִי, וְצוּר חֶבְלִי בְּעֵת צָרָה. וְהוּא נִסִּי וּמָנוֹס לִי, מְנָת כּוֹסִי בְּיוֹם אֶקְרָא. בְּיָדוֹ אַפְקִיד רוּחִי, בְּעֵת אִישַׁן וְאָעִירָה. וְעִם רוּחִי גְּוִיָּתִי, יהוה לִי וְלֹא אִירָא.

---

ized by the sixty myriads [i.e., the 600,000 battleworthy males] who emerged from Egypt. See *Commentary* in the *ArtScroll* edition of *Shir HaShirim* for the full interpretation.

יְבָרֶכְךָ ה׳ — *May HASHEM bless you.* The blessing contains sixty letters; this has significant Kabbalistic meaning in its parallel with the sixty myriads of the previous passage. [For a full exposition of this blessing, see ArtScroll *Bircas Kohanim.* See also p. 116.]

הִנֵּה לֹא יָנוּם ... — *Behold, the Guardian of Israel neither slumbers nor sleeps.* And therefore you will be able to sleep peacefully without fear of harm *(R' Hirsch).*

לִישׁוּעָתְךָ קִוִּיתִי ה׳ ... — *For Your salvation do I long, HASHEM.* The Kabbalists find in this three-

of the mighty ones of Israel. All gripping the sword, learned in warfare, each with his sword on his thigh, from fear in the nights.[1]

Recite three times— *May HASHEM bless you* and safeguard you. May HASHEM illuminate His countenance for you and be gracious to you. May HASHEM turn His face toward you and establish peace for you.*[2]

Recite three times— *Behold, the Guardian of Israel neither slumbers nor sleeps.**[3]

Recite three times— *For Your salvation do I long, HASHEM.**[4] *I do long, HASHEM, for your salvation. HASHEM, for Your salvation do I long.*

Recite three times— *In the Name of HASHEM,* God of Israel: may Michael be at my right, Gabriel at my left, Uriel before me, and Raphael behind me; and above my head the Presence of God.*

Psalm 128 (Commentary on p. 538)

שִׁיר *A song of ascents. Praiseworthy is each person who fears HASHEM, who walks in His paths. When you eat the labor of your hands, you are praiseworthy and it is well with you. Your wife shall be like a fruitful vine in the inner chambers of your home; your children like olive shoots surrounding your table. Behold! For so shall be blessed the man who fears God. May HASHEM bless you from Zion, and may you gaze upon the goodness of Jerusalem, all the days of your life. And may you see children born to your children, peace upon Israel!*

Recite three times— *Tremble and sin not.* Reflect in your hearts while on your beds, and be utterly silent. Selah.*[5]

אֲדוֹן עוֹלָם *Master of the universe, Who reigned before any form was created, At the time when His will brought all into being — then as 'King' was His Name proclaimed. After all has ceased to be, He, the Awesome one, will reign alone. It is He Who was, He Who is, and He Who shall remain, in splendor. He is One — there is no second to compare to Him, to declare as His equal. Without beginning, without conclusion — He is the power and dominion. He is my God, my living Redeemer, Rock of my pain in time of distress. He is my banner, and refuge for me, the portion in my cup on the day I call. Into His hand I shall entrust my spirit when I go to sleep — and I shall awaken! With my spirit shall my body remain, HASHEM is with me, I shall not fear.*

(1) *Song of Songs* 3:7-8. (2) *Numbers* 6:24-26. (3) *Psalms* 121:4. (4) *Genesis* 49:18. (5) *Psalms* 4:5.

word prayer mystical combinations of letters spelling the Divine Name that provides salvation against enemies. In order to arrive at the combination of letters yielding this Name, the three words of this prayer must be recited in three different orders *(R' Bachya).*

בְּשֵׁם ה' — *In the Name of HASHEM.* God's angels surround you at His command: Michael, performing His unique miracles; Gabriel, the emissary of His almighty power; Uriel, who bears the light of God before you; Raphael, who brings you healing from Him. Above your head is the Presence of God Himself *(R' Hirsch).*

רִגְזוּ וְאַל תֶּחֱטָאוּ — *Tremble and sin not.* Homiletically, this verse exhorts Israel to tremble so much at the thought of sin that the very idea of transgression becomes disturbing and traumatic *(Shaarei Teshuvah;* see *Berachos* 5a).

אֲדוֹן עוֹלָם / Adon Olam

This beautiful hymn is especially appropriate for the night because of its closing stanzas: *'Into His hand I shall entrust my spirit when I go to sleep ...'* [Commentary appears on page 12.]

תְּפִלּוֹת שַׁבָּת וְיוֹם טוֹב

Sabbath and Festival Services

הדלקת הנרות לשבת וליום טוב

OVER THE SABBATH LIGHTS:

Light the candles, then cover the eyes and recite the blessing. Uncover the eyes and gaze briefly at the candles. [When a Festival coincides with the Sabbath, recite the Festival blessings.]

בָּרוּךְ אַתָּה יהוה אֱלֹהֵינוּ מֶלֶךְ הָעוֹלָם, אֲשֶׁר קִדְּשָׁנוּ בְּמִצְוֹתָיו, וְצִוָּנוּ לְהַדְלִיק נֵר* שֶׁל שַׁבָּת.

OVER THE FESTIVAL AND YOM KIPPUR LIGHTS:

When kindling the lights of Yom Kippur, or of a Festival that coincides with the Sabbath, follow the same procedure as for the Sabbath lights. When the Festival falls on a weekday, some follow the above procedure, while others recite the blessings before lighting the candles.

If the Festival coincides with the Sabbath, the words in brackets are added.

בָּרוּךְ אַתָּה יהוה אֱלֹהֵינוּ מֶלֶךְ הָעוֹלָם, אֲשֶׁר קִדְּשָׁנוּ בְּמִצְוֹתָיו, וְצִוָּנוּ לְהַדְלִיק נֵר שֶׁל [שַׁבָּת וְשֶׁל]

on a Festival—יוֹם טוֹב.* on Yom Kippur—יוֹם הַכִּפּוּרִים.

On the seventh and eighth nights of Pesach the following blessing is omitted.

בָּרוּךְ אַתָּה יהוה אֱלֹהֵינוּ מֶלֶךְ הָעוֹלָם, שֶׁהֶחֱיָנוּ וְקִיְּמָנוּ וְהִגִּיעָנוּ לַזְּמַן הַזֶּה.

It is customary to recite the following prayer after the kindling. The words in brackets are included as they apply.

יְהִי רָצוֹן* לְפָנֶיךָ, יהוה אֱלֹהַי וֵאלֹהֵי אֲבוֹתַי, שֶׁתְּחוֹנֵן אוֹתִי [וְאֶת אִישִׁי, וְאֶת בָּנַי, וְאֶת בְּנוֹתַי, וְאֶת אָבִי, וְאֶת אִמִּי] וְאֶת כָּל קְרוֹבַי; וְתִתֶּן לָנוּ וּלְכָל יִשְׂרָאֵל חַיִּים טוֹבִים וַאֲרוּכִים; וְתִזְכְּרֵנוּ בְּזִכְרוֹן טוֹבָה וּבְרָכָה; וְתִפְקְדֵנוּ בִּפְקֻדַּת יְשׁוּעָה וְרַחֲמִים; וּתְבָרְכֵנוּ בְּרָכוֹת גְּדוֹלוֹת; וְתַשְׁלִים בָּתֵּינוּ; וְתַשְׁכֵּן שְׁכִינָתְךָ בֵּינֵינוּ. וְזַכֵּנִי לְגַדֵּל בָּנִים וּבְנֵי בָנִים חֲכָמִים וּנְבוֹנִים, אוֹהֲבֵי יהוה, יִרְאֵי אֱלֹהִים, אַנְשֵׁי אֱמֶת, זֶרַע קֹדֶשׁ, בַּיהוה דְּבֵקִים, וּמְאִירִים אֶת הָעוֹלָם בַּתּוֹרָה וּבְמַעֲשִׂים טוֹבִים, וּבְכָל מְלֶאכֶת עֲבוֹדַת הַבּוֹרֵא. אָנָּא שְׁמַע אֶת תְּחִנָּתִי בָּעֵת הַזֹּאת, בִּזְכוּת שָׂרָה וְרִבְקָה וְרָחֵל וְלֵאָה אִמּוֹתֵינוּ, וְהָאֵר נֵרֵנוּ שֶׁלֹּא יִכְבֶּה לְעוֹלָם וָעֶד, וְהָאֵר פָּנֶיךָ וְנִוָּשֵׁעָה. אָמֵן.

הַדְלָקַת הַנֵּרוֹת / KINDLING LIGHTS

The Sabbath lights are kindled approximately eighteen minutes before sunset.

Since women are generally found in the home more often than their husbands, and since women generally look after household matters, the *mitzvah* of kindling the lights has devolved upon the mistress of the house *(Rambam)*. Nevertheless, a man living alone, or with other men, is required to kindle the lights and recite the proper blessing. Similarly, if a woman is too ill to light, her husband should light the candles and recite the blessing *(Magen Avraham)*.

There should be some light in every room where it will be needed — and indeed this is a halachic requirement — nevertheless, the blessing is recited upon the flames that are kindled in the dining room *(Mishnah Berurah)*. A brightly-lit festive table represents one form of fulfillment of the prophet's instructions: *If you proclaim the Sabbath 'a delight'; the holy one of* HASHEM *'honored' ... then you shall be granted delight with* HASHEM *... (Isaiah 58:13-14)*. The lights 'honor' the Sabbath by brightening, and thereby imparting dignity and importance to, the festive meal *(Rashi)*. Additionally one's 'delight' in a festive meal is enhanced in a well-lit dining room *(Tosafos)*.

KINDLING SABBATH AND FESTIVAL LIGHTS

OVER THE SABBATH LIGHTS:

Light the candles, then cover the eyes and recite the blessing. Uncover the eyes and gaze briefly at the candles. [When a Festival coincides with the Sabbath, recite the Festival blessings.]

בָּרוּךְ *Blessed are You, HASHEM, our God, King of the universe, Who sanctified us with His commandments, and has commanded us to kindle the light* of the Sabbath.*

OVER THE FESTIVAL AND YOM KIPPUR LIGHTS:

When kindling the lights of Yom Kippur, or of a Festival that coincides with the Sabbath, follow the same procedure as for the Sabbath lights. When the Festival falls on a weekday, some follow the above procedure, while others recite the blessings before lighting the candles.

If the Festival coincides with the Sabbath, the words in brackets are added.

בָּרוּךְ *Blessed are You, HASHEM, our God, King of the universe, Who has sanctified us with His commandments, and has commanded us to kindle the light of [the Sabbath and of]*
on a Festival—*the Festival.** on Yom Kippur—*Yom Kippur.*

On the seventh and eighth days of Pesach the following blessing is omitted.

בָּרוּךְ *Blessed are you, HASHEM, our God, King of the universe, Who has kept us alive, sustained us, and brought us to this season.*

It is customary to recite the following prayer after the kindling. The words in brackets are included as they apply.

יְהִי רָצוֹן *May it be Your will* HASHEM, my God and God of my forefathers, that You show favor to me [my husband, my sons, my daughters, my father, my mother] and all my relatives; and that You grant us and all Israel a good and long life; that You remember us with a beneficent memory and blessing; that You consider us with a consideration of salvation and compassion; that You bless us with great blessings; that You make our households complete; that You cause Your Presence to dwell among us. Privilege me to raise children and grandchildren who are wise and understanding, who love HASHEM and fear God, people of truth, holy offspring, attached to HASHEM, who illuminate the world with Torah and good deeds and with every labor in the service of the Creator. Please, hear my supplication at this time, in the merit of Sarah, Rebecca, Rachel, and Leah, our mothers, and cause our light to illuminate that it be not extinguished forever, and let Your countenance shine so that we are saved. Amen.*

נֵר — *The light.* The prevalent custom calls for at least two candles to be lit. According to *Eliyah Rabbah,* the two candles symbolize man and wife. Nevertheless, since one can fulfill the *mitzvah* with a single candle [indeed, *Mishnah Berurah* advises one whose means are extremely limited to purchase one candle of good quality rather than two inferior ones] the blessing is couched in the singular form, נֵר, *light,* and not נֵרוֹת, *lights.*

שֶׁל [שַׁבָּת וְשֶׁל] יוֹם טוֹב — *Of [the Sabbath and of] the Festival.* The Sabbath is mentioned first, following the Talmudic rule that a more frequently performed *mitzvah* takes precedence over a less frequent one.

יְהִי רָצוֹן — *May it be Your will.* It is customary to recite this prayer after the kindling. Because of the Talmudic declaration, 'One who is scrupulous in the kindling of Sabbath lights will be blessed with children who are Torah scholars' (*Shabbos* 23b), the prayer stresses the supplication that the children of the home grow up learned and righteous.

שיר השירים

In some congregations each individual recites שִׁיר הַשִּׁירִים, *Song of Songs,*
on Friday afternoon before *Minchah.*

א

א **שִׁיר הַשִּׁירִים** אֲשֶׁר לִשְׁלֹמֹה. ב יִשָּׁקֵנִי מִנְּשִׁיקוֹת פִּיהוּ, כִּי טוֹבִים
דֹּדֶיךָ מִיָּיִן. ג לְרֵיחַ שְׁמָנֶיךָ טוֹבִים, שֶׁמֶן תּוּרַק שְׁמֶךָ,
עַל כֵּן עֲלָמוֹת אֲהֵבוּךָ. ד מָשְׁכֵנִי אַחֲרֶיךָ נָּרוּצָה, הֱבִיאַנִי הַמֶּלֶךְ חֲדָרָיו,
נָגִילָה וְנִשְׂמְחָה בָּךְ. נַזְכִּירָה דֹדֶיךָ מִיַּיִן, מֵישָׁרִים אֲהֵבוּךָ. ה שְׁחוֹרָה אֲנִי
וְנָאוָה, בְּנוֹת יְרוּשָׁלָיִם, כְּאָהֳלֵי קֵדָר, כִּירִיעוֹת שְׁלֹמֹה. ו אַל תִּרְאֻנִי שֶׁאֲנִי
שְׁחַרְחֹרֶת, שֶׁשֱּׁזָפַתְנִי הַשָּׁמֶשׁ, בְּנֵי אִמִּי נִחֲרוּ בִי, שָׂמֻנִי נֹטֵרָה אֶת
הַכְּרָמִים, כַּרְמִי שֶׁלִּי לֹא נָטָרְתִּי. ז הַגִּידָה לִּי, שֶׁאָהֲבָה נַפְשִׁי, אֵיכָה

שִׁיר הַשִּׁירִים / SONG OF SONGS

As the entire gamut of Talmudic and Rabbinic literature relating to *Shir HaShirim* makes clear, this highly emotional, seemingly sensuous song is an allegory. As such, a literal translation would be misleading — even false — because it would not convey the meaning intended by King Solomon, the composer. The ArtScroll translation follows the commentary of *Rashi,* and a full commentary may be found in the ArtScroll *Shir Hashirim.* The following introductory comments are adapted from *Rashi's* own introduction:

> Solomon foresaw through רוּחַ הַקֹּדֶשׁ, *the Holy Spirit,* that Israel is destined to suffer a series of exiles and will lament, nostalgically recalling her former status as God's chosen beloved. She will say, *'I shall return to my first husband* [i.e., to God] *for it was better with me then than it is now' (Hoshea* 2:9). The children of Israel will recall His beneficence and *the trespasses which they trespassed (Leviticus* 26:40). And they will recall the goodness which He promised for the End of Days.
>
> The prophets frequently likened the relationship between God and Israel to that of a loving husband angered by a straying wife who betrayed him. Solomon composed *Shir HaShirim* in the form of that same allegory. It is a passionate dialogue between the husband [God] who still loves his estranged wife [Israel], and the wife, a veritable widow of a living husband, who longs for her husband and seeks to endear herself to him once more, as she recalls her youthful love for him and admits her guilt.
>
> God, too, is *afflicted by her afflictions (Isaiah* 63:9), and He recalls the kindness of her youth, her beauty, and her skillful deeds for which He loved her [Israel] so. He proclaimed that He has *not afflicted her capriciously (Lamentations* 3:33), nor is she cast away permanently. For she is still His 'wife' and He her 'husband,' and He will yet return to her.

The custom of reciting *Shir HaShirim* before the Sabbath (or during the Sabbath if time did not permit it earlier) is based on the Kabbalistic teaching that the recitation at this time helps save one from the suffering of *Gehinnom (Siddur Arugas HaBosem).*

I

1. The song that excels all songs dedicated to God, the King to Whom peace belongs.

Israel in exile to God:

2. Communicate Your innermost wisdom to me again in loving closeness, for Your friendship is dearer than all earthly delights.
3. Like the scent of goodly oils is the spreading fame of Your great deeds; Your very name is Flowing Oil, therefore have nations loved You.
4. Upon perceiving a mere hint that You wished to draw me, we rushed with perfect faith after You into the wilderness. The King brought me into His cloud-pillared chamber; whatever our travail we shall always be glad and rejoice in Your Torah. We recall Your love more than earthly delights, unrestrainedly do they love You.

Israel to the Nations:

5. Though I am black with sin, I am comely with virtue, O nations who are destined to ascend to Jerusalem; though sullied as the tents of Kedar, I will be immaculate as the draperies of Him to Whom peace belongs.

6. Do not view me with contempt despite my swarthiness, for it is but the sun which has glared upon me. The alien children of my mother were incensed with me and made me a keeper of the vineyards of idols, but the vineyard of my own true God I did not keep.

Israel to God:

7. Tell me, You Whom my soul loves: Where

תִּרְעֶה, אֵיכָה תַּרְבִּיץ בַּצָּהֳרָיִם, שַׁלָּמָה אֶהְיֶה כְּעֹטְיָה עַל עֶדְרֵי חֲבֵרֶיךָ.
ח אִם לֹא תֵדְעִי לָךְ, הַיָּפָה בַּנָּשִׁים, צְאִי לָךְ בְּעִקְבֵי הַצֹּאן, וּרְעִי אֶת
גְּדִיֹּתַיִךְ עַל מִשְׁכְּנוֹת הָרֹעִים. ט לְסֻסָתִי בְּרִכְבֵי פַרְעֹה דִּמִּיתִיךְ, רַעְיָתִי.
י נָאווּ לְחָיַיִךְ בַּתֹּרִים, צַוָּארֵךְ בַּחֲרוּזִים. יא תּוֹרֵי זָהָב נַעֲשֶׂה לָּךְ, עִם נְקֻדּוֹת
הַכָּסֶף. יב עַד שֶׁהַמֶּלֶךְ בִּמְסִבּוֹ, נִרְדִּי נָתַן רֵיחוֹ. יג צְרוֹר הַמֹּר דּוֹדִי לִי, בֵּין
שָׁדַי יָלִין. יד אֶשְׁכֹּל הַכֹּפֶר דּוֹדִי לִי, בְּכַרְמֵי עֵין גֶּדִי. טו הִנָּךְ יָפָה, רַעְיָתִי,
הִנָּךְ יָפָה, עֵינַיִךְ יוֹנִים. טז הִנְּךָ יָפֶה, דוֹדִי, אַף נָעִים, אַף עַרְשֵׂנוּ רַעֲנָנָה.
יז קֹרוֹת בָּתֵּינוּ אֲרָזִים, רָהִיטֵנוּ בְּרוֹתִים.

ב

א אֲנִי חֲבַצֶּלֶת הַשָּׁרוֹן, שׁוֹשַׁנַּת הָעֲמָקִים. ב כְּשׁוֹשַׁנָּה בֵּין הַחוֹחִים, כֵּן
רַעְיָתִי בֵּין הַבָּנוֹת. ג כְּתַפּוּחַ בַּעֲצֵי הַיַּעַר, כֵּן דּוֹדִי בֵּין הַבָּנִים, בְּצִלּוֹ חִמַּדְתִּי
וְיָשַׁבְתִּי, וּפִרְיוֹ מָתוֹק לְחִכִּי. ד הֱבִיאַנִי אֶל בֵּית הַיָּיִן, וְדִגְלוֹ עָלַי אַהֲבָה.
ה סַמְּכוּנִי בָּאֲשִׁישׁוֹת, רַפְּדוּנִי בַּתַּפּוּחִים, כִּי חוֹלַת אַהֲבָה אָנִי. ו שְׂמֹאלוֹ
תַּחַת לְרֹאשִׁי, וִימִינוֹ תְּחַבְּקֵנִי. ז הִשְׁבַּעְתִּי אֶתְכֶם, בְּנוֹת יְרוּשָׁלַיִם,
בִּצְבָאוֹת אוֹ בְּאַיְלוֹת הַשָּׂדֶה, אִם תָּעִירוּ וְאִם תְּעוֹרְרוּ אֶת הָאַהֲבָה עַד

---

will You graze Your flock? Where will You rest them under the fiercest sun of harshest Exile? Why shall I be like one veiled in mourning among the flocks of Your fellow shepherds?

God responds to Israel:

8. If you know not where to graze, O fairest of nations, follow the footsteps of the sheep — your forefathers who traced a straight, unswerving path after My Torah. Then you can graze your tender kids even among the dwellings of foreign shepherds.
9. With My mighty steeds who battled Pharaoh's riders I revealed that you are My beloved.
10. Your cheeks are lovely with rows of gems, your neck with necklaces — My gifts to you from the splitting sea, ...
11. ... by inducing Pharaoh to engage in pursuit, to add circlets of gold to your spangles of silver.

Israel to God:

12. While the King was yet at Sinai my malodorous deed gave forth its scent as my Golden Calf defiled the covenant.
13. But my Beloved responded with a bundle of myrrh — the fragrant atonement of erecting a Tabernacle where His Presence would dwell amid the Holy Ark's staves.
14. Like a cluster of henna in Ein Gedi vineyards has my Beloved multiplied his forgiveness to me.
15. He said, 'I forgive you, My friend, for you are lovely in deed and lovely in resolve. The righteous among you are loyal as a dove.'
16. It is You Who are lovely, my Beloved, so pleasant that you pardoned my sin enabling our Temple to make me ever fresh.
17. The beams of our House are cedar, our panels are cypress.

II

1. I am but a rose of Sharon, even an ever-fresh rose of the valleys.

God to Israel:

2. Like the rose maintaining its beauty among the thorns, so is My faithful beloved among the nations.

Israel reminisces:

3. Like the fruitful, fragrant apple tree among the barren trees of the forest, so is my Beloved among the gods. In His shade I delighted and there I sat, and the fruit of His Torah was sweet to my palate.
4. He brought me to the chamber of Torah delights and clustered my encampments about Him in love.
5. I say to Him, 'Sustain me in exile with dainty cakes, spread fragrant apples about me to comfort my dispersion — for, bereft of Your Presence, I am sick with love.'
6. With memories of His loving support in the desert, of His left hand under my head, of His right hand enveloping me.

Israel to the nations:

7. I adjure you, O nations who are destined to ascend to Jerusalem — for if you violate your oath you will become as defenseless as gazelles or

שֶׁתֶּחְפָּץ. ח קוֹל דּוֹדִי הִנֵּה זֶה בָּא, מְדַלֵּג עַל הֶהָרִים, מְקַפֵּץ עַל הַגְּבָעוֹת.
ט דּוֹמֶה דוֹדִי לִצְבִי, אוֹ לְעֹפֶר הָאַיָּלִים, הִנֵּה זֶה עוֹמֵד אַחַר כָּתְלֵנוּ,
מַשְׁגִּיחַ מִן הַחַלֹּנוֹת, מֵצִיץ מִן הַחֲרַכִּים. י עָנָה דוֹדִי וְאָמַר לִי, קוּמִי לָךְ,
רַעְיָתִי, יָפָתִי, וּלְכִי לָךְ. יא כִּי הִנֵּה הַסְּתָו עָבָר, הַגֶּשֶׁם חָלַף הָלַךְ לוֹ.
יב הַנִּצָּנִים נִרְאוּ בָאָרֶץ, עֵת הַזָּמִיר הִגִּיעַ, וְקוֹל הַתּוֹר נִשְׁמַע בְּאַרְצֵנוּ.
יג הַתְּאֵנָה חָנְטָה פַגֶּיהָ, וְהַגְּפָנִים סְמָדַר נָתְנוּ רֵיחַ, קוּמִי לָךְ, רַעְיָתִי, יָפָתִי,
וּלְכִי לָךְ. יד יוֹנָתִי, בְּחַגְוֵי הַסֶּלַע, בְּסֵתֶר הַמַּדְרֵגָה, הַרְאִינִי אֶת מַרְאַיִךְ,
הַשְׁמִיעִנִי אֶת קוֹלֵךְ, כִּי קוֹלֵךְ עָרֵב, וּמַרְאֵיךְ נָאוֶה. טו אֶחֱזוּ לָנוּ שׁוּעָלִים,
שֻׁעָלִים קְטַנִּים, מְחַבְּלִים כְּרָמִים, וּכְרָמֵינוּ סְמָדַר. טז דּוֹדִי לִי, וַאֲנִי לוֹ,
הָרֹעֶה בַּשּׁוֹשַׁנִּים. יז עַד שֶׁיָּפוּחַ הַיּוֹם, וְנָסוּ הַצְּלָלִים, סֹב דְּמֵה לְךָ, דוֹדִי,
לִצְבִי אוֹ לְעֹפֶר הָאַיָּלִים, עַל הָרֵי בָתֶר.

ג

א עַל מִשְׁכָּבִי בַּלֵּילוֹת בִּקַּשְׁתִּי אֵת שֶׁאָהֲבָה נַפְשִׁי, בִּקַּשְׁתִּיו וְלֹא מְצָאתִיו.
ב אָקוּמָה נָּא וַאֲסוֹבְבָה בָעִיר, בַּשְּׁוָקִים וּבָרְחֹבוֹת, אֲבַקְשָׁה אֵת שֶׁאָהֲבָה
נַפְשִׁי, בִּקַּשְׁתִּיו וְלֹא מְצָאתִיו. ג מְצָאוּנִי הַשֹּׁמְרִים הַסֹּבְבִים בָּעִיר, אֵת
שֶׁאָהֲבָה נַפְשִׁי רְאִיתֶם. ד כִּמְעַט שֶׁעָבַרְתִּי מֵהֶם, עַד שֶׁמָּצָאתִי אֵת
שֶׁאָהֲבָה נַפְשִׁי, אֲחַזְתִּיו וְלֹא אַרְפֶּנּוּ, עַד שֶׁהֲבֵיאתִיו אֶל בֵּית אִמִּי, וְאֶל

---

hinds of the field — if you dare provoke God to hate me or disturb His love for me while He still desires it.

8. The voice of my Beloved! Behold it came suddenly to redeem me, as if leaping over mountains, skipping over hills.

9. In His swiftness to redeem me, my Beloved is like a gazelle or a young hart. I thought I would be forever alone, but behold! He was standing behind our wall, observing through the windows, peering through the lattices.

⊰ Israel reminisces:

10. When He redeemed me from Egypt, my Beloved called out and said to me, 'Arise My love, My fair one, and go forth.

11. For the winter of bondage has passed, the deluge of suffering is over and gone.

12. 'The righteous blossoms are seen in the land, the time of your song has arrived, and the voice of your guide is heard in the land.

13. 'The fig tree has formed its first small figs, ready for ascent to the Temple. The vines are in blossom, their fragrance declaring they are ready for libation. Arise, My love, My fair one, and go forth!'

14. At the sea, He said to me, 'O My dove, trapped at the sea as if in the clefts of the rock, the concealment of the terrace. Show Me your prayerful gaze, let Me hear your supplicating voice, for your voice is sweet and your countenance comely.

15. Then He told the sea, 'Seize for us the Egyptian foxes, even the small foxes who spoiled Israel's vineyards while our vineyards had just begun to blossom.'

16. My Beloved is mine, He fills all my needs and I seek from Him and none other. He grazes me in roselike bounty.

17. Until my sin blows His friendship away and sears me like the midday sun and His protection departs, my sin caused Him to turn away. I say to him, 'My Beloved, You became like a gazelle or a young hart on the distant mountains.'

III

⊰ Israel to the nations:

1. As I lay on my bed in the night of my desert travail, I sought Him Whom my soul loves. I sought Him but I found Him not, for He maintained His aloofness.

2. I resolved to arise then, and roam through the city, in the streets and squares; that I would seek through Moses, Him Whom my soul loved. I sought Him, but I found Him not.

3. They found me, Moses and Aaron, the watchmen patrolling the city. 'You have seen Him Whom my soul loves — what has He said?'

4. Scarcely had I departed from them when, in the days of Joshua, I found Him Whom my soul

חֶדֶר הוֹרָתִי. ה הִשְׁבַּעְתִּי אֶתְכֶם, בְּנוֹת יְרוּשָׁלַיִם, בִּצְבָאוֹת אוֹ בְּאַיְלוֹת
הַשָּׂדֶה, אִם תָּעִירוּ וְאִם תְּעוֹרְרוּ אֶת הָאַהֲבָה עַד שֶׁתֶּחְפָּץ. ו מִי זֹאת עֹלָה
מִן הַמִּדְבָּר, כְּתִימְרוֹת עָשָׁן, מְקֻטֶּרֶת מֹר וּלְבוֹנָה, מִכֹּל אַבְקַת רוֹכֵל.
ז הִנֵּה מִטָּתוֹ שֶׁלִּשְׁלֹמֹה, שִׁשִּׁים גִּבֹּרִים סָבִיב לָהּ, מִגִּבֹּרֵי יִשְׂרָאֵל. ח כֻּלָּם
אֲחֻזֵי חֶרֶב, מְלֻמְּדֵי מִלְחָמָה, אִישׁ חַרְבּוֹ עַל יְרֵכוֹ, מִפַּחַד בַּלֵּילוֹת.
ט אַפִּרְיוֹן עָשָׂה לוֹ הַמֶּלֶךְ שְׁלֹמֹה מֵעֲצֵי הַלְּבָנוֹן. י עַמּוּדָיו עָשָׂה כֶסֶף,
רְפִידָתוֹ זָהָב, מֶרְכָּבוֹ אַרְגָּמָן, תּוֹכוֹ רָצוּף אַהֲבָה מִבְּנוֹת יְרוּשָׁלָיִם.
יא צְאֶינָה וּרְאֶינָה, בְּנוֹת צִיּוֹן, בַּמֶּלֶךְ שְׁלֹמֹה, בַּעֲטָרָה שֶׁעִטְּרָה לּוֹ אִמּוֹ,
בְּיוֹם חֲתֻנָּתוֹ, וּבְיוֹם שִׂמְחַת לִבּוֹ.

ד

א הִנָּךְ יָפָה, רַעְיָתִי, הִנָּךְ יָפָה, עֵינַיִךְ יוֹנִים, מִבַּעַד לְצַמָּתֵךְ, שַׂעְרֵךְ כְּעֵדֶר
הָעִזִּים, שֶׁגָּלְשׁוּ מֵהַר גִּלְעָד. ב שִׁנַּיִךְ כְּעֵדֶר הַקְּצוּבוֹת שֶׁעָלוּ מִן הָרַחְצָה,
שֶׁכֻּלָּם מַתְאִימוֹת, וְשַׁכֻּלָה אֵין בָּהֶם. ג כְּחוּט הַשָּׁנִי שִׂפְתוֹתַיִךְ, וּמִדְבָּרֵיךְ
נָאוֶה, כְּפֶלַח הָרִמּוֹן רַקָּתֵךְ, מִבַּעַד לְצַמָּתֵךְ. ד כְּמִגְדַּל דָּוִיד צַוָּארֵךְ, בָּנוּי
לְתַלְפִּיּוֹת, אֶלֶף הַמָּגֵן תָּלוּי עָלָיו, כֹּל שִׁלְטֵי הַגִּבּוֹרִים. ה שְׁנֵי שָׁדַיִךְ כִּשְׁנֵי
עֳפָרִים, תְּאוֹמֵי צְבִיָּה, הָרוֹעִים בַּשּׁוֹשַׁנִּים. ו עַד שֶׁיָּפוּחַ הַיּוֹם, וְנָסוּ

---

loves. I grasped Him, determined that my deeds would never again cause me to lose hold of Him, until I brought His Presence to the Tabernacle of my mother and to the chamber of the one who conceived me.

5. I adjure you, O nations who are destined to ascend to Jerusalem — for if you violate your oath you will become as defenseless as gazelles or hinds of the field — if you dare provoke God to hate me or disturb His love for me while He still desires it.

6. You nations have asked, 'Who is this ascending from the desert, its way secured and smoothed by palmlike pillars of smoke, burning fragrant myrrh and frankincense, of all the perfumer's powders?'

7. Behold the resting place of Him to Whom peace belongs, with sixty myriads of Israel's mighty encircling it.

8. All of them gripping the sword of tradition, skilled in the battle of Torah, each with his sword ready at his side, lest he succumb in the nights of exile.

9. A Tabernacle for His presence has the King to Whom peace belongs made of the wood of Lebanon.

10. Its pillars He made of silver, His resting place was gold, its suspended curtain was purple wool, its midst was decked with implements bespeaking love by the daughters of Jerusalem.

11. Go forth and gaze, O daughters distinguished by loyalty to God, upon the King to Whom peace belongs adorned with the crown His nation made for Him, on the day His Law was given and He became one with Israel, and on the day His heart was gladdened by His Tabernacle's consecration.

IV

God to Israel:

1. Behold, you are lovely, My friend, behold you are lovely, your very appearance radiates dovelike constancy. The most common sons within your encampments are as dearly beloved as the children of Jacob in the goatlike procession descending the slopes of Mount Gilead.

2. Accountable in deed are your fiercest warriors like a well-numbered flock come up from the washing, all of them unblemished with no miscarriage of action in them.

3. Like the scarlet thread, guarantor of Rachav's safety, is the sincerity of your lips, and your word is unfeigned. As many as a pomegranate's seeds are the merits of your unworthiest within your modest veil.

4. As stately as the Tower of David is the site of your Sanhedrin built as a model to emulate, with a thousand shields of Torah armor hung upon it, all the disciple-filled quivers of the mighty.

5. Moses and Aaron, your two sustainers, are like two fawns, twins of the gazelle, who graze their sheep in roselike bounty.

6. Until My sunny benevolence was withdrawn from Shiloh and the protective shadows were

הַצְּלָלִים, אֵלֶךְ לִי אֶל הַר הַמּוֹר, וְאֶל גִּבְעַת הַלְּבוֹנָה. ז כֻּלָּךְ יָפָה, רַעְיָתִי,
וּמוּם אֵין בָּךְ. ח אִתִּי מִלְּבָנוֹן, כַּלָּה, אִתִּי מִלְּבָנוֹן תָּבוֹאִי, תָּשׁוּרִי מֵרֹאשׁ
אֲמָנָה, מֵרֹאשׁ שְׂנִיר וְחֶרְמוֹן, מִמְּעֹנוֹת אֲרָיוֹת, מֵהַרְרֵי נְמֵרִים. ט לִבַּבְתִּנִי,
אֲחֹתִי כַלָּה, לִבַּבְתִּנִי בְּאַחַת מֵעֵינַיִךְ, בְּאַחַד עֲנָק מִצַּוְּרֹנָיִךְ. י מַה יָּפוּ
דֹדַיִךְ, אֲחֹתִי כַלָּה, מַה טֹּבוּ דֹדַיִךְ מִיַּיִן, וְרֵיחַ שְׁמָנַיִךְ מִכָּל בְּשָׂמִים. יא נֹפֶת
תִּטֹּפְנָה שִׂפְתוֹתַיִךְ, כַּלָּה, דְּבַשׁ וְחָלָב תַּחַת לְשׁוֹנֵךְ, וְרֵיחַ שַׂלְמֹתַיִךְ כְּרֵיחַ
לְבָנוֹן. יב גַּן נָעוּל אֲחֹתִי כַלָּה, גַּל נָעוּל, מַעְיָן חָתוּם. יג שְׁלָחַיִךְ פַּרְדֵּס
רִמּוֹנִים, עִם פְּרִי מְגָדִים, כְּפָרִים עִם נְרָדִים. יד נֵרְדְּ וְכַרְכֹּם, קָנֶה וְקִנָּמוֹן,
עִם כָּל עֲצֵי לְבוֹנָה, מֹר וַאֲהָלוֹת, עִם כָּל רָאשֵׁי בְשָׂמִים. טו מַעְיַן גַּנִּים,
בְּאֵר מַיִם חַיִּים, וְנֹזְלִים מִן לְבָנוֹן. טז עוּרִי צָפוֹן, וּבוֹאִי תֵימָן, הָפִיחִי גַנִּי,
יִזְּלוּ בְשָׂמָיו, יָבֹא דוֹדִי לְגַנּוֹ, וְיֹאכַל פְּרִי מְגָדָיו.

ה

א בָּאתִי לְגַנִּי, אֲחֹתִי כַלָּה, אָרִיתִי מוֹרִי עִם בְּשָׂמִי, אָכַלְתִּי יַעְרִי עִם דִּבְשִׁי,
שָׁתִיתִי יֵינִי עִם חֲלָבִי, אִכְלוּ רֵעִים, שְׁתוּ וְשִׁכְרוּ דּוֹדִים. ב אֲנִי יְשֵׁנָה וְלִבִּי
עֵר, קוֹל דּוֹדִי דוֹפֵק, פִּתְחִי לִי, אֲחֹתִי, רַעְיָתִי, יוֹנָתִי, תַמָּתִי, שֶׁרֹּאשִׁי
נִמְלָא טָל, קְוֻצּוֹתַי רְסִיסֵי לָיְלָה. ג פָּשַׁטְתִּי אֶת כֻּתָּנְתִּי, אֵיכָכָה אֶלְבָּשֶׁנָּה,
רָחַצְתִּי אֶת רַגְלַי, אֵיכָכָה אֲטַנְּפֵם. ד דּוֹדִי שָׁלַח יָדוֹ מִן הַחוֹר, וּמֵעַי הָמוּ

---

dispersed by your sin. I will go to Mount Moriah and the hill of frankincense —

7. where you will be completely fair My beloved, and no blemish will be in you.

8. With Me will you be exiled from the Temple, O bride, with Me from the Temple until you return; then to contemplate the fruits of your faith from its earliest beginnings from your first arrival at the summits of Snir and of Hermon, the lands of mighty Sichon and Og, as impregnable as dens of lions, and as mountains of leopards.

9. You captured My heart, My sister, O bride; you captured My heart with but one of your virtues, with but one of the precepts that adorn you like beads of a necklace resplendent.

10. How fair was your love in so many settings, My sister, O bride; so superior is your love to wine and your spreading fame to all perfumes.

11. The sweetness of Torah drops from your lips, like honey and milk it lies under your tongue; your very garments are scented with precepts like the scent of Lebanon.

12. As chaste as a garden locked, My sister, O bride; a spring locked up, a fountain sealed.

13. Your least gifted ones are a pomegranate orchard with luscious fruit; henna with nard;

14. nard and saffron, calamus and cinnamon, with all trees of frankincense, myrrh and aloes with all the chief spices;

15. purified in a garden spring, a well of waters alive and flowing clean from Lebanon.

16. Awake from the north and come from the south! Like the winds let My exiles return to My garden, let their fragrant goodness flow in Jerusalem.

◆§ Israel to God:

Let but my Beloved come to His garden and enjoy His precious people.

V

◆§ God responds to Israel:

1. To your Tabernacle Dedication, My sister, O bride, I came as if to My garden. I gathered My myrrh with My spice from your princely incense; I accepted your unbidden as well as your bidden offerings to Me; I drank your libations pure as milk. Eat, My beloved priests! Drink and become God-intoxicated, O friends!

◆§ Israel reminisces regretfully

2. I let my devotion slumber, but the God of my heart was awake! A sound! My Beloved knocks! He said, 'Open your heart to Me, My sister, My love, My dove, My perfection; admit Me and My head is filled with dewlike memories of Abraham; spurn Me and I bear collections of punishing rains in exile-nights.'

3. And I responded, 'I have doffed my robe of devotion; how can I don it? I have washed my feet that trod Your path; how can I soil them?'

4. In anger at my recalcitrance, my Beloved sent

עָלָיו. ה קַמְתִּי אֲנִי לִפְתֹּחַ לְדוֹדִי, וְיָדַי נָטְפוּ מוֹר, וְאֶצְבְּעֹתַי מוֹר עֹבֵר, עַל
כַּפּוֹת הַמַּנְעוּל. ו פָּתַחְתִּי אֲנִי לְדוֹדִי, וְדוֹדִי חָמַק עָבָר, נַפְשִׁי יָצְאָה בְדַבְּרוֹ,
בִּקַּשְׁתִּיהוּ וְלֹא מְצָאתִיהוּ, קְרָאתִיו וְלֹא עָנָנִי. ז מְצָאֻנִי הַשֹּׁמְרִים הַסֹּבְבִים
בָּעִיר, הִכּוּנִי פְצָעוּנִי, נָשְׂאוּ אֶת רְדִידִי מֵעָלַי שֹׁמְרֵי הַחֹמוֹת. ח הִשְׁבַּעְתִּי
אֶתְכֶם, בְּנוֹת יְרוּשָׁלָיִם, אִם תִּמְצְאוּ אֶת דּוֹדִי, מַה תַּגִּידוּ לוֹ שֶׁחוֹלַת
אַהֲבָה אָנִי. ט מַה דּוֹדֵךְ מִדּוֹד, הַיָּפָה בַּנָּשִׁים, מַה דּוֹדֵךְ מִדּוֹד, שֶׁכָּכָה
הִשְׁבַּעְתָּנוּ. י דּוֹדִי צַח וְאָדוֹם, דָּגוּל מֵרְבָבָה. יא רֹאשׁוֹ כֶּתֶם פָּז, קְוֻצּוֹתָיו
תַּלְתַּלִּים, שְׁחֹרוֹת כָּעוֹרֵב. יב עֵינָיו כְּיוֹנִים עַל אֲפִיקֵי מָיִם, רֹחֲצוֹת בֶּחָלָב,
יֹשְׁבוֹת עַל מִלֵּאת. יג לְחָיָו כַּעֲרוּגַת הַבֹּשֶׂם, מִגְדְּלוֹת מֶרְקָחִים, שִׂפְתוֹתָיו
שׁוֹשַׁנִּים, נֹטְפוֹת מוֹר עֹבֵר. יד יָדָיו גְּלִילֵי זָהָב, מְמֻלָּאִים בַּתַּרְשִׁישׁ, מֵעָיו
עֶשֶׁת שֵׁן, מְעֻלֶּפֶת סַפִּירִים. טו שׁוֹקָיו עַמּוּדֵי שֵׁשׁ, מְיֻסָּדִים עַל אַדְנֵי פָז,
מַרְאֵהוּ כַּלְּבָנוֹן, בָּחוּר כָּאֲרָזִים. טז חִכּוֹ מַמְתַקִּים, וְכֻלּוֹ מַחֲמַדִּים, זֶה דוֹדִי
וְזֶה רֵעִי, בְּנוֹת יְרוּשָׁלָיִם.

ו

א אָנָה הָלַךְ דּוֹדֵךְ, הַיָּפָה בַּנָּשִׁים, אָנָה פָּנָה דוֹדֵךְ, וּנְבַקְשֶׁנּוּ עִמָּךְ. ב דּוֹדִי
יָרַד לְגַנּוֹ, לַעֲרוּגוֹת הַבֹּשֶׂם, לִרְעוֹת בַּגַּנִּים וְלִלְקֹט שׁוֹשַׁנִּים. ג אֲנִי לְדוֹדִי,

forth His Hand from the portal in wrath, and my intestines churned with longing for Him.

5. I arose to open for my Beloved and my hands dripped myrrh of repentant devotion to Torah and God, and my fingers flowing with myrrh to remove the traces of my foolish rebuke from the handles of the lock.

6. I opened for my Beloved; but, alas, my Beloved had turned His back on my plea and was gone. My soul departed at His decree! I sought His closeness but could not find it; I beseeched Him but He would not answer.

7. They found me, the enemy watchmen patrolling the city; they struck me, they bloodied me wreaking God's revenge on me. They stripped my mantle of holiness from me, the angelic watchmen of the wall.

⊷§ Israel to the nations:

8. I adjure you, O nations who are destined to ascend to Jerusalem, when you see my Beloved on the future Day of Judgment, won't you tell Him that I bore all travails for love of Him?

⊷§ The nations ask Israel:

9. With what does your beloved God excel all others that you suffer for His Name, O fairest of nations? With what does your beloved God excel all others that you dare to adjure us?

⊷§ Israel responds:

10. My Beloved is pure and purifies sin, and ruddy with vengeance to punish betrayers, surrounded with myriad angels.

11. His opening words were finest gold, His crowns hold mounds of statutes written in raven-black flame.

12. Like the gaze of doves toward their cotes, His eyes are fixed on the waters of Torah, bathing all things in clarity, established upon creation's fullness.

13. Like a bed of spices are His words at Sinai, like towers of perfume. His comforting words from the Tabernacle are roses dripping flowing myrrh.

14. The Tablets, His handiwork, are desirable above even rolls of gold; they are studded with commandments precious as gems, the Torah's innards are sparkling as ivory intricately overlaid with precious stone.

15. The Torah's columns are marble set in contexts of finest gold, its contemplation flowers like Lebanon, it is sturdy as cedars.

16. The words of His palate are sweet and He is all delight. This is my Beloved and this is my Friend, O nations who are destined to ascend to Jerusalem.

VI

⊷§ The nations derisively, to Israel:

1. Where has your Beloved gone, O forsaken fairest among women? Where has your Beloved turned to rejoin you? Let us seek Him with you and build His Temple with you.

⊷§ Israel responds:

2. My Beloved has descended to His Temple gar-

וְדוֹדִי לִי, הָרֹעֶה בַּשּׁוֹשַׁנִּים. ד יָפָה אַתְּ רַעְיָתִי כְּתִרְצָה, נָאוָה כִּירוּשָׁלָיִם,
אֲיֻמָּה כַּנִּדְגָּלוֹת. ה הָסֵבִּי עֵינַיִךְ מִנֶּגְדִּי, שֶׁהֵם הִרְהִיבֻנִי, שַׂעְרֵךְ כְּעֵדֶר
הָעִזִּים, שֶׁגָּלְשׁוּ מִן הַגִּלְעָד. ו שִׁנַּיִךְ כְּעֵדֶר הָרְחֵלִים, שֶׁעָלוּ מִן הָרַחְצָה,
שֶׁכֻּלָּם מַתְאִימוֹת, וְשַׁכֻּלָה אֵין בָּהֶם. ז כְּפֶלַח הָרִמּוֹן רַקָּתֵךְ, מִבַּעַד
לְצַמָּתֵךְ. ח שִׁשִּׁים הֵמָּה מְלָכוֹת, וּשְׁמֹנִים פִּילַגְשִׁים, וַעֲלָמוֹת אֵין מִסְפָּר.
ט אַחַת הִיא יוֹנָתִי תַמָּתִי, אַחַת הִיא לְאִמָּהּ, בָּרָה הִיא לְיוֹלַדְתָּהּ, רָאוּהָ
בָנוֹת וַיְאַשְּׁרוּהָ, מְלָכוֹת וּפִילַגְשִׁים, וַיְהַלְלוּהָ. י מִי זֹאת הַנִּשְׁקָפָה כְּמוֹ
שָׁחַר, יָפָה כַלְּבָנָה, בָּרָה כַּחַמָּה, אֲיֻמָּה כַּנִּדְגָּלוֹת. יא אֶל גִּנַּת אֱגוֹז יָרַדְתִּי
לִרְאוֹת בְּאִבֵּי הַנָּחַל, לִרְאוֹת הֲפָרְחָה הַגֶּפֶן, הֵנֵצוּ הָרִמֹּנִים. יב לֹא יָדַעְתִּי,
נַפְשִׁי שָׂמַתְנִי, מַרְכְּבוֹת עַמִּי נָדִיב.

ז

א שׁוּבִי שׁוּבִי, הַשּׁוּלַמִּית, שׁוּבִי שׁוּבִי וְנֶחֱזֶה בָּךְ, מַה תֶּחֱזוּ בַּשּׁוּלַמִּית,
כִּמְחֹלַת הַמַּחֲנָיִם. ב מַה יָּפוּ פְעָמַיִךְ בַּנְּעָלִים, בַּת נָדִיב, חַמּוּקֵי יְרֵכַיִךְ כְּמוֹ
חֲלָאִים, מַעֲשֵׂה יְדֵי אָמָּן. ג שָׁרְרֵךְ אַגַּן הַסַּהַר, אַל יֶחְסַר הַמָּזֶג, בִּטְנֵךְ
עֲרֵמַת חִטִּים, סוּגָה בַּשּׁוֹשַׁנִּים. ד שְׁנֵי שָׁדַיִךְ כִּשְׁנֵי עֳפָרִים, תָּאֳמֵי צְבִיָּה.

---

den, to His incense altar, yet still He grazes my brethren remaining in gardens of exile to gather the roseate fragrance of their words of Torah.

3. I alone am my Beloved's and my Beloved is mine, He Who grazes His sheep in roselike pastures.

God to Israel:

4. You are beautiful, My love, when your deeds are pleasing, as comely now as once you were in Jerusalem of old, hosts of angels stand in awe of you.

5. Turn your pleading eyes from Me lest I be tempted to bestow upon you holiness more than you can bear. But with all your flaws, your most common sons are as dearly beloved as the children of Jacob in the goatlike procession descending the slopes of Mount Gilead.

6. Your mighty leaders are perfect, as a flock of ewes come up from the washing, all of them unblemished with no miscarriage of action in them.

7. As many as a pomegranate's seeds are the merits of your unworthiest within your modest veil.

8. The queenly offspring of Abraham are sixty, compared to whom the eighty Noachides and all their countless nations are like mere concubines.

9. Unique is she, My constant dove, My perfect one. Unique is she, this nation striving for the truth; pure is she to Jacob who begot her. Nations saw her and acclaimed her; queens and concubines, and they praised her:

10. 'Who is this that gazes down from atop the Temple Mount, brightening like the dawn, beautiful as the moon, brilliant as the sun, awesome as the bannered hosts of kings?'

11. I descended upon the deceptively simple holiness of the Second Temple to see your moisture-laden deeds in valleys. Had your Torah scholars budded on the vine, had your merit-laden righteous flowered like the pomegranates filled with seeds?

Israel responds regretfully:

12. Alas, I knew not how to guard myself from sin! My own devices harnessed me, like chariots subject to a foreign nation's mercies.

VII

1. The nations have said to me, 'Turn away, turn away from God, O nation whose faith in Him is perfect, turn away, turn away, and we shall choose nobility from you.' But I replied to them, 'What can you bestow upon a nation whole in faith to Him commensurate even with the desert camps encircling?'

The nations to Israel:

2. But your footsteps were so lovely when shod in pilgrim's sandals, O daughter of nobles. The rounded shafts for your libations' abysslike trenches, handiwork of the Master Craftsman.

3. At earth's very center your Sanhedrin site is an ivory basin of ceaseless, flowing teaching, your national center an indispensable heap of nourishing knowledge hedged about with roses.

4. Your twin sustainers, the Tablets of the Law, are like two fawns, twins of the gazelle.

ה צַוָּארֵךְ כְּמִגְדַּל הַשֵּׁן, עֵינַיִךְ בְּרֵכוֹת בְּחֶשְׁבּוֹן, עַל שַׁעַר בַּת רַבִּים, אַפֵּךְ
כְּמִגְדַּל הַלְּבָנוֹן, צוֹפֶה פְּנֵי דַמָּשֶׂק. ו רֹאשֵׁךְ עָלַיִךְ כַּכַּרְמֶל, וְדַלַּת רֹאשֵׁךְ
כָּאַרְגָּמָן, מֶלֶךְ אָסוּר בָּרְהָטִים. ז מַה יָּפִית וּמַה נָּעַמְתְּ, אַהֲבָה בַּתַּעֲנוּגִים.
ח זֹאת קוֹמָתֵךְ דָּמְתָה לְתָמָר, וְשָׁדַיִךְ לְאַשְׁכֹּלוֹת. ט אָמַרְתִּי, אֶעֱלֶה בְתָמָר,
אֹחֲזָה בְּסַנְסִנָּיו, וְיִהְיוּ נָא שָׁדַיִךְ כְּאֶשְׁכְּלוֹת הַגֶּפֶן, וְרֵיחַ אַפֵּךְ כַּתַּפּוּחִים.
י וְחִכֵּךְ כְּיֵין הַטּוֹב, הוֹלֵךְ לְדוֹדִי לְמֵישָׁרִים, דּוֹבֵב שִׂפְתֵי יְשֵׁנִים. יא אֲנִי
לְדוֹדִי, וְעָלַי תְּשׁוּקָתוֹ. יב לְכָה דוֹדִי, נֵצֵא הַשָּׂדֶה, נָלִינָה בַּכְּפָרִים.
יג נַשְׁכִּימָה לַכְּרָמִים, נִרְאֶה אִם פָּרְחָה הַגֶּפֶן, פִּתַּח הַסְּמָדַר, הֵנֵצוּ
הָרִמּוֹנִים, שָׁם אֶתֵּן אֶת דֹּדַי לָךְ. יד הַדּוּדָאִים נָתְנוּ רֵיחַ, וְעַל פְּתָחֵינוּ כָּל
מְגָדִים, חֲדָשִׁים גַּם יְשָׁנִים, דּוֹדִי, צָפַנְתִּי לָךְ.

ח

א מִי יִתֶּנְךָ כְּאָח לִי, יוֹנֵק שְׁדֵי אִמִּי, אֶמְצָאֲךָ בַחוּץ אֶשָּׁקְךָ, גַּם לֹא יָבֻזוּ לִי.
ב אֶנְהָגְךָ, אֲבִיאֲךָ אֶל בֵּית אִמִּי, תְּלַמְּדֵנִי, אַשְׁקְךָ מִיַּיִן הָרֶקַח, מֵעֲסִיס
רִמֹּנִי. ג שְׂמֹאלוֹ תַּחַת רֹאשִׁי, וִימִינוֹ תְּחַבְּקֵנִי. ד הִשְׁבַּעְתִּי אֶתְכֶם, בְּנוֹת
יְרוּשָׁלָיִם, מַה תָּעִירוּ וּמַה תְּעֹרְרוּ אֶת הָאַהֲבָה עַד שֶׁתֶּחְפָּץ. ה מִי זֹאת

---

5. Your altar and Temple, erect and stately as an ivory tower; your wise men aflow with springs of complex wisdom at the gate of the many-peopled city, your face like a Lebanese tower, looks to your future boundary as far as Damascus.

6. The Godly name on your head is as mighty as Carmel; your crowning braid is royal purple, your King is bound in nazaritic tresses.

7. How beautiful and pleasant are you, befitting the pleasures of spiritual love.

8. Such is your stature, likened to a towering palm tree, from your teachers flow sustenance like wine-filled clusters.

God to Israel in exile:

9. I boast on High that your deeds cause Me to ascend on your palm tree, I grasp onto your branches. I beg now your teachers that they may remain like clusters of grapes from which flow strength to your weakest ones, and the fragrance of your face like apples,

10. and may your utterance be like finest wine

Israel interjects:

I shall heed Your plea to uphold my faith before my Beloved in love so upright and honest that my slumbering fathers will move their lips in approval.

11. I say to the nations, 'I am my Beloved's and He longs for my perfection.'

12. Come my Beloved, let us go to the fields where Your children serve You in want, there let us lodge with Esau's children who are blessed with plenty yet still deny.

13. Let us wake at dawn in vineyards of prayer and study. Let us see if students of Writ have budded, if students of Oral Law have blossomed, if ripened scholars have bloomed — there I will display my finest products to You.

14. All my baskets, good and bad, emit a fragrance, all at our doors have the precious fruits of comely deeds — those the Scribes have newly ordained and Your Torah's timeless wisdom, for You, Beloved, has my heart stored them.

VIII

1. If only, despite my wrongs, You could comfort me as Joseph did, like a brother nurtured at the bosom of my mother, if in the streets I found Your prophets I would kiss You and embrace You through them, nor could anyone despise me for it.

2. I would lead You, I would bring You to my mother's Temple for You to teach me as You did in Moses' Tent, to drink I'd give You spiced libations, wines like pomegranate nectar.

Israel to the nation:

3. Despite my laments in Exile, His left hand supports my head and His right hand embraces me in support.

4. I adjure you, O nations destined to ascend to Jerusalem — for if you violate your oath you will become defenseless — if you dare provoke God to hate me or disturb His love for me while He still desires it.

עֲלָה מִן הַמִּדְבָּר, מִתְרַפֶּקֶת עַל דּוֹדָהּ, תַּחַת הַתַּפּוּחַ עוֹרַרְתִּיךָ, שָׁמָּה
חִבְּלַתְךָ אִמֶּךָ, שָׁמָּה חִבְּלָה יְלָדַתְךָ. ו שִׂימֵנִי כַחוֹתָם עַל לִבֶּךָ, כַּחוֹתָם עַל
זְרוֹעֶךָ, כִּי עַזָּה כַמָּוֶת אַהֲבָה, קָשָׁה כִשְׁאוֹל קִנְאָה, רְשָׁפֶיהָ רִשְׁפֵּי אֵשׁ,
שַׁלְהֶבֶתְיָה. ז מַיִם רַבִּים לֹא יוּכְלוּ לְכַבּוֹת אֶת הָאַהֲבָה, וּנְהָרוֹת לֹא
יִשְׁטְפוּהָ, אִם יִתֵּן אִישׁ אֶת כָּל הוֹן בֵּיתוֹ בָּאַהֲבָה, בּוֹז יָבוּזוּ לוֹ. ח אָחוֹת
לָנוּ קְטַנָּה, וְשָׁדַיִם אֵין לָהּ, מַה נַּעֲשֶׂה לַאֲחוֹתֵנוּ בַּיּוֹם שֶׁיְּדֻבַּר בָּהּ. ט אִם
חוֹמָה הִיא, נִבְנֶה עָלֶיהָ טִירַת כָּסֶף, וְאִם דֶּלֶת הִיא, נָצוּר עָלֶיהָ לוּחַ אָרֶז.
י אֲנִי חוֹמָה, וְשָׁדַי כַּמִּגְדָּלוֹת, אָז הָיִיתִי בְעֵינָיו כְּמוֹצְאֵת שָׁלוֹם. יא כֶּרֶם
הָיָה לִשְׁלֹמֹה בְּבַעַל הָמוֹן, נָתַן אֶת הַכֶּרֶם לַנֹּטְרִים, אִישׁ יָבִא בְּפִרְיוֹ אֶלֶף
כָּסֶף. יב כַּרְמִי שֶׁלִּי לְפָנָי, הָאֶלֶף לְךָ שְׁלֹמֹה, וּמָאתַיִם לְנֹטְרִים אֶת פִּרְיוֹ.
יג הַיּוֹשֶׁבֶת בַּגַּנִּים, חֲבֵרִים מַקְשִׁיבִים לְקוֹלֵךְ, הַשְׁמִיעִנִי. יד בְּרַח דּוֹדִי,
וּדְמֵה לְךָ לִצְבִי, אוֹ לְעֹפֶר הָאַיָּלִים, עַל הָרֵי בְשָׂמִים.

God and the Heavenly Tribunal:

5. How worthy she is who rises from the desert bearing Torah and His Presence, clinging to her Beloved!

Israel interjects:

Under Sinai suspended above me, there I roused Your love, there was Your people born; a mother to other nations, there she endured the travail of her birth.

6. For the sake of my love, place me like a seal on Your heart, like a seal to dedicate Your strength for me, for strong till the death is my love; though their zeal for vengeance is hard as the grave, its flashes are flashes of fire from the flame of God.

God replies to Israel:

7. Many waters of heathen tribulation cannot extinguish the fire of this love, nor rivers of royal seduction or torture wash it away. Were any man to offer all the treasure of his home to entice you away from your love, they would scorn him to extreme.

The Heavenly Tribunal reflects:

8. Israel desires to cleave to us, the small and humble one, but her time of spiritual maturity has not come. What shall we do for our cleaving one on the day the nations plot against her?

9. If her faith and belief are strong as a wall withstanding incursions from without, we shall become her fortress and beauty; building her City and Holy Temple; but if she wavers like a door, succumbing to every alien knock, with fragile cedar panels shall we then enclose her.

Israel replies proudly and reminisces:

10. My faith is firm as a wall, and my nourishing synagogues and study halls are strong as towers! Then, having said so, I become in His eyes like a bride found perfect.

11. Israel was vineyard of Him to Whom peace belongs in populous Jerusalem. He gave His vineyard to harsh, cruel guardians; each one came to extort his fruit, even a thousand silver pieces.

God to the nations, on the Day of Judgment:

12. The vineyard is Mine! Your iniquities are before Me!

The nations will reply to God:

The thousand silver pieces are Yours, You to Whom peace belongs, and two hundred more to the Sages who guarded the fruit of Torah from our designs.

God to Israel:

13. O My beloved, dwelling in far-flung gardens, your fellows, the angels hearken to your voice of Torah and prayer. Let Me hear it that they may then sanctify Me.

Israel to God:

14. Flee, my Beloved, from our common Exile and be like a gazelle or a young hart in Your swiftness to redeem and rest your Presence among us on the fragrant Mount Moriah, site of Your Temple.

One who is unable to recite the entire שִׁיר הַשִּׁירִים, should recite these four verses:

יִשָּׁקֵנִי מִנְּשִׁיקוֹת פִּיהוּ, כִּי טוֹבִים דֹּדֶיךָ מִיָּיִן.[1]

עוּרִי צָפוֹן, וּבוֹאִי תֵימָן, הָפִיחִי גַנִּי, יִזְּלוּ בְשָׂמָיו, יָבֹא דוֹדִי לְגַנּוֹ, וְיֹאכַל פְּרִי מְגָדָיו.[2]

קוֹל דּוֹדִי הִנֵּה זֶה בָּא, מְדַלֵּג עַל הֶהָרִים, מְקַפֵּץ עַל הַגְּבָעוֹת.[3]

בָּאתִי לְגַנִּי, אֲחֹתִי כַלָּה, אָרִיתִי מוֹרִי עִם בְּשָׂמִי, אָכַלְתִּי יַעְרִי עִם דִּבְשִׁי, שָׁתִיתִי יֵינִי עִם חֲלָבִי, אִכְלוּ רֵעִים, שְׁתוּ וְשִׁכְרוּ דּוֹדִים.[4]

Some recite this prayer after completing שִׁיר הַשִּׁירִים.

רִבּוֹן כָּל הָעוֹלָמִים, יְהִי רָצוֹן מִלְּפָנֶיךָ, יהוה אֱלֹהַי וֵאלֹהֵי אֲבוֹתַי, שֶׁבִּזְכוּת שִׁיר הַשִּׁירִים אֲשֶׁר קָרִיתִי וְלָמַדְתִּי, שֶׁהוּא קֹדֶשׁ קָדָשִׁים, בִּזְכוּת פְּסוּקָיו, וּבִזְכוּת תֵּבוֹתָיו, וּבִזְכוּת אוֹתִיּוֹתָיו, וּבִזְכוּת נְקֻדּוֹתָיו, וּבִזְכוּת טְעָמָיו, וּבִזְכוּת שְׁמוֹתָיו, וְצֵרוּפָיו וּרְמָזָיו וְסוֹדוֹתָיו הַקְּדוֹשִׁים וְהַטְּהוֹרִים, הַנּוֹרָאִים הַיּוֹצְאִים מִמֶּנּוּ. שֶׁתְּהֵא שָׁעָה זוּ שְׁעַת רַחֲמִים, שְׁעַת הַקְשָׁבָה, שְׁעַת הַאֲזָנָה, וְנִקְרָאֲךָ וְתַעֲנֵנוּ. נַעְתִּיר לְךָ וְהֵעָתֶר לָנוּ, שֶׁיִּהְיֶה עוֹלֶה לְפָנֶיךָ קְרִיאַת וְלִמּוּד שִׁיר הַשִּׁירִים, כְּאִלּוּ הִשַּׂגְנוּ כָּל הַסּוֹדוֹת הַנִּפְלָאוֹת וְהַנּוֹרָאוֹת אֲשֶׁר הֵם חֲתוּמִים בּוֹ, בְּכָל תְּנָאָיו. וְנִזְכֶּה לְמָקוֹם שֶׁהָרוּחוֹת וְהַנְּשָׁמוֹת נֶחֱצָבוֹת מִשָּׁם. וּכְאִלּוּ עָשִׂינוּ כָּל מַה שֶּׁמּוּטָל עָלֵינוּ, לְהַשִּׂיג בֵּין בְּגִלְגּוּל זֶה בֵּין בְּגִלְגּוּל אַחֵר. וְלִהְיוֹת מִן הָעוֹלִים וְהַזּוֹכִים לָעוֹלָם הַבָּא עִם שְׁאָר צַדִּיקִים וַחֲסִידִים. וּמַלֵּא כָּל מִשְׁאֲלוֹת לִבֵּנוּ לְטוֹבָה, וְתִהְיֶה עִם לְבָבֵנוּ וְאִמְרֵי פִינוּ, בְּעֵת מַחְשְׁבוֹתֵינוּ. וְעִם יָדֵינוּ, בְּעֵת מַעְבָּדֵינוּ. וְתִשְׁלַח בְּרָכָה וְהַצְלָחָה וְהַרְוָחָה, בְּכָל מַעֲשֵׂה יָדֵינוּ. וּמֵעָפָר תְּקִימֵנוּ, וּמֵאַשְׁפּוֹת דַּלּוּתֵנוּ תְּרוֹמְמֵנוּ, וְתָשִׁיב שְׁכִינָתְךָ לְעִיר קָדְשֶׁךָ, בִּמְהֵרָה בְיָמֵינוּ. אָמֵן.

רִבּוֹן *Master of all worlds, may it be Your will,* HASHEM *my God and the God of my forefathers, that in the merit of Song of Songs which I have read and studied, and which is holy of holies — in the merit of its verses; in the merit of its words; in the merit of its letters; in the merit of its vowels; in the merit of its cantillation; in the merit of its holy, pure, awesome Names, combinations, allusions and secrets that are derived from it — that this hour be an hour of compassion, an hour of attention, an hour of hearkening, that we may call to You, and that You may answer us; that we may entreat You, and that You allow Yourself to be prevailed upon by us. May the recitation and study of Song of Songs rise before You, as if we have grasped all the wondrous and awesome secrets that are sealed into it, with all its conditions. And may we be worthy of the place from where the spirits and souls are hewn, as if we have done all that is required of us to accomplish — whether in this transmigration or in another transmigration; and may we be among those who rise and merit the World to Come along with other righteous and pious ones. May He fulfill all the requests of our hearts for goodness. May You be with our hearts and the words of our mouth, at the time of our thoughts, and with our hands at the time of our actions. May You send blessings, success and relief to all our handiwork. From the dust, stand us erect; from the trash heap of our poverty raise us; and return Your Presence to Your Holy City — speedily, in our days, Amen.*

(1) Song of Songs 1:2. (2) 4:16. (3) 2:8. (4) 5:1.

קבלת שבת

In some congregations יְדִיד נֶפֶשׁ (p. 590) is recited before *Kabbalas Shabbos.*
The regular *Kabbalas Shabbos* service begins here. When a Festival or Chol HaMoed fall on either Friday or the Sabbath, most congregations begin with מִזְמוֹר שִׁיר לְיוֹם הַשַּׁבָּת (p. 320).

תהלים צה

לְכוּ* נְרַנְּנָה לַיהוה, נָרִיעָה לְצוּר יִשְׁעֵנוּ.* נְקַדְּמָה פָנָיו בְּתוֹדָה, בִּזְמִרוֹת נָרִיעַ לוֹ. כִּי אֵל גָּדוֹל יהוה, וּמֶלֶךְ גָּדוֹל עַל כָּל אֱלֹהִים.* אֲשֶׁר בְּיָדוֹ מֶחְקְרֵי אָרֶץ,* וְתוֹעֲפוֹת הָרִים לוֹ. אֲשֶׁר לוֹ הַיָּם וְהוּא עָשָׂהוּ, וְיַבֶּשֶׁת יָדָיו יָצָרוּ. בֹּאוּ נִשְׁתַּחֲוֶה וְנִכְרָעָה, נִבְרְכָה לִפְנֵי יהוה עֹשֵׂנוּ. כִּי הוּא אֱלֹהֵינוּ וַאֲנַחְנוּ עַם מַרְעִיתוֹ וְצֹאן יָדוֹ, הַיּוֹם* אִם בְּקֹלוֹ תִשְׁמָעוּ. אַל תַּקְשׁוּ לְבַבְכֶם כִּמְרִיבָה, כְּיוֹם מַסָּה* בַּמִּדְבָּר. אֲשֶׁר נִסּוּנִי אֲבוֹתֵיכֶם, בְּחָנוּנִי גַּם רָאוּ פָעֳלִי. ❖ אַרְבָּעִים שָׁנָה אָקוּט בְּדוֹר, וָאֹמַר עַם תֹּעֵי לֵבָב הֵם,* וְהֵם לֹא יָדְעוּ דְרָכָי. אֲשֶׁר נִשְׁבַּעְתִּי בְאַפִּי, אִם יְבֹאוּן אֶל מְנוּחָתִי.

תהלים צו

שִׁירוּ לַיהוה שִׁיר חָדָשׁ,* שִׁירוּ לַיהוה כָּל הָאָרֶץ. שִׁירוּ לַיהוה בָּרְכוּ שְׁמוֹ, בַּשְּׂרוּ מִיּוֹם לְיוֹם יְשׁוּעָתוֹ.* סַפְּרוּ בַגּוֹיִם כְּבוֹדוֹ, בְּכָל הָעַמִּים נִפְלְאוֹתָיו. כִּי גָדוֹל יהוה וּמְהֻלָּל מְאֹד, נוֹרָא הוּא עַל כָּל אֱלֹהִים. כִּי כָּל אֱלֹהֵי

קַבָּלַת שַׁבָּת / KABBALAS SHABBOS

The Talmud *(Shabbos* 119a) teaches that as the Sabbath drew near, the Sages would don their finest clothing and say to one another 'Let us go out to greet the Sabbath queen.' A thousand years later, the Kabbalists of Safed embellished the Talmudic custom by actually walking out to the fields to 'welcome the incoming Sabbath.' It was there in Safed, that the קַבָּלַת שַׁבָּת, *Welcoming the Sabbath,* service was first formulated and from where it spread to the entire Jewish world. The point was that Jews regarded the Sabbath as a queen that brought majesty to their midst and that it was their privilege to usher her in.

Since this service was an innovation, many congregations wished to signify that it was not part of the established service. They did so by having the *chazzan* stand at the *bimah* (Torah reading table) until after *Lechah Dodi,* whereupon he moves to his accustomed place at the front of the synagogue.

The *Kabbalas Shabbos* service begins with six psalms [95-99 and 29], whose common theme is that God is Master of the universe. Indeed the Sabbath is the testimony that He created heaven and earth in six days and rested on the Sabbath, as we will see throughout the Sabbath prayers. In this light, many commentators teach that the six psalms allude to the six weekdays, which we elevate by dedicating them to the service of God and by preparing for the Sabbath day of spiritual elevation. These six psalms are followed by the *Lechah Dodi* song that greets the incoming queen and Psalms 92-93, the songs of not only every Sabbath, but of the eternal Sabbath of Messianic days.

לְכוּ נְרַנְּנָה / Psalm 95

This psalm is composed of two parts. The first seven verses are the Psalmist's call to his people: Come with alacrity to sing to God, to praise Him, to thank Him, to acknowledge Him as the sole Creator and Guiding Force — of the universe in general and of Israel in particular.

The second section is in the form of a direct exhortation from God to Israel, in which He recalls the disastrous results of our ancestors' sins in the Wilderness and urges us not to emulate that course.

לְכוּ — *Come* [lit. *go*]. The expression represents an enthusiastic appeal: Forget your preoccupation with material concerns and heretical beliefs, and join me in singing God's praises! *(Meiri).*

KABBALAS SHABBOS

In some congregations *Yedid Nefesh* (p. 591) is recited before *Kabbalas Shabbos*.
The regular *Kabbalas Shabbos* service begins here. When a Festival or Chol Hamoed falls on either Friday or the Sabbath, most congregations begin with Psalm 92 (p. 321).

Psalm 95

לְכוּ נְרַנְּנָה *Come!* — let us sing to* HASHEM, *let us call out to the Rock of our salvation.* Let us greet Him with thanksgiving, with praiseful songs let us call out to Him. For a great God is* HASHEM, *and a great King above all heavenly powers.* For in His power are the hidden mysteries of earth,* and the mountain summits are His. For His is the sea and He perfected it, and the dry land — His hands fashioned it. Come! — let us prostrate ourselves and bow, let us kneel before God, our Maker. For He is our God and we can be the flock He pastures, and the sheep in His charge — even today,* if we but heed His call! Do not harden your heart as at Meribah, as on the day of Massah* in the Wilderness; when Your ancestors tried Me; they tested Me, though they had seen My deed.* Chazzan— *For forty years I was angry with the generation; then I said, 'An errant-hearted people are they,* and they know not My ways. Therefore, I have sworn in My wrath that they shall not enter My land of contentment.'*

Psalm 96

שִׁירוּ לַיהוה *Sing to* HASHEM *a new song,* sing to* HASHEM, *— everyone on earth. Sing to* HASHEM, *bless His Name; announce His salvation daily.* Relate His glory among the nations, among all peoples, His wonders: that* HASHEM *is great and exceedingly lauded, awesome is He above all heavenly powers. For all the gods of*

לְצוּר יִשְׁעֵנוּ — *To the Rock of our salvation.* No matter how imminent Israel's destruction has often seemed, the Protector of Israel always prevented the 'inevitable' from happening *(Avnei Eliyahu).*

וּמֶלֶךְ גָּדוֹל עַל כָּל אֱלֹהִים — *And a great King above all heavenly powers,* i.e. the angels and other heavenly forces through whom God exercises His mastery of the universe *(Radak).*

מֶחְקְרֵי אָרֶץ — *The hidden mysteries of earth.* This verse and the next poetically describe God's power in terms of all aspects of the world's existence.

הַיּוֹם — *Even today.* If we only heed God's call, He will end our travail and suffering *even today.* If we do so, He will immediately give us the love and care that a shepherd gives his flock.

כִּמְרִיבָה כְּיוֹם מַסָּה — *As at Meribah, as on the day of Massah.* According to *Radak,* both phrases refer poetically to the place known as *Massah u'Meribah* [lit. *Testing and Strife*], where Israel made its first public complaint against God, for failing to provide sufficient fresh water (see *Exodus* 17:7).

עַם תֹּעֵי לֵבָב הֵם — *An errant-hearted people are they.* Because the Israelites who left Egypt were not wholesome at heart, they failed to recognize God's power and interest in their welfare. It was not He Who was remiss — but their perception of Him. Therefore God decreed forty years of wandering during which all the adults of the generation would die *(Radak).*

שִׁירוּ לַה׳ שִׁיר חָדָשׁ / Psalm 96

שִׁיר חָדָשׁ — *A new song.* What is new about this song? — It is the one that will be sung in honor of the future redemption of Israel as is indicated by the final verse of the psalm *(Rashi):*

— The song is *new* because, like none other in Scripture, it will come at the unique stage of history when all the nations on earth will join in acknowledging God *(R' Hirsch).*

— It is a song of renewal in honor of the national rejuvenation of the future *(Iyun Tefillah).*

בַּשְּׂרוּ מִיּוֹם לְיוֹם יְשׁוּעָתוֹ — *Announce His salvation daily.* Do not acknowledge God only for openly miraculous interventions. Recognize that even seemingly innocuous daily events are Heavenly gifts *(R' Hirsch).*

הָעַמִּים אֱלִילִים, (pause) וַיהוה* שָׁמַיִם עָשָׂה. הוֹד וְהָדָר לְפָנָיו, עֹז וְתִפְאֶרֶת בְּמִקְדָּשׁוֹ. הָבוּ לַיהוה מִשְׁפְּחוֹת עַמִּים, הָבוּ לַיהוה כָּבוֹד וָעֹז. הָבוּ לַיהוה כְּבוֹד שְׁמוֹ, שְׂאוּ מִנְחָה וּבֹאוּ לְחַצְרוֹתָיו. הִשְׁתַּחֲווּ לַיהוה בְּהַדְרַת קֹדֶשׁ,* חִילוּ מִפָּנָיו כָּל הָאָרֶץ. אִמְרוּ בַגּוֹיִם יהוה מָלָךְ, אַף תִּכּוֹן תֵּבֵל בַּל תִּמּוֹט, יָדִין עַמִּים בְּמֵישָׁרִים. ❖ יִשְׂמְחוּ הַשָּׁמַיִם* וְתָגֵל הָאָרֶץ, יִרְעַם הַיָּם וּמְלֹאוֹ. יַעֲלֹז שָׂדַי וְכָל אֲשֶׁר בּוֹ, אָז יְרַנְּנוּ כָּל עֲצֵי יָעַר. לִפְנֵי יהוה כִּי בָא, כִּי בָא* לִשְׁפֹּט הָאָרֶץ, יִשְׁפֹּט תֵּבֵל בְּצֶדֶק, וְעַמִּים בֶּאֱמוּנָתוֹ.

תהלים צז

יהוה מָלָךְ* תָּגֵל הָאָרֶץ, יִשְׂמְחוּ אִיִּים רַבִּים. עָנָן וַעֲרָפֶל סְבִיבָיו,* צֶדֶק וּמִשְׁפָּט מְכוֹן כִּסְאוֹ. אֵשׁ לְפָנָיו תֵּלֵךְ,* וּתְלַהֵט סָבִיב צָרָיו. הֵאִירוּ בְרָקָיו תֵּבֵל, רָאֲתָה וַתָּחֵל הָאָרֶץ. הָרִים כַּדּוֹנַג נָמַסּוּ* מִלִּפְנֵי יהוה, מִלִּפְנֵי אֲדוֹן כָּל הָאָרֶץ. הִגִּידוּ הַשָּׁמַיִם* צִדְקוֹ, וְרָאוּ כָל הָעַמִּים כְּבוֹדוֹ. יֵבֹשׁוּ כָּל עֹבְדֵי פֶסֶל הַמִּתְהַלְלִים בָּאֱלִילִים, הִשְׁתַּחֲווּ לוֹ כָּל אֱלֹהִים. שָׁמְעָה וַתִּשְׂמַח צִיּוֹן וַתָּגֵלְנָה בְּנוֹת יְהוּדָה,* לְמַעַן מִשְׁפָּטֶיךָ יהוה. כִּי אַתָּה יהוה עֶלְיוֹן עַל כָּל הָאָרֶץ, מְאֹד נַעֲלֵיתָ עַל כָּל אֱלֹהִים. ❖ אֹהֲבֵי יהוה שִׂנְאוּ רָע, שֹׁמֵר נַפְשׁוֹת חֲסִידָיו, מִיַּד רְשָׁעִים יַצִּילֵם. אוֹר זָרֻעַ לַצַּדִּיק,* וּלְיִשְׁרֵי לֵב שִׂמְחָה. שִׂמְחוּ צַדִּיקִים בַּיהוה, וְהוֹדוּ לְזֵכֶר קָדְשׁוֹ.

אֱלִילִים, וַה׳ — *Are nothings, but* HASHEM. One must pause slightly between the words אֱלִילִים, *nothings,* and וַה׳, *but* (lit. *and)* HASHEM. If the two Hebrew words were to be said together it would seem ח״ו as if HASHEM were being equated with the gods of the nations.

בְּהַדְרַת קֹדֶשׁ — *In His intensely holy place* [lit. *in the strength of holiness*]. This refers to the intensely holy Temple. Thus, when you bring an offering, come to the Temple and bow *(Radak).* Alternatively, [when you bring your offering] *prostrate yourselves before HASHEM with intense holiness (Ibn Ezra).*

יִשְׂמְחוּ הַשָּׁמַיִם... — *The heavens will be glad* ... The components of nature signify their joy by carrying out the functions assigned to them by God. The heavens give abundant rain and dew, the earth gives generous crops, and so on *(Ibn Ezra).*

כִּי בָא, כִּי בָא — *For He will have arrived, He will have arrived.* The repetition alludes to two aspects: First, God will manifest Himself in the functioning of nature when people recognize that the so-called laws of nature are truly the concealed Hand of God. Second, God will be perceived as the One Who judges the deeds of people *(Malbim).*

ה׳ מָלָךְ / Psalm 97

ה׳ מָלָךְ — *When* HASHEM *will reign.* Altnough the word is in past tense — מָלָךְ, *reigned,* instead of יִמְלֹךְ, *will reign* — tenses are frequently interchanged in Scripture, especially in poetry. The translation follows the context *(Meiri).* The past tense also alludes to an eternal truth: Although God's future supremacy will seem to be a shocking new phenomenon in the long course of history, the reality should not escape us — God *has always* reigned, it is only we who failed to perceive it.

עָנָן וַעֲרָפֶל סְבִיבָיו — *Cloud and dense darkness will*

the peoples are nothings — but HASHEM made heaven! Glory and majesty are before Him, might and splendor in His Sanctuary. Render unto HASHEM, O families of the peoples, render unto HASHEM honor and might. Render unto HASHEM honor worthy of His Name, take an offering and come to His courtyards. Prostrate yourselves before HASHEM in His intensely holy place,* tremble before Him, everyone on earth. Declare among the peoples, 'HASHEM reigns, indeed, the world is fixed so that it cannot falter. He will judge the peoples with fairness.'* Chazzan— *The heavens will be glad* and the earth will rejoice, the sea and its fullness will roar; the field and everything in it will exult, then all the trees of the forest will sing with joy — before HASHEM, for He will have arrived, He will have arrived* to judge the earth. He will judge the world with righteousness, and peoples with His truth.*

Psalm 97

יהוה מָלָךְ *When HASHEM will reign,* the world will rejoice; numerous islands will be glad. Cloud and dense darkness will surround Him;* righteousness and justice are His throne's foundation. Fire will advance before Him* and consume His enemies all around. His lightning bolts will light up the world, the inhabitants of the earth will see and tremble. Mountains will melt like wax* before HASHEM, before the Lord of all the earth. The heavens will declare* His righteousness, and all the peoples will see His glory. Humiliated will be all who worship idols, who pride themselves in worthless gods; to Him all the powers will bow. Zion will hear and be glad, and the daughters of Judah* will exult, because of Your judgments, HASHEM. For You, HASHEM, are supreme above all the earth; exceedingly exalted above all powers.* Chazzan— *O lovers of HASHEM — despise evil! He guards the lives of His devout ones, from the hand of the wicked He rescues them. Light is sown for the righteous;* and for the upright of heart, gladness. Be glad, O righteous, in HASHEM, and give grateful praise at the mention of His Holy Name.*

---

surround Him. We often fail to understand the justice of God's ways; it is as if His guidance of events is masked by cloud and darkness. In reality, however, *righteousness and justice* [are] *His throne's foundation;* everything He does is for a reason.

אֵשׁ לְפָנָיו תֵּלֵךְ — *Fire will advance before Him.* The reference is to the War of Gog and Magog, described in *Ezekiel* 38, during which the mortal enemies of God and Israel will attempt to destroy God's people — but will themselves be destroyed *(Rashi).*

הָרִים כַּדּוֹנַג נָמַסּוּ — *Mountains will melt like wax. Radak* and *Ibn Ezra* interpret *mountains* as a figurative reference to great and towering leaders; their pretensions of grandeur will *melt like wax* before God's wrath.

Rashi refers this to *Ezekiel* 38:20, which describes the physical upheavals that will devastate Gog and Magog.

הִגִּידוּ הַשָּׁמַיִם — *The heavens will declare.* By raining hailstones and destruction upon the wicked, the heavenly forces will, in effect, declare His glory *(Radak).*

שָׁמְעָה וַתִּשְׂמַח צִיּוֹן ... בְּנוֹת יְהוּדָה — *Zion will hear and be glad ... the daughters of Judah.* Zion and Judah represent the Holy Temple and those who mourned its destruction — they will have earned the right to rejoice in the Redemption *(R' Hirsch).*

אוֹר זָרֻעַ לַצַּדִּיק — *Light is sown for the righteous.* The spiritual light — the reward for good deeds and the personal perfection that are their natural

תהלים צח

מִזְמוֹר, שִׁירוּ לַיהוה שִׁיר חָדָשׁ, כִּי נִפְלָאוֹת עָשָׂה, הוֹשִׁיעָה לוֹ יְמִינוֹ* וּזְרוֹעַ קָדְשׁוֹ. הוֹדִיעַ יהוה יְשׁוּעָתוֹ, לְעֵינֵי הַגּוֹיִם גִּלָּה צִדְקָתוֹ. זָכַר חַסְדּוֹ וֶאֱמוּנָתוֹ לְבֵית יִשְׂרָאֵל, רָאוּ כָל אַפְסֵי אָרֶץ אֵת יְשׁוּעַת אֱלֹהֵינוּ. הָרִיעוּ לַיהוה כָּל הָאָרֶץ,* פִּצְחוּ וְרַנְּנוּ וְזַמֵּרוּ. זַמְּרוּ לַיהוה בְּכִנּוֹר, בְּכִנּוֹר וְקוֹל זִמְרָה. בַּחֲצֹצְרוֹת וְקוֹל שׁוֹפָר, הָרִיעוּ לִפְנֵי הַמֶּלֶךְ יהוה. יִרְעַם הַיָּם וּמְלֹאוֹ, תֵּבֵל וְיֹשְׁבֵי בָהּ. ❖ נְהָרוֹת יִמְחֲאוּ כָף, יַחַד הָרִים יְרַנֵּנוּ. לִפְנֵי יהוה כִּי בָא לִשְׁפֹּט הָאָרֶץ, יִשְׁפֹּט תֵּבֵל בְּצֶדֶק, וְעַמִּים בְּמֵישָׁרִים.*

תהלים צט

יהוה מָלָךְ יִרְגְּזוּ עַמִּים, יֹשֵׁב כְּרוּבִים* תָּנוּט הָאָרֶץ. יהוה בְּצִיּוֹן גָּדוֹל, וְרָם הוּא עַל כָּל הָעַמִּים. יוֹדוּ שִׁמְךָ גָּדוֹל וְנוֹרָא קָדוֹשׁ הוּא. וְעֹז מֶלֶךְ מִשְׁפָּט אָהֵב, אַתָּה כּוֹנַנְתָּ מֵישָׁרִים,* מִשְׁפָּט וּצְדָקָה בְּיַעֲקֹב אַתָּה עָשִׂיתָ. רוֹמְמוּ יהוה אֱלֹהֵינוּ, וְהִשְׁתַּחֲווּ לַהֲדֹם רַגְלָיו, קָדוֹשׁ הוּא. מֹשֶׁה וְאַהֲרֹן בְּכֹהֲנָיו,* וּשְׁמוּאֵל בְּקֹרְאֵי שְׁמוֹ,* קֹרְאִים אֶל יהוה וְהוּא יַעֲנֵם. ❖ בְּעַמּוּד עָנָן יְדַבֵּר אֲלֵיהֶם, שָׁמְרוּ עֵדֹתָיו וְחֹק נָתַן לָמוֹ. יהוה אֱלֹהֵינוּ אַתָּה עֲנִיתָם,* אֵל נֹשֵׂא הָיִיתָ לָהֶם, וְנֹקֵם עַל עֲלִילוֹתָם.* רוֹמְמוּ יהוה אֱלֹהֵינוּ וְהִשְׁתַּחֲווּ לְהַר קָדְשׁוֹ, כִּי קָדוֹשׁ יהוה אֱלֹהֵינוּ.

---

result — are like seeds sown in fertile soil *(Rashi; Radak).*

מִזְמוֹר שִׁירוּ לַה׳ שִׁיר חָדָשׁ / Psalm 98

הוֹשִׁיעָה לוֹ יְמִינוֹ — *His own right hand ... helped Him.* God requires no outside assistance. What He wants done, He accomplishes through His *right hand,* a term symbolic of power *(Radak).*

הָרִיעוּ לַה׳ כָּל הָאָרֶץ — *Call out to* HASHEM, *all inhabitants of the earth.* Everyone on earth will benefit from the new era of peace and happiness that will accompany the Messianic era. Therefore it is proper for *all* peoples to *call out* in praise and gratitude *(Radak).*

A Czarist official in Russia once asked the *Netziv,* rabbi of Volozhin, why many psalms call upon the nations to praise God for His salvation of Israel. It should be *Israel,* not its oppressors, who praise Him!

The *Netziv* replied, 'We have no way of knowing the extent of your conspiracies against us. Only you know how many times you have plotted against us, but been thwarted by God. You are far more conscious than we are, therefore, of the magnitude of God's miraculous salvations. Only *you* can appreciate the full extent of His greatness.'

בְּמֵישָׁרִים — *With fairness.* The last verse of Psalm 96 (above) is virtually identical with this one except for the last word: that psalm ends בֶּאֱמוּנָתוֹ, *with His truth. Malbim* explains that the word אֱמוּנָה, *truth* or *faith,* is a reference to the functioning of nature, as if to say that natural law is unyielding and unchanging, like a person who is totally faithful and reliable. There, in Psalm 96, the Psalmist refers to punishments of the wicked which would be effected through natural means. This verse, however, describes the Divine, miraculous judgment; though it will supersede the laws of nature, it will be carried out with absolute *fairness.*

Psalm 98

מִזְמוֹר שִׁירוּ *A Psalm! Sing to* H*ASHEM a new song for He has done wonders; His own right hand and holy arm have helped Him.* HASHEM has made known His salvation; in the sight of the nations He revealed His righteousness. He recalled His kindness and faithfulness to the House of Israel; all ends of the earth have seen the salvation of our God. Call out to HASHEM, all inhabitants of the earth,* open your mouths in joyous songs and play music. Play music to HASHEM on a harp, with harp and sound of chanted praise. With trumpets and shofar sound, call out before the King, HASHEM. The sea and its fullness will roar, the world and those who dwell therein.* Chazzan— *Rivers will clap hands, mountains will exult together — Before HASHEM, for He will have arrived to judge the earth. He will judge the world with righteousness and peoples with fairness.**

Psalm 99

יהוה מָלָךְ *When HASHEM will reign nations will tremble. Before Him Who is enthroned on Cherubim,* the earth will quake. Before HASHEM Who is great in Zion and Who is exalted above all nations. They will gratefully praise Your great and awesome Name; it is holy! Mighty is the King, Who loves justice. You founded fairness.* The justice and righteousness of Jacob, You have made. Exalt HASHEM, our God, and bow at His footstool; He is holy! Moses and Aaron were among His priests,* and Samuel among those who invoke His Name* — they called upon HASHEM and He answered them.* Chazzan— *In a pillar of cloud He spoke to them; they obeyed His testimonies and whatever decree He gave them. HASHEM, our God, You answered them.* A forgiving God were You to them — and an Avenger for their iniquities.* Exalt HASHEM, our God, and bow at His holy mountain; for holy is HASHEM, our God.*

ה׳ מָלָךְ / Psalm 99 ◆§

יֹשֵׁב כְּרוּבִים — *Who is enthroned on Cherubim.* The golden Cherubim stand atop the Ark which contains the Tablets of the Law. The holy Presence of God rests with its greatest intensity between the Cherubim in the Holy of Holies in the Temple (see *Exodus* 25:22).

אַתָּה כּוֹנַנְתָּ מֵישָׁרִים — *You founded fairness.* Although human beings have concepts of fairness, we should not delude ourselves into thinking that such ideals are of human origin. Even so-called 'human decency' was ingrained in man by his Maker — *You founded fairness.*

מֹשֶׁה וְאַהֲרֹן בְּכֹהֲנָיו — *Moses and Aaron were among His priests.* How did Israel merit the gifts of God's Torah and His Sanctuary on earth? Because it had — and was obedient to — leaders such as Moses, Aaron, and Samuel *(Iyun Tefillah).*

Although Moses was a Levite, he is described as a *Kohen* [priest] because he was the only one permitted to perform the Tabernacle service during the Seven Days of Dedication, when the newly built Tabernacle was inaugurated. Thereafter, the service became the exclusive province of the priestly family of Aaron, but Moses retained the title of priest *(Ibn Ezra).*

וּשְׁמוּאֵל בְּקֹרְאֵי שְׁמוֹ — *And Samuel among those who invoke His Name.* Samuel is singled out from among the multitude of prophets *who invoke His Name,* because he was the greatest prophet [after Moses] or because he, like Moses, was a Levite *(Radak).*

אַתָּה עֲנִיתָם — *You answered them,* i.e., You responded to the prayers of Israel.

וְנֹקֵם עַל עֲלִילוֹתָם — *And an Avenger for their iniquities.* God punished all those who wronged Israel. Even Moses, Aaron, and Samuel were punished when they criticized Israel too harshly *(Rashi).*

It is customary to stand during the recitation of the following psalm, and to recite it slowly, fervently, and aloud. Some continue standing until after the קַדִּישׁ יָתוֹם (p. 322).

תהלים כט

מִזְמוֹר לְדָוִד, הָבוּ לַיהוה בְּנֵי אֵלִים,* הָבוּ לַיהוה כָּבוֹד וָעֹז. הָבוּ לַיהוה כְּבוֹד שְׁמוֹ,* הִשְׁתַּחֲווּ לַיהוה בְּהַדְרַת קֹדֶשׁ. קוֹל יהוה* עַל הַמָּיִם, אֵל הַכָּבוֹד הִרְעִים, יהוה עַל מַיִם רַבִּים. קוֹל יהוה בַּכֹּחַ, קוֹל יהוה בֶּהָדָר. קוֹל יהוה שֹׁבֵר אֲרָזִים,* וַיְשַׁבֵּר יהוה אֶת אַרְזֵי הַלְּבָנוֹן. וַיַּרְקִידֵם כְּמוֹ עֵגֶל, לְבָנוֹן וְשִׂרְיוֹן כְּמוֹ בֶן רְאֵמִים.* קוֹל יהוה חֹצֵב לַהֲבוֹת אֵשׁ.* קוֹל יהוה יָחִיל מִדְבָּר, יָחִיל יהוה מִדְבַּר קָדֵשׁ.* ❖ קוֹל יהוה יְחוֹלֵל אַיָּלוֹת,* וַיֶּחֱשֹׂף יְעָרוֹת,* וּבְהֵיכָלוֹ, כֻּלּוֹ אֹמֵר כָּבוֹד. יהוה לַמַּבּוּל יָשָׁב, וַיֵּשֶׁב יהוה מֶלֶךְ לְעוֹלָם.* יהוה עֹז לְעַמּוֹ יִתֵּן, יהוה יְבָרֵךְ אֶת עַמּוֹ בַשָּׁלוֹם.*

אָנָּא בְּכֹחַ,* גְּדֻלַּת יְמִינְךָ, תַּתִּיר צְרוּרָה.* — אב״ג ית״ץ
קַבֵּל רִנַּת, עַמְּךָ שַׂגְּבֵנוּ, טַהֲרֵנוּ נוֹרָא. — קר״ע שט״ן
נָא גִבּוֹר, דּוֹרְשֵׁי יִחוּדְךָ,* כְּבָבַת שָׁמְרֵם. — נג״ד יכ״ש
בָּרְכֵם טַהֲרֵם, רַחֲמֵם* צִדְקָתְךָ, תָּמִיד גָּמְלֵם. — בט״ר צת״ג
חֲסִין קָדוֹשׁ, בְּרוֹב טוּבְךָ, נַהֵל עֲדָתֶךָ. — חק״ב טנ״ע
יָחִיד גֵּאֶה, לְעַמְּךָ פְּנֵה, זוֹכְרֵי קְדֻשָּׁתֶךָ. — יג״ל פז״ק
שַׁוְעָתֵנוּ קַבֵּל, וּשְׁמַע צַעֲקָתֵנוּ, יוֹדֵעַ תַּעֲלֻמוֹת. — שק״ו צי״ת
בָּרוּךְ שֵׁם כְּבוֹד מַלְכוּתוֹ לְעוֹלָם וָעֶד.

⁂ מִזְמוֹר לְדָוִד / Psalm 29

Arizal writes of many Kabbalistic allusions found in this psalm and teaches that when it is recited with intense devotion it causes profound spiritual benefit in the heavenly realms. Many commentators urge that although few are qualified to study the allusions of *Arizal*, all should recite this psalm with great joy, with as much understanding as they can muster, and with a determination to sanctify God's Name no matter what sacrifice may be necessary to achieve that goal.

בְּנֵי אֵלִים — *Sons of the powerful.* The Psalmist addresses himself to the descendants of Abraham, Isaac, and Jacob, the *powerful* men of righteousness *(Rashi; Radak).*

Rashi interprets the psalm as a reference to God's *past* graciousness to Israel, while *Radak* interprets it as directed to the Messianic era when God's power and glory will finally become unmistakably manifest.

כְּבוֹד שְׁמוֹ — *Honor worthy of His Name.* Each Name of God symbolizes a different aspect of His greatness: HASHEM represents Mercy, Elohim represents strict Judgment, and so on. Whatever Name we use, therefore, indicates reference to a specific manifestation of His greatness, and should be accompanied by appropriate honor to that particular attribute *(Etz Yosef).*

קוֹל ה׳ — *The voice of* HASHEM. Throughout Scripture, the 'voice' of God refers only to His communication with man, never to a loud natural sound, such as thunder *(R' Hirsch).*

רְאֵמִים — *Re'eimim.* See commentary on page 110.

שֹׁבֵר אֲרָזִים — *Breaks the cedars.* Alien kings stood haughty as mighty cedar trees, like the majestic cedar forests of the Lebanon mountains. They were broken by God into submission.

חֹצֵב לַהֲבוֹת אֵשׁ — *Cleaves with shafts of fire.* A reference to the Midrashic teaching that when God pronounced the Ten Commandments, the very words sprang forth like fire, so to speak, and cleaved themselves into the Tablets of the Law.

יָחִיל ... קָדֵשׁ — *Convulses ... Kadesh. Kadesh,* derived from קֹדֶשׁ, *holy,* is another name for the Wilderness of Sinai, for it was there that Israel became sanctified through accepting the Torah.

It is customary to stand during the recitation of the following psalm, and to recite it slowly, fervently and aloud. Some continue standing until after the Mourner's *Kaddish* (p. 322).

Psalm 29

מִזְמוֹר לְדָוִד *A psalm of David. Render unto* HASHEM*, you sons of the powerful;* render unto* HASHEM*, honor and might. Render unto* HASHEM *honor worthy of His Name;* prostrate yourselves before* HASHEM *in His intensely holy place. The voice of* HASHEM* *is upon the waters, the God of Glory thunders,* HASHEM *is upon vast waters. The voice of* HASHEM *is in power! The voice of* HASHEM *is in majesty! The voice of* HASHEM *breaks the cedars,** HASHEM *shatters the cedars of Lebanon! He makes them prance about like a calf; Lebanon and Siryon like young re'eimim.* The voice of* HASHEM *cleaves with shafts of fire.* The voice of* HASHEM *convulses the wilderness;* HASHEM *convulses the wilderness of Kadesh.** Chazzan— *The voice of* HASHEM *frightens the hinds,* and strips the forests bare;* while in His Temple all proclaim, 'Glory!'* HASHEM *sat enthroned at the Deluge;* HASHEM *sits enthroned as King forever.** HASHEM *will give might to His people,* HASHEM *will bless His people with peace.**

אָנָּא *We beg You! With the strength* of Your right hand's greatness, untie the bundled sins.* Accept the prayer of Your nation; strengthen us, purify us, O Awesome One. Please, O Strong One — those who foster Your Oneness,* guard them like the pupil of an eye. Bless them, purify them, show them pity,* may Your righteousness always recompense them. Powerful Holy One, with Your abundant goodness guide Your congregation. One and only Exalted One, turn to Your nation which proclaims Your holiness. Accept our entreaty and hear our cry, O Knower of mysteries.*

Blessed is the Name of His glorious kingdom for all eternity.

Just as a person reacts with trembling and awe when suddenly faced with unaccustomed holiness, the deserted wilderness became convulsed, as it were, when it became host to the awesome spectacle of God's Presence.

יְחוֹלֵל אַיָּלוֹת — *Frightens the hinds.* The Psalmist turns to the future. Nations that now stand as erect and unflinching as deer [hinds], will be made to tremble...

וַיֶּחֱשֹׂף יְעָרוֹת — *And strips the forests bare.* The mighty will be as denuded of their power and vanity as trees stripped of their bark and left *bare* to the elements.

לַמַּבּוּל ... מֶלֶךְ לְעוֹלָם — *At the Deluge ... King forever.* Seldom has God's omnipotence been as pronounced as during the Deluge in the time of Noah. Then, the universe came to a standstill and life was virtually wiped out. When the entire earth was covered with water, God reigned alone in silence, while man and beast who had disobeyed Him were washed away. That degree of sovereignty will be manifest again in Messianic times when idolatry and wickedness will be uprooted.

עֹז ... בַשָּׁלוֹם — *Might ... with peace.* When that time comes, once-lowly Israel will emerge as the repository of a human power based on spiritual attainment, and God will grant His nation the ultimate blessings of peace and harmony.

אָנָּא בְּכֹחַ — *We beg You! With the strength ...* Tradition ascribes this mystic prayer to the *tanna* R' Nechuniah ben Hakanah. It contains forty-two words, the initials of which form the secret forty-two letter Name of God. Moreover, the six initials of each of its seven verses form Divine Names. The Kabbalists teach that it should be divided into phrases of two words each, but our translation follows the division indicated by a simple reading of the phrases.

תַּתִּיר צְרוּרָה — *Untie the bundled sins.* The accumulated sins of Israel are bound together like a barrier that prevents our prayers from ascending to the Heavenly Throne. We ask God to remove this impediment *(Iyun Tefillah).*

דּוֹרְשֵׁי יִחוּדְךָ — *Those who foster Your Oneness.* The acknowledgment of God's Oneness is paramount (see commentary to שְׁמַע יִשְׂרָאֵל, p. 90). As the nation that accepts this obligation upon itself, Israel pleads for God's protection *(Iyun Tefillah).*

רַחֲמֵם — *Show them pity.* According to some versions, this phrase reads רַחֲמֵי צִדְקָתְךָ, *the mercy of Your righteousness.*

לְכָה דוֹדִי is recited responsively. In most congregations, the *chazzan* repeats each verse after the congregation. In others the procedure is reversed.

לְכָה דוֹדִי* לִקְרַאת כַּלָּה,* פְּנֵי שַׁבָּת נְקַבְּלָה.

לְכָה דוֹדִי לִקְרַאת כַּלָּה, פְּנֵי שַׁבָּת נְקַבְּלָה.

שָׁמוֹר וְזָכוֹר בְּדִבּוּר אֶחָד, הִשְׁמִיעָנוּ* אֵל הַמְּיֻחָד,
יְהוָה אֶחָד וּשְׁמוֹ אֶחָד, לְשֵׁם וּלְתִפְאֶרֶת וְלִתְהִלָּה.

לְכָה דוֹדִי לִקְרַאת כַּלָּה, פְּנֵי שַׁבָּת נְקַבְּלָה.

לִקְרַאת שַׁבָּת לְכוּ וְנֵלְכָה, כִּי הִיא מְקוֹר הַבְּרָכָה,*
מֵרֹאשׁ מִקֶּדֶם נְסוּכָה, סוֹף מַעֲשֶׂה בְּמַחֲשָׁבָה תְּחִלָּה.*

לְכָה דוֹדִי לִקְרַאת כַּלָּה, פְּנֵי שַׁבָּת נְקַבְּלָה.

מִקְדַּשׁ מֶלֶךְ* עִיר מְלוּכָה, קוּמִי צְאִי מִתּוֹךְ הַהֲפֵכָה,
רַב לָךְ שֶׁבֶת בְּעֵמֶק הַבָּכָא,* וְהוּא יַחֲמוֹל עָלַיִךְ חֶמְלָה.

לְכָה דוֹדִי לִקְרַאת כַּלָּה, פְּנֵי שַׁבָּת נְקַבְּלָה.

הִתְנַעֲרִי מֵעָפָר קוּמִי,* לִבְשִׁי בִּגְדֵי תִפְאַרְתֵּךְ עַמִּי,*
עַל יַד בֶּן יִשַׁי* בֵּית הַלַּחְמִי, קָרְבָה אֶל נַפְשִׁי גְאָלָהּ.

לְכָה דוֹדִי לִקְרַאת כַּלָּה, פְּנֵי שַׁבָּת נְקַבְּלָה.

לְכָה דוֹדִי / Lechah Dodi

This beautiful and inspiring song to the Sabbath was composed by the sixteenth century Kabbalist Rabbi Shlomo HaLevi Alkabetz. He was a brother-in-law and teacher of Rabbi Moshe Cordovero, and was a leading figure in the Safed group of scholars that included *Arizal* and Rabbi Yosef Karo, author of the *Shulchan Aruch*. The author's name, שְׁלֹמֹה הַלֵּוִי, *Shlomo HaLevi*, is formed by the acrostic of the first eight stanzas. Many similar poetic greetings to the Sabbath were extant, but only this one received the endorsement of *Arizal*, with the result that it has been adapted universally as part of *Kabbalas Shabbos*.

The song is based on the Talmud's description of the Sages' joyous greeting of the Sabbath (*Shabbos* 119a); Rabbi Chaninah would wrap himself in his cloak and say, 'Come, let us go and greet the Sabbath Queen.' Rabbi Yannai would don his garment and say, 'Enter, O bride! Enter, O bride!'

לְכָה דוֹדִי — *Come my Beloved.* Our 'Beloved' is God Himself. We invite Him to join us in ushering in the Sabbath (*Anaf Yosef; R' Hirsch*).

כַּלָּה — *The bride.* The Midrash (*Bereishis Rabbah* 11) teaches that God told the newly created Sabbath, 'Israel shall be your mate.' Accordingly, every week, Israel greets the approaching Sabbath like a groom awaiting his bride as she advances to the wedding canopy (*Etz Yosef*).

Anaf Yosef, however, interprets כַּלָּה, *bride*, as an allusion to the *Shechinah*, God's Presence, which was withdrawn from man due to Israel's sins. We ask God [דוֹדִי, *my Beloved*] to join us in greeting the *Shechinah*, signifying our prayer for an end to the Exile.

שָׁמוֹר וְזָכוֹר בְּדִבּוּר אֶחָד הִשְׁמִיעָנוּ — *'Safeguard' and 'Remember' — in a single utterance...made us hear.* The Talmud (*Shavuos* 20b) teaches, when He gave the Ten Commandments, He miraculously caused Israel to hear simultaneously the two complementary aspects of the Sabbath commandment. שָׁמוֹר, *Safeguard* (*Deut.* 5:12), is the injunction to avoid the desecration of the Sabbath, while זָכוֹר, *Remember* (*Exodus* 20:8), is the commandment to keep the Sabbath in our minds and hearts, and give verbal expression to its holiness. Although the Torah writes these commandments separately, God combined them at Sinai so that Israel would know they are inseparable. To observe the 'spirit of the Sabbath' while ignoring its practice, and vice-versa, is a travesty (*R' Hirsch*).

לִקְרַאת ... כִּי הִיא מְקוֹר הַבְּרָכָה — *To welcome ... For it is the source of blessing.* The *Zohar* teaches

לְכָה דוֹדִי, *'Come my Beloved,'* is recited responsively. In most congregations, the *chazzan* repeats each verse after the congregation. In others the procedure is reversed.

לְכָה דוֹדִי *Come my Beloved* to greet the bride—**
The Sabbath presence, let us welcome!
Come my Beloved to greet the bride—The Sabbath presence, let us welcome!

שָׁמוֹר *'Safeguard' and 'Remember' — in a single utterance*
*The One and Only God made us hear.**
HASHEM is One and His Name is One,
For renown, for splendor, and for praise.
Come my Beloved to greet the bride—The Sabbath presence, let us welcome!

לִקְרַאת *To welcome the Sabbath, come let us go,*
*For it is the source of blessing;**
From the beginning, from antiquity she was honored,
*Last in deed, but first in thought.**
Come my Beloved to greet the bride—The Sabbath presence, let us welcome!

מִקְדַּשׁ *O Sanctuary of the King,* royal City —*
Arise and depart from amid the upheaval,
*Too long have you dwelled in the valley of weeping.**
He will shower compassion upon you.
Come my Beloved to greet the bride—The Sabbath presence, let us welcome!

הִתְנַעֲרִי *Shake off the dust — arise!**
*Don your splendid clothes, My people,**
Through the son of Jesse, the Bethlehemite!*
Draw near to my soul — redeem it!
Come my Beloved to greet the bride—The Sabbath presence, let us welcome!

---

that all the weekday blessings and success come as a result of the Sabbath's holiness *(Etz Yosef);* to which *Iyun Tefillah* adds the dictum of *Shabbos* 118a that whoever brings joy to the Sabbath is rewarded with a boundless legacy of blessing.

סוֹף מַעֲשֶׂה בְּמַחֲשָׁבָה תְּחִלָּה — *Last in deed, but first in thought* [i.e., the Sabbath was the final act of Creation, but primary in God's purpose]. Whenever a great project is envisioned, a host of preparations must be made before the goal can be achieved. That there would be a day of holiness in Creation was uppermost in God's thought, but the entire universe had to be created first.

מִקְדַּשׁ מֶלֶךְ — *O Sanctuary of the King* [i.e., Jerusalem]. From this point until the last stanza, the theme shifts from the Sabbath to Israel's longing for redemption. This is a logical extension of our welcome of the Sabbath, because the Talmud *(Shabbos* 118b) teaches that the Messiah will come if Israel observes two Sabbaths properly *(Iyun Tefillah).*

הַהֲפֵכָה ... בְּעֵמֶק הַבָּכָא — *The upheaval ... in the valley of weeping.* Both are references to the suffering and woe of exile. We are speaking to Jerusalem, for she too, as it were, grieves over the exile of her children. May she rejoice again in the ingathering of Israel.

הִתְנַעֲרִי מֵעָפָר קוּמִי — *Shake off the dust — arise!* The reference is to *Isaiah* 52:2 where the prophet addresses Jerusalem as if she were a woman wallowing in the dust. He urges her to rise up, dress in her finery, and resume her noble ways *(Avodas Yisrael).*

לִבְשִׁי בִּגְדֵי תִפְאַרְתֵּךְ עַמִּי — *Don your splendid clothes, My people.* In a novel interpretation, *Iyun Tefillah* comments: 'Jerusalem — your most splendid garment is Israel. Let the redemption come so that they may inhabit you in holiness once more.'

בֶּן יִשַׁי — *The son of Jesse.* A reference to Messiah, who will be a descendant of David, son of Jesse.

הִתְעוֹרְרִי* הִתְעוֹרְרִי, כִּי בָא אוֹרֵךְ קוּמִי אוֹרִי,
עוּרִי עוּרִי שִׁיר דַּבֵּרִי, כְּבוֹד יהוה עָלַיִךְ נִגְלָה.
לְכָה דוֹדִי לִקְרַאת כַּלָּה, פְּנֵי שַׁבָּת נְקַבְּלָה.

לֹא תֵבוֹשִׁי וְלֹא תִכָּלְמִי, מַה תִּשְׁתּוֹחֲחִי וּמַה תֶּהֱמִי,
בָּךְ יֶחֱסוּ עֲנִיֵּי עַמִּי, וְנִבְנְתָה עִיר עַל תִּלָּהּ.
לְכָה דוֹדִי לִקְרַאת כַּלָּה, פְּנֵי שַׁבָּת נְקַבְּלָה.

וְהָיוּ לִמְשִׁסָּה שֹׁאסָיִךְ,* וְרָחֲקוּ כָּל מְבַלְּעָיִךְ,
יָשִׂישׂ עָלַיִךְ אֱלֹהָיִךְ, כִּמְשׂוֹשׂ חָתָן עַל כַּלָּה.
לְכָה דוֹדִי לִקְרַאת כַּלָּה, פְּנֵי שַׁבָּת נְקַבְּלָה.

יָמִין וּשְׂמֹאל תִּפְרֹוצִי,* וְאֶת יהוה תַּעֲרִיצִי,
עַל יַד אִישׁ בֶּן פַּרְצִי,* וְנִשְׂמְחָה וְנָגִילָה.
לְכָה דוֹדִי לִקְרַאת כַּלָּה, פְּנֵי שַׁבָּת נְקַבְּלָה.

Rise and face the rear of the synagogue to greet the Sabbath Bride. When saying the words בּוֹאִי כַלָּה, bow and turn, as if to acknowledge the entrance of the Sabbath.

בּוֹאִי בְשָׁלוֹם עֲטֶרֶת בַּעְלָהּ,* גַּם בְּשִׂמְחָה* וּבְצָהֳלָה,
תּוֹךְ אֱמוּנֵי עַם סְגֻלָּה, בּוֹאִי כַלָּה, בּוֹאִי כַלָּה.
לְכָה דוֹדִי לִקְרַאת כַּלָּה, פְּנֵי שַׁבָּת נְקַבְּלָה.

During the week of *shivah,* mourners enter the synagogue at this point and are greeted by the leaders of the congregation, whereupon the congregation offers these words of consolation:

הַמָּקוֹם יְנַחֵם אֶתְכֶם בְּתוֹךְ שְׁאָר אֲבֵלֵי צִיּוֹן וִירוּשָׁלָיִם.

הִתְעוֹרְרִי — *Wake up!* The poet addresses Jerusalem again, exhorting her to rise from the spiritual sluggishness of exile and exhibit the brilliance that once made her great. The stanza closes by declaring that God's glory has returned — as if the redemption has already taken place.

וְהָיוּ לִמְשִׁסָּה שֹׁאסָיִךְ — *May your oppressors be downtrodden.* Messianic times will bring a turnabout. Those who delighted in oppressing Israel will be dealt with measure for measure. But as for Israel, their erstwhile victim, *'Your God will rejoice over you ...'*

יָמִין וּשְׂמֹאל תִּפְרֹוצִי — *Rightward and leftward, you shall spread out mightily.* With the redemption will come fulfillment of Isaiah's prophecy that Jerusalem will overpower its antagonists to the right and left *(Etz Yosef).*

אִישׁ בֶּן פַּרְצִי — *The man descended from Peretz.* An allusion to Messiah, a descendant of David, whose line began with Judah's son Peretz.

בּוֹאִי בְשָׁלוֹם — *Enter in peace.* At this point, the holiness of the Sabbath enters and with it the נְשָׁמָה יְתֵרָה, *additional soul,* which enables a Jew to appreciate and benefit from the enhanced holiness of the day. Along with the Sabbath, the *Shechinah* comes among us. [For this reason, the congregation turns to face the rear of the synagogue, as if to welcome the Queen as she makes her entrance.] Therefore, this stanza should be said with intense joy and devotion *(Yesod V'Shoresh HaAvodah).*

עֲטֶרֶת בַּעְלָהּ — *O crown of her husband.* Since the Sabbath and Israel have been designated as mates, the Sabbath is given the title Solomon bestowed upon a 'woman of accomplishment' [*Proverbs* 12:4] *(Etz Yosef).*

הִתְעוֹרְרִי *Wake up!* Wake up!*
For your light has come, rise up and shine;
Awaken, awaken, utter a song,
The glory of HASHEM *is revealed on you.*
Come my Beloved to greet the bride—The Sabbath presence, let us welcome!

לֹא תֵבֹשִׁי *Feel not ashamed, be not humiliated,*
Why are you downcast? Why are you disconsolate?
In you will My people's afflicted find shelter
As the City is built upon its hilltop.
Come my Beloved to greet the bride—The Sabbath presence, let us welcome!

וְהָיוּ *May your oppressor be downtrodden,**
And may those who devoured you be cast far off.
Your God will rejoice over you
Like a groom's rejoicing over his bride.
Come my Beloved to greet the bride—The Sabbath presence, let us welcome!

יָמִין וּשְׂמֹאל *Rightward and leftward, you shall spread out mightily,**
And you shall extol the might of HASHEM,
*Through the man descended from Peretz,**
Then we shall be glad and mirthful.
Come my Beloved to greet the bride—The Sabbath presence, let us welcome!

Rise and face the rear of the synagogue to greet the Sabbath Bride. When saying the words *'Enter, O bride,'* bow and turn, as if to acknowledge the entrance of the Sabbath.

בּוֹאִי *Enter in peace,* O crown of her husband,**
Even in gladness and good cheer,*
Among the faithful of the treasured nation
Enter, O bride! Enter, O bride!
Come my Beloved to greet the bride—The Sabbath presence, let us welcome!

During the week of *shivah,* mourners enter the synagogue at this point and are greeted by the leaders of the congregation, whereupon the congregation offers these words of consolation:

הַמָּקוֹם *May the Omnipresent console you among the other mourners of Zion and Jerusalem.*

גַּם בְּשִׂמְחָה — *Even in gladness.* Not only in peace, but in gladness *(Iyun Tefillah).*

הַמָּקוֹם / The Mourners Enter

Because the Sabbath begins with the recital of the next psalm (92, see below) and public observance of the regulations of mourning are not permitted on this sacred day, mourners during the *shivah* week now enter the synagogue to pray with the congregation. In many congregations it is customary to mark this interruption of mourning with a brief ceremony. The leaders of the congregation invite the mourners to enter the synagogue whereupon they are welcomed with the traditional formula of consolation: הַמָּקוֹם יְנַחֵם ..., *May the Omnipresent console you ...*

With the recitation of Psalm 92, we accept upon ourselves the holiness of the Sabbath. When a Festival or Chol HaMoed falls on either Friday or the Sabbath, most congregations omit the earlier parts of *Kabbalas Shabbos* and begin at this point:

תהלים צב

מִזְמוֹר שִׁיר לְיוֹם הַשַּׁבָּת.* טוֹב לְהֹדוֹת לַיהוה, וּלְזַמֵּר לְשִׁמְךָ עֶלְיוֹן. לְהַגִּיד בַּבֹּקֶר חַסְדֶּךָ, וֶאֱמוּנָתְךָ בַּלֵּילוֹת.* עֲלֵי עָשׂוֹר* וַעֲלֵי נָבֶל, עֲלֵי הִגָּיוֹן בְּכִנּוֹר. כִּי שִׂמַּחְתַּנִי יהוה בְּפָעֳלֶךָ, בְּמַעֲשֵׂי יָדֶיךָ אֲרַנֵּן. מַה גָּדְלוּ מַעֲשֶׂיךָ יהוה, מְאֹד עָמְקוּ מַחְשְׁבֹתֶיךָ.* אִישׁ בַּעַר לֹא יֵדָע, וּכְסִיל לֹא יָבִין אֶת זֹאת. בִּפְרֹחַ רְשָׁעִים* כְּמוֹ עֵשֶׂב, וַיָּצִיצוּ כָּל פֹּעֲלֵי אָוֶן, לְהִשָּׁמְדָם עֲדֵי עַד.* וְאַתָּה מָרוֹם לְעֹלָם יהוה. כִּי הִנֵּה אֹיְבֶיךָ יהוה, כִּי הִנֵּה אֹיְבֶיךָ יֹאבֵדוּ, יִתְפָּרְדוּ כָּל פֹּעֲלֵי אָוֶן. וַתָּרֶם כִּרְאֵים קַרְנִי,* בַּלֹּתִי בְּשֶׁמֶן רַעֲנָן.* וַתַּבֵּט עֵינִי בְּשׁוּרָי, בַּקָּמִים עָלַי מְרֵעִים, תִּשְׁמַעְנָה אָזְנָי. ❖ צַדִּיק כַּתָּמָר יִפְרָח, כְּאֶרֶז* בַּלְּבָנוֹן יִשְׂגֶּה. שְׁתוּלִים בְּבֵית יהוה,* בְּחַצְרוֹת אֱלֹהֵינוּ יַפְרִיחוּ. עוֹד יְנוּבוּן בְּשֵׂיבָה, דְּשֵׁנִים וְרַעֲנַנִּים יִהְיוּ. לְהַגִּיד כִּי יָשָׁר יהוה, צוּרִי וְלֹא עַוְלָתָה בּוֹ.

תהלים צג

יהוה מָלָךְ גֵּאוּת לָבֵשׁ,* לָבֵשׁ יהוה עֹז הִתְאַזָּר, אַף תִּכּוֹן תֵּבֵל בַּל תִּמּוֹט. נָכוֹן כִּסְאֲךָ מֵאָז, מֵעוֹלָם אָתָּה.

⁂ מִזְמוֹר שִׁיר לְיוֹם הַשַּׁבָּת / Psalm 92

Although the recitation of the *Kabbalas Shabbos* liturgy up to this point originated with the school of *Arizal,* the custom of reciting the next two psalms is ancient. In a responsa, *Rambam (Pe'er HaDor* 116) implies clearly that it predated him by many generations. With our recitation of this song of praise to the Sabbath, we accept its holiness upon ourselves together with all its positive and negative *mitzvos.*

מִזְמוֹר שִׁיר לְיוֹם הַשַּׁבָּת — *A psalm, a song for the Sabbath day.* Although this psalm is identified as belonging particularly to the theme of the Sabbath — indeed, it was the Levites' song for the Sabbath Temple service *(Rashi)* — the text contains not a single direct reference to the Sabbath. What is the connection? Many explanations are given. Among them are:

— The psalm refers not to the weekly Sabbath, but to the World to Come, when man will achieve the spiritual perfection we only glimpse during the Sabbath. The psalm is thus well suited to the Sabbath which is a semblance of that future spiritual perfection *(Rashi).*

— Praise of God is necessary, but difficult in the weekdays when people must struggle for a livelihood. On the Sabbath when Jews are free from the strictures of the week, they can turn their minds and hearts to the perception of God's ways and His praise — which are the topics of this psalm *(Radak).*

בַּבֹּקֶר ... בַּלֵּילוֹת — *In the dawn ... in the nights.* Dawn is an allusion to redemption, while night symbolizes exile. We express our faith that even though there were times when God made us suffer, those, too, were manifestations of His *kindness,* because He did it for our ultimate benefit. Thus we *relate* His *kindness,* whether it was as clear and pleasant as the bright *dawn* or whether it was as hard to accept as the dark *night.* During the harsh night of exile, we call it אֱמוּנָתְךָ, *Your faith,* because we have faith that God is good, even if we do not understand some of the things He does.

עֲלֵי עָשׂוֹר — *Upon ten-stringed instrument.* The Sages teach that the lyre of Messianic times will be ten-stringed, representing a beautiful enhancement of music, which is now limited to the octave of eight notes. Every period in life calls for its own unique expression of praise, just

With the recitation of Psalm 92, we accept upon ourselves the holiness of the Sabbath. When a Festival or Chol HaMoed falls on either Friday or the Sabbath, most congregations omit the earlier parts of *Kabbalas Shabbos* and begin at this point.

Psalm 92

מִזְמוֹר שִׁיר *A psalm, a song for the Sabbath day.* It is good to thank HASHEM and to sing praise to Your Name, O Exalted One; to relate Your kindness in the dawn and Your faith in the nights.* Upon ten-stringed instrument* and lyre, with singing accompanied by a harp. For You have gladdened me, HASHEM, with Your deeds; at the works of Your Hands I sing glad song. How great are Your deeds, HASHEM; exceedingly profound are Your thoughts.* A boor cannot know, nor can a fool understand this: when the wicked bloom* like grass and all the doers of iniquity blossom — it is to destroy them till eternity.* But You remain exalted forever, HASHEM. For behold! — Your enemies, HASHEM, for behold! — Your enemies shall perish, dispersed shall be all doers of iniquity. As exalted as a re'eim's shall be my pride,* I will be saturated with ever-fresh oil.* My eyes have seen my vigilant foes; when those who would harm me rise up against me, my ears have heard their doom.* Chazzan— *A righteous man will flourish like a date palm, like a cedar* in the Lebanon he will grow tall. Planted in the house of HASHEM,* in the courtyards of our God they will flourish. They will still be fruitful in old age, vigorous and fresh they will be — to declare that HASHEM is just, my Rock in Whom there is no wrong.*

Psalm 93

יהוה מָלָךְ *HASHEM will have reigned, He will have donned grandeur;* HASHEM will have donned might and girded himself; even firmed the world that it should not falter. Your throne was established from of old; eternal are You.*

---

as each day has its own song of praise and each part of creation serves God in its own way. The enhanced spirituality of Messianic times will demand a heightened form of song *(Sfas Emes;* see *Overview,* ArtScroll *Tehillim).*

מַעֲשֶׂיךָ ... מַחְשְׁבֹתֶיךָ — *Your deeds ... Your thoughts.* God's *deeds* are the tangible parts of Creation and the events we perceive with our senses. His *thoughts* are His purposes and goals; they are profound beyond human comprehension *(Sfas Emes).*

בִּפְרֹחַ רְשָׁעִים — *When the wicked bloom.* Most people can find no answer to the eternal human dilemma: Why do the wicked prosper? If only these inquisitors could look beyond what their senses tell them, they would realize that ...

לְהִשָּׁמְדָם עֲדֵי עַד — *To destroy them till eternity.* God gives temporal success and happiness to the wicked as reward for whatever good deeds they may have done. Having been recompensed, they will sink to destruction, while the righteous gain eternal reward *(Rashi).*

וַתָּרֶם כִּרְאֵים קַרְנִי — *As exalted as a re'eim's shall be my pride* [lit. *my horn*]. The once-downtrodden pride of the righteous will rise and be as exalted as the upraised horns of the haughty *re'eim* [a beast of uncertain identity, see commentary, p. 110] *(Radak).*

בְּשֶׁמֶן רַעֲנָן — *With ever-fresh oil.* Oil is a common Scriptural simile for blessing, prosperity, and supremacy *(Rashi).*

כַּתָּמָר ... כְּאֶרֶז — *Like a date palm, like a cedar.* The *tzaddik* will be as fruitful as a date palm, and as sturdy in health as a cedar *(Rashi).*

שְׁתוּלִים בְּבֵית ה׳ — *Planted in the house of HASHEM.* The quality of a tree — described in the previous verse — is only half the formula for success; for maximum benefit it must be planted in luxuriant soil. The righteous will be firmly rooted in the spiritual riches of God's House. There they will blossom without limit *(Radak).*

⁂ ה׳ מָלָךְ / Psalm 93

This psalm is a direct continuation of the previous theme that God's greatness will be

נָשְׂאוּ נְהָרוֹת, יהוה, נָשְׂאוּ נְהָרוֹת קוֹלָם,* יִשְׂאוּ נְהָרוֹת דָּכְיָם. ❖ מִקֹּלוֹת מַיִם רַבִּים, אַדִּירִים מִשְׁבְּרֵי יָם, אַדִּיר בַּמָּרוֹם יהוה. עֵדֹתֶיךָ* נֶאֶמְנוּ מְאֹד לְבֵיתְךָ נַאֲוָה קֹדֶשׁ, יהוה, לְאֹרֶךְ יָמִים.*

קדיש יתום

In the presence of a *minyan,* mourners recite קַדִּישׁ יָתוֹם, the Mourner's *Kaddish* (see *Laws* §119):

יִתְגַּדַּל וְיִתְקַדַּשׁ שְׁמֵהּ רַבָּא. (.Cong —אָמֵן.) בְּעָלְמָא דִּי בְרָא כִרְעוּתֵהּ. וְיַמְלִיךְ מַלְכוּתֵהּ, בְּחַיֵּיכוֹן וּבְיוֹמֵיכוֹן וּבְחַיֵּי דְכָל בֵּית יִשְׂרָאֵל, בַּעֲגָלָא וּבִזְמַן קָרִיב. וְאִמְרוּ: אָמֵן.

(.Cong— אָמֵן. יְהֵא שְׁמֵהּ רַבָּא מְבָרַךְ לְעָלַם וּלְעָלְמֵי עָלְמַיָּא.)

יְהֵא שְׁמֵהּ רַבָּא מְבָרַךְ לְעָלַם וּלְעָלְמֵי עָלְמַיָּא.

יִתְבָּרַךְ וְיִשְׁתַּבַּח וְיִתְפָּאַר וְיִתְרוֹמַם וְיִתְנַשֵּׂא וְיִתְהַדָּר וְיִתְעַלֶּה וְיִתְהַלָּל שְׁמֵהּ דְּקֻדְשָׁא בְּרִיךְ הוּא (.Cong— בְּרִיךְ הוּא) — °לְעֵלָּא מִן כָּל (From Rosh Hashanah to Yom Kippur substitute— °לְעֵלָּא וּלְעֵלָּא מִכָּל) בִּרְכָתָא וְשִׁירָתָא תֻּשְׁבְּחָתָא וְנֶחֱמָתָא, דַּאֲמִירָן בְּעָלְמָא. וְאִמְרוּ: אָמֵן. (.Cong— אָמֵן.)

יְהֵא שְׁלָמָא רַבָּא מִן שְׁמַיָּא, וְחַיִּים עָלֵינוּ וְעַל כָּל יִשְׂרָאֵל. וְאִמְרוּ: אָמֵן. (.Cong— אָמֵן.)

Take three steps back. Bow left and say ... עֹשֶׂה; bow right and say ... הוּא; bow forward and say וְעַל כָּל ... אָמֵן. Remain standing in place for a few moments, then take three steps forward.

עֹשֶׂה שָׁלוֹם בִּמְרוֹמָיו, הוּא יַעֲשֶׂה שָׁלוֹם עָלֵינוּ, וְעַל כָּל יִשְׂרָאֵל. וְאִמְרוּ: אָמֵן. (.Cong— אָמֵן.)

❖{ במה מדליקין }❖

In most congregations בַּמֶּה מַדְלִיקִין, the second chapter of the Mishnah tractate *Shabbos,* is recited at this point. In others it is recited after *Maariv.* When a Festival or Chol HaMoed falls on either Friday or the Sabbath בַּמֶּה מַדְלִיקִין is usually omitted, and the service continues with בָּרְכוּ (p. 330).

משנה שבת פרק ב

[א] **בַּמֶּה מַדְלִיקִין** וּבַמָּה אֵין מַדְלִיקִין? אֵין מַדְלִיקִין לֹא בְלֶכֶשׁ, וְלֹא בְחֹסֶן, וְלֹא בְכַלָּךְ, וְלֹא בִפְתִילַת הָאִידָן, וְלֹא בִפְתִילַת הַמִּדְבָּר, וְלֹא בִירוֹקָה שֶׁעַל פְּנֵי הַמָּיִם. לֹא

---

recognized by all in the Messianic era. Because it describes God in His full grandeur and power as He was when He completed the six days of Creation, and because it describes Him as 'donning' grandeur and 'girding' Himself like one dressing in Sabbath finery, the psalm was designated as the Levite's song of Friday [see p. 168], when the footsteps of the Sabbath begin to be heard *(R' Yaakov Emden).*

גֵּאוּת לָבֵשׁ — *He will have donned grandeur.* The concept of *grandeur* represents God's revelation as the dominant force before whom yield the mightiest natural forces. In man, grandeur — or arrogance — is a contemptible trait, because man's power is limited at best. But to God, *grandeur* is becoming because all forces owe their existence to Him while He is dependent on nothing *(Midrash Shocher Tov).*

God 'dons' grandeur — It is similar to a person donning a garment; our comprehension of him is guided by the contours and quality of the

Like rivers they raised, O H*ASHEM, like rivers they raised their voice;* like rivers they shall raise their destructiveness.* Chazzan– *More than the roars of many waters, mightier than the waves of the sea – You are mighty on high,* H*ASHEM. Your testimonies* about Your House, the Sacred Dwelling are exceedingly trustworthy – O* H*ASHEM, may it be for lengthy days.**

MOURNER'S KADDISH

In the presence of a *minyan,* mourners recite קַדִּישׁ יָתוֹם, the Mourner's *Kaddish* (see *Laws* §119): [A transliteration of this *Kaddish* appears on page 1043, and commentary on p. 57.]

יִתְגַּדַּל *May His great Name grow exalted and sanctified* (Cong.– *Amen.*) *in the world that He created as He willed. May He give reign to His kingship in your lifetimes and in your days, and in the lifetimes of the entire Family of Israel, swiftly and soon. Now respond: Amen.*

(Cong.–*Amen. May His great Name be blessed forever and ever.*)

May His great Name be blessed forever and ever.

Blessed, praised, glorified, exalted, extolled, mighty, upraised, and lauded be the Name of the Holy One, Blessed is He (Cong.– *Blessed is He*) – (From Rosh Hashanah to Yom Kippur add: *exceedingly*) *beyond any blessing and song, praise and consolation that are uttered in the world. Now respond: Amen.* (Cong.–*Amen.*)

May there be abundant peace from Heaven, and life, upon us and upon all Israel. Now respond: Amen. (Cong.–*Amen.*)

Take three steps back. Bow left and say, *'He Who makes peace ...';* bow right and say, *'may He ...';* bow forward and say, *'and upon all Israel ...'* Remain standing in place for a few moments, then take three steps forward.

He Who makes peace in His heights, may He make peace upon us, and upon all Israel. Now respond: Amen. (Cong.–*Amen.*)

BAMEH MADLIKIN

In most congregations the second chapter of the Mishnah tractate *Shabbos* is recited at this point. In others it is recited after *Maariv.* When a Festival or Chol HaMoed falls on either Friday or the Sabbath, this chapter is usually omitted, and the service continues with *'Borchu ...'* (p. 330).

Mishnah, *Shabbos* chapter 2

[1] **בַּמֶּה מַדְלִיקִין** *With what may we light* [*the Sabbath lamp*] *and with what may we not light? We may not light with cedar bast, uncombed flax, floss-silk, willow bast, desert silk, nor seaweed. Nor* [*may we*

---

garment, but the garment is hardly his essence. No matter how much of God's greatness we think we understand, our puny intellect grasps but the minutest fraction of His infinite greatness. He does us the favor of allowing mankind this degree of perception so that we can aspire to the privilege of praising Him.

נָשְׂאוּ נְהָרוֹת קוֹלָם – *Like rivers they raised their voice.* The enemies of Israel will roar against Israel like raging rivers at flood stage *(Radak).*

The repetition of the phrase represents the destruction of the two Temples *(Etz Yosef).*

עֵדֹתֶיךָ – *Your testimonies.* The assurances of Your prophets regarding the eventual rebuilding of the Temple *(Rashi).*

ה׳ לְאֹרֶךְ יָמִים – *O* H*ASHEM, may it be for lengthy days.* The psalm closes with a plea that when the *trustworthy* prophecies about the Third Temple are finally fulfilled, may it stand for *lengthy days,* a Scriptural idiom meaning forever *(Radak).*

בַּמֶּה מַדְלִיקִין / BAMEH MADLIKIN

From the times of the Geonim, it has been customary to recite the second chapter of Mishnah *Shabbos* during *Kabbalas Shabbos.* The chapter primarily discusses the laws of providing light in the home during the Sabbath and also mentions tangentially the *eruv* requirement, which makes it permissible to carry from one domain to another, and the giving of

בְזֶפֶת, וְלֹא בְשַׁעֲוָה, וְלֹא בְשֶׁמֶן קִיק, וְלֹא בְשֶׁמֶן שְׂרֵפָה, וְלֹא בְאַלְיָה, וְלֹא בְחֵלֶב. נַחוּם הַמָּדִי אוֹמֵר: מַדְלִיקִין בְּחֵלֶב מְבֻשָּׁל. וַחֲכָמִים אוֹמְרִים: אֶחָד מְבֻשָּׁל וְאֶחָד שֶׁאֵינוֹ מְבֻשָּׁל אֵין מַדְלִיקִין בּוֹ.

[ב] אֵין מַדְלִיקִין בְּשֶׁמֶן שְׂרֵפָה בְּיוֹם טוֹב. רַבִּי יִשְׁמָעֵאל אוֹמֵר: אֵין מַדְלִיקִין בְּעִטְרָן מִפְּנֵי כְּבוֹד הַשַּׁבָּת. וַחֲכָמִים מַתִּירִין בְּכָל הַשְּׁמָנִים: בְּשֶׁמֶן שֻׁמְשְׁמִין, בְּשֶׁמֶן אֱגוֹזִים, בְּשֶׁמֶן צְנוֹנוֹת, בְּשֶׁמֶן דָּגִים, בְּשֶׁמֶן פַּקּוּעוֹת, בְּעִטְרָן, וּבְנֵפְטְ. רַבִּי טַרְפוֹן אוֹמֵר: אֵין מַדְלִיקִין אֶלָּא בְשֶׁמֶן זַיִת בִּלְבָד.

[ג] כָּל הַיּוֹצֵא מִן הָעֵץ אֵין מַדְלִיקִין בּוֹ אֶלָּא פִשְׁתָּן. וְכָל הַיּוֹצֵא מִן הָעֵץ אֵינוֹ מִטַּמֵּא טֻמְאַת אֹהָלִים אֶלָּא פִשְׁתָּן. פְּתִילַת הַבֶּגֶד שֶׁקִּפְּלָהּ וְלֹא הִבְהֲבָהּ — רַבִּי אֱלִיעֶזֶר אוֹמֵר: טְמֵאָה הִיא וְאֵין מַדְלִיקִין בָּהּ. רַבִּי עֲקִיבָא אוֹמֵר: טְהוֹרָה הִיא וּמַדְלִיקִין בָּהּ.

[ד] לֹא יִקּוֹב אָדָם שְׁפוֹפֶרֶת שֶׁל בֵּיצָה וִימַלְּאֶנָּה שֶׁמֶן וְיִתְּנֶנָּה עַל פִּי הַנֵּר בִּשְׁבִיל שֶׁתְּהֵא מְנַטֶּפֶת, וַאֲפִילוּ הִיא שֶׁל חֶרֶס. וְרַבִּי יְהוּדָה מַתִּיר. אֲבָל אִם חִבְּרָהּ הַיּוֹצֵר מִתְּחִלָּה — מֻתָּר, מִפְּנֵי שֶׁהוּא כְּלִי אֶחָד. לֹא

tithes, which provides the Levites with food and makes the remaining food permissible to its owner. These three *mitzvos* — light, *eruv*, and *maaser* — enhance the feeling of peace within the home. Light makes the meal more festive and prevents accidents and raw nerves that result from stumbling in the dark, *eruv* improves relationships with neighbors, and tithes provide for others. In consonance with this theme of peace, the Sages appended teachings in praise of the Sages, who foster peace among people *(Sh'iltos).*

Some recite the chapter after *Maariv,* in view of its subject matter which deals with the laws of the Sabbath *(Siddur R' Amram Gaon). Abudraham,* however, cites with approval a custom to recite it before *Maariv* so that, in case one's lamp, *eruv,* or *maaser* is not in order, he can rush home and make proper arrangements, assuming the Sabbath has not yet begun.

A thorough phrase-by-phrase commentary on this chapter may be found in the ArtScroll Mishnah, *Shabbos,* from which the following commentary has been abridged

1. The mishnah first lists wicks that are unacceptable because they do not burn evenly. As a result, someone may forget it is the Sabbath and tip the lamp so that more fuel will flow up the wick, an act forbidden on the Sabbath because it promotes burning.

לֶכֶשׁ — *Cedar bast,* the fibers between the bark and the wood.

כַּלָּךְ — *Floss-silk,* stray, sub-standard threads from silk.

פְּתִילַת הַמִּדְבָּר — *Desert silk,* fibers from a plant that grows in the desert.

וְלֹא בְזֶפֶת — *Nor* [*may we light*] *with pitch.* Now the mishnah lists the unacceptable fuels. Except for one of them (see below) the reason they are unfit is because they do not burn well, leading to the fear that the user may tip the lamp.

שֶׁמֶן שְׂרֵפָה — *Oil that must be destroyed by burning.* Oil of *terumah* [the priestly tithe] must be burned if it becomes *tamei* [ritually contaminated]. Even if such oil is of the sort that burns well, there is a fear that one may tip the lamp in order to more efficiently fulfill the *mitzvah* of burning the oil.

[Sheeps' fat and tallow may not be used as fuel in lamps, but they may be made into candles.]

נַחוּם הַמָּדִי — *Nachum the Mede* holds that *boiled* tallow will burn evenly enough to be acceptable, but the Rabbis disagree.

2. בְּיוֹם טוֹב — *On Yom Tov.* Although kindling (from an existing flame) is permitted on festivals, it is forbidden to burn contaminated *terumah* on *Yom Tov.*

בְּעִטְרָן — *With tar.* Although it burns well, tar has a foul odor and will cause people to dishonor the Sabbath by refusing to remain at the table.

בְּכָל הַשְּׁמָנִים — *With all* [*these*] *oils.* The Sages maintain that all the following oils, including tar,

light] with pitch, wax, cottonseed oil, oil that must be destroyed by burning, fat from sheeps' tails, nor with tallow. Nachum the Mede says: We may light with boiled tallow. But the Sages say: Whether it is boiled or it is not boiled, we may not light with it.

[2] *We may not light on Yom Tov with oil that must be destroyed by burning. Rabbi Yishmael says: We may not light with tar, out of respect for the honor due the Sabbath. But the Sages permit [lighting] with all [these] oils: with sesame oil, nut oil, radish oil, fish oil, gourd oil, tar, or naphtha. Rabbi Tarfon says: We may light only with olive oil.*

[3] *We may not light with any product of a tree, with the exception of linen. And no tree-product can contract contamination from sheltering [a contaminated object], with the exception of linen. If a wick was made from a cloth that was twisted but not singed — Rabbi Eliezer says: It accepts contamination and we may not light with it. Rabbi Akiva says: It does not accept contamination and we may light with it.*

[4] *One may not pierce an egg-shell, fill it with oil, and put it over the mouth of a lamp so that [the oil] will drip down, even if [the container is] of earthenware: Rabbi Yehudah permits this. But if the potter originally attached it, it is permitted, because it is a single vessel. One may not*

---

may be used. They are not concerned with the smell, as long as the fuel burns well.

3. The mishnah returns to discussing the wicks.

מִן הָעֵץ — *Product of a tree.* The mishnah forbids wicks made from trees because they do not burn well. Linen is the exception. Although the flax plant from which linen comes is not generally considered a tree, Scripture sometimes refers to it as a tree (see, e.g., *Joshua* 2:6), presumably because the flax bolls grow of tall woody stalks.

טֻמְאַת אֹהָלִים — *Contamination from sheltering [a contaminated object].* If a corpse is under the shelter of a roof or canopy, everything else under the shelter becomes contaminated. The shelter itself, however, does not become contaminated if it was a tree product — unless it was made of linen.

פְּתִילַת הַבֶּגֶד — *If a wick was made from a cloth ...* A cloth is not susceptible to *tumah*-contamination unless it can be used as clothing. The minimum size for this is three fingerbreadths square, for such a piece of cloth may serve as a patch. The discussion now centers on the status of a piece of cloth of minimum dimensions that has been twisted into a wick for an oil lamp. The question is whether the twisting renders the cloth smaller than the minimum size and no longer subject to contamination. [Had it been singed over a fire to facilitate its burning, the singeing would have reduced its size to below the three fingerbreadth minimum, but this had not been done.]

Our mishnah speaks of the case of a *Yom Tov* that fell on a Friday. According to Rabbi Eliezer, the twisted cloth retains the status of a garment; to insert it into a lamp on *Yom Tov* and light it would be to change it from a cloth to a wick on *Yom Tov.* Such an act makes the wick a new creation [נוֹלָד] and it may not be handled on *Yom Tov.* Rabbi Akiva disagrees. He holds that merely twisting it into a wick changes its halachic status from a cloth to a wick. If so, (a) it no longer accepts contamination and (b) it may be used for lighting.

4. לֹא יִקּוֹב — *One may not pierce.* The pierced egg-shell, in effect, becomes a spare reservoir of fuel for the lamp, increasing its oil capacity and allowing it to burn longer, but it does not become an integral part of the lamp. The Sages feared that the owner might take some oil from the shell on the Sabbath, thus decreasing the life of the flame (by denying it more oil) and causing it to become extinguished.

חֶרֶס — *Of earthenware.* Instead of using an egg-shell, he made an earthenware reservoir. Generally, earthenware is repulsive and people would not withdraw oil from it for food. Nevertheless the Sages forbade the use of such a reservoir on the Sabbath because there is still a slight chance that someone may take oil from it thus reducing the length of time that the lamp will burn.

אֲבָל אִם חִבְּרָהּ — *But if ... attached it.* If the reservoir and lamp were attached, they are regarded as a single lamp, and we do not fear that someone will remove oil from a lamp.

יְמַלֵּא אָדָם קְעָרָה שֶׁמֶן וְיִתְּנֶנָּה בְּצַד הַנֵּר וְיִתֵּן רֹאשׁ הַפְּתִילָה בְּתוֹכָהּ בִּשְׁבִיל שֶׁתְּהֵא שׁוֹאֶבֶת. וְרַבִּי יְהוּדָה מַתִּיר.

[ה] הַמְּכַבֶּה אֶת הַנֵּר מִפְּנֵי שֶׁהוּא מִתְיָרֵא מִפְּנֵי גוֹיִם, מִפְּנֵי לִסְטִים, מִפְּנֵי רוּחַ רָעָה, אוֹ בִּשְׁבִיל הַחוֹלֶה שֶׁיִּישַׁן, פָּטוּר. כְּחָס עַל הַנֵּר, כְּחָס עַל הַשֶּׁמֶן, כְּחָס עַל הַפְּתִילָה, חַיָּב. רַבִּי יוֹסֵי פּוֹטֵר בְּכֻלָּן, חוּץ מִן הַפְּתִילָה, מִפְּנֵי שֶׁהוּא עוֹשָׂה פֶּחָם.

[ו] עַל שָׁלֹשׁ עֲבֵרוֹת נָשִׁים מֵתוֹת בִּשְׁעַת לֵדָתָן: עַל שֶׁאֵינָן זְהִירוֹת בְּנִדָּה, בְּחַלָּה, וּבְהַדְלָקַת הַנֵּר.

[ז] שְׁלֹשָׁה דְבָרִים צָרִיךְ אָדָם לוֹמַר בְּתוֹךְ בֵּיתוֹ עֶרֶב שַׁבָּת עִם חֲשֵׁכָה: „עִשַּׂרְתֶּם, עֵרַבְתֶּם, הַדְלִיקוּ אֶת הַנֵּר״. סָפֵק חֲשֵׁכָה סָפֵק אֵינָהּ חֲשֵׁכָה — אֵין מְעַשְּׂרִין אֶת הַוַּדַּאי, וְאֵין מַטְבִּילִין אֶת הַכֵּלִים, וְאֵין מַדְלִיקִין אֶת הַנֵּרוֹת; אֲבָל מְעַשְּׂרִין אֶת הַדְּמַאי, וּמְעָרְבִין, וְטוֹמְנִין אֶת הַחַמִּין.

תַּנְיָא* אָמַר רַבִּי חֲנִינָא: חַיָּב אָדָם לְמַשְׁמֵשׁ* בְּגָדָיו בְּעֶרֶב שַׁבָּת עִם חֲשֵׁכָה, שֶׁמָּא יִשְׁכַּח וְיֵצֵא. אָמַר רַב יוֹסֵף: הִלְכְתָא רַבְּתָא לְשַׁבַּתָּא.[1]*

וְיִתֵּן רֹאשׁ הַפְּתִילָה בְּתוֹכָהּ — *And put the end of the wick into* [*the bowl*]. The intent is that the wick will burn longer because it has two sources of oil, the lamp and the bowl. Here, too, the Sages feared that one might withdraw oil from the bowl.

5. הַמְּכַבֶּה ... מִפְּנֵי שֶׁהוּא מִתְיָרֵא — *If one extinguishes ... because he fears.* The mishnah's first four cases involve life and death. Certain idolatrous sects did not permit fires to be kindled on their holidays except in their temples. Anyone caught violating this rule would be killed.

לִסְטִים — *Bandits.* The light may disclose his whereabouts to a band of cutthroats.

רוּחַ רָעָה — *Melancholia,* a mental illness that causes the sufferer to fear the light to a dangerous degree.

חוֹלֶה — *A sick person.* The patient's condition is critical and he must sleep.

פָּטוּר — *He is not liable.* In the context of the Sabbath laws, liability involves one of three penalties: (a) If the act was done willfully, in the presence of two acceptable witnesses, and immediately after the perpetrator had been warned of the transgression and its consequence, the act carries the death penalty; (b) if the act was commited willfully but either there were no acceptable witnesses, or there was no adequate warning, the punishment is כָּרֵת [*kares*], *spiritual excision,* carried out by the Heavenly Court; (c) if the transgression was inadvertant, it must be atoned for with the bringing of a sin-offering in the Holy Temple.

It should also be noted that the word פָּטוּר, *he is not liable,* does not necessarily mean that the act is permitted; merely that it does not entail one of the punishments mentioned above. It may, nevertheless, be prohibited by Rabbinic decree.

רַבִּי יוֹסֵי פּוֹטֵר — *Rabbi Yose absolves.* Because Rabbi Yose holds that to be culpable for desecrating the Sabbath, the prohibited labor must be performed for its primary purpose. For example, if one extinguished the flame so that he would be left with charcoal or a singed wick, he is liable.

The conflict between the Sages and Rabbi Yose concerns the question of מְלָאכָה שֶׁאֵינָהּ צְרִיכָה לְגוּפָהּ, *a labor that is not needed for its primary purpose.* For example, the purpose of digging is to make a hole; what if someone has no need for the hole, but required sand? If so, he has no need for the primary purpose of the forbidden labor in which he is engaged. The Sages hold that he is liable nonetheless, but Rabbi Yose disagrees. The primary purpose of extinguishing, in terms of the Sabbath laws, is to make charcoal. In our mishnah, there is no need for charcoal but the light is extinguished either to help a patient or to conserve the fuel or the wick.

6. עַל שָׁלֹשׁ עֲבֵרוֹת — *For three transgressions.* These three *mitzvos* are assigned to women,

fill a bowl with oil, put it next to a lamp, and put the end of the wick into [the bowl] so that it will draw [oil]. Rabbi Yehudah permits this.

[5] *If one extinguishes a lamp because he fears idolaters, bandits, melancholia, or so that a sick person can fall asleep, he is not liable. But if he does so to spare the lamp, to spare the oil, or to spare the wick, he is liable. Rabbi Yose absolves in all these cases, except that of the wick, because he makes it into charcoal.*

[6] *For three transgressions women die during childbirth: for being careless regarding [the laws of] menstruation, the tithe from dough, and kindling the [Sabbath] light.*

[7] *A person must say three things in his home on the eve of the Sabbath just before dark: 'Have you tithed? Have you prepared the eruv? Kindle the [Sabbath] lights!' If there is a doubt whether it is dark or it is not dark, we may not tithe the definitely untithed produce, we may not immerse vessels, and we may not kindle the lights; but we may tithe questionable produce, make an* eruv, *and insulate hot food.*

תַּנְיָא *It has been taught,* Rabbi Chanania said: A person is required to examine* his clothing on the eve of the Sabbath just before dark, for he may forget himself and go out. Rav Yosef said: This is a significant law regarding the Sabbath.**[1]

(1) Cf. Tractate *Shabbos* 12a.

---

therefore they bear great responsibility for neglecting them.

בִּשְׁעַת לֵדָתָן — *During childbirth.* Punishments are most likely in time of danger.

7. עִשַּׂרְתֶּם — *Have you tithed?* It is forbidden to tithe on the Sabbath and untithed food may not be eaten.

עֵרַבְתֶּם — *Have you prepared the eruv?* There are two types of *eruv,* one that enables people to carry from one domain to another [עֵרוּבֵי חֲצֵרוֹת] and a second that enables one to walk (in one direction) more than he would normally be permitted on the Sabbath [עֵרוּבֵי תְחוּמִין].

סָפֵק — *If there is a doubt.* If one is not sure whether or not the Sabbath has begun, it is forbidden to risk performing labors that are definitely forbidden on the Sabbath, even though the prohibitions are of Rabbinic, not Scriptural, origin. The time when such a doubt exists is during twilight [בֵּין הַשְּׁמָשׁוֹת], the halachic status of which is in question.

הַדְּמַאי — *Questionable produce.* Although the majority of ignorant farmers *do* tithe their produce, the Sages require one who purchases from them to set aside tithes because a minority of farmers are not observant of this *mitzvah.* Since it is only a precautionary measure, the Sages permitted such tithes to be taken on the Sabbath.

וְטוֹמְנִין — *And insulate.* Hot food may be wrapped and bundled to retain its warmth. This is permitted at twilight because food is always hot at that time. During the Sabbath day, however, it is forbidden, because the food may have become cool and the owner may forget himself and reheat it.

תַּנְיָא ☙ — *It has been taught.* This passage (*Shabbos* 12a) does not appear in all *siddurim,* but many authorities, including *Sh'lah* and *Kol Bo,* maintain that it should be recited; presumably because, like mishnah 7, it contains a requirement of the final minutes just before the Sabbath begins.

לְמַשְׁמֵשׁ — *To examine* [lit. *to tap*]. One should examine his pockets and belt, on which he may have hung things, to be sure that he is not carrying items that he may unwittingly take with him when he leaves home.

הִלְכְתָא רַבְּתָא לְשַׁבְּתָא — *This is a significant law regarding the Sabbath.* In the law of examining clothing there is a major deterrent against violating the Sabbath *(Rashi).* [The principle here is important: one should not rely on his memory or good intentions; he should make plans and institute procedures to develop habits of Sabbath observance.]

ברכות סד.

אָמַר רַבִּי אֶלְעָזָר אָמַר רַבִּי חֲנִינָא: תַּלְמִידֵי חֲכָמִים מַרְבִּים שָׁלוֹם בָּעוֹלָם.* שֶׁנֶּאֱמַר: וְכָל בָּנַיִךְ לִמּוּדֵי יהוה, וְרַב שְׁלוֹם בָּנָיִךְ.[1] אַל תִּקְרֵי* בָּנָיִךְ אֶלָּא בּוֹנָיִךְ. ❖ שָׁלוֹם רָב לְאֹהֲבֵי תוֹרָתֶךָ,* וְאֵין לָמוֹ מִכְשׁוֹל.[2] יְהִי שָׁלוֹם בְּחֵילֵךְ,* שַׁלְוָה בְּאַרְמְנוֹתָיִךְ. לְמַעַן אַחַי וְרֵעָי, אֲדַבְּרָה נָּא שָׁלוֹם בָּךְ. לְמַעַן בֵּית יהוה אֱלֹהֵינוּ, אֲבַקְשָׁה טוֹב לָךְ.[3] יהוה עֹז לְעַמּוֹ יִתֵּן, יהוה יְבָרֵךְ אֶת עַמּוֹ בַשָּׁלוֹם.[4]

קדיש דרבנן

In the presence of a *minyan,* mourners recite קַדִּישׁ דְּרַבָּנָן.

יִתְגַּדַּל וְיִתְקַדַּשׁ שְׁמֵהּ רַבָּא. (.Cong —אָמֵן.) בְּעָלְמָא דִּי בְרָא כִרְעוּתֵהּ. וְיַמְלִיךְ מַלְכוּתֵהּ, בְּחַיֵּיכוֹן וּבְיוֹמֵיכוֹן וּבְחַיֵּי דְכָל בֵּית יִשְׂרָאֵל, בַּעֲגָלָא וּבִזְמַן קָרִיב. וְאִמְרוּ: אָמֵן.

(.Cong— אָמֵן. יְהֵא שְׁמֵהּ רַבָּא מְבָרַךְ לְעָלַם וּלְעָלְמֵי עָלְמַיָּא.)

יְהֵא שְׁמֵהּ רַבָּא מְבָרַךְ לְעָלַם וּלְעָלְמֵי עָלְמַיָּא.

יִתְבָּרַךְ וְיִשְׁתַּבַּח וְיִתְפָּאַר וְיִתְרוֹמַם וְיִתְנַשֵּׂא וְיִתְהַדָּר וְיִתְעַלֶּה וְיִתְהַלָּל שְׁמֵהּ דְּקֻדְשָׁא בְּרִיךְ הוּא (.Cong— בְּרִיךְ הוּא) — °לְעֵלָּא מִן כָּל (°לְעֵלָּא וּלְעֵלָּא מִכָּל —From Rosh Hashanah to Yom Kippur substitute) בִּרְכָתָא וְשִׁירָתָא תֻּשְׁבְּחָתָא וְנֶחֱמָתָא, דַּאֲמִירָן בְּעָלְמָא. וְאִמְרוּ: אָמֵן. (.Cong— אָמֵן.)

עַל יִשְׂרָאֵל וְעַל רַבָּנָן, וְעַל תַּלְמִידֵיהוֹן וְעַל כָּל תַּלְמִידֵי תַלְמִידֵיהוֹן, וְעַל כָּל מָאן דְּעָסְקִין בְּאוֹרַיְתָא, דִּי בְאַתְרָא הָדֵין וְדִי בְכָל אֲתַר וַאֲתַר. יְהֵא לְהוֹן וּלְכוֹן שְׁלָמָא רַבָּא, חִנָּא וְחִסְדָּא וְרַחֲמִין, וְחַיִּין אֲרִיכִין, וּמְזוֹנֵי רְוִיחֵי, וּפֻרְקָנָא, מִן קֳדָם אֲבוּהוֹן דִּי בִשְׁמַיָּא (וְאַרְעָא). וְאִמְרוּ: אָמֵן. (.Cong— אָמֵן.)

יְהֵא שְׁלָמָא רַבָּא מִן שְׁמַיָּא, וְחַיִּים (טוֹבִים) עָלֵינוּ וְעַל כָּל יִשְׂרָאֵל. וְאִמְרוּ: אָמֵן. (.Cong— אָמֵן.)

Take three steps back. Bow left and say ... עֹשֶׂה; bow right and say ... הוּא; bow forward and say וְעַל כָּל ... אָמֵן. Remain standing in place for a few moments, then take three steps forward.

עֹשֶׂה שָׁלוֹם בִּמְרוֹמָיו, הוּא בְּרַחֲמָיו יַעֲשֶׂה שָׁלוֹם עָלֵינוּ, וְעַל כָּל יִשְׂרָאֵל. וְאִמְרוּ: אָמֵן. (.Cong— אָמֵן.)

⋞ אָמַר רַבִּי אֶלְעָזָר / Rabbi Elazar said

תַּלְמִידֵי חֲכָמִים מַרְבִּים שָׁלוֹם בָּעוֹלָם — *Torah scholars increase peace in the world.* As noted above in the introduction to the *Rabbis' Kaddish* (p. 52), it is customary to recite a passage of Aggadah prior to the recitation of this *Kaddish.* Why did the Sages choose this particular passage? Since mishnah 7 discusses Rabbinic enactments that increase peace in the home, the Sages appended passages that discuss the Rabbis' role in increasing peace *(Abudraham).*

Etz Yosef explains that Torah scholars increase peace in two ways: They engage in the activity for which the universe was created; and God promises peace as a reward for the diligent

Talmud, *Berachos* 64a

אָמַר *Rabbi Elazar said on behalf of Rabbi Chanina: Torah scholars increase peace in the world,* as it is said: And all your children will be students of* HASHEM *and your children will have abundant peace*[1] *— do not read** [בָּנָיִךְ] *'your children,' but* [בּוֹנָיִךְ] *'your builders.'* Chazzan— *There is abundant peace for the lovers of Your Torah,* and there is no stumbling block for them.*[2] *May there be peace within your wall,* serenity within your palaces. For the sake of my brethren and my comrades, I shall speak of peace in your midst. For the sake of the House of* HASHEM, *our God, I will request good for you.*[3] HASHEM *will give might to His nation,* HASHEM *will bless His nation with peace.*[4]

THE RABBIS' KADDISH

In the presence of a *minyan,* mourners recite the Rabbis' *Kaddish* (see *Laws* §120-121):

[A transliteration of this *Kaddish* appears on page 1042.]

יִתְגַּדַּל *May His great Name grow exalted and sanctified* (Cong.— *Amen.*) *in the world that He created as He willed. May He give reign to His kingship in your lifetimes and in your days, and in the lifetimes of the entire Family of Israel, swiftly and soon. Now respond: Amen.*

(Cong.— *Amen. May His great Name be blessed forever and ever.*)

May His great Name be blessed forever and ever.

Blessed, praised, glorified, exalted, extolled, mighty, upraised, and lauded be the Name of the Holy One, Blessed is He (Cong.— *Blessed is He*) — (From Rosh Hashanah to Yom Kippur add: *exceedingly*) *beyond any blessing and song, praise and consolation that are uttered in the world. Now respond: Amen.* (Cong.— *Amen.*)

Upon Israel, upon the teachers, their disciples and all of their disciples and upon all those who engage in the study of Torah, who are here or anywhere else; may they and you have abundant peace, grace, kindness, and mercy, long life, ample nourishment, and salvation, from before their Father Who is in Heaven (and on earth). Now respond: Amen. (Cong. — *Amen.*)

May there be abundant peace from Heaven, and (good) life, upon us and upon all Israel. Now respond: Amen. (Cong.— *Amen.*)

Take three steps back. Bow left and say, *'He Who makes peace ...';* bow right and say, *'may He ...';* bow forward and say, *'and upon all Israel ...'* Remain standing in place for a few moments, then take three steps forward.

He Who makes peace in His heights, may He, in His compassion, make peace upon us, and upon all Israel. Now respond: Amen. (Cong.— *Amen.*)

(1) *Isaiah* 54:13. (2) *Psalms* 119:165. (3) 122:7-9. (4) 29:11.

---

study of Torah (*Leviticus* 26:5, see *Rashi* to 26:3).

אַל תִּקְרֵי — *Do not read.* As in all cases where the Sages use this expression, they do *not* seek to change the Masoretic text, but to suggest an additional implication. Since the word בָּנָיִךְ, *your children,* already appears in the verse, the repetition of the same word can only be meant to introduce a new concept — that children are also builders — in this case that the students of Torah are the builders of רַב שָׁלוֹם, *abundant peace* (*Etz Yosef*).

לְאֹהֲבֵי תוֹרָתֶךָ — *For the lovers of Your Torah.* Not only those who study Torah, but those who *love* Torah share in the blessing of peace, even if they are not scholars. Thus it is that the Sages speak frequently of the reward awaiting those who support and respect Torah scholars (*Etz Yosef*).

יְהִי שָׁלוֹם בְּחֵילֵךְ — *May there be peace within your wall.* The liturgy of peace now speaks to the city of Jerusalem, wishing that its protective ramparts, its palaces, its people, and its Temple always have the blessing of peace.

מעריב לשבת ויום טוב

A commentary to *Maariv* begins on page 256. In some congregations the *chazzan* chants a melody during his recitation of בָּרְכוּ so that the congregation can then recite יִתְבָּרַךְ.

Chazzan bows at בָּרְכוּ and straightens up at ה׳.

בָּרְכוּ אֶת יהוה הַמְּבֹרָךְ.

Congregation, followed by *chazzan*, responds, bowing at בָּרוּךְ and straightening up at ה׳.

בָּרוּךְ יהוה הַמְּבֹרָךְ לְעוֹלָם וָעֶד.

יִתְבָּרַךְ וְיִשְׁתַּבַּח וְיִתְפָּאַר וְיִתְרוֹמַם וְיִתְנַשֵּׂא שְׁמוֹ שֶׁל מֶלֶךְ מַלְכֵי הַמְּלָכִים, הַקָּדוֹשׁ בָּרוּךְ הוּא. שֶׁהוּא רִאשׁוֹן וְהוּא אַחֲרוֹן, וּמִבַּלְעָדָיו אֵין אֱלֹהִים.[1] סֹלּוּ, לָרֹכֵב בָּעֲרָבוֹת, בְּיָהּ שְׁמוֹ, וְעִלְזוּ לְפָנָיו.[2] וּשְׁמוֹ מְרוֹמָם עַל כָּל בְּרָכָה וּתְהִלָּה.[3] בָּרוּךְ שֵׁם כְּבוֹד מַלְכוּתוֹ לְעוֹלָם וָעֶד. יְהִי שֵׁם יהוה מְבֹרָךְ, מֵעַתָּה וְעַד עוֹלָם.[4]

ברכות קריאת שמע

בָּרוּךְ אַתָּה יהוה אֱלֹהֵינוּ מֶלֶךְ הָעוֹלָם, אֲשֶׁר בִּדְבָרוֹ מַעֲרִיב עֲרָבִים, בְּחָכְמָה פּוֹתֵחַ שְׁעָרִים, וּבִתְבוּנָה מְשַׁנֶּה עִתִּים, וּמַחֲלִיף אֶת הַזְּמַנִּים, וּמְסַדֵּר אֶת הַכּוֹכָבִים בְּמִשְׁמְרוֹתֵיהֶם בָּרָקִיעַ כִּרְצוֹנוֹ. בּוֹרֵא יוֹם וָלָיְלָה, גּוֹלֵל אוֹר מִפְּנֵי חֹשֶׁךְ וְחֹשֶׁךְ מִפְּנֵי אוֹר. וּמַעֲבִיר יוֹם וּמֵבִיא לָיְלָה, וּמַבְדִּיל בֵּין יוֹם וּבֵין לָיְלָה, יהוה צְבָאוֹת שְׁמוֹ. ❖ אֵל חַי וְקַיָּם, תָּמִיד יִמְלוֹךְ עָלֵינוּ, לְעוֹלָם וָעֶד. בָּרוּךְ אַתָּה יהוה, הַמַּעֲרִיב עֲרָבִים.

(Cong.— אָמֵן.)

אַהֲבַת עוֹלָם בֵּית יִשְׂרָאֵל עַמְּךָ אָהָבְתָּ. תּוֹרָה וּמִצְוֹת, חֻקִּים וּמִשְׁפָּטִים, אוֹתָנוּ לִמַּדְתָּ. עַל כֵּן יהוה אֱלֹהֵינוּ, בְּשָׁכְבֵנוּ וּבְקוּמֵנוּ נָשִׂיחַ בְּחֻקֶּיךָ, וְנִשְׂמַח בְּדִבְרֵי תוֹרָתֶךָ, וּבְמִצְוֹתֶיךָ לְעוֹלָם וָעֶד. ❖ כִּי הֵם חַיֵּינוּ, וְאֹרֶךְ יָמֵינוּ, וּבָהֶם נֶהְגֶּה יוֹמָם וָלָיְלָה. וְאַהֲבָתְךָ, אַל תָּסִיר מִמֶּנּוּ לְעוֹלָמִים. בָּרוּךְ אַתָּה יהוה, אוֹהֵב עַמּוֹ יִשְׂרָאֵל.

(Cong.— אָמֵן.)

שמע

Immediately before reciting the *Shema* concentrate on fulfilling the positive commandment of reciting the *Shema* twice daily. It is important to enunciate each word clearly and not to run words together. For this reason, vertical lines have been placed between two words that are prone to be slurred into one and are not separated by a comma or a hyphen. See *Laws* §46-60.
A commentary to *Shema* begins on page 90.

When praying without a *minyan*, begin with the following three-word formula:

אֵל מֶלֶךְ נֶאֱמָן.

Recite the first verse aloud, with the right hand covering the eyes, and concentrate intensely upon accepting God's absolute sovereignty.

שְׁמַע | יִשְׂרָאֵל, יהוה | אֱלֹהֵינוּ, יהוה | אֶחָד:

In an undertone— בָּרוּךְ שֵׁם כְּבוֹד מַלְכוּתוֹ לְעוֹלָם וָעֶד.

MAARIV FOR SABBATH AND FESTIVALS

A commentary to *Maariv* begins on p. 256. In some congregations the *chazzan* chants a melody during his recitation of *Borchu*, so that the congregation can then recite *'Blessed, praised ...'*

Chazzan bows at *'Bless,'* and straightens up at *'HASHEM.'*

Bless HASHEM, the blessed One.

Congregation, followed by *chazzan*, responds, bowing at *'Blessed'* and straightening up at *'HASHEM.'*

Blessed is HASHEM, the blessed One, for all eternity.

Blessed, praised, glorified, exalted and upraised is the Name of the King Who rules over kings — the Holy One, Blessed is He. For He is the First and He is the Last and aside from Him there is no god.[1] *Extol Him — Who rides the highest heavens — with His Name, YAH, and exult before Him.*[2] *His Name is exalted beyond every blessing and praise.*[3] *Blessed is the Name of His glorious kingdom for all eternity. Blessed be the Name of HASHEM from this time and forever.*[4]

BLESSINGS OF THE SHEMA

בָּרוּךְ *Blessed are You, HASHEM, our God, King of the universe, Who by His word brings on evenings, with wisdom opens gates, with understanding alters periods, changes the seasons, and orders the stars in their heavenly constellations as He wills. He creates day and night, removing light before darkness and darkness before light. He causes day to pass and brings night, and separates between day and night — HASHEM, Master of Legions, is His Name.* Chazzan— *May the living and enduring God continuously reign over us, for all eternity. Blessed are You, HASHEM, Who brings on evenings.* (Cong.— *Amen.*)

אַהֲבַת *With an eternal love have You loved the House of Israel, Your nation. Torah and commandments, decrees and ordinances have You taught us. Therefore HASHEM, our God, upon our retiring and arising, we will discuss Your decrees and we will rejoice with the words of Your Torah and with Your commandments for all eternity.* Chazzan— *For they are our life and the length of our days and about them we will meditate day and night. May You not remove Your love from us forever. Blessed are You, HASHEM, Who loves His nation Israel.* (Cong.— *Amen.*)

THE SHEMA

Immediately before reciting the *Shema* concentrate on fulfilling the positive commandment of reciting the *Shema* twice daily. It is important to enunciate each word clearly and not to run words together. See *Laws* §46-60. A commentary to *Shema* begins on page 90.

When praying without a *minyan*, begin with the following three-word formula:

God, trustworthy King.

Recite the first verse aloud, with the right hand covering the eyes, and concentrate intensely upon accepting God's absolute sovereignty.

Hear, O Israel: HASHEM is our God, HASHEM, the One and Only.

In an undertone— *Blessed is the Name of His glorious kingdom for all eternity.*

(1) Cf. *Isaiah* 44:6. (2) *Psalms* 68:5. (3) Cf. *Nechemiah* 9:5. (4) *Psalms* 113:2.

While reciting the first paragraph (דברים ו:ה־ט), concentrate on accepting the commandment to love God.

וְאָהַבְתָּ אֵת יהוה | אֱלֹהֶיךָ, בְּכָל־לְבָבְךָ, וּבְכָל־נַפְשְׁךָ, וּבְכָל־מְאֹדֶךָ: וְהָיוּ הַדְּבָרִים הָאֵלֶּה, אֲשֶׁר | אָנֹכִי מְצַוְּךָ הַיּוֹם, עַל־לְבָבֶךָ: וְשִׁנַּנְתָּם לְבָנֶיךָ, וְדִבַּרְתָּ בָּם, בְּשִׁבְתְּךָ בְּבֵיתֶךָ, וּבְלֶכְתְּךָ בַדֶּרֶךְ, וּבְשָׁכְבְּךָ וּבְקוּמֶךָ: וּקְשַׁרְתָּם לְאוֹת | עַל־יָדֶךָ, וְהָיוּ לְטֹטָפֹת בֵּין | עֵינֶיךָ: וּכְתַבְתָּם | עַל־מְזֻזוֹת בֵּיתֶךָ, וּבִשְׁעָרֶיךָ:

While reciting the second paragraph (דברים יא:יג־כא), concentrate on accepting all the commandments and the concept of reward and punishment.

וְהָיָה, אִם־שָׁמֹעַ תִּשְׁמְעוּ אֶל־מִצְוֹתַי, אֲשֶׁר | אָנֹכִי מְצַוֶּה | אֶתְכֶם הַיּוֹם, לְאַהֲבָה אֶת־יהוה | אֱלֹהֵיכֶם וּלְעָבְדוֹ, בְּכָל־לְבַבְכֶם, וּבְכָל־נַפְשְׁכֶם: וְנָתַתִּי מְטַר־אַרְצְכֶם בְּעִתּוֹ, יוֹרֶה וּמַלְקוֹשׁ, וְאָסַפְתָּ דְגָנֶךָ וְתִירֹשְׁךָ וְיִצְהָרֶךָ: וְנָתַתִּי | עֵשֶׂב | בְּשָׂדְךָ לִבְהֶמְתֶּךָ, וְאָכַלְתָּ וְשָׂבָעְתָּ: הִשָּׁמְרוּ לָכֶם, פֶּן־יִפְתֶּה לְבַבְכֶם, וְסַרְתֶּם וַעֲבַדְתֶּם | אֱלֹהִים | אֲחֵרִים, וְהִשְׁתַּחֲוִיתֶם לָהֶם: וְחָרָה | אַף־יהוה בָּכֶם, וְעָצַר אֶת־הַשָּׁמַיִם, וְלֹא־יִהְיֶה מָטָר, וְהָאֲדָמָה לֹא תִתֵּן אֶת־יְבוּלָהּ, וַאֲבַדְתֶּם | מְהֵרָה מֵעַל הָאָרֶץ הַטֹּבָה | אֲשֶׁר | יהוה נֹתֵן לָכֶם: וְשַׂמְתֶּם | אֶת־דְּבָרַי | אֵלֶּה, עַל־לְבַבְכֶם וְעַל־נַפְשְׁכֶם, וּקְשַׁרְתֶּם | אֹתָם לְאוֹת | עַל־יֶדְכֶם, וְהָיוּ לְטוֹטָפֹת בֵּין | עֵינֵיכֶם: וְלִמַּדְתֶּם | אֹתָם | אֶת־בְּנֵיכֶם, לְדַבֵּר בָּם, בְּשִׁבְתְּךָ בְּבֵיתֶךָ, וּבְלֶכְתְּךָ בַדֶּרֶךְ, וּבְשָׁכְבְּךָ וּבְקוּמֶךָ: וּכְתַבְתָּם | עַל־מְזוּזוֹת בֵּיתֶךָ, וּבִשְׁעָרֶיךָ: לְמַעַן | יִרְבּוּ | יְמֵיכֶם וִימֵי בְנֵיכֶם, עַל הָאֲדָמָה | אֲשֶׁר נִשְׁבַּע | יהוה לַאֲבֹתֵיכֶם לָתֵת לָהֶם, כִּימֵי הַשָּׁמַיִם | עַל־הָאָרֶץ:

במדבר טו:לז־מא

וַיֹּאמֶר | יהוה | אֶל־מֹשֶׁה לֵּאמֹר: דַּבֵּר | אֶל־בְּנֵי | יִשְׂרָאֵל, וְאָמַרְתָּ אֲלֵהֶם, וְעָשׂוּ לָהֶם צִיצִת, עַל־כַּנְפֵי בִגְדֵיהֶם לְדֹרֹתָם, וְנָתְנוּ | עַל־צִיצִת הַכָּנָף, פְּתִיל תְּכֵלֶת: וְהָיָה לָכֶם לְצִיצִת, וּרְאִיתֶם | אֹתוֹ, וּזְכַרְתֶּם | אֶת־כָּל־מִצְוֹת | יהוה, וַעֲשִׂיתֶם | אֹתָם, וְלֹא תָתֻרוּ | אַחֲרֵי לְבַבְכֶם וְאַחֲרֵי | עֵינֵיכֶם, אֲשֶׁר־אַתֶּם זֹנִים | אַחֲרֵיהֶם: לְמַעַן תִּזְכְּרוּ, וַעֲשִׂיתֶם | אֶת־כָּל־

While reciting the first paragraph (*Deuteronomy* 6:5-9), concentrate on accepting the commandment to love God.

וְאָהַבְתָּ *You shall love HASHEM, your God, with all your heart, with all your soul and with all your resources. Let these matters that I command you today be upon your heart. Teach them thoroughly to your children and speak of them while you sit in your home, while you walk on the way, when you retire and when you arise. Bind them as a sign upon your arm and let them be tefillin between your eyes. And write them on the doorposts of your house and upon your gates.*

While reciting the second paragraph (*Deuteronomy* 11:13-21), concentrate on accepting all the commandments and the concept of reward and punishment.

וְהָיָה *And it will come to pass that if you continually hearken to My commandments that I command you today, to love HASHEM, your God, and to serve Him, with all your heart and with all your soul — then I will provide rain for your land in its proper time, the early and late rains, that you may gather in your grain, your wine, and your oil. I will provide grass in your field for your cattle and you will eat and be satisfied. Beware lest your heart be seduced and you turn astray and serve gods of others and bow to them. Then the wrath of HASHEM will blaze against you. He will restrain the heaven so there will be no rain and the ground will not yield its produce. And you will swiftly be banished from the goodly land which HASHEM gives you. Place these words of Mine upon your heart and upon your soul; bind them for a sign upon your arm and let them be tefillin between your eyes. Teach them to your children, to discuss them, while you sit in your home, while you walk on the way, when you retire and when you arise. And write them on the doorposts of your house and upon your gates. In order to prolong your days and the days of your children upon the ground that HASHEM has sworn to your ancestors to give them, like the days of the heaven on the earth.*

Numbers 15:37-41

וַיֹּאמֶר *And HASHEM said to Moses saying: Speak to the Children of Israel and say to them that they are to make themselves tzitzis on the corners of their garments, throughout their generations. And they are to place upon the tzitzis of each corner a thread of techeiles. And it shall constitute tzitzis for you, that you may see it and remember all the commandments of HASHEM and perform them; and not explore after your heart and after your eyes after which you stray. So that you may remember and perform all My*

Concentrate on fulfilling the commandment of remembering the Exodus from Egypt.

מִצְוֹתָי, וִהְיִיתֶם קְדֹשִׁים לֵאלֹהֵיכֶם: אֲנִי יהוה | אֱלֹהֵיכֶם, אֲשֶׁר הוֹצֵאתִי | אֶתְכֶם | מֵאֶרֶץ מִצְרַיִם, לִהְיוֹת לָכֶם לֵאלֹהִים, אֲנִי | יהוה | אֱלֹהֵיכֶם: אֱמֶת —

Although the word אֱמֶת belongs to the next paragraph, it is appended to the conclusion of the previous one, as explained in the commentary on page 95.

Chazzan repeats— **יהוה אֱלֹהֵיכֶם אֱמֶת.**

וֶאֱמוּנָה כָּל זֹאת, וְקַיָּם עָלֵינוּ, כִּי הוּא יהוה אֱלֹהֵינוּ וְאֵין זוּלָתוֹ, וַאֲנַחְנוּ יִשְׂרָאֵל עַמּוֹ. הַפּוֹדֵנוּ מִיַּד מְלָכִים, מַלְכֵּנוּ הַגּוֹאֲלֵנוּ מִכַּף כָּל הֶעָרִיצִים. הָאֵל הַנִּפְרָע לָנוּ מִצָּרֵינוּ, וְהַמְשַׁלֵּם גְּמוּל לְכָל אֹיְבֵי נַפְשֵׁנוּ. הָעֹשֶׂה גְדֹלוֹת עַד אֵין חֵקֶר, וְנִפְלָאוֹת עַד אֵין מִסְפָּר.[1] הַשָּׂם נַפְשֵׁנוּ בַּחַיִּים, וְלֹא נָתַן לַמּוֹט רַגְלֵנוּ.[2] הַמַּדְרִיכֵנוּ עַל בָּמוֹת אוֹיְבֵינוּ, וַיָּרֶם קַרְנֵנוּ עַל כָּל שֹׂנְאֵינוּ. הָעֹשֶׂה לָּנוּ נִסִּים וּנְקָמָה בְּפַרְעֹה, אוֹתוֹת וּמוֹפְתִים בְּאַדְמַת בְּנֵי חָם. הַמַּכֶּה בְעֶבְרָתוֹ כָּל בְּכוֹרֵי מִצְרָיִם, וַיּוֹצֵא אֶת עַמּוֹ יִשְׂרָאֵל מִתּוֹכָם לְחֵרוּת עוֹלָם. הַמַּעֲבִיר בָּנָיו בֵּין גִּזְרֵי יַם סוּף, אֶת רוֹדְפֵיהֶם וְאֶת שׂוֹנְאֵיהֶם בִּתְהוֹמוֹת טִבַּע. וְרָאוּ בָנָיו גְּבוּרָתוֹ, שִׁבְּחוּ וְהוֹדוּ לִשְׁמוֹ. ❖ וּמַלְכוּתוֹ בְּרָצוֹן קִבְּלוּ עֲלֵיהֶם. מֹשֶׁה וּבְנֵי יִשְׂרָאֵל לְךָ עָנוּ שִׁירָה, בְּשִׂמְחָה רַבָּה, וְאָמְרוּ כֻלָּם:

מִי כָמֹכָה בָּאֵלִם יהוה, מִי כָּמֹכָה נֶאְדָּר בַּקֹּדֶשׁ, נוֹרָא תְהִלֹּת, עֹשֵׂה פֶלֶא.[3] ❖ מַלְכוּתְךָ רָאוּ בָנֶיךָ בּוֹקֵעַ יָם לִפְנֵי מֹשֶׁה, זֶה אֵלִי[4] עָנוּ וְאָמְרוּ:

יהוה יִמְלֹךְ לְעֹלָם וָעֶד.[5] ❖ וְנֶאֱמַר: כִּי פָדָה יהוה אֶת יַעֲקֹב, וּגְאָלוֹ מִיַּד חָזָק מִמֶּנּוּ.[6] בָּרוּךְ אַתָּה יהוה, גָּאַל יִשְׂרָאֵל.

(Cong.— אָמֵן.)

הַשְׁכִּיבֵנוּ יהוה אֱלֹהֵינוּ לְשָׁלוֹם, וְהַעֲמִידֵנוּ מַלְכֵּנוּ לְחַיִּים, וּפְרוֹשׂ עָלֵינוּ סֻכַּת שְׁלוֹמֶךָ, וְתַקְּנֵנוּ בְּעֵצָה טוֹבָה מִלְּפָנֶיךָ, וְהוֹשִׁיעֵנוּ לְמַעַן שְׁמֶךָ. וְהָגֵן בַּעֲדֵנוּ, וְהָסֵר מֵעָלֵינוּ אוֹיֵב, דֶּבֶר, וְחֶרֶב, וְרָעָב, וְיָגוֹן, וְהָסֵר שָׂטָן מִלְּפָנֵינוּ וּמֵאַחֲרֵינוּ,

Concentrate on fulfilling the commandment of remembering the Exodus from Egypt.

commandments; and be holy to your God. I am HASHEM, *your God, Who has removed you from the land of Egypt to be a God to you; I am* HASHEM *your God — it is true —*

Although the word אֱמֶת, *'true,'* belongs to the next paragraph, it is appended to the conclusion of the previous one, as explained in the commentary on page 95.

Chazzan repeats: **HASHEM, your God, is true.**

וֶאֱמוּנָה *And faithful is all this, and it is firmly established for us that He is* HASHEM *our God, and there is none but Him, and we are Israel, His nation. He redeems us from the power of kings, our King Who delivers us from the hand of all the cruel tyrants. He is the God Who exacts vengeance for us from our foes and Who brings just retribution upon all enemies of our soul; Who performs great deeds that are beyond comprehension, and wonders beyond number.*[1] *Who set our soul in life and did not allow our foot to falter.*[2] *Who led us upon the heights of our enemies and raised our pride above all who hate us; Who wrought for us miracles and vengeance upon Pharaoh; signs and wonders on the land of the offspring of Ham; Who struck with His anger all the firstborn of Egypt and removed His nation Israel from their midst to eternal freedom; Who brought His children through the split parts of the Sea of Reeds while those who pursued them and hated them He caused to sink into the depths. When His children perceived His power, they lauded and gave grateful praise to His Name.* Chazzan— *And His Kingship they accepted upon themselves willingly. Moses and the Children of Israel raised their voices to You in song with abundant gladness — and said unanimously:*

מִי כָמֹכָה *Who is like You among the heavenly powers,* HASHEM! *Who is like You, mighty in holiness, too awesome for praise, doing wonders!*[3] Chazzan— *Your children beheld Your majesty, as You split the sea before Moses: 'This is my God!'*[4] *they exclaimed, then they said:*

יהוה *'*HASHEM *shall reign for all eternity!'*[5] Chazzan— *And it is further said: 'For* HASHEM *has redeemed Jacob and delivered him from a power mightier than he.'*[6] *Blessed are You* HASHEM, *Who redeemed Israel.*

(Cong.— *Amen.*)

הַשְׁכִּיבֵנוּ *Lay us down to sleep,* HASHEM *our God, in peace, raise us erect, our King, to life; and spread over us the shelter of Your peace. Set us aright with good counsel from before Your Presence, and save us for Your Name's sake. Shield us, remove from us foe, plague, sword, famine, and woe; and remove spiritual impediment from before us and behind us and*

(1) *Job* 9:10. (2) *Psalms* 66:9. (3) *Exodus* 15:11. (4) 15:2. (5) 15:18. (6) *Jeremiah* 31:10.

וּבְצֵל כְּנָפֶיךָ תַּסְתִּירֵנוּ,[1] כִּי אֵל שׁוֹמְרֵנוּ וּמַצִּילֵנוּ אָתָּה, כִּי אֵל מֶלֶךְ חַנּוּן וְרַחוּם אָתָּה.[2] ❖ וּשְׁמוֹר צֵאתֵנוּ וּבוֹאֵנוּ, לְחַיִּים וּלְשָׁלוֹם מֵעַתָּה וְעַד עוֹלָם.[3] וּפְרוֹשׂ עָלֵינוּ* סֻכַּת שְׁלוֹמֶךָ. בָּרוּךְ אַתָּה יהוה, הַפּוֹרֵשׂ סֻכַּת שָׁלוֹם עָלֵינוּ וְעַל כָּל עַמּוֹ יִשְׂרָאֵל וְעַל יְרוּשָׁלָיִם. (.Cong.— אָמֵן.)

Congregation rises and remains standing until after *Shemoneh Esrei.*

On the Sabbath, the congregation, followed by the *chazzan,* recites:

וְשָׁמְרוּ* בְנֵי יִשְׂרָאֵל אֶת הַשַּׁבָּת, לַעֲשׂוֹת אֶת הַשַּׁבָּת* לְדֹרֹתָם בְּרִית עוֹלָם. בֵּינִי וּבֵין בְּנֵי יִשְׂרָאֵל* אוֹת הִיא לְעֹלָם, כִּי שֵׁשֶׁת יָמִים עָשָׂה יהוה אֶת הַשָּׁמַיִם וְאֶת הָאָרֶץ, וּבַיּוֹם הַשְּׁבִיעִי שָׁבַת וַיִּנָּפַשׁ.*[4]

On Festivals (but not Chol HaMoed) the congregation, followed by the *chazzan,* recites:

וַיְדַבֵּר מֹשֶׁה* אֶת מֹעֲדֵי יהוה, אֶל בְּנֵי יִשְׂרָאֵל.[5]

חצי קדיש

If a *minyan* is present, the *chazzan* recites חֲצִי קַדִּישׁ.

יִתְגַּדַּל וְיִתְקַדַּשׁ שְׁמֵהּ רַבָּא. (.Cong.— אָמֵן.) בְּעָלְמָא דִּי בְרָא כִרְעוּתֵהּ, וְיַמְלִיךְ מַלְכוּתֵהּ, בְּחַיֵּיכוֹן וּבְיוֹמֵיכוֹן וּבְחַיֵּי דְכָל בֵּית יִשְׂרָאֵל, בַּעֲגָלָא וּבִזְמַן קָרִיב. וְאִמְרוּ: אָמֵן.

(.Cong.— אָמֵן. יְהֵא שְׁמֵהּ רַבָּא מְבָרַךְ לְעָלַם וּלְעָלְמֵי עָלְמַיָּא.)

יְהֵא שְׁמֵהּ רַבָּא מְבָרַךְ לְעָלַם וּלְעָלְמֵי עָלְמַיָּא.

יִתְבָּרַךְ וְיִשְׁתַּבַּח וְיִתְפָּאַר וְיִתְרוֹמַם וְיִתְנַשֵּׂא וְיִתְהַדָּר וְיִתְעַלֶּה וְיִתְהַלָּל שְׁמֵהּ דְּקֻדְשָׁא בְּרִיךְ הוּא (.Cong.— בְּרִיךְ הוּא) — °לְעֵלָּא מִן כָּל (From Rosh Hashanah to Yom Kippur substitute— °לְעֵלָּא וּלְעֵלָּא מִכָּל) בִּרְכָתָא וְשִׁירָתָא תֻּשְׁבְּחָתָא וְנֶחֱמָתָא, דַּאֲמִירָן בְּעָלְמָא. וְאִמְרוּ: אָמֵן. (.Cong.— אָמֵן.)

On ordinary Sabbaths and on the Sabbath of Chol HaMoed continue with *Shemoneh Esrei,* next page. On Festivals, even those that fall on the Sabbath, the Festival *Shemoneh Esrei* (p. 660) is recited.

וּפְרוֹשׂ עָלֵינוּ – *And spread over us.* This phrase was recited earlier in the paragraph, but it is repeated now because of its similarity to the closing of the blessing. There is a general rule that the conclusion of a blessing should be related to the content. Unlike the weekday הַשְׁכִּיבֵנוּ, the concluding blessing on the Sabbath and Festivals reflects the peace that comes with the holiness of the day *(Anaf Yosef).*

וְשָׁמְרוּ ◆§ – *And ... shall keep.* As noted above, there should be no interruption between the theme of redemption and *Shemoneh Esrei.* However, this Scriptural statement of Israel's Sabbath observance is related to the theme of redemption, because Israel will be redeemed from exile in the merit of Sabbath observance *(Abudraham).* The verse for the pilgrimage festivals alludes to the freedom from Egypt.

This chapter of Sabbath observance appears in the Torah immediately after the commandment to commence the construction of the Tabernacle. This teaches that even for the sake of building the Temple, one may not desecrate the Sabbath *(Rashi* to *Exodus* 31:13). [By logical extension,

in the shadow of Your wings shelter us[1] *— for God Who protects and rescues us are You; for God, the Gracious and Compassionate King, are You.*[2] Chazzan— *Safeguard our going and coming — for life and for peace from now to eternity.*[3] ***And spread over us* the shelter of Your peace. Blessed are You,*** *H*ASHEM, ***Who spreads the shelter of peace upon us, upon all of his people Israel and upon Jerusalem.***

(Cong.—*Amen.)*

Congregation rises and remains standing till after *Shemoneh Esrei.*

On the Sabbath, the congregation, followed by the *chazzan,* recites:

וְשָׁמְרוּ ***And the children of Israel shall keep* the Sabbath, to make the Sabbath* an eternal covenant for their generations. Between Me and the Children of Israel* it is a sign forever that in six days*** *H*ASHEM ***made heaven and earth, and on the seventh day He rested and was refreshed.****[4]

On Festivals (but not Chol Hamoed) the congregation, followed by the *chazzan,* recites:

*And Moses declared** *H*ASHEM*'s appointed festivals to the Children of Israel.*[5]

HALF-KADDISH

If a *minyan* is present, the *chazzan* recites Half-*Kaddish.*

יִתְגַּדַּל ***May His great Name grow exalted and sanctified*** (Cong.— *Amen.*) ***in the world that He created as He willed. May He give reign to His kingship in your lifetimes and in your days, and in the lifetimes of the entire Family of Israel, swiftly and soon. Now respond: Amen.***

(Cong.—*Amen. May His great Name be blessed forever and ever.*)

May His great Name be blessed forever and ever.

Blessed, praised, glorified, exalted, extolled, mighty, upraised, and lauded be the Name of the Holy One, Blessed is He (Cong.— ***Blessed is He***) — (From Rosh Hashanah to Yom Kippur add: ***exceedingly***) ***beyond any blessing and song, praise and consolation that are uttered in the world. Now respond: Amen.*** (Cong.—*Amen*).

On ordinary Sabbaths and on the Sabbath of Chol HaMoed continue with *Shemoneh Esrei,* next page. On Festivals, even those that fall on the Sabbath, the Festival *Shemoneh Esrei* (p. 660) is recited.

(1) Cf. *Psalms* 17:8. (2) Cf. *Nechemiah* 9:31. (3) Cf. *Psalms* 121:8. (4) *Exodus* 31:16-17. (5) *Leviticus* 23:44.

---

this concept refutes those who may tend to relax the observance of the Sabbath or other *mitzvos* for the sake of what they consider to be noble spiritual causes.]

לַעֲשׂוֹת אֶת הַשַּׁבָּת *— To make the Sabbath.* Each generation must *'make' the Sabbath,* by teaching its importance and holiness to those who are lax in sanctifying it because they fail to appreciate its importance *(Maor VaShemesh).*

בֵּינִי וּבֵין בְּנֵי יִשְׂרָאֵל *— Between Me and the Children of Israel.* Only Israel is commanded to observe the Sabbath, thereby bearing witness to God's creation of heaven and earth in six days. Consequently, the Sabbath is a *sign* of God's special relationship with Israel.

וַיִּנָּפַשׁ *— And was refreshed.* The translation follows *Rashi* who comments that this is an example of how God is described in human terms: God, of course, cannot become tired or refreshed, but a man would need a day of rest to refresh himself after six days of labor.

Other commentators, *Ramban* and *R' Yehudah HaChassid* among them, derive this word from נֶפֶשׁ, *soul.* They render וַיִּנָּפַשׁ: the heaven and earth just mentioned *were given a soul,* as if to say that the creation of the Sabbath gave a new spiritual dimension to the universe.

◆§ וַיְדַבֵּר מֹשֶׁה *— And Moses declared.* This verse concludes a chapter that discusses the festivals. Thus, the verse alludes to all the specific laws and teachings of each of the festivals.

שמונה עשרה — עמידה

Take three steps backward, then three steps forward. Remain standing with the feet together while reciting *Shemoneh Esrei*. It should be recited with quiet devotion and without any interruption, verbal or otherwise. Although it should not be audible to others, one must pray loudly enough to hear himself. See *Laws* §61-90 for a brief summary of its laws, including how to rectify the omission of phrases that are added at particular times of the year.

Commentary to the first three blessings of *Shemoneh Esrei* begins on p. 98; the last three, p. 110.

אֲדֹנָי שְׂפָתַי תִּפְתָּח, וּפִי יַגִּיד תְּהִלָּתֶךָ.[1]

אבות

Bend the knees at בָּרוּךְ; bow at אַתָּה; straighten up at ה׳.

בָּרוּךְ אַתָּה יהוה אֱלֹהֵינוּ וֵאלֹהֵי אֲבוֹתֵינוּ, אֱלֹהֵי אַבְרָהָם, אֱלֹהֵי יִצְחָק, וֵאלֹהֵי יַעֲקֹב, הָאֵל הַגָּדוֹל הַגִּבּוֹר וְהַנּוֹרָא, אֵל עֶלְיוֹן, גּוֹמֵל חֲסָדִים טוֹבִים וְקוֹנֵה הַכֹּל, וְזוֹכֵר חַסְדֵי אָבוֹת, וּמֵבִיא גוֹאֵל לִבְנֵי בְנֵיהֶם, לְמַעַן שְׁמוֹ בְּאַהֲבָה.

From Rosh Hashanah to Yom Kippur add:

זָכְרֵנוּ לְחַיִּים, מֶלֶךְ חָפֵץ בַּחַיִּים, וְכָתְבֵנוּ בְּסֵפֶר הַחַיִּים, לְמַעַנְךָ אֱלֹהִים חַיִּים.

[If forgotten, do not repeat *Shemoneh Esrei*. See *Laws* §61.]

Bend the knees at בָּרוּךְ; bow at אַתָּה; straighten up at ה׳.

מֶלֶךְ עוֹזֵר וּמוֹשִׁיעַ וּמָגֵן. בָּרוּךְ אַתָּה יהוה, מָגֵן אַבְרָהָם.

גבורות

אַתָּה גִּבּוֹר לְעוֹלָם אֲדֹנָי, מְחַיֵּה מֵתִים אַתָּה, רַב לְהוֹשִׁיעַ.

Between Shemini Atzeres and Pesach add the following.

מַשִּׁיב הָרוּחַ וּמוֹרִיד °הַגֶּשֶׁם [some say – °הַגָּשֶׁם].

[If forgotten, see *Laws* §70-75.]

מְכַלְכֵּל חַיִּים בְּחֶסֶד, מְחַיֵּה מֵתִים בְּרַחֲמִים רַבִּים, סוֹמֵךְ נוֹפְלִים, וְרוֹפֵא חוֹלִים, וּמַתִּיר אֲסוּרִים, וּמְקַיֵּם אֱמוּנָתוֹ לִישֵׁנֵי עָפָר. מִי כָמוֹךָ בַּעַל גְּבוּרוֹת, וּמִי דּוֹמֶה לָּךְ, מֶלֶךְ מֵמִית וּמְחַיֶּה וּמַצְמִיחַ יְשׁוּעָה.

From Rosh Hashanah to Yom Kippur add the following:

מִי כָמוֹךָ אַב הָרַחֲמִים, זוֹכֵר יְצוּרָיו לְחַיִּים בְּרַחֲמִים.

[If forgotten, do not repeat *Shemoneh Esrei*. See *Laws* §61.]

וְנֶאֱמָן אַתָּה לְהַחֲיוֹת מֵתִים. בָּרוּךְ אַתָּה יהוה, מְחַיֵּה הַמֵּתִים.

קדושת השם

אַתָּה קָדוֹשׁ וְשִׁמְךָ קָדוֹשׁ, וּקְדוֹשִׁים בְּכָל יוֹם יְהַלְלוּךָ סֶּלָה. בָּרוּךְ אַתָּה יהוה, °הָאֵל הַקָּדוֹשׁ.

°הַמֶּלֶךְ הַקָּדוֹשׁ. —From Rosh Hashanah to Yom Kippur substitute

[If forgotten, repeat *Shemoneh Esrei*. See *Laws* §62-63.]

SHEMONEH ESREI OF SHABBOS / AMIDAH

Technically, the name *Shemoneh Esrei* [lit. *eighteen*] refers to the weekday prayer which originally contained eighteen blessings. It is a misnomer for the seven-blessing Sabbath prayer, which should correctly be called the *Amidah*

SHEMONEH ESREI — AMIDAH

Take three steps backward, then three steps forward. Remain standing with the feet together while reciting *Shemoneh Esrei.* It should be recited with quiet devotion and without any interruption, verbal or otherwise. Although it should not be audible to others, one must pray loudly enough to hear himself. See *Laws* §61-90 for a brief summary of its laws, including how to rectify the omission of phrases that are added at particular times of the year.

Commentary to the first three blessings of *Shemoneh Esrei* begins on p. 98; the last three, p. 110.

My Lord, open my lips, that my mouth may declare Your praise.[1]

PATRIARCHS

Bend the knees at *'Blessed'*; bow at *'You'*; straighten up at *'HASHEM'*.

בָּרוּךְ *Blessed are You, HASHEM, our God and the God of our forefathers, God of Abraham, God of Isaac, and God of Jacob; the great, mighty, and awesome God, the supreme God, Who bestows beneficial kindnesses and creates everything, Who recalls the kindnesses of the Patriarchs and brings a Redeemer to their children's children, for His Name's sake, with love.*

From Rosh Hashanah to Yom Kippur add the following.

Remember us for life, O King Who desires life,
and inscribe us in the Book of Life — for Your sake, O Living God.

[If forgotten, do not repeat *Shemoneh Esrei.* See *Laws* §61.]

Bend the knees at *'Blessed'*; bow at *'You'*; straighten up at *'HASHEM'*.

O King, Helper, Savior, and Shield. Blessed are You, HASHEM, Shield of Abraham.

GOD'S MIGHT

אַתָּה *You are eternally mighty, my Lord, the Resuscitator of the dead are You; abundantly able to save,*

Between Shemini Atzeres and Pesach add the following.

Who makes the wind blow and makes the rain descend;

[If forgotten, see *Laws* §70-75.]

Who sustains the living with kindness, resuscitates the dead with abundant mercy, supports the fallen, heals the sick, releases the confined, and maintains His faith to those asleep in the dust. Who is like You, O Master of mighty deeds, and who is comparable to You, O King Who causes death and restores life and makes salvation sprout!

From Rosh Hashanah to Yom Kippur add the following.

Who is like You, Merciful Father, Who recalls His creatures mercifully for life!

[If forgotten, do not repeat *Shemoneh Esrei.* See *Laws* §61.]

And You are faithful to resuscitate the dead. Blessed are You, HASHEM, Who resuscitates the dead.

HOLINESS OF GOD'S NAME

אַתָּה *You are holy and Your Name is holy, and holy ones praise You every day, forever. Blessed are You, HASHEM, °the holy God.*

°From Rosh Hashanah to Yom Kippur substitute: *the holy King.*
[If forgotten, repeat *Shemoneh Esrei.* See *Laws* §62-63.]

(1) *Psalms* 51:17.

[Standing Prayer]. Nevertheless, both names are commonly used interchangeably, and we follow the popular practice in this *Siddur,* as well.

The *Shemoneh Esrei* of the Sabbath and *Yom Tov* should have been identical to the weekday one, with the inclusion of an appropriate

קדושת היום

If one erroneously began the weekday blessings, or an inappropriate Sabbath *Amidah*, see *Laws* §128-133.

אַתָּה קִדַּשְׁתָּ אֶת יוֹם הַשְּׁבִיעִי לִשְׁמֶךָ,* תַּכְלִית* מַעֲשֵׂה שָׁמַיִם וָאָרֶץ, וּבֵרַכְתּוֹ מִכָּל הַיָּמִים, וְקִדַּשְׁתּוֹ מִכָּל הַזְּמַנִּים, וְכֵן כָּתוּב* בְּתוֹרָתֶךָ:

וַיְכֻלּוּ הַשָּׁמַיִם וְהָאָרֶץ* וְכָל צְבָאָם.* וַיְכַל אֱלֹהִים בַּיּוֹם הַשְּׁבִיעִי מְלַאכְתּוֹ אֲשֶׁר עָשָׂה, וַיִּשְׁבֹּת* בַּיּוֹם הַשְּׁבִיעִי מִכָּל מְלַאכְתּוֹ אֲשֶׁר עָשָׂה. וַיְבָרֶךְ אֱלֹהִים אֶת יוֹם הַשְּׁבִיעִי, וַיְקַדֵּשׁ אֹתוֹ, כִּי בוֹ שָׁבַת מִכָּל מְלַאכְתּוֹ, אֲשֶׁר בָּרָא אֱלֹהִים לַעֲשׂוֹת.*[1]

אֱלֹהֵינוּ וֵאלֹהֵי אֲבוֹתֵינוּ רְצֵה בִמְנוּחָתֵנוּ.* קַדְּשֵׁנוּ בְּמִצְוֹתֶיךָ,* וְתֵן חֶלְקֵנוּ בְּתוֹרָתֶךָ. שַׂבְּעֵנוּ מִטּוּבֶךָ, וְשַׂמְּחֵנוּ בִּישׁוּעָתֶךָ, וְטַהֵר לִבֵּנוּ* לְעָבְדְּךָ בֶּאֱמֶת. וְהַנְחִילֵנוּ יהוה אֱלֹהֵינוּ בְּאַהֲבָה וּבְרָצוֹן שַׁבַּת קָדְשֶׁךָ, וְיָנוּחוּ בָהּ* יִשְׂרָאֵל מְקַדְּשֵׁי שְׁמֶךָ. בָּרוּךְ אַתָּה יהוה, מְקַדֵּשׁ הַשַּׁבָּת.

---

paragraph indicating the holiness of the day, as is done on Rosh Chodesh and *Chol Hamoed*. The Sages, however, wished to make the Sabbath Festival prayers simpler and less burdensome than they would be if we had to beseech God for the entire catalogue of our personal and national needs. Therefore they omitted the middle thirteen blessings, which are all requests (see commentary to the weekday *Shemoneh Esrei*, p. 98), and replaced them with a single blessing known as קְדוּשַּׁת הַיּוֹם, *Sanctity of the Day* (*Berachos* 21a). Moreover, as the Midrash (*Tanchuma, Vayeira*) explains, the thirteen middle blessings of *Shemoneh Esrei* which deal with human concerns and needs are not appropriate for the Sabbath, the sacred day on which we turn from ordinary preoccupations and occupy ourselves with spiritual values and priorities.

Because of the fact that the entire weekday *Shemoneh Esrei* would have been appropriate for the holy days as well, in the event someone erred in his prayers and began to recite the weekday blessings on the Sabbath or *Yom Tov*, he should complete whatever blessing he has begun and then begin the appropriate blessing of קְדוּשַּׁת הַיּוֹם, *Sanctity of the Day* (*Orach Chaim* 268:2). In the case of the Sabbath eve *Maariv* this would be אַתָּה קִדַּשְׁתָּ.

◆§ קְדוּשַּׁת הַיּוֹם / Sanctification of the Day

אַתָּה קִדַּשְׁתָּ ... לִשְׁמֶךָ — *You sanctified ... for Your Name's sake.* God sanctified the Sabbath as an eternal reminder that He rested on that day (*Abudraham*); and He made it clear that we are not to regard it as a humanly legislated day of rest for personal convenience, but are to dedicate it to His service, *for* [His] *Name's sake* (*R' Munk*).

תַּכְלִית — *The conclusion.* God's six days of labor ended on the Sabbath. The word תַּכְלִית has the secondary meaning of *purpose:* the purpose of Creation was so that God could allow people to enjoy the spiritual pleasure of His Presence. That will occur in its fullest sense only when the Messiah arrives; that era will be known as an unending Sabbath, because its holiness will be unlimited. Meanwhile, however, a taste of the spiritual bliss of the future is given Israel every week with the advent of the holy Sabbath. Accordingly, it is only on the Sabbath that Creation achieves its purpose (*Be'er Mayim Chaim*).

וְכֵן כָּתוּב — *And so it is written.* The passage about to be quoted proves that the Sabbath represents the *purpose of the creation* (*Tur*).

◆§ וַיְכֻלּוּ הַשָּׁמַיִם וְהָאָרֶץ — *Thus the heaven and the earth were finished.* The Talmud (*Shabbos* 119b) derives homiletically from this verse that whoever recites this passage is regarded as God's partner in Creation, because the word וַיְכֻלּוּ homiletically can be vocalized וַיְכַלּוּ, *and* **they** [i.e., God and everyone who acknowledges His Creation] *finished*. God's Creation would have fallen short of its purpose unless man

HOLINESS OF THE DAY

If one erroneously began the weekday blessings, he should complete whatever blessing he had begun and then continue with the Sabbath blessing.

אַתָּה *You sanctified the seventh day for Your Name's sake,* the conclusion* of the creation of heaven and earth. Of all days, You blessed it; and of all seasons, You sanctified it — and so it is written* in Your Torah:*

וַיְכֻלּוּ *Thus the heaven and the earth were finished,* and all their legion.* On the seventh day God completed His work which He had done, and He abstained* on the seventh day from all His work which He had done. God blessed the seventh day and sanctified it, because on it He had abstained from all His work which God created to make.**[1]

אֱלֹהֵינוּ *Our God and the God of our forefathers, may You be pleased with our rest.* Sanctify us with Your commandments* and grant our share in Your Torah; satisfy us from Your goodness and gladden us with Your salvation, and purify our heart* to serve You sincerely. O* Hashem, *our God, with love and favor grant us Your holy Sabbath as a heritage and may Israel, the sanctifiers of Your Name, rest on it.* Blessed are You,* Hashem, *Who sanctifies the Sabbath.*

(1) *Genesis* 2:1-3.

acknowledged Him as the Creator *(Maharsha).*

וְכָל צְבָאָם — *And all their legion.* The word צָבָא, *array* or *legion,* refers to an organized, disciplined group acting in unison. The heavenly bodies and spiritual beings are a *legion* because they act only according to God's plan. On earth, it is the duty of Israel, by acting according to the Torah, to be His earthly legion *(R' Bunam of P'shis'cha).*

וַיְכַל ... וַיִּשְׁבֹּת — *Completed ... and He abstained.* These two words have different connotations. *He completed* [וַיְכַל] means that the task at hand was finished, with nothing left to be done; *He abstained* [וַיִּשְׁבֹּת] implies that more is to be done, but it is set aside for another day. The Torah uses both words to teach people that even though they are still in the middle of their work, when the Sabbath arrives they should consider it completed and not think about it *(Avnei Eliyahu).*

אֲשֶׁר בָּרָא אֱלֹהִים לַעֲשׂוֹת — *Which God created to make.* People can labor long and hard to *create* something — whether it is a house, a tool, or a business. Then it is up to them to *use* it properly. God created the world for the use of humanity; the *completion* of Creation, however, He entrusted to mankind. Now it is up *to us* to *use it* as He intended *(Chasam Sofer).*

☙ אֱלֹהֵינוּ ... רְצֵה בִמְנוּחָתֵנוּ — *O God ... may You be pleased with our rest.* Even though we may concentrate more on relaxation and good food than spiritual growth, we ask that You not be displeased by our human frailty *(Etz Yosef).*

קַדְּשֵׁנוּ בְּמִצְוֹתֶיךָ — *Sanctify us with Your commandments.* The *performance* of *mitzvos* in itself elevates a person and makes him more prone to absorb sanctity. Alternatively, the word קַדְּשֵׁנוּ can be related to קִדּוּשִׁין, *betrothal.* God has *betrothed* Israel, as it were, by allowing us to perform His commandments *(Abudraham).*

וְטַהֵר לִבֵּנוּ — *And purify our heart.* The Sages assure us that הַבָּא לִיטַּהֵר מְסַיְּיעִין אוֹתוֹ, *if one comes to purify himself, Heaven helps him* *(Yoma* 38b). Therefore, we are justified in asking God to help us purify ourselves to serve Him better *(Abudraham).*

וְיָנוּחוּ בָהּ — *Rest on it.* Since the word Sabbath is feminine, the word בָהּ, in the feminine form, should be used in all the *tefillos* of the day *(Avodas Yisrael). Magen Avraham (Orach Chaim* 268:3), however, cites a custom that on Friday night we recite בָהּ, while at *Shacharis* and *Mussaf* we say וְיָנוּחוּ בוֹ, *rest on* **it** in the masculine, and at *Minchah* we say בָם, *on* **them.** The differing expressions allude to three different periods. In the evening, which represents the Sabbath of Creation, the feminine form is used because the newly created Sabbath — without a nation to observe it and realize its potential — was like a lonely woman without a husband. In the morning, which represents the Sabbath when the Torah was given, the masculine form בוֹ alludes to Israel's acceptance of the Torah, when the Sabbath became 'betrothed' to Israel, the nation that activated the latent ideals symbolized by the Sabbath.

עבודה

רְצֵה יהוה אֱלֹהֵינוּ בְּעַמְּךָ יִשְׂרָאֵל וּבִתְפִלָּתָם, וְהָשֵׁב אֶת הָעֲבוֹדָה לִדְבִיר בֵּיתֶךָ. וְאִשֵּׁי יִשְׂרָאֵל וּתְפִלָּתָם בְּאַהֲבָה תְקַבֵּל בְּרָצוֹן, וּתְהִי לְרָצוֹן תָּמִיד עֲבוֹדַת יִשְׂרָאֵל עַמֶּךָ.

On Rosh Chodesh and Chol HaMoed add the following.

אֱלֹהֵינוּ וֵאלֹהֵי אֲבוֹתֵינוּ, יַעֲלֶה, וְיָבֹא, וְיַגִּיעַ, וְיֵרָאֶה, וְיֵרָצֶה, וְיִשָּׁמַע, וְיִפָּקֵד, וְיִזָּכֵר זִכְרוֹנֵנוּ וּפִקְדוֹנֵנוּ, וְזִכְרוֹן אֲבוֹתֵינוּ, וְזִכְרוֹן מָשִׁיחַ בֶּן דָּוִד עַבְדֶּךָ, וְזִכְרוֹן יְרוּשָׁלַיִם עִיר קָדְשֶׁךָ, וְזִכְרוֹן כָּל עַמְּךָ בֵּית יִשְׂרָאֵל לְפָנֶיךָ, לִפְלֵיטָה לְטוֹבָה, לְחֵן וּלְחֶסֶד וּלְרַחֲמִים, לְחַיִּים וּלְשָׁלוֹם בְּיוֹם

on Rosh Chodesh	on Pesach	on Succos
רֹאשׁ הַחֹדֶשׁ	חַג הַמַּצּוֹת	חַג הַסֻּכּוֹת

הַזֶּה. זָכְרֵנוּ יהוה אֱלֹהֵינוּ בּוֹ לְטוֹבָה, וּפָקְדֵנוּ בוֹ לִבְרָכָה, וְהוֹשִׁיעֵנוּ בוֹ לְחַיִּים. וּבִדְבַר יְשׁוּעָה וְרַחֲמִים, חוּס וְחָנֵּנוּ וְרַחֵם עָלֵינוּ וְהוֹשִׁיעֵנוּ, כִּי אֵלֶיךָ עֵינֵינוּ, כִּי אֵל מֶלֶךְ חַנּוּן וְרַחוּם אָתָּה.[1]

[If forgotten, at *Maariv* of Rosh Chodesh, do not repeat *Shemoneh Esrei;* at *Maariv* of Chol HaMoed, repeat *Shemoneh Esrei.* See *Laws* §89.]

וְתֶחֱזֶינָה עֵינֵינוּ בְּשׁוּבְךָ לְצִיּוֹן בְּרַחֲמִים. בָּרוּךְ אַתָּה יהוה, הַמַּחֲזִיר שְׁכִינָתוֹ לְצִיּוֹן.

הודאה

Bow at מוֹדִים; straighten up at 'ה.

מוֹדִים אֲנַחְנוּ לָךְ שָׁאַתָּה הוּא יהוה אֱלֹהֵינוּ וֵאלֹהֵי אֲבוֹתֵינוּ לְעוֹלָם וָעֶד. צוּר חַיֵּינוּ, מָגֵן יִשְׁעֵנוּ אַתָּה הוּא לְדוֹר וָדוֹר. נוֹדֶה לְּךָ וּנְסַפֵּר תְּהִלָּתֶךָ[2] עַל חַיֵּינוּ הַמְּסוּרִים בְּיָדֶךָ, וְעַל נִשְׁמוֹתֵינוּ הַפְּקוּדוֹת לָךְ, וְעַל נִסֶּיךָ שֶׁבְּכָל יוֹם עִמָּנוּ, וְעַל נִפְלְאוֹתֶיךָ וְטוֹבוֹתֶיךָ שֶׁבְּכָל עֵת, עֶרֶב וָבֹקֶר וְצָהֳרָיִם. הַטּוֹב כִּי לֹא כָלוּ רַחֲמֶיךָ, וְהַמְּרַחֵם כִּי לֹא תַמּוּ חֲסָדֶיךָ,[3] מֵעוֹלָם קִוִּינוּ לָךְ.

On Chanukah add the following.

(וְ)עַל הַנִּסִּים, וְעַל הַפֻּרְקָן, וְעַל הַגְּבוּרוֹת, וְעַל הַתְּשׁוּעוֹת, וְעַל הַמִּלְחָמוֹת, שֶׁעָשִׂיתָ לַאֲבוֹתֵינוּ בַּיָּמִים הָהֵם בַּזְּמַן הַזֶּה.

בִּימֵי מַתִּתְיָהוּ בֶּן יוֹחָנָן כֹּהֵן גָּדוֹל חַשְׁמוֹנַאי וּבָנָיו, כְּשֶׁעָמְדָה מַלְכוּת יָוָן הָרְשָׁעָה עַל עַמְּךָ יִשְׂרָאֵל, לְהַשְׁכִּיחָם תּוֹרָתֶךָ, וּלְהַעֲבִירָם מֵחֻקֵּי רְצוֹנֶךָ. וְאַתָּה בְּרַחֲמֶיךָ הָרַבִּים, עָמַדְתָּ לָהֶם בְּעֵת צָרָתָם, רַבְתָּ אֶת רִיבָם, דַּנְתָּ אֶת דִּינָם, נָקַמְתָּ אֶת נִקְמָתָם.[4]

TEMPLE SERVICE

רְצֵה *Be favorable,* Hashem, *our God, toward Your people Israel and their prayer and restore the service to the Holy of Holies of Your Temple. The fire-offerings of Israel and their prayer accept with love and favor, and may the service of Your people Israel always be favorable to You.*

On Rosh Chodesh and Chol HaMoed add the following.

אֱלֹהֵינוּ *Our God and God of our forefathers, may there rise, come, reach, be noted, be favored, be heard, be considered, and be remembered — the remembrance and consideration of ourselves; the remembrance of our forefathers; the remembrance of Messiah, son of David, Your servant; the remembrance of Jerusalem, the City of Your Holiness, the remembrance of Your entire people the Family of Israel — before You, for deliverance, for goodness, for grace, for kindness, and for compassion, for life, and for peace on this day of*

on Rosh Chodesh	on Passover	on Succos
Rosh Chodesh.	*the Festival of Matzos.*	*the Succos Festival.*

Remember us on it, Hashem, *our God, for goodness; consider us on it for blessing; and help us on it for life. In the matter of salvation and compassion, pity, be gracious and compassionate with us and help us, for our eyes are turned to You, because You are God, the gracious, and compassionate King.*[1]

[If forgotten at *Maariv* of Rosh Chodesh, do not repeat *Shemoneh Esrei;* at *Maariv* of Chol HaMoed, repeat *Shemoneh Esrei.*]

וְתֶחֱזֶינָה *May our eyes behold Your return to Zion in compassion. Blessed are You,* Hashem, *Who restores His Presence to Zion.*

THANKSGIVING [MODIM]

Bow at *'We gratefully thank You';* straighten up at *'Hashem'.*

מוֹדִים *We gratefully thank You, for it is You Who are* Hashem, *our God and the God of our forefathers for all eternity; Rock of our lives, Shield of our salvation are You from generation to generation. We shall thank You and relate Your praise*[2] *— for our lives, which are committed to Your power and for our souls that are entrusted to You; for Your miracles that are with us every day; and for Your wonders and favors in every season — evening, morning, and afternoon. The Beneficent One, for Your compassions were never exhausted, and the Compassionate One, for Your kindnesses never ended*[3] *— always have we put our hope in You.*

On Chanukah add the following.

(וְ)עַל *(And) for the miracles, and for the salvation, and for the mighty deeds, and for the victories, and for the battles which You performed for our forefathers in those days, at this time.*

בִּימֵי *In the days of Mattisyahu, the son of Yochanan, the High Priest, the Hasmonean, and his sons—when the wicked Greek kingdom rose up against Your people Israel to make them forget Your Torah and compel them to stray from the statutes of Your Will—You in Your great mercy stood up for them in the time of their distress. You took up their grievance, judged their claim, and avenged their wrong.*[4]

---

(1) Cf. *Nechemiah* 9:31. (2) Cf. *Psalms* 79:13. (3) Cf. *Lamentations* 3:22. (4) Cf. *Jeremiah* 51:36.

Minchah represents the Sabbath of the future, when every day — *all* the days (plural) — will have the serenity and holiness of the Sabbath *(R' Munk).*

מָסַרְתָּ גִבּוֹרִים בְּיַד חַלָּשִׁים, וְרַבִּים בְּיַד מְעַטִּים, וּטְמֵאִים בְּיַד טְהוֹרִים, וּרְשָׁעִים בְּיַד צַדִּיקִים, וְזֵדִים בְּיַד עוֹסְקֵי תוֹרָתֶךָ. וּלְךָ עָשִׂיתָ שֵׁם גָּדוֹל וְקָדוֹשׁ בְּעוֹלָמֶךָ, וּלְעַמְּךָ יִשְׂרָאֵל עָשִׂיתָ תְּשׁוּעָה גְדוֹלָה וּפֻרְקָן כְּהַיּוֹם הַזֶּה. וְאַחַר כֵּן בָּאוּ בָנֶיךָ לִדְבִיר בֵּיתֶךָ, וּפִנּוּ אֶת הֵיכָלֶךָ, וְטִהֲרוּ אֶת מִקְדָּשֶׁךָ, וְהִדְלִיקוּ נֵרוֹת בְּחַצְרוֹת קָדְשֶׁךָ, וְקָבְעוּ שְׁמוֹנַת יְמֵי חֲנֻכָּה אֵלּוּ, לְהוֹדוֹת וּלְהַלֵּל לְשִׁמְךָ הַגָּדוֹל.

[If forgotten, do not repeat *Shemoneh Esrei.*]

וְעַל כֻּלָּם יִתְבָּרַךְ וְיִתְרוֹמַם שִׁמְךָ מַלְכֵּנוּ תָּמִיד לְעוֹלָם וָעֶד.

From Rosh Hashanah to Yom Kippur add the following.

וּכְתוֹב לְחַיִּים טוֹבִים כָּל בְּנֵי בְרִיתֶךָ.

[If forgotten, do not repeat *Shemoneh Esrei.* See *Laws* §61.]

Bend the knees at בָּרוּךְ; bow at אַתָּה; straighten up at 'ה.

וְכֹל הַחַיִּים יוֹדְוּךָ סֶּלָה, וִיהַלְלוּ אֶת שִׁמְךָ בֶּאֱמֶת, הָאֵל יְשׁוּעָתֵנוּ וְעֶזְרָתֵנוּ סֶלָה. בָּרוּךְ אַתָּה יהוה, הַטּוֹב שִׁמְךָ וּלְךָ נָאֶה לְהוֹדוֹת.

שלום

שָׁלוֹם רָב עַל יִשְׂרָאֵל עַמְּךָ תָּשִׂים לְעוֹלָם, כִּי אַתָּה הוּא מֶלֶךְ אָדוֹן לְכָל הַשָּׁלוֹם. וְטוֹב בְּעֵינֶיךָ לְבָרֵךְ אֶת עַמְּךָ יִשְׂרָאֵל בְּכָל עֵת וּבְכָל שָׁעָה בִּשְׁלוֹמֶךָ. °בָּרוּךְ אַתָּה יהוה, הַמְּבָרֵךְ אֶת עַמּוֹ יִשְׂרָאֵל בַּשָּׁלוֹם.

°From Rosh Hashanah to Yom Kippur substitute the following [see *Laws* §65]:

בְּסֵפֶר חַיִּים בְּרָכָה וְשָׁלוֹם, וּפַרְנָסָה טוֹבָה, נִזָּכֵר וְנִכָּתֵב לְפָנֶיךָ, אֲנַחְנוּ וְכָל עַמְּךָ בֵּית יִשְׂרָאֵל, לְחַיִּים טוֹבִים וּלְשָׁלוֹם. בָּרוּךְ אַתָּה יהוה, עוֹשֵׂה הַשָּׁלוֹם.

[If forgotten, do not repeat *Shemoneh Esrei.* See *Laws* §61.]

יִהְיוּ לְרָצוֹן אִמְרֵי פִי וְהֶגְיוֹן לִבִּי לְפָנֶיךָ, יהוה צוּרִי וְגֹאֲלִי.[2]

אֱלֹהַי, נְצוֹר לְשׁוֹנִי מֵרָע, וּשְׂפָתַי מִדַּבֵּר מִרְמָה,[3] וְלִמְקַלְלַי נַפְשִׁי תִדּוֹם, וְנַפְשִׁי כֶּעָפָר לַכֹּל תִּהְיֶה. פְּתַח לִבִּי בְּתוֹרָתֶךָ, וּבְמִצְוֹתֶיךָ תִּרְדּוֹף נַפְשִׁי. וְכֹל הַחוֹשְׁבִים עָלַי רָעָה, מְהֵרָה הָפֵר עֲצָתָם וְקַלְקֵל מַחֲשַׁבְתָּם. עֲשֵׂה לְמַעַן שְׁמֶךָ, עֲשֵׂה לְמַעַן יְמִינֶךָ, עֲשֵׂה לְמַעַן קְדֻשָּׁתֶךָ, עֲשֵׂה לְמַעַן תּוֹרָתֶךָ. לְמַעַן יֵחָלְצוּן יְדִידֶיךָ, הוֹשִׁיעָה יְמִינְךָ וַעֲנֵנִי.[4]

Some recite verses pertaining to their names at this point. See page 924.

יִהְיוּ לְרָצוֹן אִמְרֵי פִי וְהֶגְיוֹן לִבִּי לְפָנֶיךָ, יהוה צוּרִי וְגֹאֲלִי.[2] עֹשֶׂה שָׁלוֹם בִּמְרוֹמָיו, הוּא יַעֲשֶׂה שָׁלוֹם עָלֵינוּ, וְעַל כָּל יִשְׂרָאֵל. וְאִמְרוּ: אָמֵן.

You delivered the strong into the hands of the weak, the many into the hands of the few, the impure into the hands of the pure, the wicked into the hands of the righteous, and the wanton into the hands of the diligent students of Your Torah. For Yourself You made a great and holy Name in Your world, and for Your people Israel You worked a great victory[1] and salvation as this very day. Thereafter, Your children came to the Holy of Holies of Your House, cleansed Your Temple, purified the site of Your Holiness and kindled lights in the Courtyards of Your Sanctuary; and they established these eight days of Chanukah to express thanks and praise to Your great Name.

[If forgotten, do not repeat *Shemoneh Esrei.*]

For all these, may Your Name be blessed and exalted, our King, continually forever and ever.

From Rosh Hashanah to Yom Kippur add the following.

And inscribe all the children of Your covenant for a good life.

[If forgotten, do not repeat *Shemoneh Esrei.* See *Laws* §61.]

Bend the knees at *'Blessed'*; bow at *'You'*; straighten up at *'HASHEM'*.

Everything alive will gratefully acknowledge You, Selah! and praise Your Name sincerely, O God of our salvation and help, Selah! Blessed are You, HASHEM, Your Name is 'The Beneficent One' and to You it is fitting to give thanks.

PEACE

שָׁלוֹם רָב *Establish abundant peace upon Your people Israel forever, for You are King, Master of all peace. May it be good in Your eyes to bless Your people Israel at every time and every hour with Your peace. °Blessed are You, HASHEM, Who blesses His people Israel with peace.*

°From Rosh Hashanah to Yom Kippur substitute the following [see *Laws* §65]:

In the book of life, blessing, and peace, and good livelihood, may we be remembered and inscribed before You — we and Your entire people the Family of Israel for a good life and for peace. Blessed are You, HASHEM, Who makes peace.

[If forgotten, do not repeat *Shemoneh Esrei.* See *Laws* §61.]

May the expressions of my mouth and the thoughts of my heart find favor before You, HASHEM, my Rock and my Redeemer.[2]

אֱלֹהַי *My God, guard my tongue from evil and my lips from speaking deceitfully.*[3] *To those who curse me, let my soul be silent; and let my soul be like dust to everyone. Open my heart to Your Torah, then my soul will pursue Your commandments. As for all those who design evil against me, speedily nullify their counsel and disrupt their design. Act for Your Name's sake; act for Your right hand's sake; act for Your sanctity's sake; act for Your Torah's sake. That Your beloved ones may be given rest; let Your right hand save, and respond to me.*[4]

Some recite verses pertaining to their names at this point. See page 924.

May the expressions of my mouth and the thoughts of my heart find favor before You, HASHEM, my Rock and my Redeemer.[2]

He Who makes peace in His heights, may He make peace upon us, and upon all Israel. Now respond: Amen.

---

(1) Cf. *I Samuel* 19:5. (2) *Psalms* 19:15. (3) Cf. 34:14. (4) 60:7; 108:7.

יְהִי רָצוֹן מִלְּפָנֶיךָ יהוה אֱלֹהֵינוּ וֵאלֹהֵי אֲבוֹתֵינוּ, שֶׁיִּבָּנֶה בֵּית הַמִּקְדָּשׁ בִּמְהֵרָה בְיָמֵינוּ, וְתֵן חֶלְקֵנוּ בְּתוֹרָתֶךָ. וְשָׁם נַעֲבָדְךָ בְּיִרְאָה, כִּימֵי עוֹלָם וּכְשָׁנִים קַדְמוֹנִיּוֹת. וְעָרְבָה לַיהוה מִנְחַת יְהוּדָה וִירוּשָׁלָיִם, כִּימֵי עוֹלָם וּכְשָׁנִים קַדְמוֹנִיּוֹת.[1]

Shemoneh Esrei ends here. *Chazzan* does not repeat *Shemoneh Esrei* at *Maariv*.

All present stand and recite וַיְכֻלּוּ aloud in unison. Conversation is forbidden during the congregation's recital of וַיְכֻלּוּ, until after the אָמֵן response to the blessing מְקַדֵּשׁ הַשַּׁבָּת (p. 348).

וַיְכֻלּוּ* הַשָּׁמַיִם וְהָאָרֶץ וְכָל צְבָאָם. וַיְכַל אֱלֹהִים בַּיּוֹם הַשְּׁבִיעִי מְלַאכְתּוֹ אֲשֶׁר עָשָׂה, וַיִּשְׁבֹּת בַּיּוֹם הַשְּׁבִיעִי מִכָּל מְלַאכְתּוֹ אֲשֶׁר עָשָׂה. וַיְבָרֶךְ אֱלֹהִים אֶת יוֹם הַשְּׁבִיעִי, וַיְקַדֵּשׁ אֹתוֹ, כִּי בוֹ שָׁבַת מִכָּל מְלַאכְתּוֹ, אֲשֶׁר בָּרָא אֱלֹהִים לַעֲשׂוֹת.[2]

ברכה מעין שבע

The following three paragraphs are omitted by an individual praying alone or by an occasional *minyan* (such as that in the home of a mourner). However, even in such cases, if one wishes to, he may recite the paragraph מָגֵן אָבוֹת. The three paragraphs are also omitted on the first night of Pesach. (Some congregations recite הַלֵּל, p. 632, on the first night of Pesach.)

Chazzan continues:

בָּרוּךְ אַתָּה יהוה אֱלֹהֵינוּ וֵאלֹהֵי אֲבוֹתֵינוּ, אֱלֹהֵי אַבְרָהָם, אֱלֹהֵי יִצְחָק, וֵאלֹהֵי יַעֲקֹב, הָאֵל הַגָּדוֹל הַגִּבּוֹר וְהַנּוֹרָא, אֵל עֶלְיוֹן, קוֹנֵה שָׁמַיִם וָאָרֶץ.

Congregation, then *chazzan*:

מָגֵן אָבוֹת בִּדְבָרוֹ, מְחַיֵּה מֵתִים בְּמַאֲמָרוֹ, °הָאֵל הַקָּדוֹשׁ (°הַמֶּלֶךְ הַקָּדוֹשׁ — Rosh Hashanah to Yom Kippur) שֶׁאֵין כָּמוֹהוּ, הַמֵּנִיחַ לְעַמּוֹ בְּיוֹם שַׁבַּת קָדְשׁוֹ, כִּי בָם רָצָה לְהָנִיחַ לָהֶם. לְפָנָיו נַעֲבֹד בְּיִרְאָה וָפַחַד, וְנוֹדֶה לִשְׁמוֹ בְּכָל יוֹם תָּמִיד מֵעֵין הַבְּרָכוֹת. אֵל הַהוֹדָאוֹת, אֲדוֹן הַשָּׁלוֹם, מְקַדֵּשׁ הַשַּׁבָּת וּמְבָרֵךְ שְׁבִיעִי, וּמֵנִיחַ בִּקְדֻשָּׁה לְעַם מְדֻשְּׁנֵי עֹנֶג, זֵכֶר לְמַעֲשֵׂה בְרֵאשִׁית.

⁂ וַיְכֻלּוּ — ... *were finished.* Although וַיְכֻלּוּ has been recited as part of *Shemoneh Esrei*, it is recited again afterward, because of times when a Festival falls on a Sabbath. On such days, וַיְכֻלּוּ is not part of the Festival *Shemoneh Esrei*, so it must be said afterward. In order not to differentiate between the Sabbath and Festival services, the Rabbis ordained that it be recited after *Shemoneh Esrei* at all times (*Tos. Pesachim* 106a, זוכרהו). *Ibn Yarchi* adds that it is a form of testimony that God created heaven and earth — and witnesses must give their testimony while standing and in a loud, clear voice.

Because of this paragraph's status as a testimony, it should preferably be said with the congregation, or at least in the company of one other person. However, it may be recited by an individual as well (*Orach Chaim* 268).

⁂ בְּרָכָה מֵעֵין שֶׁבַע / **The Seven-faceted Blessing**

In Talmudic times, the synagogues were generally located outside town limits, in open fields. Since it was dangerous to walk home alone in the dark after *Maariv*, the Sages instituted an extra prayer for the congregation so that everyone would stay a little longer, in case someone was slow in finishing his own *Maariv* (*Shabbos* 24b). On weekdays, the prayer בָּרוּךְ ה' לְעוֹלָם, *Blessed is* HASHEM *forever*, alludes to the number of blessings in the weekday *Shemoneh Esrei* (see p. 265). On the eve of the Sabbath, this

יְהִי רָצוֹן *May it be Your will,* HASHEM *our God and the God of our forefathers, that the Holy Temple be rebuilt, speedily in our days. Grant us our share in Your Torah, and may we serve You there with reverence, as in days of old and in former years. Then the offering of Judah and Jerusalem will be pleasing to* HASHEM, *as in days of old and in former years.*[1]

Shemoneh Esrei ends here. *Chazzan* does not repeat *Shemoneh Esrei* at *Maariv.*

All present stand and recite וַיְכֻלּוּ, *'Thus the Heaven ...,'* aloud in unison.
Conversation is forbidden during the congregation's recital of *'Thus ...'* until after the *'Amen'* response to the *chazzan's* blessing, *'Who sanctifies the Sabbath'* (p. 348).

וַיְכֻלּוּ *Thus the heaven and the earth were finished,* and all their legion. On the seventh day God completed His work which He had done, and He abstained on the seventh day from all His work which He had done. God blessed the seventh day and sanctified it, because on it He had abstained from all His work which God created to make.*[2]

THE SEVEN-FACETED BLESSING

The following three paragraphs are omitted by an individual praying alone or by an occasional *minyan* (such as that in the home of a mourner). However, even in such cases, if one wishes to, he may recite the paragraph מָגֵן אָבוֹת, *He Who was.* The three paragraphs are also omitted on the first night of Pesach. (Some congregations recite *Hallel,* p. 632, on the first night of Pesach.)

Chazzan continues:

בָּרוּךְ *Blessed are You,* HASHEM, *our God and the God of our forefathers, God of Abraham, God of Isaac, and God of Jacob; the great, might, and awesome God, the supreme God, Creator of heaven and earth.* Possessor!

Congregation, then *chazzan:*

מָגֵן *He Who was the shield of our forefathers with His word, Who resuscitates the dead with His utterance, °the Holy God (*from Rosh Hashanah to Yom Kippur substitute: *°the Holy King) Who is unequalled, Who grants rest to His people on His holy Sabbath day, for He was pleased with them to grant them rest. Before Him we will serve with awe and dread and give thanks to His Name every day continually with appropriate blessings. God of grateful praise, Master of peace, Who sanctifies the Sabbath and blesses the seventh day, and gives rest with holiness to a people saturated with delight — in memory of the work of Creation.*

(1) *Malachi* 3:4. (2) *Genesis* 2:1-3.

---

extra prayer was formulated as a synopsis of the seven blessings of the *Shemoneh Esrei.* It begins בָּרוּךְ אַתָּה ה׳, which is very similar to the beginning of *Shemoneh Esrei.* Then it continues with מָגֵן אָבוֹת, which has seven parts, as follows:
(1) מָגֵן אָבוֹת, *Shield of our forefathers* = the blessing of אָבוֹת, *forefathers;*
(2) מְחַיֵּה מֵתִים, *Who resuscitates the dead* = the blessing of resuscitation;
(3) הָאֵל הַקָּדוֹשׁ, *The holy God* = the blessing of His holiness;
(4) הַמֵּנִיחַ לְעַמּוֹ, *Who grants rest to His people* = קְדוּשַׁת הַיּוֹם, the intermediate blessing, which discusses the Sabbath;
(5) לְפָנָיו נַעֲבוֹד, *Before Him we serve* = רְצֵה, which appeals for *acceptance* of our service;
(6) וְנוֹדֶה לִשְׁמוֹ, *And give thanks to His Name* = the blessing of מוֹדִים, which *thanks* God for His many favors;
(7) אֲדוֹן הַשָּׁלוֹם, *Master of peace* = שָׁלוֹם רָב, the last blessing, which speaks of *peace.*

If a Festival falls on the Sabbath, this prayer is recited without any mention of the Festival, because the Sages did not compose a separate seven-faceted blessing for Festivals. However, if the Seder night of Pesach falls on a Sabbath eve, only וַיְכֻלּוּ is recited. The seven-faceted blessing is omitted because Pesach is לֵיל שִׁמּוּרִים, *a night of protection,* a time when Jews are protected against ordinary dangers.

Chazzan continues:

אֱלֹהֵינוּ וֵאלֹהֵי אֲבוֹתֵינוּ רְצֵה בִמְנוּחָתֵנוּ. קַדְּשֵׁנוּ בְּמִצְוֹתֶיךָ, וְתֵן חֶלְקֵנוּ בְּתוֹרָתֶךָ. שַׂבְּעֵנוּ מִטּוּבֶךָ, וְשַׂמְּחֵנוּ בִּישׁוּעָתֶךָ, וְטַהֵר לִבֵּנוּ לְעָבְדְּךָ בֶּאֱמֶת. וְהַנְחִילֵנוּ יהוה אֱלֹהֵינוּ בְּאַהֲבָה וּבְרָצוֹן שַׁבַּת קָדְשֶׁךָ, וְיָנוּחוּ בָהּ יִשְׂרָאֵל מְקַדְּשֵׁי שְׁמֶךָ. בָּרוּךְ אַתָּה יהוה, מְקַדֵּשׁ הַשַּׁבָּת. (Cong.— אָמֵן.)

The *chazzan* recites קַדִּישׁ שָׁלֵם:

יִתְגַּדַּל וְיִתְקַדַּשׁ שְׁמֵהּ רַבָּא. (Cong.— אָמֵן.) בְּעָלְמָא דִּי בְרָא כִרְעוּתֵהּ. וְיַמְלִיךְ מַלְכוּתֵהּ, בְּחַיֵּיכוֹן וּבְיוֹמֵיכוֹן וּבְחַיֵּי דְכָל בֵּית יִשְׂרָאֵל, בַּעֲגָלָא וּבִזְמַן קָרִיב. וְאִמְרוּ: אָמֵן.

(Cong.— אָמֵן. יְהֵא שְׁמֵהּ רַבָּא מְבָרַךְ לְעָלַם וּלְעָלְמֵי עָלְמַיָּא.)

יְהֵא שְׁמֵהּ רַבָּא מְבָרַךְ לְעָלַם וּלְעָלְמֵי עָלְמַיָּא.

יִתְבָּרַךְ וְיִשְׁתַּבַּח וְיִתְפָּאַר וְיִתְרוֹמַם וְיִתְנַשֵּׂא וְיִתְהַדָּר וְיִתְעַלֶּה וְיִתְהַלָּל שְׁמֵהּ דְּקֻדְשָׁא בְּרִיךְ הוּא (Cong.— בְּרִיךְ הוּא) — °לְעֵלָּא מִן כָּל (From Rosh Hashanah to Yom Kippur substitute— °לְעֵלָּא וּלְעֵלָּא מִכָּל) בִּרְכָתָא וְשִׁירָתָא תֻּשְׁבְּחָתָא וְנֶחֱמָתָא, דַּאֲמִירָן בְּעָלְמָא. וְאִמְרוּ: אָמֵן. (Cong.— אָמֵן.)

(Cong.— קַבֵּל בְּרַחֲמִים וּבְרָצוֹן אֶת תְּפִלָּתֵנוּ.)

תִּתְקַבֵּל צְלוֹתְהוֹן וּבָעוּתְהוֹן דְּכָל בֵּית יִשְׂרָאֵל קֳדָם אֲבוּהוֹן דִּי בִשְׁמַיָּא. וְאִמְרוּ: אָמֵן. (Cong.— אָמֵן.)

(Cong.— יְהִי שֵׁם יהוה מְבֹרָךְ, מֵעַתָּה וְעַד עוֹלָם.[1])

יְהֵא שְׁלָמָא רַבָּא מִן שְׁמַיָּא, וְחַיִּים עָלֵינוּ וְעַל כָּל יִשְׂרָאֵל. וְאִמְרוּ: אָמֵן. (Cong.— אָמֵן.)

(Cong.— עֶזְרִי מֵעִם יהוה, עֹשֵׂה שָׁמַיִם וָאָרֶץ.[2])

Take three steps back. Bow left and say ... עֹשֶׂה; bow right and say ... הוּא; bow forward and say וְעַל כָּל ... אָמֵן. Remain standing in place for a few moments, then take three steps forward.

עֹשֶׂה שָׁלוֹם בִּמְרוֹמָיו, הוּא יַעֲשֶׂה שָׁלוֹם עָלֵינוּ, וְעַל כָּל יִשְׂרָאֵל. וְאִמְרוּ: אָמֵן. (Cong.— אָמֵן.)

קידוש לליל שבת בבית הכנסת

In most congregations, the *chazzan* recites *Kiddush*. The Sabbath *Kiddush* appears below; the *Kiddush* for Succos, p. 722; for other Festivals, p. 656.

סַבְרִי מָרָנָן וְרַבָּנָן וְרַבּוֹתַי.

בָּרוּךְ אַתָּה יהוה אֱלֹהֵינוּ מֶלֶךְ הָעוֹלָם, בּוֹרֵא פְּרִי הַגָּפֶן. (Cong.— אָמֵן.)

בָּרוּךְ אַתָּה יהוה אֱלֹהֵינוּ מֶלֶךְ הָעוֹלָם, אֲשֶׁר קִדְּשָׁנוּ בְּמִצְוֹתָיו, וְרָצָה בָנוּ, וְשַׁבַּת קָדְשׁוֹ בְּאַהֲבָה וּבְרָצוֹן הִנְחִילָנוּ, זִכָּרוֹן לְמַעֲשֵׂה בְרֵאשִׁית. כִּי הוּא יוֹם תְּחִלָּה לְמִקְרָאֵי קֹדֶשׁ, זֵכֶר לִיצִיאַת מִצְרָיִם. כִּי בָנוּ בָחַרְתָּ, וְאוֹתָנוּ קִדַּשְׁתָּ, מִכָּל הָעַמִּים. וְשַׁבַּת קָדְשְׁךָ בְּאַהֲבָה וּבְרָצוֹן

Chazzan continues:

אֱלֹהֵינוּ *Our God and the God of our forefathers, may You be pleased with our rest. Sanctify us with Your commandments and grant us our share in Your Torah; satisfy us from Your goodness and gladden us with Your salvation, and purify our heart to serve You sincerely. O* HASHEM, *our God, with love and favor grant us Your holy Sabbath as a heritage and may Israel, the sanctifiers of Your Name, rest on it. Blessed are You,* HASHEM, *Who sanctifies the Sabbath.* (Cong.— *Amen.*)

The chazzan recites the Full Kaddish:

יִתְגַּדַּל *May His great Name grow exalted and sanctified* (Cong.— *Amen.*) *in the world that He created as He willed. May He give reign to His kingship in your lifetimes and in your days, and in the lifetimes of the entire Family of Israel, swiftly and soon. Now respond: Amen.*

(Cong.— *Amen. May His great Name be blessed forever and ever.*)

May His great Name be blessed forever and ever.

Blessed, praised, glorified, exalted, extolled, mighty, upraised, and lauded be the Name of the Holy One, Blessed is He (Cong.— *Blessed is He*) — (From Rosh Hashanah to Yom Kippur add: *exceedingly*) *beyond any blessing and song, praise and consolation that are uttered in the world. Now respond: Amen.* (Cong.— *Amen.*)

(Cong.— *Accept our prayers with mercy and favor.*)

May the prayers and supplications of the entire Family of Israel be accepted before their Father Who is in Heaven. Now respond: Amen. (Cong.— *Amen.*)

(Cong.— *Blessed be the Name of* HASHEM, *from this time and forever.*[1])

May there be abundant peace from Heaven, and life, upon us and upon all Israel. Now respond: Amen. (Cong.— *Amen.*)

(Cong.— *My help is from* HASHEM, *Maker of heaven and earth.*[2])

Take three steps back. Bow left and say, *'He Who makes peace ...'*; bow right and say, *'may He ...'*; bow forward and say, *'and upon all Israel ...'* Remain standing in place for a few moments, then take three steps forward.

He Who makes peace in His heights, may He make peace upon us, and upon all Israel. Now respond: Amen. (Cong.— *Amen.*)

SABBATH EVE KIDDUSH IN THE SYNAGOGUE

In most congregations, the *chazzan* recites *Kiddush*. The Sabbath *Kiddush* appears below; the *Kiddush* for Succos, p. 722; for other Festivals, p. 656.

By your leave, my masters and teachers,

בָּרוּךְ *Blessed are You,* HASHEM, *our God, King of the universe, Who creates the fruit of the vine.* (Cong.— *Amen.*)

בָּרוּךְ *Blessed are You,* HASHEM, *our God, King of the universe, Who sanctified us with His commandments, took pleasure in us, and with love and favor gave us His holy Sabbath as a heritage, a remembrance of creation. For that day is the prologue to the holy convocations, a memorial of the Exodus from Egypt. For us did you choose and us did You sanctify from all the nations. And Your holy Sabbath, with love and favor*

(1) *Psalm* 113:2. (2) 121:2.

הַנְחַלְתָּנוּ. בָּרוּךְ אַתָּה יהוה, מְקַדֵּשׁ הַשַּׁבָּת. (Cong.— אָמֵן.)

The *chazzan* should not drink the *Kiddush* wine, but should give some to a child who has listened to *Kiddush* and responded אָמֵן. If no child is present, the *chazzan* himself should drink the wine. In either case, he should recite *Kiddush* again at home for the benefit of his family.

Between Pesach and Shavuos, the *Omer* is counted (p. 282).

The congregation stands while reciting עָלֵינוּ.

עָלֵינוּ לְשַׁבֵּחַ לַאֲדוֹן הַכֹּל, לָתֵת גְּדֻלָּה לְיוֹצֵר בְּרֵאשִׁית, שֶׁלֹּא עָשָׂנוּ כְּגוֹיֵי הָאֲרָצוֹת, וְלֹא שָׂמָנוּ כְּמִשְׁפְּחוֹת הָאֲדָמָה. שֶׁלֹּא שָׂם חֶלְקֵנוּ כָּהֶם, וְגוֹרָלֵנוּ כְּכָל הֲמוֹנָם. (שֶׁהֵם מִשְׁתַּחֲוִים לְהֶבֶל וָרִיק, וּמִתְפַּלְּלִים אֶל אֵל לֹא יוֹשִׁיעַ.[1]) וַאֲנַחְנוּ כּוֹרְעִים וּמִשְׁתַּחֲוִים וּמוֹדִים, לִפְנֵי מֶלֶךְ מַלְכֵי הַמְּלָכִים הַקָּדוֹשׁ בָּרוּךְ הוּא. שֶׁהוּא נוֹטֶה שָׁמַיִם וְיֹסֵד אָרֶץ,[2] וּמוֹשַׁב יְקָרוֹ בַּשָּׁמַיִם מִמַּעַל, וּשְׁכִינַת עֻזּוֹ בְּגָבְהֵי מְרוֹמִים. הוּא אֱלֹהֵינוּ, אֵין עוֹד. אֱמֶת מַלְכֵּנוּ, אֶפֶס זוּלָתוֹ, כַּכָּתוּב בְּתוֹרָתוֹ: וְיָדַעְתָּ הַיּוֹם וַהֲשֵׁבֹתָ אֶל לְבָבֶךָ, כִּי יהוה הוּא הָאֱלֹהִים בַּשָּׁמַיִם מִמַּעַל וְעַל הָאָרֶץ מִתָּחַת, אֵין עוֹד.[3]

Bow while reciting וַאֲנַחְנוּ כּוֹרְעִים וּמִשְׁתַּחֲוִים.

עַל כֵּן נְקַוֶּה לְּךָ יהוה אֱלֹהֵינוּ לִרְאוֹת מְהֵרָה בְּתִפְאֶרֶת עֻזֶּךָ, לְהַעֲבִיר גִּלּוּלִים מִן הָאָרֶץ, וְהָאֱלִילִים כָּרוֹת יִכָּרֵתוּן, לְתַקֵּן עוֹלָם בְּמַלְכוּת שַׁדַּי. וְכָל בְּנֵי בָשָׂר יִקְרְאוּ בִשְׁמֶךָ, לְהַפְנוֹת אֵלֶיךָ כָּל רִשְׁעֵי אָרֶץ. יַכִּירוּ וְיֵדְעוּ כָּל יוֹשְׁבֵי תֵבֵל, כִּי לְךָ תִּכְרַע כָּל בֶּרֶךְ, תִּשָּׁבַע כָּל לָשׁוֹן.[4] לְפָנֶיךָ יהוה אֱלֹהֵינוּ יִכְרְעוּ וְיִפֹּלוּ, וְלִכְבוֹד שִׁמְךָ יְקָר יִתֵּנוּ. וִיקַבְּלוּ כֻלָּם אֶת עוֹל מַלְכוּתֶךָ, וְתִמְלֹךְ עֲלֵיהֶם מְהֵרָה לְעוֹלָם וָעֶד. כִּי הַמַּלְכוּת שֶׁלְּךָ הִיא וּלְעוֹלְמֵי עַד תִּמְלוֹךְ בְּכָבוֹד, כַּכָּתוּב בְּתוֹרָתֶךָ: יהוה יִמְלֹךְ לְעֹלָם וָעֶד.[5] וְנֶאֱמַר: וְהָיָה יהוה לְמֶלֶךְ עַל כָּל הָאָרֶץ, בַּיּוֹם הַהוּא יִהְיֶה יהוה אֶחָד וּשְׁמוֹ אֶחָד.[6]

In some congregations the following is recited after עָלֵינוּ:

אַל תִּירָא מִפַּחַד פִּתְאֹם, וּמִשֹּׁאַת רְשָׁעִים כִּי תָבֹא.[7] עֻצוּ עֵצָה וְתֻפָר, דַּבְּרוּ דָבָר וְלֹא יָקוּם, כִּי עִמָּנוּ אֵל.[8] וְעַד זִקְנָה אֲנִי הוּא, וְעַד שֵׂיבָה אֲנִי אֶסְבֹּל, אֲנִי עָשִׂיתִי וַאֲנִי אֶשָּׂא, וַאֲנִי אֶסְבֹּל וַאֲמַלֵּט.[9]

did You give us as a heritage. Blessed are You, HASHEM, Who sanctifies the Sabbath. (Cong.— *Amen.)*

The *chazzan* should not drink the *Kiddush* wine, but should give some to a child who has listened to *Kiddush* and responded, *'Amen'.* If no child is present, the *chazzan* himself should drink the wine. In either case, he should recite *Kiddush* again at home for the benefit of his family.

Between Pesach and Shavuos, the *Omer* is counted (p. 282).

The congregation stands while reciting עָלֵינוּ, *'It is our duty ...'*

עָלֵינוּ *It is our duty to praise the Master of all, to ascribe greatness to the Molder of primeval creation, for He has not made us like the nations of the lands and has not emplaced us like the families of the earth; for He has not assigned our portion like theirs nor our lot like all their multitudes. (For they bow to vanity and emptiness and pray to a god which helps not.[1]) But we bend our knees, bow, and acknowledge our thanks before the King Who reigns over kings, the Holy One, Blessed is He. He stretches out heaven and establishes earth's foundation,[2] the seat of His homage is in the heavens above and His powerful Presence is in the loftiest heights. He is our God and there is none other. True is our King, there is nothing beside Him, as it is written in His Torah: 'You are to know this day and take to your heart that HASHEM is the only God — in heaven above and on the earth below — there is none other.'[3]*

Bow while reciting *'But we bend our knees.'*

עַל כֵּן *Therefore we put our hope in You, HASHEM our God, that we may soon see Your mighty splendor, to remove detestable idolatry from the earth, and false gods will be utterly cut off, to perfect the universe through the Almighty's sovereignty. Then all humanity will call upon Your Name, to turn all the earth's wicked toward You. All the world's inhabitants will recognize and know that to You every knee should bend, every tongue should swear.[4] Before You, HASHEM, our God, they will bend every knee and cast themselves down and to the glory of Your Name they will render homage, and they will all accept upon themselves the yoke of Your kingship that You may reign over them soon and eternally. For the kingdom is Yours and You will reign for all eternity in glory as it is written in Your Torah: HASHEM shall reign for all eternity.[5] And it is said: HASHEM will be King over all the world — on that day HASHEM will be One and His Name will be One.[6]*

In some congregations the following is recited after *Aleinu:*

אַל תִּירָא *Do not fear sudden terror, or the holocaust of the wicked when it comes.[7] Plan a conspiracy and it will be annulled; speak your piece and it shall not stand, for God is with us.[8] Even till your seniority, I remain unchanged; and even till your ripe old age, I shall endure. I created you and I shall bear you; I shall endure and rescue.[9]*

(1) *Isaiah* 45:20. (2) 51:13. (3) *Deuteronomy* 4:39. (4) Cf. *Isaiah* 45:23. (5) *Exodus* 15:18. (6) *Zechariah* 14:9. (7) *Proverbs* 3:25. (8) *Isaiah* 8:10. (9) 46:4.

קדיש יתום

In the presence of a *minyan*, mourners recite קַדִּישׁ יָתוֹם, the Mourner's *Kaddish* (see *Laws* §119):

יִתְגַּדַּל וְיִתְקַדַּשׁ שְׁמֵהּ רַבָּא. (.Cong.— אָמֵן.) בְּעָלְמָא דִּי בְרָא כִרְעוּתֵהּ. וְיַמְלִיךְ מַלְכוּתֵהּ, בְּחַיֵּיכוֹן וּבְיוֹמֵיכוֹן וּבְחַיֵּי דְכָל בֵּית יִשְׂרָאֵל, בַּעֲגָלָא וּבִזְמַן קָרִיב. וְאִמְרוּ: אָמֵן.

(.Cong.— אָמֵן. יְהֵא שְׁמֵהּ רַבָּא מְבָרַךְ לְעָלַם וּלְעָלְמֵי עָלְמַיָּא.)

יְהֵא שְׁמֵהּ רַבָּא מְבָרַךְ לְעָלַם וּלְעָלְמֵי עָלְמַיָּא.

יִתְבָּרַךְ וְיִשְׁתַּבַּח וְיִתְפָּאַר וְיִתְרוֹמַם וְיִתְנַשֵּׂא וְיִתְהַדָּר וְיִתְעַלֶּה וְיִתְהַלָּל שְׁמֵהּ דְּקֻדְשָׁא בְּרִיךְ הוּא (.Cong.— בְּרִיךְ הוּא) — °לְעֵלָּא מִן כָּל (From Rosh Hashanah to Yom Kippur substitute— °לְעֵלָּא וּלְעֵלָּא מִכָּל) בִּרְכָתָא וְשִׁירָתָא תֻּשְׁבְּחָתָא וְנֶחֱמָתָא, דַּאֲמִירָן בְּעָלְמָא. וְאִמְרוּ: אָמֵן. (.Cong.— אָמֵן.)

יְהֵא שְׁלָמָא רַבָּא מִן שְׁמַיָּא, וְחַיִּים עָלֵינוּ וְעַל כָּל יִשְׂרָאֵל. וְאִמְרוּ: אָמֵן. (.Cong.— אָמֵן.)

Take three steps back. Bow left and say ... עֹשֶׂה; bow right and say ... הוּא; bow forward and say וְעַל כָּל ... אָמֵן. Remain standing in place for a few moments, then take three steps forward.

עֹשֶׂה שָׁלוֹם בִּמְרוֹמָיו, הוּא יַעֲשֶׂה שָׁלוֹם עָלֵינוּ, וְעַל כָּל יִשְׂרָאֵל. וְאִמְרוּ: אָמֵן. (.Cong.— אָמֵן.)

Between Rosh Chodesh Elul and Shemini Atzeres, לְדָוִד (*Psalm* 27) is recited; see p. 282.

אֲדוֹן עוֹלָם* אֲשֶׁר מָלַךְ, בְּטֶרֶם כָּל יְצִיר נִבְרָא.
לְעֵת נַעֲשָׂה בְחֶפְצוֹ כֹּל, אֲזַי מֶלֶךְ שְׁמוֹ נִקְרָא.
וְאַחֲרֵי כִּכְלוֹת הַכֹּל, לְבַדּוֹ יִמְלוֹךְ נוֹרָא.
וְהוּא הָיָה וְהוּא הֹוֶה, וְהוּא יִהְיֶה בְּתִפְאָרָה.
וְהוּא אֶחָד וְאֵין שֵׁנִי, לְהַמְשִׁיל לוֹ לְהַחְבִּירָה.
בְּלִי רֵאשִׁית בְּלִי תַכְלִית, וְלוֹ הָעֹז וְהַמִּשְׂרָה.
וְהוּא אֵלִי וְחַי גֹּאֲלִי, וְצוּר חֶבְלִי בְּעֵת צָרָה.
וְהוּא נִסִּי וּמָנוֹס לִי, מְנָת כּוֹסִי בְּיוֹם אֶקְרָא.
בְּיָדוֹ אַפְקִיד רוּחִי, בְּעֵת אִישַׁן וְאָעִירָה.
וְעִם רוּחִי גְּוִיָּתִי, יהוה לִי וְלֹא אִירָא.

אֲדוֹן עוֹלָם ◆ — The theme of this beautiful poem of praise has motivated many communities to adopt it as the concluding part of *Kabbalas Shabbos. Adon Olam* proclaims God as the One and the Eternal; He existed before Creation and He will survive every form of material existence. Since observance of the Sabbath is Israel's way of bearing witness to God as the Creator, it is fitting that one leave the synagogue bearing the message of God's eternal sovereignty. The recitation of *Adon Olam* now has a further significance. During the week, we begin the day before *Shacharis* and end it after the Bedtime *Shema* by reciting *Adon Olam.* By reciting it

MOURNER'S KADDISH

In the presence of a *minyan,* mourners recite the Mourner's *Kaddish* (see *Laws* §119):

[A transliteration of this *Kaddish* appears on page 1043; commentary on page 57.]

יִתְגַּדַּל *May His great Name grow exalted and sanctified* (Cong.— *Amen.*) *in the world that He created as He willed. May He give reign to His kingship in your lifetimes and in your days, and in the lifetimes of the entire Family of Israel, swiftly and soon. Now respond: Amen.*

(Cong.— *Amen. May His great Name be blessed forever and ever.*)

May His great Name be blessed forever and ever.

Blessed, praised, glorified, exalted, extolled, mighty, upraised, and lauded be the Name of the Holy One, Blessed is He (Cong.— *Blessed is He*) — (From Rosh Hashanah to Yom Kippur add: *exceedingly*) *beyond any blessing and song, praise and consolation that are uttered in the world. Now respond: Amen.* (Cong.— *Amen.*)

May there be abundant peace from Heaven, and life, upon us and upon all Israel. Now respond: Amen. (Cong.— *Amen.*)

Take three steps back. Bow left and say, *'He Who makes peace ...';* bow right and say, *'may He ...';* bow forward and say, *'and upon all Israel ...'* Remain standing in place for a few moments, then take three steps forward.

He Who makes peace in His heights, may He make peace upon us, and upon all Israel. Now respond: Amen. (Cong.— *Amen.*)

Between Rosh Chodesh Elul and Shemini Atzeres, לְדָוִד (*Psalm* 27) is recited; see p. 282.

אֲדוֹן עוֹלָם* *Master of the universe, Who reigned*
before any form was created,
At the time when His will brought all into being —
then as 'King' was His Name proclaimed.
After all has ceased to be,
He, the Awesome One, will reign alone.
It is He Who was, He Who is,
and He Who shall remain, in splendor.
He is One — there is no second
to compare to Him, to declare as His equal.
Without beginning, without conclusion —
His is the power and dominion.
He is my God, my living Redeemer,
Rock of my pain in time of distress.
He is my banner, a refuge for me,
the portion in my cup on the day I call.
Into His hand I shall entrust my spirit
when I go to sleep — and I shall awaken!
With my spirit shall my body remain.
HASHEM is with me, I shall not fear.

---

now at the inauguration of the Sabbath, we signify that this is not the start of just one more day, but that the Sabbath is on a far higher spiritual level, and therefore represents a new beginning in our service of God (see commentary on p. 12).

ברכת הבנים

There is a widespread custom for parents to bless their children — young and old — upon returning from the synagogue on the eve of the Sabbath.

For a boy:

יְשִׂמְךָ אֱלֹהִים
כְּאֶפְרַיִם וְכִמְנַשֶּׁה.*[1]

For a girl:

יְשִׂמֵךְ אֱלֹהִים
כְּשָׂרָה רִבְקָה רָחֵל וְלֵאָה.*

יְבָרֶכְךָ יהוה* וְיִשְׁמְרֶךָ.
יָאֵר יהוה פָּנָיו אֵלֶיךָ וִיחֻנֶּךָּ.
יִשָּׂא יהוה פָּנָיו אֵלֶיךָ, וְיָשֵׂם לְךָ שָׁלוֹם.[2]

סעודת ליל שבת

The meal is opened with this greeting to the two angels that escort each Jew home from the synagogue on the Sabbath eve. Each of the four stanzas is recited three times.

שָׁלוֹם עֲלֵיכֶם, מַלְאֲכֵי הַשָּׁרֵת, מַלְאֲכֵי עֶלְיוֹן,* מִמֶּלֶךְ מַלְכֵי הַמְּלָכִים הַקָּדוֹשׁ בָּרוּךְ הוּא.

בּוֹאֲכֶם לְשָׁלוֹם,* מַלְאֲכֵי הַשָּׁלוֹם*, מַלְאֲכֵי עֶלְיוֹן, מִמֶּלֶךְ מַלְכֵי הַמְּלָכִים הַקָּדוֹשׁ בָּרוּךְ הוּא.

בָּרְכוּנִי לְשָׁלוֹם,* מַלְאֲכֵי הַשָּׁלוֹם, מַלְאֲכֵי עֶלְיוֹן, מִמֶּלֶךְ מַלְכֵי הַמְּלָכִים הַקָּדוֹשׁ בָּרוּךְ הוּא.

צֵאתְכֶם לְשָׁלוֹם, מַלְאֲכֵי הַשָּׁלוֹם, מַלְאֲכֵי עֶלְיוֹן, מִמֶּלֶךְ מַלְכֵי הַמְּלָכִים הַקָּדוֹשׁ בָּרוּךְ הוּא.

בִּרְכַּת הַבָּנִים / BLESSING OF THE CHILDREN

The flow of Divine beneficence and blessing which comes with the beginning of the Sabbath makes it a particularly auspicious time for such blessings.

When conferring the blessing, parents should have in mind a silent prayer that they should be able to raise their children and grandchildren to lives of Torah, marriage and good deeds. Both hands should be laid upon the head of the child to signify that the blessing is conveyed with complete generosity of spirit.

יְשִׂמְךָ אֱלֹהִים כְּאֶפְרַיִם וְכִמְנַשֶּׁה — *May God make you like Ephraim and Menashe.* This is the blessing that the Patriarch Jacob conferred upon his grandchildren, the two sons of Joseph and the first Jews born and raised in exile. What is more, they grew to be sources of pride to the Patriarch, despite having been raised in Pharaoh's court at a time when there was no Jewish religious life in Egypt except for the intimacy of their own family. Jacob himself indicated that this blessing should be given by Jewish parents to their children throughout history.

יְשִׂמֵךְ אֱלֹהִים כְּשָׂרָה רִבְקָה רָחֵל וְלֵאָה — *May God make you like Sarah, Rebecca, Rachel and Leah.* Unlike that of sons, this blessing is not a Scriptural quote. However, it is logical to wish Jewish girls that they be like the Matriarchs who grew up in alien surroundings and surmounted infertility and other distress to become the mothers of the nation.

יְבָרֶכְךָ ה׳ — *May HASHEM bless you.* These verses form the Priestly Blessings (see p. 116). The priests in the Temple were designated as the instruments through which God allows His blessing to rest upon Israel. Similarly, parents in their own families serve as agents to bestow God's blessing upon their children.

סְעוּדַת לֵיל שַׁבָּת / SABBATH EVE MEAL

שָׁלוֹם עֲלֵיכֶם / Shalom Aleichem

The Talmud teaches that two ministering angels — one good and one evil — escort a person home from the synagogue on the eve of the Sabbath. If a Jew arrives home and finds a kindled lamp, a set table, and a made bed, the good angel says, May it be [God's] will that it

BLESSING OF THE CHILDREN

There is a widespread custom for parents to bless their children — young and old — upon returning from the synagogue on the eve of the Sabbath.

For a boy:

May God make you like Ephraim and Menashe.[*1]

For a girl:

*May God make you like Sarah, Rebecca, Rachel and Leah.**

May HASHEM *bless you* and safeguard you.*
May HASHEM *illuminate His countenance for you and be gracious to you.*
May HASHEM *turn His countenance to you and establish peace for you.*[2]

SABBATH EVE MEAL

The meal is opened with this greeting to the two angels that escort each Jew home from the synagogue on the Sabbath eve. Each of the four stanzas is recited three times.

שָׁלוֹם עֲלֵיכֶם *Peace upon you, O ministering angels, angels of the Exalted One* — from the King Who reigns over kings, the Holy One, Blessed is He.*

בּוֹאֲכֶם לְשָׁלוֹם *May your coming be for peace,* O angels of peace,* angels of the Exalted One — from the King who reigns over kings, the Holy One, Blessed is He.*

בָּרְכוּנִי לְשָׁלוֹם *Bless me for peace,* O angels of peace, angels of the Exalted One — from the King Who reigns over kings, the Holy One, Blessed is He.*

צֵאתְכֶם לְשָׁלוֹם *May your departure be to peace, O angels of peace, angels of the Exalted One — from the King who reigns over kings, the Holy One, Blessed is He.*

(1) *Genesis* 48:20. (2) *Numbers* 6:24-26.

also be so next Sabbath.' The evil angel is compelled to answer, 'Amen.' But if not — then the evil angel says, 'May it be [God's] will that it also be so next Sabbath.' The good angel is compelled to answer, 'Amen' (*Shabbos* 119b).

The *Shalom Aleichem* song is based on the above passage. If every Jew is accompanied home by two ministering angels, then it is only proper that he greet them, bless them, and seek their blessing. The *zemer* is of comparatively recent origin, apparently composed by the Kabbalists of the seventeenth century. [For a full exposition, see the ArtScroll *Zemiroth.*]

מַלְאֲכֵי עֶלְיוֹן — *Angels of the Exalted One,* i.e., of God.

בּוֹאֲכֶם לְשָׁלוֹם — *May your coming be for peace.* If a Jewish home is worthy of the Sabbath's holiness, even the *angels* gain the blessings of peace that emanate from the meritorious deed.

מַלְאֲכֵי הַשָּׁלוֹם — *Angels of peace.* Whereas the first stanza referred to *'ministering' angels,* this one speaks to *angels of 'peace'. Rabbi Isaac of Komarna* explains that each stanza is addressed to a different set of angels. The first stanza of the song refers to the entire heavenly host, the infinite heavenly beings who stand in the service of God. This second stanza, as well as the succeeding ones, is directed specifically to the angels who accompany the Jew to his home when the Sabbath begins.

בָּרְכוּנִי לְשָׁלוֹם — *Bless me for peace.* This is not a request for an angelic blessing in the usual sense, but should be understood as follows:

If the escorting angels are pleased with the Sabbath preparations awaiting them, they extend the blessing that it may be equally so in succeeding weeks. This is in recognition of man's achievement and is a good wish for the future. In seeking this 'blessing' from the angels we do no more than express the hope that our efforts have met with their approval.

כִּי מַלְאָכָיו יְצַוֶּה לָּךְ,* לִשְׁמָרְךָ בְּכָל דְּרָכֶיךָ.[1]
יהוה יִשְׁמָר צֵאתְךָ וּבוֹאֶךָ, מֵעַתָּה וְעַד עוֹלָם.[2]

רִבּוֹן כָּל הָעוֹלָמִים,* אֲדוֹן כָּל הַנְּשָׁמוֹת, אֲדוֹן הַשָּׁלוֹם,* מֶלֶךְ אַבִּיר,* מֶלֶךְ בָּרוּךְ, מֶלֶךְ גָּדוֹל, מֶלֶךְ דּוֹבֵר שָׁלוֹם, מֶלֶךְ הָדוּר, מֶלֶךְ וָתִיק, מֶלֶךְ זָךְ, מֶלֶךְ חֵי הָעוֹלָמִים, מֶלֶךְ טוֹב וּמֵטִיב, מֶלֶךְ יָחִיד וּמְיֻחָד, מֶלֶךְ כַּבִּיר, מֶלֶךְ לוֹבֵשׁ רַחֲמִים, מֶלֶךְ מַלְכֵי הַמְּלָכִים, מֶלֶךְ נִשְׂגָּב, מֶלֶךְ סוֹמֵךְ נוֹפְלִים, מֶלֶךְ עוֹשֶׂה מַעֲשֵׂה בְרֵאשִׁית, מֶלֶךְ פּוֹדֶה וּמַצִּיל, מֶלֶךְ צַח וְאָדוֹם, מֶלֶךְ קָדוֹשׁ, מֶלֶךְ רָם וְנִשָּׂא, מֶלֶךְ שׁוֹמֵעַ תְּפִלָּה, מֶלֶךְ תָּמִים דַּרְכּוֹ.

מוֹדֶה אֲנִי לְפָנֶיךָ* יהוה אֱלֹהַי וֵאלֹהֵי אֲבוֹתַי, עַל כָּל הַחֶסֶד אֲשֶׁר עָשִׂיתָ עִמָּדִי, וַאֲשֶׁר אַתָּה עָתִיד לַעֲשׂוֹת עִמִּי וְעִם כָּל בְּנֵי בֵיתִי וְעִם כָּל בְּרִיּוֹתֶיךָ בְּנֵי בְרִיתִי. וּבְרוּכִים הֵם מַלְאָכֶיךָ הַקְּדוֹשִׁים וְהַטְּהוֹרִים שֶׁעוֹשִׂים רְצוֹנֶךָ.

אֲדוֹן הַשָּׁלוֹם, מֶלֶךְ שֶׁהַשָּׁלוֹם שֶׁלּוֹ, בָּרְכֵנִי בַשָּׁלוֹם, וְתִפְקוֹד אוֹתִי וְאֶת כָּל בְּנֵי בֵיתִי, וְכָל עַמְּךָ בֵּית יִשְׂרָאֵל, לְחַיִּים טוֹבִים וּלְשָׁלוֹם.

מֶלֶךְ עֶלְיוֹן עַל כָּל צְבָא מָרוֹם, יוֹצְרֵנוּ יוֹצֵר בְּרֵאשִׁית, אֲחַלֶּה פָנֶיךָ הַמְּאִירִים שֶׁתְּזַכֶּה אוֹתִי וְאֶת כָּל בְּנֵי בֵיתִי לִמְצוֹא חֵן וְשֵׂכֶל טוֹב בְּעֵינֶיךָ, וּבְעֵינֵי כָּל בְּנֵי אָדָם וְחַוָּה, וּבְעֵינֵי כָל רוֹאֵינוּ, לַעֲבוֹדָתֶךָ. וְזַכֵּנוּ לְקַבֵּל שַׁבָּתוֹת מִתּוֹךְ רוֹב שִׂמְחָה, וּמִתּוֹךְ עֹשֶׁר וְכָבוֹד, וּמִתּוֹךְ מִעוּט עֲוֹנוֹת. וְהָסֵר מִמֶּנִּי וּמִכָּל בְּנֵי בֵיתִי וּמִכָּל עַמְּךָ בֵּית יִשְׂרָאֵל כָּל מִינֵי חֹלִי, וְכָל מִינֵי מַדְוֶה, וְכָל מִינֵי דַלּוּת וַעֲנִיּוּת וְאֶבְיוֹנוּת. וְתֵן בָּנוּ יֵצֶר טוֹב לְעָבְדְּךָ בֶּאֱמֶת וּבְיִרְאָה וּבְאַהֲבָה. וְנִהְיֶה מְכֻבָּדִים בְּעֵינֶיךָ וּבְעֵינֵי כָל רוֹאֵינוּ, כִּי אַתָּה הוּא מֶלֶךְ הַכָּבוֹד, כִּי לְךָ נָאֶה, כִּי לְךָ יָאֶה.

אָנָּא מֶלֶךְ מַלְכֵי הַמְּלָכִים, צַוֵּה לְמַלְאָכֶיךָ מַלְאֲכֵי הַשָּׁרֵת, מְשָׁרְתֵי עֶלְיוֹן, שֶׁיִּפְקְדוּנִי בְּרַחֲמִים, וִיבָרְכוּנִי בְּבוֹאָם לְבֵיתִי בְּיוֹם קָדְשֵׁנוּ. כִּי הִדְלַקְתִּי נֵרוֹתַי, וְהִצַּעְתִּי מִטָּתִי, וְהֶחֱלַפְתִּי שִׂמְלוֹתַי לִכְבוֹד יוֹם הַשַּׁבָּת. וּבָאתִי לְבֵיתְךָ לְהַפִּיל תְּחִנָּתִי לְפָנֶיךָ, שֶׁתַּעֲבִיר אַנְחָתִי, וָאָעִיד אֲשֶׁר בָּרָאתָ בְשִׁשָּׁה יָמִים כָּל הַיְצוּר. וָאֶשְׁנֶה וַאֲשַׁלֵּשׁ עוֹד לְהָעִיד עַל כּוֹסִי בְּתוֹךְ שִׂמְחָתִי, כַּאֲשֶׁר צִוִּיתָנִי לְזָכְרוֹ, וּלְהִתְעַנֵּג בְּיֶתֶר נִשְׁמָתִי אֲשֶׁר נָתַתָּ בִּי. בּוֹ אֶשְׁבּוֹת כַּאֲשֶׁר צִוִּיתָנִי, לְשָׁרְתֶךָ, וְכֵן אַגִּיד גְּדֻלָּתְךָ בְּרִנָּה. וְשִׁוִּיתִי יהוה לִקְרָאתִי, שֶׁתְּרַחֲמֵנִי עוֹד בְּגָלוּתִי, לְגָאֳלֵנִי וּלְעוֹרֵר לִבִּי לְאַהֲבָתֶךָ, וְאָז אֶשְׁמוֹר פִּקּוּדֶיךָ וְחֻקֶּיךָ בְּלִי עֶצֶב, וְאֶתְפַּלֵּל כַּדָּת כָּרָאוּי וּכְנָכוֹן.

מַלְאֲכֵי הַשָּׁלוֹם, בּוֹאֲכֶם לְשָׁלוֹם, בָּרְכוּנִי לְשָׁלוֹם, וְאִמְרוּ בָּרוּךְ לְשֻׁלְחָנִי הֶעָרוּךְ, וְצֵאתְכֶם לְשָׁלוֹם, מֵעַתָּה וְעַד עוֹלָם. אָמֵן סֶלָה.

כִּי מַלְאָכָיו יְצַוֶּה לָּךְ — *He will charge His angels for you.* These two verses are recited following *Shalom Aleichem* because our Sages taught that one who performs many commandments will be given many angels to protect him. Therefore, upon taking leave of the angels at the conclusion of *Shalom Aleichem,* the Jew is comforted by the pledge that God will dispatch numerous other angels to safeguard him.

⊛ **רִבּוֹן כָּל־הָעוֹלָמִים** — *Master of all worlds.* This prayer, too, is of relatively recent origin. Like *Shalom Aleichem,* it was first published in 5401 (1641) and has gained widespread acceptance.

אֲדוֹן הַשָּׁלוֹם — *Lord of peace.* Rabbi Shimon bar Chalafta said: The Holy one, Blessed is He, found no vessel to contain blessing for Israel except for peace (*Uktzin* 3:12). Therefore, in praying for God's blessings upon Israel on the most blessed day of the week, God is addressed as the Lord of peace — for peace is the framework within which blessings can be bestowed.

He will charge His angels for you, to protect you in all your ways.*[1] *May HASHEM protect your going and returning, from this time and forever.*[2]

רִבּוֹן כָּל הָעוֹלָמִים *Master of all worlds,* Lord of all souls, Lord of peace* — King Who is mighty,* King Who is blessed, King Who is great, King Who bespeaks peace, King Who is glorious, King Who is faithful, King Who is pure, King Who gives life to the universe, King Who is good and beneficent, King Who is unique and Whose uniqueness is proclaimed, King Who is powerful, King Who dons mercy, King Who reigns over kings, King Who is exalted, King Who supports the fallen, King Who maintains the works of creation, King Who redeems and rescues, King Who is pure yet ruddy, King Who is holy, King Who is exalted and upraised, King Who hears prayer, King Whose way is wholesome.*

I gratefully thank You, HASHEM, my God and the God of my forefathers, for all the kindness You have done with me, and which You will do with me, with all my household, and with all Your creatures who are my fellows. Blessed are Your holy and pure angels who do Your will.*

Lord of peace, King to Whom peace belongs, bless me with peace, and consider me and my entire household, and Your entire people, Israel, for a good life and for peace.

O King Who is exalted above all the heavenly legions, our Molder, Molder of the creation, I beseech Your luminous countenance that You privilege me and all my household to find favor and good understanding — in Your Eyes, and in the eyes of all descendants of Adam and Eve, and in the eyes of all who see us — that we may perform Your service. Privilege us to receive Sabbaths amid abundant gladness, amid wealth and honor, and amid fewness of sins. Remove from me, from all my household, and from Your entire nation Israel, every manner of illness, every manner of pain, and every manner of need, poverty, and destitution. Give us a virtuous desire to serve You with honesty, with awe, and with love. May we be honored in Your eyes and in the eyes of all who see us, for You are the King of Glory — for to You it is seemly, for to You it is fitting!

Please, O King Who reigns over kings, instruct Your angels, the ministering angels, servants of the Exalted One, that they consider me with mercy and bless me when they enter my home on our holy day, for I have kindled my lights, spread my bed, and changed my clothes in honor of the Sabbath day. I have entered Your house to cast my supplication before You that You banish my sighs; I bore witness that in six days You created the entire universe. I repeated it and will again repeat it over my cup amid my gladness as You commanded me to recall it, and to take pleasure in the additional soul which You have placed within me. On it shall I rest, as You have commanded me, to serve You, and so shall I relate Your greatness with joyous song. I have set HASHEM before me that You should further show me mercy in my exile, to redeem me and to inspire my heart to Your love. Then I shall observe Your laws and Your decrees without suffering and I shall pray correctly as is fitting and right.

O, Angels of peace, may your coming be for peace. Bless me for peace. Pronounce 'Blessed' upon my prepared table. May your departure be in peace, from this time and forever. Amen. Selah.

(1) *Psalms* 91:11. (2) 121:8.

... מֶלֶךְ אַבִּיר — *King Who is mighty* ... The Poet uses the common device of listing a series of adjectives in the form of an *aleph-beis* acrostic, i.e., beginning the first with an *Aleph* and continuing until *Tav*, the last letter of the Hebrew alphabet. The formula indicates that the theme under discussion is consistent from beginning to end; that we praise God with every sound available to the organs of speech; and that the author of the prayer intended to make it easier to memorize.

מוֹדֶה אֲנִי לְפָנֶיךָ — *I gratefully thank You.* The Sabbath is the source of blessing for the entire week. Therefore, when one enjoys the spiritual beneficence of the Sabbath, he should also realize that within it is the goodness he will experience in the succeeding days as well. Much like a businessman bringing his accounts up to date and assessing his future prospects, one should take an account of past blessings and project future ones. All derive from the Sabbath and for them he should thank God *(Bais Aharon).*

אשת חיל (משלי לא:י־לא)

אֵשֶׁת חָיִל* מִי יִמְצָא, וְרָחֹק מִפְּנִינִים מִכְרָהּ.
בָּטַח בָּהּ לֵב בַּעְלָהּ, וְשָׁלָל לֹא יֶחְסָר.
גְּמָלַתְהוּ טוֹב וְלֹא רָע, כֹּל יְמֵי חַיֶּיהָ.
דָּרְשָׁה צֶמֶר וּפִשְׁתִּים, וַתַּעַשׂ בְּחֵפֶץ כַּפֶּיהָ.
הָיְתָה כָּאֳנִיּוֹת סוֹחֵר, מִמֶּרְחָק תָּבִיא לַחְמָהּ.
וַתָּקָם בְּעוֹד לַיְלָה,* וַתִּתֵּן טֶרֶף לְבֵיתָהּ, וְחֹק לְנַעֲרֹתֶיהָ.
זָמְמָה שָׂדֶה וַתִּקָּחֵהוּ, מִפְּרִי כַפֶּיהָ נָטְעָה כָּרֶם.
חָגְרָה בְעוֹז מָתְנֶיהָ, וַתְּאַמֵּץ זְרוֹעֹתֶיהָ.*
טָעֲמָה כִּי טוֹב סַחְרָהּ, לֹא יִכְבֶּה בַלַּיְלָה נֵרָהּ.
יָדֶיהָ שִׁלְּחָה בַכִּישׁוֹר, וְכַפֶּיהָ תָּמְכוּ פָלֶךְ.*
כַּפָּהּ פָּרְשָׂה לֶעָנִי, וְיָדֶיהָ שִׁלְּחָה לָאֶבְיוֹן.*
לֹא תִירָא לְבֵיתָהּ מִשָּׁלֶג, כִּי כָל בֵּיתָהּ לָבֻשׁ שָׁנִים.
מַרְבַדִּים עָשְׂתָה לָּהּ, שֵׁשׁ וְאַרְגָּמָן לְבוּשָׁהּ.
נוֹדָע בַּשְּׁעָרִים בַּעְלָהּ,* בְּשִׁבְתּוֹ עִם זִקְנֵי אָרֶץ.
סָדִין עָשְׂתָה וַתִּמְכֹּר, וַחֲגוֹר נָתְנָה לַכְּנַעֲנִי.
עוֹז וְהָדָר לְבוּשָׁהּ, וַתִּשְׂחַק לְיוֹם אַחֲרוֹן.*
פִּיהָ פָּתְחָה בְחָכְמָה, וְתוֹרַת חֶסֶד עַל לְשׁוֹנָהּ.*
צוֹפִיָּה הֲלִיכוֹת בֵּיתָהּ, וְלֶחֶם עַצְלוּת לֹא תֹאכֵל.
קָמוּ בָנֶיהָ וַיְאַשְּׁרוּהָ,* בַּעְלָהּ וַיְהַלְלָהּ.
רַבּוֹת בָּנוֹת עָשׂוּ חָיִל, וְאַתְּ עָלִית עַל כֻּלָּנָה.
שֶׁקֶר הַחֵן וְהֶבֶל הַיֹּפִי,* אִשָּׁה יִרְאַת יהוה הִיא תִתְהַלָּל.
תְּנוּ לָהּ מִפְּרִי יָדֶיהָ,* וִיהַלְלוּהָ בַשְּׁעָרִים מַעֲשֶׂיהָ.

אשת חיל — *An accomplished woman,* consists of the concluding twenty-two verses of the Book of *Proverbs,* which, on the surface, is a hymn to the perfect wife who is the mainstay of her home. Although the commentators agree that the chapter is allegorical — it is variously interpreted as a reference to the *Shechinah,* the Sabbath, the Torah, wisdom, and the soul. The very fact that the Jewish woman was chosen as the vehicle through which to describe such lofty spiritual manifestations is in itself a profound tribute to her.

חָיִל — *Accomplished.* The word חָיִל as it is used in Scripture has various connotations: organized military force, strength, wealth, skill, general competence, or devoutness. It always implies the presence of whatever skills or attributes are needed to carry out the task at hand. As is clear from the context, the wife described here is energetic, righteous, and capable, hence *an accomplished woman.*

וַתָּקָם בְּעוֹד לַיְלָה — *She arises while it is yet nighttime.* With enthusiasm and a sense of responsibility, she arises before dawn to be sure that she can prepare adequately for the needs of her household. She recognizes that only by caring for the physical well-being of her family can she be sure that they will grow spiritually.

חָגְרָה בְעוֹז מָתְנֶיהָ וַתְּאַמֵּץ זְרוֹעֹתֶיהָ — *With strength she girds her loins* to run quickly to the *mitzvah,* and *invigorates her arms* to perform it.

כִּישׁוֹר ... פָּלֶךְ — *Distaff ... spindle.* The כִּישׁוֹר, *distaff,* is a staff which holds the fibers which are fed into the פָּלֶךְ, *spindle.* The *spindle* is a rounded tapered rod on the spinning wheel which is used to twist the fibers into thread.

כַּפָּהּ פָּרְשָׂה לֶעָנִי וְיָדֶיהָ שִׁלְּחָה לָאֶבְיוֹן — *She spreads out her palm to the poor and extends her hands to the destitute.* The אֶבְיוֹן, *destitute,* is in a more desperate situation than the עָנִי, *poor person.* Even as she helps both, she recognizes that one is

AISHES CHAYIL *(Proverbs 31:10-31)*

אֵשֶׁת חַיִל *An accomplished woman,* who can find? —*
Far beyond pearls is her value.
ב *Her husband's heart relies on her and he shall lack no fortune.*
ג *She repays his good, but never his harm, all the days of her life.*
ד *She seeks out wool and linen, and her hands work willingly.*
ה *She is like a merchant's ships, from afar she brings her sustenance.*
ו *She arises while it is yet nighttime,**
and gives food to her household and a ration to her maidens.
ז *She envisions a field and buys it,*
from the fruit of her handiwork she plants a vineyard.
ח *With strength she girds her loins, and invigorates her arms.**
ט *She discerns that her enterprise is good —*
so her lamp is not snuffed out by night.
י *Her hands she stretches out to the distaff,*
*and her palms support the spindle.**
כ *She spreads out her palm to the poor,*
*and extends her hands to the destitute.**
ל *She fears not snow for her household,*
for her entire household is clothed with scarlet wool.
מ *Luxurious bedspreads she made herself,*
linen and purple wool are her clothing.
נ *Distinctive in the councils is her husband,**
when he sits with the elders of the land.
ס *She makes a cloak to sell, and delivers a belt to the peddler.*
ע *Strength and majesty are her raiment, she joyfully awaits the last day.**
פ *She opens her mouth with wisdom,*
*and a lesson of kindness is on her tongue.**
צ *She anticipates the ways of her household,*
and partakes not of the bread of laziness.
ק *Her children arise and praise her,* her husband, and he lauds her:*
ר *'Many daughters have amassed achievement, but you surpassed them all.'*
ש *False is grace and vain is beauty,**
a God-fearing woman — she should be praised.
ת *Give her the fruits of her hand**
and let her be praised in the gates by her very own deeds.

---

more needy than the other. Therefore, to the *poor* person, she opens her hand allowing him to take what he wishes, but to the *destitute* one, she takes the initiative by *extending her hands* to give him what he needs.

נוֹדָע בַּשְּׁעָרִים בַּעְלָהּ — *Distinctive in the councils* [lit. *gates*] *is her husband.* The beautiful garments she tailors for him make her husband stand out when he takes part in the councils of distinguished men. The word שְׁעָרִים, literally *gates,* is used throughout Scripture to denote gathering of elders and leaders.

וַתִּשְׂחַק לְיוֹם אַחֲרוֹן — *She joyfully awaits the last day.* She awaits the inevitable last day of life with confidence that she will have earned respect and honor.

וְתוֹרַת חֶסֶד עַל לְשׁוֹנָהּ — *And a lesson of kindness is on her tongue.* She teaches others to engage in kind deeds.

קָמוּ בָנֶיהָ וַיְאַשְּׁרוּהָ — *Her children arise and praise her,* in appreciation for, and recognition of, the qualities described above.

שֶׁקֶר הַחֵן וְהֶבֶל הַיֹּפִי — *False is grace and vain is beauty.* Grace and beauty are not attributes that are worthy of serious praise for they have no great value. Moreover, they are often only transitory and do not reflect the character and worth of a person. Only a woman's fear of God is deserving of praise.

תְּנוּ לָהּ מִפְּרִי יָדֶיהָ — *Give her the fruits of her hand.* There is no need to recite her praises; her own

קידוש לליל שבת

The following *Kiddush* is recited on Sabbath and on Sabbath Chol HaMoed.
The *Kiddush* for Succos appears on p. 722; for Rosh Hashanah, p. 766; for others Festivals, p. 656.

(וַיְהִי עֶרֶב וַיְהִי בֹקֶר —Recite Silently)

יוֹם הַשִּׁשִּׁי.* וַיְכֻלּוּ הַשָּׁמַיִם וְהָאָרֶץ וְכָל צְבָאָם. וַיְכַל אֱלֹהִים בַּיּוֹם הַשְּׁבִיעִי מְלַאכְתּוֹ אֲשֶׁר עָשָׂה, וַיִּשְׁבֹּת בַּיּוֹם הַשְּׁבִיעִי מִכָּל מְלַאכְתּוֹ אֲשֶׁר עָשָׂה. וַיְבָרֶךְ אֱלֹהִים אֶת יוֹם הַשְּׁבִיעִי וַיְקַדֵּשׁ אֹתוֹ, כִּי בוֹ שָׁבַת מִכָּל מְלַאכְתּוֹ אֲשֶׁר בָּרָא אֱלֹהִים לַעֲשׂוֹת.[1]

סַבְרִי מָרָנָן וְרַבָּנָן וְרַבּוֹתַי:

בָּרוּךְ אַתָּה יהוה אֱלֹהֵינוּ מֶלֶךְ הָעוֹלָם, בּוֹרֵא פְּרִי הַגָּפֶן.

(אָמֵן. —All present respond)

בָּרוּךְ אַתָּה יהוה אֱלֹהֵינוּ מֶלֶךְ הָעוֹלָם, אֲשֶׁר קִדְּשָׁנוּ בְּמִצְוֹתָיו וְרָצָה בָנוּ, וְשַׁבַּת קָדְשׁוֹ בְּאַהֲבָה וּבְרָצוֹן הִנְחִילָנוּ, זִכָּרוֹן לְמַעֲשֵׂה בְרֵאשִׁית. כִּי הוּא יוֹם תְּחִלָּה לְמִקְרָאֵי קֹדֶשׁ,* זֵכֶר לִיצִיאַת מִצְרָיִם.* כִּי בָנוּ בָחַרְתָּ, וְאוֹתָנוּ קִדַּשְׁתָּ, מִכָּל הָעַמִּים. וְשַׁבַּת קָדְשְׁךָ בְּאַהֲבָה וּבְרָצוֹן הִנְחַלְתָּנוּ. בָּרוּךְ אַתָּה יהוה, מְקַדֵּשׁ הַשַּׁבָּת.*

(אָמֵן. —All present respond)

On the Sabbath of Chol HaMoed Succos, in the *succah*, add:

בָּרוּךְ אַתָּה יהוה אֱלֹהֵינוּ מֶלֶךְ הָעוֹלָם, אֲשֶׁר קִדְּשָׁנוּ בְּמִצְוֹתָיו וְצִוָּנוּ לֵישֵׁב בַּסֻּכָּה.

(אָמֵן. —All present respond)

It is customary to give each person present some wine from the *Kiddush* cup.
All present wash their hands in the ritual manner and the head of the household recites the blessing for bread over two *challahs* and distributes a piece to each person.

---

deeds are the most eloquent testimony to her virtue.

קידוש / KIDDUSH

The *mitzvah* to recite — or listen to — *Kiddush* over a cup of wine is incumbent upon men and women alike.

The first paragraph of *Kiddush* is in the nature of testimony to the fact that God completed the labor of creation in six days and rested on the seventh. Thus by observing the Sabbath, we bear weekly testimony to God's creation of the universe. Although this paragraph has already been recited as part of the evening service [and for that reason it is not repeated as part of the *Kiddush* which is recited in the synagogue], it was included in the *Kiddush* for the benefit of women and children who did not recite the evening service (*Pesachim* 106a).

The head of the household, or another adult present, recites the *Kiddush* while holding a full cup of grape wine (or juice) in his right hand. He should bear in mind that his recitation is the fulfillment of the *mitzvah* of *Kiddush* for both himself and the others who are listening. Those listening should bear in mind that their listening and response is in fulfillment of the *mitzvah* of *Kiddush*, and should remain silent except when responding *'Amen.'* Some stand during *Kiddush*, others sit, and still others stand until the blessing over wine, then sit.

יום הששי — *The sixth day.* Strictly speaking, these two words, which conclude the account of

⊰ SABBATH EVE KIDDUSH ⊱

The following *Kiddush* is recited on Sabbath and on Sabbath Chol HaMoed.
The *Kiddush* for Succos appears on p. 722; for Rosh Hashanah, p. 766; for other Festivals, p. 656.
(Recite silently— *And there was evening and there was morning)*

יוֹם הַשִּׁשִּׁי *The sixth day.* Thus the heavens and earth were finished, and all their array. On the seventh day God completed His work which He had done, and He abstained on the seventh day from all His work which He had done. God blessed the seventh day and hallowed it, because on it He abstained from all His work which God created to make.*[1]

By your leave, my masters, rabbis and teachers,

בָּרוּךְ *Blessed are You,* HASHEM, *our God, King of the universe, Who creates the fruit of the vine.* (All present respond— *Amen.)*

בָּרוּךְ *Blessed are You,* HASHEM, *our God, King of the universe, Who has sanctified us with His commandments, took pleasure in us, and with love and favor gave us His holy Sabbath as a heritage, a remembrance of creation. For that day is the prologue to the holy convocations,* a memorial of the Exodus from Egypt.* For us did You choose and us did You sanctify from all the nations. And Your holy Sabbath, with love and favor did You give us as a heritage. Blessed are You,* HASHEM, *Who sanctifies the Sabbath.** (All present respond— *Amen.)*

On the Sabbath of Chol HaMoed Succos, in the *succah,* add:

בָּרוּךְ *Blessed are You,* HASHEM, *our God, King of the universe, Who has sanctified us with His commandments and has commanded us to dwell in the Succah.* (All present respond— *Amen.)*

It is customary to give each person present some wine from the *Kiddush* cup.
All present wash their hands in the ritual manner and the head of the household recites the blessing for bread over two *challahs* and distributes a piece to each person.

(1) *Genesis* 1:31-2:3.

---

the first six days of creation, do not relate to the testimony of the Sabbath's holiness and are not part of *Kiddush.* Nevertheless, they are attached to *Kiddush* because their initials together with the initials of וַיְכֻלּוּ הַשָּׁמַיִם form the Four-Letter Name of God. Because these two isolated words have no logical meaning standing alone, the Sages incorporated the preceding words: וַיְהִי עֶרֶב וַיְהִי בֹקֶר, *and there was evening and there was morning,* to form a complete thought. Those words, however, are said quietly.

תְּחִלָּה לְמִקְרָאֵי קֹדֶשׁ — *The prologue to the holy convocations.* The festivals are described as *holy convocations* because they come about as a result of the months which are proclaimed by the courts of Israel. The Sabbath, however, is independent of any proclamations of the court. As such it is not properly called a *holy convocation.* Nevertheless, *Leviticus* 23 which lists the festivals begin by mentioning the Sabbath, thus making the Sabbath *the prologue to the holy convocations.*

זֵכֶר לִיצִיאַת מִצְרָיִם — *A memorial of the Exodus from Egypt. Ramban* explains that the Sabbath and the Exodus are intertwined. The Sabbath is symbolic of God's creation; the Exodus was His demonstration to humanity that He controls nature and manipulates it as His will sees fit. In turn, the events of the Exodus bear witness to God's creation — and, hence, His mastery — of the universe. The Sabbath on the other hand, is the backdrop of the Exodus, because the concept it represents explains how the events of the Exodus were possible.

מְקַדֵּשׁ הַשַּׁבָּת — *Who sanctifies the Sabbath.* Unlike the festivals whose sanctity is dependent

זמירות לליל שבת

כל מקדש

כָּל מְקַדֵּשׁ שְׁבִיעִי כָּרָאוּי לוֹ, כָּל שׁוֹמֵר שַׁבָּת כַּדָּת מֵחַלְּלוֹ, שְׂכָרוֹ הַרְבֵּה מְאֹד עַל פִּי פָעֳלוֹ, אִישׁ עַל מַחֲנֵהוּ וְאִישׁ עַל דִּגְלוֹ.1

אוֹהֲבֵי יהוה הַמְּחַכִּים בְּבִנְיַן אֲרִיאֵל, בְּיוֹם הַשַּׁבָּת (קֹדֶשׁ) שִׂישׂוּ וְשִׂמְחוּ כִּמְקַבְּלֵי מַתַּן נַחֲלִיאֵל, גַּם שְׂאוּ יְדֵיכֶם קֹדֶשׁ וְאִמְרוּ לָאֵל, בָּרוּךְ יהוה אֲשֶׁר נָתַן מְנוּחָה לְעַמּוֹ יִשְׂרָאֵל.2

דּוֹרְשֵׁי יהוה זֶרַע אַבְרָהָם אוֹהֲבוֹ, הַמְּאַחֲרִים לָצֵאת מִן הַשַּׁבָּת וּמְמַהֲרִים לָבוֹא, וּשְׂמֵחִים לְשָׁמְרוֹ וּלְעָרֵב עֵרוּבוֹ, זֶה הַיּוֹם עָשָׂה יהוה נָגִילָה וְנִשְׂמְחָה בוֹ.3

זִכְרוּ תּוֹרַת מֹשֶׁה בְּמִצְוַת שַׁבָּת גְּרוּסָה, חֲרוּתָה לַיּוֹם הַשְּׁבִיעִי כְּכַלָּה בֵּין רֵעוֹתֶיהָ מְשֻׁבָּצָה, טְהוֹרִים יִירָשׁוּהָ וִיקַדְּשׁוּהָ בְּמַאֲמַר כָּל אֲשֶׁר עָשָׂה, וַיְכַל אֱלֹהִים בַּיּוֹם הַשְּׁבִיעִי מְלַאכְתּוֹ אֲשֶׁר עָשָׂה.4

יוֹם קָדוֹשׁ הוּא מִבּוֹאוֹ וְעַד צֵאתוֹ, כָּל זֶרַע יַעֲקֹב יְכַבְּדוּהוּ כִּדְבַר הַמֶּלֶךְ וְדָתוֹ, לָנוּחַ בּוֹ וְלִשְׂמֹחַ בְּתַעֲנוּג אָכוֹל וְשָׁתוֹ, כָּל עֲדַת יִשְׂרָאֵל יַעֲשׂוּ אֹתוֹ.5

מְשׁוֹךְ חַסְדְּךָ לְיוֹדְעֶיךָ, אֵל קַנֹּא וְנוֹקֵם, נוֹטְרֵי לַיּוֹם הַשְּׁבִיעִי זָכוֹר וְשָׁמוֹר לְהָקֵם, שַׂמְּחֵם בְּבִנְיַן שָׁלֵם, בְּאוֹר פָּנֶיךָ תַּבְהִיקֵם, יִרְוְיֻן מִדֶּשֶׁן בֵּיתֶךָ, וְנַחַל עֲדָנֶיךָ תַשְׁקֵם.6

עֲזוֹר לַשּׁוֹבְתִים בַּשְּׁבִיעִי, בֶּחָרִישׁ וּבַקָּצִיר עוֹלָמִים, פּוֹסְעִים בּוֹ פְּסִיעָה קְטַנָּה, סוֹעֲדִים בּוֹ, לְבָרֵךְ שָׁלֹשׁ פְּעָמִים, צִדְקָתָם תַּצְהִיר כְּאוֹר שִׁבְעַת הַיָּמִים, יהוה אֱלֹהֵי יִשְׂרָאֵל, הָבָה תָמִים.7 (יהוה אֱלֹהֵי יִשְׂרָאֵל אַהֲבַת תָּמִים. יהוה אֱלֹהֵי יִשְׂרָאֵל תְּשׁוּעַת עוֹלָמִים.)

מנוחה ושמחה

מְנוּחָה וְשִׂמְחָה אוֹר לַיְּהוּדִים, יוֹם שַׁבָּתוֹן יוֹם מַחֲמַדִּים, שׁוֹמְרָיו וְזוֹכְרָיו הֵמָּה מְעִידִים, כִּי לְשִׁשָּׁה כֹּל בְּרוּאִים וְעוֹמְדִים.

כָּל מְקַדֵּשׁ / Kol Mekadesh

Nothing is known of the author of this *zemer* except that his name is Moshe. The acrostic forming his name is found in the initials of the second words of the first three stiches: מְקַדֵּשׁ, שׁוֹמֵר, הַרְבֵּה. It has been surmised that his great modesty led him to 'sign' the *zemer* in second words rather than in a more conspicuous manner.

upon the proclamation of the months by courts of Israel, the Sabbath owes its sanctity solely to God Who declared its holiness at the time of creation.

זְמִירוֹת לְלֵיל שַׁבָּת / SABBATH EVE ZEMIROS

A complete selection of Zemiros with a phrase-by-phrase commentary can be found in the ArtScroll *Zemiroth.*

ZEMIROS FOR THE SABBATH EVE

KOL MEKADESH

כָּל מְקַדֵּשׁ *Whoever hallows the Sabbath as befits it, whoever safeguards the Sabbath properly from desecration, His reward is exceedingly great in accordance with his deed — 'Every man at his own camp, every man at his own banner.'*[1]

אוֹהֲבֵי *Lovers of* HASHEM *who long for the building of His leonine Temple, On the (holy) Sabbath day rejoice and be glad! — as if receiving the gift of God's heritage, raise your hands in holiness and say to God — 'Blessed is* HASHEM *Who presented tranquillity to His people, Israel.'*[2]

דּוֹרְשֵׁי *Seekers of* HASHEM, *seed of Abraham His beloved, who delay departing from the Sabbath and rush to enter, Glad to safeguard it and set its eruv — 'This is the day* HASHEM *has made; let us rejoice and be glad on it.'*[3]

זִכְרוּ *Remember Moses' Torah as its Sabbath precept is expounded, engraved with teachings for the Seventh Day, like a bride bedecked among her companions; Pure ones bequeath it and hallow it with the statement: 'All that He had made ...' — 'On the Seventh Day, God completed His work which He had done.'*[4]

יוֹם *It is a holy day from beginning to end, all Jacob's seed will honor it according to the King's word and decree To rest on it and be glad with the pleasure of food and drink — 'The entire congregation of Israel will observe it'.*[5]

מְשׁוֹךְ *Extend Your kindness to those who know You, O jealous and vengeful God, Those who await the Seventh day to uphold 'Remember' and 'Safeguard'. Gladden them with rebuilt Jerusalem, with the light of Your countenance make them radiant — 'May they be sated from the abundance of Your house and may You give them drink from the stream of Your delights.'*[6]

עֲזוֹר *Always help those who desist from plow and harvest on the Seventh, Who walk on it with short strides and feast three times on it in order to bless You. May their righteousness blaze forth like the light of the Seven Days — '*HASHEM, *God of Israel, grant completeness!'*[7] *(*HASHEM, *God of Israel — a perfect love!* HASHEM, *God of Israel — an eternal salvation!)*

MENUCHAH V'SIMCHAH

מְנוּחָה וְשִׂמְחָה *Contentment and gladness and light for the Jews, on this day of Sabbath, day of delights; those who protect and those who remember it — they bear witness, that in six days all was created and still endures.*

(1) *Numbers* 1:52. (2) *I Kings* 8:56. (3) *Psalms* 118:24. (4) *Genesis* 2:2.
(5) *Exodus* 12:47. (6) *Psalms* 36:9. (7) *I Samuel* 14:41.

Each stanza ends with a Scriptural verse. From the second stanza onward, the stiches (with the exception of the scriptural endings) follow the *aleph-beis.*

מְנוּחָה וְשִׂמְחָה / Menuchah V'Simchah

Written by an unknown composer whose name, מֹשֶׁה, *Moshe,* is found in an acrostic formed by the first words of the first three stanzas, this *zemer* first appeared in print in 1545.

The *zemer* lauds the rewards awaiting those who observe and honor the holy Sabbath properly.

שְׁמֵי שָׁמַיִם אֶרֶץ וְיַמִּים, כָּל צְבָא מָרוֹם גְּבוֹהִים וְרָמִים, תַּנִּין וְאָדָם וְחַיַּת רְאֵמִים, כִּי בְּיָהּ יהוה צוּר עוֹלָמִים.[1]

הוּא אֲשֶׁר דִּבֶּר לְעַם סְגֻלָּתוֹ, שָׁמוֹר לְקַדְּשׁוֹ מִבּוֹאוֹ וְעַד צֵאתוֹ, שַׁבַּת קֹדֶשׁ יוֹם חֶמְדָּתוֹ, כִּי בוֹ שָׁבַת אֵל מִכָּל מְלַאכְתּוֹ.[2]

בְּמִצְוַת שַׁבָּת אֵל יַחֲלִיצָךְ, קוּם קְרָא אֵלָיו יָחִישׁ לְאַמְּצָךְ, נִשְׁמַת כָּל חַי וְגַם נַעֲרִיצָךְ, אֱכוֹל בְּשִׂמְחָה כִּי כְבָר רָצָךְ.[3]

בְּמִשְׁנֶה לֶחֶם וְקִדּוּשׁ רַבָּה, בְּרֹב מַטְעַמִּים וְרוּחַ נְדִיבָה, יִזְכּוּ לְרַב טוּב הַמִּתְעַנְּגִים בָּהּ, בְּבִיאַת גּוֹאֵל לְחַיֵּי הָעוֹלָם הַבָּא.

יום זה לישראל

יוֹם זֶה לְיִשְׂרָאֵל אוֹרָה וְשִׂמְחָה, שַׁבַּת מְנוּחָה.

צִוִּיתָ פִּקּוּדִים בְּמַעֲמַד הַר סִינַי, שַׁבָּת וּמוֹעֲדִים לִשְׁמוֹר בְּכָל שָׁנַי, לַעֲרוֹךְ לְפָנַי מַשְׂאֵת וַאֲרוּחָה, שַׁבַּת מְנוּחָה.

יוֹם זֶה לְיִשְׂרָאֵל אוֹרָה וְשִׂמְחָה, שַׁבַּת מְנוּחָה.

חֶמְדַּת הַלְּבָבוֹת לְאֻמָּה שְׁבוּרָה, לִנְפָשׁוֹת נִכְאָבוֹת נְשָׁמָה יְתֵרָה, לְנֶפֶשׁ מְצֵרָה תָּסִיר אֲנָחָה, שַׁבַּת מְנוּחָה.

יוֹם זֶה לְיִשְׂרָאֵל אוֹרָה וְשִׂמְחָה, שַׁבַּת מְנוּחָה.

קִדַּשְׁתָּ בֵּרַכְתָּ אוֹתוֹ מִכָּל יָמִים, בְּשֵׁשֶׁת כִּלִּיתָ מְלֶאכֶת עוֹלָמִים, בּוֹ מָצְאוּ עֲגוּמִים הַשְׁקֵט וּבִטְחָה, שַׁבַּת מְנוּחָה.

יוֹם זֶה לְיִשְׂרָאֵל אוֹרָה וְשִׂמְחָה, שַׁבַּת מְנוּחָה.

לְאִסּוּר מְלָאכָה צִוִּיתָנוּ נוֹרָא, אֶזְכֶּה הוֹד מְלוּכָה אִם שַׁבָּת אֶשְׁמְרָה, אַקְרִיב שַׁי לַמּוֹרָא מִנְחָה מֶרְקָחָה, שַׁבַּת מְנוּחָה.

יוֹם זֶה לְיִשְׂרָאֵל אוֹרָה וְשִׂמְחָה, שַׁבַּת מְנוּחָה:

חַדֵּשׁ מִקְדָּשֵׁנוּ זָכְרָה נֶחֱרֶבֶת, טוּבְךָ מוֹשִׁיעֵנוּ תְּנָה לַנֶּעֱצֶבֶת, בְּשַׁבָּת יוֹשֶׁבֶת בְּזֶמֶר וּשְׁבָחָה, שַׁבַּת מְנוּחָה.

יוֹם זֶה לְיִשְׂרָאֵל אוֹרָה וְשִׂמְחָה, שַׁבַּת מְנוּחָה.

יה רבון

יָהּ רִבּוֹן עָלַם וְעָלְמַיָּא, אַנְתְּ הוּא מַלְכָּא מֶלֶךְ מַלְכַיָּא, עוֹבַד גְּבוּרְתֵּךְ וְתִמְהַיָּא, שְׁפַר קֳדָמָךְ לְהַחֲוָיָא.

יָהּ רִבּוֹן עָלַם וְעָלְמַיָּא, אַנְתְּ הוּא מַלְכָּא מֶלֶךְ מַלְכַיָּא.

יוֹם זֶה לְיִשְׂרָאֵל / Yom Zeh L'Yisrael

This *zemer* is generally considered to be the work of Rabbi Yitzchak Luria, better known as the *Arizal*. If so, it is one of the very few compositons which he wrote in Hebrew, rather than Aramaic. The initial letter of the first four verses spell יִצְחָק, *Yitzchak*.

יָהּ רִבּוֹן / Kah Ribon

Kah Ribon's five stanzas form the acrostic יִשְׂרָאֵל, *Yisrael*, the name of its composer, Yisrael

שְׁמֵי *The most exalted heaven, earth, and seas, all the legions of above, high and exalted, sea giant and man and mighty beasts — that the Creator,* HASHEM, *is the Rock of the Universe.*[1]

הוּא *It is He Who spoke to His treasured nation: 'Stand guard to hallow it from arrival to departure' — The holy Sabbath, day of His delight, for on it the Almighty rested from all His work.*[2]

בְּמִצְוַת *Through the Sabbath command will the Almighty strengthen you; arise! beseech Him, that He may rush to fortify you; recite 'Soul of all living' and also 'We proclaim Your strength'; eat in gladness for He has already shown you favor.*[3]

בְּמִשְׁנֶה *With double loaves and the great Kiddush, with abundant delicacies and a generous spirit; they will merit much good, those who take pleasure in it, with the redeemer's coming, for the life of the World to Come.*

YOM ZEH L'YISRAEL

יוֹם זֶה לְיִשְׂרָאֵל *This day for Israel is light and gladness — Sabbath of contentment.*

צִוִּיתָ *You commanded precepts at the Assemblage at Mount Sinai, the Sabbath and festivals to keep through all my years; to prepare before me courses and banquets — Sabbath of contentment.*

This day for Israel is light and gladness — Sabbath of contentment.

חֶמְדַּת *Hearts' beloved of the shattered nation, for suffering people an additional soul; for a troubled soul it removes moaning — Sabbath of contentment.*

This day for Israel is light and gladness — Sabbath of contentment.

קִדַּשְׁתָּ *You hallowed, You blessed it more than any days; in six You completed the labor of the universe; on it grieving people find tranquillity and trust — Sabbath of contentment.*

This day for Israel is light and gladness — Sabbath of contentment.

לְאִסּוּר *Concerning the ban of labor, the Awesome One commanded us; I shall merit kingly glory if I safeguard the Sabbath; I shall bring an offering to the Fearsome One, a perfumed meal-offering — Sabbath of contentment.*

This day for Israel is light and gladness — Sabbath of contentment.

חַדֵּשׁ *Renew our Sanctuary, remember the ruined city; Your goodness, our Savior, grant the saddened one, who spends the Sabbath in song and praise — Sabbath of contentment.*

This day for Israel is light and gladness — Sabbath of contentment.

KAH RIBON

יָהּ רִבּוֹן *O Creator, Master of this world and all worlds, You are the King who reigns over kings — Your powerful and wondrous deeds it is beautiful to declare before You.*

O Creator, Master of this world and all worlds,
You are the King who reigns over kings.

(1) *Isaiah* 26:4. (2) Cf. *Genesis* 2:3. (3) Cf. *Ecclesiastes* 9:7.

[ben Moshe of Najara]. He was a student of the *Arizal* in Safed during the sixteenth century and later became rabbi of Gaza. It is said that he composed as many as four hundred fifty

שְׁבָחִין אֲסַדֵּר צַפְרָא וְרַמְשָׁא, לָךְ אֱלָהָא קַדִּישָׁא דִּי בְרָא כָּל נַפְשָׁא, עִירִין קַדִּישִׁין וּבְנֵי אֱנָשָׁא, חֵיוַת בָּרָא וְעוֹפֵי שְׁמַיָּא.

יָהּ רִבּוֹן עָלַם וְעָלְמַיָּא, אַנְתְּ הוּא מַלְכָּא מֶלֶךְ מַלְכַיָּא.

רַבְרְבִין עוֹבְדָיךְ וְתַקִּיפִין, מָכִיךְ רְמַיָּא וְזַקִּיף כְּפִיפִין, לוּ יִחְיֶה גְבַר שְׁנִין אַלְפִין, לָא יֵעוֹל גְּבוּרְתֵּךְ בְּחֻשְׁבְּנַיָּא.

יָהּ רִבּוֹן עָלַם וְעָלְמַיָּא, אַנְתְּ הוּא מַלְכָּא מֶלֶךְ מַלְכַיָּא.

אֱלָהָא דִּי לֵהּ יְקַר וּרְבוּתָא, פְּרוֹק יַת עָנָךְ מִפּוּם אַרְיָוָתָא, וְאַפֵּיק יַת עַמֵּךְ מִגּוֹ גָלוּתָא, עַמֵּךְ דִּי בְחַרְתְּ מִכָּל אֻמַּיָּא.

יָהּ רִבּוֹן עָלַם וְעָלְמַיָּא, אַנְתְּ הוּא מַלְכָּא מֶלֶךְ מַלְכַיָּא.

לְמִקְדָּשָׁךְ תּוּב וּלְקֹדֶשׁ קֻדְשִׁין, אֲתַר דִּי בֵהּ יֶחֱדוּן רוּחִין וְנַפְשִׁין, וִיזַמְּרוּן לָךְ שִׁירִין וְרַחֲשִׁין, בִּירוּשְׁלֵם קַרְתָּא דְשׁוּפְרַיָּא.

יָהּ רִבּוֹן עָלַם וְעָלְמַיָּא, אַנְתְּ הוּא מַלְכָּא מֶלֶךְ מַלְכַיָּא.

צור משלו

צוּר מִשֶּׁלּוֹ אָכַלְנוּ בָּרְכוּ אֱמוּנַי, שָׂבַעְנוּ וְהוֹתַרְנוּ כִּדְבַר יהוה.

הַזָּן אֶת עוֹלָמוֹ רוֹעֵנוּ אָבִינוּ, אָכַלְנוּ אֶת לַחְמוֹ וְיֵינוֹ שָׁתִינוּ, עַל כֵּן נוֹדֶה לִשְׁמוֹ וּנְהַלְּלוֹ בְּפִינוּ, אָמַרְנוּ וְעָנִינוּ אֵין קָדוֹשׁ כַּיהוה.

צוּר מִשֶּׁלּוֹ אָכַלְנוּ בָּרְכוּ אֱמוּנַי, שָׂבַעְנוּ וְהוֹתַרְנוּ כִּדְבַר יהוה.

בְּשִׁיר וְקוֹל תּוֹדָה נְבָרֵךְ לֵאלֹהֵינוּ, עַל אֶרֶץ חֶמְדָּה טוֹבָה שֶׁהִנְחִיל לַאֲבוֹתֵינוּ, מָזוֹן וְצֵדָה הִשְׂבִּיעַ לְנַפְשֵׁנוּ, חַסְדּוֹ גָּבַר עָלֵינוּ וֶאֱמֶת יהוה.

צוּר מִשֶּׁלּוֹ אָכַלְנוּ בָּרְכוּ אֱמוּנַי, שָׂבַעְנוּ וְהוֹתַרְנוּ כִּדְבַר יהוה.

רַחֵם בְּחַסְדֶּךָ עַל עַמְּךָ צוּרֵנוּ, עַל צִיּוֹן מִשְׁכַּן כְּבוֹדֶךָ זְבוּל בֵּית תִּפְאַרְתֵּנוּ, בֶּן דָּוִד עַבְדֶּךָ יָבֹא וְיִגְאָלֵנוּ. רוּחַ אַפֵּינוּ מְשִׁיחַ יהוה.

צוּר מִשֶּׁלּוֹ אָכַלְנוּ בָּרְכוּ אֱמוּנַי, שָׂבַעְנוּ וְהוֹתַרְנוּ כִּדְבַר יהוה.

יִבָּנֶה הַמִּקְדָּשׁ עִיר צִיּוֹן תְּמַלֵּא, וְשָׁם נָשִׁיר שִׁיר חָדָשׁ וּבִרְנָנָה נַעֲלֶה, הָרַחֲמָן הַנִּקְדָּשׁ יִתְבָּרַךְ וְיִתְעַלֶּה, עַל כּוֹס יַיִן מָלֵא כְּבִרְכַּת יהוה.

צוּר מִשֶּׁלּוֹ אָכַלְנוּ בָּרְכוּ אֱמוּנַי, שָׂבַעְנוּ וְהוֹתַרְנוּ כִּדְבַר יהוה.

---

zemiros. Kah Ribon contains no mention of the Sabbath. Nevertheless, its simple beauty as a song of praise to God has made it one of the most universally popular *zemiros.*

צוּר מִשֶּׁלּוֹ / Tzur MiShelo

This *zemer* is an introduction to בִּרְכַּת הַמָּזוֹן, [*Bircas HaMazon*] *Grace after Meals.* The refrain, by inviting the assembled guests to join in thanking God for the food, approximates זימון, *the Invitation*, to bless together. The first three stanzas of the *zemer* follow the pattern of the first three blessings of *Bircas HaMazon*, the respective subjects of which are ordained by the Torah (see p. 182).

שְׁבָחִין *Praises shall I prepare morning and evening, to You, O Holy God, Who created all life: holy angels and sons of man, beasts of the field and birds of the sky.*

O Creator, Master of this world and all worlds,
You are the King who reigns over kings.

רַבְרְבִין *Great are Your deeds and mighty, humbling the haughty and straightening the bent; even if man lived thousands of years, he could not fathom the extent of Your powerful deeds.*

O Creator, Master of this world and all worlds,
You are the King who reigns over kings.

אֱלָהָא *God to Whom belongs honor and greatness, save Your sheep from the mouth of lions, and bring Your people out of its exile, the people that You chose from all the nations.*

O Creator, Master of this world and all worlds,
You are the King who reigns over kings.

לְמִקְדָּשָׁךְ *To Your Sanctuary return and to the Holy of Holies, the place where spirits and souls will rejoice and utter songs and praises — In Jerusalem, city of beauty.*

O Creator, Master of this world and all worlds,
You are the King who reigns over kings.

TZUR MISHELO

צוּר מִשֶּׁלּוֹ *The Rock from Whose we have eaten! Bless Him, my faithful friends — we have eaten our fill and left over — according to HASHEM's word.*

הַזָּן *He nourishes His universe, our Shepherd, our Father; we have eaten His bread and His wine we have drunk; therefore let us praise His Name and praise Him with our mouths, let us sing out loudly, 'There is none as holy as HASHEM.'*

The Rock from Whose we have eaten! Bless Him, my faithful friends —
we have eaten our fill and left over — according to HASHEM's word.

בְּשִׁיר *With song and sound of thanksgiving let us bless our God, for the land so desirable and good that He gave our forefathers as a heritage; with nourishment and sustenance He sated our souls; his kindness was mighty over us, and HASHEM is truth!*

The Rock from Whose we have eaten! Bless Him, my faithful friends —
we have eaten our fill and left over — according to HASHEM's word.

רַחֵם *Be merciful in Your kindness upon Your nation, our Rock, upon Zion resting place of Your Glory, the shrine, home of our splendor; may the son of David, Your servant, come and redeem us, breath of our nostrils, anointed of HASHEM.*

The Rock from Whose we have eaten! Bless Him, my faithful friends —
we have eaten our fill and left over — according to HASHEM's word.

יִבָּנֶה *May the Temple be rebuilt; the City of Zion replenished; there shall we sing a new song, with joyous singing ascend; may the Merciful, the Sanctified, be blessed and exalted over a full cup of wine worthy of HASHEM's blessing.*

The Rock from Whose we have eaten! Bless Him, my faithful friends —
we have eaten our fill and left over — according to HASHEM's word.

❧ פסוקי דזמרה לשבת ויום טוב ☙

The preliminary sections of *Shacharis* are the same as on weekdays (pp. 2-54).

INTRODUCTORY PSALM TO PESUKEI D'ZIMRAH

(commentary on p. 55) תהלים ל

מִזְמוֹר שִׁיר חֲנֻכַּת הַבַּיִת לְדָוִד. אֲרוֹמִמְךָ יהוה כִּי דִלִּיתָנִי, וְלֹא שִׂמַּחְתָּ אֹיְבַי לִי. יהוה אֱלֹהָי, שִׁוַּעְתִּי אֵלֶיךָ וַתִּרְפָּאֵנִי. יהוה הֶעֱלִיתָ מִן שְׁאוֹל נַפְשִׁי, חִיִּיתַנִי מִיָּרְדִי בוֹר. זַמְּרוּ לַיהוה חֲסִידָיו, וְהוֹדוּ לְזֵכֶר קָדְשׁוֹ. כִּי רֶגַע בְּאַפּוֹ, חַיִּים בִּרְצוֹנוֹ, בָּעֶרֶב יָלִין בֶּכִי וְלַבֹּקֶר רִנָּה. וַאֲנִי אָמַרְתִּי בְשַׁלְוִי, בַּל אֶמּוֹט לְעוֹלָם. יהוה בִּרְצוֹנְךָ הֶעֱמַדְתָּה לְהַרְרִי עֹז, הִסְתַּרְתָּ פָנֶיךָ הָיִיתִי נִבְהָל. אֵלֶיךָ יהוה אֶקְרָא, וְאֶל אֲדֹנָי אֶתְחַנָּן. מַה בֶּצַע בְּדָמִי, בְּרִדְתִּי אֶל שָׁחַת, הֲיוֹדְךָ עָפָר, הֲיַגִּיד אֲמִתֶּךָ. שְׁמַע יהוה וְחָנֵּנִי, יהוה הֱיֵה עֹזֵר לִי. ❖ הָפַכְתָּ מִסְפְּדִי לְמָחוֹל לִי, פִּתַּחְתָּ שַׂקִּי, וַתְּאַזְּרֵנִי שִׂמְחָה. לְמַעַן יְזַמֶּרְךָ כָבוֹד וְלֹא יִדֹּם, יהוה אֱלֹהַי לְעוֹלָם אוֹדֶךָּ.

קדיש יתום

In the presence of a *minyan,* mourners recite קַדִּישׁ יָתוֹם (see *Laws* §119):

[A commentary to this *Kaddish* appears on p. 57.]

יִתְגַּדַּל וְיִתְקַדַּשׁ שְׁמֵהּ רַבָּא. (.Cong.— אָמֵן) בְּעָלְמָא דִּי בְרָא כִרְעוּתֵהּ. וְיַמְלִיךְ מַלְכוּתֵהּ, בְּחַיֵּיכוֹן וּבְיוֹמֵיכוֹן וּבְחַיֵּי דְכָל בֵּית יִשְׂרָאֵל, בַּעֲגָלָא וּבִזְמַן קָרִיב. וְאִמְרוּ: אָמֵן.

(.Cong.— אָמֵן. יְהֵא שְׁמֵהּ רַבָּא מְבָרַךְ לְעָלַם וּלְעָלְמֵי עָלְמַיָּא.)

יְהֵא שְׁמֵהּ רַבָּא מְבָרַךְ לְעָלַם וּלְעָלְמֵי עָלְמַיָּא.

יִתְבָּרַךְ וְיִשְׁתַּבַּח וְיִתְפָּאַר וְיִתְרוֹמַם וְיִתְנַשֵּׂא וְיִתְהַדָּר וְיִתְעַלֶּה וְיִתְהַלָּל שְׁמֵהּ דְּקֻדְשָׁא בְּרִיךְ הוּא (.Cong.— בְּרִיךְ הוּא) — °לְעֵלָּא מִן כָּל (°לְעֵלָּא וּלְעֵלָּא מִכָּל —From Rosh Hashanah to Yom Kippur substitute) בִּרְכָתָא וְשִׁירָתָא תֻּשְׁבְּחָתָא וְנֶחֱמָתָא, דַּאֲמִירָן בְּעָלְמָא. וְאִמְרוּ: אָמֵן. (.Cong.— אָמֵן.)

יְהֵא שְׁלָמָא רַבָּא מִן שְׁמַיָּא, וְחַיִּים עָלֵינוּ וְעַל כָּל יִשְׂרָאֵל. וְאִמְרוּ: אָמֵן. (.Cong.— אָמֵן.)

Take three steps back. Bow left and say ... עֹשֶׂה; bow right and say ... הוּא; bow forward and say וְעַל כָּל ... אָמֵן. Remain standing in place for a few moments, then take three steps forward.

עֹשֶׂה שָׁלוֹם בִּמְרוֹמָיו, הוּא יַעֲשֶׂה שָׁלוֹם עָלֵינוּ, וְעַל כָּל יִשְׂרָאֵל. וְאִמְרוּ: אָמֵן. (.Cong.— אָמֵן.)

PESUKEI D'ZIMRAH FOR THE SABBATH AND FESTIVALS

The preliminary sections of *Shacharis* are the same as on weekdays (pp. 2-54).

INTRODUCTORY PSALM TO PESUKEI D'ZIMRAH

Psalm 30 (commentary on p. 55).

מִזְמוֹר *A psalm — a song for the inauguration of the Temple— by David. I will exalt You,* HASHEM, *for You have drawn me up and not let my foes rejoice over me.* HASHEM, *my God, I cried out to You and You healed me.* HASHEM, *You have raised my soul from the lower world, You have preserved me from my descent to the Pit. Make music to* HASHEM, *His devout ones, and give thanks to His Holy Name. For His anger endures but a moment; life results from His favor. In the evening one lies down weeping, but with dawn — a cry of joy! I had said in my serenity, 'I will never falter.' But,* HASHEM, *all is through Your favor — You supported my greatness with might; should You but conceal Your face, I would be confounded. To You,* HASHEM, *I would call and to my Lord I would appeal. What gain is there in my death, when I descend to the Pit? Will the dust acknowledge You? Will it declare Your truth? Hear,* HASHEM, *and favor me;* HASHEM, *be my Helper!* Chazzan— *You have changed for me my lament into dancing; You undid my sackcloth and girded me with gladness. So that my soul might make music to You and not be stilled,* HASHEM *my God, forever will I thank You.*

THE MOURNERS' KADDISH

In the presence of a *minyan,* mourners recite קַדִּישׁ יָתוֹם, the Mourner's *Kaddish.* (See *Laws* §119.)

[A transliteration of this *Kaddish* appears on page 1043.]

יִתְגַּדַּל *May His great Name grow exalted and sanctified* (Cong.— *Amen.*) *in the world that He created as He willed. May He give reign to His kingship in your lifetimes and in your days, and in the lifetimes of the entire Family of Israel, swiftly and soon. Now respond: Amen.*

(Cong.— *Amen. May His great Name be blessed forever and ever.*)

May His great Name be blessed forever and ever.

Blessed, praised, glorified, exalted, extolled, mighty, upraised, and lauded be the Name of the Holy One, Blessed is He (Cong.— *Blessed is He*) — (From Rosh Hashanah to Yom Kippur add: *exceedingly*) *beyond any blessing and song, praise and consolation that are uttered in the world. Now respond: Amen.* (Cong.— *Amen.*)

May there be abundant peace from Heaven, and life, upon us and upon all Israel. Now respond: Amen. (Cong.— *Amen.*)

Take three steps back. Bow left and say, *'He Who makes peace ...',* bow right and say, *'may He ...';* bow forward and say, *'and upon all Israel ...'* Remain standing in place for a few moments, then take three steps forward.

He Who makes peace in His heights, may He make peace upon us, and upon all Israel. Now respond: Amen. (Cong.— *Amen.*)

Some recite this short Kabbalistic declaration of intent before beginning *Pesukei D'zimrah:*

הֲרֵינִי מְזַמֵּן אֶת פִּי לְהוֹדוֹת וּלְהַלֵּל וּלְשַׁבֵּחַ אֶת בּוֹרְאִי. לְשֵׁם יִחוּד קוּדְשָׁא בְּרִיךְ הוּא וּשְׁכִינְתֵּיהּ עַל יְדֵי הַהוּא טָמִיר וְנֶעְלָם, בְּשֵׁם כָּל יִשְׂרָאֵל.

Pesukei D'zimrah begins with the recital of בָּרוּךְ שֶׁאָמַר.
Stand while reciting בָּרוּךְ שֶׁאָמַר. During its recitation, hold the two front *tzitzis* of the *tallis* (or *tallis kattan*) in the right hand, and at its conclusion kiss the *tzitzis* and release them.
Conversation is forbidden from this point until after *Shemoneh Esrei,*
except for certain prayer responses (see commentary, p. 59 and *Laws* §33-54).

בָּרוּךְ שֶׁאָמַר וְהָיָה הָעוֹלָם, בָּרוּךְ הוּא. בָּרוּךְ עֹשֶׂה בְרֵאשִׁית, בָּרוּךְ אוֹמֵר וְעֹשֶׂה, בָּרוּךְ גּוֹזֵר וּמְקַיֵּם, בָּרוּךְ מְרַחֵם עַל הָאָרֶץ, בָּרוּךְ מְרַחֵם עַל הַבְּרִיּוֹת, בָּרוּךְ מְשַׁלֵּם שָׂכָר טוֹב לִירֵאָיו, בָּרוּךְ חַי לָעַד וְקַיָּם לָנֶצַח, בָּרוּךְ פּוֹדֶה וּמַצִּיל, בָּרוּךְ שְׁמוֹ. בָּרוּךְ אַתָּה יהוה אֱלֹהֵינוּ מֶלֶךְ הָעוֹלָם, הָאֵל הָאָב הָרַחֲמָן הַמְּהֻלָּל בְּפֶה עַמּוֹ, מְשֻׁבָּח וּמְפֹאָר בִּלְשׁוֹן חֲסִידָיו וַעֲבָדָיו, וּבְשִׁירֵי דָוִד עַבְדֶּךָ. נְהַלֶּלְךָ יהוה אֱלֹהֵינוּ, בִּשְׁבָחוֹת וּבִזְמִרוֹת. נְגַדֶּלְךָ וּנְשַׁבֵּחֲךָ וּנְפָאֶרְךָ וְנַזְכִּיר שִׁמְךָ וְנַמְלִיכְךָ, מַלְכֵּנוּ אֱלֹהֵינוּ. ❖ יָחִיד, חֵי הָעוֹלָמִים, מֶלֶךְ מְשֻׁבָּח וּמְפֹאָר עֲדֵי עַד שְׁמוֹ הַגָּדוֹל. בָּרוּךְ אַתָּה יהוה, מֶלֶךְ מְהֻלָּל בַּתִּשְׁבָּחוֹת. (Cong.— אָמֵן.)

דברי הימים א טז:ח-לו (commentary on p. 60)

הוֹדוּ לַיהוה קִרְאוּ בִשְׁמוֹ, הוֹדִיעוּ בָעַמִּים עֲלִילֹתָיו. שִׁירוּ לוֹ, זַמְּרוּ לוֹ, שִׂיחוּ בְּכָל נִפְלְאֹתָיו. הִתְהַלְּלוּ בְּשֵׁם קָדְשׁוֹ, יִשְׂמַח לֵב מְבַקְשֵׁי יהוה. דִּרְשׁוּ יהוה וְעֻזּוֹ, בַּקְּשׁוּ פָנָיו תָּמִיד. זִכְרוּ נִפְלְאֹתָיו אֲשֶׁר עָשָׂה, מֹפְתָיו וּמִשְׁפְּטֵי פִיהוּ. זֶרַע יִשְׂרָאֵל עַבְדּוֹ, בְּנֵי יַעֲקֹב בְּחִירָיו. הוּא יהוה אֱלֹהֵינוּ, בְּכָל הָאָרֶץ מִשְׁפָּטָיו. זִכְרוּ לְעוֹלָם בְּרִיתוֹ, דָּבָר צִוָּה לְאֶלֶף דּוֹר. אֲשֶׁר כָּרַת אֶת אַבְרָהָם, וּשְׁבוּעָתוֹ לְיִצְחָק. וַיַּעֲמִידֶהָ לְיַעֲקֹב לְחֹק, לְיִשְׂרָאֵל בְּרִית עוֹלָם. לֵאמֹר, לְךָ אֶתֵּן אֶרֶץ כְּנָעַן, חֶבֶל נַחֲלַתְכֶם. בִּהְיוֹתְכֶם מְתֵי מִסְפָּר, כִּמְעַט וְגָרִים בָּהּ. וַיִּתְהַלְּכוּ מִגּוֹי אֶל גּוֹי, וּמִמַּמְלָכָה אֶל עַם אַחֵר. לֹא הִנִּיחַ לְאִישׁ לְעָשְׁקָם, וַיּוֹכַח עֲלֵיהֶם מְלָכִים. אַל תִּגְּעוּ בִּמְשִׁיחָי, וּבִנְבִיאַי אַל תָּרֵעוּ. שִׁירוּ לַיהוה כָּל הָאָרֶץ, בַּשְּׂרוּ מִיּוֹם אֶל יוֹם יְשׁוּעָתוֹ. סַפְּרוּ בַגּוֹיִם אֶת כְּבוֹדוֹ, בְּכָל הָעַמִּים נִפְלְאוֹתָיו.

Some recite this short Kabbalistic declaration of intent before beginning *Pesukei D'zimrah:*

I now prepare my mouth to thank, laud, and praise my Creator. For the sake of the unification of the Holy One, Blessed is He, and His Presence, through Him Who is hidden and inscrutable — [I pray] in the name of all Israel.

Pesukei D'zimrah begins with the recital of בָּרוּךְ שֶׁאָמַר, *'Blessed is He Who spoke ...'* Stand while reciting בָּרוּךְ שֶׁאָמַר. During its recitation, hold the two front *tzitzis* of the *tallis* (or *tallis kattan*) in the right hand, and at its conclusion kiss the *tzitzis* and release them. Conversation is forbidden from this point until after *Shemoneh Esrei,* except for certain prayer responses (see commentary, p. 59 and *Laws* §33-54).

בָּרוּךְ שֶׁאָמַר *Blessed is He Who spoke, and the world came into being — blessed is He. Blessed is He Who maintains Creation; blessed is He Who speaks and does; blessed is He Who decrees and fulfills; blessed is He Who has mercy on the earth; blessed is He Who has mercy on the creatures; blessed is He Who gives goodly reward to those who fear Him; blessed is He Who lives forever and endures to eternity; blessed is He Who redeems and rescues — blessed is His Name! Blessed are You, HASHEM, our God, King of the universe, the God, the merciful Father, Who is lauded by the mouth of His people, praised and glorified by the tongue of His devout ones and His servants and through the psalms of David Your servant. We shall laud You, HASHEM, our God, with praises and songs. We shall exalt You, praise You, glorify You, mention Your Name and proclaim Your reign, our King, our God.* Chazzan— *O Unique One, Life-giver of the worlds, King Whose great Name is eternally praised and glorified. Blessed are You, HASHEM, the King Who is lauded with praises.* (Cong.— *Amen.)*

I Chronicles 16:8-36 (commentary on p. 60).

הוֹדוּ *Give thanks to HASHEM, declare His Name, make His acts known among the peoples. Sing to Him, make music to Him, speak of all His wonders. Glory in His Holy Name, be glad of heart, you who seek HASHEM. Search out HASHEM and His might, seek His Presence always. Remember His wonders that He wrought, His marvels and the judgments of His mouth. O seed of Israel, His servant, O children of Jacob, His chosen ones — He is HASHEM, our God, over all the earth are His judgments. Remember His covenant forever — the word He commanded for a thousand generations — that He made with Abraham and His vow to Isaac. Then He established it for Jacob as a statute, for Israel as an everlasting covenant; saying, 'To you I shall give the Land of Canaan, the lot of your heritage.' When you were but few in number, hardly dwelling there, and they wandered from nation to nation, from one kingdom to another people. He let no man rob them, and He rebuked kings for their sake. 'Dare not touch My anointed ones, and to My prophets do no harm.' Sing to HASHEM, everyone on earth, announce His salvation daily. Relate His glory among the nations, among all the peoples His wonders.*

כִּי גָדוֹל יהוה וּמְהֻלָּל מְאֹד, וְנוֹרָא הוּא עַל כָּל אֱלֹהִים. ❖ כִּי כָּל אֱלֹהֵי הָעַמִּים אֱלִילִים, (pause) וַיהוה שָׁמַיִם עָשָׂה.

הוֹד וְהָדָר לְפָנָיו, עֹז וְחֶדְוָה בִּמְקֹמוֹ. הָבוּ לַיהוה מִשְׁפְּחוֹת עַמִּים, הָבוּ לַיהוה כָּבוֹד וָעֹז. הָבוּ לַיהוה כְּבוֹד שְׁמוֹ, שְׂאוּ מִנְחָה וּבֹאוּ לְפָנָיו, הִשְׁתַּחֲווּ לַיהוה בְּהַדְרַת קֹדֶשׁ. חִילוּ מִלְּפָנָיו כָּל הָאָרֶץ, אַף תִּכּוֹן תֵּבֵל בַּל תִּמּוֹט. יִשְׂמְחוּ הַשָּׁמַיִם וְתָגֵל הָאָרֶץ, וְיֹאמְרוּ בַגּוֹיִם, יהוה מָלָךְ. יִרְעַם הַיָּם וּמְלוֹאוֹ, יַעֲלֹץ הַשָּׂדֶה וְכָל אֲשֶׁר בּוֹ. אָז יְרַנְּנוּ עֲצֵי הַיָּעַר, מִלִּפְנֵי יהוה, כִּי בָא לִשְׁפּוֹט אֶת הָאָרֶץ. הוֹדוּ לַיהוה כִּי טוֹב, כִּי לְעוֹלָם חַסְדּוֹ. וְאִמְרוּ הוֹשִׁיעֵנוּ אֱלֹהֵי יִשְׁעֵנוּ, וְקַבְּצֵנוּ וְהַצִּילֵנוּ מִן הַגּוֹיִם, לְהֹדוֹת לְשֵׁם קָדְשֶׁךָ, לְהִשְׁתַּבֵּחַ בִּתְהִלָּתֶךָ. בָּרוּךְ יהוה אֱלֹהֵי יִשְׂרָאֵל מִן הָעוֹלָם וְעַד הָעֹלָם, וַיֹּאמְרוּ כָל הָעָם, אָמֵן, וְהַלֵּל לַיהוה.

❖ רוֹמְמוּ יהוה אֱלֹהֵינוּ וְהִשְׁתַּחֲווּ לַהֲדֹם רַגְלָיו, קָדוֹשׁ הוּא.[1] רוֹמְמוּ יהוה אֱלֹהֵינוּ וְהִשְׁתַּחֲווּ לְהַר קָדְשׁוֹ, כִּי קָדוֹשׁ יהוה אֱלֹהֵינוּ.[2]

וְהוּא רַחוּם יְכַפֵּר עָוֹן וְלֹא יַשְׁחִית, וְהִרְבָּה לְהָשִׁיב אַפּוֹ, וְלֹא יָעִיר כָּל חֲמָתוֹ.[3] אַתָּה יהוה, לֹא תִכְלָא רַחֲמֶיךָ מִמֶּנִּי, חַסְדְּךָ וַאֲמִתְּךָ תָּמִיד יִצְּרוּנִי.[4] זְכֹר רַחֲמֶיךָ יהוה וַחֲסָדֶיךָ, כִּי מֵעוֹלָם הֵמָּה.[5] תְּנוּ עֹז לֵאלֹהִים, עַל יִשְׂרָאֵל גַּאֲוָתוֹ, וְעֻזּוֹ בַּשְּׁחָקִים. נוֹרָא אֱלֹהִים מִמִּקְדָּשֶׁיךָ, אֵל יִשְׂרָאֵל הוּא נֹתֵן עֹז וְתַעֲצֻמוֹת לָעָם, בָּרוּךְ אֱלֹהִים.[6] אֵל נְקָמוֹת יהוה, אֵל נְקָמוֹת הוֹפִיעַ. הִנָּשֵׂא שֹׁפֵט הָאָרֶץ, הָשֵׁב גְּמוּל עַל גֵּאִים.[7] לַיהוה הַיְשׁוּעָה, עַל עַמְּךָ בִרְכָתֶךָ סֶּלָה.[8] ❖ יהוה צְבָאוֹת עִמָּנוּ, מִשְׂגָּב לָנוּ אֱלֹהֵי יַעֲקֹב סֶלָה.[9] יהוה צְבָאוֹת, אַשְׁרֵי אָדָם בֹּטֵחַ בָּךְ.[10] יהוה הוֹשִׁיעָה, הַמֶּלֶךְ יַעֲנֵנוּ בְיוֹם קָרְאֵנוּ.[11]

הוֹשִׁיעָה אֶת עַמֶּךָ, וּבָרֵךְ אֶת נַחֲלָתֶךָ, וּרְעֵם וְנַשְּׂאֵם עַד הָעוֹלָם.[12] נַפְשֵׁנוּ חִכְּתָה לַיהוה, עֶזְרֵנוּ וּמָגִנֵּנוּ הוּא. כִּי בוֹ יִשְׂמַח לִבֵּנוּ, כִּי בְשֵׁם קָדְשׁוֹ בָטָחְנוּ. יְהִי חַסְדְּךָ יהוה עָלֵינוּ, כַּאֲשֶׁר יִחַלְנוּ לָךְ.[13] הַרְאֵנוּ יהוה חַסְדֶּךָ, וְיֶשְׁעֲךָ תִּתֶּן לָנוּ.[14]

That HASHEM is great and exceedingly lauded, and awesome is He above all heavenly powers. Chazzan—*For all the gods of the peoples are nothings — but HASHEM made heaven!*

Glory and majesty are before Him, might and delight are in His place. Render to HASHEM, O families of the peoples, render to HASHEM honor and might. Render to HASHEM honor worthy of His Name, take an offering and come before Him, prostrate yourselves before HASHEM in His intensely holy place. Tremble before Him, everyone on earth, indeed, the world is fixed so that it cannot falter. The heavens will be glad and the earth will rejoice and say among the nations, 'HASHEM has reigned!' The sea and its fullness will roar, the field and everything in it will exult. Then the trees of the forest will sing with joy before HASHEM, for He will have arrived to judge the earth. Give thanks to HASHEM, for He is good, for His kindness endures forever. And say, 'Save us, O God of our salvation, gather us and rescue us from the nations, to thank Your Holy Name and to glory in Your praise!' Blessed is HASHEM, the God of Israel, from This World to the World to Come — and let the entire people say, 'Amen and praise to God!'

Chazzan— *Exalt HASHEM, our God, and bow at His footstool; He is holy!*[1] *Exalt HASHEM, our God, and bow at His holy mountain; for holy is HASHEM, our God.*[2]

He, the Merciful One, is forgiving of iniquity and does not destroy; frequently, He withdraws His anger, not arousing His entire rage.[3] *You, HASHEM — withhold not Your mercy from me; may Your kindness and Your truth always protect me.*[4] *Remember Your mercies, HASHEM, and Your kindnesses, for they are from the beginning of the world.*[5] *Render might to God, Whose majesty hovers over Israel and Whose might is in the clouds. You are awesome, O God, from Your sanctuaries, O God of Israel — it is He Who grants might and power to the people, blessed is God.*[6] *O God of vengeance, HASHEM, O God of vengeance, appear! Arise, O Judge of the earth, render recompense to the haughty.*[7] *Salvation is HASHEM's, upon Your people is Your blessing, Selah.*[8] Chazzan— *HASHEM, Master of Legions, is with us, a stronghold for us is the God of Jacob, Selah.*[9] *HASHEM, Master of Legions, praiseworthy is the person who trusts in You.*[10] *HASHEM, save! May the King answer us on the day we call.*[11]

Save Your people and bless Your heritage, tend them and elevate them forever.[12] *Our soul longed for HASHEM — our help and our shield is He. For in Him will our hearts be glad, for in His Holy Name we trusted. May Your kindness, HASHEM, be upon us, just as we awaited You.*[13] *Show us Your kindness, HASHEM, and grant us Your salvation.*[14]

---

(1) *Psalms* 99:5. (2) 99:9. (3) 78:38. (4) 40:12. (5) 25:6. (6) 68:35-36. (7) 94:1-2. (8) 3:9. (9) 46:8. (10) 84:13. (11) 20:10. (12) 28:9. (13) 33:20-22 (14) 85:8.

קוּמָה עֶזְרָתָה לָּנוּ, וּפְדֵנוּ לְמַעַן חַסְדֶּךָ.[1] אָנֹכִי יהוה אֱלֹהֶיךָ
הַמַּעַלְךָ מֵאֶרֶץ מִצְרָיִם, הַרְחֶב פִּיךָ וַאֲמַלְאֵהוּ.[2] אַשְׁרֵי הָעָם
שֶׁכָּכָה לּוֹ, אַשְׁרֵי הָעָם שֶׁיהוה אֱלֹהָיו.[3] ❖ וַאֲנִי בְּחַסְדְּךָ בָטַחְתִּי,
יָגֵל לִבִּי בִּישׁוּעָתֶךָ, אָשִׁירָה לַיהוה, כִּי גָמַל עָלָי.[4]

תהלים יט

לַמְנַצֵּחַ מִזְמוֹר לְדָוִד. הַשָּׁמַיִם מְסַפְּרִים כְּבוֹד אֵל, וּמַעֲשֵׂה יָדָיו מַגִּיד הָרָקִיעַ.* יוֹם לְיוֹם יַבִּיעַ אֹמֶר,* וְלַיְלָה לְּלַיְלָה יְחַוֶּה דָּעַת. אֵין אֹמֶר וְאֵין דְּבָרִים,* בְּלִי נִשְׁמָע קוֹלָם. בְּכָל הָאָרֶץ יָצָא קַוָּם,* וּבִקְצֵה תֵבֵל מִלֵּיהֶם,* לַשֶּׁמֶשׁ שָׂם אֹהֶל* בָּהֶם. וְהוּא כְּחָתָן יֹצֵא מֵחֻפָּתוֹ, יָשִׂישׂ כְּגִבּוֹר לָרוּץ אֹרַח.* מִקְצֵה הַשָּׁמַיִם מוֹצָאוֹ, וּתְקוּפָתוֹ עַל קְצוֹתָם, וְאֵין נִסְתָּר מֵחַמָּתוֹ. תּוֹרַת יהוה תְּמִימָה, מְשִׁיבַת נָפֶשׁ, עֵדוּת יהוה נֶאֱמָנָה,* מַחְכִּימַת פֶּתִי. פִּקּוּדֵי יהוה יְשָׁרִים, מְשַׂמְּחֵי לֵב,* מִצְוַת יהוה בָּרָה, מְאִירַת עֵינָיִם. יִרְאַת יהוה טְהוֹרָה,* עוֹמֶדֶת לָעַד, מִשְׁפְּטֵי יהוה אֱמֶת, צָדְקוּ יַחְדָּו.* הַנֶּחֱמָדִים מִזָּהָב וּמִפָּז רָב, וּמְתוּקִים מִדְּבַשׁ וְנֹפֶת צוּפִים. גַּם עַבְדְּךָ נִזְהָר בָּהֶם, בְּשָׁמְרָם עֵקֶב רָב. שְׁגִיאוֹת מִי יָבִין,* מִנִּסְתָּרוֹת נַקֵּנִי. גַּם מִזֵּדִים

⊲§ Additional Pesukei D'zimrah for the Sabbath and Festivals

The *Zohar* teaches that the prayers of the Sabbath morning symbolize the special spiritual bliss that adorns Israel on the Sabbath. The angels join in their own hymns of praise to God, they laud Israel, saying that our human spiritual elevation enables the angels themselves to rise to greater heights. This heightened holiness is expressed by the addition of psalms to the *Pesukei D'zimrah,* and hymns to the Blessings of the *Shema.* The choice of psalms is based on three fundamental concepts found in the Sabbath: the remembrance that God finished creation in six days and rested on the Sabbath (זֵכֶר לְמַעֲשֵׂה בְרֵאשִׁית); the remembrance of the Exodus from Egypt (זֵכֶר לִיצִיאַת מִצְרָיִם); and the idea that our Sabbath is a semblance of the World to Come (מֵעֵין עוֹלָם הַבָּא) *(World of Prayer).* As we come to these added psalms, the commentary will note which of these concepts are expressed by each one respectively.

⊲§ לַמְנַצֵּחַ / Psalm 19

This psalm describes how the wonders of creation are a testimony to the glory of God Who made them. Nature sings to God in the sense that each part of the universe acts as God wanted it to and in harmony with all other parts. Seen this way, the universe is like a symphony orchestra playing a continuous song of praise. But after lyrically recounting the wonders of creation, the Psalmist says that all of this is merely an example of the greatness of the Torah — the blueprint that enables man to understand God's will and fulfill it.

הַשָּׁמַיִם ... הָרָקִיעַ — *The heavens ... the expanse of the sky.* The upper reaches where the planets and stars orbit are called שָׁמַיִם, *the heavens.* The רָקִיעַ, *expanse of the sky,* contains the atmosphere and evaporated moisture that forms clouds and becomes precipitation *(Malbim).*

יוֹם לְיוֹם יַבִּיעַ אֹמֶר — *Day following day brings expressions* [*of praise*]. The daily renewed works of creation, such as the rising and setting of the sun, stir mankind to speak and express God's praises *(Rashi).*

אֵין אֹמֶר וְאֵין דְּבָרִים — *There is no speech and there are no words.* The heavens do not speak, yet the inner soul of man can discern their message clearly *(Radak).*

קַוָּם — *Their line.* The precision of the universe is likened metaphorically to a surveyor's tape stretched out to the ends of the earth. This means

Arise — assist us, and redeem us by virtue of Your kindness.[1] *I am* HASHEM, *your God, Who raised you from the land of Egypt, open wide your mouth and I will fill it.*[2] *Praiseworthy is the people for whom this is so, praiseworthy is the people whose God is* HASHEM.[3] Chazzan— *As for me, I trust in Your kindness; my heart will rejoice in Your salvation. I will sing to* HASHEM, *for He dealt kindly with me.*[4]

Psalm 19

לַמְנַצֵּחַ *For the Conductor; a song of David. The heavens declare the glory of God, and the expanse of the sky* tells of His handiwork. Day following day brings expressions of praise,* and night following night bespeaks wisdom. There is no speech and there are no words;* their sound is unheard. Their line* goes forth throughout the earth, and their words* reach the farthest ends of the land; He has set up a tent* for the sun in their midst. And it is like a groom coming forth from his bridal chamber, rejoicing like a warrior to run the course.* The end of the heavens is its source, and its circuit is to their other end; nothing is hidden from its heat. The Torah of* HASHEM *is perfect, restoring the soul; the testimony of* HASHEM *is trustworthy,* making the simple one wise. The orders of* HASHEM *are upright, gladdening the heart;* the command of* HASHEM *is clear, enlightening the eyes. The fear of* HASHEM *is pure,* enduring forever; the judgments of* HASHEM *are true, altogether righteous.* They are more desirable than gold, than even much fine gold; sweeter than honey and drippings from the combs. Even Your servant is careful of them, for in observing them there is great reward. Yet, who can discern mistakes?* From unperceived faults cleanse me. Also from intentional sins,*

(1) *Psalms* 44:27. (2) 81:11. (3) 144:15. (4) 13:6.

that the precision of the cosmos is evident all over the earth to any observer.

מִלֵּיהֶם — *Their words.* The performance of the heavenly bodies speaks of God's wisdom with greater eloquence than the spoken word *(Radak).*

אֹהֶל — *A tent.* The sky is likened to a tent with the sun affixed in its roof *(Ibn Ezra).*

יָשִׂישׂ כְּגִבּוֹר לָרוּץ אֹרַח — *Rejoicing like a warrior to run the course.* The warrior rejoices at the opportunity to go out to war, for he has confidence in his strength. So too, the sun is confident that it will run its course with no interference *(Metzudos).*

עֵדוּת ה׳ נֶאֱמָנָה — *The testimony of* HASHEM *is trustworthy.* The *mitzvos* of the Torah are called *testimony,* because they attest to the *faith* of the people who fulfill them *(Metzudos).*

מְשַׂמְּחֵי לֵב — *Gladdening the heart.* The wise man will rejoice when his intellect will dominate the passions of his body *(Radak).*

יִרְאַת ה׳ טְהוֹרָה — *The fear of* HASHEM *is pure.* This refers to the negative commandments. The person who is careful not to transgress them is pure, for he has not sullied himself with sin *(Ibn Ezra).*

צָדְקוּ יַחְדָּו — *Altogether righteous.* There is no contradiction between one law of the Torah and another, whereas in civil law one will very often find inconsistencies and conflicts between different statutes *(Ibn Ezra).*

שְׁגִיאוֹת מִי יָבִין — *Yet, who can discern mistakes?* Though I try to keep Your commands, who can be so careful that he never errs unintentionally? *(Rashi; Radak).* שְׁגִיאָה, *mistake,* denotes an error due to imperfect understanding and reasoning from which no man is immune and of which he is unaware. Only Divine assistance can protect a person from these inborn human flaws *(R' Hirsch).*

חֲשֹׂךְ עַבְדֶּךָ, אַל יִמְשְׁלוּ בִי,* אָז אֵיתָם, וְנִקֵּיתִי מִפֶּשַׁע רָב.

❖ יִהְיוּ לְרָצוֹן אִמְרֵי פִי, וְהֶגְיוֹן לִבִּי* לְפָנֶיךָ, יהוה צוּרִי וְגֹאֲלִי.

תהלים לד

לְדָוִד, בְּשַׁנּוֹתוֹ אֶת טַעְמוֹ לִפְנֵי אֲבִימֶלֶךְ, וַיְגָרְשֵׁהוּ וַיֵּלַךְ.

אֲבָרְכָה* אֶת יהוה בְּכָל עֵת, תָּמִיד תְּהִלָּתוֹ בְּפִי.

בַּיהוה תִּתְהַלֵּל נַפְשִׁי, יִשְׁמְעוּ עֲנָוִים וְיִשְׂמָחוּ.

גַּדְּלוּ לַיהוה אִתִּי,* וּנְרוֹמְמָה שְׁמוֹ יַחְדָּו.

דָּרַשְׁתִּי אֶת יהוה וְעָנָנִי, וּמִכָּל מְגוּרוֹתַי הִצִּילָנִי.

הִבִּיטוּ אֵלָיו וְנָהָרוּ,

וּפְנֵיהֶם אַל יֶחְפָּרוּ.

זֶה עָנִי* קָרָא וַיהוה שָׁמֵעַ,* וּמִכָּל צָרוֹתָיו הוֹשִׁיעוֹ.

חֹנֶה מַלְאַךְ יהוה סָבִיב לִירֵאָיו, וַיְחַלְּצֵם.

טַעֲמוּ וּרְאוּ* כִּי טוֹב יהוה, אַשְׁרֵי הַגֶּבֶר יֶחֱסֶה בּוֹ.

יְראוּ אֶת יהוה קְדֹשָׁיו,* כִּי אֵין מַחְסוֹר לִירֵאָיו.

כְּפִירִים רָשׁוּ* וְרָעֵבוּ, וְדֹרְשֵׁי יהוה לֹא יַחְסְרוּ כָל טוֹב.*

לְכוּ בָנִים* שִׁמְעוּ לִי, יִרְאַת יהוה אֲלַמֶּדְכֶם.

מִי הָאִישׁ הֶחָפֵץ חַיִּים,* אֹהֵב יָמִים לִרְאוֹת טוֹב.

אַל יִמְשְׁלוּ בִי — *Let them not rule me.* Do not let my evil inclination overpower me. For, God helps those whose hearts yearn to do what is right and proper [cf. *Yoma* 38b].

וְהֶגְיוֹן לִבִּי — *And the thoughts of my heart.* Please do not limit Your attention to the requests which I express orally. Be aware of the many inner thoughts that I am incapable of expressing *(Radak).*

⸎ לְדָוִד בְּשַׁנּוֹתוֹ / Psalm 34

Everything in creation has its place. The previous psalm spoke of the loftiest physical and spiritual forces in creation and how they sing to God. Here we see how His greatness can be perceived even in the most painful depths. David once said to God, 'All that You created is beautiful, and wisdom is the most beautiful of all. However, I fail to understand or to appreciate the value of madness. What satisfaction can You derive from having created a lunatic who walks about ripping his clothing, is chased by little children and is mocked by all?'

God replied, 'David, you will some day need this madness which you now criticize. Furthermore, you will even pray that I give this madness to you.'

A short time later, David was forced to flee for his life from King Saul. Only among the Philistines, Israel's sworn enemies, did he find safety. But even there he was recognized as Israel's greatest warrior and threatened with death. He pretended to be insane and King Abimelech — disgusted by David's lunatic behavior — drove him out. [See *I Samuel* 21:11-16.] Instead of feeling despair, David composed this beautiful and profound hymn. Its verses begin according to the letters of the *Aleph-Beis,* to show that we are to praise God with our every faculty, and to acknowledge that whatever He created — from *aleph* to *tav* — is for the good.

אֲבָרְכָה — *I shall bless.* David's frightening experiences and his miraculous escape inspired him to understand that God's ways are merciful. Hence, he responds with a blessing *(Sforno).*

גַּדְּלוּ לַה' אִתִּי — *Declare the greatness of* HASHEM *with me.* Not content merely to have been saved, he wants his salvation to be a lesson to others. Let everyone declare God's greatness.

זֶה עָנִי — *This poor man.* In his humility, David looks upon himself as poor and undeserving *(Radak).*

וַה' שָׁמֵעַ — *And* HASHEM *hears.* He hears and

restrain Your servant; let them not rule me; then I shall be perfect and cleansed of great transgression.* Chazzan– *May the expressions of my mouth and the thoughts of my heart* find favor before You, HASHEM, my Rock and my Redeemer.*

Psalm 34

לְדָוִד *Of David: When he disguised his sanity before Abimelech who drove him out and he left.*

א *I shall bless* HASHEM at all times,*
always shall His praise be in my mouth.

ב *In HASHEM does my soul glory,*
may humble ones hear and be glad.

ג *Declare the greatness of HASHEM with me,**
and let us exalt His Name together.

ד *I sought out HASHEM and He answered me,*
and from all my terror He delivered me.

ה *They look to Him and become radiant,*
ו *and their faces were not shamed.*

ז *This poor man* calls and HASHEM hears* —*
and from all his troubles He saved him.

ח *The angel of HASHEM encamps around His reverent ones*
and releases them.

ט *Contemplate and see* that HASHEM is good —*
praiseworthy is the man who takes refuge in Him.

י *Fear HASHEM, you — His holy ones* —*
for there is no deprivation for His reverent ones.

כ *Young lions may want* and hunger,*
*but those who seek HASHEM will not lack any good.**

ל *Go, O sons,* heed me,*
the fear of HASHEM will I teach you.

מ *Which man desires life,**
who loves days of seeing good?

---

responds even before the supplicant has completed his prayer *(R' Chaim Vital).*

טַעֲמוּ וּרְאוּ — *Contemplate and see. Contemplate* intellectually, by analyzing events, and *see,* by noticing God's deeds — and you will realize *that HASHEM is good (Radak).*

קְדֹשָׁיו — *His holy ones.* Holy people are those who control their lusts, even the permitted ones *(Ramban).*

כְּפִירִים רָשׁוּ — *Young lions may want.* Strong, vigorous people — like lions in the prime of life — become helpless and destitute, but God will provide for those who trust in Him.

לֹא יַחְסְרוּ כָל טוֹב — *Will not lack any good.* They may not have all the luxuries enjoyed by their neighbors, but they feel no lack of anything because they are content with their lot *(Sh'lah).*

לְכוּ בָנִים — *Go, O sons.* In this sense, go is an exhortation to accomplish a goal *(Radak).*

מִי הָאִישׁ הֶחָפֵץ חַיִּים — *Which man desires life,* i.e., in the World to Come *(Sforno).* In another vein, however, the Psalmist urged people to better their lives in This World by avoiding gossip and slander. David was the victim of constant slander and his generation suffered defeats in battle because they were not careful in their speech [*Yerushalmi Peah* 1:1] *(R' A. Ch. Feuer).*

The *Baal Shem Tov* taught that every person is allotted a given number of words during his life.

נְצֹר לְשׁוֹנְךָ מֵרָע, וּשְׂפָתֶיךָ מִדַּבֵּר מִרְמָה.* סוּר מֵרָע וַעֲשֵׂה טוֹב, בַּקֵּשׁ שָׁלוֹם וְרָדְפֵהוּ. עֵינֵי יהוה אֶל צַדִּיקִים, וְאָזְנָיו אֶל שַׁוְעָתָם. פְּנֵי יהוה בְּעֹשֵׂי רָע, לְהַכְרִית מֵאֶרֶץ זִכְרָם. צָעֲקוּ וַיהוה שָׁמֵעַ, וּמִכָּל צָרוֹתָם הִצִּילָם. קָרוֹב יהוה לְנִשְׁבְּרֵי לֵב, וְאֶת דַּכְּאֵי רוּחַ יוֹשִׁיעַ. רַבּוֹת רָעוֹת צַדִּיק,* וּמִכֻּלָּם יַצִּילֶנּוּ יהוה. שֹׁמֵר כָּל עַצְמוֹתָיו, אַחַת מֵהֵנָּה לֹא נִשְׁבָּרָה. תְּמוֹתֵת רָשָׁע רָעָה,* וְשֹׂנְאֵי צַדִּיק יֶאְשָׁמוּ. ❖ פּוֹדֶה יהוה נֶפֶשׁ עֲבָדָיו, וְלֹא יֶאְשְׁמוּ כָּל הַחֹסִים בּוֹ.

תהלים צ

תְּפִלָּה לְמֹשֶׁה אִישׁ הָאֱלֹהִים,* אֲדֹנָי מָעוֹן אַתָּה הָיִיתָ לָּנוּ בְּדֹר וָדֹר. בְּטֶרֶם הָרִים יֻלָּדוּ וַתְּחוֹלֵל אֶרֶץ וְתֵבֵל, וּמֵעוֹלָם עַד עוֹלָם אַתָּה אֵל. תָּשֵׁב אֱנוֹשׁ* עַד דַּכָּא, וַתֹּאמֶר שׁוּבוּ* בְנֵי אָדָם. כִּי אֶלֶף שָׁנִים בְּעֵינֶיךָ כְּיוֹם אֶתְמוֹל כִּי יַעֲבֹר, וְאַשְׁמוּרָה בַלָּיְלָה. זְרַמְתָּם, שֵׁנָה יִהְיוּ,* בַּבֹּקֶר כֶּחָצִיר יַחֲלֹף. בַּבֹּקֶר יָצִיץ וְחָלָף, לָעֶרֶב יְמוֹלֵל וְיָבֵשׁ. כִּי כָלִינוּ בְאַפֶּךָ, וּבַחֲמָתְךָ נִבְהָלְנוּ. שַׁתָּ עֲוֹנֹתֵינוּ לְנֶגְדֶּךָ,* עֲלֻמֵנוּ לִמְאוֹר פָּנֶיךָ. כִּי כָל יָמֵינוּ פָּנוּ* בְעֶבְרָתֶךָ, כִּלִּינוּ שָׁנֵינוּ כְמוֹ הֶגֶה. יְמֵי שְׁנוֹתֵינוּ בָהֶם* שִׁבְעִים שָׁנָה, וְאִם בִּגְבוּרֹת שְׁמוֹנִים* שָׁנָה,

---

When he has used up his quota, he dies. Thus, by guarding his tongue, one assures himself of greater longevity.

מֵרָע ... מִרְמָה — *From evil ... deceit,* i.e., slander, false testimony, and cursing. *Deceit* refers to insincere friendship that masks evil designs *(Radak).* It also includes exaggerated praise that lays the groundwork for discussing vices. 'He is a wonderful person, *but* ...' *(Chazeh Zion).*

רַבּוֹת רָעוֹת צַדִּיק — *Many are the mishaps of the righteous.* Greatness is a product of challenges, brave attempts, and many mistakes. No one becomes truly *righteous* without his share of *mishaps (Sfas Emes).*

תְּמוֹתֵת רָשָׁע רָעָה — *The death blow of the wicked is evil.* Wicked people will be destroyed by the very evil they set in motion *(Radak; Rashi).*

❧ תְּפִלָּה לְמֹשֶׁה / Psalm 90

In composing *Psalms,* David drew upon the works of ten psalmists — including Moses — in addition to his own *(Bava Basra* 14b). According to *Radak,* David found an ancient scroll written by Moses. It contained eleven psalms (90-100), which David adapted for incorporation in the Book of *Psalms.* The Talmud *(Nedarim* 39b) teaches that repentance was a prerequisite to creation, for man is the centerpoint of the universe, and unless he can free himself of sin, he will neither fulfill his purpose nor survive. Therefore, this psalm is appended to those that recall the Sabbath, the day dedicated as the memorial of creation.

אִישׁ הָאֱלֹהִים — *The man of God.* Though Moses was a flesh-and-blood man, he elevated himself to the level of a Godly being *(Devarim Rabbah* 11:4).

תָּשֵׁב אֱנוֹשׁ — *You reduce* [lit. *return*] *man.* God crushes the pride of arrogant people *(Rashi).*

וַתֹּאמֶר שׁוּבוּ — *And You say, 'Repent.'* By

נ *Guard your tongue from evil,*
*and your lips from speaking deceit.**
ס *Turn from evil and do good,*
seek peace and pursue it.
ע *The eyes of* HASHEM *are toward the righteous,*
and His ears to their cry.
פ *The face of* HASHEM *is against evildoers,*
to cut off their memory from earth.
צ *They cried out and* HASHEM *heeds,*
and from all their troubles He rescues them.
ק HASHEM *is close to the brokenhearted;*
and those crushed in spirit, He saves.
ר *Many are the mishaps of the righteous,**
but from them all HASHEM *rescues him.*
ש *He guards all his bones,*
even one of them was not broken.
ת *The death blow of the wicked is evil,**
and the haters of the righteous will be condemned.
Chazzan— HASHEM *redeems the soul of His servants,*
and all those who take refuge in Him will not be condemned.

Psalm 90

תְּפִלָּה *A prayer by Moses, the man of God:* My Lord, an abode have You been for us in all generations; before the mountains were born and You had not yet fashioned the earth and the inhabited land, and from This World to the World to Come You are God. You reduce man* to pulp and You say, 'Repent,* O sons of man.' For a thousand years in Your eyes are but a bygone yesterday, and like a watch in the night. You flood them away, they become sleeplike,* by morning they are like grass that withers. In the morning it blossoms and is rejuvenated, by evening it is cut down and brittle. For we are consumed by Your fury; and we are confounded by Your wrath. You have set our iniquities before Yourself,* our immaturity before the light of Your countenance. For all our days passed by* because of Your anger, we consumed our years like a fleeting thought. The days of our years among them* are seventy years, and if with strength, eighty* years;*

---

showing vulnerable man that he is powerless, God 'tells' him to *repent.*

זְרַמְתָּם שֵׁנָה יִהְיוּ — *You flood them away, they become sleeplike.* The Psalmist continues to describe man's transitory nature. His life is like a dream that vanishes without a trace *(Radak).*

שַׁתָּ עֲוֹנֹתֵינוּ לְנֶגְדֶּךָ — *You have set our iniquities before Yourself.* Man may forget his sins, but God's memory is eternal *(Radak).*

יָמֵינוּ פָּנוּ — *Our days passed by.* Because we incurred God's wrath, our days passed by unproductively *(Rashi).*

יְמֵי שְׁנוֹתֵינוּ בָהֶם — *The days of our years among them.* Our time on earth surrounded by the sins and immaturity mentioned above consists of seventy years, on average *(Rashi).*

שִׁבְעִים ... שְׁמוֹנִים — *Seventy ... eighty.* Although Moses, who composed this psalm, lived to one hundred twenty years, this verse speaks of average people *(Radak);* or it was inserted by

וְרָהְבָּם עָמָל וָאָוֶן, כִּי גָז חִישׁ וַנָּעֻפָה.* מִי יוֹדֵעַ עֹז אַפֶּךָ,* וּכְיִרְאָתְךָ עֶבְרָתֶךָ. לִמְנוֹת יָמֵינוּ* כֵּן הוֹדַע, וְנָבִא לְבַב חָכְמָה. שׁוּבָה יהוה עַד מָתָי,* וְהִנָּחֵם עַל עֲבָדֶיךָ. שַׂבְּעֵנוּ בַבֹּקֶר חַסְדֶּךָ, וּנְרַנְּנָה וְנִשְׂמְחָה בְּכָל יָמֵינוּ. שַׂמְּחֵנוּ כִּימוֹת עִנִּיתָנוּ,* שְׁנוֹת רָאִינוּ רָעָה. יֵרָאֶה אֶל עֲבָדֶיךָ פָעֳלֶךָ, וַהֲדָרְךָ עַל בְּנֵיהֶם. ❖ וִיהִי נֹעַם* אֲדֹנָי אֱלֹהֵינוּ עָלֵינוּ, וּמַעֲשֵׂה יָדֵינוּ כּוֹנְנָה עָלֵינוּ,* וּמַעֲשֵׂה יָדֵינוּ כּוֹנְנֵהוּ.

תהלים צא

יֹשֵׁב בְּסֵתֶר עֶלְיוֹן,* בְּצֵל שַׁדַּי יִתְלוֹנָן. אֹמַר לַיהוה מַחְסִי וּמְצוּדָתִי, אֱלֹהַי אֶבְטַח בּוֹ. כִּי הוּא יַצִּילְךָ מִפַּח יָקוּשׁ, מִדֶּבֶר הַוּוֹת. בְּאֶבְרָתוֹ יָסֶךְ לָךְ, וְתַחַת כְּנָפָיו תֶּחְסֶה, צִנָּה וְסֹחֵרָה אֲמִתּוֹ. לֹא תִירָא מִפַּחַד לָיְלָה,* מֵחֵץ יָעוּף יוֹמָם. מִדֶּבֶר בָּאֹפֶל יַהֲלֹךְ, מִקֶּטֶב יָשׁוּד צָהֳרָיִם. יִפֹּל מִצִּדְּךָ אֶלֶף, וּרְבָבָה מִימִינֶךָ,* אֵלֶיךָ לֹא יִגָּשׁ. רַק בְּעֵינֶיךָ תַבִּיט, וְשִׁלֻּמַת רְשָׁעִים תִּרְאֶה. כִּי אַתָּה יהוה מַחְסִי, עֶלְיוֹן שַׂמְתָּ מְעוֹנֶךָ. לֹא תְאֻנֶּה אֵלֶיךָ רָעָה, וְנֶגַע לֹא יִקְרַב בְּאָהֳלֶךָ.* כִּי מַלְאָכָיו יְצַוֶּה לָּךְ, לִשְׁמָרְךָ בְּכָל דְּרָכֶיךָ. עַל כַּפַּיִם יִשָּׂאוּנְךָ,* פֶּן תִּגֹּף

David [who lived seventy years], since lifespans were shorter in his time *(Tosafos).*

כִּי גָז חִישׁ וַנָּעֻפָה — *For it is cut off swiftly and we fly away.* Man's success is fleeting. When our souls fly away, life and accomplishment go with it.

מִי יוֹדֵעַ עֹז אַפֶּךָ — *Who knows the power of Your fury?* Once God's wrath is unleashed, who can guard against it? *(Radak).*

לִמְנוֹת יָמֵינוּ — *According to the count of our days.* Since our lives are so short, make the truth known to us so that we may comprehend it *(Sforno).*

שׁוּבָה ה׳ עַד מָתָי — *Return,* HASHEM, *how long?* Come back to us — how long will You abandon us? *(Radak).*

שַׂמְּחֵנוּ כִּימוֹת עִנִּיתָנוּ — *Gladden us according to the days You afflicted us.* May our joy in the future be equal in intensity to our suffering of the past.

וִיהִי נֹעַם — *May the pleasantness.* When the Tabernacle was built, Moses uttered this prayer that it might endure and be blessed by God *(Midrash).* The term נֹעַם, *pleasantness,* refers to the bliss someone feels when he has done something that achieved its purpose. When man has this feeling of accomplishment, God, too, feels satisfaction that His will has been done *(Malbim).*

וּמַעֲשֵׂה יָדֵינוּ כּוֹנְנָה עָלֵינוּ — *Our handiwork, may He establish for us.* Moses repeated the prayer for the success of *our handiwork,* once referring to the newly-built Tabernacle and once referring to man's general activities *(Rashi).* This can also be understood as a plea that we be independent of human pressures that interfere with our service of God *(R' Hirsch).*

⊱ יֹשֵׁב בְּסֵתֶר / Psalm 91

Moses continues his theme that man achieves fulfillment only through closeness to God. Moreover, God will rescue him from danger and foe. The Talmud *(Shavuos* 15b) calls this hymn *Song of Plagues,* [שִׁיר שֶׁל פְּגָעִים אוֹ שֶׁל נְגָעִים] because one who recites it with faith in God will be helped by Him in time of danger. In it, Moses speaks of the faithful believer who finds refuge in *the shadow of the Almighty.* This is the true hero whom God promises long life and salvation.

According to the Midrash, Moses composed this work on the day he completed construction of the מִשְׁכָּן, *[Mishkan], Tabernacle,* and these verses describe Moses himself, who entered the

their proudest success is but toil and pain, for it is cut off swiftly and we fly away. Who knows the power of Your fury?* As You are feared, so is Your anger. According to the count of our days,* so may You teach us; then we shall acquire a heart of wisdom. Return, HASHEM, how long?* Relent concerning Your servants. Satisfy us in the morning with Your kindness, then we shall sing out and rejoice throughout our days. Gladden us according to the days You afflicted us,* the years when we saw evil. May Your works be visible to Your servants, and Your majesty upon their children.* Chazzan— *May the pleasantness* of my Lord, our God, be upon us — our handiwork, may He establish for us;* our handiwork, may He establish.*

Psalm 91

יֹשֵׁב *Whoever sits in the refuge of the Most High,* he shall dwell in the shadow of the Almighty. I will say of HASHEM, 'He is my refuge and my fortress, my God, I will trust in Him.' For He will deliver you from the ensnaring trap, from devastating pestilence. With His pinion He will cover you, and beneath His wings you will be protected; shield and armor is His truth. You shall not fear the terror of night;* nor of the arrow that flies by day; nor the pestilence that walks in gloom; nor the destroyer who lays waste at noon. Let a thousand encamp at your side and a myriad at your right hand,* but to you they shall not approach. You will merely peer with your eyes and you will see the retribution of the wicked. Because [you said] 'You, HASHEM, are my refuge,' you have made the Most High your dwelling place. No evil will befall you, nor will any plague come near your tent.* He will charge His angels for you, to protect you in all your ways. On your palms they will carry you,* lest you strike*

Divine clouds and was enveloped *in the shadow of the Almighty*. At that moment, a great question arose: How could a Tabernacle with walls and curtains contain the Presence of the Almighty? The Master of the Universe Himself explained, 'The entire world cannot contain My glory, yet when I wish, I can concentrate My entire essence into one small spot. Indeed, I am Most High, yet I sit in a [limited, constricted] refuge — in the shadow of the Tabernacle.' God's intention in removing the nation from the Egyptian slavery was, *'You shall serve God upon this mountain' (Exodus* 3:12). And it was to this service that the *Mishkan* was dedicated.

יֹשֵׁב בְּסֵתֶר עֶלְיוֹן — *Whoever sits in the refuge of the Most High.* The person who scorns conventional forms of protection and seeks only the refuge provided by the Most High will find his faith rewarded. He will be enveloped by God's providence so that he can continue to seek holiness and wisdom without fear of those who would seek to do him harm: *He shall dwell in the shadow of the Almighty (Rashi).*

לֹא תִירָא מִפַּחַד לָיְלָה — *You shall not fear the terror of night.* If you put your faith in God, fear will be banished from your heart *(Rashi).*

יִפֹּל מִצִּדְּךָ אֶלֶף וּרְבָבָה מִימִינֶךָ — *Let a thousand encamp at your side and a myriad at your right hand.* Thousands and myriads of demons may encamp around the man who is shielded by God's truth, but they will not be able to come near to harm him *(Rashi).*

וְנֶגַע לֹא יִקְרַב בְּאָהֳלֶךָ — *Nor will any plague come near your tent.* The Talmud *(Sanhedrin* 103a) perceives this as a blessing for domestic tranquillity and that one will have worthy children and students, who will not shame him.

עַל כַּפַּיִם יִשָּׂאוּנְךָ — *On* [*your*] *palms they will carry you.* The angels created by the commandments you perform with your *palms* [i.e., giving charity and doing acts of kindness] will raise you above all dangers that lurk in your path *(Zera Yaakov).*

בְּאֶבֶן רַגְלֶךָ. עַל שַׁחַל וָפֶתֶן* תִּדְרֹךְ, תִּרְמֹס כְּפִיר וְתַנִּין. כִּי בִי חָשַׁק* וַאֲפַלְּטֵהוּ, אֲשַׂגְּבֵהוּ כִּי יָדַע שְׁמִי. יִקְרָאֵנִי וְאֶעֱנֵהוּ, עִמּוֹ אָנֹכִי בְצָרָה, אֲחַלְּצֵהוּ וַאֲכַבְּדֵהוּ. ❖ אֹרֶךְ יָמִים אַשְׂבִּיעֵהוּ, וְאַרְאֵהוּ בִּישׁוּעָתִי.* אֹרֶךְ יָמִים אַשְׂבִּיעֵהוּ, וְאַרְאֵהוּ בִּישׁוּעָתִי.

תהלים קלה

הַלְלוּיָהּ הַלְלוּ אֶת שֵׁם יהוה, הַלְלוּ עַבְדֵי יהוה.* שֶׁעֹמְדִים בְּבֵית יהוה,* בְּחַצְרוֹת בֵּית אֱלֹהֵינוּ. הַלְלוּיָהּ כִּי טוֹב יהוה, זַמְּרוּ לִשְׁמוֹ כִּי נָעִים. כִּי יַעֲקֹב בָּחַר לוֹ יָהּ, יִשְׂרָאֵל* לִסְגֻלָּתוֹ. כִּי אֲנִי יָדַעְתִּי כִּי גָדוֹל יהוה, וַאֲדֹנֵינוּ מִכָּל אֱלֹהִים. כֹּל אֲשֶׁר חָפֵץ יהוה עָשָׂה, בַּשָּׁמַיִם וּבָאָרֶץ, בַּיַּמִּים וְכָל תְּהוֹמוֹת. מַעֲלֶה נְשִׂאִים מִקְצֵה הָאָרֶץ, בְּרָקִים לַמָּטָר עָשָׂה, מוֹצֵא רוּחַ מֵאוֹצְרוֹתָיו. שֶׁהִכָּה בְּכוֹרֵי מִצְרָיִם, מֵאָדָם עַד בְּהֵמָה. שָׁלַח אוֹתֹת וּמֹפְתִים בְּתוֹכֵכִי מִצְרָיִם, בְּפַרְעֹה וּבְכָל עֲבָדָיו. שֶׁהִכָּה גּוֹיִם רַבִּים, וְהָרַג מְלָכִים עֲצוּמִים. לְסִיחוֹן מֶלֶךְ הָאֱמֹרִי, וּלְעוֹג* מֶלֶךְ הַבָּשָׁן, וּלְכֹל מַמְלְכוֹת כְּנָעַן. וְנָתַן אַרְצָם נַחֲלָה, נַחֲלָה לְיִשְׂרָאֵל עַמּוֹ. יהוה שִׁמְךָ לְעוֹלָם,* יהוה זִכְרְךָ לְדֹר וָדֹר. כִּי יָדִין יהוה* עַמּוֹ, וְעַל עֲבָדָיו יִתְנֶחָם. עֲצַבֵּי הַגּוֹיִם כֶּסֶף וְזָהָב, מַעֲשֵׂה יְדֵי אָדָם. פֶּה לָהֶם וְלֹא יְדַבֵּרוּ,* עֵינַיִם לָהֶם וְלֹא יִרְאוּ. אָזְנַיִם לָהֶם וְלֹא יַאֲזִינוּ, אַף אֵין יֶשׁ רוּחַ בְּפִיהֶם. כְּמוֹהֶם יִהְיוּ עֹשֵׂיהֶם,* כֹּל אֲשֶׁר בֹּטֵחַ בָּהֶם. ❖ בֵּית יִשְׂרָאֵל בָּרְכוּ אֶת יהוה, בֵּית אַהֲרֹן בָּרְכוּ אֶת יהוה. בֵּית הַלֵּוִי* בָּרְכוּ

עַל שַׁחַל וָפֶתֶן — *Upon the lion and the viper.* Even when confronted by ferocious beasts and poisonous reptiles, you will simply tread on them and remain unharmed.

כִּי בִי חָשַׁק — *For he has yearned for Me.* From here to the end of the psalm, God speaks in praise of and with assurances to the person who has faith in Him.

וְאַרְאֵהוּ בִּישׁוּעָתִי — *And I will show him My salvation.* He will witness the salvation I will bring about at the advent of the Messiah, at the time of the revival of the dead, and at the salvation of the World to Come *(Radak).*

Indeed, it is not God who needs salvation, but Israel; yet God calls Israel's victory, 'My salvation,' to emphasize that Israel's salvation is His as well *(Midrash Shocher Tov).*

הַלְלוּיָהּ ❧ / Psalm 135

The Exodus from Egypt complements the Sabbath. While the Sabbath testifies that God created the universe, the miracles of the Exodus testify that He continues to supervise and guide history. This psalm recounts the miracles of the Exodus and Israel's trek through the Wilderness to *Eretz Yisrael.* It ends with the conclusion that it is worthless to worship anything except HASHEM.

הַלְלוּ עַבְדֵי ה׳ — *Praise — you servants of* HASHEM. You are free from the bonds of Pharaoh or any other human ruler — you owe allegiance only to God *(Sforno).*

שֶׁעוֹמְדִים בְּבֵית ה׳ — *You who stand in the House of* HASHEM. The prime responsibility to lead Israel in God's praise falls upon the scholars and

your foot against a stone. Upon the lion and the viper you will tread; you will trample the young lion and the serpent. For he has yearned for Me* and I will deliver him; I will elevate him because he knows My Name. He will call upon Me and I will answer him, I am with him in distress, I will release him and I will honor him.* Chazzan— *With long life will I satisfy him, and I will show him My salvation.* With long life will I satisfy him, and I will show him My salvation.*

Psalm 135

הַלְלוּיָהּ *Halleluyah! Praise the Name of HASHEM! Praise — you servants of HASHEM;* you who stand in the House of HASHEM,* in the courtyards of the House of our God — praise God, for HASHEM is good. Sing to His Name, for It is pleasant. For God selected Jacob for His own, Israel* as His treasure. For I know that HASHEM is greater — our Lord — than all heavenly powers. Whatever HASHEM wished, He did, in heaven and on earth; in the seas and all the depths. He raises clouds from the end of the earth; He made lightning bolts for the rain; He brings forth wind from His treasuries. It was He who smote the firstborn of Egypt, from man to beast. He sent signs and wonders into your midst, O Egypt, upon Pharaoh and upon all of his servants. It was He who smote many nations, and slew mighty kings — Sichon, King of the Emorites, Og,* King of Bashan, and all the kingdoms of Canaan — and presented their land as a heritage, a heritage for Israel, His people. HASHEM is Your Name forever,* HASHEM is Your memorial throughout the generations. When HASHEM will judge* His people, He will relent concerning His servants. The idols of the nations are silver and gold, human handiwork. They have mouths, but they speak not;* they have eyes, but they see not; they have ears, but they heed not; neither is there any breath in their mouths. Like them shall their makers become,* everyone who trusts in them.* Chazzan— *O House of Israel, bless HASHEM; O House of Aaron, bless HASHEM. O House of Levi,* bless*

---

teachers in the synagogues and study halls *(Sforno).*

כִּי יַעֲקֹב ... יִשְׂרָאֵל — *For Jacob ... Israel.* 'Jacob' represents the multitude of Jews while 'Israel' represents the great people among them. God chooses even ordinary Jews for His Own, but 'Israel' is His *treasure (Siach Yitzchak).*

לְסִיחוֹן ... וּלְעוֹג — *Sichon ... Og.* Upon coming tc the part of *Eretz Yisrael* that lay east of the Jordan, the Jewish people encountered and defeated these two kings [*Numbers* 21:21-35]. Thus, they are symbolic of all the rulers whom Israel defeated. Also, they are singled out because of their unusual might *(Radak).*

ה' שִׁמְךָ לְעוֹלָם — *HASHEM is Your Name forever.* This Name symbolizes God's eternity. Just as He controlled history in the past, He continues to do so always *(Rashi).*

כִּי יָדִין ה' — *When HASHEM will judge.* Eventually, God will consider the plight of oppressed Israel, and then He will show mercy to His people.

פֶּה לָהֶם וְלֹא יְדַבֵּרוּ — *They have mouths, but they speak not.* Intelligent speech is man's greatest distinction, yet idolaters are foolish enough to worship mute idols! *(Ibn Ezra).*

כְּמוֹהֶם יִהְיוּ עֹשֵׂיהֶם — *Like them shall their makers become.* This can be taken as a prayer, or as a statement of fact that eventually idol-worshipers will perish and be as lifeless as the clods they worship *(Radak).*

בֵּית יִשְׂרָאֵל ... בֵּית אַהֲרֹן ... בֵּית הַלֵּוִי — *House of Israel ... House of Aaron ... House of Levi.* First comes the general call to all Jews, then the *Kohanim* [House of Aaron], who are privileged to perform the Temple service; the Levites, who sing and play the Temple songs; and finally the

אֶת יהוה, יִרְאֵי יהוה בָּרְכוּ אֶת יהוה. בָּרוּךְ יהוה מִצִּיּוֹן* שֹׁכֵן יְרוּשָׁלָיִם, הַלְלוּיָהּ.

Most congregations stand while reciting the following psalm.

תהלים קלו

הוֹדוּ לַיהוה כִּי טוֹב,* כִּי לְעוֹלָם חַסְדּוֹ.*
הוֹדוּ לֵאלֹהֵי הָאֱלֹהִים,* כִּי לְעוֹלָם חַסְדּוֹ.
הוֹדוּ לַאֲדֹנֵי הָאֲדֹנִים,* כִּי לְעוֹלָם חַסְדּוֹ.
לְעֹשֵׂה נִפְלָאוֹת גְּדֹלוֹת לְבַדּוֹ, כִּי לְעוֹלָם חַסְדּוֹ.
לְעֹשֵׂה הַשָּׁמַיִם בִּתְבוּנָה,* כִּי לְעוֹלָם חַסְדּוֹ.
לְרוֹקַע הָאָרֶץ עַל הַמָּיִם, כִּי לְעוֹלָם חַסְדּוֹ.
לְעֹשֵׂה אוֹרִים גְּדֹלִים, כִּי לְעוֹלָם חַסְדּוֹ.
אֶת הַשֶּׁמֶשׁ לְמֶמְשֶׁלֶת בַּיּוֹם, כִּי לְעוֹלָם חַסְדּוֹ.
אֶת הַיָּרֵחַ וְכוֹכָבִים לְמֶמְשְׁלוֹת בַּלָּיְלָה, כִּי לְעוֹלָם חַסְדּוֹ.
לְמַכֵּה מִצְרַיִם בִּבְכוֹרֵיהֶם,* כִּי לְעוֹלָם חַסְדּוֹ.
וַיּוֹצֵא יִשְׂרָאֵל מִתּוֹכָם, כִּי לְעוֹלָם חַסְדּוֹ.
בְּיָד חֲזָקָה וּבִזְרוֹעַ נְטוּיָה, כִּי לְעוֹלָם חַסְדּוֹ.
לְגֹזֵר יַם סוּף לִגְזָרִים,* כִּי לְעוֹלָם חַסְדּוֹ.
וְהֶעֱבִיר יִשְׂרָאֵל בְּתוֹכוֹ, כִּי לְעוֹלָם חַסְדּוֹ.
וְנִעֵר פַּרְעֹה וְחֵילוֹ בְיַם סוּף, כִּי לְעוֹלָם חַסְדּוֹ.
לְמוֹלִיךְ עַמּוֹ בַּמִּדְבָּר, כִּי לְעוֹלָם חַסְדּוֹ.
לְמַכֵּה מְלָכִים גְּדֹלִים,* כִּי לְעוֹלָם חַסְדּוֹ.
וַיַּהֲרֹג מְלָכִים אַדִּירִים,* כִּי לְעוֹלָם חַסְדּוֹ.

---

righteous people *who fear* HASHEM.

בָּרוּךְ ה׳ מִצִּיּוֹן — *Blessed is* HASHEM *from Zion.* May the end of the exile come soon — when we will be able to bless God from Zion, His holy mountain (*Sforno*).

❧ הודו לה׳ / Psalm 136

The Talmud (*Pesachim* 118a) calls this psalm הַלֵּל הַגָּדוֹל, *the Great Song of Praise,* because it lauds God for giving sustenance to every living being. Thus, although it speaks of a multitude of mighty miracles, including the Creation of the universe and the Exodus from Egypt, the psalm concludes by saying נֹתֵן לֶחֶם לְכָל בָּשָׂר, *He gives nourishment* [lit., *bread*] *to all flesh,* because God's mercy upon every creature is equal to all the 'great' miracles. The twenty-six verses of the psalm are another allusion to God's mercy, for all twenty-six generations before the Torah was given, God provided for all living things out of His mercy. Once the Torah was given, man can *earn* his keep by performing the commandments. The praises are in present tense because God renews Creation constantly.

כִּי טוֹב — *For He is good.* An aspect of His goodness is that He punishes man for his sins each according to his own level of prosperity. The rich man may lose an expensive bull while the pauper will be deprived of a crust of bread (*Pesachim* 118a).

כִּי לְעוֹלָם חַסְדּוֹ — *For His kindness endures forever.* Homiletically, this can be rendered: His kindness is for the *world.* Man's kindnesses can be prompted by selfish motives, but God acts for the sake of the *world,* not Himself (*Alshich*).

הָאֱלֹהִים — *The heavenly powers,* i.e., the angels (*Radak*).

HASHEM; O those who fear HASHEM, bless HASHEM. Blessed is HASHEM from Zion, He Who dwells in Jerusalem. Halleluyah!*

Most congregations stand while reciting the following psalm.

Psalm 136

הוֹדוּ *Give thanks to HASHEM for He is good,**
for His kindness endures forever.
*Give thanks to the God of the heavenly powers,**
for His kindness endures forever.
*Give thanks to the Lord of the lords,**
for His kindness endures forever.
To Him Who alone performs great wonders,
for His kindness endures forever.
*To Him Who makes the heavens with understanding,**
for His kindness endures forever.
To Him Who spread out the earth upon the waters,
for His kindness endures forever.
To Him Who makes great lights, for His kindness endures forever.
The sun for the reign of the day, for His kindness endures forever.
The moon and the stars for the reign of the night,
for His kindness endures forever.
*To Him Who smote Egypt through their firstborn,**
for His kindness endures forever.
And brought Israel forth from their midst,
for His kindness endures forever.
With strong hand and outstretched arm,
for His kindness endures forever.
*To Him Who divided the Sea of Reeds into parts,**
for His kindness endures forever.
And caused Israel to pass through it,
for His kindness endures forever.
And threw Pharaoh and his army into the Sea of Reeds,
for His kindness endures forever.
To Him Who led His people through the wilderness,
for His kindness endures forever.
To Him Who smote great kings, for His kindness endures forever.*
And slew mighty kings, for His kindness endures forever.*

הָאֲדֹנִים — *The lords,* i.e., the heavenly bodies *(Radak).*

בִּתְבוּנָה — *With understanding.* The solar system and the countless galaxies function with a complexity that is beyond human comprehension *(R' Hirsch).*

לְמַכֵּה מִצְרַיִם בִּבְכוֹרֵיהֶם — *Who smote Egypt through their firstborn.* Upon hearing that they would soon die, the firstborn Egyptians insisted that the Jews be set free. When their countrymen refused, the firstborn attacked and killed many of their fellow Egyptians. Thus, the plague of the first-born was a double blow *(Midrash).*

יַם סוּף לִגְזָרִים — *The Sea of Reeds into parts.* The Midrash teaches that the sea was divided into twelve parts, one for each tribe. This shows that each tribe has its own mission and deserved the miracle for its own sake *(Sfas Emes).*

מְלָכִים גְּדֹלִים — *Great kings,* i.e., the thirty-one Canaanite kings *(Rashi).*

מְלָכִים אַדִּירִים — *Mighty kings,* i.e. Pharaoh and

לְסִיחוֹן מֶלֶךְ הָאֱמֹרִי, כִּי לְעוֹלָם חַסְדּוֹ.
וּלְעוֹג מֶלֶךְ הַבָּשָׁן, כִּי לְעוֹלָם חַסְדּוֹ.
וְנָתַן אַרְצָם לְנַחֲלָה, כִּי לְעוֹלָם חַסְדּוֹ.
נַחֲלָה לְיִשְׂרָאֵל עַבְדּוֹ, כִּי לְעוֹלָם חַסְדּוֹ.
שֶׁבְּשִׁפְלֵנוּ* זָכַר לָנוּ, כִּי לְעוֹלָם חַסְדּוֹ.
וַיִּפְרְקֵנוּ מִצָּרֵינוּ, כִּי לְעוֹלָם חַסְדּוֹ.
❖ נֹתֵן לֶחֶם לְכָל בָּשָׂר, כִּי לְעוֹלָם חַסְדּוֹ.
הוֹדוּ לְאֵל הַשָּׁמָיִם, כִּי לְעוֹלָם חַסְדּוֹ.

תהלים לג

רַנְּנוּ צַדִּיקִים בַּיהוה, לַיְשָׁרִים נָאוָה תְהִלָּה. הוֹדוּ לַיהוה בְּכִנּוֹר, בְּנֵבֶל עָשׂוֹר זַמְּרוּ לוֹ. שִׁירוּ לוֹ שִׁיר חָדָשׁ, הֵיטִיבוּ נַגֵּן בִּתְרוּעָה. כִּי יָשָׁר דְּבַר יהוה, וְכָל מַעֲשֵׂהוּ בֶּאֱמוּנָה.* אֹהֵב צְדָקָה וּמִשְׁפָּט, חֶסֶד יהוה מָלְאָה הָאָרֶץ. בִּדְבַר יהוה שָׁמַיִם נַעֲשׂוּ, וּבְרוּחַ פִּיו כָּל צְבָאָם. כֹּנֵס כַּנֵּד מֵי הַיָּם, נֹתֵן בְּאוֹצָרוֹת תְּהוֹמוֹת. יִירְאוּ מֵיהוה כָּל הָאָרֶץ, מִמֶּנּוּ יָגוּרוּ כָּל יֹשְׁבֵי תֵבֵל. כִּי הוּא אָמַר וַיֶּהִי, הוּא צִוָּה וַיַּעֲמֹד.* יהוה הֵפִיר עֲצַת גּוֹיִם, הֵנִיא מַחְשְׁבוֹת עַמִּים. עֲצַת יהוה לְעוֹלָם תַּעֲמֹד, מַחְשְׁבוֹת לִבּוֹ לְדֹר וָדֹר. אַשְׁרֵי הַגּוֹי אֲשֶׁר יהוה אֱלֹהָיו, הָעָם בָּחַר לְנַחֲלָה לוֹ. מִשָּׁמַיִם הִבִּיט יהוה, רָאָה אֶת כָּל בְּנֵי הָאָדָם. מִמְּכוֹן שִׁבְתּוֹ הִשְׁגִּיחַ,* אֶל כָּל יֹשְׁבֵי הָאָרֶץ. הַיֹּצֵר יַחַד לִבָּם, הַמֵּבִין אֶל כָּל מַעֲשֵׂיהֶם. אֵין הַמֶּלֶךְ נוֹשָׁע בְּרָב חָיִל, גִּבּוֹר לֹא יִנָּצֵל בְּרָב כֹּחַ. שֶׁקֶר הַסּוּס לִתְשׁוּעָה, וּבְרֹב חֵילוֹ לֹא יְמַלֵּט. הִנֵּה עֵין יהוה אֶל יְרֵאָיו, לַמְיַחֲלִים לְחַסְדּוֹ. לְהַצִּיל מִמָּוֶת נַפְשָׁם, וּלְחַיּוֹתָם בָּרָעָב. ❖ נַפְשֵׁנוּ חִכְּתָה לַיהוה, עֶזְרֵנוּ וּמָגִנֵּנוּ הוּא. כִּי בוֹ יִשְׂמַח לִבֵּנוּ, כִּי בְשֵׁם קָדְשׁוֹ בָטָחְנוּ. יְהִי חַסְדְּךָ יהוה עָלֵינוּ, כַּאֲשֶׁר יִחַלְנוּ לָךְ.

---

his legion, who were even mightier than the combined Canaanite nations *(Rashi).*

שֶׁבְּשִׁפְלֵנוּ — *In our lowliness,* i.e., during our Egyptian enslavement *(Rashi);* or this is a prophetic reference to Israel's downtrodden condition during the periods when the Temples were destroyed *(Radak).*

⊱ רַנְּנוּ צַדִּיקִים / Psalm 33

We turn now to the celebration of the World to Come when all will recognize that God controls events. The Sabbath represents awareness of this truth, and it calls upon us to *sing Him a new song.*

וְכָל מַעֲשֵׂהוּ בֶּאֱמוּנָה — *And all His deeds are done with faithfulness.* The natural forces are reliable and consistent. Otherwise we would be in constant fear of upheaval *(Malbim).*

הוּא צִוָּה וַיַּעֲמֹד — *He commanded and it stood firm.*

Sichon, king of the Emorites, *for His kindness endures forever.*
And Og, king of Bashan, *for His kindness endures forever.*
And presented their land as a heritage,
for His kindness endures forever.
A heritage for Israel, His servant, *for His kindness endures forever.*
In our lowliness He remembered us,*
for His kindness endures forever.
And released us from our tormentors,
for His kindness endures forever.
Chazzan— *He gives nourishment to all flesh,*
for His kindness endures forever.
Give thanks to God of the heavens, *for His kindness endures forever.*

Psalm 33

רַנְּנוּ *Sing joyfully, O righteous, before* HASHEM*; for the upright, praise is fitting. Give thanks to* HASHEM *with the harp with the ten-stringed lyre make music to Him. Sing Him a new song, play well with sounds of deepest feeling. For upright is the word of* HASHEM*, and all His deeds are done with faithfulness.* He loves charity and justice, the kindness of* HASHEM *fills the earth. By the word of* HASHEM *the heavens were made, and by the breath of His mouth all their host. He assembles like a wall the waters of the sea, He places the deep waters in vaults. Fear* HASHEM*, all the earth; of Him be in dread, all inhabitants of the world. For He spoke and it came to be, He commanded and it stood firm.** HASHEM *annuls the counsel of nations, He balks the designs of peoples. The counsel of* HASHEM *will endure forever, the designs of His heart throughout the generations. Praiseworthy is the nation whose God is* HASHEM*, the people He chose for His own heritage. From heaven* HASHEM *looks down, He sees all mankind. From His dwelling place He oversees* all inhabitants of earth. He fashions their hearts all together, He comprehends all their deeds. A king is not saved by a great army, nor is a hero rescued by great strength; sham is the horse for salvation; despite its great strength it provides no escape. Behold, the eye of* HASHEM *is on those who fear Him, upon those who await His kindness, To rescue their soul from death, and to sustain them in famine.* Chazzan— *Our soul longed for* HASHEM *— our help and our shield is He. For in Him will our hearts be glad, for in His Holy Name we trusted. May Your kindness,* HASHEM*, be upon us, just as we awaited You.*

When God ordered the world to come into being, it kept expanding until it reached the size He desired; then He commanded it to stand firm (*Chagigah* 12a).

הִבִּיט ה׳ ... הִשְׁגִּיחַ — *HASHEM looks down ... He oversees.* These expressions imply the two differing forms of God's הַשְׁגָּחָה, *supervision.* There is the general supervision [הַשְׁגָּחָה כְּלָלִית] of the laws of nature; in that sense, God seems to *look down* from a distance. But God also exercises close supervision [הַשְׁגָּחָה פְּרָטִית] — *He oversees* — over each person according to his own deeds (*Malbim*).

תהלים צב (commentary on p. 320)

מִזְמוֹר שִׁיר לְיוֹם הַשַּׁבָּת. טוֹב לְהֹדוֹת לַיהוה, וּלְזַמֵּר לְשִׁמְךָ עֶלְיוֹן. לְהַגִּיד בַּבֹּקֶר חַסְדֶּךָ, וֶאֱמוּנָתְךָ בַּלֵּילוֹת. עֲלֵי עָשׂוֹר וַעֲלֵי נָבֶל, עֲלֵי הִגָּיוֹן בְּכִנּוֹר. כִּי שִׂמַּחְתַּנִי יהוה בְּפָעֳלֶךָ בְּמַעֲשֵׂי יָדֶיךָ אֲרַנֵּן. מַה גָּדְלוּ מַעֲשֶׂיךָ יהוה, מְאֹד עָמְקוּ מַחְשְׁבֹתֶיךָ. אִישׁ בַּעַר לֹא יֵדָע, וּכְסִיל לֹא יָבִין אֶת זֹאת. בִּפְרֹחַ רְשָׁעִים כְּמוֹ עֵשֶׂב, וַיָּצִיצוּ כָּל פֹּעֲלֵי אָוֶן, לְהִשָּׁמְדָם עֲדֵי עַד. וְאַתָּה מָרוֹם לְעֹלָם יהוה. כִּי הִנֵּה אֹיְבֶיךָ יהוה, כִּי הִנֵּה אֹיְבֶיךָ יֹאבֵדוּ, יִתְפָּרְדוּ כָּל פֹּעֲלֵי אָוֶן. וַתָּרֶם כִּרְאֵים קַרְנִי, בַּלֹּתִי בְּשֶׁמֶן רַעֲנָן. וַתַּבֵּט עֵינִי בְּשׁוּרָי, בַּקָּמִים עָלַי מְרֵעִים, תִּשְׁמַעְנָה אָזְנָי. ❖ צַדִּיק כַּתָּמָר יִפְרָח, כְּאֶרֶז בַּלְּבָנוֹן יִשְׂגֶּה. שְׁתוּלִים בְּבֵית יהוה, בְּחַצְרוֹת אֱלֹהֵינוּ יַפְרִיחוּ. עוֹד יְנוּבוּן בְּשֵׂיבָה, דְּשֵׁנִים וְרַעֲנַנִּים יִהְיוּ. לְהַגִּיד כִּי יָשָׁר יהוה, צוּרִי וְלֹא עַוְלָתָה בּוֹ.

תהלים צג (commentary on p. 321)

יהוה מָלָךְ גֵּאוּת לָבֵשׁ, לָבֵשׁ יהוה עֹז הִתְאַזָּר, אַף תִּכּוֹן תֵּבֵל בַּל תִּמּוֹט. נָכוֹן כִּסְאֲךָ מֵאָז, מֵעוֹלָם אָתָּה. נָשְׂאוּ נְהָרוֹת יהוה, נָשְׂאוּ נְהָרוֹת קוֹלָם, יִשְׂאוּ נְהָרוֹת דָּכְיָם. ❖ מִקֹּלוֹת מַיִם רַבִּים, אַדִּירִים מִשְׁבְּרֵי יָם, אַדִּיר בַּמָּרוֹם יהוה. עֵדֹתֶיךָ נֶאֶמְנוּ מְאֹד לְבֵיתְךָ נַאֲוָה קֹדֶשׁ, יהוה לְאֹרֶךְ יָמִים.

[ON HOSHANA RABBAH, CONTINUE יְהִי כְבוֹד OF THE WEEKDAY SERVICE ON PAGE 64.]

The following prayer should be recited with special intensity. (Commentary on page 65.)

יְהִי כְבוֹד יהוה לְעוֹלָם, יִשְׂמַח יהוה בְּמַעֲשָׂיו.[1] יְהִי שֵׁם יהוה מְבֹרָךְ, מֵעַתָּה וְעַד עוֹלָם. מִמִּזְרַח שֶׁמֶשׁ עַד מְבוֹאוֹ, מְהֻלָּל שֵׁם יהוה. רָם עַל כָּל גּוֹיִם יהוה, עַל הַשָּׁמַיִם כְּבוֹדוֹ.[2] יהוה שִׁמְךָ לְעוֹלָם, יהוה זִכְרְךָ לְדֹר וָדֹר.[3] יהוה בַּשָּׁמַיִם הֵכִין כִּסְאוֹ, וּמַלְכוּתוֹ בַּכֹּל מָשָׁלָה.[4] יִשְׂמְחוּ הַשָּׁמַיִם וְתָגֵל הָאָרֶץ, וְיֹאמְרוּ בַגּוֹיִם יהוה מָלָךְ.[5] יהוה מֶלֶךְ,[6]

(1) *Psalms* 104:31. (2) 113:2-4. (3) 135:13. (4) 103:19. (5) *I Chronicles* 16:31. (6) *Psalms* 10:16.

מִזְמוֹר שִׁיר לְיוֹם הַשַּׁבָּת / Psalm 92

מִזְמוֹר שִׁיר לְיוֹם הַשַּׁבָּת — *A psalm, a song for the Sabbath day.* This psalm is recited on festivals as well as the Sabbath because they, too, are referred to as 'a Sabbath' in the Torah. Although this psalm is identified as belonging particularly to the theme of the Sabbath — indeed, it was the Levites' song for the Sabbath Temple service *(Rashi)* — the text contains not a single direct reference to the Sabbath. One explanation is that it refers not to the weekly Sabbath, but to the World to Come, when man will achieve the spiritual perfection we only glimpse during the Sabbath. The psalm is thus well suited to the Sabbath which is a semblance of that future spiritual perfection *(Rashi).*

Psalm 92 (commentary on page 320).

מִזְמוֹר שִׁיר *A psalm, a song for the Sabbath day. It is good to thank* HASHEM *and to sing praise to Your Name, O Exalted One; to relate Your kindness in the dawn and Your faith in the nights. Upon ten-stringed instrument and lyre, with singing accompanied by a harp. For You have gladdened me,* HASHEM, *with Your deeds; at the works of Your Hands I sing glad song. How great are Your deeds,* HASHEM; *exceedingly profound are Your thoughts. A boor cannot know, nor can a fool understand this: when the wicked bloom like grass and all the doers of iniquity blossom — it is to destroy them till eternity. But You remain exalted forever,* HASHEM. *For behold! — Your enemies,* HASHEM, *for behold! — Your enemies shall perish, dispersed shall be all doers of iniquity. As exalted as a re'eim's shall be my pride, I will be saturated with ever-fresh oil. My eyes have seen my vigilant foes; when those who would harm me rise up against me, my ears have heard their doom.* Chazzan— *A righteous man will flourish like a date palm, like a cedar in the Lebanon he will grow tall. Planted in the house of* HASHEM, *in the courtyards of our God they will flourish. They will still be fruitful in old age, vigorous and fresh they will be — to declare that* HASHEM *is just, my Rock in Whom there is no wrong.*

Psalm 93 (commentary on page 321.)

יהוה מָלָךְ HASHEM *will have reigned, He will have donned grandeur;* HASHEM *will have donned might and girded Himself; even firmed the world that it should not falter. Your throne was established from of old; eternal are You. Like rivers they raised, O* HASHEM, *like rivers they raised their voice; like rivers they shall raise their destructiveness.* Chazzan— *More than the roars of many waters, mightier than the waves of the sea — You are mighty on high,* HASHEM. *Your testimonies about Your House, the Sacred Dwelling are exceedingly trustworthy — O* HASHEM, *may it be for lengthy days.*

[ON HOSHANA RABBAH, CONTINUE יְהִי כְבוֹד, *'MAY THE GLORY . . .'* OF THE WEEKDAY SERVICE ON P. 64.]

The following prayer should be recited with special intensity. (Commentary on page 65.)

יְהִי כְבוֹד *May the glory of* HASHEM *endure forever, let* HASHEM *rejoice in His works.*[1] *Blessed be the Name of* HASHEM, *from this time and forever. From the rising of the sun to its setting,* HASHEM'*s Name is praised. High above all nations is* HASHEM, *above the heavens is His glory.*[2] *'*HASHEM*' is Your Name forever, '*HASHEM*' is Your memorial throughout the generations.*[3] HASHEM *has established His throne in the heavens, and His kingdom reigns over all.*[4] *The heavens will be glad and the earth will rejoice, they will proclaim among the nations, '*HASHEM *has reigned!'*[5] HASHEM *reigns,*[6]

ה׳ מָלָךְ / Psalm 93

This psalm is a direct continuation of the previous theme that God's greatness will be recognized by all in the Messianic era. It describes God in His full grandeur and power as He was when He completed the six days of

יהוה מָלָךְ,1 יהוה יִמְלֹךְ לְעֹלָם וָעֶד.2 יהוה מֶלֶךְ עוֹלָם וָעֶד,
אָבְדוּ גוֹיִם מֵאַרְצוֹ.3 יהוה הֵפִיר עֲצַת גּוֹיִם, הֵנִיא מַחְשְׁבוֹת
עַמִּים.4 רַבּוֹת מַחֲשָׁבוֹת בְּלֶב אִישׁ, וַעֲצַת יהוה הִיא תָקוּם.5
עֲצַת יהוה לְעוֹלָם תַּעֲמֹד, מַחְשְׁבוֹת לִבּוֹ לְדֹר וָדֹר.6 כִּי הוּא
אָמַר וַיֶּהִי, הוּא צִוָּה וַיַּעֲמֹד.7 כִּי בָחַר יהוה בְּצִיּוֹן, אִוָּהּ לְמוֹשָׁב
לוֹ.8 כִּי יַעֲקֹב בָּחַר לוֹ יָהּ, יִשְׂרָאֵל לִסְגֻלָּתוֹ.9 כִּי לֹא יִטֹּשׁ יהוה
עַמּוֹ, וְנַחֲלָתוֹ לֹא יַעֲזֹב.10 ❖ וְהוּא רַחוּם יְכַפֵּר עָוֹן וְלֹא יַשְׁחִית,
וְהִרְבָּה לְהָשִׁיב אַפּוֹ, וְלֹא יָעִיר כָּל חֲמָתוֹ.11 יהוה הוֹשִׁיעָה,
הַמֶּלֶךְ יַעֲנֵנוּ בְיוֹם קָרְאֵנוּ.12

(Commentary on page 66.)

אַשְׁרֵי יוֹשְׁבֵי בֵיתֶךָ, עוֹד יְהַלְלוּךָ סֶּלָה.13 אַשְׁרֵי הָעָם שֶׁכָּכָה
לוֹ, אַשְׁרֵי הָעָם שֶׁיהוה אֱלֹהָיו.14

תהלים קמה

תְּהִלָּה לְדָוִד,

אֲרוֹמִמְךָ אֱלוֹהַי הַמֶּלֶךְ, וַאֲבָרְכָה שִׁמְךָ לְעוֹלָם וָעֶד.
בְּכָל יוֹם אֲבָרְכֶךָּ, וַאֲהַלְלָה שִׁמְךָ לְעוֹלָם וָעֶד.
גָּדוֹל יהוה וּמְהֻלָּל מְאֹד, וְלִגְדֻלָּתוֹ אֵין חֵקֶר.
דּוֹר לְדוֹר יְשַׁבַּח מַעֲשֶׂיךָ, וּגְבוּרֹתֶיךָ יַגִּידוּ.
הֲדַר כְּבוֹד הוֹדֶךָ, וְדִבְרֵי נִפְלְאֹתֶיךָ אָשִׂיחָה.
וֶעֱזוּז נוֹרְאוֹתֶיךָ יֹאמֵרוּ, וּגְדוּלָּתְךָ אֲסַפְּרֶנָּה.
זֵכֶר רַב טוּבְךָ יַבִּיעוּ, וְצִדְקָתְךָ יְרַנֵּנוּ.
חַנּוּן וְרַחוּם יהוה, אֶרֶךְ אַפַּיִם וּגְדָל חָסֶד.
טוֹב יהוה לַכֹּל, וְרַחֲמָיו עַל כָּל מַעֲשָׂיו.
יוֹדוּךָ יהוה כָּל מַעֲשֶׂיךָ, וַחֲסִידֶיךָ יְבָרְכוּכָה.
כְּבוֹד מַלְכוּתְךָ יֹאמֵרוּ, וּגְבוּרָתְךָ יְדַבֵּרוּ.
לְהוֹדִיעַ לִבְנֵי הָאָדָם גְּבוּרֹתָיו, וּכְבוֹד הֲדַר מַלְכוּתוֹ.
מַלְכוּתְךָ מַלְכוּת כָּל עֹלָמִים, וּמֶמְשַׁלְתְּךָ בְּכָל דּוֹר וָדֹר.

(1) *Psalms* 93:1 et al. (2) *Exodus* 15:18. (3) *Psalms* 10:16. (4) 33:10. (5) *Proverbs* 19:21. (6) *Psalms* 33:11. (7) 33:9. (8) 132:13. (9) 135:4. (10) 94:14. (11) 78:38. (12) 20:10. (13) 84:5. (14) 144:15.

Creation, and as 'donning grandeur and girding' Himself like one dressing in his Sabbath finery. Additional commentary to this psalm appears on p. 321.

HASHEM has reigned,[1] HASHEM shall reign for all eternity.[2] HASHEM reigns forever and ever, even when the nations will have perished from His earth.[3] HASHEM annuls the counsel of nations, He balks the designs of peoples.[4] Many designs are in man's heart, but the counsel of HASHEM — only it will prevail.[5] The counsel of HASHEM will endure forever, the designs of His heart throughout the generations.[6] For He spoke and it came to be; He commanded and it stood firm.[7] For HASHEM selected Zion, He desired it for His dwelling place.[8] For God selected Jacob as His own, Israel as His treasure.[9] For HASHEM will not cast off His people, nor will He forsake His heritage.[10] He, the Merciful One, is forgiving of iniquity and does not destroy; frequently He withdraws His anger, not arousing His entire rage.[11] Chazzan— *HASHEM, save! May the King answer us on the day we call.[12]*

(Commentary on page 66.)

אַשְׁרֵי *Praiseworthy are those who dwell in Your house; may they always praise You, Selah![13] Praiseworthy is the people for whom this is so, praiseworthy is the people whose God is HASHEM.[14]*

Psalm 145 *A psalm of praise by David:*

א *I will exalt You, my God the King,*
and I will bless Your Name forever and ever.
ב *Every day I will bless You,*
and I will laud Your Name forever and ever.
ג *HASHEM is great and exceedingly lauded,*
and His greatness is beyond investigation.
ד *Each generation will praise Your deeds to the next*
and of Your mighty deeds they will tell.
ה *The splendrous glory of Your power*
and Your wondrous deeds I shall discuss.
ו *And of Your awesome power they will speak,*
and Your greatness I shall relate.
ז *A recollection of Your abundant goodness they will utter*
and of Your righteousness they will sing exultantly.
ח *Gracious and merciful is HASHEM,*
slow to anger, and great in [bestowing] kindness.
ט *HASHEM is good to all; His mercies are on all His works.*
י *All Your works shall thank You, HASHEM,*
and Your devout ones will bless You.
כ *Of the glory of Your kingdom they will speak,*
and of Your power they will tell;
ל *To inform human beings of His mighty deeds,*
and the glorious splendor of His kingdom.
מ *Your kingdom is a kingdom spanning all eternities,*
and Your dominion is throughout every generation.

סוֹמֵךְ יהוה לְכָל הַנֹּפְלִים, וְזוֹקֵף לְכָל הַכְּפוּפִים.
עֵינֵי כֹל אֵלֶיךָ יְשַׂבֵּרוּ, וְאַתָּה נוֹתֵן לָהֶם אֶת אָכְלָם בְּעִתּוֹ.
פּוֹתֵחַ אֶת יָדֶךָ,
וּמַשְׂבִּיעַ לְכָל חַי רָצוֹן.

While reciting the verse פּוֹתֵחַ, concentrate intently on its meaning.

צַדִּיק יהוה בְּכָל דְּרָכָיו, וְחָסִיד בְּכָל מַעֲשָׂיו.
קָרוֹב יהוה לְכָל קֹרְאָיו, לְכֹל אֲשֶׁר יִקְרָאֻהוּ בֶאֱמֶת.
רְצוֹן יְרֵאָיו יַעֲשֶׂה, וְאֶת שַׁוְעָתָם יִשְׁמַע וְיוֹשִׁיעֵם.
שׁוֹמֵר יהוה אֶת כָּל אֹהֲבָיו, וְאֵת כָּל הָרְשָׁעִים יַשְׁמִיד.
❖ תְּהִלַּת יהוה יְדַבֶּר פִּי, וִיבָרֵךְ כָּל בָּשָׂר שֵׁם קָדְשׁוֹ לְעוֹלָם
וָעֶד. וַאֲנַחְנוּ נְבָרֵךְ יָהּ, מֵעַתָּה וְעַד עוֹלָם, הַלְלוּיָהּ.[1]

תהלים קמו (commentary on p. 70)

הַלְלוּיָהּ, הַלְלִי נַפְשִׁי אֶת יהוה. אֲהַלְלָה יהוה בְּחַיָּי, אֲזַמְּרָה לֵאלֹהַי בְּעוֹדִי. אַל תִּבְטְחוּ בִנְדִיבִים, בְּבֶן אָדָם שֶׁאֵין לוֹ תְשׁוּעָה. תֵּצֵא רוּחוֹ, יָשֻׁב לְאַדְמָתוֹ, בַּיּוֹם הַהוּא אָבְדוּ עֶשְׁתֹּנֹתָיו. אַשְׁרֵי שֶׁאֵל יַעֲקֹב בְּעֶזְרוֹ, שִׂבְרוֹ עַל יהוה אֱלֹהָיו. עֹשֶׂה שָׁמַיִם וָאָרֶץ, אֶת הַיָּם וְאֶת כָּל אֲשֶׁר בָּם, הַשֹּׁמֵר אֱמֶת לְעוֹלָם. עֹשֶׂה מִשְׁפָּט לַעֲשׁוּקִים, נֹתֵן לֶחֶם לָרְעֵבִים, יהוה מַתִּיר אֲסוּרִים. יהוה פֹּקֵחַ עִוְרִים, יהוה זֹקֵף כְּפוּפִים, יהוה אֹהֵב צַדִּיקִים. יהוה שֹׁמֵר אֶת גֵּרִים, יָתוֹם וְאַלְמָנָה יְעוֹדֵד, וְדֶרֶךְ רְשָׁעִים יְעַוֵּת. ❖ יִמְלֹךְ יהוה לְעוֹלָם, אֱלֹהַיִךְ צִיּוֹן, לְדֹר וָדֹר, הַלְלוּיָהּ.

תהלים קמז (commentary on p. 71)

הַלְלוּיָהּ, כִּי טוֹב זַמְּרָה אֱלֹהֵינוּ, כִּי נָעִים נָאוָה תְהִלָּה. בּוֹנֵה יְרוּשָׁלַיִם יהוה, נִדְחֵי יִשְׂרָאֵל יְכַנֵּס. הָרוֹפֵא לִשְׁבוּרֵי לֵב, וּמְחַבֵּשׁ לְעַצְּבוֹתָם. מוֹנֶה מִסְפָּר לַכּוֹכָבִים, לְכֻלָּם שֵׁמוֹת יִקְרָא. גָּדוֹל אֲדוֹנֵינוּ וְרַב כֹּחַ, לִתְבוּנָתוֹ אֵין מִסְפָּר. מְעוֹדֵד עֲנָוִים יהוה, מַשְׁפִּיל רְשָׁעִים עֲדֵי אָרֶץ. עֱנוּ לַיהוה בְּתוֹדָה, זַמְּרוּ לֵאלֹהֵינוּ בְכִנּוֹר. הַמְכַסֶּה שָׁמַיִם בְּעָבִים, הַמֵּכִין לָאָרֶץ מָטָר, הַמַּצְמִיחַ הָרִים חָצִיר. נוֹתֵן

ס *HASHEM supports all the fallen ones and straightens all the bent.*
ע *The eyes of all look to You with hope*
and You give them their food in its proper time;
פ *You open Your hand,*
and satisfy the desire
of every living thing.

While reciting the verse, *'You open ...'* concentrate intently on its meaning.

צ *Righteous is HASHEM in all His ways*
and magnanimous in all His deeds.
ק *HASHEM is close to all who call upon Him —*
to all who call upon Him sincerely.
ר *The will of those who fear Him He will do;*
and their cry He will hear, and save them.
ש *HASHEM protects all who love Him;*
but all the wicked He will destroy.
ת Chazzan— *May my mouth declare the praise of HASHEM*
and may all flesh bless His Holy Name forever and ever.
We will bless God from this time and forever, Halleluyah![1]

Psalm 146 (commentary on page 70).

הַלְלוּיָהּ *Halleluyah! Praise HASHEM, O my soul! I will praise HASHEM while I live, I will make music to my God while I exist. Do not rely on nobles, nor on a human being for he holds no salvation. When his spirit departs he returns to his earth, on that day his plans all perish. Praiseworthy is one whose help is Jacob's God, whose hope is in HASHEM, his God. He is the Maker of heaven and earth, the sea and all that is in them, Who safeguards truth forever. He does justice for the exploited; He gives bread to the hungry; HASHEM releases the bound. HASHEM gives sight to the blind; HASHEM straightens the bent; HASHEM loves the righteous. HASHEM protects strangers; orphan and widow He encourages; but the way of the wicked He contorts.* Chazzan— *HASHEM shall reign forever — your God, O Zion — from generation to generation. Halleluyah!*

Psalm 147 (commentary on page 71).

הַלְלוּיָהּ *Halleluyah! For it is good to make music to our God, for praise is pleasant and befitting. The Builder of Jerusalem is HASHEM, the outcast of Israel He will gather in. He is the Healer of the broken-hearted, and the One Who binds up their sorrows. He counts the number of the stars, to all of them He assigns names. Great is our Lord and abundant in strength, His understanding is beyond calculation. HASHEM encourages the humble, He lowers the wicked down to the ground. Call out to HASHEM with thanks, with the harp sing to our God — Who covers the heavens with clouds, Who prepares rain for the earth, Who makes mountains sprout with grass. He gives*

(1) *Psalms* 115:18.

לִבְהֵמָה לַחְמָהּ, לִבְנֵי עֹרֵב אֲשֶׁר יִקְרָאוּ. לֹא בִגְבוּרַת הַסּוּס יֶחְפָּץ, לֹא בְשׁוֹקֵי הָאִישׁ יִרְצֶה. רוֹצֶה יהוה אֶת יְרֵאָיו, אֶת הַמְיַחֲלִים לְחַסְדּוֹ. שַׁבְּחִי יְרוּשָׁלַיִם אֶת יהוה, הַלְלִי אֱלֹהַיִךְ צִיּוֹן. כִּי חִזַּק בְּרִיחֵי שְׁעָרָיִךְ, בֵּרַךְ בָּנַיִךְ בְּקִרְבֵּךְ. הַשָּׂם גְּבוּלֵךְ שָׁלוֹם, חֵלֶב חִטִּים יַשְׂבִּיעֵךְ. הַשֹּׁלֵחַ אִמְרָתוֹ אָרֶץ, עַד מְהֵרָה יָרוּץ דְּבָרוֹ. הַנֹּתֵן שֶׁלֶג כַּצָּמֶר, כְּפוֹר כָּאֵפֶר יְפַזֵּר. מַשְׁלִיךְ קַרְחוֹ כְפִתִּים, לִפְנֵי קָרָתוֹ מִי יַעֲמֹד. יִשְׁלַח דְּבָרוֹ וְיַמְסֵם, יַשֵּׁב רוּחוֹ יִזְּלוּ מָיִם. ❖ מַגִּיד דְּבָרָיו לְיַעֲקֹב, חֻקָּיו וּמִשְׁפָּטָיו לְיִשְׂרָאֵל. לֹא עָשָׂה כֵן לְכָל גּוֹי, וּמִשְׁפָּטִים בַּל יְדָעוּם, הַלְלוּיָהּ.

תהלים קמח (commentary on p. 72)

הַלְלוּיָהּ, הַלְלוּ אֶת יהוה מִן הַשָּׁמַיִם, הַלְלוּהוּ בַּמְּרוֹמִים. הַלְלוּהוּ כָל מַלְאָכָיו, הַלְלוּהוּ כָּל צְבָאָיו. הַלְלוּהוּ שֶׁמֶשׁ וְיָרֵחַ, הַלְלוּהוּ כָּל כּוֹכְבֵי אוֹר. הַלְלוּהוּ שְׁמֵי הַשָּׁמָיִם, וְהַמַּיִם אֲשֶׁר מֵעַל הַשָּׁמָיִם. יְהַלְלוּ אֶת שֵׁם יהוה, כִּי הוּא צִוָּה וְנִבְרָאוּ. וַיַּעֲמִידֵם לָעַד לְעוֹלָם, חָק נָתַן וְלֹא יַעֲבוֹר. הַלְלוּ אֶת יהוה מִן הָאָרֶץ, תַּנִּינִים וְכָל תְּהֹמוֹת. אֵשׁ וּבָרָד, שֶׁלֶג וְקִיטוֹר, רוּחַ סְעָרָה עֹשָׂה דְבָרוֹ. הֶהָרִים וְכָל גְּבָעוֹת, עֵץ פְּרִי וְכָל אֲרָזִים. הַחַיָּה וְכָל בְּהֵמָה, רֶמֶשׂ וְצִפּוֹר כָּנָף. מַלְכֵי אֶרֶץ וְכָל לְאֻמִּים, שָׂרִים וְכָל שֹׁפְטֵי אָרֶץ. בַּחוּרִים וְגַם בְּתוּלוֹת, זְקֵנִים עִם נְעָרִים. ❖ יְהַלְלוּ אֶת שֵׁם יהוה, כִּי נִשְׂגָּב שְׁמוֹ לְבַדּוֹ, הוֹדוֹ עַל אֶרֶץ וְשָׁמָיִם. וַיָּרֶם קֶרֶן לְעַמּוֹ, תְּהִלָּה לְכָל חֲסִידָיו, לִבְנֵי יִשְׂרָאֵל עַם קְרֹבוֹ, הַלְלוּיָהּ.

תהלים קמט (commentary on p. 73)

הַלְלוּיָהּ, שִׁירוּ לַיהוה שִׁיר חָדָשׁ, תְּהִלָּתוֹ בִּקְהַל חֲסִידִים. יִשְׂמַח יִשְׂרָאֵל בְּעֹשָׂיו, בְּנֵי צִיּוֹן יָגִילוּ בְמַלְכָּם. יְהַלְלוּ שְׁמוֹ בְמָחוֹל, בְּתֹף וְכִנּוֹר יְזַמְּרוּ לוֹ. כִּי רוֹצֶה יהוה בְּעַמּוֹ, יְפָאֵר עֲנָוִים בִּישׁוּעָה. יַעְלְזוּ חֲסִידִים בְּכָבוֹד, יְרַנְּנוּ עַל מִשְׁכְּבוֹתָם. רוֹמְמוֹת אֵל בִּגְרוֹנָם, וְחֶרֶב פִּיפִיּוֹת בְּיָדָם. לַעֲשׂוֹת נְקָמָה בַּגּוֹיִם, תּוֹכֵחוֹת בַּלְאֻמִּים. ❖ לֶאְסֹר מַלְכֵיהֶם בְּזִקִּים, וְנִכְבְּדֵיהֶם בְּכַבְלֵי בַרְזֶל. לַעֲשׂוֹת בָּהֶם מִשְׁפָּט כָּתוּב, הָדָר הוּא לְכָל חֲסִידָיו, הַלְלוּיָהּ.

to an animal its food, to young ravens that cry out. Not in the strength of the horse does He desire, and not in the legs of man does He favor. HASHEM favors those who fear Him, those who hope for His kindness. Praise HASHEM, O Jerusalem, laud your God, O Zion. For He has strengthened the bars of your gates, and blessed your children in your midst; He Who makes your borders peaceful, and with the cream of the wheat He sates you; He Who dispatches His utterance earthward; how swiftly His commandment runs! He Who gives snow like fleece, He scatters frost like ashes. He hurls His ice like crumbs — before His cold, who can stand? He issues His command and it melts them, He blows His wind — the waters flow Chazzan— *He relates His Word to Jacob, His statutes and judgments to Israel. He did not do so for any other nation, such judgments — they know them not. Halleluyah!*

Psalm 148 (commentary on page 72).

הַלְלוּיָהּ *Halleluyah! Praise HASHEM from the heavens; praise Him in the heights. Praise Him, all His angels; praise Him, all His legions. Praise Him, sun and moon; praise Him, all bright stars. Praise Him, the most exalted of the heavens and the waters that are above the heavens. Let them praise the Name of HASHEM, for He commanded and they were created. And He established them forever and ever, He issued a decree that will not change. Praise HASHEM from the earth, sea giants and all watery depths. Fire and hail, snow and vapor, stormy wind fulfilling His word. Mountains and all hills, fruitful trees and all cedars. Beasts and all cattle, crawling things and winged fowl. Kings of the earth and all governments, princes and all judges on earth. Young men and also maidens, old men together with youths.* Chazzan— *Let them praise the Name of HASHEM, for His Name alone will have been exalted; His glory is above earth and heaven. And He will have exalted the pride of His nation, causing praise for all His devout ones, for the Children of Israel, His intimate people. Halleluyah!*

Psalm 149 (commentary on page 73).

הַלְלוּיָהּ *Halleluyah! Sing to HASHEM a new song, let His praise be in the congregation of the devout. Let Israel exult in its Maker, let the Children of Zion rejoice in their King. Let them praise His Name with dancing, with drums and harp let them make music to Him. For HASHEM favors His nation, He adorns the humble with salvation. Let the devout exult in glory, let them sing joyously upon their beds. The lofty praises of God are in their throats, and a double-edged sword is in their hand — to execute vengeance among the nations, rebukes among the governments.* Chazzan— *To bind their kings with chains, and their nobles with fetters of iron. To execute upon them written judgment — that will be the splendor of all His devout ones. Halleluyah!*

תהלים קנ (commentary on p. 74)

הַלְלוּיָהּ, הַלְלוּ אֵל בְּקָדְשׁוֹ, הַלְלוּהוּ בִּרְקִיעַ עֻזּוֹ. הַלְלוּהוּ בִגְבוּרֹתָיו, הַלְלוּהוּ כְּרֹב גֻּדְלוֹ. הַלְלוּהוּ בְּתֵקַע שׁוֹפָר, הַלְלוּהוּ בְּנֵבֶל וְכִנּוֹר. הַלְלוּהוּ בְּתֹף וּמָחוֹל, הַלְלוּהוּ בְּמִנִּים וְעֻגָב. הַלְלוּהוּ בְצִלְצְלֵי שָׁמַע, הַלְלוּהוּ בְּצִלְצְלֵי תְרוּעָה. ❖ כֹּל הַנְּשָׁמָה תְּהַלֵּל יָהּ, הַלְלוּיָהּ. כֹּל הַנְּשָׁמָה תְּהַלֵּל יָהּ, הַלְלוּיָהּ.

בָּרוּךְ יהוה לְעוֹלָם, אָמֵן וְאָמֵן.[1] בָּרוּךְ יהוה מִצִּיּוֹן, שֹׁכֵן יְרוּשָׁלָיִם, הַלְלוּיָהּ.[2] בָּרוּךְ יהוה אֱלֹהִים אֱלֹהֵי יִשְׂרָאֵל, עֹשֵׂה נִפְלָאוֹת לְבַדּוֹ. ❖ וּבָרוּךְ שֵׁם כְּבוֹדוֹ לְעוֹלָם, וְיִמָּלֵא כְבוֹדוֹ אֶת כָּל הָאָרֶץ, אָמֵן וְאָמֵן.[3]

One must stand from וַיְבָרֶךְ דָּוִיד, until after the phrase אַתָּה הוּא ה׳ הָאֱלֹהִים, however, there is a generally accepted custom to remain standing until after completing אָז יָשִׁיר (p. 400).

דברי הימים א כט:י־יג (commentary on p. 75)

וַיְבָרֶךְ דָּוִיד אֶת יהוה לְעֵינֵי כָּל הַקָּהָל, וַיֹּאמֶר דָּוִיד: בָּרוּךְ אַתָּה יהוה, אֱלֹהֵי יִשְׂרָאֵל אָבִינוּ, מֵעוֹלָם וְעַד עוֹלָם. לְךָ יהוה הַגְּדֻלָּה וְהַגְּבוּרָה וְהַתִּפְאֶרֶת וְהַנֵּצַח וְהַהוֹד, כִּי כֹל בַּשָּׁמַיִם וּבָאָרֶץ; לְךָ יהוה הַמַּמְלָכָה וְהַמִּתְנַשֵּׂא לְכֹל לְרֹאשׁ. וְהָעֹשֶׁר וְהַכָּבוֹד מִלְּפָנֶיךָ, וְאַתָּה מוֹשֵׁל בַּכֹּל, וּבְיָדְךָ כֹּחַ וּגְבוּרָה, וּבְיָדְךָ לְגַדֵּל וּלְחַזֵּק לַכֹּל. וְעַתָּה אֱלֹהֵינוּ מוֹדִים אֲנַחְנוּ לָךְ, וּמְהַלְלִים לְשֵׁם תִּפְאַרְתֶּךָ.

נחמיה ט:ו־יא

אַתָּה הוּא יהוה לְבַדֶּךָ, אַתָּה עָשִׂיתָ אֶת הַשָּׁמַיִם, שְׁמֵי הַשָּׁמַיִם וְכָל צְבָאָם, הָאָרֶץ וְכָל אֲשֶׁר עָלֶיהָ, הַיַּמִּים וְכָל אֲשֶׁר בָּהֶם, וְאַתָּה מְחַיֶּה אֶת כֻּלָּם, וּצְבָא הַשָּׁמַיִם לְךָ מִשְׁתַּחֲוִים. ❖ אַתָּה הוּא יהוה הָאֱלֹהִים אֲשֶׁר בָּחַרְתָּ בְּאַבְרָם, וְהוֹצֵאתוֹ מֵאוּר כַּשְׂדִּים, וְשַׂמְתָּ שְׁמוֹ אַבְרָהָם. וּמָצָאתָ אֶת לְבָבוֹ נֶאֱמָן לְפָנֶיךָ —

— וְכָרוֹת עִמּוֹ הַבְּרִית לָתֵת אֶת אֶרֶץ הַכְּנַעֲנִי הַחִתִּי הָאֱמֹרִי וְהַפְּרִזִּי וְהַיְבוּסִי וְהַגִּרְגָּשִׁי, לָתֵת לְזַרְעוֹ, וַתָּקֶם אֶת דְּבָרֶיךָ, כִּי צַדִּיק אָתָּה. וַתֵּרֶא אֶת עֳנִי אֲבֹתֵינוּ בְּמִצְרָיִם, וְאֶת זַעֲקָתָם שָׁמַעְתָּ עַל יַם סוּף. וַתִּתֵּן אֹתֹת וּמֹפְתִים בְּפַרְעֹה וּבְכָל עֲבָדָיו וּבְכָל עַם אַרְצוֹ, כִּי יָדַעְתָּ כִּי הֵזִידוּ עֲלֵיהֶם, וַתַּעַשׂ לְךָ

Psalm 150 (commentary on page 74).

הַלְלוּיָהּ *Halleluyah! Praise God in His Sanctuary; praise Him in the firmament of His power. Praise Him for His mighty acts; praise Him as befits His abundant greatness. Praise Him with the blast of the shofar; praise Him with lyre and harp. Praise Him with drum and dance; praise Him with organ and flute. Praise Him with clanging cymbals; praise Him with resonant trumpets.* Chazzan— *Let all souls praise God, Halleluyah! Let all souls praise God, Halleluyah!*

בָּרוּךְ *Blessed is* HASHEM *forever, Amen and Amen.*[1] *Blessed is* HASHEM *from Zion, Who dwells in Jerusalem, Halleluyah.*[2] *Blessed is* HASHEM, *God, the God of Israel, Who alone does wonders.* Chazzan— *Blessed is His glorious Name forever, and may all the earth be filled with His glory, Amen and Amen.*[3]

One must stand from *'And David Blessed,'* until after the phrase *'It is You,* HASHEM *the God,'* however, there is a generally accepted custom to remain standing until after completing the Song at the Sea (p. 400).

I Chronicles 29:10-13 (commentary on page 75).

וַיְבָרֶךְ *And David blessed* HASHEM *in the presence of the entire congregation; David said, 'Blessed are You,* HASHEM, *the God of Israel our forefather from This World to the World to Come. Yours,* HASHEM, *is the greatness, the strength, the splendor, the triumph, and the glory, even everything in heaven and earth; Yours,* HASHEM, *is the kingdom and the sovereignty over every leader. Wealth and honor come from You and You rule everything — in Your hand is power and strength and it is in Your hand to make anyone great or strong. So now, our God, we thank You and praise Your splendrous Name.'*

Nechemiah 9:6-11

It is You alone, HASHEM, *You have made the heaven, the most exalted heaven and all their legions, the earth and everything upon it, the seas and everything in them and You give them all life; the heavenly legions bow to You.* Chazzan— *It is You,* HASHEM *the God, Who selected Abram, brought him out of Ur Kasdim and made his name Abraham. You found his heart faithful before You —*

— and You established the covenant with him to give the land of the Canaanite, Hittite, Emorite, Perizzite, Jebusite, and Girgashite to give it to his offspring; and You affirmed Your word, for You are righteous. You observed the suffering of our forefathers in Egypt and their outcry You heard at the Sea of Reeds. You imposed signs and wonders upon Pharaoh and upon all his servants, and upon all the people of his land. For You knew that they sinned flagrantly against them, and You brought Yourself renown as

(1) *Psalms* 89:53. (2) 135:21. (3) 72:18-19.

שָׁם כְּהַיּוֹם הַזֶּה. ❖ וְהַיָּם בָּקַעְתָּ לִפְנֵיהֶם, וַיַּעַבְרוּ בְתוֹךְ הַיָּם בַּיַּבָּשָׁה, וְאֶת רֹדְפֵיהֶם הִשְׁלַכְתָּ בִמְצוֹלֹת, כְּמוֹ אֶבֶן בְּמַיִם עַזִּים.

שירת הים

שמות יד:ל-טו:יט (commentary on p. 78)

וַיּוֹשַׁע יְהֹוָה בַּיּוֹם הַהוּא אֶת־יִשְׂרָאֵל מִיַּד מִצְרָיִם, וַיַּרְא יִשְׂרָאֵל אֶת־מִצְרַיִם מֵת עַל־שְׂפַת הַיָּם: ❖ וַיַּרְא יִשְׂרָאֵל אֶת־הַיָּד הַגְּדֹלָה אֲשֶׁר עָשָׂה יְהֹוָה בְּמִצְרַיִם, וַיִּירְאוּ הָעָם אֶת־יְהֹוָה, וַיַּאֲמִינוּ בַּיהֹוָה וּבְמֹשֶׁה עַבְדּוֹ:

אָז יָשִׁיר־מֹשֶׁה וּבְנֵי יִשְׂרָאֵל אֶת־הַשִּׁירָה הַזֹּאת לַיהֹוָה, וַיֹּאמְרוּ לֵאמֹר, אָשִׁירָה לַיהֹוָה כִּי־גָאֹה גָּאָה, סוּס וְרֹכְבוֹ רָמָה בַיָּם: עָזִּי וְזִמְרָת יָהּ וַיְהִי־לִי לִישׁוּעָה, זֶה אֵלִי וְאַנְוֵהוּ, אֱלֹהֵי אָבִי וַאֲרֹמְמֶנְהוּ: יְהֹוָה אִישׁ מִלְחָמָה, יְהֹוָה שְׁמוֹ: מַרְכְּבֹת פַּרְעֹה וְחֵילוֹ יָרָה בַיָּם, וּמִבְחַר שָׁלִשָׁיו טֻבְּעוּ בְיַם־סוּף: תְּהֹמֹת יְכַסְיֻמוּ, יָרְדוּ בִמְצוֹלֹת כְּמוֹ־אָבֶן: יְמִינְךָ יְהֹוָה נֶאְדָּרִי בַּכֹּחַ, יְמִינְךָ יְהֹוָה תִּרְעַץ אוֹיֵב: וּבְרֹב גְּאוֹנְךָ תַּהֲרֹס קָמֶיךָ, תְּשַׁלַּח חֲרֹנְךָ יֹאכְלֵמוֹ כַּקַּשׁ: וּבְרוּחַ אַפֶּיךָ נֶעֶרְמוּ מַיִם, נִצְּבוּ כְמוֹ־נֵד נֹזְלִים, קָפְאוּ תְהֹמֹת בְּלֶב־יָם: אָמַר אוֹיֵב, אֶרְדֹּף אַשִּׂיג אֲחַלֵּק שָׁלָל, תִּמְלָאֵמוֹ נַפְשִׁי, אָרִיק חַרְבִּי, תּוֹרִישֵׁמוֹ יָדִי: נָשַׁפְתָּ בְרוּחֲךָ כִּסָּמוֹ יָם, צָלְלוּ כַּעוֹפֶרֶת בְּמַיִם אַדִּירִים: מִי־כָמֹכָה בָּאֵלִם יְהֹוָה, מִי כָּמֹכָה נֶאְדָּר בַּקֹּדֶשׁ, נוֹרָא תְהִלֹּת עֹשֵׂה פֶלֶא: נָטִיתָ יְמִינְךָ, תִּבְלָעֵמוֹ אָרֶץ: נָחִיתָ בְחַסְדְּךָ עַם־זוּ גָּאָלְתָּ, נֵהַלְתָּ בְעָזְּךָ אֶל־נְוֵה קָדְשֶׁךָ: שָׁמְעוּ עַמִּים יִרְגָּזוּן, חִיל אָחַז יֹשְׁבֵי פְּלָשֶׁת: אָז נִבְהֲלוּ אַלּוּפֵי אֱדוֹם, אֵילֵי מוֹאָב יֹאחֲזֵמוֹ רָעַד, נָמֹגוּ כֹּל יֹשְׁבֵי כְנָעַן: תִּפֹּל עֲלֵיהֶם אֵימָתָה

clear as this very day. Chazzan— *You split the Sea before them and they crossed in the midst of the Sea on dry land; but their pursuers You hurled into the depths, like a stone into turbulent waters.*

THE SONG AT THE SEA

Exodus 14:30-15:19 (commentary on page 78).

וַיּוֹשַׁע *HASHEM saved — on that day — Israel from the hand of Egypt, and Israel saw the Egyptians dead on the seashore.* Chazzan— *Israel saw the great hand that HASHEM inflicted upon Egypt and the people feared HASHEM, and they had faith in HASHEM and in Moses, His servant.*

Then Moses and the Children of Israel chose to sing this song to HASHEM, and they said the following:

I shall sing to HASHEM for He is exalted above the arrogant, having hurled horse with its rider into the sea.

God is my might and my praise, and He was a salvation for me. This is my God, and I will build Him a Sanctuary; the God of my father, and I will exalt Him.

HASHEM is Master of war, through His Name HASHEM.

Pharaoh's chariots and army He threw into the sea; and the pick of his officers were mired in the Sea of Reeds.

Deep waters covered them; they descended in the depths like stone.

Your right hand, HASHEM, is adorned with strength; Your right hand, HASHEM, smashes the enemy.

In Your abundant grandeur You shatter Your opponents; You dispatch Your wrath, it consumes them like straw.

At a blast from Your nostrils the waters were heaped up; straight as a wall stood the running water, the deep waters congealed in the heart of the sea.

The enemy declared: 'I will pursue, I will overtake, I will divide plunder; I will satisfy my lust with them; I will unsheathe my sword, my hand will impoverish them.'

You blew with Your wind — the sea enshrouded them; the mighty ones sank like lead in the waters.

Who is like You among the heavenly powers, HASHEM! Who is like You, mighty in holiness, too awesome for praise, doing wonders!

You stretched out Your right hand — the earth swallowed them.

You guided in Your kindness this people that You redeemed; You led with Your might to Your holy abode.

Peoples heard — they were agitated; convulsive terror gripped the dwellers of Philistia.

Then the chieftains of Edom were confounded, trembling gripped the powers of Moab, all the dwellers of Canaan dissolved.

וָפַחַד, בִּגְדֹל זְרוֹעֲךָ יִדְּמוּ כָּאָבֶן, עַד־
יַעֲבֹר עַמְּךָ יהוה, עַד־יַעֲבֹר עַם־זוּ
קָנִיתָ: תְּבִאֵמוֹ וְתִטָּעֵמוֹ בְּהַר נַחֲלָתְךָ, מָכוֹן
לְשִׁבְתְּךָ פָּעַלְתָּ יהוה, מִקְּדָשׁ אֲדֹנָי כּוֹנְנוּ
יָדֶיךָ: יהוה | יִמְלֹךְ לְעֹלָם וָעֶד:

יהוה יִמְלֹךְ לְעֹלָם וָעֶד. (יהוה מַלְכוּתֵהּ קָאֵם, לְעָלַם וּלְעָלְמֵי עָלְמַיָּא.) כִּי בָא סוּס פַּרְעֹה בְּרִכְבּוֹ וּבְפָרָשָׁיו בַּיָּם, וַיָּשֶׁב יהוה עֲלֵהֶם אֶת מֵי הַיָּם, וּבְנֵי יִשְׂרָאֵל הָלְכוּ בַיַּבָּשָׁה בְּתוֹךְ הַיָּם. ❖ כִּי לַיהוה הַמְּלוּכָה, וּמשֵׁל בַּגּוֹיִם.[1] וְעָלוּ מוֹשִׁעִים בְּהַר צִיּוֹן, לִשְׁפֹּט אֶת הַר עֵשָׂו, וְהָיְתָה לַיהוה הַמְּלוּכָה.[2] וְהָיָה יהוה לְמֶלֶךְ עַל כָּל הָאָרֶץ, בַּיּוֹם הַהוּא יִהְיֶה יהוה אֶחָד וּשְׁמוֹ אֶחָד.[3]
(וּבְתוֹרָתְךָ כָּתוּב לֵאמֹר: שְׁמַע יִשְׂרָאֵל יהוה אֱלֹהֵינוּ יהוה אֶחָד.[4])

נִשְׁמַת כָּל חַי תְּבָרֵךְ אֶת שִׁמְךָ יהוה אֱלֹהֵינוּ, וְרוּחַ* כָּל בָּשָׂר תְּפָאֵר וּתְרוֹמֵם זִכְרְךָ מַלְכֵּנוּ תָּמִיד. מִן הָעוֹלָם וְעַד הָעוֹלָם אַתָּה אֵל,[5] וּמִבַּלְעָדֶיךָ אֵין לָנוּ מֶלֶךְ[6] גּוֹאֵל וּמוֹשִׁיעַ. פּוֹדֶה וּמַצִּיל וּמְפַרְנֵס וּמְרַחֵם בְּכָל עֵת צָרָה וְצוּקָה,* אֵין לָנוּ מֶלֶךְ אֶלָּא אָתָּה. אֱלֹהֵי הָרִאשׁוֹנִים וְהָאַחֲרוֹנִים,* אֱלוֹהַּ כָּל בְּרִיּוֹת, אֲדוֹן כָּל תּוֹלָדוֹת, הַמְּהֻלָּל בְּרֹב הַתִּשְׁבָּחוֹת, הַמְּנַהֵג עוֹלָמוֹ בְּחֶסֶד וּבְרִיּוֹתָיו בְּרַחֲמִים. וַיהוה לֹא יָנוּם וְלֹא יִישָׁן.[7] הַמְּעוֹרֵר יְשֵׁנִים, וְהַמֵּקִיץ נִרְדָּמִים, וְהַמֵּשִׂיחַ אִלְּמִים, וְהַמַּתִּיר אֲסוּרִים,[8] וְהַסּוֹמֵךְ נוֹפְלִים, וְהַזּוֹקֵף כְּפוּפִים.[9] לְךָ לְבַדְּךָ אֲנַחְנוּ מוֹדִים. אִלּוּ פִינוּ* מָלֵא שִׁירָה כַּיָּם, וּלְשׁוֹנֵנוּ רִנָּה כַּהֲמוֹן גַּלָּיו, וְשִׂפְתוֹתֵינוּ שֶׁבַח כְּמֶרְחֲבֵי רָקִיעַ, וְעֵינֵינוּ מְאִירוֹת כַּשֶּׁמֶשׁ

נִשְׁמַת / Nishmas

This beautiful and moving prayer is an outpouring of praise and gratitude to God. Lyrically, it depicts our utter dependency on God's mercy, our total inadequacy to laud Him properly, and our enthusiastic resolve to dedicate ourselves to His service. It is especially appropriate for recitation on the Sabbath and Festivals — although it contains no mention of the day — because the additional holiness of the Sabbath and the time it affords for extra contemplation make man better able to understand and express the message of the *Nishmas* prayer.

The Talmud (*Pesachim* 118a) calls this prayer בִּרְכַּת הַשִּׁיר, *the Blessing of the Song,* because it concludes the psalms and songs of *Pesukei D'zimrah,* and because it continues the theme of the Song of the Sea. In the Sabbath and Festival service as in the Passover Haggadah, *Nishmas* introduces the series of praises that culminate with יִשְׁתַּבַּח, *Yishtabach.* There, too, it climaxes the grateful narrative of the Exodus with an outpouring of dedication.

So highly was this prayer regarded that such great commentators as *Rabbi Yehudah HaLevi* and *Ibn Ezra* composed poetic introductions to *Nishmas.* That of *Ibn Ezra,* incidentally, צָמְאָה נַפְשִׁי לֵאלֹהִים, *My soul thirsts for God,* is sung by

May fear and terror befall them, at the greatness of Your arm may they be still as stone; until Your people passes through, HASHEM, until this people You have acquired passes through.

You shall bring them and implant them on the mount of Your heritage, the foundation of Your dwelling-place, which you, HASHEM, have made: the Sanctuary, my Lord, that Your hands established.

HASHEM shall reign for all eternity.

HASHEM shall reign for all eternity. (HASHEM — His kingdom is established forever and ever.) When Pharaoh's cavalry came — with his chariots and horsemen — into the sea and HASHEM turned back the waters of the sea upon them, the Children of Israel walked on the dry bed amid the sea. Chazzan— *For the sovereignty is HASHEM's and He rules over nations.*[1] *The saviors will ascend Mount Zion to judge Esau's mountain, and the kingdom will be HASHEM's.*[2] *Then HASHEM will be King over all the world, on that day HASHEM will be One and His Name will be One.*[3] *(And in Your Torah it is written: Hear O Israel: HASHEM is our God, HASHEM, the One and Only.*[4]*)*

נִשְׁמַת *The soul of every living being shall bless Your Name, HASHEM our God; the spirit* of all flesh shall always glorify and exalt Your remembrance, our King. From This World to the World to Come, You are God,*[5] *and other than You we have no king,*[6] *redeemer or savior. Liberator, Rescuer, Sustainer and Merciful One in every time of distress and anguish,* we have no king but You! — God of the first and of the last,* God of all creatures, Master of all generations, Who is extolled through a multitude of praises, Who guides His world with kindness and His creatures with mercy. HASHEM neither slumbers nor sleeps.*[7] *He Who rouses the sleepers and awakens the slumberers, Who makes the mute speak and releases the bound;*[8] *Who supports the fallen and straightens the bent.*[9] *To You alone we give thanks. Were our mouth* as full of song as the sea, and our tongue as full of joyous song as its multitude of waves, and our lips as full of praise as the breadth of the heavens, and our eyes as brilliant as the sun*

(1) *Psalms* 22:29. (2) *Ovadiah* 1:21. (3) *Zechariah* 14:9. (4) *Deuteronomy* 6:4. (5) Cf. *Psalms* 90:2. (6) Cf. *Isaiah* 44:6. (7) Cf. *Psalms* 121:4. (8) Cf. 146:7. (9) Cf. 145:14.

many in the Sabbath Eve *Zemiros* (see Artscroll *Zemiroth*, p. 118)

נִשְׁמַת ... רוּחַ — *The soul ... the spirit.* Essentially, these two concepts are similar, but נְשָׁמָה represents a higher degree of spiritual awareness than רוּחַ. Thus, on the Sabbath when Jews are invested with a נְשָׁמָה יְתֵרָה, a higher degree of spiritual awareness, we dedicate that, too, to bless God.

בְּכָל עֵת צָרָה וְצוּקָה — *In every time of distress and anguish.* Commonly, people express gratitude in happy times and pray for salvation in hard times. We go further, however — even when we suffer distress and anguish, we express our gratitude to God for allowing us to survive the attacks of our enemies.

אֱלֹהֵי הָרִאשׁוֹנִים וְהָאַחֲרוֹנִים — *God of the first and of the last.* When God initiates a course of action, He takes into account the results it will bring about centuries into the future. Thus He is the Master of the *first* set of events as well as of the *last (R' Moshe Cordevero).*

אִלּוּ פִינוּ — *Were our mouth ...* Having stated that God is All-powerful and All-merciful, and thus

וְכַיָּרֵחַ,* וְיָדֵינוּ פְרוּשׂוֹת כְּנִשְׁרֵי שָׁמָיִם, וְרַגְלֵינוּ קַלּוֹת כָּאַיָּלוֹת, אֵין אֲנַחְנוּ מַסְפִּיקִים לְהוֹדוֹת לְךָ, יהוה אֱלֹהֵינוּ וֵאלֹהֵי אֲבוֹתֵינוּ, וּלְבָרֵךְ אֶת שְׁמֶךָ עַל אַחַת מֵאָלֶף אֶלֶף אַלְפֵי אֲלָפִים וְרִבֵּי רְבָבוֹת פְּעָמִים הַטּוֹבוֹת שֶׁעָשִׂיתָ עִם אֲבוֹתֵינוּ וְעִמָּנוּ.* מִמִּצְרַיִם גְּאַלְתָּנוּ יהוה אֱלֹהֵינוּ, וּמִבֵּית עֲבָדִים פְּדִיתָנוּ. בְּרָעָב זַנְתָּנוּ, וּבְשָׂבָע כִּלְכַּלְתָּנוּ, מֵחֶרֶב הִצַּלְתָּנוּ, וּמִדֶּבֶר מִלַּטְתָּנוּ, וּמֵחֳלָיִם רָעִים וְנֶאֱמָנִים דִּלִּיתָנוּ. עַד הֵנָּה עֲזָרוּנוּ רַחֲמֶיךָ, וְלֹא עֲזָבוּנוּ חֲסָדֶיךָ. וְאַל תִּטְּשֵׁנוּ יהוה אֱלֹהֵינוּ לָנֶצַח. עַל כֵּן אֵבָרִים שֶׁפִּלַּגְתָּ בָּנוּ, וְרוּחַ וּנְשָׁמָה שֶׁנָּפַחְתָּ בְּאַפֵּינוּ, וְלָשׁוֹן אֲשֶׁר שַׂמְתָּ בְּפִינוּ, הֵן הֵם יוֹדוּ וִיבָרְכוּ וִישַׁבְּחוּ וִיפָאֲרוּ וִירוֹמְמוּ וְיַעֲרִיצוּ וְיַקְדִּישׁוּ וְיַמְלִיכוּ אֶת שִׁמְךָ מַלְכֵּנוּ. כִּי כָל פֶּה לְךָ יוֹדֶה, וְכָל לָשׁוֹן לְךָ תִשָּׁבַע, וְכָל בֶּרֶךְ לְךָ תִכְרַע,[1] וְכָל קוֹמָה לְפָנֶיךָ תִשְׁתַּחֲוֶה,* וְכָל לְבָבוֹת יִירָאוּךָ, וְכָל קֶרֶב וּכְלָיוֹת יְזַמְּרוּ לִשְׁמֶךָ, כַּדָּבָר שֶׁכָּתוּב: כָּל עַצְמֹתַי תֹּאמַרְנָה,* יהוה מִי כָמוֹךָ, מַצִּיל עָנִי מֵחָזָק מִמֶּנּוּ, וְעָנִי וְאֶבְיוֹן מִגֹּזְלוֹ.[2] מִי יִדְמֶה לָּךְ, וּמִי יִשְׁוֶה לָּךְ, וּמִי יַעֲרָךְ לָךְ.[3] הָאֵל הַגָּדוֹל הַגִּבּוֹר וְהַנּוֹרָא, אֵל עֶלְיוֹן, קֹנֵה שָׁמַיִם וָאָרֶץ. ❖ נְהַלֶּלְךָ וּנְשַׁבֵּחֲךָ וּנְפָאֶרְךָ וּנְבָרֵךְ אֶת שֵׁם קָדְשֶׁךָ, כָּאָמוּר: לְדָוִד, בָּרְכִי נַפְשִׁי אֶת יהוה, וְכָל קְרָבַי אֶת שֵׁם קָדְשׁוֹ.[4]

On Festivals, the *chazzan* for *Shacharis* begins here.

הָאֵל בְּתַעֲצֻמוֹת עֻזֶּךָ,* הַגָּדוֹל בִּכְבוֹד שְׁמֶךָ, הַגִּבּוֹר לָנֶצַח וְהַנּוֹרָא בְּנוֹרְאוֹתֶיךָ, הַמֶּלֶךְ הַיּוֹשֵׁב עַל כִּסֵּא רָם וְנִשָּׂא.[5]

---

worthy of our grateful thanks, the liturgist now begins to explain that no creature could do justice to this task — even if he were endowed with superhuman qualities.

מְאִירוֹת כַּשֶּׁמֶשׁ וְכַיָּרֵחַ — *As brilliant as the sun and the moon,* which see everything on earth.

עִם אֲבוֹתֵינוּ וְעִמָּנוּ — *For our ancestors and for us.* Man does not live in a vacuum. The favors done for previous generations have lasting effects that benefit us as well.

וְכָל קוֹמָה לְפָנֶיךָ תִשְׁתַּחֲוֶה — *Every erect spine shall prostrate itself before You.* One must bow to God even while he is standing erect. 'Bowing' is not only a physical action; it must also be done in the heart and mind *(R' Baruch of Mezhibozh).*

כָּל עַצְמוֹתַי תֹּאמַרְנָה — *All my bones shall say.* Having just described how each limb and organ will offer praise to God, we cite the Scriptural source for this obligation. The verse concludes with the inspiring praise that God's greatness is manifested in His rescue of the powerless from their oppressors. This is meant both literally and figuratively, for, as *Radak* explains, God rescues the seemingly overmatched good inclination from the seductions of the evil inclination.

❧ הָאֵל בְּתַעֲצֻמוֹת עֻזֶּךָ — *O God, in the omnipotence of Your strength.* This and the following verses elaborate upon the themes of *Nishmas.* The last sentence of *Nishmas* contained the four terms הָאֵל הַגָּדוֹל הַגִּבּוֹר וְהַנּוֹרָא, *O — great, mighty, and awesome God.* Now,

and the moon, and our hands as outspread as eagles of the sky and our feet as swift as hinds — we still could not thank You sufficiently, HASHEM our God and God of our forefathers, and to bless Your Name for even one of the thousand thousand, thousands of thousands and myriad myriads of favors that You performed for our ancestors and for us.* You redeemed us from Egypt, HASHEM our God, and liberated us from the house of bondage. In famine You nourished us and in plenty You sustained us. From sword You saved us; from plague You let us escape; and from severe and enduring diseases You spared us. Until now Your mercy has helped us, and Your kindness has not forsaken us. Do not abandon us, HASHEM our God, forever. Therefore, the organs that You set within us, and the spirit and soul that You breathed into our nostrils, and the tongue that You placed in our mouth — all of them shall thank and bless, praise and glorify, exalt and revere, sanctify and declare the sovereignty of Your Name, our King. For every mouth shall offer thanks to You; every tongue shall vow allegiance to You; every knee shall bend to You;[1] every erect spine shall prostrate itself before You;* all hearts shall fear You, and all innermost feelings and thoughts shall sing praises to Your name, as it is written: "All my bones shall say:* 'HASHEM, who is like You?' You save the poor man from one stronger than he, the poor and destitute from one who would rob him."[2] Who is like unto You? Who is equal to You? Who can be compared to You?[3] O great, mighty, and awesome God, the supreme God, Creator of heaven and earth.* Chazzan— *We shall laud, praise, and glorify You and bless Your holy Name, as it is said 'Of David: Bless HASHEM, O my soul, and let all my innermost being bless His holy Name!'[4]*

On Festivals, the *chazzan* for *Shacharis* begins here.

הָאֵל *O God, in the omnipotence of Your strength,* great in the glory of Your Name, mighty forever and awesome through Your awesome deeds, O King enthroned upon a high and lofty throne![5]*

(1) Cf. *Isaiah* 45:23. (2) *Psalms* 35:10. (3) Cf. 89:7; *Isaiah* 40:25. (4) *Psalms* 103:1. (5) Cf. *Isaiah* 6:1.

---

each of those terms is used and elaborated upon in a phrase lauding God:

1. הָאֵל — *O God.* This Name refers to God as the All-Powerful. Thus, God's power is expressed by the idea that He does not depend on servants, armies, or the consent of His subjects. He is omnipotent in His strength without reliance on anything else.

2. הַגָּדוֹל — *Great.* His greatness is signified by the fact that all creatures give honor to His Name.

3. הַגִּבּוֹר — *Mighty.* Unlike mighty human rulers, whose powers ebb as they grow old, God's majesty and strength are eternal and undiminished.

4. וְהַנּוֹרָא — *Awesome.* Unlike human kings who are held in awe only because they have the power to punish their detractors, God's awesomeness is obvious because the entire universe testifies to His greatness.

In many congregations it is customary to divide the Sabbath and *Yom Tov* services among several *chazzanim:* one for *Pesukei D'zimrah;* another for *Shacharis;* and a third for *Mussaf.* On the Sabbath, the *chazzan* begins שׁוֹכֵן עַד, *He Who abides forever,* because the Sabbath was the

On the Sabbath, the *chazzan* for *Shacharis* begins here:

שׁוֹכֵן עַד* מָרוֹם וְקָדוֹשׁ שְׁמוֹ.[1] וְכָתוּב: רַנְּנוּ צַדִּיקִים בַּיהוה לַיְשָׁרִים נָאוָה תְהִלָּה.[2]

❖ בְּפִי **יְ**שָׁרִים* תִּתְהַלָּל.
וּבְדִבְרֵי **צַ**דִּיקִים תִּתְבָּרַךְ.
וּבִלְשׁוֹן **חֲ**סִידִים תִּתְרוֹמָם.
וּבְקֶרֶב **קְ**דוֹשִׁים תִּתְקַדָּשׁ.

וּבְמַקְהֲלוֹת רִבְבוֹת* עַמְּךָ בֵּית יִשְׂרָאֵל, בְּרִנָּה יִתְפָּאַר שִׁמְךָ מַלְכֵּנוּ בְּכָל דּוֹר וָדוֹר. ❖ שֶׁכֵּן חוֹבַת כָּל הַיְּצוּרִים,* לְפָנֶיךָ יהוה אֱלֹהֵינוּ וֵאלֹהֵי אֲבוֹתֵינוּ, לְהוֹדוֹת לְהַלֵּל לְשַׁבֵּחַ לְפָאֵר לְרוֹמֵם לְהַדֵּר לְבָרֵךְ לְעַלֵּה וּלְקַלֵּס, עַל כָּל דִּבְרֵי שִׁירוֹת וְתִשְׁבְּחוֹת דָּוִד* בֶּן יִשַׁי עַבְדְּךָ מְשִׁיחֶךָ.

Stand while reciting יִשְׁתַּבַּח... The fifteen expressions of praise — שִׁיר וּשְׁבָחָה ... בְּרָכוֹת וְהוֹדָאוֹת — should be recited without pause, preferably in one breath.

יִשְׁתַּבַּח שִׁמְךָ לָעַד מַלְכֵּנוּ, הָאֵל הַמֶּלֶךְ הַגָּדוֹל וְהַקָּדוֹשׁ, בַּשָּׁמַיִם וּבָאָרֶץ. כִּי לְךָ נָאֶה יהוה אֱלֹהֵינוּ וֵאלֹהֵי אֲבוֹתֵינוּ, שִׁיר וּשְׁבָחָה, הַלֵּל וְזִמְרָה, עֹז וּמֶמְשָׁלָה, נֶצַח גְּדֻלָּה וּגְבוּרָה, תְּהִלָּה וְתִפְאֶרֶת, קְדֻשָּׁה וּמַלְכוּת, בְּרָכוֹת וְהוֹדָאוֹת מֵעַתָּה וְעַד עוֹלָם. ❖ בָּרוּךְ אַתָּה יהוה, אֵל מֶלֶךְ גָּדוֹל בַּתִּשְׁבָּחוֹת, אֵל הַהוֹדָאוֹת, אֲדוֹן הַנִּפְלָאוֹת, הַבּוֹחֵר בְּשִׁירֵי זִמְרָה, מֶלֶךְ אֵל חֵי הָעוֹלָמִים. (Cong.— אָמֵן.)

---

climax of creation, when God had all of creation, including man, to acknowledge and praise Him.

On Pesach, Shavuos, and Succos, the *chazzan* of *Shacharis* begins הָאֵל בְּתַעֲצֻמוֹת, *O God, in the Omnipotence,* because those three festivals testify to the Exodus, the great event when God revealed 'the omnipotence of His strength.' Thus the characteristics spoken of in this paragraph are fitting for the way in which God revealed Himself in bringing Israel to freedom and its new status as His people. However, on Rosh Hashanah and Yom Kippur when God is the 'King sitting in judgment', the *chazzan* begins הַמֶּלֶךְ, *the King (Levush).*

⊸§ **שׁוֹכֵן עַד** — *He Who abides forever.* Although God is *exalted and holy,* He nevertheless makes His abode on earth, for it is only here — through the deeds of the righteous — that His commandments can be carried out. Therefore, this paragraph goes on to say that the primary praise of God comes from such people. The key, however, is not in their rhetoric but in the 'song' of their good deeds.

בְּפִי יְשָׁרִים — *By the mouth of the upright.* Four categories of people are listed as praising God: יְשָׁרִים, צַדִּיקִים, חֲסִידִים, קְדוֹשִׁים, *upright, righteous, devout,* and *holy.* The initials of these four words spell יִצְחָק, leading some to speculate that it is the signature of the unknown author of *Nishmas.*

Rabbi Shraga Feivel Mendlowitz noted that these four categories seem to be listed in

On the Sabbath, the *chazzan* for *Shacharis* begins here:

שׁוֹכֵן עַד *He Who abides forever,* exalted and holy is His Name.*[1] *And it is written: 'Sing joyfully, O righteous, before* HASHEM*; for the upright, praise is fitting.'*[2]

Chazzan— *By the mouth of the upright * shall You be lauded;*
by the words of the righteous shall You be blessed;
by the tongue of the devout shall You be exalted;
and amid the holy shall You be sanctified.

וּבְמַקְהֲלוֹת *And in the assemblies of the myriads* of Your people, the House of Israel, with joyous song shall Your Name be glorified, our King, throughout every generation.* Chazzan— *For such is the duty of all creatures* — before You,* HASHEM*, our God, God of our forefathers, to thank, laud, praise, glorify, exalt, adore, bless, raise high, and sing praises — even beyond all expressions of the songs and praises of David* the son of Jesse, Your servant, Your anointed.*

Stand while reciting *'May Your Name be praised ...'*
The fifteen expressions of praise — *'song and praise...blessings and thanksgivings'* — should be recited without pause, preferably in one breath.

יִשְׁתַּבַּח *May Your Name be praised forever — our King, the God, the great and holy King — in heaven and on earth. Because for You is fitting — O* HASHEM*, our God, and the God of our forefathers — song and praise, lauding and hymns, power and dominion, triumph, greatness and strength, praise and splendor, holiness and sovereignty, blessings and thanksgivings from this time and forever.* Chazzan— *Blessed are You,* HASHEM*, God, King exalted through praises, God of thanksgivings, Master of wonders, Who chooses musical songs of praise — King, God, Life-giver of the world.* (Cong.— *Amen.*)

(1) Cf. *Isaiah* 57:15. (2) *Psalms* 33:1.

---

ascending order of their spiritual accomplishment, the lowest being the upright, fair-minded people and the highest being the holy ones. The higher the level of the person, the more meaningful the manner in which he praises God. While the *upright* praises God with his *mouth*, the *righteous* uses articulated *words*. The *devout* uses his *tongue*, implying that the praise comes from deeper within himself. The *holy* person, however, praises God with his very *essence* [קֶרֶב, literally, *inner being*].

☙ **וּבְמַקְהֲלוֹת רִבְבוֹת** — *And in the assemblies of the myriads.* In future times, Jews will gather in their tens of thousands to glorify God.

שֶׁכֵּן חוֹבַת כָּל הַיְצוּרִים — *For such is the duty of all creatures.* It is their duty because of the simple fact that they are God's creatures; since He fashioned them, they must feel obligated to pay Him homage.

עַל כָּל דִּבְרֵי ... דָּוִד — *Even beyond all expressions ... of David.* Although David, the נְעִים זְמִרוֹת יִשְׂרָאֵל, *sweet singer of Israel (II Samuel* 23:1), is the quintessential composer of God's praises, even he could not nearly do justice to God's greatness. Therefore we now say that we are obligated to praise Him limitlessly — even beyond the songs of David.

☙ **יִשְׁתַּבַּח** — Commentary to *Yishtabach* and *Borchu* begins on p. 82.

From Rosh Hashanah until Yom Kippur many congregations recite *Psalm* 130, שִׁיר הַמַּעֲלוֹת, at this point. Each verse is chanted aloud by the *chazzan,* then repeated by the congregation.

שִׁיר הַמַּעֲלוֹת, מִמַּעֲמַקִּים קְרָאתִיךָ יהוה. אֲדֹנָי שִׁמְעָה בְקוֹלִי, תִּהְיֶינָה אָזְנֶיךָ קַשֻּׁבוֹת, לְקוֹל תַּחֲנוּנָי. אִם עֲוֹנוֹת תִּשְׁמָר יָהּ, אֲדֹנָי מִי יַעֲמֹד. כִּי עִמְּךָ הַסְּלִיחָה, לְמַעַן תִּוָּרֵא. קִוִּיתִי יהוה קִוְּתָה נַפְשִׁי, וְלִדְבָרוֹ הוֹחָלְתִּי. נַפְשִׁי לַאדֹנָי, מִשֹּׁמְרִים לַבֹּקֶר, שֹׁמְרִים לַבֹּקֶר. יַחֵל יִשְׂרָאֵל אֶל יהוה, כִּי עִם יהוה הַחֶסֶד, וְהַרְבֵּה עִמּוֹ פְדוּת. וְהוּא יִפְדֶּה אֶת יִשְׂרָאֵל, מִכֹּל עֲוֹנוֹתָיו.

If a *minyan* is present, the *chazzan* recites חֲצִי קַדִּישׁ and בָּרְכוּ:

יִתְגַּדַּל וְיִתְקַדַּשׁ שְׁמֵהּ רַבָּא. (.Cong.— אָמֵן.) בְּעָלְמָא דִּי בְרָא כִרְעוּתֵהּ. וְיַמְלִיךְ מַלְכוּתֵהּ, בְּחַיֵּיכוֹן וּבְיוֹמֵיכוֹן וּבְחַיֵּי דְכָל בֵּית יִשְׂרָאֵל, בַּעֲגָלָא וּבִזְמַן קָרִיב. וְאִמְרוּ: אָמֵן.

(.Cong.— אָמֵן. יְהֵא שְׁמֵהּ רַבָּא מְבָרַךְ לְעָלַם וּלְעָלְמֵי עָלְמַיָּא.)

יְהֵא שְׁמֵהּ רַבָּא מְבָרַךְ לְעָלַם וּלְעָלְמֵי עָלְמַיָּא.

יִתְבָּרַךְ וְיִשְׁתַּבַּח וְיִתְפָּאַר וְיִתְרוֹמַם וְיִתְנַשֵּׂא וְיִתְהַדָּר וְיִתְעַלֶּה וְיִתְהַלָּל שְׁמֵהּ דְּקֻדְשָׁא בְּרִיךְ הוּא (.Cong.— בְּרִיךְ הוּא) — °לְעֵלָּא מִן כָּל (From Rosh Hashanah to Yom Kippur substitute— °לְעֵלָּא וּלְעֵלָּא מִכָּל) בִּרְכָתָא וְשִׁירָתָא תֻּשְׁבְּחָתָא וְנֶחֱמָתָא, דַּאֲמִירָן בְּעָלְמָא. וְאִמְרוּ: אָמֵן. (.Cong.— אָמֵן.)

In some congregations the *chazzan* chants a melody during his recitation of בָּרְכוּ, so that the congregation can then recite יִתְבָּרַךְ.

Chazzan bows at בָּרְכוּ and straightens up at ה׳.

בָּרְכוּ אֶת יהוה הַמְּבֹרָךְ.

Congregation, followed by *chazzan,* responds, bowing at בָּרוּךְ and straightening up at ה׳.

בָּרוּךְ יהוה הַמְּבֹרָךְ לְעוֹלָם וָעֶד.

יִתְבָּרַךְ וְיִשְׁתַּבַּח וְיִתְפָּאַר וְיִתְרוֹמַם וְיִתְנַשֵּׂא שְׁמוֹ שֶׁל מֶלֶךְ מַלְכֵי הַמְּלָכִים, הַקָּדוֹשׁ בָּרוּךְ הוּא. שֶׁהוּא רִאשׁוֹן וְהוּא אַחֲרוֹן, וּמִבַּלְעָדָיו אֵין אֱלֹהִים.[1] סֹלּוּ, לָרֹכֵב בָּעֲרָבוֹת, בְּיָהּ שְׁמוֹ, וְעִלְזוּ לְפָנָיו.[2] וּשְׁמוֹ מְרוֹמַם עַל כָּל בְּרָכָה וּתְהִלָּה.[3] בָּרוּךְ שֵׁם כְּבוֹד מַלְכוּתוֹ לְעוֹלָם וָעֶד. יְהִי שֵׁם יהוה מְבֹרָךְ, מֵעַתָּה וְעַד עוֹלָם.[4]

ברכות קריאת שמע

It is preferable that one sit while reciting the following series of prayers — particularly the *Kedushah* verses, קָדוֹשׁ קָדוֹשׁ קָדוֹשׁ and בָּרוּךְ כְּבוֹד — until *Shemoneh Esrei.*

בָּרוּךְ אַתָּה יהוה אֱלֹהֵינוּ מֶלֶךְ הָעוֹלָם, יוֹצֵר אוֹר וּבוֹרֵא חֹשֶׁךְ, עֹשֶׂה שָׁלוֹם וּבוֹרֵא אֶת הַכֹּל.[5]

בִּרְכוֹת קְרִיאַת שְׁמַע/Blessings of the Shema

Essentially, this part of the Sabbath *Shacharis* is no different from that of weekdays. Each contains two blessings before the *Shema* and one after it. Since the first blessing discusses the miracles of creation, and it is the Sabbath that commemorates the completion of the universe,

From Rosh Hashanah until Yom Kippur many congregations recite *Psalm* 130, *'A Song of Ascents,'* at this point. Each verse is chanted aloud by the *chazzan,* then repeated by the congregation.

שִׁיר הַמַּעֲלוֹת *A song of ascents: From the depths I called You, HASHEM. My Lord, hear my voice, may Your ears be attentive to the sound of my pleas. If You preserve iniquities, O God, my Lord, who could survive? For with You is forgiveness, that You may be feared. I put confidence in HASHEM, my soul put confidence, and I hoped for His word. I yearn for my Lord, among those longing for the dawn, those longing for the dawn. Let Israel hope for HASHEM, for with HASHEM is kindness, and with Him is abundant redemption. And He shall redeem Israel from all its iniquities.*

If a *minyan* is present, the *chazzan* recites Half-*Kaddish* and *Borchu:*

יִתְגַּדַּל *May His great Name grow exalted and sanctified* (Cong.— *Amen.*) *in the world that He created as He willed. May He give reign to His kingship in your lifetimes and in your days, and in the lifetimes of the entire Family of Israel, swiftly and soon. Now respond: Amen.*

(Cong.— *Amen. May His great Name be blessed forever and ever.*)

May His great Name be blessed forever and ever.

Blessed, praised, glorified, exalted, extolled, mighty, upraised, and lauded be the Name of the Holy One, Blessed is He (Cong.— *Blessed is He*) — (From Rosh Hashanah to Yom Kippur add: *exceedingly*) *beyond any blessing and song, praise and consolation that are uttered in the world. Now respond: Amen.* (Cong.— *Amen.*)

In some congregations the *chazzan* chants a melody during his recitation of *Borchu,* so that the congregation can then recite *'Blessed, praised ...'*

Chazzan bows at *'Bless,'* and straightens up at *'HASHEM.'*

Bless HASHEM, the blessed One.

Congregation, followed by *chazzan,* responds, bowing at *'Blessed'* and straightening up at *'HASHEM.'*

Blessed is HASHEM, the blessed One, for all eternity.

Blessed, praised, glorified, exalted and upraised is the Name of the King Who rules over kings — the Holy One, Blessed is He. For He is the First and He is the Last and aside from Him there is no god.[1] *Extol Him — Who rides the highest heavens — with His Name, YAH, and exult before Him.*[2] *His Name is exalted beyond every blessing and praise.*[3] *Blessed is the Name of His glorious kingdom for all eternity. Blessed be the Name of HASHEM from this time and forever.*[4]

BLESSINGS OF THE SHEMA

It is preferable that one sit while reciting the following series of prayers — particularly the *Kedushah* verses, *'Holy, holy, holy ...'* and *'Blessed is the glory ...'* — until *Shemoneh Esrei.*

בָּרוּךְ *Blessed are You, HASHEM, our God, King of the Universe, Who forms light and creates darkness, makes peace and creates all.*[5]

(1) Cf. *Isaiah* 44:6. (2) *Psalms* 68:5. (3) Cf. *Nechemiah* 9:5. (4) *Psalms* 113:2. (5) Cf. *Isaiah* 45:7.

this blessing is augmented on the Sabbath with additional prayers and songs of praise. Commentary to the *Shema* and its blessings appears on pp. 84-97. The commentary below is limited to the Sabbath additions.

Festivals, unlike the Sabbath, place special emphasis on events other than creation. Therefore, on weekday festivals, the regular הַמֵּאִיר לָאָרֶץ, *He Who illuminates the earth,* is recited.

When a Festival occurs on a weekday, הַמֵּאִיר לָאָרֶץ (below) is substituted:

הַכֹּל יוֹדְוּךָ,* וְהַכֹּל יְשַׁבְּחְוּךָ, וְהַכֹּל יֹאמְרוּ אֵין קָדוֹשׁ כַּיהוה.[1] הַכֹּל יְרוֹמְמְוּךָ סֶּלָה, יוֹצֵר הַכֹּל. הָאֵל הַפּוֹתֵחַ בְּכָל יוֹם דַּלְתוֹת שַׁעֲרֵי מִזְרָח, וּבוֹקֵעַ חַלּוֹנֵי רָקִיעַ,* מוֹצִיא חַמָּה מִמְּקוֹמָהּ וּלְבָנָה מִמְּכוֹן שִׁבְתָּהּ, וּמֵאִיר לָעוֹלָם כֻּלּוֹ וּלְיוֹשְׁבָיו, שֶׁבָּרָא בְּמִדַּת רַחֲמִים. הַמֵּאִיר לָאָרֶץ וְלַדָּרִים עָלֶיהָ בְּרַחֲמִים, וּבְטוּבוֹ מְחַדֵּשׁ בְּכָל יוֹם תָּמִיד מַעֲשֵׂה בְרֵאשִׁית. הַמֶּלֶךְ הַמְּרוֹמָם לְבַדּוֹ מֵאָז, הַמְּשֻׁבָּח וְהַמְּפֹאָר וְהַמִּתְנַשֵּׂא מִימוֹת עוֹלָם. אֱלֹהֵי עוֹלָם, בְּרַחֲמֶיךָ הָרַבִּים רַחֵם עָלֵינוּ, אֲדוֹן עֻזֵּנוּ, צוּר מִשְׂגַּבֵּנוּ, מָגֵן יִשְׁעֵנוּ, מִשְׂגָּב בַּעֲדֵנוּ. אֵין כְּעֶרְכֶּךָ,* וְאֵין זוּלָתֶךָ, אֶפֶס בִּלְתֶּךָ, וּמִי דּוֹמֶה לָּךְ. אֵין כְּעֶרְכְּךָ יהוה אֱלֹהֵינוּ בָּעוֹלָם הַזֶּה, וְאֵין זוּלָתְךָ מַלְכֵּנוּ לְחַיֵּי הָעוֹלָם הַבָּא. אֶפֶס בִּלְתְּךָ גּוֹאֲלֵנוּ לִימוֹת הַמָּשִׁיחַ, וְאֵין דּוֹמֶה לְּךָ מוֹשִׁיעֵנוּ לִתְחִיַּת הַמֵּתִים.

(Continue אֵל אָדוֹן, page 410)

When a Festival occurs on a weekday substitute:
(commentary on p. 85)

הַמֵּאִיר לָאָרֶץ וְלַדָּרִים עָלֶיהָ בְּרַחֲמִים, וּבְטוּבוֹ מְחַדֵּשׁ בְּכָל יוֹם תָּמִיד מַעֲשֵׂה בְרֵאשִׁית. מָה רַבּוּ מַעֲשֶׂיךָ יהוה, כֻּלָּם בְּחָכְמָה עָשִׂיתָ, מָלְאָה הָאָרֶץ קִנְיָנֶךָ.[2] הַמֶּלֶךְ הַמְּרוֹמָם לְבַדּוֹ מֵאָז, הַמְּשֻׁבָּח וְהַמְּפֹאָר וְהַמִּתְנַשֵּׂא מִימוֹת עוֹלָם. אֱלֹהֵי עוֹלָם, בְּרַחֲמֶיךָ הָרַבִּים רַחֵם עָלֵינוּ, אֲדוֹן עֻזֵּנוּ, צוּר מִשְׂגַּבֵּנוּ, מָגֵן יִשְׁעֵנוּ, מִשְׂגָּב בַּעֲדֵנוּ. **אֵל בָּרוּךְ גְּדוֹל דֵּעָה, הֵכִין וּפָעַל זָהֳרֵי חַמָּה, טוֹב יָצַר כָּבוֹד לִשְׁמוֹ, מְאוֹרוֹת נָתַן סְבִיבוֹת עֻזּוֹ, פִּנּוֹת צְבָאָיו קְדוֹשִׁים רוֹמְמֵי שַׁדַּי,** תָּמִיד מְסַפְּרִים כְּבוֹד אֵל וּקְדֻשָּׁתוֹ. תִּתְבָּרַךְ יהוה אֱלֹהֵינוּ עַל שֶׁבַח מַעֲשֵׂה יָדֶיךָ, וְעַל מְאוֹרֵי אוֹר שֶׁעָשִׂיתָ יְפָאֲרוּךָ סֶּלָה.

(Continue תִּתְבָּרַךְ, p. 412).

☙ **הַכֹּל יוֹדְוּךָ** — *All will thank You.* The word 'all' refers to the previous blessing, which ends וּבוֹרֵא אֶת הַכֹּל, *and creates all.* Thus, every facet of the universe will join in thanking and lauding God. Only man and the angels do this verbally; the rest of creation does so by carrying out its assigned tasks and inspiring man to recognize the Guiding Hand that created and orders everything.

דַּלְתוֹת שַׁעֲרֵי מִזְרָח ... חַלּוֹנֵי רָקִיעַ — *Doors of the gateways of the East ... windows of the firmament.* These expressions are given various interpretations. On the simple level, they refer poetically to the rising sun breaking through the portals of darkness. Alternatively, the phrase *doors of the gateways* refers to daybreak, which illuminates the sky long before sunrise. The *windows* are different points in the sky at which the sun rises as the seasons move to the longer days of summer and then back again to the shorter days of winter *(R' Hirsch; Iyun Tefillah).*

אֵין כְּעֶרְכֶּךָ — *There is no comparison to You.* This verse makes four statements about God that are explained in the next verse. Thus the two verses should be seen as a unit. As explained by *R' Hirsch*, the four statements are:

1. אֵין כְּעֶרְכֶּךָ — *There is no comparison to You.*

When a Festival occurs on a weekday, הַמֵּאִיר, *'He Who illuminates the earth'* (below) is substituted:

הַכֹּל יוֹדְוּךָ *All will thank You* and all will praise You — and all will declare: 'Nothing is as holy as HASHEM!',[1] All will exalt You, Selah! — You Who forms everything. The God Who opens daily the doors of the gateways of the East, and splits the windows of the firmament,* Who removes the sun from its place and the moon from the site of its dwelling, and Who illuminates all the world and its inhabitants, which He created with the attribute of mercy. He Who illuminates the earth and those who dwell upon it, with compassion; and in His goodness renews daily, perpetually, the work of creation. The King Who was exalted in solitude from before creation, Who is praised, glorified, and extolled since days of old. Eternal God, with Your abundant compassion be compassionate to us — O Master of our power, our rocklike stronghold; O Shield of our salvation, be a stronghold for us. There is no comparison to You,* there is nothing except for You, there is nothing without You, for Who is like You? There is no comparison to You, HASHEM, our God, in this world; and there will be nothing except for You, our King, in the life of the World to Come; there will be nothing without You, our Redeemer, in Messianic days; and there will be none like You, our Savior; at the Resuscitation of the Dead.* (Continue, *'God — the Master,'* p. 411.)

When a Festival occurs on a weekday substitute:
(commentary on p. 85)

הַמֵּאִיר *He Who illuminates the earth and those who dwell upon it, with compassion; and in His goodness renews daily, perpetually, the work of creation. How great are Your works, HASHEM, You make them all with wisdom, the world is full of Your possessions.[2] The King Who was exalted in solitude before creation, Who is praised, glorified, and extolled since days of old. Eternal God, with Your abundant compassion be compassionate to us — O Master of our power, our rocklike stronghold; O shield of our salvation, be a stronghold for us. The blessed God, Who is great in knowledge, prepared and worked on the rays of the sun; the Beneficent One fashioned honor for His Name, emplaced luminaries all around His power; the leaders of His legions, holy ones, exalt the Almighty, constantly relate the honor of God and His sanctity. May You be blessed, HASHEM, our God, beyond the praises of Your handiwork and beyond the brilliant luminaries that You have made — may they themselves glorify You — Selah!* (Continue, *'May You be blessed ...,'* p. 413.)

(1) *I Samuel* 2:2. (2) *Psalms* 104:24.

Although we have expressed our gratitude for the heavenly bodies and the various forces of the universe, we hasten to affirm that none of them can even be compared to God's power on earth.

2. וְאֵין זוּלָתְךָ — *There is nothing except for You.* In the World to Come, even the most beneficial aspects of life in this material world will not exist. In the blissful state of that world, nothing will exist except for God and those whose lives on earth have made them worthy of His spiritual grandeur.

3. אֶפֶס בִּלְתְּךָ — *There is nothing without You.* On earth, too, there will be a state of bliss with the coming of the Messiah — but that redemption is impossible without God, despite the earthly factors that will seem to contribute to it.

4. וּמִי דּוֹמֶה לָּךְ — *For who is like You?* Nothing will so clearly reveal God's absolute mastery as the Resuscitation of the Dead. That is the ultimate redemption, for it will demonstrate that not only slavery and freedom, but even life and death depend on Him.

The following liturgical song is recited responsively in most congregations. In some congregations, the *chazzan* and congregation sing the stanzas together.

אֵל אָדוֹן* עַל כָּל הַמַּעֲשִׂים, **בָּ**רוּךְ וּמְבֹרָךְ* בְּפִי כָּל נְשָׁמָה,
גָּדְלוֹ וְטוּבוֹ מָלֵא עוֹלָם, **דַּ**עַת וּתְבוּנָה סוֹבְבִים אֹתוֹ.
הַמִּתְגָּאֶה* עַל חַיּוֹת הַקֹּדֶשׁ, **וְ**נֶהְדָּר בְּכָבוֹד עַל הַמֶּרְכָּבָה,
זְכוּת וּמִישׁוֹר לִפְנֵי כִסְאוֹ, **חֶ**סֶד וְרַחֲמִים לִפְנֵי כְבוֹדוֹ.
טוֹבִים מְאוֹרוֹת שֶׁבָּרָא אֱלֹהֵינוּ, **יְ**צָרָם בְּדַעַת בְּבִינָה וּבְהַשְׂכֵּל,
כֹּחַ וּגְבוּרָה נָתַן בָּהֶם, **לִ**הְיוֹת מוֹשְׁלִים בְּקֶרֶב תֵּבֵל.
מְלֵאִים זִיו וּמְפִיקִים נֹגַהּ, **נָ**אֶה זִיוָם בְּכָל הָעוֹלָם,
שְׂמֵחִים בְּצֵאתָם* וְשָׂשִׂים בְּבוֹאָם, **ע**וֹשִׂים בְּאֵימָה רְצוֹן קוֹנָם.
פְּאֵר וְכָבוֹד* נוֹתְנִים לִשְׁמוֹ, **צָ**הֳלָה וְרִנָּה לְזֵכֶר מַלְכוּתוֹ,
קָרָא לַשֶּׁמֶשׁ וַיִּזְרַח אוֹר, **רָ**אָה וְהִתְקִין צוּרַת הַלְּבָנָה.*
שֶׁבַח נוֹתְנִים לוֹ כָּל צְבָא מָרוֹם,
תִּפְאֶרֶת וּגְדֻלָּה, שְׂרָפִים וְאוֹפַנִּים וְחַיּוֹת הַקֹּדֶשׁ—

לָאֵל אֲשֶׁר שָׁבַת* מִכָּל הַמַּעֲשִׂים, בַּיּוֹם הַשְּׁבִיעִי הִתְעַלָּה וְיָשַׁב עַל כִּסֵּא כְבוֹדוֹ, תִּפְאֶרֶת עָטָה לְיוֹם הַמְּנוּחָה, עֹנֶג קָרָא לְיוֹם הַשַּׁבָּת. זֶה שֶׁבַח שֶׁל יוֹם הַשְּׁבִיעִי,* שֶׁבּוֹ שָׁבַת אֵל מִכָּל מְלַאכְתּוֹ. וְיוֹם הַשְּׁבִיעִי מְשַׁבֵּחַ וְאוֹמֵר: מִזְמוֹר שִׁיר לְיוֹם הַשַּׁבָּת, טוֹב לְהוֹדוֹת לַיהוה.[1] לְפִיכָךְ יְפָאֲרוּ* וִיבָרְכוּ לָאֵל כָּל יְצוּרָיו. שֶׁבַח יְקָר וּגְדֻלָּה יִתְּנוּ לָאֵל מֶלֶךְ יוֹצֵר כֹּל, הַמַּנְחִיל מְנוּחָה לְעַמּוֹ יִשְׂרָאֵל בִּקְדֻשָּׁתוֹ בְּיוֹם שַׁבַּת קֹדֶשׁ. שִׁמְךָ יהוה

☙ **אֵל אָדוֹן** — *God — the Master.* This poetic prayer comprises twenty-two phrases, the initial letters of which form the *Aleph-Beis.* It is parallel to the alphabetical prayer אֵל בָּרוּךְ גְּדוֹל דֵּעָה of the weekday *Shacharis;* but the weekday prayer contains only twenty-two words. The *Vilna Gaon* explains that the lesser holiness of the weekdays is expressed not only in the shorter version, but in the content. There, the praise concentrates on God's greatness as we perceive it in the form of the heavenly bodies. Here, the greater holiness of the Sabbath enables us to perceive more — though clearly not all — of His greatness.

בָּרוּךְ וּמְבֹרָךְ — *The blessed One — and He is blessed,* i.e., God is the source of all blessing. In addition, His creatures bless Him in their prayers and through their obedience to His will *(Vilna Gaon).*

הַמִּתְגָּאֶה — *He Who exalts Himself.* The *Chayos* are the highest category of angels and the Chariot [מֶרְכָּבָה] refers to the order of angelic praises of God. Both were seen by Ezekiel in his *Ma'aseh Merkavah* prophecy (Ch. 1). Thus they represent the highest degree of holiness accessible to human understanding. Nevertheless, God is exalted far above even this.

שְׂמֵחִים בְּצֵאתָם — *Glad as they go forth.* The heavenly bodies are likened to a loyal servant entrusted with an important mission. He is proud and happy when he sets out, but is even more joyous when he returns to his master.

פְּאֵר וְכָבוֹד — *Splendor and glory.* The exact movements of the heavenly bodies inspire people to praise the One Who created them.

צוּרַת הַלְּבָנָה — *The form of the moon.* With insight, God shaped the phases of the moon so that it would enable Israel to order the calendar as commanded by the Torah.

☙ **לָאֵל אֲשֶׁר שָׁבַת** — *To the God Who rested.* To Whom are directed the praises mentioned above?

The following liturgical song is recited responsively in most congregations. In some congregations, the *chazzan* and congregation sing the stanzas together.

אֵל אָדוֹן *God — the Master* over all works; the Blessed One —*
and He is blessed by the mouth of every soul;*
His greatness and goodness fill the world,
wisdom and insight surround Him.
He Who exalts Himself over the holy Chayos*
and is splendrous in glory above the Chariot;
Merit and fairness are before His throne,
kindness and mercy are before His glory.
Good are the luminaries that our God has created,
He has fashioned them with wisdom,
with insight and discernment;
Strength and power has He granted them,
to be dominant within the world.
Filled with luster and radiating brightness,
their luster is beautiful throughout the world;
Glad as they go forth and exultant as they return,*
they do with awe their Creator's will.
Splendor and glory they bestow upon His Name,*
jubilation and glad song upon the mention of His reign —
He called out to the sun and it glowed with light,
*He saw and fashioned the form of the moon.**
All the host above bestows praise on Him,
splendor and greatness — the Seraphim, Ophanim,
and holy Chayos —

לָאֵל *To the God Who rested* from all works, Who ascended on the Seventh Day and sat on the Throne of His Glory. With splendor He enwrapped the Day of Contentment — He declared the Sabbath day a delight! This is the praise of the Sabbath Day:* that on it God rested from all His work. And the Seventh Day gives praise saying: 'A psalm, a song for the Sabbath Day. It is good to thank* HASHEM *...'*[1] *Therefore let all that He has fashioned glorify* and bless God. Praise, honor, and greatness let them render to God, the King Who fashioned everything, Who gives a heritage of contentment to His People, Israel, in His holiness on the holy Sabbath Day. May Your Name,* HASHEM

(1) *Psalms* 92:1-2.

— to the God Who rested on the Sabbath from His six days of creation. We say that He 'ascended on the Seventh Day' in the sense that His Presence is no longer obvious, on earth. Nevertheless, He left us with the Sabbath as an eternal testimony to His six days of activity and the Sabbath of His rest.

זֶה שֶׁבַח שֶׁל יוֹם הַשְּׁבִיעִי — *This is the praise of the Sabbath Day.* The glory of the Sabbath is not in the leisure it offers, but in its witness to the Creator and its stimulus to man to join it in praising God. In this sense, the very existence of the Sabbath is a praise to God; alternatively, the 'praise' can be understood as the Song of the Day for the Sabbath.

לְפִיכָךְ יְפָאֲרוּ — *Therefore let all ... glorify.* As the prayer goes on to say, the reason that Creation glorifies God is because He has given the

אֱלֹהֵינוּ יִתְקַדַּשׁ, וְזִכְרְךָ מַלְכֵּנוּ יִתְפָּאַר, בַּשָּׁמַיִם מִמַּעַל וְעַל הָאָרֶץ מִתָּחַת. תִּתְבָּרַךְ מוֹשִׁיעֵנוּ עַל שֶׁבַח מַעֲשֵׂה יָדֶיךָ, וְעַל מְאוֹרֵי אוֹר שֶׁעָשִׂיתָ, יְפָאֲרוּךָ, סֶּלָה.

Commentary to the following appears on pp. 86-97.

תִּתְבָּרַךְ צוּרֵנוּ מַלְכֵּנוּ וְגוֹאֲלֵנוּ, בּוֹרֵא קְדוֹשִׁים. יִשְׁתַּבַּח שִׁמְךָ לָעַד מַלְכֵּנוּ, יוֹצֵר מְשָׁרְתִים, וַאֲשֶׁר מְשָׁרְתָיו כֻּלָּם עוֹמְדִים בְּרוּם עוֹלָם, וּמַשְׁמִיעִים בְּיִרְאָה יַחַד בְּקוֹל דִּבְרֵי אֱלֹהִים חַיִּים וּמֶלֶךְ עוֹלָם.[1] כֻּלָּם אֲהוּבִים, כֻּלָּם בְּרוּרִים, כֻּלָּם גִּבּוֹרִים, וְכֻלָּם עֹשִׂים בְּאֵימָה וּבְיִרְאָה רְצוֹן קוֹנָם. ❖ וְכֻלָּם פּוֹתְחִים אֶת פִּיהֶם בִּקְדֻשָּׁה וּבְטָהֳרָה, בְּשִׁירָה וּבְזִמְרָה, וּמְבָרְכִים וּמְשַׁבְּחִים וּמְפָאֲרִים וּמַעֲרִיצִים וּמַקְדִּישִׁים וּמַמְלִיכִים —

אֶת שֵׁם הָאֵל הַמֶּלֶךְ הַגָּדוֹל הַגִּבּוֹר וְהַנּוֹרָא קָדוֹשׁ הוּא.[2] ❖ וְכֻלָּם מְקַבְּלִים עֲלֵיהֶם עֹל מַלְכוּת שָׁמַיִם זֶה מִזֶּה, וְנוֹתְנִים רְשׁוּת זֶה לָזֶה, לְהַקְדִּישׁ לְיוֹצְרָם, בְּנַחַת רוּחַ בְּשָׂפָה בְרוּרָה וּבִנְעִימָה. קְדֻשָּׁה כֻּלָּם כְּאֶחָד עוֹנִים וְאוֹמְרִים בְּיִרְאָה:

— Congregation recites aloud.

קָדוֹשׁ קָדוֹשׁ קָדוֹשׁ יהוה צְבָאוֹת, מְלֹא כָל הָאָרֶץ כְּבוֹדוֹ.[3]

❖ וְהָאוֹפַנִּים וְחַיּוֹת הַקֹּדֶשׁ בְּרַעַשׁ גָּדוֹל מִתְנַשְּׂאִים לְעֻמַּת שְׂרָפִים. לְעֻמָּתָם מְשַׁבְּחִים וְאוֹמְרִים:

—Congregation recites aloud **בָּרוּךְ כְּבוֹד יהוה מִמְּקוֹמוֹ.**[4]

לְאֵל בָּרוּךְ נְעִימוֹת יִתֵּנוּ. לְמֶלֶךְ אֵל חַי וְקַיָּם, זְמִרוֹת יֹאמֵרוּ, וְתִשְׁבָּחוֹת יַשְׁמִיעוּ. כִּי הוּא לְבַדּוֹ פּוֹעֵל גְּבוּרוֹת, עֹשֶׂה חֲדָשׁוֹת, בַּעַל מִלְחָמוֹת, זוֹרֵעַ צְדָקוֹת, מַצְמִיחַ יְשׁוּעוֹת, בּוֹרֵא רְפוּאוֹת, נוֹרָא תְהִלּוֹת, אֲדוֹן הַנִּפְלָאוֹת. הַמְּחַדֵּשׁ בְּטוּבוֹ בְּכָל יוֹם תָּמִיד מַעֲשֵׂה בְרֵאשִׁית. כָּאָמוּר: לְעֹשֵׂה אוֹרִים גְּדֹלִים, כִּי לְעוֹלָם חַסְדּוֹ.[5] ❖ אוֹר חָדָשׁ עַל צִיּוֹן תָּאִיר, וְנִזְכֶּה כֻלָּנוּ מְהֵרָה לְאוֹרוֹ. בָּרוּךְ אַתָּה יהוה, יוֹצֵר הַמְּאוֹרוֹת. (.Cong— אָמֵן)

אַהֲבָה רַבָּה אֲהַבְתָּנוּ יהוה אֱלֹהֵינוּ, חֶמְלָה גְדוֹלָה וִיתֵרָה חָמַלְתָּ עָלֵינוּ. אָבִינוּ מַלְכֵּנוּ, בַּעֲבוּר אֲבוֹתֵינוּ שֶׁבָּטְחוּ

our God, be sanctified and may Your remembrance, Our King, be glorified in the heaven above and upon the earth below. May You be blessed, our Savior, beyond the praises of Your handiwork and beyond the brilliant luminaries that You have made — may they glorify You — Selah.

Commentary to the following appears on pp. 86-97.

תִּתְבָּרַךְ *May You be blessed, our Rock, our King and Redeemer, Creator of holy ones; may Your Name be praised forever, our King, O Fashioner of ministering angels; all of Whose ministering angels stand at the summit of the universe and proclaim — with awe, together, loudly — the words of the living God and King of the universe.*[1] *They are all beloved; they are all flawless; they are all mighty, they all do the will of their Maker with dread and reverence.* Chazzan— *And they all open their mouth in holiness and purity, in song and hymn — and bless, praise, glorify, revere, sanctify and declare the kingship of —*

אֶת שֵׁם *The Name of God, the great, mighty, and awesome King; holy is He.*[2] Chazzan— *Then they all accept upon themselves the yoke of heavenly sovereignty from one another, and grant permission to one another to sanctify the One Who formed them, with tranquillity, with clear articulation, and with sweetness. All of them as one proclaim His holiness and say with awe:*

Congregation recites aloud: **'Holy, holy, holy is HASHEM, Master of Legions, the whole world is filled with His glory.'**[3]

Chazzan— *Then the Ofanim and the holy Chayos with great noise raise themselves towards the Seraphim. Facing them they give praise saying:*

Cong. recites aloud: **'Blessed is the glory of HASHEM from His place.'**[4]

לְאֵל *To the blessed God they shall offer sweet melodies; to the King, the living and enduring God, they shall sing hymns and proclaim praises. For He alone effects mighty deeds, makes new things, is Master of wars, sows kindnesses, makes salvations flourish, creates cures, is too awesome for praise, is Lord of wonders. In His goodness He renews daily, perpetually, the work of creation. As it is said: '[Give thanks] to Him Who makes the great luminaries, for His kindness endures forever.'*[5] Chazzan— *May You shine a new light on Zion, and may we all speedily merit its light. Blessed are You, HASHEM, Who fashions the luminaries.* (Cong.— *Amen*)

אַהֲבָה *With an abundant love have You loved us, HASHEM, our God; with exceedingly great pity have You pitied us. Our Father, our King, for the sake of our forefathers who trusted*

(1) Cf. *Jeremiah* 10:10. (2) Cf. *Deuteronomy* 10:17; *Psalms* 99:3. (3) *Isaiah* 6:3. (4) *Ezekiel* 3:12. (5) *Psalms* 136:7.

Sabbath to Israel. By observing the Sabbath and absorbing its holiness, Israel brings a higher degree of fulfillment and holiness to the entire universe.

בְּךָ, וַתְּלַמְּדֵם חֻקֵּי חַיִּים, כֵּן תְּחָנֵּנוּ וּתְלַמְּדֵנוּ. אָבִינוּ הָאָב הָרַחֲמָן הַמְרַחֵם, רַחֵם עָלֵינוּ, וְתֵן בְּלִבֵּנוּ לְהָבִין וּלְהַשְׂכִּיל, לִשְׁמֹעַ לִלְמוֹד וּלְלַמֵּד, לִשְׁמֹר וְלַעֲשׂוֹת וּלְקַיֵּם אֶת כָּל דִּבְרֵי תַלְמוּד תּוֹרָתֶךָ בְּאַהֲבָה. וְהָאֵר עֵינֵינוּ בְּתוֹרָתֶךָ, וְדַבֵּק לִבֵּנוּ בְּמִצְוֹתֶיךָ, וְיַחֵד לְבָבֵנוּ לְאַהֲבָה וּלְיִרְאָה אֶת שְׁמֶךָ,[1] וְלֹא נֵבוֹשׁ לְעוֹלָם וָעֶד. כִּי בְשֵׁם קָדְשְׁךָ הַגָּדוֹל וְהַנּוֹרָא בָּטָחְנוּ, נָגִילָה וְנִשְׂמְחָה בִּישׁוּעָתֶךָ. וַהֲבִיאֵנוּ לְשָׁלוֹם מֵאַרְבַּע כַּנְפוֹת הָאָרֶץ, וְתוֹלִיכֵנוּ קוֹמְמִיּוּת לְאַרְצֵנוּ. כִּי אֵל פּוֹעֵל יְשׁוּעוֹת אָתָּה, וּבָנוּ בָחַרְתָּ מִכָּל עַם וְלָשׁוֹן. ❖ וְקֵרַבְתָּנוּ לְשִׁמְךָ הַגָּדוֹל סֶלָה בֶּאֱמֶת, לְהוֹדוֹת לְךָ וּלְיַחֶדְךָ בְּאַהֲבָה. בָּרוּךְ אַתָּה יהוה, הַבּוֹחֵר בְּעַמּוֹ יִשְׂרָאֵל בְּאַהֲבָה.

At this point, gather the four *tzitzis* between the fourth and fifth fingers of the left hand. Hold *tzitzis* in this manner throughout שְׁמַע.

(—Cong. אָמֵן.)

שמע

Immediately before reciting the *Shema* concentrate on fulfilling the positive commandment of reciting the *Shema* every morning. It is important to enunciate each word clearly and not to run words together. See *Laws* §46-60. A commentary to *Shema* appears on pp. 90-94.

When praying without a *minyan,* begin with the following three-word formula:

אֵל מֶלֶךְ נֶאֱמָן.

Recite the first verse aloud, with the right hand covering the eyes, and concentrate intensely upon accepting God's absolute sovereignty.

שְׁמַע | יִשְׂרָאֵל, יהוה | אֱלֹהֵינוּ, יהוה | אֶחָד:[2]

—In an undertone בָּרוּךְ שֵׁם כְּבוֹד מַלְכוּתוֹ לְעוֹלָם וָעֶד.

While reciting the first paragraph (דברים ו:ה-ט), concentrate on accepting the commandment to love God.

וְאָהַבְתָּ אֵת | יהוה | אֱלֹהֶיךָ, בְּכָל-לְבָבְךָ, וּבְכָל-נַפְשְׁךָ, וּבְכָל-מְאֹדֶךָ: וְהָיוּ הַדְּבָרִים הָאֵלֶּה, אֲשֶׁר | אָנֹכִי מְצַוְּךָ הַיּוֹם, עַל-לְבָבֶךָ: וְשִׁנַּנְתָּם לְבָנֶיךָ, וְדִבַּרְתָּ בָּם, בְּשִׁבְתְּךָ בְּבֵיתֶךָ, וּבְלֶכְתְּךָ בַדֶּרֶךְ, וּבְשָׁכְבְּךָ וּבְקוּמֶךָ: וּקְשַׁרְתָּם לְאוֹת | עַל-יָדֶךָ, וְהָיוּ לְטֹטָפֹת בֵּין | עֵינֶיךָ: וּכְתַבְתָּם | עַל-מְזֻזוֹת בֵּיתֶךָ, וּבִשְׁעָרֶיךָ:

While reciting the second paragraph (דברים יא:יג-כא), concentrate on accepting all the commandments and the concept of reward and punishment.

וְהָיָה, אִם-שָׁמֹעַ תִּשְׁמְעוּ אֶל-מִצְוֹתַי, אֲשֶׁר | אָנֹכִי מְצַוֶּה | אֶתְכֶם הַיּוֹם, לְאַהֲבָה אֶת-יהוה | אֱלֹהֵיכֶם וּלְעָבְדוֹ, בְּכָל-לְבַבְכֶם, וּבְכָל-נַפְשְׁכֶם: וְנָתַתִּי מְטַר-אַרְצְכֶם בְּעִתּוֹ, יוֹרֶה

in You and whom You taught the decrees of life, may You be equally gracious to us and teach us. Our Father, the merciful Father, Who acts mercifully, have mercy upon us, instill in our hearts to understand and elucidate, to listen, learn, teach, safeguard, perform, and fulfill all the words of Your Torah's teaching with love. Enlighten our eyes in Your Torah, attach our hearts to Your commandments, and unify our hearts to love and fear Your Name,[1] *and may we not feel inner shame for all eternity. Because we have trusted in Your great and awesome holy Name, may we exult and rejoice in Your salvation. Bring us in peacefulness from the four corners of the earth and lead us with upright pride to our land. For You effect salvations, O God; You have chosen us from among every people and tongue.* Chazzan— *And You have brought us close to Your great Name forever in truth, to offer praiseful thanks to You, and proclaim Your Oneness with love. Blessed are You, HASHEM, Who chooses His people Israel with love.*

At this point, gather the four *tzitzis* between the fourth and fifth fingers of the left hand. Hold *tzitzis* in this manner throughout the *Shema.*

(Cong.—*Amen.*)

THE SHEMA

Immediately before reciting the *Shema* concentrate on fulfilling the positive commandment of reciting the *Shema* every morning. It is important to enunciate each word clearly and not to run words together. See *Laws* §46-60. A commentary to *Shema* appears on pp. 90-94.

When praying without a *minyan,* begin with the following three-word formula:

God, trustworthy King.

Recite the first verse aloud, with the right hand covering the eyes, and concentrate intensely upon accepting God's absolute sovereignty.

Hear, O Israel: HASHEM is our God, HASHEM, the One and Only.[2]

In an undertone— *Blessed is the Name of His glorious kingdom for all eternity.*

While reciting the first paragraph (*Deuteronomy* 6:5-9), concentrate on accepting the commandment to love God.

וְאָהַבְתָּ *You shall love HASHEM, your God, with all your heart, with all your soul and with all your resources. Let these matters that I command you today be upon your heart. Teach them thoroughly to your children and speak of them while you sit in your home, while you walk on the way, when you retire and when you arise. Bind them as a sign upon your arm and let them be tefillin between your eyes. And write them on the doorposts of your house and upon your gates.*

While reciting the second paragraph (*Deuteronomy* 11:13-21), concentrate on accepting all the commandments and the concept of reward and punishment.

וְהָיָה *And it will come to pass that if you continually hearken to My commandments that I command you today, to love HASHEM, your God, and to serve Him, with all your heart and with all your soul — then I will provide rain for your land in its proper time, the early*

(1) Cf. *Psalms* 86:11. (2) *Deuteronomy* 6:4.

וּמַלְקוֹשׁ, וְאָסַפְתָּ דְגָנֶךָ וְתִירֹשְׁךָ וְיִצְהָרֶךָ: וְנָתַתִּי | עֵשֶׂב | בְּשָׂדְךָ לִבְהֶמְתֶּךָ, וְאָכַלְתָּ וְשָׂבָעְתָּ: הִשָּׁמְרוּ לָכֶם, פֶּן־יִפְתֶּה לְבַבְכֶם, וְסַרְתֶּם וַעֲבַדְתֶּם | אֱלֹהִים | אֲחֵרִים, וְהִשְׁתַּחֲוִיתֶם לָהֶם: וְחָרָה | אַף־יהוה בָּכֶם, וְעָצַר | אֶת־הַשָּׁמַיִם, וְלֹא־יִהְיֶה מָטָר, וְהָאֲדָמָה לֹא תִתֵּן אֶת־יְבוּלָהּ, וַאֲבַדְתֶּם | מְהֵרָה מֵעַל הָאָרֶץ הַטֹּבָה | אֲשֶׁר | יהוה נֹתֵן לָכֶם: וְשַׂמְתֶּם | אֶת־דְּבָרַי | אֵלֶּה, עַל־לְבַבְכֶם וְעַל־נַפְשְׁכֶם, וּקְשַׁרְתֶּם | אֹתָם לְאוֹת | עַל־יֶדְכֶם, וְהָיוּ לְטוֹטָפֹת בֵּין | עֵינֵיכֶם: וְלִמַּדְתֶּם | אֹתָם | אֶת־בְּנֵיכֶם, לְדַבֵּר בָּם, בְּשִׁבְתְּךָ בְּבֵיתֶךָ, וּבְלֶכְתְּךָ בַדֶּרֶךְ, וּבְשָׁכְבְּךָ וּבְקוּמֶךָ: וּכְתַבְתָּם | עַל־מְזוּזוֹת בֵּיתֶךָ, וּבִשְׁעָרֶיךָ: לְמַעַן | יִרְבּוּ | יְמֵיכֶם וִימֵי בְנֵיכֶם, עַל הָאֲדָמָה | אֲשֶׁר נִשְׁבַּע | יהוה לַאֲבֹתֵיכֶם לָתֵת לָהֶם, כִּימֵי הַשָּׁמַיִם | עַל־הָאָרֶץ:

Before reciting the third paragraph (במדבר טו:לז־מא) the *tzitzis,* which have been held in the left hand, are taken in the right hand also. The *tzitzis* are kissed at each mention of the word and at the end of the paragraph, and are passed before the eyes at וּרְאִיתֶם אֹתוֹ.

וַיֹּאמֶר | יהוה | אֶל־מֹשֶׁה לֵּאמֹר: דַּבֵּר | אֶל־בְּנֵי | יִשְׂרָאֵל, וְאָמַרְתָּ אֲלֵהֶם, וְעָשׂוּ לָהֶם צִיצִת, עַל־כַּנְפֵי בִגְדֵיהֶם לְדֹרֹתָם, וְנָתְנוּ | עַל־צִיצִת הַכָּנָף, פְּתִיל תְּכֵלֶת: וְהָיָה לָכֶם לְצִיצִת, וּרְאִיתֶם | אֹתוֹ, וּזְכַרְתֶּם | אֶת־כָּל־מִצְוֹת | יהוה, וַעֲשִׂיתֶם | אֹתָם, וְלֹא תָתוּרוּ | אַחֲרֵי לְבַבְכֶם וְאַחֲרֵי | עֵינֵיכֶם, אֲשֶׁר־אַתֶּם זֹנִים | אַחֲרֵיהֶם: לְמַעַן תִּזְכְּרוּ, וַעֲשִׂיתֶם | אֶת־כָּל־מִצְוֹתָי, וִהְיִיתֶם קְדֹשִׁים לֵאלֹהֵיכֶם: אֲנִי יהוה | אֱלֹהֵיכֶם, אֲשֶׁר הוֹצֵאתִי | אֶתְכֶם | מֵאֶרֶץ מִצְרַיִם, לִהְיוֹת לָכֶם לֵאלֹהִים, אֲנִי | יהוה | אֱלֹהֵיכֶם: אֱמֶת —

Concentrate on fulfilling the commandment of remembering the Exodus from Egypt.

Although the word אֱמֶת belongs to the next paragraph, it is appended to the conclusion of the previous one, as explained in the commentary on p. 94.

Chazzan repeats— **יהוה אֱלֹהֵיכֶם אֱמֶת.**

וְיַצִּיב וְנָכוֹן וְקַיָּם וְיָשָׁר וְנֶאֱמָן וְאָהוּב וְחָבִיב וְנֶחְמָד וְנָעִים וְנוֹרָא וְאַדִּיר וּמְתֻקָּן וּמְקֻבָּל וְטוֹב וְיָפֶה הַדָּבָר הַזֶּה עָלֵינוּ לְעוֹלָם וָעֶד. אֱמֶת אֱלֹהֵי עוֹלָם מַלְכֵּנוּ צוּר יַעֲקֹב, מָגֵן יִשְׁעֵנוּ, לְדֹר וָדֹר הוּא קַיָּם, וּשְׁמוֹ קַיָּם, וְכִסְאוֹ נָכוֹן, וּמַלְכוּתוֹ וֶאֱמוּנָתוֹ לָעַד קַיֶּמֶת. וּדְבָרָיו חָיִים וְקַיָּמִים, נֶאֱמָנִים וְנֶחֱמָדִים לָעַד (kiss the *tzitzis* and release them) וּלְעוֹלְמֵי עוֹלָמִים. ❖ עַל אֲבוֹתֵינוּ

and late rains, that you may gather in your grain, your wine, and your oil. I will provide grass in your field for your cattle and you will eat and be satisfied. Beware lest your heart be seduced and you turn astray and serve gods of others and bow to them. Then the wrath of HASHEM will blaze against you. He will restrain the heaven so there will be no rain and the ground will not yield its produce. And you will swiftly be banished from the goodly land which HASHEM gives you. Place these words of Mine upon your heart and upon your soul; bind them for a sign upon your arm and let them be tefillin between your eyes. Teach them to your children, to discuss them, while you sit in your home, while you walk on the way, when you retire and when you arise. And write them on the doorposts of your house and upon your gates. In order to prolong your days and the days of your children upon the ground that HASHEM has sworn to your ancestors to give them, like the days of the heaven on the earth.

Before reciting the third paragraph (*Numbers* 15:37-41) the *tzitzis,* which have been held in the left hand, are taken in the right hand also. The *tzitzis* are kissed at each mention of the word and at the end of the paragraph, and are passed before the eyes at *'that you may see it'.*

וַיֹּאמֶר *And HASHEM said to Moses saying: Speak to the Children of Israel and say to them that they are to make themselves tzitzis on the corners of their garments, throughout their generations. And they are to place upon the tzitzis of each corner a thread of techeiles. And it shall constitute tzitzis for you, that you may see it and remember all the commandments of HASHEM and perform them; and not explore after your heart and after your eyes after which you stray. So that you may remember and perform all My commandments; and be holy to your God. I am HASHEM, your God, Who has removed you from the land of Egypt to be a God to you. I am HASHEM your God — it is true —*

Concentrate on fulfiling the commandment of remembering the Exodus from Egypt.

Although the word אֱמֶת, *'it is true',* belongs to the next paragraph, it is appended to the conclusion of the previous one, as explained in the commentary on p. 94.

Chazzan repeats: **HASHEM, your God, is true.**

וְיַצִּיב *And certain, established and enduring, fair and faithful, beloved and cherished, delightful and pleasant, awesome and powerful, correct and accepted, good and beautiful is this affirmation to us forever and ever. True — the God of the universe is our King; the Rock of Jacob is the Shield of our salvation. From generation to generation He endures and His Name endures and His throne is well established; His sovereignty and faithfulness endure forever. His words are living and enduring, faithful and delightful forever* (kiss the *tzitzis* and release them) *and to all eternity;* Chazzan— *for our forefathers*

וְעָלֵינוּ, עַל בָּנֵינוּ וְעַל דּוֹרוֹתֵינוּ, וְעַל כָּל דּוֹרוֹת זֶרַע יִשְׂרָאֵל עֲבָדֶיךָ.

עַל הָרִאשׁוֹנִים וְעַל הָאַחֲרוֹנִים, דָּבָר טוֹב וְקַיָּם לְעוֹלָם וָעֶד, אֱמֶת וֶאֱמוּנָה חֹק וְלֹא יַעֲבֹר. אֱמֶת שָׁאַתָּה הוּא יהוה אֱלֹהֵינוּ וֵאלֹהֵי אֲבוֹתֵינוּ, ❖ מַלְכֵּנוּ מֶלֶךְ אֲבוֹתֵינוּ, גֹּאֲלֵנוּ גֹּאֵל אֲבוֹתֵינוּ, יוֹצְרֵנוּ צוּר יְשׁוּעָתֵנוּ, פּוֹדֵנוּ וּמַצִּילֵנוּ מֵעוֹלָם שְׁמֶךָ, אֵין אֱלֹהִים זוּלָתֶךָ.

עֶזְרַת אֲבוֹתֵינוּ אַתָּה הוּא מֵעוֹלָם, מָגֵן וּמוֹשִׁיעַ לִבְנֵיהֶם אַחֲרֵיהֶם בְּכָל דּוֹר וָדוֹר. בְּרוּם עוֹלָם מוֹשָׁבֶךָ, וּמִשְׁפָּטֶיךָ וְצִדְקָתְךָ עַד אַפְסֵי אָרֶץ. אַשְׁרֵי אִישׁ שֶׁיִּשְׁמַע לְמִצְוֹתֶיךָ, וְתוֹרָתְךָ וּדְבָרְךָ יָשִׂים עַל לִבּוֹ. אֱמֶת אַתָּה הוּא אָדוֹן לְעַמֶּךָ וּמֶלֶךְ גִּבּוֹר לָרִיב רִיבָם. אֱמֶת אַתָּה הוּא רִאשׁוֹן וְאַתָּה הוּא אַחֲרוֹן, וּמִבַּלְעָדֶיךָ אֵין לָנוּ מֶלֶךְ[1] גּוֹאֵל וּמוֹשִׁיעַ. מִמִּצְרַיִם גְּאַלְתָּנוּ יהוה אֱלֹהֵינוּ, וּמִבֵּית עֲבָדִים פְּדִיתָנוּ. כָּל בְּכוֹרֵיהֶם הָרָגְתָּ, וּבְכוֹרְךָ גָּאָלְתָּ, וְיַם סוּף בָּקַעְתָּ, וְזֵדִים טִבַּעְתָּ, וִידִידִים הֶעֱבַרְתָּ, וַיְכַסּוּ מַיִם צָרֵיהֶם, אֶחָד מֵהֶם לֹא נוֹתָר.[2] עַל זֹאת שִׁבְּחוּ אֲהוּבִים וְרוֹמְמוּ אֵל, וְנָתְנוּ יְדִידִים זְמִרוֹת שִׁירוֹת וְתִשְׁבָּחוֹת, בְּרָכוֹת וְהוֹדָאוֹת, לְמֶלֶךְ אֵל חַי וְקַיָּם, רָם וְנִשָּׂא, גָּדוֹל וְנוֹרָא, מַשְׁפִּיל גֵּאִים, וּמַגְבִּיהַּ שְׁפָלִים, מוֹצִיא אֲסִירִים, וּפוֹדֶה עֲנָוִים, וְעוֹזֵר דַּלִּים, וְעוֹנֶה לְעַמּוֹ בְּעֵת שַׁוְּעָם אֵלָיו.

Rise for *Shemoneh Esrei.* Some take three steps backward at this point; others do so before צוּר יִשְׂרָאֵל.

❖ תְּהִלּוֹת לְאֵל עֶלְיוֹן, בָּרוּךְ הוּא וּמְבֹרָךְ. מֹשֶׁה וּבְנֵי יִשְׂרָאֵל לְךָ עָנוּ שִׁירָה בְּשִׂמְחָה רַבָּה וְאָמְרוּ כֻלָּם:

מִי כָמֹכָה בָּאֵלִם יהוה, מִי כָּמֹכָה נֶאְדָּר בַּקֹּדֶשׁ, נוֹרָא תְהִלֹּת עֹשֵׂה פֶלֶא.[3] ❖ שִׁירָה חֲדָשָׁה שִׁבְּחוּ גְאוּלִים לְשִׁמְךָ עַל שְׂפַת הַיָּם, יַחַד כֻּלָּם הוֹדוּ וְהִמְלִיכוּ וְאָמְרוּ:

יהוה יִמְלֹךְ לְעֹלָם וָעֶד.[4]

It is forbidden to interrupt or pause between גָּאַל יִשְׂרָאֵל and *Shemoneh Esrei,* even for prayer responses. [However, many authorities permit responses to *Kaddish, Kedushah* and *Borchu,* on the Sabbath (see *Mishnah Berurah* 111:9).]

and for us, for our children and for our generations, and for all the generations of Your servant Israel's offspring.

עַל הָרִאשׁוֹנִים *Upon the earlier and upon later generations, this affirmation is good and enduring forever. True and faithful, it is an unbreachable decree. It is true that You are* HASHEM, *our God and the God of our forefathers,* Chazzan— *our King and the King of our forefathers, our Redeemer, the Redeemer of our forefathers; our Molder, the Rock of our salvation; our Liberator and our Rescuer — this has ever been Your Name. There is no God but You.*

עֶזְרַת *The Helper of our forefathers are You alone, forever, Shield and Savior for their children after them in every generation. At the zenith of the universe is Your dwelling, and Your justice and Your righteousness extend to the ends of the earth. Praiseworthy is the person who obeys Your commandments and takes to his heart Your teaching and Your word. True — You are the Master for Your people and a mighty King to take up their grievance. True — You are the First and You are the Last, and other than You we have no king,[1] redeemer, or savior. From Egypt You redeemed us,* HASHEM, *our God, and from the house of slavery You liberated us. All their firstborn You slew, but Your firstborn You redeemed; the Sea of Reeds You split; the wanton sinners You drowned; the dear ones You brought across; and the water covered their foes — not one of them was left.[2] For this, the beloved praised and exalted God; the dear ones offered hymns, songs, praises, blessings, and thanksgivings to the King, the living and enduring God — exalted and uplifted, great and awesome, Who humbles the haughty and lifts the lowly; withdraws the captive, liberates the humble, and helps the poor; Who responds to His people upon their outcry to Him.*

Rise for *Shemoneh Esrei.* Some take three steps backward at this point; others do so before צוּר יִשְׂרָאֵל, *'Rock of Israel.'*

Chazzan— *Praises to the Supreme God, the blessed One Who is blessed. Moses and the children of Israel exclaimed a song to You with great joy and they all said:*

'Who is like You among the heavenly powers, HASHEM*! Who is like You, mighty in holiness, too awesome for praise, doing wonders.'[3]* Chazzan— *With a new song the redeemed ones praised Your Name at the seashore, all of them in unison gave thanks, acknowledged [Your] sovereignty, and said:*

'HASHEM shall reign for all eternity.'[4]

It is forbidden to interrupt or pause between *'Who redeemed Israel'* and *Shemoneh Esrei,* even for prayer responses. [However, many authorities permit responses to *Kaddish, Kedushah* and *Borchu,* on the Sabbath (see *Mishnah Berurah* 111:9).]

---

(1) Cf. *Isaiah* 44:6. (2) *Psalms* 106:11. (3) *Exodus* 15:11. (4) 15:18.

❖ **צוּר יִשְׂרָאֵל,** קוּמָה בְּעֶזְרַת יִשְׂרָאֵל, וּפְדֵה כִנְאֻמֶךָ יְהוּדָה וְיִשְׂרָאֵל. גֹּאֲלֵנוּ יהוה צְבָאוֹת שְׁמוֹ, קְדוֹשׁ יִשְׂרָאֵל.[1] °°בָּרוּךְ אַתָּה יהוה, גָּאַל יִשְׂרָאֵל.

On regular Sabbaths and on the Sabbath of Chol HaMoed, continue with *Shemoneh Esrei* below. On Festivals, even those that fall on the Sabbath, the Festival *Shemoneh Esrei* (p. 660) is recited.

שמונה עשרה — עמידה

Take three steps backward, then three steps forward. Remain standing with the feet together while reciting *Shemoneh Esrei.* It should be recited with quiet devotion and without any interruption, verbal or otherwise. Although it should not be audible to others, one must pray loudly enough to hear himself. See *Laws* §61-90 for a brief summary of its laws, including how to rectify the omission of phrases that are added at particular times of the year.

אֲדֹנָי שְׂפָתַי תִּפְתָּח, וּפִי יַגִּיד תְּהִלָּתֶךָ.[2]

אבות

Bend the knees at בָּרוּךְ; bow at אַתָּה; straighten up at 'ה.

בָּרוּךְ אַתָּה יהוה אֱלֹהֵינוּ וֵאלֹהֵי אֲבוֹתֵינוּ, אֱלֹהֵי אַבְרָהָם, אֱלֹהֵי יִצְחָק, וֵאלֹהֵי יַעֲקֹב, הָאֵל הַגָּדוֹל הַגִּבּוֹר וְהַנּוֹרָא, אֵל עֶלְיוֹן, גּוֹמֵל חֲסָדִים טוֹבִים וְקוֹנֵה הַכֹּל, וְזוֹכֵר חַסְדֵי אָבוֹת, וּמֵבִיא גוֹאֵל לִבְנֵי בְנֵיהֶם, לְמַעַן שְׁמוֹ בְּאַהֲבָה.

From Rosh Hashanah to Yom Kippur add:

זָכְרֵנוּ לְחַיִּים, מֶלֶךְ חָפֵץ בַּחַיִּים, וְכָתְבֵנוּ בְּסֵפֶר הַחַיִּים, לְמַעַנְךָ אֱלֹהִים חַיִּים.

[If forgotten, do not repeat *Shemoneh Esrei.* See *Laws* §61.]

Bend the knees at בָּרוּךְ; bow at אַתָּה; straighten up at 'ה.

מֶלֶךְ עוֹזֵר וּמוֹשִׁיעַ וּמָגֵן. בָּרוּךְ אַתָּה יהוה, מָגֵן אַבְרָהָם.

גבורות

אַתָּה גִּבּוֹר לְעוֹלָם אֲדֹנָי, מְחַיֵּה מֵתִים אַתָּה, רַב לְהוֹשִׁיעַ.

Between Succos and Pesach add:

מַשִּׁיב הָרוּחַ וּמוֹרִיד הַגֶּשֶׁם.

[If forgotten, see *Laws* §70-75.]

מְכַלְכֵּל חַיִּים בְּחֶסֶד, מְחַיֵּה מֵתִים בְּרַחֲמִים רַבִּים, סוֹמֵךְ נוֹפְלִים, וְרוֹפֵא חוֹלִים, וּמַתִּיר אֲסוּרִים, וּמְקַיֵּם אֱמוּנָתוֹ לִישֵׁנֵי עָפָר. מִי כָמוֹךָ בַּעַל גְּבוּרוֹת, וּמִי דּוֹמֶה לָּךְ, מֶלֶךְ מֵמִית וּמְחַיֶּה וּמַצְמִיחַ יְשׁוּעָה.

From Rosh Hashanah to Yom Kippur add:

מִי כָמוֹךָ אַב הָרַחֲמִים, זוֹכֵר יְצוּרָיו לְחַיִּים בְּרַחֲמִים.

[If forgotten, do not repeat *Shemoneh Esrei.* See *Laws* §61.]

❖ שְׁמֹנֶה עֶשְׂרֵה / SHEMONEH ESREI ❖

Commentary to the first three blessings of *Shemoneh Esrei* appears on pp. 98-102; to the last three blessings, on pp. 110-119.

צוּר יִשְׂרָאֵל Chazzan— *Rock of Israel, arise to the aid of Israel and liberate, as You pledged, Judah and Israel. Our Redeemer — HASHEM, Master of Legions, is His Name — is the Holy One of Israel.*[1] °°*Blessed are You HASHEM, Who redeemed Israel.*

On regular Sabbaths and on the Sabbath of Chol HaMoed, continue with *Shemoneh Esrei* below. On Festivals, even those that fall on the Sabbath, the Festival *Shemoneh Esrei* (p. 660) is recited.

SHEMONEH ESREI — AMIDAH

Take three steps backward, then three steps forward. Remain standing with the feet together while reciting *Shemoneh Esrei.* It should be recited with quiet devotion and without any interruption, verbal or otherwise. Although it should not be audible to others, one must pray loudly enough to hear himself. See *Laws* §61-90 for a brief summary of its laws, including how to rectify the omission of phrases that are added at particular times of the year.

My Lord, open my lips, that my mouth may declare Your praise.[2]

PATRIARCHS

Bend the knees at *'Blessed'*; bow at *'You'*; straighten up at *'HASHEM'*.

בָּרוּךְ *Blessed are You, HASHEM, our God and the God of our forefathers, God of Abraham, God of Isaac, and God of Jacob; the great, mighty, and awesome God, the supreme God, Who bestows beneficial kindnesses and creates everything, Who recalls the kindnesses of the Patriarchs and brings a Redeemer to their children's children, for His Name's sake, with love.*

From Rosh Hashanah to Yom Kippur add the following.
Remember us for life, O King Who desires life,
and inscribe us in the Book of Life — for Your sake, O Living God.
[If forgotten, do not repeat *Shemoneh Esrei.* See *Laws* §61.]

Bend the knees at *'Blessed'*; bow at *'You'*; straighten up at 'HASHEM'.

O King, Helper, Savior, and Shield. Blessed are You, HASHEM, Shield of Abraham.

GOD'S MIGHT

אַתָּה *You are eternally mighty, my Lord, the Resuscitator of the dead are You; abundantly able to save.*

Between Shemini Atzeres and Pesach add the following.
He makes the wind blow and He makes the rain descend.
[If forgotten, see *Laws* §70-75.]

He sustains the living with kindness, resuscitates the dead with abundant mercy, supports the fallen, heals the sick, releases the confined, and maintains His faith to those asleep in the dust. Who is like You, O Master of mighty deeds, and who is comparable to You, O King Who causes death and restores life and makes salvation sprout!

From Rosh Hashanah to Yom Kippur add the following.
Who is like You, Merciful Father, Who recalls His creatures mercifully for life!
[If forgotten, do not repeat *Shemoneh Esrei.* See *Laws* §61.]

(1) *Isaiah* 47:4. (2) *Psalms* 51:17.

°° On Pesach, some congregations recite בְּרַח דּוֹדִי (p. 710) and יוֹם לְיַבָּשָׁה (p. 712) at this point.

וְנֶאֱמָן אַתָּה לְהַחֲיוֹת מֵתִים. בָּרוּךְ אַתָּה יהוה, מְחַיֵּה הַמֵּתִים.

During the silent *Shemoneh Esrei* continue with אַתָּה קָדוֹשׁ.
During the *chazzan's* repetition, *Kedushah* is recited at this point.

קדושת השם

אַתָּה קָדוֹשׁ וְשִׁמְךָ קָדוֹשׁ, וּקְדוֹשִׁים בְּכָל יוֹם יְהַלְלְוּךָ סֶּלָה. בָּרוּךְ אַתָּה יהוה, °הָאֵל הַקָּדוֹשׁ.

°הַמֶּלֶךְ הַקָּדוֹשׁ. —From Rosh Hashanah to Yom Kippur substitute
[If forgotten, repeat *Shemoneh Esrei.* See *Laws* §62-63.]

קדושה

When reciting *Kedushah,* one must stand with his feet together, and avoid any interruptions. One should rise to his toes when saying the words קָדוֹשׁ, קָדוֹשׁ, קָדוֹשׁ; בָּרוּךְ (of בָּרוּךְ כְּבוֹד); and יִמְלֹךְ.

—Cong. then *Chazzan*: **נְקַדֵּשׁ** אֶת שִׁמְךָ בָּעוֹלָם, כְּשֵׁם שֶׁמַּקְדִּישִׁים אוֹתוֹ בִּשְׁמֵי מָרוֹם, כַּכָּתוּב עַל יַד נְבִיאֶךָ, וְקָרָא זֶה אֶל זֶה וְאָמַר:

—All: קָדוֹשׁ קָדוֹשׁ קָדוֹשׁ יהוה צְבָאוֹת, מְלֹא כָל הָאָרֶץ כְּבוֹדוֹ.[1]

—Cong. then *Chazzan*: אָז בְּקוֹל* רַעַשׁ גָּדוֹל אַדִּיר וְחָזָק מַשְׁמִיעִים קוֹל, מִתְנַשְּׂאִים לְעֻמַּת שְׂרָפִים, לְעֻמָּתָם בָּרוּךְ יֹאמֵרוּ:

—All: בָּרוּךְ כְּבוֹד יהוה, מִמְּקוֹמוֹ.*[2]

—Cong. then *Chazzan*: מִמְּקוֹמְךָ* מַלְכֵּנוּ תוֹפִיעַ, וְתִמְלֹךְ עָלֵינוּ, כִּי מְחַכִּים אֲנַחְנוּ לָךְ. מָתַי תִּמְלֹךְ בְּצִיּוֹן, בְּקָרוֹב בְּיָמֵינוּ, לְעוֹלָם וָעֶד תִּשְׁכּוֹן. תִּתְגַּדַּל וְתִתְקַדַּשׁ בְּתוֹךְ יְרוּשָׁלַיִם עִירְךָ, לְדוֹר וָדוֹר וּלְנֵצַח נְצָחִים. וְעֵינֵינוּ תִרְאֶינָה מַלְכוּתֶךָ, כַּדָּבָר הָאָמוּר בְּשִׁירֵי עֻזֶּךָ, עַל יְדֵי דָוִד מְשִׁיחַ צִדְקֶךָ:

—All: יִמְלֹךְ יהוה לְעוֹלָם, אֱלֹהַיִךְ צִיּוֹן, לְדֹר וָדֹר, הַלְלוּיָהּ.[3]

—*Chazzan* continues: לְדוֹר וָדוֹר נַגִּיד גָּדְלֶךָ וּלְנֵצַח נְצָחִים קְדֻשָּׁתְךָ נַקְדִּישׁ, וְשִׁבְחֲךָ אֱלֹהֵינוּ מִפִּינוּ לֹא יָמוּשׁ לְעוֹלָם וָעֶד, כִּי אֵל מֶלֶךְ גָּדוֹל וְקָדוֹשׁ אָתָּה. בָּרוּךְ אַתָּה יהוה, °הָאֵל הַקָּדוֹשׁ.

°הַמֶּלֶךְ הַקָּדוֹשׁ. —From Rosh Hashanah to Yom Kippur substitute

Chazzan continues ... יִשְׂמַח מֹשֶׁה.

קדושה / Kedushah

Commentary to the daily *Kedushah* appears on p. 100.

The *Kedushah* of the Sabbath is expanded to indicate the special significance of the Sabbath in attaining the goal of sanctification. The home of God's Presence was — and will be again — the Temple in Jerusalem. If we properly appreciate the great holiness of the Sabbath, we can better comprehend the song of the angels and elevate ourselves to the level where we are worthy for the coming of Messiah and the return of the Temple. Therefore, these two themes are stressed in the Sabbath additions to *Kedushah.*

אָז בְּקוֹל — *Then with a sound.* This narrative describing the song of the angels is based on *Ezekiel* Ch. 1 and is also found in a different form in the morning Blessings of the *Shema* and *Uva Le'Tzion.* See pp. 86-88.

מִמְּקוֹמוֹ — *From His place.* Rambam (*Moreh*

And You are faithful to resuscitate the dead. Blessed are You, HASHEM, Who resuscitates the dead.

During the silent *Shemoneh Esrei* continue with *'You are holy'*.
During the *chazzan's* repetition, *Kedushah* is recited at this point.

HOLINESS OF GOD'S NAME

אַתָּה *You are holy and Your Name is holy, and holy ones praise You every day, forever. Blessed are You, HASHEM, °the holy God.*

°From Rosh Hashanah to Yom Kippur substitute: *the holy King.*
[If forgotten, repeat *Shemoneh Esrei.* See *Laws* §62-63.]

KEDUSHAH

When reciting *Kedushah,* one must stand with his feet together and avoid any interruptions. One should rise to his toes when saying the words *Holy, holy, holy; Blessed; HASHEM shall reign.*

Cong.— then Chazzan **נְקַדֵּשׁ** *We shall sanctify Your Name in this world, just as they sanctify It in heaven above, as it is written by Your prophet, "And one [angel] will call another and say:*

All— *'Holy, holy, holy is HASHEM, Master of Legions, the whole world is filled with His glory.'"*[1]

Cong.— then Chazzan *Then, with a sound* of great noise, mighty and powerful, they make heard a voice, raising themselves toward the Seraphim; those facing them say 'Blessed ...':*

All— *'Blessed is the glory of HASHEM from His place.'**[2]

Cong.— then Chazzan *From Your place,* our King, You will appear and reign over us, for we await You. When will You reign in Zion? Soon, in our days — forever and ever — may You dwell there. May You be exalted and sanctified within Jerusalem, Your city, from generation to generation and for all eternity. May our eyes see Your kingdom, as it is expressed in the songs of Your might, written by David, Your righteous anointed:*

All— *'HASHEM shall reign forever — your God, O Zion — from generation to generation, Halleluyah!'*[3]

Chazzan continues— *From generation to generation we shall relate Your greatness and for infinite eternities we shall proclaim Your holiness. Your praise, our God, shall not leave our mouth forever and ever, for You O God, are a great and holy King. Blessed are You HASHEM, °the holy God.*

°From Rosh Hashanah to Yom Kippur substitute: *the holy King.*

Chazzan continues יִשְׂמַח מֹשֶׁה, *Moses rejoiced ...*

(1) *Isaiah* 6:3. (2) *Ezekiel* 3:12. (3) *Psalms* 146:10.

Nevuchim 1:8) interprets *place* figuratively as meaning 'level' or 'degree,' in the sense that we say that someone takes his father's 'place.' However, even the angels do not know what God's 'place' really is — He is beyond all understanding. Therefore, when we say that God's glory comes *from His place,* we are purposely being vague because we cannot know the extent of His true glory. We are saying that whatever the true level of God's perfection may be, let it be implicit in the limited words with which we praise Him *(Nefesh HaChaim).*

מִמְּקוֹמְךָ — *From Your place.* As noted above, God's 'place' is the infinity of His perfection. We beg and confidently hope that He will reveal Himself to us by returning His Presence to Jerusalem with the final and eternal Redemption.

קדושת היום

יִשְׂמַח מֹשֶׁה* בְּמַתְּנַת חֶלְקוֹ, כִּי עֶבֶד נֶאֱמָן קָרָאתָ לּוֹ. כְּלִיל תִּפְאֶרֶת* בְּרֹאשׁוֹ נָתַתָּ (לוֹ), בְּעָמְדוֹ לְפָנֶיךָ עַל הַר סִינָי. וּשְׁנֵי לוּחוֹת אֲבָנִים הוֹרִיד בְּיָדוֹ,[1] וְכָתוּב בָּהֶם שְׁמִירַת שַׁבָּת. וְכֵן כָּתוּב בְּתוֹרָתֶךָ:

וְשָׁמְרוּ בְנֵי יִשְׂרָאֵל אֶת הַשַּׁבָּת, לַעֲשׂוֹת אֶת הַשַּׁבָּת לְדֹרֹתָם בְּרִית עוֹלָם. בֵּינִי וּבֵין בְּנֵי יִשְׂרָאֵל אוֹת הִיא לְעֹלָם, כִּי שֵׁשֶׁת יָמִים עָשָׂה יהוה אֶת הַשָּׁמַיִם וְאֶת הָאָרֶץ, וּבַיּוֹם הַשְּׁבִיעִי שָׁבַת וַיִּנָּפַשׁ.[2]

וְלֹא נְתַתּוֹ* יהוה אֱלֹהֵינוּ לְגוֹיֵי הָאֲרָצוֹת, וְלֹא הִנְחַלְתּוֹ מַלְכֵּנוּ לְעוֹבְדֵי פְסִילִים, וְגַם בִּמְנוּחָתוֹ לֹא יִשְׁכְּנוּ עֲרֵלִים. כִּי לְיִשְׂרָאֵל עַמְּךָ נְתַתּוֹ בְּאַהֲבָה, לְזֶרַע יַעֲקֹב* אֲשֶׁר בָּם בָּחָרְתָּ. עַם מְקַדְּשֵׁי שְׁבִיעִי, כֻּלָּם יִשְׂבְּעוּ וְיִתְעַנְּגוּ מִטּוּבֶךָ. וּבַשְּׁבִיעִי רָצִיתָ בּוֹ וְקִדַּשְׁתּוֹ חֶמְדַּת יָמִים* אוֹתוֹ קָרָאתָ, זֵכֶר לְמַעֲשֵׂה בְרֵאשִׁית.

אֱלֹהֵינוּ וֵאלֹהֵי אֲבוֹתֵינוּ, רְצֵה בִמְנוּחָתֵנוּ, קַדְּשֵׁנוּ בְּמִצְוֹתֶיךָ, וְתֵן חֶלְקֵנוּ בְּתוֹרָתֶךָ, שַׂבְּעֵנוּ מִטּוּבֶךָ, וְשַׂמְּחֵנוּ בִּישׁוּעָתֶךָ, וְטַהֵר לִבֵּנוּ לְעָבְדְּךָ בֶּאֱמֶת. וְהַנְחִילֵנוּ יהוה אֱלֹהֵינוּ בְּאַהֲבָה וּבְרָצוֹן שַׁבַּת קָדְשֶׁךָ, וְיָנוּחוּ בוֹ יִשְׂרָאֵל מְקַדְּשֵׁי שְׁמֶךָ. בָּרוּךְ אַתָּה יהוה, מְקַדֵּשׁ הַשַּׁבָּת.

⚜ יִשְׂמַח מֹשֶׁה — *Moses rejoiced* that God considered him a faithful servant [*Numbers* 12:7] and that, in reward for Moses' dedication, God chose him to receive the tablets of the Ten Commandments, which included the *mitzvah* of the Sabbath.

Why is Moses singled out for mention in connection with the Sabbath and why only in the morning *Amidah*? Among the reasons are:

— The Ten Commandments were given to Moses on the morning of the Sabbath.

— When he was still a child growing up in Pharaoh's palace, Moses asked the king to proclaim the Sabbath as a day of rest for the enslaved Jews.

— God told Moses in Marah, before Israel came to Mount Sinai, 'I have a precious gift called Sabbath. Teach the Jews about it.'

כְּלִיל תִּפְאֶרֶת — *A crown of splendor.* When Moses descended from Sinai, his face glowed with a Divine radiance, signifying that he was worthy to be a bearer of God's splendor. [See *Exodus* 34:29.]

⚜ וְלֹא נְתַתּוֹ — *You did not give it.* If the Sabbath were nothing more than a day of rest, it could be the equal property of all nations. But the Sabbath is a day of holiness and, as such, it could be given only to the nation that accepts the mission of sanctity. God did not give the Sabbath to such

HOLINESS OF THE DAY

יִשְׂמַח *Moses rejoiced* in the gift of his portion: that You called him a faithful servant. A crown of splendor* You placed on his head when he stood before You on Mount Sinai. He brought down two stone tablets in his hand,[1] on which is inscribed the observance of the Sabbath. So it is written in Your Torah:*

וְשָׁמְרוּ *And the Children of Israel shall keep the Sabbath, to make the Sabbath an eternal covenant for their generations. Between Me and the Children of Israel it is a sign forever that in six days HASHEM made heaven and earth, and on the seventh day He rested and was refreshed.[2]*

וְלֹא נְתַתּוֹ *You did not give it,* HASHEM, our God, to the nations of the lands, nor did You make it the inheritance, our King, of the worshipers of graven idols. And in its contentment the uncircumcised shall not abide — for to Israel, Your people, have You given it in love, to the seed of Jacob,* whom You have chosen. The people that sanctifies the Seventh — they will all be satisfied and delighted from Your goodness. And the Seventh — You found favor in it and sanctified it! 'Most coveted of days,'* You called it, a remembrance of the act of creation.*

אֱלֹהֵינוּ *Our God and the God of our fathers, may You be pleased with our rest. Sanctify us with Your commandments and grant our share in Your Torah; satisfy us from Your goodness and gladden us with Your salvation, and purify our heart to serve You sincerely. O HASHEM, our God, with love and favor grant us Your holy Sabbath as a heritage, and may Israel, the sanctifiers of Your Name, rest on it. Blessed are You, HASHEM, Who sanctifies the Sabbath.*

---

(1) Cf. *Exodus* 32:15. (2) 31:16-17.

---

unworthy nations as גּוֹיֵי הָאֲרָצוֹת, *nations of the lands,* who worship the 'land' and the power its possession implies; nor to עוֹבְדֵי פְסִילִים, *the worshipers of graven idols,* who ascribe mastery of the world to such natural forces as the heavenly bodies, fertility, nature and so on that they symbolize by means of idols; nor to עֲרֵלִים, *uncircumcised people,* who are unwilling to curb their lusts for the sake of a higher goal *(R' Hirsch).*

לְזֶרַע יַעֲקֹב — *To the seed of Jacob.* God's blessings for those who observe the Sabbath are uniquely connected to Jacob. When God promised *Eretz Yisrael* to Abraham and Isaac, He set boundaries on the land their descendants would receive, but in Jacob's promise, He specified no limits. Therefore, the Jew who honors the Sabbath without limitations is worthy of the sort of blessing promised Jacob *(Shabbos* 118a; see *Maharsha).*

חֶמְדַּת יָמִים — *Most coveted of days.* In telling that God completed the labor of Creation, the Torah says וַיְכַל אֱלֹהִים בַּיּוֹם הַשְּׁבִיעִי, *on the seventh day God completed (Genesis* 2:2). *Targum Yerushalmi* translates וַיְכַל as וְחַמִּיד, *He coveted;* thus we are told that God coveted the Sabbath, a statement made about no other day *(Abudraham).*

עבודה

רְצֵה יהוה אֱלֹהֵינוּ בְּעַמְּךָ יִשְׂרָאֵל וּבִתְפִלָּתָם, וְהָשֵׁב אֶת הָעֲבוֹדָה לִדְבִיר בֵּיתֶךָ. וְאִשֵּׁי יִשְׂרָאֵל וּתְפִלָּתָם בְּאַהֲבָה תְקַבֵּל בְּרָצוֹן, וּתְהִי לְרָצוֹן תָּמִיד עֲבוֹדַת יִשְׂרָאֵל עַמֶּךָ.

On Rosh Chodesh and Chol HaMoed add the following paragraph:
(During the *chazzan's* repetition, the congregation responds אָמֵן as indicated).

אֱלֹהֵינוּ וֵאלֹהֵי אֲבוֹתֵינוּ, יַעֲלֶה, וְיָבֹא, וְיַגִּיעַ, וְיֵרָאֶה, וְיֵרָצֶה, וְיִשָּׁמַע, וְיִפָּקֵד, וְיִזָּכֵר זִכְרוֹנֵנוּ וּפִקְדוֹנֵנוּ, וְזִכְרוֹן אֲבוֹתֵינוּ, וְזִכְרוֹן מָשִׁיחַ בֶּן דָּוִד עַבְדֶּךָ, וְזִכְרוֹן יְרוּשָׁלַיִם עִיר קָדְשֶׁךָ, וְזִכְרוֹן כָּל עַמְּךָ בֵּית יִשְׂרָאֵל לְפָנֶיךָ, לִפְלֵיטָה לְטוֹבָה, לְחֵן וּלְחֶסֶד וּלְרַחֲמִים, לְחַיִּים וּלְשָׁלוֹם בְּיוֹם

on Rosh Chodesh	on Pesach	on Succos
רֹאשׁ הַחֹדֶשׁ	חַג הַמַּצּוֹת	חַג הַסֻּכּוֹת

הַזֶּה. זָכְרֵנוּ יהוה אֱלֹהֵינוּ בּוֹ לְטוֹבָה (.Cong—אָמֵן), וּפָקְדֵנוּ בוֹ לִבְרָכָה (.Cong—אָמֵן), וְהוֹשִׁיעֵנוּ בוֹ לְחַיִּים (.Cong—אָמֵן). וּבִדְבַר יְשׁוּעָה וְרַחֲמִים, חוּס וְחָנֵּנוּ וְרַחֵם עָלֵינוּ וְהוֹשִׁיעֵנוּ, כִּי אֵלֶיךָ עֵינֵינוּ, כִּי אֵל מֶלֶךְ חַנּוּן וְרַחוּם אָתָּה.[1]

[If forgotten, repeat *Shemoneh Esrei.* See *Laws* §89.]

וְתֶחֱזֶינָה עֵינֵינוּ בְּשׁוּבְךָ לְצִיּוֹן בְּרַחֲמִים. בָּרוּךְ אַתָּה יהוה, הַמַּחֲזִיר שְׁכִינָתוֹ לְצִיּוֹן.

הודאה

Bow at מוֹדִים; straighten up at 'ה. In his repetition the *chazzan* should recite the entire מוֹדִים aloud, while the congregation recites מוֹדִים דְּרַבָּנָן softly.

מוֹדִים אֲנַחְנוּ לָךְ שָׁאַתָּה הוּא יהוה אֱלֹהֵינוּ וֵאלֹהֵי אֲבוֹתֵינוּ לְעוֹלָם וָעֶד. צוּר חַיֵּינוּ, מָגֵן יִשְׁעֵנוּ אַתָּה הוּא לְדוֹר וָדוֹר. נוֹדֶה לְּךָ וּנְסַפֵּר תְּהִלָּתֶךָ[2] עַל חַיֵּינוּ הַמְּסוּרִים בְּיָדֶךָ, וְעַל נִשְׁמוֹתֵינוּ הַפְּקוּדוֹת לָךְ, וְעַל נִסֶּיךָ שֶׁבְּכָל יוֹם עִמָּנוּ, וְעַל נִפְלְאוֹתֶיךָ וְטוֹבוֹתֶיךָ שֶׁבְּכָל עֵת, עֶרֶב וָבֹקֶר וְצָהֳרָיִם. הַטּוֹב כִּי לֹא כָלוּ רַחֲמֶיךָ, וְהַמְרַחֵם כִּי לֹא תַמּוּ חֲסָדֶיךָ,[3] מֵעוֹלָם קִוִּינוּ לָךְ.

מודים דרבנן

מוֹדִים אֲנַחְנוּ לָךְ, שָׁאַתָּה הוּא יהוה אֱלֹהֵינוּ וֵאלֹהֵי אֲבוֹתֵינוּ, אֱלֹהֵי כָל בָּשָׂר, יוֹצְרֵנוּ, יוֹצֵר בְּרֵאשִׁית. בְּרָכוֹת וְהוֹדָאוֹת לְשִׁמְךָ הַגָּדוֹל וְהַקָּדוֹשׁ, עַל שֶׁהֶחֱיִיתָנוּ וְקִיַּמְתָּנוּ. כֵּן תְּחַיֵּנוּ וּתְקַיְּמֵנוּ, וְתֶאֱסוֹף גָּלֻיּוֹתֵינוּ לְחַצְרוֹת קָדְשֶׁךָ, לִשְׁמוֹר חֻקֶּיךָ וְלַעֲשׂוֹת רְצוֹנֶךָ, וּלְעָבְדְּךָ בְּלֵבָב שָׁלֵם, עַל שֶׁאֲנַחְנוּ מוֹדִים לָךְ. בָּרוּךְ אֵל הַהוֹדָאוֹת.

(1) Cf. *Nechemiah* 9:31. (2) Cf. *Psalms* 79:13. (3) Cf. *Lamentations* 3:22.

TEMPLE SERVICE

רְצֵה *Be favorable, HASHEM, our God, toward Your people Israel and their prayer and restore the service to the Holy of Holies of Your Temple. The fire-offerings of Israel and their prayer accept with love and favor, and may the service of Your people Israel always be favorable to You.*

On Rosh Chodesh and Chol HaMoed add the following paragraph:
(During the *chazzan's* repetition, the congregation responds *Amen* as indicated.)

אֱלֹהֵינוּ *Our God and God of our forefathers, may there rise, come, reach, be noted, be favored, be heard, be considered, and be remembered — the remembrance and consideration of ourselves; the remembrance of our forefathers; the remembrance of Messiah, son of David, Your servant; the remembrance of Jerusalem, the City of Your Holiness, the remembrance of Your entire people the Family of Israel — before You, for deliverance, for goodness, for grace, for kindness, and for compassion, for life, and for peace on this day of*

on Rosh Chodesh	on Passover	on Succos
Rosh Chodesh.	*the Festival of Matzos.*	*the Succos Festival.*

Remember us on it, HASHEM, our God, for goodness (Cong.— *Amen*)*; consider us on it for blessing* (Cong.— *Amen*)*; and help us on it for life* (Cong.— *Amen*)*. In the matter of salvation and compassion, pity, be gracious and compassionate with us and help us, for our eyes are turned to You, because You are God, the gracious and compassionate King.*[1] [If forgotten, repeat *Shemoneh Esrei*. See *Laws*, §89.]

וְתֶחֱזֶינָה *May our eyes behold Your return to Zion in compassion. Blessed are You, HASHEM, Who restores His Presence to Zion.*

THANKSGIVING [MODIM]

Bow at *'We gratefully thank You'*; straighten up at *'HASHEM.'* In his repetition the *chazzan* should recite the entire *Modim* aloud, while the congregation recites *Modim of the Rabbis* softly.

מוֹדִים *We gratefully thank You, for it is You Who are HASHEM, our God and the God of our forefathers for all eternity; Rock of our lives, Shield of our salvation are You from generation to generation. We shall thank You and relate Your praise*[2] *— for our lives, which are committed to Your power and for our souls that are entrusted to You; for Your miracles that are with us every day; and for Your wonders and favors in every season — evening, morning, and afternoon. The Beneficent One, for Your compassions were never exhausted, and the Compassionate One, for Your kindnesses never ended*[3] *— always have we put our hope in You.*

MODIM OF THE RABBIS

מוֹדִים *We gratefully thank You, for it is You Who are HASHEM, our God and the God of our forefathers, the God of all flesh, our Molder, the Molder of the universe. Blessings and thanks are due Your great and holy Name for You have given us life and sustained us. So may You continue to give us life and sustain us and gather our exiles to the Courtyards of Your Sanctuary, to observe Your decrees, to do Your will and to serve You wholeheartedly. [We thank You] for inspiring us to thank You. Blessed is the God of thanksgivings.*

On Chanukah add:

(וְ)עַל הַנִּסִּים, וְעַל הַפֻּרְקָן, וְעַל הַגְּבוּרוֹת, וְעַל הַתְּשׁוּעוֹת, וְעַל הַמִּלְחָמוֹת, שֶׁעָשִׂיתָ לַאֲבוֹתֵינוּ בַּיָּמִים הָהֵם בַּזְּמַן הַזֶּה.

בִּימֵי מַתִּתְיָהוּ בֶּן יוֹחָנָן כֹּהֵן גָּדוֹל חַשְׁמוֹנַאי וּבָנָיו, כְּשֶׁעָמְדָה מַלְכוּת יָוָן הָרְשָׁעָה עַל עַמְּךָ יִשְׂרָאֵל, לְהַשְׁכִּיחָם תּוֹרָתֶךָ, וּלְהַעֲבִירָם מֵחֻקֵּי רְצוֹנֶךָ. וְאַתָּה בְּרַחֲמֶיךָ הָרַבִּים, עָמַדְתָּ לָהֶם בְּעֵת צָרָתָם, רַבְתָּ אֶת רִיבָם, דַּנְתָּ אֶת דִּינָם, נָקַמְתָּ אֶת נִקְמָתָם.[1] מָסַרְתָּ גִבּוֹרִים בְּיַד חַלָּשִׁים, וְרַבִּים בְּיַד מְעַטִּים, וּטְמֵאִים בְּיַד טְהוֹרִים, וּרְשָׁעִים בְּיַד צַדִּיקִים, וְזֵדִים בְּיַד עוֹסְקֵי תוֹרָתֶךָ. וּלְךָ עָשִׂיתָ שֵׁם גָּדוֹל וְקָדוֹשׁ בְּעוֹלָמֶךָ, וּלְעַמְּךָ יִשְׂרָאֵל עָשִׂיתָ תְּשׁוּעָה גְדוֹלָה[2] וּפֻרְקָן כְּהַיּוֹם הַזֶּה. וְאַחַר כֵּן בָּאוּ בָנֶיךָ לִדְבִיר בֵּיתֶךָ, וּפִנּוּ אֶת הֵיכָלֶךָ, וְטִהֲרוּ אֶת מִקְדָּשֶׁךָ, וְהִדְלִיקוּ נֵרוֹת בְּחַצְרוֹת קָדְשֶׁךָ, וְקָבְעוּ שְׁמוֹנַת יְמֵי חֲנֻכָּה אֵלּוּ, לְהוֹדוֹת וּלְהַלֵּל לְשִׁמְךָ הַגָּדוֹל.

[If forgotten, do not repeat *Shemoneh Esrei*. See *Laws* §90.]

וְעַל כֻּלָּם יִתְבָּרַךְ וְיִתְרוֹמַם שִׁמְךָ מַלְכֵּנוּ תָּמִיד לְעוֹלָם וָעֶד.

From Rosh Hashanah to Yom Kippur add:

וּכְתוֹב לְחַיִּים טוֹבִים כָּל בְּנֵי בְרִיתֶךָ.

[If forgotten, do not repeat *Shemoneh Esrei*. See *Laws* §61.]

Bend the knees at בָּרוּךְ; bow at אַתָּה; straighten up at 'ה.

וְכֹל הַחַיִּים יוֹדוּךָ סֶּלָה, וִיהַלְלוּ אֶת שִׁמְךָ בֶּאֱמֶת, הָאֵל יְשׁוּעָתֵנוּ וְעֶזְרָתֵנוּ סֶלָה. בָּרוּךְ אַתָּה יהוה, הַטּוֹב שִׁמְךָ וּלְךָ נָאֶה לְהוֹדוֹת.

ברכת כהנים

The *chazzan* recites בִּרְכַּת כֹּהֲנִים during his repetition. *Chazzan* faces the Ark while reciting 'יְבָרֶכְךָ ה, then turns to the right and says וְיִשְׁמְרֶךָ; faces the Ark while reciting 'יָאֵר ה, then turns to the left and says פָּנָיו אֵלֶיךָ וִיחֻנֶּךָּ; faces the Ark while reciting the entire last verse.

אֱלֹהֵינוּ, וֵאלֹהֵי אֲבוֹתֵינוּ, בָּרְכֵנוּ בַבְּרָכָה הַמְּשֻׁלֶּשֶׁת, בַּתּוֹרָה הַכְּתוּבָה עַל יְדֵי מֹשֶׁה עַבְדֶּךָ, הָאֲמוּרָה מִפִּי אַהֲרֹן וּבָנָיו, כֹּהֲנִים עַם קְדוֹשֶׁךָ, כָּאָמוּר:

יְבָרֶכְךָ יהוה, וְיִשְׁמְרֶךָ. (Cong.— כֵּן יְהִי רָצוֹן.)

יָאֵר יהוה פָּנָיו אֵלֶיךָ וִיחֻנֶּךָּ. (Cong.— כֵּן יְהִי רָצוֹן.)

יִשָּׂא יהוה פָּנָיו אֵלֶיךָ וְיָשֵׂם לְךָ שָׁלוֹם.[3] (Cong.— כֵּן יְהִי רָצוֹן.)

שלום

שִׂים שָׁלוֹם, טוֹבָה, וּבְרָכָה, חֵן, וָחֶסֶד וְרַחֲמִים עָלֵינוּ וְעַל כָּל יִשְׂרָאֵל עַמֶּךָ. בָּרְכֵנוּ אָבִינוּ, כֻּלָּנוּ כְּאֶחָד בְּאוֹר פָּנֶיךָ, כִּי בְאוֹר פָּנֶיךָ נָתַתָּ לָּנוּ, יהוה אֱלֹהֵינוּ, תּוֹרַת חַיִּים וְאַהֲבַת חֶסֶד, וּצְדָקָה, וּבְרָכָה, וְרַחֲמִים, וְחַיִּים, וְשָׁלוֹם. וְטוֹב בְּעֵינֶיךָ לְבָרֵךְ

On Chanukah add:

(וְ)עַל *(And) for the miracles, and for the salvation, and for the mighty deeds, and for the victories, and for the battles which You performed for our forefathers in those days, at this time.*

בִּימֵי *In the days of Mattisyahu, the son of Yochanan, the High Priest, the Hasmonean, and his sons — when the wicked Greek kingdom rose up against Your people Israel to make them forget Your Torah and compel them to stray from the statutes of Your Will—You in Your great mercy stood up for them in the time of their distress. You took up their grievance, judged their claim, and avenged their wrong.*[1] *You delivered the strong into the hands of the weak, the many into the hands of the few, the impure into the hands of the pure, the wicked into the hands of the righteous, and the wanton into the hands of the diligent students of Your Torah. For Yourself You made a great and holy Name in Your world, and for Your people Israel You worked a great victory*[2] *and salvation as this very day. Thereafter, Your children came to the Holy of Holies of Your House, cleansed Your Temple, purified the site of Your Holiness and kindled lights in the Courtyards of Your Sanctuary; and they established these eight days of Chanukah to express thanks and praise to Your great Name.*

[If forgotten, do not repeat *Shemoneh Esrei*. See *Laws* §90.]

For all these, may Your Name be blessed and exalted, our King, continually forever and ever.

From Rosh Hashanah to Yom Kippur add the following.

And inscribe all the children of Your covenant for a good life.

If forgotten, do not repeat *Shemoneh Esrei*. See *Laws* §61.]

Bend the knees at *'Blessed'*; bow at *'You'*; straighten up at *'HASHEM'*.

Everything alive will gratefully acknowledge You, Selah! and praise Your Name sincerely, O God of our salvation and help, Selah! Blessed are You, HASHEM, Your Name is 'The Beneficent One' and to You it is fitting to give thanks.

THE PRIESTLY BLESSING

The *chazzan* recites the Priestly Blessing during his repetition.

אֱלֹהֵינוּ *Our God and the God of our forefathers, bless us with the three-verse blessing in the Torah that was written by the hand of Moses, Your servant, that was said by Aaron and his sons, the Kohanim, Your holy people, as it is said:*

May HASHEM bless you and safeguard you. (Cong.— *So may it be.*)

May HASHEM illuminate His countenance for you and be gracious to you. (Cong.— *So may it be.*)

May HASHEM turn His countenance to you and establish peace for you.[3] (Cong.— *So may it be.*)

PEACE

שִׂים *Establish peace, goodness, blessing, graciousness, kindness, and compassion upon us and upon all of Your people Israel. Bless us, our Father, all of us as one, with the light of Your countenance, for with the light of Your countenance You gave us, HASHEM, our God, the Torah of life and a love of kindness, righteousness, blessing, compassion, life, and peace. And may it be good in Your eyes to bless*

(1) Cf. *Jeremiah* 51:36. (2) Cf. *I Samuel* 19:5. (3) *Numbers* 6:24-26.

אֶת עַמְּךָ יִשְׂרָאֵל, בְּכָל עֵת וּבְכָל שָׁעָה בִּשְׁלוֹמֶךָ. °בָּרוּךְ אַתָּה יהוה, הַמְּבָרֵךְ אֶת עַמּוֹ יִשְׂרָאֵל בַּשָּׁלוֹם.

°From Rosh Hashanah to Yom Kippur substitute the following [see *Laws* §65]:

בְּסֵפֶר חַיִּים בְּרָכָה וְשָׁלוֹם, וּפַרְנָסָה טוֹבָה, נִזָּכֵר וְנִכָּתֵב לְפָנֶיךָ, אֲנַחְנוּ וְכָל עַמְּךָ בֵּית יִשְׂרָאֵל, לְחַיִּים טוֹבִים וּלְשָׁלוֹם. בָּרוּךְ אַתָּה יהוה, עֹשֵׂה הַשָּׁלוֹם.

[If forgotten, do not repeat *Shemoneh Esrei*. See *Laws* §61.]

The *chazzan's* repetition of *Shemoneh Esrei* ends here. See below for further instructions.

Many hold that the following verse should be recited here by individuals and the *Chazzan:*

יִהְיוּ לְרָצוֹן אִמְרֵי פִי וְהֶגְיוֹן לִבִּי לְפָנֶיךָ, יהוה צוּרִי וְגֹאֲלִי.[1]

See p. 119 for permissible responses while reciting this final paragraph of *Shemoneh Esrei.*

אֱלֹהַי, נְצוֹר לְשׁוֹנִי מֵרָע, וּשְׂפָתַי מִדַּבֵּר מִרְמָה,[2] וְלִמְקַלְלַי נַפְשִׁי תִדּוֹם, וְנַפְשִׁי כֶּעָפָר לַכֹּל תִּהְיֶה. פְּתַח לִבִּי בְּתוֹרָתֶךָ, וּבְמִצְוֹתֶיךָ תִּרְדּוֹף נַפְשִׁי. וְכֹל הַחוֹשְׁבִים עָלַי רָעָה, מְהֵרָה הָפֵר עֲצָתָם וְקַלְקֵל מַחֲשַׁבְתָּם. עֲשֵׂה לְמַעַן שְׁמֶךָ, עֲשֵׂה לְמַעַן יְמִינֶךָ, עֲשֵׂה לְמַעַן קְדֻשָּׁתֶךָ, עֲשֵׂה לְמַעַן תּוֹרָתֶךָ. לְמַעַן יֵחָלְצוּן יְדִידֶיךָ, הוֹשִׁיעָה יְמִינְךָ וַעֲנֵנִי.[3]

Some recite verses pertaining to their names at this point. See page 924.

יִהְיוּ לְרָצוֹן אִמְרֵי פִי וְהֶגְיוֹן לִבִּי לְפָנֶיךָ, יהוה צוּרִי וְגֹאֲלִי.[1]

Bow and take three steps back. Bow left and say ... עֹשֶׂה; bow right and say ... הוּא יַעֲשֶׂה; bow forward and say וְעַל כָּל ... אָמֵן. Remain standing in place while reciting יְהִי רָצוֹן.

עֹשֶׂה שָׁלוֹם בִּמְרוֹמָיו, הוּא יַעֲשֶׂה שָׁלוֹם עָלֵינוּ, וְעַל כָּל יִשְׂרָאֵל. וְאִמְרוּ: אָמֵן.

יְהִי רָצוֹן מִלְּפָנֶיךָ יהוה אֱלֹהֵינוּ וֵאלֹהֵי אֲבוֹתֵינוּ, שֶׁיִּבָּנֶה בֵּית הַמִּקְדָּשׁ בִּמְהֵרָה בְיָמֵינוּ, וְתֵן חֶלְקֵנוּ בְּתוֹרָתֶךָ. וְשָׁם נַעֲבָדְךָ בְּיִרְאָה, כִּימֵי עוֹלָם וּכְשָׁנִים קַדְמוֹנִיּוֹת. וְעָרְבָה לַיהוה מִנְחַת יְהוּדָה וִירוּשָׁלָיִם, כִּימֵי עוֹלָם וּכְשָׁנִים קַדְמוֹנִיּוֹת.[4]

THE INDIVIDUAL'S RECITATION OF שְׁמוֹנֶה עֶשְׂרֵה ENDS HERE.

The individual remains standing in place until the chazzan reaches *Kedushah* — or at least until the chazzan begins his repetition — then he takes three steps forward. The chazzan himself, or one praying alone, should remain in place for a few moments before taking three steps forward.

On Rosh Chodesh, Chanukah and Chol Hamoed, הַלֵּל, *Hallel* (p. 632) is recited at this point.

קדיש שלם

The *chazzan* recites קַדִּישׁ שָׁלֵם:

יִתְגַּדַּל וְיִתְקַדַּשׁ שְׁמֵהּ רַבָּא. (.Cong — אָמֵן.) בְּעָלְמָא דִּי בְרָא כִרְעוּתֵהּ. וְיַמְלִיךְ מַלְכוּתֵהּ, בְּחַיֵּיכוֹן וּבְיוֹמֵיכוֹן וּבְחַיֵּי דְכָל בֵּית יִשְׂרָאֵל, בַּעֲגָלָא וּבִזְמַן קָרִיב. וְאִמְרוּ: אָמֵן.

(.Cong — אָמֵן. יְהֵא שְׁמֵהּ רַבָּא מְבָרַךְ לְעָלַם וּלְעָלְמֵי עָלְמַיָּא.)

יְהֵא שְׁמֵהּ רַבָּא מְבָרַךְ לְעָלַם וּלְעָלְמֵי עָלְמַיָּא.

יִתְבָּרַךְ וְיִשְׁתַּבַּח וְיִתְפָּאַר וְיִתְרוֹמַם וְיִתְנַשֵּׂא וְיִתְהַדָּר וְיִתְעַלֶּה

Your people Israel, in every season and in every hour with Your Peace. °*Blessed are You, HASHEM, Who blesses His people Israel with peace.*

°From Rosh Hashanah to Yom Kippur substitute the following [see *Laws* §65]:

In the book of life, blessing, and peace, good livelihood, may we be remembered and inscribed before You — we and Your entire people the Family of Israel for a good life and for peace. Blessed are You, HASHEM, Who makes peace.

[If forgotten, do not repeat *Shemoneh Esrei.* See *Laws* §61.]

The *chazzan's* repetition of *Shemoneh Esrei* ends here. see below for further instructions.

Many hold that the following verse should be recited here by individuals and the *chazzan:*

May the expressions of my mouth and the thoughts of my heart find favor before You, HASHEM, my Rock and my Redeemer.[1]

See p. 119 for permissible responses while reciting this final paragraph of *Shemoneh Esrei.*

אֱלֹהַי *My God, guard my tongue from evil and my lips from speaking deceitfully.*[2] *To those who curse me, let my soul be silent; and let my soul be like dust to everyone. Open my heart to Your Torah, then my soul will pursue Your commandments. As for all those who design evil against me, speedily nullify their counsel and disrupt their design. Act for Your Name's sake; act for Your right hand's sake; act for Your sanctity's sake; act for Your Torah's sake. That Your beloved ones may be given rest; let Your right hand save, and respond to me.*[3]

Some recite verses pertaining to their names at this point. See page 924.

May the expressions of my mouth and the thoughts of my heart find favor before You, HASHEM, my Rock and my Redeemer.[1]

Bow and take three steps back. Bow left and say, *'He Who makes peace ...';* bow right and say, *'may He make peace ...';* bow forward and say, *'and upon ... Amen.'*

He Who makes peace in His heights, may He make peace upon us, and upon all Israel. Now respond: Amen.

יְהִי רָצוֹן *May it be Your will, HASHEM our God and the God of our forefathers, that the Holy Temple be rebuilt, speedily in our days. Grant us our share in Your Torah, and may we serve You there with reverence, as in days of old and in former years. Then the offering of Judah and Jerusalem will be pleasing to HASHEM, as in days of old and in former years.*[4]

THE INDIVIDUAL'S RECITATION OF *SHEMONEH ESREI* ENDS HERE.

The individual remains standing in place until the *chazzan* reaches *Kedushah* — or at least until the *chazzan* begins his repetition — then he takes three steps forward. The *chazzan* himself, or one praying alone, should remain in place for a few moments before taking three steps forward.

On Rosh Chodesh, Chanukah and Chol HaMoed, *Hallel* (p. 632) is recited at this point.

FULL-KADDISH

The *chazzan* recites the Full *Kaddish:*

יִתְגַּדַּל *May His great Name grow exalted and sanctified* (Cong.— *Amen.*) *in the world that He created as He willed. May He give reign to His kingship in your lifetimes and in your days, and in the lifetimes of the entire Family of Israel, swiftly and soon. Now respond: Amen.*

(Cong.— *Amen. May His great Name be blessed forever and ever.*)

May His great Name be blessed forever and ever.

Blessed, praised, glorified, exalted, extolled, mighty, upraised, and

(1) *Psalms* 19:15. (2) Cf. 34:14. (3) 60:7; 108:7. (4) *Malachi* 3:4.

וְיִתְהַלָּל שְׁמֵהּ דְּקֻדְשָׁא בְּרִיךְ הוּא (.Cong — בְּרִיךְ הוּא) — °לְעֵלָּא מִן כָּל (From Rosh Hashanah to Yom Kippur substitute— °לְעֵלָּא וּלְעֵלָּא מִכָּל) בִּרְכָתָא וְשִׁירָתָא תֻּשְׁבְּחָתָא וְנֶחֱמָתָא, דַּאֲמִירָן בְּעָלְמָא. וְאִמְרוּ: אָמֵן. (.Cong— אָמֵן.)

(.Cong—קַבֵּל בְּרַחֲמִים וּבְרָצוֹן אֶת תְּפִלָּתֵנוּ.)

תִּתְקַבֵּל צְלוֹתְהוֹן וּבָעוּתְהוֹן דְּכָל בֵּית יִשְׂרָאֵל קֳדָם אֲבוּהוֹן דִּי בִשְׁמַיָּא. וְאִמְרוּ: אָמֵן. (.Cong — אָמֵן.)

(.Cong—יְהִי שֵׁם יהוה מְבֹרָךְ, מֵעַתָּה וְעַד עוֹלָם.)

יְהֵא שְׁלָמָא רַבָּא מִן שְׁמַיָּא, וְחַיִּים עָלֵינוּ וְעַל כָּל יִשְׂרָאֵל. וְאִמְרוּ: אָמֵן. (.Cong— אָמֵן.)

(.Cong—עֶזְרִי מֵעִם יהוה, עֹשֵׂה שָׁמַיִם וָאָרֶץ.)

Take three steps back. Bow left and say ... עֹשֶׂה; bow right and say ... הוּא; bow forward and say וְעַל כָּל ... אָמֵן. Remain standing in place for a few moments, then take three steps forward.

עֹשֶׂה שָׁלוֹם בִּמְרוֹמָיו, הוּא יַעֲשֶׂה שָׁלוֹם עָלֵינוּ, וְעַל כָּל יִשְׂרָאֵל. וְאִמְרוּ: אָמֵן. (.Cong— אָמֵן.)

הוצאת ספר תורה

From the moment the Ark is opened until the Torah is returned to it, one must conduct himself with the utmost respect, and avoid unnecessary conversation. It is commendable to kiss the Torah as it is carried to the *bimah* [reading table] and back to the Ark.

All rise and remain standing until the Torah is placed on the *bimah*. The congregation recites:

אֵין כָּמוֹךָ* בָאֱלֹהִים אֲדֹנָי, וְאֵין כְּמַעֲשֶׂיךָ.*[1] מַלְכוּתְךָ מַלְכוּת כָּל עֹלָמִים, וּמֶמְשַׁלְתְּךָ בְּכָל דּוֹר וָדֹר.[2] יהוה מֶלֶךְ,[3] יהוה מָלָךְ,[4] יהוה יִמְלֹךְ לְעֹלָם וָעֶד.[5] יהוה עֹז לְעַמּוֹ יִתֵּן, יהוה יְבָרֵךְ אֶת עַמּוֹ בַשָּׁלוֹם.[6]

אַב הָרַחֲמִים, הֵיטִיבָה בִרְצוֹנְךָ אֶת צִיּוֹן,* תִּבְנֶה חוֹמוֹת יְרוּשָׁלָיִם.[7] כִּי בְךָ לְבַד בָּטָחְנוּ, מֶלֶךְ אֵל רָם וְנִשָּׂא, אֲדוֹן עוֹלָמִים.

The Ark is opened; before the Torah is removed the congregation recites:

וַיְהִי בִּנְסֹעַ הָאָרֹן* וַיֹּאמֶר מֹשֶׁה, קוּמָה יהוה וְיָפֻצוּ אֹיְבֶיךָ וְיָנֻסוּ מְשַׂנְאֶיךָ מִפָּנֶיךָ.[8] כִּי מִצִּיּוֹן תֵּצֵא תוֹרָה, וּדְבַר יהוה מִירוּשָׁלָיִם.[9] בָּרוּךְ שֶׁנָּתַן תּוֹרָה לְעַמּוֹ יִשְׂרָאֵל בִּקְדֻשָּׁתוֹ.

הוֹצָאַת סֵפֶר תּוֹרָה / Removal of the Torah

אֵין כָּמוֹךָ — *There is none like You.* On the Sabbath and Festivals when people have more time than on weekdays, the service of removing the Torah from the Ark and bringing it to the *bimah* is expanded. First comes an introductory series of verses that emphasize God's greatness and plead for the rebuilding of Zion and Jerusalem. Since we are about to read from God's word to Israel, it is fitting that we first call to mind that the One Who speaks to us is our All-powerful King.

וְאֵין כְּמַעֲשֶׂיךָ — *And there is nothing like Your works.* This refers to the work of creation. It

lauded be the Name of the Holy One, Blessed is He (Cong.— *Blessed is He*) — (From Rosh Hashanah to Yom Kippur add: *exceedingly*) *beyond any blessing and song, praise and consolation that are uttered in the world. Now respond: Amen.* (Cong.— *Amen*).

(*Cong.— Accept our prayers with mercy and favor.*)

May the prayers and supplications of the entire Family of Israel be accepted before their Father Who is in Heaven. Now respond: Amen. (Cong.— *Amen.*)

(Cong.— *May the Name of HASHEM, be blessed from now to eternity.*)

May there be abundant peace from Heaven, and life, upon us and upon all Israel. Now respond: Amen. (Cong.— *Amen.*)

(Cong.— *My help is from HASHEM, Maker of heaven and earth.*)

Take three steps back. Bow left and say, *'He Who makes peace ...'*; bow right and say, *'may He ...'*; bow forward and say, *'and upon all Israel ...'* Remain standing in place for a few moments, then take three steps forward.

He Who makes peace in His heights, may He make peace upon us, and upon all Israel. Now respond: Amen. (Cong.— *Amen.*)

REMOVAL OF THE TORAH FROM THE ARK

From the moment the Ark is opened until the Torah is returned to it, one must conduct himself with the utmost respect, and avoid unnecessary conversation. It is commendable to kiss the Torah as it is carried to the *bimah* [reading table] and back to the Ark.

All rise and remain standing until the Torah is placed on the *bimah*. The congregation recites:

אֵין כָּמְוֹךָ *There is none like You* among the gods, my Lord, and there is nothing like Your works.*[1] Your kingdom is a kingdom spanning all eternities, and Your dominion is throughout every generation.[2] HASHEM reigns,[3] HASHEM has reigned,[4] HASHEM shall reign for all eternity.[5] HASHEM will give might to His people; HASHEM will bless His people with peace.[6]*

אַב הָרַחֲמִים *Father of compassion, do good with Zion* according to Your will; rebuild the walls of Jerusalem.[7] For we trust in You alone, O King, God, exalted and uplifted, Master of worlds.*

The Ark is opened; before the Torah is removed the congregation recites:

וַיְהִי בִּנְסְעַ *When the Ark would travel,* Moses would say, 'Arise, HASHEM, and let Your foes be scattered, let those who hate You flee from You.'[8] For from Zion the Torah will come forth and the word of HASHEM from Jerusalem.[9] Blessed is He Who gave the Torah to His people Israel in His holiness.*

(1) *Psalms* 86:8. (2) 145:13. (3) 10:16. (4) 93:1 et al. (5) *Exodus* 15:18. (6) *Psalms* 29:11. (7) 51:20. (8) *Numbers* 10:35. (9) *Isaiah* 2:3.

follows, therefore, that since God is the Creator of the universe, He was and remains its King.

הֵטִיבָה ... אֶת צִיּוֹן — *Do good with Zion.* Only in God's chosen Sanctuary can His kingdom come to full flower among mankind. Only there can the Torah reading attain its greatest meaning.

וַיְהִי בִּנְסֹעַ הָאָרֹן — *When the Ark would travel.* When the Ark is opened we declare, as Moses did when the Ark traveled, that God's word is invincible. Having acknowledged this, we can read from the Torah with the proper awareness. We continue that it is God's will that the Torah's message go forth to the entire world, and by blessing Him for having given us the Torah, we accept our responsibility to carry out its commands and spread its message *(R' Hirsch).*

On Festivals that occur on weekdays (in many congregations from Rosh Hashanah to Yom Kippur and on Hoshana Rabbah) the following prayer is added.

The Thirteen Attributes of Mercy (bold type) are recited three times:

יהוה, יהוה, אֵל, רַחוּם, וְחַנּוּן, אֶֽרֶךְ אַפַּֽיִם, וְרַב חֶֽסֶד, וֶאֱמֶת, נֹצֵר חֶֽסֶד לָאֲלָפִים, נֹשֵׂא עָוֹן, וָפֶֽשַׁע, וְחַטָּאָה, וְנַקֵּה.[1]

On Festival days of Pesach, Shavuos and Succos continue:

רִבּוֹנוֹ שֶׁל עוֹלָם מַלֵּא מִשְׁאֲלוֹת לִבִּי לְטוֹבָה,* וְהָפֵק רְצוֹנִי, וְתֵן שְׁאֵלָתִי, לִי עַבְדְּךָ (name) בֶּן/בַּת (mother's name) אֲמָתֶֽךָ,* וְזַכֵּנִי

וְאֶת — Insert the appropriate phrase(s) אִשְׁתִּי/בַּעְלִי, וּבְנִי/וּבָנַי, וּבִתִּי/וּבְנוֹתַי

וְכָל בְּנֵי בֵיתִי לַעֲשׂוֹת רְצוֹנְךָ בְּלֵבָב שָׁלֵם. וּמַלְּטֵֽנוּ מִיֵּֽצֶר הָרָע, וְתֵן חֶלְקֵֽנוּ בְּתוֹרָתֶֽךָ. וְזַכֵּֽנוּ שֶׁתִּשְׁרֶה שְׁכִינָתְךָ עָלֵֽינוּ, וְהוֹפַע עָלֵֽינוּ רֽוּחַ חָכְמָה וּבִינָה. וְיִתְקַיֵּם בָּֽנוּ מִקְרָא שֶׁכָּתוּב: וְנָחָה עָלָיו רֽוּחַ יהוה, רֽוּחַ חָכְמָה וּבִינָה, רֽוּחַ עֵצָה וּגְבוּרָה, רֽוּחַ דַּֽעַת וְיִרְאַת יהוה.[2] וְכֵן יְהִי רָצוֹן מִלְּפָנֶֽיךָ, יהוה אֱלֹהֵֽינוּ וֵאלֹהֵי אֲבוֹתֵֽינוּ, שֶׁתְּזַכֵּֽנוּ לַעֲשׂוֹת מַעֲשִׂים טוֹבִים בְּעֵינֶֽיךָ, וְלָלֶֽכֶת בְּדַרְכֵי יְשָׁרִים לְפָנֶֽיךָ. וְקַדְּשֵֽׁנוּ בְּמִצְוֹתֶֽיךָ כְּדֵי שֶׁנִּזְכֶּה לְחַיִּים טוֹבִים וַאֲרוּכִים לִימוֹת הַמָּשִֽׁיחַ וּלְחַיֵּי הָעוֹלָם הַבָּא. וְתִשְׁמְרֵֽנוּ מִמַּעֲשִׂים רָעִים, וּמִשָּׁעוֹת רָעוֹת הַמִּתְרַגְּשׁוֹת לָבֹא לָעוֹלָם. וְהַבּוֹטֵֽחַ בַּיהוה חֶֽסֶד יְסוֹבְּבֶֽנְהוּ,[3] אָמֵן.

From Rosh Hashanah to Yom Kippur; and on Hoshana Rabbah* continue:

רִבּוֹנוֹ שֶׁל עוֹלָם, מַלֵּא מִשְׁאֲלוֹתַי לְטוֹבָה, וְהָפֵק רְצוֹנִי, וְתֵן שְׁאֵלָתִי, וּמְחוֹל לִי עַל כָּל עֲוֹנוֹתַי, וְעַל כָּל עֲוֹנוֹת אַנְשֵׁי בֵיתִי, מְחִילָה בְּחֶֽסֶד, מְחִילָה בְּרַחֲמִים, וְטַהֲרֵֽנִי מֵחֲטָאַי וּמֵעֲוֹנוֹתַי וּמִפְּשָׁעַי. וְזָכְרֵֽנִי בְּזִכָּרוֹן טוֹב לְפָנֶֽיךָ, וּפָקְדֵֽנִי בִּפְקֻדַּת יְשׁוּעָה וְרַחֲמִים, וְזָכְרֵֽנִי לְחַיִּים אֲרוּכִים לְחַיִּים טוֹבִים וּלְשָׁלוֹם, וּפַרְנָסָה טוֹבָה וְכַלְכָּלָה, וְלֶֽחֶם לֶאֱכוֹל, וּבֶֽגֶד לִלְבּוֹשׁ, וְעֹֽשֶׁר וְכָבוֹד וַאֲרִיכוּת יָמִים לַהֲגוֹת בְּתוֹרָתֶֽךָ וּבְמִצְוֹתֶֽיךָ, וְשֵֽׂכֶל וּבִינָה לְהָבִין וּלְהַשְׂכִּיל עִמְקֵי סוֹדוֹתֶֽיךָ. וְהָפֵק רְפוּאָה שְׁלֵמָה לְכָל מַכְאוֹבֵֽינוּ, וּתְבָרֵךְ אֶת כָּל מַעֲשֵׂה יָדֵֽינוּ. וְתִגְזוֹר עָלֵֽינוּ גְּזֵרוֹת טוֹבוֹת יְשׁוּעוֹת וְנֶחָמוֹת. וּתְבַטֵּל מֵעָלֵֽינוּ כָּל גְּזֵרוֹת קָשׁוֹת וְרָעוֹת, וְתֵן בְּלֵב מַלְכוּת וְיוֹעֲצָיו וְשָׂרָיו עָלֵֽינוּ לְטוֹבָה. אָמֵן וְכֵן יְהִי רָצוֹן.

יִהְיוּ לְרָצוֹן אִמְרֵי פִי, וְהֶגְיוֹן לִבִּי לְפָנֶֽיךָ, יהוה צוּרִי וְגוֹאֲלִי.[4]

Recite the following verse three times:

וַאֲנִי תְפִלָּתִי לְךָ* יהוה עֵת רָצוֹן, אֱלֹהִים בְּרָב חַסְדֶּֽךָ, עֲנֵֽנִי בֶּאֱמֶת יִשְׁעֶֽךָ.[5]

◆§ Special Festival Prayers / Thirteen Attributes of Mercy

On Pesach, Shavuos, and Succos, a special prayer is inserted before בְּרִיךְ שְׁמֵהּ, *Blessed is the Name*, requesting God's help in attaining His goals for us. Similarly, on Rosh Hashanah, Yom Kippur, and Hoshana Rabbah, a prayer is recited that reflects the theme of repentance and forgiveness. Each of these prayers is preceded by the י״ג מִדּוֹת הָרַחֲמִים, *Thirteen Attributes of Mercy*, the prayer that God Himself taught Moses after Israel worshiped the Golden Calf. Although Moses, quite understandably, thought that no prayers could help the nation that had bowed to and danced around an idol less than six weeks after hearing the Ten Commandments, God showed him that it was never too late for prayer and repentance. Instead, Moses was given a Divine covenant that 'the Thirteen Attributes are never turned back unanswered' (*Rosh Hashanah* 17b).

A commentary on the Thirteen Attributes may be found in the *Selichos* section; p. 817. There, as in the Yom Kippur services, the Thirteen Attributes are the leitmotif of the supplications.

Like all personal supplications, this one is not recited on the Sabbath or Festivals that fall on the Sabbath.

On Festivals that occur on weekdays (in many congregations from Rosh Hashanah to Yom Kippur and on Hoshana Rabbah) the following prayer is added.

The Thirteen Attributes of Mercy (bold type) are recited three times:

HASHEM, HASHEM, God, Compassionate and Gracious, Slow to anger, and Abundant in Kindness and Truth. Preserver of kindness for thousands of generations, Forgiver of iniquity, willful sin, and error, and Who cleanses.[1]

On Festival days of Pesach, Shavuos and Succos continue:

רִבּוֹנוֹ *Master of the universe, fulfill my heartfelt requests for good,* satisfy my desire and grant my request, me — Your servant* (name) *son/daughter of* (mother's name) *Your maid-servant* — and privilege me*

Insert the appropriate phrase(s): *and my wife/husband, my son(s), my daughter(s)*

and everyone in my household to do Your will wholeheartedly. Rescue us from the Evil Inclination and grant our share in Your Torah. Privilege us that You may rest Your Presence upon us and radiate upon us a spirit of wisdom and insight. Let there be fulfilled in us the verse that is written: The spirit of HASHEM shall rest upon him, the spirit of wisdom and insight, the spirit of counsel and strength, the spirit of knowledge and fear of HASHEM.[2] *Similarly may it be Your will, HASHEM, our God and the God of our forefathers, that You privilege us to do deeds that are good in Your eyes and to walk before You in upright paths. Sanctify us with Your commandments so that we may be worthy of a good and long life, to the days of the Messiah and to the life of the World to Come. May You protect us against evil deeds and from bad times that surge upon the world. He who trusts in HASHEM — may kindness surround him.*[3] *Amen.*

From Rosh Hashanah to Yom Kippur; and on Hoshana Rabbah* continue:

רִבּוֹנוֹ *Master of the universe, fulfill my requests for good, satisfy my desire and grant my request, pardon all my iniquities and all the iniquities of my household — a pardon of kindness, a pardon of compassion — and purify me of my errors, my iniquities, and my willful sins. Remember me with a favorable memory before You and consider me for salvation and compassion. Remember me for long life, for good life and for peace, good livelihood and sustenance, bread to eat, clothes to wear, wealth, honor, a long life engaged in Your Torah and Your commandments; and intelligence and insight to understand and discern the depths of Your mysteries. Grant a complete recovery to all our sufferings and bless all our handiwork. Decree upon us good decrees, salvations and consolations. Nullify all harsh and evil decrees against us and dispose the feelings of the government, its counselors and ministers upon us for good. Amen, and so be Your will.*

May the expressions of my mouth and the thoughts of my heart find favor before You, HASHEM, my Rock and my Redeemer.[4]

Recite the following verse three times:

As for me, may my prayer to You,* HASHEM, be at an opportune time; O God, in Your abundant kindness, answer me with the truth of Your salvation.[5]

(1) *Exodus* 34:6-7. (2) *Isaiah* 11:2. (3) Cf. *Psalms* 32:10. (4) 19:15. (5) 69:14.

⌘ רִבּוֹנוֹ שֶׁל עוֹלָם / Master of the Universe

מַלֵּא מִשְׁאֲלוֹת לִבִּי לְטוֹבָה — *Fulfill my heartfelt requests for good.* Often man's personal goals are not to his real benefit. May my requests be filled in a way that will be truly good.

עַבְדְּךָ בֶּן אֲמָתֶךָ — *Your servant son of Your maidservant.* This formulation is taken from David's prayer in *Hallel* (*Psalms* 116:16). A slave born to a maidservant has never tasted freedom and is instinctively more submissive (*Rashi; Sforno*). By using this expression, we impress upon ourselves our dependency on God.

⌘ **Hoshana Rabbah** is the climax of the judgment process that began on Rosh Hashanah. Therefore, this prayer streses that we want not only forgiveness, but God's help in living a worthwhile, spiritually fulfilling life.

⌘ וַאֲנִי תְפִלָּתִי לְךָ — *As for me, may my prayer to You.* This verse makes three declarations: Our prayers are to God alone; we hope that the time is proper in His eyes; and we know full well that only through His abundant kindness can we expect His salvation.

On all Sabbaths and Festivals:

בְּרִיךְ שְׁמֵהּ* דְּמָרֵא עָלְמָא, בְּרִיךְ כִּתְרָךְ וְאַתְרָךְ. יְהֵא רְעוּתָךְ עִם עַמָּךְ יִשְׂרָאֵל לְעָלַם, וּפֻרְקַן יְמִינָךְ אַחֲזֵי לְעַמָּךְ בְּבֵית מַקְדְּשָׁךְ, וּלְאַמְטוּיֵי לָנָא מִטּוּב נְהוֹרָךְ, וּלְקַבֵּל צְלוֹתָנָא בְּרַחֲמִין. יְהֵא רַעֲוָא קֳדָמָךְ, דְּתוֹרִיךְ לָן חַיִּין בְּטִיבוּתָא, וְלֶהֱוֵי אֲנָא פְקִידָא בְּגוֹ צַדִּיקַיָּא, לְמִרְחַם עָלַי וּלְמִנְטַר יָתִי וְיַת כָּל דִּי לִי, וְדִי לְעַמָּךְ יִשְׂרָאֵל. אַנְתְּ הוּא זָן לְכֹלָּא, וּמְפַרְנֵס לְכֹלָּא, אַנְתְּ הוּא שַׁלִּיט עַל כֹּלָּא. אַנְתְּ הוּא דְּשַׁלִּיט עַל מַלְכַיָּא, וּמַלְכוּתָא דִּילָךְ הִיא. אֲנָא עַבְדָּא דְקֻדְשָׁא בְּרִיךְ הוּא, דְּסָגִידְנָא קַמֵּהּ וּמִקַּמָּא דִּיקַר אוֹרַיְתֵהּ בְּכָל עִדָּן וְעִדָּן. לָא עַל אֱנָשׁ רָחִיצְנָא, וְלָא עַל בַּר אֱלָהִין סָמִיכְנָא, אֶלָּא בֶּאֱלָהָא דִשְׁמַיָּא, דְּהוּא אֱלָהָא קְשׁוֹט, וְאוֹרַיְתֵהּ קְשׁוֹט, וּנְבִיאוֹהִי קְשׁוֹט, וּמַסְגֵּא לְמֶעְבַּד טַבְוָן וּקְשׁוֹט. בֵּהּ אֲנָא רָחִיץ, וְלִשְׁמֵהּ קַדִּישָׁא יַקִּירָא אֲנָא אֵמַר תֻּשְׁבְּחָן. יְהֵא רַעֲוָא קֳדָמָךְ, דְּתִפְתַּח לִבָּאִי בְּאוֹרַיְתָא, וְתַשְׁלִים מִשְׁאֲלִין דְּלִבָּאִי, וְלִבָּא דְכָל עַמָּךְ יִשְׂרָאֵל, לְטַב וּלְחַיִּין וְלִשְׁלָם. (אָמֵן.)

The Torah is removed from the Ark and presented to the *chazzan,* who accepts it in his right arm. Facing the congregation the *chazzan* raises the Torah and, followed by congregation, recites:

שְׁמַע יִשְׂרָאֵל* יהוה אֱלֹהֵינוּ יהוה אֶחָד.[1]

Still facing the congregation, the *chazzan* raises the Torah and, followed by congregation, recites:

אֶחָד (הוּא) אֱלֹהֵינוּ גָּדוֹל אֲדוֹנֵינוּ,
קָדוֹשׁ (On Hoshana Rabbah—**וְנוֹרָא) שְׁמוֹ.**

The *chazzan* turns to Ark, bows and raises the Torah, and recites:

גַּדְּלוּ* לַיהוה אִתִּי וּנְרוֹמְמָה שְׁמוֹ יַחְדָּו.[2]

The *chazzan* turns to his right and carries the Torah to the *bimah,* as the congregation responds:

לְךָ יהוה הַגְּדֻלָּה* וְהַגְּבוּרָה וְהַתִּפְאֶרֶת וְהַנֵּצַח וְהַהוֹד כִּי כֹל בַּשָּׁמַיִם וּבָאָרֶץ, לְךָ יהוה הַמַּמְלָכָה וְהַמִּתְנַשֵּׂא לְכֹל לְרֹאשׁ.[3] רוֹמְמוּ יהוה אֱלֹהֵינוּ, וְהִשְׁתַּחֲווּ לַהֲדֹם רַגְלָיו,* קָדוֹשׁ הוּא. רוֹמְמוּ יהוה אֱלֹהֵינוּ, וְהִשְׁתַּחֲווּ לְהַר קָדְשׁוֹ, כִּי קָדוֹשׁ יהוה אֱלֹהֵינוּ.[4]

בְּרִיךְ שְׁמֵהּ — *Blessed is the Name.* The *Zohar* declares that when the congregation prepares to read from the Torah, the heavenly gates of mercy are opened and God's love for Israel is aroused. Therefore, it is an auspicious occasion for the recital of this prayer which asks for God's compassion; pleads that He display His salvation in the finally rebuilt Holy Temple; declares our faith in Him and His Torah; and asks that He make us receptive to its wisdom.

שְׁמַע יִשְׂרָאֵל — *Hear, O Israel.* Holding the Torah Scroll and facing the congregation, the

On all Sabbaths and Festivals:

בְּרִיךְ שְׁמֵהּ *Blessed is the Name* of the Master of the universe, blessed is Your crown and Your place. May Your favor remain with Your people Israel forever; may You display the salvation of Your right hand to Your people in Your Holy Temple, to benefit us with the goodness of Your luminescence and to accept our prayers with mercy. May it be Your will that You extend our lives with goodness and that I be numbered among the righteous; that You have mercy on me and protect me, all that is mine and that is Your people Israel's. It is You Who nourishes all and sustains all; You control everything. It is You Who control kings, and kingship is Yours. I am a servant of the Holy One Blessed is He, and I prostrate myself before Him and before the glory of His Torah at all times. Not in any man do I put trust, nor on any angel do I rely — only on the God of heaven Who is the God of truth, Whose Torah is truth and Whose prophets are true and Who acts liberally with kindness and truth. In Him do I trust, and to His glorious and holy Name do I declare praises. May it be Your will that You open my heart to the Torah and that You fulfill the wishes of my heart and the heart of Your entire people Israel for good, for life, and for peace. (Amen.)*

The Torah is removed from the Ark and presented to the *chazzan,* who accepts it in his right arm. Facing the congregation the *chazzan* raises the Torah and, followed by congregation, recites:

Hear, O Israel:* HASHEM is our God, HASHEM, the One and Only.[1]

Still facing the congregation, the *chazzan* raises the Torah and, followed by congregation, recites:

One is our God, great is our Master, Holy [on Hoshana Rabbah: **and awesome**] **is His Name.**

The *chazzan* turns to Ark, bows and raises the Torah, and recites:

Declare the greatness* of HASHEM with me, and let us exalt His Name together.[2]

The *chazzan* turns to his right and carries the Torah to the *bimah,* as the congregation responds:

לְךָ *Yours, HASHEM, is the greatness,* the strength, the splendor, the triumph, and the glory; even everything in heaven and earth; Yours, HASHEM, is the kingdom, and the sovereignty over every leader.*[3] *Exalt HASHEM, our God, and bow at His footstool;* He is Holy! Exalt HASHEM, our God, and bow to His holy mountain; for holy is HASHEM, our God.*[4]

(1) *Deuteronomy* 6:4. (2) *Psalms* 34:4. (3) *I Chronicles* 29:11. (4) *Psalms* 99:5,9.

chazzan leads them in reciting three verses that help set the majestic tone of reading publicly from the word of God. The verses form a logical progression: God is One; He is great and holy; therefore we join in declaring His greatness.

גַּדְּלוּ — *Declare the greatness.* Our rejoicing in the Torah manifests itself in praise of its Giver. The *chazzan* calls upon the congregation to join him in praising God.

לְךָ ה׳ הַגְּדֻלָּה — *Yours, HASHEM, is the greatness.* This praise was first uttered by David in his ecstasy at seeing how wholeheartedly the people contributed their riches toward the eventual building of the Temple. He ascribed the greatness of that and every other achievement to God's graciousness.

As the *chazzan* carries the Torah to the *bimah* the congregation recites:

עַל הַכֹּל,* יִתְגַּדַּל וְיִתְקַדַּשׁ וְיִשְׁתַּבַּח וְיִתְפָּאַר וְיִתְרוֹמַם וְיִתְנַשֵּׂא שְׁמוֹ שֶׁל מֶלֶךְ מַלְכֵי הַמְּלָכִים הַקָּדוֹשׁ בָּרוּךְ הוּא, בָּעוֹלָמוֹת שֶׁבָּרָא, הָעוֹלָם הַזֶּה וְהָעוֹלָם הַבָּא, כִּרְצוֹנוֹ,* וְכִרְצוֹן יְרֵאָיו, וְכִרְצוֹן כָּל בֵּית יִשְׂרָאֵל. צוּר הָעוֹלָמִים, אֲדוֹן כָּל הַבְּרִיּוֹת, אֱלוֹהַּ כָּל הַנְּפָשׁוֹת, הַיּוֹשֵׁב בְּמֶרְחֲבֵי מָרוֹם, הַשּׁוֹכֵן בִּשְׁמֵי שְׁמֵי קֶדֶם. קְדֻשָּׁתוֹ עַל הַחַיּוֹת, וּקְדֻשָּׁתוֹ עַל כִּסֵּא הַכָּבוֹד. וּבְכֵן יִתְקַדַּשׁ שִׁמְךָ בָּנוּ* יהוה אֱלֹהֵינוּ לְעֵינֵי כָּל חָי. וְנֹאמַר לְפָנָיו שִׁיר חָדָשׁ, כַּכָּתוּב: שִׁירוּ לֵאלֹהִים זַמְּרוּ שְׁמוֹ, סֹלּוּ לָרֹכֵב בָּעֲרָבוֹת בְּיָהּ שְׁמוֹ,* וְעִלְזוּ לְפָנָיו.[1] וְנִרְאֵהוּ עַיִן בְּעַיִן בְּשׁוּבוֹ אֶל נָוֵהוּ, כַּכָּתוּב: כִּי עַיִן בְּעַיִן יִרְאוּ בְּשׁוּב יהוה צִיּוֹן.[2] וְנֶאֱמַר: וְנִגְלָה כְּבוֹד יהוה, וְרָאוּ כָל בָּשָׂר יַחְדָּו כִּי פִּי יהוה דִּבֵּר.[3]

אַב הָרַחֲמִים הוּא יְרַחֵם עַם עֲמוּסִים,* וְיִזְכֹּר בְּרִית אֵיתָנִים,* וְיַצִּיל נַפְשׁוֹתֵינוּ מִן הַשָּׁעוֹת הָרָעוֹת, וְיִגְעַר בְּיֵצֶר הָרָע מִן הַנְּשׂוּאִים, וְיָחֹן אוֹתָנוּ לִפְלֵיטַת עוֹלָמִים, וִימַלֵּא מִשְׁאֲלוֹתֵינוּ בְּמִדָּה טוֹבָה יְשׁוּעָה וְרַחֲמִים.

The Torah is placed on the *bimah* and prepared for reading.
The *gabbai* uses the following formula to call a *Kohen* to the Torah:

וְיַעֲזוֹר וְיָגֵן וְיוֹשִׁיעַ לְכָל הַחוֹסִים בּוֹ, וְנֹאמַר, אָמֵן. הַכֹּל הָבוּ גֹדֶל* לֵאלֹהֵינוּ וּתְנוּ כָבוֹד לַתּוֹרָה, כֹּהֵן° קְרָב,* יַעֲמֹד* (name) בֶּן (father's name) הַכֹּהֵן.

°If no *Kohen* is present, the *gabbai* says:
"אֵין כַּאן כֹּהֵן, יַעֲמֹד (insert name) יִשְׂרָאֵל (לֵוִי) בִּמְקוֹם כֹּהֵן."

לַהֲדֹם רַגְלָיו — *At His footstool,* i.e., the Temple, as if to say that God's Heavenly Presence extends earthward, like a footstool helping support a monarch sitting on his throne. In a further sense, this represents our resolve to live in such a way that we are worthy of His Presence resting upon us *(R' Hirsch).*

☙ **עַל הַכֹּל** — *For all this.* All the praises that we have uttered heretofore are inadequate to describe God's greatness. May His Name continue to grow exalted *(Kol Bo).*

This paragraph is intended to express the majesty of God especially now that we are about to read from the Torah. We say that although He is sanctified in the heavens and by the spiritual beings, we long to become worthy vehicles through which His greatness can be manifested on earth, as well.

כִּרְצוֹנוֹ — *According to His will.* May He be *exalted, sanctified, praised* ... as He wishes to be. God created the universe so that His glory could be appreciated and emulated by man (see *Isaiah* 43:7). We now pray that this will indeed take place.

וּבְכֵן יִתְקַדַּשׁ שִׁמְךָ בָּנוּ — *Similarly, may Your Name be sanctified within us.* The goal of people should be to demonstrate that God's greatness should not be reserved for the 'higher, spiritual' spheres. Rather, the most noble purpose of life is for mortal man to become a bearer of Godliness. When that comes about, we will have an infinitely clearer insight into God's greatness than we have now. Thus, our song of praise will be a *new song* — one that is qualitatively of an entirely different order than anything we are now capable of expressing.

בְּיָהּ שְׁמוֹ — *With His Name* YAH. The Talmud teaches that the Name יָהּ refers to God as the Creator. With the letter י, He created the heavens, and with the letter ה, He created the earth *(Menachos* 29b).

As the *chazzan* carries the Torah to the *bimah* the congregation recites:

עַל הַכֹּל *For all this,* let the Name of the King of kings, the Holy One, Blessed is He, grow exalted, sanctified, praised, glorified, exalted, and extolled in the worlds that He has created — This World and the World to Come — according to His will,* the will of those who fear Him, and the will of the entire House of Israel. Rock of the eternities, Master of all creatures, God of all souls, He Who sits in the expanses on high, Who rests in the loftiest primeval heavens. His holiness is upon the Chayos; His holiness is upon the Throne of Glory. Similarly, may Your Name be sanctified within us,* HASHEM, our God, in the sight of all the living. May we chant before Him a new song as it is written: 'Sing to God, make music for His Name, extol the One Who rides in the highest heavens with His Name YAH,* and exult before Him.'*[1] *May we see Him with a perceptive view upon His return to His Abode, as is written: 'For they shall see with a perceptive view as HASHEM returns to Zion.'*[2] *And it is said: 'The glory of HASHEM shall be revealed and all flesh together shall see that the mouth of HASHEM has spoken.'*[3]

אַב הָרַחֲמִים *May the Father of compassion have mercy on the nation that is borne by Him,* and may He remember the covenant of the spiritually mighty.* May He rescue our souls from the bad times, and upbraid the Evil Inclination to leave those borne by Him, graciously make us an eternal remnant, and fulfill our requests in good measure, for salvation and mercy.*

The Torah is placed on the *bimah* and prepared for reading.
The *gabbai* uses the following formula to call a *Kohen* to the Torah:

וְיַעֲזוֹר *May He help, shield, and save all who take refuge in Him — Now let us respond: Amen. All of you ascribe greatness* to our God and give honor to the Torah. Kohen,°* *approach.* Arise** (name) *son of* (father's name) *the Kohen.*

°If no *Kohen* is present, the *gabbai* says: *'There is no Kohen present, stand* (name) *son of* (father's name) *an Israelite (Levite) in place of the Kohen.*

(1) *Psalms* 68:5. (2) *Isaiah* 52:8. (3) 40:5.

אַב הָרַחֲמִים ◆§ / Father of Compassion

עַם עֲמוּסִים — *The nation that is borne by Him,* i.e., the nation that God bears upon Himself as His personal responsibility *(Etz Yosef).* Alternatively, this phrase may be translated: *the nation that is burdened* [with suffering] *(R' Hirsch).*

אֵיתָנִים — *The spiritually mighty* is a frequently used term for Abraham, Isaac, and Jacob.

הַכֹּל הָבוּ גֹדֶל — *All of you ascribe greatness.* Addressing the congregation, the *gabbai* calls upon them to show honor to God by giving honor to His Word — the Torah — which is about to be read.

כֹּהֵן קְרָב — *Kohen, approach.* It should be noted that only when a *Kohen* is called to the Torah do we use the expression קְרָב, *approach.* In Scripture, this term is used generally for *Kohanim* who 'approach' to perform the Divine sacrificial service (see e.g., *Leviticus* 1:5). Thus, its use here is in the sense that today's synagogue service is in place of the sacrifices *(Iyun Tefillah).*

The priestly family is granted the privilege of going first in all sacred matters *(Gittin* 59b). Since Levites assist the *Kohanim* in the Temple service, and they, too, devote themselves to God's service, a Levite is called to the Torah after the *Kohen.* If no Levite is present, the same *Kohen* reads the Levite's portion as well, and the *Kohen* repeats the blessings over the Levite's portion. If no *Kohen* is present, either an Israelite or a Levite is called to the Torah (ibid.).

יַעֲמֹד — *Arise.* The person called to read from the

בָּרוּךְ שֶׁנָּתַן תּוֹרָה לְעַמּוֹ יִשְׂרָאֵל בִּקְדֻשָּׁתוֹ. (תּוֹרַת יהוה* תְּמִימָה מְשִׁיבַת נָפֶשׁ, עֵדוּת יהוה נֶאֱמָנָה מַחְכִּימַת פֶּתִי. פִּקּוּדֵי יהוה יְשָׁרִים מְשַׂמְּחֵי לֵב, מִצְוַת יהוה בָּרָה מְאִירַת עֵינָיִם.[1] יהוה עֹז לְעַמּוֹ יִתֵּן, יהוה יְבָרֵךְ אֶת עַמּוֹ בַשָּׁלוֹם.[2] הָאֵל תָּמִים דַּרְכּוֹ, אִמְרַת יהוה צְרוּפָה, מָגֵן הוּא לְכֹל הַחֹסִים בּוֹ.[3])

Congregation then *gabbai* recite:

וְאַתֶּם הַדְּבֵקִים בַּיהוה* אֱלֹהֵיכֶם, חַיִּים כֻּלְּכֶם הַיּוֹם.[4]

קריאת התורה

[See *Laws* §97-114.] The reader shows the *oleh* (person called to the Torah) the place in the Torah. The *oleh* touches the Torah with a corner of his *tallis,* or the belt or mantle of the Torah, and kisses it. He then begins the blessing, bowing at בָּרְכוּ, and straightening up at ה׳.

בָּרְכוּ אֶת יהוה* הַמְּבֹרָךְ.

Congregation, followed by *oleh,* responds, bowing at בָּרוּךְ, and straightening up at ה׳.

בָּרוּךְ יהוה הַמְּבֹרָךְ לְעוֹלָם וָעֶד.

Oleh continues:

בָּרוּךְ אַתָּה יהוה אֱלֹהֵינוּ מֶלֶךְ הָעוֹלָם, אֲשֶׁר בָּחַר בָּנוּ מִכָּל הָעַמִּים, וְנָתַן לָנוּ אֶת תּוֹרָתוֹ. בָּרוּךְ אַתָּה יהוה, נוֹתֵן הַתּוֹרָה. (Cong.— אָמֵן.)

After his Torah portion has been read, the *oleh* recites:

בָּרוּךְ אַתָּה יהוה אֱלֹהֵינוּ מֶלֶךְ הָעוֹלָם, אֲשֶׁר נָתַן לָנוּ תּוֹרַת אֱמֶת, וְחַיֵּי עוֹלָם* נָטַע בְּתוֹכֵנוּ. בָּרוּךְ אַתָּה יהוה, נוֹתֵן הַתּוֹרָה. (Cong.— אָמֵן.)

Torah is told to rise because it is forbidden to sit while reading for the congregation *(Iyun Tefillah).*

תּוֹרַת ה׳ — *The Torah of* HASHEM. Authoritative *siddurim* and many halachic authorities include the four verses that we have given in parentheses. They total forty words to allude to the forty days Moses spent on Mount Sinai when he received the Torah. However, most congregations over the centuries have omitted these verses. Many authorities give only the last verse in this group — הָאֵל, *the God* — because it contains forty letters.

וְאַתֶּם הַדְּבֵקִים בַּה׳ — *You who cling to* HASHEM. The congregation responds with a blessing to all who are called to the Torah and who are loyal to it.

קְרִיאַת הַתּוֹרָה / Reading of the Torah

Moses and his court ordained that the Torah be read publicly on the mornings of the Sabbath, Monday and Thursday so that no three-day period would ever go by without a minimum of Torah study. This enactment was in response to a historical event. Scripture tells that the Jewish people traveled for three days וְלֹא מָצְאוּ מָיִם, *and they did not find water,* whereupon they complained against God *(Exodus* 15:22-24). The Sages teach that *water* is a symbolic term for Torah, and, as a result of their strenuous travel, the people did not study Torah for three days, with the result that they rebelled against God. To prevent such happenings in the future, Moses and his colleagues instituted the regular Torah reading.

The Talmud *(Bava Kamma* 82a) teaches that, in the early years of the Second Temple Era, Ezra the Scribe instituted the Sabbath *Minchah* reading so that people should not wile away the day idly. He also instituted that on Mondays and Thursdays, three people be called to the Torah to read a total of at least ten verses. Prior to that, the weekday reading had required that one man read three verses or that three men read at least one verse each. It is noteworthy that the minimum

Blessed is He Who gave the Torah to His people Israel in His holiness. (The Torah of HASHEM is perfect, restoring the soul; the testimony of HASHEM is trustworthy, making the simple one wise. The orders of HASHEM are upright, gladdening the heart; the command of HASHEM is clear, enlightening the eyes.[1] HASHEM will give might to His people; HASHEM will bless his people with peace.[2] The God Whose way is perfect, the promise of HASHEM is flawless, He is a shield for all who take refuge in Him.[3])*

Congregation then *gabbai,* recite:

You who cling to HASHEM,* your God, you are all alive today.[4]

READING OF THE TORAH

[See *Laws* §97-114.] The reader shows the *oleh* (person called to the Torah) the place in the Torah. The *oleh* touches the Torah with a corner of his *tallis,* or the belt or mantle of the Torah, and kisses it. He then begins the blessing, bowing at *'Bless,'* and straightening up at 'HASHEM.'

Bless HASHEM,* the blessed One.

Congregation, followed by *oleh,* responds, bowing at 'Blessed,' and straightening up at 'HASHEM.'

Blessed is HASHEM, the blessed One, for all eternity.

Oleh continues:

בָּרוּךְ *Blessed are You, HASHEM, our God, King of the universe, Who selected us from all the peoples and gave us His Torah. Blessed are You, HASHEM, Giver of the Torah.* (Cong.—*Amen.*)

After his Torah portion has been read, the *oleh* recites:

בָּרוּךְ *Blessed are You, HASHEM, our God, King of the universe, Who gave us the Torah of truth and implanted eternal life* within us. Blessed are You, HASHEM, Giver of the Torah.* (Cong.—*Amen.*)

(1) *Psalms* 19:8-9. (2) 29:11. (3) 18:31. (4) *Deuteronomy* 4:4.

---

number of verses instituted by Ezra — ten — is in honor of עֲשָׂרָה בַּטְלָנִים, ten people who should be supported by the community in order that they be free to dedicate themselves to Torah study and service, and be in the synagogue so that there would always be a *minyan* for services.

There is a basic difference between the reading of the Torah and the prayers. When we pray, *we* call upon *God;* that is why the *chazzan* stands in front of the congregation as its representative. But the Torah reading is reminiscent of God's revelation to Israel, when the nation gathered around Mount Sinai to hear Him communicate His word to Israel. That is why the Torah is read from a *bimah,* platform, usually elevated and in the center of the congregation, like Israel gathered around the mountain.

The number of people called to the Torah varies in accordance with the sanctity of the day. Thus, on Monday and Thursday, fast days, Purim and Chanukah, three people are called; on Rosh Chodesh and Chol HaMoed, four are called; on Festivals and Rosh Hashanah, five; on Yom Kippur, six; and on the Sabbath, seven. (It should be noted that *Maftir* is not included in the above number since *Maftir* is attached to the *Haftarah* reading. See p. 446.) Only three are called on Sabbath afternoons since the Torah has already been read in the morning.

☙ בָּרְכוּ אֶת ה׳ — *Bless HASHEM.* This call to the congregation to bless God prior to the Torah reading is based on the practice of Ezra (*Nechemiah* 8:6). Before he read from the Torah to the multitude, he blessed God and they responded in kind. Similarly, the Sages (*Berachos* 21a) derive the Scriptural requirement to recite a blessing before Torah study from the verse, *When I proclaim the Name of HASHEM, ascribe greatness to our God* (*Deuteronomy* 32:3). The implication is that the public study of Torah requires a blessing.

תּוֹרַת אֱמֶת ... וְחַיֵּי עוֹלָם — *A Torah of truth ... eternal life. Torah of truth* refers to the Written Torah, and *eternal life* to the Oral Law. The Oral Law is described as *implanted within us,* because Jews constantly expand their Torah knowledge through their personal study and analysis (*Tur Orach Chaim* 139).

מי שברך לעולה לתורה

מִי שֶׁבֵּרַךְ אֲבוֹתֵינוּ אַבְרָהָם יִצְחָק וְיַעֲקֹב, הוּא יְבָרֵךְ אֶת (name) בֶּן (father's name) בַּעֲבוּר שֶׁעָלָה לִכְבוֹד הַמָּקוֹם, לִכְבוֹד הַתּוֹרָה, [On the Sabbath— לִכְבוֹד הַשַּׁבָּת,] [On Pesach, Shavuos and Succos— לִכְבוֹד הָרֶגֶל,] בִּשְׂכַר זֶה, הַקָּדוֹשׁ בָּרוּךְ הוּא יִשְׁמְרֵהוּ וְיַצִּילֵהוּ מִכָּל צָרָה וְצוּקָה, וּמִכָּל נֶגַע וּמַחֲלָה, וְיִשְׁלַח בְּרָכָה וְהַצְלָחָה בְּכָל מַעֲשֵׂה יָדָיו, [On Pesach, Shavuos and Succos— וְיִזְכֶּה לַעֲלוֹת לְרֶגֶל,] עִם כָּל יִשְׂרָאֵל אֶחָיו. וְנֹאמַר: אָמֵן. (Cong.— אָמֵן.)

מי שברך ליולדת (וקריאת שם)

The bracketed passage is included only at the naming of the baby.

מִי שֶׁבֵּרַךְ אֲבוֹתֵינוּ אַבְרָהָם יִצְחָק וְיַעֲקֹב, הוּא יְבָרֵךְ אֶת הָאִשָּׁה הַיּוֹלֶדֶת (new mother's name) בַּת (her father's name) וְאֶת

for a girl

בִּתָּהּ הַנּוֹלְדָה לָהּ בְּמַזָּל טוֹב, [וְיִקָּרֵא שְׁמָהּ בְּיִשְׂרָאֵל (baby's name) בַּת (baby's father's name)] בַּעֲבוּר שֶׁבַּעְלָהּ וְאָבִיהָ יִתֵּן לִצְדָקָה.* בִּשְׂכַר זֶה יְגַדְּלָהּ (לְתוֹרָה) לְחֻפָּה וּלְמַעֲשִׂים טוֹבִים. וְנֹאמַר: אָמֵן. (Cong.— אָמֵן.)

for a boy

בְּנָהּ הַנּוֹלָד לָהּ בְּמַזָּל טוֹב, בַּעֲבוּר שֶׁבַּעְלָהּ וְאָבִיו יִתֵּן לִצְדָקָה.* בִּשְׂכַר זֶה, יְגַדְּלוּ לְתוֹרָה, וּלְחֻפָּה, וּלְמַעֲשִׂים טוֹבִים. (וְיַכְנִיסוּ בִּבְרִיתוֹ שֶׁל אַבְרָהָם אָבִינוּ בִּזְמַנּוֹ) וְנֹאמַר: אָמֵן. (Cong.— אָמֵן.)

מי שברך לחולה

מִי שֶׁבֵּרַךְ אֲבוֹתֵינוּ אַבְרָהָם יִצְחָק וְיַעֲקֹב, מֹשֶׁה אַהֲרֹן דָּוִד וּשְׁלֹמֹה,

for a man

הוּא יְבָרֵךְ וִירַפֵּא אֶת הַחוֹלֶה (patient's name) בֶּן (mother's name) בַּעֲבוּר שֶׁ(name of supplicant) יִתֵּן לִצְדָקָה* בַּעֲבוּרוֹ.°° בִּשְׂכַר זֶה, הַקָּדוֹשׁ בָּרוּךְ הוּא יִמָּלֵא רַחֲמִים עָלָיו, לְהַחֲלִימוֹ וּלְרַפֹּאתוֹ וּלְהַחֲזִיקוֹ וּלְהַחֲיוֹתוֹ, וְיִשְׁלַח לוֹ מְהֵרָה רְפוּאָה שְׁלֵמָה מִן הַשָּׁמַיִם, לִרְמַ״ח אֵבָרָיו, וּשְׁסָ״ה גִּידָיו, בְּתוֹךְ שְׁאָר חוֹלֵי יִשְׂרָאֵל, רְפוּאַת הַנֶּפֶשׁ, וּרְפוּאַת הַגּוּף,

for a woman

הוּא יְבָרֵךְ וִירַפֵּא אֶת הַחוֹלָה (patient's name) בַּת (mother's name) בַּעֲבוּר שֶׁ(name of supplicant) יִתֵּן לִצְדָקָה* בַּעֲבוּרָהּ.°° בִּשְׂכַר זֶה, הַקָּדוֹשׁ בָּרוּךְ הוּא יִמָּלֵא רַחֲמִים עָלֶיהָ, לְהַחֲלִימָהּ וּלְרַפֹּאתָהּ וּלְהַחֲזִיקָהּ וּלְהַחֲיוֹתָהּ, וְיִשְׁלַח לָהּ מְהֵרָה רְפוּאָה שְׁלֵמָה מִן הַשָּׁמַיִם, לְכָל אֵבָרֶיהָ, וּלְכָל גִּידֶיהָ, בְּתוֹךְ שְׁאָר חוֹלֵי יִשְׂרָאֵל, רְפוּאַת הַנֶּפֶשׁ, וּרְפוּאַת הַגּוּף,

[On the Sabbath— שַׁבָּת הִיא מִלִּזְעֹק, וּרְפוּאָה קְרוֹבָה לָבֹא,]
[On a Festival— יוֹם טוֹב הוּא מִלִּזְעֹק, וּרְפוּאָה קְרוֹבָה לָבֹא,]

הַשְׁתָּא, בַּעֲגָלָא וּבִזְמַן קָרִיב. וְנֹאמַר: אָמֵן. (Cong.— אָמֵן.)

°°Many congregations substitute:
בַּעֲבוּר שֶׁכָּל הַקָּהָל מִתְפַּלְּלִים בַּעֲבוּרוֹ (בַּעֲבוּרָהּ)

PRAYER FOR THE OLEH

מִי שֶׁבֵּרַךְ *He Who blessed our forefathers Abraham, Isaac, and Jacob — may He bless* (Hebrew name) *son of* (father's Hebrew name) *because he has come up to the Torah in honor of the Omnipresent, in honor of the Torah, [in honor of the Sabbath/in honor of the pilgrimage festival]. As reward for this, may the Holy One, Blessed is He, protect him and rescue him from every trouble and distress, from every plague and illness; and may He send blessing and success in his every endeavor* (on Pesach, Shavuos and Succos add: *and may he be privileged to ascend to Jerusalem for the pilgrimage*) *together with all Israel, his brethren. Now let us respond: Amen.* (Cong.— *Amen.*)

PRAYER FOR MOTHER AND NEWBORN CHILD (AND NAMING A BABY GIRL)

The bracketed passage is included only at the naming of the baby.

מִי שֶׁבֵּרַךְ *He Who blessed our forefathers Abraham, Isaac, and Jacob — may He bless the woman who has given birth* (new mother's *Hebrew name*) *daughter of* (her father's Hebrew name) *with her*

for a girl

daughter who has been born at an auspicious time, [and may her name be called in Israel (baby's Hebrew name) *daughter of* (baby's father's Hebrew name)*] for her husband, the infant's father, will contribute to charity* on their behalf. In reward for this, may they raise her to (Torah), marriage and good deeds. Now let us respond: Amen.* (Cong.— *Amen.*)

for a boy

son who has been born at an auspicious time, for her husband, the infant's father, will contribute to charity on their behalf. In reward for this may they raise him to Torah, chupah, and good deeds (and bring him into the covenant of Abraham, our forefather, in the proper time). Now let us respond: Amen.* (Cong.— *Amen.*)

PRAYER FOR A SICK PERSON

מִי שֶׁבֵּרַךְ *He Who blessed our forefathers Abraham, Isaac and Jacob, Moses and Aaron, David and Solomon — may He bless and heal the sick person* (patient's Hebrew name) *son/daughter of* (patient's mother's Hebrew name) *because* (name of supplicant) *will contribute to charity on*

for a man

his behalf.°° In reward for this, may the Holy One, Blessed is He, be filled with compassion for him to restore his health, to heal him, to strengthen him, and to revivify him. And may He send him speedily a complete recovery from heaven for his two hundred forty-eight organs and three hundred sixty-five blood vessels,

for a woman

her behalf.°° In reward for this, may the Holy One, Blessed is He, be filled with compassion for her to restore her health, to heal her, to strengthen her, and to revivify her. And may He send her speedily a complete recovery from heaven for all her organs and all her blood vessels,

among the other sick people of Israel, a recovery of the body and a recovery of the spirit (on the Sabbath and Festivals add: *though the Sabbath/Festival prohibits us from crying out, may a recovery come speedily*)*, swiftly and soon. Now let us respond: Amen.* (Cong.— *Amen.*)

°°Many congregations substitute:

because the entire congregation prays for him (her)

מִי שֶׁבֵּרַךְ / He Who blessed

בַּעֲבוּר שֶׁיִּתֵּן לִצְדָקָה — *For ... will contribute to charity.* The custom of blessing those who ascend to read from the Torah is centuries old, and it has become customary for these blessings

מי שברך לחילי צה"ל

מִי שֶׁבֵּרַךְ אֲבוֹתֵינוּ אַבְרָהָם יִצְחָק וְיַעֲקֹב, הוּא יְבָרֵךְ אֶת חַיָּלֵי צְבָא הֲגַנָּה לְיִשְׂרָאֵל, הָעוֹמְדִים עַל מִשְׁמַר אַרְצֵנוּ וְעָרֵי אֱלֹהֵינוּ, מִגְּבוּל הַלְּבָנוֹן וְעַד מִדְבַּר מִצְרַיִם, וּמִן הַיָּם הַגָּדוֹל עַד לְבוֹא הָעֲרָבָה, בַּיַּבָּשָׁה בָּאֲוִיר וּבַיָּם. יִתֵּן יהוה אֶת אוֹיְבֵינוּ הַקָּמִים עָלֵינוּ נִגָּפִים לִפְנֵיהֶם. הַקָּדוֹשׁ בָּרוּךְ הוּא יִשְׁמֹר וְיַצִּיל אֶת חַיָּלֵינוּ מִכָּל צָרָה וְצוּקָה, וּמִכָּל נֶגַע וּמַחֲלָה, וְיִשְׁלַח בְּרָכָה וְהַצְלָחָה בְּכָל מַעֲשֵׂה יְדֵיהֶם. יַדְבֵּר שׂוֹנְאֵינוּ תַּחְתֵּיהֶם, וִיעַטְּרֵם בְּכֶתֶר יְשׁוּעָה וּבַעֲטֶרֶת נִצָּחוֹן. וִיקֻיַּם בָּהֶם הַכָּתוּב: כִּי יהוה אֱלֹהֵיכֶם הַהֹלֵךְ עִמָּכֶם, לְהִלָּחֵם לָכֶם עִם אֹיְבֵיכֶם לְהוֹשִׁיעַ אֶתְכֶם. וְנֹאמַר: אָמֵן. (—Cong. אָמֵן.)

ברכת הגומל

The following is recited by one who has survived a dangerous situation. See p. 142.

בָּרוּךְ אַתָּה יהוה אֱלֹהֵינוּ מֶלֶךְ הָעוֹלָם, הַגּוֹמֵל לְחַיָּבִים* טוֹבוֹת, שֶׁגְּמָלַנִי כָּל טוֹב.

Congregation responds:

אָמֵן. מִי שֶׁגְּמָלְךָ כָּל טוֹב, הוּא יִגְמָלְךָ כָּל טוֹב, סֶלָה.

ברוך שפטרני

After a *bar mitzvah* boy completes his first *aliyah,* his father recites the following. See p. 145.

בָּרוּךְ (אַתָּה יהוה אֱלֹהֵינוּ מֶלֶךְ הָעוֹלָם), שֶׁפְּטָרַנִי מֵעָנְשׁוֹ* שֶׁלָּזֶה.

When the Torah reading has been completed the reader recites חֲצִי קַדִּישׁ, Half-*Kaddish** (p. 138). Then the Torah is raised for all to see. Each person looks at the Torah and recites aloud:

וְזֹאת הַתּוֹרָה* אֲשֶׁר שָׂם מֹשֶׁה לִפְנֵי בְּנֵי יִשְׂרָאֵל,[1] עַל פִּי יהוה בְּיַד מֹשֶׁה.[2]

Some add the following verses:

עֵץ חַיִּים הִיא לַמַּחֲזִיקִים בָּהּ, וְתֹמְכֶיהָ מְאֻשָּׁר.[3] דְּרָכֶיהָ דַרְכֵי נֹעַם, וְכָל נְתִיבוֹתֶיהָ שָׁלוֹם.[4] אֹרֶךְ יָמִים בִּימִינָהּ, בִּשְׂמֹאלָהּ עֹשֶׁר וְכָבוֹד.[5] יהוה חָפֵץ לְמַעַן צִדְקוֹ, יַגְדִּיל תּוֹרָה וְיַאְדִּיר.[6]

---

to include pledges to charitable causes. Although the formula most often used is בַּעֲבוּר שֶׁנָּדַר, *for he has pledged,* it is preferable to use the formula בַּעֲבוּר שֶׁיִּתֵּן, *for he will contribute.* This is based on the Talmudic teaching *(Beitzah* 36b) that it is improper to make certain types of monetary pledges on Festivals, and this latter formula does not have the status of a vow. Variations of the מִי שֶׁבֵּרַךְ blessing express prayers for the congregation as a whole or individual members of it, sick people, or new mothers and their infants. In all cases, the concept behind the prayer is that the merit of the Torah reading and of the person who has read from it is a source of blessing.

חֲצִי קַדִּישׁ ☙ — *Half*-Kaddish. Half-*Kaddish* is recited after the Torah reading is completed to signify that this unit of the service is over. On days when someone is called to *Maftir,* the Half-Kaddish is recited *before* his reading because, as explained below, the *Maftir* and *Haftarah* are not

PRAYER FOR MEMBERS OF THE ISRAEL DEFENSE FORCE

מִי שֶׁבֵּרַךְ *He Who blessed our forefathers Abraham, Isaac and Jacob — may He bless the fighters of the Israel Defense Force, who stand guard over our land and the cities of our God from the border of the Lebanon to the desert of Egypt, and from the Great Sea unto the approach of the Arabah, on the land, in the air, and on the sea. May* Hashem *cause the enemies who rise up against us to be struck down before them. May the Holy One, Blessed is He, preserve and rescue our fighting men from every trouble and distress and from every plague and illness, and may He send blessing and success in their every endeavor. May He lead our enemies under their sway and may He grant them salvation and crown them with victory. And may there be fulfilled for them the verse: For it is* Hashem, *your God, Who goes with you to battle your enemies for you to save you. Now let us respond: Amen.*

THANKSGIVING BLESSING

The following is recited by one who has survived a dangerous situation. See p. 142.

בָּרוּךְ *Blessed are You* Hashem, *King of the universe, Who bestows good things upon the guilty,* Who has bestowed every goodness upon me.*

Congregation responds:

Amen. May He Who has bestowed goodness upon you continue to bestow every goodness upon you forever.

BAR MITZVAH BLESSING

After a *bar mitzvah* boy completes his first *aliyah,* his father recites the following. See p. 145.

בָּרוּךְ *Blessed is the One (are You,* Hashem, *our God, King of the universe) Who has freed me from the punishment* due this boy.*

When the Torah reading has been completed the reader recites Half-*Kaddish* (p. 138). Then the Torah is raised for all to see. Each person looks at the Torah and recites aloud:

This is the Torah* that Moses placed before the Children of Israel,[1] upon the command of Hashem, through Moses' hand.[2]

Some add the following verses:

עֵץ *It is a tree of life for those who grasp it, and its supporters are praiseworthy.*[3] *Its ways are ways of pleasantness and all its paths are peace.*[4] *Lengthy days are at its right; at its left are wealth and honor.*[5] Hashem *desired, for the sake of its [Israel's] righteousness, that the Torah be made great and glorious.*[6]

(1) *Deuteronomy* 4:44. (2) *Numbers* 9:23. (3) *Proverbs* 3:18. (4) 3:17. (5) 3:16. (6) *Isaiah* 42:21.

part of the Torah reading as it was originally instituted. However, on fast days when the third person called to the Torah is also assigned the reading of the *Haftarah, Kaddish* cannot be recited before his reading because he is one of the minimum number of readers. Also, when the Torah reading immediately precedes *Shemoneh Esrei,* i.e., when the Torah is read at *Minchah,* the Half-*Kaddish* is recited after the Torah is returned to the Ark.

וְזֹאת הַתּוֹרָה — *This is the Torah.* As the congregation looks at the words and columns of the unrolled, upheld Torah Scroll, it declares the

ברכות ההפטרה

After the Torah Scroll has been tied and covered the *Maftir* recites the *Haftarah* blessings.

בָּרוּךְ אַתָּה יהוה אֱלֹהֵינוּ מֶלֶךְ הָעוֹלָם, אֲשֶׁר בָּחַר בִּנְבִיאִים טוֹבִים,* וְרָצָה בְדִבְרֵיהֶם* הַנֶּאֱמָרִים בֶּאֱמֶת, בָּרוּךְ אַתָּה יהוה,* הַבּוֹחֵר בַּתּוֹרָה וּבְמֹשֶׁה עַבְדּוֹ, וּבְיִשְׂרָאֵל עַמּוֹ, וּבִנְבִיאֵי הָאֱמֶת וָצֶדֶק: (Cong.— אָמֵן.)

The *Haftarah* is read, after which the *oleh* recites the following blessings.

בָּרוּךְ אַתָּה יהוה אֱלֹהֵינוּ מֶלֶךְ הָעוֹלָם, צוּר כָּל הָעוֹלָמִים, צַדִּיק בְּכָל הַדּוֹרוֹת,* הָאֵל הַנֶּאֱמָן הָאוֹמֵר וְעֹשֶׂה, הַמְּדַבֵּר וּמְקַיֵּם, שֶׁכָּל דְּבָרָיו אֱמֶת וָצֶדֶק. נֶאֱמָן* אַתָּה הוּא יהוה אֱלֹהֵינוּ, וְנֶאֱמָנִים דְּבָרֶיךָ, וְדָבָר אֶחָד מִדְּבָרֶיךָ אָחוֹר לֹא יָשׁוּב רֵיקָם, כִּי אֵל מֶלֶךְ נֶאֱמָן (וְרַחֲמָן) אָתָּה. בָּרוּךְ אַתָּה יהוה, הָאֵל הַנֶּאֱמָן בְּכָל דְּבָרָיו. (Cong.— אָמֵן.)

רַחֵם עַל צִיּוֹן* כִּי הִיא בֵּית חַיֵּינוּ, וְלַעֲלוּבַת נֶפֶשׁ תּוֹשִׁיעַ בִּמְהֵרָה בְיָמֵינוּ. בָּרוּךְ אַתָּה יהוה, מְשַׂמֵּחַ צִיּוֹן בְּבָנֶיהָ. (Cong.— אָמֵן.)

שַׂמְּחֵנוּ יהוה אֱלֹהֵינוּ בְּאֵלִיָּהוּ הַנָּבִיא עַבְדֶּךָ, וּבְמַלְכוּת בֵּית דָּוִד* מְשִׁיחֶךָ, בִּמְהֵרָה יָבֹא וְיָגֵל לִבֵּנוּ, עַל

---

cardinal tenet of faith that the Torah now in our hands is the same one that God transmitted to Moses.

◆§ The Haftarah

The practice of reading from the Prophets — today known as the *Haftarah* — was introduced during the reign of the infamous Syrian-Greek King Antiochus, who ruled and persecuted Israel prior to the time of the Chanukah miracle [165 B.C.E.]. In his attempts to rid the Jewish people of their religion, he forbade the public reading from the Torah. Unable to refresh their spiritual thirst from the Torah itself, the people resorted to readings from the Prophets, calling seven people to read at least three verses each. Later, when the ban was lifted, the people retained their custom of having someone read from the Prophets. However, in order not to let it seem as though the reading from the Prophets had equal standing with the reading from the Torah, the Sages decreed that the person reading the *Haftarah* must first read a portion from the Torah. The *Haftarah* selection is always one that is related to the subject of the weekly Torah reading or the festival or event being celebrated.

The word *Haftarah* comes from פטר, *to dismiss*, to *complete*. The dessert of a meal is known in the Talmud as *haftarah* because it is the end of the meal, just as the Prophetic reading completes the Torah reading part of the service. The person doing this 'completing,' therefore, is called the *Maftir*.

Generally, the last group of verses from the week's Torah reading are read for the *Maftir* and the *Haftarah* is on a subject related to the Torah portion. On festivals and other special days, the *Maftir* portion is read from a second Torah scroll, on a topic related to the particular day. The *Haftarah*, too, is related to the theme of the day. [See *Orach Chaim* 284.]

◆§ Blessing before the Haftarah

The theme of the *Haftarah* blessings is the integrity of the prophets and their teachings. The person called up as *Maftir* recites a total of seven

BLESSINGS OF THE HAFTARAH

After the Torah Scroll has been tied and covered the *Maftir* recites the *Haftarah* blessings.

בָּרוּךְ *Blessed are You, HASHEM, our God, King of the universe, Who has chosen good prophets* and was pleased with their words that were uttered with truth. Blessed are You, HASHEM,* Who chooses the Torah; Moses, His servant; Israel, His nation; and the prophets of truth and righteousness.* (Cong.— *Amen.)*

The *Haftarah* is read, after which the *Maftir* recites the following blessings.

בָּרוּךְ *Blessed are You, HASHEM, our God, King of the universe, Rock of all eternities, Righteous in all generations,* the trustworthy God, Who says and does, Who speaks and fulfills, all of Whose words are true and righteous. Trustworthy* are You HASHEM, our God, and trustworthy are Your words, not one of Your words is turned back to its origin unfulfilled, for You are God, trustworthy (and compassionate) King. Blessed are You, HASHEM, the God Who is trustworthy in all His words.* (Cong.— *Amen.)*

רַחֵם *Have mercy on Zion* for it is the source of our life; to the one who is deeply humiliated bring salvation speedily, in our days. Blessed are You, HASHEM, Who gladdens Zion through her children.* (Cong.— *Amen.)*

שַׂמְּחֵנוּ *Gladden us, HASHEM, our God, with Elijah the prophet, Your servant, and with the kingdom of the House of David,* Your anointed, may he come speedily and cause our heart to exult. On his*

---

blessings — two for the Torah reading, one before the *Haftarah* and four after the *Haftarah* — corresponding to the seven people who are required to read from the Torah.

בִּנְבִיאִים טוֹבִים — *Good prophets.* They are good to the Jewish people, even when it is their mission to criticize and threaten. Also, they are chosen because they are *good* people: learned, righteous, impressive, and so on. Our tradition does not accept prophets who had been lacking in any of the attributes of Jewish greatness.

וְרָצָה בְדִבְרֵיהֶם — *And was pleased with their words.* The words of the prophets are as authoritative to us as the Torah itself. Alternatively, God is especially pleased (a) with the prophecies of Israel's future good; (b) that the prophets adhere scrupulously to His mission; and (c) with what the prophets do on their own initiative.

בָּרוּךְ אַתָּה ה' — *Blessed are You HASHEM.* Not a new blessing, this is a summing up of the previous points: God has chosen the Torah, which owes its authority to our absolute faith in the prophecy of Moses (see the seventh Principle of Faith, p. 178), and gave it Israel, whom He instructs and chastises through His truthful and righteous prophets.

◆§ Blessings after the Haftarah

צַדִּיק בְּכָל הַדּוֹרוֹת — *Righteous in all generations.* Whether a generation enjoys good fortune or suffers tragic oppression, God is righteous and His judgments are justified.

נֶאֱמָן — *Trustworthy.* Although in most *siddurim* it is printed as a new paragraph, this is not the beginning of a new blessing. The reason for the new paragraph is that in ancient times congregations would insert optional praises at this point *(Abudraham; Machzor Vitry).*

רַחֵם עַל צִיּוֹן — *Have mercy on Zion.* The holiness of the Temple on Mount Zion is the source of our spiritual life. Exiled and without it, we are humiliated. Without her children, Zion, too, is despondent.

בְּאֵלִיָּהוּ ... בֵּית דָּוִד — *With Elijah ... the House of David.* Elijah will be the herald of the Messiah, a descendant of the Davidic dynasty.

כִּסְאוֹ לֹא יֵשֶׁב זָר וְלֹא יִנְחֲלוּ עוֹד אֲחֵרִים אֶת כְּבוֹדוֹ, כִּי בְשֵׁם קָדְשְׁךָ נִשְׁבַּעְתָּ לּוֹ, שֶׁלֹּא יִכְבֶּה נֵרוֹ לְעוֹלָם וָעֶד. בָּרוּךְ אַתָּה יהוה, מָגֵן דָּוִד.* (.אָמֵן —Cong.)

[ON FAST DAYS THE *HAFTARAH* BLESSINGS END HERE.]

On an ordinary Sabbath (including the Sabbath of Chol HaMoed Pesach) continue:°

עַל הַתּוֹרָה,* וְעַל הָעֲבוֹדָה, וְעַל הַנְּבִיאִים, וְעַל יוֹם הַשַּׁבָּת הַזֶּה, שֶׁנָּתַתָּ לָּנוּ יהוה אֱלֹהֵינוּ, לִקְדֻשָּׁה וְלִמְנוּחָה, לְכָבוֹד וּלְתִפְאָרֶת. עַל הַכֹּל יהוה אֱלֹהֵינוּ, אֲנַחְנוּ מוֹדִים לָךְ, וּמְבָרְכִים אוֹתָךְ, יִתְבָּרַךְ שִׁמְךָ בְּפִי כָּל חַי תָּמִיד לְעוֹלָם וָעֶד. בָּרוּךְ אַתָּה יהוה, מְקַדֵּשׁ הַשַּׁבָּת. (.אָמֵן —Cong.)

°On a Festival and on a Sabbath that coincides with a Festival (including the Sabbath of Chol HaMoed Succos) continue here (the words in brackets are inserted on the Sabbath):

עַל הַתּוֹרָה, וְעַל הָעֲבוֹדָה, וְעַל הַנְּבִיאִים וְעַל יוֹם [הַשַּׁבָּת הַזֶּה וְיוֹם]

On Pesach	On Shavuos	On Succos	On Shemini Atzeres/Simchas Torah
חַג הַמַּצּוֹת	חַג הַשָּׁבֻעוֹת	חַג הַסֻּכּוֹת	הַשְּׁמִינִי חַג הָעֲצֶרֶת

הַזֶּה, שֶׁנָּתַתָּ לָּנוּ יהוה אֱלֹהֵינוּ, [לִקְדֻשָּׁה וְלִמְנוּחָה] לְשָׂשׂוֹן וּלְשִׂמְחָה, לְכָבוֹד וּלְתִפְאָרֶת. עַל הַכֹּל יהוה אֱלֹהֵינוּ, אֲנַחְנוּ מוֹדִים לָךְ, וּמְבָרְכִים אוֹתָךְ, יִתְבָּרַךְ שִׁמְךָ בְּפִי כָּל חַי תָּמִיד לְעוֹלָם וָעֶד. בָּרוּךְ אַתָּה יהוה, מְקַדֵּשׁ [הַשַּׁבָּת וְ]יִשְׂרָאֵל וְהַזְּמַנִּים. (.אָמֵן —Cong.)

יקום פרקן

On every Sabbath of the year continue with יְקוּם פֻּרְקָן (below).
On a weekday Festival (except when *Yizkor* is recited) continue with יָהּ אֵלִי (p. 672),
followed by אַשְׁרֵי (p. 456).
On the final day of Pesach, of Shavuos, and on Shemini Atzeres,
Yizkor (p. 810) is recited (on the Sabbath, after יְקוּם פֻּרְקָן).

יְקוּם פֻּרְקָן* מִן שְׁמַיָּא, חִנָּא וְחִסְדָּא וְרַחֲמֵי, וְחַיֵּי אֲרִיכֵי, וּמְזוֹנֵי רְוִיחֵי, וְסִיַּעְתָּא דִשְׁמַיָּא, וּבַרְיוּת גּוּפָא, וּנְהוֹרָא מַעַלְיָא, זַרְעָא חַיָּא וְקַיָּמָא, זַרְעָא דִּי לָא יִפְסוּק וְדִי לָא יִבְטוּל מִפִּתְגָּמֵי אוֹרַיְתָא. לְמָרָנָן וְרַבָּנָן חֲבוּרָתָא קַדִּישָׁתָא דִּי

מָגֵן דָּוִד — *Shield of David.* In *II Samuel* (22:36) and *Psalms* (18:36), David praised God for shielding him against defeat.

עַל הַתּוֹרָה — *For the Torah.* This final blessing sums up the entire Torah reading service: not only the reading from the Prophets, but also the Torah reading, the prayers and the holiness of the Sabbath or Festival day.

יְקוּם פֻּרְקָן — *May salvation arise.* Very fittingly, the reading from the Torah is followed by a series of prayers for those who uphold the Torah — by teaching, study, and support, and

*throne let no stranger sit nor let others continue to inherit his honor, for by Your holy Name You swore to him that his heir will not be extinguished forever and ever. Blessed are You, HASHEM, Shield of David.** (Cong.— *Amen.*)

[ON FAST DAYS THE *HAFTARAH* BLESSINGS END HERE.]

On an ordinary Sabbath (including the Sabbath of Chol HaMoed Pesach) continue:°

עַל הַתּוֹרָה *For the Torah reading, for the prayer service, for the reading from the Prophets and for this Sabbath day that You, HASHEM, our God, have given us for holiness and contentment, for glory and splendor — for all this, HASHEM, our God, we gratefully thank You and bless You. May Your Name be blessed by the mouth of all the living always, for all eternity. Blessed are You, HASHEM, Who sanctifies the Sabbath.* (Cong.—*Amen.*)

°On a Festival and on a Sabbath that coincides with a Festival (including the Sabbath of Chol HaMoed Succos) continue here (the words in brackets are inserted on the Sabbath):

For the Torah reading, for the prayer service, for the reading from the Prophets, and for this [Sabbath day and this] day of the

On Pesach	On Shavuos	On Succos	On Shemini Atzeres/Simchas Torah
Festival of Matzos	*Shavuos Festival*	*Succos Festival*	*Shemini Atzeres Festival*

that You, HASHEM, our God, have given us [for holiness and contentment] for gladness and joy, for glory and splendor. For all this, HASHEM, our God, we gratefully thank You and bless You. May Your Name be blessed by the mouth of all the living, always, for all eternity. Blessed are You, HASHEM, Who sanctifies [the Sabbath], Israel and the festival seasons.

(Cong.— *Amen.*)

YEKUM PURKAN

On every Sabbath of the year continue with יְקוּם פֻּרְקָן, *Yekum Purkan* (below).
On a weekday Festival (except when *Yizkor* is recited) continue with יָהּ אֵלִי, *Kah Keili* (p. 672) followed by אַשְׁרֵי, *Ashrei* (p. 456).
On the final day of Pesach, of Shavuos, and on Shemini Atzeres, *Yizkor* (p. 810) is recited (on the Sabbath, after *Yekum Purkan*).

יְקוּם פֻּרְקָן *May salvation arise* from heaven — grace, kindness, compassion, long life, abundant sustenance, heavenly assistance, physical health, lofty vision, living and surviving offspring, offspring who will neither interrupt nor cease from words of the Torah — for our masters and sages, the holy fellowships that*

---

especially by undertaking the difficult responsibilities of leadership. The first יְקוּם פֻּרְקָן is a general prayer for all such people wherever they may be; consequently, it is recited even by people praying alone at home. The second יְקוּם פֻּרְקָן and the מִי שֶׁבֵּרַךְ are prayers for the congregation with which one is praying; consequently someone praying alone does not recite those two prayers. The two יְקוּם פֻּרְקָן prayers were composed by the Babylonian *geonim* after the close of the Talmudic period; therefore they were written in Aramaic, the

בְּאַרְעָא דְיִשְׂרָאֵל וְדִי בְּבָבֶל,* לְרֵישֵׁי כַלֵּי,* וּלְרֵישֵׁי גַלְוָתָא,* וּלְרֵישֵׁי מְתִיבָתָא, וּלְדַיָּנֵי דִי בָבָא,* לְכָל תַּלְמִידֵיהוֹן, וּלְכָל תַּלְמִידֵי תַלְמִידֵיהוֹן, וּלְכָל מָן דְּעָסְקִין בְּאוֹרַיְתָא. מַלְכָּא דְעָלְמָא יְבָרֵךְ יַתְהוֹן, יַפִּישׁ חַיֵּיהוֹן, וְיַסְגֵּא יוֹמֵיהוֹן, וְיִתֵּן אַרְכָה לִשְׁנֵיהוֹן, וְיִתְפָּרְקוּן וְיִשְׁתֵּזְבוּן מִן כָּל עָקָא וּמִן כָּל מַרְעִין בִּישִׁין. מָרָן דִּי בִשְׁמַיָּא יְהֵא בְסַעְדְּהוֹן, כָּל זְמַן וְעִדָּן. וְנֹאמַר: אָמֵן. (Cong.— אָמֵן.)

The next two paragraphs are only recited when praying with a congregation. An individual praying alone omits them.

יְקוּם פֻּרְקָן* מִן שְׁמַיָּא, חִנָּא וְחִסְדָּא וְרַחֲמֵי, וְחַיֵּי אֲרִיכֵי, וּמְזוֹנֵי רְוִיחֵי, וְסִיַּעְתָּא דִשְׁמַיָּא, וּבַרְיוּת גּוּפָא, וּנְהוֹרָא מַעַלְיָא, זַרְעָא חַיָּא וְקַיָּמָא, זַרְעָא דִּי לָא יִפְסוּק וְדִי לָא יִבְטוּל מִפִּתְגָּמֵי אוֹרַיְתָא. לְכָל קְהָלָא קַדִּישָׁא הָדֵין, רַבְרְבַיָּא עִם זְעֵרַיָּא, טַפְלָא וּנְשַׁיָּא, מַלְכָּא דְעָלְמָא יְבָרֵךְ יַתְכוֹן, יַפִּישׁ חַיֵּיכוֹן, וְיַסְגֵּא יוֹמֵיכוֹן, וְיִתֵּן אַרְכָה לִשְׁנֵיכוֹן, וְתִתְפָּרְקוּן וְתִשְׁתֵּזְבוּן מִן כָּל עָקָא וּמִן כָּל מַרְעִין בִּישִׁין, מָרָן דִּי בִשְׁמַיָּא יְהֵא בְסַעְדְּכוֹן, כָּל זְמַן וְעִדָּן. וְנֹאמַר: אָמֵן. (Cong.— אָמֵן.)

מִי שֶׁבֵּרַךְ* אֲבוֹתֵינוּ אַבְרָהָם יִצְחָק וְיַעֲקֹב, הוּא יְבָרֵךְ אֶת כָּל הַקָּהָל הַקָּדוֹשׁ הַזֶּה, עִם כָּל קְהִלּוֹת הַקֹּדֶשׁ, הֵם, וּנְשֵׁיהֶם, וּבְנֵיהֶם, וּבְנוֹתֵיהֶם, וְכָל אֲשֶׁר לָהֶם. וּמִי שֶׁמְּיַחֲדִים בָּתֵּי כְנֵסִיּוֹת לִתְפִלָּה, וּמִי שֶׁבָּאִים בְּתוֹכָם לְהִתְפַּלֵּל, וּמִי שֶׁנּוֹתְנִים נֵר לַמָּאוֹר, וְיַיִן לְקִדּוּשׁ וּלְהַבְדָּלָה, וּפַת לָאוֹרְחִים, וּצְדָקָה לָעֲנִיִּים, וְכָל מִי שֶׁעוֹסְקִים בְּצָרְכֵי צִבּוּר בֶּאֱמוּנָה, הַקָּדוֹשׁ בָּרוּךְ הוּא יְשַׁלֵּם שְׂכָרָם, וְיָסִיר מֵהֶם כָּל מַחֲלָה, וְיִרְפָּא לְכָל גּוּפָם, וְיִסְלַח לְכָל עֲוֹנָם, וְיִשְׁלַח בְּרָכָה וְהַצְלָחָה בְּכָל מַעֲשֵׂה יְדֵיהֶם, עִם כָּל יִשְׂרָאֵל אֲחֵיהֶם. וְנֹאמַר: אָמֵן. (Cong.— אָמֵן.)

---

spoken language of the country. These prayers were instituted specifically for the Sabbath; not for Festivals, except those that fall on the Sabbath.

דִּי בְאַרְעָא דְיִשְׂרָאֵל וְדִי בְּבָבֶל — *That are in Eretz Yisrael and that are in the Diaspora* [lit. *Babylonia*]. Although the Jewish community in *Eretz Yisrael* at that time was comparatively insignificant, the *geonim* gave honor and precedence to the Holy Land. The original text of the prayer has been maintained throughout the centuries of exile — even when the great masses of Jewry no longer lived in Babylonia. By extension, however, this timeless prayer refers to all Jewish communities; the word Babylonia is a general term for all Jewish communities outside of *Eretz Yisrael.*

לְרֵישֵׁי כַלֵּי — *The leaders of the Torah*

are in Eretz Yisrael and that are in the Diaspora: for the leaders of the Torah assemblages,* the leaders of the exile communities,* the leaders of the academies, the judges at the gateways,* and all their students and to all the students of their students, and to everyone who engages in Torah study. May the King of the universe bless them, make their lives fruitful, increase their days and grant length to their years. May He save them and rescue them from every distress and from all serious ailments. May the Master in heaven come to their assistance at every season and time. Now let us respond: Amen.* (Cong.—*Amen.*)

The next two paragraphs are only recited when praying with a congregation. An individual praying alone omits them.

יְקוּם פֻּרְקָן *May salvation arise* from heaven — grace, kindness, compassion, long life, abundant sustenance, heavenly assistance, physical health, lofty vision, living and surviving offspring, offspring who will neither interrupt nor cease from the words of the Torah — to this entire holy congregation, adults along with children, infants and women. May the King of the universe bless you, make your lives fruitful, increase your days, and grant length to your years. May He save you and rescue you from every distress and from all serious ailments. May the Master in heaven come to your assistance at every season and time. Now let us respond: Amen.* (Cong.—*Amen.*)

מִי שֶׁבֵּרַךְ *He Who blessed* our forefathers, Abraham, Isaac, and Jacob — may He bless this entire holy congregation along with all the holy congregations; them, their wives, sons, and daughters and all that is theirs; and those who dedicate synagogues for prayer and those who enter them to pray, and those who give lamps for illumination and wine for Kiddush and Havdalah, bread for guests and charity for the poor; and all who are involved faithfully in the needs of the community — may the Holy One, Blessed is He, pay their reward and remove from them every affliction, heal their entire body and forgive their every iniquity, and send blessing and success to all their handiwork, along with all Israel, their brethren. And let us say: Amen.* (Cong.—*Amen.*)

---

assemblages. These were the scholars who delivered Torah lectures on Sabbaths and Festivals to mass gatherings of the people.

לְרֵישֵׁי גַלְוָתָא — *The leaders of the exile communities.* The רֵישׁ גָּלוּתָא, *Exilarch,* was the leader of the Jewish nation, equivalent to the *Nassi* in earlier times. His headquarters was in Babylonia.

וּלְדַיָּנֵי דִי בָבָא — *The judges at the gateways.* In ancient times, courts were usually headquartered at the city gates, because they were the centers of commerce and social activity — the places where disputes would tend to arise.

יְקוּם פֻּרְקָן — *May salvation arise.* This prayer is virtually identical to the previous one with one difference: This one refers specifically to the congregation with whom one is praying. Therefore it omits mention of national teachers and leaders, and it is written in the second person. It also mentions all segments of the congregation, young and old, man and woman, because it prays for the welfare of each member of the community.

מִי שֶׁבֵּרַךְ — *He Who blessed.* This is a prayer

תפלה בעד שלום המדינה

הַנּוֹתֵן תְּשׁוּעָה לַמְּלָכִים וּמֶמְשָׁלָה לַנְּסִיכִים, מַלְכוּתוֹ מַלְכוּת כָּל עוֹלָמִים, הַפּוֹצֶה אֶת דָּוִד עַבְדּוֹ מֵחֶרֶב רָעָה, הַנּוֹתֵן בַּיָּם דֶּרֶךְ וּבְמַיִם עַזִּים נְתִיבָה, הוּא יְבָרֵךְ אֶת הַנָּשִׂיא וְאֶת מִשְׁנֵהוּ וְאֶת כָּל שָׂרֵי הַמְּדִינוֹת הָאֵלּוּ.

מֶלֶךְ מַלְכֵי הַמְּלָכִים, בְּרַחֲמָיו יְחַיֵּם וְיִשְׁמְרֵם, וּמִכָּל צָרָה וְיָגוֹן וָנֶזֶק יַצִּילֵם. וְיִתֵּן בְּלִבָּם וּבְלֵב כָּל יוֹעֲצֵיהֶם וְשָׂרֵיהֶם לַעֲשׂוֹת טוֹבוֹת עִמָּנוּ וְעִם כָּל יִשְׂרָאֵל אַחֵינוּ. בִּימֵיהֶם וּבְיָמֵינוּ תִּוָּשַׁע יְהוּדָה, וְיִשְׂרָאֵל יִשְׁכּוֹן לָבֶטַח. וּבָא לְצִיּוֹן גּוֹאֵל. וְכֵן יְהִי רָצוֹן. וְנֹאמַר: אָמֵן. (.Cong—אָמֵן.)

תפלה בעד שלום מדינת ישראל

אָבִינוּ שֶׁבַּשָּׁמַיִם, צוּר יִשְׂרָאֵל וְגוֹאֲלוֹ, בָּרֵךְ אֶת מְדִינַת יִשְׂרָאֵל, רֵאשִׁית צְמִיחַת גְּאֻלָּתֵנוּ. הָגֵן עָלֶיהָ בְּאֶבְרַת חַסְדֶּךָ, וּפְרֹשׂ עָלֶיהָ סֻכַּת שְׁלוֹמֶךָ, וּשְׁלַח אוֹרְךָ וַאֲמִתְּךָ לְרָאשֶׁיהָ שָׂרֶיהָ וְיוֹעֲצֶיהָ, וְתַקְּנֵם בְּעֵצָה טוֹבָה מִלְּפָנֶיךָ. חַזֵּק אֶת יְדֵי מְגִנֵּי אֶרֶץ קָדְשֵׁנוּ, וְהַנְחִילֵם אֱלֹהֵינוּ יְשׁוּעָה, וַעֲטֶרֶת נִצָּחוֹן תְּעַטְּרֵם, וְנָתַתָּ שָׁלוֹם בָּאָרֶץ וְשִׂמְחַת עוֹלָם לְיוֹשְׁבֶיהָ.

וְאֶת אַחֵינוּ כָּל בֵּית יִשְׂרָאֵל, פְּקָד נָא בְּכָל אַרְצוֹת פְּזוּרֵיהֶם, וְתוֹלִיכֵם מְהֵרָה קוֹמְמִיּוּת לְצִיּוֹן עִירֶךָ, וְלִירוּשָׁלַיִם מִשְׁכַּן שְׁמֶךָ, כַּכָּתוּב בְּתוֹרַת מֹשֶׁה עַבְדֶּךָ: אִם יִהְיֶה נִדַּחֲךָ בִּקְצֵה הַשָּׁמָיִם, מִשָּׁם יְקַבֶּצְךָ יהוה אֱלֹהֶיךָ, וּמִשָּׁם יִקָּחֶךָ. וֶהֱבִיאֲךָ יהוה אֱלֹהֶיךָ אֶל הָאָרֶץ אֲשֶׁר יָרְשׁוּ אֲבֹתֶיךָ וִירִשְׁתָּהּ, וְהֵיטִבְךָ וְהִרְבְּךָ מֵאֲבֹתֶיךָ.[1]

וְיַחֵד לְבָבֵנוּ לְאַהֲבָה וּלְיִרְאָה אֶת שְׁמֶךָ, וְלִשְׁמֹר אֶת כָּל דִּבְרֵי תוֹרָתֶךָ, וּשְׁלַח לָנוּ מְהֵרָה בֶּן דָּוִד מְשִׁיחַ צִדְקֶךָ, לִפְדּוֹת מְחַכֵּי קֵץ יְשׁוּעָתֶךָ.

וְהוֹפַע בַּהֲדַר גְּאוֹן עֻזֶּךָ, עַל כָּל יוֹשְׁבֵי תֵבֵל אַרְצֶךָ, וְיֹאמַר כֹּל אֲשֶׁר נְשָׁמָה בְאַפּוֹ: יהוה אֱלֹהֵי יִשְׂרָאֵל מֶלֶךְ, וּמַלְכוּתוֹ בַּכֹּל מָשָׁלָה. אָמֵן, סֶלָה.

---

that God bless this and all other congregations. It also singles out the people who provide the means and services for the general good. *Bais Yosef* (284) notes that these charitable causes are

PRAYER FOR THE WELFARE OF THE GOVERNMENT

הַנּוֹתֵן *He Who grants salvation to kings and dominion to rulers, Whose kingdom is a kingdom spanning all eternities; Who releases David, His servant, from the evil sword; Who places a road in the sea and a path in the mighty waters — may He bless the President, the Vice President, and all the constituted officers of government of this land.*

The King Who reigns over kings, in His mercy may He sustain them and protect them; from every trouble, woe and injury, may He rescue them; and put into their heart and into the heart of all their counselors compassion to do good with us and with all Israel, our brethren. In their days and in ours, may Judah be saved and may Israel dwell securely, and may the Redeemer come to Zion. So may it be His will. Now let us respond: Amen. (Cong.— *Amen.*)

PRAYER FOR THE WELFARE OF THE STATE OF ISRAEL

אָבִינוּ *Our Father in heaven, Protector and Redeemer of Israel, bless the State of Israel, the first flowering of our redemption. Shield her beneath the wings of Your kindness, and spread over her Your canopy of peace. Send Your light and truth to her leaders, officers and counselors, and direct them with Your good counsel. Strengthen the defenders of our Holy Land; grant them salvation; crown them with victory. Establish peace in the land and everlasting joy for its inhabitants.*

Remember our brothers, the whole House of Israel, in all the lands of their dispersion. Speedily bring them to Zion, Your city, to Jerusalem, Your dwelling place, as it is written in the Torah of Moses, Your servant: Even if your outcasts are at the ends of the world, from there HASHEM, *your God, will gather you, from there He will fetch you. And* HASHEM, *your God, will bring you to the land which your fathers occupied, and you shall occupy it; and He will make you more prosperous and more numerous than your fathers.*[1]

Unite our hearts to love and revere Your Name and to observe all the precepts of Your Torah. Speedily send us Your righteous Messiah of the House of David to redeem those who long for Your salvation.

Reflect Your glorious majesty upon all the inhabitants of the Earth and let everyone who breathes declare: HASHEM, *God of Israel, is King and His dominion rules over all. Amen. Selah.*

(1) *Deuteronomy* 30:4-5.

---

stressed so that the entire community will hear how great is the reward of those who study Torah and provide for others. Knowing this, others will emulate their deeds.

ברכת החודש

On the Sabbath preceding Rosh Chodesh, a special blessing for the new month is recited. The *chazzan* stands at the *bimah* and he or a congregant next to him holds the Torah Scroll.

The congregation, standing, recites יְהִי רָצוֹן, which is then repeated by the *chazzan*.

יְהִי רָצוֹן* מִלְּפָנֶיךָ, יהוה אֱלֹהֵינוּ וֵאלֹהֵי אֲבוֹתֵינוּ, שֶׁתְּחַדֵּשׁ עָלֵינוּ אֶת הַחֹדֶשׁ הַזֶּה לְטוֹבָה וְלִבְרָכָה. וְתִתֶּן לָנוּ חַיִּים אֲרוּכִים, חַיִּים שֶׁל שָׁלוֹם, חַיִּים שֶׁל טוֹבָה, חַיִּים שֶׁל בְּרָכָה, חַיִּים שֶׁל פַּרְנָסָה, חַיִּים שֶׁל חִלּוּץ עֲצָמוֹת, חַיִּים שֶׁיֵּשׁ בָּהֶם יִרְאַת שָׁמַיִם וְיִרְאַת חֵטְא,* חַיִּים שֶׁאֵין בָּהֶם בּוּשָׁה וּכְלִמָּה, חַיִּים שֶׁל עֹשֶׁר וְכָבוֹד, חַיִּים שֶׁתְּהֵא בָנוּ אַהֲבַת תּוֹרָה וְיִרְאַת שָׁמַיִם,* חַיִּים שֶׁיִּמָּלְאוּ מִשְׁאֲלוֹת לִבֵּנוּ לְטוֹבָה. אָמֵן, סֶלָה.

The congregation is informed of the *molad** and then recites מִי שֶׁעָשָׂה, after which the *chazzan* takes the Torah Scroll in his arms and repeats:

מִי שֶׁעָשָׂה נִסִּים* לַאֲבוֹתֵינוּ, וְגָאַל אוֹתָם מֵעַבְדוּת לְחֵרוּת, הוּא יִגְאַל אוֹתָנוּ בְּקָרוֹב, וִיקַבֵּץ נִדָּחֵינוּ מֵאַרְבַּע כַּנְפוֹת הָאָרֶץ, חֲבֵרִים כָּל יִשְׂרָאֵל. וְנֹאמַר: אָמֵן.

Chazzan then congregation:

רֹאשׁ חֹדֶשׁ (name of month) יִהְיֶה בְּיוֹם* (day of the week°)
הַבָּא עָלֵינוּ וְעַל כָּל יִשְׂרָאֵל לְטוֹבָה.

°If Rosh Chodesh is on Sunday, insert the word רִאשׁוֹן; Monday, שֵׁנִי; Tuesday, שְׁלִישִׁי; Wednesday, רְבִיעִי; Thursday, חֲמִישִׁי; Friday, שִׁשִּׁי; Saturday, שַׁבַּת קֹדֶשׁ.
If Rosh Chodesh is two days this formula is substituted: Sunday, Monday, בְּיוֹם רִאשׁוֹן וּבְיוֹם שֵׁנִי; Monday, Tuesday, בְּיוֹם שֵׁנִי וּבְיוֹם שְׁלִישִׁי; Tuesday, Wednesday, בְּיוֹם שְׁלִישִׁי וּבְיוֹם רְבִיעִי; Wednesday, Thursday, בְּיוֹם רְבִיעִי וּבְיוֹם חֲמִישִׁי; Thursday, Friday, בְּיוֹם חֲמִישִׁי וּבְיוֹם שִׁשִּׁי; Friday, Sabbath, בְּיוֹם שִׁשִּׁי וּבְיוֹם שַׁבַּת קֹדֶשׁ; Sabbath, Sunday, בְּיוֹם שַׁבַּת קֹדֶשׁ וּלְמָחֳרָתוֹ בְּיוֹם רִאשׁוֹן.

Congregation then *chazzan:*

יְחַדְּשֵׁהוּ הַקָּדוֹשׁ בָּרוּךְ הוּא עָלֵינוּ וְעַל כָּל עַמּוֹ בֵּית יִשְׂרָאֵל, לְחַיִּים וּלְשָׁלוֹם, לְשָׂשׂוֹן וּלְשִׂמְחָה, לִישׁוּעָה וּלְנֶחָמָה. וְנֹאמַר: אָמֵן.

בִּרְכַּת הַחֹדֶשׁ / Blessing of the New Month

On the Sabbath before the new month begins, we pray that it be a good and blessed month for all Israel. The purpose of this blessing is not to sanctify the month as was done in ancient times; that task was the sole prerogative of the *Beis Din.* Rather, this blessing is intended to inform the congregation of the date of Rosh Chodesh, so that the people will keep track of the calendar. It is done on the Sabbath simply because that is when the greatest number of people are congregated.

It is customary to stand during this ritual in commemoration of the sanctification of the *Beis Din,* during which everyone stood (*Magen Avraham* 417:1).

יְהִי רָצוֹן — *May it be Your will.* With minor variations, this is the prayer that the Talmudic sage Rav used to recite at the conclusion of his *Shemoneh Esrei* (*Berachos* 16b). Since it contains a full gamut of people's spiritual and physical needs, the phrase 'that You inaugurate this month upon us' was added so that the prayer could serve as our supplication for a blessed new month.

יִרְאַת שָׁמַיִם וְיִרְאַת חֵטְא — *Fear of heaven and fear*

❧ BLESSING OF THE NEW MONTH ☙

On the Sabbath preceding Rosh Chodesh, a special blessing for the new month is recited. The *chazzan* stands at the *bimah* and he or a congregant next to him holds the Torah Scroll.

Congregation, standing, recites יְהִי רָצוֹן, *May it be Your will ...,* which is repeated by the *chazzan*.

יְהִי רָצוֹן *May it be Your will,* HASHEM, our God and the God of our forefathers, that You inaugurate this month upon us for goodness and for blessing. May You give us long life — a life of peace, a life of goodness, a life of blessing, a life of sustenance, a life of physical health, a life in which there is fear of heaven and fear of sin,* a life in which there is no shame nor humiliation, a life of wealth and honor, a life in which we will have love of Torah and fear of heaven,* a life in which our heartfelt requests will be fulfilled for the good. Amen, Selah.*

The congregation is informed of the *molad** and then recites מִי שֶׁעָשָׂה, *He Who performed miracles ...,* after which the *chazzan* takes the Torah Scroll in his arms and repeats:

מִי שֶׁעָשָׂה *He Who performed miracles* for our forefathers and redeemed them from slavery to freedom — may He redeem us soon and gather in our dispersed from the four corners of the earth; all Israel becoming comrades. Now let us respond: Amen.*

Chazzan then congregation:

The new month (name of month) *will be on the* (day of the week) *day* which is coming to us and all Israel for goodness.*

Congregation then *chazzan:*

יְחַדְּשֵׁהוּ *May the Holy One, Blessed is He, renew it upon us and upon all His people, the Family of Israel, for life and for peace, for joy and for gladness, for salvation and for consolation. Now let us respond: Amen.*

---

of sin. In Rav's prayer, the phrase *fear of heaven* does not appear at this point. The reason for its inclusion may be that 'fear of heaven' adds a dimension to 'fear of sin.' *Fear of heaven* refers to the shame one should feel at the very thought that he could contemplate sin against God. *Fear of sin* represents the disgust someone should feel at the thought that he could defile himself with the spiritual filth of sin. Thus, these two concepts complement one another.

אַהֲבַת תּוֹרָה וְיִרְאַת שָׁמַיִם — *Love of Torah and fear of heaven.* Knowledge and appreciation of Torah enhances a person's feeling of reverence and awe of God.

⁂ Announcement of the Molad

It is customary — but not obligatory — to announce the precise time at which the new moon begins to appear in Jerusalem. The time, following the ancient tradition, gives the hour, minute and *chelek* [literally *portion;* one-eighteenth of a minute, or 3⅓ seconds].

It is noteworthy that Rosh Chodesh was the first commandment given to Israel as a nation and that its observance was prohibited by the Syrian-Greek King Antiochus and by the Romans, respectively, when they ruled *Eretz Yisrael.* The cycle of the moon is symbolic of renewal and it teaches that Israel's glory may fade and disappear, but the nation will always re-emerge and grow to fullness, as does the moon. Thus, the sanctification of the month by the *Beis Din* and the monthly blessing of the new month in all Jewish congregations are events of inspiration and significance.

⁂ מִי שֶׁעָשָׂה נִסִּים — *He Who performed miracles.* Since the *mitzvah* of Rosh Chodesh and its symbolism of national renewal are related to the Exodus and every Jewish redemption, the blessing of the new month is, in effect, a prayer for the sequence of salvation. As given in this prayer, that sequence is a miraculous deliverance from oppression and an ingathering of exiles climaxed by Jewish unity, 'all Israel becoming comrades.' Only then can the final Redemption come.

יִהְיֶה בְּיוֹם — *Will be on the ... day.* The day of the week is not given as 'Sunday', 'Monday', etc., but as 'the first day', 'the second day', etc., in

On the last day of each Festival and on Yom Kippur, *Yizkor*, p. 810, is recited at this point.

In many congregations אֵל מָלֵא רַחֲמִים is recited at this point for those who have passed away during the year and, in many congregations, for those whose *yahrzeit* falls during the coming week. The one reciting the prayer holds or touches the Torah while doing so.

אֵל מָלֵא רַחֲמִים, שׁוֹכֵן בַּמְּרוֹמִים, הַמְצֵא מְנוּחָה נְכוֹנָה עַל כַּנְפֵי הַשְּׁכִינָה, בְּמַעֲלוֹת קְדוֹשִׁים וּטְהוֹרִים כְּזֹהַר הָרָקִיעַ מַזְהִירִים,

for a man

אֶת נִשְׁמַת (name of deceased) בֶּן (his father's name) שֶׁהָלַךְ לְעוֹלָמוֹ, בַּעֲבוּר שֶׁ(name of supplicant) יִתֵּן צְדָקָה בְּעַד הַזְכָּרַת נִשְׁמָתוֹ, בְּגַן עֵדֶן תְּהֵא מְנוּחָתוֹ, לָכֵן בַּעַל הָרַחֲמִים יַסְתִּירֵהוּ בְּסֵתֶר כְּנָפָיו לְעוֹלָמִים, וְיִצְרוֹר בִּצְרוֹר הַחַיִּים אֶת נִשְׁמָתוֹ, יהוה הוּא נַחֲלָתוֹ, וְיָנוּחַ בְּשָׁלוֹם עַל מִשְׁכָּבוֹ, וְנֹאמַר: אָמֵן. (Cong.— אָמֵן.)

for a woman

אֶת נִשְׁמַת (name of deceased) בַּת (her father's name) שֶׁהָלְכָה לְעוֹלָמָהּ, בַּעֲבוּר שֶׁ(name of supplicant) יִתֵּן צְדָקָה בְּעַד הַזְכָּרַת נִשְׁמָתָהּ, בְּגַן עֵדֶן תְּהֵא מְנוּחָתָהּ, לָכֵן בַּעַל הָרַחֲמִים יַסְתִּירֶהָ בְּסֵתֶר כְּנָפָיו לְעוֹלָמִים, וְיִצְרוֹר בִּצְרוֹר הַחַיִּים אֶת נִשְׁמָתָהּ, יהוה הוּא נַחֲלָתָהּ, וְתָנוּחַ בְּשָׁלוֹם עַל מִשְׁכָּבָהּ, וְנֹאמַר: אָמֵן. (Cong.— אָמֵן.)

Except on certain festive Sabbaths described in the commentary, the following prayer, in memory of the departed, is recited.

אַב הָרַחֲמִים,* שׁוֹכֵן מְרוֹמִים, בְּרַחֲמָיו הָעֲצוּמִים הוּא יִפְקוֹד בְּרַחֲמִים, הַחֲסִידִים וְהַיְּשָׁרִים וְהַתְּמִימִים, קְהִלּוֹת הַקֹּדֶשׁ שֶׁמָּסְרוּ נַפְשָׁם עַל קְדֻשַּׁת הַשֵּׁם, הַנֶּאֱהָבִים וְהַנְּעִימִים בְּחַיֵּיהֶם, וּבְמוֹתָם לֹא נִפְרָדוּ. מִנְּשָׁרִים קַלּוּ, וּמֵאֲרָיוֹת גָּבֵרוּ, לַעֲשׂוֹת רְצוֹן קוֹנָם וְחֵפֶץ צוּרָם. יִזְכְּרֵם אֱלֹהֵינוּ לְטוֹבָה, עִם שְׁאָר צַדִּיקֵי עוֹלָם, וְיִנְקוֹם* לְעֵינֵינוּ נִקְמַת דַּם עֲבָדָיו הַשָּׁפוּךְ, כַּכָּתוּב בְּתוֹרַת מֹשֶׁה אִישׁ הָאֱלֹהִים: הַרְנִינוּ גוֹיִם עַמּוֹ כִּי דַם עֲבָדָיו יִקּוֹם, וְנָקָם יָשִׁיב לְצָרָיו, וְכִפֶּר אַדְמָתוֹ עַמּוֹ.[1] וְעַל יְדֵי עֲבָדֶיךָ הַנְּבִיאִים כָּתוּב לֵאמֹר: וְנִקֵּיתִי דָּמָם לֹא נִקֵּיתִי, וַיהוה שֹׁכֵן בְּצִיּוֹן.[2] וּבְכִתְבֵי הַקֹּדֶשׁ נֶאֱמַר: לָמָּה יֹאמְרוּ הַגּוֹיִם, אַיֵּה אֱלֹהֵיהֶם, יִוָּדַע בַּגּוֹיִם לְעֵינֵינוּ, נִקְמַת

---

fulfillment of the Torah's command to always remember the Sabbath. By counting the days of the week with references to the Sabbath we tie our existence to the Sabbath. This is in sharp contrast to the non-Jewish custom of assigning names to the days in commemoration of events or gods, such as Sunday for the sun, Monday for the moon and so on *(Ramban, Exodus* 20:8).

אַב הָרַחֲמִים — *Father of compassion.* This is a memorial prayer, as the text makes clear, for the martyrs who died to sanctify God's Name. The halachic basis for this memorial is explained by *Levush* (Ch. 284): The Sabbath is a day of complete rest and a semblance of the World to Come, a day on which the dead have respite from judgment and punishment. Therefore, it is proper that prayers be said for the peace of their souls. As a general rule, the memorial prayer is omitted on occasions when *Tachanun* would not be said on weekdays, but there are any number of varying customs in this matter and each

On the last day of each Festival and on Yom Kippur, *Yizkor*, p. 810, is recited at this point.

In many congregations אֵל מָלֵא רַחֲמִים, *'O God, full of mercy,'* is recited at this point for those who have passed away during the year and, in many congregations, for those whose *yahrzeit* falls during the coming week. The one reciting the prayer holds or touches the Torah while doing so.

אֵל *O God, full of mercy, Who dwells on high, grant proper rest on the wings of the Divine Presence — in the lofty levels of the holy and the pure ones, who shine like the glow of the firmament — for the soul of*

for a man

(name of deceased) *son of* (name of his father)*, who went on to his world, for* (name of supplicant) *will contribute to charity in remembrance of his soul. May his resting place be in the Garden of Eden — therefore may the Master of mercy shelter him in the shelter of His wings for eternity; and may He bind his soul in the Bond of Life.* HASHEM *is his heritage, and may he repose in peace on his resting place. Now let us respond: Amen.* (Cong.— *Amen.*)

for a woman

(name of deceased) *daughter of* (name of her father)*, who went on to her world, for* (name of supplicant) *will contribute to charity in remembrance of her soul. May her resting place be in the Garden of Eden — therefore may the Master of mercy shelter her in the shelter of His wings for eternity; and may He bind her soul in the Bond of Life.* HASHEM *is her heritage, and may she repose in peace on her resting place. Now let us respond: Amen.* (Cong.— *Amen.*)

Except on certain festive Sabbaths described in the commentary, the following prayer, in memory of the departed, is recited.

אַב הָרַחֲמִים *Father of compassion,* Who dwells on high, in His powerful compassion may He recall with compassion the devout, the upright, and the perfect ones; the holy congregations who gave their lives for the Sanctification of the Name — who were beloved and pleasant in their lifetime and in their death were not parted [from God]. They were quicker than eagles and stronger than lions to do their Creator's will and their Rock's desire. May our God remember them for good with the other righteous of the world. May He, before our eyes, exact retribution* for the spilled blood of His servants, as is written in the Torah of Moses, the man of God: 'O nations, sing the praise of His people for He will avenge the blood of His servants and He will bring retribution upon His foes; and He will appease His land and His people.'*[1] *And by Your servants, the prophets, is written saying: 'Though I cleanse [the enemy] — their bloodshed I will not cleanse when* HASHEM *dwells in Zion.'*[2] *And in the Holy Writings it is said: "Why should the nations say, 'Where is their God?' Let there be known among the nations, before our eyes, revenge for*

(1) *Deuteronomy* 32:43. (2) *Joel* 4:21.

---

congregation should follow its own practice. During *Sefirah*, however, all agree that אַב הָרַחֲמִים is recited even on Sabbaths when it would ordinarily be omitted, because many bloody massacres took place during that period in the time of the Crusades. Here, too, there are varying customs, and each congregation should follow its own.

וְיִנְקוֹם — *May He exact retribution.* We do not

דַּם עֲבָדֶיךָ הַשָּׁפוּךְ.[1] וְאוֹמֵר: כִּי דֹרֵשׁ דָּמִים אוֹתָם זָכָר, לֹא שָׁכַח צַעֲקַת עֲנָוִים.[2] וְאוֹמֵר: יָדִין בַּגּוֹיִם* מָלֵא גְוִיּוֹת, מָחַץ רֹאשׁ עַל אֶרֶץ רַבָּה. מִנַּחַל בַּדֶּרֶךְ יִשְׁתֶּה, עַל כֵּן יָרִים רֹאשׁ.[3]

אַשְׁרֵי יוֹשְׁבֵי בֵיתֶךָ, עוֹד יְהַלְלוּךָ סֶּלָה.[4] אַשְׁרֵי הָעָם שֶׁכָּכָה לּוֹ, אַשְׁרֵי הָעָם שֶׁיהוה אֱלֹהָיו.[5]

תהלים קמה

תְּהִלָּה לְדָוִד,

אֲרוֹמִמְךָ אֱלוֹהַי הַמֶּלֶךְ, וַאֲבָרְכָה שִׁמְךָ לְעוֹלָם וָעֶד.
בְּכָל יוֹם אֲבָרְכֶךָּ, וַאֲהַלְלָה שִׁמְךָ לְעוֹלָם וָעֶד.
גָּדוֹל יהוה וּמְהֻלָּל מְאֹד, וְלִגְדֻלָּתוֹ אֵין חֵקֶר.
דּוֹר לְדוֹר יְשַׁבַּח מַעֲשֶׂיךָ, וּגְבוּרֹתֶיךָ יַגִּידוּ.
הֲדַר כְּבוֹד הוֹדֶךָ, וְדִבְרֵי נִפְלְאֹתֶיךָ אָשִׂיחָה.
וֶעֱזוּז נוֹרְאוֹתֶיךָ יֹאמֵרוּ, וּגְדוּלָּתְךָ אֲסַפְּרֶנָּה.
זֵכֶר רַב טוּבְךָ יַבִּיעוּ, וְצִדְקָתְךָ יְרַנֵּנוּ.
חַנּוּן וְרַחוּם יהוה, אֶרֶךְ אַפַּיִם וּגְדָל חָסֶד.
טוֹב יהוה לַכֹּל, וְרַחֲמָיו עַל כָּל מַעֲשָׂיו.
יוֹדוּךָ יהוה כָּל מַעֲשֶׂיךָ, וַחֲסִידֶיךָ יְבָרְכוּכָה.
כְּבוֹד מַלְכוּתְךָ יֹאמֵרוּ, וּגְבוּרָתְךָ יְדַבֵּרוּ.
לְהוֹדִיעַ לִבְנֵי הָאָדָם גְּבוּרֹתָיו, וּכְבוֹד הֲדַר מַלְכוּתוֹ.
מַלְכוּתְךָ מַלְכוּת כָּל עֹלָמִים, וּמֶמְשַׁלְתְּךָ בְּכָל דּוֹר וָדֹר.
סוֹמֵךְ יהוה לְכָל הַנֹּפְלִים, וְזוֹקֵף לְכָל הַכְּפוּפִים.
עֵינֵי כֹל אֵלֶיךָ יְשַׂבֵּרוּ, וְאַתָּה נוֹתֵן לָהֶם אֶת אָכְלָם בְּעִתּוֹ.
פּוֹתֵחַ אֶת יָדֶךָ,
וּמַשְׂבִּיעַ לְכָל חַי רָצוֹן.

While reciting the verse פּוֹתֵחַ, concentrate intently on its meaning.

צַדִּיק יהוה בְּכָל דְּרָכָיו, וְחָסִיד בְּכָל מַעֲשָׂיו.
קָרוֹב יהוה לְכָל קֹרְאָיו, לְכֹל אֲשֶׁר יִקְרָאֻהוּ בֶאֱמֶת.

יָדִין בַּגּוֹיִם — *He will judge the ... nations.* God intervenes against the nations who seek to slaughter the Jews. He turns their army into a mass of corpses and crushes their leader. Figuratively, enemy blood flows like a river from which the rescued fugitives can 'drink.' Spared from danger and shame, Israel 'may proudly lift his head.'

pray that we be strong enough to avenge our martyrs; Jews are not motivated by a lust to repay violence and murder with violence and murder. Rather we pray that God choose how and when to atone for the blood of His fallen martyrs. For the living, decency and integrity remain the primary goals of social life *(R' Hirsch).*

Your servants' spilled blood.''[1] And it says: 'For the Avenger of blood has remembered them; He has not forgotten the cry of the humble.'[2] And it says: 'He will judge the corpse-filled nations, He will crush the leader of the mighty land. From a river along the way he shall drink — therefore he may proudly lift his head.'[3]*

אַשְׁרֵי *Praiseworthy are those who dwell in Your house; may they always praise You, Selah![4] Praiseworthy is the people for whom this is so, praiseworthy is the people whose God is HASHEM.[5]*

Psalm 145

A psalm of praise by David:

א *I will exalt You, my God the King,*
and I will bless Your Name forever and ever.

ב *Every day I will bless You,*
and I will laud Your Name forever and ever.

ג *HASHEM is great and exceedingly lauded,*
and His greatness is beyond investigation.

ד *Each generation will praise Your deeds to the next*
and of Your mighty deeds they will tell.

ה *The splendrous glory of Your power*
and Your wondrous deeds I shall discuss.

ו *And of Your awesome power they will speak,*
and Your greatness I shall relate.

ז *A recollection of Your abundant goodness they will utter*
and of Your righteousness they will sing exultantly.

ח *Gracious and merciful is HASHEM,*
slow to anger, and great in [bestowing] kindness.

ט *HASHEM is good to all; His mercies are on all His works.*

י *All Your works shall thank You, HASHEM,*
and Your devout ones will bless You.

כ *Of the glory of Your kingdom they will speak,*
and of Your power they will tell;

ל *To inform human beings of His mighty deeds,*
and the glorious splendor of His kingdom.

מ *Your kingdom is a kingdom spanning all eternities,*
and Your dominion is throughout every generation.

ס *HASHEM supports all the fallen ones and straightens all the bent.*

ע *The eyes of all look to You with hope*
and You give them their food in its proper time;

פ *You open Your hand,*
and satisfy the desire
of every living thing.

While reciting the verse, *'You open ...'* concentrate intently on its meaning.

צ *Righteous is HASHEM in all His ways*
and magnanimous in all His deeds.

ק *HASHEM is close to all who call upon Him —*
to all who call upon Him sincerely.

---

(1) *Psalms* 79:10. (2) 9:13. (3) 110:6-7. (4) 84:5. (5) 144:15.

רְצוֹן יְרֵאָיו יַעֲשֶׂה, וְאֶת שַׁוְעָתָם יִשְׁמַע וְיוֹשִׁיעֵם. שׁוֹמֵר יהוה אֶת כָּל אֹהֲבָיו, וְאֵת כָּל הָרְשָׁעִים יַשְׁמִיד. ❖ תְּהִלַּת יהוה יְדַבֶּר פִּי, וִיבָרֵךְ כָּל בָּשָׂר שֵׁם קָדְשׁוֹ לְעוֹלָם וָעֶד. וַאֲנַחְנוּ נְבָרֵךְ יָהּ, מֵעַתָּה וְעַד עוֹלָם, הַלְלוּיָהּ.[1]

הכנסת ספר תורה

The *chazzan* takes the Torah in his right arm and recites:

יְהַלְלוּ אֶת שֵׁם יהוה, כִּי נִשְׂגָּב שְׁמוֹ לְבַדּוֹ —

Congregation responds:

— הוֹדוֹ עַל אֶרֶץ וְשָׁמָיִם. וַיָּרֶם קֶרֶן לְעַמּוֹ, תְּהִלָּה לְכָל חֲסִידָיו, לִבְנֵי יִשְׂרָאֵל עַם קְרֹבוֹ, הַלְלוּיָהּ.[2]

On the first Sabbath after Rosh Chodesh Cheshvan and Iyar, the *chazzan* or *gabbai* recites the following prayer for those who will fast on Monday, Thursday, and Monday (בה״ב).

מִי שֶׁבֵּרַךְ* אֲבוֹתֵינוּ אַבְרָהָם יִצְחָק וְיַעֲקֹב, מֹשֶׁה וְאַהֲרֹן, דָּוִד וּשְׁלֹמֹה, הוּא יְבָרֵךְ אֶת כָּל מִי שֶׁיְּקַבֵּל עָלָיו לְהִתְעַנּוֹת שֵׁנִי וַחֲמִישִׁי וְשֵׁנִי. בִּשְׂכַר זֶה הַקָּדוֹשׁ בָּרוּךְ הוּא יִשְׁמְרֵהוּ וְיַצִּילֵהוּ מִכָּל צָרָה וְצוּקָה, וּמִכָּל נֶגַע וּמַחֲלָה, וְיִשְׁלַח בְּרָכָה וְהַצְלָחָה בְּכָל מַעֲשֵׂה יְדֵיהֶם וִיקַבֵּל תְּפִלּוֹתֵיהֶם וְיַאֲזִין שַׁוְעוֹתֵיהֶם עִם כָּל יִשְׂרָאֵל אֲחֵיהֶם. וְנֹאמַר: אָמֵן.

As the Torah is carried to the Ark after the ordinary Sabbath morning reading, the congregation recites the following psalm. (For weekday Festivals, see next page.)

תהלים כט (commentary on p. 314)

מִזְמוֹר לְדָוִד, הָבוּ לַיהוה בְּנֵי אֵלִים, הָבוּ לַיהוה כָּבוֹד וָעֹז. הָבוּ לַיהוה כְּבוֹד שְׁמוֹ, הִשְׁתַּחֲווּ לַיהוה בְּהַדְרַת קֹדֶשׁ. קוֹל יהוה עַל הַמָּיִם, אֵל הַכָּבוֹד הִרְעִים, יהוה עַל מַיִם רַבִּים. קוֹל יהוה בַּכֹּחַ, קוֹל יהוה בֶּהָדָר. קוֹל יהוה שֹׁבֵר אֲרָזִים, וַיְשַׁבֵּר יהוה אֶת אַרְזֵי הַלְּבָנוֹן. וַיַּרְקִידֵם כְּמוֹ עֵגֶל, לְבָנוֹן וְשִׂרְיוֹן כְּמוֹ בֶן רְאֵמִים. קוֹל יהוה חֹצֵב לַהֲבוֹת אֵשׁ. קוֹל יהוה יָחִיל מִדְבָּר, יָחִיל יהוה מִדְבַּר קָדֵשׁ. ❖ קוֹל יהוה יְחוֹלֵל אַיָּלוֹת, וַיֶּחֱשֹׂף יְעָרוֹת, וּבְהֵיכָלוֹ, כֻּלּוֹ אֹמֵר כָּבוֹד. יהוה לַמַּבּוּל יָשָׁב, וַיֵּשֶׁב יהוה מֶלֶךְ לְעוֹלָם. יהוה עֹז לְעַמּוֹ יִתֵּן, יהוה יְבָרֵךְ אֶת עַמּוֹ בַשָּׁלוֹם.

מִי שֶׁבֵּרַךְ — *He Who blessed.* During the long period of festivities on Pesach and Succos, it is possible that one may have sinned due to excessive levity. (On the very brief Shavuos festival and the somber days of awe, there is no fear of this.) Consequently it is considered meritorious for righteous people to fast and repent for three days after Pesach and Succos. The days of fasting are Monday, Thursday, and Monday since those are days of judgment (see p. 124). These fasts are not observed during the festive months of Nissan and Tishrei, nor is the public prayer announcing them made during these months. They are scheduled for the following months, Cheshvan and Iyar. This prayer is recited on the first Sabbath of

ר *The will of those who fear Him He will do;*
and their cry He will hear, and save them.
ש *HASHEM protects all who love Him;*
but all the wicked He will destroy.
ת Chazzan— *May my mouth declare the praise of HASHEM*
and may all flesh bless His Holy Name forever and ever.
We will bless God from this time and forever, Halleluyah![1]

RETURNING THE TORAH

The *chazzan* takes the Torah in his right arm and recites:

Let them praise the Name of HASHEM, for His Name alone will have been exalted —

Congregation responds:

— His glory is above earth and heaven. And He will have exalted the pride of His people, causing praise for all His devout ones, for the Children of Israel, His intimate people. Halleluyah![2]

On the first Sabbath after Rosh Chodesh Cheshvan and Iyar, the *chazzan* or *gabbai* recites the following prayer for those who will fast on Monday, Thursday, and Monday.

מִי שֶׁבֵּרַךְ *He Who blessed* our forefathers, Abraham, Isaac, and Jacob, Moses and Aaron, David and Solomon — may He bless everyone who takes upon himself to fast on Monday, Thursday, and Monday. In reward for this, may the Holy One, Blessed is He, protect him and rescue him from every distress and travail and from every disease and illness, and may He send blessing and success to their every undertaking; and accept their prayers and be attentive to their cries, together with all Israel, their brethren. And let us say: Amen.*

As the Torah is carried to the Ark after the ordinary Sabbath morning reading, the Congregation recites the following psalm. (For weekday Festivals, see next page.)

Psalm 29 (commentary on p. 314).

מִזְמוֹר לְדָוִד *A psalm of David. Ascribe for HASHEM, you sons of the powerful; ascribe for HASHEM, honor and might. Ascribe for HASHEM the honor due His Name, bow to HASHEM in His intensely holy place. The voice of HASHEM is upon the waters, the God of Glory thunders, HASHEM is upon vast waters. The voice of HASHEM is in power! The voice of HASHEM is in majesty! The voice of HASHEM breaks the cedars, HASHEM shatters the cedars of Lebanon! He makes them prance about like a calf; Lebanon and Siryon like young re'eimim. The voice of HASHEM cleaves with shafts of fire. The voice of HASHEM convulses the wilderness. HASHEM convulses the wilderness of Kadesh.* Chazzan— *The voice of HASHEM frightens the hinds, and strips the forests bare; while in His Temple all proclaim, 'Glory!' HASHEM sat enthroned at the Deluge; HASHEM sits enthroned as King forever. HASHEM will give might to His people, HASHEM will bless His people with peace.*

(1) *Psalms* 115:18. (2) 148:13-14.

Cheshvan and Iyar, unless Rosh Chodesh is on the Sabbath, in which case the prayer and fasts are postponed for a week. The prayer serves a dual purpose: it invokes God's blessing on those

At all times other than Sabbath morning, the congregation recites *Psalm 24,* לְדָוִד מִזְמוֹר.

לְדָוִד מִזְמוֹר, לַיהוה הָאָרֶץ וּמְלוֹאָהּ, תֵּבֵל וְיֹשְׁבֵי בָהּ. כִּי הוּא עַל יַמִּים יְסָדָהּ, וְעַל נְהָרוֹת יְכוֹנְנֶהָ. מִי יַעֲלֶה בְהַר יהוה, וּמִי יָקוּם בִּמְקוֹם קָדְשׁוֹ. נְקִי כַפַּיִם וּבַר לֵבָב, אֲשֶׁר לֹא נָשָׂא לַשָּׁוְא נַפְשִׁי וְלֹא נִשְׁבַּע לְמִרְמָה. יִשָּׂא בְרָכָה מֵאֵת יהוה, וּצְדָקָה מֵאֱלֹהֵי יִשְׁעוֹ. זֶה דּוֹר דֹּרְשָׁיו, מְבַקְשֵׁי פָנֶיךָ, יַעֲקֹב, סֶלָה. שְׂאוּ שְׁעָרִים רָאשֵׁיכֶם, וְהִנָּשְׂאוּ פִּתְחֵי עוֹלָם, וְיָבוֹא מֶלֶךְ הַכָּבוֹד. מִי זֶה מֶלֶךְ הַכָּבוֹד, יהוה עִזּוּז וְגִבּוֹר, יהוה גִּבּוֹר מִלְחָמָה. שְׂאוּ שְׁעָרִים רָאשֵׁיכֶם, וּשְׂאוּ פִּתְחֵי עוֹלָם, וְיָבֹא מֶלֶךְ הַכָּבוֹד. מִי הוּא זֶה מֶלֶךְ הַכָּבוֹד, יהוה צְבָאוֹת הוּא מֶלֶךְ הַכָּבוֹד, סֶלָה.

As the Torah is placed into the Ark, the congregation recites the following verses:

וּבְנֻחֹה יֹאמַר,* שׁוּבָה יהוה רִבְבוֹת אַלְפֵי יִשְׂרָאֵל.[1] קוּמָה יהוה* לִמְנוּחָתֶךָ, אַתָּה וַאֲרוֹן עֻזֶּךָ. כֹּהֲנֶיךָ יִלְבְּשׁוּ צֶדֶק, וַחֲסִידֶיךָ יְרַנֵּנוּ. בַּעֲבוּר דָּוִד עַבְדֶּךָ, אַל תָּשֵׁב פְּנֵי מְשִׁיחֶךָ.[2] כִּי לֶקַח טוֹב* נָתַתִּי לָכֶם, תּוֹרָתִי אַל תַּעֲזֹבוּ.[3] ❖ עֵץ חַיִּים הִיא לַמַּחֲזִיקִים בָּהּ, וְתֹמְכֶיהָ מְאֻשָּׁר.[4] דְּרָכֶיהָ דַרְכֵי נֹעַם, וְכָל נְתִיבוֹתֶיהָ שָׁלוֹם.[5] הֲשִׁיבֵנוּ* יהוה אֵלֶיךָ וְנָשׁוּבָה, חַדֵּשׁ יָמֵינוּ כְּקֶדֶם.[6]

In the presence of a *minyan,* the *chazzan* recites חֲצִי קַדִּישׁ:

יִתְגַּדַּל וְיִתְקַדַּשׁ שְׁמֵהּ רַבָּא. (—Cong. אָמֵן.) בְּעָלְמָא דִּי בְרָא כִרְעוּתֵהּ. וְיַמְלִיךְ מַלְכוּתֵהּ, בְּחַיֵּיכוֹן וּבְיוֹמֵיכוֹן וּבְחַיֵּי דְכָל בֵּית יִשְׂרָאֵל, בַּעֲגָלָא וּבִזְמַן קָרִיב. וְאִמְרוּ: אָמֵן.

(—Cong. אָמֵן. יְהֵא שְׁמֵהּ רַבָּא מְבָרַךְ לְעָלַם וּלְעָלְמֵי עָלְמַיָּא.)

יְהֵא שְׁמֵהּ רַבָּא מְבָרַךְ לְעָלַם וּלְעָלְמֵי עָלְמַיָּא.

יִתְבָּרַךְ וְיִשְׁתַּבַּח וְיִתְפָּאַר וְיִתְרוֹמַם וְיִתְנַשֵּׂא וְיִתְהַדָּר וְיִתְעַלֶּה וְיִתְהַלָּל שְׁמֵהּ דְּקֻדְשָׁא בְּרִיךְ הוּא (—Cong. בְּרִיךְ הוּא) — °לְעֵלָּא מִן כָּל (°לְעֵלָּא וּלְעֵלָּא מִכָּל —From Rosh Hashanah to Yom Kippur substitute) בִּרְכָתָא וְשִׁירָתָא תֻּשְׁבְּחָתָא וְנֶחֱמָתָא, דַּאֲמִירָן בְּעָלְמָא. וְאִמְרוּ: אָמֵן. (—Cong. אָמֵן.)

On an ordinary Sabbath and Sabbath-Rosh Chodesh, continue with *Mussaf,* next page. On Festivals and Chol HaMoed (even when they fall on the Sabbath) recite the Festival *Mussaf,* p. 674.

---

who will fast, and it serves as their formal acceptance upon themselves of the obligation by responding *Amen* to the prayer; but if one does not intend to fast, his *Amen* does not constitute an obligation.

☙ **וּבְנֻחֹה יֹאמַר** — *And when it rested he would say.* This is the companion verse to וַיְהִי בִּנְסֹעַ הָאָרֹן, *When the Ark would travel,* above (p. 432), which Moses said when the Ark began to journey. When it came to rest, he expressed this hope that God's Presence would find comfortable repose among the multitudes of the Jewish people; in other words, that Israel should be worthy of being host to God's holiness.

The rest of this paragraph is a selection of

At all times other than Sabbath morning, the congregation recites *Psalm* 24.

לְדָוִד *Of David a psalm.* HASHEM*'s is the earth and its fullness, the inhabited land and those who dwell in it. For He founded it upon seas, and established it upon rivers. Who may ascend the mountain of* HASHEM*, and who may stand in the place of His sanctity? One with clean hands and pure heart, who has not sworn in vain by My soul and has not sworn deceitfully. He will receive a blessing from* HASHEM *and just kindness from the God of his salvation. This is the generation of those who seek Him, those who strive for Your Presence — Jacob, Selah. Raise up your heads, O gates, and be uplifted, you everlasting entrances, so that the King of Glory may enter. Who is this King of Glory? —* HASHEM*, the mighty and strong,* HASHEM*, the strong in battle. Raise up your heads, O gates, and raise up, you everlasting entrances, so that the King of Glory may enter. Who then is the King of Glory?* HASHEM*, Master of Legions, He is the King of Glory. Selah!*

As the Torah is placed into the Ark, the congregation recites the following verses:

וּבְנֻחֹה *And when it rested he would say,* 'Return* HASHEM *to the myriad thousands of Israel.'*[1] *Arise,* HASHEM*,* to Your resting place, You and the Ark of Your strength. Let Your priests be clothed in righteousness, and Your devout ones will sing joyously. For the sake of David, Your servant, turn not away the face of Your anointed.*[2] *For I have given you a good teaching,* do not forsake My Torah.*[3] Chazzan— *It is a tree of life for those who grasp it, and its supporters are praiseworthy.*[4] *Its ways are ways of pleasantness and all its paths are peace.*[5] *Bring us back* to You,* HASHEM*, and we shall return, renew our days as of old.*[6]

In the presence of a *minyan,* the *chazzan* recites Half-*Kaddish.*

יִתְגַּדַּל *May His great Name grow exalted and sanctified* (Cong.— *Amen.*) *in the world that He created as He willed. May He give reign to His kingship in your lifetimes and in your days, and in the lifetimes of the entire Family of Israel, swiftly and soon. Now respond: Amen.*

(Cong.— *Amen. May His great Name be blessed forever and ever.*)

May His great Name be blessed forever and ever.

Blessed, praised, glorified, exalted, extolled, mighty, upraised, and lauded be the Name of the Holy One, Blessed is He (Cong.— *Blessed is He*) — (From Rosh Hashanah to Yom Kippur add: *exceedingly*) *beyond any blessing and song, praise and consolation that are uttered in the world. Now respond: Amen.* (Cong.— *Amen.*)

On an ordinary Sabbath and Sabbath-Rosh Chodesh, continue with *Mussaf,* next page. On Festivals and Chol HaMoed (even when they fall on the Sabbath) recite the Festival *Mussaf,* p. 674.

(1) *Numbers* 10:36. (2) *Psalms* 132:8-10. (3) *Proverbs* 4:2. (4) 3:18. (5) 3:17. (6) *Lamentations* 5:21.

verses from Scripture on the themes of a resting place for God's Law, the greatness of the Torah, and the hope that God will see fit to draw us closer to His service.

קוּמָה ה׳ — *Arise,* HASHEM. The following three verses were recited by Solomon, with minor variations, when he dedicated the Temple (*II Chronicles* 6:41-42). The first verse asks that God establish His resting place among Israel. The next verse refers to the *priests* who dedicate themselves to God's service, and the Levites whose song accompanies the Temple ritual. Finally, David prayed that the site chosen for the Temple — a choice that was made by David and the prophet Nathan — not be spurned, but that it remain eternally holy (*Radak; Ibn Ezra*).

כִּי לֶקַח טוֹב — *For ... a good teaching.* The next three verses, all from *Proverbs,* are a call to Israel: The Torah is God's most precious gift. It benefits those who are loyal to it; and it results in pleasantness and peace.

הֲשִׁיבֵנוּ — *Bring us back.* Finally, the Jewish soul

מוסף לשבת ולשבת ראש חדש

Take three steps backward, then three steps forward. Remain standing with the feet together while reciting *Shemoneh Esrei*. It should be recited with quiet devotion and without any interruption, verbal or otherwise. Although it should not be audible to others, one must pray loudly enough to hear himself. See *Laws* §61-90 for a brief summary of its laws, including how to rectify the omission of phrases that are added at particular times of the year.

כִּי שֵׁם יהוה אֶקְרָא, הָבוּ גֹדֶל לֵאלֹהֵינוּ.[1]
אֲדֹנָי שְׂפָתַי תִּפְתָּח, וּפִי יַגִּיד תְּהִלָּתֶךָ.[2]

אבות

Bend the knees at בָּרוּךְ; bow at אַתָּה; straighten up at ה׳.

בָּרוּךְ אַתָּה יהוה אֱלֹהֵינוּ וֵאלֹהֵי אֲבוֹתֵינוּ, אֱלֹהֵי אַבְרָהָם, אֱלֹהֵי יִצְחָק, וֵאלֹהֵי יַעֲקֹב, הָאֵל הַגָּדוֹל הַגִּבּוֹר וְהַנּוֹרָא, אֵל עֶלְיוֹן, גּוֹמֵל חֲסָדִים טוֹבִים וְקוֹנֵה הַכֹּל, וְזוֹכֵר חַסְדֵי אָבוֹת, וּמֵבִיא גוֹאֵל לִבְנֵי בְנֵיהֶם, לְמַעַן שְׁמוֹ בְּאַהֲבָה.

From Rosh Hashanah to Yom Kippur add:

זָכְרֵנוּ לְחַיִּים, מֶלֶךְ חָפֵץ בַּחַיִּים, וְכָתְבֵנוּ בְּסֵפֶר הַחַיִּים, לְמַעַנְךָ אֱלֹהִים חַיִּים.

[If forgotten, do not repeat *Shemoneh Esrei*. See *Laws* §61.]

Bend the knees at בָּרוּךְ; bow at אַתָּה; straighten up at ה׳.

מֶלֶךְ עוֹזֵר וּמוֹשִׁיעַ וּמָגֵן. בָּרוּךְ אַתָּה יהוה, מָגֵן אַבְרָהָם.

גבורות

אַתָּה גִּבּוֹר לְעוֹלָם אֲדֹנָי, מְחַיֵּה מֵתִים אַתָּה, רַב לְהוֹשִׁיעַ.

Between Shemini Atzeres and Pesach add:

מַשִּׁיב הָרוּחַ וּמוֹרִיד הַגֶּשֶׁם.

[If forgotten, see *Laws* §70-75.]

מְכַלְכֵּל חַיִּים בְּחֶסֶד, מְחַיֵּה מֵתִים בְּרַחֲמִים רַבִּים, סוֹמֵךְ נוֹפְלִים, וְרוֹפֵא חוֹלִים, וּמַתִּיר אֲסוּרִים, וּמְקַיֵּם אֱמוּנָתוֹ לִישֵׁנֵי עָפָר. מִי כָמוֹךָ בַּעַל גְּבוּרוֹת, וּמִי דּוֹמֶה לָּךְ, מֶלֶךְ מֵמִית וּמְחַיֶּה וּמַצְמִיחַ יְשׁוּעָה.

From Rosh Hashanah to Yom Kippur add:

מִי כָמוֹךָ אַב הָרַחֲמִים, זוֹכֵר יְצוּרָיו לְחַיִּים בְּרַחֲמִים.

[If forgotten, do not repeat *Shemoneh Esrei*. See *Laws* §61.]

וְנֶאֱמָן אַתָּה לְהַחֲיוֹת מֵתִים. בָּרוּךְ אַתָּה יהוה, מְחַיֵּה הַמֵּתִים.

---

cries out that it wants to find its way back to the spiritual greatness of yore. If only God will help us begin, we will continue with alacrity.

Mussaf

Shacharis and *Minchah* respectively are in place of the morning and afternoon *tamid* (continual) Temple offerings. The *Mussaf* [lit. additional] prayer commemorates the special communal offerings that were brought in the Temple on days of enhanced holiness (*Numbers* ch. 28 and 29). These additions to the daily

MUSSAF FOR SABBATH AND SABBATH-ROSH CHODESH

Take three steps backward, then three steps forward. Remain standing with the feet together while reciting *Shemoneh Esrei.* It should be recited with quiet devotion and without any interruption, verbal or otherwise. Although it should not be audible to others, one must pray loudly enough to hear himself. See *Laws* §61-90 for a brief summary of its laws, including how to rectify the omission of phrases that are added at particular times of the year.

When I call out the Name of HASHEM, ascribe greatness to our God.[1]
My Lord, open my lips, that my mouth may declare Your praise.[2]

PATRIARCHS

Bend the knees at *'Blessed'*; bow at *'You'*; straighten up at *'HASHEM'*.

בָּרוּךְ *Blessed are You, HASHEM, our God and the God of our forefathers, God of Abraham, God of Isaac, and God of Jacob; the great, mighty, and awesome God, the supreme God, Who bestows beneficial kindnesses and creates everything, Who recalls the kindnesses of the Patriarchs and brings a Redeemer to their children's children, for His Name's sake, with love.*

From Rosh Hashanah to Yom Kippur add the following.
Remember us for life, O King Who desires life,
and inscribe us in the Book of Life — for Your sake, O Living God.
[If forgotten, do not repeat *Shemoneh Esrei.* See *Laws* §61.]

Bend the knees at *'Blessed'*; bow at *'You'*; straighten up at *'HASHEM'*.

O King, Helper, Savior, and Shield. Blessed are You, HASHEM, Shield of Abraham.

GOD'S MIGHT

אַתָּה *You are eternally mighty, my Lord, the Resuscitator of the dead are You; abundantly able to save.*

Between Shemini Atzeres and Pesach add the following.
He makes the wind blow and He makes the rain descend.
[If forgotten, see *Laws* §70-75.]

He sustains the living with kindness, resuscitates the dead with abundant mercy, supports the fallen, heals the sick, releases the confined, and maintains His faith to those asleep in the dust. Who is like You, O Master of mighty deeds, and who is comparable to You, O King Who causes death and restores life and makes salvation sprout!

From Rosh Hashanah to Yom Kippur add the following.
Who is like You, Merciful Father, Who recalls His creatures mercifully for life!
[If forgotten, do not repeat *Shemoneh Esrei.* See *Laws* §61.]

And You are faithful to resuscitate the dead. Blessed are You, HASHEM, Who resuscitates the dead.

(1) *Deuteronomy* 32:3. (2) *Psalms* 51:17.

Temple service symbolized the added holiness and joy of the Sabbath or festival. This is reflected in the emphasis on joy that is found in the *Mussaf Shemoneh Esrei* and in the expanded version of the *Mussaf Kedushah.* The commentary to the first three blessings of *Shemoneh Esrei* may be found beginning p. 98; the last three, p. 110.

During the *chazzan's* repetition, *Kedushah* (below) is recited at this point.

קדושת השם

אַתָּה קָדוֹשׁ וְשִׁמְךָ קָדוֹשׁ, וּקְדוֹשִׁים בְּכָל יוֹם יְהַלְלוּךָ סֶּלָה. בָּרוּךְ אַתָּה יהוה, °הָאֵל הַקָּדוֹשׁ.

°הַמֶּלֶךְ הַקָּדוֹשׁ. —From Rosh Hashanah to Yom Kippur substitute
[If forgotten, repeat *Shemoneh Esrei.* See *Laws* §62-63.]

קדושה

When reciting *Kedushah,* one must stand with his feet together, and avoid any interruptions. One should rise to his toes when saying the words קָדוֹשׁ, קָדוֹשׁ, קָדוֹשׁ; בָּרוּךְ (of בָּרוּךְ כְּבוֹד); and יִמְלֹךְ.

—Cong. then *Chazzan*: **נַעֲרִיצְךָ** וְנַקְדִּישְׁךָ* כְּסוֹד שִׂיחַ שַׂרְפֵי קֹדֶשׁ, הַמַּקְדִּישִׁים שִׁמְךָ בַּקֹּדֶשׁ, כַּכָּתוּב עַל יַד נְבִיאֶךָ, וְקָרָא זֶה אֶל זֶה וְאָמַר:

—All: קָדוֹשׁ קָדוֹשׁ קָדוֹשׁ יהוה צְבָאוֹת, מְלֹא כָל הָאָרֶץ כְּבוֹדוֹ.*[1]

—Cong. then *Chazzan*: כְּבוֹדוֹ מָלֵא עוֹלָם,* מְשָׁרְתָיו שׁוֹאֲלִים זֶה לָזֶה, אַיֵּה מְקוֹם כְּבוֹדוֹ,* לְעֻמָּתָם בָּרוּךְ יֹאמֵרוּ:

—All: בָּרוּךְ כְּבוֹד יהוה, מִמְּקוֹמוֹ.[2]

—Cong. then *Chazzan*: מִמְּקוֹמוֹ הוּא יִפֶן בְּרַחֲמִים,* וְיָחוֹן עַם הַמְיַחֲדִים שְׁמוֹ, עֶרֶב וָבֹקֶר בְּכָל יוֹם תָּמִיד, פַּעֲמַיִם בְּאַהֲבָה שְׁמַע אוֹמְרִים.*

—All: שְׁמַע יִשְׂרָאֵל, יהוה אֱלֹהֵינוּ, יהוה אֶחָד.[3]

—Cong. then *Chazzan*: הוּא אֱלֹהֵינוּ,* הוּא אָבִינוּ, הוּא מַלְכֵּנוּ, הוּא מוֹשִׁיעֵנוּ, וְהוּא יַשְׁמִיעֵנוּ בְּרַחֲמָיו שֵׁנִית,* לְעֵינֵי כָּל חָי, לִהְיוֹת לָכֶם לֵאלֹהִים,* אֲנִי יהוה אֱלֹהֵיכֶם.[4]

—*Chazzan*: וּבְדִבְרֵי קָדְשְׁךָ כָּתוּב לֵאמֹר:

—All: יִמְלֹךְ יהוה לְעוֹלָם, אֱלֹהַיִךְ צִיּוֹן, לְדֹר וָדֹר, הַלְלוּיָהּ.[5]

—*Chazzan* continues: לְדוֹר וָדוֹר נַגִּיד גָּדְלֶךָ וּלְנֵצַח נְצָחִים קְדֻשָּׁתְךָ נַקְדִּישׁ, וְשִׁבְחֲךָ אֱלֹהֵינוּ מִפִּינוּ לֹא יָמוּשׁ לְעוֹלָם וָעֶד, כִּי אֵל מֶלֶךְ גָּדוֹל וְקָדוֹשׁ אָתָּה. בָּרוּךְ אַתָּה יהוה, °הָאֵל הַקָּדוֹשׁ.

°הַמֶּלֶךְ הַקָּדוֹשׁ. —From Rosh Hashanah to Yom Kippur substitute

Chazzan continues ... תִּכַּנְתָּ שַׁבָּת (or אַתָּה יָצַרְתָּ).

קְדוּשָּׁה / Kedushah

The *Kedushah* of *Mussaf* is based on *Pirkei D'Rabbi Eliezer's* narrative of the angelic praises. Indicative of the higher spirituality of *Mussaf,* Israel joins the angels by proclaiming שְׁמַע יִשְׂרָאֵל, our own declaration of God's greatness.

נַעֲרִיצְךָ וְנַקְדִּישְׁךָ — *We will revere You and sanctify You. Revere* refers to our recognition of God's outward greatness as displayed in His deeds. *Sanctify* refers to our attempt to express the idea that God's essence is elevated beyond man's capacity to comprehend.

כְּבוֹדוֹ מָלֵא עוֹלָם — *His glory fills the world.* The material nature of the earth is no barrier to His glory; it is everywhere.

אַיֵּה מְקוֹם כְּבוֹדוֹ — *Where is the place of His glory?* God's glory is infinite and unbounded. Can anyone say that His glory is limited to any one place and unable to enter another? The Kabbalists comment that the letters of אַיֵּה, *where,* are the initials of אֶת יוֹם הַשַּׁבָּת, *the Sabbath day,* i.e., the Sabbath is the 'place,' of His glory in the sense that God's glory is revealed on the Sabbath to the greatest extent perceivable by man.

הוּא יִפֶן בְּרַחֲמִים — *May He turn with compassion.* God's mercy causes Him to move from the throne of judgment to the throne of compassion.

עַם הַמְיַחֲדִים שְׁמוֹ ... שְׁמַע אוֹמְרִים — *The people who declare the Oneness of His Name ... they proclaim 'Shema.'* With its twice-a-day declara-

During the *chazzan's* repetition, *Kedushah* (below) is recited at this point.

HOLINESS OF GOD'S NAME

אַתָּה *You are holy and Your Name is holy, and holy ones praise You every day, forever. Blessed are You,* HASHEM, °*the holy God.*

°From Rosh Hashanah to Yom Kippur substitute: *the holy King.* [If forgotten, repeat *Shemoneh Esrei.* See Laws §62-63.]

KEDUSHAH

When reciting *Kedushah,* one must stand with his feet together and avoid any interruptions. One should rise to his toes when saying the words *'Holy, holy, holy; Blessed is;* and HASHEM *shall reign.'*

Cong.— then Chazzan — נַעֲרִיצְךָ *We will revere You and sanctify You* according to the counsel of the holy Seraphim, who sanctify Your Name in the Sanctuary, as it is written by Your prophet: "And one will call another and say:*

All— *'Holy, holy, holy is* HASHEM, *Master of Legions, the whole world is filled with His glory.' "*[1]

Cong.— then Chazzan — *His glory fills the world.* His ministering angels ask one another, 'Where is the place of His glory?'* Those facing them say 'Blessed':*

All— *'Blessed is the glory of* HASHEM *from His place.'*[2]

Cong.— then Chazzan — *From His place may He turn with compassion* and be gracious to the people who declare the Oneness of His Name; evening and morning, every day constantly, twice, with love, they proclaim 'Shema.'**

All— *'Hear O Israel:* HASHEM *is our God,* HASHEM *the One and Only.'*[3]

Cong. then Chazzan— *He is our God;* He is our Father; He is our King; He is our Savior; and He will let us hear, in His compassion, for a second time* in the presence of all the living,' ... to be a God to you,* I am* HASHEM, *your God.'*[4]

Chazzan— *And in Your holy Writings the following is written:*

All— *'*HASHEM *shall reign forever — your God, O Zion — from generation to generation, Halleluyah!'*[5]

Chazzan continues— *From generation to generation we shall relate Your greatness and for infinite eternities we shall proclaim Your holiness. Your praise, our God, shall not leave our mouth forever and ever, for You O God, are a great and holy King. Blessed are You* HASHEM, °*the holy God.*

°From Rosh Hashanah to Yom Kippur substitute: *the holy King.*

Chazzan continues ... תִּכַּנְתָּ שַׁבָּת, *You instituted the Sabbath* (or אַתָּה יָצַרְתָּ, *You fashioned).*

(1) *Isaiah* 6:3. (2) *Ezekiel* 3:12. (3) *Deuteronomy* 6:4. (4) *Numbers* 15:41. (5) *Psalms* 146:10.

---

tion of the *Shema,* Israel joins in the sacred chorus of the angels — and this is merit enough to win God's compassion.

As explained more fully in the commentary to קָרְבָּנוֹת (see p. 28), the fifth-century Persian king Yezdegerd forbade the recitation of *Shema.* They had to comply during the morning when guards were present, but the Jews partially circumvented the decree by incorporating *Shema* into the *Mussaf Kedushah.*

הוּא אֱלֹהֵינוּ — *He is our God,* i.e., He controls nature; He is our merciful Father, the Ruler of all peoples, and our only hope for salvation.

שֵׁנִית — *For a second time.* The prophet *Isaiah* (11:11) foretold that God would redeem Israel from its final exile in as miraculous a manner as He did at the time of the Exodus from Egypt. Thus, the *second time* refers to the concept of a complete and total redemption, unlike the limited one that ended the Babylonian exile and led to the building of the Second Temple

לִהְיוֹת לָכֶם לֵאלֹהִים — *To be a God to you.* When redeeming Israel from Egypt, God said that His purpose in doing so was to be a God to the Jewish people. The purpose of the *second* and ultimate redemption will be the same.

קדושת היום

On an ordinary Sabbath, except on Sabbath-Rosh Chodesh, recite:

תִּכַּנְתָּ שַׁבָּת* רָצִיתָ קָרְבְּנוֹתֶיהָ, צִוִּיתָ פֵּרוּשֶׁיהָ* עִם סִדּוּרֵי נְסָכֶיהָ,* מְעַנְּגֶיהָ לְעוֹלָם כָּבוֹד יִנְחָלוּ, טוֹעֲמֶיהָ חַיִּים זָכוּ, וְגַם הָאוֹהֲבִים דְּבָרֶיהָ* גְּדֻלָּה בָּחָרוּ, אָז מִסִּינַי נִצְטַוּוּ עָלֶיהָ, וַתְּצַוֵּנוּ יהוה אֱלֹהֵינוּ, לְהַקְרִיב בָּהּ קָרְבַּן מוּסַף שַׁבָּת כָּרָאוּי. יְהִי רָצוֹן מִלְּפָנֶיךָ, יהוה אֱלֹהֵינוּ וֵאלֹהֵי אֲבוֹתֵינוּ, שֶׁתַּעֲלֵנוּ בְשִׂמְחָה לְאַרְצֵנוּ, וְתִטָּעֵנוּ בִּגְבוּלֵנוּ, וְשָׁם נַעֲשֶׂה לְפָנֶיךָ אֶת קָרְבְּנוֹת חוֹבוֹתֵינוּ, תְּמִידִים כְּסִדְרָם וּמוּסָפִים כְּהִלְכָתָם. וְאֶת מוּסַף יוֹם הַשַּׁבָּת הַזֶּה נַעֲשֶׂה וְנַקְרִיב לְפָנֶיךָ בְּאַהֲבָה, כְּמִצְוַת רְצוֹנֶךָ, כְּמוֹ שֶׁכָּתַבְתָּ עָלֵינוּ בְּתוֹרָתֶךָ, עַל יְדֵי מֹשֶׁה עַבְדֶּךָ, מִפִּי כְבוֹדֶךָ כָּאָמוּר:

⊷ **תִּכַּנְתָּ שַׁבָּת** — *You established the Sabbath.* This paragraph introduces the concept of the special service in the Temple and concludes with the prayer that we be enabled to offer the Sabbath *Mussaf* offering. The first twenty-two words begin with the letters of the *Aleph-Beis* in reverse order, from ת to א. This Kabbalistic device symbolizes that after man reaches the full extent of his understanding — ת representing completion — he must realize that he should go back to the beginning and deepen his spiritual understanding even more. [For a discussion of this concept, see R' M.L. Munk's *Wisdom of the Hebrew Alphabet, p. 221.*]

צִוִּיתָ פֵּרוּשֶׁיהָ — [You] *instructed regarding its*

On Sabbath-Rosh Chodesh, the following is substituted:

אַתָּה יָצַרְתָּ עוֹלָמְךָ מִקֶּדֶם,* כִּלִּיתָ מְלַאכְתְּךָ בַּיּוֹם הַשְּׁבִיעִי, אָהַבְתָּ אוֹתָנוּ וְרָצִיתָ בָּנוּ, וְרוֹמַמְתָּנוּ מִכָּל הַלְּשׁוֹנוֹת,* וְקִדַּשְׁתָּנוּ בְּמִצְוֹתֶיךָ, וְקֵרַבְתָּנוּ מַלְכֵּנוּ לַעֲבוֹדָתֶךָ, וְשִׁמְךָ הַגָּדוֹל וְהַקָּדוֹשׁ עָלֵינוּ קָרָאתָ. וַתִּתֶּן לָנוּ יהוה אֱלֹהֵינוּ בְּאַהֲבָה, שַׁבָּתוֹת לִמְנוּחָה וְרָאשֵׁי חֳדָשִׁים לְכַפָּרָה.* וּלְפִי שֶׁחָטָאנוּ לְפָנֶיךָ אֲנַחְנוּ וַאֲבוֹתֵינוּ, חָרְבָה עִירֵנוּ, וְשָׁמֵם בֵּית מִקְדָּשֵׁנוּ, וְגָלָה יְקָרֵנוּ, וְנִטַּל כָּבוֹד מִבֵּית חַיֵּינוּ, וְאֵין אֲנַחְנוּ יְכוֹלִים לַעֲשׂוֹת חוֹבוֹתֵינוּ בְּבֵית בְּחִירָתֶךָ, בַּבַּיִת הַגָּדוֹל וְהַקָּדוֹשׁ שֶׁנִּקְרָא שִׁמְךָ עָלָיו, מִפְּנֵי הַיָּד שֶׁנִּשְׁתַּלְּחָה בְּמִקְדָּשֶׁךָ. יְהִי רָצוֹן מִלְּפָנֶיךָ יהוה אֱלֹהֵינוּ וֵאלֹהֵי אֲבוֹתֵינוּ, שֶׁתַּעֲלֵנוּ בְשִׂמְחָה לְאַרְצֵנוּ, וְתִטָּעֵנוּ בִּגְבוּלֵנוּ, וְשָׁם נַעֲשֶׂה לְפָנֶיךָ אֶת קָרְבְּנוֹת חוֹבוֹתֵינוּ, תְּמִידִים כְּסִדְרָם, וּמוּסָפִים כְּהִלְכָתָם. וְאֶת מוּסְפֵי יוֹם הַשַּׁבָּת הַזֶּה וְיוֹם רֹאשׁ הַחֹדֶשׁ הַזֶּה נַעֲשֶׂה וְנַקְרִיב לְפָנֶיךָ בְּאַהֲבָה, כְּמִצְוַת רְצוֹנֶךָ, כְּמוֹ שֶׁכָּתַבְתָּ עָלֵינוּ בְּתוֹרָתֶךָ, עַל יְדֵי מֹשֶׁה עַבְדֶּךָ, מִפִּי כְבוֹדֶךָ כָּאָמוּר:

⊷ **אַתָּה יָצַרְתָּ עוֹלָמְךָ מִקֶּדֶם** — *You fashioned Your world from of old. The Mussaf* of Sabbath-Rosh Chodesh is the only *Shemoneh Esrei* that stresses God's role as the Creator. The monthly rebirth of the moon recalls the notion of the early idolaters that the heavenly bodies had powers of their own. On the other hand, the Sabbath is the eternal testimony that God alone created heaven and earth from an absolute vacuum. Consequently, the Sages ordained that we declare our faith in God's creation on the occasion of Sabbath-Rosh Chodesh *(Iyun Tefillah).*

וְרוֹמַמְתָּנוּ מִכָּל הַלְּשׁוֹנוֹת — *And raised us above all tongues.* Unlike the Sabbath service, the *Shemoneh Esrei* of the Festivals and Rosh

HOLINESS OF THE DAY

On an ordinary Sabbath, except on Sabbath-Rosh Chodesh, recite:

תִּכַּנְתָּ שַׁבָּת *You established the Sabbath; found favor in its offerings; instructed regarding its commentaries* along with the order of its showbreads.* Those who delight in it will inherit eternal honor, whose who savor it will merit life and also those who love the speech that befits it* have chosen greatness. Then — from Sinai — they were instructed about it, when You commanded us,* HASHEM, *our God, to offer on it the Sabbath mussaf offering properly. May it be Your will,* HASHEM, *our God and the God of our forefathers, that You bring us up in gladness to our land and plant us within our boundaries. There we will perform before You the rite of our required offerings, the continual offerings in their order and the mussaf offerings according to their laws. And the mussaf of this Sabbath day we will perform and offer to You with love according to the commandment of Your will, as You have written for us in Your Torah, through Moses, Your servant, from Your glorious expression, as is said·*

commentaries. The numerous and complex laws of Sabbath labor are not clear from the verses of the Torah. We know them because God *instructed* [Moses] *regarding its commentaries,* meaning that He taught Moses how the Scriptural verses should be understood and interpreted.

סִדּוּרֵי נְסָכֶיהָ — *The order of its showbreads.* Although the literal translation would seem to be *drink-offerings,* many commentators interpret this to refer to the twelve showbreads, which had to be set out in the Sanctuary every Sabbath (*Leviticus* 24:5-9). This is logical because the showbread service — not the drink-offerings — was performed only on the Sabbath.

דְּבָרֶיהָ — *The speech that befits it.* Because on the

On Sabbath-Rosh Chodesh, the following is substituted:

אַתָּה יָצַרְתָּ *You fashioned Your world from of old;* You completed Your work on the Seventh Day. You loved us, found favor in us, and raised us above all tongues,* sanctified us through Your commandments and drew us near to Your service, our King, and Your great and holy Name You proclaimed upon us. And You gave us,* HASHEM, *our God, with love, Sabbaths for contentment and New Moons for atonement.* But because we sinned before You — we and our forefathers — our City was destroyed and our Holy Temple was made desolate, our honor was exiled and glory was taken from the House of our life. So we cannot fulfill our responsibilities in Your chosen House, in the great and holy House upon which Your Name was called, because of the hand that was sent against Your Sanctuary. May it be Your will,* HASHEM, *our God and the God of our forefathers, that You bring us up in gladness to our land and plant us within our boundaries. There we will perform before You the rite of our required offerings, the continual offerings in their order and the mussaf offerings according to their laws. And the mussaf offerings of this Sabbath day and this day of the New Moon we will perform and bring near to You with love according to the commandment of Your will, as You have written for us in Your Torah, through Moses, Your servant, from Your glorious expression, as is said:*

Chodesh contains the idea that the Jewish people were given special status among the nations. The distinction suggested by these festive days is the authority to regulate the calendar, a function that the Torah confers upon the *Beis Din.* In effect, by proclaiming when the months will begin, the Jewish people control the very existence of the Festivals. The Sabbath, on the other hand, comes every seventh day, independent of the Jewish people and the calendar.

וְרָאשֵׁי חֳדָשִׁים לְכַפָּרָה — *And New Moons for atonement.* The sin-offering of the Rosh Chodesh *mussaf* atoned for carelessness that resulted in contamination of the Sanctuary and for whatever sins may be responsible for preventing the coming of the Messiah and the renewal of the Davidic dynasty, which is symbolized by the moon. [This symbolism is discussed in the introduction to *Kiddush Levanah,* Blessing of the Moon, p. 612.]

On a regular Sabbath continue:

וּבְיוֹם הַשַּׁבָּת* שְׁנֵי כְבָשִׂים בְּנֵי שָׁנָה, תְּמִימִם, וּשְׁנֵי עֶשְׂרֹנִים סֹלֶת מִנְחָה בְּלוּלָה בַשֶּׁמֶן וְנִסְכּוֹ. עֹלַת שַׁבַּת בְּשַׁבַּתּוֹ,* עַל עֹלַת הַתָּמִיד וְנִסְכָּהּ.[1]

יִשְׂמְחוּ בְמַלְכוּתְךָ* שׁוֹמְרֵי שַׁבָּת וְקוֹרְאֵי עֹנֶג, עַם מְקַדְּשֵׁי שְׁבִיעִי, כֻּלָּם יִשְׂבְּעוּ וְיִתְעַנְּגוּ מִטּוּבֶךָ, וּבַשְּׁבִיעִי רָצִיתָ בּוֹ וְקִדַּשְׁתּוֹ, חֶמְדַּת יָמִים אוֹתוֹ קָרָאתָ, זֵכֶר לְמַעֲשֵׂה בְרֵאשִׁית.

אֱלֹהֵינוּ וֵאלֹהֵי אֲבוֹתֵינוּ רְצֵה בִמְנוּחָתֵנוּ, קַדְּשֵׁנוּ בְּמִצְוֹתֶיךָ, וְתֵן חֶלְקֵנוּ בְּתוֹרָתֶךָ, שַׂבְּעֵנוּ מִטּוּבֶךָ, וְשַׂמְּחֵנוּ בִּישׁוּעָתֶךָ, וְטַהֵר לִבֵּנוּ לְעָבְדְּךָ בֶּאֱמֶת, וְהַנְחִילֵנוּ יהוה אֱלֹהֵינוּ בְּאַהֲבָה וּבְרָצוֹן שַׁבַּת קָדְשֶׁךָ, וְיָנוּחוּ בוֹ יִשְׂרָאֵל מְקַדְּשֵׁי שְׁמֶךָ. בָּרוּךְ אַתָּה יהוה, מְקַדֵּשׁ הַשַּׁבָּת.

On Sabbath-Rosh Chodesh continue:

וּבְיוֹם הַשַּׁבָּת שְׁנֵי כְבָשִׂים בְּנֵי שָׁנָה תְּמִימִם, וּשְׁנֵי עֶשְׂרֹנִים סֹלֶת מִנְחָה בְּלוּלָה בַשֶּׁמֶן וְנִסְכּוֹ. עֹלַת שַׁבַּת בְּשַׁבַּתּוֹ, עַל עֹלַת הַתָּמִיד וְנִסְכָּהּ.[1] (some add— זֶה קָרְבַּן שַׁבָּת, וְקָרְבַּן הַיּוֹם כָּאָמוּר:)

וּבְרָאשֵׁי חָדְשֵׁיכֶם תַּקְרִיבוּ עֹלָה לַיהוה, פָּרִים בְּנֵי בָקָר שְׁנַיִם, וְאַיִל אֶחָד, כְּבָשִׂים בְּנֵי שָׁנָה שִׁבְעָה, תְּמִימִם.[2]

וּמִנְחָתָם* וְנִסְכֵּיהֶם כִּמְדֻבָּר, שְׁלשָׁה עֶשְׂרֹנִים לַפָּר, וּשְׁנֵי עֶשְׂרֹנִים לָאָיִל, וְעִשָּׂרוֹן לַכֶּבֶשׂ, וְיַיִן כְּנִסְכּוֹ, וְשָׂעִיר לְכַפֵּר, וּשְׁנֵי תְמִידִים כְּהִלְכָתָם.[3]

יִשְׂמְחוּ בְמַלְכוּתְךָ, שׁוֹמְרֵי שַׁבָּת וְקוֹרְאֵי עֹנֶג, עַם מְקַדְּשֵׁי שְׁבִיעִי, כֻּלָּם יִשְׂבְּעוּ וְיִתְעַנְּגוּ מִטּוּבֶךָ, וּבַשְּׁבִיעִי רָצִיתָ בּוֹ וְקִדַּשְׁתּוֹ, חֶמְדַּת יָמִים אוֹתוֹ קָרָאתָ, זֵכֶר לְמַעֲשֵׂה בְרֵאשִׁית.

During the *chazzan's* repetition, congregation responds אָמֵן as indicated (see comm. on p. 648).

אֱלֹהֵינוּ וֵאלֹהֵי אֲבוֹתֵינוּ רְצֵה בִמְנוּחָתֵנוּ, וְחַדֵּשׁ עָלֵינוּ בְּיוֹם הַשַּׁבָּת הַזֶּה אֶת הַחֹדֶשׁ הַזֶּה לְטוֹבָה וְלִבְרָכָה (אָמֵן), לְשָׂשׂוֹן וּלְשִׂמְחָה (אָמֵן), לִישׁוּעָה וּלְנֶחָמָה (אָמֵן), לְפַרְנָסָה וּלְכַלְכָּלָה (אָמֵן), לְחַיִּים וּלְשָׁלוֹם (אָמֵן), לִמְחִילַת חֵטְא וְלִסְלִיחַת עָוֹן (אָמֵן). [During a Jewish leap year, add— וּלְכַפָּרַת פָּשַׁע (אָמֵן)] כִּי בְעַמְּךָ יִשְׂרָאֵל בָּחַרְתָּ מִכָּל הָאֻמּוֹת, וְשַׁבַּת קָדְשְׁךָ לָהֶם הוֹדָעְתָּ,[4] וְחֻקֵּי רָאשֵׁי חֳדָשִׁים לָהֶם קָבָעְתָּ. בָּרוּךְ אַתָּה יהוה, מְקַדֵּשׁ הַשַּׁבָּת וְיִשְׂרָאֵל וְרָאשֵׁי חֳדָשִׁים.

וּמִנְחָתָם — *And their meal-offerings.* All elevation- and peace-offerings were accompanied by a meal-offering, and by a wine-libation that was poured into pipes set into the Altar. Each category of animal has a different prescribed amount for its meal-offering and libation. Since the *tamid* and *mussaf* offerings of Sabbath-Rosh Chodesh contain all three categories of animals, the respective amounts are listed.

On a regular Sabbath continue:

וּבְיוֹם הַשַּׁבָּת *On the Sabbath day,* two [male] first-year lambs, unblemished, two tenth-ephah of fine flour for a meal-offering, mixed with olive oil, and its wine-libation. The elevation-offering of the Sabbath must be on its particular Sabbath in addition to the continual elevation-offering and its wine-libation.*[1]

יִשְׂמְחוּ *They shall rejoice in Your kingship* — those who observe the Sabbath and call it a delight. The people that sanctifies the Seventh — they will all be satisfied and delighted from Your goodness, And the Seventh — You found favor in it and sanctified it. 'Most coveted of days,' You called it, a remembrance of creation.*

אֱלֹהֵינוּ *Our God and the God of our fathers, may You be pleased with our rest. Sanctify us with Your commandments and grant our share in Your Torah; satisfy us from Your goodness and gladden us with Your salvation, and purify our heart to serve You sincerely. O* Hashem, *our God, with love and favor grant us Your holy Sabbath as a heritage, and may Israel, the sanctifiers of Your Name, rest on it. Blessed are You,* Hashem, *Who sanctifies the Sabbath.*

Sabbath one should discuss spiritual matters and not business and other mundane affairs.

וּבְיוֹם הַשַּׁבָּת — *And on the Sabbath day.* This is the *mussaf* offering of the Sabbath.

יִשְׂמְחוּ בְמַלְכוּתְךָ — *They shall rejoice in Your kingship.* The Sabbath reaches its pinnacle when all Jews not only perform God's will, but *rejoice* in it. Furthermore, they will find their joy not in the physical pleasures of the Sabbath, but in the fact that they exist to serve and obey God.

On Sabbath-Rosh Chodesh continue:

וּבְיוֹם הַשַּׁבָּת *And on the Sabbath day: two [male] first-year lambs, unblemished, and two tenth-ephah of fine flour for a meal-offering mixed with olive oil, and its wine-libation. The elevation-offering of a Sabbath must be on its particular Sabbath, besides the continual elevation-offering and its wine-libation.*[1] (Some add— *The above is the Sabbath offering; the offering of the Rosh Chodesh day is as follows:)*

וּבְרָאשֵׁי *On the first days of your months you are to bring an elevation-offering to* Hashem, *two young bulls, one ram, seven [male] first-year lambs, unblemished.*[2]

וּמִנְחָתָם *And their meal-offerings* and their wine-libations as mentioned: three tenth-ephah for each bull; two tenth-ephah for the ram; one tenth-ephah for each lamb; and wine for its wine-libations. A he-goat for atonement and two continual offerings according to their law.*[3]

יִשְׂמְחוּ *They shall rejoice in Your kingship — those who observe the Sabbath and call it a delight. The people that sanctifies the Seventh — they will all be satisfied and delighted from Your goodness. And the Seventh — You found favor in it and sanctified it. 'Most coveted of days,' You called it, a remembrance of creation.*

During the *chazzan's* repetition, congregation responds *Amen* as indicated (see comm. p. 648).

אֱלֹהֵינוּ *Our God and the God of our forefathers, may You be pleased with our rest, and on this Sabbath day inaugurate this month for good and for blessing (Amen), for joy and for gladness (Amen), for salvation and for consolation (Amen), for sustenance and for support (Amen), for life and for peace (Amen), for pardon of sin and forgiveness of iniquity (Amen)* [During a Jewish leap year, add: *and for atonement of willful sin (Amen)*], *for You have chosen Your people Israel from all the nations, and You made Your holy Sabbath known to them*[4] *and You set forth the decrees of the New Moons for them. Blessed are You,* Hashem, *Who sanctifies the Sabbath, Israel and the New Moons.*

(1) *Numbers* 28:9-10. (2) 28:11. (3) Cf. 28:12-15 (4) Cf. *Nechemiah* 9:14.

עבודה

רְצֵה יהוה אֱלֹהֵינוּ בְּעַמְּךָ יִשְׂרָאֵל וּבִתְפִלָּתָם, וְהָשֵׁב אֶת הָעֲבוֹדָה לִדְבִיר בֵּיתֶךָ. וְאִשֵּׁי יִשְׂרָאֵל וּתְפִלָּתָם בְּאַהֲבָה תְקַבֵּל בְּרָצוֹן, וּתְהִי לְרָצוֹן תָּמִיד עֲבוֹדַת יִשְׂרָאֵל עַמֶּךָ.

וְתֶחֱזֶינָה עֵינֵינוּ בְּשׁוּבְךָ לְצִיּוֹן בְּרַחֲמִים. בָּרוּךְ אַתָּה יהוה, הַמַּחֲזִיר שְׁכִינָתוֹ לְצִיּוֹן.

הודאה

Bow at מוֹדִים; straighten up at 'ה. In his repetition the *chazzan* should recite the entire מוֹדִים aloud, while the congregation recites מוֹדִים דְּרַבָּנָן softly.

מוֹדִים אֲנַחְנוּ לָךְ שָׁאַתָּה הוּא יהוה אֱלֹהֵינוּ וֵאלֹהֵי אֲבוֹתֵינוּ לְעוֹלָם וָעֶד. צוּר חַיֵּינוּ, מָגֵן יִשְׁעֵנוּ אַתָּה הוּא לְדוֹר וָדוֹר. נוֹדֶה לְּךָ וּנְסַפֵּר תְּהִלָּתֶךָ[1] עַל חַיֵּינוּ הַמְּסוּרִים בְּיָדֶךָ, וְעַל נִשְׁמוֹתֵינוּ הַפְּקוּדוֹת לָךְ, וְעַל נִסֶּיךָ שֶׁבְּכָל יוֹם עִמָּנוּ, וְעַל נִפְלְאוֹתֶיךָ וְטוֹבוֹתֶיךָ שֶׁבְּכָל עֵת, עֶרֶב וָבֹקֶר וְצָהֳרָיִם. הַטּוֹב כִּי לֹא כָלוּ רַחֲמֶיךָ, וְהַמְּרַחֵם כִּי לֹא תַמּוּ חֲסָדֶיךָ,[2] מֵעוֹלָם קִוִּינוּ לָךְ.

מודים דרבנן

מוֹדִים אֲנַחְנוּ לָךְ, שָׁאַתָּה הוּא יהוה אֱלֹהֵינוּ וֵאלֹהֵי אֲבוֹתֵינוּ, אֱלֹהֵי כָל בָּשָׂר, יוֹצְרֵנוּ, יוֹצֵר בְּרֵאשִׁית. בְּרָכוֹת וְהוֹדָאוֹת לְשִׁמְךָ הַגָּדוֹל וְהַקָּדוֹשׁ, עַל שֶׁהֶחֱיִיתָנוּ וְקִיַּמְתָּנוּ. כֵּן תְּחַיֵּנוּ וּתְקַיְּמֵנוּ, וְתֶאֱסוֹף גָּלֻיּוֹתֵינוּ לְחַצְרוֹת קָדְשֶׁךָ, לִשְׁמוֹר חֻקֶּיךָ וְלַעֲשׂוֹת רְצוֹנֶךָ, וּלְעָבְדְּךָ בְּלֵבָב שָׁלֵם, עַל שֶׁאֲנַחְנוּ מוֹדִים לָךְ. בָּרוּךְ אֵל הַהוֹדָאוֹת.

On Chanukah add:

(וְ)עַל הַנִּסִּים, וְעַל הַפֻּרְקָן, וְעַל הַגְּבוּרוֹת, וְעַל הַתְּשׁוּעוֹת, וְעַל הַמִּלְחָמוֹת, שֶׁעָשִׂיתָ לַאֲבוֹתֵינוּ בַּיָּמִים הָהֵם בַּזְּמַן הַזֶּה.

בִּימֵי מַתִּתְיָהוּ בֶּן יוֹחָנָן כֹּהֵן גָּדוֹל חַשְׁמוֹנַאי וּבָנָיו, כְּשֶׁעָמְדָה מַלְכוּת יָוָן הָרְשָׁעָה עַל עַמְּךָ יִשְׂרָאֵל, לְהַשְׁכִּיחָם תּוֹרָתֶךָ, וּלְהַעֲבִירָם מֵחֻקֵּי רְצוֹנֶךָ. וְאַתָּה בְּרַחֲמֶיךָ הָרַבִּים, עָמַדְתָּ לָהֶם בְּעֵת צָרָתָם, רַבְתָּ אֶת רִיבָם, דַּנְתָּ אֶת דִּינָם, נָקַמְתָּ אֶת נִקְמָתָם.[3] מָסַרְתָּ גִבּוֹרִים בְּיַד חַלָּשִׁים, וְרַבִּים בְּיַד מְעַטִּים, וּטְמֵאִים בְּיַד טְהוֹרִים, וּרְשָׁעִים בְּיַד צַדִּיקִים, וְזֵדִים בְּיַד עוֹסְקֵי תוֹרָתֶךָ. וּלְךָ עָשִׂיתָ שֵׁם גָּדוֹל וְקָדוֹשׁ בְּעוֹלָמֶךָ, וּלְעַמְּךָ יִשְׂרָאֵל עָשִׂיתָ תְּשׁוּעָה גְדוֹלָה[4] וּפֻרְקָן כְּהַיּוֹם הַזֶּה. וְאַחַר כֵּן בָּאוּ בָנֶיךָ לִדְבִיר בֵּיתֶךָ, וּפִנּוּ אֶת הֵיכָלֶךָ, וְטִהֲרוּ אֶת מִקְדָּשֶׁךָ, וְהִדְלִיקוּ נֵרוֹת בְּחַצְרוֹת קָדְשֶׁךָ, וְקָבְעוּ שְׁמוֹנַת יְמֵי חֲנֻכָּה אֵלּוּ, לְהוֹדוֹת וּלְהַלֵּל לְשִׁמְךָ הַגָּדוֹל.

[If forgotten, do not repeat *Shemoneh Esrei*. See *Laws* §90.]

TEMPLE SERVICE

רְצֵה *Be favorable, HASHEM, our God, toward Your people Israel and their prayer and restore the service to the Holy of Holies of Your Temple. The fire-offerings of Israel and their prayer accept with love and favor, and may the service of Your people Israel always be favorable to You.*

וְתֶחֱזֶינָה *May our eyes behold Your return to Zion in compassion. Blessed are You, HASHEM, Who restores His Presence to Zion.*

THANKSGIVING [MODIM]

Bow at *'We gratefully thank You'*; straighten up at *'HASHEM'*. In his repetition the chazzan should recite the entire *Modim* aloud, while the congregation recites *Modim of the Rabbis* softly.

מוֹדִים *We gratefully thank You, for it is You Who are HASHEM, our God and the God of our forefathers for all eternity; Rock of our lives, Shield of our salvation are You from generation to generation. We shall thank You and relate Your praise[1] — for our lives, which are committed to Your power and for our souls that are entrusted to You; for Your miracles that are with us every day; and for Your wonders and favors in every season — evening, morning, and afternoon. The Beneficent One, for Your compassions were never exhausted, and the Compassionate One, for Your kindnesses never ended[2] — always have we put our hope in You.*

MODIM OF THE RABBIS

מוֹדִים *We gratefully thank You, for it is You Who are HASHEM, our God and the God of our forefathers, the God of all flesh, our Molder, the Molder of the universe. Blessings and thanks are due Your great and holy Name for You have given us life and sustained us. So may You continue to give us life and sustain us and gather our exiles to the Courtyards of Your Sanctuary, to observe Your decrees, to do Your will and to serve You wholeheartedly. [We thank You] for inspiring us to thank You. Blessed is the God of thanksgivings.*

On Chanukah add:

(וְ)עַל *(And) for the miracles, and for the salvation, and for the mighty deeds, and for the victories, and for the battles which You performed for our forefathers in those days, at this time.*

בִּימֵי *In the days of Mattisyahu, the son of Yochanan, the High Priest, the Hasmonean, and his sons — when the wicked Greek kingdom rose up against Your people Israel to make them forget Your Torah and compel them to stray from the statutes of Your Will—You in Your great mercy stood up for them in the time of their distress. You took up their grievance, judged their claim, and avenged their wrong.[3] You delivered the strong into the hands of the weak, the many into the hands of the few, the impure into the hands of the pure, the wicked into the hands of the righteous, and the wanton into the hands of the diligent students of Your Torah. For Yourself You made a great and holy Name in Your world, and for Your people Israel You worked a great victory[4] and salvation as this very day. Thereafter, Your children came to the Holy of Holies of Your House, cleansed Your Temple, purified the site of Your Holiness and kindled lights in the Courtyards of Your Sanctuary; and they established these eight days of Chanukah to express thanks and praise to Your great Name.*

[If forgotten, do not repeat *Shemoneh Esrei*. See *Laws* §90.]

(1) Cf. *Psalms* 79:13. (2) Cf. *Lamentations* 3:22. (3) Cf. *Jeremiah* 51:36. (4) Cf. *I Samuel* 19:5.

וְעַל כֻּלָּם יִתְבָּרַךְ וְיִתְרוֹמַם שִׁמְךָ מַלְכֵּנוּ תָּמִיד לְעוֹלָם וָעֶד.

From Rosh Hashanah to Yom Kippur add:

וּכְתוֹב לְחַיִּים טוֹבִים כָּל בְּנֵי בְרִיתֶךָ.

[If forgotten, do not repeat *Shemoneh Esrei*. See *Laws* §61.]

Bend the knees at בָּרוּךְ; bow at אַתָּה; straighten up at ה׳.

וְכֹל הַחַיִּים יוֹדְוּךָ סֶּלָה, וִיהַלְּלוּ אֶת שִׁמְךָ בֶּאֱמֶת, הָאֵל יְשׁוּעָתֵנוּ וְעֶזְרָתֵנוּ סֶלָה. בָּרוּךְ אַתָּה יהוה, הַטּוֹב שִׁמְךָ וּלְךָ נָאֶה לְהוֹדוֹת.

ברכת כהנים

The *chazzan* recites בִּרְכַּת כֹּהֲנִים during his repetition. *Chazzan* faces the Ark while reciting יְבָרֶכְךָ ה׳, then turns to the right and says וְיִשְׁמְרֶךָ; faces the Ark while reciting יָאֵר ה׳, then turns to the left and says פָּנָיו אֵלֶיךָ וִיחֻנֶּךָּ; faces the Ark while reciting the entire last verse.

אֱלֹהֵינוּ, וֵאלֹהֵי אֲבוֹתֵינוּ, בָּרְכֵנוּ בַבְּרָכָה הַמְּשֻׁלֶּשֶׁת, בַּתּוֹרָה הַכְּתוּבָה עַל יְדֵי מֹשֶׁה עַבְדֶּךָ, הָאֲמוּרָה מִפִּי אַהֲרֹן וּבָנָיו, כֹּהֲנִים עַם קְדוֹשֶׁךָ, כָּאָמוּר:

יְבָרֶכְךָ יהוה, וְיִשְׁמְרֶךָ. (Cong.— כֵּן יְהִי רָצוֹן.)

יָאֵר יהוה פָּנָיו אֵלֶיךָ וִיחֻנֶּךָּ. (Cong.— כֵּן יְהִי רָצוֹן.)

יִשָּׂא יהוה פָּנָיו אֵלֶיךָ וְיָשֵׂם לְךָ שָׁלוֹם.[1] (Cong.— כֵּן יְהִי רָצוֹן.)

שלום

שִׂים שָׁלוֹם, טוֹבָה, וּבְרָכָה, חֵן, וָחֶסֶד וְרַחֲמִים עָלֵינוּ וְעַל כָּל יִשְׂרָאֵל עַמֶּךָ. בָּרְכֵנוּ אָבִינוּ, כֻּלָּנוּ כְּאֶחָד בְּאוֹר פָּנֶיךָ, כִּי בְאוֹר פָּנֶיךָ נָתַתָּ לָּנוּ, יהוה אֱלֹהֵינוּ, תּוֹרַת חַיִּים וְאַהֲבַת חֶסֶד, וּצְדָקָה, וּבְרָכָה, וְרַחֲמִים, וְחַיִּים, וְשָׁלוֹם. וְטוֹב בְּעֵינֶיךָ לְבָרֵךְ אֶת עַמְּךָ יִשְׂרָאֵל, בְּכָל עֵת וּבְכָל שָׁעָה בִּשְׁלוֹמֶךָ. °בָּרוּךְ אַתָּה יהוה, הַמְּבָרֵךְ אֶת עַמּוֹ יִשְׂרָאֵל בַּשָּׁלוֹם.

°From Rosh Hashanah to Yom Kippur substitute the following [see *Laws* §65]:

בְּסֵפֶר חַיִּים בְּרָכָה וְשָׁלוֹם, וּפַרְנָסָה טוֹבָה, נִזָּכֵר וְנִכָּתֵב לְפָנֶיךָ, אֲנַחְנוּ וְכָל עַמְּךָ בֵּית יִשְׂרָאֵל, לְחַיִּים טוֹבִים וּלְשָׁלוֹם. בָּרוּךְ אַתָּה יהוה, עֹשֵׂה הַשָּׁלוֹם.

[If forgotten, do not repeat *Shemoneh Esrei*. See *Laws* §61.]

The *chazzan's* repetition of *Shemoneh Esrei* ends here. Individuals continue until next page.

Many hold that the following verse should be recited here by individuals and the *chazzan*:

יִהְיוּ לְרָצוֹן אִמְרֵי פִי וְהֶגְיוֹן לִבִּי לְפָנֶיךָ, יהוה צוּרִי וְגֹאֲלִי.[2]

אֱלֹהַי, נְצוֹר לְשׁוֹנִי מֵרָע, וּשְׂפָתַי מִדַּבֵּר מִרְמָה,[3] וְלִמְקַלְלַי נַפְשִׁי תִדּוֹם, וְנַפְשִׁי כֶּעָפָר לַכֹּל תִּהְיֶה. פְּתַח לִבִּי בְּתוֹרָתֶךָ, וּבְמִצְוֹתֶיךָ תִּרְדּוֹף נַפְשִׁי. וְכֹל הַחוֹשְׁבִים עָלַי רָעָה, מְהֵרָה הָפֵר עֲצָתָם וְקַלְקֵל מַחֲשַׁבְתָּם. עֲשֵׂה לְמַעַן שְׁמֶךָ, עֲשֵׂה

For all these, may Your Name be blessed and exalted, our King, continually forever and ever.

From Rosh Hashanah to Yom Kippur add the following.
And inscribe all the children of Your covenant for a good life.
If forgotten, do not repeat *Shemoneh Esrei.* See *Laws* §61.]

Bend the knees at *'Blessed'*; bow at *'You'*; straighten up at *'HASHEM'*.

Everything alive will gratefully acknowledge You, Selah! and praise Your Name sincerely, O God of our salvation and help, Selah! Blessed are You, HASHEM, Your Name is 'The Beneficent One' and to You it is fitting to give thanks.

THE PRIESTLY BLESSING
The *chazzan* recites the Priestly Blessing during his repetition.

אֱלֹהֵינוּ *Our God and the God of our forefathers, bless us with the three-verse blessing in the Torah that was written by the hand of Moses, Your servant, that was said by Aaron and his sons, the Kohanim, Your holy people, as it is said:*
May HASHEM bless you and safeguard you. (Cong.— *So may it be.*)
May HASHEM illuminate His countenance for you and be gracious to you. (Cong.— *So may it be.*)
May HASHEM turn His countenance to you and establish peace for you.[1] (Cong.— *So may it be.*)

PEACE

שִׂים *Establish peace, goodness, blessing, graciousness, kindness, and compassion upon us and upon all of Your people Israel. Bless us, our Father, all of us as one, with the light of Your countenance, for with the light of Your countenance You gave us, HASHEM, our God, the Torah of life and a love of kindness, righteousness, blessing, compassion, life, and peace. And may it be good in Your eyes to bless Your people Israel, in every season and in every hour with Your Peace.* °*Blessed are You, HASHEM, Who blesses His people Israel with peace.*

°From Rosh Hashanah to Yom Kippur substitute the following [see *Laws* §65]:
In the book of life, blessing, and peace, good livelihood, may we be remembered and inscribed before You — we and Your entire people the Family of Israel for a good life and for peace. Blessed are You, HASHEM, Who makes peace.
[If forgotten, do not repeat *Shemoneh Esrei.* See *Laws* §61.]

The *chazzan's* repetition of *Shemoneh Esrei* ends here. Individuals continue until next page.
Many hold that the following verse should be recited here by individuals and the *chazzan:*
May the expressions of my mouth and the thoughts of my heart find favor before You, HASHEM, my Rock and my Redeemer.[2]

אֱלֹהַי *My God, guard my tongue from evil and my lips from speaking deceitfully.*[3] *To those who curse me, let my soul be silent; and let my soul be like dust to everyone. Open my heart to Your Torah, then my soul will pursue Your commandments. As for all those who design evil against me, speedily nullify their counsel and disrupt their design. Act for Your Name's sake; act for*

(1) *Numbers* 6:24-26. (2) *Psalms* 19:15. (3) Cf. 34:14.

לְמַעַן יְמִינֶךָ, עֲשֵׂה לְמַעַן קְדֻשָּׁתֶךָ, עֲשֵׂה לְמַעַן תּוֹרָתֶךָ. לְמַעַן יֵחָלְצוּן יְדִידֶיךָ, הוֹשִׁיעָה יְמִינְךָ וַעֲנֵנִי.[1]

Some recite verses pertaining to their names at this point. See page 924.

יִהְיוּ לְרָצוֹן אִמְרֵי פִי וְהֶגְיוֹן לִבִּי לְפָנֶיךָ, יהוה צוּרִי וְגֹאֲלִי.[2]

Bow and take three steps back. Bow left and say ... עֹשֶׂה; bow right and say ... הוּא יַעֲשֶׂה; bow forward and say וְעַל כָּל ... אָמֵן. Remain standing in place while reciting יְהִי רָצוֹן.

עֹשֶׂה שָׁלוֹם בִּמְרוֹמָיו, הוּא יַעֲשֶׂה שָׁלוֹם עָלֵינוּ, וְעַל כָּל יִשְׂרָאֵל. וְאִמְרוּ: אָמֵן.

יְהִי רָצוֹן מִלְּפָנֶיךָ יהוה אֱלֹהֵינוּ וֵאלֹהֵי אֲבוֹתֵינוּ, שֶׁיִּבָּנֶה בֵּית הַמִּקְדָּשׁ בִּמְהֵרָה בְיָמֵינוּ, וְתֵן חֶלְקֵנוּ בְּתוֹרָתֶךָ. וְשָׁם נַעֲבָדְךָ בְּיִרְאָה, כִּימֵי עוֹלָם וּכְשָׁנִים קַדְמוֹנִיּוֹת. וְעָרְבָה לַיהוה מִנְחַת יְהוּדָה וִירוּשָׁלָיִם, כִּימֵי עוֹלָם וּכְשָׁנִים קַדְמוֹנִיּוֹת.[3]

THE INDIVIDUAL'S RECITATION OF שְׁמוֹנֶה עֶשְׂרֵה ENDS HERE.

The individual remains standing in place until the *chazzan* reaches *Kedushah* — or at least until the *chazzan* begins his repetition — then he takes three steps forward. The *chazzan* himself, or one praying alone, should remain in place for a few moments before taking three steps forward.

קדיש שלם

The *chazzan* recites קַדִּישׁ שָׁלֵם:

יִתְגַּדַּל וְיִתְקַדַּשׁ שְׁמֵהּ רַבָּא. (.Cong— אָמֵן.) בְּעָלְמָא דִּי בְרָא כִרְעוּתֵהּ. וְיַמְלִיךְ מַלְכוּתֵהּ, בְּחַיֵּיכוֹן וּבְיוֹמֵיכוֹן וּבְחַיֵּי דְכָל בֵּית יִשְׂרָאֵל, בַּעֲגָלָא וּבִזְמַן קָרִיב. וְאִמְרוּ: אָמֵן.

(.Cong— אָמֵן. יְהֵא שְׁמֵהּ רַבָּא מְבָרַךְ לְעָלַם וּלְעָלְמֵי עָלְמַיָּא.)

יְהֵא שְׁמֵהּ רַבָּא מְבָרַךְ לְעָלַם וּלְעָלְמֵי עָלְמַיָּא.

יִתְבָּרַךְ וְיִשְׁתַּבַּח וְיִתְפָּאַר וְיִתְרוֹמַם וְיִתְנַשֵּׂא וְיִתְהַדָּר וְיִתְעַלֶּה וְיִתְהַלָּל שְׁמֵהּ דְּקֻדְשָׁא בְּרִיךְ הוּא (.Cong— בְּרִיךְ הוּא) — °לְעֵלָּא מִן כָּל (°From Rosh Hashanah to Yom Kippur substitute— לְעֵלָּא וּלְעֵלָּא מִכָּל) בִּרְכָתָא וְשִׁירָתָא תֻּשְׁבְּחָתָא וְנֶחֱמָתָא, דַּאֲמִירָן בְּעָלְמָא. וְאִמְרוּ: אָמֵן. (.Cong— אָמֵן.)

(.Cong— קַבֵּל בְּרַחֲמִים וּבְרָצוֹן אֶת תְּפִלָּתֵנוּ.)

תִּתְקַבֵּל צְלוֹתְהוֹן וּבָעוּתְהוֹן דְּכָל בֵּית יִשְׂרָאֵל קֳדָם אֲבוּהוֹן דִּי בִשְׁמַיָּא. וְאִמְרוּ: אָמֵן. (.Cong— אָמֵן.)

(.Cong— יְהִי שֵׁם יהוה מְבֹרָךְ, מֵעַתָּה וְעַד עוֹלָם.)

יְהֵא שְׁלָמָא רַבָּא מִן שְׁמַיָּא, וְחַיִּים עָלֵינוּ וְעַל כָּל יִשְׂרָאֵל. וְאִמְרוּ: אָמֵן. (.Cong— אָמֵן.)

(.Cong— עֶזְרִי מֵעִם יהוה, עֹשֵׂה שָׁמַיִם וָאָרֶץ.)

Take three steps back. Bow left and say ... עֹשֶׂה; bow right and say ... הוּא; bow forward and say וְעַל כָּל ... אָמֵן. Remain standing in place for a few moments, then take three steps forward.

עֹשֶׂה שָׁלוֹם בִּמְרוֹמָיו, הוּא יַעֲשֶׂה שָׁלוֹם עָלֵינוּ, וְעַל כָּל יִשְׂרָאֵל. וְאִמְרוּ: אָמֵן. (.Cong— אָמֵן.)

Your right hand's sake; act for Your sanctity's sake; act for Your Torah's sake. That Your beloved ones may be given rest; let Your right hand save, and respond to me.[1]

Some recite verses pertaining to their names at this point. See page 924.

May the expressions of my mouth and the thoughts of my heart find favor before You, HASHEM, my Rock and my Redeemer.[2]

Bow and take three steps back. Bow left and say, *'He Who makes peace ...';* bow right and say, *'may He make peace ...';* bow forward and say, *'and upon ... Amen.'*

He Who makes peace in His heights, may He make peace upon us, and upon all Israel. Now respond: Amen.

יְהִי רָצוֹן *May it be Your will, HASHEM our God and the God of our forefathers, that the Holy Temple be rebuilt, speedily in our days. Grant us our share in Your Torah, and may we serve You there with reverence, as in days of old and in former years. Then the offering of Judah and Jerusalem will be pleasing to HASHEM, as in days of old and in former years.*[3]

THE INDIVIDUAL'S RECITATION OF *SHEMONEH ESREI* ENDS HERE.

The individual remains standing in place until the *chazzan* reaches *Kedushah* — or at least until the *chazzan* begins his repetition — then he takes three steps forward. The *chazzan* himself, or one praying alone, should remain in place for a few moments before taking three steps forward.

FULL-KADDISH

Chazzan recites the Full-*Kaddish:*

יִתְגַּדַּל *May His great Name grow exalted and sanctified* (Cong.— *Amen.*) *in the world that He created as He willed. May He give reign to His kingship in your lifetimes and in your days, and in the lifetimes of the entire Family of Israel, swiftly and soon. Now respond: Amen.*

(Cong.— *Amen. May His great Name be blessed forever and ever.*)

May His great Name be blessed forever and ever.

Blessed, praised, glorified, exalted, extolled, mighty, upraised, and lauded be the Name of the Holy One, Blessed is He (Cong.— *Blessed is He*) — (From Rosh Hashanah to Yom Kippur add: *exceedingly*) *beyond any blessing and song, praise and consolation that are uttered in the world. Now respond: Amen.* (Cong.— *Amen.*)

(Cong.— *Accept our prayers with mercy and favor.*)

May the prayers and supplications of the entire Family of Israel be accepted before their Father Who is in Heaven. Now respond: Amen. (Cong.— *Amen.*)

(Cong.— *May the Name of HASHEM, be blessed from now to eternity*[4].)

May there be abundant peace from Heaven, and life, upon us and upon all Israel. Now respond: Amen. (Cong.— *Amen.*)

(Cong.— *My help is from HASHEM, Maker of heaven and earth.*[5])

Take three steps back. Bow left and say, *'He Who makes peace ...';* bow right and say, *'may He ...';* bow forward and say, *'and upon all Israel ...'* Remain standing in place for a few moments, then take three steps forward.

He Who makes peace in His heights, may He make peace upon us, and upon all Israel. Now respond: Amen. (Cong.— *Amen.*)

---

(1) *Psalms* 60:7; 108:7. (2) 19:15. (3) *Malachi* 3:4. (4) *Psalms* 113:2. (5) 121:2.

קַוֵּה אֶל יהוה, חֲזַק וְיַאֲמֵץ לִבֶּךָ, וְקַוֵּה אֶל יהוה.[1] אֵין קָדוֹשׁ כַּיהוה, כִּי אֵין בִּלְתֶּךָ, וְאֵין צוּר כֵּאלֹהֵינוּ.[2] כִּי מִי אֱלוֹהַּ מִבַּלְעֲדֵי יהוה, וּמִי צוּר זוּלָתִי אֱלֹהֵינוּ.[3]

אֵין כֵּאלֹהֵינוּ,* אֵין כַּאדוֹנֵינוּ, אֵין כְּמַלְכֵּנוּ, אֵין כְּמוֹשִׁיעֵנוּ. מִי כֵאלֹהֵינוּ, מִי כַאדוֹנֵינוּ, מִי כְמַלְכֵּנוּ, מִי כְמוֹשִׁיעֵנוּ. נוֹדֶה לֵאלֹהֵינוּ, נוֹדֶה לַאדוֹנֵינוּ, נוֹדֶה לְמַלְכֵּנוּ, נוֹדֶה לְמוֹשִׁיעֵנוּ. בָּרוּךְ אֱלֹהֵינוּ, בָּרוּךְ אֲדוֹנֵינוּ, בָּרוּךְ מַלְכֵּנוּ, בָּרוּךְ מוֹשִׁיעֵנוּ. אַתָּה הוּא אֱלֹהֵינוּ, אַתָּה הוּא אֲדוֹנֵינוּ, אַתָּה הוּא מַלְכֵּנוּ, אַתָּה הוּא מוֹשִׁיעֵנוּ. אַתָּה הוּא שֶׁהִקְטִירוּ אֲבוֹתֵינוּ לְפָנֶיךָ אֶת קְטֹרֶת הַסַּמִּים.

כריתות ו.

פִּטּוּם הַקְּטֹרֶת:* (א) הַצֳּרִי, (ב) וְהַצִּפֹּרֶן, (ג) הַחֶלְבְּנָה,* (ד) וְהַלְּבוֹנָה, מִשְׁקַל שִׁבְעִים שִׁבְעִים מָנֶה; (ה) מוֹר, (ו) וּקְצִיעָה, (ז) שִׁבֹּלֶת נֵרְדְּ, (ח) וְכַרְכֹּם, מִשְׁקַל שִׁשָּׁה עָשָׂר שִׁשָּׁה עָשָׂר מָנֶה; (ט) הַקֹּשְׁטְ שְׁנֵים עָשָׂר, (י) וְקִלּוּפָה שְׁלֹשָׁה, (יא) וְקִנָּמוֹן תִּשְׁעָה. בֹּרִית כַּרְשִׁינָה תִּשְׁעָה קַבִּין, יֵין קַפְרִיסִין סְאִין תְּלָתָא וְקַבִּין תְּלָתָא; וְאִם אֵין לוֹ יֵין קַפְרִיסִין, מֵבִיא חֲמַר חִוַּרְיָן עַתִּיק; מֶלַח סְדוֹמִית רֹבַע הַקָּב; מַעֲלֶה עָשָׁן כָּל שֶׁהוּא. רַבִּי נָתָן הַבַּבְלִי אוֹמֵר: אַף כִּפַּת הַיַּרְדֵּן כָּל שֶׁהוּא. וְאִם נָתַן בָּהּ דְּבַשׁ פְּסָלָהּ. וְאִם חִסַּר אַחַת מִכָּל סַמָּנֶיהָ, חַיָּב מִיתָה.

רַבָּן שִׁמְעוֹן בֶּן גַּמְלִיאֵל אוֹמֵר: הַצֳּרִי אֵינוֹ אֶלָּא שְׂרָף הַנּוֹטֵף מֵעֲצֵי הַקְּטָף. בֹּרִית כַּרְשִׁינָה שֶׁשָּׁפִין בָּהּ אֶת הַצִּפֹּרֶן כְּדֵי שֶׁתְּהֵא נָאָה; יֵין קַפְרִיסִין שֶׁשּׁוֹרִין בּוֹ

אֵין כֵּאלֹהֵינוּ — *There is none like our God.* The declaration of faith made in this hymn was formulated in response to a particular need of Sabbaths and Festivals. The Sages teach that it is meritorious to recite a hundred blessings every day. On weekdays, the bulk of this total is accounted for by the three-times-a-day recitation of *Shemoneh Esrei,* which contains nineteen blessings. On the Sabbath and Festivals, however, each *Shemoneh Esrei* contains only seven blessings. One means of filling this gap is the recitation of אֵין כֵּאלֹהֵינוּ, because each declaration of faith — *there is none like our God … who is like our God,* etc. — is regarded as a blessing of sorts. Furthermore, the initial letters of the words אֵין, מִי, and נוֹדֶה spell אָמֵן, a further allusion to the concept of blessing. Thus the recitation of this paragraph is equivalent to twenty blessings *(Kol Bo).*

Responsa Noda B'Yehudah (1:10) offers a

קַוֵּה *Hope to HASHEM, strengthen yourself and He will give you courage; and hope to HASHEM.*[1] *There is none holy as HASHEM, for there is none beside You, and there is no Rock like our God.*[2] *For who is a god beside HASHEM, and who is a Rock except for our God.*[3]

אֵין *There is none like our God;* there is none like our Master;*
there is none like our King; there is none like our Savior.
Who is like our God? Who is like our Master?*
Who is like our King? Who is like our Savior?
Let us thank our God; let us thank our Master;
let us thank our King; let us thank our Savior.
Blessed is our God; blessed is our Master;
blessed is our King; blessed is our Savior.
It is You Who is our God; it is You Who is our Master;
it is You Who is our King; it is You Who is our Savior.
It is You before Whom our forefathers burned the spice-incense.

Talmud, *Kereisos* 6a

פִּטּוּם הַקְּטֹרֶת *The incense mixture* was formulated of [eleven spices]: (1) stacte, (2) onycha, (3) galbanum,* (4) frankincense — each weighing seventy maneh; (5) myrrh, (6) cassia, (7) spikenard, (8) saffron — each weighing sixteen maneh; (9) costus — twelve maneh; (10) aromatic bark — three; and (11) cinnamon — nine. [Additionally] Carshina lye — nine kab; Cyprus wine, three se'ah and three kab — if he has no Cyprus wine, he brings old white wine; Sodom salt, a quarter kab; and a minute amount of smoke-raising herb. Rabbi Nassan the Babylonian says: Also a minute amount of Jordan amber. If he placed honey into it, he invalidated it. And if he left out any of its spices, he is liable to the death penalty.*

רַבָּן שִׁמְעוֹן *Rabban Shimon ben Gamliel says: The stacte is simply the sap that drips from balsam trees. Carshina lye is used to bleach the onycha to make it pleasing. Cyprus wine is used to soak*

---

(1) *Psalms* 27:14. (2) *I Samuel* 2:2. (3) *Psalms* 18:32.

---

novel reason for reciting אֵין כֵּאלֹהֵינוּ before the passage about the incense offering. The Talmud teaches that any *Kohen* who prepared the incense would become wealthy. Thus, before speaking about the incense ritual, we declare our absolute faith in God, acknowledging that wealth comes from Him, not through our own talent or effort.

אֵין ... מִי — *There is none ... Who is like?* First we declare unequivocally our recognition that nothing compares to our God. Then we ask the rhetorical question, can anyone or anything compare to Him?

פִּטּוּם הַקְּטֹרֶת — *The incense mixture.* Although the Temple incense was burned after the morning *tamid,* before the *mussaf* offering, this passage describing the incense preparation is recited here so that a portion of Talmudic law will be studied at the conclusion of the service. It should be noted that we cannot be certain of the exact translation of the spices included in the incense. For commentary and discussion, see p. 34-38.

הַחֶלְבְּנָה — *Galbanum.* The Talmud (*Kerisus* 6a) notes that galbanum has a foul odor, yet is included in the incense mixture to teach that even

אֶת הַצִּפֹּרֶן כְּדֵי שֶׁתְּהֵא עַזָּה; וַהֲלֹא מֵי רַגְלַיִם יָפִין לָהּ, אֶלָּא שֶׁאֵין מַכְנִיסִין מֵי רַגְלַיִם בָּעֲזָרָה מִפְּנֵי הַכָּבוֹד.

משנה, תמיד ז:ד

הַשִּׁיר* שֶׁהַלְּוִיִּם הָיוּ אוֹמְרִים בְּבֵית הַמִּקְדָּשׁ. בַּיּוֹם הָרִאשׁוֹן הָיוּ אוֹמְרִים: לַיהוה הָאָרֶץ וּמְלוֹאָהּ, תֵּבֵל וְיֹשְׁבֵי בָהּ.[1] בַּשֵּׁנִי הָיוּ אוֹמְרִים: גָּדוֹל יהוה וּמְהֻלָּל מְאֹד, בְּעִיר אֱלֹהֵינוּ הַר קָדְשׁוֹ.[2] בַּשְּׁלִישִׁי הָיוּ אוֹמְרִים: אֱלֹהִים נִצָּב בַּעֲדַת אֵל, בְּקֶרֶב אֱלֹהִים יִשְׁפֹּט.[3] בָּרְבִיעִי הָיוּ אוֹמְרִים: אֵל נְקָמוֹת יהוה, אֵל נְקָמוֹת הוֹפִיעַ.[4] בַּחֲמִישִׁי הָיוּ אוֹמְרִים: הַרְנִינוּ לֵאלֹהִים עוּזֵּנוּ, הָרִיעוּ לֵאלֹהֵי יַעֲקֹב.[5] בַּשִּׁשִּׁי הָיוּ אוֹמְרִים: יהוה מָלָךְ גֵּאוּת לָבֵשׁ, לָבֵשׁ יהוה עֹז הִתְאַזָּר, אַף תִּכּוֹן תֵּבֵל בַּל תִּמּוֹט.[6] בַּשַּׁבָּת הָיוּ אוֹמְרִים: מִזְמוֹר שִׁיר לְיוֹם הַשַּׁבָּת.[7] מִזְמוֹר שִׁיר לֶעָתִיד לָבֹא, לְיוֹם שֶׁכֻּלּוֹ שַׁבָּת וּמְנוּחָה לְחַיֵּי הָעוֹלָמִים.

מגילה כח:

תָּנָא דְבֵי אֵלִיָּהוּ:* כָּל הַשּׁוֹנֶה הֲלָכוֹת בְּכָל יוֹם, מֻבְטָח לוֹ שֶׁהוּא בֶּן עוֹלָם הַבָּא, שֶׁנֶּאֱמַר: הֲלִיכוֹת עוֹלָם לוֹ,[8] אַל תִּקְרֵי* הֲלִיכוֹת, אֶלָּא הֲלָכוֹת.

ברכות סד.

אָמַר רַבִּי אֶלְעָזָר* אָמַר רַבִּי חֲנִינָא: תַּלְמִידֵי חֲכָמִים מַרְבִּים שָׁלוֹם בָּעוֹלָם, שֶׁנֶּאֱמַר: וְכָל בָּנַיִךְ לִמּוּדֵי יהוה, וְרַב שְׁלוֹם בָּנָיִךְ,[9] אַל תִּקְרֵי בָּנָיִךְ אֶלָּא בּוֹנָיִךְ. ❖ שָׁלוֹם רָב לְאֹהֲבֵי תוֹרָתֶךָ, וְאֵין לָמוֹ מִכְשׁוֹל.[10] יְהִי שָׁלוֹם בְּחֵילֵךְ, שַׁלְוָה בְּאַרְמְנוֹתָיִךְ. לְמַעַן אַחַי וְרֵעָי, אֲדַבְּרָה נָּא שָׁלוֹם בָּךְ. לְמַעַן בֵּית יהוה אֱלֹהֵינוּ, אֲבַקְשָׁה טוֹב לָךְ.[11] יהוה עֹז לְעַמּוֹ יִתֵּן, יהוה יְבָרֵךְ אֶת עַמּוֹ בַשָּׁלוֹם.[12]

---

non-observant people should be welcomed to participate in the service of God.

☙ הַשִּׁיר ❧ — *The* [*daily*] *song.* This mishnah (*Tamid* 7:4) is recited here because the daily song was chanted by the Levites at the conclusion of the incense service. [For the text and commentary to each of the daily songs, see pages 162-169.]

☙ תָּנָא דְבֵי אֵלִיָּהוּ ❧ — *The Academy of Elijah taught.* This homiletical teaching likens the ways of the world to the laws that govern a Jew's life on earth. Only by studying, knowing and practicing the laws of the Torah can a Jew insure himself of ultimate success.

☙ אָמַר רַבִּי אֶלְעָזָר ❧ — *Rabbi Elazar said.* This famous teaching is the concluding statement of

the onycha to make it pungent. Even though urine is suitable for that, nevertheless they do not bring urine into the Temple out of respect.

Mishnah, *Tamid* 7:4

הַשִּׁיר *The daily song* that the Levites would recite in the Temple was as follows: On the first day [of the week] they would say: 'HASHEM's is the earth and its fullness, the inhabited land and those who dwell in it.'*[1] *On the second day they would say: 'Great is HASHEM and much praised, in the city of our God, Mount of His Holiness.'*[2] *On the third day they would say: 'God stands in the Divine assembly, in the midst of judges shall He judge.'*[3] *On the fourth day they would say: 'O God of vengeance, HASHEM, O God of vengeance, appear.'*[4] *On the fifth day they would say: 'Sing joyously to the God of our might, call out to the God of Jacob.'*[5] *On the sixth day they would say: 'HASHEM will have reigned, He will have donned grandeur; He will have donned might and girded Himself; He even made the world firm so that it should not falter.'*[6] *On the Sabbath they would say: 'A psalm, a song for the Sabbath day.'*[7] *A psalm, a song for the time to come, to the day that will be entirely Sabbath and contentment for the eternal life.*

Talmud, *Megillah* 28b

תָּנָא *The Academy of Elijah taught:* He who studies Torah laws every day, has the assurance that he will be in the World to Come, as it is said, 'The ways of the world are His'*[8] *— do not read* [הֲלִיכוֹת] *'ways,' but* [הֲלָכוֹת] *'laws.'*

Talmud, *Berachos* 64a

אָמַר *Rabbi Elazar said* on behalf of Rabbi Chanina: Torah scholars increase peace in the world, as it is said: 'And all your children will be students of HASHEM, and your children will have peace'*[9] *— do not read** [בָּנָיִךְ] *'your children,' but* [בּוֹנָיִךְ] *'your builders.'* Chazzan— *There is abundant peace for the lovers of your Torah, and there is no stumbling block for them.*[10] *May there be peace within your wall, serenity within your palaces. For the sake of my brethren and comrades I shall speak of peace in your midst. For the sake of the House of HASHEM, our God, I will request your good.*[11] *HASHEM will give might to His nation, HASHEM will bless His nation with peace.*[12]

(1) *Psalms* 24:1. (2) 48:2. (3) 82:1. (4) 94:1. (5) 81:2. (6) 93:1. (7) 92:1.
(8) *Habakkuk* 3:6. (9) *Isaiah* 54:13. (10) *Psalms* 119:165. (11) 122:7-9. (12) 29:11.

---

tractate *Berachos. Maharsha* there, in a comment that applies here as well, explains that the tractate dealt with prayers and blessings that had been instituted by the Sages. The reason they promulgated these expressions of devotion was to increase the harmony in the universe between man and his Maker.

אַל תִּקְרֵי — *Do not read.* The intention is not to change the accepted reading of Scripture. Whenever such a statement appears in Rabbinic literature it means that the verse contains an allusion in addition to its literal meaning, *as if* it were pronounced differently. [See further commentary, page 329.]

קדיש דרבנן

In the presence of a *minyan,* mourners recite קַדִּישׁ דְּרַבָּנָן:

יִתְגַּדַּל וְיִתְקַדַּשׁ שְׁמֵהּ רַבָּא. (.Cong — אָמֵן.) בְּעָלְמָא דִּי בְרָא כִרְעוּתֵהּ. וְיַמְלִיךְ מַלְכוּתֵהּ, בְּחַיֵּיכוֹן וּבְיוֹמֵיכוֹן וּבְחַיֵּי דְכָל בֵּית יִשְׂרָאֵל, בַּעֲגָלָא וּבִזְמַן קָרִיב. וְאִמְרוּ: אָמֵן.

(.Cong — אָמֵן. יְהֵא שְׁמֵהּ רַבָּא מְבָרַךְ לְעָלַם וּלְעָלְמֵי עָלְמַיָּא.)

יְהֵא שְׁמֵהּ רַבָּא מְבָרַךְ לְעָלַם וּלְעָלְמֵי עָלְמַיָּא.

יִתְבָּרַךְ וְיִשְׁתַּבַּח וְיִתְפָּאַר וְיִתְרוֹמַם וְיִתְנַשֵּׂא וְיִתְהַדָּר וְיִתְעַלֶּה וְיִתְהַלָּל שְׁמֵהּ דְּקֻדְשָׁא בְּרִיךְ הוּא (.Cong — בְּרִיךְ הוּא) — °לְעֵלָּא מִן כָּל (From Rosh Hashanah to Yom Kippur substitute— °לְעֵלָּא וּלְעֵלָּא מִכָּל) בִּרְכָתָא וְשִׁירָתָא תֻּשְׁבְּחָתָא וְנֶחֱמָתָא, דַּאֲמִירָן בְּעָלְמָא. וְאִמְרוּ: אָמֵן. (.Cong — אָמֵן.)

עַל יִשְׂרָאֵל וְעַל רַבָּנָן, וְעַל תַּלְמִידֵיהוֹן וְעַל כָּל תַּלְמִידֵי תַלְמִידֵיהוֹן, וְעַל כָּל מָאן דְּעָסְקִין בְּאוֹרַיְתָא, דִּי בְאַתְרָא הָדֵין וְדִי בְכָל אֲתַר וַאֲתַר. יְהֵא לְהוֹן וּלְכוֹן שְׁלָמָא רַבָּא, חִנָּא וְחִסְדָּא וְרַחֲמִין, וְחַיִּין אֲרִיכִין, וּמְזוֹנֵי רְוִיחֵי, וּפֻרְקָנָא, מִן קֳדָם אֲבוּהוֹן דִּי בִשְׁמַיָּא (וְאַרְעָא). וְאִמְרוּ: אָמֵן. (.Cong — אָמֵן.)

יְהֵא שְׁלָמָא רַבָּא מִן שְׁמַיָּא, וְחַיִּים (טוֹבִים) עָלֵינוּ וְעַל כָּל יִשְׂרָאֵל. וְאִמְרוּ: אָמֵן. (.Cong — אָמֵן.)

Take three steps back. Bow left and say ... עֹשֶׂה; bow right and say ... הוּא; bow forward and say וְעַל כָּל ... אָמֵן. Remain standing in place for a few moments, then take three steps forward.

עֹשֶׂה שָׁלוֹם בִּמְרוֹמָיו, הוּא בְּרַחֲמָיו יַעֲשֶׂה שָׁלוֹם עָלֵינוּ, וְעַל כָּל יִשְׂרָאֵל. וְאִמְרוּ: אָמֵן. (.Cong — אָמֵן.)

Stand while reciting עָלֵינוּ.

עָלֵינוּ לְשַׁבֵּחַ לַאֲדוֹן הַכֹּל, לָתֵת גְּדֻלָּה לְיוֹצֵר בְּרֵאשִׁית, שֶׁלֹּא עָשָׂנוּ כְּגוֹיֵי הָאֲרָצוֹת, וְלֹא שָׂמָנוּ כְּמִשְׁפְּחוֹת הָאֲדָמָה. שֶׁלֹּא שָׂם חֶלְקֵנוּ כָּהֶם, וְגוֹרָלֵנוּ כְּכָל הֲמוֹנָם. (שֶׁהֵם מִשְׁתַּחֲוִים לְהֶבֶל וָרִיק, וּמִתְפַּלְּלִים אֶל אֵל לֹא יוֹשִׁיעַ.[1]) וַאֲנַחְנוּ כּוֹרְעִים וּמִשְׁתַּחֲוִים וּמוֹדִים, לִפְנֵי מֶלֶךְ מַלְכֵי הַמְּלָכִים הַקָּדוֹשׁ בָּרוּךְ הוּא. שֶׁהוּא נוֹטֶה שָׁמַיִם וְיֹסֵד אָרֶץ,[2] וּמוֹשַׁב יְקָרוֹ בַּשָּׁמַיִם מִמַּעַל, וּשְׁכִינַת עֻזּוֹ בְּגָבְהֵי מְרוֹמִים. הוּא אֱלֹהֵינוּ, אֵין עוֹד. אֱמֶת מַלְכֵּנוּ, אֶפֶס זוּלָתוֹ, כַּכָּתוּב בְּתוֹרָתוֹ: וְיָדַעְתָּ הַיּוֹם וַהֲשֵׁבֹתָ אֶל לְבָבֶךָ, כִּי יהוה הוּא הָאֱלֹהִים בַּשָּׁמַיִם מִמַּעַל וְעַל הָאָרֶץ מִתָּחַת, אֵין עוֹד.[3]

Bow while reciting וַאֲנַחְנוּ כּוֹרְעִים וּמִשְׁתַּחֲוִים.

THE RABBIS' KADDISH

In the presence of a *minyan,* mourners recite the Rabbis' *Kaddish* (see *Laws* §120-121):
[A transliteration of this *Kaddish* appears on page 1042.]

יִתְגַּדַּל *May His great Name grow exalted and sanctified* (Cong.— *Amen.*) *in the world that He created as He willed. May He give reign to His kingship in your lifetimes and in your days, and in the lifetimes of the entire Family of Israel, swiftly and soon. Now respond: Amen.*

(Cong.— *Amen. May His great Name be blessed forever and ever.*)
May His great Name be blessed forever and ever.

Blessed, praised, glorified, exalted, extolled, mighty, upraised, and lauded be the Name of the Holy One, Blessed is He (Cong.— *Blessed is He*) — (From Rosh Hashanah to Yom Kippur add: *exceedingly*) *beyond any blessing and song, praise and consolation that are uttered in the world. Now respond: Amen.* (Cong.— *Amen.*)

Upon Israel, upon the teachers, their disciples and all of their disciples and upon all those who engage in the study of Torah, who are here or anywhere else; may they and you have abundant peace, grace, kindness, and mercy, long life, ample nourishment, and salvation, from before their Father Who is in Heaven (and on earth). Now respond: Amen. (Cong. — *Amen.*)

May there be abundant peace from Heaven, and (good) life, upon us and upon all Israel. Now respond: Amen. (Cong.— *Amen.*)

Take three steps back. Bow left and say, *'He Who makes peace ...';* bow right and say, *'may He ...';* bow forward and say, *'and upon all Israel ...'* Remain standing in place for a few moments, then take three steps forward.

He Who makes peace in His heights, may He, in His compassion, make peace upon us, and upon all Israel. Now respond: Amen. (Cong.— *Amen.*)

Stand while reciting *Aleinu.*

עָלֵינוּ *It is our duty to praise the Master of all, to ascribe greatness to the Molder of primeval creation, for He has not made us like the nations of the lands and has not emplaced us like the families of the earth; for He has not assigned our portion like theirs nor our lot like all their multitudes. (For they bow to vanity and emptiness and pray to a god which helps not.*[1]*) But we bend our knees, bow, and acknowledge our thanks before the King Who reigns over kings, the Holy One, Blessed is He. He stretches out heaven and establishes earth's foundation,*[2] *the seat of His homage is in the heavens above and His powerful Presence is in the loftiest heights. He is our God and there is none other. True is our King, there is nothing beside Him, as it is written in His Torah: 'You are to know this day and take to your heart* that* HASHEM *is the only God — in heaven above and on the earth below — there is none other.'*[3]

Bow while reciting *'But we bend our knees.'*

(1) *Isaiah* 45:20. (2) 51:13. (3) *Deuteronomy* 4:39.

עַל כֵּן נְקַוֶּה לְּךָ יהוה אֱלֹהֵינוּ לִרְאוֹת מְהֵרָה בְּתִפְאֶרֶת עֻזֶּךָ, לְהַעֲבִיר גִּלּוּלִים מִן הָאָרֶץ, וְהָאֱלִילִים כָּרוֹת יִכָּרֵתוּן, לְתַקֵּן עוֹלָם בְּמַלְכוּת שַׁדַּי. וְכָל בְּנֵי בָשָׂר יִקְרְאוּ בִשְׁמֶךָ, לְהַפְנוֹת אֵלֶיךָ כָּל רִשְׁעֵי אָרֶץ. יַכִּירוּ וְיֵדְעוּ כָּל יוֹשְׁבֵי תֵבֵל, כִּי לְךָ תִּכְרַע כָּל בֶּרֶךְ, תִּשָּׁבַע כָּל לָשׁוֹן.[1] לְפָנֶיךָ יהוה אֱלֹהֵינוּ יִכְרְעוּ וְיִפֹּלוּ, וְלִכְבוֹד שִׁמְךָ יְקָר יִתֵּנוּ. וִיקַבְּלוּ כֻלָּם אֶת עוֹל מַלְכוּתֶךָ, וְתִמְלֹךְ עֲלֵיהֶם מְהֵרָה לְעוֹלָם וָעֶד. כִּי הַמַּלְכוּת שֶׁלְּךָ הִיא וּלְעוֹלְמֵי עַד תִּמְלוֹךְ בְּכָבוֹד, כַּכָּתוּב בְּתוֹרָתֶךָ: יהוה יִמְלֹךְ לְעֹלָם וָעֶד.[2] ❖ וְנֶאֱמַר: וְהָיָה יהוה לְמֶלֶךְ עַל כָּל הָאָרֶץ, בַּיּוֹם הַהוּא יִהְיֶה יהוה אֶחָד וּשְׁמוֹ אֶחָד.[3]

Some congregations recite the following after עָלֵינוּ:

אַל תִּירָא מִפַּחַד פִּתְאֹם, וּמִשֹּׁאַת רְשָׁעִים כִּי תָבֹא.[4] עֻצוּ עֵצָה וְתֻפָר, דַּבְּרוּ דָבָר וְלֹא יָקוּם, כִּי עִמָּנוּ אֵל.[5] וְעַד זִקְנָה אֲנִי הוּא, וְעַד שֵׂיבָה אֲנִי אֶסְבֹּל, אֲנִי עָשִׂיתִי וַאֲנִי אֶשָּׂא, וַאֲנִי אֶסְבֹּל וַאֲמַלֵּט.[6]

קדיש יתום

In the presence of a *minyan,* mourners recite קַדִּישׁ יָתוֹם, the Mourner's *Kaddish* (see *Laws* §119):

יִתְגַּדַּל וְיִתְקַדַּשׁ שְׁמֵהּ רַבָּא. (.Cong.— אָמֵן) בְּעָלְמָא דִּי בְרָא כִרְעוּתֵהּ. וְיַמְלִיךְ מַלְכוּתֵהּ, בְּחַיֵּיכוֹן וּבְיוֹמֵיכוֹן וּבְחַיֵּי דְכָל בֵּית יִשְׂרָאֵל, בַּעֲגָלָא וּבִזְמַן קָרִיב. וְאִמְרוּ: אָמֵן.

(.Cong.— אָמֵן. יְהֵא שְׁמֵהּ רַבָּא מְבָרַךְ לְעָלַם וּלְעָלְמֵי עָלְמַיָּא.)

יְהֵא שְׁמֵהּ רַבָּא מְבָרַךְ לְעָלַם וּלְעָלְמֵי עָלְמַיָּא.

יִתְבָּרַךְ וְיִשְׁתַּבַּח וְיִתְפָּאַר וְיִתְרוֹמַם וְיִתְנַשֵּׂא וְיִתְהַדָּר וְיִתְעַלֶּה וְיִתְהַלָּל שְׁמֵהּ דְּקֻדְשָׁא בְּרִיךְ הוּא (.Cong.— בְּרִיךְ הוּא) — °לְעֵלָּא מִן כָּל (From Rosh Hashanah to Yom Kippur substitute— °לְעֵלָּא וּלְעֵלָּא מִכָּל) בִּרְכָתָא וְשִׁירָתָא תֻּשְׁבְּחָתָא וְנֶחֱמָתָא, דַּאֲמִירָן בְּעָלְמָא. וְאִמְרוּ: אָמֵן. (.Cong.— אָמֵן.)

יְהֵא שְׁלָמָא רַבָּא מִן שְׁמַיָּא, וְחַיִּים עָלֵינוּ וְעַל כָּל יִשְׂרָאֵל. וְאִמְרוּ: אָמֵן. (.Cong.— אָמֵן.)

Take three steps back. Bow left and say ... עֹשֶׂה; bow right and say ... הוּא; bow forward and say וְעַל כָּל ... אָמֵן. Remain standing in place for a few moments, then take three steps forward.

עֹשֶׂה שָׁלוֹם בִּמְרוֹמָיו, הוּא יַעֲשֶׂה שָׁלוֹם עָלֵינוּ, וְעַל כָּל יִשְׂרָאֵל. וְאִמְרוּ: אָמֵן. (.Cong.— אָמֵן.)

עַל כֵּן *Therefore we put our hope in You, HASHEM our God, that we may soon see Your mighty splendor, to remove detestable idolatry from the earth, and false gods will be utterly cut off, to perfect the universe through the Almighty's sovereignty. Then all humanity will call upon Your Name, to turn all the earth's wicked toward You. All the world's inhabitants will recognize and know that to You every knee should bend, every tongue should swear.*[1] *Before You, HASHEM, our God, they will bend every knee and cast themselves down and to the glory of Your Name they will render homage, and they will all accept upon themselves the yoke of Your kingship that You may reign over them soon and eternally. For the kingdom is Yours and You will reign for all eternity in glory as it is written in Your Torah: HASHEM shall reign for all eternity.*[2] Chazzan—*And it is said: HASHEM will be King over all the world — on that day HASHEM will be One and His Name will be One.*[3]

Some congregations recite the following after *Aleinu.*

אַל תִּירָא *Do not fear sudden terror, or the holocaust of the wicked when it comes.*[4] *Plan a conspiracy and it will be annulled; speak your piece and it shall not stand, for God is with us.*[5] *Even till your seniority, I remain unchanged; and even till your ripe old age, I shall endure. I created you and I shall bear you; I shall endure and rescue.*[6]

MOURNER'S KADDISH

In the presence of a *minyan,* mourners recite קַדִּישׁ יָתוֹם, the Mourner's *Kaddish* (see *Laws* §119):

[A transliteration of this *Kaddish* appears on page 1043, and commentary on p. 57.]

יִתְגַּדַּל *May His great Name grow exalted and sanctified* (Cong.— *Amen.*) *in the world that He created as He willed. May He give reign to His kingship in your lifetimes and in your days, and in the lifetimes of the entire Family of Israel, swiftly and soon. Now respond: Amen.*

(Cong.— *Amen. May His great Name be blessed forever and ever.*)

May His great Name be blessed forever and ever.

Blessed, praised, glorified, exalted, extolled, mighty, upraised, and lauded be the Name of the Holy One, Blessed is He (Cong.— *Blessed is He*) — (From Rosh Hashanah to Yom Kippur add: *exceedingly*) *beyond any blessing and song, praise and consolation that are uttered in the world. Now respond: Amen.* (Cong.—*Amen*).

May there be abundant peace from Heaven, and life, upon us and upon all Israel. Now respond: Amen. (Cong.— *Amen.*)

Take three steps back. Bow left and say, *'He Who makes peace ...';*
bow right and say, *'may He ...';* bow forward and say, *'and upon all Israel ...'*
Remain standing in place for a few moments, then take three steps forward.

He Who makes peace in His heights, may He make peace upon us, and upon all Israel. Now respond: Amen. (Cong.—*Amen.*)

---

(1) Cf. *Isaiah* 45:23. (2) *Exodus* 15:18. (3) *Zechariah* 14:9. (4) *Proverbs* 3:25. (5) *Isaiah* 8:10. (6) 46:4.

שיר הכבוד

The Ark is opened and שִׁיר הַכָּבוֹד, *The Song of Glory,* is recited responsively — the *chazzan* reciting the first verse, the congregation reciting the second and so on.

אַנְעִים זְמִירוֹת וְשִׁירִים אֶאֱרוֹג,* כִּי אֵלֶיךָ נַפְשִׁי תַעֲרוֹג.

—All **נַ**פְשִׁי חָמְדָה בְּצֵל יָדֶךָ, לָדַעַת כָּל רָז סוֹדֶךָ.

—Chazzan מִדֵּי דַבְּרִי בִּכְבוֹדֶךָ, הוֹמֶה לִבִּי אֶל דּוֹדֶיךָ.

—All עַל כֵּן אֲדַבֵּר בְּךָ נִכְבָּדוֹת, וְשִׁמְךָ אֲכַבֵּד בְּשִׁירֵי יְדִידוֹת.

—Chazzan **אֲ**סַפְּרָה כְבוֹדְךָ וְלֹא רְאִיתִיךָ,*
אֲדַמְּךָ אֲכַנְּךָ וְלֹא יְדַעְתִּיךָ.

—All **בְּ**יַד נְבִיאֶיךָ* בְּסוֹד עֲבָדֶיךָ, דִּמִּיתָ הֲדַר כְּבוֹד הוֹדֶךָ.

—Chazzan **גְּ**דֻלָּתְךָ וּגְבוּרָתֶךָ, כִּנּוּ לְתֹקֶף פְּעֻלָּתֶךָ.

—All **דִּ**מּוּ אוֹתְךָ וְלֹא כְּפִי יֶשְׁךָ, וַיְשַׁוּוּךָ לְפִי מַעֲשֶׂיךָ.*

—Chazzan **הִ**מְשִׁילוּךָ בְּרֹב חֶזְיוֹנוֹת, הִנְּךָ אֶחָד* בְּכָל דִּמְיוֹנוֹת.

—All **וַ**יֶּחֱזוּ בְךָ זִקְנָה וּבַחֲרוּת,
וּשְׂעַר רֹאשְׁךָ בְּשֵׂיבָה וְשַׁחֲרוּת.

—Chazzan **זִ**קְנָה* בְּיוֹם דִּין וּבַחֲרוּת בְּיוֹם קְרָב,
כְּאִישׁ מִלְחָמוֹת יָדָיו לוֹ רָב.

—All **חָ**בַשׁ כֹּבַע יְשׁוּעָה בְּרֹאשׁוֹ,
הוֹשִׁיעָה לּוֹ יְמִינוֹ* וּזְרוֹעַ קָדְשׁוֹ.

—Chazzan **טַ**לְלֵי אוֹרוֹת* רֹאשׁוֹ נִמְלָא, קְוֻצּוֹתָיו רְסִיסֵי לָיְלָה.

—All **יִ**תְפָּאֵר בִּי כִּי חָפֵץ בִּי. וְהוּא יִהְיֶה לִּי לַעֲטֶרֶת צְבִי.

—Chazzan **כֶּ**תֶם טָהוֹר פָּז דְּמוּת רֹאשׁוֹ,
וְחַק עַל מֵצַח כְּבוֹד שֵׁם קָדְשׁוֹ.*

—All **לְ**חֵן וּלְכָבוֹד* צְבִי תִפְאָרָה, אֻמָּתוֹ לוֹ עִטְּרָה עֲטָרָה.

⁂ שִׁיר הַכָּבוֹד / Song of Glory

This beautiful sacred song has been ascribed to R' Yehudah HaChassid, the twelfth century German scholar and Kabbalist. Due to the song's great holiness, the Ark is opened when it is recited, and it is not recited daily so that it not become too familiar *(Levush).* Most congregations recite it every Sabbath and on all Festivals. The *Vilna Gaon* held that it should be recited only on Festivals, and some congregations recite it only on Rosh Hashanah and Yom Kippur.

וְשִׁירִים אֶאֱרוֹג — *And weave hymns.* Just as a weaver unifies countless threads to make a finished garment, so does the *paytan* [liturgical poet] weave together words and phrases to compose beautiful songs of praise.

וְלֹא רְאִיתִיךָ — *Though I see You not.* This stich of the song introduces much of what comes later. We cannot see God, nor can we know His essence. The best we can do is to imagine and describe Him in human terms.

בְּיַד נְבִיאֶיךָ — *Through the hand of Your prophets.* The precedent for describing God in human, physical terminology comes from Him — for He described Himself to the prophets in such terms.

לְפִי מַעֲשֶׂיךָ — *According to Your deeds.* It is a familiar truth that we cannot conceive of what

SONG OF GLORY

The Ark is opened and the *Song of Glory* is recited responsively — the *chazzan* reciting the first verse, the congregation reciting the second and so on.

אַנְעִים זְמִירוֹת *I shall compose pleasant psalms and weave hymns,* because for You shall my soul pine.*

All— *My soul desired the shelter of Your hand, to know every mystery of Your secret.*

Chazzan— *As I speak of Your glory, my heart yearns for Your love.*

All— *Therefore I shall speak of Your glories, and Your Name I shall honor with loving songs.*

Chazzan— *I shall relate Your glory, though I see You not;* I shall allegorize You, I shall describe You, though I know You not.*

All— *Through the hand of Your prophets,* through the counsel of Your servants; You allegorized the splendrous glory of Your power.*

Chazzan— *Your greatness and Your strength, they described the might of Your works.*

All— *They allegorized You, but not according to Your reality, and they portrayed You according to Your deeds.**

Chazzan— *They symbolized You in many varied visions; yet You are a Unity* containing all the allegories.*

All— *They envisioned in You agedness and virility, and the hair of Your head as hoary and jet black.*

Chazzan— *Aged* on judgment day and virile on the day of battle, like a man of war whose powers are many.*

All— *The hat of salvation He put on His head; salvation for Him, His right hand* and His sacred arm.*

Chazzan— *With illuminating dew drops* His head is filled, His locks are the rains of the night.*

All— *He shall glory in me for He desires me, and He shall be for me a crown of pride.*

Chazzan— *A form of the very finest gold upon his head, and carved on his forehead is His glorious, sacred Name.**

All— *For grace and for glory* the pride of His splendor; His nation crowns Him with its prayers.*

God *is;* we can only know something of Him through His deeds.

הִנְּךָ אֶחָד — *Yet You are a Unity.* God is One though He appears in many guises: merciful, judgmental, old, young, warrior and so on.

זִקְנָה — *Aged.* This stich expounds on the previous one. Since the song now begins an extensive discussion of God in human terms, it changes to third person out of respect.

הוֹשִׁיעָה לוֹ יְמִינוֹ — *Salvation for Him, His right hand.* God was like a warrior winning victory through his powerful arm.

טַלְלֵי אוֹרוֹת — *[With] illuminating dew drops. Dew* refers to the illumination of the Torah and the life-giving dew that resuscitates the dead. *Rain* refers to the flow of heavenly blessings.

כֶּתֶם ...שֵׁם קָדְשׁוֹ — *A form ... sacred Name.* A reference to the headplate of the *Kohen Gadol* [High Priest], upon which was inscribed God's sacred Name.

לְחֵן וּלְכָבוֹד ... — *... For grace and for glory.* It is a mark of God's esteem for Israel that He desires its prayers and that He takes them, as it were, as a crown on His head.

—Chazzan מַחְלְפוֹת רֹאשׁוֹ* כְּבִימֵי בְחֻרוֹת, קְוֻצּוֹתָיו תַּלְתַּלִּים שְׁחוֹרוֹת.

—All נְוֵה הַצֶּדֶק צְבִי תִפְאַרְתּוֹ, יַעֲלֶה נָּא עַל רֹאשׁ שִׂמְחָתוֹ.

—Chazzan סְגֻלָּתוֹ תְּהִי בְיָדוֹ עֲטֶרֶת, וּצְנִיף מְלוּכָה צְבִי תִפְאֶרֶת.

—All עֲמוּסִים נְשָׂאָם עֲטֶרֶת עִנְּדָם, מֵאֲשֶׁר יָקְרוּ בְעֵינָיו כִּבְּדָם.

—Chazzan פְּאֵרוֹ* עָלַי וּפְאֵרִי עָלָיו, וְקָרוֹב אֵלַי בְּקָרְאִי אֵלָיו.

—All צַח וְאָדוֹם* לִלְבוּשׁוֹ אָדוֹם, פּוּרָה בְדָרְכוֹ בְּבוֹאוֹ מֵאֱדוֹם.

—Chazzan קֶשֶׁר תְּפִלִּין* הֶרְאָה לֶעָנָו, תְּמוּנַת יהוה לְנֶגֶד עֵינָיו.

—All רוֹצֶה בְעַמּוֹ עֲנָוִים יְפָאֵר, יוֹשֵׁב תְּהִלּוֹת בָּם לְהִתְפָּאֵר.

—Chazzan רֹאשׁ דְּבָרְךָ אֱמֶת קוֹרֵא מֵרֹאשׁ,* דּוֹר וָדוֹר עַם דּוֹרֶשְׁךָ דְּרוֹשׁ.

—All שִׁית הֲמוֹן שִׁירַי נָא עָלֶיךָ, וְרִנָּתִי תִּקְרַב אֵלֶיךָ.

—Chazzan תְּהִלָּתִי תְּהִי לְרֹאשְׁךָ עֲטֶרֶת, וּתְפִלָּתִי תִּכּוֹן קְטֹרֶת.

—All תִּיקַר שִׁירַת רָשׁ בְּעֵינֶיךָ, כַּשִּׁיר יוּשַׁר עַל קָרְבָּנֶיךָ.

—Chazzan בִּרְכָתִי תַעֲלֶה לְרֹאשׁ מַשְׁבִּיר, מְחוֹלֵל וּמוֹלִיד צַדִּיק כַּבִּיר.

—All וּבְבִרְכָתִי תְנַעֲנַע לִי רֹאשׁ, וְאוֹתָהּ קַח לְךָ כִּבְשָׂמִים רֹאשׁ.

—Chazzan יֶעֱרַב נָא שִׂיחִי עָלֶיךָ, כִּי נַפְשִׁי תַעֲרוֹג אֵלֶיךָ.

לְךָ יהוה הַגְּדֻלָּה וְהַגְּבוּרָה וְהַתִּפְאֶרֶת וְהַנֵּצַח וְהַהוֹד, כִּי כֹל בַּשָּׁמַיִם וּבָאָרֶץ; לְךָ יהוה הַמַּמְלָכָה וְהַמִּתְנַשֵּׂא לְכֹל לְרֹאשׁ.[1] מִי יְמַלֵּל גְּבוּרוֹת יהוה, יַשְׁמִיעַ כָּל תְּהִלָּתוֹ.[2]

If a mourner is present, he recites קַדִּישׁ יָתוֹם, page 482.

מַחְלְפוֹת רֹאשׁוֹ — *The tresses of His head.* God does not change with the passage of time. His 'youth' remains with Him, just as the 'maturity of age' was always with Him.

פְּאֵרוֹ — *His tefillin-splendor.* Just as Israel takes pride in God, so God takes pride in Israel. The Talmud (*Berachos* 6a) expresses this idea by saying that just as Israel wears *tefillin* in which are written the praises of God, so does God wear *tefillin,* described as His *splendor,* which contain Scriptural verses that praise Israel.

צַח וְאָדוֹם — *He is white and crimson.* God is both compassionate, symbolized by white, and strict, symbolized by crimson. He is kind or harsh, depending on the need. When the final Redemption comes, God will execute judgment against Edom for that nation's outrages against Israel. God is metaphorically portrayed as a

Chazzan— *The tresses of His head* are like His youthful days; His locks are jet-black ringlets.*

All— *The Abode of righteousness is the pride of His splendor; may He elevate it to His foremost joy.*

Chazzan— *May His treasured nation be in His hand like a crown, and like a royal tiara the pride of His splendor.*

All— *From infancy He bore them and affixed them as a crown, because they are precious in His eyes He honored them.*

Chazzan— *His tefillin-splendor* is upon me and my tefillin-splendor is upon Him, and He is near to me when I call to Him.*

All— *He is white and crimson; His garment will be bloody red, when He tramples as in a press on His coming from Edom.*

Chazzan— *He showed the tefillin-knot* to the humble [Moses], the likeness of* HASHEM *before his eyes*

All— *He desires His people, He will glorify the humble; enthroned upon praises, He glories with them.*

Chazzan— *The very beginning of Your word is truth — one reads it from the Torah's start;* the people that seeks You expounds each generation's fate.*

All— *Place the multitude of my songs before You, please; and my glad song bring near to You.*

Chazzan— *May my praise be a crown for Your head, and may my prayer be accepted like incense.*

All— *May the poor man's song be dear in Your eyes, like the song that is sung over Your offerings.*

Chazzan— *May my blessing rise up upon the head of the Sustainer — Creator, Giver of life, mighty Righteous One.*

All— *And to my blessing, nod Your head to me, and take it to Yourself like the finest incense.*

Chazzan— *May my prayer be sweet to You, for my soul shall pine for You.*

לְךָ *Yours,* HASHEM, *is the greatness, the strength, the splendor, the triumph, and the glory; even everything in heaven and earth; Yours,* HASHEM, *is the kingdom, and the sovereignty over every leader.*[1] *Who can express the mighty acts of* HASHEM*? Who can declare all His praise?*[2]

If a mourner is present, he recites the Mourner's *Kaddish,* page 482.

(1) *I Chronicles* 29:11. (2) *Psalms* 106:2.

warrior whose clothing becomes soaked with blood as he kills his adversary. [See *Isaiah* 63:1, *Rashi*:]

קֶשֶׁר תְּפִלִּין — *The tefillin-knot.* When Moses asked to see [i.e., understand] God, He showed him, in the simile of the Sages, the *tefillin*-knot at the back of His 'head,' as it were. This indicated two things: that not even Moses could have a clear vision of God's ways, and that God wished to be attached — symbolized by a knot — to His humble prophet.

קוֹרֵא מֵרֹאשׁ — *One reads it from the Torah's start.* That God's seal is truth is implied from the first three words of the Torah, בְּרֵאשִׁית בָּרָא אֱלֹקִים, the last letters of which spell אֱמֶת, *truth.*

שיר של יום

On the Sabbath, *Psalm* 92, below, is recited. On a Festival that falls on a weekday, the appropriate *Song of the Day* (pp. 162-168) is recited.

הַיּוֹם יוֹם שַׁבַּת קֹדֶשׁ שֶׁבּוֹ הָיוּ הַלְוִיִּם אוֹמְרִים בְּבֵית הַמִּקְדָּשׁ.

תהלים צב (commentary on page 320)

מִזְמוֹר שִׁיר לְיוֹם הַשַּׁבָּת. טוֹב לְהֹדוֹת לַיהוה, וּלְזַמֵּר לְשִׁמְךָ עֶלְיוֹן. לְהַגִּיד בַּבֹּקֶר חַסְדֶּךָ, וֶאֱמוּנָתְךָ בַּלֵּילוֹת. עֲלֵי עָשׂוֹר וַעֲלֵי נָבֶל, עֲלֵי הִגָּיוֹן בְּכִנּוֹר. כִּי שִׂמַּחְתַּנִי יהוה בְּפָעֳלֶךָ, בְּמַעֲשֵׂי יָדֶיךָ אֲרַנֵּן. מַה גָּדְלוּ מַעֲשֶׂיךָ יהוה, מְאֹד עָמְקוּ מַחְשְׁבֹתֶיךָ. אִישׁ בַּעַר לֹא יֵדָע, וּכְסִיל לֹא יָבִין אֶת זֹאת. בִּפְרֹחַ רְשָׁעִים כְּמוֹ עֵשֶׂב, וַיָּצִיצוּ כָּל פֹּעֲלֵי אָוֶן, לְהִשָּׁמְדָם עֲדֵי עַד. וְאַתָּה מָרוֹם לְעֹלָם יהוה. כִּי הִנֵּה אֹיְבֶיךָ יהוה, כִּי הִנֵּה אֹיְבֶיךָ יֹאבֵדוּ, יִתְפָּרְדוּ כָּל פֹּעֲלֵי אָוֶן. וַתָּרֶם כִּרְאֵים קַרְנִי, בַּלֹּתִי בְּשֶׁמֶן רַעֲנָן. וַתַּבֵּט עֵינִי בְּשׁוּרָי, בַּקָּמִים עָלַי מְרֵעִים, תִּשְׁמַעְנָה אָזְנָי. ❖ צַדִּיק כַּתָּמָר יִפְרָח, כְּאֶרֶז בַּלְּבָנוֹן יִשְׂגֶּה. שְׁתוּלִים בְּבֵית יהוה, בְּחַצְרוֹת אֱלֹהֵינוּ יַפְרִיחוּ. עוֹד יְנוּבוּן בְּשֵׂיבָה, דְּשֵׁנִים וְרַעֲנַנִּים יִהְיוּ. לְהַגִּיד כִּי יָשָׁר יהוה, צוּרִי וְלֹא עַוְלָתָה בּוֹ.

If a mourner is present, he recites קַדִּישׁ יָתוֹם, page 482.

From Rosh Chodesh Elul through Shemini Atzeres, *Psalm* 27, לְדָוִד is recited.

לְדָוִד, יהוה אוֹרִי וְיִשְׁעִי, מִמִּי אִירָא, יהוה מָעוֹז חַיַּי, מִמִּי אֶפְחָד. בִּקְרֹב עָלַי מְרֵעִים לֶאֱכֹל אֶת בְּשָׂרִי, צָרַי וְאֹיְבַי לִי, הֵמָּה כָּשְׁלוּ וְנָפָלוּ. אִם תַּחֲנֶה עָלַי מַחֲנֶה, לֹא יִירָא לִבִּי, אִם תָּקוּם עָלַי מִלְחָמָה, בְּזֹאת אֲנִי בוֹטֵחַ. אַחַת שָׁאַלְתִּי מֵאֵת יהוה, אוֹתָהּ אֲבַקֵּשׁ, שִׁבְתִּי בְּבֵית יהוה כָּל יְמֵי חַיַּי, לַחֲזוֹת בְּנֹעַם יהוה, וּלְבַקֵּר בְּהֵיכָלוֹ. כִּי יִצְפְּנֵנִי בְּסֻכֹּה בְּיוֹם רָעָה, יַסְתִּירֵנִי בְּסֵתֶר אָהֳלוֹ, בְּצוּר יְרוֹמְמֵנִי. וְעַתָּה יָרוּם רֹאשִׁי עַל אֹיְבַי סְבִיבוֹתַי, וְאֶזְבְּחָה בְאָהֳלוֹ זִבְחֵי תְרוּעָה, אָשִׁירָה וַאֲזַמְּרָה לַיהוה. שְׁמַע יהוה קוֹלִי אֶקְרָא, וְחָנֵּנִי וַעֲנֵנִי. לְךָ אָמַר לִבִּי בַּקְּשׁוּ פָנָי, אֶת פָּנֶיךָ יהוה אֲבַקֵּשׁ. אַל תַּסְתֵּר פָּנֶיךָ מִמֶּנִּי, אַל תַּט בְּאַף עַבְדֶּךָ, עֶזְרָתִי הָיִיתָ, אַל תִּטְּשֵׁנִי וְאַל תַּעַזְבֵנִי, אֱלֹהֵי יִשְׁעִי. כִּי אָבִי וְאִמִּי עֲזָבוּנִי, וַיהוה יַאַסְפֵנִי. הוֹרֵנִי יהוה דַּרְכֶּךָ, וּנְחֵנִי בְּאֹרַח מִישׁוֹר, לְמַעַן שׁוֹרְרָי. אַל תִּתְּנֵנִי בְּנֶפֶשׁ צָרָי, כִּי קָמוּ בִי עֵדֵי שֶׁקֶר, וִיפֵחַ חָמָס. ❖ לוּלֵא הֶאֱמַנְתִּי לִרְאוֹת בְּטוּב יהוה בְּאֶרֶץ חַיִּים. קַוֵּה אֶל יהוה, חֲזַק וְיַאֲמֵץ לִבֶּךָ, וְקַוֵּה אֶל יהוה.

If a mourner is present, he recites קַדִּישׁ יָתוֹם, page 482.

On Rosh Chodesh many congregations recite בָּרְכִי נַפְשִׁי (p. 172); on Chanukah, מִזְמוֹר שִׁיר (p. 54).

SONG OF THE DAY

On the Sabbath, *Psalm* 92, below, is recited. On a Festival that falls on a weekday, the appropriate *Song of the Day* (pp. 163-169) is recited.

Today is the Holy Sabbath, on which the Levites would sing in the Holy Temple.

Psalm 92 (commentary on page 320)

מִזְמוֹר שִׁיר *A psalm, a song for the Sabbath day. It is good to thank HASHEM and to sing praise to Your Name, O Exalted One; to relate Your kindness in the dawn and Your faith in the nights. Upon ten-stringed instrument and lyre, with singing accompanied by a harp. For You have gladdened me, HASHEM, with Your deeds; at the works of Your Hands I sing glad song. How great are Your deeds, HASHEM; exceedingly profound are Your thoughts. A boor cannot know, nor can a fool understand this: when the wicked bloom like grass and all the doers of iniquity blossom — it is to destroy them till eternity. But You remain exalted forever, HASHEM. For behold! — Your enemies, HASHEM, for behold! — Your enemies shall perish, dispersed shall be all doers of iniquity. As exalted as a re'eim's shall be my pride, I will be saturated with ever-fresh oil. My eyes have seen my vigilant foes; when those who would harm me rise up against me, my ears have heard their doom.* Chazzan— *A righteous man will flourish like a date palm, like a cedar in the Lebanon he will grow tall. Planted in the house of HASHEM, in the courtyards of our God they will flourish. They will still be fruitful in old age, vigorous and fresh they will be — to declare that HASHEM is just, my Rock in Whom there is no wrong.*

If a mourner is present, he recites the Mourner's *Kaddish*, page 482.

From Rosh Chodesh Elul through Shemini Atzeres, *Psalm* 27, *'Of David'*, is recited.

לְדָוִד *Of David; HASHEM is my light and my salvation, whom shall I fear? HASHEM is my life's strength, whom shall I dread? When evildoers approach me to devour my flesh, my tormentors and my foes against me — it is they who stumble and fall. Though an army would besiege me, my heart would not fear; though war would arise against me, in this I trust. One thing I asked of HASHEM, that shall I seek: That I dwell in the House of HASHEM all the days of my life; to behold the sweetness of HASHEM and to contemplate in His Sanctuary. Indeed, He will hide me in His Shelter on the day of evil; He will conceal me in the concealment of His Tent, He will lift me upon a rock. Now my head is raised above my enemies around me, and I will slaughter offerings in His Tent accompanied by joyous song; I will sing and make music to HASHEM. HASHEM, hear my voice when I call, be gracious toward me and answer me. In Your behalf, my heart has said, 'Seek My Presence'; Your Presence, HASHEM, do I seek. Conceal not Your Presence from me, repel not Your servant in anger. You have been my Helper, abandon me not, forsake me not, O God of my salvation. Though my father and mother have forsaken me, HASHEM will gather me in. Teach me Your way, HASHEM, and lead me on the path of integrity, because of my watchful foes. Deliver me not to the wishes of my tormentors, for there have arisen against me false witnesses who breathe violence.* Chazzan— *Had I not trusted that I would see the goodness of HASHEM in the land of life! Hope to HASHEM, strengthen yourself and He will give you courage; and hope to HASHEM.*

If a mourner is present, he recites the Mourner's *Kaddish*, page 482.

Many congregations recite *Psalm* 104, (p. 173) Rosh Chodesh; and *Psalm* 30 (p. 54) on Chanukah.

סעודת יום השבת

חי ה׳

חַי יהוה וּבָרוּךְ צוּרִי, בַּיהוה תִּתְהַלֵּל נַפְשִׁי, כִּי יהוה יָאִיר נֵרִי, בְּהִלּוֹ נֵרוֹ עֲלֵי רֹאשִׁי.

יהוה רֹעִי לֹא אֶחְסָר, עַל מֵי מְנֻחוֹת יְנַהֲלֵנִי, נוֹתֵן לֶחֶם לְכָל בָּשָׂר, לֶחֶם חֻקִּי הַטְרִיפֵנִי.

יְהִי רָצוֹן מִלְּפָנֶיךָ, אַתָּה אֱלֹהֵי קְדוֹשִׁי, תַּעֲרֹךְ לְפָנַי שֻׁלְחָנֶךָ, תְּדַשֵּׁן בַּשֶּׁמֶן רֹאשִׁי.

מִי יִתֵּן מְנוּחָתִי, לִפְנֵי אֲדוֹן הַשָּׁלוֹם, וְהָיְתָה שְׁלֵמָה מִטָּתִי, הַחַיִּים וְהַשָּׁלוֹם.

יִשְׁלַח מַלְאָכוֹ לְפָנַי, לְלַוּוֹתִי לְוָיָה, בְּכוֹס יְשׁוּעוֹת אֶשָּׂא פָנַי, מְנָת כּוֹסִי רְוָיָה.

צָמְאָה נַפְשִׁי אֶל יהוה, יְמַלֵּא שֹׂבַע אֲסָמַי, אֶל הֶהָרִים אֶשָּׂא עֵינַי, כְּהִלֵּל וְלֹא כְשַׁמַּאי.

חֶדְוַת יָמִים וּשְׁנוֹת עוֹלָמִים, עוּרָה כְבוֹדִי עוּרָה, וְעַל רֹאשִׁי יִהְיוּ תַמִּים, נֵר מִצְוָה וְאוֹר תּוֹרָה.

קוּמָה יהוה לִמְנוּחָתִי. אַתָּה וַאֲרוֹן עֻזֶּךָ, קַח נָא אֵל אֶת בִּרְכָתִי, וְהַחֲזֵק מָגֵן חוֹזֶךָ.

תהלים כג

מִזְמוֹר לְדָוִד, יהוה רֹעִי* לֹא אֶחְסָר.* בִּנְאוֹת דֶּשֶׁא* יַרְבִּיצֵנִי, עַל מֵי מְנֻחוֹת יְנַהֲלֵנִי. נַפְשִׁי יְשׁוֹבֵב, יַנְחֵנִי בְמַעְגְּלֵי צֶדֶק* לְמַעַן שְׁמוֹ. גַּם כִּי אֵלֵךְ בְּגֵיא צַלְמָוֶת,* לֹא אִירָא רָע כִּי אַתָּה עִמָּדִי, שִׁבְטְךָ וּמִשְׁעַנְתֶּךָ* הֵמָּה יְנַחֲמֻנִי. תַּעֲרֹךְ לְפָנַי שֻׁלְחָן נֶגֶד צֹרְרָי, דִּשַּׁנְתָּ בַשֶּׁמֶן רֹאשִׁי, כּוֹסִי רְוָיָה. אַךְ טוֹב וָחֶסֶד* יִרְדְּפוּנִי כָּל יְמֵי חַיָּי, וְשַׁבְתִּי בְּבֵית יהוה לְאֹרֶךְ יָמִים.

סעודת יום השבת / SABBATH DAY MEAL

A complete selection of Zemiros with a phrase by phrase commentary can be found in the ArtScroll Zemiroth.

חַי ה׳ / Chai HASHEM

This *zemer* was composed by חַיִּים יִצְחָק, *Chaim Yitzchak*, whose name is formed by the acrostic. Virtually nothing is known about him except that he apparently lived in the seventeenth century. The first five stanzas of the *zemer* refer to the five items which must be prepared before the Sabbath begins: candles, two loaves, a set table, made beds, and the cup of *Kiddush*.

מִזְמוֹר לְדָוִד / Psalm 23

רֹעִי — *My Shepherd.* God is described as a *Shepherd* because He provides and cares for us. Without His benevolence we would be as helpless as sheep.

לֹא אֶחְסָר — *I shall not lack.* Just as sheep feel no anxiety, because their shepherd sees to their every need, so do we express our complete contentment in the knowledge that God will not deny us any legitimate need.

בִּנְאוֹת דֶּשֶׁא — *In lush meadows,* i.e., the pasture land which is a sheep's natural habitat. Thus, God, the Shepherd, seeks out suitable places for His flock, Israel.

SABBATH DAY MEAL

CHAI HASHEM

חַי יהוה *HASHEM lives — blessed is my Rock! In HASHEM does my soul glory, for HASHEM gives light to my lamp when He lights His lamp over my head.*

יהוה *HASHEM is my Shepherd I shall not lack, beside tranquil waters He leads me. He Who gives bread for all flesh — feed me my allotted bread.*

יְהִי *May it be Your will — You, my Sacred God — prepare Your table before me, anoint my head with oil.*

מִי *O who can place my contentment, before the Lord of Peace that my progeny be perfect, with life and peace!*

יִשְׁלַח *May He send His angel before me as my accompanying escort. Then I shall raise my face with a cup of salvations, the portion of my cup overflows.*

צָמְאָה *My soul thirsts for HASHEM, may He fill my storehouses with abundance. To the teachers I shall raise my eyes, like Hillel, not like Shammai.*

חֶדְוַת *So give me days of delight and eternal years — 'Wake up, my soul, wake up!' — Then above my head, will unite as twins, the lamp of precepts and the light of Torah.*

קוּמָה *Rise up, HASHEM, be present in my contentment, You and the ark of Your strength. Please accept, O God, my blessing and strengthen the shield of Your seer.*

Psalm 23

מִזְמוֹר לְדָוִד *A psalm of David: HASHEM is my Shepherd,* I shall not lack.* In lush meadows* He lays me down, beside tranquil waters He leads me. He restores my soul. He leads me on paths of justice* for His Name's sake. Though I walk in the valley overshadowed by death,* I will fear no evil, for You are with me. Your rod and Your staff,* they comfort me. You prepare a table before me in full view of my tormentors. You anointed my head with oil, my cup overflows. May only goodness and kindness* pursue me all the days of my life, and may I dwell in the House of HASHEM for long days.*

יַנְחֵנִי בְמַעְגְּלֵי צֶדֶק — *He leads me on paths of justice.* The shepherd chooses his path carefully to avoid overstraining his sheep. Similarly, righteous people are granted a significant degree of Divine protection which helps prevent them from straying from the just path.

בְּגֵיא צַלְמָוֶת — *The valley overshadowed by death.* The morbid *valley* is a characterization of all exiles. Alternatively, it is a place so dangerous that it is as dark and forbidding as the grave.

שִׁבְטְךָ וּמִשְׁעַנְתֶּךָ — *Your rod and Your staff.* God's *rod* represents His strict punishment for sin, while His *staff* is His support for me in times of my affliction. Both are equally comforting, for a Jew's greatest consolation is that he is not an insignificant straw blown about by chance winds. Rather, God is cognizant of his behavior, and rewards or punishes accordingly.

טוֹב וָחֶסֶד — *Goodness and kindness. Goodness* refers to spiritual enrichment while *kindness* refers to concern for the spirituality of others. The combination of the two terms expresses a desire that one will experience personal growth while not neglecting to help others.

❧ קידושא רבא לשבת ויום טוב ❧

On the Sabbath, including Festivals that fall on the Sabbath, begin here:

אִם תָּשִׁיב* מִשַּׁבָּת רַגְלֶךָ, עֲשׂוֹת חֲפָצֶךָ בְּיוֹם קָדְשִׁי, וְקָרָאתָ לַשַּׁבָּת עֹנֶג,* לִקְדוֹשׁ יהוה מְכֻבָּד, וְכִבַּדְתּוֹ מֵעֲשׂוֹת דְּרָכֶיךָ, מִמְּצוֹא חֶפְצְךָ וְדַבֵּר דָּבָר.* אָז תִּתְעַנַּג עַל יהוה, וְהִרְכַּבְתִּיךָ עַל בָּמֳתֵי אָרֶץ, וְהַאֲכַלְתִּיךָ נַחֲלַת יַעֲקֹב אָבִיךָ,* כִּי פִּי יהוה דִּבֵּר.[1]

וְשָׁמְרוּ* בְנֵי יִשְׂרָאֵל אֶת הַשַּׁבָּת, לַעֲשׂוֹת אֶת הַשַּׁבָּת לְדֹרֹתָם בְּרִית עוֹלָם. בֵּינִי וּבֵין בְּנֵי יִשְׂרָאֵל אוֹת הִיא לְעֹלָם, כִּי שֵׁשֶׁת יָמִים עָשָׂה יהוה אֶת הַשָּׁמַיִם וְאֶת הָאָרֶץ, וּבַיּוֹם הַשְּׁבִיעִי שָׁבַת וַיִּנָּפַשׁ.[2]

זָכוֹר* אֶת יוֹם הַשַּׁבָּת לְקַדְּשׁוֹ. שֵׁשֶׁת יָמִים תַּעֲבֹד* וְעָשִׂיתָ כָּל מְלַאכְתֶּךָ. וְיוֹם הַשְּׁבִיעִי שַׁבָּת לַיהוה אֱלֹהֶיךָ, לֹא תַעֲשֶׂה כָל מְלָאכָה, אַתָּה וּבִנְךָ וּבִתֶּךָ עַבְדְּךָ וַאֲמָתְךָ וּבְהֶמְתֶּךָ,* וְגֵרְךָ אֲשֶׁר בִּשְׁעָרֶיךָ. כִּי שֵׁשֶׁת יָמִים עָשָׂה יהוה אֶת הַשָּׁמַיִם וְאֶת הָאָרֶץ אֶת הַיָּם וְאֶת כָּל אֲשֶׁר בָּם, וַיָּנַח בַּיּוֹם הַשְּׁבִיעִי —

עַל כֵּן בֵּרַךְ יהוה אֶת יוֹם הַשַּׁבָּת וַיְקַדְּשֵׁהוּ.[3]

On weekday Festivals, begin here:

(אֵלֶּה מוֹעֲדֵי יהוה מִקְרָאֵי קֹדֶשׁ אֲשֶׁר תִּקְרְאוּ אֹתָם בְּמוֹעֲדָם[4])
וַיְדַבֵּר מֹשֶׁה אֶת מֹעֲדֵי יהוה, אֶל בְּנֵי יִשְׂרָאֵל.[5]

On Rosh Hashanah add:

תִּקְעוּ בַחֹדֶשׁ שׁוֹפָר, בַּכֶּסֶה לְיוֹם חַגֵּנוּ.
כִּי חֹק לְיִשְׂרָאֵל הוּא, מִשְׁפָּט לֵאלֹהֵי יַעֲקֹב.[6]

סַבְרִי מָרָנָן וְרַבָּנָן וְרַבּוֹתַי:

בָּרוּךְ אַתָּה יהוה אֱלֹהֵינוּ מֶלֶךְ הָעוֹלָם, בּוֹרֵא פְּרִי הַגָּפֶן.

On Succos, in the *succah,* add:

בָּרוּךְ אַתָּה יהוה אֱלֹהֵינוּ מֶלֶךְ הָעוֹלָם, אֲשֶׁר קִדְּשָׁנוּ בְּמִצְוֹתָיו וְצִוָּנוּ לֵישֵׁב בַּסֻּכָּה.

קִידוּשָׁא רַבָּא / The Morning Kiddush

The morning *Kiddush* was introduced by the Sages, and its status is inferior to the Sabbath Eve *Kiddush* which is Scriptural in origin (*Pesachim* 106b). Therefore, it is euphemistically called קִידוּשָׁא רַבָּא, the *Great Kiddush.* Originally, the *Kiddush* consisted only of the blessing over wine (*Pesachim* 106b). The Scriptural verses were added over the centuries. However, not all the verses are said in all communities. In some, only the last fragment of the last verse (*beginning* עַל כֵּן) is recited.

אִם תָּשִׁיב — *If you restrain.* These verses conclude a chapter that urges a variety of good

KIDDUSHA RABBA FOR THE SABBATH AND FESTIVALS

On the Sabbath, including Festivals that fall on the Sabbath, begin here:

אִם תָּשִׁיב *If you restrain,* because of the Sabbath, your feet, refrain from accomplishing your own needs on My holy day; if you proclaim the Sabbath, 'a delight', the holy one of HASHEM, 'honored one,' and you honor it by not doing your own ways, from seeking your needs or discussing the forbidden. Then you shall be granted pleasure with HASHEM and I shall mount you astride the heights of the world, and provide you the heritage of your forefather Jacob* — for the mouth of HASHEM has spoken.*[1]

וְשָׁמְרוּ *And the Children of Israel observed* the Sabbath, to make the Sabbath for their generations an eternal covenant. Between Me and the Children of Israel it is a sign forever, that in six days did HASHEM make the heaven and the earth, and on the seventh day He rested and was refreshed.*[2]

זָכוֹר *Always remember* the Sabbath day to hallow it. For six days you may labor and do all your work. But the seventh day is the Sabbath for HASHEM, Your God; you may do no work — you, your son and your daughter, your slave and your maidservant, your animal, and the stranger who is in your gates. For in six days did HASHEM make the heaven and the earth, the sea and all that is in them and He rested on the seventh day;*

therefore HASHEM blessed the Sabbath day and sanctified it.[3]

On weekday Festivals, begin here:

(These are the appointed festivals of HASHEM, holy convocations, which you are to proclaim in their appointed times.[4]*)*
And Moses declared HASHEM's appointed festivals to the Children of Israel.[5]

On Rosh Hashanah add:

Blow the shofar at the moon's renewal, at the time appointed for our festive day. Because it is a decree for Israel, a judgment day for the God of Jacob.[6]

By your leave my masters and teachers:

בָּרוּךְ *Blessed are You, HASHEM, our God, King of the universe, Who creates the fruit of the vine.*

On Succos, in the *succah,* add:

בָּרוּךְ *Blessed are You, HASHEM, our God, King of the universe, Who has sanctified us with His commandments and has commanded us to dwell in the Succah.*

(1) *Isaiah* 58:13-14. (2) *Exodus* 31:16-17. (3) 20:8-11. (4) *Leviticus* 23:4. (5) 23:44. (6) *Psalms* 81:4-5.

---

practices upon people and assures them of God's blessings in return for compliance.

נַחֲלַת יַעֲקֹב אָבִיךָ — *The heritage of your forefather Jacob.* The land promised Abraham and Isaac was delineated by borders, but Jacob's blessing had no limitation.

וְשָׁמְרוּ — *And ... observed.* See comm. p. 336.

זָכוֹר — *Always remember.* The fourth of the Ten Commandments, this passage implies the positive commandments of the day.

זמירות ליום שבת

ברוך ה׳ יום יום

בָּרוּךְ אֲדֹנָי יוֹם יוֹם, יַעֲמָס לָנוּ יֶשַׁע וּפִדְיוֹם,1 וּבִשְׁמוֹ נָגִיל כָּל הַיּוֹם, וּבִישׁוּעָתוֹ נָרִים רֹאשׁ עֶלְיוֹן. כִּי הוּא מָעוֹז לַדָּל, וּמַחֲסֶה לָאֶבְיוֹן.2

שִׁבְטֵי יָהּ לְיִשְׂרָאֵל עֵדוּת, בְּצָרָתָם לוֹ צָר בְּסִבְלוּת וּבְעַבְדוּת, בְּלִבְנַת הַסַּפִּיר הֶרְאָם עֹז יְדִידוּת, וְנִגְלָה לְהַעֲלוֹתָם מֵעֹמֶק בּוֹר וָדוּת. כִּי עִם יהוה הַחֶסֶד, וְהַרְבֵּה עִמּוֹ פְדוּת.3

מַה יָּקָר חַסְדּוֹ בְּצִלּוֹ לְגוֹנְנֵמוֹ, בְּגָלוּת בָּבֶלָה שֻׁלַּח לְמַעֲנֵמוֹ, לְהוֹרִיד בָּרִיחִים נִמְנָה בֵינֵימוֹ. וַיִּתְּנֵם לְרַחֲמִים לִפְנֵי שׁוֹבֵימוֹ. כִּי לֹא יִטֹּשׁ יהוה אֶת עַמּוֹ, בַּעֲבוּר הַגָּדוֹל שְׁמוֹ.4

עֵילָם שָׁת כִּסְאוֹ לְהַצִּיל יְדִידָיו, לְהַאֲבִיד מִשָּׁם מָעֻזְנֵי מוֹרְדָיו,5 מֵעֲבוֹר בַּשֶּׁלַח פָּדָה אֶת עֲבָדָיו, קֶרֶן לְעַמּוֹ יָרִים תְּהִלָּה לְכָל חֲסִידָיו. כִּי אִם הוֹגָה וְרִחַם, כְּרַחֲמָיו וּכְרֹב חֲסָדָיו.6

וּצְפִיר הָעִזִּים הִגְדִּיל עֲצוּמָיו, וְגַם חָזוּת אַרְבַּע עָלוּ לִמְרוֹמָיו, וּבְלִבָּם דִּמּוּ לְהַשְׁחִית אֶת רְחוּמָיו, עַל יְדֵי כֹהֲנָיו מִגֵּר מִתְקוֹמְמָיו. חַסְדֵי יהוה כִּי לֹא תָמְנוּ, כִּי לֹא כָלוּ רַחֲמָיו.7

נִסְגַּרְתִּי לֶאֱדוֹם בְּיַד רֵעַי מְדָנַי, שֶׁבְּכָל יוֹם וָיוֹם מְמַלְּאִים כְּרֵשָׂם מֵעֲדָנַי, עֶזְרָתוֹ עִמִּי לִסְמוֹךְ אֶת אֲדָנַי, וְלֹא נְטַשְׁתַּנִי כָּל יְמֵי עִדָּנַי. כִּי לֹא יִזְנַח לְעוֹלָם אֲדֹנָי.8

בְּבֹאוֹ מֵאֱדוֹם חֲמוּץ בְּגָדִים, זֶבַח לוֹ בְּבָצְרָה וְטֶבַח לוֹ בְּבוֹגְדִים, וְיֵז נִצְחָם מַלְבּוּשָׁיו לְהַאְדִּים,9 בְּכֹחוֹ הַגָּדוֹל יִבְצֹר רוּחַ נְגִידִים. הָגָה בְּרוּחוֹ הַקָּשָׁה, בְּיוֹם קָדִים.10

רְאוֹתוֹ כִּי כֵן אֲדוֹמִי הָעוֹצֵר, יַחֲשׁוֹב לוֹ בְּבָצְרָה תִּקְלוֹט כְּבֶצֶר, וּמַלְאָךְ כְּאָדָם בְּתוֹכָהּ יִנָּצֵר, וּמֵזִיד כַּשּׁוֹגֵג בְּמִקְלָט יֵעָצֵר. אֶהֱבוּ אֶת יהוה כָּל חֲסִידָיו, אֱמוּנִים נֹצֵר.11

בָּרוּךְ ה׳ יוֹם יוֹם / Baruch Hashem Yom Yom

The composer of the *zemer* was Shimon bar Yitzchak, whose name is found in the acrostic of the second through the eighth stanzas, which contains the name *Shimon bar,* while the initial letters of the first four words of the ninth stanza spell *Yitzchak*. He lived in tenth century Mainz, Germany, and was also known as Rabbi Shimon HaGadol [the Great].

The *zemer* is based on the teaching of the Sages that God's Presence goes with Israel to all its various exiles, redeeming His people from them all, including the final one. Specifically the second stanza speaks of the redemption from Egypt; the third, of the Babylonian exile; the fourth, the Persian exile; the fifth, the Greek persecution; and the sixth the Roman exile. The next two foretell of the downfall of Edom, and the final four stanzas are prayers for the nation's future. There are various customs regarding the

ZEMIROS FOR THE SABBATH DAY

BARUCH HASHEM YOM YOM

בָּרוּךְ אֲדֹנָי יוֹם יוֹם *Blessed is My Lord for every single day, He will bear fo*ı *us salvation and redemption.*[1] *Then in His Name we wil*ı *sing glad song all the day and in His salvation we will raise our head to the heights — For He is a stronghold for the sick and a refuge for the needy.*[2]

שִׁבְטֵי *That the tribes are God's He bore witness to Israel. Amid their distress is His distress, in oppression and slavery. Through a sapphire brick, he showed them the strength of His love. He was then revealed to lift them from the depth of pit and dungeon — For with God is the kindness and abundant with Him is redemption.*[3]

מַה *How precious is His kindness to shield them with His protection. Into Babylonian Exile was He dispatched for their sake; when their ships went down He was included among them; then He made them inspire mercy before their captors — For* H*ASHEM* *will not forsake His people because of His great Name.*[4]

עֵילָם *In Elam He placed His throne to rescue His loved ones, to destroy from there the strongholds of His rebels.*[5] *From passage under the sword He redeemed His servants. Pride for His nation shall He raise, praise for all His devout ones — For although He afflicts, He then pities, according to His mercy and His abundant kindness.*[6]

וּצְפִיר *Then the he-goat exalted itself over mighty ones, and the semblance of the four ascended even to His heights. In their hearts they intended to destroy the objects of His mercy, but through His priests He laid low those who rose up against Him —* H*ASHEM*'s *kindness surely has not ended, nor are His mercies exhausted.*[7]

נִסְגַּרְתִּי *I was handed over to Edom through my contentious brothers, who daily filled their bellies from my treasures. His help stayed with me to support my pillars. But He will not forsake me all the days of my times — For My Lord does not reject forever.*[8]

בְּבֹאוֹ *When He comes from Edom with bloodied clothes, He will have a slaughter in Bozrah, an execution of traitors. The dripping of their lifeblood will redden His garments.*[9] *With His great strength He will cut down the spirit of the nobles — Sweeping away with His powerful blast like the day of the east wind.*[10]

רְאוֹתוֹ *When he sees how it is, the Edomite oppressor, he will think that Bozrah can give refuge like Bezer; that angel, like man, is protected within it; and that the willful, like the unintentional one, is detained in the refuge — Love* H*ASHEM*, *all his devout ones, His faithful ones He safeguards.*[11]

(1) Cf. *Psalms* 68:20. (2) Cf. *Isaiah* 25:4. (3) *Psalms* 130:7. (4) Cf. *I Samuel* 12:22. (5) Cf. *Jeremiah* 49:38. (6) Cf. *Lamentations* 3:32. (7) 3:22. (8) 3:31. (9) Cf. *Isaiah* 63:1-3. (10) 27:8. (11) *Psalms* 31:24.

recitation of this *zemer*. Some recite it in its entirety at the daytime meal. Others recite either the first six or the first eight stanzas. The remaining stanzas are recited at *Seudah Shlishis* (see p. 588). For a stanza-by-stanza commentary, see the ArtScroll *Zemiroth*.

יְצַוֶּה צוּר חַסְדּוֹ קְהִלּוֹתָיו לְקַבֵּץ, מֵאַרְבַּע רוּחוֹת עָדָיו לְהִקָּבֵץ, וּבְהַר מְרוֹם הָרִים אוֹתָנוּ לְהַרְבֵּץ, וְאִתָּנוּ יָשׁוּב נִדָּחִים קוֹבֵץ. יָשִׁיב לֹא נֶאֱמַר, כִּי אִם וְשָׁב וְקִבֵּץ.

בָּרוּךְ הוּא אֱלֹהֵינוּ אֲשֶׁר טוֹב גְּמָלָנוּ, כְּרַחֲמָיו וּכְרֹב חֲסָדָיו הִגְדִּיל לָנוּ, אֵלֶּה וְכָאֵלֶּה יוֹסֵף עִמָּנוּ, לְהַגְדִּיל שְׁמוֹ הַגָּדוֹל הַגִּבּוֹר וְהַנּוֹרָא שֶׁנִּקְרָא עָלֵינוּ.

בָּרוּךְ הוּא אֱלֹהֵינוּ שֶׁבְּרָאָנוּ לִכְבוֹדוֹ, לְהַלְלוֹ וּלְשַׁבְּחוֹ וּלְסַפֵּר הוֹדוֹ, מִכָּל אֹם גָּבַר עָלֵינוּ חַסְדּוֹ, לָכֵן בְּכָל לֵב וּבְכָל נֶפֶשׁ וּבְכָל מְאוֹדוֹ, נַמְלִיכוֹ וּנְיַחֲדוֹ.[1]

שֶׁהַשָּׁלוֹם שֶׁלּוֹ יָשִׂים עָלֵינוּ בְּרָכָה וְשָׁלוֹם, מִשְּׂמֹאל וּמִיָּמִין עַל יִשְׂרָאֵל שָׁלוֹם, הָרַחֲמָן הוּא יְבָרֵךְ אֶת עַמּוֹ בַשָּׁלוֹם,[2] וְיִזְכּוּ לִרְאוֹת בָּנִים וּבְנֵי בָנִים עוֹסְקִים בַּתּוֹרָה וּבְמִצְוֹת, עַל יִשְׂרָאֵל שָׁלוֹם. יוֹעֵץ אֵל גִּבּוֹר אֲבִי עַד שַׂר שָׁלוֹם.[3]

ברוך אל עליון

בָּרוּךְ אֵל עֶלְיוֹן אֲשֶׁר נָתַן מְנוּחָה, לְנַפְשֵׁנוּ פִּדְיוֹן מִשֵּׁאת וַאֲנָחָה, וְהוּא יִדְרוֹשׁ לְצִיּוֹן עִיר הַנִּדָּחָה, עַד אָנָה תּוּגְיוֹן נֶפֶשׁ נֶאֱנָחָה.[4]

הַשּׁוֹמֵר שַׁבָּת, הַבֵּן עִם הַבַּת, לָאֵל יֵרָצוּ כְּמִנְחָה עַל מַחֲבַת.

רוֹכֵב בָּעֲרָבוֹת מֶלֶךְ עוֹלָמִים, אֶת עַמּוֹ לִשְׁבּוֹת אִזֵּן בַּנְּעִימִים, בְּמַאֲכָלֵי עֲרֵבוֹת בְּמִינֵי מַטְעַמִּים, בְּמַלְבּוּשֵׁי כָבוֹד זֶבַח מִשְׁפָּחָה.

הַשּׁוֹמֵר שַׁבָּת, הַבֵּן עִם הַבַּת, לָאֵל יֵרָצוּ כְּמִנְחָה עַל מַחֲבַת.

וְאַשְׁרֵי כָּל חוֹכֶה לְתַשְׁלוּמֵי כֵפֶל, מֵאֵת כָּל סוֹכֶה שׁוֹכֵן בָּעֲרָפֶל, נַחֲלָה לוֹ יִזְכֶּה בָּהָר וּבַשָּׁפֶל, נַחֲלָה וּמְנוּחָה כַּשֶּׁמֶשׁ לוֹ זָרְחָה.

הַשּׁוֹמֵר שַׁבָּת, הַבֵּן עִם הַבַּת, לָאֵל יֵרָצוּ כְּמִנְחָה עַל מַחֲבַת.

כָּל שׁוֹמֵר שַׁבָּת כַּדָּת מֵחַלְּלוֹ, הֵן הֶכְשַׁר חִבַּת קֹדֶשׁ גּוֹרָלוֹ, וְאִם יָצָא חוֹבַת הַיּוֹם אַשְׁרֵי לוֹ, אֶל אֵל אָדוֹן מְחוֹלְלוֹ מִנְחָה הִיא שְׁלוּחָה.

הַשּׁוֹמֵר שַׁבָּת, הַבֵּן עִם הַבַּת, לָאֵל יֵרָצוּ כְּמִנְחָה עַל מַחֲבַת.

חֶמְדַּת הַיָּמִים קְרָאוֹ אֵלִי צוּר, וְאַשְׁרֵי לִתְמִימִים אִם יִהְיֶה נָצוּר, כֶּתֶר הִלּוּמִים עַל רֹאשָׁם יָצוּר, צוּר הָעוֹלָמִים רוּחוֹ בָּם נָחָה.

הַשּׁוֹמֵר שַׁבָּת, הַבֵּן עִם הַבַּת, לָאֵל יֵרָצוּ כְּמִנְחָה עַל מַחֲבַת.

בָּרוּךְ אֵל עֶלְיוֹן / Baruch Kel Elyon

The presumed author, R' Baruch ben Shmuel, lived in Mainz, Germany, where he died in 4981 (1221 C.E.). The acrostic forms the name *Baruch Chazak*. In addition to being a prolific *paytan*, he was one of the prominent *Tosafists*. He is credited by some with authorship of the *Tosafos*

יְצַוֶּה *May the Rock command His kindness to gather in His congregations; from the four winds to be gathered up to Him, upon the loftiest mountain to set us down. He shall return with us, the Gatherer of outcasts — 'He shall bring back' is not said; but 'He shall return' and gather in.*

בָּרוּךְ *Blessed is our God Who did us good. According to His mercy and His abundant kindness He did great things for us. Both these and those may He increase with us — to magnify His great, mighty, and awesome Name Which was proclaimed upon us.*

בָּרוּךְ *Blessed is our God Who created us for His glory; to praise Him, laud Him and relate His majesty. More than any nation He strengthened His kindness over us. Therefore with complete heart, with complete soul, and with complete resources, let us proclaim Him King and proclaim Him Unique.*[1]

שֶׁהַשָּׁלוֹם *May He to Whom peace belongs set upon us blessing and peace — from left and from right, peace upon Israel. May the Merciful One bless His people with peace;*[2] *and may they merit to see children and grandchildren engaging in Torah and precepts, bringing peace upon Israel. Adviser, Mighty God, Eternal Father, Prince of Peace.*[3]

BARUCH KEL ELYON

בָּרוּךְ אֵל עֶלְיוֹן *Blessed is the Most Exalted God who gave contentment; for our souls it is relief from ravage and groaning. May He seek out Zion the outcast city, how long, the grieving for the groaning soul!*[4]

Whoever keeps the Sabbath — man and woman alike —
may they find God's favor like a meal-offering in a sacred pan.

רוֹכֵב *He Who rides atop the heavens, the King of the universe — that His nation rest on the Sabbath He made it hear with pleasantness, with tasty foods and every manner of delicacy, with elegant garments and a family feast.*

Whoever keeps the Sabbath — man and woman alike —
may they find God's favor like a meal-offering in a sacred pan.

וְאַשְׁרֵי *Praiseworthy is everyone who awaits a double reward from the One Who sees all but dwells in dense darkness. He will grant him an inheritance in mountain and valley, a heritage and a resting place like his upon whom the sun shone.*

Whoever keeps the Sabbath — man and woman alike —
may they find God's favor like a meal-offering in a sacred pan.

כָּל *Whoever safeguards the Sabbath properly from desecration, behold — worthiness for beloved holiness is his lot. And if he fulfills the day's obligation, praises are due him; to God, the Lord Who fashioned him it is sent as a gift.*

Whoever keeps the Sabbath — man and woman alike —
may they find God's favor like a meal-offering in a sacred pan.

חֶמְדַּת *'The most beloved of days' is what my God and Rock called it. Praises are due the wholesome ones if it is protected; a fitting crown is fashioned on their heads. As for the Rock of the universe, His spirit will be content with them.*

Whoever keeps the Sabbath — man and woman alike —
may they find God's favor like a meal-offering in a sacred pan.

---

(1) Cf. *Deuteronomy* 6:4-5. (2) *Psalms* 29:11. (3) *Isaiah* 9:5. (4) cf. *Job* 19:2.

זָכוֹר אֶת יוֹם הַשַּׁבָּת לְקַדְּשׁוֹ,[1] קַרְנוֹ כִּי גָבְהָה נֵזֶר עַל רֹאשׁוֹ, עַל כֵּן יִתֵּן הָאָדָם לְנַפְשׁוֹ, עֹנֶג וְגַם שִׂמְחָה בָּהֶם לְמָשְׁחָה.

הַשּׁוֹמֵר שַׁבָּת, הַבֵּן עִם הַבַּת, לָאֵל יֵרָצוּ כְּמִנְחָה עַל מַחֲבַת.

קֹדֶשׁ הִיא לָכֶם שַׁבָּת הַמַּלְכָּה,[2] אֶל תּוֹךְ בָּתֵּיכֶם לְהָנִיחַ בְּרָכָה, בְּכָל מוֹשְׁבוֹתֵיכֶם לֹא תַעֲשׂוּ מְלָאכָה, בְּנֵיכֶם וּבְנוֹתֵיכֶם עֶבֶד וְגַם שִׁפְחָה.[3]

הַשּׁוֹמֵר שַׁבָּת, הַבֵּן עִם הַבַּת, לָאֵל יֵרָצוּ כְּמִנְחָה עַל מַחֲבַת.

יום זה מכבד

יוֹם זֶה מְכֻבָּד מִכָּל יָמִים, כִּי בוֹ שָׁבַת צוּר* עוֹלָמִים.

שֵׁשֶׁת יָמִים תַּעֲשֶׂה מְלַאכְתֶּךָ, וְיוֹם הַשְּׁבִיעִי לֵאלֹהֶיךָ, שַׁבָּת לֹא תַעֲשֶׂה בוֹ מְלָאכָה, כִּי כֹל עָשָׂה שֵׁשֶׁת יָמִים.[4]

יוֹם זֶה מְכֻבָּד מִכָּל יָמִים, כִּי בוֹ שָׁבַת צוּר עוֹלָמִים.

רִאשׁוֹן הוּא לְמִקְרָאֵי קֹדֶשׁ, יוֹם שַׁבָּתוֹן יוֹם שַׁבַּת קֹדֶשׁ, עַל כֵּן כָּל אִישׁ בְּיֵינוֹ יְקַדֵּשׁ, עַל שְׁתֵּי לֶחֶם יִבְצְעוּ תְמִימִים.

יוֹם זֶה מְכֻבָּד מִכָּל יָמִים, כִּי בוֹ שָׁבַת צוּר עוֹלָמִים.

אֱכוֹל מַשְׁמַנִּים שְׁתֵה מַמְתַּקִּים,[5] כִּי אֵל יִתֵּן לְכָל בּוֹ דְבֵקִים, בֶּגֶד לִלְבּוֹשׁ לֶחֶם חֻקִּים,[6] בָּשָׂר וְדָגִים וְכָל מַטְעַמִּים.

יוֹם זֶה מְכֻבָּד מִכָּל יָמִים, כִּי בוֹ שָׁבַת צוּר עוֹלָמִים.

לֹא תֶחְסַר כֹּל בּוֹ וְאָכַלְתָּ וְשָׂבָעְתָּ, וּבֵרַכְתָּ אֶת יהוה אֱלֹהֶיךָ[7] אֲשֶׁר אָהַבְתָּ, כִּי בֵרַכְךָ מִכָּל הָעַמִּים.

יוֹם זֶה מְכֻבָּד מִכָּל יָמִים, כִּי בוֹ שָׁבַת צוּר עוֹלָמִים.

הַשָּׁמַיִם מְסַפְּרִים כְּבוֹדוֹ, וְגַם הָאָרֶץ מָלְאָה חַסְדּוֹ, רְאוּ כִּי כָל אֵלֶּה עָשְׂתָה יָדוֹ, כִּי הוּא הַצּוּר פָּעֳלוֹ תָמִים.

יוֹם זֶה מְכֻבָּד מִכָּל יָמִים, כִּי בוֹ שָׁבַת צוּר עוֹלָמִים.

יום שבתון

יוֹם שַׁבָּתוֹן אֵין לִשְׁכּוֹחַ, זִכְרוֹ כְּרֵיחַ הַנִּיחֹחַ, יוֹנָה מָצְאָה בוֹ מָנוֹחַ, וְשָׁם יָנוּחוּ יְגִיעֵי כֹחַ.[8]

יוֹנָה מָצְאָה בוֹ מָנוֹחַ, וְשָׁם יָנוּחוּ יְגִיעֵי כֹחַ.

---

to tractate *Sotah*. The *zemer* speaks in praise of the Sabbath observer and lyrically portrays the rewards awaiting him.

יוֹם זֶה מְכֻבָּד / Yom Zeh Mechubad

Nothing is known about the *zemer's* author except that his name Yisrael is formed by the acrostic. The *zemer* urges one to honor the Sabbath and gives him the assurance that God will more than replenish whatever he expends.

צוּר — *He Who fashioned.* Although the word צוּר is generally translated as *Rock*, as a reference to God's strength and stability, the Sages occasionally give to it the connotation of צַיָּר, *the*

זָכוֹר *He who remembers the Sabbath day to hallow it,*[1] *his honor will rise like a diadem on his head. Therefore, let each man give himself, delight and also gladness with which to exalt himself.*

Whoever keeps the Sabbath — man and woman alike —
may they find God's favor like a meal-offering in a sacred pan.

קֹדֶשׁ *She is holy to you, the Sabbath Queen,*[2] *within your homes to deposit blessing. In all your dwellings do no work — your sons and daughters, slave and even maidservant.*[3]

Whoever keeps the Sabbath — man and woman alike —
may they find God's favor like a meal-offering in a sacred pan.

YOM ZEH MECHUBAD

יוֹם זֶה מְכֻבָּד *This day is honored from among all days, for on it rested He Who fashioned* the universe.*

שֵׁשֶׁת *For six days you may do your work, but the seventh day is your God's. On the Sabbath, do no work, for He completed all in six days.*[4]

This day is honored from among all days,
for on it rested He Who fashioned the universe.

רִאשׁוֹן *It is the first of the holy convocations, a day of rest, the holy Sabbath day. Therefore let every man recite Kiddush with his wine, and over two complete loaves let him slice.*

This day is honored from among all days,
for on it rested He Who fashioned the universe.

אֱכוֹל *Eat rich foods, drink sweet drinks,*[5] *for God will give to all who cleave to Him clothes to wear and allotted bread,*[6] *meat and fish and all the dainties.*

This day is honored from among all days,
for on it rested He Who fashioned the universe.

לֹא *You will lack nothing on it, you will eat, be satisfied, and bless* HASHEM, *your God,*[7] *Whom you love, for He has blessed you beyond all peoples.*

This day is honored from among all days,
for on it rested He Who fashioned the universe.

הַשָּׁמַיִם *The heavens declare His glory, and the earth as well is full of His kindness. Perceive that all these have His hand made, for He is the Molder — His work is perfect.*

This day is honored from among all days,
for on it rested He Who fashioned the universe.

YOM SHABBASON

יוֹם שַׁבָּתוֹן *The day of rest should not be forgotten, its memory is like a satisfying aroma. On it the dove found rest, there shall rest exhausted ones.*[8] *On it the dove found rest, there shall rest exhausted ones.*

---

(1) *Exodus* 20:8. (2) Cf. 31:14. (3) Cf. 20:10. (4) Cf. 31:15-17. (5) Cf. *Nechemiah* 8:10.
(6) Cf. *Genesis* 28:20. (7) *Deuteronomy* 8:10. (8) *Job* 3:17.

Molder (see *Berachos* 10a). Our translation follows this interpretation since it better fits the context.

יוֹם שַׁבָּתוֹן / Yom Shabbason

The acrostic of this *zemer* spells *Yehudah*, presumed by many to be Rabbi Yehudah Halevi,

הַיּוֹם נִכְבָּד לִבְנֵי אֱמוּנִים, זְהִירִים לְשָׁמְרוֹ אָבוֹת וּבָנִים, חָקוּק בִּשְׁנֵי לֻחוֹת אֲבָנִים, מֵרֹב אוֹנִים וְאַמִּיץ כֹּחַ.[1]

יוֹנָה מָצְאָה בוֹ מָנוֹחַ,* וְשָׁם יָנוּחוּ יְגִיעֵי כֹחַ.

וּבָאוּ כֻלָּם בִּבְרִית יַחַד, נַעֲשֶׂה וְנִשְׁמַע[2] אָמְרוּ כְּאֶחָד, וּפָתְחוּ וְעָנוּ יהוה אֶחָד, בָּרוּךְ הַנֹּתֵן לַיָּעֵף כֹּחַ.[3]

יוֹנָה מָצְאָה בוֹ מָנוֹחַ, וְשָׁם יָנוּחוּ יְגִיעֵי כֹחַ.

דִּבֶּר בְּקָדְשׁוֹ בְּהַר הַמּוֹר, יוֹם הַשְּׁבִיעִי זָכוֹר וְשָׁמוֹר, וְכָל פִּקֻּדָיו יַחַד לִגְמוֹר, חַזֵּק מָתְנַיִם וְאַמֵּץ כֹּחַ.[4]

יוֹנָה מָצְאָה בוֹ מָנוֹחַ, וְשָׁם יָנוּחוּ יְגִיעֵי כֹחַ.

הָעָם אֲשֶׁר נָע כַּצֹּאן תָּעָה, יִזְכּוֹר לְפָקְדוֹ בְּרִית וּשְׁבוּעָה, לְבַל יַעֲבָר בָּם מִקְרֵה רָעָה, כַּאֲשֶׁר נִשְׁבַּעְתָּ עַל מֵי נֹחַ.[5]

יוֹנָה מָצְאָה בוֹ מָנוֹחַ, וְשָׁם יָנוּחוּ יְגִיעֵי כֹחַ.

דרור יקרא

דְּרוֹר יִקְרָא לְבֵן עִם בַּת, **וְ**יִנְצָרְכֶם כְּמוֹ בָבַת, **נְ**עִים שִׁמְכֶם וְלֹא יֻשְׁבַּת, **שְׁ**בוּ וְנוּחוּ בְּיוֹם שַׁבָּת.

דְּרוֹשׁ נָוִי וְאוּלָמִי, **וְ**אוֹת יֶשַׁע עֲשֵׂה עִמִּי, **נְ**טַע שׂוֹרֵק בְּתוֹךְ כַּרְמִי, **שְׁ**עֵה שַׁוְעַת בְּנֵי עַמִּי.

דְּרוֹךְ פּוּרָה בְּתוֹךְ בָּצְרָה, **וְ**גַם בָּבֶל אֲשֶׁר גָּבְרָה, **נְ**תוֹץ צָרַי בְּאַף וְעֶבְרָה, **שְׁ**מַע קוֹלִי בְּיוֹם אֶקְרָא.

אֱלֹהִים תֵּן בַּמִּדְבָּר הַר, **הֲ**דַס שִׁטָּה בְּרוֹשׁ תִּדְהָר, **וְ**לַמַּזְהִיר וְלַנִּזְהָר, **שְׁ**לוֹמִים תֵּן כְּמֵי נָהָר.

הֲדוֹךְ קָמַי אֵל קַנָּא, **בְּ**מוֹג לֵבָב וּבַמְּגִנָּה, **וְ**נַרְחִיב פֶּה וּנְמַלְּאֶנָּה, **לְ**שׁוֹנֵנוּ לְךָ רִנָּה.

דְּעֵה חָכְמָה לְנַפְשֶׁךָ, **וְ**הִיא כֶתֶר לְרֹאשֶׁךָ, **נְ**צוֹר מִצְוַת קְדוֹשֶׁךָ, **שְׁ**מוֹר שַׁבַּת קָדְשֶׁךָ.

It is customary to repeat some of the Sabbath eve *zemiros* at the daytime meal — notably *Kah Ribon* and *Tzur Mishelo* (pp. 364-367).

---

author of *Kuzari* and one of the most famous and prolific of all *paytanim.* He was born in Toledo, Spain and lived from 4835-4900 (1075-1140 C.E.). As indicated by most of his poetry, he had a passionate love for *Eretz Yisrael* and eventually decided to settle there. In his journey to *Eretz Yisrael* Rabbi Yehudah is known to have reached Egypt and Damascus, but no further documentation of his trip is available. According to popular belief, he did actually reach Jerusalem where he fell to the ground in a state of ecstasy. As he was kissing the soil of the Holy City, he was trampled and killed by an Arab horseman.

The *zemer* depicts the honor given the

הַיּוֹם *This day is honored by the faithful ones who are scrupulous to safeguard it, parents and children. Engraved in the two stone tablets given by the Abundantly Potent and Vigorously Strong.*[1]

On it the dove found rest, there shall rest exhausted ones.*

וּבָאוּ *Then they all joined together in a covenant — 'We will do and we will listen,'*[2] *they said as one. Then they opened their mouths and called out, 'HASHEM is One'! Blessed is He Who gives strength to the exhausted.*[3]

On it the dove found rest, there shall rest exhausted ones.

דִּבֵּר *He spoke amid His holiness at the mountain of teaching, 'The Seventh day — remember and safeguard.' And all His precepts should equally be studied. Strengthen loins and be vigorously strong!*[4]

On it the dove found rest, there shall rest exhausted ones.

הָעָם *The nation which wandered like bewildered sheep — may He remember for them His covenant and oath. Lest evil happenings pass among them — as He swore at the Waters of Noah.*[5]

On it the dove found rest, there shall rest exhausted ones.

DROR YIKRA

דְּרוֹר יִקְרָא *Freedom shall He proclaim for man and woman, and protect you like the pupil of the eye. Pleasant will be your reputation, never to cease. Rest and be content on the Sabbath day.*

דְּרוֹשׁ *Seek my Temple and my Hall, and show me a sign of salvation. Plant a branch within my vineyard; turn to the outcry of my people!*

דְּרוֹךְ *Tread the press in Bozrah, and also Babylon which overpowered. Smash my foes with wrathful anger; hear my voice on the day I call.*

אֱלֹהִים *O God let bloom on the desert-like mountain, myrtle, acacia, cypress, and box tree. To the exhorters and to the scrupulous give peace as flowing as a river's waters.*

הֲדוֹךְ *Crush my foes, O jealous God, with melting heart and grief. May we open our mouth and fill it, our tongue sing Your joyful song.*

דְּעֶה *Let your soul know Torah then it will be a crown on your head. Observe the precepts of your Holy One; observe your holy Sabbath.*

It is customary to repeat some of the Sabbath eve *zemiros* at the daytime meal — notably *Kah Ribon* and *Tzur Mishelo* (pp. 364-367).

(1) *Isaiah* 40:26. (2) *Exodus* 24:7. (3) Cf. *Isaiah* 40:29. (4) *Nachum* 2:2. (5) Cf. *Isaiah* 54:9.

Sabbath by God at Sinai, Israel's love of the day, and describes it as the day of rest from weekday travail.

יוֹנָה מָצְאָה בוֹ מָנוֹחַ — *On it the dove found rest.* After the waters of the Deluge had subsided, Noah's dove found rest on the seventh day. In our *zemer,* that occurrence is used as an allegory for Israel's love of the Sabbath. Israel, which is frequently likened to a dove [see, for example, *Shir HaShirim* 4:1], finds its own rest on the seventh day.

◆§ דְּרוֹר יִקְרָא / Dror Yikra

The composer is Donash ben Labrat, the famed medieval grammarian and *paytan* from Baghdad who lived from 4680-4750 (920-990 C.E.). He is frequently cited by *Rashi* and *Ibn Ezra.* His name, דוֹנָשׁ, appears four times as the acrostic of the stiches in stanzas 1, 2, 3 and 6. The *zemer* is a plea to God to protect Israel, destroy its oppressors, and bring it peace and redemption.

מנחה
לשבת ויום טוב

אַשְׁרֵי יוֹשְׁבֵי בֵיתֶךָ, עוֹד יְהַלְלְוּךָ סֶּלָה.[1] אַשְׁרֵי הָעָם שֶׁכָּכָה לּוֹ, אַשְׁרֵי הָעָם שֶׁיהוה אֱלֹהָיו.[2]

תהלים קמה

תְּהִלָּה לְדָוִד,

אֲרוֹמִמְךָ אֱלוֹהַי הַמֶּלֶךְ, וַאֲבָרְכָה שִׁמְךָ לְעוֹלָם וָעֶד.
בְּכָל יוֹם אֲבָרְכֶךָּ, וַאֲהַלְלָה שִׁמְךָ לְעוֹלָם וָעֶד.
גָּדוֹל יהוה וּמְהֻלָּל מְאֹד, וְלִגְדֻלָּתוֹ אֵין חֵקֶר.
דּוֹר לְדוֹר יְשַׁבַּח מַעֲשֶׂיךָ, וּגְבוּרֹתֶיךָ יַגִּידוּ.
הֲדַר כְּבוֹד הוֹדֶךָ, וְדִבְרֵי נִפְלְאֹתֶיךָ אָשִׂיחָה.
וֶעֱזוּז נוֹרְאוֹתֶיךָ יֹאמֵרוּ, וּגְדוּלָּתְךָ אֲסַפְּרֶנָּה.
זֵכֶר רַב טוּבְךָ יַבִּיעוּ, וְצִדְקָתְךָ יְרַנֵּנוּ.
חַנּוּן וְרַחוּם יהוה, אֶרֶךְ אַפַּיִם וּגְדָל חָסֶד.
טוֹב יהוה לַכֹּל, וְרַחֲמָיו עַל כָּל מַעֲשָׂיו.
יוֹדְוּךָ יהוה כָּל מַעֲשֶׂיךָ, וַחֲסִידֶיךָ יְבָרְכוּכָה.
כְּבוֹד מַלְכוּתְךָ יֹאמֵרוּ, וּגְבוּרָתְךָ יְדַבֵּרוּ.
לְהוֹדִיעַ לִבְנֵי הָאָדָם גְּבוּרֹתָיו, וּכְבוֹד הֲדַר מַלְכוּתוֹ.
מַלְכוּתְךָ מַלְכוּת כָּל עֹלָמִים, וּמֶמְשַׁלְתְּךָ בְּכָל דּוֹר וָדֹר.
סוֹמֵךְ יהוה לְכָל הַנֹּפְלִים, וְזוֹקֵף לְכָל הַכְּפוּפִים.
עֵינֵי כֹל אֵלֶיךָ יְשַׂבֵּרוּ, וְאַתָּה נוֹתֵן לָהֶם אֶת אָכְלָם בְּעִתּוֹ.

While reciting the verse פּוֹתֵחַ, concentrate intently on its meaning.

פּוֹתֵחַ אֶת יָדֶךָ,
וּמַשְׂבִּיעַ לְכָל חַי רָצוֹן.
צַדִּיק יהוה בְּכָל דְּרָכָיו, וְחָסִיד בְּכָל מַעֲשָׂיו.
קָרוֹב יהוה לְכָל קֹרְאָיו, לְכֹל אֲשֶׁר יִקְרָאֻהוּ בֶאֱמֶת.

⁂ מִנְחָה לְשַׁבָּת וְיוֹם טוֹב /
Minchah for the Sabbath and Festivals

The climax of the Sabbath is described in Kabbalistic literature as a time when God receives our prayers with favor, and Himself yearns for the Redemption, an aspect of the day that is reflected by the *Minchah* service. After *Ashrei*, which is recited at every *Minchah*, we recite וּבָא לְצִיּוֹן גּוֹאֵל, *A redeemer shall come to Zion*, which confidently looks ahead to the coming of the Messiah. The Sabbath *Minchah* *Shemoneh Esrei* speaks of the spiritual bliss that will prevail in that time of perfection and universal recognition of God's sovereignty.

The Torah reading during the Sabbath *Minchah* includes the calling to the Torah of *Kohen*, Levite, and Israelite. The reading is identical to the reading on the following Monday and Thursday. This reading was ordained by Ezra for the benefit of people who would not be able to attend the Monday and Thursday services. In another sense, however, the Torah

MINCHAH

FOR SABBATH AND FESTIVALS

אַשְׁרֵי *Praiseworthy are those who dwell in Your house; may they always praise You, Selah!*[1] *Praiseworthy is the people for whom this is so, praiseworthy is the people whose God is* HASHEM.[2]

Psalm 145 *A psalm of praise by David:*

א *I will exalt You, my God the King,*
and I will bless Your Name forever and ever.

ב *Every day I will bless You,*
and I will laud Your Name forever and ever.

ג HASHEM *is great and exceedingly lauded,*
and His greatness is beyond investigation.

ד *Each generation will praise Your deeds to the next*
and of Your mighty deeds they will tell.

ה *The splendrous glory of Your power*
and Your wondrous deeds I shall discuss.

ו *And of Your awesome power they will speak,*
and Your greatness I shall relate.

ז *A recollection of Your abundant goodness they will utter*
and of Your righteousness they will sing exultantly.

ח *Gracious and merciful is* HASHEM,
slow to anger, and great in [bestowing] kindness.

ט HASHEM *is good to all; His mercies are on all His works.*

י *All Your works shall thank You,* HASHEM,
and Your devout ones will bless You.

כ *Of the glory of Your kingdom they will speak,*
and of Your power they will tell;

ל *To inform human beings of His mighty deeds,*
and the glorious splendor of His kingdom.

מ *Your kingdom is a kingdom spanning all eternities,*
and Your dominion is throughout every generation.

ס HASHEM *supports all the fallen ones and straightens all the bent.*

ע *The eyes of all look to You with hope*
and You give them their food in its proper time;

פ *You open Your hand,*
and satisfy the desire
of every living thing.

While reciting the verse, *'You open ...'* concentrate intently on its meaning.

צ *Righteous is* HASHEM *in all His ways*
and magnanimous in all His deeds.

ק HASHEM *is close to all who call upon Him —*
to all who call upon Him sincerely.

---
(1) Psalms 84:5. (2) 144:15.

רְצוֹן יְרֵאָיו יַעֲשֶׂה, וְאֶת שַׁוְעָתָם יִשְׁמַע וְיוֹשִׁיעֵם. שׁוֹמֵר יהוה אֶת כָּל אֹהֲבָיו, וְאֵת כָּל הָרְשָׁעִים יַשְׁמִיד. ❖ תְּהִלַּת יהוה יְדַבֶּר פִּי, וִיבָרֵךְ כָּל בָּשָׂר שֵׁם קָדְשׁוֹ לְעוֹלָם וָעֶד. וַאֲנַחְנוּ נְבָרֵךְ יָהּ, מֵעַתָּה וְעַד עוֹלָם, הַלְלוּיָהּ.[1]

The primary part of וּבָא לְצִיּוֹן is the *Kedushah* recited by the angels. These verses are presented in bold type and it is preferable that the congregation recite them aloud and in unison. However, the interpretive translation in Aramaic (which follows the verses in bold type) should be recited softly.

וּבָא לְצִיּוֹן גּוֹאֵל, וּלְשָׁבֵי פֶשַׁע בְּיַעֲקֹב, נְאֻם יהוה. וַאֲנִי, זֹאת בְּרִיתִי אוֹתָם, אָמַר יהוה, רוּחִי אֲשֶׁר עָלֶיךָ, וּדְבָרַי אֲשֶׁר שַׂמְתִּי בְּפִיךָ, לֹא יָמוּשׁוּ מִפִּיךָ וּמִפִּי זַרְעֲךָ וּמִפִּי זֶרַע זַרְעֲךָ, אָמַר יהוה, מֵעַתָּה וְעַד עוֹלָם:[2] ❖ וְאַתָּה קָדוֹשׁ יוֹשֵׁב תְּהִלּוֹת יִשְׂרָאֵל.[3] וְקָרָא זֶה אֶל זֶה וְאָמַר:

קָדוֹשׁ, קָדוֹשׁ, קָדוֹשׁ יהוה צְבָאוֹת, מְלֹא כָל הָאָרֶץ כְּבוֹדוֹ.[4]

וּמְקַבְּלִין דֵּין מִן דֵּין וְאָמְרִין:
קַדִּישׁ בִּשְׁמֵי מְרוֹמָא עִלָּאָה בֵּית שְׁכִינְתֵּהּ,
קַדִּישׁ עַל אַרְעָא עוֹבַד גְּבוּרְתֵּהּ,
קַדִּישׁ לְעָלַם וּלְעָלְמֵי עָלְמַיָּא, יהוה צְבָאוֹת,
מַלְיָא כָל אַרְעָא זִיו יְקָרֵהּ.[5]

❖ וַתִּשָּׂאֵנִי רוּחַ, וָאֶשְׁמַע אַחֲרַי קוֹל רַעַשׁ גָּדוֹל:

בָּרוּךְ כְּבוֹד יהוה מִמְּקוֹמוֹ.[6]

וּנְטָלַתְנִי רוּחָא, וּשְׁמִעֵית בַּתְרַי קָל זִיעַ סַגִּיא דִּמְשַׁבְּחִין וְאָמְרִין:
בְּרִיךְ יְקָרָא דַיהוה מֵאֲתַר בֵּית שְׁכִינְתֵּהּ.[7]

יהוה יִמְלֹךְ לְעֹלָם וָעֶד.[8]

יהוה מַלְכוּתֵהּ קָאֵם לְעָלַם וּלְעָלְמֵי עָלְמַיָּא.[9]

יהוה אֱלֹהֵי אַבְרָהָם יִצְחָק וְיִשְׂרָאֵל אֲבֹתֵינוּ, שָׁמְרָה זֹּאת* לְעוֹלָם, לְיֵצֶר מַחְשְׁבוֹת לְבַב עַמֶּךָ, וְהָכֵן לְבָבָם אֵלֶיךָ.[10] וְהוּא רַחוּם, יְכַפֵּר עָוֹן וְלֹא יַשְׁחִית, וְהִרְבָּה לְהָשִׁיב אַפּוֹ, וְלֹא יָעִיר כָּל חֲמָתוֹ.[11] כִּי אַתָּה אֲדֹנָי טוֹב וְסַלָּח, וְרַב חֶסֶד לְכָל

---

reading just before the end of the Sabbath symbolizes that we will take the Torah-imbued spirit of the Sabbath with us into the next week.

Commentary to אַשְׁרֵי can be found on p. 66; to וּבָא לְצִיּוֹן on p. 154; to the *Kedushah* recited by the angels on p. 88.

ר *The will of those who fear Him He will do;*
and their cry He will hear, and save them.
ש *HASHEM protects all who love Him;*
but all the wicked He will destroy.
ת Chazzan— *May my mouth declare the praise of HASHEM*
and may all flesh bless His Holy Name forever and ever.
We will bless God from this time and forever, Halleluyah![1]

The primary part of וּבָא לְצִיּוֹן, *'A redeemer shall come ...',* is the *Kedushah* recited by the angels. These verses are presented in bold type and it is preferable that the congregation recite them aloud and in unison. However, the interpretive translation in Aramaic (which follows the verses in bold type) should be recited softly.

וּבָא לְצִיּוֹן *'A redeemer shall come to Zion and to those of Jacob who repent from willful sin,' the words of HASHEM. 'And as for Me, this is My covenant with them,' said HASHEM, 'My spirit that is upon you and My words that I have placed in your mouth shall not be withdrawn from your mouth, nor from the mouth of your offspring, nor from the mouth of your offspring's offspring,' said HASHEM, 'from this moment and forever.'*[2] Chazzan— *You are the Holy One, enthroned upon the praises of Israel.*[3] *And one [angel] will call another and say:*

'Holy, holy, holy is HASHEM, Master of Legions,
the whole world is filled with His glory.'[4]
And they receive permission from one another and say:
'Holy in the most exalted heaven, the abode of His Presence;
holy on earth, product of His strength;
holy forever and ever is HASHEM, Master of Legions —
the entire world is filled with the radiance of His glory.'[5]
Chazzan— *And a wind lifted me; and I heard behind me*
the sound of a great noise:
'Blessed is the glory of HASHEM from His place.'[6]
And a wind lifted me and I heard behind me the sound
of the powerful movement of those who praised saying:
'Blessed is the honor of HASHEM
from the place of the abode of His Presence.'[7]
HASHEM shall reign for all eternity.[8]
HASHEM — His kingdom is established forever and ever.[9]

HASHEM, God of Abraham, Isaac, and Israel, our forefathers, may You preserve this forever as the realization of the thoughts in Your people's heart, and may You direct their heart to You.[10] *He, the Merciful One, is forgiving of iniquity and does not destroy; frequently He withdraws His anger, not arousing His entire rage.*[11] *For You, my Lord, are good and forgiving, and abundantly kind to all*

(1) *Psalms* 115:18. (2) *Isaiah* 59:20-21. (3) *Psalms* 22:4. (4) *Isaiah* 6:3. (5) *Targum Yonasan* to *Isaiah* 6:3. (6) *Ezekiel* 3:12. (7) *Targum Yonasan* to *Ezekiel* 3:12. (8) *Exodus* 15:18. (9) *Targum Onkelos* to *Exodus* 15:18. (10) *I Chronicles* 29:18. (11) *Psalms* 78:38.

קָרְאֵיךָ.[1] צִדְקָתְךָ צֶדֶק לְעוֹלָם, וְתוֹרָתְךָ אֱמֶת.[2] תִּתֵּן אֱמֶת לְיַעֲקֹב, חֶסֶד לְאַבְרָהָם, אֲשֶׁר נִשְׁבַּעְתָּ לַאֲבֹתֵינוּ מִימֵי קֶדֶם.[3] בָּרוּךְ אֲדֹנָי יוֹם יוֹם יַעֲמָס לָנוּ, הָאֵל יְשׁוּעָתֵנוּ סֶלָה.[4] יהוה צְבָאוֹת עִמָּנוּ, מִשְׂגָּב לָנוּ אֱלֹהֵי יַעֲקֹב סֶלָה.[5] יהוה צְבָאוֹת, אַשְׁרֵי אָדָם בֹּטֵחַ בָּךְ.[6] יהוה הוֹשִׁיעָה, הַמֶּלֶךְ יַעֲנֵנוּ בְיוֹם קָרְאֵנוּ.[7]

בָּרוּךְ הוּא אֱלֹהֵינוּ שֶׁבְּרָאָנוּ לִכְבוֹדוֹ, וְהִבְדִּילָנוּ מִן הַתּוֹעִים, וְנָתַן לָנוּ תּוֹרַת אֱמֶת, וְחַיֵּי עוֹלָם נָטַע בְּתוֹכֵנוּ. הוּא יִפְתַּח לִבֵּנוּ בְּתוֹרָתוֹ, וְיָשֵׂם בְּלִבֵּנוּ אַהֲבָתוֹ וְיִרְאָתוֹ וְלַעֲשׂוֹת רְצוֹנוֹ וּלְעָבְדוֹ בְּלֵבָב שָׁלֵם, לְמַעַן לֹא נִיגַע לָרִיק, וְלֹא נֵלֵד לַבֶּהָלָה.[8]

יְהִי רָצוֹן מִלְּפָנֶיךָ יהוה אֱלֹהֵינוּ וֵאלֹהֵי אֲבוֹתֵינוּ, שֶׁנִּשְׁמֹר חֻקֶּיךָ בָּעוֹלָם הַזֶּה, וְנִזְכֶּה וְנִחְיֶה וְנִרְאֶה וְנִירַשׁ טוֹבָה וּבְרָכָה לִשְׁנֵי יְמוֹת הַמָּשִׁיחַ וּלְחַיֵּי הָעוֹלָם הַבָּא. לְמַעַן יְזַמֶּרְךָ כָבוֹד וְלֹא יִדֹּם, יהוה אֱלֹהַי לְעוֹלָם אוֹדֶךָּ.[9] בָּרוּךְ הַגֶּבֶר אֲשֶׁר יִבְטַח בַּיהוה,* וְהָיָה יהוה מִבְטַחוֹ.[10] בִּטְחוּ בַיהוה עֲדֵי עַד, כִּי בְּיָהּ יהוה צוּר עוֹלָמִים.[11] ❖ וְיִבְטְחוּ בְךָ יוֹדְעֵי שְׁמֶךָ, כִּי לֹא עָזַבְתָּ דֹרְשֶׁיךָ, יהוה.[12] יהוה חָפֵץ לְמַעַן צִדְקוֹ, יַגְדִּיל תּוֹרָה וְיַאְדִּיר.[13]

The *chazzan* recites Half-*Kaddish*.

יִתְגַּדַּל וְיִתְקַדַּשׁ שְׁמֵהּ רַבָּא. (.Cong.— אָמֵן.) בְּעָלְמָא דִּי בְרָא כִרְעוּתֵהּ. וְיַמְלִיךְ מַלְכוּתֵהּ, בְּחַיֵּיכוֹן וּבְיוֹמֵיכוֹן וּבְחַיֵּי דְכָל בֵּית יִשְׂרָאֵל, בַּעֲגָלָא וּבִזְמַן קָרִיב. וְאִמְרוּ: אָמֵן.

(.Cong.— אָמֵן. יְהֵא שְׁמֵהּ רַבָּא מְבָרַךְ לְעָלַם וּלְעָלְמֵי עָלְמַיָּא.)

יְהֵא שְׁמֵהּ רַבָּא מְבָרַךְ לְעָלַם וּלְעָלְמֵי עָלְמַיָּא.

יִתְבָּרַךְ וְיִשְׁתַּבַּח וְיִתְפָּאַר וְיִתְרוֹמַם וְיִתְנַשֵּׂא וְיִתְהַדָּר וְיִתְעַלֶּה וְיִתְהַלָּל שְׁמֵהּ דְּקֻדְשָׁא בְּרִיךְ הוּא (.Cong.— בְּרִיךְ הוּא) — °לְעֵלָּא מִן כָּל (From Rosh Hashanah to Yom Kippur substitute— °לְעֵלָּא וּלְעֵלָּא מִכָּל) בִּרְכָתָא וְשִׁירָתָא תֻּשְׁבְּחָתָא וְנֶחֱמָתָא, דַּאֲמִירָן בְּעָלְמָא. וְאִמְרוּ: אָמֵן. (.Cong.— אָמֵן.)

On the Sabbath continue below. On Festivals (other than those that coincide with the Sabbath), the Festival *Shemoneh Esrei*, page 660, is recited at this point.

Congregation, then *chazzan*:

וַאֲנִי תְפִלָּתִי לְךָ יהוה עֵת רָצוֹן, אֱלֹהִים בְּרָב חַסְדֶּךָ, עֲנֵנִי בֶּאֱמֶת יִשְׁעֶךָ.[14]

who call upon You.[1] *Your righteousness remains righteous forever, and Your Torah is truth.*[2] *Grant truth to Jacob, kindness to Abraham, as You swore to our forefathers from ancient times.*[3] *Blessed is my Lord for every single day, He burdens us with blessings, the God of our salvation, Selah.*[4] *HASHEM, Master of Legions, is with us, a stronghold for us is the God of Jacob, Selah.*[5] *HASHEM, Master of Legions, praiseworthy is the man who trusts in You.*[6] *HASHEM, save! May the King answer us on the day we call.*[7]

Blessed is He, our God, Who created us for His glory, separated us from those who stray, gave us the Torah of truth and implanted eternal life within us. May He open our heart through His Torah and imbue our heart with love and awe of Him and that we may do His will and serve Him wholeheartedly, so that we do not struggle in vain nor produce for futility.[8]

May it be Your will, HASHEM, our God and the God of our forefathers, that we observe Your decrees in This World, and merit that we live and see and inherit goodness and blessing in the years of Messianic times and for the life of the World to Come. So that my soul might sing to You and not be stilled, HASHEM, my God, forever will I thank You.[9] *Blessed is the man who trusts in HASHEM, then HASHEM will be his security.*[10] *Trust in HASHEM forever, for in God, HASHEM, is the strength of the worlds.*[11] Chazzan— *Those knowing Your Name will trust in You, and You forsake not those Who seek You, HASHEM.*[12] *HASHEM desired, for the sake of its [Israel's] righteousness, that the Torah be made great and glorious.*[13]

The *chazzan* recites Half-*Kaddish.*

יִתְגַּדַּל *May His great Name grow exalted and sanctified* (Cong.— *Amen.*) *in the world that He created as He willed. May He give reign to His kingship in your lifetimes and in your days, and in the lifetimes of the entire Family of Israel, swiftly and soon. Now respond: Amen.*

(Cong.— *Amen. May His great Name be blessed forever and ever.*)

May His great Name be blessed forever and ever.

Blessed, praised, glorified, exalted, extolled, mighty, upraised, and lauded be the Name of the Holy One, Blessed is He (Cong.— *Blessed is He*) — (From Rosh Hashanah to Yom Kippur add: *exceedingly*) *beyond any blessing and song, praise and consolation that are uttered in the world. Now respond: Amen.* (Cong.— *Amen.*)

On the Sabbath continue below. On Festivals (other than those that coincide with the Sabbath), the Festival *Shemoneh Esrei,* page 660, is recited at this point.

Congregation, then *chazzan:*

וַאֲנִי תְפִלָּתִי *As for me, may my prayer to You, HASHEM, be at an opportune time; O God, in Your abundant kindness, answer me with the truth of Your salvation.*[14]

(1) *Psalms* 86:5. (2) 119:142. (3) *Micah* 7:20. (4) *Psalms* 68:20. (5) 46:8. (6) 84:13. (7) 20:10. (8) Cf. *Isaiah* 65:23. (9) *Psalms* 30:13. (10) *Jeremiah* 17:7. (11) *Isaiah* 26:4. (12) *Psalms* 9:11. (13) *Isaiah* 42:21. (14) *Psalms* 69:14.

הוצאת ספר תורה

From the moment the Ark is opened until the Torah is returned to it, one must conduct himself with the utmost respect, and avoid unnecessary conversation. It is commendable to kiss the Torah as it is carried to the *bimah* [reading table] and back to the Ark.

All rise and remain standing until the Torah is placed on the *bimah*.
The Ark is opened; before the Torah is removed the congregation recites:

וַיְהִי בִּנְסֹעַ הָאָרֹן, וַיֹּאמֶר מֹשֶׁה, קוּמָה יהוה וְיָפֻצוּ אֹיְבֶיךָ, וְיָנֻסוּ מְשַׂנְאֶיךָ מִפָּנֶיךָ.[1] כִּי מִצִּיּוֹן תֵּצֵא תוֹרָה, וּדְבַר יהוה מִירוּשָׁלָיִם.[2] בָּרוּךְ שֶׁנָּתַן תּוֹרָה לְעַמּוֹ יִשְׂרָאֵל בִּקְדֻשָּׁתוֹ.

זוהר ויקהל שסט:א

בְּרִיךְ שְׁמֵהּ דְּמָרֵא עָלְמָא, בְּרִיךְ כִּתְרָךְ וְאַתְרָךְ. יְהֵא רְעוּתָךְ עִם עַמָּךְ יִשְׂרָאֵל לְעָלַם, וּפֻרְקַן יְמִינָךְ אַחֲזֵי לְעַמָּךְ בְּבֵית מַקְדְּשָׁךְ, וּלְאַמְטוּיֵי לָנָא מִטּוּב נְהוֹרָךְ, וּלְקַבֵּל צְלוֹתָנָא בְּרַחֲמִין. יְהֵא רַעֲוָא קֳדָמָךְ, דְּתוֹרִיךְ לָן חַיִּין בְּטִיבוּתָא, וְלֶהֱוֵי אֲנָא פְקִידָא בְּגוֹ צַדִּיקַיָּא, לְמִרְחַם עָלַי וּלְמִנְטַר יָתִי וְיַת כָּל דִּי לִי וְדִי לְעַמָּךְ יִשְׂרָאֵל. אַנְתְּ הוּא זָן לְכֹלָּא, וּמְפַרְנֵס לְכֹלָּא, אַנְתְּ הוּא שַׁלִּיט עַל כֹּלָּא. אַנְתְּ הוּא דְּשַׁלִּיט עַל מַלְכַיָּא, וּמַלְכוּתָא דִּילָךְ הִיא. אֲנָא עַבְדָּא דְקֻדְשָׁא בְּרִיךְ הוּא, דְּסָגִידְנָא קַמֵּהּ וּמִקַּמָּא דִּיקַר אוֹרַיְתֵהּ בְּכָל עִדָּן וְעִדָּן. לָא עַל אֱנָשׁ רָחִיצְנָא, וְלָא עַל בַּר אֱלָהִין סָמִיכְנָא, אֶלָּא בֶּאֱלָהָא דִשְׁמַיָּא, דְּהוּא אֱלָהָא קְשׁוֹט, וְאוֹרַיְתֵהּ קְשׁוֹט, וּנְבִיאוֹהִי קְשׁוֹט, וּמַסְגֵּא לְמֶעְבַּד טַבְוָן וּקְשׁוֹט. בֵּהּ אֲנָא רָחִיץ, וְלִשְׁמֵהּ קַדִּישָׁא יַקִּירָא אֲנָא אֵמַר תֻּשְׁבְּחָן. יְהֵא רַעֲוָא קֳדָמָךְ, דְּתִפְתַּח לִבָּאִי בְּאוֹרַיְתָא, וְתַשְׁלִים מִשְׁאֲלִין דְּלִבָּאִי, וְלִבָּא דְכָל עַמָּךְ יִשְׂרָאֵל, לְטַב וּלְחַיִּין וְלִשְׁלָם. (אָמֵן.)

The Torah is removed from the Ark and presented to the *chazzan,* who accepts it in his right arm. He then turns to the Ark and raises the Torah slightly as he bows and recites:

גַּדְּלוּ לַיהוה אִתִּי, וּנְרוֹמְמָה שְׁמוֹ יַחְדָּו.[3]

The *chazzan* turns to his right and carries the Torah to the *bimah,* as the congregation responds:

לְךָ יהוה הַגְּדֻלָּה וְהַגְּבוּרָה וְהַתִּפְאֶרֶת וְהַנֵּצַח וְהַהוֹד, כִּי כֹל בַּשָּׁמַיִם וּבָאָרֶץ, לְךָ יהוה הַמַּמְלָכָה וְהַמִּתְנַשֵּׂא לְכֹל לְרֹאשׁ.[4] רוֹמְמוּ יהוה אֱלֹהֵינוּ וְהִשְׁתַּחֲווּ לַהֲדֹם רַגְלָיו, קָדוֹשׁ הוּא. רוֹמְמוּ יהוה אֱלֹהֵינוּ וְהִשְׁתַּחֲווּ לְהַר קָדְשׁוֹ, כִּי קָדוֹשׁ יהוה אֱלֹהֵינוּ.[5]

אַב הָרַחֲמִים הוּא יְרַחֵם עַם עֲמוּסִים, וְיִזְכֹּר בְּרִית אֵיתָנִים, וְיַצִּיל נַפְשׁוֹתֵינוּ מִן הַשָּׁעוֹת הָרָעוֹת, וְיִגְעַר בְּיֵצֶר הָרָע מִן הַנְּשׂוּאִים, וְיָחֹן אוֹתָנוּ לִפְלֵיטַת עוֹלָמִים, וִימַלֵּא מִשְׁאֲלוֹתֵינוּ בְּמִדָּה טוֹבָה יְשׁוּעָה וְרַחֲמִים.

The Torah is placed on the *bimah* and prepared for reading.

REMOVAL OF THE TORAH FROM THE ARK

From the moment the Ark is opened until the Torah is returned to it, one must conduct himself with the utmost respect, and avoid unnecessary conversation. It is commendable to kiss the Torah as it is carried to the *bimah* [reading table] and back to the Ark.

All rise and remain standing until the Torah is placed on the *bimah*.
The Ark is opened; before the Torah is removed the congregation recites:

וַיְהִי בִּנְסֹעַ *When the Ark would travel, Moses would say, 'Arise, HASHEM, and let Your foes be scattered, let those who hate You flee from You.'[1] For from Zion will the Torah come forth and the word of HASHEM from Jerusalem.[2] Blessed is He Who gave the Torah to His people Israel in His holiness.*

Zohar, *Vayakhel* 369a

בְּרִיךְ שְׁמֵהּ *Blessed is the Name of the Master of the universe, blessed is Your crown and Your place. May Your favor remain with Your people Israel forever; may You display the salvation of Your right hand to Your people in Your Holy Temple, to benefit us with the goodness of Your luminescence and to accept our prayers with mercy. May it be Your will that You extend our lives with goodness and that I be numbered among the righteous; that You have mercy on me and protect me, all that is mine and that is Your people Israel's. It is You Who nourishes all and sustains all, You control everything. It is You Who control kings, and kingship is Yours. I am a servant of the Holy One, Blessed is He, and I prostrate myself before Him and before the glory of His Torah at all times. Not in any man do I put trust, nor on any angel do I rely — only on the God of heaven Who is the God of truth, Whose Torah is truth and Whose prophets are true and Who acts liberally with kindness and truth. In Him do I trust, and to His glorious and holy Name do I declare praises. May it be Your will that You open my heart to the Torah and that You fulfill the wishes of my heart and the heart of Your entire people Israel for good, for life, and for peace. (Amen.)*

The Torah is removed from the Ark and presented to the *chazzan,* who accepts it in his right arm. He then turns to the Ark and raises the Torah slightly as he bows and recites:

Declare the greatness of HASHEM with me, and let us exalt His Name together.[3]

The *chazzan* turns to his right and carries the Torah to the *bimah,* as the congregation responds:

לְךָ *Yours, HASHEM, is the greatness, the strength, the splendor, the triumph, and the glory; even everything in heaven and earth; Yours, HASHEM, is the kingdom, and the sovereignty over every leader.[4] Exalt HASHEM, our God, and bow at His footstool; He is Holy! Exalt HASHEM, our God, and bow at His holy mountain; for holy is HASHEM, our God.[5]*

אַב הָרַחֲמִים *May the Father of mercy have mercy on the nation that is borne by Him, and may He remember the covenant of the spiritually mighty. May He rescue our souls from the bad times, and upbraid the evil inclination to leave those borne by Him, graciously make us an eternal remnant, and fulfill our requests in good measure, for salvation and mercy.*

The Torah is placed on the *bimah* and prepared for reading.

---

(1) *Numbers* 10:35. (2) *Isaiah* 2:3. (3) *Psalms* 34:4. (4) *I Chronicles* 29:11. (5) *Psalms* 99:5,9.

The *gabbai* uses the following formula to call a *Kohen* to the Torah:

וְתִגָּלֶה וְתֵרָאֶה מַלְכוּתוֹ עָלֵינוּ בִּזְמַן קָרוֹב, וְיָחֹן פְּלֵיטָתֵנוּ וּפְלֵיטַת עַמּוֹ בֵּית יִשְׂרָאֵל לְחֵן וּלְחֶסֶד וּלְרַחֲמִים וּלְרָצוֹן. וְנֹאמַר אָמֵן. הַכֹּל הָבוּ גֹדֶל לֵאלֹהֵינוּ וּתְנוּ כָבוֹד לַתּוֹרָה. כֹּהֵן° קְרָב, יַעֲמֹד (insert name) הַכֹּהֵן.

°If no *Kohen* is present, the *gabbai* says: "אֵין כַּאן כֹּהֵן, יַעֲמֹד (insert name) יִשְׂרָאֵל (לֵוִי) בִּמְקוֹם כֹּהֵן".

בָּרוּךְ שֶׁנָּתַן תּוֹרָה לְעַמּוֹ יִשְׂרָאֵל בִּקְדֻשָּׁתוֹ. (תּוֹרַת יהוה תְּמִימָה מְשִׁיבַת נָפֶשׁ, עֵדוּת יהוה נֶאֱמָנָה מַחְכִּימַת פֶּתִי. פִּקּוּדֵי יהוה יְשָׁרִים מְשַׂמְּחֵי לֵב, מִצְוַת יהוה בָּרָה מְאִירַת עֵינָיִם.[1] יהוה עֹז לְעַמּוֹ יִתֵּן, יהוה יְבָרֵךְ אֶת עַמּוֹ בַשָּׁלוֹם.[2] הָאֵל תָּמִים דַּרְכּוֹ, אִמְרַת יהוה צְרוּפָה, מָגֵן הוּא לְכֹל הַחֹסִים בּוֹ.[3])

Congregation, then *gabbai:*

וְאַתֶּם הַדְּבֵקִים בַּיהוה אֱלֹהֵיכֶם, חַיִּים כֻּלְּכֶם הַיּוֹם:[4]

קריאת התורה

[See *Laws* §97-114.] A commentary appears on p. 440.
The appropriate portions for the *Minchah* readings may be found beginning on p. 927-03.

The reader shows the *oleh* (person called to the Torah) the place in the Torah. The *oleh* touches the Torah with a corner of his *tallis,* or the belt or mantle of the Torah, and kisses it. He then begins the blessing, bowing at בָּרְכוּ, and straightening up at 'ה.

בָּרְכוּ אֶת יהוה הַמְבֹרָךְ.

Congregation, followed by *oleh,* responds, bowing at בָּרוּךְ, and straightening up at 'ה:

בָּרוּךְ יהוה הַמְבֹרָךְ לְעוֹלָם וָעֶד.

Oleh continues:

בָּרוּךְ אַתָּה יהוה אֱלֹהֵינוּ מֶלֶךְ הָעוֹלָם, אֲשֶׁר בָּחַר בָּנוּ מִכָּל הָעַמִּים, וְנָתַן לָנוּ אֶת תּוֹרָתוֹ. בָּרוּךְ אַתָּה יהוה, נוֹתֵן הַתּוֹרָה.

(.Cong.— אָמֵן)

After his Torah portion has been read, the *oleh* recites:

בָּרוּךְ אַתָּה יהוה אֱלֹהֵינוּ מֶלֶךְ הָעוֹלָם, אֲשֶׁר נָתַן לָנוּ תּוֹרַת אֱמֶת, וְחַיֵּי עוֹלָם נָטַע בְּתוֹכֵנוּ. בָּרוּךְ אַתָּה יהוה, נוֹתֵן הַתּוֹרָה.

(.Cong.— אָמֵן)

THE VARIOUS מִי שֶׁבֵּרַךְ PRAYERS APPEAR ON P. 442.

When the Torah reading has been completed, the Torah is raised for all to see.
Each person looks at the Torah and recites aloud:

וְזֹאת הַתּוֹרָה אֲשֶׁר שָׂם מֹשֶׁה לִפְנֵי בְּנֵי יִשְׂרָאֵל,[5]
עַל פִּי יהוה בְּיַד מֹשֶׁה.[6]

Some add the following verses:

עֵץ חַיִּים הִיא לַמַּחֲזִיקִים בָּהּ, וְתֹמְכֶיהָ מְאֻשָּׁר.[7] דְּרָכֶיהָ דַרְכֵי נֹעַם, וְכָל נְתִיבוֹתֶיהָ שָׁלוֹם.[8] אֹרֶךְ יָמִים בִּימִינָהּ, בִּשְׂמֹאלָהּ עֹשֶׁר וְכָבוֹד.[9] יהוה חָפֵץ לְמַעַן צִדְקוֹ, יַגְדִּיל תּוֹרָה וְיַאְדִּיר.[10]

The *gabbai* uses the following formula to call a *Kohen* to the Torah:

וְתִגָּלֶה *And may His kingship over us be revealed and become visible soon, and may He be gracious to our remnant and the remnant of His people the Family of Israel, for graciousness, kindness, mercy, and favor. And let us respond, Amen. All of you ascribe greatness to our God and give honor to the Torah. Kohen,*° *approach. Stand* (name) *son of* (father's name) *the Kohen.*

°If no *Kohen* is present, the *gabbai* says: *'There is no Kohen present, stand* (name) *son of* (father's name) *an Israelite (Levite) in place of the Kohen.'*

Blessed is He Who gave the Torah to His people Israel in His holiness. (The Torah of HASHEM is perfect, restoring the soul; the testimony of HASHEM is trustworthy, making the simple one wise. The orders of HASHEM are upright, gladdening the heart; the command of HASHEM is clear, enlightening the eyes.[1] *HASHEM will give might to His people; HASHEM will bless His people with peace.*[2] *The God Whose way is perfect, the promise of HASHEM is flawless, He is a shield for all who take refuge in Him.*[3]*)*

Congregation, then *gabbai:*

You who cling to HASHEM, your God — you are all alive today.[4]

READING OF THE TORAH

[See *Laws* §97-114.] A commentary appears on p. 440.
The appropriate portions for the *Minchah* readings may be found beginning on p. 927.

The reader shows the *oleh* (person called to the Torah) the place in the Torah. The *oleh* touches the Torah with a corner of his *tallis,* or the belt or mantle of the Torah, and kisses it. He then begins the blessing, bowing at *'Bless',* and straightening up at 'HASHEM':

Bless HASHEM, the blessed One.

Congregation, followed by *oleh,* responds, bowing at 'Blessed,' and straightening up at 'HASHEM'.

Blessed is HASHEM, the blessed One, for all eternity.

Oleh continues:

בָּרוּךְ *Blessed are You, HASHEM, our God, King of the universe, Who selected us from all the peoples and gave us His Torah. Blessed are You, HASHEM, Giver of the Torah.* (Cong.— *Amen.)*

After his Torah portion has been read, the *oleh* recites:

בָּרוּךְ *Blessed are You, HASHEM, our God, King of the universe, Who gave us the Torah of truth and implanted eternal life within us. Blessed are You, HASHEM, Giver of the Torah.* (Cong.— *Amen.)*

THE VARIOUS *MI SHEBEIRACH* PRAYERS APPEAR ON P. 442.

When the Torah reading has been completed, the Torah is raised for all to see. Each person looks at the Torah and recites aloud:

This is the Torah that Moses placed before the Children of Israel,[5] **upon the command of HASHEM, through Moses' hand.**[6]

Some add the following verses:

עֵץ *It is a tree of life for those who grasp it, and its supporters are praiseworthy.*[7] *Its ways are ways of pleasantness and all its paths are peace.*[8] *Lengthy days are at its right; at its left are wealth and honor.*[9] *HASHEM desired, for the sake of its [Israel's] righteousness, that the Torah be made great and glorious.*[10]

(1) *Psalms* 19:8-9. (2) 29:11. (3) 18:31. (4) *Deuteronomy* 4:4. (5) 4:44.
(6) *Numbers* 9:23. (7) *Proverbs* 3:18. (8) 3:17. (9) 3:16. (10) *Isaiah* 42:21.

In many congregations the *gabbai* recites אֵל מָלֵא רַחֲמִים, *O God, full of mercy,* in memory of the deceased, either on or prior to the *Yahrzeit.*

אֵל מָלֵא רַחֲמִים, שׁוֹכֵן בַּמְּרוֹמִים, הַמְצֵא מְנוּחָה נְכוֹנָה עַל כַּנְפֵי הַשְּׁכִינָה, בְּמַעֲלוֹת קְדוֹשִׁים וּטְהוֹרִים כְּזֹהַר הָרָקִיעַ מַזְהִירִים, אֶת נִשְׁמַת

for a man

(name of deceased) **בֶּן** (his father's name) שֶׁהָלַךְ לְעוֹלָמוֹ, בַּעֲבוּר שֶׁ(name of supplicant) יִתֵּן צְדָקָה בְּעַד הַזְכָּרַת נִשְׁמָתוֹ, בְּגַן עֵדֶן תְּהֵא מְנוּחָתוֹ, לָכֵן בַּעַל הָרַחֲמִים יַסְתִּירֵהוּ בְּסֵתֶר כְּנָפָיו לְעוֹלָמִים, וְיִצְרוֹר בִּצְרוֹר הַחַיִּים אֶת נִשְׁמָתוֹ, יהוה הוּא נַחֲלָתוֹ, וְיָנוּחַ בְּשָׁלוֹם עַל מִשְׁכָּבוֹ, וְנֹאמַר: אָמֵן. (Cong.— אָמֵן.)

for a woman

(name of deceased) **בַּת** (her father's name) שֶׁהָלְכָה לְעוֹלָמָהּ, בַּעֲבוּר שֶׁ(name of supplicant) יִתֵּן צְדָקָה בְּעַד הַזְכָּרַת נִשְׁמָתָהּ, בְּגַן עֵדֶן תְּהֵא מְנוּחָתָהּ, לָכֵן בַּעַל הָרַחֲמִים יַסְתִּירֶהָ בְּסֵתֶר כְּנָפָיו לְעוֹלָמִים, וְיִצְרוֹר בִּצְרוֹר הַחַיִּים אֶת נִשְׁמָתָהּ, יהוה הוּא נַחֲלָתָהּ, וְתָנוּחַ בְּשָׁלוֹם עַל מִשְׁכָּבָהּ, וְנֹאמַר: אָמֵן. (Cong.— אָמֵן.)

The *chazzan* takes the Torah in his right arm and recites:

יְהַלְלוּ אֶת שֵׁם יהוה, כִּי נִשְׂגָּב שְׁמוֹ לְבַדּוֹ —

Congregation responds:

— הוֹדוֹ עַל אֶרֶץ וְשָׁמָיִם. וַיָּרֶם קֶרֶן לְעַמּוֹ, תְּהִלָּה לְכָל חֲסִידָיו, לִבְנֵי יִשְׂרָאֵל עַם קְרֹבוֹ, הַלְלוּיָהּ.[1]

As the Torah is carried to the Ark, congregation recites Psalm 24, לְדָוִד מִזְמוֹר.

לְדָוִד מִזְמוֹר, לַיהוה הָאָרֶץ וּמְלוֹאָהּ, תֵּבֵל וְיֹשְׁבֵי בָהּ. כִּי הוּא עַל יַמִּים יְסָדָהּ, וְעַל נְהָרוֹת יְכוֹנְנֶהָ. מִי יַעֲלֶה בְהַר יהוה, וּמִי יָקוּם בִּמְקוֹם קָדְשׁוֹ. נְקִי כַפַּיִם וּבַר לֵבָב, אֲשֶׁר לֹא נָשָׂא לַשָּׁוְא נַפְשִׁי וְלֹא נִשְׁבַּע לְמִרְמָה. יִשָּׂא בְרָכָה מֵאֵת יהוה, וּצְדָקָה מֵאֱלֹהֵי יִשְׁעוֹ. זֶה דּוֹר דֹּרְשָׁיו, מְבַקְשֵׁי פָנֶיךָ, יַעֲקֹב, סֶלָה. שְׂאוּ שְׁעָרִים רָאשֵׁיכֶם, וְהִנָּשְׂאוּ פִּתְחֵי עוֹלָם, וְיָבוֹא מֶלֶךְ הַכָּבוֹד. מִי זֶה מֶלֶךְ הַכָּבוֹד, יהוה עִזּוּז וְגִבּוֹר, יהוה גִּבּוֹר מִלְחָמָה. שְׂאוּ שְׁעָרִים רָאשֵׁיכֶם, וּשְׂאוּ פִּתְחֵי עוֹלָם, וְיָבֹא מֶלֶךְ הַכָּבוֹד. מִי הוּא זֶה מֶלֶךְ הַכָּבוֹד, יהוה צְבָאוֹת הוּא מֶלֶךְ הַכָּבוֹד, סֶלָה.

As the Torah is placed into the Ark, congregation recites the following verses:

וּבְנֻחֹה יֹאמַר, שׁוּבָה יהוה רִבְבוֹת אַלְפֵי יִשְׂרָאֵל.[2] קוּמָה יהוה לִמְנוּחָתֶךָ, אַתָּה וַאֲרוֹן עֻזֶּךָ. כֹּהֲנֶיךָ יִלְבְּשׁוּ צֶדֶק, וַחֲסִידֶיךָ יְרַנֵּנוּ. בַּעֲבוּר דָּוִד עַבְדֶּךָ אַל תָּשֵׁב פְּנֵי מְשִׁיחֶךָ.[3] כִּי לֶקַח טוֹב נָתַתִּי לָכֶם, תּוֹרָתִי אַל תַּעֲזֹבוּ.[4] ❖ עֵץ חַיִּים הִיא לַמַּחֲזִיקִים בָּהּ, וְתֹמְכֶיהָ מְאֻשָּׁר.[5] דְּרָכֶיהָ דַרְכֵי נֹעַם, וְכָל נְתִיבוֹתֶיהָ שָׁלוֹם.[6] הֲשִׁיבֵנוּ יהוה אֵלֶיךָ וְנָשׁוּבָה, חַדֵּשׁ יָמֵינוּ כְּקֶדֶם.[7]

In many congregations the *gabbai* recites אֵל מָלֵא רַחֲמִים, *O God, full of mercy,* in memory of the deceased, either on or prior to the *Yahrzeit.*

אֵל *O God, full of mercy, Who dwells on high, grant proper rest on the wings of the Divine Presence — in the lofty levels of the holy and the pure ones, who shine like the glow of the firmament — for the soul of*

for a man

(name of deceased) *son of* (name of his father), *who went on to his world, for* (name of supplicant) *will contribute to charity in remembrance of his soul. May his resting place be in the Garden of Eden — therefore may the Master of mercy shelter him in the shelter of His wings for eternity; and may He bind his soul in the Bond of Life.* HASHEM *is his heritage, and may he repose in peace on his resting place. Now let us respond: Amen.* (Cong.— *Amen.*)

for a woman

(name of deceased) *daughter of* (name of her father), *who went on to her world, for* (name of supplicant) *will contribute to charity in remembrance of her soul. May her resting place be in the Garden of Eden — therefore may the Master of mercy shelter her in the shelter of His wings for eternity; and may He bind her soul in the Bond of Life.* HASHEM *is her heritage, and may she repose in peace on her resting place. Now let us respond: Amen.* (Cong.— *Amen.*)

The *chazzan* takes the Torah in his right arm and recites:

Let them praise the Name of HASHEM, for His Name alone will have been exalted —

Congregation responds:

— His glory is above earth and heaven. And He will have exalted the pride of His people, causing praise for all His devout ones, for the Children of Israel, His intimate nation. Halleluyah![1]

As the Torah is carried to the Ark, congregation recites Psalm 24, *'Of David a psalm.'*

לְדָוִד *Of David a psalm.* HASHEM*'s is the earth and its fullness, the inhabited land and those who dwell in it. For He founded it upon seas, and established it upon rivers. Who may ascend the mountain of* HASHEM*, and who may stand in the place of His sanctity? One with clean hands and pure heart, who has not sworn in vain by My soul and has not sworn deceitfully. He will receive a blessing from* HASHEM *and just kindness from the God of his salvation. This is the generation of those who seek Him, those who strive for Your Presence — Jacob, Selah. Raise up your heads, O gates, and be uplifted, you everlasting entrances, so that the King of Glory may enter. Who is this King of Glory? —* HASHEM*, the mighty and strong,* HASHEM*, the strong in battle. Raise up your heads, O gates, and raise up, you everlasting entrances, so that the King of Glory may enter. Who then is the King of Glory?* HASHEM*, Master of Legions, He is the King of Glory. Selah!*

As the Torah is placed into the Ark, congregation recites the following verses:

וּבְנֻחֹה *And when it rested he would say, 'Return* HASHEM *to the myriad thousands of Israel.'*[2] *Arise,* HASHEM*, to Your resting place, You and the Ark of Your strength. Let Your priests be clothed in righteousness, and Your devout ones will sing joyously. For the sake of David, Your servant, turn not away the face of Your anointed.*[3] *For I have given you a good teaching, do not forsake My Torah.*[4] Chazzan— *It is a tree of life for those who grasp it, and its supporters are praiseworthy.*[5] *Its ways are ways of pleasantness and all its paths are peace.*[6] *Bring us back to You,* HASHEM*, and we shall return, renew our days as of old.*[7]

(1) *Psalms* 148:13-14. (2) *Numbers* 10:36. (3) *Psalms* 132:8-10.
(4) *Proverbs* 4:2. (5) 3:18. (6) 3:17. (7) *Lamentations* 5:21.

In the presence of a *minyan,* the *chazzan* recites חֲצִי קַדִּישׁ. [See comment on p. 445.]

יִתְגַּדַּל וְיִתְקַדַּשׁ שְׁמֵהּ רַבָּא. (.Cong.— אָמֵן.) בְּעָלְמָא דִּי בְרָא כִרְעוּתֵהּ. וְיַמְלִיךְ מַלְכוּתֵהּ, בְּחַיֵּיכוֹן וּבְיוֹמֵיכוֹן וּבְחַיֵּי דְכָל בֵּית יִשְׂרָאֵל, בַּעֲגָלָא וּבִזְמַן קָרִיב. וְאִמְרוּ: אָמֵן.

(.Cong.— אָמֵן. יְהֵא שְׁמֵהּ רַבָּא מְבָרַךְ לְעָלַם וּלְעָלְמֵי עָלְמַיָּא.)

יְהֵא שְׁמֵהּ רַבָּא מְבָרַךְ לְעָלַם וּלְעָלְמֵי עָלְמַיָּא.

יִתְבָּרַךְ וְיִשְׁתַּבַּח וְיִתְפָּאַר וְיִתְרוֹמַם וְיִתְנַשֵּׂא וְיִתְהַדָּר וְיִתְעַלֶּה וְיִתְהַלָּל שְׁמֵהּ דְּקֻדְשָׁא בְּרִיךְ הוּא (.Cong.— בְּרִיךְ הוּא) — °לְעֵלָּא מִן כָּל (°לְעֵלָּא וּלְעֵלָּא מִכָּל —From Rosh Hashanah to Yom Kippur substitute) בִּרְכָתָא וְשִׁירָתָא תֻּשְׁבְּחָתָא וְנֶחֱמָתָא, דַּאֲמִירָן בְּעָלְמָא. וְאִמְרוּ: אָמֵן. (.Cong.— אָמֵן.)

On an ordinary Sabbath and Sabbath Chol HaMoed, continue *Shemoneh Esrei* below.
On Festivals (even when they fall on the Sabbath) the Festival *Shemoneh Esrei* (p. 660) is recited.

שמונה עשרה — עמידה

Take three steps backward, then three steps forward. Remain standing with the feet together while reciting *Shemoneh Esrei.* It should be recited with quiet devotion and without any interruption, verbal or otherwise. Although its recitation should not be audible to others, one must pray loudly enough to hear himself. See *Laws* §61-96 for a brief summary of its laws, including how to rectify the omission of phrases that are added at particular times of the year.

כִּי שֵׁם יהוה אֶקְרָא, הָבוּ גֹדֶל לֵאלֹהֵינוּ.[1]

אֲדֹנָי שְׂפָתַי תִּפְתָּח, וּפִי יַגִּיד תְּהִלָּתֶךָ.[2]

אבות

Bend the knees at בָּרוּךְ; bow at אַתָּה; straighten up at ה׳.

בָּרוּךְ אַתָּה יהוה אֱלֹהֵינוּ וֵאלֹהֵי אֲבוֹתֵינוּ, אֱלֹהֵי אַבְרָהָם, אֱלֹהֵי יִצְחָק, וֵאלֹהֵי יַעֲקֹב, הָאֵל הַגָּדוֹל הַגִּבּוֹר וְהַנּוֹרָא, אֵל עֶלְיוֹן, גּוֹמֵל חֲסָדִים טוֹבִים וְקוֹנֵה הַכֹּל, וְזוֹכֵר חַסְדֵי אָבוֹת, וּמֵבִיא גוֹאֵל לִבְנֵי בְנֵיהֶם, לְמַעַן שְׁמוֹ בְּאַהֲבָה.

From Rosh Hashanah to Yom Kippur add:

זָכְרֵנוּ לְחַיִּים, מֶלֶךְ חָפֵץ בַּחַיִּים, וְכָתְבֵנוּ בְּסֵפֶר הַחַיִּים, לְמַעַנְךָ אֱלֹהִים חַיִּים.

[If forgotten, do not repeat *Shemoneh Esrei.* See *Laws* §61.]

Bend the knees at בָּרוּךְ; bow at אַתָּה; straighten up at ה׳.

מֶלֶךְ עוֹזֵר וּמוֹשִׁיעַ וּמָגֵן. בָּרוּךְ אַתָּה יהוה, מָגֵן אַבְרָהָם.

גבורות

אַתָּה גִּבּוֹר לְעוֹלָם אֲדֹנָי, מְחַיֵּה מֵתִים אַתָּה, רַב לְהוֹשִׁיעַ.

Between Succos and Pesach add:

מַשִּׁיב הָרוּחַ וּמוֹרִיד °הַגֶּשֶׁם [some say – °הַגָּשֶׁם].

[If forgotten, see *Laws* §70-75.]

עֲמִידָה / Amidah
Commentary to the first three blessings of *Shemoneh Esrei* appears on pp. 98-102; to the last three blessings, on pp. 110-119.

In the presence of a *minyan,* the *chazzan* recites Half-*Kaddish.* [See comment on p. 445.]

יִתְגַּדַּל *May His great Name grow exalted and sanctified* (Cong.— *Amen.*) *in the world that He created as He willed. May He give reign to His kingship in your lifetimes and in your days, and in the lifetimes of the entire Family of Israel, swiftly and soon. Now respond: Amen.*

(Cong.– *Amen. May His great Name be blessed forever and ever.*)

May His great Name be blessed forever and ever.

Blessed, praised, glorified, exalted, extolled, mighty, upraised, and lauded be the Name of the Holy One, Blessed is He (Cong.— *Blessed is He*) — (From Rosh Hashanah to Yom Kippur add: *exceedingly*) *beyond any blessing and song, praise and consolation that are uttered in the world. Now respond: Amen.*

(Cong.— *Amen.*)

On an ordinary Sabbath and Sabbath Chol HaMoed, continue *Shemoneh Esrei* below. On Festivals (even when they fall on the Sabbath) the Festival *Shemoneh Esrei* (p. 660) is recited.

SHEMONEH ESREI — AMIDAH

Take three steps backward, then three steps forward. Remain standing with the feet together while reciting *Shemoneh Esrei.* It should be recited with quiet devotion and without any interruption, verbal or otherwise. Although its recitation should not be audible to others, one must pray loudly enough to hear himself. See *Laws* §61-96 for a brief summary of its laws including how to rectify the omission of phrases that are added at particular times of the year.

When I call out the Name of Hashem, *ascribe greatness to our God.*[1]

My Lord, open my lips, that my mouth may declare Your praise.[2]

PATRIARCHS

Bend the knees at *'Blessed';* bow at *'You';* straighten up at *'Hashem'.*

בָּרוּךְ *Blessed are You,* Hashem, *our God and the God of our forefathers, God of Abraham, God of Isaac, and God of Jacob; the great, mighty, and awesome God, the supreme God, Who bestows beneficial kindnesses and creates everything, Who recalls the kindnesses of the Patriarchs and brings a Redeemer to their children's children, for His Name's sake, with love.*

From Rosh Hashanah to Yom Kippur add the following.

Remember us for life, O King Who desires life,

and inscribe us in the Book of Life — for Your sake, O Living God.

[If forgotten, do not repeat *Shemoneh Esrei.* See *Laws* §61.]

Bend the knees at *'Blessed';* bow at *'You';* straighten up at *'Hashem'.*

O King, Helper, Savior, and Shield. Blessed are You, Hashem, *Shield of Abraham.*

GOD'S MIGHT

אַתָּה *You are eternally mighty, my Lord, the Resuscitator of the dead are You; abundantly able to* ***save,***

Between Shemini Atzeres and Pesach add the following.

Who makes the wind blow and makes the rain descend;

[If forgotten, see *Laws* §70-75.]

---

(1) *Deuteronomy* 32:3. (2) *Psalms* 51:17.

מְכַלְכֵּל חַיִּים בְּחֶסֶד, מְחַיֵּה מֵתִים בְּרַחֲמִים רַבִּים, סוֹמֵךְ נוֹפְלִים, וְרוֹפֵא חוֹלִים, וּמַתִּיר אֲסוּרִים, וּמְקַיֵּם אֱמוּנָתוֹ לִישֵׁנֵי עָפָר. מִי כָמוֹךָ בַּעַל גְּבוּרוֹת, וּמִי דּוֹמֶה לָּךְ, מֶלֶךְ מֵמִית וּמְחַיֶּה וּמַצְמִיחַ יְשׁוּעָה.

From Rosh Hashanah to Yom Kippur add:

מִי כָמוֹךְ אַב הָרַחֲמִים, זוֹכֵר יְצוּרָיו לְחַיִּים בְּרַחֲמִים.

[If forgotten, do not repeat *Shemoneh Esrei.* See *Laws* §61.]

וְנֶאֱמָן אַתָּה לְהַחֲיוֹת מֵתִים. בָּרוּךְ אַתָּה יהוה, מְחַיֵּה הַמֵּתִים.

During the *chazzan's* repetition, *Kedushah* (below) is recited at this point.

קדושת השם

אַתָּה קָדוֹשׁ וְשִׁמְךָ קָדוֹשׁ, וּקְדוֹשִׁים בְּכָל יוֹם יְהַלְלוּךָ סֶּלָה. בָּרוּךְ אַתָּה יהוה, °הָאֵל הַקָּדוֹשׁ.

°הַמֶּלֶךְ הַקָּדוֹשׁ. —From Rosh Hashanah to Yom Kippur substitute

[If forgotten, repeat *Shemoneh Esrei.* See *Laws* §62-63.]

קדושת היום

אַתָּה אֶחָד* וְשִׁמְךָ אֶחָד, וּמִי כְּעַמְּךָ יִשְׂרָאֵל* גּוֹי אֶחָד בָּאָרֶץ,[1] תִּפְאֶרֶת גְּדֻלָּה,* וַעֲטֶרֶת יְשׁוּעָה, יוֹם

קדושה

When reciting *Kedushah,* one must stand with his feet together, and avoid any interruptions. One should rise to his toes when saying the words קָדוֹשׁ, קָדוֹשׁ, קָדוֹשׁ; בָּרוּךְ (of בָּרוּךְ כְּבוֹד); and יִמְלֹךְ.

—Cong. then *Chazzan* **נְקַדֵּשׁ** אֶת שִׁמְךָ בָּעוֹלָם, כְּשֵׁם שֶׁמַּקְדִּישִׁים אוֹתוֹ בִּשְׁמֵי מָרוֹם, כַּכָּתוּב עַל יַד נְבִיאֶךָ, וְקָרָא זֶה אֶל זֶה וְאָמַר:

—All קָדוֹשׁ קָדוֹשׁ קָדוֹשׁ יהוה צְבָאוֹת, מְלֹא כָל הָאָרֶץ כְּבוֹדוֹ.[2]

—*Chazzan* לְעֻמָּתָם בָּרוּךְ יֹאמֵרוּ:

—All בָּרוּךְ כְּבוֹד יהוה, מִמְּקוֹמוֹ.[3]

—*Chazzan* וּבְדִבְרֵי קָדְשְׁךָ כָּתוּב לֵאמֹר:

—All יִמְלֹךְ יהוה לְעוֹלָם, אֱלֹהַיִךְ צִיּוֹן לְדֹר וָדֹר, הַלְלוּיָהּ.[4]

—*Chazzan* concludes לְדוֹר וָדוֹר נַגִּיד גָּדְלֶךָ וּלְנֵצַח נְצָחִים קְדֻשָּׁתְךָ נַקְדִּישׁ, וְשִׁבְחֲךָ אֱלֹהֵינוּ מִפִּינוּ לֹא יָמוּשׁ לְעוֹלָם וָעֶד, כִּי אֵל מֶלֶךְ גָּדוֹל וְקָדוֹשׁ אָתָּה. בָּרוּךְ אַתָּה יהוה, °הָאֵל הַקָּדוֹשׁ.

°הַמֶּלֶךְ הַקָּדוֹשׁ. —From Rosh Hashanah to Yom Kippur substitute

Chazzan continues ... אַתָּה אֶחָד.

⚜ **אַתָּה אֶחָד** — *You are One.* The opening verse is a clear reference to the verse (*Zechariah* 14:9) stating that when the final redemption comes, all the world will recognize the Oneness of God, meaning that there are no contradictions in His behavior. As noted above, the Sabbath *Minchah* alludes to the long-awaited day when history will attain God's goal of perfection. Thus the

Who sustains the living with kindness, resuscitates the dead with abundant mercy, supports the fallen, heals the sick, releases the confined, and maintains His faith to those asleep in the dust. Who is like You, O Master of mighty deeds, and who is comparable to You, O King Who causes death and restores life and makes salvation sprout!

From Rosh Hashanah to Yom Kippur add the following.
Who is like You, Merciful Father, Who recalls His creatures mercifully for life!
[If forgotten, do not repeat *Shemoneh Esrei.* See *Laws* §61.]

And You are faithful to resuscitate the dead. Blessed are You, HASHEM, Who resuscitates the dead.

During the *chazzan's* repetition, *Kedushah* (below) is recited at this point.

HOLINESS OF GOD'S NAME

אַתָּה *You are holy and Your Name is holy, and holy ones praise You every day, forever. Blessed are You, HASHEM, °the holy God.*

°From Rosh Hashanah to Yom Kippur substitute: *the holy King.*
[If forgotten, repeat *Shemoneh Esrei.* See *Laws* §62-63.]

HOLINESS OF THE DAY

אַתָּה אֶחָד *You are One* and Your Name is One; and who is like Your people Israel,* one nation on earth.*[1] *The splendor of greatness* and the crown of salvation, the day of*

KEDUSHAH

When reciting *Kedushah,* one must stand with his feet together and avoid any interruptions. One should rise to his toes when saying the words, *Holy, holy, holy; Blessed;* and *HASHEM shall reign.*

Cong.— then Chazzan— **נְקַדֵּשׁ** *We shall sanctify Your Name in this world, just as they sanctify it in heaven above, as it is written by Your prophet, 'And one [angel] will call another and say:*

All— *'Holy, holy, holy is HASHEM, Master of Legions, the whole world is filled with His glory.'*[2]

Chazzan— *Those facing them say 'Blessed':*

All— *'Blessed is the glory of HASHEM from His place.'*[3]

Chazzan— *And in Your holy Writings the following is written:*

All— *'HASHEM shall reign forever — your God, O Zion — from generation to generation, Halleluyah!'*[4]

Chazzan concludes— *From generation to generation we shall relate Your greatness and for infinite eternities we shall proclaim Your holiness. Your praise, our God, shall not leave our mouth forever and ever, for You O God, are a great and holy King. Blessed are You HASHEM, °the holy God.*

°From Rosh Hashanah to Yom Kippur substitute: *the holy King.*

Chazzan continues אַתָּה אֶחָד, *You are One ...*

(1) Cf. *II Samuel* 7:23. (2) *Isaiah* 6:3. (3) *Ezekiel* 3:12. (4) *Psalms* 146:10.

Minchah Shemoneh Esrei directs our focus not only to the holiness of the Sabbath day, but to the spiritual bliss of the future.

וּמִי כְּעַמְּךָ יִשְׂרָאֵל — *And who is like Your people Israel.* Israel is unique because it alone accepted the Torah and dedicated itself to God's service. Consequently, God awarded Israel the spiritual gifts cited in the next verse.

תִּפְאֶרֶת גְּדֻלָּה — *The splendor of greatness.* Some interpret this to mean the Temple. Others

מְנוּחָה וּקְדֻשָּׁה לְעַמְּךָ נָתָתָּ, אַבְרָהָם יָגֵל, יִצְחָק יְרַנֵּן, יַעֲקֹב וּבָנָיו יָנוּחוּ בוֹ,* מְנוּחַת אַהֲבָה וּנְדָבָה, מְנוּחַת אֱמֶת וֶאֱמוּנָה, מְנוּחַת שָׁלוֹם וְשַׁלְוָה וְהַשְׁקֵט וָבֶטַח, מְנוּחָה שְׁלֵמָה שָׁאַתָּה רוֹצֶה בָּהּ, יַכִּירוּ בָנֶיךָ וְיֵדְעוּ כִּי מֵאִתְּךָ הִיא מְנוּחָתָם,* וְעַל מְנוּחָתָם יַקְדִּישׁוּ אֶת שְׁמֶךָ.

אֱלֹהֵינוּ וֵאלֹהֵי אֲבוֹתֵינוּ רְצֵה בִמְנוּחָתֵנוּ. קַדְּשֵׁנוּ בְּמִצְוֹתֶיךָ, וְתֵן חֶלְקֵנוּ בְּתוֹרָתֶךָ. שַׂבְּעֵנוּ מִטּוּבֶךָ, וְשַׂמְּחֵנוּ בִּישׁוּעָתֶךָ, וְטַהֵר לִבֵּנוּ לְעָבְדְּךָ בֶּאֱמֶת. וְהַנְחִילֵנוּ יהוה אֱלֹהֵינוּ בְּאַהֲבָה וּבְרָצוֹן שַׁבַּת קָדְשֶׁךָ, וְיָנוּחוּ בָם* יִשְׂרָאֵל מְקַדְּשֵׁי שְׁמֶךָ. בָּרוּךְ אַתָּה יהוה, מְקַדֵּשׁ הַשַּׁבָּת.

עבודה

רְצֵה יהוה אֱלֹהֵינוּ בְּעַמְּךָ יִשְׂרָאֵל וּבִתְפִלָּתָם, וְהָשֵׁב אֶת הָעֲבוֹדָה לִדְבִיר בֵּיתֶךָ. וְאִשֵּׁי יִשְׂרָאֵל וּתְפִלָּתָם בְּאַהֲבָה תְקַבֵּל בְּרָצוֹן, וּתְהִי לְרָצוֹן תָּמִיד עֲבוֹדַת יִשְׂרָאֵל עַמֶּךָ.

On Rosh Chodesh and Chol HaMoed add the following paragraph:
(During the *chazzan's* repetition, the congregation responds אָמֵן as indicated.)

אֱלֹהֵינוּ וֵאלֹהֵי אֲבוֹתֵינוּ, יַעֲלֶה, וְיָבֹא, וְיַגִּיעַ, וְיֵרָאֶה, וְיֵרָצֶה, וְיִשָּׁמַע, וְיִפָּקֵד, וְיִזָּכֵר זִכְרוֹנֵנוּ וּפִקְדוֹנֵנוּ, וְזִכְרוֹן אֲבוֹתֵינוּ, וְזִכְרוֹן מָשִׁיחַ בֶּן דָּוִד עַבְדֶּךָ, וְזִכְרוֹן יְרוּשָׁלַיִם עִיר קָדְשֶׁךָ, וְזִכְרוֹן כָּל עַמְּךָ בֵּית יִשְׂרָאֵל לְפָנֶיךָ, לִפְלֵיטָה לְטוֹבָה, לְחֵן וּלְחֶסֶד וּלְרַחֲמִים, לְחַיִּים וּלְשָׁלוֹם בְּיוֹם

on Rosh Chodesh	on Pesach	on Succos
רֹאשׁ הַחֹדֶשׁ	חַג הַמַּצּוֹת	חַג הַסֻּכּוֹת

הַזֶּה. זָכְרֵנוּ יהוה אֱלֹהֵינוּ בּוֹ לְטוֹבָה (Cong.— אָמֵן), וּפָקְדֵנוּ בוֹ לִבְרָכָה (Cong.— אָמֵן), וְהוֹשִׁיעֵנוּ בוֹ לְחַיִּים (Cong.— אָמֵן). וּבִדְבַר יְשׁוּעָה וְרַחֲמִים, חוּס וְחָנֵּנוּ וְרַחֵם עָלֵינוּ וְהוֹשִׁיעֵנוּ, כִּי אֵלֶיךָ עֵינֵינוּ, כִּי אֵל מֶלֶךְ חַנּוּן וְרַחוּם אָתָּה.[1]

[If forgotten, repeat *Shemoneh Esrei*. See *Laws* §89.]

וְתֶחֱזֶינָה עֵינֵינוּ בְּשׁוּבְךָ לְצִיּוֹן בְּרַחֲמִים. בָּרוּךְ אַתָּה יהוה, הַמַּחֲזִיר שְׁכִינָתוֹ לְצִיּוֹן.

---

interpret this phrase and the others in this verse as references to various aspects of Messianic times.

יַעֲקֹב וּבָנָיו יָנוּחוּ בוֹ — *Jacob and his children would rest on it.* The Sages derive from Scriptural verses that all three Patriarchs observed the Sabbath, even before the Torah was given. Only of Jacob, however, could it be said that all his children joined him in observing the day, because Abraham's Ishmael and Isaac's Esau were not righteous.

כִּי מֵאִתְּךָ הִיא מְנוּחָתָם — *That from You comes their contentment and holiness have You given to Your people. Abraham would rejoice, Isaac would exult, Jacob and his children would rest on it,* a rest of love and magnanimity, a rest of truth and faith, a rest of peace and serenity and tranquility and security, a perfect rest in which You find favor. May Your children recognize and know that from You comes their rest,* and through their rest, they will sanctify Your Name.*

אֱלֹהֵינוּ *Our God and the God of our forefathers, may You be pleased with our rest. Sanctify us with Your commandments and grant us our share in Your Torah; satisfy us from Your goodness and gladden us with Your salvation, and purify our heart to serve You sincerely. O* HASHEM, *our God, with love and favor grant us Your holy Sabbath as a heritage and may Israel, the sanctifiers of Your Name, rest on them.* Blessed are You,* HASHEM, *Who sanctifies the Sabbath.*

TEMPLE SERVICE

רְצֵה *Be favorable,* HASHEM, *our God, toward Your people Israel and their prayer and restore the service to the Holy of Holies of Your Temple. The fire-offerings of Israel and their prayer accept with love and favor, and may the service of Your people Israel always be favorable to You.*

On Rosh Chodesh and Chol HaMoed add the following paragraph:
(During the *chazzan's* repetition, the congregation responds *Amen* as indicated.)

אֱלֹהֵינוּ *Our God and God of our forefathers, may there rise, come, reach, be noted, be favored, be heard, be considered, and be remembered — the remembrance and consideration of ourselves; the remembrance of our forefathers; the remembrance of Messiah, son of David, Your servant; the remembrance of Jerusalem, the City of Your Holiness, the remembrance of Your entire people the Family of Israel — before You, for deliverance, for goodness, for grace, for kindness, and for compassion, for life, and for peace on this day of*

on Rosh Chodesh	on Passover	on Succos
Rosh Chodesh.	*the Festival of Matzos.*	*the Succos Festival.*

Remember us on it, HASHEM, *our God, for goodness* (Cong.— *Amen*); *consider us on it for blessing* (Cong.— *Amen*); *and help us on it for life* (Cong.— *Amen*). *In the matter of salvation and compassion, pity, be gracious and compassionate with us and help us, for our eyes are turned to You, because You are God, the gracious, and compassionate King.*[1]

[If forgotten, repeat *Shemoneh Esrei.* See Laws, §89.]

וְתֶחֱזֶינָה *May our eyes behold Your return to Zion in compassion. Blessed are You,* HASHEM, *Who restores His Presence to Zion.*

(1) Cf. *Nechemiah* 9:31.

rest. The quality of our Sabbath rest, as we have just described it, is God-given; and this is because God Himself rested on the Sabbath.

וְיָנוּחוּ בָם — *And* [*they*] *will rest on them.* As noted on p. 341, the plural form בָם, *them,* appears only in the *Minchah Shemoneh Esrei,* because in the ideal life of the World to Come, all days will have the serenity and holiness we now sense only on the Sabbath.

הודאה

Bow at מוֹדִים; straighten up at ה׳. In his repetition the *chazzan* should recite the entire מוֹדִים aloud, while the congregation recites מוֹדִים דְּרַבָּנָן softly.

מוֹדִים אֲנַחְנוּ לָךְ שָׁאַתָּה הוּא יהוה אֱלֹהֵינוּ וֵאלֹהֵי אֲבוֹתֵינוּ לְעוֹלָם וָעֶד. צוּר חַיֵּינוּ, מָגֵן יִשְׁעֵנוּ אַתָּה הוּא לְדוֹר וָדוֹר. נוֹדֶה לְּךָ וּנְסַפֵּר תְּהִלָּתֶךָ[1] עַל חַיֵּינוּ הַמְּסוּרִים בְּיָדֶךָ, וְעַל נִשְׁמוֹתֵינוּ הַפְּקוּדוֹת לָךְ, וְעַל נִסֶּיךָ שֶׁבְּכָל יוֹם עִמָּנוּ, וְעַל נִפְלְאוֹתֶיךָ וְטוֹבוֹתֶיךָ שֶׁבְּכָל עֵת, עֶרֶב וָבֹקֶר וְצָהֳרָיִם. הַטּוֹב כִּי לֹא כָלוּ רַחֲמֶיךָ, וְהַמְרַחֵם כִּי לֹא תַמּוּ חֲסָדֶיךָ,[2] מֵעוֹלָם קִוִּינוּ לָךְ.

מודים דרבנן

מוֹדִים אֲנַחְנוּ לָךְ, שָׁאַתָּה הוּא יהוה אֱלֹהֵינוּ וֵאלֹהֵי אֲבוֹתֵינוּ, אֱלֹהֵי כָל בָּשָׂר, יוֹצְרֵנוּ, יוֹצֵר בְּרֵאשִׁית. בְּרָכוֹת וְהוֹדָאוֹת לְשִׁמְךָ הַגָּדוֹל וְהַקָּדוֹשׁ, עַל שֶׁהֶחֱיִיתָנוּ וְקִיַּמְתָּנוּ. כֵּן תְּחַיֵּנוּ וּתְקַיְּמֵנוּ, וְתֶאֱסוֹף גָּלֻיּוֹתֵינוּ לְחַצְרוֹת קָדְשֶׁךָ, לִשְׁמוֹר חֻקֶּיךָ וְלַעֲשׂוֹת רְצוֹנֶךָ, וּלְעָבְדְּךָ בְּלֵבָב שָׁלֵם, עַל שֶׁאֲנַחְנוּ מוֹדִים לָךְ. בָּרוּךְ אֵל הַהוֹדָאוֹת.

On Chanukah add:

(וְ)עַל הַנִּסִּים, וְעַל הַפֻּרְקָן, וְעַל הַגְּבוּרוֹת, וְעַל הַתְּשׁוּעוֹת, וְעַל הַמִּלְחָמוֹת, שֶׁעָשִׂיתָ לַאֲבוֹתֵינוּ בַּיָּמִים הָהֵם בַּזְּמַן הַזֶּה.

בִּימֵי מַתִּתְיָהוּ בֶּן יוֹחָנָן כֹּהֵן גָּדוֹל חַשְׁמוֹנַאי וּבָנָיו, כְּשֶׁעָמְדָה מַלְכוּת יָוָן הָרְשָׁעָה עַל עַמְּךָ יִשְׂרָאֵל, לְהַשְׁכִּיחָם תּוֹרָתֶךָ, וּלְהַעֲבִירָם מֵחֻקֵּי רְצוֹנֶךָ. וְאַתָּה בְּרַחֲמֶיךָ הָרַבִּים, עָמַדְתָּ לָהֶם בְּעֵת צָרָתָם, רַבְתָּ אֶת רִיבָם, דַּנְתָּ אֶת דִּינָם, נָקַמְתָּ אֶת נִקְמָתָם.[3] מָסַרְתָּ גִבּוֹרִים בְּיַד חַלָּשִׁים, וְרַבִּים בְּיַד מְעַטִּים, וּטְמֵאִים בְּיַד טְהוֹרִים, וּרְשָׁעִים בְּיַד צַדִּיקִים, וְזֵדִים בְּיַד עוֹסְקֵי תוֹרָתֶךָ. וּלְךָ עָשִׂיתָ שֵׁם גָּדוֹל וְקָדוֹשׁ בְּעוֹלָמֶךָ, וּלְעַמְּךָ יִשְׂרָאֵל עָשִׂיתָ תְּשׁוּעָה גְדוֹלָה[4] וּפֻרְקָן כְּהַיּוֹם הַזֶּה. וְאַחַר כֵּן בָּאוּ בָנֶיךָ לִדְבִיר בֵּיתֶךָ, וּפִנּוּ אֶת הֵיכָלֶךָ, וְטִהֲרוּ אֶת מִקְדָּשֶׁךָ, וְהִדְלִיקוּ נֵרוֹת בְּחַצְרוֹת קָדְשֶׁךָ, וְקָבְעוּ שְׁמוֹנַת יְמֵי חֲנֻכָּה אֵלּוּ, לְהוֹדוֹת וּלְהַלֵּל לְשִׁמְךָ הַגָּדוֹל.

[If forgotten, do not repeat *Shemoneh Esrei.* See *Laws* §90.]

וְעַל כֻּלָּם יִתְבָּרַךְ וְיִתְרוֹמַם שִׁמְךָ מַלְכֵּנוּ תָּמִיד לְעוֹלָם וָעֶד.

From Rosh Hashanah to Yom Kippur add:

וּכְתוֹב לְחַיִּים טוֹבִים כָּל בְּנֵי בְרִיתֶךָ.

[If forgotten, do not repeat *Shemoneh Esrei.* See *Laws* §61.]

THANKSGIVING [MODIM]

Bow at *'We gratefully thank You'*; straighten up at *'HASHEM'*. In his repetition the chazzan should recite the entire *Modim* aloud, while the congregation recites *Modim of the Rabbis* softly.

מוֹדִים *We gratefully thank You, for it is You Who are HASHEM, our God and the God of our forefathers for all eternity; Rock of our lives, Shield of our salvation are You from generation to generation. We shall thank You and relate Your praise[1] — for our lives, which are committed to Your power and for our souls that are entrusted to You; for Your miracles that are with us every day; and for Your wonders and favors in every season — evening, morning, and afternoon. The Beneficent One, for Your compassions were never exhausted, and the Compassionate One, for Your kindnesses never ended[2] — always have we put our hope in You.*

MODIM OF THE RABBIS

מוֹדִים *We gratefully thank You, for it is You Who are HASHEM, our God and the God of our forefathers, the God of all flesh, our Molder, the Molder of the universe. Blessings and thanks are due Your great and holy Name for You have given us life and sustained us. So may You continue to give us life and sustain us and gather our exiles to the Courtyards of Your Sanctuary, to observe Your decrees, to do Your will and to serve You wholeheartedly. [We thank You] for inspiring us to thank You. Blessed is the God of thanksgivings.*

On Chanukah add:

(וְ)עַל *(And) for the miracles, and for the salvation, and for the mighty deeds, and for the victories, and for the battles which You performed for our forefathers in those days, at this time.*

בִּימֵי *In the days of Mattisyahu, the son of Yochanan, the High Priest, the Hasmonean, and his sons — when the wicked Greek kingdom rose up against Your people Israel to make them forget Your Torah and compel them to stray from the statutes of Your Will — You in Your great mercy stood up for them in the time of their distress. You took up their grievance, judged their claim, and avenged their wrong.[3] You delivered the strong into the hands of the weak, the many into the hands of the few, the impure into the hands of the pure, the wicked into the hands of the righteous, and the wanton into the hands of the diligent students of Your Torah. For Yourself You made a great and holy Name in Your world, and for Your people Israel You worked a great victory[4] and salvation as this very day. Thereafter, Your children came to the Holy of Holies of Your House, cleansed Your Temple, purified the site of Your Holiness and kindled lights in the Courtyards of Your Sanctuary; and they established these eight days of Chanukah to express thanks and praise to Your great Name.*

[If forgotten, do not repeat *Shemoneh Esrei*. See *Laws* §90.]

For all these, may Your Name be blessed and exalted, our King, continually forever and ever.

From Rosh Hashanah to Yom Kippur add the following.

And inscribe all the children of Your covenant for a good life.

If forgotten, do not repeat *Shemoneh Esrei*. See *Laws* §61.]

(1) Cf. *Psalms* 79:13. (2) Cf. *Lamentations* 3:22. (3) Cf. *Jeremiah* 51:36. (4) Cf. *I Samuel* 19:5.

Bend the knees at בָּרוּךְ; bow at אַתָּה; straighten up at ה׳.

וְכֹל הַחַיִּים יוֹדְוּךָ סֶּלָה, וִיהַלְלוּ אֶת שִׁמְךָ בֶּאֱמֶת, הָאֵל יְשׁוּעָתֵנוּ וְעֶזְרָתֵנוּ סֶלָה. בָּרוּךְ אַתָּה יהוה, הַטּוֹב שִׁמְךָ וּלְךָ נָאֶה לְהוֹדוֹת.

שלום

שָׁלוֹם רָב עַל יִשְׂרָאֵל עַמְּךָ תָּשִׂים לְעוֹלָם, כִּי אַתָּה הוּא מֶלֶךְ אָדוֹן לְכָל הַשָּׁלוֹם. וְטוֹב בְּעֵינֶיךָ לְבָרֵךְ אֶת עַמְּךָ יִשְׂרָאֵל בְּכָל עֵת וּבְכָל שָׁעָה בִּשְׁלוֹמֶךָ. °בָּרוּךְ אַתָּה יהוה, הַמְּבָרֵךְ אֶת עַמּוֹ יִשְׂרָאֵל בַּשָּׁלוֹם.

°From Rosh Hashanah to Yom Kippur substitute the following [see *Laws* §65]:

בְּסֵפֶר חַיִּים בְּרָכָה וְשָׁלוֹם, וּפַרְנָסָה טוֹבָה, נִזָּכֵר וְנִכָּתֵב לְפָנֶיךָ, אֲנַחְנוּ וְכָל עַמְּךָ בֵּית יִשְׂרָאֵל, לְחַיִּים טוֹבִים וּלְשָׁלוֹם. בָּרוּךְ אַתָּה יהוה, עֹשֵׂה הַשָּׁלוֹם.

[If forgotten, do not repeat *Shemoneh Esrei*. See *Laws* §61.]

The *chazzan's* repetition of *Shemoneh Esrei* ends here. See below for further instructions.

יִהְיוּ לְרָצוֹן אִמְרֵי פִי וְהֶגְיוֹן לִבִּי לְפָנֶיךָ, יהוה צוּרִי וְגֹאֲלִי.[1]

אֱלֹהַי, נְצוֹר לְשׁוֹנִי מֵרָע, וּשְׂפָתַי מִדַּבֵּר מִרְמָה,[2] וְלִמְקַלְלַי נַפְשִׁי תִדּוֹם, וְנַפְשִׁי כֶּעָפָר לַכֹּל תִּהְיֶה. פְּתַח לִבִּי בְּתוֹרָתֶךָ, וּבְמִצְוֹתֶיךָ תִּרְדּוֹף נַפְשִׁי. וְכֹל הַחוֹשְׁבִים עָלַי רָעָה, מְהֵרָה הָפֵר עֲצָתָם וְקַלְקֵל מַחֲשַׁבְתָּם. עֲשֵׂה לְמַעַן שְׁמֶךָ, עֲשֵׂה לְמַעַן יְמִינֶךָ, עֲשֵׂה לְמַעַן קְדֻשָּׁתֶךָ, עֲשֵׂה לְמַעַן תּוֹרָתֶךָ. לְמַעַן יֵחָלְצוּן יְדִידֶיךָ, הוֹשִׁיעָה יְמִינְךָ וַעֲנֵנִי.[3]

Some recite verses pertaining to their names at this point. See page 924.

יִהְיוּ לְרָצוֹן אִמְרֵי פִי וְהֶגְיוֹן לִבִּי לְפָנֶיךָ, יהוה צוּרִי וְגֹאֲלִי.[1] עֹשֶׂה שָׁלוֹם בִּמְרוֹמָיו, הוּא יַעֲשֶׂה שָׁלוֹם עָלֵינוּ, וְעַל כָּל יִשְׂרָאֵל. וְאִמְרוּ: אָמֵן.

יְהִי רָצוֹן מִלְּפָנֶיךָ יהוה אֱלֹהֵינוּ וֵאלֹהֵי אֲבוֹתֵינוּ, שֶׁיִּבָּנֶה בֵּית הַמִּקְדָּשׁ בִּמְהֵרָה בְיָמֵינוּ, וְתֵן חֶלְקֵנוּ בְּתוֹרָתֶךָ. וְשָׁם נַעֲבָדְךָ בְּיִרְאָה, כִּימֵי עוֹלָם וּכְשָׁנִים קַדְמוֹנִיּוֹת. וְעָרְבָה לַיהוה מִנְחַת יְהוּדָה וִירוּשָׁלָיִם, כִּימֵי עוֹלָם וּכְשָׁנִים קַדְמוֹנִיּוֹת.[4]

THE INDIVIDUAL'S RECITATION OF שְׁמוֹנֶה עֶשְׂרֵה ENDS HERE.

The individual remains standing in place until the *chazzan* reaches *Kedushah* — or at least until the *chazzan* begins his repetition — then he takes three steps forward. The *chazzan* himself, or one praying alone, should remain in place for a few moments before taking three steps forward.

Bend the knees at *'Blessed'*; bow at *'You'*; straighten up at *'HASHEM'*.

Everything alive will gratefully acknowledge You, Selah! and praise Your Name sincerely, O God of our salvation and help, Selah! Blessed are You, HASHEM, Your Name is 'The Beneficent One' and to You it is fitting to give thanks.

PEACE

שָׁלוֹם רָב *Establish abundant peace upon Your people Israel forever, for You are King, Master of all peace. May it be good in Your eyes to bless Your people Israel at every time and every hour with Your peace. °Blessed are You, HASHEM, Who blesses His people Israel with peace.*

°From Rosh Hashanah to Yom Kippur substitute the following [see *Laws* §65]:
In the book of life, blessing, and peace, good livelihood, may we be remembered and inscribed before You — we and Your entire people the Family of Israel for a good life and for peace. Blessed are You, HASHEM, Who makes peace.
[If forgotten, do not repeat *Shemoneh Esrei*. See *Laws* §61.]

The *chazzan's* repetition of *Shemoneh Esrei* ends here. See below for further instructions.

May the expressions of my mouth and the thoughts of my heart find favor before You, HASHEM, my Rock and my Redeemer.[1]

אֱלֹהַי *My God, guard my tongue from evil and my lips from speaking deceitfully.*[2] *To those who curse me, let my soul be silent; and let my soul be like dust to everyone. Open my heart to Your Torah, then my soul will pursue Your commandments. As for all those who design evil against me, speedily nullify their counsel and disrupt their design. Act for Your Name's sake; act for Your right hand's sake; act for Your sanctity's sake; act for Your Torah's sake. That Your beloved ones may be given rest; let Your right hand save, and respond to me.*[3]

Some recite verses pertaining to their names at this point. See page 924.

May the expressions of my mouth and the thoughts of my heart find favor before You, HASHEM, my Rock and my Redeemer.[1] *He Who makes peace in His heights, may He make peace upon us, and upon all Israel. Now respond: Amen.*

יְהִי רָצוֹן *May it be Your will, HASHEM our God and the God of our forefathers, that the Holy Temple be rebuilt, speedily in our days. Grant us our share in Your Torah, and may we serve You there with reverence, as in days of old and in former years. Then the offering of Judah and Jerusalem will be pleasing to HASHEM, as in days of old and in former years.*[4]

THE INDIVIDUAL'S RECITATION OF *SHEMONEH ESREI* ENDS HERE.

The individual remains standing in place until the *chazzan* reaches *Kedushah* — or at least until the *chazzan* begins his repetition — then he takes three steps forward. The *chazzan* himself, or one praying alone, should remain in place for a few moments before taking three steps forward.

---

(1) *Psalms* 19:15. (2) Cf. 34:14. (3) 60:7; 108:7. (4) *Malachi* 3:4.

See commentary for days on which the following three verses are omitted.

צִדְקָתְךָ צֶדֶק לְעוֹלָם,* וְתוֹרָתְךָ אֱמֶת.*[1] וְצִדְקָתְךָ אֱלֹהִים עַד מָרוֹם* אֲשֶׁר עָשִׂיתָ גְדֹלוֹת,* אֱלֹהִים מִי כָמוֹךָ.[2] צִדְקָתְךָ כְּהַרְרֵי אֵל* מִשְׁפָּטֶיךָ תְּהוֹם רַבָּה, אָדָם וּבְהֵמָה תוֹשִׁיעַ, יהוה.*[3]

קדיש שלם

The *chazzan* recites קַדִּישׁ שָׁלֵם:

יִתְגַּדַּל וְיִתְקַדַּשׁ שְׁמֵהּ רַבָּא. (—Cong. אָמֵן.) בְּעָלְמָא דִּי בְרָא כִרְעוּתֵהּ. וְיַמְלִיךְ מַלְכוּתֵהּ, בְּחַיֵּיכוֹן וּבְיוֹמֵיכוֹן וּבְחַיֵּי דְכָל בֵּית יִשְׂרָאֵל, בַּעֲגָלָא וּבִזְמַן קָרִיב. וְאִמְרוּ: אָמֵן.

(—Cong. אָמֵן. יְהֵא שְׁמֵהּ רַבָּא מְבָרַךְ לְעָלַם וּלְעָלְמֵי עָלְמַיָּא.)

יְהֵא שְׁמֵהּ רַבָּא מְבָרַךְ לְעָלַם וּלְעָלְמֵי עָלְמַיָּא.

יִתְבָּרַךְ וְיִשְׁתַּבַּח וְיִתְפָּאַר וְיִתְרוֹמַם וְיִתְנַשֵּׂא וְיִתְהַדָּר וְיִתְעַלֶּה וְיִתְהַלָּל שְׁמֵהּ דְּקֻדְשָׁא בְּרִיךְ הוּא (—Cong. בְּרִיךְ הוּא) — °לְעֵלָּא מִן כָּל (—From Rosh Hashanah to Yom Kippur substitute °לְעֵלָּא וּלְעֵלָּא מִכָּל) בִּרְכָתָא וְשִׁירָתָא תֻּשְׁבְּחָתָא וְנֶחֱמָתָא, דַּאֲמִירָן בְּעָלְמָא. וְאִמְרוּ: אָמֵן. (—Cong. אָמֵן.)

☙ צִדְקָתְךָ / Your Righteousness

As the Sabbath draws to a close, the Jew becomes conscious of the ebbing of holiness and the onset of the six days of labor with their relative absence of holiness and their abundance of cares. Furthermore, according to the *Zohar*, Moses, Joseph, and David died on the Sabbath at *Minchah* time. As such thoughts and memories dampen our spirit of Sabbath joy, we recite three verses, each of which begins with the word צִדְקָתְךָ, *Your righteousness.* These verses were selected to show us how to accept the harsher manifestations of God's justice, the *righteousness* that is not only fair, but essential to man's mission on earth. The significance of the respective verses will be explained below.

Given the nature of these verses, they are omitted when an extra note of festivity joins that of the Sabbath. Thus, if the Sabbath *Minchah* period coincides with an occasion when *Tachanun* would not be recited even on weekdays — such as a festival or the afternoon before Rosh Chodesh — the צִדְקָתְךָ verses are omitted. The double joy of the Sabbath and the other times of gladness are sufficient to banish the fears that normally accompany the waning of the Sabbath.

צִדְקָתְךָ צֶדֶק לְעוֹלָם — *Your righteousness is an everlasting righteousness.* If God, in His righteousness, makes a promise to benefit an individual or nation, His word is everlasting; nothing can nullify His will *(Midrash Shocher Tov).*

וְתוֹרָתְךָ אֱמֶת — *And Your Torah is truth.* The Torah is the source of creation, and the universe continues to exist only by virtue of continued Torah study and performance of its commandments. Moreover, because the Torah is the expression of God's wisdom, it is the only true basis for such elemental necessities of society as decency, morality, and honesty *(Radak).*

On the other hand, the righteousness and truth expressed in this verse have another aspect: They imply that even the harsh judgment that God sometimes imposes on man and society also emanates from His knowledge of what creation requires. Thus, we can face the oncoming week with at least the partial comfort that events are not haphazard and without justification.

וְצִדְקָתְךָ אֱלֹהִים עַד מָרוֹם — *Your righteousness, O God, is unto the high heavens.* According to *Pesikta Rabbasi* (47:1) God's righteousness is seen not only in His kindness to earthbound creatures, but also in His treatment of the *"high heavens."* Since the moon had no light of its own, it would have seemed doomed to a dark oblivion. But God mercifully placed it in the sky so that it would reflect the sun's brilliance and thus assume a prominence of its own.

In another sense, God's righteousness is expressed in lofty spheres because He allows human repentance to ascend even as high as His

See comm... ..ich the following three verses are omitted.

צִדְקָתְךָ *Your ri... ...ess is an everlasting righteousness,* and Your Tora... ... truth.*[1] And Your righteousness, O God, is unto the high heavens,* You, Who have done great things,* O God, Who is like You?[2] Your righteousness is like the mighty mountains* — Your judgment is like the vast deep waters. Man and beast You save, HASHEM.*[3]*

FULL-KADDISH

The *chazzan* recites the Full *Kaddish:*

יִתְגַּדַּל *May His great Name grow exalted and sanctified* (Cong.— *Amen.*) *in the world that He created as He willed. May He give reign to His kingship in your lifetimes and in your days, and in the lifetimes of the entire Family of Israel, swiftly and soon. Now respond: Amen.*

(Cong.— *Amen. May His great Name be blessed forever and ever.*)

May His great Name be blessed forever and ever.

Blessed, praised, glorified, exalted, extolled, mighty, upraised, and lauded be the Name of the Holy One, Blessed is He (Cong.— *Blessed is He*) — (From Rosh Hashanah to Yom Kippur add: *exceedingly*) *beyond any blessing and song, praise and consolation that are uttered in the world. Now respond: Amen.* (Cong.— *Amen.*)

(1) *Psalms* 119:142. (2) 71:19. (3) 36:7.

heavenly throne (*Yoma* 86b).

אֲשֶׁר עָשִׂיתָ גְדֹלוֹת — *You, Who have done great things.* God's accomplishments are so great that they defy specific description (*Alshich*).

Psalm 71, where this verse appears, describes one of the lowest points in David's life, when in his old age he was forced to flee for his life from his son Absalom, who had usurped the throne. Even then, however, David did not cease his praises of God, for he understood that even God's harsh judgment is for the sake of man's ultimate good — although man seldom understands how. This explains the choice of this passage for the waning hours of the Sabbath. The twilight period of life is no less constructive in its way than is the rising sun of the morning hours.

צִדְקָתְךָ כְּהַרְרֵי אֵל — *Your righteousness is like the mighty mountains.* This verse describes two contrasts: God's righteousness like a mighty mountain, and His judgment like the vast depths. Indeed, both manifestations are apparent in the world; there are times when God's kindness is unbounded, surpassing even the mightiest land masses, as it were. On the other hand, the punishments earned by the wicked are equally unbounded. This implies choice, for God must differentiate between the opposites on earth and between the complex mixtures of good and bad within individual human beings. This form of judgment is as essential to human welfare as is His unbounded mercy. Thus, with their blurring of good and their frequent premium on the less sublime aspects of human character, the weekdays provide the arena for this choice. They represent man's challenge and his opportunity for greatness.

אָדָם וּבְהֵמָה תוֹשִׁיעַ ה' — *Man and beast You save, HASHEM. Malbim* comments that every human being combines within himself both *man* and *beast.* He has an animal body and a Divine soul. Since his soul is encased in a body, God's Presence is hidden from him to a significant degree. The challenge facing man is to discern

Occasions and Days on which צִדְקָתְךָ, 'Your Righteousness' Is Omitted

(a) In the presence of a bridegroom during the *Sheva Berachos* week (if both bride and groom have been previously married, their period of celebration extends for only three days);

(b) On a Sabbath that immediately precedes or that coincides with: a Festival (including Chol Hamoed); Rosh Chodesh; the entire month of Nissan; (in some congregations Pesach Sheni, 14 Iyar); Lag B'Omer; from Rosh Chodesh Sivan until the day after Shavuos (some congregations do not resume until 14 Sivan); Tishah B'Av; 15 Av; between Yom Kippur and the day after Succos (some congregations do not resume until 2 Cheshvan); Chanukah; Tu B'Shevat; Purim and Shushan Purim (in a leap year this applies also to 14-15 Adar I).

(Cong.—קַבֵּל בְּרַחֲמִים וּבְרָצוֹן אֶת תְּפִלָּתֵנוּ.)

תִּתְקַבֵּל צְלוֹתְהוֹן וּבָעוּתְהוֹן דְּכָל בֵּית יִשְׂרָאֵל קֳדָם אֲבוּהוֹן דִּי בִשְׁמַיָּא. וְאִמְרוּ: אָמֵן. (Cong.— אָמֵן.)

(Cong.— יְהִי שֵׁם יהוה מְבֹרָךְ, מֵעַתָּה וְעַד עוֹלָם.[1])

יְהֵא שְׁלָמָא רַבָּא מִן שְׁמַיָּא, וְחַיִּים עָלֵינוּ וְעַל כָּל יִשְׂרָאֵל. וְאִמְרוּ: אָמֵן. (Cong.— אָמֵן.)

(Cong.—עֶזְרִי מֵעִם יהוה, עֹשֵׂה שָׁמַיִם וָאָרֶץ.[2])

Take three steps back. Bow left and say ... עֹשֶׂה; bow right and say ... הוּא; bow forward and say וְעַל כָּל ... אָמֵן. Remain standing in place for a few moments, then take three steps forward.

עֹשֶׂה שָׁלוֹם בִּמְרוֹמָיו, הוּא יַעֲשֶׂה שָׁלוֹם עָלֵינוּ, וְעַל כָּל יִשְׂרָאֵל. וְאִמְרוּ: אָמֵן. (Cong.— אָמֵן.)

From the Sabbath after Pesach until the Sabbath before Rosh Hashanah, many congregations recite (or study) פִּרְקֵי אָבוֹת, *Pirkei Avos* (beginning on page 544), at this point.

From the Sabbath after Succos until two Sabbaths before Pesach, many congregations recite Psalm 104, בָּרְכִי נַפְשִׁי, and Psalms 120-134, שִׁיר הַמַּעֲלוֹת (beginning on page 530), at this point.

On the Sabbath before Pesach, many congregations recite part of the Haggadah (from עֲבָדִים הָיִינוּ, *We were slaves* ..., until רַבָּן גַּמְלִיאֵל, *Rabban Gamliel),* at this point.

The congregation stands while reciting עָלֵינוּ.

עָלֵינוּ לְשַׁבֵּחַ לַאֲדוֹן הַכֹּל, לָתֵת גְּדֻלָּה לְיוֹצֵר בְּרֵאשִׁית, שֶׁלֹּא עָשָׂנוּ כְּגוֹיֵי הָאֲרָצוֹת, וְלֹא שָׂמָנוּ כְּמִשְׁפְּחוֹת הָאֲדָמָה. שֶׁלֹּא שָׂם חֶלְקֵנוּ כָּהֶם, וְגוֹרָלֵנוּ כְּכָל הֲמוֹנָם. (שֶׁהֵם מִשְׁתַּחֲוִים לְהֶבֶל וָרִיק, וּמִתְפַּלְּלִים אֶל אֵל לֹא יוֹשִׁיעַ.[3]) וַאֲנַחְנוּ כּוֹרְעִים וּמִשְׁתַּחֲוִים וּמוֹדִים, לִפְנֵי מֶלֶךְ מַלְכֵי הַמְּלָכִים הַקָּדוֹשׁ בָּרוּךְ הוּא. שֶׁהוּא נוֹטֶה שָׁמַיִם וְיֹסֵד אָרֶץ,[4] וּמוֹשַׁב יְקָרוֹ בַּשָּׁמַיִם מִמַּעַל, וּשְׁכִינַת עֻזּוֹ בְּגָבְהֵי מְרוֹמִים. הוּא אֱלֹהֵינוּ, אֵין עוֹד. אֱמֶת מַלְכֵּנוּ, אֶפֶס זוּלָתוֹ, כַּכָּתוּב בְּתוֹרָתוֹ: וְיָדַעְתָּ הַיּוֹם וַהֲשֵׁבֹתָ אֶל לְבָבֶךָ, כִּי יהוה הוּא הָאֱלֹהִים בַּשָּׁמַיִם מִמַּעַל וְעַל הָאָרֶץ מִתָּחַת, אֵין עוֹד.[5]

Bow while reciting וַאֲנַחְנוּ כּוֹרְעִים וּמִשְׁתַּחֲוִים.

עַל כֵּן נְקַוֶּה לְּךָ יהוה אֱלֹהֵינוּ לִרְאוֹת מְהֵרָה בְּתִפְאֶרֶת עֻזֶּךָ, לְהַעֲבִיר גִּלּוּלִים מִן הָאָרֶץ, וְהָאֱלִילִים כָּרוֹת יִכָּרֵתוּן, לְתַקֵּן עוֹלָם בְּמַלְכוּת שַׁדַּי. וְכָל בְּנֵי בָשָׂר יִקְרְאוּ בִשְׁמֶךָ, לְהַפְנוֹת אֵלֶיךָ כָּל רִשְׁעֵי אָרֶץ. יַכִּירוּ וְיֵדְעוּ כָּל יוֹשְׁבֵי תֵבֵל, כִּי

God's judgment and control even in the *vast deep waters* — i.e., the murkiness of this material world — and thus come to discover the Godly soul within himself.

The Talmud *(Chullin* 5b) interprets this phrase homiletically as referring to righteous people. They have the intellectual capacity of a *man*, but they humble themselves before God.

(Cong.— *Accept our prayers with mercy and favor.*)

May the prayers and supplications of the entire Family of Israel be accepted before their Father Who is in Heaven. Now respond: Amen. (Cong.— *Amen.*)

(Cong.— *Blessed be the Name of* HASHEM, *from this moment and forever.*[1])

May there be abundant peace from Heaven, and life, upon us and upon all Israel. Now respond: Amen. (Cong.— *Amen.*)

(Cong.— *My help is from* HASHEM, *Maker of heaven and earth.*[2])

Take three steps back. Bow left and say, *'He Who makes peace ...'*; bow right and say, *'may He ...'*; bow forward and say, *'and upon all Israel ...'* Remain standing in place for a few moments, then take three steps forward.

He Who makes peace in His heights, may He make peace upon us, and upon all Israel. Now respond: Amen. (Cong.— *Amen.*)

From the Sabbath after Pesach until the Sabbath before Rosh Hashanah, many congregations recite (or study) פִּרְקֵי אָבוֹת, *Pirkei Avos* (beginning on page 544), at this point.

From the Sabbath after Succos until two Sabbaths before Pesach, many congregations recite Psalm 104, בָּרְכִי נַפְשִׁי, and Psalms 120-134, שִׁיר הַמַּעֲלוֹת, *A Song of Ascents* (beginning on page 530), at this point.

On the Sabbath before Pesach, many congregations recite part of the Haggadah (from עֲבָדִים הָיִינוּ, *We were slaves ...*, until רַבָּן גַּמְלִיאֵל, *Rabban Gamliel*), at this point.

The congregation stands while reciting *Aleinu.*

עָלֵינוּ *It is our duty to praise the Master of all, to ascribe greatness to the Molder of primeval creation, for He has not made us like the nations of the lands and has not emplaced us like the families of the earth; for He has not assigned our portion like theirs nor our lot like all their multitudes. (For they bow to vanity and emptiness and pray to a god which helps not.*[3]*) But we bend our knees, bow, and acknowledge our thanks before the King Who reigns over kings, the Holy One, Blessed is He. He stretches out heaven and establishes earth's foundation,*[4] *the seat of His homage is in the heavens above and His powerful Presence is in the loftiest heights. He is our God and there is none other. True is our King, there is nothing beside Him, as it is written in His Torah: 'You are to know this day and take to your heart* that* HASHEM *is the only God — in heaven above and on the earth below — there is none other.'*[5]

Bow while reciting 'But we bend our knees.'

עַל כֵּן *Therefore we put our hope in You,* HASHEM *our God, that we may soon see Your mighty splendor, to remove detestable idolatry from the earth, and false gods will be utterly cut off, to perfect the universe through the Almighty's sovereignty. Then all humanity will call upon Your Name, to turn all the earth's wicked toward You. All the world's inhabitants will recognize and know that*

(1) *Psalms* 113:2. (2) 121:2. (3) *Isaiah* 45:20. (4) 51:13. (5) *Deuteronomy* 4:39.

לְךָ תִּכְרַע כָּל בֶּרֶךְ, תִּשָּׁבַע כָּל לָשׁוֹן.[1] לְפָנֶיךָ יהוה אֱלֹהֵינוּ יִכְרְעוּ וְיִפֹּלוּ, וְלִכְבוֹד שִׁמְךָ יְקָר יִתֵּנוּ. וִיקַבְּלוּ כֻלָּם אֶת עוֹל מַלְכוּתֶךָ, וְתִמְלֹךְ עֲלֵיהֶם מְהֵרָה לְעוֹלָם וָעֶד. כִּי הַמַּלְכוּת שֶׁלְּךָ הִיא וּלְעוֹלְמֵי עַד תִּמְלוֹךְ בְּכָבוֹד, כַּכָּתוּב בְּתוֹרָתֶךָ: יהוה יִמְלֹךְ לְעֹלָם וָעֶד.[2] ❖ וְנֶאֱמַר: וְהָיָה יהוה לְמֶלֶךְ עַל כָּל הָאָרֶץ, בַּיּוֹם הַהוּא יִהְיֶה יהוה אֶחָד וּשְׁמוֹ אֶחָד.[3]

In some congregations the following is recited after עָלֵינוּ:

אַל תִּירָא מִפַּחַד פִּתְאֹם, וּמִשֹּׁאַת רְשָׁעִים כִּי תָבֹא.[4] עֻצוּ עֵצָה וְתֻפָר, דַּבְּרוּ דָבָר וְלֹא יָקוּם, כִּי עִמָּנוּ אֵל.[5] וְעַד זִקְנָה אֲנִי הוּא, וְעַד שֵׂיבָה אֲנִי אֶסְבֹּל, אֲנִי עָשִׂיתִי וַאֲנִי אֶשָּׂא, וַאֲנִי אֶסְבֹּל וַאֲמַלֵּט.[6]

קדיש יתום

In the presence of a *minyan,* mourners recite קַדִּישׁ יָתוֹם, the Mourner's *Kaddish* (see *Laws* §119):

יִתְגַּדַּל וְיִתְקַדַּשׁ שְׁמֵהּ רַבָּא. (Cong. – אָמֵן.) בְּעָלְמָא דִּי בְרָא כִרְעוּתֵהּ. וְיַמְלִיךְ מַלְכוּתֵהּ, בְּחַיֵּיכוֹן וּבְיוֹמֵיכוֹן וּבְחַיֵּי דְכָל בֵּית יִשְׂרָאֵל, בַּעֲגָלָא וּבִזְמַן קָרִיב. וְאִמְרוּ: אָמֵן.

(Cong. – אָמֵן. יְהֵא שְׁמֵהּ רַבָּא מְבָרַךְ לְעָלַם וּלְעָלְמֵי עָלְמַיָּא.)

יְהֵא שְׁמֵהּ רַבָּא מְבָרַךְ לְעָלַם וּלְעָלְמֵי עָלְמַיָּא.

יִתְבָּרַךְ וְיִשְׁתַּבַּח וְיִתְפָּאַר וְיִתְרוֹמַם וְיִתְנַשֵּׂא וְיִתְהַדָּר וְיִתְעַלֶּה וְיִתְהַלָּל שְׁמֵהּ דְּקֻדְשָׁא בְּרִיךְ הוּא (Cong. – בְּרִיךְ הוּא) – °לְעֵלָּא מִן כָּל (—From Rosh Hashanah to Yom Kippur substitute °לְעֵלָּא וּלְעֵלָּא מִכָּל) בִּרְכָתָא וְשִׁירָתָא תֻּשְׁבְּחָתָא וְנֶחֱמָתָא, דַּאֲמִירָן בְּעָלְמָא. וְאִמְרוּ: אָמֵן. (Cong. – אָמֵן.)

יְהֵא שְׁלָמָא רַבָּא מִן שְׁמַיָּא, וְחַיִּים עָלֵינוּ וְעַל כָּל יִשְׂרָאֵל. וְאִמְרוּ: אָמֵן. (Cong. – אָמֵן.)

Take three steps back. Bow left and say ... עֹשֶׂה; bow right and say ... הוּא; bow forward and say וְעַל כָּל ... אָמֵן. Remain standing in place for a few moments, then take three steps forward.

עֹשֶׂה שָׁלוֹם בִּמְרוֹמָיו, הוּא יַעֲשֶׂה שָׁלוֹם עָלֵינוּ, וְעַל כָּל יִשְׂרָאֵל. וְאִמְרוּ: אָמֵן. (Cong. – אָמֵן.)

to You every knee should bend, every tongue should swear.[1] *Before You,* HASHEM*, our God, they will bend every knee and cast themselves down and to the glory of Your Name they will render homage, and they will all accept upon themselves the yoke of Your kingship that You may reign over them soon and eternally. For the kingdom is Yours and You will reign for all eternity in glory as it is written in Your Torah:* HASHEM *shall reign for all eternity.*[2] Chazzan — *And it is said:* HASHEM *will be King over all the world — on that day* HASHEM *will be One and His Name will be One.*[3]

In some congregations the following is recited after *Aleinu:*

אַל תִּירָא *Do not fear sudden terror, or the holocaust of the wicked when it comes.*[4] *Plan a conspiracy and it will be annulled; speak your piece and it shall not stand, for God is with us.*[5] *Even till your seniority, I remain unchanged; and even till your ripe old age, I shall endure. I created you and I shall bear you; I shall endure and rescue.*[6]

MOURNER'S KADDISH

In the presence of a *minyan,* mourners recite קַדִּישׁ יָתוֹם, the Mourner's *Kaddish* (see *Laws* §119):

[A transliteration of this *Kaddish* appears on page 1043, and commentary on p. 57.]

יִתְגַּדַּל *May His great Name grow exalted and sanctified* (Cong.— *Amen.*) *in the world that He created as He willed. May He give reign to His kingship in your lifetimes and in your days, and in the lifetimes of the entire Family of Israel, swiftly and soon. Now respond: Amen.*

(Cong.— *Amen. May His great Name be blessed forever and ever.*)

May His great Name be blessed forever and ever.

Blessed, praised, glorified, exalted, extolled, mighty, upraised, and lauded be the Name of the Holy One, Blessed is He (Cong.— *Blessed is He*) — (From Rosh Hashanah to Yom Kippur add: *exceedingly*) *beyond any blessing and song, praise and consolation that are uttered in the world. Now respond: Amen.* (Cong.— *Amen.*)

May there be abundant peace from Heaven, and life, upon us and upon all Israel. Now respond: Amen. (Cong.— *Amen.*)

Take three steps back. Bow left and say, *'He Who makes peace ...';* bow right and say, *'may He ...';* bow forward and say, *'and upon all Israel ...'* Remain standing in place for a few moments, then take three steps forward.

He Who makes peace in His heights, may He make peace upon us, and upon all Israel. Now respond: Amen. (Cong.— *Amen.*)

(1) Cf. *Isaiah* 45:23. (2) *Exodus* 15:18. (3) *Zechariah* 14:9. (4) *Proverbs* 3:25. (5) *Isaiah* 8:10. (6) 46:4.

ברכי נפשי

The following psalms are recited after *Minchah* every Sabbath between Succos and Shabbos HaGadol (the Sabbath before Pesach).

תהלים קד

בָּרְכִי נַפְשִׁי אֶת יהוה,* יהוה אֱלֹהַי גָּדַלְתָּ מְּאֹד,* הוֹד וְהָדָר לָבָשְׁתָּ. עֹטֶה אוֹר כַּשַּׂלְמָה, נוֹטֶה שָׁמַיִם כַּיְרִיעָה. הַמְּקָרֶה בַמַּיִם עֲלִיּוֹתָיו,* הַשָּׂם עָבִים רְכוּבוֹ, הַמְּהַלֵּךְ עַל כַּנְפֵי רוּחַ. עֹשֶׂה מַלְאָכָיו רוּחוֹת, מְשָׁרְתָיו אֵשׁ לֹהֵט.* יָסַד אֶרֶץ עַל מְכוֹנֶיהָ, בַּל תִּמּוֹט עוֹלָם וָעֶד. תְּהוֹם כַּלְּבוּשׁ כִּסִּיתוֹ, עַל הָרִים יַעַמְדוּ מָיִם. מִן גַּעֲרָתְךָ יְנוּסוּן,* מִן קוֹל רַעַמְךָ יֵחָפֵזוּן. יַעֲלוּ הָרִים, יֵרְדוּ בְקָעוֹת, אֶל מְקוֹם זֶה יָסַדְתָּ לָהֶם. גְּבוּל שַׂמְתָּ בַּל יַעֲבֹרוּן, בַּל יְשׁוּבוּן לְכַסּוֹת הָאָרֶץ. הַמְּשַׁלֵּחַ מַעְיָנִים בַּנְּחָלִים,* בֵּין הָרִים יְהַלֵּכוּן. יַשְׁקוּ כָּל חַיְתוֹ שָׂדָי, יִשְׁבְּרוּ פְרָאִים צְמָאָם. עֲלֵיהֶם עוֹף הַשָּׁמַיִם יִשְׁכּוֹן, מִבֵּין עֳפָאיִם יִתְּנוּ קוֹל. מַשְׁקֶה הָרִים מֵעֲלִיּוֹתָיו, מִפְּרִי מַעֲשֶׂיךָ תִּשְׂבַּע הָאָרֶץ. מַצְמִיחַ חָצִיר לַבְּהֵמָה,* וְעֵשֶׂב לַעֲבֹדַת הָאָדָם, לְהוֹצִיא לֶחֶם מִן הָאָרֶץ. וְיַיִן יְשַׂמַּח לְבַב אֱנוֹשׁ,* לְהַצְהִיל פָּנִים מִשָּׁמֶן, וְלֶחֶם לְבַב אֱנוֹשׁ יִסְעָד. יִשְׂבְּעוּ עֲצֵי יהוה, אַרְזֵי לְבָנוֹן אֲשֶׁר נָטָע. אֲשֶׁר שָׁם צִפֳּרִים יְקַנֵּנוּ, חֲסִידָה בְּרוֹשִׁים בֵּיתָהּ.* הָרִים הַגְּבֹהִים לַיְּעֵלִים,* סְלָעִים מַחְסֶה לַשְׁפַנִּים.

בָּרְכִי נַפְשִׁי / Psalm 104

Beginning with the Sabbath after Succos [on which the weekly portion *Bereishis,* describing the creation of the world, is read] we recite Psalm 104, the beautiful lyrical song of tribute to the Creator and His universe. The fifteen Songs of Ascents [שִׁיר הַמַּעֲלוֹת — *psalms* 120-134] are also recited for these psalms are related to the creation.

The Talmud *(Sukkah* 53a) relates that David prepared the foundations for the future Temple and deep pits beneath the site of the Altar, into which the wine and water libations would flow. David dug so deep that he penetrated the תְּהוֹם, *subterranean reservoirs,* of water that had been stored beneath the earth's crust since creation. The waters erupted from the reservoir and threatened to inundate the world, whereupon David inscribed a Divine Name on a shard and cast it into the waters, which then receded sixteen thousand cubits. When he saw that they had receded too far, he said, 'The closer the waters are to the surface, the more fertile the land will be.' He recited the fifteen Songs of Ascents and the deep waters rose fifteen thousand cubits, to remain one thousand cubits beneath the earth's surface.

The deeper meaning of this incident is that the Temple was intended as a microcosm of the world, permeated by the Divine Spirit. The process of constructing it paralleled the six days of Creation, when God's spirit permeated the world. Originally, water covered the entire surface of the earth; later, the water was contained within the seas and the vast depths, but was positioned so as to promote the flourishing of vegetation [see *Genesis* 1:9-11]. What David did at the time of establishing the Temple's foundations reenacted the primeval containment of the waters.

By reciting these psalms, we bear weekly testimony that God created heaven and earth.

This recitation continues through two weeks before Pesach. On the Sabbath before Pesach *(Shabbos HaGadol),* portions of the *Haggadah* are read in anticipation of the Festival. From Pesach until the Sabbath before Rosh Hashanah, we recite *Pirkei Avos,* beginning on page 544, as we focus on the spiritual creation symbolized by the giving of the Torah.

בָּרְכִי נַפְשִׁי אֶת ה׳ — *Bless HASHEM, O my soul.* By calling upon his soul to bless God, the Psalmist suggests that the human soul is God's great gift to man and, in effect, thanks God for the ability to reason, articulate, and rise to spiritual heights.

ה׳ אֱלֹהַי גָּדַלְתָּ מְּאֹד — *HASHEM, my God, You are very great.* We cannot define the extent of God's greatness; we say only that God is very great. Man can merely begin a recital of God's blessings, which are truly innumerable *(Ibn Ezra).*

BORCHI NAFSHI

The following psalms are recited after *Minchah* every Sabbath between Succos and Shabbos HaGadol (the Sabbath before Pesach).

Psalm 104

בָּרְכִי נַפְשִׁי *Bless* HASHEM, *O my soul.* HASHEM, my God, You are very great;* You have donned majesty and splendor; cloaked in light as with a garment, stretching out the heavens like a curtain. He Who roofs His upper chambers with water;* He Who makes clouds His chariot; He Who walks on winged wind; He makes the winds His messengers, the flaming fire His attendants;* He established the earth upon its foundations, that it falter not forever and ever.*

The watery deep, as with a garment You covered it; upon the mountains, water would stand. From Your rebuke they flee, from the sound of Your thunder they rush away. They ascend mountains, they descend to valleys, to the special place You founded for them. You set a boundary they cannot overstep, they cannot return to cover the earth.*

He sends the springs into the streams, they flow between the mountains. They water every beast of the field, they quench the wild creatures' thirst. Near them dwell the heaven's birds, from among the branches they give forth song. He waters the mountains from His upper chambers, from the fruit of Your works the earth is sated.*

He causes vegetation to sprout for the cattle, and plants through man's labor, to bring forth bread from the earth; and wine that gladdens man's heart,* to make the face glow from oil, and bread that sustains the heart of man. The trees of* HASHEM *are sated, the cedars of Lebanon that He has planted; there where the birds nest, the chassidah with its home among cypresses;* high mountains for the wild goats,* rocks as refuge for the gophers.*

הַמְקָרֶה בַמַּיִם עֲלִיּוֹתָיו — *He Who roofs His upper chambers with water.* This refers to the clouds which are stretched out across the sky like beams and rafters [to shield the earth from the blazing sun] *(Radak; Ibn Yachya).*

מְשָׁרְתָיו אֵשׁ לֹהֵט — *The flaming fire His attendants,* i.e., the blazing flashes of lightning that streak through the sky *(Radak).*

מִן גַּעֲרָתְךָ יְנוּסוּן — *From Your rebuke they flee.* At the beginning of Creation, water covered the entire surface of the earth. When God cried out יִקָּווּ הַמַּיִם, *Let the waters gather (Genesis* 1:9), they all fled from where they were spread out and concentrated into seas and oceans *(Rashi).*

הַמְשַׁלֵּחַ מַעְיָנִים בַּנְּחָלִים — *He sends the springs into the streams.* The Psalmist describes poetically how God instituted a natural system whereby the earth would be watered to provide for people and vegetation.

מַצְמִיחַ חָצִיר לַבְּהֵמָה ... — *He causes vegetation to sprout for the cattle ...* For animals, which cannot engage in agriculture, God causes vegetation to sprout. Man, however, must labor to earn his daily bread. Before he can partake of food, he must first sow thresh, knead, and bake his bread *(R' Yoseif Titzak; see Pesachim* 118a).

וְיַיִן יְשַׂמַּח לְבַב אֱנוֹשׁ — *And wine that gladdens man's heart.* God creates the grapes from which wine is pressed. When drunk in sensible proportions, wine gladdens the heart and drives away melancholy. It heightens the intellect and even prepares the mind for prophecy *(Radak).*

חֲסִידָה בְּרוֹשִׁים בֵּיתָהּ — *The chassidah with its home among cypresses.* [Although the exact meaning of חֲסִידָה, *chassidah,* is uncertain, most translations use *stork.*] The Psalmist singles out the *chassidah* because it nests only in tall trees like the cedar or cypress *(Radak).*

הָרִים הַגְּבֹהִים לַיְּעֵלִים — *High mountains for the wild goats.* At first glance, the remote and barren mountains appear to serve no purpose; but in fact they were created to provide a habitat for the wild mountain goats *(Rashi; Radak).*

Contrary to the theory that species survived only by adapting themselves to hostile environments, the Psalmist says that God created the setting to suit the needs of the species.

עָשָׂה יָרֵחַ לְמוֹעֲדִים,* שֶׁמֶשׁ יָדַע מְבוֹאוֹ. תָּשֶׁת חֹשֶׁךְ וִיהִי לָיְלָה, בּוֹ תִרְמֹשׂ כָּל חַיְתוֹ יָעַר. הַכְּפִירִים שֹׁאֲגִים לַטָּרֶף, וּלְבַקֵּשׁ מֵאֵל אָכְלָם. תִּזְרַח הַשֶּׁמֶשׁ יֵאָסֵפוּן,* וְאֶל מְעוֹנֹתָם יִרְבָּצוּן. יֵצֵא אָדָם לְפָעֳלוֹ, וְלַעֲבֹדָתוֹ עֲדֵי עָרֶב.

מָה רַבּוּ מַעֲשֶׂיךָ יהוה,* כֻּלָּם בְּחָכְמָה עָשִׂיתָ,* מָלְאָה הָאָרֶץ קִנְיָנֶךָ.* זֶה הַיָּם, גָּדוֹל וּרְחַב יָדָיִם, שָׁם רֶמֶשׂ וְאֵין מִסְפָּר, חַיּוֹת קְטַנּוֹת עִם גְּדֹלוֹת. שָׁם אֳנִיּוֹת יְהַלֵּכוּן, לִוְיָתָן* זֶה יָצַרְתָּ לְשַׂחֶק בּוֹ. כֻּלָּם אֵלֶיךָ יְשַׂבֵּרוּן, לָתֵת אָכְלָם בְּעִתּוֹ.* תִּתֵּן לָהֶם, יִלְקֹטוּן, תִּפְתַּח יָדְךָ, יִשְׂבְּעוּן טוֹב. תַּסְתִּיר פָּנֶיךָ יִבָּהֵלוּן, תֹּסֵף רוּחָם יִגְוָעוּן, וְאֶל עֲפָרָם יְשׁוּבוּן. תְּשַׁלַּח רוּחֲךָ יִבָּרֵאוּן,* וּתְחַדֵּשׁ פְּנֵי אֲדָמָה.

יְהִי כְבוֹד יהוה לְעוֹלָם, יִשְׂמַח יהוה בְּמַעֲשָׂיו. הַמַּבִּיט לָאָרֶץ וַתִּרְעָד, יִגַּע בֶּהָרִים וְיֶעֱשָׁנוּ. אָשִׁירָה לַיהוה בְּחַיָּי, אֲזַמְּרָה לֵאלֹהַי בְּעוֹדִי. יֶעֱרַב עָלָיו שִׂיחִי, אָנֹכִי אֶשְׂמַח בַּיהוה. יִתַּמּוּ חַטָּאִים מִן הָאָרֶץ, וּרְשָׁעִים עוֹד אֵינָם,* בָּרְכִי נַפְשִׁי אֶת יהוה, הַלְלוּיָהּ.

תהלים קכ

שִׁיר הַמַּעֲלוֹת, אֶל יהוה בַּצָּרָתָה לִּי, קָרָאתִי וַיַּעֲנֵנִי. יהוה הַצִּילָה נַפְשִׁי מִשְּׂפַת שֶׁקֶר,* מִלָּשׁוֹן רְמִיָּה. מַה יִּתֵּן לְךָ,* וּמַה יֹּסִיף לָךְ, לָשׁוֹן רְמִיָּה. חִצֵּי גִבּוֹר שְׁנוּנִים,* עִם גַּחֲלֵי רְתָמִים.* אוֹיָה לִי כִּי גַרְתִּי מֶשֶׁךְ,* שָׁכַנְתִּי עִם אָהֳלֵי קֵדָר.* רַבַּת שָׁכְנָה לָּהּ נַפְשִׁי, עִם שׂוֹנֵא שָׁלוֹם. אֲנִי שָׁלוֹם,* וְכִי אֲדַבֵּר, הֵמָּה לַמִּלְחָמָה.*

עָשָׂה יָרֵחַ לְמוֹעֲדִים — *He made the moon for festivals,* i.e., the moon and its cycles were made to facilitate the lunar calendar, upon which the Torah bases the dating of the festivals.

תִּזְרַח הַשֶּׁמֶשׁ יֵאָסֵפוּן — *The sun rises and they are gathered in.* When the night ends and daylight emerges, the wild beasts come back to their caves to hide from people *(Rashi; Radak).*

מָה רַבּוּ מַעֲשֶׂיךָ ה׳ — *How abundant are Your works, HASHEM.* מָה רַבּוּ, *how abundant,* has both a quantitative meaning, *how numerous,* and a qualitative meaning, *how great (Radak).*

כֻּלָּם בְּחָכְמָה עָשִׂיתָ — *With wisdom You made them all.* No creature evolved by chance; every one was designed by God in His *wisdom* and demonstrates His omnipotence *(Sforno).*

מָלְאָה הָאָרֶץ קִנְיָנֶךָ — *The earth is full of Your possessions.* God did not allow a single inch to go to waste. Every spot is full of wondrous creations which testify to Hashem's absolute mastery over the world *(Radak).*

לִוְיָתָן — *Leviathan.* Scripture *(Genesis* 1:21) states: *HASHEM created the great* תַּנִּינִם, *sea-giants.* The *Talmud (Bava Basra* 74b) identifies the *sea-giants* as the *Leviathan* and its mate. *Rashba* and *Maharal* interpret the Leviathan allegorically, maintaining that all references to it refer to spiritual concepts that the Sages chose to disguise in tales of a monster fish. A discussion of these concepts may be found in the Overview to the ArtScroll *Succos.*

לָתֵת אָכְלָם בְּעִתּוֹ — *To provide their food in its [proper] time.* Every species of life has a different feeding schedule, and You carefully provide each one with its food at the proper time *(Radak).*

תְּשַׁלַּח רוּחֲךָ יִבָּרֵאוּן — *When You send forth Your breath, they are created.* When man dies, God snatches the breath of life from him, but He will return it at the time of תְּחִיַּת הַמֵּתִים, *the resuscitation of the dead.* Then the dead bodies will be recreated, and their souls restored *(Radak).*

יִתַּמּוּ חַטָּאִים מִן הָאָרֶץ וּרְשָׁעִים עוֹד אֵינָם — *Sinners will cease from the earth, and the wicked will be no more.* In Hebrew the word for *sinner* has two forms: חוֹטְאִים and חַטָּאִים. The latter form may be homiletically interpreted as חֲטָאִים, *sins.* Thus, the Talmud *(Berachos* 10a) teaches that when sin will cease to be perpetrated, the wicked will be no more, for then everyone will be righteous.

⁂ שִׁיר הַמַּעֲלוֹת / The Song of Ascents

The fifteen psalms (120-134), known as the Songs of Ascents, were sung in the Temple, for it

He made the moon for festivals, the sun knows its destination. You make darkness and it is night, in which every forest beast stirs. The young lions roar after their prey, and to seek their food from God. The sun rises and they are gathered in,* and in their dens they crouch. Man goes forth to his work, and to his labor until evening.*

How abundant are Your works, HASHEM; with wisdom You made them all,* the earth is full of Your possessions.* Behold this sea — great and of broad measure; there are creeping things without number, small creatures and great ones. There ships travel, this Leviathan* You fashioned to sport with. Everything looks to You with hope, to provide their food in its proper time.* You give to them, they gather it in; You open Your hand, they are sated with good. When You hide Your face, they are dismayed; when You retrieve their spirit, they perish and to their dust they return. When You send forth Your breath, they are created,* and You renew the surface of the earth.*

May the glory of HASHEM endure forever, let HASHEM rejoice in His works. He peers toward the earth and it trembles, He touches the mountains and they smoke. I will sing to HASHEM while I live, I will sing praises to my God while I endure. May my words be sweet to Him — I will rejoice in HASHEM. Sinners will cease from the earth, and the wicked will be no more — Bless HASHEM, O my soul. Halleluyah!*

Psalm 120

שִׁיר הַמַּעֲלוֹת *A song of ascents. To HASHEM, in my distress I cried and He answered me. HASHEM, rescue my soul from lying lips,* from a deceitful tongue. What can He give you,* and what will it profit you, O deceitful tongue? You are like the sharp arrows of the mighty;* with coals of rotem-wood.* Woe unto me, for my drawn-out sojourn;* I dwelt with those who inhabit the tents of Kedar.* Long has my soul dwelt with those who hate peace. I am peace* — but when I speak, they are for war.**

---

was in that sacred location that the Jew was catapulted toward successively higher spiritual summits. In the Temple, Israel declared that man must not be spiritually stagnant; the world is composed of infinite degrees of goodness, and man's mission is to scale the מַעֲלוֹת, *spiritual heights,* which rise from earth heavenward.

These psalms do not begin, שִׁיר הַמַּעֲלָה, *A song of ascent* (singular), but שִׁיר הַמַּעֲלוֹת, *A song of ascents* (plural), because when the Children of Israel are worthy to ascend, they do not climb one step at a time; rather, they mount many rungs at once. As Scripture *(Deuteronomy* 28:13) states: וְהָיִיתָ רַק לְמַעְלָה, *And you shall be in constant ascent (Midrash Shocher Tov).*

⁂ Psalm 120

מִשְּׂפַת שֶׁקֶר — *From lying lips ...* This refers to someone who spreads slander behind another's back, whereas *deceitful tongue* refers to a traitor who feigns friendship while his heart seethes with malice and hatred *(Malbim).*

מַה יִּתֵּן לְךָ — *What can He give you?* The Psalmist addresses the tongue: What can the Almighty do, tongue, to restrain you from doing further damage? Has He not already placed you behind two walls? *(Rashi).*

חִצֵּי גִבּוֹר שְׁנוּנִים — [*You are like*] *the sharp arrows of the mighty.* The tongue is like a bow that shoots arrows of slander. Just as a bow inflicts its damage far from its source, so does the evil spread by the tongue attack its victim at a distance *(Rashi).*

עִם גַּחֲלֵי רְתָמִים — [*You are to be compared*] *with coals of rotem-wood.* Charcoals of *rotem*-wood are especially dangerous, because long after they appear to be dead on the surface, they continue to burn within *(Rashi).*

אוֹיָה לִי כִּי גַרְתִּי מֶשֶׁךְ — *Woe unto me, for my drawn-out sojourn,* i.e., the long exile of the Jewish people *(Radak).*

שָׁכַנְתִּי עִם אָהֳלֵי קֵדָר — *I dwelt with* [*those who inhabit*] *the tents of Kedar.* Kedar is the Arab empire of Ishmael, the great power that would persecute Israel in exile *(Radak; Ibn Ezra).*

אֲנִי שָׁלוֹם — *I am peace.* Uppermost in my mind is a constant desire to make peace, even when circumstances force me to act belligerently *(Rav Yitzchak Arma'ah).*

וְכִי אֲדַבֵּר הֵמָּה לַמִּלְחָמָה — *But when I speak, they are for war.* The more I speak of peace, the more they clamor for war, because they view my

תהלים קכא

שִׁיר לַמַּעֲלוֹת,* אֶשָּׂא עֵינַי אֶל הֶהָרִים, מֵאַיִן יָבֹא עֶזְרִי. עֶזְרִי מֵעִם יהוה, עֹשֵׂה שָׁמַיִם וָאָרֶץ. אַל יִתֵּן לַמּוֹט רַגְלֶךָ, אַל יָנוּם שֹׁמְרֶךָ. הִנֵּה לֹא יָנוּם וְלֹא יִישָׁן, שׁוֹמֵר יִשְׂרָאֵל. יהוה שֹׁמְרֶךָ, יהוה צִלְּךָ עַל יַד יְמִינֶךָ. יוֹמָם הַשֶּׁמֶשׁ לֹא יַכֶּכָּה וְיָרֵחַ בַּלָּיְלָה. יהוה יִשְׁמָרְךָ מִכָּל רָע,* יִשְׁמֹר אֶת נַפְשֶׁךָ. יהוה יִשְׁמָר צֵאתְךָ וּבוֹאֶךָ,* מֵעַתָּה וְעַד עוֹלָם.

תהלים קכב

שִׁיר הַמַּעֲלוֹת, לְדָוִד,* שָׂמַחְתִּי בְּאֹמְרִים לִי, בֵּית יהוה נֵלֵךְ. עֹמְדוֹת הָיוּ רַגְלֵינוּ, בִּשְׁעָרַיִךְ יְרוּשָׁלָיִם. יְרוּשָׁלַיִם הַבְּנוּיָה,* כְּעִיר שֶׁחֻבְּרָה לָּהּ יַחְדָּו. שֶׁשָּׁם עָלוּ שְׁבָטִים, שִׁבְטֵי יָהּ עֵדוּת לְיִשְׂרָאֵל, לְהֹדוֹת לְשֵׁם יהוה. כִּי שָׁמָּה יָשְׁבוּ כִסְאוֹת לְמִשְׁפָּט, כִּסְאוֹת לְבֵית דָּוִד.* שַׁאֲלוּ שְׁלוֹם יְרוּשָׁלָיִם,* יִשְׁלָיוּ אֹהֲבָיִךְ. יְהִי שָׁלוֹם בְּחֵילֵךְ, שַׁלְוָה בְּאַרְמְנוֹתָיִךְ. לְמַעַן אַחַי וְרֵעָי, אֲדַבְּרָה נָּא שָׁלוֹם בָּךְ. לְמַעַן בֵּית יהוה אֱלֹהֵינוּ, אֲבַקְשָׁה טוֹב לָךְ.*

תהלים קכג

שִׁיר הַמַּעֲלוֹת, אֵלֶיךָ נָשָׂאתִי אֶת עֵינַי, הַיֹּשְׁבִי בַּשָּׁמָיִם. הִנֵּה כְעֵינֵי עֲבָדִים אֶל יַד אֲדוֹנֵיהֶם, כְּעֵינֵי שִׁפְחָה אֶל יַד גְּבִרְתָּהּ, כֵּן עֵינֵינוּ אֶל יהוה אֱלֹהֵינוּ, עַד שֶׁיְּחָנֵּנוּ. חָנֵּנוּ יהוה חָנֵּנוּ,* כִּי רַב שָׂבַעְנוּ בוּז.* רַבַּת שָׂבְעָה לָּהּ נַפְשֵׁנוּ הַלַּעַג הַשַּׁאֲנַנִּים, הַבּוּז לִגְאֵי יוֹנִים.*

---

attempt at rapprochement as a sign of weakness and vulnerability.

Psalm 121

שִׁיר לַמַּעֲלוֹת — *A song to the ascents.* This song differs from all others in this series because it is not called שִׁיר הַמַּעֲלוֹת, *a song* **of** *ascents;* but is dedicated **לַמַּעֲלוֹת, to** *the ascents.* It describes the means whereby Israel finds the strength to attain godly heights and ascend to His glorious Presence.

ה׳ יִשְׁמָרְךָ מִכָּל רָע — *HASHEM will protect you from every evil,* both physical and spiritual.

ה׳ יִשְׁמָר צֵאתְךָ וּבוֹאֶךָ — *HASHEM will guard your departure and your arrival.* Upon your departure from the House of Torah Study in order to pursue your business affairs, God will guard you; and He will continue to do so until your arrival back in the House of Torah study *(Targum).*

Furthermore, Hashem will supervise *the departure* of Israel from exile and He will assure Israel's *arrival* in the Holy Land *(Radak).*

Psalm 122

This psalm describes Jerusalem as a city where the individual experiences a personal encounter with holiness. No matter how many pilgrims come, each feels a sense of worth and elevation.

שִׁיר הַמַּעֲלוֹת לְדָוִד — *A song of ascents, by David.* David composed this psalm with the intention that it be recited in the Temple after it was built *(Ibn Ezra).*

Others maintain that this song refers specifically to the reconstruction of the Third (and final) Temple, which will be built through the efforts of the Messiah, the scion of David.

יְרוּשָׁלַיִם הַבְּנוּיָה — *The built-up Jerusalem.* David foresaw that his son Solomon would 'build up' the spiritual nature of Jerusalem by constructing its most imposing edifice — the Temple. There, the *Shechinah* (Divine Presence) would dwell in the Holy City.

כִּסְאוֹת לְבֵית דָּוִד — *Thrones for the House of David.* The seat of David's kingdom was in Jerusalem, the capital city *(Rashi).*

Psalm 121

שִׁיר לַמַּעֲלוֹת *A song to the ascents.* I raise my eyes to the mountains; whence will come my help? My help is from* HASHEM, *Maker of heaven and earth. He will not allow your foot to falter; your Guardian will not slumber. Behold, He neither slumbers nor sleeps — the Guardian of Israel.* HASHEM *is your Guardian;* HASHEM *is your Shade at your right hand. By day the sun will not harm you, nor the moon by night.* HASHEM *will protect you from every evil;* He will guard your soul.* HASHEM *will guard your departure and your arrival,* from this time and forever.*

Psalm 122

שִׁיר הַמַּעֲלוֹת *A song of ascents, by David.* I rejoiced when they said to me, 'Let us go to the House of* HASHEM.' *Immobile stood our feet, within your gates, O Jerusalem. The built-up Jerusalem* is like a city that is united together. For there the tribes ascended — the tribes of God, who are a testimony for Israel — to give thanks to the Name of* HASHEM. *For there sat thrones of judgment, thrones for the House of David.* Pray for the peace of Jerusalem;* those who love you will be serene. May there be peace within your wall, serenity within your palaces. For the sake of my brethren and my comrades, I shall speak of peace in your midst. For the sake of the House of* HASHEM, *our God, I will request good for you.**

Psalm 123

שִׁיר הַמַּעֲלוֹת *A song of ascents. To You I raised my eyes, O You Who dwell in the heavens. Behold! Like the eyes of servants unto their masters' hand, like the eyes of a maid unto her mistress' hand, so are our eyes unto* HASHEM, *our God, until He will favor us. Favor us,* HASHEM, *favor us,* for we are fully sated with contempt.* Our soul is fully sated with the mockery of the complacent ones, with the contempt of the arrogant.**

שַׁאֲלוּ שְׁלוֹם יְרוּשָׁלָיִם — *Pray for the peace of Jerusalem.* This is an exhortation to the monarchs who sit on the thrones of the House of David. Whenever you offer supplication to God, pray for the peace of Jerusalem *(Sforno).*

The Jews in exile exclaim: 'Pray to God for the peace of Jerusalem.' Permanent peace will come to the world only with the ingathering of the exiles from the four corners of the earth. Until then Jerusalem will never experience true peace, because many nations will war over this city. The exiled Jews, those who love her, mourn over the destruction of Jerusalem and pine to see her glory renewed *(Radak).*

לְמַעַן בֵּית ה׳ אֱלֹהֵינוּ אֲבַקְשָׁה טוֹב לָךְ — *For the sake of the House of* HASHEM, *our God, I will request good for you.* More than the Jews need Jerusalem, Jerusalem needs the Jews. Of what value is the Holy City and the House of HASHEM if there are no people to absorb their sacred spirit? God's Spirit dwells only where there are people who will benefit from His Presence.

Psalm 123

The Psalmist writes from the perspective of Jews in exile, whose tragic experience has taught them that only God can help them.

חָנֵּנוּ ה׳ חָנֵּנוּ — *Favor us,* HASHEM, *favor us.* The double request reflects the double threat of exile, for Israel is endangered both physically and spiritually in the Diaspora where it is surrounded by hostile nations *(R' Vidal HaTzarfati).*

כִּי רַב שָׂבַעְנוּ בוּז — *For we are fully sated with contempt.* There is no point in continuing the exile, because we have already experienced every possible form of disgrace and contempt; there is nothing more to add *(R' Feuer).*

הַלַּעַג הַשַּׁאֲנַנִּים הַבּוּז לִגְאֵי יוֹנִים — *With the mockery of the complacent ones, with the contempt of the arrogant.* Israel's attempt at spiritual fulfillment and its effort to teach that life must have a spiritual goal are greeted with derision by those who are content with and proud of their material and hedonistic successes.

תהלים קכד

שִׁיר הַמַּעֲלוֹת, לְדָוִד, לוּלֵי יהוה שֶׁהָיָה לָנוּ, יֹאמַר נָא יִשְׂרָאֵל.* לוּלֵי יהוה שֶׁהָיָה לָנוּ, בְּקוּם עָלֵינוּ אָדָם. אֲזַי חַיִּים בְּלָעוּנוּ, בַּחֲרוֹת אַפָּם בָּנוּ. אֲזַי הַמַּיִם שְׁטָפוּנוּ, נַחְלָה עָבַר עַל נַפְשֵׁנוּ. אֲזַי עָבַר עַל נַפְשֵׁנוּ, הַמַּיִם הַזֵּידוֹנִים. בָּרוּךְ יהוה, שֶׁלֹּא נְתָנָנוּ טֶרֶף לְשִׁנֵּיהֶם. נַפְשֵׁנוּ כְּצִפּוֹר נִמְלְטָה* מִפַּח יוֹקְשִׁים, הַפַּח נִשְׁבָּר וַאֲנַחְנוּ נִמְלָטְנוּ. עֶזְרֵנוּ בְּשֵׁם יהוה, עֹשֵׂה שָׁמַיִם וָאָרֶץ.

תהלים קכה

שִׁיר הַמַּעֲלוֹת, הַבֹּטְחִים בַּיהוה, כְּהַר צִיּוֹן* לֹא יִמּוֹט לְעוֹלָם יֵשֵׁב. יְרוּשָׁלַיִם הָרִים סָבִיב לָהּ,* וַיהוה סָבִיב לְעַמּוֹ, מֵעַתָּה וְעַד עוֹלָם. כִּי לֹא יָנוּחַ שֵׁבֶט הָרֶשַׁע עַל גּוֹרַל הַצַּדִּיקִים,* לְמַעַן לֹא יִשְׁלְחוּ הַצַּדִּיקִים בְּעַוְלָתָה יְדֵיהֶם.* הֵיטִיבָה יהוה לַטּוֹבִים,* וְלִישָׁרִים בְּלִבּוֹתָם. וְהַמַּטִּים עֲקַלְקַלּוֹתָם* יוֹלִיכֵם יהוה אֶת פֹּעֲלֵי הָאָוֶן, שָׁלוֹם עַל יִשְׂרָאֵל.*

תהלים קכו

שִׁיר הַמַּעֲלוֹת, בְּשׁוּב יהוה אֶת שִׁיבַת צִיּוֹן* הָיִינוּ כְּחֹלְמִים.* אָז יִמָּלֵא שְׂחוֹק פִּינוּ, וּלְשׁוֹנֵנוּ רִנָּה,* אָז יֹאמְרוּ בַגּוֹיִם, הִגְדִּיל יהוה לַעֲשׂוֹת עִם אֵלֶּה. הִגְדִּיל יהוה לַעֲשׂוֹת עִמָּנוּ, הָיִינוּ שְׂמֵחִים. שׁוּבָה יהוה אֶת שְׁבִיתֵנוּ, כַּאֲפִיקִים בַּנֶּגֶב.* הַזֹּרְעִים בְּדִמְעָה*

Psalm 124

לוּלֵי ה׳ שֶׁהָיָה לָנוּ יֹאמַר נָא יִשְׂרָאֵל — *Had not HASHEM been with us — let Israel declare it now!* Let us now declare that had He not appeared as HASHEM, i.e., in His aspect as the Dispenser of Kindness, and offered compassionate protection, Israel could not have survived the terrible exile. As is common in Scripture, the dire alternative is left unsaid *(Sforno).*

נַפְשֵׁנוּ ... נִמְלְטָה — *Our soul escaped* — unharmed from our enemies — like a bird from the hunter's snare.

Psalm 125

הַבֹּטְחִים בַּה׳ כְּהַר צִיּוֹן — *Those who trust in HASHEM are like Mount Zion.* Although Mount Zion is situated south of Mount Moriah in Jerusalem, Zion is often used poetically as a title for Mount Moriah, the site of the Holy Temple.

The righteous are likened to Mount Zion in that God's spirit will always remain with them just as it does with Mount Zion.

יְרוּשָׁלַיִם הָרִים סָבִיב לָהּ — *Jerusalem — mountains enwrap it.* Though Jerusalem is surrounded by protective mountains that afford a tremendous strategic advantage, the Psalmist cautions the people that the city is defenseless unless God Himself guards it. Only when HASHEM enwraps His nation are the people truly secure *(Radak).*

כִּי לֹא יָנוּחַ שֵׁבֶט הָרֶשַׁע עַל גּוֹרַל הַצַּדִּיקִים — *For the rod of wickedness shall not rest upon the lot of the righteous.* Jerusalem is the lot where the righteous are destined to settle. The enemies of Israel will attempt to wrest the city from Jewish rule, but they will fail.

לְמַעַן לֹא יִשְׁלְחוּ הַצַּדִּיקִים בְּעַוְלָתָה יְדֵיהֶם — *So that the righteous shall not stretch their hands into iniquity.* The wicked will not be able to gain ascendancy among the righteous of Jerusalem, lest the righteous learn from their evil ways *(Rashi).*

הֵיטִיבָה ה׳ לַטּוֹבִים — *Do good, HASHEM, to good people.* In the bitter darkness of the exile, it is easy to lose sight of the glorious Divine Presence. Therefore, the Psalmist now prays for the righteous who strive to be free of moral degradation, 'May these men of pure spirit fathom the secret of Divinity, which is the highest goodness man can achieve.

וְהַמַּטִּים עֲקַלְקַלּוֹתָם — *But those who turn to their perverseness.* The opposite of the upright, who are sincere, are those who are inherently crooked

Psalm 124

שִׁיר הַמַּעֲלוֹת *A song of ascents, by David. Had not HASHEM been with us — let Israel declare it now!* Had not HASHEM been with us when men rose up against us, then they would have swallowed us alive, when their anger was kindled against us. Then the waters would have inundated us; the current would have surged across our soul. Then they would have surged across our soul — the treacherous waters. Blessed is HASHEM, Who did not present us as prey for their teeth. Our soul escaped* like a bird from the hunters' snare; the snare broke and we escaped. Our help is through the Name of HASHEM, Maker of heaven and earth.*

Psalm 125

שִׁיר הַמַּעֲלוֹת *A song of ascents. Those who trust in HASHEM are like Mount Zion,* that falters not but abides forever. Jerusalem — mountains enwrap it,* and HASHEM enwraps His nation, from this time and forever. For the rod of wickedness shall not rest upon the lot of the righteous,* so that the righteous shall not stretch their hands into iniquity.* Do good, HASHEM, to good people,* and to the upright in their hearts. But those who turn to their perverseness* — HASHEM will lead them with the workers of iniquity — peace upon Israel.**

Psalm 126

שִׁיר הַמַּעֲלוֹת *A song of ascents. When HASHEM will return the captivity of Zion,* we will be like dreamers.* Then our mouth will be filled with laughter and our tongue with glad song.* Then will they declare among the nations, 'HASHEM has done greatly with these.' HASHEM has done greatly with us, we were gladdened. O HASHEM — return our captivity like springs in the desert.* Those who tearfully sow**

---

and distort the truth. Unscrupulously, they resort to dishonesty whenever the truth will impede their plans. Thus, they turn to their perverseness, and ignore the truth.

שָׁלוֹם עַל יִשְׂרָאֵל — *Peace upon Israel.* When the corrupt element is removed from Israel, there will be no one to disturb the internal harmony of the nation. In addition to inner serenity, the nation will enjoy external peace and security *(Radak).*

◆§ Psalm 126

בְּשׁוּב ה׳ אֶת שִׁיבַת צִיּוֹן — *When HASHEM will return the captivity of Zion.* The Psalmist wrote prophetically about the return from the Babylonian exile — an event that would take place about five hundred years later.

הָיִינוּ כְּחֹלְמִים — *We will be like dreamers.* When the long-awaited return to Zion finally comes to pass, the recollection of the past oppression of the exile will swiftly fade away and seem like a bad dream *(Radak).*

אָז יִמָּלֵא שְׂחוֹק פִּינוּ וּלְשׁוֹנֵנוּ רִנָּה — *Then our mouth will be filled with laughter and our tongue with glad song.* We will explode with happy laughter at the unexpected miraculous turn of events *(R' Hirsch).*

R' Yochanan said in the name of R' Shimon bar Yochai that a Jew is forbidden to fill his mouth with laughter in this world [i.e., to experience unadulterated happiness] until the day when all nations declare הִגְדִּיל ה׳ לַעֲשׂוֹת עִם אֵלֶּה, *HASHEM has done greatly with these* — for our verse says אָז, *then,* meaning only then, when there is a general recognition of God's love for Israel, may we exult fully *(Berachos* 31a).

שׁוּבָה ה׳ אֶת שְׁבִיתֵנוּ כַּאֲפִיקִים בַּנֶּגֶב — *O HASHEM — return our captivity like springs in the desert.* Just as water turns a seemingly barren desert into a flourishing garden, so will we be transformed and gladdened when God delivers us from our exile *(Rashi).*

הַזֹּרְעִים בְּדִמְעָה — *Those who tearfully sow.* The Psalmist continues by comparing those whose primary concern is with the study of Torah and the performance of the commandments to farmers. The seeds of Israel's spiritual mission may become drenched in tears of unbearable suffering, but the crop, the eventual harvest of homage to righteousness and truth, will be

בְּרִנָּה יִקְצֹרוּ. הָלוֹךְ יֵלֵךְ וּבָכֹה נֹשֵׂא מֶשֶׁךְ הַזָּרַע,* בֹּא יָבֹא בְרִנָּה נֹשֵׂא אֲלֻמֹּתָיו.

תהלים קכז

שִׁיר הַמַּעֲלוֹת, לִשְׁלֹמֹה,* אִם יהוה לֹא יִבְנֶה בַיִת, שָׁוְא עָמְלוּ בוֹנָיו בּוֹ,* אִם יהוה לֹא יִשְׁמָר עִיר, שָׁוְא שָׁקַד שׁוֹמֵר. שָׁוְא לָכֶם מַשְׁכִּימֵי קוּם מְאַחֲרֵי שֶׁבֶת* אֹכְלֵי לֶחֶם הָעֲצָבִים, כֵּן יִתֵּן לִידִידוֹ שֵׁנָא. הִנֵּה נַחֲלַת יהוה בָּנִים,* שָׂכָר פְּרִי הַבָּטֶן. כְּחִצִּים בְּיַד גִּבּוֹר כֵּן בְּנֵי הַנְּעוּרִים.* אַשְׁרֵי הַגֶּבֶר אֲשֶׁר מִלֵּא אֶת אַשְׁפָּתוֹ מֵהֶם, לֹא יֵבֹשׁוּ, כִּי יְדַבְּרוּ אֶת אוֹיְבִים בַּשָּׁעַר.*

תהלים קכח

שִׁיר הַמַּעֲלוֹת, אַשְׁרֵי כָּל יְרֵא יהוה,* הַהֹלֵךְ בִּדְרָכָיו. יְגִיעַ כַּפֶּיךָ כִּי תֹאכֵל,* אַשְׁרֶיךָ וְטוֹב לָךְ. אֶשְׁתְּךָ כְּגֶפֶן פֹּרִיָּה בְּיַרְכְּתֵי בֵיתֶךָ,* בָּנֶיךָ כִּשְׁתִלֵי זֵיתִים,* סָבִיב לְשֻׁלְחָנֶךָ. הִנֵּה כִי כֵן יְבֹרַךְ גָּבֶר יְרֵא יהוה. יְבָרֶכְךָ יהוה מִצִּיּוֹן, וּרְאֵה בְּטוּב יְרוּשָׁלָיִם, כֹּל יְמֵי חַיֶּיךָ.* וּרְאֵה בָנִים לְבָנֶיךָ, שָׁלוֹם עַל יִשְׂרָאֵל.

---

reaped in joy *(R' Hirsch).*

הָלוֹךְ יֵלֵךְ וּבָכֹה נֹשֵׂא מֶשֶׁךְ הַזָּרַע — *He who bears the measure of seeds walks along weeping.* The poor man carrying seeds weeps in fear that his precious seeds may be lost and go to waste. God sees his plight and has mercy on him, enabling him to reap a bountiful crop. So, too, exiled Israel carries the burden of spiritual seeds in a hostile world, fearful lest its efforts be wasted. Yet, God will reward its sacrifice with the bounty of the World to Come *(Ibn Ezra).*

◆§ Psalm 127

שִׁיר הַמַּעֲלוֹת לִשְׁלֹמֹה — *A song of ascents for Solomon.* David dedicated this psalm to Solomon, who was to build the Temple.

אִם ה׳ לֹא יִבְנֶה בַיִת שָׁוְא עָמְלוּ בוֹנָיו בּוֹ — *If HASHEM will not build the house, in vain do its builders labor on it.* The success of man's plans is totally dependent upon the will of God. Although David amassed resources for the construction of the Temple, God gave the privilege of carrying out the sacred project to David's son *(Ibn Ezra; Radak).*

שָׁוְא לָכֶם מַשְׁכִּימֵי קוּם מְאַחֲרֵי שֶׁבֶת — *It is vain for you who rise early, who sit up late.* Without God's help, builders will fail, though they work early and late and deprive themselves of food, rest, and tranquility. To His beloved ones, however, who trust in Him, and whose primary goal is spiritual growth, God will give restful sleep.

הִנֵּה נַחֲלַת ה׳ בָּנִים — *Behold! The heritage of HASHEM is children.* Previously, the Psalmist emphasized that human effort is in vain and that all depends upon the will of God. Nowhere is this more evident than in the bearing of children. The Talmud *(Taanis* 24a) teaches that although God granted control of many natural phenomena to the angels, He reserved for Himself the key of the womb, i.e., control over fertility. Thus, a woman does not conceive until the precise moment that God Himself has ordained, for God bequeaths the precious heritage of children to whomever He desires *(Ibn Ezra).*

Even after a healthy baby is born, God's constant vigilance and assistance are essential, for parents cannot train a child properly and imbue him with deep faith and strong character without Divine guidance *(Malbim).*

Some selfish people view each additional child as an unwelcome burden. Wise parents, however, realize that every newborn infant is a precious gift from God, which enables them to participate in the process of creation. Such a parent considers himself privileged to have been chosen as God's agent to raise a child, and he has unreserved confidence in God's ability and desire to assist him in his role as parent *(R' Hirsch).*

כְּחִצִּים בְּיַד גִּבּוֹר כֵּן בְּנֵי הַנְּעוּרִים — *Like arrows in the hand of a warrior* [lit. *mighty person*], *so are the children of youth.* When a father is still young, he possesses the patience and energy to give painstaking attention to developing his child's personality. The son becomes a sharpened arrow, i.e., a weapon in the legions of the Lord to wage

will reap in glad song. He who bears the measure of seeds walks along weeping, but will return in exultation, a bearer of his sheaves.*

Psalm 127

שִׁיר הַמַּעֲלוֹת *A song of ascents for Solomon.* If HASHEM will not build the house, in vain do its builders labor on it;* if HASHEM will not guard the city, in vain is the watchman vigilant. It is vain for you who rise early, who sit up late,* who eat the bread of sorrows — for indeed, He gives His beloved ones restful sleep. Behold! The heritage of HASHEM is children;* a reward, the fruit of the womb. Like arrows in the hand of a warrior, so are the children of youth.* Praiseworthy is the man who fills his quiver with them, they shall not be shamed, when they speak with enemies in the gate.**

Psalm 128

שִׁיר הַמַּעֲלוֹת *A song of ascents. Praiseworthy is each person who fears HASHEM,* who walks in His paths. When you eat the labor of your hands,* you are praiseworthy, and it is well with you. Your wife shall be like a fruitful vine in the inner chambers of your home;* your children shall be like olive shoots* surrounding your table. Behold! For so is blessed the man who fears HASHEM. May HASHEM bless you from Zion, and may you gaze upon the goodness of Jerusalem, all the days of your life.* And may you see children born to your children, peace upon Israel.*

---

ideological battles against the enemies of our faith *(Sforno).*

לֹא יֵבֹשׁוּ כִּי יְדַבְּרוּ אֶת אוֹיְבִים בַּשָּׁעַר — *They shall not be shamed, when they speak with enemies in the gate.* When the youthful father [or teacher] has taught his children properly, he can proudly and confidently display them in the gate, i.e., in public, for they will valiantly voice their support of what is right *(Sforno).*

☙ Psalm 128

אַשְׁרֵי כָּל יְרֵא ה׳ — *Praiseworthy is each person who fears HASHEM.* This verse presents a verbal portrait of the genuinely righteous Jew. Since he fears only God no mortal can intimidate him, not even the hostile conqueror who holds him captive in exile *(Maharam Arama).*

יְגִיעַ כַּפֶּיךָ כִּי תֹאכֵל — *When you eat the labor of your hands.* The Rabbis repeatedly praise honest labor. The merit of personal toil and effort exceeds זְכוּת אָבוֹת, *the merit of ancestors* ... Let no man say, 'I will eat, and drink, and enjoy life, without bothering to support myself. I have nothing to fear, for surely they will have mercy on me in heaven' [and provide for all my expenses]. As a rebuttal to this distorted thinking, Scripture states: *You bless the fruit of the labor of his hands (Job* 1:10), indicating that a man must toil and produce results with his own two hands. Only after man exerts effort does God send His blessing *(Tanchuma, Vayeitzei).*

אֶשְׁתְּךָ כְּגֶפֶן פֹּרִיָּה בְּיַרְכְּתֵי בֵיתֶךָ — *Your wife shall be like a fruitful vine in the inner chambers of your home.* The Jewish woman finds her palace and her paradise in the privacy of her home. There, she blossoms with contentment and raises children rich in vigor and health. When she is happy, her husband can go out to his work with an easy heart and his labors do not weigh upon him like a crushing burden. Thus the Psalmist compares the good-hearted wife to the grapevine, the noble plant whose fruits *gladden God and mankind (Judges* 9:13; *R' Hirsch).*

בָּנֶיךָ כִּשְׁתִלֵי זֵיתִים — *Your children shall be like olive shoots.* The olive tree is unique in that it is not affected by the changing seasons. It remains green and fresh all year round. Similarly, the children of the good wife and mother are of consistent high quality, their perfection never fails *(Radak).*

וּרְאֵה בְּטוּב יְרוּשָׁלָיִם כֹּל יְמֵי חַיֶּיךָ — *And may you gaze upon the goodness of Jerusalem, all the days of your life.* May you be among those privileged to be redeemed from exile and may you gaze upon the goodness of Jerusalem, as you return home to the Holy City. But even if you do not have the opportunity to return from exile, may you experience as much goodness as possible, all the days of your life, wherever you are *(Radak).*

This verse also alludes to the obligation to always view the holy city of Jerusalem in a positive way. One should try to see the good of Jerusalem at all times.

תהלים קכט

שִׁיר הַמַּעֲלוֹת, רַבַּת צְרָרְוּנִי מִנְּעוּרָי יֹאמַר נָא יִשְׂרָאֵל.* רַבַּת צְרָרְוּנִי מִנְּעוּרָי, גַּם לֹא יָכְלוּ לִי. עַל גַּבִּי חָרְשׁוּ חֹרְשִׁים, הֶאֱרִיכוּ לְמַעֲנִיתָם.* יהוה צַדִּיק, קִצֵּץ עֲבוֹת רְשָׁעִים. יֵבֹשׁוּ וְיִסֹּגוּ אָחוֹר כֹּל שֹׂנְאֵי צִיּוֹן.* יִהְיוּ כַּחֲצִיר גַּגּוֹת שֶׁקַּדְמַת שָׁלַף יָבֵשׁ. שֶׁלֹּא מִלֵּא כַפּוֹ קוֹצֵר, וְחִצְנוֹ מְעַמֵּר. וְלֹא אָמְרוּ הָעֹבְרִים, בִּרְכַּת יהוה אֲלֵיכֶם,* בֵּרַכְנוּ אֶתְכֶם בְּשֵׁם יהוה.

תהלים קל

שִׁיר הַמַּעֲלוֹת, מִמַּעֲמַקִּים קְרָאתִיךָ יהוה. אֲדֹנָי שִׁמְעָה בְקוֹלִי,* תִּהְיֶינָה אָזְנֶיךָ קַשֻּׁבוֹת לְקוֹל תַּחֲנוּנָי. אִם עֲוֹנוֹת תִּשְׁמָר יָהּ,* אֲדֹנָי מִי יַעֲמֹד. כִּי עִמְּךָ הַסְּלִיחָה, לְמַעַן תִּוָּרֵא. קִוִּיתִי יהוה קִוְּתָה נַפְשִׁי,* וְלִדְבָרוֹ הוֹחָלְתִּי. נַפְשִׁי לַאדֹנָי, מִשֹּׁמְרִים לַבֹּקֶר,* שֹׁמְרִים לַבֹּקֶר. יַחֵל יִשְׂרָאֵל אֶל יהוה, כִּי עִם יהוה הַחֶסֶד, וְהַרְבֵּה עִמּוֹ פְדוּת. וְהוּא יִפְדֶּה אֶת יִשְׂרָאֵל, מִכֹּל עֲוֹנוֹתָיו.

תהלים קלא

שִׁיר הַמַּעֲלוֹת, לְדָוִד, יהוה לֹא גָבַהּ לִבִּי, וְלֹא רָמוּ עֵינַי,* וְלֹא הִלַּכְתִּי בִּגְדֹלוֹת וּבְנִפְלָאוֹת מִמֶּנִּי. אִם לֹא שִׁוִּיתִי וְדוֹמַמְתִּי נַפְשִׁי,* כְּגָמֻל עֲלֵי אִמּוֹ, כַּגָּמֻל עָלַי נַפְשִׁי. יַחֵל יִשְׂרָאֵל אֶל יהוה, מֵעַתָּה וְעַד עוֹלָם.

תהלים קלב

שִׁיר הַמַּעֲלוֹת, זְכוֹר יהוה לְדָוִד, אֵת כָּל עֻנּוֹתוֹ.* אֲשֶׁר נִשְׁבַּע לַיהוה, נָדַר לַאֲבִיר יַעֲקֹב. אִם אָבֹא בְּאֹהֶל בֵּיתִי,* אִם אֶעֱלֶה עַל עֶרֶשׂ יְצוּעָי. אִם אֶתֵּן שְׁנָת לְעֵינָי, לְעַפְעַפַּי תְּנוּמָה. עַד

☙ Psalm 129

יֹאמַר נָא יִשְׂרָאֵל — *Let Israel declare now.* Now, after centuries and millennia have elapsed, Israel looks back at its history. The Jews' ability to survive all efforts to destroy them attests that the hand of God guides the course of Israel's history and shelters the Jews from all danger *(Radak).*

הֶאֱרִיכוּ לְמַעֲנִיתָם — *They lengthened their furrow.* The plowman never pauses while he is in the middle of a furrow, but waits until he reaches the end of the line. Thus, the longer the furrow, the longer the oxen must toil, without any respite. This alludes to Israel in exile who suffered over a lengthy period, without relief *(Radak).*

יֵבֹשׁוּ וְיִסֹּגוּ אָחוֹר כֹּל שֹׂנְאֵי צִיּוֹן — *Ashamed and turned back, will be all who hate Zion.* When God tears the 'ropes of the wicked ... who hate Zion,' their schemes against Israel will be frustrated and they will be shamed *(Radak).*

וְלֹא אָמְרוּ הָעֹבְרִים בִּרְכַּת ה׳ אֲלֵיכֶם — *And passers-by have never said, 'HASHEM's blessing to you.'* It was customary for passers-by to greet the reapers by invoking God's blessing upon them. Boaz, for example, told the reapers, ה׳ עִמָּכֶם, *HASHEM be with you (Ruth 2:4).* However, these greetings are extended only when the harvest is a bountiful blessing. The plucking of withered grass warrants no such benediction *(Radak).*

☙ Psalm 130

אֲדֹנָי שִׁמְעָה בְקוֹלִי — *My Lord, hear my voice.* Although I am extremely distant from You, and I have sunk to the most remote depths, please hear my voice *(Ibn Ezra).*

When a supplicant has the presence of mind to articulate his requests, he need not shout. But when misery robs him of his equanimity, he cries out in anguish *(Pri Tzaddik).*

אִם עֲוֹנוֹת תִּשְׁמָר יָהּ — *If You preserve iniquities, O God.* We cannot deny that we have sinned abundantly, but if God preserves our sins and refuses to forgive them unless we are totally deserving, we could not survive *(Ibn Ezra).*

Psalm 129

שִׁיר הַמַּעֲלוֹת *A song of ascents. Much have they distressed me since my youth, let Israel declare now.* Much have they distressed me since my youth, but they never conquered me. On my back the plowers plowed, they lengthened their furrow.* HASHEM is righteous, He cut the ropes of the wicked. Ashamed and turned back, will be all who hate Zion.* They shall be like the grass on rooftops, that, even before it is plucked, withers — with which the reaper cannot fill his hand, nor the binder of sheaves his arm. And passers-by have never said, 'HASHEM's blessing to you;* we bless you in the Name of HASHEM.'*

Psalm 130

שִׁיר הַמַּעֲלוֹת *A song of ascents. From the depths I called You, HASHEM. My Lord, hear my voice,* may Your ears be attentive to the sound of my pleas. If You preserve iniquities, O God,* my Lord, who could survive? For with You is forgiveness, that You may be feared. I put confidence in HASHEM, my soul put confidence,* and I hoped for His word. I yearn for my Lord, among those longing for the dawn,* those longing for the dawn. Let Israel hope for HASHEM, for with HASHEM is kindness, and with Him is abundant redemption. And He shall redeem Israel from all its iniquities.*

Psalm 131

שִׁיר הַמַּעֲלוֹת *A song of ascents, by David. HASHEM, my heart was not proud, and my eyes were not haughty,* nor did I pursue matters too great and too wondrous for me. I swear that I stilled and silenced my soul,* like a suckling child at his mother's side, like the suckling child is my soul. Let Israel hope to HASHEM, from this time and forever.*

Psalm 132

שִׁיר הַמַּעֲלוֹת *A song of ascents. O HASHEM, remember unto David all his suffering.* How he swore to HASHEM, and vowed to the Strong One of Jacob. 'If I enter the tent of my home;* if I go upon the bed that is spread for me; if I allow sleep to my eyes, slumber to my eyelids; before*

קִוִּיתִי ה׳ קִוְּתָה נַפְשִׁי — *I put confidence in HASHEM, my soul put confidence.* My body put confidence in HASHEM for physical security in This World, and *my soul placed confidence* in Him to merit the glory and spiritual bliss of the World to Come *(Radak; Ibn Yachya).*

נַפְשִׁי לַאדֹנָי מִשֹּׁמְרִים לַבֹּקֶר — *I yearn* [lit. *my soul*] *for my Lord, among those longing for the dawn.* I am among those who constantly look out for the first signs of the dawn of redemption. The phrase שֹׁמְרִים לַבֹּקֶר is repeated for emphasis: I have not been discouraged by hopeful signs which proved to be unfounded. Rather, I persistently watched for the morning, time and time again *(Rashi).*

Psalm 131

ה׳ לֹא גָבַהּ לִבִּי וְלֹא רָמוּ עֵינַי — *HASHEM, my heart was not proud, and my eyes were not haughty.* David conquered mighty kings, yet he banished pride from his heart, for whenever he had the inclination to be haughty, he was overwhelmed by a sense of fear and awe in the presence of God. And when David strode among his own people as their sovereign, his eyes never became lofty and arrogant, because he was constantly engrossed in Torah study *(Zohar, Mishpatim).*

אִם לֹא שִׁוִּיתִי וְדוֹמַמְתִּי נַפְשִׁי — *I swear that I stilled and silenced my soul.* The phrase אִם לֹא [literally, *if not*] is a form of oath; implying that if this is not so, let dire consequences occur *(Radak).*

Literally, שִׁוִּיתִי means *I equalized.* Thus: I have accepted everything with calm equanimity, and I am silent and composed because of my complete faith in God.

Psalm 132

זְכוֹר ה׳ לְדָוִד אֵת כָּל עֻנּוֹתוֹ — *O HASHEM, remember unto David all his suffering.* This refers to David's longing to build the Temple and, when God told him he could not do so, his sincere and unselfish labor to prepare the way for Solomon to accomplish the task.

אִם אָבֹא בְּאֹהֶל בֵּיתִי — *If I enter the tent of my home.* David vowed that he would not enjoy the

אֶמְצָא מָקוֹם לַיהוה,* מִשְׁכָּנוֹת לַאֲבִיר יַעֲקֹב. הִנֵּה שְׁמַעֲנוּהָ בְאֶפְרָתָה,* מְצָאנוּהָ בִּשְׂדֵי יָעַר. נָבוֹאָה לְמִשְׁכְּנוֹתָיו,* נִשְׁתַּחֲוֶה לַהֲדֹם רַגְלָיו. קוּמָה יהוה לִמְנוּחָתֶךָ,* אַתָּה וַאֲרוֹן עֻזֶּךָ. כֹּהֲנֶיךָ יִלְבְּשׁוּ צֶדֶק, וַחֲסִידֶיךָ יְרַנֵּנוּ. בַּעֲבוּר דָּוִד עַבְדֶּךָ, אַל תָּשֵׁב פְּנֵי מְשִׁיחֶךָ. נִשְׁבַּע יהוה לְדָוִד, אֱמֶת לֹא יָשׁוּב מִמֶּנָּה, מִפְּרִי בִטְנְךָ אָשִׁית לְכִסֵּא לָךְ. אִם יִשְׁמְרוּ בָנֶיךָ בְּרִיתִי, וְעֵדֹתִי זוֹ אֲלַמְּדֵם, גַּם בְּנֵיהֶם עֲדֵי עַד, יֵשְׁבוּ לְכִסֵּא לָךְ.* כִּי בָחַר יהוה בְּצִיּוֹן, אִוָּהּ לְמוֹשָׁב לוֹ. זֹאת מְנוּחָתִי עֲדֵי עַד, פֹּה אֵשֵׁב כִּי אִוִּתִיהָ. צֵידָהּ בָּרֵךְ אֲבָרֵךְ, אֶבְיוֹנֶיהָ אַשְׂבִּיעַ לָחֶם. וְכֹהֲנֶיהָ אַלְבִּישׁ יֶשַׁע, וַחֲסִידֶיהָ רַנֵּן יְרַנֵּנוּ. שָׁם אַצְמִיחַ קֶרֶן לְדָוִד,* עָרַכְתִּי נֵר לִמְשִׁיחִי. אוֹיְבָיו אַלְבִּישׁ בֹּשֶׁת, וְעָלָיו יָצִיץ נִזְרוֹ.

תהלים קלג

שִׁיר הַמַּעֲלוֹת, לְדָוִד, הִנֵּה מַה טּוֹב וּמַה נָּעִים, שֶׁבֶת אַחִים גַּם יָחַד.* כַּשֶּׁמֶן הַטּוֹב עַל הָרֹאשׁ* יֹרֵד עַל הַזָּקָן, זְקַן אַהֲרֹן שֶׁיֹּרֵד עַל פִּי מִדּוֹתָיו. כְּטַל חֶרְמוֹן שֶׁיֹּרֵד עַל הַרְרֵי צִיּוֹן, כִּי שָׁם צִוָּה יהוה אֶת הַבְּרָכָה, חַיִּים עַד הָעוֹלָם.

תהלים קלד

שִׁיר הַמַּעֲלוֹת, הִנֵּה בָּרְכוּ אֶת יהוה כָּל עַבְדֵי יהוה, הָעֹמְדִים בְּבֵית יהוה בַּלֵּילוֹת.* שְׂאוּ יְדֵכֶם קֹדֶשׁ, וּבָרְכוּ אֶת יהוה. יְבָרֶכְךָ יהוה מִצִּיּוֹן,* עֹשֵׂה שָׁמַיִם וָאָרֶץ.*

In the presence of a *minyan*, mourners recite קַדִּישׁ יָתוֹם (p. 528).
Then, the congregation continues with עָלֵינוּ (p. 526).

---

comforts of his own home until he prepared a home for God as he said *(II Samuel* 7:2): *Behold, please,* [how can] *I dwell in a cedar palace, when the Ark of God rests within a mere curtain? (Radak).*

עַד אֶמְצָא מָקוֹם לַה׳ — *Before I find a place for* HASHEM. David's first task was to find the place where God wished the Temple to be built.

הִנֵּה שְׁמַעֲנוּהָ בְאֶפְרָתָה — *Behold! We heard of it in Ephras.* When we were in Ephras, we heard the news of the Temple's eventual location. Ephras is a title of honor referring to a place where nobles and aristocrats gather *(Rashi).*

נָבוֹאָה לְמִשְׁכְּנוֹתָיו — *We will arrive at His Tabernacles.* The plural form מִשְׁכְּנוֹתָיו refers to the fact that the Temple erected on earth corresponded to a Temple of the Spirit, which was directly above it in heaven *(Alshich).*

קוּמָה ה׳ לִמְנוּחָתֶךָ — *Arise,* HASHEM, *to Your resting place.* The following three verses [by David] were repeated by Solomon [with minor variations] when he dedicated the Temple *(II Chronicles* 6:41-42). With these words, God was invited to change His dwelling place, so to speak, from His temporary abode in the מִשְׁכָּן, *Tabernacle,* to His permanent מְנוּחָה, *resting place,* in the Temple *(Radak).*

גַּם בְּנֵיהֶם עֲדֵי עַד יֵשְׁבוּ לְכִסֵּא לָךְ — *Then their sons, too, forever and ever, shall sit upon your throne.* The royal privilege belongs to David and to his seed for all generations. Anyone who believes in the truth of the Torah given by Moses, the master of all prophets, must believe that only those who descend from Solomon are fit for royalty. Anyone who is not of Solomon's distinguished seed is considered a total foreigner and alien to royalty, just as anyone who is not of Aaron's seed is totally alien to the priesthood and Temple service *(Ramban, Sefer HaMitzvos* 362).

שָׁם אַצְמִיחַ קֶרֶן לְדָוִד — *There I shall cause pride to sprout for David.* Pride refers to the power of kingship *(Targum).* The spiritual revival of the Messianic era is compared to the sprouting of a tree, because in exile Israel resembled a tree which withered and died *(Radak).*

☙ Psalm 133

שֶׁבֶת אַחִים גַּם יָחַד — *The dwelling of brothers, moreover, in unity.* Having spoken in the previous psalm of the Temple, David goes on to laud the idyllic state that will exist when all Jews live together in brotherly love — and unity will be in their hearts as well.

I find a place for HASHEM, resting places for the Strong One of Jacob.' Behold! We heard of it in Ephras,* we found it in the forested field. We will arrive at His Tabernacles,* we will prostrate ourselves at His footstool. Arise, HASHEM, to Your resting place,* You and the Ark of Your strength. Let Your priests be clothed in righteousness, and Your devout ones will sing joyously. For the sake of David, Your servant, turn not away the face of Your anointed. HASHEM has sworn to David, a truth from which He will never retreat: 'From the fruit of your issue I will place upon your throne. If your sons keep My covenant, and this, My testament, that I shall teach them, then their sons, too, forever and ever, shall sit upon your throne.'* For HASHEM has chosen Zion, He has desired it for His habitation. This is My resting place forever and ever, here I will dwell, for I have desired it. Her sustenance I will bless abundantly; her needy I will satisfy with food. I will clothe her priests with salvation; her devout ones will always sing joyously. There I shall cause pride to sprout for David;* I have prepared a lamp for My anointed. His enemies I will clothe with shame, but upon him, his crown will shine.*

Psalm 133

שִׁיר הַמַּעֲלוֹת *A song of ascents, by David. Behold, how good and how pleasant is the dwelling of brothers, moreover, in unity.* Like the precious oil upon the head* running down upon the beard, the beard of Aaron, running down over the hem of his garments. Like the dew of Hermon descending upon the mountains of Zion, for there HASHEM has commanded the blessing. May there be life forever!*

Psalm 134

שִׁיר הַמַּעֲלוֹת *A song of ascents. Behold, bless HASHEM, all you servants of HASHEM, who stand in the House of HASHEM in the nights.* Lift your hands in the Sanctuary and bless HASHEM. May HASHEM bless you from Zion,* Maker of heaven and earth.**

In the presence of a *minyan,* mourners recite קַדִּישׁ יָתוֹם, the Mourner's *Kaddish* (p. 528). Then the congregation continues with עָלֵינוּ, *Aleinu* (p. 526).

בְּשֶׁמֶן הַטּוֹב עַל הָרֹאשׁ — *Like the precious oil upon the head.* The Psalmist likens the flow of heavenly blessing to the precious oil with which High Priests and kings were anointed. Because Aaron was the first Jew to be anointed, he is used as the example. The oil ran from his head to his beard and clothing. So, too, when Jews are united in brotherhood, God's blessing will flow like a stream from Mount Hermon, the lofty mountain in the north, down to every nook and cranny of the land.

◆§ Psalm 134

הָעֹמְדִים בְּבֵית ה׳ בַּלֵּילוֹת — *Who stand in the House of HASHEM in the nights.* The genuine servant of HASHEM never abandons his post. Not only does he act as a guardian of the faith by day, i.e., in times of ease and success, but even at night, i.e., in times of adversity and gloom, he remains on guard and refuses to fall asleep at his post *(Malbim).*

The Talmud *(Menachos* 110a) says that this stich refers to the dedicated Torah scholars who arise to study in the middle of the night. God deems their self-sacrifice equal to service in His Holy Temple.

יְבָרֶכְךָ ה׳ מִצִּיּוֹן — *May HASHEM bless you from Zion.* This refers to the priestly blessing which was offered every day in the Holy Temple, and which drew the blessing of God upon all of Israel. Also, this refers to prayer in general. The Psalmist declares that whenever God responds to a Jew's prayer, He sends forth His blessings from Zion *(Radak).*

עֹשֵׂה שָׁמַיִם וָאָרֶץ — *Maker of heaven and earth.* When man is truly deserving, God will dispense blessings upon the earth directly from Zion, where God's Presence dwells on earth *(Malbim).*

This psalm is dedicated to the diligent Torah scholar. If his studies are purely for the sake of God, he has the power to remake heaven and earth. The Psalmist assures such a scholar that Hashem, Who is the Maker of heaven and earth, will readily bless him for helping return heaven and earth to their primeval purity through Torah and *mitzvos (Alshich).*

פרקי אבות

The chapters of *Pirkei Avos* are studied successively, one chapter each Sabbath, from Pesach until Rosh Hashanah.

פרק ראשון

כָּל יִשְׂרָאֵל יֵשׁ לָהֶם חֵלֶק לָעוֹלָם הַבָּא, שֶׁנֶּאֱמַר: „וְעַמֵּךְ כֻּלָּם צַדִּיקִים, לְעוֹלָם יִירְשׁוּ אָרֶץ, נֵצֶר מַטָּעַי, מַעֲשֵׂה יָדַי לְהִתְפָּאֵר.״[1]

❁ ❁ ❁

[א] **מֹשֶׁה** קִבֵּל תּוֹרָה מִסִּינַי, וּמְסָרָהּ לִיהוֹשֻׁעַ, וִיהוֹשֻׁעַ לִזְקֵנִים, וּזְקֵנִים לִנְבִיאִים, וּנְבִיאִים מְסָרוּהָ לְאַנְשֵׁי כְנֶסֶת הַגְּדוֹלָה. הֵם אָמְרוּ שְׁלשָׁה דְבָרִים: הֱווּ מְתוּנִים בַּדִּין, וְהַעֲמִידוּ תַלְמִידִים הַרְבֵּה, וַעֲשׂוּ סְיָג לַתּוֹרָה.

[ב] שִׁמְעוֹן הַצַּדִּיק הָיָה מִשְּׁיָרֵי כְנֶסֶת הַגְּדוֹלָה. הוּא הָיָה אוֹמֵר: עַל שְׁלשָׁה דְבָרִים הָעוֹלָם עוֹמֵד: עַל הַתּוֹרָה, וְעַל הָעֲבוֹדָה, וְעַל גְּמִילוּת חֲסָדִים.

[ג] אַנְטִיגְנוֹס אִישׁ סוֹכוֹ קִבֵּל מִשִּׁמְעוֹן הַצַּדִּיק. הוּא הָיָה אוֹמֵר: אַל תִּהְיוּ כַּעֲבָדִים הַמְשַׁמְּשִׁין אֶת הָרַב עַל מְנָת לְקַבֵּל פְּרָס; אֶלָּא הֱווּ כַּעֲבָדִים הַמְשַׁמְּשִׁין אֶת הָרַב שֶׁלֹּא עַל מְנָת לְקַבֵּל פְּרָס; וִיהִי מוֹרָא שָׁמַיִם עֲלֵיכֶם.

[ד] יוֹסֵי בֶּן יוֹעֶזֶר אִישׁ צְרֵדָה וְיוֹסֵי בֶּן יוֹחָנָן אִישׁ יְרוּשָׁלַיִם קִבְּלוּ מֵהֶם. יוֹסֵי בֶּן יוֹעֶזֶר אִישׁ צְרֵדָה אוֹמֵר: יְהִי בֵיתְךָ בֵּית וַעַד לַחֲכָמִים, וֶהֱוֵי

פִּרְקֵי אָבוֹת / ETHICS OF THE FATHERS

The Torah comprises the entire code of Jewish life — civil, religious, ritual law and ethical behavior as well. It is with the last area that the tractate *Avos* is primarily, though not exclusively, concerned. It contains the moral and practical teachings and exhortations of about sixty sages whose lives embraced nearly five centuries. But though their sayings would seem to carry no greater weight than that of their own considerable stature, the very first mishnah of the tractate teaches that this is not so. 'Moses received the Torah from Sinai and transmitted it,' we are told. The tradition contained in *Avos* originated no less at Sinai than did the Ten Commandments. Judaism melds ethics and morality with ritual and civil law into the total code of behavior contained in the Torah, expounded by the Sages, and embodied in practice into a living expression of God's will. The first five chapters of *Avos* constitute one of the Mishnaic tractates; the sixth chapter, too, is of Tannaitic authorship (see p. 580).

The Talmud *(Bava Kamma* 30a) teaches that one who wishes to be a devout and pious person should fulfill the dicta of *Avos*. Clearly, therefore, 'piety' refers to the full range of human behavior, and it is quite understandable that Jewish communities stressed the recitation and study of *Avos*. The custom of reciting it on Sabbath afternoons began in Gaonic times. In many communities, it was recited only from Pesach to Shavuos, as a preparation for the festival of the Revelation at Sinai. For that reason, too, the sixth chapter, which deals with Torah study, was appended to the five chapters of *Avos* as a fitting recitation for the Sabbath just before Shavuos. The prevalent custom nowadays is to continue the weekly recitation until Rosh Hashanah, so that the long summertime Sabbath afternoons can be filled with shared Torah study. Another reason for the summer study is that the pleasant weather tends to stimulate man's physical appetites; the study of *Avos* helps rein and direct them.

In many congregations, the chapter of the week is recited in unison after *Minchah* on the Sabbath, and followed by the Rabbis' *Kaddish*. In others, the recitation is left to the individual.

CHAPTER ONE

Prologue

כָּל יִשְׂרָאֵל — *All Israel.* This maxim is taken from the Mishnah, *Sanhedrin* 90a. It is read as an introduction to each chapter of *Avos* because it increases our incentive to apply ourselves to the teachings of this tractate. Since our ultimate reward in the World to Come is within reach, why should we not pursue the ways to attain it?

PIRKEI AVOS

The chapters of *Pirkei Avos* are studies successively, one chapter each Sabbath, from Pesach to Rosh Hashanah.

CHAPTER ONE

All Israel has a share in the World to Come, as it is said: 'And your people are all righteous; they shall inherit the land forever; they are the branch of My planting, My handiwork, in which to take pride.'[1]

❀ ❀ ❀

[1] **מֹשֶׁה** *Moses received the Torah from Sinai and transmitted it to Joshua; Joshua to the Elders; the Elders to the Prophets; and the Prophets transmitted it to the Men of the Great Assembly. They [the Men of the Great Assembly] said three things: Be deliberate in judgment; develop many disciples; and make a fence for the Torah.*

[2] *Shimon the Righteous was among the survivors of the Great Assembly. He used to say: The world depends on three things — on Torah study, on the service [of God], and on kind deeds.*

[3] *Antigonus, leader of Socho, received the tradition from Shimon the Righteous. He used to say: Be not like servants who serve their master for the sake of receiving a reward; instead be like servants who serve their master not for the sake of receiving a reward. And let the awe of Heaven be upon you.*

[4] *Yose ben Yoezer, leader of Tz'redah and Yose ben Yochanan, leader of Jerusalem, received the tradition from them. Yose ben Yoezer, leader of Tz'redah, says: Let your house be a meeting place for sages; sit in the*

(1) *Isaiah* 60:21.

The term *Israel* refers to any individual who has not utterly divorced himself from Israel's lofty spiritual and ethical destiny. His portion in the World to Come will vary according to his merit, but as long as he remains part of 'Israel,' he will never lose it entirely *(R' Hirsch).*

1. תּוֹרָה — *Torah.* The term Torah includes the Written Law (תּוֹרָה שֶׁבִּכְתָב, i.e., the Five Books of Moses), and the accompanying Oral Law (תּוֹרָה שֶׁבְּעַל פֶּה) — the interpretation of the Text as divinely handed down to Moses in its entirety and expounded by successive generations of Sages. Moses received the Torah from God at Sinai in full view of all the people. The mishnah describes this as מִסִּינַי, *from Sinai,* meaning, from God Who appeared at Sinai. Moses expounded the Torah to them during the forty years of their wanderings through the desert, and before he died he 'transferred' the tradition to Joshua to ensure its perpetuation.

אַנְשֵׁי כְנֶסֶת הַגְּדוֹלָה — *The Men of the Great Assembly.* This group of one hundred and twenty Sages led the Jewish people at the beginning of the Second Temple era. It included the last prophets, among them Ezra, Mordechai, Haggai, Zechariah and Malachi. As the Sages put it, the Assembly 'restored the crown of the Torah to its pristine splendor.' They laid the foundation of the liturgy, edited several of the Scriptural Books, provided for the intensified study of the Oral Law, and enacted many ordinances designed to prevent laxity in observance of the commandments.

סְיָג לַתּוֹרָה — *A fence* [protective bounds] *for the Torah.* Enact provisions and cautionary rules to safeguard against transgression of the laws of the Torah itself. For example, the Rabbis forbade even the handling of certain utensils on the Sabbath (מוּקְצֶה), lest one use them to perform a labor forbidden by the Torah.

2. הָעֲבוֹדָה — *The service* [*of God*], i.e., the sacrificial service in the Temple and, in the absence of the Temple, study of the laws regarding the service. In its broader sense, *service* refers to prayer and the performance of the commandments.

גְּמִילוּת חֲסָדִים — *Kind deeds,* i.e., the performance of benevolent acts between man and his fellow.

3. אַל תִּהְיוּ כַּעֲבָדִים — *Be not like servants* i.e., serve God out of love for Him, not merely because your good deeds will be rewarded.

מוֹרָא שָׁמַיִם — *Awe of Heaven.* This reverence must be maintained even though one has great love for God, for awe will inhibit one from transgressing His laws, while love not complemented by fear can sometimes lead one to take excessive liberties.

מִתְאַבֵּק בַּעֲפַר רַגְלֵיהֶם, וֶהֱוֵי שׁוֹתֶה בַצָּמָא אֶת דִּבְרֵיהֶם.

[ה] יוֹסֵי בֶּן יוֹחָנָן אִישׁ יְרוּשָׁלַיִם אוֹמֵר: יְהִי בֵיתְךָ פָּתוּחַ לִרְוָחָה, וְיִהְיוּ עֲנִיִּים בְּנֵי בֵיתֶךָ, וְאַל תַּרְבֶּה שִׂיחָה עִם הָאִשָּׁה. בְּאִשְׁתּוֹ אָמְרוּ, קַל וָחֹמֶר בְּאֵשֶׁת חֲבֵרוֹ. מִכָּאן אָמְרוּ חֲכָמִים: כָּל הַמַּרְבֶּה שִׂיחָה עִם הָאִשָּׁה — גּוֹרֵם רָעָה לְעַצְמוֹ, וּבוֹטֵל מִדִּבְרֵי תוֹרָה, וְסוֹפוֹ יוֹרֵשׁ גֵּיהִנֹּם.

[ו] יְהוֹשֻׁעַ בֶּן פְּרַחְיָה וְנִתַּאי הָאַרְבֵּלִי קִבְּלוּ מֵהֶם. יְהוֹשֻׁעַ בֶּן פְּרַחְיָה אוֹמֵר: עֲשֵׂה לְךָ רַב, וּקְנֵה לְךָ חָבֵר, וֶהֱוֵי דָן אֶת כָּל הָאָדָם לְכַף זְכוּת.

[ז] נִתַּאי הָאַרְבֵּלִי אוֹמֵר: הַרְחֵק מִשָּׁכֵן רָע, וְאַל תִּתְחַבֵּר לָרָשָׁע, וְאַל תִּתְיָאֵשׁ מִן הַפֻּרְעָנוּת.

[ח] יְהוּדָה בֶּן טַבַּאי וְשִׁמְעוֹן בֶּן שָׁטַח קִבְּלוּ מֵהֶם. יְהוּדָה בֶּן טַבַּאי אוֹמֵר: אַל תַּעַשׂ עַצְמְךָ כְּעוֹרְכֵי הַדַּיָּנִין; וּכְשֶׁיִּהְיוּ בַּעֲלֵי הַדִּין עוֹמְדִים לְפָנֶיךָ, יִהְיוּ בְעֵינֶיךָ כִּרְשָׁעִים; וּכְשֶׁנִּפְטָרִים מִלְּפָנֶיךָ, יִהְיוּ בְעֵינֶיךָ כְּזַכָּאִין, כְּשֶׁקִּבְּלוּ עֲלֵיהֶם אֶת הַדִּין.

[ט] שִׁמְעוֹן בֶּן שָׁטַח אוֹמֵר: הֱוֵי מַרְבֶּה לַחֲקוֹר אֶת הָעֵדִים; וֶהֱוֵי זָהִיר בִּדְבָרֶיךָ, שֶׁמָּא מִתּוֹכָם יִלְמְדוּ לְשַׁקֵּר.

[י] שְׁמַעְיָה וְאַבְטַלְיוֹן קִבְּלוּ מֵהֶם. שְׁמַעְיָה אוֹמֵר: אֱהֹב אֶת הַמְּלָאכָה, וּשְׂנָא אֶת הָרַבָּנוּת, וְאַל תִּתְוַדַּע לָרָשׁוּת.

[יא] אַבְטַלְיוֹן אוֹמֵר: חֲכָמִים, הִזָּהֲרוּ בְדִבְרֵיכֶם, שֶׁמָּא תָחוֹבוּ חוֹבַת גָּלוּת וְתִגְלוּ לִמְקוֹם מַיִם הָרָעִים, וְיִשְׁתּוּ הַתַּלְמִידִים הַבָּאִים אַחֲרֵיכֶם וְיָמוּתוּ, וְנִמְצָא שֵׁם שָׁמַיִם מִתְחַלֵּל.

[יב] הִלֵּל וְשַׁמַּאי קִבְּלוּ מֵהֶם. הִלֵּל אוֹמֵר: הֱוֵי מִתַּלְמִידָיו שֶׁל אַהֲרֹן, אוֹהֵב שָׁלוֹם וְרוֹדֵף שָׁלוֹם, אוֹהֵב אֶת הַבְּרִיּוֹת וּמְקָרְבָן לַתּוֹרָה.

---

4. וֶהֱוֵי מִתְאַבֵּק בַּעֲפַר רַגְלֵיהֶם — *Sit in the dust of their feet.* Attend to their needs *(Rav).* In Mishnaic times, the teacher sat on a bench and his pupils sat on the ground. Thus, Yose ben Yoezer exhorts us to become loyal disciples of the sages.

5. לִרְוָחָה — *Wide.* Make your home a center of hospitality. Some render לִרְוָחָה in the sense of *relief,* meaning that anyone who needs help of any sort can be sure of getting it from you.

וְאַל תַּרְבֶּה שִׂיחָה — *And do not converse excessively.* The Mishnah warns us against idle chatter and too much of it. A man who truly respects his wife will value her views and counsel and not overburden their conversation with frivolous chatter. Moreover, this sort of bantering with other women can loosen the bounds of morality and lead to sin *(R' Hirsch).*

גֵּיהִנֹּם — *Gehinnom.* The place where the souls of the wicked are punished.

6. עֲשֵׂה לְךָ רַב — *Accept a teacher upon yourself,* i.e., a competent mentor who can correctly transmit the tradition, and thereby avoid error. Be willing to submit to his direction, for without a mentor to respect, a person is directionless.

חָבֵר — *A friend,* with whom to jointly engage in Torah study. 'Either companionship or death', said the Talmudic sage, Choni [*Taanis* 23a]. *Rashi* suggests that our Mishnah means that one should acquire *books* — they are the best companions and are essential for acquiring Torah knowledge.

7. וְאַל תִּתְיָאֵשׁ מִן הַפֻּרְעָנוּת — *And do not despair of retribution.* The doctrine of Divine Retribution — that God eventually punishes the wicked — is one of the foundations of the Faith. Even though it seems slow in coming, one must remain confident that there will be a time of judgment; otherwise a good person may come to feel that evil and dishonesty will always be ascendant. This passage can also be interpreted: *Do not*

dust of their feet; and drink in their words thirstily.

[5] Yose ben Yochanan, leader of Jerusalem, says: Let your house be open wide; treat the poor as members of your household; and do not converse excessively with a woman. They said this even about one's own wife; surely it applies to another's wife. Consequently, the Sages said: Anyone who converses excessively with a woman causes evil to himself, neglects Torah study and will eventually inherit Gehinnom.

[6] Yehoshua ben Perachyah and Nittai of Arbel received the tradition from them. Yehoshua ben Perachyah says: Accept a teacher upon yourself; acquire a friend for yourself, and judge everyone favorably.

[7] Nittai of Arbel says: Distance yourself from a bad neighbor; do not associate with a wicked person; and do not despair of retribution.

[8] Yehudah ben Tabbai and Shimon ben Shatach received the tradition from them. Yehudah ben Tabbai says: [When serving as a judge] do not act as a lawyer; when the litigants stand before you, consider them both as guilty; but when they are dismissed from you, consider them both as innocent, provided they have accepted the judgment.

[9] Shimon ben Shatach says: Interrogate the witnesses extensively; and be cautious with your words, lest they learn to lie.

[10] Shemayah and Avtalyon received the tradition from them. Shemayah says: Love work; despise lordliness; and do not become overly familiar with the government.

[11] Avtalyon says: Scholars, be cautious with your words, for you may incur the penalty of exile and be banished to a place of evil waters [heresy]. The disciples who follow you there may drink and die, and consequently the Name of Heaven will be desecrated.

[12] Hillel and Shammai received the tradition from them. Hillel says: Be among the disciples of Aaron, loving peace and pursuing peace, loving people, and bringing them closer to the Torah.

---

despair because of punishment: Even though you have been punished, remain hopeful; you can repent in sincerity and be forgiven.

8. כְּעוֹרְכֵי הַדַּיָּנִין — *As a lawyer.* This is addressed to judges: In your role of impartial arbiter, do not counsel litigants how to plead their case. Even if you are convinced of an individual's righteousness, maintain your impartiality *(Rashi; R' Hirsch).*

כִּרְשָׁעִים — *As guilty.* Not that the judge assumes the litigant to be literally *guilty*, but that he must make every effort to establish the authenticity of every statement made before him. Only through rigorous probing will he ferret out the truth.

כְּזַכָּאִין — *As innocent.* Once the verdict has been accepted, even the guilty litigant is to be regarded as having pleaded and sworn truthfully according to his own interpretation of the facts. Or, he should be viewed as having repented *(R' Yonah).*

9. יִלְמְדוּ לְשַׁקֵּר — *Learn to lie.* Speak carefully to witnesses and litigants, lest the direction of your interrogation give them a hint on how to fabricate their testimony to tell you what they think you are looking for.

10. וּשְׂנָא אֶת הָרַבָּנוּת — *Despise lordliness,* i.e., do your utmost to avoid holding positions of dominance and leadership, for they shorten a man's life *(Rashi);* shun pompousness and rank.

לָרָשׁוּת — *The government,* i.e., tyrannical authorities, who merely exploit people for their own ends. Such associations cause one to neglect religion; one cannot be a servant to two masters.

11. חֲכָמִים, הִזָּהֲרוּ — *Scholars, be cautious.* The mishnah speaks allegorically of the dangerous results of unclear teachings that lend themselves to misinterpretation. Do not express yourself in a way that can be misunderstood by students other than your own. You may be forced into exile where unworthy students may sin, based on a misinterpretation of your teaching. If they die as a result of their sins, God's Name will have been desecrated.

12. אַהֲרֹן — *Aaron.* In Talmudic literature Aaron

[יג] הוּא הָיָה אוֹמֵר: נְגִיד שְׁמָא אֲבַד שְׁמֵהּ, וּדְלָא מוֹסִיף יָסֵף, וּדְלָא יַלִּיף קְטָלָא חַיָּב, וּדְאִשְׁתַּמֵּשׁ בְּתָגָא חֲלָף.

[יד] הוּא הָיָה אוֹמֵר: אִם אֵין אֲנִי לִי, מִי לִי? וּכְשֶׁאֲנִי לְעַצְמִי, מָה אֲנִי? וְאִם לֹא עַכְשָׁו, אֵימָתָי?

[טו] שַׁמַּאי אוֹמֵר: עֲשֵׂה תוֹרָתְךָ קֶבַע, אֱמֹר מְעַט וַעֲשֵׂה הַרְבֵּה, וֶהֱוֵי מְקַבֵּל אֶת כָּל הָאָדָם בְּסֵבֶר פָּנִים יָפוֹת.

[טז] רַבָּן גַּמְלִיאֵל הָיָה אוֹמֵר: עֲשֵׂה לְךָ רַב, וְהִסְתַּלֵּק מִן הַסָּפֵק, וְאַל תַּרְבֶּה לְעַשֵּׂר אֻמָּדוֹת.

[יז] שִׁמְעוֹן בְּנוֹ אוֹמֵר: כָּל יָמַי גָּדַלְתִּי בֵּין הַחֲכָמִים, וְלֹא מָצָאתִי לְגוּף טוֹב אֶלָּא שְׁתִיקָה. וְלֹא הַמִּדְרָשׁ הוּא הָעִקָּר, אֶלָּא הַמַּעֲשֶׂה. וְכָל הַמַּרְבֶּה דְבָרִים מֵבִיא חֵטְא.

[יח] רַבָּן שִׁמְעוֹן בֶּן גַּמְלִיאֵל אוֹמֵר: עַל שְׁלֹשָׁה דְבָרִים הָעוֹלָם קַיָּם — עַל הַדִּין וְעַל הָאֱמֶת וְעַל הַשָּׁלוֹם, שֶׁנֶּאֱמַר: „אֱמֶת וּמִשְׁפַּט שָׁלוֹם שִׁפְטוּ בְּשַׁעֲרֵיכֶם."[1]

❧ ❧ ❧

רַבִּי חֲנַנְיָא בֶּן עֲקַשְׁיָא אוֹמֵר: רָצָה הַקָּדוֹשׁ בָּרוּךְ הוּא לְזַכּוֹת אֶת יִשְׂרָאֵל, לְפִיכָךְ הִרְבָּה לָהֶם תּוֹרָה וּמִצְוֹת, שֶׁנֶּאֱמַר: „יהוה חָפֵץ לְמַעַן צִדְקוֹ, יַגְדִּיל תּוֹרָה וְיַאְדִּיר."[2]

In the presence of a *minyan,* mourners recite קַדִּישׁ דְּרַבָּנָן, the Rabbis' *Kaddish* (p. 52). Then the congregation continues with עָלֵינוּ (p. 526).

---

is described as the great peacemaker who went to any ends to make peace between man and wife and between feuding Jews.

13. אֲבַד שְׁמֵהּ — *Loses his reputation.* Selfish ambition to attain fame often results in one losing his reputation entirely.

יָסֵף — *Decreases it,* because he eventually forgets what he has learned previously. The translation follows *Rashi.* By refusing to share his Torah knowledge with others, one demonstrates his selfishness and his lack of concern for Torah learning, the paramount *mitzvah. R' Yonah* interprets that the mishnah refers to someone who is totally ignorant of the Torah's wisdom. Since he lacks the precious teaching that is the Jew's primary distinction, of what value is his life?

וּדְאִשְׁתַּמֵּשׁ בְּתָגָא חֲלָף — *And he who exploits the crown of Torah shall fade away.* This refers to one who abuses his Torah knowledge by using it as a common tool for selfish gains. *Rashi* explains that such a person forfeits reward for his Torah study in the Hereafter since he has already gained materially from it in the present.

14. This three-fold dictum refers to man's spiritual goals.

אִם אֵין אֲנִי לִי — *If I am not for myself,* i.e., if I do not rouse my soul to higher things, who will rouse it? If I do not fulfill the commandments, who will fulfill them for me?

וּכְשֶׁאֲנִי לְעַצְמִי — *And if I am for myself.* Even if I make the successful effort to grow spiritually, there is still so much more for me to do; consequently, I can never be satisfied with myself. Some comment that although man must work hard to perfect himself, he must not forget that he is part of a group that both helps him and should share in his accomplishments.

15. קֶבַע — *A fixed practice.* The study of Torah must be one's main occupation, and a regular time and schedule must be set aside for it. It must not be relegated to a secondary, casual, position in man's daily life, for Torah study determines the extent to which we will understand and fulfill our duties to God. In the ultimate sense every other pursuit is superfluous. Moreover, one should set a goal for his studies to maintain the discipline.

[13] *He used to say: He who seeks renown loses his reputation; he who does not increase [his Torah learning] decreases it; he who refuses to teach [Torah] deserves death; and he who exploits the crown of Torah shall fade away.*

[14] *He used to say: If I am not for myself, who will be for me? And if I am for myself, what am I? And if not now, when?*

[15] *Shammai says: Make your Torah study a fixed practice; say little and do much; and receive everyone with a cheerful face.*

[16] *Rabban Gamliel used to say: Accept a teacher upon yourself and remove yourself from uncertainty; and do not give excess tithes by estimating [instead of measuring].*

[17] *Shimon his son says: All my days I have been raised among the Sages and I found nothing better for oneself than silence; not study, but practice is the main thing; and one who talks excessively brings on sin.*

[18] *Rabban Shimon ben Gamliel says: The world endures on three things — justice, truth, and peace, as it is said: 'Truth and the verdict of peace are you to adjudicate in your gates.'*[1]

❀ ❀ ❀

Rabbi Chanania ben Akashia says: The Holy One, Blessed is He, wished to confer merit upon Israel; therefore He gave them Torah and mitzvos in abundance, as it is said: 'HASHEM desired, for the sake of its [Israel's] righteousness, that the Torah be made great and glorious.'[2]

In the presence of a *minyan,* mourners recite קַדִּישׁ דְּרַבָּנָן, the Rabbis' *Kaddish* (p. 52). Then the congregation continues with עָלֵינוּ, *Aleinu* (p. 526).

(1) *Zechariah* 8:16. (2) *Isaiah* 60:21.

וַעֲשֵׂה הַרְבֵּה — *And do much.* The righteous promise little but do much; the wicked make grandiose promises but do little.

16. עֲשֵׂה לְךָ רַב — *Accept a teacher upon yourself.* The same advice occurs in Mishnah 6. There the reference is to a teacher of Torah study, here to a teacher in practical matters of *halachah,* Torah Law. Alternatively this dictum is addressed to one who is himself an authority; even he needs another authority to consult in matters of practical halachic decisions.

וְהִסְתַּלֵּק מִן הַסָּפֵק — *And remove yourself from uncertainty,* i.e., in matters pertaining to Torah law. Moreover, avoid such things which may possibly be forbidden *(Machzor Vitry).*

אֻמָּדוֹת — *Estimating* [instead of measuring]. Tithes from the harvest must be exactly one-tenth; the allocation is to be precise, not made by guess work. *Meiri* perceives this in the broader sense as a caution against rendering halachic decisions by conjecture; one must meticulously examine the law until it is entirely clear to him, or let him consult others.

17. אֶלָּא הַמַּעֲשֶׂה — *But practice.* Though Torah study is paramount in importance beyond all other pursuits, it is the *performance* of the Torah's commandments for which man is rewarded. One must study with the intention of putting his knowledge into practice. Judaism is not a theology; it is a system of laws. The Torah's primary purpose is to regulate conduct.

18. הָעוֹלָם קַיָּם — *The world endures.* This is different from the maxim in mishnah 2. There, the Sages speak of the initial act of Creation, and the three things for which the world was created; here the reference is to the spiritual forces by which the social order is held together and civilization sustained.

רַבִּי חֲנַנְיָא בֶּן עֲקַשְׁיָא — *R' Chanania ben Akashia.* This excerpt is from the last mishnah in tractate *Makkos.* The Talmud teaches that the Rabbis' *Kaddish* (p. 52) is recited only after the public study of *Aggadah.* For this reason a standard portion of the Talmud was chosen for recitation after every public study session. Although *Avos* is Aggadic material, the universal custom of reciting this passage is maintained. The message of this excerpt is the reason it was chosen: Torah study and *mitzvah* performance are a Divinely-conferred privilege.

הַרְבָּה — *Gave ... in abundance.* That is, by giving Israel the opportunity of performing so many commandments, God graciously provided them with the means of acquiring abundant merit.

פרק שני

כָּל יִשְׂרָאֵל יֵשׁ לָהֶם חֵלֶק לָעוֹלָם הַבָּא, שֶׁנֶּאֱמַר: „וְעַמֵּךְ כֻּלָּם צַדִּיקִים, לְעוֹלָם יִירְשׁוּ אָרֶץ, נֵצֶר מַטָּעַי, מַעֲשֵׂה יָדַי לְהִתְפָּאֵר."[1]

❀ ❀ ❀

[א] **רַבִּי** אוֹמֵר: אֵיזוֹ הִיא דֶרֶךְ יְשָׁרָה שֶׁיָּבֹר לוֹ הָאָדָם? כָּל שֶׁהִיא תִפְאֶרֶת לְעֹשֶׂה וְתִפְאֶרֶת לוֹ מִן הָאָדָם. וֶהֱוֵי זָהִיר בְּמִצְוָה קַלָּה כְּבַחֲמוּרָה, שֶׁאֵין אַתָּה יוֹדֵעַ מַתַּן שְׂכָרָן שֶׁל מִצְוֹת. וֶהֱוֵי מְחַשֵּׁב הֶפְסֵד מִצְוָה כְּנֶגֶד שְׂכָרָהּ, וּשְׂכַר עֲבֵרָה כְּנֶגֶד הֶפְסֵדָהּ. הִסְתַּכֵּל בִּשְׁלשָׁה דְבָרִים, וְאֵין אַתָּה בָא לִידֵי עֲבֵרָה; דַּע מַה לְּמַעְלָה מִמְּךָ — עַיִן רוֹאָה, וְאֹזֶן שׁוֹמַעַת, וְכָל מַעֲשֶׂיךָ בַּסֵּפֶר נִכְתָּבִים.

[ב] רַבָּן גַּמְלִיאֵל בְּנוֹ שֶׁל רַבִּי יְהוּדָה הַנָּשִׂיא אוֹמֵר: יָפֶה תַלְמוּד תּוֹרָה עִם דֶּרֶךְ אֶרֶץ, שֶׁיְּגִיעַת שְׁנֵיהֶם מְשַׁכַּחַת עָוֹן. וְכָל תּוֹרָה שֶׁאֵין עִמָּהּ מְלָאכָה, סוֹפָהּ בְּטֵלָה וְגוֹרֶרֶת עָוֹן. וְכָל הָעוֹסְקִים עִם הַצִּבּוּר, יִהְיוּ עוֹסְקִים עִמָּהֶם לְשֵׁם שָׁמַיִם, שֶׁזְּכוּת אֲבוֹתָם מְסַיַּעְתָּם, וְצִדְקָתָם עוֹמֶדֶת לָעַד. וְאַתֶּם, מַעֲלֶה אֲנִי עֲלֵיכֶם שָׂכָר הַרְבֵּה כְּאִלּוּ עֲשִׂיתֶם.

[ג] הֱווּ זְהִירִין בָּרָשׁוּת, שֶׁאֵין מְקָרְבִין לוֹ לְאָדָם אֶלָּא לְצֹרֶךְ עַצְמָן; נִרְאִין כְּאוֹהֲבִין בִּשְׁעַת הֲנָאָתָן, וְאֵין עוֹמְדִין לוֹ לְאָדָם בִּשְׁעַת דָּחְקוֹ.

[ד] הוּא הָיָה אוֹמֵר: עֲשֵׂה רְצוֹנוֹ כִּרְצוֹנֶךָ, כְּדֵי שֶׁיַּעֲשֶׂה רְצוֹנְךָ כִּרְצוֹנוֹ. בַּטֵּל רְצוֹנְךָ מִפְּנֵי רְצוֹנוֹ, כְּדֵי שֶׁיְּבַטֵּל רְצוֹן אֲחֵרִים מִפְּנֵי רְצוֹנֶךָ.

[ה] הִלֵּל אוֹמֵר: אַל תִּפְרוֹשׁ מִן הַצִּבּוּר, וְאַל תַּאֲמִין בְּעַצְמְךָ עַד יוֹם מוֹתְךָ, וְאַל תָּדִין אֶת חֲבֵרְךָ עַד שֶׁתַּגִּיעַ לִמְקוֹמוֹ, וְאַל תֹּאמַר דָּבָר שֶׁאִי אֶפְשַׁר לִשְׁמוֹעַ, שֶׁסּוֹפוֹ לְהִשָּׁמַע. וְאַל תֹּאמַר לִכְשֶׁאֶפָּנֶה אֶשְׁנֶה, שֶׁמָּא לֹא תִפָּנֶה.

CHAPTER TWO

1. רַבִּי — *Rabbi.* This refers to R' Yehudah HaNassi ['the Prince'] (135-219 C.E.), redactor of the Mishnah, who was reverently referred to as *Rabbi,* teacher par excellence, and *Rabbeinu HaKadosh,* our Holy Teacher.

שֶׁאֵין אַתָּה יוֹדֵעַ מַתַּן שְׂכָרָן — *For you do not know the reward given.* God did not reveal the specific rewards for performance of the respective commandments lest everyone strive to observe only those that will earn him a greater reward.

וֶהֱוֵי מְחַשֵּׁב — *Calculate the cost.* Disregard the cost in time or money in fulfilling a *mitzvah.* Likewise, do not be misled by the pleasure or profit of a sin. Instead, calculate the eternal reward for a *mitzvah* against the temporary loss it may cause, and the eternal cost of a sin against the temporary benefit it may bring.

הִסְתַּכֵּל בִּשְׁלשָׁה דְבָרִים — *Consider three things.* Consider three aspects of *what is above you* and you will avoid sin. The three aspects are: (a) Man's deeds are observed; (b) his words are heard; (c) he cannot escape the consequences of his behavior because everything he does and says is indelibly recorded.

2. עִם דֶּרֶךְ אֶרֶץ — *With an occupation.* The ideal for spiritual reflection is a synthesis of diligent Torah study combined with an honest occupation for support. If a man's day is thereby filled, idleness that leads to sin is avoided. Others render דֶּרֶךְ אֶרֶץ in the familiar sense of *proper social conduct* which combined with Torah study is a deterrent to sin.

סוֹפָהּ בְּטֵלָה וְגוֹרֶרֶת עָוֹן — *Will cease in the end, and leads to sin.* Without a means of support, a scholar will find it impossible to continue his studies, and the press of his needs may lead him to dishonesty.

מַעֲלֶה אֲנִי עֲלֵיכֶם — *I [God] will bestow upon you.*

CHAPTER TWO

All Israel has a share in the World to Come, as it is said: 'And your people are all righteous; they shall inherit the land forever; they are the branch of My planting, My handiwork, in which to take pride.'[1]

❦ ❦ ❦

[1] **רַבִּי** *Rabbi said: Which is the proper path that a man should choose for himself? Whatever is a credit to himself and earns him the esteem of fellow men. Be as scrupulous in performing a 'minor' mitzvah as in a 'major' one, for you do not know the reward given for the respective mitzvos. Calculate the cost of a mitzvah against its reward, and the reward of a sin against its cost. Consider three things and you will not come into the grip of sin: Know what is above you — a watchful Eye, an attentive Ear and all your deeds are recorded in a Book.*

[2] *Rabban Gamliel, the son of Rabbi Judah HaNassi, says: Torah study is good together with an occupation, for the exertion of them both makes sin forgotten. All Torah study that is not joined with work will cease in the end, and leads to sin. All who exert themselves for the community should exert themselves for the sake of Heaven, for then the merit of the community's forefathers aids them and their righteousness endures forever. Nevertheless, as for you, I [God] will bestow upon you as great a reward as if you had accomplished it on your own.*

[3] *Beware of rulers, for they befriend someone only for their own benefit; they act friendly when it benefits them, but they do not stand by someone in his time of need.*

[4] *He used to say: Treat His will as if it were your own will, so that He will treat your will as if it were His will. Nullify your will before His will, so that He will nullify the will of others before your will.*

[5] *Hillel said: Do not separate yourself from the community; do not believe in yourself until the day you die; do not judge your fellow until you have reached his place; do not make a statement that cannot be easily understood on the ground that it will be understood eventually; and do not say, 'When I am free I will study,' for perhaps you will not become free.*

(1) *Isaiah* 60:21.

Although your success was due in great measure to the ancestral merit of the community you serve, God will reward your unselfish efforts as if you alone were responsible for your accomplishments.

3. בְּרָשׁוּת — *Of rulers.* Although servants of the community must often deal with the government, they should always be vigilant, for the interests of rulers and those of the community may not coincide.

4. עֲשֵׂה רְצוֹנוֹ כִּרְצוֹנְךָ — ***Treat His will as if it were your own will.*** Devote as much time and money to *mitzvos* as to your own desires. In return, God will help you beyond all expectations.

5. אַל תִּפְרוֹשׁ מִן הַצִּבּוּר — *Do not separate yourself from the community.* Share its woes and do nothing to undermine its solidarity.

וְאַל תַּאֲמִין בְּעַצְמְךָ — *Do not believe in yourself.* Piety must never be taken for granted. One must remain on guard against sin throughout his life.

עַד שֶׁתַּגִּיעַ לִמְקוֹמוֹ — *Until you have reached his place.* You never know how you would react if you were in the same predicament. You cannot condemn a person who succumbed to temptation unless you have overcome a similar challenge.

וְאַל תֹּאמַר — *And do not say.* One's words must be immediately understandable to the listener. Unless a teacher makes himself clear, his doctrine may be misinterpreted and cause harm.

לִכְשֶׁאֶפָּנֶה — *When I am free.* The Evil Inclination always urges you to wait for a more opportune time. Rather, every available moment, no matter how short and seemingly insignificant, should be utilized for Torah study.

[ו] הוּא הָיָה אוֹמֵר: אֵין בּוּר יְרֵא חֵטְא, וְלֹא עַם הָאָרֶץ חָסִיד, וְלֹא הַבַּיְשָׁן לָמֵד, וְלֹא הַקַּפְּדָן מְלַמֵּד, וְלֹא כָל הַמַּרְבֶּה בִסְחוֹרָה מַחְכִּים, וּבִמְקוֹם שֶׁאֵין אֲנָשִׁים הִשְׁתַּדֵּל לִהְיוֹת אִישׁ.

[ז] אַף הוּא רָאָה גֻלְגֹּלֶת אַחַת שֶׁצָּפָה עַל פְּנֵי הַמָּיִם. אָמַר לָהּ: „עַל דַּאֲטֵפְתְּ אַטְפוּךְ, וְסוֹף מְטַיְּפַיִךְ יְטוּפוּן.״

[ח] הוּא הָיָה אוֹמֵר: מַרְבֶּה בָשָׂר, מַרְבֶּה רִמָּה; מַרְבֶּה נְכָסִים, מַרְבֶּה דְאָגָה; מַרְבֶּה נָשִׁים, מַרְבֶּה כְשָׁפִים; מַרְבֶּה שְׁפָחוֹת, מַרְבֶּה זִמָּה; מַרְבֶּה עֲבָדִים, מַרְבֶּה גָזֵל. מַרְבֶּה תוֹרָה, מַרְבֶּה חַיִּים; מַרְבֶּה יְשִׁיבָה, מַרְבֶּה חָכְמָה; מַרְבֶּה עֵצָה, מַרְבֶּה תְבוּנָה; מַרְבֶּה צְדָקָה, מַרְבֶּה שָׁלוֹם. קָנָה שֵׁם טוֹב, קָנָה לְעַצְמוֹ; קָנָה לוֹ דִבְרֵי תוֹרָה, קָנָה לוֹ חַיֵּי הָעוֹלָם הַבָּא.

[ט] רַבָּן יוֹחָנָן בֶּן זַכַּאי קִבֵּל מֵהִלֵּל וּמִשַּׁמַּאי. הוּא הָיָה אוֹמֵר: אִם לָמַדְתָּ תּוֹרָה הַרְבֵּה, אַל תַּחֲזִיק טוֹבָה לְעַצְמְךָ, כִּי לְכַךְ נוֹצָרְתָּ.

[י] חֲמִשָּׁה תַלְמִידִים הָיוּ לוֹ לְרַבָּן יוֹחָנָן בֶּן זַכַּאי, וְאֵלּוּ הֵן: רַבִּי אֱלִיעֶזֶר בֶּן הֻרְקְנוֹס, רַבִּי יְהוֹשֻׁעַ בֶּן חֲנַנְיָא, רַבִּי יוֹסֵי הַכֹּהֵן, רַבִּי שִׁמְעוֹן בֶּן נְתַנְאֵל, וְרַבִּי אֶלְעָזָר בֶּן עֲרָךְ.

[יא] הוּא הָיָה מוֹנֶה שִׁבְחָן: רַבִּי אֱלִיעֶזֶר בֶּן הֻרְקְנוֹס, בּוֹר סוּד שֶׁאֵינוֹ מְאַבֵּד טִפָּה; רַבִּי יְהוֹשֻׁעַ בֶּן חֲנַנְיָא, אַשְׁרֵי יוֹלַדְתּוֹ; רַבִּי יוֹסֵי הַכֹּהֵן, חָסִיד; רַבִּי שִׁמְעוֹן בֶּן נְתַנְאֵל, יְרֵא חֵטְא; וְרַבִּי אֶלְעָזָר בֶּן עֲרָךְ, כְּמַעְיָן הַמִּתְגַּבֵּר.

[יב] הוּא הָיָה אוֹמֵר: אִם יִהְיוּ כָּל חַכְמֵי יִשְׂרָאֵל בְּכַף מֹאזְנַיִם, וֶאֱלִיעֶזֶר בֶּן הֻרְקְנוֹס בְּכַף שְׁנִיָּה, מַכְרִיעַ אֶת כֻּלָּם. אַבָּא שָׁאוּל אוֹמֵר מִשְּׁמוֹ: אִם יִהְיוּ כָּל חַכְמֵי יִשְׂרָאֵל בְּכַף מֹאזְנַיִם, וְרַבִּי אֱלִיעֶזֶר בֶּן הֻרְקְנוֹס אַף עִמָּהֶם, וְרַבִּי אֶלְעָזָר בֶּן עֲרָךְ בְּכַף שְׁנִיָּה, מַכְרִיעַ אֶת כֻּלָּם.

[יג] אָמַר לָהֶם: צְאוּ וּרְאוּ אֵיזוֹ הִיא דֶּרֶךְ טוֹבָה שֶׁיִּדְבַּק בָּהּ הָאָדָם. רַבִּי אֱלִיעֶזֶר אוֹמֵר: עַיִן טוֹבָה. רַבִּי יְהוֹשֻׁעַ אוֹמֵר: חָבֵר טוֹב. רַבִּי יוֹסֵי

---

6. בּוּר — *Boor.* An uncultivated and uncivilized person has little regard for right and wrong.

עַם הָאָרֶץ — *Unlearned person,* i.e., unlearned in Torah. The term חָסִיד, *scrupulously pious,* refers to someone who goes further than the minimum requirements of the law. An unlearned person remains blind to the requirements of the law, and so cannot be pious.

הַקַּפְּדָן — *The quick, impatient person.* Because he will not tolerate questions, students will be afraid to seek clarification.

שֶׁאֵין אֲנָשִׁים — *Where there are no leaders* [lit. *men*]. Where there is no one to accept communal and spiritual responsibility and provide leadership, we are bidden to rise to the occasion and fill the role. The implication, however, is that where there are competent 'men,' we are to stand aside and devote ourselves to the study of Torah *(Rashi).* According to *R' Yonah,* the 'leader' is someone to direct us upon the proper path of God's service. In the absence of such a person, we must strive to improve ourselves.

7. עַל דַּאֲטֵפְתְּ — *Because you drowned others.* Moved by this sight of a floating skull that had been deprived of proper burial *(Tiferes Yisrael),* Hillel remarked aloud about the justice of Divine retribution: God punishes man 'measure for measure.' Nothing man experiences in life is without reason. The commentators agree that Hillel meant his statement only in *general* terms, but he did not mean that every corpse was that of

[6] *He used to say: A boor cannot be fearful of sin; an unlearned person cannot be scrupulously pious; the bashful person cannot learn, and the quick, impatient person cannot teach; anyone excessively occupied in business cannot become a scholar; and in a place where there are no leaders, strive to be a leader.*

[7] *He also saw a skull floating on the water; he said to it: 'Because you drowned others, they drowned you; and those who drowned you will be drowned eventually.'*

[8] *He used to say: The more flesh, the more worms; the more possessions, the more worry; the more wives, the more witchcraft; the more maidservants, the more lewdness; the more manservants, the more thievery. [However] the more Torah, the more life; the more study, the more wisdom; the more counsel, the more understanding; the more charity, the more peace. One who has gained a good reputation, has gained it for his own benefit; one who has gained himself Torah knowledge, has gained himself the life of the World to Come.*

[9] *Rabban Yochanan ben Zakkai received the tradition from Hillel and Shammai. He used to say: If you have studied much Torah, do not take credit for yourself, because that is what you were created to do.*

[10] *Rabban Yochanan ben Zakkai had five [primary] disciples. They were: Rabbi Eliezer ben Hyrkanos, Rabbi Yehoshua ben Chanania, Rabbi Yose the Kohen, Rabbi Shimon ben Nesanel, and Rabbi Elazar ben Arach.*

[11] *He used to enumerate their praises: Rabbi Eliezer ben Hyrkanos is like a cemented cistern that loses not a drop; Rabbi Yehoshua ben Chanania, praiseworthy is she who bore him; Rabbi Yose the Kohen is a scrupulously pious person; Rabbi Shimon ben Nesanel fears sin; and Rabbi Elazar ben Arach is like a spring flowing stronger and stronger.*

[12] *He used to say: If all the sages of Israel were on one pan of a balance-scale, and Eliezer ben Hyrkanos were on the other, he would outweigh them all. Abba Shaul said in his name: If all the sages of Israel, with even Rabbi Eliezer ben Hyrkanos among them, were on one pan of the balance-scale, and Rabbi Elazar ben Arach were on the other, he would outweigh them all.*

[13] *He said to them: Go out and discern which is the proper way to which a man should cling. Rabbi Eliezer says: A good eye. Rabbi Yehoshua says:*

---

a murderer. Many victims had never committed such a crime, but Hillel's point was that there is always justice in God's scheme.

יְטוּפוּן — *Will be drowned.* Those who drowned you, too, were not guiltless, and therefore God used them as His tools to perpetrate this illegal act [מְגַלְגְּלִין חוֹב עַל יְדֵי חַיָּב]. Accordingly they will also be punished.

8. The dicta in this mishnah denounce excess and overindulgence in life; only extensive Torah study and piety bring beneficial results. While other things might *seem* desirable to many, they can have an adverse affect on those who pursue them.

רִמָּה — *Worms.* One's corpulent body becomes food for maggots in the grave; a denunciation of gluttony.

כְּשָׁפִים — *Witchcraft.* This condemnation of polygamy focuses upon the jealousy between rival wives. They may resort to anything — even witchcraft — to gain their husband's affection.

9. כִּי לְכַךְ נוֹצָרְתָּ — *Because that is what you were created to do.* Intelligence was given you only for the purpose of acquiring knowledge, and you may not become arrogant for having utilized this knowledge any more than a bird may for utilizing his wings to fly *(Mesilas Yesharim).*

11. שֶׁאֵינוֹ מְאַבֵּד טִפָּה — *That loses not a drop.* He retained everything he ever learned.

13. אָמַר לָהֶם — *He said to them.* Rabban Yochanan to his disciples.

שֶׁיִּדְבַּק — *Should cling.* In order to live meritoriously and inherit the life of the World to Come.

אוֹמֵר: שָׁכֵן טוֹב. רַבִּי שִׁמְעוֹן אוֹמֵר: הָרוֹאֶה אֶת הַנּוֹלָד. רַבִּי אֶלְעָזָר אוֹמֵר: לֵב טוֹב. אָמַר לָהֶם: רוֹאֶה אֲנִי אֶת דִּבְרֵי אֶלְעָזָר בֶּן עֲרָךְ מִדִּבְרֵיכֶם, שֶׁבִּכְלַל דְּבָרָיו דִּבְרֵיכֶם.

[יד] אָמַר לָהֶם: צְאוּ וּרְאוּ אֵיזוֹ הִיא דֶּרֶךְ רָעָה שֶׁיִּתְרַחֵק מִמֶּנָּה הָאָדָם. רַבִּי אֱלִיעֶזֶר אוֹמֵר: עַיִן רָעָה. רַבִּי יְהוֹשֻׁעַ אוֹמֵר: חָבֵר רָע. רַבִּי יוֹסֵי אוֹמֵר: שָׁכֵן רָע. רַבִּי שִׁמְעוֹן אוֹמֵר: הַלֹּוֶה וְאֵינוֹ מְשַׁלֵּם. אֶחָד הַלֹּוֶה מִן הָאָדָם כְּלֹוֶה מִן הַמָּקוֹם, שֶׁנֶּאֱמַר: „לֹוֶה רָשָׁע וְלֹא יְשַׁלֵּם, וְצַדִּיק חוֹנֵן וְנוֹתֵן."[1] רַבִּי אֶלְעָזָר אוֹמֵר: לֵב רָע. אָמַר לָהֶם: רוֹאֶה אֲנִי אֶת דִּבְרֵי אֶלְעָזָר בֶּן עֲרָךְ מִדִּבְרֵיכֶם, שֶׁבִּכְלַל דְּבָרָיו דִּבְרֵיכֶם.

[טו] הֵם אָמְרוּ שְׁלֹשָׁה דְבָרִים. רַבִּי אֱלִיעֶזֶר אוֹמֵר: יְהִי כְבוֹד חֲבֵרְךָ חָבִיב עָלֶיךָ כְּשֶׁלָּךְ, וְאַל תְּהִי נוֹחַ לִכְעוֹס; וְשׁוּב יוֹם אֶחָד לִפְנֵי מִיתָתְךָ; וֶהֱוֵי מִתְחַמֵּם כְּנֶגֶד אוּרָן שֶׁל חֲכָמִים, וֶהֱוֵי זָהִיר בְּגַחַלְתָּן שֶׁלֹּא תִכָּוֶה — שֶׁנְּשִׁיכָתָן נְשִׁיכַת שׁוּעָל, וַעֲקִיצָתָן עֲקִיצַת עַקְרָב, וּלְחִישָׁתָן לְחִישַׁת שָׂרָף, וְכָל דִּבְרֵיהֶם כְּגַחֲלֵי אֵשׁ.

[טז] רַבִּי יְהוֹשֻׁעַ אוֹמֵר: עַיִן הָרָע, וְיֵצֶר הָרָע, וְשִׂנְאַת הַבְּרִיּוֹת מוֹצִיאִין אֶת הָאָדָם מִן הָעוֹלָם.

[יז] רַבִּי יוֹסֵי אוֹמֵר: יְהִי מָמוֹן חֲבֵרְךָ חָבִיב עָלֶיךָ כְּשֶׁלָּךְ; וְהַתְקֵן עַצְמְךָ לִלְמוֹד תּוֹרָה, שֶׁאֵינָהּ יְרֻשָּׁה לָךְ; וְכָל מַעֲשֶׂיךָ יִהְיוּ לְשֵׁם שָׁמָיִם.

[יח] רַבִּי שִׁמְעוֹן אוֹמֵר: הֱוֵי זָהִיר בִּקְרִיאַת שְׁמַע וּבִתְפִלָּה; וּכְשֶׁאַתָּה מִתְפַּלֵּל, אַל תַּעַשׂ תְּפִלָּתְךָ קֶבַע, אֶלָּא רַחֲמִים וְתַחֲנוּנִים לִפְנֵי הַמָּקוֹם, שֶׁנֶּאֱמַר: „כִּי חַנּוּן וְרַחוּם הוּא אֶרֶךְ אַפַּיִם וְרַב חֶסֶד וְנִחָם עַל הָרָעָה"[2]; וְאַל תְּהִי רָשָׁע בִּפְנֵי עַצְמֶךָ.

[יט] רַבִּי אֶלְעָזָר אוֹמֵר: הֱוֵי שָׁקוּד לִלְמוֹד תּוֹרָה, וְדַע מַה שֶׁתָּשִׁיב לְאֶפִּיקוֹרוֹס; וְדַע לִפְנֵי מִי אַתָּה עָמֵל; וְנֶאֱמָן הוּא בַּעַל מְלַאכְתְּךָ, שֶׁיְּשַׁלֶּם לְךָ שְׂכַר פְּעֻלָּתֶךָ.

עַיִן טוֹבָה — *A good eye.* An attitude of tolerance and benevolence toward others.

חָבֵר טוֹב — *A good friend.* Both *being* one and *acquiring* one. [See note to 1:6.]

שָׁכֵן טוֹב — *A good neighbor,* even more influential than a *good friend.* Because of his close proximity, one has more opportunity to learn from his good behavior.

הָרוֹאֶה אֶת הַנּוֹלָד — *One who considers the outcome of a deed.* This does not refer to prophetic foresight, but to one who foresees the consequences of his actions.

לֵב טוֹב — *A good heart.* The *heart* symbolizes the emotion and desire that are at the root of every endeavor, aspiration, spiritual tendency, and achievement. Thus the term לֵב טוֹב includes all the stimuli that lead people toward goodness, provided they obey the dictates of their noble instincts.

14. עַיִן רָעָה — *An evil eye,* i.e., greed, ill will; the opposite of a 'good eye' in the previous mishnah.

כְּלֹוֶה מִן הַמָּקוֹם — *Is like one who borrows from the Omnipresent.* When a borrower betrays the lender who trusted him, God Himself — צַדִּיק, the *Righteous One* — recompenses the lender. Thus, it is as if the borrower took the money from God.

15. הֵם אָמְרוּ — *They each* [i.e., each of the five disciples mentioned in Mishnah 10] *said three things* on the subject of ethics.

וְשׁוּב יוֹם אֶחָד לִפְנֵי מִיתָתְךָ — *Repent one day before*

A good friend. Rabbi Yose says: A good neighbor. Rabbi Shimon says: One who considers the outcome of a deed. Rabbi Elazar says: A good heart. He [Rabban Yochanan ben Zakkai] said to them: I prefer the words of Elazar ben Arach to your words, for your words are included in his words.

[14] *He said to them: Go out and discern which is the evil path from which a man should distance himself. Rabbi Eliezer says: An evil eye. Rabbi Yehoshua says: A wicked friend. Rabbi Yose says: A wicked neighbor. Rabbi Shimon says: One who borrows and does not repay; one who borrows from man is like one who borrows from the Omnipresent, as it is said: 'The wicked one borrows and does not repay, but the Righteous One is gracious and gives.'*[1] *Rabbi Elazar said: A wicked heart. He [Rabban Yochanan ben Zakkai] said to them: I prefer the words of Elazar ben Arach to your words, for your words are included in his words.*

[15] *They each said three things. Rabbi Eliezer says: (a) Let your fellow's honor be as dear to you as your own and do not anger easily; (b) repent one day before your death; and (c) warm yourself by the fire of the sages, but beware of their glowing coal lest you be burnt — for their bite is the bite of a fox, their sting is the sting of a scorpion, their hiss is the hiss of a serpent, and all their words are like fiery coals.*

[16] *Rabbi Yehoshua says: (a) An evil eye, (b) the evil inclination, and (c) hatred of other people remove a person from the world.*

[17] *Rabbi Yose says: (a) Let your fellow's money be as dear to you as your own; (b) apply yourself to study Torah, for it is not yours by inheritance; and (c) let all your deeds be for the sake of Heaven.*

[18] *Rabbi Shimon says: (a) Be meticulous in reading the Shema and in prayer; (b) when you pray, do not make your prayer a set routine, but rather [beg for] compassion and supplication before the Omnipresent, as it is said: 'For He is gracious and compassionate, slow to anger, abounding in kindness, and relentful of punishment;'*[2] *and (c) do not judge yourself to be a wicked person.*

[19] *Rabbi Elazar says: (a) Be diligent in the study of Torah and know what to answer a heretic; (b) know before Whom you toil; and (c) know that your Employer can be relied upon to pay you the wage of your labor.*

(1) *Psalms* 37:21. (2) *Joel* 2:13.

---

your death. R' Eliezer's disciples asked, 'But does one know the day of his death?' He explained, 'Let him repent each day lest he die on the morrow.'

וֶהֱוֵי מִתְחַמֵּם כְּנֶגֶד אוּרָן שֶׁל חֲכָמִים — *Warm yourself by the fire of the sages.* One should keep in close contact with Torah scholars to learn from their ways. However, if he becomes too close, to the point where he becomes casual and disrespectful, they may burn him with a stinging admonition.

17. שֶׁאֵינָהּ יְרֻשָּׁה לָךְ — *For it is not yours by inheritance.* One cannot attain scholarship on the merit of his father's studies; everyone must acquire knowledge by personal effort.

לְשֵׁם שָׁמָיִם — *For the sake of Heaven.* For the sake of God, i.e., with pure purpose and good intentions. Every action, however mundane and secular, should be consecrated to the service of God, and not merely done for personal benefit. For example, one should always intend that even his eating, sleeping, etc., are for the purpose of strengthening his body for serving God.

18. וְאַל תְּהִי רָשָׁע בִּפְנֵי עַצְמָךְ — *And do not judge yourself to be a wicked person.* This teaches the obligation for self-esteem. Do not consider yourself so beyond help that you lose hope for Divine mercy, and as a result you do not pray properly and repent. If you give up on yourself, you will fall.

19. וְדַע מַה שֶּׁתָּשִׁיב לְאֶפִּיקוֹרוֹס — *And know what to answer a heretic.* Immerse yourself in Torah knowledge and laws so you can defend the Torah against malicious opponents.

[כ] רַבִּי טַרְפוֹן אוֹמֵר: הַיּוֹם קָצֵר, וְהַמְּלָאכָה מְרֻבָּה, וְהַפּוֹעֲלִים עֲצֵלִים, וְהַשָּׂכָר הַרְבֵּה, וּבַעַל הַבַּיִת דּוֹחֵק.

[כא] הוּא הָיָה אוֹמֵר: לֹא עָלֶיךָ הַמְּלָאכָה לִגְמוֹר, וְלֹא אַתָּה בֶן חוֹרִין לְהִבָּטֵל מִמֶּנָּה. אִם לָמַדְתָּ תּוֹרָה הַרְבֵּה, נוֹתְנִים לְךָ שָׂכָר הַרְבֵּה; וְנֶאֱמָן הוּא בַּעַל מְלַאכְתְּךָ, שֶׁיְּשַׁלֶּם לְךָ שְׂכַר פְּעֻלָּתֶךָ. וְדַע שֶׁמַּתַּן שְׂכָרָן שֶׁל צַדִּיקִים לֶעָתִיד לָבֹא.

❀ ❀ ❀

רַבִּי חֲנַנְיָא בֶּן עֲקַשְׁיָא אוֹמֵר: רָצָה הַקָּדוֹשׁ בָּרוּךְ הוּא לְזַכּוֹת אֶת יִשְׂרָאֵל, לְפִיכָךְ הִרְבָּה לָהֶם תּוֹרָה וּמִצְוֹת, שֶׁנֶּאֱמַר: „יהוה חָפֵץ לְמַעַן צִדְקוֹ, יַגְדִּיל תּוֹרָה וְיַאְדִּיר."[1]

In the presence of a *minyan*, mourners recite קַדִּישׁ דְּרַבָּנָן, the Rabbis' *Kaddish* (p. 52). Then the congregation continues with עָלֵינוּ (p. 526).

פרק שלישי

כָּל יִשְׂרָאֵל יֵשׁ לָהֶם חֵלֶק לָעוֹלָם הַבָּא, שֶׁנֶּאֱמַר: „וְעַמֵּךְ כֻּלָּם צַדִּיקִים, לְעוֹלָם יִירְשׁוּ אָרֶץ, נֵצֶר מַטָּעַי, מַעֲשֵׂה יָדַי לְהִתְפָּאֵר."[2]

❀ ❀ ❀

[א] **עֲקַבְיָא** בֶּן מַהֲלַלְאֵל אוֹמֵר: הִסְתַּכֵּל בִּשְׁלֹשָׁה דְבָרִים וְאֵין אַתָּה בָא לִידֵי עֲבֵרָה: דַּע מֵאַיִן בָּאתָ, וּלְאָן אַתָּה הוֹלֵךְ, וְלִפְנֵי מִי אַתָּה עָתִיד לִתֵּן דִּין וְחֶשְׁבּוֹן. מֵאַיִן בָּאתָ? מִטִּפָּה סְרוּחָה. וּלְאָן אַתָּה הוֹלֵךְ? לִמְקוֹם עָפָר, רִמָּה וְתוֹלֵעָה. וְלִפְנֵי מִי אַתָּה עָתִיד לִתֵּן דִּין וְחֶשְׁבּוֹן? לִפְנֵי מֶלֶךְ מַלְכֵי הַמְּלָכִים, הַקָּדוֹשׁ בָּרוּךְ הוּא.

[ב] רַבִּי חֲנִינָא סְגַן הַכֹּהֲנִים אוֹמֵר: הֱוֵי מִתְפַּלֵּל בִּשְׁלוֹמָהּ שֶׁל מַלְכוּת, שֶׁאִלְמָלֵא מוֹרָאָהּ, אִישׁ אֶת רֵעֵהוּ חַיִּים בְּלָעוֹ.

[ג] רַבִּי חֲנִינָא בֶּן תְּרַדְיוֹן אוֹמֵר: שְׁנַיִם שֶׁיּוֹשְׁבִין וְאֵין בֵּינֵיהֶם דִּבְרֵי תוֹרָה, הֲרֵי זֶה מוֹשַׁב לֵצִים, שֶׁנֶּאֱמַר: „וּבְמוֹשַׁב לֵצִים לֹא יָשָׁב."[3] אֲבָל שְׁנַיִם שֶׁיּוֹשְׁבִין וְיֵשׁ בֵּינֵיהֶם דִּבְרֵי תוֹרָה, שְׁכִינָה שְׁרוּיָה בֵינֵיהֶם, שֶׁנֶּאֱמַר: „אָז נִדְבְּרוּ יִרְאֵי יהוה אִישׁ אֶל רֵעֵהוּ, וַיַּקְשֵׁב יהוה וַיִּשְׁמָע, וַיִּכָּתֵב סֵפֶר זִכָּרוֹן לְפָנָיו, לְיִרְאֵי יהוה וּלְחֹשְׁבֵי שְׁמוֹ."[4] אֵין לִי אֶלָּא שְׁנַיִם; מִנַּיִן שֶׁאֲפִילוּ אֶחָד שֶׁיּוֹשֵׁב וְעוֹסֵק בַּתּוֹרָה, שֶׁהַקָּדוֹשׁ בָּרוּךְ הוּא קוֹבֵעַ לוֹ שָׂכָר?

---

20. הַיּוֹם – *The day,* i.e., man's lifespan.

וְהַמְּלָאכָה – *[And] the task,* i.e., of utilizing one's life in acquiring Torah knowledge and serving God. Therefore time is too precious to waste.

וּבַעַל הַבַּיִת – *And the Master of the house,* i.e., God – Master of the universe.

21. הַמְּלָאכָה – *The task.* See comment to Mishnah 20. Do not be discouraged at the magnitude of what remains to be accomplished; God does not expect one individual to complete it alone. Man is required only to do as much as his abilities allow.

CHAPTER THREE

1. וְאֵין אַתָּה בָא לִידֵי עֲבֵרָה – *And you will not come into the grip of sin.* Reflection upon one's origins will induce humility, the lack of which results in pride and sinfulness. Similarly, man's contemplation of his physical end will help him put his sensual lusts into perspective, for it is only man's spiritual and moral element that will remain eternal. And to constantly recall the day

[20] *Rabbi Tarfon says: The day is short, the task is abundant, the laborers are lazy, the wage is great, and the Master of the house is insistent.*

[21] *He used to say: You are not required to complete the task, yet you are not free to withdraw from it. If you have studied much Torah, they will give you great reward; and your Employer can be relied upon to pay you the wage for your labor, but be aware that the reward of the righteous will be given in the World to Come.*

❀ ❀ ❀

Rabbi Chanania ben Akashia says: The Holy One, Blessed is He, wished to confer merit upon Israel; therefore He gave them Torah and mitzvos in abundance, as it is said: 'HASHEM desired, for the sake of its [Israel's] righteousness, that the Torah be made great and glorious.'[1]

In the presence of a *minyan*, mourners recite קַדִּישׁ דְּרַבָּנָן, the Rabbis' *Kaddish* (p. 52). Then the congregation continues with עָלֵינוּ, *Aleinu* (p. 526).

CHAPTER THREE

All Israel has a share in the World to Come, as it is said: 'And your people are all righteous; they shall inherit the land forever; they are the branch of My planting, My handiwork, in which to take pride.'[2]

❀ ❀ ❀

[1] **עֲקַבְיָא** *Akavia ben Mahalalel said: Consider three things and you will not come into the grip of sin: Know whence you came, whither you go, and before Whom you will give justification and reckoning. 'Whence you came?' — from a putrid drop; 'whither you go?' — to a place of dust, worms and maggots; 'and before Whom you will give justification and reckoning?' — before the King Who reigns over kings, the Holy One, Blessed is He.*

[2] *Rabbi Chanina, the deputy Kohen Gadol [High Priest], says: Pray for the welfare of the government, because if people did not fear it, a person would swallow his fellow alive.*

[3] *Rabbi Chanina ben Tradyon says: If two sit together and there are no words of Torah between them, it is a session of scorners, as it is said: 'In the session of scorners he does not sit.'*[3] *But if two sit together and words of Torah are between them, the Divine Presence rests between them, as it is said: 'Then those who fear HASHEM spoke to one another, and HASHEM listened and heard, and a book of remembrance was written before Him for those who fear HASHEM and give thought to His Name.'*[4] *From this verse we would know this only about two people; how do we know that if even one person sits and occupies himself with Torah the Holy One, Blessed is He, determines a reward for him?*

(1) *Isaiah* 42:21. (2) 60:21. (3) *Psalms* 1:1. (4) *Malachi* 3:16.

of reckoning will inspire man with the true fear of God.

2. מַלְכוּת — *Government.* The government maintains social order and peace, and by instilling fear of the law it prevents anarchy and wanton crime from destroying the fabric of society.

3. The main subject of the rest of this chapter is the importance of Torah study and, conversely, the grave seriousness of failure to study and value it properly.

הֲרֵי זֶה מוֹשַׁב לֵצִים — *It is a session of scorners.* They are scorners not in the usual sense of someone who slanders or harms someone, but in the sense that they imply contempt for the Torah, by not utilizing an opportunity to study (*R' Yonah*). As the commentators explain, we know that these *scorners* are people who do not study because the very next verse (*Psalms* 1:2) says that the opposite of the scorner is one whose *desire is in the Torah of HASHEM.*

אָז נִדְבְּרוּ יִרְאֵי ה' אִישׁ אֶל רֵעֵהוּ — *Then those who fear HASHEM spoke to one another.* The verse implies that only two people are speaking

שֶׁנֶּאֱמַר: „יֵשֵׁב בָּדָד וְיִדֹּם, כִּי נָטַל עָלָיו."[1]

[ד] רַבִּי שִׁמְעוֹן אוֹמֵר: שְׁלשָׁה שֶׁאָכְלוּ עַל שֻׁלְחָן אֶחָד וְלֹא אָמְרוּ עָלָיו דִּבְרֵי תוֹרָה, כְּאִלּוּ אָכְלוּ מִזִּבְחֵי מֵתִים, שֶׁנֶּאֱמַר: „כִּי כָּל שֻׁלְחָנוֹת מָלְאוּ קִיא צוֹאָה, בְּלִי מָקוֹם."[2] אֲבָל שְׁלשָׁה שֶׁאָכְלוּ עַל שֻׁלְחָן אֶחָד וְאָמְרוּ עָלָיו דִּבְרֵי תוֹרָה, כְּאִלּוּ אָכְלוּ מִשֻּׁלְחָנוֹ שֶׁל מָקוֹם, שֶׁנֶּאֱמַר: „וַיְדַבֵּר אֵלַי, זֶה הַשֻּׁלְחָן אֲשֶׁר לִפְנֵי יהוה."[3]

[ה] רַבִּי חֲנִינָא בֶּן חֲכִינַאי אוֹמֵר: הַנֵּעוֹר בַּלַּיְלָה, וְהַמְּהַלֵּךְ בַּדֶּרֶךְ יְחִידִי, וּמְפַנֶּה לִבּוֹ לְבַטָּלָה — הֲרֵי זֶה מִתְחַיֵּב בְּנַפְשׁוֹ.

[ו] רַבִּי נְחוּנְיָא בֶּן הַקָּנָה אוֹמֵר: כָּל הַמְּקַבֵּל עָלָיו עֹל תּוֹרָה, מַעֲבִירִין מִמֶּנּוּ עֹל מַלְכוּת וְעֹל דֶּרֶךְ אֶרֶץ; וְכָל הַפּוֹרֵק מִמֶּנּוּ עֹל תּוֹרָה, נוֹתְנִין עָלָיו עֹל מַלְכוּת וְעֹל דֶּרֶךְ אֶרֶץ.

[ז] רַבִּי חֲלַפְתָּא בֶּן דּוֹסָא אִישׁ כְּפַר חֲנַנְיָא אוֹמֵר: עֲשָׂרָה שֶׁיּוֹשְׁבִין וְעוֹסְקִין בַּתּוֹרָה, שְׁכִינָה שְׁרוּיָה בֵינֵיהֶם, שֶׁנֶּאֱמַר: „אֱלֹהִים נִצָּב בַּעֲדַת אֵל."[4] וּמִנַּיִן אֲפִילוּ חֲמִשָּׁה? שֶׁנֶּאֱמַר: „וַאֲגֻדָּתוֹ עַל אֶרֶץ יְסָדָהּ."[5] וּמִנַּיִן אֲפִילוּ שְׁלשָׁה? שֶׁנֶּאֱמַר: „בְּקֶרֶב אֱלֹהִים יִשְׁפֹּט."[6] וּמִנַּיִן אֲפִילוּ שְׁנַיִם? שֶׁנֶּאֱמַר: „אָז נִדְבְּרוּ יִרְאֵי יהוה אִישׁ אֶל רֵעֵהוּ וַיַּקְשֵׁב יהוה וַיִּשְׁמָע."[7] וּמִנַּיִן אֲפִילוּ אֶחָד? שֶׁנֶּאֱמַר: „בְּכָל הַמָּקוֹם אֲשֶׁר אַזְכִּיר אֶת שְׁמִי, אָבוֹא אֵלֶיךָ וּבֵרַכְתִּיךָ."[8]

[ח] רַבִּי אֶלְעָזָר אִישׁ בַּרְתּוֹתָא אוֹמֵר: תֶּן לוֹ מִשֶּׁלּוֹ, שֶׁאַתָּה וְשֶׁלְּךָ שֶׁלּוֹ; וְכֵן בְּדָוִד הוּא אוֹמֵר: „כִּי מִמְּךָ הַכֹּל, וּמִיָּדְךָ נָתַנּוּ לָךְ."[9]

---

together [to *one another*], but because they speak of matters that express their fear of God, their deed is so precious that God Himself listens and records their words as an eternal keepsake for Himself.

יֵשֵׁב בָּדָד וְיִדֹּם — *Let one sit in solitude and be still.* One who studies alone tends to do so quietly. Nevertheless, even a solitary individual studying Torah is valuable in God's eyes.

4. שְׁלשָׁה שֶׁאָכְלוּ — *If three have eaten.* By taking in spiritual nourishment while he eats, a person consecrates his table. Then it may be truly said that he ate at God's table. This obligation of Torah study may be fulfilled by the recitation of the Grace After Meals since it contains Scriptural passages, although it is meritorious to engage in additional Torah discourses during meals.

The mishnah deduces from the verse in *Isaiah* that three people shared the meal, because the prophet had been discussing the activities of three people: a scholar, a prophet, and a *Kohen.* Had there been only two people, perhaps they would not have been judged so harshly, but in a group of three at least one of them should have reminded his colleagues to stop their idle chatter *(Tos. Yom Tov).*

וַיְדַבֵּר אֵלַי, זֶה הַשֻּׁלְחָן — *'And he said to me, "This is the table ..." '* Although the table of the verse refers to the Temple Altar that an angel had been showing to the prophet Ezekiel, the Sages understand it also to be an allusion to the table of human beings. Thus, it teaches that we can give our dining table a sanctity that makes it like a sacred vessel that is *before* HASHEM.

5. הַנֵּעוֹר בַּלַּיְלָה — *One who stays awake at night.* This person wastes his nights on idle thoughts rather than utilizing them to study Torah, for which the quiet of night is particularly suited. Not only does he fail to utilize the time best suited for spiritual elevation, he also spurns the Torah's protective powers against the dangers of the night.

וְהַמְּהַלֵּךְ בַּדֶּרֶךְ יְחִידִי — *Or who travels alone on the road.* He is unaccompanied by a companion with whom to study Torah, and at the same time is exposed to the perils of the way because he lacks the protection afforded by Torah study. By not utilizing those solitary times to engage in study,

For it is said: 'Let one sit in solitude and be still, for he will have received [a reward] for it.'[1]

[4] *Rabbi Shimon said: If three have eaten at the same table and have not spoken words of Torah there, it is as if they have eaten of offerings to the dead idols, as it is said: 'For all tables are full of vomit and filth, without the Omnipresent.'*[2] *But if three have eaten at the same table and have spoken words of Torah there, it is as if they have eaten from the table of the Omnipresent, as it is said: 'And he said to me, "This is the table that is before* HASHEM*." '*[3]

[5] *Rabbi Chanina ben Chachinai says: One who stays awake at night or who travels alone on the road, but turns his heart to idleness — indeed, he bears guilt for his soul.*

[6] *Rabbi Nechunia ben Hakanah says: If someone takes upon himself the yoke of Torah — the yoke of government and the yoke of worldly responsibilities are removed from him. But if someone throws off the yoke of Torah from himself — the yoke of government and the yoke of worldly responsibilities are placed upon him.*

[7] *Rabbi Chalafta ben Dosa of Kfar Chanania says: If ten people sit together and engage in Torah study, the Divine Presence rests among them, as it is said: 'God stands in the assembly of God.'*[4] *How do we know this even of five? For it is said: 'He has established His bundle upon earth.'*[5] *How do we know this even of three? For it is said: 'In the midst of judges He shall judge.'*[6] *How do we know this even of two? For it is said: 'Then those who fear* HASHEM *spoke to one another, and* HASHEM *listened and heard.'*[7] *How do we know this even of one? For it is said: 'In every place where I cause My Name to be mentioned, I will come to you and bless you.'*[8]

[8] *Rabbi Elazar of Bartosa says: Give Him from His Own, for you and your possessions are His. And so has David said, 'For everything is from You, and from Your Own we have given You.'*[9]

(1) *Lamentations* 3:28. (2) *Isaiah* 28:8. (3) *Ezekiel* 41:22. (4) *Psalms* 82:1.
(5) *Amos* 9:6. (6) *Psalms* 82:1. (7) *Malachi* 3:16. (8) *Exodus* 20:21. (9) *I Chronicles* 29:14.

he exposes himself to danger — and has only himself to blame.

6. מְעֲבִירִין מִמֶּנּוּ — *Are removed from him.* One who devotes himself primarily to the 'burden' of Torah acquires endurance, serenity, and contentment. In effect, he frees himself from being adversely affected by the rigors and anxieties of earthly cares. He does not feel pressured by the burdens of the government and of everyday secular living. The converse is also true. The *Chofetz Chaim* used to counsel that everyone must have cares in his life; we have the choice of being burdened with spiritual strivings, or with mundane cares that drain us but do not offer blessings.

7. Rabbi Chalafta teaches that God's Presence joins those who study Torah. His concluding words are that even a solitary student merits this blessing — why then need he enumerate groups of ten, five, three, and two? The more people join in performing a good deed, the greater its cumulative value; a multitude studying Torah together is better than a group of unrelated individuals *(R' Yonah;* Cf. *Berachos* 6a).

בַּעֲדַת אֵל — *In the assembly of God.* The Sages *(Berachos* 21b) derive from Scripture that the term עֵדָה, *assembly,* refers to at least ten people.

חֲמִשָּׁה ... אֲגֻדָּתוֹ — *Five? ... His bundle.* The word אֲגֻדָּה usually refers to a quantity of sheaves or other articles that can be grasped in the five fingers of one hand. The word is also used for the hand or any other group of five *(Rambam).*

שְׁלֹשָׁה ... אֱלֹהִים — *Three ... judges.* The minimum number of judges that can constitute a *beis din* is three.

8. תֶּן לוֹ מִשֶּׁלוֹ — *Give Him from His Own.* An inspiring exhortation to be generous in dispensing charity. Man should withhold neither himself nor his wealth from the wishes of Heaven. All that he is and has belongs to God, and he should be ready to dedicate all his faculties in fulfillment of God's will. [For R' Elazar's own lavish generosity in alms giving, see *Taanis* 24a.]

[ט] רַבִּי יַעֲקֹב אוֹמֵר: הַמְּהַלֵּךְ בַּדֶּרֶךְ וְשׁוֹנֶה, וּמַפְסִיק מִמִּשְׁנָתוֹ, וְאוֹמֵר: „מַה נָּאֶה אִילָן זֶה! וּמַה נָּאֶה נִיר זֶה!" — מַעֲלֶה עָלָיו הַכָּתוּב כְּאִלּוּ מִתְחַיֵּב בְּנַפְשׁוֹ.

[י] רַבִּי דוֹסְתָּאִי בַּר יַנַּאי מִשּׁוּם רַבִּי מֵאִיר אוֹמֵר: כָּל הַשּׁוֹכֵחַ דָּבָר אֶחָד מִמִּשְׁנָתוֹ, מַעֲלֶה עָלָיו הַכָּתוּב כְּאִלּוּ מִתְחַיֵּב בְּנַפְשׁוֹ, שֶׁנֶּאֱמַר: „רַק הִשָּׁמֶר לְךָ, וּשְׁמֹר נַפְשְׁךָ מְאֹד, פֶּן תִּשְׁכַּח אֶת הַדְּבָרִים אֲשֶׁר רָאוּ עֵינֶיךָ."[1] יָכוֹל אֲפִילוּ תָּקְפָה עָלָיו מִשְׁנָתוֹ? תַּלְמוּד לוֹמַר: „וּפֶן יָסְוּרוּ מִלְּבָבְךָ כֹּל יְמֵי חַיֶּיךָ"; הָא אֵינוֹ מִתְחַיֵּב בְּנַפְשׁוֹ עַד שֶׁיֵּשֵׁב וִיסִירֵם מִלִּבּוֹ.

[יא] רַבִּי חֲנִינָא בֶּן דּוֹסָא אוֹמֵר: כֹּל שֶׁיִּרְאַת חֶטְאוֹ קוֹדֶמֶת לְחָכְמָתוֹ, חָכְמָתוֹ מִתְקַיֶּמֶת; וְכֹל שֶׁחָכְמָתוֹ קוֹדֶמֶת לְיִרְאַת חֶטְאוֹ, אֵין חָכְמָתוֹ מִתְקַיֶּמֶת.

[יב] הוּא הָיָה אוֹמֵר: כֹּל שֶׁמַּעֲשָׂיו מְרֻבִּין מֵחָכְמָתוֹ, חָכְמָתוֹ מִתְקַיֶּמֶת; וְכֹל שֶׁחָכְמָתוֹ מְרֻבָּה מִמַּעֲשָׂיו, אֵין חָכְמָתוֹ מִתְקַיֶּמֶת.

[יג] הוּא הָיָה אוֹמֵר: כֹּל שֶׁרְוּחַ הַבְּרִיּוֹת נוֹחָה הֵימֶנּוּ, רְוּחַ הַמָּקוֹם נוֹחָה הֵימֶנּוּ; וְכֹל שֶׁאֵין רְוּחַ הַבְּרִיּוֹת נוֹחָה הֵימֶנּוּ, אֵין רְוּחַ הַמָּקוֹם נוֹחָה הֵימֶנּוּ.

[יד] רַבִּי דוֹסָא בֶּן הָרְכִּינַס אוֹמֵר: שֵׁנָה שֶׁל שַׁחֲרִית, וְיַיִן שֶׁל צָהֳרַיִם, וְשִׂיחַת הַיְלָדִים, וִישִׁיבַת בָּתֵּי כְנֵסִיּוֹת שֶׁל עַמֵּי הָאָרֶץ — מוֹצִיאִין אֶת הָאָדָם מִן הָעוֹלָם.

[טו] רַבִּי אֶלְעָזָר הַמּוֹדָעִי אוֹמֵר: הַמְּחַלֵּל אֶת הַקֳּדָשִׁים, וְהַמְּבַזֶּה אֶת הַמּוֹעֲדוֹת, וְהַמַּלְבִּין פְּנֵי חֲבֵרוֹ בָּרַבִּים, וְהַמֵּפֵר בְּרִיתוֹ שֶׁל אַבְרָהָם אָבִינוּ, וְהַמְּגַלֶּה פָנִים בַּתּוֹרָה שֶׁלֹּא כַהֲלָכָה, אַף עַל פִּי שֶׁיֵּשׁ בְּיָדוֹ תּוֹרָה וּמַעֲשִׂים טוֹבִים — אֵין לוֹ חֵלֶק לָעוֹלָם הַבָּא.

[טז] רַבִּי יִשְׁמָעֵאל אוֹמֵר: הֱוֵי קַל לְרֹאשׁ, וְנוֹחַ לְתִשְׁחֹרֶת, וֶהֱוֵי מְקַבֵּל אֶת כָּל הָאָדָם בְּשִׂמְחָה.

[יז] רַבִּי עֲקִיבָא אוֹמֵר: שְׂחוֹק וְקַלּוּת רֹאשׁ מַרְגִּילִין אֶת הָאָדָם לְעֶרְוָה. מַסּוֹרֶת סְיָג לַתּוֹרָה; מַעְשְׂרוֹת סְיָג לָעֹשֶׁר; נְדָרִים סְיָג לַפְּרִישׁוּת; סְיָג לַחָכְמָה שְׁתִיקָה.

---

9. וּמַפְסִיק מִמִּשְׁנָתוֹ — *But interrupts his review.* It is not the expression of praise for the beauty of God's creation that is condemned here, but the interruption of one's studies. The point is that during Torah study, one's attention should not be diverted to common things — however noble. Moreover, one who journeys is exposed to harm, and if one interrupts his study of Torah, which is his safeguard, he incurs danger.

10. כָּל הַשּׁוֹכֵחַ — *Whoever forgets,* i.e., due to negligence, laziness, or indifference. One is obligated to review his studies regularly to minimize the natural process of forgetfulness. The mishnah condemns one who fails to make every attempt to retain what he has learned. This is the implication of וּפֶן יָסוּרוּ מִלְּבָבְךָ, *and lest they be removed from your heart,* i.e., you had mastered this knowledge, but allowed yourself to forget it.

11-12. Man's acquired wisdom can endure only

[9] *Rabbi Yaakov said: One who walks on the road while reviewing [a Torah lesson] but interrupts his review and exclaims, 'How beautiful is this tree! How beautiful is this plowed field!' — Scripture considers it as if he bears guilt for his soul.*

[10] *Rabbi Dostai bar Yannai says in the name of Rabbi Meir: Whoever forgets anything of his Torah learning, Scripture considers it as if he bears guilt for his soul, for it is said: 'But beware and guard your soul exceedingly lest you forget the things your eyes have seen.'*[1] *Does this apply even if [he forgot because] his studies were too difficult for him? [This is not so, for] Scripture says, 'And lest they be removed from your heart all the days of your life.'*[1] *Thus, one does not bear guilt for his soul unless he sits [idly] and [through lack of concentration and review] removes them from his consciousness.*

[11] *Rabbi Chanina ben Dosa says: Anyone whose fear of sin takes priority over his wisdom, his wisdom will endure; but anyone whose wisdom takes priority over his fear of sin, his wisdom will not endure.*

[12] *He used to say: Anyone whose good deeds exceed his wisdom, his wisdom will endure; but anyone whose wisdom exceeds his good deeds, his wisdom will not endure.*

[13] *He used to say: If the spirit of one's fellows is pleased with him, the spirit of the Omnipresent is pleased with him; but if the spirit of one's fellows is not pleased with him, the spirit of the Omnipresent is not pleased with him.*

[14] *Rabbi Dosa ben Harkinas said: Late morning sleep, midday wine, children's chatter, and sitting in the assemblies of the ignorant, remove a man from the world.*

[15] *Rabbi Elazar the Moda'ite said: One who desecrates sacred things, who disgraces the Festivals, who humiliates his fellow in public, who nullifies the covenant of our forefather Abraham, or who perverts the Torah contrary to the halachah — though he may have Torah and good deeds, he has no share in the World to Come.*

[16] *Rabbi Yishmael said: Be yielding to a superior, pleasant to the young, and receive every person cheerfully.*

[17] *Rabbi Akiva said: Mockery and levity accustom a man to immorality. The transmitted Oral Torah is a protective fence around the Torah; tithes are a protective fence for wealth; vows are a protective fence for abstinence; a protective fence for wisdom is silence.*

(1) *Deuteronomy* 4:9.

---

if it is secondary to his fear of God; if wisdom is made an end unto itself, it lacks a moral foundation and it must fail. Similarly, one's performance of the Torah must exceed his wisdom; wisdom without observance cannot endure; see on 1:17.

13. כֹּל שֶׁרוּחַ הַבְּרִיּוֹת נוֹחָה הֵימֶנּוּ — *If the spirit of one's fellows is pleased with him.* If someone behaves in a courteous, ethical, trustworthy manner, he sanctifies God's Name by gaining the affection of his peers.

14. שֵׁנָה שֶׁל שַׁחֲרִית —*Late morning sleep.* Beyond the time prescribed for the saying of the Shema and of prayer. The idle pursuits mentioned by the mishnah represent a squandering of time that should be used to carry out one's mission on earth.

15. וְהַמֵּפֵר בְּרִיתוֹ — *Who nullifies the covenant.* By refusing to circumcise himself; or by surgically concealing his circumcision.

אֵין לוֹ חֵלֶק לָעוֹלָם הַבָּא — *He has no share in the World to Come,* because he demonstrates contempt for sanctity.

17. מַעַשְׂרוֹת סְיָג לָעֹשֶׁר — *Tithes are a protective fence for wealth.* The discipline of contributing

[יח] הוּא הָיָה אוֹמֵר: חָבִיב אָדָם שֶׁנִּבְרָא בְצֶלֶם; חִבָּה יְתֵרָה נוֹדַעַת לוֹ שֶׁנִּבְרָא בְּצֶלֶם, שֶׁנֶּאֱמַר: „כִּי בְּצֶלֶם אֱלֹהִים עָשָׂה אֶת הָאָדָם."[1] חֲבִיבִין יִשְׂרָאֵל, שֶׁנִּקְרְאוּ בָנִים לַמָּקוֹם; חִבָּה יְתֵרָה נוֹדַעַת לָהֶם שֶׁנִּקְרְאוּ בָנִים לַמָּקוֹם, שֶׁנֶּאֱמַר: „בָּנִים אַתֶּם לַיהוה אֱלֹהֵיכֶם."[2] חֲבִיבִין יִשְׂרָאֵל, שֶׁנִּתַּן לָהֶם כְּלִי חֶמְדָּה; חִבָּה יְתֵרָה נוֹדַעַת לָהֶם, שֶׁנִּתַּן לָהֶם כְּלִי חֶמְדָּה, שֶׁנֶּאֱמַר: „כִּי לֶקַח טוֹב נָתַתִּי לָכֶם, תּוֹרָתִי אַל תַּעֲזֹבוּ."[3]

[יט] הַכֹּל צָפוּי, וְהָרְשׁוּת נְתוּנָה. וּבְטוּב הָעוֹלָם נָדוֹן, וְהַכֹּל לְפִי רוֹב הַמַּעֲשֶׂה.

[כ] הוּא הָיָה אוֹמֵר: הַכֹּל נָתוּן בָּעֵרָבוֹן, וּמְצוּדָה פְּרוּסָה עַל כָּל הַחַיִּים. הֶחָנוּת פְּתוּחָה, וְהַחֶנְוָנִי מַקִּיף, וְהַפִּנְקָס פָּתוּחַ, וְהַיָּד כּוֹתֶבֶת, וְכָל הָרוֹצֶה לִלְווֹת יָבֹא וְיִלְוֶה. וְהַגַּבָּאִים מַחֲזִירִין תָּדִיר בְּכָל יוֹם וְנִפְרָעִין מִן הָאָדָם, מִדַּעְתּוֹ וְשֶׁלֹּא מִדַּעְתּוֹ, וְיֵשׁ לָהֶם עַל מַה שֶּׁיִּסְמֹכוּ. וְהַדִּין דִּין אֱמֶת, וְהַכֹּל מְתֻקָּן לִסְעוּדָה.

[כא] רַבִּי אֶלְעָזָר בֶּן עֲזַרְיָה אוֹמֵר: אִם אֵין תּוֹרָה, אֵין דֶּרֶךְ אֶרֶץ; אִם אֵין דֶּרֶךְ אֶרֶץ, אֵין תּוֹרָה. אִם אֵין חָכְמָה, אֵין יִרְאָה; אִם אֵין יִרְאָה, אֵין חָכְמָה. אִם אֵין דַּעַת, אֵין בִּינָה; אִם אֵין בִּינָה, אֵין דַּעַת. אִם אֵין קֶמַח, אֵין תּוֹרָה; אִם אֵין תּוֹרָה, אֵין קֶמַח.

[כב] הוּא הָיָה אוֹמֵר: כֹּל שֶׁחָכְמָתוֹ מְרֻבָּה מִמַּעֲשָׂיו, לְמָה הוּא דוֹמֶה? לְאִילָן שֶׁעֲנָפָיו מְרֻבִּין וְשָׁרָשָׁיו מוּעָטִין, וְהָרוּחַ בָּאָה וְעוֹקַרְתּוֹ וְהוֹפַכְתּוֹ עַל פָּנָיו, שֶׁנֶּאֱמַר: „וְהָיָה כְּעַרְעָר בָּעֲרָבָה, וְלֹא יִרְאֶה כִּי יָבוֹא טוֹב, וְשָׁכַן חֲרֵרִים בַּמִּדְבָּר, אֶרֶץ מְלֵחָה וְלֹא תֵשֵׁב."[4] אֲבָל כֹּל שֶׁמַּעֲשָׂיו מְרֻבִּין מֵחָכְמָתוֹ, לְמָה הוּא דוֹמֶה? לְאִילָן שֶׁעֲנָפָיו מוּעָטִין וְשָׁרָשָׁיו מְרֻבִּין, שֶׁאֲפִילוּ כָּל הָרוּחוֹת שֶׁבָּעוֹלָם בָּאוֹת וְנוֹשְׁבוֹת בּוֹ, אֵין מְזִיזִין אוֹתוֹ מִמְּקוֹמוֹ, שֶׁנֶּאֱמַר: „וְהָיָה כְּעֵץ שָׁתוּל עַל מַיִם, וְעַל יוּבַל יְשַׁלַּח שָׁרָשָׁיו, וְלֹא יִרְאֶה כִּי יָבֹא חֹם, וְהָיָה עָלֵהוּ רַעֲנָן, וּבִשְׁנַת בַּצֹּרֶת לֹא יִדְאָג, וְלֹא יָמִישׁ מֵעֲשׂוֹת פֶּרִי."[5]

---

tithes to charity makes the owner cognizant of the true Owner of all wealth; thereby it makes him worthy of even greater fortune. On the words עַשֵּׂר תְּעַשֵּׂר, literally, *you are to give tithes* [*Deut.* 14:22], the Sages homiletically expound עַשֵּׂר בִּשְׁבִיל שֶׁתִּתְעַשֵּׁר, *Give tithes so you will become wealthy (Taanis* 9a).

שְׁתִיקָה — *Silence.* Not *total* silence, but moderation in ordinary conversation. See 1:17 By doing so, a person avoids being drawn into sin and controversy, which would detract from his pursuit of Torah wisdom.

18. חִבָּה יְתֵרָה — *A greater love.* By letting Israel know its privileged status, God not only gave it cause for pride, but let it know what its spiritual goals should be.

19. הַכֹּל צָפוּי, וְהָרְשׁוּת נְתוּנָה — *Everything is foreseen, yet the freedom of choice is given.* This is a fundamental concept of Divine Providence. Although God foresees the path a man will adopt, this in no way restricts man's complete freedom of choice. Nothing is imposed upon man, and God's foreknowledge and man's free will are not contradictory.

וְהַכֹּל לְפִי רוֹב הַמַּעֲשֶׂה — *And everything depends on the abundance of good deeds.* Man is condemned or acquitted according to the *preponderance* of his good or bad deeds. Alternatively, one should accustom himself to repeating good deeds over and over again.

[18] *He used to say: Beloved is man, for he was created in God's image; it is indicative of a greater love that it was made known to him that he was created in God's image, as it is said: 'For in the image of God He made man.'* [1] *Beloved are the people Israel, for they are described as children of the Omnipresent; it is indicative of a greater love that it was made known to them that they are described as children of the Omnipresent, as it is said: 'You are children to* HASHEM *Your God.'*[2] *Beloved are the people Israel, for a cherished utensil was given to them; it is indicative of a greater love that it was made known to them that they were given a cherished utensil, as it is said: 'For I have given you a good teaching; do not forsake My Torah.'*[3]

[19] *Everything is foreseen, yet the freedom of choice is given. The world is judged with goodness, and everything depends on the abundance of good deeds.*

[20] *He used to say: Everything is given on collateral and a net is spread over all the living. The shop is open; the Merchant extends credit; the ledger is open; the hand writes; and whoever wishes to borrow, let him come and borrow. The collectors make their rounds constantly, every day, and collect payment from the person whether he realizes it or not. They have proof to rely upon; the judgment is a truthful judgment; and everything is prepared for the [final festive] banquet.*

[21] *Rabbi Elazar ben Azariah says: If there is no Torah, there is no worldly occupation; if there is no worldly occupation, there is no Torah. If there is no wisdom, there is no fear of God; if there is no fear of God, there is no wisdom. If there is no knowledge, there is no understanding; if there is no understanding, there is no knowledge. If there is no flour there is no Torah; if there is no Torah, there is no flour.*

[22] *He used to say: Anyone whose wisdom exceeds his good deeds, to what is he likened? — to a tree whose branches are numerous but whose roots are few; then the wind comes and uproots it and turns it upside down; as it is said: 'And he shall be like an isolated tree in an arid land and shall not see when good comes; he shall dwell on parched soil in the wilderness, on a salted land, uninhabited.'* [4] *But one whose good deeds exceed his wisdom, to what is he likened? — to a tree whose branches are few but whose roots are numerous; even if all the winds in the world were to come and blow against it, they could not budge it from its place; as it is said: 'And he shall be like a tree planted by waters, toward the stream spreading its roots, and it shall not notice the heat's arrival, and its foliage shall be fresh; in the year of drought it shall not worry, nor shall it cease from yielding fruit.'*[5]

(1) *Genesis* 9:6. (2) *Deuteronomy* 14:1. (3) *Proverbs* 4:2. (4) *Jeremiah* 17:6. (5) 17:8.

20. הַכֹּל נָתוּן בָּעֵרָבוֹן — *Everything is given on collateral.* The metaphor is that God's conduct of the world is likened to a business: He grants man the goodness of this world, freedom and opportunities on the 'pledge' that he will utilize them properly. No unpaid debt — however long term — is ever cancelled, and no one can evade his responsibilities.

לִסְעוּדָה — *For the [final festive] banquet.* To be enjoyed by the righteous in the World to Come.

21. אֵין דֶּרֶךְ אֶרֶץ — *There is no worldly occupation.* See note on 2:2. The laws of the Torah regulate commerce and business ethics; therefore, without Torah knowledge and fidelity to its laws, one's business practices may well be improper.

דַּעַת ... בִּינָה — *Knowledge ... understanding.* Both are necessary. Mere accumulation of knowledge is sterile without the reasoning and understanding which enables it to be integrated and applied.

אִם אֵין קֶמַח — *If there is no flour,* i.e., sustenance.

[כג] רַבִּי אֶלְעָזָר בֶּן חִסְמָא אוֹמֵר: קִנִּין וּפִתְחֵי נִדָּה הֵן הֵן גּוּפֵי הֲלָכוֹת; תְּקוּפוֹת וְגִמַטְרִיָּאוֹת — פַּרְפְּרָאוֹת לַחָכְמָה.

❀ ❀ ❀

רַבִּי חֲנַנְיָא בֶּן עֲקַשְׁיָא אוֹמֵר: רָצָה הַקָּדוֹשׁ בָּרוּךְ הוּא לְזַכּוֹת אֶת יִשְׂרָאֵל, לְפִיכָךְ הִרְבָּה לָהֶם תּוֹרָה וּמִצְוֹת, שֶׁנֶּאֱמַר: „יהוה חָפֵץ לְמַעַן צִדְקוֹ, יַגְדִּיל תּוֹרָה וְיַאְדִּיר."[1]

In the presence of a *minyan,* mourners recite קַדִּישׁ דְּרַבָּנָן, the Rabbis' *Kaddish* (p. 52). Then the congregation continues with עָלֵינוּ (p. 526).

פרק רביעי

כָּל יִשְׂרָאֵל יֵשׁ לָהֶם חֵלֶק לָעוֹלָם הַבָּא, שֶׁנֶּאֱמַר: „וְעַמֵּךְ כֻּלָּם צַדִּיקִים, לְעוֹלָם יִירְשׁוּ אָרֶץ, נֵצֶר מַטָּעַי, מַעֲשֵׂה יָדַי לְהִתְפָּאֵר."[2]

❀ ❀ ❀

[א] **בֶּן זוֹמָא** אוֹמֵר: אֵיזֶהוּ חָכָם? הַלּוֹמֵד מִכָּל אָדָם, שֶׁנֶּאֱמַר: „מִכָּל מְלַמְּדַי הִשְׂכַּלְתִּי."[3] אֵיזֶהוּ גִבּוֹר? הַכּוֹבֵשׁ אֶת יִצְרוֹ, שֶׁנֶּאֱמַר: „טוֹב אֶרֶךְ אַפַּיִם מִגִּבּוֹר, וּמֹשֵׁל בְּרוּחוֹ מִלֹּכֵד עִיר."[4] אֵיזֶהוּ עָשִׁיר? הַשָּׂמֵחַ בְּחֶלְקוֹ, שֶׁנֶּאֱמַר: „יְגִיעַ כַּפֶּיךָ כִּי תֹאכֵל אַשְׁרֶיךָ וְטוֹב לָךְ."[5] „אַשְׁרֶיךָ" — בָּעוֹלָם הַזֶּה, „וְטוֹב לָךְ" — לָעוֹלָם הַבָּא. אֵיזֶהוּ מְכֻבָּד? הַמְּכַבֵּד אֶת הַבְּרִיּוֹת, שֶׁנֶּאֱמַר: „כִּי מְכַבְּדַי אֲכַבֵּד, וּבֹזַי יֵקָלּוּ."[6]

[ב] בֶּן עַזַּאי אוֹמֵר: הֱוֵי רָץ לְמִצְוָה קַלָּה, וּבוֹרֵחַ מִן הָעֲבֵרָה; שֶׁמִּצְוָה גוֹרֶרֶת מִצְוָה, וַעֲבֵרָה גוֹרֶרֶת עֲבֵרָה, שֶׁשְּׂכַר מִצְוָה מִצְוָה, וּשְׂכַר עֲבֵרָה עֲבֵרָה.

[ג] הוּא הָיָה אוֹמֵר: אַל תְּהִי בָז לְכָל אָדָם, וְאַל תְּהִי מַפְלִיג לְכָל דָּבָר, שֶׁאֵין לְךָ אָדָם שֶׁאֵין לוֹ שָׁעָה, וְאֵין לְךָ דָבָר שֶׁאֵין לוֹ מָקוֹם.

[ד] רַבִּי לְוִיטַס אִישׁ יַבְנֶה אוֹמֵר: מְאֹד מְאֹד הֱוֵי שְׁפַל רוּחַ, שֶׁתִּקְוַת אֱנוֹשׁ רִמָּה.

[ה] רַבִּי יוֹחָנָן בֶּן בְּרוֹקָא אוֹמֵר: כָּל הַמְּחַלֵּל שֵׁם שָׁמַיִם בְּסֵתֶר, נִפְרָעִין מִמֶּנּוּ בְגָלוּי. אֶחָד שׁוֹגֵג וְאֶחָד מֵזִיד בְּחִלּוּל הַשֵּׁם.

The body must be nourished properly in order to function effectively; without nourishment, one cannot study properly. Conversely, physical nourishment — the acquisition of material things only — is not enough: man's intellect must be nourished with Torah as well.

23. קִנִּין וּפִתְחֵי נִדָּה — *The laws of bird-offerings* [see *Leviticus* 12:8], *and the laws regarding the beginning of menstrual periods.* These are areas of study which may appear to be an unworthy or unattractive subject for the true scholar. The mishnah therefore emphasizes that no study of Torah law is to be taken lightly — such laws are essential. Similarly, other pursuits such as astronomy and mathematics — or, according to some, the mystical study of numerical values of Hebrew letters — are 'seasonings of wisdom.' These disciplines should be studied only after one has 'filled his stomach' with the study of Torah and Talmud.

CHAPTER FOUR

1. אֵיזֶהוּ חָכָם — *Who is wise?* Ben Zoma does not mean to say that people cannot be wise, strong, rich, happy, or honored unless they comply with his definitions. Rather, he is telling us that people are entitled to take pride in their achievements only if they are attained and exercised in accordance with the moral teachings of the Torah.

[23] *Rabbi Eliezer ben Chisma said: The laws of bird-offerings, and the laws regarding the beginning of menstrual periods — these are the essential laws; astronomy and mathematics are like the seasonings of wisdom.*

❀ ❀ ❀

Rabbi Chanania ben Akashia says: The Holy One, Blessed is He, wished to confer merit upon Israel; therefore He gave them Torah and mitzvos in abundance, as it is said: 'HASHEM desired, for the sake of its [Israel's] righteousness, that the Torah be made great and glorious.'[1]

In the presence of a *minyan,* mourners recite קַדִּישׁ דְּרַבָּנָן, the Rabbis' *Kaddish* (p. 52). Then the congregation continues with עָלֵינוּ, *Aleinu* (p. 526).

CHAPTER FOUR

All Israel has a share in the World to Come, as it is said: 'And your people are all righteous; they shall inherit the land forever; they are the branch of My planting, My handiwork, in which to take pride.[2]

❀ ❀ ❀

[1] **בֶּן זוֹמָא** *Ben Zoma says: Who is wise? He who learns from every person, as it is said: 'From all my teachers I grew wise.'*[3] *Who is strong? He who subdues his personal inclination, as it is said: 'He who is slow to anger is better than the strong man, and a master of his passions is better than a conqueror of a city.'*[4] *Who is rich? He who is happy with his lot, as it is said: 'When you eat of the labor of your hands, you are praiseworthy and all is well with you.'*[5] *'You are praiseworthy' — in this world; 'and all is well with you' — in the World to Come. Who is honored? He who honors others, as it is said: "For those who honor Me I will honor, and those who scorn Me shall be degraded.'*[6]

[2] *Ben Azzai said: Run to perform even a 'minor' mitzvah, and flee from sin; for one mitzvah leads to another mitzvah, and one sin leads to another sin; for the consequence of a mitzvah is a mitzvah, and the consequence of a sin is a sin.*

[3] *He used to say: Do not be scornful of any person and do not be disdainful of anything, for you have no person without his hour and no thing without its place.*

[4] *Rabbi Levitas of Yavneh said: Be exceedingly humble in spirit, for the anticipated end of mortal man is worms.*

[5] *Rabbi Yochanan ben Beroka said: Whoever desecrates the Name of Heaven in secret, they will exact punishment from him in public; unintentional or intentional, both are alike regarding desecration of the Name.*

(1) *Isaiah* 42:21. (2) 60:21. (3) *Psalms* 119:99. (4) *Proverbs* 16:32. (5) *Psalms* 128:2. (6) *I Samuel* 2:30.

הַלּוֹמֵד מִכָּל אָדָם — *He who learns from every person.* One who truly values wisdom will seek it wherever it can be found. For a person to refuse to learn from someone because he dislikes or disapproves of that someone is to elevate his feelings — however justified — over his pursuit of knowledge.

אֵיזֶהוּ עָשִׁיר — *Who is rich?* What good is wealth if it does not provide happiness? Therefore, the truly wealthy person is the contented one.

אֵיזֶהוּ מְכֻבָּד — *Who is honored?* A person with the above virtues is truly worthy of honor whether or not his neighbors acknowledge it. But how does one gain the recognition of others as well? — by honoring *them.* If even God repays honor with honor, surely people will do the same.

2. שֶׁמִּצְוָה גוֹרֶרֶת מִצְוָה — *For one mitzvah leads to another mitzvah.* When someone performs a *mitzvah* he becomes conditioned to obey God's will; conversely, each wrongful act dulls the conscience.

5. חִלּוּל הַשֵּׁם — *Desecration of the Name* involves

[ו] רַבִּי יִשְׁמָעֵאל בַּר רַבִּי יוֹסֵי אוֹמֵר: הַלּוֹמֵד עַל מְנָת לְלַמֵּד, מַסְפִּיקִין בְּיָדוֹ לִלְמוֹד וּלְלַמֵּד; וְהַלּוֹמֵד עַל מְנָת לַעֲשׂוֹת, מַסְפִּיקִין בְּיָדוֹ לִלְמוֹד וּלְלַמֵּד, לִשְׁמוֹר וְלַעֲשׂוֹת.

[ז] רַבִּי צָדוֹק אוֹמֵר: אַל תִּפְרוֹשׁ מִן הַצִּבּוּר; וְאַל תַּעַשׂ עַצְמְךָ כְּעוֹרְכֵי הַדַּיָּנִין; וְאַל תַּעֲשֶׂהָ עֲטָרָה לְהִתְגַּדֵּל בָּהּ, וְלֹא קַרְדֹּם לַחְפָּר בָּהּ. וְכָךְ הָיָה הִלֵּל אוֹמֵר: וְדִאִשְׁתַּמֵּשׁ בְּתָגָא חֲלָף. הָא לָמַדְתָּ: כָּל הַנֶּהֱנֶה מִדִּבְרֵי תוֹרָה, נוֹטֵל חַיָּיו מִן הָעוֹלָם.

[ח] רַבִּי יוֹסֵי אוֹמֵר: כָּל הַמְּכַבֵּד אֶת הַתּוֹרָה, גּוּפוֹ מְכֻבָּד עַל הַבְּרִיּוֹת; וְכָל הַמְּחַלֵּל אֶת הַתּוֹרָה, גּוּפוֹ מְחֻלָּל עַל הַבְּרִיּוֹת.

[ט] רַבִּי יִשְׁמָעֵאל בְּנוֹ אוֹמֵר: הַחוֹשֵׂךְ עַצְמוֹ מִן הַדִּין, פּוֹרֵק מִמֶּנּוּ אֵיבָה וְגָזֵל וּשְׁבוּעַת שָׁוְא. וְהַגַּס לִבּוֹ בְּהוֹרָאָה, שׁוֹטֶה רָשָׁע וְגַס רוּחַ.

[י] הוּא הָיָה אוֹמֵר: אַל תְּהִי דָן יְחִידִי, שֶׁאֵין דָּן יְחִידִי אֶלָּא אֶחָד. וְאַל תֹּאמַר: „קַבְּלוּ דַעְתִּי!" שֶׁהֵן רַשָּׁאִין וְלֹא אָתָּה.

[יא] רַבִּי יוֹנָתָן אוֹמֵר: כָּל הַמְּקַיֵּם אֶת הַתּוֹרָה מֵעֹנִי, סוֹפוֹ לְקַיְּמָהּ מֵעֹשֶׁר; וְכָל הַמְּבַטֵּל אֶת הַתּוֹרָה מֵעֹשֶׁר, סוֹפוֹ לְבַטְּלָהּ מֵעֹנִי.

[יב] רַבִּי מֵאִיר אוֹמֵר: הֱוֵי מְמַעֵט בְּעֵסֶק, וַעֲסֹק בַּתּוֹרָה; וֶהֱוֵי שְׁפַל רוּחַ בִּפְנֵי כָל אָדָם; וְאִם בָּטַלְתָּ מִן הַתּוֹרָה, יֶשׁ לְךָ בְּטֵלִים הַרְבֵּה כְּנֶגְדְּךָ; וְאִם עָמַלְתָּ בַּתּוֹרָה, יֶשׁ לוֹ שָׂכָר הַרְבֵּה לִתֶּן לָךְ.

[יג] רַבִּי אֱלִיעֶזֶר בֶּן יַעֲקֹב אוֹמֵר: הָעוֹשֶׂה מִצְוָה אַחַת קוֹנֶה לוֹ פְּרַקְלִיט אֶחָד; וְהָעוֹבֵר עֲבֵרָה אַחַת, קוֹנֶה לוֹ קַטֵּיגוֹר אֶחָד. תְּשׁוּבָה וּמַעֲשִׂים טוֹבִים כִּתְרִיס בִּפְנֵי הַפֻּרְעָנוּת.

[יד] רַבִּי יוֹחָנָן הַסַּנְדְּלָר אוֹמֵר: כָּל כְּנֵסִיָּה שֶׁהִיא לְשֵׁם שָׁמַיִם, סוֹפָהּ לְהִתְקַיֵּם; וְשֶׁאֵינָהּ לְשֵׁם שָׁמַיִם, אֵין סוֹפָהּ לְהִתְקַיֵּם.

---

the sort of conduct that makes onlookers think or say that people who claim to be observant Jews act in an unworthy manner. For some of the great Talmudic sages, even to take a few paces without studying Torah constituted a desecration. For ordinary people, rudeness, dishonesty and the like would be a desecration. One who does things that bring God's Name into disrepute ח״ו shows contempt for God and this is the most serious of all sins, especially because of the effect it has on others. Even an unintentional desecration is most serious, if it is the result of insufficient care or concern. Just as people cannot justify carelessness where the health and life of their loved ones are involved, so too one who is truly concerned with the honor of God will not permit an unintentional desecration to take place. Because it is so serious a sin, one who could have avoided or prevented it has no right to excuse himself by saying it was unintended.

6. Learning is of great importance; using this knowledge to teach others is even greater, while the ultimate purpose of all study is performance.

7. אַל תִּפְרוֹשׁ ... אַל תַּעַשׂ — *Do not separate yourself ... do not act* — R' Tzadok apparently took these sayings of Hillel [2:5] and Yehudah ben Tabbai [1:8] as his motto.

8. וְכָל הַמְּחַלֵּל אֶת הַתּוֹרָה — *And whoever disgraces the Torah,* by using it for personal gain, or by living a debased life.

9. הַחוֹשֵׂךְ עַצְמוֹ מִן הַדִּין — *One who withdraws from judgment.* If more competent judges are available, one should withdraw in their favor; otherwise, the most qualified judge has a responsibility to accept the case *(R' Yonah). Rashi* interprets that a judge should attempt to bring about compromises rather than render definitive judgments.

[6] *Rabbi Yishmael bar Rabbi Yose said: One who studies Torah in order to teach, is given the means to study and to teach; and one who studies in order to practice, is given the means to study and to teach, to observe and to practice.*

[7] *Rabbi Tzadok said: Do not separate yourself from the community; [when serving as a judge] do not act as a lawyer; do not make the Torah a crown for self-glorification, nor a spade with which to dig. So too Hillel used to say: He who exploits the crown [of Torah for personal benefit] shall fade away. From this you derive that whoever seeks personal benefit from the words of Torah removes his life from the world.*

[8] *Rabbi Yose said: Whoever honors the Torah is himself honored by people; and whoever disgraces the Torah is himself disgraced by people.*

[9] *Rabbi Yishmael his son said: One who withdraws from judgment removes from himself hatred, robbery, and [the responsibility for] an unnecessary oath; but one who is too self-confident in handing down legal decisions is a fool, wicked and arrogant of spirit.*

[10] *He used to say: Do not act as judge alone, for none judges alone except One; and do not say, 'Accept my view,' for they are permitted to, but not you.*

[11] *Rabbi Yonasan said: Whoever fulfills the Torah despite poverty, will ultimately fulfill it in wealth; but whoever neglects the Torah because of wealth, will ultimately neglect it in poverty.*

[12] *Rabbi Meir said: Reduce your business activities and engage in Torah study. Be of humble spirit before every person. If you should neglect the [study of] Torah, you will come upon many excuses to neglect it; but if you labor in the Torah, God has ample reward to give you.*

[13] *Rabbi Eliezer ben Yaakov said: He who fulfills even a single mitzvah gains himself a single advocate, and he who commits even a single transgression gains himself a single accuser. Repentance and good deeds are like a shield against retribution.*

[14] *Rabbi Yochanan the Sandler said: Every assembly that is dedicated to the sake of Heaven will have an enduring effect, but one that is not for the sake of Heaven will not have an enduring effect.*

וְגָזֵל — *robbery.* As the result of an erroneous legal decision whereby the innocent litigant is deprived of what is legally his.

10. יְחִידִי — *Alone.* Rather, always endeavor to be part of a tribunal, so you will be able to discuss all aspects of the case and render proper judgment.

וְאַל תֹּאמַר — *And do not say.* If you are in the minority, do not insist that your colleagues give in to you, for they, as the majority, can impose their will, and you must accede.

12. בְּטֵלִים הַרְבֵּה — *Many excuses to neglect it.* There are always 'compelling reasons' why it is impossible for someone to study Torah. If he weakens his resolve and gives in to 'necessity,' he will find it harder and harder to study with diligence.

13. קוֹנֶה לוֹ פְּרַקְלִיט אֶחָד — *Gains himself a single advocate,* to plead on his behalf on the day of judgment.

תְּשׁוּבָה וּמַעֲשִׂים טוֹבִים כִּתְרִיס — *Repentance and good deeds are like a shield.* Life is full of hard times, but if someone constantly seeks to improve himself, God gives him protection from such natural hazards.

14. כָּל כְּנֵסִיָּה שֶׁהִיא לְשֵׁם שָׁמַיִם — *Every assembly that is dedicated to the sake of Heaven.* If the participants sincerely mean to serve God, their undertakings will have eventual success, even though they began on a pessimistic, inauspicious note. Conversely, there is no such guarantee if the motives of the participants are not pure. Consequently, earnest people should not fear failure and criticism — if their intentions are elevated, they will have *ultimate* success.

[טו] רַבִּי אֶלְעָזָר בֶּן שַׁמּוּעַ אוֹמֵר: יְהִי כְבוֹד תַּלְמִידְךָ חָבִיב עָלֶיךָ כְּשֶׁלָּךְ; וּכְבוֹד חֲבֵרְךָ כְּמוֹרָא רַבָּךְ; וּמוֹרָא רַבָּךְ כְּמוֹרָא שָׁמַיִם.

[טז] רַבִּי יְהוּדָה אוֹמֵר: הֱוֵי זָהִיר בְּתַלְמוּד, שֶׁשִּׁגְגַת תַּלְמוּד עוֹלָה זָדוֹן.

[יז] רַבִּי שִׁמְעוֹן אוֹמֵר: שְׁלֹשָׁה כְתָרִים הֵם: כֶּתֶר תּוֹרָה, וְכֶתֶר כְּהֻנָּה, וְכֶתֶר מַלְכוּת; וְכֶתֶר שֵׁם טוֹב עוֹלֶה עַל גַּבֵּיהֶן.

[יח] רַבִּי נְהוֹרָאִי אוֹמֵר: הֱוֵי גוֹלֶה לִמְקוֹם תּוֹרָה, וְאַל תֹּאמַר שֶׁהִיא תָבוֹא אַחֲרֶיךָ, שֶׁחֲבֵרֶיךָ יְקַיְּמוּהָ בְיָדֶךָ. וְאֶל בִּינָתְךָ אַל תִּשָּׁעֵן.[1]

[יט] רַבִּי יַנַּאי אוֹמֵר: אֵין בְּיָדֵינוּ לֹא מִשַּׁלְוַת הָרְשָׁעִים וְאַף לֹא מִיִּסּוּרֵי הַצַּדִּיקִים.

[כ] רַבִּי מַתְיָא בֶּן חָרָשׁ אוֹמֵר: הֱוֵי מַקְדִּים בִּשְׁלוֹם כָּל אָדָם, וֶהֱוֵי זָנָב לָאֲרָיוֹת, וְאַל תְּהִי רֹאשׁ לְשׁוּעָלִים.

[כא] רַבִּי יַעֲקֹב אוֹמֵר: הָעוֹלָם הַזֶּה דּוֹמֶה לִפְרוֹזְדוֹר בִּפְנֵי הָעוֹלָם הַבָּא, הַתְקֵן עַצְמְךָ בַּפְּרוֹזְדוֹר, כְּדֵי שֶׁתִּכָּנֵס לַטְּרַקְלִין.

[כב] הוּא הָיָה אוֹמֵר: יָפָה שָׁעָה אַחַת בִּתְשׁוּבָה וּמַעֲשִׂים טוֹבִים בָּעוֹלָם הַזֶּה מִכֹּל חַיֵּי הָעוֹלָם הַבָּא; וְיָפָה שָׁעָה אַחַת שֶׁל קוֹרַת רוּחַ בָּעוֹלָם הַבָּא מִכֹּל חַיֵּי הָעוֹלָם הַזֶּה.

[כג] רַבִּי שִׁמְעוֹן בֶּן אֶלְעָזָר אוֹמֵר: אַל תְּרַצֶּה אֶת חֲבֵרְךָ בִּשְׁעַת כַּעְסוֹ; וְאַל תְּנַחֲמֵהוּ בְּשָׁעָה שֶׁמֵּתוֹ מֻטָּל לְפָנָיו; וְאַל תִּשְׁאַל לוֹ בִּשְׁעַת נִדְרוֹ; וְאַל תִּשְׁתַּדֵּל לִרְאוֹתוֹ בִּשְׁעַת קַלְקָלָתוֹ.

[כד] שְׁמוּאֵל הַקָּטָן אוֹמֵר: „בִּנְפֹל אוֹיִבְךָ אַל תִּשְׂמָח, וּבִכָּשְׁלוֹ אַל יָגֵל לִבֶּךָ. פֶּן יִרְאֶה יהוה וְרַע בְּעֵינָיו, וְהֵשִׁיב מֵעָלָיו אַפּוֹ."[2]

[כה] אֱלִישָׁע בֶּן אֲבוּיָה אוֹמֵר: הַלּוֹמֵד יֶלֶד, לְמָה הוּא דוֹמֶה? לִדְיוֹ כְתוּבָה עַל נְיָר חָדָשׁ. וְהַלּוֹמֵד זָקֵן, לְמָה הוּא דוֹמֶה? לִדְיוֹ כְתוּבָה עַל נְיָר מָחוּק.

---

15. כְּבוֹד תַּלְמִידְךָ — *The honor of your student.* Rendering honor to others is so important that one should always treat them as though they are on a higher level than they really are. The comparison of a teacher to God means that one should accept his teacher's opinions even though he disagrees, just as we do not question God's word *(Tiferes Yisrael).*

16. שֶׁשִּׁגְגַת תַּלְמוּד — *For a careless misinterpretation.* A misinterpretation is judged so harshly only if it was due to the student's failure to apply himself according to his capacity. A sincere mistake is regarded as an unintentional error.

17. וְכֶתֶר שֵׁם טוֹב — *But the crown of a good name.* This crown adorns someone whose deeds and behavior earn him the respect and affection of his fellows. Even scholars, priests, and kings are lacking if they fail to earn this crown.

18. הֱוֵי גוֹלֶה לִמְקוֹם תּוֹרָה — *Exile yourself to a place of Torah.* One should uproot himself and move to a place where there are Torah scholars from whom to learn and be stimulated.

שֶׁהִיא תָבוֹא אַחֲרֶיךָ — *That it will come after you.* That the Torah [i.e., scholars] will follow you if you move to a place currently devoid of Torah.

שֶׁחֲבֵרֶיךָ יְקַיְּמוּהָ בְיָדֶךָ — *For it is your colleagues* [through stimulating debate] *who will cause it to remain with you.* According to *Rashi,* this explains the beginning of the mishnah: One must live in a Torah environment because it is only in association with fellow students that Torah can be properly studied.

[15] *Rabbi Elazar ben Shamua said: Let the honor of your student be as dear to you as your own; the honor of your colleague as the reverence for your teacher; and the reverence for your teacher as the reverence of Heaven.*

[16] *Rabbi Yehudah said: Be meticulous in study, for a careless misinterpretation is considered tantamount to willful transgression.*

[17] *Rabbi Shimon said: There are three crowns — the crown of Torah, the crown of priesthood, and the crown of kingship; but the crown of a good name surpasses them all.*

[18] *Rabbi Nehorai said: Exile yourself to a place of Torah — and do not assume that it will come after you — for it is your colleagues who will cause it to remain with you; 'and do not rely on your own understanding.'*[1]

[19] *Rabbi Yannai said: It is not in our power to explain either the tranquility of the wicked or the suffering of the righteous.*

[20] *Rabbi Masya ben Charash said: Initiate a greeting to every person; and be a tail to lions rather than a head to foxes.*

[21] *Rabbi Yaakov said: This world is like a lobby before the World to Come; prepare yourself in the lobby so that you may enter the banquet hall.*

[22] *He used to say: Better one hour of repentance and good deeds in This World than the entire life of the World to Come; and better one hour of spiritual bliss in the World to Come than the entire life of This World.*

[23] *Rabbi Shimon ben Elazar says: Do not appease your fellow in the time of his anger; do not console him while his dead lies before him; do not question him about his vow at the time he makes it; and do not attempt to see him at the time of his degradation.*

[24] *Shmuel HaKattan says: 'When your enemy falls be not glad, and when he stumbles let your heart not be joyous. Lest* HASHEM *see and it displease Him, and He will turn His wrath from him [to you].'*[2]

[25] *Elisha ben Avuya said: One who studies Torah as a child, to what can he be likened? — to ink written on fresh paper. And one who studies Torah as an old man, to what can he be likened? — to ink written on smudged paper.*

(1) *Proverbs* 3:5. (2) 24:17-18.

אַל תִּשָּׁעֵן — *Do not rely,* by studying alone, in an environment devoid of Torah scholarship.

19. אֵין בְּיָדֵינוּ — *It is not in our power.* We cannot know for sure if what befalls each of them is indeed a blessing or a calamity. We must therefore abstain from passing judgment in either case and not permit our own short-sighted view of events to influence our decisions *(R' Hirsch).*

20. וֶהֱוֵי זָנָב לַאֲרָיוֹת — *And be a tail to lions.* Better to be a follower of the righteous (from whom you can learn) than a leader of common people.

21. In the Talmud *(Avodah Zarah* 3a) there is a similar saying: 'This world is like the eve of Sabbath, and the World to Come is like Sabbath. He who prepares on the eve of Sabbath will have food to eat on Sabbath.'

22. יָפָה שָׁעָה אַחַת — *Better one hour.* The Mishnah deals with two different concepts. Only in This World can one elevate himself spiritually; in the World to Come he can only enjoy the reward for his accomplishments here. On the other hand, all the bliss of all the generations in the history of the world cannot equal an hour of bliss in the World to Come.

23. אַל תְּרַצֶּה — *Do not appease.* R' Shimon ben Elazar's message concerns the importance of proper timing. To reason with or appease someone at a time of great passion is counterproductive.

24. בִּנְפֹל אוֹיִבְךָ — *When your enemy falls.* This entire dictum is a quotation from the Book of *Proverbs.* Shmuel HaKattan apparently was in the habit of quoting it when admonishing people.

25. נְיָר חָדָשׁ — *Fresh paper,* which retains ink legibly and permanently. This is a lesson on a

[כו] רַבִּי יוֹסֵי בַּר יְהוּדָה אִישׁ כְּפַר הַבַּבְלִי אוֹמֵר: הַלּוֹמֵד מִן הַקְּטַנִּים, לְמָה הוּא דוֹמֶה? לְאוֹכֵל עֲנָבִים קֵהוֹת, וְשׁוֹתֶה יַיִן מִגִּתּוֹ. וְהַלּוֹמֵד מִן הַזְּקֵנִים, לְמָה הוּא דוֹמֶה? לְאוֹכֵל עֲנָבִים בְּשׁוּלוֹת, וְשׁוֹתֶה יַיִן יָשָׁן.

[כז] רַבִּי מֵאִיר אוֹמֵר: אַל תִּסְתַּכֵּל בַּקַּנְקַן, אֶלָּא בְּמַה שֶּׁיֵּשׁ בּוֹ; יֵשׁ קַנְקַן חָדָשׁ מָלֵא יָשָׁן, וְיָשָׁן שֶׁאֲפִילוּ חָדָשׁ אֵין בּוֹ.

[כח] רַבִּי אֶלְעָזָר הַקַּפָּר אוֹמֵר: הַקִּנְאָה וְהַתַּאֲוָה וְהַכָּבוֹד מוֹצִיאִין אֶת הָאָדָם מִן הָעוֹלָם.

[כט] הוּא הָיָה אוֹמֵר: הַיִּלּוֹדִים לָמוּת, וְהַמֵּתִים לְחִיוֹת, וְהַחַיִּים לִדּוֹן — לֵידַע לְהוֹדִיעַ וּלְהִוָּדַע שֶׁהוּא אֵל, הוּא הַיּוֹצֵר, הוּא הַבּוֹרֵא, הוּא הַמֵּבִין, הוּא הַדַּיָּן, הוּא הָעֵד, הוּא בַּעַל דִּין, הוּא עָתִיד לָדוּן. בָּרוּךְ הוּא, שֶׁאֵין לְפָנָיו לֹא עַוְלָה, וְלֹא שִׁכְחָה, וְלֹא מַשּׂוֹא פָנִים, וְלֹא מִקַּח שֹׁחַד; שֶׁהַכֹּל שֶׁלּוֹ. וְדַע, שֶׁהַכֹּל לְפִי הַחֶשְׁבּוֹן. וְאַל יַבְטִיחֲךָ יִצְרְךָ שֶׁהַשְּׁאוֹל בֵּית מָנוֹס לָךְ — שֶׁעַל כָּרְחֲךָ אַתָּה נוֹצָר; וְעַל כָּרְחֲךָ אַתָּה נוֹלָד; וְעַל כָּרְחֲךָ אַתָּה חַי; וְעַל כָּרְחֲךָ אַתָּה מֵת; וְעַל כָּרְחֲךָ אַתָּה עָתִיד לִתֵּן דִּין וְחֶשְׁבּוֹן לִפְנֵי מֶלֶךְ מַלְכֵי הַמְּלָכִים, הַקָּדוֹשׁ בָּרוּךְ הוּא.

❀ ❀ ❀

רַבִּי חֲנַנְיָא בֶּן עֲקַשְׁיָא אוֹמֵר: רָצָה הַקָּדוֹשׁ בָּרוּךְ הוּא לְזַכּוֹת אֶת יִשְׂרָאֵל, לְפִיכָךְ הִרְבָּה לָהֶם תּוֹרָה וּמִצְוֹת, שֶׁנֶּאֱמַר: „יהוה חָפֵץ לְמַעַן צִדְקוֹ, יַגְדִּיל תּוֹרָה וְיַאְדִּיר.״[2]

In the presence of a *minyan,* mourners recite קַדִּישׁ דְּרַבָּנָן, the Rabbis' *Kaddish* (p. 52). Then the congregation continues with עָלֵינוּ (p. 526).

פרק חמישי

כָּל יִשְׂרָאֵל יֵשׁ לָהֶם חֵלֶק לָעוֹלָם הַבָּא, שֶׁנֶּאֱמַר: „וְעַמֵּךְ כֻּלָּם צַדִּיקִים, לְעוֹלָם יִירְשׁוּ אָרֶץ, נֵצֶר מַטָּעַי, מַעֲשֵׂה יָדַי לְהִתְפָּאֵר.״[2]

❀ ❀ ❀

[א] **בַּעֲשָׂרָה** מַאֲמָרוֹת נִבְרָא הָעוֹלָם. וּמַה תַּלְמוּד לוֹמַר? וַהֲלֹא בְּמַאֲמָר אֶחָד יָכוֹל לְהִבָּרְאוֹת? אֶלָּא לְהִפָּרַע מִן הָרְשָׁעִים, שֶׁמְּאַבְּדִין אֶת הָעוֹלָם שֶׁנִּבְרָא בַּעֲשָׂרָה מַאֲמָרוֹת, וְלִתֵּן שָׂכָר טוֹב לַצַּדִּיקִים, שֶׁמְּקַיְּמִין אֶת הָעוֹלָם שֶׁנִּבְרָא בַּעֲשָׂרָה מַאֲמָרוֹת.

[ב] עֲשָׂרָה דוֹרוֹת מֵאָדָם וְעַד נֹחַ, לְהוֹדִיעַ כַּמָּה אֶרֶךְ אַפַּיִם לְפָנָיו; שֶׁכָּל הַדּוֹרוֹת הָיוּ מַכְעִיסִין וּבָאִין, עַד שֶׁהֵבִיא עֲלֵיהֶם אֶת מֵי הַמַּבּוּל.

---

person's duty to learn Torah while he is young and his mind is fresh and receptive.

27. אַל תִּסְתַּכֵּל בַּקַּנְקַן — *Do not look at the vessel.* This contrasts with the view in Mishnah 26. Do not draw general conclusions based on age. Some young men have achieved greater levels of learning than older men; nor should one judge others by their appearance only.

28. הַקִּנְאָה וְהַתַּאֲוָה וְהַכָּבוֹד — *Jealousy, lust and glory.* These base instincts and appetites prevent

[26] *Rabbi Yose bar Yehudah of Kfar HaBavli says: One who learns Torah from the young, to what can he be likened? — to one who eats unripe grapes or drinks unfermented wine from his vat. But one who learns Torah from the old, to what can he be likened? — to one who eats ripe grapes or drinks aged wine.*

[27] *Rabbi Meir says: Do not look at the vessel, but what is in it; there is a new vessel filled with old wine and an old vessel that does not even contain new wine.*

[28] *Rabbi Elazar HaKappar says: Jealousy, lust and glory remove a man from the world.*

[29] *He used to say: The newborn will die; the dead will live again; the living will be judged — in order that they know, teach, and become aware that He is God, He is the Fashioner, He is the Creator, He is the Discerner, He is the Judge, He is the Witness, He is the Plaintiff, He will judge. Blessed is He, before Whom there is no iniquity, no forgetfulness, no favoritism, and no acceptance of bribery, for everything is His. Know that everything is according to the reckoning. And let not your evil inclination promise you that the grave will be an escape for you — for against your will you were created; against your will you were born; against your will you live; against your will you die, and against your will you are destined to give an account before the King Who rules over kings, the Holy One, Blessed is He.*

❀ ❀ ❀

Rabbi Chanania ben Akashia says: The Holy One, Blessed is He, wished to confer merit upon Israel; therefore He gave them Torah and mitzvos in abundance, as it is said: 'HASHEM desired, for the sake of its [Israel's] righteousness, that the Torah be made great and glorious.'[1]

In the presence of a *minyan,* mourners recite קַדִּישׁ דְּרַבָּנָן, the Rabbis' *Kaddish* (p. 52). Then the congregation continues with עָלֵינוּ, *Aleinu* (p. 526).

CHAPTER FIVE

All Israel has a share in the World to Come, as it is said: 'And your people are all righteous; they shall inherit the land forever; they are the branch of My planting, My handiwork, in which to take pride.'[2]

❀ ❀ ❀

[1] **בַּעֲשָׂרָה** *With ten utterances the world was created. What does this come to teach us? Indeed, could it not have been created with one utterance? This was to exact punishment from the wicked who destroy the world that was created with ten utterances, and to bestow goodly reward upon the righteous who sustain the world that was created by ten utterances.*

[2] *There were ten generations from Adam to Noah — to show the degree of His patience; for all those generations angered Him increasingly, until He brought upon them the waters of the Flood.*

---

(1) *Isaiah* 41:21. (2) 60:21.

---

a person from enjoying life.

CHAPTER FIVE

1. בַּעֲשָׂרָה מַאֲמָרוֹת — *With ten utterances.* The Divine utterances are recorded in *Genesis* 1 and 2:18.

2. עֲשָׂרָה דוֹרוֹת — *Ten generations.* They are enumerated in *Genesis* 5.

[ג] עֲשָׂרָה דוֹרוֹת מִנֹּחַ וְעַד אַבְרָהָם, לְהוֹדִיעַ כַּמָּה אֶרֶךְ אַפַּיִם לְפָנָיו; שֶׁכָּל הַדּוֹרוֹת הָיוּ מַכְעִיסִין וּבָאִין, עַד שֶׁבָּא אַבְרָהָם אָבִינוּ וְקִבֵּל שְׂכַר כֻּלָּם.

[ד] עֲשָׂרָה נִסְיוֹנוֹת נִתְנַסָּה אַבְרָהָם אָבִינוּ וְעָמַד בְּכֻלָּם, לְהוֹדִיעַ כַּמָּה חִבָּתוֹ שֶׁל אַבְרָהָם אָבִינוּ.

[ה] עֲשָׂרָה נִסִּים נַעֲשׂוּ לַאֲבוֹתֵינוּ בְּמִצְרַיִם וַעֲשָׂרָה עַל הַיָּם. עֶשֶׂר מַכּוֹת הֵבִיא הַקָּדוֹשׁ בָּרוּךְ הוּא עַל הַמִּצְרִים בְּמִצְרַיִם וְעֶשֶׂר עַל הַיָּם.

[ו] עֲשָׂרָה נִסְיוֹנוֹת נִסּוּ אֲבוֹתֵינוּ אֶת הַקָּדוֹשׁ בָּרוּךְ הוּא בַּמִּדְבָּר, שֶׁנֶּאֱמַר: „וַיְנַסּוּ אֹתִי זֶה עֶשֶׂר פְּעָמִים, וְלֹא שָׁמְעוּ בְּקוֹלִי.״[1]

[ז] עֲשָׂרָה נִסִּים נַעֲשׂוּ לַאֲבוֹתֵינוּ בְּבֵית הַמִּקְדָּשׁ: לֹא הִפִּילָה אִשָּׁה מֵרֵיחַ בְּשַׂר הַקֹּדֶשׁ; וְלֹא הִסְרִיחַ בְּשַׂר הַקֹּדֶשׁ מֵעוֹלָם; וְלֹא נִרְאָה זְבוּב בְּבֵית הַמִּטְבְּחַיִם; וְלֹא אִירַע קֶרִי לְכֹהֵן גָּדוֹל בְּיוֹם הַכִּפּוּרִים; וְלֹא כִבּוּ הַגְּשָׁמִים אֵשׁ שֶׁל עֲצֵי הַמַּעֲרָכָה; וְלֹא נִצְּחָה הָרוּחַ אֶת עַמּוּד הֶעָשָׁן; וְלֹא נִמְצָא פְסוּל בָּעֹמֶר, וּבִשְׁתֵּי הַלֶּחֶם, וּבְלֶחֶם הַפָּנִים; עוֹמְדִים צְפוּפִים, וּמִשְׁתַּחֲוִים רְוָחִים; וְלֹא הִזִּיק נָחָשׁ וְעַקְרָב בִּירוּשָׁלַיִם מֵעוֹלָם; וְלֹא אָמַר אָדָם לַחֲבֵרוֹ: „צַר לִי הַמָּקוֹם שֶׁאָלִין בִּירוּשָׁלַיִם.״

[ח] עֲשָׂרָה דְבָרִים נִבְרְאוּ בְּעֶרֶב שַׁבָּת בֵּין הַשְּׁמָשׁוֹת, וְאֵלוּ הֵן: פִּי הָאָרֶץ, וּפִי הַבְּאֵר, פִּי הָאָתוֹן, וְהַקֶּשֶׁת, וְהַמָּן, וְהַמַּטֶּה, וְהַשָּׁמִיר, הַכְּתָב, וְהַמִּכְתָּב, וְהַלּוּחוֹת. וְיֵשׁ אוֹמְרִים: אַף הַמַּזִּיקִין, וּקְבוּרָתוֹ שֶׁל מֹשֶׁה, וְאֵילוֹ שֶׁל אַבְרָהָם אָבִינוּ. וְיֵשׁ אוֹמְרִים: אַף צְבָת בִּצְבָת עֲשׂוּיָה.

---

3. עֲשָׂרָה דוֹרוֹת — *Ten generations.* See *Genesis* 11:10. The count begins with Shem, Noah's son.

וְקִבֵּל שְׂכַר כֻּלָּם — *And received the reward of them all.* Abraham's righteousness was so great that he received the total reward that would have gone to the ten generations, had they not been sinful.

4. עֲשָׂרָה נִסְיוֹנוֹת — *Ten trials.* See footnote to ArtScroll *Bereishis* 12:1, page 424.

5. עֲשָׂרָה נִסִּים — *Ten miracles ... for our ancestors in Egypt,* i.e., by being saved from the ten plagues which were brought upon the Egyptians. Thus, each plague was accompanied by the miracle of Jewish salvation.

7. בְּבֵית הַמִּקְדָּשׁ — *In the Holy Temple,* the abode of the Divine Presence, where the laws of Nature were transcended.

בְּשַׂר הַקֹּדֶשׁ — *Sacrificial meat.* Flesh of the offerings was burned constantly on the Altar and for the meals of the *Kohanim.* The miracle was that no pregnant woman ever craved to eat this meat, for it would not be permitted her and she might otherwise miscarry if her craving were not satisfied.

קֶרִי — *Seminal emission,* which would have rendered the priest ritually contaminated and unfit to officiate in the Temple.

בָּעֹמֶר — *In the Omer* [see *Leviticus* 23:19]. The sheaf of barley offered in the Temple on the morning of the 16th of Nissan, after which people were allowed to eat the new grain crop. A limited amount of barley was cut on the night before [the second night of Passover] and offered the following morning. Had a ritual defect been found in the barley, the offering could not be brought that year.

וּבִשְׁתֵּי הַלֶּחֶם — *Or in the Two Loaves* [see *Leviticus* 23:17]. These had to be baked before the onset of Shavuos, and offered on the festival itself. If they became disqualified by a defect, replacements could not be baked.

וּבְלֶחֶם הַפָּנִים — *Or in the Showbread.* [See *Exodus* 25:30; *Leviticus* 24:5.] Twelve loaves were baked each Friday and placed on the Table in the Temple on the Sabbath, where they remained until new loaves replaced them on the following Sabbath. If a defect were found, the *mitzvah* could not be performed because new loaves could not be baked on the Sabbath.

[3] *There were ten generations from Noah to Abraham — to show the degree of His patience; for all those generations angered Him increasingly, until our forefather Abraham came and received the reward of them all.*

[4] *Our forefather Abraham was tested with ten trials, and he withstood them all — to show the degree of our forefather Abraham's love for God.*

[5] *Ten miracles were performed for our ancestors in Egypt and ten at the Sea. Ten plagues did the Holy One, Blessed is He, bring upon the Egyptians in Egypt and ten at the Sea.*

[6] *With ten trials did our ancestors test the Holy One, Blessed is He, in the Wilderness, as it is said: 'They have tested Me these ten times and did not heed My voice.'*[1]

[7] *Ten miracles were performed for our ancestors in the Holy Temple: No woman miscarried because of the aroma of the sacrificial meat; the sacrificial meat never became putrid; no fly was seen in the place where the meat was butchered; no seminal emission occurred to the High Priest on Yom Kippur; the rains did not extinguish the fire on the altar-pyre; the wind did not disperse the vertical column of smoke from the altar; no disqualification was found in the Omer, or in the Two Loaves, or in the Showbread; the people stood crowded together, yet prostrated themselves in ample space; neither serpent nor scorpion ever caused injury in Jerusalem; nor did any man say to his fellow, 'The space is insufficient for me to stay overnight in Jerusalem.'*

[8] *Ten things were created on Sabbath eve, at twilight. They are: The mouth of the earth; the mouth of the well; the mouth of the donkey; the rainbow [which was Noah's sign that there would be no future floods]; the manna; the staff; the shamir worm; the script; the inscription; and the Tablets. Some say also destructive spirits, Moses' grave, and the ram of our forefather Abraham. And some say also tongs, which are made with tongs.*

(1) *Numbers* 14:22.

צְפוּפִים — *Crowded together.* Throngs of pilgrims gathered in the Temple court on the Festivals and Yom Kippur, filling it to capacity. Yet miraculously, though there was not even enough room to stand, each person had ample room to prostrate himself and confess his sins on Yom Kippur or recite private prayers on the Festivals without being overheard by his neighbor.

צַר לִי הַמָּקוֹם — *The space is insufficient for me,* i.e., there is no room for me. Though throngs of people came to Jerusalem, especially for the festivals, there were sufficient accommodations for them all. Moreover, because of the holiness of the city, God provided for all residents of Jerusalem so that no one ever had to move to another city to seek a livelihood.

8. Even the provision for future miracles and exceptions to God's natural order were provided for in advance when He created the world, immediately prior to the first Sabbath.

פִּי הָאָרֶץ — *The mouth of the earth,* which engulfed Korach and his fellow conspirators [*Numbers* 16:32].

וּפִי הַבְּאֵר — *The mouth of the well,* which provided water for Israel in the Wilderness.

פִּי הָאָתוֹן — *The mouth of the donkey,* which spoke to Balaam [*Numbers* 22:28].

וְהַמַּטֶּה — *The staff,* with which Moses performed the signs in Egypt [*Exodus* 4:17]. According to Rabbinic tradition it belonged to Adam and was transmitted through the generations to Moses. The Four Letter divine Name was engraved on it.

וְהַשָּׁמִיר — *The shamir,* a small worm that, according to the Mishnah, split large stones as it crawled on them. Since no sword or iron — symbols of violence — could be used to hew the stones for the Temple's construction, the shamir took the place of conventional tools.

הַכְּתָב — *The script,* the form of the Hebrew alphabet *(Rashi).*

וְהַמִּכְתָּב — *The inscription,* the instrument used by God to engrave the לוחות, *Tablets,* of the Ten Commandments, which were miraculously 'written on both their sides' [*Exodus* 32:15]. The first Tablets were created then, but the second ones were carved by Moses.

אַף צְבָת בִּצְבָת עֲשׂוּיָה — *Also tongs, which are made*

[ט] שִׁבְעָה דְבָרִים בְּגֹלֶם, וְשִׁבְעָה בְּחָכָם. חָכָם אֵינוֹ מְדַבֵּר לִפְנֵי מִי שֶׁגָּדוֹל מִמֶּנּוּ בְּחָכְמָה וּבְמִנְיָן; וְאֵינוֹ נִכְנָס לְתוֹךְ דִּבְרֵי חֲבֵרוֹ; וְאֵינוֹ נִבְהָל לְהָשִׁיב; שׁוֹאֵל כְּעִנְיָן, וּמֵשִׁיב כַּהֲלָכָה; וְאוֹמֵר עַל רִאשׁוֹן רִאשׁוֹן, וְעַל אַחֲרוֹן אַחֲרוֹן; וְעַל מַה שֶּׁלֹּא שָׁמַע אוֹמֵר: „לֹא שָׁמַעְתִּי;" וּמוֹדֶה עַל הָאֱמֶת. וְחִלּוּפֵיהֶן בְּגֹלֶם.

[י] שִׁבְעָה מִינֵי פֻרְעָנִיּוֹת בָּאִין לָעוֹלָם עַל שִׁבְעָה גוּפֵי עֲבֵרָה: מִקְצָתָן מְעַשְּׂרִין וּמִקְצָתָן אֵינָן מְעַשְּׂרִין, רָעָב שֶׁל בַּצֹּרֶת בָּא, מִקְצָתָן רְעֵבִים וּמִקְצָתָן שְׂבֵעִים; גָּמְרוּ שֶׁלֹּא לְעַשֵּׂר, רָעָב שֶׁל מְהוּמָה וְשֶׁל בַּצֹּרֶת בָּא; וְשֶׁלֹּא לִטֹּל אֶת הַחַלָּה, רָעָב שֶׁל כְּלָיָה בָּא;

[יא] דֶּבֶר בָּא לָעוֹלָם — עַל מִיתוֹת הָאֲמוּרוֹת בַּתּוֹרָה שֶׁלֹּא נִמְסְרוּ לְבֵית דִּין, וְעַל פֵּרוֹת שְׁבִיעִית; חֶרֶב בָּאָה לָעוֹלָם — עַל עִנּוּי הַדִּין, וְעַל עִוּוּת הַדִּין, וְעַל הַמּוֹרִים בַּתּוֹרָה שֶׁלֹּא כַהֲלָכָה; חַיָּה רָעָה בָּאָה לָעוֹלָם — עַל שְׁבוּעַת שָׁוְא, וְעַל חִלּוּל הַשֵּׁם; גָּלוּת בָּאָה לָעוֹלָם — עַל עוֹבְדֵי עֲבוֹדָה זָרָה, וְעַל גִּלּוּי עֲרָיוֹת, וְעַל שְׁפִיכוּת דָּמִים, וְעַל שְׁמִטַּת הָאָרֶץ.

[יב] בְּאַרְבָּעָה פְרָקִים הַדֶּבֶר מִתְרַבֶּה: בָּרְבִיעִית, וּבַשְּׁבִיעִית, וּבְמוֹצָאֵי שְׁבִיעִית, וּבְמוֹצָאֵי הֶחָג שֶׁבְּכָל שָׁנָה וְשָׁנָה. בָּרְבִיעִית, מִפְּנֵי מַעֲשַׂר עָנִי שֶׁבַּשְּׁלִישִׁית; בַּשְּׁבִיעִית, מִפְּנֵי מַעֲשַׂר עָנִי שֶׁבַּשִּׁשִּׁית; בְּמוֹצָאֵי שְׁבִיעִית, מִפְּנֵי פֵּרוֹת שְׁבִיעִית; בְּמוֹצָאֵי הֶחָג שֶׁבְּכָל שָׁנָה וְשָׁנָה, מִפְּנֵי גֶזֶל מַתְּנוֹת עֲנִיִּים.

[יג] אַרְבַּע מִדּוֹת בָּאָדָם. הָאוֹמֵר: „שֶׁלִּי שֶׁלִּי וְשֶׁלְּךָ שֶׁלָּךְ," זוֹ מִדָּה בֵינוֹנִית, וְיֵשׁ אוֹמְרִים: זוֹ מִדַּת סְדוֹם; „שֶׁלִּי שֶׁלָּךְ וְשֶׁלְּךָ שֶׁלִּי," עַם הָאָרֶץ; "שֶׁלִּי שֶׁלָּךְ וְשֶׁלְּךָ שֶׁלָּךְ," חָסִיד; „שֶׁלְּךָ שֶׁלִּי וְשֶׁלִּי שֶׁלִּי," רָשָׁע.

[יד] אַרְבַּע מִדּוֹת בְּדֵעוֹת: נוֹחַ לִכְעוֹס וְנוֹחַ לִרְצוֹת, יָצָא שְׂכָרוֹ בְּהֶפְסֵדוֹ; קָשֶׁה לִכְעוֹס וְקָשֶׁה לִרְצוֹת, יָצָא הֶפְסֵדוֹ בִשְׂכָרוֹ; קָשֶׁה לִכְעוֹס וְנוֹחַ לִרְצוֹת, חָסִיד; נוֹחַ לִכְעוֹס וְקָשֶׁה לִרְצוֹת, רָשָׁע.

---

with tongs. Tongs are made with another pair which holds the red-hot metal for the smith. According to this view, God provided man with the original pair of tongs with which to make others.

9. רִאשׁוֹן רִאשׁוֹן — *First things first.* His mind works in an orderly, organized fashion.

לֹא שָׁמַעְתִּי — *'I have not heard.'* He does not fabricate false sources, nor is he ashamed to admit his ignorance.

וּמוֹדֶה עַל הָאֱמֶת — *And he acknowledges the truth.* He readily admits an error.

10-11. Seven forms of Divine retribution — 'measure for measure' — for seven sins. Every calamity that befalls mankind is a punishment for sin.

12. This mishnah elaborates on one of the themes of the preceding one, the sending of Plague [דֶּבֶר, *pestilence*] upon the earth. As noted previously, pestilence strikes the world for a variety of sins. Even at such times, however, the people dare not neglect their responsibilities to the poor. If they do, the pestilence would intensify. The special times of responsibility to the poor are at the harvests of the third and sixth years, when a tithe is to be given to the poor, and during the Sabbatical year, when everyone, including the poor, are entitled to take whatever grew in the fields during the year.

[9] *Seven traits characterize an uncultivated person and seven a learned one. A learned person does not begin speaking before one who is greater than he in wisdom or in years; he does not interrupt the words of his fellow; he does not answer impetuously; he questions with relevance to the subject and he replies accurately; he discusses first things first and last things last; about something he has not heard he says, 'I have not heard'; and he acknowledges the truth. And the reverse of these characterize an uncultivated person.*

[10] *Seven kinds of punishment come to the world for seven kinds of transgressions. (a) If some people tithe and others do not, a famine caused by lack of rain ensues, some go hungry and others are satisfied; (b) if all decided not to tithe, general famine caused by both armed bands and drought ensues; and (c) [if they also decided] not to separate the challah, a famine caused by destructive drought ensues;*

[11] *(d) pestilence comes to the world for the death penalties prescribed by the Torah that were not carried out by the court, and for illegally using the fruits of the Sabbatical year; (e) the sword of war comes to the world for the delay of justice, for the perversion of justice and for interpreting the Torah decision in opposition to the halachah; (f) wild beasts come upon the world for vain oaths and for Desecration of God's Name; (g) exile comes to the world for idolatry, for immorality, for bloodshed, and for working the earth during the Sabbatical year.*

[12] *At four periods [of the seven-year Sabbatical cycle] pestilence increases — in the fourth year, in the seventh year, in the year following the Sabbatical year, and annually following the Succos festival. In the fourth year, for [neglecting] the tithe of the poor in the third; in the seventh year, for [neglecting] the tithe of the poor in the sixth; in the year following the Sabbatical year, for [violating the laws of] the Sabbatical produce; annually, at the conclusion of the festival of Succos, for robbing the poor of their gifts.*

[13] *There are four character types among people: (a) One who says, 'My property is mine and yours is yours,' is an average character type, but some say this is characteristic of Sodom; (b) 'Mine is yours and yours is mine,' is an unlearned person; (c) 'Mine is yours and yours is yours,' is scrupulously pious; (d) 'Yours is mine and mine is mine,' is wicked.*

[14] *There are four types of temperament: (a) One who is angered easily and pacified easily, his gain is offset by his loss; (b) one who is hard to anger and hard to pacify, his loss is offset by his gain; (c) one who is hard to anger and easy to pacify is pious; (d) one who is easily angered and hard to pacify is wicked.*

גֶּזֶל מַתְּנוֹת עֲנִיִּים — *For robbing the poor of their gifts.* At harvest time, which is before Succos, the Torah requires farmers to leave dropped and forgotten sheaves and a corner of the field for the poor.

13. זוֹ מִדַּת סְדוֹם — *This is characteristic of Sodom,* whose residents displayed the epitome of selfishness — *'She did not strengthen the hand of the needy'* [*Ezekiel* 16:49]. According to this view, having an attitude of 'each man for himself' is not merely average, but unethical, since it negates the entire concept of charity and benevolence.

14. נוֹחַ לִכְעוֹס ... יָצָא שְׂכָרוֹ בְּהֶפְסֵדוֹ — *One who is angered easily ... his gain is offset by his loss.* [This is the version cited by *Rashi.*] The positive aspect of such a person's character is offset by the negative aspect of his being easily provoked; a moment of anger causes damage that cannot be erased easily by subsequent appeasement.

[טו] אַרְבַּע מִדּוֹת בְּתַלְמִידִים: מָהִיר לִשְׁמוֹעַ וּמָהִיר לְאַבֵּד, יָצָא שְׂכָרוֹ בְּהֶפְסֵדוֹ; קָשֶׁה לִשְׁמוֹעַ וְקָשֶׁה לְאַבֵּד, יָצָא הֶפְסֵדוֹ בִשְׂכָרוֹ; מָהִיר לִשְׁמוֹעַ וְקָשֶׁה לְאַבֵּד, זֶה חֵלֶק טוֹב; קָשֶׁה לִשְׁמוֹעַ וּמָהִיר לְאַבֵּד, זֶה חֵלֶק רָע.

[טז] אַרְבַּע מִדּוֹת בְּנוֹתְנֵי צְדָקָה: הָרוֹצֶה שֶׁיִּתֵּן וְלֹא יִתְּנוּ אֲחֵרִים, עֵינוֹ רָעָה בְּשֶׁל אֲחֵרִים; יִתְּנוּ אֲחֵרִים וְהוּא לֹא יִתֵּן, עֵינוֹ רָעָה בְּשֶׁלּוֹ; יִתֵּן וְיִתְּנוּ אֲחֵרִים, חָסִיד; לֹא יִתֵּן וְלֹא יִתְּנוּ אֲחֵרִים, רָשָׁע.

[יז] אַרְבַּע מִדּוֹת בְּהוֹלְכֵי בֵית הַמִּדְרָשׁ: הוֹלֵךְ וְאֵינוֹ עוֹשֶׂה, שְׂכַר הֲלִיכָה בְּיָדוֹ; עוֹשֶׂה וְאֵינוֹ הוֹלֵךְ, שְׂכַר מַעֲשֶׂה בְּיָדוֹ; הוֹלֵךְ וְעוֹשֶׂה, חָסִיד; לֹא הוֹלֵךְ וְלֹא עוֹשֶׂה, רָשָׁע.

[יח] אַרְבַּע מִדּוֹת בְּיוֹשְׁבִים לִפְנֵי חֲכָמִים: סְפוֹג, וּמַשְׁפֵּךְ, מְשַׁמֶּרֶת, וְנָפָה. סְפוֹג, שֶׁהוּא סוֹפֵג אֶת הַכֹּל; וּמַשְׁפֵּךְ, שֶׁמַּכְנִיס בְּזוֹ וּמוֹצִיא בְזוֹ; מְשַׁמֶּרֶת, שֶׁמּוֹצִיאָה אֶת הַיַּיִן וְקוֹלֶטֶת אֶת הַשְּׁמָרִים; וְנָפָה, שֶׁמּוֹצִיאָה אֶת הַקֶּמַח וְקוֹלֶטֶת אֶת הַסֹּלֶת.

[יט] כָּל אַהֲבָה שֶׁהִיא תְלוּיָה בְדָבָר, בָּטֵל דָּבָר, בְּטֵלָה אַהֲבָה; וְשֶׁאֵינָהּ תְּלוּיָה בְדָבָר, אֵינָהּ בְּטֵלָה לְעוֹלָם. אֵיזוֹ הִיא אַהֲבָה שֶׁהִיא תְלוּיָה בְדָבָר? זוֹ אַהֲבַת אַמְנוֹן וְתָמָר. וְשֶׁאֵינָהּ תְּלוּיָה בְדָבָר? זוֹ אַהֲבַת דָּוִד וִיהוֹנָתָן.

[כ] כָּל מַחֲלֹקֶת שֶׁהִיא לְשֵׁם שָׁמַיִם, סוֹפָהּ לְהִתְקַיֵּם; וְשֶׁאֵינָהּ לְשֵׁם שָׁמַיִם, אֵין סוֹפָהּ לְהִתְקַיֵּם. אֵיזוֹ הִיא מַחֲלֹקֶת שֶׁהִיא לְשֵׁם שָׁמַיִם? זוֹ מַחֲלֹקֶת הִלֵּל וְשַׁמַּאי. וְשֶׁאֵינָהּ לְשֵׁם שָׁמַיִם? זוֹ מַחֲלֹקֶת קֹרַח וְכָל עֲדָתוֹ.

[כא] כָּל הַמְּזַכֶּה אֶת הָרַבִּים, אֵין חֵטְא בָּא עַל יָדוֹ; וְכָל הַמַּחֲטִיא אֶת הָרַבִּים, אֵין מַסְפִּיקִין בְּיָדוֹ לַעֲשׂוֹת תְּשׁוּבָה. מֹשֶׁה זָכָה וְזִכָּה אֶת הָרַבִּים, זְכוּת הָרַבִּים תָּלוּי בּוֹ, שֶׁנֶּאֱמַר: „צִדְקַת יהוה עָשָׂה, וּמִשְׁפָּטָיו עִם

---

16. עֵינוֹ רָעָה בְּשֶׁל אֲחֵרִים — *He begrudges* [lit. *his eye is evil with regard to*] *others.* He does not want them to accrue merit and blessing for their charitable act; alternatively: he begrudges the needy any extra charity.

עֵינוֹ רָעָה בְּשֶׁלּוֹ — *He begrudges himself.* He begrudges himself the merit that would accrue to him from giving alms: he is more concerned about holding onto his wealth than about the greater blessing that he would receive for giving charity.

18. סוֹפֵג אֶת הַכֹּל — *Absorbs everything.* Though he remembers everything, he is not capable of distinguishing between the true and the false, the meaningful and the trivial.

he learns.

שֶׁמּוֹצִיאָה אֶת הַיַּיִן — *Which lets the wine flow through.* He retains only the minor, trivial points, and forgets the major, basic points.

שֶׁמּוֹצִיאָה אֶת הַקֶּמַח — *Which allows the flour dust to pass through and retains the fine flour.* The ideal is a sieve which is so constructed that it lets the coarse grain pass through and retains in a receptacle only the fine flour. The reference is to a student who retains the essence of his studies and ignores the superfluous.

19. שֶׁהִיא תְלוּיָה בְדָבָר — *That depends on a specific cause,* i.e., something material or sensual such as wealth or beauty, rather than an unselfish union based on mutual respect and affection, and an interest in the good of the

[15] *There are four types of students: (a) One who grasps quickly and forgets quickly, his gain is offset by his loss; (b) one who grasps slowly and forgets slowly, his loss is offset by his gain; (c) one who grasps quickly and forgets slowly, this is a good portion; (d) one who grasps slowly and forgets quickly, this is a bad portion.*

[16] *There are four types of donors to charity: (a) One who wishes to give himself but wants others not to give, he begrudges others; (b) that others should give but that he should not give, he begrudges himself; (c) that he should give and that others should give is pious; (d) that he should not give and that others should not give is wicked.*

[17] *There are four types among those who go to the house of study: (a) One who goes but does not study, has the reward for going; (b) one who studies [at home] but does not attend [the house of study], has the reward for accomplishment; (c) one who goes and studies is pious; (d) one who does not go and does not study is wicked.*

[18] *There are four types among students who sit before the sages: A sponge, a funnel, a strainer and a sieve: a sponge, which absorbs everything; a funnel, which lets in from one end and lets out from the other; a strainer, which lets the wine flow through and retains the sediment; and a sieve, which allows the flour dust to pass through and retains the fine flour.*

[19] *Any love that depends on a specific cause, when that cause is gone, the love is gone; but if it does not depend on a specific cause, it will never cease. What sort of love depended upon a specific cause? — The love of Amnon for Tamar. And what did not depend upon a specific cause? — The love of David and Jonathan.*

[20] *Any dispute that is for the sake of Heaven will have a constructive outcome; but one that is not for the sake of Heaven will not have a constructive outcome. What sort of dispute was for the sake of Heaven? — The dispute between Hillel and Shammai. And which was not for the sake of Heaven? — The dispute of Korach and his entire company.*

[21] *Whoever influences the masses to become meritorious shall not be the cause of sin; but one who influences the masses to sin will not be given the means to repent. Moses was meritorious and influenced the masses to be meritorious, so the merit of the masses was to his credit, as it is said: 'He performed the righteousness of* H*ASHEM, and His laws together with*

אַמְנוֹן וְתָמָר — *Amnon for Tamar.* Amnon's love was motivated by Tamar's beauty. See *II Samuel* 13.

דָּוִד וִיהוֹנָתָן — *David and Jonathan* whose souls were bound up with one another. Even though each knew that the other stood in the way of his succession to the throne, their love for one another was not affected. See *I Samuel* 18.

20. סוֹפָהּ לְהִתְקַיֵּם — *Will have a constructive outcome.* There are several interpretations: their respective views will be remembered, even those of the one whose opinion is not adopted *(Rambam);* since their disputes result in a clearer understanding of the Torah, they will continue to have such disputes *(R' Yonah);* the disputants will live and survive, unlike Korach's company that perished *(Rav);* the disputants will succeed in their goal of finding and clarifying the truth *(Rav).*

הִלֵּל וְשַׁמַּאי — *Hillel and Shammai.* Though they had disputes regarding Halachah, they were concerned not with triumph but with a sincere search for truth in the exposition of Torah.

קֹרַח וְכָל עֲדָתוֹ — *Korach and his entire company.* Their dispute was merely a rebellion against authority, and accordingly met a tragic end. See *Numbers* 16.

21. אֵין מַסְפִּיקִין בְּיָדוֹ — *Will not be given the means to repent.* As a general rule, God helps those who seek to repent. But in the case of

יִשְׂרָאֵל."[1] יָרָבְעָם בֶּן נְבָט חָטָא וְהֶחֱטִיא אֶת הָרַבִּים, חֵטְא הָרַבִּים תָּלוּי בּוֹ, שֶׁנֶּאֱמַר: „עַל חַטֹּאות יָרָבְעָם אֲשֶׁר חָטָא, וַאֲשֶׁר הֶחֱטִיא אֶת יִשְׂרָאֵל."[2]

[כב] כָּל מִי שֶׁיֵּשׁ בְּיָדוֹ שְׁלֹשָׁה דְבָרִים הַלָּלוּ, הוּא מִתַּלְמִידָיו שֶׁל אַבְרָהָם אָבִינוּ; וּשְׁלֹשָׁה דְבָרִים אֲחֵרִים, הוּא מִתַּלְמִידָיו שֶׁל בִּלְעָם הָרָשָׁע. עַיִן טוֹבָה, וְרוּחַ נְמוּכָה, וְנֶפֶשׁ שְׁפָלָה, תַּלְמִידָיו שֶׁל אַבְרָהָם אָבִינוּ. עַיִן רָעָה, וְרוּחַ גְּבוֹהָה, וְנֶפֶשׁ רְחָבָה, תַּלְמִידָיו שֶׁל בִּלְעָם הָרָשָׁע. מַה בֵּין תַּלְמִידָיו שֶׁל אַבְרָהָם אָבִינוּ לְתַלְמִידָיו שֶׁל בִּלְעָם הָרָשָׁע? תַּלְמִידָיו שֶׁל אַבְרָהָם אָבִינוּ אוֹכְלִין בָּעוֹלָם הַזֶּה, וְנוֹחֲלִין הָעוֹלָם הַבָּא, שֶׁנֶּאֱמַר: „לְהַנְחִיל אֹהֲבַי יֵשׁ, וְאֹצְרֹתֵיהֶם אֲמַלֵּא."[3] אֲבָל תַּלְמִידָיו שֶׁל בִּלְעָם הָרָשָׁע יוֹרְשִׁין גֵּיהִנֹּם, וְיוֹרְדִין לִבְאֵר שַׁחַת, שֶׁנֶּאֱמַר: „וְאַתָּה אֱלֹהִים תּוֹרִדֵם לִבְאֵר שַׁחַת, אַנְשֵׁי דָמִים וּמִרְמָה לֹא יֶחֱצוּ יְמֵיהֶם, וַאֲנִי אֶבְטַח בָּךְ."[4]

[כג] יְהוּדָה בֶּן תֵּימָא אוֹמֵר: הֱוֵי עַז כַּנָּמֵר, וְקַל כַּנֶּשֶׁר, רָץ כַּצְּבִי, וְגִבּוֹר כָּאֲרִי לַעֲשׂוֹת רְצוֹן אָבִיךָ שֶׁבַּשָּׁמָיִם.

[כד] הוּא הָיָה אוֹמֵר: עַז פָּנִים לְגֵיהִנֹּם, וּבֹשֶׁת פָּנִים לְגַן עֵדֶן. יְהִי רָצוֹן מִלְּפָנֶיךָ יהוה אֱלֹהֵינוּ וֵאלֹהֵי אֲבוֹתֵינוּ שֶׁיִּבָּנֶה בֵּית הַמִּקְדָּשׁ בִּמְהֵרָה בְיָמֵינוּ וְתֵן חֶלְקֵנוּ בְּתוֹרָתֶךָ.

[כה] הוּא הָיָה אוֹמֵר: בֶּן חָמֵשׁ שָׁנִים לַמִּקְרָא, בֶּן עֶשֶׂר שָׁנִים לַמִּשְׁנָה, בֶּן שְׁלֹשׁ עֶשְׂרֵה לַמִּצְוֹת, בֶּן חֲמֵשׁ עֶשְׂרֵה לַגְּמָרָא, בֶּן שְׁמוֹנֶה עֶשְׂרֵה לַחֻפָּה, בֶּן עֶשְׂרִים לִרְדּוֹף, בֶּן שְׁלֹשִׁים לַכֹּחַ, בֶּן אַרְבָּעִים לַבִּינָה, בֶּן חֲמִשִּׁים לְעֵצָה, בֶּן שִׁשִּׁים לְזִקְנָה, בֶּן שִׁבְעִים לְשֵׂיבָה, בֶּן שְׁמוֹנִים לִגְבוּרָה, בֶּן תִּשְׁעִים לָשׁוּחַ, בֶּן מֵאָה כְּאִלּוּ מֵת וְעָבַר וּבָטֵל מִן הָעוֹלָם.

[כו] בֶּן בַּג בַּג אוֹמֵר: הֲפָךְ בָּהּ וַהֲפָךְ בָּהּ, דְּכֹלָּה בָהּ; וּבָהּ תֶּחֱזֵי, וְסִיב

---

someone who is responsible for the spiritual downfall of others, it would be unfair to help him escape punishment while his victims must suffer for their sins. However, even so egregious a sinner *can* repent, though he will not receive Divine assistance.

24. וּבֹשֶׁת פָּנִים — *But the shamefaced,* i.e., those who feel a sense of shame when thinking about sin. Such people will not sin habitually and will be rewarded with Gan Eden.

יְהִי רָצוֹן — *May it be Your will.* According to the *Vilna Gaon,* this prayer belongs at the end of the chapter.

25. בֶּן עֶשְׂרִים לִרְדּוֹף — *A twenty-year-old begins pursuit [of a livelihood].* Most familiarly understood to refer to the pursuit of a livelihood, which naturally follows soon after marriage. *Rashi* cites an opinion that it refers to the age when the Heavenly court *pursues* man for his actions — holding him liable for Divine punishment for his sins.

בֶּן חֲמִשִּׁים לְעֵצָה — *A fifty-year-old can offer counsel.* Fifty was the age at which Levites were no longer considered fit for heavy work, but continued to act as guides and counselors to the younger Levites [*Numbers* 8:25]. At this age one can draw on his life experience and intellect to advise others.

בֶּן שִׁשִּׁים לְזִקְנָה — *A sixty-year-old attains seniority* [literally *old age*]. This denotes one's appearance at that age, or it refers to intellectual maturity [זָקֵן=זֶה שֶׁקָּנָה חָכְמָה].

בֶּן שִׁבְעִים לְשֵׂיבָה — *A seventy-year-old attains a ripe old age.* This was the age at which David died, of whom it was said: *he died in fullness of years* [בְּשֵׂיבָה טוֹבָה] (*I Chronicles* 29:28).

Israel.'[1] *Jeroboam ben Nebat sinned and caused the masses to sin, so the sin of the masses is charged against him, as it is said: 'For the sins of Jeroboam which he committed and which he caused Israel to commit.'*[2]

[22] *Whoever has the following three traits is among the disciples of our forefather Abraham; and [whoever has] three different traits is among the disciples of the wicked Balaam. Those who have a good eye, a humble spirit, and a meek soul are among the disciples of our forefather Abraham. Those who have an evil eye, an arrogant spirit, and a greedy soul are among the disciples of the wicked Balaam. How are the disciples of our forefather Abraham different from the disciples of the wicked Balaam? The disciples of our forefather Abraham enjoy [the fruits of their good deeds] in this world and inherit the World to Come, as is said: 'To cause those who love Me to inherit an everlasting possession [the World to Come], and I will fill their storehouses [in this world]'.*[3] *But the disciples of the wicked Balaam inherit Gehinnom and descend into the well of destruction, as is said: 'And You, O God, shall lower them into the well of destruction, men of bloodshed and deceit shall not live out half their days; but as for me, I will trust in You.'*[4]

[23] *Yehudah ben Tema said: Be bold as a leopard, light as an eagle, swift as a deer, and strong as a lion, to carry out the will of your Father in Heaven.*

[24] *He used to say: The brazen goes to Gehinnom, but the shamefaced goes to the Garden of Eden. May it be Your will,* HASHEM, *our God and the God of our forefathers, that the Holy Temple be rebuilt, speedily in our days, and grant us our share in Your Torah.*

[25] *He used to say: A five-year-old begins Scripture; a ten-year-old begins Mishnah; a thirteen-year-old becomes obliged to observe the commandments; a fifteen-year-old begins the study of Gemara; an eighteen-year-old goes to the marriage canopy; a twenty-year-old begins pursuit [of a livelihood]; a thirty-year-old attains full strength; a forty-year-old attains understanding; a fifty-year-old can offer counsel; a sixty year-old attains seniority; a seventy-year-old attains a ripe old age; an eighty-year-old shows strength; a ninety-year-old becomes stooped over; a hundred-year-old is as if he were dead, passed away and ceased from the world.*

[26] *Ben Bag Bag says: Delve in it [the Torah] and continue to delve in it [the Torah] for everything is in it; look deeply into it; grow old and*

---

(1) *Deuteronomy* 33:21. (2) *I Kings* 15:30. (3) *Proverbs* 8:21. (4) *Psalms* 55:24.

בֶּן שְׁמוֹנִים לִגְבוּרָה — *An eighty-year-old shows strength.* This follows *Psalms* 90:10: *The days of our years — among them are seventy years, and if with strength — eighty years.* When one lives to be over eighty, it is because God has granted him special natural strength and vigor; it is an age invested with an abundance of spiritual vigor as well.

בֶּן מֵאָה כְּאִלּוּ מֵת — *A hundred-year-old is as if he were dead.* He has lost most of his natural faculties.

26. בֶּן בַּג בַּג ... בֶּן הֵא הֵא — *Ben Bag Bag ... Ben Hei Hei.* The former's full name was R' Yochanan ben Bag Bag [*Kiddushin* 10b]. Both Bag Bag and Hei Hei were descendants of proselytes whose names were disguised to protect them from informers who would have turned them over to the Romans. Some interpret בַּג בַּג as an abbreviation for בֶּן גֵּר בֶּן גִּיוֹרֶת, *the son of male and female proselytes.* There is a view that the name *Hei Hei* alludes to the first 'proselytes,' Abraham and Sarah, to each of whose names God added the letter ה, *hei.* Thus the name אַבְרָם became אַבְרָהָם and שָׂרַי became שָׂרָה. The name Bag Bag also contains this allusion because the numerical value of בַּג (2 and 3) equals ה (5). See *Tosafos Chagigah* 9b.

הֲפָךְ בָּהּ — *Delve in it* [the Torah; lit. *turn over in it*]. Study the Torah from all sides.

דְּכֹלָּה בָהּ — *For everything is in it.* The Torah is a

וּבְלֵה בָהּ, וּמִנַּהּ לָא תָזוּעַ, שֶׁאֵין לְךָ מִדָּה טוֹבָה הֵימֶנָּה. בֶּן הֵא הֵא אוֹמֵר: לְפוּם צַעֲרָא אַגְרָא.

❀ ❀ ❀

רַבִּי חֲנַנְיָא בֶּן עֲקַשְׁיָא אוֹמֵר: רָצָה הַקָּדוֹשׁ בָּרוּךְ הוּא לְזַכּוֹת אֶת יִשְׂרָאֵל, לְפִיכָךְ הִרְבָּה לָהֶם תּוֹרָה וּמִצְוֹת, שֶׁנֶּאֱמַר: „יהוה חָפֵץ לְמַעַן צִדְקוֹ יַגְדִּיל תּוֹרָה וְיַאְדִּיר.״[1]

In the presence of a *minyan,* mourners recite קַדִּישׁ דְּרַבָּנָן, the Rabbis' *Kaddish* (p. 52). Then the congregation continues with עָלֵינוּ (p. 526).

פרק ששי

כָּל יִשְׂרָאֵל יֵשׁ לָהֶם חֵלֶק לָעוֹלָם הַבָּא, שֶׁנֶּאֱמַר: „וְעַמֵּךְ כֻּלָּם צַדִּיקִים, לְעוֹלָם יִירְשׁוּ אָרֶץ, נֵצֶר מַטָּעַי, מַעֲשֵׂה יָדַי לְהִתְפָּאֵר.״[2]

❀ ❀ ❀

שָׁנוּ חֲכָמִים בִּלְשׁוֹן הַמִּשְׁנָה. בָּרוּךְ שֶׁבָּחַר בָּהֶם וּבְמִשְׁנָתָם.

[א] רַבִּי מֵאִיר אוֹמֵר: כָּל הָעוֹסֵק בַּתּוֹרָה לִשְׁמָהּ זוֹכֶה לִדְבָרִים הַרְבֵּה; וְלֹא עוֹד, אֶלָּא שֶׁכָּל הָעוֹלָם כֻּלּוֹ כְּדַאי הוּא לוֹ. נִקְרָא רֵעַ, אָהוּב. אוֹהֵב אֶת הַמָּקוֹם, אוֹהֵב אֶת הַבְּרִיּוֹת, מְשַׂמֵּחַ אֶת הַמָּקוֹם, מְשַׂמֵּחַ אֶת הַבְּרִיּוֹת. וּמַלְבַּשְׁתּוֹ עֲנָוָה וְיִרְאָה; וּמַכְשַׁרְתּוֹ לִהְיוֹת צַדִּיק, חָסִיד, יָשָׁר, וְנֶאֱמָן; וּמְרַחַקְתּוֹ מִן הַחֵטְא, וּמְקָרַבְתּוֹ לִידֵי זְכוּת. וְנֶהֱנִין מִמֶּנּוּ עֵצָה וְתוּשִׁיָּה, בִּינָה וּגְבוּרָה, שֶׁנֶּאֱמַר: „לִי עֵצָה וְתוּשִׁיָּה, אֲנִי בִינָה, לִי גְבוּרָה״.[3] וְנוֹתֶנֶת לוֹ מַלְכוּת, וּמֶמְשָׁלָה, וְחִקּוּר דִּין; וּמְגַלִּין לוֹ רָזֵי תוֹרָה; וְנַעֲשֶׂה כְּמַעְיָן הַמִּתְגַּבֵּר, וּכְנָהָר שֶׁאֵינוֹ פוֹסֵק; וְהֹוֶה צָנוּעַ, וְאֶרֶךְ רוּחַ, וּמוֹחֵל עַל עֶלְבּוֹנוֹ. וּמְגַדַּלְתּוֹ וּמְרוֹמַמְתּוֹ עַל כָּל הַמַּעֲשִׂים.

[ב] אָמַר רַבִּי יְהוֹשֻׁעַ בֶּן לֵוִי: בְּכָל יוֹם וָיוֹם בַּת קוֹל יוֹצֵאת מֵהַר חוֹרֵב, וּמַכְרֶזֶת וְאוֹמֶרֶת: „אוֹי לָהֶם לַבְּרִיּוֹת, מֵעֶלְבּוֹנָהּ שֶׁל תּוֹרָה!״ שֶׁכָּל מִי שֶׁאֵינוֹ עוֹסֵק בַּתּוֹרָה נִקְרָא נָזוּף, שֶׁנֶּאֱמַר: „נֶזֶם זָהָב בְּאַף חֲזִיר,

---

self-contained guide to life; all of the world's wisdom is contained in it.

This and the following paragraph are quoted in Aramaic, the vernacular of Mishnaic times, since they were popular folk-sayings.

לְפוּם צַעֲרָא אַגְרָא — *The reward is in proportion to the exertion.* The reward for observing God's commandment is increased in proportion to the effort and discomfort one experiences in its performance.

CHAPTER SIX

שָׁנוּ חֲכָמִים — *The Sages taught.* This phrase is the Hebrew equivalent of the familiar Aramaic תָּנוּ רַבָּנָן which the Talmud uses to introduce a *baraisa.* The word *baraisa,* literally *outside,* refers to tannaitic teachings that were not selected for inclusion in the Mishnah, but were preserved 'outside' of it. They were written in the style of the Mishnah and supplement it.

This chapter is not part of the tractate *Avos,* but is a collection of *baraisos (Kallah* 8). Its inclusion brings to six the number of chapters in *Avos,* corresponding to the six Sabbaths between Pesach and Shavuos, during which one cycle of *Pirkei Avos* is read, one chapter each Sabbath. Thus, this chapter is studied on the Sabbath preceding Shavuos, the Festival commemorating the giving of the Torah. Dealing as it does with acquiring Torah knowledge, this final added chapter has been named קִנְיַן תּוֹרָה, *Acquisition of Torah.* It is also called *Baraisa of R' Meir* since it opens with a *baraisa* attributed to him.

1. On the qualities acquired from Torah study.

לִשְׁמָהּ — *For its own sake.* From pure love of God,

gray over it, and do not stir from it, for you can have no better portion than it. Ben Hei Hei says: The reward is in proportion to the exertion.

❀ ❀ ❀

Rabbi Chanania ben Akashia says: The Holy One, Blessed is He, wished to confer merit upon Israel; therefore He gave them Torah and mitzvos in abundance, as it is said: 'HASHEM desired, for the sake of its [Israel's] righteousness, that the Torah be made great and glorious.'[1]

In the presence of a *minyan,* mourners recite קַדִּישׁ דְּרַבָּנָן, the Rabbis' *Kaddish* (p. 52). Then the congregation continues with עָלֵינוּ, *Aleinu* (p. 526).

CHAPTER SIX

All Israel has a share in the World to Come, as it is said: 'And your people are all righteous; they shall inherit the land forever; they are the branch of My planting, My handiwork, in which to take pride.'[2]

❀ ❀ ❀

שָׁנוּ חֲכָמִים *The Sages taught [this chapter] in the language of the Mishnah. Blessed is He who chose them and their teaching.*

[1] *Rabbi Meir said: Whoever engages in Torah study for its own sake merits many things; furthermore, [the creation of] the entire world is worthwhile for his sake alone. He is called, 'Friend, Beloved.' He loves the Omnipresent, he loves [His] creatures, he gladdens the Omnipresent, he gladdens [His] creatures. [The Torah] clothes him in humility and fear [of God]; it makes him fit to be righteous, devout, fair and faithful. It moves him away from sin and draws him near to merit. From him people enjoy counsel and wisdom, understanding and strength, as it is said: 'Mine are counsel and wisdom, I am understanding, mine is strength.'*[3] *[The Torah] gives him kingship and dominion and analytical judgment; the secrets of the Torah are revealed to him; he becomes like a steadily strengthening fountain and like an unceasing river. He becomes modest, patient, and forgiving of insult to himself. [The Torah] makes him great and exalts him above all things.*

[2] *Rabbi Yehoshua ben Levi said: Every single day a heavenly voice emanates from Mount Horeb, proclaiming and saying, 'Woe to them, to the people, because of [their] insult to the Torah!' For whoever does not occupy himself with the Torah is called, 'Rebuked,' as it is said: 'Like a golden ring in a swine's*

(1) *Isaiah* 42:21. (2) 60:21. (3) *Proverbs* 8:14.

---

and for the sole motive of acquiring a knowledge of God's will, and fulfilling His commandments without any ulterior motive.

זוֹכֶה לִדְבָרִים הַרְבֵּה — *Merits many things.* The blessings awaiting this person are too bountiful to be specified.

כְּדַאי הוּא לוֹ — *Is worthwhile for his sake alone.* The entire world was created for such a person since its purpose is realized through him.

אוֹהֵב אֶת הַבְּרִיּוֹת — *He loves [His] creatures,* without distinction, cynicism or malice of any kind, because they are God's creation.

לִי עֵצָה וְתוּשִׁיָּה — *Mine are counsel and wisdom.* The 'speaker' is the Torah. It tells its adherents that it provides not only wisdom, but the spiritual *strength* to prevail over adversity. Furthermore it gives kings and scholars the guidance in law and behavior to exercise moral power.

2. מֵהַר חוֹרֵב — *From Mount Horeb.* Another name for Mount Sinai, where the Torah was given. This voice from Mount Horeb denotes the perpetual witness of the Torah to man's actions.

נֶזֶם זָהָב בְּאַף חֲזִיר — *Like a golden ring in a swine's snout.* In our context the Torah is represented by a golden ring which becomes degraded and sullied when the 'pig' wallows in dirt. This proof verse is related by means of the Rabbinic exposition of *notarikon* [abbreviated shorthand], whereby the initial letters of **נֶזֶם זָהָב** are combined with the last letter of **בְּאַף** to form **נזף**.

אִשָּׁה יָפָה וְסָרַת טָעַם.״[1] וְאוֹמֵר: ,,וְהַלֻּחֹת מַעֲשֵׂה אֱלֹהִים הֵמָּה וְהַמִּכְתָּב מִכְתַּב אֱלֹהִים הוּא חָרוּת עַל הַלֻּחֹת״.[2] אַל תִּקְרָא ,,חָרוּת״ אֶלָּא ,,חֵרוּת,״ שֶׁאֵין לְךָ בֶּן חוֹרִין אֶלָּא מִי שֶׁעוֹסֵק בְּתַלְמוּד תּוֹרָה. וְכָל מִי שֶׁעוֹסֵק בְּתַלְמוּד תּוֹרָה הֲרֵי זֶה מִתְעַלֶּה, שֶׁנֶּאֱמַר: ,,וּמִמַּתָּנָה נַחֲלִיאֵל, וּמִנַּחֲלִיאֵל בָּמוֹת.״[3]

[ג] הַלּוֹמֵד מֵחֲבֵרוֹ פֶּרֶק אֶחָד, אוֹ הֲלָכָה אַחַת, אוֹ פָּסוּק אֶחָד, אוֹ דִבּוּר אֶחָד, אוֹ אֲפִילוּ אוֹת אַחַת — צָרִיךְ לִנְהָג בּוֹ כָּבוֹד. שֶׁכֵּן מָצִינוּ בְּדָוִד מֶלֶךְ יִשְׂרָאֵל, שֶׁלֹּא לָמַד מֵאֲחִיתֹפֶל אֶלָּא שְׁנֵי דְבָרִים בִּלְבָד, וּקְרָאוֹ רַבּוֹ, אַלּוּפוֹ, וּמְיֻדָּעוֹ, שֶׁנֶּאֱמַר: ,,וְאַתָּה אֱנוֹשׁ כְּעֶרְכִּי, אַלּוּפִי וּמְיֻדָּעִי.״[4] וַהֲלֹא דְבָרִים קַל וָחֹמֶר: וּמַה דָּוִד מֶלֶךְ יִשְׂרָאֵל, שֶׁלֹּא לָמַד מֵאֲחִיתֹפֶל אֶלָּא שְׁנֵי דְבָרִים בִּלְבָד, קְרָאוֹ רַבּוֹ אַלּוּפוֹ וּמְיֻדָּעוֹ — הַלּוֹמֵד מֵחֲבֵרוֹ פֶּרֶק אֶחָד, אוֹ הֲלָכָה אַחַת, אוֹ פָּסוּק אֶחָד, אוֹ דִבּוּר אֶחָד, אוֹ אֲפִילוּ אוֹת אַחַת, עַל אַחַת כַּמָּה וְכַמָּה שֶׁצָּרִיךְ לִנְהָג בּוֹ כָּבוֹד! וְאֵין כָּבוֹד אֶלָּא תוֹרָה, שֶׁנֶּאֱמַר: ,,כָּבוֹד חֲכָמִים יִנְחָלוּ״;[5] ,,וּתְמִימִים יִנְחֲלוּ טוֹב״[6] וְאֵין טוֹב אֶלָּא תוֹרָה, שֶׁנֶּאֱמַר: ,,כִּי לֶקַח טוֹב נָתַתִּי לָכֶם, תּוֹרָתִי אַל תַּעֲזֹבוּ.״[7]

[ד] כַּךְ הִיא דַרְכָּהּ שֶׁל תּוֹרָה: פַּת בְּמֶלַח תֹּאכֵל, וּמַיִם בַּמְּשׂוּרָה תִּשְׁתֶּה, וְעַל הָאָרֶץ תִּישָׁן, וְחַיֵּי צַעַר תִּחְיֶה, וּבַתּוֹרָה אַתָּה עָמֵל; אִם אַתָּה עוֹשֶׂה כֵּן, ,,אַשְׁרֶיךָ וְטוֹב לָךְ״:[8] ,,אַשְׁרֶיךָ״ — בָּעוֹלָם הַזֶּה, ,,וְטוֹב לָךְ״ — לָעוֹלָם הַבָּא.

[ה] אַל תְּבַקֵּשׁ גְּדֻלָּה לְעַצְמְךָ, וְאַל תַּחְמֹד כָּבוֹד; יוֹתֵר מִלִּמּוּדְךָ עֲשֵׂה. וְאַל תִּתְאַוֶּה לְשֻׁלְחָנָם שֶׁל מְלָכִים, שֶׁשֻּׁלְחָנְךָ גָּדוֹל מִשֻּׁלְחָנָם, וְכִתְרְךָ גָּדוֹל מִכִּתְרָם; וְנֶאֱמָן הוּא בַּעַל מְלַאכְתְּךָ, שֶׁיְּשַׁלֶּם לְךָ שְׂכַר פְּעֻלָּתֶךָ.

[ו] גְּדוֹלָה תוֹרָה יוֹתֵר מִן הַכְּהֻנָּה וּמִן הַמַּלְכוּת, שֶׁהַמַּלְכוּת נִקְנֵית בִּשְׁלֹשִׁים מַעֲלוֹת, וְהַכְּהֻנָּה נִקְנֵית בְּעֶשְׂרִים וְאַרְבָּעָה, וְהַתּוֹרָה נִקְנֵית בְּאַרְבָּעִים וּשְׁמוֹנָה דְבָרִים, וְאֵלּוּ הֵן: בְּתַלְמוּד, בִּשְׁמִיעַת הָאֹזֶן, בַּעֲרִיכַת שְׂפָתַיִם, בְּבִינַת הַלֵּב, בְּשִׂכְלוּת הַלֵּב, בְּאֵימָה, בְּיִרְאָה, בַּעֲנָוָה, בְּשִׂמְחָה, בְּטָהֳרָה, בְּשִׁמּוּשׁ חֲכָמִים, בְּדִקְדּוּק חֲבֵרִים, בְּפִלְפּוּל הַתַּלְמִידִים, בְּיִשּׁוּב, בְּמִקְרָא, בְּמִשְׁנָה, בְּמִעוּט סְחוֹרָה, בְּמִעוּט דֶּרֶךְ אֶרֶץ, בְּמִעוּט תַּעֲנוּג,

---

וְאוֹמֵר — *And it says:* The *baraisa* now teaches another lesson regarding those who are committed to Torah; it is the source of true freedom.

אַל תִּקְרָא חָרוּת אֶלָּא חֵרוּת — *Do not read 'charus'* (engraved) *but 'cherus'* (freedom). The Torah is unvowelized, and the Rabbis often employ this interpretive method of reading a word with different vowels to elicit a homiletic thought. Nevertheless, the simple meaning of the verse remains unchanged.

וּמִמַּתָּנָה נַחֲלִיאֵל ... בָּמוֹת — *Mattanah ... Nachaliel ... Bamos.* These are place names which are homiletically interpreted here in their literal sense — מַתָּנָה, *gift* ... נַחֲלִיאֵל, *divine heritage* ... בָּמוֹת, *heights* — rendering the verse: *From the gift of Torah man gains a divine heritage which elevates him and leads him to lofty spiritual heights.*

3. שְׁנֵי דְבָרִים — *Two things.* They were: that one should not study Torah alone but with a colleague; and that when going to the House of God one should walk with reverence — or according to another interpretation: run with exuberance and vigor.

4. כַּךְ הִיא דַרְכָּהּ — *This is the way.* Asceticism is

snout is a beautiful woman who turns away from good judgment.'[1] *And it says: 'The Tablets are God's handiwork and the script was God's script charus (engraved) on the Tablets.'*[2] *Do not read 'charus' (engraved) but 'cherus' (freedom), for you can have no freer man than one who engages in the study of the Torah. And anyone who engages in the study of the Torah becomes elevated, as it is said: 'From Mattanah to Nachaliel, and from Nachaliel to Bamos.'*[3]

[3] *He who learns from his fellowman a single chapter, a single halachah, a single verse, a single Torah statement, or even a single letter, must treat him with honor. For thus we find in the case of David, King of Israel, who learned nothing from Achitophel except for two things, yet called him his teacher, his guide, his intimate, as it is said: 'You are a man of my measure, my guide and my intimate.'*[4] *One can derive from this the following: If David, King of Israel, who learned nothing from Achitophel except for two things, called him his teacher, his guide, his intimate — one who learns from his fellowman a single chapter, a single halachah, a single verse, a single statement, or even a single letter, how much more must he treat him with honor! And honor is due only for Torah, as it is said: 'The wise shall inherit honor,'*[5] *'... and the perfect shall inherit good.'*[6] *And only Torah is truly good, as it is said: 'I have given you a good teaching, do not forsake My Torah.'*[7]

[4] *This is the way of Torah: Eat bread with salt, drink water in small measure, sleep on the ground, live a life of deprivation — but toil in the Torah! If you do this, 'You are praiseworthy, and all is well with you.'*[8] *'You are praiseworthy' — in this world; 'and all is well with you' — in the World to Come.*

[5] *Do not seek greatness for yourself, and do not crave honor; let your performance exceed your learning. Do not lust for the table of kings, for your table is greater than theirs, and your crown is greater than their crown; and your Employer is trustworthy to pay you remuneration for your deeds.*

[6] *Torah is even greater than priesthood or royalty; for royalty is acquired along with thirty prerogatives, and the priesthood with twenty-four [gifts], but the Torah is acquired by means of forty-eight qualities, which are: Study, attentive listening, articulate speech, intuitive understanding, discernment, awe, reverence, modesty, joy, purity, ministering to the sages, closeness with colleagues, sharp discussion with students, deliberation, [knowledge of] Scripture, Mishnah, limited business activity, limited sexual activity, limited*

(1) *Proverbs* 11:22. (2) *Exodus* 32:16. (3) *Numbers* 21:19. (4) *Psalms* 55:14.
(5) *Proverbs* 3:35. (6) 28:10. (7) 4:2. (8) *Psalms* 128:2.

not being advocated here; one who is wealthy is not expected to cast away his wealth in the pursuit of Torah. Rather, this is a general call for moderation and an address to the poor person: Even if you are poverty-stricken do not neglect Torah study to pursue tangible wealth. The serenity of Torah can be experienced even in privation, and one must always be prepared to sacrifice his personal comfort on behalf of Torah.

5. וְאַל תַּחְמֹד כָּבוֹד — *And do not crave honor* for your scholarly attainments in Torah study, for you will thereby negate the pure motives required for study of Torah for its own sake [see Mishnah 1].

שֶׁשֻּׁלְחָנְךָ — *For your table,* i.e., spiritually in the World to Come.

6. בִּשְׁלֹשִׁים מַעֲלוֹת — *Along with thirty prerogatives.* These are privileges that go with the office. They are enumerated in *Sanhedrin* 18a. See also *I Samuel* 8:11*ff* and *Deut.* 17:5*ff.*

בְּעֶשְׂרִים וְאַרְבָּעָה — *With twenty-four.* The twenty-four priestly gifts are deduced from *Leviticus* 21 and *Numbers* 18.

בְּמִעוּט שֵׁנָה, בְּמִעוּט שִׂיחָה, בְּמִעוּט שְׂחוֹק, בְּאֶרֶךְ אַפַּיִם, בְּלֵב טוֹב, בֶּאֱמוּנַת חֲכָמִים, בְּקַבָּלַת הַיִּסּוּרִין, הַמַּכִּיר אֶת מְקוֹמוֹ, וְהַשָּׂמֵחַ בְּחֶלְקוֹ, וְהָעוֹשֶׂה סְיָג לִדְבָרָיו, וְאֵינוֹ מַחֲזִיק טוֹבָה לְעַצְמוֹ, אָהוּב, אוֹהֵב אֶת הַמָּקוֹם, אוֹהֵב אֶת הַבְּרִיּוֹת, אוֹהֵב אֶת הַצְּדָקוֹת, אוֹהֵב אֶת הַמֵּישָׁרִים, אוֹהֵב אֶת הַתּוֹכָחוֹת, וּמִתְרַחֵק מִן הַכָּבוֹד, וְלֹא מֵגִיס לִבּוֹ בְּתַלְמוּדוֹ, וְאֵינוֹ שָׂמֵחַ בְּהוֹרָאָה, נוֹשֵׂא בְעֹל עִם חֲבֵרוֹ, וּמַכְרִיעוֹ לְכַף זְכוּת, וּמַעֲמִידוֹ עַל הָאֱמֶת, וּמַעֲמִידוֹ עַל הַשָּׁלוֹם, וּמִתְיַשֵּׁב לִבּוֹ בְּתַלְמוּדוֹ, שׁוֹאֵל וּמֵשִׁיב, שׁוֹמֵעַ וּמוֹסִיף, הַלּוֹמֵד עַל מְנָת לְלַמֵּד, וְהַלּוֹמֵד עַל מְנָת לַעֲשׂוֹת, הַמַּחְכִּים אֶת רַבּוֹ, וְהַמְכַוֵּן אֶת שְׁמוּעָתוֹ, וְהָאוֹמֵר דָּבָר בְּשֵׁם אוֹמְרוֹ. הָא לָמַדְתָּ, כָּל הָאוֹמֵר דָּבָר בְּשֵׁם אוֹמְרוֹ, מֵבִיא גְאֻלָּה לָעוֹלָם, שֶׁנֶּאֱמַר: „וַתֹּאמֶר אֶסְתֵּר לַמֶּלֶךְ בְּשֵׁם מָרְדְּכָי.״[1]

[ז] גְּדוֹלָה תוֹרָה, שֶׁהִיא נוֹתֶנֶת חַיִּים לְעוֹשֶׂיהָ בָּעוֹלָם הַזֶּה וּבָעוֹלָם הַבָּא, שֶׁנֶּאֱמַר: „כִּי חַיִּים הֵם לְמֹצְאֵיהֶם, וּלְכָל בְּשָׂרוֹ מַרְפֵּא״.[2] וְאוֹמֵר: „רִפְאוּת תְּהִי לְשָׁרֶּךָ, וְשִׁקּוּי לְעַצְמוֹתֶיךָ״.[3] וְאוֹמֵר: „עֵץ חַיִּים הִיא לַמַּחֲזִיקִים בָּהּ וְתֹמְכֶיהָ מְאֻשָּׁר״.[4] וְאוֹמֵר: „כִּי לִוְיַת חֵן הֵם לְרֹאשֶׁךָ, וַעֲנָקִים לְגַרְגְּרֹתֶיךָ״.[5] וְאוֹמֵר: „תִּתֵּן לְרֹאשְׁךָ לִוְיַת חֵן, עֲטֶרֶת תִּפְאֶרֶת תְּמַגְּנֶךָּ״.[6] וְאוֹמֵר: „כִּי בִי יִרְבּוּ יָמֶיךָ, וְיוֹסִיפוּ לְךָ שְׁנוֹת חַיִּים״.[7] וְאוֹמֵר: „אֹרֶךְ יָמִים בִּימִינָהּ, בִּשְׂמֹאולָהּ עֹשֶׁר וְכָבוֹד״.[8] וְאוֹמֵר: „כִּי אֹרֶךְ יָמִים וּשְׁנוֹת חַיִּים, וְשָׁלוֹם יוֹסִיפוּ לָךְ.״[9]

[ח] רַבִּי שִׁמְעוֹן בֶּן יְהוּדָה מִשּׁוּם רַבִּי שִׁמְעוֹן בֶּן יוֹחָאי אוֹמֵר: הַנּוֹי, וְהַכֹּחַ, וְהָעֹשֶׁר, וְהַכָּבוֹד, וְהַחָכְמָה, וְהַזִּקְנָה, וְהַשֵּׂיבָה, וְהַבָּנִים — נָאֶה לַצַּדִּיקִים וְנָאֶה לָעוֹלָם, שֶׁנֶּאֱמַר: „עֲטֶרֶת תִּפְאֶרֶת שֵׂיבָה, בְּדֶרֶךְ צְדָקָה תִּמָּצֵא״.[10] וְאוֹמֵר: „עֲטֶרֶת זְקֵנִים בְּנֵי בָנִים, וְתִפְאֶרֶת בָּנִים אֲבוֹתָם״.[11] וְאוֹמֵר: „תִּפְאֶרֶת בַּחוּרִים כֹּחָם, וַהֲדַר זְקֵנִים שֵׂיבָה״.[12] וְאוֹמֵר „וְחָפְרָה הַלְּבָנָה וּבוֹשָׁה הַחַמָּה, כִּי מָלַךְ יהוה צְבָאוֹת בְּהַר צִיּוֹן וּבִירוּשָׁלַיִם, וְנֶגֶד זְקֵנָיו כָּבוֹד.״[13] רַבִּי שִׁמְעוֹן בֶּן מְנַסְיָא אוֹמֵר: אֵלּוּ שֶׁבַע מִדּוֹת, שֶׁמָּנוּ חֲכָמִים לַצַּדִּיקִים, כֻּלָּם נִתְקַיְּמוּ בְּרַבִּי וּבְבָנָיו.

[ט] אָמַר רַבִּי יוֹסֵי בֶּן קִסְמָא: פַּעַם אַחַת הָיִיתִי מְהַלֵּךְ בַּדֶּרֶךְ, וּפָגַע בִּי אָדָם אֶחָד. וְנָתַן לִי שָׁלוֹם, וְהֶחֱזַרְתִּי לוֹ שָׁלוֹם. אָמַר לִי: „רַבִּי, מֵאֵיזֶה מָקוֹם אַתָּה״? אָמַרְתִּי לוֹ: „מֵעִיר גְּדוֹלָה שֶׁל חֲכָמִים וְשֶׁל סוֹפְרִים אָנִי״.

בֶּאֱמוּנַת חֲכָמִים — *Faith in the sages,* i.e., in the authenticity of their teachings as representing the Oral Law transmitted to Moses at Sinai.

הַמַּחְכִּים אֶת רַבּוֹ — *Making his teacher wiser,* by sharpening his mind through asking incisive questions and seeking constant clarification of his teachings. Compare the Rabbinic maxim: 'Much have I learned from my teachers, more from my colleagues, but most of all from my students' *(Taanis* 7a).

וְהָאוֹמֵר דָּבָר בְּשֵׁם אוֹמְרוֹ — *And repeating a saying in the name of the one who said it,* thus not falsely taking credit for someone else's statement. One must display indebtedness to a source and mention him by name. The mention of Mordechai's name in *Esther 6:2* eventually led to the miracle of Purim and the salvation of the Jews in Persia.

7. The Biblical verses in this *baraisa* are taken from *Proverbs,* where the subject is the wisdom

pleasure, limited sleep, limited conversation, limited laughter, slowness to anger, a good heart, faith in the sages, acceptance of suffering, knowing one's place, being happy with one's lot, making a protective fence around his personal matters, claiming no credit for himself, being beloved, loving the Omnipresent, loving [His] creatures, loving righteous ways, loving justice, loving reproof, keeping far from honor, not being arrogant with his learning, not enjoying halachic decison-making, sharing his fellow's yoke, judging him favorably, setting him on the truthful course, setting him on the peaceful course, thinking deliberately in his study, asking and answering, listening and contributing to the discussion, learning in order to teach, learning in order to practice, making his teacher wiser, pondering over what he has learned, and repeating a saying in the name of the one who said it. For you have learned this: Whoever repeats a thing in the name of the one who said it brings redemption to the world, as it is said: 'And Esther said to the king in the name of Mordechai.'[1]

[7] *Great is Torah, for it confers life upon its practitioners, both in this world and in the World to Come, as it is said: 'For they [the teachings of the Torah] are life to those who find them, and a healing to his entire flesh.'*[2] *And it says: 'It shall be healing to your body, and marrow to your bones.'*[3] *And it says: 'It is a tree of life to those who grasp it, and its supporters are praiseworthy.'*[4] *And it says: 'They are a garland of grace for your head, and necklaces for your neck.'*[5] *And it says: 'It will give to your head a garland of grace, a crown of glory it will deliver to you.'*[6] *And it says: 'Indeed, through me [the Torah] your days shall be increased, and years of life shall be added to you.'*[7] *And it says: 'Lengthy days are at its right, and at its left are wealth and honor.'*[8] *And it says: 'For lengthy days and years of life, and peace shall they add to you.'*[9]

[8] *Rabbi Shimon ben Yehudah says in the name of Rabbi Shimon ben Yochai: Beauty, strength, wealth, honor, wisdom, old age, hoary age, and children — these befit the righteous and befit the world, as it is said: 'Ripe old age is a crown of splendor, it can be found in the path of righteousness.'*[10] *And it says: 'The crown of the aged is grandchildren, and the splendor of children is their fathers.'*[11] *And it says: 'The splendor of young men is their strength, and the glory of old men is hoary age.'*[12] *And it says: 'The moon will grow pale and the sun be shamed, when* HASHEM, *Master of Legions, will have reigned on Mount Zion and in Jerusalem, and honor shall be before His elders.'*[13] *Rabbi Shimon ben Menasya said: These seven qualities that the Sages attributed to the righteous were all realized in Rabbi and his sons.*

[9] *Rabbi Yose ben Kisma said: Once I was walking on the road, when a certain man met me. He greeted me and I returned his greeting. He said to me, 'Rabbi, from what place are you?' I said to him, 'I am from a great city of*

(1) *Esther* 2:22. (2) *Proverbs* 4:22. (3) 3:8. (4) 3:18. (5) 1:9. (6) 4:9. (7) 9:11. (8) 3:16. (9) 3:2. (10) 16:31. (11) 17:6. (12) 20:29. (13) *Isaiah* 24:23.

of the Torah.

8. נָאֶה לַצַּדִּיקִים — *Befit the righteous.* They can be instruments for attaining righteousness or secular worldliness, depending upon how their possessor utilizes these adornments.

שֶׁבַע — *Seven.* Actually *eight* adornments appear to be enumerated in this *baraisa*. The *Vilna Gaon* omits 'wisdom' as it is not referred to in the proof texts cited, while the parallel dictum in *Yerushalmi Sanhedrin* 11:3 omits 'old age.'

בְּרַבִּי — *In Rabbi,* Rabbi Yehudah the Prince. See 2:1.

אָמַר לִי: ,,רַבִּי, רְצוֹנְךָ שֶׁתָּדוּר עִמָּנוּ בִּמְקוֹמֵנוּ? וַאֲנִי אֶתֵּן לְךָ אֶלֶף אֲלָפִים דִּינְרֵי זָהָב וַאֲבָנִים טוֹבוֹת וּמַרְגָּלִיּוֹת״. אָמַרְתִּי לוֹ: ,,אִם אַתָּה נוֹתֵן לִי כָּל כֶּסֶף וְזָהָב וַאֲבָנִים טוֹבוֹת וּמַרְגָּלִיּוֹת שֶׁבָּעוֹלָם, אֵינִי דָר אֶלָּא בִּמְקוֹם תּוֹרָה״. וְכֵן כָּתוּב בְּסֵפֶר תְּהִלִּים עַל יְדֵי דָוִד מֶלֶךְ יִשְׂרָאֵל: ,,טוֹב לִי תוֹרַת פִּיךָ מֵאַלְפֵי זָהָב וָכָסֶף״.[1] וְלֹא עוֹד אֶלָּא שֶׁבִּשְׁעַת פְּטִירָתוֹ שֶׁל אָדָם אֵין מְלַוִּין לוֹ לְאָדָם לֹא כֶסֶף וְלֹא זָהָב וְלֹא אֲבָנִים טוֹבוֹת וּמַרְגָּלִיּוֹת, אֶלָּא תּוֹרָה וּמַעֲשִׂים טוֹבִים בִּלְבָד, שֶׁנֶּאֱמַר: ,,בְּהִתְהַלֶּכְךָ תַּנְחֶה אֹתָךְ, בְּשָׁכְבְּךָ תִּשְׁמֹר עָלֶיךָ, וַהֲקִיצוֹתָ הִיא תְשִׂיחֶךָ.״[2] ,,בְּהִתְהַלֶּכְךָ תַּנְחֶה אֹתָךְ״ — בָּעוֹלָם הַזֶּה; ,,בְּשָׁכְבְּךָ תִּשְׁמֹר עָלֶיךָ״ — בַּקֶּבֶר; ,,וַהֲקִיצוֹתָ הִיא תְשִׂיחֶךָ״ — לָעוֹלָם הַבָּא. וְאוֹמֵר: ,,לִי הַכֶּסֶף וְלִי הַזָּהָב, נְאֻם יהוה צְבָאוֹת.״[3]

[י] חֲמִשָּׁה קִנְיָנִים קָנָה הַקָּדוֹשׁ בָּרוּךְ הוּא בְּעוֹלָמוֹ, וְאֵלּוּ הֵן: תּוֹרָה — קִנְיָן אֶחָד, שָׁמַיִם וָאָרֶץ — קִנְיָן אֶחָד, אַבְרָהָם — קִנְיָן אֶחָד, יִשְׂרָאֵל — קִנְיָן אֶחָד, בֵּית הַמִּקְדָּשׁ — קִנְיָן אֶחָד. תּוֹרָה מִנַּיִן? דִּכְתִיב: ,,יהוה קָנָנִי רֵאשִׁית דַּרְכּוֹ, קֶדֶם מִפְעָלָיו מֵאָז.״[4] שָׁמַיִם וָאָרֶץ מִנַּיִן? דִּכְתִיב: ,,כֹּה אָמַר יהוה, הַשָּׁמַיִם כִּסְאִי, וְהָאָרֶץ הֲדֹם רַגְלָי, אֵי זֶה בַיִת אֲשֶׁר תִּבְנוּ לִי, וְאֵי זֶה מָקוֹם מְנוּחָתִי״;[5] וְאוֹמֵר: ,,מָה רַבּוּ מַעֲשֶׂיךָ יהוה, כֻּלָּם בְּחָכְמָה עָשִׂיתָ, מָלְאָה הָאָרֶץ קִנְיָנֶךָ.״[6] אַבְרָהָם מִנַּיִן? דִּכְתִיב: ,,וַיְבָרְכֵהוּ וַיֹּאמַר, בָּרוּךְ אַבְרָם לְאֵל עֶלְיוֹן, קֹנֵה שָׁמַיִם וָאָרֶץ.״[7] יִשְׂרָאֵל מִנַּיִן? דִּכְתִיב: ,,עַד יַעֲבֹר עַמְּךָ יהוה, עַד יַעֲבֹר עַם זוּ קָנִיתָ״;[8] וְאוֹמֵר: ,,לִקְדוֹשִׁים אֲשֶׁר בָּאָרֶץ הֵמָּה, וְאַדִּירֵי כָּל חֶפְצִי בָם.״[9] בֵּית הַמִּקְדָּשׁ מִנַּיִן? דִּכְתִיב: ,,מָכוֹן לְשִׁבְתְּךָ פָּעַלְתָּ יהוה, מִקְּדָשׁ אֲדֹנָי כּוֹנְנוּ יָדֶיךָ״;[10] וְאוֹמֵר: ,,וַיְבִיאֵם אֶל גְּבוּל קָדְשׁוֹ, הַר זֶה קָנְתָה יְמִינוֹ.״[11]

[יא] כָּל מַה שֶּׁבָּרָא הַקָּדוֹשׁ בָּרוּךְ הוּא בְּעוֹלָמוֹ לֹא בְרָאוֹ אֶלָּא לִכְבוֹדוֹ, שֶׁנֶּאֱמַר:[12] ,,כֹּל הַנִּקְרָא בִשְׁמִי וְלִכְבוֹדִי בְּרָאתִיו, יְצַרְתִּיו אַף עֲשִׂיתִיו״; וְאוֹמֵר: ,,יהוה יִמְלֹךְ לְעֹלָם וָעֶד.״[13]

❦ ❦ ❦

רַבִּי חֲנַנְיָא בֶּן עֲקַשְׁיָא אוֹמֵר: רָצָה הַקָּדוֹשׁ בָּרוּךְ הוּא לְזַכּוֹת אֶת יִשְׂרָאֵל, לְפִיכָךְ הִרְבָּה לָהֶם תּוֹרָה וּמִצְוֹת, שֶׁנֶּאֱמַר: ,,יהוה חָפֵץ לְמַעַן צִדְקוֹ יַגְדִּיל תּוֹרָה וְיַאְדִּיר.״[14]

In the presence of a *minyan,* mourners recite קַדִּישׁ דְּרַבָּנָן, the Rabbis' *Kaddish* (p. 52). Then the congregation continues with עָלֵינוּ (p. 526).

---

10. קָנָה — *Acquire for Himself.* Of all the infinite universe, God singled out five things that uniquely advance the goals of creation.

תּוֹרָה — *Torah.* The Torah reveals God's will and purpose. Only by studying and obeying it can man fulfill the mission set forth for him by God.

שָׁמַיִם וָאָרֶץ — *Heaven and earth.* The domain on which Torah is to be fulfilled.

אַבְרָהָם — *Abraham.* The man who showed the way to the recognition of God.

יִשְׂרָאֵל — *Israel.* The Jewish people — bearers of the Covenant.

בֵּית הַמִּקְדָּשׁ — *The Holy Temple,* the 'dwelling place' of the Divine Presence on this world.

11. After six chapters of teaching and exhortation, *Avos* concludes with the stirring and inspirational declaration that everything in creation is a tool for His glory. Clearly, since God

scholars and sages.' He said to me, 'Rabbi, would you be willing to live with us in our place? I would give you thousands upon thousands of golden dinars, precious stones and pearls.' I replied, 'Even if you were to give me all the silver and gold, precious stones and pearls in the world, I would dwell nowhere but in a place of Torah.' And so it is written in the Book of Psalms by David, King of Israel: 'I prefer the Torah of Your mouth above thousands in gold and silver.'[1] *Furthermore, when a man departs from this world, neither silver, nor gold, nor precious stones nor pearls escort him, but only Torah study and good deeds, as it is said: 'When you walk, it shall guide you; when you lie down, it shall guard you; and when you awake, it shall speak on your behalf.'*[2] *'When you walk, it shall guide you' — in this world; 'when you lie down, it shall guard you' — in the grave; 'and when you awake, it shall speak on your behalf' — in the World to Come. And it says: 'Mine is the silver, and Mine is the gold, says* HASHEM, *Master of Legions.'*[3]

[10] *Five possessions did the Holy One, Blessed is He, acquire for Himself in His world, and they are: Torah, one possession; heaven and earth, one possession; Abraham, one possession; Israel, one possession; the Holy Temple, one possession. From where do we know this about the Torah? Since it is written: '*HASHEM *acquired me [the Torah] at the beginning of His way, before His works in time of yore.'*[4] *From where do we know this about heaven and earth? Since it is written: 'So says* HASHEM. *The heaven is My throne, and the earth is My footstool; what House can you build for Me, and where is the place of My rest?'*[5] *And it says: 'How abundant are Your works,* HASHEM, *with wisdom You made them all, the earth is full of Your possessions.'*[6] *From where do we know this about Abraham? Since it is written: 'And He blessed him and said: Blessed is Abram of God the Most High, Who acquired heaven and earth.'*[7] *From where do we know this about the people Israel? Since it is written: 'Until Your people passes through,* HASHEM, *until it passes through — this people You acquired,'*[8] *and it [also] says 'But for the holy ones who are in the earth and for the mighty all my desires are due to them.'*[9] *From where do we know this about the Holy Temple? Since it is written: 'Your dwelling-place which You,* HASHEM, *have made; the Sanctuary, my Lord, that Your hands established.'*[10] *And it says: 'And He brought them to His sacred boundary, to this mountain which His right hand acquired.'*[11]

[11] *All that the Holy One, Blessed is He, created in His world, He created solely for His glory, as it is said: 'All that is called by My Name, indeed, it is for My glory that I have created it, formed it, and made it.'*[12] *And it says: '*HASHEM *shall reign for all eternity.'*[13]

❀ ❀ ❀

*Rabbi Chanania ben Akashia says: The Holy One, Blessed is He, wished to confer merit upon Israel; therefore He gave them Torah and mitzvos in abundance, as it is said: '*HASHEM *desired, for the sake of its [Israel's] righteousness, that the Torah be made great and glorious.'*[14]

In the presence of a *minyan,* mourners recite קַדִּישׁ דְּרַבָּנָן, the Rabbis' *Kaddish* (p. 52).
Then the congregation continues with עָלֵינוּ, *Aleinu* (p. 526).

(1) *Psalms* 119:72. (2) *Proverbs* 6:22. (3) *Chaggai* 2:8. (4) *Proverbs* 8:22. (5) *Isaiah* 66:1. (6) *Psalms* 104:24. (7) *Genesis* 14:19. (8) *Exodus* 15:16. (9) *Psalms* 16:3. (10) *Exodus* 15:17. (11) *Psalms* 78:54. (12) *Isaiah* 43:7. (13) *Exodus* 15:18. (14) *Isaiah* 42:21.

created the universe for His service, no force can prevent man from utilizing it properly. God has shown us the way; it is for us to supply the will and the wisdom.

שלש סעודות

אתקינו סעודתא

אַתְקִינוּ סְעוּדָתָא דִמְהֵימְנוּתָא שְׁלֵימָתָא, חֶדְוָתָא דְּמַלְכָּא קַדִּישָׁא. אַתְקִינוּ סְעוּדָתָא דְמַלְכָּא, דָּא הִיא סְעוּדָתָא דִּזְעֵיר אַנְפִּין.* וְעַתִּיקָא קַדִּישָׁא* וַחֲקַל תַּפּוּחִין קַדִּישִׁין* אַתְיָן לְסַעֲדָא בַּהֲדֵיהּ.

בְּנֵי הֵיכָלָא,* דִּכְסִיפִין, לְמֶחֱזֵי זִיו דִּזְעֵיר אַנְפִּין.
יְהוֹן הָכָא, בְּהַאי תַּכָּא, דְּבֵהּ מַלְכָּא בְּגִלּוּפִין.
צְבוּ לַחֲדָא, בְּהַאי וַעֲדָא, בְּגוֹ עִירִין וְכָל גַּדְפִין.
חֲדוּ הַשְׁתָּא, בְּהַאי שַׁעְתָּא, דְּבֵהּ רַעֲוָא וְלֵית זַעֲפִין.
קְרִיבוּ לִי,* חֲזוּ חֵילִי, דְּלֵית דִּינִין דִּתְקִיפִין.
לְבַר נַטְלִין, וְלָא עָאלִין, הָנֵי כַּלְבִין דַּחֲצִיפִין.*
וְהָא אַזְמִין, עַתִּיק יוֹמִין, לְמִנְחָה עֲדֵי יְהוֹן חָלְפִין.
רְעוּ דִילֵהּ, דְּגַלֵּי לֵהּ, לְבַטָּלָא בְּכָל קְלִיפִין.*

סְעוּדָה שְׁלִישִׁית / SHALOSH SEUDOS

The requirement to eat three meals on the Sabbath is based on the commandment concerning the preparations for the Sabbath. The word הַיּוֹם, *this day,* is used three times in the same verse (*Exodus* 16:25); from this the Sages derive the obligation to eat three meals in honor of the Sabbath.

The three meals of the Sabbath symbolize the three Patriarchs; the three divisions of Scripture: Torah, Prophets and Hagiographa; and the three manna meals that were provided every Sabbath in the wilderness. Many matters of awesome spiritual significance are dependent on the Third Meal as *Zohar* discusses frequently (*Aruch HaShulchan* 291:1).

In Kabbalistic literature, the time of the Third Meal is referred to as רַעֲוָא דְרַעֲוִין, *the* [*time of*] *favor of favors,* i.e., it is the time when God is most kindly disposed toward Israel, and the time when He most sympathetically receives Israel's efforts toward spiritual growth.

Strangely, although the Hebrew term for the Third Meal is properly סְעוּדָה שְׁלִישִׁית, *Seudah Shlishis,* it is commonly called שָׁלֹשׁ סְעוּדוֹת, *Shalosh Seudos,* literally *Three Meals,* as if all three meals of the day were included in this one. *Divrei Emes* explains that the first two meals of the Sabbath are eaten at normal mealtimes when people are hungry. Thus the eating is not obviously in honor of the Sabbath — who would not enjoy a delicious repast when he is hungry? But the Third Meal comes at a time when people are not hungry; often they would not eat at all were it not a *mitzvah* to do so. That they eat the Third Meal is indicative of their general attitude: they eat not because the food tempts them, but because God commands that this meal be eaten. Thus, the act of eating the Third Meal sanctifies the earlier two meals as well; it is truly as if all three meals were now being eaten in a spirit of dedication.

There are a host of customs regarding the selections of *Shalosh Seudos Zemiros.* Here we present only those that are not recited at either of the previous meals.

אַתְקִינוּ סְעוּדָתָא / Askinu Seudasa

This brief paragraph, based on the *Zohar,* is used to introduce the sacred songs composed by the holy *Arizal, Rabbi Yitzchak Luria,* for each Sabbath meal. It begins with this exhortation to those present that they prepare for the spiritual experience of the Sabbath feast, the virtues of

SHALOSH SEUDOS

ASKINU SEUDASA

אַתְקִינוּ סְעוּדָתָא *I shall prepare the feast of perfect faith, the joy of the Holy King. I shall prepare the feast of the King. This is the feast of the Miniature Presence.* The Ancient Holy One* and the Field of Sacred Apples* come to feast with it.*

בְּנֵי הֵיכָלָא *Members of the Sanctuary* who yearn*
to see the glow of the Miniature Presence,

י *May they be here at this table*
in which is inscribed the King in joy.

צ *Long to be part of this assemblage*
among many-winged angels.

ח *Be exultant now at this very time*
in which there is favor, but no anger.

ק *Approach me,* see my strength,*
when there are no powerful judgments.

ל *Outside, let them remain, never to arise —*
*those brazen dogs.**

ו *But I invite the Ancient Holy One*
at Minchah, the time when they fade away,

ר *His favor — when it is revealed —*
*will negate all impure shells.**

---

which will be extolled in this paragraph and in the succeeding *zemer*. The commentary is based on *Minchas Yaakov*.

דִּזְעֵיר אַנְפִּין — *Of the Miniature Presence.* Although God's Presence is everywhere, it is not readily discernible on earth where events can be understood as a result of natural causes rather than as emanating from Him. The lack of clarity in our perception of His Presence is as if we observed an event through אִסְפַּקְלַרְיָא שֶׁאֵינָהּ מְאִירָה, *a blurred, cloudy lens.* The result is that we have diminished appreciation of God's greatness. This unclear lens through which we attempt to perceive His influence is referred to as the Miniature Presence of God.

וְעַתִּיקָא קַדִּישָׁא — *The Ancient Holy One*, i.e., God Who is timeless and infinite.

וַחֲקַל תַּפּוּחִין קַדִּישִׁין — *And the Field of Sacred Apples.* This expression is frequently found in Kabbalistic literature to refer to the *Shechinah* [Divine Presence].

בְּנֵי הֵיכָלָא — *Members of the Sanctuary.* These are the righteous scholars who long for a glimpse of the *Shechinah's* splendor.

קְרִיבוּ לִי — *Approach me.* The composer, representing the righteous scholars who are seated at God's table, urges all Jews to join them by living up to the high responsibilities imposed by one's presence at such an assemblage.

הֲנֵי כַלְבִּין דַּחֲצִיפִין — *Those brazen dogs.* Those who seek to accuse and persecute Israel before God are likened to dogs in their brazenness. At this hour of Divine favor, they are given no leave to come before the Divine Presence.

קְלִיפִּין — [*Impure*] *shells.* This term is a synonym for evil. *Kabbalistic* literature teaches that nothing can exist unless it has within it at least an infinitesimal spark of good. Often, however, this good is enclosed by an overlay of evil, materialism, or apathy which makes it imperceptible and inaccessible. This overlay is

יְשַׁוֵּי לוֹן, בְּנוּקְבֵיהוֹן, וִיטַמְּרוּן בְּגוֹ כֵפִין.
אֲרֵי הַשְׁתָּא, בְּמִנְחָתָא,* בְּחֶדְוָתָא דִזְעֵיר אַנְפִּין.

תהלים כג (commentary on p. 490)

מִזְמוֹר לְדָוִד, יהוה רֹעִי לֹא אֶחְסָר. בִּנְאוֹת דֶּשֶׁא יַרְבִּיצֵנִי, עַל מֵי מְנֻחוֹת יְנַהֲלֵנִי. נַפְשִׁי יְשׁוֹבֵב, יַנְחֵנִי בְמַעְגְּלֵי צֶדֶק לְמַעַן שְׁמוֹ. גַּם כִּי אֵלֵךְ בְּגֵיא צַלְמָוֶת, לֹא אִירָא רָע כִּי אַתָּה עִמָּדִי, שִׁבְטְךָ וּמִשְׁעַנְתֶּךָ הֵמָּה יְנַחֲמֻנִי. תַּעֲרֹךְ לְפָנַי שֻׁלְחָן נֶגֶד צֹרְרָי, דִּשַּׁנְתָּ בַשֶּׁמֶן רֹאשִׁי, כּוֹסִי רְוָיָה. אַךְ טוֹב וָחֶסֶד יִרְדְּפוּנִי כָּל יְמֵי חַיָּי, וְשַׁבְתִּי בְּבֵית יהוה לְאֹרֶךְ יָמִים.

ידיד נפש

יְדִיד נֶפֶשׁ אָב הָרַחֲמָן, מְשׁוֹךְ עַבְדְּךָ אֶל רְצוֹנֶךָ, יָרוּץ עַבְדְּךָ כְּמוֹ אַיָּל, יִשְׁתַּחֲוֶה אֶל מוּל הֲדָרֶךָ, יֶעֱרַב לוֹ יְדִידוֹתֶיךָ, מִנֹּפֶת צוּף וְכָל טָעַם.

הָדוּר נָאֶה זִיו הָעוֹלָם, נַפְשִׁי חוֹלַת אַהֲבָתֶךָ, אָנָּא אֵל נָא רְפָא נָא לָהּ, בְּהַרְאוֹת לָהּ נֹעַם זִיוֶךָ, אָז תִּתְחַזֵּק וְתִתְרַפֵּא, וְהָיְתָה לָהּ שִׂמְחַת עוֹלָם.

וָתִיק יֶהֱמוּ נָא רַחֲמֶיךָ, וְחוּסָה נָּא עַל בֵּן אֲהוּבֶךָ, כִּי זֶה כַּמָּה נִכְסֹף נִכְסַפְתִּי, לִרְאוֹת מְהֵרָה בְּתִפְאֶרֶת עֻזֶּךָ, אֵלֶּה חָמְדָה לִבִּי, וְחוּסָה נָּא וְאַל תִּתְעַלָּם.

הִגָּלֶה נָא וּפְרֹשׂ חֲבִיבִי עָלַי, אֶת סֻכַּת שְׁלוֹמֶךָ, תָּאִיר אֶרֶץ מִכְּבוֹדֶךָ, נָגִילָה וְנִשְׂמְחָה בָּךְ. מַהֵר אֱהֹב כִּי בָא מוֹעֵד, וְחָנֵּנוּ כִּימֵי עוֹלָם.

---

called a קְלִיפָּה, *shell,* since it is similar to the covering of a fruit or a nut which conceals the edible matter within. Man's task is to achieve spiritual growth and thereby to peel away the shell which prevents him from realizing his spiritual potential. A Jew's exposure to the holiness of the Sabbath and the Divine favor which is manifest on it can assist him in negating the harmful influence of these impure shells.

אֲרֵי הַשְׁתָּא בְּמִנְחָתָא — [*I ask this*] *now at* Minchah *time.* All my previous prayers for my own elevation and for the destruction or banishment of evil, I express now, at the time of *Minchah,* because it is God's period of favor and

י *May He place them in their nether holes*
and hide them among rocks.

א *I ask this now, at Minchah time,**
during the exultation of the Miniature Presence.

Psalm 23 (commentary on p. 490).

מִזְמוֹר לְדָוִד *A psalm of David: HASHEM is my shepherd, I shall not lack. In lush meadows He lays me down, beside tranquil waters He leads me. He restores my soul. He leads me on paths of righteousness for His Name's sake. Though I walk in the valley overshadowed by death, I will fear no evil, for You are with me. Your rod and Your staff, they comfort me. You prepare a table before me in full view of my tormentors. You anointed my head with oil, my cup overflows. May only goodness and kindness pursue me all the days of my life, and I shall dwell in the House of HASHEM for long days.*

YEDID NEFESH

יְדִיד נֶפֶשׁ *Beloved of the soul, Compassionate Father, draw Your servant to Your will. Then Your servant will hurry like a hart to bow before Your majesty. To him Your friendship will be sweeter than the dripping of the honeycomb and any taste.*

הָדוּר ***Majestic, Beautiful, Radiance of the universe — my soul pines for Your love. Please, O God, heal her now by showing her the pleasantness of Your radiance. Then she will be strengthened and healed, and eternal gladness will be hers.***

וָתִיק *All-worthy One — may Your mercy be aroused and please take pity on the son of Your beloved, because it is so very long that I have yearned intensely to see the splendor of Your strength. Only these my heart desired, so please take pity and do not conceal Yourself.*

הִגָּלֶה *Please be revealed and spread upon me, my Beloved, the shelter of Your peace. Illuminate the world with Your glory that we may rejoice and be glad with You. Hasten, show love, for the time has come, and show us grace as in days of old.*

---

exultation. Now is the moment when such prayers are particularly acceptable before Him.

✤ יְדִיד נֶפֶשׁ / Yedid Nefesh

The composer of *Yedid Nefesh* is R' Eliezer Azikri, one of the great kabbalists and halachists of the sixteenth century in *Eretz Yisrael*, whose major work was *Sefer Charedim*. A central theme of his moral and liturgical writings was the intense love one must feel for God. This theme is readily apparent in *Yedid Nefesh*.

סדר מוצאי שבת

מזמורים קודם מעריב

Many congregations recite the following psalms before *Maariv:*

תהלים קמד

לְדָוִד בָּרוּךְ יהוה צוּרִי,* הַמְלַמֵּד יָדַי לַקְרָב, אֶצְבְּעוֹתַי לַמִּלְחָמָה.* חַסְדִּי וּמְצוּדָתִי מִשְׂגַּבִּי וּמְפַלְטִי לִי מָגִנִּי וּבוֹ חָסִיתִי,* הָרוֹדֵד עַמִּי תַחְתָּי.* יהוה מָה אָדָם וַתֵּדָעֵהוּ,* בֶּן אֱנוֹשׁ וַתְּחַשְּׁבֵהוּ. אָדָם לַהֶבֶל דָּמָה, יָמָיו כְּצֵל עוֹבֵר. יהוה הַט שָׁמֶיךָ וְתֵרֵד, גַּע בֶּהָרִים וְיֶעֱשָׁנוּ. בְּרוֹק בָּרָק וּתְפִיצֵם, שְׁלַח חִצֶּיךָ וּתְהֻמֵּם.* שְׁלַח יָדֶיךָ מִמָּרוֹם, פְּצֵנִי וְהַצִּילֵנִי מִמַּיִם רַבִּים,* מִיַּד בְּנֵי נֵכָר. אֲשֶׁר פִּיהֶם דִּבֶּר שָׁוְא, וִימִינָם יְמִין שָׁקֶר. אֱלֹהִים שִׁיר חָדָשׁ אָשִׁירָה לָּךְ,* בְּנֵבֶל עָשׂוֹר אֲזַמְּרָה לָּךְ. הַנּוֹתֵן תְּשׁוּעָה לַמְּלָכִים, הַפּוֹצֶה אֶת דָּוִד עַבְדּוֹ מֵחֶרֶב רָעָה.* פְּצֵנִי וְהַצִּילֵנִי מִיַּד בְּנֵי נֵכָר אֲשֶׁר פִּיהֶם דִּבֶּר שָׁוְא וִימִינָם יְמִין שָׁקֶר. אֲשֶׁר בָּנֵינוּ כִּנְטִעִים,* מְגֻדָּלִים בִּנְעוּרֵיהֶם, בְּנוֹתֵינוּ כְזָוִיֹּת, מְחֻטָּבוֹת תַּבְנִית הֵיכָל.* מְזָוֵינוּ מְלֵאִים, מְפִיקִים מִזַּן אֶל זַן, צֹאנֵנוּ מַאֲלִיפוֹת מְרֻבָּבוֹת בְּחוּצוֹתֵינוּ. אַלּוּפֵינוּ מְסֻבָּלִים אֵין פֶּרֶץ וְאֵין יוֹצֵאת,* וְאֵין צְוָחָה בִּרְחֹבֹתֵינוּ. אַשְׁרֵי הָעָם שֶׁכָּכָה לּוֹ,* אַשְׁרֵי הָעָם שֶׁיהוה אֱלֹהָיו.

תהלים כט (commentary on page 314)

מִזְמוֹר לְדָוִד, הָבוּ לַיהוה בְּנֵי אֵלִים, הָבוּ לַיהוה כָּבוֹד וָעֹז. הָבוּ לַיהוה כְּבוֹד שְׁמוֹ, הִשְׁתַּחֲווּ לַיהוה בְּהַדְרַת קֹדֶשׁ.
קוֹל יהוה עַל הַמָּיִם, אֵל הַכָּבוֹד הִרְעִים, יהוה עַל מַיִם רַבִּים. קוֹל יהוה

Psalm 144

לְדָוִד בָּרוּךְ ה׳ צוּרִי — *By David. Blessed is* HASHEM, *my Rock.* God provided a strong refuge for David, as if David were surrounded by a secure, impregnable fortress hewn from solid rock.

הַמְלַמֵּד יָדַי לַקְרָב אֶצְבְּעוֹתַי לַמִּלְחָמָה — *Who trains my hands for battle, my fingers for war.* David refers to his battle with Goliath, when he chose from the river bed five smooth pebbles *(I Samuel* 17:40), corresponding to the five fingers of his hand to demonstrate that with God's help, he needed only to lift his little finger to slay the giant. This encounter with Goliath trained him for even greater wars against vast armies *(Alshich).*

חַסְדִּי וּמְצוּדָתִי מִשְׂגַּבִּי וּמְפַלְטִי לִי מָגִנִּי וּבוֹ חָסִיתִי — *My Benefactor, my Fortress, my Stronghold, my own Rescuer, my Shield — in Him I take refuge.* This list of titles reflects the gamut of praises which David expressed throughout the Book of Psalms. All serve to emphasize that David takes no credit for his military prowess, but attributes his successes to God alone *(Radak).*

הָרוֹדֵד עַמִּי תַחְתָּי — *He Who subjugates my nation to me.* David refers to his own Jewish subjects who remained hostile and refused to accept his sovereignty. Their stubborn resistance to David melted when they witnessed his extraordinary success. God transformed their unyielding obstinacy into smooth, pliant obedience to David *(R' Hirsch).*

ה׳ מָה אָדָם וַתֵּדָעֵהוּ — HASHEM, *what is man that You recognize him?* David is overwhelmed by the scope of God's involvement in the events of human history. Realizing that God controls every minute detail of world events David wonders why the Almighty should concern Himself with frail man.

שְׁלַח חִצֶּיךָ וּתְהֻמֵּם — *Shoot Your arrows and panic them.* Lightning bolts and arrows are figurative expressions for the Divine decrees which God hurls down from heaven against His enemies *(Radak).*

וְהַצִּילֵנִי מִמַּיִם רַבִּים — *And rescue me from great waters.* The great waters are the hordes of enemies and the overwhelming misfortunes which threaten to drown us *(Radak; Ibn Yachya).*

SABBATH CONCLUSION

PRELIMINARY PRAYERS

Many congregations recite the following psalms before *Maariv:*

Psalm 144

לְדָוִד *By David. Blessed is HASHEM, my Rock,* Who trains my hands for battle, my fingers for war.* My Benefactor, my Fortress, my Stronghold, my own Rescuer, my Shield — in Him I take refuge* — He Who subjugates my nation to me.* HASHEM, what is man that You recognize him;* the son of a frail human that You reckon with him? Man is like a breath; his days are like a passing shadow. HASHEM! Bend Your heavens and descend; touch the mountains and they will go up in smoke. Flash a lightning bolt and scatter them; shoot Your arrows and panic them.* Stretch out Your hands from above, release me and rescue me from great waters,* from the hand of strangers; whose mouth speaks vanity, and whose right hand is a right hand of falsehood. O God, a new song will I sing to You,* on a ten-stringed harp will I play to You. He Who grants salvation to the kings, He Who releases David, His servant, from the evil sword.* Release me and rescue me from the hand of the strangers, whose mouth speaks vanity and whose right hand is a right hand of falsehood. For our sons are like saplings,* nurtured from their youth, our daughters are like cornerstones, crafted in palatial form.* Our storehouses overflow to their very corners, providing from harvest to harvest; our sheep increase by the thousands, by the myriads in our open spaces. Our oxen are laden; there is neither defection, nor outburst,* nor wailing in our streets. Praiseworthy is the people for whom this is so;* praiseworthy is the people whose God is HASHEM.*

Psalm 29 (commentary on page 314):

מִזְמוֹר לְדָוִד *A psalm of David. Render unto HASHEM, you sons of the powerful; render unto HASHEM, honor and might. Render unto HASHEM, honor worthy of His Name; prostrate yourselves before HASHEM in His intensely holy place. The voice of HASHEM is upon the waters, the God of Glory thunders, HASHEM is upon vast waters. The voice of HASHEM is in power! The voice of HASHEM is in majesty! The voice of HASHEM*

אֱלֹהִים שִׁיר חָדָשׁ אָשִׁירָה לָּךְ — *O God, a new song will I sing to You.* Whenever You renew Your miracles on my behalf, I pledge to compose new songs of thanksgiving for You, with new lyrics and new musical accompaniment *(Radak).*

מֵחֶרֶב רָעָה — *From the evil sword.* David refers to Saul's weapon as the evil [i.e., extremely dangerous] sword because David was defenseless against it. David could not strike back because Saul was his sovereign *(Radak).* Alternatively, this is a reference to the sword of Goliath. Whereas some heroes fight to achieve a worthy, lofty purpose, Goliath's sole purpose was to wreak evil and destruction *(Sforno).*

אֲשֶׁר בָּנֵינוּ כִּנְטִעִים — *For our sons are like saplings.* It is essential that God deliver David from his enemies, because so much is at stake! Not only does the Jewish nation enjoy the heritage of a glorious past, the best is yet to come. This is evident in the superb quality and high caliber of our sons, who are like hardy plants, free of all blemishes and infirmities, innocent of any sin *(Rashi).*

מְחֻטָּבוֹת תַּבְנִית הֵיכָל — *Crafted in palatial form.* In their palaces, Jewish wives and mothers reign as queens over their families, which they fashion in accordance with Jewish tradition.

אֵין פֶּרֶץ וְאֵין יוֹצֵאת — *There is neither defection, nor outburst.* These words reflect national solidarity. There is no defection [i.e., dissension] in our ranks; morale is high, friendships are strong, and we are not shamed by an outburst of vituperation or embarrassing behavior *(Rashi).*

When God blesses the Jewish people with tranquillity, the cycles of life proceed smoothly, without interruption. The livestock are productive and no miscarriage interrupts the birth process. Moreover, the serenity of the people is not disturbed by a breach in our outer defenses. No enemy infiltrates our borders to capture man or beast *(Radak).*

אַשְׁרֵי הָעָם שֶׁכָּכָה לּוֹ — *Praiseworthy is the people for whom this is so,* i.e., the nation which enjoys all these elements of good fortune. The reason why the nation merits such good fortune is that its God is HASHEM *(Radak).*

בַּכֹּחַ, קוֹל יהוה בֶּהָדָר. קוֹל יהוה שֹׁבֵר אֲרָזִים, וַיְשַׁבֵּר יהוה אֶת אַרְזֵי הַלְּבָנוֹן. וַיַּרְקִידֵם כְּמוֹ עֵגֶל, לְבָנוֹן וְשִׂרְיוֹן כְּמוֹ בֶן רְאֵמִים. קוֹל יהוה חֹצֵב לַהֲבוֹת אֵשׁ. קוֹל יהוה יָחִיל מִדְבָּר, יָחִיל יהוה מִדְבַּר קָדֵשׁ. קוֹל יהוה יְחוֹלֵל אַיָּלוֹת, וַיֶּחֱשֹׂף יְעָרוֹת, וּבְהֵיכָלוֹ, כֻּלּוֹ אֹמֵר כָּבוֹד. יהוה לַמַּבּוּל יָשָׁב, וַיֵּשֶׁב יהוה מֶלֶךְ לְעוֹלָם. יהוה עֹז לְעַמּוֹ יִתֵּן, יהוה יְבָרֵךְ אֶת עַמּוֹ בַשָּׁלוֹם.

תהלים סז

לַמְנַצֵּחַ בִּנְגִינֹת* מִזְמוֹר שִׁיר. אֱלֹהִים יְחָנֵּנוּ וִיבָרְכֵנוּ,* יָאֵר פָּנָיו אִתָּנוּ סֶלָה.* לָדַעַת בָּאָרֶץ דַּרְכֶּךָ,* בְּכָל גּוֹיִם יְשׁוּעָתֶךָ. יוֹדוּךָ עַמִּים אֱלֹהִים, יוֹדוּךָ עַמִּים כֻּלָּם.* יִשְׂמְחוּ וִירַנְּנוּ לְאֻמִּים,* כִּי תִשְׁפֹּט עַמִּים מִישֹׁר, וּלְאֻמִּים בָּאָרֶץ תַּנְחֵם סֶלָה. יוֹדוּךָ עַמִּים אֱלֹהִים, יוֹדוּךָ עַמִּים כֻּלָּם. אֶרֶץ נָתְנָה יְבוּלָהּ, יְבָרְכֵנוּ אֱלֹהִים אֱלֹהֵינוּ. יְבָרְכֵנוּ אֱלֹהִים, וְיִירְאוּ אוֹתוֹ כָּל אַפְסֵי אָרֶץ.

מעריב למוצאי שבת

The regular weekday *Maariv* is recited until the end of *Shemoneh Esrei,* pages 256-278. After *Shemoneh Esrei, chazzan* recites Half-*Kaddish* and service continues below with וִיהִי נֹעַם.

If a Festival or *Erev* Pesach falls before the coming Sabbath, the *chazzan* recites קַדִּישׁ שָׁלֵם, the Full-*Kaddish* (p. 598) and the Service continues there.

On Purim the *Megillah* is read here, and on Tishah B'Av, *Eichah* and *Kinos* are read here. Both are followed by וְאַתָּה קָדוֹשׁ (p. 596) and עָלֵינוּ (p. 608).

תפילות אחר מעריב

וִיהִי נֹעַם אֲדֹנָי אֱלֹהֵינוּ עָלֵינוּ, וּמַעֲשֵׂה יָדֵינוּ כּוֹנְנָה עָלֵינוּ, וּמַעֲשֵׂה יָדֵינוּ כּוֹנְנֵהוּ.[1]

תהלים צא (commentary on p. 380)

יֹשֵׁב בְּסֵתֶר עֶלְיוֹן, בְּצֵל שַׁדַּי יִתְלוֹנָן. אֹמַר לַיהוה, מַחְסִי וּמְצוּדָתִי, אֱלֹהַי אֶבְטַח בּוֹ. כִּי הוּא יַצִּילְךָ מִפַּח יָקוּשׁ, מִדֶּבֶר הַוּוֹת. בְּאֶבְרָתוֹ יָסֶךְ לָךְ, וְתַחַת כְּנָפָיו תֶּחְסֶה, צִנָּה וְסֹחֵרָה אֲמִתּוֹ. לֹא תִירָא מִפַּחַד לָיְלָה, מֵחֵץ יָעוּף יוֹמָם. מִדֶּבֶר

Psalm 67

בִּנְגִינֹת — *Upon Neginos,* a type of musical instrument *(Radak).*

אֱלֹהִים יְחָנֵּנוּ וִיבָרְכֵנוּ — *May God favor us and bless us.* Favor us although we are undeserving; bless us with fertility, for the persecutions of exile have decreased our population *(Sforno).*

יָאֵר פָּנָיו אִתָּנוּ סֶלָה — *May He illuminate His countenance with us, Selah.* May He illuminate our minds so that we may perceive the wondrous lessons of Torah *(Sforno).*

לָדַעַת בָּאָרֶץ דַּרְכֶּךָ — *To make known Your way on earth.* We ask for intellectual enlightenment so that we can spread Your teachings throughout the world. We yearn to guide mankind to an appreciation of Your *way* of kindness and mercy *(Rashi; Sforno).*

יוֹדוּךָ עַמִּים כֻּלָּם — *The peoples will acknowledge You, all of them.* Ultimately, God's message will penetrate every corner of the world and all nations will worship Him *(R' Hirsch).*

יִשְׂמְחוּ וִירַנְּנוּ לְאֻמִּים — *Nations will be glad and sing for joy.* לְאֹם refers to the *state* that governs a people and represents its particular striving. So long as nations are selfish and acquisitive, their nationalistic posture will reflect selfishness; but ultimately, all national governments will discard selfish isolation and recognize that the welfare of all men depends on a harmonious community of nations joyously united in the worship of God.

breaks the cedars, HASHEM shatters the cedars of Lebanon! He makes them prance about like a calf; Lebanon and Siryon like young re'eimim. The voice of HASHEM cleaves with shafts of fire. The voice of HASHEM convulses the wilderness; HASHEM convulses the wilderness of Kadesh. The voice of HASHEM frightens the hinds, and strips the forests bare; while in His Temple all proclaim, 'Glory!' HASHEM sat enthroned at the Deluge; HASHEM sits enthroned as King forever. HASHEM will give might to His people, HASHEM will bless His people with peace.

Psalm 67

לַמְנַצֵּחַ *For the Conductor, upon Neginos,* a psalm, a song. May God favor us and bless us,* may He illuminate His countenance with us, Selah.* To make known Your way on earth,* among all the nations Your salvation. The peoples will acknowledge You, O God, the peoples will acknowledge You, all of them.* Nations will be glad and sing for joy,* because You will judge the peoples fairly and guide the nations on earth, Selah. The peoples will acknowledge You, O God, the peoples will acknowledge You, all of them. The earth has yielded its produce, may God, our own God, bless us. May God bless us and may all the ends of the earth fear Him.*

MAARIV FOR THE CONCLUSION OF SABBATH

The regular weekday *Maariv* is recited until the end of *Shemoneh Esrei*, pages 256-278. After *Shemoneh Esrei*, the *chazzan* recites Half-*Kaddish* and the service continues below with וִיהִי נֹעַם, *'May the pleasantness ....*

If a Festival or *Erev* Pesach falls before the coming Sabbath, the *chazzan* recites Full-*Kaddish* (p. 598) and the service continues there.

On Purim the *Megillah* is read here, and on Tishah B'Av, *Eichah* and *Kinos* are read here. Both are followed by וְאַתָּה קָדוֹשׁ, *You are the Holy One* (p. 596) and *Aleinu* (p. 608).

PRAYERS FOLLOWING MAARIV

וִיהִי נֹעַם *May the pleasantness of my Lord, our God, be upon us — may He establish our handiwork for us; our handiwork may He establish.*[1]

Psalm 91 (commentary on p. 380)

יֹשֵׁב *Whoever sits in the refuge of the Most High, he shall dwell in the shadow of the Almighty. I will say of HASHEM, 'He is my refuge and my fortress, my God, I will trust in Him.' That He will deliver you from the ensnaring trap and from devastating pestilence. With His pinion He will cover you, and beneath His wings you will be protected; shield and armor is His truth. You shall not be afraid of the terror of night, nor of the arrow that flies by day; nor the pestilence*

(1) *Psalms* 90:17.

עַם, *a people,* describes a national community that keeps itself separate from all other peoples. International animosity is inevitable so long as each people seeks only its own welfare *(R' Hirsch).*

⇜ Maariv at the Conclusion of the Sabbath

After *Shemoneh Esrei,* two additional prayers are recited: וִיהִי נֹעַם and וְאַתָּה קָדוֹשׁ, both of which set the tone for the transition from the Sabbath to the weekdays.

The verse וִיהִי נֹעַם contains two aspects of our concept of blessing. On the one hand we ask that God give us the satisfaction of 'pleasantness in our handiwork,' meaning that we have the freedom to be productive. On the other hand, we ask God Himself to 'establish our handiwork,' meaning that we give up our independence to the will and law of God. We ask that this declaration become the framework of the work week that now begins — may we be free to enjoy our handiwork, but may it always be done according to the laws of the Torah.

We then go on to Psalm 91, another of the psalms composed by Moses. The Talmud *(Shavuos* 150) calls it שִׁיר שֶׁל פְּגָעִים, *Song of Afflictions,* because it expresses prayerful confidence that God will protect us from the

בְּאֹפֶל יַהֲלֹךְ, מִקֶּטֶב יָשׁוּד צָהֳרָיִם. יִפֹּל מִצִּדְּךָ אֶלֶף, וּרְבָבָה מִימִינֶךָ, אֵלֶיךָ לֹא יִגָּשׁ. רַק בְּעֵינֶיךָ תַבִּיט, וְשִׁלֻּמַת רְשָׁעִים תִּרְאֶה. כִּי אַתָּה יהוה מַחְסִי, עֶלְיוֹן שַׂמְתָּ מְעוֹנֶךָ. לֹא תְאֻנֶּה אֵלֶיךָ רָעָה, וְנֶגַע לֹא יִקְרַב בְּאָהֳלֶךָ. כִּי מַלְאָכָיו יְצַוֶּה לָּךְ, לִשְׁמָרְךָ בְּכָל דְּרָכֶיךָ. עַל כַּפַּיִם יִשָּׂאוּנְךָ, פֶּן תִּגֹּף בָּאֶבֶן רַגְלֶךָ. עַל שַׁחַל וָפֶתֶן תִּדְרֹךְ, תִּרְמֹס כְּפִיר וְתַנִּין. כִּי בִי חָשַׁק וַאֲפַלְּטֵהוּ, אֲשַׂגְּבֵהוּ, כִּי יָדַע שְׁמִי. יִקְרָאֵנִי וְאֶעֱנֵהוּ, עִמּוֹ אָנֹכִי בְצָרָה, אֲחַלְּצֵהוּ וַאֲכַבְּדֵהוּ. אֹרֶךְ יָמִים אַשְׂבִּיעֵהוּ, וְאַרְאֵהוּ בִּישׁוּעָתִי. אֹרֶךְ יָמִים אַשְׂבִּיעֵהוּ, וְאַרְאֵהוּ בִּישׁוּעָתִי.

The verses in bold type are the *Kedushah* of the angels.
It is preferable that the congregation recite them aloud and in unison.

❖ **וְאַתָּה קָדוֹשׁ** יוֹשֵׁב תְּהִלּוֹת יִשְׂרָאֵל.[1] וְקָרָא זֶה אֶל זֶה וְאָמַר:

קָדוֹשׁ, קָדוֹשׁ, קָדוֹשׁ יהוה צְבָאוֹת, מְלֹא כָל הָאָרֶץ כְּבוֹדוֹ.[2]

וּמְקַבְּלִין דֵּין מִן דֵּין וְאָמְרִין:

קַדִּישׁ בִּשְׁמֵי מְרוֹמָא עִלָּאָה בֵּית שְׁכִינְתֵּהּ,

קַדִּישׁ עַל אַרְעָא עוֹבַד גְּבוּרְתֵּהּ,

קַדִּישׁ לְעָלַם וּלְעָלְמֵי עָלְמַיָּא, יהוה צְבָאוֹת,

מַלְיָא כָל אַרְעָא זִיו יְקָרֵהּ.[3]

❖ וַתִּשָּׂאֵנִי רוּחַ, וָאֶשְׁמַע אַחֲרַי קוֹל רַעַשׁ גָּדוֹל:

בָּרוּךְ כְּבוֹד יהוה מִמְּקוֹמוֹ.[4]

וּנְטָלַתְנִי רוּחָא, וְשִׁמְעֵת בַּתְרַי קָל זִיעַ סַגִּיא דִּמְשַׁבְּחִין וְאָמְרִין:

בְּרִיךְ יְקָרָא דַיהוה מֵאֲתַר בֵּית שְׁכִינְתֵּהּ.[5]

יהוה יִמְלֹךְ לְעֹלָם וָעֶד.[6]

יהוה מַלְכוּתֵהּ קָאֵם לְעָלַם וּלְעָלְמֵי עָלְמַיָּא.[7]

יהוה אֱלֹהֵי אַבְרָהָם יִצְחָק וְיִשְׂרָאֵל אֲבֹתֵינוּ, שָׁמְרָה זֹּאת לְעוֹלָם, לְיֵצֶר מַחְשְׁבוֹת לְבַב עַמֶּךָ, וְהָכֵן לְבָבָם אֵלֶיךָ.[8] וְהוּא

---

dangers and afflictions of life. *Tur (Orach Chaim* 294) calls it מִזְמוֹר שֶׁל בְּרָכָה, *Psalm of Blessing*, a more positive way of expressing the same idea. As the protective holiness of the Sabbath leaves us, we ask God to continue His protection over us throughout the work week.

Avudraham notes that *Psalm* 91 contains 124 words and that a repetition of the psalm would yield 248 words, a number equivalent to the organs and limbs of the body, thus symbolizing God's protection of every part of those who serve Him. Rather than trouble the congregation to repeat the psalm, it has become customary to repeat the last verse אֹרֶךְ יָמִים, *With long life*. For

that walks in gloom, nor the destroyer who lays waste at noon. Let a thousand encamp at your side and a myriad at your right hand, but to you they shall not approach. You will merely peer with your eyes and you will see the retribution of the wicked. Because You, HASHEM, *are my refuge; You have made the Most High Your dwelling place. No evil will befall you, nor will any plague come near your tent. He will charge His angels for you, to protect you in all your ways. On your palms they will carry you, lest you strike your foot against a stone. Upon the lion and the viper you will tread; you will trample the young lion and the serpent. For he has yearned for Me and I will deliver him; I will elevate him because he knows My Name. He will call upon Me and I will answer him, I am with him in distress, I will release him and I will honor him. With long life will I satisfy him, and I will show him My salvation. With long life will I satisfy him, and I will show him My salvation.*

✧ **וְאַתָּה קָדוֹשׁ** *You are the Holy One, enthroned upon the praises of Israel.*[1] *And one [angel] will call another and say:*

'Holy, holy, holy is HASHEM, Master of Legions,
the whole world is filled with His glory.'[2]

And they receive permission from one another and say:
'Holy in the most exalted heaven, the abode of His Presence;
holy on earth, product of His strength;
holy forever and ever is HASHEM, *Master of Legions —*
the entire world is filled with the radiance of His glory.'[3]

Chazzan— *And a wind lifted me; and I heard behind me*
the sound of a great noise:

'Blessed is the glory of HASHEM from His place.'[4]

And a wind lifted me and I heard behind me the sound
of the powerful movement of those who praised saying:
'Blessed is the honor of HASHEM
from the place of the abode of His Presence.'[5]

HASHEM shall reign for all eternity.[6]

HASHEM *— His kingdom is established forever and ever.*[7]

HASHEM, *God of Abraham, Isaac, and Israel, our forefathers, may You preserve this forever as the realization of the thoughts in Your people's heart, and may You direct their heart to You.*[8] *He,*

(1) *Psalms* 22:4. (2) *Isaiah* 6:3. (3) *Targum Yonasan* to *Isaiah* 6:3.
(4) *Ezekiel* 3:12. (5) *Targum Yonasan* to *Ezekiel* 3:12. (6) *Exodus* 15:18.
(7) *Targum Onkelos* to *Exodus* 15:18. (8) *I Chronicles* 29:18.

commentary to this psalm, see page 380.

וְאַתָּה קָדוֹשׁ / You are the Holy One

Having requested God's blessings during the forthcoming week, we now ask that the Sabbath holiness remain with us, and afford us spiritual protection throughout the week, even though the day itself is departing. Therefore we recite the

רַחוּם, יְכַפֵּר עָוֹן וְלֹא יַשְׁחִית, וְהִרְבָּה לְהָשִׁיב אַפּוֹ, וְלֹא יָעִיר כָּל חֲמָתוֹ.[1] כִּי אַתָּה אֲדֹנָי טוֹב וְסַלָּח, וְרַב חֶסֶד לְכָל קֹרְאֶיךָ.[2] צִדְקָתְךָ צֶדֶק לְעוֹלָם, וְתוֹרָתְךָ אֱמֶת.[3] תִּתֵּן אֱמֶת לְיַעֲקֹב, חֶסֶד לְאַבְרָהָם, אֲשֶׁר נִשְׁבַּעְתָּ לַאֲבֹתֵינוּ מִימֵי קֶדֶם.[4] בָּרוּךְ אֲדֹנָי יוֹם יוֹם יַעֲמָס לָנוּ, הָאֵל יְשׁוּעָתֵנוּ סֶלָה.[5] יהוה צְבָאוֹת עִמָּנוּ, מִשְׂגָּב לָנוּ אֱלֹהֵי יַעֲקֹב סֶלָה.[6] יהוה צְבָאוֹת, אַשְׁרֵי אָדָם בֹּטֵחַ בָּךְ.[7] יהוה הוֹשִׁיעָה, הַמֶּלֶךְ יַעֲנֵנוּ בְיוֹם קָרְאֵנוּ.[8]

בָּרוּךְ הוּא אֱלֹהֵינוּ שֶׁבְּרָאָנוּ לִכְבוֹדוֹ, וְהִבְדִּילָנוּ מִן הַתּוֹעִים, וְנָתַן לָנוּ תּוֹרַת אֱמֶת, וְחַיֵּי עוֹלָם נָטַע בְּתוֹכֵנוּ. הוּא יִפְתַּח לִבֵּנוּ בְּתוֹרָתוֹ, וְיָשֵׂם בְּלִבֵּנוּ אַהֲבָתוֹ וְיִרְאָתוֹ וְלַעֲשׂוֹת רְצוֹנוֹ וּלְעָבְדוֹ בְּלֵבָב שָׁלֵם, לְמַעַן לֹא נִיגַע לָרִיק, וְלֹא נֵלֵד לַבֶּהָלָה.[9]

יְהִי רָצוֹן מִלְּפָנֶיךָ יהוה אֱלֹהֵינוּ וֵאלֹהֵי אֲבוֹתֵינוּ, שֶׁנִּשְׁמֹר חֻקֶּיךָ בָּעוֹלָם הַזֶּה, וְנִזְכֶּה וְנִחְיֶה וְנִרְאֶה וְנִירַשׁ טוֹבָה וּבְרָכָה לִשְׁנֵי יְמוֹת הַמָּשִׁיחַ וּלְחַיֵּי הָעוֹלָם הַבָּא. לְמַעַן יְזַמֶּרְךָ כָבוֹד וְלֹא יִדֹּם, יהוה אֱלֹהַי לְעוֹלָם אוֹדֶךָּ.[10] בָּרוּךְ הַגֶּבֶר אֲשֶׁר יִבְטַח בַּיהוה, וְהָיָה יהוה מִבְטַחוֹ.[11] בִּטְחוּ בַיהוה עֲדֵי עַד, כִּי בְּיָהּ יהוה צוּר עוֹלָמִים.[12] ❖ וְיִבְטְחוּ בְךָ יוֹדְעֵי שְׁמֶךָ, כִּי לֹא עָזַבְתָּ דֹּרְשֶׁיךָ, יהוה.[13] יהוה חָפֵץ לְמַעַן צִדְקוֹ, יַגְדִּיל תּוֹרָה וְיַאְדִּיר.[14]

The *chazzan* recites קַדִּישׁ שָׁלֵם:

יִתְגַּדַּל וְיִתְקַדַּשׁ שְׁמֵהּ רַבָּא. (.Cong —אָמֵן.) בְּעָלְמָא דִּי בְרָא כִרְעוּתֵהּ. וְיַמְלִיךְ מַלְכוּתֵהּ, בְּחַיֵּיכוֹן וּבְיוֹמֵיכוֹן וּבְחַיֵּי דְכָל בֵּית יִשְׂרָאֵל, בַּעֲגָלָא וּבִזְמַן קָרִיב. וְאִמְרוּ: אָמֵן.

(.Cong— אָמֵן. יְהֵא שְׁמֵהּ רַבָּא מְבָרַךְ לְעָלַם וּלְעָלְמֵי עָלְמַיָּא.)

יְהֵא שְׁמֵהּ רַבָּא מְבָרַךְ לְעָלַם וּלְעָלְמֵי עָלְמַיָּא.

יִתְבָּרַךְ וְיִשְׁתַּבַּח וְיִתְפָּאַר וְיִתְרוֹמַם וְיִתְנַשֵּׂא וְיִתְהַדָּר וְיִתְעַלֶּה וְיִתְהַלָּל שְׁמֵהּ דְּקֻדְשָׁא בְּרִיךְ הוּא (.Cong— בְּרִיךְ הוּא) — °לְעֵלָּא מִן כָּל (From Rosh Hashanah to Yom Kippur substitute— °לְעֵלָּא וּלְעֵלָּא מִכָּל) בִּרְכָתָא וְשִׁירָתָא תֻּשְׁבְּחָתָא וְנֶחֱמָתָא, דַּאֲמִירָן בְּעָלְמָא. וְאִמְרוּ: אָמֵן. (.Cong— אָמֵן.)

---

verses that proclaim God's holiness on earth as well as heaven. Then we go on to acknowledge that we were created to glorify Him and we pray that we be capable of absorbing the teachings of the Torah. For commentary see page 154.

Since these prayers refer to the six days of labor, they are not recited if a Festival (Pesach,

the Merciful One, is forgiving of iniquity and does not destroy; frequently He withdraws His anger, not arousing His entire rage.[1] *For You, my Lord, are good and forgiving, and abundantly kind to all who call upon You.*[2] *Your righteousness remains righteous forever, and Your Torah is truth.*[3] *Grant truth to Jacob, kindness to Abraham, as You swore to our forefathers from ancient times.*[4] *Blessed is my Lord for every single day, He burdens us with blessings, the God of our salvation, Selah.*[5] *HASHEM, Master of Legions, is with us, a stronghold for us is the God of Jacob, Selah.*[6] *HASHEM, Master of Legions, praiseworthy is the man who trusts in You.*[7] *HASHEM, save! May the King answer us on the day we call.*[8]

Blessed is He, our God, Who created us for His glory, separated us from those who stray, gave us the Torah of truth and implanted eternal life within us. May He open our heart through His Torah and imbue our heart with love and awe of Him and that we may do His will and serve Him wholeheartedly, so that we do not struggle in vain nor produce for futility.[9]

May it be Your will, HASHEM, our God and the God of our forefathers, that we observe Your decrees in This World, and merit that we live and see and inherit goodness and blessing in the years of Messianic times and for the life of the World to Come. So that my soul might sing to You and not be stilled, HASHEM, my God, forever will I thank You.[10] *Blessed is the man who trusts in HASHEM, then HASHEM will be his security.*[11] *Trust in HASHEM forever, for in God, HASHEM, is the strength of the worlds.*[12] Chazzan– *Those knowing Your Name will trust in You, and You forsake not those Who seek You, HASHEM.*[13] *HASHEM desired, for the sake of its [Israel's] righteousness, that the Torah be made great and glorious.*[14]

The *chazzan* recites the Full *Kaddish:*

יִתְגַּדַּל *May His great Name grow exalted and sanctified* (Cong.— *Amen.*) *in the world that He created as He willed. May He give reign to His kingship in your lifetimes and in your days, and in the lifetimes of the entire Family of Israel, swiftly and soon. Now respond: Amen.*

(Cong.— *Amen. May His great Name be blessed forever and ever.*)

May His great Name be blessed forever and ever.

Blessed, praised, glorified, exalted, extolled, mighty, upraised, and lauded be the Name of the Holy One, Blessed is He (Cong.— *Blessed is He*) — (From Rosh Hashanah to Yom Kippur add: *exceedingly*) *beyond any blessing and song, praise and consolation that are uttered in the world. Now respond: Amen.* (Cong.— *Amen.*)

(1) *Psalms* 78:38. (2) 86:5. (3) 119:142. (4) *Micah* 7:20. (5) *Psalms* 68:20.
(6) 46:8. (7) 84:13. (8) 20:10. (9) Cf. *Isaiah* 65:23. (10) *Psalms* 30:13.
(11) *Jeremiah* 17:7. (12) *Isaiah* 26:4. (13) *Psalms* 9:11. (14) *Isaiah* 42:21.

Shavuos, Rosh Hashanah, Yom Kippur, Succos) will occur during the coming week. In that case, the holiness of the Festival suffices to infuse the week with the sanctity we long for.

On Purim and Tishah B'Av continue יְהֵי שְׁלָמָא, below.

(Cong.—קַבֵּל בְּרַחֲמִים וּבְרָצוֹן אֶת תְּפִלָּתֵנוּ.)

תִּתְקַבֵּל צְלוֹתְהוֹן וּבָעוּתְהוֹן דְּכָל בֵּית יִשְׂרָאֵל קֳדָם אֲבוּהוֹן דִּי בִשְׁמַיָּא. וְאִמְרוּ: אָמֵן. (Cong.— אָמֵן.)

(Cong.—יְהִי שֵׁם יהוה מְבֹרָךְ, מֵעַתָּה וְעַד עוֹלָם.)

יְהֵא שְׁלָמָא רַבָּא מִן שְׁמַיָּא, וְחַיִּים עָלֵינוּ וְעַל כָּל יִשְׂרָאֵל. וְאִמְרוּ: אָמֵן. (Cong.— אָמֵן.)

(Cong.—עֶזְרִי מֵעִם יהוה, עֹשֵׂה שָׁמַיִם וָאָרֶץ.)

Take three steps back. Bow left and say ... עֹשֶׂה; bow right and say ... הוּא; bow forward and say וְעַל כָּל ... אָמֵן. Remain standing in place for a few moments, then take three steps forward.

עֹשֶׂה שָׁלוֹם בִּמְרוֹמָיו, הוּא יַעֲשֶׂה שָׁלוֹם עָלֵינוּ, וְעַל כָּל יִשְׂרָאֵל. וְאִמְרוּ: אָמֵן. (Cong.— אָמֵן.)

During Chanukah the synagogue *menorah* is lit (page 782).
Between Pesach and Shavuos, the *Omer* is counted (p. 282).

פסוקי ברכה

וְיִתֶּן לְךָ* הָאֱלֹהִים מִטַּל הַשָּׁמַיִם וּמִשְׁמַנֵּי הָאָרֶץ, וְרֹב דָּגָן וְתִירֹשׁ. יַעַבְדוּךָ עַמִּים, וְיִשְׁתַּחֲווּ לְךָ לְאֻמִּים, הֱוֵה גְבִיר לְאַחֶיךָ, וְיִשְׁתַּחֲווּ לְךָ בְּנֵי אִמֶּךָ, אֹרְרֶיךָ אָרוּר, וּמְבָרְכֶיךָ בָּרוּךְ.[1] וְאֵל שַׁדַּי יְבָרֵךְ אֹתְךָ* וְיַפְרְךָ וְיַרְבֶּךָ, וְהָיִיתָ לִקְהַל עַמִּים. וְיִתֶּן לְךָ אֶת בִּרְכַּת אַבְרָהָם, לְךָ וּלְזַרְעֲךָ אִתָּךְ, לְרִשְׁתְּךָ אֶת אֶרֶץ מְגֻרֶיךָ, אֲשֶׁר נָתַן אֱלֹהִים לְאַבְרָהָם.[2] מֵאֵל אָבִיךָ וְיַעְזְרֶךָּ, וְאֵת שַׁדַּי וִיבָרְכֶךָּ, בִּרְכֹת שָׁמַיִם מֵעָל, בִּרְכֹת תְּהוֹם רֹבֶצֶת תָּחַת, בִּרְכֹת שָׁדַיִם וָרָחַם. בִּרְכֹת אָבִיךָ* גָּבְרוּ עַל בִּרְכֹת הוֹרַי, עַד תַּאֲוַת גִּבְעֹת עוֹלָם, תִּהְיֶיןָ לְרֹאשׁ יוֹסֵף, וּלְקָדְקֹד נְזִיר אֶחָיו.[3] וַאֲהֵבְךָ* וּבֵרַכְךָ וְהִרְבֶּךָ, וּבֵרַךְ פְּרִי בִטְנְךָ וּפְרִי אַדְמָתֶךָ, דְּגָנְךָ וְתִירֹשְׁךָ וְיִצְהָרֶךָ, שְׁגַר אֲלָפֶיךָ וְעַשְׁתְּרֹת צֹאנֶךָ, עַל הָאֲדָמָה אֲשֶׁר נִשְׁבַּע לַאֲבֹתֶיךָ לָתֶת לָךְ. בָּרוּךְ תִּהְיֶה מִכָּל הָעַמִּים,

---

וְיִתֶּן לְךָ הָאֱלֹהִים / Verses of Blessing

After *Maariv,* this collection of Scriptural passages is recited. Although most congregations recite them in the synagogue, in some communities it is customary for individuals to recite them at home after *Havdalah.* This is primarily an anthology of blessings, beginning with that given by Isaac to Jacob. By reciting them now, on the threshold of a new week, we invoke God's blessing on the labor of the coming six days.

Siddur Avodas Yisrael divides the Scriptural selections into seven topics: (1) בְּרָכָה, *blessing;* (2) גְּאוּלָּה, *redemption;* (3) יְשׁוּעָה, *salvation;* (4) דַּעַת ה׳, *knowledge of God;* (5) פִּדְיוֹן, *rescue;* (6) הִפּוּךְ צָרָה, *transformation of distress to relief;* and (7) שָׁלוֹם, *peace.* He notes also that the order of the verses as they are quoted here does not always follow the order in which they appear in the Torah. This is simply because in וְיִתֶּן לְךָ they are placed in logical sequence according to topics, as will be evident when one follows the text.

וְיִתֶּן לְךָ — *And may* [*God*] *give you.* The first two verses comprise the blessing given by Isaac to Jacob at the time that Jacob posed as Esau.

וְאֵל שַׁדַּי יְבָרֵךְ אֹתְךָ — *And may El Shaddai bless you.* The Name *El Shaddai* has been translated the *All-Sufficient One* or the *Almighty.* It refers to the aspect of God that determines how much or how little blessing a person needs, how much suffering he can endure and so on. God

(Cong.— Accept our prayers with mercy and favor.)

May the prayers and supplications of the entire Family of Israel be accepted before their Father Who is in Heaven. Now respond: Amen. (Cong.—*Amen.*)

(Cong.— *May the Name of* HASHEM, *be blessed from now to eternity.*)

May there be abundant peace from Heaven, and life, upon us and upon all Israel. Now respond: Amen. (Cong.— *Amen.*)

(Cong.— *My help is from* HASHEM, *Maker of heaven and earth.)*

Take three steps back. Bow left and say, *'He Who makes peace ...'*; bow right and say, *'may He ...'*; bow forward and say, *'and upon all Israel ...'* Remain standing in place for a few moments, then take three steps forward.

He Who makes peace in His heights, may He make peace upon us, and upon all Israel. Now respond: Amen. (Cong.—*Amen.*)

During Chanukah the synagogue *menorah* is lit (page 782).
Between Pesach and Shavuos, the *Omer* is counted (page 282).

VERSES OF BLESSING

וְיִתֶּן *And may God give you* of the dew of the heavens and of the fatness of the earth, and abundant grain and wine. Peoples will serve you, and regimes will prostrate themselves to you; be a lord to your kinsmen, and your mother's sons will prostrate themselves to you; they who curse you are cursed, and they who bless you are blessed.*[1] *And may El Shaddai bless you,* make you fruitful and make you numerous, and may you be a congregation of peoples. May He grant you the blessing of Abraham, to you and to your offspring with you, that you may possess the land of your sojourns which God gave to Abraham.*[2] *It is from the God of your father and He will help you, and with Shaddai and He will bless you — blessings of heaven from above, blessings of the deep crouching below, blessings of the bosom and womb. The blessings of your father* surpassed the blessings of my fathers, to the endless bounds of the world's hills; let them be upon Joseph's head and upon the head of the one separated from his brothers.*[3] *And He shall love you,* and He shall bless you, and He shall make you numerous; may He bless the fruit of your womb and the fruit of your land, your grain, your wine and your oil, the offspring of your cattle and the flocks of your sheep, on the land that He swore to your forefathers to give to you. Blessed shall you be above all peoples;*

(1) *Genesis* 27:28-29. (2) 28:3-4. (3) 49:25-26.

determines what is דַּי, *enough,* and has the absolute power to see that only this and neither more nor less comes into being.

This verse and the next one are the blessing given by Isaac to Jacob just before Jacob was sent to Paddan Aram to escape the wrath of the murderous Esau and to find himself a wife.

בִּרְכֹת אָבִיךָ — *The blessings of your father.* This verse is the climax of Jacob's blessing to Joseph, who earned the distinction of primacy among his brothers. Although all of Jacob's blessings had awesome significance, that given to Joseph is cited here because Jacob described it as surpassing all others and because he wanted it to be unbounded by any limits.

וַאֲהֵבְךָ — *And He shall love you.* In the last weeks of Moses' life, he exhorted and taught, warned and blessed. From here to the end of the paragraph is one of many blessings Moses pronounced as the Divine reward for Israel's

לֹא יִהְיֶה בְךָ עָקָר וַעֲקָרָה, וּבִבְהֶמְתֶּךָ. וְהֵסִיר יהוה מִמְּךָ כָּל חֹלִי, וְכָל מַדְוֵי מִצְרַיִם הָרָעִים אֲשֶׁר יָדַעְתָּ, לֹא יְשִׂימָם בָּךְ, וּנְתָנָם בְּכָל שֹׂנְאֶיךָ.[1]

הַמַּלְאָךְ* הַגֹּאֵל אֹתִי מִכָּל רָע יְבָרֵךְ אֶת הַנְּעָרִים וְיִקָּרֵא בָהֶם שְׁמִי, וְשֵׁם אֲבֹתַי אַבְרָהָם וְיִצְחָק, וְיִדְגּוּ לָרֹב בְּקֶרֶב הָאָרֶץ.[2] יהוה אֱלֹהֵיכֶם הִרְבָּה אֶתְכֶם, וְהִנְּכֶם הַיּוֹם כְּכוֹכְבֵי הַשָּׁמַיִם לָרֹב. יהוה אֱלֹהֵי אֲבוֹתֵכֶם יֹסֵף עֲלֵיכֶם כָּכֶם אֶלֶף פְּעָמִים, וִיבָרֵךְ אֶתְכֶם כַּאֲשֶׁר דִּבֶּר לָכֶם.[3]

בָּרוּךְ אַתָּה בָּעִיר,* וּבָרוּךְ אַתָּה בַּשָּׂדֶה. בָּרוּךְ אַתָּה בְּבֹאֶךָ, וּבָרוּךְ אַתָּה בְּצֵאתֶךָ. בָּרוּךְ טַנְאֲךָ וּמִשְׁאַרְתֶּךָ. בָּרוּךְ פְּרִי בִטְנְךָ וּפְרִי אַדְמָתְךָ וּפְרִי בְהֶמְתֶּךָ, שְׁגַר אֲלָפֶיךָ וְעַשְׁתְּרוֹת צֹאנֶךָ.[4] יְצַו יהוה אִתְּךָ אֶת הַבְּרָכָה בַּאֲסָמֶיךָ וּבְכֹל מִשְׁלַח יָדֶךָ, וּבֵרַכְךָ בָּאָרֶץ אֲשֶׁר יהוה אֱלֹהֶיךָ נֹתֵן לָךְ. יִפְתַּח יהוה לְךָ אֶת אוֹצָרוֹ הַטּוֹב, אֶת הַשָּׁמַיִם, לָתֵת מְטַר אַרְצְךָ בְּעִתּוֹ, וּלְבָרֵךְ אֵת כָּל מַעֲשֵׂה יָדֶךָ, וְהִלְוִיתָ גּוֹיִם רַבִּים, וְאַתָּה לֹא תִלְוֶה.[5] כִּי יהוה אֱלֹהֶיךָ בֵּרַכְךָ* כַּאֲשֶׁר דִּבֶּר לָךְ, וְהַעֲבַטְתָּ גּוֹיִם רַבִּים, וְאַתָּה לֹא תַעֲבֹט, וּמָשַׁלְתָּ בְּגוֹיִם רַבִּים, וּבְךָ לֹא יִמְשֹׁלוּ.[6] אַשְׁרֶיךָ יִשְׂרָאֵל,* מִי כָמוֹךָ, עַם נוֹשַׁע בַּיהוה, מָגֵן עֶזְרֶךָ, וַאֲשֶׁר חֶרֶב גַּאֲוָתֶךָ, וְיִכָּחֲשׁוּ אֹיְבֶיךָ לָךְ, וְאַתָּה עַל בָּמוֹתֵימוֹ תִדְרֹךְ.[7]

גאולה

מָחִיתִי* כָעָב פְּשָׁעֶיךָ וְכֶעָנָן חַטֹּאתֶיךָ, שׁוּבָה אֵלַי כִּי גְאַלְתִּיךָ. רָנּוּ שָׁמַיִם, כִּי עָשָׂה יהוה, הָרִיעוּ תַּחְתִּיּוֹת

---

loyalty to God and His commandments.

☙ הַמַּלְאָךְ — [*May*] *the angel.* This paragraph is devoted to blessings given by aged leaders who took pride in the growth of a young and thriving new generation. The first verse has become one of the classic blessings conferred upon children. It was given by Jacob on his deathbed to Menashe and Ephraim, the Egyptian-born children of Joseph. The last two verses, beginning ה' אֱלֹהֵיכֶם, *HASHEM, your God,* were Moses' proud description of the nation that he had led out of Egypt and his blessing that their future greatness should dwarf anything that had happened in the past.

☙ בָּרוּךְ אַתָּה בָּעִיר — *Blessed are you in the city.* Moses pronounced this stirring series of blessings upon his people, telling them that if they observed the Torah, there would be no area of their lives that would be untouched by God's generosity. These blessings were the introduction to Moses' תּוֹכֵחָה, *chastisement,* in which he warned the people of the woes that would befall them if they neglected the Torah. This long blessing seems to be entirely material in nature, without mention of spiritual growth. This is one of the great miracles of creation. We would expect people to attain spiritual riches in return for spiritual service of God; the Torah has no need to mention that. But it is miraculous and inspiring that in return for the study of Torah and the performance of *mitzvos,* God promises *there shall not be among you a barren man or woman, nor among your cattle. HASHEM shall remove from you all illness; and all the evil sufferings of Egypt that you knew, He will not place upon you, but He will set them upon all your enemies.*[1]

הַמַּלְאָךְ *May the angel* who redeems me from all evil bless the lads, and may my name be declared upon them — and the names of my forefathers Abraham and Isaac — and may they proliferate abundantly like fish within the land.*[2] *HASHEM, Your God, has made you numerous, and behold! you are today like the stars of heaven in abundance. May HASHEM, the God of your forefathers, increase you a thousandfold and bless you as He spoke to you.*[3]

בָּרוּךְ *Blessed are you in the city;* blessed are you in the field. Blessed are you upon your arrival; blessed are you upon your departure. Blessed is your fruit basket and your kneading trough. Blessed is the fruit of your womb, the fruit of your land and the fruit of your animal, the offspring of your cattle and the flocks of your sheep.*[4] *May HASHEM command that the blessing accompany you in your storehouse and wherever you set your hand, and may He bless you in the land that HASHEM, your God, gives you. May HASHEM open for you His good treasury, the heaven, to give you rain for your land in its time and to bless your every handiwork; and may you lend many nations, but may you not borrow.*[5] *For HASHEM, your God, will have blessed you* as He spoke to you; and may you make many nations indebted to you, but may you not become indebted; and you will dominate many nations, but they will not dominate you.*[6] *Praiseworthy are you, O Israel,* who is like you! — a people saved by God, Who is the Shield of your help, and Who is the Sword of your majesty. Your enemies will be false with you, but you will tread upon their heights.*[7]

REDEMPTION

מָחִיתִי *I have blotted out* your willful sins like a thick mist and your errors like a cloud — return to Me for I have redeemed you. Sing gladly, O heaven, for HASHEM has done so; exult O depths of the*

(1) *Deuteronomy* 7:13-15. (2) *Genesis* 48:16. (3) *Deuteronomy* 1:10-11.
(4) 28:3,6,5,4. (5) 28:8,12. (6) 15:6. (7) 33:29.

His people health, wealth and physical security *(Ramban).*

כִּי ה׳ אֱלֹהֶיךָ בֵּרַכְךָ — *For HASHEM, your God, will have blessed you.* This verse, from a different part of *Deuteronomy,* is inserted here because it is very similar to the one cited just before. The term וְהַעֲבַטְתָּ, *you will make indebted,* comes from the word עֲבֹט, *collateral.* Although it is similar in meaning to תַּלְוֶה, *may you lend,* it is a stronger term because it implies a continuing moral and legal obligation.

אַשְׁרֶיךָ יִשְׂרָאֵל — *Praiseworthy are you, O Israel.* These two verses are Moses' last words to his people. Though they had tried him sorely during the forty years in the Wilderness and though their provocation had caused him to be denied the privilege of ever setting foot in *Eretz Yisrael,* Moses ended his life with love and praise of the nation that meant more to him than life and glory.

☙ מָחִיתִי — *I have blotted out.* The section of redemption makes clear that the basis of

אָֽרֶץ, פִּצְחוּ הָרִים רִנָּה, יַֽעַר וְכָל עֵץ בּוֹ, כִּי גָאַל יהוה יַֽעֲקֹב וּבְיִשְׂרָאֵל יִתְפָּאָר.[1] גֹּאֲלֵנוּ יהוה צְבָאוֹת שְׁמוֹ, קְדוֹשׁ יִשְׂרָאֵל.[2]

ישועה

יִשְׂרָאֵל נוֹשַׁע* בַּיהוה תְּשׁוּעַת עוֹלָמִים, לֹא תֵבֹֽשׁוּ וְלֹא תִכָּלְמוּ* עַד עוֹלְמֵי עַד.[3] וַאֲכַלְתֶּם אָכוֹל וְשָׂבֽוֹעַ, וְהִלַּלְתֶּם אֶת שֵׁם יהוה אֱלֹהֵיכֶם אֲשֶׁר עָשָׂה עִמָּכֶם לְהַפְלִיא, וְלֹא יֵבֹֽשׁוּ עַמִּי לְעוֹלָם. וִידַעְתֶּם כִּי בְקֶֽרֶב יִשְׂרָאֵל אָֽנִי, וַאֲנִי יהוה אֱלֹהֵיכֶם, וְאֵין עוֹד, וְלֹא יֵבֹֽשׁוּ עַמִּי לְעוֹלָם.[4] כִּי בְשִׂמְחָה תֵצֵֽאוּ וּבְשָׁלוֹם תּוּבָלוּן, הֶהָרִים וְהַגְּבָעוֹת יִפְצְחוּ לִפְנֵיכֶם רִנָּה, וְכָל עֲצֵי הַשָּׂדֶה יִמְחֲאוּ כָף.[5] הִנֵּה אֵל יְשׁוּעָתִי, אֶבְטַח וְלֹא אֶפְחָד, כִּי עָזִּי וְזִמְרָת יָהּ יהוה וַיְהִי לִי לִישׁוּעָה. וּשְׁאַבְתֶּם מַֽיִם בְּשָׂשׂוֹן, מִמַּעַיְנֵי הַיְשׁוּעָה. וַאֲמַרְתֶּם בַּיּוֹם הַהוּא, הוֹדוּ לַיהוה קִרְאוּ בִשְׁמוֹ, הוֹדִֽיעוּ בָעַמִּים עֲלִילֹתָיו, הַזְכִּֽירוּ כִּי נִשְׂגָּב שְׁמוֹ. זַמְּרוּ יהוה כִּי גֵאוּת עָשָׂה, מוּדַֽעַת זֹאת בְּכָל הָאָֽרֶץ. צַהֲלִי וָרֹֽנִּי יוֹשֶֽׁבֶת צִיּוֹן, כִּי גָדוֹל בְּקִרְבֵּךְ קְדוֹשׁ יִשְׂרָאֵל.[6] וְאָמַר בַּיּוֹם הַהוּא, הִנֵּה אֱלֹהֵֽינוּ זֶה, קִוִּֽינוּ לוֹ וְיוֹשִׁיעֵֽנוּ, זֶה יהוה קִוִּֽינוּ לוֹ, נָגִֽילָה וְנִשְׂמְחָה בִּישׁוּעָתוֹ.[7]

דעת ה'

בֵּית יַֽעֲקֹב,* לְכוּ וְנֵלְכָה בְּאוֹר יהוה.[8] וְהָיָה אֱמוּנַת עִתֶּֽיךָ חֹֽסֶן יְשׁוּעֹת חָכְמַת וָדָֽעַת, יִרְאַת יהוה הִיא אוֹצָרוֹ.[9] וַיְהִי דָוִד לְכָל דְּרָכָיו מַשְׂכִּיל, וַיהוה עִמּוֹ.[10]

פדיום

פָּדָה* בְשָׁלוֹם נַפְשִׁי מִקְּרָב לִי, כִּי בְרַבִּים הָיוּ עִמָּדִי.[11] וַיֹּֽאמֶר הָעָם אֶל שָׁאוּל, הֲיוֹנָתָן יָמוּת אֲשֶׁר עָשָׂה הַיְשׁוּעָה הַגְּדוֹלָה הַזֹּאת בְּיִשְׂרָאֵל, חָלִֽילָה, חַי יהוה, אִם יִפֹּל מִשַּׂעֲרַת

---

redemption is repentance and a return to God, which brings forgiveness of sin.

יִשְׂרָאֵל נוֹשַׁע — *Israel is saved.* The first few verses of salvation give an interesting insight into the nature of exile from which Israel is to be saved. Each of the first three verses promises that Israel will no longer be ashamed.

לֹא תֵבֹשׁוּ וְלֹא תִכָּלְמוּ — *They will not be shamed nor humiliated.* These two terms refer respectively to the shame that is felt inwardly and the humiliation that is inflicted publicly by others. In exile, Israel suffers from both. The outer humiliation is obvious; the inner shame is caused by becoming subject to more powerful nations and by being forced to adopt alien cultures and values. With the salvation of redemption and the resultant sovereignty of God's will, Israel will feel joy and pride.

בֵּית יַעֲקֹב — *O House of Jacob.* These three verses provide a definition of the salvation of which we have just spoken: salvation is meaningless unless it includes knowledge of God's Torah. This concept is expressed in the

earth; break out, O mountains, in glad song, forest and every tree within it, for HASHEM has redeemed Jacob and will take pride in Israel.[1] *Our Redeemer — HASHEM, Master of Legions, is His Name — is the Holy One of Israel.*[2]

SALVATION

יִשְׂרָאֵל *Israel is saved* by God in an everlasting salvation; they will not be shamed nor humiliated* forever and ever.*[3] *You shall eat food and be satisfied, and you shall praise the Name of HASHEM, your God, Who has done wondrously with you, and My people shall not be shamed forever. And you shall know that in the midst of Israel am I, and I am HASHEM, your God — there is none other; and My people shall not be shamed forever.*[4] *For in gladness shall you go out and in peace shall you arrive; the mountains and the hills will break out before you in glad song and all the trees of the field will clap hands.*[5] *Behold! God is my help, I shall trust and not fear — for God is my might and my praise — HASHEM — and He was a salvation to me. You can draw water in joy, from the springs of salvation. And you shall say on that day, 'Give thanks to HASHEM, declare His name, make His acts known among the peoples;' remind one another, for His Name is powerful. Make music to HASHEM for He has established grandeur — this is known throughout the earth. Exult and sing for joy, O inhabitant of Zion, for the Holy One of Israel has done greatly among you.*[6] *And he shall say on that day, 'Behold! this is our God, we have hoped for Him, that He would save us — this is HASHEM, we have hoped for Him, we shall rejoice and be glad at His salvation.*[7]

KNOWLEDGE OF GOD

בֵּית *O House of Jacob* — come let us go by the light of HASHEM.*[8] *The stability of your times, the strength of your salvations shall be through knowledge and wisdom, fear of God — that is one's treasure.*[9] *And David was successful in all his ways, and HASHEM was with him.*[10]

RESCUE

פָּדָה *He redeemed* my soul in peace from the battles that were upon me, for the sake of the multitudes who were with me.*[11] *And the people said to Saul, 'Shall Jonathan die, who performed this great salvation for Israel? A sacrilege! — as HASHEM lives, if a hair of his head*

(1) *Isaiah* 44:22-23. (2) 47:4. (3) 45:17. (4) *Joel* 2:26-27. (5) *Isaiah* 55:12. (6) 12:2-6. (7) 25:9. (8) 2:5. (9) 33:6. (10) *I Samuel* 18:14. (11) *Psalms* 55:19.

Talmudic dictum that there is no truly free person except for one who occupies himself with the Torah. As the second of these verses teaches, one's treasure is knowledge, wisdom, and fear of God, and as the third verse teaches, success comes through God's help. A further allusion to the necessity of Torah knowledge is the passage in *Shabbos* 31a that expounds the second verse as symbolic of the Six Orders of the Mishnah. Thus, the first verse refers to the Written Torah, the second to the Oral Law, and the third expresses the assurance that knowledge of the Torah is the key to success.

פָּדָה — *He redeemed.* The inclusion of the next nine verses is based on *Berachos* 55b. There the

רֹאשׁוֹ אַרְצָה, כִּי עִם אֱלֹהִים עָשָׂה הַיּוֹם הַזֶּה, וַיִּפְדּוּ הָעָם אֶת יוֹנָתָן וְלֹא מֵת.[1] וּפְדוּיֵי יהוה יְשֻׁבוּן, וּבָאוּ צִיּוֹן בְּרִנָּה, וְשִׂמְחַת עוֹלָם עַל רֹאשָׁם, שָׂשׂוֹן וְשִׂמְחָה יַשִּׂיגוּ וְנָסוּ יָגוֹן וַאֲנָחָה.[2]

הפוך צרה

הָפַכְתָּ מִסְפְּדִי לְמָחוֹל לִי, פִּתַּחְתָּ שַׂקִּי, וַתְּאַזְּרֵנִי שִׂמְחָה.[3] וְלֹא אָבָה יהוה אֱלֹהֶיךָ לִשְׁמֹעַ אֶל בִּלְעָם, וַיַּהֲפֹךְ יהוה אֱלֹהֶיךָ לְּךָ אֶת הַקְּלָלָה לִבְרָכָה, כִּי אֲהֵבְךָ יהוה אֱלֹהֶיךָ.[4] אָז תִּשְׂמַח בְּתוּלָה בְּמָחוֹל, וּבַחֻרִים וּזְקֵנִים יַחְדָּו, וְהָפַכְתִּי אֶבְלָם לְשָׂשׂוֹן, וְנִחַמְתִּים וְשִׂמַּחְתִּים מִיגוֹנָם.[5]

שלום

בּוֹרֵא נִיב שְׂפָתָיִם, שָׁלוֹם שָׁלוֹם לָרָחוֹק וְלַקָּרוֹב, אָמַר יהוה וּרְפָאתִיו.[6] וְרוּחַ לָבְשָׁה אֶת עֲמָשַׂי, רֹאשׁ הַשָּׁלִישִׁים, לְךָ דָוִיד וְעִמְּךָ בֶן יִשַׁי שָׁלוֹם, שָׁלוֹם לְךָ, וְשָׁלוֹם לְעֹזְרֶךָ כִּי עֲזָרְךָ אֱלֹהֶיךָ וַיְקַבְּלֵם דָּוִיד וַיִּתְּנֵם בְּרָאשֵׁי הַגְּדוּד.[7] וַאֲמַרְתֶּם, כֹּה לֶחָי, וְאַתָּה שָׁלוֹם וּבֵיתְךָ שָׁלוֹם וְכֹל אֲשֶׁר לְךָ שָׁלוֹם.[8] יהוה עֹז לְעַמּוֹ יִתֵּן יהוה יְבָרֵךְ אֶת עַמּוֹ בַשָּׁלוֹם.[9]

מסכת מגילה לא.

אָמַר רַבִּי יוֹחָנָן:* בְּכָל מָקוֹם שֶׁאַתָּה מוֹצֵא גְּדֻלָּתוֹ שֶׁל הַקָּדוֹשׁ בָּרוּךְ הוּא, שָׁם אַתָּה מוֹצֵא עַנְוְתָנוּתוֹ. דָּבָר זֶה כָּתוּב בַּתּוֹרָה, וְשָׁנוּי בַּנְּבִיאִים, וּמְשֻׁלָּשׁ בַּכְּתוּבִים. כָּתוּב בַּתּוֹרָה: כִּי יהוה אֱלֹהֵיכֶם הוּא אֱלֹהֵי הָאֱלֹהִים וַאֲדֹנֵי הָאֲדֹנִים, הָאֵל הַגָּדֹל הַגִּבֹּר וְהַנּוֹרָא אֲשֶׁר לֹא יִשָּׂא פָנִים וְלֹא יִקַּח שֹׁחַד.[10] וּכְתִיב בַּתְרֵהּ: עֹשֶׂה מִשְׁפַּט יָתוֹם וְאַלְמָנָה, וְאֹהֵב גֵּר לָתֶת לוֹ לֶחֶם וְשִׂמְלָה.[11] שָׁנוּי בַּנְּבִיאִים, דִּכְתִיב: כִּי כֹה אָמַר רָם וְנִשָּׂא שֹׁכֵן עַד וְקָדוֹשׁ שְׁמוֹ, מָרוֹם וְקָדוֹשׁ אֶשְׁכּוֹן, וְאֶת דַּכָּא וּשְׁפַל רוּחַ, לְהַחֲיוֹת רוּחַ שְׁפָלִים וּלְהַחֲיוֹת לֵב נִדְכָּאִים.[12]

Talmud teaches that if one has had a very disturbing dream and he continues to be depressed by it, he should come before three people and tell them he has had such a dream. They are to reply with the wish that God change the implication of the dream from bad to good. Then they are to recite the following nine verses that, in effect, express the prayer that the dream's evil omen be transformed to the good, that the dreamer be rescued from distress, and he know only peace. In the context of the conclusion of the Sabbath, we change the order of the three sections. Since there is no actual distress at this moment, we begin with the verses of rescue, asking God to save us from the weekday challenges to the spiritual elevation we have absorbed during the Sabbath.

אָמַר רַבִּי יוֹחָנָן — *Rabbi Yochanan said.* Although this Talmudic passage has no direct relationship to the above prayers for the coming week, the commentators note that it provides

falls to the ground, for with HASHEM has he acted this day!' And the people redeemed Jonathan and he did not die.[1] *Those redeemed by God will return and arrive at Zion with glad song and eternal gladness on their heads; joy and gladness shall they attain, and sorrow and groan shall flee.*[2]

TRANSFORMATION OF DISTRESS TO RELIEF

הָפַכְתָּ *You have changed for me my lament into dancing; You undid my sackcloth and girded me with gladness.*[3] *HASHEM, your God, did not wish to pay heed to Balaam, and HASHEM, your God, transformed for you the curse to blessing, for HASHEM, your God, loves you.*[4] *Then the maiden shall rejoice in a dance, and lads and elders together; and I shall change their mourning to joy, and I shall console them and gladden them from their sorrow.*[5]

PEACE

בּוֹרֵא *I create fruit of the lips: 'Peace, peace, for far and near,' says HASHEM, 'and I shall heal him.'*[6] *A spirit clothed Amasai, head of the officers, 'For your sake, David, and to be with you, son of Jesse; peace, peace to you, and peace to him who helps you, for your God has helped you.' David accepted them and appointed them heads of the band.*[7] *And you shall say: 'So may it be as long as you live; peace for you, peace for your household and peace for all that is with you.*[8] *HASHEM will give might to His people, HASHEM will bless His people with peace.*[9]

Talmud, Tractate *Megillah* 31a

אָמַר ***Rabbi Yochanan said:* Wherever you find the greatness of the Holy One, Blessed is He, there you find His humility. This phenomenon is written in the Torah, repeated in the Prophets and stated a third time in the Writings. It is written in the Torah: 'For HASHEM, your God, He is the God of heavenly forces and the Master of masters, the great, mighty and awesome God, Who shows no favoritism and accepts no bribe.'***[10] ***Afterwards it is written: 'He performs justice for orphan and widow, and loves the stranger, to give him food and clothing.'***[11] ***It is repeated in the Prophets, as it is written: "For so says the exalted and uplifted One, Who abides forever, and Whose Name is holy, 'I abide in exaltedness and holiness — but am with the contrite and lowly of spirit, to revive the spirit of the lowly and to revive the heart of the contrite.' "***[12] ***And it is stated a third time***

(1) *I Samuel* 14:45. (2) *Isaiah* 35:10. (3) *Psalms* 30:12. (4) *Deuteronomy* 23:6. (5) *Jeremiah* 31:12. (6) *Isaiah* 57:19. (7) *I Chronicles* 12:19. (8) *I Samuel* 25:6. (9) *Psalms* 29:11. (10) *Deuteronomy* 10:17. (11) 10:18. (12) *Isaiah* 57:15.

perspective in the following ways:

— Rabbi Yochanan's teaching gives us confidence to pray. People have always expressed a fear, a sense of inadequacy to pray to God: what are we and who are we that we ask God to take notice of us? To this concern, Rabbi Yochanan replies with a host of Scriptural passages that even when God's grandeur is most apparent, He reveals His humility, meaning that He is concerned with the needs and fears of even

מִשְׁלָּשׁ בַּכְּתוּבִים, דִּכְתִיב: שִׁירוּ לֵאלֹהִים, זַמְּרוּ שְׁמוֹ, סֹלּוּ לָרֹכֵב בָּעֲרָבוֹת, בְּיָהּ שְׁמוֹ, וְעִלְזוּ לְפָנָיו.[1] וּכְתִיב בַּתְרֵהּ: אֲבִי יְתוֹמִים וְדַיַּן אַלְמָנוֹת, אֱלֹהִים בִּמְעוֹן קָדְשׁוֹ.[2]

יְהִי יהוה אֱלֹהֵינוּ עִמָּנוּ* כַּאֲשֶׁר הָיָה עִם אֲבֹתֵינוּ, אַל יַעַזְבֵנוּ וְאַל יִטְּשֵׁנוּ.[3] וְאַתֶּם הַדְּבֵקִים בַּיהוה אֱלֹהֵיכֶם חַיִּים כֻּלְּכֶם הַיּוֹם.[4] כִּי נִחַם יהוה צִיּוֹן, נִחַם כָּל חָרְבֹתֶיהָ, וַיָּשֶׂם מִדְבָּרָהּ כְּעֵדֶן וְעַרְבָתָהּ כְּגַן יהוה, שָׂשׂוֹן וְשִׂמְחָה יִמָּצֵא בָהּ, תּוֹדָה וְקוֹל זִמְרָה.[5] יהוה חָפֵץ לְמַעַן צִדְקוֹ, יַגְדִּיל תּוֹרָה וְיַאְדִּיר.[6]

תהלים קכח (commentary on p. 539)

שִׁיר הַמַּעֲלוֹת* אַשְׁרֵי כָּל יְרֵא יהוה, הַהֹלֵךְ בִּדְרָכָיו. יְגִיעַ כַּפֶּיךָ כִּי תֹאכֵל, אַשְׁרֶיךָ וְטוֹב לָךְ. אֶשְׁתְּךָ כְּגֶפֶן פֹּרִיָּה בְּיַרְכְּתֵי בֵיתֶךָ, בָּנֶיךָ כִּשְׁתִלֵי זֵיתִים, סָבִיב לְשֻׁלְחָנֶךָ. הִנֵּה כִי כֵן יְבֹרַךְ גָּבֶר יְרֵא יהוה. יְבָרֶכְךָ יהוה מִצִּיּוֹן וּרְאֵה בְּטוּב יְרוּשָׁלָיִם, כֹּל יְמֵי חַיֶּיךָ. וּרְאֵה בָנִים לְבָנֶיךָ, שָׁלוֹם עַל יִשְׂרָאֵל.

In some congregations mourners recite קַדִּישׁ יָתוֹם (page 610) at this point.
In the synagogue, *Havdalah* is recited before *Aleinu*.

The congregation stands while reciting עָלֵינוּ.

עָלֵינוּ לְשַׁבֵּחַ לַאֲדוֹן הַכֹּל, לָתֵת גְּדֻלָּה לְיוֹצֵר בְּרֵאשִׁית, שֶׁלֹּא עָשָׂנוּ כְּגוֹיֵי הָאֲרָצוֹת, וְלֹא שָׂמָנוּ כְּמִשְׁפְּחוֹת הָאֲדָמָה. שֶׁלֹּא שָׂם חֶלְקֵנוּ כָּהֶם, וְגוֹרָלֵנוּ כְּכָל הֲמוֹנָם. (שֶׁהֵם מִשְׁתַּחֲוִים לְהֶבֶל וָרִיק, וּמִתְפַּלְלִים אֶל אֵל לֹא יוֹשִׁיעַ.[7]) וַאֲנַחְנוּ כּוֹרְעִים וּמִשְׁתַּחֲוִים וּמוֹדִים, לִפְנֵי מֶלֶךְ מַלְכֵי הַמְּלָכִים הַקָּדוֹשׁ בָּרוּךְ הוּא. שֶׁהוּא נוֹטֶה שָׁמַיִם וְיֹסֵד אָרֶץ,[8] וּמוֹשַׁב יְקָרוֹ בַּשָּׁמַיִם מִמַּעַל, וּשְׁכִינַת עֻזּוֹ בְּגָבְהֵי מְרוֹמִים. הוּא אֱלֹהֵינוּ, אֵין עוֹד. אֱמֶת מַלְכֵּנוּ, אֶפֶס זוּלָתוֹ, כַּכָּתוּב בְּתוֹרָתוֹ: וְיָדַעְתָּ הַיּוֹם וַהֲשֵׁבֹתָ אֶל לְבָבֶךָ, כִּי יהוה הוּא הָאֱלֹהִים בַּשָּׁמַיִם מִמַּעַל וְעַל הָאָרֶץ מִתָּחַת, אֵין עוֹד.[9]

Bow while reciting וַאֲנַחְנוּ כּוֹרְעִים וּמִשְׁתַּחֲוִים.

---

the humblest man *(Avodas Yisrael).*

— Judaism teaches that a Jew should always seek to emulate God's compassion, generosity and other traits. Consequently, as we leave the rarefied spiritual atmosphere of the Sabbath, we are reminded that God remains near to the weak. This give us encouragement in our own lives and it provides both an inspiration and a warning: an inspiring call to the privileged that they be concerned with the weak — as God is; and a warning not to take advantage of the defenseless, for God is the Father of orphans and the Judge of

in the Writings, as it is written: 'Sing to God, make music for His Name, extol Him Who rides in the highest heaven, with His Name — God — and exult before Him.'[1] Afterwards it is written: 'Father of orphans and Judge of widows, God in the habitation of His holiness.'[2]

May HASHEM, our God be with us as He was with our forefathers, may He not forsake us nor cast us off.[3] You who cling to HASHEM, our God, are all alive today.[4] For HASHEM comforts Zion, He comforts all her ruins, He will make her wilderness like Eden and her wastes like a garden of HASHEM — joy and gladness will be found there, thanksgiving and the sound of music.[5] HASHEM desired, for the sake of its [Israel's] righteousness, that the Torah be made great and glorious.[6]*

Psalm 128 (commentary on p. 539)

שִׁיר הַמַּעֲלוֹת *A song of ascents.* Praiseworthy is each person who fears HASHEM, who walks in His paths. When you eat the labor of your hands, you are praiseworthy, and it is well with you. Your wife shall be like a fruitful vine in the inner chambers of your home; your children shall be like olive shoots surrounding your table. Behold! For so is blessed the man who fears HASHEM. May HASHEM bless you from Zion, and may you gaze upon the goodness of Jerusalem, all the days of your life. And may you see children born to children, peace upon Israel.*

In some congregations mourners recite the Mourner's *Kaddish* (page 610) at this point.
In the synagogue, *Havdalah* is recited before *Aleinu*.

The congregation stands while reciting *Aleinu*.

עָלֵינוּ ***It is our duty to praise the Master of all, to ascribe greatness to the Molder of primeval creation, for He has not made us like the nations of the lands and has not emplaced us like the families of the earth; for He has not assigned our portion like theirs nor our lot like all their multitudes. (For they bow to vanity and emptiness and pray to a god which helps not.[7]) But we bend our knees, bow, and acknowledge our thanks before the King Who reigns over kings, the Holy One, Blessed is He. He stretches out heaven and establishes earth's foundation,[8] the seat of His homage is in the heavens above and His powerful Presence is in the loftiest heights. He is our God and there is none other. True is our King, there is nothing beside Him, as it is written in His Torah: 'You are to know this day and take to your heart that HASHEM is the only God — in heaven above and on the earth below — there is none other.'[9]***

Bow while reciting 'But we bend our knees'.

(1) *Psalms* 68:5. (2) v. 6. (3) *I Kings* 8:57. (4) *Deuteronomy* 4:4.
(5) *Isaiah* 51:3. (6) 42:21. (7) 45:20. (8) 51:13. (9) *Deuteronomy* 4:39.

widows *(World of Prayer).*

יְהִי ה׳ אֱלֹהֵינוּ עִמָּנוּ — *May HASHEM, our God, be with us.* The following verses are not part of Rabbi Yochanan's dictum. They are verses of consolation and reassurance, which are added to this prayer in order to renew our confidence that exile is not eternal and that the Redemption may have been long delayed, but it will come no matter what.

☙ שִׁיר הַמַּעֲלוֹת — *A song of ascents.* This psalm, which extols the economic and family life of one who fears God, is recited here as an exhortation

עַל כֵּן נְקַוֶּה לְּךָ יהוה אֱלֹהֵינוּ לִרְאוֹת מְהֵרָה בְּתִפְאֶרֶת עֻזֶּךָ, לְהַעֲבִיר גִּלּוּלִים מִן הָאָרֶץ, וְהָאֱלִילִים כָּרוֹת יִכָּרֵתוּן, לְתַקֵּן עוֹלָם בְּמַלְכוּת שַׁדַּי. וְכָל בְּנֵי בָשָׂר יִקְרְאוּ בִשְׁמֶךָ, לְהַפְנוֹת אֵלֶיךָ כָּל רִשְׁעֵי אָרֶץ. יַכִּירוּ וְיֵדְעוּ כָּל יוֹשְׁבֵי תֵבֵל, כִּי לְךָ תִּכְרַע כָּל בֶּרֶךְ, תִּשָּׁבַע כָּל לָשׁוֹן.[1] לְפָנֶיךָ יהוה אֱלֹהֵינוּ יִכְרְעוּ וְיִפֹּלוּ, וְלִכְבוֹד שִׁמְךָ יְקָר יִתֵּנוּ. וִיקַבְּלוּ כֻלָּם אֶת עוֹל מַלְכוּתֶךָ, וְתִמְלֹךְ עֲלֵיהֶם מְהֵרָה לְעוֹלָם וָעֶד. כִּי הַמַּלְכוּת שֶׁלְּךָ הִיא וּלְעוֹלְמֵי עַד תִּמְלוֹךְ בְּכָבוֹד, כַּכָּתוּב בְּתוֹרָתֶךָ: יהוה יִמְלֹךְ לְעֹלָם וָעֶד.[2] ❖ וְנֶאֱמַר: וְהָיָה יהוה לְמֶלֶךְ עַל כָּל הָאָרֶץ, בַּיּוֹם הַהוּא יִהְיֶה יהוה אֶחָד וּשְׁמוֹ אֶחָד.[3]

In some congregations the following is recited after עָלֵינוּ:

אַל תִּירָא מִפַּחַד פִּתְאֹם, וּמִשֹּׁאַת רְשָׁעִים כִּי תָבֹא.[4] עֻצוּ עֵצָה וְתֻפָר, דַּבְּרוּ דָבָר וְלֹא יָקוּם, כִּי עִמָּנוּ אֵל.[5] וְעַד זִקְנָה אֲנִי הוּא, וְעַד שֵׂיבָה אֲנִי אֶסְבֹּל, אֲנִי עָשִׂיתִי וַאֲנִי אֶשָּׂא, וַאֲנִי אֶסְבֹּל וַאֲמַלֵּט.[6]

קדיש יתום

In the presence of a *minyan,* mourners recite קַדִּישׁ יָתוֹם the Mourner's *Kaddish* (see *Laws* §119):

יִתְגַּדַּל וְיִתְקַדַּשׁ שְׁמֵהּ רַבָּא. (Cong. — אָמֵן.) בְּעָלְמָא דִּי בְרָא כִרְעוּתֵהּ. וְיַמְלִיךְ מַלְכוּתֵהּ, בְּחַיֵּיכוֹן וּבְיוֹמֵיכוֹן וּבְחַיֵּי דְכָל בֵּית יִשְׂרָאֵל, בַּעֲגָלָא וּבִזְמַן קָרִיב. וְאִמְרוּ: אָמֵן.

(Cong. — אָמֵן. יְהֵא שְׁמֵהּ רַבָּא מְבָרַךְ לְעָלַם וּלְעָלְמֵי עָלְמַיָּא.)

יְהֵא שְׁמֵהּ רַבָּא מְבָרַךְ לְעָלַם וּלְעָלְמֵי עָלְמַיָּא.

יִתְבָּרַךְ וְיִשְׁתַּבַּח וְיִתְפָּאַר וְיִתְרוֹמַם וְיִתְנַשֵּׂא וְיִתְהַדָּר וְיִתְעַלֶּה וְיִתְהַלָּל שְׁמֵהּ דְּקֻדְשָׁא בְּרִיךְ הוּא (Cong. — בְּרִיךְ הוּא) — °לְעֵלָּא מִן כָּל (From Rosh Hashanah to Yom Kippur substitute — °לְעֵלָּא וּלְעֵלָּא מִכָּל) בִּרְכָתָא וְשִׁירָתָא תֻּשְׁבְּחָתָא וְנֶחֱמָתָא, דַּאֲמִירָן בְּעָלְמָא. וְאִמְרוּ: אָמֵן. (Cong. — אָמֵן.)

יְהֵא שְׁלָמָא רַבָּא מִן שְׁמַיָּא, וְחַיִּים עָלֵינוּ וְעַל כָּל יִשְׂרָאֵל. וְאִמְרוּ: אָמֵן. (Cong. — אָמֵן.)

Take three steps back. Bow left and say ... עֹשֶׂה; bow right and say ... הוּא; bow forward and say וְעַל כָּל ... אָמֵן. Remain standing in place for a few moments, then take three steps forward.

עֹשֶׂה שָׁלוֹם בִּמְרוֹמָיו, הוּא יַעֲשֶׂה שָׁלוֹם עָלֵינוּ, וְעַל כָּל יִשְׂרָאֵל. וְאִמְרוּ: אָמֵן. (Cong. — אָמֵן.)

From Rosh Chodesh Elul through Shemini Atzeres *Psalm 27,* לְדָוִד is recited (p. 488).

עַל כֵּן *Therefore we put our hope in You, HASHEM our God, that we may soon see Your mighty splendor, to remove detestable idolatry from the earth, and false gods will be utterly cut off, to perfect the universe through the Almighty's sovereignty. Then all humanity will call upon Your Name, to turn all the earth's wicked toward You. All the world's inhabitants will recognize and know that to You every knee should bend, every tongue should swear.*[1] *Before You, HASHEM, our God, they will bend every knee and cast themselves down and to the glory of Your Name they will render homage, and they will all accept upon themselves the yoke of Your kingship that You may reign over them soon and eternally. For the kingdom is Yours and You will reign for all eternity in glory as it is written in Your Torah: HASHEM shall reign for all eternity.*[2] Chazzan — *And it is said: HASHEM will be King over all the world — on that day HASHEM will be One and His Name will be One.*[3]

In some congregations the following is recited after *Aleinu:*

אַל תִּירָא *Do not fear sudden terror, or the holocaust of the wicked when it comes.*[4] *Plan a conspiracy and it will be annulled; speak your piece and it shall not stand, for God is with us.*[5] *Even till your seniority, I remain unchanged; and even till your ripe old age, I shall endure. I created you and I shall bear you; I shall endure and rescue.*[6]

THE MOURNER'S KADDISH

In the presence of a *minyan,* mourners recite the Mourner's *Kaddish* (see *Laws* §119):

[A transliteration of this *Kaddish* appears on page 1043.]

יִתְגַּדַּל *May His great Name grow exalted and sanctified* (Cong.— *Amen.*) *in the world that He created as He willed. May He give reign to His kingship in your lifetimes and in your days, and in the lifetimes of the entire Family of Israel, swiftly and soon. Now respond: Amen.*

(Cong.— *Amen. May His great Name be blessed forever and ever.*)

May His great Name be blessed forever and ever.

Blessed, praised, glorified, exalted, extolled, mighty, upraised, and lauded be the Name of the Holy One, Blessed is He (Cong.— *Blessed is He*) — (From Rosh Hashanah to Yom Kippur add: *exceedingly*) *beyond any blessing and song, praise and consolation that are uttered in the world. Now respond: Amen.* (Cong.— *Amen.*)

May there be abundant peace from Heaven, and life, upon us and upon all Israel. Now respond: Amen. (Cong.— *Amen.*)

Take three steps back. Bow left and say, *'He Who makes peace ...';* bow right and say, *'may He ...';* bow forward and say, *'and upon all Israel ...'* Remain standing in place for a few moments, then take three steps forward.

He Who makes peace in His heights, may He, in His compassion, make peace upon us, and upon all Israel. Now respond: Amen. (Cong.— *Amen.*)

From Rosh Chodesh Elul through Shemini Atzeres, *Psalm 27, 'Of David,'* is recited (p. 488).

(1) Cf. *Isaiah* 45:23. (2) *Exodus* 15:18. (3) *Zechariah* 14:9. (4) *Proverbs* 3:25. (5) *Isaiah* 8:10. (6) 46:4.

to honesty and compassion during the ensuing week *(Avodas Yisrael).*

The Talmud (Berachos 8a) expounds this psalm to teach that one who enjoys the fruits of his own labor is assured of God's blessing in This World as well as in the World to Come.

קידוש לבנה

תהלים קמח:א־ו

הַלְלוּיָהּ, הַלְלוּ אֶת יהוה מִן הַשָּׁמַיִם,* הַלְלוּהוּ בַּמְּרוֹמִים. הַלְלוּהוּ כָל מַלְאָכָיו, הַלְלוּהוּ כָּל צְבָאָיו. הַלְלוּהוּ שֶׁמֶשׁ וְיָרֵחַ, הַלְלוּהוּ כָּל כּוֹכְבֵי אוֹר. הַלְלוּהוּ שְׁמֵי הַשָּׁמָיִם, וְהַמַּיִם אֲשֶׁר מֵעַל הַשָּׁמָיִם. יְהַלְלוּ אֶת שֵׁם יהוה, כִּי הוּא צִוָּה וְנִבְרָאוּ. וַיַּעֲמִידֵם לָעַד לְעוֹלָם, חָק נָתַן וְלֹא יַעֲבוֹר.

One should look at the moon before reciting this blessing:

בָּרוּךְ אַתָּה יהוה, אֱלֹהֵינוּ מֶלֶךְ הָעוֹלָם, אֲשֶׁר בְּמַאֲמָרוֹ בָּרָא* שְׁחָקִים, וּבְרוּחַ פִּיו כָּל צְבָאָם. חֹק וּזְמַן נָתַן לָהֶם* שֶׁלֹּא יְשַׁנּוּ אֶת תַּפְקִידָם. שָׂשִׂים וּשְׂמֵחִים* לַעֲשׂוֹת רְצוֹן קוֹנָם, פּוֹעֵל אֱמֶת שֶׁפְּעֻלָּתוֹ אֱמֶת. וְלַלְּבָנָה אָמַר שֶׁתִּתְחַדֵּשׁ עֲטֶרֶת תִּפְאֶרֶת לַעֲמוּסֵי בָטֶן,* שֶׁהֵם עֲתִידִים לְהִתְחַדֵּשׁ כְּמוֹתָהּ,* וּלְפָאֵר לְיוֹצְרָם עַל שֵׁם כְּבוֹד מַלְכוּתוֹ. בָּרוּךְ אַתָּה יהוה, מְחַדֵּשׁ חֳדָשִׁים.

קידוש לְבָנָה / SANCTIFICATION OF THE MOON

The Sanctification of the Moon, [*Kiddush Levanah*] should not be confused with the Sanhedrin's קִידּוּשׁ הַחֹדֶשׁ, *Sanctification of the Month,* by which the court pronounced the appropriate day as the beginning of a new month. That proclamation was the sole province of the court and affected the calendar; the Sanctification of the *Moon* — not the month — has no calendrical significance.

There are two bases for this ritual. Rabbi Yochanan taught that one who blesses the new moon in its proper time is regarded like one who greets the *Shechinah* [God's Presence] *(Sanhedrin* 42a). This is because the only way we can recognize the existence of God is through His works. This is seen in history through the miracles and revelations to Israel. In nature it is seen through the orderly functioning of the enormously complex heavenly bodies. We may note that as science unfolds more and more of the vastness of the universe, the presence of a Creator becomes more and more obvious to one who wishes to see; indeed, to deny Him is ludicrous. This phenomenon is most apparent in the cycles of the moon, because its changes are more visible than those of any other body. Thus, when we greet the moon, we greet its Maker and Guide *(Rabbeinu Yonah, Berachos* 4).

The second aspect of the prayer is its significance for the history of Israel. Just as the moon is reborn after a period of decline and total disappearance so, too, Israel's decline will end and its light will once again blaze to fullness. As an example, the Midrash *(Shemos Rabbah* 15) states, when Israel is worthy of God's favor it is like the waxing moon, but when it is not worthy, it is like the declining moon. In this vein, ancient Israel's rise and fall paralleled the phases of the moon. There were fifteen generations from Abraham to Solomon, during which Israel rose to the zenith of its greatness. The decline began during Solomon's reign; there were fifteen generations from then (including Solomon) to the reign of Zedekiah, when the First Temple was destroyed. This corresponds to the twenty-nine day cycle of the moon.

Because the moon is such a significant allusion to God as the Creator and to Israel's rebirth, *Kiddush Levanah* should be recited joyously, preferably at the conclusion of the Sabbath when people are still dressed in their finest clothes. Conversely, it is not recited on the Sabbath or a festival (except under unusual circumstances), because we do not set two different causes for joy in competition with one another *(World of Prayer).* It is also customary to defer *Kiddush Levanah* until after Tishah B'Av and Yom Kippur because the sadness of Av and the dread of the Days of Judgment are inappropriate to the joy required during *Kiddush Levanah.*

הַלְלוּיָהּ הַלְלוּ אֶת ה׳ מִן הַשָּׁמַיִם — *Halleluyah! Praise HASHEM from the heavens.* The first six verses of Psalm 148 describe how the heavens

SANCTIFICATION OF THE MOON/KIDDUSH LEVANAH

Psalms 148:1-6

הַלְלוּיָהּ *Halleluyah! Praise HASHEM from the heavens;* praise Him in the heights. Praise Him, all His angels; praise Him, all His legions. Praise Him, sun and moon; praise Him, all bright stars. Praise Him, the most exalted of the heavens and the waters that are above the heavens. Let them praise the Name of HASHEM, for He commanded and they were created. And He established them forever and ever, He issued a decree that will not change.*

One should look at the moon before reciting this blessing:

בָּרוּךְ *Blessed are You, HASHEM, our God, King of the Universe, Who with His utterance created* the heavens, and with the breath of His mouth all their legion. A decree and a schedule did He give them* that they not alter their assigned task. They are joyous and glad* to perform the will of their Owner — the Worker of truth Whose work is truth. To the moon He said that it should renew itself as a crown of splendor for those borne [by Him] from the womb,* those who are destined to renew themselves like it,* and to glorify their Molder for the name of His glorious kingdom. Blessed are You, HASHEM, Who renews the months.*

---

praise God, and they are therefore used as the preface to *Kiddush Levanah.* The rest of the psalm, however, deals with man's praise of God.

בָּרוּךְ ... אֲשֶׁר בְּמַאֲמָרוֹ בָּרָא — *Blessed ... Who with His utterance created.* God created heaven and its infinite bodies with nothing more than His word. The very existence of so many galaxies and solar systems testifies undeniably to creation because so huge and complex a universe could not have come about by chance.

חֹק וּזְמַן נָתַן לָהֶם — *A decree and a schedule did He give them.* After creating the heavenly bodies, God set them in their specified orbits, giving each an unchangeable role in the cosmos.

שָׂשִׂים וּשְׂמֵחִים — *They are joyous and glad.* Despite the apparent tedium of their permanently assigned tasks, the heavenly bodies joyously serve their Maker because they know that by doing His will they have a role in creation. This is a lesson to man to revel in his opportunity to serve God.

לַעֲמוּסֵי בָטֶן — *For those borne [by Him] from the womb.* The Jewish nation is thus described (*Isaiah* 46:3) because God carries them, as it were, providing for and protecting them.

לְהִתְחַדֵּשׁ כְּמוֹתָהּ — *To renew themselves like it.* The majesty of the Jewish people will be renewed, and the nation will render praise to God

---

Laws of Kiddush Levanah

It is preferable that *Kiddush Levanah* be recited: (a) under the open sky; (b) with a *minyan;* (c) at the departure of the Sabbath. When these optimal conditions are not feasible, they may be waived (e.g., a shut-in, if he can see the moon through a window or door; one who cannot form a *minyan;* the sky is cloudy at the departure of the Sabbath).

The earliest time for *Kiddush Levanah* is seventy-two hours after the *molad* (new moon, see p. 452), although some authorities delay it until seven full days after the *molad.*

The latest time for *Kiddush Levanah* is mid-month, i.e., fourteen days, eighteen hours and twenty-two minutes (some authorities extend this limit to fifteen full days) after the *molad.*

Kiddush Levanah should not be recited on a Sabbath or a Festival unless it is the last remaining night before the mid-month deadline.

If one cannot recite *Kiddush Levanah* with a *minyan,* he should try to do so in the presence of at least three others with whom to exchange the *Shalom Aleichem* greeting. If this, too, is not possible, one may recite *Kiddush Levanah* by himself.

During Tishrei, *Kiddush Levanah* is generally postponed until after Yom Kippur; during Av, until after Tishah B'Av.

—Recite three times בָּרוּךְ יוֹצְרֵךְ,* בָּרוּךְ עוֹשֵׂךְ, בָּרוּךְ קוֹנֵךְ, בָּרוּךְ בּוֹרְאֵךְ.

Upon reciting the next verse, rise on the toes as if in dance:

—Recite three times כְּשֵׁם שֶׁאֲנִי רוֹקֵד* כְּנֶגְדֵּךְ וְאֵינִי יָכוֹל לִנְגּוֹעַ בָּךְ כַּךְ לֹא יוּכְלוּ כָּל אוֹיְבַי לִנְגּוֹעַ בִּי לְרָעָה.

—Recite three times תִּפֹּל עֲלֵיהֶם* אֵימָתָה וָפַחַד, בִּגְדֹל זְרוֹעֲךָ יִדְּמוּ כָּאָבֶן.[1]

—Recite three times כָּאָבֶן יִדְּמוּ* זְרוֹעֲךָ בִּגְדֹל וָפַחַד אֵימָתָה עֲלֵיהֶם תִּפֹּל.

—Recite three times דָּוִד מֶלֶךְ יִשְׂרָאֵל* חַי וְקַיָּם.

—Extend greetings to three different people שָׁלוֹם עֲלֵיכֶם* —

—who, in turn, respond עֲלֵיכֶם שָׁלוֹם.

—Recite three times סִמָּן טוֹב וּמַזָּל טוֹב יְהֵא לָנוּ וּלְכָל יִשְׂרָאֵל. אָמֵן.

קוֹל דּוֹדִי* הִנֵּה זֶה בָּא מְדַלֵּג עַל הֶהָרִים מְקַפֵּץ עַל הַגְּבָעוֹת. דּוֹמֶה דוֹדִי לִצְבִי אוֹ לְעֹפֶר הָאַיָּלִים הִנֵּה זֶה עוֹמֵד אַחַר כָּתְלֵנוּ, מַשְׁגִּיחַ מִן הַחַלֹּנוֹת, מֵצִיץ מִן הַחֲרַכִּים.[2]

תהלים קכא (commentary on page 534)

שִׁיר לַמַּעֲלוֹת, אֶשָּׂא עֵינַי אֶל הֶהָרִים, מֵאַיִן יָבֹא עֶזְרִי. עֶזְרִי מֵעִם יהוה, עֹשֵׂה שָׁמַיִם וָאָרֶץ. אַל יִתֵּן לַמּוֹט רַגְלֶךָ, אַל יָנוּם שֹׁמְרֶךָ. הִנֵּה לֹא יָנוּם וְלֹא יִישָׁן, שׁוֹמֵר יִשְׂרָאֵל. יהוה שֹׁמְרֶךָ, יהוה צִלְּךָ עַל יַד יְמִינֶךָ. יוֹמָם הַשֶּׁמֶשׁ לֹא יַכֶּכָּה וְיָרֵחַ בַּלָּיְלָה. יהוה יִשְׁמָרְךָ מִכָּל רָע, יִשְׁמֹר אֶת נַפְשֶׁךָ. יהוה יִשְׁמָר צֵאתְךָ וּבוֹאֶךָ, מֵעַתָּה וְעַד עוֹלָם.

---

and the glories of His kingdom. Alternatively, this refers to the dead who will be resuscitated after the Redemption *(R'ah)*.

בָּרוּךְ יוֹצְרֵךְ — *Blessed is your Molder.* The initials of these four titles of God spell יַעֲקֹב, *Jacob.* Just as the moon is called הַמָּאוֹר הַקָּטֹן, *the smaller luminary (Genesis* 1:16) in relation to the sun, so Jacob was called בְּנָהּ הַקָּטָן, *her younger* [lit. *smaller*] *son (Genesis* 27:15,42), because he was the younger of Rebecca's two sons. This verse alludes to *Isaiah* 43:1 (as explained by *Vayikra Rabbah* 36) that God created the universe for the sake of Jacob and his offspring *(Sh'lah)*.

This verse and the following ones are repeated three times to give special emphasis to their message.

כְּשֵׁם שֶׁאֲנִי רוֹקֵד — *Just as I dance.* Often in Scripture, a prophecy is accompanied by a physical act. This has the effect of making the prophecy irreversible. Here, too, we, in a symbolic way, exert ourselves to touch the moon while remaining on earth, and we pray that, in like fashion, the exertions of our enemies against us will be of no avail. Thus, we reinforce the point by a physical act *(Dover Shalom)*.

תִּפֹּל עֲלֵיהֶם — *Let fall upon them.* This verse, taken from the Song at the Sea *(Exodus* 15:16), follows naturally upon the previous one. Having said that our foes will be unable to harm us, we now declare that they will be terror-stricken.

כָּאָבֶן יִדְּמוּ — *As stone let them be still.* We now

Recite three times— *Blessed is your Molder;* blessed is your Maker; blessed is your Owner; blessed is your Creator.*

Upon reciting the next verse, rise on the toes as if in dance:

Recite three times— *Just as I dance* toward you but cannot touch you, so may none of my enemies be able to touch me for evil.*

Recite three times— *Let fall upon them* fear and terror; at the greatness of Your arm, let them be still as stone.*[1]

Recite three times— *As stone let them be still,* at Your arm's greatness; terror and fear, upon them let fall.*

Recite three times— *David, King of Israel,* is alive and enduring.*

Extend greetings to three different people— *Peace upon you*—*

who, in turn, respond— *Upon you, peace.*

Recite three times— *May there be a good sign and a good fortune for us and for all Israel. Amen.*

קוֹל *The voice of my beloved* — Behold! It came suddenly, leaping over mountains, skipping over hills. My beloved is like a gazelle or a young hart. Behold! He was standing behind our wall, observing through the windows, peering through the lattices.*[2]

Psalm 121 (commentary on page 534)

שִׁיר לַמַּעֲלוֹת *A song to the ascents. I raise my eyes to the mountains; whence will come my help? My help is from* HASHEM, *Maker of heaven and earth. He will not allow your foot to falter; your Guardian will not slumber. Behold, He neither slumbers nor sleeps — the Guardian of Israel.* HASHEM *is your Guardian;* HASHEM *is your Shade at your right hand. By day the sun will not harm you, nor the moon by night.* HASHEM *will protect you from every evil; He will guard your soul.* HASHEM *will guard your departure and your arrival, from this time and forever.*

(1) *Exodus* 15:16. (2) *Song of Songs* 2:8-9.

repeat the previous verse, but we reverse the order of the words. This reversal implies that the natural order of nature, too, may sometimes be reversed. In other words, God will sometimes protect us through the natural order of events; at other times He will perform open miracles to thwart those who seek our harm (*World of Prayer*).

דָּוִד מֶלֶךְ יִשְׂרָאֵל — *David, King of Israel.* As noted above, the phases of the moon allude to the Davidic dynasty. Thus, we include this confident expression of faith that David's reign endures and will shine again. This verse was composed by Rabbi Yehudah *HaNassi* (*Rosh Hashanah* 25a).

שָׁלוֹם עֲלֵיכֶם — *Peace upon you.* Various reasons are given for the inclusion of this greeting in *Kiddush Levanah:*

— Having greeted the *Shechinah,* we joyously wish the blessing of peace upon one another (*Levush*).

— After cursing our enemies, we make clear that we wish no ill to our brethren (*Mateh Moshe*).

— At the beginning of creation, as recorded in the Talmud (*Chullin* 60b), the sun and moon were of equal size. When the moon complained that two kings cannot wear the same crown, i.e., it should be larger than the sun, the moon was made smaller. Nevertheless, the sun continues to shine its brilliant light upon the moon, thus providing a lesson to man not to harbor a grudge against others who have wronged him. We express this resolve by wishing peace upon our fellow Jews (*Anaf Yosef*).

קול דודי — *The voice of my beloved.* The inclusion of these two verses is based on the

(commentary on page 74) תהלים קנ

הַלְלוּיָהּ, הַלְלוּ אֵל בְּקָדְשׁוֹ, הַלְלְוּהוּ בִּרְקִיעַ עֻזּוֹ. הַלְלְוּהוּ בִגְבוּרֹתָיו, הַלְלְוּהוּ כְּרֹב גֻּדְלוֹ. הַלְלְוּהוּ בְּתֵקַע שׁוֹפָר, הַלְלְוּהוּ בְּנֵבֶל וְכִנּוֹר. הַלְלְוּהוּ בְּתֹף וּמָחוֹל, הַלְלְוּהוּ בְּמִנִּים וְעֻגָב. הַלְלְוּהוּ בְצִלְצְלֵי שָׁמַע, הַלְלְוּהוּ בְּצִלְצְלֵי תְרוּעָה. כֹּל הַנְּשָׁמָה תְּהַלֵּל יָהּ, הַלְלוּיָהּ.

תָּנָא דְבֵי רַבִּי יִשְׁמָעֵאל:* אִלְמָלֵי לֹא זָכוּ יִשְׂרָאֵל אֶלָּא לְהַקְבִּיל פְּנֵי אֲבִיהֶם שֶׁבַּשָּׁמַיִם פַּעַם אַחַת בַּחֹדֶשׁ, דַּיָּם. אָמַר אַבַּיֵי: הִלְכָּךְ צָרִיךְ לְמֵימְרָא מְעֻמָּד.* מִי זֹאת עֹלָה* מִן הַמִּדְבָּר מִתְרַפֶּקֶת עַל דּוֹדָהּ.[1]

וִיהִי רָצוֹן מִלְּפָנֶיךָ יהוה אֱלֹהַי וֵאלֹהֵי אֲבוֹתַי, לְמַלֹּאת פְּגִימַת הַלְּבָנָה,* וְלֹא יִהְיֶה בָּהּ שׁוּם מִעוּט, וִיהִי אוֹר הַלְּבָנָה כְּאוֹר הַחַמָּה, וּכְאוֹר שִׁבְעַת יְמֵי בְרֵאשִׁית[2] כְּמוֹ שֶׁהָיְתָה קוֹדֶם מִעוּטָהּ, שֶׁנֶּאֱמַר: אֶת שְׁנֵי הַמְּאֹרֹת הַגְּדֹלִים.[3] וְיִתְקַיֵּם בָּנוּ מִקְרָא שֶׁכָּתוּב: וּבִקְשׁוּ אֶת יהוה אֱלֹהֵיהֶם, וְאֵת דָּוִיד מַלְכָּם.[4] אָמֵן.

(commentary on page 594) תהלים סז

לַמְנַצֵּחַ בִּנְגִינֹת מִזְמוֹר שִׁיר. אֱלֹהִים יְחָנֵּנוּ וִיבָרְכֵנוּ, יָאֵר פָּנָיו אִתָּנוּ סֶלָה. לָדַעַת בָּאָרֶץ דַּרְכֶּךָ, בְּכָל גּוֹיִם יְשׁוּעָתֶךָ. יוֹדְוּךָ עַמִּים אֱלֹהִים, יוֹדְוּךָ עַמִּים כֻּלָּם. יִשְׂמְחוּ וִירַנְּנוּ לְאֻמִּים, כִּי תִשְׁפֹּט עַמִּים מִישֹׁר, וּלְאֻמִּים בָּאָרֶץ תַּנְחֵם סֶלָה. יוֹדְוּךָ עַמִּים אֱלֹהִים, יוֹדְוּךָ עַמִּים כֻּלָּם. אֶרֶץ נָתְנָה יְבוּלָהּ, יְבָרְכֵנוּ אֱלֹהִים אֱלֹהֵינוּ. יְבָרְכֵנוּ אֱלֹהִים, וְיִירְאוּ אוֹתוֹ כָּל אַפְסֵי אָרֶץ.

In most congregations, עָלֵינוּ, *Aleinu** (page 608), followed by the Mourner's *Kaddish,* is repeated at this point.

Yalkut which interprets them as an allusion to the Messiah. When the Messiah [i.e., *my beloved*] announces the month of the redemption, Israel will protest disbelievingly that there are so many obstacles in his path. The Messiah will reply that he will hurdle all the barriers like a gazelle leaping over mountains. He goes on to say that God was never oblivious to our plight — though we felt abandoned, God was *standing ... observing* ... and *peering* to see our needs and plan for our salvation.

◆§ תָּנָא דְבֵי רַבִּי יִשְׁמָעֵאל — *The Academy of Rabbi Yishmael taught.* This Talmudic passage (*Sanhedrin* 42a) is based on the concept discussed in the prefatory remarks, that the Sanctification of the Moon constitutes Israel's recognition of and greeting to the *Shechinah.* We long to do this always, but we are grateful for the privilege of doing so at least this once a month.

מְעֻמָּד — *While standing.* Since *Kiddush Levanah* involves a greeting to God's Presence, it is proper

Psalm 150 (commentary on page 74)

הַלְלוּיָהּ *Halleluyah! Praise God in His Sanctuary; praise Him in the firmament of His power. Praise Him for His mighty acts; praise Him as befits His abundant greatness. Praise Him with the blast of the shofar; praise Him with lyre and harp. Praise Him with drum and dance; praise Him with organ and flute. Praise Him with clanging cymbals; praise him with resonant trumpets. Let all souls praise God, Halleluyah!*

תָּנָא *The Academy of Rabbi Yishmael taught:* Had Israel not been privileged to greet the countenance of their Father in Heaven except for once a month — it would have sufficed them. Abaye said: Therefore one must recite it while standing.**

Who is this who rises from the desert clinging to her Beloved!*[1]

וִיהִי *May it be Your will,* HASHEM, *my God and the God of my forefathers, to fill the flaw of the moon* that there be no diminution in it. May the light of the moon be like the light of the sun and like the light of the seven days of creation,*[2] *as it was before it was diminished, as it is said: 'The two great luminaries.'*[3] *And may there be fulfilled upon us the verse that is written: They shall seek* HASHEM, *their God, and David, their king.*[4] *Amen.*

Psalm 67 (commentary on p. 594)

לַמְנַצֵּחַ *For the Conductor, upon Neginos, a psalm, a song. May God favor us and bless us, may He illuminate His countenance with us, Selah. To make known Your way on earth, among all the nations Your salvation. The peoples will acknowledge You, O God, the peoples will acknowledge You, all of them. Nations will be glad and sing for joy, because You will judge the peoples fairly and guide the nations on earth, Selah. Then peoples will acknowledge You, O God, the peoples will acknowledge You, all of them. The earth has yielded its produce, may God, our own God, bless us. May God bless us and may all the ends of the earth fear Him.*

In most congregations, עָלֵינוּ, *Aleinu** (page 608), followed by the Mourner's *Kaddish,* is repeated at this point.

(1) *Song of Songs* 8:5. (2) Cf. *Isaiah* 30:26. (3) *Genesis* 1:16. (4) *Hoshea* 3:5.

that it be recited while standing.

מִי זֹאת עֹלָה — *Who is this who rises.* This verse expresses Israel's yearning to greet the *Shechinah (Iyun Tefillah).*

לְמַלֹּאת פְּגִימַת הַלְּבָנָה — *To fill the flaw of the moon.* The references to diminution of the moon and its restoration to its primeval status refer to spiritual concepts. The Sages teach that the spiritual illumination of those earliest days was concealed because God knew that man would prove unworthy of it. That was only a temporary phenomenon, however. When the final Redemption comes, that splendor will be returned to the earth, thus removing the stigma from the moon. Since the moon symbolizes Israel and the House of David, it is natural that man's lack of spiritual fulfillment — the concealment of the light — should be expressed in the smallness of the moon.

עָלֵינוּ — *Aleinu.* Lest our ecstatic greeting of the moon be interpreted as worship of a heavenly body, God forbid, we recite עָלֵינוּ, which is our declaration that we worship only God and none other *(Mishnah Berurah* 426:2).

﴾ הבדלה למוצאי שבת ויום טוב ﴿

At the departure of Sabbath, one recites *Havdalah* holding a cup of wine. Either he or someone else holds a multi-wicked candle or two ordinary candles with their flames touching each other. Aromatic spices are held in the left hand preferably, or they may be placed on the table.

At the departure of a weekday Festival (and when *Havdalah* is recited Sunday night — such as after Tishah B'Av) the introductory verses (beginning הִנֵּה), the candle, and the spices are omitted.

Havdalah is recited either standing or sitting, depending on one's custom.

At the departure of Yom Kippur [that does not coincide with the Sabbath] the introductory verses and spices are omitted. However the blessing over the flame is said over a candle lit from a fire that had burned throughout Yom Kippur. If such a fire is not available, the blessing over the flame is omitted.

At the departure of the Sabbath begin here. In the synagogue, the first paragraph is omitted.

הִנֵּה אֵל יְשׁוּעָתִי אֶבְטַח* וְלֹא אֶפְחָד, כִּי עָזִּי וְזִמְרָת יָהּ יהוה, וַיְהִי לִי לִישׁוּעָה. וּשְׁאַבְתֶּם מַיִם בְּשָׂשׂוֹן,* מִמַּעַיְנֵי הַיְשׁוּעָה.[1] לַיהוה הַיְשׁוּעָה, עַל עַמְּךָ בִרְכָתֶךָ סֶּלָה.[2] יהוה צְבָאוֹת עִמָּנוּ, מִשְׂגָּב לָנוּ אֱלֹהֵי יַעֲקֹב סֶלָה.[3] יהוה צְבָאוֹת, אַשְׁרֵי אָדָם בֹּטֵחַ בָּךְ.[4] יהוה הוֹשִׁיעָה, הַמֶּלֶךְ יַעֲנֵנוּ בְיוֹם קָרְאֵנוּ.[5] לַיְּהוּדִים הָיְתָה אוֹרָה וְשִׂמְחָה, וְשָׂשׂן וִיקָר,[6] כֵּן תִּהְיֶה לָּנוּ. כּוֹס יְשׁוּעוֹת* אֶשָּׂא, וּבְשֵׁם יהוה אֶקְרָא.[7]

At the departure of a Festival begin here:

סַבְרִי מָרָנָן וְרַבָּנָן וְרַבּוֹתַי:

בָּרוּךְ אַתָּה יהוה אֱלֹהֵינוּ מֶלֶךְ הָעוֹלָם, בּוֹרֵא פְּרִי הַגָּפֶן.

(—all present respond — אָמֵן.)

After the following blessing smell the spices:

בָּרוּךְ אַתָּה יהוה אֱלֹהֵינוּ מֶלֶךְ הָעוֹלָם, בּוֹרֵא מִינֵי בְשָׂמִים.*

(—all present respond — אָמֵן.)

After the following blessing hold fingers up to the flame to see the reflected light:

בָּרוּךְ אַתָּה יהוה אֱלֹהֵינוּ מֶלֶךְ הָעוֹלָם, בּוֹרֵא מְאוֹרֵי הָאֵשׁ.*

(—all present respond — אָמֵן.)

﴾ HAVDALAH / הַבְדָּלָה ﴿

As noted in the commentary to צִדְקָתְךָ, *Your righteousness* (p. 524), the concluding moments of the Sabbath are a time of foreboding, as holiness wanes and travail looms. Consequently, the *Havdalah* after the Sabbath includes symbols of blessing. Among them are the optimistic verses of blessing that introduce the post-Sabbath *Havdalah* and the custom to fill the cup until it overflows.

The concept of *Havdalah*, literally, *distinction*, is ordained by the Torah as part of the general commandment to 'Remember the Sabbath,' the implication being that its differentiation from other days must be verbalized *(Rambam)*.

With the departure of the holy Sabbath and the onset of the work week, it is essential to be conscious of the differences between sanctity and secularity. In explaining why the first mention of this separation is made in the *Shemoneh Esrei* blessing for wisdom, the Sages explain: אִם אֵין דֵּעָה הַבְדָּלָה מִנַּיִן, *If there is no wisdom, how can one differentiate?* Clearly, then, to distinguish is a function of intelligent reasoning. It is incumbent, therefore, upon each Jew to be conscious of the sharp difference between the holiness he has just been experiencing and the sharply lower level of spirituality to which he is about to descend.

⊰ **הִנֵּה אֵל יְשׁוּעָתִי אֶבְטַח** — *Behold! God is my*

HAVDALAH AFTER THE SABBATH AND FESTIVALS

At the departure of Sabbath, one recites *Havdalah* holding a cup of wine. Either he or someone else holds a multi-wicked candle or two ordinary candles with their flames touching each other. Aromatic spices are held in the left hand preferably, or they may be placed on the table. At the departure of a weekday Festival (and when *Havdalah* is recited Sunday night — such as after Tishah B'Av) the introductory verses (beginning הִנֵּה), the candle, and the spices are omitted.

At the departure of Yom Kippur [that does not coincide with the Sabbath] the introductory verses and spices are omitted. However the blessing over the flame is said over a candle lit from a fire that had burned throughout Yom Kippur. If such a fire is not available, the blessing over the flame is omitted.

At the departure of the Sabbath begin here. In the synagogue, the first paragraph is omitted.

הִנֵּה *Behold! God is my salvation, I shall trust* and not fear — for God is my might and my praise — HASHEM — and He was a salvation for me. You can draw water with joy,* from the springs of salvation.*[1] *Salvation is HASHEM's, upon Your people is Your blessing, Selah.*[2] *HASHEM, Master of legions, is with us, a stronghold for us is the God of Jacob, Selah.*[3] *HASHEM, Master of legions, praised is the man who trusts in You.*[4] *HASHEM save! May the King answer us on the day we call.*[5] *For the Jews there was light, gladness, joy, and honor*[6] *— so may it be for us. I will raise the cup of salvations,* and I shall invoke the Name of HASHEM.*[7]

At the departure of a Festival begin here:

By your leave, my masters and teachers:

בָּרוּךְ *Blessed are You, HASHEM, our God, King of the universe, Who creates the fruit of the vine.* (All present respond—*Amen.*)

After the following blessing smell the spices:

בָּרוּךְ *Blessed are You, HASHEM, our God, King of the universe, Who creates species of fragrance.** (All present respond—*Amen.*)

After the following blessing hold fingers up to the flame to see the reflected light:

בָּרוּךְ *Blessed are You, HASHEM, our God, King of the universe, Who creates the illuminations of the fire.** (All present respond—*Amen.*)

---

(1) *Isaiah* 12:2-3. (2) *Psalms* 3:9. (3) 46:12. (4) 84:13. (5) 20:10. (6) *Esther* 8:16. (7) *Psalms* 116:13.

---

salvation, I shall trust. Since I know that *God is my salvation* and He will not forsake me, I can trust in Him always and never fear.

וּשְׁאַבְתֶּם מַיִם בְּשָׂשׂוֹן — *You can draw water with joy.* When one has a מַעְיָן, *spring,* from which to draw, he never doubts his water supply because a spring always flows with fresh, bubbling water. Such a fortunate person is always happy. Similarly, we are always joyous no matter what our predicament, because our salvation comes from God — a never-ending *spring* of compassion, miracles, and salvation.

כּוֹס יְשׁוּעוֹת — *The cup of salvations.* When one expresses his gratitude to God, he lifts a cup of wine symbolizing his joy at the salvations that God has granted. The upraised cup is called *the cup of salvations.*

בּוֹרֵא מִינֵי בְשָׂמִים — *Who creates species of fragrance.* The reason for smelling the pleasant odor of spices at the end of the Sabbath is to assuage oneself for the loss of the departing נְשָׁמָה יְתֵרָה, *additional* [Sabbath] *soul (Abudraham).*

Additionally, the fires of *Gehinnom* begin to rage after having been dormant during the Sabbath. The pain of knowing that sinners are beginning to endure new punishments is eased by the spices *(Bach; Tosafos).*

בּוֹרֵא מְאוֹרֵי הָאֵשׁ — *Who creates the illuminations of the fire.* The Talmud *(Pesachim*

בָּרוּךְ אַתָּה יהוה אֱלֹהֵינוּ מֶלֶךְ הָעוֹלָם, הַמַּבְדִּיל בֵּין קֹדֶשׁ לְחוֹל,* בֵּין אוֹר לְחֹשֶׁךְ,* בֵּין יִשְׂרָאֵל לָעַמִּים, בֵּין יוֹם הַשְּׁבִיעִי לְשֵׁשֶׁת יְמֵי הַמַּעֲשֶׂה. בָּרוּךְ אַתָּה יהוה, הַמַּבְדִּיל בֵּין קֹדֶשׁ לְחוֹל.

(all present respond— אָמֵן.)

The one who recited *Havdalah,* or someone else present for *Havdalah,* should drink most of the wine from the cup, then extinguish the flame by pouring leftover wine over it into a dish.
It is customary to dip the fingers into the wine-dish and touch the eyelids and inner pockets with them. This symbolizes that the 'light of the *mitzvah*' will guide us and it invokes blessing for the week.

גאט פון אברהם

In some communities, women recite the following before *Havdalah*. See commentary.

גאט פון אַבְרָהָם* און פון יִצְחָק און פון יַעֲקֹב, בַּאהִיט דַיין פָאלְק יִשְׂרָאֵל פון אַלֶעם בֵּייזִין אִין דַיינֶעם לויב, אַז דֶער לִיבֶּער שַׁבָּת קוֹדֶשׁ גֵייט אַוֶועק, אַז דִיא וָואךְ זָאל אוּנְז קוּמֶען צוּ אֱמוּנָה שְׁלֵימָה, צוּ אֱמוּנַת חֲכָמִים, צוּ אַהֲבַת וְדִבּוּק חֲבֵרִים טוֹבִים, צוּ דְבֵיקוּת הַבּוֹרֵא בָּרוּךְ הוּא, מַאֲמִין צוּ זַיין בִּשְׁלֹשָׁה עָשָׂר עִיקָּרִים שֶׁלְּךָ, וּבִגְאוּלָה שְׁלֵמָה וּקְרוֹבָה בִּמְהֵרָה בְּיָמֵינוּ, וּבִתְחִיַּת הַמֵּתִים, וּבִנְבוּאַת מֹשֶׁה רַבֵּינוּ עָלָיו הַשָּׁלוֹם.

רִבּוֹנוֹ שֶׁל עוֹלָם דוּא בִּיסְט דָאךְ הַנּוֹתֵן לַיָּעֵף כֹּחַ, גִיבּ דֵיינֶע לִיבֶּע אִידִישֶׁע קִינְדֶערְלֶעךְ אוֹיךְ כֹּחַ דִיךְ צוּ לוֹיבִּין, און דִיךְ צוּ דִינֶען און וַוייטֶער קֵיינֶעם נִישְׁט.

און דִיא וָואךְ זָאל אוּנְז קוּמֶען צוּ חֶסֶד, און צוּ מַזָּל, און צוּ בְרָכָה, און צוּ הַצְלָחָה, און צוּ גֶזוּנְט, און צוּ עוֹשֶׁר וְכָבוֹד, און צוּ בָּנֵי חַיֵּי וּמְזוֹנֵי, לָנוּ וּלְכָל יִשְׂרָאֵל. אָמֵן.

54a) gives the reason for the institution of this blessing. Fire was created at the end of Adam's first Sabbath on earth. Then, God gave Adam the instinctive understanding to rub stones together in order to bring forth a fire for light and heat. *Midrash Rabbah* (11:2) elaborates that God did so in response to Adam's fear when he saw darkness falling. He was terrified lest, having been banished from the Garden of Eden, he would be faced with mortal danger that he could not even see. As in the case of all such blessings, one must enjoy the thing for which he thanks God, in this case, the illumination. Therefore, we hold our fingers up to the flame and gaze at its light upon our nails.

חול — *Secular.* [Although the more familiar translation is *profane,* we have chosen not to use it. The word *profane* has the general connotation of blasphemy and impurity. The message of Sabbath, however, is not limited to avoidance of the blasphemous and impure; rather it involves the need to recognize that even ordinary, *secular,* pursuits are deficient if they are not imbued with holiness.]

בין קדש לחול בין אור לחשך ... — *Between holy and secular, between light and darkness...* The *holy* represents sanctity, while חול is the קְלִפָּה, *shell,* i.e., the outer barrier that prevents people from perceiving holiness. By recognizing the difference between *light* and *darkness* one is able to discern God's wisdom, and thereby make one's own distinction between good, represented by

בָּרוּךְ *Blessed are You,* HASHEM *our God, King of the universe, Who separates between holy and secular,* between light and darkness,* between Israel and the nations, between the seventh day and the six days of labor. Blessed are You,* HASHEM, *Who separates between holy and secular.* (All present respond— *Amen.*)

The one who recited *Havdalah,* or someone else present for *Havdalah,* should drink most of the wine from the cup, then extinguish the flame by pouring leftover wine over it into a dish.
It is customary to dip the fingers into the wine-dish and touch the eyelids and inner pockets with them. This symbolizes that the 'light of the *mitzvah'* will guide us and it invokes blessing for the week.

GOTT FUN AVROHOM

In some communities, women recite the following before *Havdalah.* See commentary.

גָאט *God of Abraham,* of Isaac, and of Jacob, protect Your people, Israel, from all evil in Your praise — as the beloved, Holy Sabbath takes leave — that the coming week may arrive to bring perfect faith, faith in scholars, love of and attachment to good friends, attachment to the Creator, Blessed is He, to have faith in Your Thirteen Principles, and in the complete and close Redemption, speedily in our days, in the Resuscitation of the Dead and in the prophecy of our teacher, Moses, peace is upon him.*

Master of the universe, since You are the One Who gives strength to the exhausted — give Your beloved Jewish children the strength to praise You, and to serve only You and no other.

May this week arrive for kindness, for good fortune, for blessing, for success, for good health, for wealth and honor, and for children, life, and sustenance, for us and for all Israel. Amen.

---

light, and evil, represented by darkness. The awareness that God took Israel to Himself as His Chosen Nation should cause inexpressible joy. Finally, the last cause of intense joy is the realization that Sabbath is God's special day of holiness and, as the *Zohar* teaches, He presented it as a gift to Israel *(Yesod v'Shoresh Ha'Avodah).*

☙ **גָאט פוּן אַבְרָהָם** — *Gott fun Avrohom.* It was customary in many European communities for the women to recite the following prayer for a successful week, before *Havdalah.* Since women generally did not recite the *Maariv* service, they would follow this prayer with בָּרוּךְ הַמַּבְדִּיל בֵּין קֹדֶשׁ לְחוֹל, *Blessed is He Who separates between holy and secular,* as a substitute for אַתָּה חוֹנַנְתָּנוּ, *You have graciously given us,* which is inserted into the *Shemoneh Esrei* to proclaim the distinction between the sanctity represented by the Sabbath, and the secularity represented by the weekdays. Today, many women maintain the custom of reciting *Gott fun Avrohom* before *Havdalah.* Rabbi Levi Yitzchak of Berditchev, traditionally recognized as the author of this prayer, however, wrote that it should be recited three times by men, women, and children, and that this recitation would help assure success in the ensuing week. Because it was designed both as a prayer, and as a source of inspiration, it was composed in Yiddish, the prevailing language among Eastern European Jews.

זמירות למוצאי שבת

המבדיל

הַמַּבְדִּיל בֵּין קֹדֶשׁ לְחוֹל, חַטֹּאתֵינוּ הוּא יִמְחוֹל,
זַרְעֵנוּ וְכַסְפֵּנוּ יַרְבֶּה כַחוֹל, וְכַכּוֹכָבִים בַּלָּיְלָה.

יוֹם פָּנָה כְּצֵל תֹּמֶר, אֶקְרָא לָאֵל עָלַי גֹּמֵר,[1]
אָמַר שֹׁמֵר, אָתָא בֹקֶר וְגַם לָיְלָה.[2]

צִדְקָתְךָ כְּהַר תָּבוֹר, עַל חֲטָאַי עָבוֹר תַּעֲבוֹר,
כְּיוֹם אֶתְמוֹל כִּי יַעֲבֹר, וְאַשְׁמוּרָה בַלָּיְלָה.[3]

חָלְפָה עוֹנַת מִנְחָתִי, מִי יִתֵּן מְנוּחָתִי,
יָגַעְתִּי בְאַנְחָתִי, אַשְׂחֶה בְכָל לָיְלָה.[4]

קוֹלִי בַּל יֻנְטָל, פְּתַח לִי שַׁעַר הַמְּנֻטָּל,
שֶׁרֹּאשִׁי נִמְלָא טָל, קְוֻצּוֹתַי רְסִיסֵי לָיְלָה.[5]

הֵעָתֵר נוֹרָא וְאָיוֹם, אֲשַׁוֵּעַ תְּנָה פִדְיוֹם,
בְּנֶשֶׁף בְּעֶרֶב יוֹם, בְּאִישׁוֹן לָיְלָה.[6]

קְרָאתִיךָ יָהּ הוֹשִׁיעֵנִי, אֹרַח חַיִּים תּוֹדִיעֵנִי,[7]
מִדַּלָּה תְבַצְּעֵנִי, מִיּוֹם וְעַד לָיְלָה.[8]

טַהֵר טִנּוּף מַעֲשַׂי, פֶּן יֹאמְרוּ מַכְעִיסַי,
אַיֵּה (נָא) אֱלוֹהַּ עֹשָׂי, נֹתֵן זְמִרוֹת בַּלָּיְלָה.[9]

נַחְנוּ בְיָדְךָ כַּחֹמֶר, סְלַח נָא עַל קַל וָחֹמֶר,
יוֹם לְיוֹם יַבִּיעַ אֹמֶר, וְלַיְלָה לְּלָיְלָה.[10]

הַמַּבְדִּיל בֵּין קֹדֶשׁ לְחוֹל, חַטֹּאתֵינוּ הוּא יִמְחוֹל,
זַרְעֵנוּ וְכַסְפֵּנוּ יַרְבֶּה כַחוֹל, וְכַכּוֹכָבִים בַּלָּיְלָה.

במוצאי

בְּמוֹצָאֵי יוֹם מְנוּחָה, הַמְצֵא לְעַמְּךָ רְוָחָה,
שְׁלַח תִּשְׁבִּי לְנֶאֱנָחָה, וְנָס יָגוֹן וַאֲנָחָה.

יָאֲתָה לְךָ צוּרִי, לְקַבֵּץ עַם מְפֻזָּרִי,
מִיַּד גּוֹי אַכְזָרִי, אֲשֶׁר כָּרָה לִי שׁוּחָה.

עֵת דּוֹדִים תְּעוֹרֵר אֵל, לְמַלֵּט עַם אֲשֶׁר שׁוֹאֵל,
רְאוֹת טוּבְךָ בְּבֹא גוֹאֵל, לְשֶׂה פְזוּרָה נִדָּחָה.

ZEMIROS / זְמִירוֹת

HaMavdil / הַמַּבְדִּיל

This *zemer* was composed by the unknown יִצְחָק הַקָּטָן, *Yitzchak HaKatan,* whose name is formed by the acrostic of the stanzas. With the Sabbath having departed, we begin the new week with a prayer for forgiveness. Although *HaMavdil* is universally recited after *Havdalah, Chasam Sofer* maintains that it was orginally

ZEMIROS FOR THE DEPARTURE OF THE SABBATH

HAMAVDIL

הַמַּבְדִּיל *He Who separates between holy and secular, may He forgive our sins; our offspring and wealth may He increase like dust and like the nighttime stars.*

יוֹם *The day moved on like a date-palm's shadow — I shall cry out to God that He fulfill for me*[1] *what the Watchman said: 'The dawn has come, and also night.'*[2]

צִדְקָתְךָ *Your righteousness is lofty as Mount Tabor. As for my sins, may You overlook them, like a bygone day that passes on, and like a watch of the night.*[3]

חָלְפָה *The time of my afternoon offering has passed — who will grant me contentment? I am wearied with my sigh, I drench with tears each night.*[4]

קוֹלִי *May my voice be not withdrawn! Open the lofty gate for me! For my head is saturated as if with dew, my locks with the dewdrops of the night.*[5]

הֵעָתֵר *Be receptive, Awesome and Fearsome One! When I cry out, grant redemption — at night, when daylight wanes, in the darkness of night.*[6]

קְרָאתִיךָ *I called upon You, O God, help me. The way of life make known to me.*[7] *To my poverty bring an end as quickly as from day to night.*[8]

טַהֵר *Render pure the filth of my deeds, lest my tormentors ask, 'Where is the God Who made me, Who gives cause for song at night?'*[9]

נַחְנוּ *In Your hands we are but like clay, please forgive sins small and great. Day after day brings expressions of praise, and night after night.*[10]

הַמַּבְדִּיל *He Who separates between holy and secular, may He forgive our sins; our offspring and wealth may He increase like dust and like the nighttime stars.*

B'MOTZAEI

בְּמוֹצָאֵי *At the departure of the day of contentment, provide relief for Your people; send the Tishbi to the groaning one, and let groans and sorrow flee.*

יָאֲתָה *It is seemly for You, my Rock, to gather in the scattered people from the hand of a cruel nation that has dug me a pit.*

עֵת *Arouse the time of love, O God, to rescue the people who are praying to see Your goodness at the redeemer's advent, for the sheep, scattered and cast out.*

---

(1) Cf. *Psalms* 57:3. (2) *Isaiah* 21:12. (3) *Psalms* 90:3. (4) 6:7. (5) *Song of Songs* 5:2. (6) *Proverbs* 7:9. (7) Cf. *Psalms* 16:11. (8) Cf. *Isaiah* 38:12. (9) *Job* 35:10. (10) *Psalms* 19:3.

---

composed for the conclusion of Yom Kippur. This explains the frequent reference to forgiveness.

The concluding stich of each stanza is a Scriptural verse-fragment ending with the word לָיְלָה, *night.*

בְּמוֹצָאֵי / B'Motzaei

This *zemer* is of early origin, being found in *Machzor Vitry*. Its composer is יַעֲקֹב מְנוּי, *Yaakov*

קְרָא יֶשַׁע לְעַם נִדְבָּה, אֵל דָּגוּל מֵרְבָבָה,
יְהִי הַשָּׁבְוּעַ הַבָּא, לִישׁוּעָה וְלִרְוָחָה.

בַּת צִיּוֹן הַשְּׁכוּלָה, אֲשֶׁר הִיא הַיּוֹם גְּעוּלָה,
מְהֵרָה תִּהְיֶה בְעוּלָה, בְּאֵם הַבָּנִים שְׂמֵחָה.

מַעְיָנוֹת אֲזַי יְזוּבוּן, וּפְדוּיֵי יהוה יְשׁוּבוּן,
וּמֵי יֶשַׁע יִשְׁאֲבוּן, וְהַצָּרָה נִשְׁכָּחָה.

נְחֵה עַמְּךָ כְּאָב רַחֲמָן, יְצַפְצְפוּ עִם לֹא אַלְמָן,
דְּבַר יהוה אֲשֶׁר נֶאֱמָן, בַּהֲקִימְךָ הַבְטָחָה.

וִידִידִים פְּלֵיטֵי חֶרֶץ, נְגִינָתָם יִפְצְחוּ בְּמֶרֶץ,
בְּלִי צְוָחָה וּבְלִי פֶּרֶץ, אֵין יוֹצֵאת וְאֵין צְוָחָה.

יְהִי הַחֹדֶשׁ הַזֶּה, כִּנְבוּאַת אֲבִי חוֹזֶה,
וְיִשָּׁמַע בְּבַיִת זֶה, קוֹל שָׂשׂוֹן וְקוֹל שִׂמְחָה.

חָזָק יְמַלֵּא מִשְׁאֲלוֹתֵינוּ, אַמִּיץ יַעֲשֶׂה בַּקָּשָׁתֵנוּ,
וְהוּא יִשְׁלַח בְּמַעֲשֵׂה יָדֵינוּ, בְּרָכָה וְהַצְלָחָה.

בְּמוֹצָאֵי יוֹם גִּילָה, שִׁמְךָ נוֹרָא עֲלִילָה,
שְׁלַח תִּשְׁבִּי לְעַם סְגֻלָּה, רֶוַח שָׂשׂוֹן וַהֲנָחָה.

קוֹל צָהֳלָה וְרִנָּה, שְׂפָתֵינוּ אָז תְּרַנֵּנָּה,
אָנָּא יהוה הוֹשִׁיעָה נָּא, אָנָּא יהוה הַצְלִיחָה נָא.

אמר ה׳ ליעקב

אָמַר יהוה לְיַעֲקֹב,[1] אַל תִּירָא עַבְדִּי יַעֲקֹב.
בָּחַר יהוה בְּיַעֲקֹב,[2] אַל תִּירָא עַבְדִּי יַעֲקֹב.
גָּאַל יהוה אֶת יַעֲקֹב,[3] אַל תִּירָא עַבְדִּי יַעֲקֹב.
דָּרַךְ כּוֹכָב מִיַּעֲקֹב,[4] אַל תִּירָא עַבְדִּי יַעֲקֹב.
הַבָּאִים יַשְׁרֵשׁ יַעֲקֹב,[5] אַל תִּירָא עַבְדִּי יַעֲקֹב.
וְיֵרְדְּ מִיַּעֲקֹב,[6] אַל תִּירָא עַבְדִּי יַעֲקֹב.
זְכֹר זֹאת לְיַעֲקֹב,[7] אַל תִּירָא עַבְדִּי יַעֲקֹב.
חֶדְוַת יְשׁוּעוֹת יַעֲקֹב,[8] אַל תִּירָא עַבְדִּי יַעֲקֹב.
טֹבוּ אֹהָלֶיךָ יַעֲקֹב,[9] אַל תִּירָא עַבְדִּי יַעֲקֹב.
יוֹרוּ מִשְׁפָּטֶיךָ לְיַעֲקֹב,[10] אַל תִּירָא עַבְדִּי יַעֲקֹב.
כִּי לֹא נַחַשׁ בְּיַעֲקֹב,[11] אַל תִּירָא עַבְדִּי יַעֲקֹב.
לֹא הִבִּיט אָוֶן בְּיַעֲקֹב,[12] אַל תִּירָא עַבְדִּי יַעֲקֹב.

Manui, whose name is spelled in the acrostic beginning with the second stanza. The *zemer* begins with a plea that God gather Israel together from its exile during the coming week. It asks that He redeem Israel from its current state of degradation and bring it, in uninterrupted joy, to

קְרָא *Proclaim salvation for the generous people, O God, Who is bannered with myriad angels. May the coming week be one of salvation and relief.*

בַּת *The bereaved daughter of Zion, who is now despised, may she soon be wed, a joyous mother of children.*

מַעְיָנוֹת *The wellsprings then will flow as HASHEM's redeemed will return and draw the waters of salvation — then the torment will be forgotten.*

נְחֵה *Guide Your people like a merciful father. The unabandoned nation will speak the word of HASHEM Who is faithful, when You uphold the promise.*

וִידִידִים *The dear ones surviving the decree will sing their song robustly, without a scream and without defeat. There will be no captive and no scream.*

יְהִי *May this month be like the prophecy of [Moses] the father of seers. And may there be heard in this house the sound of joy and the sound of gladness.*

חָזָק *The Strong One will fill our requests; the Firm One will implement our prayers; and He will send into our handiwork, blessing and success.*

בְּמוֹצָאֵי *At the departure of the day of delight, You Whose Name is 'Awesome Accomplishment,' dispatch the Tishbi to the treasured people with relief and joy and respite.*

קוֹל *With sound of cheer and joyous song our lips will then exult. Please, HASHEM, save now! Please, HASHEM, bring success now!*

AMAR HASHEM L'YAAKOV

א	*HASHEM said to Jacob*[1]	*— fear not, My servant Jacob.*
ב	*HASHEM chose Jacob*[2]	*— fear not, My servant Jacob.*
ג	*HASHEM will redeem Jacob*[3]	*— fear not, My servant Jacob.*
ד	*A star will emerge from Jacob*[4]	*— fear not, My servant Jacob.*
ה	*In time to come Jacob will strike roots*[5]	*— fear not, My servant Jacob.*
ו	*A ruler will arise from Jacob*[6]	*— fear not, My servant Jacob.*
ז	*Remember this for Jacob's sake*[7]	*— fear not, My servant Jacob.*
ח	*Delight will come with Jacob's salvation*[8]	*— fear not, My servant Jacob.*
ט	*Your tents are goodly, Jacob*[9]	*— fear not, My servant Jacob.*
י	*They shall teach Your ordinances to Jacob*[10]	*— fear not, My servant Jacob.*
כ	*For there is no sorcery in Jacob*[11]	*— fear not, My servant Jacob.*
ל	*He perceives no wrong in Jacob*[12]	*— fear not, My servant Jacob.*

(1) Cf. *Isaiah* 29:22. (2) Cf. *Psalms* 135:4. (3) Cf. *Isaiah* 44:23. (4) *Numbers* 24:17. (5) *Isaiah* 27:6. (6) *Numbers* 24:19. (7) Cf. *Isaiah* 44:21. (8) Cf. 25:9. (9) *Numbers* 24:5. (10) *Deuteronomy* 33:10. (11) *Numbers* 23:23. (12) 23:21.

the Temple. The *zemer* opens and closes with a prayer for the coming of the prophet Elijah the Tishbi, traditionally the herald of the Messiah.

אָמַר ה׳ לְיַעֲקֹב / Amar HASHEM L'Yaakov

This *zemer*, of unknown authorship, follows the *Aleph-Beis*. The first stich of each stanza is, in nearly all cases, a Scriptural fragment; where it is not a direct quote, it is a close paraphrase of a verse. Each stanza concludes with the urging to the Jewish people: *Fear not, my servant Jacob* — a phrase that appears no less than four times in Scripture *(Isaiah* 44:2; *Jeremiah* 30:10; 46:27,28). The general theme is that Israel, based

מִי מָנָה עֲפַר יַעֲקֹב,[1] אַל תִּירָא עַבְדִּי יַעֲקֹב.
נִשְׁבַּע יהוה לְיַעֲקֹב,[2] אַל תִּירָא עַבְדִּי יַעֲקֹב.
סְלַח נָא לַעֲוֹן יַעֲקֹב,[3] אַל תִּירָא עַבְדִּי יַעֲקֹב.
עַתָּה הָשֵׁב שְׁבוּת יַעֲקֹב,[4] אַל תִּירָא עַבְדִּי יַעֲקֹב.
פָּדָה יהוה אֶת יַעֲקֹב,[5] אַל תִּירָא עַבְדִּי יַעֲקֹב.
צַוֵּה יְשׁוּעוֹת יַעֲקֹב,[6] אַל תִּירָא עַבְדִּי יַעֲקֹב.
קוֹל קוֹל יַעֲקֹב,[7] אַל תִּירָא עַבְדִּי יַעֲקֹב.
רָנִּי וְשִׂמְחִי לְיַעֲקֹב,[8] אַל תִּירָא עַבְדִּי יַעֲקֹב.
שָׁב יהוה אֶת גְּאוֹן יַעֲקֹב,[9] אַל תִּירָא עַבְדִּי יַעֲקֹב.
תִּתֵּן אֱמֶת לְיַעֲקֹב,[10] אַל תִּירָא עַבְדִּי יַעֲקֹב.

אליהו הנביא

אֵלִיָּהוּ הַנָּבִיא אֵלִיָּהוּ הַתִּשְׁבִּי אֵלִיָּהוּ הַגִּלְעָדִי.*
בִּמְהֵרָה יָבוֹא אֵלֵינוּ עִם מָשִׁיחַ בֶּן דָּוִד.

אִישׁ **אֲ**שֶׁר קִנֵּא לְשֵׁם הָאֵל.
אִישׁ **בֻּ**שַּׂר שָׁלוֹם עַל יַד יְקוּתִיאֵל.*
אִישׁ **גָּ**שׁ וַיְכַפֵּר עַל בְּנֵי יִשְׂרָאֵל.[11]

אֵלִיָּהוּ הַנָּבִיא אֵלִיָּהוּ הַתִּשְׁבִּי אֵלִיָּהוּ הַגִּלְעָדִי.
בִּמְהֵרָה יָבוֹא אֵלֵינוּ עִם מָשִׁיחַ בֶּן דָּוִד.

אִישׁ **דּ**וֹרוֹת שְׁנֵים עָשָׂר* רָאוּ עֵינָיו.
אִישׁ **הַ**נִּקְרָא בַּעַל שֵׂעָר בְּסִמָּנָיו.
אִישׁ **וְ**אֵזוֹר עוֹר אָזוּר בְּמָתְנָיו.[12]

אֵלִיָּהוּ הַנָּבִיא אֵלִיָּהוּ הַתִּשְׁבִּי אֵלִיָּהוּ הַגִּלְעָדִי.
בִּמְהֵרָה יָבוֹא אֵלֵינוּ עִם מָשִׁיחַ בֶּן דָּוִד.

אִישׁ **זָ**עַף עַל עוֹבְדֵי חַמָּנִים.
אִישׁ **חָ**שׁ וְנִשְׁבַּע מֵהְיוֹת גִּשְׁמֵי מְעוֹנִים.
אִישׁ **טַ**ל וּמָטָר עָצַר שָׁלֹשׁ שָׁנִים.[13]

אֵלִיָּהוּ הַנָּבִיא אֵלִיָּהוּ הַתִּשְׁבִּי אֵלִיָּהוּ הַגִּלְעָדִי.
בִּמְהֵרָה יָבוֹא אֵלֵינוּ עִם מָשִׁיחַ בֶּן דָּוִד.

אִישׁ **יָ**צָא לִמְצוֹא לְנַפְשׁוֹ נַחַת.
אִישׁ **כִּ**לְכְּלוּהוּ הָעֹרְבִים וְלֹא מֵת לַשַּׁחַת.
אִישׁ **לְ**מַעֲנוֹ נִתְבָּרְכוּ כַּד וְצַפַּחַת.[14]

אֵלִיָּהוּ הַנָּבִיא אֵלִיָּהוּ הַתִּשְׁבִּי אֵלִיָּהוּ הַגִּלְעָדִי.
בִּמְהֵרָה יָבוֹא אֵלֵינוּ עִם מָשִׁיחַ בֶּן דָּוִד.

---

(1) *Numbers* 23:10. (2) Cf. *Amos* 8:7. (3) Cf. *Numbers* 14:19. (4) Cf. *Ezekiel* 39:25. (5) *Jeremiah* 31:10. (6) *Psalms* 44:5. (7) *Genesis* 27:22. (8) Cf. *Zechariah* 2:14. (9) Cf. *Deuteronomy* 30:3. (10) *Michah* 7:20. (11) See *Numbers* 25:1-15. (12) Cf. *II Kings* 1:8. (13) See *I Kings* 17:1; 18:1-18. (14) See 17:2-16.

מ *Who can count the dust of Jacob?*[1] — *fear not, My servant Jacob.*
נ *HASHEM swore to Jacob*[2] — *fear not, My servant Jacob.*
ס *Please forgive the sin of Jacob*[3] — *fear not, My servant Jacob.*
ע *Bring back, now, the captivity of Jacob*[4] — *fear not, My servant Jacob.*
פ *God will redeem Jacob*[5] — *fear not, My servant Jacob.*
צ *Command salvations for Jacob*[6] — *fear not, My servant Jacob.*
ק *The voice is the voice of Jacob*[7] — *fear not, My servant Jacob.*
ר *Bring song and gladness for Jacob*[8] — *fear not, My servant Jacob.*
ש *HASHEM will return the captivity of Jacob*[9] — *fear not, My servant Jacob.*
ת *You will grant truth to Jacob*[10] — *fear not, My servant Jacob.*

ELIYAHU HANAVI

אֵלִיָּהוּ הַנָּבִיא *Elijah the prophet, Elijah the Tishbi, Elijah the Giladi* —*
May he quickly come to us with Messiah, son of David.

א *The man who was zealous in defense of God's Name;*
ב *the man who was promised peace by the symbol of hope in God;**
ג *the man who approached sinners and atoned for Israel.*[11]

Elijah the prophet, Elijah the Tishbi, Elijah the Giladi —
May he quickly come to us with Messiah, son of David.

ד *The man whose eyes saw twelve generations;**
ה *the man called 'Hairy One' because of his appearance;*
ו *the man with leather belt girdling his loins.*[12]

Elijah the prophet, Elijah the Tishbi, Elijah the Giladi —
May he quickly come to us with Messiah, son of David.

ז *The man who raged against worshipers of the sun;*
ח *the man who rushed and swore that there would be no rains from heaven;*
ט *the man who withheld dew and rain three years.*[13]

Elijah the prophet, Elijah the Tishbi, Elijah the Giladi —
May he quickly come to us with Messiah, son of David.

י *The man who left to find himself tranquillity;*
כ *the man nourished by ravens not to die for the grave;*
ל *the man on whose behalf the jug and jar were blessed.*[14]

Elijah the prophet, Elijah the Tishbi, Elijah the Giladi —
May he quickly come to us with Messiah, son of David.

---

on the Scriptural assurances which are respectively cited, need have no fear that it is, God forbid, doomed.

אֵלִיָּהוּ הַנָּבִיא / Eliyahu HaNavi

This *zemer,* of unknown authorship, is devoted exclusively to the praise of Elijah the prophet. It also includes references to Phineas son of Elazar, the High Priest, because the *Midrash* identifies him with Elijah.

After the first stanza, which is repeated as the refrain between succeeding stanzas, are twenty-two stiches that begin with the word אִישׁ, *man.* The second words of these stiches contain an alphabetic acrostic.

הַתִּשְׁבִּי ... הַגִּלְעָדִי — *The Tishbi ... the Giladi.* Elijah was a native of Toshav and he later moved to Gilad. Therefore, he is known as both *Tishbi* and *Giladi.*

יְקוּתִיאֵל — *The symbol of hope in God.* Moses is called יְקוּתִיאֵל from יְקַוֶּה, *he will hope,* and אֵל, *God.* Thus, Moses, the symbol of hope in God, promised the blessing of peace to Phineas who approached sinners [Zimri and Kozbi] and atoned for Israel *(Numbers* 25).

שְׁנֵים עָשָׂר — *Twelve generations.* According to the Midrash, Phineas/Elijah lived for many centuries. He lived in the time of twelve generations of the Davidic family: Nachshon, Salmon, Boaz,

אִישׁ **מ**וּסָרָיו הִקְשִׁיבוּ כְּמֵהִים.
אִישׁ **נ**ֶעֱנָה בָאֵשׁ מִשְּׁמֵי גְבוֹהִים.
אִישׁ **ס**ָחוּ אַחֲרָיו יהוה הוּא הָאֱלֹהִים.[1]
אֵלִיָּהוּ הַנָּבִיא אֵלִיָּהוּ הַתִּשְׁבִּי אֵלִיָּהוּ הַגִּלְעָדִי.
בִּמְהֵרָה יָבוֹא אֵלֵינוּ עִם מָשִׁיחַ בֶּן דָּוִד.

אִישׁ **ע**ָתִיד לְהִשְׁתַּלֵּחַ מִשְּׁמֵי עֲרָבוֹת.
אִישׁ **פ**ָּקִיד עַל כָּל בְּשׂוֹרוֹת טוֹבוֹת.
אִישׁ **צ**ִיר נֶאֱמָן לְהָשִׁיב לֵב בָּנִים עַל אָבוֹת.[2]
אֵלִיָּהוּ הַנָּבִיא אֵלִיָּהוּ הַתִּשְׁבִּי אֵלִיָּהוּ הַגִּלְעָדִי.
בִּמְהֵרָה יָבוֹא אֵלֵינוּ עִם מָשִׁיחַ בֶּן דָּוִד.

אִישׁ **ק**ָרָא קַנֹּא קִנֵּאתִי לַיהוה[3] בְּתִפְאָרָה.
אִישׁ **ר**ָכַב עַל סוּסֵי אֵשׁ בִּסְעָרָה.
אִישׁ **שֶׁ**לֹּא טָעַם טַעַם מִיתָה וּקְבוּרָה.[4]
אֵלִיָּהוּ הַנָּבִיא אֵלִיָּהוּ הַתִּשְׁבִּי אֵלִיָּהוּ הַגִּלְעָדִי.
בִּמְהֵרָה יָבוֹא אֵלֵינוּ עִם מָשִׁיחַ בֶּן דָּוִד.

אִישׁ **ת**ִּשְׁבִּי עַל שְׁמוֹ נִקְרָא.
תַּצְלִיחֵנוּ עַל יָדוֹ בַּתּוֹרָה.*
תַּשְׁמִיעֵנוּ מִפִּיו בְּשׂוֹרָה טוֹבָה בִּמְהֵרָה.
תּוֹצִיאֵנוּ מֵאֲפֵלָה לְאוֹרָה.
אֵלִיָּהוּ הַנָּבִיא אֵלִיָּהוּ הַתִּשְׁבִּי אֵלִיָּהוּ הַגִּלְעָדִי.
בִּמְהֵרָה יָבוֹא אֵלֵינוּ עִם מָשִׁיחַ בֶּן דָּוִד.

אִישׁ **ת**ִּשְׁבִּי תַּצִּילֵנוּ מִפִּי אֲרָיוֹת.
תְּבַשְּׂרֵנוּ בְּשׂוֹרוֹת טוֹבוֹת.
תְּשַׂמְּחֵנוּ בָּנִים עַל אָבוֹת. בְּמוֹצָאֵי שַׁבָּתוֹת.*
אֵלִיָּהוּ הַנָּבִיא אֵלִיָּהוּ הַתִּשְׁבִּי אֵלִיָּהוּ הַגִּלְעָדִי.
בִּמְהֵרָה יָבוֹא אֵלֵינוּ עִם מָשִׁיחַ בֶּן דָּוִד.

כַּכָּתוּב: הִנֵּה אָנֹכִי שֹׁלֵחַ לָכֶם אֵת אֵלִיָּה הַנָּבִיא
לִפְנֵי בּוֹא יוֹם יהוה הַגָּדוֹל וְהַנּוֹרָא.
וְהֵשִׁיב לֵב אָבוֹת עַל בָּנִים וְלֵב בָּנִים עַל אֲבוֹתָם.[5]
אֵלִיָּהוּ הַנָּבִיא אֵלִיָּהוּ הַתִּשְׁבִּי אֵלִיָּהוּ הַגִּלְעָדִי.
בִּמְהֵרָה יָבוֹא אֵלֵינוּ עִם מָשִׁיחַ בֶּן דָּוִד.

אַשְׁרֵי מִי שֶׁרָאָה פָנָיו בַּחֲלוֹם.
אַשְׁרֵי מִי שֶׁנָּתַן לוֹ שָׁלוֹם. וְהֶחֱזִיר לוֹ שָׁלוֹם
יהוה יְבָרֵךְ אֶת עַמּוֹ בַשָּׁלוֹם.[6]
אֵלִיָּהוּ הַנָּבִיא אֵלִיָּהוּ הַתִּשְׁבִּי אֵלִיָּהוּ הַגִּלְעָדִי.
בִּמְהֵרָה יָבוֹא אֵלֵינוּ עִם מָשִׁיחַ בֶּן דָּוִד.

מ *The man whose admonitions attracted people longing for God;*
נ *the man answered with fire from the high heavens;*
ס *the man after whom they said, 'HASHEM — only He is God'.*[1]

Elijah the prophet, Elijah the Tishbi, Elijah the Giladi —
May he quickly come to us with Messiah, son of David.

ע *The man destined to be sent from the heavens;*
פ *the man appointed over all good tidings;*
צ *the man who is the trusty agent to return children's hearts to their parents.*[2]

Elijah the prophet, Elijah the Tishbi, Elijah the Giladi —
May he quickly come to us with Messiah, son of David.

ק *The man who proclaimed in splendor, 'I acted zealously for HASHEM's sake';*[3]
ר *the man who rode fiery horses in a stormy wind;*
ש *the man who never felt the taste of death and burial.*[4]

Elijah the prophet, Elijah the Tishbi, Elijah the Giladi —
May he quickly come to us with Messiah, son of David.

ת *The man called 'Tishbi' in addition to his name;*
ת *make our Torah study successful* through him;*
ת *let us hear speedily from his mouth the good tidings;*
ת *may he remove us from darkness to light.*

Elijah the prophet, Elijah the Tishbi, Elijah the Giladi —
May he quickly come to us with Messiah, son of David.

ת *The man, Tishbi, may he rescue us from the lions' mouth;*
ת *may he herald good tidings for us;*
ת *may he gladden children with parents at the departure of Sabbaths.**

Elijah the prophet, Elijah the Tishbi, Elijah the Giladi —
May he quickly come to us with Messiah, son of David.

כַּכָּתוּב *As it is written, 'Behold! I send you Elijah the prophet,*
before the arrival of the great and awesome day of HASHEM;
and He shall return the heart of parents to children
and the heart of children to their parents.'[5]

Elijah the prophet, Elijah the Tishbi, Elijah the Giladi —
May he quickly come to us with Messiah, son of David.

אַשְׁרֵי *Fortunate is he who has seen his face in a dream,*
fortunate is he who greeted him with 'Peace'
and to whom he responded 'Peace,'
may HASHEM bless His people with peace.[6]

Elijah the prophet, Elijah the Tishbi, Elijah the Giladi —
May he quickly come to us with Messiah, son of David.

---

(1) See *I Kings* 18:19-40. (2) Cf. *Malachi* 3:24. (3) *I Kings* 19:10.
(4) See *II Kings* 2:11. (5) *Malachi* 3:23-24. (6) *Psalms* 29:11.

Oved, Jesse, David, Solomon, Rehoboam, Abiah, Asa, Jehoshafat, and Jehoram.

תַּצְלִיחֵנוּ ... בַּתּוֹרָה — *Make our Torah study successful.* The Sages teach that when Elijah comes to herald the redemption, he will also resolve all difficulties in the area of Torah study.

Further, scholars of great saintly merit have been privileged to be taught by Elijah.

בְּמוֹצָאֵי שַׁבָּתוֹת — *At the departure of Sabbaths.* Since the observance of Sabbath helps bring the redemption, the departure of the day is an auspicious time for Elijah to come.

נטילת לולב

Many recite the following declaration of intent before taking the Four Species:

יְהִי רָצוֹן מִלְּפָנֶיךָ, יהוה אֱלֹהַי וֵאלֹהֵי אֲבוֹתַי, בִּפְרִי עֵץ הָדָר,* וְכַפּוֹת תְּמָרִים,* וַעֲנַף עֵץ עָבוֹת,* וְעַרְבֵי נָחַל,[1] אוֹתִיּוֹת שִׁמְךָ הַמְּיֻחָד* תְּקָרֵב אֶחָד אֶל אֶחָד, וְהָיוּ לַאֲחָדִים בְּיָדִי, וְלֵידַע אֵיךְ שִׁמְךָ נִקְרָא עָלַי, וְיִירְאוּ מִגֶּשֶׁת אֵלָי. וּבְנַעֲנוּעִי אוֹתָם תַּשְׁפִּיעַ שֶׁפַע בְּרָכוֹת מִדַּעַת עֶלְיוֹן לִנְוֵה אַפִּרְיוֹן, לִמְכוֹן בֵּית אֱלֹהֵינוּ. וּתְהֵא חֲשׁוּבָה לְפָנֶיךָ מִצְוַת אַרְבָּעָה מִינִים אֵלּוּ, כְּאִלּוּ קִיַּמְתִּיהָ בְּכָל פְּרָטוֹתֶיהָ וְשָׁרָשֶׁיהָ וְתַרְיַ״ג מִצְוֹת הַתְּלוּיִם בָּהּ. כִּי כַוָּנָתִי* לְיַחֲדָא שְׁמָא דְקֻדְשָׁא בְּרִיךְ הוּא וּשְׁכִינְתֵּהּ, בִּדְחִילוּ וּרְחִימוּ, לְיַחֵד שֵׁם י״ה בְּו״ה בְּיִחוּדָא שְׁלִים, בְּשֵׁם כָּל יִשְׂרָאֵל. אָמֵן. בָּרוּךְ יהוה לְעוֹלָם, אָמֵן, וְאָמֵן.[2]

The Four Species — *lulav, hadasim, aravos, esrog* — are taken in hand every day of Succos — through *Hoshana Rabbah* — except on the Sabbath. The *lulav*-bundle is picked up with the right hand, then the *esrog* (with the *pitam* facing down) with the left. After the blessings are recited, the *esrog* is turned over and the Four Species are waved in the six directions. (See *Laws* on facing page).

בָּרוּךְ אַתָּה יהוה אֱלֹהֵינוּ מֶלֶךְ הָעוֹלָם, אֲשֶׁר קִדְּשָׁנוּ בְּמִצְוֹתָיו, וְצִוָּנוּ עַל נְטִילַת לוּלָב.*

The following blessing is added only on the first day that the Four Species are taken.

בָּרוּךְ אַתָּה יהוה אֱלֹהֵינוּ מֶלֶךְ הָעוֹלָם, שֶׁהֶחֱיָנוּ* וְקִיְּמָנוּ וְהִגִּיעָנוּ לַזְּמַן הַזֶּה.

נְטִילַת לוּלָב / THE FOUR SPECIES

The Torah commands the taking of the Four Species and concludes: *You shall be joyous before* HASHEM ... *(Leviticus* 23:40). The Midrash explains the connection between this *mitzvah* and joyousness:

In earlier days if a litigant's claim before the royal court was decided in his favor, he would receive a spear from the king. When he left the palace holding the king's spear aloft all knew that he had been victorious in his suit. Similarly, during the Days of Awe, the Jewish people were on trial before the Heavenly Court. On Succos, the season of joy,' we celebrate our happiness that God has accepted our repentance — a confidence symbolized by the *lulav* held aloft.

בִּפְרִי עֵץ הָדָר — *Through the fruit of the esrog* [lit. *beautiful*] *tree.* The Torah does not specify the *esrog* by name, but uses this descriptive phrase. *Targum* renders הָדָר, *beautiful,* as אֶתְרוֹגִין, *esrogim.*

וְכַפּוֹת תְּמָרִים — *Date-palm branches,* i.e., *the lulav.* In the Scriptural verse, the terms for *esrog* and *lulav* are not connected by the conjunctive ו, *and.* However, conjunctions do connect the terms for *lulav, hadasim* (myrtle), and *aravos* (willow). From this it is derived that the species be held in two groups: the *esrog* by itself; and a bundle containing the *lulav, hadasim* and *aravos (Succah* 24b).

וַעֲנַף עֵץ עָבוֹת — *Twigs of the myrtle tree,* i.e., *hadasim.* Literally, עֵץ עָבוֹת means a *thick* or *braided* tree. The Talmud *(Succah* 32b) understands this to refer to a species whose leaf coverage is thick, completely covering the twig, and whose leaves overlap each other, as if they were braided — and identify it as the *myrtle.*

אוֹתִיּוֹת שִׁמְךָ הַמְּיֻחָד — *The letters of Your unified Name.* Kabbalah teaches that each of the Four Species is identified with another of the letters of the Four-Letter Name of God. Rabbi Michael Ber Weissmandl (in *Toras Chemed)* adduces a complex series of calculations to prove that the *aravos, lulav, hadasim,* and *esrog* correspond, in that order, with the four letters of the Name.

כַּוָּנָתִי — *My intention.* Even one who has spent much time and money on perfect species should not taint the performance of his *mitzvah* by pride in his acquisition. Rather, his intention in fulfilling the *mitzvah* should be above personal considerations. It is not coincidental that the initials of the verse *(Psalms* 36:12): אַל תְּבוֹאֵנִי רֶגֶל גַּאֲוָה, *Bring me not* [*to*] *the foot of arrogance,* form the word אֶתְרֹג *(Baal Shem Tov).*

THE FOUR SPECIES/LULAV AND ESROG

Many recite the following declaration of intent before taking the Four Species:

יְהִי רָצוֹן *May it be Your will,* HASHEM, *my God and the God of my forefathers, that through the fruit of the esrog tree,* date-palm branches,* twigs of the myrtle tree,* and brook willows,*[1] *the letters of Your unified Name* may become close to one another, that they may become united in my hand; and to make known that Your Name is called upon me, that [evil forces] may be fearful of approaching me. And when I wave them, may an abundant outpouring of blessings flow from the wisdom of the Most High to the abode of the tabernacle, to the prepared place of the House of our God. And may the mitzvah of these Four Species be reckoned before You as if I had fulfilled it with all its particulars, roots, and the six hundred thirteen mitzvos dependent on it. For my intention* is to unify the Name of the Holy One, Blessed is He, and His Presence, in awe and in love, to unify the Name Yud-Kei with Vav-Kei in perfect unity, in the name of all Israel; Amen. Blessed is* HASHEM *forever, Amen and Amen.*[2]

The Four Species — *lulav, hadasim, aravos, esrog* — are taken in hand every day of Succos — through *Hoshana Rabbah* — except on the Sabbath. The *lulav*-bundle is picked up with the right hand, then the *esrog* (with the *pitam* facing down) with the left. After the blessings are recited, the *esrog* is turned over and the Four Species are waved in the six directions. (See *Laws* below).

בָּרוּךְ *Blessed are You,* HASHEM, *our God, King of the universe, Who has sanctified us with His commandments and has commanded us concerning the taking of a palm branch.**

The following blessing is added only on the first day that the Four Species are taken.

בָּרוּךְ *Blessed are You,* HASHEM, *our God, King of the universe, Who has kept us alive,* sustained us, and brought us to this season.*

(1) Cf. *Leviticus* 23:40. (2) *Psalms* 89:53.

נְטִילַת לוּלָב — *Taking of a palm branch.* The Talmud *(Succah* 37b) explains that only the *lulav* is mentioned in the benediction since the date-palm tree, of which the *lulav* is a branch, is taller than any of the other species.

Laws of the Four Species

If at all possible one should not eat or drink before taking the Species.

Most *siddurim* place the blessings of the Four Species just before *Hallel,* in accordance with the ruling of *Shulchan Aruch* (644:1) that the Species be taken between *Shemoneh Esrei* and *Hallel.* However, many follow *Arizal's* view that these blessings should be recited in the *succah,* and therefore, recite them before entering the synagogue for *Shacharis.*

The שֶׁהֶחֱיָנוּ blessing is recited on the first day that the Four Species are taken. Thus, if the first day of Succos coincides with the Sabbath, this blessing is recited on Sunday. Additionally, if one was unable to take the Four Species on the first day of Succos, he recites this blessing the first time he is able to, regardless of which day of Succos it is. [A full exposition of the significance and laws of the *mitzvah* may be found in the ArtScroll *Succos.*]

In addition to holding the Four Species together — which is sufficient for performance of the commandment — one should also perform נַעֲנוּעִים, the *waving,* (or *shaking*) of the Species in six directions — the four points of the compass, up and down. It is preferable that one face east while waving the Species. The sequence followed in most Ashkenaz congregations is: straight ahead (i.e., east), right (south), back (west), left (north), up and down.

The generally followed manner of waving is to stretch out the arms and shake strongly enough to rustle the *lulav's* leaves, and then to draw the Species close to the chest and shake again. This is repeated three times in each direction *(Rama, Orach Chaim* 651:9).

The Species are also held during the recitation of *Hallel* and *Hoshanos.* During certain verses of *Hallel,* they are waved again in the manner described above. Although one should follow the custom of his own congregation, the customary rule is to wave the Species each time the verses הוֹדוּ לַה׳ כִּי טוֹב and אָנָּא ה׳ הוֹשִׁיעָה נָּא are recited (ibid. 651:8).

❧ הלל ☙

Hallel is recited after the *Shemoneh Esrei* of *Shacharis* on Festivals (with the exception of Rosh Hashanah, Yom Kippur, and Purim) and on Chanukah and Rosh Chodesh. (Some congregations also recite it following the *Maariv Shemoneh Esrei* on *Seder* nights.) On Rosh Chodesh and the last six days of Pesach, two paragraphs (as indicated in the text) are omitted. [Those who wear *tefillin* on Chol HaMoed remove them at this point before reciting *Hallel*.]

The chazzan recites the blessing. The congregation, after responding אָמֵן, repeats it, and continues with the first psalm. Regarding the blessing for one praying alone, see *Laws* §37.

בָּרוּךְ אַתָּה יהוה אֱלֹהֵינוּ מֶלֶךְ הָעוֹלָם, אֲשֶׁר קִדְּשָׁנוּ בְּמִצְוֹתָיו, וְצִוָּנוּ לִקְרוֹא אֶת הַהַלֵּל. (.Cong.— אָמֵן)

תהלים קיג

הַלְלוּיָהּ הַלְּלוּ עַבְדֵי יהוה,* הַלְּלוּ אֶת שֵׁם יהוה. יְהִי שֵׁם יהוה מְבֹרָךְ, מֵעַתָּה וְעַד עוֹלָם. מִמִּזְרַח שֶׁמֶשׁ עַד מְבוֹאוֹ, מְהֻלָּל שֵׁם יהוה. רָם עַל כָּל גּוֹיִם יהוה, עַל הַשָּׁמַיִם כְּבוֹדוֹ. מִי כַּיהוה אֱלֹהֵינוּ, הַמַּגְבִּיהִי לָשָׁבֶת. הַמַּשְׁפִּילִי לִרְאוֹת, בַּשָּׁמַיִם וּבָאָרֶץ.* ❖ מְקִימִי מֵעָפָר דָּל, מֵאַשְׁפֹּת יָרִים אֶבְיוֹן. לְהוֹשִׁיבִי עִם נְדִיבִים,* עִם נְדִיבֵי עַמּוֹ. מוֹשִׁיבִי עֲקֶרֶת הַבַּיִת,* אֵם הַבָּנִים שְׂמֵחָה, הַלְלוּיָהּ.

תהלים קיד

בְּצֵאת יִשְׂרָאֵל מִמִּצְרָיִם,* בֵּית יַעֲקֹב מֵעַם לֹעֵז.* הָיְתָה יְהוּדָה לְקָדְשׁוֹ,* יִשְׂרָאֵל מַמְשְׁלוֹתָיו. הַיָּם רָאָה וַיָּנֹס, הַיַּרְדֵּן יִסֹּב לְאָחוֹר. הֶהָרִים רָקְדוּ כְאֵילִים,* גְּבָעוֹת כִּבְנֵי צֹאן. ❖ מַה לְּךָ הַיָּם כִּי תָנוּס, הַיַּרְדֵּן תִּסֹּב לְאָחוֹר.* הֶהָרִים תִּרְקְדוּ

⊰ Hallel

The prophets ordained that the six psalms of *Hallel* [literally, *praise*] be recited on each Festival, and to commemorate times of national deliverance from peril. Moreover, before David redacted and incorporated these psalms into the Book of Psalms, *Hallel* was already known to the nation: Moses and Israel recited it after being saved from the Egyptians at the sea; Joshua, after defeating the Kings of Canaan; Deborah and Barak, after defeating Sisera; Hezekiah, after defeating Sennacherib; Chananyah, Mishael and Azariah, after being saved from the wicked Nebuchadnezzar; and Mordechai and Esther, after the defeat of the wicked Haman (*Pesachim* 117a).

These psalms were singled out as the unit of praise because they contain five fundamental themes of Jewish faith: the Exodus, the Splitting of the Sea, the Giving of the Torah at Sinai, the future Resuscitation of the dead, and the coming of the Messiah (ibid. 118a).

Hallel is omitted on Rosh Hashanah and Yom Kippur because they are days of judgment and it is inappropriate to sing joyful praises on days when our very survival is being weighed on the scales of judgment. It is omitted on Purim, because, despite the miracle of the day, the Jewish people remained in exile as servants of Ahasuerus, and thus the deliverance was only partial. On Chanukah, however, not only was the military victory more complete, the *Hallel* also commemorates the miracle of the lights, which marked the renewal of the Temple.

⊰ **הַלְלוּיָהּ הַלְּלוּ עַבְדֵי ה׳** — *Halleluyah! Give praise, you servants of* HASHEM! Only after their liberation from Pharaoh's bondage could the Jews be considered the *servants of* HASHEM, because they no longer vowed allegiance to any ruler.

הַמַּשְׁפִּילִי לִרְאוֹת בַּשָּׁמַיִם וּבָאָרֶץ — *Yet deigns to look* [lit. *bends down low to see*] *upon the heaven and the earth?* This is the challenging and exciting aspect of God's relationship to man: as we act towards God, so does He react to us. If we ignore His presence, He withdraws high *above the*

❧ HALLEL ☙

Hallel is recited after the *Shemoneh Esrei* of *Shacharis* on Festivals (with the exception of Rosh Hashanah, Yom Kippur, and Purim) and on Chanukah and Rosh Chodesh. (Some congregations also recite it following the *Maariv Shemoneh Esrei* on *Seder* nights.) On Rosh Chodesh and the last six days of Pesach, two paragraphs (as indicated in the text) are omitted. [Those who wear *tefillin* on Chol HaMoed remove them at this point before reciting *Hallel.*]

The *chazzan* recites the blessing. The congregation, after responding *Amen,* repeats it, and continues with the first psalm. Regarding the blessing for one praying alone, see *Laws* §37.

בָּרוּךְ *Blessed are You* H*ASHEM*, *our God, King of the universe, Who has sanctified us with His commandments and has commanded us to read the Hallel.* (Cong.— *Amen.)*

Psalm 113

הַלְלוּיָהּ *Halleluyah! Give praise, you servants of* H*ASHEM*;* *praise the Name of* H*ASHEM*! *Blessed be the Name of* H*ASHEM*, *from this time and forever. From the rising of the sun to its setting,* H*ASHEM*'s *Name is praised. High above all nations is* H*ASHEM*, *above the heavens is His glory. Who is like* H*ASHEM*, *our God, Who is enthroned on high — yet deigns to look upon the heaven and the earth?** Chazzan— *He raises the needy from the dust, from the trash heaps He lifts the destitute. To seat them with nobles,* with the nobles of His people. He transforms the barren wife* into a glad mother of children. Halleluyah!*

Psalm 114

בְּצֵאת *When Israel went out of Egypt,* Jacob's household from a people of alien tongue* — Judah became His sanctuary,* Israel His dominions. The sea saw and fled: the Jordan turned backward. The mountains skipped like rams,* the hills like young lambs.* Chazzan— *What ails you, O sea, that you flee? O Jordan, that you turn backward?* O mountains, that you skip*

---

heavens; but if we welcome His proximity, He lovingly involves Himself in every phase of our lives *(R' A.C. Feuer).*

לְהוֹשִׁיבִי עִם נְדִיבִים — *To seat them with nobles.* God does not merely lift the poor and needy out of degradation; He also elevates them to the highest ranks of nobility.

מוֹשִׁיבִי עֲקֶרֶת הַבַּיִת — *He transforms the barren wife.* The Creator exercises complete control over nature. This control is vividly demonstrated when God suddenly transforms a barren woman into a mother *(Radak).*

☙ **בְּצֵאת יִשְׂרָאֵל מִמִּצְרָיִם** — *When Israel went out of Egypt.* This second chapter of Hallel continues the theme of the first chapter, which praises God for raising up the needy and destitute. Israel was thus elevated when they left Egypt and risked their lives by entering the sea at God's command.

בֵּית יַעֲקֹב מֵעַם לֹעֵז — *Jacob's household from a people of alien tongue.* Even the Jews who were forced to communicate with the Egyptians in the language of the land did so only under duress. Among themselves, however, they spoke only the Holy Tongue and regarded Egyptian as a foreign language.

הָיְתָה יְהוּדָה לְקָדְשׁוֹ — *Judah became His sanctuary.* God singled out the tribe of Judah to be the family of royalty, because they sanctified God's Name at the Sea of Reeds. Led by their prince, Nachshon ben Aminadav, this tribe was the first to jump into the threatening waters *(Rosh).*

הֶהָרִים רָקְדוּ כְאֵילִים — *The mountains skipped like rams.* When Israel received the Torah, Sinai and the neighboring mountains and hills shook and trembled at the manifestation of God's Presence and the thunder and lightning that accompanied it.

מַה לְּךָ הַיָּם כִּי תָנוּס הַיַּרְדֵּן תִּסֹּב לְאָחוֹר — *What ails you, O sea, that you flee? O Jordan, that you turn backward?* The Psalmist captures the sense of awe and bewilderment which then seized mankind.

כְּאֵילִים, גְּבָעוֹת כִּבְנֵי צֹאן. מִלִּפְנֵי אָדוֹן חוּלִי אָרֶץ, מִלִּפְנֵי אֱלוֹהַּ יַעֲקֹב. הַהֹפְכִי הַצּוּר אֲגַם מָיִם,* חַלָּמִישׁ לְמַעְיְנוֹ מָיִם.

An abridged version of Hallel is recited on the last six days of Pesach* and on Rosh Chodesh.* On these days, omit the following paragraph and continue with ה' זְכָרָנוּ.

תהלים קטו:א-יא

לֹא לָנוּ* יהוה לֹא לָנוּ, כִּי לְשִׁמְךָ תֵּן כָּבוֹד,* עַל חַסְדְּךָ עַל אֲמִתֶּךָ. לָמָּה יֹאמְרוּ הַגּוֹיִם, אַיֵּה נָא אֱלֹהֵיהֶם. וֵאלֹהֵינוּ בַשָּׁמָיִם, כֹּל אֲשֶׁר חָפֵץ עָשָׂה. עֲצַבֵּיהֶם כֶּסֶף וְזָהָב, מַעֲשֵׂה יְדֵי אָדָם. פֶּה לָהֶם וְלֹא יְדַבֵּרוּ,* עֵינַיִם לָהֶם וְלֹא יִרְאוּ. אָזְנַיִם לָהֶם וְלֹא יִשְׁמָעוּ, אַף לָהֶם וְלֹא יְרִיחוּן. יְדֵיהֶם וְלֹא יְמִישׁוּן, רַגְלֵיהֶם וְלֹא יְהַלֵּכוּ, לֹא יֶהְגּוּ בִּגְרוֹנָם. כְּמוֹהֶם יִהְיוּ עֹשֵׂיהֶם, כֹּל אֲשֶׁר בֹּטֵחַ בָּהֶם. ❖ יִשְׂרָאֵל בְּטַח בַּיהוה,* עֶזְרָם וּמָגִנָּם הוּא.* בֵּית אַהֲרֹן בִּטְחוּ בַיהוה, עֶזְרָם וּמָגִנָּם הוּא. יִרְאֵי יהוה בִּטְחוּ בַיהוה, עֶזְרָם וּמָגִנָּם הוּא.

תהלים קטו:יב-יח

יהוה זְכָרָנוּ יְבָרֵךְ,* יְבָרֵךְ אֶת בֵּית יִשְׂרָאֵל, יְבָרֵךְ אֶת בֵּית אַהֲרֹן. יְבָרֵךְ יִרְאֵי יהוה, הַקְּטַנִּים עִם הַגְּדֹלִים. יֹסֵף יהוה עֲלֵיכֶם, עֲלֵיכֶם וְעַל בְּנֵיכֶם.* בְּרוּכִים אַתֶּם לַיהוה, עֹשֵׂה שָׁמַיִם וָאָרֶץ. ❖ הַשָּׁמַיִם שָׁמַיִם לַיהוה, וְהָאָרֶץ נָתַן

הַהֹפְכִי הַצּוּר אֲגַם מָיִם — *Who turns the rock into a pond of water.* When the Jews thirsted for water in the wilderness, God instructed Moses (*Exodus* 17:6), *'You shall smite the rock and water shall come out of it, so that the people may drink.'*

◆§ Abridged Hallel/ Pesach and Rosh Chodesh

The Talmud (*Arachin* 10b) teaches that a festival day with a *mussaf* offering different from that of the day before is cause for the recitation of the full *Hallel.* Each new offering is an indication of a new spiritual manifestation, which is commemorated through *Hallel.* On Succos, therefore, when each of the eight days has a different *mussaf* offering (see p. 682), the full *Hallel* is recited each day. On the other hand, the *mussaf* offering on Passover is identical every day; consequently, only the 'abridged' or 'half' *Hallel* is recited on the last six days.

Another reason the shorter version of *Hallel* is recited during the latter days of Pesach is that the Jewish people did not attain their full level of holiness until they accepted the Torah on Shavuos. To signify this incompleteness without the Torah, we abbreviate Hallel (*Sh'lah*).

The prophets did not ordain that *Hallel* be recited on Rosh Chodesh because it is neither a Festival nor a day on which a miracle occurred (*Arachin* 10b).

Nevertheless, the custom developed — first in Babylonia and later in *Eretz Yisrael* — to recite an abridged version on Rosh Chodesh (*Taanis* 28b). The commentators explain that *Hallel* alludes to the kingship of David and, as noted in the commentary to *Kiddush Levanah* (p. 612), Rosh Chodesh recalls the renewal of the Davidic dynasty. Nevertheless, in order to demonstrate that the *Hallel* of Rosh Chodesh is not of the same status as that of Festivals, an abridged version is recited.

In the abridged form, the first eleven verses of both *Psalms* 115 [לֹא לָנוּ] and *Psalm* 116 [אָהַבְתִּי] are omitted. The reason these two half-psalms were chosen to be skipped is that their general themes are repeated in their second halves [ה' זְכָרָנוּ and מָה אָשִׁיב], so nothing essential is lost by their omission (*Eliah Rabbah*).

◆§ **לֹא לָנוּ** — *Not for our sake.* The preceding psalm depicts the awe inspired by God's miracles. Here the Psalmist describes the aftermath of that inspiration. Although Israel remained imbued with faith, our oppressors soon

like rams? O hills, like young lambs? Before the Lord's Presence — did I, the earth, tremble — before the presence of the God of Jacob, Who turns the rock into a pond of water, the flint into a flowing fountain.*

An abridged version of Hallel is recited on the last six days of Pesach* and on Rosh Chodesh.* On these days, omit the following paragraph and continue with *'HASHEM Who has remembered ...'*

Psalms 115:1-11

לֹא לָנוּ *Not for our sake,* HASHEM, not for our sake, but for Your Name's sake give glory,* for Your kindness and for Your truth! Why should the nations say, 'Where is their God now?' Our God is in the heavens; whatever He pleases, He does! Their idols are silver and gold, the handiwork of man. They have a mouth, but cannot speak;* they have eyes, but cannot see. They have ears, but cannot hear; they have a nose, but cannot smell. Their hands — they cannot feel; their feet — they cannot walk; they cannot utter a sound from their throat. Those who make them should become like them, whoever trusts in them!* Chazzan— *O Israel, trust in HASHEM;* — their help and their shield is He!* House of Aaron, trust in HASHEM; their help and their shield is He! You who fear HASHEM, trust in HASHEM; their help and their shield is He!*

Psalm 115:12-18

יהוה *HASHEM Who has remembered us will bless* — He will bless the House of Israel; He will bless the House of Aaron; He will bless those who fear HASHEM, the small as well as the great. May HASHEM increase upon you, upon you and upon your children!* You are blessed of HASHEM, maker of heaven and earth.* Chazzan— *As for the heavens — the heavens are HASHEM's, but the earth He has given*

---

began to scoff, 'Where is their God?' We pray that God will intervene again in the affairs of man, not for our sake, but for His.

לֹא לָנוּ ה׳ ... כִּי לְשִׁמְךָ תֵּן כָּבוֹד — *Not for our sake, HASHEM ... but for Your Name's sake give glory.* We beg You to redeem us, but not because we are personally worthy, nor because of the merit of our forefathers *(Iyun Tefillah).* Rather we urgently strive to protect Your glorious Name, so that no one can deny Your mastery and dominion *(Radak).*

פֶּה לָהֶם וְלֹא יְדַבֵּרוּ — *They have a mouth, but cannot speak.* These illustrations emphasize the complete impotence of man-made idols, which even lack the senses that every ordinary man possesses.

יִשְׂרָאֵל בְּטַח בַּה׳ — *O Israel, trust in HASHEM.* The psalm now contrasts the Children of Israel, who trust in God alone, with those described in the previous verse, who trust in the lifeless and helpless idols *(Ibn Ezra).*

The Psalmist speaks of three kinds of Jews, each with a different motive for serving God. Some Jews cling to God simply because they feel that He is their Father, and they are His devoted sons. These are called יִשְׂרָאֵל, *Israel,* God's chosen, beloved nation. The second group serves God out of love. They resemble the *House of Aaron,* the *Kohanim*-priests who never betrayed God and were therefore designated to stand in His presence, in the Temple, for all time. Finally, *you who fear HASHEM* refers to a third group of Jews, who serve God out of fear and awe *(Maharal).*

עֶזְרָם וּמָגִנָּם הוּא — *Their help and their shield is He!* This is thrice repeated. Since each successive group possesses a different level of faith, it deserves a totally different degree of divine protection. Thus God's reaction to each group is mentioned separately.

☙ ה׳ זְכָרָנוּ יְבָרֵךְ — *HASHEM Who has remembered us will bless.* The Psalmist expresses confidence that just as God has blessed His people in the past, so He will bless them in the future.

יֹסֵף ה׳ עֲלֵיכֶם, עֲלֵיכֶם וְעַל בְּנֵיכֶם — *May HASHEM increase upon you, upon you and upon your children.* The true nature of בְּרָכָה, *blessing,* means increase and abundance *(Ibn Ezra).*

לִבְנֵי אָדָם.* לֹא הַמֵּתִים יְהַלְלוּ יָהּ,* וְלֹא כָּל יֹרְדֵי דוּמָה. וַאֲנַחְנוּ נְבָרֵךְ יָהּ, מֵעַתָּה וְעַד עוֹלָם, הַלְלוּיָהּ.

On Rosh Chodesh and on the last six days of Pesach, omit the following paragraph and continue with מָה אָשִׁיב.

תהלים קטז:א-יא

אָהַבְתִּי* כִּי יִשְׁמַע יהוה, אֶת קוֹלִי תַּחֲנוּנָי. כִּי הִטָּה אָזְנוֹ לִי, וּבְיָמַי אֶקְרָא. אֲפָפוּנִי חֶבְלֵי מָוֶת,* וּמְצָרֵי שְׁאוֹל מְצָאוּנִי, צָרָה וְיָגוֹן אֶמְצָא. וּבְשֵׁם יהוה אֶקְרָא, אָנָּה יהוה מַלְּטָה נַפְשִׁי. חַנּוּן יהוה וְצַדִּיק, וֵאלֹהֵינוּ מְרַחֵם. שֹׁמֵר פְּתָאִים יהוה, דַּלּוֹתִי וְלִי יְהוֹשִׁיעַ. שׁוּבִי נַפְשִׁי לִמְנוּחָיְכִי,* כִּי יהוה גָּמַל עָלָיְכִי. כִּי חִלַּצְתָּ נַפְשִׁי מִמָּוֶת, אֶת עֵינִי מִן דִּמְעָה, אֶת רַגְלִי מִדֶּחִי. ❖ אֶתְהַלֵּךְ לִפְנֵי יהוה, בְּאַרְצוֹת הַחַיִּים.* הֶאֱמַנְתִּי כִּי אֲדַבֵּר, אֲנִי עָנִיתִי מְאֹד. אֲנִי אָמַרְתִּי בְחָפְזִי, כָּל הָאָדָם כֹּזֵב.*

תהלים קטז:יב-יט

מָה אָשִׁיב לַיהוה,* כָּל תַּגְמוּלוֹהִי עָלָי. כּוֹס יְשׁוּעוֹת אֶשָּׂא,* וּבְשֵׁם יהוה אֶקְרָא. נְדָרַי לַיהוה אֲשַׁלֵּם,* נֶגְדָה נָּא לְכָל עַמּוֹ. יָקָר בְּעֵינֵי יהוה, הַמָּוְתָה לַחֲסִידָיו. אָנָּה יהוה כִּי אֲנִי עַבְדֶּךָ, אֲנִי עַבְדְּךָ, בֶּן אֲמָתֶךָ,* פִּתַּחְתָּ לְמוֹסֵרָי.

Abarbanel explains that the Psalmist foresaw that Israel would suffer from attrition in exile and they would fear eventual extinction. Therefore, he offers the assurance that, at the advent of Messiah, their numbers will increase dramatically.

הַשָּׁמַיִם שָׁמַיִם לַה׳, וְהָאָרֶץ נָתַן לִבְנֵי אָדָם — *As for the heavens — the heavens are HASHEM's, but the earth He has given to mankind.* Since the heavens remain under God's firm control, all celestial bodies are forced to act in accordance with His will without freedom of choice. On earth, however, man was granted the freedom to determine his own actions and beliefs *(Maharit).*

Many commentators explain this verse homiletically. Man need not perfect heaven because it is already dedicated to the holiness of God. But the earth is man's province. We are bidden to perfect it and transform its material nature into something spiritual. Indeed, we were created to make the earth heavenly.

לֹא הַמֵּתִים יְהַלְלוּ יָהּ — *Neither the dead can praise God.* The people who fail to recognize God's omnipresence and influence over the world resemble the dead, who are insensitive to all external stimuli and who are oblivious to reality *(R' Azariah Figo).* However, the souls of the righteous continue to praise God even after they depart from their bodies *(Ibn Ezra).*

A dried-out, bleached, or brittle *lulav* is invalid for use during the Festival of Succos, because the *lulav* symbolizes the human spine, which enables man to lead an active life. Thus the *lulav* must be fresh and supple, for the dead cannot praise God *(Yalkut Shimoni* 873).

☙ אָהַבְתִּי — *I love* [*Him*]. The Psalmist foresaw that Israel would feel completely alone in exile. The nations would taunt them, 'Your prayers and pleas are worthless, because God has turned a deaf ear to you.' Therefore, he composed this psalm to encourage the downcast exiles with the assurance that indeed: *HASHEM hears my voice, my supplications.*

The Talmud *(Rosh Hashanah* 16b-17a) explains that this psalm describes the day of Final Judgment at the time of תְּחִיַּת הַמֵּתִים, *the Resurrection of the Dead.* The average people, who are neither completely righteous nor completely wicked, will be saved from Gehinnom because God will hear their cries, and He will forgive them. In gratitude, they will sing, *'I love Him, for HASHEM hears my voice, my supplications.'*

חֶבְלֵי מָוֶת — *The pains of death.* This is an apt

to mankind. Neither the dead can praise God,* nor any who descend into silence; but we will bless God from this time and forever. Halleluyah!*

On Rosh Chodesh and on the last six days of Pesach, omit the following paragraph and continue with *'How can I repay ...'*

Psalm 116:1-11

אָהַבְתִּי *I love Him,* for HASHEM hears my voice, my supplications. As He has inclined His ear to me, so in my days shall I call. The pains of death* encircled me; the confines of the grave have found me; trouble and sorrow I would find. Then I would invoke the Name of HASHEM: 'Please HASHEM, save my soul.' Gracious is HASHEM and righteous, our God is merciful. HASHEM protects the simple; I was brought low, but He saved me. Return, my soul, to your rest;* for HASHEM has been kind to you. For You have delivered my soul from death, my eyes from tears, my feet from stumbling.* Chazzan— *I shall walk before HASHEM in the lands of the living.* I have kept faith although I say: 'I suffer exceedingly.' I said in my haste: 'All mankind is deceitful.'**

Psalm 116:12-19

מָה אָשִׁיב *How can I repay HASHEM* for all His kindness to me? I will raise the cup of salvations* and the Name of HASHEM I will invoke. My vows to HASHEM I will pay,* in the presence, now, of His entire people. Difficult in the eyes of HASHEM is the death of His devout ones. Please, HASHEM — for I am Your servant, I am Your servant, son of Your handmaid* — You have released my bonds.*

---

description of the exile, when Israel is encircled by violent enemies who seek to kill them *(Abarbanel).*

שׁוּבִי נַפְשִׁי לִמְנוּחָיְכִי — *Return, my soul, to your rest.* When misery and persecution upset me, I told my soul that it would find peace and comfort only if it would *return* to God *(Radak).*

אֶתְהַלֵּךְ לִפְנֵי ה׳ בְּאַרְצוֹת הַחַיִּים — *I shall walk before HASHEM in the lands of the living.* How I yearn to return to *Eretz Yisrael* where the very air makes men healthy and robust and the holy atmosphere grants the mind renewed vitality and alertness! *(Radak). Eretz Yisrael* is identified as the *land of the living* because the dead are destined to be resurrected there. This is why the Patriarchs and the righteous of all generations yearned to be buried there.

אֲנִי אָמַרְתִּי בְחָפְזִי כָּל הָאָדָם כֹּזֵב — *I said in my haste: 'All mankind is deceitful.'* This bitter comment was originally uttered by David when the people of Zif betrayed his hiding place to King Saul [see *I Samuel* 23:19-29] *(Rashi).* It is also a reference to the bleak, dismal exile [for the exile discourages the Jews and leads them to the hasty, premature conclusion that all the prophets' promises concerning redemption were *deceitful*] *(Abarbanel).*

☙ מָה אָשִׁיב לַה׳ — *How can I repay HASHEM?* What gift can I give to the King who owns everything? *(Ibn Ezra).* How can I possibly repay His acts of kindness for they are too numerous to recount? *(Radak).* How can I even approach Him? He is eternal and I am finite; He is the highest, and I am the lowest! *(Ibn Yachya).*

כּוֹס יְשׁוּעוֹת אֶשָּׂא — *I will raise the cup of salvations.* This refers to the wine libations that will accompany the thanksgiving offerings of the returning exiles *(Rashi).*

נְדָרַי לַה׳ אֲשַׁלֵּם — *My vows to HASHEM I will pay.* As I was fleeing and wandering in exile, I vowed that if God would return me safely to *Eretz Yisrael,* I would render thanksgiving offerings to His Name; now I will make good on my vows *(Radak).*

אֲנִי עַבְדְּךָ בֶּן אֲמָתֶךָ — *I am Your servant, son of Your handmaid.* The slave who is born to a *handmaid* is far more submissive than a slave who was born free *(Rashi).* The former serves his master naturally and instinctively, whereas the

❖ לְךָ אֶזְבַּח זֶבַח תּוֹדָה, וּבְשֵׁם יהוה אֶקְרָא. נְדָרַי לַיהוה אֲשַׁלֵּם, נֶגְדָה נָּא לְכָל עַמּוֹ. בְּחַצְרוֹת בֵּית יהוה, בְּתוֹכֵכִי יְרוּשָׁלָיִם הַלְלוּיָהּ.

Congregation, then *chazzan:*

תהלים קיז

הַלְלוּ אֶת יהוה,* כָּל גּוֹיִם, שַׁבְּחוּהוּ כָּל הָאֻמִּים.* כִּי גָבַר עָלֵינוּ חַסְדּוֹ,* וֶאֱמֶת יהוה לְעוֹלָם, הַלְלוּיָהּ.

Each of the following four verses is recited aloud by the *chazzan.* After each verse, the congregation responds הוֹדוּ לַה׳ כִּי טוֹב, כִּי לְעוֹלָם חַסְדּוֹ, and then recites the succeeding verse. On Succos, the Four Species are waved. See page 631.

תהלים קיח

הוֹדוּ לַיהוה כִּי טוֹב,* כִּי לְעוֹלָם חַסְדּוֹ.

יֹאמַר נָא יִשְׂרָאֵל, כִּי לְעוֹלָם חַסְדּוֹ.

יֹאמְרוּ נָא בֵית אַהֲרֹן, כִּי לְעוֹלָם חַסְדּוֹ.

יֹאמְרוּ נָא יִרְאֵי יהוה, כִּי לְעוֹלָם חַסְדּוֹ.

מִן הַמֵּצַר* קָרָאתִי יָּהּ, עָנָנִי בַמֶּרְחָב יָהּ. יהוה לִי לֹא אִירָא, מַה יַּעֲשֶׂה לִי אָדָם. יהוה לִי בְּעֹזְרָי,* וַאֲנִי אֶרְאֶה בְשֹׂנְאָי. טוֹב לַחֲסוֹת בַּיהוה, מִבְּטֹחַ בָּאָדָם.* טוֹב לַחֲסוֹת בַּיהוה, מִבְּטֹחַ בִּנְדִיבִים. כָּל גּוֹיִם סְבָבוּנִי, בְּשֵׁם יהוה כִּי אֲמִילַם. סַבּוּנִי גַם סְבָבוּנִי, בְּשֵׁם יהוה כִּי אֲמִילַם. סַבּוּנִי כִדְבֹרִים דֹּעֲכוּ כְּאֵשׁ קוֹצִים, בְּשֵׁם יהוה כִּי אֲמִילַם. דָּחֹה דְחִיתַנִי לִנְפֹּל, וַיהוה עֲזָרָנִי.* עָזִּי וְזִמְרָת יָהּ, וַיְהִי לִי לִישׁוּעָה. קוֹל רִנָּה וִישׁוּעָה בְּאָהֳלֵי צַדִּיקִים,* יְמִין יהוה עֹשָׂה חָיִל. יְמִין

---

latter serves him only in response to external threats *(Sforno).*

❧ הַלְלוּ אֶת ה׳ — *Praise* HASHEM. This psalm, containing only two verses, is the shortest chapter in all of Scripture. *Radak* explains that its brevity symbolizes the simplicity of the world order which will prevail after the advent of the Messiah.

גּוֹיִם ... הָאֻמִּים — *Nations ... the states.* הָאֻמִּים, *the states,* is written with the definite article, whereas גּוֹיִם, *nations,* is spelled without it. This teaches that הָאֻמִּים refers to large nations that are well known and powerful; whereas גּוֹיִם refers to small, backward nations that have no prominence *(Iyun Tefillah).*

כִּי גָבַר עָלֵינוּ חַסְדּוֹ — *For His kindness has overwhelmed us.* Why should non-Jewish peoples and nations praise God for overwhelming Israel with Divine kindness? Israel will merit God's kindness because of the extraordinary service they rendered to Him. Recognizing Israel's distinction, the nations will consider it a privilege to become subservient to God's chosen ones, and will praise Him for His kindness to the Jews *(Yaavetz Hadoresh).*

❧ הוֹדוּ לַה׳ כִּי טוֹב — *Give thanks to* HASHEM, *for He is good.* This is a general expression of thanks to God. No matter what occurs, God is always good and everything He does is for the best, even though this may not be immediately apparent to man *(Abarbanel).*

❧ מִן הַמֵּצַר — *From the straits.* This psalm expresses gratitude and confidence. Just as David himself was catapulted from his personal straits to a reign marked by accomplishment and glory, so too Israel can look forward to Divine

Chazzan— *To You I will sacrifice thanksgiving offerings, and the name of HASHEM I will invoke. My vows to HASHEM I will pay, in the presence, now, of His entire people. In the courtyards of the House of HASHEM, in your midst, O Jerusalem, Halleluyah!*

Congregation, then *chazzan:*

Psalm 117

הַלְלוּ *Praise HASHEM,* all nations; praise Him, all the states!* For His kindness has overwhelmed us,* and the truth of HASHEM is eternal, Halleluyah!*

Each of the following four verses is recited aloud by the *chazzan*. After each verse, the congregation responds, *'Give thanks to HASHEM for He is good; His kindness endures forever,'* and then recites the succeeding verse.

On Succos, the Four Species are waved. See page 631.

Psalm 118

הוֹדוּ *Give thanks to HASHEM for He is good;**	*His kindness endures forever!*
Let Israel say:	*His kindness endures forever!*
Let the House of Aaron say:	*His kindness endures forever!*
Let those who fear HASHEM say:	*His kindness endures forever!*

מִן הַמֵּצַר *From the straits* did I call upon God; God answered me with expansiveness. HASHEM is with me, I have no fear; how can man affect me? HASHEM is with me through my helpers;* therefore I can face my foes. It is better to take refuge in HASHEM than to rely on man.* It is better to take refuge in HASHEM than to rely on nobles. All the nations surround me; in the Name of HASHEM I cut them down! They encircle me, they also surround me; in the Name of HASHEM, I cut them down! They encircle me like bees, but they are extinguished as a fire does thorns; in the Name of HASHEM I cut them down! You pushed me hard that I might fall, but HASHEM assisted me.* God is my might and my praise, and He was a salvation for me. The sound of rejoicing and salvation is in the tents of the righteous:* 'HASHEM's right hand does valiantly. HASHEM's right hand*

---

redemption from the straits of exile and oppression.

ה׳ לִי בְּעֹזְרָי — *HASHEM is with me, through my helpers.* I have many helpers, but I place confidence in them only because HASHEM is with them. If my helpers were not granted strength by God, their assistance would be futile *(Ibn Ezra; Radak).*

טוֹב לַחֲסוֹת בַּה׳ מִבְּטֹחַ בָּאָדָם — *It is better to take refuge in HASHEM than to rely on man.* חִסָּיוֹן, here translated *taking refuge,* denotes absolute confidence even though no guarantees have been given; בִּטָּחוֹן, *reliance,* however, presupposes a promise of protection. The Psalmist says that it is far better to put one's trust in God's protection, even without a pledge from Him, than to rely on the most profuse assurances of human beings *(R' Bachya; Vilna Gaon).*

דָּחֹה דְחִיתַנִי לִנְפֹּל וַה׳ עֲזָרָנִי — *You pushed me hard that I might fall, but HASHEM assisted me.* In the preceding verses, the Psalmist speaks of his enemy indirectly; now, however, he addresses the foe directly.

קוֹל רִנָּה וִישׁוּעָה בְּאָהֳלֵי צַדִּיקִים — *The sound of rejoicing and salvation is in the tents of the righteous.* When HASHEM's right hand does valiantly for the sake of His chosen people, then the righteous will respond by filling their tents with sounds of rejoicing over this salvation *(Radak).*

יהוה רוֹמֵמָה, יְמִין יהוה עֹשָׂה חָיִל. לֹא אָמוּת כִּי אֶחְיֶה, וַאֲסַפֵּר מַעֲשֵׂי יָהּ.* יַסֹּר יִסְּרַנִּי יָּהּ, וְלַמָּוֶת לֹא נְתָנָנִי.* ❖ פִּתְחוּ לִי שַׁעֲרֵי צֶדֶק, אָבֹא בָם אוֹדֶה יָהּ. זֶה הַשַּׁעַר לַיהוה, צַדִּיקִים יָבֹאוּ בוֹ. (—Each of the following four verses is recited twice.) אוֹדְךָ* כִּי עֲנִיתָנִי, וַתְּהִי לִי לִישׁוּעָה. אֶבֶן מָאֲסוּ הַבּוֹנִים, הָיְתָה לְרֹאשׁ פִּנָּה.* מֵאֵת יהוה הָיְתָה זֹּאת, הִיא נִפְלָאת בְּעֵינֵינוּ.* זֶה הַיּוֹם עָשָׂה יהוה, נָגִילָה וְנִשְׂמְחָה בוֹ.

The next four lines are recited responsively — *chazzan,* then congregation.
On Succos, the Four Species are waved during the next two verses. See page 631.

אָנָּא יהוה הוֹשִׁיעָה נָּא.
אָנָּא יהוה הוֹשִׁיעָה נָּא.
אָנָּא יהוה הַצְלִיחָה נָא.
אָנָּא יהוה הַצְלִיחָה נָא.

Each of the following four verses is recited twice:
On Succos, the Four Species are waved each time the verse הודו is recited. See page 631.

בָּרוּךְ הַבָּא בְּשֵׁם יהוה, בֵּרַכְנוּכֶם מִבֵּית יהוה. אֵל יהוה וַיָּאֶר לָנוּ, אִסְרוּ חַג בַּעֲבֹתִים, עַד קַרְנוֹת הַמִּזְבֵּחַ. אֵלִי אַתָּה וְאוֹדֶךָּ, אֱלֹהַי אֲרוֹמְמֶךָּ. הוֹדוּ לַיהוה כִּי טוֹב, כִּי לְעוֹלָם חַסְדּוֹ.

יְהַלְלוּךָ יהוה אֱלֹהֵינוּ כָּל מַעֲשֶׂיךָ,* וַחֲסִידֶיךָ צַדִּיקִים* עוֹשֵׂי רְצוֹנֶךָ,* וְכָל עַמְּךָ בֵּית יִשְׂרָאֵל בְּרִנָּה יוֹדוּ וִיבָרְכוּ וִישַׁבְּחוּ וִיפָאֲרוּ וִירוֹמְמוּ וְיַעֲרִיצוּ וְיַקְדִּישׁוּ וְיַמְלִיכוּ אֶת

לֹא אָמוּת כִּי אֶחְיֶה וַאֲסַפֵּר מַעֲשֵׂי יָהּ — *I shall not die! But I shall live and relate the deeds of God.* I will survive the assassination attempts of my enemies and live to recount the deeds of God, Who saved me from my foes *(Radak).*

יַסֹּר יִסְּרַנִּי יָּהּ וְלַמָּוֶת לֹא נְתָנָנִי — *God has chastened me exceedingly, but He did not let me die.* Throughout the duration of the exile, I survived because whatever suffering God decreed was only to atone for my sins *(Rashi).*

זֶה הַשַּׁעַר לַה׳ צַדִּיקִים יָבֹאוּ בוֹ — *This is the gate of HASHEM; the righteous shall enter through it.* This refers to the gate of the Temple. When the exile is over, the righteous will enter through this gate, and they will thank God for answering their plea for redemption *(Targum; Rashi).*

Repetition of Verses

אוֹדְךָ — *I thank You.* From this point until the end of the Scriptural part of *Hallel* — i.e., the nine verses until יְהַלְלוּךָ — each verse is recited twice.

This entire psalm, which begins with הוֹדוּ לַה׳, *Give thanks to HASHEM,* follows a pattern, namely, that each new theme is repeated in the next verse or two in the same or slightly different words. Therefore the custom was introduced to follow through on this repetition by repeating each of these verses as well *(Rashi* to *Succah* 38a).

Another reason for repeating each verse is based upon the Talmud *(Pesachim* 119a) which relates that these verses were recited in a responsive dialogue between Samuel, Jesse, David, and David's brothers when the prophet announced that the young shepherd would be the future king of Israel. To honor these distinguished personages, we repeat each one's statement, as if it were a full chapter.

is raised triumphantly; HASHEM's right hand does valiantly!' I shall not die! But I shall live and relate the deeds of God. God has chastened me exceedingly, but He did not let me die.** Chazzan— *Open for me the gates of righteousness, I will enter them and thank God. This is the gate of HASHEM; the righteous shall enter through it.** (Each of the following four verses is recited twice—) *I thank You* for You have answered me and become my salvation. The stone the builders despised has become the cornerstone.* This emanated from HASHEM; it is wondrous in our eyes.* This is the day HASHEM has made; let us rejoice and be glad on it.*

The next four lines are recited responsively — *chazzan,* then congregation.
On Succos, the Four Species are waved during the next two verses. See page 631.

אָנָּא *Please, HASHEM, save now!*
Please, HASHEM, save now!
Please, HASHEM, bring success now!
Please, HASHEM, bring success now!

Each of the following four verses is recited twice:
On Succos, the Four Species are waved each time *'Give thanks ...,'* is recited. See page 631.

בָּרוּךְ *Blessed is he who comes in the Name of HASHEM; we bless you from the House of HASHEM. HASHEM is God, He illuminated for us; bind the festival offering with cords until the corners of the Altar. You are my God, and I will thank You; my God, I will exalt You. Give thanks to HASHEM, for He is good; His kindness endures forever.*

יְהַלְלוּךָ *All Your works shall praise You,* HASHEM our God. And Your devout ones, the righteous,* who do Your will,* and Your entire people, the House of Israel, with glad song will thank, bless, praise, glorify, exalt, extol, sanctify, and proclaim the*

אֶבֶן מָאֲסוּ הַבּוֹנִים הָיְתָה לְרֹאשׁ פִּנָּה — *The stone the builders despised has become the cornerstone.* This verse refers to David, who was rejected by his own father and brothers *(Targum).* When the prophet Samuel announced that one of Jesse's sons was to be anointed king, no one even thought of summoning David, who was out with the sheep [see *I Samuel* 16:4-13].

Israel too is called אֶבֶן, *stone (Genesis* 49:24), for Israel is the cornerstone of God's design for the world. The world endures only by virtue of Israel's observance of God's laws, a fact that has influenced all nations to appreciate and accept certain aspects of God's commands. If not for the order and meaning that Israel has brought to the world, it would long ago have sunk into chaos. But the builders, i.e., the rulers of the nations, despised the Jews, claiming that they were parasites who made no contribution to the common good. When the dawn of redemption arrives, however, all nations will realize that Israel is indeed the cornerstone of the world *(Radak).*

מֵאֵת ה׳ הָיְתָה זֹּאת · הִיא נִפְלָאת בְּעֵינֵינוּ — *This emanated from HASHEM; it is wondrous in our eyes.* When David was crowned, all were amazed. But David said, 'This is even more surprising and wondrous to me than it is to anyone else!'

Similarly, when Israel is catapulted to glory and tranquillity in the future, the nations who persecuted the Jews will ask in surprise, 'Aren't these the very Jews who were once despised and afflicted?'

The Jews will respond, 'We are even more amazed than you are, for only we know the depths of degradation we suffered!'

Then a heavenly voice will proclaim, 'This has emanated from HASHEM!'

⁂ יְהַלְלוּךָ ... כָּל מַעֲשֶׂיךָ — *All Your works shall praise You.* This paragraph is not part of Psalms,

שִׁמְךָ מַלְכֵּנוּ, ❖ כִּי לְךָ טוֹב לְהוֹדוֹת וּלְשִׁמְךָ נָאֶה לְזַמֵּר, כִּי מֵעוֹלָם וְעַד עוֹלָם אַתָּה אֵל. בָּרוּךְ אַתָּה יהוה, מֶלֶךְ מְהֻלָּל בַּתִּשְׁבָּחוֹת. (.Cong.— אָמֵן)

On Rosh Chodesh many people recite the following verse after Hallel:

וְאַבְרָהָם זָקֵן בָּא בַּיָּמִים, וַיהוה בֵּרַךְ אֶת אַבְרָהָם בַּכֹּל.[1]

The *chazzan* recites *Kaddish:*

יִתְגַּדַּל וְיִתְקַדַּשׁ שְׁמֵהּ רַבָּא. (.Cong.— אָמֵן) בְּעָלְמָא דִּי בְרָא כִרְעוּתֵהּ. וְיַמְלִיךְ מַלְכוּתֵהּ, בְּחַיֵּיכוֹן וּבְיוֹמֵיכוֹן וּבְחַיֵּי דְכָל בֵּית יִשְׂרָאֵל, בַּעֲגָלָא וּבִזְמַן קָרִיב. וְאִמְרוּ: אָמֵן.

(.Cong.— אָמֵן. יְהֵא שְׁמֵהּ רַבָּא מְבָרַךְ לְעָלַם וּלְעָלְמֵי עָלְמַיָּא.)

יְהֵא שְׁמֵהּ רַבָּא מְבָרַךְ לְעָלַם וּלְעָלְמֵי עָלְמַיָּא.

יִתְבָּרַךְ וְיִשְׁתַּבַּח וְיִתְפָּאַר וְיִתְרוֹמַם וְיִתְנַשֵּׂא וְיִתְהַדָּר וְיִתְעַלֶּה וְיִתְהַלָּל שְׁמֵהּ דְּקֻדְשָׁא בְּרִיךְ הוּא (.Cong.— בְּרִיךְ הוּא) — לְעֵֽלָּא מִן כָּל בִּרְכָתָא וְשִׁירָתָא תֻּשְׁבְּחָתָא וְנֶחֱמָתָא, דַּאֲמִירָן בְּעָלְמָא. וְאִמְרוּ: אָמֵן. (.Cong.— אָמֵן)

During Chanukah (except on the Sabbath or Rosh Chodesh), the *Kaddish* ends here.
At other times, *Kaddish* continues:

(.Cong.— קַבֵּל בְּרַחֲמִים וּבְרָצוֹן אֶת תְּפִלָּתֵנוּ)

תִּתְקַבֵּל צְלוֹתְהוֹן וּבָעוּתְהוֹן דְּכָל בֵּית יִשְׂרָאֵל קֳדָם אֲבוּהוֹן דִּי בִשְׁמַיָּא. וְאִמְרוּ: אָמֵן. (.Cong.— אָמֵן)

(.Cong.— יְהִי שֵׁם יהוה מְבֹרָךְ, מֵעַתָּה וְעַד עוֹלָם.[2])

יְהֵא שְׁלָמָא רַבָּא מִן שְׁמַיָּא, וְחַיִּים עָלֵינוּ וְעַל כָּל יִשְׂרָאֵל. וְאִמְרוּ: אָמֵן. (.Cong.— אָמֵן)

(.Cong.— עֶזְרִי מֵעִם יהוה, עֹשֵׂה שָׁמַיִם וָאָרֶץ.[3])

Take three steps back. Bow left and say ... עֹשֶׂה; bow right and say ... הוּא; bow forward and say וְעַל כָּל ... אָמֵן. Remain standing in place for a few moments, then take three steps forward.

עֹשֶׂה שָׁלוֹם בִּמְרוֹמָיו, הוּא יַעֲשֶׂה שָׁלוֹם עָלֵינוּ, וְעַל כָּל יִשְׂרָאֵל. וְאִמְרוּ: אָמֵן. (.Cong.— אָמֵן)

The service continues with the Torah reading.
On Festivals, Hoshana Rabbah and the Sabbath, turn to page 432. At other times, turn to page 138.
On Seder night the service continues with עָלֵינוּ (p. 350).

---

but is a concluding blessing that sums up the broad theme of *Hallel* — that Israel and the entire universe will join in praising God. *All Your works shall praise You* means that in the perfect world of the future, the entire universe, including the vast variety of human beings, will function harmoniously according to God's will. This is the highest form of praise, for without it all the beautiful spoken and sung words and songs of praise are insincere and meaningless.

וַחֲסִידֶיךָ צַדִּיקִים — *Your devout ones, the righteous.* The word חָסִיד, *devout one,* refers to one who serves God beyond the minimum requirement of the Halachah. The word is derived from חֶסֶד, *kindness,* as if to say that such people do acts of

sovereignty of Your Name, our King. Chazzan— *For to You it is fitting to give thanks, and unto Your Name it is proper to sing praises, for from This World to the World to Come You are God. Blessed are You* HASHEM, *the King Who is lauded with praises.* (Cong.— *Amen.)*

On Rosh Chodesh many people recite the following verse after Hallel:

Now Abraham was old, well on in years, and HASHEM *had blessed Abraham with everything.*[1]

The chazzan recites *Kaddish:*

יִתְגַּדַּל *May His great Name grow exalted and sanctified* (Cong.— *Amen.*) *in the world that He created as He willed. May He give reign to His kingship in your lifetimes and in your days, and in the lifetimes of the entire Family of Israel, swiftly and soon. Now respond: Amen.*

(Cong.— *Amen. May His great Name be blessed forever and ever.)*

May His great Name be blessed forever and ever.

Blessed, praised, glorified, exalted, extolled, mighty, upraised, and lauded be the Name of the Holy One, Blessed is He (Cong.— *Blessed is He*) — *beyond any blessing and song, praise and consolation that are uttered in the world. Now respond: Amen.* (Cong.—*Amen.)*

During Chanukah (except on the Sabbath or Rosh Chodesh), the *Kaddish* ends here.
At other times *Kaddish* continues:

(Cong.— Accept our prayers with mercy and favor.)

May the prayers and supplications of the entire Family of Israel be accepted before their Father Who is in Heaven. Now respond: Amen. (Cong.— *Amen.*)

(Cong.— *Blessed be the Name of* HASHEM, *from this time and forever.*[2])

May there be abundant peace from Heaven, and life, upon us and upon all Israel. Now respond: Amen. (Cong.— *Amen.*)

(Cong.— *My help is from* HASHEM, *Maker of heaven and earth.*[3])

Take three steps back. Bow left and say, *'He Who makes peace ...';*
bow right and say, *'may He ...';* bow forward and say, *'and upon all Israel ...'*
Remain standing in place for a few moments, then take three steps forward.

He Who makes peace in His heights, may He make peace upon us, and upon all Israel. Now respond: Amen. (Cong.— *Amen.)*

The service continues with the Torah reading.
On Festivals, Hoshana Rabbah and the Sabbath, turn to page 432. At other times, turn to page 138.

On Seder night the *chazzan* recites Kiddush (p. 658), followed by עָלֵינוּ, *'it is our duty'* (p. 350).

(1) *Genesis* 24:1. (2) *Psalms* 113:2. (3) 121:2.

kindness for God's sake. They serve as an example for the *righteous* people, who fulfill all the requirements of the Law, and for the masses of Israel, whose goal is to serve God, even though they may not equal the spiritual accomplishments of the *devout* and the *righteous.*

עוֹשֵׂי רְצוֹנֶךָ — *Who do Your will.* In an inspiring homiletical interpretation, *Yismach Yisrael* interprets that the good deeds of the righteous can remake God's will, as it were. In other words, when Jews serve Him properly, God responds by lavishing kindness and a sense of fulfillment upon the world. Then, *Hallel* will become not only a song of thanksgiving for the miracles of the past, but also a song of praise for the longed-for redemption.

מוסף לראש חדש

Tefillin must be removed before *Mussaf.* (It is preferable that they be removed after *Kaddish*). This should be done quickly and the *tefillin* should not be rolled up in order not to cause undue delay between *Kaddish* and *Mussaf.* Since the *minyan* should begin *Shemoneh Esrei* together, it is advisable that someone signal the congregation to begin the silent *Shemoneh Esrei* in unison.

Take three steps backward, then three steps forward. Remain standing with the feet together while reciting *Shemoneh Esrei.* It should be recited with quiet devotion and without any interruption, verbal or otherwise. Although it should not be audible to others, one must pray loudly enough to hear himself. See *Laws* §61-90 for a brief summary of its laws, including how to rectify the omission of phrases that are added at particular times of the year.

כִּי שֵׁם יהוה אֶקְרָא, הָבוּ גֹדֶל לֵאלֹהֵינוּ.[1]
אֲדֹנָי שְׂפָתַי תִּפְתָּח, וּפִי יַגִּיד תְּהִלָּתֶךָ.[2]

אבות

Bend the knees at בָּרוּךְ; bow at אַתָּה; straighten up at 'ה.

בָּרוּךְ אַתָּה יהוה אֱלֹהֵינוּ וֵאלֹהֵי אֲבוֹתֵינוּ, אֱלֹהֵי אַבְרָהָם, אֱלֹהֵי יִצְחָק, וֵאלֹהֵי יַעֲקֹב, הָאֵל הַגָּדוֹל הַגִּבּוֹר וְהַנּוֹרָא, אֵל עֶלְיוֹן, גּוֹמֵל חֲסָדִים טוֹבִים וְקוֹנֵה הַכֹּל, וְזוֹכֵר חַסְדֵי אָבוֹת, וּמֵבִיא גוֹאֵל לִבְנֵי בְנֵיהֶם, לְמַעַן שְׁמוֹ בְּאַהֲבָה.

Bend the knees at בָּרוּךְ; bow at אַתָּה; straighten up at 'ה.

מֶלֶךְ עוֹזֵר וּמוֹשִׁיעַ וּמָגֵן. בָּרוּךְ אַתָּה יהוה, מָגֵן אַבְרָהָם.

גבורות

אַתָּה גִּבּוֹר לְעוֹלָם אֲדֹנָי, מְחַיֵּה מֵתִים אַתָּה, רַב לְהוֹשִׁיעַ.

Between Succos and Pesach add:

מַשִּׁיב הָרוּחַ וּמוֹרִיד °הַגֶּשֶׁם [some say – °הַגָּשֶׁם].

[If forgotten, see *Laws* §70-75.]

מְכַלְכֵּל חַיִּים בְּחֶסֶד, מְחַיֵּה מֵתִים בְּרַחֲמִים רַבִּים, סוֹמֵךְ נוֹפְלִים, וְרוֹפֵא חוֹלִים, וּמַתִּיר אֲסוּרִים, וּמְקַיֵּם אֱמוּנָתוֹ לִישֵׁנֵי עָפָר. מִי כָמוֹךָ בַּעַל גְּבוּרוֹת, וּמִי דּוֹמֶה לָּךְ, מֶלֶךְ מֵמִית וּמְחַיֶּה וּמַצְמִיחַ יְשׁוּעָה. וְנֶאֱמָן אַתָּה לְהַחֲיוֹת מֵתִים. בָּרוּךְ אַתָּה יהוה, מְחַיֵּה הַמֵּתִים.

◈§ Mussaf

The *Mussaf* [lit. additional] prayer commemorates the special communal offering that was brought on Rosh Chodesh (*Numbers* 28:11-15) to mark its special holiness. Commentary to the beginning of *Shemoneh Esrei* may be found on pp. 98-102.

Such authors as *Sh'lah* and *Yesod V'Shoresh HaAvodah* attach special importance to the need for repentance and intense concentration during *Mussaf.* As the text of *Mussaf* says, Rosh

MUSSAF OF ROSH CHODESH

Tefillin must be removed before *Mussaf.* (It is preferable that they be removed after *Kaddish.*) This should be done quickly and the *tefillin* should not be rolled up in order not to cause undue delay between *Kaddish* and *Mussaf.* Since the *minyan* should begin *Shemoneh Esrei* together, it is advisable that someone signal the congregation to begin the silent *Shemoneh Esrei* in unison.

Take three steps backward, then three steps forward. Remain standing with the feet together while reciting *Shemoneh Esrei.* It should be recited with quiet devotion and without any interruption, verbal or otherwise. Although it should not be audible to others, one must pray loudly enough to hear himself. See *Laws* §61-90 for a brief summary of its laws, including how to rectify the omission of phrases that are added at particular times of the year.

When I call out the Name of HASHEM, ascribe greatness to our God.[1]
My Lord, open my lips, that my mouth may declare Your praise.[2]

PATRIARCHS

Bend the knees at *'Blessed'*; bow at *'You'*; straighten up at *'HASHEM'*.

בָּרוּךְ *Blessed are You, HASHEM, our God and the God of our forefathers, God of Abraham, God of Isaac, and God of Jacob; the great, mighty, and awesome God, the supreme God, Who bestows beneficial kindnesses and creates everything, Who recalls the kindnesses of the Patriarchs and brings a Redeemer to their children's children, for His Name's sake, with love.*

Bend the knees at *'Blessed'*; bow at *'You'*; straighten up at 'HASHEM.'

O King, Helper, Savior, and Shield. Blessed are You, HASHEM, Shield of Abraham.

GOD'S MIGHT

אַתָּה *You are eternally mighty, my Lord, the Resuscitator of the dead are You; abundantly able to save,*

Between Succos and Pesach add the following.

Who makes the wind blow and makes the rain descend;

[If forgotten, see *Laws* §70-75.]

Who sustains the living with kindness, resuscitates the dead with abundant mercy, supports the fallen, heals the sick, releases the confined, and maintains His faith to those asleep in the dust. Who is like You, O Master of mighty deeds, and who is comparable to You, O King Who causes death and restores life and makes salvation sprout! And You are faithful to resuscitate the dead. Blessed are You, HASHEM, Who resuscitates the dead.

(1) *Deuteronomy* 32:3. (2) *Psalms* 51:17.

Chodesh is a זְמַן כַּפָּרָה, *time of atonement.* The fact that the prayer commemorates a Temple offering that we cannot now offer makes it incumbent upon us that we plead fervently for God's mercy and an end of the exile. The commentators add that a *Shemoneh Esrei* can hardly take the place of an offering unless it is prayed with sincere devotion.

During the *chazzan's* repetition, *Kedushah* (below) is recited at this point.

קדושת השם

אַתָּה קָדוֹשׁ וְשִׁמְךָ קָדוֹשׁ, וּקְדוֹשִׁים בְּכָל יוֹם יְהַלְּלְוּךָ סֶּלָה. בָּרוּךְ אַתָּה יהוה, הָאֵל הַקָּדוֹשׁ.

קדושת היום

רָאשֵׁי חֳדָשִׁים לְעַמְּךָ נָתָתָּ,* זְמַן כַּפָּרָה* לְכָל תּוֹלְדוֹתָם,* בִּהְיוֹתָם מַקְרִיבִים לְפָנֶיךָ זִבְחֵי רָצוֹן, וּשְׂעִירֵי חַטָּאת* לְכַפֵּר בַּעֲדָם. זִכָּרוֹן לְכֻלָּם יִהְיוּ, וּתְשׁוּעַת נַפְשָׁם* מִיַּד שׂוֹנֵא. מִזְבֵּחַ חָדָשׁ בְּצִיּוֹן תָּכִין, וְעוֹלַת רֹאשׁ חֹדֶשׁ נַעֲלֶה עָלָיו, וּשְׂעִירֵי עִזִּים נַעֲשֶׂה בְרָצוֹן.* וּבַעֲבוֹדַת בֵּית הַמִּקְדָּשׁ נִשְׂמַח כֻּלָּנוּ, וּבְשִׁירֵי דָוִד עַבְדֶּךָ הַנִּשְׁמָעִים בְּעִירֶךָ, הָאֲמוּרִים לִפְנֵי מִזְבְּחֶךָ. אַהֲבַת עוֹלָם תָּבִיא לָהֶם, וּבְרִית אָבוֹת לַבָּנִים תִּזְכּוֹר.

קדושה

When reciting *Kedushah,* one must stand with his feet together, and avoid any interruptions. One should rise to his toes when saying the words קָדוֹשׁ, קָדוֹשׁ, קָדוֹשׁ; בָּרוּךְ (of בָּרוּךְ כְּבוֹד); and יִמְלֹךְ.
(A commentary to *Kedushah* appears on p. 100.)

—Cong. then *Chazzan* **נְקַדֵּשׁ** אֶת שִׁמְךָ בָּעוֹלָם, כְּשֵׁם שֶׁמַּקְדִּישִׁים אוֹתוֹ בִּשְׁמֵי מָרוֹם, כַּכָּתוּב עַל יַד נְבִיאֶךָ, וְקָרָא זֶה אֶל זֶה וְאָמַר:

—All קָדוֹשׁ קָדוֹשׁ קָדוֹשׁ יהוה צְבָאוֹת, מְלֹא כָל הָאָרֶץ כְּבוֹדוֹ.[1]

—*Chazzan* לְעֻמָּתָם בָּרוּךְ יֹאמֵרוּ:

—All בָּרוּךְ כְּבוֹד יהוה, מִמְּקוֹמוֹ.[2]

—*Chazzan* וּבְדִבְרֵי קָדְשְׁךָ כָּתוּב לֵאמֹר:

—All יִמְלֹךְ יהוה לְעוֹלָם, אֱלֹהַיִךְ צִיּוֹן לְדֹר וָדֹר, הַלְלוּיָהּ.[3]

—*Chazzan* only concludes לְדוֹר וָדוֹר נַגִּיד גָּדְלֶךָ וּלְנֵצַח נְצָחִים קְדֻשָּׁתְךָ נַקְדִּישׁ, וְשִׁבְחֲךָ אֱלֹהֵינוּ מִפִּינוּ לֹא יָמוּשׁ לְעוֹלָם וָעֶד, כִּי אֵל מֶלֶךְ גָּדוֹל וְקָדוֹשׁ אָתָּה. בָּרוּךְ אַתָּה יהוה, הָאֵל הַקָּדוֹשׁ.

Chazzan continues ... רָאשֵׁי חֳדָשִׁים [above].

רָאשֵׁי חֳדָשִׁים לְעַמְּךָ נָתָתָּ — *New Moons have You given Your people.* The first commandment given to the Jewish nation as a whole was that of proclaiming the new months *(Exodus* 12:2). This *mitzvah* gave the Jewish people, through its courts, the authority to determine the calendar. It also provides an insight into the nature of the people: like the moon, Jews can become great and then seem to disappear, but they always renew themselves; and by means of regulating the calendar, Jews constantly renew their consciousness of God's control over the universe. [See also commentary to *Mussaf* of Sabbath-Rosh Chodesh (p. 466) and *Kiddush Levanah* (p. 612).]

זְמַן כַּפָּרָה — *A time of atonement.* The offerings of Rosh Chodesh — and the prayers that take their place in the absence of the Temple — atone for unintentional contamination of the Temple and its offerings [טֻמְאַת מִקְדָּשׁ וְקָדָשָׁיו] *(Shevuos* 2b); for sins that can bring epidemics, specifically diphtheria, upon children *(Daas Zekeinim* to *Numbers* 28:9); and for general sins that prevent the coming of Messiah *(Iyun Tefillah).*

לְכָל תּוֹלְדוֹתָם — *For all their offspring,* i.e. the Jewish people, the offspring of the nation to whom the Rosh Chodesh commandment was originally given. Additionally it refers to the children who are spared from serious illness by the offerings and prayers of the day (see above comment). In a novel comment, *Kuzari* writes that this refers to the month's offspring, i.e., the

During the *chazzan's* repetition, *Kedushah* (below) is recited at this point.

HOLINESS OF GOD'S NAME

אַתָּה *You are holy and Your Name is holy, and holy ones praise You every day, forever. Blessed are You,* HASHEM, *the holy God.*

HOLINESS OF THE DAY

רָאשֵׁי *New Moons have You given Your people,* a time of atonement* for all their offspring,* when they would bring before You offerings for favor and goats of sin-offering* to atone on their behalf. They would serve as a remembrance for them all and a salvation for their soul* from the hand of the enemy. May You establish a new Altar in Zion, and may we bring up upon it the elevation-offering of the new moon, and prepare he-goats with favor.* In the service of the Holy Temple may we all rejoice and in the songs of Your servant David that are heard in Your City, when they are recited before Your Altar. May Your bring them an eternal love and the covenant of the forefathers may You recall upon the children.*

KEDUSHAH

When reciting *Kedushah,* one must stand with his feet together and avoid any interruptions. One should rise to his toes when saying the words *'Holy, holy, holy'; 'Blessed (is the glory)';* and *'*HASHEM *shall reign.'* (A commentary to *Kedushah* appears on p. 100.)

Cong. then Chazzan— **נְקַדֵּשׁ** *We shall sanctify Your Name in this world, just as they sanctify it in heaven above, as it is written by Your prophet, 'And one [angel] will call another and say:*

All— *'Holy, holy, holy is* HASHEM, *Master of Legions, the whole world is filled with His glory.'*[1]

Chazzan— *Those facing them say 'Blessed':*

All— *'Blessed is the glory of* HASHEM *from His place.'*[2]

Chazzan— *And in Your holy Writings the following is written:*

All— *'*HASHEM *shall reign forever — your God, O Zion — from generation to generation, Halleluyah!'*[3]

Chazzan only concludes— *From generation to generation we shall relate Your greatness and for infinite eternities we shall proclaim Your holiness. Your praise, our God, shall not leave our mouth forever and ever, for You O God, are a great and holy King. Blessed are You* HASHEM, *the holy God.*

Chazzan continues רָאשֵׁי חֳדָשִׁים, *'New Moons'* [above].

(1) *Isaiah* 6:3. (2) *Ezekiel* 3:12. (3) *Psalms* 146:10.

---

events that will take place during the ensuing month.

זִבְחֵי רָצוֹן וּשְׂעִירֵי חַטָּאת — *Offerings for favor and goats of sin-offering.* The *Mussaf,* or additional offering, of Rosh Chodesh is enumerated later in the *Shemoneh Esrei.* It includes several animals as elevation-offerings which are intended to gain God's favor, and a goat as a sin-offering, which atones for sin.

זִכָּרוֹן ... וּתְשׁוּעַת נַפְשָׁם — *A remembrance ... and a salvation for their soul.* The Torah describes the offerings of the festivals and Rosh Chodesh as Israel's 'remembrance' before God *(Numbers* 10:10). It is axiomatic that Israel's devotion to God's service brings salvation from human and spiritual enemies.

וּשְׂעִירֵי עִזִּים נַעֲשֶׂה בְרָצוֹן — *And prepare he-goats with favor.* The prescribed communal sin-offerings are brought even when no sins have been committed. At such longed-for times, these offerings are sources of spiritual elevation. Here, we express the hope that in the Temple of the future, sin-offerings will come only for that purpose *(Maharit Algazi).*

וַהֲבִיאֵנוּ לְצִיּוֹן עִירְךָ בְּרִנָּה, וְלִירוּשָׁלַיִם בֵּית מִקְדָּשְׁךָ בְּשִׂמְחַת עוֹלָם. וְשָׁם נַעֲשֶׂה לְפָנֶיךָ אֶת קָרְבְּנוֹת חוֹבוֹתֵינוּ, תְּמִידִים כְּסִדְרָם, וּמוּסָפִים כְּהִלְכָתָם, וְאֶת מוּסַף יוֹם רֹאשׁ הַחֹדֶשׁ הַזֶּה נַעֲשֶׂה וְנַקְרִיב לְפָנֶיךָ בְּאַהֲבָה כְּמִצְוַת רְצוֹנֶךָ,* כְּמוֹ שֶׁכָּתַבְתָּ עָלֵינוּ בְּתוֹרָתֶךָ, עַל יְדֵי מֹשֶׁה עַבְדֶּךָ, מִפִּי כְבוֹדֶךָ, כָּאָמוּר:

וּבְרָאשֵׁי חָדְשֵׁיכֶם* תַּקְרִיבוּ עֹלָה לַיהוה, פָּרִים בְּנֵי בָקָר שְׁנַיִם, וְאַיִל אֶחָד, כְּבָשִׂים בְּנֵי שָׁנָה שִׁבְעָה תְּמִימִם.[1] וּמִנְחָתָם וְנִסְכֵּיהֶם כִּמְדֻבָּר, שְׁלֹשָׁה עֶשְׂרֹנִים לַפָּר, וּשְׁנֵי עֶשְׂרֹנִים לָאָיִל, וְעִשָּׂרוֹן לַכֶּבֶשׂ וְיַיִן כְּנִסְכּוֹ, וְשָׂעִיר לְכַפֵּר, וּשְׁנֵי תְמִידִים כְּהִלְכָתָם.[2]

During *chazzan's* repetition, congregation, responds אָמֵן, as indicated.

אֱלֹהֵינוּ* וֵאלֹהֵי אֲבוֹתֵינוּ, חַדֵּשׁ עָלֵינוּ אֶת הַחֹדֶשׁ הַזֶּה לְטוֹבָה וְלִבְרָכָה (אָמֵן), לְשָׂשׂוֹן וּלְשִׂמְחָה (אָמֵן), לִישׁוּעָה וּלְנֶחָמָה (אָמֵן), לְפַרְנָסָה וּלְכַלְכָּלָה (אָמֵן), לְחַיִּים וּלְשָׁלוֹם (אָמֵן), לִמְחִילַת חֵטְא וְלִסְלִיחַת עָוֹן (אָמֵן). [during a leap year add— וּלְכַפָּרַת פָּשַׁע (אָמֵן)]. כִּי בְעַמְּךָ יִשְׂרָאֵל בָּחַרְתָּ מִכָּל הָאֻמּוֹת,* וְחֻקֵּי רָאשֵׁי חֳדָשִׁים לָהֶם קָבָעְתָּ. בָּרוּךְ אַתָּה יהוה, מְקַדֵּשׁ יִשְׂרָאֵל וְרָאשֵׁי חֳדָשִׁים.*

עבודה

רְצֵה יהוה אֱלֹהֵינוּ בְּעַמְּךָ יִשְׂרָאֵל וּבִתְפִלָּתָם, וְהָשֵׁב אֶת הָעֲבוֹדָה לִדְבִיר בֵּיתֶךָ. וְאִשֵּׁי יִשְׂרָאֵל וּתְפִלָּתָם בְּאַהֲבָה תְקַבֵּל בְּרָצוֹן, וּתְהִי לְרָצוֹן תָּמִיד עֲבוֹדַת יִשְׂרָאֵל עַמֶּךָ.

וְתֶחֱזֶינָה עֵינֵינוּ בְּשׁוּבְךָ לְצִיּוֹן בְּרַחֲמִים. בָּרוּךְ אַתָּה יהוה, הַמַּחֲזִיר שְׁכִינָתוֹ לְצִיּוֹן.

כְּמִצְוַת רְצוֹנֶךָ — *According to the commandment of Your favor.* The offerings are desired by God and they are a means for Israel to gain His favor *(Etz Yosef).*

וּבְרָאשֵׁי חָדְשֵׁיכֶם — *And on your New Moons.* The New Moons are described as 'yours' because the authority to proclaim them is vested in Israel through its rabbinical courts. As is done in every *Mussaf Shemoneh Esrei,* the special offering of the day is set forth, including its animals, meal-offerings and drink-offerings.

אֱלֹהֵינוּ — *Our God.* Having set forth the characteristics and the service of Rosh Chodesh, we conclude with a final plea that God fill the new month with every form of happiness and blessing. Since the year has twelve months, we specify twelve sorts of blessing. They are grouped in six pairs and the congregation answers *Amen* after each of them. [In a Jewish leap year, which has a thirteenth month, a thirteenth term of blessing is added: וּלְכַפָּרַת פָּשַׁע, *and for atonement of willful sin.* Most congregations recite the additional phrase only until the Second Adar, the extra month, while some recite it all year long.]

May You bring us to Zion, Your city, in glad song and to Jerusalem, Your Holy Temple, in eternal gladness. There we shall perform before You our obligated offerings, the continual offerings according to their order and the additional offerings according to their law. And the additional offering of this New Moon day we shall perform and bring before You with love according to the commandment of Your favor, as You have written for us in Your Torah, through Moses Your servant, from Your glorious expression, as it is said:*

וּבְרָאשֵׁי *And on your New Moons* you are to bring an elevation-offering to* HASHEM*: two young bulls; one ram; seven [male] first-year lambs — unblemished.*[1] *And their meal-offerings and their drink-offerings as specified: three tenth-ephah for each bull; two tenth-ephah for the ram; one tenth-ephah for each lamb; and wine for its drink offering. A he-goat for atonement and two continual daily offerings according to their law.*[2]

During *chazzan's* repetition, congregation responds *'Amen,'* as indicated.

אֱלֹהֵינוּ *Our God* and the God of our forefathers, inaugurate for us this month for good and for blessing (Amen), for joy and for gladness (Amen), for salvation and for consolation (Amen), for sustenance and for support (Amen), for life and for peace (Amen), for pardon of sin and forgiveness of iniquity (Amen)* [during a leap year add: *and for atonement of willful sin (Amen)*]. *For You have chosen Your people Israel from all the nations,* and You have set forth the decrees of the New Moons for them. Blessed are You* HASHEM*, Who sanctifies Israel and the New Moons.**

TEMPLE SERVICE

רְצֵה *Be favorable,* HASHEM*, our God, toward Your people Israel and their prayer and restore the service to the Holy of Holies of Your Temple. The fire-offerings of Israel and their prayer accept with love and favor, and may the service of Your people Israel always be favorable to You.*

וְתֶחֱזֶינָה *May our eyes behold Your return to Zion in compassion. Blessed are You,* HASHEM*, Who restores His Presence to Zion.*

(1) *Numbers* 28:11. (2) Cf. 28:12-15

בָּחַרְתָּ מִכָּל הָאֻמּוֹת — *You have chosen* [*Israel*] *from all the nations.* Unlike most nations, we calculate our calendar by the moon as well as the sun. Israel is likened to the moon in several ways. Like the moon, we are assured of a return to our past glory even after periods of utter decline. Additionally, unlike the sun that sets at night, the moon is in the sky by day as well as at night. Thus, even though our glow is sometimes not noticeable, it is like that of the moon when the sun holds sway; it is there nonetheless *(R' Yaakov Emden).*

מְקַדֵּשׁ יִשְׂרָאֵל וְרָאשֵׁי חֳדָשִׁים — *Who sanctifies Israel and the New Moons.* Israel is mentioned before the New Moons because the sanctity of the new moon depends on the prior sanctification of the Jewish people and the declaration of its court. In the blessing of the Sabbath (מְקַדֵּשׁ הַשַּׁבָּת, *Who sanctifies the Sabbath*), however, Israel is not

הודאה

Bow at מוֹדִים; straighten up at 'ה. In his repetition the *chazzan* should recite the entire מוֹדִים aloud, while the congregation recites מוֹדִים דְּרַבָּנָן softly.

מוֹדִים אֲנַחְנוּ לָךְ שָׁאַתָּה הוּא יהוה אֱלֹהֵינוּ וֵאלֹהֵי אֲבוֹתֵינוּ לְעוֹלָם וָעֶד. צוּר חַיֵּינוּ, מָגֵן יִשְׁעֵנוּ אַתָּה הוּא לְדוֹר וָדוֹר. נוֹדֶה לְּךָ וּנְסַפֵּר תְּהִלָּתֶךָ[1] עַל חַיֵּינוּ הַמְּסוּרִים בְּיָדֶךָ, וְעַל נִשְׁמוֹתֵינוּ הַפְּקוּדוֹת לָךְ, וְעַל נִסֶּיךָ שֶׁבְּכָל יוֹם עִמָּנוּ, וְעַל נִפְלְאוֹתֶיךָ וְטוֹבוֹתֶיךָ שֶׁבְּכָל עֵת, עֶרֶב וָבֹקֶר וְצָהֳרָיִם. הַטּוֹב כִּי לֹא כָלוּ רַחֲמֶיךָ, וְהַמְרַחֵם כִּי לֹא תַמּוּ חֲסָדֶיךָ,[2] מֵעוֹלָם קִוִּינוּ לָךְ:

מודים דרבנן

מוֹדִים אֲנַחְנוּ לָךְ, שָׁאַתָּה הוּא יהוה אֱלֹהֵינוּ וֵאלֹהֵי אֲבוֹתֵינוּ, אֱלֹהֵי כָל בָּשָׂר, יוֹצְרֵנוּ, יוֹצֵר בְּרֵאשִׁית. בְּרָכוֹת וְהוֹדָאוֹת לְשִׁמְךָ הַגָּדוֹל וְהַקָּדוֹשׁ, עַל שֶׁהֶחֱיִיתָנוּ וְקִיַּמְתָּנוּ. כֵּן תְּחַיֵּנוּ וּתְקַיְּמֵנוּ, וְתֶאֱסוֹף גָּלֻיּוֹתֵינוּ לְחַצְרוֹת קָדְשֶׁךָ, לִשְׁמוֹר חֻקֶּיךָ וְלַעֲשׂוֹת רְצוֹנֶךָ, וּלְעָבְדְּךָ בְּלֵבָב שָׁלֵם, עַל שֶׁאֲנַחְנוּ מוֹדִים לָךְ. בָּרוּךְ אֵל הַהוֹדָאוֹת.

On Chanukah add:

(וְ)עַל הַנִּסִּים, וְעַל הַפֻּרְקָן, וְעַל הַגְּבוּרוֹת, וְעַל הַתְּשׁוּעוֹת, וְעַל הַמִּלְחָמוֹת, שֶׁעָשִׂיתָ לַאֲבוֹתֵינוּ בַּיָּמִים הָהֵם בַּזְּמַן הַזֶּה.

בִּימֵי מַתִּתְיָהוּ בֶּן יוֹחָנָן כֹּהֵן גָּדוֹל חַשְׁמוֹנָאִי וּבָנָיו, כְּשֶׁעָמְדָה מַלְכוּת יָוָן הָרְשָׁעָה עַל עַמְּךָ יִשְׂרָאֵל, לְהַשְׁכִּיחָם תּוֹרָתֶךָ, וּלְהַעֲבִירָם מֵחֻקֵּי רְצוֹנֶךָ. וְאַתָּה בְּרַחֲמֶיךָ הָרַבִּים, עָמַדְתָּ לָהֶם בְּעֵת צָרָתָם, רַבְתָּ אֶת רִיבָם, דַּנְתָּ אֶת דִּינָם, נָקַמְתָּ אֶת נִקְמָתָם.[3] מָסַרְתָּ גִבּוֹרִים בְּיַד חַלָּשִׁים, וְרַבִּים בְּיַד מְעַטִּים, וּטְמֵאִים בְּיַד טְהוֹרִים, וּרְשָׁעִים בְּיַד צַדִּיקִים, וְזֵדִים בְּיַד עוֹסְקֵי תוֹרָתֶךָ. וּלְךָ עָשִׂיתָ שֵׁם גָּדוֹל וְקָדוֹשׁ בְּעוֹלָמֶךָ, וּלְעַמְּךָ יִשְׂרָאֵל עָשִׂיתָ תְּשׁוּעָה גְדוֹלָה[4] וּפֻרְקָן כְּהַיּוֹם הַזֶּה. וְאַחַר כֵּן בָּאוּ בָנֶיךָ לִדְבִיר בֵּיתֶךָ, וּפִנּוּ אֶת הֵיכָלֶךָ, וְטִהֲרוּ אֶת מִקְדָּשֶׁךָ, וְהִדְלִיקוּ נֵרוֹת בְּחַצְרוֹת קָדְשֶׁךָ, וְקָבְעוּ שְׁמוֹנַת יְמֵי חֲנֻכָּה אֵלּוּ, לְהוֹדוֹת וּלְהַלֵּל לְשִׁמְךָ הַגָּדוֹל.

[If forgotten, do not repeat *Shemoneh Esrei*. See Laws §90.]

וְעַל כֻּלָּם יִתְבָּרַךְ וְיִתְרוֹמַם שִׁמְךָ מַלְכֵּנוּ תָּמִיד לְעוֹלָם וָעֶד.

Bend the knees at בָּרוּךְ; bow at אַתָּה; straighten up at 'ה.

וְכֹל הַחַיִּים יוֹדוּךָ סֶּלָה, וִיהַלְלוּ אֶת שִׁמְךָ בֶּאֱמֶת, הָאֵל יְשׁוּעָתֵנוּ וְעֶזְרָתֵנוּ סֶלָה. בָּרוּךְ אַתָּה יהוה, הַטּוֹב שִׁמְךָ וּלְךָ נָאֶה לְהוֹדוֹת.

---

mentioned in the blessing of sanctification because the holiness of the Sabbath preceded and is independent of the existence of the Jewish people.

THANKSGIVING [MODIM]

Bow at *'We gratefully thank You'*; straighten up at *'HASHEM'*. In his repetition the *chazzan* should recite the entire *Modim* aloud, while the congregation recites *Modim of the Rabbis* softly.

מוֹדִים *We gratefully thank You, for it is You Who are HASHEM, our God and the God of our forefathers for all eternity; Rock of our lives, Shield of our salvation are You from generation to generation. We shall thank You and relate Your praise*[1] *— for our lives, which are committed to Your power and for our souls that are entrusted to You; for Your miracles that are with us every day; and for Your wonders and favors in every season — evening, morning, and afternoon. The Beneficent One, for Your compassions were never exhausted, and the Compassionate One, for Your kindnesses never ended*[2] *— always have we put our hope in You.*

MODIM OF THE RABBIS

מוֹדִים *We gratefully thank You, for it is You Who are HASHEM, our God and the God of our forefathers, the God of all flesh, our Molder, the Molder of the universe. Blessings and thanks are due Your great and holy Name for You have given us life and sustained us. So may You continue to give us life and sustain us and gather our exiles to the Courtyards of Your Sanctuary, to observe Your decrees, to do Your will and to serve You wholeheartedly. [We thank You] for inspiring us to thank You. Blessed is the God of thanksgivings.*

On Chanukah add:

(וְ)עַל *(And) for the miracles, and for the salvation, and for the mighty deeds, and for the victories, and for the battles which You performed for our forefathers in those days, at this time.*

בִּימֵי *In the days of Mattisyahu, the son of Yochanan, the High Priest, the Hasmonean, and his sons — when the wicked Greek kingdom rose up against Your people Israel to make them forget Your Torah and compel them to stray from the statutes of Your Will—You in Your great mercy stood up for them in the time of their distress. You took up their grievance, judged their claim, and avenged their wrong.*[3] *You delivered the strong into the hands of the weak, the many into the hands of the few, the impure into the hands of the pure, the wicked into the hands of the righteous, and the wanton into the hands of the diligent students of Your Torah. For Yourself You made a great and holy Name in Your world, and for Your people Israel You worked a great victory*[4] *and salvation as this very day. Thereafter, Your children came to the Holy of Holies of Your House, cleansed Your Temple, purified the site of Your Holiness and kindled lights in the Courtyards of Your Sanctuary; and they established these eight days of Chanukah to express thanks and praise to Your great Name.*

[If forgotten, do not repeat *Shemoneh Esrei*. See *Laws* §90.]

For all these, may Your Name be blessed and exalted, our King, continually forever and ever.

Bend the knees at *'Blessed'*; bow at *'You'*; straighten up at *'HASHEM.'*

Everything alive will gratefully acknowledge You, Selah! and praise Your Name sincerely, O God of our salvation and help, Selah! Blessed are You, HASHEM, Your Name is 'The Beneficent One' and to You it is fitting to give thanks.

---

(1) Cf. *Psalms* 79:13. (2) Cf. *Lamentations* 3:22. (3) Cf. *Jeremiah* 51:36. (4) Cf. *I Samuel* 19:5.

ברכת כהנים

The *chazzan* recites בִּרְכַּת כֹּהֲנִים during his repetition, except in a house of mourning. *Chazzan* faces to the right at וְיִשְׁמְרֶךָ and to the left at פָּנָיו אֵלֶיךָ וִיחֻנֶּךָּ.

אֱלֹהֵינוּ, וֵאלֹהֵי אֲבוֹתֵינוּ, בָּרְכֵנוּ בַבְּרָכָה הַמְּשֻׁלֶּשֶׁת, בַּתּוֹרָה הַכְּתוּבָה עַל יְדֵי מֹשֶׁה עַבְדֶּךָ, הָאֲמוּרָה מִפִּי אַהֲרֹן וּבָנָיו, כֹּהֲנִים עַם קְדוֹשֶׁךָ, כָּאָמוּר: יְבָרֶכְךָ יהוה, וְיִשְׁמְרֶךָ. (Cong.— כֵּן יְהִי רָצוֹן.)
יָאֵר יהוה פָּנָיו אֵלֶיךָ וִיחֻנֶּךָּ. (Cong.— כֵּן יְהִי רָצוֹן.)
יִשָּׂא יהוה פָּנָיו אֵלֶיךָ וְיָשֵׂם לְךָ שָׁלוֹם.[1] (Cong.— כֵּן יְהִי רָצוֹן.)

שלום

שִׂים שָׁלוֹם, טוֹבָה, וּבְרָכָה, חֵן, וָחֶסֶד וְרַחֲמִים עָלֵינוּ וְעַל כָּל יִשְׂרָאֵל עַמֶּךָ. בָּרְכֵנוּ אָבִינוּ, כֻּלָּנוּ כְּאֶחָד בְּאוֹר פָּנֶיךָ, כִּי בְאוֹר פָּנֶיךָ נָתַתָּ לָּנוּ, יהוה אֱלֹהֵינוּ, תּוֹרַת חַיִּים וְאַהֲבַת חֶסֶד, וּצְדָקָה, וּבְרָכָה, וְרַחֲמִים, וְחַיִּים, וְשָׁלוֹם. וְטוֹב בְּעֵינֶיךָ לְבָרֵךְ אֶת עַמְּךָ יִשְׂרָאֵל, בְּכָל עֵת וּבְכָל שָׁעָה בִּשְׁלוֹמֶךָ. בָּרוּךְ אַתָּה יהוה, הַמְּבָרֵךְ אֶת עַמּוֹ יִשְׂרָאֵל בַּשָּׁלוֹם.

Chazzan's repetition of *Shemoneh Esrei* ends here. Individuals continue to end of page.

יִהְיוּ לְרָצוֹן אִמְרֵי פִי וְהֶגְיוֹן לִבִּי לְפָנֶיךָ, יהוה צוּרִי וְגֹאֲלִי.[2]

אֱלֹהַי, נְצוֹר לְשׁוֹנִי מֵרָע, וּשְׂפָתַי מִדַּבֵּר מִרְמָה,[3] וְלִמְקַלְלַי נַפְשִׁי תִדּוֹם, וְנַפְשִׁי כֶּעָפָר לַכֹּל תִּהְיֶה. פְּתַח לִבִּי בְּתוֹרָתֶךָ, וּבְמִצְוֹתֶיךָ תִּרְדּוֹף נַפְשִׁי. וְכֹל הַחוֹשְׁבִים עָלַי רָעָה, מְהֵרָה הָפֵר עֲצָתָם וְקַלְקֵל מַחֲשַׁבְתָּם. עֲשֵׂה לְמַעַן שְׁמֶךָ, עֲשֵׂה לְמַעַן יְמִינֶךָ, עֲשֵׂה לְמַעַן קְדֻשָּׁתֶךָ, עֲשֵׂה לְמַעַן תּוֹרָתֶךָ. לְמַעַן יֵחָלְצוּן יְדִידֶיךָ, הוֹשִׁיעָה יְמִינְךָ וַעֲנֵנִי.[4]

Some recite verses pertaining to their names at this point. See page 924.

יִהְיוּ לְרָצוֹן אִמְרֵי פִי וְהֶגְיוֹן לִבִּי לְפָנֶיךָ, יהוה צוּרִי וְגֹאֲלִי.[2]

Bow and take three steps back. Bow left and say ... עֹשֶׂה; bow right and say ... הוּא יַעֲשֶׂה; bow forward and say וְעַל כָּל ... אָמֵן. Remain standing in place while reciting יְהִי רָצוֹן.

עֹשֶׂה שָׁלוֹם בִּמְרוֹמָיו, הוּא יַעֲשֶׂה שָׁלוֹם עָלֵינוּ, וְעַל כָּל יִשְׂרָאֵל. וְאִמְרוּ: אָמֵן.

יְהִי רָצוֹן מִלְּפָנֶיךָ יהוה אֱלֹהֵינוּ וֵאלֹהֵי אֲבוֹתֵינוּ, שֶׁיִּבָּנֶה בֵּית הַמִּקְדָּשׁ בִּמְהֵרָה בְיָמֵינוּ, וְתֵן חֶלְקֵנוּ בְּתוֹרָתֶךָ. וְשָׁם נַעֲבָדְךָ בְּיִרְאָה, כִּימֵי עוֹלָם וּכְשָׁנִים קַדְמוֹנִיּוֹת. וְעָרְבָה לַיהוה מִנְחַת יְהוּדָה וִירוּשָׁלָיִם, כִּימֵי עוֹלָם וּכְשָׁנִים קַדְמוֹנִיּוֹת.[5]

THE INDIVIDUAL'S RECITATION OF שְׁמוֹנֶה עֶשְׂרֵה ENDS HERE.

The *chazzan* recites the Full *Kaddish* (p. 156) and *Shacharis* is continued with *Aleinu* (p. 158).

THE PRIESTLY BLESSING

The *chazzan* recites the Priestly Blessing during his repetition, except in a house of mourning.

אֱלֹהֵינוּ *Our God and the God of our forefathers, bless us with the three-verse blessing in the Torah that was written by the hand of Moses, Your servant, that was said by Aaron and his sons, the Kohanim, Your holy people, as it is said:*

May HASHEM *bless you and safeguard you.* (Cong.— *So may it be.*)

May HASHEM *illuminate His countenance for you and be gracious to you.* (Cong.— *So may it be.*)

May HASHEM *turn His countenance to you and establish peace for you.*[1] (Cong.— *So may it be.*)

PEACE

שִׂים *Establish peace, goodness, blessing, graciousness, kindness, and compassion upon us and upon all of Your people Israel. Bless us, our Father, all of us as one, with the light of Your countenance, for with the light of Your countenance You gave us,* HASHEM, *our God, the Torah of life and a love of kindness, righteousness, blessing, compassion, life, and peace. And may it be good in Your eyes to bless Your people Israel, in every season and in every hour with Your Peace. Blessed are You,* HASHEM, *Who blesses His people Israel with peace.*

Chazzan's repetition of *Shemoneh Esrei* ends here. Individuals continue to end of page.

May the expressions of my mouth and the thoughts of my heart find favor before You, HASHEM, *my Rock and my Redeemer.*[2]

אֱלֹהַי *My God, guard my tongue from evil and my lips from speaking deceitfully.*[3] *To those who curse me, let my soul be silent; and let my soul be like dust to everyone. Open my heart to Your Torah, then my soul will pursue Your commandments. As for all those who design evil against me, speedily nullify their counsel and disrupt their design. Act for Your Name's sake; act for Your right hand's sake; act for Your sanctity's sake; act for Your Torah's sake. That Your beloved ones may be given rest; let Your right hand save, and respond to me.*[4]

Some recite verses pertaining to their names at this point. See page 924.

May the expressions of my mouth and the thoughts of my heart find favor before You, HASHEM, *my Rock and my Redeemer.*[2]

Bow and take three steps back. Bow left and say, *'He Who makes peace ...';* bow right and say, *'may He make peace ...';* bow forward and say, *'and upon ... Amen.'*

He Who makes peace in His heights, may He make peace upon us, and upon all Israel. Now respond: Amen.

יְהִי רָצוֹן *May it be Your will,* HASHEM *our God and the God of our forefathers, that the Holy Temple be rebuilt, speedily in our days. Grant us our share in Your Torah, and may we serve You there with reverence, as in days of old and in former years. Then the offering of Judah and Jerusalem will be pleasing to* HASHEM, *as in days of old and in former years.*[4]

THE INDIVIDUAL'S RECITATION OF *SHEMONEH ESREI* ENDS HERE.

The *chazzan* recites the Full *Kaddish* (p. 156) and *Shacharis* is continued with *Aleinu* (p. 158).

---

(1) *Numbers* 6:24-26. (2) *Psalms* 19:15. (3) Cf. 34:14. (4) 60:7; 108:7. (5) *Malachi* 3:4.

בדיקת חמץ

On the night of 14 Nissan, the night before the Pesach *Seder,* the search for *chametz* (leaven) is made. It should be done with a candle as soon as possible after nightfall. [When the first *Seder* is on Saturday night, the search is conducted on Thursday night (13 Nissan).]

Before the search is begun, the following blessing is recited. If several people assist in the search, only one recites the blessing for all.

בָּרוּךְ אַתָּה יהוה אֱלֹהֵינוּ מֶלֶךְ הָעוֹלָם, אֲשֶׁר קִדְּשָׁנוּ בְּמִצְוֹתָיו, וְצִוָּנוּ עַל בִּעוּר חָמֵץ.*

After the search, the *chametz* is wrapped and put aside in a safe place to be burned in the morning. Then the following declaration is made:

כָּל חֲמִירָא* וַחֲמִיעָא דְּאִכָּא בִרְשׁוּתִי* דְּלָא חֲמִתֵּהּ וּדְלָא בִעַרְתֵּהּ וּדְלָא יְדַעְנָא לֵהּ לִבָּטֵל וְלֶהֱוֵי הֶפְקֵר כְּעַפְרָא דְאַרְעָא.

In the morning, after the *chametz* has been burned, the following declaration is made:

כָּל חֲמִירָא וַחֲמִיעָא דְּאִכָּא בִרְשׁוּתִי,* דַּחֲזִתֵּהּ וּדְלָא חֲזִתֵּהּ, דַּחֲמִתֵּהּ וּדְלָא חֲמִתֵּהּ, דְּבִעַרְתֵּהּ וּדְלָא בִעַרְתֵּהּ, לִבָּטֵל וְלֶהֱוֵי הֶפְקֵר כְּעַפְרָא דְאַרְעָא.

ערוב תבשילין

The *eruv*-foods (see commentary) are held while the following blessing and declaration are recited:

בָּרוּךְ אַתָּה יהוה אֱלֹהֵינוּ מֶלֶךְ הָעוֹלָם, אֲשֶׁר קִדְּשָׁנוּ בְּמִצְוֹתָיו, וְצִוָּנוּ עַל מִצְוַת עֵרוּב.

בַּהֲדֵין עֵרוּבָא יְהֵא שָׁרֵא לָנָא לַאֲפוּיֵי וּלְבַשּׁוּלֵי וּלְאַטְמוּנֵי וּלְאַדְלוּקֵי שְׁרָגָא וּלְתַקָּנָא וּלְמֶעְבַּד כָּל צָרְכָּנָא, מִיּוֹמָא טָבָא לְשַׁבְּתָא (לָנָא וּלְכָל יִשְׂרָאֵל הַדָּרִים בָּעִיר הַזֹּאת).

בְּדִיקַת חָמֵץ / THE SEARCH FOR CHAMETZ

בִּעוּר חָמֵץ — *The removal of chametz.* Since the Torah forbids a Jew to have *chametz* in his possession during Pesach, the Rabbis ordained a search of all homes, shops, and any other places where *chametz* may have been brought during the year. The Talmud derives from Scriptural implications that the search be made by candle light and therefore it should be done at night when a candle's flame is noticeable *(Pesachim* 2a). The primary *mitzvah* is the destruction of the *chametz* that will take place on the next morning, but the blessing is made now because the search is in preparation for, and part of the *mitzvah* of, the destruction. It is customary that ten bits of bread be hidden so that the searcher will truly search and the quest for *chametz* will not be in vain.

כָּל חֲמִירָא — *Any chametz.* It is essential that all *chametz* be declared ownerless so that one not be in possession of *chametz* without knowing it. The evening declaration carefully omits any *chametz* that one wishes to retain for the next day's breakfast, the *chametz* that will be burned the next morning, and the *chametz* that will be sold to a non-Jew in the morning.

This is a *legal* declaration, not a prayer; therefore it must be understood. If one does not understand the Aramaic, he should recite it in a language he understands. It should be recited by all members of the family.

דְּאִכָּא בִרְשׁוּתִי — *That is in my possession.* If one

THE SEARCH FOR CHAMETZ/LEAVEN

On the night of 14 Nissan, the night before the Pesach *Seder,* the search for *chametz* (leaven) is made. It should be done with a candle as soon as possible after nightfall. [When the first *Seder* is on Saturday night, the search is conducted on Thursday night (13 Nissan).]
Before the search is begun, the following blessing is recited.
If several people assist in the search, only one recites the blessing for all.

בָּרוּךְ *Blessed are You, HASHEM, our God, King of the universe, Who has sanctified us with His commandments and has commanded us concerning the removal of chametz.**

After the search, the *chametz* is wrapped and put aside in a safe place to be burned in the morning. Then the following declaration is made:

כָּל חֲמִירָא *Any chametz* or leaven that is in my possession* which I have not seen, have not removed and do not know about, should be annulled and become ownerless, like dust of the earth.*

In the morning, after the *chametz* has been burned, the following declaration is made:

כָּל חֲמִירָא *Any chametz or leaven that is in my possession,* whether I have recognized it or not, whether I have seen it or not, whether I have removed it or not, should be annulled and become ownerless, like dust of the earth.*

ERUV TAVSHILIN

The *eruv*-foods (see commentary) are held while the following blessing and declaration are recited:

בָּרוּךְ *Blessed are You, HASHEM, our God, King of the universe, Who has sanctified us with His commandments and has commanded us concerning the mitzvah of eruv.*

בַּהֲדֵין עֵרוּבָא *Through this eruv may we be permitted to bake, cook, insulate, kindle flame, prepare and do anything necessary on the Festival for the sake of the Sabbath (for ourselves and for all Jews who live in this city).*

---

has appointed an agent to conduct the search or to burn his *chametz,* the agent should say, '... *that is in so-and-so's possession ...'* Nevertheless, it is preferable that the owner of the *chametz* recite the declaration, wherever he may be.

ERUV TAVSHILIN / עֵרוּב תַּבְשִׁילִין

The Biblical prohibition against the performance of labor on the festivals (*Exodus* 12:16) does not apply to preparation of food. Although it is forbidden to perform work on a Festival in preparation for a weekday, food preparation for the next day would be permitted by Scriptural law because, in the event guests were to come unexpectedly on the Festival, the food would be used for them — thus the preparation could be considered to be for Festival use. However, the Rabbis forbade such preparation for another day as as demeaning to the Festival.

Since the prohibition is of Rabbinic origin, the Sages instituted the following device to permit preparation of food for the Sabbath if a Festival falls on a Friday. The Sabbath food preparation must begin before the Festival starts. Then the Sages permitted the preparation to be continued on Friday. Thus, on the day before the Festival, one takes a *challah* or *matzah* along with another cooked food (such as fish, meat, or an egg). These foods are held while the blessing and declaration are recited, and are then set aside to be eaten on the Sabbath. This is known as *Eruv Tavshilin,* literally, *mingling of cooked foods,* since these foods become part of the Sabbath food, whose preparation has already begun and may be continued on Friday (*Orach Chaim* 527:1-2 according to *Mishnah Berurah;* cf. *Aruch HaShulchan*).

ערובי חצרות

The *eruv*-foods (see commentary) are held while the following blessing and declaration are recited:

בָּרוּךְ אַתָּה יהוה אֱלֹהֵינוּ מֶלֶךְ הָעוֹלָם, אֲשֶׁר קִדְּשָׁנוּ בְּמִצְוֹתָיו, וְצִוָּנוּ עַל מִצְוַת עֵרוּב.

בַּהֲדֵין עֵרוּבָא יְהֵא שָׁרֵא לָנָא לְאַפּוּקֵי וּלְעַיּוּלֵי מִן הַבָּתִּים לֶחָצֵר, וּמִן הֶחָצֵר לְבָתִּים, וּמִבַּיִת לְבַיִת, וּמֵחָצֵר לְחָצֵר, וּמִגַּג לְגַג, כָּל מַאי דִצְרִיךְ לָן, וּלְכָל יִשְׂרָאֵל הַדָּרִים בַּשְּׁכוּנָה זוּ [וּלְכָל מִי שֶׁיִּתּוֹסֵף בָּהּ, לְכָל שַׁבְּתוֹת הַשָּׁנָה, וּלְכָל יָמִים טוֹבִים].

ערובי תחומין

The *eruv*-food is put in a safe place and the following blessing and declaration are recited. The appropriate bracketed phrases should be added.

בָּרוּךְ אַתָּה יהוה אֱלֹהֵינוּ מֶלֶךְ הָעוֹלָם אֲשֶׁר קִדְּשָׁנוּ בְּמִצְוֹתָיו וְצִוָּנוּ עַל מִצְוַת עֵרוּב.

בְּזֶה הָעֵרוּב יְהֵא מֻתָּר [לִי/לָנוּ] לֵילֵךְ מִמָּקוֹם זֶה אַלְפַּיִם אַמָּה לְכָל רוּחַ [בְּשַׁבָּת/יוֹם טוֹב/יוֹם כִּיפּוּר] זֶה.

קידוש לליל יום טוב

The following *Kiddush* is recited on Festivals (*Kiddush* for Succos appears on page 722). On the Sabbath of Chol HaMoed the regular Sabbath *Kiddush* (p. 360), is recited.

When the Festival falls on Friday night, begin here:

(וַיְהִי עֶרֶב וַיְהִי בֹקֶר—Recite silently)

יוֹם הַשִּׁשִּׁי. וַיְכֻלּוּ הַשָּׁמַיִם וְהָאָרֶץ וְכָל צְבָאָם. וַיְכַל אֱלֹהִים בַּיּוֹם הַשְּׁבִיעִי מְלַאכְתּוֹ אֲשֶׁר עָשָׂה, וַיִּשְׁבֹּת בַּיּוֹם הַשְּׁבִיעִי מִכָּל מְלַאכְתּוֹ אֲשֶׁר עָשָׂה. וַיְבָרֶךְ אֱלֹהִים אֶת יוֹם הַשְּׁבִיעִי וַיְקַדֵּשׁ אֹתוֹ, כִּי בוֹ שָׁבַת מִכָּל מְלַאכְתּוֹ אֲשֶׁר בָּרָא אֱלֹהִים לַעֲשׂוֹת.[1]

עֵרוּבֵי חֲצֵרוֹת / MERGING OF COURTYARDS

The Sages forbade carrying from the private domain of one person to that of another on the Sabbath. A courtyard, hall or staircase shared by the residents of houses or apartments is regarded as a separate domain, and it is forbidden to carry from private dwellings into the shared area. The Sages provided a procedure — *eruvei chatzeiros* — to remove this prohibition. This procedure merges all the houses opening into the shared area into one ownership. This is done by collecting a loaf of bread or a matzah from each of the families and placing all the loaves in one of the dwelling units, to symbolize that all the contributors are residents of that unit. Consequently, the entire area is regarded as a single dwelling and all the residents may carry in all its parts on the Sabbath, as long as the breads are intact and edible at the onset of Sabbath. [The declaration given here is not valid if the *eruv* area includes a public thoroughfare. The procedure for such an area should not be undertaken by a layman.]

עֵרוּבֵי תְּחוּמִין / MERGING OF BOUNDARIES

On the Sabbath and Festivals, a person is forbidden to go more than 2,000 cubits from his

ERUVEI CHATZEIROS

The *eruv*-foods (see commentary) are held while the following blessing and declaration are recited:

בָּרוּךְ *Blessed are You,* Hashem, *our God, King of the universe, Who has sanctified us with His commandments and has commanded us concerning the mitzvah of eruv.*

בַּהֲדֵין עֵרוּבָא *Through this eruv may we be permitted to carry out or to carry in from the houses to the courtyard, and from the courtyard to the houses, from house to house, from courtyard to courtyard, and from roof to roof, all that we require, for ourselves and for all Jews who live in this area [and to all who will move into this area, for all the Sabbaths and Festivals of the year].*

ERUVEI TECHUMIN

The *eruv*-food is put in a safe place and the following blessing and declaration are recited. The appropriate bracketed phrases should be added.

בָּרוּךְ *Blessed are You,* Hashem, *our God, King of the universe, Who has sanctified us with His commandments and has commanded us concerning the mitzvah of eruv.*

בְּזֶה הָעֵרוּב *Through this eruv may [I/we] be permitted to walk two thousand cubits in every direction from this place during this [Sabbath/Festival/Yom Kippur].*

FESTIVAL EVE KIDDUSH

The following *Kiddush* is recited on Festivals (*Kiddush* for Succos appears on page 722). On the Sabbath of Chol HaMoed the regular Sabbath *Kiddush* (p. 360) is recited.

When the festival falls on Friday night, begin here:

(Recite silently— *And there was evening and there was morning)*

יוֹם הַשִּׁשִּׁי *The sixth day. Thus the heavens and earth were finished, and all their array. On the seventh day God completed His work which He had done, and He abstained on the seventh day from all His work which He had done. God blessed the seventh day and hallowed it, because on it He abstained from all His work which God created to make.*[1]

(1) *Genesis* 1:31-2:3.

halachically defined dwelling. This limit is called his תְּחוּם, *boundary*. Ordinarily, this 'dwelling' is the person's residence, but a person has the option of establishing his dwelling elsewhere. By placing a sufficient amount of food for two Sabbath meals in a place as much as 2,000 cubits from his residence, one establishes *that* place as his residence, and his 2,000 cubit radius is reckoned from there. [For a full discussion of *Eruvei Chatzeiros* and *Techumin*, see the Introduction to the ArtScroll *Mishnah Eruvin.*]

קִידּוּשׁ לְלֵיל יוֹם טוֹב / FESTIVAL EVE KIDDUSH

Commentary to the introductory passage (יוֹם הַשִּׁשִּׁי, *The sixth day*) recited on Friday evening appears on page 360. The main body of the sanctification blessing is an abridgement of the central blessing of the Festival *Shemoneh Esrei* and the commentary to *Shemoneh Esrei* (page 664) applies to *Kiddush* as well. On Saturday night, the blessing over the flame and the *Havdalah* blessing are added (commentary, page 618). Finally, on Festivals, *Kiddush* is concluded with the שֶׁהֶחֱיָנוּ blessing, except on the last two days of Pesach. Since those days are not a new Festival, but a continuation of Pesach, the blessing is inappropriate. Shemini Atzeres and *Simchas Torah*, however, have the status of a new Festival, not merely an extension of Succos; consequently שֶׁהֶחֱיָנוּ is recited then.

On all nights other than Friday begin here (on Friday night include all words in brackets):

סַבְרִי מָרָנָן וְרַבָּנָן וְרַבּוֹתַי:

בָּרוּךְ אַתָּה יהוה אֱלֹהֵינוּ מֶלֶךְ הָעוֹלָם, בּוֹרֵא פְּרִי הַגָּפֶן.

(All present respond— אָמֵן.)

בָּרוּךְ אַתָּה יהוה אֱלֹהֵינוּ מֶלֶךְ הָעוֹלָם, אֲשֶׁר בָּחַר בָּנוּ מִכָּל עָם, וְרוֹמְמָנוּ מִכָּל לָשׁוֹן, וְקִדְּשָׁנוּ בְּמִצְוֹתָיו. וַתִּתֶּן לָנוּ יהוה אֱלֹהֵינוּ בְּאַהֲבָה [שַׁבָּתוֹת לִמְנוּחָה וּ]מוֹעֲדִים לְשִׂמְחָה חַגִּים וּזְמַנִּים לְשָׂשׂוֹן, אֶת יוֹם [הַשַּׁבָּת הַזֶּה וְאֶת יוֹם]

Pesach	Shavuos	Shemini Atzeres/Simchas Torah
חַג הַמַּצּוֹת הַזֶּה, זְמַן חֵרוּתֵנוּ	חַג הַשָּׁבֻעוֹת הַזֶּה, זְמַן מַתַּן תּוֹרָתֵנוּ	הַשְּׁמִינִי חַג הָעֲצֶרֶת הַזֶּה, זְמַן שִׂמְחָתֵנוּ

[בְּאַהֲבָה] מִקְרָא קֹדֶשׁ, זֵכֶר לִיצִיאַת מִצְרָיִם. כִּי בָנוּ בָחַרְתָּ וְאוֹתָנוּ קִדַּשְׁתָּ מִכָּל הָעַמִּים, [וְשַׁבָּת] וּמוֹעֲדֵי קָדְשֶׁךָ [בְּאַהֲבָה וּבְרָצוֹן] בְּשִׂמְחָה וּבְשָׂשׂוֹן הִנְחַלְתָּנוּ. בָּרוּךְ אַתָּה יהוה, מְקַדֵּשׁ [הַשַּׁבָּת וְ]יִשְׂרָאֵל וְהַזְּמַנִּים.

(All present respond— אָמֵן.)

On Saturday night, add the following two *Havdalah* blessings. A multi-wicked candle or two ordinary candles with flames touching each other should be held before the person reciting the *Havdalah*. After the first blessing, hold the fingers up to the flames to see the reflected light.

בָּרוּךְ אַתָּה יהוה אֱלֹהֵינוּ מֶלֶךְ הָעוֹלָם, בּוֹרֵא מְאוֹרֵי הָאֵשׁ.

(All present respond— אָמֵן.)

בָּרוּךְ אַתָּה יהוה אֱלֹהֵינוּ מֶלֶךְ הָעוֹלָם, הַמַּבְדִּיל בֵּין קֹדֶשׁ לְחוֹל, בֵּין אוֹר לְחֹשֶׁךְ, בֵּין יִשְׂרָאֵל לָעַמִּים, בֵּין יוֹם הַשְּׁבִיעִי לְשֵׁשֶׁת יְמֵי הַמַּעֲשֶׂה. בֵּין קְדֻשַּׁת שַׁבָּת לִקְדֻשַּׁת יוֹם טוֹב הִבְדַּלְתָּ, וְאֶת יוֹם הַשְּׁבִיעִי מִשֵּׁשֶׁת יְמֵי הַמַּעֲשֶׂה קִדַּשְׁתָּ, הִבְדַּלְתָּ וְקִדַּשְׁתָּ אֶת עַמְּךָ יִשְׂרָאֵל בִּקְדֻשָּׁתֶךָ. בָּרוּךְ אַתָּה יהוה, הַמַּבְדִּיל בֵּין קֹדֶשׁ לְקֹדֶשׁ.

(All present respond— אָמֵן.)

The following blessing is omitted on the last two nights of Pesach:

בָּרוּךְ אַתָּה יהוה אֱלֹהֵינוּ מֶלֶךְ הָעוֹלָם, שֶׁהֶחֱיָנוּ* וְקִיְּמָנוּ וְהִגִּיעָנוּ לַזְּמַן הַזֶּה.

(All present respond— אָמֵן.)

The daytime *Kiddush* for Festivals appears on page 492.

הַבְדָּלָה / Havdalah

The blessing is made over the flame just as it is on an ordinary *Motza'ei* Shabbos (the conclusion of the Sabbath), because this blessing recalls the fact that Adam learned to make fire at the end of his first Sabbath in the Garden of Eden. However, there is one vital difference between this *Havdalah* and the ordinary one. On a Festival, although fire may be used and a flame

On all nights other than Friday begin here (on Friday night include all passages in brackets):

By your leave, my masters and teachers:

בָּרוּךְ *Blessed are you, HASHEM, our God, King of the universe, Who creates the fruit of the vine.* (All present respond— *Amen.*)

בָּרוּךְ *Blessed are you, HASHEM, our God, King of the universe, Who has chosen us from every people, exalted us above every tongue, and sanctified us with His commandments. And You gave us, HASHEM, our God, with love* [*Sabbaths for rest*], *appointed festivals for gladness, festivals and times for joy,* [*this day of Sabbath and*]

Pesach	Shavuos	Shemini Atzeres/Simchas Torah
this day of the Festival of Matzos, the time of our freedom	*this day of the Festival of Shavuos, the time of the giving of our Torah*	*the eighth day, this Festival of Assembly, the time of our gladness*

[*with love*] *a holy convocation, a memorial of the Exodus from Egypt. For You have chosen us and You have sanctified us above all the peoples,* [*and the Sabbath*] *and Your holy Festivals* [*in love and in favor*] *in gladness and in joy have You granted us as a heritage. Blessed are You, HASHEM, Who sanctifies* [*the Sabbath and*] *Israel and the festive seasons.*

(All present respond— *Amen.*)

On Saturday night, add the following two *Havdalah* blessings. A multi-wicked candle or two ordinary candles with flames touching each other, should be held before the person reciting the *Havdalah.* After the first blessing, hold the fingers up to the flames to see the reflected light.

בָּרוּךְ *Blessed are you, HASHEM, our God, King of the universe, Who creates the illumination of the fire.* (All present respond— *Amen.*)

בָּרוּךְ *Blessed are you, HASHEM, our God, King of the universe, Who distinguishes between the sacred and secular, between light and darkness, between Israel and the peoples, between the seventh day and the six days of labor. Between sanctity of the Sabbaths and the sanctity of the holidays You have distinguished, and the seventh day, from among the six days of labor You have sanctified. You have distinguished and You have sanctified Your people Israel with Your holiness. Blessed are You, HASHEM, Who distinguishes between holiness and holiness.* (All present respond— *Amen.*)

The following blessing is omitted on the last two nights of Pesach:

בָּרוּךְ *Blessed are you, HASHEM, our God, King of the universe, Who has kept us alive, sustained us, and brought us to this season.*

(All present respond— *Amen.*)

The daytime *Kiddush* for Festivals appears on page 492.

---

may be lit from an existing fire, it is forbidden to make a *new* flame. Therefore, one may not strike a match to light the *Havdalah* candle, nor may it be extinguished. The candles must be lit from another flame or the candles from the candelabrum may be held together, and after *Havdalah,* the candles must be left to burn themselves out.

שֶׁהֶחֱיָנוּ — *Who has kept us alive.* We have given the reading לִזְּמַן because it is the version found in virtually all siddurim. However, *Magen Avraham,* the Lubavitcher Siddur, and *Mishnah Berurah* (676:1) vocalize it as לַזְּמַן.

שמונה עשרה לשלש רגלים

This *Shemoneh Esrei* is recited at *Maariv, Shacharis* and *Minchah* on the Festival days of Pesach, Shavuos and Succos. On *Chol HaMoed* the weekday (or Sabbath) *Shemoneh Esrei* is recited. The *Shemoneh Esrei* for *Mussaf* may be found on p. 674.

Take three steps backward, then three steps forward. Remain standing with the feet together during *Shemoneh Esrei.* Recite it with quiet devotion and without any interruption, verbal or otherwise. Although it should not be audible to others, one must pray loudly enough to hear himself.

(At *Minchah*— כִּי שֵׁם יהוה אֶקְרָא, הָבוּ גֹדֶל לֵאלֹהֵינוּ.[1])

אֲדֹנָי שְׂפָתַי תִּפְתָּח, וּפִי יַגִּיד תְּהִלָּתֶךָ.[2]

אבות

Bend the knees at בָּרוּךְ; bow at אַתָּה; straighten up at ה׳.

בָּרוּךְ אַתָּה יהוה אֱלֹהֵינוּ וֵאלֹהֵי אֲבוֹתֵינוּ, אֱלֹהֵי אַבְרָהָם, אֱלֹהֵי יִצְחָק, וֵאלֹהֵי יַעֲקֹב, הָאֵל הַגָּדוֹל הַגִּבּוֹר וְהַנּוֹרָא, אֵל עֶלְיוֹן, גּוֹמֵל חֲסָדִים טוֹבִים וְקוֹנֵה הַכֹּל, וְזוֹכֵר חַסְדֵי אָבוֹת, וּמֵבִיא גוֹאֵל לִבְנֵי בְנֵיהֶם, לְמַעַן שְׁמוֹ בְּאַהֲבָה.

Bend the knees at בָּרוּךְ; bow at אַתָּה; straighten up at ה׳.

מֶלֶךְ עוֹזֵר וּמוֹשִׁיעַ וּמָגֵן. בָּרוּךְ אַתָּה יהוה, מָגֵן אַבְרָהָם.

גבורות

אַתָּה גִּבּוֹר לְעוֹלָם אֲדֹנָי, מְחַיֵּה מֵתִים אַתָּה, רַב לְהוֹשִׁיעַ.

At *Minchah* of Shemini Atzeres; all prayers of Simchas Torah; and *Maariv* and *Shacharis* of the first day of Pesach, add the following phrase.

מַשִּׁיב הָרוּחַ וּמוֹרִיד °הַגֶּשֶׁם [some say – °הַגָּשֶׁם].

[If forgotten, see *Laws* §68-75.]

מְכַלְכֵּל חַיִּים בְּחֶסֶד, מְחַיֵּה מֵתִים בְּרַחֲמִים רַבִּים, סוֹמֵךְ נוֹפְלִים, וְרוֹפֵא חוֹלִים, וּמַתִּיר אֲסוּרִים, וּמְקַיֵּם אֱמוּנָתוֹ לִישֵׁנֵי עָפָר. מִי כָמוֹךָ בַּעַל גְּבוּרוֹת, וּמִי דּוֹמֶה לָּךְ, מֶלֶךְ מֵמִית וּמְחַיֶּה וּמַצְמִיחַ יְשׁוּעָה. וְנֶאֱמָן אַתָּה לְהַחֲיוֹת מֵתִים. בָּרוּךְ אַתָּה יהוה, מְחַיֵּה הַמֵּתִים.

◆§ The Festival Prayers

Unlike the *Shemoneh Esrei* prayers of the Sabbath that concentrate primarily on the sanctity of the day, the Festival prayers stress Israel's status as God's Chosen People. The Sabbath derives its holiness from God Who rested on the seventh day of creation; its holiness predated Israel and is in no way dependent on the Jewish people. The Festivals, on the other hand, commemorate the history of Israel. Although the Sabbath, as the testimony to God the Creator, could exist without the Jewish people, there could be no Festivals unless there had been a nation that was freed from Egypt, given the Torah and sheltered in the Wilderness. This emphasis is apparent from the very start of the middle section of the Festival *Shemoneh Esrei,* which declares that God has chosen Israel from among the nations, a concept that is absent from the Sabbath *Shemoneh Esrei.*

Furthermore, since the Festivals are dependent on the calendar and the sanctification of the months — which the Torah assigns to the Jewish people through their courts — the Festivals are creatures of the Jewish people, as it were. (This concept has been discussed in *Kiddush Levanah* and *Mussaf* of Rosh Chodesh, p. 646.) Another

SHEMONEH ESREI FOR THE FESTIVALS

This *Shemoneh Esrei* is recited at *Maariv, Shacharis* and *Minchah* on the Festival days of Pesach, Shavuos and Succos. On *Chol HaMoed* the weekday (or Sabbath) *Shemoneh Esrei* is recited. The *Shemoneh Esrei* for *Mussaf* may be found on page 674.

Take three steps backward, then three steps forward. Remain standing with the feet together during *Shemoneh Esrei*. Recite it with quiet devotion and without any interruption, verbal or otherwise. Although it should not be audible to others, one must pray loudly enough to hear himself.

(At *Minchah— When I call out the Name of* HASHEM, *ascribe greatness to our God.*[1])
My Lord, open my lips, that my mouth may declare Your praise.[2]

PATRIARCHS

Bend the knees at *'Blessed'*; bow at *'You'*; straighten up at *'HASHEM'*.

בָּרוּךְ *Blessed are You,* HASHEM, *our God and the God of our forefathers, God of Abraham, God of Isaac, and God of Jacob; the great, mighty, and awesome God, the supreme God, Who bestows beneficial kindnesses and creates everything, Who recalls the kindnesses of the Patriarchs and brings a Redeemer to their children's children, for His Name's sake, with love.*

Bend the knees at *'Blessed'*; bow at *'You'*; straighten up at 'HASHEM.'

O King, Helper, Savior, and Shield. Blessed are You, HASHEM, *Shield of Abraham.*

GOD'S MIGHT

אַתָּה *You are eternally mighty, my Lord, the Resuscitator of the dead are You; abundantly able to* ***save,***

At *Minchah* of Shemini Atzeres; all prayers of Simchas Torah; and *Maariv* and *Shacharis* of the first day of Pesach, add the following phrase.

Who makes the wind blow and makes the rain descend;

[If forgotten, see *Laws* §68-75.]

Who sustains the living with kindness, *resuscitates the dead with abundant mercy, supports the fallen, heals the sick, releases the confined, and maintains His faith to those asleep in the dust. Who is like You, O Master of mighty deeds, and who is comparable to You, O King Who causes death and restores life and makes salvation sprout! And You are faithful to resuscitate the dead. Blessed are You,* HASHEM, *Who resuscitates the dead.*

(1) *Deuteronomy* 32:3. (2) *Psalms* 51:17.

---

feature unique to the Festivals is that joy is an integral part of their observance. Both of these features are reflected in the Festival *Shemoneh Esrei*.

The basic structure of the Festival *Shemoneh Esrei* is similar to that of the Sabbath in that it consists of seven blessings: the same three-blessing introduction and conclusion as those of every other *Shemoneh Esrei* all year round, and a single-blessing mid-section that contains the prayers of the day. As explained in the commentary to the Sabbath prayers, each *Shemoneh Esrei* of the Sabbath refers to a different aspect of the day, and is therefore unique. These differences do not apply on Festivals with the result that all the *Shemoneh Esrei* services (with the exception of *Mussaf*, of course) are identical.

☙ The commentary for the first section of *Shemoneh Esrei* and the shorter version of *Kedushah* may be found on page 98. The commentary for the longer version of *Kedushah* may be found on page 422.

During the *chazzan's* repetition, *Kedushah* (below) is recited at this point.

קדושת השם

אַתָּה קָדוֹשׁ וְשִׁמְךָ קָדוֹשׁ, וּקְדוֹשִׁים בְּכָל יוֹם יְהַלְלְוּךָ סֶּלָה. בָּרוּךְ אַתָּה יהוה, הָאֵל הַקָּדוֹשׁ.

קדושת היום

אַתָּה בְחַרְתָּנוּ* מִכָּל הָעַמִּים, אָהַבְתָּ אוֹתָנוּ, וְרָצִיתָ בָּנוּ, וְרוֹמַמְתָּנוּ מִכָּל הַלְּשׁוֹנוֹת,* וְקִדַּשְׁתָּנוּ בְּמִצְוֹתֶיךָ,* וְקֵרַבְתָּנוּ מַלְכֵּנוּ לַעֲבוֹדָתֶךָ, וְשִׁמְךָ הַגָּדוֹל וְהַקָּדוֹשׁ עָלֵינוּ קָרָאתָ.*

קדושה

When reciting *Kedushah,* one must stand with his feet together, and avoid any interruptions. One should rise to his toes when saying the words קָדוֹשׁ, קָדוֹשׁ, קָדוֹשׁ; בָּרוּךְ; (of בָּרוּךְ כְּבוֹד); and יִמְלֹךְ.

—Cong. then *Chazzan* **נְקַדֵּשׁ** אֶת שִׁמְךָ בָּעוֹלָם, כְּשֵׁם שֶׁמַּקְדִּישִׁים אוֹתוֹ בִּשְׁמֵי מָרוֹם, כַּכָּתוּב עַל יַד נְבִיאֶךָ, וְקָרָא זֶה אֶל זֶה וְאָמַר:

—All קָדוֹשׁ קָדוֹשׁ קָדוֹשׁ יהוה צְבָאוֹת, מְלֹא כָל הָאָרֶץ כְּבוֹדוֹ.[1]

AT SHACHARIS

Cong. then *chazzan:*

אָז בְּקוֹל רַעַשׁ גָּדוֹל אַדִּיר וְחָזָק מַשְׁמִיעִים קוֹל, מִתְנַשְּׂאִים לְעֻמַּת שְׂרָפִים, לְעֻמָּתָם בָּרוּךְ יֹאמֵרוּ:

—All בָּרוּךְ כְּבוֹד יהוה, מִמְּקוֹמוֹ.[2]

Cong. then *chazzan:*

מִמְּקוֹמְךָ מַלְכֵּנוּ תוֹפִיעַ, וְתִמְלוֹךְ עָלֵינוּ, כִּי מְחַכִּים אֲנַחְנוּ לָךְ. מָתַי תִּמְלוֹךְ בְּצִיּוֹן, בְּקָרוֹב בְּיָמֵינוּ, לְעוֹלָם וָעֶד תִּשְׁכּוֹן. תִּתְגַּדַּל וְתִתְקַדַּשׁ בְּתוֹךְ יְרוּשָׁלַיִם עִירְךָ, לְדוֹר וָדוֹר וּלְנֵצַח נְצָחִים. וְעֵינֵינוּ תִרְאֶינָה מַלְכוּתֶךָ, כַּדָּבָר הָאָמוּר בְּשִׁירֵי עֻזֶּךָ, עַל יְדֵי דָוִד מְשִׁיחַ צִדְקֶךָ:

AT MINCHAH

Chazzan:

לְעֻמָּתָם בָּרוּךְ יֹאמֵרוּ:

All:

בָּרוּךְ כְּבוֹד יהוה, מִמְּקוֹמוֹ.[2]

Chazzan:

וּבְדִבְרֵי קָדְשְׁךָ כָּתוּב לֵאמֹר:

—All יִמְלֹךְ יהוה לְעוֹלָם, אֱלֹהַיִךְ צִיּוֹן, לְדֹר וָדֹר, הַלְלוּיָהּ.[3]

—*Chazzan* only concludes לְדוֹר וָדוֹר נַגִּיד גָּדְלֶךָ וּלְנֵצַח נְצָחִים קְדֻשָּׁתְךָ נַקְדִּישׁ, וְשִׁבְחֲךָ אֱלֹהֵינוּ מִפִּינוּ לֹא יָמוּשׁ לְעוֹלָם וָעֶד, כִּי אֵל מֶלֶךְ גָּדוֹל וְקָדוֹשׁ אָתָּה. בָּרוּךְ אַתָּה יהוה, הָאֵל הַקָּדוֹשׁ.

Chazzan continues ... אַתָּה בְחַרְתָּנוּ.

❧ **אַתָּה בְחַרְתָּנוּ** – *You have chosen us.* As noted above, the theme of the *Shemoneh Esrei* is that God has chosen Israel to be the bearers of His mission on earth.

מִכָּל הַלְּשׁוֹנוֹת – *Above all the tongues.* Human language is capable of capturing sublime thoughts and complex ideas, but Israel was granted the language of the Torah, which encompasses God's own wisdom and which is uniquely suited to expressing concepts of holiness.

וְקִדַּשְׁתָּנוּ בְּמִצְוֹתֶיךָ – *And You sanctified us with Your commandments.* Unlike the laws of human legislatures and monarchs, the laws of the Torah

During the *chazzan's* repetition, *Kedushah* (below) is recited at this point.

HOLINESS OF GOD'S NAME

אַתָּה *You are holy and Your Name is holy, and holy ones praise You every day, forever. Blessed are You,* HASHEM, *the holy God.*

SANCTIFICATION OF THE DAY

אַתָּה בְחַרְתָּנוּ *You have chosen us* from all the peoples; You loved us and found favor in us; You exalted us above all the tongues* and You sanctified us with Your commandments.* You drew us close, our King, to Your service and proclaimed Your great and Holy Name upon us.**

KEDUSHAH

When reciting *Kedushah,* one must stand with his feet together and avoid any interruptions. One should rise to his toes when saying the words *Holy, holy, holy; Blessed;* and HASHEM *shall reign.*

Cong.— then Chazzan **נְקַדֵּשׁ** *We shall sanctify Your Name in this world, just as they sanctify it in heaven above, as it is written by Your prophet, "And one [angel] will call another and say:*

All— *'Holy, holy, holy is* HASHEM, *Master of Legions, the whole world is filled with His glory.' "*[1]

AT SHACHARIS

Cong. then *chazzan:*

Then, with a sound of great noise, mighty and powerful, they make heard a voice, raising themselves toward the seraphim; *those facing them say 'Blessed ...':*

All— *'Blessed is the glory of* HASHEM *from His place.'*[2]

Cong. then *chazzan:*

From Your place, our King, You will appear and reign over us, for we await You. When will You reign in Zion? Soon, in our days — forever and ever — may You dwell there. May You be exalted and sanctified within Jerusalem, Your city, from generation to generation and for all eternity. May our eyes see Your Kingdom, as it is expressed in the songs of Your might, written by David, Your righteous anointed:

AT MINCHAH

Chazzan:

Those facing them say 'Blessed':

All—

'Blessed is the glory of HASHEM *from His place.'*[2]

Chazzan—

And in Your holy Writings the following is written:

All— *'*HASHEM *shall reign forever — your God, O Zion — from generation to generation, Halleluyah!'*[3]

Chazzan only concludes— *From generation to generation we shall relate Your greatness and for infinite eternities we shall proclaim Your holiness. Your praise, our God, shall not leave our mouth forever and ever, for You, O God, are a great and holy King. Blessed are You* HASHEM, *the holy God.*

Chazzan continues ... אַתָּה בְחַרְתָּנוּ, *'You have chosen us ...'*

(1) *Isaiah* 6:3. (2) *Ezekiel* 3:12. (3) *Psalms* 146:10.

---

infuse holiness into those who observe them.

וְשִׁמְךָ ... עָלֵינוּ קָרָאתָ — *And proclaimed Your ... Name upon us.* We are proud and grateful that God wished to be known as the God of Israel.

The three expressions at the beginning of this paragraph — *chosen, loved,* and *found favor* — allude to the respective historical characteristics

The following is recited when the Festival falls on Saturday night:

וַתּוֹדִיעֵנוּ* יהוה אֱלֹהֵינוּ אֶת מִשְׁפְּטֵי צִדְקֶךָ, וַתְּלַמְּדֵנוּ לַעֲשׂוֹת (בָּהֶם) חֻקֵּי רְצוֹנֶךָ. וַתִּתֶּן לָנוּ* יהוה אֱלֹהֵינוּ מִשְׁפָּטִים יְשָׁרִים וְתוֹרוֹת אֱמֶת חֻקִּים וּמִצְוֹת טוֹבִים. וַתַּנְחִילֵנוּ זְמַנֵּי שָׂשׂוֹן וּמוֹעֲדֵי קֹדֶשׁ וְחַגֵּי נְדָבָה.* וַתּוֹרִישֵׁנוּ קְדֻשַּׁת שַׁבָּת וּכְבוֹד מוֹעֵד וַחֲגִיגַת הָרֶגֶל. וַתַּבְדֵּל* יהוה אֱלֹהֵינוּ בֵּין קֹדֶשׁ לְחוֹל, בֵּין אוֹר לְחֹשֶׁךְ, בֵּין יִשְׂרָאֵל לָעַמִּים, בֵּין יוֹם הַשְּׁבִיעִי לְשֵׁשֶׁת יְמֵי הַמַּעֲשֶׂה. בֵּין קְדֻשַּׁת שַׁבָּת לִקְדֻשַּׁת יוֹם טוֹב הִבְדַּלְתָּ, וְאֶת יוֹם הַשְּׁבִיעִי מִשֵּׁשֶׁת יְמֵי הַמַּעֲשֶׂה קִדַּשְׁתָּ, הִבְדַּלְתָּ וְקִדַּשְׁתָּ אֶת עַמְּךָ יִשְׂרָאֵל בִּקְדֻשָּׁתֶךָ.

On the Sabbath add the words in brackets. If forgotten, *Shemoneh Esrei must* be repeated. The same is true if the festival names are omitted or transposed. However, if one said the Succos phrase on Shemini Atzeres, no repetition is necessary.

וַתִּתֶּן לָנוּ* יהוה אֱלֹהֵינוּ בְּאַהֲבָה [שַׁבָּתוֹת לִמְנוּחָה וּ]מוֹעֲדִים* לְשִׂמְחָה חַגִּים* וּזְמַנִּים לְשָׂשׂוֹן, אֶת יוֹם [הַשַּׁבָּת הַזֶּה וְאֶת יוֹם]

On Shemini Atzeres/Simchas Torah	On Succos	On Shavuos	On Pesach
הַשְּׁמִינִי חַג הָעֲצֶרֶת הַזֶּה, זְמַן שִׂמְחָתֵנוּ	חַג הַסֻּכּוֹת הַזֶּה, זְמַן שִׂמְחָתֵנוּ	חַג הַשָּׁבֻעוֹת הַזֶּה, זְמַן מַתַּן תּוֹרָתֵנוּ	חַג הַמַּצּוֹת הַזֶּה, זְמַן חֵרוּתֵנוּ

[בְּאַהֲבָה*] מִקְרָא קֹדֶשׁ,* זֵכֶר לִיצִיאַת מִצְרָיִם.

---

of the three pilgrimage festivals, which will be named in וַתִּתֶּן לָנוּ, *You gave us.* On Pesach, God chose us from among the Egyptians; on Shavuos He showed His love for us by giving us His Torah; and on Succos, He showed us favor by forgiving the sin of the Golden Calf and bringing us under the Divine shelter which is symbolized by the *succah*-booth *(Siach Yitzchak).*

These three terms are suited to their respective festivals. The term "choose" implies that one selects one person or thing over others — not that it is perfect, but because it is the best of the lot, or because of its potential. Thus, Pesach marks the "choice" of an imperfect Israel that had enormous potential for good. One "loves" another because he is compatible emotionally or in deed. God showed His love on Shavuos by giving us the Torah. "Favor" is the highest of all levels, because it transcends logic. Even after Israel sinned with the Golden Calf, God had "found favor" in Israel to such a degree that He forgave the sin on Yom Kippur and ushered in Succos, the most joyous of all the festivals *(Poras Yosef).*

וַתּוֹדִיעֵנוּ — *You made known to us.* This paragraph, which was composed by the Talmudic sages, Rav and Shmuel *(Berachos* 33b), takes the place of אַתָּה חוֹנַנְתָּנוּ, *You have graced us,* the insertion at the conclusion of the regular Sabbath that draws the distinction between the holy and the secular (see p. 268). Despite the great sanctity of the Festivals, they are less holy than the Sabbath, hence the requirement that *Havdalah* be recited here in *Shemoneh Esrei* and as part of the *Kiddush.*

וַתִּתֶּן לָנוּ — *You gave us.* God gave us many commandments of various kinds — some that are comprehensible to the human mind, some that teach us to perceive our proper role in creation, some decrees that are above our comprehension, and commandments to regulate all facets of our behavior in a manner that will bring us closer to His service. The Sabbaths and Festivals are uniquely suited to inspire us with renewed sanctity to strive toward the fulfillment of the tasks God has set for us *(R' Hirsch).*

זְמַנֵּי שָׂשׂוֹן וּמוֹעֲדֵי קֹדֶשׁ וְחַגֵּי נְדָבָה — *Seasons of joy, appointed Festivals of holiness, and free-willed festive offerings.* These three terms refer to three aspects of the Festivals. Firstly, they are seasons of joy as regards the agricultural cycle: Pesach comes in springtime; Shavuos ushers in the time of the first fruits; and Succos is the festive season of harvest. Secondly, they are appointed

The following is recited when the Festival falls on Saturday night:

וַתּוֹדִיעֵנוּ *You made known to us,* HASHEM, our God, Your righteous ordinances, and You taught us to do the decrees of Your will. You gave us,* HASHEM, our God, fair laws and true teachings, good decrees and commandments. As a heritage You gave us seasons of joy, appointed Festivals of holiness, and free-willed festive offerings.* You made us heir to the Sabbath holiness, the appointed Festival glory, and festive offering of the pilgrimage. You distinguished,* O HASHEM, our God between the sacred and secular, between light and darkness, between Israel and the peoples, between the seventh day and the six days of labor. Between the sanctity of the Sabbath and the sanctity of the holiday You have distinguished, and the seventh day, from among the six days of labor You have sanctified. You have distinguished and You have sanctified Your people Israel with Your holiness.*

On the Sabbath add the words in brackets. If forgotten, *Shemoneh Esrei must* be repeated. The same is true if the festival names are omitted or transposed. However, if one said the Succos phrase on Shemini Atzeres, no repetition is necessary.

וַתִּתֶּן *And You gave us,* HASHEM, our God, with love [Sabbaths for rest], appointed festivals* for gladness, Festivals* and times for joy, [this day of Sabbath and]*

On Pesach	On Shavuos	On Succos	On Shemini Atzeres and Simchas Torah
this day of the Festival of Matzos, the time of our freedom	*this day of the Festival of Shavuos, the time of the giving of our Torah*	*this day of the Festival of Succos, the time of our gladness*	*the eighth day, this Festival of Assembly, the time of our gladness*

[with love] a holy convocation,* a memorial of the Exodus from Egypt.*

---

as Festivals because of their historical significance: Pesach commemorates the Exodus; Shavuos recalls the Revelation at Sinai; and Succos reminds us that God sheltered us in the Wilderness. Finally these three terms recall the three kinds of offerings, expressing both devotion and joy, that were offered by the multitudes of Jews who came to Jerusalem for each of the three annual pilgrimage Festivals *(R' Hirsch).*

וַתַּבְדֵּל — *You distinguished.* The following list parallels the one found in the weekday *Shemoneh Esrei* recited at the conclusion of the Sabbath, except, of course, that this one includes the distinction between the Sabbath and Festival holiness.

☙ וַתִּתֶּן לָנוּ — *And You gave us.* Having chosen us, God gave us this special day. If the Festival falls on a Sabbath, that day, too, is mentioned here specifically. The difference in description between the Sabbath and the Festivals expresses a major difference between them. Although there is rest on the Festivals and gladness on the Sabbath, their primary features are, as we say here, Sabbath for *rest* and Festivals for *gladness.*

מוֹעֲדִים — *Appointed Festivals.* This term for the Festivals has the connotation of meeting, i.e., God has designated times when Israel can greet His Presence.

חַגִּים — *Festivals.* The word חַג is sometimes used for the Festival day and sometimes to refer to the קָרְבַּן חֲגִיגָה, *festive offering,* that pilgrims brought in celebration of the day.

בְּאַהֲבָה — *With love.* This extra expression of love, referring only to the Sabbath, denotes the particular affection with which Israel accepted the commandments of the Sabbath. Whereas the Festival observance represents our acknowledgment of God's kindness to our ancestors, the Sabbath shows our desire to honor Him as the Creator.

מִקְרָא קֹדֶשׁ — *A holy convocation.* On these days, the nation is called upon to gather for the pursuit of holiness, and to sanctify the Festival through prayer and praise to God *(Ramban; Sforno).*

During the *chazzan's* repetition, the congregation responds אָמֵן as indicated.

אֱלֹהֵינוּ וֵאלֹהֵי אֲבוֹתֵינוּ, יַעֲלֶה, וְיָבֹא,* וְיַגִּיעַ, וְיֵרָאֶה, וְיֵרָצֶה, וְיִשָּׁמַע, וְיִפָּקֵד, וְיִזָּכֵר זִכְרוֹנֵנוּ וּפִקְדוֹנֵנוּ, וְזִכְרוֹן אֲבוֹתֵינוּ, וְזִכְרוֹן מָשִׁיחַ בֶּן דָּוִד עַבְדֶּךָ, וְזִכְרוֹן יְרוּשָׁלַיִם עִיר קָדְשֶׁךָ, וְזִכְרוֹן כָּל עַמְּךָ בֵּית יִשְׂרָאֵל לְפָנֶיךָ, לִפְלֵיטָה לְטוֹבָה לְחֵן וּלְחֶסֶד וּלְרַחֲמִים, לְחַיִּים וּלְשָׁלוֹם בְּיוֹם

On Pesach	On Shavuos	On Succos	On Shemini Atzeres/Simchas Torah
חַג הַמַּצּוֹת	חַג הַשָּׁבֻעוֹת	חַג הַסֻּכּוֹת	הַשְּׁמִינִי חַג הָעֲצֶרֶת*

הַזֶּה. זָכְרֵנוּ יהוה אֱלֹהֵינוּ בּוֹ לְטוֹבָה (Cong. — אָמֵן), וּפָקְדֵנוּ בוֹ לִבְרָכָה (Cong. — אָמֵן), וְהוֹשִׁיעֵנוּ בוֹ לְחַיִּים (Cong. — אָמֵן). וּבִדְבַר יְשׁוּעָה וְרַחֲמִים, חוּס וְחָנֵּנוּ וְרַחֵם עָלֵינוּ וְהוֹשִׁיעֵנוּ, כִּי אֵלֶיךָ עֵינֵינוּ, כִּי אֵל מֶלֶךְ חַנּוּן וְרַחוּם אָתָּה.[1]

Add the words in brackets on the Sabbath.

וְהַשִּׂיאֵנוּ* יהוה אֱלֹהֵינוּ אֶת בִּרְכַּת מוֹעֲדֶיךָ לְחַיִּים וּלְשָׁלוֹם, לְשִׂמְחָה וּלְשָׂשׂוֹן, כַּאֲשֶׁר רָצִיתָ* וְאָמַרְתָּ לְבָרְכֵנוּ. [אֱלֹהֵינוּ וֵאלֹהֵי אֲבוֹתֵינוּ רְצֵה בִמְנוּחָתֵנוּ] קַדְּשֵׁנוּ בְּמִצְוֹתֶיךָ וְתֵן חֶלְקֵנוּ בְּתוֹרָתֶךָ, שַׂבְּעֵנוּ מִטּוּבֶךָ וְשַׂמְּחֵנוּ בִּישׁוּעָתֶךָ, וְטַהֵר לִבֵּנוּ לְעָבְדְּךָ בֶּאֱמֶת, וְהַנְחִילֵנוּ יהוה אֱלֹהֵינוּ [בְּאַהֲבָה וּבְרָצוֹן] בְּשִׂמְחָה וּבְשָׂשׂוֹן [שַׁבָּת וּ]מוֹעֲדֵי קָדְשֶׁךָ, וְיִשְׂמְחוּ בְךָ יִשְׂרָאֵל מְקַדְּשֵׁי שְׁמֶךָ. בָּרוּךְ אַתָּה יהוה, מְקַדֵּשׁ [הַשַּׁבָּת וְ]יִשְׂרָאֵל וְהַזְּמַנִּים.*

יַעֲלֶה וְיָבֹא ☙ — *May there rise, come.* Our exultant recollection of the Festivals as testament to Israel's chosenness brings home the poignant reality that we still lack the opportunity to ascend to the Temple and serve God as He commanded us. Therefore, we pray that He will bring an end to the exile and reunite Israel, Jerusalem, and the Temple. For commentary, see page 111.

הַשְּׁמִינִי חַג הָעֲצֶרֶת — *The eighth day ... Festival of Assembly.* Although it is the eighth day of Succos, Shemini Atzeres is regarded as an independent Festival, as is indicated by the uniqueness of its *Mussaf* offering (see *Mussaf Shemoneh Esrei,* p. 674). Nevertheless, it is also an extension of Succos, as indicated by the designation, 'time of our gladness.' The word עֲצֶרֶת means *assembly,* as if to say that a loving God has asked His people Israel to remain with Him for an extra day after Succos. All during Succos, the *Mussaf* service had included sacrifices in honor of the seventy nations of the world, but on Shemini Atzeres the *Mussaf* was a smaller one symbolizing only the Jewish nation, because this day is a time of private communion, as it were, between God and Israel *(Rashi, Leviticus* 23:36).

During the *chazzan's* repetition, the congregation responds *Amen* as indicated.

אֱלֹהֵינוּ *Our God and God of our forefathers, may there rise, come,* reach, be noted, be favored, be heard, be considered, and be remembered — the remembrance and consideration of ourselves; the remembrance of our forefathers; the remembrance of Messiah, son of David, Your servant; the remembrance of Jerusalem, the City of Your Holiness; the remembrance of Your entire people the Family of Israel — before You for deliverance, for goodness, for grace, for kindness, and for compassion, for life, and for peace on*

On Pesach	On Shavuos	On Succos	On Shemini Atzeres and Simchas Torah
this day of the Festival of Matzos,	*this day of the Festival of Shavuos,*	*this day of the Festival of Succos,*	*the eighth day, this Festival of Assembly,**

Remember us on it, H*ASHEM*, *our God, for goodness* (Cong.— *Amen*), *consider us on it for blessing* (Cong.— *Amen*), *and help us on it for life* (Cong.— *Amen*). *In the matter of salvation and compassion, pity, be gracious and compassionate with us and help us, for our eyes are turned to You, because You are God, the gracious, and compassionate King.*[1]

Add the words in brackets on the Sabbath.

וְהַשִּׂיאֵנוּ *Bestow upon us,* O* H*ASHEM*, *our God, the blessing of Your appointed Festivals for life and for peace, for gladness and for joy, as You desired* and promised to bless us. [Our God and the God of our forefathers, may You be pleased with our rest.] Sanctify us with Your commandments and grant us our share in Your Torah; satisfy us from Your goodness and gladden us with Your salvation, and purify our heart to serve You sincerely. And grant us a heritage, O* H*ASHEM our God — [with love and with favor] with gladness and with joy — [the Sabbath and] the appointed festivals of Your holiness, and may Israel, the sanctifiers of Your Name, rejoice in You. Blessed are you,* H*ASHEM*, *Who sanctifies [the Sabbath] Israel and the festive seasons.**

(1) Cf. *Nechemiah* 9:31.

❧ וְהַשִּׂיאֵנוּ — *Bestow upon us.* In concluding the central portion of the *Shemoneh Esrei,* we ask God to give all the joyous blessings of the day and season.

כַּאֲשֶׁר רָצִיתָ — *As You desired.* God wishes to bless and help His people; it remains for us to be worthy of His blessings.

מְקַדֵּשׁ יִשְׂרָאֵל וְהַזְּמַנִּים — *Who sanctifies Israel and the festive seasons.* The use of the word זְמַנִּים, *festive seasons,* rather than the Scriptural term מוֹעֲדִים, *appointed Festivals,* alludes to a special feature of the Jewish calendar. The Torah ordains that Pesach must fall in the springtime, thus the court must take the זְמַנִּים, *seasons,* into account in formulating the calendar *(R' Bachya).*

עבודה

רְצֵה יהוה אֱלֹהֵינוּ בְּעַמְּךָ יִשְׂרָאֵל וּבִתְפִלָּתָם, וְהָשֵׁב אֶת הָעֲבוֹדָה לִדְבִיר בֵּיתֶךָ. וְאִשֵּׁי יִשְׂרָאֵל וּתְפִלָּתָם בְּאַהֲבָה תְקַבֵּל בְּרָצוֹן, וּתְהִי לְרָצוֹן תָּמִיד עֲבוֹדַת יִשְׂרָאֵל עַמֶּךָ.

וְתֶחֱזֶינָה עֵינֵינוּ בְּשׁוּבְךָ לְצִיּוֹן בְּרַחֲמִים. בָּרוּךְ אַתָּה יהוה, הַמַּחֲזִיר שְׁכִינָתוֹ לְצִיּוֹן.

הודאה

Bow at מוֹדִים; straighten up at ה׳. In his repetition the *chazzan* should recite the entire מוֹדִים aloud, while the congregation recites מוֹדִים דְּרַבָּנָן softly.

מוֹדִים אֲנַחְנוּ לָךְ שָׁאַתָּה הוּא יהוה אֱלֹהֵינוּ וֵאלֹהֵי אֲבוֹתֵינוּ לְעוֹלָם וָעֶד. צוּר חַיֵּינוּ, מָגֵן יִשְׁעֵנוּ אַתָּה הוּא לְדוֹר וָדוֹר. נוֹדֶה לְּךָ וּנְסַפֵּר תְּהִלָּתֶךָ[1] עַל חַיֵּינוּ הַמְּסוּרִים בְּיָדֶךָ, וְעַל נִשְׁמוֹתֵינוּ הַפְּקוּדוֹת לָךְ, וְעַל נִסֶּיךָ שֶׁבְּכָל יוֹם עִמָּנוּ, וְעַל נִפְלְאוֹתֶיךָ וְטוֹבוֹתֶיךָ שֶׁבְּכָל עֵת, עֶרֶב וָבֹקֶר וְצָהֳרָיִם. הַטּוֹב כִּי לֹא כָלוּ רַחֲמֶיךָ, וְהַמְרַחֵם כִּי לֹא תַמּוּ חֲסָדֶיךָ,[2] מֵעוֹלָם קִוִּינוּ לָךְ.

מודים דרבנן

מוֹדִים אֲנַחְנוּ לָךְ, שָׁאַתָּה הוּא יהוה אֱלֹהֵינוּ וֵאלֹהֵי אֲבוֹתֵינוּ, אֱלֹהֵי כָל בָּשָׂר, יוֹצְרֵנוּ, יוֹצֵר בְּרֵאשִׁית. בְּרָכוֹת וְהוֹדָאוֹת לְשִׁמְךָ הַגָּדוֹל וְהַקָּדוֹשׁ, עַל שֶׁהֶחֱיִיתָנוּ וְקִיַּמְתָּנוּ. כֵּן תְּחַיֵּנוּ וּתְקַיְּמֵנוּ, וְתֶאֱסוֹף גָּלֻיּוֹתֵינוּ לְחַצְרוֹת קָדְשֶׁךָ, לִשְׁמוֹר חֻקֶּיךָ וְלַעֲשׂוֹת רְצוֹנֶךָ, וּלְעָבְדְּךָ בְּלֵבָב שָׁלֵם, עַל שֶׁאֲנַחְנוּ מוֹדִים לָךְ. בָּרוּךְ אֵל הַהוֹדָאוֹת.

וְעַל כֻּלָּם יִתְבָּרַךְ וְיִתְרוֹמַם שִׁמְךָ מַלְכֵּנוּ תָּמִיד לְעוֹלָם וָעֶד.

Bend the knees at בָּרוּךְ; bow at אַתָּה; straighten up at ה׳.

וְכֹל הַחַיִּים יוֹדוּךָ סֶּלָה, וִיהַלְלוּ אֶת שִׁמְךָ בֶּאֱמֶת, הָאֵל יְשׁוּעָתֵנוּ וְעֶזְרָתֵנוּ סֶלָה. בָּרוּךְ אַתָּה יהוה, הַטּוֹב שִׁמְךָ וּלְךָ נָאֶה לְהוֹדוֹת.

ברכת כהנים

At *Shacharis,* the *chazzan* recites בִּרְכַּת כֹּהֲנִים during his repetition. He faces right at וְיִשְׁמְרֶךָ; faces left at אֵלֶיךָ וִיחֻנֶּךָּ; faces the Ark for the rest of the blessings.

אֱלֹהֵינוּ, וֵאלֹהֵי אֲבוֹתֵינוּ, בָּרְכֵנוּ בַבְּרָכָה הַמְּשֻׁלֶּשֶׁת, בַּתּוֹרָה הַכְּתוּבָה עַל יְדֵי מֹשֶׁה עַבְדֶּךָ, הָאֲמוּרָה מִפִּי אַהֲרֹן וּבָנָיו, כֹּהֲנִים עַם קְדוֹשֶׁךָ, כָּאָמוּר:

יְבָרֶכְךָ יהוה, וְיִשְׁמְרֶךָ. (—Cong. כֵּן יְהִי רָצוֹן.)

יָאֵר יהוה פָּנָיו אֵלֶיךָ וִיחֻנֶּךָּ. (—Cong. כֵּן יְהִי רָצוֹן.)

יִשָּׂא יהוה פָּנָיו אֵלֶיךָ וְיָשֵׂם לְךָ שָׁלוֹם.[3] (—Cong. כֵּן יְהִי רָצוֹן.)

TEMPLE SERVICE

רְצֵה *Be favorable, HASHEM, our God, toward Your people Israel and their prayer and restore the service to the Holy of Holies of Your Temple. The fire-offerings of Israel and their prayer accept with love and favor, and may the service of Your people Israel always be favorable to You.*

וְתֶחֱזֶינָה *May our eyes behold Your return to Zion in compassion. Blessed are You, HASHEM, Who restores His Presence to Zion.*

THANKSGIVING [MODIM]

Bow at *'We gratefully thank You'*; straighten up at *'HASHEM.'* In his repetition the *chazzan* should recite the entire *Modim* aloud, while the congregation recites *Modim of the Rabbis* softly.

מוֹדִים *We gratefully thank You, for it is You Who are HASHEM, our God and the God of our forefathers for all eternity; Rock of our lives, Shield of our salvation are You from generation to generation. We shall thank You and relate Your praise[1] — for our lives, which are committed to Your power and for our souls that are entrusted to You; for Your miracles that are with us every day; and for Your wonders and favors in every season — evening, morning, and afternoon. The Beneficent One, for Your compassions were never exhausted, and the Compassionate One, for Your kindnesses never ended[2] — always have we put our hope in You.*

MODIM OF THE RABBIS

מוֹדִים *We gratefully thank You, for it is You Who are HASHEM, our God and the God of our forefathers, the God of all flesh, our Molder, the Molder of the universe. Blessings and thanks are due Your great and holy Name for You have given us life and sustained us. So may You continue to give us life and sustain us and gather our exiles to the Courtyards of Your Sanctuary, to observe Your decrees, to do Your will and to serve You wholeheartedly. [We thank You] for inspiring us to thank You. Blessed is the God of thanksgivings.*

For all these, may Your Name be blessed and exalted, our King, continually forever and ever.

Bend the knees at *'Blessed'*; bow at *'You'*; straighten up at *'HASHEM.'*

Everything alive will gratefully acknowledge You, Selah! and praise Your Name sincerely, O God of our salvation and help, Selah! Blessed are You, HASHEM, Your Name is 'The Beneficent One' and to You it is fitting to give thanks.

THE PRIESTLY BLESSING

At *Shacharis,* the *chazzan* recites the Priestly Blessing during his repetition.

אֱלֹהֵינוּ *Our God and the God of our forefathers, bless us with the three-verse blessing in the Torah that was written by the hand of Moses, Your servant, that was said by Aaron and his sons, the Kohanim, Your holy people, as it is said:*

May HASHEM bless you and safeguard you. (Cong.— *So may it be.*)

May HASHEM illuminate His countenance for you and be gracious to you. (Cong.— *So may it be.*)

May HASHEM turn His countenance to you and establish peace for you.[3] (Cong.— *So may it be.*)

(1) Cf. *Psalms* 79:13. (2) Cf. *Lamentations* 3:22. (3) *Numbers* 6:24-26.

שלום

At *Shacharis:*

שִׂים שָׁלוֹם, טוֹבָה, וּבְרָכָה, חֵן, וָחֶסֶד וְרַחֲמִים עָלֵינוּ וְעַל כָּל יִשְׂרָאֵל עַמֶּךָ. בָּרְכֵנוּ אָבִינוּ, כֻּלָּנוּ כְּאֶחָד בְּאוֹר פָּנֶיךָ, כִּי בְאוֹר פָּנֶיךָ נָתַתָּ לָּנוּ, יהוה אֱלֹהֵינוּ, תּוֹרַת חַיִּים וְאַהֲבַת חֶסֶד, וּצְדָקָה, וּבְרָכָה, וְרַחֲמִים, וְחַיִּים, וְשָׁלוֹם. וְטוֹב

At *Minchah/Maariv:*

שָׁלוֹם רָב עַל יִשְׂרָאֵל עַמְּךָ תָּשִׂים לְעוֹלָם, כִּי אַתָּה הוּא מֶלֶךְ אָדוֹן לְכָל הַשָּׁלוֹם. וְטוֹב

בְּעֵינֶיךָ לְבָרֵךְ אֶת עַמְּךָ יִשְׂרָאֵל, בְּכָל עֵת וּבְכָל שָׁעָה בִּשְׁלוֹמֶךָ. בָּרוּךְ אַתָּה יהוה, הַמְּבָרֵךְ אֶת עַמּוֹ יִשְׂרָאֵל בַּשָּׁלוֹם.

The *chazzan's* repetition of *Shemoneh Esrei* ends here. See below for further instructions.

יִהְיוּ לְרָצוֹן אִמְרֵי פִי וְהֶגְיוֹן לִבִּי לְפָנֶיךָ, יהוה צוּרִי וְגֹאֲלִי.[1]

אֱלֹהַי, נְצוֹר לְשׁוֹנִי מֵרָע, וּשְׂפָתַי מִדַּבֵּר מִרְמָה,[2] וְלִמְקַלְלַי נַפְשִׁי תִדּוֹם, וְנַפְשִׁי כֶּעָפָר לַכֹּל תִּהְיֶה. פְּתַח לִבִּי בְּתוֹרָתֶךָ, וּבְמִצְוֹתֶיךָ תִּרְדּוֹף נַפְשִׁי. וְכֹל הַחוֹשְׁבִים עָלַי רָעָה, מְהֵרָה הָפֵר עֲצָתָם וְקַלְקֵל מַחֲשַׁבְתָּם. עֲשֵׂה לְמַעַן שְׁמֶךָ, עֲשֵׂה לְמַעַן יְמִינֶךָ, עֲשֵׂה לְמַעַן קְדֻשָּׁתֶךָ, עֲשֵׂה לְמַעַן תּוֹרָתֶךָ. לְמַעַן יֵחָלְצוּן יְדִידֶיךָ, הוֹשִׁיעָה יְמִינְךָ וַעֲנֵנִי.[3]

Some recite verses pertaining to their names at this point. See page 924.

יִהְיוּ לְרָצוֹן אִמְרֵי פִי וְהֶגְיוֹן לִבִּי לְפָנֶיךָ, יהוה צוּרִי וְגֹאֲלִי.[1] עֹשֶׂה שָׁלוֹם בִּמְרוֹמָיו, הוּא יַעֲשֶׂה שָׁלוֹם עָלֵינוּ, וְעַל כָּל יִשְׂרָאֵל. וְאִמְרוּ: אָמֵן.

יְהִי רָצוֹן מִלְּפָנֶיךָ יהוה אֱלֹהֵינוּ וֵאלֹהֵי אֲבוֹתֵינוּ, שֶׁיִּבָּנֶה בֵּית הַמִּקְדָּשׁ בִּמְהֵרָה בְיָמֵינוּ, וְתֵן חֶלְקֵנוּ בְּתוֹרָתֶךָ. וְשָׁם נַעֲבָדְךָ בְּיִרְאָה, כִּימֵי עוֹלָם וּכְשָׁנִים קַדְמוֹנִיּוֹת. וְעָרְבָה לַיהוה מִנְחַת יְהוּדָה וִירוּשָׁלָיִם, כִּימֵי עוֹלָם וּכְשָׁנִים קַדְמוֹנִיּוֹת.[4]

THE INDIVIDUAL'S RECITATION OF שְׁמוֹנֶה עֶשְׂרֵה ENDS HERE.

At *Shacharis* continue with *Hallel* (p. 632).
At *Minchah,* the *chazzan* recites קַדִּישׁ שָׁלֵם (p. 348), followed by *Aleinu* (p. 350).
At *Maariv* (except on the Sabbath and on *Seder* nights), the *chazzan* recites קַדִּישׁ שָׁלֵם (p. 348), followed by *Kiddush.*
At *Maariv* of a Festival that coincides with the Sabbath continue with וַיְכֻלּוּ, (p. 346).
On *Seder* nights [some congregations recite *Hallel* (p. 632), then] the *chazzan* recites קַדִּישׁ שָׁלֵם (348), followed by עָלֵינוּ (p. 350).

PEACE

At *Shacharis:*

שִׂים *Establish peace, goodness, blessing, graciousness, kindness, and compassion upon us and upon all of Your people Israel. Bless us, our Father, all of us as one, with the light of Your countenance, for with the light of Your countenance You gave us, HASHEM, our God, the Torah of life and a love of kindness, righteousness, blessing, compassion, life, and peace. And may it be good in Your eyes to bless Your*

At *Minchah/Maariv:*

שָׁלוֹם *Establish abundant peace upon Your people Israel forever, for You are King, Master of all peace. May it be good in Your eyes to bless Your*

people Israel at every time and every hour with Your peace. Blessed are You, HASHEM, Who blesses His people Israel with peace.

The *chazzan's* repetition of *Shemoneh Esrei* ends here. See below for further instructions.

May the expressions of my mouth and the thoughts of my heart find favor before You, HASHEM, my Rock and my Redeemer.[1]

אֱלֹהַי *My God, guard my tongue from evil and my lips from speaking deceitfully.*[2] *To those who curse me, let my soul be silent; and let my soul be like dust to everyone. Open my heart to Your Torah, then my soul will pursue Your commandments. As for all those who design evil against me, speedily nullify their counsel and disrupt their design. Act for Your Name's sake; act for Your right hand's sake; act for Your sanctity's sake; act for Your Torah's sake. That Your beloved ones may be given rest; let Your right hand save, and respond to me.*[3]

Some recite verses pertaining to their names at this point. See page 924.

May the expressions of my mouth and the thoughts of my heart find favor before You, HASHEM, my Rock and my Redeemer.[1] *He Who makes peace in His heights, may He make peace upon us, and upon all Israel. Now respond: Amen.*

יְהִי רָצוֹן *May it be Your will, HASHEM our God and the God of our forefathers, that the Holy Temple be rebuilt, speedily in our days. Grant us our share in Your Torah, and may we serve You there with reverence, as in days of old and in former years. Then the offering of Judah and Jerusalem will be pleasing to HASHEM, as in days of old and in former years.*[4]

THE INDIVIDUAL'S RECITATION OF *SHEMONEH ESREI* ENDS HERE.

At *Shacharis* continue with *Hallel* (p. 632).

At *Minchah,* the *chazzan* recites the Full *Kaddish* (p. 348), followed by *Aleinu* (p. 350).

At *Maariv* (except on the Sabbath), the *chazzan* recites the Full *Kaddish* (p. 348), followed by *Kiddush.*

At *Maariv* of a Festival that coincides with the Sabbath continue with *'Thus the heaven ...'* (p. 346). On *Seder* nights [some congregations recite *Hallel* (p. 632), then] the *chazzan* recites the full *Kaddish* (p. 348), followed by *Aleinu* (p. 350).

(1) *Psalms* 19:15. (2) Cf. 34:14. (3) 60:7; 108:7. (4) *Malachi* 3:4.

יה אלי

On Festivals, in most congregations, the *chazzan* chants יָהּ אֵלִי, *O God, my God,* after the *Haftarah* blessings (p. 448). On days when *Yizkor* is recited, this song is usually omitted.

יָהּ אֵלִי* וְגוֹאֲלִי אֶתְיַצְּבָה לִקְרָאתֶךָ, הָיָה וְיִהְיֶה, הָיָה וְהֹוֶה, כָּל גּוֹי אַדְמָתֶךָ.* וְתוֹדָה,* וְלָעוֹלָה, וְלַמִּנְחָה, וְלַחַטָּאת, וְלָאָשָׁם, וְלַשְּׁלָמִים, וְלַמִּלּוּאִים כָּל קָרְבָּנֶךָ. זְכוֹר נִלְאָה* אֲשֶׁר נָשְׂאָה וְהָשִׁיבָהּ לְאַדְמָתֶךָ. סֶלָה אֲהַלְלֶךָ,* בְּאַשְׁרֵי יוֹשְׁבֵי בֵיתֶךָ.

דַּק עַל דַּק,* עַד אֵין נִבְדַּק, וְלִתְבוּנָתוֹ אֵין חֵקֶר. הָאֵל נוֹרָא, בְּאַחַת סְקִירָה,* בֵּין טוֹב לָרַע יְבַקֵּר. וְתוֹדָה, וְלָעוֹלָה, וְלַמִּנְחָה, וְלַחַטָּאת, וְלָאָשָׁם, וְלַשְּׁלָמִים, וְלַמִּלּוּאִים כָּל קָרְבָּנֶךָ. זְכוֹר נִלְאָה אֲשֶׁר נָשְׂאָה וְהָשִׁיבָהּ לְאַדְמָתֶךָ. סֶלָה אֲהַלְלֶךָ, בְּאַשְׁרֵי יוֹשְׁבֵי בֵיתֶךָ.

אֲדוֹן צְבָאוֹת,* בְּרוֹב פְּלָאוֹת, חִבֵּר כָּל אָהֳלוֹ. בִּנְתִיבוֹת לֵב לְבַלֵּב, הַצּוּר תָּמִים פָּעֳלוֹ. וְתוֹדָה, וְלָעוֹלָה, וְלַמִּנְחָה, וְלַחַטָּאת, וְלָאָשָׁם, וְלַשְּׁלָמִים, וְלַמִּלּוּאִים כָּל קָרְבָּנֶךָ. זְכוֹר נִלְאָה אֲשֶׁר נָשְׂאָה וְהָשִׁיבָהּ לְאַדְמָתֶךָ. סֶלָה אֲהַלְלֶךָ, בְּאַשְׁרֵי יוֹשְׁבֵי בֵיתֶךָ.

The congregation recites *Ashrei* (p. 456) and continues with the *Mussaf* service.

יָהּ אֵלִי — *O God, my God.* Since *Ashrei* is one of the most prominent of all the psalms (see p. 66), its recitation before the Festival *Mussaf* is introduced with a joyous prayer that longs for the opportunity to sing it before God in the rebuilt Temple, along with the order of sacrificial offerings. This is in keeping with the literal meaning of אַשְׁרֵי יוֹשְׁבֵי בֵיתֶךָ, *Praiseworthy are those who dwell in Your house.* Although, in the Siddur, God's 'house' has the broad meaning of the synagogue or any other place where one can serve God, it also refers specifically to the Temple, where the *Kohanim* and Levites have the good fortune to serve God (*Radak* and *Ibn Ezra* to *Psalms* 84:5). The spiritual elevation of the Festival, especially before *Mussaf* when we are about to cite the unique offering of the Festival, is a logical time for this prayer that combines joy in the Temple service and longing that we will soon be able to perform it in actuality as well as in aspiration. In view of the somber nature of *Yizkor,* this *piyut* is omitted on *Yizkor* days.

הָיָה וְיִהְיֶה — *Who was and Who will be.* God's Four-letter Name contains the letters that form the words indicating past, present, and future. Thus, this Name represents Him as the One Who creates and controls history — and Who will sooner or later return our service to the Temple.

כָּל גּוֹי אַדְמָתֶךָ — *With the entire nation on Your soil.* May all Israel be united in *Eretz Yisrael,* there to praise and thank God by offering all the prescribed offerings listed below.

וְתוֹדָה — *And the thanksgiving-offering.* We ask for the privilege of being in the Temple on God's soil so that we may bring him all the offerings mentioned in the Torah.

The order of the offerings is difficult since the thanksgiving offering has less holiness than the next four on the list. Also, the meal offering consists of flour and oil, yet it is inserted between the animal offerings. Perhaps the order can be explained this way: first comes the thanksgiving offering because the very fact that we will have been returned to *Eretz Yisrael* and the rebuilt Temple will be cause for an enormous sense of thanksgiving. The elevation offering, which is

PRE-MUSSAF PIYUT

On Festivals, in most congregations, the *chazzan* chants יָהּ אֵלִי, *O God, my God,* after the *Haftarah* blessings (p. 448). On days when *Yizkor* is recited, this song is usually omitted.

יָהּ אֵלִי *O God, my God* and Redeemer, I shall stand to greet You — Who was and Who will be,* Who was and Who is — with the entire nation on Your soil;* and the thanksgiving-,* elevation-, meal-, sin-, guilt-, peace-, and inauguration-offerings — Your every offering. Remember the exhausted [nation]* that won [Your favor], and return her to Your soil. Eternally will I laud You,* saying, 'Praiseworthy are those who dwell in Your House.'*

דַּק *Painstakingly exact,* beyond calculation — to His intelligence there is no limit. The awesome God — with a single stripe,* He differentiates the good from bad. And the thanksgiving-, elevation-, meal-, sin-, guilt-, peace-, and inauguration-offerings — Your every offering. Remember the exhausted [nation] that won [Your favor], and return her to Your soil. Eternally will I laud You, saying, 'Praiseworthy are those who dwell in Your House.'*

אֲדוֹן *The Lord of Legions,* with abundant miracles He connected His entire Tabernacle; in the paths of the heart may it blossom — the Rock, His work is perfect! And the thanksgiving-, elevation-, meal-, sin-, guilt-, peace-, and inauguration-offerings — Your every offering. Remember the exhausted [nation] that won [Your favor], and return her to Your soil. Eternally will I laud You, saying, 'Praiseworthy are those who dwell in Your House.'*

The congregation recites *Ashrei* (p. 456) and continues with the *Mussaf* service.

---

consumed entirely on the altar, represents Israel's longing for elevation in God's service and dedication to Him; thus it takes precedence over offerings that come to atone for sin. Of the meal offering, the Sages derive from Scripture (see *Rashi, Leviticus* 2:1) that God heaps particular praise upon a poor man who can afford no more than a bit of flour and oil, yet wishes to bring an offering to express His dedication to God. The sin and guilt offerings are of greater holiness than the peace offering. The inauguration offerings are mentioned last because they will be offered only once — when the Temple is dedicated — and then will never be needed, because the Third Temple will be eternal.

זְכוֹר נִלְאָה — *Remember the exhausted* [*nation*]. Israel has been exhausted by long exile and much travail, but she won God's favor long ago and therefore longs for her return from exile.

סֶלָה אֲהַלְלֶךָּ — *Eternally will I laud You.* This verse is a rearrangement of the first verse of *Ashrei.* It expresses our resolve to praise God by declaring our pride at being able to serve Him.

דַּק עַל דַּק — *Painstakingly exact.* This verse and the next describe the inscrutable greatness of God's awesome judgment.

בְּאַחַת סְקִירָה — *With a single stripe.* This phrase is based on the Talmudic expression that on the Day of Judgment, 'All who walk the earth pass before Him כִּבְנֵי מָרוֹן, *like young sheep' (Rosh Hashanah* 16a, 18a). When sheep were tithed, they were released one by one through a small opening in a corral. Each tenth one was marked with a single stripe, identifying it as a tithe animal that would become an Altar offering. In the context of this prayer, it refers to God differentiating between the sinful and the righteous.

צְבָאוֹת — *Legions.* God's Legions are the entire host of the universe's components. He weaves them together to create the complex harmony of Creation. We pray that realization of His greatness will blossom in our hearts so that we will recognize His greatness and be worthy to serve Him in the rebuilt Temple.

מוסף לשלש רגלים

Take three steps backward, then three steps forward. Remain standing with the feet together while reciting *Shemoneh Esrei.* It should be recited with quiet devotion and without any interruption, verbal or otherwise. Although its recitation should not be audible to others, one must pray loudly enough to hear himself. See *Laws* §65-75, 89 for a brief summary of its laws.

On the first day of Pesach the *chazzan's* repetition begins with the Prayer for Dew, page 702. On Shemini Atzeres the *chazzan's* repetition begins with the Prayer for Rain, page 704.

כִּי שֵׁם יהוה אֶקְרָא, הָבוּ גֹדֶל לֵאלֹהֵינוּ.[1]

אֲדֹנָי שְׂפָתַי תִּפְתָּח, וּפִי יַגִּיד תְּהִלָּתֶךָ.[2]

אבות

Bend the knees at בָּרוּךְ; bow at אַתָּה; straighten up at 'ה.

בָּרוּךְ אַתָּה יהוה אֱלֹהֵינוּ וֵאלֹהֵי אֲבוֹתֵינוּ, אֱלֹהֵי אַבְרָהָם, אֱלֹהֵי יִצְחָק, וֵאלֹהֵי יַעֲקֹב, הָאֵל הַגָּדוֹל הַגִּבּוֹר וְהַנּוֹרָא, אֵל עֶלְיוֹן, גּוֹמֵל חֲסָדִים טוֹבִים וְקוֹנֵה הַכֹּל, וְזוֹכֵר חַסְדֵי אָבוֹת, וּמֵבִיא גוֹאֵל לִבְנֵי בְנֵיהֶם, לְמַעַן שְׁמוֹ בְּאַהֲבָה.

Bend the knees at בָּרוּךְ; bow at אַתָּה; straighten up at 'ה.

מֶלֶךְ עוֹזֵר וּמוֹשִׁיעַ וּמָגֵן. בָּרוּךְ אַתָּה יהוה, מָגֵן אַבְרָהָם.

גבורות

אַתָּה גִּבּוֹר לְעוֹלָם אֲדֹנָי, מְחַיֵּה מֵתִים אַתָּה, רַב לְהוֹשִׁיעַ.

On Shemini Atzeres, Simchas Torah; and the silent *Shemoneh Esrei* of the first day of Pesach, add the following phrase. [If forgotten, see *Laws* §70-75.]

מַשִּׁיב הָרוּחַ וּמוֹרִיד °הַגֶּשֶׁם [some say – °הַגָּשֶׁם].

מְכַלְכֵּל חַיִּים בְּחֶסֶד, מְחַיֵּה מֵתִים בְּרַחֲמִים רַבִּים, סוֹמֵךְ נוֹפְלִים, וְרוֹפֵא חוֹלִים, וּמַתִּיר אֲסוּרִים, וּמְקַיֵּם אֱמוּנָתוֹ לִישֵׁנֵי עָפָר. מִי כָמוֹךָ בַּעַל גְּבוּרוֹת, וּמִי דּוֹמֶה לָּךְ, מֶלֶךְ מֵמִית וּמְחַיֶּה וּמַצְמִיחַ יְשׁוּעָה. וְנֶאֱמָן אַתָּה לְהַחֲיוֹת מֵתִים. בָּרוּךְ אַתָּה יהוה, מְחַיֵּה הַמֵּתִים.

מוסף / MUSSAF

Just as *Shacharis* and *Minchah* respectively correspond to the morning and afternoon continual offerings in the Temple, so does *Mussaf* correspond to the *mussaf*, or additional, offerings of the Festivals, Rosh Chodesh and the Sabbath. Thus, it is natural that these offerings be enumerated in the *Shemoneh Esrei* of *Mussaf.* This is especially true in view of the fact that the Festivals do not all have identical *mussaf* offerings. Moreover, the additional offerings of Succos vary from day to day. This is because part of the Succos offerings symbolize the seventy primary nations of the world. Thus, thirteen bulls are offered on the first day of Succos; twelve, on the second; and one less each day, until seven are offered on the last day, for a total of seventy bulls.

The necessity of enumerating the offerings of each day is the point of a halachic dispute between the *Rishonim* (medieval rabbinic authorities). In detailing the various offerings of each day, we follow the view of *Rabbeinu Tam*

❧ MUSSAF FOR THE FESTIVALS ☙

Take three steps backward, then three steps forward. Remain standing with the feet together while reciting *Shemoneh Esrei.* It should be recited with quiet devotion and without any interruption, verbal or otherwise. Although its recitation should not be audible to others, one must pray loudly enough to hear himself. See *Laws* §65-75, 89 for a brief summary of its laws.

On the first day of Pesach the *chazzan's* repetition begins with the Prayer for Dew, page 702.
On Shemini Atzeres the *chazzan's* repetition begins with the Prayer for Rain, page 704.

When I call out the Name of HASHEM, ascribe greatness to our God.[1]
My Lord, open my lips, that my mouth may declare Your praise.[2]

PATRIARCHS

Bend the knees at *'Blessed'*; bow at *'You'*; straighten up at *'HASHEM.'*

בָּרוּךְ *Blessed are You, HASHEM, our God and the God of our forefathers, God of Abraham, God of Isaac, and God of Jacob; the great, mighty, and awesome God, the supreme God, Who bestows beneficial kindnesses and creates everything, Who recalls the kindnesses of the Patriarchs and brings a Redeemer to their children's children, for His Name's sake, with love. O King, Helper, Savior, and Shield.*

Bend the knees at *'Blessed'*; bow at *'You'*; straighten up at 'HASHEM.'

Blessed are You, HASHEM, Shield of Abraham.

GOD'S MIGHT

אַתָּה *You are eternally mighty, my Lord, the Resuscitator of the dead are You; abundantly able to save,*

On Shemini Atzeres, Simchas Torah, and the silent *Shemoneh Esrei* of the first day of Pesach, add the following phrase. [If forgotten, see *Laws* §70-75.]

Who makes the wind blow and makes the rain descend;

Who sustains the living with kindness, resuscitates the dead with abundant mercy, supports the fallen, heals the sick, releases the confined, and maintains His faith to those asleep in the dust. Who is like You, O Master of mighty deeds, and who is comparable to You, O King Who causes death and restores life and makes salvation sprout! And You are faithful to resuscitate the dead. Blessed are You, HASHEM, Who resuscitates the dead.

(1) *Deuteronomy* 32:3. (2) *Psalms* 51:17.

(Rosh Hashana 35a). However, if one omitted the description of the offering, or recited the wrong day's offering, and has already completed the blessing ... *Who sanctifies Israel and the seasons,* he may continue *Shemoneh Esrei* and is not required to rectify his error *(Mishnah Berurah* 488:13). This is in accord with *Rashi's* view that it is sufficient merely to recite the general statement, נַעֲשֶׂה וְנַקְרִיב ... בְּתוֹרָתֶךָ, *We will perform and bring near to You, according to the commandment of Your will, as You have written for us in Your Torah,'* and the offerings need not be enumerated.

❧ The commentary for the first section of *Shemoneh Esrei* and the shorter version of *Kedushah* may be found on page 98. The commentary for the longer version of *Kedushah* may be found on page 464.

During the *chazzan's* repetition, *Kedushah* (below) is recited at this point.

קדושת השם

אַתָּה קָדוֹשׁ וְשִׁמְךָ קָדוֹשׁ, וּקְדוֹשִׁים בְּכָל יוֹם יְהַלְּלוּךָ סֶּלָה.
בָּרוּךְ אַתָּה יהוה, הָאֵל הַקָּדוֹשׁ.

קדושה

When reciting *Kedushah,* one must stand with his feet together, and avoid any interruptions. One should rise to his toes when saying the words קָדוֹשׁ, קָדוֹשׁ, קָדוֹשׁ; בָּרוּךְ (of בָּרוּךְ כְּבוֹד); and יִמְלֹךְ.

FESTIVAL/SHABBOS CHOL HAMOED/HOSHANA RABBAH

Cong. then *chazzan:*

נַעֲרִיצְךָ וְנַקְדִּישְׁךָ כְּסוֹד שִׂיחַ שַׂרְפֵי קֹדֶשׁ, הַמַּקְדִּישִׁים שִׁמְךָ בַּקֹּדֶשׁ, כַּכָּתוּב עַל יַד נְבִיאֶךָ, וְקָרָא זֶה אֶל זֶה וְאָמַר:

All—קָדוֹשׁ קָדוֹשׁ קָדוֹשׁ יהוה צְבָאוֹת, מְלֹא כָל הָאָרֶץ כְּבוֹדוֹ.[1] ❖ כְּבוֹדוֹ מָלֵא עוֹלָם, מְשָׁרְתָיו שׁוֹאֲלִים זֶה לָזֶה, אַיֵּה מְקוֹם כְּבוֹדוֹ, לְעֻמָּתָם בָּרוּךְ יֹאמֵרוּ:

All—בָּרוּךְ כְּבוֹד יהוה, מִמְּקוֹמוֹ.[2] ❖ מִמְּקוֹמוֹ הוּא יִפֶן בְּרַחֲמִים, וְיָחֹן עַם הַמְיַחֲדִים שְׁמוֹ, עֶרֶב וָבֹקֶר בְּכָל יוֹם תָּמִיד, פַּעֲמַיִם בְּאַהֲבָה שְׁמַע אוֹמְרִים.

All—שְׁמַע יִשְׂרָאֵל, יהוה אֱלֹהֵינוּ, יהוה אֶחָד.[3] ❖ הוּא אֱלֹהֵינוּ, הוּא אָבִינוּ, הוּא מַלְכֵּנוּ, הוּא מוֹשִׁיעֵנוּ, וְהוּא יַשְׁמִיעֵנוּ בְּרַחֲמָיו שֵׁנִית, לְעֵינֵי כָּל חָי, לִהְיוֹת לָכֶם לֵאלֹהִים, אֲנִי יהוה אֱלֹהֵיכֶם.[4]

Most congregations omit the following paragraph on Shabbos Chol Hamoed:

All—אַדִּיר אַדִּירֵנוּ,* יהוה אֲדֹנֵינוּ, מָה אַדִּיר שִׁמְךָ בְּכָל הָאָרֶץ.[5] וְהָיָה יהוה לְמֶלֶךְ עַל כָּל הָאָרֶץ, בַּיּוֹם הַהוּא יִהְיֶה יהוה אֶחָד וּשְׁמוֹ אֶחָד.[6]

Chazzan—וּבְדִבְרֵי קָדְשְׁךָ כָּתוּב לֵאמֹר:

All—יִמְלֹךְ יהוה לְעוֹלָם, אֱלֹהַיִךְ צִיּוֹן, לְדֹר וָדֹר, הַלְלוּיָהּ.[7]

CHOL HAMOED

Cong. then *chazzan:*

נְקַדֵּשׁ אֶת שִׁמְךָ בָּעוֹלָם, כְּשֵׁם שֶׁמַּקְדִּישִׁים אוֹתוֹ בִּשְׁמֵי מָרוֹם, כַּכָּתוּב עַל יַד נְבִיאֶךָ, וְקָרָא זֶה אֶל זֶה וְאָמַר:

All:

קָדוֹשׁ קָדוֹשׁ קָדוֹשׁ יהוה צְבָאוֹת, מְלֹא כָל הָאָרֶץ כְּבוֹדוֹ.[1]

Chazzan:

לְעֻמָּתָם בָּרוּךְ יֹאמֵרוּ:

All:

בָּרוּךְ כְּבוֹד יהוה, מִמְּקוֹמוֹ.[2]

Chazzan:

וּבְדִבְרֵי קָדְשְׁךָ כָּתוּב לֵאמֹר:

All:

יִמְלֹךְ יהוה לְעוֹלָם, אֱלֹהַיִךְ צִיּוֹן לְדֹר וָדֹר, הַלְלוּיָהּ.[7]

Chazzan only concludes— לְדוֹר וָדוֹר נַגִּיד גָּדְלֶךָ וּלְנֵצַח נְצָחִים קְדֻשָּׁתְךָ נַקְדִּישׁ, וְשִׁבְחֲךָ אֱלֹהֵינוּ מִפִּינוּ לֹא יָמוּשׁ לְעוֹלָם וָעֶד, כִּי אֵל מֶלֶךְ גָּדוֹל וְקָדוֹשׁ אָתָּה. בָּרוּךְ אַתָּה יהוה, הָאֵל הַקָּדוֹשׁ.

Chazzan continues אַתָּה בְחַרְתָּנוּ.

---

(1) *Isaiah* 6:3. (2) *Ezekiel* 3:12. (3) *Deuteronomy* 6:4.
(4) *Numbers* 15:41. (5) *Psalms* 8:2. (6) *Zechariah* 14:9. (7) *Psalms* 146:10.

During the *chazzan's* repetition, *Kedushah* (below) is recited at this point.

HOLINESS OF GOD'S NAME

אַתָּה *You are holy and Your Name is holy, and holy ones praise You every day, forever. Blessed are You,* HASHEM, *the holy God.*

KEDUSHAH

When reciting *Kedushah*, one must stand with his feet together and avoid any interruptions. One should rise to his toes when saying the words *'Holy, holy, holy; Blessed is;* HASHEM *shall reign.'*

FESTIVAL/SHABBOS CHOL HAMOED/HOSHANA RABBAH

Cong. then *chazzan:*

נַעֲרִיצְךָ *We will revere You and sanctify You according to the counsel of the holy Seraphim, who sanctify Your Name in the Sanctuary, as it is written by Your prophet: "And one [angel] will call another and say:*

All — *'Holy, holy, holy is* HASHEM, *Master of Legions, the whole world is filled with His glory.' "*[1] ❖ *His glory fills the world. His ministering angels ask one another, 'Where is the place of His glory?' Those facing them say 'Blessed':*

All — *'Blessed is the glory of* HASHEM *from His place.'*[2] ❖ *From His place may He turn with compassion and be gracious to the people who declare the Oneness of His Name; evening and morning, every day constantly, twice, with love, they proclaim 'Shema.'*

All — *'Hear O Israel:* HASHEM *is our God,* HASHEM *the One and Only.'*[3] ❖ *He is our God; He is our Father; He is our King; He is our Savior; and He will let us hear, in His compassion, for a second time in the presence of all the living,' ... to be a God to you, I am* HASHEM, *your God.'*[4]

Most congregations omit the following paragraph on Shabbos Chol Hamoed:

All — *Mighty is our Mighty One,** HASHEM, *our Master — how mighty is Your name throughout the earth!*[5] HASHEM *will be King over all the world — on that day* HASHEM *will be One and His Name will be One.*[6]

Chazzan — *And in Your holy Writings the following is written:*

All — *'*HASHEM *shall reign forever — your God, O Zion — from generation to generation, Halleluyah!'*[7]

CHOL HAMOED

Cong. then *chazzan:*

נְקַדֵּשׁ *We shall sanctify Your Name in this world, just as they sanctify it in heaven above, as it is written by Your prophet, "And one [angel] will call another and say:*

All:

'Holy, holy, holy is HASHEM, *Master of Legions, the whole world is filled with His glory.' "*[1]

Chazzan:

Those facing them say 'Blessed':

All:

'Blessed is the glory of HASHEM *from His place.'*[2]

Chazzan:

And in Your holy Writings the following is written:

All:

*'*HASHEM *shall reign forever — your God, O Zion — from generation to generation, Halleluyah!'*[7]

Chazzan concludes— *From generation to generation we shall relate Your greatness and for infinite eternities we shall proclaim Your holiness. Your praise, our God, shall not leave our mouth forever and ever, for You O God, are a great and holy King. Blessed are You* HASHEM, *the holy God.*

Chazzan continues אַתָּה בְחַרְתָּנוּ, *You have chosen us ...*

☙ אַדִּיר אַדִּירֵנוּ — *Mighty is our Mighty One.* This brief selection is added to *Kedushah* only on Festivals, because, as discussed elsewhere, they are times of special closeness between God and Israel. In this brief prayer, we exclaim our confidence that God's absolute power will

קדושת היום

אַתָּה בְחַרְתָּנוּ מִכָּל הָעַמִּים, אָהַבְתָּ אוֹתָנוּ, וְרָצִיתָ בָּנוּ, וְרוֹמַמְתָּנוּ מִכָּל הַלְּשׁוֹנוֹת, וְקִדַּשְׁתָּנוּ בְּמִצְוֹתֶיךָ, וְקֵרַבְתָּנוּ מַלְכֵּנוּ לַעֲבוֹדָתֶךָ, וְשִׁמְךָ הַגָּדוֹל וְהַקָּדוֹשׁ עָלֵינוּ קָרָאתָ.

On the Sabbath, add the words in brackets.

וַתִּתֶּן לָנוּ* יהוה אֱלֹהֵינוּ בְּאַהֲבָה [שַׁבָּתוֹת לִמְנוּחָה וּ]מוֹעֲדִים* לְשִׂמְחָה חַגִּים וּזְמַנִּים לְשָׂשׂוֹן, אֶת יוֹם [הַשַּׁבָּת הַזֶּה וְאֶת יוֹם]

On Pesach	On Shavuos	On Succos	On Shemini Atzeres/Simchas Torah
חַג הַמַּצּוֹת הַזֶּה, זְמַן חֵרוּתֵנוּ	חַג הַשָּׁבֻעוֹת הַזֶּה, זְמַן מַתַּן תּוֹרָתֵנוּ	חַג הַסֻּכּוֹת הַזֶּה, זְמַן שִׂמְחָתֵנוּ	הַשְּׁמִינִי חַג הָעֲצֶרֶת הַזֶּה, זְמַן שִׂמְחָתֵנוּ

[בְּאַהֲבָה] מִקְרָא קֹדֶשׁ, זֵכֶר לִיצִיאַת מִצְרָיִם.

וּמִפְּנֵי חֲטָאֵינוּ* גָּלִינוּ מֵאַרְצֵנוּ, וְנִתְרַחַקְנוּ מֵעַל אַדְמָתֵנוּ.* וְאֵין אֲנַחְנוּ יְכוֹלִים לַעֲלוֹת וְלֵרָאוֹת וּלְהִשְׁתַּחֲוֹת לְפָנֶיךָ, וְלַעֲשׂוֹת חוֹבוֹתֵינוּ בְּבֵית בְּחִירָתֶךָ, בַּבַּיִת הַגָּדוֹל וְהַקָּדוֹשׁ שֶׁנִּקְרָא שִׁמְךָ עָלָיו, מִפְּנֵי הַיָּד שֶׁנִּשְׁתַּלְּחָה בְּמִקְדָּשֶׁךָ. יְהִי רָצוֹן מִלְּפָנֶיךָ יהוה אֱלֹהֵינוּ וֵאלֹהֵי אֲבוֹתֵינוּ, מֶלֶךְ רַחֲמָן, שֶׁתָּשׁוּב וּתְרַחֵם עָלֵינוּ וְעַל מִקְדָּשְׁךָ בְּרַחֲמֶיךָ הָרַבִּים, וְתִבְנֵהוּ מְהֵרָה וּתְגַדֵּל כְּבוֹדוֹ.* אָבִינוּ מַלְכֵּנוּ, גַּלֵּה כְּבוֹד מַלְכוּתְךָ עָלֵינוּ מְהֵרָה, וְהוֹפַע וְהִנָּשֵׂא עָלֵינוּ לְעֵינֵי כָּל חָי. וְקָרֵב פְּזוּרֵינוּ מִבֵּין הַגּוֹיִם, וּנְפוּצוֹתֵינוּ כַּנֵּס מִיַּרְכְּתֵי אָרֶץ. וַהֲבִיאֵנוּ לְצִיּוֹן עִירְךָ בְּרִנָּה, וְלִירוּשָׁלַיִם בֵּית מִקְדָּשְׁךָ בְּשִׂמְחַת עוֹלָם. וְשָׁם נַעֲשֶׂה לְפָנֶיךָ אֶת קָרְבְּנוֹת חוֹבוֹתֵינוּ, תְּמִידִים כְּסִדְרָם, וּמוּסָפִים כְּהִלְכָתָם. וְאֶת

---

ultimately be recognized by the entire human race.

וּמִפְּנֵי חֲטָאֵינוּ — *But because of our sins.* This is a cardinal principle of Jewish faith. History is not haphazard; Israel's exile and centuries-long distress is a result of its sins. It is axiomatic, therefore, that only repentance can reverse this process.

מֵאַרְצֵנוּ ... מֵאַדְמָתֵנוּ — *From our land ... from our soil.* The term אֶרֶץ, *land,* refers to the entire country from which the nation as a whole was exiled; אֲדָמָה, *soil,* refers to the individual parcels of land. These two conditions involve halachic differences. Some commandments, such as the laws of the Jubilee Year and the laws of Jewish indentured servants, cannot be observed unless the nation as a whole lives in *Eretz Yisrael.* Other commandments, such as those relating to tithes and the use of fruits during a tree's first four

HOLINESS OF THE DAY

אַתָּה בְחַרְתָּנוּ *You have chosen us from all the peoples; You loved us and found favor in us; You exalted us above all the tongues and You sanctified us with Your commandments. You drew us close, our King, to Your service and proclaimed Your great and Holy Name upon us.*

On the Sabbath, add the words in brackets.

וַתִּתֶּן *And You gave us, HASHEM, our God, with love [Sabbaths for rest], appointed Festivals for gladness, Festivals and times for joy, [this day of Sabbath and]*

On Pesach	On Shavuos	On Succos	On Shemini Atzeres and Simchas Torah
this day of the Festival of Matzos, the time of our freedom	*this day of the Festival of Shavuos, the time of the giving of our Torah*	*this day of the Festival of Succos, the time of our gladness*	*the eighth day, this Festival of Assembly, the time of our gladness*

[with love] a holy convocation, a memorial of the Exodus from Egypt.

וּמִפְּנֵי חֲטָאֵינוּ *But because of our sins* we have been exiled from our land and sent far from our soil.* We cannot ascend to appear and to prostrate ourselves before You, and to perform our obligations in the House of Your choice, in the great and holy House upon which Your Name was proclaimed, because of the hand that was dispatched against Your Sanctuary. May it be Your will, HASHEM, our God and the God of our forefathers, O merciful King, that You once more be compassionate upon us and upon Your Sanctuary in Your abundant mercy, and rebuild it soon and magnify its glory.* Our Father, our King, reveal the glory of Your Kingship upon us, speedily; appear and be uplifted over us before the eyes of all the living. Draw our scattered ones near, from among the nations, and bring in our dispersions from the ends of the earth. Bring us to Zion, Your City, in glad song, and to Jerusalem, home of Your Sanctuary, in eternal joy. There we will perform before You our obligatory offerings, the continual offerings according to their order and the additional offerings according to their law. And*

---

years, are observed by Jewish landowners in *Eretz Yisrael* even if the country is under foreign rule. We now say that the exile has deprived all or most of our people of these two categories of commandments. Then, we go on to mention a third category that we are deprived of in exile — the performance of the Temple service.

וְתִבְנֵהוּ מְהֵרָה וּתְגַדֵּל כְּבוֹדוֹ — *And rebuild it soon and magnify its glory. Eretz Yisrael* and the Temple are more than geographical or architectural concepts. There is a spiritual Presence that complements the material places on earth. When Israel sinned the spiritual Presence withdrew because it could not tolerate the nearness of

[Weekdays— מוּסַף יוֹם] [Sabbath— מוּסְפֵי יוֹם הַשַּׁבָּת הַזֶּה וְיוֹם]

On Pesach	On Shavuos	On Succos	On Shemini Atzeres/Simchas Torah
חַג הַמַּצּוֹת הַזֶּה	חַג הַשָּׁבֻעוֹת הַזֶּה	חַג הַסֻּכּוֹת הַזֶּה	הַשְּׁמִינִי חַג הָעֲצֶרֶת הַזֶּה

נַעֲשֶׂה וְנַקְרִיב לְפָנֶיךָ בְּאַהֲבָה כְּמִצְוַת רְצוֹנֶךָ, כְּמוֹ שֶׁכָּתַבְתָּ עָלֵינוּ בְּתוֹרָתֶךָ, עַל יְדֵי מֹשֶׁה עַבְדֶּךָ, מִפִּי כְבוֹדֶךָ כָּאָמוּר:

On the Sabbath:

וּבְיוֹם הַשַּׁבָּת שְׁנֵי כְבָשִׂים בְּנֵי שָׁנָה תְּמִימִם, וּשְׁנֵי עֶשְׂרֹנִים סֹלֶת מִנְחָה בְּלוּלָה בַשֶּׁמֶן, וְנִסְכּוֹ. עֹלַת שַׁבַּת בְּשַׁבַּתּוֹ, עַל עֹלַת הַתָּמִיד וְנִסְכָּהּ.[1] (זֶה קָרְבַּן שַׁבָּת. וְקָרְבַּן הַיּוֹם כָּאָמוּר:)

ON THE FIRST TWO DAYS OF PESACH

וּבַחֹדֶשׁ הָרִאשׁוֹן בְּאַרְבָּעָה עָשָׂר יוֹם לַחֹדֶשׁ, פֶּסַח לַיהוה. וּבַחֲמִשָּׁה עָשָׂר יוֹם לַחֹדֶשׁ הַזֶּה, חָג, שִׁבְעַת יָמִים מַצּוֹת יֵאָכֵל. בַּיּוֹם הָרִאשׁוֹן מִקְרָא קֹדֶשׁ, כָּל מְלֶאכֶת עֲבֹדָה לֹא תַעֲשׂוּ. וְהִקְרַבְתֶּם אִשֶּׁה עֹלָה לַיהוה, פָּרִים בְּנֵי בָקָר שְׁנַיִם, וְאַיִל אֶחָד, וְשִׁבְעָה כְבָשִׂים בְּנֵי שָׁנָה, תְּמִימִם יִהְיוּ לָכֶם.[2] וּמִנְחָתָם וְנִסְכֵּיהֶם כִּמְדֻבָּר, שְׁלֹשָׁה עֶשְׂרֹנִים לַפָּר, וּשְׁנֵי עֶשְׂרֹנִים לָאָיִל, וְעִשָּׂרוֹן לַכֶּבֶשׂ, וְיַיִן כְּנִסְכּוֹ. וְשָׂעִיר לְכַפֵּר, וּשְׁנֵי תְמִידִים כְּהִלְכָתָם.

On the Sabbath continue יִשְׂמְחוּ, on weekdays continue אֱלֹהֵינוּ (page 686).

ON CHOL HAMOED PESACH AND THE LAST TWO DAYS OF PESACH

וְהִקְרַבְתֶּם אִשֶּׁה עֹלָה לַיהוה, פָּרִים בְּנֵי בָקָר שְׁנַיִם, וְאַיִל אֶחָד, וְשִׁבְעָה כְבָשִׂים בְּנֵי שָׁנָה, תְּמִימִם יִהְיוּ לָכֶם.[3] וּמִנְחָתָם וְנִסְכֵּיהֶם כִּמְדֻבָּר, שְׁלֹשָׁה עֶשְׂרֹנִים לַפָּר, וּשְׁנֵי עֶשְׂרֹנִים לָאָיִל, וְעִשָּׂרוֹן לַכֶּבֶשׂ, וְיַיִן כְּנִסְכּוֹ. וְשָׂעִיר לְכַפֵּר, וּשְׁנֵי תְמִידִים כְּהִלְכָתָם.

On the Sabbath continue יִשְׂמְחוּ, on weekdays continue אֱלֹהֵינוּ (page 686).

sinners. Consequently, the Jewish people were exiled from the land that they had spiritually contaminated. Conversely, Jewish return to the land is incomplete unless we can also bring about the return of the Divine holiness to the country and the Temple Mount. Thus we now pray that *God* rebuild the Temple in the sense that He return His Presence to the land, a condition that can come about only when God's sovereignty is accepted by all, and the Jewish people are returned to their land. Then will come the climax of our longing: that we will deserve to serve God in His Temple as He ordained in the Torah *(Sh'lah).*

the additional offering[s of this day of Sabbath and] of

On Pesach	On Shavuos	On Succos	On Shemini Atzeres and Simchas Torah
this day of the Festival of Matzos,	*this day of the Festival of Shavuos,*	*this day of the Festival of Succos,*	*this day of the Shemini Atzeres,*

we will perform and bring near to You with love, according to the commandment of Your will, as You have written for us in Your Torah, through Moses, Your servant, from Your glorious expression, as it is said:

On the Sabbath:

וּבְיוֹם הַשַּׁבָּת *On the Sabbath day: two [male] first-year lambs, unblemished; and two tenth-ephah of fine flour for a meal-offering, mixed with olive oil, and its wine-libation. The elevation-offering of the Sabbath must be on its particular Sabbath, in addition to the continual elevation-offering and its wine-libation.*[1] *(This is the offering of the Sabbath. And the offering of the day is as it is said:)*

ON THE FIRST TWO DAYS OF PESACH

וּבַחֹדֶשׁ הָרִאשׁוֹן *And in the first month on the fourteenth day of the month — the Pesach offering to* HASHEM. *And on the fifteenth day of this month — a festival; for seven days, matzos are to be eaten. On the first day is a holy convocation, you may not do any laborious work. You are to bring a fire-offering, an elevation-offering to* HASHEM, *two young bulls, one ram and seven [male] first-year lambs, they shall be unblemished for you.*[2] *And their meal-offerings and their wine-libations as mentioned: three tenth-ephah for each bull; two tenth-ephah for each ram; one tenth-ephah for each lamb; and wine for its libation. A he-goat for atonement, and two continual offerings according to their law.*

On the Sabbath continue, *'They shall rejoice ...'*; on weekdays continue, *'Our God ...,'*; page 686.

ON CHOL HAMOED PESACH AND THE LAST TWO DAYS OF PESACH

וְהִקְרַבְתֶּם *You are to bring a fire-offering, an elevation-offering to* HASHEM, *two young bulls, one ram, and seven [male] first-year lambs, they shall be unblemished for you.*[3] *And their meal-offerings and their wine-libations as mentioned: three tenth-ephah for each bull; two tenth-ephah for each ram; one tenth-ephah for each lamb; and wine for its libation. A he-goat for atonement, and two continual offerings according to their law.*

On the Sabbath continue, *'They shall rejoice ...'*; on weekdays continue, *'Our God ...,'*; page 686.

---

(1) *Numbers* 28:9-10. (2) 28:16-19. (3) 28:19.

ON SHAVUOS

וּבְיוֹם הַבִּכּוּרִים, בְּהַקְרִיבְכֶם מִנְחָה חֲדָשָׁה לַיהוה, בְּשָׁבֻעֹתֵיכֶם, מִקְרָא קֹדֶשׁ יִהְיֶה לָכֶם, כָּל מְלֶאכֶת עֲבֹדָה לֹא תַעֲשׂוּ. וְהִקְרַבְתֶּם עוֹלָה לְרֵיחַ נִיחֹחַ לַיהוה, פָּרִים בְּנֵי בָקָר שְׁנַיִם, אַיִל אֶחָד, שִׁבְעָה כְבָשִׂים בְּנֵי שָׁנָה.1 וּמִנְחָתָם וְנִסְכֵּיהֶם כִּמְדֻבָּר, שְׁלֹשָׁה עֶשְׂרֹנִים לַפָּר, וּשְׁנֵי עֶשְׂרֹנִים לָאָיִל, וְעִשָּׂרוֹן לַכֶּבֶשׂ, וְיַיִן כְּנִסְכּוֹ. וְשָׂעִיר לְכַפֵּר, וּשְׁנֵי תְמִידִים כְּהִלְכָתָם.

On the Sabbath continue יִשְׂמְחוּ, on weekdays continue אֱלֹהֵינוּ (page 686).

ON THE FIRST TWO DAYS OF SUCCOS

וּבַחֲמִשָּׁה עָשָׂר יוֹם לַחֹדֶשׁ הַשְּׁבִיעִי, מִקְרָא קֹדֶשׁ יִהְיֶה לָכֶם, כָּל מְלֶאכֶת עֲבֹדָה לֹא תַעֲשׂוּ, וְחַגֹּתֶם חַג לַיהוה שִׁבְעַת יָמִים. וְהִקְרַבְתֶּם עֹלָה אִשֵּׁה רֵיחַ נִיחֹחַ לַיהוה, פָּרִים בְּנֵי בָקָר שְׁלֹשָׁה עָשָׂר, אֵילִם שְׁנָיִם, כְּבָשִׂים בְּנֵי שָׁנָה אַרְבָּעָה עָשָׂר, תְּמִימִם יִהְיוּ.2 וּמִנְחָתָם וְנִסְכֵּיהֶם כִּמְדֻבָּר, שְׁלֹשָׁה עֶשְׂרֹנִים לַפָּר, וּשְׁנֵי עֶשְׂרֹנִים לָאָיִל, וְעִשָּׂרוֹן לַכֶּבֶשׂ, וְיַיִן כְּנִסְכּוֹ. וְשָׂעִיר לְכַפֵּר, וּשְׁנֵי תְמִידִים כְּהִלְכָתָם.

On the Sabbath continue יִשְׂמְחוּ, on weekdays continue אֱלֹהֵינוּ (page 686).

ON THE FIRST DAY CHOL HAMOED SUCCOS

וּבַיּוֹם הַשֵּׁנִי, פָּרִים בְּנֵי בָקָר שְׁנֵים עָשָׂר, אֵילִם שְׁנָיִם, כְּבָשִׂים בְּנֵי שָׁנָה אַרְבָּעָה עָשָׂר, תְּמִימִם.3 וּמִנְחָתָם וְנִסְכֵּיהֶם כִּמְדֻבָּר, שְׁלֹשָׁה עֶשְׂרֹנִים לַפָּר, וּשְׁנֵי עֶשְׂרֹנִים לָאָיִל, וְעִשָּׂרוֹן לַכֶּבֶשׂ, וְיַיִן כְּנִסְכּוֹ. וְשָׂעִיר לְכַפֵּר, וּשְׁנֵי תְמִידִים כְּהִלְכָתָם. וּבַיּוֹם הַשְּׁלִישִׁי, פָּרִים עַשְׁתֵּי עָשָׂר, אֵילִם שְׁנָיִם, כְּבָשִׂים בְּנֵי שָׁנָה אַרְבָּעָה עָשָׂר, תְּמִימִם.4 וּמִנְחָתָם וְנִסְכֵּיהֶם כִּמְדֻבָּר, שְׁלֹשָׁה עֶשְׂרֹנִים לַפָּר, וּשְׁנֵי עֶשְׂרֹנִים לָאָיִל, וְעִשָּׂרוֹן לַכֶּבֶשׂ, וְיַיִן כְּנִסְכּוֹ. וְשָׂעִיר לְכַפֵּר, וּשְׁנֵי תְמִידִים כְּהִלְכָתָם.

On the Sabbath continue יִשְׂמְחוּ, on weekdays continue אֱלֹהֵינוּ (page 686).

ON THE SECOND DAY CHOL HAMOED SUCCOS

וּבַיּוֹם הַשְּׁלִישִׁי, פָּרִים עַשְׁתֵּי עָשָׂר, אֵילִם שְׁנָיִם, כְּבָשִׂים בְּנֵי שָׁנָה אַרְבָּעָה עָשָׂר, תְּמִימִם.4 וּמִנְחָתָם וְנִסְכֵּיהֶם כִּמְדֻבָּר, שְׁלֹשָׁה עֶשְׂרֹנִים לַפָּר, וּשְׁנֵי עֶשְׂרֹנִים לָאָיִל,

ON SHAVUOS

וּבְיוֹם הַבִּכּוּרִים *And on the day of the first fruits, when your bring a new meal-offering to HASHEM, on your Festival of Weeks; there shall be a holy convocation for you, you may not do any laborious work. You are to bring an elevation-offering for a satisfying aroma to HASHEM; two young bulls, one ram, seven [male] first-year lambs.*[1] *And their meal-offerings and their wine-libations as mentioned: three tenth-ephah for each bull; two tenth-ephah for each ram; one tenth-ephah for each lamb; and wine for its libation. A he-goat for atonement, and two continual offerings according to their law.*

On the Sabbath continue, *'They shall rejoice ...'*; on weekdays continue, *'Our God ...,'*; page 687.

ON THE FIRST TWO DAYS OF SUCCOS

וּבַחֲמִשָּׁה עָשָׂר *And on the fifteenth day of the seventh month, there shall be a holy convocation for you; you may not do any laborious work; and you shall celebrate a festival to HASHEM for seven days. You are to bring an elevation-offering, a fire-offering, a satisfying aroma to HASHEM; thirteen young bulls, two rams, fourteen [male] first-year lambs, they are to be unblemished.*[2] *And their meal-offerings and their wine-libations as mentioned: three tenth-ephah for each bull; two tenth-ephah for each ram; one tenth-ephah for each lamb; and wine for its libation. A he-goat for atonement, and two continual offerings according to their law.*

On the Sabbath continue, *'They shall rejoice ...'*; on weekdays continue, *'Our God ...,'*; page 687.

ON THE FIRST DAY CHOL HAMOED SUCCOS

וּבַיּוֹם הַשֵּׁנִי *And on the second day: twelve young bulls, two rams, fourteen [male] first-year lambs, unblemished.*[3] *And their meal-offerings and their wine-libations as mentioned: three tenth-ephah for each bull; two tenth-ephah for each ram; one tenth-ephah for each lamb; and wine for its libation. A he-goat for atonement, and two continual offerings according to their law. And on the third day: eleven bulls, two rams, fourteen [male] first-year lambs, unblemished.*[4] *And their meal-offerings and their wine-libations as mentioned: three tenth-ephah for each bull; two tenth-ephah for each ram; one tenth-ephah for each lamb; and wine for its libation. A he-goat for atonement, and two continual offerings according to their law.*

On the Sabbath continue, *'They shall rejoice ...'*; on weekdays continue, *'Our God ...,'*; page 687.

ON THE SECOND DAY CHOL HAMOED SUCCOS

וּבַיּוֹם הַשְּׁלִישִׁי *And on the third day: eleven bulls, two rams, fourteen [male] first-year lambs, unblemished.*[4] *And their meal-offerings and their wine-libations as mentioned: three tenth-ephah for each bull; two tenth-ephah for each ram;*

---

(1) *Numbers* 28:26-27. (2) 29:12-13. (3) 29:17. (4) 29:20.

וְעִשָּׂרוֹן לַכֶּבֶשׂ, וְיַיִן כְּנִסְכּוֹ. וְשָׂעִיר לְכַפֵּר, וּשְׁנֵי תְמִידִים כְּהִלְכָתָם. וּבַיּוֹם הָרְבִיעִי פָּרִים עֲשָׂרָה, אֵילִם שְׁנָיִם, כְּבָשִׂים בְּנֵי שָׁנָה אַרְבָּעָה עָשָׂר, תְּמִימִם.[1] וּמִנְחָתָם וְנִסְכֵּיהֶם כִּמְדֻבָּר, שְׁלֹשָׁה עֶשְׂרֹנִים לַפָּר, וּשְׁנֵי עֶשְׂרֹנִים לָאָיִל, וְעִשָּׂרוֹן לַכֶּבֶשׂ, וְיַיִן כְּנִסְכּוֹ. וְשָׂעִיר לְכַפֵּר, וּשְׁנֵי תְמִידִים כְּהִלְכָתָם.

Continue אֱלֹהֵינוּ (page 686).

ON THE THIRD DAY CHOL HAMOED SUCCOS

וּבַיּוֹם הָרְבִיעִי פָּרִים עֲשָׂרָה, אֵילִם שְׁנָיִם, כְּבָשִׂים בְּנֵי שָׁנָה אַרְבָּעָה עָשָׂר, תְּמִימִם.[1] וּמִנְחָתָם וְנִסְכֵּיהֶם כִּמְדֻבָּר, שְׁלֹשָׁה עֶשְׂרֹנִים לַפָּר, וּשְׁנֵי עֶשְׂרֹנִים לָאָיִל, וְעִשָּׂרוֹן לַכֶּבֶשׂ, וְיַיִן כְּנִסְכּוֹ. וְשָׂעִיר לְכַפֵּר, וּשְׁנֵי תְמִידִים כְּהִלְכָתָם. וּבַיּוֹם הַחֲמִישִׁי, פָּרִים תִּשְׁעָה, אֵילִם שְׁנָיִם, כְּבָשִׂים בְּנֵי שָׁנָה אַרְבָּעָה עָשָׂר, תְּמִימִם.[2] וּמִנְחָתָם וְנִסְכֵּיהֶם כִּמְדֻבָּר, שְׁלֹשָׁה עֶשְׂרֹנִים לַפָּר, וּשְׁנֵי עֶשְׂרֹנִים לָאָיִל, וְעִשָּׂרוֹן לַכֶּבֶשׂ, וְיַיִן כְּנִסְכּוֹ. וְשָׂעִיר לְכַפֵּר, וּשְׁנֵי תְמִידִים כְּהִלְכָתָם.

On the Sabbath continue יִשְׂמְחוּ, on weekdays continue אֱלֹהֵינוּ (page 686).

ON THE FOURTH DAY CHOL HAMOED SUCCOS

וּבַיּוֹם הַחֲמִישִׁי פָּרִים תִּשְׁעָה, אֵילִם שְׁנָיִם, כְּבָשִׂים בְּנֵי שָׁנָה אַרְבָּעָה עָשָׂר, תְּמִימִם.[2] וּמִנְחָתָם וְנִסְכֵּיהֶם כִּמְדֻבָּר, שְׁלֹשָׁה עֶשְׂרֹנִים לַפָּר, וּשְׁנֵי עֶשְׂרֹנִים לָאָיִל, וְעִשָּׂרוֹן לַכֶּבֶשׂ, וְיַיִן כְּנִסְכּוֹ. וְשָׂעִיר לְכַפֵּר, וּשְׁנֵי תְמִידִים כְּהִלְכָתָם. וּבַיּוֹם הַשִּׁשִּׁי, פָּרִים שְׁמֹנָה, אֵילִם שְׁנָיִם, כְּבָשִׂים בְּנֵי שָׁנָה אַרְבָּעָה עָשָׂר, תְּמִימִם.[3] וּמִנְחָתָם וְנִסְכֵּיהֶם כִּמְדֻבָּר, שְׁלֹשָׁה עֶשְׂרֹנִים לַפָּר, וּשְׁנֵי עֶשְׂרֹנִים לָאָיִל, וְעִשָּׂרוֹן לַכֶּבֶשׂ, וְיַיִן כְּנִסְכּוֹ. וְשָׂעִיר לְכַפֵּר, וּשְׁנֵי תְמִידִים כְּהִלְכָתָם.

On the Sabbath continue יִשְׂמְחוּ, on weekdays continue אֱלֹהֵינוּ (page 686).

ON HOSHANA RABBAH

וּבַיּוֹם הַשִּׁשִּׁי פָּרִים שְׁמֹנָה, אֵילִם שְׁנָיִם, כְּבָשִׂים בְּנֵי שָׁנָה אַרְבָּעָה עָשָׂר, תְּמִימִם.[3] וּמִנְחָתָם וְנִסְכֵּיהֶם כִּמְדֻבָּר, שְׁלֹשָׁה עֶשְׂרֹנִים לַפָּר, וּשְׁנֵי עֶשְׂרֹנִים לָאָיִל, וְעִשָּׂרוֹן לַכֶּבֶשׂ, וְיַיִן כְּנִסְכּוֹ. וְשָׂעִיר לְכַפֵּר, וּשְׁנֵי תְמִידִים כְּהִלְכָתָם. וּבַיּוֹם הַשְּׁבִיעִי, פָּרִים שִׁבְעָה, אֵילִם שְׁנָיִם, כְּבָשִׂים בְּנֵי שָׁנָה אַרְבָּעָה עָשָׂר, תְּמִימִם.[4] וּמִנְחָתָם וְנִסְכֵּיהֶם כִּמְדֻבָּר, שְׁלֹשָׁה

one tenth-ephah for each lamb; and wine for its libation. A he-goat for atonement, and two continual offerings according to their law. And on the fourth day: ten bulls, two rams, fourteen [male] first-year lambs, unblemished.[1] *And their meal-offerings and their wine-libations as mentioned: three tenth-ephah for each bull; two tenth-ephah for each ram; one tenth-ephah for each lamb; and wine for its libation. A he-goat for atonement, and two continual offerings according to their law.*

Continue *'Our God...'* (page 687).

ON THE THIRD DAY CHOL HAMOED SUCCOS

וּבַיּוֹם הָרְבִיעִי *And on the fourth day: ten bulls, two rams, fourteen [male] first-year lambs, unblemished.*[1] *And their meal-offerings and their wine-libations as mentioned: three tenth-ephah for each bull; two tenth-ephah for each ram; one tenth-ephah for each lamb; and wine for its libation. A he-goat for atonement, and two continual offerings according to their law. And on the fifth day: nine bulls, two rams, fourteen [male] first-year lambs, unblemished.*[2] *And their meal-offerings and their wine-libations as mentioned: three tenth-ephah for each bull; two tenth-ephah for each ram; one tenth-ephah for each lamb; and wine for its libation. A he-goat for atonement, and two continual offerings according to their law.*

On the Sabbath continue, *'They shall rejoice ...'*; on weekdays continue, *'Our God ...,'*; page 687.

ON THE FOURTH DAY CHOL HAMOED SUCCOS

וּבַיּוֹם הַחֲמִישִׁי *And on the fifth day: nine bulls, two rams, fourteen [male] first-year lambs, unblemished.*[2] *And their meal-offerings and their wine-libations as mentioned: three tenth-ephah for each bull; two tenth-ephah for each ram; one tenth-ephah for each lamb; and wine for its libation. A he-goat for atonement, and two continual offerings according to their law. And on the sixth day: eight bulls, two rams, fourteen [male] first-year lambs, unblemished.*[3] *And their meal-offerings and their wine-libations as mentioned: three tenth-ephah for each bull; two tenth-ephah for each ram; one tenth-ephah for each lamb; and wine for its libation. A he-goat for atonement, and two continual offerings according to their law.*

On the Sabbath continue, *'They shall rejoice ...'*; on weekdays continue, *'Our God ...,'*; page 687.

ON HOSHANA RABBAH

וּבַיּוֹם הַשִּׁשִּׁי *And on the sixth day: eight bulls, two rams, fourteen [male] first-year lambs, unblemished.*[3] *And their meal-offerings and their wine-libations as mentioned: three tenth-ephah for each bull; two tenth-ephah for each ram; one tenth-ephah for each lamb; and wine for its libation. A he-goat for atonement, and two continual offerings according to their law. And on the seventh day: seven bulls, two rams, fourteen [male] first-year lambs, unblemished.*[4] *And their meal-offerings and their wine-libations as mentioned:*

---

(1) *Numbers* 29:23. (2) 29:26. (3) 29:29. (4) 29:32.

עֶשְׂרֹנִים לַפָּר, וּשְׁנֵי עֶשְׂרֹנִים לָאָיִל, וְעִשָּׂרוֹן לַכֶּבֶשׂ, וְיַיִן כְּנִסְכּוֹ. וְשָׂעִיר לְכַפֵּר, וּשְׁנֵי תְמִידִים כְּהִלְכָתָם.

Continue אֱלֹהֵינוּ (below).

ON SHEMINI ATZERES/SIMCHAS TORAH

בַּיּוֹם הַשְּׁמִינִי, עֲצֶרֶת תִּהְיֶה לָכֶם, כָּל מְלֶאכֶת עֲבֹדָה לֹא תַעֲשׂוּ. וְהִקְרַבְתֶּם עֹלָה אִשֵּׁה רֵיחַ נִיחֹחַ לַיהוה, פַּר אֶחָד, אַיִל אֶחָד, כְּבָשִׂים בְּנֵי שָׁנָה שִׁבְעָה, תְּמִימִם.[1] וּמִנְחָתָם וְנִסְכֵּיהֶם כִּמְדֻבָּר, שְׁלֹשָׁה עֶשְׂרֹנִים לַפָּר, וּשְׁנֵי עֶשְׂרֹנִים לָאָיִל, וְעִשָּׂרוֹן לַכֶּבֶשׂ, וְיַיִן כְּנִסְכּוֹ. וְשָׂעִיר לְכַפֵּר, וּשְׁנֵי תְמִידִים כְּהִלְכָתָם.

On the Sabbath:

יִשְׂמְחוּ בְמַלְכוּתְךָ שׁוֹמְרֵי שַׁבָּת וְקוֹרְאֵי עֹנֶג, עַם מְקַדְּשֵׁי שְׁבִיעִי, כֻּלָּם יִשְׂבְּעוּ וְיִתְעַנְּגוּ מִטּוּבֶךָ, וּבַשְּׁבִיעִי רָצִיתָ בּוֹ וְקִדַּשְׁתּוֹ, חֶמְדַּת יָמִים אוֹתוֹ קָרָאתָ, זֵכֶר לְמַעֲשֵׂה בְרֵאשִׁית.

On all days continue [on the Sabbath add the words in brackets]:

אֱלֹהֵינוּ וֵאלֹהֵי אֲבוֹתֵינוּ, [רְצֵה בִמְנוּחָתֵנוּ] מֶלֶךְ רַחֲמָן רַחֵם עָלֵינוּ, טוֹב וּמֵטִיב* הִדָּרֶשׁ לָנוּ, שׁוּבָה אֵלֵינוּ בַּהֲמוֹן רַחֲמֶיךָ, בִּגְלַל אָבוֹת שֶׁעָשׂוּ רְצוֹנֶךָ. בְּנֵה בֵיתְךָ כְּבַתְּחִלָּה, וְכוֹנֵן מִקְדָּשְׁךָ עַל מְכוֹנוֹ, וְהַרְאֵנוּ בְּבִנְיָנוֹ, וְשַׂמְּחֵנוּ בְּתִקּוּנוֹ. וְהָשֵׁב כֹּהֲנִים לַעֲבוֹדָתָם, וּלְוִיִּם לְשִׁירָם וּלְזִמְרָם, וְהָשֵׁב יִשְׂרָאֵל לִנְוֵיהֶם. וְשָׁם נַעֲלֶה וְנֵרָאֶה* וְנִשְׁתַּחֲוֶה לְפָנֶיךָ, בְּשָׁלֹשׁ פַּעֲמֵי רְגָלֵינוּ, כַּכָּתוּב בְּתוֹרָתֶךָ: שָׁלוֹשׁ פְּעָמִים בַּשָּׁנָה, יֵרָאֶה כָל זְכוּרְךָ אֶת פְּנֵי יהוה אֱלֹהֶיךָ, בַּמָּקוֹם אֲשֶׁר יִבְחָר, בְּחַג הַמַּצּוֹת, וּבְחַג הַשָּׁבֻעוֹת, וּבְחַג הַסֻּכּוֹת, וְלֹא יֵרָאֶה אֶת פְּנֵי יהוה רֵיקָם.* אִישׁ כְּמַתְּנַת יָדוֹ, כְּבִרְכַּת יהוה אֱלֹהֶיךָ, אֲשֶׁר נָתַן לָךְ.[2]

וְהַשִּׂיאֵנוּ יהוה אֱלֹהֵינוּ אֶת בִּרְכַּת מוֹעֲדֶיךָ לְחַיִּים וּלְשָׁלוֹם, לְשִׂמְחָה וּלְשָׂשׂוֹן, כַּאֲשֶׁר רָצִיתָ וְאָמַרְתָּ לְבָרְכֵנוּ.

אֱלֹהֵינוּ ... טוֹב וּמֵטִיב — *Our God ... O good and beneficent One.* In the case of human beings, someone may be good, but not have the resources to benefit others. On the other hand, someone may benefit others by helping them do good deeds, but for himself he may prefer to indulge his sinful nature. God, however, is perfect — He is both good and beneficent *(Iyun Tefillah).*

וְשָׁם נַעֲלֶה וְנֵרָאֶה — *And there we will ascend and appear.* Having been returned to *Eretz Yisrael,* we will be able to fulfill the commandment of going up to the Temple to appear before God.

רֵיקָם — *Emptyhanded.* During the pilgrimages, each Jew must offer elevation-offerings and peace-offerings in honor of the Festivals. However, though no one may come empty-

three tenth-ephah for each bull; two tenth-ephah for each ram; one tenth-ephah for each lamb; and wine for its libation. A he-goat for atonement, and two continual offerings according to their law.

Continue *'Our God...'* (below).

ON SHEMINI ATZERES/SIMCHAS TORAH

בַּיּוֹם הַשְּׁמִינִי *On the eighth day, there shall be an Assembly for you, you may not do any laborious work. You are to bring an elevation-offering, a fire-offering, a satisfying aroma to* HASHEM, *one bull, one ram, seven [male] first-year lambs, unblemished.*[1] *And their meal-offerings and their wine-libations as mentioned: three tenth-ephah for each bull; two tenth-ephah for each ram; one tenth-ephah for each lamb; and wine for its libation. A he-goat for atonement, and two continual offerings according to their law.*

On the Sabbath:

יִשְׂמְחוּ *They shall rejoice in Your Kingship — those who observe the Sabbath and call it a delight. The people that sanctifies the Seventh — they will all be satisfied and delighted from Your goodness. And the Seventh — You found favor in it and sanctified it. 'Most coveted of days' You called it, a remembrance of creation.*

On all days continue [on the Sabbath add the words in brackets]:

אֱלֹהֵינוּ *Our God and the God of our forefathers, [may You be pleased with our rest] O merciful King, have mercy on us; O good and beneficent One,* let Yourself be sought out by us; return to us in Your yearning mercy for the sake of the forefathers who did Your will. Rebuild Your House as it was at first, and establish Your Sanctuary on its prepared site; show us its rebuilding and gladden us in its perfection Restore the Kohanim to their service and the Levites to their song and music; and restore Israel to their dwellings. And there we will ascend and appear* and prostrate ourselves before You, during our three pilgrimage seasons, as it is written in Your Torah: Three times a year all your males are to appear before* HASHEM, *your God, in the place He shall choose, on the Festival of Matzos, on the Festival of Shavuos, and on the Festival of Succos, and they shall not appear before* HASHEM *empty-handed.* Every man according to the gift of his hand, according to the blessing of* HASHEM, *your God, that He gave you.*[2]

וְהַשִּׂיאֵנוּ *Bestow upon us, O* HASHEM, *our God, the blessing of Your appointed Festivals for life and for peace, for gladness and for joy, as You desired and promised to bless us.*

(1) *Numbers* 29:35-36. (2) *Deuteronomy* 16:16-17.

---

handed — without offerings — he should give only as much as he can afford, but not more, *according to the gift of his hand,* i.e., depending on how much God has blessed him with *(Rashi).*

On the Sabbath, add the words in brackets.

[אֱלֹהֵינוּ וֵאלֹהֵי אֲבוֹתֵינוּ רְצֵה בִמְנוּחָתֵנוּ] קַדְּשֵׁנוּ בְּמִצְוֹתֶיךָ וְתֵן חֶלְקֵנוּ בְּתוֹרָתֶךָ, שַׂבְּעֵנוּ מִטּוּבֶךָ וְשַׂמְּחֵנוּ בִּישׁוּעָתֶךָ, וְטַהֵר לִבֵּנוּ לְעָבְדְּךָ בֶּאֱמֶת, וְהַנְחִילֵנוּ יהוה אֱלֹהֵינוּ [בְּאַהֲבָה וּבְרָצוֹן] בְּשִׂמְחָה וּבְשָׂשׂוֹן [שַׁבָּת וּ]מוֹעֲדֵי קָדְשֶׁךָ, וְיִשְׂמְחוּ בְךָ יִשְׂרָאֵל מְקַדְּשֵׁי שְׁמֶךָ. בָּרוּךְ אַתָּה יהוה, מְקַדֵּשׁ [הַשַּׁבָּת וְ]יִשְׂרָאֵל וְהַזְּמַנִּים.

עבודה

רְצֵה יהוה אֱלֹהֵינוּ בְּעַמְּךָ יִשְׂרָאֵל וּבִתְפִלָּתָם, וְהָשֵׁב אֶת הָעֲבוֹדָה לִדְבִיר בֵּיתֶךָ. וְאִשֵּׁי יִשְׂרָאֵל וּתְפִלָּתָם בְּאַהֲבָה תְקַבֵּל בְּרָצוֹן, וּתְהִי לְרָצוֹן תָּמִיד עֲבוֹדַת יִשְׂרָאֵל עַמֶּךָ.

On Festivals when the *Kohanim* ascend the *duchan* to pronounce *Bircas Kohanim* [the Priestly Blessing], the *chazzan's* repetition continues on page 692.

During Chol HaMoed, or if no *Kohen* is present on the Festival, the *chazzan* continues here.

וְתֶחֱזֶינָה עֵינֵינוּ בְּשׁוּבְךָ לְצִיּוֹן בְּרַחֲמִים. בָּרוּךְ אַתָּה יהוה, הַמַּחֲזִיר שְׁכִינָתוֹ לְצִיּוֹן.

הודאה

Bow at מוֹדִים; straighten up at 'ה. In his repetition the *chazzan* should recite the entire מוֹדִים aloud, while the congregation recites מוֹדִים דְּרַבָּנָן softly.

מוֹדִים אֲנַחְנוּ לָךְ שָׁאַתָּה הוּא יהוה אֱלֹהֵינוּ וֵאלֹהֵי אֲבוֹתֵינוּ לְעוֹלָם וָעֶד. צוּר חַיֵּינוּ, מָגֵן יִשְׁעֵנוּ אַתָּה הוּא לְדוֹר וָדוֹר. נוֹדֶה לְּךָ וּנְסַפֵּר תְּהִלָּתֶךָ[1] עַל חַיֵּינוּ הַמְּסוּרִים בְּיָדֶךָ, וְעַל נִשְׁמוֹתֵינוּ הַפְּקוּדוֹת לָךְ, וְעַל נִסֶּיךָ שֶׁבְּכָל יוֹם עִמָּנוּ, וְעַל נִפְלְאוֹתֶיךָ וְטוֹבוֹתֶיךָ שֶׁבְּכָל עֵת, עֶרֶב וָבֹקֶר וְצָהֳרָיִם. הַטּוֹב כִּי לֹא כָלוּ רַחֲמֶיךָ, וְהַמְּרַחֵם כִּי לֹא תַמּוּ חֲסָדֶיךָ,[2] מֵעוֹלָם קִוִּינוּ לָךְ:

מודים דרבנן

מוֹדִים אֲנַחְנוּ לָךְ, שָׁאַתָּה הוּא יהוה אֱלֹהֵינוּ וֵאלֹהֵי אֲבוֹתֵינוּ, אֱלֹהֵי כָל בָּשָׂר, יוֹצְרֵנוּ, יוֹצֵר בְּרֵאשִׁית. בְּרָכוֹת וְהוֹדָאוֹת לְשִׁמְךָ הַגָּדוֹל וְהַקָּדוֹשׁ, עַל שֶׁהֶחֱיִיתָנוּ וְקִיַּמְתָּנוּ. כֵּן תְּחַיֵּנוּ וּתְקַיְּמֵנוּ, וְתֶאֱסוֹף גָּלֻיּוֹתֵינוּ לְחַצְרוֹת קָדְשֶׁךָ, לִשְׁמוֹר חֻקֶּיךָ וְלַעֲשׂוֹת רְצוֹנֶךָ, וּלְעָבְדְּךָ בְּלֵבָב שָׁלֵם, עַל שֶׁאֲנַחְנוּ מוֹדִים לָךְ. בָּרוּךְ אֵל הַהוֹדָאוֹת.

וְעַל כֻּלָּם יִתְבָּרַךְ וְיִתְרוֹמַם שִׁמְךָ מַלְכֵּנוּ תָּמִיד לְעוֹלָם וָעֶד.

On the Sabbath, add the words in brackets.

[Our God and the God of our forefathers, may You be pleased with our rest.] Sanctify us with Your commandments and grant us our share in Your Torah; satisfy us from Your goodness and gladden us with Your salvation, and purify our heart to serve You sincerely. And grant us a heritage, O HASHEM *our God — [with love and with favor] with gladness and with joy — [the Sabbath and] the appointed festivals of Your holiness, and may Israel, the sanctifiers of Your Name, rejoice in You. Blessed are you,* HASHEM, *Who sanctifies [the Sabbath] Israel and the festive seasons.*

TEMPLE SERVICE

רְצֵה *Be favorable,* HASHEM, *our God, toward Your people Israel and their prayer and restore the service to the Holy of Holies of Your Temple. The fire-offerings of Israel and their prayer accept with love and favor, and may the service of Your people Israel always be favorable to You.*

On Festivals when the *Kohanim* ascend the *duchan* to pronounce *Bircas Kohanim* [the Priestly Blessing], the *chazzan's* repetition continues on page 692.

During Chol HaMoed, or if no *Kohen* is present on the Festival, the *chazzan* continues here.

וְתֶחֱזֶינָה *May our eyes behold Your return to Zion in compassion. Blessed are You,* HASHEM, *Who restores His Presence to Zion.*

THANKSGIVING [MODIM]

Bow at *'We gratefully thank You'*; straighten up at *'HASHEM.'* In his repetition the *chazzan* should recite the entire *Modim* aloud, while the congregation recites *Modim of the Rabbis* softly.

מוֹדִים *We gratefully thank You, for it is You Who are* HASHEM, *our God and the God of our forefathers for all eternity; Rock of our lives, Shield of our salvation are You from generation to generation. We shall thank You and relate Your praise[1] — for our lives, which are committed to Your power and for our souls that are entrusted to You; for Your miracles that are with us every day; and for Your wonders and favors in every season — evening, morning, and afternoon. The Beneficent One, for Your compassions were never exhausted, and the Compassionate One, for Your kindnesses never ended[2] — always have we put our hope in You.*

MODIM OF THE RABBIS

מוֹדִים *We gratefully thank You, for it is You Who are* HASHEM, *our God and the God of our forefathers, the God of all flesh, our Molder, the Molder of the universe. Blessings and thanks are due Your great and holy Name for You have given us life and sustained us. So may You continue to give us life and sustain us and gather our exiles to the Courtyards of Your Sanctuary, to observe Your decrees, to do Your will and to serve You wholeheartedly. [We thank You] for inspiring us to thank You. Blessed is the God of thanksgivings.*

For all these, may Your Name be blessed and exalted, our King, continually forever and ever.

(1) Cf. *Psalms* 79:13. (2) Cf. *Lamentations* 3:22.

Bend the knees at בָּרוּךְ; bow at אַתָּה; straighten up at ה׳.

וְכֹל הַחַיִּים יוֹדְוּךָ סֶּלָה, וִיהַלְּלוּ אֶת שִׁמְךָ בֶּאֱמֶת, הָאֵל יְשׁוּעָתֵנוּ וְעֶזְרָתֵנוּ סֶלָה. בָּרוּךְ אַתָּה יהוה, הַטּוֹב שִׁמְךָ וּלְךָ נָאֶה לְהוֹדוֹת.

If the *Kohanim* do not ascend the *duchan,*
the *chazzan* recites the following during his repetition.
He faces right at וְיִשְׁמְרֶךָ; faces left at אֵלֶיךָ וִיחֻנֶּךָּ; faces the Ark for the rest of the blessings:

אֱלֹהֵינוּ, וֵאלֹהֵי אֲבוֹתֵינוּ, בָּרְכֵנוּ בַבְּרָכָה הַמְּשֻׁלֶּשֶׁת, בַּתּוֹרָה הַכְּתוּבָה עַל יְדֵי מֹשֶׁה עַבְדֶּךָ, הָאֲמוּרָה מִפִּי אַהֲרֹן וּבָנָיו, כֹּהֲנִים עַם קְדוֹשֶׁךָ, כָּאָמוּר:

יְבָרֶכְךָ יהוה, וְיִשְׁמְרֶךָ. (.Cong.—כֵּן יְהִי רָצוֹן)

יָאֵר יהוה פָּנָיו אֵלֶיךָ וִיחֻנֶּךָּ. (.Cong.—כֵּן יְהִי רָצוֹן)

יִשָּׂא יהוה פָּנָיו אֵלֶיךָ וְיָשֵׂם לְךָ שָׁלוֹם.[1] (.Cong.—כֵּן יְהִי רָצוֹן)

שלום

שִׂים שָׁלוֹם, טוֹבָה, וּבְרָכָה, חֵן, וָחֶסֶד וְרַחֲמִים עָלֵינוּ וְעַל כָּל יִשְׂרָאֵל עַמֶּךָ. בָּרְכֵנוּ אָבִינוּ, כֻּלָּנוּ כְּאֶחָד בְּאוֹר פָּנֶיךָ, כִּי בְאוֹר פָּנֶיךָ נָתַתָּ לָּנוּ, יהוה אֱלֹהֵינוּ, תּוֹרַת חַיִּים וְאַהֲבַת חֶסֶד, וּצְדָקָה, וּבְרָכָה, וְרַחֲמִים, וְחַיִּים, וְשָׁלוֹם. וְטוֹב בְּעֵינֶיךָ לְבָרֵךְ אֶת עַמְּךָ יִשְׂרָאֵל, בְּכָל עֵת וּבְכָל שָׁעָה בִּשְׁלוֹמֶךָ. בָּרוּךְ אַתָּה יהוה, הַמְּבָרֵךְ אֶת עַמּוֹ יִשְׂרָאֵל בַּשָּׁלוֹם.

The *chazzan's* repetition of *Shemoneh Esrei* ends here. The individual continues until next page.

יִהְיוּ לְרָצוֹן אִמְרֵי פִי וְהֶגְיוֹן לִבִּי לְפָנֶיךָ, יהוה צוּרִי וְגֹאֲלִי.[2]

אֱלֹהַי, נְצוֹר לְשׁוֹנִי מֵרָע, וּשְׂפָתַי מִדַּבֵּר מִרְמָה,[3] וְלִמְקַלְּלַי נַפְשִׁי תִדּוֹם, וְנַפְשִׁי כֶּעָפָר לַכֹּל תִּהְיֶה. פְּתַח לִבִּי בְּתוֹרָתֶךָ, וּבְמִצְוֹתֶיךָ תִּרְדּוֹף נַפְשִׁי. וְכֹל הַחוֹשְׁבִים עָלַי רָעָה, מְהֵרָה הָפֵר עֲצָתָם וְקַלְקֵל מַחֲשַׁבְתָּם. עֲשֵׂה לְמַעַן שְׁמֶךָ, עֲשֵׂה לְמַעַן יְמִינֶךָ, עֲשֵׂה לְמַעַן קְדֻשָּׁתֶךָ, עֲשֵׂה לְמַעַן תּוֹרָתֶךָ. לְמַעַן יֵחָלְצוּן יְדִידֶיךָ, הוֹשִׁיעָה יְמִינְךָ וַעֲנֵנִי.[4]

Some recite verses pertaining to their names at this point. See page 924.

יִהְיוּ לְרָצוֹן אִמְרֵי פִי וְהֶגְיוֹן לִבִּי לְפָנֶיךָ, יהוה צוּרִי וְגֹאֲלִי.[2] עֹשֶׂה שָׁלוֹם בִּמְרוֹמָיו, הוּא יַעֲשֶׂה שָׁלוֹם עָלֵינוּ, וְעַל כָּל יִשְׂרָאֵל. וְאִמְרוּ: אָמֵן.

Bend the knees at *'Blessed'*; bow at *'You'*; straighten up at *'HASHEM.'*

Everything alive will gratefully acknowledge You, Selah! and praise Your Name sincerely, O God of our salvation and help, Selah! Blessed are You, HASHEM, Your Name is 'The Beneficent One' and to You it is fitting to give thanks.

If the *Kohanim* do not ascend the *duchan*, the *chazzan* recites the following during his repetition.

אֱלֹהֵינוּ *Our God and the God of our forefathers, bless us with the three-verse blessing in the Torah that was written by the hand of Moses, Your servant, that was said by Aaron and his sons, the Kohanim, Your holy people, as it is said:*

May HASHEM bless you and safeguard you. (Cong.— *So may it be.*)

May HASHEM illuminate His countenance for you and be gracious to you. (Cong.— *So may it be.*)

May HASHEM turn His countenance to you and establish peace for you.[1] (Cong.— *So may it be.*)

PEACE

שִׂים *Establish peace, goodness, blessing, graciousness, kindness, and compassion upon us and upon all of Your people Israel. Bless us, our Father, all of us as one, with the light of Your countenance, for with the light of Your countenance You gave us, HASHEM, our God, the Torah of life and a love of kindness, righteousness, blessing, compassion, life, and peace. And may it be good in Your eyes to bless Your people Israel, in every season and in every hour with Your peace. Blessed are You, HASHEM, Who blesses His people Israel with peace.*

The *chazzan's* repetition of *Shemoneh Esrei* ends here. The individual continues until next page.

May the expressions of my mouth and the thoughts of my heart find favor before You, HASHEM, my Rock and my Redeemer.[2]

אֱלֹהַי *My God, guard my tongue from evil and my lips from speaking deceitfully.*[3] *To those who curse me, let my soul be silent; and let my soul be like dust to everyone. Open my heart to Your Torah, then my soul will pursue Your commandments. As for all those who design evil against me, speedily nullify their counsel and disrupt their design. Act for Your Name's sake; act for Your right hand's sake; act for Your sanctity's sake; act for Your Torah's sake. That Your beloved ones may be given rest; let Your right hand save, and respond to me.*[4]

Some recite verses pertaining to their names at this point. See page 924.

May the expressions of my mouth and the thoughts of my heart find favor before You, HASHEM, my Rock and my Redeemer.[2] *He Who makes peace in His heights, may He make peace upon us, and upon all Israel. Now respond: Amen.*

---

(1) *Numbers* 6:24-26. (2) *Psalms* 19:15. (3) Cf. 34:14. (4) 60:7; 108:7.

יְהִי רָצוֹן מִלְּפָנֶיךָ יהוה אֱלֹהֵינוּ וֵאלֹהֵי אֲבוֹתֵינוּ, שֶׁיִּבָּנֶה בֵּית הַמִּקְדָּשׁ בִּמְהֵרָה בְיָמֵינוּ, וְתֵן חֶלְקֵנוּ בְּתוֹרָתֶךָ. וְשָׁם נַעֲבָדְךָ בְּיִרְאָה, כִּימֵי עוֹלָם וּכְשָׁנִים קַדְמוֹנִיּוֹת. וְעָרְבָה לַיהוה מִנְחַת יְהוּדָה וִירוּשָׁלָיִם, כִּימֵי עוֹלָם וּכְשָׁנִים קַדְמוֹנִיּוֹת.[1]

THE INDIVIDUAL'S RECITATION OF *SHEMONEH ESREI* ENDS HERE.

During Succos, the *Hoshana* prayers (p. 726) are recited.
On Festival days (and the Sabbath of Chol HaMoed) other than Succos, the *chazzan* recites the Full *Kaddish* (p. 474) and the service continues from there (pp. 476-488).
During Chol HaMoed Pesach, the *chazzan* recites the Full *Kaddish* (p. 156) and the service continues from there (pp. 158-168).

ברכת כהנים

When the *Kohanim* ascend the *duchan* to pronounce *Bircas Kohanim* [the Priestly Blessing], the *chazzan's* repetition of *Shemoneh Esrei* continues here from page 689.

Congregation and *Kohanim,* then *chazzan.*

וְתֶעָרֵב לְפָנֶיךָ עֲתִירָתֵנוּ* כְּעוֹלָה וּכְקָרְבָּן. אָנָּא, רַחוּם, בְּרַחֲמֶיךָ הָרַבִּים הָשֵׁב שְׁכִינָתְךָ לְצִיּוֹן עִירֶךָ, וְסֵדֶר הָעֲבוֹדָה לִירוּשָׁלָיִם. וְתֶחֱזֶינָה עֵינֵינוּ בְּשׁוּבְךָ לְצִיּוֹן בְּרַחֲמִים, וְשָׁם נַעֲבָדְךָ בְּיִרְאָה כִּימֵי עוֹלָם וּכְשָׁנִים קַדְמוֹנִיּוֹת.

—*Chazzan* concludes בָּרוּךְ אַתָּה יהוה, שֶׁאוֹתְךָ לְבַדְּךָ בְּיִרְאָה נַעֲבוֹד.

(—Cong. and *Kohanim* אָמֵן.)

Chazzan recites the entire מוֹדִים aloud, while the congregation and *Kohanim* recite מוֹדִים דְּרַבָּנָן softly. Bow at מוֹדִים; straighten up at ה׳.

מוֹדִים אֲנַחְנוּ לָךְ שָׁאַתָּה הוּא יהוה אֱלֹהֵינוּ וֵאלֹהֵי אֲבוֹתֵינוּ לְעוֹלָם וָעֶד. צוּר חַיֵּינוּ, מָגֵן יִשְׁעֵנוּ אַתָּה הוּא לְדוֹר וָדוֹר. נוֹדֶה לְּךָ וּנְסַפֵּר תְּהִלָּתֶךָ[2] עַל חַיֵּינוּ הַמְּסוּרִים בְּיָדֶךָ, וְעַל נִשְׁמוֹתֵינוּ הַפְּקוּדוֹת לָךְ, וְעַל נִסֶּיךָ שֶׁבְּכָל יוֹם עִמָּנוּ, וְעַל נִפְלְאוֹתֶיךָ וְטוֹבוֹתֶיךָ שֶׁבְּכָל עֵת, עֶרֶב וָבֹקֶר וְצָהֳרָיִם. הַטּוֹב כִּי לֹא כָלוּ רַחֲמֶיךָ, וְהַמְּרַחֵם כִּי לֹא תַמּוּ חֲסָדֶיךָ,[3] מֵעוֹלָם קִוִּינוּ לָךְ:

מודים דרבנן

מוֹדִים אֲנַחְנוּ לָךְ, שָׁאַתָּה הוּא יהוה אֱלֹהֵינוּ וֵאלֹהֵי אֲבוֹתֵינוּ, אֱלֹהֵי כָל בָּשָׂר, יוֹצְרֵנוּ, יוֹצֵר בְּרֵאשִׁית. בְּרָכוֹת וְהוֹדָאוֹת לְשִׁמְךָ הַגָּדוֹל וְהַקָּדוֹשׁ, עַל שֶׁהֶחֱיִיתָנוּ וְקִיַּמְתָּנוּ. כֵּן תְּחַיֵּנוּ וּתְקַיְּמֵנוּ, וְתֶאֱסוֹף גָּלֻיּוֹתֵינוּ לְחַצְרוֹת קָדְשֶׁךָ, לִשְׁמוֹר חֻקֶּיךָ וְלַעֲשׂוֹת רְצוֹנֶךָ, וּלְעָבְדְּךָ בְּלֵבָב שָׁלֵם, עַל שֶׁאֲנַחְנוּ מוֹדִים לָךְ. בָּרוּךְ אֵל הַהוֹדָאוֹת.

וְעַל כֻּלָּם יִתְבָּרַךְ וְיִתְרוֹמַם שִׁמְךָ מַלְכֵּנוּ תָּמִיד לְעוֹלָם וָעֶד.

יְהִי רָצוֹן *May it be Your will,* HASHEM *our God and the God of our forefathers, that the Holy Temple be rebuilt, speedily in our days. Grant us our share in Your Torah, and may we serve You there with reverence, as in days of old and in former years. Then the offering of Judah and Jerusalem will be pleasing to* HASHEM, *as in days of old and in former years.*[1]

THE INDIVIDUAL'S RECITATION OF *SHEMONEH ESREI* ENDS HERE.

During Succos, the *Hoshana* prayers (p. 726) are recited.
On Festival days (and the Sabbath of Chol HaMoed) other than Succos, the *chazzan* recites the Full *Kaddish* (p. 474) and the service continues from there (pp. 476-488).
During Chol HaMoed Pesach, the *chazzan* recites the Full *Kaddish* (p. 156) and the service continues from there (pp. 158-168).

BIRCAS KOHANIM

When the *Kohanim* ascend the *duchan* to pronounce *Bircas Kohanim* [the Priestly Blessing], the *chazzan's* repetition of *Shemoneh Esrei* continues here from page 689.

Congregation and *Kohanim,* then *chazzan.*

וְתֶעֱרַב *May our entreaty be pleasing unto You as an elevation-offering and as a sacrifice. Please, O Merciful One, in Your abounding mercy return Your Shechinah to Zion, Your city, and the order of the Temple service to Jerusalem. And may our eyes behold when You return to Zion in mercy, that we may there serve You with awe as in days of old and as in earlier years.*

Chazzan concludes— *Blessed are You* HASHEM, *for You alone do we serve with awe.* (Cong. and *Kohanim*— *Amen.)*

Chazzan recites the entire *Modim* aloud, while the congregation and *Kohanim* recite *Modim of the Rabbis* softly. Bow at *'We gratefully thank You';* straighten up at *'HASHEM.'*

מוֹדִים *We gratefully thank You, for it is You Who are* HASHEM, *our God and the God of our forefathers for all eternity; Rock of our lives, Shield of our salvation are You from generation to generation. We shall thank You and relate Your praise*[2] *— for our lives, which are committed to Your power and for our souls that are entrusted to You; for Your miracles that are with us every day; and for Your wonders and favors in every season — evening, morning, and afternoon. The Beneficent One, for Your compassions were never exhausted, and the Compassionate One, for Your kindnesses never ended*[3] *— always have we put our hope in You.*

MODIM OF THE RABBIS

מוֹדִים *We gratefully thank You, for it is You Who are* HASHEM, *our God and the God of our forefathers, the God of all flesh, our Molder, the Molder of the universe. Blessings and thanks are due Your great and holy Name for You have given us life and sustained us. So may You continue to give us life and sustain us and gather our exiles to the Courtyards of Your Sanctuary, to observe Your decrees, to do Your will and to serve You wholeheartedly. [We thank You] for inspiring us to thank You. Blessed is the God of thanksgivings.*

For all these, may Your Name be blessed and exalted, our King, continually forever and ever.

(1) *Malachi* 3:4. (2) Cf. *Psalms* 79:13. (3) Cf. *Lamentations* 3:22.

When the *chazzan* recites וְכֹל הַחַיִּים, the *Kohanim* recite יְהִי רָצוֹן.

וְכֹל הַחַיִּים יוֹדְוּךָ סֶּלָה, וִיהַלְלוּ אֶת שִׁמְךָ בֶּאֱמֶת, הָאֵל יְשׁוּעָתֵנוּ וְעֶזְרָתֵנוּ סֶלָה. בָּרוּךְ אַתָּה יהוה, הַטּוֹב שִׁמְךָ וּלְךָ נָאֶה לְהוֹדוֹת. (—Cong. and *Kohanim*—אָמֵן.)

יְהִי רָצוֹן מִלְּפָנֶיךָ, יהוה אֱלֹהֵינוּ וֵאלֹהֵי אֲבוֹתֵינוּ, שֶׁתְּהֵא הַבְּרָכָה הַזֹּאת שֶׁצִּוִּיתָנוּ לְבָרֵךְ אֶת עַמְּךָ יִשְׂרָאֵל בְּרָכָה שְׁלֵמָה, וְלֹא יִהְיֶה בָּהּ שׁוּם מִכְשׁוֹל וְעָוֹן מֵעַתָּה וְעַד עוֹלָם.

The *chazzan* recites the following in an undertone but says the word כֹּהֲנִים aloud as a formal summons to the *Kohanim** to bless the people. In some communities the congregation, but not the *Kohanim,* responds עַם קְדוֹשֶׁךָ כָּאָמוּר, aloud.

אֱלֹהֵינוּ וֵאלֹהֵי אֲבוֹתֵינוּ, בָּרְכֵנוּ בַבְּרָכָה* הַמְּשֻׁלֶּשֶׁת,* בַּתּוֹרָה הַכְּתוּבָה עַל יְדֵי מֹשֶׁה עַבְדֶּךָ, הָאֲמוּרָה מִפִּי אַהֲרֹן וּבָנָיו,

כֹּהֲנִים

עַם קְדוֹשֶׁךָ* — כָּאָמוּר:

Facing the Ark, the *Kohanim* raise their hands and begin to recite the following blessing aloud and in unison. Upon reaching וְצִוָּנוּ, they turn to face the congregation and complete the blessing. The congregation, but not the *chazzan,* responds *Amen.*

בָּרוּךְ אַתָּה יהוה, אֱלֹהֵינוּ מֶלֶךְ הָעוֹלָם, אֲשֶׁר קִדְּשָׁנוּ בִּקְדֻשָּׁתוֹ שֶׁל אַהֲרֹן,* וְצִוָּנוּ לְבָרֵךְ אֶת עַמּוֹ יִשְׂרָאֵל בְּאַהֲבָה.* (—Cong.—אָמֵן.)

Laws of Bircas Kohanim

After *Kedushah,* a Levite pours water from a utensil over the *Kohen's* hands. When the *chazzan* begins רְצֵה, the *Kohanim* slip off their shoes (the laces should be loosened before the hands are washed) and ascend the *duchan* [platform in front of the Ark] where they stand facing the Ark.

When the *chazzan* recites וְכֹל הַחַיִּים, the *Kohanim* quietly recite the יְהִי רָצוֹן supplication, concluding it to coincide with the ending of the *chazzan's* blessing, so that the congregational *Amen* will be in response to their prayer as well as the *chazzan's.*

In most congregations, the *chazzan* quietly recites ... אֱלֹהֵינוּ וֵאלֹהֵי אֲבוֹתֵינוּ בָּרְכֵנוּ *'Our God ... bless us ...'* until the word כֹּהֲנִים, *Kohanim,* which he calls out in a loud voice. Then, resuming his undertone, he recites the next words עַם קְדוֹשֶׁךָ כָּאָמוּר, *'Your holy people, as it is said.'* Even if only one *Kohen* is present, the *chazzan* uses the word *Kohanim* in plural, since it is the established form of the prayer. In some congregations, however, the *chazzan* merely calls out *'Kohanim'* without reciting the introductory prayer. In these places the *chazzan* calls out the plural word *Kohanim* only if two or more *Kohanim* ascend the *duchan.* If only one *Kohen* is present, however, that *Kohen* does not wait for a call, but raises his hands and begins his blessing immediately.

From this point until the *chazzan* begins שִׂים שָׁלוֹם, the congregation stands, facing the *Kohanim* attentively. Neither the *Kohanim* nor the congregation may gaze at the *Kohanim's* raised hands.

Those standing behind the *Kohanim* do not receive the benefits of the blessing. Therefore, people behind them should move up during *Bircas Kohanim.*

The *chazzan* reads each word of *Bircas Kohanim* aloud and the *Kohanim* repeat it after him. The congregation may not respond אָמֵן until the *Kohanim* have completed the initial blessing; the *chazzan* may not call out יְבָרֶכְךָ until the congregation has finished its אָמֵן; the *Kohanim* may not repeat יְבָרֶכְךָ until the *chazzan* has read the full word; etc., etc.

When the *chazzan* recites וְכֹל הַחַיִּים, *Everything alive,* the *Kohanim* recite יְהִי רָצוֹן, *May it be ...*

וְכֹל *Everything alive will gratefully acknowledge You, Selah! and praise Your Name sincerely, O God of our salvation and help, Selah! Blessed are You,* HASHEM, *Your Name is 'The Beneficent One' and to You it is fitting to give thanks.*

(Cong. and *Kohanim*— *Amen.*)

יְהִי רָצוֹן *May it be Your will,* HASHEM, *our God and the God of our fathers, that this blessing which You have commanded us to bestow upon Your nation Israel be a full blessing, that there be in it neither stumbling block nor sin from now and forever.*

The *chazzan* recites the following in an undertone but says the word *'Kohanim'* aloud as a formal summons to the *Kohanim** to bless the people. In some communities the congregation, but not the *Kohanim,* responds, *'Your holy people — as it is said,'* aloud.

אֱלֹהֵינוּ *Our God and the God of our forefathers, bless us with the three-verse* blessing* in the Torah that was written by the hand of Moses, Your servant, that was said by Aaron and his sons, the*

Kohanim,

Your holy people — as it is said:*

Facing the Ark, the *Kohanim* raise their hands and begin to recite the following blessing aloud and in unison. Upon reaching וְצִוָּנוּ, they turn to face the congregation and complete the blessing. The congregation, but not the *chazzan,* responds *Amen.*

בָּרוּךְ *Blessed are You* HASHEM, *our God, King of the universe, Who has sanctified us with the holiness of Aaron,* and has commanded us to bless His people Israel with love.** (Cong.— *Amen.*)

בִּרְכַּת כֹּהֲנִים / THE PRIESTLY BLESSING

The Midrash (*Bamidbar Rabbah* 11:2) teaches that until the time of the Patriarchs, God Himself retained the power to bless people. With the advent of the Patriarchs, He gave this awesome power to them. After they died, God declared that henceforth the *Kohanim* would bless the Jewish people. Thus, the upraised hands of the *Kohanim* are the vehicle through which God's blessing flows upon His chosen people.

The laws and commentary presented here are abridged from ArtScroll's volume, *Bircas Kohanim/The Priestly Blessings,* by Rabbi Avie Gold, which contains a full treatment of all aspects of *Bircas Kohanim.*

אֱלֹהֵינוּ ... בָּרְכֵנוּ בַבְּרָכָה — *Our God ... bless us with the ... blessing.* We ask God, not the *Kohanim* to bless us, because, although the *Kohanim* pronounce the words, they are merely conduits through which the blessing descends from God to the nation below (*Chullin* 49a). This is made clear in the Scriptural commandment, which ends with God's pledge וַאֲנִי אֲבָרְכֵם, *and I will bless them* (*Numbers* 2:27).

הַמְשֻׁלֶּשֶׁת — *Three-verse.* The Priestly Blessing contains three verses, and it is found בַּתּוֹרָה ... הַכְּתוּבָה, *in the Torah that was written by the hand of Moses.*

עַם קְדוֹשֶׁךָ — *Your holy people.* The *Kohanim* are described as a holy people (*I Chronicles* 23:13) because they were designated to serve God and bless Israel.

בָּרוּךְ ... בִּקְדֻשָּׁתוֹ שֶׁל אַהֲרֹן — *Blessed ... with the holiness of Aaron.* Just as the selection of Israel as the Holy Nation is not dependent solely upon the deeds of each individual member, but on the holiness of their forebears — indeed, it is the very sanctity of the Patriarchs which imbued their descendants with a capacity for holiness — so is the sanctity of the *Kehunah* [priesthood] unique among the descendants of Aaron.

בְּאַהֲבָה — *With love.* The *Kohanim* are to feel love for the congregation when they pronounce the blessings. The addition of the phrase *with love* is based upon *Zohar* (*Naso* 147b): Any *Kohen* who does not have love for the congregation or for whom the congregation has no love, may not raise his hands to bless the congregation ...

On his first day as *Kohen Gadol,* when he completed the service, *Aaron raised his hands toward the nation and blessed them* (*Leviticus* 9:22), but we are not told what he said (*Ramban*).

See commentary regarding the related verses* in small print that appears beside the words of the *Kohanim's* blessing.

יְבָרֶכְךָ יְבָרֶכְךָ יהוה מִצִּיּוֹן, עֹשֵׂה שָׁמַיִם וָאָרֶץ.[1]

יהוה* יהוה אֲדֹנֵינוּ, מָה אַדִּיר שִׁמְךָ בְּכָל הָאָרֶץ.[2]

וְיִשְׁמְרֶךָ.* שָׁמְרֵנִי, אֵל, כִּי חָסִיתִי בָךְ.[3]

The *Kohanim* sing an extended chant before saying וְיִשְׁמְרֶךָ, and the congregation recites the following supplication in an undertone. (On the Sabbath this supplication is omitted.) When the *Kohanim* conclude וְיִשְׁמְרֶךָ, the congregation and *chazzan* respond אָמֵן.

רִבּוֹנוֹ שֶׁל עוֹלָם,* אֲנִי שֶׁלָּךְ וַחֲלוֹמוֹתַי שֶׁלָּךְ. חֲלוֹם חָלַמְתִּי וְאֵינִי יוֹדֵעַ מַה הוּא.* יְהִי רָצוֹן מִלְּפָנֶיךָ, יהוה אֱלֹהַי וֵאלֹהֵי אֲבוֹתַי, שֶׁיִּהְיוּ כָּל חֲלוֹמוֹתַי עָלַי וְעַל כָּל יִשְׂרָאֵל לְטוֹבָה — בֵּין שֶׁחָלַמְתִּי עַל עַצְמִי, וּבֵין שֶׁחָלַמְתִּי עַל אֲחֵרִים, וּבֵין שֶׁחָלְמוּ אֲחֵרִים עָלָי. אִם טוֹבִים הֵם, חַזְּקֵם וְאַמְּצֵם, וְיִתְקַיְּמוּ בִי וּבָהֶם כַּחֲלוֹמוֹתָיו שֶׁל יוֹסֵף הַצַּדִּיק. וְאִם צְרִיכִים רְפוּאָה, רְפָאֵם כְּחִזְקִיָּהוּ מֶלֶךְ יְהוּדָה מֵחָלְיוֹ, וּכְמִרְיָם הַנְּבִיאָה מִצָּרַעְתָּהּ, וּכְנַעֲמָן מִצָּרַעְתּוֹ, וּכְמֵי מָרָה עַל יְדֵי מֹשֶׁה רַבֵּנוּ, וּכְמֵי יְרִיחוֹ עַל יְדֵי אֱלִישָׁע. וּכְשֵׁם שֶׁהָפַכְתָּ אֶת קִלְלַת בִּלְעָם הָרָשָׁע מִקְּלָלָה לִבְרָכָה, כֵּן תַּהֲפוֹךְ כָּל חֲלוֹמוֹתַי עָלַי וְעַל כָּל יִשְׂרָאֵל לְטוֹבָה, וְתִשְׁמְרֵנִי וּתְחָנֵּנִי וְתִרְצֵנִי. אָמֵן.

יָאֵר אֱלֹהִים יְחָנֵּנוּ וִיבָרְכֵנוּ, יָאֵר פָּנָיו אִתָּנוּ, סֶלָה.[4]

יהוה יהוה יהוה, אֵל רַחוּם וְחַנּוּן, אֶרֶךְ אַפַּיִם וְרַב חֶסֶד וֶאֱמֶת.[5]

פָּנָיו פְּנֵה אֵלַי וְחָנֵּנִי, כִּי יָחִיד וְעָנִי אָנִי.[6]

אֵלֶיךָ* אֵלֶיךָ יהוה נַפְשִׁי אֶשָּׂא.[7]

This teaches that a person must rejoice in his fellow Jew's good fortune until his heart becomes filled with love, joy and blessing — a blessing so great that mere words cannot express it. His blessing must be so overflowing with love that the very movements of his hands must express his joy and love.

Raising the hands is a symbol of a heart pouring forth blessing and joy from a treasure trove of happiness. Raising the hands is not a sterile act — it must be a wholehearted expression of the hope and blessing which are hidden in the soul. An ocean of inexpressible joy issues from a pure soul; and the purer the soul, the purer the blessing *(Ohr Chadash).*

☙ **יְבָרֶכְךָ ה׳** — *May HASHEM bless you,* with increasing wealth *(Rashi)* and long lives *(Ibn Ezra).*

וְיִשְׁמְרֶךָ — *And safeguard you.* May the above blessings be preserved against loss or attack. Only God can guarantee that no one or nothing can tamper with the gifts He confers upon His loved ones *(Midrash Rabbah).*

☙ **Related verses** appear alongside the fifteen words of *Bircas Kohanim* in most *Siddurim.* The function of these verses and the propriety of reciting them presents a difficulty already dealt with in the Talmud *(Sotah* 39b,40a). Most authorities agree that no verses should be recited at all. Some permit the verses to be read in an undertone while the *chazzan* calls out the words of the blessing. In any case, the practice of the masses who read these verses aloud — and especially of those who repeat the words of *Bircas Kohanim* after the *chazzan* — is wrong and has no halachic basis *(Mishnah Berurah* 128:103).

See commentary regarding the related verses* in small print that appears beside the words of the *Kohanim's* blessing.

May [He] bless you	*May* HASHEM *bless you from Zion, Maker of heaven and earth.*[1]
— HASHEM* —	HASHEM, *our Master, how mighty is Your Name throughout the earth!*[2]
and safeguard you.*	*Safeguard me, O God, for in You have I taken refuge.*[3]

The *Kohanim* sing an extended chant and the congregation recites the following supplication in an undertone. (On the Sabbath this supplication is omitted.) When the *Kohanim* conclude וְיִשְׁמְרֶךָ, *'and safeguard you,'* the congregation and *chazzan* respond *Amen.*

רִבּוֹנוֹ שֶׁל עוֹלָם *Master of the world,* I am Yours and my dreams are Yours. I have dreamed a dream but I do not know what it indicates.* May it be Your will,* HASHEM, *my God and the God of my fathers, that all my dreams regarding myself and regarding all of Israel be good ones — those I have dreamed about myself, those I have dreamed about others, and those that others dreamed about me. If they are good, strengthen them, fortify them, make them endure in me and in them like the dreams of the righteous Joseph. But if they require healing, heal them like Hezekiah, King of Judah, from his sickness; like Miriam the prophetess from her tzaraas; like Naaman from his tzaraas; like the waters of Marah through the hand of Moses our teacher; and like the waters of Jericho through the hand of Elisha. And just as You transformed the curse of the wicked Balaam from a curse to a blessing, so may You transform all of my dreams regarding myself and regarding all of Israel for goodness. May You protect me, may You be gracious to me, may You accept me. Amen.*

May [He] illuminate	*May God favor us and bless us, may He illuminate His countenance with us, Selah.*[4]
— HASHEM —	HASHEM, HASHEM, *God, Compassionate and Gracious, Slow to anger, and Abundant in Kindness and Truth.*[5]
His countenance	*Turn Your face to me and be gracious to me, for alone and afflicted am I.*[6]
for you*	*To You,* HASHEM, *I raise my soul.*[7]

(1) *Psalms* 134:3. (2) 8:10. (3) 16:1. (4) 67:2. (5) *Exodus* 34:6. (6) *Psalms* 25:16. (7) 25:1.

רבונו של עולם — *Master of the world.* Between the verses of *Bircas Kohanim* it is customary to recite a supplication regarding dreams. The currently prevalent version of this supplication is virtually unchanged from the text appearing in the Talmud. There it appears with the following introduction:

If one had a dream but is uncertain whether the dream forebode good or evil let him stand before the *Kohanim* at the time they spread their hands in blessing, and let him say, *Master of the world! I am Yours and my dreams are Yours ... (Berachos* 55b).

חֲלוֹם חָלַמְתִּי וְאֵינִי יוֹדֵעַ מַה הוּא — *I have dreamed a dream but I do not know what it indicates.* During sleep the soul divests itself of the corporeal garb which inhibits its free movement during the day. Thus, in his dreams, one is able to soar above his body and attain the higher spiritual forces of eternal life, yet upon awakening he will be unaware of the implications of what he has attained *(Maggid Meisharim).*

יָאֵר ה' פָּנָיו אֵלֶיךָ — *May* HASHEM *illuminate His countenance for you.* This is the blessing of spiritual growth, the light of Torah, which is symbolized by God's 'countenance' *(Sifre).*

וִיחֻנֶּֽךָּ.* הִנֵּה כְעֵינֵי עֲבָדִים אֶל יַד אֲדוֹנֵיהֶם, כְּעֵינֵי שִׁפְחָה אֶל יַד גְּבִרְתָּהּ, כֵּן עֵינֵינוּ אֶל יהוה אֱלֹהֵינוּ עַד שֶׁיְּחָנֵּנוּ.[1]

The *Kohanim* sing an extended chant and the congregation recites the following supplication in an undertone. (On the Sabbath this supplication is omitted.) When the *Kohanim* conclude וִיחֻנֶּֽךָּ, the congregation and *chazzan* respond אָמֵן.

רִבּוֹנוֹ שֶׁל עוֹלָם, אֲנִי שֶׁלָּךְ וַחֲלוֹמוֹתַי שֶׁלָּךְ. חֲלוֹם חָלַמְתִּי וְאֵינִי יוֹדֵעַ מַה הוּא. יְהִי רָצוֹן מִלְּפָנֶיךָ, יהוה אֱלֹהַי וֵאלֹהֵי אֲבוֹתַי, שֶׁיִּהְיוּ כָּל חֲלוֹמוֹתַי עָלַי וְעַל כָּל יִשְׂרָאֵל לְטוֹבָה — בֵּין שֶׁחָלַמְתִּי עַל עַצְמִי, וּבֵין שֶׁחָלַמְתִּי עַל אֲחֵרִים, וּבֵין שֶׁחָלְמוּ אֲחֵרִים עָלָי. אִם טוֹבִים הֵם, חַזְּקֵם וְאַמְּצֵם, וְיִתְקַיְּמוּ בִי וּבָהֶם כַּחֲלוֹמוֹתָיו שֶׁל יוֹסֵף הַצַּדִּיק. וְאִם צְרִיכִים רְפוּאָה, רְפָאֵם כְּחִזְקִיָּהוּ מֶלֶךְ יְהוּדָה מֵחָלְיוֹ, וּכְמִרְיָם הַנְּבִיאָה מִצָּרַעְתָּהּ, וּכְנַעֲמָן מִצָּרַעְתּוֹ, וּכְמֵי מָרָה עַל יְדֵי מֹשֶׁה רַבֵּנוּ, וּכְמֵי יְרִיחוֹ עַל יְדֵי אֱלִישָׁע. וּכְשֵׁם שֶׁהָפַכְתָּ אֶת קִלְלַת בִּלְעָם הָרָשָׁע מִקְּלָלָה לִבְרָכָה, כֵּן תַּהֲפוֹךְ כָּל חֲלוֹמוֹתַי עָלַי וְעַל כָּל יִשְׂרָאֵל לְטוֹבָה, וְתִשְׁמְרֵנִי וּתְחָנֵּנִי וְתִרְצֵנִי. אָמֵן.

יִשָּׂא יִשָּׂא בְרָכָה מֵאֵת יהוה, וּצְדָקָה מֵאֱלֹהֵי יִשְׁעוֹ.[2] וּמְצָא חֵן וְשֵׂכֶל טוֹב בְּעֵינֵי אֱלֹהִים וְאָדָם.[3]

יהוה יהוה, חָנֵּנוּ, לְךָ קִוִּינוּ, הֱיֵה זְרֹעָם לַבְּקָרִים, אַף יְשׁוּעָתֵנוּ בְּעֵת צָרָה.[4]

פָּנָיו אַל תַּסְתֵּר פָּנֶיךָ מִמֶּנִּי בְּיוֹם צַר לִי, הַטֵּה אֵלַי אָזְנֶךָ, בְּיוֹם אֶקְרָא מַהֵר עֲנֵנִי.[5]

אֵלֶיךָ* אֵלֶיךָ נָשָׂאתִי אֶת עֵינַי, הַיֹּשְׁבִי בַּשָּׁמָיִם.[6]

וְיָשֵׂם וְשָׂמוּ אֶת שְׁמִי עַל בְּנֵי יִשְׂרָאֵל, וַאֲנִי אֲבָרְכֵם.[7]

לְךָ לְךָ יהוה, הַגְּדֻלָּה וְהַגְּבוּרָה וְהַתִּפְאֶרֶת וְהַנֵּצַח וְהַהוֹד, כִּי כֹל בַּשָּׁמַיִם וּבָאָרֶץ, לְךָ יהוה, הַמַּמְלָכָה וְהַמִּתְנַשֵּׂא לְכֹל לְרֹאשׁ.[8]

שָׁלוֹם.* שָׁלוֹם שָׁלוֹם לָרָחוֹק וְלַקָּרוֹב, אָמַר יהוה, וּרְפָאתִיו.[9]

The *Kohanim* sing an extended chant before saying שָׁלוֹם, and the congregation recites the following supplication in an undertone. [The twenty-two letter Divine Name appears here in brackets and bold type. This Name should be scanned with the eyes but not spoken.] (On the Sabbath this supplication is omitted.) When the *Kohanim* conclude שָׁלוֹם, the congregation and *chazzan* respond אָמֵן.

יְהִי רָצוֹן מִלְּפָנֶיךָ, יהוה אֱלֹהַי וֵאלֹהֵי אֲבוֹתַי, שֶׁתַּעֲשֶׂה לְמַעַן קְדֻשַּׁת חֲסָדֶיךָ וְגֹדֶל רַחֲמֶיךָ הַפְּשׁוּטִים, וּלְמַעַן טָהֳרַת שִׁמְךָ הַגָּדוֹל הַגִּבּוֹר וְהַנּוֹרָא, בֶּן עֶשְׂרִים וּשְׁתַּיִם אוֹתִיּוֹת הַיּוֹצְאִים מִן הַפְּסוּקִים שֶׁל בִּרְכַּת כֹּהֲנִים **[אנקת״ם פסת״ם פספסי״ם דיונסי״ם]** הָאֲמוּרָה מִפִּי אַהֲרֹן

וִיחֻנֶּֽךָּ — *And be gracious to you.* May you find favor in God's eyes *(Ramban);* or, may you find favor in the eyes of others, for all a person's talents and qualities will avail him little if others dislike him *(Ohr HaChaim).*

יִשָּׂא ה׳ פָּנָיו אֵלֶיךָ — *May [He] HASHEM turn His countenance to you.* May He suppress His anger against you, even if you are sinful and deserve to be punished *(Rashi).* One's face is indicative of his attitude toward someone else. If he is angry, he will turn away from the one he dislikes. God 'turns His face' *toward* Israel to show that He loves them *(Maharzu).*

וְיָשֵׂם לְךָ שָׁלוֹם — *And establish for you peace.* Peace is the seal of all blessings, because without peace — prosperity, health, food, and drink are

and be gracious to you.* *Behold! Like the eyes of servants unto their master's hand, like the eyes of a maid unto her mistress's hand, so are our eyes unto HASHEM, our God, until He will favor us.*[1]

The *Kohanim* sing an extended chant and the congregation recites the following supplication in an undertone. (On the Sabbath this supplication is omitted.) When the *Kohanim* conclude וִיחֻנֶּךָ, *'and be gracious to you,'* the congregation and *chazzan* respond *Amen.*

רִבּוֹנוֹ שֶׁל עוֹלָם *Master of the world, I am Yours and my dreams are Yours. I have dreamed a dream but I do not know what it indicates. May it be Your will, HASHEM, my God and the God of my fathers, that all my dreams regarding myself and regarding all of Israel be good ones — those I have dreamed about myself, those I have dreamed about others, and those that others dreamed about me. If they are good, strengthen them, fortify them, make them endure in me and in them like the dreams of the righteous Joseph. But if they require healing, heal them like Hezekiah, King of Judah, from his sickness; like Miriam the prophetess from her tzaraas; like Naaman from his tzaraas; like the waters of Marah through the hand of Moses our teacher; and like the waters of Jericho through the hand of Elisha. And just as You transformed the curse of the wicked Balaam from a curse to a blessing, so may You transform all of my dreams regarding myself and regarding all of Israel for goodness. May You protect me, may You be gracious to me, may You accept me. Amen.*

May [He] turn *May he receive a blessing from HASHEM, and just kindness from the God of his salvation.*[2] *And he will find favor and good understanding in the eyes of God and man.*[3]

— HASHEM — *HASHEM, find favor with us, for You have we hoped! Be their power in the mornings, and our salvation in times of distress.*[4]

His countenance *Do not hide Your countenance from me in a day that is distressing to me; lean Your ear toward me; in the day that I call, speedily answer me.*[5]

to you* *To You I raised my eyes, O You Who dwell in the Heavens.*[6]

and establish *And they shall place My Name upon the Children of Israel, and I shall bless them.*[7]

for you *Yours, HASHEM, is the greatness, the strength, the splendor, the triumph, and the glory, even all that is in heaven and earth; Yours, HASHEM, is the kingdom and the sovereignty over every leader.*[8]

peace.* *'Peace, peace, for far and near,' says HASHEM, 'and I shall heal him.'*[9]

The *Kohanim* sing an extended chant and the congregation recites the following supplication in an undertone. [The twenty-two letter Divine Name appears here in brackets and bold type. This Name should be scanned with the eyes but not spoken.] (On the Sabbath this supplication is omitted.) When the *Kohanim* conclude שָׁלוֹם, *'peace,'* the congregation and *chazzan* respond *Amen.*

יְהִי רָצוֹן *May it be Your will, HASHEM, my God and the God of my forefathers, that You act for the sake of the holiness of Your kindness and the greatness of Your mercies which reach out, and for the sake of the sanctity of Your Name — the great, the mighty and the awesome; composed of twenty-two letters which derive from the verses of Bircas Kohanim* **[אנקת״ם פסת״ם פספסי״ם דיונסי״ם]**; *spoken by Aaron*

(1) *Psalms* 123:2. (2) 24:5. (3) *Proverbs* 3:4. (4) *Isaiah* 33:2. (5) *Psalms* 102:3.
(6) 123:1. (7) *Numbers* 6:27. (8) *I Chronicles* 29:11. (9) *Isaiah* 57:19.

וּבָנָיו עַם קְדוֹשֶׁךָ, שֶׁתִּהְיֶה קָרוֹב לִי בְּקָרְאִי לָךְ, וְתִשְׁמַע תְּפִלָּתִי נַאֲקָתִי וְאֶנְקָתִי תָּמִיד, כְּשֵׁם שֶׁשָּׁמַעְתָּ **אֶנְקַת** יַעֲקֹב תְּמִימֶךָ הַנִּקְרָא אִישׁ **תָּם**. וְתִתֶּן לִי וּלְכָל נַפְשׁוֹת בֵּיתִי מְזוֹנוֹתֵינוּ וּפַרְנָסָתֵנוּ — בְּרֶוַח וְלֹא בְצִמְצוּם, בְּהֶתֵּר וְלֹא בְאִסּוּר, בְּנַחַת וְלֹא בְצַעַר, — מִתַּחַת יָדְךָ הָרְחָבָה, כְּשֵׁם שֶׁנָּתַתָּ **פִּסַּת** לֶחֶם לֶאֱכוֹל וּבֶגֶד לִלְבּוֹשׁ לְיַעֲקֹב אָבִינוּ הַנִּקְרָא אִישׁ **תָּם**. וְתִתְּנֵנוּ לְאַהֲבָה, לְחֵן וּלְחֶסֶד וּלְרַחֲמִים בְּעֵינֶיךָ וּבְעֵינֵי כָל רוֹאֵינוּ, וְיִהְיוּ דְבָרַי נִשְׁמָעִים לַעֲבוֹדָתֶךָ, כְּשֵׁם שֶׁנָּתַתָּ אֶת יוֹסֵף צַדִּיקֶךָ — בְּשָׁעָה שֶׁהִלְבִּישׁוֹ אָבִיו כְּתֹנֶת **פַּסִּים** — לְחֵן וּלְחֶסֶד וּלְרַחֲמִים בְּעֵינֶיךָ וּבְעֵינֵי כָל רוֹאָיו. וְתַעֲשֶׂה עִמִּי נִפְלָאוֹת **וְנִסִּים**,* וּלְטוֹבָה אוֹת, וְתַצְלִיחֵנִי בִּדְרָכַי, וְתֵן בְּלִבִּי בִּינָה לְהָבִין וּלְהַשְׂכִּיל וּלְקַיֵּם אֶת כָּל דִּבְרֵי תַלְמוּד תּוֹרָתֶךָ וְסוֹדוֹתֶיהָ, וְתַצִּילֵנִי מִשְּׁגִיאוֹת, וּתְטַהֵר רַעְיוֹנַי וְלִבִּי לַעֲבוֹדָתֶךָ וּלְיִרְאָתֶךָ. וְתַאֲרִיךְ יָמַי (insert the appropriate words— וִימֵי אָבִי וְאִמִּי וְאִשְׁתִּי וּבָנַי וּבְנוֹתַי) בְּטוֹב וּבִנְעִימוֹת, בְּרֹב עֹז וְשָׁלוֹם, אָמֵן סֶלָה.

The *chazzan* immediately begins שִׂים שָׁלוֹם; the *Kohanim* turn back to the Ark, lower their hands and recite their concluding prayer רִבּוֹנוֹ שֶׁל עוֹלָם; and the congregation recites אַדִּיר בַּמָּרוֹם. All should conclude their respective prayers simultaneously with the *chazzan's* conclusion of שִׂים שָׁלוֹם.

Kohanim:

רִבּוֹנוֹ שֶׁל עוֹלָם, עָשִׂינוּ מַה שֶּׁגָּזַרְתָּ עָלֵינוּ, אַף אַתָּה עֲשֵׂה עִמָּנוּ כְּמָה שֶׁהִבְטַחְתָּנוּ: הַשְׁקִיפָה מִמְּעוֹן קָדְשְׁךָ, מִן הַשָּׁמַיִם, וּבָרֵךְ אֶת עַמְּךָ אֶת יִשְׂרָאֵל, וְאֵת הָאֲדָמָה אֲשֶׁר נָתַתָּה לָנוּ — כַּאֲשֶׁר נִשְׁבַּעְתָּ לַאֲבוֹתֵינוּ — אֶרֶץ זָבַת חָלָב וּדְבָשׁ.[1]

Congregation:

אַדִּיר בַּמָּרוֹם, שׁוֹכֵן בִּגְבוּרָה, אַתָּה שָׁלוֹם וְשִׁמְךָ שָׁלוֹם. יְהִי רָצוֹן שֶׁתָּשִׂים עָלֵינוּ וְעַל כָּל עַמְּךָ בֵּית יִשְׂרָאֵל חַיִּים וּבְרָכָה לְמִשְׁמֶרֶת שָׁלוֹם.

Chazzan:

שִׂים שָׁלוֹם, טוֹבָה, וּבְרָכָה, חֵן, וָחֶסֶד וְרַחֲמִים עָלֵינוּ וְעַל כָּל יִשְׂרָאֵל עַמֶּךָ. בָּרְכֵנוּ אָבִינוּ, כֻּלָּנוּ כְּאֶחָד בְּאוֹר פָּנֶיךָ, כִּי בְאוֹר פָּנֶיךָ נָתַתָּ לָּנוּ, יהוה אֱלֹהֵינוּ, תּוֹרַת חַיִּים וְאַהֲבַת חֶסֶד, וּצְדָקָה, וּבְרָכָה, וְרַחֲמִים, וְחַיִּים, וְשָׁלוֹם. וְטוֹב בְּעֵינֶיךָ לְבָרֵךְ אֶת עַמְּךָ יִשְׂרָאֵל, בְּכָל עֵת וּבְכָל שָׁעָה בִּשְׁלוֹמֶךָ. בָּרוּךְ אַתָּה יהוה, הַמְּבָרֵךְ אֶת עַמּוֹ יִשְׂרָאֵל בַּשָּׁלוֹם.

(Cong. and *Kohanim*— אָמֵן.)

יִהְיוּ לְרָצוֹן אִמְרֵי פִי וְהֶגְיוֹן לִבִּי לְפָנֶיךָ, יהוה צוּרִי וְגֹאֲלִי.[2]

During Succos, the *Hoshana* prayers (p. 726) are recited at this point.
On other Festivals *chazzan* recites Full *Kaddish* (p. 474), and the service continues there.

---

worthless *(Sifre).*

וְתַעֲשֶׂה עִמִּי נִפְלָאוֹת וְנִסִּים — *May You perform wonders and miracles with me.* It is unseemly for an individual to request miraculous intervention in his personal affairs, for what assurance does he have that he is deserving?

There are two classifications of miracle — overt [e.g., the splitting of the Sea of Reeds; Joshua's stopping the sun] and covert [e.g., the seeming historic simplicity of the Purim story]. It

and his sons, Your holy people — that You be near to me when I call to You; that You listen to my prayer, my plea and my cry at all times, just as You listened to the cry [אֶנְקַת] *of Jacob, Your perfect one, who is called 'a wholesome man'* [תָּם]. *And may You bestow upon me and upon all the souls of my household, our food and our sustenance — generously and not sparsely, honestly and not in forbidden fashion, pleasurably and not in pain — from beneath Your generous hand, just as You gave a portion* [פִּסַּת] *of bread to eat and clothing to wear to our father Jacob who is called 'a wholesome man'* [תָּם]. *And may You grant that we find love, favor, kindness and mercy in Your eyes and in the eyes of all who behold us; and that my words in Your service be heard; just as You granted Joseph, Your righteous one — at the time that his father garbed him in a fine woolen tunic* [פַּסִּים] *— that he find favor, kindness and mercy in Your eyes and in the eyes of all who beheld him. May You perform wonders and miracles* [וְנִסִּים] *with me,* and a goodly sign; grant me success in my ways; place in my heart the power of understanding, to understand, to be wise, to fulfill all the words of Your Torah's teaching and its mysteries; save me from errors; and purify my thinking and my heart for Your service and Your awe. May You prolong my days* [insert the appropriate words— *and the days of my father, my mother, my wife, my son(s), my daughter(s)*] *with goodness, with sweetness, with an abundance of strength and peace. Amen: Selah.*

The *chazzan* immediately begins שִׂים שָׁלוֹם, *Establish peace;* the *Kohanim* turn back to the Ark, lower their hands and recite their concluding prayer רִבּוֹנוֹ שֶׁל עוֹלָם, *Master of the World;* and the congregation recites אַדִּיר, *Mighty One.* All should conclude their respective prayers simultaneously with the *chazzan's* conclusion of שִׂים שָׁלוֹם.

Kohanim:

רִבּוֹנוֹ שֶׁל עוֹלָם *Master of the world, we have done what You have decreed upon us, now may You also do as You have promised us: Look down from Your sacred dwelling, from the heavens, and bless Your people, Israel, and the earth which You have given us — just as You have sworn to our fathers — a land that flows with milk and honey.*[1]

Congregation:

אַדִּיר *Mighty One on high, He Who dwells in power! You are Peace and Your Name is Peace! May it be acceptable that You grant us and all of Your people, the house of Israel, life and blessing for a safeguard of peace.*

Chazzan:

שִׂים שָׁלוֹם *Establish peace, goodness, blessing, graciousness, kindness, and compassion upon us and upon all of Your people Israel. Bless us, our Father, all of us as one, with the light of Your countenance, for with the light of Your countenance You gave us,* HASHEM, *our God, the Torah of life and a love of kindness, righteousness, blessing, compassion, life, and peace. And may it be good in Your eyes to bless Your people Israel, in every season and in every hour with Your Peace. Blessed are You,* HASHEM, *Who blesses His people Israel with peace.* (Cong. and *Kohanim*— *Amen.*)

May the expressions of my mouth and the thoughts of my heart find favor before You, HASHEM, *my Rock and my Redeemer.*[2]

During Succos, the *Hoshana* prayers (p. 726) are recited at this point. On other Festivals *chazzan* recites Full *Kaddish* (p. 474), and the service continues there.

(1) *Deuteronomy* 26:15. (2) *Psalms* 19:15.

is wrong for an individual to request *obvious* miracles, but he may pray for covert miracles, because they are disguised as natural phenomena *(Bechor Shor).*

✤ תפלת טל ✤

This prayer for dew is recited by the *chazzan* on the first day of Pesach during his repetition of *Mussaf*. The Ark is opened and the congregation stands until the conclusion of the prayer.

כִּי שֵׁם יהוה אֶקְרָא, הָבוּ גֹדֶל לֵאלֹהֵינוּ.[1]
אֲדֹנָי שְׂפָתַי תִּפְתָּח, וּפִי יַגִּיד תְּהִלָּתֶךָ.[2]

Bend the knees at בָּרוּךְ; bow at אַתָּה; straighten up at 'ה.

בָּרוּךְ אַתָּה יהוה אֱלֹהֵינוּ וֵאלֹהֵי אֲבוֹתֵינוּ, אֱלֹהֵי אַבְרָהָם, אֱלֹהֵי יִצְחָק, וֵאלֹהֵי יַעֲקֹב, הָאֵל הַגָּדוֹל הַגִּבּוֹר וְהַנּוֹרָא, אֵל עֶלְיוֹן, גּוֹמֵל חֲסָדִים טוֹבִים וְקוֹנֵה הַכֹּל, וְזוֹכֵר חַסְדֵי אָבוֹת, וּמֵבִיא גוֹאֵל לִבְנֵי בְנֵיהֶם, לְמַעַן שְׁמוֹ בְּאַהֲבָה. מֶלֶךְ עוֹזֵר וּמוֹשִׁיעַ וּמָגֵן.

בְּדַעְתּוֹ אַבִּיעָה חִידוֹת,* בְּעַם זוּ בְּזוּ* בְּטַל לְהַחֲדוֹת.
טַל גֵּיא וּדְשָׁאֶיהָ לַחֲדוֹת, דָּצִים בְּצִלּוֹ לְהֵחָדוֹת.
אוֹת יַלְדוּת* טַל לְהָגֵן לְתוֹלָדוֹת.

Bend the knees at בָּרוּךְ; bow at אַתָּה; straighten up at 'ה.

בָּרוּךְ אַתָּה יהוה, מָגֵן אַבְרָהָם.

אַתָּה גִּבּוֹר לְעוֹלָם אֲדֹנָי, מְחַיֵּה מֵתִים אַתָּה, רַב לְהוֹשִׁיעַ.

תְּהוֹמוֹת הֲדוֹם* לִרְסִיסוֹ כְּסוּפִים, וְכָל נְאוֹת דֶּשֶׁא לוֹ נִכְסָפִים.
טַל זִכְרוֹ גְּבוּרוֹת מוֹסִיפִים,* חָקוּק בְּגִישַׁת מוּסָפִים,
טַל לְהַחֲיוֹת בּוֹ* נְקוּקֵי סְעִיפִים.

אֱלֹהֵינוּ וֵאלֹהֵי אֲבוֹתֵינוּ,

טַל תֵּן לִרְצוֹת אַרְצָךְ, שִׁיתֵנוּ בְרָכָה בְּדִיצָךְ,
רֹב דָּגָן וְתִירוֹשׁ בְּהַפְרִיצָךְ, קוֹמֵם עִיר בָּהּ חֶפְצָךְ,* בְּטָל.

✤ THE PRAYER FOR DEW / תְּפִלַּת טַל ✤

When Isaac bestowed the Patriarchal blessing upon his son Jacob (*Genesis* ch. 27), he declared that Pesach, the time of redemption and of praise for God, is the time when the Heavenly chambers of dew and blessing are open (*Pirkei deR'Eliezer*, ch. 32). Thus, the first day of Pesach is an auspicious time to pray for dew (*Mateh Moshe*, 662). Moreover, the prayer and the season suggest the principle that Creation was designed to accommodate the dictates of the Torah: Spring, the season of gentle dew and the rejuvenation of nature, is also the time when the Jewish nation was redeemed and began to blossom.

✤ **בְּדַעְתּוֹ אַבִּיעָה חִידוֹת** — *With His consent I shall speak of mysteries.* The references to dew throughout this prayer have two meanings: (a) The moisture that makes plant growth possible; and (b) what the Sages call טַל שֶׁל תְּחִיָּה, *the dew of life*, i.e., the invigorating spiritual property that gives life to people and that can even resuscitate the dead (*Chagigah* 12b). Thus, the references to dew contain both simple meanings and deep mysteries.

בְּעַם זוּ בְּזוּ — *Among this people, through this* [*prayer*], i.e., may the Jewish people merit the blessing of dew, for which we now pray in this *Mussaf* prayer.

אוֹת יַלְדוּת — *A symbol of youth*[*ful promise*]. The

⁂ PRAYER FOR DEW ⁂

This prayer for dew is recited by the *chazzan* on the first day of Pesach during his repetition of *Mussaf*. The Ark is opened and the congregation stands until the conclusion of the prayer.

When I call out the Name of HASHEM, *ascribe greatness to our God.*[1]
My Lord, open my lips, that my mouth may declare Your praise.[2]

Bend the knees at *'Blessed'*; bow at *'You'*; straighten up at *'HASHEM'*.

בָּרוּךְ *Blessed are You,* HASHEM, *our God and the God of our forefathers, God of Abraham, God of Isaac, and God of Jacob; the great, mighty, and awesome God, the supreme God, Who bestows beneficial kindnesses and creates everything, Who recalls the kindnesses of the Patriarchs and brings a Redeemer to their children's children, for His Name's sake, with love. O King, Helper, Savior, and Shield.*

בְּדַעְתּוֹ *With His consent I shall speak of mysteries.* Among this people, through this prayer,* may they be made exultant by the dew. Dew — bringing joy to valley and its herbage; taking pleasure in His shelter to be made exultant. Dew is a symbol of youthful promise,* may it protect the generations.*

Bend the knees at *'Blessed'*; bow at *'You'*; straighten up at 'HASHEM.'

Blessed are You, HASHEM, *Shield of Abraham.*

אַתָּה *You are eternally mighty, my Lord, the Resuscitator of the dead are You; abundantly able to save.*

תְּהוֹמוֹת *The depths of the footstool* yearn for His droplet, and every lush meadow yearns for it. Dew — its mention enhances His powers,* it is inscribed in the Mussaf prayer. Dew — to resuscitate with it* those buried in the cleft of rocks.*

Our God and the God of our forefathers

טַל *Dew — give it to favor Your land;*
establish us for blessing in Your pleasure;
with abundant grain and wine may You strengthen us;
*establish the City containing Your delight** — *with dew.*

(1) *Deuteronomy* 32:3. (2) *Psalms* 51:17.

Psalmist compares the sweet and gentle righteousness of Abraham's youth with the sweetness and gentleness of dew *(Rashi* to *Psalms* 110:39). The Patriarch's deeds serve to protect the generations of his offspring.

⁂ **תְּהוֹמוֹת הֲדוֹם** — *The depths of the footstool.* The earth is referred to as God's footstool *(Isaiah* 66:1).

זִכְרוֹ גְּבוּרוֹת מוֹסִיפִים — *Its mention enhances* [*His*] *powers.* The אַתָּה גִּבּוֹר verse in *Shemoneh Esrei* is called גְּבוּרוֹת גְּשָׁמִים, *the powers of rain,* because it describes God's mastery over precipitation. In a deeper sense, man's recognition of God's omnipotence increases holiness — hence, God's perceived power — on earth.

לְהַחֲיוֹת בּוֹ — *To resuscitate with it.* As noted above, the dead will be resuscitated with a spiritual force referred to as 'dew.' In ancient *Eretz Yisrael* it was common to bury the dead in openings carved out of solid rock, thus the reference to clefts of rocks.

קוֹמֵם עִיר בָּהּ חֶפְצָךְ — *Establish the city containing Your delight.* No prayer for success and prosperity is complete without a plea for the rebuilding of Jerusalem and, within it, God's delight, i.e., the Temple.

טל צַוֵּה שָׁנָה טוֹבָה וּמְעֻטֶּרֶת, פְּרִי הָאָרֶץ* לְגָאוֹן וּלְתִפְאֶרֶת,
עִיר כַּסֻּכָּה נוֹתֶרֶת,* שִׂימָהּ בְּיָדְךָ עֲטֶרֶת, בְּטָל.

טל נוֹפֵף עָלֵי אֶרֶץ בְּרוּכָה, מִמֶּגֶד שָׁמַיִם שַׂבְּעֵנוּ בְרָכָה,
לְהָאִיר מִתּוֹךְ חֲשֵׁכָה, כַּנָּה* אַחֲרֶיךָ מְשׁוּכָה, בְּטָל.

טל יַעֲסִיס צוּף הָרִים, טְעֵם בִּמְאוֹדֶךָ מֻבְחָרִים,
חֲנוּנֶיךָ חַלֵּץ מִמַּסְגֵּרִים, זִמְרָה נַנְעִים וְקוֹל נָרִים, בְּטָל.

טל וְשׂוֹבַע מַלֵּא אֲסָמֵינוּ, הֲבָעַת תְּחַדֵּשׁ יָמֵינוּ,
דּוֹד כְּעֶרְכְּךָ הַעֲמֵד שְׁמֵנוּ, גַּן רָוֶה שִׂימֵנוּ, בְּטָל.

טל בּוֹ תְבָרֵךְ מָזוֹן, בְּמִשְׁמַנֵּינוּ אַל יְהִי רָזוֹן,
אֲיֻמָּה אֲשֶׁר הִסַּעְתָּ כַּצֹּאן, אָנָּא תָּפֵק לָהּ רָצוֹן, בְּטָל.

שָׁאַתָּה הוּא יהוה אֱלֹהֵינוּ, מַשִּׁיב הָרְוּחַ וּמוֹרִיד הַטָּל.

—Cong. then *chazzan* לִבְרָכָה וְלֹא לִקְלָלָה. (Cong.— אָמֵן.)

—Cong. then *chazzan* לְחַיִּים וְלֹא לְמָוֶת. (Cong.— אָמֵן.)

—Cong. then *chazzan* לְשׂוֹבַע וְלֹא לְרָזוֹן. (Cong.— אָמֵן.)

The Ark is closed, and the *chazzan* continues, מְכַלְכֵּל חַיִּים, p. 674.

❦ תפלת גשם ❦

This prayer for rain is recited by the *chazzan* on Shemini Atzeres during his repetition of *Mussaf*. The Ark is opened and the congregation stands until the conclusion of the prayer.

כִּי שֵׁם יהוה אֶקְרָא, הָבוּ גֹדֶל לֵאלֹהֵינוּ.[1]
אֲדֹנָי שְׂפָתַי תִּפְתָּח,* וּפִי יַגִּיד תְּהִלָּתֶךָ.[2]

Bend the knees at בָּרוּךְ; bow at אַתָּה; straighten up at ה׳.

בָּרוּךְ אַתָּה יהוה אֱלֹהֵינוּ וֵאלֹהֵי אֲבוֹתֵינוּ, אֱלֹהֵי אַבְרָהָם, אֱלֹהֵי יִצְחָק, וֵאלֹהֵי יַעֲקֹב, הָאֵל הַגָּדוֹל הַגִּבּוֹר וְהַנּוֹרָא, אֵל עֶלְיוֹן, גּוֹמֵל חֲסָדִים טוֹבִים וְקוֹנֵה הַכֹּל, וְזוֹכֵר חַסְדֵּי אָבוֹת, וּמֵבִיא גוֹאֵל לִבְנֵי בְנֵיהֶם, לְמַעַן שְׁמוֹ בְּאַהֲבָה. מֶלֶךְ עוֹזֵר וּמוֹשִׁיעַ וּמָגֵן.

פְּרִי הָאָרֶץ — *The fruit of the earth. Isaiah* (4:2) likens the redeemed Jews of the future to the fruit of the earth.

עִיר כַּסֻּכָּה נוֹתֶרֶת — *The City deserted like a booth.* This refers to the booth put up by field hands for shade. Once the harvest is over, it has no utility and is deserted.

כַּנָּה — *The fundamental nation.* Since Israel is the nation charged with the mission of upholding the Torah and carrying out God's plan for creation, it is the 'foundation' of the universe.

❦ תְּפִלַּת גֶּשֶׁם / PRAYER FOR RAIN ❦

Since the fall and winter are the rainy season in *Eretz Yisrael,* and it is a country that depends on rainfall more than most, the Sages ordained that the prayer for rain be recited on Succos, the

טַל *Dew — decree it for a year that is good and crowned;*
may the fruit of the earth be proud and splendrous;*
the City deserted like a booth —*
let Your hand make it a crown — *with dew.*

טַל *Dew — let it drop sweetly on the blessed land,*
with the delicacies of heaven sate us with blessing,
to enlighten from amid the darkness
the fundamental nation that is drawn after You* — *with dew.*

טַל *Dew — let it sweeten the honey of the mountains,*
let the chosen people savor Your plenty.
Free Your favored ones from bondage;
sweetly we will sing and raise our voice! — *with dew.*

טַל *Dew and plenty, may they fill our granaries —*
if only You would now rejuvenate our days!
Beloved One, make our names enduring like Your own,
make us like a well-watered garden — *with dew.*

טַל *Dew — may You bless our sustenance with it,*
in our abundance may there be no scarcity.
This nation that You led like sheep —
please, fulfill her desire — *with dew.*

For You are HASHEM, our God,
Who makes the wind blow and makes the dew descend.

Cong. then *chazzan*— *For blessing and not for curse.* (Cong.— *Amen.*)
Cong. then *chazzan*— *For life and not for death.* (Cong.— *Amen.*)
Cong. then *chazzan*— *For plenty and not for scarcity.* (Cong.— *Amen.*)

The Ark is closed and the *chazzan* continues, *'He sustains the living ...'* p. 674.

PRAYER FOR RAIN

This prayer for rain is recited by the *chazzan* on Shemini Atzeres during his repetition of *Mussaf*. The Ark is opened and the congregation stands until the conclusion of the prayer.

When I call out the Name of HASHEM, ascribe greatness to our God.[1]
My Lord, open my lips, that my mouth may declare Your praise.[2]

Bend the knees at *'Blessed'*; bow at *'You'*; straighten up at *'HASHEM.'*

בָּרוּךְ *Blessed are You, HASHEM, our God and the God of our forefathers, God of Abraham, God of Isaac, and God of Jacob; the great, mighty, and awesome God, the supreme God, Who bestows beneficial kindnesses and creates everything, Who recalls the kindnesses of the Patriarchs and brings a Redeemer to their children's children, for His Name's sake, with love. O King, Helper, Savior, and Shield.*

(1) *Deuteronomy* 32:3. (2) *Psalms* 51:17.

אַף־בְּרִי* אֻתַּת שֵׁם שַׂר מָטָר, לְהַעֲבִיב וּלְהַעֲנִין לְהָרִיק וּלְהַמְטַר,
מַיִם אִבִּים בָּם גֵּיא לַעֲטַר, לְבַל יֻעֲצְרוּ בְּנִשְׁיוֹן שְׁטָר,*
אֱמוּנִים גְּנוֹן בָּם שׁוֹאֲלֵי מָטָר.

Bend the knees at בָּרוּךְ; bow at אַתָּה; straighten up at 'ה.

בָּרוּךְ אַתָּה יהוה, מָגֵן אַבְרָהָם.

אַתָּה גִּבּוֹר לְעוֹלָם אֲדֹנָי, מְחַיֵּה מֵתִים אַתָּה, רַב לְהוֹשִׁיעַ.

יַטְרִיחַ לְפַלֵּג מִפֶּלֶג גֶּשֶׁם,* לְמוֹגֵג פְּנֵי נֶשִׁי בְּצַחוּת לֶשֶׁם,
מַיִם לְאַדֶּרְךָ כִּנִּיתָ בְּרֶשֶׁם,* לְהַרְגִּיעַ בְּרַעְפָּם לְנִפְוּחֵי נֶשֶׁם,
לְהַחֲיוֹת מַזְכִּירִים גְּבוּרוֹת הַגֶּשֶׁם.

אֱלֹהֵינוּ וֵאלֹהֵי אֲבוֹתֵינוּ,

זְכוֹר* אָב* נִמְשַׁךְ אַחֲרֶיךָ כַּמַּיִם, בֵּרַכְתּוֹ כְּעֵץ שָׁתוּל עַל פַּלְגֵי מָיִם,
גְּנַנְתּוֹ, הִצַּלְתּוֹ מֵאֵשׁ וּמִמַּיִם,* דְּרַשְׁתּוֹ בְּזָרְעוֹ עַל כָּל מָיִם.*

Cong.— בַּעֲבוּרוֹ אַל תִּמְנַע מָיִם.

זְכוֹר הַנּוֹלָד בִּבְשׂוֹרַת* יֻקַּח נָא מְעַט מַיִם,
וְשַׂחְתָּ לְהוֹרוֹ לְשָׁחֲטוֹ, לִשְׁפּוֹךְ דָּמוֹ כַּמַּיִם,
זִהֵר גַּם הוּא לִשְׁפּוֹךְ לֵב כַּמַּיִם, חָפַר וּמָצָא בְּאֵרוֹת מָיִם.*

Cong.— בְּצִדְקוֹ חֹן חַשְׁרַת מָיִם.

זְכוֹר טָעַן מַקְלוֹ* וְעָבַר יַרְדֵּן מַיִם, יִחַד לֵב* וְגָל אֶבֶן מִפִּי בְּאֵר מַיִם,

---

pilgrimage festival closest to the rainy season. Because the festival itself is spent primarily in the *succah*, and it is regarded as a symbol of Divine displeasure for rain to prevent people from eating and living there, it would be incongruous to pray for rain at a time when we do not want it to fall. Therefore, the prayer is recited on Shemini Atzeres, after the Scriptural commandment of *succah*-dwelling is over.

אַף־בְּרִי — *Af-Bri,* the name of the angel appointed over the rainclouds *(Rashi* to *Job* 37:11), is formed from the two words אַף, *anger,* and בְּרִי, *health.* This name alludes to the two ways in which rain may fall. Sometimes it comes in harsh torrents and is a sign of Divine anger (אַף); at other times it falls in a beneficial manner and brings health (בְּרִי) and prosperity in its wake *(Mateh Levi).* The responsibilities of this angel are described in the first two stanzas of this prayer.

נִשְׁיוֹן שְׁטָר — *Unredeemed debt* [lit. *document*]. A long list of our sins is recorded in God's ledger.

מִפֶּלֶג גֶּשֶׁם — *Of the segregated rain.* God separated between the heavenly water and the earthly water *(Genesis* 1:6). Here the segregated rain, i.e., the heavenly water, is used as a metaphor for the spiritual flow of blessing from on high.

מַיִם לְאַדֶּרְךָ כִּנִּיתָ בְּרֶשֶׁם — *With water You symbolized Your might in Scripture.* The Prophet *(Ezekiel* 43:2) compares God's voice to *the sound of great waters (Maaseh Oreg).*

זְכוֹר — *Remember.* The next six stanzas respectively speak of Abraham, Isaac, Jacob, Moses, Aaron and the twelve tribes. Each stanza is followed by a prayer that for their sake water not be withheld; instead abundant rain should fall in their righteous merit.

אָב — *The Patriarch.* Abraham was called אַב הֲמוֹן גּוֹיִם, *the father* [or, *Patriarch*] *of a multitude of nations (Genesis* 17:5).

מֵאֵשׁ וּמִמַּיִם — *From fire and from water.* The Talmud *(Pesachim* 118a) and Midrash *(Bereishis Rabbah* 38) relate how Abraham allowed himself to be thrown into a fiery furnace when he

אַף־בְּרִי *Af-Bri* is designated as the name of the angel of rain;*
to thicken and to form clouds, to empty them and to cause rain.
Water with which to crown the valley's vegetation
*— may it not be withheld because of our unredeemed debt.**
In the merit of the faithful Patriarchs protect the ones who pray for rain.

Bend the knees at *'Blessed'*; bow at *'You'*; straighten up at 'HASHEM'.

Blessed are You, HASHEM, Shield of Abraham.

אַתָּה *You are eternally mighty, my Lord, the Resuscitator of the dead are You; abundantly able to save.*

יַטְרִיחַ *May He obligate [the Angel Af-Bri] to give us portions of the segregated rain,* to soften the wasteland's face when it is dry as rock.*
*With water You symbolized Your might in Scripture,**
to soothe with its drops those in whom was blown a soul,
to keep alive the ones who recall the strengths of the rain.

Our God and the God of our forefathers:

זְכוֹר *Remember* the Patriarch [Abraham],**
who was drawn behind You like water.
You blessed him like a tree replanted alongside streams of water.
*You shielded him, You rescued him from fire and from water.**
*You tested him when he sowed upon all waters.**
Cong.— *For his sake, do not hold water back!*

זְכוֹר *Remember the one [Isaac] born with the tidings of,**
'Let some water be brought.'
You told his father to slaughter him — to spill his blood like water.
He too was scrupulous to pour his heart like water.
*He dug and discovered wells of water.**
Cong.— *For the sake of his righteousness, grant abundant water!*

זְכוֹר *Remember the one [Jacob] who carried his staff**
and crossed the Jordan's water.
He dedicated his heart and rolled a stone*
off the mouth of a well of water,

---

refused to bow before Nimrod's idols. Another Midrash *(Tanchuma)* describes how Satan, in the guise of a wide and deep river, attempted to drown Abraham and Isaac on their way to the *Akeidah* (see p. 22) on Mount Moriah *(Maaseh Oreg).*

בְּזָרְעוֹ עַל כָּל מָיִם — *When he sowed upon all waters.* The Talmud *(Bava Kamma* 17a) applies the words of the Prophet — *Praiseworthy are those who sow upon all waters (Isaiah* 32:20) — to those who perform kind and charitable deeds *(Maaseh Oreg).* Abraham is the epitome of kindness and his generosity was based on the rules of the Torah, which is likened to water.

הַנּוֹלָד בְּבְשׂוֹרַת — *The one born with the tidings of ...* The birth of Isaac was prophesied to Abraham after he began his hospitality to the three angels by saying, *'Let some water be brought and wash your feet ...' (Genesis* 18:4).

בְּאֵרוֹת מָיִם — *Wells of water.* Scripture *(Genesis* 26:18-22) relates that Isaac dug no less than five wells.

טָעַן מַקְלוֹ ... — *The one who carried his staff ...* Upon returning to Canaan from Aram, Jacob offered a prayer in which he declared, *'For with my staff I crossed this Jordan' (Genesis* 32:11). *Rashi* cites the Midrashic teaching that when Jacob had reached the Jordan River, he had placed his staff in the waters of the river and it split for him, allowing him to pass through.

יִחֵד לֵב — *He dedicated his heart.* Jacob's steadfast

כְּנֶאֱבַק לוֹ שַׂר בָּלוּל מֵאֵשׁ וּמִמַּיִם,*
לָכֵן הִבְטַחְתּוֹ הֱיוֹת עִמּוֹ בָּאֵשׁ וּבַמָּיִם.*

—Cong. בַּעֲבוּרוֹ אַל תִּמְנַע מָיִם.

זְכוֹר מָשׁוּי* בְּתֵבַת גֹּמֶא מִן הַמַּיִם, נָמוּ* דָּלֹה דָלָה וְהִשְׁקָה צֹאן מַיִם,
סְגוּלֶיךָ עֵת צָמְאוּ לַמַּיִם, עַל הַסֶּלַע הָךְ* וַיֵּצְאוּ מָיִם.

—Cong. בְּצִדְקוֹ חֹן חַשְׁרַת מָיִם.

זְכוֹר פְּקִיד* שָׁתוֹת* טוֹבֵל חָמֵשׁ טְבִילוֹת* בַּמַּיִם,
צוֹעֶה וּמַרְחִיץ כַּפָּיו בְּקִדּוּשׁ מַיִם,
קוֹרֵא וּמַזֶּה* טָהֳרַת מַיִם, רֻחַק* מֵעַם פַּחַז כַּמָּיִם.

—Cong. בַּעֲבוּרוֹ אַל תִּמְנַע מָיִם.

זְכוֹר שְׁנֵים עָשָׂר שְׁבָטִים שֶׁהֶעֱבַרְתָּ בְּגִזְרַת מַיִם,*
שֶׁהִמְתַּקְתָּ לָמוֹ מְרִירוּת מַיִם,
תּוֹלְדוֹתָם* נִשְׁפַּךְ דָּמָם עָלֶיךָ כַּמַּיִם,
תֵּפֶן כִּי נַפְשֵׁנוּ אָפְפוּ מָיִם.

—Cong. בְּצִדְקָם חֹן חַשְׁרַת מָיִם.

—chazzan **שָׁאַתָּה הוּא יהוה אֱלֹהֵינוּ, מַשִּׁיב הָרוּחַ וּמוֹרִיד הַגָּשֶׁם.**

—Cong. then *chazzan* לִבְרָכָה וְלֹא לִקְלָלָה. (Cong.— אָמֵן.)

—Cong. then *chazzan* לְחַיִּים וְלֹא לְמָוֶת. (Cong.— אָמֵן.)

—Cong. then *chazzan* לְשֹׂבַע וְלֹא לְרָזוֹן. (Cong.— אָמֵן.)

The Ark is closed and the *chazzan* continues, מְכַלְכֵּל חַיִּים, p. 674.

---

faith in God enabled him singlehandedly to roll a huge boulder off the mouth of the well — a chore that usually required the cooperative efforts of a large number of shepherds — in order to water Laban's sheep (see *Genesis* 29:11).

בָּלוּל מֵאֵשׁ וּמִמַּיִם — *Composed of fire and water.* Angels are composed of fire and water *(Yerushalmi, Rosh Hashanah* 2:5). The episode of Jacob's wrestling with an angel is told in *Genesis* (32:25-31).

הִבְטַחְתּוֹ ... בָּאֵשׁ וּבַמָּיִם. — *You pledged ... fire and water.* The Prophet *(Isaiah* 43:1-2) proclaimed: *'And now,' so said* HASHEM, *your Creator ... 'when you pass through water, I am with you ... when you go through fire, you shall not be burned ...'*

מָשׁוּי — *The one drawn forth.* When Pharaoh's daughter found a Jewish baby among the reeds, she named him מֹשֶׁה, *Moses,* because מִן הַמַּיִם מְשִׁיתִהוּ, *'I have drawn him from the water' (Exodus* 2:10).

נָמוּ — *They said.* The daughters of Jethro reported to their father how 'an Egyptian man' [Moses] drew water for them (see *Exodus* 2:16-19).

עַל הַסֶּלַע הָךְ ... — *He struck the rock ...* When Israel cried for water in the Wilderness, God ordered Moses to smite a stone from which water would issue forth (see *Exodus* 17:6).

פְּקִיד — *The appointee.* This word refers to the holder of a high office, in this case, Aaron, the first *Kohen Gadol (Mateh Levi).*

שָׁתוֹת — *The Temple.* The Holy Temple is called the אֶבֶן שְׁתִיָּה, *Foundation Stone,* after a stone located at the center of the Holy of Holies upon

*as when he was wrestled by an angel composed of fire and water.**
*Therefore You pledged to remain with him through fire and water.**
Cong.— *For his sake, do not hold water back!*

זְכוֹר *Remember the one [Moses] drawn forth**
in a bulrush basket from the water.
They said, 'He drew water and provided the sheep with water.'*
At the time Your treasured people thirsted for water,
he struck the rock and out came water.*
Cong.— *For the sake of his righteousness, grant abundant water!*

זְכוֹר *Remember the appointee* [Aaron] over the Temple,**
who made five immersions in the water.*
He went to cleanse his hands through sanctification with water.
He called out and sprinkled [blood bringing] purity as with water.*
He remained apart from a people of waterlike impetuosity.*
Cong.— *For his sake, do not hold water back!*

זְכוֹר *Remember the twelve tribes You caused*
*to cross through the split waters,**
for whom You sweetened the water's bitter taste.
Their offspring whose blood was spilt for You like water.*
Turn to us — for woes engulf our souls like water.
Cong.— *For the sake of their righteousness, grant abundant water!*

Chazzan— **For You are HASHEM, our God,**
Who makes the wind blow and makes the rain descend.

Cong. then *chazzan*— *For blessing and not for curse.* (Cong.— *Amen.)*
Cong. then *chazzan*— *For life and not for death.* (Cong.— *Amen.)*
Cong. then *chazzan*— *For plenty and not for scarcity.* (Cong.— *Amen.)*

The Ark is closed and the *chazzan* continues, *'He sustains the living ...'* p. 674.

---

which stood the Ark of the Covenant. According to the Talmud *(Yoma* 53b) this stone was the first part of the earth to be created by God, and from it the planet as we know it expanded.

חָמֵשׁ טְבִילוֹת ... — *Five immersions.* The Mishnah *(Yoma* 3:3, based on *Leviticus,* ch. 16) teaches that the *Kohen Gadol* must immerse himself five times during the Yom Kippur Temple service. Before and after each immersion he would wash his hands and feet in a ritually prescribed manner with water that had been sanctified in a sacred vessel.

קוֹרֵא וּמַזֶּה — *He called out and sprinkled.* During the Yom Kippur service, the *Kohen Gadol* would sprinkle the blood of various offerings in various parts of the Temple (see *Leviticus* 16:145). To ensure that the proper number of sprinklings were performed, the *Kohen Gadol* would count aloud as he sprinkled the blood (see *Yoma* 5:3-4).

רָחַק — *He remained apart.* Aaron's personal sanctity was much greater than that of the rest of Israel, as Scripture states: *And Aaron was set apart that he be sanctified* [as] *holy of holies ... (I Chronicles* 23:13).

שֶׁהֶעֱבַרְתָּ בְּגִזְרַת מַיִם — *You caused to cross through the split waters ...* The Splitting of the Sea is described in *Exodus* (14:15-15:21), and is followed by the story of the sweetening of the waters of Marah (15:22-26).

תּוֹלְדוֹתָם — *Their offspring,* i.e., the generations of Jews whose blood has been spilled in Sanctification of the Holy Name. Alternatively, this refers to the supplicants, the descendants of the twelve tribes, who pour out their hearts in prayer.

ברח דודי

In some congregations, the following *piyutim* are recited in the Pesach *Shacharis* just before the blessing גָּאַל יִשְׂרָאֵל that precedes *Shemoneh Esrei.*

FIRST DAY OF PESACH:

בְּרַח דּוֹדִי עַד שֶׁתְּחְפַּץ אַהֲבַת כְּלוּלֵינוּ, שׁוּב לְרַחֵם כִּי כְּלוּנוּ מַלְכֵי זֵדִים שׁוֹבֵינוּ תּוֹלָלֵינוּ, הֲרוֹס וְקַעְקַע בֵּיצָתָם מִתִּלֵּנוּ, הָקֵם טוּרָךְ נַגֵּן שְׁתִילֵינוּ, הִנֵּה זֶה עוֹמֵד אַחַר כָּתְלֵנוּ.[1]

בְּרַח דּוֹדִי עַד שֶׁיָּפוּחַ קֵץ מַחֲזֶה, חִישׁ וְנָסוּ הַצְּלָלִים מִזֶּה, יָרוּם וְנִשָּׂא וְגָבַהּ נִבְזֶה, יַשְׂכִּיל וְיוֹכִיחַ וְגוֹיִם רַבִּים יַזֶּה, חֲשׂוֹף זְרוֹעֲךָ קָרוֹא כָּזֶה, קוֹל דּוֹדִי הִנֵּה זֶה.[2]

בְּרַח דּוֹדִי וּדְמֵה לְךָ לִצְבִי, יָגֵל יִגַּשׁ קֵץ קִצְבִי, דְּלוּתִי מִשְּׁבִי לַעֲטֶרֶת צְבִי, תְּעוּבִים תְּאֵבִים הַר צְבִי, וְאֵין מֵבִיא וְנָבִיא, וְלֹא תְשַׁבִּי מְשׁוּי מְשִׁיבִי, רִיבָה רִיבִי, הָסֵר חוֹבִי וּכְאֵבִי, וְיֵרֶא וְיֵבוֹשׁ אוֹיְבִי, וְאָשִׁיבָה חוֹרְפִי בְּנִיבִי, זֶה דוֹדִי, גּוֹאֲלִי קְרוֹבִי, רֵעִי וַאֲהוּבִי, אֵל אֱלֹהֵי אָבִי.

בִּגְלַל אָבוֹת תּוֹשִׁיעַ בָּנִים, וְתָבִיא גְאֻלָּה לִבְנֵי בְנֵיהֶם.

בָּרוּךְ אַתָּה, יהוה, גָּאַל יִשְׂרָאֵל.

Turn to page 660 for *Shemoneh Esrei.*

SECOND DAY OF PESACH:

בְּרַח דּוֹדִי אֶל מָכוֹן לְשִׁבְתָּךְ, וְאִם עָבַרְנוּ אֶת בְּרִיתָךְ, אָנָּא זְכוֹר אִוּוּי חֶפְצָתָךְ, הָקֵם קוֹשְׁטְ מִלָּתָךְ, כּוֹנֵן מְשׂוֹשׂ קִרְיָתָךְ, הַעֲלוֹתָהּ עַל רֹאשׁ שִׂמְחָתָךְ.

בְּרַח דּוֹדִי אֶל שָׁלֵם סֻכָּךְ, וְאִם תָּעִינוּ מִדַּרְכָּךְ, אָנָּא הָצֵץ מֵחֲרַכָּךְ, וְתוֹשִׁיעַ עַם עָנִי וּמֻתְכָּךְ, חֲמָתְךָ מֵהֶם לְשַׁכָּךְ, וּבְאֶבְרָתְךָ סֶלָה לְהִסְתּוֹכָךְ.

בְּרַח דּוֹדִי אֶל לִבְּךָ וְעֵינֶיךָ שָׁם, וְאִם זָנַחְנוּ טוֹב מְדֻשָּׁן, אָנָּא שְׁמַע שַׁאֲגַת קוֹל צוֹרְרֶיךָ וְרִגְשָׁם, רַוֵּה מִדָּם גּוּשָׁם, וַעֲפָרָם מֵחֵלֶב יְדֻשַּׁן, וּפִגְרֵיהֶם יַעֲלֶה בָאְשָׁם.

בְּרַח דּוֹדִי אֶל מָרוֹם מֵרִאשׁוֹן, וְאִם בָּגַדְנוּ בְּכַחֲשׁוֹן, אָנָּא סְכוּת צְקוּן לַחֲשׁוֹן, דְּלוּתִי מִטְּבוּעַ רִפְשׁוֹן, גְּאַל נְצוּרֵי כְּאִישׁוֹן, כְּאָז בַּחֹדֶשׁ הָרִאשׁוֹן.

בִּגְלַל אָבוֹת תּוֹשִׁיעַ בָּנִים, וְתָבִיא גְאֻלָּה לִבְנֵי בְנֵיהֶם.

בָּרוּךְ אַתָּה, יהוה, גָּאַל יִשְׂרָאֵל.

Turn to page 660 for *Shemoneh Esrei.*

SHABBOS CHOL HAMOED:

בְּרַח דּוֹדִי אֶל שַׁאֲנָן נָוֶה, וְאִם הֶלְאֵינוּ דֶּרֶךְ הָעִוֶּה, הִנֵּה לָקִינוּ בְּכָל מַדְוֶה, וְאַתָּה יהוה מָעוֹז וּמִקְוֶה, עָלֶיךָ כָּל הַיּוֹם נְקַוֶּה, לְגָאֳלֵנוּ וּלְשִׁיתֵנוּ כְּגַן רָוֶה.

בְּרַח דּוֹדִי / FLEE MY BELOVED

Three liturgical hymns, all beginning בְּרַח דּוֹדִי, were composed for insertion in the *Shacharis* of the first and second days and Shabbos Chol Hamoed of Pesach. Their theme is based on the last verse of *Shir HaShirim,* in which Israel pleads to God, its *Beloved,* to flee from His exile and renew their relationship. The first day's *piyut* [hymn] is ascribed to Rabbi Shlomo HaBavli of tenth century Italy; the second day's, to his student Rabbi Meshullam of Lucca, Italy,

BRACH DODI

In some congregations, the following *piyutim* are recited in the Pesach *Shacharis* just before the blessing '... *Who redeemed Israel,*' that precedes *Shemoneh Esrei.*

FIRST DAY OF PESACH:

בְּרַח דּוֹדִי *Flee, my Beloved [from Your estrangement], while the love of our betrothal still gratifies; return and be merciful for we are being destroyed by the wanton rulers — our captors and mockers; tear down and uproot their swampy growth from our mountain. Put up the walls of Your Temple and let our children sing: 'Behold — He is standing behind our wall!'*[1]

Flee, my Beloved [and bring the Messiah] before the appointed deadline blows by, hurry and let the clouds of exile disperse from here. May he [the Messiah] be raised and uplifted, and lofty, he who is now debased; may he cleverly reprove and purify many nations. Bare Your arm and proclaim the following: 'The voice of my Beloved, behold it [has come]!'[2]

Flee, my Beloved, and be like a deer, reveal and bring near our appointed time, draw me from captivity to be a crown of pride. The abominated [Jews] covet the cherished [Temple] Mount — but there is neither leader nor prophet, nor [Elijah the] Tishbite to resolve [disputes] and reconcile [generations]. O take up my grievance, remove my guilt and pain, let my enemy see and be shamed, may I answer my abusers by saying: 'This is my Beloved, my Redeemer Who is close to me, my Friend Whom I adore — God, the God of my father!'

For the sake of the forefathers may You save the offspring,
and bring redemption to their children's children.
Blessed are You, HASHEM, *Who redeemed Israel.*

Turn to page 661 for *Shemoneh Esrei.*

SECOND DAY OF PESACH:

בְּרַח דּוֹדִי *Flee, my Beloved, to the foundation of Your dwelling place. If we have violated Your covenant, please remember Your coveted canopy [the Temple], affirm the truth of Your word, establish Your city of joy, raise her to the peak of Your gladness.*

Flee, my Beloved, to Jerusalem Your abode. If we have strayed from Your path, please peer [at us] through Your lattice and save the poor and bruised people. Calm Your anger against them and may Your wing always shelter them.

Flee, my Beloved, to [the Temple] where Your heart and eyes are directed. Though we have foresaken the goodly, abundant [Temple], please listen to the roar of our enemies' voice and their tumult; sate [Your sword] from the blood of their corpulence and may their dust grow oily from their fat, may their corpses raise a stench.

Flee, my Beloved, to Your lofty home [the Temple] from of old. Though we have rebelled treacherously, please hear the outpouring of whispered prayer, draw me from sinking into the muck, redeem those who are protected like the pupil of the eye as then [in Egypt] in the first month.

For the sake of the forefathers may You save the offspring,
and bring redemption to their children's children.
Blessed are You, HASHEM, *Who redeemed Israel.*

Turn to page 661 for *Shemoneh Esrei.*

SHABBOS CHOL HAMOED:

בְּרַח דּוֹדִי *Flee, my Beloved, to the tranquil abode. Though we have grown weary on a perverted path, behold we have been afflicted with every sort of pain. You,* HASHEM, *are power and hope; upon You we hope all the day to redeem us and to make us a fertile garden.*

(1) Song of Songs 2:9. (2) 2:8.

בְּרַח דּוֹדִי אֶל מְקוֹם מִקְדָּשֵׁנוּ, וְאִם עֲוֹנוֹת עָבְרוּ רֹאשֵׁנוּ, הִנֵּה בָאָה בְּבַרְזֶל נַפְשֵׁנוּ, וְאַתָּה יהוה גֹּאֲלֵנוּ קְדוֹשֵׁנוּ, עָלֶיךָ נִשְׁפֹּךְ שִׂיחַ רַחֲשֵׁנוּ, לְגָאֳלֵנוּ מִמְּעוֹן קָדְשְׁךָ לְהַחְפִּישֵׁנוּ.

בְּרַח דּוֹדִי אֶל עִיר צִדְקֵנוּ, וְאִם לֹא שָׁמַעְנוּ לְקוֹל מַצְדִּיקֵינוּ, הִנֵּה אֲכָלוּנוּ בְּכָל פֶּה מַדִּיקֵינוּ, וְאַתָּה יהוה שׁוֹפְטֵנוּ מְחֹקְקֵנוּ, עָלֶיךָ נַשְׁלִיךְ יְהַב חֶלְקֵנוּ, לְגָאֳלֵנוּ בְּהַשְׁקֵט וּבְבִטְחָה לְהַחֲזִיקֵנוּ.

בְּרַח דּוֹדִי אֶל וַעַד הַזְּבוּל, וְאִם עָלֶךָ שָׁבַרְנוּ בְּלִי סָבוּל, הִנֵּה לָקִינוּ בְּכָל מִינֵי חִבּוּל, וְאַתָּה יהוה מְשַׂמֵּחַ אָבוּל, עָלֶיךָ נַסְבִּיר לְהַתִּיר כָּבוּל, לְגָאֳלֵנוּ לְהִתְגַּדֵּל מֵעַל לִגְבוּל.

בְּרַח דּוֹדִי אֶל נִשָּׂא מִגְּבָעוֹת, וְאִם זַדְנוּ בִּפְרֹעַ פְּרָעוֹת, הִנֵּה הִשִּׂיגוּנוּ צָרוֹת רַבּוֹת וְרָעוֹת, וְאַתָּה יהוה אֵל לְמוֹשָׁעוֹת, עָלֶיךָ נִשְׁפֹּךְ שִׂיחַ שְׁוָעוֹת, לְגָאֳלֵנוּ וּלְעַטְּרֵנוּ כּוֹבַע יְשׁוּעוֹת.

בִּגְלַל אָבוֹת תּוֹשִׁיעַ בָּנִים, וְתָבִיא גְאֻלָּה לִבְנֵי בְנֵיהֶם.
בָּרוּךְ אַתָּה, יהוה, גָּאַל יִשְׂרָאֵל.

Turn to page 420 for *Shemoneh Esrei*.

SEVENTH DAY PESACH:

יוֹם לְיַבָּשָׁה נֶהֶפְכוּ מְצוּלִים, שִׁירָה חֲדָשָׁה שִׁבְּחוּ גְאוּלִים.

הִטְבַּעְתָּ בְּתַרְמִית רַגְלֵי בַּת עֲנָמִית, וּפַעֲמֵי שׁוּלַמִּית
יָפוּ בַּנְּעָלִים. שִׁירָה חֲדָשָׁה שִׁבְּחוּ גְאוּלִים.

וְכָל רוֹאֵי יְשׁוּרוּן, בְּבֵית הוֹדִי יְשׁוֹרְרוּן, אֵין כָּאֵל יְשׁוּרוּן,
וְאוֹיְבֵינוּ פְּלִילִים. שִׁירָה חֲדָשָׁה שִׁבְּחוּ גְאוּלִים.

דְּגָלַי כֵּן תָּרִים, עַל הַנִּשְׁאָרִים, וּתְלַקֵּט נִפְזָרִים, כִּמְלַקֵּט שִׁבֳּלִים.
שִׁירָה חֲדָשָׁה שִׁבְּחוּ גְאוּלִים.

הַבָּאִים עִמְּךָ, בִּבְרִית חוֹתָמְךָ, וּמִבֶּטֶן לִשְׁמְךָ, הֵמָּה נְמוּלִים.
שִׁירָה חֲדָשָׁה שִׁבְּחוּ גְאוּלִים.

הַרְאֵה אוֹתוֹתָם, לְכָל רוֹאֵי אוֹתָם, וְעַל כַּנְפֵי כְסוּתָם, יַעֲשׂוּ גְדִילִים.
שִׁירָה חֲדָשָׁה שִׁבְּחוּ גְאוּלִים.

לְמִי זֹאת נִרְשֶׁמֶת, הַכֶּר נָא דְּבַר אֱמֶת, לְמִי הַחוֹתֶמֶת, וּלְמִי הַפְּתִילִים.
שִׁירָה חֲדָשָׁה שִׁבְּחוּ גְאוּלִים.

וְשׁוּב שֵׁנִית לְקַדְּשָׁהּ, וְאַל תּוֹסִיף לְגָרְשָׁהּ, וְהַעֲלֵה אוֹר שִׁמְשָׁהּ,
וְנָסוּ הַצְּלָלִים. שִׁירָה חֲדָשָׁה שִׁבְּחוּ גְאוּלִים.

יְדִידִים רוֹמְמוּךָ, בְּשִׁירָה קִדְּמוּךָ, מִי כָמֹכָה, יהוה בָּאֵלִים.
שִׁירָה חֲדָשָׁה שִׁבְּחוּ גְאוּלִים.

בִּגְלַל אָבוֹת תּוֹשִׁיעַ בָּנִים, וְתָבִיא גְאוּלָה לִבְנֵי בְנֵיהֶם.
בָּרוּךְ אַתָּה, יהוה, גָּאַל יִשְׂרָאֵל.

Turn to page 660 for *Shemoneh Esrei*.

[later of Mainz]; and the *piyut* for Shabbos Chol HaMoed, to Rabbi Shimon HaGadol of Mainz.

☙ יוֹם — *The day.* This prayer is also recited at the circumcision feast, see page 214.

Flee, my Beloved, to the site of our Sanctuary. Though sins have overflowed our head, behold our lives are fettered in an iron exile. You, HASHEM, are our Redeemer, our Holy One, to You we pour out the words of our prayer, to redeem us — from Your holy abode — and to set us free.

Flee, my Beloved, to our righteous City. Though we have not listened to the voice of those [the prophets] who would make us righteous, behold our foes have devoured and ground us down. You HASHEM, our Judge and Lawgiver, upon You we cast our granted portion, to redeem us quietly and to strengthen us in security.

Flee, my Beloved, to the appointed abode. Though we have broken Your yoke, unwilling to endure it, behold we have been struck with every manner of assault. You, HASHEM, gladden the aggrieved; upon You is our hope to release the chained, to redeem us and make us unboundedly great.

Flee, my Beloved, to the most exalted mountain. Though we sinned wantonly in breaching [the faith], behold we have been overtaken by abundant and evil travails. You, HASHEM, God of salvations, upon You we pour our prayerful cries, to redeem us and crown us with the cap of salvations.

For the sake of the forefathers may You save the offspring,
and bring redemption to their children's children.
Blessed are You, HASHEM, Who redeemed Israel.

Turn to page 421 for *Shemoneh Esrei.*

SEVENTH DAY OF PESACH:

יוֹם לְיַבָּשָׁה *The day the depths turned to dry land,*
the redeemed ones sang a new song.
Because of her deceitfulness, You caused the Anamite daughter's feet to sink;
but the footsteps of the wholesome one were beautiful in shoes —
the redeemed ones sang a new song.
All who see Jeshurun will sing in My Majestic Home:
'There is none like the God of Jeshurun', and our enemies are judged —
the redeemed ones sang a new song.
May You raise my banners over the survivors;
and may You gather the scattered ones as one gathers sheaves —
the redeemed ones sang a new song.
Those who come with You into the covenant of Your seal,
and from the womb they are circumcised for Your Name's sake —
the redeemed ones sang a new song.
Display their signs to all who see them,
and on the corners of their garments they will make fringes —
the redeemed ones sang a new song.
Whose is this Torah, inscribed with commandments? — Please recognize the truth!
Whose is the signet and Whose are the threads? —
the redeemed ones sang a new song.
Betroth her again and drive her out no more;
let her sunlight rise and let the shadows flee —
the redeemed ones sang a new song.
The beloved ones exalt You, with song they come and greet You;
who is like You, HASHEM, among the mighty ones —
the redeemed ones sang a new song.

For the sake of the forefathers may You save the offspring,
and bring redemption to their children's children.
Blessed are You, HASHEM, Who redeemed Israel.

Turn to page 661 for *Shemoneh Esrei.*

סדר אקדמות

On the first day of Shavuos, after the *Kohen* has been called to the Torah, but before he recites his blessing, *Akdamus* is read responsively, the *chazzan* chanting two verses and the congregation chanting the next two. It was composed as an introduction to the Ten Commandments.

אַקְדָּמוּת מִלִּין,* וְשָׁרָיוּת שׁוּ תָא.
אַוְלָא שָׁקֵילְנָא, הַרְמָן וּרְשׁוּ תָא.
בְּבָבֵי תְּרֵי וּתְלָת,* דְּאֶפְתַּח בְּנַקְשׁוּ תָא.
בְּבָרֵי דְבָרֵי וְטָרֵי, עֲדֵי לְקַשִּׁישׁוּ תָא.
גְּבוּרָן עָלְמִין לֵיהּ, וְלָא סִפֵּק פְּרִישׁוּ תָא.
גְּוִיל אִלּוּ רְקִיעֵי,* קְנֵי כָּל חוּרְשָׁא תָא.
דְּיוֹ אִלּוּ יַמֵּי, וְכָל מֵי כְנִישׁוּ תָא.
דָּיְרֵי אַרְעָא סָפְרֵי, וְרָשְׁמֵי רַשְׁוָן תָא.*
הֲדַר* מָרֵי שְׁמַיָּא, וְשַׁלִּיט בְּיַבֶּשְׁתָּא תָא.
הָקֵים עָלְמָא יְחִידָאֵי, וְכַבְּשֵׁיהּ בְּכַבְּשׁוּ תָא.*
וּבְלָא לֵאוּ שַׁכְלְלֵיהּ, וּבְלָא תְשָׁשׁוּ תָא.
וּבְאָתָא קַלִּילָא,* דְּלֵית בַּהּ מְשָׁשׁוּ תָא.
זַמֵּן כָּל עֲבִידְתֵּיהּ, בְּהַךְ יוֹמֵי שִׁ תָא.
זְהוֹר יְקָרֵיהּ עֲלִי, עֲלֵי כָרְסְיֵהּ דְּאֶשָּׁ תָא.
חֲיָל* אֱלֶף אַלְפִין, וְרִבּוֹא לְשַׁמְשׁוּ תָא.
חַדְתִּין נְבוֹט לְצַפְרִין, סַגִּיאָה טְרָשׁוּ תָא.*
טְפֵי יְקִידִין שְׂרָפִין, כְּלוֹל גַּפֵּי שִׁ תָא.
טְעֵם עַד יִתְיְהֵב לְהוֹן,* שְׁתִיקִין בְּאַדִּשְׁ תָא.
יְקַבְּלוּן דֵּין מִן דֵּין,* שָׁוֵי דְלָא בְשַׁשְׁ תָא.
יְקַר מְלֵי כָל אַרְעָא, לְתְלוּתֵי קְדוּשְׁ תָא.
כְּקָל מִן קֳדָם שַׁדַּי, כְּקָל מֵי נְפִישׁוּ תָא.
כְּרוּבִין קֳבֵל גַּלְגַּלִּין, מְרוֹמְמִין בְּאַוְשָׁ תָא.
לְמֶחֱזֵי בְּאַנְפָּא עֵין, כְּוָת גִּירֵי קַשְׁ תָא.
לְכָל אֲתַר דְּמִשְׁתַּלְּחִין, זְרִיזִין בְּאַשְׁוָ תָא.

אַקְדָּמוּת / AKDAMUS

Composed by Rabbi Meir ben Yitzchak (11th cent., Worms, Germany), *Akdamus* may well be Judaism's best-known and most beloved *piyut* [liturgical poem]. In its ninety verses, written in a terse, difficult Aramaic, *Akdamus* leads the reader through the great heights and depths of mystical understanding — from a description of God's creation of the world to a close look at the splendors of the World to Come; from the angels' praise of the Almighty to the greatness and the suffering of the Jewish people. The first forty-four verses form a double acrostic of the *Aleph-Beis*, while the first letters of the remaining verses spell the author's name and a blessing: מֵאִיר בְּרַבִּי יִצְחָק יִגְדַּל בְּתוֹרָה וּבְמַעֲשִׂים טוֹבִים אָמֵן וְחָזַק וֶאֱמָץ, *Meir, the son of Rabbi Yitzchak, may he grow in Torah and in good deeds. Amen. Be strong and of good courage.*

Each verse concludes with the suffix תא, the last and first letters of the Hebrew alphabet, to signify that the cycle of Torah study is endless, and that as soon as one completes the Torah, he should begin anew *(Sefer HaToda'ah).*

[A full commentary dealing with every word in this *piyut* appears in the ArtScroll *Akdamus Millin* by R' Avrohom Y. Salamon.]

מִלִּין — *The Words,* i.e., the Ten Commandments, which are to be read after the recital of this poem. The first four verses are the poet's request for *permission,* from God and from his listeners, to explain the Torah's words.

⁂ AKDAMUS ⁂

On the first day of Shavuos, after the *Kohen* has been called to the Torah, but before he recites his blessing, *Akdamus* is read responsively, the *chazzan* chanting two verses and the congregation chanting the next two. It was composed as an introduction to the Ten Commandments.

אַקְדָמוּת *In introduction to the Words,* and commencement of my speech, I begin by taking authorization and permission.*

ב *In two and three sections,* I shall commence with trembling,*

ב *With permission from Him Who created everything and shields it till its hoary age.*

ג *His is eternal strength that could not be described —*

ג *Even if the heavens were parchment,* and the forests quills,*

ד *If all oceans were ink, as well as every gathered water,*

ד *If the earth's inhabitants were scribes and recorders of initials* —*

ה *The glory* of the Master of heaven and the Ruler of earth.*

ה *In isolation He established the earth and controlled [its expansion] with constraint,**

ו *He perfected it without fatigue and without weariness,*

ו *And with a letter, slight* and lacking substance.*

ז *He readied all His work in those six days.*

ז *Then the splendor of His majesty ascended upon His fiery throne.*

ח *A host* of a thousand thousands and tens of thousands serve Him*

ח *New ones flow forth every morning — How great is Your faithfulness!**

ט *Even greater are the flaming Seraphim, each one six winged,*

ט *Until permission is granted them,* they must be still, in total silence.*

י *Upon receiving [permission] from one another,* in unison with no delay [they chant]:*

י *'All the world is filled with His glory' — after three times chanting 'Holy.'*

כ *Like the sound emanating from the Almighty, like the sound of torrential waters,*

כ *Cherubim responding to galgalim, exalting in a crescendo.*

ל *Seeming to the human eye like arrows flashing from a bow,*

ל *To every place that they are sent, they hasten anxiously.*

בְּבָבֵי תְּרֵי וּתְלָת — *In two and three sections.* The poem is divided into two major themes: (a) God's greatness; and (b) Jewish faith in God and obedience to the Torah, despite the oppression and ridicule; — and three subordinate themes: (a) the angels praising God; (b) the Torah's greatness; and (c) the reward awaiting the righteous for upholding the Torah *(T'yul B'gan).*

גְּוִיל אִלּוּ רְקִיעֵי — *Even if the heavens were parchment.* The next three verses are a parenthetical elaboration on God's glory. Even were unlimited resources available, it would nevertheless be impossible to describe fully God's greatness.

וְרָשְׁמֵי רַשְׁוָתָא — *And recorders of initials.* Were all the world's inhabitants scribes, writing only the initials of chapters depicting God's greatness, it would still be impossible to record all His praises.

הֲדַר — *The glory.* The poet proceeds to speak of God's greatness after having stated that an adequate description is impossible.

וְכַבְשֵׁיהּ בְּכַבְּשׁוּתָא — *And controlled [its expansion] with constraint.* The Talmud *(Chagigah* 12a) teaches that the first rock of the earth proceeded to expand until it reached the size God desired. Thereupon, He halted its growth *(M'vo HaShir).*

וּבְאָתָא קְלִילָא — *And with a letter, slight.* God created the world as effortlessly as a person pronounces the letter ה, which requires but an exhalation of breath *(Midrash Tehillim* 62:1).

חֵיל — *A host.* The next sixteen verses describe angels, and their awe in praising God.

חַדְתִּין נְבוֹט לְצַפְרִין סַגִּיאָה טְרָשׁוּתָא — *New ones* [i.e., angels] *flow forth every morning — How great is Your faithfulness!* Hosts of angels are created daily to praise God only on that day, as is stated *(Lamentations* 3:23): *New ones are created every morning (Chagigah* 14a).

טְעֵם עַד יִתְיְהֵב לְהוֹן — *Until permission is granted them.* The angels are not permitted to offer their daily hymns to God, until Israel has completed its psalms of praise *(Pirkei Heichalos).*

יְקַבְּלוּן דֵּין מִן דֵּין — *Upon receiving [permission]*

מְבָרְכִין בְּרִיךְ יְקָרֵיהּ, בְּכָל לִשָּׁן לְחִישׁוּ   תָּא.

מֵאֲתַר בֵּית שְׁכִינְתֵּיהּ, דְּלָא צְרִיךְ בְּחִישׁוּ   תָּא.*

נְהִים כָּל חֵיל מְרוֹמָא, מְקַלְּסִין בַּחֲשַׁשׁ   תָּא.

נְהִירָא מַלְכוּתֵיהּ, לְדָר וְדָר לְאַפְרָשׁ   תָּא.

סְדִירָא בְּהוֹן קְדוּשְׁתָּא, וְכַד חָלְפָא שַׁעְ   תָּא.

סִיּוּמָא דְלְעָלַם,* וְאוֹף לָא לִשְׁבוּעְ   תָּא.

עֲדַב יְקָר אַחֲסַנְתֵּיהּ,* חֲבִיבִין דִּבְקַבַּעְ   תָּא.

עֲבִידִין לֵיהּ חֲטִיבָה, בְּדִנַח וּשְׁקַעְ   תָּא.

פְּרִישָׁן לְמָנָתֵיהּ, לְמֶעְבַּד לֵיהּ רְעוּ   תָּא.

פְּרִישׁוּתֵיהּ שְׁבָחֵיהּ, יְחַוּוֹן בִּשְׁעוּ   תָּא.

צְבִי וְחָמִיד וְרָגִיג, דִּילְאוֹן בְּלָעוּ   תָּא.*

צְלוֹתְהוֹן בְּכֵן מְקַבֵּל, וְהַנְיָא בָּעוּ   תָּא.

קְטִירָא* לְחַי עָלְמָא, בְּתַגָּא בִּשְׁבוּעְ   תָּא.

קָבֵל יְקָר טוֹטַפְתָּא,* יְתִיבָא בִּקְבִיעוּ   תָּא.

רְשִׁימָא הִיא גוּפָא, בְּחָכְמְתָא וּבְדַעְ   תָּא.

רְבוּתְהוֹן דְּיִשְׂרָאֵל, קְרָאֵי בִּשְׁמַעְ   תָּא.

שְׁבַח* רִבּוֹן עָלְמָא, אֲמִירָא דַכְן   תָּא.

שְׁפַר עֲלֵי לְחַווֹיֵהּ, בְּאַפֵּי מַלְכָּן   תָּא.

תָּאִין וּמִתְכַּנְּשִׁין, כְּחֵזוּ אַדְן   תָּא.

תְּמֵהִין וְשָׁיְלִין לֵיהּ, בְּעֵסֶק אָתְן   תָּא.*

מִנָּן וּמָאן הוּא רְחִימָךְ, שַׁפִּירָא בְּרֵין   תָּא.*

אֲרוּם בְּגִינֵיהּ סָפִית, מְדוֹר אַרְיָן   תָּא.

יְקָרָא וְיָאָה אַתְּ, אִין תַּעַרְבִי לְמַרְן   תָּא.

רְעוּתֵךְ נַעֲבִיד לִיךְ, בְּכָל אַתְרָן   תָּא.

בְּחָכְמְתָא מְתִיבָתָא לְהוֹן, קְצָת לְהוֹדָעוּ   תָּא.

יְדַעְתּוּן חַכְּמִין לֵיהּ, בְּאִשְׁתְּמוֹדָעוּ   תָּא.

רְבוּתְכוֹן מָה חֲשִׁיבָא, קֳבֵל הַהִיא שְׁבַח   תָּא.

רְבוּתָא דְּיַעֲבֵד לִי, כַּד מַטְיָא יְשׁוּעְ   תָּא.

בְּמֵיתֵי לִי נְהוֹרָא, וְתַחֲפֵי לְכוֹן בַּהֲ   תָּא.

יְקָרֵיהּ כַּד אִתְגְּלֵי, בְּתָקְפָּא וּבְגֵין   תָּא.

יְשַׁלֵּם גְּמֻלַיָּא, לְסָנְאֵי וְנָגְן   תָּא.*

צִדְקָתָא לְעַם חָבִיב, וְסַגִּיא זָכְן   תָּא.

חֲדוּ שְׁלָמָא בְּמֵיתֵי, וּמְנֵי דַכְי   תָּא.

---

from one another. The next twelve verses describe in minute detail the angels' daily recitation of *Kedushah*. (See pages 86 and 100.)

דְּלָא צְרִיךְ בְּחִישׁוּתָא — *Which requires no searching.* The *Shechinah*, Divine Presence of God, need not be sought, since He is everywhere.

סִיּוּמָא דְלְעָלַם — *It is forever at an end.* Unlike Israel which always praises God, angels praise Him only once a day, once a week, or even but once in seven years (*Chullin* 91b).

יְקָר אַחֲסַנְתֵּיהּ — *His precious inheritance.* This refers to Israel, which is God's own portion,

מ *They chant the blessing: 'Blessed is His glory' — in every spoken tongue —*
מ *'From the place where His Presence dwells' — which requires no searching**
נ *Roaring, the entire heavenly legion, praises in trepidation:*
נ *'May His kingdom glow eternally from generation to generation.'*
ס *Scheduled among them is the Kedushah service, and when the time is over,*
ס *It is forever at an end,* not repeated, even after seven years.*
ע *But the portion of His precious inheritance* is better, for with regularity*
ע *They make Him their sole desire, at sunrise and sunset.*
פ *Designated as His portion to carry out His will,*
פ *His wonders and His praises they recount at every hour.*
צ *He desired, longed, and coveted that they toil in Torah study* —*
צ *Therefore He accepts their prayers; their prayer is efficacious.*
ק *They are wreathed* with an oath into a crown for the Eternally Living.*
ק *Beside His precious tefillin,* it rests with regularity.*
ר *This is inscribed therein, with wisdom and with knowledge:*
ר *The magnitude of Israel, reciters of the Shema.*
ש *This praise* of the Master of the Universe is a pure statement*
ש *That it behooves me to declare in the presence of kings.*
ת *The wicked come and gather, appearing like sea waves,*
ת *With wonderment they inquire of Israel regarding proofs:**
מ *'Whence and Who is your Beloved, O nation of beautiful appearance,**
א *That for His sake you perish in a lions' den?*
י *Honored and comely would you be, if you would blend into our dominion;*
ר *We would grant your wish in every place.'*
ב *With wisdom she responds to them in part — to let them know:*
י *'If your wise men could but know Him with full awareness!*
ר *What value has your greatness compared to His praise?*
ר *Of the great things He will do for me when redemption shall arrive;*
ב *When He will bring me light, and you will be covered with shame;*
י *When His glory will be revealed with power and with grandeur,*
י *He will repay in kind to the haters and the isles.**
צ *But righteousness to the people who are beloved and, abundantly meritorious,*
ח *When He brings total joy, and pure vessels*

---

selected from all the nations of the world.

דְּיִלְאוּן בְּלָעוּתָא — *That they toil in* [Torah] *study.* Because Israel must toil to understand the Torah, it merits reward for its labors. The angels, however, are neither obligated to study the Torah, nor need they exert themselves to do so *(Yad Aharon).*

קְטִירָא — *Wreathed.* The praises are symbolically woven into a crown that places itself upon God's head, as it were *(Chagigah* 13b).

קֳבֵל יְקָר טוֹטַפְתָּא — *Beside His precious tefillin.* The Talmud *(Berachos* 6a) states that God wears *tefillin,* as it were, in which are inscribed praises of Israel. The crown that has been wreathed from Israel's prayers rests in its permanently preassigned place alongside God's *tefillin.*

שְׁבַח — *Praise.* The next fourteen verses laud Israel for its firm and adamant stand against the attempts of the nations of the world to convert it to other religions. Specifically, it refers to the many religious disputations that the Christians forced on the Jews during medieval times.

תְּמֵהִין וְשָׁיְלִין לֵיהּ בְּעֵסֶק אָתְוָתָא — *With wonderment, they inquire of Israel regarding proofs.* The Christians ask for proof that God watches and protects Israel and that their hoped-for Messiah would ever come. Surely the very opposite seemed to be true, with Israel being murdered and tortured without God's intercession *(M'vo HaShir).*

שַׁפִּירָא בְּרֵוָתָא — *O nation of beautiful appearance.* So the heathens ask Israel. Their questioning is mocking and derisive.

לְסָנְאֵי וְנַגְוָתָא — *To the haters and the isles.* In Scripture the term *islands* often denotes an enemy of Israel, and the poet here uses the word

קִרְיְתָא דִירוּשְׁלֵם, כַּד יְכַנֵּשׁ גַּלְוָן   תָּא.
יְקָרֵיהּ מַטִּיל עֲלַהּ, בְּיוֹמֵי וְלֵילְוָן   תָּא.
גְּנוּנֵיהּ לְמֶעְבַּד בַּהּ,* בְּתוּשְׁבְּחָן כְּלִילָן   תָּא.
דְּזֵיהוֹר עֲנָנַיָּא, לְמִשְׁפַּר כִּילָן   תָּא.*
לְפוּמֵיהּ דַּעֲבִידְתָּא, עֲבִידָן מְטַלַּל   תָּא.
בְּתַכְתְּקֵי דְהַב פִּיזָא, וּשְׁבַע מַעֲלָן   תָּא.*
תְּחִימִין צַדִּיקֵי, קֳדָם רַב פָּעֳלָן   תָּא.
וְרֵיוֵיהוֹן דָּמֵי, לְשַׁבְעָא חֶדְוָן   תָּא.
רְקִיעָא בְּזֵיהוֹרֵיהּ, וְכוֹכְּבֵי זִינָן   תָּא.
הֲדָרָא דְלָא אֶפְשַׁר, לְמִפְרַט בִּשְׂפָוָן   תָּא.
וְלָא אִשְׁתְּמַע וְחָמֵי, נְבִיאָן חֶזְוָן   תָּא.
בְּלָא שָׁלְטָא בֵּיהּ עֵין,* בְּגוֹ עֵדֶן גִּנָן   תָּא.
מְטַיְּלֵי בֵי חִנְגָּא, לְבַהֲדֵי דִשְׁכִינָן   תָּא.
עֲלֵיהּ רָמְזֵי דֵין הוּא, בְּרַם בְּאֵמְתָּנוּ   תָּא.
שַׂבַּרְנָא לֵיהּ בְּשִׁבְיָן, תְּקוֹף הֵמָנוּ   תָּא.
יַדְבַּר לָן עָלְמִין, עֲלֵמִין מְדַמּוּ   תָּא.
מְנָת דִּילָן דְּמִלְּקַדְמִין, פָּרֵשׁ בַּאֲרָמוּ   תָּא.
טְלוּלָא דְלִוְיָתָן,* וְתוֹר טוּר רָמוּ   תָּא.
וְחַד בְּחַד כִּי סָבִיךְ, וְעָבֵד קְרָבוּ   תָּא.
בְּקַרְנוֹהִי מְנַגַּח בְּהֵמוֹת,* בְּרְבוּ   תָּא.
יְקַרְטַע נוּן לְקִבְלֵיהּ, בְּצִיצוֹי בִּגְבוּר   תָּא.
מְקָרֵב לֵיהּ בָּרְיֵהּ, בְּחַרְבֵּיהּ רַבְרְבוּ   תָּא.
אֲרִסְטוֹן לְצַדִּיקֵי יְתַקֵּן, וְשֵׁרוּ   תָּא.
מְסַחֲרִין עֲלֵי תַכֵּי, דְּכַדְכֹּד וְגוּמַר   תָּא.
נְגִידִין קַמֵּיהוֹן, אֲפַרְסְמוֹן נַהֲרָ   תָּא.
וּמִתְפַּנְּקִין וְרָווּ, בְּכַסֵּי רְוָיָ   תָּא.
חֲמַר מְרַת דְּמִבְּרֵאשִׁית,* נְטִיר בֵּי נַעֲוָ   תָּא.
זַכָּאִין* כַּד שְׁמַעְתּוּן, שְׁבַח דָּא שִׁירָ   תָּא.
קְבִיעִין כֵּן תֶּהֱווּן, בְּהַנְהוּ חֲבוּרָ   תָּא.
וְתִזְכּוּן דִּי תֵיתְּבוּן, בְּעֵלָּא דָרָ   תָּא.
אֲרֵי תְצִיתוּן לְמִלּוֹי, דְּנָפְקִין בְּהַדְרָ   תָּא.
מְרוֹמָם הוּא אֱלָהִין, בְּקַדְמָא וּבַתְרָי   תָּא.
צְבִי וְאִתְרְעִי בָן, וּמְסַר לָן אוֹרָי   תָּא.

---

broadly to designate all haters of Jews.

גְּנוּנֵיהּ לְמֶעְבַּד בַּהּ — *His bridal canopy to be built in her* [i.e., Jerusalem]. The canopy is an allegorical reference to the Temple which will once again be erected when the Messiah will come. The Temple will be like the canopy in the allegorical wedding of God and Israel *(Kinyan Tov).*

לְמִשְׁפַּר כִּילָתָא — *To beautify the canopy.* This verse refers to the *canopy* that God will make for each righteous person as part of his reward in the World-to-Come. Each person's reward will be in proportion to the amount of labor and toil that

ק *To the city of Jerusalem as He gathers in the Exile.*
י *His Shechinah will shelter her during days and nights,*
ג *His bridal canopy to be built in her* crowned with praises —*
ד *With brilliant clouds to beautify the canopy.**
ל *For each according to his sacred toil, they will make a shelter.*
ב *Upon armchairs of purest gold and seven elevations**
ת *Will the righteous be emplaced before Him of many achievements,*
ו *And their appearance will resemble one as sated with joy*
ר *As the heavenly expanse in its splendor and the sparkling stars —*
ה *Beauty that cannot be detailed with lips,*
ו *That was neither heard nor seen in prophetic visions,*
ב *Over which no eye has reigned:* the inside of the Garden of Eden.*
מ *In it they will find joy in a circle-dance before the Shechinah.*
ע *To Him, they will point: "That is He!" — but with trepidation —*
ש *"We hoped for Him in our captivity, with a powerful faith."*
י *He will lead us forever — we will be youthfully vigorous —*
מ *Our predetermined portions having been set aside with elevation.*
ט *The sport with the Leviathan* and the ox of lofty mountains —*
ו *When they will interlock with one another and engage in combat,*
ב *With his horns the Behemoth* will gore with strength,*
י *The fish will leap to meet him with his fins, with power.*
מ *Their Creator will approach them with His mighty sword.*
א *A banquet for the righteous will He prepare, and feast.*
מ *They will sit around tables of precious stones and gems,*
נ *Before them will be flowing rivers of balsam.*
ו *They will delight and drink their fill from overflowing goblets*
ח *Of sweet wine that since Creation* was preserved in pressing tanks.'*
ז *O righteous ones,* just as you heard the praise within this song,*
ק *So may you be appointed among that company,*
ו *Being privileged to be seated in the foremost row —*
א *If you listen to His words that emanate in majesty.*
מ *He is exalted — God — in the beginning and when all is done,*
צ *He desired and selected us, and He gave us the Torah!*

---

he devotes to the studying and upholding of the Torah.

וּשְׁבַע מַעֲלָתָא — *And seven elevations.* The righteous in Paradise will be classified into one of seven categories, according to their merit *(Yad Aharon).*

בְּלָא שָׁלְטָא בֵּיהּ עֵין — *Over which no eye has reigned.* No living creature has ever seen Eden.

⤳§ Leviathan and Behemoth

According to the Talmud and Midrash, the Leviathan is a giant fish, created on the fifth day of Creation, and the ruler of all the creatures of the sea. The Behemoth is a gigantic bull, created on the sixth day of Creation, that, like the Leviathan, possesses enormous strength. The Talmud and Midrash tell of the huge size and appetite of these monsters. The commentators explain that these accounts, as well as the description of their violent battle to the deaths, are allegorical and refer to spiritual values.

From the beautiful skin of the Leviathan, God will construct canopies to shelter the righteous, who will eat the meat of the Behemoth and the Leviathan amid great joy and merriment, at a huge banquet that will be given for them.

חֲמַר מְרַת דְּמִבְּרֵאשִׁית — *Of sweet wine that since Creation.* The righteous will delight in cups overflowing with the wine that was preserved since the six days of Creation *(Berachos* 34b).

זַכָּאִין — *O righteous ones.* Having completed the narrative and descriptive portions of his poem, the poet now concludes his words with a blessing for his audience. He tells them that, as a reward for their having listened to and also recited the praises of God in this poem, may they be privileged to be among the righteous in Paradise.

אושפיזין

Upon entering the *succah* we invite the *Ushpizin*-guests [see commentary] to join us, and we offer prayers that our fulfillment of the *mitzvah* of *succah* be found worthy of Divine favor.

הֲרֵינִי מוּכָן וּמְזֻמָּן לְקַיֵּם מִצְוַת סֻכָּה כַּאֲשֶׁר צִוַּנִי הַבּוֹרֵא יִתְבָּרַךְ שְׁמוֹ: בַּסֻּכֹּת תֵּשְׁבוּ שִׁבְעַת יָמִים, כָּל הָאֶזְרָח בְּיִשְׂרָאֵל יֵשְׁבוּ בַּסֻּכֹּת. לְמַעַן יֵדְעוּ דֹרֹתֵיכֶם, כִּי בַסֻּכּוֹת הוֹשַׁבְתִּי אֶת בְּנֵי יִשְׂרָאֵל, בְּהוֹצִיאִי אוֹתָם מֵאֶרֶץ מִצְרָיִם.[1]

תִּיבוּ תִּיבוּ אוּשְׁפִּיזִין עִילָּאִין, תִּיבוּ תִּיבוּ אוּשְׁפִּיזִין קַדִּישִׁין, תִּיבוּ תִּיבוּ אוּשְׁפִּיזִין דִּמְהֵימְנוּתָא, תִּיבוּ בְּצִלָּא דְקוּדְשָׁא בְּרִיךְ הוּא. זַכָּאָה חוּלְקָנָא, וְזַכָּאָה חוּלְקֵיהוֹן דְּיִשְׂרָאֵל, דִּכְתִיב: כִּי חֵלֶק יהוה עַמּוֹ, יַעֲקֹב חֶבֶל נַחֲלָתוֹ.[2] לְשֵׁם יִחוּד קוּדְשָׁא בְּרִיךְ הוּא וּשְׁכִינְתֵּהּ, לְיַחֲדָא שֵׁם י״ה בְּו״ה בְּיִחוּדָא שְׁלִים עַל יְדֵי הַהוּא טָמִיר וְנֶעְלָם, בְּשֵׁם כָּל יִשְׂרָאֵל.

וִיהִי נֹעַם אֲדֹנָי אֱלֹהֵינוּ עָלֵינוּ, וּמַעֲשֵׂה יָדֵינוּ כּוֹנְנָה עָלֵינוּ, וּמַעֲשֵׂה יָדֵינוּ כּוֹנְנֵהוּ.[3]

יְהִי רָצוֹן מִלְּפָנֶיךָ, יהוה אֱלֹהַי וֵאלֹהֵי אֲבוֹתַי, שֶׁתַּשְׁרֶה שְׁכִינָתְךָ בֵּינֵינוּ, וְתִפְרוֹשׂ עָלֵינוּ סֻכַּת שְׁלוֹמֶךָ — בִּזְכוּת מִצְוַת סֻכָּה שֶׁאָנוּ מְקַיְּמִין — לְיַחֲדָא שְׁמָא דְקוּדְשָׁא בְּרִיךְ הוּא וּשְׁכִינְתֵּהּ, בִּדְחִילוּ וּרְחִימוּ, לְיַחֲדָא שֵׁם י״ה בְּו״ה בְּיִחוּדָא שְׁלִים, בְּשֵׁם כָּל יִשְׂרָאֵל, וּלְהַקִּיף אוֹתָנוּ מִזִּיו כְּבוֹדְךָ הַקָּדוֹשׁ וְהַטָּהוֹר, נָטוּי עַל רָאשֵׁינוּ מִלְמַעְלָה כְּנֶשֶׁר יָעִיר קִנּוֹ;[4] וּמִשָּׁם יַשְׁפַּע שֶׁפַע הַחַיִּים לְעַבְדְּךָ (Hebrew name) בֶּן (mother's Hebrew name) אֲמָתֶךָ. וּבִזְכוּת צֵאתִי מִבֵּיתִי הַחוּצָה — וְדֶרֶךְ מִצְוֹתֶיךָ אָרוּצָה[5] — יֵחָשֵׁב לִי בְּזֹאת כְּאִלּוּ הִרְחַקְתִּי נְדוֹד.[6] וְהֶרֶב כַּבְּסֵנִי מֵעֲוֹנִי, וּמֵחַטָּאתִי טַהֲרֵנִי.[7] וּמֵאוּשְׁפִּיזִין עִילָּאִין, אוּשְׁפִּיזִין דִּמְהֵימְנוּתָא, תִּהְיֶינָה אָזְנֶיךָ קַשֻּׁבוֹת רַב בְּרָכוֹת. (וְלָרְעֵבִים גַּם צְמֵאִים תֵּן לַחְמָם וּמֵימָם הַנֶּאֱמָנִים.) וְתִתֶּן לִי זְכוּת לָשֶׁבֶת וְלַחֲסוֹת בְּסֵתֶר צֵל כְּנָפֶיךָ — בְּעֵת פְּטִירָתִי מִן הָעוֹלָם — וְלַחֲסוֹת מִזֶּרֶם וּמִמָּטָר,[8] כִּי תַמְטִיר עַל רְשָׁעִים פַּחִים.[9] וּתְהֵא חֲשׁוּבָה מִצְוַת סֻכָּה זוּ שֶׁאֲנִי מְקַיֵּם כְּאִלּוּ קִיַּמְתִּיהָ בְּכָל פְּרָטֶיהָ וְדִקְדּוּקֶיהָ וּתְנָאֶיהָ וְכָל מִצְוֹת הַתְּלוּיִם בָּהּ. וְתֵיטִיב לָנוּ הַחֲתִימָה. וּתְזַכֵּנוּ לֵישֵׁב יָמִים רַבִּים עַל הָאֲדָמָה, אַדְמַת קֹדֶשׁ, בַּעֲבוֹדָתְךָ וּבְיִרְאָתֶךָ. בָּרוּךְ יהוה לְעוֹלָם, אָמֵן וְאָמֵן.[10]

רִבּוֹן כָּל הָעוֹלָמִים, יְהִי רָצוֹן מִלְּפָנֶיךָ שֶׁיְּהֵא חָשׁוּב לְפָנֶיךָ מִצְוַת יְשִׁיבַת סֻכָּה זוּ, כְּאִילוּ קִיַּמְתִּיהָ בְּכָל פְּרָטֶיהָ וְדִקְדּוּקֶיהָ וְתַרְיַ״ג מִצְוֹת הַתְּלוּיִם בָּהּ, וּכְאִילוּ כִּוַּנְתִּי בְּכָל הַכַּוָּנוֹת שֶׁכִּוְּנוּ בָהּ אַנְשֵׁי כְּנֶסֶת הַגְּדוֹלָה.

אושפיזין / USHPIZIN

The *Zohar* teaches that for dwelling faithfully in their *succos*, the people of Israel merit the privilege of inviting and welcoming the *Shechinah* [God's Presence] and the seven 'faithful shepherds' who descend from their heavenly abode in Gan Eden and enter these *succos* as exalted *ushpizin*, or guests. There they observe how their descendants fulfill the *mitzvah* of *succah* dwelling under God's protection.

These seven faithful shepherds of Israel are: Abraham, Isaac, Jacob, Joseph, Moses, Aaron and King David. All seven are guests in every *succah* throughout the seven days of the Festival, but on each day one of them leads the others as the guest of honor.

For example, on the first day Abraham leads the other six, and that day is referred to as the '*Ushpizin* of Abraham.' On the second day Isaac leads the others, the day being referred to as the '*Ushpizin* of Isaac.' And so on until Hoshana Rabbah when King David is the guest of honor.

Customs regarding the invitation and associated prayers differ. Some recite the full text as presented here, while others include or omit various paragraphs. Additionally, some repeat the invitations and prayers before each meal,

USHPIZIN

Upon entering the *succah* we invite the *Ushpizin*-guests [see commentary] to join us, and we offer prayers that our fulfillment of the *mitzvah* of *succah* be found worthy of Divine favor.

הֲרֵינִי *Behold, I am prepared and ready to perform the commandment of succah as the Creator, Blessed is His Name, commanded me: In succos shall you dwell for seven days; every citizen in Israel shall dwell in succos; in order that your generations may know that I caused the Children of Israel to dwell in succos when I brought them forth from the land of Egypt.*[1]

Be seated, be seated, exalted guests; be seated, be seated, holy guests; be seated, be seated, guests of faithfulness; be seated in the shade of the Holy One, Blessed is He. Worthy is our portion, worthy is the portion of Israel, as it is written: For HASHEM*'s portion is His people, Jacob the lot of His heritage.*[2] *For the sake of the unification of the Holy One, Blessed is He, and His Presence, to unify the Name Yud-Kei with Vav-Kei in perfect unity through Him Who is hidden and inscrutable — [I pray] in the name of all Israel.*

May the pleasantness of my Lord, our God, be upon us — may He establish our handiwork for us; our handiwork may He establish.[3]

יְהִי רָצוֹן *May it be Your will,* HASHEM *my God and the God of my forefathers, that You cause Your Presence to reside among us; that You spread over us the succah of Your peace — in the merit of the mitzvah of succah that we are fulfilling — to unify the Name of the Holy One, Blessed is He, and His Presence, in fear and love, to unify the Name Yud-Kei with Vav-Kei in perfect unity, in the name of all Israel; and to surround us with the aura of Your honor, holy and pure, spread over our heads from above like an eagle arousing its brood;*[4] *and from there cause an abundant outpouring of life for Your servant* (Hebrew name) *son of* (mother's Hebrew name) *Your handmaid. And in the merit of my leaving my house to go out — and I will enthusiastically pursue the path of Your commandments*[5] *— may this be reckoned for me as if I have wandered afar.*[6] *Cleanse me thoroughly from my iniquity, and from my sin purify me.*[7] *From the exalted guests, the guests of faithfulness, may Your ears hear abundant blessings. (To the hungry and thirsty, may You give their food and their unfailing supply of water.) May you endow me with the privilege to dwell and take refuge in the sheltering protection of Your wings — at the time of my departure from the world — to take refuge from the stream [of fire] and the [fiery] rain,*[8] *when You rain coals upon the wicked.*[9] *May this mitzvah of succah that I perform be reckoned as if I had fulfilled it in all its details, implications and specifications, as well as all the mitzvos dependent on it. May You seal [the Book of Life] for our benefit, and allow us the opportunity to dwell many days upon the land, the Holy Land, in Your service and in Your reverence. Blessed is* HASHEM *forever, Amen and Amen.*[10]

רִבּוֹן *Master of all the worlds, may it be Your will that this mitzvah of dwelling in the succah be reckoned before You as if I had fulfilled it in all its details and implications, as well as the six hundred thirteen mitzvos that are dependent upon it; and as if I had concentrated upon all the intentions which the Men of the Great Assembly concentrated upon regarding it.*

(1) *Leviticus* 23:42-43. (2) *Deuteronomy* 32:9. (3) *Psalms* 90:17. (4) *Deuteronomy* 32:11. (5) Cf. *Psalms* 119:32. (6) Cf. 55:8. (7) 51:4. (8) Cf. *Isaiah* 4:6. (9) Cf. *Psalms* 11:6. (10) 89:53.

while others recite them only once each day.

A third difference concerns the order of the *ushpizin*. The order given here follows the *Sh'lah* who places the *ushpizin* in chronological order, Joseph preceding Moses and Aaron. According to the Kabbalistic teaching of *Arizal*, Moses and Aaron should precede Joseph. Thus, on the fourth day, Moses is the leader of the *ushpizin;* on the fifth day, Aaron; on the sixth day, Joseph; the wording of the invitations are altered accordingly.

[A full commentary on the *ushpizin* appears in the ArtScroll *Succos — Its Significance, Laws and Prayers.*]

Each day — אֻזַּמִּן לִסְעֻדָּתִי אֻשְׁפִּיזִין עִלָּאִין: אַבְרָהָם יִצְחָק יַעֲקֹב יוֹסֵף מֹשֶׁה אַהֲרֹן וְדָוִד.

On the first day — בְּמָטוּ מִנָּךְ אַבְרָהָם אֻשְׁפִּיזִי עִלָּאִי, דְיֵתְבוּ עִמִּי וְעִמָּךְ כָּל אֻשְׁפִּיזֵי עִלָּאֵי, יִצְחָק יַעֲקֹב יוֹסֵף מֹשֶׁה אַהֲרֹן וְדָוִד.

On the second day — בְּמָטוּ מִנָּךְ יִצְחָק אֻשְׁפִּיזִי עִלָּאִי, דְיֵתְבוּ עִמִּי וְעִמָּךְ כָּל אֻשְׁפִּיזֵי עִלָּאֵי, אַבְרָהָם יַעֲקֹב יוֹסֵף מֹשֶׁה אַהֲרֹן וְדָוִד.

On the third day — בְּמָטוּ מִנָּךְ יַעֲקֹב אֻשְׁפִּיזִי עִלָּאִי, דְיֵתְבוּ עִמִּי וְעִמָּךְ כָּל אֻשְׁפִּיזֵי עִלָּאֵי, אַבְרָהָם יִצְחָק יוֹסֵף מֹשֶׁה אַהֲרֹן וְדָוִד.

On the fourth day — בְּמָטוּ מִנָּךְ יוֹסֵף אֻשְׁפִּיזִי עִלָּאִי, דְיֵתְבוּ עִמִּי וְעִמָּךְ כָּל אֻשְׁפִּיזֵי עִלָּאֵי, אַבְרָהָם יִצְחָק יַעֲקֹב מֹשֶׁה אַהֲרֹן וְדָוִד.

On the fifth day — בְּמָטוּ מִנָּךְ מֹשֶׁה אֻשְׁפִּיזִי עִלָּאִי, דְיֵתְבוּ עִמִּי וְעִמָּךְ כָּל אֻשְׁפִּיזֵי עִלָּאֵי, אַבְרָהָם יִצְחָק יַעֲקֹב יוֹסֵף אַהֲרֹן וְדָוִד.

On the sixth day — בְּמָטוּ מִנָּךְ אַהֲרֹן אֻשְׁפִּיזִי עִלָּאִי, דְיֵתְבוּ עִמִּי וְעִמָּךְ כָּל אֻשְׁפִּיזֵי עִלָּאֵי, אַבְרָהָם יִצְחָק יַעֲקֹב יוֹסֵף מֹשֶׁה וְדָוִד.

On Hoshana Rabbah — בְּמָטוּ מִנָּךְ דָּוִד אֻשְׁפִּיזִי עִלָּאִי, דְיֵתְבוּ עִמִּי וְעִמָּךְ כָּל אֻשְׁפִּיזֵי עִלָּאֵי, אַבְרָהָם יִצְחָק יַעֲקֹב יוֹסֵף מֹשֶׁה וְאַהֲרֹן.

קידוש לליל סוכות

The following *Kiddush* is recited on the first two nights of Succos.
(*Kiddush* for other Festivals appears on p. 656.)
On the Sabbath of Chol HaMoed the regular Sabbath *Kiddush* (p. 360), is recited.

When the Festival falls on Friday night, begin here:

(וַיְהִי עֶרֶב וַיְהִי בֹקֶר —Recite silently)

יוֹם הַשִּׁשִּׁי. וַיְכֻלּוּ הַשָּׁמַיִם וְהָאָרֶץ וְכָל צְבָאָם. וַיְכַל אֱלֹהִים בַּיּוֹם הַשְּׁבִיעִי מְלַאכְתּוֹ אֲשֶׁר עָשָׂה, וַיִּשְׁבֹּת בַּיּוֹם הַשְּׁבִיעִי מִכָּל מְלַאכְתּוֹ אֲשֶׁר עָשָׂה. וַיְבָרֶךְ אֱלֹהִים אֶת יוֹם הַשְּׁבִיעִי וַיְקַדֵּשׁ אֹתוֹ, כִּי בוֹ שָׁבַת מִכָּל מְלַאכְתּוֹ אֲשֶׁר בָּרָא אֱלֹהִים לַעֲשׂוֹת.[1]

On all nights other than Friday begin here (on Friday night include all words in brackets):

סַבְרִי מָרָנָן וְרַבָּנָן וְרַבּוֹתַי:

בָּרוּךְ אַתָּה יהוה אֱלֹהֵינוּ מֶלֶךְ הָעוֹלָם, בּוֹרֵא פְּרִי הַגָּפֶן.

(אָמֵן.—All present respond)

Each day: *I invite to my meal the exalted guests: Abraham, Isaac, Jacob, Joseph, Moses, Aaron and David.*

On the first day: *May it please you, Abraham, my exalted guest, that all the other exalted guests dwell here with me and with you — Isaac, Jacob, Joseph, Moses, Aaron and David.*

On the second day: *May it please you, Isaac, my exalted guest, that all the other exalted guests dwell here with me and with you — Abraham, Jacob, Joseph, Moses, Aaron and David.*

On the third day: *May it please you, Jacob, my exalted guest, that all the other exalted guests dwell here with me and with you — Abraham, Isaac, Joseph, Moses, Aaron and David.*

On the fourth day: *May it please you, Joseph, my exalted guest, that all the other exalted guests dwell here with me and with you — Abraham, Isaac, Jacob, Moses, Aaron and David.*

On the fifth day: *May it please you, Moses, my exalted guest, that all the other exalted guests dwell here with me and with you — Abraham, Isaac, Jacob, Joseph, Aaron and David.*

On the sixth day: *May it please you, Aaron, my exalted guest, that all the other exalted guests dwell here with me and with you — Abraham, Isaac, Jacob, Joseph, Moses and David.*

On Hoshana Rabbah: *May it please you, David, my exalted guest, that all the other exalted guests dwell here with me and with you — Abraham, Isaac, Jacob, Joseph, Moses and Aaron.*

KIDDUSH FOR SUCCOS

The following *Kiddush* is recited on the first two nights of Succos.
(*Kiddush* for other Festivals appears on p. 656.)
On the Sabbath of Chol HaMoed the regular Sabbath *Kiddush* (p. 360), is recited.

When the festival falls on Friday night, begin here:
(Recite silently— *And there was evening and there was morning)*

יוֹם הַשִּׁשִּׁי *The sixth day. Thus the heavens and earth were finished, and all their array. On the seventh day God completed His work which He had done, and He abstained on the seventh day from all His work which He had done. God blessed the seventh day and hallowed it, because on it He abstained from all His work which God created to make.*[1]

On all nights other than Friday begin here (on Friday night include all words in brackets):
By your leave, my masters, rabbis and teachers:

בָּרוּךְ *Blessed are you, HASHEM, our God, King of the universe, Who creates the fruit of the vine.* (All present respond— *Amen.)*

(1) *Genesis* 1:31-2:3.

בָּרוּךְ אַתָּה יהוה אֱלֹהֵינוּ מֶלֶךְ הָעוֹלָם, אֲשֶׁר בָּחַר בָּנוּ מִכָּל עָם, וְרוֹמְמָנוּ מִכָּל לָשׁוֹן, וְקִדְּשָׁנוּ בְּמִצְוֹתָיו. וַתִּתֶּן לָנוּ יהוה אֱלֹהֵינוּ בְּאַהֲבָה [שַׁבָּתוֹת לִמְנוּחָה וּ]מוֹעֲדִים לְשִׂמְחָה חַגִּים וּזְמַנִּים לְשָׂשׂוֹן, אֶת יוֹם [הַשַּׁבָּת הַזֶּה וְאֶת יוֹם] חַג הַסֻּכּוֹת הַזֶּה, זְמַן שִׂמְחָתֵנוּ [בְּאַהֲבָה] מִקְרָא קֹדֶשׁ, זֵכֶר לִיצִיאַת מִצְרָיִם. כִּי בָנוּ בָחַרְתָּ וְאוֹתָנוּ קִדַּשְׁתָּ מִכָּל הָעַמִּים, [וְשַׁבָּת] וּמוֹעֲדֵי קָדְשֶׁךָ [בְּאַהֲבָה וּבְרָצוֹן] בְּשִׂמְחָה וּבְשָׂשׂוֹן הִנְחַלְתָּנוּ. בָּרוּךְ אַתָּה יהוה, מְקַדֵּשׁ [הַשַּׁבָּת וְ]יִשְׂרָאֵל וְהַזְּמַנִּים. (All present respond— אָמֵן.)

On Saturday night, add the following two *Havdalah* blessings. A multi-wicked candle or two ordinary candles with flames touching each other should be held before the person reciting the *Havdalah*. After the first blessing, hold the fingers up to the flames to see the reflected light.

בָּרוּךְ אַתָּה יהוה אֱלֹהֵינוּ מֶלֶךְ הָעוֹלָם, בּוֹרֵא מְאוֹרֵי הָאֵשׁ.

(All present respond— אָמֵן.)

בָּרוּךְ אַתָּה יהוה אֱלֹהֵינוּ מֶלֶךְ הָעוֹלָם, הַמַּבְדִּיל בֵּין קֹדֶשׁ לְחוֹל, בֵּין אוֹר לְחֹשֶׁךְ, בֵּין יִשְׂרָאֵל לָעַמִּים, בֵּין יוֹם הַשְּׁבִיעִי לְשֵׁשֶׁת יְמֵי הַמַּעֲשֶׂה. בֵּין קְדֻשַּׁת שַׁבָּת לִקְדֻשַּׁת יוֹם טוֹב הִבְדַּלְתָּ, וְאֶת יוֹם הַשְּׁבִיעִי מִשֵּׁשֶׁת יְמֵי הַמַּעֲשֶׂה קִדַּשְׁתָּ, הִבְדַּלְתָּ וְקִדַּשְׁתָּ אֶת עַמְּךָ יִשְׂרָאֵל בִּקְדֻשָּׁתֶךָ. בָּרוּךְ אַתָּה יהוה, הַמַּבְדִּיל בֵּין קֹדֶשׁ לְקֹדֶשׁ.

(All present respond— אָמֵן.)

If, for whatever the reason, one does not recite *Kiddush* in a *succah,* the following blessing is omitted. On the second night of Succos, some reverse the order of the following two blessings.

בָּרוּךְ אַתָּה יהוה אֱלֹהֵינוּ מֶלֶךְ הָעוֹלָם, אֲשֶׁר קִדְּשָׁנוּ בְּמִצְוֹתָיו וְצִוָּנוּ לֵישֵׁב בַּסֻּכָּה. (All present respond— אָמֵן.)

בָּרוּךְ אַתָּה יהוה אֱלֹהֵינוּ מֶלֶךְ הָעוֹלָם, שֶׁהֶחֱיָנוּ וְקִיְּמָנוּ וְהִגִּיעָנוּ לַזְּמַן הַזֶּה. (All present respond— אָמֵן.)

The daytime *Kiddush* appears on page 492.

יציאה מן הסוכה

Before leaving the *succah* for the last time one says:

יְהִי רָצוֹן מִלְּפָנֶיךָ,* יהוה אֱלֹהֵינוּ וֵאלֹהֵי אֲבוֹתֵינוּ, כְּשֵׁם שֶׁקִּיַּמְתִּי וְיָשַׁבְתִּי בַּסֻּכָּה זוֹ, כֵּן אֶזְכֶּה לְשָׁנָה הַבָּאָה לֵישֵׁב בְּסֻכַּת עוֹרוֹ שֶׁל לִוְיָתָן.* לְשָׁנָה הַבָּאָה בִּירוּשָׁלָיִם.

יְצִיאָה מִן הַסֻּכָּה / FAREWELL TO THE SUCCAH

יְהִי רָצוֹן מִלְּפָנֶיךָ — *May it be Your will.* We take leave of the *succah* with a prayer that next year we can experience the joy of deliverance, so that all the symbolic holiness of the *Succos* can be realized in our national and personal lives. These symbols are discussed at length in the ArtScroll *Succah*, particularly the Overview. In this brief prayer we specify only the '*succah* of the skin of

בָּרוּךְ *Blessed are you, HASHEM, our God, King of the universe, Who has chosen us from every people, exalted us above every tongue, and sanctified us with His commandments. And You gave us, HASHEM, our God, with love [Sabbaths for rest], appointed festivals for gladness, festivals and times for joy, [this day of Sabbath and] Succos, the time of our gladness [with love] a holy convocation, a memorial of the Exodus from Egypt. For You have chosen us and You have sanctified us above all the peoples, [and the Sabbath] and Your holy festivals [in love and in favor] in gladness and in joy have You granted us as a heritage. Blessed are You, HASHEM, Who sanctifies [the Sabbath and] Israel and the seasons.* (All present respond—*Amen.*)

On Saturday night, add the following two *Havdalah* blessings. A multi-wicked candle or two ordinary candles with flames touching each other should be held before the person reciting the *Havdalah*. After the first blessing, hold the fingers up to the flames to see the reflected light.

בָּרוּךְ *Blessed are you, HASHEM, our God, King of the universe, Who creates the illumination of the fire.* (All present respond—*Amen.*)

בָּרוּךְ *Blessed are you, HASHEM, our God, King of the universe, Who distinguishes between the sacred and secular, between light and darkness, between Israel and the peoples, between the seventh day and the six days of labor. Between sanctity of the Sabbaths and the sanctity of the holidays You have distinguished, and the seventh day, from among the six days of labor You have sanctified. You have distinguished and You have sanctified Your people Israel with Your holiness. Blessed are You, HASHEM, Who distinguishes between holiness and holiness.* (All present respond—*Amen.*)

If, for whatever the reason, one does not recite *Kiddush* in a *succah*, the following blessing is omitted. On the second night of Succos, some reverse the order of the following two blessings.

בָּרוּךְ *Blessed are You HASHEM, our God, King of the universe, Who has sanctified us with His commandments and has commanded us to dwell in the Succah.* (All present respond—*Amen.*)

בָּרוּךְ *Blessed are you, HASHEM, our God, King of the universe, Who has kept us alive, sustained us, and brought us to this season.* (All present respond—*Amen.*)

The daytime *Kiddush* appears on page 492.

FAREWELL TO THE SUCCAH

Before leaving the *succah* for the last time one says:

יְהִי רָצוֹן *May it be Your will,* HASHEM, our God and the God of our forefathers, that just as I have fulfilled [the mitzvah] and dwelled in this succah, so may I merit in the coming year to dwell in the succah of the skin of Leviathan.* Next year in Jerusalem.*

---

the Leviathan' and the hope that we soon be in Jerusalem upon the coming of Messiah.

בְּסֻכַּת עוֹרוֹ שֶׁל לִוְיָתָן — *In the succah of the skin of Leviathan.* The Leviathan was a monstrous fish created on the fifth day of Creation. Its story is related at length in the Talmud (*Bava Basra* 74b), where it is told that the Leviathan will be slain and its flesh served as a feast to the righteous in Time to Come, and its skin used to cover the tent where the banquet will take place. [See commentary to *Akdamus*, p. 719.]

﴾ סדר הושענות ﴿

Each day's *Hoshana* service begins with this introductory stanza chanted responsively.

הוֹשַׁעְנָא,* לְמַעַנְךָ אֱלֹהֵינוּ, הוֹשַׁעְנָא.
הוֹשַׁעְנָא, לְמַעַנְךָ בּוֹרְאֵנוּ, הוֹשַׁעְנָא.
הוֹשַׁעְנָא, לְמַעַנְךָ גּוֹאֲלֵנוּ, הוֹשַׁעְנָא.
הוֹשַׁעְנָא, לְמַעַנְךָ דּוֹרְשֵׁנוּ, הוֹשַׁעְנָא.

למען אמתך

לְמַעַן אֲמִתָּךְ. לְמַעַן בְּרִיתָךְ. לְמַעַן גָּדְלָךְ וְתִפְאַרְתָּךְ. לְמַעַן דָּתָךְ.
לְמַעַן הוֹדָךְ. לְמַעַן וִעוּדָךְ. לְמַעַן זִכְרָךְ. לְמַעַן חַסְדָּךְ.

◆§ The Hoshana Service

On each day of Succos, immediately after the *chazzan's* repetition of the *Shemoneh Esrei* of *Mussaf,* special prayers called *Hoshanos* are recited. The Ark is opened and a Torah scroll is removed and carried to the *bimah* where one member of the congregation holds it. The Ark remains open and the Torah is held at the *bimah* until the conclusion of the *Hoshana* service. The *lulav* and *esrog* are held during the entire service.

Four introductory stiches are recited responsively — *chazzan* then congregation — each day. Upon completing the introductory verses the *chazzan* leads all males who are carrying *lulav* and *esrog* around the *bimah* as he reads the day's *Hoshana* [see below] responsively with the congregation. He should time his steps to complete the circuit as he recites the last verse of the *Hoshana.*

Two factors determine which *Hoshana* is recited: (a) the day of the week; and (b) the day of the month. The accompanying diagrams record the four calendrical possibilites for the Festival of Succos, and the *Hoshana* recited in each case.

On the Sabbath three changes are made in the service: (a) Although the Ark is opened, a Torah is not removed; (b) the *bimah* is not circled; and (c) the *lulav* and *esrog* are omitted.

Hoshana Rabbah: On Hoshana Rabbah, the seventh day of Succos, all the Torah scrolls in the Ark are brought to the *bimah,* held by a member of the congregation. On this day the *bimah* is circled seven times, as seven *Hoshana* prayers are recited. After each *Hoshana,* a Scriptural verse related to the *Sefirah*-emanation [see commentary p. 728] of that *hakafah*-circuit is recited. When the seven circuits have been completed, additional prayers, beginning on page 740, are recited.

First Day Succos on Monday

S	M	T	W	T	F	S
14	**15** p. 726 למען אמתך FOR THE SAKE OF YOUR TRUTH	**16** p. 728 אבן שתיה FOUNDATION STONE	**17** p. 734 אערוך שועי I SHALL ARRANGE MY PRAYER	**18** p. 728 אום אני חומה NATION THAT DECLARES, 'I AM A WALL!'	**19** p. 734 אל למושעות O GOD! BRING ABOUT SALVATIONS	**20** p. 736 אום נצורה NATION PROTECTED
21 הושענא רבה **HOSHANA RABBAH**	**22**	**23**	**24**	**25**	**26**	**27**

First Day Succos on Tuesday

S	M	T	W	T	F	S
13	**14**	**15** p. 726 למען אמתך FOR THE SAKE OF YOUR TRUTH	**16** p. 728 אבן שתיה FOUNDATION STONE	**17** p. 734 אערוך שועי I SHALL ARRANGE MY PRAYER	**18** *p. 734 אל למושעות O GOD! BRING ABOUT SALVATIONS	**19** p. 736 אום נצורה NATION PROTECTED
20 p. 728 אדון המושיע LORD WHO SAVES	**21** הושענא רבה **HOSHANA RABBAH**	**22**	**23**	**24**	**25**	**26**

*Some congregations substitute אוֹם אֲנִי חוֹמָה, *Nation That Declares (p. 728).*

HOSHANOS

Each day's *Hoshana* service begins with this introductory stanza chanted responsively.

הוֹשַׁעְנָא *Please save* — for Your sake, our God! Please save!*
Please save — for Your sake, our Creator! Please save!
Please save — for Your sake, our Redeemer! Please save!
Please save — for Your sake, our Attender! Please save!

FOR THE SAKE OF YOUR TRUTH

לְמַעַן אֲמִתָּךְ *For the sake of Your Truth; for the sake of Your Covenant; for the sake of Your Greatness and Your Splendor; for the sake of Your Mandate; for the sake of Your Glory; for the sake of Your Meeting House; for the sake of Your Mention; for the sake of Your Kindness; for*

First Day Succos on Thursday

S	M	T	W	T	F	S
11	12	13	14	15 p. 726 למען אמתך FOR THE SAKE OF YOUR TRUTH	16 p. 728 אבן שתיה FOUNDATION STONE	17 p. 736 אום נצורה NATION PROTECTED
18 p. 734 אערוך שועי I SHALL ARRANGE MY PRAYER	19 p. 734 אל למושעות O GOD! BRING ABOUT SALVATIONS	20 p. 728 אדון המושיע LORD WHO SAVES	21 הושענא רבה HOSHANA RABBAH	22	23	24

First Day Succos on the Sabbath

S	M	T	W	T	F	S
9	10	11	12	13	14	15 p. 736 אום נצורה NATION PROTECTED
16 p. 726 למען אמתך FOR THE SAKE OF YOUR TRUTH	17 p. 734 אערוך שועי I SHALL ARRANGE MY PRAYER	18 p. 728 אבן שתיה FOUNDATION STONE	19 p. 734 אל למושעות O GOD! BRING ABOUT SALVATIONS	20 p. 728 אדון המושיע LORD WHO SAVES	21 הושענא רבה HOSHANA RABBAH	22

הוֹשַׁעְנוֹת / HOSHANOS

[The commentary below is abridged from the ArtScroll *Hoshanos*, by Rabbi Avie Gold, which contains commentary to every phrase of the *Hoshana* prayers.]

הוֹשַׁעְנָא — *Please save.* This word is compounded of the words הוֹשַׁע, *save,* and נָא, *please.* Indeed, many *siddurim* give it as two words. נָא may also be translated *now;* thus, הוֹשַׁעְנָא would mean *save now.*

In the introductory stanza each verse begins and ends with the word הוֹשַׁעְנָא. Although it does not appear in the *siddurim,* most congregations add the word הוֹשַׁעְנָא, *please save,* to each verse of each *Hoshana,* either:
—before it (הוֹשַׁעְנָא לְמַעַן אֲמִתָּךְ);
—after it (לְמַעַן אֲמִתָּךְ הוֹשַׁעְנָא);
—or both (הוֹשַׁעְנָא לְמַעַן אֲמִתָּךְ הוֹשַׁעְנָא).

לְמַעַן אֲמִתָּךְ / For the Sake of Your Truth

Each of the *Hoshanos* comprises twenty-two verses or stanzas which follow an alphabetical pattern. In this first *Hoshana,* each verse begins with the word לְמַעַן, *for the sake of,* followed by one of many attributes of God; accordingly, it may be considered an extension of the introductory stanza which directly precedes it *(Rashi).* It is recited on the first day of the festival (unless that day is a Sabbath). It is recited again during the first *hakafah*-circuit of *Hoshana Rabbah,* when the final verdict which was written on *Rosh Hashanah* and sealed on *Yom Kippur* is given its final seal. Since the seal of God is אֱמֶת, *Truth (Shabbos* 55a), it is fitting that the *hakafah*-circuits on the day of the final seal begin by calling upon the attribute of אֱמֶת, *Truth (Bnei Yisas'char).*

לְמַעַן טוּבָךְ. לְמַעַן יִחוּדָךְ. לְמַעַן **כְּ**בוֹדָךְ. לְמַעַן **לִ**מּוּדָךְ. לְמַעַן **מַ**לְכוּתָךְ. לְמַעַן **נִ**צְחָךְ. לְמַעַן **ס**וֹדָךְ. לְמַעַן **עֻ**זָּךְ. לְמַעַן **פְּ**אֵרָךְ. לְמַעַן **צִ**דְקָתָךְ. לְמַעַן **קְ**דֻשָּׁתָךְ. לְמַעַן **רַ**חֲמֶיךָ הָרַבִּים. לְמַעַן **שְׁ**כִינָתָךְ. לְמַעַן **תְּ**הִלָּתָךְ.

During the first six days of Succos continue אֲנִי וָהוֹ (p. 734). On Hoshana Rabbah continue:

כִּי אָמַרְתִּי עוֹלָם חֶסֶד יִבָּנֶה.[1]

אבן שתיה

אֶבֶן שְׁתִיָּה. **בֵּ**ית הַבְּחִירָה. **גֹּ**רֶן אָרְנָן. **דְּ**בִיר הַמֻּצְנָע. **הַ**ר הַמּוֹרִיָּה. **וְ**הַר יֵרָאֶה. **זְ**בוּל תִּפְאַרְתֶּךָ. **חָ**נָה דָוִד. **טוֹ**ב הַלְּבָנוֹן. **יְ**פֵה נוֹף מְשׂוֹשׂ כָּל הָאָרֶץ. **כְּ**לִילַת יֹפִי. **לִ**ינַת הַצֶּדֶק. **מָ**כוֹן לְשִׁבְתֶּךָ. **נָ**וֶה שַׁאֲנָן. **סֻ**כַּת שָׁלֵם. **עֲ**לִיַּת שְׁבָטִים. **פִּ**נַּת יִקְרַת. **צִ**יּוֹן הַמְּצֻיֶּנֶת. **קֹ**דֶשׁ הַקֳּדָשִׁים. **רָ**צוּף אַהֲבָה. **שְׁ**כִינַת כְּבוֹדֶךָ. **תֵּ**ל תַּלְפִּיּוֹת.

During the first six days of Succos continue אֲנִי וָהוֹ (p. 734). On Hoshana Rabbah continue:

לְךָ זְרוֹעַ עִם גְּבוּרָה, תָּעֹז יָדְךָ תָּרוּם יְמִינֶךָ.[2]

אום אני חומה

אוֹם אֲנִי חוֹמָה. **בָּ**רָה כַּחַמָּה. **גּ**וֹלָה וְסוּרָה. **דָּ**מְתָה לְתָמָר. **הַ**הֲרוּגָה עָלֶיךָ. **וְ**נֶחְשֶׁבֶת כְּצֹאן טִבְחָה. **זְ**רוּיָה בֵּין מַכְעִיסֶיהָ. **חֲ**בוּקָה וּדְבוּקָה בָךְ. **טוֹ**עֶנֶת עֻלָּךְ. **יְ**חִידָה לְיַחֲדָךְ. **כְּ**בוּשָׁה בַּגּוֹלָה. **לוֹ**מֶדֶת יִרְאָתָךְ. **מְ**רוּטַת לֶחִי. **נְ**תוּנָה לְמַכִּים. **ס**וֹבֶלֶת סִבְלָךְ. **עֲ**נִיָּה סֹעֲרָה. **פְּ**דוּיַת טוֹבִיָּה. **צֹ**אן קָדָשִׁים. **קְ**הִלּוֹת יַעֲקֹב. **רְ**שׁוּמִים בִּשְׁמֶךָ. **שׁוֹ**אֲגִים הוֹשַׁעְנָא. **תְּ**מוּכִים עָלֶיךָ.

During the first six days of Succos continue אֲנִי וָהוֹ (p. 734). On Hoshana Rabbah continue:

תִּתֵּן אֱמֶת לְיַעֲקֹב, חֶסֶד לְאַבְרָהָם.[3]

אדון המושיע

אָדוֹן הַמּוֹשִׁיעַ. **בִּ**לְתְּךָ אֵין לְהוֹשִׁיעַ. **גִּ**בּוֹר וְרַב לְהוֹשִׁיעַ. **דַּ**לּוֹתִי וְלִי יְהוֹשִׁיעַ. **הָ**אֵל הַמּוֹשִׁיעַ. **וּ**מַצִּיל וּמוֹשִׁיעַ. **ז**וֹעֲקֶיךָ

Hakafah-circuits and Sefirah-emanations

Man can have no conception of God Himself, for His true Being is beyond human intelligence. All we can know are His manifestations such as mercy, power, and judgment, and even these can come to us only through intermediaries. These intermediaries are called *Sefiros,* generally translated *emanations.*

Each of the seven *hakafah*-circuits of *Hoshana Rabbah* is related to one of seven *Sefirah*-emanations. A Scriptural passage which mentions the applicable *Sefirah* is recited after each *hakafah.* The seven *Sefiros* are: חֶסֶד, *Kindness;* גְּבוּרָה, *Strength;* תִּפְאֶרֶת, *Splendor;* נֶצַח, *Triumph;* הוֹד, *Glory;* יְסוֹד, *Foundation;* and מַלְכוּת, *Kingship.* These *Sefiros* are in turn assigned as the attributes of the seven patriarchs who serve as the *ushpizin*-guests on *Succos* (see page 720): Abraham, Isaac, Jacob, Moses, Aaron, Joseph and King David.

אֶבֶן שְׁתִיָּה / Foundation Stone

All twenty-two verses of this prayer are allusions to either the Holy Temple or the city of Jerusalem in which it was located. Most of the descriptive expressions are of Scriptural derivation; the remainder are of Talmudic origin.

The intent of all these verses is the same, namely: Please save (i.e., redeem) the *Beis HaMidkash* from its present desolation and desecration; from the wild foxes that prowl over it [see *Lamentations* 5:18] *(Beis Avraham);* that it may be rebuilt, speedily in our days *(Shaar HaShamayim).*

the sake of Your Goodness; for the sake of Your Oneness; for the sake of Your Honor; for the sake of Your Teaching; for the sake of Your Kingship; for the sake of Your Triumph; for the sake of Your Counsel; for the sake of Your Power; for the sake of Your Beauty; for the sake of Your Righteousness; for the sake of Your Sanctity; for the sake of Your numerous Mercies; for the sake of Your Shechinah; for the sake of Your Praise.

During the first six days of Succos continue *Ani Vaho* (p. 735). On Hoshana Rabbah continue:

For I have said: The world shall be built with kindness.[1]

FOUNDATION STONE

אֶבֶן שְׁתִיָּה *Foundation stone; chosen Temple; Arnan's granary; hidden rendezvous; Mount Moriah; Mount He-is-seen; residence of Your Splendor; where David resided; goodness of Lebanon; fairest of brides; joy of all the earth; perfectly beautiful; lodge of righteousness; prepared for Your dwelling; tranquil abode; Tabernacle of Salem; pilgrimage of the tribes; valuable cornerstone; the distinguished Zion; Holy of Holies; decked with love; resting place of Your Honor; hill of Talpios.*

During the first six days of Succos continue *Ani Vaho* (p. 735). On Hoshana Rabbah continue:

Yours is the arm with strength, show us the power of Your hand,
raise high Your right hand.[2]

NATION THAT DECLARES

אוֹם אֲנִי חוֹמָה *Nation that declares, 'I am a wall!' Brilliant as the sun — yet exiled and displaced; likened to a palm tree — yet murdered for Your sake and regarded like a sheep for slaughter; although scattered among her provocateurs, she hugs and cleaves to You and bears Your yoke — unique in declaring Your Oneness. While vanquished in exile, she learns Your awesomeness. Plucked of cheek, given over to the whippers, she shoulders Your burden. A storm-tossed pauper is she who was redeemed by Moses. Sacred sheep, congregations of Jacob, inscribed with Your Name, they cry, 'Please save us!' — they rely upon You!*

During the first six days of Succos continue *Ani Vaho* (p. 735). On Hoshana Rabbah continue:

Grant truth to Jacob, kindness to Abraham.[3]

LORD WHO SAVES

אָדוֹן הַמּוֹשִׁיעַ *Lord Who saves, other than You there is no savior. You are powerful and abundantly able to save. I am impoverished, yet You shall save me. God is the Savior, He delivers and saves. Those who cry to*

(1) *Psalms* 89:3. (2) 89:14. (3) *Michah* 7:20.

אוֹם אֲנִי חוֹמָה / Nation That Declares

Many metaphors are used in Scripture and Rabbinic writing to describe the nation of Israel. During the third *hakafah*-circuit, which corresponds to the Patriarch Jacob (Israel), from whom the nation derived its name, an alphabetical catalogue of such metaphors is chanted in prayer for the nation's redemption and salvation *(Bnei Yisas'char).*

Most of the epithets in this *Hoshana* are particularly applicable to Israel during its decline and exile. Material poverty is juxtaposed with spiritual wealth as the *paytan* paints a word-picture depicting the firm faith of God's chosen people.

אָדוֹן הַמּוֹשִׁיעַ / Lord Who Saves

Every part of Creation may be assigned to one

תּוֹשִׁיעַ. **ח**וֹכֶיךָ הוֹשִׁיעַ. **ט**ְלָאֶיךָ תַּשְׂבִּיעַ. **י**ְבוּל לְהַשְׁפִּיעַ. **כּ**ָל שִׂיחַ תַּדְשֵׁא וְתוֹשִׁיעַ. **ל**ְגֵיא בַּל תַּרְשִׁיעַ. **מ**ְגָדִים תַּמְתִּיק וְתוֹשִׁיעַ. **נ**ְשִׂיאִים לְהַסִּיעַ. **שׂ**ְעִירִים לְהָנִיעַ. **ע**ֲנָנִים מִלְּהַמְנִיעַ. **פּ**וֹתֵחַ יָד וּמַשְׂבִּיעַ. **צ**ְמֵאֶיךָ תַּשְׂבִּיעַ. **ק**וֹרְאֶיךָ תּוֹשִׁיעַ. **ר**ְחוּמֶיךָ תּוֹשִׁיעַ. **שׁ**וֹחֲרֶיךָ הוֹשִׁיעַ. **ת**ְּמִימֶיךָ תּוֹשִׁיעַ.

During the first six days of Succos continue אֲנִי וָהוֹ (p. 734). On Hoshana Rabbah continue:

נְעִמוֹת בִּימִינְךָ נֶצַח.[1]

אדם ובהמה

אָדָם וּבְהֵמָה. **בָּ**שָׂר וְרוּחַ וּנְשָׁמָה. **גִּ**יד וְעֶצֶם וְקָרְמָה. **דְּ**מוּת וְצֶלֶם וְרִקְמָה. **הוֹ**ד לַהֶבֶל דָּמָה. **וְ**נִמְשַׁל כַּבְּהֵמוֹת נִדְמָה. **זִ**יו וְתֹאַר וְקוֹמָה. **חִ**דּוּשׁ פְּנֵי אֲדָמָה. **טִ**יעַת עֲצֵי נְשַׁמָּה. **יְ**קָבִים וְקָמָה. **כְּ**רָמִים וְשִׁקְמָה. לְתֵבֵל הַמְּסֻיָּמָה. **מִ**טְרוֹת עֹז לְסַמְּמָה. **נְ**שִׁיָּה לְקַיְּמָה. **שִׂ**יחִים לְקוֹמְמָה. **עֲ**דָנִים לְעָצְמָה. **פְּ**רָחִים לְהַעֲצִימָה. **צְ**מָחִים לְגָשְׁמָה. **קָ**רִים לְזָרְמָה. **רְ**בִיבִים לְשַׁלְּמָה. **שְׁ**תִיָּה לְרוֹמְמָה. **תְּ**לוּיָה עַל בְּלִימָה.

יהוה אֲדֹנֵינוּ מָה אַדִּיר שִׁמְךָ בְּכָל הָאָרֶץ, אֲשֶׁר תְּנָה הוֹדְךָ עַל הַשָּׁמָיִם.[2]

אדמה מארר

אֲדָמָה מֵאֶרֶר. **בְּ**הֵמָה מִמְּשַׁכֶּלֶת. **גֹּ**רֶן מִגָּזָם. **דָּ**גָן מִדַּלֶּקֶת. **הוֹ**ן מִמְּאֵרָה. **וְ**אֹכֶל מִמְּהוּמָה. **זַ**יִת מִנֶּשֶׁל. **חִ**טָּה מֵחָגָב. **טֶ**רֶף מִגּוֹבַי. **יֶ**קֶב מִיֶּלֶק. **כֶּ**רֶם מִתּוֹלַעַת. **לֶ**קֶשׁ מֵאַרְבֶּה. **מֶ**גֶד מִצְּלָצַל. **נֶ**פֶשׁ מִבֶּהָלָה. **שֹׂ**בַע מִסָּלְעָם. **עֲ**דָרִים מִדַּלּוּת. **פֵּ**רוֹת מִשִּׁדָּפוֹן. **צֹ**אן מִצַּמִּיתוּת. **קָ**צִיר מִקְּלָלָה. **רֹ**ב מֵרָזוֹן. **שִׁ**בֹּלֶת מִצִּנָּמוֹן. **תְּ**בוּאָה מֵחָסִיל.

צַדִּיק יהוה בְּכָל דְּרָכָיו, וְחָסִיד בְּכָל מַעֲשָׂיו.[3]

למען איתן

לְמַעַן אֵיתָן* הַנִּזְרָק בְּלַהַב אֵשׁ.
לְמַעַן **בֵּ**ן הַנֶּעֱקַד עַל עֵצִים וָאֵשׁ.

---

of four kingdoms or categories of existence. In ascending spiritual order they are: דוֹמֵם, *mineral* [lit. *silent*]; צוֹמֵחַ, *vegetable* [lit. *sprouting*]; חַי, *animal* [lit. *living*]; and מְדַבֵּר, *human* [lit. *speaking*].

In the Divine plan for the world, each member of one realm is capable of becoming elevated to a higher one. Indeed, this is the purpose of its existence. The minerals in the soil, water, and air are absorbed by plants, which in turn, serve as food for the animals. Finally, these become the fare of Man. Scripture alludes to this system of elevation: *And I shall give grass* [*vegetable*] *in your field* [*mineral*] *for your cattle* [*animal*] *and you* [*Man*] *shall eat and be sated (Deuteronomy* 11:15).

But does this process of uplifting end with man? Is man the perfect being? Certainly not. Man must raise himself from the evil which fills his heart. The last words of the above verse, *and you shall eat and be sated,* tell how. This same phrase also appears as the opening of another verse which continues: *and you shall bless* HASHEM, *your God.* Recitation of a blessing is the fulfillment of a *mitzvah,* and, as Kabbalah teaches, while study of Torah provides the soul's sustenance, the performance of *mitzvos* supplies its raiment. Man must use the baser elements of

You — save; those who yearn for You — save. Satiate Your lambs, cause an abundance of crops, of trees, of vegetation — save. Do not condemn the ground, but sweeten the luscious fruits — save. Let the wind bring the soaring clouds, let the stormy rains be emplaced, let the clouds not be withheld, He Who opens a hand and satisfies Your thirsty ones — satisfy; Your callers — save; Your beloved — save; Your seekers — save; Your wholesome ones — save.

During the first six days of Succos continue *Ani Vaho* (p. 735). On Hoshana Rabbah continue:

There is delight at Your right hand for triumph.[1]

MAN AND BEAST

אָדָם וּבְהֵמָה *Man and beast: Flesh, spirit and soul; sinew, bone and skin; likeness and image — a tapestry; splendor resembling futility, compared to the likeness of beasts — luster, figure and stature. Renew the face of the earth — planting trees in desolate lands, winepresses and stands of grain, vineyards and sycamores. To the demarcated land — to heal with powerful rains, to give life to forsaken wastes, to sustain with vegetation, to enhance with sweet fruits, to invigorate with flowers. To rain on the sproutings — to pour a stream of cool waters, to cloak with droplets, to elevate the thirsty earth which is suspended upon silence.*

HASHEM, our Lord, how mighty is Your Name throughout the earth; for it were fit that You place Your splendor above the heavens.[2]

GROUND FROM ACCURSEDNESS

אֲדָמָה מֵאֶרֶר *Ground from accursedness; beast from aborting; granary from gazam; grain from scorch; wealth from affliction; food from confusion; olives from dropping; wheat from chagav; nourishment from govai; wine-press from yelek; vineyard from worms; late crop from arbeh; fruit from tzlatzal; soul from panic; satiety from salam; flocks from leanness; fruits from the east wind; sheep from extermination; harvest from curse; abundance from emaciation; grain spikes from withering; crops from chasil.*

HASHEM is righteous in all His ways; virtuous in all His deeds.[3]

IN THE MERIT OF THE COURAGEOUS ONE

לְמַעַן אֵיתָן *In the merit of the courageous one [Abraham]**
who was hurled into flaming fire.
In the merit of the son [Isaac] who was bound upon the wood near the fire.

(1) *Psalms* 16:11. (2) 8:2. (3) 145:17.

---

creation in the fulfillment of *mitzvos*, but he needs guidance to use them wisely.

In the next three *Hoshanos* we invoke Divine protection for all of these realms, and we pray for our own welfare — *Lord Who saves ... save now man and beast ... the ground [and its produce] from accursedness.*

אֲדָמָה מֵאֶרֶר / Ground from Accursedness

This *Hoshana* enumerates a whole litany of destructive forces that could destroy the world's food supply. Appearing on the list are eight species of locust — *gazam, chagav, govai, yelek, arbeh, tzlatzal, salam* and *chasil.*

לְמַעַן אֵיתָן / In the Merit of the Courageous One

Who planted the seeds of superhuman fortitude and dignity with which millennia of Jews have endured hardship and privation? From

לְמַעַן **גִּ**בּוֹר הַנֶּאֱבַק עִם שַׂר אֵשׁ.
לְמַעַן **דְּ**גָלִים נָחִיתָ בְּאוֹר וַעֲנַן אֵשׁ.
לְמַעַן **הֹ**עֲלָה לַמָּרוֹם וְנִתְעַלָּה כְּמַלְאֲכֵי אֵשׁ.
לְמַעַן **וְ**הוּא לָךְ כְּסֶגֶן בְּאֶרְאֶלֵּי אֵשׁ.
לְמַעַן **זֶ**בֶד דִּבְּרוֹת הַנִּתּוּנוֹת מֵאֵשׁ.
לְמַעַן **חִ**פּוּי יְרִיעוֹת עֲנַן אֵשׁ.
לְמַעַן **טֶ**כֶס הַר יָרַדְתָּ עָלָיו בָּאֵשׁ.
לְמַעַן **יְ**דִידוּת בַּיִת אֲשֶׁר אָהַבְתָּ מִשְּׁמֵי אֵשׁ.
לְמַעַן **כָּ**מַהּ עַד שָׁקְעָה הָאֵשׁ.
לְמַעַן **לָ**קַח מַחְתַּת אֵשׁ וְהֵסִיר חֲרוֹן אֵשׁ.
לְמַעַן **מְ**קַנֵּא קִנְאָה גְדוֹלָה בָּאֵשׁ.
לְמַעַן **נָ**ף יָדוֹ וְיָרְדוּ אַבְנֵי אֵשׁ.
לְמַעַן **שָׂ**ם טְלֵה חָלָב כְּלִיל אֵשׁ.
לְמַעַן **עָ**מַד בַּגֹּרֶן וְנִתְרַצָּה בָאֵשׁ.
לְמַעַן **פִּ**לֵּל בָּעֲזָרָה וְיָרְדָה הָאֵשׁ.
לְמַעַן **צִ**יר עָלָה וְנִתְעַלָּה בְּרֶכֶב וְסוּסֵי אֵשׁ.
לְמַעַן **קְ**דוֹשִׁים מֻשְׁלָכִים בָּאֵשׁ.
לְמַעַן **רִ**בּוֹ רִבְּבָן חָז וְנַהֲרֵי אֵשׁ.
לְמַעַן **שְׁ**מְמוֹת עִירְךָ הַשְּׂרוּפָה בָאֵשׁ.
לְמַעַן **תּ**וֹלְדוֹת אַלּוּפֵי יְהוּדָה תָּשִׂים כְּכִיּוֹר אֵשׁ.

לְךָ יהוה הַגְּדֻלָּה וְהַגְּבוּרָה וְהַתִּפְאֶרֶת וְהַנֵּצַח וְהַהוֹד כִּי כֹל בַּשָּׁמַיִם וּבָאָרֶץ, לְךָ יהוה הַמַּמְלָכָה וְהַמִּתְנַשֵּׂא לְכֹל לְרֹאשׁ.[1] וְהָיָה יהוה לְמֶלֶךְ עַל כָּל הָאָרֶץ, בַּיּוֹם הַהוּא יִהְיֶה יהוה אֶחָד וּשְׁמוֹ אֶחָד.[2] וּבְתוֹרָתְךָ כָּתוּב לֵאמֹר: שְׁמַע יִשְׂרָאֵל יהוה אֱלֹהֵינוּ יהוה אֶחָד.[3] בָּרוּךְ שֵׁם כְּבוֹד מַלְכוּתוֹ לְעוֹלָם וָעֶד.

On Hoshana Rabbah continue אֲנִי וָהוֹ (p. 734).

---

whom did Israel inherit the ability to remain holy even amid holocaust? *Ramban* provides the answer: כָּל מַה שֶּׁאֵירַע לְאָבוֹת סִמָּן לְבָנִים, *all that happened to the Patriarchs is of prophetic significance to their descendants.* For this reason, too, the Torah often relates seemingly unimportant events in the lives of our forebears.

Not only did the deeds of the Patriarchs insure the posterity of Israel, but they also inculcated into the nation's fiber the traits which engendered those deeds. A Talmudic dictum teaches: תַּמָּה זְכוּת אָבוֹת, *the merits of the Patriarchs have expired (Shabbos* 55a); nevertheless, the qualities of character with which their merits have imbued their offspring have not expired. Because we still exhibit Abraham's kindness, Isaac's courage, and Jacob's adherence to truth, because we follow the trails blazed by Moses and Aaron, Joshua and Samuel, David and Solomon, because we

In the merit of the strong one [Jacob] who wrestled with a prince of *fire.*
In the merit of the tribal banners which You guided with a light — and a cloud — of *fire.*
In the merit of him [Moses] who was raised to the heavens and became as exalted as angels of *fire.*
In the merit of him [Aaron] who was to You like a deputy at the Altars of *fire.*
In the merit of the gift of Commandments presented from a *fire.*
In the merit of the canopy of curtains — a cloud of *fire.*
In the merit of the array at the mountain upon which You descended in *fire.*
In the merit of the love of the Temple which You adored beyond heavens made of *fire.*
In the merit of him [Moses] who yearned until the sinking of the *fire.*
In the merit of him [Aaron] who took a fire pan and removed an anger burning like *fire.*
In the merit of him [Elijah] who zealously took great vengeance with *fire.*
In the merit of him [Joshua] who raised his hand in prayer — and down came stones of *fire.*
In the merit of him [Samuel] who offered a nursing ewe to be completely consumed by *fire.*
In the merit of him [David] who stood in the granary and was shown favor with *fire.*
In the merit of him [Solomon] who prayed in the Courtyard and down came *fire.*
In the merit of the agent [Elijah] who ascended to heaven and was exalted, through a chariot and horses of *fire.*
In the merit of holy ones [Chananiah, Mishael, and Azariah] who were cast into the *fire.*
In the merit of him [Daniel] who saw myriad myriads and streams of *fire.*
In the merit of the ruins of Your city which was devoured in *fire.*
In the merit of the descendants of Judah's princes whom You will set as a flaming *fire.*

לְךָ *Yours,* H*ASHEM*, *is the greatness, the strength, the splendor, the triumph, and the glory, even everything in heaven and earth; Yours,* H*ASHEM*, *is the kingdom, and the sovereignty over every leader.*[1] H*ASHEM* *will be King over all the earth, on that day* H*ASHEM* *will be One and His Name will be One.*[2] *And in Your Torah is written as follows: Hear, O Israel,* H*ASHEM* *is our God,* H*ASHEM* *is the One and Only.*[3] *Blessed is the Name of His glorious kingdom for all eternity.*

On Hoshana Rabbah continue *Ani Vaho* (p. 735).

(1) *II Chronicles* 29:11. (2) *Zechariah* 14:9. (3) *Deuteronomy* 6:4.

maintain and display the unwavering faith of Daniel and his companions, we are able to pray for salvation.

This *Hoshana* traces the achievements of our spiritual models as they were tested with fire, and appeals for salvation in the merit of their indelible imprint upon Israel's national character.

אערוך שועי

אֶעֱרוֹךְ שׁוּעִי. בְּבֵית שַׁוְעִי. גִּלִּיתִי בַצּוֹם פִּשְׁעִי. דְּרַשְׁתִּיךָ בּוֹ לְהוֹשִׁיעִי. הַקְשִׁיבָה לְקוֹל שַׁוְעִי. וְקוּמָה וְהוֹשִׁיעִי. זְכוֹר וְרַחֵם מוֹשִׁיעִי. חַי כֵּן תְּשַׁעְשְׁעִי. טוֹב בְּאֶנֶק שְׁעִי. יָחִישׁ מוֹשִׁיעִי. כַּלֵּה מַרְשִׁיעִי. לְבַל עוֹד תַּרְשִׁיעִי. מַהֵר אֱלֹהֵי יִשְׁעִי. נֶצַח לְהוֹשִׁיעִי. שָׂא נָא עֲוֹן רִשְׁעִי. עֲבוֹר עַל פִּשְׁעִי. פְּנֵה נָא לְהוֹשִׁיעִי. צוּר צַדִּיק מוֹשִׁיעִי. קַבֵּל נָא שַׁוְעִי. רוֹמֵם קֶרֶן יִשְׁעִי. שַׁדַּי מוֹשִׁיעִי. תּוֹפִיעַ וְתוֹשִׁיעִי.

Continue אֲנִי וָהוֹ, below.

אל למושעות

אֵל לְמוֹשָׁעוֹת. בְּאַרְבַּע שְׁבֻעוֹת. גָּשִׁים בְּשַׁוְעוֹת. דּוֹפְקֵי עֶרֶךְ שׁוּעוֹת. הוֹגֵי שַׁעֲשֻׁעוֹת. וְחִידָתָם מִשְׁתַּעַשְׁעוֹת. זוֹעֲקִים לְהַשְׁעוֹת. חוֹכֵי יְשׁוּעוֹת. טְפוּלִים בָּךְ שְׁעוֹת. יוֹדְעֵי בִּין שָׁעוֹת. כּוֹרְעֶיךָ בְּשַׁוְעוֹת. לְהָבִין שְׁמוּעוֹת. מֵפִיק נִשְׁמָעוֹת. נוֹתֵן תְּשׁוּעוֹת. סְפוּרוֹת מַשְׁמָעוֹת. עֵדוֹת מַשְׁמִיעוֹת. פּוֹעֵל יְשׁוּעוֹת. צַדִּיק נוֹשָׁעוֹת. קִרְיַת תְּשׁוּעוֹת. רֶגֶשׁ תְּשֻׁאוֹת. שָׁלֹשׁ שָׁעוֹת. תָּחִישׁ לִתְשׁוּעוֹת.

כהושעת אלים

After each day's *hakafah*-circuit (except on the Sabbath), the following *Hoshana* is recited:

אֲנִי וָהוֹ הוֹשִׁיעָה נָּא.*

כְּהוֹשַׁעְתָּ אֵלִים בְּלוּד עִמָּךְ, בְּצֵאתְךָ לְיֵשַׁע עַמָּךְ, כֵּן הוֹשַׁעְנָא.
כְּהוֹשַׁעְתָּ גּוֹי וֵאלֹהִים,
דְּרוּשִׁים לְיֵשַׁע אֱלֹהִים, כֵּן הוֹשַׁעְנָא.
כְּהוֹשַׁעְתָּ הֲמוֹן צְבָאוֹת,
וְעִמָּם מַלְאֲכֵי צְבָאוֹת, כֵּן הוֹשַׁעְנָא.
כְּהוֹשַׁעְתָּ זַכִּים מִבֵּית עֲבָדִים,
חַנּוּן בְּיָדָם מַעֲבִידִים, כֵּן הוֹשַׁעְנָא.

אֶעֱרוֹךְ שׁוּעִי / I Shall Arrange My Prayer

One must always anticipate troublesome situations and pray for salvation before oppressive times arrive (*Sanhedrin* 44b). When is the opportune time for such prayer?

Seek HASHEM when He may be found; call to Him when He is near (Isaiah 55:6). The Talmud asks, 'When may He be found? When is He near?' and answers, 'During the Ten Days [of Awe] beginning with Rosh Hashanah and culminating with Yom Kippur' (*Rosh HaShanah* 18a).

Now Israel prays that God recall its repentance during the period when God called for it. In response to my having *bared my transgression* before You on Yom Kippur, may You *pardon the iniquity of my wickedness* and *overlook my transgression*. Just as *I sought You on that day, for salvation*, You, in turn *arise ... remember and be merciful, my Savior*. Because this *Hoshana* refers to Yom Kippur it is recited on the third day of Succos [unless that day is the Sabbath], the same day of the week as Yom Kippur.

אֵל לְמוֹשָׁעוֹת / O God! Bring About Salvations

Although the Psalmist uses the phrase אֵל לְמוֹשָׁעוֹת, *God of salvations*, while contrasting God's salvation of Israel with His destruction of its enemies, here it is used to introduce a description of the Jews' clinging to God, and their observance of His *mitzvos*, despite their exile.

I SHALL ARRANGE MY PRAYER

אֶעֱרוֹךְ שׁוּעִי *I shall arrange my prayer in the house of prayer: I have bared, on the fast day, my transgression; I have sought You on that day for salvation. Harken to the sound of my outcry; arise and save me; remember and be merciful, my Savior. Living God — in Your faithfulness let me rejoice. Goodly One — turn to my groan, may my savior hasten. Destroy the one who tempts me to sin, that he may no longer incriminate me. Hasten, God of my salvation, eternally to save me. Please, pardon the iniquity of my wickedness, overlook my transgression, turn, now, and save me. Rock, Righteous One, Who is my Savior — accept now my prayer, elevate the pride of my salvation. Almighty — my Savior, shine Your countenance upon me and save me.*

Continue *Ani Vaho,* below.

O GOD! BRING ABOUT SALVATIONS

אֵל לְמוֹשָׁעוֹת *O God! Bring about salvations because of the four oaths of those who approach with pleas. They knock on the doors where prayers are arranged; they meditate upon the beloved Torah and their riddles are beloved; they cry for attention; they yearn for salvation; they cling to You, to You they turn. They know the understanding of the hours, yet they kneel before You pleading that they may understand the lessons which were heard from Your mouth. O Grantor of salvations, gather the counters that teach the testimony. O Worker of salvations, send the righteous one who will find salvation. For the city of salvations, swarming with masses, during the three hours, hasten the time of salvations.*

AS YOU SAVED THE TEREBINTHS

After each day's *hakafah*-circuit (except on the Sabbath), the following *Hoshana* is recited:

ANI VAHO, bring salvation now.*

כְּהוֹשַׁעְתָּ אֵלִים *As You saved the terebinths in Lud along with Yourself when You went forth to save the nation — so save now.*

As You saved the nation and its leaders who sought the salvations of God — so save now.

As You saved the multitudes of hosts and with them the hosts of angels — so save now.

As You saved pure ones from the house of slavery, Gracious One, from those who forced manual labor upon them — so save now.

⤛§ כְּהוֹשַׁעְתָּ אֵלִים / As You Saved the Terebinths

This *Hoshana,* which is recited after each day's circuit [except on the Sabbath], contains various poetical allusions to the Exodus from Egypt and other incidents of God's salvation of Israel, and pleads that we be granted similar salvation.

אֲנִי וָהוֹ הוֹשִׁיעָה נָּא — *ANI VAHO, bring salvation now.* The obscure terms אֲנִי וָהוֹ, *ANI VAHO,* are identified by *Rashi (Succah* 45a) as two in a series of seventy-two Divine Names, each containing three letters. The complete series is composed of the letters which make up three consecutive verses of *Exodus* (14:19-21), each of which contains exactly seventy-two letters. In the mystical formula by which these Names are formed, verses 19 and 21 are read in their proper order, while verse 20 is read backwards. The first of these seven-two Names is והו, and the thirty-seventh Name is אני.

The particular aptness of these two Names in the *Hoshana* service stems from their *gematria* [*numerical value*], seventy-eight, which is equal to that of אָנָּא ה׳, *please, HASHEM (Rashi).*

כְּהוֹשַׁעְתָּ טְבוּעִים בְּצוּל גְּזָרִים,
יְקָרְךָ עִמָּם מַעֲבִירִים, כֵּן הוֹשַׁעְנָא.
כְּהוֹשַׁעְתָּ כַּנָּה מְשׁוֹרֶרֶת וַיּוֹשַׁע,
לְגוֹחָהּ מְצַיֶּנֶת וַיִּוָּשַׁע, כֵּן הוֹשַׁעְנָא.
כְּהוֹשַׁעְתָּ מַאֲמַר וְהוֹצֵאתִי אֶתְכֶם,
נָקוּב וְהוּצֵאתִי אִתְּכֶם, כֵּן הוֹשַׁעְנָא.
כְּהוֹשַׁעְתָּ סוֹבְבֵי מִזְבֵּחַ,
עוֹמְסֵי עֲרָבָה לְהַקִּיף מִזְבֵּחַ, כֵּן הוֹשַׁעְנָא.
כְּהוֹשַׁעְתָּ פִּלְאֵי אָרוֹן כְּהֻפְשַׁע,
צִעֵר פְּלֶשֶׁת בַּחֲרוֹן אַף וְנוֹשַׁע, כֵּן הוֹשַׁעְנָא.
כְּהוֹשַׁעְתָּ קְהִלּוֹת בָּבֶלָה שִׁלַּחְתָּ,
רַחוּם לְמַעֲנָם שֻׁלַּחְתָּ, כֵּן הוֹשַׁעְנָא.
כְּהוֹשַׁעְתָּ שְׁבוּת שִׁבְטֵי יַעֲקֹב,
תָּשׁוּב וְתָשִׁיב שְׁבוּת אָהֳלֵי יַעֲקֹב, וְהוֹשִׁיעָה נָּא.
כְּהוֹשַׁעְתָּ שׁוֹמְרֵי מִצְוֹת,
וְחוֹכֵי יְשׁוּעוֹת, אֵל לְמוֹשָׁעוֹת, וְהוֹשִׁיעָה נָּא.

אֲנִי וָהוֹ הוֹשִׁיעָה נָּא.

On Hoshana Rabbah continue תִּתְּנֵנוּ (p. 740). During the first six days of Succos continue:

הוֹשִׁיעָה אֶת עַמֶּךָ, וּבָרֵךְ אֶת נַחֲלָתֶךָ, וּרְעֵם וְנַשְּׂאֵם עַד הָעוֹלָם.[1] וְיִהְיוּ דְבָרַי אֵלֶּה אֲשֶׁר הִתְחַנַּנְתִּי לִפְנֵי יהוה, קְרֹבִים אֶל יהוה אֱלֹהֵינוּ יוֹמָם וָלָיְלָה, לַעֲשׂוֹת מִשְׁפַּט עַבְדּוֹ וּמִשְׁפַּט עַמּוֹ יִשְׂרָאֵל, דְּבַר יוֹם בְּיוֹמוֹ. לְמַעַן דַּעַת כָּל עַמֵּי הָאָרֶץ, כִּי יהוה הוּא הָאֱלֹהִים, אֵין עוֹד.[2]

The Torah Scroll is returned to the Ark.
On the first two days of Succos the *chazzan* recites the Full *Kaddish* (p. 474) and the service continues from there (pp. 476-488).
During Chol HaMoed the *chazzan* recites the Full *Kaddish* (p. 156) and the service continues from there (pp. 158-170).

אום נצורה

On Shabbos the following *Hoshana* until אֵין עוֹד (p. 740) is recited:

אוֹם נְצוּרָה כְּבָבַת. **ב**ּוֹנֶנֶת בְּדַת נֶפֶשׁ מְשִׁיבַת. **ג**ּוֹמֶרֶת הִלְכוֹת שַׁבָּת. **ד**ּוֹרֶשֶׁת מַשְׂאַת שַׁבָּת. **ה**ַקּוֹבַעַת אַלְפַּיִם תְּחוּם שַׁבָּת. **ו**ּמְשִׁיבַת רֶגֶל מִשַּׁבָּת. **ז**ָכוֹר וְשָׁמוֹר מְקַיֶּמֶת בַּשַּׁבָּת. **ח**ָשָׁה לְמַהֵר בִּיאַת שַׁבָּת. **ט**וֹרַחַת כֹּל מִשִּׁשָּׁה לַשַּׁבָּת. **י**וֹשֶׁבֶת וּמַמְתֶּנֶת עַד כְּלוֹת שַׁבָּת. **כָּ**בוֹד וָעֹנֶג קוֹרְאָה לַשַּׁבָּת. **ל**ְבוּשׁ וּכְסוּת מְחַלֶּפֶת בַּשַּׁבָּת. **מ**ַאֲכָל וּמִשְׁתֶּה מְכִינָה לַשַּׁבָּת. **נ**ְעַם מְגָדִים מַנְעֶמֶת לַשַּׁבָּת. **ס**ְעוּדוֹת שָׁלֹשׁ מְקַיֶּמֶת בַּשַּׁבָּת. **עַ**ל

אוֹם נְצוּרָה / Nation Protected

The Four Species are not taken on the Sabbath, because the Sages declare them to be מֻקְצֶה, *set apart,* thereby forbidding their use, or even moving them from place to place. This

As You saved those sinking in the depths of the rifts, Your honor was with them when they crossed — so save now.
As You saved the garden which sang 'He delivered,' regarding Him Who draws forth it is pronounced 'He was delivered' — so save now.
As You saved with the declaration 'I shall bring you forth,' which may be interpreted, 'I shall be brought forth with you' — so save now.
As You saved those who went roundabout with the altar, those who carry the willow to encircle the altar — so save now.
As You saved the Ark of the Name, captured as a result of sin, when you punished Philistia with flaming anger, and it was saved — so save now.
As You saved the congregations which You had sent to Babylon, Merciful One, for their sake were You also sent — so save now.
As You saved the captivity of the tribes of Jacob, return and restore the captivity of the tents of Jacob, and bring salvation now.
As You saved those observant of mitzvos, and hopeful for salvation — O God Who brings about salvation, bring salvation now.

ANI VAHO, bring salvation now.

On Hoshana Rabbah continue תְּתְּנֵנוּ, *Establish us* (p. 741).
During the first six days of Succos continue:

הוֹשִׁיעָה *Save Your people and bless Your heritage, tend them and elevate them forever.*[1] *May these words of mine, which I have supplicated before* HASHEM, *be near to* HASHEM, *our God, by day and by night; that He bring about justice for His servant and justice for His people, Israel, each day's need in its day; that all the peoples of the earth shall know that* HASHEM *is God, there is no other.*[2]

The Torah Scroll is returned to the Ark.
On the first two days of Succos the *chazzan* recites the Full *Kaddish* (p. 474) and the service continues from there (pp. 476-488).
During Chol HaMoed the *chazzan* recites the Full *Kaddish* (p. 156) and the service continues from there (pp. 158-170).

NATION PROTECTED

On Shabbos the following *Hoshana* until, '... *there is no other*' (p. 741), is recited:

אוֹם נְצוּרָה *Nation protected like the pupil of the eye — she seeks understanding of the law which restores the soul: She studies the laws of the Sabbath, explicates the burdens of the Sabbath, establishes two thousand as the boundary of the Sabbath, and restrains her foot because of the Sabbath. 'Remember' and 'Safeguard' she fulfills on the Sabbath by rushing to hasten the onset of the Sabbath; by toiling throughout the six for the Sabbath; by sitting, patiently waiting until the end of the Sabbath; 'Honor' and 'Delight' she proclaims the Sabbath: clothing and raiment she changes for the Sabbath; food and drink she prepares for the Sabbath; of the sweetness of delicate fruits she partakes on the Sabbath; three meals she fulfills on the Sabbath; over*

(1) *Psalms* 28:9. (2) *I Kings* 8:59-60.

decree was issued to prevent the unlearned and from bringing their *lulav* and *esrog* to a learned neighbor's home for instruction in their use. Such carrying through a public thoroughfare would constitute a desecration of the Sabbath (*Succah* 42b, 43a). Since the Four Species are not

שְׁתֵּי כִכָּרוֹת בּוֹצַעַת בַּשַּׁבָּת. **פּ**וֹרֶטֶת אַרְבַּע רְשֻׁיּוֹת בַּשַּׁבָּת. **צִ**וּוּי הַדְלָקַת נֵר מַדְלֶקֶת בַּשַּׁבָּת. **ק**ְדוֹשׁ הַיּוֹם מְקַדֶּשֶׁת בַּשַּׁבָּת. **ר**ֶנֶן שֶׁבַע מְפַלֶּלֶת בַּשַּׁבָּת. **ש**ִׁבְעָה בַּדָּת קוֹרְאָה בַּשַּׁבָּת. **ת**ַּנְחִילֶנָּה לְיוֹם שֶׁכֻּלּוֹ שַׁבָּת.

כהושעת אדם

אֲנִי וָהוֹ הוֹשִׁיעָה נָּא:

כְּהוֹשַׁעְתָּ אָדָם יְצִיר כַּפֶּיךָ לְגוֹנְנָה,
בְּשַׁבַּת קֹדֶשׁ הִמְצֵאתוֹ כֹּפֶר וַחֲנִינָה, כֵּן הוֹשַׁעְנָא.

כְּהוֹשַׁעְתָּ **ג**ּוֹי מְצֻיָּן מְקַוִּים חֹפֶשׁ,
דֵּעָה כִּוְּנוּ לָבוּר שְׁבִיעִי לְנֹפֶשׁ, כֵּן הוֹשַׁעְנָא.

כְּהוֹשַׁעְתָּ **ה**ָעָם נִהַגְתָּ כַּצֹּאן לְהַנְחוֹת,
וְחֹק שַׂמְתָּ בְּמָרָה עַל מֵי מְנֻחוֹת, כֵּן הוֹשַׁעְנָא.

כְּהוֹשַׁעְתָּ **ז**ְבוּדֶיךָ בְּמִדְבַּר סִין בַּמַּחֲנֶה,
חָכְמוּ וְלָקְטוּ בַּשִּׁשִּׁי לֶחֶם מִשְׁנֶה, כֵּן הוֹשַׁעְנָא.

כְּהוֹשַׁעְתָּ **ט**ְפוּלֶיךָ הוֹרוּ הֲכָנָה בְּמַדָּעָם,
יִשֵּׁר כֹּחָם וְהוֹדָה לָמוֹ רוֹעָם, כֵּן הוֹשַׁעְנָא.

כְּהוֹשַׁעְתָּ **כ**ֻּלְכְּלוּ בְּעֹנֶג מָן הַמְּשֻׁמָּר,
לֹא הָפַךְ עֵינוֹ וְרֵיחוֹ לֹא נָמָר, כֵּן הוֹשַׁעְנָא.

כְּהוֹשַׁעְתָּ **מ**ִשְׁפְּטֵי מַשְׂאוֹת שַׁבָּת גָּמָרוּ,
נָחוּ וְשָׁבְתוּ רְשֻׁיּוֹת וּתְחוּמִים שָׁמָרוּ, כֵּן הוֹשַׁעְנָא.

כְּהוֹשַׁעְתָּ **ס**ִינַי הֻשְׁמְעוּ בְּדִבּוּר רְבִיעִי,
עִנְיַן זָכוֹר וְשָׁמוֹר לְקַדֵּשׁ שְׁבִיעִי, כֵּן הוֹשַׁעְנָא.

כְּהוֹשַׁעְתָּ **פ**ֻּקְּדוּ יְרִיחוֹ שֶׁבַע לְהַקֵּף,
צָרוּ עַד רִדְתָּהּ בַּשַּׁבָּת לְתַקֵּף, כֵּן הוֹשַׁעְנָא.

כְּהוֹשַׁעְתָּ **ק**ֹהֶלֶת וְעַמּוֹ בְּבֵית עוֹלָמִים,
רִצּוּךָ בְּחָגְגָם שִׁבְעָה וְשִׁבְעָה יָמִים, כֵּן הוֹשַׁעְנָא.

כְּהוֹשַׁעְתָּ **שָׁ**בִים עוֹלֵי גוֹלָה לְפִדְיוֹם,
תּוֹרָתְךָ בְּקָרְאָם בֶּחָג יוֹם יוֹם, כֵּן הוֹשַׁעְנָא.

כְּהוֹשַׁעְתָּ **מ**ְשַׂמְּחֶיךָ בְּבִנְיַן שֵׁנִי הַמְּחֻדָּשׁ,
נוֹטְלִין לוּלָב כָּל שִׁבְעָה בַּמִּקְדָּשׁ, כֵּן הוֹשַׁעְנָא.

כְּהוֹשַׁעְתָּ **ח**ִבּוּט עֲרָבָה שַׁבָּת מַדְחִים,
מְרַבִּיּוֹת מוֹצָא לִיסוֹד מִזְבֵּחַ מַנִּיחִים, כֵּן הוֹשַׁעְנָא.

---

taken on the Sabbath, *hakafah*-circuits are omitted on that day *(Rashi*, cited by *Tur* 660).

As would be expected, the *Hoshana* recited on the Sabbath contains allusions to the observance of various *mitzvos* related to the Sabbath.

כְּהוֹשַׁעְתָּ אָדָם / As You Saved Adam

Unlike the other *Hoshanos* which were composed by Rabbi Elazar HaKalir, this *Hoshana* is by Rabbi Menachem ben Rabbi Machir. While the others all follow an alphabetical scheme, this *Hoshana* also bears an acrostic of the author's name, מְנַחֵם בְּרַבִּי מָכִיר, with a blessing appended to it, חֲזַק לָעַד אָמֵן, *may he be strengthened forever, amen*, in the style common to most *paytanim*. Like the preceding *Hoshana* this one

two loaves she breaks bread on the Sabbath. She distinguishes four domains on the Sabbath. The command of kindling the light she fulfills for the Sabbath. The Sanctification of the day she recites on the Sabbath. A seven-part prayer she prays on the Sabbath. Seven portions of the Torah she reads on the Sabbath. Cause her to inherit the day which will be completely a Sabbath.

AS YOU SAVED ADAM

Ani Vaho, bring salvation now.

כְּהוֹשַׁעְתָּ אָדָם *As You saved Adam, Your handiwork, to be his shield; on the holy Sabbath You brought forth for him forgiveness and grace — so save now.*

As You saved the distinctive nation which sought freedom; with wisdom they anticipated the choice of the seventh for rest — so save now.

As You saved the people whom You guided like a flock to contentment; and You issued a statute at Marah beside tranquil waters — so save now.

As You saved Your portion in the encampment at the Wilderness of Sin; they acted wisely and gathered double bread on the sixth — so save now.

As You saved those who clung to You, who derived the rules of preparation through their wisdom; their shepherd blessed their talent and deferred to them — so save now.

As You saved those You sustained on the day of delight with the guarded manna, whose appearance did not change and whose aroma did not sour — so save now.

As You saved those who study the laws regarding the burdens of the Sabbath; they are content and they rest, guarding domains and boundaries — so save now.

As You saved those permitted to hear the fourth pronouncement at Sinai; the theme of 'Remember' and 'Safeguard' to sanctify the seventh — so save now.

As You saved those bidden at Jericho to encircle seven times; they besieged it until its downfall on the Sabbath, to strengthen them — so save now.

As You saved Koheles [Solomon] and his nation in the eternal Temple, they pleased You when they celebrated seven and another seven days — so save now.

As You saved those who returned arising from exile to redemption; as they read Your Torah on the Festival, every day — so save now.

As You saved those who brought You joy with the renewed Second Temple; who took up the lulav all seven days in the Sanctuary — so save now.

As You saved those for whom the beating of the willow overrode the Sabbath; those who placed Motza's branches at the base of the altar — so save now.

כְּהוֹשַֽׁעְתָּ **בְּ**רַכּוֹת וַאֲרוּכוֹת וּגְבוֹהוֹת מְעֻלָּסִים,
בְּפְטִירָתָן **יֹ**פִי לְךָ מִזְבֵּחַ מְקַלְּסִים, כֵּן הוֹשַׁעְנָא.

כְּהוֹשַֽׁעְתָּ **מ**וֹדִים וּמְיַחֲלִים וְלֹא מְשַׁנִּים,
כֻּלָּנוּ אָנוּ לְיָהּ וְעֵינֵינוּ לְיָהּ שׁוֹנִים, כֵּן הוֹשַׁעְנָא.

כְּהוֹשַֽׁעְתָּ **יֶ**קֶב מַחְצָבֶיךָ סוֹבְבִים בִּרְעָנָנָה,
רוֹנְנִים אֲנִי וָהוֹ הוֹשִֽׁיעָה נָּא, כֵּן הוֹשַׁעְנָא.

כְּהוֹשַֽׁעְתָּ **חֵ**יל **זְ**רִיזִים מְשָׁרְתִים בִּמְנוּחָה,
קָרְבַּן שַׁבָּת כָּפוּל עוֹלָה וּמִנְחָה, כֵּן הוֹשַׁעְנָא.

כְּהוֹשַֽׁעְתָּ **לְ**וִיֶּיךָ **עַל ד**וּכָנָם לְהַרְבַּת,
אוֹמְרִים **מִ**זְמוֹר שִׁיר לְיוֹם הַשַּׁבָּת, כֵּן הוֹשַׁעְנָא.

כְּהוֹשַֽׁעְתָּ **נ**ְחוּמֶיךָ בְּמִצְוֹתֶיךָ תָּמִיד יִשְׁתַּעְשְׁעוּן, וּרְצֵם וְהַחֲלִיצֵם בְּשׁוּבָה וָנַחַת יִוָּשֵׁעוּן, כֵּן הוֹשַׁעְנָא.

כְּהוֹשַֽׁעְתָּ **שְׁ**בוּת שִׁבְטֵי יַעֲקֹב, תָּשׁוּב וְתָשִׁיב שְׁבוּת אָהֳלֵי יַעֲקֹב, וְהוֹשִֽׁיעָה נָּא.

כְּהוֹשַֽׁעְתָּ **שׁ**וֹמְרֵי **מִ**צְוֹת,
וְחוֹכֵי יְשׁוּעוֹת, **אֵ**ל **לְ**מוֹשָׁעוֹת, וְהוֹשִֽׁיעָה נָּא.

אֲנִי וָהוֹ הוֹשִֽׁיעָה נָּא.

הוֹשִֽׁיעָה אֶת עַמֶּךָ, וּבָרֵךְ אֶת נַחֲלָתֶךָ, וּרְעֵם וְנַשְּׂאֵם עַד הָעוֹלָם.[1] וְיִהְיוּ דְבָרַי אֵלֶּה אֲשֶׁר הִתְחַנַּנְתִּי לִפְנֵי יהוה, קְרֹבִים אֶל יהוה אֱלֹהֵינוּ יוֹמָם וָלָיְלָה, לַעֲשׂוֹת מִשְׁפַּט עַבְדּוֹ וּמִשְׁפַּט עַמּוֹ יִשְׂרָאֵל, דְּבַר יוֹם בְּיוֹמוֹ. לְמַעַן דַּעַת כָּל עַמֵּי הָאָרֶץ, כִּי יהוה הוּא הָאֱלֹהִים, אֵין עוֹד.[2]

The Ark is closed, the *chazzan* recites the Full *Kaddish* (p. 474), and the service continues there.

ADDITIONAL PRAYERS FOR HOSHANA RABBAH

תתננו

On Hoshana Rabbah continue here. In most congregations the introductory passages (bold type) of the following prayers are recited responsively — *chazzan,* then congregation. The prayers themselves are recited by both *chazzan* and congregation, with the *chazzan* reciting the last line or two aloud.

תְּתְּנֵנוּ לְשֵׁם וְלִתְהִלָּה. **תְּ**שִׁיתֵנוּ אֶל הַחֶבֶל וְאֶל הַנַּחֲלָה. **תְּ**רוֹמְמֵנוּ לְמַעְלָה לְמָעְלָה. **תְּ**קַבְּצֵנוּ לְבֵית הַתְּפִלָּה. **תַּ**צִּיבֵנוּ כְּעֵץ עַל פַּלְגֵי מַיִם שְׁתוּלָה. **תְּ**פְדֵּנוּ מִכָּל נֶגַע וּמַחֲלָה. **תְּ**עַטְּרֵנוּ בְּאַהֲבָה כְּלוּלָה. **תְּ**שַׂמְּחֵנוּ בְּבֵית הַתְּפִלָּה. **תְּ**נַהֲלֵנוּ עַל מֵי מְנוּחוֹת סֶלָה. **תְּ**מַלְּאֵנוּ חָכְמָה וְשִׂכְלָה. **תַּ**לְבִּישֵׁנוּ עֹז וּגְדֻלָּה. **תַּ**כְתִּירֵנוּ בְּכֶתֶר כְּלוּלָה. **תְּ**יַשְּׁרֵנוּ בְּאֹרַח סְלוּלָה. **תִּ**טָּעֵנוּ בְּיֹשֶׁר מְסִלָּה. **תְּ**חָנֵּנוּ בְּרַחֲמִים

תְּתְּנֵנוּ / Establish Us

Although all the *Hoshanos* (except one of this one was written specifically for the Sabbath and contains many allusions to the *mitzvos* and customs of that day.

As You saved those who praised with supple, long and tall willows; who departed while extolling, 'Beauty becomes you, O Altar'
— so save now.

As You saved those who thanked and hoped, but never exchanged; like them we all cry out, 'We are God's and our eyes are to God'
— so save now.

As You saved those who encircled the wine cellar of Your hewing with greenery; singing, 'ANI VAHO, bring salvation now'
— so save now.

As You saved the army of speedy ones who serve on the day of contentment, with the doubled Sabbath offering, of burnt and meal offering
— so save now.

As You saved Your Levites who sang upon their platform, saying, 'A psalm, a song, for the Sabbath day' — so save now.

As You saved those whom You comforted, those who constantly find joy in Your mitzvos; so may You favor them and give them rest, and tranquility, and contentedly may they attain salvation
— so save now.

As You saved the captivity of the tribes of Jacob, return and restore the captivity of Jacob's tents and bring salvation now.

As You saved those observing mitzvos, and hoping for salvation — O God Who brings salvations bring salvation now.

ANI VAHO, bring salvation now.

הוֹשִׁיעָה *Save Your people and bless Your heritage, tend them and elevate them forever.*[1] *May these words of mine, which I have supplicated before HASHEM, be near to HASHEM, our God, by day and by night; that He bring about justice for His servant and justice for His people, Israel, each day's need in its day; that all the peoples of the earth shall know that HASHEM is God, there is no other.*[2]

The Ark is closed, the *chazzan* recites the Full *Kaddish* (p. 474), and the service continues there.

ADDITIONAL PRAYERS FOR HOSHANA RABBAH

ESTABLISH US

On Hoshana Rabbah continue here. In most congregations the introductory passages (bold type) of the following prayers are recited responsively — *chazzan,* then congregation. The prayers themselves are recited by both *chazzan* and congregation, with the *chazzan* reciting the last line or two aloud.

תְּתְּנֵנוּ *Establish us for fame and renown, place us upon our measured heritage; raise us ever higher; gather us to the House of Prayer, stand us erect, like a tree embedded by streams of water; redeem us from every plague and sickness; envelop us with perfect love; gladden us in the House of Prayer; lead us beside tranquil waters, forever; fill us with wisdom and sense; clothe us with strength and greatness; crown us with the perfect crown; set us right on the level road; plant us on the straight path; grace us with mercy*

(1) *Psalm* 28:9. (2) *I Kings* 8:59-60.

those recited on the Sabbath) are attributed to Rabbi Elazar HaKalir, only this *Hoshana* bears his signature. The second letters of each verse form the twenty-two letters of the *aleph-beis* in

וּבְחֶמְלָה. תַּזְכִּירֵנוּ בְּמִי זֹאת עוֹלָה. תּוֹשִׁיעֵנוּ לְקֵץ הַגְּאֻלָּה. תְּהַדְּרֵנוּ בְּזִיו הַמּוּלָה. תַּדְבִּיקֵנוּ כְּאֵזוֹר חֲתוּלָה. תְּגַדְּלֵנוּ בְּיָד הַגְּדוֹלָה. תְּבִיאֵנוּ לְבֵיתְךָ בְּרִנָּה וְצָהֳלָה. תְּאַמְּצֵנוּ בְּרֶוַח וְהַצָּלָה. תְּאַדְּרֵנוּ בְּאֶבֶן תְּלוּלָה. תְּלַבְּבֵנוּ בְּבִנְיַן עִירְךָ כְּבַתְּחִלָּה. תְּעוֹרְרֵנוּ לְצִיּוֹן בְּשִׁכְלוּלָה. תְּזַכֵּנוּ בְּבִנְבְּנָתָה הָעִיר עַל תִּלָּהּ. תַּרְבִּיצֵנוּ בְּשָׂשׂוֹן וְגִילָה. תְּחַזְּקֵנוּ אֱלֹהֵי יַעֲקֹב סֶלָה.

אנא אזון

אָנָּא הוֹשִׁיעָה נָּא.

אָנָּא אֱזוֹן חִין תְּאֵבֵי יִשְׁעָךְ,
בְּעָרְבֵי נַחַל לְשַׁעְשְׁעָךְ, וְהוֹשִׁיעָה נָּא.
אָנָּא **גְּ**אַל כַּנַּת נִטְעָךְ,
דּוּמָה בְּטַאטְאָךְ, וְהוֹשִׁיעָה נָּא.
אָנָּא **הַ**בֵּט לַבְּרִית טִבְעָךְ,
וּמַחֲשַׁכֵּי אֶרֶץ בְּהַטְבִּיעָךְ, וְהוֹשִׁיעָה נָּא.
אָנָּא **זְ**כָר לָנוּ אָב יְדָעָךְ,
חַסְדְּךָ לָמוֹ בְּהוֹדִיעָךְ, וְהוֹשִׁיעָה נָּא.
אָנָּא **טְ**הוֹרֵי לֵב בְּהַפְלִיאָךְ,
יִוָּדַע כִּי הוּא פִלְאָךְ, וְהוֹשִׁיעָה נָּא.
אָנָּא **כַּ**בִּיר כֹּחַ תֶּן לָנוּ יִשְׁעָךְ,
לַאֲבוֹתֵינוּ כְּהִשָּׁבְעָךְ, וְהוֹשִׁיעָה נָּא.
אָנָּא **מַ**לֵּא מִשְׁאֲלוֹת עַם מְשַׁוְּעָךְ,
נֶעֱקַד בְּהַר מוֹר כְּמוֹ שִׁוְּעָךְ, וְהוֹשִׁיעָה נָּא.
אָנָּא **סַ**גֵּב אֶשְׁלֵי נִטְעָךְ,
עֲרִיצִים בְּהַנִּיעָךְ, וְהוֹשִׁיעָה נָּא.
אָנָּא **פְּ**תַח לָנוּ אוֹצְרוֹת רִבְעָךְ,
צִיָּה מֵהֶם בְּהַרְבִּיעָךְ, וְהוֹשִׁיעָה נָּא.
אָנָּא **קוֹ**רְאֶיךָ אֶרֶץ בְּרוֹעֲעָךְ,
רְעֵם בְּטוּב מִרְעָךְ, וְהוֹשִׁיעָה נָּא.
אָנָּא **שְׁ**עָרֶיךָ תַּעַל מִמַּשּׁוּאָךְ,
תֵּל תַּלְפִּיּוֹת בְּהַשִּׂיאָךְ, וְהוֹשִׁיעָה נָּא.

אל נא

אָנָּא אֵל נָא, הוֹשַׁעְנָא וְהוֹשִׁיעָה נָּא.

אֵל נָא תָּעִינוּ כְּשֶׂה אֹבֵד,
שְׁמֵנוּ מִסִּפְרְךָ אַל תְּאַבֵּד, הוֹשַׁעְנָא וְהוֹשִׁיעָה נָּא.

תְּחַזְּקֵנוּ, *Establish us,* is the first in a series of additional *Hoshanos* chanted on Hoshana

reverse order, followed by אֶלְעָזָר חֲזַק, *Elazar, may he be strengthened.*

and pity; remember us with 'How worthy is she!'; save us for the final End of Redemption; beautify us with the radiance of angels; cause us to cleave to You like a tightly wrapped sash; make us great with Your great hand; bring us to Your Temple with joyous song and cheer; strengthen us with relief and rescue; adorn us with the elevated stone; hearten us with the rebuilding of Your city as of old; awaken us to Zion in its completeness; let us merit the rebuilding of the City on its hill; let us recline with joy and gladness; strengthen us, O God of Jacob, Selah.

PLEASE HEARKEN

Please bring salvation now.

אָנָּא אֱזוֹן *Please hearken to the plea of those who long for Your salvation;*
with brook willows they bring You joy — and bring salvation now.
Please redeem the garden of Your planting,
as You sweep away Dumah — and bring salvation now.
Please gaze upon the covenant of Your signet ring,
even as You sink the ones who darken the earth
— and bring salvation now.
Please recall on our behalf the Patriarch who perceived You;
may Your loving-kindness be upon them, for he made You known
— and bring salvation now.
Please when you set aside the pure of heart it will be known
that this is Your wonder — and bring salvation now.
Please Almighty One, grant us Your salvation,
as You swore to our fathers — and bring salvation now.
Please fulfill the requests of Your entreating nation
as the bound one on the myrrh mountain entreated You
— and bring salvation now.
Please strengthen the tamarisks of Your planting
as You cause the idolaters to wander — and bring salvation now.
Please open the treasure troves of Your rains for us
as You water the parched earth from them — and bring salvation now.
Please — those who call to You, when You bring the earth destruction,
shepherd them in Your goodly pastures — and bring salvation now.
Please raise Your gates in the wake of Your desolation
when You exalt the Hill of Talpios — and bring salvation now.

PLEASE GOD

Please God, please! Save now and bring salvation now.

אֵל נָא *Please God! We have strayed like lost sheep; do not cause our name to be lost from Your Book*
— save now and bring salvation now.

Rabbah after the completion of the seven *hakafah*-circuits.

אָנָּא אֱזוֹן / Please Hearken

The rainy season in *Eretz Yisrael* begins almost immediately after Succos. For this reason special prayers for rain (p. 704) are recited on Shemini Atzeres. Additionally, the *Hoshanos* service of Hoshana Rabbah centers on the *aravos*, or brook-willows, a species which both

אֵל נָא רְעֵה אֶת צֹאן הַהֲרֵגָה,
קְצוּפָה וְעָלֶיךָ הֲרוּגָה, הוֹשַׁעְנָא וְהוֹשִׁיעָה נָּא.
אֵל נָא צֹאנְךָ וְצֹאן מַרְעִיתֶךָ,
פְּעֻלָּתְךָ וְרַעְיָתֶךָ, הוֹשַׁעְנָא וְהוֹשִׁיעָה נָּא.
אֵל נָא עֲנִיֵּי הַצֹּאן,
שִׂיחָם עֲנֵה בְּעֵת רָצוֹן, הוֹשַׁעְנָא וְהוֹשִׁיעָה נָּא.
אֵל נָא נוֹשְׂאֵי לְךָ עַיִן,
מִתְקוֹמְמֵיהֶם יִהְיוּ כְּאַיִן, הוֹשַׁעְנָא וְהוֹשִׁיעָה נָּא.
אֵל נָא לִמְנַסְּכֵי לְךָ מַיִם,
כְּמִמַּעַיְנֵי הַיְשׁוּעָה יִשְׁאֲבוּן מַיִם, הוֹשַׁעְנָא וְהוֹשִׁיעָה נָּא.
אֵל נָא יַעֲלוּ לְצִיּוֹן מוֹשִׁיעִים,
טְפוּלִים בְּךָ וּבְשִׁמְךָ נוֹשָׁעִים, הוֹשַׁעְנָא וְהוֹשִׁיעָה נָּא.
אֵל נָא חֲמוּץ בְּגָדִים,
זְעוֹם לְנַעֵר כָּל בּוֹגְדִים, הוֹשַׁעְנָא וְהוֹשִׁיעָה נָּא.
אֵל נָא וְזָכוֹר תִּזְכּוֹר,
הַנִּכּוּרֵי בִּלְתְּךָ וָכוֹר, הוֹשַׁעְנָא וְהוֹשִׁיעָה נָּא.
אֵל נָא דּוֹרְשֶׁיךָ בְּעַנְפֵי עֲרָבוֹת,
גַּעְיָם שְׁעֵה מֵעֲרָבוֹת, הוֹשַׁעְנָא וְהוֹשִׁיעָה נָּא.
אֵל נָא בָּרֵךְ בְּעִטּוּר שָׁנָה,
אֲמָרֵי רְצֵה בְּפִלּוּלִי בְּיוֹם הוֹשַׁעְנָא, הוֹשַׁעְנָא וְהוֹשִׁיעָה נָּא.

למען תמים

אָנָּא אֵל נָא, הוֹשַׁעְנָא וְהוֹשִׁיעָה נָּא, אָבִינוּ אָתָּה.

לְמַעַן תָּמִים בְּדוֹרוֹתָיו, הַנִּמְלָט בְּרוֹב צִדְקוֹתָיו,
מֻצָּל מִשֶּׁטֶף בְּבֹא מַבּוּל מָיִם.
לְאוֹם אֲנִי חוֹמָה, הוֹשַׁעְנָא וְהוֹשִׁיעָה נָּא, אָבִינוּ אָתָּה.
לְמַעַן שָׁלֵם בְּכָל מַעֲשִׂים, הַמְּנֻסֶּה בַּעֲשָׂרָה נִסִּים,
כְּשַׂר מַלְאָכִים נָם יֻקַּח נָא מְעַט מַיִם.
לְבָרָה כַּחַמָּה, הוֹשַׁעְנָא וְהוֹשִׁיעָה נָּא, אָבִינוּ אָתָּה.
לְמַעַן רַךְ וְיָחִיד נֶחְנַט פְּרִי לְמֵאָה, זָעַק אַיֵּה הַשֶּׂה לְעוֹלָה,
בִּשְּׂרוּהוּ עֲבָדָיו מָצָאנוּ מָיִם.
לְגוֹלָה וְסוּרָה, הוֹשַׁעְנָא וְהוֹשִׁיעָה נָּא, אָבִינוּ אָתָּה.

---

depends upon and is identified with water.

The Talmud teaches that during Succos the Heavenly Tribunal judges the world with regard to its water supply for the following year. God ordained the water-libations of Succos as a source of merit; as if He said, 'Pour water before Me on this Festival, that you be blessed with the year's rains' *(Rosh Hashanah* 16a). These prayers for rain are not recited until the last day of the festival because 'rain is but a symptom of curse during Succos,' for it makes it impossible to sit in the *succah (Taanis* 2a).

Please God! Graze the sheep of the slaughter, who are the victims of wrath and are killed for Your sake — save now and bring salvation now.
Please God! Your sheep and the sheep of Your pasture, Your accomplishment and Your beloved — save now and bring salvation now.
Please God! The poorest of the sheep, answer their prayers at an opportune time — save now and bring salvation now.
Please God! Those who raise their eyes to You, may those who rise against them be as naught — save now and bring salvation now.
Please God! Those who pour water before You, from the springs of salvation may they draw water — save now and bring salvation now.
Please God! May saviors arise from Zion; those who cling to You and are saved in Your Name — save now and bring salvation now.
Please God! With bloodied clothes, be enraged to shake out all the rebels — save now and bring salvation now.
Please God! Remember may You remember, those purchased for a lesech and a kor — save now and bring salvation now.
Please God! Those who seek You with willow branches, to their cries turn, from Aravos — save now and bring salvation now.
Please God! With a crown bless this year. May you find my words favorable as I pray on this day of Hoshana — save now and bring salvation now.

IN THE MERIT OF HIM WHO WAS PERFECT

Please God, please! Save now and bring salvation now, for You are our Father.

לְמַֽעַן תָּמִים *In the merit of him [Noah] who was perfect in his generations, he escaped by his abundant righteousness, and was rescued from inundation upon the arrival of the Flood of water*
— for the sake of the nation that declares, 'I am a wall,'
may You save now and bring salvation now, for You are our Father.
In the merit of him [Abraham] who was perfect in all deeds, who was proven through ten trials; upon seeing the angels he said, 'Let them be brought some water
— for the sake of the people brilliant as the sun,
may You save now and bring salvation now, for You are our Father.
In the merit of the tender and only fruit [Isaac] which blossomed at one hundred, who cried, 'Where is the lamb for the offering?' His servants informed him, 'We have found water'
— for the sake of the exiled and displaced,
may You save now and bring salvation now, for You are our Father.

☙ לְמַֽעַן תָּמִים / In the Merit of Him who was Perfect

In a style reminiscent of the *Hoshana* beginning לְמַֽעַן אֵיתָן, *In the merit of the courageous one*, this *Hoshana* recounts the love for God which was the hallmark of the righteous people of old. Since that *Hoshana* was a prayer for an

לְמַעַן **קְ**דַם שְׂאֵת בְּרָכָה, הַנִּשְׁטָם וּלְשִׁמְךָ חִכָּה,
מְיַחֵם בְּמַקְלוֹת בְּשִׁקְתוֹת הַמָּיִם.
לְ**דָ**מְתָה לְתָמָר, הוֹשַׁעְנָא וְהוֹשִׁיעָה נָּא, אָבִינוּ אָתָּה.

לְמַעַן **צָ**דֵק הֱיוֹת לְךָ לְכַהֵן, כְּחָתָן פְּאֵר יְכַהֵן,
מְנֻסֶּה בְּמַסָּה בְּמֵי מְרִיבַת מָיִם.
לְ**הָ**הָר הַטּוֹב, הוֹשַׁעְנָא וְהוֹשִׁיעָה נָּא, אָבִינוּ אָתָּה.

לְמַעַן **פְּ**אֵר הֱיוֹת גְּבִיר לְאֶחָיו, יְהוּדָה אֲשֶׁר גָּבַר בְּאֶחָיו,
מִסְפַּר רֹבַע מִדָּלְיָו יִזַּל מָיִם.
לְ**וֹ**א לָנוּ כִּי אִם לְמַעַנְךָ, הוֹשַׁעְנָא וְהוֹשִׁיעָה נָּא, אָבִינוּ אָתָּה.

לְמַעַן **עָ**נָיו מִכֹּל וְנֶאֱמָן, אֲשֶׁר בְּצִדְקוֹ כִּלְכֵּל הַמָּן,
מָשׁוּךְ לְגוֹאֵל וּמָשׁוּי מִמָּיִם.
לְ**זֹ**את הַנִּשְׁקָפָה, הוֹשַׁעְנָא וְהוֹשִׁיעָה נָּא, אָבִינוּ אָתָּה.

לְמַעַן **שַׂ**מְתּוֹ כְּמַלְאֲכֵי מְרוֹמִים, הַלּוֹבֵשׁ אוּרִים וְתֻמִּים,
מְצֻוֶּה לָבֹא בַּמִּקְדָּשׁ בְּקִדּוּשׁ יָדַיִם וְרַגְלַיִם וּרְחִיצַת מָיִם.
לְ**ח**וֹלַת אַהֲבָה, הוֹשַׁעְנָא וְהוֹשִׁיעָה נָּא, אָבִינוּ אָתָּה.

לְמַעַן **נְ**בִיאָה מְחוֹלַת מַחֲנַיִם, לִכְמֵהֵי לֵב הוּשְׂמָה עֵינַיִם,
לְרַגְלָהּ רָצָה עֲלוֹת וָרֶדֶת בְּאֵר מָיִם.
לְ**טֹ**בוּ אֹהָלָיו, הוֹשַׁעְנָא וְהוֹשִׁיעָה נָּא, אָבִינוּ אָתָּה.

לְמַעַן **מְ**שָׁרֵת לֹא מָשׁ מֵאֹהֶל, וְרוּחַ הַקֹּדֶשׁ עָלָיו אִהֵל,
בְּעָבְרוֹ בַּיַּרְדֵּן נִכְרְתוּ הַמָּיִם.
לְ**יָ**פָה וּבָרָה, הוֹשַׁעְנָא וְהוֹשִׁיעָה נָּא, אָבִינוּ אָתָּה.

לְמַעַן **לָ**מַד רְאוֹת לְטוֹבָה אוֹת, זָעַק אַיֵּה נִפְלָאוֹת,
מִצָּה טַל מִגִּזָּה מְלֹא הַסֵּפֶל מָיִם.
לְ**כַ**לַּת לְבָנוֹן, הוֹשַׁעְנָא וְהוֹשִׁיעָה נָּא, אָבִינוּ אָתָּה.

לְמַעַן **כְּ**לוּלֵי עֲשׂוֹת מִלְחַמְתֶּךָ, אֲשֶׁר בְּיָדָם תַּתָּה יְשׁוּעָתֶךָ,
צְרוּפֵי מִגּוֹי בְּלָקְקָם בְּיָדָם מָיִם.
לְ**לֹ**א בָגְדוּ בָךְ, הוֹשַׁעְנָא וְהוֹשִׁיעָה נָּא, אָבִינוּ אָתָּה.

לְמַעַן **יָ**חִיד צוֹרְרִים דָּשׁ, אֲשֶׁר מֵרֶחֶם לְנָזִיר הֻקְדָּשׁ,
מִמַּכְתֵּשׁ לֶחִי הִבְקַעְתָּ לּוֹ מָיִם.

---

end to Israel's suffering in exile, it mentioned an incident involving fire in the life of each Patriarch. This *Hoshana* is a prayer for rain, so the biographical events are related to water.

A double acrostic is used by the *paytan*. Each verse is divided into four parts. The first word of each verse is לְמַעַן, *In the merit of*, followed by an allusion to the righteousness of one of Israel's progenitors. These allusions are contained in the first two parts of each verse and form a reverse alphabetical acrostic going from ת to א. The third section of each stich is reference to a water-

In the merit of the one [Jacob] who was first with gift for the blessing, who was hated but who yearned for Your Name, he stimulated with rods at the troughs of water
— for the sake of those likened to a palm tree,
may You save now and bring salvation now, for You are our Father.

In the merit of the one [Levi] worthy of being Your Kohen adorned like a bridegroom he would serve, he was proven at Massah, at Merivah's water
— for the sake of the good mountain,
may You save now and bring salvation now, for You are our Father.

In the merit of the splendrous one who would be master over his brothers, Judah who ruled over his brothers though he was fourth, from his buckets shall pour water
— not for our sake but for Yours,
may You save now and bring salvation now, for You are our Father.

In the merit of the humblest of all [Moses], and most trusted, for whose righteousness He supplied manna, he was drawn to be a redeemer and pulled from the water
— for the sake of the one who gazes down,
may You save now and bring salvation now, for You are our Father.

In the merit of the one [Aaron] You emplaced like exalted angels, he who, wearing the Urim and Tumim, is commanded to come to the Temple with sanctified hands and feet, and an immersion in water
— for the sake of the one sick with love,
may You save now and bring salvation now, for You are our Father.

In the merit of the prophetess [Miriam] of the dance of the camps, to those of thirsting heart she was an inspiration, at her feet ran, rising and descending, the well of water
— for the sake of the one of goodly tents,
may You save now and bring salvation now, for You are our Father.

In the merit of the servant [Joshua] who moved not from the tent, upon him the Holy Spirit rested, when he crossed the Jordan, cut was the water
— for the sake of the beautiful and brilliant,
may You save now and bring salvation now, for You are our Father.

In the merit of him [Gideon] who showed how to perceive a good omen, he cried, 'Where are Your wonders,' from a fleece he pressed, a bowl full of water
— for the sake of the bride of Lebanon,
may You save now and bring salvation now, for You are our Father.

In the merit of the dedicated fighters [Gideon's army] in Your war, into whose hands You placed Your salvation, proven purest of the nation by having lapped from their hand water
— for the sake of those that did not rebel against You,
may You save now and bring salvation now, for You are our Father.

In the merit of the only child [Samson], who thrashed the oppressors, sanctified from the womb as a Nazir; from the hollow of a jawbone You brought him water

לְמַעַן שֵׁם קָדְשֶׁךָ, הוֹשַׁעְנָא וְהוֹשִׁיעָה נָּא, אָבִינוּ אָתָּה.

לְמַעַן **ט**וֹב הוֹלֵךְ וְגָדֵל, אֲשֶׁר מֵעֹשֶׁק עֵדָה חָדֵל,
בְּשׁוּב עָם מֵחֵטְא צָו שְׁאָב מָיִם.
לְ**נָ**אוָה כִּירוּשָׁלָיִם, הוֹשַׁעְנָא וְהוֹשִׁיעָה נָּא, אָבִינוּ אָתָּה.

לְמַעַן **חַ**יָּךְ מְכַרְכֵּר בְּשִׁיר, הַמְּלַמֵּד תּוֹרָה בְּכָל כְּלֵי שִׁיר,
מְנַסֵּךְ לְפָנָיו כְּתָאֵב שְׁתוֹת מָיִם.
לְ**שָׂ**מוּ בְךָ סִבְרָם, הוֹשַׁעְנָא וְהוֹשִׁיעָה נָּא, אָבִינוּ אָתָּה.

לְמַעַן **זָ**ךְ עָלָה בִסְעָרָה, הַמְּקַנֵּא וּמֵשִׁיב עֶבְרָה,
לִפְלוּלוֹ יָרְדָה אֵשׁ וְלִחֲכָה עָפָר וּמָיִם.
לְ**עֵ**ינֶיהָ בְּרֵכוֹת, הוֹשַׁעְנָא וְהוֹשִׁיעָה נָּא, אָבִינוּ אָתָּה.

לְמַעַן **וְ**שֵׁרֵת בֶּאֱמֶת לְרַבּוֹ, פִּי שְׁנַיִם בְּרוּחוֹ נֶאֱצַל בּוֹ,
בְּקַחְתּוֹ מְנַגֵּן נִתְמַלְּאוּ גֵבִים מָיִם.
לְ**פָ**צוּ מִי כָמֹכָה, הוֹשַׁעְנָא וְהוֹשִׁיעָה נָּא, אָבִינוּ אָתָּה.

לְמַעַן **הִ**רְהֵר עֲשׂוֹת רְצוֹנֶךָ, הַמַּכְרִיז תְּשׁוּבָה לְצֹאנֶךָ,
אָז בְּבֹא מְחָרֵף סָתַם עֵינוֹת מָיִם.
לְ**צִ**יּוֹן מִכְלַל יֹפִי, הוֹשַׁעְנָא וְהוֹשִׁיעָה נָּא, אָבִינוּ אָתָּה.

לְמַעַן **דָּ**רְשׁוּךָ בְּתוֹךְ הַגּוֹלָה, וְסוֹדְךָ לָמוֹ נִגְלָה,
בְּלִי לְהִתְגָּאֵל דָּרְשׁוּ זֵרְעוֹנִים וּמָיִם.
לְ**קוֹ**רְאֶיךָ בַּצָּר, הוֹשַׁעְנָא וְהוֹשִׁיעָה נָּא, אָבִינוּ אָתָּה.

לְמַעַן **גְּ**מַר חָכְמָה וּבִינָה, סוֹפֵר מָהִיר מְפַלֵּשׁ אֲמָנָה,
מְחַכְּמֵנוּ אֲמָרִים הַמְּשׁוּלִים בְּרַחֲבֵי מָיִם.
לְ**רַ**בָּתִי עָם, הוֹשַׁעְנָא וְהוֹשִׁיעָה נָּא, אָבִינוּ אָתָּה.

לְמַעַן **בָּ**אֵי לְךָ הַיּוֹם בְּכָל לֵב, שׁוֹפְכִים לְךָ שִׂיחַ בְּלֹא לֵב וָלֵב,
שׁוֹאֲלִים מִמְּךָ עוֹז מִטְרוֹת מָיִם.
לְ**שׁוֹ**רְרוּךָ בַּיָּם, הוֹשַׁעְנָא וְהוֹשִׁיעָה נָּא, אָבִינוּ אָתָּה.

לְמַעַן **א**וֹמְרֵי יִגְדַּל שְׁמֶךָ, וְהֵם נַחֲלָתְךָ וְעַמֶּךָ,
צְמֵאִים לְיֶשְׁעֲךָ. כְּאֶרֶץ עֲיֵפָה לַמָּיִם.
לְ**תַ**רְתָּ לָמוֹ מְנוּחָה, הוֹשַׁעְנָא וְהוֹשִׁיעָה נָּא, אָבִינוּ אָתָּה.

---

related incident. The final lines of the verses form a straight alphabetical acrostic, beginning with **א**, and listing praises of Israel, the nation, or of *Eretz Yisrael*.

— for the sake of Your Holy Name,
may You save now and bring salvation now, for You are our Father.

In the merit of the good and increasingly exalted one [Samuel] who restrained himself from robbing the flock, when the nation repented he bade them draw water
— for the sake of the one as beautiful as Jerusalem,
may You save now and bring salvation now, for You are our Father.

In the merit of the one [David] who caused You joy, dancing with song, who teaches Torah accompanied by every sort of instrument, he poured libations before Him though he thirsted to drink water
— for the sake of those who place their hope in You,
may You save now and bring salvation now, for You are our Father.

In the merit of the pure one [Elijah] who ascended in a storm wind, who avenged and turned back fury, at his prayer there descended fire which consumed dust and water
— for the sake of the one whose eyes are like pools,
may You save now and bring salvation now, for You are our Father.

In the merit of the one [Elisha] who served his master earnestly, a double measure of his spirit was vested in him, when he summoned a musician the cisterns were filled with water
— for the sake of those who exclaimed, 'Who is like You?',
may You save now and bring salvation now, for You are our Father.

In the merit of the one [Hezekiah] who meant to do Your will, he cried out, 'Repentance,' to Your sheep, then when the blasphemer came he sealed the springs of water
— for the sake of Zion, perfect in beauty,
may You save now and bring salvation now, for You are our Father.

In the merit of those [Daniel, Chananiah, Mishael, and Azariah] who sought You in midst of the exile, your secret was uncovered to them. Not to defile themselves they requested pulse and water
— for the sake of those who call in distress,
may You save now and bring salvation now, for You are our Father.

In the merit of the one [Ezra] who studied wisdom and understanding, a skillful scribe, expounder of faith, he made us wise with sayings that are likened to expanses of water
— for the sake of the city great with people,
may You save now and bring salvation now, for You are our Father.

For the sake of those [the present congregation] who came to You today with all their heart, pouring prayer before You with undivided heart, asking You for powerful rains of water
— for the sake of those who sang to You at the Sea,
may You save now and bring salvation now, for You are our Father.

For the sake of those [Israel] who say, 'May Your Name be exalted!' they are Your heritage and Your nation; they thirst for Your salvation as does a land that thirsts for water
— for the sake of those for whom You scouted a resting place,
may You save now and bring salvation now, for You are our Father.

תענה אמונים

Some put aside the *lulav* and *esrog* and take up the *hoshana*-bundle of five willow twigs. This is held until it is beaten at the end of the service. Others retain the *lulav* and *esrog* and do not take up the *hoshana*-bundle until it is to be beaten.

הוֹשַׁעְנָא, אֵל נָא, אָנָּא הוֹשִׁיעָה נָּא.
הוֹשַׁעְנָא, סְלַח נָא, וְהַצְלִיחָה נָא,
וְהוֹשִׁיעֵנוּ אֵל מָעֻזֵּנוּ.

תַּעֲנֶה אֱמוּנִים שׁוֹפְכִים לְךָ לֵב כַּמַּיִם, וְהוֹשִׁיעָה נָּא,
לְמַעַן **בָּא** בָּאֵשׁ וּבַמַּיִם,
גָּזַר וְנָם יֻקַּח נָא מְעַט מַיִם, וְהַצְלִיחָה נָא, וְהוֹשִׁיעֵנוּ אֵל מָעֻזֵּנוּ.

תַּעֲנֶה **דְ**גָלִים גָּזוּ גִּזְרֵי מַיִם, וְהוֹשִׁיעָה נָּא,
לְמַעַן **הַ**נֶּעֱקַד בְּשַׁעַר הַשָּׁמַיִם,
וְשָׁב וְחָפַר בְּאֵרוֹת מַיִם, וְהַצְלִיחָה נָא, וְהוֹשִׁיעֵנוּ אֵל מָעֻזֵּנוּ.

תַּעֲנֶה **זַ**כִּים חוֹנִים עֲלֵי מַיִם, וְהוֹשִׁיעָה נָּא,
לְמַעַן **חָ**לָק מְפַצֵּל מַקְלוֹת בְּשִׁקֲתוֹת הַמַּיִם,
טָעַן וְגָל אֶבֶן מִבְּאֵר מַיִם, וְהַצְלִיחָה נָא, וְהוֹשִׁיעֵנוּ אֵל מָעֻזֵּנוּ.

תַּעֲנֶה **יְ**דִידִים נוֹחֲלֵי דָת מְשׁוּלַת מַיִם, וְהוֹשִׁיעָה נָּא,
לְמַעַן **כָּ**רוּ בְּמִשְׁעֲנוֹתָם מַיִם.
לְהָכִין לָמוֹ וּלְצֶאֱצָאֵימוֹ מַיִם, וְהַצְלִיחָה נָא, וְהוֹשִׁיעֵנוּ אֵל מָעֻזֵּנוּ.

תַּעֲנֶה **מִ**תְחַנְּנִים כְּבִישִׁימוֹן עֲלֵי מַיִם, וְהוֹשִׁיעָה נָּא,
לְמַעַן **נֶ**אֱמַן בַּיִת מַסְפִּיק לָעָם מַיִם,
סֶלַע הָךְ וַיָּזוּבוּ מַיִם, וְהַצְלִיחָה נָא, וְהוֹשִׁיעֵנוּ אֵל מָעֻזֵּנוּ.

תַּעֲנֶה **עוֹ**נִים עֲלֵי בְאֵר מַיִם, וְהוֹשִׁיעָה נָּא,
לְמַעַן **פֻּ**קַד בְּמֵי מְרִיבַת מַיִם,
צְמֵאִים לְהַשְׁקוֹתָם מַיִם, וְהַצְלִיחָה נָא, וְהוֹשִׁיעֵנוּ אֵל מָעֻזֵּנוּ.

תַּעֲנֶה **קְ**דוֹשִׁים מְנַסְּכִים לְךָ מַיִם, וְהוֹשִׁיעָה נָּא,
לְמַעַן **רֹ**אשׁ מְשׁוֹרְרִים כְּתָאַב שְׁתוֹת מַיִם,
שָׁב וְנָסַךְ לְךָ מַיִם, וְהַצְלִיחָה נָא, וְהוֹשִׁיעֵנוּ אֵל מָעֻזֵּנוּ.

תַּעֲנֶה **שׁוֹ**אֲלִים בְּרִבּוּעַ אֶשְׁלֵי מַיִם, וְהוֹשִׁיעָה נָּא,
לְמַעַן **תֵּ**ל תַּלְפִּיּוֹת מוֹצָא מַיִם,
תִּפְתַּח אֶרֶץ וְתַרְעִיף שָׁמַיִם, וְהַצְלִיחָה נָא, וְהוֹשִׁיעֵנוּ אֵל מָעֻזֵּנוּ.

תַּעֲנֶה אֱמוּנִים / Answer the Faithful
Following the theme of the preceding *Hoshana,* we again ask for rain in the merit of our righteous forbears.

ANSWER THE FAITHFUL

Some put aside the *lulav* and *esrog* and take up the *hoshana*-bundle of five willow twigs. This is held until it is beaten at the end of the service. Others retain the *lulav* and *esrog* and do not take up the *hoshana*-bundle until it is to be beaten.

Save now, please God, please bring salvation now.
Save now, forgive now, bring success now,
and save us, God, our Fortress.

תַּעֲנֶה אֱמוּנִים *Answer the faithful who pour out their heart to You like water — and bring salvation now,*
in the merit of the one [Abraham] who entered fire and water — who decreed saying, 'Let there now be taken some water;'
and bring success now and save us, God, our Fortress.
Answer the banners [the Twelve Tribes] who passed through divisions of water — and bring salvation now,
in the merit of the one [Isaac] bound at the gateway of Heaven, who returned and dug wells of water;
and bring success now and save us, God, our Fortress.
Answer the pure ones [Israelites] who encamped near the water — and bring salvation now,
in the merit of the smooth-skinned one [Jacob] who peeled rods at the trough of water, who lifted and rolled away a boulder from a well of water; and bring success now and save us, God, our Fortress.
Answer the beloved heirs of the mandate likened to water — and bring salvation now,
in the merit of those who dug with their staffs for water, to prepare, for themselves and for their offspring, water;
and bring success now and save us, God, our Fortress.
Answer those who beseech as in the Wilderness for water — and bring salvation now,
in the merit of the most trusted of the household [Moses], who supplied the people with water, who struck the rock and there flowed water,
and bring success now and save us, God, our Fortress.
Answer those who responded, 'Ascend, O well of water' — and bring salvation now,
in the merit of the one [Aaron] assigned at Merivah's waters, to give drink to those thirsting for water;
and bring success now and save us, God, our Fortress.
Answer the holy ones who pour before You libations of water — and bring salvation now,
in the merit of the foremost singer [David], who, though thirsting to drink water, poured before You a libation of water;
and bring success now and save us, God, our Fortress.
Answer those who ask with a quartet of species planted near water — and bring salvation now,
in the merit of the Hill of Talpios [the Temple], source of water, may the earth open wide and the heavens give rain;
and bring success now and save us, God, our Fortress.

אז כעיני עבדים

רַחֵם נָא קְהַל עֲדַת יְשֻׁרוּן, סְלַח וּמְחַל עֲוֹנָם, וְהוֹשִׁיעֵנוּ אֱלֹהֵי יִשְׁעֵנוּ.

אָז כְּעֵינֵי עֲבָדִים אֶל יַד אֲדוֹנִים,
בָּאנוּ לְפָנֶיךָ נְדוֹנִים, וְהוֹשִׁיעֵנוּ אֱלֹהֵי יִשְׁעֵנוּ.
גֵּאָה אֲדוֹנֵי הָאֲדוֹנִים, נִתְגָּרוּ בָנוּ מְדָנִים,
דְּשׁוּנוּ וּבְעָלוּנוּ זוּלָתְךָ אֲדוֹנִים, וְהוֹשִׁיעֵנוּ אֱלֹהֵי יִשְׁעֵנוּ.
הֵן גַּשְׁנוּ הַיּוֹם בְּתַחֲנוּן, עָדֶיךָ רַחוּם וְחַנּוּן,
וּסִפַּרְנוּ נִפְלְאוֹתֶיךָ בְּשִׁנּוּן, וְהוֹשִׁיעֵנוּ אֱלֹהֵי יִשְׁעֵנוּ.
זָבַת חָלָב וּדְבָשׁ, נָא אַל תִּיבָשׁ,
חֶשְׁרַת מַיִם בְּאִבֶּיהָ תֶּחְבָּשׁ, וְהוֹשִׁיעֵנוּ אֱלֹהֵי יִשְׁעֵנוּ.
טְעֵנוּ בִּשְׁמֹנָה, בְּיַד שִׁבְעָה וּשְׁמוֹנָה,
יָשָׁר צַדִּיק אֵל אֱמוּנָה, וְהוֹשִׁיעֵנוּ אֱלֹהֵי יִשְׁעֵנוּ.
כָּרַתָּ בְרִית לָאָרֶץ, עוֹד כָּל יְמֵי הָאָרֶץ,
לְבִלְתִּי פְרָץ בָּהּ פֶּרֶץ, וְהוֹשִׁיעֵנוּ אֱלֹהֵי יִשְׁעֵנוּ.
מִתְחַנְּנִים עֲלֵי מַיִם, כַּעֲרָבִים עַל יִבְלֵי מָיִם,
נָא זְכָר לָמוֹ נִסּוּךְ הַמַּיִם, וְהוֹשִׁיעֵנוּ אֱלֹהֵי יִשְׁעֵנוּ.
שִׂיחִים בְּדֶרֶךְ מַטָּעָתָם, עוֹמְסִים בְּשַׁוְעָתָם,
עֱנֵם בְּקוֹל פְּגִיעָתָם, וְהוֹשִׁיעֵנוּ אֱלֹהֵי יִשְׁעֵנוּ.
פּוֹעֵל יְשׁוּעוֹת, פְּנֵה לְפִלּוּלָם שְׁעוֹת,
צַדְּקֵם אֵל לְמוֹשָׁעוֹת, וְהוֹשִׁיעֵנוּ אֱלֹהֵי יִשְׁעֵנוּ.
קוֹל רִגְשָׁם תֶּשַׁע, תִּפְתַּח אֶרֶץ וְיִפְרוּ יֶשַׁע,
רַב לְהוֹשִׁיעַ וְלֹא חָפֵץ רֶשַׁע, וְהוֹשִׁיעֵנוּ אֱלֹהֵי יִשְׁעֵנוּ.

שַׁעֲרֵי שָׁמַיִם פְּתַח, וְאוֹצָרְךָ הַטּוֹב לָנוּ תִפְתַּח, תּוֹשִׁיעֵנוּ וְרִיב אַל תִּמְתַּח, וְהוֹשִׁיעֵנוּ אֱלֹהֵי יִשְׁעֵנוּ.

קול מבשר

קוֹל מְבַשֵּׂר מְבַשֵּׂר וְאוֹמֵר:

אֹמֶץ יֶשְׁעֲךָ בָּא, קוֹל דּוֹדִי הִנֵּה זֶה בָּא, מְבַשֵּׂר וְאוֹמֵר.
קוֹל בָּא בְּרִבְבוֹת כִּתִּים, לַעֲמוֹד עַל הַר הַזֵּיתִים, מְבַשֵּׂר וְאוֹמֵר.

אָז כְּעֵינֵי עֲבָדִים / Then, Like the Eyes of Slaves.

Slaves have no avenues of support other than the largesse of their master. Likewise, Israel has no source of sustenance other than its faith in God to whom it turns its eyes (*Radak* to *Psalms* 123:2).

THEN, LIKE THE EYES OF SLAVES

Be Merciful, please, with the congregation of Jeshurun's flock; forgive and pardon their iniquities; and save us, God of our salvation.

אָז כְּעֵינֵי עֲבָדִים *Then, like the eyes of slaves looking to their master's hand, so did we come before You for judgment — so save us, God of our salvation.*

Proud One, Lord of lords, they have stirred up strife within us; lords have trodden upon us and become our masters, excluding You — so save us, God of our salvation.

Indeed we have approached with supplication today, before You, O merciful and gracious One. And we have recounted, and repeated Your wonders — so save us, God of our salvation.

Where milk and honey flow please make not arid. With watering clouds clothe her produce — and save us, God of our salvation.

Plant us in the fertile land, by the hand of seven and eight; O just and righteous One, O trustworthy God — and save us, God of our salvation.

You have made a covenant with the earth, continuously, all the days of the earth, not to cause a breach in it — so save us, God of our salvation.

Those who supplicate for water like willows alongside streams of water; please, remember for their sake the libations of water — and save us, God of our salvation.

Trees, in the direction of their growth, they carry as they supplicate — respond to the sound of their entreaties — and save us, God of our salvation.

Worker of salvations, heed their prayers and turn to them, adjudge them righteous, O God of salvations — and save us, God of our salvation.

To the voices of their multitudes turn, open the earth and let salvation sprout, O He Who is bounteous in salvation, and desires not wickedness — and save us, God of our salvation.

Open the gates of heaven, and Your goodly treasure trove may You open for us. Save us, do not let accusations be drawn out, and save us, God of our salvation.

THE VOICE OF THE HERALD

The voice of the herald heralds and proclaims:

אֹמֶץ יְשְׁעֲךָ *The strength of Your salvations comes, a voice — my Beloved, behold He comes — heralds and proclaims.*

A voice — He comes among myriad bands, to stand upon the Mount of Olives — heralds and proclaims.

קוֹל מְבַשֵּׂר / The Voice of the Herald ◆§

Upon concluding the prayers for rain we proclaim our faith in תְּחִיַּת הַמֵּתִים, *the resuscitation of the dead,* which will follow the coming of the Messiah.

This juxtaposition is based upon the Talmud and the Midrash: Greater is the day of the rains

קוֹל גִּשְׁתּוֹ בְּשׁוֹפָר לִתְקַע, תַּחְתָּיו הַר יִבָּקַע, מְבַשֵּׂר וְאוֹמֵר.
קוֹל דָּפַק וְהֵצִיץ וְזָרַח, וּמָשׁ חֲצִי הָהָר מִמִּזְרָח, מְבַשֵּׂר וְאוֹמֵר.
קוֹל הֵקִים מִלּוּל נְאָמוֹ, וּבָא הוּא וְכָל קְדוֹשָׁיו עִמּוֹ, מְבַשֵּׂר וְאוֹמֵר.
קוֹל וּלְכָל בָּאֵי הָעוֹלָם, בַּת קוֹל יִשָּׁמַע בָּעוֹלָם, מְבַשֵּׂר וְאוֹמֵר.
קוֹל זֶרַע עֲמוּסֵי רְחָמוֹ, נוֹלְדוּ כְּיֶלֶד מִמְּעֵי אִמּוֹ, מְבַשֵּׂר וְאוֹמֵר.
קוֹל חָלָה וְיָלְדָה מִי זֹאת, מִי שָׁמַע כָּזֹאת, מְבַשֵּׂר וְאוֹמֵר.
קוֹל טָהוֹר פָּעַל כָּל אֵלֶּה, וּמִי רָאָה כָּאֵלֶּה, מְבַשֵּׂר וְאוֹמֵר.
קוֹל יֶשַׁע וּזְמַן הוּחַד, הֲיוּחַל אֶרֶץ בְּיוֹם אֶחָד, מְבַשֵּׂר וְאוֹמֵר.
קוֹל כַּבִּיר רוּם וָתַחַת, אִם יִוָּלֵד גּוֹי פַּעַם אֶחָת, מְבַשֵּׂר וְאוֹמֵר.
קוֹל לְעֵת יִגְאַל עַמּוֹ נָאוֹר, וְהָיָה לְעֵת עֶרֶב יִהְיֶה אוֹר, מְבַשֵּׂר וְאוֹמֵר.
קוֹל מוֹשִׁיעִים יַעֲלוּ לְהַר צִיּוֹן, כִּי חָלָה גַּם יָלְדָה צִיּוֹן, מְבַשֵּׂר וְאוֹמֵר.
קוֹל נִשְׁמַע בְּכָל גְּבוּלֵךְ, הַרְחִיבִי מְקוֹם אָהֳלֵךְ, מְבַשֵּׂר וְאוֹמֵר.
קוֹל שִׂימִי עַד דַּמֶּשֶׂק מִשְׁכְּבוֹתָיִךְ, קַבְּלִי בָנַיִךְ וּבְנוֹתָיִךְ, מְבַשֵּׂר וְאוֹמֵר.
קוֹל עִלְזִי חֲבַצֶּלֶת הַשָּׁרוֹן, כִּי קָמוּ יְשֵׁנֵי חֶבְרוֹן, מְבַשֵּׂר וְאוֹמֵר.
קוֹל פְּנוּ אֵלַי וְהִוָּשְׁעוּ, הַיּוֹם אִם בְּקוֹלִי תִשְׁמָעוּ, מְבַשֵּׂר וְאוֹמֵר.
קוֹל צָמַח אִישׁ צֶמַח שְׁמוֹ, הוּא דָוִד בְּעַצְמוֹ, מְבַשֵּׂר וְאוֹמֵר.
קוֹל קוּמוּ כְּפוּשֵׁי עָפָר, הָקִיצוּ וְרַנְּנוּ שׁוֹכְנֵי עָפָר, מְבַשֵּׂר וְאוֹמֵר.
קוֹל רַבָּתִי עָם בְּהַמְלִיכוֹ, מִגְדּוֹל יְשׁוּעוֹת מַלְכּוֹ, מְבַשֵּׂר וְאוֹמֵר.
קוֹל שֵׁם רְשָׁעִים לְהַאֲבִיד, עֹשֶׂה חֶסֶד לִמְשִׁיחוֹ לְדָוִד, מְבַשֵּׂר וְאוֹמֵר.
קוֹל תְּנָה יְשׁוּעוֹת לְעַם עוֹלָם, לְדָוִד וּלְזַרְעוֹ עַד עוֹלָם, מְבַשֵּׂר וְאוֹמֵר.

The *chazzan* calls out loudly three times, followed by the congregation:

קוֹל מְבַשֵּׂר מְבַשֵּׂר וְאוֹמֵר.
קוֹל מְבַשֵּׂר מְבַשֵּׂר וְאוֹמֵר.
קוֹל מְבַשֵּׂר מְבַשֵּׂר וְאוֹמֵר.

הוֹשִׁיעָה אֶת עַמֶּךָ וּבָרֵךְ אֶת נַחֲלָתֶךָ, וּרְעֵם וְנַשְּׂאֵם עַד הָעוֹלָם.[1] וְיִהְיוּ דְבָרַי אֵלֶּה אֲשֶׁר הִתְחַנַּנְתִּי לִפְנֵי יהוה, קְרֹבִים אֶל יהוה אֱלֹהֵינוּ יוֹמָם וָלָיְלָה, לַעֲשׂוֹת מִשְׁפַּט עַבְדּוֹ וּמִשְׁפַּט עַמּוֹ יִשְׂרָאֵל, דְּבַר יוֹם בְּיוֹמוֹ. לְמַעַן דַּעַת כָּל עַמֵּי הָאָרֶץ, כִּי יהוה הוּא הָאֱלֹהִים, אֵין עוֹד.[2]

(1) *Psalms* 28:9. (2) *I Kings* 8:59-60.

than the resuscitation of the dead. The resuscitation will benefit only the righteous, while the rains benefit both the righteous and the wicked *(Taanis* 7a); the resuscitation will benefit only man, while the rains benefit both man and beast *(Bereishis Rabbah* 13:6).

A voice — To the blast of the shofar, He draws near, beneath Him the mountain shall be split — heralds and proclaims.

A voice — He knocks, He peers and He shines, and half the mountain moves from the east — heralds and proclaims.

A voice — He has verified the words of His utterance, He has come, and all His holy ones with Him — heralds and proclaims.

A voice — To all who walk the earth, a heavenly voice is heard on the earth — heralds and proclaims.

A voice — The seed borne by Him from the womb, born like a child from its mother's innards — heralds and proclaims.

A voice — She delivered and gave birth: 'Who is this? Who has heard the likes of this?' — heralds and proclaims.

A voice — The pure One has done all these; and who has seen the likes of these? — heralds and proclaims.

A voice — Salvation and its moment were ordained. Can the earth deliver issue in a single day? — heralds and proclaims.

A voice — He Who is mighty above and below, can a nation be born in a trice? — heralds and proclaims.

A voice — when the resplendent One redeems His nation, at evening time there will be light — heralds and proclaims.

A voice — Saviors shall ascend upon Mount Zion, for Zion has delivered and given birth — heralds and proclaims.

A voice — It is heard within all your boundaries, 'Expand the area of your tents!' — heralds and proclaims.

A voice — Set up your dwellings until Damasek, receive your sons and your daughters — heralds and proclaims.

A voice — Be joyous, O rose of Sharon, for those sleeping in Hebron have arisen — heralds and proclaims.

A voice — Turn to Me and you shall be saved this very day — if you will but heed My voice — heralds and proclaims.

A voice — A man has sprouted, Tzemach is his name, He is David himself — heralds and proclaims.

A voice — Arise, you who are covered with dust; awake and sing, you who lie in the dust — heralds and proclaims.

A voice — When He rules the city great with people, His king shall be a tower of salvations — heralds and proclaims.

A voice — The name of the wicked He will cause to be lost, but He will show kindness to His anointed, to David — heralds and proclaims.

A voice — Grant salvations to the eternal people, to David and to his descendants, forever — heralds and proclaims.

The chazzan calls out loudly three times, followed by the congregation:

The voice of the herald heralds and proclaims.
The voice of the herald heralds and proclaims.
The voice of the herald heralds and proclaims.

הוֹשִׁיעָה *Save Your nation and bless Your heritage, tend them and elevate them forever.*[1] *May these words of mine, which I have supplicated before* HASHEM, *be near to* HASHEM, *our God, by day and by night; that He bring about justice for His servant and justice for His people, Israel, each day's need in its day; that all the peoples of the earth shall know that* HASHEM *is God, there is no other.*[2]

חביטת הערבה

The Torah Scrolls are returned to the Ark and it is closed. The *hoshana*-bundle is beaten on the ground, after which the יְהִי רָצוֹן is recited, followed by the Full *Kaddish*. In some congregations the order is reversed, with *Kaddish* being recited before the *hoshana*-bundle is beaten.

יְהִי רָצוֹן מִלְּפָנֶיךָ יהוה אֱלֹהֵינוּ וֵאלֹהֵי אֲבוֹתֵינוּ, הַבּוֹחֵר בִּנְבִיאִים טוֹבִים וּבְמִנְהֲגֵיהֶם הַטּוֹבִים,* שֶׁתְּקַבֵּל בְּרַחֲמִים וּבְרָצוֹן אֶת תְּפִלָּתֵנוּ וְהַקָּפוֹתֵינוּ, וּזְכָר לָנוּ זְכוּת שִׁבְעַת תְּמִימֶיךָ, וְתָסִיר מְחִיצַת הַבַּרְזֶל* הַמַּפְסֶקֶת בֵּינֵינוּ וּבֵינֶיךָ, וְתַאֲזִין שַׁוְעָתֵנוּ, וְתֵיטִיב לָנוּ הַחֲתִימָה,* תְּלֵה אֶרֶץ עַל בְּלִימָה. וְחָתְמֵנוּ בְּסֵפֶר חַיִּים טוֹבִים. וְהַיּוֹם הַזֶּה תִּתֵּן בִּשְׁכִינַת עֻזֶּךָ. חֲמִשָּׁה גְבוּרוֹת מְמֻתָּקוֹת עַל יְדֵי חֲבִיטַת עֲרָבָה מִנְהַג נְבִיאֶיךָ הַקְּדוֹשִׁים. וְתִתְעוֹרֵר הָאַהֲבָה בֵּינֵיהֶם, וּתְנַשְּׁקֵנוּ מִנְּשִׁיקוֹת פִּיךָ, מַמְתֶּקֶת כָּל הַגְּבוּרוֹת וְכָל הַדִּינִין, וְתָאִיר לִשְׁכִינַת עֻזֶּךָ בְּשֵׁם יו״ד הֵ״א וָא״ו שֶׁהוּא טַל אוֹרֹת טַלֶּךָ, וּמִשָּׁם תַּשְׁפִּיעַ שֶׁפַע לְעַבְדְּךָ הַמִּתְנַפֵּל לְפָנֶיךָ, מְחִילָה, שֶׁתַּאֲרִיךְ יָמַי וְתִמְחַל לִי חֲטָאַי וַעֲוֹנוֹתַי וּפְשָׁעַי, וְתִפְשׁוֹט יְמִינְךָ וְיָדְךָ לְקַבְּלֵנִי בִּתְשׁוּבָה שְׁלֵמָה לְפָנֶיךָ, וְאוֹצָרְךָ הַטּוֹב תִּפְתַּח לְהַשְׂבִּיעַ מַיִם נֶפֶשׁ שׁוֹקֵקָה, כְּמוֹ שֶׁכָּתוּב: יִפְתַּח יהוה לְךָ אֶת אוֹצָרוֹ הַטּוֹב אֶת הַשָּׁמַיִם, לָתֵת מְטַר אַרְצְךָ בְּעִתּוֹ וּלְבָרֵךְ אֶת כָּל מַעֲשֵׂה יָדֶךָ.[1] אָמֵן.

קדיש שלם

The *chazzan* recites קַדִּישׁ שָׁלֵם, the Full *Kaddish*:

יִתְגַּדַּל וְיִתְקַדַּשׁ שְׁמֵהּ רַבָּא. (.Cong —אָמֵן.) בְּעָלְמָא דִּי בְרָא כִרְעוּתֵהּ. וְיַמְלִיךְ מַלְכוּתֵהּ, בְּחַיֵּיכוֹן וּבְיוֹמֵיכוֹן וּבְחַיֵּי דְכָל בֵּית יִשְׂרָאֵל, בַּעֲגָלָא וּבִזְמַן קָרִיב. וְאִמְרוּ: אָמֵן.

(.Cong —אָמֵן. יְהֵא שְׁמֵהּ רַבָּא מְבָרַךְ לְעָלַם וּלְעָלְמֵי עָלְמַיָּא.)

יְהֵא שְׁמֵהּ רַבָּא מְבָרַךְ לְעָלַם וּלְעָלְמֵי עָלְמַיָּא.

יִתְבָּרַךְ וְיִשְׁתַּבַּח וְיִתְפָּאַר וְיִתְרוֹמַם וְיִתְנַשֵּׂא וְיִתְהַדָּר וְיִתְעַלֶּה וְיִתְהַלָּל שְׁמֵהּ דְּקֻדְשָׁא בְּרִיךְ הוּא (.Cong —בְּרִיךְ הוּא) — לְעֵלָּא מִן כָּל בִּרְכָתָא וְשִׁירָתָא תֻּשְׁבְּחָתָא וְנֶחֱמָתָא, דַּאֲמִירָן בְּעָלְמָא. וְאִמְרוּ: אָמֵן. (.Cong —אָמֵן.)

(.Cong —קַבֵּל בְּרַחֲמִים וּבְרָצוֹן אֶת תְּפִלָּתֵנוּ.)

תִּתְקַבֵּל צְלוֹתְהוֹן וּבָעוּתְהוֹן דְּכָל בֵּית יִשְׂרָאֵל קֳדָם אֲבוּהוֹן דִּי בִשְׁמַיָּא. וְאִמְרוּ: אָמֵן. (.Cong —אָמֵן.)

(.Cong —יְהִי שֵׁם יהוה מְבֹרָךְ, מֵעַתָּה וְעַד עוֹלָם.[2])

יְהֵא שְׁלָמָא רַבָּא מִן שְׁמַיָּא, וְחַיִּים עָלֵינוּ וְעַל כָּל יִשְׂרָאֵל. וְאִמְרוּ: אָמֵן. (.Cong —אָמֵן.)

(.Cong —עֶזְרִי מֵעִם יהוה, עֹשֵׂה שָׁמַיִם וָאָרֶץ.[3])

עֹשֶׂה שָׁלוֹם בִּמְרוֹמָיו, הוּא יַעֲשֶׂה שָׁלוֹם עָלֵינוּ, וְעַל כָּל יִשְׂרָאֵל. וְאִמְרוּ: אָמֵן. (.Cong —אָמֵן.)

The service continues with קַוֵּה אֶל ה׳ (p. 476).

(1) *Deuteronomy* 28:12 (2) *Psalms* 113:2. (3) 121:2.

BEATING THE HOSHANA-BUNDLE

The Torah Scrolls are returned to the Ark and it is closed. The *hoshana*-bundle is beaten on the ground, after which the יְהִי רָצוֹן prayer is recited, followed by קַדִּישׁ שָׁלֵם. In some congregations the order is reversed, with *Kaddish* being recited before the *hoshana*-bundle is beaten.

יְהִי רָצוֹן *May it be favorable before You, HASHEM, our God and God of our fathers, He Who opts for good prophets and their good customs,* that You accept with mercy and favor our prayers and our hakafah-circuits. Remember for our sake the merit of Your seven perfect ones. Remove the iron partition* separating us from You. Hearken to our pleas and grant us the good seal,* He Who suspends the earth upon silence. Seal us in the Book of Good Life. Today may You place, with the manifestation of Your strength, five strict powers which have been sweetened through the beating of willows, the custom ordained by Your holy prophets. May You awaken love among them and kiss us with the kisses of Your mouth, which sweeten all the strict powers and all the harsh judgments. bmay you illuminate the manifestation of Your strength with the Name Yud Kei Vav which corresponds to the dew — Your dew is the dew of lights. From there endow Your servant, who prostrates himself before You, with forgiveness, that my days may be lengthened. Forgive me my sins, my iniquities, and my transgressions. Spread wide Your right arm and Your hand to accept me, with my wholehearted repentance before You. Open Your goodly treasure trove to satisfy with water a thirsty soul — as it is written: May HASHEM open for you His goodly treasure trove, the heavens, to give your land rain in its season and to bless all of your handiwork.*[1] *Amen.*

The *chazzan* recites the Full *Kaddish:*

יִתְגַּדַּל *May His great Name grow exalted and sanctified* (Cong.— *Amen.*) *in the world that He created as He willed. May He give reign to His kingship in your lifetimes and in your days, and in the lifetimes of the entire Family of Israel, swiftly and soon. Now respond: Amen.*

(Cong.— *Amen. May His great Name be blessed forever and ever.*)

May His great Name be blessed forever and ever.

Blessed, praised, glorified, exalted, extolled, mighty, upraised, and lauded be the Name of the Holy One, Blessed is He (Cong.— *Blessed is He*) — *beyond any blessing and song, praise and consolation that are uttered in the world. Now respond: Amen.* (Cong.— *Amen.*)

(Cong.— *Accept our prayers with mercy and favor.*)

May the prayers and supplications of the entire Family of Israel be accepted before their Father Who is in Heaven. Now respond: Amen. (Cong.— *Amen.*)

(Cong.— *May the Name of HASHEM, be blessed from now to eternity*[2].)

May there be abundant peace from Heaven, and life, upon us and upon all Israel. Now respond: Amen. (Cong.— *Amen.*)

(Cong.— *My help is from HASHEM, Maker of heaven and earth.*[3])

He Who makes peace in His heights, may He make peace upon us, and upon all Israel. Now respond: Amen. (Cong.— *Amen.*)

The service continues with קַוֵּה אֶל ה׳, *'Hope to HASHEM ...'* (p. 476).

יְהִי רָצוֹן / May It Be Favorable

וּבְמִנְהֲגֵיהֶם הַטּוֹבִים — *And their good customs.* The beating of the willow is a custom ordained by the prophets.

מְחִיצַת הַבַּרְזֶל — *The iron partition.* Sinful acts build a partition between the sinner and the spark of holiness, which is the source of spiritual life. As one plunges deeper into sin, the partition strengthens until it is strong as iron, while the spark of holiness becomes virtually inaccessible. Only repentance can breach the partition and extricate that spark of holiness (see *Tanya* 1:17).

הַחֲתִימָה — *The seal.* On Hoshana Rabbah the final seal is placed on the verdict issued on Rosh Hashanah and tentatively sealed on Yom Kippur.

הקפות לשמחת תורה

Before the Ark is opened on *Simchas Torah,* the following selection of verses is recited responsively:

אַתָּה הָרְאֵתָ לָדַעַת, כִּי יהוה הוּא הָאֱלֹהִים, אֵין עוֹד מִלְּבַדּוֹ.[1]
לְעֹשֵׂה נִפְלָאוֹת גְּדֹלוֹת לְבַדּוֹ, כִּי לְעוֹלָם חַסְדּוֹ.[2]
אֵין כָּמוֹךָ בָאֱלֹהִים, אֲדֹנָי, וְאֵין כְּמַעֲשֶׂיךָ.[3]
יְהִי כְבוֹד יהוה לְעוֹלָם, יִשְׂמַח יהוה בְּמַעֲשָׂיו.[4]
יְהִי שֵׁם יהוה מְבֹרָךְ, מֵעַתָּה וְעַד עוֹלָם.[5]
יְהִי יהוה אֱלֹהֵינוּ עִמָּנוּ, כַּאֲשֶׁר הָיָה עִם אֲבֹתֵינוּ,
אַל יַעַזְבֵנוּ וְאַל יִטְּשֵׁנוּ.[6]
וְאִמְרוּ, הוֹשִׁיעֵנוּ, אֱלֹהֵי יִשְׁעֵנוּ, וְקַבְּצֵנוּ וְהַצִּילֵנוּ מִן הַגּוֹיִם,
לְהֹדוֹת לְשֵׁם קָדְשֶׁךָ, לְהִשְׁתַּבֵּחַ בִּתְהִלָּתֶךָ.[7]
יהוה מֶלֶךְ,[8] יהוה מָלָךְ,[9] יהוה יִמְלֹךְ לְעוֹלָם וָעֶד.[10]
יהוה עֹז לְעַמּוֹ יִתֵּן, יהוה יְבָרֵךְ אֶת עַמּוֹ בַשָּׁלוֹם.[11]
וְיִהְיוּ נָא אֲמָרֵינוּ לְרָצוֹן, לִפְנֵי אֲדוֹן כֹּל.[12]

The ark is opened and the responsive recitation continues:

וַיְהִי בִּנְסֹעַ הָאָרֹן, וַיֹּאמֶר מֹשֶׁה, קוּמָה יהוה, וְיָפֻצוּ אֹיְבֶיךָ,
וְיָנֻסוּ מְשַׂנְאֶיךָ מִפָּנֶיךָ.[13]
קוּמָה יהוה לִמְנוּחָתֶךָ, אַתָּה וַאֲרוֹן עֻזֶּךָ.
כֹּהֲנֶיךָ יִלְבְּשׁוּ צֶדֶק, וַחֲסִידֶיךָ יְרַנֵּנוּ.
בַּעֲבוּר דָּוִד עַבְדֶּךָ, אַל תָּשֵׁב פְּנֵי מְשִׁיחֶךָ.[14]
וְאָמַר בַּיּוֹם הַהוּא, הִנֵּה אֱלֹהֵינוּ זֶה, קִוִּינוּ לוֹ וְיוֹשִׁיעֵנוּ,
זֶה יהוה קִוִּינוּ לוֹ, נָגִילָה וְנִשְׂמְחָה בִּישׁוּעָתוֹ.[15]
מַלְכוּתְךָ מַלְכוּת כָּל עֹלָמִים, וּמֶמְשַׁלְתְּךָ בְּכָל דּוֹר וָדֹר.[16]
כִּי מִצִּיּוֹן תֵּצֵא תוֹרָה, וּדְבַר יהוה מִירוּשָׁלָיִם.[17]

אַב הָרַחֲמִים, הֵיטִיבָה בִרְצוֹנְךָ אֶת צִיּוֹן, תִּבְנֶה חוֹמוֹת יְרוּשָׁלָיִם.[18]
כִּי בְךָ לְבַד בָּטָחְנוּ, מֶלֶךְ אֵל רָם וְנִשָּׂא, אֲדוֹן עוֹלָמִים.

SIMCHAS TORAH

Simchas Torah is unique among the Festivals. Technically, in the Diaspora, it is the second-day extension of Shemini Atzeres and should no more have a separate identity than the eighth day of Pesach or the second day of Shavuos. Nevertheless, the special nature of Simchas Torah — literally, celebration of the Torah — has caused it to be given a name that emphasizes the joyous nature of the day.

Besamim Rosh cites two Midrashic passages as reasons for the name and nature of the day: When God promised unsurpassed wisdom to the newly crowned Solomon, the young king celebrated with a feast for all his dear ones (*II Kings* 3:15). From this the Sages derive that one should make a feast upon completing a section of the Torah — as we do on Simchas Torah when we complete the reading of the Five Books of the Torah.

Another Midrash teaches that Satan complains before God that the Jewish people do not always complete their Torah studies. And even if they do, they show a degree of disdain by not going back for further review. But on Simchas Torah, when we not only complete the *Chumash* but immediately begin *Bereishis* anew, God triumphantly silences Satan and Israel is vindicated.

THE HAKAFAH-CIRCUITS OF SIMCHAS TORAH

Before the Ark is opened on *Simchas Torah,* the following selection of verses is recited responsively:

אַתָּה הָרְאֵתָ *You have been shown to know, that HASHEM, He is the God, there is none beside Him.*[1]

To Him Who alone performs great wonders, for His kindness endures forever.[2]

There is none like You among the gods, my Lord,
and there is nothing like Your works.[3]

May the glory of HASHEM endure forever, let HASHEM rejoice in His works.[4]

Blessed be the Name of HASHEM, from this time and forever.[5]

May HASHEM, our God, be with us, as He was with our forefathers,
may He not forsake us nor cast us off.[6]

Say: 'Save us, O God of our salvation,
gather us and rescue us from the nations,
to thank Your Holy Name and to glory in Your praise.'[7]

HASHEM reigns,[8] *HASHEM has reigned,*[9] *HASHEM shall reign for all eternity.*[10]

HASHEM will give might to His people,
HASHEM will bless His people with peace.[11]

May our words find favor, we pray, before the Lord of everything.[12]

The Ark is opened and the responsive recitation continues:

וַיְהִי בִּנְסֹעַ *When the Ark would travel, Moses would say,*
'Arise, HASHEM, and let Your foes be scattered;
let those who hate You flee from You.'[13]

Arise, HASHEM, to Your resting place, You and the Ark of Your strength.

Let your priests be clothed in righteousness, and Your devout ones will sing joyously.

For the sake of David, Your servant, turn not away the face of Your anointed.[14]

He shall say on that day, 'Behold! — this is our God,
we hoped to Him and He saved us; this is HASHEM to whom we hoped,
let us exult and be glad in His salvation.'[15]

Your kingdom is a kingdom spanning all eternities,
and Your dominion is throughout every generation.[16]

For from Zion the Torah will come forth,
and the word of HASHEM from Jerusalem.[17]

אַב הָרַחֲמִים *Father of compassion, do good to Zion according to Your will; rebuild the walls of Jerusalem. For we trust in You alone, O King, God, exalted and uplifted, Master of worlds.*[18]

(1) *Deuteronomy* 4:35. (2) *Psalms* 136:4. (3) 86:8. (4) 104:31. (5) 113:2. (6) *I Kings* 8:57. (7) *I Chronicles* 16:35. (8) *Psalms* 10:16. (9) 93:1 et al. (10) *Exodus* 15:18. (11) *Psalms* 29:11. (12) Cf. 19:15. (13) *Numbers* 10:35. (14) *Psalms* 132:8-10. (15) *Isaiah* 25:9. (16) *Psalms* 145:13. (17) *Isaiah* 2:3. (18) *Psalms* 51:20.

Symbolic of this joy, we celebrate Simchas Torah by removing all the Torah scrolls from the Ark and making seven *Hakafos* (circuits) around the *bimah,* the table from which the Torah is read. This is done in the evening after *Maariv* and in the morning before the Torah reading. In many congregations, *Hakafos* are also made on the night of Shemini Atzeres to commemorate the fact that that night is celebrated in Israel as Simchas Torah.

The number seven represents spiritual completion, similar to the seventh day of the week as the Sabbath and the seven circuits around the *bimah* on Hoshana Rabbah. Thus,

As the Torah Scrolls are carried around the *bimah,* the following verses are recited responsively:

—First *Hakafah*-circuit

אָנָּא יהוה, הוֹשִׁיעָה נָּא. אָנָּא יהוה, הַצְלִיחָה נָא.[1]
אָנָּא יהוה, עֲנֵנוּ בְיוֹם קָרְאֵנוּ.[2]

אֱלֹהֵי הָרוּחוֹת, הוֹשִׁיעָה נָּא. **בּ**וֹחֵן לְבָבוֹת, הַצְלִיחָה נָא.
גּוֹאֵל חָזָק, עֲנֵנוּ בְיוֹם קָרְאֵנוּ.

—Second *Hakafah*-circuit

דּוֹבֵר צְדָקוֹת, הוֹשִׁיעָה נָּא. **הָ**דוּר בִּלְבוּשׁוֹ, הַצְלִיחָה נָא.
וָתִיק וְחָסִיד, עֲנֵנוּ בְיוֹם קָרְאֵנוּ.

—Third *Hakafah*-circuit

זַךְ וְיָשָׁר, הוֹשִׁיעָה נָּא. **ח**וֹמֵל דַּלִּים, הַצְלִיחָה נָא.
טוֹב וּמֵטִיב, עֲנֵנוּ בְיוֹם קָרְאֵנוּ.

—Fourth *Hakafah*-circuit

יוֹדֵעַ מַחֲשָׁבוֹת, הוֹשִׁיעָה נָּא. **כַּ**בִּיר וְנָאוֹר, הַצְלִיחָה נָא.
לוֹבֵשׁ צְדָקוֹת, עֲנֵנוּ בְיוֹם קָרְאֵנוּ.

—Fifth *Hakafah*-circuit

מֶלֶךְ עוֹלָמִים, הוֹשִׁיעָה נָּא. **נָ**אוֹר וְאַדִּיר, הַצְלִיחָה נָא.
סוֹמֵךְ נוֹפְלִים, עֲנֵנוּ בְיוֹם קָרְאֵנוּ.

—Sixth *Hakafah*-circuit

עוֹזֵר דַּלִּים, הוֹשִׁיעָה נָּא. **פּ**וֹדֶה וּמַצִּיל, הַצְלִיחָה נָא.
צוּר עוֹלָמִים, עֲנֵנוּ בְיוֹם קָרְאֵנוּ.

—Seventh *Hakafah*-circuit

קָדוֹשׁ וְנוֹרָא, הוֹשִׁיעָה נָּא. **רַ**חוּם וְחַנּוּן, הַצְלִיחָה נָא.
שׁוֹמֵר הַבְּרִית, עֲנֵנוּ בְיוֹם קָרְאֵנוּ.

תּוֹמֵךְ תְּמִימִים, הוֹשִׁיעָה נָּא. **תַּ**קִּיף לָעַד, הַצְלִיחָה נָא.
תָּמִים בְּמַעֲשָׂיו, עֲנֵנוּ בְיוֹם קָרְאֵנוּ.

After the *Hakafos,* the scrolls (except for those needed for the Torah reading) are returned to the Ark. On the night of *Simchas Torah,* the reading is from the final portion of the Torah, וְזֹאת הַבְּרָכָה. Some congregations call three people to the Torah, others call five. In the morning, all of וְזֹאת הַבְּרָכָה, as well as the first section of *Bereishis* and *Maftir,* are read.

In most congregations, it is customary to chant the following song at one or more points during the Simchas Torah *Hakafah*-circuits or after the Torah reading:

שִׂישׂוּ וְשִׂמְחוּ בְּשִׂמְחַת תּוֹרָה, וּתְנוּ כָבוֹד לַתּוֹרָה,
כִּי טוֹב סַחְרָהּ מִכָּל סְחוֹרָה, מִפָּז וּמִפְּנִינִים יְקָרָה.
נָגִיל וְנָשִׂישׂ בְּזֹאת הַתּוֹרָה, כִּי הִיא לָנוּ עֹז וְאוֹרָה.
אֲהַלְלָה אֱלֹהַי וְאֶשְׂמְחָה בוֹ, וְאָשִׂימָה תִקְוָתִי בּוֹ,
אֲהוֹדֶנּוּ בְּסוֹד עַם קְרוֹבוֹ, אֱלֹהֵי צוּרִי אֶחֱסֶה בּוֹ.
נָגִיל וְנָשִׂישׂ בְּזֹאת הַתּוֹרָה, כִּי הִיא לָנוּ עֹז וְאוֹרָה.
בְּכָל לֵב אֲרַנֵּן צִדְקוֹתֶיךָ, וַאֲסַפְּרָה תְּהִלָּתֶךָ,
בְּעוֹדִי אַגִּיד נִפְלְאוֹתֶיךָ, עַל חַסְדְּךָ וְעַל אֲמִתֶּךָ.
נָגִיל וְנָשִׂישׂ בְּזֹאת הַתּוֹרָה, כִּי הִיא לָנוּ עֹז וְאוֹרָה.

---

our seven *Hakafos* on Simchas Torah symbolize the completeness of our joy in the Torah.

Before the Torah Scrolls are removed, the congregation responsively recites the collection of Scriptural verses beginning with אַתָּה הָרְאֵתָ, *You have been shown.* This is the regular service for removal of the Torah scrolls, with the augmentation of additional verses.

As the Torah Scrolls are carried around the *bimah,* the following verses are recited responsively:

First—*Hakafah*-circuit

אָנָּא *Please, HASHEM, save now!*
Please, HASHEM, bring success now![1]
Please, HASHEM, answer us on the day we call.[2]

אֱלֹהֵי *God of the spirits, save now!*
Tester of hearts, bring success now!
O Powerful Redeemer, answer us on the day we call!

Second—*Hakafah*-circuit

דּוֹבֵר *Speaker of righteousness, save now!*
Majestic One in His garb, bring success now!
Faithful and Devout One, answer us on the day we call!

Third—*Hakafah*-circuit

זַךְ *Pure and Just One, save now!*
He Who pities the poor, bring success now!
Good and Beneficent One, answer us on the day we call!

Fourth—*Hakafah*-circuit

יוֹדֵעַ *Knower of thoughts, save now!*
Powerful and illustrious One, bring success now!
He Who garbs Himself in righteousness, answer us on the day we call!

Fifth—*Hakafah*-circuit

מֶלֶךְ *Eternal King, save now!*
Illustrious and mighty One, bring success now!
Supporter of the fallen, answer us on the day we call!

Sixth—*Hakafah*-circuit

עוֹזֵר *Helper of the destitute, save now!*
Redeemer and rescuer, bring success now!
Eternal Rock, answer us on the day we call!

Seventh—*Hakafah*-circuit

קָדוֹשׁ *Holy and awesome One, save now!*
Merciful and gracious One, bring success now!
Keeper of the covenant, answer us on the day we call!

תּוֹמֵךְ *Supporter of the wholesome, save now!*
Eternally strong One, bring success now!
Perfect in His deeds, answer us on the day we call!

After the *Hakafos,* the scrolls (except for those needed for the Torah reading) are returned to the Ark. On the night of *Simchas Torah,* the reading is from the final portion of the Torah, וְזֹאת הַבְּרָכָה. Some congregations call three people to the Torah, others call five. In the morning, all of וְזֹאת הַבְּרָכָה, as well as the first section of *Bereishis* and *Maftir,* are read.

In most congregations, it is customary to chant the following song at one or more points during the Simchas Torah *Hakafah*-circuits or after the Torah reading:

שִׂישׂוּ *Rejoice and be glad with the celebration of the Torah, and pay homage to the Torah, for it is better than any commerce, more precious than finest gold and jewels.*

Let us exult and rejoice with this Torah, for it is our strength and light.
I shall laud my God and be glad with Him, and place my hope in Him.
I shall praise Him in the counsel of His intimate people — the God Who formed me — I take refuge in Him.

Let us exult and rejoice with this Torah, for it is our strength and light.
Wholeheartedly I exalt Your righteousness and I relate Your praise.
While I live I will tell Your wonders, of Your kindness and Your truth.

Let us exult and rejoice with this Torah, for it is our strength and light.

(1) *Psalms* 118:25. (2) Cf. 20:10.

סדר התרת נדרים

It is meritorious to annul vows on the morning before Rosh Hashanah (see commentary). The three 'judges' sit while the petitioner seeking annulment stands before them and states:

שִׁמְעוּ נָא רַבּוֹתַי דַּיָּנִים מוּמְחִים. כָּל נֶדֶר אוֹ שְׁבוּעָה אוֹ אִסּוּר אוֹ קוֹנָם אוֹ חֵרֶם שֶׁנָּדַרְתִּי אוֹ נִשְׁבַּעְתִּי בְּהָקִיץ אוֹ בַחֲלוֹם, אוֹ נִשְׁבַּעְתִּי בְּשֵׁמוֹת הַקְּדוֹשִׁים שֶׁאֵינָם נִמְחָקִים, וּבְשֵׁם הוי״ה בָּרוּךְ הוּא, וְכָל מִינֵי נְזִירוּת שֶׁקִּבַּלְתִּי עָלַי, חוּץ מִנְּזִירוּת שִׁמְשׁוֹן, וְכָל שׁוּם אִסּוּר, וַאֲפִילוּ אִסּוּר הֲנָאָה שֶׁאָסַרְתִּי עָלַי אוֹ עַל אֲחֵרִים, בְּכָל לָשׁוֹן שֶׁל אִסּוּר, בֵּין בִּלְשׁוֹן אִסּוּר אוֹ חֵרֶם אוֹ קוֹנָם, וְכָל שׁוּם קַבָּלָה אֲפִילוּ שֶׁל מִצְוָה שֶׁקִּבַּלְתִּי עָלַי בֵּין בִּלְשׁוֹן נֶדֶר, בֵּין בִּלְשׁוֹן נְדָבָה, בֵּין בִּלְשׁוֹן שְׁבוּעָה, בֵּין בִּלְשׁוֹן נְזִירוּת, בֵּין בְּכָל לָשׁוֹן, וְגַם הַנַּעֲשֶׂה בִּתְקִיעַת כָּף, בֵּין כָּל נֶדֶר, וּבֵין כָּל נְדָבָה, וּבֵין שׁוּם מִנְהָג שֶׁל מִצְוָה שֶׁנָּהַגְתִּי אֶת עַצְמִי, וְכָל מוֹצָא שְׂפָתַי שֶׁיָּצָא מִפִּי, אוֹ שֶׁנָּדַרְתִּי וְגָמַרְתִּי בְלִבִּי לַעֲשׂוֹת שׁוּם מִצְוָה מֵהַמִּצְוֹת, אוֹ אֵיזֶה הַנְהָגָה טוֹבָה אוֹ אֵיזֶה דָבָר טוֹב, שֶׁנָּהַגְתִּי שָׁלֹשׁ פְּעָמִים, וְלֹא הִתְנֵיתִי שֶׁיְּהֵא בְּלִי נֶדֶר, הֵן דָּבָר שֶׁעָשִׂיתִי, הֵן עַל עַצְמִי, הֵן עַל אֲחֵרִים, הֵן אוֹתָן הַיְּדוּעִים לִי, הֵן אוֹתָן שֶׁכְּבָר שָׁכַחְתִּי, בְּכֻלְּהוֹן אִתְחֲרַטְנָא בְהוֹן מֵעִקָּרָא, וְשׁוֹאֵל וּמְבַקֵּשׁ אֲנִי מִמַּעֲלַתְכֶם הַתָּרָה עֲלֵיהֶם. כִּי יָרֵאתִי פֶּן אֶכָּשֵׁל וְנִלְכַּדְתִּי, חַס וְשָׁלוֹם, בַּעֲוֹן נְדָרִים וּשְׁבוּעוֹת וּנְזִירוּת וַחֲרָמוֹת וְאִסּוּרִין וְקוֹנָמוֹת וְהַסְכָּמוֹת.

וְאֵין אֲנִי תוֹהֵא, חַס וְשָׁלוֹם, עַל קִיּוּם הַמַּעֲשִׂים הַטּוֹבִים הָהֵם שֶׁעָשִׂיתִי. רַק אֲנִי מִתְחָרֵט עַל קַבָּלַת הָעִנְיָנִים בִּלְשׁוֹן נֶדֶר אוֹ שְׁבוּעָה אוֹ נְזִירוּת אוֹ אִסּוּר אוֹ חֵרֶם אוֹ קוֹנָם אוֹ הַסְכָּמָה אוֹ קַבָּלָה בְלֵב, וּמִתְחָרֵט אֲנִי עַל זֶה שֶׁלֹּא אָמַרְתִּי, הִנְנִי עוֹשֶׂה דָּבָר זֶה בְּלִי נֶדֶר וּשְׁבוּעָה וּנְזִירוּת וְחֵרֶם וְאִסּוּר וְקוֹנָם וְקַבָּלָה בְלֵב.

הַתָּרַת נְדָרִים / ANNULMENT OF VOWS

The Torah permits people to accept upon themselves personal obligations and prohibitions, and it gives an owner the right to forbid others to enjoy his property. Such undertakings, known as שְׁבוּעוֹת וּנְדָרִים, *oaths and vows*, must be carried out and have the force of a positive com-

ANNULMENT OF VOWS

It is meritorious to annul vows on the morning before Rosh Hashanah (see commentary). The three 'judges' sit while the petitioner seeking annulment stands before them and states:

שִׁמְעוּ *Listen, please, my masters, expert judges — every vow or oath or prohibition, or prohibition that I adopted by use of the slang term 'konam' or the term 'cherem'; that I vowed or swore while I was awake or in a dream; or that I swore by means of God's Holy Names that it is forbidden to erase or by means of the Name* HASHEM, *Blessed is He; or any form of nazirism that I accepted upon myself, except the nazirism of Samson [which does not include a prohibition against contact with the dead]; or any prohibition, even a prohibition to derive enjoyment that I imposed upon myself or upon others by means of any expression of prohibition, whether by specifying the term 'prohibition' or by use of the terms 'konam' or 'cherem'; or any commitment — even to perform a mitzvah — that I accepted upon myself, whether the acceptance was in terms of a vow, a voluntary gift, an oath, nazirism, or by means of any other sort of expression, or whether it was made final through a handshake; any form of vow or voluntary gift, or any custom that constitutes a good deed to which I have accustomed myself; and any utterance that escaped my mouth or that I vowed in my heart to perform any of the various optional good deeds, or good practices, or any good thing that I have performed three times but without specifying that the practice does not have the force of a vow; whether the thing I did related to myself or to others; both regarding vows that are known to me and those that I have already forgotten — regarding all of them I regret retroactively and I ask and request of your eminences an annulment of them. [My reason is that] I am fearful that I will stumble and become entrapped, Heaven forbid, in the sin of vows, oaths, nazirism, cherems, prohibitions, konams, and [violation of] agreements.*

I do not regret, Heaven forbid, the performance of the good deeds I have done, rather I regret only having accepted them upon myself with an expression of a vow or oath or nazirism or prohibition or cherem or konam or agreement or acceptance in my heart, and I regret not having said, 'Behold I do this without [adopting it in terms of] a vow, oath, nazirism, cherem, prohibition, konam, or acceptance in my heart.'

---

mandment, כְּכָל הַיֹּצֵא מִפִּיו יַעֲשֶׂה, *he shall do whatever he has uttered*, and its violation carries the penalty of a negative commandment, לֹא יַחֵל דְּבָרוֹ, *he shall not desecrate his word (Numbers* 30:3). So serious are these matters that they are the primary subject of three tractates: *Nedarim, Nazir,* and *Shevuos.*

That a person's freely chosen wishes can have the force of Torah law is a striking indication of the sanctity that God attaches to a person's word. Consequently, it is considered a fearsome sin for one to violate his vows and oaths and the Sages

לָכֵן אֲנִי שׁוֹאֵל הַתָּרָה בְּכֻלְּהוֹן. אֲנִי מִתְחָרֵט עַל כָּל הַנִּזְכָּר, בֵּין אִם הָיוּ הַמַּעֲשִׂים מֵהַדְּבָרִים הַנּוֹגְעִים בְּמָמוֹן, בֵּין מֵהַדְּבָרִים הַנּוֹגְעִים בְּגוּף, בֵּין מֵהַדְּבָרִים הַנּוֹגְעִים אֶל הַנְּשָׁמָה. בְּכֻלְּהוֹן אֲנִי מִתְחָרֵט עַל לְשׁוֹן נֶדֶר וּשְׁבוּעָה וּנְזִירוּת וְאִסּוּר וְחֵרֶם וְקוֹנָם וְקַבָּלָה בְלֵב.

וְהִנֵּה מִצַּד הַדִּין הַמִּתְחָרֵט וְהַמְבַקֵּשׁ הַתָּרָה צָרִיךְ לִפְרוֹט הַנֶּדֶר, אַךְ דְּעוּ נָא רַבּוֹתַי, כִּי אִי אֶפְשָׁר לְפוֹרְטָם כִּי רַבִּים הֵם. וְאֵין אֲנִי מְבַקֵּשׁ הַתָּרָה עַל אוֹתָם הַנְּדָרִים שֶׁאֵין לְהַתִּיר אוֹתָם. עַל כֵּן יִהְיוּ נָא בְעֵינֵיכֶם כְּאִלּוּ הָיִיתִי פוֹרְטָם.

The judges repeat three times:

הַכֹּל יִהְיוּ מֻתָּרִים לָךְ, הַכֹּל מְחוּלִים לָךְ, הַכֹּל שְׁרוּיִם לָךְ, אֵין כַּאן לֹא נֶדֶר וְלֹא שְׁבוּעָה וְלֹא נְזִירוּת וְלֹא חֵרֶם וְלֹא אִסּוּר וְלֹא קוֹנָם וְלֹא נִדּוּי וְלֹא שַׁמְתָּא וְלֹא אָרוּר. אֲבָל יֵשׁ כַּאן מְחִילָה וּסְלִיחָה וְכַפָּרָה. וּכְשֵׁם שֶׁמַּתִּירִים בְּבֵית דִּין שֶׁל מַטָּה, כַּךְ יִהְיוּ מֻתָּרִים בְּבֵית דִּין שֶׁל מַעְלָה.

The petitioner makes the following declaration:

הֲרֵי אֲנִי מוֹסֵר מוֹדָעָה לִפְנֵיכֶם, וַאֲנִי מְבַטֵּל מִכַּאן וּלְהַבָּא כָּל הַנְּדָרִים וְכָל שְׁבוּעוֹת וּנְזִירוּת וְאִסּוּרִין וְקוֹנָמוֹת וַחֲרָמוֹת וְהַסְכָּמוֹת וְקַבָּלָה בְלֵב שֶׁאֲקַבֵּל עָלַי בְּעַצְמִי, הֵן בְּהָקִיץ, הֵן בַּחֲלוֹם, חוּץ מִנִּדְרֵי תַעֲנִית בִּשְׁעַת מִנְחָה. וּבְאִם שֶׁאֶשְׁכַּח לִתְנַאי מוֹדָעָה הַזֹּאת, וְאֶדּוֹר מֵהַיּוֹם עוֹד, מֵעַתָּה אֲנִי מִתְחָרֵט עֲלֵיהֶם, וּמַתְנֶה עֲלֵיהֶם, שֶׁיִּהְיוּ כֻּלָּן בְּטֵלִין וּמְבֻטָּלִין, לָא שְׁרִירִין וְלָא קַיָּמִין, וְלָא יְהוֹן חָלִין כְּלָל וּכְלָל. בְּכֻלָּן אִתְחֲרַטְנָא בְּהוֹן מֵעַתָּה וְעַד עוֹלָם.

---

regard it as an extremely serious matter for one to approach the Days of Judgment with such violation in hand.

However, the Torah provides a means for one to release himself from such obligations. A 'court' composed of three knowledgeable people has the authority to decide that the oath or vow was undertaken under a mistaken impression and they may annul the obligation retroactively. [This is a very oversimplified explanation of the process of annulment, but the key is that the court has this retroactive power.] One of the pleas that one can make to the court is that he regrets ever having undertaken the obligation as a vow or oath.

In order to free oneself of the sin of such violations before being judged on Rosh Hashanah and Yom Kippur, the Halachic

Therefore I request annulment for them all. I regret all the aforementioned, whether they were matters relating to money, or whether they are matters relating to the body or whether they were matters relating to the soul. Regarding them all, I regret the terminology of vow, oath, nazirism, prohibition, cherem, konam and acceptance in the heart.

Now behold, according to the law, one who regrets and seeks annulment must specify the vow, but please be informed, my masters, that it is impossible to specify them because they are many. Nor do I seek annulment of those vows that cannot be annulled, therefore may you consider as if I had specified them.

The judges repeat three times:

הַכֹּל *May everything be permitted you, may everything be forgiven you, may everything be allowed you. There does not exist any vow, oath, nazirism, cherem, prohibition, konam, ostracism, excommunication, or curse. But there does exist pardon, forgiveness, and atonement. And just as the earthly court permits them, so may they be permitted in the Heavenly Court.*

The petitioner makes the following declaration:

הֲרֵי *Behold I make formal declaration before you and I cancel from this time onward all vows and all oaths, nazirism, prohibitions, konams, cherems, agreements, and acceptances of the heart that I myself will accept upon myself, whether while I am awake or in a dream, except for vows to fast that I undertake during Minchah. In case I forget the conditions of this declaration and I make a vow from this day onward, from this moment I retroactively regret them and declare of them that they are all totally null and void, without effect and without validity, and they shall not take effect at all. Regarding them all, I regret them from this time and forever.*

---

authorities urge that one convene a court of at least three people — preferably ten — and seek release from his vows and oaths. However, as the declaration makes clear, this annulment applies only to vows for which the *halachah* permits annulments and for which there is a halachically acceptable reason for doing so. Likewise, annulment is valid only if the vows involve only oneself. If, however, the vows were adopted for the sake of, or involve, someone else, they cannot be annulled without the consent of the other party.

A second aspect of the Annulment of Vows is the concluding declaration, in which one makes the legal declaration that his future undertakings should not have the force of a vow or oath. While this does not free him from the obligation to keep his word, it does remove the severity of sin that attaches to formally proclaimed vows and oaths.

קידוש לליל ראש השנה

When Rosh Hashanah falls on Friday night, begin here:

(וַיְהִי עֶרֶב וַיְהִי בֹקֶר —Recite silently)

יוֹם הַשִּׁשִּׁי. וַיְכֻלּוּ הַשָּׁמַיִם וְהָאָרֶץ וְכָל צְבָאָם. וַיְכַל אֱלֹהִים בַּיּוֹם הַשְּׁבִיעִי מְלַאכְתּוֹ אֲשֶׁר עָשָׂה, וַיִּשְׁבֹּת בַּיּוֹם הַשְּׁבִיעִי מִכָּל מְלַאכְתּוֹ אֲשֶׁר עָשָׂה. וַיְבָרֶךְ אֱלֹהִים אֶת יוֹם הַשְּׁבִיעִי וַיְקַדֵּשׁ אֹתוֹ, כִּי בוֹ שָׁבַת מִכָּל מְלַאכְתּוֹ אֲשֶׁר בָּרָא אֱלֹהִים לַעֲשׂוֹת.[1]

On all nights other than Friday begin here (on Friday night include all words in brackets):

סַבְרִי מָרָנָן וְרַבָּנָן וְרַבּוֹתַי:

בָּרוּךְ אַתָּה יהוה אֱלֹהֵינוּ מֶלֶךְ הָעוֹלָם, בּוֹרֵא פְּרִי הַגָּפֶן.

(אָמֵן. —All present respond)

בָּרוּךְ אַתָּה יהוה אֱלֹהֵינוּ מֶלֶךְ הָעוֹלָם, אֲשֶׁר בָּחַר בָּנוּ מִכָּל עָם, וְרוֹמְמָנוּ מִכָּל לָשׁוֹן, וְקִדְּשָׁנוּ בְּמִצְוֹתָיו. וַתִּתֶּן לָנוּ יהוה אֱלֹהֵינוּ בְּאַהֲבָה אֶת יוֹם [הַשַּׁבָּת הַזֶּה וְאֶת יוֹם] הַזִּכָּרוֹן הַזֶּה, יוֹם [זִכְרוֹן] תְּרוּעָה [בְּאַהֲבָה] מִקְרָא קֹדֶשׁ, זֵכֶר לִיצִיאַת מִצְרָיִם. כִּי בָנוּ בָחַרְתָּ וְאוֹתָנוּ קִדַּשְׁתָּ מִכָּל הָעַמִּים, וּדְבָרְךָ אֱמֶת וְקַיָּם לָעַד. בָּרוּךְ אַתָּה יהוה, מֶלֶךְ עַל כָּל הָאָרֶץ, מְקַדֵּשׁ [הַשַּׁבָּת וְ]יִשְׂרָאֵל וְיוֹם הַזִּכָּרוֹן.

(אָמֵן. —All present respond)

On Saturday night, add the following two *Havdalah* blessings. A multi-wicked candle or two ordinary candles with flames touching each other should be held before the person reciting the *Havdalah*. After the first blessing, hold the fingers up to the flames to see the reflected light.

בָּרוּךְ אַתָּה יהוה אֱלֹהֵינוּ מֶלֶךְ הָעוֹלָם, בּוֹרֵא מְאוֹרֵי הָאֵשׁ.

(אָמֵן. —All present respond)

בָּרוּךְ אַתָּה יהוה אֱלֹהֵינוּ מֶלֶךְ הָעוֹלָם, הַמַּבְדִּיל בֵּין קֹדֶשׁ לְחוֹל, בֵּין אוֹר לְחֹשֶׁךְ, בֵּין יִשְׂרָאֵל לָעַמִּים, בֵּין יוֹם הַשְּׁבִיעִי לְשֵׁשֶׁת יְמֵי הַמַּעֲשֶׂה. בֵּין קְדֻשַּׁת שַׁבָּת לִקְדֻשַּׁת יוֹם טוֹב הִבְדַּלְתָּ, וְאֶת יוֹם הַשְּׁבִיעִי מִשֵּׁשֶׁת יְמֵי הַמַּעֲשֶׂה קִדַּשְׁתָּ, הִבְדַּלְתָּ וְקִדַּשְׁתָּ אֶת עַמְּךָ יִשְׂרָאֵל בִּקְדֻשָּׁתֶךָ. בָּרוּךְ אַתָּה יהוה, הַמַּבְדִּיל בֵּין קֹדֶשׁ לְקֹדֶשׁ.

(אָמֵן. —All present respond)

The following blessing is recited on both nights:

בָּרוּךְ אַתָּה יהוה אֱלֹהֵינוּ מֶלֶךְ הָעוֹלָם, שֶׁהֶחֱיָנוּ וְקִיְּמָנוּ וְהִגִּיעָנוּ לַזְּמַן הַזֶּה.

(אָמֵן. —All present respond)

ROSH HASHANAH EVENING KIDDUSH

When Rosh Hashanah falls on Friday night, begin here:
(Recite silently— *And there was evening and there was morning)*

יוֹם הַשִּׁשִּׁי *The sixth day. Thus the heavens and earth were finished, and all their array. On the seventh day God completed His work which He had done, and He abstained on the seventh day from all His work which He had done. God blessed the seventh day and hallowed it, because on it He abstained from all His work which God created to make.*[1]

On all nights other than Friday begin here (on Friday night include all passages in brackets):
By your leave, my masters and teachers:

בָּרוּךְ *Blessed are you, HASHEM, our God, King of the universe, Who creates the fruit of the vine.* (All present respond— *Amen.)*

בָּרוּךְ *Blessed are you, HASHEM, our God, King of the universe, Who has chosen us from every people, exalted us above every tongue, and sanctified us with His commandments. And You gave us, HASHEM, our God, with love,* [this Sabbath day and] *this Day of Remembrance, a day of* [remembrance of] *shofar blowing* [with love] *a holy convocation, a memorial of the Exodus from Egypt. For You have chosen us and You have sanctified us above all the peoples, and Your word is true and established forever. Blessed are You, HASHEM, King over the entire earth, Who sanctifies* [the Sabbath and] *Israel and the Day of Remembrance.* (All present respond— *Amen.)*

On Saturday night, add the following two *Havdalah* blessings. A multi-wicked candle or two ordinary candles with flames touching each other, should be held before the person reciting the *Havdalah.* After the first blessing, hold the fingers up to the flames to see the reflected light.

בָּרוּךְ *Blessed are you, HASHEM, our God, King of the universe, Who creates the illumination of the fire.* (All present respond— *Amen.)*

בָּרוּךְ *Blessed are you, HASHEM, our God, King of the universe, Who distinguishes between the sacred and secular, between light and darkness, between Israel and the peoples, between the seventh day and the six days of labor. Between the sanctity of the Sabbaths and the sanctity of the holidays You have distinguished, and the seventh day, from among the six days of labor You have sanctified. You have distinguished and You have sanctified Your people Israel with Your holiness. Blessed are You, HASHEM, Who distinguishes between holiness and holiness.*
(All present respond— *Amen.)*

The following blessing is recited on both nights:

בָּרוּךְ *Blessed are you, HASHEM, our God, King of the universe, Who has kept us alive, sustained us, and brought us to this season.*
(All present respond— *Amen.)*

---

(1) *Genesis* 1:31-2:3.

⸨ סימנא מילתא ⸩

On the night of Rosh Hashanah there is an almost universal custom of dipping the first piece of *challah* into honey. After the *challah* has been eaten, a piece of apple sweetened with honey is given to each participant and the blessing is recited:

בָּרוּךְ אַתָּה יהוה אֱלֹהֵינוּ מֶלֶךְ הָעוֹלָם, בּוֹרֵא פְּרִי הָעֵץ.

A small piece of the apple is eaten and the following prayer is recited before the apple is finished.

יְהִי רָצוֹן מִלְּפָנֶיךָ, יהוה אֱלֹהֵינוּ וֵאלֹהֵי אֲבוֹתֵינוּ,
שֶׁתְּחַדֵּשׁ עָלֵינוּ שָׁנָה טוֹבָה וּמְתוּקָה.

The following symbolic foods are mentioned in the Talmud, *Shulchan Aruch* or other authorities. The list follows no particular order.

Carrots:

יְהִי רָצוֹן מִלְּפָנֶיךָ, יהוה אֱלֹהֵינוּ וֵאלֹהֵי אֲבוֹתֵינוּ, שֶׁיִּרְבּוּ זְכֻיּוֹתֵינוּ.

Leek or cabbage:

יְהִי רָצוֹן מִלְּפָנֶיךָ, יהוה אֱלֹהֵינוּ וֵאלֹהֵי אֲבוֹתֵינוּ, שֶׁיִּכָּרְתוּ שׂוֹנְאֵינוּ.

Beets:

יְהִי רָצוֹן מִלְּפָנֶיךָ, יהוה אֱלֹהֵינוּ וֵאלֹהֵי אֲבוֹתֵינוּ, שֶׁיִּסְתַּלְּקוּ אוֹיְבֵינוּ.

Dates:

יְהִי רָצוֹן מִלְּפָנֶיךָ, יהוה אֱלֹהֵינוּ וֵאלֹהֵי אֲבוֹתֵינוּ, שֶׁיִּתַּמּוּ שׂוֹנְאֵינוּ.

Gourd:

יְהִי רָצוֹן מִלְּפָנֶיךָ, יהוה אֱלֹהֵינוּ וֵאלֹהֵי אֲבוֹתֵינוּ,
שֶׁיִּקָּרַע גְּזַר דִּינֵנוּ וְיִקָּרְאוּ לְפָנֶיךָ זְכֻיּוֹתֵינוּ.

Pomegranate:

יְהִי רָצוֹן מִלְּפָנֶיךָ, יהוה אֱלֹהֵינוּ וֵאלֹהֵי אֲבוֹתֵינוּ, שֶׁנִּרְבֶּה זְכֻיּוֹת כְּרִמּוֹן.

Fish:

יְהִי רָצוֹן מִלְּפָנֶיךָ, יהוה אֱלֹהֵינוּ וֵאלֹהֵי אֲבוֹתֵינוּ, שֶׁנִּפְרֶה וְנִרְבֶּה כְּדָגִים.

Head of a sheep (or fish):

יְהִי רָצוֹן מִלְּפָנֶיךָ, יהוה אֱלֹהֵינוּ וֵאלֹהֵי אֲבוֹתֵינוּ,
שֶׁנִּהְיֶה לְרֹאשׁ וְלֹא לְזָנָב.

⸨ סִימָנָא מִילְתָא / SYMBOLIC FOODS ⸩

Various symbolic foods are eaten at the festive meal on the first night of Rosh Hashanah (some also eat them on the second night), and a short prayer alluding to the symbolism is recited for each food.

The custom of eating symbolic foods on Rosh Hashanah is based on a Talmudic teaching: Omens are significant, therefore each person should habituate himself to eat, at the beginning of the year, gourds, leeks, beets and dates (*Horayos* 12a; *Kerisus* 6a).

The symbolism of the different foods falls into various groupings. Some are sweet tasting and indicate a sweet year *(Rashi)*, while others allude

SYMBOLIC FOODS

On the night of Rosh Hashanah there is an almost universal custom of dipping the first piece of *challah* into honey. After the *challah* has been eaten, a piece of apple sweetened with honey is given to each participant and the blessing is recited:

בָּרוּךְ *Blessed are You, HASHEM, our God, King of the universe, Who creates the fruit of the tree.*

A small piece of the apple is eaten and the following prayer is recited before the apple is finished.

May it be Your will, HASHEM, our God and the God of our forefathers, that You renew for us a good and a sweet year.

The following symbolic foods are mentioned in the Talmud, *Shulchan Aruch* or other authorities. The list follows no particular order.

Carrots:

May it be Your will, HASHEM, our God and the God of our forefathers, that our merits increase.

Leek or cabbage:

May it be Your will, HASHEM, our God and the God of our forefathers, that our enemies be decimated.

Beets:

May it be Your will, HASHEM, our God and the God of our forefathers, that our adversaries be removed.

Dates:

May it be Your will, HASHEM, our God and the God of our forefathers, that our enemies be consumed.

Gourd:

May it be Your will, HASHEM, our God and the God of our forefathers,
that the decree of our sentence be torn asunder;
and may our merits be proclaimed before You.

Pomegranate:

May it be Your will, HASHEM, our God and the God of our forefathers, that our merits increase as [the seeds of] a pomegranate.

Fish:

May it be Your will, HASHEM, our God and the God of our forefathers, that we be fruitful and multiply like fish.

Head of a sheep (or fish):

May it be Your will, HASHEM, our God and the God of our forefathers, that we be as the head and not as the tail.

---

to abundance and symbolize an increase of Israel's *mitzvah* performance; others allude to destruction and eradication and are applied to Israel's sins and enemies *(Mordechai; Or Zarua).*

תשליך

יהוה יהוה אל רחום וחנון ארך
[א]מִי אֵל כָּמוֹךָ [ב] נֹשֵׂא עָוֹן [ג] וְעֹבֵר עַל פֶּשַׁע [ד] לִשְׁאֵרִית
אפים ורב חסד ואמת
נַחֲלָתוֹ [ה] לֹא הֶחֱזִיק לָעַד אַפּוֹ [ו] כִּי חָפֵץ חֶסֶד הוּא. [ז] יָשׁוּב
נצר חסד לאלפים
יְרַחֲמֵנוּ [ח] יִכְבֹּשׁ עֲוֹנֹתֵינוּ [ט] וְתַשְׁלִיךְ בִּמְצֻלוֹת יָם כָּל חַטֹּאתָם.

(וְכָל חַטֹּאת עַמְּךָ בֵּית יִשְׂרָאֵל, תַּשְׁלִיךְ בְּמָקוֹם אֲשֶׁר לֹא יִזָּכְרוּ, וְלֹא יִפָּקְדוּ, וְלֹא יַעֲלוּ עַל לֵב לְעוֹלָם.)

נשא עון ופשע וחטאה
[י] תִּתֵּן אֱמֶת, לְיַעֲקֹב [יא] חֶסֶד לְאַבְרָהָם [יב] אֲשֶׁר נִשְׁבַּעְתָּ
ונקה
לַאֲבֹתֵינוּ [יג] מִימֵי קֶדֶם.[1]

יהוה ארך אפים ורב חסד נשא
[א] מִן הַמֵּצַר, קָרָאתִי יָּהּ [ב] עָנָנִי בַמֶּרְחָב יָהּ. [ג] יהוה לִי [ד] לֹא
עון ופשע ונקה לא ינקה
אִירָא [ה] מַה יַּעֲשֶׂה לִי אָדָם. [ו] יהוה לִי בְּעֹזְרָי [ז] וַאֲנִי אֶרְאֶה
פקד עון אבות על בנים
בְשֹׂנְאָי. [ח] טוֹב לַחֲסוֹת בַּיהוה, מִבְּטֹחַ בָּאָדָם. [ט] טוֹב לַחֲסוֹת
על שלשים ועל רבעים
בַּיהוה, מִבְּטֹחַ בִּנְדִיבִים.[2]

תהלים לג (Commentary, p. 386)

רַנְּנוּ צַדִּיקִים בַּיהוה, לַיְשָׁרִים נָאוָה תְהִלָּה. הוֹדוּ לַיהוה בְּכִנּוֹר, בְּנֵבֶל עָשׂוֹר זַמְּרוּ לוֹ. שִׁירוּ לוֹ שִׁיר חָדָשׁ, הֵיטִיבוּ נַגֵּן בִּתְרוּעָה. כִּי יָשָׁר דְּבַר יהוה, וְכָל מַעֲשֵׂהוּ בֶּאֱמוּנָה. אֹהֵב צְדָקָה וּמִשְׁפָּט, חֶסֶד יהוה מָלְאָה הָאָרֶץ. בִּדְבַר יהוה שָׁמַיִם נַעֲשׂוּ, וּבְרוּחַ פִּיו כָּל צְבָאָם. כֹּנֵס כַּנֵּד מֵי הַיָּם,

---

TASHLICH / תַּשְׁלִיךְ

The custom of reciting *Tashlich* began during medieval times. As the Scriptural passage in *Micah* implies clearly, it symbolizes our hope that God will dismiss our sins on this day of judgment. However, two other reasons are given:

— When Abraham and Isaac went to the *Akeidah*, the Satan tried to deter them by causing a raging flood that threatened to drown them. In their devotion to God they ignored the impediments. Thus, by praying at the water's edge we recall the merit of the Patriarchs and imply that we attempt to emulate their righteousness *(Sh'lah; Levush)*.

— In ancient times, kings were crowned on a river bank. Similarly, on Rosh Hashanah, when we proclaim God's kingship at the water's edge, we acknowledge our dependence on His mercy.

The essential parts of *Tashlich* are the two passages מִי אֵל כָּמוֹךָ, *Who, O God, is like You,* and מִן הַמֵּצַר, *From the straights.* The Kabbalists teach that these passages allude to the two times when Moses invoked God's merciful attributes to pray for His forgiveness after grievous sins committed by the Jewish people. When Israel worshiped the Golden Calf, Moses intervened with God by means of the Thirteen Attributes of Mercy *(Exodus 34:6-7; see p. 434)*. Later when the people sinned by believing the spies' report that *Eretz Yisrael* could not be conquered, Moses

TASHLICH

HASHEM, HASHEM, GOD MERCIFUL

[1] **Who, O God is like You,** [2] **Who pardons iniquity** [3] **And**

COMPASSIONATE SLOW

overlooks transgression [4] **for the remnant of His heritage?**

TO ANGER ABUNDANT IN

[5] **Who has not retained His wrath eternally,** [6] **for He desires**

KINDNESS (ABUNDANT IN) TRUTH PRESERVER OF

kindness! [7] **He will again be merciful to us;** [8] **He will suppress**

KINDNESS FOR THOUSANDS OF GENERATIONS

our iniquities. [9] **And cast into the depths of the sea all their sins.**

(And all the sins of Your nation, the House of Israel, cast away to a place where they will neither be remembered, considered, nor brought to mind—ever.)

FORGIVER OF INIQUITY (FORGIVER OF) TRANSGRESSION

[10] **Grant truth to Jacob,** [11] **kindness to Abraham,**

(FORGIVER OF) SIN AND WHO CLEANSES

[12] **As You swore to our forefathers** [13] **from ancient times.**[1]

HASHEM, SLOW TO ANGER

[1] **From the straits did I call upon God,** [2] **God answered me with**

ABUNDANT IN KINDNESS BEARER OF INIQUITY

expansiveness. [3] **HASHEM is with me,** [4] **I have no fear —** [5] **how**

(BEARER OF) TRANSGRESSION AND WHO CLEANSES

can man affect me? [6] **HASHEM is with me, through my helpers,**

AND HE DOES NOT ERASE HE ACCOUNTS THE INIQUITY OF THE

[7] **therefore I can face my foes.** [8] **It is better to take refuge in**

FATHERS TO THE SONS TO THE THIRD AND THE FOURTH

HASHEM than to rely on man. [9] **It is better to take refuge in HASHEM**

GENERATIONS

than to rely on nobles.[2]

Psalm 33 (Commentary, p. 386)

רַנְּנוּ *Sing joyfully, O righteous, before HASHEM; for the upright, praise is fitting. Give thanks to HASHEM with the harp, with the ten-stringed lyre make music to Him. Sing Him a new song, play well with sounds of deepest feeling. For upright is the word of HASHEM, and all His deeds are done with faithfulness. He loves charity and justice, the kindness of HASHEM fills the earth. By the word of HASHEM the heavens were made, and by the breath of His mouth all their host. He assembles like a wall the waters of the sea,*

(1) *Micah* 7:18-20. (2) *Psalms* 118:5-9.

Laws of Tashlich

On the first afternoon of Rosh Hashanah, after *Minchah,* it is customary to go to a body of water — preferably one that contains living fish — and recite the *Tashlich* prayer. If there is no such water within walking distance, or in case of inclement weather, *Tashlich* may be recited during the Ten Days of Repentance, or even until Hoshana Rabbah. If the first day of Rosh Hashanah is on the Sabbath, the *Tashlich* service is postponed until the second day.

נֹתֵן בְּאוֹצָרוֹת תְּהוֹמוֹת. יִירְאוּ מֵיהוה כָּל הָאָרֶץ, מִמֶּנּוּ יָגוּרוּ כָּל יֹשְׁבֵי תֵבֵל. כִּי הוּא אָמַר וַיֶּהִי, הוּא צִוָּה וַיַּעֲמֹד. יהוה הֵפִיר עֲצַת גּוֹיִם, הֵנִיא מַחְשְׁבוֹת עַמִּים. עֲצַת יהוה לְעוֹלָם תַּעֲמֹד, מַחְשְׁבוֹת לִבּוֹ לְדֹר וָדֹר. אַשְׁרֵי הַגּוֹי אֲשֶׁר יהוה אֱלֹהָיו, הָעָם בָּחַר לְנַחֲלָה לוֹ. מִשָּׁמַיִם הִבִּיט יהוה, רָאָה אֶת כָּל בְּנֵי הָאָדָם. מִמְּכוֹן שִׁבְתּוֹ הִשְׁגִּיחַ, אֶל כָּל יֹשְׁבֵי הָאָרֶץ. הַיֹּצֵר יַחַד לִבָּם, הַמֵּבִין אֶל כָּל מַעֲשֵׂיהֶם. אֵין הַמֶּלֶךְ נוֹשָׁע בְּרָב חָיִל, גִּבּוֹר לֹא יִנָּצֵל בְּרָב כֹּחַ. שֶׁקֶר הַסּוּס לִתְשׁוּעָה, וּבְרֹב חֵילוֹ לֹא יְמַלֵּט. הִנֵּה עֵין יהוה אֶל יְרֵאָיו, לַמְיַחֲלִים לְחַסְדּוֹ. לְהַצִּיל מִמָּוֶת נַפְשָׁם, וּלְחַיּוֹתָם בָּרָעָב. נַפְשֵׁנוּ חִכְּתָה לַיהוה, עֶזְרֵנוּ וּמָגִנֵּנוּ הוּא. כִּי בוֹ יִשְׂמַח לִבֵּנוּ, כִּי בְשֵׁם קָדְשׁוֹ בָטָחְנוּ. יְהִי חַסְדְּךָ יהוה עָלֵינוּ, כַּאֲשֶׁר יִחַלְנוּ לָךְ.

לֹא יָרֵעוּ וְלֹא יַשְׁחִיתוּ בְּכָל הַר קָדְשִׁי, כִּי מָלְאָה הָאָרֶץ דֵּעָה אֶת יהוה, כַּמַּיִם לַיָּם מְכַסִּים.[1]

תהלים קל (Commentary p. 540)

שִׁיר הַמַּעֲלוֹת, מִמַּעֲמַקִּים קְרָאתִיךָ יהוה. אֲדֹנָי שִׁמְעָה בְקוֹלִי, תִּהְיֶינָה אָזְנֶיךָ קַשֻּׁבוֹת, לְקוֹל תַּחֲנוּנָי. אִם עֲוֹנוֹת תִּשְׁמָר יָהּ, אֲדֹנָי מִי יַעֲמֹד. כִּי עִמְּךָ הַסְּלִיחָה, לְמַעַן תִּוָּרֵא. קִוִּיתִי יהוה קִוְּתָה נַפְשִׁי, וְלִדְבָרוֹ הוֹחָלְתִּי. נַפְשִׁי לַאדֹנָי, מִשֹּׁמְרִים לַבֹּקֶר, שֹׁמְרִים לַבֹּקֶר. יַחֵל יִשְׂרָאֵל אֶל יהוה, כִּי עִם יהוה הַחֶסֶד, וְהַרְבֵּה עִמּוֹ פְדוּת. וְהוּא יִפְדֶּה אֶת יִשְׂרָאֵל, מִכֹּל עֲוֹנוֹתָיו.

כפרות

Take the chicken [or money] in the right hand (some say נֶפֶשׁ תַּחַת נֶפֶשׁ, *A life for a life,* as they do so), and recite the following paragraph. Then — while reciting the appropriate paragraph on the next page — revolve the chicken or the money around the head (some do this three times). Follow this procedure three times. [Alternatively, recite the following paragraph three times. Then — while revolving the chicken or the money around the head — recite the appropriate paragraph on the next page three times.]

בְּנֵי אָדָם יֹשְׁבֵי חֹשֶׁךְ וְצַלְמָוֶת, אֲסִירֵי עֳנִי וּבַרְזֶל. יוֹצִיאֵם מֵחֹשֶׁךְ וְצַלְמָוֶת, וּמוֹסְרוֹתֵיהֶם יְנַתֵּק. אֱוִלִים מִדֶּרֶךְ פִּשְׁעָם, וּמֵעֲוֹנֹתֵיהֶם יִתְעַנּוּ. כָּל אֹכֶל תְּתַעֵב נַפְשָׁם, וַיַּגִּיעוּ עַד שַׁעֲרֵי מָוֶת. וַיִּזְעֲקוּ אֶל יהוה בַּצַּר לָהֶם, מִמְּצֻקוֹתֵיהֶם יוֹשִׁיעֵם. יִשְׁלַח דְּבָרוֹ וְיִרְפָּאֵם, וִימַלֵּט מִשְּׁחִיתוֹתָם. יוֹדוּ לַיהוה חַסְדּוֹ, וְנִפְלְאוֹתָיו לִבְנֵי אָדָם.[2] אִם יֵשׁ עָלָיו מַלְאָךְ מֵלִיץ אֶחָד מִנִּי אָלֶף, לְהַגִּיד לְאָדָם יָשְׁרוֹ. וַיְחֻנֶּנּוּ וַיֹּאמֶר, פְּדָעֵהוּ מֵרֶדֶת שַׁחַת, מָצָאתִי כֹפֶר.[3]

---

again prayed, but that time he invoked only nine of the Attributes (*Numbers* 14:18). In our text of *Tashlich*, we indicate, by means of superscript, how, according to the Kabbalistic interpretation, the respective phrases of the *Tashlich* passage refer to the respective attributes. These attributes should not be pronounced during the *Tashlich* service. [The ArtScroll *Tashlich* gives a full explanation of all the above.]

ATONEMENT / כַּפָּרוֹת

There is an ancient custom to take a white rooster for males and a white hen for females on the day before Yom Kippur and perform the *Kaparos* [Atonement] ritual. Money may be substituted for the fowl, and the ritual may be performed before Erev Yom Kippur if necessary. It is most important to realize, however, that the atonement results from giving the bird (or its

He places the deep waters in vaults. Fear HASHEM, *all the earth; of Him be in dread, all inhabitants of the world. For He spoke and it came to be, He commanded and it stood firm.* HASHEM *annuls the counsel of nations, He balks the designs of peoples. The counsel of* HASHEM *will endure forever, the designs of His heart throughout the generations. Praiseworthy is the nation whose God is* HASHEM, *the people He chose for His own heritage. From heaven* HASHEM *looks down, He sees all mankind. From His dwelling place He oversees all inhabitants of earth. He fashions their hearts all together, He comprehends all their deeds. A king is not saved by a great army, nor is a hero rescued by great strength; sham is the horse for salvation; despite its great strength it provides no escape. Behold, the eye of* HASHEM *is on those who fear Him, upon those who await His kindness, to rescue their soul from death, and to sustain them in famine. Our soul longed for* HASHEM *— our help and our shield is He. For in Him will our hearts be glad, for in His Holy Name we trusted. May Your kindness,* HASHEM, *be upon us, just as we awaited You.*

They shall neither injure nor destroy in all of My sacred mount, for the earth shall be filled with knowledge of HASHEM, *as water covers the sea.*[1]

Psalm 130 (Commentary, p. 540)

שִׁיר הַמַּעֲלוֹת *A song of ascents: From the depths I called You,* HASHEM. *My Lord, hear my voice, may Your ears be attentive to the sound of my pleas. If You preserve iniquities, O God, my Lord, who could survive? For with You is forgiveness, that You may be feared. I put confidence in* HASHEM, *my soul put confidence, and I hoped for His word. I yearn for my Lord, among those longing for the dawn, those longing for the dawn. Let Israel hope for* HASHEM, *for with* HASHEM *is kindness, and with Him is abundant redemption. And He shall redeem Israel from all its iniquities.*

❧ KAPOROS / ATONEMENT ❧

Take the chicken [or money] in the right hand (some say נֶפֶשׁ תַּחַת נֶפֶשׁ, *A life for a life,* as they do so), and recite the following paragraph. Then — while reciting th apopropriate paragraph on the next page — revolve the chicken or money around the head (some do this three times). Follow this procedure three times. [Alternatively, recite the following paragraph three times. Then — while revolving the chicken or the money around the head — recite the appropriate paragraph on the next page three times.]

בְּנֵי *Children of Man, who sit in darkness and the shadow of death, shackled in affliction and iron. He removed them from darkness and the shadow of death, and broke open their shackles. The fools — because of their sinful path and their iniquities they were afflicted. Their soul abhorred all food, and they reached the portals of death. Then they cried out to* HASHEM *in their distress; from their woes He spared them. He dispatched His word and cured them, and let them escape their destruction. Let them thank* HASHEM *for His kindness and for His wonders to mankind.*[2] *If there will be for someone but a single defending angel out of a thousand to declare a man's uprightness on his behalf, then He will be gracious to him and say, 'Redeem him from descending to the Pit; I have found atonement.'*[3]

(1) *Isaiah* 11:9. (2) *Psalms* 107:10,14,17-21. (3) *Job* 33:23-24.

value) to the poor. Only that, as part of repentance, gives meaning to the ceremony. Some use a different chicken for each person, while others use a single rooster for many men or a single hen for many women.

A pregnant woman customarily takes both a hen and a rooster, a hen for herself and a rooster in case she is carrying a male. Those who use a

Recite the applicable paragraph.
[When money is used, substitute the bracketed phrase for the phrase preceding it.]
Each time the paragraph is recited the bird or money is circled around the head.

—A man performing the ritual for himself

זֶה חֲלִיפָתִי, זֶה תְּמוּרָתִי, זֶה כַּפָּרָתִי. זֶה הַתַּרְנְגוֹל יֵלֵךְ לְמִיתָה, [זֶה הַכֶּסֶף יֵלֵךְ לִצְדָקָה] וַאֲנִי אֶכָּנֵס וְאֵלֵךְ לְחַיִּים טוֹבִים אֲרוּכִים וּלְשָׁלוֹם.

—Two or more men performing the ritual for themselves

זֶה חֲלִיפָתֵנוּ, זֶה תְּמוּרָתֵנוּ, זֶה כַּפָּרָתֵנוּ. זֶה הַתַּרְנְגוֹל יֵלֵךְ לְמִיתָה, [זֶה הַכֶּסֶף יֵלֵךְ לִצְדָקָה] וַאֲנַחְנוּ נִכָּנֵס וְנֵלֵךְ לְחַיִּים טוֹבִים אֲרוּכִים וּלְשָׁלוֹם.

—One performing the ritual for a man

זֶה חֲלִיפָתְךָ, זֶה תְּמוּרָתְךָ, זֶה כַּפָּרָתְךָ. זֶה הַתַּרְנְגוֹל יֵלֵךְ לְמִיתָה, [זֶה הַכֶּסֶף יֵלֵךְ לִצְדָקָה] וְאַתָּה תִּכָּנֵס וְתֵלֵךְ לְחַיִּים טוֹבִים אֲרוּכִים וּלְשָׁלוֹם.

—One performing the ritual for two or more men

זֶה חֲלִיפַתְכֶם, זֶה תְּמוּרַתְכֶם, זֶה כַּפָּרַתְכֶם. זֶה הַתַּרְנְגוֹל יֵלֵךְ לְמִיתָה, [זֶה הַכֶּסֶף יֵלֵךְ לִצְדָקָה] וְאַתֶּם תִּכָּנְסוּ וְתֵלְכוּ לְחַיִּים טוֹבִים אֲרוּכִים וּלְשָׁלוֹם.

—A woman performing the ritual for herself

זֹאת חֲלִיפָתִי, זֹאת תְּמוּרָתִי, זֹאת כַּפָּרָתִי. זֹאת הַתַּרְנְגֹלֶת תֵּלֵךְ לְמִיתָה, [זֶה הַכֶּסֶף יֵלֵךְ לִצְדָקָה] וַאֲנִי אֶכָּנֵס וְאֵלֵךְ לְחַיִּים טוֹבִים אֲרוּכִים וּלְשָׁלוֹם.

—Two or more women performing the ritual for themselves

זֹאת חֲלִיפָתֵנוּ, זֹאת תְּמוּרָתֵנוּ, זֹאת כַּפָּרָתֵנוּ. זֹאת הַתַּרְנְגֹלֶת תֵּלֵךְ לְמִיתָה, [זֶה הַכֶּסֶף יֵלֵךְ לִצְדָקָה] וַאֲנַחְנוּ נִכָּנֵס וְנֵלֵךְ לְחַיִּים טוֹבִים אֲרוּכִים וּלְשָׁלוֹם.

—One performing the ritual for a woman

זֹאת חֲלִיפָתֵךְ, זֹאת תְּמוּרָתֵךְ, זֹאת כַּפָּרָתֵךְ. זֹאת הַתַּרְנְגֹלֶת תֵּלֵךְ לְמִיתָה, [זֶה הַכֶּסֶף יֵלֵךְ לִצְדָקָה] וְאַתְּ תִּכָּנְסִי וְתֵלְכִי לְחַיִּים טוֹבִים אֲרוּכִים וּלְשָׁלוֹם.

—One performing the ritual for two or more women

זֹאת חֲלִיפַתְכֶן, זֹאת תְּמוּרַתְכֶן, זֹאת כַּפָּרַתְכֶן. זֹאת הַתַּרְנְגֹלֶת תֵּלֵךְ לְמִיתָה, [זֶה הַכֶּסֶף יֵלֵךְ לִצְדָקָה] וְאַתֶּן תִּכָּנַסְנָה וְתֵלַכְנָה לְחַיִּים טוֹבִים אֲרוּכִים וּלְשָׁלוֹם.

—A pregnant woman performing the ritual for herself

אֵלּוּ חֲלִיפוֹתֵינוּ, אֵלּוּ תְּמוּרוֹתֵינוּ, אֵלּוּ כַּפָּרוֹתֵינוּ. אֵלּוּ הַתַּרְנְגוֹלִים יֵלְכוּ לְמִיתָה, [זֶה הַכֶּסֶף יֵלֵךְ לִצְדָקָה] וַאֲנַחְנוּ נִכָּנֵס וְנֵלֵךְ לְחַיִּים טוֹבִים אֲרוּכִים וּלְשָׁלוֹם.

—One performing the ritual for a pregnant woman

אֵלּוּ חֲלִיפוֹתֵיכֶם, אֵלּוּ תְּמוּרוֹתֵיכֶם, אֵלּוּ כַּפָּרוֹתֵיכֶם. אֵלּוּ הַתַּרְנְגוֹלִים יֵלְכוּ לְמִיתָה, [זֶה הַכֶּסֶף יֵלֵךְ לִצְדָקָה] וְאַתֶּם תִּכָּנְסוּ וְתֵלְכוּ לְחַיִּים טוֹבִים אֲרוּכִים וּלְשָׁלוֹם.

Recite the applicable paragraph. [When money is used, substitute the bracketed phrase for the phrase preceding it.] Each time the paragraph is recited the bird or money is circled around the head.

A man performing the ritual for himself— *This is my exchange, this is my substitute, this is my atonement. This rooster will go to its death [this money will go to charity] while I will enter and go to a good, long life, and to peace.*

Two or more men performing the ritual for themselves— *This is our exchange, this is our substitute, this is our atonement. This rooster will go to its death [this money will go to charity] while we will enter and go to a good, long life, and to peace.*

One performing the ritual for a man— *This is your exchange, this is your substitute, this is your atonement. This rooster will go to its death [this money will go to charity] while you will enter and go to a good, long life, and to peace.*

One performing the ritual for two or more men— *This is your exchange, this is your substitute, this is your atonement. This rooster will go to its death [this money will go to charity], while you will enter and go to a good, long life, and to peace.*

A woman performing the ritual for herself— *This is my exchange, this is my substitute, this is my atonement. This hen will go to its death [this money will go to charity] while I will enter and go to a good, long life, and to peace.*

Two or more women performing the ritual for themselves— *This is our exchange, this is our substitute, this is our atonement. This hen will go to its death [this money will go to charity] while we will enter and go to a good, long life, and to peace.*

One performing the ritual for a woman— *This is your exchange, this is your substitute, this is your atonement. This hen will go to its death [this money will go to charity] while you will enter and go to a good, long life, and to peace.*

One performing the ritual for two or more women— *This is your exchange, this is your substitute, this is your atonement. This hen will go to its death [this money will go to charity], while you will enter and go to a good, long life, and to peace.*

A pregnant woman performing the ritual for herself— *This is our exchange, this is our substitute, this is our atonement. These chickens will go to their death [this money will go to charity] while we will enter and go to a good, long life, and to peace.*

One performing the ritual for a pregnant woman— *This is your exchange, this is your substitute, this is your atonement. These chickens will go to their death [this money will go to charity] while you will enter and go to a good, long life, and to peace.*

---

separate bird for each person take three birds for a pregnant women, two hens, one for herself and one in case she is carrying a female, and a rooster in case she is carrying a male.

מנחה לערב יום כפור

At the Minchah service of Erev Yom Kippur the regular silent *Shemoneh Esrei* (pp. 234-248) is recited. Before אֱלֹהַי נְצוֹר, the following וִדּוּי, *confessional,* is then recited. The *chazzan* does not repeat the confessional during his repetition of *Shemoneh Esrei.* A full commentary of this basic component of the Yom Kippur repentance liturgy may be found in the ArtScroll *Machzor.*

יִהְיוּ לְרָצוֹן אִמְרֵי פִי, וְהֶגְיוֹן לִבִּי לְפָנֶיךָ, יהוה צוּרִי וְגֹאֲלִי.[1]

אֱלֹהֵינוּ וֵאלֹהֵי אֲבוֹתֵינוּ, תָּבֹא לְפָנֶיךָ תְּפִלָּתֵנוּ,[2] וְאַל תִּתְעַלַּם מִתְּחִנָּתֵנוּ,[3] שֶׁאֵין אֲנַחְנוּ עַזֵּי פָנִים וּקְשֵׁי עֹרֶף, לוֹמַר לְפָנֶיךָ יהוה אֱלֹהֵינוּ וֵאלֹהֵי אֲבוֹתֵינוּ, צַדִּיקִים אֲנַחְנוּ וְלֹא חָטָאנוּ, אֲבָל אֲנַחְנוּ וַאֲבוֹתֵינוּ חָטָאנוּ.[4]

Strike the left side of the chest with the right fist while reciting each of the sins of the following confessional litany:

אָשַׁמְנוּ, בָּגַדְנוּ, גָּזַלְנוּ, דִּבַּרְנוּ דֹפִי. הֶעֱוִינוּ, וְהִרְשַׁעְנוּ, זַדְנוּ, חָמַסְנוּ, טָפַלְנוּ שֶׁקֶר. יָעַצְנוּ רָע, כִּזַּבְנוּ, לַצְנוּ, מָרַדְנוּ, נִאַצְנוּ, סָרַרְנוּ, עָוִינוּ, פָּשַׁעְנוּ, צָרַרְנוּ, קִשִּׁינוּ עֹרֶף. רָשַׁעְנוּ, שִׁחַתְנוּ, תִּעַבְנוּ, תָּעִינוּ, תִּעְתָּעְנוּ.

סַרְנוּ מִמִּצְוֹתֶיךָ וּמִמִּשְׁפָּטֶיךָ הַטּוֹבִים, וְלֹא שָׁוָה לָנוּ.[5] וְאַתָּה צַדִּיק עַל כָּל הַבָּא עָלֵינוּ, כִּי אֱמֶת עָשִׂיתָ וַאֲנַחְנוּ הִרְשָׁעְנוּ.[6]

מַה נֹּאמַר לְפָנֶיךָ יוֹשֵׁב מָרוֹם, וּמַה נְּסַפֵּר לְפָנֶיךָ שׁוֹכֵן שְׁחָקִים, הֲלֹא כָּל הַנִּסְתָּרוֹת וְהַנִּגְלוֹת אַתָּה יוֹדֵעַ.

אַתָּה יוֹדֵעַ רָזֵי עוֹלָם, וְתַעֲלוּמוֹת סִתְרֵי כָּל חָי. אַתָּה חוֹפֵשׂ כָּל חַדְרֵי בָטֶן,[7] וּבֹחֵן כְּלָיוֹת וָלֵב.[8] אֵין דָּבָר נֶעְלָם מִמֶּךָּ, וְאֵין נִסְתָּר מִנֶּגֶד עֵינֶיךָ. וּבְכֵן יְהִי רָצוֹן מִלְּפָנֶיךָ, יהוה אֱלֹהֵינוּ וֵאלֹהֵי אֲבוֹתֵינוּ, שֶׁתִּסְלַח לָנוּ עַל כָּל חַטֹּאתֵינוּ, וְתִמְחַל לָנוּ עַל כָּל עֲוֹנוֹתֵינוּ, וּתְכַפֵּר לָנוּ עַל כָּל פְּשָׁעֵינוּ.

Strike the left side of the chest with the right fist each time the word שֶׁחָטָאנוּ is said.

עַל חֵטְא שֶׁחָטָאנוּ לְפָנֶיךָ בְּאֹנֶס וּבְרָצוֹן,
וְעַל חֵטְא שֶׁחָטָאנוּ לְפָנֶיךָ בְּאִמּוּץ הַלֵּב.
עַל חֵטְא שֶׁחָטָאנוּ לְפָנֶיךָ בִּבְלִי דָעַת,
וְעַל חֵטְא שֶׁחָטָאנוּ לְפָנֶיךָ בְּבִטּוּי שְׂפָתָיִם.

MINCHAH EREV YOM KIPPUR

As found several times in the Torah and as codified by *Rambam* in the Laws of Repentance, the confession of sins is an essential part of repentance. It is human nature for people to rationalize their shortcomings in their own minds as unavoidable or even to define them as virtues. As long as someone refuses to acknowledge his wrongdoing, he cannot repent sincerely. So important is the confession, not only to the process of repentance but also to the Jew's chance to survive the Heavenly judgment, that the Sages ordained that the confessional be recited the afternoon before Yom Kippur, lest illness or death prevent someone from praying on Yom Kippur itself.

MINCHAH OF THE AFTERNOON BEFORE YOM KIPPUR

At the Minchah service of Erev Yom Kippur the regular silent *Shemoneh Esrei* (pp. 234-248) is recited. Before אֱלֹהַי נְצוֹר, *'My God, guard ...,'* the following וִדּוּי, *confessional,* is then recited. The *chazzan* does not repeat the confessional during his repetition of *Shemoneh Esrei.* A full commentary of this basic component of the Yom Kippur repentance liturgy may be found in the ArtScroll *Machzor.*

May the expressions of my mouth and the thoughts of my heart find favor before You, HASHEM, my Rock and my Redeemer.[1]

אֱלֹהֵינוּ *Our God and the God of our forefathers, may our prayer come before You,*[2] *and do not ignore our supplication*[3] *for we are not so brazen and obstinate as to say before You, HASHEM, our God, and the God of our forefathers, that we are righteous and have not sinned — rather, we and our forefathers have sinned.*[4]

Strike the left side of the chest with the right fist while reciting each of the sins of the following confessional litany:

אָשַׁמְנוּ *We have become guilty, we have betrayed, we have robbed, we have spoken slander. We have caused perversion, we have caused wickedness, we have sinned willfully, we have extorted, we have accused falsely. We have given evil counsel, we have been deceitful, we have scorned, we have rebelled, we have provoked, we have turned away, we have been perverse, we have acted wantonly, we have persecuted, we have been obstinate. We have been wicked, we have corrupted, we have been abominable, we have strayed, You have let us go astray.*

סַרְנוּ *We have turned away from Your commandments and from Your good laws but to no avail.*[5] *But You are righteous in all that has come upon us, for You have acted truthfully while we have caused wickedness.*[6]

מַה *What can we say before You, Who dwells on high, and what can we relate to You, Who abides in the highest heavens — for indeed, everything that is hidden and revealed You know.*

אַתָּה יוֹדֵעַ *You know the secrets of the universe, and the hiddenmost mysteries of all the living. You probe all innermost chambers*[7] *and test thoughts and emotions.*[8] *Nothing is hidden from You and nothing is concealed from Your eyes. And so may it be Your will, HASHEM, our God and the God of our forefathers, that You forgive us all our errors, and You pardon us all our iniquities, and You atone for us all our willful sins.*

Strike the left side of the chest with the right fist each time the phrase *'we have sinned'* is said.

עַל חֵטְא א *For the sin that we have sinned before You under duress and willingly;*
and for the sin that we have sinned before You through hardness of the heart.

ב *For the sin that we have sinned before You without knowledge;*
and for the sin that we have sinned before You with the utterance of the lips.

---

(1) *Psalms* 19:15. (2) Cf. 88:3. (3) Cf. 55:2. (4) Cf. 106:6. (5) Cf. *Job* 33:27. (6) *Nechemiah* 9:33. (7) *Proverbs* 20:27. (8) *Jeremiah* 11:20.

עַל חֵטְא שֶׁחָטָאנוּ לְפָנֶיךָ בְּגָלוּי וּבַסָּתֶר,
וְעַל חֵטְא שֶׁחָטָאנוּ לְפָנֶיךָ בְּגִלּוּי עֲרָיוֹת.
עַל חֵטְא שֶׁחָטָאנוּ לְפָנֶיךָ **בְּד**ִבּוּר פֶּה,
וְעַל חֵטְא שֶׁחָטָאנוּ לְפָנֶיךָ **בְּד**ַעַת וּבְמִרְמָה.
עַל חֵטְא שֶׁחָטָאנוּ לְפָנֶיךָ **בְּה**ַרְהוֹר הַלֵּב,
וְעַל חֵטְא שֶׁחָטָאנוּ לְפָנֶיךָ **בְּה**וֹנָאַת רֵעַ.
עַל חֵטְא שֶׁחָטָאנוּ לְפָנֶיךָ **בְּו**ִדּוּי פֶּה,
וְעַל חֵטְא שֶׁחָטָאנוּ לְפָנֶיךָ **בְּו**ְעִידַת זְנוּת.
עַל חֵטְא שֶׁחָטָאנוּ לְפָנֶיךָ **בְּז**ָדוֹן וּבִשְׁגָגָה,
וְעַל חֵטְא שֶׁחָטָאנוּ לְפָנֶיךָ **בְּז**ִלְזוּל הוֹרִים וּמוֹרִים.
עַל חֵטְא שֶׁחָטָאנוּ לְפָנֶיךָ **בְּח**ֹזֶק יָד,
וְעַל חֵטְא שֶׁחָטָאנוּ לְפָנֶיךָ **בְּח**ִלּוּל הַשֵּׁם.
עַל חֵטְא שֶׁחָטָאנוּ לְפָנֶיךָ **בְּט**ִפְשׁוּת פֶּה,
וְעַל חֵטְא שֶׁחָטָאנוּ לְפָנֶיךָ **בְּט**ֻמְאַת שְׂפָתָיִם.
עַל חֵטְא שֶׁחָטָאנוּ לְפָנֶיךָ **בְּי**ֵצֶר הָרָע,
וְעַל חֵטְא שֶׁחָטָאנוּ לְפָנֶיךָ **בְּי**וֹדְעִים וּבְלֹא יוֹדְעִים.

וְעַל כֻּלָּם, אֱלוֹהַּ סְלִיחוֹת, סְלַח לָנוּ, מְחַל לָנוּ, כַּפֶּר לָנוּ.

עַל חֵטְא שֶׁחָטָאנוּ לְפָנֶיךָ **בְּכ**ַפַּת שֹׁחַד,
וְעַל חֵטְא שֶׁחָטָאנוּ לְפָנֶיךָ **בְּכ**ַחַשׁ וּבְכָזָב.
עַל חֵטְא שֶׁחָטָאנוּ לְפָנֶיךָ **בְּל**ָשׁוֹן הָרָע,
וְעַל חֵטְא שֶׁחָטָאנוּ לְפָנֶיךָ **בְּל**ָצוֹן.
עַל חֵטְא שֶׁחָטָאנוּ לְפָנֶיךָ **בְּמ**ַשָּׂא וּבְמַתָּן,
וְעַל חֵטְא שֶׁחָטָאנוּ לְפָנֶיךָ **בְּמ**ַאֲכָל וּבְמִשְׁתֶּה.
עַל חֵטְא שֶׁחָטָאנוּ לְפָנֶיךָ **בְּנ**ֶשֶׁךְ וּבְמַרְבִּית,
וְעַל חֵטְא שֶׁחָטָאנוּ לְפָנֶיךָ **בְּנ**ְטִיַּת גָּרוֹן.
עַל חֵטְא שֶׁחָטָאנוּ לְפָנֶיךָ **בְּש**ִׂקּוּר עָיִן,
וְעַל חֵטְא שֶׁחָטָאנוּ לְפָנֶיךָ **בְּש**ִׂיחַ שִׂפְתוֹתֵינוּ.
עַל חֵטְא שֶׁחָטָאנוּ לְפָנֶיךָ **בְּע**ֵינַיִם רָמוֹת,
וְעַל חֵטְא שֶׁחָטָאנוּ לְפָנֶיךָ **בְּע**ַזּוּת מֵצַח.

וְעַל כֻּלָּם, אֱלוֹהַּ סְלִיחוֹת, סְלַח לָנוּ, מְחַל לָנוּ, כַּפֶּר לָנוּ.

עַל חֵטְא שֶׁחָטָאנוּ לְפָנֶיךָ **בְּפ**ְרִיקַת עֹל,
וְעַל חֵטְא שֶׁחָטָאנוּ לְפָנֶיךָ **בְּפ**ְלִילוּת.

The confessional includes a very wide range of sins, far more than any individual could have committed. This is because it contains not only the sins of the individual supplicant, but also those of the entire Jewish people. It is axiomatic that had the nation as a whole repented sufficiently the final redemption would have come by now. Thus, we share responsibility not only for our own sins, but for those of the past. Furthermore, the principle 'all Jews are responsible for one another' makes us all partners in the failures of our brethren.

ג *For the sin that we have sinned before You in public or in private;*
and for the sin that we have sinned before You through immorality.

ד *For the sin that we have sinned before You through harsh speech;*
and for the sin that we have sinned before You
with knowledge and with deceit.

ה *For the sin that we have sinned before You through inner thoughts;*
and for the sin that we have sinned before You
through wronging a neighbor.

ו *For the sin that we have sinned before You with insincere confession;*
and for the sin that we have sinned before You in a session of vice.

ז *For the sin that we have sinned before You willfully and carelessly;*
and for the sin that we have sinned before You
by showing contempt for parents and teachers.

ח *For the sin that we have sinned before You by exercising power;*
and for the sin that we have sinned before You
through desecration of the Name.

ט *For the sin that we have sinned before You through foolish speech;*
and for the sin that we have sinned before You through impure lips.

י *For the sin that we have sinned before You with the Evil Inclination;*
and for the sin that we have sinned before You
against those who know and against those who do not know.

For them all, O God of forgiveness,
forgive us, pardon us, atone for us.

כ *For the sin that we have sinned before You*
by causing subservience through bribery;
and for the sin that we have sinned before You
through denial and false promises.

ל *For the sin that we have sinned before You through evil talk;*
and for the sin that we have sinned before You through scorning.

מ *For the sin that we have sinned before You in commercial dealings;*
and for the sin that we have sinned before You with food and drink.

נ *For the sin that we have sinned before You through interest and extortion;*
and for the sin that we have sinned before You through haughtiness.

ש *For the sin that we have sinned before You with prying eyes;*
and for the sin that we have sinned before You
with the idle chatter of our lips.

ע *For the sin that we have sinned before You with haughty eyes;*
and for the sin that we have sinned before You with brazenness.

For them all, O God of forgiveness,
forgive us, pardon us, atone for us.

פ *For the sin that we have sinned before You in throwing off [Your] yoke;*
and for the sin that we have sinned before You in judgment.

Despite the wide range of sins enumerated in this long confessional, there are many individual sins that are not specified. The confessional should be seen not as a complete and exhaustive list of all possible sins, but as a list of categories and causes. For example, the sins of 'abusing parents and teachers' and of 'foolish speech' are the direct cause of many other misdeeds. Seen in this light, the confessional is a means of introspective soul searching to discover the shortcomings of our personality as well as to set forth individual sins.

עַל חֵטְא שֶׁחָטָאנוּ לְפָנֶיךָ בִּצְדִיַּת רֵעַ,
וְעַל חֵטְא שֶׁחָטָאנוּ לְפָנֶיךָ בְּצָרוּת עָיִן.
עַל חֵטְא שֶׁחָטָאנוּ לְפָנֶיךָ בְּקַלּוּת רֹאשׁ,
וְעַל חֵטְא שֶׁחָטָאנוּ לְפָנֶיךָ בְּקַשְׁיוּת עֹרֶף.
עַל חֵטְא שֶׁחָטָאנוּ לְפָנֶיךָ בְּרִיצַת רַגְלַיִם לְהָרַע,
וְעַל חֵטְא שֶׁחָטָאנוּ לְפָנֶיךָ בִּרְכִילוּת.
עַל חֵטְא שֶׁחָטָאנוּ לְפָנֶיךָ בִּשְׁבוּעַת שָׁוְא,
וְעַל חֵטְא שֶׁחָטָאנוּ לְפָנֶיךָ בְּשִׂנְאַת חִנָּם.
עַל חֵטְא שֶׁחָטָאנוּ לְפָנֶיךָ בִּתְשׂוּמֶת יָד,
וְעַל חֵטְא שֶׁחָטָאנוּ לְפָנֶיךָ בְּתִמְהוֹן לֵבָב.

וְעַל כֻּלָּם, אֱלוֹהַּ סְלִיחוֹת, סְלַח לָנוּ, מְחַל לָנוּ, כַּפֶּר לָנוּ.

וְעַל חֲטָאִים שֶׁאָנוּ חַיָּבִים עֲלֵיהֶם עוֹלָה.
וְעַל חֲטָאִים שֶׁאָנוּ חַיָּבִים עֲלֵיהֶם חַטָּאת.
וְעַל חֲטָאִים שֶׁאָנוּ חַיָּבִים עֲלֵיהֶם קָרְבָּן עוֹלֶה וְיוֹרֵד.
וְעַל חֲטָאִים שֶׁאָנוּ חַיָּבִים עֲלֵיהֶם אָשָׁם וַדַּאי וְתָלוּי.
וְעַל חֲטָאִים שֶׁאָנוּ חַיָּבִים עֲלֵיהֶם מַכַּת מַרְדּוּת.
וְעַל חֲטָאִים שֶׁאָנוּ חַיָּבִים עֲלֵיהֶם מַלְקוּת אַרְבָּעִים.
וְעַל חֲטָאִים שֶׁאָנוּ חַיָּבִים עֲלֵיהֶם מִיתָה בִּידֵי שָׁמָיִם.
וְעַל חֲטָאִים שֶׁאָנוּ חַיָּבִים עֲלֵיהֶם כָּרֵת וַעֲרִירִי.
וְעַל חֲטָאִים שֶׁאָנוּ חַיָּבִים עֲלֵיהֶם אַרְבַּע מִיתוֹת בֵּית דִּין —
סְקִילָה, שְׂרֵפָה, הֶרֶג, וְחֶנֶק.

עַל מִצְוַת עֲשֵׂה וְעַל מִצְוַת לֹא תַעֲשֶׂה, בֵּין שֶׁיֵּשׁ בָּהּ קוּם עֲשֵׂה, וּבֵין שֶׁאֵין בָּהּ קוּם עֲשֵׂה. אֶת הַגְּלוּיִם לָנוּ וְאֶת שֶׁאֵינָם גְּלוּיִם לָנוּ, אֶת הַגְּלוּיִם לָנוּ כְּבָר אֲמַרְנוּם לְפָנֶיךָ, וְהוֹדִינוּ לְךָ עֲלֵיהֶם, וְאֶת שֶׁאֵינָם גְּלוּיִם לָנוּ, לְפָנֶיךָ הֵם גְּלוּיִם וִידוּעִים, כַּדָּבָר שֶׁנֶּאֱמַר, הַנִּסְתָּרֹת לַיהוה אֱלֹהֵינוּ, וְהַנִּגְלֹת לָנוּ וּלְבָנֵינוּ עַד עוֹלָם, לַעֲשׂוֹת אֶת כָּל דִּבְרֵי הַתּוֹרָה הַזֹּאת.[1] כִּי אַתָּה סָלְחָן לְיִשְׂרָאֵל וּמָחֳלָן לְשִׁבְטֵי יְשֻׁרוּן בְּכָל דּוֹר וָדוֹר, וּמִבַּלְעָדֶיךָ אֵין לָנוּ מֶלֶךְ מוֹחֵל וְסוֹלֵחַ אֶלָּא אָתָּה.

אֱלֹהַי, עַד שֶׁלֹּא נוֹצַרְתִּי אֵינִי כְדַאי, וְעַכְשָׁו שֶׁנּוֹצַרְתִּי כְּאִלּוּ לֹא נוֹצַרְתִּי, עָפָר אֲנִי בְּחַיָּי, קַל וָחֹמֶר בְּמִיתָתִי.[2] הֲרֵי אֲנִי לְפָנֶיךָ כִּכְלִי מָלֵא בוּשָׁה וּכְלִמָּה. יְהִי רָצוֹן מִלְּפָנֶיךָ, יהוה אֱלֹהַי וֵאלֹהֵי אֲבוֹתַי, שֶׁלֹּא אֶחֱטָא עוֹד וּמַה שֶּׁחָטָאתִי לְפָנֶיךָ מָרֵק בְּרַחֲמֶיךָ הָרַבִּים, אֲבָל לֹא עַל יְדֵי יִסּוּרִים וָחֳלָיִם רָעִים.

Return to אֱלֹהַי נְצוֹר (p. 248) for the conclusion of *Shemoneh Esrei.*

---

(1) *Deuteronomy* 29:28. (2) Cf. *Genesis* 3:19.

צ *For the sin that we have sinned before You through entrapping a neighbor; and for the sin that we have sinned before You through a begrudging eye.*

ק *For the sin that we have sinned before You through light-headedness; and for the sin that we have sinned before You with obstinacy.*

ר *For the sin that we have sinned before You with legs that run to do evil; and for the sin that we have sinned before You by gossip-mongering.*

ש *For the sin that we have sinned before You through vain oath-taking; and for the sin that we have sinned before You through baseless hatred.*

ת *For the sin that we have sinned before You in the matter of extending a hand; and for the sin that we have sinned before You through confusion of heart.*

For them all, O God of forgiveness, forgive us, pardon us, atone for us.

And for the sins for which we are liable to bring an elevation-offering.
And for the sins for which we are liable to bring a sin-offering.
And for the sins for which we are liable to bring a variable-offering.
And for the sins for which we are liable to bring a guilt-offering for a definite or a possible sin.
And for the sins for which we are liable to lashes for rebelliousness.
And for the sins for which we are liable to forty lashes.
And for the sins for which we are liable to the death penalty at the hands of the Heavenly Court.
And for the sins for which we are liable to spiritual excision and childlessness.
And for the sins for which we are liable to the four death-penalties of the human court: stoning, burning, beheading, and strangling.

For a positive commandment and for a negative commandment, whether it can be remedied by a positive act or whether it cannot be remedied by a positive act; those that are revealed to us and those that are not revealed to us. Those that are revealed to us we have already declared before You and confessed them to You; and those that are not revealed to us are revealed and known to You, as it is said, 'The concealed [sins] are for HASHEM*, our God, but the revealed [sins] are ours and our children's forever, [that we may] fulfill all the words of this Torah.'*[1] *For You are the Forgiver of Israel and the Pardoner of the tribes of Jeshurun in every generation, and beside You we have no king Who pardons and forgives — only You.*

אֱלֹהַי *My God, before I was formed I was unworthy, and now that I have been formed, it is as if I had not been formed. I am dust in my life and will surely be so in my death.*[2] *Behold — before You I am like a vessel filled with shame and humiliation. May it be Your will,* HASHEM*, my God and the God of my forefathers, that I not sin again. And what I have sinned before You, may You cleanse with Your abundant mercy, but not through suffering or serious illness.*

Return to אֱלֹהַי נְצוֹר (p. 248) for the conclusion of *Shemoneh Esrei.*

הדלקת נר חנוכה

All three blessings are pronounced before kindling the Chanukah *menorah* for the first time. On all subsequent nights, the third blessing, שֶׁהֶחֱיָנוּ, is omitted.

בָּרוּךְ אַתָּה יהוה אֱלֹהֵינוּ מֶלֶךְ הָעוֹלָם, אֲשֶׁר קִדְּשָׁנוּ בְּמִצְוֹתָיו, וְצִוָּנוּ לְהַדְלִיק נֵר שֶׁל חֲנֻכָּה.

בָּרוּךְ אַתָּה יהוה אֱלֹהֵינוּ מֶלֶךְ הָעוֹלָם, שֶׁעָשָׂה נִסִּים לַאֲבוֹתֵינוּ, בַּיָּמִים הָהֵם בַּזְּמַן הַזֶּה.

בָּרוּךְ אַתָּה יהוה אֱלֹהֵינוּ מֶלֶךְ הָעוֹלָם, שֶׁהֶחֱיָנוּ וְקִיְּמָנוּ וְהִגִּיעָנוּ לַזְּמַן הַזֶּה.

On the first night, the light to the extreme right is kindled. On each subsequent night, a new light is added to the left of the previous night's lights. The new light is always kindled first, the one to its right second, and so on. After one light has been kindled, הַנֵּרוֹת הַלָּלוּ is recited. The additional lights are kindled during its recitation.

הַנֵּרוֹת הַלָּלוּ אֲנַחְנוּ מַדְלִיקִין עַל הַנִּסִּים וְעַל הַנִּפְלָאוֹת,* וְעַל הַתְּשׁוּעוֹת וְעַל הַמִּלְחָמוֹת, שֶׁעָשִׂיתָ לַאֲבוֹתֵינוּ בַּיָּמִים הָהֵם בַּזְּמַן הַזֶּה, עַל יְדֵי כֹּהֲנֶיךָ הַקְּדוֹשִׁים. וְכָל שְׁמוֹנַת יְמֵי חֲנֻכָּה, הַנֵּרוֹת הַלָּלוּ קֹדֶשׁ הֵם. וְאֵין לָנוּ רְשׁוּת לְהִשְׁתַּמֵּשׁ בָּהֶם,* אֶלָּא לִרְאוֹתָם בִּלְבָד, כְּדֵי לְהוֹדוֹת וּלְהַלֵּל לְשִׁמְךָ הַגָּדוֹל* עַל נִסֶּיךָ וְעַל נִפְלְאוֹתֶיךָ וְעַל יְשׁוּעָתֶךָ.

After the proper number of lights have been kindled, מָעוֹז צוּר is chanted:

מָעוֹז צוּר* יְשׁוּעָתִי לְךָ נָאֶה לְשַׁבֵּחַ,
תִּכּוֹן בֵּית תְּפִלָּתִי וְשָׁם תּוֹדָה נְזַבֵּחַ,
לְעֵת תָּכִין מַטְבֵּחַ מִצָּר הַמְנַבֵּחַ,
אָז אֶגְמוֹר בְּשִׁיר מִזְמוֹר חֲנֻכַּת הַמִּזְבֵּחַ.

נֵר חֲנֻכָּה / CHANUKAH MENORAH

הַנֵּרוֹת הַלָּלוּ / Haneiros Halalu

[See ArtScroll *Chanukah* for full commentary.]

עַל הַנִּסִּים וְעַל הַנִּפְלָאוֹת — *Upon the miracles,* [*and upon*] *the wonders.* The word נִסִּים, *miracles,* refers to the obvious acts of intervention of His Divine Providence. This word can also mean *banners* or *signposts,* for God's miracles are meant to be signposts and symbols that stand out to teach and to guide us.

The term נִפְלָאוֹת, *wonders,* describes these extraordinary occurrences in terms of their independence from the regular order of things (*R' Hirsch*).

וְאֵין לָנוּ רְשׁוּת לְהִשְׁתַּמֵּשׁ בָּהֶם — *These lights are sacred, and we are not permitted to make ordinary use of them.* It is forbidden to use the Chanukah lights for any personal purpose — such as reading or doing work by their illumination 'lest one slight the *mitzvos*' (*Shabbos* 21b). The prohibition against enjoying the lights makes it manifestly clear to all that they were kindled for the sole purpose of commemorating the miracle.

In compliance with the prohibition against enjoying the lights, we light a *shamash* [lit. *servant*] flame, which is not holy, so that any

KINDLING THE CHANUKAH MENORAH

All three blessings are pronounced before kindling the Chanukah *menorah* for the first time. On all subsequent nights, the third blessing, שֶׁהֶחֱיָנוּ, *'Who has kept us alive,'* is omitted.

בָּרוּךְ *Blessed are You, HASHEM our God, King of the universe, Who has sanctified us with His commandments, and has commanded us to kindle the Chanukah light.*

בָּרוּךְ *Blessed are You, HASHEM our God, King of the universe, Who has wrought miracles for our forefathers, in those days at this season.*

בָּרוּךְ *Blessed are You, HASHEM our God, King of the universe, Who has kept us alive, sustained us, and brought us to this season.*

On the first night, the light to the extreme right is kindled. On each subsequent night, a new light is added to the left of the previous night's lights. The new light is always kindled first, the one to its right second, and so on. After one light has been kindled, *'These lights we kindle'* is recited. The additional lights are kindled during its recitation.

הַנֵּרוֹת הַלָּלוּ *These lights we kindle upon the miracles, the wonders,* the salvations, and the battles which you performed for our forefathers in those days at this season through Your holy priests. During all eight days of Chanukah these lights are sacred, and we are not permitted to make ordinary use of them,* but to look at them in order to express thanks and praise to Your great Name* for Your miracles, Your wonders and Your salvations.*

After the proper number of lights have been kindled, *Maoz Tzur* is chanted:

מָעוֹז צוּר *O mighty Rock* of my salvation,*
to praise You is a delight.
Restore my House of Prayer
and there we will bring a thanksgiving offering.
When You will have prepared the slaughter
for the blaspheming foe,
Then I shall complete with a song of hymn
the dedication of the Altar.

---

incidental pleasure that comes from the lights can be considered as coming from the *shamash.*

כְּדֵי לְהוֹדוֹת וּלְהַלֵּל לְשִׁמְךָ הַגָּדוֹל — *In order to express thanks and praise to Your great Name.* That is, by refraining from utilizing the Chanukah lights for anything but the *mitzvah* itself and contemplating them while they burn we make it apparent to all that our intent is to popularize the miracle and to praise God's great Name in acknowledgment of His great miracles.

מָעוֹז צוּר / Ma'oz Tzur

Following the kindling of the lights and recital of *HaNeiros Hallalu* it is customary to recite the following *zemer.*

The author's name, Mordechai [מָרְדְּכַי], appears in the acrostic of the initial letters of the first five stanzas. It was apparently composed in the mid-thirteenth century.

In the *zemer* the *paytan* [liturgical poet] recalls various exiles that the Jewish people endured, praises God for redeeming us from each of them, and prays for the restoration of the Temple and for the dawn of the Messianic Redemption.

Shem MiShmuel notes that each of the earlier periods of servitude — the Egyptian bondage and the Babylonian, Persian and Greek exiles — served to prepare the nation for the tribulations it would encounter in the subsequent exiles.

מָעוֹז צוּר — *O mighty Rock.* This opening stanza is a plea for the reestablishment of the Temple, our House of Prayer; the rededication of the Altar; and the renewal of the services there.

רָעוֹת שָׂבְעָה נַפְשִׁי,* בְּיָגוֹן כֹּחִי כִּלָּה,
חַיַּי מֵרְרוּ בְקֹשִׁי בְּשִׁעְבּוּד מַלְכוּת עֶגְלָה,
וּבְיָדוֹ הַגְּדוֹלָה הוֹצִיא אֶת הַסְּגֻלָּה,
חֵיל פַּרְעֹה וְכָל זַרְעוֹ יָרְדוּ כְּאֶבֶן בִּמְצוּלָה.

דְּבִיר קָדְשׁוֹ* הֱבִיאַנִי וְגַם שָׁם לֹא שָׁקַטְתִּי,
וּבָא נוֹגֵשׂ וְהִגְלַנִי כִּי זָרִים עָבַדְתִּי,
וְיֵין רַעַל מָסַכְתִּי כִּמְעַט שֶׁעָבַרְתִּי,
קֵץ בָּבֶל, זְרֻבָּבֶל, לְקֵץ שִׁבְעִים נוֹשָׁעְתִּי.

כְּרוֹת קוֹמַת בְּרוֹשׁ* בִּקֵּשׁ אֲגָגִי בֶּן הַמְּדָתָא,
וְנִהְיְתָה לוֹ לְפַח וּלְמוֹקֵשׁ וְגַאֲוָתוֹ נִשְׁבָּתָה,
רֹאשׁ יְמִינִי נִשֵּׂאתָ וְאוֹיֵב שְׁמוֹ מָחִיתָ,
רֹב בָּנָיו וְקִנְיָנָיו עַל הָעֵץ תָּלִיתָ.

יְוָנִים* נִקְבְּצוּ עָלַי אֲזַי בִּימֵי חַשְׁמַנִּים,
וּפָרְצוּ חוֹמוֹת מִגְדָּלַי וְטִמְּאוּ כָּל הַשְּׁמָנִים,
וּמִנּוֹתַר קַנְקַנִּים נַעֲשָׂה נֵס לַשּׁוֹשַׁנִּים,
בְּנֵי בִינָה יְמֵי שְׁמוֹנָה קָבְעוּ שִׁיר וּרְנָנִים.

חֲשׂוֹף זְרוֹעַ קָדְשֶׁךָ* וְקָרֵב קֵץ הַיְשׁוּעָה,
נְקוֹם נִקְמַת דַּם עֲבָדֶיךָ מֵאֻמָּה הָרְשָׁעָה,
כִּי אָרְכָה לָנוּ הַיְשׁוּעָה וְאֵין קֵץ לִימֵי הָרָעָה,
דְּחֵה אַדְמוֹן* בְּצֵל צַלְמוֹן הָקֵם לָנוּ רוֹעִים שִׁבְעָה.*

רָעוֹת שָׂבְעָה נַפְשִׁי — *Troubles sated my soul,* during the bondage in Egypt. Scripture *(Jeremiah* 46:20) describes the Egyptians as עֶגְלָה יְפֵה פִיָּה, *a very fair calf.*

דְּבִיר קָדְשׁוֹ — [To] *the abode of His holiness,* i.e., the Holy of Holies in King Solomon's Temple. The oppressor is Babylonia, who exiled the nation from its land when Israel drank the 'wine of sin' and her sensitivity to holiness was numbed.

כְּרוֹת קוֹמַת בְּרוֹשׁ — *To sever the towering cypress.* The Talmud *(Megillah* 10b) expounds on an obscure prophecy of *Isaiah* (55:13): *In place of the thorn shall come up the cypress* — the prickly, useless 'thorn' is Haman who attempted to destroy Mordechai, the stately 'cypress.' But Haman's own sinister plans ensnared him and he was hung on the gallows he had prepared for Mordechai.

יְוָנִים — *Greeks.* This refers to the Syrian-Greeks, especially Antiochus IV Epiphanes, the monarch who attempted to Hellenize [i.e., impose Greek culture] *Eretz Yisrael* through force.

חֲשׂוֹף זְרוֹעַ קָדְשֶׁךָ — *Bare Your holy arm.* This final stanza is generally regarded to be a later addition [about 1500] by a different author. The initial letters of the first three words form the acrostic חָזָק, *be strong.* Since it contains a strong plea for Divine vengeance against Israel's foes, this stanza was subject to much censorship by Christian authorities. Accordingly some *siddurim* have replaced certain stiches with others less offensive to the censors. The *Red One* refers to Esau/Edom, whose descendants

רָעוֹת *Troubles sated my soul,**
when with grief my strength was consumed.
They had embittered my life with hardship,
with the calf-like kingdom's bondage.
But with His great power
He brought forth the treasured ones,
Pharaoh's army and all his offspring
went down like a stone into the deep.

דְּבִיר *To the abode of His holiness* He brought me.*
But there, too, I had no rest
And an oppressor came and exiled me.
For I had served aliens,
And had drunk benumbing wine.
Scarcely had I departed [my land]
When at Babylonia's demise Zerubabel came —
At the end of seventy years I was saved.

כְּרוֹת *To sever the towering cypress**
sought the Aggagite, son of Hammedatha,
But it became a snare and a stumbling block to him
and his arrogance was stilled.
The head of the Benjaminite You lifted
and the enemy, his name You blotted out
His numerous progeny — his possessions —
on the gallows You hanged.

יְוָנִים *Greeks* gathered against me*
then in Hasmonean days.
They breached the walls of my towers
and they defiled all the oils;
And from the one remnant of the flasks
a miracle was wrought for the roses.
Men of insight — eight days
established for song and jubilation

חֲשׂוֹף *Bare Your holy arm**
and hasten the End for salvation —
Avenge the vengeance of Your servant's blood
from the wicked nation.
For the triumph is too long delayed for us,
and there is no end to days of evil,
Repel the Red One in the nethermost shadow*
*and establish for us the seven shepherds.**

---

brought the current exile. The *seven shepherds* (*Micah* 5:4) who will conquer Israel's oppressors are David, Adam, Seth, Methuselah, Abraham, Jacob and Moses (*Succah* 52b).

קריאת המגילה

Before reading the *Megillah,* the reader recites the following three blessings. The congregation should answer *Amen* only [not בָּרוּךְ הוּא וּבָרוּךְ שְׁמוֹ] after each and have in mind that they wish to fulfill the obligation of reciting the blessings themselves.
[These blessings are recited whether or not a *minyan* is present for the reading.]

בָּרוּךְ אַתָּה יהוה אֱלֹהֵינוּ מֶלֶךְ הָעוֹלָם, אֲשֶׁר קִדְּשָׁנוּ בְּמִצְוֹתָיו, וְצִוָּנוּ עַל מִקְרָא מְגִלָּה. (Cong.— אָמֵן.)

בָּרוּךְ אַתָּה יהוה אֱלֹהֵינוּ מֶלֶךְ הָעוֹלָם, שֶׁעָשָׂה נִסִּים לַאֲבוֹתֵינוּ, בַּיָּמִים הָהֵם, בַּזְּמַן הַזֶּה. (Cong.— אָמֵן.)

בָּרוּךְ אַתָּה יהוה אֱלֹהֵינוּ מֶלֶךְ הָעוֹלָם, שֶׁהֶחֱיָנוּ, וְקִיְּמָנוּ, וְהִגִּיעָנוּ לַזְּמַן הַזֶּה. (Cong.— אָמֵן.)

[THE MEGILLAH IS READ]

After the *Megillah* reading each member of the congregation recites the following blessing.
[This blessing is not recited unless a *minyan* is present for the reading.]

בָּרוּךְ אַתָּה יהוה אֱלֹהֵינוּ מֶלֶךְ הָעוֹלָם, הָרָב אֶת רִיבֵנוּ, וְהַדָּן אֶת דִּינֵנוּ, וְהַנּוֹקֵם אֶת נִקְמָתֵנוּ, וְהַמְּשַׁלֵּם גְּמוּל לְכָל אֹיְבֵי נַפְשֵׁנוּ, וְהַנִּפְרָע לָנוּ מִצָּרֵינוּ. בָּרוּךְ אַתָּה יהוה, הַנִּפְרָע לְעַמּוֹ יִשְׂרָאֵל מִכָּל צָרֵיהֶם, הָאֵל הַמּוֹשִׁיעַ.

The following is recited only after the evening *Megillah* reading. After the morning reading continue with שׁוֹשַׁנַּת יַעֲקֹב, next page.

אֲשֶׁר הֵנִיא עֲצַת גּוֹיִם, וַיָּפֶר מַחְשְׁבוֹת עֲרוּמִים.
בְּקוּם עָלֵינוּ אָדָם רָשָׁע, נֵצֶר זָדוֹן, מִזֶּרַע עֲמָלֵק.
גָּאָה בְעָשְׁרוֹ, וְכָרָה לוֹ בּוֹר, וּגְדֻלָּתוֹ יָקְשָׁה לוֹ לָכֶד.
דִּמָּה בְנַפְשׁוֹ לִלְכֹּד, וְנִלְכַּד, בִּקֵּשׁ לְהַשְׁמִיד, וְנִשְׁמַד מְהֵרָה.
הָמָן הוֹדִיעַ אֵיבַת אֲבוֹתָיו, וְעוֹרֵר שִׂנְאַת אַחִים לַבָּנִים.
וְלֹא זָכַר רַחֲמֵי שָׁאוּל, כִּי בְחֶמְלָתוֹ עַל אֲגָג נוֹלַד אוֹיֵב.
זָמַם רָשָׁע לְהַכְרִית צַדִּיק, וְנִלְכַּד טָמֵא, בִּידֵי טָהוֹר.
חֶסֶד גָּבַר עַל שִׁגְגַת אָב, וְרָשָׁע הוֹסִיף חֵטְא עַל חֲטָאָיו.
טָמַן בְּלִבּוֹ מַחְשְׁבוֹת עֲרוּמָיו, וַיִּתְמַכֵּר לַעֲשׂוֹת רָעָה.
יָדוֹ שָׁלַח בִּקְדוֹשֵׁי אֵל, כַּסְפּוֹ נָתַן לְהַכְרִית זִכְרָם.
כִּרְאוֹת מָרְדְּכַי, כִּי יָצָא קֶצֶף, וְדָתֵי הָמָן נִתְּנוּ בְשׁוּשָׁן.
לָבַשׁ שַׂק וְקָשַׁר מִסְפֵּד, וְגָזַר צוֹם, וַיֵּשֶׁב עַל הָאֵפֶר.
מִי זֶה יַעֲמֹד לְכַפֵּר שְׁגָגָה, וְלִמְחֹל חַטַּאת עֲוֹן אֲבוֹתֵינוּ.

אֲשֶׁר הֵנִיא — *Who balked.* This poetic summary of the Purim story is based on the narrative of the Megillah itself and follows the order of the *Aleph Beis.*

READING OF THE MEGILLAH

Before reading the *Megillah,* the reader recites the following three blessings. The congregation should answer *Amen* only after each and have in mind that they wish to fulfill the obligation of reciting the blessings themselves. [These blessings are recited whether or not a *minyan* is present for the reading.]

בָּרוּךְ *Blessed are You,* HASHEM, *our God, King of the universe, Who has sanctified us with His commandments and has commanded us regarding the reading of the Megillah.* (Cong.— *Amen.)*

בָּרוּךְ *Blessed are You,* HASHEM, *our God, King of the universe, Who has wrought miracles for our forefathers, in those days at this season.* (Cong.— *Amen.)*

בָּרוּךְ *Blessed are You,* HASHEM, *our God, King of the universe, Who has kept us alive, sustained us, and brought us to this season.* (Cong.— *Amen.)*

[THE MEGILLAH IS READ]

After the *Megillah* reading, each member of the congregation recites the following blessing. [This blessing is not recited unless a *minyan* is present for the reading.]

בָּרוּךְ *Blessed are You,* HASHEM, *our God, King of the universe, Who takes up our grievance, judges our claim, avenges our wrong; Who brings just retribution upon all enemies of our soul, and exacts vengeance for us from our foes. Blessed are you* HASHEM, *Who exacts vengeance for His people Israel from all their foes, the God Who brings salvation.*

The following is recited only after the evening *Megillah* reading. After the morning reading continue with שׁוֹשַׁנַּת יַעֲקֹב, *'The rose of Jacob,'* next page.

אֲשֶׁר הֵנִיא *Who balked the counsel of the nations*
and annulled the designs of the cunning,
ב *When a wicked man stood up against us,*
a wantonly evil branch of Amalek's offspring.
ג *Haughty with his wealth he dug himself a grave,*
and his very greatness snared him in a trap.
ד *Fancying to trap, he became entrapped;*
attempting to destroy, he was swiftly destroyed.
ה *Haman showed his forebears' enmity,*
and aroused the brotherly hate of Esau on the children.
ו *He would not remember Saul's compassion,*
that through his pity on Agag the foe was born.
ז *The wicked one conspired to cut away the righteous,*
but the impure one was trapped in the pure one's hands.
ח *Kindness overcame the father's error, and the wicked one piled sin on sins.*
ט *In his heart he hid his cunning thoughts, and devoted himself to evildoing.*
י *He stretched his hand against God's holy ones,*
he spent his silver to destroy their memory.
כ *When Mordecai saw the wrath commence,*
and Haman's decrees be issued in Shushan,
ל *He put on sackcloth and bound himself in mourning,*
decreed a fast and sat on ashes:
מ *'Who would arise to atone for error, to gain forgiveness for our ancestors' sins?'*

נֵץ פָּרַח מְלוּלָב, הֵן הֲדַסָּה עָמְדָה לְעוֹרֵר יְשֵׁנִים.
סָרִיסֶיהָ הִבְהִילוּ לְהָמָן, לְהַשְׁקוֹתוֹ יֵין חֲמַת תַּנִּינִים.
עָמַד בְּעָשְׁרוֹ, וְנָפַל בְּרִשְׁעוֹ, עָשָׂה לוֹ עֵץ, וְנִתְלָה עָלָיו.
פִּיהֶם פָּתְחוּ, כָּל יוֹשְׁבֵי תֵבֵל, כִּי פוּר הָמָן נֶהְפַּךְ לְפוּרֵנוּ.
צַדִּיק נֶחֱלַץ מִיַּד רָשָׁע, אוֹיֵב נִתַּן תַּחַת נַפְשׁוֹ.
קִיְּמוּ עֲלֵיהֶם, לַעֲשׂוֹת פּוּרִים, וְלִשְׂמֹחַ בְּכָל שָׁנָה וְשָׁנָה.
רָאִיתָ אֶת תְּפִלַּת מָרְדְּכַי וְאֶסְתֵּר, הָמָן וּבָנָיו עַל הָעֵץ תָּלִיתָ.

The following is recited after both *Megillah* readings.

שׁוֹשַׁנַּת יַעֲקֹב צָהֲלָה וְשָׂמֵחָה, בִּרְאוֹתָם יַחַד תְּכֵלֶת מָרְדְּכָי. תְּשׁוּעָתָם הָיִיתָ לָנֶצַח, וְתִקְוָתָם בְּכָל דּוֹר וָדוֹר. לְהוֹדִיעַ, שֶׁכָּל קֹוֶיךָ לֹא יֵבֹשׁוּ, וְלֹא יִכָּלְמוּ לָנֶצַח כָּל הַחוֹסִים בָּךְ. אָרוּר הָמָן, אֲשֶׁר בִּקֵּשׁ לְאַבְּדִי, בָּרוּךְ מָרְדְּכַי הַיְּהוּדִי. אֲרוּרָה זֶרֶשׁ, אֵשֶׁת מַפְחִידִי, בְּרוּכָה אֶסְתֵּר בַּעֲדִי, וְגַם חַרְבוֹנָה זָכוּר לַטּוֹב.

After the evening reading, *Maariv* continues with וְאַתָּה קָדוֹשׁ and the Full *Kaddish* (p. 596), followed by עָלֵינוּ and the Mourner's *Kaddish* (p. 608).
On Saturday evening, *Maariv* continues with וִיהִי נֹעַם (p. 594).
After the morning reading, *Shacharis* continues with אַשְׁרֵי (p. 150).

קרובץ לפורים

Many congregations recite *Krovetz* during the *chazzan's* repetition of *Shemoneh Esrei* on the morning of Purim. See commentary.

The *Chazzan* begins his repetition (p. 98) and continues through וּמוֹשִׁיעַ וּמָגֵן. Then all recite:

וַיֶּאֱהַב אוֹמֵן יְתוֹמַת הֶגֶן, אֲמָנָהּ שִׁבְעִים וְחָמֵשׁ בַּעֲדָה לְהָגֵן,
אָז מֵאָז כְּחָז יוֹדֵעַ נַגֵּן, אַרְיֵה בֶּן זְאֵב לְיֶשַׁע הוֹגֵן,
אָץ לְהַזְכִּיר אוֹתוֹ מְנַגֵּן,* **וּמָרְדְּכַי** אִמֵּץ בְּאֶלֶף הַמָּגֵן.

Chazzan concludes the blessing:

בָּרוּךְ אַתָּה יהוה, מָגֵן אַבְרָהָם.

KROVETZ FOR PURIM

The title *Krovetz,* קְרוּבֶץ, is the initials of קוֹל רִנָּה וִישׁוּעָה בְּאָהֳלֵי צַדִּיקִים, *The sound of rejoicing and salvation is in the tents of the righteous (Psalms* 118:15), a verse that expresses perfectly the joy and celebration of the Purim miracle.

The *Krovetz* is recited during *Shacharis* on Purim. It consists of poetic stanzas that are inserted just before the conclusion of the blessings of *Shemoneh Esrei* during the *chazzan's* repetition. The only blessing where this is not done is אֶת צֶמַח דָּוִד, *The offspring of ... David,* since the Purim miracle came about through descendants of King Saul. The eighteen stanzas of the liturgy begin, respectively, with the words of the Book of *Esther* that tell of Esther's rise to power: וַיֶּאֱהַב הַמֶּלֶךְ אֶת אֶסְתֵּר מִכָּל הַנָּשִׁים וַתִּשָּׂא חֵן וָחֶסֶד לְפָנָיו מִכָּל הַבְּתוּלוֹת וַיָּשֶׂם כֶּתֶר מַלְכוּת בְּרֹאשָׁהּ וַיַּמְלִיכֶהָ תַּחַת וַשְׁתִּי, *The king loved Esther more than all the women, and she won more of his grace and favor than all the other girls; so he set the royal crown upon her head, and made her queen in place of Vashti (Esther* 2:17)

A second key verse from the Book of *Esther* is interspersed among the stanzas. In our text its words appear in bold type: וּמָרְדְּכַי יָצָא מִלִּפְנֵי הַמֶּלֶךְ

נ *A blossom bloomed from a lulav branch — behold!*
Hadassah stood up to arouse the sleeping.
ס *Her servants hastened Haman, to serve him wine of serpent's poison.*
ע *He stood tall through his wealth and toppled through his evil —*
he built the gallows on which he was hung.
פ *The earth's inhabitants opened their mouths, for Haman's lot became our Purim,*
צ *The righteous man was saved from the wicked's hand;*
the foe was substituted for him.
ק *They undertook to establish Purim, to rejoice in every single year.*
ר *You noted the prayer of Mordechai and Esther;*
Haman and his sons You hung on the gallows.

The following is recited after both *Megillah* readings.

שׁוֹשַׁנַּת יַעֲקֹב *The rose of Jacob was cheerful and glad, when they jointly saw Mordechai robed in royal blue.*

You have been their eternal salvation, and their hope throughout generations. To make known that all who hope in You will not be shamed; nor ever be humiliated, those taking refuge in You. Accursed be Haman who sought to destroy me, blessed be Mordechai the Yehudi. Accursed be Zeresh the wife of my terrorizer, blessed be Esther [who sacrificed] for me — and Charvonah, too, be remembered for good.

After the evening reading, *Maariv* continues with וְאַתָּה קָדוֹשׁ, *'You are the Holy One,'* and the Full *Kaddish* (p. 596), followed by עָלֵינוּ, *'It is our duty,'* and the Mourner's *Kaddish* (p. 608).
On Saturday evening, *Maariv* continues with וִיהִי נֹעַם, *'May the pleasantness'* (p. 594).
After the morning reading, *Shacharis* continues with אַשְׁרֵי, *'Praiseworthy'* (p. 150).

KROVETZ TO PURIM

Many congregations recite *Krovetz* during the *chazzan's* repetition of *Shemoneh Esrei* on the morning of Purim. See commentary.

The *chazzan* begins his repetition (p. 98) and continues through וּמוֹשִׁיעַ וּמָגֵן. Then all recite:

וַיֶּאֱהַב *[Mordechai] loved and raised the worthy orphan [Esther].*
The faith displayed by Abraham at seventy-five protected her.
Then [Mordechai] carried out the mission foreseen by [David] the skilled musician;
descended from the lion-like Judah and the wolf-like Benjamin,
[Mordechai] was the worthy savior.
*The musician [David] exerted himself to allude to him.**
And Mordechai was strengthened by the thousand shields [promised Abraham].

Chazzan concludes the blessing:
Blessed are You, HASHEM, shield of Abraham.

בִּלְבוּשׁ מַלְכוּת תְּכֵלֶת וָחוּר וַעֲטֶרֶת זָהָב גְּדוֹלָה וְתַכְרִיךְ בּוּץ וְאַרְגָּמָן וְהָעִיר שׁוּשָׁן צָהֲלָה וְשָׂמֵחָה, *Mordechai left the king's presence clad in royal apparel of blue and white with a large gold crown and a robe of fine linen and purple, then the city of Shushan was cheerful and glad* (8:15).

There are two further motifs hidden in the poetry of this song. Each word following the words of the above verse begins with an initial of the composer's name אֶלְעָזָר בִּירַבִּי קַלִּיר חֲזַק. Also, the successive stanzas accentuate words beginning with the order of the *aleph-beis*. These letters appear in bold type.

לְהַזְכִּיר אוֹתוֹ מְנַגֵּן — *The musician ... to allude to him.* David, 'the sweet singer of Israel,' would not let the traitor Shimi be harmed because Mordechai was destined to descend from him *(II Samuel* 19:23, *Megillah* 12b).

Chazzan continues from אַתָּה גִּבּוֹר through לְהַחֲיוֹת מֵתִים. Then all recite:

הַמֶּלֶךְ **בְּ**כֶס יָהּ חַק לְזֶרַע כֹּה יִהְיֶה, **בְּ**קָמִים כָּל גֶּשֶׁם לֹא תְחַיֶּה,
בֶּן בְּכוֹרַת חַל דְּבַר אֶהְיֶה, **בְּ**קוֹץ אֲשֶׁר נִכְמַר וַיְּחַיֶּה,
בְּכֵן צִפְעוֹ צָץ לְצַדִּים שֶׁיִּהְיֶה, **יָצָא לְ**מָרְרוֹ מוֹר בִּגְשָׁמִים מְחַיֶּה.

Chazzan concludes the blessing:

בָּרוּךְ אַתָּה יהוה, מְחַיֵּה הַמֵּתִים.

KEDUSHAH (P. 100) IS RECITED AT THIS POINT.

Chazzan continues from לְדוֹר וָדוֹר through וְקָדוֹשׁ אַתָּה. Then all recite:

אֶת אֶסְתֵּר **גַּ**ל מְמַסְתִּיר לְגוֹאֵל, **גּוֹ**י כְּנוֹאֵשׁ מִלְּהִגָּאֵל,
גּוֹזֵר אִם אֵין לָאִישׁ גּוֹאֵל, **גַּ**ף מִיִּשְׁפֵּה תַּבְנִית הַגּוֹאֵל,
גָּשׁ כְּאָח לְצָרָה לְצַחְצֵחַ הַגּוֹאֵל, **מִלְּפְנֵי עִיר** וְקַדִּישׁ לְהַקְדִּישׁ אָאֵל.

Chazzan concludes the blessing:

בָּרוּךְ אַתָּה יהוה, הָאֵל הַקָּדוֹשׁ.

Chazzan continues from אַתָּה חוֹנֵן through בִּינָה וְהַשְׂכֵּל. Then all recite:

מִכָּל **דּ**וֹרוֹ בָּן לְהִתְבּוֹנֵן, **דַּ**עַת מֵאֵיזֶה חֵטְא צָג צָר שׁוֹנֵן,
דִּבְרַת אָב כְּזָכַר אוֹנֵן, **דַּ**לְתֵי צוּר כְּנֵסָה דָפַק וְחִנֵּן,
דְּגָלִים לְשַׁלֵּשׁ תָּעַן וּלְחַנֵּן, **הַמֶּלֶךְ** **זַ**עֲקָם בָּן דֵּעָה חוֹנֵן.

Chazzan concludes the blessing:

בָּרוּךְ אַתָּה יהוה, חוֹנֵן הַדָּעַת.

Chazzan continues from הֲשִׁיבֵנוּ through שְׁלֵמָה לְפָנֶיךָ. Then all recite:

הַנָּשִׁים **הַ**הֲגוּנוֹת לְכֵס יְשִׁיבָה, **הוּ**כְעֲרוּ וּסְעָרָה בָם נָשָׁבָה,
הֲדַסָּה זֹאת כְּגַע לָהּ תּוֹר וּמַחֲשָׁבָה, **הִ**לְּלָה לְכָל רוֹאֶיהָ וְעֵזֶר לוֹ שִׁוָּה,
הֶדֵּר יְמִינִי לְשׁוֹבֵב שׁוֹבֵבָה, **בִּלְבוּשׁ** **רַ**צּוֹת רוֹצֶה בִּתְשׁוּבָה.

Chazzan concludes the blessing:

בָּרוּךְ אַתָּה יהוה, הָרוֹצֶה בִּתְשׁוּבָה.

Chazzan continues from סְלַח לָנוּ through וְסוֹלֵחַ אָתָּה. Then all recite:

וַתִּשָּׂא **וַ**תָּבֹא בֶּאֱלוֹהַּ, **וְ**לֹא יָדְעָה כִּי זֹאת עָשְׂתָה יַד אֱלוֹהַּ,
וַיִּבְעַר חָנֵף בְּכָל גְּבוּל לִשְׁלוֹחַ, **וּ**בְהַגִּיעַ תּוֹר בִּנְיָן לִצְלוֹחַ,
וּבַת אֲבִיחַיִל לָבְשָׁה צָלוֹחַ,* **מַלְכוּת** **בָּ**הּ רַבָּה מַרְבֶּה לִסְלוֹחַ.

Chazzan concludes the blessing:

בָּרוּךְ אַתָּה יהוה, חַנּוּן הַמַּרְבֶּה לִסְלוֹחַ.

Chazzan continues from רְאֵה through גּוֹאֵל חָזָק אָתָּה. Then all recite:

חֵן **זְ**בֻדָה מֵהַרְרֵי אֵל, **זְ**כוּתָהּ עִמְּעֵם בְּיַד בֶּן אֲבִיאֵל,
זֹאת בְּבוֹאָהּ הֲלוֹם נָשְׂאָה עַיִן לָאֵל, **זָ**כְרָה נָּא לִי צִדְקַת הַרְרֵי אֵל,
זֶה הֱכִינָהּ לְאוֹת לְתִקּוּן אֲרִיאֵל, **תְּכֵלֶת** **יָ**דָהּ עֲשׂוֹת לִגְאוּלֵי אֵל.

וּבַת אֲבִיחַיִל לָבְשָׁה צָלוֹחַ — *[Esther] the daughter of Avichail donned success.* Esther became the mother of King Darius who authorized the construction of the Second Temple.

Chazzan continues from אַתָּה גִּבּוֹר through לְהַחֲיוֹת מֵתִים. Then all recite:

הַמֶּלֶךְ *The King [HASHEM] swore by God's throne, about [Abraham's] offspring,*
which would be [numerous as the stars],
that none who rise against them should live!
The first Jewish king [Saul] desecrated the word of the Everlasting One
by being compassionate and allowing the Amalekite thorn to live.
Therefore his offspring [Haman] flourished to become a thorn —
until Mordechai overcame him
with the aid of the Fragrant One Whose life-giving rains will resuscitate.

Chazzan concludes the blessing:

Blessed are You, HASHEM, Who resuscitates the dead.

KEDUSHAH (P. 100) IS RECITED AT THIS POINT.

Chazzan continues from לְדוֹר וָדוֹר through וְקָדוֹשׁ אַתָּה. Then all recite:

אֶת אֶסְתֵּר *[God] revealed Esther from concealment to be a redeemer*
of the nation when it had despaired of being redeemed.
He decreed that when someone had no redeemer,
He would fashion a redeemer from yashpheh [the tribe of Benjamin].
Mordechai approached like a brother in distress to polish away abomination of sin,
with a desire to sanctify the Name even before the angels did so.

Chazzan concludes the blessing:

Blessed are You, HASHEM, the holy God.

Chazzan continues from אַתָּה חוֹנֵן through בִּינָה וְהַשְׂכֵּל. Then all recite:

מִכָּל *Of all his generation [Mordechai] attempted to understand*
and identify the sin for which the foe could approach with sharpened fang;
in his distress he recalled Jacob's confident word [that Benjamin would prevail].
He pounded on the synagogue doors and supplicated the Rock of Israel;
on Israel's bannered tribes be decreed a three-day fast to supplicate —
the King Who grants wisdom understood their cry.

Chazzan concludes the blessing:

Blessed are You, HASHEM, gracious Giver of Wisdom.

Chazzan continues from הֲשִׁיבֵנוּ through שְׁלֵמָה לְפָנֶיךָ. Then all recite:

הַנָּשִׁים *All the women eligible to sit on the queenly throne*
were deemed ugly and driven away by [Ahasuerus'] stormy anger;
but when Hadassah's [Esther's] turn came for consideration,
she was praised by all who saw her and he made her his helpmeet.
The Benjaminite circulated to bring rebellious Israel to repent
by wearing sackcloth and appeasing God Who desires repentance.

Chazzan concludes the blessing:

Blessed are You, HASHEM, Who desires repentance.

Chazzan continues from סְלַח לָנוּ through וְסוֹלֵחַ אָתָּה. Then all recite:

וַתִּשָּׂא *She came to the king with eyes raised to God,*
without realizing that the hand of God had acted
in enthusing the hypocritical Ahasuerus to dispatch agents throughout his boundaries [to seek beautiful women].
When the time came for the Temple to flourish,
*[Esther] the daughter of Avichail donned success**
then the One Who pardons abundantly gave her abundant sovereignty.

Chazzan concludes the blessing:

Blessed are You, HASHEM, the gracious One Who pardons abundantly.

Chazzan continues from רְאֵה through גּוֹאֵל חָזָק אָתָּה. Then all recite:

חֵן *She [Esther] was apportioned grace from the godly Patriarchs,*
her merit united with that of [Mordechai] the descendant of Aviel.
When she arrived there she raised her eyes to God, [praying]:
'Recall for me the righteousness of the godly Patriarchs.'
[God] prepared Esther as a symbol that the Temple would yet be built
she made the techeiles-blue garment [of freedom] for those to be redeemed by God.

Chazzan concludes the blessing:

בָּרוּךְ אַתָּה יהוה, גּוֹאֵל יִשְׂרָאֵל.

Chazzan continues from רְפָאֵנוּ through וְרַחֲמָן אָתָּה. Then all recite:

וָחֶסֶד **חִ**סְדָּהּ חָסִיד הַמְּחוֹלְלִי, **חוּר** וְכַרְפַּס וְכֶתֶם וַחֲלִי,
חִיְּלָהּ רוֹץ רֹאשׁ פֶּתֶן מִגַּחֲלִי, **חָ**רוֹן בּוֹ לְשַׁלֵּחַ עוֹד מִלְּאַכְּלִי,
חִלַּת פְּנֵי אֱלֹהִים יהוה חֵילִי, **וְחוּר רַב** חִתְּלִי רוֹפֵא חָוֹלִי.

Chazzan concludes the blessing:

בָּרוּךְ אַתָּה יהוה, רוֹפֵא חוֹלֵי עַמּוֹ יִשְׂרָאֵל.

Chazzan continues from בָּרֵךְ עָלֵינוּ through כַּשָּׁנִים הַטּוֹבוֹת. Then all recite:

לְפָנָיו **טָ**בַע הוֹד אַבְרֵךְ, **טָ**בוּעַ הָיָה וּמוּכָן לְהַאֲרֵךְ,
טְמֻנָה וְסֻתְּרָה מִפְּרוֹעַ יָרֵךְ, **טָ**מֵא כְּהֶגְרֵל גַּפְנָהּ לְהַבְרֵךְ,
טוֹב פָּץ לָהּ קוּמִי אוֹרִי כִּי בָא אוֹרֵךְ, **וַעֲטֶרֶת בִּ**שְׁנַת טוֹבָתְךָ בְּגֶשֶׁם אֲבָרֵךְ.

Chazzan concludes the blessing:

בָּרוּךְ אַתָּה יהוה, מְבָרֵךְ הַשָּׁנִים.

Chazzan continues from תְּקַע through כַּנְפוֹת הָאָרֶץ. Then all recite:

מִכָּל **יוֹ**דְעֵי דָת שְׂפָתַי מַרְבֵּץ, **יְ**קַר יְמִינִי בְּדָת יָמִין רוֹבֵץ,
יְפִי עֲדִי עֲדָיִים מַשְׁבֵּץ, **יָ**צָא מְלֻבָּשׁ עַל יַד קוֹבֵץ,
יָרַשׁ מַתַּן שְׁאֵלוֹת יַעְבֵּץ, **זָהָב יְ**מֵן לֶאֱסוֹף נִדָּחִים מְקַבֵּץ.

Chazzan concludes the blessing:

בָּרוּךְ אַתָּה יהוה, מְקַבֵּץ נִדְחֵי עַמּוֹ יִשְׂרָאֵל.

Chazzan continues from הָשִׁיבָה through בַּמִּשְׁפָּט. Then all recite:

הַבְּתוּלוֹת **בְּ**הִקָּבֵץ שֵׁנִית בְּמַאֲהֵב, **כְּ**בוּדָה בַּת מֶלֶךְ הִשְׁלִיכָה יְהָב,
כִּי צַדִּיק יהוה צְדָקוֹת אָהֵב, **כְּ**מַס דּוֹב רִשְׁפֵּי לַהַב, מַלְהִיב לְלַהֵב,
כָּרָה שׁוּחָה לָעַד לְחוּמוֹ לְהַבְהֵב, **גְּדוֹלָה קָ**פַץ בְּדִין מִשְׁפָּט אָהֵב.

Chazzan concludes the blessing:

בָּרוּךְ אַתָּה יהוה, מֶלֶךְ אוֹהֵב צְדָקָה וּמִשְׁפָּט.

Chazzan continues from וְלַמַּלְשִׁינִים through בִּמְהֵרָה בְיָמֵינוּ. Then all recite:

וַיָּשֶׂם **לַ**יְלָה וּתְנוּמָה הִמְנִיעַ, **לֵ**יל אֲשֶׁר תִּבֵּן וְיָרֵב הֵנִיעַ,
לַדּוֹרוֹת אוֹתוֹ הִצְנִיעַ, **לִ**הְיוֹת לְפִלְאוֹ צָנוּעַ,
לְכַד זֵד יָהִיר וּבְאַשְׁמוּרוֹ הִכְנִיעַ, **וְתַכְרִיךְ** יְחוּמָיו שַׁח זֵדִים מַכְנִיעַ.

Chazzan concludes the blessing:

בָּרוּךְ אַתָּה יהוה, שׁוֹבֵר אֹיְבִים וּמַכְנִיעַ זֵדִים.

Chazzan continues from עַל הַצַּדִּיקִים through בְּךָ בָטָחְנוּ. Then all recite:

כֶּתֶר **מְ**לוּכָה מֵאָז הָיָה מֻבְטָח, **מֵ**אֵלָיו הָיָה לְהִנָּתֵן לְבַת הָבְטַח,
מְלָכוֹת כְּשָׁרוּהָ מַרְאָם הוּטַח, **מְ**טוּבַּת זִיו הוֹד מִבְטָח,

Chazzan concludes the blessing:

Blessed are You, HASHEM, Redeemer of Israel.

Chazzan continues from רְפָאֵנוּ through וְרַחֲמָן אָתָּה. Then all recite:

וְחֶסֶד *The Kind One [God] Who created me [Israel] extended kindness to her,*
draping her in white, fine cotton, prints, and jewelry.
She prayed to crush the head of the serpent [Haman] who poured burning coals on me,
to send Heavenly wrath upon him that he not consume me.
Because I prayed to God, HASHEM was my army,
and my large wound was cured by the Healer of disease.

Chazzan concludes the blessing:

Blessed are You, HASHEM, Who heals the sick of His people Israel.

Chazzan continues from בָּרֵךְ עָלֵינוּ through כַּשָּׁנִים הַטּוֹבוֹת. Then all recite:

לְפָנָיו *Centuries earlier, God stamped the glorious visage of Avrech [Joseph],*
it was permanent and ready to heal [Israel];
she covered and concealed her body not to reveal a thigh,
but it became her lot to graft her vine to the impure Ahasuerus.
The Good One said to her, 'Rise up and shine for your light has come —
I will crown the year of your goodness and bless it with generous rain.'

Chazzan concludes the blessing:

Blessed are You, HASHEM, Who blesses the years.

Chazzan continues from תְּקַע through כַּנְפוֹת הָאָרֶץ. Then all recite:

מִכָּל *More than all who know the law and crouch in rows [before their teachers],*
the Benjaminite was worthy in spreading the law given by God's right hand;
he was beautifully bedecked in jewelry when he left Ahasuerus,
dressed in finery was this gatherer [of Torah knowledge].
He inherited the gift of Yabetz's requests [for Torah knowledge].
He Who gathers in the dispersed induced [Haman] to collect gold.

Chazzan concludes the blessing:

Blessed are You, HASHEM, Who gathers in the dispersed of His people Israel.

Chazzan continues from הָשִׁיבָה through בְּמִשְׁפָּט. Then all recite:

הַבְּתוּלוֹת *When they gathered maidens a second time to make Esther jealous,*
the honorable [Jewish] princess cast her lot [upon God],
for HASHEM is righteous and He loves righteousness.
The bear [Ahasuerus] harbored a flaming love [for Esther]
that would consume the one who sought to consume [Israel],
the one who dug a pit for Israel — to burn his flesh to eternity.
The great attribute of mercy of the One Who loves judgment sprang to the defense.

Chazzan concludes the blessing:

Blessed are You, HASHEM, the King Who loves righteousness and judgment.

Chazzan continues from וְלַמַּלְשִׁינִים through בִּמְהֵרָה בְיָמֵינוּ. Then all recite:

וַיָּשֶׂם *He [God] made the night but deprived him [Ahasuerus] of sleep,*
as at night He disturbed the sleep of the serpent [Pharaoh]
and the aggressor [Sennacherib];
For generations He preserved that [Pesach night] for His miracles
on behalf of the modest nation,
He conquered the arrogant sinner [Haman] and humbled him at night's end;
the whole gang of his offspring were brought down
by Him Who humbles the wanton.

Chazzan concludes the blessing:

Blessed are You, HASHEM, Who breaks enemies and humbles wanton sinners.

Chazzan continues from עַל הַצַּדִּיקִים through בְּךָ בָּטָחְנוּ. Then all recite:

כֶּתֶר *The crown of kingship was promised [to Benjamin] from of old,*
from him it was meant to be promised to his descendant [Esther];
when princesses saw her their faces paled
at the goodness of the glorious splendor promised her.

מֵרֹאשׁ עַד עָקֵב לִבָּהּ בָּטַח, **בּוּץ** לְהַאֲמִירָהּ בְּמָעוֹז וּמִבְטָח.

Chazzan concludes the blessing:

בָּרוּךְ אַתָּה יהוה, מִשְׁעָן וּמִבְטָח לַצַּדִּיקִים.

Chazzan continues from וְלִירוּשָׁלַיִם through לְתוֹכָהּ תָּכִין. Then all recite:

מַלְכוּת **נֶחְפָּזָה** כְּחָזוּ רְבִיד, **נָבָל**, נָתוּן עַל יְדִיד, מִיַּד מַעֲבִיד,
נִשְּׂאוֹ מֵעַל כֹּל וְטָרְחוֹ הִכְבִּיד, **נִינָיו** כְּתִרְזוּ לְהַאֲבִיד,
נְשׂוּאֵי רַחַם זֶבֶד טוֹב הִזְבִּיד, **וְאַרְגָּמָן** **יִמְּנָם** לְכוֹנֵן עִיר דָּוִד.

Chazzan concludes the blessing:

בָּרוּךְ אַתָּה יהוה, בּוֹנֵה יְרוּשָׁלָיִם.

Chazzan continues with the entire blessing of אֶת צֶמַח, and from שְׁמַע קוֹלֵנוּ through יִשְׂרָאֵל בְּרַחֲמִים. Then all recite:

בְּרֹאשָׁהּ **סִיֵּם** זֵר אֲשֶׁר הִפְלָא, **סֶגֶּת** שׁוֹשָׁן עֲלוֹת מִשְׁפְּלָה,
שִׂיחַת רְדוּמִים עֲלוֹת מִמַּכְפֵּלָה, **שֵׂעִיר** וְאֶת שְׂרִידָיו לְשַׁחַת הִפִּילָה,
סְגוּרֵי כֶלֶא הֶפֶן מֵאֲפֵלָה, **וְהָעִיר** **רוֹן** כָּפְלָה לְשׁוֹמֵעַ תְּפִלָּה.

Chazzan concludes the blessing:

בָּרוּךְ אַתָּה יהוה, שׁוֹמֵעַ תְּפִלָּה.

Chazzan continues from רְצֵה through לְצִיּוֹן בְּרַחֲמִים. Then all recite:

וַיַּמְלִיכֶהָ **עָזוּר** לְאוֹם מוֹרָאָה, **עֲצוּרָה** הָיְתָה לָכֵן מֵעֵת נִבְרָאָה,
עֲמִיתָהּ הִפְגִּיעַ בַּעֲדָהּ קְרִיאָה, **עַד** עֵת בֹּא דְבָרוֹ אֲשֶׁר רָאָה,
עֱנוּתָם לַחוֹזִים שַׁדַּי הֶרְאָה, **שׁוֹשָׁן** **חוֹחִים** לְעָבְדוֹ בְּיִרְאָה.

Chazzan concludes the blessing:

בָּרוּךְ אַתָּה יהוה, הַמַּחֲזִיר שְׁכִינָתוֹ לְצִיּוֹן.

Chazzan continues from מוֹדִים through וְעֶזְרָתֵנוּ סֶלָה. Then all recite:

תַּחַת **פִּלְפּוּל** יְגִיעַ לֶקַח טוֹב, **פְּעֻלַּת** צַדִּיק פָּעֳלָם לַטּוֹב,
פְּאֵר אוֹמֵר אֲשֶׁר הוּא טוֹב, **פּוּר** הָפַךְ לְמִשְׁתֶּה וְיוֹם טוֹב,
פְּדוּת כֵּן תָּחִישׁ לְהַר הַטּוֹב, **צָהֲלָה** **וְזִמְרָה** לְהוֹדוֹת לְאֵל טוֹב.

Chazzan concludes the blessing:

בָּרוּךְ אַתָּה יהוה, הַטּוֹב שִׁמְךָ וּלְךָ נָאֶה לְהוֹדוֹת.

Chazzan continues from אֱלֹהֵינוּ וֵאלֹהֵי אֲבוֹתֵינוּ through בִּשְׁלוֹמֶךָ. Then all recite:

וַשְׁתִּי **צוֹאֲנָה** לְמַעֲרָכוֹת, **קְצִינוּת** כְּהִכְתָּרָה מִמְּלָכוֹת,
רַגְלֵי אַיֶּלֶת בָּמוֹת דּוֹרְכוֹת, **שִׁבְעִים** יְמֵי צָר עֲלוֹת לָהּ אֲרוּכוֹת,
תָּקְפָּה עִם דּוֹד לְעֵינֶיהָ בְּרֵכוֹת, **וְשִׂמְחָה** **קוֹל** נִשְׁמַע מֶחֲרָכוֹת, וְדוֹבֵר שָׁלוֹם מִמְּעוֹן הַבְּרָכוֹת.

Chazzan concludes the blessing:

בָּרוּךְ אַתָּה יהוה, הַמְּבָרֵךְ אֶת עַמּוֹ יִשְׂרָאֵל בַּשָּׁלוֹם.

Chazzan recites Half-*Kaddish* (p. 138) and the service continues with the Torah reading.

From beginning to end her heart trusted
that she would be set apart in linen robes by the Stronghold and Assurance.

Chazzan concludes the blessing:

Blessed are You, HASHEM, Mainstay and Assurance of the righteous.

Chazzan continues from וְלִירוּשָׁלַיִם through לְתוֹכָהּ תָּכִין. Then all recite:

מַלְכוּת *The kingdom was startled when they saw the degenerate's [Haman] necklace*
placed upon the beloved [Mordechai] thanks to the One Who subjugates all.
Though He had elevated him [Haman] above everyone
and made him heavily burdensome,
Haman's children trickled away to oblivion.
[But as for Israel] — who are borne [by God] from the womb —
He presented them with a goodly portion,
preparing for them royal purple, to establish the City of David.

Chazzan concludes the blessing:

Blessed are You, HASHEM, Who rebuilds Jerusalem.

Chazzan continues with the entire blessing of אֶת צֶמַח, and from שְׁמַע קוֹלֵנוּ through יִשְׂרָאֵל בְּרַחֲמִים. Then all recite:

בְּרֹאשָׁהּ *On her was fitted a designated crown,*
[through it the nation] nestled in a hedge of roses stood up from degradation.
The prayer of the slumbering [Patriarchs] went up from Machpelah,
and through it Seir and his successors were cast down to destruction.
Those imprisoned in chains turned away from darkness,
and the city [of Shushan] sang many glad songs to the One Who hears prayer.

Chazzan concludes the blessing:

Blessed are You, HASHEM, Who hears prayer.

Chazzan continues from רְצֵה through לְצִיּוֹן בְּרַחֲמִים. Then all recite:

וַיַּמְלִיכֶהָ *He made her [Esther] queen to aid the nation that was abominated;*
she was safeguarded for that purpose from the time she was created.
Her companion [Mordechai] called out in prayer for her
until the time when the dream he saw became fulfilled.
The Almighty showed their screams to the prophets,
the nation hedged by roses that serves Him with reverence.

Chazzan concludes the blessing:

Blessed are You, HASHEM, Who restores His Presence to Zion.

Chazzan continues from מוֹדִים though וְעֶזְרָתֵנוּ סֶלָה. Then all recite:

תְּחַת *Because Mordechai toiled in expounding the goodly gift [of Torah],*
like the efforts of the righteous who accomplish good,
through the splendor of his prayer that was good,
he transformed [Haman's] lot to feast and festival.
So may You hasten deliverance to the goodly [Temple] Mount,
that it may give thanks to the good God with exultation and song of praise.

Chazzan concludes the blessing:

Blessed are You, HASHEM, Your Name is 'The Beneficent One'
and to You it is fitting to give thanks.

Chazzan continues with the Priestly Blessing through בַּשָּׁלוֹם. Then all recite:

וַשְׁתִּי *Vashti was brought to judgment with fanfare*
just when she was crowned above all queens,
because the feet of the morning star [Esther] strode up to the heights.
[Israel endured] seventy days of distress while remedies emerged for it.
Together with her uncle, Esther wrote of God's power to the one [the Jewish nation]
aflow with springs of wisdom.
It [the city of Shushan] rejoiced with a voice heard in the heavens,
and with him [Mordechai] who spoke of peace from the abode of blessings.

Chazzan concludes the blessing:

Blessed are You, HASHEM, Who blesses His people Israel with peace.

Chazzan recites Half-*Kaddish* (p. 138) and the service continues with the Torah reading.

עִנְיָנֵי שְׂמָחוֹת

Death and Bereavement

❧{ ודוי של שכיב מרע }❧

The following confession is recited by or with a person near death, Heaven forbid. See commentary.

מוֹדֶה אֲנִי לְפָנֶיךָ יהוה אֱלֹהַי וֵאלֹהֵי אֲבוֹתַי, שֶׁרְפוּאָתִי וּמִיתָתִי בְיָדֶךָ. יְהִי רָצוֹן מִלְּפָנֶיךָ שֶׁתְּרַפְּאֵנִי רְפוּאָה שְׁלֵמָה, וְאִם אָמוּת, תְּהֵא מִיתָתִי כַפָּרָה עַל כָּל חֲטָאִים עֲוֹנוֹת וּפְשָׁעִים שֶׁחָטָאתִי וְשֶׁעָוִיתִי וְשֶׁפָּשַׁעְתִּי לְפָנֶיךָ. וְתֵן חֶלְקִי בְּגַן עֵדֶן, וְזַכֵּנִי לְעוֹלָם הַבָּא הַצָּפוּן לַצַּדִּיקִים.

❧{ הלוית המת }❧

The mourners recite the following blessing when they rip their outer garments.

בָּרוּךְ אַתָּה יהוה אֱלֹהֵינוּ מֶלֶךְ הָעוֹלָם, דַּיַּן הָאֱמֶת.*

Those who have not seen a cemetery for thirty days recite the following blessing when coming there:

בָּרוּךְ אַתָּה יהוה אֱלֹהֵינוּ מֶלֶךְ הָעוֹלָם, אֲשֶׁר יָצַר* אֶתְכֶם בַּדִּין,* וְזָן וְכִלְכֵּל אֶתְכֶם בַּדִּין, וְהֵמִית אֶתְכֶם בַּדִּין, וְיוֹדֵעַ מִסְפַּר כֻּלְּכֶם בַּדִּין,* וְהוּא עָתִיד לְהַחֲיוֹתְכֶם וּלְקַיֵּם אֶתְכֶם בַּדִּין. בָּרוּךְ אַתָּה יהוה, מְחַיֵּה הַמֵּתִים.

אַתָּה גִּבּוֹר לְעוֹלָם* אֲדֹנָי, מְחַיֵּה מֵתִים אַתָּה, רַב לְהוֹשִׁיעַ. מְכַלְכֵּל חַיִּים בְּחֶסֶד, מְחַיֵּה מֵתִים בְּרַחֲמִים רַבִּים, סוֹמֵךְ נוֹפְלִים, וְרוֹפֵא חוֹלִים, וּמַתִּיר אֲסוּרִים, וּמְקַיֵּם אֱמוּנָתוֹ לִישֵׁנֵי עָפָר. מִי כָמוֹךָ בַּעַל גְּבוּרוֹת, וּמִי דּוֹמֶה לָּךְ, מֶלֶךְ מֵמִית וּמְחַיֶּה וּמַצְמִיחַ יְשׁוּעָה, וְנֶאֱמָן אַתָּה לְהַחֲיוֹת מֵתִים.

❧{ וִדּוּי שֶׁל שְׁכִיב מְרַע/DEATHBED CONFESSION }❧

If a sick person is near death, Heaven forbid, someone should recite the following confession with him. However, it is required that this be done in such a way that his morale not be broken because this may even hasten death. He should be told, 'Many have confessed and did not die and many who did not confess died anyway. In reward for your having confessed, may you live, but everyone who confesses has a share in the World to Come.' If the patient cannot speak, he should confess in his heart. One who is unsophisticated should not be asked to confess because it may break his spirit and cause him to weep.

The text here contains the minimum confession as recorded in *Shulchan Aruch (Yoreh De'ah* 337:2); if one wishes, he may add the text of the Yom Kippur confession (p. 776).

❧{ הַלְוָיַת הַמֵּת / FUNERAL SERVICES }❧

The ritual of burial combines grief with consolation, mourning with acceptance. The grief and mourning aspects are obvious: the tearful eulogies, ripping of garments, the restrictive laws of the various periods of mourning. The consolation and acceptance are reflected in the prayers and blessings of this difficult period. For one theme runs through them all: God judges righteously. His righteousness was the controlling factor in the sunshine of life, health, growth, and happiness. It is no less so in the somber days of illness, suffering, and death. And His righteousness provides the ultimate consolation that the souls of the departed live on in a better place and will return to reborn bodies after the final Redemption when the dead are resuscitated.

דַּיַּן הָאֱמֶת — *The true Judge.* Truth is the very seal of God *(Shabbos* 55a) and as such it characterizes His every deed. In acknowledging God's judgment as a manifestation of truth, we proclaim that even the Divine deeds that we find hardest to understand are no different at their source than the acts of mercy and kindness that we so crave. Indeed, the Talmud teaches that in time to come people will be privileged to understand God's ways more clearly, and the

CONFESSIONAL ON THE DEATH BED

The following confession is recited by or with a person near death, Heaven forbid. See commentary.

מוֹדֶה אֲנִי *I acknowledge before You, HASHEM, my God and the God of my forefathers, that my recovery and death are in Your hand. May it be Your will that You heal me with total recovery, but, if I die, may my death be an atonement for all the errors, iniquities, and willful sins that I have erred, sinned and transgressed before You. May You grant my share in the Garden of Eden, and privilege me for the World to Come that is concealed for the righteous.*

FUNERAL SERVICES

The mourners recite the following blessing when they rip their outer garments.

בָּרוּךְ *Blessed are You, HASHEM, our God, King of the universe, the true Judge.*

Those who have not seen a cemetery for thirty days recite the following blessing when coming there:

בָּרוּךְ *Blessed are You, HASHEM, our God, King of the universe, Who fashioned* you with justice,* nourished and sustained you with justice, took your lives with justice,* knows the sum total of you all with justice, and will restore and resuscitate you with judgment. Blessed are You, HASHEM, Who resuscitates the dead.*

You are eternally mighty, my Lord, the Resuscitator of the dead are You; abundantly able to save. He sustains the living with kindness, resuscitates the dead with abundant mercy, supports the fallen, heals the sick, releases the confined, and maintains His faith to those asleep in the dust. Who is like You, O Master of mighty deeds, and who is comparable to You, O King Who causes death and restores life and makes salvation sprout. And You are faithful to resuscitate the dead.*

---

blessing in times of tragedy, as in times of good fortune, will be הַטּוֹב וְהַמֵּטִיב, the *Good and Beneficent One,* in recognition that all God's deeds are equally merciful.

בָּרוּךְ ... אֲשֶׁר יָצַר — *Blessed ... Who fashioned.* This blessing is not part of the burial service *per se.* It is recited by anyone who sees Jewish graves for the first time in thirty or more days. Death is a shattering and moving experience. When a month has gone by, the impact lessens and a new visit to a cemetery becomes a new emotional experience. We respond by acknowledging anew the sentiments expressed in this prayer. [Authorities differ regarding the frequency with which this blessing is recited. Some maintain that it may not be recited more than once in thirty days, even when different cemeteries are visited. Others hold that the blessing is recited whenever the particular graves have not been seen during the past thirty days (see *Mishnah Berurah* 224:17).]

אֲשֶׁר יָצַר אֶתְכֶם בַּדִּין — *Who fashioned you with justice.* The implication is plain that 'justice' in this context refers not to reward and punishment, because we speak here of justice with regard to the fashioning of the newborn. Rather, the term justice refers to God's total plan for creation.

וְיוֹדֵעַ מִסְפַּר כֻּלְּכֶם בַּדִּין — *Knows the sum total of you all with justice.* The souls of the departed remain important to God. He keeps account of them and waits for the day when the dead will be brought back to life.

אַתָּה גִּבּוֹר לְעוֹלָם — *You are eternally mighty.* From this point to its end, the prayer is taken from the portion of *Shemoneh Esrei* (p. 98) that describes God as the Giver of Life.

צדוק הדין

When the deceased is brought to the cemetery, the following is recited. However, it is omitted when *Tachanun* is not recited (see p. 125).

הַצּוּר תָּמִים פָּעֳלוֹ,* כִּי כָל דְּרָכָיו מִשְׁפָּט, אֵל אֱמוּנָה וְאֵין עָוֶל, צַדִּיק וְיָשָׁר הוּא.[1]

הַצּוּר תָּמִים בְּכָל פֹּעַל, מִי יֹאמַר לוֹ מַה תִּפְעָל,* הַשַּׁלִּיט בְּמַטָּה וּבְמַעַל, מֵמִית וּמְחַיֶּה,* מוֹרִיד שְׁאוֹל וַיָּעַל.[2]

הַצּוּר תָּמִים בְּכָל מַעֲשֶׂה, מִי יֹאמַר אֵלָיו מַה תַּעֲשֶׂה, הָאוֹמֵר וְעֹשֶׂה, חֶסֶד חִנָּם לָנוּ תַעֲשֶׂה, וּבִזְכוּת הַנֶּעֱקַד כְּשֶׂה,* הַקְשִׁיבָה וַעֲשֵׂה.

צַדִּיק בְּכָל דְּרָכָיו הַצּוּר תָּמִים, אֶרֶךְ אַפַּיִם וּמָלֵא רַחֲמִים, חֲמָל נָא וְחוּס נָא עַל אָבוֹת וּבָנִים, כִּי לְךָ אָדוֹן הַסְּלִיחוֹת וְהָרַחֲמִים.

צַדִּיק אַתָּה יהוה לְהָמִית וּלְהַחֲיוֹת, אֲשֶׁר בְּיָדְךָ פִּקְדוֹן כָּל רוּחוֹת, חָלִילָה לְּךָ זִכְרוֹנֵנוּ לִמְחוֹת,* וְיִהְיוּ נָא עֵינֶיךָ בְּרַחֲמִים עָלֵינוּ פְקוּחוֹת, כִּי לְךָ אָדוֹן הָרַחֲמִים וְהַסְּלִיחוֹת.

אָדָם אִם בֶּן שָׁנָה יִהְיֶה,* אוֹ אֶלֶף שָׁנִים יִחְיֶה, מַה יִּתְרוֹן לוֹ, כְּלֹא הָיָה יִהְיֶה, בָּרוּךְ דַּיַּן הָאֱמֶת, מֵמִית וּמְחַיֶּה.

בָּרוּךְ הוּא, כִּי אֱמֶת דִּינוֹ, וּמְשׁוֹטֵט הַכֹּל בְּעֵינוֹ,[3] וּמְשַׁלֵּם* לְאָדָם חֶשְׁבּוֹנוֹ וְדִינוֹ, וְהַכֹּל לִשְׁמוֹ הוֹדָיָה יִתֵּנוּ.

יָדַעְנוּ יהוה כִּי צֶדֶק מִשְׁפָּטֶךָ, תִּצְדַּק בְּדָבְרֶךָ וְתִזְכֶּה בְּשָׁפְטֶךָ,[4] וְאֵין לְהַרְהֵר אַחַר מִדַּת שָׁפְטֶךָ, צַדִּיק אַתָּה יהוה, וְיָשָׁר מִשְׁפָּטֶיךָ.[5]

דַּיַּן אֱמֶת, שׁוֹפֵט צֶדֶק וֶאֱמֶת, בָּרוּךְ דַּיַּן הָאֱמֶת, שֶׁכָּל מִשְׁפָּטָיו צֶדֶק וֶאֱמֶת.

נֶפֶשׁ כָּל חַי בְּיָדֶךָ,[6] צֶדֶק מָלְאָה יְמִינְךָ[7] וְיָדֶךָ, רַחֵם עַל פְּלֵיטַת צֹאן יָדֶךָ, וְתֹאמַר לַמַּלְאָךְ הֶרֶף יָדֶךָ.[8]

צִדּוּק הַדִּין / Acceptance of Judgment

הַצּוּר תָּמִים פָּעֳלוֹ — *The Rock! — perfect is His work.* In this moving prayer, the mourners declare their acceptance of the Divine judgment and also plead with God to be merciful upon the living. As noted elsewhere, the word צוּר has the dual connotation of *Rock*, in the sense that God is impregnable and unchanging, and *Molder* (from צַיָּר, *one who fashions)*, in the sense that He is the Creator Who molds people and events to suit His purposes. In this prayer as in many others, both connotations are equally appropriate.

His work is תָּמִים, *perfect*, meaning that the totality of His deeds forms a harmonious whole. Man's intelligence is incapable of comprehending how all the pieces of God's puzzle fit together, but we have faith that this is so.

מִי יֹאמַר לוֹ מַה תִּפְעָל — *Who can say to Him, 'What have You done?'* The first step in learning to accept God's justice is to recognize that we have no power to question His ways.

מֵמִית וּמְחַיֶּה — *Brings death and resuscitates.* Life and death are in God's hands, but death is not eternal; it is a principle of our faith that God will resuscitate the dead. Having said that He is a *God of faith* Who carries out His word, we console ourselves with the knowledge that death is not eternal.

וּבִזְכוּת הַנֶּעֱקַד כְּשֶׂה — *In the merit of him who was*

ACCEPTANCE OF JUDGMENT

When the deceased is brought to the cemetery, the following is recited. However, it is omitted when *Tachanun* is not recited (p. 125).

הַצּוּר *The Rock! — perfect is His work,* for all His paths are justice; a God of faith without iniquity, righteous and fair is He.*[1]

הַצּוּר *The Rock! — perfect in every work. Who can say to Him, 'What have You done?'* He rules below and above, brings death and resuscitates, brings down to the grave and raises up.*[2]

הַצּוּר *The Rock! — perfect in every deed. Who can say to Him, 'What do You do?' O He Who says and does, do undeserved kindness with us. In the merit of him [Isaac] who was bound like a lamb,* hearken and act.*

צַדִּיק *O righteous One in all His ways, O Rock who is perfect — slow to anger and full of mercy — take pity and please spare parents and children, for Yours, O master, are forgiveness and mercy.*

צַדִּיק *Righteous are You, HASHEM, to bring death and to resuscitate, for in Your hand is the safekeeping of all spirits. It would be sacrilegious for You to erase our memory.* May Your eyes mercifully take cognizance of us, for Yours, O Master, are mercy and forgiveness.*

אָדָם *A man, whether he be a year old,* or whether he lives a thousand years, what does it profit him? — As if he has never been shall he be. Blessed is the true Judge, Who brings death and resuscitates.*

בָּרוּךְ *Blessed is He, for His judgment is true, He scans everything with His eye,*[3] *and He recompenses* man according to his account and his just sentence. All must give His Name acknowledgment.*

יָדַעְנוּ *We know, HASHEM, that Your judgment is righteous, You are righteous when You speak and pure when You judge;*[4] *and there is no complaining about the attribute of Your judgment. Righteous are You, HASHEM, and Your judgments are fair.*[5]

דַּיַּן *O true Judge, Judge of righteousness and truth. Blessed is the true Judge, for all of His judgments are righteous and true.*

נֶפֶשׁ *The soul of all the living is in Your hand,*[6] *righteousness fills Your right hand*[7] *and Your power. Have mercy on the remnant of the sheep of Your hand, and say to the Angel [of Death], 'Hold back your hand!'*[8]

---

(1) *Deuteronomy* 32:4. (2) *I Samuel* 2:6. (3) Cf. *II Chronicles* 16:9; *Zechariah* 4:10. (4) Cf. *Psalms* 51:6. (5) 119:137. (6) Cf. *Job* 12:10. (7) Cf. *Psalms* 48:11. (8) Cf. *II Samuel* 24:16.

---

bound like a lamb. Isaac was ready to let himself be slaughtered if such was God's will. In the merit of the trait of acceptance of God's will that our people has inherited from him, may God answer our prayers.

חָלִילָה לְךָ זִכְרוֹנֵנוּ לִמְחוֹת — *It would be sacrilegious for You to erase our memory.* In a paraphrase of Abraham's prayer for the sinful people of Sodom and its surrounding cities *(Genesis* 18:25), we beg God to have mercy on His people.

אָדָם אִם בֶּן שָׁנָה יִהְיֶה — *A man, whether he be a year old.* No matter how long man lives and how much wealth and fame he amasses, he leaves earth with none of it. The only thing that matters is the degree to which he recognizes and serves God.

וּמְשׁוֹטֵט הַכֹּל בְּעֵינוֹ וּמְשַׁלֵּם — *He scans everything with His eye, and He recompenses.* God sees all that man does, and rewards and punishes justly. Consequently we must accept His judgment.

גָּדֹל הָעֵצָה וְרַב הָעֲלִילִיָּה, אֲשֶׁר עֵינֶיךָ פְּקֻחוֹת עַל כָּל דַּרְכֵי בְּנֵי אָדָם, לָתֵת לְאִישׁ כִּדְרָכָיו וְכִפְרִי מַעֲלָלָיו.[1]

לְהַגִּיד כִּי יָשָׁר יהוה, צוּרִי וְלֹא עַוְלָתָה בּוֹ.[2]

יהוה נָתַן, וַיהוה לָקָח, יְהִי שֵׁם יהוה מְבֹרָךְ.[3]

וְהוּא רַחוּם, יְכַפֵּר עָוֹן וְלֹא יַשְׁחִית, וְהִרְבָּה לְהָשִׁיב אַפּוֹ, וְלֹא יָעִיר כָּל חֲמָתוֹ.[4]

קדיש אחר הקבורה

יִתְגַּדַּל וְיִתְקַדַּשׁ שְׁמֵהּ רַבָּא. (.Cong— אָמֵן.) בְּעָלְמָא דִּי הוּא עָתִיד לְאִתְחַדָּתָא, וּלְאַחֲיָאָה מֵתַיָּא, וּלְאַסָּקָא יָתְהוֹן לְחַיֵּי עָלְמָא, וּלְמִבְנֵא קַרְתָּא דִּי יְרוּשְׁלֵם, וּלְשַׁכְלָלָא הֵיכְלֵהּ בְּגַוַּהּ, וּלְמֶעְקַר פָּלְחָנָא נֻכְרָאָה מִן אַרְעָא, וְלַאֲתָבָא פָּלְחָנָא דִשְׁמַיָּא לְאַתְרֵהּ, וְיַמְלִיךְ קֻדְשָׁא בְּרִיךְ הוּא בְּמַלְכוּתֵהּ וִיקָרֵהּ, בְּחַיֵּיכוֹן וּבְיוֹמֵיכוֹן וּבְחַיֵּי דְכָל בֵּית יִשְׂרָאֵל, בַּעֲגָלָא וּבִזְמַן קָרִיב. וְאִמְרוּ: אָמֵן.

(.Cong— אָמֵן. יְהֵא שְׁמֵהּ רַבָּא מְבָרַךְ לְעָלַם וּלְעָלְמֵי עָלְמַיָּא.)

יְהֵא שְׁמֵהּ רַבָּא מְבָרַךְ לְעָלַם וּלְעָלְמֵי עָלְמַיָּא.

יִתְבָּרַךְ וְיִשְׁתַּבַּח וְיִתְפָּאַר וְיִתְרוֹמַם וְיִתְנַשֵּׂא וְיִתְהַדָּר וְיִתְעַלֶּה וְיִתְהַלָּל שְׁמֵהּ דְּקֻדְשָׁא בְּרִיךְ הוּא (.Cong— בְּרִיךְ הוּא) — °לְעֵלָּא מִן כָּל (From Rosh Hashanah to Yom Kippur substitute— °לְעֵלָּא וּלְעֵלָּא מִכָּל) בִּרְכָתָא וְשִׁירָתָא תֻּשְׁבְּחָתָא וְנֶחֱמָתָא, דַּאֲמִירָן בְּעָלְמָא. וְאִמְרוּ: אָמֵן. (.Cong— אָמֵן.)

יְהֵא שְׁלָמָא רַבָּא מִן שְׁמַיָּא, וְחַיִּים עָלֵינוּ וְעַל כָּל יִשְׂרָאֵל. וְאִמְרוּ: אָמֵן. (.Cong— אָמֵן.)

Take three steps back. Bow left and say ... עֹשֶׂה; bow right and say ... הוּא; bow forward and say וְעַל כָּל ... אָמֵן. Remain standing in place for a few moments, then take three steps forward.

עֹשֶׂה שָׁלוֹם בִּמְרוֹמָיו, הוּא יַעֲשֶׂה שָׁלוֹם עָלֵינוּ, וְעַל כָּל יִשְׂרָאֵל. וְאִמְרוּ: אָמֵן. (.Cong— אָמֵן.)

Those present at the burial form two rows through which the mourners walk. As the mourners pass them, those forming the rows recite the traditional prayer of consolation.

הַמָּקוֹם* יְנַחֵם אֶתְכֶם בְּתוֹךְ שְׁאָר אֲבֵלֵי צִיּוֹן וִירוּשָׁלָיִם.

As the participants leave the cemetery, they tear out some blades of grass and toss them over their right shoulders as they recite:

וְיָצִיצוּ* מֵעִיר כְּעֵשֶׂב הָאָרֶץ.[5] זָכוּר כִּי עָפָר אֲנָחְנוּ.[6]

קַדִּישׁ אַחַר הַקְּבוּרָה/KADDISH AFTER BURIAL

More directly than any other text of *Kaddish*, this one refers to the state of perfection which will come with the Redemption and the End of Days. The first such blessing to be mentioned in this special addition to *Kaddish* is the Divine promise that God will resuscitate the dead. It goes on to list other Divine gifts that will shower upon earth during that period of spiritual beneficence. There can be no greater consolation at a burial than to recall God's guarantee that the dead will live again, and that life has a meaning and purpose that survive an essentially

גְּדֹל *Great in counsel and abundant in deed, Your eyes are open upon all the ways of the children of man, to give man according to his ways and according to the fruit of his deeds.*[1]

לְהַגִּיד *To declare that HASHEM is just, my Rock, in Whom there is no wrong.*[2]

יהוה *HASHEM gave and HASHEM took, Blessed be the Name of HASHEM.*[3]

וְהוּא *He, the Merciful One, is forgiving of iniquity and does not destroy, frequently withdrawing His anger, not arousing His entire rage.*[4]

KADDISH AFTER A BURIAL

יִתְגַּדַּל *May His great Name grow exalted and sanctified* (Cong.— *Amen.*) *in the world which will be renewed, and where He will resuscitate the dead and raise them up to eternal life, and rebuild the city of Jerusalem and complete His Temple within it, and uproot alien worship from the earth, and return the service of Heaven to its place and where the Holy One, Blessed is He, will reign in His sovereignty and splendor, in your lifetimes and in your days, and in the lifetimes of the entire Family of Israel, swiftly and soon. Now respond: Amen.*

(Cong.— *Amen. May His great Name be blessed forever and ever.*)

May His great Name be blessed forever and ever.

Blessed, praised, glorified, exalted, extolled, mighty, upraised, and lauded be the Name of the Holy One, Blessed is He (Cong.— *Blessed is He*) — (From Rosh Hashanah to Yom Kippur add: *exceedingly*) *beyond any blessing and song, praise and consolation that are uttered in the world. Now respond: Amen.* (Cong.— *Amen.*)

May there be abundant peace from Heaven, and life, upon us and upon all Israel. Now respond: Amen. (Cong.— *Amen.*)

Take three steps back. Bow left and say, *'He Who makes peace ...'*; bow right and say, *'may He ...'*; bow forward and say, *'and upon all Israel ...'* Remain standing in place for a few moments, then take three steps forward.

He Who makes peace in His heights, may He make peace upon us, and upon all Israel. Now respond: Amen. (Cong.—*Amen.*)

Those present at the burial form two rows through which the mourners walk. As the mourners pass them, those forming the rows recite the traditional prayer of consolation.

הַמָּקוֹם *May the Omnipresent* console you among the other mourners of Zion and Jerusalem.*

As the participants leave the cemetery, they tear out some blades of grass and toss them over their right shoulders as they recite:

וְיָצִיצוּ *May they blossom forth* from the city like the grass of the earth.*[5] *Remember that we are but dust.*[6]

(1) *Jeremiah* 32:19. (2) *Psalms* 92:16. (3) *Job* 1:21. (4) *Psalms* 78:38. (5) *Psalms* 72:16. (6) 103:14.

temporary death.

הַמָּקוֹם — [*May the*] *Omnipresent.* At the climax of the burial service, those who have come to share the mourners' grief, and to render the final honor to the departed, form two rows and express their prayerful wish that the mourners be consoled. This is an expression of Jewish brotherhood, symbolized by the mourners walking through the midst of their brethren and by the prayer that includes all those who mourn the national tragedy of Zion and Jerusalem in the category of those who have now become bereaved.

וְיָצִיצוּ — *May they blossom forth.* This verse concludes the portrayal given in Psalm 72 of the happy and blessed life that flourishes under the wise leadership of a God-inspired leader. The idea is that God provides the necessary elements

After leaving the cemetery, one washes his hands ritually and recites:

בִּלַּע הַמָּוֶת* לָנֶצַח, וּמָחָה אֲדֹנָי יֱהֹוִה דִּמְעָה מֵעַל כָּל פָּנִים, וְחֶרְפַּת עַמּוֹ יָסִיר מֵעַל כָּל הָאָרֶץ, כִּי יהוה דִּבֵּר.[1]

❦ לימוד משניות לזכר הנפטרים ❦

מקואות פרק ז

[א] **יֵשׁ מַעֲלִין** אֶת הַמִּקְוֶה וְלֹא פוֹסְלִין, פּוֹסְלִין וְלֹא מַעֲלִין, לֹא מַעֲלִין וְלֹא פוֹסְלִין. אֵלּוּ מַעֲלִין וְלֹא פוֹסְלִין: הַשֶּׁלֶג, וְהַבָּרָד, וְהַכְּפוֹר, וְהַגְּלִיד, וְהַמֶּלַח, וְהַטִּיט הַנָּרוֹק. אָמַר רַבִּי עֲקִיבָא: הָיָה רַבִּי יִשְׁמָעֵאל דָּן כְּנֶגְדִּי לוֹמַר: הַשֶּׁלֶג אֵינוֹ מַעֲלֶה אֶת הַמִּקְוֶה. וְהֵעִידוּ אַנְשֵׁי מֵידְבָא מִשְּׁמוֹ, שֶׁאָמַר לָהֶם: צְאוּ וְהָבִיאוּ שֶׁלֶג וַעֲשׂוּ מִקְוֶה בַּתְּחִלָּה. רַבִּי יוֹחָנָן בֶּן נוּרִי אוֹמֵר: אֶבֶן הַבָּרָד כְּמַיִם.

---

for a successful human society just as He provides all the nutrients needed for vegetable life. By throwing grass over our shoulders as we depart the burial field and return to the land of the living, we symbolize our faith in God's benevolent providence for society *(R' Hirsch).*

❧ בִּלַּע הַמָּוֶת — *May He swallow up death.* The ritual cleansing of the hands symbolizes our resolve to improve ourselves and our lives, and put thoughts of death and decay behind us. To express this idea, we recite the verse that prophesies the end of death, tears, and scorn.

❦ MISHNAYOS STUDY / לימוד מִשְׁנָיוֹת ❦

It is customary to study mishnayos as a source of merit for the souls of the departed. An allusion to this custom is found in the letters of the Hebrew word מִשְׁנָה, *Mishnah,* which — as *Arizal* and *Sh'lah* point out — can be rearranged to form the word נְשָׁמָה, *neshamah* or soul.

Four periods are set aside for the study of Mishnayos as a merit for the departed: (a) the *shivah,* seven-day mourning period, during which time those visiting the mourners study aloud, usually between *Minchah* and *Maariv* [the mourners themselves are prohibited from most areas of Torah study on their own during this period]; (b) the remainder of the *shloshim* (or thirty-day period commencing from the burial), during which time the mourners themselves also study either on their own and by taking part in group study and discussion; (c) during the entire first year, until the first *yahrzeit,* anniversary of death [as recorded in the Jewish calendar]; and (d) each year on the *yahrzeit.*

Although any section of the six orders of Mishnah may be studied for this purpose, there are two primary traditions. One custom is to study a group of chapters, the initial letters of which form the name of the deceased. Thus if the deceased's name was מֹשֶׁה, first a chapter beginning with the letter מ would be studied, then a chapter beginning with ש, followed by a chapter beginning with ה (many sets of Mishnah have an alphabetical listing of chapters to facilitate such study).

Another tradition calls for the study of *Seder Taharos.* Two chapters of *Taharos* are preferred: (a) chapter twenty-four of tractate *Keilim,* because each mishnah in it concludes with the word טָהוֹר, *pure;* and (b) chapter seven of tractate *Mikvaos* — according to R' Yitzchak Isaac of Komarna's Mishnah commentary — because the initial letters of its final four mishnayos spell the word נְשָׁמָה, *neshamah* or soul. Since the second custom has gained widespread acceptance, we include it below. Some study the entire chapter while others study only the last four mishnayos.

YAD AVRAHAM/יד אברהם

[A full treatment of these and all relevant Mishnayos may be found in the ArtScroll Mishnah with the *Yad Avraham* commentary.]

❧ Mikvaos / Chapter 7

A מִקְוֶה, *mikveh* [pl. *mikvaos*], is a body of water used for the cleansing of the *tamei,* ritually unclean person or object. Among the requirements that must be met for a body of water to be a valid *mikveh* is that it contain at least forty *se'ah* — approximately 200 gallons — of water. Additionally, the initial forty *se'ah* must be (a) *mechubarin,* or 'attached' (i.e., a body of water attached to the ground), and not (b) *she'uvin,* 'drawn' (i.e, water that has been drawn, carried or merely stored in a utensil or other container).

On a Scriptural level, once a body of water contains more than half the required volume of *mechubarin* (i.e., more than twenty *se'ah*), then even if *she'uvin* are added to bring the volume to forty *se'ah,* the body constitutes a valid *mikveh.* However, the Sages decreed that *she'uvin* may not be used to complete the forty *se'ah.* Moreover, they decreed that if even three לוֹג, *log,*

After leaving the cemetery, one washes his hands ritually and recites:

בִּלַּע *May He swallow up death* forever, and may HASHEM the God wipe away tears from every face and remove the scorn of His people from throughout the world, for the mouth of HASHEM has spoken.*[1]

MISHNAYOS STUDY IN MEMORY OF THE DECEASED

MIKVAOS, CHAPTER 7

[1] **יֵשׁ מַעֲלִין** *Some [substances] complete a mikveh and [certainly] do not invalidate [it]; [some] invalidate [a mikveh] and do not complete [it]; [and some] neither complete nor invalidate [it]. These complete and do not invalidate: snow, hail, sleet, ice, salt and liquid mud. Said Rabbi Akiva: "Rabbi Yishmael argued with me saying: 'Snow cannot complete a mikveh.' " But the citizens of Meidva testified in his [i.e., Rabbi Yishmael's] name that he said to them, "Go and bring snow and make a mikveh from the beginning." Rabbi Yochanan ben Nuri says: Hailstones are like water.*

(1) *Isaiah* 25:8.

YAD AVRAHAM

(approximately 36 fluid ounces) of *she'uvin* fall or are poured into a body of less than forty *se'ah* of *mechubarin,* the body is permanently invalidated and may never be used as a *mikveh* even if enough water is later added to it to bring it up to the required forty *se'ah.* The first five *mishnayos* discuss various details and ramifications of this rabbinic decree.

1. There are three categories of substances which differ in the way they affect the validity of a *mikveh:*

יֵשׁ מַעֲלִין אֶת הַמִּקְוֶה ... — *Some [substances] complete a mikveh* ... The substances in this category (enumerated below) can be used to complete the minimum forty *se'ah* volume of a body of water which already contains more than twenty *se'ah* of *mechubarin.* Since they can even validate a *mikveh,* it is obvious that three *log* of any of these substances do not invalidate a body which contains less than forty *se'ah.*

פּוֹסְלִין וְלֹא מַעֲלִין — *[Some] invalidate a* mikveh *and do not complete [it].* If three *log* of any of the substances in this category (enumerated in mishnah 2) fall into a body of less than forty *se'ah,* they invalidate that body from ever becoming a *mikveh.* Additionally, if a *mikveh* lacks less than three *log* to complete the forty *se'ah* minimum, these substances cannot be used to make up the difference [although being less than three *log,* they would not invalidate the *mikveh*].

לֹא מַעֲלִין וְלֹא פּוֹסְלִין — *[Some] neither complete nor invalidate [it].* If an amount of less than three *log* is necessary to complete the forty *se'ah,* and that amount of one of the substances in this category (enumerated in mishnah 2) falls in, the body is not considered a valid *mikveh.* Nevertheless, if the body is missing more than three *log* of *mechubarin,* and three *log* of these substances fall in, the body does not become invalidated. It may still become a *mikveh* if the proper amount of *mechubarin* is subsequently added.

אֵלּוּ מַעֲלִין וְלֹא פוֹסְלִין — *These complete and do not invalidate.* The mishnah now lists the substances of the first category. The principle underlying this category is that these substances are legally considered water with regard to completing the Scriptural requirement that a *mikveh* contain at least forty *se'ah.* However, they are not considered water with regard to the disqualification of *she'uvin* for completing a *mikveh.*

וְהַטִּיט הַנָּרוֹק — *Liquid mud,* i.e., mud thin enough to be poured. Although it is considered water with regard to completing a *mikveh* which has more than twenty *se'ah* of proper water, it is not classified as water with regard to the disqualification of *she'uvin;* thicker mud certainly does not invalidate in this respect.

אָמַר רַבִּי עֲקִיבָא ... וְהֵעִידוּ אַנְשֵׁי מֵידְבָא ... — *Said Rabbi Akiva ... But the citizens of Meidva ...* The people of Meidva testified that only for the sake of discussion and debate did Rabbi Yishmael disagree with Rabbi Akiva regarding the status of snow. In actual practice, however, Rabbi Yishmael also ruled that snow can complete a *mikveh.* Indeed, not only did Rabbi Yishmael permit snow to be used to complete the minimum volume of forty *se'ah,* he also permitted snow — even snow that had been contained in a utensil — to make up the *entire* forty *se'ah* (from the beginning.)

Moreover, the term snow refers to all the forms of frozen water listed in the mishnah. This is the view accepted as halachah. [However, according to most authorities, immersion may not take place until the snow actually melts.]

אֶבֶן הַבָּרָד כַּמַּיִם — *Hailstones are like water,* regarding the disqualification of *she'uvin.* This view is not accepted by the halachah.

כֵּיצַד מַעֲלִין וְלֹא פוֹסְלִין? מִקְוֶה שֶׁיֵּשׁ בּוֹ אַרְבָּעִים סְאָה חָסֵר אַחַת, נָפַל מֵהֶם סְאָה לְתוֹכוֹ, וְהֶעֱלָהוּ, נִמְצְאוּ — מַעֲלִין וְלֹא פוֹסְלִין.

[ב] אֵלּוּ פוֹסְלִין וְלֹא מַעֲלִין: הַמַּיִם בֵּין טְמֵאִים בֵּין טְהוֹרִים, וּמֵי כְבָשִׁים, וּמֵי שְׁלָקוֹת, וְהַתֶּמֶד עַד שֶׁלֹּא הֶחֱמִיץ. כֵּיצַד פּוֹסְלִין וְלֹא מַעֲלִין? מִקְוֶה שֶׁיֵּשׁ בּוֹ אַרְבָּעִים סְאָה חָסֵר קוֹרְטוֹב, וְנָפַל מֵהֶן קוֹרְטוֹב לְתוֹכוֹ — לֹא הֶעֱלָהוּ; פּוֹסְלוֹ בִּשְׁלֹשָׁה לֻגִּין.

אֲבָל שְׁאָר הַמַּשְׁקִין, וּמֵי פֵרוֹת, וְהַצִּיר, וְהַמֻּרְיָס, וְהַתֶּמֶד מִשֶּׁהֶחֱמִיץ — פְּעָמִים מַעֲלִין וּפְעָמִים שֶׁאֵינָן מַעֲלִין. כֵּיצַד? מִקְוֶה שֶׁיֵּשׁ בּוֹ אַרְבָּעִים סְאָה חָסֵר אַחַת נָפַל לְתוֹכוֹ סְאָה מֵהֶם — לֹא הֶעֱלָהוּ. הָיוּ בוֹ אַרְבָּעִים סְאָה, נָתַן סְאָה וְנָטַל סְאָה, הֲרֵי זֶה כָּשֵׁר.

[ג] הֵדִיחַ בּוֹ סַלֵּי זֵיתִים וְסַלֵּי עֲנָבִים, וְשִׁנּוּ אֶת מַרְאָיו — כָּשֵׁר. רַבִּי יוֹסֵי אוֹמֵר: מֵי הַצֶּבַע פּוֹסְלִין אוֹתוֹ בִּשְׁלֹשָׁה לֻגִּין, וְאֵינָן פּוֹסְלִין אוֹתוֹ בְּשִׁנּוּי מַרְאֶה.

נָפַל לְתוֹכוֹ יַיִן וּמֹחַל, וְשִׁנּוּ אֶת מַרְאָיו — פָּסוּל. כֵּיצַד יַעֲשֶׂה? יַמְתִּין לוֹ עַד שֶׁיֵּרְדוּ גְשָׁמִים, וְיַחְזְרוּ מַרְאֵיהֶן לְמַרְאֵה הַמַּיִם. הָיוּ בוֹ אַרְבָּעִים סְאָה, מְמַלֵּא בְכָתֵף וְנוֹתֵן לְתוֹכוֹ, עַד שֶׁיַּחְזְרוּ מַרְאֵיהֶן לְמַרְאֵה הַמַּיִם.

יד אברהם

נִמְצְאוּ מַעֲלִין וְלֹא פוֹסְלִין — *Thus they complete but do not invalidate.* Even if the additional *se'ah* is of *she'uvin,* it completes the *mikveh.* Since a *se'ah* (which contains twenty-four *log)* of *she'uvin* does not disqualify the *mechubarin,* it is obvious that a mere three *log* of *she'uvin* cannot invalidate them.

2. The mishnah now enumerates the substances in the second category mentioned in the previous mishnah. These substances are considered as water in all respects. Thus, if they are *she'uvin,* they cannot be used to complete a *mikveh;* moreover, three *log* invalidate the *mechubarin* of an incomplete *mikveh.*

הַמַּיִם — *Water* which has been drawn or placed in a utensil, i.e., *she'uvin.*

בֵּין טְמֵאִים בֵּין טְהוֹרִים — *Whether* [*ritually*] *contaminated or not contaminated.* This phrase is included in the mishnah because there are certain areas of *tumah*-contamination in which the rules applying to contaminated and non-contaminated water differ.

וְהַתֶּמֶד — *Marc-wine,* i.e., wine made by soaking the residue (skins, pulp, pips) of the wine press in water. Before fermentation, this liquid is still considered water; after fermentation (see below) it is considered wine.

קוֹרְטוֹב — *Kortov.* One sixty-fourth of a *log.*

לֹא הֶעֱלָהוּ — *It has not completed* [*the mikveh*]. An incomplete *mikveh* can never be completed with *she'uvin,* no matter how minute the amount.

אֲבָל שְׁאָר מַשְׁקִין — *But other liquids.* The mishnah now turns to the third category mentioned in the previous mishnah. This category includes seven substances that are classified *(Machshirin 6:4)* by the halachic term מַשְׁקֶה, *liquid:* (a) dew, (b) water, (c) grape wine, (d) olive oil, (e) blood, (f) milk, and (g) bee honey. Since dew and water were included in the first two categories, for they are forms of water and subject to the disqualification of *she'uvin,* the mishnah's phrase *other liquids* refers to the remaining five.

וְהַצִּיר וְהַמֻּרְיָס — *Fish-water, fish-oil.* This refers to the watery and oily liquids that ooze from salted fish.

פְּעָמִים מַעֲלִין — *Sometimes complete* [*a mikveh*]. Even though they are not classified as water.

וּפְעָמִים שֶׁאֵינָן מַעֲלִין — *And sometimes do not complete* [*a mikveh*]. Nevertheless, they do not invalidate it either.

הָיוּ בוֹ אַרְבָּעִים סְאָה נָתַן סְאָה וְנָטַל סְאָה — *If* [*the mikveh*] *contained forty se'ah, and he put in a se'ah* [*of one of these substances*], *then removed a se'ah.* A *se'ah* of one of these substances was added to a valid *mikveh* of exactly forty *se'ah,* bringing its volume to forty-one *se'ah.* Then a *se'ah* of the combined liquid was removed from the *mikveh,* bringing the volume back to forty *se'ah.* Although the removed *se'ah* contains approximately forty parts water and one part other liquid, and the total volume of water

In what instance do they complete and not invalidate? If a mikveh contains forty se'ah less one and a se'ah of [one of] these [substances] falls into it, it has completed [the mikveh]; thus they complete but do not invalidate.

[2] *These [substances] invalidate [a mikveh] and do not complete [it]: water, whether contaminated or not contaminated; water in which fruits or vegetables have been soaked; water in which fruits and vegetables have been cooked; and marc-wine which has not yet fermented. In what instance do they invalidate and not complete? If a mikveh contains forty se'ah less one kortov and a kortov of [one of] these [substances] falls into it, it has not completed [the mikveh], but it invalidates, with three log.*

But other liquids, fruit juices, fish-water, fish-oil, and marc-wine which has fermented, sometimes complete [a mikveh], and sometimes do not complete [a mikveh]. In what instances? If a mikveh contains forty se'ah less one and a se'ah of [one of] these [substances] falls into it, it has not completed [the mikveh]. If [the mikveh] contained forty se'ah, and he put in a se'ah [of one of these substances], then removed a se'ah, it [the mikveh] is valid.

[3] *If one rinsed olive baskets or grape baskets in it [a valid mikveh] thus changing its color, it is valid. Rabbi Yose says: Dye-water invalidates [a mikveh] if there are three log, but does not invalidate it by change of color.*

If wine or olive-water fell into it [the mikveh] and changed its color, it is invalid. What should one do? One should wait until rain falls and restores its color to the color of water. If it contained forty se'ah, he may draw [water, carry it] on his shoulder and place it into it [the mikveh], until its color returns to the color of water.

YAD AVRAHAM

remaining in the *mikveh* is less than the required forty *se'ah*, nevertheless the *mikveh* remains valid.

הֲרֵי זֶה כָּשֵׁר — *It [the mikveh] is valid.* This process can be repeated several times and the *mikveh* will remain valid, but only if we can be sure that more than twenty *se'ah* of water remain in the *mikveh*.

3. Besides by the addition of *she'uvin*, the waters of a *mikveh* may become invalidated by שִׁנּוּי מַרְאֶה, *a change of color*. Unlike the disqualification of *she'uvin*, which only invalidates an incomplete *mikveh*, change of color can invalidate even a complete *mikveh*.

הֵדִיחַ בּוֹ סַלֵּי זֵיתִים וְסַלֵּי עֲנָבִים ... כָּשֵׁר — *If one rinsed olive baskets or grape baskets ... it is valid.* The disqualification of change of color applies only if the substances from which that color derives is actually present in the *mikveh*. But the baskets that are rinsed in the *mikveh* do not contain the olives or grapes, only stains from them. This residue is not significant enough to invalidate the *mikveh*.

מֵי הַצֶּבַע — *Dye-water.* This refers to water in which dyestuffs have been soaked, thereby imparting their color to the water, and then removed. Since the dyestuffs are not present when the dye-water falls into the *mikveh*, the *mikveh* is not invalidated by change of color. Moreover, the dye-water retains the status of water insofar as the disqualification of *she'uvin* is concerned, and it therefore invalidates the *mikveh* if it contains three *log* of *she'uvin*. This view is accepted as halachah.

מֹחַל — *Olive-water*, i.e., a dark watery liquid that oozes out of ripe olives.

פָּסוּל — *It is invalid.* Since the color is an intrinsic part of the wine or olive-water, the presence of that liquid in the discolored *mikveh* invalidates the *mikveh*.

כֵּיצַד יַעֲשֶׂה — *What should one do?* How can the disqualification be removed from (a) the discolored *mechubarin* in an incomplete *mikveh?* and (b) a discolored complete *mikveh?*

גְּשָׁמִים — *Rain.* For an incomplete *mikveh* one may not use *she'uvin* to restore the original color, for three *log* would invalidate the water. Therefore, one must wait for natural water (rain) to sufficiently dilute the colored water so that it gains the appearance of water.

הָיָה בּוֹ אַרְבָּעִים סְאָה — *If it contained forty se'ah* it does not become invalid by the addition of *she'uvin*. Therefore, one may add any kind of water to it in order to dilute the color.

[ד] **נָ**פַל לְתוֹכוֹ יַיִן אוֹ מֹחַל, וְשִׁנּוּ מִקְצָת מַרְאָיו: אִם אֵין בּוֹ מַרְאֵה מַיִם אַרְבָּעִים סְאָה, הֲרֵי זֶה לֹא יִטְבֹּל בּוֹ.

[ה] **שְׁ**לֹשָׁה לֻגִּין מַיִם, וְנָפַל לְתוֹכָן קוֹרְטוֹב יַיִן, וַהֲרֵי מַרְאֵיהֶן כְּמַרְאֵה הַיַּיִן, וְנָפְלוּ לַמִּקְוֶה, לֹא פְסָלוּהוּ.

שְׁלֹשָׁה לֻגִּין מַיִם חָסֵר קוֹרְטוֹב, וְנָפַל לְתוֹכָן קוֹרְטוֹב חָלָב, וַהֲרֵי מַרְאֵיהֶן כְּמַרְאֵה הַמַּיִם, וְנָפְלוּ לַמִּקְוֶה — לֹא פְסָלוּהוּ. רַבִּי יוֹחָנָן בֶּן נוּרִי אוֹמֵר: הַכֹּל הוֹלֵךְ אַחַר הַמַּרְאֶה.

[ו] **מִ**קְוֶה שֶׁיֵּשׁ בּוֹ אַרְבָּעִים סְאָה מְכֻוָּנוֹת, יָרְדוּ שְׁנַיִם וְטָבְלוּ זֶה אַחַר זֶה — הָרִאשׁוֹן טָהוֹר, וְהַשֵּׁנִי טָמֵא. רַבִּי יְהוּדָה אוֹמֵר: אִם הָיוּ רַגְלָיו שֶׁל רִאשׁוֹן נוֹגְעוֹת בַּמַּיִם, אַף הַשֵּׁנִי טָהוֹר. הִטְבִּיל בּוֹ אֶת הַסָּגוֹס וְהֶעֱלָהוּ, מִקְצָתוֹ נוֹגֵעַ בַּמַּיִם — טָהוֹר.

הַכַּר וְהַכֶּסֶת שֶׁל עוֹר, כֵּיוָן שֶׁהִגְבִּיהַּ שִׂפְתוֹתֵיהֶם מִן הַמַּיִם — הַמַּיִם שֶׁבְּתוֹכָן שְׁאוּבִין. כֵּיצַד יַעֲשֶׂה? מַטְבִּילָן וּמַעֲלֶה אוֹתָן דֶּרֶךְ שׁוּלֵיהֶם.

[ז] **הִ**טְבִּיל בּוֹ אֶת הַמִּטָּה, אַף עַל פִּי שֶׁרַגְלֶיהָ שׁוֹקְעוֹת בְּטִיט הֶעָבֶה — טְהוֹרָה, מִפְּנֵי שֶׁהַמַּיִם מְקַדְּמִין.

מִקְוֶה שֶׁמֵּימָיו מְרֻדָּדִין, כּוֹבֵשׁ אֲפִילוּ חֲבִילֵי עֵצִים, אֲפִילוּ חֲבִילֵי קָנִים, כְּדֵי שֶׁיִּתְפְּחוּ הַמַּיִם, וְיוֹרֵד וְטוֹבֵל.

מַחַט שֶׁהִיא נְתוּנָה עַל מַעֲלוֹת הַמְּעָרָה, הָיָה מוֹלִיךְ וּמֵבִיא בַּמַּיִם, כֵּיוָן שֶׁעָבַר עָלֶיהָ הַגַּל — טְהוֹרָה.

If the *Mishnayos* were studied in the presence of a *minyan,* קַדִּישׁ דְּרַבָּנָן (p. 52) is recited.

יד אברהם

4. This mishnah begins with the letter נ of נְשָׁמָה.

לֹא יִטְבֹּל — *One may not immerse in it,* even in the part that has not been discolored (since that part by itself does not contain the required forty *se'ah.* If one does immerse in this *mikveh,* his immersion is invalid.

5. This mishnah begins with the letter ש of נְשָׁמָה.

כְּמַרְאֵה הַיַּיִן — *Like the color of wine.* Since the three *log* have taken on the color of wine, they are no longer considered water, and are not subject to the disqualification of *she'uvin.* Thus, they do not invalidate the *mechubarin* of an incomplete *mikveh.*

כְּמַרְאֵה הַמַּיִם — *Like the color of water.* Although the three *log* appear to be all water, since they in fact are not, only the actual water in them is subject to the disqualification of *she'uvin,* but not the milk. [A drop of milk is not sufficient to discolor water, whereas a drop of wine is.]

הַכֹּל הוֹלֵךְ אַחַר הַמַּרְאֶה — *Everything follows the color.* Wine-colored water is considered as wine and is not subject to the disqualification of *she'uvin.* Water-colored milk is considered as water and is subject to the *she'uvin* disqualification. This view is not accepted as halachah.

6. This mishnah begins with the letter מ of נְשָׁמָה.

וְהַשֵּׁנִי טָמֵא — *But the second* [*remains*] *contaminated.* When the first person stepped out of the *mikveh* a small amount of *mikveh* water remained on his body. Thus the *mikveh,* which originally contained exactly forty *se'ah,* was incomplete when the second person immersed.

אִם הָיוּ רַגְלָיו שֶׁל רִאשׁוֹן נוֹגְעוֹת בַּמַּיִם — *If the feet of the first were* [*still*] *touching the water* when the second immersed himself. Rabbi Yehudah applies the halachic principle of גּוּד אַחִית, *gud achis* [lit. *extend downward;* this principle allows us to view certain types of objects suspended above a surface as extending down to that surface. It is applied primarily to suspended partitions in regard to the law of Sabbath] to the water on the first person's body. Thus, the *mikveh* is considered full, despite the fact that part of the forty *se'ah* has been removed. This view is not accepted as halachah.

סָגוֹס — *A thick cloth* [lit. *a burnoose*]. According to some commentaries, this rule is a continuation of Rabbi Yehudah's opinion and is also based on the principle of *gud achis.* Thus, this view is also rejected by halachah. Other commentaries maintain that this ruling is not based on *gud*

[4] *If wine or olive-water fell into it [a mikveh] and changed the color of part [of the mikveh], if there are no longer forty se'ah with the color of water, one may not immerse in it.*

[5] *If three log of water — into which a kortov of wine had fallen and their color became like the color of wine — fell into a mikveh, they did not invalidate it.*

If three log less a kortov of water — into which a kortov of milk had fallen and their color was like the color of water — fell into a mikveh, they did not invalidate it. Rabbi Yochanan ben Nuri says: Everything follows the color.

[6] *If a mikveh contained exactly forty se'ah and two people immersed in it one after the other, the first is cleansed but the second [remains] contaminated. Rabbi Yehudah says: If the feet of the first were [still] touching the water, even the second is cleansed. If one immersed a thick cloth in it [a mikveh of exactly forty se'ah] and lifted it out, [as long as] part of it touches the water [one who immerses in the mikveh] is cleansed.*

[If] a mattress or a cushion of leather [is immersed in such a mikveh], as soon as one lifts their edges from the water, the water within them is she'uvin. What should one do? One should immerse them and remove them holding their bottoms upward.

[7] *If one immersed a bed in it, then even if the legs sink into the thick mud it is cleansed, because the water comes first.*

A mikveh of shallow water: he may press down [material on one side of the mikveh], even bundles of wood, even bundles of reeds, to raise the water [level], then he goes down and immerses.

If a needle was placed on the steps of a cave and one moved the water to and fro, as soon as a wave passes over it [the needle] is cleansed.

If the *Mishnayos* were studied in the presence of a *minyan,* the Rabbis' *Kaddish,* (p. 52) is recited.

YAD AVRAHAM

achis for, unlike the water on a person's body, the water absorbed by the thick cloth has not been completely removed from the larger body of water. Consequently the person who immersed in this *mikveh* before the cloth was fully removed is cleansed. According to this interpretation, this view is accepted as halachah.

הַכַּר וְהַכֶּסֶת שֶׁל עוֹר — *A mattress or a cushion of leather.* These are leather sacks, open on one side, that are filled with stuffing when they are used. If one of these sacks is immersed in the *mikveh* and removed open side up, the water that has entered the sack becomes *she'uvin.* Since the *mikveh* in question originally contained exactly forty *se'ah,* if the *she'uvin* were poured back into the *mikveh,* it would become invalid.

דֶּרֶךְ שׁוּלֵיהֶם — *Holding their bottoms upward.* Water that enters the immersed cushion will remain in the *mikveh* and will not be lifted out with the cushion. Thus the water will not become *she'uvin.* Nevertheless, since some small amount of water must adhere to the leather and be removed from the *mikveh,* the *mikveh* is no longer valid until its *minimum* volume is restored.

7. This mishnah begins with the letter ה of נְשָׁמָה.

אֶת הַמִּטָּה — *A bed.* The mishnah refers to a bed with tall posts that is immersed in a shallow *mikveh,* the bottom of which is covered with thick mud. It is impossible for the entire bed to fit into the *mikveh's* water at one time unless the legs sink into the mud. But all parts of a utensil must be immersed at the same time if it is to be cleansed. Thus, the immersion of this bed in a shallow *mikveh* presents a halachic problem.

טְהוֹרָה מִפְּנֵי שֶׁהַמַּיִם מְקַדְּמִין — *It is cleansed, because the water comes first,* i.e., the legs of the bed became wet with *mikveh* water before sinking into the mud. Since the legs are still wet when the topmost part of the bed is immersed, and since that wetness is still connected to the water of the *mikveh,* the immersion is valid.

מִקְוֶה שֶׁמֵּימָיו מְרוּדָּדִין — *A mikveh of shallow water,* i.e., a body of water that covered a very large area but was too shallow for a person or utensil to be completely submerged at one time.

כּוֹבֵשׁ — *He may press down [material].* Since wood or reeds float on top of the *mikveh* and do not raise its level, stones may be placed on the bundles to press them down and hold them in place.

אֲפִילוּ חֲבִילֵי עֵצִים אֲפִילוּ חֲבִילֵי קָנִים — *Even bundles of wood, even bundles of reeds.* Although the bundles may seem to divide the *mikveh* into two bodies, thus invalidating it, since the water can

תפלה אחר למוד משניות על הנפטר

It is customary to recite this prayer whenever *Mishnayos* are studied in memory of a deceased.

אָנָּא יהוה מָלֵא רַחֲמִים, אֲשֶׁר בְּיָדְךָ נֶפֶשׁ כָּל חָי, וְרוּחַ כָּל בְּשַׂר אִישׁ.[1] יְהִיֶה נָא לְרָצוֹן לְפָנֶיךָ תּוֹרָתֵנוּ וּתְפִלָּתֵנוּ בַּעֲבוּר נִשְׁמַת (deceased's Hebrew name) בֶּן/בַּת (father's Hebrew name) וּגְמוֹל נָא עִמָּה בְּחַסְדְּךָ הַגָּדוֹל, לִפְתּוֹחַ לָהּ שַׁעֲרֵי רַחֲמִים וָחֶסֶד, וְשַׁעֲרֵי גַּן עֵדֶן.* וּתְקַבֵּל אוֹתָהּ בְּאַהֲבָה וּבְחִבָּה, וּשְׁלַח לָהּ מַלְאָכֶיךָ הַקְּדוֹשִׁים וְהַטְּהוֹרִים, לְהוֹלִיכָהּ וּלְהוֹשִׁיבָהּ תַּחַת עֵץ הַחַיִּים,* אֵצֶל נִשְׁמַת הַצַּדִּיקִים וְהַצִּדְקָנִיּוֹת, חֲסִידִים וַחֲסִידוֹת, לֵהָנוֹת מִזִּיו שְׁכִינָתְךָ, לְהַשְׂבִּיעָהּ מִטּוּבְךָ הַצָּפוּן לַצַּדִּיקִים. וְהַגּוּף יָנוּחַ בַּקֶּבֶר בִּמְנוּחָה נְכוֹנָה, בְּחֶדְוָה וּבְשִׂמְחָה וְשָׁלוֹם, כִּדְכְתִיב: יָבוֹא שָׁלוֹם, יָנוּחוּ עַל מִשְׁכְּבוֹתָם, הֹלֵךְ נְכֹחוֹ.[2] וּכְתִיב: יַעְלְזוּ חֲסִידִים בְּכָבוֹד, יְרַנְּנוּ עַל מִשְׁכְּבוֹתָם.[3] וּכְתִיב: אִם תִּשְׁכַּב לֹא תִפְחָד, וְשָׁכַבְתָּ וְעָרְבָה שְׁנָתֶךָ.[4]

for a male:

וְתִשְׁמוֹר אוֹתוֹ מֵחִבּוּט הַקֶּבֶר,* וּמֵרִמָּה וְתוֹלֵעָה. וְתִסְלַח וְתִמְחוֹל לוֹ עַל כָּל פְּשָׁעָיו, כִּי אָדָם אֵין צַדִּיק בָּאָרֶץ, אֲשֶׁר יַעֲשֶׂה טּוֹב וְלֹא יֶחֱטָא.[5] וּזְכוֹר לוֹ זְכֻיּוֹתָיו וְצִדְקוֹתָיו אֲשֶׁר עָשָׂה. וְתַשְׁפִּיעַ לוֹ מִנִּשְׁמָתוֹ לְדַשֵּׁן עַצְמוֹתָיו בַּקֶּבֶר מֵרֹב טוּב הַצָּפוּן לַצַּדִּיקִים, דִּכְתִיב: מָה רַב טוּבְךָ אֲשֶׁר צָפַנְתָּ לִּירֵאֶיךָ.[6] וּכְתִיב: שֹׁמֵר כָּל עַצְמֹתָיו, אַחַת מֵהֵנָּה לֹא נִשְׁבָּרָה.[7] וְיִשְׁכּוֹן בֶּטַח בָּדָד[8] וְשַׁאֲנַן מִפַּחַד רָעָה, וְאַל יִרְאֶה פְּנֵי גֵיהִנֹּם.* וְנִשְׁמָתוֹ תְּהֵא צְרוּרָה בִּצְרוֹר הַחַיִּים,*[9] וּלְהַחֲיוֹתוֹ בִּתְחִיַּת הַמֵּתִים עִם כָּל מֵתֵי עַמְּךָ יִשְׂרָאֵל בְּרַחֲמִים. אָמֵן.

for a female:

וְתִשְׁמוֹר אוֹתָהּ מֵחִבּוּט הַקֶּבֶר,* וּמֵרִמָּה וְתוֹלֵעָה. וְתִסְלַח וְתִמְחוֹל לָהּ עַל כָּל פְּשָׁעֶיהָ, כִּי אָדָם אֵין צַדִּיק בָּאָרֶץ, אֲשֶׁר יַעֲשֶׂה טּוֹב וְלֹא יֶחֱטָא.[5] וּזְכוֹר לָהּ זְכֻיּוֹתֶיהָ וְצִדְקוֹתֶיהָ אֲשֶׁר עָשְׂתָה. וְתַשְׁפִּיעַ לָהּ מִנִּשְׁמָתָהּ לְדַשֵּׁן עַצְמוֹתֶיהָ בַּקֶּבֶר מֵרֹב טוּב הַצָּפוּן לַצַּדִּיקִים, דִּכְתִיב: מָה רַב טוּבְךָ אֲשֶׁר צָפַנְתָּ לִּירֵאֶיךָ.[6] וּכְתִיב: שֹׁמֵר כָּל עַצְמֹתָיו, אַחַת מֵהֵנָּה לֹא נִשְׁבָּרָה.[7] וְתִשְׁכּוֹן בֶּטַח בָּדָד[8] וְשַׁאֲנַן מִפַּחַד רָעָה, וְאַל תִּרְאֶה פְּנֵי גֵיהִנֹּם.* וְנִשְׁמָתָהּ תְּהֵא צְרוּרָה בִּצְרוֹר הַחַיִּים,*[9] וּלְהַחֲיוֹתָהּ בִּתְחִיַּת הַמֵּתִים עִם כָּל מֵתֵי עַמְּךָ יִשְׂרָאֵל בְּרַחֲמִים. אָמֵן.

יד אברהם

flow freely through the bundles the water is considered as one body. Obviously stones that sink into the mud and raise the water's level may be used for this purpose. However, a dam that divides the pool into two bodies of water would create two incomplete *mikvaos*.

מַחַט — *A needle* became contaminated, but the person who was to immerse it was apprehensive lest it slip from his hand and be lost in the *mikveh*. He therefore placed the needle on the steps leading to a *mikveh*, and swished the water until it passed over the needle. As long as the

PRAYER AFTER THE STUDY OF MISHNAH FOR THE DECEASED

It is customary to recite this prayer whenever *Mishnayos* are studied in memory of a deceased.

אָנָּא *Please, O* HASHEM, *full of mercy, for in Your hand is the soul of all the living and the spirit of every human being,*[1] *may You find favor in our Torah study and prayer for the soul of* (deceased's Hebrew name) *son/daughter of* (father's Hebrew name) *and do with it according to Your great kindness to open for it the gates of mercy and kindness and the gates of the Garden of Eden.* Accept it with love and affection and send it Your holy and pure angels to lead it and to settle it under the Tree of Life* near the souls of the righteous and devout men and women, to enjoy the radiance of Your Presence, to satiate it from Your good that is concealed for the righteous. May the body repose in the grave with proper contentment, pleasure, gladness and peace, as it is written: 'Let him enter in peace, let them rest on their beds — everyone who has lived in his proper way.'*[2] *And it is written: 'Let the devout exult in glory, let them sing joyously upon their beds.'*[3] *And it is written: 'If you lay down, you will not fear; when you lay down, your sleep will be sweet.'*[4] *And protect him/her from the tribulations of the grave* and from worms and maggots. Forgive and pardon him/her for all his/her sins, for there is no man so wholly righteous on earth that he does good and never sins.*[5] *Remember for him/her the merits and righteous deeds that he/she performed, and cause a spiritual flow from his/her soul to keep his/her bones fresh in the grave from the abundant good that is concealed for the righteous, as it is written: 'How abundant is Your goodness that You have concealed for Your reverent ones,'*[6] *and it is written: 'He guards all his bones, even one of them was not broken.'*[7] *May it rest secure, alone,*[8] *and serene, from fear of evil and may it not see the threshold of Gehinnom.* May his/her soul be bound in the Bond of Life.**[9] *And may it be brought back to life with the Resuscitation of the Dead with all the dead of Your people Israel, with mercy. Amen.*

(1) Cf. *Job* 12:10. (2) *Isaiah* 57:2. (3) *Psalms* 149:5. (4) *Proverbs* 3:24. (5) *Ecclesiastes* 7:20. (6) *Psalms* 31:20. (7) 34:21. (8) Cf. *Deuteronomy* 33:28. (9) Cf. *I Samuel* 25:29.

water did not become detached from the main body, the needle is cleansed.

הַמְּעָרָה — *A cave.* The bodies of water found in many of the caves dotting the Judean hills are often valid *mikvaos* and were frequently used as such in earlier times. Thus a *mikveh* is often referred to as a cave.

PRAYER AFTER MISHNAYOS FOR THE DECEASED

גַּן עֵדֶן — *Garden of Eden.* The term Garden of Eden is widely used in traditional literature to denote the spiritual reward of the righteous in the World to Come. It is not identical with the Garden of Eden mentioned in the Creation as the dwelling place of Adam. As *Ramban* puts it *(Comm.* to *Genesis* 3:22): 'The Garden of Eden is on this earth as is the Tree of Life ... but just as they are on the earth so do they have their Heavenly counterparts which are called by the same names and which are the foundations of those on earth ...'

עֵץ הַחַיִּים — *The Tree of Life.* One of the many phases of the Eternal Life; see above, s.v. גַּן עֵדֶן.

חִבּוּט הַקֶּבֶר — *Tribulations of the grave* [lit. *beating of the grave*]. A metaphor for the suffering of the body in its grave. R' Eliyahu de Vidas in his classic *Reshis Chachmah* reproduces a small midrash which describes graphically the pain one may be subjected to in this phase of retribution.

גֵּיהִנֹּם — *Gehinnom.* So named after the Valley of Hinnom *(Joshua* 18:16) near Jerusalem. One of the seven names for the place designated for the punishment of sinners *(Eruvin* 19a) and their ultimate rehabilitation and entry into the Garden of Eden.

צְרוֹר הַחַיִּים — *Bond of Life.* One of the Scriptural metaphors for the spiritual reward in the World to Come (see *I Samuel* 25:29).

סדר הזכרת נשמות

Yizkor, the memorial service for the departed, is recited before אַב הָרַחֲמִים on the eighth day of Pesach, the second day of Shavuos, Yom Kippur and Shemini Atzeres.

Those congregants whose both parents are living do not participate in the *Yizkor* service, but leave the synagogue and return when the congregation begins אַב הָרַחֲמִים after *Yizkor.*

Although the following verses are not part of the traditional *Yizkor* service, some congregations have adopted the custom of responsively reciting them before *Yizkor:*

יהוה, מָה אָדָם וַתֵּדָעֵהוּ, בֶּן אֱנוֹשׁ וַתְּחַשְּׁבֵהוּ.
אָדָם לַהֶבֶל דָּמָה, יָמָיו כְּצֵל עוֹבֵר.[1]
בַּבֹּקֶר יָצִיץ וְחָלָף, לָעֶרֶב יְמוֹלֵל וְיָבֵשׁ.[2]
לִמְנוֹת יָמֵינוּ כֵּן הוֹדַע, וְנָבִא לְבַב חָכְמָה.[3]
שְׁמָר תָּם וּרְאֵה יָשָׁר, כִּי אַחֲרִית לְאִישׁ שָׁלוֹם.[4]
אַךְ אֱלֹהִים יִפְדֶּה נַפְשִׁי מִיַּד שְׁאוֹל, כִּי יִקָּחֵנִי סֶלָה.[5]
כָּלָה שְׁאֵרִי וּלְבָבִי, צוּר לְבָבִי וְחֶלְקִי אֱלֹהִים לְעוֹלָם.[6]
וְיָשֹׁב הֶעָפָר עַל הָאָרֶץ כְּשֶׁהָיָה, וְהָרוּחַ תָּשׁוּב אֶל הָאֱלֹהִים אֲשֶׁר נְתָנָהּ.[7]

תהלים צא (Commentary on p. 380)

יֹשֵׁב בְּסֵתֶר עֶלְיוֹן, בְּצֵל שַׁדַּי יִתְלוֹנָן. אֹמַר לַיהוה, מַחְסִי וּמְצוּדָתִי, אֱלֹהַי אֶבְטַח בּוֹ. כִּי הוּא יַצִּילְךָ מִפַּח יָקוּשׁ, מִדֶּבֶר הַוּוֹת. בְּאֶבְרָתוֹ יָסֶךְ לָךְ, וְתַחַת כְּנָפָיו תֶּחְסֶה, צִנָּה וְסֹחֵרָה אֲמִתּוֹ. לֹא תִירָא מִפַּחַד לָיְלָה, מֵחֵץ יָעוּף יוֹמָם. מִדֶּבֶר בָּאֹפֶל יַהֲלֹךְ, מִקֶּטֶב יָשׁוּד צָהֳרָיִם. יִפֹּל מִצִּדְּךָ אֶלֶף, וּרְבָבָה מִימִינֶךָ, אֵלֶיךָ לֹא יִגָּשׁ. רַק בְּעֵינֶיךָ תַבִּיט, וְשִׁלֻּמַת רְשָׁעִים תִּרְאֶה. כִּי אַתָּה יהוה מַחְסִי, עֶלְיוֹן שַׂמְתָּ מְעוֹנֶךָ. לֹא תְאֻנֶּה אֵלֶיךָ רָעָה, וְנֶגַע לֹא יִקְרַב בְּאָהֳלֶךָ. כִּי מַלְאָכָיו יְצַוֶּה לָּךְ, לִשְׁמָרְךָ בְּכָל דְּרָכֶיךָ. עַל כַּפַּיִם יִשָּׂאוּנְךָ, פֶּן תִּגֹּף בָּאֶבֶן רַגְלֶךָ. עַל שַׁחַל וָפֶתֶן תִּדְרֹךְ, תִּרְמֹס כְּפִיר וְתַנִּין. כִּי בִי חָשַׁק וַאֲפַלְּטֵהוּ, אֲשַׂגְּבֵהוּ, כִּי יָדַע שְׁמִי. יִקְרָאֵנִי וְאֶעֱנֵהוּ, עִמּוֹ אָנֹכִי בְצָרָה, אֲחַלְּצֵהוּ וַאֲכַבְּדֵהוּ. אֹרֶךְ יָמִים אַשְׂבִּיעֵהוּ, וְאַרְאֵהוּ בִּישׁוּעָתִי. אֹרֶךְ יָמִים אַשְׂבִּיעֵהוּ, וְאַרְאֵהוּ בִּישׁוּעָתִי.

Whenever the name of the deceased is mentioned in the *Yizkor* service, it is given in the following form: the Hebrew name of the deceased followed by the word בֶּן, *son of* — or, בַּת, *daughter of* — and then the deceased's father's Hebrew name.

FOR ONE'S FATHER

יִזְכֹּר אֱלֹהִים* נִשְׁמַת אָבִי מוֹרִי (name of the deceased) שֶׁהָלַךְ לְעוֹלָמוֹ, בַּעֲבוּר שֶׁבְּלִי נֶדֶר אֶתֵּן צְדָקָה בַּעֲדוֹ. בִּשְׂכַר זֶה תְּהֵא נַפְשׁוֹ צְרוּרָה בִּצְרוֹר הַחַיִּים* עִם נִשְׁמוֹת אַבְרָהָם יִצְחָק וְיַעֲקֹב, שָׂרָה רִבְקָה רָחֵל וְלֵאָה, וְעִם שְׁאָר צַדִּיקִים וְצִדְקָנִיּוֹת שֶׁבְּגַן עֵדֶן.* וְנֹאמַר: אָמֵן.

YIZKOR / יִזְכּוֹר

The ancient custom of recalling the souls of the departed and contributing to charity in their memory is rooted in the fundamental Jewish belief in the eternity of the soul. When physical life ends, only the body dies, but the soul ascends to the realm of the spirit where it regularly attains higher levels of purity and holiness.

When this life is over, the soul can no longer perform good deeds; that method of attaining merit is the sole province of mortal man who must struggle with the baseness and selfishness of his animal nature. But there is a way that the disembodied soul can derive new sources of merit. History is a continuum. If we, the living, give charity or do good deeds due to the lasting influence or in memory of a departed parent or other loved one, the merit is truly that of the soul in its spiritual realm. Moreover, God in His mercy credits our deed to the departed one because he or she too would have done the same were it possible. But mere intentions do not suffice; only accomplishment can achieve this purpose. The intention to give and the fulfillment of that intention are both necessary.

The earliest source of the *Yizkor* custom is *Midrash Tanchuma, Haazinu,* which cites the custom of recalling the departed and pledging charity on their behalf on Yom Kippur.

YIZKOR

Yizkor, the memorial service for the departed, is recited before אַב הָרַחֲמִים, *Father of Compassion,* on the eighth day of Pesach, the second day of Shavuos, Yom Kippur and Shemini Atzeres.

Those congregants whose both parents are living do not participate in the *Yizkor* service, but leave the synagogue and return when the congregation begins אַב הָרַחֲמִים, *Father of Compassion,* after *Yizkor.*

Although the following verses are not part of the traditional *Yizkor* service, some congregations have adopted the custom of responsively reciting them before *Yizkor:*

יהוה *HASHEM, what is man that You recognize him? The son of a frail human that You reckon with him?*

Man is like a breath, his days are like a passing shadow.[1]

In the morning it blossoms and is rejuvenated, by evening it is cut down and brittle.[2]

According to the count of our days, so may You teach us;
then we shall acquire a heart of wisdom.[3]

Safeguard the perfect and watch the upright, for the destiny of that man is peace.[4]

But God will redeem my soul from the grip of the Lower World,
for He will take me, Selah![5]

My flesh and my heart yearn — Rock of my heart, and my portion is God, forever.[6]

Thus the dust returns to the ground as it was, and the spirit returns to God who gave it.[7]

Psalm 91 (Commentary on p. 380.)

יֹשֵׁב *Whoever sits in the refuge of the Most High, he shall dwell in the shadow of the Almighty. I will say of HASHEM, 'He is my refuge and my fortress, my God, I will trust in Him.' That He will deliver you from the ensnaring trap and from devastating pestilence. With His pinion He will cover you, and beneath His wings you will be protected; shield and armor is His truth. You shall not be afraid of the terror of night, nor of the arrow that flies by day; nor the pestilence that walks in gloom, nor the destroyer who lays waste at noon. Let a thousand encamp at your side and a myriad at your right hand, but to you they shall not approach. You will merely peer with your eyes and you will see the retribution of the wicked. Because [you said], 'You, HASHEM, are my refuge'; you have made the Most High your dwelling place. No evil will befall you, nor will any plague come near your tent. He will charge His angels for you, to protect you in all your ways. On your palms they will carry you, lest you strike your foot against a stone. Upon the lion and the viper you will tread; you will trample the young lion and the serpent. For he has yearned for Me and I will deliver him; I will elevate him because he knows My Name. He will call upon Me and I will answer him, I am with him in distress, I will release him and I will honor him I will satisfy him with long life and show him My salvation. I will satisfy him with long life and show him My salvation.*

Whenever the name of the deceased is mentioned in the *Yizkor* service, it is given in the following form: the Hebrew name of the deceased followed by בֶּן, *son of* — or, בַּת, *daughter of* — and then the deceased's father's Hebrew name.

FOR ONE'S FATHER

יִזְכֹּר *May God remember* the soul of my father, my teacher,* (name of the deceased) *who has gone on to his world, because, without making a vow, I shall give to charity on his behalf. As reward for this, may his soul be bound in the Bond of Life,* together with the souls of Abraham, Isaac, and Jacob; Sarah, Rebecca, Rachel, and Leah; and together with the other righteous men and women in the Garden of Eden.* Now let us respond: Amen.*

(1) *Psalms* 144:3-4. (2) 90:6. (3) 90:12. (4) 37:37. (5) 49:16. (6) 73:26. (7) *Ecclesiastes* 12:7.

Ashkenazic Jewry's custom of reciting *Yizkor* on the three pilgrimage festivals is of a later origin, possibly the time of the Crusades when bloody massacres wiped out many Jewish communities and seriously hurt many others. The three festivals, which the Torah ordains as times of charity, were chosen as times to remember the dead and pray that the generosity of the living should be a source of merit for their souls.

It should be noted that a נֶדֶר, *vow, is a* very serious matter in Jewish law, and one must be scrupulous in fulfilling his vows. In order to avoid the possibility that one may make a pledge and then forget to carry it out, we follow the practice of many *siddurim* in not using the word נֶדֶר, *vow,* in the *Yizkor* text. Instead, we use the form שֶׁבְּלִי נֶדֶר אֶתֵּן, *without making a vow I shall give.*

יִזְכּוֹר אֱלֹהִים — *May God remember.* In calling

FOR ONE'S MOTHER

יִזְכֹּר אֱלֹהִים* נִשְׁמַת אִמִּי מוֹרָתִי (name of the deceased) שֶׁהָלְּכָה לְעוֹלָמָהּ, בַּעֲבוּר שֶׁבְּלִי נֶדֶר אֶתֵּן צְדָקָה בַּעֲדָהּ. בִּשְׂכַר זֶה תְּהֵא נַפְשָׁהּ צְרוּרָה בִּצְרוֹר הַחַיִּים* עִם נִשְׁמוֹת אַבְרָהָם יִצְחָק וְיַעֲקֹב, שָׂרָה רִבְקָה רָחֵל וְלֵאָה, וְעִם שְׁאָר צַדִּיקִים וְצִדְקָנִיּוֹת שֶׁבְּגַן עֵדֶן.* וְנֹאמַר: אָמֵן.

FOR A MALE RELATIVE

husband	son	brother	uncle	grandfather
בַּעְלִי	בְּנִי	אָחִי	דּוֹדִי	זְקֵנִי

יִזְכֹּר אֱלֹהִים* נִשְׁמַת (name of the deceased) שֶׁהָלַךְ לְעוֹלָמוֹ, בַּעֲבוּר שֶׁבְּלִי נֶדֶר אֶתֵּן צְדָקָה בַּעֲדוֹ. בִּשְׂכַר זֶה תְּהֵא נַפְשׁוֹ צְרוּרָה בִּצְרוֹר הַחַיִּים* עִם נִשְׁמוֹת אַבְרָהָם יִצְחָק וְיַעֲקֹב, שָׂרָה רִבְקָה רָחֵל וְלֵאָה, וְעִם שְׁאָר צַדִּיקִים וְצִדְקָנִיּוֹת שֶׁבְּגַן עֵדֶן.* וְנֹאמַר: אָמֵן.

FOR A FEMALE RELATIVE

wife	daughter	sister	aunt	grandmother
אִשְׁתִּי	בִּתִּי	אֲחוֹתִי	דּוֹדָתִי	זְקֶנְתִּי

יִזְכֹּר אֱלֹהִים* נִשְׁמַת (name of the deceased) שֶׁהָלְּכָה לְעוֹלָמָהּ, בַּעֲבוּר שֶׁבְּלִי נֶדֶר אֶתֵּן צְדָקָה בַּעֲדָהּ. בִּשְׂכַר זֶה תְּהֵא נַפְשָׁהּ צְרוּרָה בִּצְרוֹר הַחַיִּים* עִם נִשְׁמוֹת אַבְרָהָם יִצְחָק וְיַעֲקֹב, שָׂרָה רִבְקָה רָחֵל וְלֵאָה, וְעִם שְׁאָר צַדִּיקִים וְצִדְקָנִיּוֹת שֶׁבְּגַן עֵדֶן.* וְנֹאמַר: אָמֵן.

FOR ONE'S EXTENDED FAMILY

יִזְכֹּר אֱלֹהִים* נִשְׁמוֹת זְקֵנַי וּזְקֵנוֹתַי, דּוֹדַי וְדוֹדוֹתַי, אַחַי וְאַחְיוֹתַי, הֵן מִצַּד אָבִי, הֵן מִצַּד אִמִּי, שֶׁהָלְּכוּ לְעוֹלָמָם, בַּעֲבוּר שֶׁבְּלִי נֶדֶר אֶתֵּן צְדָקָה בַּעֲדָם. בִּשְׂכַר זֶה תִּהְיֶינָה נַפְשׁוֹתֵיהֶם צְרוּרוֹת בִּצְרוֹר הַחַיִּים* עִם נִשְׁמוֹת אַבְרָהָם יִצְחָק וְיַעֲקֹב, שָׂרָה רִבְקָה רָחֵל וְלֵאָה, וְעִם שְׁאָר צַדִּיקִים וְצִדְקָנִיּוֹת שֶׁבְּגַן עֵדֶן.* וְנֹאמַר: אָמֵן.

FOR MARTYRS

יִזְכֹּר אֱלֹהִים* נִשְׁמוֹת (כָּל קְרוֹבַי וּקְרוֹבוֹתַי, הֵן מִצַּד אָבִי, הֵן מִצַּד אִמִּי) הַקְּדוֹשִׁים וְהַטְּהוֹרִים שֶׁהוּמְתוּ וְשֶׁנֶּהֶרְגוּ וְשֶׁנִּשְׁחֲטוּ וְשֶׁנִּשְׂרְפוּ וְשֶׁנִּטְבְּעוּ וְשֶׁנֶּחְנְקוּ עַל קִדּוּשׁ הַשֵּׁם, בַּעֲבוּר שֶׁבְּלִי נֶדֶר אֶתֵּן צְדָקָה בְּעַד הַזְכָּרַת נִשְׁמוֹתֵיהֶם. בִּשְׂכַר זֶה תִּהְיֶינָה נַפְשׁוֹתֵיהֶם צְרוּרוֹת בִּצְרוֹר הַחַיִּים* עִם נִשְׁמוֹת אַבְרָהָם יִצְחָק וְיַעֲקֹב, שָׂרָה רִבְקָה רָחֵל וְלֵאָה, וְעִם שְׁאָר צַדִּיקִים וְצִדְקָנִיּוֹת שֶׁבְּגַן עֵדֶן.* וְנֹאמַר: אָמֵן.

FOR MEMBERS OF THE ISRAEL DEFENSE FORCE

יִזְכֹּר אֱלֹהִים אֶת נִשְׁמוֹת חַיָּלֵי צְבָא הֲגָנָּה לְיִשְׂרָאֵל שֶׁמָּסְרוּ נַפְשָׁם עַל קְדֻשַּׁת הַשֵּׁם, הָעָם וְהָאָרֶץ, וְנָפְלוּ מוֹת גִּבּוֹרִים בְּתַפְקִידֵי שִׁחְרוּר, הֲגָנָּה וּבִטָּחוֹן. מִנְּשָׁרִים קַלּוּ, וּמֵאֲרָיוֹת גָּבֵרוּ, בְּהֵחָלְצָם לְעֶזְרַת הָעָם, וְהִרְווּ בְּדָמָם הַטָּהוֹר אֶת רִגְבֵי אַדְמַת קָדְשֵׁנוּ. זֵכֶר עֲקֵדָתָם וּמַעֲשֵׂי גְבוּרָתָם לֹא יָסוּפוּ מֵאִתָּנוּ לְעוֹלָמִים. תִּהְיֶינָה נִשְׁמוֹתֵיהֶם צְרוּרוֹת בִּצְרוֹר הַחַיִּים עִם נִשְׁמוֹת אַבְרָהָם יִצְחָק וְיַעֲקֹב, וְעִם נִשְׁמוֹת שְׁאָר גִּבּוֹרֵי יִשְׂרָאֵל וּקְדוֹשָׁיו שֶׁבְּגַן עֵדֶן. אָמֵן.

FOR ONE'S MOTHER

יִזְכֹּר *May God remember* the soul of my Mother, my teacher,* (name of the deceased) *who has gone on to her world, because, without making a vow, I shall give to charity on her behalf. As reward for this, may her soul be bound in the Bond of Life,* together with the souls of Abraham, Isaac, and Jacob; Sarah, Rebecca, Rachel, and Leah; and together with the other righteous men and women in the Garden of Eden.* Now let us respond: Amen.*

FOR A RELATIVE

יִזְכֹּר *May God remember* the soul of my grandfather/grandmother/uncle/aunt/brother/sister/son/daughter/husband/wife* (name of the deceased) *who has gone on to his/her world, because, without making a vow, I shall give to charity on his/her behalf. As reward for this, may his/her soul be bound in the Bond of Life,* together with the souls of Abraham, Isaac, and Jacob; Sarah, Rebecca, Rachel, and Leah; and together with the other righteous men and women in the Garden of Eden.* Now let us respond: Amen.*

FOR ONE'S EXTENDED FAMILY

יִזְכֹּר *May God remember* the souls of my grandfathers and grandmothers, uncles and aunts, brothers and sisters both on my father's side and on my mother's side, who went on to their world, because, without making a vow, I shall give to charity on their behalf. As reward for this, may their souls be bound in the Bond of Life,* together with the souls of Abraham, Isaac, and Jacob; Sarah, Rebecca, Rachel, and Leah; and together with the other righteous men and women in the Garden of Eden.* Now let us respond: Amen.*

FOR MARTYRS

יִזְכֹּר *May God remember* the souls of (all my relatives, both on my father's side and on my mother's side), the holy and pure one who were killed, murdered, slaughtered, burned, drowned and strangled for the sanctification of the Name, because, without making a vow, I shall give to charity on their behalf. As reward for this, may their souls be bound in the Bond of Life,* together with the souls of Abraham, Isaac, and Jacob; Sarah, Rebecca, Rachel, and Leah; and together with the other righteous men and women in the Garden of Eden.* Now let us respond: Amen.*

FOR MEMBERS OF THE ISRAEL DEFENSE FORCE

יִזְכֹּר *May God remember the souls of the fighters of the Israel Defense Force who gave their lives for the sanctification of the Name, the People and the Land; who died a heroic death in missions of liberation, defense and security. They were quicker than eagles and stronger than lions as they volunteered to assist the people and with their pure blood soaked the clods of our holy earth. The memory of their self-sacrifice and heroic deeds will never perish from us. May their souls be bound in the Bond of Life with the souls of Abraham, Isaac and Jacob, and with the souls of the other Jewish heroes and martyrs who are in the Garden of Eden. Amen.*

---

upon God to 'remember' the soul of the departed, we do not suggest that the possibility of forgetting exists before the All-Knowing One. Rather we pray that in return for our devotion and generosity, God should take cognizance of the new source of merit for the soul whose memory is now influencing our conduct.

בִּצְרוֹר הַחַיִּים — *In the Bond of Life.* The ultimate life is that of the spirit, which is eternal and which is unlimited by the constraints of time and space and the weakness of flesh. The greater the merit achieved by a soul during its time on earth — or as a result of our good deeds in its memory — the more it is bound together with the souls of the Patriarchs and Matriarchs.

בְּגַן עֵדֶן — *In the Garden of Eden.* Although literally this is the place where Adam and Eve lived until their sin caused them to be driven out, it is also used to refer to the spiritual paradise

After reciting *Yizkor* it is customary to recite the following prayer(s).

אֵל מָלֵא רַחֲמִים, שׁוֹכֵן בַּמְּרוֹמִים, הַמְצֵא מְנוּחָה נְכוֹנָה* עַל כַּנְפֵי הַשְּׁכִינָה,* בְּמַעֲלוֹת קְדוֹשִׁים וּטְהוֹרִים* כְּזֹהַר הָרָקִיעַ מַזְהִירִים,

for a man

אֶת נִשְׁמַת (name of the deceased) שֶׁהָלַךְ לְעוֹלָמוֹ, בַּעֲבוּר שֶׁבְּלִי נֶדֶר אֶתֵּן צְדָקָה בְּעַד הַזְכָּרַת נִשְׁמָתוֹ, בְּגַן עֵדֶן תְּהֵא מְנוּחָתוֹ, לָכֵן בַּעַל הָרַחֲמִים יַסְתִּירֵהוּ בְּסֵתֶר כְּנָפָיו לְעוֹלָמִים, וְיִצְרוֹר בִּצְרוֹר הַחַיִּים אֶת נִשְׁמָתוֹ, יהוה הוּא נַחֲלָתוֹ, וְיָנוּחַ בְּשָׁלוֹם עַל מִשְׁכָּבוֹ. וְנֹאמַר: אָמֵן.

for a woman

אֶת נִשְׁמַת (name of the deceased) שֶׁהָלְכָה לְעוֹלָמָהּ, בַּעֲבוּר שֶׁבְּלִי נֶדֶר אֶתֵּן צְדָקָה בְּעַד הַזְכָּרַת נִשְׁמָתָהּ, בְּגַן עֵדֶן תְּהֵא מְנוּחָתָהּ, לָכֵן בַּעַל הָרַחֲמִים יַסְתִּירֶהָ בְּסֵתֶר כְּנָפָיו לְעוֹלָמִים, וְיִצְרוֹר בִּצְרוֹר הַחַיִּים אֶת נִשְׁמָתָהּ, יהוה הוּא נַחֲלָתָהּ, וְתָנוּחַ בְּשָׁלוֹם עַל מִשְׁכָּבָהּ. וְנֹאמַר: אָמֵן.

FOR MARTYRS

אֵל מָלֵא רַחֲמִים, שׁוֹכֵן בַּמְּרוֹמִים, דַּיַּן אַלְמָנוֹת וַאֲבִי יְתוֹמִים, הַמְצֵא מְנוּחָה נְכוֹנָה* עַל כַּנְפֵי הַשְּׁכִינָה,* בְּמַעֲלוֹת קְדוֹשִׁים וּטְהוֹרִים* כְּזֹהַר הָרָקִיעַ מַזְהִירִים, לְנִשְׁמוֹת רִבְבוֹת אַלְפֵי יִשְׂרָאֵל, אֲנָשִׁים נָשִׁים וָטַף, שֶׁנֶּהֶרְגוּ וְשֶׁנִּשְׁחֲטוּ, שֶׁנֶּחְנְקוּ וְשֶׁנִּשְׂרְפוּ וְשֶׁנִּקְבְּרוּ חַיִּים, עַל קִדּוּשׁ הַשֵּׁם. כֻּלָּם קְדוֹשִׁים וּטְהוֹרִים, וּבָהֶם גְּאוֹנִים וְצַדִּיקִים, אַרְזֵי הַלְּבָנוֹן וְאַדִּירֵי הַתּוֹרָה. בַּעַל הָרַחֲמִים יַסְתִּירֵם בְּסֵתֶר כְּנָפָיו לְעוֹלָמִים, וְיִצְרוֹר בִּצְרוֹר הַחַיִּים אֶת נִשְׁמוֹתֵיהֶם, בְּגַן עֵדֶן תְּהֵא מְנוּחָתָם, יהוה הוּא נַחֲלָתָם, יִזְכֹּר עֲקֵדָתָם וְתַעֲמוֹד לָנוּ וּלְכָל יִשְׂרָאֵל צִדְקָתָם. אֶרֶץ אַל תְּכַסִּי דָמָם וְאַל יְהִי מָקוֹם לְזַעֲקָתָם, בִּזְכוּתָם יָשׁוּבוּ נִדְחֵי יִשְׂרָאֵל לַאֲחֻזָּתָם, וְהַקְּדוֹשִׁים לְזִכְרוֹן תָּמִיד נֶגֶד יהוה יַעַמְדוּ לְגוֹרָלָם, יָבוֹאוּ שָׁלוֹם וְיָנוּחוּ עַל מִשְׁכְּבוֹתָם, וְיָקוּמוּ לְקֵץ הַיָּמִין לְחַיּוּתָם, וְנֹאמַר: אָמֵן.

FOR MEMBERS OF THE ISRAEL DEFENSE FORCE

אֵל מָלֵא רַחֲמִים, שׁוֹכֵן בַּמְּרוֹמִים, הַמְצֵא מְנוּחָה נְכוֹנָה* עַל כַּנְפֵי הַשְּׁכִינָה,* בְּמַעֲלוֹת קְדוֹשִׁים וּטְהוֹרִים* כְּזֹהַר הָרָקִיעַ מַזְהִירִים, לְנִשְׁמוֹת חַיָּלֵי צְבָא הַהֲגַנָּה לְיִשְׂרָאֵל אֲשֶׁר מָסְרוּ נַפְשָׁם עַל קְדֻשַּׁת הַשֵּׁם וְעַל כִּבּוּשׁ הָאָרֶץ. בַּעַל הָרַחֲמִים יַסְתִּירֵם בְּסֵתֶר כְּנָפָיו לְעוֹלָמִים, וְיִצְרוֹר בִּצְרוֹר הַחַיִּים אֶת נִשְׁמוֹתֵיהֶם, יהוה הוּא נַחֲלָתָם, בְּגַן עֵדֶן תְּהֵא מְנוּחָתָם, וְיָנוּחוּ בְּשָׁלוֹם עַל מִשְׁכְּבוֹתָם. וְנֹאמַר: אָמֵן.

---

because it implies spiritual perfection and bliss.

☙ אֵל ... הַמְצֵא מְנוּחָה נְכוֹנָה — *O God, ... grant proper rest.* The fact that a soul is in Paradise does not guarantee it complete contentment. Its level there depends on its prior achievements here on earth, consequently there are as many degrees there as there are degrees of righteousness on earth. Through our prayers and deeds, we hope to earn God's compassion upon the departed soul.

עַל כַּנְפֵי הַשְּׁכִינָה — *On the wings of the Divine Presence.* When this term is used to mean

After reciting *Yizkor* it is customary to recite the following prayer(s).

אֵל *O God, full of mercy, Who dwells on high, grant proper rest* on the wings of the Divine Presence* — in the lofty levels of the holy and the pure ones,* who shine like the glow of the firmament — for the soul of*

for a man

(name of the deceased) *who went on to his world, because, without making a vow, I will contribute to charity in remembrance of his soul. May his resting place be in the Garden of Eden — therefore may the Master of mercy shelter him in the shelter of His wings for eternity; and may He bind his soul in the Bond of Life. HASHEM is his heritage, and may he repose in peace on his resting place. Now let us respond: Amen.*

for a woman

(name of the deceased) *who went on to her world, because, without making a vow, I will contribute to charity in remembrance of her soul. May her resting place be in the Garden of Eden — therefore may the Master of mercy shelter her in the shelter of His wings for eternity; and may He bind her soul in the Bond of Life. HASHEM is her heritage, and may she repose in peace on her resting place. Now let us respond: Amen.*

FOR MARTYRS

אֵל *O God, full of mercy, Who dwells on high, Defender of widows and Father of orphans, grant proper rest* on the wings of the Divine Presence* — in the lofty levels of the holy and the pure ones,* who shine like the glow of the firmament — for the souls of millions of Jews, men, women and children, who were brutally and tortuously murdered, gassed and cremated, or buried alive, for the sanctification of Your Name. Holy and pure were they all, among them scholars and saints as majestic in Torah as the cedars of Lebanon. May the Master of Mercy shelter them in the shelter of His wings for eternity and may He bind their souls in the Bond of Life. May their resting place be in the Garden of Eden. HASHEM is their heritage. May He remember their martyrdom, and may their righteousness stand in merit for us and all Israel. Earth, do not cover their blood! Do not silence their cries! In their merit may the scattered ones of Israel be gathered to their possession. May the martyrs' righteousness forever be before HASHEM. May they repose in peace in their resting places and rise at the end of days to life. Now let us respond: Amen.*

FOR MEMBERS OF THE ISRAEL DEFENSE FORCE

אֵל *O God, full of mercy, Who dwells on high, grant proper rest* on the wings of the Divine Presence* — in the lofty levels of the holy and the pure ones,* who shine like the glow of the firmament — for the souls of the members of the Israel Defense Force, who gave up their lives for the sanctification of Your Name and for the conquest of the Land. May the Master of Mercy shelter them in the shelter of His wings for eternity and may he bind their souls in the Bond of Life. HASHEM is their heritage. May their resting place be in the Garden of Eden. May they repose in peace in their resting places. Now let us respond: Amen.*

Heavenly protection from danger, we say תַּחַת, *under* the wings, using the analogy of a bird spreading its protective wings over its young. In this prayer, where we speak of spiritual elevation, we reverse the analogy, comparing God's Presence to a soaring eagle that puts its young on top of its wings and carries them aloft.

קְדוֹשִׁים וּטְהוֹרִים — *The holy and the pure ones,* a reference to the angels.

סְלִיחוֹת וְיוֹצְרוֹת

Selichos and Yotzros

סליחות

Selichos are recited immediately after the *chazzan's* repetition of *Shemoneh Esrei* on the appropriate fast days: the Fasts of *Behab,* the Tenth of Teves, the Fast of Esther and the Seventeenth of Tammuz. (On the Ninth of Av, *Kinos* are recited; on the Fast of Gedaliah, the *Selichos* of the Ten Days of Repentance are recited.) Even those not fasting should join the congregation in reciting *Selichos.* Though it is preferable to stand during *Selichos,* those who find it difficult to do so should stand at least during אֵל מֶלֶךְ, אֵל אֶרֶךְ אַפַּיִם, the Thirteen Attributes, and שְׁמַע קוֹלֵנוּ.

The introductory portion of *Selichos* is identical on all fast days.

סְלַח לָנוּ אָבִינוּ, כִּי בְרוֹב אִוַּלְתֵּנוּ שָׁגִינוּ,
מְחַל לָנוּ מַלְכֵּנוּ, כִּי רַבּוּ עֲוֹנֵינוּ.

אֵל אֶרֶךְ אַפַּיִם אַתָּה, וּבַעַל הָרַחֲמִים נִקְרֵאתָ, וְדֶרֶךְ תְּשׁוּבָה הוֹרֵיתָ.
גְּדֻלַּת רַחֲמֶיךָ וַחֲסָדֶיךָ, תִּזְכּוֹר הַיּוֹם וּבְכָל יוֹם לְזֶרַע יְדִידֶיךָ.
תֵּפֶן אֵלֵינוּ בְּרַחֲמִים, כִּי אַתָּה הוּא בַּעַל הָרַחֲמִים.
בְּתַחֲנוּן וּבִתְפִלָּה פָּנֶיךָ נְקַדֵּם, כְּהוֹדַעְתָּ לֶעָנָיו מִקֶּדֶם.
מֵחֲרוֹן אַפְּךָ שׁוּב, כְּמוֹ בְתוֹרָתְךָ כָּתוּב.
וּבְצֵל כְּנָפֶיךָ נֶחֱסֶה וְנִתְלוֹנָן, כְּיוֹם וַיֵּרֶד יהוה בֶּעָנָן.
❖ תַּעֲבוֹר עַל פֶּשַׁע וְתִמְחֶה אָשָׁם, כְּיוֹם וַיִּתְיַצֵּב עִמּוֹ שָׁם.
תַּאֲזִין שַׁוְעָתֵנוּ וְתַקְשִׁיב מֶנּוּ מַאֲמַר, כְּיוֹם וַיִּקְרָא בְשֵׁם יהוה,[1]* וְשָׁם נֶאֱמַר.

Congregation and *chazzan* recite loudly and in unison:

וַיַּעֲבֹר יהוה עַל פָּנָיו וַיִּקְרָא:

יהוה, יהוה, אֵל, רַחוּם, וְחַנּוּן, אֶרֶךְ אַפַּיִם, וְרַב חֶסֶד, וֶאֱמֶת, נֹצֵר חֶסֶד לָאֲלָפִים, נֹשֵׂא עָוֹן, וָפֶשַׁע, וְחַטָּאָה, וְנַקֵּה.[2] וְסָלַחְתָּ

סליחות / SELICHOS

In introducing the laws of fasts, *Rambam* sets forth the principle that the Torah requires us to gather, pray, repent, and beg for Heavenly mercy whenever the community is threatened by a natural or human calamity. On the other hand, for one to maintain that catastrophe is inevitable or that it can be avoided only by recourse to human remedy is 'cruel,' for not only will such a course never lead people to improve themselves and thereby merit God's mercy, it will result in further Divine punishment. One means of bringing about repentance is fasting, and therefore the Sages ordained that public fasts be proclaimed in times of calamity *(Rambam, Hil. Taaniyos* 1:1-4). Similarly, they ordained permanent public fast days to commemorate times of national tragedy. The purpose of these fasts is to bring the nation to repentance, because the exile and other suffering that flowed from the misdeeds of yore are still with us (ibid. 5:1).

Within the framework of the *Siddur,* this mood of repentance is expressed in the *Selichos* or prayers of supplication. They are of ancient origin; some of them are even mentioned in the *mishnayos* describing to prayers for rain *(Taanis* ch. 2), but nearly all of them were composed between the 8th and 16th centuries. The reader will note that several of the more prominent *Selichos* are recited not only on a fast day, but also in the *Selichos* that are recited in conjunction with the Days of Awe and the Ten Days of Repentance.

[It should be noted that Tishah B'Av is unique. Since it commemorates the Destruction, an event of overpowering sorrow, it has a prayer order, *Kinos* (Elegies), all its own.]

The central theme of all the *Selichos,* as well as of the Yom Kippur *Maariv* and *Neilah* services, is the שְׁלֹשׁ עֶשְׂרֵה מִדּוֹת שֶׁל רַחֲמִים, the *Thirteen Attributes of Mercy.* This passage appears in the Torah *(Exodus* 34:6-7) at the time when God proclaimed His readiness to do away with the Jewish people after the sin of the Golden Calf. According to R' Yochanan's interpretation *(Rosh Hashanah* 17b), Moses felt that Israel's sin was so grievous that there was no possibility of his intercession on their behalf. Thereupon, God appeared to him in the form of a *chazzan* wrapped in a *tallis* and taught him the Thirteen Attributes, saying, 'Whenever Israel sins, let them recite this in its proper order and I will forgive them.' Thus, this appeal to God's mercy reassures us both that repentance is always

SELICHOS

Selichos are recited immediately after the *chazzan's* repetition of *Shemoneh Esrei* on the appropriate fast days: the Fasts of *Behab,* the Tenth of Teves, the Fast of Esther and the Seventeenth of Tammuz. (On the Ninth of Av, *Kinos* are recited; on the Fast of Gedaliah, the *Selichos* of the Ten Days of Repentance are recited.) Even those not fasting should join the congregation in reciting *Selichos.* Though it is preferable to stand during *Selichos,* those who find it difficult to do so should stand at least during אֵל מֶלֶךְ ,אֵל אֶרֶךְ אַפַּיִם, the Thirteen Attributes, and שְׁמַע קוֹלֵנוּ.

The introductory portion of *Selichos* is identical on all fast days.

סְלַח *Forgive us, our Father, for in our abundant folly we have erred,*
pardon us, our King, for our iniquities are many.

אֵל *O God — You are slow to anger, You are called the Master of Mercy,*
and You have taught the way of repentance.
May You remember this day and every day the greatness of Your mercy and
Your kindness to the offspring of Your beloved Ones.
Turn to us in mercy for You are the Master of Mercy.
With supplication and prayer we approach Your Presence
in the manner that You made known to the humble one [Moses] in ancient times.
Turn back from Your fierce anger as it is written in Your Torah.
In the shadow of Your wings may we find shelter and lodging
as on the day 'HASHEM descended in a cloud' [to appear to Moses on Sinai].
∴ *Overlook sin and erase guilt as on the day 'He [God] stood there with him [Moses].'*
Give heed to our cry and hearken to our declaration
as on day 'He called out with the Name HASHEM,'[1] *and there it was said:*

Congregation and *chazzan* recite loudly and in unison:

And HASHEM passed before him [Moses] and proclaimed:

יהוה *HASHEM, HASHEM, God, Compassionate and Gracious, Slow to anger, and Abundant in Kindness and Truth. Preserver of kindness for thousands of generations, Forgiver of iniquity, willful sin, and error, and Who cleanses.*[2] *May You forgive*

(1) *Exodus* 34:5. (2) 34:6-7.

possible and that God always awaits our return to Him. The implication is also plain that if we emulate God's merciful ways, He will treat us mercifully in return.

When it appears in the *Selichos,* the Thirteen Attributes is introduced by one of two prayers: the first time on each fast day (or day of repentance), it is introduced by אֵל אֶרֶךְ אַפַּיִם, *O God — You are slow to anger,* and thereafter, it is always introduced by אֵל מֶלֶךְ יוֹשֵׁב, *O God — King Who sits ...* Brief explanations of these introductions, as well as of the Thirteen Attributes appear below. After the Thirteen Attributes there is always a direct prayer for forgiveness, following the example of Moses who, after being taught the Thirteen Attributes, pleaded that God forgive Israel *(Exodus* 34:8-9).

On all the Rabbinically ordained fast days, the *Selichos* follow the same framework: first there is a common introductory section (pages 816-820); this is followed by two supplications recited by the congregation and concluded by the *chazzan,* and a פִּזְמוֹן [*pizmon*], a prayer that is recited responsively — each of these supplications and the *pizmon* is followed by אֵל מֶלֶךְ יוֹשֵׁב and the Thirteen Attributes; and finally another section (pages 828-836) common to all *Selichos,* which includes, among other prayers, an appeal that God recall the merit of the Patriarchs, pleas that He answer us, and a confession of sins.

◆ אֵל אֶרֶךְ אַפַּיִם / O God — You are Slow to Anger

After declaring that God's patience with sinful people and His boundless mercy are our primary hope, we beg Him to be as merciful to us now as He was on the day He taught the Thirteen Attributes to Moses, the epitome of humility, on Mount Sinai. On that day, God assured Moses that He would continue to protect Israel despite the nation's grievous sin. So may He heed and protect us, and be merciful to us now.

וַיִּקְרָא בְשֵׁם ה׳ — *He called out with the Name HASHEM.* According to *Mizrachi's* understanding of *Rashi (Exodus* 34:5), Moses called out God's Name. However, *Gur Aryeh's* interpretation of *Rashi, Ibn Ezra* and *Sforno* comment that God called out His Own Name, teaching Moses the order of the Thirteen Attributes.

◆ The Thirteen Attributes of Mercy

[The enumeration and brief explanation of the Thirteen Attributes follows the generally accepted opinion of *Rabbeinu Tam (Rosh Hashanah* 17b). A full commentary can be found in ArtScroll's *Tashlich and the Thirteen Attributes.*]

1. ה׳ — *HASHEM.* This Name denotes mercy: God

לַעֲוֺנֵנוּ וּלְחַטָּאתֵנוּ וּנְחַלְתָּנוּ.[1] סְלַח לָנוּ אָבִינוּ כִּי חָטָאנוּ, מְחַל לָנוּ מַלְכֵּנוּ כִּי פָשָׁעְנוּ. כִּי אַתָּה אֲדֹנָי טוֹב וְסַלָּח, וְרַב חֶסֶד לְכָל קֹרְאֶיךָ.[2]

—On First Monday of *Behab* recite

הוֹשִׁיעָה יהוה כִּי גָמַר חָסִיד, כִּי פַסּוּ אֱמוּנִים מִבְּנֵי אָדָם.[3] לוּלֵי יהוה שֶׁהָיָה לָנוּ, בְּקוּם עָלֵינוּ אָדָם. אֲזַי חַיִּים בְּלָעוּנוּ, בַּחֲרוֹת אַפָּם בָּנוּ.[4]

—On Thursday of *Behab* recite

הַאֲזִינָה יהוה תְּפִלָּתֵנוּ, הַקְשִׁיבָה לְקוֹל תַּחֲנוּנוֹתֵינוּ.[5] הַקְשִׁיבָה לְקוֹל שַׁוְעֵנוּ מַלְכֵּנוּ וֵאלֹהֵינוּ, כִּי אֵלֶיךָ נִתְפַּלָּל.[6] שְׁמַע יהוה וְחָנֵּנוּ, יהוה הֱיֵה עוֹזֵר לָנוּ.[7]

—On the Second Monday of *Behab* recite

אַל תִּקְצֹף יהוה עַד מְאֹד, וְאַל לָעַד תִּזְכֹּר עָוֺן, הֵן הַבֶּט נָא עַמְּךָ כֻלָּנוּ. הַעַל אֵלֶּה תִתְאַפַּק יהוה, תֶּחֱשֶׁה וּתְעַנֵּנוּ עַד מְאֹד.[8] שׁוּבָה יהוה עַד מָתָי, וְהִנָּחֵם עַל עֲבָדֶיךָ.[9]

—On the Tenth of Teves recite

כִּי עִם יהוה הַחֶסֶד, וְהַרְבֵּה עִמּוֹ פְדוּת.[10] פְּדֵה אֱלֹהִים אֶת יִשְׂרָאֵל, מִכֹּל צָרוֹתָיו.[11] וְהוּא יִפְדֶּה אֶת יִשְׂרָאֵל, מִכֹּל עֲוֺנוֹתָיו.[12] פּוֹדֶה יהוה נֶפֶשׁ עֲבָדָיו, וְלֹא יֶאְשְׁמוּ כָּל הַחוֹסִים בּוֹ.[13]

—On the Fast of Esther recite

קַוֵּה קִוִּינוּ אֶל יהוה, וַיֵּט אֵלֵינוּ וַיִּשְׁמַע שַׁוְעָתֵנוּ.[14] אַף אֹרַח מִשְׁפָּטֶיךָ יהוה קִוִּינוּךָ, לְשִׁמְךָ וּלְזִכְרְךָ תַּאֲוַת נָפֶשׁ.[15]

—On the Seventeenth of Tammuz recite

אַל תִּתְּנוּ דֳמִי לוֹ, עַד יְכוֹנֵן וְעַד יָשִׂים אֶת יְרוּשָׁלַיִם תְּהִלָּה בָּאָרֶץ.[16] כִּי עִמְּךָ מְקוֹר חַיִּים, בְּאוֹרְךָ נִרְאֶה אוֹר.[17] אֱלֹהֵינוּ, בֹּשְׁנוּ בְּמַעֲשֵׂינוּ וְנִכְלַמְנוּ בַּעֲוֺנֵינוּ.[18]

On all days continue:

כְּרַחֵם אָב עַל בָּנִים, כֵּן תְּרַחֵם יהוה עָלֵינוּ.[19] לַיהוה הַיְשׁוּעָה, עַל עַמְּךָ בִרְכָתֶךָ סֶּלָה.[20] יהוה צְבָאוֹת עִמָּנוּ, מִשְׂגָּב לָנוּ אֱלֹהֵי יַעֲקֹב סֶלָה.[21] יהוה צְבָאוֹת, אַשְׁרֵי אָדָם בֹּטֵחַ בָּךְ.[22] יהוה הוֹשִׁיעָה, הַמֶּלֶךְ יַעֲנֵנוּ בְיוֹם קָרְאֵנוּ.[23]

---

is merciful before a person sins, even though He knows that future evil lies dormant in the person.

2. 'ה — *HASHEM*. God is merciful after the sinner has gone astray.

3. אֵל — *God*. This Name denotes power: God's mercy sometimes surpasses even the degree indicated by the Name *HASHEM*.

4. רַחוּם — *Compassionate*. God eases the punishment of the guilty; and He does not put people into extreme temptation.

5. וְחַנּוּן — *and Gracious*, even to the undeserving.

our iniquities and our errors and make us Your heritage.[1] *Forgive us, our Father, for we have erred; pardon us, our King, for we have willfully sinned; for You, my Lord, are good and forgiving and abundantly kind to all who call upon You.*[2]

On First Monday of Behab recite— **הוֹשִׁיעָה** *Save, O HASHEM, for the devout is no more, for the faithful have vanished from mankind.*[3] *Had not HASHEM been with us when men rose up against us; then they would have swallowed us alive when their anger was kindled against us.*[4]

On Thursday of Behab recite— **הַאֲזִינָה** *Give ear, O HASHEM, to our prayer, and heed the sound of our supplications.*[5] *Heed the sound of our outcry, our King and our God, for to you alone do we pray.*[6] *Hear, HASHEM, and favor us; HASHEM, be our helper.*[7]

On the Second Monday of Behab recite— **אַל** *O HASHEM, be not exceedingly wrathful, do not eternally remember iniquity — behold, please look, all of us are Your people. Will you restrain Yourself, HASHEM, despite all this [suffering]? Will You remain silent? Will You afflict us so exceedingly?*[8] *Return, HASHEM, how long? — concerning upon Your servants.*[9]

On the Tenth of Teves recite— **כִּי** *For with HASHEM is kindness, and with Him is abundant redemption.*[10] *Redeem Israel, O God, from all its distress.*[11] *And He shall redeem Israel from all its inquities.*[12] *HASHEM redeems the soul of His servants; and all who take refuge in Him will not be condemned.*[13]

On the Fast of Esther recite— **קַוֵּה** *We have continually hoped for HASHEM, so He inclined to us and heard our cry.*[14] *Even when we are on the path of Your judgment, we hope in You; our soul's desire is for Your Name and Your remembrance.*[15]

On the Seventeenth of Tammuz recite— **אַל** *Allow Him no respite until He re-establishes and makes Jerusalem the praise of the earth.*[16] *For with You is the source of life — by Your light shall we see light.*[17] *Our God, we are shamed by our deeds and humiliated by our iniquities.*[18]

On all days continue:

כְּרַחֵם *As a father has mercy on his children, so, HASHEM, may You have mercy on us.*[19] *Salvation is HASHEM's, upon Your people is Your blessing, Selah.*[20] *HASHEM, Master of Legions, is with us, a stronghold for us is the God of Jacob, Selah.*[21] *HASHEM, Master of Legions, praiseworthy is the person who trusts in You.*[22] *HASHEM, save! May the King answer us on the day we call.*[23]

(1) *Exodus* 34:9. (2) *Psalms* 86:5. (3) 12:2. (4) 124:2,3. (5) Cf. 86:6. (6) Cf. 5:3. (7) Cf. 30:11. (8) *Isaiah* 64:8, 11. (9) *Psalms* 90:13. (10) 130:7. (11) 25:22. (12) 130:8. (13) 34:23. (14) Cf. 40:2. (15) *Isaiah* 26:8. (16) 62:7. (17) *Psalms* 36:10 (18) Cf. *Ezra* 9:6. (19) Cf. *Psalms* 103:13. (20) 3:9. (21) 46:8. (22) 84:13. (23) 20:10.

---

6. אֶרֶךְ אַפַּיִם — *Slow to anger,* so that the sinner can reconsider long before it is too late.

7. וְרַב חֶסֶד — *and Abundant in Kindness,* toward those who lack personal merits. Also, if the scales of good and evil are evenly balanced, He tips them to the good.

8. וֶאֱמֶת — *and Truth.* God never reneges on His word.

9. נֹצֵר חֶסֶד לָאֲלָפִים — *Preserver of kindness for thousands of generations.* The deeds of the righteous benefit their offspring far into the future.

10. נֹשֵׂא עָוֹן — *Forgiver of iniquity.* God forgives the intentional sinner, if he repents.

11. וָפֶשַׁע — *[Forgiver of] willful sin.* Even those who purposely anger God are allowed to repent.

12. וְחַטָּאָה — *and [Forgiver of] error.* This is a sin committed out of carelessness or apathy.

13. וְנַקֵּה — *and Who cleanses.* God wipes away the sins of those who repent.

In some congregations, the following two verses are recited responsively — the *chazzan* reciting סְלַח, and the congregation responding, וַיֹּאמֶר. In other congregations these verses are recited silently.

סְלַח נָא לַעֲוֹן הָעָם הַזֶּה כְּגֹדֶל חַסְדֶּךָ, וְכַאֲשֶׁר נָשָׂאתָה לָעָם הַזֶּה מִמִּצְרַיִם וְעַד הֵנָּה,[1] וְשָׁם נֶאֱמַר.

וַיֹּאמֶר יהוה סָלַחְתִּי כִּדְבָרֶךָ.[2]

All continue:

הַטֵּה אֱלֹהַי אָזְנְךָ וּשְׁמָע, פְּקַח עֵינֶיךָ וּרְאֵה שֹׁמְמֹתֵינוּ, וְהָעִיר אֲשֶׁר נִקְרָא שִׁמְךָ עָלֶיהָ, כִּי לֹא עַל צִדְקֹתֵינוּ אֲנַחְנוּ מַפִּילִים תַּחֲנוּנֵינוּ לְפָנֶיךָ, כִּי עַל רַחֲמֶיךָ הָרַבִּים. אֲדֹנָי שְׁמָעָה, אֲדֹנָי סְלָחָה, אֲדֹנָי הַקְשִׁיבָה, וַעֲשֵׂה אַל תְּאַחַר, לְמַעַנְךָ אֱלֹהַי, כִּי שִׁמְךָ נִקְרָא עַל עִירְךָ וְעַל עַמֶּךָ.[3]

Continue with the *Selichos* of the respective fast days: First Monday of *Behab,* below; Thursday of *Behab,* p. 836; Second Monday of *Behab,* p. 842; Tenth of Teves, p. 848; Fast of Esther, p. 854; Seventeenth of Tammuz, p. 862.

❧ סליחות לשני קמא ❧

Begin *Selichos* on page 816. Then continue here:

אֱלֹהֵינוּ וֵאלֹהֵי אֲבוֹתֵינוּ

יִשְׂרָאֵל עַמְּךָ תְּחִנָּה עוֹרְכִים, שֶׁהֵם מְצֵרִים וּלְהִוָּשֵׁעַ צְרִיכִים,
צָרֵיהֶם עֲלֵיהֶם עוֹל מַאֲרִיכִים, כָּל זֹאת הַגַּעְתָּם וְשִׁמְךָ מְבָרְכִים.
חָלִי וּמַכְאוֹב לְהִכָּתֵב לֹא נִמְסַר, עֲלוּבִים מִנֹּעַר וּמֵהֶם לֹא הוּסַר,
קָדוֹשׁ בְּיָדְךָ לְפַתֵּחַ מוּסָר, כְּאֱמוּנָתְךָ הַנְּקִיָּה וְלֹא כְּאֱמוּנוֹת בָּשָׂר.
הַלּוֹבֵשׁ צְדָקָה וְלוֹ כַּמְּעִיל עֲטוּיָה, וּמִמַּכָּה עַצְמָה מְתַקֵּן רְטִיָּה,
קוֹמֵם עֲדָתְךָ מִנְּפִילָתָהּ הַמֻּטוּיָה, בְּכֹחֲךָ הַגָּדוֹל וּבִזְרוֹעֲךָ הַנְּטוּיָה.
טוֹעִים הָאוֹמְרִים נַחֲלָתְךָ לְחַבֵּל, כְּבוֹדְךָ לְהָמִיר וּבַהֶבֶל לְהִתְהַבֵּל.
נְטוֹת מִדְּרָכֶיךָ וְתֹהוּ לְקַבֵּל, וְיִרְאָתְךָ הַקְּדוֹשָׁה לִנְטוֹשׁ וּלְנַבֵּל.
בְּאַהֲבָתְךָ וּבְחֶמְלָתְךָ מְנַשֵּׂא וּמְנַטֵּל,
עֲצַת צוֹרְרֶיךָ תְּסַכֵּל וּמַחְשְׁבוֹתָם תְּבַטֵּל,
רַבָּה מְהוּמָה בֵּינֵיהֶם הַטֵּל, וּמַלְאַךְ אַכְזָרִי דּוֹחֶה וּמְטַלְטֵל.
בַּעֲבוּר כְּבוֹד עַצְמְךָ וְשֵׁם קָדְשְׁךָ הַמְּהֻלָּל,
נוֹרְאוֹת הַפְלֵא לְבַל בַּגּוֹיִם יִתְחַלָּל.
יוֹעֲצֵיהֶם וְאֵיתָנֵיהֶם תּוֹלִיךְ שׁוֹלָל, וּבָהֶם תְּעוֹלֵל כַּאֲשֶׁר בִּי הִתְעוֹלָל.
מֵקִים מֵעָפָר דָּל וְאֶבְיוֹן מֵאַשְׁפָּה, כְּנֵסָתְךָ אַל תִּתֵּן לְכָלָה וּלְחֶרְפָּה,
אִם בְּפִקּוּדֶיךָ מִתְעַצֶּלֶת וּמִרְפָּה, עַל כָּל פְּשָׁעֶיהָ אַהֲבָתְךָ תְּהֵא מְחַפָּה.

❧ שֵׁנִי קַמָּא / FIRST MONDAY OF BEHAB ❧

The acronym בְּהַ״ב stands for Monday (ב, the second day of the week), Thursday (ה, the fifth day), and Monday. It is an ancient custom going back to Temple times that some people would fast on three days — Monday, Thursday, and Monday — after Pesach and Succos to atone for the possibility that they may have become excessively frivolous and sinned during the long festival of eating and drinking. During Shavuos, which is only a one-day festival, there was little chance of such an occurrence, so no fasts were adopted after Shavuos. Since it is not proper to fast unnecessarily during the festive months of

In some congregations, the following two verses are recited responsively — the *chazzan* reciting סְלַח, *'Please forgive ...,'* and the congregation responding, *'And HASHEM said ...'.* In other congregations these verses are recited silently.

סְלַח ❖ *Please forgive the iniquity of this people according to the greatness of Your kindness and as You have forgiven this people from Egypt until now,*[1] *and there it was said:*

And HASHEM said, 'I have forgiven according to your words!'[2]

All continue:

הַטֵּה *Incline Your ear, my God, and listen, open Your eyes and see our desolation and that of the city upon which Your Name is proclaimed; for not because of our righteousness do we cast down our supplications before You, rather because of Your abundant compassion. O my Lord, heed; O my Lord, forgive; O my Lord, be attentive and act, do not delay; for Your sake, my God, for Your Name is proclaimed upon Your city and upon Your people.*[3]

Continue with the *Selichos* of the respective fast days: First Monday of *Behab,* below; Thursday of *Behab,* p. 836; Second Monday of *Behab,* p. 842; Tenth of Teves, p. 848; Fast of Esther, p. 854; Seventeenth of Tammuz, p. 862.

SELICHOS FOR FIRST MONDAY OF BEHAB

Begin *Selichos* on page 816, then continue here:

Our God and the God of our forefathers.

יִשְׂרָאֵל *Israel, Your people, prepares supplication,*
because they are distressed and need to be helped.
Their oppressors prolong the yoke upon them —
all this has befallen them, but they bless Your Name.
The disease and pain cannot be committed to writing,
degraded from youth and not removed from them.
O holy One, it is in Your power to open the bonds
according to Your pure craft, and not according to human craftsmanship.
He Who dons righteousness and it is draped on Him like a cloak,
and from the very affliction He fashions the salve.
raise up Your congregation from its abject downfall,
with Your great strength and Your outstretched arm.
Misguided ones who say they will destroy Your heritage,
to exchange Your glory and integrate themselves with vanity,
leave Your ways to accept desolate idols
and to abandon and abominate Your holy reverence.
With Your love and compassion You bear and uplift [us],
turn the counsel of Your enemies to folly and nullify their intentions,
Impose much confusion among them;
and repulse and give no rest to the cruel angel.
For the sake of Your honor and Your lauded holy Name,
perform wondrously awesome deeds that it not be desecrated among the nations.
Lead their advisers and strong men into foolishness,
wreak evil upon them as it was wrought upon me.
You Who raise the needy from the dust and the destitute from the trash heap,
do not deliver Your congregation to destruction and disgrace.
Though it be slothful and lax regarding Your commands,
let Your love cover up all their willfulness.

(1) *Numbers* 14:19. (2) 14:20. (3) *Daniel* 9:18-19.

Nissan and Tishrei, the fasts were deferred until Iyar and Cheshvan. On the first Sabbath, in these months, a public prayer (p. 458) is recited before *Mussaf* for the benefit of those who will fast, and on the next Monday, the fasts begin. Monday and Thursday were chosen because, they are days of judgment (see p. 124).

יִשְׂרָאֵל ❧ — *Israel.* The acrostic spells the author's name, יִצְחָק הַקָּטָן בְּרַבִּי מֵאִיר, *Yitzchak the*

יְתֵרָה חִבָּתָם לְפָנֶיךָ אֲדוֹנֵי הָאֲדוֹנִים, בֵּין כַּךְ וּבֵין כַּךְ קְרוּאִים לְךָ בָּנִים,
רַחֲמֶיךָ יְקַדְּמוּנוּ אֱלֹהֵי עֶלְיוֹנִים וְתַחְתּוֹנִים,
טֶרֶם יִשְׁטְפוּנוּ הַמַּיִם הַזֵּידוֹנִים.
חֲפֵצֵי קִרְבָתְךָ עַל כָּל הַבָּאוֹת, הָחִישָׁה לָמוֹ יְשׁוּעוֹת הַנִּבָּאוֹת,
❖ קָדוֹשׁ, עֲשֵׂה עִמָּם לְטוֹבָה אוֹת, חָזָק וְאַמִּיץ גּוֹאֲלָם יהוה צְבָאוֹת.

אֵל מֶלֶךְ יוֹשֵׁב עַל כִּסֵּא רַחֲמִים, מִתְנַהֵג בַּחֲסִידוּת, מוֹחֵל עֲוֹנוֹת עַמּוֹ, מַעֲבִיר רִאשׁוֹן רִאשׁוֹן, מַרְבֶּה מְחִילָה לְחַטָּאִים וּסְלִיחָה לַפּוֹשְׁעִים, עֹשֶׂה צְדָקוֹת עִם כָּל בָּשָׂר וָרוּחַ, לֹא כְרָעָתָם תִּגְמוֹל. ❖ אֵל הוֹרֵיתָ לָּנוּ לוֹמַר שְׁלֹשׁ עֶשְׂרֵה, וּזְכוֹר לָנוּ הַיּוֹם בְּרִית שְׁלֹשׁ עֶשְׂרֵה, כְּמוֹ שֶׁהוֹדַעְתָּ לֶעָנָיו מִקֶּדֶם, כְּמוֹ שֶׁכָּתוּב, וַיֵּרֶד יהוה בֶּעָנָן וַיִּתְיַצֵּב עִמּוֹ שָׁם, וַיִּקְרָא בְשֵׁם יהוה.

Congregation and *chazzan* recite loudly and in unison:

וַיַּעֲבֹר יהוה עַל פָּנָיו וַיִּקְרָא:

יהוה, יהוה, אֵל, רַחוּם, וְחַנּוּן, אֶרֶךְ אַפַּיִם, וְרַב חֶסֶד, וֶאֱמֶת, נֹצֵר חֶסֶד לָאֲלָפִים, נֹשֵׂא עָוֹן, וָפֶשַׁע, וְחַטָּאָה, וְנַקֵּה. וְסָלַחְתָּ לַעֲוֹנֵנוּ וּלְחַטָּאתֵנוּ וּנְחַלְתָּנוּ. סְלַח לָנוּ אָבִינוּ כִּי חָטָאנוּ, מְחַל לָנוּ מַלְכֵּנוּ כִּי פָשָׁעְנוּ. כִּי אַתָּה אֲדֹנָי טוֹב וְסַלָּח, וְרַב חֶסֶד לְכָל קֹרְאֶיךָ.

All continue:

נִשָּׂא לְבָבֵנוּ אֶל כַּפָּיִם אֶל אֵל בַּשָּׁמָיִם.[1] תָּבוֹא לְפָנֶיךָ אֶנְקַת אָסִיר כְּגֹדֶל זְרוֹעֲךָ, הוֹתֵר בְּנֵי תְמוּתָה.[2] לַאדֹנָי אֱלֹהֵינוּ הָרַחֲמִים וְהַסְּלִיחוֹת, כִּי מָרַדְנוּ בּוֹ.[3]

כְּרַחֵם אָב עַל בָּנִים, כֵּן תְּרַחֵם יהוה עָלֵינוּ. לַיהוה הַיְשׁוּעָה, עַל עַמְּךָ בִרְכָתֶךָ סֶּלָה. יהוה צְבָאוֹת עִמָּנוּ, מִשְׂגָּב לָנוּ אֱלֹהֵי יַעֲקֹב סֶלָה. יהוה צְבָאוֹת, אַשְׁרֵי אָדָם בֹּטֵחַ בָּךְ. יהוה הוֹשִׁיעָה, הַמֶּלֶךְ יַעֲנֵנוּ בְיוֹם קָרְאֵנוּ.

(Many congregations repeat, סְלַח נָא . . . וְעַל עַמְּךָ [p. 820] here.)

אֱלֹהִים בְּיִשְׂרָאֵל גָּדוֹל נוֹדַעְתָּ, אַתָּה יהוה אָבִינוּ אָתָּה.
בְּכָל קָרְאֵנוּ אֵלֶיךָ קָרַבְנוּ, רָם וְנִשָּׂא אַתָּה בְּקִרְבֵּנוּ.
גְּמַלְתָּנוּ הַטּוֹבוֹת גַּם בְּחוֹבֵינוּ, לֹא בְּצִדְקוֹתֵינוּ וּבְיֹשֶׁר לְבָבֵנוּ.
דּוֹדֵנוּ גַּם כִּי זָנַחְנוּ, גְּאָלֵנוּ כִּי עֲבָדִים אֲנָחְנוּ.
הִנְּנוּ בַּעֲוֹנֵינוּ עַד דַּכָּא, וַתִּקְצַר נֶפֶשׁ לְךָ מְחַכָּה.
וְאַיֵּה חֲסָדֶיךָ הָרִאשׁוֹנִים עִמָּנוּ, מֵעוֹלָם וְעַד עוֹלָם נֶאֱמָנוּ.
זַעַף נִשָּׂא וַתַּשׁ כֹּחֵנוּ, יהוה אַל בְּאַפְּךָ תוֹכִיחֵנוּ.
חַלְחָלוֹת רַבּוֹת בִּלּוּ בְשָׂרֵנוּ, נָא אַל בַּחֲמָתְךָ תְיַסְּרֵנוּ.

---

lesser, son of Rabbi Meir (France, about 1090-1130). He was a grandson of Rashi and a brother and colleague of the well-known Tosafists Rashbam and Rabbeinu Tam.

May Your affection for them abound, O Lord of lords,
no matter what [they do], they are called Your children.
May Your mercy advance toward us, O God of the upper and lower worlds —
before the surging waters inundate us.
To those who are anxious for Your nearness whatever befalls them —
hasten for them the prophesied salvations;
∴ *O Holy One, perform for us a token of goodness;*
O strong and powerful one, their Redeemer, HASHEM, Master of Legions.

אֵל מֶלֶךְ *O God, King Who sits on the throne of mercy; Who acts with kindness, pardons the sins of His people, removes sins one by one, increasingly grants pardon to careless sinners and forgiveness to willful ones, performs acts of generosity with every living being — You do not repay them in accord with their evil.* ∴ *O God, You taught us to recite the Thirteen [Attributes of Mercy], so remember for us today the covenant of these Thirteen, as You made known to the humble one [Moses] in ancient times, as it is written: And HASHEM descended in a cloud and stood with him there, and He called out with the Name HASHEM.*

Congregation and *chazzan* recite loudly and in unison:

And HASHEM passed before him [Moses] and proclaimed:

יהוה *HASHEM, HASHEM, God, Compassionate and Gracious, Slow to anger, and Abundant in Kindness and Truth. Preserver of kindness for thousands of generations, Forgiver of iniquity, willful sin, and error, and Who cleanses. May You forgive our iniquities and our errors and make us Your heritage. Forgive us, our Father, for we have erred; pardon us, our King, for we have willfully sinned; for You, my Lord, are good and forgiving and abundantly kind to all who call upon You.*

All continue:

נִשָּׂא *Let us lift our hearts with our hands to God in heaven.*[1] *Let the groan of the prisoner come before You, as befits the greatness of Your power, release those condemned to die.*[2] *My Lord our God's is the compassion and forgiveness, for we have rebelled against Him.*[3]

כְּרַחֵם *As a father has mercy on his children, so, HASHEM, may You have mercy on us. Salvation is HASHEM's, upon Your people is Your blessing, Selah. HASHEM, Master of Legions, is with us, a stronghold for us is the God of Jacob, Selah. HASHEM, Master of Legions, praiseworthy is the person who trusts in You. HASHEM, save! May the King answer us on the day we call.*

(Many congregations repeat, *'Please forgive . . . Your people,'* [p. 820] here.)

אֱלֹהִים *O God, You are known in Israel to be great.*
You are HASHEM, our Father are You.
ב *Whenever we call upon You, draw us close;*
You are exalted and uplifted among us.
ג *You have done us favors despite our guilt,*
not because of our righteousness and the uprightness of our heart.
ד *Our Beloved, though we have been forsaken, redeem us for You are our servants.*
ה *Our sins have brought us the point of disintegration,*
our soul is impatiently awaiting You.
ו *Where are Your earlier kindnesses with us — that were faithful forever and ever?*
ז *We have borne anger and our strength has ebbed —*
O God, do not rebuke us in Your anger.
ח *Many convulsions have withered our flesh, please do not rebuke us in Your anger.*

אֵל מֶלֶךְ יוֹשֵׁב / O God, King Who Sits

God, Who is all powerful, chooses to exercise mercy even when people are undeserving of it. With infinite kindness He chooses to forgive sins one by one, until a person's merits outnumber his wrongs. Since He knows that people are but mortal, He deals kindly with them. As an additional kindness, He taught us the Thirteen Attributes so that we can recite them and gain His forgiveness.

טְרַח הַצָּרוֹת אֵין לְהַסְפֵּר, אַיֵּה שׁוֹקֵל וְאַיֵּה סוֹפֵר.
יָדַעְנוּ רִשְׁעֵנוּ כִּי פָשָׁעְנוּ, כִּי אֱמֶת עָשִׂיתָ וַאֲנַחְנוּ הִרְשָׁעְנוּ.
כַּעַס וְחָרוֹן מֶנּוּ יֶחְדַּל, כִּי קָטֹן יַעֲקֹב וָדָל.
לַחַץ יוֹסֵר וְעוֹל מֶנּוּ יְחֻבַּל, כִּי כָשַׁל כֹּחַ הַסַּבָּל.
מְנָת מְדָּתֵנוּ לֹא תִגְבֶּה, כִּי נִשְׁאַרְנוּ מְעַט מֵהַרְבֵּה.
נָחֵם עַל הָרָעָה לַאֲיֻמָּתֶךָ, מַטֵּה כְלַפֵּי חֶסֶד אֱמוּנָתֶךָ.
סְלִיחָה אִם עֲוֹנֵינוּ עָנוּ בָנוּ, עָזְרֵנוּ כִּי עָלֶיךָ נִשְׁעָנוּ.
עֲרֵפֵנוּ כֹּף לְךָ לְהִשְׁתַּעְבֵּד, בְּאַהֲבָה וּבְיִרְאָה אוֹתְךָ לַעֲבוֹד וּלְכַבֵּד.
פּוֹקְדֶיךָ קִדְּשׁוּ צוֹמוֹת לִקְבּוֹעַ, דַּעְתָּם קְצָרָה צָרְכָּם לִתְבּוֹעַ.
צְקוֹן לַחֲשָׁם אֵלֶיךָ תָבֹא, חַתֵּל לְאִישׁ אִישׁ נִגְעוֹ וּמַכְאוֹבוֹ.
קוֹל יַעֲקֹב נוֹהֵם מִתְּהוֹמוֹתֶיךָ, תִּשְׁמַע הַשָּׁמַיִם מְכוֹן שִׁבְתֶּךָ.
רוֹדֶה רוֹדֵף בְּאַף תְּכַלֶּה, שְׁנַת שִׁלּוּמִים לְרִיב צִיּוֹן תְּגַלֶּה.
שַׁרְתָּ וְרָדְתָּ מִנֹּעַר קְנוּתֵנוּ, וְאַל תַּשְׁלִיכֵנוּ לְעֵת זִקְנָתֵנוּ.
תָּעֵינוּ לִשְׂמֹאל וִימִינְךָ תְּקָרְבֵנוּ, כִּכְלוֹת כֹּחֵנוּ אַל תַּעַזְבֵנוּ.
תַּבִּיט וְתָצִיץ וְתַשְׁגִּיחַ לִרְחוּמֶיךָ, תִּתְאַזֵּר בַּחֲנִינוּתֶיךָ תִּתְלַבֵּשׁ בִּצְדְקוֹתֶיךָ,
❖ תִּתְכַּסֶּה בְּרַחֲמֶיךָ וְתִתְעַטֵּף בַּחֲסִידוּתֶךָ,
וְתָבֹא לְפָנֶיךָ מִדַּת טוּבְךָ וְעַנְוְתָנוּתֶךָ.

אֵל מֶלֶךְ יוֹשֵׁב עַל כִּסֵּא רַחֲמִים, מִתְנַהֵג בַּחֲסִידוּת, מוֹחֵל עֲוֹנוֹת עַמּוֹ, מַעֲבִיר רִאשׁוֹן רִאשׁוֹן, מַרְבֶּה מְחִילָה לְחַטָּאִים וּסְלִיחָה לַפּוֹשְׁעִים, עֹשֶׂה צְדָקוֹת עִם כָּל בָּשָׂר וָרוּחַ, לֹא כְרָעָתָם תִּגְמוֹל. ❖ אֵל הוֹרֵיתָ לָּנוּ לוֹמַר שְׁלֹשׁ עֶשְׂרֵה, וּזְכוֹר לָנוּ הַיּוֹם בְּרִית שְׁלֹשׁ עֶשְׂרֵה, כְּמוֹ שֶׁהוֹדַעְתָּ לֶעָנָיו מִקֶּדֶם, כְּמוֹ שֶׁכָּתוּב, וַיֵּרֶד יהוה בֶּעָנָן וַיִּתְיַצֵּב עִמּוֹ שָׁם, וַיִּקְרָא בְשֵׁם יהוה.

Congregation and *chazzan* recite loudly and in unison:

וַיַּעֲבֹר יהוה עַל פָּנָיו וַיִּקְרָא:

יהוה, יהוה, אֵל, רַחוּם, וְחַנּוּן, אֶרֶךְ אַפַּיִם, וְרַב חֶסֶד, וֶאֱמֶת, נֹצֵר חֶסֶד לָאֲלָפִים, נֹשֵׂא עָוֹן, וָפֶשַׁע, וְחַטָּאָה, וְנַקֵּה. וְסָלַחְתָּ לַעֲוֹנֵנוּ וּלְחַטָּאתֵנוּ וּנְחַלְתָּנוּ. סְלַח לָנוּ אָבִינוּ כִּי חָטָאנוּ, מְחַל לָנוּ מַלְכֵּנוּ כִּי פָשָׁעְנוּ. כִּי אַתָּה אֲדֹנָי טוֹב וְסַלָּח, וְרַב חֶסֶד לְכָל קֹרְאֶיךָ.

The following prayer is recited responsively by the *chazzan* and congregation.

מַלְאֲכֵי רַחֲמִים מְשָׁרְתֵי עֶלְיוֹן, חַלּוּ נָא פְּנֵי אֵל בְּמֵיטַב הִגָּיוֹן,
אוּלַי יָחוֹס עַם עָנִי וְאֶבְיוֹן, אוּלַי יְרַחֵם.

מַלְאֲכֵי — *O angels.* The acrostic spells שְׁמוּאֵל כֹּהֵן יְחִי, *Shmuel the Kohen, may he live.*

ט *The burden of the distresses cannot be calculated,*
who can weigh it and who can count it?

י *We know our wickedness for we have sinned willfully,*
for You have acted truthfully while we have caused wickedness.

כ *Let anger and fury cease from us, for Jacob is small and needy.*

ל *Remove oppression and may the yoke be broken off us,*
for the ability to bear them has failed.

מ *Do not exact the full measure [of our sins] from us, for we remain few out of many.*

נ *Relent from the evil to Your nation, Your craft is to tip the scale toward kindness.*

ס *Forgive though our sins testify against us, help us, for we depend on You.*

ע *Bend our stiff neck to be subservient to You,*
so that we can serve and honor You with love and reverence.

פ *Those who think of You have sanctified designated fasts,*
their awareness is too limited to request their needs.

צ *May their whispered prayer come to You, heal every person's wound and pain.*

ק *The voice of Jacob moans from Your depths,*
may You hear in heaven the abode of Your dwelling.

ר *May You destroy the pursuing tyrant in Your anger,*
reveal a year of restitution for Zion's grievance.

ש *You saw [the Egyptian oppression] and descended to acquire us from our youth,*
but do not cast us off in time of our old age.

ת *We strayed to the left, but let Your right hand draw us close,*
when our strength is gone do not abandon us.

ת *Gaze, peer, oversee the objects of Your mercy,*
gird Yourself in Your graciousness, garb Yourself in Your righteousness,

ת ∴ *Cover Yourself in Your mercy, wrap Yourself in Your kindness,*
and may Your attribute of goodness and humility come before You.

אֵל מֶלֶךְ *O God, King Who sits on the throne of mercy; Who acts with kindness, pardons the sins of His people, removes sins one by one, increasingly grants pardon to careless sinners and forgiveness to willful ones, performs acts of generosity with every living being — You do not repay them in accord with their evil.* ∴ *O God, You taught us to recite the Thirteen [Attributes of Mercy], so remember for us today the covenant of these Thirteen, as You made known to the humble one [Moses] in ancient times, as it is written: And* HASHEM *descended in a cloud and stood with him there, and He called out with the Name* HASHEM.

Congregation and *chazzan* recite loudly and in unison:

And HASHEM *passed before him [Moses] and proclaimed:*

יהוה HASHEM, HASHEM, *God, Compassionate and Gracious, Slow to anger, and Abundant in Kindness and Truth. Preserver of kindness for thousands of generations, Forgiver of iniquity, willful sin, and error, and Who cleanses. May You forgive our iniquities and our errors and make us Your heritage. Forgive us, our Father, for we have erred; pardon us, our King, for we have willfully sinned; for You, my Lord, are good and forgiving and abundantly kind to all who call upon You.*

The following prayer is recited responsively by the *chazzan* and congregation.

מַלְאֲכֵי *O angels of mercy, servants of the Supreme, please entreat before God with eloquent expression —*
perhaps He will pity the poor and destitute people; perhaps He will have mercy.

---

(1) *Lamentations* 3:41. (2) *Psalms* 79:11. (3) *Daniel* 9:9.

אוּלַי יְרַחֵם **שְׁ**אֵרִית יוֹסֵף, **שְׁ**פָלִים וּנְבֻזִים פְּשׁוּחֵי שֶׁסֶף,
שְׁבוּיֵי חִנָּם מְכוּרֵי בְּלֹא כֶסֶף, **שׁוֹ**אֲגִים בִּתְפִלָּה וּמְבַקְשִׁים רִשְׁיוֹן,
אוּלַי יָחוּס עַם עָנִי וְאֶבְיוֹן, אוּלַי יְרַחֵם.

אוּלַי יְרַחֵם **מְ**עֻנֵּי כֶבֶל, **מְ**לֻמָּדֵי מַכּוֹת בְּעִנּוּי סֵבֶל,
מְנוֹד רֹאשׁ נְתוּנִים בְּיוֹשְׁבֵי תֵבֵל, **מָ**שָׁל בָּעַמִּים בְּקֶצֶף וּבִזָּיוֹן,
אוּלַי יָחוּס עַם עָנִי וְאֶבְיוֹן, אוּלַי יְרַחֵם.

אוּלַי יְרַחֵם **וְ**יֵרֶא בָּעֳנִי עַמּוֹ, **וְ**יַקְשֵׁב וְיִשְׁמַע הַצָּגִים לְעֻמּוֹ,
וְעוֹדִים בְּלַחַשׁ מוּסָר לָמוֹ, **וְ**עֵינֵיהֶם תּוֹלִים לִמְצוֹא רִצָּיוֹן,
אוּלַי יָחוּס עַם עָנִי וְאֶבְיוֹן, אוּלַי יְרַחֵם.

אוּלַי יְרַחֵם **אוֹ**מְרֵי סְלַח נָא, **אוֹ**מְצֵי שִׁבְחוֹ בְּכָל עֵת וְעוֹנָה,
אֲגוּדִים בַּצָּרָה לִשְׁפּוֹךְ תְּחִנָּה, **אֶ**ת פְּנֵי אֱלֹהֵיהֶם שׁוֹפְכִים לֵב דִּוָּיוֹן,
אוּלַי יָחוּס עַם עָנִי וְאֶבְיוֹן, אוּלַי יְרַחֵם.

אוּלַי יְרַחֵם **לָ**קָתָה בְּכִפְלַיִם, **לְ**עוּטָה אֲרָיוֹת כְּמוֹ בְּפִי שַׁחֲלַיִם,
לְקָה וּמִשְׁתַּלֶּמֶת בַּעֲוֹן שׁוּלַיִם, **לֹא** שָׁכְחָה בְּכָל זֹאת מִכְתַּב עוֹז חֶבְיוֹן,
אוּלַי יָחוּס עַם עָנִי וְאֶבְיוֹן, אוּלַי יְרַחֵם.

אוּלַי יְרַחֵם **כְּ**בוּשֵׁי פָנִים, **הַ**שּׁוֹמְעִים חֶרְפָּתָם וְלֹא מְשִׁיבִים וְעוֹנִים,
נִצְחוֹ מְקַוִּים וְלִישְׁעוֹ נִשְׁעָנִים, כִּי לֹא כָלוּ רַחֲמָיו בְּכִלָּיוֹן,
אוּלַי יָחוּס עַם עָנִי וְאֶבְיוֹן, אוּלַי יְרַחֵם.

אוּלַי **יְ**רַחֵם יְחַלֵּץ עָנִי בְּעָנְיוֹ, **חֲ**בוּשׁוֹ יַתִּיר מֵאֶרֶץ שִׁבְיוֹ,
יִגְהֶה מְזוֹרוֹ וַיַחְבּוֹשׁ חָלְיוֹ, **צַ**עֲקָתוֹ יִשְׁמַע וְיָחִישׁ עֵת פִּדְיוֹן,
אוּלַי יָחוּס עַם עָנִי וְאֶבְיוֹן, אוּלַי יְרַחֵם.

אֵל מֶלֶךְ יוֹשֵׁב עַל כִּסֵּא רַחֲמִים, מִתְנַהֵג בַּחֲסִידוּת, מוֹחֵל עֲוֹנוֹת עַמּוֹ, מַעֲבִיר רִאשׁוֹן רִאשׁוֹן, מַרְבֶּה מְחִילָה לְחַטָּאִים וּסְלִיחָה לַפּוֹשְׁעִים, עֹשֶׂה צְדָקוֹת עִם כָּל בָּשָׂר וָרוּחַ, לֹא כְרָעָתָם תִּגְמוֹל. ❖ אֵל הוֹרֵיתָ לָּנוּ לוֹמַר שְׁלֹשׁ עֶשְׂרֵה, וּזְכוֹר לָנוּ הַיּוֹם בְּרִית שְׁלֹשׁ עֶשְׂרֵה, כְּמוֹ שֶׁהוֹדַעְתָּ לֶעָנָיו מִקֶּדֶם, כְּמוֹ שֶׁכָּתוּב, וַיֵּרֶד יהוה בֶּעָנָן וַיִּתְיַצֵּב עִמּוֹ שָׁם, וַיִּקְרָא בְשֵׁם יהוה.

Congregation and *chazzan* recite loudly and in unison:

וַיַּעֲבֹר יהוה עַל פָּנָיו וַיִּקְרָא:

יהוה, יהוה, אֵל, רַחוּם, וְחַנּוּן, אֶרֶךְ אַפַּיִם, וְרַב חֶסֶד, וֶאֱמֶת, נֹצֵר חֶסֶד לָאֲלָפִים, נֹשֵׂא עָוֹן, וָפֶשַׁע, וְחַטָּאָה, וְנַקֵּה. וְסָלַחְתָּ לַעֲוֹנֵנוּ וּלְחַטָּאתֵנוּ וּנְחַלְתָּנוּ. סְלַח לָנוּ אָבִינוּ כִּי חָטָאנוּ, מְחַל לָנוּ מַלְכֵּנוּ כִּי פָשָׁעְנוּ. כִּי אַתָּה אֲדֹנָי טוֹב וְסַלָּח, וְרַב חֶסֶד לְכָל קֹרְאֶיךָ.

Perhaps He will have mercy on the remnant of Joseph,
degraded and disgraced, torn and ripped,
taken captive without reason, sold for no money,
shouting in prayer and pleading for permission —
perhaps He will pity the poor and destitute people; perhaps He will have mercy.
Perhaps He will have mercy on those tortured by chains,
accustomed to blows in the suffering of hard labor,
their heads made to tremble by all inhabitants of the world,
a slogan among the peoples for wrath and disgrace —
perhaps He will pity the poor and destitute people; perhaps He will have mercy.
Perhaps He will have mercy and see the suffering of His people,
and hearken and hear those assembled before Him,
gathered in silent prayer when they are chastised
and their eyes are raised to find favor —
perhaps He will pity the poor and destitute people; perhaps He will have mercy.
Perhaps He will have mercy on those who say, 'Please forgive,'
who intensify His praise at every time and season,
gathered in distress to pour out supplication,
before their God they pour out their anguished heart —
perhaps He will pity the poor and destitute people; perhaps He will have mercy.
Perhaps He will have mercy on the nation that was doubly assaulted,
devoured by lions as by the mouth of vicious lions,
beaten and forced to pay for her obvious sin,
despite all this, she will not forget the mighty, hidden Written Law —
perhaps He will pity the poor and destitute people; perhaps He will have mercy.
Perhaps He will have mercy on those who hide their face,
who hear their shame and neither respond nor call out;
for His triumph they hope and on His salvation they rely,
for His mercy has not come to a total end —
perhaps He will pity the poor and destitute people; perhaps He will have mercy.
Perhaps He will have mercy and deliver the afflicted from his affliction,
release His prisoner from the land of his captivity,
cure his wound and heal his disease,
hear his outcry and hasten the time of his redemption —
perhaps He will pity the poor and destitute people; perhaps He will have mercy.

אֵל מֶלֶךְ *O God, King Who sits on the throne of mercy; Who acts with kindness, pardons the sins of His people, removes sins one by one, increasingly grants pardon to careless sinners and forgiveness to willful ones, performs acts of generosity with every living being — You do not repay them in accord with their evil. ∴ O God, You taught us to recite the Thirteen [Attributes of Mercy], so remember for us today the covenant of these Thirteen, as You made known to the humble one [Moses] in ancient times, as it is written: And HASHEM descended in a cloud and stood with him there, and He called out with the Name HASHEM.*

Congregation and chazzan recite loudly and in unison:

And HASHEM passed before him [Moses] and proclaimed:

יהוה *HASHEM, HASHEM, God, Compassionate and Gracious, Slow to anger, and Abundant in Kindness and Truth. Preserver of kindness for thousands of generations, Forgiver of iniquity, willful sin, and error, and Who cleanses. May You forgive our iniquities and our errors and make us Your heritage. Forgive us, our Father, for we have erred; pardon us, our King, for we have willfully sinned; for You, my Lord, are good and forgiving and abundantly kind to all who call upon You.*

On all fast days continue here:

זְכוֹר רַחֲמֶיךָ יהוה וַחֲסָדֶיךָ, כִּי מֵעוֹלָם הֵמָּה.[1] זָכְרֵנוּ יהוה בִּרְצוֹן עַמֶּךָ, פָּקְדֵנוּ בִּישׁוּעָתֶךָ.[2] זְכֹר עֲדָתְךָ קָנִיתָ קֶּדֶם, גָּאַלְתָּ שֵׁבֶט נַחֲלָתֶךָ, הַר צִיּוֹן זֶה שָׁכַנְתָּ בּוֹ.[3] זְכוֹר יהוה חִבַּת יְרוּשָׁלָיִם, אַהֲבַת צִיּוֹן אַל תִּשְׁכַּח לָנֶצַח. אַתָּה תָקוּם תְּרַחֵם צִיּוֹן כִּי עֵת לְחֶנְנָהּ, כִּי בָא מוֹעֵד.[4] זְכֹר יהוה לִבְנֵי אֱדוֹם, אֵת יוֹם יְרוּשָׁלָיִם, הָאֹמְרִים עָרוּ עָרוּ עַד הַיְסוֹד בָּהּ.[5] זְכֹר לְאַבְרָהָם לְיִצְחָק וּלְיִשְׂרָאֵל עֲבָדֶיךָ, אֲשֶׁר נִשְׁבַּעְתָּ לָהֶם בָּךְ וַתְּדַבֵּר אֲלֵיהֶם, אַרְבֶּה אֶת זַרְעֲכֶם כְּכוֹכְבֵי הַשָּׁמָיִם, וְכָל הָאָרֶץ הַזֹּאת אֲשֶׁר אָמַרְתִּי, אֶתֵּן לְזַרְעֲכֶם, וְנָחֲלוּ לְעֹלָם.[6] זְכֹר לַעֲבָדֶיךָ לְאַבְרָהָם לְיִצְחָק וּלְיַעֲקֹב, אַל תֵּפֶן אֶל קְשִׁי הָעָם הַזֶּה וְאֶל רִשְׁעוֹ וְאֶל חַטָּאתוֹ.[7]

סליחות לתחלואי ילדים ר״ל

Most congregations omit the following *Selichos for children's illness* and continue with זְכוֹר לָנוּ, page 830. These congregations recite this special prayer only if there is an acutal epidemic afflicting children. Other congregations recite this prayer on every fast day.

The following two verses are recited responsively:

אַל נָא תָשֵׁת עָלֵינוּ חַטָּאת, אֲשֶׁר נוֹאַלְנוּ וַאֲשֶׁר חָטָאנוּ.[8]

חָטָאנוּ צוּרֵנוּ, סְלַח לָנוּ יוֹצְרֵנוּ.

אֵל נָא רְפָא נָא תַּחֲלוּאֵי גֶּפֶן פּוֹרִיָּה, **בּ**וֹשָׁה וַחֲפוּרָה וְאֻמְלַל פִּרְיָהּ,
גְּאָלֶנָּה מִשַּׁחַת וּמִמַּכָּה טְרִיָּה,
עֲנֵנוּ כְּשֶׁעָנִיתָ לְאַבְרָהָם אָבִינוּ בְּהַר הַמּוֹרִיָּה. חָטָאנוּ צוּרֵנוּ, סְלַח לָנוּ יוֹצְרֵנוּ.

דִּגְלֵי עַם פְּדוּיֵי בִּזְרוֹעַ חָשׂוּף, **הַ**צֵּל מִנֶּגֶף וְאַל יִהְיוּ לִשְׂסוּף,
וְתַעֲנֶה קְרִיאָתֵנוּ לְמַעֲשֵׂה יָדֶיךָ תִּכְסוֹף,
עֲנֵנוּ כְּשֶׁעָנִיתָ לַאֲבוֹתֵינוּ עַל יַם סוּף. חָטָאנוּ צוּרֵנוּ, סְלַח לָנוּ יוֹצְרֵנוּ.

זְכוּת צוּר חֻצַּב הַיּוֹם לָנוּ תְגַל, **חָ**שְׁכֵנוּ מֵאֶנֶף וּנְחֵנוּ בְּיֹשֶׁר מַעְגָּל,
טַהֵר טֻמְאָתֵנוּ וְלִמְאוֹר תּוֹרָתְךָ עֵינֵינוּ גַּל,
עֲנֵנוּ כְּשֶׁעָנִיתָ לִיהוֹשֻׁעַ בַּגִּלְגָּל. חָטָאנוּ צוּרֵנוּ, סְלַח לָנוּ יוֹצְרֵנוּ.

יָהּ רְאֵה דֶּשֶׁן עָקוּד וְהַצְמַח לָנוּ תְרוּפָה, **כַּ**לֵּה שׁוֹד וָשֶׁבֶר סַעַר וְסוּפָה,
לַמְּדֵנוּ וְחַכְּמֵנוּ אִמְרָתְךָ הַצְּרוּפָה,
עֲנֵנוּ כְּשֶׁעָנִיתָ לִשְׁמוּאֵל בַּמִּצְפָּה. חָטָאנוּ צוּרֵנוּ, סְלַח לָנוּ יוֹצְרֵנוּ.

מְתֻמָּם מֵרֶחֶם שָׁרָשָׁיו אַל תְּקַמֵּל, **נַ**קֵּנוּ מִכֶּתֶם וָשֶׁמֶץ וְלֹא נֶאֱמַל,
סְעָדֵנוּ וְנִוָּשֵׁעָה וְאָרְחוֹת חֲסָדֶיךָ נִגָּמֵל,
עֲנֵנוּ כְּשֶׁעָנִיתָ לְאֵלִיָּהוּ בְּהַר הַכַּרְמֶל. חָטָאנוּ צוּרֵנוּ, סְלַח לָנוּ יוֹצְרֵנוּ.

עוֹדְדֵנוּ בְּצֶדֶק מָשׁוּי מִמַּיִם וְכַפֵּר זָדוֹן וּמְשׁוּגָה,
פְּדֵנוּ מִמְּהוּמַת מָוֶת וְאָחוֹר כָּל נְסוֹגָה,
צַוֵּה יְשׁוּעָתֵנוּ וּבַעֲוֹנוֹתֵינוּ אַל נִתְמוֹגָגָה,
עֲנֵנוּ כְּשֶׁעָנִיתָ לְיוֹנָה בִּמְעֵי הַדָּגָה. חָטָאנוּ צוּרֵנוּ, סְלַח לָנוּ יוֹצְרֵנוּ.

קְדֻשַּׁת אִישׁ חֲסִידֶךָ זְכוֹר לִיפַת פְּעָמִים,

On all fast days continue here:

זְכוֹר *Remember Your mercies, O HASHEM, and Your kindnesses, for they are from the beginning of the world.*[1] *Remember us, HASHEM, when You show Your nation favor and recall us with Your salvation.*[2] *Remember Your congregation that You acquired of old, You redeemed the tribe of Your heritage, this Mount of Zion where You dwelled.*[3] *Remember, O HASHEM, the affection of Zion, may You never forget the love of Jerusalem. You will arise and show Zion mercy, for it will be the time to favor her, for the appointed time will have come.*[4] *Remember, HASHEM, for the offspring of Edom, the day of Jerusalem — for those who said, 'Destroy! Destroy! to its very foundation.'*[5] *Remember for Abraham, Isaac, and Israel, Your servants, to whom You swore by Your Being, and You said to them, 'I shall increase your offspring like the stars of the heavens; and this entire land of which I spoke I will give to your offspring and they will inherit it forever.'*[6] *Remember for Your servants, for Abraham, for Isaac, and for Jacob; ignore the stubbornness of this people, its wickedness and its sinfulness.*[7]

SELICHOS FOR CHILDREN'S ILLNESS

Most congregations omit the following *Selichos for Children's Illness* and continue with זְכוֹר לָנוּ, *Remember for us*, page 830. These congregations recite this special prayer only if there is an actual epidemic afflicting children. Other congregations recite this prayer on every fast day.

Please, do not place sin upon us,
that we have foolishly done and that we have committed.[8]

We have erred, our Rock; forgive us, our Molder.

אֵל *O God, please cure the illnesses of the fruitful vine;*
shamed, disgraced, and feeble is its fruit,
redeem it from ruin and festering wound,
answer us as You answered our father Abraham on Mount Moriah —
We have erred, our Rock; forgive us, our Molder.
The formations of the people who were redeemed with a bare arm,
rescue them from plague and let them not be dismembered;
answer our call and yearn for Your handiwork,
answer us as You answered our forefathers by the Sea of Reeds —
We have erred, our Rock; forgive us, our Molder.
The merit of the hewn rock [Abraham], reveal for us today,
withhold us from anger and guide us on a straight path,
cleanse our contamination and reveal the light of Your Torah to our eyes,
answer us as You answered Joshua in Gilgal —
We have erred, our Rock; forgive us, our Molder.
O God, see the ashes of him [Isaac] who was bound and let a cure sprout for us,
bring an end to plunder, destruction, storm, and tempest,
teach us and make us wise through Your pure word,
answer us as You answered Samuel in Mitzpah —
We have erred, our Rock; forgive us, our Molder.
Do not shrivel the roots of him [Jacob] who was perfect from the womb,
cleanse us from stain and blemish, and let us not be miserable,
support us that we may be saved and let us benefit from Your ways of kindness,
answer us as You answered Elijah on Mount Carmel —
We have erred, our Rock; forgive us, our Molder.
Encourage us through the righteousness of him [Moses] who was drawn from the water and atone for willful and unintentional sin,
redeem us from panic of death and let us not retreat backward,
command our salvation and let us not disintegrate in our iniquities,
answer us as You answered Jonah in the innards of the fish —
We have erred, our Rock; forgive us, our Molder.
Remember the holiness of Your devout one [Aaron]
for the people with lovely footsteps [making the pilgrimage to Jerusalem],

(1) *Psalms* 25:6. (2) Cf. 106:4. (3) 74:2. (4) 102:14. (5) 137:7.
(6) *Exodus* 32:13. (7) *Deuteronomy* 9:27. (8) *Numbers* 12:11.

רַחֲמֶיךָ תְּעוֹרֵר כִּי לְקִינוּ בְּכִפְלַיִם, שׁוּבֵנוּ תֹּקֶף לְיִרְאָתֶךָ, וְלֹא נֶחְשַׁף שׁוּלַיִם, עֲנֵנוּ כְּשֶׁעָנִיתָ לְדָוִד וְלִשְׁלֹמֹה בְנוֹ בִּירוּשָׁלָיִם. חָטָאנוּ צוּרֵנוּ, סְלַח לָנוּ יוֹצְרֵנוּ.

Some congregations add (either on all fast days, or only on the Fast of Esther):

(תַּעֲנֶה לְקוֹרְאֶיךָ, וְהַסְכֵּת מִמְּעוֹנִים,
תִּשְׁמַע שַׁוְעַת צוֹעֲקֶיךָ, שׁוֹמֵעַ אֶל אֶבְיוֹנִים,
תְּרַחֵם עַל בָּנֶיךָ, כְּרַחֵם אָב עַל בָּנִים,
עֲנֵנוּ כְּשֶׁעָנִיתָ לְמָרְדְּכַי וְאֶסְתֵּר, וְתָלוּ עַל הָעֵץ חֲמִשִּׁים הָאָב עִם הַבָּנִים.
חָטָאנוּ צוּרֵנוּ, סְלַח לָנוּ יוֹצְרֵנוּ.)

All continue:

זְכוֹר לָנוּ בְּרִית אָבוֹת, כַּאֲשֶׁר אָמַרְתָּ: וְזָכַרְתִּי אֶת בְּרִיתִי יַעֲקוֹב, וְאַף אֶת בְּרִיתִי יִצְחָק, וְאַף אֶת בְּרִיתִי אַבְרָהָם אֶזְכֹּר, וְהָאָרֶץ אֶזְכֹּר.[1] זְכוֹר לָנוּ בְּרִית רִאשׁוֹנִים, כַּאֲשֶׁר אָמַרְתָּ: וְזָכַרְתִּי לָהֶם בְּרִית רִאשׁוֹנִים, אֲשֶׁר הוֹצֵאתִי אֹתָם מֵאֶרֶץ מִצְרַיִם לְעֵינֵי הַגּוֹיִם, לִהְיוֹת לָהֶם לֵאלֹהִים, אֲנִי יהוה.[2] עֲשֵׂה עִמָּנוּ כְּמָה שֶׁהִבְטַחְתָּנוּ: וְאַף גַּם זֹאת בִּהְיוֹתָם בְּאֶרֶץ אֹיְבֵיהֶם, לֹא מְאַסְתִּים וְלֹא גְעַלְתִּים לְכַלֹּתָם לְהָפֵר בְּרִיתִי אִתָּם, כִּי אֲנִי יהוה אֱלֹהֵיהֶם.[3]

הָשֵׁב שְׁבוּתֵנוּ וְרַחֲמֵנוּ, כְּמָה שֶּׁכָּתוּב: וְשָׁב יהוה אֱלֹהֶיךָ אֶת שְׁבוּתְךָ וְרִחֲמֶךָ, וְשָׁב וְקִבֶּצְךָ מִכָּל הָעַמִּים אֲשֶׁר הֱפִיצְךָ יהוה אֱלֹהֶיךָ שָׁמָּה.[4] קַבֵּץ נִדָּחֵינוּ, כְּמָה שֶּׁכָּתוּב: אִם יִהְיֶה נִדַּחֲךָ בִּקְצֵה הַשָּׁמָיִם, מִשָּׁם יְקַבֶּצְךָ יהוה אֱלֹהֶיךָ, וּמִשָּׁם יִקָּחֶךָ.[5] מְחֵה פְשָׁעֵינוּ כָּעָב וְכֶעָנָן, כְּמָה שֶּׁכָּתוּב: מָחִיתִי כָעָב פְּשָׁעֶיךָ וְכֶעָנָן חַטֹּאתֶיךָ, שׁוּבָה אֵלַי כִּי גְאַלְתִּיךָ.[6] מְחֵה פְשָׁעֵינוּ לְמַעַנְךָ, כַּאֲשֶׁר אָמַרְתָּ: אָנֹכִי אָנֹכִי הוּא מֹחֶה פְשָׁעֶיךָ לְמַעֲנִי, וְחַטֹּאתֶיךָ לֹא אֶזְכֹּר.[7]

הַלְבֵּן חֲטָאֵינוּ כַּשֶּׁלֶג וְכַצֶּמֶר, כְּמָה שֶּׁכָּתוּב: לְכוּ נָא וְנִוָּכְחָה, יֹאמַר יהוה, אִם יִהְיוּ חֲטָאֵיכֶם כַּשָּׁנִים כַּשֶּׁלֶג יַלְבִּינוּ, אִם יַאְדִּימוּ כַתּוֹלָע, כַּצֶּמֶר יִהְיוּ.[8] זְרוֹק עָלֵינוּ מַיִם טְהוֹרִים וְטַהֲרֵנוּ, כְּמָה שֶּׁכָּתוּב: וְזָרַקְתִּי עֲלֵיכֶם מַיִם טְהוֹרִים וּטְהַרְתֶּם, מִכֹּל טֻמְאוֹתֵיכֶם וּמִכָּל גִּלּוּלֵיכֶם אֲטַהֵר אֶתְכֶם.[9] רַחֵם עָלֵינוּ וְאַל תַּשְׁחִיתֵנוּ, כְּמָה שֶּׁכָּתוּב: כִּי אֵל רַחוּם יהוה אֱלֹהֶיךָ, לֹא יַרְפְּךָ וְלֹא יַשְׁחִיתֶךָ, וְלֹא יִשְׁכַּח אֶת בְּרִית אֲבֹתֶיךָ אֲשֶׁר נִשְׁבַּע לָהֶם.[10]

מוֹל אֶת לְבָבֵנוּ לְאַהֲבָה אֶת שְׁמֶךָ, כְּמָה שֶּׁכָּתוּב: וּמָל יהוה אֱלֹהֶיךָ אֶת לְבָבְךָ וְאֶת לְבַב זַרְעֶךָ, לְאַהֲבָה אֶת יהוה אֱלֹהֶיךָ, בְּכָל לְבָבְךָ וּבְכָל נַפְשְׁךָ, לְמַעַן חַיֶּיךָ.[11] הִמָּצֵא לָנוּ בְּבַקָּשָׁתֵנוּ, כְּמָה שֶּׁכָּתוּב: וּבִקַּשְׁתֶּם מִשָּׁם אֶת יהוה אֱלֹהֶיךָ וּמָצָאתָ, כִּי תִדְרְשֶׁנּוּ בְּכָל לְבָבְךָ וּבְכָל נַפְשֶׁךָ.[12] ❖ תְּבִיאֵנוּ אֶל הַר קָדְשֶׁךָ, וְשַׂמְּחֵנוּ בְּבֵית תְּפִלָּתֶךָ, כְּמָה שֶּׁכָּתוּב: וַהֲבִיאוֹתִים אֶל הַר קָדְשִׁי, וְשִׂמַּחְתִּים בְּבֵית תְּפִלָּתִי, עוֹלֹתֵיהֶם וְזִבְחֵיהֶם לְרָצוֹן עַל מִזְבְּחִי, כִּי בֵיתִי בֵּית תְּפִלָּה יִקָּרֵא לְכָל הָעַמִּים.[13]

arouse Your mercy for we have been doubly smitten,
return us forcefully to Your reverence, and let our shame not be exposed,
answer us as You answered David and his son Solomon in Jerusalem —
We have erred, our Rock; forgive us, our Molder.

Some congregations add (either on all fast days, or only on the Fast of Esther):

(Respond to those who call You and listen from the heavens,
hear the cry of those who entreat You,
You Who hear the destitute
have mercy on Your children as a father has mercy on his children,
answer us as You answered Mordechai and Esther
so they could hang on a fifty-cubit gallows father and sons —
We have erred, our Rock; forgive us, our Molder.)

All continue:

זכור *Remember for us the covenant of the Patriarchs, as You said: 'And I will remember My covenant with Jacob, and also My covenant with Isaac, and also My covenant with Abraham will I remember; and the Land will I remember.'*[1] *Remember for us the covenant of the ancestors, as You said: 'And I will remember for them the covenant of the ancestors whom I removed from the land of Egypt in the very sight of the nations, to be a God to them; I am* HASHEM.*'*[2] *Do with us as You promised us: 'And even with all that when they will be in the land of their enemies, I will not have despised them nor abhorred them to destroy them, to annul my covenant with them, for I am* HASHEM, *their God.'*[3]

*Bring back our captivity and have mercy on us, as it is written: '*HASHEM, *your God will bring back your captivity and have mercy on you, and He will again gather you in from all the peoples where* HASHEM, *your God, has scattered you.'*[4] *Gather in our dispersed ones, as it is written: 'If your dispersed were to be at the ends of heaven, from there* HASHEM, *your God, will gather you in and from there He will take you.'*[5] *Wipe away our willful sins like a cloud and like a mist, as it is written: 'I will have wiped away your willful sins like a cloud and your errors like a mist — repent to Me, for I will have redeemed you.'*[6] *Wipe away our willful sins for Your sake, as You have said: 'I, only I, am the One Who wipes away your willful sins for My sake, and I shall not recall your errors.'*[7]

Whiten our errors like snow and like wool, as it is written: 'Come now, let us reason together, says HASHEM, *though your errors will be like scarlet, they will become white as snow; though they will be red as crimson, they will become like wool.'*[8] *Pour pure water upon us and purify us, as it is written: 'I shall pour pure water upon you and purify you, of all your contaminations and of all your abominations I will purify you.'*[9] *Have mercy on us and do not destroy us, as it is written: 'For a merciful God is* HASHEM, *your God, He will not relinquish you nor destroy you, and He will not forget the covenant with your forefathers, which He swore to them.'*[10]

*Circumcise [thus removing the barrier from] our hearts to love your Name, as it is written: '*HASHEM, *your God, will circumcise your heart and the heart of your offspring, to love* HASHEM, *your God, with all your heart and with all your soul, that you may live.'*[11] *Be accessible to us in our quest, as it is written: 'From there you will seek* HASHEM, *your God, and you will find, when you search Him out with all your heart and with all your soul.'*[12] ∴ *Bring us to Your holy mountain and gladden us in Your house of prayer, as it is written: 'And I will bring them to My holy mountain, and I will gladden them in My house of prayer; their elevation offerings and their feast-offerings will find favor on My Altar, for My House will be called a house of prayer, for all nations.'*[13]

(1) *Leviticus* 26:42. (2) 26:45. (3) 26:44. (4) *Deuteronomy* 30:3. (5) 30:4. (6) *Isaiah* 44:22. (7) 43:25. (8) 1:18. (9) *Ezekiel* 36:25. (10) *Deuteronomy* 4:31. (11) 30:6. (12) 4:29. (13) *Isaiah* 56:7.

The Ark is opened. The first four verses of the next prayer are recited responsively:

שְׁמַע קוֹלֵנוּ יהוה אֱלֹהֵינוּ, חוּס וְרַחֵם עָלֵינוּ, וְקַבֵּל בְּרַחֲמִים וּבְרָצוֹן אֶת תְּפִלָּתֵנוּ.
הֲשִׁיבֵנוּ יהוה אֵלֶיךָ וְנָשׁוּבָה, חַדֵּשׁ יָמֵינוּ כְּקֶדֶם.[1]
אַל תַּשְׁלִיכֵנוּ מִלְּפָנֶיךָ, וְרוּחַ קָדְשְׁךָ אַל תִּקַּח מִמֶּנּוּ.[2]
אַל תַּשְׁלִיכֵנוּ לְעֵת זִקְנָה, כִּכְלוֹת כֹּחֵנוּ אַל תַּעַזְבֵנוּ.[3]
אַל תַּעַזְבֵנוּ יהוה, אֱלֹהֵינוּ אַל תִּרְחַק מִמֶּנּוּ.[4]

עֲשֵׂה עִמָּנוּ אוֹת לְטוֹבָה, וְיִרְאוּ שׂוֹנְאֵינוּ וְיֵבֹשׁוּ, כִּי אַתָּה יהוה עֲזַרְתָּנוּ וְנִחַמְתָּנוּ.[5] אֲמָרֵינוּ הַאֲזִינָה יהוה, בִּינָה הֲגִיגֵנוּ.[6] יִהְיוּ לְרָצוֹן אִמְרֵי פִינוּ וְהֶגְיוֹן לִבֵּנוּ לְפָנֶיךָ, יהוה צוּרֵנוּ וְגוֹאֲלֵנוּ.[7] כִּי לְךָ יהוה הוֹחָלְנוּ, אַתָּה תַעֲנֶה אֲדֹנָי אֱלֹהֵינוּ.[8]

The ark is closed and each individual continues until the end of *Selichos* (p. 836).

אֱלֹהֵינוּ וֵאלֹהֵי אֲבוֹתֵינוּ, תָּבֹא לְפָנֶיךָ תְּפִלָּתֵנוּ. וְאַל תִּתְעַלַּם מִתְּחִנָּתֵנוּ שֶׁאֵין אֲנוּ עַזֵּי פָנִים וּקְשֵׁי עֹרֶף, לוֹמַר לְפָנֶיךָ יהוה אֱלֹהֵינוּ וֵאלֹהֵי אֲבוֹתֵינוּ, צַדִּיקִים אֲנַחְנוּ וְלֹא חָטָאנוּ, אֲבָל אֲנַחְנוּ וַאֲבוֹתֵינוּ חָטָאנוּ.

Strike the left side of the chest with the right fist when reciting each term in the following confession.

אָשַׁמְנוּ, **בָּ**גַדְנוּ, **גָּ**זַלְנוּ, **דִּ**בַּרְנוּ דֹפִי. **הֶ**עֱוִינוּ, **וְ**הִרְשַׁעְנוּ, **זַ**דְנוּ, **חָ**מַסְנוּ, **טָ**פַלְנוּ שֶׁקֶר. **יָ**עַצְנוּ רָע, **כִּ**זַּבְנוּ, **לַ**צְנוּ, **מָ**רַדְנוּ, **נִ**אַצְנוּ, **סָ**רַרְנוּ, **עָ**וִינוּ, **פָּ**שַׁעְנוּ, **צָ**רַרְנוּ, **קִ**שִּׁינוּ עֹרֶף. **רָ**שַׁעְנוּ, **שִׁ**חַתְנוּ, **תִּ**עַבְנוּ, **תָּ**עִינוּ, **תִּ**עְתָּעְנוּ.

סַרְנוּ מִמִּצְוֹתֶיךָ וּמִמִּשְׁפָּטֶיךָ הַטּוֹבִים וְלֹא שָׁוָה לָנוּ.[9] וְאַתָּה צַדִּיק עַל כָּל הַבָּא עָלֵינוּ, כִּי אֱמֶת עָשִׂיתָ וַאֲנַחְנוּ הִרְשָׁעְנוּ.[10]

הִרְשַׁעְנוּ וּפָשַׁעְנוּ, לָכֵן לֹא נוֹשָׁעְנוּ. וְתֵן בְּלִבֵּנוּ לַעֲזוֹב דֶּרֶךְ רֶשַׁע, וְחִישׁ לָנוּ יֶשַׁע, כַּכָּתוּב עַל יַד נְבִיאֶךָ: יַעֲזֹב רָשָׁע דַּרְכּוֹ, וְאִישׁ אָוֶן מַחְשְׁבֹתָיו, וְיָשֹׁב אֶל יהוה וִירַחֲמֵהוּ, וְאֶל אֱלֹהֵינוּ כִּי יַרְבֶּה לִסְלוֹחַ.[11]

מְשִׁיחַ צִדְקֶךָ אָמַר לְפָנֶיךָ, שְׁגִיאוֹת מִי יָבִין, מִנִּסְתָּרוֹת נַקֵּנִי.[12] נַקֵּנוּ יהוה אֱלֹהֵינוּ מִכָּל פְּשָׁעֵינוּ, וְטַהֲרֵנוּ מִכָּל טֻמְאוֹתֵינוּ, וּזְרוֹק עָלֵינוּ מַיִם טְהוֹרִים וְטַהֲרֵנוּ, כַּכָּתוּב עַל יַד נְבִיאֶךָ: וְזָרַקְתִּי עֲלֵיכֶם מַיִם טְהוֹרִים וּטְהַרְתֶּם, מִכֹּל טֻמְאוֹתֵיכֶם וּמִכָּל גִּלּוּלֵיכֶם אֲטַהֵר אֶתְכֶם.[13] עַמְּךָ וְנַחֲלָתְךָ, רְעֵבֵי טוּבְךָ, צְמֵאֵי חַסְדֶּךָ, תְּאֵבֵי יִשְׁעֶךָ, יַכִּירוּ וְיֵדְעוּ כִּי לַיהוה אֱלֹהֵינוּ הָרַחֲמִים וְהַסְּלִיחוֹת.

אֵל רַחוּם שְׁמֶךָ, אֵל חַנּוּן שְׁמֶךָ, בָּנוּ נִקְרָא שְׁמֶךָ. יהוה עֲשֵׂה לְמַעַן שְׁמֶךָ, עֲשֵׂה לְמַעַן **אֲ**מִתֶּךָ, עֲשֵׂה לְמַעַן **בְּ**רִיתֶךָ, עֲשֵׂה לְמַעַן **גָּ**דְלְךָ וְתִפְאַרְתֶּךָ, עֲשֵׂה לְמַעַן **דָּ**תֶךָ, עֲשֵׂה לְמַעַן **הוֹ**דֶךָ, עֲשֵׂה לְמַעַן

The Ark is opened. The first four verses of the next prayer are recited responsively:

שְׁמַע קוֹלֵנוּ *Hear our voice, HASHEM, our God, pity and be compassionate to us, and accept — with compassion and favor — our prayer.*

Bring us back to You, HASHEM, and we shall return,
renew our days as of old.[1]
Do not cast us away from Yourself,
and do not remove Your holy spirit from us.[2]
Do not cast us away in old age,
when our strength gives out do not forsake us.[3]
Do not forsake us, HASHEM, our God,
be not distant from us.[4]

Display for us a sign for good, so that our enemies may see it and be ashamed, for You, HASHEM, will have helped and consoled us.[5] *To our sayings give ear, HASHEM, perceive our thoughts.*[6] *May the expressions of our mouth and the thoughts of our heart find favor before You, HASHEM, our Rock and our Redeemer.*[7] *Because for You, HASHEM, we waited, You will answer, my Lord, our God.*[8]

The ark is closed and each individual continues until the end of Selichos (p. 836).

אֱלֹהֵינוּ *Our God and the God of our forefathers, may our prayer come before You. Do not ignore our supplication for we are not so brazen and obstinate as to say before You, HASHEM, our God, and the God of our forefathers, that we are righteous and have not erred — rather, we and our forefathers have erred.*

Strike the left side of the chest with the right fist
when reciting each term in the following confession:

אָשַׁמְנוּ *We have become guilty, we have betrayed, we have robbed, we have spoken slander. We have caused perversion, we have caused wickedness, we have sinned willfully, we have been violent, we have falsely accused. We have counseled evil, we have been unfaithful, we have scorned, we have rebelled, we have provoked, we have turned away, we have been perverse, we have acted wantonly, we have persecuted, we have been obstinate. We have been wicked, we have corrupted, we have been abominable, we have strayed, we have led others astray.*

סַרְנוּ *We have turned away from Your commandments and from Your good laws but to no avail.*[9] *But You are righteous in all that has come upon us, for You have acted truthfully while we have caused wickedness.*[10]

הִרְשַׁעְנוּ *We have caused wickedness and sinned willfully, therefore we have not been helped. Inspire us to abandon the path of wickedness and hasten salvation to us. As it is written by Your prophet: 'May the wicked one abandon his way and the iniquitous one his thoughts; may he return to HASHEM and He will have mercy on him, and to our God for He will forgive abundantly.'*[11]

מְשִׁיחַ *Your righteous anointed [King David] said before You: 'Who can discern mistakes? — Cleanse me from unperceived faults.'*[12] *Cleanse us, O HASHEM, my God, of all our willful sins and purify us of all our contaminations. Pour pure water upon us and purify us, as it is written by Your prophet: 'I shall pour pure water upon you and purify you, of all your contaminations and of all your abominations I will purify you.'*[13] *Your people and Your heritage, who hunger for Your goodness, thirst for Your kindness, and long for Your salvation, may they recognize and know that to HASHEM, our God, belong mercy and forgiveness.*

אֵל רַחוּם *'Merciful God' is Your Name, 'Gracious God' is Your Name, Your Name is called upon us — O HASHEM, act for Your Name's sake. Act for the sake of Your truth; act for the sake of Your covenant; act for the sake of Your greatness and splendor; act for the sake of Your law; act for the sake of Your glory, act for the sake*

(1) *Lamentations* 5:21. (2) *Psalms* 51:13. (3) Cf. 71:9. (4) Cf. 38:22. (5) Cf. 86:17. (6) Cf. 5:2. (7) Cf. 19:15. (8) Cf. 38:16. (9) Cf. *Job* 33:27. (10) *Nechemiah* 9:33. (11) *Isaiah* 55:7. (12) *Psalms* 19:13. (13) *Ezekiel* 36:25.

וְעוּדֶךָ, עֲשֵׂה לְמַעַן **זִ**כְרֶךָ, עֲשֵׂה לְמַעַן **חַ**סְדֶּךָ, עֲשֵׂה לְמַעַן **טוּ**בֶךָ, עֲשֵׂה לְמַעַן **יִ**חוּדֶךָ, עֲשֵׂה לְמַעַן **כְּ**בוֹדֶךָ, עֲשֵׂה לְמַעַן **לִ**מּוּדֶךָ, עֲשֵׂה לְמַעַן **מַ**לְכוּתֶךָ, עֲשֵׂה לְמַעַן **נִ**צְחֶךָ, עֲשֵׂה לְמַעַן **סוֹ**דֶךָ, עֲשֵׂה לְמַעַן **עֻ**זֶּךָ, עֲשֵׂה לְמַעַן **פְּ**אֵרֶךָ, עֲשֵׂה לְמַעַן **צִ**דְקָתֶךָ, עֲשֵׂה לְמַעַן **קְ**דֻשָּׁתֶךָ, עֲשֵׂה לְמַעַן **רַ**חֲמֶיךָ הָרַבִּים, עֲשֵׂה לְמַעַן **שְׁ**כִינָתֶךָ, עֲשֵׂה לְמַעַן **תְּ**הִלָּתֶךָ, עֲשֵׂה לְמַעַן אוֹהֲבֶיךָ שׁוֹכְנֵי עָפָר, עֲשֵׂה לְמַעַן אַבְרָהָם יִצְחָק וְיַעֲקֹב, עֲשֵׂה לְמַעַן מֹשֶׁה וְאַהֲרֹן, עֲשֵׂה לְמַעַן דָּוִד וּשְׁלֹמֹה, עֲשֵׂה לְמַעַן יְרוּשָׁלַיִם עִיר קָדְשֶׁךָ, עֲשֵׂה לְמַעַן צִיּוֹן מִשְׁכַּן כְּבוֹדֶךָ, עֲשֵׂה לְמַעַן שִׁמְמוֹת הֵיכָלֶךָ, עֲשֵׂה לְמַעַן הֲרִיסוּת מִזְבְּחֶךָ, עֲשֵׂה לְמַעַן הֲרוּגִים עַל שֵׁם קָדְשֶׁךָ, עֲשֵׂה לְמַעַן טְבוּחִים עַל יִחוּדֶךָ, עֲשֵׂה לְמַעַן בָּאֵי בָאֵשׁ וּבַמַּיִם עַל קִדּוּשׁ שְׁמֶךָ, עֲשֵׂה לְמַעַן יוֹנְקֵי שָׁדַיִם שֶׁלֹּא חָטְאוּ, עֲשֵׂה לְמַעַן גְּמוּלֵי חָלָב שֶׁלֹּא פָשְׁעוּ, עֲשֵׂה לְמַעַן תִּינוֹקוֹת שֶׁל בֵּית רַבָּן, עֲשֵׂה לְמַעַנְךָ אִם לֹא לְמַעֲנֵנוּ, עֲשֵׂה לְמַעַנְךָ וְהוֹשִׁיעֵנוּ.

עֲנֵנוּ יהוה עֲנֵנוּ, עֲנֵנוּ אֱלֹהֵינוּ עֲנֵנוּ, עֲנֵנוּ **אָ**בִינוּ עֲנֵנוּ, עֲנֵנוּ **בּוֹ**רְאֵנוּ עֲנֵנוּ, עֲנֵנוּ **גּוֹ**אֲלֵנוּ עֲנֵנוּ, עֲנֵנוּ **דּוֹ**רְשֵׁנוּ עֲנֵנוּ, עֲנֵנוּ **הָ**אֵל הַנֶּאֱמָן עֲנֵנוּ, עֲנֵנוּ **וָ**תִיק וְחָסִיד עֲנֵנוּ, עֲנֵנוּ **זַ**ךְ וְיָשָׁר עֲנֵנוּ, עֲנֵנוּ **חַ**י וְקַיָּם עֲנֵנוּ, עֲנֵנוּ **טוֹ**ב וּמֵטִיב עֲנֵנוּ, עֲנֵנוּ **יוֹ**דֵעַ יֵצֶר עֲנֵנוּ, עֲנֵנוּ **כּוֹ**בֵשׁ כְּעָסִים עֲנֵנוּ, עֲנֵנוּ **לוֹ**בֵשׁ צְדָקוֹת עֲנֵנוּ, עֲנֵנוּ **מֶ**לֶךְ מַלְכֵי הַמְּלָכִים עֲנֵנוּ, עֲנֵנוּ **נוֹ**רָא וְנִשְׂגָּב עֲנֵנוּ, עֲנֵנוּ **סוֹ**לֵחַ וּמוֹחֵל עֲנֵנוּ, עֲנֵנוּ **עוֹ**נֶה בְּעֵת צָרָה עֲנֵנוּ, עֲנֵנוּ **פּוֹ**דֶה וּמַצִּיל עֲנֵנוּ, עֲנֵנוּ **צַ**דִּיק וְיָשָׁר עֲנֵנוּ, עֲנֵנוּ **קָ**רוֹב לְקוֹרְאָיו עֲנֵנוּ, עֲנֵנוּ **קָ**שֶׁה לִכְעוֹס עֲנֵנוּ, עֲנֵנוּ **רַ**ךְ לִרְצוֹת עֲנֵנוּ, עֲנֵנוּ **רַ**חוּם וְחַנּוּן עֲנֵנוּ, עֲנֵנוּ **שׁוֹ**מֵעַ אֶל אֶבְיוֹנִים עֲנֵנוּ, עֲנֵנוּ **תּוֹ**מֵךְ תְּמִימִים עֲנֵנוּ, עֲנֵנוּ אֱלֹהֵי אֲבוֹתֵינוּ עֲנֵנוּ, עֲנֵנוּ אֱלֹהֵי אַבְרָהָם עֲנֵנוּ, עֲנֵנוּ פַּחַד יִצְחָק עֲנֵנוּ, עֲנֵנוּ אֲבִיר יַעֲקֹב עֲנֵנוּ, עֲנֵנוּ עֶזְרַת הַשְּׁבָטִים עֲנֵנוּ, עֲנֵנוּ מִשְׂגַּב אִמָּהוֹת עֲנֵנוּ, עֲנֵנוּ עוֹנֶה בְּעֵת רָצוֹן עֲנֵנוּ, עֲנֵנוּ אֲבִי יְתוֹמִים עֲנֵנוּ, עֲנֵנוּ דַּיַּן אַלְמָנוֹת עֲנֵנוּ.

מִי שֶׁעָנָה לְאַבְרָהָם אָבִינוּ בְּהַר הַמּוֹרִיָּה — **הוּא יַעֲנֵנוּ.**
מִי שֶׁעָנָה לְיִצְחָק בְּנוֹ כְּשֶׁנֶּעֱקַד עַל גַּב הַמִּזְבֵּחַ — **הוּא יַעֲנֵנוּ.**
מִי שֶׁעָנָה לְיַעֲקֹב בְּבֵית אֵל — **הוּא יַעֲנֵנוּ.**
מִי שֶׁעָנָה לְיוֹסֵף בְּבֵית הָאֲסוּרִים — **הוּא יַעֲנֵנוּ.**
מִי שֶׁעָנָה לַאֲבוֹתֵינוּ עַל יַם סוּף — **הוּא יַעֲנֵנוּ.**
מִי שֶׁעָנָה לְמֹשֶׁה בְּחוֹרֵב — **הוּא יַעֲנֵנוּ.**
מִי שֶׁעָנָה לְאַהֲרֹן בַּמַּחְתָּה — **הוּא יַעֲנֵנוּ.**
מִי שֶׁעָנָה לְפִינְחָס בְּקוּמוֹ מִתּוֹךְ הָעֵדָה — **הוּא יַעֲנֵנוּ.**
מִי שֶׁעָנָה לִיהוֹשֻׁעַ בַּגִּלְגָּל — **הוּא יַעֲנֵנוּ.**
מִי שֶׁעָנָה לִשְׁמוּאֵל בַּמִּצְפָּה — **הוּא יַעֲנֵנוּ.**
מִי שֶׁעָנָה לְדָוִד וּשְׁלֹמֹה בְנוֹ בִּירוּשָׁלָיִם — **הוּא יַעֲנֵנוּ.**
מִי שֶׁעָנָה לְאֵלִיָּהוּ בְּהַר הַכַּרְמֶל — **הוּא יַעֲנֵנוּ.**

of Your Meeting House; act for the sake of Your remembrance; act for the sake of Your kindness; act for the sake of Your goodness; act for the sake of Your Oneness; act for the sake of Your honor; act for the sake of Your teaching; act for the sake of Your kingship; act for the sake of Your triumph; act for the sake of Your counsel; act for the sake of Your power; act for the sake of Your beauty; act for the sake of Your righteousness; act for the sake of Your sanctity; act for the sake of Your abundant mercy; act for the sake of Your Presence, act for the sake of Your praise; act for the sake of Your beloved ones who rest in the dust; act for the sake of Abraham, Isaac, and Jacob; act for the sake of Moses and Aaron; act for the sake of David and Solomon; act for the sake of Jerusalem, Your holy city; act for the sake of Zion, the abode of Your glory; act for the sake of the desolation of Your Temple; act for the sake of the ruin of Your Altar; act for the sake of the martyrs for Your holy Name; act for the sake of those slaughtered for Your Oneness; act for the sake of those who entered fire and water for the sanctification of Your Name; act for the nursing infants who did not err; act for the sake of the weaned babes who did not sin; act for the sake of children at the schoolroom; act for Your sake if not for ours; act for Your sake and save us.

עֲנֵנוּ *Answer us,* HASHEM*, answer us; Answer us, our God, answer us; answer us, our Father, answer us; answer us, our Creator, answer us; answer us, our Redeemer, answer us; answer us, You Who searches us out, answer us; answer us, faithful God, answer us; answer us, steadfast and kind One, answer us; answer us, pure and upright One, answer us; answer us, living and enduring One, answer us; answer us, good and beneficent One, answer us; answer us, You Who knows inclinations, answer us; answer us, You Who suppresses wrath, answer us; answer us, You Who dons righteousness, answer us; answer us, King Who reigns over kings, answer us; answer us, awesome and powerful One, answer us; answer us, You Who forgives and pardons, answer us; answer us, You Who answers in time of distress, answer us; answer us, Redeemer and Rescuer, answer us; answer us, righteous and upright One, answer us; answer us, He Who is close to those who call upon Him, answer us; answer us, You Who are is hard to anger, answer us; answer us, You Who are easy to pacify, answer us; answer us, merciful and gracious One, answer us; answer us, You Who hears the destitute, answer us; answer us, You Who supports the wholesome, answer us; answer us, God of our forefathers, answer us; answer us, God of Abraham, answer us; answer us, Dread of Isaac, answer us; answer us, Mighty One of Jacob, answer us; answer us, Helper of the tribes, answer us; answer us, Stronghold of the Matriarchs, answer us; answer us, You Who answers in a time of favor, answer us; answer us, Father of orphans, answer us; answer us, Judge of widows, answer us.*

מִי שֶׁעָנָה *He who answered our father Abraham on Mount Moriah, may He answer us.*
He Who answered his son Isaac when he was bound atop the altar, may He answer us.
He Who answered Jacob in Bethel, may He answer us.
He Who answered Joseph in the prison, may He answer us.
He Who answered our forefathers at the Sea of Reeds, may He answer us.
He Who answered Moses in Horeb, may He answer us.
He Who answered Aaron when he offered the censer, may He answer us.
He Who answered Phineas when he arose from amid the congregation, may He answer us.
He Who answered Joshua in Gilgal, may He answer us.
He Who answered Samuel in Mitzpah, may He answer us.
He Who answered David and his son Solomon in Jerusalem, may He answer us.
He Who answered Elijah on Mount Carmel, may He answer us.

מִי שֶׁעָנָה לֶאֱלִישָׁע בִּירִיחוֹ **הוּא יַעֲנֵנוּ.**

מִי שֶׁעָנָה לְיוֹנָה בִּמְעֵי הַדָּגָה **הוּא יַעֲנֵנוּ.**

מִי שֶׁעָנָה לְחִזְקִיָּהוּ מֶלֶךְ יְהוּדָה בְּחָלְיוֹ **הוּא יַעֲנֵנוּ.**

מִי שֶׁעָנָה לַחֲנַנְיָה מִישָׁאֵל וַעֲזַרְיָה בְּתוֹךְ כִּבְשַׁן הָאֵשׁ **הוּא יַעֲנֵנוּ.**

מִי שֶׁעָנָה לְדָנִיֵּאל בְּגוֹב הָאֲרָיוֹת **הוּא יַעֲנֵנוּ.**

מִי שֶׁעָנָה לְמָרְדְּכַי וְאֶסְתֵּר בְּשׁוּשַׁן הַבִּירָה **הוּא יַעֲנֵנוּ.**

מִי שֶׁעָנָה לְעֶזְרָא בַגּוֹלָה **הוּא יַעֲנֵנוּ.**

מִי שֶׁעָנָה לְכָל הַצַּדִּיקִים וְהַחֲסִידִים וְהַתְּמִימִים וְהַיְשָׁרִים **הוּא יַעֲנֵנוּ.**

רַחֲמָנָא דְּעָנֵי לַעֲנִיֵּי, עֲנֵינָן. רַחֲמָנָא דְּעָנֵי לִתְבִירֵי לִבָּא, עֲנֵינָן. רַחֲמָנָא דְּעָנֵי לְמַכִּיכֵי רוּחָא, עֲנֵינָן. רַחֲמָנָא עֲנֵינָן. רַחֲמָנָא חוּס. רַחֲמָנָא פְּרוֹק. רַחֲמָנָא שְׁזִיב. רַחֲמָנָא רְחַם עֲלָן, הַשְׁתָּא בַּעֲגָלָא וּבִזְמַן קָרִיב.

Shacharis continues with אָבִינוּ מַלְכֵּנוּ, page 120.

סליחות לחמישי

Begin *Selichos* on page 816, then continue here:

אֱלֹהֵינוּ וֵאלֹהֵי אֲבוֹתֵינוּ

תַּעֲנִית צִבּוּר קָבְעוּ תְּבוֹעַ צְרָכִים,\
שׁוּב עָדֶיךָ חַפֵּשׂ וְלַחֲקוֹר דְּרָכִים,\
רַךְ לִרְצוֹת בִּשְׁלֹשׁ עֶשְׂרֵה עֲרָכִים,\
קָשֶׁה לִכְעוֹס תֵּת לְאַפַּיִם אֲרֻכִּים.\
צְדָדֶיךָ מְקֻשָּׁטִים עֲדָיִם בְּלִי תַפְשִׁיט,\
פְּאֵר הָרַחֲמִים וְהַסְּלִיחוֹת הוֹד תַּכְשִׁיט,\
עֶרֶךְ שַׁוְעָתֵנוּ לְךָ לְבַד נוֹשִׁיט,\
סֶדֶר חַיִּים וּפַרְנָסָה לִיצוּרִים תּוֹשִׁיט.\
נִסְתְּמָה הַבִּירָה וְנִתְרוֹקַן טְהַר הַשֻּׁלְחָן,\
מֵזִין וּמֵזִיחַ סֶתֶר מֵעֲבֹדַת פָּלְחָן,\
לְשְׁפִיכַת הַנֶּפֶשׁ חָשׁוּב כְּבַשִׂית זָלְחָן,\
כִּמְעַטֵּר וּמַשְׂבִּיעַ גּוֹאֵל וְרוֹפֵא וְסָלְחָן.\
יֵאוֹת לְךָ יַעַן מִמְּנָתְךָ נִשְׁנֶסֶת,\
טוֹב רְוָחֲךָ הֱיוֹת נִזּוֹנֶת וּמִתְפַּרְנֶסֶת,\
חֵלֶף (לְךָ) שׁוֹאֶלֶת קוֹבֶלֶת וּמִתְנוֹסֶסֶת,\
זֵכֶר דַּאֲגוֹתֶיהָ לְפָנֶיךָ מְשִׂיחָה וּמַכְנֶסֶת.\
וְאֵלֶיךָ הִיא נְשׂוּיָה וּבְךָ חָסָיָה,\
הַוּוֹתֶיהָ הַעֲבֵר מִי כָמוֹךָ חֲסִין יָהּ,\
דֶּרֶךְ אֱמוּנָתְךָ בְּחֶלְקְךָ לִלְגִיוֹנְךָ אַפְסַנְיָא,\
גְּמוֹל חֶסֶד לַעֲלוּבָה הַלֵּזוּ אַכְסַנְיָא.\
בְּקִיאִים וּמְיֻשָּׁבִים לְרַצּוֹתְךָ בִּדְבָרִים עֲרֵבִים,\
אָפְסוּ פַּסּוּ בְּכֹחָם קַטֵּגוֹר מְעַרְבְּבִים,

He Who answered Elisha in Jericho, *may He answer us.*
He Who answered Jonah in the innards of the fish, *may He answer us.*
He Who answered Hezekiah, King of Judah, in his illness, *may He answer us.*
He Who answered Chananiah, Mishael, and Azariah in the fiery oven,
may He answer us.
He Who answered Daniel in the lions' den, *may He answer us.*
He Who answered Mordechai and Esther in Shushan the capital, *may He answer us.*
He Who answered Ezra in the exile, *may He answer us.*
He Who answered all the righteous, the devout, the wholesome, and the upright,
may He answer us.

רַחֲמָנָא *The Merciful One who answers the poor, may He answer us. The Merciful One Who answers the brokenhearted, may He answer us. The Merciful One Who answers the humble of spirit, may He answer us. O Merciful One, answer us. O Merciful One, pity. O Merciful One, redeem. O Merciful One, deliver. O Merciful One, have mercy on us — now, swiftly and soon.*

Shacharis continues with אָבִינוּ מַלְכֵּנוּ, 'Our Father, our King,' page 120.

SELICHOS FOR THURSDAY

Begin *Selichos* on page 816, then continue here:

Our God and the God of our forefathers

תַּעֲנִית *A public fast they designated, to petition for our necessities,*
ש *to repent to You through searching and examining our ways,*
ר *You Who are easily appeased through the formula*
of the Thirteen Attributes [of Mercy] —
ק *You Who are hard to anger, be patient in Your wrath.*
צ *You are adorned on all sides with ornaments [of mercy] — do not remove them;*
פ *the splendor of mercy and forgiveness are a glorious ornament;*
ע *adorn Yourself with a diadem of our praise and prayer,*
ס *extend orderly life and livelihood to Your creatures.*
נ *The capital city [Jerusalem] was shut down*
and the Table was emptied of its purity,
מ *the giver of sustenance and forgiveness [the Altar]*
is deprived of its Divine service,
ל *let the soulful outpouring of prayer be reckoned like the libations*
that drained into the [Altar's] pipe —
כ *be our Protector, Sustainer, Redeemer, Healer, and Forgiver.*
י *This befits You because Israel is girded by Your [Torah] portion,*
ט *from Your goodly spirit may she be nourished and sustained,*
ח *because (only to You) she does entreat, complain, and take pride;*
ז *the expression of her worries she expresses and presents to You.*
ו *To You does she lift her gaze and in You does she take refuge;*
ה *remove treacheries from her, for who is like You, O powerful God;*
ד *in Your customary manner of apportioning reward to Your legions,*
ג *do kindness to this disgraced abode [the soul].*
ב *Those knowledgeable and tactful in placating You with pleasant words —*
א *they have vanished, gone are those with the power*
to confound the accuser [Satan],

תַּעֲנִית — *A public fast they designated.* The verses of this supplication form a reverse alphabetical acrostic from ת to א. The last ten verses bear the author's signature, מֵאִיר הַצָּעִיר חָזָק בְּתוֹרָה וּבְמַעֲשִׂים טוֹבִים, *Meir, the Younger, may he be strong in Torah and good deeds.*

מְאַהֲבֵי לַאֲבִיהֶם שֶׁבַּשָּׁמַיִם זְרִיזִים וּמְעָרְבָבִים,
יְרֵאָיו נִדְבָּרִים דָּתוֹ שְׁחָרִים וַעֲרָבִים.
הִקְדַּשְׁנוּ **צוֹם עוֹ**לְלִים וְזִקְנֵי אֲסֻפּוֹת,
יִשַּׁרְנוּ **רִנָּ**ה וּתְפִלָּה וְשָׁקַדְנוּ סִפּוֹת,
חֲשׁוֹךְ לְמַטָּה מֵעָוֹן, וּשְׁלוֹמֵנוּ תִשְׁפּוֹת,
זְקוֹף דַּל מֵעָפָר וְאֶבְיוֹן מֵאַשְׁפּוֹת.
❖ **בְּתוֹר הַ**מַּעֲלָה **וּבְמִ**דּוֹת הֲגוּנוֹת תְּרוּמוֹת,
עֲרְבָתֵנוּ **שִׂים טוֹב יוֹ**שֵׁב **מְ**רוֹמוֹת,
וּבְמִקְוֵה טֹהַר תָּדִיחַ קַלּוֹת וְרָמוֹת,
מְצוֹא תְּפִלָּתֵנוּ חֶסֶד לְאַדֶּרֶךְ רוֹמֵמוֹת.

אֵל מֶלֶךְ יוֹשֵׁב עַל כִּסֵּא רַחֲמִים, מִתְנַהֵג בַּחֲסִידוּת, מוֹחֵל עֲוֹנוֹת עַמּוֹ, מַעֲבִיר רִאשׁוֹן רִאשׁוֹן, מַרְבֶּה מְחִילָה לְחַטָּאִים וּסְלִיחָה לַפּוֹשְׁעִים, עֹשֶׂה צְדָקוֹת עִם כָּל בָּשָׂר וָרוּחַ, לֹא כְרָעָתָם תִּגְמוֹל. ❖ אֵל הוֹרֵיתָ לָּנוּ לוֹמַר שְׁלֹשׁ עֶשְׂרֵה, וּזְכוֹר לָנוּ הַיּוֹם בְּרִית שְׁלֹשׁ עֶשְׂרֵה, כְּמוֹ שֶׁהוֹדַעְתָּ לֶעָנָיו מִקֶּדֶם, כְּמוֹ שֶׁכָּתוּב, וַיֵּרֶד יהוה בֶּעָנָן וַיִּתְיַצֵּב עִמּוֹ שָׁם, וַיִּקְרָא בְשֵׁם יהוה.

Congregation and *chazzan* recite loudly and in unison:

וַיַּעֲבֹר יהוה עַל פָּנָיו וַיִּקְרָא.

יהוה, יהוה, אֵל, רַחוּם, וְחַנּוּן, אֶרֶךְ אַפַּיִם, וְרַב חֶסֶד, וֶאֱמֶת, נֹצֵר חֶסֶד לָאֲלָפִים, נֹשֵׂא עָוֹן, וָפֶשַׁע, וְחַטָּאָה, וְנַקֵּה. וְסָלַחְתָּ לַעֲוֹנֵנוּ וּלְחַטָּאתֵנוּ וּנְחַלְתָּנוּ. סְלַח לָנוּ אָבִינוּ כִּי חָטָאנוּ, מְחַל לָנוּ מַלְכֵּנוּ כִּי פָשָׁעְנוּ. כִּי אַתָּה אֲדֹנָי טוֹב וְסַלָּח, וְרַב חֶסֶד לְכָל קֹרְאֶיךָ.

All continue:

הוֹשִׁיעָה יהוה כִּי גָמַר חָסִיד, כִּי פַסּוּ אֱמוּנִים מִבְּנֵי אָדָם.[1] כִּי אָדָם אֵין צַדִּיק בָּאָרֶץ, אֲשֶׁר יַעֲשֶׂה טּוֹב וְלֹא יֶחֱטָא.[2] הוֹשַׁע יהוה אֶת עַמְּךָ אֵת שְׁאֵרִית יִשְׂרָאֵל.[3] יִשְׂרָאֵל נוֹשַׁע בַּיהוה תְּשׁוּעַת עוֹלָמִים.[4]

כְּרַחֵם אָב עַל בָּנִים, כֵּן תְּרַחֵם יהוה עָלֵינוּ. לַיהוה הַיְשׁוּעָה, עַל עַמְּךָ בִרְכָתֶךָ סֶּלָה. יהוה צְבָאוֹת עִמָּנוּ, מִשְׂגָּב לָנוּ אֱלֹהֵי יַעֲקֹב סֶלָה. יהוה צְבָאוֹת, אַשְׁרֵי אָדָם בֹּטֵחַ בָּךְ. יהוה הוֹשִׁיעָה, הַמֶּלֶךְ יַעֲנֵנוּ בְיוֹם קָרְאֵנוּ.

(Many congregations repeat, סְלַח נָא . . . וְעַל עַמְּךָ [p. 820] here.)

אֱלֹהֵינוּ וֵאלֹהֵי אֲבוֹתֵינוּ

אַנְשֵׁי אֱמָנָה אָבָדוּ, **בָּ**אִים בְּכֹחַ מַעֲשֵׂיהֶם. **גִּ**בּוֹרִים לַעֲמוֹד בַּפֶּרֶץ, **ד**וֹחִים אֶת הַגְּזֵרוֹת. **הָ**יוּ לָנוּ לְחוֹמָה, **וּ**לְמַחֲסֶה בְּיוֹם זָעַם. **ז**וֹעֲכִים אַף בְּלַחֲשָׁם, **ח**ֵמָה עוֹצְרִים בְּשַׁוְעָם. **טֶ**רֶם קְרָאוּךָ עֲנִיתָם, **י**וֹדְעִים לַעְתֵּר וּלְרַצֵּךְ. **כְּ**אָב רִחַמְתָּ לְמַעֲנָם, **לֹ**א הֱשִׁיבוֹתָ פְּנֵיהֶם רֵיקָם. **מֵ**רוֹב עֲוֹנֵינוּ אֲבַדְנוּם, **נֶ**אֶסְפוּ מֶנּוּ בַּחֲטָאֵינוּ. **סָ**עוּ הֵמָּה לִמְנוּחוֹת, **עָ**זְבוּ אוֹתָנוּ לַאֲנָחוֹת.

those who made me beloved to my Father in heaven,
who were alacritous and pleasant,
who revered Him and discussed His law morning and evening.
We consecrated a fast day, gathering young and old,
with well-ordered chant and prayer we surge to Your gates;
restrain Yourself — [punish us] below the level of our sin
and increase our well being,
raise the needy erect from the dust and the destitute from the trash heaps.
∴ *With a sublime appearance, and with proper and lofty traits,*
endow us for the good, our Guarantor Who dwells in the heights,
and in a cleansing pool cleanse our minor and serious sins —
may our prayer elicit kindness to glorify You with exaltation.

אֵל מֶלֶךְ *O God, King Who sits on the throne of mercy; Who acts with kindness, pardons the sins of His people, removes sins one by one, increasingly grants pardon to careless sinners and forgiveness to willful ones, performs acts of generosity with every living being — You do not repay them in accord with their evil.* ∴ *O God, You taught us to recite the Thirteen [Attributes of Mercy], so remember for us today the covenant of these Thirteen, as You made known to the humble one [Moses] in ancient times, as it is written: And HASHEM descended in a cloud and stood with him there, and He called out with the Name HASHEM:*

Congregation and chazzan recite loudly and in unison:

And HASHEM passed before him [Moses] and proclaimed:

יהוה *HASHEM, HASHEM, God, Compassionate and Gracious, Slow to anger, and Abundant in Kindness and Truth. Preserver of kindness for thousands of generations, Forgiver of iniquity, willful sin, and error, and Who cleanses. May You forgive our iniquities and our errors and make us Your heritage. Forgive us, our Father, for we have erred; pardon us, our King, for we have willfully sinned; for You, my Lord, are good and forgiving and abundantly kind to all who call upon You.*

All continue:

הוֹשִׁיעָה *Save, HASHEM, for the devout is no more, for the faithful have vanished from mankind.*[1] *For no man is so wholly righteous on earth that he does good and never sins.*[2] *Save, O HASHEM, Your people, the remnant of Israel.*[3] *Israel is saved by HASHEM, with an eternal salvation.*[4]

כְּרַחֵם *As a father has mercy on his children, so, HASHEM, may You have mercy on us. Salvation is HASHEM's, upon Your people is Your blessing, Selah. HASHEM, Master of Legions, is with us, a stronghold for us is the God of Jacob, Selah. HASHEM, Master of Legions, praiseworthy is the person who trusts in You. HASHEM, save! May the King answer us on the day we call.*

(Many congregations repeat, *'Please forgive . . . Your people,'* [p. 820] here.)

Our God and the God of our Forefathers

אַנְשֵׁי *Lost are the men of faith, who would come in the merit of their deeds. Heroic to stand in the breach, they repulsed harsh decrees. They were our wall and a refuge in the day of wrath. With their prayer they extinguished fiery wrath, with their outcry they restrained fury. Before they called You, You answered them; they knew how to entreat and appease You. For their sake You showed mercy like a father, You did not turn them back empty-handed. For our abundant sins we lost them, they were taken from us because of our sins. They journeyed away to their rests, but us they left to groans.*

(1) *Psalms* 12:2. (2) *Ecclesiastes* 7:20. (3) *Jeremiah* 31:6. (4) *Isaiah* 45:17.

פַּסּוּ גּוֹדְרֵי פֶּרֶץ, צִמְּתוּ מְשִׁיבֵי חֵמָה. קָמֵי בַּפֶּרֶץ אַיִן, רְאוּיִם לְרַצּוֹתְךָ בְּעֶתֶר. שֻׁטַּטְנוּ בְּאַרְבַּע פִּנּוֹת, תְּרוּפָה לֹא מָצָאנוּ. ❖ שַׁבְנוּ אֵלֶיךָ בְּבֹשֶׁת פָּנִים, לְשַׁחֶרְךָ אֵל בְּעֵת צָרוֹתֵינוּ.

אֵל מֶלֶךְ יוֹשֵׁב עַל כִּסֵּא רַחֲמִים, מִתְנַהֵג בַּחֲסִידוּת, מוֹחֵל עֲוֹנוֹת עַמּוֹ, מַעֲבִיר רִאשׁוֹן רִאשׁוֹן, מַרְבֶּה מְחִילָה לְחַטָּאִים וּסְלִיחָה לַפּוֹשְׁעִים, עֹשֶׂה צְדָקוֹת עִם כָּל בָּשָׂר וָרוּחַ, לֹא כְרָעָתָם תִּגְמוֹל. ❖ אֵל הוֹרֵיתָ לָּנוּ לוֹמַר שְׁלֹשׁ עֶשְׂרֵה, וּזְכוֹר לָנוּ הַיּוֹם בְּרִית שְׁלֹשׁ עֶשְׂרֵה, כְּמוֹ שֶׁהוֹדַעְתָּ לֶעָנָיו מִקֶּדֶם, כְּמוֹ שֶׁכָּתוּב, וַיֵּרֶד יהוה בֶּעָנָן וַיִּתְיַצֵּב עִמּוֹ שָׁם, וַיִּקְרָא בְשֵׁם יהוה.

Congregation and *chazzan* recite loudly and in unison:

וַיַּעֲבֹר יהוה עַל פָּנָיו וַיִּקְרָא.

יהוה, יהוה, אֵל, רַחוּם, וְחַנּוּן, אֶרֶךְ אַפַּיִם, וְרַב חֶסֶד, וֶאֱמֶת, נֹצֵר חֶסֶד לָאֲלָפִים, נֹשֵׂא עָוֹן, וָפֶשַׁע, וְחַטָּאָה, וְנַקֵּה. וְסָלַחְתָּ לַעֲוֹנֵנוּ וּלְחַטָּאתֵנוּ וּנְחַלְתָּנוּ. סְלַח לָנוּ אָבִינוּ כִּי חָטָאנוּ, מְחַל לָנוּ מַלְכֵּנוּ כִּי פָשָׁעְנוּ. כִּי אַתָּה אֲדֹנָי טוֹב וְסַלָּח, וְרַב חֶסֶד לְכָל קֹרְאֶיךָ.

The following prayer is recited responsively by *chazzan* and congregation:

יִשְׂרָאֵל נוֹשַׁע בַּיהוה תְּשׁוּעַת עוֹלָמִים,[1]
גַּם הַיּוֹם יִוָּשְׁעוּ מִפִּיךָ שׁוֹכֵן מְרוֹמִים,
כִּי אַתָּה רַב סְלִיחוֹת וּבַעַל הָרַחֲמִים.

שְׁעָרֶיךָ הֵם דּוֹפְקִים כַּעֲנִיִּים וְדַלִּים,
צָקוּן לַחֲשָׁם קְשׁוֹב יָהּ שׁוֹכֵן מְעָלִים,
כִּי אַתָּה רַב סְלִיחוֹת וּבַעַל הָרַחֲמִים.

פְּחוּדִים הֵם מִכָּל צָרוֹת, מִמְּחָרְפֵיהֶם וּמִלּוֹחֲצֵיהֶם,
נָא אַל תַּעַזְבֵם יהוה אֱלֹהֵי אֲבוֹתֵיהֶם,
כִּי אַתָּה רַב סְלִיחוֹת וּבַעַל הָרַחֲמִים.

טוֹבוֹתֶיךָ יְקַדְּמוּ לָהֶם בְּיוֹם תּוֹכֵחָה,
וּמִתּוֹךְ צָרָה הַמְצִיאֵם פְּדוּת וּרְוָחָה,
כִּי אַתָּה רַב סְלִיחוֹת וּבַעַל הָרַחֲמִים.

יִוָּשְׁעוּ לְעֵין כֹּל וְאַל יִמְשְׁלוּ בָם רְשָׁעִים,
כַּלֵּה שֵׂעִיר וְחוֹתְנוּ וְיַעֲלוּ לְצִיּוֹן מוֹשִׁיעִים,[2]
כִּי אַתָּה רַב סְלִיחוֹת וּבַעַל הָרַחֲמִים.

הַקְשִׁיבָה אָדוֹן לְקוֹל שַׁוְעָתָם,
וְלִמְכוֹן שִׁבְתְּךָ הַשָּׁמַיִם תַּעֲלֶה תְפִלָּתָם,
כִּי אַתָּה רַב סְלִיחוֹת וּבַעַל הָרַחֲמִים.

Turn to page 826 for אֵל מֶלֶךְ, and continue until the conclusion of *Selichos*.

(1) *Isaiah* 45:17. (2) Cf. *Obadiah* 1:21.

Vanished are those who erected fences, cut off are those who turned back wrath. Those who stood in the breach are gone, who were worthy to appease You with entreaty. We were scattered to the four corners [of the earth], but we found no relief. ∴ *We have returned to You shamefacedly, to greet You in early morning, O God, in time of our distress.*

אֵל מֶלֶךְ *O God, King Who sits on the throne of mercy; Who acts with kindness, pardons the sins of His people, removes sins one by one, increasingly grants pardon to careless sinners and forgiveness to willful ones, performs acts of generosity with every living being — You do not repay them in accord with their evil.* ∴ *O God, You taught us to recite the Thirteen [Attributes of Mercy], so remember for us today the covenant of these Thirteen, as You made known to the humble one [Moses] in ancient times, as it is written: And HASHEM descended in a cloud and stood with him there, and He called out with the Name HASHEM:*

Congregation and chazzan recite loudly and in unison:

And HASHEM passed before him [Moses] and proclaimed:

יהוה *HASHEM, HASHEM, God, Compassionate and Gracious, Slow to anger, and Abundant in Kindness and Truth. Preserver of kindness for thousands of generations, Forgiver of iniquity, willful sin, and error, and Who cleanses. May You forgive our iniquities and our errors and make us Your heritage. Forgive us, our Father, for we have erred; pardon us, our King, for we have willfully sinned; for You, my Lord, are good and forgiving and abundantly kind to all who call upon You.*

The following prayer is recited responsively by the *chazzan* and congregation:

יִשְׂרָאֵל *Israel is saved by HASHEM with an eternal salvation;*[1]
today, too, may they be saved by Your word,
You Who dwells in the heights —
for You are abundantly forgiving and the Master of mercies.

They knock on Your gates like poor and destitute people;
hearken to the quiet outpouring of their heart, O God Who dwells aloft —
for You are abundantly forgiving and the Master of mercies.

They are made afraid by all the woes, of those who disgrace and oppress them;
please do not forsake them, O HASHEM, the God of their forefathers —
for You are abundantly forgiving and the Master of mercies.

May Your goodness precede them on the day of admonishment,
and from amid distress remove them to deliverance and relief —
for You are abundantly forgiving and the Master of mercies.

May they be saved in the sight of everyone and let not the wicked dominate them,
destroy Seir [Esau] and his father-in-law [Ishmael]
and let saviors go up to Zion[2] *—*
for You are abundantly forgiving and the Master of mercies.

Hearken, O Master, to the sound of their outcry;
and to the heavenly place of Your dwelling, may their prayer ascend —
for You are abundantly forgiving and the Master of mercies.

Turn to page 826 for אֵל מֶלֶךְ, *'O God, King,'* and continue until the conclusion of *Selichos.*

יִשְׂרָאֵל — *Israel.* The acrostic spells the author's name, שְׁפַטְיָה, *Shephatiah,* a well-known Kabbalist who lived in Oria, Italy. When the Byzantine emperor Basil I issued anti-Jewish decrees (about 873 C.E.), Rabbi Shephatiah traveled to Constantinople in an attempt to convince the emperor to annul his decrees. Although unsuccessful in his overall mission, while he was in Basil's court Rabbi Shephatiah cured a daughter of the emperor who had been 'possessed.' As a reward, Basil released the Jews of Oria, as well as four other Jewish communities, from his decrees. Both Rabbi Shephatiah and his son and successor, Rabbi

סליחות לשני תנינא

Begin *Selichos* on page 816, then continue here:

אֱלֹהֵינוּ וֵאלֹהֵי אֲבוֹתֵינוּ

אֲפָפוּנוּ מַיִם עַד נֶפֶשׁ,[1] **בָּ**אנוּ בְּעִמְקֵי מְצוּלָה, **גַּ**לֵּי יַם עָבְרוּ עָלֵינוּ, **דָּ**כְיוֹת תְּהוֹם כִּסָּתְנוּ. **הוֹ**דֵנוּ נֶהְפַּךְ לְמַשְׁחִית, **וְ**עוֹד לֹא עָצַרְנוּ כֹּחַ,[2] **זָ**לְעָפְנוּ עַל חַטֹּאתֵינוּ, **חָ**לְחָלְנוּ עַל רוֹב פְּשָׁעֵינוּ. **טָ**כַסְנוּ עֵצָה מַה לַּעֲשׂוֹת, **יוֹ**עֵץ בְּקִרְבֵּנוּ אָיִן, **כּ**וֹנַנּוּ בְּלֵב מַחֲשָׁבוֹת, **לְ**מֵרָחוֹק שְׂאֵת דֵּעָה.[3] **מַ**סֹּרֶת בְּיָדֵינוּ מֵאֲבוֹתֵינוּ, **נְ**אָקָה תְּשׁוּבָה וּצְדָקָה, **סוֹ**תְּרוֹת רוֹעַ גְּזֵרוֹת, **עוֹד** מְעֻנּוֹת עָם. **פָּ**צְנוּ בְּהַסְכָּמָה אַחַת, **צוֹם** שֵׁנִי וַחֲמִישִׁי וְשֵׁנִי, **קָ**דוֹשׁ אוּלַי יַשְׁקִיף, **רַ**חֲמָיו לְקַדֵּם לְרֹגֶז. **שַׁ**דַּי עָשִׂינוּ אֶת שֶׁלָּנוּ, **תַּ**קִּיף עֲשֵׂה אֶת שֶׁלָּךְ. ❖ אַל תֵּשֵׁב עִמָּנוּ בַּדִּין, מִדֶּבֶר וּמֵחֶרֶב וּמֵרָעָב מַלְּטֵנוּ, **תִּ**יקַר נַפְשֵׁנוּ בְּעֵינֶיךָ, יָהּ סְלַח לָנוּ, מְחַל לָנוּ, כַּפֵּר לָנוּ, כְּיוֹם רְדִתְּךָ בֶּעָנָן.

אֵל מֶלֶךְ יוֹשֵׁב עַל כִּסֵּא רַחֲמִים, מִתְנַהֵג בַּחֲסִידוּת, מוֹחֵל עֲוֹנוֹת עַמּוֹ, מַעֲבִיר רִאשׁוֹן רִאשׁוֹן, מַרְבֶּה מְחִילָה לְחַטָּאִים וּסְלִיחָה לַפּוֹשְׁעִים, עֹשֶׂה צְדָקוֹת עִם כָּל בָּשָׂר וָרוּחַ, לֹא כְרָעָתָם תִּגְמוֹל. ❖ אֵל הוֹרֵיתָ לָּנוּ לוֹמַר שְׁלֹשׁ עֶשְׂרֵה, וּזְכוֹר לָנוּ הַיּוֹם בְּרִית שְׁלֹשׁ עֶשְׂרֵה, כְּמוֹ שֶׁהוֹדַעְתָּ לֶעָנָיו מִקֶּדֶם, כְּמוֹ שֶׁכָּתוּב, וַיֵּרֶד יהוה בֶּעָנָן וַיִּתְיַצֵּב עִמּוֹ שָׁם, וַיִּקְרָא בְשֵׁם יהוה.

Congregation and *chazzan* recite loudly and in unison:

וַיַּעֲבֹר יהוה עַל פָּנָיו וַיִּקְרָא.

יהוה, יהוה, אֵל, רַחוּם, וְחַנּוּן, אֶרֶךְ אַפַּיִם, וְרַב חֶסֶד, וֶאֱמֶת, נֹצֵר חֶסֶד לָאֲלָפִים, נֹשֵׂא עָוֹן, וָפֶשַׁע, וְחַטָּאָה, וְנַקֵּה. וְסָלַחְתָּ לַעֲוֹנֵנוּ וּלְחַטָּאתֵנוּ וּנְחַלְתָּנוּ. סְלַח לָנוּ אָבִינוּ כִּי חָטָאנוּ, מְחַל לָנוּ מַלְכֵּנוּ כִּי פָשָׁעְנוּ. כִּי אַתָּה אֲדֹנָי טוֹב וְסַלָּח, וְרַב חֶסֶד לְכָל קֹרְאֶיךָ.

All continue:

הַאֲזִינָה יהוה תְּפִלָּתֵנוּ, וְהַקְשִׁיבָה בְּקוֹל תַּחֲנוּנוֹתֵינוּ.[4] שְׁמַע יהוה קוֹלֵנוּ, נִקְרָא חָנֵּנוּ וַעֲנֵנוּ.[5] שִׁמְעָה יהוה צֶדֶק, הַקְשִׁיבָה רִנָּתֵנוּ, הַאֲזִינָה תְּפִלָּתֵנוּ.[6] שְׁמַע יהוה וְחָנֵּנוּ, יהוה הֱיֵה עוֹזֵר לָנוּ.[7]

כְּרַחֵם אָב עַל בָּנִים, כֵּן תְּרַחֵם יהוה עָלֵינוּ. לַיהוה הַיְשׁוּעָה, עַל עַמְּךָ בִרְכָתֶךָ סֶּלָה. יהוה צְבָאוֹת עִמָּנוּ, מִשְׂגָּב לָנוּ אֱלֹהֵי יַעֲקֹב סֶלָה. יהוה צְבָאוֹת, אַשְׁרֵי אָדָם בֹּטֵחַ בָּךְ. יהוה הוֹשִׁיעָה, הַמֶּלֶךְ יַעֲנֵנוּ בְיוֹם קָרְאֵנוּ.

(Many congregations repeat, סְלַח נָא . . . וְעַל עַמֶּךָ [p. 820] here.)

---

(1) Cf. *Jonah* 2:6. (2) Cf. *Daniel* 10:8. (3) Cf. *Job* 36:3.
(4) Cf. *Psalms* 86:8. (5) Cf. 27:7. (6) Cf. 17:1. (7) Cf. 30:11.

SELICHOS FOR THE SECOND MONDAY

Begin *Selichos* on page 816, then continue here:

Our God and the God of our forefathers

אֲפָפְוּנוּ *Waters encompass us to our very soul;*[1] *we have arrived at the furthest depths; the waves of the sea poured over us; the roaring waves of the deep cover us. Our majesty has changed to corruption, and we have no more strength;*[2] *we tremble because of our sins; we are deeply distressed because of the multitude of our willful sins. We sought counsel what to do; there is no counselor among us; we pondered thoughts in our heart, bearing knowledge from afar.*[3] *We hold the tradition of our forefathers, that prayer, repentance, and charity shatter evil decrees, that the nation may no longer suffer. We proclaimed unanimously the fast of Monday, Thursday, and Monday, hoping that the Holy One would peer down on us, to precede the wrath with His mercy. Almighty One, we have done ours; O Powerful One, do Yours.* ∴ *Do not sit with us in judgment; spare us from plague, sword and famine; may our souls be precious in Your eyes; O God, please forgive us, pardon us, atone for us, as on the day You descended in a cloud.*

אֵל מֶלֶךְ *O God, King Who sits on the throne of mercy; Who acts with kindness, pardons the sins of His people, removes sins one by one, increasingly grants pardon to careless sinners and forgiveness to willful ones, performs acts of generosity with every living being — You do not repay them in accord with their evil.* ∴ *O God, You taught us to recite the Thirteen [Attributes of Mercy], so remember for us today the covenant of these Thirteen, as You made known to the humble one [Moses] in ancient times, as it is written: And HASHEM descended in a cloud and stood with him there, and He called out with the Name HASHEM:*

Congregation and *chazzan* recite loudly and in unison:

And HASHEM passed before him [Moses] and proclaimed:

יהוה *HASHEM, HASHEM, God, Compassionate and Gracious, Slow to anger, and Abundant in Kindness and Truth. Preserver of kindness for thousands of generations, Forgiver of iniquity, willful sin, and error, and Who cleanses. May You forgive our iniquities and our errors and make us Your heritage. Forgive us, our Father, for we have erred; pardon us, our King, for we have willfully sinned; for You, my Lord, are good and forgiving and abundantly kind to all who call upon You.*

All continue:

הַאֲזִינָה *Give ear, O HASHEM, to our prayer, and heed the sound of our supplications.*[4] *Hear, HASHEM, our voice when we call; favor us and answer us.*[5] *Hear, HASHEM, what is righteous, hearken to our cry, give ear to our prayer.*[6] *Hear, HASHEM, and favor us, HASHEM, be our Helper.*[7]

כְּרַחֵם *As a father has mercy on his children, so, HASHEM, may You have mercy on us. Salvation is HASHEM's, upon Your people is Your blessing, Selah. HASHEM, Master of Legions, is with us, a stronghold for us is the God of Jacob, Selah. HASHEM, Master of Legions, praiseworthy is the person who trusts in You. HASHEM, save! May the King answer us on the day we call.*

(Many congregations repeat, *'Please forgive . . . Your people,'* [p. 820] here.)

Amittai (see below), often allude to the persecutions and forced conversions that Basil inflicted upon the Jews.

אֲפָפְוּנוּ מַיִם — *Waters encompass us.* The *paytan* signed his name אֲמִתַּי, *Amittai,* as the acrostic of the four stiches of the final verse. He was the son and successor to his father, Rabbi Shephatiah (see above), as leader of the Jewish community in Oria.

אֱלֹהֵינוּ וֵאלֹהֵי אֲבוֹתֵינוּ

אֱזוֹן תַּחַן וְהַסְכֵּת עֲתִירָה, אַף הָפֵר וְשַׁכֵּךְ עֶבְרָה,
בָּאֵי לְחַלּוֹתְךָ בְּנֶפֶשׁ מָרָה, בְּשִׁמְךָ הַגָּדוֹל יִמְצְאוּ עֶזְרָה.
גַּעְיַת נֶאֱנָחִים עֱנוּתָם חֲזֵה, גְּחִינַת קוֹמָתָם אַל תִּבְזֶה,
דְּרוֹשׁ עֶלְבּוֹנָם מִצַּר וּבוֹזֶה, דְּרוֹךְ פּוּרָה וְנִצְחָם יַזֶּה.[1]
הֲלֹא אַתָּה הָיִיתָ וְהִנְּךָ, הָיוֹ תִהְיֶה בַּהֲדַר גְּאוֹנֶךָ,
וְנַמְתָּ יִכּוֹן זֶרַע אֱמוּנֶיךָ, וְהִנָּם כָּלִים מִתִּגְרַת חֲרוֹנֶךָ.
זוֹעֲמוּ בְּעִוּוּיָם וּמִמַּאֲוַיָּם נִסָּחוּ, זוֹרוּ בָּאֲפָסִים וְלֹא נָחוּ,
חֻבְּלָה רוּחָם וְלֶעָפָר שָׁחוּ, חָרְשׁוּ חוֹרְשִׁים וּמַעֲנִית הִמְתִּיחוּ.[2]
טָבְעוּ בַּבּוֹץ וְאֵין פּוֹצֶה, טוֹרְפֵיהֶם שָׁלוּ מִקָּצֶה אֶל קָצֶה,
יוֹם יוֹם לוֹחֲמָם מְנַצֵּחַ, יַד פּוֹרְשִׂים מִלַּחַץ לֵיצֵא.
כָּלוּ חַיֵּיהֶם בְּיָגוֹן וַאֲנָחָה, כָּשַׁל רַבָּה וְעָרְבָה שִׂמְחָה,
לְיֶשַׁע חוֹכִים וְהִנֵּה צְוָחָה, לִבְּטוּם קָמִים וְכָרוּ שׁוּחָה.
מַעֲרִימִים סוֹד מִמְּךָ לְהַדִּיחָם, מַכְבִּידִים עוֹל לְהַכְשִׁיל כֹּחָם,
נוֹאֲקִים אֵלֶיךָ בְּהִתְעַטֵּף רוּחָם, נַחַת לִמְצוֹא מִכֹּבֶד טָרְחָם.
שִׂיחַ צָקִים בְּמַעֲמַד צָפוּף, סְלִיחָה מְבַקְשִׁים בְּקָדְקֹד כָּפוּף,
עוֹשְׁקֵיהֶם הִקְנִיאוּם וּנְתָנוּם לְשִׁסּוּף, עִוְעִים יִמְסְכוּ וְיִהְיוּ לְסִפּוּף.
פְּדֵה דְבֵקֶיךָ מֵחֶרֶץ וְכִלּוּי, פַּלְּטֵם מִצּוֹרֵר וּתְנֵם לְעִלּוּי,
צַוֵּה יְשׁוּעוֹת מְשַׁחֲרֶיךָ בְּחִלּוּי, צוּר עוֹלָמִים הוֹשִׁיעֵנוּ בְּגָלוּי.
קַנָּא וְנוֹקֵם קַנֵּא לִשְׁמֶךָ, קַצֵּץ עֻלָּם מְצַוֵּאר עַמֶּךָ,
רְאֵה עֲמָלֵנוּ וְשׁוּב מִזַּעְמֶךָ, רִיבָה רִיבֵנוּ מֵעִם חֶרְמֶךָ.
שְׁכִינָתְךָ הָשֵׁב לְחֵיק אַרְמוֹנַי, שַׁאֲנָן הוֹשֵׁב לְוִיַּי וְכֹהֲנַי,
❖ תַּטֶּה אָזְנְךָ לְקוֹל תַּחֲנוּנַי, תִּרְצֵנִי בְּקָרְאִי יהוה יהוה.

אֵל מֶלֶךְ יוֹשֵׁב עַל כִּסֵּא רַחֲמִים, מִתְנַהֵג בַּחֲסִידוּת, מוֹחֵל עֲוֹנוֹת עַמּוֹ, מַעֲבִיר רִאשׁוֹן רִאשׁוֹן, מַרְבֶּה מְחִילָה לְחַטָּאִים וּסְלִיחָה לַפּוֹשְׁעִים, עֹשֶׂה צְדָקוֹת עִם כָּל בָּשָׂר וָרוּחַ, לֹא כְרָעָתָם תִּגְמוֹל. ❖ אֵל הוֹרֵיתָ לָּנוּ לוֹמַר שְׁלֹשׁ עֶשְׂרֵה, וּזְכוֹר לָנוּ הַיּוֹם בְּרִית שְׁלֹשׁ עֶשְׂרֵה, כְּמוֹ שֶׁהוֹדַעְתָּ לֶעָנָיו מִקֶּדֶם, כְּמוֹ שֶׁכָּתוּב, וַיֵּרֶד יהוה בֶּעָנָן וַיִּתְיַצֵּב עִמּוֹ שָׁם, וַיִּקְרָא בְשֵׁם יהוה.

(1) Cf. *Isaiah* 63:3. (2) Cf. *Psalms* 129:3.

Our God and the God of our forefathers

אֱזוֹן *Give ear to supplication and heed entreaty, annul anger and calm fury,*
ב *may those who come to implore You with embittered soul*
find help through Your Great Name.
ג *Note the wail of those who groan in their affliction,*
do not disgrace their body hunched in prayer,
ד *avenge their humiliation from oppressor and scorner,*
trample him as in a winepress and let his blood spurt out.[1]
ה *Have You not always existed and still exist?*
You shall always exist in Your splendrous pride,
ו *and You declared that the offspring of Your faithful ones would be steadfast —*
but behold they are consumed by the force of Your anger.
ז *They have enraged You with their iniquities and became distanced from their delightful Temple,*
they were scattered to all corners and rested not,
ח *their spirit is broken and they are bowed to the dust,*
the plowers plowed [on them] and lengthened their furrow.[2]
ט *They sunk into the mire and no one releases [them],*
those who devour them are at ease from end to end,
י *every day their attackers provoke,*
while they extend a pleading hand to escape oppression.
כ *Their lives are consumed in grief and groaning;*
the collapse is great and gladness is darkened;
ל *they hope for salvation, but behold there is shrieking,*
their adversaries perplexed them and dug a pit.
מ *They scheme deceitfully to turn them away from You,*
they weigh down the yoke to weaken them,
נ *they cry out to You when their spirit grows faint,*
to find relief from their burdensome weight.
ס *They pour forth prayers in crowded quarters,*
they implore forgiveness with head bowed down,
ע *their tormentors provoke them and deliver them to slaughter —*
may confusion confound them and let them be destroyed.
פ *Redeem those who cling to You from the decree of destruction,*
rescue them from the oppressor and place them on the ascent,
צ *command salvations for those who seek You with entreaty —*
O Rock of the Worlds, save us openly.
ק *O zealous and avenging One, be zealous for Your Name,*
slice off the yoke from the neck of Your people,
ר *see our toil and turn back from Your anger,*
take up our grievance against the people that blasphemes You.
ש *Return Your presence to the bosom of my palaces,*
return the tranquillity of my Levites and Kohanim,
ת ∴ *incline Your ear to the sound of my supplications,*
favor me when I call out, 'HASHEM, HASHEM!'

אֵל מֶלֶךְ *O God, King Who sits on the throne of mercy; Who acts with kindness, pardons the sins of His people, removes sins one by one, increasingly grants pardon to careless sinners and forgiveness to willful ones, performs acts of generosity with every living being — You do not repay them in accord with their evil. ∴ O God, You taught us to recite the Thirteen [Attributes of Mercy], so remember for us today the covenant of these Thirteen, as You made known to the humble one [Moses] in ancient times, as it is written: And HASHEM descended in a cloud and stood with him there, and He called out with the Name HASHEM:*

Congregation and *chazzan* recite loudly and in unison:

וַיַּעֲבֹר יהוה עַל פָּנָיו וַיִּקְרָא.

יהוה, יהוה, אֵל, רַחוּם, וְחַנּוּן, אֶרֶךְ אַפַּיִם, וְרַב חֶסֶד, וֶאֱמֶת, נֹצֵר חֶסֶד לָאֲלָפִים, נֹשֵׂא עָוֹן, וָפֶשַׁע, וְחַטָּאָה, וְנַקֵּה. וְסָלַחְתָּ לַעֲוֹנֵנוּ וּלְחַטָּאתֵנוּ וּנְחַלְתָּנוּ. סְלַח לָנוּ אָבִינוּ כִּי חָטָאנוּ, מְחַל לָנוּ מַלְכֵּנוּ כִּי פָשָׁעְנוּ. כִּי אַתָּה אֲדֹנָי טוֹב וְסַלָּח, וְרַב חֶסֶד לְכָל קֹרְאֶיךָ.

The following prayer is recited responsively by the *chazzan* and congregation:

יהוה יהוה אֵל, רַחוּם, וְחַנּוּן, אֶרֶךְ אַפַּיִם, וְרַב חֶסֶד, וֶאֱמֶת.
נֹצֵר חֶסֶד לָאֲלָפִים, נֹשֵׂא עָוֹן, וָפֶשַׁע, וְחַטָּאָה, וְנַקֵּה.[1]
וְסָלַחְתָּ לַעֲוֹנֵנוּ וּלְחַטָּאתֵנוּ וּנְחַלְתָּנוּ.[2]

אֶזְכְּרָה אֱלֹהִים וְאֶהֱמָיָה,[3] בִּרְאוֹתִי כָּל עִיר עַל תִּלָּהּ בְּנוּיָה,
וְעִיר הָאֱלֹהִים מֻשְׁפֶּלֶת עַד שְׁאוֹל תַּחְתִּיָּה,
וּבְכָל זֹאת, אָנוּ לְיָהּ וְעֵינֵינוּ לְיָהּ.
מִדַּת הָרַחֲמִים עָלֵינוּ הִתְגַּלְגְּלִי, וְלִפְנֵי קוֹנֵךְ תְּחִנָּתֵנוּ הַפִּילִי,
וּבְעַד עַמֵּךְ רַחֲמִים שַׁאֲלִי, כִּי כָל לֵבָב דַּוָּי וְכָל רֹאשׁ לָחֳלִי.[4]
תָּמַכְתִּי יְתֵדוֹתַי בִּשְׁלֹשׁ עֶשְׂרֵה תֵבוֹת, וּבְשַׁעֲרֵי דְמָעוֹת כִּי לֹא נִשְׁלָבוֹת,
לָכֵן שָׁפַכְתִּי שִׂיחַ פְּנֵי בוֹחֵן לִבּוֹת,
בָּטוּחַ אֲנִי בְּאֵלֶּה וּבִזְכוּת שְׁלֹשֶׁת אָבוֹת.
יְהִי רָצוֹן מִלְּפָנֶיךָ שׁוֹמֵעַ קוֹל בְּכִיּוֹת, שֶׁתָּשִׂים דִּמְעוֹתֵינוּ בְּנֹאדְךָ לִהְיוֹת,[5]
וְתַצִּילֵנוּ מִכָּל גְּזֵרוֹת אַכְזָרִיּוֹת, כִּי לְךָ לְבַד עֵינֵינוּ תְלוּיוֹת.

אֵל מֶלֶךְ יוֹשֵׁב עַל כִּסֵּא רַחֲמִים, מִתְנַהֵג בַּחֲסִידוּת, מוֹחֵל עֲוֹנוֹת עַמּוֹ, מַעֲבִיר רִאשׁוֹן רִאשׁוֹן, מַרְבֶּה מְחִילָה לְחַטָּאִים וּסְלִיחָה לַפּוֹשְׁעִים, עֹשֶׂה צְדָקוֹת עִם כָּל בָּשָׂר וָרוּחַ, לֹא כְרָעָתָם תִּגְמוֹל. ❖ אֵל הוֹרֵיתָ לָּנוּ לוֹמַר שְׁלֹשׁ עֶשְׂרֵה, וּזְכוֹר לָנוּ הַיּוֹם בְּרִית שְׁלֹשׁ עֶשְׂרֵה, כְּמוֹ שֶׁהוֹדַעְתָּ לֶעָנָיו מִקֶּדֶם, כְּמוֹ שֶׁכָּתוּב, וַיֵּרֶד יהוה בֶּעָנָן וַיִּתְיַצֵּב עִמּוֹ שָׁם, וַיִּקְרָא בְשֵׁם יהוה.

Congregation and *chazzan* recite loudly and in unison:

וַיַּעֲבֹר יהוה עַל פָּנָיו וַיִּקְרָא.

יהוה, יהוה, אֵל, רַחוּם, וְחַנּוּן, אֶרֶךְ אַפַּיִם, וְרַב חֶסֶד, וֶאֱמֶת, נֹצֵר חֶסֶד לָאֲלָפִים, נֹשֵׂא עָוֹן, וָפֶשַׁע, וְחַטָּאָה, וְנַקֵּה. וְסָלַחְתָּ לַעֲוֹנֵנוּ וּלְחַטָּאתֵנוּ וּנְחַלְתָּנוּ. סְלַח לָנוּ אָבִינוּ כִּי חָטָאנוּ, מְחַל לָנוּ מַלְכֵּנוּ כִּי פָשָׁעְנוּ. כִּי אַתָּה אֲדֹנָי טוֹב וְסַלָּח, וְרַב חֶסֶד לְכָל קֹרְאֶיךָ.

Turn to page 828 for זְכוֹר רַחֲמֶיךָ, and the conclusion of *Selichos*.

Congregation and *chazzan* recite loudly and in unison:

And HASHEM passed before him [Moses] and proclaimed:

יהוה *HASHEM, HASHEM, God, Compassionate and Gracious, Slow to anger, and Abundant in Kindness and Truth. Preserver of kindness for thousands of generations, Forgiver of iniquity, willful sin, and error, and Who cleanses. May You forgive our iniquities and our errors and make us Your heritage. Forgive us, our Father, for we have erred; pardon us, our King, for we have willfully sinned; for You, my Lord, are good and forgiving and abundantly kind to all who call upon You.*

The following prayer is recited responsively by the *chazzan* and congregation:

יהוה יהוה *HASHEM, HASHEM, God, Compassionate and Gracious,*
Slow to anger, and Abundant in Kindness and Truth.
Preserver of kindness for thousands of generations,
Forgiver of iniquity, willful sin, and error, and Who cleanses.[1]
May You forgive our iniquities and our errors and make us Your heritage.[2]

I shall remember, O God, and I shall moan,[3] *when I see every city built on its hilltop,*
while the City of God is lowered to the nethermost depth.
But despite all this, we are God's and our eyes look to God.

O attribute of Mercy, overflow upon us,
and cast our supplication before your Creator;
for the sake of Your people request mercy,
for every heart is pained and every head is ill.[4]

I have placed my reliance on the Thirteen Attributes
and on the gates of tears for they are never closed,
therefore I have poured out my prayer to Him Who tests hearts.
I trust in these and in the merit of the three Patriarchs.

May it be Your will, You who hears the sound of weeping,
that You place our tears in Your flask permanently,[5]
and that You rescue us from all cruel decrees,
for on You alone are our eyes fixed.

אֵל מֶלֶךְ *O God, King Who sits on the throne of mercy; Who acts with kindness, pardons the sins of His people, removes sins one by one, increasingly grants pardon to careless sinners and forgiveness to willful ones, performs acts of generosity with every living being — You do not repay them in accord with their evil. ∴ O God, You taught us to recite the Thirteen [Attributes of Mercy], so remember for us today the covenant of these Thirteen, as You made known to the humble one [Moses] in ancient times, as it is written: And HASHEM descended in a cloud and stood with him there, and He called out with the Name HASHEM:*

Congregation and *chazzan* recite loudly and in unison:

And HASHEM passed before him [Moses] and proclaimed:

יהוה *HASHEM, HASHEM, God, Compassionate and Gracious, Slow to anger, and Abundant in Kindness and Truth. Preserver of kindness for thousands of generations, Forgiver of iniquity, willful sin, and error, and Who cleanses. May You forgive our iniquities and our errors and make us Your heritage. Forgive us, our Father, for we have erred; pardon us, our King, for we have willfully sinned; for You, my Lord, are good and forgiving and abundantly kind to all who call upon You.*

Turn to page 828 for זְכוֹר רַחֲמֶיךָ, *Remember Your mercies,* and the conclusion of *Selichos.*

(1) *Exodus* 34:6-7. (2) 34:9. (3) *Psalms* 77:4. (4) Cf. *Isaiah* 1:5. (5) Cf. *Psalms* 56:9.

⊰ה׳ ה׳ — *HASHEM, HASHEM*. The acrostic spells the author's name אֲמִתַּי. See commentary p. 843.

סליחות לעשרה בטבת

Begin *Selichos* on page 816, then continue here:

אֱלֹהֵינוּ וֵאלֹהֵי אֲבוֹתֵינוּ

אֶזְכְּרָה מָצוֹק אֲשֶׁר קְרָאַנִי, **בְּ**שָׁלֹשׁ מַכּוֹת בַּחֹדֶשׁ הַזֶּה הִכַּנִי,
גְּדָעַנִי הֱנִיאַנִי הִכְאַנִי, אַךְ עַתָּה הֶלְאָנִי.[1]
דְּעָכַנִי בִּשְׁמוֹנָה בוֹ שְׂמֹאלִית וִימָנִית, **הֲ**לֹא שְׁלָשְׁתָּן קָבַעְתִּי תַעֲנִית,
וּמֶלֶךְ יָוָן אִנְּסַנִי לִכְתּוֹב דַּת יְוָנִית,
עַל גַּבִּי חָרְשׁוּ חוֹרְשִׁים, הֶאֱרִיכוּ מַעֲנִית.[2]
זוֹעַמְתִּי בְּתִשְׁעָה בוֹ בִּכְלִמָּה וָחֵפֶר, **חָ**שַׁךְ מֵעָלַי מְעִיל הוֹד וָצֶפֶר,
טָרֹף טֹרַף בּוֹ הַנּוֹתֵן אִמְרֵי שֶׁפֶר, הוּא עֶזְרָא הַסּוֹפֵר.
יוֹם עֲשִׂירִי צֻוָּה בֶּן בּוּזִי הַחוֹזֶה, **כְּ**תָב לְךָ בְּסֵפֶר הַמַּחֲזֶה,
לְזִכָּרוֹן לְעַם נָמֵס וְנִבְזֶה, אֶת עֶצֶם הַיּוֹם הַזֶּה.[3]
מִנְיַן סֵדֶר חֳדָשִׁים בַּעֲשָׂרָה בּוֹ הֵעִיר, **נְ**הִי וִילֵל בְּמוֹ פִי אַפְעִיר,
סֵדֶר פֻּרְעָנִיּוֹת בְּתוֹךְ לְבָבִי יַבְעִיר,
בְּבֹא אֵלַי הַפָּלִיט לֵאמֹר הֻכְּתָה הָעִיר.[4]
עַל אֵלֶּה עַל פָּנַי אָבָק זֵרִיתִי, **פָּ**צְתִּי עַל אַרְבַּעְתָּן לוּ חֵץ בְּלִבִּי יָרִיתִי,
צָרוֹת עַל אֵלֶּה קֶבֶר לִי כָּרִיתִי, צַדִּיק הוּא יהוה כִּי פִיהוּ מָרִיתִי.[5]
קָרָאתִי שִׁמְךָ מִתְנַחֵם עַל רָעָתִי, **רְ**אֵה עָנְיִי וּשְׁמַע קוֹל פְּגִיעָתִי,
שְׁמַע תְּחִנָּתִי חִישׁ נָא יְשׁוּעָתִי, אַל תַּעְלֵם אָזְנְךָ לְרַוְחָתִי לְשַׁוְעָתִי.[6]
❖ **יֶ**רַח טֵבֵת מְאֹד לָקִיתִי בוֹ, **וְ**נִשְׁתַּנּוּ עָלַי סִדְרֵי נְתִיבוֹ,
סָרַרְתִּי פְּשָׁעָתִי, יְגַלֶּה לִי טוּבוֹ, **הָ**אוֹמֵר לַיָּם עַד פֹּה תָבֹא.[7]

אֵל מֶלֶךְ יוֹשֵׁב עַל כִּסֵּא רַחֲמִים, מִתְנַהֵג בַּחֲסִידוּת, מוֹחֵל עֲוֹנוֹת עַמּוֹ, מַעֲבִיר רִאשׁוֹן רִאשׁוֹן, מַרְבֶּה מְחִילָה לְחַטָּאִים וּסְלִיחָה לַפּוֹשְׁעִים, עֹשֶׂה צְדָקוֹת עִם כָּל בָּשָׂר וָרוּחַ, לֹא כְרָעָתָם תִּגְמוֹל. ❖ אֵל הוֹרֵיתָ לָּנוּ לוֹמַר שְׁלֹשׁ עֶשְׂרֵה, וּזְכוֹר לָנוּ הַיּוֹם בְּרִית שְׁלֹשׁ עֶשְׂרֵה, כְּמוֹ שֶׁהוֹדַעְתָּ לֶעָנָיו מִקֶּדֶם, כְּמוֹ שֶׁכָּתוּב, וַיֵּרֶד יהוה בֶּעָנָן וַיִּתְיַצֵּב עִמּוֹ שָׁם, וַיִּקְרָא בְשֵׁם יהוה.

Congregation and *chazzan* recite loudly and in unison:

וַיַּעֲבֹר יהוה עַל פָּנָיו וַיִּקְרָא:

יהוה, יהוה, אֵל, רַחוּם, וְחַנּוּן, אֶרֶךְ אַפַּיִם, וְרַב חֶסֶד, וֶאֱמֶת, נֹצֵר חֶסֶד לָאֲלָפִים, נֹשֵׂא עָוֹן, וָפֶשַׁע, וְחַטָּאָה, וְנַקֵּה. וְסָלַחְתָּ לַעֲוֹנֵנוּ וּלְחַטָּאתֵנוּ וּנְחַלְתָּנוּ. סְלַח לָנוּ אָבִינוּ כִּי חָטָאנוּ, מְחַל לָנוּ מַלְכֵּנוּ כִּי פָשָׁעְנוּ. כִּי אַתָּה אֲדֹנָי טוֹב וְסַלָּח, וְרַב חֶסֶד לְכָל קֹרְאֶיךָ.

All continue:

אֱלֹהִים בָּאוּ גוֹיִם בְּנַחֲלָתֶךָ, טִמְּאוּ אֶת הֵיכַל קָדְשֶׁךָ, שָׂמוּ אֶת יְרוּשָׁלַיִם לְעִיִּים.[8] אֱלֹהִים זֵדִים קָמוּ עָלֵינוּ, וַעֲדַת עָרִיצִים בִּקְשׁוּ נַפְשֵׁנוּ, וְלֹא שָׂמוּךָ לְנֶגְדָּם.[9]

SELICHOS FOR THE TENTH OF TEVES

Begin *Selichos* on page 816, then continue here:

Our God and the God of our forefathers

אֶזְכְּרָה *I recall the distress that befell me,*
ב *with three blows He struck me in this month —*
ג *He cut me down, pushed me away, caused me pain, but now He has exhausted me.*[1]
ד *He surrounded me on its eighth day with darkness left and right,*
ה *for these three events I instituted a fast:*
ו *the Grecian king forced me to translate the Torah into Greek,*
on my back the plowers plowed and lengthened their furrow.[2]
ז *I was reproached on the ninth [of this month] with humiliation and disgrace,*
ח *removed from me was the mantle of majesty and my diadem,*
ט *on this day was torn away the giver of beautiful works, Ezra the Scribe.*
י *On the tenth day, [Ezekiel] ben Buzi the Seer was commanded,*
כ *'Record for yourself in the book of prophecy —*
ל *as a remembrance for the decaying and disgraced people — this very date.'*[3]
מ *In the count of the monthly cycle, the tenth month inspired me*
נ *to open my mouth in wailing and lament;*
ס *the sequence of punishments kindles fire within my heart —*
as the fugitive came to me and said, 'The city is vanquished!'[4]
ע *For these I spread ashes on my face,*
פ *for these four tragedies [the translation of the Torah, the death of Ezra, the siege of Jerusalem, and its fall] I exclaimed, 'Had only an arrow pierced my heart,*
צ *for these misfortunes I would dig myself a grave,*
it is HASHEM Who is righteous, for I disobeyed His utterance.'[5]
ק *I called out Your Name, You Who relents over the evil that struck me;*
ר *see my affliction and hear the sound of my prayer;*
ש *hear my supplication, please hasten my salvation,*
ת *do not avert Your ear from my sigh, from my cry.*[6]
∴ *In the month of Teves I was exceedingly smitten,*
and its normal course was altered to my detriment.
I strayed, I rebelled; may He reveal to me His goodness —
the One Who told the sea, 'Thus far may you come!'[7]

אֵל מֶלֶךְ *O God, King Who sits on the throne of mercy; Who acts with kindness, pardons the sins of His people, removes sins one by one, increasingly grants pardon to careless sinners and forgiveness to willful ones, performs acts of generosity with every living being — You do not repay them in accord with their evil.* ∴ *O God, You taught us to recite the Thirteen [Attributes of Mercy], so remember for us today the covenant of these Thirteen, as You made known to the humble one [Moses] in ancient times, as it is written: And HASHEM descended in a cloud and stood with him there, and He called out with the Name HASHEM:*

Congregation and *chazzan* recite loudly and in unison:

And HASHEM passed before him [Moses] and proclaimed:

יהוה *HASHEM, HASHEM, God, Compassionate and Gracious, Slow to anger, and Abundant in Kindness and Truth. Preserver of kindness for thousands of generations, Forgiver of iniquity, willful sin, and error, and Who cleanses. May You forgive our iniquities and our errors and make us Your heritage. Forgive us, our Father, for we have erred; pardon us, our King, for we have willfully sinned; for You, my Lord, are good and forgiving and abundantly kind to all who call upon You.*

All continue:

אֱלֹהִים *O God! The nations have entered Your heritage, they defiled the Sanctuary of Your holiness, they turned Jerusalem into heaps of rubble.*[8] *O God! Transgressors have risen up against me, a company of ruthless men sought my soul and they have not set You before them.*[9]

---

(1) *Job* 16:7. (2) Cf. *Psalms* 129:3. (3) *Ezekiel* 24:2. (4) Cf. 33:21. (5) *Lamentations* 1:18. (6) 3:56. (7) Cf. *Job* 38:11. (8) *Psalms* 79:1. (9) Cf. 86:14.

כְּרַחֵם אָב עַל בָּנִים, כֵּן תְּרַחֵם יהוה עָלֵינוּ. לַיהוה הַיְשׁוּעָה, עַל עַמְּךָ בִרְכָתֶךָ סֶּלָה. יהוה צְבָאוֹת עִמָּנוּ, מִשְׂגָּב לָנוּ אֱלֹהֵי יַעֲקֹב סֶלָה. יהוה צְבָאוֹת, אַשְׁרֵי אָדָם בֹּטֵחַ בָּךְ. יהוה הוֹשִׁיעָה, הַמֶּלֶךְ יַעֲנֵנוּ בְיוֹם קָרְאֵנוּ.

(Many congregations repeat, סְלַח נָא . . . וְעַל עַמְּךָ [p. 820] here.)

אֱלֹהֵינוּ וֵאלֹהֵי אֲבוֹתֵינוּ

אֶבֶן הָרֹאשָׁה, לְעִיִּים וְלַחֲרִישָׁה, וְנוֹחֲלֵי מוֹרָשָׁה, מְנוֹד רֹאשׁ בַּלְאֻמִּים.[1]
בְּקִרְבִּי לֵב נִכְאָב, נִדְוֶה וְנִדְאָב, נִשְׁאַרְנוּ כְּאֵין אָב, וְהָיִינוּ כִּיתוֹמִים.[2]
רַכָּה וַעֲנֻגָּה, בַּשּׁוֹשַׁנִּים סוּגָה, וְעַתָּה הִיא נוּגָה, מְסוּרָה בְּיַד קָמִים.
הָיְתָה כְּאַלְמָנָה, קִרְיָה נֶאֱמָנָה, וְזֶרַע מִי מָנָה, נִמְכְּרוּ בְּלֹא דָמִים.
מְעֻנָּגָה וְרַכָּה, צָלְחָה לִמְלוּכָה, וּמַעֲנִיתָהּ אָרְכָה, זֶה כַּמֶּה שָׁנִים וְיָמִים.
בֵּית יַעֲקֹב לְבִזָּה, לְלַעַג וּלְעִזָּה, וְהָעִיר הָעַלִּיזָה, לְמַטָּעֵי כְרָמִים.
רְוּיָה תַּרְעֵלָה, בְּיַד בְּנֵי עַוְלָה, הָרְצוּיָה כְּעוֹלָה, וְכִקְטֹרֶת הַסַּמִּים.
מָאֲסָה לִזְנוֹחַ, תּוֹרַת אֲבִי זָנוֹחַ, וְלֹא מָצְאָה מָנוֹחַ, לֵילוֹת וְגַם יָמִים.
נוֹרָא אֵל עֶלְיוֹן, מִמְּךָ יְהִי צִבְיוֹן, לְהָשִׁיב לְרִיב צִיּוֹן, שְׁנַת שִׁלּוּמִים.
חַדֵּשׁ יָמֵינוּ כְּקֶדֶם,[4] **מְעֹנָה** אֱלֹהֵי קֶדֶם,[5] וְלַבֵּן כַּצֶּמֶר אֹדֶם, וְכַשֶּׁלֶג כְּתָמִים.[6]
❖ חַזְּקֵנוּ בְּיִרְאָתֶךָ, וּבְקִיּוּם תּוֹרָתֶךָ, וּפָקְדֵנוּ בִּישׁוּעָתֶךָ, אֵל מָלֵא רַחֲמִים.

אֵל מֶלֶךְ יוֹשֵׁב עַל כִּסֵּא רַחֲמִים, מִתְנַהֵג בַּחֲסִידוּת, מוֹחֵל עֲוֹנוֹת עַמּוֹ, מַעֲבִיר רִאשׁוֹן רִאשׁוֹן, מַרְבֶּה מְחִילָה לְחַטָּאִים וּסְלִיחָה לַפּוֹשְׁעִים, עֹשֶׂה צְדָקוֹת עִם כָּל בָּשָׂר וָרוּחַ, לֹא כְרָעָתָם תִּגְמוֹל. ❖ אֵל הוֹרֵיתָ לָּנוּ לוֹמַר שְׁלֹשׁ עֶשְׂרֵה, וּזְכוֹר לָנוּ הַיּוֹם בְּרִית שְׁלֹשׁ עֶשְׂרֵה, כְּמוֹ שֶׁהוֹדַעְתָּ לֶעָנָיו מִקֶּדֶם, כְּמוֹ שֶׁכָּתוּב, וַיֵּרֶד יהוה בֶּעָנָן וַיִּתְיַצֵּב עִמּוֹ שָׁם, וַיִּקְרָא בְשֵׁם יהוה.

Congregation and *chazzan* recite loudly and in unison:

וַיַּעֲבֹר יהוה עַל פָּנָיו וַיִּקְרָא.

יהוה, יהוה, אֵל, רַחוּם, וְחַנּוּן, אֶרֶךְ אַפַּיִם, וְרַב חֶסֶד, וֶאֱמֶת, נֹצֵר חֶסֶד לָאֲלָפִים, נֹשֵׂא עָוֹן, וָפֶשַׁע, וְחַטָּאָה, וְנַקֵּה. וְסָלַחְתָּ לַעֲוֹנֵנוּ וּלְחַטָּאתֵנוּ וּנְחַלְתָּנוּ. סְלַח לָנוּ אָבִינוּ כִּי חָטָאנוּ, מְחַל לָנוּ מַלְכֵּנוּ כִּי פָשָׁעְנוּ. כִּי אַתָּה אֲדֹנָי טוֹב וְסַלָּח, וְרַב חֶסֶד לְכָל קֹרְאֶיךָ.

The following prayer is recited responsively by the *chazzan* and congregation.

אֲבוֹתַי, כִּי בָטְחוּ בְּשֵׁם אֱלֹהֵי צוּרִי, גָּדְלוּ וְהִצְלִיחוּ וְגַם עָשׂוּ פֶּרִי,
וּמֵעֵת הֻדְּחוּ וְהָלְכוּ עִמּוֹ קֶרִי,
הָיוּ הָלוֹךְ וְחָסוֹר עַד הַחֹדֶשׁ הָעֲשִׂירִי.[7]

◆§ עֲשָׂרָה בְּטֵבֵת / The Tenth of Teves

Three tragedies occurred in Teves, but in order to avoid serious hardship on the people, the prophets decreed only one fast day, on the anniversary of the most tragic of the occurences. The three events were:

8 Teves — On the orders of the Egyptian King Ptolemy II (285-246 B.C.E.), seventy Jewish sages were forced to translate the Torah into Greek. Though miracles guided their work on this book, called the Septuagint, the Talmud says 'three days of darkness descended on the world,' because it was now possible for the unlearned to

כְּרַחֵם *As a father has mercy on his children, so, HASHEM, may You have mercy on us. Salvation is HASHEM's, upon Your people is Your blessing, Selah. HASHEM, Master of Legions, is with us, a stronghold for us is the God of Jacob, Selah. HASHEM, Master of Legions, praiseworthy is the person who trusts in You. HASHEM, save! May the King answer us on the day we call.*

(Many congregations repeat, *'Please forgive . . . Your people,'* [p. 820] here.)

Our God and the God of our forefathers

אֶבֶן *The leading stone [the Temple] has become rubble and plowed under,*
and the heirs of the [Torah] heritage
have become a cause for nations to shake their heads.[1]
Within me is an aching heart, pained and anguished;
we were left as if fatherless and became like orphans.[2]
Tender and delicate [Israel], hedged about with rose-like commandments,
now she is aggrieved and given over to the power of her foes.
She became like a widow, this faithful city [Jerusalem],
and the uncountable children [Israel] were sold for no money.
Delicate and tender [Babylonia] succeeded to sovereignty
and lengthened her tenure these many years.
The House of Jacob has become an object of loot, scorn, and slander;
and the jubilant city [Jerusalem] has become a plantation of vineyards.
Made drunk with poison at the hands of the iniquitous
[is the city that was] as favored as an elevation-offering and as a mixture of incense.
She disdained to forsake the Torah of Avi-Zanoach [Moses],
so she found no rest in days or nights.
O awesome, supreme God, may the desire emanate from You,
to compensate the grievance of Zion with a year of retribution.[3]
Renew our days as of old,[4] *O eternal God Who dwells in the heavens;*[5]
make crimson sin white as wool and make stains snow white.[6]
∵ *Strengthen us in Your reverence and in fulfillment of Your Torah;*
recall us with Your salvation, O God Who is filled with mercy.

אֵל מֶלֶךְ *O God, King Who sits on the throne of mercy; Who acts with kindness, pardons the sins of His people, removes sins one by one, increasingly grants pardon to careless sinners and forgiveness to willful ones, performs acts of generosity with every living being — You do not repay them in accord with their evil.* ∵ *O God, You taught us to recite the Thirteen [Attributes of Mercy], so remember for us today the covenant of these Thirteen, as You made known to the humble one [Moses] in ancient times, as it is written: And HASHEM descended in a cloud and stood with him there, and He called out with the Name HASHEM:*

Congregation and chazzan recite loudly and in unison:

And HASHEM passed before him [Moses] and proclaimed:

יהוה *HASHEM, HASHEM, God, Compassionate and Gracious, Slow to anger, and Abundant in Kindness and Truth. Preserver of kindness for thousands of generations, Forgiver of iniquity, willful sin, and error, and Who cleanses. May You forgive our iniquities and our errors and make us Your heritage. Forgive us, our Father, for we have erred; pardon us, our King, for we have willfully sinned; for You, my Lord, are good and forgiving and abundantly kind to all who call upon You.*

The following is recited responsively by the *chazzan* and congregation:

אֲבוֹתַי *When my forefathers trusted in the Name of my Rock-like God,*
they became great and successful, and also fruitful,
but from the time they went astray and treated Him casually,
they were progressively diminished until the tenth month.[7]

(1) *Psalms* 44:15. (2) Cf. *Lamentations* 5:3. (3) Cf. *Isaiah* 34:8. (4) *Lamentations* 5:21. (5) *Deuteronomy* 33:27. (6) Cf. *Isaiah* 1:18. (7) *Genesis* 8:5.

boast of a superficial, usually erroneous, understanding of the Torah.

9 Teves — Ezra the Scribe and his colleague Nechemiah both died on this date. They led the Jewish people in the rebuilding of the Temple and Jerusalem and forged it into a nation at a

בַּעֲשִׂירִי לַחֹדֶשׁ סָמַךְ מֶלֶךְ בָּבֶל,[1] וְצָר עַל עִיר הַקֹּדֶשׁ, וְנִקְרַב רַב הַחוֹבֵל,
נְתַתִּי הָדֵשׁ וְעֻנֵּיתִי בַּכֶּבֶל, וְהָיָה מִדֵּי חֹדֶשׁ לְאֵבֶל כִּנּוֹרִי.
רֵאשִׁית בְּכוּרָה לְרֵאשִׁית הַחֵרֶם. שֵׁם אֲחֵרִים הִזְכִּירָה וְהֶעָוֹן גּוֹרֵם,
אֵל לֹא הִכִּירָה וְשִׁטְּפָה בְּזֶרֶם, צָרָה כְּמַבְכִּירָה כָּעֵת בַּמָּרוֹם תַּמְרִיא.[2]
הָאֱלֹהִים הֵבִיא יוֹם רָעָה וּמָצוֹר, צִוָּה צָרַי סְבִיבַי,[3] עוֹלָלַי לִבְצוֹר,
יוֹם הֵרַךְ לְבָבִי, וְאֵין כֹּחַ לַעֲצוֹר, וְדִבֶּר אֶל נָבִיא, מְשׁוֹל אֶל בֵּית הַמֶּרִי.[4]
מִיּוֹשְׁבֵי שַׂעַר, הֶעֱבִיר אַדֶּרֶת, חֲמָתוֹ כָּאֵשׁ בָּעַר, וְהֵרִים עֲטֶרֶת,
וּמִלְּבָנוֹן יַעַר הִשְׁלִיךְ תִּפְאֶרֶת, וְרוּחַ סוֹעָה וָסַעַר, תְּסַמֵּר שַׂעֲרַת בְּשָׂרִי.
יָפְיָפִית נִמְשַׁלְתְּ, וְעַתָּה קְדוֹרַנִּית, בֶּעָוֹן כִּי כָשַׁלְתְּ,[5] וְלִבֵּךְ אֲחוֹרַנִּית,
זֻנַּבוּךְ וְנֶחֱשַׁלְתְּ, רִאשׁוֹנָה וְשֵׁנִית, וְהָחְתֵּל לֹא חֻתָּלְתְּ,[6] מְעַט צָרִי.
צַדִּיק הַצּוּר תָּם נְשׂוֹא עָוֹן נִלְאָה, מִכָּרוּב לְמִפְתָּן, לְפִנַּת גַּג דָּאָה,
מֵעָוֹן הַנִּכְתָּם, וְצַעֲקָתָם בָּאָה, רַבָּה רָעָתָם, כְּעֵץ עֹשֶׂה פֶּרִי.
חִזֵּק כָּל קָמַי תּוֹכֵן הָעֲלִילוֹת, כִּי מָלְאוּ יָמַי בְּרוֹעַ מִפְעָלוֹת,
וּמִבֹּשֶׁת עֲלוּמַי שָׁכַחְתִּי גְמוּלוֹת,[7] נוֹתֵן לַחְמִי וּמֵימַי פִּשְׁתִּי וְצַמְרִי.[8]
קָמַי פִּיהֶם פָּעֲרוּ, וְנַחֲלָתִי בִּלְּעוּ, מְאֹד עָלַי גָּבְרוּ, וְדָמִי שָׁתוּ וְלָעוּ,
נָכְרִים עָלַי צָרוּ, וְאֶת אַחַי הֵרֵעוּ, הָאוֹמְרִים עָרוּ עָרוּ, בְּנֵי שֵׂעִיר הַחֹרִי.[9]
אָמְרוּ לְכוּ נְכַלֵּם, וְנַשְׁבִּיתָה זִכְרָם, אֵל קַנֹּא וְנוֹקֵם גָּמְלֵם יִשְׂאוּ אֶת שִׁבְרָם,
כְּמַעֲשֵׂיהֶם שַׁלֵּם, וְיֵבְשׁוּ מִשְׁבָּרָם,
כְּאִישׁ חֲלוֹם חוֹלֵם, שְׁלֹשָׁה סַלֵּי חֹרִי.[10]
פִּצְעַי לֹא רֻכְּכָה וְחַבּוּרוֹתַי רֶצַח,[11] וְעֵינַי הִכְהֲתָה, צוֹפָה לְדוֹדִי צַח,
הַעוֹד לֹא שָׁכְכָה חֲמָתוֹ לָנֶצַח, עַל מֶה עָשָׂה כָּכָה, וּמֶה חֳרִי.[12]
רַחוּם זֶה אֵלִי, אַל לָעַד תִּזְנַח, אָרְכוּ יְמֵי אֶבְלִי, וְעוֹד לִבִּי נֶאֱנַח,
שׁוּבָה אֵל לְאָהֳלִי, מְקוֹמְךָ אַל תַּנַּח,[13]
שַׁלֵּם יְמֵי אֶבְלִי,[14] כִּי תָבֹא עַל שִׁבְרִי.
יהוה מְנָת חֶלְקִי,[15] חוּשָׁה לִי לְעֶזְרָה,[16] וּפִתַּחְתָּ שַׂקִּי, שִׂמְחָה לִי לְאַזְּרָה,[17]
וְתַגִּיהַּ אֶת חָשְׁכִּי, בְּאוֹרְךָ לְהָאִירָה, אֶת נֶשֶׁף חִשְׁקִי, כִּי אַתָּה נֵירִי.[18]
מִיָּגוֹן וַאֲנָחָה, פְּדֵה אֵל אֶת נַפְשִׁי, עֲשֵׂה לְעַמְּךָ הֲנָחָה מַלְכִּי וּקְדוֹשִׁי,
תַּהֲפוֹךְ לִרְוָחָה אֶת צוֹם הַחֲמִישִׁי,
לְשָׂשׂוֹן וּלְשִׂמְחָה, צוֹם הָרְבִיעִי וְצוֹם הָעֲשִׂירִי.[19]

Turn to page 826 for אֵל מֶלֶךְ, and the conclusion of *Selichos*.

---

time of difficulty and turbulence. Their loss left a tragic void.

10 Teves — On this fateful day King Nebuchadnezzar began the siege of Jerusalem that resulted in the destruction of the First Temple eighteen months later.

Although the fast's primary focus is on the siege, the other two events are alluded to as well in the *Selichos*.

אֶזְכְּרָה — *I remember.* The author signed his name, יוֹסֵף, *Yoseph*, in the acrostic of the final stanza.

אֶבֶן — *The leading stone.* The acrostic spells the author's name, אַבְרָהָם בַּר מְנַחֵם חֲזַק, *Avraham ben Menachem, may he be strong.*

אֲבוֹתַי — *When my forefathers.* The author of this prayer, the Tosafist Rabbi Ephraim of Regensburg, Germany (died 1175), included his grandfather's name, אַבְרָהָם, his father's name, יִצְחָק, and his own name, אֶפְרַיִם, in the acrostic.

ב *On the tenth of the month the king of Babylon approached*[1]
and besieged the Holy City, his captain [Nevuzaradan] drew near
and I was given over for trampling and was tortured with fetters;
whenever this month recurs, my harp turns to mourning.

ד *Her first fruits were first to be destroyed,*
because she mentioned the names of other gods and that iniquity caused it;
she did not recognize God's Presence, so she was washed away by the stream;
suffering pain like a woman's first birth, and still she rebels against the Most High.[2]

ה *God brought a day of evil and siege,*
He commanded my surrounding enemies[3] *to harvest my infants,*
on the day my heart grew faint and there was no strength to resist —
then He told the prophet [Ezekiel]: 'Compose a parable for the rebellious family.'[4]

מ *From those who sat at the gates [the Sanhedrin] He removed the mantle,*
He kindled His wrath like fire and lifted off the crown,
from the forest of Lebanon [the Temple] He cast down splendor,
with an angry wind and tempest He stood up the hair of my flesh.

י *You were likened to a beauty, but now you are blackened,*
because you stumbled into sin[5] *and your heart retreated.*
You were anguished and weakened in the first and second destructions,
and your wound was not bandaged[6] *with even a bit of balm.*

צ *The Righteous One, the Perfect Rock was weary of forgiving iniquity;*
[His Presence flew] from cherub to threshold to the corner of the roof
because their sin was indelible and their sinful shouting reached Him,
their evil abounded like a fruit-bearing tree.

ח *He Who totals all actions has strengthened my adversaries,*
for my days were filled with evil activities,
because of the sins of my youthfulness I forgot the benefits[7]
of the Giver of my bread, my water, my flax, and my wool.[8]

ק *My adversaries opened their mouths and swallowed my heritage,*
they overpowered me mightily and drank and swallowed my blood;
strangers besieged me and treated my brethren wrongly —
those who said, 'Destroy, destroy,' the offspring of Seir the Horite [Esau].[9]

א *They said, 'Let us go and destroy them and obliterate their memory.'*
O jealous and avenging God requite them, let them bear their destruction;
pay them according to their deeds and let them be ashamed of their hope,
like the one who dreamt of three wicker baskets [Pharaoh's baker].[10]

פ *My bruise has not been softened nor have my murderous wounds,*[11]
my eye grows weak with looking for my sparkling Beloved —
will His wrath never again be calmed?
Why has He done this and why this wrath?[12]

ר *O Merciful One, my God, do not abandon forever.*
The days of my mourning grow long and still my heart groans.
Return, O God, to my Tent; do not forsake Your place,[13]
repay me for my days of mourning[14] *when You came for my reward.*

י *HASHEM, the Portion of my heritage,*[15] *hasten to my aid,*[16]
untie my sackcloth to gird me with joy.[17]
Brighten my darkness by illuminating with Your light
the night I longed for — for You are my light.[18]

מ *From sorrow and groaning redeem my soul, O God,*
grant Your people relief, my King, my Holy One;
change to relief the fast of the fifth month [Tishah B'Av], and to joy and gladness
the fast of the fourth month [Tammuz] and the fast of the tenth month [Teves].[19]

Turn to page 826 for אֵל מֶלֶךְ, *'O God, King,'* and continue until the conclusion of *Selichos.*

---

(1) Cf. *Ezekiel* 24:2. (2) *Job* 39:18. (3) Cf. *Lamentations* 1:17. (4) *Ezekiel* 24:3. (5) Cf. *Hoshea* 14:2. (6) *Ezekiel* 16:4. (7) Cf. *Isaiah* 54:4. (8) Cf. *Hoshea* 2:7. (9) *Psalms* 137:7; *Genesis* 36:20. (10) 40:16. (11) Cf. *Isaiah* 1:6. (12) Cf. *Deuteronomy* 29:23. (13) *Ecclesiastes* 7:4. (14) Cf. *Isaiah* 60:20. (15) *Psalms* 16:5. (16) Cf. 38:23. (17) Cf. 30:12. (18) *Isaiah* 21:4; *II Samuel* 22:29. (19) Cf. *Zechariah* 8:19.

סליחות לתענית אסתר

Begin *Selichos* on page 816, then continue here:

אֱלֹהֵינוּ וֵאלֹהֵי אֲבוֹתֵינוּ

אָדָם בְּקוּם עָלֵינוּ,[1] חִיל אֲחָזָתְנִי לִרְעוֹד,
בְּהִסְתַּפְּחוֹ לְמַלְכוּת חָנֵף, כִּמְעַט כָּשַׁלְנוּ לִמְעוֹד,
גָּמְרוּ לְמָכְרֵנוּ כְּתֵל וְחָרִיץ בְּלִי מִסְעוֹד,
אָמְרוּ לְכוּ וְנַכְחִידֵם מִגּוֹי, וְלֹא יִזָּכֵר שֵׁם יִשְׂרָאֵל עוֹד.[2]

דַּלּוּ עֵינַי לַמָּרוֹם קְרָאתִיךָ אוֹיְבַי לָקוֹב,[3]
הַכְרֵת שֵׁם וּשְׁאָר וּמְחֵה שֵׁם לִרְקוֹב,[4]
וְצָר צוֹרְרַי בְּנִכְלֵיהֶם אֲשֶׁר נִכְּלוּ לַעֲקוֹב,[5]
וַיֹּאמְרוּ לֹא יִרְאֶה יָּהּ, וְלֹא יָבִין אֱלֹהֵי יַעֲקֹב.[6]

זְרוּיִם עִנָּה וַיַּגֶּה וְלֹא מִלֵּב לְכַלּוֹתָם,
חָבוּ לְפָנִים וְרֻדָּם בַּהֲסָרַת טַבַּעַת לְהַחֲלוֹתָם,
טוֹב דְּבָרוֹ הֵקִים לְעֵינֵי הַגּוֹיִם לְהַעֲלוֹתָם,
בְּאֶרֶץ אֹיְבֵיהֶם לֹא מְאַסְתִּים וְלֹא גְעַלְתִּים לְכַלֹּתָם.[7]

יִדַּע רֶמֶז הַקּוֹרוֹת לְעַם מְעֻפָּר וּמְהֻדָּס,
כְּתָב הַסְּתֵר אַסְתִּיר וּמָר דְּרוֹר מְפֻרְדָּס,
לִשְׁבּוֹת הָמָן מִמָּחֳרָת, הֲמִן הָעֵץ קֻנְדָּס,
תַּחַת הַנַּעֲצוּץ יַעֲלֶה בְרוֹשׁ, וְתַחַת הַסִּרְפָּד יַעֲלֶה הֲדַס.[8]

מַקְשִׁיב דְּבַר שָׁקֶר[9] כָּתַב שִׂטְנָה וָעֶצֶב,
נִתְעַטֵּף בְּבִגְדֵי שְׂרָד כְּטָעָה בְּמִנְיַן קֶצֶב,
סָדַר לְהִשְׁתַּמֵּשׁ בְּשׁוֹנִים כְּלֵי הַמַּחְצֵב, **וַיָּבוֹא גַם הַשָּׂטָן בְּתֹכָם לְהִתְיַצֵּב.**[10]

עַם הַנִּמְצָאִים בְּשׁוּשָׁן בְּאָכְלָם מִזֶּבַח עָכְרָם,
פָּעַר פִּיו לְהַשְׂטִינָם וּלְהַסְגִּירָם בְּיַד נוֹתֵן מִכְרָם,
צוּר הִסְכִּים לִכְתּוֹב אִגֶּרֶת לְאַבֵּד שִׁבְרָם,
אָמַרְתִּי אַפְאֵיהֶם, אַשְׁבִּיתָה מֵאֱנוֹשׁ זִכְרָם.[11]

קְדוֹשִׁים מַלְאֲכֵי הַשָּׁרֵת מַר יִבְכָּיוּן בִּצְעָקָה,[12]
רַחוּם הַבֵּט לַבְּרִית וְאַל תָּפֵר לְהַרְחִיקָה,
שָׁמְעָה מוֹרָשָׁה וַתִּלְבַּשׁ בִּגְדֵי אַלְמְנוּת וּמוּעָקָה,
וַתָּשֶׂם יָדָהּ עַל רֹאשָׁהּ וַתֵּלֶךְ הָלוֹךְ וְזָעָקָה.[13]

תִּשְׁבִּי שָׂם אֵזוֹר שַׂק בְּמָתְנָיו תַּחְבֹּשֶׁת,
מִהֵר וְהוֹדִיעַ יְשֵׁנֵי מַכְפֵּל אָבוֹת שְׁלֹשֶׁת,
נָחַץ לְרוֹעֶה מַה לְּךָ נִרְדָּם לְהִתְעַשֵּׁת,
קוּם קְרָא אֶל אֱלֹהֶיךָ, אוּלַי יִתְעַשֵּׁת.[14]

---

(1) Cf. *Psalms* 124:2. (2) 83:5. (3) Cf. *Numbers* 24:10. (4) Cf. *Proverbs* 10:4. (5) Cf. *Numbers* 25:18. (6) *Psalms* 94:7. (7) *Leviticus* 26:44. (8) *Isaiah* 55:13. (9) Cf. *Proverbs* 29:12. (10) *Job* 2:1. (11) *Deuteronomy* 32:26. (12) Cf. *Isaiah* 33:7. (13) *II Samuel* 13:19. (14) *Jonah* 1:6.

SELICHOS FOR THE FAST OF ESTHER

Begin *Selichos* on page 816, then continue here:

Our God and the God of our forefathers

אָדָם *When a man [Haman] rose up against us,*[1] *fear and trembling seized us,*
ב *when he clung to the flattery-loving kingship [of Ahasuerus],*
we nearly tripped and tottered;
ג *they decided to sell us as if we were a defenseless hill or ditch,*
they said, 'Come let us obliterate them from nationhood
that the name Israel no longer be remembered.'[2]
ד *My eyes rose heavenward; I called You to curse my enemies,*[3]
ה *cut off their name and remnant and erase their name that it may rot,*[4]
ו *oppress my enemies with their own evils that they conspired to pervert,*[5]
when they said, 'God will not see and the God of Jacob will not discern.'[6]
ז *He afflicted and aggrieved the scattered [people] but had not the heart to destroy them;*
ח *they sinned on the surface, He chastised them through*
[Ahasuerus'] removal of the signet ring to terrify them;
ט *but the Good One maintained His word to elevate them in the sight of the nations,*
'I will not despise them nor abhor them to destroy them in the land of their enemies.'[7]
י *The Torah alluded to the experience of this soiled and staggered people:*
כ *it writes* haster astir* *and* mor deror *of the orchard,*
ל *to nullify Haman the next day —* hamin ha'etz *hanging from the mast:*
so instead of the thorn [Haman], the cypress [Mordechai] will rise,
and instead of the nettle [Vashti] the myrtle [Esther] will rise.[8]
מ *He who hearkened to falsehood [Ahasuerus]*[9] *wrote a hateful and depressing edict;*
נ *he robed himself in priestly garments when he miscalculated the [exile's] duration,*
ס *he planned [a banquet] to use various of the Temple vessels,*
and the Satan came too, to stand among them.[10]
ע *When Shushan's Jews partook from the feast of the one who abhorred them,*
פ *[Satan] opened his mouth to condemn and deliver them to the one who paid for them;*
צ *the Rock agreed that a document be written to destroy their hope:*
'I said I will annihiliate them, I will bring an end of their memory among mankind.[11]
ק *The holy ones, the angels of peace, wept with bitter outcry,*[12]
ר *'O Merciful One, look to the covenant and do not annul it to reject it;'*
ש *the heritage [Torah] heard and donned garments of widowhood and depression,*
placed her hand on her head and went forth, crying out as she went.[13]
ת *The Tishbite [Elijah] wrapped a sackcloth girdle around his loins,*
מ *he hurried to inform the three Patriarchs who slumber in Machpelah,*
נ *he rushed to the shepherd [Moses] 'Why do you sleep passively? —*
Get up, call to your God, perhaps He will pay us mind!'[14]

The Fast of Esther

Taanis Esther, the Fast of Esther, is unique among the fasts in that it commemorates a triumph instead of a tragedy. The miracle that is commemorated by Purim took place on the thirteenth of Adar, when the Jewish people fought and defeated those who had plotted their extermination. It is a foregone conclusion that our ancestors fasted on that day, because the Jewish people never went to war without fasting and repenting in order to be worthy of God's assistance. The fast was named for Queen Esther because the miracle came about through her and as a reminder that she requested that the people fast for her when she risked her life to intervene with King Ahasuerus.

אָדָם — *When a man.* After twenty-two verses following the *Aleph Beis,* the acrostic spells מְנַחֵם בְּרַבִּי מָכִיר יִחְיֶה אָמֵן וְאָמֵן, *Menachem, son of Rabbi Machir, may he live, Amen and Amen.* Rabbi Menachem (Germany; 11th-12th cent.) also authored the *Hoshana* prayer for the Sabbath of Succos (p. 738), and אֲמָרֵר, *I am embittered,* recited on the seventeenth of Tammuz (p. 864).

הַסְתֵּר אַסְתִּיר — *Haster Astir.* The Talmud *(Chullin* 139b), in a play on words, teaches that there are phrases in the Torah that both sound like the names of the characters in the Purim story and allude to them. Esther, who reigned in

חוֹתָם טִיט אֲשֶׁר נַעֲשָׂה לְבִלְשַׁן סִפֵּר,
מְנִינָיוֹ לְמָדוּ לְאַחַר גְּזֵרָה כַּעַס לְהָפֵר,
בֶּן קִישׁ הִקִּישׁ דַּלְתוֹת בֵּית הַסֵּפֶר, וַיִּלְבַּשׁ שַׂק וַיֵּשֶׁב עַל הָאֵפֶר.[1]
רִבֵּץ תִּינוֹקוֹת לְפָנָיו יָמִים שְׁלֹשָׁה צָמִים וּמְכַפְּנִים,
בְּקוֹל יַעֲקֹב לַחֲלוֹשׁ יְדֵי עַז פָּנִים,
יָדָיו אֱמוּנָה לָאֵל הַצִּילֵנִי מֵעֶלְבּוֹנִים,
פֶּן יָבוֹא וְהִכַּנִי אֵם עַל בָּנִים.[2]

מִזֶּה אֵלֶּה וּמִזֶּה אֵלֶּה בְּנֵי אֵיתָנֵי וְרַבָּנַי,
כֻּלָּם צָעֲקוּ וַתַּעַל שַׁוְעָתָם אֶל יהוה.[3]
יָהּ לְקוֹל רִנּוּן כְּבוֹא שָׁאַל לִפְנַי,
וּמֶה קוֹל הַצֹּאן הַזֶּה בְּאָזְנָי.[4]

רוֹעֶה הֱשִׁיבוּ הֵם קְטַנֵּי קֹדֶשׁ זֶרַע,
יָהּ הַצֵּל לְקוּחֵי לַמָּוֶת מֵאוֹיֵב הָרַע,
חַנּוּן נִכְמְרוּ רַחֲמָיו וַיְבַקֵּשׁ לִבְכּוֹת הַמְּאוֹרָע,
וַיְהִי כִּקְרֹא מֶלֶךְ יִשְׂרָאֵל אֶת הַסֵּפֶר וַיִּקְרַע.[5]
יְהוּדִי **הו**ֹקִיעַ יְלָדָיו לְמַטָּה וַאֲבִיהֶם לְמַעְלָה,
אִישׁ אִישׁ בְּשָׁלֹשׁ אַמּוֹת וְהָרְבִיעִית אֲוִיר מְגֻלָּה,
מִשְׁנֶה **נָ**קַם חָזָה וְשָׂמַח וְשָׁח תְּהִלָּה,
אִתִּי הֵשִׁיב עַל כַּנִּי וְאֹתוֹ תָלָה.[6]

❖ **וַ**תִּכְתֹּב **אֶ**סְתֵּר תְּקֶף[7] לִקְרֹא כִּבְהִלֵּל מְהוֹדִים,
מִלְמַעְלָה קִיְּמוּ מַה שֶּׁקִּבְּלוּ לְמַטָּה[8] דוֹדִים,
נֵס יְנוֹסֵס לְפַרְסֵם כְּאָז פִּלְאוֹ מַסְהִידִים,
בָּעֵת הַזֹּאת רֶוַח וְהַצָּלָה יַעֲמֹד לַיְּהוּדִים.[9]

אֵל מֶלֶךְ יוֹשֵׁב עַל כִּסֵּא רַחֲמִים, מִתְנַהֵג בַּחֲסִידוּת, מוֹחֵל עֲוֹנוֹת עַמּוֹ, מַעֲבִיר רִאשׁוֹן רִאשׁוֹן, מַרְבֶּה מְחִילָה לְחַטָּאִים וּסְלִיחָה לַפּוֹשְׁעִים, עֹשֶׂה צְדָקוֹת עִם כָּל בָּשָׂר וָרוּחַ, לֹא כְרָעָתָם תִּגְמוֹל. ❖ אֵל הוֹרֵיתָ לָנוּ לוֹמַר שְׁלֹשׁ עֶשְׂרֵה, וּזְכוֹר לָנוּ הַיּוֹם בְּרִית שְׁלֹשׁ עֶשְׂרֵה, כְּמוֹ שֶׁהוֹדַעְתָּ לֶעָנָיו מִקֶּדֶם, כְּמוֹ שֶׁכָּתוּב, וַיֵּרֶד יהוה בֶּעָנָן וַיִּתְיַצֵּב עִמּוֹ שָׁם, וַיִּקְרָא בְשֵׁם יהוה.

Congregation and *chazzan* recite loudly and in unison:

וַיַּעֲבֹר יהוה עַל פָּנָיו וַיִּקְרָא.

יהוה, יהוה, אֵל, רַחוּם, וְחַנּוּן, אֶרֶךְ אַפַּיִם, וְרַב חֶסֶד, וֶאֱמֶת, נֹצֵר חֶסֶד לָאֲלָפִים, נֹשֵׂא עָוֹן, וָפֶשַׁע, וְחַטָּאָה, וְנַקֵּה. וְסָלַחְתָּ לַעֲוֹנֵנוּ וּלְחַטָּאתֵנוּ וּנְחַלְתָּנוּ. סְלַח לָנוּ אָבִינוּ כִּי חָטָאנוּ, מְחַל לָנוּ מַלְכֵּנוּ כִּי פָשָׁעְנוּ. כִּי אַתָּה אֲדֹנָי טוֹב וְסַלָּח, וְרַב חֶסֶד לְכָל קֹרְאֶיךָ.

ה *He told the linguist [Mordechai] that the decree was sealed with nothing but clay;*
ס *from Nineveh they learned to annul His anger even after the decree,*
ב *the descendant of Kish [Mordechai] pounded at the doors of the study house,*
covered himself with sackcloth and sat on ashes.[1]
ר *He set down children for three days before him, thirsty and hungry,*
ב *to weaken the power of the brazen [Haman] with the voice of Jacob.*
י *With hands lifted faithfully [in prayer] to God: 'Rescue me from disgraces,*
lest he come and strike me down, mother with children.'[2]
מ *On this side and that were the children of my Patriarchs and masters,*
כ *all cried out and their outcry went up to HASHEM.*[3]
י *And God — when the sound of prayer arrived — He asked in His inner chamber,*
'What is this sound of sheep in My ears?'[4]
ר *The shepherd responded, 'They are the small and sacred offspring —*
O God, rescue those being taken to death from the evil foe;
the Compassionate One's mercy was aroused and He wished to beweep the calamity,
so it was that when the King of Israel read the chronicle, he tore it up.[5]
Then the Jew Mordechai hung Haman's sons below and their father above,
each man took up three cubits with the fourth cubit left open;
the viceroy [Mordechai] saw the vengeance, rejoiced and uttered praise:
'Me He restored to my post and him He hanged.'[6]
∴ *Esther recorded the mighty*[7] *[miracle] to be read by the grateful like Hallel,*
in heaven above they ratified what the beloved ones adopted below;[8]
let God raise a banner to make known like then His wonders to which we testify —
at this time let relief and deliverance come to the Jews.[9]

אֵל מֶלֶךְ *O God, King Who sits on the throne of mercy; Who acts with kindness, pardons the sins of His people, removes sins one by one, increasingly grants pardon to careless sinners and forgiveness to willful ones, performs acts of generosity with every living being — You do not repay them in accord with their evil.* ∴ *O God, You taught us to recite the Thirteen [Attributes of Mercy], so remember for us today the covenant of these Thirteen, as You made known to the humble one [Moses] in ancient times, as it is written: And HASHEM descended in a cloud and stood with him there, and He called out with the Name HASHEM:*

Congregation and chazzan recite loudly and in unison:
And HASHEM passed before him [Moses] and proclaimed:

יהוה *HASHEM, HASHEM, God, Compassionate and Gracious, Slow to anger, and Abundant in Kindness and Truth. Preserver of kindness for thousands of generations, Forgiver of iniquity, willful sin, and error, and Who cleanses. May You forgive our iniquities and our errors and make us Your heritage. Forgive us, our Father, for we have erred; pardon us, our King, for we have willfully sinned; for You, my Lord, are good and forgiving and abundantly kind to all who call upon You.*

(1) *Jonah* 3:6. (2) *Genesis* 32:12. (3) Cf. *Exodus* 2:23. (4) *I Samuel* 15:14. (5) *II Kings* 5:7. (6) *Genesis* 41:13. (7) Cf. *Esther* 9:29. (8) Cf. 9:27. (9) 4:14.

a time when God seemed to forsake Israel, is alluded to when God says הַסְתֵּר אַסְתִּיר, *I will conceal my countenance (Deuteronomy* 31:18). Mordechai, who was pure and pleasant, is alluded to in one of the spices used in the Temple incense מָר דְּרוֹר, *pure myrrh,* which the Targum renders מֵירָא דַכְיָא, *meira dachya (Exodus* 30:23). The allusion to Haman who was hung on a gallows is from הֲמִן הָעֵץ, *from this tree (Genesis* 3:11).

All continue:

כִּי עִמְּךָ מְקוֹר חַיִּים, בְּאוֹרְךָ נִרְאֶה אוֹר.[1] בְּקָרְאֵנוּ עֲנֵנוּ אֱלֹהֵי צִדְקֵנוּ, בַּצָּר הִרְחַבְתָּ לָּנוּ, חָנֵּנוּ וּשְׁמַע תְּפִלָּתֵנוּ.[2] וְעַתָּה יִגְדַּל נָא כֹּחַ אֲדֹנָי, כַּאֲשֶׁר דִּבַּרְתָּ לֵאמֹר.[3]

כְּרַחֵם אָב עַל בָּנִים, כֵּן תְּרַחֵם יהוה עָלֵינוּ. לַיהוה הַיְשׁוּעָה, עַל עַמְּךָ בִרְכָתֶךָ סֶּלָה. יהוה צְבָאוֹת עִמָּנוּ, מִשְׂגָּב לָנוּ אֱלֹהֵי יַעֲקֹב סֶלָה. יהוה צְבָאוֹת, אַשְׁרֵי אָדָם בֹּטֵחַ בָּךְ. יהוה הוֹשִׁיעָה, הַמֶּלֶךְ יַעֲנֵנוּ בְיוֹם קָרְאֵנוּ.

(Many congregations repeat, סְלַח נָא . . . וְעַל עַמְּךָ [p. 820] here.)

אֱלֹהֵינוּ וֵאלֹהֵי אֲבוֹתֵינוּ

אַתָּה הָאֵל עוֹשֵׂה פְלָאוֹת, **בָּ**עַמִּים הוֹדַעְתָּ עוֹז נוֹרָאוֹת,[4]
גָּאַלְתָּ בִּזְרוֹעַ עַמְּךָ[5] מִתְּלָאוֹת, **דִּ**כִּיתָ צָרֵיהֶם בְּמוֹתֵי תַחֲלוּאוֹת.
הָאוֹיֵב בְּקוּמוֹ לְעוֹרֵר מְדָנִים, **וְ**דִמָּה לְהַכְרִית פִּרְחֵי שׁוֹשַׁנִּים,
זָמַם לִשְׁקוֹל לְגִנְזֵי אֲדוֹנִים. **חֲ**לִיפֵי מְאַת כִּכְּרֵי אֲדָנִים.[6]
טְלָאֶיךָ הִזְהַרְתָּ שִׁקְלֵיהֶם לְהַקְדִּים, **יָ**דַעְתָּ הָעֲתִידוֹת וְדָרַשְׁתָּ נִשְׁקָדִים,
כְּבוּי לְהַמְצִיא לְלַהַב יוֹקְדִים, **לְ**קוּחִים לַמָּוֶת לְתֶחִי נִפְקָדִים.
מַסֵּכָה צָרָה בְּעָבְדָם לְפָנִים, **נִ**מְסְרוּ לְהָתֵז קְנוּקָנוֹת וּגְפָנִים,
סְבָבוּם מוֹקְשִׁים בְּכָל דְּפָנִים, **עֵ**ינֵיהֶם לְךָ תּוֹלִים וּבְסִתְרְךָ נִצְפָּנִים.
פּוּר נֶהְפַּךְ בְּאוֹיְבִים לִשְׁלוֹט,[7] **צְ**לִיבָה הוּכַן אֲגָגִי לִקְלוֹט,
קַלַע וּבִלַּע פְּנֵי הַלּוֹט הַלּוֹט,[8] **רִ**יבֵי עָם בְּאַשְׁמַנִּים לַעֲלוֹט.
שָׁלוֹם וֶאֱמֶת נִכְתַּב מִכָּל צַד, **תְּ**קֶף יֶשַׁע סֶלַע וּמְצַד,
שׁוֹדֵד הָשְׁדַּד וּבְרִשְׁתּוֹ נוֹצַד, **מְ**לָשְׁנִי נִסְחַף נִצְמַת וְנִרְצַד.
עָשׂוּ שְׂמָחוֹת וְלַדּוֹרוֹת קְבָעוּם, **וּ**מִקְרָאוֹת שִׁלְּשׁוּם וְלֹא רִבְּעוּם,
נִסְכְּמוּ מִמַּעַל וּלְמַטָּה טִבְּעוּם, **בַּ**סֵּפֶר נֶחֱקַק עַל מַה קְבָעוּם.
רָמָה יָדְךָ לִסְלוֹחַ לַפּוֹשְׁעִים, **יְ**הוּדִי וַהֲדַסָּה הֲקַמְתָּ מוֹשִׁיעִים,
צִדְקָתָם עוֹמֶדֶת לָעַד[9] לְשַׁעֲשׁוּעִים, **חֲ**קֹר כְּבוֹדָם לְהִזָּכֵר לְנוֹשָׁעִים.
קַנֵּא לְשִׁמְךָ נוֹרָא וְנִקְדָּשׁ, **חֲ**זֵה כַּרְמְּךָ נֶהֱרַס וְנִדָּשׁ,
זְרוּיֵינוּ קַבֵּץ וְשִׁיר לְךָ יְחֻדָּשׁ, **קַ**יְּמֵם וְהַחֲיֵם בְּבִנְיַן בֵּית הַמִּקְדָּשׁ.
❖ **וְ**כַעֲשׂוֹתְךָ נוֹרָאוֹת בְּאוֹתָן הַיָּמִים, **אִ**תָּנוּ הַפְלֵא תְּשׁוּעַת עוֹלָמִים,
מְצוֹא לְפָנֶיךָ כֹּפֶר וְתַנְחוּמִים, **אֵ**ל מֶלֶךְ יוֹשֵׁב עַל כִּסֵּא רַחֲמִים.

אַתָּה ◆ — *You.* The author's name שִׁמְעוֹן בַּר יִצְחָק, *Shimon bar Yitzchak,* and the blessing חֲזַק וֶאֱמָץ, *may he be strong and persevere,* appear after the alphabet in the acrostic. Also known as Rabbi Shimon *HaGadol* (the Great), he lived in Mainz, Germany (about 950-1020) where he served on the rabbinical court alongside Rabbeinu Gershom *Meor HaGolah.* More than a dozen of his liturgical compositions have entered the *Siddur* and *Machzor,* among them בָּרוּךְ ה׳ יוֹם יוֹם (p. 494), and בְּרַח דּוֹדִי, recited on Chol HaMoed Pesach (p. 710).

All continue:

כִּי *For with You is the source of life — by Your light we shall see light.*[1] *When we call, answer us, O God of my salvation; in distress You gave me boundless relief, be gracious to me and hear my prayer.*[2] *And now let the power of my Lord be great, as You have spoken saying.*[3]

כְּרַחֵם *As a father has mercy on his children, so,* HASHEM, *may You have mercy on us. Salvation is* HASHEM*'s, upon Your people is Your blessing, Selah.* HASHEM, *Master of Legions, is with us, a stronghold for us is the God of Jacob, Selah.* HASHEM, *Master of Legions, praiseworthy is the person who trusts in You.* HASHEM, *save! May the King answer us on the day we call.*

(Many congregations repeat, '*Please forgive . . . Your people,*' [p. 820] here.)

Our God and the God of our forefathers

אַתָּה *You, O God, Doer of wonders,*
You made known among the nations the power of Your awesome deeds,[4]
with Your arm You redeemed Your people[5] *from hardships,*
You crushed their foes with fatal diseases.
When the enemy [Haman] arose to arouse contention,
and imagined he could cut down Israel's growing roses,
he conspired to weigh off for the treasury of his master
[silver] equal to the hundred kikar-weight sockets [of the Tabernacle].[6]
You warned Your flock to advance their own shekels,
since You knew the future, You besought the zealous ones
to provide a means to quench the wrathful flame —
that those designed for death be remembered for life.
For pretending to worship [Nevuchadnezzar's] graven image,
both young and mature grapes were handed over for chopping down,
snares encircled them on every side,
their eyes were fixed on You and they were sheltered in Your concealment.
The lot was reversed and they [the Jews] controlled their enemies,[7]
the gallows was readied to snare the Aggagite,
God casts him away and consumes his protective shelter,[8]
to blanket in darkness the enemies of His people.
Words of peace and truth were inscribed from every direction,
about the Mighty salvation of the Rock and Fortress;
the plunderer was plundered and trapped in his net,
my slanderer was swept away, cut down, and made to flee.
The Jews made celebrations and set them up for all generations —
though Scripture implied only three generations, not even four —
It was ratified from Above and established below,
in the Torah was found inscribed why they should establish it.
You raised Your hand to forgive the sinners,
the Judean [Mordechai] and Hadassah [Esther] You designated as saviors,
their righteousness endures for eternal delight,[9]
their profound honor will be remembered by the saved.
Avenge your Name, O Awesome and Sacred One;
behold Your vineyeard, shattered and trampled;
gather in our scattered ones and let a new song be sung to You,
preserve them and give them life in the rebuilt Temple.
∴ *Like You did awesome deeds in those days,*
do wonders with us, an eternal salvation,
may there be found before You atonement and comfort —
O God, King, Who sits on the throne of mercy.

(1) *Psalms* 36:10. (2) Cf. 4:2. (3) *Numbers* 14:17. (4) Cf. *Psalms* 77:15. (5) 77:16.
(6) Cf. *Exodus* 38:27. (7) Cf. *Esther* 9:1. (8) Cf. *Isaiah* 25:7. (9) Cf. *Psalms* 112:9.

אֵל מֶלֶךְ יוֹשֵׁב עַל כִּסֵּא רַחֲמִים, מִתְנַהֵג בַּחֲסִידוּת, מוֹחֵל עֲוֹנוֹת עַמּוֹ, מַעֲבִיר רִאשׁוֹן רִאשׁוֹן, מַרְבֶּה מְחִילָה לְחַטָּאִים וּסְלִיחָה לַפּוֹשְׁעִים, עֹשֶׂה צְדָקוֹת עִם כָּל בָּשָׂר וָרוּחַ, לֹא כְרָעָתָם תִּגְמוֹל. ❖ אֵל הוֹרֵיתָ לָּנוּ לוֹמַר שְׁלֹשׁ עֶשְׂרֵה, וּזְכוֹר לָנוּ הַיּוֹם בְּרִית שְׁלֹשׁ עֶשְׂרֵה, כְּמוֹ שֶׁהוֹדַעְתָּ לֶעָנָיו מִקֶּדֶם, כְּמוֹ שֶׁכָּתוּב, וַיֵּרֶד יהוה בֶּעָנָן וַיִּתְיַצֵּב עִמּוֹ שָׁם, וַיִּקְרָא בְשֵׁם יהוה.

Congregation and *chazzan* recite loudly and in unison:

וַיַּעֲבֹר יהוה עַל פָּנָיו וַיִּקְרָא.

יהוה, יהוה, אֵל, רַחוּם, וְחַנּוּן, אֶרֶךְ אַפַּיִם, וְרַב חֶסֶד, וֶאֱמֶת, נֹצֵר חֶסֶד לָאֲלָפִים, נֹשֵׂא עָוֹן, וָפֶשַׁע, וְחַטָּאָה, וְנַקֵּה. וְסָלַחְתָּ לַעֲוֹנֵנוּ וּלְחַטָּאתֵנוּ וּנְחַלְתָּנוּ. סְלַח לָנוּ אָבִינוּ כִּי חָטָאנוּ, מְחַל לָנוּ מַלְכֵּנוּ כִּי פָשָׁעְנוּ. כִּי אַתָּה אֲדֹנָי טוֹב וְסַלָּח, וְרַב חֶסֶד לְכָל קֹרְאֶיךָ.

The following prayer is recited responsively by the *chazzan* and congregation.

בִּמְתֵי מִסְפָּר חִלִּינוּ פָּנֶיךָ, לְשַׁוְעַת נְכֵאִים אַל תַּעְלֵם אָזְנֶךָ,
הַקְשֵׁב תְּחִנָּתָם מִשְּׁמֵי מְעוֹנֶךָ, כְּבִימֵי מוֹר וַהֲדַס הוֹשַׁעְתָּ בָנֶיךָ.
תְּהִלּוֹת יִשְׂרָאֵל אַתָּה יוֹשֵׁב, שַׁוְעָתָם מַאֲזִין וְרִנָּתָם קוֹשֵׁב,
רְפָאוּת לְמַחַץ מַקְדִּים וּמְחַשֵּׁב, קְנוּיֶיךָ לְהֵיטִיב וְנָוֵיהֶם לְיַשֵּׁב.
צָר וְאוֹיֵב הִלְטִישׁ עֵינָיו, פִּיהוּ פָּעַר לִשְׁאוֹף עֲנָיו,
עָשַׁת בְּשִׁלּוֹ לְהַשְׁמִיד קְהַל הֲמוֹנָיו, סֶגֶל לְאַבֵּד חָרַת בְּנִשְׁתְּוָנָיו.
נוֹקֵם לְצָרִים וְנוֹטֵר לְאוֹיְבִים, מָדַדְתָּ מִדָּתָם כָּזֶדוּ לַאֲהוּבִים,
לוֹחֵם וּנִינָיו הָתְלוּ מְצֻלָּבִים, כְּבַחֲרֹזֶת דָּגִים חוֹרְזוּ תְּחוּבִים.
יוֹם אֲשֶׁר שִׂבְּרוּ צוֹרְרִים, טִבְחָה לָשִׁית בְּעַם נְצוּרִים,
חָלְפָה הַדָּת וְנָפְלוּ פְגָרִים, זָלְעֲפוּ זוֹעֲמוּ מוּבָסִים מְגָרִים.
וּבְכֵן יִתְעַלֶּה שִׁמְךָ וְיִתְנַשֵּׂא, הוֹדְךָ שְׁמֵי שָׁמַיִם כִּסָּה,
דַּכִּים בְּרוֹמְמְךָ נְתוּנִים לִמְשִׁסָּה, גֵּיא וְאַפְסֶיהָ תְּהִלָּתְךָ מְכַסָּה.
בִּינָה הֲגִיגֵנוּ עַתָּה וּרְאֵה בַצָּר, הֲשִׁיבֵנוּ לִמְנוּחָתֶךָ כִּי יָדְךָ לֹא תִקְצָר,
אָדוֹן קְרָאנוּךָ מִן הַמֵּצַר, אָנָּא הוֹצִיאֵנוּ לַמֶּרְחָב וְחַלְּצֵנוּ מִצָּר.
מְאֹד תַּרְבֶּה לָנוּ מְחִילָה, שְׁמַע תְּפִלָּה וְהַעֲבֵר תִּפְלָה,
לוֹחֲצֵינוּ יַשְׁלִימוּ אִתָּנוּ וַעֲוֹנוֹתֵינוּ תַּשְׁלִיךְ בִּמְצוּלָה,
מִמֶּנּוּ רַחֲמֶיךָ לֹא תִכְלָא.

Turn to page 826 for אֵל מֶלֶךְ, and continue until the conclusion of *Selichos.*

⊱ בִּמְתֵי — *Though few.* Rabbi Meshullam ben Klonimos (Lucca, Italy, about 950-1020) signed his name, מְשֻׁלָּם, after a reverse alphabetical acrostic. Among his other compositions that have entered the *Siddur* is בְּרַח דּוֹדִי, recited on the second day of Pesach (p. 710).

אֵל מֶלֶךְ *O God, King Who sits on the throne of mercy; Who acts with kindness, pardons the sins of His people, removes sins one by one, increasingly grants pardon to careless sinners and forgiveness to willful ones, performs acts of generosity with every living being — You do not repay them in accord with their evil.* ∴ *O God, You taught us to recite the Thirteen [Attributes of Mercy], so remember for us today the covenant of these Thirteen, as You made known to the humble one [Moses] in ancient times, as it is written: And* HASHEM *descended in a cloud and stood with him there, and He called out with the Name* HASHEM*:*

Congregation and *chazzan* recite loudly and in unison:

And HASHEM *passed before him [Moses] and proclaimed:*

יהוה HASHEM, HASHEM, *God, Compassionate and Gracious, Slow to anger, and Abundant in Kindness and Truth. Preserver of kindness for thousands of generations, Forgiver of iniquity, willful sin, and error, and Who cleanses. May You forgive our iniquities and our errors and make us Your heritage. Forgive us, our Father, for we have erred; pardon us, our King, for we have willfully sinned; for You, my Lord, are good and forgiving and abundantly kind to all who call upon You.*

The following prayer is recited responsively by the *chazzan* and congregation:

בִּמְתֵי *Though few in number we plead before You:*
Let not Your ear ignore the cry of the crippled;
from Your heavenly abode heed their supplication,
as You saved Your children in the days of Mor [Mordechai] and Hadas [Esther].

You Who are enthroned upon the praises of Israel,
Who gives ear to their outcry and hearkens to their prayer,
Who considers and anticipates the cure before the wound,
do good to Your creatures that their homes may be settled.

The oppressor and foe [Haman] sharpened his glare,
he opened His mouth to swallow the humble,
using His [God's] wealth he plotted to destroy His assembled congregation,
he inscribed in his edicts to destroy His treasured people.

You Who wreaks vengeance on oppressors and remembers foes,
You measured their misdeed as they schemed against the beloved,
the aggressor and his offspring were hung, suspended from a gallows,
like a string of fish they were threaded and strung.

The day for which the oppressors hoped, to inflict a slaughter on the guarded people,
the decree was reversed and the corpses fell dead,
they were terrified, the objects of fury, trampled, dragged about.

Therefore, let Your Name be elevated and exalted, Your glory covers the loftiest heavens,
when You raised up the crushed, those consigned to plunder,
Your praise covers each valley to the ends of the earth.

Understand now our meditation, and see our distress,
return us to Your resting place for Your power is not limited,
O Lord, we called You from the straits —
please remove us to expansiveness and release us from distress.

Increase our pardon most abundantly, hear prayer and remove impropriety,
may our oppressors make peace with us,
and may You cast our iniquities into the deep;
do not withhold Your mercy from us.

Turn to page 826 for אֵל מֶלֶךְ, *'O God, King,'* and continue until the conclusion of *Selichos.*

סליחות לשבעה עשר בתמוז

Begin *Selichos* on page 816, then continue here:

אֱלֹהֵינוּ וֵאלֹהֵי אֲבוֹתֵינוּ

אֲתָאֲנוּ לְךָ יוֹצֵר רוּחוֹת,
בְּרוֹב עֲוֹנֵינוּ כָּבְדוּ אֲנָחוֹת, גְּזֵרוֹת עָצְמוּ וְרַבּוּ צְרִיחוֹת,
כִּי בְּשִׁבְעָה עָשָׂר בְּתַמּוּז נִשְׁתַּבְּרוּ הַלּוּחוֹת.

גָּלִינוּ מִבֵּית הַבְּחִירָה,
דִּנְּנוּ נֶחְתַּם וְנִגְזְרָה גְזֵרָה, וְחָשַׁךְ בַּעֲדֵנוּ אוֹרָה,
כִּי בְּשִׁבְעָה עָשָׂר בְּתַמּוּז נִשְׂרְפָה הַתּוֹרָה.

הָרְסוּ אוֹיְבֵינוּ הַהֵיכָל, וּבָרְחָה שְׁכִינָה מִזָּוִית הֵיכָל,
וְנִמְסַרְנוּ בְּיַד זֵדִים לְהִתְאַכָּל,
כִּי בְּשִׁבְעָה עָשָׂר בְּתַמּוּז הָעֳמַד צֶלֶם בְּהֵיכָל.

זֹרוּנוּ מֵעִיר אֶל עִיר, וְנִלְכַּד מִמֶּנּוּ רַב וְצָעִיר,
חָרְבָה מְשׂוֹשֵׂנוּ וְאֵשׁ בָּהּ הִבְעִיר,
כִּי בְּשִׁבְעָה עָשָׂר בְּתַמּוּז הָבְקְעָה הָעִיר.

טָפַשׁ מִקְדָּשֵׁנוּ צַר הַמַּשְׁמִיד, וְנֻטַּל מֵחָתָן וְכַלָּה אֶצְעָדָה וְצָמִיד,
יַעַן כְּעַסְנוּךָ נִתַּנּוּ לְהַשְׁמִיד, כִּי בְּשִׁבְעָה עָשָׂר בְּתַמּוּז בָּטֵל הַתָּמִיד.

כָּלָה מִמֶּנּוּ כָּל הוֹד וָשֶׁבַח, חַרְבּוֹ שָׁלַף אוֹיֵב עָלֵינוּ לָאֶבַח,
לִהְיוֹת עוֹלָלִים וְיוֹנְקִים מוּכָנִים לַטֶּבַח,
כִּי בְּשִׁבְעָה עָשָׂר בְּתַמּוּז בָּטְלוּ עוֹלָה וָזֶבַח.

מָרַדְנוּ לְשׁוֹכֵן מְעוֹנוֹת, לָכֵן נִתְפַּזַּרְנוּ בְּכָל פִּנּוֹת,
נֶהְפַּךְ מְחוֹלֵנוּ לְקִינוֹת, כִּי בְּשִׁבְעָה עָשָׂר בְּתַמּוּז בָּטְלוּ קָרְבָּנוֹת.

סָרַרְנוּ לְפָנֶיךָ מֵרִיב לְשׁוֹנוֹת, לָכֵן לָמְדָה לְשׁוֹנֵנוּ לוֹמַר קִינוֹת,
עֻזַּבְנוּ בְּלִי לְהִמָּנוֹת, כִּי בְּשִׁבְעָה עָשָׂר בְּתַמּוּז גָּרְמוּ לָנוּ עֲוֹנוֹת.

פֻּזַּרְנוּ בְּלִי מְצוֹא רְוָחָה, לָכֵן רָבְתָה בָּנוּ אֲנָחָה,
צוּר רְאֵה נַפְשֵׁנוּ כִּי שָׁחָה,
וְשִׁבְעָה עָשָׂר בְּתַמּוּז הֲפָךְ לָנוּ לְשָׂשׂוֹן וּלְשִׂמְחָה.

קְשֵׁינוּ עֹרֶף וְרָבְתָה בָּנוּ אָסוֹן, לָכֵן נִתַּנּוּ לִמְשִׁסָּה וְרִפְשׁוֹן,
רְאֵה יהוה וְחַלְּצֵנוּ מֵאָסוֹן,
וְשִׁבְעָה עָשָׂר בְּתַמּוּז הֲפָךְ לָנוּ לְשִׂמְחָה וּלְשָׂשׂוֹן.

❖ שְׁעֵנוּ שׁוֹכֵן רוּמָה, וְקַבֵּץ נְפוּצוֹתֵינוּ מִקַּצְוֹות אֲדָמָה,
תּוֹסִיף יָדְךָ שֵׁנִית לִקְנוֹת אֲיוּמָה, וְתֹאמַר לְצִיּוֹן קוּמָה,
וְשִׁבְעָה עָשָׂר בְּתַמּוּז הֲפָךְ לָנוּ לְיוֹם יְשׁוּעָה וְנֶחָמָה.

Seventeenth of Tammuz

The Seventeenth of Tammuz is second only to Tishah B'Av as a day of national tragedy. Although the prophets ordained it as a fast day to commemorate its role in the destruction of the Temple, it simultaneously recalls four other sad events, all of which are mentioned in the

SELICHOS FOR THE SEVENTEENTH OF TAMMUZ

Begin *Selichos* on page 816, then continue here:

Our God and the God of our forefathers

אֶתָאנוּ *We have come to You, O Molder of spirits,*
ב *our groans grew heavy with our abundant iniquities,*
strong are the decrees and many the shrieks,
for on the Seventeenth of Tammuz the Tablets were smashed.
ג *We were exiled from the Chosen House,*
ד *— our judgment was sealed and the decree was issued —*
and its light was darkened for us
for on the Seventeenth of Tammuz the Torah was burned.
ה *Our enemies tore down the Sanctuary and God's Presence fled*
from the Sanctuary's corner,
ו *we were consigned to the hands of wanton ones to be consumed —*
for on the Seventeenth of Tammuz, an idol was set up in the Sanctuary.
ז *We were scattered from city to city, old and young among us were taken captive,*
ח *[The site of] our joy [Jerusalem] was destroyed and set afire —*
for on the Seventeenth of Tammuz the City [wall] was breached.
ט *The destroying oppressor behaved insanely in the Sanctuary,*
from groom and bride armband and bracelet were taken,
י *because they angered You they were delivered to destruction —*
for on the Seventeenth of Tammuz the continual daily offering ceased.
כ *Every splendor and praise ceased from us,*
the foe unsheathed his sword to exterminate us,
ל *that babies and sucklings be prepared for the slaughter —*
for on the Seventeenth of Tammuz the elevation-offering and sacrifice ceased.
מ *We rebelled against Him Who dwells in the loftiest heavens,*
therefore we were scattered to all corners,
נ *Our dances were turned to dirges,*
for on the Seventeenth of Tammuz the offerings ceased.
ס *We strayed in Your very Presence through contentious talk,*
therefore our tongues were taught to utter dirges,
ע *we were foresaken without being counted —*
for on the Seventeenth of Tammuz the iniquities brought us their consequences.
פ *We were scattered without finding relief, therefore our groaning was increased,*
צ *O Rock, see that our soul is prostrate —*
and transform the Seventeenth of Tammuz for us to joy and gladness.
ק *We were stubborn so catastrophe increased among us,*
therefore we were consigned to be trampled and sullied,
ר *O* HASHEM*, see and spare us from catastrophe —*
and transform the Seventeenth of Tammuz for us to gladness and joy.
ש ∴ *Turn to us, You Who dwells on high,*
gather in our dispersion from the ends of the earth,
ת *may Your hand once more acquire this awe-struck nation, and may You say to Zion 'Rise!' — and transform the Seventeenth of Tammuz for us to a day of salvation and consolation.*

Selichos. The five tragedies of this day are:

1. In the Wilderness, Moses broke the first Tablets of the Covenant when he came down from Mount Sinai and found the people worshiping the Golden Calf.

2. During the siege of the First Temple, the Babylonians breached the wall of Jerusalem in Tammuz, but could not break into the Temple until 7 Av. However on 17 Tammuz, the *Kohanim* ran out of sheep for the daily continual [*Tamid*] offering.

3. During the siege of the Second Temple, the Romans breached Jerusalem's defenses on 17 Tammuz and began their bloody carnage in the city. According to *Yerushalmi (Taanis* 4) this was the anniversary of the breaching in the First

אֵל מֶלֶךְ יוֹשֵׁב עַל כִּסֵּא רַחֲמִים, מִתְנַהֵג בַּחֲסִידוּת, מוֹחֵל עֲוֹנוֹת עַמּוֹ, מַעֲבִיר רִאשׁוֹן רִאשׁוֹן, מַרְבֶּה מְחִילָה לְחַטָּאִים וּסְלִיחָה לַפּוֹשְׁעִים, עֹשֶׂה צְדָקוֹת עִם כָּל בָּשָׂר וָרוּחַ, לֹא כְרָעָתָם תִּגְמוֹל. ❖ אֵל הוֹרֵיתָ לָּנוּ לוֹמַר שְׁלשׁ עֶשְׂרֵה, וּזְכוֹר לָנוּ הַיּוֹם בְּרִית שְׁלשׁ עֶשְׂרֵה, כְּמוֹ שֶׁהוֹדַעְתָּ לֶעָנָיו מִקֶּדֶם, כְּמוֹ שֶׁכָּתוּב, וַיֵּרֶד יהוה בֶּעָנָן וַיִּתְיַצֵּב עִמּוֹ שָׁם, וַיִּקְרָא בְשֵׁם יהוה.

Congregation and *chazzan* recite loudly and in unison:

וַיַּעֲבֹר יהוה עַל פָּנָיו וַיִּקְרָא.

יהוה, יהוה, אֵל, רַחוּם, וְחַנּוּן, אֶרֶךְ אַפַּיִם, וְרַב חֶסֶד, וֶאֱמֶת, נֹצֵר חֶסֶד לָאֲלָפִים, נֹשֵׂא עָוֹן, וָפֶשַׁע, וְחַטָּאָה, וְנַקֵּה. וְסָלַחְתָּ לַעֲוֹנֵנוּ וּלְחַטָּאתֵנוּ וּנְחַלְתָּנוּ. סְלַח לָנוּ אָבִינוּ כִּי חָטָאנוּ, מְחַל לָנוּ מַלְכֵּנוּ כִּי פָשָׁעְנוּ. כִּי אַתָּה אֲדֹנָי טוֹב וְסַלָּח וְרַב חֶסֶד לְכָל קֹרְאֶיךָ.

All continue:

אֱלֹהִים אַל דֳּמִי לָךְ, אַל תֶּחֱרַשׁ וְאַל תִּשְׁקֹט אֵל. כִּי הִנֵּה אוֹיְבֶיךָ יֶהֱמָיוּן, וּמְשַׂנְאֶיךָ נָשְׂאוּ רֹאשׁ.[1] אֵל נְקָמוֹת יהוה, אֵל נְקָמוֹת הוֹפִיעַ.[2]

כְּרַחֵם אָב עַל בָּנִים, כֵּן תְּרַחֵם יהוה עָלֵינוּ. לַיהוה הַיְשׁוּעָה, עַל עַמְּךָ בִרְכָתֶךָ סֶּלָה. יהוה צְבָאוֹת עִמָּנוּ, מִשְׂגָּב לָנוּ אֱלֹהֵי יַעֲקֹב סֶלָה. יהוה צְבָאוֹת, אַשְׁרֵי אָדָם בֹּטֵחַ בָּךְ. יהוה הוֹשִׁיעָה, הַמֶּלֶךְ יַעֲנֵנוּ בְיוֹם קָרְאֵנוּ.

(Many congregations repeat, סְלַח נָא . . . וְעַל עַמֶּךָ [p. 820] here.)

אֱלֹהֵינוּ וֵאלֹהֵי אֲבוֹתֵינוּ

אֲמָרֵר בִּבְכִי מִפְּנֵי יָד שְׁלוּחָה בְּעִי,
בְּנָאֲצִי בְּתוֹךְ בֵּיתוֹ בִּבְגְדִי וְקָבְעִי,
גָּח וּבָרַח וְנָסַע עֶשֶׂר וְעָלָה לַשְּׁבִיעִי,
דִּמְּנִי הִצִּיקַנִי הֱסִיקַנִי בַּחֹדֶשׁ הָרְבִיעִי.
הֵבִיא מוֹעֵד בִּמְלֵאָתוֹ לִשְׁבּוֹר בַּחוּרֵי גִמּוּז,
וְרִבָּה בוֹ פַּעֲמַיִם בְּמִסְמוּס וּמִזְמוּז,
זְבוּלוֹ כְּשֶׁר שַׁאֲנַנּוֹת מְבַכּוֹת אֶת הַתַּמּוּז,[3]
חִיְּבָנִי אִיְּבָנִי אֲזַי בְּיֶרַח תַּמּוּז.
טָמְנוּ פַּחִים חֲמִשָּׁה בְּמִקְרָא תְּלָאוֹת מִשְׁלָחוֹת,
יָכְלוּ לִי בְּשִׁבְעָה עָשָׂר בּוֹ בַּאֲלִיחוֹת,
כִּי נוֹקַשְׁתִּי כְּכַלָּה עֲלוּבָה בְּחֻפַּת שַׁלְוָה וְהַצְלָחוֹת,
לְרוֹעִי לֹא הִמְתַּנְתִּי שֵׁשׁ וְנִשְׁתַּבְּרוּ הַלֻּחוֹת.
מִיָּדוֹ עָדִיתִי חֲלִי וָכֶתֶם אֶצְעָדָה וְצָמִיד,

(1) *Psalms* 83:2-3. (2) 94:1. (3) *Ezekiel* 8:14.

אֵל מֶלֶךְ *O God, King Who sits on the throne of mercy; Who acts with kindness, pardons the sins of His people, removes sins one by one, increasingly grants pardon to careless sinners and forgiveness to willful ones, performs acts of generosity with every living being — You do not repay them in accord with their evil. ∴ O God, You taught us to recite the Thirteen [Attributes of Mercy], so remember for us today the covenant of these Thirteen, as You made known to the humble one [Moses] in ancient times, as it is written: And* HASHEM *descended in a cloud and stood with him there, and He called out with the Name* HASHEM*:*

Congregation and chazzan recite loudly and in unison:

And HASHEM *passed before him [Moses] and proclaimed:*

יהוה HASHEM, HASHEM, *God, Compassionate and Gracious, Slow to anger, and Abundant in Kindness and Truth. Preserver of kindness for thousands of generations, Forgiver of iniquity, willful sin, and error, and Who cleanses. May You forgive our iniquities and our errors and make us Your heritage. Forgive us, our Father, for we have erred; pardon us, our King, for we have willfully sinned; for You, my Lord, are good and forgiving and abundantly kind to all who call upon You.*

All continue:

אֱלֹהִים *O God, do not hold Yourself silent; be not deaf and be not still, O God. For behold, Your foes are in an uproar and those who hate You have raised their head.*[1] *O God of vengeance,* HASHEM, *O God of vengeance, appear!*[2]

כְּרַחֵם *As a father has mercy on his children, so,* HASHEM, *may You have mercy on us. Salvation is* HASHEM*'s, upon Your people is Your blessing, Selah.* HASHEM, *Master of Legions, is with us, a stronghold for us is the God of Jacob, Selah.* HASHEM, *Master of Legions, praiseworthy is the person who trusts in You.* HASHEM, *save! May the King answer us on the day we call.*

(Many congregations repeat, *'Please forgive . . . Your people,'* [p. 820] here.)

Our God and the God of our forefathers

אֲמָרֵר *I am embittered with weeping at the hand stretched out in destruction,*
ב *for I angered God amid His Temple through treachery and robbery,*
ג *He swiftly fled in ten stages and ascended to the seventh heaven,*
ד *He cut me down, distressed me, and consumed me in this fourth month.*
ה *He brought the appointed time with full severity*
to break my blossoming youth,
ו *twice He inflicted him with crippling and infirmity,*
ז *when tranquil women in His Temple bewailed the Tammuz idol,*[3]
ח *He condemned me and opposed me then in the month of Tammuz.*
ט *They laid five traps, for You proclaimed that calamities be dispatched,*
י *on the seventeenth they could perpetrate depravities against me,*
כ *for I let myself be snared like a shameless bride*
under a calm and auspicious wedding canopy,
ל *because I did not wait six hours longer for my shephered Moses,*
the Tablets were broken.
מ *I was adorned from His hand with golden ornaments, armband and bracelet*

Temple period as well.

4. During the terror-filled years before the destruction of the Second Temple, a Roman officer named Apostomos shocked the Jewish people by publicly burning a Torah scroll, the first atrocity of this sort.

5. An idol was placed in the Temple. According to some, this was part of the disgrace perpetrated by Apostomos; others say it was done by Menashe, the idol-worshiping king of Judah during the time of the first Temple.

⇘ **אֲמָרֵר** — *I am embittered.* The first twenty-two verses follow an alphabetical scheme. The second

נגָּרוֹת בְּיוֹם אַפּוֹ כְּשִׁחַתִּי דְּרָכַי לְהַשְׁמִיד,
סֵדֶר עֲבוֹדָתוֹ וְקִיץ מִזְבְּחוֹ קָצְתִּי לְהַעֲמִיד,
עַל כֵּן מִלִּשְׁכַּת הַטְּלָאִים בֻּטַּל הַתָּמִיד.
פּוּר הִתְפּוֹרְרָה וְנִתְפַּזְּרָה סוֹעֲרָה עֲנִיָּה,
צִיָּה נִמְשְׁלָה מִבְּלִי חוֹבֵל וְנִטְרְפָה כָּאֳנִיָּה,
קַחְתָּה בְּחַטָּאתָהּ בְּרֹאשָׁהּ, וּבְכֶפֶל תַּאֲנִיָּה וַאֲנִיָּה,
רִיבוּהָ צָרֶיהָ כְּהַיּוֹם וְהָבְקְעָה הָעִיר בַּשְּׁנִיָּה.
שְׁלוּחָה כַּצְּבִי מֻדָּח מֵאֵין דּוֹרֵשׁ לְהַסְתִּירָה,
שָׁנְנוּ לְשׁוֹנָם וּנְתָנוּהָ כְּשֶׂה צְמָרָהּ וְחֶלְבָּהּ לְהַתִּירָה,
תִּצְעַק עַל כְּלִי חֶמְדָּה שֶׁבּוֹ נִכְתָּרָה,
תַּחְמוּד עֵינֶיהָ נֻצַּל כְּשָׂרַף אַפּוֹסְטְמוֹס הַתּוֹרָה.
חֵרֵף עֲשׁוּקִים וּרְצוּצִים בַּעֲבוּר הָרְעִימָה סָכָל,
יְרוּדִים בְּוַהֲיָה לֶאֱכוֹל וּבְהַסְתֵּר פָּנִים מִלְּהִסְתַּכָּל,
יַד הִשְׁלִים מִכְּנַף שִׁקּוּצִים נֶאֱכָל,
עֵת צָרָה כְּהִתְכַּנֵּס וְהָעֳמַד צֶלֶם בְּהֵיכָל.
דְּוּוּיִם סְגוּפִים בָּנִים הֱיוּ מִקֶּדֶם רִאשׁוֹנִים,
סְמוּכוֹת צָרוֹתֵיהֶם זוֹ לְזוֹ כַּמֶּה שָׁנִים,
לוֹקִים כַּאֲשֶׁר תַּעֲשֶׂינָה הַדְּבוֹרִים וְהָעַקְרַבִּים שׁוֹנִים,
הוֹגִים אָבַד שִׁבְרָם וּבָטֵל סִכּוּיָם בְּאִישׁוֹנִים.
❖ **אֵל** קַנָּא, בְּהִתְאַפֵּק בִּמְקַנְאֶיךָ דְּשֵׁנִים רְטוּבִים,
מְחַכִּים תְּקִים עוֹמְדִים לְעוֹלָמִים,
כִּנְטִיעִים מְחֻטָּבִים בַּאֲהָבִים, הָאֱמֶת וְהַשָּׁלוֹם בְּצוֹמוֹת חֲטוּבִים,
נֶצַח הֱיוֹתָם לְשִׂמְחָה וּלְשָׂשׂוֹן וּלְמוֹעֲדִים טוֹבִים.

אֵל מֶלֶךְ יוֹשֵׁב עַל כִּסֵּא רַחֲמִים, מִתְנַהֵג בַּחֲסִידוּת, מוֹחֵל עֲוֹנוֹת עַמּוֹ, מַעֲבִיר רִאשׁוֹן רִאשׁוֹן, מַרְבֶּה מְחִילָה לְחַטָּאִים וּסְלִיחָה לַפּוֹשְׁעִים, עֹשֶׂה צְדָקוֹת עִם כָּל בָּשָׂר וָרוּחַ, לֹא כְרָעָתָם תִּגְמוֹל. ❖ אֵל הוֹרֵיתָ לָנוּ לוֹמַר שְׁלֹשׁ עֶשְׂרֵה, וּזְכוֹר לָנוּ הַיּוֹם בְּרִית שְׁלֹשׁ עֶשְׂרֵה, כְּמוֹ שֶׁהוֹדַעְתָּ לֶעָנָיו מִקֶּדֶם, כְּמוֹ שֶׁכָּתוּב, וַיֵּרֶד יהוה בֶּעָנָן וַיִּתְיַצֵּב עִמּוֹ שָׁם, וַיִּקְרָא בְשֵׁם יהוה.

Congregation and *chazzan* recite loudly and in unison:

וַיַּעֲבֹר יהוה עַל פָּנָיו וַיִּקְרָא.

יהוה, יהוה, אֵל, רַחוּם, וְחַנּוּן, אֶרֶךְ אַפַּיִם, וְרַב חֶסֶד, וֶאֱמֶת, נֹצֵר חֶסֶד לָאֲלָפִים, נֹשֵׂא עָוֹן, וָפֶשַׁע, וְחַטָּאָה, וְנַקֵּה. וְסָלַחְתָּ לַעֲוֹנֵנוּ וּלְחַטָּאתֵנוּ וּנְחַלְתָּנוּ. סְלַח לָנוּ אָבִינוּ כִּי חָטָאנוּ, מְחַל לָנוּ מַלְכֵּנוּ כִּי פָשָׁעְנוּ. כִּי אַתָּה אֲדֹנָי טוֹב וְסַלָּח וְרַב חֶסֶד לְכָל קֹרְאֶיךָ.

נ *that were brushed away on the day of His wrath,*
when my corrupted ways brought destruction,
ס *I hated to maintain the order of Temple service*
and the regular elevation-offerings on the Altar,
ע *therefore the daily offering stopped coming from the chamber of sheep.*
פ *Shattered and dispersed is the storm-tossed indigent,*
צ *likened to a captainless boat and a wrecked vessel,*
ק *punished for her sin and then again, with mourning and lamentation;*
ר *her tormentors attacked her this day*
and the City [wall] was breached in the Second Commonwealth.
ש *She was exiled like an outcast deer that no one cared to shelter,*
ש *they sharpened their tongue and treated her like a sheep*
whose wool and fat are free for the taking,
ת *she cried out over the precious vessel [the Torah] with which she had been crowned,*
ת *the darling of her eyes was removed when Apostomos burned the Torah.*
The foolish conqueror reviled the robbed and crushed victims to frustrate them,
the vanquished ones felt the curses of 'It will be devoured'
and the concealment of God's Face, not taking notice of them;
a hand was broken off of the wasted idols [that King Menashe placed in the Temple],
at the time of distress when an idol was brought in and set up in the Sanctuary.
Pained and tortured were the children who once were leaders,
for years their woes came one after another,
hurt as if by all sorts of bees and scorpions,
who said, 'Their hope is lost and their potential nullified in night of exile.'
∴ *O jealous God who restrains Himself*
against the provocations of the fat and prosperous,
may You raise up those who stand by You forever,
like plants cared for lovingly, let the truth and peace that are inscribed in the fasts
become eternal gladness and joy, and beneficent festivals.

אֵל מֶלֶךְ *O God, King Who sits on the throne of mercy; Who acts with kindness, pardons the sins of His people, removes sins one by one, increasingly grants pardon to careless sinners and forgiveness to willful ones, performs acts of generosity with every living being — You do not repay them in accord with their evil.* ∴ *O God, You taught us to recite the Thirteen [Attributes of Mercy], so remember for us today the covenant of these Thirteen, as You made known to the humble one [Moses] in ancient times, as it is written: And* HASHEM *descended in a cloud and stood with him there, and He called out with the Name* HASHEM*:*

Congregation and chazzan recite loudly and in unison:
And HASHEM *passed before him [Moses] and proclaimed:*

יהוה HASHEM, HASHEM, *God, Compassionate and Gracious, Slow to anger, and Abundant in Kindness and Truth. Preserver of kindness for thousands of generations, Forgiver of iniquity, willful sin, and error, and Who cleanses. May You forgive our iniquities and our errors and make us Your heritage. Forgive us, our Father, for we have erred; pardon us, our King, for we have willfully sinned; for You, my Lord, are good and forgiving and abundantly kind to all who call upon You.*

---

letters of these verses along with the initial letters of the remaining verses spell מְנַחֵם בְּרַבִּי מָכִיר יִגְדַּל וִיחִי לָנֶצַח חַיֵּי עַד סֶלָה אָמֵן, *Menachem, son of Rabbi Machir, may he become great and live triumphantly, an everlasting life. Selah. Amen* (see page 854.)

The following prayer is recited responsively by the *chazzan* and congregation.

שְׁעֵה נֶאֱסַר, אֲשֶׁר נִמְסַר, בְּיַד בָּבֶל וְגַם שֵׂעִיר,
לְךָ יֶהֱמֶה, זֶה כַּמֶּה, וְיִתְחַנֵּן כְּבֵן צָעִיר,
יוֹם גָּבַר הָאוֹיֵב וַתִּבָּקַע הָעִיר.

לְזֹאת אִכַּף, וְאֶסְפּוֹק כַּף, בְּיוֹם חֲמֵשׁ פִּזְרוֹנִי,
וְעַל רֶגֶל, הָעֵגֶל, הַלּוּחוֹת יְצָאוּנִי,
וְגַם הִשְׁמִיד, הַתָּמִיד, וּבַסּוּגַר הֱבִיאָנִי,
וְהוּשַׂם אֱלִיל, בְּהֵיכַל כְּלִיל, וּמֵעֲצָתוֹ, כְּלָאָנִי,
וְהַמִּנְחָה הוּנָחָה, וְדָתְךָ, צָר בָּאֵשׁ הִבְעִיר.
יוֹם גָּבַר הָאוֹיֵב וַתִּבָּקַע הָעִיר.

מְאֹד אֶתְחַל, וָאֶתְחַלְחַל, בְּיוֹם שַׁדַּי דְחָפַנִי,
מְאוֹר חָשַׁךְ, וְגַם שֵׁשַׁךְ, כְּמוֹ כַּדּוּר צְנָפַנִי,
וְהַשְּׂפִיפוֹן מִצָּפוֹן, כְּשִׁבֹּלֶת שְׁטָפַנִי,
וְהַצַּיָּד, שָׁלַח יָד, וְהַצָּפִיר וְהַשָּׂעִיר.
יוֹם גָּבַר הָאוֹיֵב וַתִּבָּקַע הָעִיר.

הוֹד לִבִּי, וּמִשְׂגַּבִּי, הֲלָעַד אַפְּךָ יֶעְשַׁן,
הֲלֹא תִרְאֶה, עַם נִלְאֶה, אֲשֶׁר הָשְׁחַר כְּמוֹ כִבְשָׁן,
גְּדוֹר פִּרְצִי, בְּבֶן פַּרְצִי, וּמֵחֶדֶק לְקוֹט שׁוֹשָׁן,
בְּנֵה בֵּית זְבוּל, לְהָשִׁיב גְּבוּל, הַכַּרְמֶל וְהַבָּשָׁן.
וְעַיִן פְּקַח, וְנָקָם קַח, מֵאֶצֶר וּמִדִּישָׁן,
שְׁפוֹט אִלֵּם, וְאָז יְשַׁלֵּם, הַמַּבְעֶה וְהַמַּבְעִיר,
יוֹם גָּבַר הָאוֹיֵב וַתִּבָּקַע הָעִיר.

אֵל מֶלֶךְ יוֹשֵׁב עַל כִּסֵּא רַחֲמִים, מִתְנַהֵג בַּחֲסִידוּת מוֹחֵל עֲוֹנוֹת עַמּוֹ, מַעֲבִיר רִאשׁוֹן רִאשׁוֹן, מַרְבֶּה מְחִילָה לְחַטָּאִים וּסְלִיחָה לַפּוֹשְׁעִים, עֹשֶׂה צְדָקוֹת עִם כָּל בָּשָׂר וָרוּחַ, לֹא כְרָעָתָם תִּגְמוֹל. ❖ אֵל הוֹרֵיתָ לָּנוּ לוֹמַר שְׁלֹשׁ עֶשְׂרֵה, וּזְכוֹר לָנוּ הַיּוֹם בְּרִית שְׁלֹשׁ עֶשְׂרֵה, כְּמוֹ שֶׁהוֹדַעְתָּ לֶעָנָיו מִקֶּדֶם, כְּמוֹ שֶׁכָּתוּב, וַיֵּרֶד יהוה בֶּעָנָן וַיִּתְיַצֵּב עִמּוֹ שָׁם, וַיִּקְרָא בְשֵׁם יהוה.

Congregation and *chazzan* recite loudly and in unison:

וַיַּעֲבֹר יהוה עַל פָּנָיו וַיִּקְרָא.

יהוה, יהוה, אֵל, רַחוּם, וְחַנּוּן, אֶרֶךְ אַפַּיִם, וְרַב חֶסֶד, וֶאֱמֶת, נֹצֵר חֶסֶד לָאֲלָפִים, נֹשֵׂא עָוֹן, וָפֶשַׁע, וְחַטָּאָה, וְנַקֵּה. וְסָלַחְתָּ לַעֲוֹנֵנוּ וּלְחַטָּאתֵנוּ וּנְחַלְתָּנוּ. סְלַח לָנוּ אָבִינוּ כִּי חָטָאנוּ, מְחַל לָנוּ מַלְכֵּנוּ כִּי פָשָׁעְנוּ. כִּי אַתָּה אֲדֹנָי טוֹב וְסַלָּח, וְרַב חֶסֶד לְכָל קֹרְאֶיךָ.

Turn to page 828 for זְכוֹר רַחֲמֶיךָ, and continue until the conclusion of Selichos.

The following prayer is recited responsively by the *chazzan* and congregation:

שְׁעֵה *Turn to the captive nation that was delivered to Babylon and Seir,*
for You it yearns for so very long, supplicating like a young child —
On the day when the enemy overpowered and the City was breached.

For this I am bowed and clap my hands on the day five tragedies dispersed me:
because of the Golden Calf, the Tablets left me;
the daily offering was abolished, the enemy put me into chains;
an idol was placed in the beautiful Sanctuary, He denied me His counsel;
the meal offering came to a stop, and the enemy burned Your law in flames —
On the day when the enemy overpowered and the City was breached.

I became exceedingly ill and terrified on the day the Almighty pushed me away,
the light grew dark, and Sheshach [Babylonia] tossed me like a ball,
the serpent from the north [Nebuchadnezzar] flooded me like a raging flood;
the hunter [Edom/Rome] put out his grasping hand,
as did the hairy he-goat [Greece] —
On the day when the enemy overpowered and the City was breached.

O Glory of my heart, my Fortress, will Your wrath burn forever?
Have You not seen the exhausted people that was blackened like a furnace?
Fence in my breach through the offspring of Peretz [the Messiah]
and pluck the rose from among the thorns.
Build Your Dwelling Place, to return the rewarded nation to Carmel and Bashan,
open Your eyes and take revenge from Ezer and Dishan [Edomite nobles];
judge for the benefit of speechless Israel and thus will be requited
the nation that consumed and burned [Israel] —
On the day when the enemy overpowered and the City was breached.

אֵל מֶלֶךְ *O God, King Who sits on the throne of mercy; Who acts with kindness, pardons the sins of His people, removes sins one by one, increasingly grants pardon to careless sinners and forgiveness to willful ones, performs acts of generosity with every living being — You do not repay them in accord with their evil.* ❖ *O God, You taught us to recite the Thirteen Attributes of Mercy, so remember for us today the covenant of these Thirteen as You made known to the humble one [Moses] in ancient times, as it is written, and* HASHEM *descended in a cloud and stood with him there, and He called out with the Name* HASHEM*:*

Congregation and *chazzan* recite loudly and in unison:
And HASHEM *passed before him [Moses] and proclaimed:*

יהוה HASHEM, HASHEM, *God, Compassionate and Gracious, Slow to anger, and Abundant in Kindness and Truth. Preserver of kindness for thousands of generations, Forgiver of iniquity, willful sin, and error, and Who cleanses. May You forgive our iniquities and our errors and make us Your heritage. Forgive us, our Father, for we have erred; pardon us, our King, for we have willfully sinned; for You, my Lord, are good and forgiving and abundantly kind to all who call upon You.*

Turn to page 828 for זְכוֹר רַחֲמֶיךָ, *'Remember Your mercies,'*
and continue until the conclusion of Selichos.

⚜ **שְׁעֵה** — *Turn.* The acrostic spells the author's name שְׁלֹמֹה, *Shlomo.*

יוצר לפרשת שקלים

The *chazzan* begins his repetition of the *Shacharis Shemoneh Esrei:*

אֲדֹנָי שְׂפָתַי תִּפְתָּח, וּפִי יַגִּיד תְּהִלָּתֶךָ.

בָּרוּךְ אַתָּה יהוה אֱלֹהֵינוּ וֵאלֹהֵי אֲבוֹתֵינוּ, אֱלֹהֵי אַבְרָהָם, אֱלֹהֵי יִצְחָק, וֵאלֹהֵי יַעֲקֹב, הָאֵל הַגָּדוֹל הַגִּבּוֹר וְהַנּוֹרָא, אֵל עֶלְיוֹן, גּוֹמֵל חֲסָדִים טוֹבִים וְקוֹנֵה הַכֹּל, וְזוֹכֵר חַסְדֵי אָבוֹת, וּמֵבִיא גוֹאֵל לִבְנֵי בְנֵיהֶם, לְמַעַן שְׁמוֹ בְּאַהֲבָה. מֶלֶךְ עוֹזֵר וּמוֹשִׁיעַ וּמָגֵן.

Congregation, followed by *chazzan,* recites:

מִסּוֹד חֲכָמִים וּנְבוֹנִים, וּמִלֶּמֶד דַּעַת מְבִינִים.
אֶפְתְּחָה פִּי בְּשִׁיר וּרְנָנִים. לְהוֹדוֹת וּלְהַלֵּל פְּנֵי שׁוֹכֵן מְעוֹנִים.

All continue:

אָז מֵאָז זַמּוֹתָ בְּכָל פּוֹעַל, **בְּ**מִסְפָּר בְּמִשְׁקָל כֹּל לְךָ לְהַעַל,
גָּדְרְתָּ בְּכֵן לְמָשׁוּי מִמֵּי שַׁעַל, **דָּ**עַת מִפְקַד יוֹפִי פַּעֲמֵי נָעַל.
הַעַל הֶמִירוּ כְּבוֹד רֶעַ בְּבַעַל, **וְ**זֶה לְלֹא זֶה פָּצְחוּ בְּמַעַל,
זָנְחוּ בַּחֲרוֹן אַף לְנֶגֶף וָגַעַל, **חָ**ל בַּעֲדָם חֶבֶר וְהַצָּרִי תַּעַל.
טְוֹרַח מַשָּׂאָם הֻגַּד לוֹ שְׂאֵת, **יָ**שְׁרָם לְהָלִיץ תְּלוּי רֹאשׁ לָשֵׂאת.
❖ **כָּ**פְרָם פָּץ תֵּת לְאֻמִּים מַשְׂאֵת, **לְ**נַטְּלָם לְנַשְּׂאָם בְּכִי תִשָּׂא אֶת:

All continue:

רָאשֵׁי עַל כָּל רֹאשׁ נִשֵּׂאתָ, גֵּוִי עַל גַּפֵּי מְרוֹמֵי קֶרֶת הִתְנַשֵּׂאתָ,
❖ אַהֲבָה עַל כָּל פֶּשַׁע כִּסִּיתָ, בְּגִין צֵל יְמִינְךָ לְגוֹנְנֵי הִתְנַשֵּׂאתָ.

Chazzan continues:

בָּרוּךְ אַתָּה יהוה מָגֵן אַבְרָהָם.

אַתָּה גִּבּוֹר לְעוֹלָם אֲדֹנָי, מְחַיֵּה מֵתִים אַתָּה, רַב לְהוֹשִׁיעַ. מַשִּׁיב הָרוּחַ וּמוֹרִיד הַגֶּשֶׁם. מְכַלְכֵּל חַיִּים בְּחֶסֶד, מְחַיֵּה מֵתִים בְּרַחֲמִים רַבִּים, סוֹמֵךְ נוֹפְלִים, וְרוֹפֵא חוֹלִים, וּמַתִּיר אֲסוּרִים, וּמְקַיֵּם אֱמוּנָתוֹ לִישֵׁנֵי עָפָר. מִי כָמוֹךָ בַּעַל גְּבוּרוֹת, וּמִי דּוֹמֶה לָּךְ, מֶלֶךְ מֵמִית וּמְחַיֶּה וּמַצְמִיחַ יְשׁוּעָה. וְנֶאֱמָן אַתָּה לְהַחֲיוֹת מֵתִים.

YOTZROS

The insertion of *piyutim* (liturgical poems) into the prayers dates back to ancient times, at least as early as the second century, the time of the first known *paytan* (liturgical poet), Elazar HaKalir. [According to *Tosafos (Chagigah* 13a) and *Rosh (Berachos* 5:21), he was the Tanna Rabbi Elazar son of Rabbi Shimon bar Yochai.] The *piyutim* captured the mood, *mitzvos*, significance, and history of the particular day or festival they commemorated. They are commonly known as יוֹצְרוֹת, *yotzros*, but this is a misnomer. Actually, only those intended for insertion in *Shacharis* between the יוֹצֵר אוֹר blessing and *Shemoneh Esrei* are called *yotzros*, after the name of the blessing. Those recited during the *chazzan's Shemoneh Esrei* are קְרוֹבוֹת, a word that means 'the one who presents the prayers' (i.e. the *chazzan).* Nevertheless, all of the morning *piyutim* are commonly known as *yotzros*.

Many prominent halachic authorities from medieval times onward have opposed the insertion of *piyutim* into the prayer order, primarily on the grounds that they are an interference with and a change in the words of the prayers as they were set forth by the Sages. The *Vilna Gaon* ruled that the *piyutim* should be recited in their entirety after the *chazzan's Shemoneh Esrei* has been concluded. Most congregations, though by no means all, follow

YOTZER FOR PARASHAS SHEKALIM

The *chazzan* begins his repetition of the *Shacharis Shemoneh Esrei:*

My Lord, open my lips, that my mouth may declare Your praise.

בָּרוּךְ *Blessed are You, HASHEM, our God and the God of our forefathers, God of Abraham, God of Isaac, and God of Jacob; the great, mighty, and awesome God, the supreme God, Who bestows beneficial kindnesses and creates everything, Who recalls the kindnesses of the Patriarchs and brings a Redeemer to their children's children, for His Name's sake, with love. O King, Helper, Savior, and Shield.*

Congregation, followed by *chazzan,* recites:

מִסּוֹד *Based on the tradition* of our wise and discerning teachers,*
and the teaching derived from the knowledge of the discerning,
I open my mouth in song to praise Him Who dwells on high.

All continue:

אָז *Then, at the time of Creation, You [God] thought of*
the proper measure of each thing that You brought into being.
Accordingly You told Moses, who had been drawn from the water,
to take a census of the Jews who would be beautifully shod in pilgrim's sandals.
Because they betrayed the honor of their Friend [God] in favor of the Golden Calf,
and brazenly declared "This is your god,"
they were set aside for punishment and disdain by God's wrath.
Moses prayed and brought a cure.
He was told to bear their burden, to defend them and raise their level.
∴ *As a redemption You said the other nations would be Israel's servants,*
and that Israel would be uplifted through giving shekalim.

All continue:

רֹאשִׁי *You raised my head above all heads*
and raised my body above all high cities.
∴ *Your love covered for every sin;*
You raised us through the protection of Your right hand.

Chazzan continues:

Blessed are You, HASHEM, Shield of Abraham.

אַתָּה *You are eternally mighty, my Lord, the Resuscitator of the dead are You; abundantly able to save,* ***Who makes the wind blow and makes the rain descend;*** *Who sustains the living with kindness, resuscitates the dead with abundant mercy, supports the fallen, heals the sick, releases the confined, and maintains His faith to those asleep in the dust. Who is like You, O Master of mighty deeds, and who is comparable to You, O King Who causes death and restores life and makes salvation sprout! And You are faithful to resuscitate the dead.*

Rama (Orach Chaim 68 and 112) who permits the recitation of *piyutim.*

Our text of the *piyutim* includes the selections that are most commonly recited by most congregations. Rather than a lengthy commentary, we offer an interpretative translation of each *piyut.*

מסוד — *Based on the tradition.* To justify our recitation of *piyutim,* all of those that are recited during the *chazzan's Shemoneh Esrei* begin with the same formula. It begins מסוד חֲכָמִים וּנְבוֹנִים, *Based on the tradition of our wise and discerning teachers,* meaning that we dare to interrupt the prayer service only because these *piyutim* were transmitted to us by the great sages of yore, based on the 'foundation' of their great wisdom and piety.

YOTZER FOR PARASHAS SHEKALIM

During the Temple era, public announcements were made every year at the beginning of Adar that people were to contribute a half-*shekel* per capita to pay for the communal offerings of the Temple. To recall this *mitzvah* and to stimulate our longing for the rebuilding of the Temple, the Torah's commandment to set aside these half-*shekels* is read every year on the Sabbath before Rosh Chodesh Adar.

All continue:

מַעְתִּיק פְּלוּסִים צָר וּבוֹרֵא רוּחַ, מְמַדֵּד וּמְשַׁקֵּל גֵּזֶל עִם רוּחַ,
נֶגֶף לְבַל יַזִּיק לְנִדְכְּאֵי רוּחַ, נוֹבַבְתָּם תֵּת פִּדְיוֹן לְכָל רוּחַ.
שְׂרִיג זֵד שֵׂעִיר טֶרֶם עָמַד, סָקַרְתָּ כִּי לְמוֹקֵשׁ וְלִצְנִין יָעֳמַד,
עֲצַתְּ זֶה לָזֶה שֶׁמַע בְּמַעֲמַד, עָתוּד שְׁקָלִים מֵרֹאשׁ חֹדֶשׁ לִלְמַד.
פָּרָשָׁה זֹאת לַהֲגוֹת בְּקֵץ זֶה, פְּלָסֶיהָ לְהַקְדִּים לְפֶלֶס צַר וּבוֹזֶה.
✣ צוּרַת מַטְבֵּעַ כְּחָז אֲבִי חוֹזֶה, צִוָּה צוּר לְצִיר כֵּן תֵּת מַתָּן זֶה.

All continue:

שְׁמוֹ מִשְׁתַּתֵּף בְּעַם לוֹ עֲמוּתִים, וְעָלָיו כָּל הַיּוֹם הֵם מוּמָתִים.
✣ יָעִיר וְיַחֲשׂוֹף זְרוֹעַ וְיַד מְמִתִים, בְּזִיל נִטְפֵי לֶקֶשׁ לְהַחֲיוֹת מֵתִים.

Chazzan continues:

בָּרוּךְ אַתָּה יהוה מְחַיֵּה הַמֵּתִים.

All continue:

קְצוּבָה הִיא זֹאת לְשׁוֹעִים וְקַלִּים, קְצִינִים וְרָשִׁים יַחַד בָּהּ שְׁקוּלִים,
קָצִין לְבַל יָעוֹז מוּל מַקְהֵלִים,
קְרֹא לוֹמַר הוֹנִי פְּדָאֻנִי מֵעִקּוּלִים.
רוֹב עָם אֲשֶׁר לֹא יִסָּפֵר, רַב עִם צָעִיר מֵעֶשְׂרִים לְהִסָּפֵר,
רְאוּיִם לְעוֹנֶשׁ וְזֻהַר בְּסֵדֶר לְהִתָּפֵר,
רֶשַׁע וְכָל פֶּשַׁע לְכַפֵּר וּלְהָפֵר.
שְׁעוּרִים בְּזֶה שִׁעוּר בְּמִפְקַד לְהַגְבֵּר,
שְׁתִילֵימוֹ לִנְשִׂיאַת רֹאשׁ אוֹתָם לְחַבֵּר.
✣ שִׁקְלֵי כֶסֶף כִּפּוּרִים כָּפְרָם לְהַדְבֵּר, שְׁמוּרִים לְזִכָּרוֹן תֵּת כָּל הָעֹבֵר.

All continue:

תָּמְדוּ מֵאָז כָּל עֲדַת קְדוֹשִׁים, תְּרוֹם בִּשְׁלֹשָׁה פְּרָקִים תְּרוּמַת קָדָשִׁים.
✣ תְּכוּנָה לְבֶדֶק הַבַּיִת וְכָל אִשִּׁים,
תֵּת בְּיַד הַכֹּהֲנִים כֶּסֶף הַקֳּדָשִׁים.

All continue:

תֵּפֶן בְּאוֹן פִּיד טִיט רִפְשֵׁנוּ, תַּבִּיט בְּדָכְיֵנוּ וְעוֹד בַּל תַּכְפִּישֵׁנוּ.
✣ תִּקְרָא דְרוֹר כְּמֵאָז בּוֹ לְהַחְפִּישֵׁנוּ,
תֵּת הֲמוֹן לְאֻמִּים תַּחַת נַפְשֵׁנוּ.

All continue:

תִּזְכּוֹר לְהַעֲלוֹת נְשׂוּאֵי רַחַם מְדַכְיָם, תְּמוּכִים נְזוּרִים בְּהוֹד טוֹב עֲדָיִם.
✣ תּוֹקֶף עוֹז אַדִּירְךָ עַל יָם, תִּזְכּוֹר לְעָם מִסְפָּרָם כְּחוֹל הַיָּם.

Congregation, followed by *chazzan*, recites aloud:

יִמְלֹךְ יהוה לְעוֹלָם אֱלֹהַיִךְ צִיּוֹן לְדֹר וָדֹר הַלְלוּיָהּ.
וְאַתָּה קָדוֹשׁ יוֹשֵׁב תְּהִלּוֹת יִשְׂרָאֵל אֵל נָא.

All continue:

מַעְתִּיק *God moves and fashions mountains and creates wind,*
measures and weighs rain and wind,
prevents plague from harming the depressed —
You told them to give relief to everyone.
Before Haman, the wanton branch of Esau arose,
You saw that he would be a snare and thorn;
You advised Jews to announce to one another publicly
that they should give shekels from Rosh Chodesh.
The chapter of shekels is read at this time,
so that our contribution would come before that of our degraded foe.
∴ *Moses, father of prophets, had a vision of the half-shekel coin,*
and the Creator commanded that that amount be contributed.

All continue:

שְׁמוֹ *God's Name* [אֵל] *is contained in the name of the nation that clings to Him* [יִשְׂרָאֵל]
and that is ready to die for Him always.
∴ *God arouses Himself and bares His arm to avenge the murders of His people,*
and will cause life-giving rain to resuscitate the dead.

Chazzan continues:

Blessed are You, HASHEM, Who resuscitates the dead.

All continue:

קְצוּבָה *The half-shekel is the same for rich and poor,*
wealthy and impoverished contribute equally —
so that the wealthy not arrogantly proclaim to the masses,
"My wealth redeemed my sins."
The great nation that may not be counted by head,
young and old are counted by shekels from twenty and up,
the age when they are eligible for Heavenly punishment and warning —
and to join the ranks of war —
by means of the half-shekel contribution, to annul their evil and sins.
The Jews are reckoned to grow stronger by being counted through this coin,
but you may also contribute for children to join them in this privilege.
∴ *The silver shekels of atonement caused the nations to submit to Israel*
and were kept by God as a remembrance for each Jew.

All continue:

תָּמִידוּ *Always, in Temple times, the entire holy congregation*
would remove funds from the accumulated shekels three times yearly,
∴ *to pay for repairs to the Temple and for the sacrifices.*
The sacred funds were entrusted to the Kohanim.

All continue:

תֵּפֶן *Please, God, take note of our downfall, how we are mired in deep mud,*
look at our downtroddenness and do not leave us in the dust.
∴ *Proclaim freedom and make us independent as the Exodus.*
Make the multitude of nations subject to our will.

All continue:

תִּזְכּוֹר *Remember to raise up from downfall this nation that You carried since its birth;*
they depend on You, they are set apart from the nations
because of the glorious, goodly ornament: the Torah.
∴ *They glorified You at the Sea by praising Your power —*
so remember the nation whose number is like the sand of the sea.

Congregation, followed by *chazzan*, recites aloud:

HASHEM shall reign forever — your God, O Zion —
from generation to generation, Halleluyah!

You, O Holy One, are enthroned upon Israel's praises —
please, O God.

All continue:

מִי יוּכַל לְשַׁעֵר כָּל הַפְּקוּדִים, אֲשֶׁר בְּחֶבֶל וּבְחֶלֶשׁ לֹא נִפְקָדִים,
בְּרִית כְּרוּתָה לָמוֹ מֵאָז בִּפְקוּדִים, לְבַל יֶחְסַר הַמֶּזֶג מֵחוּמֶשׁ פְּקוּדִים.
וְאִם כְּתוֹרֶן וְכַנֵּס יוּשְׁרְדוּ מְפֻקָּדִים, לֹא יְמְעֲטוּ מִשִּׁשִּׁים רִבּוֹא מְנֻקָּדִים,
וְאִם לְנֶגֶף וָאֶנֶף בְּאַף מְפֻקָּדִים, כֶּסֶף תֵּת כּוֹפֶר הֵם מְפֻקָּדִים,
וּבְכָל עֶרֶב נִשְׁמָתָם בְּיָדְךָ מַפְקִידִים, וּבְכָל רִגְעֵי בֹקֶר נִבְחָנִים וְנִפְקָדִים,
וְלִי מַה יָּקְרוּ עָלַי הַפְּקוּדִים, אֵלֶּה הַפְּקוּדִים וְהַמִּתְפַּקְּדִים,
✤ שְׁמוֹר פְּקוּדִים וְנִפְקָדִים, וְשׁוֹקְדִים לִהְיוֹת מְשֻׁקָּדִים, וּלְךָ קוֹדִים.

Congregation, followed by *chazzan,* recites aloud:

חַי וְקַיָּם נוֹרָא וּמָרוֹם וְקָדוֹשׁ.

All continue:

אוֹמֵן בְּשָׁמְעוֹ כִּי תִשָּׂא אֶת רֹאשׁ, חָל וַיֵּחַת אֵיךְ אוֹתָם דְּרוֹשׁ.
לְעָם אֲשֶׁר לֹא יִמַּד וְלֹא יִסָּפֵר,
אֵיכָכָה אֶסְפְּרֵם וְלֹא נִתְּנוּ לְהִסָּפֵר.
עִקָּרָם כְּנֶאֱמַר לוֹ הַבֵּט וּסְפוֹר, שָׁב וַיּוֹשַׁב אִם תּוּכַל לִסְפּוֹר.
זַרְעָם כְּחוֹל יַמִּים וְכוֹכָבִים סְפוּרִים, וַאֲנִי אֵיךְ אֶסְפְּרֵם וְלָעַד פָּרִים.
רָם חִוָּה לוֹ אוֹת מִסְפָּרָם, אֵיךְ לִמְנוֹתָם וְלַעֲמוֹד עַל סִפְרָם.
בְּקוֹר רָאשֵׁי שְׁמוֹתָם לְחֶשְׁבּוֹן תַּעֲלֶה, וּמִדַּת מִנְיָנָם בְּיָדְךָ אָז תַּעֲלֶה.*
יָקָר שְׁלִישִׁי בְּתוֹכָם לֹא הָפְקַד, כִּי לִגְיוֹן מֶלֶךְ לְבַדּוֹ נִפְקָד.
רָשׁוּם מִבֶּטֶן לְהִפָּקֵד בְּמִשְׁמֶרֶת הַקּוֹדֶשׁ,
וּצְבָאוֹ וּפְקוּדָיו נִמְנִים מִבֶּן חוֹדֶשׁ.
בְּשָׁמְעוֹ אוֹמֵר וְנָתְנוּ אִישׁ כּוֹפֶר, פָּץ בַּמֶּה יִתְרַצֶּה אֶשְׁכּוֹל הַכֹּפֶר.
יְצִיר מַה יִתֵּן פִּדְיוֹן נַפְשׁוֹ, וְיִמְצָא חֲנִינָה פְּנֵי שָׁם נַפְשׁוֹ.
קָדוֹשׁ כְּחָפֵץ לְהַצְדִּיק עַם זֶה, כְּמִין מַטְבֵּעַ אֵשׁ הֶרְאָהוּ בַּמַּחֲזֶה.
לִמְּדוֹ זֶה יִתְּנוּ וְלֹא יִתְמַהְמְהוּ, וְלַכֹּל יִתְּנוּ אֵת אֲשֶׁר נָתָנוּ.
יָהּ לֹא מְצָאנוּךָ שַׂגִּיא כֹחַ, כַּאֲשֶׁר נִקֵּיתָ חֵטְא גִּבּוֹרֵי כֹחַ.
✤ רַחוּם כְּרַחֲמְתָּ נְשׂוּאֶיךָ בְּכֶסֶף כִּפּוּרִים,
כֵּן שְׁעֵה שְׂפָתֵינוּ בְּשִׁלּוּם פָּרִים.

Chazzan continues:

אֵל נָא לְעוֹלָם תֻּעֲרָץ, וּלְעוֹלָם תֻּקְדָּשׁ, וּלְעוֹלְמֵי עוֹלָמִים תִּמְלוֹךְ וְתִתְנַשֵּׂא, הָאֵל מֶלֶךְ נוֹרָא מָרוֹם וְקָדוֹשׁ, כִּי אַתָּה הוּא מֶלֶךְ מַלְכֵי הַמְּלָכִים, מַלְכוּתוֹ נֶצַח. נוֹרְאוֹתָיו שִׂיחוּ, סַפְּרוּ עֻזּוֹ, פָּאֲרוּהוּ צְבָאָיו, קַדְּשׁוּהוּ רוֹמְמוּהוּ, רוֹן שִׁיר וָשֶׁבַח, תֹּוקֶף תְּהִלּוֹת תִּפְאַרְתּוֹ.

וּמִדַּת מִנְיָנָם בְּיָדְךָ אָז תַּעֲלֶה — *And you will arrive at their census.* The numerical value of the initials of the tribes — Reuben, Simeon, Judah, Dan, Naftali, Gad, Asher, Issachar, Zebulun, Joseph, and Benjamin — add up to 597. [Since the Levites were counted separately, they are not included in this calculation.] There were 600,000 adult males who left Egypt, minus 3,000 who died because of

All continue:

מִי *Who can calculate the census of Israel, who were not counted at random.*
God made a covenant with them from the time He gave the commandments
that their numbers would be no fewer than those in the Book of Numbers.
Even if they suffer a plague and relatively few remain,
they will not be fewer than 600,000;
and if they are handed over wrathfully to be murdered,
they are commanded to gain atonement by contributing silver.
Every night they entrust their soul in Your hand
and every morning they are tested and remembered.
To me the commandments are so precious!
These counted Israelites and counted Levites —
∴*please guard them and also those who are no longer among us,*
and those who anxiously wish to be distinguished and bow to You —

Congregation, followed by *chazzan,* recites aloud:

Living and Enduring One, Awesome, Exalted, and Holy!

All continue:

אוֹמֶן *When Moses, the nurturer, heard he was to count the people,*
he worried and feared how he could do so:
"The people that is beyond measure or count —
how can I count them when it is forbidden to do so?
When their progenitor, Abraham, was told to look at the stars and count,
God added, 'if you can count them.'
Their offspring are numerous as the sand by the seas and the stars —
how can I count them when they constantly multiply?"
The One Above showed Moses a way to calculate their number,
how to count them and arrive at their total:
*"Add up the value of their initials and you will arrive at their census."**
The third tribe, Levi, was not counted among them,
because the "King's legion" is counted separately.
From the womb, Levi was destined to be counted for its holy mission,
so the Levite legion was counted from the age of a month.
When Moses heard that everyone was to give an atonement for himself,
he exclaimed, "With what can God be made to find favor?
What can a man give to redeem himself
and attain the grace of Him Who gave him his soul?"
The Holy One, wanting to justify this people
showed Moses a fiery coin in a vision;
He taught him they should give that coin without delay,
and tell them all what they should give.
God, You did not burden us too heavily;
similarly You cleansed Your strong nation's sin.
∴ *Merciful One, as You had mercy on Israel through the silver of atonement,*
so incline to our lips as we pray in place of offerings.

Chazzan continues:

אֵל נָא *O God, may You always be lauded and always be sanctified, and forever reign and be uplifted, the God, King, awesome, exalted, and holy, for You are the King Who reigns over kings, Whose sovereignty is eternal. Speak of His wonders, declare His strength, glorify Him, O His legions; sanctify Him, exalt Him. Sing song and praise, glorify Him with powerful psalms of praise.*

---

the Golden Calf; thus there were 597,000, as indicated by the initials.

אומן ❧. The initials of this *piyut* spell the name of the composer, אלעזר ברבי קליר.

Chazzan, followed by congregation, recites the following two verses aloud:

עַד אֶשָּׂא רֹאשׁ, כְּמוֹ מֵרֹאשׁ, לְהַקְדִּישׁ לְקָדוֹשׁ.
עַד בְּמֹאזְנֵי צֶדֶק, יַכְרִיעֵנוּ לְצֶדֶק, נוֹרָא וְקָדוֹשׁ.

All continue:

אֵלֶּה אֶזְכְּרָה אֵת אֲשֶׁר נַעֲשָׂה, **בִּ**הְיוֹתִי בֶּטַח וְשָׁקֵט בְּנָכוֹן וְנִשָּׂא,
גוֹעַלְתִּי בְּעֵבֶר וְשִׁקְלֵי אֵיךְ אֶשָּׂא.
דֵּי שִׁקְלֵי עַד לֹא שָׁקַלְתִּי, **הִ**נָּם לְמַס עוֹבֵד הַיּוֹם שֻׁקַּלְתִּי,
וּבְחֵטְא עִוּוּל שֶׁקֶל לָרֶשַׁע נִשְׁקַלְתִּי.
זוּזֵי לְלֹא תָתִי לְשָׁכְנֵי בְגִילָה, **חָ**בְתִּי לְתַשְׁלוּם דַּרְכְּמוֹן לְעוּלֵי גוֹלָה,
טְבְעוּ גַם הֵם וְהוּעֲרַמְתִּי מְגִלָּה.
יוֹשֶׁר שָׁלֹשׁ קֻפּוֹת מִשְׁלָשׁוֹת סְאִים, **כְּ**נוּסוֹת לְמִקַּח שַׁי מְרִיאִים וְשֵׂיִים,
לֻקְּחוּ וְאֵין עוֹד בְּצִעֵי נוֹשְׂאִים.
מִדַּת שׁוֹפָרוֹת תִּקְלִין חַדְתִּין וְעַתִּיקִין, **נְ**דָבוֹת אֲשֶׁר בָּם הָיוּ מְעַתְּקִין,
סָרוּ כַּמֶּה מֶנִי וְהַדְּבָרִים עַתִּיקִין.
עוֹצֶם הֲמוֹן חוֹגֵג וְשׁוֹטֵף כַּנָּהָר, **פֻּ**זַּר וְנוֹתַרְתִּי כְּתֹרֶן בְּרֹאשׁ הָהָר,
צֶדֶק מְלוֹנִי שֶׁעֲרַר כְּתֵל הָר.
קַן צִפּוֹר קָרָא לִמְרוֹם הָרִים, **רֹ**אשׁ נְשׂוּאֵיךְ כְּמֵאָז בּוֹ לְהָרִים,
שִׁבְעָה וּשְׁמוֹנָה עֲלֵיהֶם לְרֹאשׁ **תָּ**רִים.
∴ עַד אֶשָּׂא רֹאשׁ, כְּמוֹ מֵרֹאשׁ, לְהַקְדִּישׁ לְקָדוֹשׁ.

Chazzan and congregation recite together:

וּבְכֵן וּלְךָ תַעֲלֶה קְדֻשָּׁה כִּי אַתָּה קְדוֹשׁ יִשְׂרָאֵל וּמוֹשִׁיעַ.

Turn to page 422 for *Kedushah* and the continuation of *Shacharis*.

מוסף לפרשת שקלים

The *Chazzan* begins his repetition (p. 462) and continues through וּמוֹשִׁיעַ וּמָגֵן. Then all recite:

אֶשְׁכּוֹל, **א**וּוּי תַּאֲוַת כָּל נֶפֶשׁ, **בְּ**צִלּוֹ חִמַּדְתִּי שֶׁבֶת מְצֹא נוֹפֶשׁ,
בִּקַּשְׁתִּיו וְלֹא מְצָאתִיו וּפַצְתִּי בְּטֶפֶשׁ,
חָמַק עָבַר מִלְּהַדְרִיר לִי חוֹפֶשׁ,
גָּזַלְתִּי שִׁקְלֵי מִתֵּת כּוֹפֶר נֶפֶשׁ, וְטָבַעְתִּי בְּמֵי צוּל בְּטִיט וָרֶפֶשׁ.
∴ אוֹר פָּנֶיךָ עָלֵינוּ אָדוֹן נְסָה, וְשֶׁקֶל אֶשָּׂא בְּבַיִת נָכוֹן וְנִשָּׂא,
וּבְצֶדֶק הֶגֶה עֶרְךְּ כִּי תִשָּׂא, גּוֹנְנֵנוּ בְּמָגֵן אֵל רָם וְנִשָּׂא.

Chazzan concludes the first blessing:

בָּרוּךְ אַתָּה יהוה מָגֵן אַבְרָהָם.

MUSSAF FOR PARASHAS SHEKALIM

The *piyut* for *Mussaf* contains seven stanzas, one to be recited before each of the blessings of the *chazzan's* repetition of *Shemoneh Esrei*. The stanzas begin with the seven words of *Shir*

Chazzan, followed by congregation, recites the following two verses aloud:

**Until I can lift my head as in early times
to sanctify offerings to the Holy One.**

**Until I can be adjudged righteous in the scales of righteousness
— O Awesome and Holy One.**

All continue:

אֵלֶה *This mitzvah I shall recall as it was done
when I was safe and tranquil, secure and elevated;
but I was debased with sin — how can I bring my shekels?
I did not weigh off enough shekels for God's service,
therefore, as a servant of foreigners I must weigh my money for taxes,
and for my sin in not weighing it, I was delivered to the wicked.
Because I did not give but* two zuzim *[half-shekel] when I lived happily in Jerusalem,
I had to give* darkemons *[a larger coin] to build the Second Temple
for those returning from exile —
but those coins, too, sunk into the ground,
and I was stripped naked when the Second Temple was destroyed.
The shekels were carefully divided in three cases, each one of three* se'ahs
*that were gathered to purchase sheep and lambs —
they were taken from us and no longer atone for my sins.
There were chests labeled "new shekels" and "old shekels,"
in the merit of such gifts Israel was strong in battle,
but these things have long since left us.
A powerful flood of yearning people came on pilgrimage to Jerusalem —
it was dispersed and I am left like a solitary pole on a mountaintop,
the righteous Temple-dwelling was destroyed like a desolate mountain.
Like a nestful of birds, Israel called to the exalted Temple Mount,
pleading that You appoint leaders like the seven shepherds
[i.e. Abraham, Isaac, Jacob, Moses, Aaron, Joseph, and David]
and the eight lords
[i.e. Adam, Seth, Methuselah, Jesse, Saul, Zephaniah, Amos and Michah].
∴ Until I can lift my head as in early times
to sanctify offerings to the Holy One.*

Chazzan and congregation recite together:

**So now, the Kedushah prayer will ascend to You,
for You are the Holy One and Savior of Israel.**

Turn to page 423 for *Kedushah* and the continuation of *Shacharis*.

MUSSAF FOR PARASHAS SHEKALIM

The *chazzan* begins his repetition (p. 462) and continues through *'Savior and Shield.'* Then all recite:

אֶשְׁכּוֹל *God is like a desirable cluster, desired by everyone.
I longed to sit in His shelter, there to find refreshment,
I sought Him but found him not, and I foolishly said [that the Golden Calf was a god].
God left me and concealed Himself, no longer giving me freedom.
I stole my shekels instead of using them for atonement
and I became mired in the muck and mud of suffering.
∴ O Master, raise the light of Your face upon us,
and let me raise a shekel in the firm and exalted Temple.
In the merit of the Torah reading in* Ki Sisa,
protect us as with a shield, O exalted and uplifted God.

Chazzan concludes the first blessing:

Blessed are You, HASHEM, *Shield of Abraham.*

Chazzan continues from אַתָּה גִּבּוֹר through לְהַחֲיוֹת מֵתִים. Then all recite:

הַכּוֹפֶר, דְּעוּ דִּרְשׁוּ מֵעַל סֵפֶר, כְּמוֹ הוּא חָרוּת בְּאִמְרֵי שֶׁפֶר,
הַתְשִׁירוּ בּוֹ פְּנֵי נִדְמָה לְעוֹפֶר,
וְיִזְכּוֹר לָכֶם זְכוּת נָם אָנֹכִי עָפָר וָאֵפֶר,
וְלֹא יִהְיֶה בָכֶם נֶגֶף וָחֵפֶר, בְּתִתְּכֶם מַתָּן זֶה לְשֵׁם כּוֹפֶר.
❖ אוֹר פָּנֶיךָ עָלֵינוּ אָדוֹן נְסָה, וְשֶׁקֶל אֶשָּׂא בְּבֵית נָכוֹן וְנִשָּׂא,
וּבְצֶדֶק הֶגֵה עֶרְכְּךָ כִּי תִשָּׂא, הַחֲיֵנוּ בְּגֶשֶׁם אֵל רָם וְנִשָּׂא.

Chazzan concludes the second blessing:

בָּרוּךְ אַתָּה יהוה מְחַיֵּה הַמֵּתִים.

Kedushah (p. 464) is recited at this point.
Chazzan continues from לְדוֹר וָדוֹר through וְקָדוֹשׁ אָתָּה. Then all recite:

דּוֹדִי, זְכָר לִי שִׁקְלֵי עֶפְרוֹן, אֲשֶׁר שָׁקַל אָב בְּמַכְפֵּל חֶבְרוֹן,
חֵקֶר שִׁקְלֵי יְבוּסִי מַשְׁבִּיתֵי חָרוֹן, זָכְרָה לִי עַד לְדוֹר אַחֲרוֹן,
טַעַם חִין אֲשֶׁר אֶקְרָא בְגָרוֹן, שְׁעֵה מִנִּי אֵל בְּשׁוּבִי שׁוּבִי לְבִצָּרוֹן.
❖ אוֹר פָּנֶיךָ עָלֵינוּ אָדוֹן נְסָה, וְשֶׁקֶל אֶשָּׂא בְּבֵית נָכוֹן וְנִשָּׂא,
וּבְצֶדֶק הֶגֵה עֶרְכְּךָ כִּי תִשָּׂא, וְנַקְדִּישְׁךָ קָדוֹשׁ אֵל רָם וְנִשָּׂא.

Chazzan concludes the third blessing:

בָּרוּךְ אַתָּה יהוה הָאֵל הַקָּדוֹשׁ.

Chazzan continues from תִּכַּנְתָּ שַׁבָּת through מְקַדְּשֵׁי שְׁמֶךָ;
on Rosh Chodesh from אַתָּה יָצַרְתָּ through לָהֶם קָבָעְתָּ. Then all recite:

לִי, יִשָּׂא עַל אֶבְרַת נֶשֶׁר, כִּי יַגִּיד מֵלִיץ עָלַי שִׂיחַ יוֹשֶׁר,
כּוֹפֶר מִשֶּׁלּוֹ אֶתֵּן לוֹ חֶשֶׁר, כִּי מִלְּפָנָיו הוֹן וְכָבוֹד וָעוֹשֶׁר,
לְהַצְדִּיק אֱנוֹשׁ וּלְהַמְצִיא לוֹ כּוֹשֶׁר, שָׁת לוֹ פִּדְיוֹן לִמְצֹא אוֹשֶׁר.
❖ אוֹר פָּנֶיךָ עָלֵינוּ אָדוֹן נְסָה, וְשֶׁקֶל אֶשָּׂא בְּבֵית נָכוֹן וְנִשָּׂא,
וּבְצֶדֶק הֶגֵה עֶרְכְּךָ כִּי תִשָּׂא, עַנְּגֵנוּ בְנוֹפֶשׁ אֵל רָם וְנִשָּׂא.

Chazzan concludes the fourth blessing:

בָּרוּךְ אַתָּה יהוה מְקַדֵּשׁ הַשַּׁבָּת (on Rosh Chodesh—וְיִשְׂרָאֵל וְרָאשֵׁי חֳדָשִׁים).

Chazzan continues from רְצֵה through לְצִיּוֹן בְּרַחֲמִים. Then all recite:

בְּכַרְמֵי, מְלוֹן בֵּין שְׁנֵי שָׁדַי, אַרְבַּע מֵאוֹת וָעֶשֶׂר הֲלִינוֹתִי שַׁדַּי,
נָח בְּשָׁכְנָם וְנָם יֵשׁ דַּי, וּבְכֵס וַהֲדוֹם לֹא נָם שֵׁדַי,
סָע וְעָף בְּבֶצַע שִׁקְלֵי חֲשָׁדַי, וְנָשְׂאוּ אֶת רְדִידֵי מֵעָלַי שׁוֹדְדָי.
❖ אוֹר פָּנֶיךָ עָלֵינוּ אָדוֹן נְסָה, וְשֶׁקֶל אֶשָּׂא בְּבֵית נָכוֹן וְנִשָּׂא,
וּבְצֶדֶק הֶגֵה עֶרְכְּךָ כִּי תִשָּׂא, רְצֵנוּ כְּשַׁי אֵל רָם וְנִשָּׂא.

The last four stiches of the stanzas are identical, except for the last stich which refers to the subject of the particular blessing.

Hashirim 1:14 ,אֶשְׁכֹּל הַכֹּפֶר דּוֹדִי לִי בְּכַרְמֵי עֵין גֶּדִי, *Like a cluster of henna in Ein Gedi vineyards has my Beloved multiplied His forgiveness to me.*

Chazzan continues from *'You are...mighty'* through *'to resuscitate the dead.'* Then all recite:

הַכֹּפֶר *Know and expound from the Torah on the commandment*
of shekel-atonement as it is written in the Torah
according to the way it is interpreted in the beautiful words of the Oral Law.
Present it as a gift before the One Who rushes like a hart [to help Israel],
and He will recall for you the merit of Abraham
who said "I am like dust and ashes,"
then you will have neither plague nor shame, when you give this for atonement.
∴ *O Master, raise the light of Your face upon us,*
and let me raise a shekel in the firm and exalted Temple
in the merit of the Torah reading in Ki Sisa,
resuscitate us with life-giving rain, O exalted and uplifted God.

Chazzan concludes the second blessing:

Blessed are You, HASHEM, *Who resuscitates the dead.*

Kedushah (p. 464) is recited at this point.

Chazzan continues from *'From generation...'* through *'and holy King.'* Then all recite:

דּוֹדִי *My Beloved, recall for my merit the shekels Abraham gave Ephron,*
that the Patriarch weighed for the Cave of Machpelah;
consider the shekels David paid the Jebusite [to purchase the Temple Mount]
whose sacrifices still the Heavenly wrath; recall to the end of time
the supplications I call forth from my throat;
accept my prayer, O God, that I be returned to the stronghold of Jerusalem.
∴ *O Master, raise the light of Your face upon us,*
and let me raise a shekel in the firm and exalted Temple.
In the merit of the Torah reading in Ki Sisa,
let us sanctify You with the Kedushah *prayer, O exalted and uplifted God.*

Chazzan concludes the third blessing:

Blessed are You, HASHEM, *the holy God.*

Chazzan continues from *'You established the Sabbath'* through *'the sanctifiers of Your Name'*; on Rosh Chodesh from *'You fashioned'* through *'New Moons for them.'* Then all recite:

לִי *God will carry us on eagle's wings,*
because a sympathetic angel will speak good of us,
from God's own property I will give Him a present,
for possessions, honor, and wealth come from Him
to justify man and lead him to improvement;
You provided man with the redemptive shekel that he might find good fortune.
∴ *O Master, raise the light of Your face upon us,*
and let me raise a shekel in the firm and exalted Temple.
In the merit of the Torah reading in Ki Sisa,
let us enjoy refreshment, O exalted and uplifted God.

Chazzan concludes the fourth blessing:

Blessed are You, HASHEM, *Who sanctifies the Sabbath*
(on Rosh Chodesh add: *Israel and the New Moons).*

Chazzan continues from *'Be favorable'* through *'to Zion in compassion.'* Then all recite:

בְּכַרְמֵי *In the Temple, God's Presence was between the two staves of the Ark;*
for 410 years the Almighty rested with me,
God was satisfied there and said it is enough for Him —
of heaven and earth He did not say they are enough for Him.
But God journeyed and flew away from the Temple
because of the sin that I could not be trusted with the shekels,
and my conqueror lifted my ornament from me.
∴ *O Master, raise the light of Your face upon us,*
and let me raise a shekel in the firm and exalted Temple.
In the merit of the Torah reading in Ki Sisa,
Find favor in us as in an offering, O exalted and uplifted God.

Chazzan concludes the fifth blessing:

בָּרוּךְ אַתָּה יהוה, הַמַּחֲזִיר שְׁכִינָתוֹ לְצִיּוֹן.

Chazzan continues from מוֹדִים through וְעֶזְרָתֵנוּ סֶלָה. Then all recite:

עַיִן, עוֹצֵם הֲמוֹן מִסְפַּר שְׁנֵי עֳפָרִים, מִי מָנָה וּפָקַד בְּחֹלֶשׁ וּפוּרִים,
פִּקְדָם פּוֹקֵד בְּחִמּוּשׁ סְפָרִים, וְגַם עוֹד חָמֵשׁ בְּכָל הַסְּפָרִים,
צַחוֹת נִיב שְׂפָתֵינוּ יְשַׁלֵּם פָּרִים, כִּי אֶפֶס כֶּסֶף שִׁקְלֵי כִפּוּרִים.
❖ אוֹר פָּנֶיךָ עָלֵינוּ אָדוֹן נְסָה, וְשֶׁקֶל אֶשָּׂא בְּבֵית נָכוֹן וְנִשָּׂא.
וּבְצֶדֶק הֶגֶה עֶרְךְ כִּי תִשָּׂא, וְתֵיטִיב לָנוּ בְּטוּבְךָ אֵל רָם וְנִשָּׂא.

Chazzan concludes the sixth blessing:

בָּרוּךְ אַתָּה יהוה, הַטּוֹב שִׁמְךָ וּלְךָ נָאֶה לְהוֹדוֹת.

Chazzan continues from בִּרְכַּת כֹּהֲנִים through בִּשְׁלוֹמֶךָ. Then all recite:

גְּדִי, קְשׁוּר יָדַיִם בְּרָכוֹת לָשֵׂאת, בְּאַהַב עוֹר גְּדָיָו שְׁכִינָה נִתְעַלְּסָה,
רֵעֶה גְדִיּוֹתָיו עַל אֶבֶן מַעֲמָסָה, צֹאנוֹ עַל שֶׁכֶם וְחוּצָן נֶעֱמָסָה,
שְׁחוּחַ בְּנֵי מְעַנֶּיהָ בְּאַף מַעֲשָׂה, תִּלְבֹּשֶׁת הוֹד עֲדִי עֲדָיִים טְכוּסָה.
❖ אוֹר פָּנֶיךָ עָלֵינוּ אָדוֹן נְסָה. וְשֶׁקֶל אֶשָּׂא בְּבֵית נָכוֹן וְנִשָּׂא.
וּבְצֶדֶק הֶגֶה עֶרְךְ כִּי תִשָּׂא, בָּרְכֵנוּ בַשָּׁלוֹם אֵל רָם וְנִשָּׂא.

Chazzan concludes the seventh blessing:

בָּרוּךְ אַתָּה יהוה הַמְבָרֵךְ אֶת עַמּוֹ יִשְׂרָאֵל בַּשָּׁלוֹם.

Chazzan recites Full-*Kaddish* (p. 474) and *Mussaf* is continued (p. 476).

❦ יוצר לפרשת זכור ❦

The *chazzan* begins his repetition of the *Shacharis Shemoneh Esrei:*

אֲדֹנָי שְׂפָתַי תִּפְתָּח, וּפִי יַגִּיד תְּהִלָּתֶךָ.

בָּרוּךְ אַתָּה יהוה אֱלֹהֵינוּ וֵאלֹהֵי אֲבוֹתֵינוּ, אֱלֹהֵי אַבְרָהָם, אֱלֹהֵי יִצְחָק, וֵאלֹהֵי יַעֲקֹב, הָאֵל הַגָּדוֹל הַגִּבּוֹר וְהַנּוֹרָא, אֵל עֶלְיוֹן, גּוֹמֵל חֲסָדִים טוֹבִים וְקוֹנֵה הַכֹּל, וְזוֹכֵר חַסְדֵי אָבוֹת, וּמֵבִיא גוֹאֵל לִבְנֵי בְנֵיהֶם, לְמַעַן שְׁמוֹ בְּאַהֲבָה. מֶלֶךְ עוֹזֵר וּמוֹשִׁיעַ וּמָגֵן.

Congregation, followed by *chazzan,* recites:

מִסּוֹד חֲכָמִים וּנְבוֹנִים, וּמִלֶּמֶד דַּעַת מְבִינִים.
אֶפְתְּחָה פִּי בְּשִׁיר וּרְנָנִים. לְהוֹדוֹת וּלְהַלֵּל פְּנֵי שׁוֹכֵן מְעוֹנִים.

All continue:

אַזְכִּיר סֶלָה זִכְרוֹן מַעֲשִׂים, בַּיָּמִים הָאֵלֶּה נִזְכָּרִים וְנַעֲשִׂים,
גָּחוֹן גָּח מִבֵּין עֲכָסִים, דֵּרָאוֹנוֹ לְהַזְכִּיר לְרֶקֶב כְּעָסִים.
הַחוֹחַ הֵנֵץ מִגַּלְגַּל וְדַרְדַּר, וּמִדּוֹר לְדוֹר גִּלְגַּל וְדַרְדַּר,
זֵכֶר עֲוֹן אֲבוֹתָיו הַקְדֵּר, חַטַּאת אִמּוֹ בְּלִי לְהַעְדֵּר.

❦ YOTZER FOR PARASHAS ZACHOR ❦

The Torah commands us to remember Amalek's cowardly attack upon Israel in the Wilderness and further commands that the very memory of the Amalekite nation be obliterated

Chazzan concludes the fifth blessing:

Blessed are You, HASHEM, Who restores His Presence to Zion.

Chazzan continues from *'We gratefully thank'* through *'and help, selah!'* Then all recite:

עַיִן *The powerful vision of the multitude that is likened to the harts — with what manner of lot can they be counted?*
They are counted in the Five Books of Moses and a census is mentioned five more times in the other books.
May the pure words of our lips be like offerings of bullocks, for the atoning silver shekels are gone.
∴ *O Master, raise the light of Your face upon us, and let me raise a shekel in the firm and exalted Temple.*
In the merit of the Torah reading in Ki Sisa, *benefit us with Your goodness, O exalted and uplifted God.*

Chazzan concludes the sixth blessing:

Blessed are You, HASHEM, Your Name is 'The Beneficent One' and to You it is fitting to give thanks.

Chazzan continues from the Priestly Blessings through *'with Your peace.'* Then all recite:

גְדִי *In the merit of Jacob who bound kids [for his father's meal] in order to obtain [Isaac's] blessings.*
In reward for his love, the Tabernacle was covered with the hide of kids and kids were grazed in Jerusalem.
God's sheep [Israel] will be honored as if carried on the shoulders of their admirers.
Those who oppressed them will walk with shoulders hunched, anger will be directed against their subjugators.
Israel will wear splendid clothing and be decorated with ornaments.
∴ *O Master, raise the light of Your face upon us, and let me raise a shekel in the firm and exalted Temple.*
In the merit of the Torah reading in Ki Sisa, *bless us with peace, O exalted and uplifted God.*

Chazzan concludes the seventh blessing:

Blessed are You, HASHEM, Who blesses His people Israel with peace.

Chazzan recites Full-*Kaddish* (p. 474) and *Mussaf* is continued (p. 476).

YOTZER FOR PARASHAS ZACHOR

The *chazzan* begins his repetition of the *Shacharis Shemoneh Esrei:*

My Lord, open my lips, that my mouth may declare Your praise.

בָּרוּךְ *Blessed are You, HASHEM, our God and the God of our forefathers, God of Abraham, God of Isaac, and God of Jacob; the great, mighty, and awesome God, the supreme God, Who bestows beneficial kindnesses and creates everything, Who recalls the kindnesses of the Patriarchs and brings a Redeemer to their children's children, for His Name's sake, with love. O King, Helper, Savior, and Shield.*

Congregation, followed by *chazzan,* recites:

מְסוֹד *Based on the tradition of our wise and discerning teachers, and the teaching derived from the knowledge of the discerning, I open my mouth in song to praise Him Who dwells on high.*

All continue:

אֶזְכִּיר *I will always recall the deeds that were done and recollected on these Purim days,*
A snake [Haman] descended from serpents [Amalek], when his vileness is recalled, may his memory decay for angering God.
That thorny enemy blossomed from the nation that was a constant thorn to Israel, and generation after generation kept doing so,
let us recall the sin of Esau who blackened his fathers' lives, and let us not conceal the sin of Amalek's mother Timna.

טָרַף אַף וַיַּשְׁחֵת רַחַם, **יְ**חוּמָתוֹ מִקְלוֹט בְּהֵרָיוֹן יָחַם,
כְּהָפְקַד לְשָׁלִישׁוֹ חֵטְא נוֹחַם. **לְ**בַט לְהִלָּחֵם בְּלוֹחֲמֵי לָחֶם.
מַהֲלַךְ אַרְבַּע מֵאוֹת פַּרְסָה, **נָ**ע וָנָד מִכְּמוֹרֶת לְפָרְשָׁה,
סָע מִשֵּׂעִיר וְהִכְמִין פְּרוּסָה, **עָ**יֵף וְיָגֵעַ מְבוּשָׁיו לְסָרְסָה.
פּוֹעַל שְׂטִימַת בְּכוֹרָה לַעֲכוֹר, **צְ**מִיתוּת צֹאן קָדָשִׁים לִמְכּוֹר,
קְלוֹנוֹ הֶחָרֵט בְּעֵט לִזְכּוֹר, **רֵ**אשִׁית גּוֹיִם לְגַלַּע בְּזָכוֹר.
שַׁדַּי זָכַר לֵילָה חוֹלֵק, **שֹׁ**רֶשׁ וְעָנָף בַּחֲלַקְלַק לְהַחֲלֵק.
❖ **תְּ**מוּר כִּי חֲשָׁלָיו הִמְלֵק, **תָּ**בַע לְהִזָּכֵר מַעַשׂ עֲמָלֵק.

All continue:

לָאַחֲרוֹנָה יִסְעוּ שֶׁבָּם שָׁלַט. כִּי הֶעָנָן מַטָּם פָּלַט.
❖ לְעֵת יִמָּחֶה לֹא יְמַלֵּט, יְגוֹנֵן עַם גָּנוֹן וּמְפַלֵּט.

Chazzan continues:

בָּרוּךְ אַתָּה יהוה מָגֵן אַבְרָהָם.

אַתָּה גִּבּוֹר לְעוֹלָם אֲדֹנָי, מְחַיֵּה מֵתִים אַתָּה, רַב לְהוֹשִׁיעַ. מַשִּׁיב הָרוּחַ וּמוֹרִיד הַגֶּשֶׁם. מְכַלְכֵּל חַיִּים בְּחֶסֶד, מְחַיֵּה מֵתִים בְּרַחֲמִים רַבִּים, סוֹמֵךְ נוֹפְלִים, וְרוֹפֵא חוֹלִים, וּמַתִּיר אֲסוּרִים, וּמְקַיֵּם אֱמוּנָתוֹ לִישֵׁנֵי עָפָר. מִי כָמְוֹךָ בַּעַל גְּבוּרוֹת, וּמִי דּוֹמֶה לָּךְ, מֶלֶךְ מֵמִית וּמְחַיֶּה וּמַצְמִיחַ יְשׁוּעָה. וְנֶאֱמָן אַתָּה לְהַחֲיוֹת מֵתִים.

All continue:

תְּמִימִים בְּעוֹדָם בְּסִין רְפוּדִים, **שְׁ**בוּץ עֲדִי עֲדָיִים אֲפוּדִים,
רָצוּ שְׁלוֹל מַתַּן לַפִּידִים, **קָ**פְצוּ יָדַיִם רָפוֹת בִּרְפִידִים.
צוֹרֵר אִסֵּף כָּל אֲסַפְסוּף, **פּ**וֹשֵׁעַ סְבִיבוֹת מַחֲנָם אָסוּף,
עֲלוֹת פְּעָמֵימוֹ מִמְּצוּלוֹת סוּף, **סִ**בֵּר לְקָמְלָם כְּקָנֶה וָסוּף.
נֶדֶד וַיָּעַף שָׁלֹשׁ פְּעָמִים, **מְ**חַזֵּר בְּנִינֵי חֲמִשָּׁה עֲמָמִים,
לֵץ הִכָּה וּפֶתִי הֶעֱמִים, **כְּ**לַל לְהִתְיַחֵס נְדִיבֵי עַמִּים.
יָהַר לֵץ וְהֶעֱמִיד מְסִלָּה, **טִ**כּוּס בַּחוּרֵי בְּזִמָּה סֶלָה,
חֲמוּקֵי יְרֵכַי בָּם לְפָסְלָה, **זֶ**רַע לְהַרְבִּיעַ וּלְהַתְעִיב סְגֻלָּה.
וַיִּשְׂטוֹם שְׂטִימַת יְשִׁישׁוֹ הַמְחֻבָּא, **הֵ**חֵל לָבוֹא מֵרֹאשׁ בְּמַחְבָּא,
דָּגַר שֵׁנִית בְּחֶרֶב לְחוּבָה, **גָּ**שׁ בַּשְּׁלִישִׁי בַּעֲלִיל בְּחוּבָה.
בְּמָשְׁלוֹ שֶׁשְּׁכֵי בְּאוֹם מוֹשְׁלִים, **בְּ**פֶרֶק עָמַד מְסוֹר נְשׁוּלִים,
❖ **אָ**מְרוּ לְכוּ וְנַכְחִיד נִכְשָׁלִים, **אָ**ז כְּמֵאָז זִנֵּב כָּל הַנֶּחֱשָׁלִים.

---

after God gives Israel tranquility from all its enemies (*Deuteronomy* 25:17-19). This commandment to remember is fulfilled by a special reading of the above paragraph once a year. The Sabbath before Purim was chosen for this reading because the Jewish struggle for survival

When Esau was born, he tore angrily and destroyed his mother's womb,
preventing her from conceiving again.
When his grandson Amalek recalled the "sin" of Jacob,
he strengthened himself to attack the warriors of Torah.
Amalek traveled a distance of four hundred parasongs wandering about to set an ambush for Israel;
he traveled from Seir and concealed a trap to castrate the weary Jews.
Amalek's dastardly act grew from its hatred over Jacob's gaining the birthright;
forever, Amalek tried to sell out the holy flock,
his baseness is inscribed in the Torah to be remembered —
to recall the shame of this premier nation of evil.
O Almighty, remember the merit of Abraham who triumphed at midnight,
help us uproot the growth of those who tried to beguile the Jews.
∴ *Because Amalek murdered weaklings, God required that its act be remembered.*

All continue:

לָאַחֲרוֹנָה *The hindmost tribe, Dan, was the one that Amalek overpowered*
because the protective cloud expelled them
[i.e. the members of Dan who carried with them the idol of Michah];
∴ *but when Amalek will be blotted out and not saved —*
then God will protect and rescue the nation that takes shelter in Him.

Chazzan continues:

Blessed are You, HASHEM, Shield of Abraham.

אַתָּה *You are eternally mighty, my Lord, the Resuscitator of the dead are You; abundantly able to save,* ***Who makes the wind blow and makes the rain descend;*** *Who sustains the living with kindness, resuscitates the dead with abundant mercy, supports the fallen, heals the sick, releases the confined, and maintains His faith to those asleep in the dust. Who is like You, O Master of mighty deeds, and who is comparable to You, O King Who causes death and restores life and makes salvation sprout! And You are faithful to resuscitate the dead.*

All continue:

תְּמִימִים *When the wholesome Jewish nation was strengthened at Sinai,*
they were decorated with beautiful ornaments.
They wished to hasten the giving of the Torah that was presented amid flame,
but in Refidim they shut their hands having weakened their resolve
to study the Torah.
The Amalekite enemy gathered an assortment of allies,
the wanton one surrounded the Israelite camp
soon after they stepped from the sea's depths, hoping to smash them like reeds.
Three times Amalek retreated and returned,
recruiting allies from five Canaanite nations;
the scornful Pharaoh was struck but foolish Amalek still hid in ambush,
pretending he was proud to associate with aristocratic Israel.
The scorner arrogantly embarked on the road
to contaminate my illustrious young men through immorality,
and to make my modest women impure
through abominable seduction of God's treasured nation.
He bore the hidden hatred of his ancestor Esau, originally he kept his hatred concealed,
but later he pounced with sharpened sword,
the third time he came openly because Israel sinned.
When Sheshach [Nebuchadnezzar] conquered the dominant nation,
Amalek seized the chance to imprison the exiles.
∴ *They said, "Let us go and destroy the stragglers,"*
then as of old, they cut down all the weaklings.

All continue:

שׂוֹנְאֶיךָ הֵם יִלְבְּשׁוּ בֹשֶׁת, כְּמוֹ בְצַלְעֵי שָׂמְחוּ בַּיַּבֶּשֶׁת.
✧ בַּעֲטוֹתְךָ עֲטֶרֶת עֲדָיֵי תִלְבּוֹשֶׁת.
לְהַגְשִׁים תְּחִי לְצוֹלַעַת תַּחְבּוֹשֶׁת

Chazzan continues:

בָּרוּךְ אַתָּה יהוה מְחַיֵּה הַמֵּתִים.

All continue:

אֲצִילֵי מֵרֵעִי נֶגֶד שֵׂעִיר, תּוֹלְדוֹת אֵלֶּה בְּנֵי שֵׂעִיר,
בְּקַשָּׁם אָצוּ אִשִּׁי לְהַבְעִיר, שְׁאוֹנָם חָרְשׁוּ כִּשְׂדֵה עִיר.
גּוֹי גָּדוֹל שֶׁלֹּא הִזְכַּרְתָּ, רִשְׁיוֹנוֹתָיו לָמָּה אָז זָכַרְתָּ,
דְּגָלִים בְּלֹא הוֹן מָכַרְתָּ, קְדוֹשִׁים בַּזּוֹנָה וּבַיַּיִן הִמְכַּרְתָּ.
הִזָּכֵר לָאֲדוֹמִים נָוֶה נִאֲרוּ, צָרִים אֲשֶׁר חוֹמוֹת עִרְעֲרוּ,
וְעַד הַיְסוֹד עָרוּ עָרוּ, פִּימוּ דִּבְּרוּ בְּגֵאוּת וּפָעֲרוּ.
זֶה אֵין לְפָנֶיךָ שִׁכְחָה, עֶבְרָתָם שְׁמָרָה נֶצַח מִלְּשַׁכְּחָה,
חֵלֶף לֹא יָדְעוּ עֲשׂוֹת נְכוֹחָה, סִפְרָם חָתוּם לְיוֹם תּוֹכֵחָה.
טַעַם חוֹק בְּדַת מוּכָח, נִזְכַּר כִּי לֹא תִשָּׁכַח.
✧ יוֹם בֹּא עִמָּם לְהִתְוַכַּח, מִכַּאן צִוִּיתָ לְעַמְּךָ לֹא תִשְׁכָּח.

All continue:

יָקַשׁ לֵץ לְחָרֵף צְבָאוֹת, הַחֲתוּמֵי בְרִית בְּצָבָא וָאוֹת.
וְהֻפְקַד מִדָּה בְּמִדָּה לְתוֹצָאוֹת.
✧ דַּעַת כִּי לְעֵת הַמְּצִיאוֹת, הוּא יִפָּקֵד בְּשֵׁם יהוה צְבָאוֹת.

Congregation, followed by *chazzan*, recites aloud:

יִמְלֹךְ יהוה לְעוֹלָם אֱלֹהַיִךְ צִיּוֹן לְדֹר וָדֹר הַלְלוּיָהּ.
וְאַתָּה קָדוֹשׁ יוֹשֵׁב תְּהִלּוֹת יִשְׂרָאֵל אֵל נָא.

All continue:

(אֵל נָא) בְּלָשׁוֹן אֲשֶׁר הִזְכַּרְתָּ לְזוֹכְרֶיךָ זָכוֹר,
בּוֹ בְלָשׁוֹן הִזְכִּירוּךָ נָא אַתָּה זְכוֹר,
וְאִם הֵמָּה כְּאָדָם עָבְרוּ בְרִית מִלִּזְכּוֹר,
וְאַתָּה אֵל וְלֹא אִישׁ לָמָּה לֹא תִזְכּוֹר.
בְּזֹאת יָדַעְתִּי כִּי יֶשׁ לְךָ לִזְכּוֹר, אֲבָל תָּשׁוּחַ עָלַי נַפְשִׁי עַד זָכוֹר תִּזְכּוֹר,
וּמַה כֹּחִי כִּי אֲיַחֵל לְקֵץ זָכוֹר, וּמַה קִּצִּי כִּי אַאֲרִיךְ נַפְשִׁי עַד שֶׁתִּזְכּוֹר.
אִם לֹא לְמַעֲנִי תִזְכּוֹר, לְמַעַנְךָ וּלְמַעַן יְרוּשָׁלַיִם זְכוֹר,
חוֹק כִּי לֹא תִשָּׁכַח עֵדוּת זָכוֹר, וְאוֹמֵר אִם אֶשְׁכָּחֵךְ עַתָּה לָהּ זְכוֹר,
וְתִפְקוֹד וְתִזְכּוֹר, כְּאֵב צָר לַעֲכוֹר, פִּיהוּ לִסְכּוֹר, לָנוּעַ כַּשִּׁכּוֹר,
וְעוֹד בַּל תִּמְכּוֹר, נְקוּבֵי בֵּן בְּכוֹר.
✧ נְכוּרֵי בְלֶתֶךְ וָכוֹר,* וּפְאֵרְךָ אֶזְכּוֹר, וַאֲרַצְּךָ לִזְכּוֹר, בְּפָרָשַׁת זָכוֹר.

---

on Purim was fought against Haman, who was a descendant of Amalek.

בְלֶתֶךְ וָכוֹר — *for a lesech and a kor.* These are two measures containing a total of forty-five *se'ah.*

All continue:

שׂוֹנְאֶיךָ *Your enemies will be clothed in shame*
just as they rejoiced at my distress when my water dried out,
∴ *when You don the ten garments of vengeance*
and rain lifegiving waters of healing upon the crippled Israel.

Chazzan continues:

Blessed are You, Hashem, *Who resuscitates the dead.*

All continue:

אֲצִילֵי *The nobles who befriended me, the grandson of Seir, the offspring of*
these children of Seir, with their straw they rush to set me afire,
their multitude plowed the Holy City like a field.
If You chose not to remember that You called Israel a "great nation,"
why did You remember its sins?
You sold its tribes for nothing,
and its holy ones You sold for a harlot's hire and for wine.
Remember that Edom destroyed Your Abode, the foes who shattered its walls;
until its very foundation they destroyed completely,
their mouths spoke with brazen arrogance.
Concerning this let there be no forgetfulness, recall their anger always, never to forget;
because they know not how to do right, seal their book for the day of rebuke.
Since You commanded us in the Torah to remember Amalek,
the time will come when it will be remembered, never to be forgotten.
∴ *Because a day will come when God will bring Amalek to account,*
therefore You commanded Your people not to forget.

All continue:

יָקֹשׁ *The scornful Amalek degraded God's legions,*
that are sealed in the covenant of unity and circumcision.
Their cruelty was punished measure for measure,
∴ *in order that people should know that when the time of the Messiah comes,*
Amalek will be repaid in the Name of Hashem, *God of Legions.*

Congregation, followed by *chazzan*, recites aloud:

Hashem shall reign forever — your God, O Zion —
from generation to generation, Halleluyah!

You, O Holy One, are enthroned upon Israel's praises —
please, O God.

(אֵל נָא) ***Please, O God, just as You told Israel, which always remembers You,***
that they are to remember Amalek,
with the same word they remind You that You, too, should remember his evil.
But if Israel — with human weakness — violated the covenant to remember;
You, Who are God and not a human, why do You not remember?
Though I know that You are to remember,
my soul is despondent until You finally do remember.
Do I have the strength to hope until the time of remembering?
And when will my life end that I can survive until You remember?
If You don't remember for my sake,
remember for Your sake and for the sake of Jerusalem.
For the sake of the Torah that will never be forgotten — remember!
You declared that You would not forget, Jerusalem — remember her now!
Consider and remember to intensify the pain of the foe,
to gag his mouth, may he tremble like a drunk —
and may those designated as Your firstborn never again be sold;
∴*Israel, which God acquired for Himself for a* lesech *and a* kor*
I shall remember through reading the chapter of Zachor.

Congregation, followed by *chazzan,* recites aloud:

חַי וְקַיָּם נוֹרָא וּמָרוֹם וְקָדוֹשׁ.

All continue:

אָץ קוֹצֵץ בֶּן קוֹצֵץ, קְצוּצֵי לְקַצֵּץ,
בְּדִבּוּר מְפוֹצֵץ, רְצוּצֵי לְרַצֵּץ.
לֵץ בְּבֹא לְלוֹצֵץ, פִּלֵּץ וְנִתְלוֹצֵץ,
כְּעֵץ מְחַצְּצִים לְחַצֵּץ, כְּנֵץ עַל צִפּוֹר לְנַצֵּץ.
עָב בָּקַע מֵרֹאשׁ, יְחִידִים מֶנּוּ גְרוֹשׁ,
חָל וַיֵּלֶךְ וַיִּפְרוֹשׁ, וַיָּשָׁב עַל גַּבֵּי חֲרוֹשׁ.
זִמֵּן וְהֻנְקַב לְרֹאשׁ, רֵאשִׁית גּוֹיִם לָרַע לִדְרוֹשׁ,
הֱיוֹת לְכָל בּוֹגְדִים רֹאשׁ, וְצִפְּעוֹ תְּלוֹת בְּמִבְחַר בְּרוֹשׁ.
רָץ וְהָקְרָה בַּדֶּרֶךְ, עֲיֵפֵי טַרְחוּת דֶּרֶךְ,
וּפָץ לֹא זוּ הַדֶּרֶךְ, תָּעוּ בַּמִּדְבָּר בִּישִׁימוֹן דֶּרֶךְ.
בְּנָחָשׁ עֲלֵי דֶרֶךְ, שָׁלַח יָד בְּחַמּוּקֵי יָרֵךְ,
וְעַל כָּל רֹאשׁ דֶּרֶךְ, זִנֵּב כָּל עוֹבְרֵי דֶרֶךְ.
יָעַף וְעָף וְחָשׁ, וּמֵחוּר פֶּתֶן רָחַשׁ,
וְנוֹדַע כִּי הוּחַשׁ, מִשּׁוֹרֶשׁ נָחָשׁ.
רָגַשׁ וְלָחַשׁ, וְעֵת לֵדָתוֹ נִחֵשׁ,
וּבִכְשָׁפָיו הִכְחַשׁ, וּבְחַלָּשׁ נֶחֱלַשׁ וְלֹא חָשׁ.
בִּכְשָׁפָיו הִלְלוֹ, וּבִקְסָמָיו חִלְּלוֹ,
יוֹם הֶעֱמִיד וְזִלְלוֹ, שֶׁמֶשׁ הִדְמִים וְזִלְזְלוֹ.
יָגַע וְלֹא הוּנַח לוֹ, וְלַחֲרָפוֹת נִחֲלוֹ,
עַד בֹּא הַשֶּׁמֶשׁ הִזְחִילוֹ, לְהִמָּחוֹת הוּא וְכָל חֵילוֹ.
קָט וְשֵׁן חָרַק, וְנֶאָצוֹת שָׁרַק,
וְזְמוֹרָה בְּאַפּוֹ הֵרַק, וְחַרְבּוֹ הִבְרַק.
לַמִּילָה פֵּרַק, וּכְלַפֵּי מַעְלָה זָרַק.
וּלְשֵׁם שֶׁמֶן תּוּרַק, בְּעַזּוּת יָרוֹק יָרַק.
יָהּ אֶשְׁכּוֹל הַכֹּפֶר, צִוָּה אֶל מְשׁוֹל עוֹפֶר,
זִכְרוֹן מִשְּׁלֵי אֵפֶר, כְּתוֹב זֹאת זִכָּרוֹן בַּסֵּפֶר.
❖ **רֻשַּׁם** בְּזֶה סֵפֶר, בַּתּוֹרָה וּבַנְּבִיאִים וּבַכְּתוּבִים לְחַפֵּר,
לְהִמָּחוֹת מִסֵּפֶר, וְלֹא יִכָּתֵב עִם כָּל הַכָּתוּב לַחַיִּים בַּסֵּפֶר.

Chazzan continues:

אֵל נָא לְעוֹלָם תֻּעֲרָץ, וּלְעוֹלָם תֻּקְדָּשׁ, וּלְעוֹלְמֵי עוֹלָמִים תִּמְלוֹךְ וְתִתְנַשֵּׂא, הָאֵל מֶלֶךְ נוֹרָא מָרוֹם וְקָדוֹשׁ, כִּי אַתָּה הוּא מֶלֶךְ מַלְכֵי הַמְּלָכִים, מַלְכוּתוֹ נֶצַח. נוֹרְאוֹתָיו שִׂיחוּ, סַפְּרוּ עֻזּוֹ, פָּאֲרוּהוּ צְבָאָיו, קַדְּשׁוּהוּ רוֹמְמוּהוּ, רוֹן שִׁיר וָשֶׁבַח, תֹּקֶף תְּהִלּוֹת תִּפְאַרְתּוֹ.

Congregation, followed by *chazzan,* recites aloud:

Living and Enduring One, Awesome, Exalted, and Holy!

All continue:

אֵץ *The wicked reaper Amalek descendant of the wicked reaper*
rushed to cut down the circumcised nation
because it neglected Torah study, to trample my trampled people.
When the scornful Amalek came to ridicule,
he was defeated by Joshua and held up to scorn;
when he conspired to shoot arrows at the charitable nation,
like a hawk seizing its prey.
First he attacked the tribe of Dan that the cloud-pillar expelled,
and the individuals that it chased away;
he began by spreading out his forces and then plowed into my back.
He prepared and was designated by the Torah as Israel's first attacker,
the premier nation that sought evil,
to be the leader of all traitors,
but his serpentine offspring were hung on the finest gallows.
He ran to intercept those who were exhausted by travel;
he called out, "This is the wrong path,
they are wandering in the wilderness on a path of desolation."
Like a snake on the road, they attacked the modestly attired Jews,
and on all highways, they attached themselves to all wayfarers.
Amalek exerted himself, flew, and hurried; he slithered from a dragon's lair;
it was known to Moses that Amalek rushed from snake-like origins.
Moses was frightened and prayed,
Amalek's sorcery showed that he would be strong on his birthday
and with his magic he betrayed Israel, but despite Amalek's choice of days
Joshua weakened him and he knew not why.
Moses made Amalek's sorcery foolish and his magic foolish,
the day Moses stopped the sun he disgraced Amalek,
the sun fell silent and disgraced him.
Amalek tried but had no success, he was led to disgrace,
the battle went on till sundown, to wipe out Amalek and all his army.
He was furious and ground his teeth and shrieked curses,
in the anger he flung shame and sharpened his sword.
He cut off the sign of circumcision and hurled it skyward
and at the Name of God Whose reputation is like fragrant oil, he brazenly spat.
God, Who is like a cluster of spices,
gave a command to Moses who is likened to a hart
to remember the merit of the Patriarchs whose humility was likened to ashes —
write this triumph as a remembrance in the Torah scroll.
∴ *Recorded in this scroll,*
in the Torah, Prophets, and Writings as a disgrace to Amalek,
that he be erased from the Book
and he will not be written with those who are in the Book of Life.

Chazzan continues:

אֵל נָא *O God, may You always be lauded and always be sanctified, and forever reign and be uplifted, the God, King, awesome, exalted, and holy, for You are the King Who reigns over kings, Whose sovereignty is eternal. Speak of His wonders, declare His strength, glorify Him, O His legions; sanctify Him, exalt Him. Sing song and praise, glorify Him with powerful psalms of praise.*

The *paytan* alludes to the forty-five days from the Exodus to Israel's arrival at Sinai.

אֵץ ☙. The initials of this *piyut* spell the name of the composer, אלעזר בירבי קליר.

Chazzan recites:

וּבְכֵן זָכוֹר אֵת אֲשֶׁר עָשָׂה לְךָ עֲמָלֵק.

Chazzan, followed by congregation, recites the following two verses aloud:

וּמַח שְׁמוֹ וְזִכְרוֹ, וְנִמַּח זִכּוּרוֹ, מִלְּהַזְכִּירוֹ, בְּזִכְרוֹן קָדוֹשׁ.
יַעַן אֲשֶׁר לֹא זָכַר, וְנֶחֱשַׁב כַּנֵּכָר, מִלְּהִזָּכֵר, בְּזִכְרוֹן קָדוֹשׁ.

All continue:

זָכוֹר אִישׁ אֲשֶׁר הִגְוִיעַ אָב לְלֹא עִתּוֹ, **בְּ**רָצוֹחַ וְגָנוֹב וְנָאוֹף בְּעִתּוֹ,
גָּרַע חָמֵשׁ שָׁנִים מִמִּחְיָתוֹ.
זָכוֹר **בּ**וֹזֶה עַל גְּמִילוּת חֶסֶד, **גּ**וֹעֵל אָח עָשׂ לִזְקֵנוֹ חֶסֶד,
דוֹמֶה לַמָּס מֵרֵעֵהוּ חָסֶד.
זָכוֹר **גִּ**לָּה עֶרְוַת מְצוּאַת שָׂדֶה, **דָּ**ם שָׁפַךְ בְּבוֹאוֹ מִן הַשָּׂדֶה,
הָפַךְ לֵב אָב שָׂח בַּשָּׂדֶה.
זָכוֹר **דָּ**חוּי בְּאוֹזֶן הָעֲרֵלָה, **הַ**בּוֹזֶה בְכוֹרָה בְּכוֹס הַתַּרְעֵלָה,
וּפָרַק מֶנּוּ עוֹל וּמָשַׁךְ לוֹ עָרְלָה.
זָכוֹר **הֲ**פַכְפַּךְ דֶּרֶךְ אִישׁ וָזָר, **וְ**הִכְהָה מְאוֹר אָב בַּעֲשַׁן עֲבוֹדַת זָר,
זָמַם בְּלֵב הֱיוֹת לְאָח לְאַכְזָר.
זָכוֹר **וְ**נִתְעוֹלַל לְרֶבַע כְּאִשָּׁה, **זְ**דוֹן לִבּוֹ הִשִּׁיאוֹ בָּאִשָּׁה,
חַתּוּ גִבּוֹרָיו לִהְיוֹת כְּלֵב אִשָּׁה.
זָכוֹר **זֶ**רַע מְרֵעִים נִתְעַב וְנֶאֱלָח, **חָ**לַק לְהַשְׁחִית וְלוֹמַר הֶאָח,
טָמְנוּ גֵאִים פַּח לְחַבֵּל אָח.
זָכוֹר **חָ**נַט מֶנּוּ עֲמָלֵקִי, **טָ**שׁ כַּיֶּלֶק לְאַבֵּד חֶלְקִי,
יָרוֹעַ כַּבִּירִים לְעֵין כֹּל לְלוֹקְקִי.
זָכוֹר **טָ**פַשׁ מֵהַעֲרִימָה, **יָ**רַד וְכִתֵּת עַמִּי עַד חָרְמָה,
כְּמוֹ כֵן חַיָּב לְהַחֲרִימָה.
זָכוֹר **י**וֹשֵׁב הַנֶּגֶב בְּלִי עוֹל כַּעֲרָד, **כְּ**סוּת וְלָשׁוֹן שִׁנָּה הֱיוֹת מֶלֶךְ עֲרָד,
לְשִׁבּוּת שְׁבִי מָרַד וְחָרָד.
זָכוֹר **כְּ**סִיל שׁוֹנֶה בְאִוַּלְתּוֹ, **לְ**תַעֲרוּבַת מִדְיָן בַּעֲלוֹתוֹ,
מִהֵר יְרֶבֶשֶׁת וְגִלָּה נַבְלוּתוֹ.
זָכוֹר **לְ**קַעֲקֵעַ בִּצָּתוֹ מִשּׁוֹרֶשׁ, **מִ**לַּעֲזוֹב לוֹ עָנָף וְגַם שׁוֹרֶשׁ,
נֶעֱנַשׁ קִישִׁי כִּי הִשְׁאִיר לוֹ שׁוֹרֶשׁ.
זָכוֹר **מַ**עֲשֵׂה אֲגַג מַעֲדַנּוֹת, **נָ**שִׁים כְּשִׁכְּלָה חַרְבּוֹ לְעַנּוֹת,
סוֹרֵס שְׁאֵרוֹ לְשִׁסּוּף יַעֲנוֹת.
זָכוֹר **נָ**גִיד לְחָמְלוֹ הִסְכִּים, **סָ**ר מִמְּלוּכָה מִבֵּין נְסִיכִים,
עוֹלֵל הַנּוֹתָר עָמַד לְשַׂכִּים.

Chazzan recites:

And therefore, remember what Amalek did to You.

Chazzan, followed by congregation, recites the following two verses aloud:

Erase his name and his memory, and may his memory be obliterated from being recalled in the memory of the Holy One.

Because he did not remember to be kind and acted like a stranger, may he not be recalled in the memory of the Holy One.

All continue:

זָכוֹר *Remember Esau who caused Abraham to die before his time,*
with murder, thievery, and adultery Esau frightened him —
he diminished five years from Abraham's life.

ב *Remember Esau who scorned his brother for being kind to their bereaved father,*
Esau disdained his brother for doing kindness with his grandfather,
like someone who prevents his friend from enjoying kindness.

ג *Remember Esau who assaulted women found in the field,*
he shed blood upon returning from the field,
and deceived his father who prayed in the field.

ד *Remember Esau who was rejected from the World to Come because his ear would not listen to remonstrance,*
who spurned the birthright for a bitter cup,
and threw off the yoke of God and extended his foreskin.

ה *Remember the one whose way was the reverse of an honest man and who was a stranger to truth,*
who blinded his father with incense of idolatry,
he planned inwardly to be cruel to his brother.

ו *Remember his sexual perversion with men,*
the wantonness of his heart seduced him to degeneracy,
but his strong followers were broken and became weak like women.

ז *Remember Esau who was evil, abominable, and corrupt,*
glibly he hoped to destroy Jacob and enjoy his downfall,
the arrogant Ishmael and Esau hid a trap to harm their brother, Jacob.

ח *Remember Esau from whom blossomed Amalek,*
who flew like a locust to destroy my portion,
he publicly broke my heroes and licked my blood.

ט *Remember Amalek that lacked true wisdom*
and descended and struck my people until their desolation,
similarly he deserves to be made desolate.

י *Remember Amalek that dwelled in the south without a yoke like a poisonous snake,*
it changed its clothes and language to resemble the Canaanite king of Arad;
to take captives he hurriedly rebelled against God.

כ *Remember the fool who repeats his foolishness,*
when he went up to involve himself in Israel's war with Midian;
Gideon hurried and revealed Amalek's baseness.

ל *Remember to uproot his future entirely,*
without leaving him a branch or a root;
Saul son of Kish was punished for allowing Agag to survive.

מ *Remember the murderous deeds of Agag who was raised on delicacies,*
Samuel called out that Agag would die just as his sword had widowed women;
then he cut him apart as food for birds of prey.

נ *Remember King Saul who agreed to show pity on Agag,*
he was removed from kingship among the nobles,
because the survivor Agag made it possible for the future Haman to be born.

זָכוֹר סִבֵּב צִקְלַג וָנֶגֶב, עֲמָלֵק יוֹשֵׁב בְּאֶרֶץ הַנֶּגֶב,
פִּגְרוֹ טוֹב רוֹאִי מְנַשֵּׁף בָּעָגֶב.
זָכוֹר עָרִיץ בָּעַמּוֹנִים נֶחְבָּא, פֶּרֶץ כַּרְמֵי עֵין גֶּדִי כְּהוּבָא,
צוֹרְבוֹ אִישׁ בְּאָחִיו בְּחֶרֶב לְהוּבָה.
זָכוֹר פְּלֵיטִים אֲשֶׁר בְּאַף הִסְעִיר, צְבָאַי בְּלֶכְתָּם אֶל הַר שֵׂעִיר,
קִנֵּא לִנְקוֹם עֲיָרוֹת שֵׂעִיר.
זָכוֹר צָג בַּפֶּרֶק לְהַסְגִּיר שְׂרִידַי, קָם בְּרֹאשׁ דְּרָכִים לִסְעוֹד אֶת רוֹדַי,
רָדַף וּמָסַר בְּיָדָם פְּרוּדֵי רְפוּדַי.
זָכוֹר קָפַץ לְשַׁעַר הַשָּׁמַיִם, רָעַשׁ וְשָׁאַג מִי לִי בַשָּׁמַיִם,
שָׁלַט וַיִּגְדַּל עַד לַשָּׁמָיִם.
זָכוֹר רָד אֶל חָנֵף לְהַחֲנִיף מַמְלֶכֶת, שִׁמְשַׁי אֲשֶׁר שִׁמְשׁוֹ מְאַמֶּשֶׁת
וְהוֹלֶכֶת, תַּמָּה הַלָּשׁוֹן לְרַפּוֹתָהּ מִמְּלָאכֶת.
זָכוֹר שָׁקַל אֲלָפִים עֲשָׂרָה, שְׁתִילִים מֵאָה הֶחֱנִיט לְסַבְרָה,
שִׁעֵר מֵהֶם עֲשָׂרָה לִשְׂרָרָה.
❖ זָכוֹר תָּבַע לְהָפֵר חֲמִשִּׁים, תְּמִימָה קָצַב לְכַלּוֹת חֲמִשִּׁים,
תַּכְלִית שִׁבְעִים נִתְלָה עַל חֲמִשִּׁים.

Chazzan and congregation recite together:

וּבְכֵן וּלְךָ תַעֲלֶה קְדֻשָּׁה כִּי אַתָּה קְדוֹשׁ יִשְׂרָאֵל וּמוֹשִׁיעַ.

Turn to page 422 for *Kedushah* and the continuation of *Shacharis.*

❦ יוצר לפרשת פרה ❦

The *chazzan* begins his repetition of the *Shacharis Shemoneh Esrei:*

אֲדֹנָי שְׂפָתַי תִּפְתָּח, וּפִי יַגִּיד תְּהִלָּתֶךָ.

בָּרוּךְ אַתָּה יהוה אֱלֹהֵינוּ וֵאלֹהֵי אֲבוֹתֵינוּ, אֱלֹהֵי אַבְרָהָם, אֱלֹהֵי יִצְחָק, וֵאלֹהֵי יַעֲקֹב, הָאֵל הַגָּדוֹל הַגִּבּוֹר וְהַנּוֹרָא, אֵל עֶלְיוֹן, גּוֹמֵל חֲסָדִים טוֹבִים וְקוֹנֵה הַכֹּל, וְזוֹכֵר חַסְדֵי אָבוֹת, וּמֵבִיא גוֹאֵל לִבְנֵי בְנֵיהֶם, לְמַעַן שְׁמוֹ בְּאַהֲבָה. מֶלֶךְ עוֹזֵר וּמוֹשִׁיעַ וּמָגֵן.

Congregation, followed by *chazzan,* recites:

מִסּוֹד חֲכָמִים וּנְבוֹנִים, וּמִלֶּמֶד דַּעַת מְבִינִים.
אֶפְתְּחָה פִּי בְּשִׁיר וּרְנָנִים. לְהוֹדוֹת וּלְהַלֵּל פְּנֵי שׁוֹכֵן מְעוֹנִים.

All continue:

אֲצוּלַת אוֹמֶן בְּצֵרוּף זְקוּקָה, בִּנְבָכֶיהָ זֹאת בַּלֵּט פְּקוּקָה,
גְּלוּמָה עֲלוּמָה וּנְקוּקָה, דְּבוּרָה עַל אָפֶן חֲקוּקָה,

❦ YOTZER OF PARASHAS PARAH ❦

The Torah teaches that the only way a person can remove from himself the contamination resulting from contact with a dead body is through a ritual that includes sprinkling with a mixture of water and ashes from an unblemished פָּרָה אֲדֻמָּה, *Red Cow (Numbers* 19:1-22). Such

ס *Remember David who surrounded Ziklag in the Negev*
to battle Amalek that dwelt in the southland,
he killed Amalek — he who was handsome to see and whose harp strummed with praises to God.

ע *Remember the wicked Amalek that concealed itself to join the attacking Ammonites,*
they came to destroy the vineyards of Ein Gedi,
but the enemies turned against one another with a flaming sword.

פ *Remember the Jewish refugees who fled Nebuchadnezzar and sought refuge on Mount Seir,*
but Esau's offspring angrily drove them off,
he zealously avenged the anger of Esau.

צ *Remember Amalek who stood by the borders to turn in my survivors,*
he stood at crossroads to aid my conquerors,
he chased and hauled in my dispersed ones and those who fell to the ground.

ק *Remember Titus who sprang to the gate of the Temple*
and roared "What care I about the God of heaven,"
he dominated and held himself great up to the heaven.

ר *Remember Haman who went down to flatter the king who was himself a flatterer,*
Haman's son Shimshai whose sun became darkened and diminished —
he slandered the wholesome nation Israel and caused the work on the Temple to be halted.

ש *Remember Haman who weighed out ten thousand silver talents,*
he put hope in the hundred children he had caused to blossom,
and chose ten of them for high office.

ת *Remember Haman who requested that the Five Books of Moses be annulled,*
he drew lots for the best day of the year to destroy those that left Egypt armed with supplies.
At the end of seventy verses of the Megillah telling of his greatness he was hung on a fifty-cubit gallows.

Chazzan and congregation recite together:

So now, the Kedushah prayer will ascend to You,
for You are the Holy One and Savior of Israel.

Turn to page 423 for *Kedushah* and the continuation of *Shacharis.*

YOTZER FOR PARASHAS PARAH

The *chazzan* begins his repetition of the *Shacharis Shemoneh Esrei:*

My Lord, open my lips, that my mouth may declare Your praise.

בָּרוּךְ *Blessed are You, HASHEM, our God and the God of our forefathers, God of Abraham, God of Isaac, and God of Jacob; the great, mighty, and awesome God, the supreme God, Who bestows beneficial kindnesses and creates everything, Who recalls the kindnesses of the Patriarchs and brings a Redeemer to their children's children, for His Name's sake, with love. O King, Helper, Savior, and Shield.*

Congregation, followed by *chazzan,* recites:

מִסּוֹד *Based on the tradition of our wise and discerning teachers,*
and the teaching derived from the knowledge of the discerning,
I open my mouth in song to praise Him Who dwells on high.

All continue:

אֲצוּלַת *The Torah that emanated from God,*
His tool to create the world, is completely pure and refined.
In its depths, the reason for this commandment of the Red Cow is closed in concealment,
like an unformed vessel, hidden as if in a crevice.
[The Torah's] every word is inscribed in its proper place,

הַמְּסֻקָּלָה וְהַמְּעֻזָּקָה, **וְ**דִשּׁוּנָהּ דִּשּׁוּן לְמִשְׁמָר חֻקָּה,
זֵר שִׁבְעָתַיִם מְזֻקָּקָה, **ח**וֹק טָהוֹר מְטַמֵּא מְחֻזָּקָה,
טְבוּעָה בְּלֹא רְחוּקָה, וְהִיא רְחוּקָה, **יְ**חוּסָה אֲטוּרָה וּדְחוּקָה.
❖ **כּ**תְמַת חֲמוּקָה בָּהּ מְחוּקָה, **לְ**טָהֳרַת חֲשׁוּקָה, נֶחְקְקָה זֹאת חֻקָּה.

All continue:

מְקוֹמָהּ יְגֻלֶּה, מַעֲמַקֶּיהָ יִדְלֶה. ❖ לְעֵת יְגָלֶה, גְּנוּנָיו יַעֲלֶה.

Chazzan continues:

בָּרוּךְ אַתָּה יהוה מָגֵן אַבְרָהָם.

אַתָּה גִּבּוֹר לְעוֹלָם אֲדֹנָי, מְחַיֵּה מֵתִים אַתָּה, רַב לְהוֹשִׁיעַ. מַשִּׁיב הָרְוּחַ וּמוֹרִיד הַגֶּשֶׁם. מְכַלְכֵּל חַיִּים בְּחֶסֶד, מְחַיֵּה מֵתִים בְּרַחֲמִים רַבִּים, סוֹמֵךְ נוֹפְלִים, וְרוֹפֵא חוֹלִים, וּמַתִּיר אֲסוּרִים, וּמְקַיֵּם אֱמוּנָתוֹ לִישֵׁנֵי עָפָר. מִי כָמְוֹךָ בַּעַל גְּבוּרוֹת, וּמִי דְּוֹמֶה לָּךְ, מֶלֶךְ מֵמִית וּמְחַיֶּה וּמַצְמִיחַ יְשׁוּעָה. וְנֶאֱמָן אַתָּה לְהַחֲיוֹת מֵתִים.

All continue:

מִמָּרָה חֻקָּהּ גָּזָר, **מִ**גַּבְנוּן אִמְרָהּ נִגְזָר,
נֶאֱמָן לְאָזְנָהּ נִתְאַזָּר, **נֶ**צַח עֲדֵי כֵן בְּנִזְרָהּ נָזָר,
סְלוּל צְפוּנֶיהָ חֶלֶץ אָזָר, **שֶׁ**קֶר בְּאִבֶּיהָ וְנֶחֱשַׁב לְמוּזָר,
עָרַךְ בָּהּ חוּק לְעַם מְפֻזָּר, **עָ**בוּר מִלְּפַתֵּל עִקֵּשׁ כְּמִין וָזָר,
פְּאֵר בִּקְוּרֶיהָ בְּאֶגֶד מְשֻׁזָּר, **פְּ**עֻלָּתָהּ בְּסֶגֶן בַּעֲדֵי מָשְׁזָר.
❖ **צְ**פוּנָה לְטָהֳרַת עַם אֵל עָזָר, **צִ**וָּה צוּר לְצִיר, **צוּ**ר צְרוּרָה לְאֶלְעָזָר.

All continue:

עוֹלָם וּמְלֹאוֹ שֶׁלָּךְ, חָפַצְתָּ לְהַצְדִּיק קְהָלָךְ.
❖ עַל כֵּן אוֹחִיל לָךְ, לְהַגְשִׁים תְּחִי אֲטוּמֵי פָעֳלָךְ.

Chazzan continues:

בָּרוּךְ אַתָּה יהוה מְחַיֵּה הַמֵּתִים.

All continue:

קִפְאוֹן חוֹק אֱלְפַּת הַיְקָר, לוּטָה בְּאוֹר יָקָר,
חָשׂוּף לְעַם מְיֻקָּר, לַעֲמוֹד עַל עִקָּר.
רְעֵבִים לְפַעְנֵחַ דָּתֶיהָ, פִּעְנַח מִדּוֹתֶיהָ,
צְמֵאִים גְּמוּת חִידוֹתֶיהָ, גִּלָּה לָהֶם עֵדוֹתֶיהָ.
שֶׁמֶץ דְּגָלִים טַהֵר, מְצָרֵף וּמְטַהֵר,
הֶרֶב לְכַבְּסָם תְּמַהֵר, מְעוּוִּים אוֹתָם לְטַהֵר.
תִּקָּרֵא כֹּהֵן. בְּחַטְאָךְ בְּאֵזוֹב מִתְכַּהֵן.
❖ טְהוֹרִים זְרוֹק כִּמְכַהֵן, תְּמוּר דַּם מִקַּח אֶלְעָזָר הַכֹּהֵן.

---

perfectly red cows were so rare that from the time of Moses until the destruction of the Second Temple only seven such animals were found and offered in the manner prescribed by the Torah. The Sages ordained that the chapter of the Red Cow be read on the Sabbath before *Parashas*

obstacles are removed and the commandments fenced in to avoid transgression.
The ashes of Moses' Red Cow are an eternal keepsake for the commandment,
the Cow had sevenfold purifications.
Its most striking law is that it transforms pure to impure and impure to pure.
Though this commandment is in the Torah that is near to our understanding,
this commandment itself is far from our logic:
it is distinguished in that it is hidden and unknown.
∴ *The stain of the modest nation's sin is wiped away through it —*
for the purity of the nation that God desires, this commandment is inscribed.

All continue:

מְקוֹמָהּ *The hiding place of its ashes will be revealed,*
from its deep mystery we will draw knowledge,
at the time when God will reveal, He will raise up the nation He protects.

Chazzan continues:

Blessed are You, HASHEM, Shield of Abraham.

אַתָּה *You are eternally mighty, my Lord, the Resuscitator of the dead are You; abundantly able to save,* ***Who makes the wind blow and makes the rain descend; Who*** *sustains the living with kindness, resuscitates the dead with abundant mercy, supports the fallen, heals the sick, releases the confined, and maintains His faith to those asleep in the dust. Who is like You, O Master of mighty deeds, and who is comparable to You, O King Who causes death and restores life and makes salvation sprout! And You are faithful to resuscitate the dead.*

All continue:

מִמָּרָה *The commandment was decreed in Marah at Sinai; its details were enumerated.*
Because faithful Moses exerted himself to understand,
it is forever described as Moses' Cow.
He girded his loins to make a path toward understanding it;
he investigated its aspects but he was regarded as a stranger to it.
Therefore he presented it as an unexplained decree to the scattered Jewish people
so that they would refrain from sophistic challenges as do heretics and Satan.
God gave splendor to the sages who examined a calf by enabling to recognize
from its twisted hairs that a yoke had been on it.
Its service was performed by the Deputy High Priest wearing spun linen garments.
∴ *Its ashes were put away for the purity of the people helped by God.*
The Rock commanded his emissary [Moses]
to wrap up all details of the mitzvah for transmission to Elazar.

All continue:

עוֹלָם *The earth and its fullness are Yours,*
You wished to make Your congregation righteous.
∴ *Therefore I hope that You will bring life-giving rain*
upon Your handiwork that is interred in the grave.

Chazzan continues:

Blessed are You, HASHEM, Who resuscitates the dead.

All continue:

קִפְאוֹן *Uncover the mysterious reason for this costly cow,*
which is enwrapped in the precious light of the Torah;
uncover it for the dear people, that it may attain the main principle.
They hunger to uncover its mandates, may You reveal the ways to expound it;
they are thirsty to drink in its riddles, may You reveal to them its symbols.
May You cleanse the blotch of the tribal encampments, You Who refines and purifies,
may You hasten to wash them abundantly, to cleanse them of their iniquity.
May You be called a Kohen
when you purify with the hyssop this nation that has the mission of serving You,
∴ *pour pure water as does a Kohen, instead of the blood that Elazar the Kohen took.*

Congregation, followed by *chazzan,* recites aloud:

יִמְלֹךְ יהוה לְעוֹלָם אֱלֹהַיִךְ צִיּוֹן לְדֹר וָדֹר הַלְלוּיָהּ.
וְאַתָּה קָדוֹשׁ יוֹשֵׁב תְּהִלּוֹת יִשְׂרָאֵל אֵל נָא.

All continue:

אָמַרְתִּי אֶחְכָּמָה וְהִיא רְחוֹקָה, שָׂח אִיתִיאֵל עֲדֵי זֹאת חֻקָּה, בְּלֹא נִפְלֵאת הִיא וְלֹא רְחוֹקָה. זֹאת פְּלִיאָה הִיא וּמְרֻחָקָה, מִלְּפָנֶיהָ מִשְׁפָּט וְחֻקָּה, וּמֵאַחֲרֶיהָ תּוֹרָה וְחֻקָּה, בְּחָרוּת חֲקוּקָה, וּבְלוּחַ לֵב מְחֻקָּה, מְדוּק תְּלוּלָה וּמִשְּׁאוֹל עֲמוּקָה, וּמִדְּיְרֵי אַרְקָא, מְסִלָּתָהּ חֲמוּקָה. בְּכֵן אֵין לַעֲמוֹד בְּסוֹדָהּ, וְאֵין לְהַגִּיעַ יְסוֹדָהּ. וְאֵין לַחֲקוֹר חֻקָּהּ, וְאֵין לְהַחֲלִישׁ חֶלְקָהּ, וְאֵין לֵידַע עֶרְכָּהּ, וְאֵין לְהָבִין דַּרְכָּהּ, אֱלֹהִים הֵבִין דַּרְכָּהּ.

Congregation, followed by *chazzan,* recites aloud:

חַי וְקַיָּם נוֹרָא וּמָרוֹם וְקָדוֹשׁ.

All continue:

אֲצוּרָה וּמְפֹרְשָׁה, עֲצוּרָה וְלֹא מְפוֹרָשָׁה,
זֹאת חֻקַּת הַפָּרָשָׁה, בְּכָל שָׁנָה מִתְפָּרְשָׁה.
לְבַעֲלֵי אֲסוּפוֹת, חִידוֹתֶיהָ חֲשׂוּפוֹת,
וְכָל צְרוּרוֹת כְּסוּפוֹת, דִּקְדּוּקֶיהָ סְפוּת.
עֲרוּכָה וּשְׁמוּרָה, קְצוּבָה וּגְמוּרָה,
דְּרוּשָׁה וַאֲמוּרָה, בְּקַלָּה וַחֲמוּרָה.
זִיְּנָהּ לֶעָנָיו, בִּפְנִינֵי מְעוֹנָיו,
וְהִגִּיהַּ עֵינָיו, בְּפוּץ מַעְיָנָיו.
רָעַד כְּהִסְכִּית טַעַם תְּחִלַּת מִשְׁנָתָהּ,
פָּרָה בַּת שְׁתַּיִם עֶגְלָה בַּת שְׁנָתָהּ,
בְּצַר צִיר תַּחַן כְּקָשַׁב שְׁמוּעָתָהּ,
נָא מֶנִּי יִפְרֶה מוֹרֶה הֲלָכָה לְשַׁעְתָּהּ.
יִדְעוּ בָהּ הֲלִיכוֹת, וְשִׁנּוּן הֲלָכוֹת,
אֵלֶּה הַנֶּעֱרָכוֹת, וְאֵלֶּה הַמִּתְהַלְּכוֹת.
רְאִיָּתָהּ אֵיךְ לַחֲזוֹת, דָּמָהּ אֵיךְ לְהַזּוֹת,
בְּאוּרָהּ מִלְּהַבְזוֹת, לְחַוּוֹת לְמִי זֹאת.
בְּדִבּוּר אֱמוֹר אֶל הַכֹּהֲנִים שֶׁנָּא עוֹז פָּנָיו,
שָׁב וַיַּעֲרוֹךְ זֹאת לְפָנָיו, וְהֵאִיר עֵינָיו.
יַעַן כְּנֶאֱמַר לוֹ וְלָקְחוּ לַטָּמֵא,
פַּלָּצוּת בְּעַתַתּוּ וְשָׂח מִי יִתֵּן טָהוֹר מִטָּמֵא.
קוֹשְׁטְ אִמְרֵי פָּרָה, כָּל טָהוֹר מְטַמְּאָה,
וְאֵיךְ הִיא תַּעֲבִיר רוּחַ הַטֻּמְאָה.

HaChodesh as a reminder that all Jews should purify themselves before Pesach in order to be qualified to participate in the Pesach offering on the afternoon before the festival. According to

Congregation, followed by *chazzan,* recites aloud:

HASHEM shall reign forever — your God, O Zion — from generation to generation, Halleluyah!

You, O Holy One, are enthroned upon Israel's praises — please, O God.

All continue:

אָמַרְתִּי *"I said I would be wise [enough to understand the reason for the Red Cow], but it is far from me" — thus said Issiel [Solomon] regarding this decree that is written in the Torah that is "not too hard nor too far." But this commandment indeed is hard and far, before the Torah was given, this commandment was called a law and a decree, and thereafter it was called a teaching and decree; though it is inscribed in the tablets of the Torah, but its understanding is erased from the heart; it is higher than the heavens and deeper than the depths, and from the dwellers of the earth its way is hidden. Therefore no one can understand its secret nor penetrate its basis, nor plumb its essence, nor draw its lot, nor know its worth, nor understand its way — only God can understand its way.*

Congregation, followed by *chazzan,* recites aloud:

Living and Enduring One, Awesome, Exalted, and Holy!

All continue:

אֲצוּרָה *The commandment is sealed and separated, kept apart and incomprehensible:*
"This is the decree" of the chapter;
though the chapter containing this decree is translated every year.
To the ancient gatherings of scholars, its riddles were uncovered,
the beloved righteous ones whose souls are bound up for eternal life
fill themselves with its details.
The laws ordered and observed, specific and traditional,
expounded and stated, in its leniencies and stringencies.
With His teachings God armed the humble Moses in His innermost heavens,
and illuminated his vision to spread the teaching of His wellsprings.
Moses shuddered when he heard God Himself repeat the first mishnah:
A 'cow' is in its second year, a 'calf' is in its first year,
upon hearing this utterance, Moses the emissary expressed the supplication:
'Please may the eventual teacher of this law descend from me.'
God taught him its ways and intricate laws,
some are theoretical and some are performed.
How it should look, how to pour its blood,
to beware of belittling its explanations,
to make it clear to this longed-for nation.
At God's statement 'Tell the Kohanim not to become impure,'
Moses' strong features grew pale,
until He taught this chapter of how to cleanse impurity,
and Moses' eyes lit up.
When it was said to him, 'Let them take for the impure one'
[from the ashes of the Red Cow],
a shudder and fright gripped him and he exclaimed,
'Who can bring forth purity from impurity?
The truthful words of the Cow are that it contaminates the pure —
so how can it remove a spirit of impurity?'

---

some authorities, this public reading is required by the Torah.

אֲצוּרָה ◆§. The acrostic of this *piyut* spells the name of the composer אלעזר בירבי קליר.

לוֹ הִגִּיד אֵל חֻקָּה חֻקַּתִּי.
וּמַה תִּיַגַּע לֵידַע, עֲמוּקָּה מִשְּׁאוֹל מַה תֵּדַע.
יָבֹא אֵפֶר פָּרָה, לְהַלְבִּין טִנּוּף בֶּן פָּרָה,
הֱיוֹת כַּפָּרָה, לְסוֹרֵרָה כִּפָּרָה.
∴ **ר**ֶמֶז בְּוְיִקְחוּ אֵלֶיךָ פָּרָה, הֱיוֹת פָּרָתוֹ מִתְמֶדֶת,
שֶׁכָּל הַפָּרוֹת כָּלוֹת וְשֶׁלְּךָ לָעַד עוֹמֶדֶת.

Chazzan continues:

אֵל נָא לְעוֹלָם תֻּעֲרָץ, וּלְעוֹלָם תֻּקְדָּשׁ, וּלְעוֹלְמֵי עוֹלָמִים תִּמְלוֹךְ וְתִתְנַשֵּׂא, הָאֵל מֶלֶךְ נוֹרָא מָרוֹם וְקָדוֹשׁ, כִּי אַתָּה הוּא מֶלֶךְ מַלְכֵי הַמְּלָכִים, מַלְכוּתוֹ נֶצַח. נוֹרְאוֹתָיו שִׂיחוּ, סַפְּרוּ עֻזּוֹ, פָּאֲרוּהוּ צְבָאָיו, קַדְּשׁוּהוּ רוֹמְמוּהוּ, רוֹן שִׁיר וָשֶׁבַח, תֹּקֶף תְּהִלּוֹת תִּפְאַרְתּוֹ.

Chazzan, followed by congregation, recites aloud:

לְטַהֵר טְמֵאִים, לְטַמֵּא טְהוֹרִים, בְּאֹמֶר קָדוֹשׁ.

All continue:

אִמְרָה סְנוּנָה וּצְרוּפָה, **בְּ**דוּלָה בְּדָתָהּ מֵעֲרוּפָה,*
גְּדֵלָה כְּרַעֲנָן לִתְרוּפָה.
דְּרוּשָׁה בְּזִקּוּק שִׁבְעָה מִשִּׁבְעָה, **הַ**זָּיוֹת טְבִילוֹת וּכִבּוּסִים שִׁבְעָה,
וּפָרוֹת וְכֹהֲנִים טְהוֹרִים וּטְמֵאִים שִׁבְעָה.
זִקְנֵי גָזִית תְּמִימִים מִמּוּם, **חֲ**בוּאֶיהָ יְבַקְּרוּ לְבַל הֱיוֹת בָּהּ מוּם,
טְהוֹרָה תִּהְיֶה לַאֲדֻמּוֹת כְּמִמּוּם.
יַעֲשֶׂה מְהוֹן כֹּהֵן כֶּבֶשׁ* פָּרָה, **כִּ**פָּה מוּל אוֹטֶם בְּהוֹד תִּפְאָרָה,
לְהוֹצִיא בָהּ תְּמִימָה חֵטְא תַּמָּה מְפִירָה.
מְסַעֲדָיו אִתּוֹ יָצְאוּ לְהַר הַמִּשְׁחָה, **נָ**חַץ טְבוּל שֵׁנִית עֲבוּר כּוֹרֶה שׁוּחָה,
סִדֵּר מַעֲרֶכֶת וְלֹא שָׁהָה.
עָמַד מִקֶּדֶם וּפָנָיו לְמַעֲרָב, **פָּ**רָה שָׁחַט וְדָם לֹא עֵרַב,
צָת בָּהּ חֲרָיוֹת וּמוֹקְדָהּ הֵרַב.
קָם מוּל שַׁעַר אֵיתוֹן וְדָם שֶׁבַע יַזֶּה, **רַ**עֲנָן אֶרֶז וְאֵזוֹב וּשְׁנִי יֶחֱזֶה,
שְׁמַע לַכֹּל עֵץ אֶרֶז זֶה וְאֵזוֹב זֶה.
∴ **תִּ**רְגֵּל וְחִלְּקָהּ לִשְׁלֹשָׁה חֲלָקִים, כָּל מִשְׁמָרוֹת הָיוּ מֻנָּה מְחַלְּקִים,
תְּכוּנָה לְמִשְׁמֶרֶת עַד נְקוּקִים יָקִים.

Chazzan and congregation recite together:

וּבְכֵן וּלְךָ תַעֲלֶה קְדֻשָּׁה כִּי אַתָּה קְדוֹשׁ יִשְׂרָאֵל וּמוֹשִׁיעַ.

Turn to page 422 for *Kedushah* and the continuation of *Shacharis.*

מֵעֲרוּפָה — *The heifer whose neck was cut.* See *Deuteronomy* 21:1-9. The heifer atones for the murder of a defenseless traveler. Like the Red Cow no work may have been done with the heifer, but the Cow must be in its third year and the heifer in its first or second.

God told him 'I have decreed its law;
why do you struggle to know what is deeper than the Pit —
what can you know?'
Let the ashes of the Cow come to whiten the filth of the calf,
to be an atonement for the one that strayed like a cow.
∴ *It was alluded in the phrase: 'They are to take a cow for you'*
that Moses' Red Cow would be eternal,
for all the other cows would be used up, but yours will last forever.

Chazzan continues:

אֵל נָא *O God, may You always be lauded and always be sanctified, and forever reign and be uplifted, the God, King, awesome, exalted, and holy, for You are the King Who reigns over kings, Whose sovereignty is eternal. Speak of His wonders, declare His strength, glorify Him, O His legions; sanctify Him, exalt Him. Sing song and praise, glorify Him with powerful psalms of praise.*

Chazzan, followed by congregation, recites aloud:

To cleanse the contaminated and to contaminate the pure, through the word of the Holy One.

All continue:

אִמְרָה *The utterance regarding the Red Cow is clarified and purified,*
*its law is different from that of the heifer whose neck is cut,**
for it is grown like a flourishing tree giving healthy shade.
Its laws are expounded with seven times sevenfold diligence,
seven tosses and seven dippings of the Kohen's finger in its blood,
seven washings of his clothing,
seven cows brought throughout Jewish history,
seven pure Kohanim participate in the service and become impure in the process.
The elders of the Sanhedrin free of blemish
examine the cow's hidden parts to be sure it has no blemish;
it must be as perfectly red as it is free of blemish.
From the Kohen Gadol's personal wealth a causeway was built for the cow,*
each arch above a lower pier with splendid glory,
upon which to lead the unblemished cow
that annulled the sin of the wholesome nation.
His aides accompanied him to the Mount of Olives,
he hastened to immerse himself a second time
to refute the false teaching of the treacherous Sadducees,
then he prepared the pyre without delay.
He stood to the east facing west; he slaughtered the cow but did not use all its blood,
he ignited the pyre with twigs and nourished its flame.
He stood opposite the Iron Gate of the Temple and tossed blood seven times;
he looked at the fresh cedar wood, the hyssop, and the crimson wool
and said audibly to everyone: 'Is this cedar wood? Is this hyssop?'
∴ *The ashes would customarily be divided into three parts,*
each shift of Kohanim took a portion of it,
and a part was kept for safekeeping until God resuscitates those buried in the clefts.

Chazzan and congregation recite together:

So now, the Kedushah prayer will ascend to You, for You are the Holy One and Savior of Israel.

Turn to page 423 for *Kedushah* and the continuation of *Shacharis.*

כֶּבֶשׁ — *A causeway.* Elaborate preparations were made to insure that there would be no possibility of the people tending the cow to become contaminated.

❦ יוצר לפרשת החדש ❦

The *chazzan* begins his repetition of the *Shacharis Shemoneh Esrei:*

אֲדֹנָי שְׂפָתַי תִּפְתָּח, וּפִי יַגִּיד תְּהִלָּתֶךָ.

בָּרוּךְ אַתָּה יהוה אֱלֹהֵינוּ וֵאלֹהֵי אֲבוֹתֵינוּ, אֱלֹהֵי אַבְרָהָם, אֱלֹהֵי יִצְחָק, וֵאלֹהֵי יַעֲקֹב, הָאֵל הַגָּדוֹל הַגִּבּוֹר וְהַנּוֹרָא, אֵל עֶלְיוֹן, גּוֹמֵל חֲסָדִים טוֹבִים וְקוֹנֵה הַכֹּל, וְזוֹכֵר חַסְדֵי אָבוֹת, וּמֵבִיא גוֹאֵל לִבְנֵי בְנֵיהֶם, לְמַעַן שְׁמוֹ בְּאַהֲבָה. מֶלֶךְ עוֹזֵר וּמוֹשִׁיעַ וּמָגֵן.

Congregation, followed by *chazzan,* recites:

מִסּוֹד חֲכָמִים וּנְבוֹנִים, וּמִלֶּמֶד דַּעַת מְבִינִים.
אֶפְתְּחָה פִּי בְּשִׁיר וּרְנָנִים. לְהוֹדוֹת וּלְהַלֵּל פְּנֵי שׁוֹכֵן מְעוֹנִים.

All continue:

אֲתִיַּת עֵת דּוֹדִים כְּגָעָה, **בְּ**אַחַת וְעֶשֶׂר פּוּט נֶגְּעָה,
גִּישַׁת צִקּוּן מַכְפֵּל כְּפָגְעָה, **דִּ**לֵּג פַּעַם וְזֹאת רָגְעָה.
הִשְׁגִּיחַ עוֹפֶר מֶחֱרֶךְ אֲרֻבּוֹת, **וְ**חִתֵּל אֶרֶךְ בְּתֶבֶס תַּעֲרוּבוֹת,
זְמַן קָפַץ עֲשׂוֹת רַבּוֹת, **חֲ**דָשִׁים וְגַם יְשָׁנִים לְהַרְבּוֹת.
טָשׁ וַיֵּדֶא וְעִדָּן שְׁנָה, **יָ**קַץ כְּיָשֵׁן וְעֵר כְּמִשְׁנֶה.
❖ **כָּ**סַף וְדָפַק בְּפִתְחֵי יְשֵׁנָה, **לְ**חַפְּשָׂהּ בָּרִאשׁוֹן לְחָדְשֵׁי הַשָּׁנָה.

All continue:

לִי עוֹד תִּגְנוֹן, בְּפָסוֹחַ וְגָנוֹן. ❖ בְּגוֹנְנָךְ לְבָנוֹן, בְּמָגִנַּת יִנּוֹן.

Chazzan continues:

בָּרוּךְ אַתָּה יהוה מָגֵן אַבְרָהָם.

אַתָּה גִּבּוֹר לְעוֹלָם אֲדֹנָי, מְחַיֵּה מֵתִים אַתָּה, רַב לְהוֹשִׁיעַ. מַשִּׁיב הָרוּחַ וּמוֹרִיד הַגֶּשֶׁם. מְכַלְכֵּל חַיִּים בְּחֶסֶד, מְחַיֵּה מֵתִים בְּרַחֲמִים רַבִּים, סוֹמֵךְ נוֹפְלִים, וְרוֹפֵא חוֹלִים, וּמַתִּיר אֲסוּרִים, וּמְקַיֵּם אֱמוּנָתוֹ לִישֵׁנֵי עָפָר. מִי כָמוֹךָ בַּעַל גְּבוּרוֹת, וּמִי דּוֹמֶה לָּךְ, מֶלֶךְ מֵמִית וּמְחַיֶּה וּמַצְמִיחַ יְשׁוּעָה. וְנֶאֱמָן אַתָּה לְהַחֲיוֹת מֵתִים.

All continue:

מְרִימֵי עוֹל עֶגְלָה לְהַלְאוֹת, **מִ**כְּאֵב הֲגִתָּה לְהַרְאוֹת אוֹת,
נְאָקָה הֵחִישָׁה קֵץ הַפְּלָאוֹת,
נֶחֱצוּ לְמָאתַיִם וָעֶשֶׂר אַרְבַּע מֵאוֹת.
שֶׂה הַמְּסֻבָּךְ לְעֵקֶד צוּר, **סִ**יֵּם זִכְרוֹ בְּפֶקֶד נָצוּר,
עֲמוּסִים כְּאֶחָיו לְעֵת בִּצּוּר, **עֲ**דָיְמוֹ לְשַׁי יְהִי עָצוּר.
פֶּלֶא עֲשׂוֹת נֶגֶד אָבוֹת, **פָּ**ץ מִבֶּעָשׂוֹר לְאָסְרוֹ בַּעֲבוֹת.
❖ **צְ**לִיחַת יַרְדֵּן בּוֹ לְהִתְוֹת, **צְ**פִיַּת שֶׂה לְבֵית אָבוֹת.

❦ YOTZER OF PARASHAS HACHODESH ❦

The Sages ordained that, on the Sabbath before the beginning of Nissan or on a Sabbath that falls on the first of Nissan, the chapter of the new moon be read (*Exodus* 12:1-20). In that

YOTZER FOR PARASHAS HACHODESH

The *chazzan* begins his repetition of the *Shacharis Shemoneh Esrei:*

My Lord, open my lips, that my mouth may declare Your praise.

בָּרוּךְ *Blessed are You,* HASHEM, *our God and the God of our forefathers, God of Abraham, God of Isaac, and God of Jacob; the great, mighty, and awesome God, the supreme God, Who bestows beneficial kindnesses and creates everything, Who recalls the kindnesses of the Patriarchs and brings a Redeemer to their children's children, for His Name's sake, with love. O King, Helper, Savior, and Shield.*

Congregation, followed by *chazzan,* recites:

מְסוֹד *Based on the tradition of our wise and discerning teachers,*
and the teaching derived from the knowledge of the discerning,
I open my mouth in song to praise Him Who dwells on high.

All continue:

אֲתִיַּת *With the coming and arrival of the season of God's love,*
the land of Put [Egypt] was struck eleven times,
thanks to the many prayers of the Patriarch of Machpelah [Abraham],
God skipped 190 years of slavery and this calmed Israel.
The gazelle [God] observed through latticed windows
and applied a cure to the bloodied nation
[Israel, covered with blood of circumcision and blood of Pesach],
He leaped across time to perform wonders,
and to multiply new commandments upon the old.
He flew swiftly and altered the schedule of redemption,
He woke up like a sleeper and was aroused as if from sleep.
∴ *He yearned to redeem Israel and knocked on the doors of the sleeping nation,*
to free her in the first month of the year [Nissan].

All continue:

לִי *Your will shield me again, as You passed over and shielded me in Egypt,*
∴ *when You shield the Temple Mount [known as Lebanon]*
through the salvation of Messiah [who is known as Yenon].

Chazzan continues:

Blessed are You, HASHEM, *Shield of Abraham.*

אַתָּה *You are eternally mighty, my Lord, the Resuscitator of the dead are You; abundantly able to save,* ***Who makes the wind blow and makes the rain descend;*** *Who sustains the living with kindness, resuscitates the dead with abundant mercy, supports the fallen, heals the sick, releases the confined, and maintains His faith to those asleep in the dust. Who is like You, O Master of mighty deeds, and who is comparable to You, O King Who causes death and restores life and makes salvation sprout! And You are faithful to resuscitate the dead.*

All continue:

מְרִימֵי *You lifted from me the exhausting yoke of Egypt,*
You removed us from servile pain to show us a sign of favor,
the Jewish outcry hastened the wondrous deadline,
and cut down the four hundred years to two hundred ten.
The ram that was caught was offered on the Akedah by the rock-like Abraham,
its memory was inscribed in the protected recollection;
when this nation borne by God comes to a time of prayer,
that ram will be safeguarded as its offering to God.
He did wonders for the sake of the Patriarchs,
He said that the Pesach lamb should be bound from the tenth of Nissan
∴ *— as a symbol of the future crossing of the Jordan on that date —*
for examination of each lamb for a family.

All continue:

לְךָ עוֹד נַקְשִׁיבָה, מִמַּעַיְנֵי הַיְשׁוּעָה נִשְׁאָבָה.
✣ שָׂשׂוֹן יֶשְׁעֲךָ לָנוּ הָשִׁיבָה, וּבִתְחִיַּת גֶּשֶׁם נֵחָשֵׁבָה.

Chazzan continues:

בָּרוּךְ אַתָּה יהוה מְחַיֵּה הַמֵּתִים.

All continue:

קִיחַת עֲלִיַּת עֶקֶד, הִיא נִצְּבָה בְּפֶקֶד,
תְּוִיכַת בְּתְרֵי שָׁקֵד, רִשְׁפֵּי לוּד לְיַקֵּד.
רַחַשׁ יְשֵׁנִים כְּעָרֶב, דַּם תְּבוּסָה כְּעֹרֶב,
קֵץ חָשׁ וְקָרַב, לְעוֹרֵר בְּתַנִּין קְרָב.
שֵׁמַע מִכְסַת פְּסָחִים, אֲשֶׁר כִּסּוּ פְסוּחִים,
הִיא צִמְּתָה כַּסְלוּחִים, לְהַצִּיתָם כְּקוֹצִים כְּסוּחִים.
תְּרָפִים כְּדֵי לַמְעַט, מְנוּיֵי מְתֵי מְעַט.
✣ תּוֹקֶף הַדְרַת מֶלֶךְ מִלְּהַמְעַט, הָרְשַׁם לְהִמָּנוֹת בְּוְאֹם יִמְעַט.

All continue:

הַחֹדֶשׁ הַזֶּה לָכֶם לִשְׁמוֹר, בְּסֵכֶם אֲסוּפֵי הַר מוֹר,
✣ וְאִתָּם אֵל יִגְמוֹר, שְׁלֹשֶׁת אוֹתוֹת בּוֹ לִשְׁמוֹר.

All continue:

דּוֹרֵשׁ זֶה חֹדֶשׁ בְּחָדְשׁוֹ, לְאוֹת וּלְמוֹפֵת קָדְשׁוֹ.
✣ יְדִידֵי עַם קְדוֹשׁוֹ, הוֹשִׁיעָה לּוֹ יְמִינוֹ וּזְרוֹעַ קָדְשׁוֹ.

All continue:

הַדּוֹם אֲשֶׁר מֻגַּר וְהוּדַשׁ, כְּהַיּוֹם הַזֶּה יְחֻדַּשׁ בְּגוֹדֶשׁ.
✣ וְנוֹבִיל שַׁי בַּקֹּדֶשׁ, בָּרִאשׁוֹן בְּאֶחָד לַחֹדֶשׁ.

Congregation, followed by *chazzan,* recites aloud:

יִמְלֹךְ יהוה לְעוֹלָם אֱלֹהַיִךְ צִיּוֹן לְדֹר וָדֹר הַלְלוּיָהּ.
וְאַתָּה קָדוֹשׁ יוֹשֵׁב תְּהִלּוֹת יִשְׂרָאֵל אֵל נָא.

All continue:

רִבּוֹת עָשִׂיתָ וְחָשַׁבְתָּ וְסִפַּרְתָּ, מִפְּעֲלוֹתֶיךָ פְּעוֹל בְּסַהַר סָפַרְתָּ,
לְאוֹתוֹת וּלְמוֹעֲדִים חֲבָלוֹ שִׁפַּרְתָּ,
לִתְקוּפוֹת וּמַחֲזוֹרוֹת קִצּוֹ צָפַרְתָּ,
לְאַלְפַּיִם וְאַרְבַּע מֵאוֹת וְאַרְבָּעִים וּשְׁמוֹנָה זְמַנּוֹ בֵּאַרְתָּ,
וּבְתֵשַׁע מֵאוֹת עִבּוּרִים עָדָיו עִבַּרְתָּ, וְהַיּוֹם הוֹרֵיתָ לָעָם אֲשֶׁר בָּחַרְתָּ,
לָכֵן עַל כָּל חֹדֶשׁ חָדְשׁוֹ הִגְבַּרְתָּ, סִפְרוֹ בִּקַּרְתָּ, קִצְבּוֹ חָקַרְתָּ,
✣ נִזְלוֹ הֵקַרְתָּ, פִּלְאוֹ סָקַרְתָּ, מוֹעֲדוֹ יִקַּרְתָּ, וּבוֹ יָקַרְתָּ וְנִתְיַקַּרְתָּ.

---

chapter, God proclaims Nissan as the premier month of the year, because it was the month of redemption. Both because it was the month of the Exodus in ancient times and because the future redemption will be associated with it, the Sages chose to give added distinction to Nissan

All continue:

לְךָ *We will always heed You and draw from the wellsprings of salvation;*
∴ return to us the joy of Your salvation
and we will be worthy of the rain of resuscitation.

Chazzan continues:

Blessed are You, HASHEM, Who resuscitates the dead.

All continue:

קִיחַת *The taking of Isaac who was lifted upon the altar remains as our remembrance;*
in the merit of Abraham's enthusiasm at the Covenant between the Parts,
flames devoured Lud [Egypt].
As the prayers of the slumbering Patriarchs were sweet to God,
and the blood of Israel's Pesach and circumcision was sweetly meritorious,
He hastened and brought the redemption time near,
to provoke battle with serpentine Pharaoh.
The knowledge of the registrants on Pesach offerings
that were slaughtered by the Jews whom the plague passed over —
that merit cut down the Casluchim [Egypt], to ignite them like severed thorns.
In order to diminish the numbers of idols in Egypt,
the small Jewish nation registered to eat the Pesach sheep
[which the Egyptians worshiped],
in order that the mighty glory of the King not be decreased,
∴ He authorized them to add registrants
if a family was too small to consume every morsel of the Pesach.

All continue:

הַחֹדֶשׁ *You are to observe the commandments of this month*
that was sanctified by the assembled Sanhedrin on Mount Moriah,
∴ and God ratifies it with them,
for they consider the three indications of when to make a leap year.

All continue:

דּוֹרֵשׁ *God sought out this month when it was inaugurated in Egypt,*
∴ to sanctify it with signs and wonders;
His beloved, sacred nation — God saved with His right hand and holy arm.

All continue:

הֲדוֹם *His Footstool [the Temple] that was laid low and plowed under,*
may it be renewed on this day in greater measure than ever,
∴ and we shall deliver a gift to the Sanctuary, on the first day of this first month.

Congregation, followed by chazzan, recites aloud:

HASHEM shall reign forever — your God, O Zion —
from generation to generation, Halleluyah!

You, O Holy One, are enthroned upon Israel's praises —
please, O God.

All continue:

רַבּוֹת *Many miracles have You done and You continue to think of us and relate them,*
You counted the deeds You did during nights,
for You beautified the night's lot by making the sign for determining the festivals;
You crowned Nissan as the starting point of seasons and cycles,
in the year 2448 [the Exodus] You explained its time-status,
and up to then You declared nine hundred leap years,
but on that day You taught Your chosen people to do it,
therefore You made Nissan the most important of the new moons.
You examined the number of its days, You plumbed the number of its hours and seconds,
∴ You cooled its springs of water, You took note of its miracles,
You esteemed its festival,
and on it You brought esteem to Israel and gained esteem Yourself.

Congregation, followed by *chazzan,* recites aloud:

חַי וְקַיָּם נוֹרָא וּמָרוֹם וְקָדוֹשׁ.

All continue:

אֲבִי כָּל חוֹזֶה, חָל בּוֹ בְּמַחֲזֶה,
כְּנֶאֱמַר לוֹ חֲזֵה, תַּבְנִית הַחֹדֶשׁ הַזֶּה.
לְהָבִין קֶצֶב מוֹלַדְתּוֹ, מִתְּחִלָּתוֹ,
וְאֹרֶךְ מְלֵאָתוֹ, עַד תַּכְלִיתוֹ.
עִמְּתוֹ לְהַרְאֵהוּ, וְלֹא הִכִּיר מַרְאֵהוּ,
עַד בְּאֶצְבַּע הֶרְאָהוּ, אָז בָּן וְרָאָהוּ.
זֹהַר לְשָׁעוֹת שֵׁשׁ, תָּאֳרוֹ לְהִתְאַשֵּׁשׁ,
פָּחוֹת מִשֵּׁשׁ, כָּל עַיִן יְעַשֵּׁשׁ.
רוֹאָיו לְבַקֵּר, עֵדָיו לְחַקֵּר,
מַאֲמִירָיו לְיַקֵּר, מְמִירָיו לְעַקֵּר.
בְּמֶדֶד לוֹ שַׁעַר, עָבְיוֹ אֵיךְ לְשַׁעֵר,
עַד שְׁטִיפַת שַׂעַר, יְקַבְּלוּ יוֹשְׁבֵי שָׁעַר.
יָדְעוּ תְבוּנָה, לְחַוּוֹת לְאוֹם נְכוֹנָה,
לְהוֹרוֹת לְיוֹדְעֵי בִינָה, עֵרֶךְ לְבָנָה.
רְגָלִים לְיַשֵּׁב, זְמַנִּים לְחַשֵּׁב,
בְּעִבּוּר אֵיךְ לֵישֵׁב, וְסוֹד מָה לְהַקְשֵׁב.
בְּפָנָיו צָגוּ אֵילֵי קֹדֶשׁ, לְהָעִיד עֵדוּת חֹדֶשׁ,
וְאֵל נִתְעַטֵּף בַּקֹּדֶשׁ, כְּמַקְדִּישֵׁי חֹדֶשׁ.
יָהּ בְּדָקָם לְעֵינוֹ, וְעֵדוּתָם דִּקְדֵּק בְּמַחֲנוֹ,
וְהַכֹּל צִוְּחוּ בִּמְעוֹנוֹ, מְקֻדָּשׁ הַחֹדֶשׁ בִּזְמַנּוֹ.
קֵץ מוֹלַדְתּוֹ חָל לְהַקְצוֹת, בְּיוֹם רְבִיעִי בְּחָצוֹת,
וְעַד שְׁלֹשִׁים מְרוּצוֹת, לֹא נִכַּר בַּחוּצוֹת.
לָאָה צִיר וּפָחַד, וְתָר מְעַט לְעֵת סִפּוּר אֶחָד,
וְצוּר פָּץ לוֹ וַיִּחַד, מֵעֶרֶב וְעַד עֶרֶב מְנוֹת אֶחָד.
יַלְדוּת חֶרֶס וְסַהַר בּוֹ בַּיּוֹם חֶשְׁבּוֹן מִצּוּ,
וּכְתְחִלַּת בְּרִיָּתָם בְּחַלּוֹן אֶחָד נִמְצָאוּ.
✣ **רֵ**עִים כְּנִתַּן לָמוֹ מַסּוֹרֶת אָמָּצוּ,
לְחַשֵּׁב לְעַבֵּר וּלְקַדֵּשׁ סְפוּרוֹת כְּמָצָאוּ.

Chazzan continues:

אֵל נָא לְעוֹלָם תֻּעֲרָץ, וּלְעוֹלָם תֻּקְדָּשׁ, וּלְעוֹלְמֵי עוֹלָמִים תִּמְלוֹךְ וְתִתְנַשֵּׂא, הָאֵל מֶלֶךְ נוֹרָא מָרוֹם וְקָדוֹשׁ, כִּי אַתָּה הוּא מֶלֶךְ מַלְכֵי הַמְּלָכִים, מַלְכוּתוֹ נֶצַח. נוֹרְאוֹתָיו שִׂיחוּ, סַפְּרוּ עֻזּוֹ, פָּאֲרוּהוּ צְבָאָיו, קַדְּשׁוּהוּ רוֹמְמוּהוּ, רוֹן שִׁיר וָשֶׁבַח, תֹּוֹקֶף תְּהִלּוֹת תִּפְאַרְתּוֹ.

Congregation, followed by *chazzan,* recites aloud:

Living and Enduring One, Awesome, Exalted, and Holy!

All continue:

אֲבִי *Moses, the father of all prophets, prayed regarding the vision of the moon,*
when he was told by God to see the form of the new moon.
To discern the dimension that constitutes its rebirth from its beginning,
and how long it is full, until it disappears.
God befriended him to whom He showed it, but he did not recognize its appearance
until He pointed with His finger — then he understood and saw it.
Six hours after its rebirth its glow is recognizeably strong;
but less than six hours, the naked eye is too weak.
Through this calculation those claiming to have seen it can be tested,
its witnesses can be investigated
to give credit to those testifying truthfully and to uproot the testimony of liars.
In estimating its size, how to measure its width,
if it was even a hairbreadth wide, the judges at the gate would accept testimony.
God taught Moses discernment, for him to teach the worthy nation,
to teach the extent of the moon to those who know understanding.
To establish festivals, to calculate seasons,
to know how many judges to seat to consider leap years,
and the secret on which to base the decision.
Before God were arrayed the holy angels, to testify regarding the month,
and God wrapped Himself in holiness, like the judges who sanctify the month.
God interrogated them in Moses' presence,
and examined their testimony in His abode,
and all called out in His heaven, the month is sanctified in its proper time.
In that month the time of the moon's rebirth, which ended Adar,
occurred on Wednesday noon,
but for thirty consecutive hours, the moon was not visible outdoors.
Moses, the emissary, grew weary calculating and became fearful,
and assumed that twenty-four hours from that rebirth was a single day
[i.e. the month should begin at noon],
then the Rock told him — and he rejoiced —
that only from evening to evening could be counted as a day.
That year the sun's new cycle and the new moon were calculated on one day
just as at the start of their creation
when both were found to be in the same heavenly period.
∴ *God's friends, the Jewish people,*
firmly resolved to maintain the tradition that was given them, to calculate,
to intercalate [declare leap years], and to sanctify months as they occur.

Chazzan continues:

אֵל נָא *O God, may You always be lauded and always be sanctified, and forever reign and be uplifted, the God, King, awesome, exalted, and holy, for You are the King Who reigns over kings, Whose sovereignty is eternal. Speak of His wonders, declare His strength, glorify Him, O His legions; sanctify Him, exalt Him. Sing song and praise, glorify Him with powerful psalms of praise.*

---

by means of the special reading. In addition, the reading serves further to alert the people to the approach of Pesach and the need to prepare for the festival. In Temple times this was especially important because of the obligation for people to travel to Jerusalem and to offer the Pesach sacrifice on the day before the festival.

אֲבִי ◆§. The acrostic of this *piyut* spells the name of the composer אלעזר בירבי קליר

Chazzan, followed by congregation, recites the following two verses aloud:

רִאשׁוֹן הוּא לָכֶם, לִפְסוֹחַ עֲלֵיכֶם, לְהִתְקַדֵּשׁ בְּתוֹכְכֶם, קָדוֹשׁ.

לָכֶם הוּא רִאשׁוֹן, נְצוּרֵי כְּאִישׁוֹן,
לְהַעֲרִיץ לְאֵל אַחֲרוֹן וְרִאשׁוֹן, קָדוֹשׁ.

All continue:

אָדוֹן מִקֶּדֶם תִּכְּנוֹ רֹאשׁ, **בִּ**ינוֹ לֹא גָל בְּסֵפֶר תּוֹלְדוֹת רֹאשׁ,
גִּלָּהוּ תְּחִלָּה לָכֶם לִדְרוֹשׁ.
דּוֹרֵשׁ לְהַשְׁווֹת בּוֹ גִּיהָ וְאִישׁוֹן, **הִ**פְלָא מִכָּל עַם וְלָשׁוֹן,
וְלֹא הָמְסַר לְאָדָם הָרִאשׁוֹן.
זְמַן עֶדְנָה בּוֹ בְּשָׂרָה, **חָ**נוּט לְקִצּוֹ עָקוּד לְמוֹסֵרָה,
טַפֶּיהָ בְּכֵן בּוֹ בִּשְּׂרוּ בְשׂוֹרָה.
יֶרַח אֲשֶׁר לֹא פִּעֲנַח לָרִאשׁוֹנִים, **כָּ**מוּס לִצְפּוֹן חֲדָשִׁים וְגַם יְשָׁנִים,
לְרֹאשׁ הוּשַׂם לְאַרְבָּעָה רָאשֵׁי שָׁנִים.
מוֹעֲדִים מְזֻמִּין לִנְדְגָּלִים, **נ**וֹעֲדִים בּוֹ עֵינֵימוֹ צִירֵי רוֹגְלִים,
סָפוּר הוּא לִמְלָכִים וְלִרְגָלִים.
עִבּוּר מְעַבְּרִים לְשָׁמְרוֹ בְּמוֹעֲדוֹ, **פֶּ**רַח וְאָבִיב תְּקוּפָה בָּם לְוַעֲדוֹ,
צִיּוּן שְׁלָשְׁתָּם יְצָרְפוּ לְסַעֲדוֹ.
קִדֵּשׁ בְּרֹאשׁוֹ וּשְׁלִישׁוֹ חֶצְיוֹ וְרֻבּוֹ לִשְׁמוֹר,
לְקַדֵּשׁ לָקַחַת לְחָגֵג לִקְצוֹר וְלִגְמוֹר,
רֻשַּׁם בְּכָל דּוֹר, **שָׁ**מוּר הוּא לָרוֹכֵב עַל חֲמוֹר.
שְׁמִירַת שְׁלִישׁוֹ בַּיַּרְדֵּן עָמְדָה, **שַׁ**לְהֶבֶת חֶצְיוֹ שְׁאוֹן פּוּל הִשְׁמִידָה,
תְּשׁוּעַת קְצִירוֹ יְמִינִי הֶעֱמִידָה.

Chazzan and congregation recite together:

וּבְכֵן וּלְךָ תַעֲלֶה קְדֻשָּׁה כִּי אַתָּה קְדוֹשׁ יִשְׂרָאֵל וּמוֹשִׁיעַ.

Turn to page 422 for *Kedushah* and the continuation of *Shacharis.*

מוסף לפרשת החדש

The *chazzan* begins his repetition (p. 462) and continues through וּמוֹשִׁיעַ וּמָגֵן. Then all recite:

רִאשׁוֹן, **אִ**מַּצְתָּ לְפֶרַח שׁוֹשַׁנִּים, **אִ**מַּץ לְעוֹרֵר מֵרֶדֶם יְשֵׁנִים,
בְּזָכְרְךָ בְּרִית רִאשׁוֹנִים, **בִּ**צְפּוֹן חֲדָשִׁים וְגַם יְשָׁנִים,
גִּלּוּתוֹ בְּדָת שְׁנוּנִים, **גָּ**זַר רֹאשׁ לְאַרְבָּעָה רָאשֵׁי שָׁנִים.
❖ אַרְבָּעָה רָאשֵׁי שָׁנִים בְּמַחֲזֶה, בֵּאַרְתָּ זֶה מִזֶּה לַחוֹזֶה,
כַּאֲשֶׁר שָׁמַעְנוּ כֵּן עוֹד נֶחֱזֶה, גוֹנְנֵנוּ בְּמָגֵן בַּחֹדֶשׁ הַזֶּה.

MUSSAF FOR PARASHAS HACHODESH

The *piyut* for *Mussaf* contains seven stanzas, one to be recited before each blessing of the *chazzan's* repetition of *Shemoneh Esrei.* The stanzas begin with the words of *Isaiah* 41:7, which speaks of the time of the first glimmerings of redemption after the Babylonian exile. The verse prophecies that when King Darius would give permission to rebuild the Temple, the Jewish elders, at the urging of the prophets Chaggai and Zechariah, would rejoice.

Chazzan, followed by congregation, recites the following two verses aloud:

Nissan is the first month for you, for God to pass over you,
to be sanctified among you — the Holy One!
For you it is the first month, You Who are guarded like the apple of the eye,
to exalt God Who is last and first — the Holy One!

All continue:

אָדוֹן *From the beginning the Lord established Nissan as the first,*
but He did not reveal its understanding in the book possessed by Adam —
He first revealed it only to You [Israel] to expound.
The calculation must reconcile the movements of the brilliant sun and the dark moon,
this was hidden from every people and tongue
and not transmitted to Adam, the first man.
In this month Sarah regained her youth and was informed that she would give birth,
the ripening Isaac who was born at year's end and was bound to the altar with a rope,
in this merit her offspring were promised redemption.
This month that was not revealed to the ancients
was reserved to contain new miracles as well as old ones,
it was set as the first of the four new years.
It ushers in the Festivals for the people that encamped around four banners;
concerning it the Sanhedrin, the eyes of the people,
assemble and dispatch witnesses to spy out the moon;
it is counted as the new year for kings and pilgrimage festivals.
The court inserts a month to maintain Nissan in its proper season:
if crops and fruits are not ripe or the seasons will not be timely,
for if only one of these occurs, it may be used in conjunction with another need.
It was sanctified at its beginning, after a third [the tenth of Nissan],
in its middle, and after its majority to observe:
to sanctify the new moon, to take a lamb for the Pesach, to celebrate Pesach,
to cut barley for the Omer, and to complete the month in holiness;
its beginning is reserved in every generation
for the coming of the pauper riding on a donkey [Messiah].
In observance of a third, Israel stood that day in the bed of the Jordan,
in the merit of the Pesach flame of the middle of Nissan
the army of Sennacherib of Pul was destroyed,
the salvation resulting from the cutting of the Omer stood by
Mordechai the Benjaminite [for Haman was hung on the day of the Omer].

Chazzan and congregation recite together:

So now, the Kedushah prayer will ascend to You,
for You are the Holy One and Savior of Israel.

Turn to page 423 for *Kedushah* and the continuation of *Shacharis.*

❧ MUSSAF FOR PARASHAS HACHODESH ☙

The *chazzan* begins his repetition (p. 462) and continues through *'Savior and Shield.'* Then all recite:

ראשון *You established the first month to enhance the bloom of the rose-like nation,*
it was established to arouse the slumbering dead from their sleep
when You recall the covenant of the early ones,
and You conceal from notice the new sins as well as the old.
You revealed it in the much-reviewed Law,
which sets down Nissan as primary among the four new years.
∴ *Four new years were taught in the vision,*
You—of Whom we say 'This is my God'—explained it to the seer in this Torah;
as we heard of Your past miracles, so may we see them once again.
Protect us with Your shield in this month.

Chazzan concludes the first blessing:

בָּרוּךְ אַתָּה יהוה מָגֵן אַבְרָהָם.

Chazzan continues from אַתָּה גִּבּוֹר through לְהַחֲיוֹת מֵתִים. Then all recite:

לְצִיּוֹן, דְּרוֹר חֲשֹׁתָ בּוֹ קְפוּת, דְּבַר אוֹר יְקָרוֹת לְקִפּוּת,
הַחֹדֶשׁ אֲשֶׁר יְשׁוּעוֹת בּוֹ מַקִּיפוֹת, הַחוֹסִים בּוֹ מַתְקִיפוֹת,
וּמֵנּוּ מַתְחִילוֹת וְתוֹקְפוֹת, וְעַד רֹאשׁ לְאַרְבַּע תְּקוּפוֹת.
❖ אַרְבַּע תְּקוּפוֹת בַּשָּׁנָה, תְּחַדֵּשׁ אוֹרָם כְּבָרִאשׁוֹנָה,
כַּאֲשֶׁר שָׁמַעְנוּ כֵּן עוֹד חִישׁ נָא, הַחֲיֵנוּ בְּגֶשֶׁם בָּרִאשׁוֹן לְחָדְשֵׁי הַשָּׁנָה.

Chazzan concludes the second blessing:

בָּרוּךְ אַתָּה יהוה מְחַיֵּה הַמֵּתִים.

Kedushah (p. 464) is recited at this point.
Chazzan continues from לְדוֹר וָדוֹר through וְקָדוֹשׁ אַתָּה. Then all recite:

הִנֵּה, זֶה בָּא לִפְרָקִים, זִמּוּן לִגְאוֹל רְצוּצִים מֵאֲרָקִים,
הַחֹדֶשׁ אֲשֶׁר רְבִיבִים בּוֹ מְרִיקִים, חַשְׁרַת מַיִם לְמַלֹּאת רֵקִים,
טִיעוֹת לְרַוּוֹת וִירָקִים, טְלָאִים בּוֹ לְהָקִים בְּאַרְבָּעָה פְרָקִים.
❖ אַרְבָּעָה פְרָקִים כְּבַמַּחֲזֶה, בְּאַרְתָּ זֶה מִזֶּה לַחוֹזֶה,
כַּאֲשֶׁר שָׁמַעְנוּ כֵּן עוֹד נֶחֱזֶה, וְנַעֲרִיצְךָ קָדוֹשׁ בַּחֹדֶשׁ הַזֶּה.

Chazzan concludes the third blessing:

בָּרוּךְ אַתָּה יהוה הָאֵל הַקָּדוֹשׁ.

Chazzan continues from תִּכַּנְתָּ שַׁבָּת through מְקַדְּשֵׁי שְׁמֶךָ;
on Rosh Chodesh from אַתָּה יָצַרְתָּ through לָהֶם קָבָעְתָּ. Then all recite:

הִנָּם, יָמִים הַמְבוֹרָכִים, יוֹרֶה וּמַלְקוֹשׁ בְּאִבָּם פּוֹרְכִים,
כֹּחַ תֵּת בַּאֲבִיבִים רַכִּים, כַּרְמֶל לְהַקְלִיא אָבִיב פֵּרוּכִים,
לְשַׁנֵּן מִפְעָלוֹת מֵצִיץ מֵחֲרַכִּים, לְפָנָיו קוֹרְאִים עִנְיַן אַרְבָּעָה עֲרָכִים.
❖ אַרְבָּעָה עֲרָכִים אֲשַׁנְּנָה, סִפּוּר מִסּוֹת פִּרְחֵי שׁוֹשַׁנָּה,
כַּאֲשֶׁר שָׁמַעְנוּ כֵּן עוֹד חִישׁ נָא, עַנְּגֵנוּ בְּנֶפֶשׁ בָּרִאשׁוֹן לְחָדְשֵׁי הַשָּׁנָה.

Chazzan concludes the fourth blessing:

בָּרוּךְ אַתָּה יהוה מְקַדֵּשׁ הַשַּׁבָּת (on Rosh Chodesh—וְיִשְׂרָאֵל וְרָאשֵׁי חֳדָשִׁים).

Chazzan continues from רְצֵה through לְצִיּוֹן בְּרַחֲמִים. Then all recite:

וְלִירוּשָׁלַיִם, מוֹפֵת הוּחַק בּוֹ כַּסּוֹת, מֵעֵין כָּל חַי לְהִתְכַּסּוֹת,
נְקָמוֹת אֲשֶׁר בְּלֵב מְכֻסּוֹת,
נִתְכְּנוּ בְּמוֹעֵד זֶה הֱיוֹת טְכוּסוֹת,
שֶׂה לְבֵית אָבוֹת מְנוֹת בְּמִכְסוֹת, סַבּוֹת עָלָיו עָסִיס אַרְבָּעָה כּוֹסוֹת.
❖ אַרְבָּעָה כּוֹסוֹת כְּבַמַּחֲזֶה, בֵּאַרְתָּ זֶה מִזֶּה לַחוֹזֶה.
כַּאֲשֶׁר שָׁמַעְנוּ כֵּן עוֹד נֶחֱזֶה, רַצֵּנוּ כְּשֵׂי בַּחֹדֶשׁ הַזֶּה.

This is appropriate to the month of Nissan, which is the month of redemption. The verse reads: רִאשׁוֹן לְצִיּוֹן הִנֵּה הִנָּם וְלִירוּשָׁלַיִם מְבַשֵּׂר אֶתֵּן, *When the first one cares about Zion* [i.e. Darius], *they* [i.e., the elders] *will be ready, and for Jerusalem I will appoint a bearer of good tidings.*

Chazzan concludes the first blessing:

Blessed are You, HASHEM, Shield of Abraham.

Chazzan continues from *'You are...mighty'* through *'to resuscitate the dead.'* Then all recite:

לְצִיּוֹן *In this month You hastened Israel's freedom to bring it near to Zion,*
and to reveal the precious light of the Word,
this month in which salvations follow quickly upon one another,
They grow ever stronger for those who trust in Him,
and from it grow increasingly stronger;
it was appointed as the head of the four seasons.
∵ *There are four seasons in the year—may You renew their light as at creation,*
as we heard of Your past miracles, may You hasten to do them again.
Resuscitate us with life-giving rain in this first of the year's months.

Chazzan concludes the second blessing:

Blessed are You, HASHEM, Who resuscitates the dead.

Kedushah (p. 464) is recited at this point.

Chazzan continues from *'From generation...'* through *'and holy King.'* Then all recite:

הִנֵּה *Behold, the Messiah can come at specific intervals,*
ready to redeem the broken nation from the countries,
in this month when the clouds empty their springtime rains,
assembled waters filling cisterns,.
watering trees and greens,
to stand up Your sheep [Israel] in the four annual periods of judgment.
∵ *Four new years were taught in the vision,*
You—of Whom we say 'This is my God'—explained it to the seer in this Torah;
as we heard of Your past miracles, so may we see them once again.
And we shall revere You, O Holy One, in this month.

Chazzan concludes the third blessing:

Blessed are You, HASHEM, the holy God.

Chazzan continues from *'You established the Sabbath'* through *'the sanctifiers of Your Name';* on Rosh Chodesh from *'You fashioned'* through *'New Moons for them.'* Then all recite:

הִנָּם *These are blessed days, the early and late rains break into the growing crops,*
giving strength to the delicate stalks,
the kernels that will be roasted until crunchy and brittle,
days in which to recount the deed of the One Who peers through lattices,
before Him Jews read the subjects of the four ordered chapters.
∵ *I will repeat the four chapters,*
relating the gifts given by the blossoming rose-like nation;
as we heard of Your past miracles, so may You hasten to do them again
to delight us with tranquility in this first of the year's months.

Chazzan concludes the fourth blessing:

Blessed are You, HASHEM, Who sanctifies the Sabbath
(on Rosh Chodesh add: *Israel and the New Moons).*

Chazzan continues from *'Be favorable'* through *'to Zion in compassion.'* Then all recite:

וְלִירוּשָׁלַיִם *The future miracles of Jerusalem are inscribed but hidden,*
as Daniel was commanded to conceal that secret from all the living,
the vengeances that are concealed in God's heart,
readied for this festival to come about in the foreordained sequence.
The sheep for a family group had its members registered
and, reclining, they drank four cups of wine.
∵ *Four cups as in the dream of Pharaoh's wine steward,*
You—of Whom we say 'This is my God'—explained it to the seer in this Torah
[that they allude to the bitter cups of punishment that will befall Israel's enemies,]
As we heard of Your past miracles, so may we see them once again.
Find favor in us as in a Temple offering in this month.

Chazzan concludes the fifth blessing:

בָּרוּךְ אַתָּה יהוה הַמַּחֲזִיר שְׁכִינָתוֹ לְצִיּוֹן.

Chazzan continues from מוֹדִים through וְעֶזְרָתֵנוּ סֶלָה. Then all recite:

מְבַשֵּׂר, עִם זְכִיּוֹת, עֲצוּרִים לְהַעֲלוֹת מִצּוּל דָּכְיוֹת,
פְּדוּיִם חִוָּה בְּמַשְׂכִּיּוֹת, **פְּ**צוֹחַ שִׁירִים תְּמוּר בְּכִיּוֹת,
צִבְאוֹת כָּל חֶמְדַּת שְׂכִיּוֹת, **צֵ**את לַמֶּרְחָב מִלַּחַץ אַרְבַּע מַלְכֻיּוֹת.
❖ אַרְבַּע מַלְכֻיּוֹת נָדוּשׁ נָא, בְּמַדּוּתְךָ פָּעֳלָתָם כְּבָרִאשׁוֹנָה,
כַּאֲשֶׁר שָׁמַעְנוּ כֵּן עוֹד חִישׁ נָא,
וְתֵיטִיב לָנוּ בְּטוּבְךָ בָּרִאשׁוֹן לְחָדְשֵׁי הַשָּׁנָה.

Chazzan concludes the sixth blessing:

בָּרוּךְ אַתָּה יהוה הַטּוֹב שִׁמְךָ וּלְךָ נָאֶה לְהוֹדוֹת.

Chazzan continues from ברכת כהנים through בִּשְׁלוֹמֶךָ. Then all recite:

אֶתֵּן קוֹל כְּשׁוֹרְרוּ רָאשִׁים, **קְ**רֹא בְגָרוֹן בְּגֵיא הַחֲרָשִׁים,
רָאשֵׁי תַנִּינִים אֲשֶׁר עַל גַּבֵּי חוֹרְשִׁים, **רְ**אוּתָם בְּזֶה חֹדֶשׁ מְגֹרָשִׁים,
שִׁיר חָדָשׁ וְהֶגֶה מִדְרָשִׁים, **תְּ**רַנֵּנָּה שְׂפָתֵי בְּשׁוּרֵי אַרְבָּעָה חֲרָשִׁים.
❖ אַרְבָּעָה חָרָשִׁים כְּבְמַחֲזֶה, בֶּאֱרַתָּ זֶה מִזֶּה לַחוֹזֶה,
כַּאֲשֶׁר שָׁמַעְנוּ כֵּן עוֹד נֶחֱזֶה, בָּרְכֵנוּ בַשָּׁלוֹם בַּחֹדֶשׁ הַזֶּה.

Chazzan concludes the seventh blessing:

בָּרוּךְ אַתָּה יהוה הַמְבָרֵךְ אֶת עַמּוֹ יִשְׂרָאֵל בַּשָּׁלוֹם.

Chazzan recites Full-*Kaddish* (p. 474) and *Mussaf* is continued (p. 476).

יוצר לשבת הגדול

The *chazzan* begins his repetition of the *Shacharis Shemoneh Esrei:*

אֲדֹנָי שְׂפָתַי תִּפְתָּח, וּפִי יַגִּיד תְּהִלָּתֶךָ.

בָּרוּךְ אַתָּה יהוה אֱלֹהֵינוּ וֵאלֹהֵי אֲבוֹתֵינוּ, אֱלֹהֵי אַבְרָהָם, אֱלֹהֵי יִצְחָק, וֵאלֹהֵי יַעֲקֹב, הָאֵל הַגָּדוֹל הַגִּבּוֹר וְהַנּוֹרָא, אֵל עֶלְיוֹן, גּוֹמֵל חֲסָדִים טוֹבִים וְקוֹנֵה הַכֹּל, וְזוֹכֵר חַסְדֵי אָבוֹת, וּמֵבִיא גוֹאֵל לִבְנֵי בְנֵיהֶם, לְמַעַן שְׁמוֹ בְּאַהֲבָה. מֶלֶךְ עוֹזֵר וּמוֹשִׁיעַ וּמָגֵן.

Congregation, followed by *chazzan,* recites:

מִסּוֹד חֲכָמִים וּנְבוֹנִים, וּמִלֶּמֶד דַּעַת מְבִינִים.
אֶפְתְּחָה פִּי בְּשִׁיר וּרְנָנִים. לְהוֹדוֹת וּלְהַלֵּל פְּנֵי שׁוֹכֵן מְעוֹנִים.

All continue:

אֱלֹהִים בְּצַעְדְּךָ הַכּוֹת פַּתְרוֹס, **בְּ**תָקְעַתָּ חֵילָם מִבְצָרֵיהֶם לַהֲרוֹס,
גָּאַלְתָּ עַמְּךָ בְּנֵבֶל קַתְרוֹס, **דְּ**רַרְתָּם וְהִבְרַרְתָּם כְּסֹלֶת לָרוֹס.

שַׁבָּת הַגָּדוֹל / The Great Sabbath

On the tenth of Nissan just prior to the Exodus, a day that fell on the Sabbath, the Jewish people took the lambs for the Pesach offering that they would bring on Erev Pesach. Sheep were worshiped by the Egyptians, but the infuriated people of Egypt were helpless to

Chazzan concludes the fifth blessing:

Blessed are You, HASHEM, Who restores His Presence to Zion.

Chazzan continues from *'We gratefully thank'* through *'and help, selah!'* Then all recite:

מְבַשֵּׂר *God will bring good tidings to the people with merits,*
to elevate the captives from the depth of oppression,
to tell His redeemed through His visionaries, breaking out in songs instead of tears,
giving His legions all exquisite treasures,
going to expansiveness from the oppression of the Four Kingdoms.
∴ *Please trample the Four Kingdoms*
in the measure of their acts as You did in early times;
as we heard of Your miracles, so may You hasten to do them again,
and benefit us with Your good in this first of the year's months.

Chazzan concludes the sixth blessing:

Blessed are You, HASHEM, Your Name is 'The Beneficent One'
and to You it is fitting to give thanks.

Chazzan continues from the Priestly Blessings through *'with Your peace.'* Then all recite:

אֶתֵּן *I will raise my voice as the early leaders Moses and Aaron did at the Sea,*
calling out from the throat in the plowed-under valley of Jerusalem.
The Egyptian sea-serpent's leaders plowed on my enslaved back,
but in this month we saw them driven out,
so too, a new song and the ideas that are expounded
will my lips sing joyously when I see the four artisans of spiritual redemption
[Messiah son of David, Messiah son of Joseph, Elijah, and Shem son of Noah].
∴ *The four artisans as in the vision, You — of Whom we say 'This is my God' —*
explained it to the prophet Zachariah in this Torah,
as we heard of Your miracles so may we see them again.
Bless us with peace in this month.

Chazzan concludes the seventh blessing:

Blessed are You, HASHEM, Who blesses His people Israel with peace.

Chazzan recites Full-*Kaddish* (p. 474) and *Mussaf* is continued (p. 476).

YOTZER FOR SHABBOS HAGADOL

The *chazzan* begins his repetition of the *Shacharis Shemoneh Esrei:*

My Lord, open my lips, that my mouth may declare Your praise.

בָּרוּךְ *Blessed are You, HASHEM, our God and the God of our forefathers, God of Abraham, God of Isaac, and God of Jacob; the great, mighty, and awesome God, the supreme God, Who bestows beneficial kindnesses and creates everything, Who recalls the kindnesses of the Patriarchs and brings a Redeemer to their children's children, for His Name's sake, with love. O King, Helper, Savior, and Shield.*

Congregation, followed by *chazzan,* recites:

מִסּוֹד *Based on the tradition of our wise and discerning teachers,*
and the teaching derived from the knowledge of the discerning,
I open my mouth in song to praise Him Who dwells on high.

All continue:

אֱלֹהִים *O God, when You stepped forth to smite Pasros [Egypt],*
You punctured their army to smash their fortresses,
You redeemed Your people with lyre and tambourine,
You proclaimed their freedom and chose them like the finest flour for kneading.

---

prevent the Jewish people from slaughtering the animals. This miracle demonstrated openly that God was protecting Israel, and its anniversary has remained a day of celebration. However, since Miriam the Prophetess died on 10 Nissan forty years later, it would have been

הִגַּרְתָּ לַגַּי הֲמוֹן פִּיבֶסֶת, **וְ**נִקְּתָה לָאָרֶץ בִּטְרִיָּה נֶחְבֶּסֶת,
זְנוּחָה זָרְחָה בְּדַם מִתְבּוֹסֶסֶת, **חֲ**לָצָהּ וְנִגְהָצָה בִּרְחִיצָה וְתִכְבּוֹסֶת.
טֶרֶם מֵרוֹר מִמְּעַנִּים יֶשְׁבַּת, **יְ**שׁוּעָה צָמְחָה לִנְצוּרֵי כְּבָבַת.
❖ **כִּ**תַּרְתָּ כְּלִיל לְנֶפֶשׁ מְשִׁיבַת, **לְ**שֶׁעָבַר קִדַּמְתָּ מַתַּן שַׁבָּת.

All continue:

סֶלָה אֲרוֹמִמְךָ מוֹשִׁיעַ וְשַׁלִּיט, מוֹצִיאִי לְחָפְשִׁי מִבֵּית מַעֲלִיט.
❖ סַכּוֹתָה לְרָאשִׁי לְהַשְׁאִיר פָּלִיט, גָּנוֹן וְהַצִּיל פָּסוֹחַ וְהִמְלִיט.

Chazzan continues:

בָּרוּךְ אַתָּה יהוה מָגֵן אַבְרָהָם.

אַתָּה גִּבּוֹר לְעוֹלָם אֲדֹנָי, מְחַיֵּה מֵתִים אַתָּה, רַב לְהוֹשִׁיעַ. מַשִּׁיב הָרוּחַ וּמוֹרִיד הַגֶּשֶׁם. מְכַלְכֵּל חַיִּים בְּחֶסֶד, מְחַיֵּה מֵתִים בְּרַחֲמִים רַבִּים, סוֹמֵךְ נוֹפְלִים, וְרוֹפֵא חוֹלִים, וּמַתִּיר אֲסוּרִים, וּמְקַיֵּם אֱמוּנָתוֹ לִישֵׁנֵי עָפָר. מִי כָמוֹךָ בַּעַל גְּבוּרוֹת, וּמִי דּוֹמֶה לָּךְ, מֶלֶךְ מֵמִית וּמְחַיֶּה וּמַצְמִיחַ יְשׁוּעָה. וְנֶאֱמָן אַתָּה לְהַחֲיוֹת מֵתִים.

All continue:

מִמַּסְגֵּר אַסִּיר בְּצֵאת לְחוֹפֶשׁ, **נ**ִתְנוֹסֵס נֵס בִּטְבִיעַת רֶפֶשׁ,
סְגַבְתָּם חוֹק מַרְגּוֹעַ וָנוֹפֶשׁ, **עָ**רוֹךְ תְּחִלָּה לִמְשִׁיבַת נֶפֶשׁ.
פֵּרוּשׁוֹ וְטַעְמוֹ צִוִּיתָהּ בְּמָרָה, **צִ**חֲצוּחַ דָּתוֹ לְהָבִין וּלְגָמְרָה,
קְבִיעַת קְדֻשָּׁתוֹ בִּזְכִירָה וּשְׁמִירָה, **ר**וֹן לְהָפִיק בְּתוֹדָה וְזִמְרָה.
שְׁפָטִים גְּדוֹלִים עָשִׂיתָ בְּצוֹעַן, **שִׁ**פְרַרְתָּ אֹהֶל בַּל יִצְעָן.
❖ **תְּ**עוּבִים פַּסּוּ בְּאַף לְהַכְנִיעָן, **תָּ**קְפָה חֲרָדָה בֶּאֱדוֹם וּכְנָעַן.

All continue:

לִבְּךָ וְעֵינֶיךָ לְהֵיכָלְךָ תְּשׁוֹבֵב, דָּשֵׁן וְשָׁמֵן לְעַמְּךָ יְנוֹבֵב.
❖ תְּכוֹנֵן אֻלָמְךָ מִזְבֵּחַ וְסוֹבֵב, לְהַגְשִׁים תֶּחִי יְשֵׁנִים דּוֹבֵב.

Chazzan continues:

בָּרוּךְ אַתָּה יהוה מְחַיֵּה הַמֵּתִים.

All continue:

יִשְׁעִי וּכְבוֹדִי מִשְׂגַּבִּי וּמְנוּסִי, **וְ**נִצָּב לָרִיב עַל אוֹנְסִי,
סוֹכְכִי בְּאֶבְרָתוֹ יהוה נִסִּי.
פּוֹרֵעַ וְגוֹבֶה דִּין קְנָסִי, **בְּ**הִלּוֹ נֵרוֹ עֲלֵי רֹאשִׁי,
רָכַב עַל עָב קַל מֵעִנּוּי לְגָרְשִׁי.
שַׁחַת מִבְצָר מַחֲלִישִׁי וְחוֹרְשִׁי, **מְ**לוֹן קִצּוֹ נָחֲנֵי דוֹרְשִׁי,
וּמִמְּעוֹן קָדְשׁוֹ חָבַשׁ כְּאֵבִי.
❖ **אָ**דוֹן מִמַּעַיְנֵי הַיְשׁוּעָה הִשְׁאִיבִי, **לִ**מְּדַנִי לָנוּחַ בַּשַּׁבָּת מֵהַדְאִיבִי,
לְהַאֲכִילִי נַחֲלַת יַעֲקֹב אָבִי.

---

inappropriate to celebrate on that date, therefore the event was marked on the Sabbath before Pesach, which became known as *Shabbos HaGadol*, the Great Sabbath.

You cast down into a valley the host of Pi-Beses [Egypt],
and it lay on the ground emptied of its wealth, with many open wounds,
while the once-forlorn Israel is marked with blood [of circumcision and Pesach].
She is released and well-groomed, cleansed in spirit and laundered without.
Even before the afflicted nation won rest from bitter labor,
salvation began to sprout for the nation guarded like the apple of an eye,
∴ when You crowned them with a crown that refreshes the soul,
for before they were freed You gave them the gift of the Sabbath.

All continue:

סֶלָה *Forever will I exalt You, O Savior and Master,*
Who delivered me to freedom from the house of darkness.
∴ You sheltered my head to let me survive,
You protected and rescued, passed over and removed.

Chazzan continues:

Blessed are You, HASHEM, Shield of Abraham.

אַתָּה *You are eternally mighty, my Lord, the Resuscitator of the dead are You; abundantly able to save, Who makes the wind blow and makes the rain descend; Who sustains the living with kindness, resuscitates the dead with abundant mercy, supports the fallen, heals the sick, releases the confined, and maintains His faith to those asleep in the dust. Who is like You, O Master of mighty deeds, and who is comparable to You, O King Who causes death and restores life and makes salvation sprout! And You are faithful to resuscitate the dead.*

All continue:

מִמַּסְגֵּר *When the prisoner left his dungeon for freedom,*
You had given them a proud banner while in the muck —
You strengthened them with the Sabbath, a decree of refreshment and rest,
to observe even before receiving the Torah that restores the soul.
Its explanation and reason You taught at Marah;
then its law was burnished with understanding and completion
when its holiness was established at Sinai with commandments to remember
and observe, uttering glad songs of thanksgiving and praise.
You performed great judgment against Tzoan [Egypt],
but You beautified Israel with Your sacred cloud that they not become nomads.
∴ The abominable Egyptians vanished in wrath that subjugated them,
and trembling overcame Edom and Canaan.

All continue:

לִבְּךָ *Return Your heart and eyes to Your Sanctuary,*
may luscious fruit and oil blossom for Your people.
∴ Re-establish Your Temple with the Altar and its walkway,
to bring life-giving rain to return speech to the sleeping dead.

Chazzan continues:

Blessed are You, HASHEM, Who resuscitates the dead.

All continue:

יִשְׁעִי *My salvation and my honor, my fortress and my refuge,*
He takes up the grievance against those who overpower me,
He shelters me with His pinion, HASHEM, my banner.
He will pay me and collect from my foes the just penalty due me,
when He will kindle His flame above my head.
He rode to Egypt on a swift cloud to drive me away from affliction.
He destroyed the fortress of those who weakened me and plowed me under;
to my ultimate destination, Jerusalem, He Who sought me out guided me,
and from His holy heavenly abode He healed my hurt.
∴ The Lord made me draw from the wellsprings of salvation.
He taught to rest on the Sabbath and not to aggravate myself,
to feed me from the boundless heritage of Jacob, my father.

Congregation, followed by *chazzan*, recites aloud:

יִמְלֹךְ יהוה לְעוֹלָם אֱלֹהַיִךְ צִיּוֹן לְדֹר וָדֹר הַלְלוּיָהּ.
וְאַתָּה קָדוֹשׁ יוֹשֵׁב תְּהִלּוֹת יִשְׂרָאֵל אֵל נָא.

All continue:

כֶּרֶם חֶמֶד נֶטַע שַׁעֲשׁוּעִים, בְּלוּסָה וּמְכֻסְכֶּסֶת שִׁנֵּי רְשָׁעִים,
וְנִגְלֵיתָ לְחַלְּצָהּ מִבֵּין פּוֹשְׁעִים, בְּחֵיל אֲלָפִים רִבָבוֹת תִּשְׁעִים,
וּבְצֶדֶק נִפְקַד לְתֶשַׁע וְתִשְׁעִים, הָעֲמֻסָה מַשָּׂא פְּרָדִים תִּשְׁעִים,
פָּנִיתָ לְפָנֶיהָ מְלָכִים וְשׁוֹעִים, שִׁלְּחָה קְצִירֶיהָ וְעָלוּ מוֹשִׁיעִים,
וּלְחֶלְקָהּ נָטְלָה שִׁבְעָה מִשִּׁבְעִים, שֶׁעִשּׂוּר נְכָסִים לְבָנוֹת קְבוּעִים,
וּבִישִׁימוֹן דֶּרֶךְ הָלְכוּ אַרְבָּעִים,
❖ מַעֲדַנֵּי מֶלֶךְ אוֹכְלִים וּשְׂבֵעִים, קָדְשָׁתוֹ מְתַנִּים וְרֶנֶן מַבִּיעִים.

Congregation, followed by *chazzan*, recites aloud:

חַי וְקַיָּם נוֹרָא וּמָרוֹם וְקָדוֹשׁ.

All continue:

יָרַדְתָּ לְהַצִּיל עַמֶּךָ, לְהוֹדִיעָם אֹרַח נָעֳמֶךָ,
לְמַשּׂאוֹת תָּרִים פְּעָמֶיךָ, לְהַכְנִיעַ רוֹדִים בְּזַעְמֶךָ.
וּכְהָתֵם הֲמוֹן שׁוֹדְדִים, כָּלוּ שָׂרִים וּגְדוּדִים.
וְהִגָּעָה עֵת דּוֹדִים, צָמְחָה יְשׁוּעָה לִידִידִים.
סוֹד כְּיָצָא בְּהַנְוָיָה, צֵאת עֲגוּמִים לָרְוָיָה,
נֶחֱצוּ צִירִים לִשְׁבִיָּה, שְׁנֵי תָאֳמֵי צִבְיָּה.
פְּרוּס כֵּרָה שֶׁל מֶלֶךְ, אֵרְעוּ לְשַׂר פֶּלֶךְ,
כָּל הַבָּא לַמֶּלֶךְ, אֶשְׁכָּר לְפָנָיו מְהַלֵּךְ.
בְּשַׁעַר בַּת כַּסְלוּחַ, נִצָּבִים מַלְאֲכֵי שִׁלּוּחַ,
נִסְתַּכְּלוּ קוֹטְפֵי מַלּוּחַ, בְּאֵין קוֹמֶץ וְקִלּוּחַ.
רַהַב לֵבָב גִּנָּה, לִלְגְיוֹנָיו קָפַץ וּמִנָּה,
יִכָּנֵס הַבָּא בְּמָנָה, וְאֵלֶּה לְבַד בָּאַחֲרוֹנָה.
שָׁאַל פֶּתֶן חֵרֵשׁ, מִי נִדְרָשׁ וְהַדּוֹרֵשׁ,
הֱשִׁיבוּהוּ הָפַךְ מְשׁוֹרֵשׁ, כָּלָה גָּרֵשׁ יְגָרֵשׁ.
מָרַד זֵד בְּעִקּוּלוֹ, מַה לִּי וּלְקוּלוֹ,
וְלֹא הִרְצָנִי בְּשִׁקְלוֹ, כְּנִשְׁעָן עַל מַקְלוֹ.
וְאָז צִפָּה בָּאֱלִילִים, הֲיֵשׁ יָדָיו גְּלִילִים,
צָגוּ עָלָיו בִּפְלִילִים, אֵין פְּנוּת בַּחֲלָלִים.
אֱוִיל מוּכָן לַעֲבָרוֹת, מַה לַּכֹּהֵן בִּקְבָרוֹת,
הֲלֹא בְּתֵכֶל הַדִּבְּרוֹת, נוֹדַע בַּעַל גְּבוּרוֹת.
לוֹבֵשׁ צֶדֶק נֶאְזָר, לְהָשִׁיב גְּמוּל לְאַכְזָר,
הָפַךְ דֶּרֶךְ אִישׁ וָזָר, עֲמָלוֹ בְּרֹאשׁוֹ חָזָר.

Congregation, followed by *chazzan*, recites aloud:

HASHEM shall reign forever — your God, O Zion — from generation to generation, Halleluyah!
You, O Holy One, are enthroned upon Israel's praises — please, O God.

All continue:

כֶּרֶם *Israel — a desireable vineyard, a delightful plant —*
was soiled and mangled by the teeth of the wicked,
but You appeared to rescue it from the wanton with a force of ninety myriads.
In the merit of Abraham who was promised a son at the age of ninety-nine,
each Jew took along ninety loaded mules [from Egypt].
Before Israel You swept away thirty-one kings and wealthy rulers.
Israel spread its boughs to the Sea and saviors ascended
and for its portion took the seven Canaanite nations out of the seventy nations,
like a tenth of an inheritance that is set aside for each daughter,
on a path of desolation they traveled forty years,
∴ *eating with satisfaction the monarch's delicacies,*
they speak of His holiness and utter glad song.

Congregation, followed by *chazzan*, recites aloud:

Living and Enduring One, Awesome, Exalted, and Holy!

All continue:

יָרַדְתָּ *You descended to rescue Your nation, to inform them of Your pleasant way,*
You lifted Your footsteps to wreak ruin, to subjugate oppressors with Your fury.
When the plundering multitude was done in
its angels above and military bands below were destroyed,
the time of love came when the Torah was given
and salvation sprouted for the beloved.
When the secret was declared in heaven that the time of redemption had come,
and the mournful ones should go out to satiety,
to the captive nation hastened the two emissaries,
Moses and Aaron, [with the swiftness of] two twins of the gazelle.
A kingly repast had been spread out for Pharaoh the head of the region,
and whoever came to the king was preceded by a gift.
In the gate of the Casluchite [Egyptian] palace stood God's emissaries,
the mindless guards stared at them for they bore no gifts,
not even a handful of something or a cabbage stalk.
The arrogant-hearted Pharaoh disparaged them;
to his legions he burst out with a command:
'Whoever comes with a gift may enter, but these should be alone and last.'
The uncomprehending viper [Pharaoh] asked: 'What is requested and Who requests?'
Moses and Aaron answered him: 'He Who turns over mountains by their roots
demands that His entire people be driven out.'
Perversely the willful Pharaoh rebelled: 'What care I about Him or His voice?
He has not appeased me with His monetary gift,
but comes like a pauper leaning on his stick.'
He looked in his registry of idols:
'Does it list HASHEM *Whose arms are like rolls of fine gold?'*
Moses and Aaron presented their arguments: 'Do not seek God among the dead.
Fool who is destined for the grave, what business has a Kohen in a cemetery?
When our words are completed, you will know Who is the One with power!
He Who dons righteousness is girded to requite the cruel one;
one who reverses the proper way of a man and a stranger,
his trouble will come back upon his head.

❖ חֲנָמַל בָּרָד וּרְשָׁפִים, זִלְעֵף בַּעֲלֵי כְשָׁפִים,
קָרְסוּ כָּרְעוּ כְּשׁוּפִים, עֲפַר אֶרֶץ שׁוֹאֲפִים.

Chazzan continues:

אֵל נָא לְעוֹלָם תֻּעֲרָץ, וּלְעוֹלָם תְּקֻדָּשׁ, וּלְעוֹלְמֵי עוֹלָמִים תִּמְלוֹךְ וְתִתְנַשֵּׂא, הָאֵל מֶלֶךְ נוֹרָא מָרוֹם וְקָדוֹשׁ, כִּי אַתָּה הוּא מֶלֶךְ מַלְכֵי הַמְּלָכִים, מַלְכוּתוֹ נֶצַח. נוֹרְאוֹתָיו שִׂיחוּ, סַפְּרוּ עֻזּוֹ, פָּאֲרוּהוּ צְבָאָיו, קַדְּשׁוּהוּ רוֹמְמוּהוּ, רוֹן שִׁיר וָשֶׁבַח, תֹּקֶף תְּהִלּוֹת תִּפְאַרְתּוֹ.

Chazzan, followed by congregation, recites aloud:

יוֹצְאֵי חִפָּזוֹן, סִפְּקָם מָזוֹן, לְשׂוֹבַע וְלֹא לְרָזוֹן, קָדוֹשׁ.

All continue:

אֱמָנָה גְּדוֹלָה הָיְתָה בָעָם, **בְּ**לִי לְהִתְלוֹנֵן זֹאת הַפַּעַם
גּוֹעָה לֵאמֹר מַה נִּטְעַם.
דֶּרֶךְ שְׁלֹשָׁה נֵלֵךְ בַּמִּדְבָּר, **הִ**גִּיד מֵאָז מַנְהִיג וְדַבָּר **וְ**לֹא כִחֵד מֵהֶם דָּבָר.
זְרִיזִים חָשׁוּ לְהַקְדִּישׁ קְרוּאָיו, **חָ**סוּ בְּמַטְרִיף כָּל בְּרוּאָיו
טוֹב אֵין מַחְסוֹר לִירֵאָיו.
יָחִיד שְׁמָרָהּ לְמִדָּה שְׂרוּעָה, **כְּ**לוּלוֹתַיִךְ אֶזְכּוֹר חֶסֶד לְפָרְעָה
לֶכְתֵּךְ אַחֲרַי בַּמִּדְבָּר בְּאֶרֶץ לֹא זְרוּעָה.
מְקוֹם צִפְעוֹנִים נָחָשׁ שָׂרָף וְעַקְרָב, **נָ**סְעוּ קְדוֹשִׁים לְשֶׁמֶשׁ וְשָׁרָב
שָׁב וְעוֹלֵל וּמִקְנֶה רָב.
עֲדָרִים הִשְׂכִּילוּ מַדָּע לְהַחְכִּימָם, **פְּ**סַח מִשְׁאֲרוֹת נָשְׂאוּ בְּהַשְׁכִּימָם
צְרוּרוֹת בְּשִׂמְלוֹתָם עַל שִׁכְמָם.
קִטּוּף הָעִסָּה בַּחֲרָרָה קְמוּצָה, **רְ**צוּפָה בְּרָאשֵׁיהֶם שֶׁלֹּא חֻמָּצָה
שֶׁמֶשׁ שְׁזָפַתָּה וַאֲכָלוּהָ מַצָּה.
❖ **תֻּ**פִינֵי שִׁשִּׁים וְאַחַת בְּמִשְׁטָר, טָעֲמוּ וְאָרְחוּ בְּשִׁיּוּר הַמְּנֻטָּר
עַד לֶחֶם מִשָּׁמַיִם הֻמְטָר.

All continue:

וּבְכֵן וַיְהִי בַּחֲצִי הַלַּיְלָה.

אָז רוֹב נִסִּים הִפְלֵאתָ בַּלַּיְלָה,
בְּרֹאשׁ אַשְׁמוֹרֶת זֶה הַלַּיְלָה,
גֵּר צֶדֶק נִצַּחְתּוֹ כְּנֶחֱלַק לוֹ לַיְלָה, — וַיְהִי בַּחֲצִי הַלַּיְלָה.
דַּנְתָּ מֶלֶךְ גְּרָר בַּחֲלוֹם הַלַּיְלָה,
הִפְחַדְתָּ אֲרַמִּי בְּאֶמֶשׁ לַיְלָה,
וַיָּשַׂר יִשְׂרָאֵל לְמַלְאָךְ וַיּוּכַל לוֹ לַיְלָה, — וַיְהִי בַּחֲצִי הַלַּיְלָה.
זֶרַע בְּכוֹרֵי פַתְרוֹס מָחַצְתָּ בַּחֲצִי הַלַּיְלָה,
חֵילָם לֹא מָצְאוּ בְּקוּמָם בַּלַּיְלָה,
טִיסַת נְגִיד חֲרֹשֶׁת סִלִּיתָ בְכוֹכְבֵי לַיְלָה, — וַיְהִי בַּחֲצִי הַלַּיְלָה.

∴ *Locusts, hail, and flames will terrify the sorcerous nation.*
They will bend and fall to their knees in humiliation,
swallowing the dust of the earth.'

Chazzan continues:

אֵל *O God, may You always be lauded and always be sanctified, and forever reign and be uplifted, the God, King, awesome, exalted, and holy, for You are the King Who reigns over kings, Whose sovereignty is eternal. Speak of His wonders, declare His strength, glorify Him, O His legions; sanctify Him, exalt Him. Sing song and praise, glorify Him with powerful psalms of praise.*

Chazzan, followed by congregation, recites aloud:

Israel, which left Egypt hurriedly — He supplied them with food for satiety and not for hunger, the Holy One!

All continue:

אֲמָנָה *The people possessed great faith — this time they did not complain,*
saying bleatingly: 'What will we eat?'
'We will take a three-day trip in the Wilderness,'
they were told at the start by the leader, Moses, and the spokesman, Aaron,
who did not withhold any information from them.
Those alacritous two hastened to sanctify God's summoned ones,
who took shelter in the One Who feeds all His creatures,
the Good One Whose reverent ones feel no deprivation.
The Unique One preserved this expanding trait of faith:
'I shall remember your loving devotion and reward it,
your going after me in the Wilderness, in an unsown land.
A place of vipers, snakes, fiery serpents, and scorpions;
the holy ones journeyed through sun and burning heat:
old, young, and abundant herds.'
The Jewish flocks used knowledge intelligently to become wise,
when they stood up they carried some of their dough,
bound in their garments on their shoulder.
The prepared dough, in the form of small cakes,
laid out on their heads remaining unleavened,
the sun baked it and they ate it as matzah.
∴ *From the baking they ate sixty-one straight meals,*
they tasted and dined on these safeguarded leftovers
until food rained down from heaven.

All continue:

It came to pass* at midnight.

אָז *Of old, You performed many miracles by night.*
At the beginning of the first watch of this night.
To the righteous convert [Abraham] You gave victories
when the night was divided for him. *It came to pass at midnight.*
You judged the King of Gerar [Abimelech with death] in a dream by night.
You frightened the Aramean [Laban] in the dark of night.
Israel [Jacob] fought with an angel and overcame him by night.
It came to pass at midnight.
The first-born children of Pasros [the Egyptians] You crushed at midnight.
They did not find their host when they arose at night.
You routed the army of the prince of Charoshes [Sisera] with the stars of night.
It came to pass at midnight.

⁂ וּבְכֵן וַיְהִי — *It came to pass.* Pesach night is לֵיל שִׁמּוּרִים, *a night for protection,* because on it God has performed many miracles for the Jewish people. This poem lists thirteen of them.

יָעַץ מְחָרֵף לְנוֹפֵף אִוּוּי הוֹבַשְׁתָּ פְגָרָיו בַּלַּיְלָה,
כָּרַע בֵּל וּמַצָּבוֹ בְּאִשׁוֹן לַיְלָה,
לְאִישׁ חֲמוּדוֹת נִגְלָה רָז חֲזוֹת לַיְלָה, וַיְהִי בַּחֲצִי הַלַּיְלָה.

מִשְׁתַּכֵּר בִּכְלֵי קֹדֶשׁ נֶהֱרַג בּוֹ בַּלַּיְלָה,
נוֹשַׁע מִבּוֹר אֲרָיוֹת פּוֹתֵר בִּעֲתוּתֵי לַיְלָה,
שִׂנְאָה נָטַר אֲגָגִי וְכָתַב סְפָרִים בַּלַּיְלָה, וַיְהִי בַּחֲצִי הַלַּיְלָה.

עוֹרַרְתָּ נִצְחֲךָ עָלָיו בְּנֶדֶר שְׁנַת לַיְלָה,
פּוּרָה תִדְרוֹךְ לְשׁוֹמֵר מַה מִּלַּיְלָה,
צָרַח כַּשּׁוֹמֵר וְשָׂח אָתָא בֹקֶר וְגַם לַיְלָה, וַיְהִי בַּחֲצִי הַלַּיְלָה.

❖קָרֵב יוֹם אֲשֶׁר הוּא לֹא יוֹם וְלֹא לַיְלָה,
רָם הוֹדַע כִּי לְךָ הַיּוֹם אַף לְךָ הַלַּיְלָה,
שׁוֹמְרִים הַפְקֵד לְעִירְךָ כָּל הַיּוֹם וְכָל הַלַּיְלָה,
תָּאִיר כְּאוֹר יוֹם חֶשְׁכַּת לַיְלָה, וַיְהִי בַּחֲצִי הַלַּיְלָה.

All continue:

וּבְכֵן כָּל מַחֲמֶצֶת לֹא תֹאכֵלוּ.

אָבֹא בְּחִיל לְהִתְיַצְּבָה, בְּמַעֲמַד פְּנֵי תֵבָה,
גַּשְׁתִּי לְרוֹמֵם וּלְשַׂגְּבָה, מֵרְשׁוּת דָּגוּל מֵרְבָבָה.
הִלּוּל קוֹנִי אַקְשִׁיבָה, וּבְחֵקֶר דָּתוֹ אֶתְיַשְּׁבָה,
זֹאת לָדַעַת אֲחַשְּׁבָה, מִטַּעַם חַכְמֵי יְשִׁיבָה.
טוֹעַן עוֹלָם אַמְלִיכָה, יְהָבִי עָלָיו אַשְׁלִיכָה,
כֹּרַע לְפָנָיו אֶתְהַלְּכָה, לִפְתּוֹחַ בִּדְבַר הֲלָכָה.
מִלַּת פִּי גְדוּשָׁה, נוֹצֵר חֶסֶד אַקְדִּישָׁה,
סַלְסֵל בְּדָת חֲדָשָׁה, מֵרְשׁוּת עֵדָה הַקְּדוֹשָׁה.
פְּנֵי יְשָׁרִים דּוֹבֵר, צַחְצוּחַ אֲמָרִים אֲגַבֵּר,
קִדַּמְתִּי לִטּוֹל בְּסֵבֶר, רְשׁוּת מֵרַב וְחָבֵר.
❖שַׁדַּי חֵילִי תְּאַמֵּץ, תַּעְדִּיף קֹט וְקוֹמֶץ,
לְבָאֵר בְּלִי שֶׁמֶץ, הִלְכוֹת בִּעוּר חָמֵץ.

The following is a poetic summary of the laws of *chametz, matzah,* and the *Seder.* Though it is authoritative, not all of its points are accepted by the Halachah.

אֱלֹהֵי הָרוּחוֹת לְכָל בָּשָׂר, חוֹק לְעַמּוֹ מָסַר,
וְהִזְהִירָם בִּכְתָב מוּסָר, לִבְדּוֹק חָמֵץ אוֹר לְאַרְבָּעָה עָשָׂר.
בְּשָׁעָה שֶׁאֵין בְּנֵי אָדָם מְצוּיִים בְּשׁוּקָא, וְאוֹר הַנֵּר יָפֶה לִבְדִיקָה,
אֵין בּוֹדְקִין לֹא לְאוֹר הַחַמָּה וְלֹא לְאוֹר הַלְּבָנָה וְלֹא לְאוֹר הָאֲבוּקָה,
וְצָרִיךְ לְבָרֵךְ עַל בִּעוּר חָמֵץ כְּחֻקָּה.

The blasphemer [Sennacherib] had planned to raise his hand against Jerusalem;
You laid low his dead by night.
The idol Bel was overthrown, with its pedestal, in the darkness of the night.
To the man [Daniel] in whom You delighted, the secret vision was revealed at night.
It came to pass at midnight.
He who caroused from the holy vessels [Belshazar] was slain that night.
Rescued from the lions' den was the one [Daniel] who interpreted the meaning of the terrors of the night.
Haman bore hatred in his heart and wrote proscriptions at night.
It came to pass at midnight.
You began Your triumph over him by disturbing his king's sleep at night.
You will tread the wine-press to help those who ask the watchman,
'Ah, when will there be an end to the long night?'
Like a watchman he will exclaim and say, 'Morning will come after this night.'
It came to pass at midnight.
Bring near the day [of the coming of Messiah], that is neither day nor night.
Show, Most High, that Yours is the day as well as the night.
Appoint watchmen to Your city [Jerusalem] by day and by night.
Illumine as with the light of day, the darkness of the night.
It came to pass at midnight.

All continue:

And so, you may not eat any leavened food.

אָבֹא *I come fearfully to stand erect, in position before the lectern,*
I approach to exalt and declare God's power,
with the permission of the One declared supreme by myriad angels.
I will make my listeners hear the lauding of my Maker
and I will study intently the profundity of His law,
to know this I will meditate
according to the guidance of the wise men of the academy.
I seek the counself of Him Who bears the world, I will cast my burden upon Him.
Like a pauper I will walk before Him, as I commence relating the laws of Pesach.
May my words be crammed with significance,
I will sanctify Him Who preserves kindness,
glorifying Him through the ever-new law,
with permission of this holy congregation.
In the presence of Him Who speaks upright words,
I will confidently set forth pure words,
I will confidently set forth pure words, with a genial expression
I have first sought permission from master and scholar.
Almighty, may You strengthen my ability, enhance this puny and small person,
enabling him to clarify without blunder the laws of removal of chametz.

The following is a poetic summary of the laws of *chametz, matzah,* and the *Seder.* Though it is authoritative, not all of its points are accepted by the Halachah.

אֱלֹהֵי *God, Who knows the spirits of all living beings,*
transmitted a decree to His people
and cautioned them in the Torah whose explanation is transmitted to the Sages
to search for chametz on the evening of the fourteenth of Nissan.
The time is when people are no longer in the marketplace,
and candlelight is best for the search;
one should not search by sunlight, moonlight nor torchlight,
and one must recite the blessing, 'concerning the removal of chametz.

גְּמַר מְנַטְרֵהּ עַד דְּבַתְרָא, וּמִיַּד צָרִיךְ לְבַטֵּל הַשְּׂאֹר בַּאֲמִירָה,
וְלֵימָא הָכֵי כָּל חֲמִירָא דְּאִכָּא בְּהָדָא דִירָה,
דְּלָא חֲמִיתֵּיהּ וּדְלָא בְעַרְתֵּיהּ לִבָּטֵל וְלֶהֱוֵי כְּעַפְרָא.
דְּאִי מִשְׁתַּכַּח לְאַחַר אוֹתָהּ שָׁעָה, אֵינוֹ חַיָּב בְּבַל יֵרָאֶה וּבְבַל יִמָּצֵא לְפָשְׁעָה,
וְהָרוֹצֶה אַחַר בְּדִיקָתוֹ לֶאֱכוֹל חָמֵץ וּלְשָׂבְעָה
מַה שֶּׁמְּשַׁיֵּר יַנִּיחֶנּוּ בְּצִנְעָה.
הֵיכָא דִבְדַק בְּחוֹרֵי בֵיתָא, וְהִנִּיחַ אַרְבַּע אוֹ חָמֵשׁ רִפְתָּא,
וְאִשְׁכַּח דְחָדָא מִנַּיְהוּ פַּחֲתָא, לִבְדּוֹק מֵרֵישָׁא שֶׁמָּא חֻלְדָּה לְקָחֲתָהּ.
וְכֵן תָּנוּ רַבָּנָן בְּפִרְקִין, דְּחוֹרֵי בֵיתָא וּנְקִיקִין,
עִלָּאֵי וְתַתָּאֵי אֵינָן נִבְדָּקִין, וְאֶמְצָעִים זְקוּקִין.
זְהֵרוּ גַּג הַיָּצִיעַ וְגַג מִגְדְּלִין, וְרֶפֶת בָּקָר וּמַתְבֵּן וְלוּלִין,
וְאוֹצְרוֹת יַיִן וְשֶׁמֶן הַנְּעוּלִין, לִבְדּוֹק חָמֵץ בְּלִי עוֹלִין.
חוֹר שֶׁבֵּין אָדָם לַחֲבֵרוֹ, זֶה וָזֶה בּוֹדֵק עַד שֶׁמַּגִּיעַ וּמְבַטֵּל שְׂאָרוֹ,
וְכֵן בֵּין יְהוּדִי וְעוֹבֵד כּוֹכָבִים חַיָּב לְבַעֲרוֹ,
פְּלֵימוֹ מֵקַל שֶׁמָּא יֹאמַר הָעוֹבֵד כּוֹכָבִים כְּשָׁפוֹ וַחֲבָרוֹ.
טָעֲנוּ הַמְפָרֵשׁ וְהַיּוֹצֵא בְשַׁיָּרָא, וְאֵין דַּעְתּוֹ קוֹדֶם פֶּסַח לַחֲזָרָה,
תּוֹךְ שְׁלֹשִׁים יוֹם בָּעֵי לְבַעֵר חֲמִירָא,
לִפְנֵי שְׁלֹשִׁים יוֹם אֵין זָקוּק לְבַעֲרָה.
יִשְׂרָאֵל דְּחָמֵץ אִתְפַּקֵּד לֵיהּ, וְלֵיתֵיהּ לְמָרֵיהּ לְמִשְׁקְלֵיהּ,
נַטְרֵהּ עַד אַרְבַּע דְּחָזֵי לְאָכְלֵהּ,
שְׁלִים אַרְבַּע וְלָא אָתָא לְנָכְרִי מְזַבִּין לֵיהּ.
כְּשֶׁנָּפְלָה מַפּוֹלֶת עַל חָמֵץ בְּעַרְבֵי פְסָחִים,
וְכֶלֶב אֵין יָכוֹל לְחַפֵּשׂ אַחֲרָיו בְּטוּחִים,
הֲרֵי הוּא כִּמְבוֹעָר לְרֵעִים פִּקְחִים,
וְכַמָּה חֲפִישַׁת הַכֶּלֶב שְׁלֹשָׁה טְפָחִים.
לִמְדוּ בֵּי מִלְחֵי וּבֵי קִירֵי נְקוּבִים, וּבֵי תְמָרִים וְצִיבִים,
לִבְדּוֹק אוֹתָם חַיָּבִים, וְחָצֵר פְּטוּרָה מִפְּנֵי הָעוֹרְבִים.
מוֹצֵא חָמֵץ בַּפֶּסַח בְּתוֹךְ בֵּיתוֹ, כּוֹפֶה עָלָיו כְּלִי בְּלִי רְאוּתוֹ,
וְאִם שֶׁל הֶקְדֵּשׁ הוּא אֵין צָרִיךְ לְכַסּוֹתוֹ, לְפִי שֶׁבְּדֵלִין מֵאוֹתוֹ.
נָפֵי וּפַטִּילֵי וְיוֹרָה, דְּאִשְׁתַּמֵּשׁ בְּהוּ חַמִּין חֲמִירָא,
צָרִיךְ לְגַעֲלִינְהוּ וְיַנִּיחַ בְּגוֹ רַבָּא זְעֵירָא,
וּלְרַבָּא לֶעֱבַד גַּדְנְפָא וּלְרַתְחֵיהּ בְּנוּרָא.
סַכִּינֵי דְאִשְׁתַּמֵּשׁ בְּהוּ חֲמִירָא לַאֲרוּחִין,
אִם אֶפְשָׁר לַעֲשׂוֹתָן חֲדָשִׁים הֵם מְשֻׁבָּחִין, וְאִי לָא מַגְעִילָן בְּרוֹתְחִין,
וּבִכְלֵי רִאשׁוֹן הֵם מְצַחְצָחִין, וְעֵץ פָּרוּר מַגְעִילָן בְּרוֹתְחִין.
עִנְדוּ אַגָּנֵי וְקַצִּיעֵי דְקוּנְיָא וּפַחְרָא,
אַף עַל גַּב דְּמַפְלִיט לְהוּ שַׁפִּיר, לְאִשְׁתַּמּוּשֵׁי בְהוּ אֲסִירָא,
וְאַף עַל גַּב דְּרְוִיחָן וְאִכָּא לְמֵימַר דְּשַׁלִּיט בְּהוּ אַוִּירָא,
אֲפִילוּ הָכֵי קַיְמָא אִסּוּרָא.

Upon completion, one should safeguard what he has found until the next day,
and immediately nullify any remaining chametz with a declaration,
and say as follows: 'Any chametz in this dwelling
that I did not see and did not remove is hereby nullified and becomes like dust.'
Accordingly, if it is found after that time, one will not have willfully
transgressed the prohibitions that chametz may neither be seen nor found;
one who wishes to eat his fill of chametz after the search
should hide what he has set aside for that purpose.
In the event one has searched the holes of the house —
but he set aside four or five pieces of bread
and found that one of them is missing,
he must search anew lest a weasel moved it from its original place.
And thus did the Rabbis teach in this chapter, that the holes and crevices of the house
that are too high or too low for convenient use need not be searched,
but those in between require it.
They cautioned that the slanty roof of a porch or tower,
stall of cattle, storage of straw, coops,
locked pantries of wine or oil, do not require one to climb and search them.
A hole between the property of someone and his neighbor,
each one searches as far as he can reach and nullifies the rest;
similarly, in the space between a Jew and a non-Jew, he must [search and] nullify it;
Pleimo [the name of a sage] ruled leniently in this case because the non-Jew
might suspect the Jew of sorcery and injure him.
The Sages debated and ruled that someone who goes to sea or journeys in a caravan
and does not intend to return home before Pesach —
if it is within thirty days before Pesach he must remove the chametz,
but if more than thirty days, he need not remove it.
A Jew with whom chametz has been left for safekeeping
and the owner is not present to claim it,
he must hold it until the fourth hour of Erev Pesach when it may still be eaten,
but if the owner has not come after the fourth hour, he should sell it to a non-Jew.
If there was a cave-in atop chametz on Erev Pesach
and it is certain that a dog cannot uncover it,
than the wise, comradely Sages consider it as if removed;
and until what depth can a dog uncover it? — until three handbreadths.
They taught that places known as salt storage, candle storage,
date and wood storage
must be searched, but a courtyard is exempt because ravens eat the chametz.
One who finds chametz in his home during Pesach
should cover it with a vessel so that it will remain unseen;
but if the chametz belongs to the Sanctuary, it need not be covered
because people stay away from it.
Iron strainers, iron woven baskets, and pots used with hot chametz,
one must kosher them in boiling water by placing them in a large pot.
To kosher a large pot, one should build a clay border over its rim
and cook it over a flame [so that boiling water will cover its rim].
Knives that were used with chametz meals,
it is best to make them like new [by koshering in the fire],
but if not they may be koshered in boiling water
and in a vessel once removed from the fire they become acceptable;
and a wooden spoon, too, may be koshered in boiling water.
They crowned us with this teaching: earthenware and glazed earthenware dishes,
even though one has koshered them thoroughly, it is forbidden to use them;
even though they are so wide that air circulation would seem to prevent
chametz from entering the pores, nevertheless they remain forbidden.

פּחַר קְדֵרוֹת אֵין צָרִיךְ לְפַלְּחָא, אֲבָל מַשְׁהֵי לֵיהּ עַד בָּתַר פִּסְחָא,
וּקְעָרוֹת מֻתָּרוֹת כִּי שָׁקִיל מְדוּדָא עֲלַיְהוּ לְאַנָּחָא,
וּבוּרְמֵי דִגְלָלָא שַׁרְיָן בַּהֲדָחָה.
צָעֵי דְמַשְׁהֵי בְהוּ חֲמִירָא בִּשְׁאָר יוֹמֵי, כְּבֵית שְׂאוֹר שֶׁחִמּוּצוֹ קָשֶׁה דָּמֵי,
וְאִי אַקְרָאֵי אוֹתִיבֵיהּ וְלָא אִשְׁתְּהֵי עִמֵּיהּ, לְאִשְׁתַּמּוּשֵׁי בְהוּ שַׁפִּיר דָּמֵי.
קִטּוּף בְּיַיִן וְשֶׁמֶן עֲבִידִין, מִלְּמֵילַשׁ בְּהוּ לֵילֵי קַמָּאֵי קַפְּדִין,
וְאַמְהָן דְּלָא טְבִילָן וְעַבְדִּין, דְּלָא לְמֵילַשׁ בְּהוּ הוּא הַדִּין.
רְקִיקֵי מַצּוֹת עוֹשִׂין זֵכֶר לְעִגּוּן, וְלִשְׁמָן צָרִיךְ לְשָׁמְרָן מֵחִמּוּץ כְּהָגוּן,
וְחֵרֵשׁ שׁוֹטֶה וְקָטָן אֵין לָשִׁין דִּלְמָא יִשְׁגּוּן,
אַף עַל גַּב דְּאַפְיֵהּ יִשְׂרָאֵל בַּר דֵּעָה לָא יִנְהֲגוּן.
שָׁנוּ שֶׁאֵין לָשִׁין בְּבַת אַחַת לְמַעְלָה, מֵחֲמֵשֶׁת רְבָעִים קֶמַח וְכֵן לְחַלָּה,
וְהֵן בֵּיצִים כְּמִנְיַן חַלָּה וְהָעֹמֶר מוּכָח לָהּ,
וְהָאִשָּׁה לֹא תָלוּשׁ אֶלָּא בְּמַיִם שֶׁלָּנוּ הַלַּיְלָה.
תְּמִימִים שָׁנוּ בְּמִשְׁנָה הַמְּהֻלָּלָה,
מֵי תַשְׁמִישׁוֹ שֶׁל נַחְתּוֹם יִשָּׁפְכוּ מִפְּנֵי שֶׁמַּחֲמִיצִין סֶלָה,
וְאָמְרִינַן שָׁדֵי לְהוּ בְּמְקוֹם מוּדְרָן דְּלָא לֵיתֵי בְהוּ לִידֵי תַקָּלָה.
תַּמּוּ הִלְכוֹת בִּעוּר וְהַגְעָלָה.

יַיִן כִּי יִתְאַדֵּם, לְמִצְוָה הוּא מְקֻדָּם,
לָצֵאת בּוֹ חוֹבַת יְדֵי אָדָם, אִם אֵין קוֹנְדִּיטוֹן וּמְבֻשָּׁל נֶגְדָּם.
וְאַרְבָּעָה כּוֹסוֹת הַלָּלוּ, צָרִיךְ שֶׁיְּהֵא בָהֶן כְּדֵי רְבִיעִית בְּלִי יָקֵלּוּ,
אֶחָד אֲנָשִׁים וְאֶחָד נָשִׁים אֵלּוּ כָּאֵלּוּ,
וּמְחַלְּקִין לְתִינוֹקוֹת קְלָיוֹת וֶאֱגוֹזִין כְּדֵי שֶׁיִּשְׁאֲלוּ.
סָחוּ שֶׁהַנָּשִׁים צְרִיכוֹת לְאַמְּצָה, בְּכָל מִילֵי דְפִסְחָא בְּלִי שִׁמְצָה,
אַף עַל גַּב דְּמִצְוַת עֲשֵׂה שֶׁהַזְּמַן גְּרָמָא בָּם לָא נִמְצָא,
שֶׁכָּל שֶׁיֶּשְׁנוֹ בְּבַל תֹּאכַל חָמֵץ יֶשְׁנוֹ בְּקוּם אֱכוֹל מַצָּה.
פֵּרְשׁוּ בְּשָׂפָה נְדִיבָה, מַצָּה וְיַיִן צָרִיךְ הֲסִבָּה,
מָרוֹר אֵין בּוֹ כֵּן חוֹבָה, וּמִבָּעֵי לֵיהּ לְכַסְכּוּסֵי טוּבָא.
הֲסִבַּת יָמִין הֲסִבָּה אֵינָהּ,
וְלֹא עוֹד אֶלָּא שֶׁמָּא יַקְדִּים קָנֶה לָוֶשֶׁט וְיָבֹא לִידֵי סַכָּנָה,
פְּרַקְדָּן לָא מִן חֶשְׁבְּנָא, וְאִשָּׁה אֵינָהּ צְרִיכָה וְאִם חֲשׁוּבָה הִיא נִדּוֹנָה.
קַמֵּי אָב מֵסֵב הַבֵּן בִּרְדִיצָה, תַּלְמִיד בִּפְנֵי רַבּוֹ אֵין רָאוּי לְפָרְצָה,
אֲבָל בְּשׁוּלְיָא דְנַגָּרֵי צָרִיךְ לְהָסֵב בִּמְרוּצָה,
וְהַשַּׁמָּשׁ שֶׁאָכַל כְּזַיִת מַצָּה כְּשֶׁהוּא מֵסֵב יָצָא.
טָעֲנוּ לַחֲטוֹף מַצָּה בְּלֵילֵי פְסָחִים, כְּדֵי שֶׁלֹּא יִישְׁנוּ הַפְּרָחִים,
וְחַיָּבִים בְּרֶגֶל לִהְיוֹת שְׂמֵחִים, בְּמִקְדָּשׁ בְּבָשָׂר וְהַשְׁתָּא בְּיַיִן רְקוּחִים.
נָשִׁים חַיָּבוֹת לִשְׂמוֹחַ וּלְהַרְנִין, בְּבָבֶל בְּבִגְדֵי צִבְעוֹנִין,
בְּאֶרֶץ יִשְׂרָאֵל בְּבִגְדֵי פִשְׁתָּן הַמְּלֻבָּנִין, וְהָאֲנָשִׁים בְּיַיִן מִתְעַדְּנִין.
בְּעֶרֶב הַפֶּסַח סָמוּךְ לְמִנְחַת רִאשׁוֹן, לֹא יֹאכַל אָדָם עַד הָאִישׁוֹן,

Earthenware pots need not be broken, but they must be set aside until after Pesach.
Dishes are permitted if one pours water from a pot resting on the fire;
and stoneware is permissible upon washing [with boiling water].
Dishes used for sour dough all year are like a utensil in which
sour dough is soaked, which has an intense degree of chametz;
but if the sour dough was put on the dish only occasionally, it is proper to use it.
Smearing of matzah with wine or oil is permitted,
but we object to doing so on the first nights.
Maidservants and slaves who were not converted through immersion,
the law is that they should not knead matzos.
Matzah cakes are made in memory of the bondage,
but they must be guarded properly against leavening for the sake of matzah;
a deaf mute, an imbecile, and child should not knead because they may be careless,
even though an adult Israelite does the baking, it is not customary to do so.
They taught that at one time one does not knead more
than five logs of flour, the same amount that obligates one to take challah,
this means a volume of eggs equal to the numerical value of challah [=43]
— the omer is the standard for challah —
and a woman should knead only with water that has been left overnight.
The perfect Sages taught in the lauded mishnah: water that a baker used
to cool his hands is poured out because it always becomes chametz,
and they say it should be poured down a slope
so it should not collect and cause a mishap.
This ends the laws of removal and koshering.

יַיִן *Wine made red has preference for the Seder mitzvah*
for a person to discharge his obligation,
but if unavailable, spiced and cooked are acceptable.
These four cups must contain a revi'is each without leniency,
men and women have the same requirement;
roasted kernels and nuts are distributed to the children so that they will inquire.
The Sages said that women must exert themselves
in all matters of Pesach without blemish,
even though time-related positive commandments generally do not apply to them,
because anyone obligated not to eat chametz is included in the positive categories of eating matzah.
The Sages explained with their gifted speech
that matzah and wine require reclining when being eaten,
but maror does not have this obligation; and it must be well chewed.
Reclining on the right side is not a proper reclining,
moreover one's windpipe may swallow before the esophagus and endanger his life;
reclining on the back does not come under consideration;
a woman does not require reclining, but if she is distinguished,
she is deemed to require it.
Before his father a son may recline with alacrity;
a student before his teacher may not breach propriety;
but a carpenter's apprentice must recline without hesitation,
and a servant who eats an olive's volume of matzah as he reclines
has fulfilled his obligation.
They lift up and remove the tray of matzos on the nights of Pesach
so that the little children will not fall asleep;
all must be joyous on the pilgrimage festival,
in the Sanctuary this was through sacrificial meal and now it is with spiced wine.
Women must rejoice and celebrate, in Babylonia they did so with colored clothing
and in Eretz Yisrael with bleached linen garments, and men take delight in wine.
On Erev Pesach, near the time of Minchah preceding the first Seder,
a person may no longer eat until dark;

וּבְבֹאוֹ מִבֵּית רַחֲשׁוֹן, מוֹזְגִין לוֹ כּוֹס רִאשׁוֹן.

רִאשׁוֹן מְבָרֵךְ עַל הַיַּיִן, וְאַחַר כַּךְ קִדּוּשׁ וּזְמַן וְאֵינוֹ אוֹמֵר נֵס עֲדַיִן,
שֶׁצָּרִיךְ לְאָמְרוֹ בַּאֲגָדָה וְרָאוּי לְכָפְלוֹ אַיִן,
וְשָׁתֵי וּמָשֵׁי יָדֵיהּ וְאֵינוֹ מְבָרֵךְ עַל נְטִילַת יָדַיִם.
שָׁקֵל גַּרְגִּירָא אוֹ כַּרְפְּסָא אוֹ כֻסְבַּרְתָּא אוֹ חַסָּא,
וְיִטְבּוֹל בַּחֲרוֹסֶת וִיבָרֵךְ בּוֹרֵא פְּרִי הָאֲדָמָה,
וְכַד אָכֵל יֶחֱצֶה אַחַת מִשָּׁלֹשׁ מַצּוֹת וְאֵין בְּרָכָה עִמָּה,
מֶחֱצָה בִקְעָרָה וּמֶחֱצָה בְּשֻׁלְחָן לְהָשִׂימָה.
מוֹשֵׁךְ מֵהַקְּעָרָה שְׁנֵי תַבְשִׁילֵי, דְּאִנּוּן בִּשְׂרָא וְכוּוְרָא צְלִילֵי,
אִי נַמִּי גַּרְמָא וּבְשׁוּלֵי, וּמַגְבְּהַהּ קְעָרָה וְלֵימָא הָא לַחְמָא עַנְיָא כְּלֵיהּ.
וּמוֹזְגִים לוֹ כּוֹס שֵׁנִי מֵאַרְבַּעַת הָאֵל, וְכָאן הַבֵּן מֵאָבִיו שׁוֹאֵל,
מַה נִּשְׁתַּנָּה מִלֵּילוֹת זֶה לֵיל, וְגוֹמֵר הָאֲגָדָה עַד גָּאַל יִשְׂרָאֵל.
אַחַר דְּשָׁתֵי מָשֵׁי יְדֵהּ, וּמְבָרֵךְ עַל נְטִילַת יָדַיִם לְחוּדֵיהּ,
וְשָׁרֵי הַמּוֹצִיא עַל הַשְּׁלֵמָה דְּעִלָּוֵי תַּרְתֵּי דִידֵיהּ,
וְלָא אָכֵיל מִנֵּיהּ אַכַּתֵּי מִדֵּי.
לוֹקֵחַ פְּרוּסָה וּמְבָרֵךְ לֶאֱכוֹל מַצָּה בְּמֶלֶל, וּבַהֲדֵי דְּהַהִיא דְהַמּוֹצִיא אוֹכֵל וְכוֹלֵל,
וּמְבָרֵךְ בַּחֲזֶרֶת לֶאֱכוֹל מָרוֹר וְטוֹבֵל וּבוֹלֵל,
וְהָדַר אָכֵיל מַצָּה וּמָרוֹר בְּלֹא בְרָכָה וְכוֹרְכָן בְּבַת אַחַת כְּהִלֵּל.
חָלִיף לְכַמָּה בָתֵּי וְעָבֵיד כִּי הַאי גַּוְנָא עַד הָכָא,
וְאַחַר כַּךְ עוֹשִׂים סְעוּדָתָן כָּל צָרְכָּהּ,
וְכַזַּיִת מַצָּה בָּאַחֲרוֹנָה צְרִיכִין לְבָרְכָה,
וְנוֹטְלִין וְלָא מְבָרְכִין שֶׁמַּיִם אַחֲרוֹנִים חוֹבָה וְאֵין טְעוּנִין בְּרָכָה.
זוֹכֵר בַּשְּׁלִישִׁי בְּרָכַּת מְזוֹנוֹ, וְלִשְׁאָר הַבָּתִּים תְּחִלָּה וְטוֹעֵם הַכּוֹס עַד מִשֶּׁלוֹ אֵינוֹ,
וּבָרְבִיעִי הַלֵּל מִצְרִי לְתַנּוֹ, בַּל יִטְעוֹם כְּלוּם בְּאִישׁוֹנוֹ.
קִמְעָא לִשְׁתּוֹת מַיִם יְכַנֵּס, אִם חוֹלֶה הוּא אוֹ אִסְטְנֵס,
וּבָעֵי לְמִשְׁתֵּי חַמְרָא מִשּׁוּם אוֹנֶס, לוֹמַר בַּחֲמִישִׁי הַלֵּל הַגָּדוֹל יִשְׁתַּנֵּס.

חֲסַל סִדּוּר פֶּסַח כְּהִלְכָתוֹ, כְּכָל מִשְׁפָּטוֹ וְחֻקָּתוֹ,
כַּאֲשֶׁר זָכִינוּ לְסַדֵּר אוֹתוֹ כֵּן נִזְכֶּה לַעֲשׂוֹתוֹ.
זָךְ שׁוֹכֵן מְעוֹנָה, קוֹמֵם קְהַל עֲדַת מִי מָנָה,
בְּקָרוֹב נַהֵל נִטְעֵי כַנָּה, פְּדוּיִם לְצִיּוֹן בְּרִנָּה.

Chazzan and congregation recite together:

וּבְכֵן וּלְךָ תַעֲלֶה קְדֻשָּׁה כִּי אַתָּה קְדוֹשׁ יִשְׂרָאֵל וּמוֹשִׁיעַ.

Turn to page 422 for *Kedushah* and the continuation of *Shacharis.*

חֲסַל סִדּוּר פֶּסַח — *The order of the Pesach is now concluded.* This concluding paragraph of R' Yosef Tuv Elem's *piyut* has been inserted toward the end of the Pesach Seder. Having given a detailed summary of the laws of Pesach, the composer concludes with a prayer that just as we have been privileged to study, know, and teach them, so may we be granted the supreme privilege of actually carrying out all the laws — including those of the Pesach offering in the rebuilt Temple. Obviously, the term סִדּוּר פֶּסַח, *the order of the Pesach,* as it is used here has a slightly different connotation than the one it has in the Pesach Seder. Here, it refers to the entirely theoretical recitation of the laws. In the Seder, we have fulfilled the laws of the evening; we pray

and when he returns from the house of prayer, they pour him the first cup.
First he pronounces the blessing over the wine and then Kiddush and Shehecheyanu,
but he does not recite a blessing for the miracle as yet,
because he will discuss it in the Haggadah and it is not proper to repeat it.
He drinks from the cup, then washes his hands
but does not recite the blessing 'regarding washing the hands';
he takes cress, parsley, coriander, or horseradish
and dips it in charoses and makes the blessing 'Who creates the fruit of the ground';
after eating it he divides one of the three matzos without a blessing:
half goes back to the Seder plate and half is placed on the table.
He removes the two cooked dishes from the Seder plate,
which are roasted meat and fish, or one of roast meat and one of cooked meat,
then lifts up the Seder plate and says the entire text of 'This is the bread of affliction.'
They pour him the second of these four cups and then the child inquires of his father:
'How is this night different from other nights?'
and he concludes the Haggadah until 'Who redeemed Israel.'
After drinking, he washes his hands
and recites only the blessing 'regarding the washing of the hands.'
For Hamotzi he breaks the whole matzah that is atop his other two,
but does not eat from it as yet.
He takes the broken piece and recites 'to eat matzah,'
and with the matzah of Hamotzi he eats them both together;
over the lettuce he blesses 'to eat maror' and dips it thoroughly and eats;
then he eats matzah and maror without a blessing and
wraps them together as did Hillel.
Then he may go about to many houses to perform the Seder to this point
for unlearned people, then they have their full meal,
but they must eat an olive's volume at the end;
then they wash their hands without a blessing
because the final water is a requirement but does not call for a blessing.
Upon the third cup, he recites grace for his meal,
but should do so first for the other houses,
however he does not drink the third cup until he returns to his own;
upon the fourth cup he recites Hallel in honor of the miracles in Egypt,
and may no longer taste food that night.
He may go in to drink a bit of water, but if he is ill or delicate
and is only able to drink wine [but not water],
he may exert himself to recite the Great Hallel [Psalm 136] over a fifth cup.

חֲסַל *The order of the Pesach is now concluded* in accordance with its laws,*
with all its ordinances and statutes.
Just as we were privileged to arrange it, so may we merit to perform it.
O Pure One, Who dwells on high, raise up the countless congregation,
soon — guide the offshoots of Your plants, redeemed, to Zion with glad song.

Chazzan and congregation recite together:

So now, the Kedushah prayer will ascend to You,
for You are the Holy One and Savior of Israel.

Turn to page 423 for *Kedushah* and the continuation of *Shacharis.*

---

only that we be found worthy to carry out even those that require the Temple and its service. Therefore, this prayer at the Seder is concluded with the plea לְשָׁנָה הַבָּאָה בִּירוּשָׁלָיִם, *Next year in Jerusalem.*

On the afternoon of *Shabbos Hagadol,* it is customary to recite the first half of the Haggadah, from עֲבָדִים הָיִינוּ, *we were slaves,* to Rabban Gamliel's listing of the three primary commandments of the Seder: Pesach, matzah and *maror.* Thus on the Sabbath commemorating the beginning of freedom — when the Egyptians were powerless to prevent our ancestors from taking lambs as their offerings — we read the narrative of the Pesach redemption. Rabban Gamliel's recitation, however, is inappropriate for this day, because it discusses *mitzvos* of the Seder itself.

VERSES FOR PEOPLE'S NAMES / פסוקים לשמות אנשים

Kitzur Shelah teaches that it is a source of merit to recite a scriptural verse symbolizing one's name before יִהְיוּ לְרָצוֹן at the end of *Shemoneh Esrei*. The verse should either contain the person's name, or else begin and end with the first and last letters of the name.

Following is a selection of first and last letters of names, with appropriate verses:

א...א אָנָּא יהוה הוֹשִׁיעָה נָּא, אָנָּא יהוה הַצְלִיחָה נָּא.[1]

א...ה אַשְׁרֵי מַשְׂכִּיל אֶל דָּל, בְּיוֹם רָעָה יְמַלְּטֵהוּ יהוה.[2]

א...ו אַשְׁרֵי שֶׁאֵל יַעֲקֹב בְּעֶזְרוֹ, שִׂבְרוֹ עַל יהוה אֱלֹהָיו.[3]

א...י אֲמָרַי הַאֲזִינָה יהוה, בִּינָה הֲגִיגִי.[4]

א...ך אָמַרְתְּ לַיהוה, אֲדֹנָי אָתָּה, טוֹבָתִי בַּל עָלֶיךָ.[5]

א...ל אֶרֶץ רָעָשָׁה, אַף שָׁמַיִם נָטְפוּ מִפְּנֵי אֱלֹהִים; זֶה סִינַי, מִפְּנֵי אֱלֹהִים אֱלֹהֵי יִשְׂרָאֵל.[6]

א...ם אַתָּה הוּא יהוה הָאֱלֹהִים, אֲשֶׁר בָּחַרְתָּ בְּאַבְרָם, וְהוֹצֵאתוֹ מֵאוּר כַּשְׂדִּים, וְשַׂמְתָּ שְׁמוֹ אַבְרָהָם.[7]

א...ן אֵלֶיךָ יהוה אֶקְרָא, וְאֶל אֲדֹנָי אֶתְחַנָּן.[8]

א...ע אָמַר בְּלִבּוֹ בַּל אֶמּוֹט, לְדֹר וָדֹר אֲשֶׁר לֹא בְרָע.[9]

א...ר אֵלֶּה בָרֶכֶב וְאֵלֶּה בַסּוּסִים, וַאֲנַחְנוּ בְּשֵׁם יהוה אֱלֹהֵינוּ נַזְכִּיר.[10]

ב...א בְּרִיתִי הָיְתָה אִתּוֹ הַחַיִּים וְהַשָּׁלוֹם, וָאֶתְּנֵם לוֹ מוֹרָא וַיִּירָאֵנִי, וּמִפְּנֵי שְׁמִי נִחַת הוּא.[11]

ב...ה בַּעֲבוּר יִשְׁמְרוּ חֻקָּיו, וְתוֹרֹתָיו יִנְצֹרוּ, הַלְלוּיָהּ.[12]

ב...ז בְּיוֹם קָרָאתִי וַתַּעֲנֵנִי, תַּרְהִבֵנִי בְנַפְשִׁי עֹז.[13]

ב...ך בָּרוּךְ אַתָּה יהוה, לַמְּדֵנִי חֻקֶּיךָ.[14]

ב...ל בְּמַקְהֵלוֹת בָּרְכוּ אֱלֹהִים, אֲדֹנָי מִמְּקוֹר יִשְׂרָאֵל.[15]

ב...ן בָּרוּךְ יהוה אֱלֹהֵי יִשְׂרָאֵל מֵהָעוֹלָם וְעַד הָעוֹלָם, אָמֵן וְאָמֵן.[16]

ב...ע בְּחֶסֶד וֶאֱמֶת יְכֻפַּר עָוֹן, וּבְיִרְאַת יהוה סוּר מֵרָע.[17]

ג...ה גּוֹל עַל יהוה דַּרְכֶּךָ, וּבְטַח עָלָיו וְהוּא יַעֲשֶׂה.[18]

ג...ל גַּם אֲנִי אוֹדְךָ בִכְלִי נֶבֶל אֲמִתְּךָ אֱלֹהָי, אֲזַמְּרָה לְךָ בְכִנּוֹר, קְדוֹשׁ יִשְׂרָאֵל.[19]

ג...ן גַּם בְּנֵי אָדָם גַּם בְּנֵי אִישׁ, יַחַד עָשִׁיר וְאֶבְיוֹן.[20]

ד...ב דִּרְשׁוּ יהוה בְּהִמָּצְאוֹ, קְרָאֻהוּ בִּהְיוֹתוֹ קָרוֹב.[21]

ד...ד דִּרְשׁוּ יהוה וְעֻזּוֹ, בַּקְּשׁוּ פָנָיו תָּמִיד.[22]

ד...ה דְּאָגָה בְלֶב אִישׁ יַשְׁחֶנָּה, וְדָבָר טוֹב יְשַׂמְּחֶנָּה.[23]

ד...ל דָּן יָדִין עַמּוֹ, כְּאַחַד שִׁבְטֵי יִשְׂרָאֵל.[24]

ה...א הַצּוּר תָּמִים פָּעֳלוֹ, כִּי כָל דְּרָכָיו מִשְׁפָּט, אֵל אֱמוּנָה וְאֵין עָוֶל, צַדִּיק וְיָשָׁר הוּא.[25]

ה...ה הַסְתֵּר פָּנֶיךָ מֵחֲטָאָי, וְכָל עֲוֹנֹתַי מְחֵה.[26]

ה...ל הַקְשִׁיבָה לְקוֹל שַׁוְעִי מַלְכִּי וֵאלֹהָי, כִּי אֵלֶיךָ אֶתְפַּלָּל.[27]

ז...ב זֵכֶר צַדִּיק לִבְרָכָה, וְשֵׁם רְשָׁעִים יִרְקָב.[28]

ז...ה זֹאת מְנוּחָתִי עֲדֵי עַד, פֹּה אֵשֵׁב כִּי אִוִּתִיהָ.[29]

ז...ח זָכַרְתִּי יָמִים מִקֶּדֶם, הָגִיתִי בְכָל פָּעֳלֶךָ, בְּמַעֲשֵׂה יָדֶיךָ אֲשׂוֹחֵחַ.[30]

ז...ן זְבוּלֻן לְחוֹף יַמִּים יִשְׁכֹּן, וְהוּא לְחוֹף אֳנִיֹּת, וְיַרְכָתוֹ עַל צִידֹן.[31]

ח..ה חָגְרָה בְעוֹז מָתְנֶיהָ, וַתְּאַמֵּץ זְרוֹעֹתֶיהָ.[32]

(1) *Psalms* 118:25. (2) 41:2. (3) 146:5. (4) 5:2. (5) 16:2. (6) 68:9. (7) *Nehemiah* 9:7. (8) *Psalms* 30:9. (9) 10:6. (10) 20:8. (11) *Malachi* 2:5. (12) *Psalms* 105:45. (13) 138:3. (14) 119:12. (15) 68:27. (16) 41:14. (17) *Proverbs* 16:6. (18) *Psalms* 37:5. (19) 71:22. (20) 49:3. (21) *Isaiah* 55:6. (22) *Psalms* 105:4. (23) *Proverbs* 12:25. (24) *Genesis* 49:16. (25) *Deuteronomy* 32:4. (26) *Psalms* 51:11. (27) 5:3. (28) *Proverbs* 10:7. (29) *Psalms* 132:14. (30) 143:5. (31) *Genesis* 49:13. (32) *Proverbs* 31:17.

ח...ך חֲצוֹת לַיְלָה אָקוּם לְהוֹדוֹת לָךְ, עַל מִשְׁפְּטֵי צִדְקֶךָ.[1]

ח...ל חָדְלוּ פְרָזוֹן בְּיִשְׂרָאֵל חָדֵלּוּ, עַד שַׁקַּמְתִּי דְּבוֹרָה, שַׁקַּמְתִּי אֵם בְּיִשְׂרָאֵל.[2]

ח...ם חֹנֶה מַלְאַךְ יהוה סָבִיב לִירֵאָיו, וַיְחַלְּצֵם.[3]

ט...א טוֹב יַנְחִיל בְּנֵי בָנִים, וְצָפוּן לַצַּדִּיק חֵיל חוֹטֵא.[4]

ט...ה טָמְנוּ גֵאִים פַּח לִי וַחֲבָלִים, פָּרְשׂוּ רֶשֶׁת לְיַד מַעְגָּל, מֹקְשִׁים שָׁתוּ לִי סֶלָה.[5]

י...א יִשְׂרָאֵל בְּטַח בַּיהוה, עֶזְרָם וּמָגִנָּם הוּא.[6]

י...ב יַעַנְךָ יהוה בְּיוֹם צָרָה, יְשַׂגֶּבְךָ שֵׁם אֱלֹהֵי יַעֲקֹב.[7]

י...ד יָסַד אֶרֶץ עַל מְכוֹנֶיהָ, בַּל תִּמּוֹט עוֹלָם וָעֶד.[8]

י...ה יהוה הַצִּילָה נַפְשִׁי מִשְּׂפַת שֶׁקֶר, מִלָּשׁוֹן רְמִיָּה.[9]

י...י יהוה לִי בְּעֹזְרָי, וַאֲנִי אֶרְאֶה בְשֹׂנְאָי.[10]

י...ל יְמִין יהוה רוֹמֵמָה, יְמִין יהוה עֹשָׂה חָיִל.[11]

י...ם יַעְלְזוּ חֲסִידִים בְּכָבוֹד, יְרַנְּנוּ עַל מִשְׁכְּבוֹתָם.[12]

י...ן יָשֵׂם נְהָרוֹת לְמִדְבָּר, וּמֹצָאֵי מַיִם לְצִמָּאוֹן.[13]

י...ע יָחֹס עַל דַּל וְאֶבְיוֹן, וְנַפְשׁוֹת אֶבְיוֹנִים יוֹשִׁיעַ.[14]

י...ף יהוה יִגְמֹר בַּעֲדִי, יהוה חַסְדְּךָ לְעוֹלָם, מַעֲשֵׂי יָדֶיךָ אַל תֶּרֶף.[15]

י...ץ יְבָרְכֵנוּ אֱלֹהִים, וְיִירְאוּ אוֹתוֹ כָּל אַפְסֵי אָרֶץ.[16]

י..ק יוֹצִיאֵם מֵחֹשֶׁךְ וְצַלְמָוֶת, וּמוֹסְרוֹתֵיהֶם יְנַתֵּק.[17]

י...ר יהוה שִׁמְךָ לְעוֹלָם, יהוה זִכְרְךָ לְדֹר וָדֹר.[18]

י...ת יהוה שֹׁמֵר אֶת גֵּרִים, יָתוֹם וְאַלְמָנָה יְעוֹדֵד, וְדֶרֶךְ רְשָׁעִים יְעַוֵּת.[19]

כ...ב כִּי לֹא יִטֹּשׁ יהוה עַמּוֹ, וְנַחֲלָתוֹ לֹא יַעֲזֹב.[20]

כ...ל כִּי מֶלֶךְ כָּל הָאָרֶץ אֱלֹהִים זַמְּרוּ מַשְׂכִּיל.[21]

ל...א לֹא תִהְיֶה מְשַׁכֵּלָה וַעֲקָרָה בְּאַרְצֶךָ, אֶת מִסְפַּר יָמֶיךָ אֲמַלֵּא.[22]

ל...ה לְדָוִד, בָּרוּךְ יהוה צוּרִי, הַמְלַמֵּד יָדַי לַקְרָב, אֶצְבְּעוֹתַי לַמִּלְחָמָה.[23]

ל...י לוּלֵי תוֹרָתְךָ שַׁעֲשֻׁעָי, אָז אָבַדְתִּי בְעָנְיִי.[24]

ל...ת לַמְנַצֵּחַ עַל שֹׁשַׁנִּים לִבְנֵי קֹרַח, מַשְׂכִּיל שִׁיר יְדִידֹת.[25]

מ..א מִי כָמֹכָה בָּאֵלִם יהוה, מִי כָּמֹכָה נֶאְדָּר בַּקֹּדֶשׁ, נוֹרָא תְהִלֹּת עֹשֵׂה פֶלֶא.[26]

מ...ה מַחֲשָׁבוֹת בְּעֵצָה תִכּוֹן, וּבְתַחְבֻּלוֹת עֲשֵׂה מִלְחָמָה.[27]

מ...ו מַה דּוֹדֵךְ מִדּוֹד הַיָּפָה בַּנָּשִׁים, מַה דּוֹדֵךְ מִדּוֹד שֶׁכָּכָה הִשְׁבַּעְתָּנוּ.[28]

מ...י מָה אָהַבְתִּי תוֹרָתֶךָ, כָּל הַיּוֹם הִיא שִׂיחָתִי.[29]

מ...ל מַה טֹּבוּ אֹהָלֶיךָ יַעֲקֹב, מִשְׁכְּנֹתֶיךָ יִשְׂרָאֵל.[30]

מ...ם מְאוֹר עֵינַיִם יְשַׂמַּח לֵב, שְׁמוּעָה טוֹבָה תְּדַשֶּׁן עָצֶם.[31]

מ...ר מִי זֶה הָאִישׁ יְרֵא יהוה, יוֹרֶנּוּ בְּדֶרֶךְ יִבְחָר.[32]

נ...א נַפְשֵׁנוּ חִכְּתָה לַיהוה עֶזְרֵנוּ וּמָגִנֵּנוּ הוּא.[33]

נ...ה נָחַלְתִּי עֵדְוֹתֶיךָ לְעוֹלָם, כִּי שְׂשׂוֹן לִבִּי הֵמָּה.[34]

נ...י נִדְבוֹת פִּי רְצֵה נָא יהוה, וּמִשְׁפָּטֶיךָ לַמְּדֵנִי.[35]

נ...ל נֶחְשַׁבְתִּי עִם יוֹרְדֵי בוֹר, הָיִיתִי כְּגֶבֶר אֵין אֱיָל.[36]

נ...ם נַחֲמוּ נַחֲמוּ עַמִּי, יֹאמַר אֱלֹהֵיכֶם.[37]

נ...ן נֵר יהוה נִשְׁמַת אָדָם, חֹפֵשׂ כָּל חַדְרֵי בָטֶן.[38]

---

(1) *Psalms* 119:62. (2) *Judges* 5:7. (3) *Psalms* 34:8. (4) *Proverbs* 13:22. (5) *Psalms* 140:6. (6) 115:9. (7) 20:2. (8) 104:5. (9) 120:2. (10) 118:7. (11) 118:16. (12) 149:5. (13) 107:33. (14) 72:13. (15) 138:8. (16) 67:8. (17) 107:14. (18) 135:13. (19) 146:9. (20) 94:14. (21) 47:8. (22) *Exodus* 23:26. (23) *Psalms* 144:1. (24) 119:92. (25) 45:1. (26) *Exodus* 15:11. (27) *Proverbs* 20:18. (28) *Song of Songs* 5:9. (29) *Psalms* 119:97. (30) *Numbers* 24:5. (31) *Proverbs* 15:30. (32) *Psalms* 25:12. (33) 33:20. (34) 119:111. (35) 119:108. (36) 88:5. (37) *Isaiah* 40:1. (38) *Proverbs* 20:27.

ס...ה סֹבּוּ צִיּוֹן וְהַקִּיפְוּהָ, סִפְרוּ מִגְדָּלֶיהָ.[1]

ס...י סֵעֲפִים שָׂנֵאתִי, וְתוֹרָתְךָ אָהָבְתִּי.[2]

ע...א עַתָּה אָקוּם, יֹאמַר יהוה, עַתָּה אֵרוֹמָם, עַתָּה אֶנָּשֵׂא.[3]

ע...ב עַד אֶמְצָא מָקוֹם לַיהוה, מִשְׁכָּנוֹת לַאֲבִיר יַעֲקֹב.[4]

ע...ה עָזִּי וְזִמְרָת יָהּ, וַיְהִי לִי לִישׁוּעָה.[5]

ע...ל עַל דַּעְתְּךָ כִּי לֹא אֶרְשָׁע, וְאֵין מִיָּדְךָ מַצִּיל.[6]

ע...ם עֲרֹב עַבְדְּךָ לְטוֹב, אַל יַעַשְׁקֻנִי זֵדִים.[7]

ע...ר עֹשֶׂה גְדֹלוֹת וְאֵין חֵקֶר, נִפְלָאוֹת עַד אֵין מִסְפָּר.[8]

פ...ה פִּתְחוּ לִי שַׁעֲרֵי צֶדֶק, אָבֹא בָם אוֹדֶה יָהּ.[9]

פ...ל פֶּן יִטְרֹף כְּאַרְיֵה נַפְשִׁי, פֹּרֵק וְאֵין מַצִּיל.[10]

פ...ס פֶּלֶס וּמֹאזְנֵי מִשְׁפָּט לַיהוה, מַעֲשֵׂהוּ כָּל אַבְנֵי כִיס.[11]

פ...ץ פִּנִּיתָ לְפָנֶיהָ, וַתַּשְׁרֵשׁ שָׁרָשֶׁיהָ, וַתְּמַלֵּא אָרֶץ.[12]

צ...ה צִיּוֹן בְּמִשְׁפָּט תִּפָּדֶה, וְשָׁבֶיהָ בִּצְדָקָה.[13]

צ...ח צִיּוֹן יִשְׁאָלוּ דֶּרֶךְ הֵנָּה פְנֵיהֶם, בֹּאוּ וְנִלְווּ אֶל יהוה, בְּרִית עוֹלָם לֹא תִשָּׁכֵחַ.[14]

צ...י צַר וּמָצוֹק מְצָאוּנִי, מִצְוֹתֶיךָ שַׁעֲשֻׁעָי.[15]

צ...ל צַהֲלִי וָרֹנִּי יוֹשֶׁבֶת צִיּוֹן, כִּי גָדוֹל בְּקִרְבֵּךְ קְדוֹשׁ יִשְׂרָאֵל.[16]

ק...א קָרַבְתָּ בְּיוֹם אֶקְרָאֶךָּ, אָמַרְתָּ אַל תִּירָא.[17]

ק...ל קַמְתִּי אֲנִי לִפְתֹּחַ לְדוֹדִי, וְיָדַי נָטְפוּ מוֹר וְאֶצְבְּעֹתַי מוֹר עֹבֵר עַל כַּפּוֹת הַמַּנְעוּל.[18]

ק...ן קוֹלִי אֶל יהוה אֶזְעָק, קוֹלִי אֶל יהוה אֶתְחַנָּן.[19]

ק...ת קָרוֹב אַתָּה יהוה, וְכָל מִצְוֹתֶיךָ אֱמֶת.[20]

ר...ה רִגְזוּ וְאַל תֶּחֱטָאוּ, אִמְרוּ בִלְבַבְכֶם עַל מִשְׁכַּבְכֶם, וְדֹמּוּ סֶלָה.[21]

ר...ל רְאוּ עַתָּה כִּי אֲנִי אֲנִי הוּא, וְאֵין אֱלֹהִים עִמָּדִי, אֲנִי אָמִית וַאֲחַיֶּה, מָחַצְתִּי וַאֲנִי אֶרְפָּא, וְאֵין מִיָּדִי מַצִּיל.[22]

ר...ן רְאֵה זֶה מָצָאתִי, אָמְרָה קֹהֶלֶת, אַחַת לְאַחַת לִמְצֹא חֶשְׁבּוֹן.[23]

ר...ת רָאוּךָ מַּיִם אֱלֹהִים, רָאוּךָ מַּיִם יָחִילוּ, אַף יִרְגְּזוּ תְהֹמוֹת.[24]

ש...א שַׂמֵּחַ נֶפֶשׁ עַבְדֶּךָ, כִּי אֵלֶיךָ אֲדֹנָי נַפְשִׁי אֶשָּׂא.[25]

ש...ה שְׂאוּ יְדֵכֶם קֹדֶשׁ, וּבָרְכוּ אֶת יהוה.[26]

ש...ח שָׁמַע יהוה תְּחִנָּתִי, יהוה תְּפִלָּתִי יִקָּח.[27]

ש...י שָׂנֵאתִי הַשֹּׁמְרִים הַבְלֵי שָׁוְא, וַאֲנִי אֶל יהוה בָּטָחְתִּי.[28]

ש...ל שָׁלוֹם רָב לְאֹהֲבֵי תוֹרָתֶךָ, וְאֵין לָמוֹ מִכְשׁוֹל.[29]

ש...ם שְׁמָר תָּם וּרְאֵה יָשָׁר, כִּי אַחֲרִית לְאִישׁ שָׁלוֹם.[30]

ש...ן שִׁיתוּ לִבְּכֶם לְחֵילָה, פַּסְּגוּ אַרְמְנוֹתֶיהָ, לְמַעַן תְּסַפְּרוּ לְדוֹר אַחֲרוֹן.[31]

ש...ר שְׂפַת אֱמֶת תִּכּוֹן לָעַד, וְעַד אַרְגִּיעָה לְשׁוֹן שָׁקֶר.[32]

ש...ת שִׁיר הַמַּעֲלוֹת, הִנֵּה בָּרְכוּ אֶת יהוה כָּל עַבְדֵי יהוה, הָעֹמְדִים בְּבֵית יהוה בַּלֵּילוֹת.[33]

ת...ה תַּעֲרֹךְ לְפָנַי שֻׁלְחָן נֶגֶד צֹרְרָי, דִּשַּׁנְתָּ בַשֶּׁמֶן רֹאשִׁי, כּוֹסִי רְוָיָה.[34]

ת...י תּוֹצִיאֵנִי מֵרֶשֶׁת זוּ, טָמְנוּ לִי, כִּי אַתָּה מָעוּזִּי.[35]

ת...ם תְּנוּ עֹז לֵאלֹהִים, עַל יִשְׂרָאֵל גַּאֲוָתוֹ, וְעֻזּוֹ בַּשְּׁחָקִים.[36]

---

(1) *Psalms* 48:13. (2) 119:113. (3) *Isaiah* 33:10. (4) *Psalms* 132:5. (5) 118:14. (6) *Job* 10:7. (7) *Psalms* 119:122. (8) *Job* 5:9. (9) *Psalms* 118:19. (10) 7:3. (11) *Proverbs* 16:11. (12) *Psalms* 80:10. (13) *Isaiah* 1:27. (14) *Jeremiah* 50:5. (15) *Psalms* 119:143. (16) *Isaiah* 12:6. (17) *Lamentations* 3:57. (18) *Song of Songs* 5:5. (19) *Psalms* 142:2. (20) 119:151. (21) 4:5. (22) *Deuteronomy* 32:39. (23) *Ecclesiastes* 7:27. (24) *Psalms* 77:7. (25) 86:4. (26) 134:2. (27) 6:10. (28) 31:7. (29) 119:165. (30) 37:37. (31) 48:14. (32) *Proverbs* 12:19. (33) *Psalms* 134:1. (34) 23:5. (35) 31:5. (36) 68:35.

סֵדֶר הַפָּרָשִׁיּוֹת

Torah Readings

סדר הפרשיות TORAH READINGS

קריאת התורה למנחה בשבת ולשני וחמישי
Sabbath Afternoon, Monday and Thursday Mornings

פ׳ בראשית / BEREISHIS
(*Genesis* 1:1-13)

בְּרֵאשִׁית בָּרָא אֱלֹהִים אֵת הַשָּׁמַיִם וְאֵת הָאָרֶץ: וְהָאָרֶץ הָיְתָה תֹהוּ וָבֹהוּ וְחֹשֶׁךְ עַל־פְּנֵי תְהוֹם וְרוּחַ אֱלֹהִים מְרַחֶפֶת עַל־פְּנֵי הַמָּיִם: וַיֹּאמֶר אֱלֹהִים יְהִי אוֹר וַיְהִי־אוֹר: וַיַּרְא אֱלֹהִים אֶת־הָאוֹר כִּי־טוֹב וַיַּבְדֵּל אֱלֹהִים בֵּין הָאוֹר וּבֵין הַחֹשֶׁךְ: וַיִּקְרָא אֱלֹהִים | לָאוֹר יוֹם וְלַחֹשֶׁךְ קָרָא לָיְלָה וַיְהִי־עֶרֶב וַיְהִי־בֹקֶר יוֹם אֶחָד:

לוי וַיֹּאמֶר אֱלֹהִים יְהִי רָקִיעַ בְּתוֹךְ הַמָּיִם וִיהִי מַבְדִּיל בֵּין מַיִם לָמָיִם: וַיַּעַשׂ אֱלֹהִים אֶת־הָרָקִיעַ וַיַּבְדֵּל בֵּין הַמַּיִם אֲשֶׁר מִתַּחַת לָרָקִיעַ וּבֵין הַמַּיִם אֲשֶׁר מֵעַל לָרָקִיעַ וַיְהִי־כֵן: וַיִּקְרָא אֱלֹהִים לָרָקִיעַ שָׁמָיִם וַיְהִי־עֶרֶב וַיְהִי־בֹקֶר יוֹם שֵׁנִי:

ישראל וַיֹּאמֶר אֱלֹהִים יִקָּווּ הַמַּיִם מִתַּחַת הַשָּׁמַיִם אֶל־מָקוֹם אֶחָד וְתֵרָאֶה הַיַּבָּשָׁה וַיְהִי־כֵן: וַיִּקְרָא אֱלֹהִים | לַיַּבָּשָׁה אֶרֶץ וּלְמִקְוֵה הַמַּיִם קָרָא יַמִּים וַיַּרְא אֱלֹהִים כִּי־טוֹב: וַיֹּאמֶר אֱלֹהִים תַּדְשֵׁא הָאָרֶץ דֶּשֶׁא עֵשֶׂב מַזְרִיעַ זֶרַע עֵץ פְּרִי עֹשֶׂה פְּרִי לְמִינוֹ אֲשֶׁר זַרְעוֹ־בוֹ עַל־הָאָרֶץ וַיְהִי־כֵן: וַתּוֹצֵא הָאָרֶץ דֶּשֶׁא עֵשֶׂב מַזְרִיעַ זֶרַע לְמִינֵהוּ וְעֵץ עֹשֶׂה־פְּרִי אֲשֶׁר זַרְעוֹ־בוֹ לְמִינֵהוּ וַיַּרְא אֱלֹהִים כִּי־טוֹב: וַיְהִי־עֶרֶב וַיְהִי־בֹקֶר יוֹם שְׁלִישִׁי:

פ׳ נח / NOACH
(*Genesis* 6:9-22)

אֵלֶּה תּוֹלְדֹת נֹחַ נֹחַ אִישׁ צַדִּיק תָּמִים הָיָה בְּדֹרֹתָיו אֶת־הָאֱלֹהִים הִתְהַלֶּךְ־נֹחַ: וַיּוֹלֶד נֹחַ שְׁלֹשָׁה בָנִים אֶת־שֵׁם אֶת־חָם וְאֶת־יָפֶת: וַתִּשָּׁחֵת הָאָרֶץ לִפְנֵי הָאֱלֹהִים וַתִּמָּלֵא הָאָרֶץ חָמָס: וַיַּרְא אֱלֹהִים אֶת־הָאָרֶץ וְהִנֵּה נִשְׁחָתָה כִּי־הִשְׁחִית כָּל־בָּשָׂר אֶת־דַּרְכּוֹ עַל־הָאָרֶץ: וַיֹּאמֶר אֱלֹהִים לְנֹחַ קֵץ כָּל־בָּשָׂר בָּא לְפָנַי כִּי־מָלְאָה הָאָרֶץ חָמָס מִפְּנֵיהֶם וְהִנְנִי מַשְׁחִיתָם אֶת־הָאָרֶץ: עֲשֵׂה לְךָ תֵּבַת עֲצֵי־גֹפֶר קִנִּים תַּעֲשֶׂה אֶת־הַתֵּבָה וְכָפַרְתָּ אֹתָהּ מִבַּיִת וּמִחוּץ בַּכֹּפֶר: וְזֶה אֲשֶׁר תַּעֲשֶׂה אֹתָהּ שְׁלֹשׁ מֵאוֹת אַמָּה אֹרֶךְ הַתֵּבָה חֲמִשִּׁים אַמָּה רָחְבָּהּ וּשְׁלֹשִׁים אַמָּה קוֹמָתָהּ: צֹהַר | תַּעֲשֶׂה לַתֵּבָה וְאֶל־אַמָּה תְּכַלֶּנָּה מִלְמַעְלָה וּפֶתַח הַתֵּבָה בְּצִדָּהּ תָּשִׂים תַּחְתִּיִּם שְׁנִיִּם וּשְׁלִשִׁים תַּעֲשֶׂהָ:

לוי וַאֲנִי הִנְנִי מֵבִיא אֶת־הַמַּבּוּל מַיִם עַל־הָאָרֶץ לְשַׁחֵת כָּל־בָּשָׂר אֲשֶׁר־בּוֹ רוּחַ חַיִּים מִתַּחַת הַשָּׁמָיִם כֹּל אֲשֶׁר־בָּאָרֶץ יִגְוָע: וַהֲקִמֹתִי אֶת־בְּרִיתִי אִתָּךְ וּבָאתָ אֶל־הַתֵּבָה אַתָּה וּבָנֶיךָ וְאִשְׁתְּךָ וּנְשֵׁי־בָנֶיךָ אִתָּךְ: וּמִכָּל־הָחַי מִכָּל־בָּשָׂר שְׁנַיִם מִכֹּל תָּבִיא אֶל־הַתֵּבָה לְהַחֲיֹת אִתָּךְ זָכָר וּנְקֵבָה יִהְיוּ:

ישראל מֵהָעוֹף לְמִינֵהוּ וּמִן־הַבְּהֵמָה לְמִינָהּ מִכֹּל רֶמֶשׂ הָאֲדָמָה לְמִינֵהוּ שְׁנַיִם מִכֹּל יָבֹאוּ אֵלֶיךָ לְהַחֲיוֹת: וְאַתָּה קַח־לְךָ מִכָּל־מַאֲכָל אֲשֶׁר יֵאָכֵל וְאָסַפְתָּ אֵלֶיךָ וְהָיָה לְךָ וְלָהֶם לְאָכְלָה: וַיַּעַשׂ נֹחַ כְּכֹל אֲשֶׁר צִוָּה אֹתוֹ אֱלֹהִים כֵּן עָשָׂה:

פ׳ לך לך / LECH LECHA
(*Genesis* 12:1-13)

וַיֹּאמֶר יהוה אֶל־אַבְרָם לֶךְ־לְךָ מֵאַרְצְךָ וּמִמּוֹלַדְתְּךָ וּמִבֵּית אָבִיךָ אֶל־הָאָרֶץ אֲשֶׁר אַרְאֶךָּ: וְאֶעֶשְׂךָ לְגוֹי גָּדוֹל וַאֲבָרֶכְךָ וַאֲגַדְּלָה שְׁמֶךָ וֶהְיֵה בְּרָכָה: וַאֲבָרְכָה מְבָרְכֶיךָ וּמְקַלֶּלְךָ אָאֹר וְנִבְרְכוּ בְךָ כֹּל מִשְׁפְּחֹת הָאֲדָמָה:

לוי וַיֵּלֶךְ אַבְרָם כַּאֲשֶׁר דִּבֶּר אֵלָיו יהוה וַיֵּלֶךְ אִתּוֹ לוֹט וְאַבְרָם בֶּן־חָמֵשׁ שָׁנִים וְשִׁבְעִים שָׁנָה בְּצֵאתוֹ מֵחָרָן: וַיִּקַּח אַבְרָם אֶת־שָׂרַי אִשְׁתּוֹ וְאֶת־לוֹט בֶּן־אָחִיו וְאֶת־כָּל־רְכוּשָׁם אֲשֶׁר רָכָשׁוּ וְאֶת־הַנֶּפֶשׁ אֲשֶׁר־עָשׂוּ בְחָרָן וַיֵּצְאוּ לָלֶכֶת אַרְצָה כְּנַעַן וַיָּבֹאוּ אַרְצָה כְּנָעַן: וַיַּעֲבֹר אַבְרָם בָּאָרֶץ עַד מְקוֹם שְׁכֶם עַד אֵלוֹן מוֹרֶה וְהַכְּנַעֲנִי אָז בָּאָרֶץ: וַיֵּרָא יהוה אֶל־אַבְרָם וַיֹּאמֶר לְזַרְעֲךָ אֶתֵּן

את־הארץ הזאת ויבן שם מזבח ליהוה הנראה אליו: ויעתק משם ההרה מקדם לבית־אל ויט אהלה בית־אל מים והעי מקדם ויבן־שם מזבח ליהוה ויקרא בשם יהוה: ויסע אברם הלוך ונסוע הנגבה:

ישראל ויהי רעב בארץ וירד אברם מצרימה לגור שם כי־כבד הרעב בארץ: ויהי כאשר הקריב לבוא מצרימה ויאמר אל־שרי אשתו הנה־נא ידעתי כי אשה יפת־מראה את: והיה כי־יראו אתך המצרים ואמרו אשתו זאת והרגו אתי ואתך יחיו: אמרי־נא אחתי את למען ייטב־לי בעבורך וחיתה נפשי בגללך:

VAYERA / פ׳ וירא

(*Genesis* 18:1-14)

וירא אליו יהוה באלני ממרא והוא ישב פתח־האהל כחם היום: וישא עיניו וירא והנה שלשה אנשים נצבים עליו וירא וירץ לקראתם מפתח האהל וישתחו ארצה: ויאמר אדני אם־נא מצאתי חן בעיניך אל־נא תעבר מעל עבדך: יקח־נא מעט־מים ורחצו רגליכם והשענו תחת העץ: ואקחה פת־לחם וסעדו לבכם אחר תעברו כי־על־כן עברתם על־עבדכם ויאמרו כן תעשה כאשר דברת:

לוי וימהר אברהם האהלה אל־שרה ויאמר מהרי שלש סאים קמח סלת לושי ועשי עגות: ואל־הבקר רץ אברהם ויקח בן־בקר רך וטוב ויתן אל־הנער וימהר לעשות אתו: ויקח חמאה וחלב ובן־הבקר אשר עשה ויתן לפניהם והוא עמד עליהם תחת העץ ויאכלו:

ישראל ויאמרו אליו איה שרה אשתך ויאמר הנה באהל: ויאמר שוב אשוב אליך כעת חיה והנה־בן לשרה אשתך ושרה שמעת פתח האהל והוא אחריו: ואברהם ושרה זקנים באים בימים חדל להיות לשרה ארח כנשים: ותצחק שרה בקרבה לאמר אחרי בלתי היתה־לי עדנה ואדני זקן: ויאמר יהוה אל־אברהם למה זה צחקה שרה לאמר האף אמנם אלד ואני זקנתי: היפלא מיהוה דבר למועד אשוב אליך כעת חיה ולשרה בן:

CHAYEI SARAH / פ׳ חיי שרה

(*Genesis* 23:1-16)

ויהיו חיי שרה מאה שנה ועשרים שנה ושבע שנים שני חיי שרה: ותמת שרה בקרית ארבע הוא חברון בארץ כנען ויבא אברהם לספד לשרה ולבכתה: ויקם אברהם מעל פני מתו וידבר אל־בני־חת לאמר: גר־ותושב אנכי עמכם תנו לי אחזת־קבר עמכם ואקברה מתי מלפני: ויענו בני־חת את־אברהם לאמר לו: שמענו | אדני נשיא אלהים | אתה בתוכנו במבחר קברינו קבר את־מתך איש ממנו את־קברו לא־יכלה ממך מקבר מתך: ויקם אברהם וישתחו לעם־הארץ לבני־חת:

לוי וידבר אתם לאמר אם־יש את־נפשכם לקבר את־מתי מלפני שמעוני ופגעו־לי בעפרון בן־צחר: ויתן־לי את־מערת המכפלה אשר־לו אשר בקצה שדהו בכסף מלא יתננה לי בתוככם לאחזת־קבר: ועפרון ישב בתוך בני־חת ויען עפרון החתי את־אברהם באזני בני־חת לכל באי שער־עירו לאמר: לא־אדני שמעני השדה נתתי לך והמערה אשר־בו לך נתתיה לעיני בני־עמי נתתיה לך קבר מתך: וישתחו אברהם לפני עם־הארץ:

ישראל וידבר אל־עפרון באזני עם־הארץ לאמר אך אם־אתה לו שמעני נתתי כסף השדה קח ממני ואקברה את־מתי שמה: ויען עפרון את־אברהם לאמר לו: אדני שמעני ארץ ארבע מאת שקל־כסף ביני ובינך מה־הוא ואת־מתך קבר: וישמע אברהם אל־עפרון וישקל אברהם לעפרן את־הכסף אשר דבר באזני בני־חת ארבע מאות שקל כסף עבר לסחר:

TOLDOS / פ׳ תולדת

(*Genesis* 25:19—26:5)

ואלה תולדת יצחק בן־אברהם אברהם הוליד את־יצחק: ויהי יצחק בן־ארבעים שנה בקחתו את־רבקה בת־בתואל הארמי מפדן ארם אחות לבן הארמי לו לאשה: ויעתר יצחק ליהוה לנכח אשתו כי עקרה הוא ויעתר לו יהוה ותהר

רִבְקָה אִשְׁתּוֹ: וַיִּתְרֹצֲצוּ הַבָּנִים בְּקִרְבָּהּ
וַתֹּאמֶר אִם־כֵּן לָמָּה זֶּה אָנֹכִי וַתֵּלֶךְ לִדְרֹשׁ
אֶת־יְהוָֹה:

לוי וַיֹּאמֶר יְהוָֹה לָהּ שְׁנֵי גוֹיִם בְּבִטְנֵךְ וּשְׁנֵי
לְאֻמִּים מִמֵּעַיִךְ יִפָּרֵדוּ וּלְאֹם מִלְאֹם יֶאֱמָץ
וְרַב יַעֲבֹד צָעִיר: וַיִּמְלְאוּ יָמֶיהָ לָלֶדֶת וְהִנֵּה
תוֹמִם בְּבִטְנָהּ: וַיֵּצֵא הָרִאשׁוֹן אַדְמוֹנִי כֻּלּוֹ
כְּאַדֶּרֶת שֵׂעָר וַיִּקְרְאוּ שְׁמוֹ עֵשָׂו: וְאַחֲרֵי־כֵן
יָצָא אָחִיו וְיָדוֹ אֹחֶזֶת בַּעֲקֵב עֵשָׂו וַיִּקְרָא
שְׁמוֹ יַעֲקֹב וְיִצְחָק בֶּן־שִׁשִּׁים שָׁנָה בְּלֶדֶת
אֹתָם:

ישראל וַיִּגְדְּלוּ הַנְּעָרִים וַיְהִי עֵשָׂו אִישׁ יֹדֵעַ
צַיִד אִישׁ שָׂדֶה וְיַעֲקֹב אִישׁ תָּם יֹשֵׁב
אֹהָלִים: וַיֶּאֱהַב יִצְחָק אֶת־עֵשָׂו כִּי־צַיִד
בְּפִיו וְרִבְקָה אֹהֶבֶת אֶת־יַעֲקֹב: וַיָּזֶד יַעֲקֹב
נָזִיד וַיָּבֹא עֵשָׂו מִן־הַשָּׂדֶה וְהוּא עָיֵף:
וַיֹּאמֶר עֵשָׂו אֶל־יַעֲקֹב הַלְעִיטֵנִי נָא מִן־
הָאָדֹם הָאָדֹם הַזֶּה כִּי עָיֵף אָנֹכִי עַל־כֵּן
קָרָא־שְׁמוֹ אֱדוֹם: וַיֹּאמֶר יַעֲקֹב מִכְרָה כַיּוֹם
אֶת־בְּכֹרָתְךָ לִי: וַיֹּאמֶר עֵשָׂו הִנֵּה אָנֹכִי
הוֹלֵךְ לָמוּת וְלָמָּה־זֶּה לִי בְּכֹרָה: וַיֹּאמֶר
יַעֲקֹב הִשָּׁבְעָה לִּי כַּיּוֹם וַיִּשָּׁבַע לוֹ וַיִּמְכֹּר
אֶת־בְּכֹרָתוֹ לְיַעֲקֹב: וְיַעֲקֹב נָתַן לְעֵשָׂו לֶחֶם
וּנְזִיד עֲדָשִׁים וַיֹּאכַל וַיֵּשְׁתְּ וַיָּקָם וַיֵּלַךְ וַיִּבֶז
עֵשָׂו אֶת־הַבְּכֹרָה: וַיְהִי רָעָב בָּאָרֶץ מִלְּבַד
הָרָעָב הָרִאשׁוֹן אֲשֶׁר הָיָה בִּימֵי אַבְרָהָם
וַיֵּלֶךְ יִצְחָק אֶל־אֲבִימֶלֶךְ מֶלֶךְ־פְּלִשְׁתִּים
גְּרָרָה: וַיֵּרָא אֵלָיו יְהוָֹה וַיֹּאמֶר אַל־תֵּרֵד
מִצְרָיְמָה שְׁכֹן בָּאָרֶץ אֲשֶׁר אֹמַר אֵלֶיךָ: גּוּר
בָּאָרֶץ הַזֹּאת וְאֶהְיֶה עִמְּךָ וַאֲבָרְכֶךָּ כִּי־לְךָ
וּלְזַרְעֲךָ אֶתֵּן אֶת־כָּל־הָאֲרָצֹת הָאֵל
וַהֲקִמֹתִי אֶת־הַשְּׁבֻעָה אֲשֶׁר נִשְׁבַּעְתִּי
לְאַבְרָהָם אָבִיךָ: וְהִרְבֵּיתִי אֶת־זַרְעֲךָ
כְּכוֹכְבֵי הַשָּׁמַיִם וְנָתַתִּי לְזַרְעֲךָ אֵת כָּל־
הָאֲרָצֹת הָאֵל וְהִתְבָּרֲכוּ בְזַרְעֲךָ כֹּל גּוֹיֵי
הָאָרֶץ: עֵקֶב אֲשֶׁר־שָׁמַע אַבְרָהָם בְּקֹלִי
וַיִּשְׁמֹר מִשְׁמַרְתִּי מִצְוֹתַי חֻקּוֹתַי וְתוֹרֹתָי:

פ׳ ויצא / VAYETZEI

(Genesis 28:10-22)

וַיֵּצֵא יַעֲקֹב מִבְּאֵר שָׁבַע וַיֵּלֶךְ חָרָנָה: וַיִּפְגַּע
בַּמָּקוֹם וַיָּלֶן שָׁם כִּי־בָא הַשֶּׁמֶשׁ וַיִּקַּח
מֵאַבְנֵי הַמָּקוֹם וַיָּשֶׂם מְרַאֲשֹׁתָיו וַיִּשְׁכַּב
בַּמָּקוֹם הַהוּא: וַיַּחֲלֹם וְהִנֵּה סֻלָּם מֻצָּב
אַרְצָה וְרֹאשׁוֹ מַגִּיעַ הַשָּׁמָיְמָה וְהִנֵּה
מַלְאֲכֵי אֱלֹהִים עֹלִים וְיֹרְדִים בּוֹ:

לוי וְהִנֵּה יְהוָֹה נִצָּב עָלָיו וַיֹּאמַר אֲנִי יְהוָֹה
אֱלֹהֵי אַבְרָהָם אָבִיךָ וֵאלֹהֵי יִצְחָק הָאָרֶץ
אֲשֶׁר אַתָּה שֹׁכֵב עָלֶיהָ לְךָ אֶתְּנֶנָּה וּלְזַרְעֶךָ:
וְהָיָה זַרְעֲךָ כַּעֲפַר הָאָרֶץ וּפָרַצְתָּ יָמָּה
וָקֵדְמָה וְצָפֹנָה וָנֶגְבָּה וְנִבְרֲכוּ בְךָ כָּל־
מִשְׁפְּחֹת הָאֲדָמָה וּבְזַרְעֶךָ: וְהִנֵּה אָנֹכִי
עִמָּךְ וּשְׁמַרְתִּיךָ בְּכֹל אֲשֶׁר־תֵּלֵךְ וַהֲשִׁבֹתִיךָ
אֶל־הָאֲדָמָה הַזֹּאת כִּי לֹא אֶעֱזָבְךָ עַד אֲשֶׁר
אִם־עָשִׂיתִי אֵת אֲשֶׁר־דִּבַּרְתִּי לָךְ: וַיִּיקַץ
יַעֲקֹב מִשְּׁנָתוֹ וַיֹּאמֶר אָכֵן יֵשׁ יְהוָֹה בַּמָּקוֹם
הַזֶּה וְאָנֹכִי לֹא יָדָעְתִּי: וַיִּירָא וַיֹּאמַר מַה־
נּוֹרָא הַמָּקוֹם הַזֶּה אֵין זֶה כִּי אִם־בֵּית
אֱלֹהִים וְזֶה שַׁעַר הַשָּׁמָיִם:

ישראל וַיַּשְׁכֵּם יַעֲקֹב בַּבֹּקֶר וַיִּקַּח אֶת־הָאֶבֶן
אֲשֶׁר־שָׂם מְרַאֲשֹׁתָיו וַיָּשֶׂם אֹתָהּ מַצֵּבָה
וַיִּצֹק שֶׁמֶן עַל־רֹאשָׁהּ: וַיִּקְרָא אֶת־שֵׁם־
הַמָּקוֹם הַהוּא בֵּית־אֵל וְאוּלָם לוּז שֵׁם־
הָעִיר לָרִאשֹׁנָה: וַיִּדַּר יַעֲקֹב נֶדֶר לֵאמֹר
אִם־יִהְיֶה אֱלֹהִים עִמָּדִי וּשְׁמָרַנִי בַּדֶּרֶךְ
הַזֶּה אֲשֶׁר אָנֹכִי הוֹלֵךְ וְנָתַן־לִי לֶחֶם לֶאֱכֹל
וּבֶגֶד לִלְבֹּשׁ: וְשַׁבְתִּי בְשָׁלוֹם אֶל־בֵּית אָבִי
וְהָיָה יְהוָֹה לִי לֵאלֹהִים: וְהָאֶבֶן הַזֹּאת
אֲשֶׁר־שַׂמְתִּי מַצֵּבָה יִהְיֶה בֵּית אֱלֹהִים וְכֹל
אֲשֶׁר תִּתֶּן־לִי עַשֵּׂר אֲעַשְּׂרֶנּוּ לָךְ:

פ׳ וישלח / VAYISHLACH

(Genesis 32:4-13)

וַיִּשְׁלַח יַעֲקֹב מַלְאָכִים לְפָנָיו אֶל־עֵשָׂו
אָחִיו אַרְצָה שֵׂעִיר שְׂדֵה אֱדוֹם: וַיְצַו אֹתָם
לֵאמֹר כֹּה תֹאמְרוּן לַאדֹנִי לְעֵשָׂו כֹּה אָמַר
עַבְדְּךָ יַעֲקֹב עִם־לָבָן גַּרְתִּי וָאֵחַר עַד־עָתָּה:
וַיְהִי־לִי שׁוֹר וַחֲמוֹר צֹאן וְעֶבֶד וְשִׁפְחָה
וָאֶשְׁלְחָה לְהַגִּיד לַאדֹנִי לִמְצֹא־חֵן בְּעֵינֶיךָ:
לוי וַיָּשֻׁבוּ הַמַּלְאָכִים אֶל־יַעֲקֹב לֵאמֹר
בָּאנוּ אֶל־אָחִיךָ אֶל־עֵשָׂו וְגַם הֹלֵךְ
לִקְרָאתְךָ וְאַרְבַּע־מֵאוֹת אִישׁ עִמּוֹ: וַיִּירָא
יַעֲקֹב מְאֹד וַיֵּצֶר לוֹ וַיַּחַץ אֶת־הָעָם אֲשֶׁר־
אִתּוֹ וְאֶת־הַצֹּאן וְאֶת־הַבָּקָר וְהַגְּמַלִּים
לִשְׁנֵי מַחֲנוֹת: וַיֹּאמֶר אִם־יָבוֹא עֵשָׂו אֶל־
הַמַּחֲנֶה הָאַחַת וְהִכָּהוּ וְהָיָה הַמַּחֲנֶה
הַנִּשְׁאָר לִפְלֵיטָה:
ישראל וַיֹּאמֶר יַעֲקֹב אֱלֹהֵי אָבִי אַבְרָהָם

וֵאלֹהֵי אָבִי יִצְחָק יהוה הָאֹמֵר אֵלַי שׁוּב לְאַרְצְךָ וּלְמוֹלַדְתְּךָ וְאֵיטִיבָה עִמָּךְ: קָטֹנְתִּי מִכֹּל הַחֲסָדִים וּמִכָּל־הָאֱמֶת אֲשֶׁר עָשִׂיתָ אֶת־עַבְדֶּךָ כִּי בְמַקְלִי עָבַרְתִּי אֶת־הַיַּרְדֵּן הַזֶּה וְעַתָּה הָיִיתִי לִשְׁנֵי מַחֲנוֹת: הַצִּילֵנִי נָא מִיַּד אָחִי מִיַּד עֵשָׂו כִּי־יָרֵא אָנֹכִי אֹתוֹ פֶּן־יָבוֹא וְהִכַּנִי אֵם עַל־בָּנִים: וְאַתָּה אָמַרְתָּ הֵיטֵב אֵיטִיב עִמָּךְ וְשַׂמְתִּי אֶת־זַרְעֲךָ כְּחוֹל הַיָּם אֲשֶׁר לֹא־יִסָּפֵר מֵרֹב:

פ׳ וישב / VAYESHEV

(*Genesis* 37:1-11)

וַיֵּשֶׁב יַעֲקֹב בְּאֶרֶץ מְגוּרֵי אָבִיו בְּאֶרֶץ כְּנָעַן: אֵלֶּה | תֹּלְדוֹת יַעֲקֹב יוֹסֵף בֶּן־שְׁבַע־עֶשְׂרֵה שָׁנָה הָיָה רֹעֶה אֶת־אֶחָיו בַּצֹּאן וְהוּא נַעַר אֶת־בְּנֵי בִלְהָה וְאֶת־בְּנֵי זִלְפָּה נְשֵׁי אָבִיו וַיָּבֵא יוֹסֵף אֶת־דִּבָּתָם רָעָה אֶל־אֲבִיהֶם: וְיִשְׂרָאֵל אָהַב אֶת־יוֹסֵף מִכָּל־בָּנָיו כִּי־בֶן־זְקֻנִים הוּא לוֹ וְעָשָׂה לוֹ כְּתֹנֶת פַּסִּים:

לוי וַיִּרְאוּ אֶחָיו כִּי־אֹתוֹ אָהַב אֲבִיהֶם מִכָּל־אֶחָיו וַיִּשְׂנְאוּ אֹתוֹ וְלֹא יָכְלוּ דַּבְּרוֹ לְשָׁלֹם: וַיַּחֲלֹם יוֹסֵף חֲלוֹם וַיַּגֵּד לְאֶחָיו וַיּוֹסִפוּ עוֹד שְׂנֹא אֹתוֹ: וַיֹּאמֶר אֲלֵיהֶם שִׁמְעוּ־נָא הַחֲלוֹם הַזֶּה אֲשֶׁר חָלָמְתִּי: וְהִנֵּה אֲנַחְנוּ מְאַלְּמִים אֲלֻמִּים בְּתוֹךְ הַשָּׂדֶה וְהִנֵּה קָמָה אֲלֻמָּתִי וְגַם־נִצָּבָה וְהִנֵּה תְסֻבֶּינָה אֲלֻמֹּתֵיכֶם וַתִּשְׁתַּחֲוֶיןָ לַאֲלֻמָּתִי:

ישראל וַיֹּאמְרוּ לוֹ אֶחָיו הֲמָלֹךְ תִּמְלֹךְ עָלֵינוּ אִם־מָשׁוֹל תִּמְשֹׁל בָּנוּ וַיּוֹסִפוּ עוֹד שְׂנֹא אֹתוֹ עַל־חֲלֹמֹתָיו וְעַל־דְּבָרָיו: וַיַּחֲלֹם עוֹד חֲלוֹם אַחֵר וַיְסַפֵּר אֹתוֹ לְאֶחָיו וַיֹּאמֶר הִנֵּה חָלַמְתִּי חֲלוֹם עוֹד וְהִנֵּה הַשֶּׁמֶשׁ וְהַיָּרֵחַ וְאַחַד עָשָׂר כּוֹכָבִים מִשְׁתַּחֲוִים לִי: וַיְסַפֵּר אֶל־אָבִיו וְאֶל־אֶחָיו וַיִּגְעַר־בּוֹ אָבִיו וַיֹּאמֶר לוֹ מָה הַחֲלוֹם הַזֶּה אֲשֶׁר חָלָמְתָּ הֲבוֹא נָבוֹא אֲנִי וְאִמְּךָ וְאַחֶיךָ לְהִשְׁתַּחֲוֹת לְךָ אָרְצָה: וַיְקַנְאוּ־בוֹ אֶחָיו וְאָבִיו שָׁמַר אֶת־הַדָּבָר:

פ׳ מקץ / MIKEITZ

(*Genesis* 41:1-14)

וַיְהִי מִקֵּץ שְׁנָתַיִם יָמִים וּפַרְעֹה חֹלֵם וְהִנֵּה עֹמֵד עַל־הַיְאֹר: וְהִנֵּה מִן־הַיְאֹר עֹלֹת שֶׁבַע פָּרוֹת יְפוֹת מַרְאֶה וּבְרִיאֹת בָּשָׂר וַתִּרְעֶינָה בָּאָחוּ: וְהִנֵּה שֶׁבַע פָּרוֹת אֲחֵרוֹת עֹלוֹת אַחֲרֵיהֶן מִן־הַיְאֹר רָעוֹת מַרְאֶה וְדַקּוֹת בָּשָׂר וַתַּעֲמֹדְנָה אֵצֶל הַפָּרוֹת עַל־שְׂפַת הַיְאֹר: וַתֹּאכַלְנָה הַפָּרוֹת רָעוֹת הַמַּרְאֶה וְדַקֹּת הַבָּשָׂר אֵת שֶׁבַע הַפָּרוֹת יְפֹת הַמַּרְאֶה וְהַבְּרִיאֹת וַיִּיקַץ פַּרְעֹה:

לוי וַיִּישָׁן וַיַּחֲלֹם שֵׁנִית וְהִנֵּה | שֶׁבַע שִׁבֳּלִים עֹלוֹת בְּקָנֶה אֶחָד בְּרִיאוֹת וְטֹבוֹת: וְהִנֵּה שֶׁבַע שִׁבֳּלִים דַּקּוֹת וּשְׁדוּפֹת קָדִים צֹמְחוֹת אַחֲרֵיהֶן: וַתִּבְלַעְנָה הַשִּׁבֳּלִים הַדַּקּוֹת אֵת שֶׁבַע הַשִּׁבֳּלִים הַבְּרִיאוֹת וְהַמְּלֵאוֹת וַיִּיקַץ פַּרְעֹה וְהִנֵּה חֲלוֹם:

ישראל וַיְהִי בַבֹּקֶר וַתִּפָּעֶם רוּחוֹ וַיִּשְׁלַח וַיִּקְרָא אֶת־כָּל־חַרְטֻמֵּי מִצְרַיִם וְאֶת־כָּל־חֲכָמֶיהָ וַיְסַפֵּר פַּרְעֹה לָהֶם אֶת־חֲלֹמוֹ וְאֵין־פּוֹתֵר אוֹתָם לְפַרְעֹה: וַיְדַבֵּר שַׂר הַמַּשְׁקִים אֶת־פַּרְעֹה לֵאמֹר אֶת־חֲטָאַי אֲנִי מַזְכִּיר הַיּוֹם: פַּרְעֹה קָצַף עַל־עֲבָדָיו וַיִּתֵּן אֹתִי בְּמִשְׁמַר בֵּית שַׂר הַטַּבָּחִים אֹתִי וְאֵת שַׂר הָאֹפִים: וַנַּחַלְמָה חֲלוֹם בְּלַיְלָה אֶחָד אֲנִי וָהוּא אִישׁ כְּפִתְרוֹן חֲלֹמוֹ חָלָמְנוּ: וְשָׁם אִתָּנוּ נַעַר עִבְרִי עֶבֶד לְשַׂר הַטַּבָּחִים וַנְּסַפֶּר־לוֹ וַיִּפְתָּר־לָנוּ אֶת־חֲלֹמֹתֵינוּ אִישׁ כַּחֲלֹמוֹ פָּתָר: וַיְהִי כַּאֲשֶׁר פָּתַר־לָנוּ כֵּן הָיָה אֹתִי הֵשִׁיב עַל־כַּנִּי וְאֹתוֹ תָלָה: וַיִּשְׁלַח פַּרְעֹה וַיִּקְרָא אֶת־יוֹסֵף וַיְרִיצֻהוּ מִן־הַבּוֹר וַיְגַלַּח וַיְחַלֵּף שִׂמְלֹתָיו וַיָּבֹא אֶל־פַּרְעֹה:

פ׳ ויגש / VAYIGASH

(*Genesis* 44:18-30)

וַיִּגַּשׁ אֵלָיו יְהוּדָה וַיֹּאמֶר בִּי אֲדֹנִי יְדַבֶּר־נָא עַבְדְּךָ דָבָר בְּאָזְנֵי אֲדֹנִי וְאַל־יִחַר אַפְּךָ בְּעַבְדֶּךָ כִּי כָמוֹךָ כְּפַרְעֹה: אֲדֹנִי שָׁאַל אֶת־עֲבָדָיו לֵאמֹר הֲיֵשׁ־לָכֶם אָב אוֹ־אָח: וַנֹּאמֶר אֶל־אֲדֹנִי יֶשׁ־לָנוּ אָב זָקֵן וְיֶלֶד זְקֻנִים קָטָן וְאָחִיו מֵת וַיִּוָּתֵר הוּא לְבַדּוֹ לְאִמּוֹ וְאָבִיו אֲהֵבוֹ:

לוי וַתֹּאמֶר אֶל־עֲבָדֶיךָ הוֹרִדֻהוּ אֵלָי וְאָשִׂימָה עֵינִי עָלָיו: וַנֹּאמֶר אֶל־אֲדֹנִי לֹא־יוּכַל הַנַּעַר לַעֲזֹב אֶת־אָבִיו וְעָזַב אֶת־אָבִיו וָמֵת: וַתֹּאמֶר אֶל־עֲבָדֶיךָ אִם־לֹא יֵרֵד אֲחִיכֶם הַקָּטֹן אִתְּכֶם לֹא תֹסִפוּן לִרְאוֹת פָּנָי: וַיְהִי כִּי עָלִינוּ אֶל־עַבְדְּךָ אָבִי וַנַּגֶּד־לוֹ אֵת דִּבְרֵי אֲדֹנִי:

ישראל וַיֹּאמֶר אָבִינוּ שֻׁבוּ שִׁבְרוּ־לָנוּ מְעַט־

אֹכֶל: וַנֹּאמֶר לֹא נוּכַל לָרֶדֶת אִם־יֵשׁ
אָחִינוּ הַקָּטֹן אִתָּנוּ וְיָרַדְנוּ כִּי־לֹא נוּכַל
לִרְאוֹת פְּנֵי הָאִישׁ וְאָחִינוּ הַקָּטֹן אֵינֶנּוּ
אִתָּנוּ: וַיֹּאמֶר עַבְדְּךָ אָבִי אֵלֵינוּ אַתֶּם
יְדַעְתֶּם כִּי שְׁנַיִם יָלְדָה־לִּי אִשְׁתִּי: וַיֵּצֵא
הָאֶחָד מֵאִתִּי וָאֹמַר אַךְ טָרֹף טֹרָף וְלֹא
רְאִיתִיו עַד־הֵנָּה: וּלְקַחְתֶּם גַּם־אֶת־זֶה
מֵעִם פָּנַי וְקָרָהוּ אָסוֹן וְהוֹרַדְתֶּם אֶת־
שֵׂיבָתִי בְּרָעָה שְׁאֹלָה: וְעַתָּה כְּבֹאִי אֶל־
עַבְדְּךָ אָבִי וְהַנַּעַר אֵינֶנּוּ אִתָּנוּ וְנַפְשׁוֹ
קְשׁוּרָה בְנַפְשׁוֹ:

פ׳ ויחי / VAYECHI
(*Genesis* 47:28—48:9)

וַיְחִי יַעֲקֹב בְּאֶרֶץ מִצְרַיִם שְׁבַע עֶשְׂרֵה
שָׁנָה וַיְהִי יְמֵי־יַעֲקֹב שְׁנֵי חַיָּיו שֶׁבַע שָׁנִים
וְאַרְבָּעִים וּמְאַת שָׁנָה: וַיִּקְרְבוּ יְמֵי־יִשְׂרָאֵל
לָמוּת וַיִּקְרָא | לִבְנוֹ לְיוֹסֵף וַיֹּאמֶר לוֹ אִם־
נָא מָצָאתִי חֵן בְּעֵינֶיךָ שִׂים־נָא יָדְךָ תַּחַת
יְרֵכִי וְעָשִׂיתָ עִמָּדִי חֶסֶד וֶאֱמֶת אַל־נָא
תִקְבְּרֵנִי בְּמִצְרָיִם: וְשָׁכַבְתִּי עִם־אֲבֹתַי
וּנְשָׂאתַנִי מִמִּצְרַיִם וּקְבַרְתַּנִי בִּקְבֻרָתָם
וַיֹּאמַר אָנֹכִי אֶעֱשֶׂה כִדְבָרֶךָ: וַיֹּאמֶר
הִשָּׁבְעָה לִי וַיִּשָּׁבַע לוֹ וַיִּשְׁתַּחוּ יִשְׂרָאֵל עַל־
רֹאשׁ הַמִּטָּה:
לוי וַיְהִי אַחֲרֵי הַדְּבָרִים הָאֵלֶּה וַיֹּאמֶר
לְיוֹסֵף הִנֵּה אָבִיךָ חֹלֶה וַיִּקַּח אֶת־שְׁנֵי בָנָיו
עִמּוֹ אֶת־מְנַשֶּׁה וְאֶת־אֶפְרָיִם: וַיַּגֵּד לְיַעֲקֹב
וַיֹּאמֶר הִנֵּה בִּנְךָ יוֹסֵף בָּא אֵלֶיךָ וַיִּתְחַזֵּק
יִשְׂרָאֵל וַיֵּשֶׁב עַל־הַמִּטָּה: וַיֹּאמֶר יַעֲקֹב
אֶל־יוֹסֵף אֵל שַׁדַּי נִרְאָה־אֵלַי בְּלוּז בְּאֶרֶץ
כְּנָעַן וַיְבָרֶךְ אֹתִי:
ישראל וַיֹּאמֶר אֵלַי הִנְנִי מַפְרְךָ וְהִרְבִּיתִךָ
וּנְתַתִּיךָ לִקְהַל עַמִּים וְנָתַתִּי אֶת־הָאָרֶץ
הַזֹּאת לְזַרְעֲךָ אַחֲרֶיךָ אֲחֻזַּת עוֹלָם: וְעַתָּה
שְׁנֵי־בָנֶיךָ הַנּוֹלָדִים לְךָ בְּאֶרֶץ מִצְרַיִם עַד־
בֹּאִי אֵלֶיךָ מִצְרַיְמָה לִי־הֵם אֶפְרַיִם וּמְנַשֶּׁה
כִּרְאוּבֵן וְשִׁמְעוֹן יִהְיוּ־לִי: וּמוֹלַדְתְּךָ אֲשֶׁר־
הוֹלַדְתָּ אַחֲרֵיהֶם לְךָ יִהְיוּ עַל שֵׁם אֲחֵיהֶם
יִקָּרְאוּ בְּנַחֲלָתָם: וַאֲנִי | בְּבֹאִי מִפַּדָּן מֵתָה
עָלַי רָחֵל בְּאֶרֶץ כְּנַעַן בַּדֶּרֶךְ בְּעוֹד כִּבְרַת־
אֶרֶץ לָבֹא אֶפְרָתָה וָאֶקְבְּרֶהָ שָּׁם בְּדֶרֶךְ
אֶפְרָת הִוא בֵּית לָחֶם: וַיַּרְא יִשְׂרָאֵל אֶת־
בְּנֵי יוֹסֵף וַיֹּאמֶר מִי־אֵלֶּה: וַיֹּאמֶר יוֹסֵף אֶל־
אָבִיו בָּנַי הֵם אֲשֶׁר־נָתַן־לִי אֱלֹהִים בָּזֶה
וַיֹּאמַר קָחֶם־נָא אֵלַי וַאֲבָרֲכֵם:

פ׳ שמות / SH'MOS
(*Exodus* 1:1-17)

וְאֵלֶּה שְׁמוֹת בְּנֵי יִשְׂרָאֵל הַבָּאִים מִצְרָיְמָה
אֵת יַעֲקֹב אִישׁ וּבֵיתוֹ בָּאוּ: רְאוּבֵן שִׁמְעוֹן
לֵוִי וִיהוּדָה: יִשָּׂשכָר זְבוּלֻן וּבִנְיָמִן: דָּן
וְנַפְתָּלִי גָּד וְאָשֵׁר: וַיְהִי כָּל־נֶפֶשׁ יֹצְאֵי יֶרֶךְ־
יַעֲקֹב שִׁבְעִים נָפֶשׁ וְיוֹסֵף הָיָה בְמִצְרָיִם:
וַיָּמָת יוֹסֵף וְכָל־אֶחָיו וְכֹל הַדּוֹר הַהוּא:
וּבְנֵי יִשְׂרָאֵל פָּרוּ וַיִּשְׁרְצוּ וַיִּרְבּוּ וַיַּעַצְמוּ
בִּמְאֹד מְאֹד וַתִּמָּלֵא הָאָרֶץ אֹתָם:
לוי וַיָּקָם מֶלֶךְ־חָדָשׁ עַל־מִצְרָיִם אֲשֶׁר לֹא־
יָדַע אֶת־יוֹסֵף: וַיֹּאמֶר אֶל־עַמּוֹ הִנֵּה עַם בְּנֵי
יִשְׂרָאֵל רַב וְעָצוּם מִמֶּנּוּ: הָבָה נִתְחַכְּמָה
לוֹ פֶּן־יִרְבֶּה וְהָיָה כִּי־תִקְרֶאנָה מִלְחָמָה
וְנוֹסַף גַּם־הוּא עַל־שֹׂנְאֵינוּ וְנִלְחַם־בָּנוּ
וְעָלָה מִן־הָאָרֶץ: וַיָּשִׂימוּ עָלָיו שָׂרֵי מִסִּים
לְמַעַן עַנֹּתוֹ בְּסִבְלֹתָם וַיִּבֶן עָרֵי מִסְכְּנוֹת
לְפַרְעֹה אֶת־פִּתֹם וְאֶת־רַעַמְסֵס: וְכַאֲשֶׁר
יְעַנּוּ אֹתוֹ כֵּן יִרְבֶּה וְכֵן יִפְרֹץ וַיָּקֻצוּ מִפְּנֵי
בְּנֵי יִשְׂרָאֵל:
ישראל וַיַּעֲבִדוּ מִצְרַיִם אֶת־בְּנֵי יִשְׂרָאֵל
בְּפָרֶךְ: וַיְמָרְרוּ אֶת־חַיֵּיהֶם בַּעֲבֹדָה קָשָׁה
בְּחֹמֶר וּבִלְבֵנִים וּבְכָל־עֲבֹדָה בַּשָּׂדֶה אֵת
כָּל־עֲבֹדָתָם אֲשֶׁר־עָבְדוּ בָהֶם בְּפָרֶךְ:
וַיֹּאמֶר מֶלֶךְ מִצְרַיִם לַמְיַלְּדֹת הָעִבְרִיֹּת
אֲשֶׁר שֵׁם הָאַחַת שִׁפְרָה וְשֵׁם הַשֵּׁנִית
פּוּעָה: וַיֹּאמֶר בְּיַלֶּדְכֶן אֶת־הָעִבְרִיּוֹת
וּרְאִיתֶן עַל־הָאָבְנָיִם אִם־בֵּן הוּא וַהֲמִתֶּן
אֹתוֹ וְאִם־בַּת הִוא וָחָיָה: וַתִּירֶאןָ הַמְיַלְּדֹת
אֶת־הָאֱלֹהִים וְלֹא עָשׂוּ כַּאֲשֶׁר דִּבֶּר אֲלֵיהֶן
מֶלֶךְ מִצְרָיִם וַתְּחַיֶּיןָ אֶת־הַיְלָדִים:

פ׳ וארא / VAERA
(*Exodus* 6:2-13)

וַיְדַבֵּר אֱלֹהִים אֶל־מֹשֶׁה וַיֹּאמֶר אֵלָיו אֲנִי
יהוה: וָאֵרָא אֶל־אַבְרָהָם אֶל־יִצְחָק וְאֶל־
יַעֲקֹב בְּאֵל שַׁדָּי וּשְׁמִי יהוה לֹא נוֹדַעְתִּי
לָהֶם: וְגַם הֲקִמֹתִי אֶת־בְּרִיתִי אִתָּם לָתֵת
לָהֶם אֶת־אֶרֶץ כְּנָעַן אֵת אֶרֶץ מְגֻרֵיהֶם
אֲשֶׁר־גָּרוּ בָהּ: וְגַם | אֲנִי שָׁמַעְתִּי אֶת־נַאֲקַת
בְּנֵי יִשְׂרָאֵל אֲשֶׁר מִצְרַיִם מַעֲבִדִים אֹתָם
וָאֶזְכֹּר אֶת־בְּרִיתִי:

לוי לָכֵן אֱמֹר לִבְנֵי־יִשְׂרָאֵל אֲנִי יהוה וְהוֹצֵאתִי אֶתְכֶם מִתַּחַת סִבְלֹת מִצְרַיִם וְהִצַּלְתִּי אֶתְכֶם מֵעֲבֹדָתָם וְגָאַלְתִּי אֶתְכֶם בִּזְרוֹעַ נְטוּיָה וּבִשְׁפָטִים גְּדֹלִים: וְלָקַחְתִּי אֶתְכֶם לִי לְעָם וְהָיִיתִי לָכֶם לֵאלֹהִים וִידַעְתֶּם כִּי אֲנִי יהוה אֱלֹהֵיכֶם הַמּוֹצִיא אֶתְכֶם מִתַּחַת סִבְלוֹת מִצְרָיִם: וְהֵבֵאתִי אֶתְכֶם אֶל־הָאָרֶץ אֲשֶׁר נָשָׂאתִי אֶת־יָדִי לָתֵת אֹתָהּ לְאַבְרָהָם לְיִצְחָק וּלְיַעֲקֹב וְנָתַתִּי אֹתָהּ לָכֶם מוֹרָשָׁה אֲנִי יהוה: וַיְדַבֵּר מֹשֶׁה כֵּן אֶל־בְּנֵי יִשְׂרָאֵל וְלֹא שָׁמְעוּ אֶל־מֹשֶׁה מִקֹּצֶר רוּחַ וּמֵעֲבֹדָה קָשָׁה:

ישראל וַיְדַבֵּר יהוה אֶל־מֹשֶׁה לֵּאמֹר: בֹּא דַבֵּר אֶל־פַּרְעֹה מֶלֶךְ מִצְרָיִם וִישַׁלַּח אֶת־בְּנֵי־יִשְׂרָאֵל מֵאַרְצוֹ: וַיְדַבֵּר מֹשֶׁה לִפְנֵי יהוה לֵאמֹר הֵן בְּנֵי־יִשְׂרָאֵל לֹא־שָׁמְעוּ אֵלַי וְאֵיךְ יִשְׁמָעֵנִי פַרְעֹה וַאֲנִי עֲרַל שְׂפָתָיִם: וַיְדַבֵּר יהוה אֶל־מֹשֶׁה וְאֶל־אַהֲרֹן וַיְצַוֵּם אֶל־בְּנֵי יִשְׂרָאֵל וְאֶל־פַּרְעֹה מֶלֶךְ מִצְרָיִם לְהוֹצִיא אֶת־בְּנֵי־יִשְׂרָאֵל מֵאֶרֶץ מִצְרָיִם:

פ׳ בא / BO

(*Exodus* 10:1-11)

וַיֹּאמֶר יהוה אֶל־מֹשֶׁה בֹּא אֶל־פַּרְעֹה כִּי־אֲנִי הִכְבַּדְתִּי אֶת־לִבּוֹ וְאֶת־לֵב עֲבָדָיו לְמַעַן שִׁתִי אֹתֹתַי אֵלֶּה בְּקִרְבּוֹ: וּלְמַעַן תְּסַפֵּר בְּאָזְנֵי בִנְךָ וּבֶן־בִּנְךָ אֵת אֲשֶׁר הִתְעַלַּלְתִּי בְּמִצְרַיִם וְאֶת־אֹתֹתַי אֲשֶׁר־שַׂמְתִּי בָם וִידַעְתֶּם כִּי־אֲנִי יהוה: וַיָּבֹא מֹשֶׁה וְאַהֲרֹן אֶל־פַּרְעֹה וַיֹּאמְרוּ אֵלָיו כֹּה־אָמַר יהוה אֱלֹהֵי הָעִבְרִים עַד־מָתַי מֵאַנְתָּ לֵעָנֹת מִפָּנָי שַׁלַּח עַמִּי וְיַעַבְדֻנִי:

לוי כִּי אִם־מָאֵן אַתָּה לְשַׁלֵּחַ אֶת־עַמִּי הִנְנִי מֵבִיא מָחָר אַרְבֶּה בִּגְבֻלֶךָ: וְכִסָּה אֶת־עֵין הָאָרֶץ וְלֹא יוּכַל לִרְאֹת אֶת־הָאָרֶץ וְאָכַל | אֶת־יֶתֶר הַפְּלֵטָה הַנִּשְׁאֶרֶת לָכֶם מִן־הַבָּרָד וְאָכַל אֶת־כָּל־הָעֵץ הַצֹּמֵחַ לָכֶם מִן־הַשָּׂדֶה: וּמָלְאוּ בָתֶּיךָ וּבָתֵּי כָל־עֲבָדֶיךָ וּבָתֵּי כָל־מִצְרַיִם אֲשֶׁר לֹא־רָאוּ אֲבֹתֶיךָ וַאֲבוֹת אֲבֹתֶיךָ מִיּוֹם הֱיוֹתָם עַל־הָאֲדָמָה עַד הַיּוֹם הַזֶּה וַיִּפֶן וַיֵּצֵא מֵעִם פַּרְעֹה:

ישראל וַיֹּאמְרוּ עַבְדֵי פַרְעֹה אֵלָיו עַד־מָתַי יִהְיֶה זֶה לָנוּ לְמוֹקֵשׁ שַׁלַּח אֶת־הָאֲנָשִׁים וְיַעַבְדוּ אֶת־יהוה אֱלֹהֵיהֶם הֲטֶרֶם תֵּדַע כִּי אָבְדָה מִצְרָיִם: וַיּוּשַׁב אֶת־מֹשֶׁה וְאֶת־אַהֲרֹן אֶל־פַּרְעֹה וַיֹּאמֶר אֲלֵהֶם לְכוּ עִבְדוּ אֶת־יהוה אֱלֹהֵיכֶם מִי וָמִי הַהֹלְכִים: וַיֹּאמֶר מֹשֶׁה בִּנְעָרֵינוּ וּבִזְקֵנֵינוּ נֵלֵךְ בְּבָנֵינוּ וּבִבְנוֹתֵנוּ בְּצֹאנֵנוּ וּבִבְקָרֵנוּ נֵלֵךְ כִּי חַג־יהוה לָנוּ: וַיֹּאמֶר אֲלֵהֶם יְהִי כֵן יהוה עִמָּכֶם כַּאֲשֶׁר אֲשַׁלַּח אֶתְכֶם וְאֶת־טַפְּכֶם רְאוּ כִּי רָעָה נֶגֶד פְּנֵיכֶם: לֹא כֵן לְכוּ־נָא הַגְּבָרִים וְעִבְדוּ אֶת־יהוה כִּי אֹתָהּ אַתֶּם מְבַקְשִׁים וַיְגָרֶשׁ אֹתָם מֵאֵת פְּנֵי פַרְעֹה:

פ׳ בשלח / BESHALACH

(*Exodus* 13:17—14:8)

וַיְהִי בְּשַׁלַּח פַּרְעֹה אֶת־הָעָם וְלֹא־נָחָם אֱלֹהִים דֶּרֶךְ אֶרֶץ פְּלִשְׁתִּים כִּי קָרוֹב הוּא כִּי | אָמַר אֱלֹהִים פֶּן־יִנָּחֵם הָעָם בִּרְאֹתָם מִלְחָמָה וְשָׁבוּ מִצְרָיְמָה: וַיַּסֵּב אֱלֹהִים | אֶת־הָעָם דֶּרֶךְ הַמִּדְבָּר יַם־סוּף וַחֲמֻשִׁים עָלוּ בְנֵי־יִשְׂרָאֵל מֵאֶרֶץ מִצְרָיִם: וַיִּקַּח מֹשֶׁה אֶת־עַצְמוֹת יוֹסֵף עִמּוֹ כִּי הַשְׁבֵּעַ הִשְׁבִּיעַ אֶת־בְּנֵי יִשְׂרָאֵל לֵאמֹר פָּקֹד יִפְקֹד אֱלֹהִים אֶתְכֶם וְהַעֲלִיתֶם אֶת־עַצְמֹתַי מִזֶּה אִתְּכֶם: וַיִּסְעוּ מִסֻּכֹּת וַיַּחֲנוּ בְאֵתָם בִּקְצֵה הַמִּדְבָּר: וַיהוה הֹלֵךְ לִפְנֵיהֶם יוֹמָם בְּעַמּוּד עָנָן לַנְחֹתָם הַדֶּרֶךְ וְלַיְלָה בְּעַמּוּד אֵשׁ לְהָאִיר לָהֶם לָלֶכֶת יוֹמָם וָלָיְלָה: לֹא־יָמִישׁ עַמּוּד הֶעָנָן יוֹמָם וְעַמּוּד הָאֵשׁ לָיְלָה לִפְנֵי הָעָם:

לוי וַיְדַבֵּר יהוה אֶל־מֹשֶׁה לֵּאמֹר: דַּבֵּר אֶל־בְּנֵי יִשְׂרָאֵל וְיָשֻׁבוּ וְיַחֲנוּ לִפְנֵי פִּי הַחִירֹת בֵּין מִגְדֹּל וּבֵין הַיָּם לִפְנֵי בַּעַל צְפֹן נִכְחוֹ תַחֲנוּ עַל־הַיָּם: וְאָמַר פַּרְעֹה לִבְנֵי יִשְׂרָאֵל נְבֻכִים הֵם בָּאָרֶץ סָגַר עֲלֵיהֶם הַמִּדְבָּר: וְחִזַּקְתִּי אֶת־לֵב־פַּרְעֹה וְרָדַף אַחֲרֵיהֶם וְאִכָּבְדָה בְּפַרְעֹה וּבְכָל־חֵילוֹ וְיָדְעוּ מִצְרַיִם כִּי־אֲנִי יהוה וַיַּעֲשׂוּ־כֵן:

ישראל וַיֻּגַּד לְמֶלֶךְ מִצְרַיִם כִּי בָרַח הָעָם וַיֵּהָפֵךְ לְבַב פַּרְעֹה וַעֲבָדָיו אֶל־הָעָם וַיֹּאמְרוּ מַה־זֹּאת עָשִׂינוּ כִּי־שִׁלַּחְנוּ אֶת־יִשְׂרָאֵל מֵעָבְדֵנוּ: וַיֶּאְסֹר אֶת־רִכְבּוֹ וְאֶת־עַמּוֹ לָקַח עִמּוֹ: וַיִּקַּח שֵׁשׁ־מֵאוֹת רֶכֶב בָּחוּר וְכֹל רֶכֶב מִצְרָיִם וְשָׁלִשִׁם עַל־כֻּלּוֹ: וַיְחַזֵּק יהוה אֶת־לֵב פַּרְעֹה מֶלֶךְ מִצְרַיִם

וַיִּרְדֹּף אַחֲרֵי בְּנֵי יִשְׂרָאֵל וּבְנֵי יִשְׂרָאֵל יֹצְאִים בְּיָד רָמָה׃

פ׳ יתרו / YISRO
(*Exodus* 18:1-12)

וַיִּשְׁמַע יִתְרוֹ כֹהֵן מִדְיָן חֹתֵן מֹשֶׁה אֵת כָּל־אֲשֶׁר עָשָׂה אֱלֹהִים לְמֹשֶׁה וּלְיִשְׂרָאֵל עַמּוֹ כִּי־הוֹצִיא יְהֹוָה אֶת־יִשְׂרָאֵל מִמִּצְרָיִם׃ וַיִּקַּח יִתְרוֹ חֹתֵן מֹשֶׁה אֶת־צִפֹּרָה אֵשֶׁת מֹשֶׁה אַחַר שִׁלּוּחֶיהָ׃ וְאֵת שְׁנֵי בָנֶיהָ אֲשֶׁר שֵׁם הָאֶחָד גֵּרְשֹׁם כִּי אָמַר גֵּר הָיִיתִי בְּאֶרֶץ נָכְרִיָּה׃ וְשֵׁם הָאֶחָד אֱלִיעֶזֶר כִּי־אֱלֹהֵי אָבִי בְּעֶזְרִי וַיַּצִּלֵנִי מֵחֶרֶב פַּרְעֹה׃

לוי וַיָּבֹא יִתְרוֹ חֹתֵן מֹשֶׁה וּבָנָיו וְאִשְׁתּוֹ אֶל־מֹשֶׁה אֶל־הַמִּדְבָּר אֲשֶׁר־הוּא חֹנֶה שָׁם הַר הָאֱלֹהִים׃ וַיֹּאמֶר אֶל־מֹשֶׁה אֲנִי חֹתֶנְךָ יִתְרוֹ בָּא אֵלֶיךָ וְאִשְׁתְּךָ וּשְׁנֵי בָנֶיהָ עִמָּהּ׃ וַיֵּצֵא מֹשֶׁה לִקְרַאת חֹתְנוֹ וַיִּשְׁתַּחוּ וַיִּשַּׁק־לוֹ וַיִּשְׁאֲלוּ אִישׁ־לְרֵעֵהוּ לְשָׁלוֹם וַיָּבֹאוּ הָאֹהֱלָה׃ וַיְסַפֵּר מֹשֶׁה לְחֹתְנוֹ אֵת כָּל־אֲשֶׁר עָשָׂה יְהֹוָה לְפַרְעֹה וּלְמִצְרַיִם עַל אוֹדֹת יִשְׂרָאֵל אֵת כָּל־הַתְּלָאָה אֲשֶׁר מְצָאָתַם בַּדֶּרֶךְ וַיַּצִּלֵם יְהֹוָה׃

ישראל וַיִּחַדְּ יִתְרוֹ עַל כָּל־הַטּוֹבָה אֲשֶׁר־עָשָׂה יְהֹוָה לְיִשְׂרָאֵל אֲשֶׁר הִצִּילוֹ מִיַּד מִצְרָיִם׃ וַיֹּאמֶר יִתְרוֹ בָּרוּךְ יְהֹוָה אֲשֶׁר הִצִּיל אֶתְכֶם מִיַּד מִצְרַיִם וּמִיַּד פַּרְעֹה אֲשֶׁר הִצִּיל אֶת־הָעָם מִתַּחַת יַד־מִצְרָיִם׃ עַתָּה יָדַעְתִּי כִּי־גָדוֹל יְהֹוָה מִכָּל־הָאֱלֹהִים כִּי בַדָּבָר אֲשֶׁר זָדוּ עֲלֵיהֶם׃ וַיִּקַּח יִתְרוֹ חֹתֵן מֹשֶׁה עֹלָה וּזְבָחִים לֵאלֹהִים וַיָּבֹא אַהֲרֹן וְכֹל ׀ זִקְנֵי יִשְׂרָאֵל לֶאֱכָל־לֶחֶם עִם־חֹתֵן מֹשֶׁה לִפְנֵי הָאֱלֹהִים׃

פ׳ משפטים / MISHPATIM
(*Exodus* 21:1-19)

וְאֵלֶּה הַמִּשְׁפָּטִים אֲשֶׁר תָּשִׂים לִפְנֵיהֶם׃ כִּי תִקְנֶה עֶבֶד עִבְרִי שֵׁשׁ שָׁנִים יַעֲבֹד וּבַשְּׁבִעִת יֵצֵא לַחָפְשִׁי חִנָּם׃ אִם־בְּגַפּוֹ יָבֹא בְּגַפּוֹ יֵצֵא אִם־בַּעַל אִשָּׁה הוּא וְיָצְאָה אִשְׁתּוֹ עִמּוֹ׃ אִם־אֲדֹנָיו יִתֶּן־לוֹ אִשָּׁה וְיָלְדָה־לוֹ בָנִים אוֹ בָנוֹת הָאִשָּׁה וִילָדֶיהָ תִּהְיֶה לַאדֹנֶיהָ וְהוּא יֵצֵא בְגַפּוֹ׃ וְאִם־אָמֹר יֹאמַר הָעֶבֶד אָהַבְתִּי אֶת־אֲדֹנִי אֶת־אִשְׁתִּי וְאֶת־בָּנָי לֹא אֵצֵא חָפְשִׁי׃ וְהִגִּישׁוֹ אֲדֹנָיו אֶל־הָאֱלֹהִים וְהִגִּישׁוֹ אֶל־הַדֶּלֶת אוֹ אֶל־הַמְּזוּזָה וְרָצַע אֲדֹנָיו אֶת־אָזְנוֹ בַּמַּרְצֵעַ וַעֲבָדוֹ לְעֹלָם׃

לוי וְכִי־יִמְכֹּר אִישׁ אֶת־בִּתּוֹ לְאָמָה לֹא תֵצֵא כְּצֵאת הָעֲבָדִים׃ אִם־רָעָה בְּעֵינֵי אֲדֹנֶיהָ אֲשֶׁר־לֹו יְעָדָהּ וְהֶפְדָּהּ לְעַם נָכְרִי לֹא־יִמְשֹׁל לְמָכְרָהּ בְּבִגְדוֹ־בָהּ׃ וְאִם־לִבְנוֹ יִיעָדֶנָּה כְּמִשְׁפַּט הַבָּנוֹת יַעֲשֶׂה־לָּהּ׃ אִם־אַחֶרֶת יִקַּח־לוֹ שְׁאֵרָהּ כְּסוּתָהּ וְעֹנָתָהּ לֹא יִגְרָע׃ וְאִם־שְׁלָשׁ־אֵלֶּה לֹא יַעֲשֶׂה לָהּ וְיָצְאָה חִנָּם אֵין כָּסֶף׃

ישראל מַכֵּה אִישׁ וָמֵת מוֹת יוּמָת׃ וַאֲשֶׁר לֹא צָדָה וְהָאֱלֹהִים אִנָּה לְיָדוֹ וְשַׂמְתִּי לְךָ מָקוֹם אֲשֶׁר יָנוּס שָׁמָּה׃ וְכִי־יָזִד אִישׁ עַל־רֵעֵהוּ לְהָרְגוֹ בְעָרְמָה מֵעִם מִזְבְּחִי תִּקָּחֶנּוּ לָמוּת׃ וּמַכֵּה אָבִיו וְאִמּוֹ מוֹת יוּמָת׃ וְגֹנֵב אִישׁ וּמְכָרוֹ וְנִמְצָא בְיָדוֹ מוֹת יוּמָת׃ וּמְקַלֵּל אָבִיו וְאִמּוֹ מוֹת יוּמָת׃ וְכִי־יְרִיבֻן אֲנָשִׁים וְהִכָּה־אִישׁ אֶת־רֵעֵהוּ בְּאֶבֶן אוֹ בְאֶגְרֹף וְלֹא יָמוּת וְנָפַל לְמִשְׁכָּב׃ אִם־יָקוּם וְהִתְהַלֵּךְ בַּחוּץ עַל־מִשְׁעַנְתּוֹ וְנִקָּה הַמַּכֶּה רַק שִׁבְתּוֹ יִתֵּן וְרַפֹּא יְרַפֵּא׃

פ׳ תרומה / TERUMAH
(*Exodus* 25:1-16)

וַיְדַבֵּר יְהֹוָה אֶל־מֹשֶׁה לֵּאמֹר׃ דַּבֵּר אֶל־בְּנֵי יִשְׂרָאֵל וְיִקְחוּ־לִי תְּרוּמָה מֵאֵת כָּל־אִישׁ אֲשֶׁר יִדְּבֶנּוּ לִבּוֹ תִּקְחוּ אֶת־תְּרוּמָתִי׃ וְזֹאת הַתְּרוּמָה אֲשֶׁר תִּקְחוּ מֵאִתָּם זָהָב וָכֶסֶף וּנְחֹשֶׁת׃ וּתְכֵלֶת וְאַרְגָּמָן וְתוֹלַעַת שָׁנִי וְשֵׁשׁ וְעִזִּים׃ וְעֹרֹת אֵילִם מְאָדָּמִים וְעֹרֹת תְּחָשִׁים וַעֲצֵי שִׁטִּים׃

לוי שֶׁמֶן לַמָּאֹר בְּשָׂמִים לְשֶׁמֶן הַמִּשְׁחָה וְלִקְטֹרֶת הַסַּמִּים׃ אַבְנֵי־שֹׁהַם וְאַבְנֵי מִלֻּאִים לָאֵפֹד וְלַחֹשֶׁן׃ וְעָשׂוּ לִי מִקְדָּשׁ וְשָׁכַנְתִּי בְּתוֹכָם׃ כְּכֹל אֲשֶׁר אֲנִי מַרְאֶה אוֹתְךָ אֵת תַּבְנִית הַמִּשְׁכָּן וְאֵת תַּבְנִית כָּל־כֵּלָיו וְכֵן תַּעֲשׂוּ׃

ישראל וְעָשׂוּ אֲרוֹן עֲצֵי שִׁטִּים אַמָּתַיִם וָחֵצִי אָרְכּוֹ וְאַמָּה וָחֵצִי רָחְבּוֹ וְאַמָּה וָחֵצִי קֹמָתוֹ׃ וְצִפִּיתָ אֹתוֹ זָהָב טָהוֹר מִבַּיִת וּמִחוּץ תְּצַפֶּנּוּ וְעָשִׂיתָ עָלָיו זֵר זָהָב סָבִיב׃ וְיָצַקְתָּ לּוֹ אַרְבַּע טַבְּעֹת זָהָב וְנָתַתָּה עַל אַרְבַּע פַּעֲמֹתָיו וּשְׁתֵּי טַבָּעֹת עַל־צַלְעוֹ

הָאֶחָת וּשְׁתֵּי טַבָּעֹת עַל־צַלְעוֹ הַשֵּׁנִית: וְעָשִׂיתָ בַדֵּי עֲצֵי שִׁטִּים וְצִפִּיתָ אֹתָם זָהָב: וְהֵבֵאתָ אֶת־הַבַּדִּים בַּטַּבָּעֹת עַל צַלְעֹת הָאָרֹן לָשֵׂאת אֶת־הָאָרֹן בָּהֶם: בְּטַבְּעֹת הָאָרֹן יִהְיוּ הַבַּדִּים לֹא יָסֻרוּ מִמֶּנּוּ: וְנָתַתָּ אֶל־הָאָרֹן אֵת הָעֵדֻת אֲשֶׁר אֶתֵּן אֵלֶיךָ:

פ׳ תצוה / TETZAVEH

(*Exodus* 27:20—28:12)

וְאַתָּה תְּצַוֶּה | אֶת־בְּנֵי יִשְׂרָאֵל וְיִקְחוּ אֵלֶיךָ שֶׁמֶן זַיִת זָךְ כָּתִית לַמָּאוֹר לְהַעֲלֹת נֵר תָּמִיד: בְּאֹהֶל מוֹעֵד מִחוּץ לַפָּרֹכֶת אֲשֶׁר עַל־הָעֵדֻת יַעֲרֹךְ אֹתוֹ אַהֲרֹן וּבָנָיו מֵעֶרֶב עַד־בֹּקֶר לִפְנֵי יהוה חֻקַּת עוֹלָם לְדֹרֹתָם מֵאֵת בְּנֵי יִשְׂרָאֵל: וְאַתָּה הַקְרֵב אֵלֶיךָ אֶת־אַהֲרֹן אָחִיךָ וְאֶת־בָּנָיו אִתּוֹ מִתּוֹךְ בְּנֵי יִשְׂרָאֵל לְכַהֲנוֹ־לִי אַהֲרֹן נָדָב וַאֲבִיהוּא אֶלְעָזָר וְאִיתָמָר בְּנֵי אַהֲרֹן: וְעָשִׂיתָ בִגְדֵי־קֹדֶשׁ לְאַהֲרֹן אָחִיךָ לְכָבוֹד וּלְתִפְאָרֶת: וְאַתָּה תְּדַבֵּר אֶל־כָּל־חַכְמֵי־לֵב אֲשֶׁר מִלֵּאתִיו רוּחַ חָכְמָה וְעָשׂוּ אֶת־בִּגְדֵי אַהֲרֹן לְקַדְּשׁוֹ לְכַהֲנוֹ־לִי: וְאֵלֶּה הַבְּגָדִים אֲשֶׁר יַעֲשׂוּ חֹשֶׁן וְאֵפוֹד וּמְעִיל וּכְתֹנֶת תַּשְׁבֵּץ מִצְנֶפֶת וְאַבְנֵט וְעָשׂוּ בִגְדֵי־קֹדֶשׁ לְאַהֲרֹן אָחִיךָ וּלְבָנָיו לְכַהֲנוֹ־לִי: וְהֵם יִקְחוּ אֶת־הַזָּהָב וְאֶת־הַתְּכֵלֶת וְאֶת־הָאַרְגָּמָן וְאֶת־תּוֹלַעַת הַשָּׁנִי וְאֶת־הַשֵּׁשׁ:

לוי וְעָשׂוּ אֶת־הָאֵפֹד זָהָב תְּכֵלֶת וְאַרְגָּמָן תּוֹלַעַת שָׁנִי וְשֵׁשׁ מָשְׁזָר מַעֲשֵׂה חֹשֵׁב: שְׁתֵּי כְתֵפֹת חֹבְרֹת יִהְיֶה־לּוֹ אֶל־שְׁנֵי קְצוֹתָיו וְחֻבָּר: וְחֵשֶׁב אֲפֻדָּתוֹ אֲשֶׁר עָלָיו כְּמַעֲשֵׂהוּ מִמֶּנּוּ יִהְיֶה זָהָב תְּכֵלֶת וְאַרְגָּמָן וְתוֹלַעַת שָׁנִי וְשֵׁשׁ מָשְׁזָר: וְלָקַחְתָּ אֶת־שְׁתֵּי אַבְנֵי־שֹׁהַם וּפִתַּחְתָּ עֲלֵיהֶם שְׁמוֹת בְּנֵי יִשְׂרָאֵל:

ישראל שִׁשָּׁה מִשְּׁמֹתָם עַל הָאֶבֶן הָאֶחָת וְאֶת־שְׁמוֹת הַשִּׁשָּׁה הַנּוֹתָרִים עַל־הָאֶבֶן הַשֵּׁנִית כְּתוֹלְדֹתָם: מַעֲשֵׂה חָרַשׁ אֶבֶן פִּתּוּחֵי חֹתָם תְּפַתַּח אֶת־שְׁתֵּי הָאֲבָנִים עַל־שְׁמֹת בְּנֵי יִשְׂרָאֵל מֻסַבֹּת מִשְׁבְּצוֹת זָהָב תַּעֲשֶׂה אֹתָם: וְשַׂמְתָּ אֶת־שְׁתֵּי הָאֲבָנִים עַל כִּתְפֹת הָאֵפֹד אַבְנֵי זִכָּרֹן לִבְנֵי יִשְׂרָאֵל וְנָשָׂא אַהֲרֹן אֶת־שְׁמוֹתָם לִפְנֵי יהוה עַל־שְׁתֵּי כְתֵפָיו לְזִכָּרֹן:

פ׳ כי תשא / KI SISA

(*Exodus* 30:11-21)

וַיְדַבֵּר יהוה אֶל־מֹשֶׁה לֵּאמֹר: כִּי תִשָּׂא אֶת־רֹאשׁ בְּנֵי־יִשְׂרָאֵל לִפְקֻדֵיהֶם וְנָתְנוּ אִישׁ כֹּפֶר נַפְשׁוֹ לַיהוה בִּפְקֹד אֹתָם וְלֹא־יִהְיֶה בָהֶם נֶגֶף בִּפְקֹד אֹתָם: זֶה | יִתְּנוּ כָּל־הָעֹבֵר עַל־הַפְּקֻדִים מַחֲצִית הַשֶּׁקֶל בְּשֶׁקֶל הַקֹּדֶשׁ עֶשְׂרִים גֵּרָה הַשֶּׁקֶל מַחֲצִית הַשֶּׁקֶל תְּרוּמָה לַיהוה:

לוי כֹּל הָעֹבֵר עַל־הַפְּקֻדִים מִבֶּן עֶשְׂרִים שָׁנָה וָמָעְלָה יִתֵּן תְּרוּמַת יהוה: הֶעָשִׁיר לֹא־יַרְבֶּה וְהַדַּל לֹא יַמְעִיט מִמַּחֲצִית הַשָּׁקֶל לָתֵת אֶת־תְּרוּמַת יהוה לְכַפֵּר עַל־נַפְשֹׁתֵיכֶם: וְלָקַחְתָּ אֶת־כֶּסֶף הַכִּפֻּרִים מֵאֵת בְּנֵי יִשְׂרָאֵל וְנָתַתָּ אֹתוֹ עַל־עֲבֹדַת אֹהֶל מוֹעֵד וְהָיָה לִבְנֵי יִשְׂרָאֵל לְזִכָּרוֹן לִפְנֵי יהוה לְכַפֵּר עַל־נַפְשֹׁתֵיכֶם:

ישראל וַיְדַבֵּר יהוה אֶל־מֹשֶׁה לֵּאמֹר: וְעָשִׂיתָ כִּיּוֹר נְחֹשֶׁת וְכַנּוֹ נְחֹשֶׁת לְרָחְצָה וְנָתַתָּ אֹתוֹ בֵּין־אֹהֶל מוֹעֵד וּבֵין הַמִּזְבֵּחַ וְנָתַתָּ שָׁמָּה מָיִם: וְרָחֲצוּ אַהֲרֹן וּבָנָיו מִמֶּנּוּ אֶת־יְדֵיהֶם וְאֶת־רַגְלֵיהֶם: בְּבֹאָם אֶל־אֹהֶל מוֹעֵד יִרְחֲצוּ־מַיִם וְלֹא יָמֻתוּ אוֹ בְגִשְׁתָּם אֶל־הַמִּזְבֵּחַ לְשָׁרֵת לְהַקְטִיר אִשֶּׁה לַיהוה: וְרָחֲצוּ יְדֵיהֶם וְרַגְלֵיהֶם וְלֹא יָמֻתוּ וְהָיְתָה לָהֶם חָק־עוֹלָם לוֹ וּלְזַרְעוֹ לְדֹרֹתָם:

פ׳ ויקהל / VAYAKHEL

(*Exodus* 35:1-20)

וַיַּקְהֵל מֹשֶׁה אֶת־כָּל־עֲדַת בְּנֵי יִשְׂרָאֵל וַיֹּאמֶר אֲלֵהֶם אֵלֶּה הַדְּבָרִים אֲשֶׁר־צִוָּה יהוה לַעֲשֹׂת אֹתָם: שֵׁשֶׁת יָמִים תֵּעָשֶׂה מְלָאכָה וּבַיּוֹם הַשְּׁבִיעִי יִהְיֶה לָכֶם קֹדֶשׁ שַׁבַּת שַׁבָּתוֹן לַיהוה כָּל־הָעֹשֶׂה בוֹ מְלָאכָה יוּמָת: לֹא־תְבַעֲרוּ אֵשׁ בְּכֹל מֹשְׁבֹתֵיכֶם בְּיוֹם הַשַּׁבָּת:

לוי וַיֹּאמֶר מֹשֶׁה אֶל־כָּל־עֲדַת בְּנֵי־יִשְׂרָאֵל לֵאמֹר זֶה הַדָּבָר אֲשֶׁר־צִוָּה יהוה לֵאמֹר: קְחוּ מֵאִתְּכֶם תְּרוּמָה לַיהוה כֹּל נְדִיב לִבּוֹ יְבִיאֶהָ אֵת תְּרוּמַת יהוה זָהָב וָכֶסֶף וּנְחֹשֶׁת: וּתְכֵלֶת וְאַרְגָּמָן וְתוֹלַעַת שָׁנִי וְשֵׁשׁ וְעִזִּים: וְעֹרֹת אֵילִם מְאָדָּמִים וְעֹרֹת תְּחָשִׁים וַעֲצֵי שִׁטִּים: וְשֶׁמֶן לַמָּאוֹר וּבְשָׂמִים לְשֶׁמֶן הַמִּשְׁחָה וְלִקְטֹרֶת הַסַּמִּים:

וְאַבְנֵי־שֹׁהַם וְאַבְנֵי מִלֻּאִים לָאֵפוֹד וְלַחֹשֶׁן: וְכָל־חֲכַם־לֵב בָּכֶם יָבֹאוּ וְיַעֲשׂוּ אֵת כָּל־אֲשֶׁר צִוָּה יהוה:

ישראל אֶת־הַמִּשְׁכָּן אֶת־אָהֳלוֹ וְאֶת־מִכְסֵהוּ אֶת־קְרָסָיו וְאֶת־קְרָשָׁיו אֶת־בְּרִיחָו אֶת־עַמֻּדָיו וְאֶת־אֲדָנָיו: אֶת־הָאָרֹן וְאֶת־בַּדָּיו אֶת־הַכַּפֹּרֶת וְאֵת פָּרֹכֶת הַמָּסָךְ: אֶת־הַשֻּׁלְחָן וְאֶת־בַּדָּיו וְאֶת־כָּל־כֵּלָיו וְאֵת לֶחֶם הַפָּנִים: וְאֶת־מְנֹרַת הַמָּאוֹר וְאֶת־כֵּלֶיהָ וְאֶת־נֵרֹתֶיהָ וְאֵת שֶׁמֶן הַמָּאוֹר: וְאֶת־מִזְבַּח הַקְּטֹרֶת וְאֶת־בַּדָּיו וְאֵת שֶׁמֶן הַמִּשְׁחָה וְאֵת קְטֹרֶת הַסַּמִּים וְאֶת־מָסַךְ הַפֶּתַח לְפֶתַח הַמִּשְׁכָּן: אֵת ׀ מִזְבַּח הָעֹלָה וְאֶת־מִכְבַּר הַנְּחֹשֶׁת אֲשֶׁר־לוֹ אֶת־בַּדָּיו וְאֶת־כָּל־כֵּלָיו אֶת־הַכִּיֹּר וְאֶת־כַּנּוֹ: אֵת קַלְעֵי הֶחָצֵר אֶת־עַמֻּדָיו וְאֶת־אֲדָנֶיהָ וְאֵת מָסַךְ שַׁעַר הֶחָצֵר: אֶת־יִתְדֹת הַמִּשְׁכָּן וְאֶת־יִתְדֹת הֶחָצֵר וְאֶת־מֵיתְרֵיהֶם: אֶת־בִּגְדֵי הַשְּׂרָד לְשָׁרֵת בַּקֹּדֶשׁ אֶת־בִּגְדֵי הַקֹּדֶשׁ לְאַהֲרֹן הַכֹּהֵן וְאֶת־בִּגְדֵי בָנָיו לְכַהֵן: וַיֵּצְאוּ כָּל־עֲדַת בְּנֵי־יִשְׂרָאֵל מִלִּפְנֵי מֹשֶׁה:

PEKUDEI / פ׳ פקודי

(*Exodus* 38:21—39:1)

אֵלֶּה פְקוּדֵי הַמִּשְׁכָּן מִשְׁכַּן הָעֵדֻת אֲשֶׁר פֻּקַּד עַל־פִּי מֹשֶׁה עֲבֹדַת הַלְוִיִּם בְּיַד אִיתָמָר בֶּן־אַהֲרֹן הַכֹּהֵן: וּבְצַלְאֵל בֶּן־אוּרִי בֶן־חוּר לְמַטֵּה יְהוּדָה עָשָׂה אֵת כָּל־אֲשֶׁר־צִוָּה יהוה אֶת־מֹשֶׁה: וְאִתּוֹ אָהֳלִיאָב בֶּן־אֲחִיסָמָךְ לְמַטֵּה־דָן חָרָשׁ וְחֹשֵׁב וְרֹקֵם בַּתְּכֵלֶת וּבָאַרְגָּמָן וּבְתוֹלַעַת הַשָּׁנִי וּבַשֵּׁשׁ:

לוי כָּל־הַזָּהָב הֶעָשׂוּי לַמְּלָאכָה בְּכֹל מְלֶאכֶת הַקֹּדֶשׁ וַיְהִי ׀ זְהַב הַתְּנוּפָה תֵּשַׁע וְעֶשְׂרִים כִּכָּר וּשְׁבַע מֵאוֹת וּשְׁלֹשִׁים שֶׁקֶל בְּשֶׁקֶל הַקֹּדֶשׁ: וְכֶסֶף פְּקוּדֵי הָעֵדָה מְאַת כִּכָּר וְאֶלֶף וּשְׁבַע מֵאוֹת וַחֲמִשָּׁה וְשִׁבְעִים שֶׁקֶל בְּשֶׁקֶל הַקֹּדֶשׁ: בֶּקַע לַגֻּלְגֹּלֶת מַחֲצִית הַשֶּׁקֶל בְּשֶׁקֶל הַקֹּדֶשׁ לְכֹל הָעֹבֵר עַל־הַפְּקֻדִים מִבֶּן עֶשְׂרִים שָׁנָה וָמַעְלָה לְשֵׁשׁ־מֵאוֹת אֶלֶף וּשְׁלֹשֶׁת אֲלָפִים וַחֲמֵשׁ מֵאוֹת וַחֲמִשִּׁים: וַיְהִי מְאַת כִּכַּר הַכֶּסֶף לָצֶקֶת אֵת אַדְנֵי הַקֹּדֶשׁ וְאֵת אַדְנֵי הַפָּרֹכֶת מְאַת אֲדָנִים לִמְאַת הַכִּכָּר כִּכָּר לָאָדֶן:

ישראל וְאֶת־הָאֶלֶף וּשְׁבַע הַמֵּאוֹת וַחֲמִשָּׁה וְשִׁבְעִים עָשָׂה וָוִים לָעַמּוּדִים וְצִפָּה רָאשֵׁיהֶם וְחִשַּׁק אֹתָם: וּנְחֹשֶׁת הַתְּנוּפָה שִׁבְעִים כִּכָּר וְאַלְפַּיִם וְאַרְבַּע־מֵאוֹת שָׁקֶל: וַיַּעַשׂ בָּהּ אֶת־אַדְנֵי פֶּתַח אֹהֶל מוֹעֵד וְאֵת מִזְבַּח הַנְּחֹשֶׁת וְאֶת־מִכְבַּר הַנְּחֹשֶׁת אֲשֶׁר־לוֹ וְאֵת כָּל־כְּלֵי הַמִּזְבֵּחַ: וְאֶת־אַדְנֵי הֶחָצֵר סָבִיב וְאֶת־אַדְנֵי שַׁעַר הֶחָצֵר וְאֵת כָּל־יִתְדֹת הַמִּשְׁכָּן וְאֶת־כָּל־יִתְדֹת הֶחָצֵר סָבִיב: וּמִן־הַתְּכֵלֶת וְהָאַרְגָּמָן וְתוֹלַעַת הַשָּׁנִי עָשׂוּ בִגְדֵי־שְׂרָד לְשָׁרֵת בַּקֹּדֶשׁ וַיַּעֲשׂוּ אֶת־בִּגְדֵי הַקֹּדֶשׁ אֲשֶׁר לְאַהֲרֹן כַּאֲשֶׁר צִוָּה יהוה אֶת־מֹשֶׁה:

VAYIKRA / פ׳ ויקרא

(*Leviticus* 1:1-13)

וַיִּקְרָא אֶל־מֹשֶׁה וַיְדַבֵּר יהוה אֵלָיו מֵאֹהֶל מוֹעֵד לֵאמֹר: דַּבֵּר אֶל־בְּנֵי יִשְׂרָאֵל וְאָמַרְתָּ אֲלֵהֶם אָדָם כִּי־יַקְרִיב מִכֶּם קָרְבָּן לַיהוה מִן־הַבְּהֵמָה מִן־הַבָּקָר וּמִן־הַצֹּאן תַּקְרִיבוּ אֶת־קָרְבַּנְכֶם: אִם־עֹלָה קָרְבָּנוֹ מִן־הַבָּקָר זָכָר תָּמִים יַקְרִיבֶנּוּ אֶל־פֶּתַח אֹהֶל מוֹעֵד יַקְרִיב אֹתוֹ לִרְצֹנוֹ לִפְנֵי יהוה: וְסָמַךְ יָדוֹ עַל רֹאשׁ הָעֹלָה וְנִרְצָה לוֹ לְכַפֵּר עָלָיו:

לוי וְשָׁחַט אֶת־בֶּן הַבָּקָר לִפְנֵי יהוה וְהִקְרִיבוּ בְּנֵי אַהֲרֹן הַכֹּהֲנִים אֶת־הַדָּם וְזָרְקוּ אֶת־הַדָּם עַל־הַמִּזְבֵּחַ סָבִיב אֲשֶׁר־פֶּתַח אֹהֶל מוֹעֵד: וְהִפְשִׁיט אֶת־הָעֹלָה וְנִתַּח אֹתָהּ לִנְתָחֶיהָ: וְנָתְנוּ בְּנֵי אַהֲרֹן הַכֹּהֵן אֵשׁ עַל־הַמִּזְבֵּחַ וְעָרְכוּ עֵצִים עַל־הָאֵשׁ: וְעָרְכוּ בְּנֵי אַהֲרֹן הַכֹּהֲנִים אֵת הַנְּתָחִים אֶת־הָרֹאשׁ וְאֶת־הַפָּדֶר עַל־הָעֵצִים אֲשֶׁר עַל־הָאֵשׁ אֲשֶׁר עַל־הַמִּזְבֵּחַ: וְקִרְבּוֹ וּכְרָעָיו יִרְחַץ בַּמָּיִם וְהִקְטִיר הַכֹּהֵן אֶת־הַכֹּל הַמִּזְבֵּחָה עֹלָה אִשֵּׁה רֵיחַ־נִיחוֹחַ לַיהוה:

ישראל וְאִם־מִן־הַצֹּאן קָרְבָּנוֹ מִן־הַכְּשָׂבִים אוֹ מִן־הָעִזִּים לְעֹלָה זָכָר תָּמִים יַקְרִיבֶנּוּ: וְשָׁחַט אֹתוֹ עַל יֶרֶךְ הַמִּזְבֵּחַ צָפֹנָה לִפְנֵי יהוה וְזָרְקוּ בְּנֵי אַהֲרֹן הַכֹּהֲנִים אֶת־דָּמוֹ עַל־הַמִּזְבֵּחַ סָבִיב: וְנִתַּח אֹתוֹ לִנְתָחָיו וְאֶת־רֹאשׁוֹ וְאֶת־פִּדְרוֹ וְעָרַךְ הַכֹּהֵן אֹתָם עַל־הָעֵצִים אֲשֶׁר עַל־הָאֵשׁ אֲשֶׁר עַל־הַמִּזְבֵּחַ: וְהַקֶּרֶב וְהַכְּרָעַיִם יִרְחַץ בַּמָּיִם וְהִקְרִיב הַכֹּהֵן אֶת־הַכֹּל וְהִקְטִיר הַמִּזְבֵּחָה עֹלָה הוּא אִשֵּׁה רֵיחַ נִיחֹחַ לַיהוה:

TZAV / פ׳ צו

(*Leviticus* 6:1-11)

וַיְדַבֵּר יהוה אֶל־מֹשֶׁה לֵּאמֹר: צַו אֶת־אַהֲרֹן וְאֶת־בָּנָיו לֵאמֹר זֹאת תּוֹרַת הָעֹלָה הִוא הָעֹלָה עַל מוֹקְדָה עַל־הַמִּזְבֵּחַ כָּל־הַלַּיְלָה עַד־הַבֹּקֶר וְאֵשׁ הַמִּזְבֵּחַ תּוּקַד בּוֹ: וְלָבַשׁ הַכֹּהֵן מִדּוֹ בַד וּמִכְנְסֵי־בַד יִלְבַּשׁ עַל־בְּשָׂרוֹ וְהֵרִים אֶת־הַדֶּשֶׁן אֲשֶׁר תֹּאכַל הָאֵשׁ אֶת־הָעֹלָה עַל־הַמִּזְבֵּחַ וְשָׂמוֹ אֵצֶל הַמִּזְבֵּחַ:

לוי וּפָשַׁט אֶת־בְּגָדָיו וְלָבַשׁ בְּגָדִים אֲחֵרִים וְהוֹצִיא אֶת־הַדֶּשֶׁן אֶל־מִחוּץ לַמַּחֲנֶה אֶל־מָקוֹם טָהוֹר: וְהָאֵשׁ עַל־הַמִּזְבֵּחַ תּוּקַד־בּוֹ לֹא תִכְבֶּה וּבִעֵר עָלֶיהָ הַכֹּהֵן עֵצִים בַּבֹּקֶר בַּבֹּקֶר וְעָרַךְ עָלֶיהָ הָעֹלָה וְהִקְטִיר עָלֶיהָ חֶלְבֵי הַשְּׁלָמִים: אֵשׁ תָּמִיד תּוּקַד עַל־הַמִּזְבֵּחַ לֹא תִכְבֶּה:

ישראל וְזֹאת תּוֹרַת הַמִּנְחָה הַקְרֵב אֹתָהּ בְּנֵי־אַהֲרֹן לִפְנֵי יהוה אֶל־פְּנֵי הַמִּזְבֵּחַ: וְהֵרִים מִמֶּנּוּ בְּקֻמְצוֹ מִסֹּלֶת הַמִּנְחָה וּמִשַּׁמְנָהּ וְאֵת כָּל־הַלְּבֹנָה אֲשֶׁר עַל־הַמִּנְחָה וְהִקְטִיר הַמִּזְבֵּחַ רֵיחַ נִיחֹחַ אַזְכָּרָתָהּ לַיהוה: וְהַנּוֹתֶרֶת מִמֶּנָּה יֹאכְלוּ אַהֲרֹן וּבָנָיו מַצּוֹת תֵּאָכֵל בְּמָקוֹם קָדֹשׁ בַּחֲצַר אֹהֶל־מוֹעֵד יֹאכְלוּהָ: לֹא תֵאָפֶה חָמֵץ חֶלְקָם נָתַתִּי אֹתָהּ מֵאִשָּׁי קֹדֶשׁ קָדָשִׁים הִוא כַּחַטָּאת וְכָאָשָׁם: כָּל־זָכָר בִּבְנֵי אַהֲרֹן יֹאכְלֶנָּה חָק־עוֹלָם לְדֹרֹתֵיכֶם מֵאִשֵּׁי יהוה כֹּל אֲשֶׁר־יִגַּע בָּהֶם יִקְדָּשׁ:

SHMINI / פ׳ שמיני

(*Leviticus* 9:1-16)

וַיְהִי בַּיּוֹם הַשְּׁמִינִי קָרָא מֹשֶׁה לְאַהֲרֹן וּלְבָנָיו וּלְזִקְנֵי יִשְׂרָאֵל: וַיֹּאמֶר אֶל־אַהֲרֹן קַח־לְךָ עֵגֶל בֶּן־בָּקָר לְחַטָּאת וְאַיִל לְעֹלָה תְּמִימִם וְהַקְרֵב לִפְנֵי יהוה: וְאֶל־בְּנֵי יִשְׂרָאֵל תְּדַבֵּר לֵאמֹר קְחוּ שְׂעִיר־עִזִּים לְחַטָּאת וְעֵגֶל וָכֶבֶשׂ בְּנֵי־שָׁנָה תְּמִימִם לְעֹלָה: וְשׁוֹר וָאַיִל לִשְׁלָמִים לִזְבֹּחַ לִפְנֵי יהוה וּמִנְחָה בְּלוּלָה בַשָּׁמֶן כִּי הַיּוֹם יהוה נִרְאָה אֲלֵיכֶם: וַיִּקְחוּ אֵת אֲשֶׁר צִוָּה מֹשֶׁה אֶל־פְּנֵי אֹהֶל מוֹעֵד וַיִּקְרְבוּ כָּל־הָעֵדָה וַיַּעַמְדוּ לִפְנֵי יהוה: וַיֹּאמֶר מֹשֶׁה זֶה הַדָּבָר אֲשֶׁר־צִוָּה יהוה תַּעֲשׂוּ וְיֵרָא אֲלֵיכֶם כְּבוֹד יהוה:

לוי וַיֹּאמֶר מֹשֶׁה אֶל־אַהֲרֹן קְרַב אֶל־הַמִּזְבֵּחַ וַעֲשֵׂה אֶת־חַטָּאתְךָ וְאֶת־עֹלָתֶךָ וְכַפֵּר בַּעַדְךָ וּבְעַד הָעָם וַעֲשֵׂה אֶת־קָרְבַּן הָעָם וְכַפֵּר בַּעֲדָם כַּאֲשֶׁר צִוָּה יהוה: וַיִּקְרַב אַהֲרֹן אֶל־הַמִּזְבֵּחַ וַיִּשְׁחַט אֶת־עֵגֶל הַחַטָּאת אֲשֶׁר־לוֹ: וַיַּקְרִבוּ בְּנֵי אַהֲרֹן אֶת־הַדָּם אֵלָיו וַיִּטְבֹּל אֶצְבָּעוֹ בַּדָּם וַיִּתֵּן עַל־קַרְנוֹת הַמִּזְבֵּחַ וְאֶת־הַדָּם יָצַק אֶל־יְסוֹד הַמִּזְבֵּחַ: וְאֶת־הַחֵלֶב וְאֶת־הַכְּלָיֹת וְאֶת־הַיֹּתֶרֶת מִן־הַכָּבֵד מִן־הַחַטָּאת הִקְטִיר הַמִּזְבֵּחָה כַּאֲשֶׁר צִוָּה יהוה אֶת־מֹשֶׁה:

ישראל וְאֶת־הַבָּשָׂר וְאֶת־הָעוֹר שָׂרַף בָּאֵשׁ מִחוּץ לַמַּחֲנֶה: וַיִּשְׁחַט אֶת־הָעֹלָה וַיַּמְצִאוּ בְּנֵי אַהֲרֹן אֵלָיו אֶת־הַדָּם וַיִּזְרְקֵהוּ עַל־הַמִּזְבֵּחַ סָבִיב: וְאֶת־הָעֹלָה הִמְצִיאוּ אֵלָיו לִנְתָחֶיהָ וְאֶת־הָרֹאשׁ וַיַּקְטֵר עַל־הַמִּזְבֵּחַ: וַיִּרְחַץ אֶת־הַקֶּרֶב וְאֶת־הַכְּרָעָיִם וַיַּקְטֵר עַל־הָעֹלָה הַמִּזְבֵּחָה: וַיַּקְרֵב אֵת קָרְבַּן הָעָם וַיִּקַּח אֶת־שְׂעִיר הַחַטָּאת אֲשֶׁר לָעָם וַיִּשְׁחָטֵהוּ וַיְחַטְּאֵהוּ כָּרִאשׁוֹן: וַיַּקְרֵב אֶת־הָעֹלָה וַיַּעֲשֶׂהָ כַּמִּשְׁפָּט:

TAZRIA / פ׳ תזריע

(*Leviticus* 12:1—13:5)

וַיְדַבֵּר יהוה אֶל־מֹשֶׁה לֵּאמֹר: דַּבֵּר אֶל־בְּנֵי יִשְׂרָאֵל לֵאמֹר אִשָּׁה כִּי תַזְרִיעַ וְיָלְדָה זָכָר וְטָמְאָה שִׁבְעַת יָמִים כִּימֵי נִדַּת דְּוֹתָהּ תִּטְמָא: וּבַיּוֹם הַשְּׁמִינִי יִמּוֹל בְּשַׂר עָרְלָתוֹ: וּשְׁלֹשִׁים יוֹם וּשְׁלֹשֶׁת יָמִים תֵּשֵׁב בִּדְמֵי טָהֳרָה בְּכָל־קֹדֶשׁ לֹא־תִגָּע וְאֶל־הַמִּקְדָּשׁ לֹא תָבֹא עַד־מְלֹאת יְמֵי טָהֳרָהּ:

לוי וְאִם־נְקֵבָה תֵלֵד וְטָמְאָה שְׁבֻעַיִם כְּנִדָּתָהּ וְשִׁשִּׁים יוֹם וְשֵׁשֶׁת יָמִים תֵּשֵׁב עַל־דְּמֵי טָהֳרָה: וּבִמְלֹאת ׀ יְמֵי טָהֳרָהּ לְבֵן אוֹ לְבַת תָּבִיא כֶּבֶשׂ בֶּן־שְׁנָתוֹ לְעֹלָה וּבֶן־יוֹנָה אוֹ־תֹר לְחַטָּאת אֶל־פֶּתַח אֹהֶל־מוֹעֵד אֶל־הַכֹּהֵן: וְהִקְרִיבוֹ לִפְנֵי יהוה וְכִפֶּר עָלֶיהָ וְטָהֲרָה מִמְּקֹר דָּמֶיהָ זֹאת תּוֹרַת הַיֹּלֶדֶת לַזָּכָר אוֹ לַנְּקֵבָה: וְאִם־לֹא תִמְצָא יָדָהּ דֵּי שֶׂה וְלָקְחָה שְׁתֵּי־תֹרִים אוֹ שְׁנֵי בְּנֵי יוֹנָה אֶחָד לְעֹלָה וְאֶחָד לְחַטָּאת וְכִפֶּר עָלֶיהָ הַכֹּהֵן וְטָהֵרָה:

ישראל וַיְדַבֵּר יהוה אֶל־מֹשֶׁה וְאֶל־אַהֲרֹן לֵאמֹר: אָדָם כִּי־יִהְיֶה בְעוֹר־בְּשָׂרוֹ שְׂאֵת אוֹ־סַפַּחַת אוֹ בַהֶרֶת וְהָיָה בְעוֹר־בְּשָׂרוֹ

לְנֶגַע צָרָעַת וְהוּבָא אֶל־אַהֲרֹן הַכֹּהֵן אוֹ אֶל־אַחַד מִבָּנָיו הַכֹּהֲנִים׃ וְרָאָה הַכֹּהֵן אֶת־הַנֶּגַע בְּעוֹר־הַבָּשָׂר וְשֵׂעָר בַּנֶּגַע הָפַךְ ׀ לָבָן וּמַרְאֵה הַנֶּגַע עָמֹק מֵעוֹר בְּשָׂרוֹ נֶגַע צָרַעַת הוּא וְרָאָהוּ הַכֹּהֵן וְטִמֵּא אֹתוֹ׃ וְאִם־בַּהֶרֶת לְבָנָה הִוא בְּעוֹר בְּשָׂרוֹ וְעָמֹק אֵין־מַרְאֶהָ מִן־הָעוֹר וּשְׂעָרָה לֹא־הָפַךְ לָבָן וְהִסְגִּיר הַכֹּהֵן אֶת־הַנֶּגַע שִׁבְעַת יָמִים׃ וְרָאָהוּ הַכֹּהֵן בַּיּוֹם הַשְּׁבִיעִי וְהִנֵּה הַנֶּגַע עָמַד בְּעֵינָיו לֹא־פָשָׂה הַנֶּגַע בָּעוֹר וְהִסְגִּירוֹ הַכֹּהֵן שִׁבְעַת יָמִים שֵׁנִית׃

METZORA / פ׳ מצורע
(*Leviticus* 14:1-12)

וַיְדַבֵּר יְהוָה אֶל־מֹשֶׁה לֵּאמֹר׃ זֹאת תִּהְיֶה תּוֹרַת הַמְּצֹרָע בְּיוֹם טָהֳרָתוֹ וְהוּבָא אֶל־הַכֹּהֵן׃ וְיָצָא הַכֹּהֵן אֶל־מִחוּץ לַמַּחֲנֶה וְרָאָה הַכֹּהֵן וְהִנֵּה נִרְפָּא נֶגַע־הַצָּרַעַת מִן־הַצָּרוּעַ׃ וְצִוָּה הַכֹּהֵן וְלָקַח לַמִּטַּהֵר שְׁתֵּי־צִפֳּרִים חַיּוֹת טְהֹרוֹת וְעֵץ אֶרֶז וּשְׁנִי תוֹלַעַת וְאֵזֹב׃ וְצִוָּה הַכֹּהֵן וְשָׁחַט אֶת־הַצִּפּוֹר הָאֶחָת אֶל־כְּלִי־חֶרֶשׂ עַל־מַיִם חַיִּים׃

לוי אֶת־הַצִּפֹּר הַחַיָּה יִקַּח אֹתָהּ וְאֶת־עֵץ הָאֶרֶז וְאֶת־שְׁנִי הַתּוֹלַעַת וְאֶת־הָאֵזֹב וְטָבַל אוֹתָם וְאֵת ׀ הַצִּפֹּר הַחַיָּה בְּדַם הַצִּפֹּר הַשְּׁחֻטָה עַל הַמַּיִם הַחַיִּים׃ וְהִזָּה עַל הַמִּטַּהֵר מִן־הַצָּרַעַת שֶׁבַע פְּעָמִים וְטִהֲרוֹ וְשִׁלַּח אֶת־הַצִּפֹּר הַחַיָּה עַל־פְּנֵי הַשָּׂדֶה׃ וְכִבֶּס הַמִּטַּהֵר אֶת־בְּגָדָיו וְגִלַּח אֶת־כָּל־שְׂעָרוֹ וְרָחַץ בַּמַּיִם וְטָהֵר וְאַחַר יָבוֹא אֶל־הַמַּחֲנֶה וְיָשַׁב מִחוּץ לְאָהֳלוֹ שִׁבְעַת יָמִים׃ וְהָיָה בַיּוֹם הַשְּׁבִיעִי יְגַלַּח אֶת־כָּל־שְׂעָרוֹ אֶת־רֹאשׁוֹ וְאֶת־זְקָנוֹ וְאֵת גַּבֹּת עֵינָיו וְאֶת־כָּל־שְׂעָרוֹ יְגַלֵּחַ וְכִבֶּס אֶת־בְּגָדָיו וְרָחַץ אֶת־בְּשָׂרוֹ בַּמַּיִם וְטָהֵר׃

ישראל וּבַיּוֹם הַשְּׁמִינִי יִקַּח שְׁנֵי־כְבָשִׂים תְּמִימִם וְכַבְשָׂה אַחַת בַּת־שְׁנָתָהּ תְּמִימָה וּשְׁלֹשָׁה עֶשְׂרֹנִים סֹלֶת מִנְחָה בְּלוּלָה בַשֶּׁמֶן וְלֹג אֶחָד שָׁמֶן׃ וְהֶעֱמִיד הַכֹּהֵן הַמְטַהֵר אֵת הָאִישׁ הַמִּטַּהֵר וְאֹתָם לִפְנֵי יְהוָה פֶּתַח אֹהֶל מוֹעֵד׃ וְלָקַח הַכֹּהֵן אֶת־הַכֶּבֶשׂ הָאֶחָד וְהִקְרִיב אֹתוֹ לְאָשָׁם וְאֶת־לֹג הַשָּׁמֶן וְהֵנִיף אֹתָם תְּנוּפָה לִפְנֵי יְהוָה׃

ACHAREI MOS / פ׳ אחרי מות
(*Leviticus* 16:1-17)

וַיְדַבֵּר יְהוָה אֶל־מֹשֶׁה אַחֲרֵי מוֹת שְׁנֵי בְּנֵי אַהֲרֹן בְּקָרְבָתָם לִפְנֵי־יְהוָה וַיָּמֻתוּ׃ וַיֹּאמֶר יְהוָה אֶל־מֹשֶׁה דַּבֵּר אֶל־אַהֲרֹן אָחִיךָ וְאַל־יָבֹא בְכָל־עֵת אֶל־הַקֹּדֶשׁ מִבֵּית לַפָּרֹכֶת אֶל־פְּנֵי הַכַּפֹּרֶת אֲשֶׁר עַל־הָאָרֹן וְלֹא יָמוּת כִּי בֶּעָנָן אֵרָאֶה עַל־הַכַּפֹּרֶת׃ בְּזֹאת יָבֹא אַהֲרֹן אֶל־הַקֹּדֶשׁ בְּפַר בֶּן־בָּקָר לְחַטָּאת וְאַיִל לְעֹלָה׃ כְּתֹנֶת־בַּד קֹדֶשׁ יִלְבָּשׁ וּמִכְנְסֵי־בַד יִהְיוּ עַל־בְּשָׂרוֹ וּבְאַבְנֵט בַּד יַחְגֹּר וּבְמִצְנֶפֶת בַּד יִצְנֹף בִּגְדֵי־קֹדֶשׁ הֵם וְרָחַץ בַּמַּיִם אֶת־בְּשָׂרוֹ וּלְבֵשָׁם׃ וּמֵאֵת עֲדַת בְּנֵי יִשְׂרָאֵל יִקַּח שְׁנֵי־שְׂעִירֵי עִזִּים לְחַטָּאת וְאַיִל אֶחָד לְעֹלָה׃ וְהִקְרִיב אַהֲרֹן אֶת־פַּר הַחַטָּאת אֲשֶׁר־לוֹ וְכִפֶּר בַּעֲדוֹ וּבְעַד בֵּיתוֹ׃

לוי וְלָקַח אֶת־שְׁנֵי הַשְּׂעִירִם וְהֶעֱמִיד אֹתָם לִפְנֵי יְהוָה פֶּתַח אֹהֶל מוֹעֵד׃ וְנָתַן אַהֲרֹן עַל־שְׁנֵי הַשְּׂעִירִם גֹּרָלוֹת גּוֹרָל אֶחָד לַיהוָה וְגוֹרָל אֶחָד לַעֲזָאזֵל׃ וְהִקְרִיב אַהֲרֹן אֶת־הַשָּׂעִיר אֲשֶׁר עָלָה עָלָיו הַגּוֹרָל לַיהוָה וְעָשָׂהוּ חַטָּאת׃ וְהַשָּׂעִיר אֲשֶׁר עָלָה עָלָיו הַגּוֹרָל לַעֲזָאזֵל יָעֳמַד־חַי לִפְנֵי יְהוָה לְכַפֵּר עָלָיו לְשַׁלַּח אֹתוֹ לַעֲזָאזֵל הַמִּדְבָּרָה׃ וְהִקְרִיב אַהֲרֹן אֶת־פַּר הַחַטָּאת אֲשֶׁר־לוֹ וְכִפֶּר בַּעֲדוֹ וּבְעַד בֵּיתוֹ וְשָׁחַט אֶת־פַּר הַחַטָּאת אֲשֶׁר־לוֹ׃

ישראל וְלָקַח מְלֹא־הַמַּחְתָּה גַּחֲלֵי־אֵשׁ מֵעַל הַמִּזְבֵּחַ מִלִּפְנֵי יְהוָה וּמְלֹא חָפְנָיו קְטֹרֶת סַמִּים דַּקָּה וְהֵבִיא מִבֵּית לַפָּרֹכֶת׃ וְנָתַן אֶת־הַקְּטֹרֶת עַל־הָאֵשׁ לִפְנֵי יְהוָה וְכִסָּה ׀ עֲנַן הַקְּטֹרֶת אֶת־הַכַּפֹּרֶת אֲשֶׁר עַל־הָעֵדוּת וְלֹא יָמוּת׃ וְלָקַח מִדַּם הַפָּר וְהִזָּה בְאֶצְבָּעוֹ עַל־פְּנֵי הַכַּפֹּרֶת קֵדְמָה וְלִפְנֵי הַכַּפֹּרֶת יַזֶּה שֶׁבַע־פְּעָמִים מִן־הַדָּם בְּאֶצְבָּעוֹ׃ וְשָׁחַט אֶת־שְׂעִיר הַחַטָּאת אֲשֶׁר לָעָם וְהֵבִיא אֶת־דָּמוֹ אֶל־מִבֵּית לַפָּרֹכֶת וְעָשָׂה אֶת־דָּמוֹ כַּאֲשֶׁר עָשָׂה לְדַם הַפָּר וְהִזָּה אֹתוֹ עַל־הַכַּפֹּרֶת וְלִפְנֵי הַכַּפֹּרֶת׃ וְכִפֶּר עַל־הַקֹּדֶשׁ מִטֻּמְאֹת בְּנֵי יִשְׂרָאֵל וּמִפִּשְׁעֵיהֶם לְכָל־חַטֹּאתָם וְכֵן יַעֲשֶׂה לְאֹהֶל מוֹעֵד הַשֹּׁכֵן אִתָּם בְּתוֹךְ טֻמְאֹתָם׃ וְכָל־אָדָם לֹא־יִהְיֶה ׀ בְּאֹהֶל מוֹעֵד בְּבֹאוֹ

לְכַפֵּר בַּקֹּדֶשׁ עַד־צֵאתוֹ וְכִפֶּר בַּעֲדוֹ וּבְעַד בֵּיתוֹ וּבְעַד כָּל־קְהַל יִשְׂרָאֵל:

פ׳ קדשים / KEDOSHIM

(*Leviticus* 19:1-14)

וַיְדַבֵּר יהוה אֶל־מֹשֶׁה לֵּאמֹר: דַּבֵּר אֶל־כָּל־עֲדַת בְּנֵי־יִשְׂרָאֵל וְאָמַרְתָּ אֲלֵהֶם קְדֹשִׁים תִּהְיוּ כִּי קָדוֹשׁ אֲנִי יהוה אֱלֹהֵיכֶם: אִישׁ אִמּוֹ וְאָבִיו תִּירָאוּ וְאֶת־שַׁבְּתֹתַי תִּשְׁמֹרוּ אֲנִי יהוה אֱלֹהֵיכֶם: אַל־תִּפְנוּ אֶל־הָאֱלִילִם וֵאלֹהֵי מַסֵּכָה לֹא תַעֲשׂוּ לָכֶם אֲנִי יהוה אֱלֹהֵיכֶם:

לוי וְכִי תִזְבְּחוּ זֶבַח שְׁלָמִים לַיהוה לִרְצֹנְכֶם תִּזְבָּחֻהוּ: בְּיוֹם זִבְחֲכֶם יֵאָכֵל וּמִמָּחֳרָת וְהַנּוֹתָר עַד־יוֹם הַשְּׁלִישִׁי בָּאֵשׁ יִשָּׂרֵף: וְאִם הֵאָכֹל יֵאָכֵל בַּיּוֹם הַשְּׁלִישִׁי פִּגּוּל הוּא לֹא יֵרָצֶה: וְאֹכְלָיו עֲוֺנוֹ יִשָּׂא כִּי־אֶת־קֹדֶשׁ יהוה חִלֵּל וְנִכְרְתָה הַנֶּפֶשׁ הַהִוא מֵעַמֶּיהָ: וּבְקֻצְרְכֶם אֶת־קְצִיר אַרְצְכֶם לֹא תְכַלֶּה פְּאַת שָׂדְךָ לִקְצֹר וְלֶקֶט קְצִירְךָ לֹא תְלַקֵּט: וְכַרְמְךָ לֹא תְעוֹלֵל וּפֶרֶט כַּרְמְךָ לֹא תְלַקֵּט לֶעָנִי וְלַגֵּר תַּעֲזֹב אֹתָם אֲנִי יהוה אֱלֹהֵיכֶם:

ישראל לֹא תִּגְנֹבוּ וְלֹא־תְכַחֲשׁוּ וְלֹא־תְשַׁקְּרוּ אִישׁ בַּעֲמִיתוֹ: וְלֹא־תִשָּׁבְעוּ בִשְׁמִי לַשָּׁקֶר וְחִלַּלְתָּ אֶת־שֵׁם אֱלֹהֶיךָ אֲנִי יהוה: לֹא־תַעֲשֹׁק אֶת־רֵעֲךָ וְלֹא תִגְזֹל לֹא־תָלִין פְּעֻלַּת שָׂכִיר אִתְּךָ עַד־בֹּקֶר: לֹא־תְקַלֵּל חֵרֵשׁ וְלִפְנֵי עִוֵּר לֹא תִתֵּן מִכְשֹׁל וְיָרֵאתָ מֵּאֱלֹהֶיךָ אֲנִי יהוה:

פ׳ אמור / EMOR

(*Leviticus* 21:1-15)

וַיֹּאמֶר יהוה אֶל־מֹשֶׁה אֱמֹר אֶל־הַכֹּהֲנִים בְּנֵי אַהֲרֹן וְאָמַרְתָּ אֲלֵהֶם לְנֶפֶשׁ לֹא־יִטַּמָּא בְּעַמָּיו: כִּי אִם־לִשְׁאֵרוֹ הַקָּרֹב אֵלָיו לְאִמּוֹ וּלְאָבִיו וְלִבְנוֹ וּלְבִתּוֹ וּלְאָחִיו: וְלַאֲחֹתוֹ הַבְּתוּלָה הַקְּרוֹבָה אֵלָיו אֲשֶׁר לֹא־הָיְתָה לְאִישׁ לָהּ יִטַּמָּא: לֹא יִטַּמָּא בַּעַל בְּעַמָּיו לְהֵחַלּוֹ: לֹא־יִקְרְחוּ קָרְחָה בְּרֹאשָׁם וּפְאַת זְקָנָם לֹא יְגַלֵּחוּ וּבִבְשָׂרָם לֹא יִשְׂרְטוּ שָׂרָטֶת: קְדֹשִׁים יִהְיוּ לֵאלֹהֵיהֶם וְלֹא יְחַלְּלוּ שֵׁם אֱלֹהֵיהֶם כִּי אֶת־אִשֵּׁי יהוה לֶחֶם אֱלֹהֵיהֶם הֵם מַקְרִיבִם וְהָיוּ קֹדֶשׁ:

לוי אִשָּׁה זֹנָה וַחֲלָלָה לֹא יִקָּחוּ וְאִשָּׁה גְּרוּשָׁה מֵאִישָׁהּ לֹא יִקָּחוּ כִּי־קָדֹשׁ הוּא לֵאלֹהָיו: וְקִדַּשְׁתּוֹ כִּי־אֶת־לֶחֶם אֱלֹהֶיךָ הוּא מַקְרִיב קָדֹשׁ יִהְיֶה־לָּךְ כִּי קָדוֹשׁ אֲנִי יהוה מְקַדִּשְׁכֶם: וּבַת אִישׁ כֹּהֵן כִּי תֵחֵל לִזְנוֹת אֶת־אָבִיהָ הִיא מְחַלֶּלֶת בָּאֵשׁ תִּשָּׂרֵף: וְהַכֹּהֵן הַגָּדוֹל מֵאֶחָיו אֲשֶׁר־יוּצַק עַל־רֹאשׁוֹ | שֶׁמֶן הַמִּשְׁחָה וּמִלֵּא אֶת־יָדוֹ לִלְבֹּשׁ אֶת־הַבְּגָדִים אֶת־רֹאשׁוֹ לֹא יִפְרָע וּבְגָדָיו לֹא יִפְרֹם: וְעַל כָּל־נַפְשֹׁת מֵת לֹא יָבֹא לְאָבִיו וּלְאִמּוֹ לֹא יִטַּמָּא: וּמִן־הַמִּקְדָּשׁ לֹא יֵצֵא וְלֹא יְחַלֵּל אֵת מִקְדַּשׁ אֱלֹהָיו כִּי נֵזֶר שֶׁמֶן מִשְׁחַת אֱלֹהָיו עָלָיו אֲנִי יהוה:

ישראל וְהוּא אִשָּׁה בִבְתוּלֶיהָ יִקָּח: אַלְמָנָה וּגְרוּשָׁה וַחֲלָלָה זֹנָה אֶת־אֵלֶּה לֹא יִקָּח כִּי אִם־בְּתוּלָה מֵעַמָּיו יִקַּח אִשָּׁה: וְלֹא־יְחַלֵּל זַרְעוֹ בְּעַמָּיו כִּי אֲנִי יהוה מְקַדְּשׁוֹ:

פ׳ בהר / BEHAR

(*Leviticus* 25:1-13)

וַיְדַבֵּר יהוה אֶל־מֹשֶׁה בְּהַר סִינַי לֵאמֹר: דַּבֵּר אֶל־בְּנֵי יִשְׂרָאֵל וְאָמַרְתָּ אֲלֵהֶם כִּי תָבֹאוּ אֶל־הָאָרֶץ אֲשֶׁר אֲנִי נֹתֵן לָכֶם וְשָׁבְתָה הָאָרֶץ שַׁבָּת לַיהוה: שֵׁשׁ שָׁנִים תִּזְרַע שָׂדֶךָ וְשֵׁשׁ שָׁנִים תִּזְמֹר כַּרְמֶךָ וְאָסַפְתָּ אֶת־תְּבוּאָתָהּ:

לוי וּבַשָּׁנָה הַשְּׁבִיעִת שַׁבַּת שַׁבָּתוֹן יִהְיֶה לָאָרֶץ שַׁבָּת לַיהוה שָׂדְךָ לֹא תִזְרָע וְכַרְמְךָ לֹא תִזְמֹר: אֵת סְפִיחַ קְצִירְךָ לֹא תִקְצוֹר וְאֶת־עִנְּבֵי נְזִירֶךָ לֹא תִבְצֹר שְׁנַת שַׁבָּתוֹן יִהְיֶה לָאָרֶץ: וְהָיְתָה שַׁבַּת הָאָרֶץ לָכֶם לְאָכְלָה לְךָ וּלְעַבְדְּךָ וְלַאֲמָתֶךָ וְלִשְׂכִירְךָ וּלְתוֹשָׁבְךָ הַגָּרִים עִמָּךְ: וְלִבְהֶמְתְּךָ וְלַחַיָּה אֲשֶׁר בְּאַרְצֶךָ תִּהְיֶה כָל־תְּבוּאָתָהּ לֶאֱכֹל:

ישראל וְסָפַרְתָּ לְךָ שֶׁבַע שַׁבְּתֹת שָׁנִים שֶׁבַע שָׁנִים שֶׁבַע פְּעָמִים וְהָיוּ לְךָ יְמֵי שֶׁבַע שַׁבְּתֹת הַשָּׁנִים תֵּשַׁע וְאַרְבָּעִים שָׁנָה: וְהַעֲבַרְתָּ שׁוֹפַר תְּרוּעָה בַּחֹדֶשׁ הַשְּׁבִעִי בֶּעָשׂוֹר לַחֹדֶשׁ בְּיוֹם הַכִּפֻּרִים תַּעֲבִירוּ שׁוֹפָר בְּכָל־אַרְצְכֶם: וְקִדַּשְׁתֶּם אֵת שְׁנַת הַחֲמִשִּׁים שָׁנָה וּקְרָאתֶם דְּרוֹר בָּאָרֶץ לְכָל־יֹשְׁבֶיהָ יוֹבֵל הִוא תִּהְיֶה לָכֶם וְשַׁבְתֶּם אִישׁ אֶל־אֲחֻזָּתוֹ וְאִישׁ אֶל־מִשְׁפַּחְתּוֹ תָּשֻׁבוּ: יוֹבֵל הִוא שְׁנַת הַחֲמִשִּׁים שָׁנָה תִּהְיֶה לָכֶם לֹא תִזְרָעוּ וְלֹא תִקְצְרוּ אֶת־סְפִיחֶיהָ וְלֹא תִבְצְרוּ אֶת־נְזִרֶיהָ: כִּי יוֹבֵל הִוא קֹדֶשׁ תִּהְיֶה לָכֶם מִן־הַשָּׂדֶה תֹּאכְלוּ

אֶת־תְּבוּאָתָהּ׃ בִּשְׁנַת הַיּוֹבֵל הַזֹּאת תָּשֻׁבוּ אִישׁ אֶל־אֲחֻזָּתוֹ׃

BECHUKOSAI / פ׳ בחקתי

(*Leviticus* 26:3-13)

אִם־בְּחֻקֹּתַי תֵּלֵכוּ וְאֶת־מִצְוֹתַי תִּשְׁמְרוּ וַעֲשִׂיתֶם אֹתָם׃ וְנָתַתִּי גִשְׁמֵיכֶם בְּעִתָּם וְנָתְנָה הָאָרֶץ יְבוּלָהּ וְעֵץ הַשָּׂדֶה יִתֵּן פִּרְיוֹ׃ וְהִשִּׂיג לָכֶם דַּיִשׁ אֶת־בָּצִיר וּבָצִיר יַשִּׂיג אֶת־זָרַע וַאֲכַלְתֶּם לַחְמְכֶם לָשֹׂבַע וִישַׁבְתֶּם לָבֶטַח בְּאַרְצְכֶם׃

לוי וְנָתַתִּי שָׁלוֹם בָּאָרֶץ וּשְׁכַבְתֶּם וְאֵין מַחֲרִיד וְהִשְׁבַּתִּי חַיָּה רָעָה מִן־הָאָרֶץ וְחֶרֶב לֹא־תַעֲבֹר בְּאַרְצְכֶם׃ וּרְדַפְתֶּם אֶת־אֹיְבֵיכֶם וְנָפְלוּ לִפְנֵיכֶם לֶחָרֶב׃ וְרָדְפוּ מִכֶּם חֲמִשָּׁה מֵאָה וּמֵאָה מִכֶּם רְבָבָה יִרְדֹּפוּ וְנָפְלוּ אֹיְבֵיכֶם לִפְנֵיכֶם לֶחָרֶב׃ וּפָנִיתִי אֲלֵיכֶם וְהִפְרֵיתִי אֶתְכֶם וְהִרְבֵּיתִי אֶתְכֶם וַהֲקִימֹתִי אֶת־בְּרִיתִי אִתְּכֶם׃

ישראל וַאֲכַלְתֶּם יָשָׁן נוֹשָׁן וְיָשָׁן מִפְּנֵי חָדָשׁ תּוֹצִיאוּ׃ וְנָתַתִּי מִשְׁכָּנִי בְּתוֹכְכֶם וְלֹא־תִגְעַל נַפְשִׁי אֶתְכֶם׃ וְהִתְהַלַּכְתִּי בְּתוֹכְכֶם וְהָיִיתִי לָכֶם לֵאלֹהִים וְאַתֶּם תִּהְיוּ־לִי לְעָם׃ אֲנִי יהוה אֱלֹהֵיכֶם אֲשֶׁר הוֹצֵאתִי אֶתְכֶם מֵאֶרֶץ מִצְרַיִם מִהְיֹת לָהֶם עֲבָדִים וָאֶשְׁבֹּר מֹטֹת עֻלְּכֶם וָאוֹלֵךְ אֶתְכֶם קוֹמְמִיּוּת׃

BAMIDBAR / פ׳ במדבר

(*Numbers* 1:1-19)

וַיְדַבֵּר יהוה אֶל־מֹשֶׁה בְּמִדְבַּר סִינַי בְּאֹהֶל מוֹעֵד בְּאֶחָד לַחֹדֶשׁ הַשֵּׁנִי בַּשָּׁנָה הַשֵּׁנִית לְצֵאתָם מֵאֶרֶץ מִצְרַיִם לֵאמֹר׃ שְׂאוּ אֶת־רֹאשׁ כָּל־עֲדַת בְּנֵי־יִשְׂרָאֵל לְמִשְׁפְּחֹתָם לְבֵית אֲבֹתָם בְּמִסְפַּר שֵׁמוֹת כָּל־זָכָר לְגֻלְגְּלֹתָם׃ מִבֶּן עֶשְׂרִים שָׁנָה וָמַעְלָה כָּל־יֹצֵא צָבָא בְּיִשְׂרָאֵל תִּפְקְדוּ אֹתָם לְצִבְאֹתָם אַתָּה וְאַהֲרֹן׃ וְאִתְּכֶם יִהְיוּ אִישׁ אִישׁ לַמַּטֶּה אִישׁ רֹאשׁ לְבֵית־אֲבֹתָיו הוּא׃

לוי וְאֵלֶּה שְׁמוֹת הָאֲנָשִׁים אֲשֶׁר יַעַמְדוּ אִתְּכֶם לִרְאוּבֵן אֱלִיצוּר בֶּן־שְׁדֵיאוּר׃ לְשִׁמְעוֹן שְׁלֻמִיאֵל בֶּן־צוּרִישַׁדָּי׃ לִיהוּדָה נַחְשׁוֹן בֶּן־עַמִּינָדָב׃ לְיִשָּׂשכָר נְתַנְאֵל בֶּן־צוּעָר׃ לִזְבוּלֻן אֱלִיאָב בֶּן־חֵלֹן׃ לִבְנֵי יוֹסֵף לְאֶפְרַיִם אֱלִישָׁמָע בֶּן־עַמִּיהוּד לִמְנַשֶּׁה גַּמְלִיאֵל בֶּן־פְּדָהצוּר׃ לְבִנְיָמִן אֲבִידָן בֶּן־גִּדְעֹנִי׃ לְדָן אֲחִיעֶזֶר בֶּן־עַמִּישַׁדָּי׃ לְאָשֵׁר פַּגְעִיאֵל בֶּן־עָכְרָן׃ לְגָד אֶלְיָסָף בֶּן־דְּעוּאֵל׃ לְנַפְתָּלִי אֲחִירַע בֶּן־עֵינָן׃ אֵלֶּה קְרוּאֵי הָעֵדָה נְשִׂיאֵי מַטּוֹת אֲבוֹתָם רָאשֵׁי אַלְפֵי יִשְׂרָאֵל הֵם׃

ישראל וַיִּקַּח מֹשֶׁה וְאַהֲרֹן אֵת הָאֲנָשִׁים הָאֵלֶּה אֲשֶׁר נִקְּבוּ בְּשֵׁמוֹת׃ וְאֵת כָּל־הָעֵדָה הִקְהִילוּ בְּאֶחָד לַחֹדֶשׁ הַשֵּׁנִי וַיִּתְיַלְדוּ עַל־מִשְׁפְּחֹתָם לְבֵית אֲבֹתָם בְּמִסְפַּר שֵׁמוֹת מִבֶּן עֶשְׂרִים שָׁנָה וָמַעְלָה לְגֻלְגְּלֹתָם׃ כַּאֲשֶׁר צִוָּה יהוה אֶת־מֹשֶׁה וַיִּפְקְדֵם בְּמִדְבַּר סִינָי׃

NASSO / פ׳ נשא

(*Numbers* 4:21-37)

וַיְדַבֵּר יהוה אֶל־מֹשֶׁה לֵּאמֹר׃ נָשֹׂא אֶת־רֹאשׁ בְּנֵי גֵרְשׁוֹן גַּם־הֵם לְבֵית אֲבֹתָם לְמִשְׁפְּחֹתָם׃ מִבֶּן שְׁלֹשִׁים שָׁנָה וָמַעְלָה עַד בֶּן־חֲמִשִּׁים שָׁנָה תִּפְקֹד אוֹתָם כָּל־הַבָּא לִצְבֹא צָבָא לַעֲבֹד עֲבֹדָה בְּאֹהֶל מוֹעֵד׃ זֹאת עֲבֹדַת מִשְׁפְּחֹת הַגֵּרְשֻׁנִּי לַעֲבֹד וּלְמַשָּׂא׃

לוי וְנָשְׂאוּ אֶת־יְרִיעֹת הַמִּשְׁכָּן וְאֶת־אֹהֶל מוֹעֵד מִכְסֵהוּ וּמִכְסֵה הַתַּחַשׁ אֲשֶׁר־עָלָיו מִלְמָעְלָה וְאֶת־מָסַךְ פֶּתַח אֹהֶל מוֹעֵד׃ וְאֵת קַלְעֵי הֶחָצֵר וְאֶת־מָסַךְ ׀ פֶּתַח ׀ שַׁעַר הֶחָצֵר אֲשֶׁר עַל־הַמִּשְׁכָּן וְעַל־הַמִּזְבֵּחַ סָבִיב וְאֵת מֵיתְרֵיהֶם וְאֶת־כָּל־כְּלֵי עֲבֹדָתָם וְאֵת כָּל־אֲשֶׁר יֵעָשֶׂה לָהֶם וְעָבָדוּ׃ עַל־פִּי אַהֲרֹן וּבָנָיו תִּהְיֶה כָּל־עֲבֹדַת בְּנֵי הַגֵּרְשֻׁנִּי לְכָל־מַשָּׂאָם וּלְכֹל עֲבֹדָתָם וּפְקַדְתֶּם עֲלֵהֶם בְּמִשְׁמֶרֶת אֵת כָּל־מַשָּׂאָם׃ זֹאת עֲבֹדַת מִשְׁפְּחֹת בְּנֵי הַגֵּרְשֻׁנִּי בְּאֹהֶל מוֹעֵד וּמִשְׁמַרְתָּם בְּיַד אִיתָמָר בֶּן־אַהֲרֹן הַכֹּהֵן׃

ישראל בְּנֵי מְרָרִי לְמִשְׁפְּחֹתָם לְבֵית־אֲבֹתָם תִּפְקֹד אֹתָם׃ מִבֶּן שְׁלֹשִׁים שָׁנָה וָמַעְלָה וְעַד בֶּן־חֲמִשִּׁים שָׁנָה תִּפְקְדֵם כָּל־הַבָּא לַצָּבָא לַעֲבֹד אֶת־עֲבֹדַת אֹהֶל מוֹעֵד׃ וְזֹאת מִשְׁמֶרֶת מַשָּׂאָם לְכָל־עֲבֹדָתָם בְּאֹהֶל מוֹעֵד קַרְשֵׁי הַמִּשְׁכָּן וּבְרִיחָיו וְעַמּוּדָיו וַאֲדָנָיו׃ וְעַמּוּדֵי הֶחָצֵר סָבִיב וְאַדְנֵיהֶם וִיתֵדֹתָם וּמֵיתְרֵיהֶם לְכָל־כְּלֵיהֶם וּלְכֹל עֲבֹדָתָם וּבְשֵׁמֹת תִּפְקְדוּ אֶת־כְּלֵי מִשְׁמֶרֶת מַשָּׂאָם׃ זֹאת עֲבֹדַת מִשְׁפְּחֹת בְּנֵי מְרָרִי לְכָל־עֲבֹדָתָם בְּאֹהֶל מוֹעֵד בְּיַד אִיתָמָר בֶּן־אַהֲרֹן הַכֹּהֵן׃ (Some stop here.)

(Others continue.) וַיִּפְקֹד מֹשֶׁה וְאַהֲרֹן וּנְשִׂיאֵי הָעֵדָה אֶת־בְּנֵי הַקְּהָתִי לְמִשְׁפְּחֹתָם וּלְבֵית

אֲבֹתָֽם׃ מִבֶּ֨ן שְׁלֹשִׁ֤ים שָׁנָה֙ וָמַ֔עְלָה וְעַ֖ד בֶּן־חֲמִשִּׁ֣ים שָׁנָ֑ה כָּל־הַבָּא֙ לַצָּבָ֔א לַעֲבֹדָ֖ה בְּאֹ֥הֶל מוֹעֵֽד׃ וַיִּהְי֧וּ פְקֻדֵיהֶ֛ם לְמִשְׁפְּחֹתָ֖ם אַלְפַּ֕יִם שְׁבַ֥ע מֵא֖וֹת וַחֲמִשִּֽׁים׃ אֵ֤לֶּה פְקוּדֵי֙ מִשְׁפְּחֹ֣ת הַקְּהָתִ֔י כָּל־הָעֹבֵ֖ד בְּאֹ֣הֶל מוֹעֵ֑ד אֲשֶׁ֨ר פָּקַ֤ד מֹשֶׁה֙ וְאַהֲרֹ֔ן עַל־פִּ֥י יְהוָ֖ה בְּיַד־מֹשֶֽׁה׃

פ׳ בהעלתך / BEHA'ALOSCHA

(*Numbers* 8:1-14)

וַיְדַבֵּ֥ר יְהוָ֖ה אֶל־מֹשֶׁ֥ה לֵּאמֹֽר׃ דַּבֵּר֙ אֶֽל־אַהֲרֹ֔ן וְאָמַרְתָּ֖ אֵלָ֑יו בְּהַעֲלֹֽתְךָ֙ אֶת־הַנֵּרֹ֔ת אֶל־מוּל֙ פְּנֵ֣י הַמְּנוֹרָ֔ה יָאִ֖ירוּ שִׁבְעַ֥ת הַנֵּרֽוֹת׃ וַיַּ֤עַשׂ כֵּן֙ אַהֲרֹ֔ן אֶל־מוּל֙ פְּנֵ֣י הַמְּנוֹרָ֔ה הֶעֱלָ֖ה נֵרֹתֶ֑יהָ כַּאֲשֶׁ֛ר צִוָּ֥ה יְהוָ֖ה אֶת־מֹשֶֽׁה׃ וְזֶ֨ה מַעֲשֵׂ֤ה הַמְּנֹרָה֙ מִקְשָׁ֣ה זָהָ֔ב עַד־יְרֵכָ֥הּ עַד־פִּרְחָ֖הּ מִקְשָׁ֣ה הִ֑וא כַּמַּרְאֶ֗ה אֲשֶׁ֨ר הֶרְאָ֤ה יְהוָה֙ אֶת־מֹשֶׁ֔ה כֵּ֥ן עָשָׂ֖ה אֶת־הַמְּנֹרָֽה׃

לוי וַיְדַבֵּ֥ר יְהוָ֖ה אֶל־מֹשֶׁ֥ה לֵּאמֹֽר׃ קַ֚ח אֶת־הַלְוִיִּ֔ם מִתּ֖וֹךְ בְּנֵ֣י יִשְׂרָאֵ֑ל וְטִהַרְתָּ֖ אֹתָֽם׃ וְכֹֽה־תַעֲשֶׂ֤ה לָהֶם֙ לְטַֽהֲרָ֔ם הַזֵּ֥ה עֲלֵיהֶ֖ם מֵ֣י חַטָּ֑את וְהֶעֱבִ֤ירוּ תַ֙עַר֙ עַל־כָּל־בְּשָׂרָ֔ם וְכִבְּס֥וּ בִגְדֵיהֶ֖ם וְהִטֶּהָֽרוּ׃ וְלָֽקְחוּ֙ פַּ֣ר בֶּן־בָּקָ֔ר וּמִנְחָת֔וֹ סֹ֖לֶת בְּלוּלָ֣ה בַשָּׁ֑מֶן וּפַר־שֵׁנִ֥י בֶן־בָּקָ֖ר תִּקַּ֥ח לְחַטָּֽאת׃ וְהִקְרַבְתָּ֙ אֶת־הַלְוִיִּ֔ם לִפְנֵ֖י אֹ֣הֶל מוֹעֵ֑ד וְהִ֨קְהַלְתָּ֔ אֶֽת־כָּל־עֲדַ֖ת בְּנֵ֥י יִשְׂרָאֵֽל׃

ישראל וְהִקְרַבְתָּ֥ אֶת־הַלְוִיִּ֖ם לִפְנֵ֣י יְהוָ֑ה וְסָמְכ֧וּ בְנֵי־יִשְׂרָאֵ֛ל אֶת־יְדֵיהֶ֖ם עַל־הַלְוִיִּֽם׃ וְהֵנִיף֩ אַהֲרֹ֨ן אֶת־הַלְוִיִּ֤ם תְּנוּפָה֙ לִפְנֵ֣י יְהוָ֔ה מֵאֵ֖ת בְּנֵ֣י יִשְׂרָאֵ֑ל וְהָי֕וּ לַעֲבֹ֖ד אֶת־עֲבֹדַ֥ת יְהוָֽה׃ וְהַלְוִיִּם֙ יִסְמְכ֣וּ אֶת־יְדֵיהֶ֔ם עַ֖ל רֹ֣אשׁ הַפָּרִ֑ים וַעֲשֵׂ֠ה אֶת־הָאֶחָ֨ד חַטָּ֜את וְאֶת־הָאֶחָ֤ד עֹלָה֙ לַֽיהוָ֔ה לְכַפֵּ֖ר עַל־הַלְוִיִּֽם׃ וְהַֽעֲמַדְתָּ֙ אֶת־הַלְוִיִּ֔ם לִפְנֵ֥י אַהֲרֹ֖ן וְלִפְנֵ֣י בָנָ֑יו וְהֵנַפְתָּ֥ אֹתָ֛ם תְּנוּפָ֖ה לַיהוָֽה׃ וְהִבְדַּלְתָּ֙ אֶת־הַלְוִיִּ֔ם מִתּ֖וֹךְ בְּנֵ֣י יִשְׂרָאֵ֑ל וְהָ֥יוּ לִ֖י הַלְוִיִּֽם׃

פ׳ שלח / SH'LACH

(*Numbers* 13:1-20)

וַיְדַבֵּ֥ר יְהוָ֖ה אֶל־מֹשֶׁ֥ה לֵּאמֹֽר׃ שְׁלַח־לְךָ֣ אֲנָשִׁ֗ים וְיָתֻ֙רוּ֙ אֶת־אֶ֣רֶץ כְּנַ֔עַן אֲשֶׁר־אֲנִ֥י נֹתֵ֖ן לִבְנֵ֣י יִשְׂרָאֵ֑ל אִ֣ישׁ אֶחָד֩ אִ֨ישׁ אֶחָ֜ד לְמַטֵּ֤ה אֲבֹתָיו֙ תִּשְׁלָ֔חוּ כֹּ֖ל נָשִׂ֥יא בָהֶֽם׃ וַיִּשְׁלַ֨ח אֹתָ֥ם מֹשֶׁ֛ה מִמִּדְבַּ֥ר פָּארָ֖ן עַל־פִּ֣י יְהוָ֑ה כֻּלָּ֣ם אֲנָשִׁ֔ים רָאשֵׁ֥י בְנֵֽי־יִשְׂרָאֵ֖ל הֵֽמָּה׃

לוי וְאֵ֖לֶּה שְׁמוֹתָ֑ם לְמַטֵּ֣ה רְאוּבֵ֔ן שַׁמּ֖וּעַ בֶּן־זַכּֽוּר׃ לְמַטֵּ֣ה שִׁמְע֔וֹן שָׁפָ֖ט בֶּן־חוֹרִֽי׃ לְמַטֵּ֣ה יְהוּדָ֔ה כָּלֵ֖ב בֶּן־יְפֻנֶּֽה׃ לְמַטֵּ֣ה יִשָּׂשכָ֔ר יִגְאָ֖ל בֶּן־יוֹסֵֽף׃ לְמַטֵּ֥ה אֶפְרָ֖יִם הוֹשֵׁ֥עַ בִּן־נֽוּן׃ לְמַטֵּ֥ה בִנְיָמִ֖ן פַּלְטִ֥י בֶּן־רָפֽוּא׃ לְמַטֵּ֣ה זְבוּלֻ֔ן גַּדִּיאֵ֖ל בֶּן־סוֹדִֽי׃ לְמַטֵּ֥ה יוֹסֵ֖ף לְמַטֵּ֣ה מְנַשֶּׁ֑ה גַּדִּ֖י בֶּן־סוּסִֽי׃ לְמַטֵּ֣ה דָ֔ן עַמִּיאֵ֖ל בֶּן־גְּמַלִּֽי׃ לְמַטֵּ֣ה אָשֵׁ֔ר סְת֖וּר בֶּן־מִיכָאֵֽל׃ לְמַטֵּ֣ה נַפְתָּלִ֔י נַחְבִּ֖י בֶּן־וָפְסִֽי׃ לְמַטֵּ֣ה גָ֔ד גְּאוּאֵ֖ל בֶּן־מָכִֽי׃ אֵ֚לֶּה שְׁמ֣וֹת הָֽאֲנָשִׁ֔ים אֲשֶׁר־שָׁלַ֥ח מֹשֶׁ֖ה לָת֣וּר אֶת־הָאָ֑רֶץ וַיִּקְרָ֥א מֹשֶׁ֛ה לְהוֹשֵׁ֥עַ בִּן־נ֖וּן יְהוֹשֻֽׁעַ׃

ישראל וַיִּשְׁלַ֤ח אֹתָם֙ מֹשֶׁ֔ה לָת֖וּר אֶת־אֶ֣רֶץ כְּנָ֑עַן וַיֹּ֣אמֶר אֲלֵהֶ֗ם עֲל֥וּ זֶה֙ בַּנֶּ֔גֶב וַעֲלִיתֶ֖ם אֶת־הָהָֽר׃ וּרְאִיתֶ֥ם אֶת־הָאָ֖רֶץ מַה־הִ֑וא וְאֶת־הָעָם֙ הַיֹּשֵׁ֣ב עָלֶ֔יהָ הֶחָזָ֥ק הוּא֙ הֲרָפֶ֔ה הַמְעַ֥ט ה֖וּא אִם־רָֽב׃ וּמָ֣ה הָאָ֗רֶץ אֲשֶׁר־הוּא֙ יֹשֵׁ֣ב בָּ֔הּ הֲטוֹבָ֥ה הִ֖וא אִם־רָעָ֑ה וּמָ֣ה הֶעָרִ֗ים אֲשֶׁר־הוּא֙ יוֹשֵׁ֣ב בָּהֵ֔נָּה הַבְּמַֽחֲנִ֖ים אִ֥ם בְּמִבְצָרִֽים׃ וּמָ֣ה הָ֠אָרֶץ הַשְּׁמֵנָ֨ה הִ֜וא אִם־רָזָ֗ה הֲיֵֽשׁ־בָּ֥הּ עֵץ֙ אִם־אַ֔יִן וְהִ֨תְחַזַּקְתֶּ֔ם וּלְקַחְתֶּ֖ם מִפְּרִ֣י הָאָ֑רֶץ וְהַ֨יָּמִ֔ים יְמֵ֖י בִּכּוּרֵ֥י עֲנָבִֽים׃

פ׳ קרח / KORACH

(*Numbers* 16:1-13)

וַיִּקַּ֣ח קֹ֔רַח בֶּן־יִצְהָ֥ר בֶּן־קְהָ֖ת בֶּן־לֵוִ֑י וְדָתָ֨ן וַאֲבִירָ֜ם בְּנֵ֧י אֱלִיאָ֛ב וְא֥וֹן בֶּן־פֶּ֖לֶת בְּנֵ֥י רְאוּבֵֽן׃ וַיָּקֻ֙מוּ֙ לִפְנֵ֣י מֹשֶׁ֔ה וַאֲנָשִׁ֥ים מִבְּנֵֽי־יִשְׂרָאֵ֖ל חֲמִשִּׁ֣ים וּמָאתָ֑יִם נְשִׂיאֵ֥י עֵדָ֛ה קְרִאֵ֥י מוֹעֵ֖ד אַנְשֵׁי־שֵֽׁם׃ וַיִּֽקָּהֲל֞וּ עַל־מֹשֶׁ֣ה וְעַֽל־אַהֲרֹ֗ן וַיֹּאמְר֣וּ אֲלֵהֶם֮ רַב־לָכֶם֒ כִּ֤י כָל־הָֽעֵדָה֙ כֻּלָּ֣ם קְדֹשִׁ֔ים וּבְתוֹכָ֖ם יְהוָ֑ה וּמַדּ֥וּעַ תִּֽתְנַשְּׂא֖וּ עַל־קְהַ֥ל יְהוָֽה׃

לוי וַיִּשְׁמַ֣ע מֹשֶׁ֔ה וַיִּפֹּ֖ל עַל־פָּנָֽיו׃ וַיְדַבֵּ֨ר אֶל־קֹ֜רַח וְאֶֽל־כָּל־עֲדָתוֹ֮ לֵאמֹר֒ בֹּ֠קֶר וְיֹדַ֨ע יְהוָ֧ה אֶת־אֲשֶׁר־ל֛וֹ וְאֶת־הַקָּד֖וֹשׁ וְהִקְרִ֣יב אֵלָ֑יו וְאֵ֛ת אֲשֶׁ֥ר יִבְחַר־בּ֖וֹ יַקְרִ֥יב אֵלָֽיו׃ זֹ֖את עֲשׂ֑וּ קְחוּ־לָכֶ֣ם מַחְתּ֔וֹת קֹ֖רַח וְכָל־עֲדָתֽוֹ׃ וּתְנ֣וּ בָהֵ֣ן ׀ אֵ֡שׁ וְשִׂ֩ימוּ֩ עֲלֵיהֶ֨ן ׀ קְטֹ֜רֶת לִפְנֵ֤י יְהוָה֙ מָחָ֔ר וְהָיָ֗ה הָאִ֛ישׁ אֲשֶׁר־יִבְחַ֥ר יְהוָ֖ה ה֣וּא הַקָּד֑וֹשׁ רַב־לָכֶ֖ם בְּנֵ֥י לֵוִֽי׃

ישראל וַיֹּאמֶר מֹשֶׁה אֶל־קֹרַח שִׁמְעוּ־נָא בְּנֵי לֵוִי: הַמְעַט מִכֶּם כִּי־הִבְדִּיל אֱלֹהֵי יִשְׂרָאֵל אֶתְכֶם מֵעֲדַת יִשְׂרָאֵל לְהַקְרִיב אֶתְכֶם אֵלָיו לַעֲבֹד אֶת־עֲבֹדַת מִשְׁכַּן יהוה וְלַעֲמֹד לִפְנֵי הָעֵדָה לְשָׁרְתָם: וַיַּקְרֵב אֹתְךָ וְאֶת־כָּל־אַחֶיךָ בְנֵי־לֵוִי אִתָּךְ וּבִקַּשְׁתֶּם גַּם־כְּהֻנָּה: לָכֵן אַתָּה וְכָל־עֲדָתְךָ הַנֹּעָדִים עַל־יהוה וְאַהֲרֹן מַה־הוּא כִּי תַלִּינוּ עָלָיו: וַיִּשְׁלַח מֹשֶׁה לִקְרֹא לְדָתָן וְלַאֲבִירָם בְּנֵי אֱלִיאָב וַיֹּאמְרוּ לֹא נַעֲלֶה: הַמְעַט כִּי הֶעֱלִיתָנוּ מֵאֶרֶץ זָבַת חָלָב וּדְבַשׁ לַהֲמִיתֵנוּ בַּמִּדְבָּר כִּי־תִשְׂתָּרֵר עָלֵינוּ גַּם־הִשְׂתָּרֵר:

CHUKAS / פ׳ חקת

(*Numbers* 19:1-17)

וַיְדַבֵּר יהוה אֶל־מֹשֶׁה וְאֶל־אַהֲרֹן לֵאמֹר: זֹאת חֻקַּת הַתּוֹרָה אֲשֶׁר־צִוָּה יהוה לֵאמֹר דַּבֵּר | אֶל־בְּנֵי יִשְׂרָאֵל וְיִקְחוּ אֵלֶיךָ פָרָה אֲדֻמָּה תְּמִימָה אֲשֶׁר אֵין־בָּהּ מוּם אֲשֶׁר לֹא־עָלָה עָלֶיהָ עֹל: וּנְתַתֶּם אֹתָהּ אֶל־אֶלְעָזָר הַכֹּהֵן וְהוֹצִיא אֹתָהּ אֶל־מִחוּץ לַמַּחֲנֶה וְשָׁחַט אֹתָהּ לְפָנָיו: וְלָקַח אֶלְעָזָר הַכֹּהֵן מִדָּמָהּ בְּאֶצְבָּעוֹ וְהִזָּה אֶל־נֹכַח פְּנֵי אֹהֶל־מוֹעֵד מִדָּמָהּ שֶׁבַע פְּעָמִים: וְשָׂרַף אֶת־הַפָּרָה לְעֵינָיו אֶת־עֹרָהּ וְאֶת־בְּשָׂרָהּ וְאֶת־דָּמָהּ עַל־פִּרְשָׁהּ יִשְׂרֹף: וְלָקַח הַכֹּהֵן עֵץ אֶרֶז וְאֵזוֹב וּשְׁנִי תוֹלָעַת וְהִשְׁלִיךְ אֶל־תּוֹךְ שְׂרֵפַת הַפָּרָה:

לוי וְכִבֶּס בְּגָדָיו הַכֹּהֵן וְרָחַץ בְּשָׂרוֹ בַּמַּיִם וְאַחַר יָבֹא אֶל־הַמַּחֲנֶה וְטָמֵא הַכֹּהֵן עַד־הָעָרֶב: וְהַשֹּׂרֵף אֹתָהּ יְכַבֵּס בְּגָדָיו בַּמַּיִם וְרָחַץ בְּשָׂרוֹ בַּמָּיִם וְטָמֵא עַד־הָעָרֶב: וְאָסַף | אִישׁ טָהוֹר אֵת אֵפֶר הַפָּרָה וְהִנִּיחַ מִחוּץ לַמַּחֲנֶה בְּמָקוֹם טָהוֹר וְהָיְתָה לַעֲדַת בְּנֵי־יִשְׂרָאֵל לְמִשְׁמֶרֶת לְמֵי נִדָּה חַטָּאת הִוא:

ישראל וְכִבֶּס הָאֹסֵף אֶת־אֵפֶר הַפָּרָה אֶת־בְּגָדָיו וְטָמֵא עַד־הָעָרֶב וְהָיְתָה לִבְנֵי יִשְׂרָאֵל וְלַגֵּר הַגָּר בְּתוֹכָם לְחֻקַּת עוֹלָם: הַנֹּגֵעַ בְּמֵת לְכָל־נֶפֶשׁ אָדָם וְטָמֵא שִׁבְעַת יָמִים: הוּא יִתְחַטָּא־בוֹ בַּיּוֹם הַשְּׁלִישִׁי וּבַיּוֹם הַשְּׁבִיעִי יִטְהָר וְאִם־לֹא יִתְחַטָּא בַּיּוֹם הַשְּׁלִישִׁי וּבַיּוֹם הַשְּׁבִיעִי לֹא יִטְהָר: כָּל־הַנֹּגֵעַ בְּמֵת בְּנֶפֶשׁ הָאָדָם אֲשֶׁר־יָמוּת וְלֹא יִתְחַטָּא אֶת־מִשְׁכַּן יהוה טִמֵּא וְנִכְרְתָה הַנֶּפֶשׁ הַהִוא מִיִּשְׂרָאֵל כִּי מֵי נִדָּה לֹא־זֹרַק עָלָיו טָמֵא יִהְיֶה עוֹד טֻמְאָתוֹ בוֹ: זֹאת הַתּוֹרָה אָדָם כִּי־יָמוּת בְּאֹהֶל כָּל־הַבָּא אֶל־הָאֹהֶל וְכָל־אֲשֶׁר בָּאֹהֶל יִטְמָא שִׁבְעַת יָמִים: וְכֹל כְּלִי פָתוּחַ אֲשֶׁר אֵין־צָמִיד פָּתִיל עָלָיו טָמֵא הוּא: וְכֹל אֲשֶׁר־יִגַּע עַל־פְּנֵי הַשָּׂדֶה בַּחֲלַל־חֶרֶב אוֹ בְמֵת אוֹ־בְעֶצֶם אָדָם אוֹ בְקָבֶר יִטְמָא שִׁבְעַת יָמִים: וְלָקְחוּ לַטָּמֵא מֵעֲפַר שְׂרֵפַת הַחַטָּאת וְנָתַן עָלָיו מַיִם חַיִּים אֶל־כֶּלִי:

BALAK / פ׳ בלק

(*Numbers* 22:2-12)

וַיַּרְא בָּלָק בֶּן־צִפּוֹר אֵת כָּל־אֲשֶׁר־עָשָׂה יִשְׂרָאֵל לָאֱמֹרִי: וַיָּגָר מוֹאָב מִפְּנֵי הָעָם מְאֹד כִּי רַב־הוּא וַיָּקָץ מוֹאָב מִפְּנֵי בְּנֵי יִשְׂרָאֵל: וַיֹּאמֶר מוֹאָב אֶל־זִקְנֵי מִדְיָן עַתָּה יְלַחֲכוּ הַקָּהָל אֶת־כָּל־סְבִיבֹתֵינוּ כִּלְחֹךְ הַשּׁוֹר אֵת יֶרֶק הַשָּׂדֶה וּבָלָק בֶּן־צִפּוֹר מֶלֶךְ לְמוֹאָב בָּעֵת הַהִוא:

לוי וַיִּשְׁלַח מַלְאָכִים אֶל־בִּלְעָם בֶּן־בְּעֹר פְּתוֹרָה אֲשֶׁר עַל־הַנָּהָר אֶרֶץ בְּנֵי־עַמּוֹ לִקְרֹא־לוֹ לֵאמֹר הִנֵּה עַם יָצָא מִמִּצְרַיִם הִנֵּה כִסָּה אֶת־עֵין הָאָרֶץ וְהוּא יֹשֵׁב מִמֻּלִי: וְעַתָּה לְכָה־נָּא אָרָה־לִּי אֶת־הָעָם הַזֶּה כִּי־עָצוּם הוּא מִמֶּנִּי אוּלַי אוּכַל נַכֶּה־בּוֹ וַאֲגָרְשֶׁנּוּ מִן־הָאָרֶץ כִּי יָדַעְתִּי אֵת אֲשֶׁר־תְּבָרֵךְ מְבֹרָךְ וַאֲשֶׁר תָּאֹר יוּאָר: וַיֵּלְכוּ זִקְנֵי מוֹאָב וְזִקְנֵי מִדְיָן וּקְסָמִים בְּיָדָם וַיָּבֹאוּ אֶל־בִּלְעָם וַיְדַבְּרוּ אֵלָיו דִּבְרֵי בָלָק:

ישראל וַיֹּאמֶר אֲלֵיהֶם לִינוּ פֹה הַלַּיְלָה וַהֲשִׁבֹתִי אֶתְכֶם דָּבָר כַּאֲשֶׁר יְדַבֵּר יהוה אֵלָי וַיֵּשְׁבוּ שָׂרֵי־מוֹאָב עִם־בִּלְעָם: וַיָּבֹא אֱלֹהִים אֶל־בִּלְעָם וַיֹּאמֶר מִי הָאֲנָשִׁים הָאֵלֶּה עִמָּךְ: וַיֹּאמֶר בִּלְעָם אֶל־הָאֱלֹהִים בָּלָק בֶּן־צִפֹּר מֶלֶךְ מוֹאָב שָׁלַח אֵלָי: הִנֵּה הָעָם הַיֹּצֵא מִמִּצְרַיִם וַיְכַס אֶת־עֵין הָאָרֶץ עַתָּה לְכָה קָבָה־לִּי אֹתוֹ אוּלַי אוּכַל לְהִלָּחֶם בּוֹ וְגֵרַשְׁתִּיו: וַיֹּאמֶר אֱלֹהִים אֶל־בִּלְעָם לֹא תֵלֵךְ עִמָּהֶם לֹא תָאֹר אֶת־הָעָם כִּי בָרוּךְ הוּא:

PINCHAS / פ׳ פינחס

(*Numbers* 25:10—26:4)

וַיְדַבֵּר יהוה אֶל־מֹשֶׁה לֵּאמֹר: פִּינְחָס בֶּן־אֶלְעָזָר בֶּן־אַהֲרֹן הַכֹּהֵן הֵשִׁיב אֶת־חֲמָתִי מֵעַל בְּנֵי־יִשְׂרָאֵל בְּקַנְאוֹ אֶת־קִנְאָתִי

בְּתוֹכָם וְלֹא־כִלִּיתִי אֶת־בְּנֵי־יִשְׂרָאֵל בְּקִנְאָתִי: לָכֵן אֱמֹר הִנְנִי נֹתֵן לוֹ אֶת־בְּרִיתִי שָׁלוֹם:

לוי וְהָיְתָה לּוֹ וּלְזַרְעוֹ אַחֲרָיו בְּרִית כְּהֻנַּת עוֹלָם תַּחַת אֲשֶׁר קִנֵּא לֵאלֹהָיו וַיְכַפֵּר עַל־בְּנֵי יִשְׂרָאֵל: וְשֵׁם אִישׁ יִשְׂרָאֵל הַמֻּכֶּה אֲשֶׁר הֻכָּה אֶת־הַמִּדְיָנִית זִמְרִי בֶּן־סָלוּא נְשִׂיא בֵית־אָב לַשִּׁמְעֹנִי: וְשֵׁם הָאִשָּׁה הַמֻּכָּה הַמִּדְיָנִית כָּזְבִּי בַת־צוּר רֹאשׁ אֻמּוֹת בֵּית־אָב בְּמִדְיָן הוּא:

ישראל וַיְדַבֵּר יהוה אֶל־מֹשֶׁה לֵּאמֹר: צָרוֹר אֶת־הַמִּדְיָנִים וְהִכִּיתֶם אוֹתָם: כִּי־צֹרְרִים הֵם לָכֶם בְּנִכְלֵיהֶם אֲשֶׁר־נִכְּלוּ לָכֶם עַל־דְּבַר פְּעוֹר וְעַל־דְּבַר כָּזְבִּי בַת־נְשִׂיא מִדְיָן אֲחֹתָם הַמֻּכָּה בְיוֹם־הַמַּגֵּפָה עַל־דְּבַר פְּעוֹר: וַיְהִי אַחֲרֵי הַמַּגֵּפָה וַיֹּאמֶר יהוה אֶל־מֹשֶׁה וְאֶל אֶלְעָזָר בֶּן־אַהֲרֹן הַכֹּהֵן לֵאמֹר: שְׂאוּ אֶת־רֹאשׁ | כָּל־עֲדַת בְּנֵי־יִשְׂרָאֵל מִבֶּן עֶשְׂרִים שָׁנָה וָמַעְלָה לְבֵית אֲבֹתָם כָּל־יֹצֵא צָבָא בְּיִשְׂרָאֵל: וַיְדַבֵּר מֹשֶׁה וְאֶלְעָזָר הַכֹּהֵן אֹתָם בְּעַרְבֹת מוֹאָב עַל־יַרְדֵּן יְרֵחוֹ לֵאמֹר: מִבֶּן עֶשְׂרִים שָׁנָה וָמָעְלָה כַּאֲשֶׁר צִוָּה יהוה אֶת־מֹשֶׁה וּבְנֵי יִשְׂרָאֵל הַיֹּצְאִים מֵאֶרֶץ מִצְרָיִם:

פ׳ מטות / MATOS
(*Numbers* 30:2-17)

וַיְדַבֵּר מֹשֶׁה אֶל־רָאשֵׁי הַמַּטּוֹת לִבְנֵי יִשְׂרָאֵל לֵאמֹר זֶה הַדָּבָר אֲשֶׁר צִוָּה יהוה: אִישׁ כִּי־יִדֹּר נֶדֶר לַיהוה אוֹ־הִשָּׁבַע שְׁבֻעָה לֶאְסֹר אִסָּר עַל־נַפְשׁוֹ לֹא יַחֵל דְּבָרוֹ כְּכָל־הַיֹּצֵא מִפִּיו יַעֲשֶׂה: וְאִשָּׁה כִּי־תִדֹּר נֶדֶר לַיהוה וְאָסְרָה אִסָּר בְּבֵית אָבִיהָ בִּנְעֻרֶיהָ: וְשָׁמַע אָבִיהָ אֶת־נִדְרָהּ וֶאֱסָרָהּ אֲשֶׁר אָסְרָה עַל־נַפְשָׁהּ וְהֶחֱרִישׁ לָהּ אָבִיהָ וְקָמוּ כָּל־נְדָרֶיהָ וְכָל־אִסָּר אֲשֶׁר־אָסְרָה עַל־נַפְשָׁהּ יָקוּם: וְאִם־הֵנִיא אָבִיהָ אֹתָהּ בְּיוֹם שָׁמְעוֹ כָּל־נְדָרֶיהָ וֶאֱסָרֶיהָ אֲשֶׁר־אָסְרָה עַל־נַפְשָׁהּ לֹא יָקוּם וַיהוה יִסְלַח־לָהּ כִּי־הֵנִיא אָבִיהָ אֹתָהּ: וְאִם־הָיוֹ תִהְיֶה לְאִישׁ וּנְדָרֶיהָ עָלֶיהָ אוֹ מִבְטָא שְׂפָתֶיהָ אֲשֶׁר אָסְרָה עַל־נַפְשָׁהּ: וְשָׁמַע אִישָׁהּ בְּיוֹם שָׁמְעוֹ וְהֶחֱרִישׁ לָהּ וְקָמוּ נְדָרֶיהָ וֶאֱסָרֶהָ אֲשֶׁר־אָסְרָה עַל־נַפְשָׁהּ יָקֻמוּ: וְאִם בְּיוֹם שְׁמֹעַ אִישָׁהּ יָנִיא אוֹתָהּ וְהֵפֵר אֶת־נִדְרָהּ אֲשֶׁר עָלֶיהָ וְאֵת מִבְטָא שְׂפָתֶיהָ אֲשֶׁר אָסְרָה עַל־נַפְשָׁהּ וַיהוה יִסְלַח־לָהּ:

לוי וְנֵדֶר אַלְמָנָה וּגְרוּשָׁה כֹּל אֲשֶׁר־אָסְרָה עַל־נַפְשָׁהּ יָקוּם עָלֶיהָ: וְאִם־בֵּית אִישָׁהּ נָדָרָה אוֹ־אָסְרָה אִסָּר עַל־נַפְשָׁהּ בִּשְׁבֻעָה: וְשָׁמַע אִישָׁהּ וְהֶחֱרִשׁ לָהּ לֹא הֵנִיא אֹתָהּ וְקָמוּ כָּל־נְדָרֶיהָ וְכָל־אִסָּר אֲשֶׁר־אָסְרָה עַל־נַפְשָׁהּ יָקוּם: וְאִם־הָפֵר יָפֵר אֹתָם | אִישָׁהּ בְּיוֹם שָׁמְעוֹ כָּל־מוֹצָא שְׂפָתֶיהָ לִנְדָרֶיהָ וּלְאִסַּר נַפְשָׁהּ לֹא יָקוּם אִישָׁהּ הֲפֵרָם וַיהוה יִסְלַח־לָהּ:

ישראל כָּל־נֵדֶר וְכָל־שְׁבֻעַת אִסָּר לְעַנֹּת נָפֶשׁ אִישָׁהּ יְקִימֶנּוּ וְאִישָׁהּ יְפֵרֶנּוּ: וְאִם־הַחֲרֵשׁ יַחֲרִישׁ לָהּ אִישָׁהּ מִיּוֹם אֶל־יוֹם וְהֵקִים אֶת־כָּל־נְדָרֶיהָ אוֹ אֶת־כָּל־אֱסָרֶיהָ אֲשֶׁר עָלֶיהָ הֵקִים אֹתָם כִּי־הֶחֱרִשׁ לָהּ בְּיוֹם שָׁמְעוֹ: וְאִם־הָפֵר יָפֵר אֹתָם אַחֲרֵי שָׁמְעוֹ וְנָשָׂא אֶת־עֲוֺנָהּ: אֵלֶּה הַחֻקִּים אֲשֶׁר צִוָּה יהוה אֶת־מֹשֶׁה בֵּין אִישׁ לְאִשְׁתּוֹ בֵּין־אָב לְבִתּוֹ בִּנְעֻרֶיהָ בֵּית אָבִיהָ:

פ׳ מסעי / MASEI
(*Numbers* 33:1-10)

אֵלֶּה מַסְעֵי בְנֵי־יִשְׂרָאֵל אֲשֶׁר יָצְאוּ מֵאֶרֶץ מִצְרַיִם לְצִבְאֹתָם בְּיַד־מֹשֶׁה וְאַהֲרֹן: וַיִּכְתֹּב מֹשֶׁה אֶת־מוֹצָאֵיהֶם לְמַסְעֵיהֶם עַל־פִּי יהוה וְאֵלֶּה מַסְעֵיהֶם לְמוֹצָאֵיהֶם: וַיִּסְעוּ מֵרַעְמְסֵס בַּחֹדֶשׁ הָרִאשׁוֹן בַּחֲמִשָּׁה עָשָׂר יוֹם לַחֹדֶשׁ הָרִאשׁוֹן מִמָּחֳרַת הַפֶּסַח יָצְאוּ בְנֵי־יִשְׂרָאֵל בְּיָד רָמָה לְעֵינֵי כָּל־מִצְרָיִם:

לוי וּמִצְרַיִם מְקַבְּרִים אֵת אֲשֶׁר הִכָּה יהוה בָּהֶם כָּל־בְּכוֹר וּבֵאלֹהֵיהֶם עָשָׂה יהוה שְׁפָטִים: וַיִּסְעוּ בְנֵי־יִשְׂרָאֵל מֵרַעְמְסֵס וַיַּחֲנוּ בְּסֻכֹּת: וַיִּסְעוּ מִסֻּכֹּת וַיַּחֲנוּ בְאֵתָם אֲשֶׁר בִּקְצֵה הַמִּדְבָּר:

ישראל וַיִּסְעוּ מֵאֵתָם וַיָּשָׁב עַל־פִּי הַחִירֹת אֲשֶׁר עַל־פְּנֵי בַּעַל צְפוֹן וַיַּחֲנוּ לִפְנֵי מִגְדֹּל: וַיִּסְעוּ מִפְּנֵי הַחִירֹת וַיַּעַבְרוּ בְתוֹךְ־הַיָּם הַמִּדְבָּרָה וַיֵּלְכוּ דֶּרֶךְ שְׁלֹשֶׁת יָמִים בְּמִדְבַּר אֵתָם וַיַּחֲנוּ בְּמָרָה: וַיִּסְעוּ מִמָּרָה וַיָּבֹאוּ אֵילִמָה וּבְאֵילִם שְׁתֵּים עֶשְׂרֵה עֵינֹת מַיִם וְשִׁבְעִים תְּמָרִים וַיַּחֲנוּ־שָׁם: וַיִּסְעוּ מֵאֵילִם וַיַּחֲנוּ עַל־יַם־סוּף:

DEVARIM / פ׳ דברים

(*Deuteronomy* 1:1-11)

אֵלֶּה הַדְּבָרִים אֲשֶׁר דִּבֶּר מֹשֶׁה אֶל־כָּל־יִשְׂרָאֵל בְּעֵבֶר הַיַּרְדֵּן בַּמִּדְבָּר בָּעֲרָבָה מוֹל סוּף בֵּין־פָּארָן וּבֵין־תֹּפֶל וְלָבָן וַחֲצֵרֹת וְדִי זָהָב׃ אַחַד עָשָׂר יוֹם מֵחֹרֵב דֶּרֶךְ הַר־שֵׂעִיר עַד קָדֵשׁ בַּרְנֵעַ׃ וַיְהִי בְּאַרְבָּעִים שָׁנָה בְּעַשְׁתֵּי־עָשָׂר חֹדֶשׁ בְּאֶחָד לַחֹדֶשׁ דִּבֶּר מֹשֶׁה אֶל־בְּנֵי יִשְׂרָאֵל כְּכֹל אֲשֶׁר צִוָּה יהוה אֹתוֹ אֲלֵהֶם׃

לוי אַחֲרֵי הַכֹּתוֹ אֵת סִיחֹן מֶלֶךְ הָאֱמֹרִי אֲשֶׁר יוֹשֵׁב בְּחֶשְׁבּוֹן וְאֵת עוֹג מֶלֶךְ הַבָּשָׁן אֲשֶׁר־יוֹשֵׁב בְּעַשְׁתָּרֹת בְּאֶדְרֶעִי׃ בְּעֵבֶר הַיַּרְדֵּן בְּאֶרֶץ מוֹאָב הוֹאִיל מֹשֶׁה בֵּאֵר אֶת־הַתּוֹרָה הַזֹּאת לֵאמֹר׃ יהוה אֱלֹהֵינוּ דִּבֶּר אֵלֵינוּ בְּחֹרֵב לֵאמֹר רַב־לָכֶם שֶׁבֶת בָּהָר הַזֶּה׃ פְּנוּ | וּסְעוּ לָכֶם וּבֹאוּ הַר הָאֱמֹרִי וְאֶל־כָּל־שְׁכֵנָיו בָּעֲרָבָה בָהָר וּבַשְּׁפֵלָה וּבַנֶּגֶב וּבְחוֹף הַיָּם אֶרֶץ הַכְּנַעֲנִי וְהַלְּבָנוֹן עַד־הַנָּהָר הַגָּדֹל נְהַר־פְּרָת׃

ישראל רְאֵה נָתַתִּי לִפְנֵיכֶם אֶת־הָאָרֶץ בֹּאוּ וּרְשׁוּ אֶת־הָאָרֶץ אֲשֶׁר נִשְׁבַּע יהוה לַאֲבֹתֵיכֶם לְאַבְרָהָם לְיִצְחָק וּלְיַעֲקֹב לָתֵת לָהֶם וּלְזַרְעָם אַחֲרֵיהֶם׃ וָאֹמַר אֲלֵכֶם בָּעֵת הַהִוא לֵאמֹר לֹא־אוּכַל לְבַדִּי שְׂאֵת אֶתְכֶם׃ יהוה אֱלֹהֵיכֶם הִרְבָּה אֶתְכֶם וְהִנְּכֶם הַיּוֹם כְּכוֹכְבֵי הַשָּׁמַיִם לָרֹב׃ יהוה אֱלֹהֵי אֲבוֹתֵכֶם יֹסֵף עֲלֵיכֶם כָּכֶם אֶלֶף פְּעָמִים וִיבָרֵךְ אֶתְכֶם כַּאֲשֶׁר דִּבֶּר לָכֶם׃

VA'ESCHANAN / פ׳ ואתחנן

(*Deuteronomy* 3:23—4:8)

וָאֶתְחַנַּן אֶל־יהוה בָּעֵת הַהִוא לֵאמֹר׃ אֲדֹנָי יֱהוִה אַתָּה הַחִלּוֹתָ לְהַרְאוֹת אֶת־עַבְדְּךָ אֶת־גָּדְלְךָ וְאֶת־יָדְךָ הַחֲזָקָה אֲשֶׁר מִי־אֵל בַּשָּׁמַיִם וּבָאָרֶץ אֲשֶׁר־יַעֲשֶׂה כְמַעֲשֶׂיךָ וְכִגְבוּרֹתֶךָ׃ אֶעְבְּרָה־נָּא וְאֶרְאֶה אֶת־הָאָרֶץ הַטּוֹבָה אֲשֶׁר בְּעֵבֶר הַיַּרְדֵּן הָהָר הַטּוֹב הַזֶּה וְהַלְּבָנֹן׃

לוי וַיִּתְעַבֵּר יהוה בִּי לְמַעַנְכֶם וְלֹא שָׁמַע אֵלָי וַיֹּאמֶר יהוה אֵלַי רַב־לָךְ אַל־תּוֹסֶף דַּבֵּר אֵלַי עוֹד בַּדָּבָר הַזֶּה׃ עֲלֵה | רֹאשׁ הַפִּסְגָּה וְשָׂא עֵינֶיךָ יָמָּה וְצָפֹנָה וְתֵימָנָה וּמִזְרָחָה וּרְאֵה בְעֵינֶיךָ כִּי־לֹא תַעֲבֹר אֶת־הַיַּרְדֵּן הַזֶּה׃ וְצַו אֶת־יְהוֹשֻׁעַ וְחַזְּקֵהוּ וְאַמְּצֵהוּ כִּי־הוּא יַעֲבֹר לִפְנֵי הָעָם הַזֶּה וְהוּא יַנְחִיל אוֹתָם אֶת־הָאָרֶץ אֲשֶׁר תִּרְאֶה׃ וַנֵּשֶׁב בַּגָּיְא מוּל בֵּית פְּעוֹר׃ וְעַתָּה יִשְׂרָאֵל שְׁמַע אֶל־הַחֻקִּים וְאֶל־הַמִּשְׁפָּטִים אֲשֶׁר אָנֹכִי מְלַמֵּד אֶתְכֶם לַעֲשׂוֹת לְמַעַן תִּחְיוּ וּבָאתֶם וִירִשְׁתֶּם אֶת־הָאָרֶץ אֲשֶׁר יהוה אֱלֹהֵי אֲבֹתֵיכֶם נֹתֵן לָכֶם׃ לֹא תֹסִפוּ עַל־הַדָּבָר אֲשֶׁר אָנֹכִי מְצַוֶּה אֶתְכֶם וְלֹא תִגְרְעוּ מִמֶּנּוּ לִשְׁמֹר אֶת־מִצְוֹת יהוה אֱלֹהֵיכֶם אֲשֶׁר אָנֹכִי מְצַוֶּה אֶתְכֶם׃ עֵינֵיכֶם הָרֹאוֹת אֵת אֲשֶׁר־עָשָׂה יהוה בְּבַעַל פְּעוֹר כִּי כָל־הָאִישׁ אֲשֶׁר הָלַךְ אַחֲרֵי בַעַל־פְּעוֹר הִשְׁמִידוֹ יהוה אֱלֹהֶיךָ מִקִּרְבֶּךָ׃ וְאַתֶּם הַדְּבֵקִים בַּיהוה אֱלֹהֵיכֶם חַיִּים כֻּלְּכֶם הַיּוֹם׃

ישראל רְאֵה | לִמַּדְתִּי אֶתְכֶם חֻקִּים וּמִשְׁפָּטִים כַּאֲשֶׁר צִוַּנִי יהוה אֱלֹהָי לַעֲשׂוֹת כֵּן בְּקֶרֶב הָאָרֶץ אֲשֶׁר אַתֶּם בָּאִים שָׁמָּה לְרִשְׁתָּהּ׃ וּשְׁמַרְתֶּם וַעֲשִׂיתֶם כִּי הִוא חָכְמַתְכֶם וּבִינַתְכֶם לְעֵינֵי הָעַמִּים אֲשֶׁר יִשְׁמְעוּן אֵת כָּל־הַחֻקִּים הָאֵלֶּה וְאָמְרוּ רַק עַם־חָכָם וְנָבוֹן הַגּוֹי הַגָּדוֹל הַזֶּה׃ כִּי מִי־גוֹי גָּדוֹל אֲשֶׁר־לוֹ אֱלֹהִים קְרֹבִים אֵלָיו כַּיהוה אֱלֹהֵינוּ בְּכָל־קָרְאֵנוּ אֵלָיו׃ וּמִי גּוֹי גָּדוֹל אֲשֶׁר־לוֹ חֻקִּים וּמִשְׁפָּטִים צַדִּיקִם כְּכֹל הַתּוֹרָה הַזֹּאת אֲשֶׁר אָנֹכִי נֹתֵן לִפְנֵיכֶם הַיּוֹם׃

EIKEV / פ׳ עקב

(*Deuteronomy* 7:12—8:10)

וְהָיָה | עֵקֶב תִּשְׁמְעוּן אֵת הַמִּשְׁפָּטִים הָאֵלֶּה וּשְׁמַרְתֶּם וַעֲשִׂיתֶם אֹתָם וְשָׁמַר יהוה אֱלֹהֶיךָ לְךָ אֶת־הַבְּרִית וְאֶת־הַחֶסֶד אֲשֶׁר נִשְׁבַּע לַאֲבֹתֶיךָ׃ וַאֲהֵבְךָ וּבֵרַכְךָ וְהִרְבֶּךָ וּבֵרַךְ פְּרִי־בִטְנְךָ וּפְרִי־אַדְמָתֶךָ דְּגָנְךָ וְתִירֹשְׁךָ וְיִצְהָרֶךָ שְׁגַר־אֲלָפֶיךָ וְעַשְׁתְּרֹת צֹאנֶךָ עַל הָאֲדָמָה אֲשֶׁר־נִשְׁבַּע לַאֲבֹתֶיךָ לָתֶת לָךְ׃ בָּרוּךְ תִּהְיֶה מִכָּל־הָעַמִּים לֹא־יִהְיֶה בְךָ עָקָר וַעֲקָרָה וּבִבְהֶמְתֶּךָ׃ וְהֵסִיר יהוה מִמְּךָ כָּל־חֹלִי וְכָל־מַדְוֵי מִצְרַיִם הָרָעִים אֲשֶׁר יָדַעְתָּ לֹא יְשִׂימָם בָּךְ וּנְתָנָם בְּכָל־שֹׂנְאֶיךָ׃ וְאָכַלְתָּ אֶת־כָּל־הָעַמִּים אֲשֶׁר יהוה אֱלֹהֶיךָ נֹתֵן לָךְ לֹא־תָחוֹס עֵינְךָ עֲלֵיהֶם וְלֹא תַעֲבֹד אֶת־אֱלֹהֵיהֶם כִּי־מוֹקֵשׁ הוּא לָךְ׃ כִּי תֹאמַר בִּלְבָבְךָ רַבִּים הַגּוֹיִם

הָאֵלֶּה מִמֶּנִּי אֵיכָה אוּכַל לְהוֹרִישָׁם׃ לֹא תִירָא מֵהֶם זָכֹר תִּזְכֹּר אֵת אֲשֶׁר־עָשָׂה יְהוָה אֱלֹהֶיךָ לְפַרְעֹה וּלְכָל־מִצְרָיִם׃ הַמַּסֹּת הַגְּדֹלֹת אֲשֶׁר־רָאוּ עֵינֶיךָ וְהָאֹתֹת וְהַמֹּפְתִים וְהַיָּד הַחֲזָקָה וְהַזְּרֹעַ הַנְּטוּיָה אֲשֶׁר הוֹצִאֲךָ יְהוָה אֱלֹהֶיךָ כֵּן־יַעֲשֶׂה יְהוָה אֱלֹהֶיךָ לְכָל־הָעַמִּים אֲשֶׁר־אַתָּה יָרֵא מִפְּנֵיהֶם׃ וְגַם אֶת־הַצִּרְעָה יְשַׁלַּח יְהוָה אֱלֹהֶיךָ בָּם עַד־אֲבֹד הַנִּשְׁאָרִים וְהַנִּסְתָּרִים מִפָּנֶיךָ׃ לֹא תַעֲרֹץ מִפְּנֵיהֶם כִּי־יְהוָה אֱלֹהֶיךָ בְּקִרְבֶּךָ אֵל גָּדוֹל וְנוֹרָא׃

לוי וְנָשַׁל יְהוָה אֱלֹהֶיךָ אֶת־הַגּוֹיִם הָאֵל מִפָּנֶיךָ מְעַט מְעָט לֹא תוּכַל כַּלֹּתָם מַהֵר פֶּן־תִּרְבֶּה עָלֶיךָ חַיַּת הַשָּׂדֶה׃ וּנְתָנָם יְהוָה אֱלֹהֶיךָ לְפָנֶיךָ וְהָמָם מְהוּמָה גְדֹלָה עַד הִשָּׁמְדָם׃ וְנָתַן מַלְכֵיהֶם בְּיָדֶךָ וְהַאֲבַדְתָּ אֶת־שְׁמָם מִתַּחַת הַשָּׁמָיִם לֹא־יִתְיַצֵּב אִישׁ בְּפָנֶיךָ עַד הִשְׁמִדְךָ אֹתָם׃ פְּסִילֵי אֱלֹהֵיהֶם תִּשְׂרְפוּן בָּאֵשׁ לֹא־תַחְמֹד כֶּסֶף וְזָהָב עֲלֵיהֶם וְלָקַחְתָּ לָךְ פֶּן תִּוָּקֵשׁ בּוֹ כִּי תוֹעֲבַת יְהוָה אֱלֹהֶיךָ הוּא׃ וְלֹא־תָבִיא תוֹעֵבָה אֶל־בֵּיתֶךָ וְהָיִיתָ חֵרֶם כָּמֹהוּ שַׁקֵּץ | תְּשַׁקְּצֶנּוּ וְתַעֵב | תְּתַעֲבֶנּוּ כִּי־חֵרֶם הוּא׃ כָּל־הַמִּצְוָה אֲשֶׁר אָנֹכִי מְצַוְּךָ הַיּוֹם תִּשְׁמְרוּן לַעֲשׂוֹת לְמַעַן תִּחְיוּן וּרְבִיתֶם וּבָאתֶם וִירִשְׁתֶּם אֶת־הָאָרֶץ אֲשֶׁר־נִשְׁבַּע יְהוָה לַאֲבֹתֵיכֶם׃ וְזָכַרְתָּ אֶת־כָּל־הַדֶּרֶךְ אֲשֶׁר הוֹלִיכֲךָ יְהוָה אֱלֹהֶיךָ זֶה אַרְבָּעִים שָׁנָה בַּמִּדְבָּר לְמַעַן עַנֹּתְךָ לְנַסֹּתְךָ לָדַעַת אֶת־אֲשֶׁר בִּלְבָבְךָ הֲתִשְׁמֹר מִצְוֹתָו אִם־לֹא׃ וַיְעַנְּךָ וַיַּרְעִבֶךָ וַיַּאֲכִלְךָ אֶת־הַמָּן אֲשֶׁר לֹא־יָדַעְתָּ וְלֹא יָדְעוּן אֲבֹתֶיךָ לְמַעַן הוֹדִיעֲךָ כִּי לֹא עַל־הַלֶּחֶם לְבַדּוֹ יִחְיֶה הָאָדָם כִּי עַל־כָּל־מוֹצָא פִי־יְהוָה יִחְיֶה הָאָדָם׃

ישראל שִׂמְלָתְךָ לֹא בָלְתָה מֵעָלֶיךָ וְרַגְלְךָ לֹא בָצֵקָה זֶה אַרְבָּעִים שָׁנָה׃ וְיָדַעְתָּ עִם־לְבָבֶךָ כִּי כַּאֲשֶׁר יְיַסֵּר אִישׁ אֶת־בְּנוֹ יְהוָה אֱלֹהֶיךָ מְיַסְּרֶךָּ׃ וְשָׁמַרְתָּ אֶת־מִצְוֹת יְהוָה אֱלֹהֶיךָ לָלֶכֶת בִּדְרָכָיו וּלְיִרְאָה אֹתוֹ׃ כִּי יְהוָה אֱלֹהֶיךָ מְבִיאֲךָ אֶל־אֶרֶץ טוֹבָה אֶרֶץ נַחֲלֵי מָיִם עֲיָנֹת וּתְהֹמֹת יֹצְאִים בַּבִּקְעָה וּבָהָר׃ אֶרֶץ חִטָּה וּשְׂעֹרָה וְגֶפֶן וּתְאֵנָה וְרִמּוֹן אֶרֶץ־זֵית שֶׁמֶן וּדְבָשׁ׃ אֶרֶץ אֲשֶׁר לֹא בְמִסְכֵּנֻת תֹּאכַל־בָּהּ לֶחֶם לֹא־תֶחְסַר כֹּל בָּהּ אֶרֶץ אֲשֶׁר אֲבָנֶיהָ בַרְזֶל וּמֵהֲרָרֶיהָ תַּחְצֹב נְחֹשֶׁת׃ וְאָכַלְתָּ וְשָׂבָעְתָּ וּבֵרַכְתָּ אֶת־יְהוָה אֱלֹהֶיךָ עַל־הָאָרֶץ הַטֹּבָה אֲשֶׁר נָתַן־לָךְ׃

פ׳ ראה / RE'EH

(*Deuteronomy* 11:26—12:10)

רְאֵה אָנֹכִי נֹתֵן לִפְנֵיכֶם הַיּוֹם בְּרָכָה וּקְלָלָה׃ אֶת־הַבְּרָכָה אֲשֶׁר תִּשְׁמְעוּ אֶל־מִצְוֹת יְהוָה אֱלֹהֵיכֶם אֲשֶׁר אָנֹכִי מְצַוֶּה אֶתְכֶם הַיּוֹם׃ וְהַקְּלָלָה אִם־לֹא תִשְׁמְעוּ אֶל־מִצְוֹת יְהוָה אֱלֹהֵיכֶם וְסַרְתֶּם מִן־הַדֶּרֶךְ אֲשֶׁר אָנֹכִי מְצַוֶּה אֶתְכֶם הַיּוֹם לָלֶכֶת אַחֲרֵי אֱלֹהִים אֲחֵרִים אֲשֶׁר לֹא־יְדַעְתֶּם׃ וְהָיָה כִּי יְבִיאֲךָ יְהוָה אֱלֹהֶיךָ אֶל־הָאָרֶץ אֲשֶׁר־אַתָּה בָא־שָׁמָּה לְרִשְׁתָּהּ וְנָתַתָּה אֶת־הַבְּרָכָה עַל־הַר גְּרִזִּים וְאֶת־הַקְּלָלָה עַל־הַר עֵיבָל׃ הֲלֹא־הֵמָּה בְּעֵבֶר הַיַּרְדֵּן אַחֲרֵי דֶּרֶךְ מְבוֹא הַשֶּׁמֶשׁ בְּאֶרֶץ הַכְּנַעֲנִי הַיֹּשֵׁב בָּעֲרָבָה מוּל הַגִּלְגָּל אֵצֶל אֵלוֹנֵי מֹרֶה׃ כִּי אַתֶּם עֹבְרִים אֶת־הַיַּרְדֵּן לָבֹא לָרֶשֶׁת אֶת־הָאָרֶץ אֲשֶׁר־יְהוָה אֱלֹהֵיכֶם נֹתֵן לָכֶם וִירִשְׁתֶּם אֹתָהּ וִישַׁבְתֶּם־בָּהּ׃

לוי וּשְׁמַרְתֶּם לַעֲשׂוֹת אֵת כָּל־הַחֻקִּים וְאֶת־הַמִּשְׁפָּטִים אֲשֶׁר אָנֹכִי נֹתֵן לִפְנֵיכֶם הַיּוֹם׃ אֵלֶּה הַחֻקִּים וְהַמִּשְׁפָּטִים אֲשֶׁר תִּשְׁמְרוּן לַעֲשׂוֹת בָּאָרֶץ אֲשֶׁר נָתַן יְהוָה אֱלֹהֵי אֲבֹתֶיךָ לְךָ לְרִשְׁתָּהּ כָּל־הַיָּמִים אֲשֶׁר־אַתֶּם חַיִּים עַל־הָאֲדָמָה׃ אַבֵּד תְּאַבְּדוּן אֶת־כָּל־הַמְּקֹמוֹת אֲשֶׁר עָבְדוּ־שָׁם הַגּוֹיִם אֲשֶׁר אַתֶּם יֹרְשִׁים אֹתָם אֶת־אֱלֹהֵיהֶם עַל־הֶהָרִים הָרָמִים וְעַל־הַגְּבָעוֹת וְתַחַת כָּל־עֵץ רַעֲנָן׃ וְנִתַּצְתֶּם אֶת־מִזְבְּחֹתָם וְשִׁבַּרְתֶּם אֶת־מַצֵּבֹתָם וַאֲשֵׁרֵיהֶם תִּשְׂרְפוּן בָּאֵשׁ וּפְסִילֵי אֱלֹהֵיהֶם תְּגַדֵּעוּן וְאִבַּדְתֶּם אֶת־שְׁמָם מִן־הַמָּקוֹם הַהוּא׃ לֹא־תַעֲשׂוּן כֵּן לַיהוָה אֱלֹהֵיכֶם׃ כִּי אִם־אֶל־הַמָּקוֹם אֲשֶׁר־יִבְחַר יְהוָה אֱלֹהֵיכֶם מִכָּל־שִׁבְטֵיכֶם לָשׂוּם אֶת־שְׁמוֹ שָׁם לְשִׁכְנוֹ תִדְרְשׁוּ וּבָאתָ שָׁמָּה׃

ישראל וַהֲבֵאתֶם שָׁמָּה עֹלֹתֵיכֶם וְזִבְחֵיכֶם וְאֵת מַעְשְׂרֹתֵיכֶם וְאֵת תְּרוּמַת יֶדְכֶם וְנִדְרֵיכֶם וְנִדְבֹתֵיכֶם וּבְכֹרֹת בְּקַרְכֶם וְצֹאנְכֶם׃ וַאֲכַלְתֶּם־שָׁם לִפְנֵי יְהוָה

אֱלֹֽהֵיכֶ֑ם וּשְׂמַחְתֶּם֙ בְּכֹל֙ מִשְׁלַ֣ח יֶדְכֶ֔ם
אַתֶּ֖ם וּבָתֵּיכֶ֑ם אֲשֶׁ֥ר בֵּרַכְךָ֖ יהו֥ה אֱלֹהֶֽיךָ:
לֹ֣א תַעֲשׂ֔וּן כְּ֠כֹל אֲשֶׁ֨ר אֲנַ֧חְנוּ עֹשִׂ֛ים פֹּ֖ה
הַיּ֑וֹם אִ֖ישׁ כָּל־הַיָּשָׁ֥ר בְּעֵינָֽיו: כִּ֥י לֹא־בָאתֶ֖ם
עַד־עָ֑תָּה אֶל־הַמְּנוּחָה֙ וְאֶל־הַֽנַּחֲלָ֔ה אֲשֶׁר־
יהו֥ה אֱלֹהֶ֖יךָ נֹתֵ֥ן לָֽךְ: וַעֲבַרְתֶּם֘ אֶת־הַיַּרְדֵּן֒
וִֽישַׁבְתֶּ֣ם בָּאָ֔רֶץ אֲשֶׁר־יהו֥ה אֱלֹהֵיכֶ֖ם
מַנְחִ֣יל אֶתְכֶ֑ם וְהֵנִ֨יחַ לָכֶ֧ם מִכָּל־אֹיְבֵיכֶ֛ם
מִסָּבִ֖יב וִֽישַׁבְתֶּם־בֶּֽטַח:

⁂ פ' שֹׁפְטִים / SHOFTIM
(Deuteronomy 16:18—17:13)

שֹׁפְטִ֣ים וְשֹֽׁטְרִ֗ים תִּֽתֶּן־לְךָ֙ בְּכָל־שְׁעָרֶ֔יךָ
אֲשֶׁ֨ר יהו֧ה אֱלֹהֶ֛יךָ נֹתֵ֥ן לְךָ֖ לִשְׁבָטֶ֑יךָ
וְשָׁפְט֥וּ אֶת־הָעָ֖ם מִשְׁפַּט־צֶֽדֶק: לֹא־תַטֶּ֣ה
מִשְׁפָּ֗ט לֹ֤א תַכִּיר֙ פָּנִ֔ים וְלֹא־תִקַּ֖ח שֹׁ֑חַד כִּ֣י
הַשֹּׁ֗חַד יְעַוֵּר֙ עֵינֵ֣י חֲכָמִ֔ים וִֽיסַלֵּ֖ף דִּבְרֵ֥י
צַדִּיקִֽם: צֶ֥דֶק צֶ֖דֶק תִּרְדֹּ֑ף לְמַ֤עַן תִּֽחְיֶה֙
וְיָרַשְׁתָּ֣ אֶת־הָאָ֔רֶץ אֲשֶׁר־יהו֥ה אֱלֹהֶ֖יךָ
נֹתֵ֥ן לָֽךְ:

לוי לֹֽא־תִטַּ֥ע לְךָ֛ אֲשֵׁרָ֖ה כָּל־עֵ֑ץ אֵ֕צֶל
מִזְבַּ֛ח יהו֥ה אֱלֹהֶ֖יךָ אֲשֶׁ֥ר תַּֽעֲשֶׂה־לָּֽךְ: וְלֹֽא־
תָקִ֥ים לְךָ֖ מַצֵּבָ֑ה אֲשֶׁ֥ר שָׂנֵ֖א יהו֥ה אֱלֹהֶֽיךָ:
לֹא־תִזְבַּח֩ לַֽיהו֨ה אֱלֹהֶ֜יךָ שׁ֣וֹר וָשֶׂ֗ה אֲשֶׁ֨ר
יִֽהְיֶ֥ה בוֹ֙ מ֔וּם כֹּ֖ל דָּבָ֣ר רָ֑ע כִּ֧י תֽוֹעֲבַ֛ת יהו֥ה
אֱלֹהֶ֖יךָ הֽוּא: כִּֽי־יִמָּצֵ֤א בְקִרְבְּךָ֙ בְּאַחַ֣ד
שְׁעָרֶ֔יךָ אֲשֶׁר־יהו֥ה אֱלֹהֶ֖יךָ נֹתֵ֣ן לָ֑ךְ אִ֣ישׁ
אֽוֹ־אִשָּׁ֗ה אֲשֶׁ֨ר יַעֲשֶׂ֧ה אֶת־הָרַ֛ע בְּעֵינֵ֥י
יהו֥ה־אֱלֹהֶ֖יךָ לַעֲבֹ֥ר בְּרִיתֽוֹ: וַיֵּ֗לֶךְ וַֽיַּעֲבֹד֙
אֱלֹהִ֣ים אֲחֵרִ֔ים וַיִּשְׁתַּ֖חוּ לָהֶ֑ם וְלַשֶּׁ֣מֶשׁ | א֣וֹ
לַיָּרֵ֗חַ א֛וֹ לְכָל־צְבָ֥א הַשָּׁמַ֖יִם אֲשֶׁ֥ר לֹא־
צִוִּֽיתִי: וְהֻֽגַּד־לְךָ֖ וְשָׁמָ֑עְתָּ וְדָרַשְׁתָּ֣ הֵיטֵ֔ב
וְהִנֵּ֤ה אֱמֶת֙ נָכ֣וֹן הַדָּבָ֔ר נֶֽעֶשְׂתָ֛ה הַתּוֹעֵבָ֥ה
הַזֹּ֖את בְּיִשְׂרָאֵֽל: וְהֽוֹצֵאתָ֣ אֶת־הָאִ֣ישׁ
הַה֡וּא א֣וֹ אֶת־הָֽאִשָּׁ֡ה הַהִ֡וא אֲשֶׁ֣ר עָ֠שׂוּ
אֶת־הַדָּבָ֨ר הָרָ֤ע הַזֶּה֙ אֶל־שְׁעָרֶ֔יךָ אֶת־
הָאִ֕ישׁ א֖וֹ אֶת־הָֽאִשָּׁ֑ה וּסְקַלְתָּ֥ם בָּאֲבָנִ֖ים
וָמֵֽתוּ: עַל־פִּ֣י | שְׁנַ֣יִם עֵדִ֗ים א֛וֹ שְׁלֹשָׁ֥ה עֵדִ֖ים
יוּמַ֣ת הַמֵּ֑ת לֹ֣א יוּמַ֔ת עַל־פִּ֖י עֵ֥ד אֶחָֽד: יַ֣ד
הָעֵדִ֞ים תִּֽהְיֶה־בּ֤וֹ בָרִֽאשֹׁנָה֙ לַהֲמִית֔וֹ וְיַ֥ד
כָּל־הָעָ֖ם בָּאַחֲרֹנָ֑ה וּבִֽעַרְתָּ֥ הָרָ֖ע מִקִּרְבֶּֽךָ:
כִּ֣י יִפָּלֵא֩ מִמְּךָ֨ דָבָ֜ר לַמִּשְׁפָּ֗ט בֵּֽין־דָּ֨ם | לְדָ֜ם
בֵּֽין־דִּ֣ין לְדִ֗ין וּבֵ֥ין נֶ֙גַע֙ לָנֶ֔גַע דִּבְרֵ֥י רִיבֹ֖ת
בִּשְׁעָרֶ֑יךָ וְקַמְתָּ֣ וְעָלִ֔יתָ אֶל־הַמָּק֔וֹם אֲשֶׁ֥ר
יִבְחַ֛ר יהו֥ה אֱלֹהֶ֖יךָ בּֽוֹ: וּבָאתָ֗ אֶל־הַכֹּהֲנִים֙

הַלְוִיִּ֗ם וְאֶל־הַשֹּׁפֵ֔ט אֲשֶׁ֥ר יִהְיֶ֖ה בַּיָּמִ֣ים הָהֵ֑ם
וְדָֽרַשְׁתָּ֙ וְהִגִּ֣ידוּ לְךָ֔ אֵ֖ת דְּבַ֥ר הַמִּשְׁפָּֽט:
וְעָשִׂ֗יתָ עַל־פִּ֤י הַדָּבָר֙ אֲשֶׁ֣ר יַגִּ֣ידוּ לְךָ֔ מִן־
הַמָּק֣וֹם הַה֔וּא אֲשֶׁ֖ר יִבְחַ֣ר יהו֑ה וְשָֽׁמַרְתָּ֣
לַעֲשׂ֔וֹת כְּכֹ֖ל אֲשֶׁ֥ר יוֹרֽוּךָ:

ישראל עַל־פִּ֨י הַתּוֹרָ֜ה אֲשֶׁ֣ר יוֹר֗וּךָ וְעַל־
הַמִּשְׁפָּ֛ט אֲשֶׁר־יֹאמְר֥וּ לְךָ֖ תַּעֲשֶׂ֑ה לֹ֣א
תָס֗וּר מִן־הַדָּבָ֛ר אֲשֶׁר־יַגִּ֥ידֽוּ לְךָ֖ יָמִ֥ין
וּשְׂמֹֽאל: וְהָאִ֞ישׁ אֲשֶׁר־יַעֲשֶׂ֣ה בְזָד֗וֹן לְבִלְתִּ֨י
שְׁמֹ֤עַ אֶל־הַכֹּהֵן֙ הָעֹמֵ֞ד לְשָׁ֤רֶת שָׁם֙ אֶת־
יהו֣ה אֱלֹהֶ֔יךָ א֖וֹ אֶל־הַשֹּׁפֵ֑ט וּמֵת֙ הָאִ֣ישׁ
הַה֔וּא וּבִֽעַרְתָּ֥ הָרָ֖ע מִיִּשְׂרָאֵֽל: וְכָל־הָעָ֖ם
יִשְׁמְע֣וּ וְיִרָ֑אוּ וְלֹ֥א יְזִיד֖וּן עֽוֹד:

⁂ פ' כי תצא / KI SEITZEI
(Deuteronomy 21:10-21)

כִּֽי־תֵצֵ֥א לַמִּלְחָמָ֖ה עַל־אֹיְבֶ֑יךָ וּנְתָנ֞וֹ יהו֧ה
אֱלֹהֶ֛יךָ בְּיָדֶ֖ךָ וְשָׁבִ֥יתָ שִׁבְיֽוֹ: וְרָאִ֙יתָ֙ בַּשִּׁבְיָ֔ה
אֵ֖שֶׁת יְפַת־תֹּ֑אַר וְחָשַׁקְתָּ֣ בָ֔הּ וְלָקַחְתָּ֥ לְךָ֖
לְאִשָּֽׁה: וַהֲבֵאתָ֖הּ אֶל־תּ֣וֹךְ בֵּיתֶ֑ךָ וְגִלְּחָה֙
אֶת־רֹאשָׁ֔הּ וְעָשְׂתָ֖ה אֶת־צִפָּרְנֶֽיהָ: וְהֵסִ֩ירָה֩
אֶת־שִׂמְלַ֨ת שִׁבְיָ֜הּ מֵעָלֶ֗יהָ וְיָֽשְׁבָה֙ בְּבֵיתֶ֔ךָ
וּבָֽכְתָ֛ה אֶת־אָבִ֥יהָ וְאֶת־אִמָּ֖הּ יֶ֣רַח יָמִ֑ים
וְאַ֨חַר כֵּ֜ן תָּב֤וֹא אֵלֶ֙יהָ֙ וּבְעַלְתָּ֔הּ וְהָיְתָ֥ה לְךָ֖
לְאִשָּֽׁה: וְהָיָ֞ה אִם־לֹ֧א חָפַ֣צְתָּ בָּ֗הּ וְשִׁלַּחְתָּהּ֙
לְנַפְשָׁ֔הּ וּמָכֹ֤ר לֹֽא־תִמְכְּרֶ֙נָּה֙ בַּכָּ֔סֶף לֹֽא־
תִתְעַמֵּ֣ר בָּ֔הּ תַּ֖חַת אֲשֶׁ֥ר עִנִּיתָֽהּ:

לוי כִּֽי־תִהְיֶ֤ין לְאִישׁ֙ שְׁתֵּ֣י נָשִׁ֔ים הָֽאַחַ֥ת
אֲהוּבָ֖ה וְהָאַחַ֣ת שְׂנוּאָ֑ה וְיָֽלְדוּ־ל֣וֹ בָנִ֗ים
הָאֲהוּבָ֣ה וְהַשְּׂנוּאָ֔ה וְהָיָ֛ה הַבֵּ֥ן הַבְּכֹ֖ר
לַשְּׂנִיאָֽה: וְהָיָ֗ה בְּיוֹם֙ הַנְחִיל֣וֹ אֶת־בָּנָ֔יו אֵ֠ת
אֲשֶׁר־יִֽהְיֶ֣ה ל֗וֹ לֹ֤א יוּכַל֙ לְבַכֵּ֣ר אֶת־בֶּן־
הָ֣אֲהוּבָ֔ה עַל־פְּנֵ֥י בֶן־הַשְּׂנוּאָ֖ה הַבְּכֹֽר: כִּי֩
אֶת־הַבְּכֹ֨ר בֶּן־הַשְּׂנוּאָ֜ה יַכִּ֗יר לָ֤תֶת לוֹ֙ פִּ֣י
שְׁנַ֔יִם בְּכֹ֥ל אֲשֶׁר־יִמָּצֵ֖א ל֑וֹ כִּי־הוּא֙ רֵאשִׁ֣ית
אֹנ֔וֹ ל֖וֹ מִשְׁפַּ֥ט הַבְּכֹרָֽה:

ישראל כִּֽי־יִהְיֶ֣ה לְאִ֗ישׁ בֵּ֚ן סוֹרֵ֣ר וּמוֹרֶ֔ה
אֵינֶ֣נּוּ שֹׁמֵ֔עַ בְּק֥וֹל אָבִ֖יו וּבְק֣וֹל אִמּ֑וֹ וְיִסְּר֣וּ
אֹת֔וֹ וְלֹ֥א יִשְׁמַ֖ע אֲלֵיהֶֽם: וְתָ֥פְשׂוּ ב֖וֹ אָבִ֣יו וְאִמּ֑וֹ
וְהוֹצִ֧יאוּ אֹת֛וֹ אֶל־זִקְנֵ֥י עִיר֖וֹ וְאֶל־
שַׁ֥עַר מְקֹמֽוֹ: וְאָמְר֞וּ אֶל־זִקְנֵ֣י עִיר֗וֹ בְּנֵ֤נוּ זֶה֙
סוֹרֵ֣ר וּמֹרֶ֔ה אֵינֶ֥נּוּ שֹׁמֵ֖עַ בְּקֹלֵ֑נוּ זוֹלֵ֖ל
וְסֹבֵֽא: וּ֠רְגָמֻ֠הוּ כָּל־אַנְשֵׁ֨י עִיר֤וֹ בָֽאֲבָנִים֙
וָמֵ֔ת וּבִֽעַרְתָּ֥ הָרָ֖ע מִקִּרְבֶּ֑ךָ וְכָל־יִשְׂרָאֵ֖ל
יִשְׁמְע֥וּ וְיִרָֽאוּ:

פ' כי תבוא / KI SAVO

(*Deuteronomy* 26:1-15)

וְהָיָה֙ כִּֽי־תָב֣וֹא אֶל־הָאָ֔רֶץ אֲשֶׁר֙ יְהוָ֣ה
אֱלֹהֶ֔יךָ נֹתֵ֥ן לְךָ֖ נַחֲלָ֑ה וִֽירִשְׁתָּ֖הּ וְיָשַׁ֥בְתָּ בָּֽהּ׃
וְלָקַחְתָּ֞ מֵרֵאשִׁ֣ית ׀ כָּל־פְּרִ֣י הָאֲדָמָ֗ה אֲשֶׁ֨ר
תָּבִ֧יא מֵֽאַרְצְךָ֛ אֲשֶׁ֨ר יְהוָ֧ה אֱלֹהֶ֛יךָ נֹתֵ֥ן לָ֖ךְ
וְשַׂמְתָּ֣ בַטֶּ֑נֶא וְהָֽלַכְתָּ֙ אֶל־הַמָּק֔וֹם אֲשֶׁ֤ר
יִבְחַר֙ יְהוָ֣ה אֱלֹהֶ֔יךָ לְשַׁכֵּ֥ן שְׁמ֖וֹ שָֽׁם׃ וּבָאתָ֙
אֶל־הַכֹּהֵ֔ן אֲשֶׁ֥ר יִהְיֶ֖ה בַּיָּמִ֣ים הָהֵ֑ם וְאָמַרְתָּ֣
אֵלָ֗יו הִגַּ֤דְתִּי הַיּוֹם֙ לַיהוָ֣ה אֱלֹהֶ֔יךָ כִּי־בָ֙אתִי֙
אֶל־הָאָ֔רֶץ אֲשֶׁ֨ר נִשְׁבַּ֧ע יְהוָ֛ה לַאֲבֹתֵ֖ינוּ
לָ֥תֶת לָֽנוּ׃
לוי וְלָקַ֧ח הַכֹּהֵ֛ן הַטֶּ֖נֶא מִיָּדֶ֑ךָ וְהִ֨נִּיח֔וֹ לִפְנֵ֕י
מִזְבַּ֖ח יְהוָ֥ה אֱלֹהֶֽיךָ׃ וְעָנִ֨יתָ וְאָמַרְתָּ֜ לִפְנֵ֣י ׀
יְהוָ֣ה אֱלֹהֶ֗יךָ אֲרַמִּי֙ אֹבֵ֣ד אָבִ֔י וַיֵּ֣רֶד
מִצְרַ֔יְמָה וַיָּ֥גָר שָׁ֖ם בִּמְתֵ֣י מְעָ֑ט וַֽיְהִי־שָׁ֕ם
לְג֥וֹי גָּד֖וֹל עָצ֥וּם וָרָֽב׃ וַיָּרֵ֧עוּ אֹתָ֛נוּ הַמִּצְרִ֖ים
וַיְעַנּ֑וּנוּ וַיִּתְּנ֥וּ עָלֵ֖ינוּ עֲבֹדָ֥ה קָשָֽׁה׃ וַנִּצְעַ֕ק
אֶל־יְהוָ֖ה אֱלֹהֵ֣י אֲבֹתֵ֑ינוּ וַיִּשְׁמַ֤ע יְהוָה֙ אֶת־
קֹלֵ֔נוּ וַיַּ֧רְא אֶת־עָנְיֵ֛נוּ וְאֶת־עֲמָלֵ֖נוּ וְאֶת־
לַחֲצֵֽנוּ׃ וַיּוֹצִאֵ֤נוּ יְהוָה֙ מִמִּצְרַ֔יִם בְּיָ֤ד חֲזָקָה֙
וּבִזְרֹ֣עַ נְטוּיָ֔ה וּבְמֹרָ֖א גָּדֹ֑ל וּבְאֹת֖וֹת
וּבְמֹפְתִֽים׃ וַיְבִאֵ֖נוּ אֶל־הַמָּק֣וֹם הַזֶּ֑ה וַיִּתֶּן־
לָ֙נוּ֙ אֶת־הָאָ֣רֶץ הַזֹּ֔את אֶ֛רֶץ זָבַ֥ת חָלָ֖ב
וּדְבָֽשׁ׃ וְעַתָּ֗ה הִנֵּ֤ה הֵבֵ֙אתִי֙ אֶת־רֵאשִׁית֙
פְּרִ֣י הָֽאֲדָמָ֔ה אֲשֶׁר־נָתַ֥תָּה לִּ֖י יְהוָ֑ה וְהִנַּחְתּ֗וֹ
לִפְנֵי֙ יְהוָ֣ה אֱלֹהֶ֔יךָ וְהִֽשְׁתַּחֲוִ֔יתָ לִפְנֵ֖י יְהוָ֥ה
אֱלֹהֶֽיךָ׃ וְשָׂמַחְתָּ֣ בְכָל־הַטּ֗וֹב אֲשֶׁ֧ר נָֽתַן־לְךָ֛
יְהוָ֥ה אֱלֹהֶ֖יךָ וּלְבֵיתֶ֑ךָ אַתָּה֙ וְהַלֵּוִ֔י וְהַגֵּ֖ר
אֲשֶׁ֥ר בְּקִרְבֶּֽךָ׃
ישראל כִּ֣י תְכַלֶּ֞ה לַ֠עְשֵׂר אֶת־כָּל־מַעְשַׂ֧ר
תְּבוּאָתְךָ֛ בַּשָּׁנָ֥ה הַשְּׁלִישִׁ֖ת שְׁנַ֣ת הַֽמַּעֲשֵׂ֑ר
וְנָתַתָּ֣ה לַלֵּוִ֗י לַגֵּר֙ לַיָּת֣וֹם וְלָאַלְמָנָ֔ה וְאָכְל֥וּ
בִשְׁעָרֶ֖יךָ וְשָׂבֵֽעוּ׃ וְאָמַרְתָּ֡ לִפְנֵי֩ יְהוָ֨ה
אֱלֹהֶ֜יךָ בִּעַ֧רְתִּי הַקֹּ֣דֶשׁ מִן־הַבַּ֗יִת וְגַ֨ם נְתַתִּ֤יו
לַלֵּוִי֙ וְלַגֵּר֙ לַיָּת֣וֹם וְלָאַלְמָנָ֔ה כְּכָל־מִצְוָתְךָ֖
אֲשֶׁ֣ר צִוִּיתָ֑נִי לֹֽא־עָבַ֥רְתִּי מִמִּצְוֺתֶ֖יךָ וְלֹ֥א
שָׁכָֽחְתִּי׃ לֹֽא־אָכַ֨לְתִּי בְאֹנִ֜י מִמֶּ֗נּוּ וְלֹֽא־
בִעַ֤רְתִּי מִמֶּ֙נּוּ֙ בְּטָמֵ֔א וְלֹא־נָתַ֥תִּי מִמֶּ֖נּוּ לְמֵ֑ת
שָׁמַ֗עְתִּי בְּקוֹל֙ יְהוָ֣ה אֱלֹהָ֔י עָשִׂ֕יתִי כְּכֹ֖ל
אֲשֶׁ֥ר צִוִּיתָֽנִי׃ הַשְׁקִ֩יפָה֩ מִמְּע֨וֹן קָדְשְׁךָ֜ מִן־
הַשָּׁמַ֗יִם וּבָרֵ֤ךְ אֶֽת־עַמְּךָ֙ אֶת־יִשְׂרָאֵ֔ל וְאֵת֙
הָאֲדָמָ֔ה אֲשֶׁ֥ר נָתַ֖תָּה לָ֑נוּ כַּאֲשֶׁ֤ר נִשְׁבַּ֙עְתָּ֙
לַאֲבֹתֵ֔ינוּ אֶ֛רֶץ זָבַ֥ת חָלָ֖ב וּדְבָֽשׁ׃

פ' נצבים / NITZAVIM

(*Deuteronomy* 29:9-28)

אַתֶּ֨ם נִצָּבִ֤ים הַיּוֹם֙ כֻּלְּכֶ֔ם לִפְנֵ֖י יְהוָ֣ה
אֱלֹהֵיכֶ֑ם רָאשֵׁיכֶ֣ם שִׁבְטֵיכֶ֗ם זִקְנֵיכֶם֙
וְשֹׁ֣טְרֵיכֶ֔ם כֹּ֖ל אִ֥ישׁ יִשְׂרָאֵֽל׃ טַפְּכֶ֣ם נְשֵׁיכֶ֔ם
וְגֵ֣רְךָ֔ אֲשֶׁ֖ר בְּקֶ֣רֶב מַחֲנֶ֑יךָ מֵחֹטֵ֣ב עֵצֶ֔יךָ עַ֖ד
שֹׁאֵ֥ב מֵימֶֽיךָ׃ לְעָבְרְךָ֗ בִּבְרִ֛ית יְהוָ֥ה אֱלֹהֶ֖יךָ
וּבְאָלָת֑וֹ אֲשֶׁר֙ יְהוָ֣ה אֱלֹהֶ֔יךָ כֹּרֵ֥ת עִמְּךָ֖
הַיּֽוֹם׃
לוי לְמַ֣עַן הָקִֽים־אֹתְךָ֩ הַיּ֨וֹם ׀ ל֜וֹ לְעָ֗ם וְה֤וּא
יִֽהְיֶה־לְּךָ֙ לֵֽאלֹהִ֔ים כַּאֲשֶׁ֖ר דִּבֶּר־לָ֑ךְ וְכַאֲשֶׁ֤ר
נִשְׁבַּע֙ לַאֲבֹתֶ֔יךָ לְאַבְרָהָ֥ם לְיִצְחָ֖ק וּֽלְיַעֲקֹֽב׃
וְלֹ֥א אִתְּכֶ֖ם לְבַדְּכֶ֑ם אָנֹכִ֗י כֹּרֵת֙ אֶת־הַבְּרִ֣ית
הַזֹּ֔את וְאֶת־הָאָלָ֖ה הַזֹּֽאת׃ כִּי֩ אֶת־אֲשֶׁ֨ר
יֶשְׁנ֜וֹ פֹּ֗ה עִמָּ֙נוּ֙ עֹמֵ֣ד הַיּ֔וֹם לִפְנֵ֖י יְהוָ֣ה
אֱלֹהֵ֑ינוּ וְאֵ֨ת אֲשֶׁ֥ר אֵינֶ֛נּוּ פֹּ֖ה עִמָּ֥נוּ הַיּֽוֹם׃
ישראל כִּֽי־אַתֶּ֣ם יְדַעְתֶּ֔ם אֵ֥ת אֲשֶׁר־יָשַׁ֖בְנוּ
בְּאֶ֣רֶץ מִצְרָ֑יִם וְאֵ֧ת אֲשֶׁר־עָבַ֛רְנוּ בְּקֶ֥רֶב
הַגּוֹיִ֖ם אֲשֶׁ֥ר עֲבַרְתֶּֽם׃ וַתִּרְאוּ֙ אֶת־
שִׁקּ֣וּצֵיהֶ֔ם וְאֵ֖ת גִּלֻּלֵיהֶ֑ם עֵ֣ץ וָאֶ֔בֶן כֶּ֥סֶף
וְזָהָ֖ב אֲשֶׁ֥ר עִמָּהֶֽם׃ פֶּן־יֵ֣שׁ בָּ֠כֶם אִ֣ישׁ אוֹ־
אִשָּׁ֞ה א֧וֹ מִשְׁפָּחָ֣ה אוֹ־שֵׁ֗בֶט אֲשֶׁר֩ לְבָב֨וֹ
פֹנֶ֤ה הַיּוֹם֙ מֵעִם֙ יְהוָ֣ה אֱלֹהֵ֔ינוּ לָלֶ֣כֶת לַעֲבֹ֔ד
אֶת־אֱלֹהֵ֖י הַגּוֹיִ֣ם הָהֵ֑ם פֶּן־יֵ֣שׁ בָּכֶ֗ם שֹׁ֛רֶשׁ
פֹּרֶ֥ה רֹ֖אשׁ וְלַעֲנָֽה׃ וְהָיָ֡ה בְּשָׁמְעוֹ֩ אֶת־דִּבְרֵ֨י
הָאָלָ֜ה הַזֹּ֗את וְהִתְבָּרֵ֨ךְ בִּלְבָב֤וֹ לֵאמֹר֙
שָׁל֣וֹם יִֽהְיֶה־לִּ֔י כִּ֛י בִּשְׁרִר֥וּת לִבִּ֖י אֵלֵ֑ךְ
לְמַ֛עַן סְפ֥וֹת הָרָוָ֖ה אֶת־הַצְּמֵאָֽה׃ לֹֽא־יֹאבֶ֣ה
יְהוָה֮ סְלֹ֣חַ לוֹ֒ כִּ֣י אָ֠ז יֶעְשַׁ֨ן אַף־יְהוָ֤ה
וְקִנְאָתוֹ֙ בָּאִ֣ישׁ הַה֔וּא וְרָ֤בְצָה בּוֹ֙ כָּל־הָ֣אָלָ֔ה
הַכְּתוּבָ֖ה בַּסֵּ֣פֶר הַזֶּ֑ה וּמָחָ֤ה יְהוָה֙ אֶת־שְׁמ֔וֹ
מִתַּ֖חַת הַשָּׁמָֽיִם׃ וְהִבְדִּיל֤וֹ יְהוָה֙ לְרָעָ֔ה
מִכֹּ֖ל שִׁבְטֵ֣י יִשְׂרָאֵ֑ל כְּכֹל֙ אָל֣וֹת הַבְּרִ֔ית
הַכְּתוּבָ֕ה בְּסֵ֥פֶר הַתּוֹרָ֖ה הַזֶּֽה׃ וְאָמַ֞ר הַדּ֣וֹר
הָאַֽחֲר֗וֹן בְּנֵיכֶם֙ אֲשֶׁ֤ר יָק֙וּמוּ֙ מֵאַ֣חֲרֵיכֶ֔ם
וְהַ֨נָּכְרִ֔י אֲשֶׁ֥ר יָבֹ֖א מֵאֶ֣רֶץ רְחוֹקָ֑ה וְ֠רָאוּ
אֶת־מַכּ֞וֹת הָאָ֤רֶץ הַהִוא֙ וְאֶת־תַּ֣חֲלֻאֶ֔יהָ
אֲשֶׁר־חִלָּ֥ה יְהוָ֖ה בָּֽהּ׃ גָּפְרִ֣ית וָמֶלַח֮ שְׂרֵפָ֣ה
כָל־אַרְצָהּ֒ לֹ֤א תִזָּרַע֙ וְלֹ֣א תַצְמִ֔חַ וְלֹא־
יַעֲלֶ֥ה בָ֖הּ כָּל־עֵ֑שֶׂב כְּֽמַהְפֵּכַ֞ת סְדֹ֤ם וַעֲמֹרָה֙
אַדְמָ֣ה וּצְבוֹיִ֔ם אֲשֶׁר֙ הָפַ֣ךְ יְהוָ֔ה בְּאַפּ֖וֹ
וּבַחֲמָתֽוֹ׃ וְאָמְרוּ֙ כָּל־הַגּוֹיִ֔ם עַל־מֶ֨ה עָשָׂ֧ה
יְהוָ֛ה כָּ֖כָה לָאָ֣רֶץ הַזֹּ֑את מֶ֥ה חֳרִ֛י הָאַ֥ף
הַגָּד֖וֹל הַזֶּֽה׃ וְאָ֣מְר֔וּ עַ֚ל אֲשֶׁ֣ר עָזְב֔וּ אֶת־

בְּרִית יהוה אֱלֹהֵי אֲבֹתָם אֲשֶׁר כָּרַת עִמָּם בְּהוֹצִיאוֹ אֹתָם מֵאֶרֶץ מִצְרָיִם: וַיֵּלְכוּ וַיַּעַבְדוּ אֱלֹהִים אֲחֵרִים וַיִּשְׁתַּחֲווּ לָהֶם אֱלֹהִים אֲשֶׁר לֹא־יְדָעוּם וְלֹא חָלַק לָהֶם: וַיִּחַר־אַף יהוה בָּאָרֶץ הַהִוא לְהָבִיא עָלֶיהָ אֶת־כָּל־הַקְּלָלָה הַכְּתוּבָה בַּסֵּפֶר הַזֶּה: וַיִּתְּשֵׁם יהוה מֵעַל אַדְמָתָם בְּאַף וּבְחֵמָה וּבְקֶצֶף גָּדוֹל וַיַּשְׁלִכֵם אֶל־אֶרֶץ אַחֶרֶת כַּיּוֹם הַזֶּה: הַנִּסְתָּרֹת לַיהוה אֱלֹהֵינוּ וְהַנִּגְלֹת לָנוּ וּלְבָנֵינוּ עַד־עוֹלָם לַעֲשׂוֹת אֶת־כָּל־דִּבְרֵי הַתּוֹרָה הַזֹּאת:

VAYEILECH / פ׳ וילך

(*Deuteronomy* 31:1-13)

וַיֵּלֶךְ מֹשֶׁה וַיְדַבֵּר אֶת־הַדְּבָרִים הָאֵלֶּה אֶל־כָּל־יִשְׂרָאֵל: וַיֹּאמֶר אֲלֵהֶם בֶּן־מֵאָה וְעֶשְׂרִים שָׁנָה אָנֹכִי הַיּוֹם לֹא־אוּכַל עוֹד לָצֵאת וְלָבוֹא וַיהוה אָמַר אֵלַי לֹא תַעֲבֹר אֶת־הַיַּרְדֵּן הַזֶּה: יהוה אֱלֹהֶיךָ הוּא | עֹבֵר לְפָנֶיךָ הוּא־יַשְׁמִיד אֶת־הַגּוֹיִם הָאֵלֶּה מִלְּפָנֶיךָ וִירִשְׁתָּם יְהוֹשֻׁעַ הוּא עֹבֵר לְפָנֶיךָ כַּאֲשֶׁר דִּבֶּר יהוה:

לוי וְעָשָׂה יהוה לָהֶם כַּאֲשֶׁר עָשָׂה לְסִיחוֹן וּלְעוֹג מַלְכֵי הָאֱמֹרִי וּלְאַרְצָם אֲשֶׁר הִשְׁמִיד אֹתָם: וּנְתָנָם יהוה לִפְנֵיכֶם וַעֲשִׂיתֶם לָהֶם כְּכָל־הַמִּצְוָה אֲשֶׁר צִוִּיתִי אֶתְכֶם: חִזְקוּ וְאִמְצוּ אַל־תִּירְאוּ וְאַל־תַּעַרְצוּ מִפְּנֵיהֶם כִּי | יהוה אֱלֹהֶיךָ הוּא הַהֹלֵךְ עִמָּךְ לֹא יַרְפְּךָ וְלֹא יַעַזְבֶךָּ:

ישראל וַיִּקְרָא מֹשֶׁה לִיהוֹשֻׁעַ וַיֹּאמֶר אֵלָיו לְעֵינֵי כָל־יִשְׂרָאֵל חֲזַק וֶאֱמָץ כִּי אַתָּה תָּבוֹא אֶת־הָעָם הַזֶּה אֶל־הָאָרֶץ אֲשֶׁר נִשְׁבַּע יהוה לַאֲבֹתָם לָתֵת לָהֶם וְאַתָּה תַּנְחִילֶנָּה אוֹתָם: וַיהוה הוּא | הַהֹלֵךְ לְפָנֶיךָ הוּא יִהְיֶה עִמָּךְ לֹא יַרְפְּךָ וְלֹא יַעַזְבֶךָּ לֹא תִירָא וְלֹא תֵחָת: וַיִּכְתֹּב מֹשֶׁה אֶת־הַתּוֹרָה הַזֹּאת וַיִּתְּנָהּ אֶל־הַכֹּהֲנִים בְּנֵי לֵוִי הַנֹּשְׂאִים אֶת־אֲרוֹן בְּרִית יהוה וְאֶל־כָּל־זִקְנֵי יִשְׂרָאֵל: וַיְצַו מֹשֶׁה אוֹתָם לֵאמֹר מִקֵּץ | שֶׁבַע שָׁנִים בְּמֹעֵד שְׁנַת הַשְּׁמִטָּה בְּחַג הַסֻּכּוֹת: בְּבוֹא כָל־יִשְׂרָאֵל לֵרָאוֹת אֶת־פְּנֵי יהוה אֱלֹהֶיךָ בַּמָּקוֹם אֲשֶׁר יִבְחָר תִּקְרָא אֶת־הַתּוֹרָה הַזֹּאת נֶגֶד כָּל־יִשְׂרָאֵל בְּאָזְנֵיהֶם: הַקְהֵל אֶת־הָעָם הָאֲנָשִׁים וְהַנָּשִׁים וְהַטַּף וְגֵרְךָ אֲשֶׁר בִּשְׁעָרֶיךָ לְמַעַן יִשְׁמְעוּ וּלְמַעַן יִלְמְדוּ וְיָרְאוּ אֶת־יהוה אֱלֹהֵיכֶם וְשָׁמְרוּ לַעֲשׂוֹת אֶת־כָּל־דִּבְרֵי הַתּוֹרָה הַזֹּאת: וּבְנֵיהֶם אֲשֶׁר לֹא־יָדְעוּ יִשְׁמְעוּ וְלָמְדוּ לְיִרְאָה אֶת־יהוה אֱלֹהֵיכֶם כָּל־הַיָּמִים אֲשֶׁר אַתֶּם חַיִּים עַל־הָאֲדָמָה אֲשֶׁר אַתֶּם עֹבְרִים אֶת־הַיַּרְדֵּן שָׁמָּה לְרִשְׁתָּהּ:

HA'AZINU / פ׳ האזינו

(*Deuteronomy* 32:1-12)

הַאֲזִינוּ הַשָּׁמַיִם וַאֲדַבֵּרָה וְתִשְׁמַע הָאָרֶץ אִמְרֵי־פִי: יַעֲרֹף כַּמָּטָר לִקְחִי תִּזַּל כַּטַּל אִמְרָתִי כִּשְׂעִירִם עֲלֵי־דֶשֶׁא וְכִרְבִיבִים עֲלֵי־עֵשֶׂב: כִּי שֵׁם יהוה אֶקְרָא הָבוּ גֹדֶל לֵאלֹהֵינוּ:

לוי הַצּוּר תָּמִים פָּעֳלוֹ כִּי כָל־דְּרָכָיו מִשְׁפָּט אֵל אֱמוּנָה וְאֵין עָוֶל צַדִּיק וְיָשָׁר הוּא: שִׁחֵת לוֹ לֹא בָּנָיו מוּמָם דּוֹר עִקֵּשׁ וּפְתַלְתֹּל: הַ לַיהוה תִּגְמְלוּ־זֹאת עַם נָבָל וְלֹא חָכָם הֲלוֹא־הוּא אָבִיךָ קָּנֶךָ הוּא עָשְׂךָ וַיְכֹנְנֶךָ:

ישראל זְכֹר יְמוֹת עוֹלָם בִּינוּ שְׁנוֹת דֹּר־וָדֹר שְׁאַל אָבִיךָ וְיַגֵּדְךָ זְקֵנֶיךָ וְיֹאמְרוּ לָךְ: בְּהַנְחֵל עֶלְיוֹן גּוֹיִם בְּהַפְרִידוֹ בְּנֵי אָדָם יַצֵּב גְּבֻלֹת עַמִּים לְמִסְפַּר בְּנֵי יִשְׂרָאֵל: כִּי חֵלֶק יהוה עַמּוֹ יַעֲקֹב חֶבֶל נַחֲלָתוֹ: יִמְצָאֵהוּ בְּאֶרֶץ מִדְבָּר וּבְתֹהוּ יְלֵל יְשִׁמֹן יְסֹבְבֶנְהוּ יְבוֹנְנֵהוּ יִצְּרֶנְהוּ כְּאִישׁוֹן עֵינוֹ: כְּנֶשֶׁר יָעִיר קִנּוֹ עַל־גּוֹזָלָיו יְרַחֵף יִפְרֹשׂ כְּנָפָיו יִקָּחֵהוּ יִשָּׂאֵהוּ עַל־אֶבְרָתוֹ: יהוה בָּדָד יַנְחֶנּוּ וְאֵין עִמּוֹ אֵל נֵכָר:

V'ZOS HABRACHA / פ׳ וזאת הברכה

(*Deuteronomy* 33:1-17)

וְזֹאת הַבְּרָכָה אֲשֶׁר בֵּרַךְ מֹשֶׁה אִישׁ הָאֱלֹהִים אֶת־בְּנֵי יִשְׂרָאֵל לִפְנֵי מוֹתוֹ: וַיֹּאמַר יהוה מִסִּינַי בָּא וְזָרַח מִשֵּׂעִיר לָמוֹ הוֹפִיעַ מֵהַר פָּארָן וְאָתָה מֵרִבְבֹת קֹדֶשׁ מִימִינוֹ אֵשׁ דָּת לָמוֹ: אַף חֹבֵב עַמִּים כָּל־קְדֹשָׁיו בְּיָדֶךָ וְהֵם תֻּכּוּ לְרַגְלֶךָ יִשָּׂא מִדַּבְּרֹתֶיךָ: תּוֹרָה צִוָּה־לָנוּ מֹשֶׁה מוֹרָשָׁה קְהִלַּת יַעֲקֹב: וַיְהִי בִישֻׁרוּן מֶלֶךְ בְּהִתְאַסֵּף רָאשֵׁי עָם יַחַד שִׁבְטֵי יִשְׂרָאֵל: יְחִי רְאוּבֵן וְאַל־יָמֹת וִיהִי מְתָיו מִסְפָּר: וְזֹאת לִיהוּדָה וַיֹּאמַר שְׁמַע יהוה קוֹל יְהוּדָה וְאֶל־עַמּוֹ תְּבִיאֶנּוּ יָדָיו רָב לוֹ וְעֵזֶר מִצָּרָיו תִּהְיֶה:

לוי וּלְלֵוִי אָמַר תֻּמֶּיךָ וְאוּרֶיךָ לְאִישׁ חֲסִידֶךָ אֲשֶׁר נִסִּיתוֹ בְּמַסָּה תְּרִיבֵהוּ עַל־מֵי מְרִיבָה: הָאֹמֵר לְאָבִיו וּלְאִמּוֹ לֹא רְאִיתִיו וְאֶת־אֶחָיו לֹא הִכִּיר וְאֶת־בָּנָו לֹא יָדָע כִּי שָׁמְרוּ אִמְרָתֶךָ וּבְרִיתְךָ יִנְצֹרוּ: יוֹרוּ מִשְׁפָּטֶיךָ לְיַעֲקֹב וְתוֹרָתְךָ לְיִשְׂרָאֵל יָשִׂימוּ קְטוֹרָה בְּאַפֶּךָ וְכָלִיל עַל־מִזְבְּחֶךָ: בָּרֵךְ יהוה חֵילוֹ וּפֹעַל יָדָיו תִּרְצֶה מְחַץ מָתְנַיִם קָמָיו וּמְשַׂנְאָיו מִן־יְקוּמוּן: לְבִנְיָמִן אָמַר יְדִיד יהוה יִשְׁכֹּן לָבֶטַח עָלָיו חֹפֵף עָלָיו כָּל־הַיּוֹם וּבֵין כְּתֵפָיו שָׁכֵן:

ישראל וּלְיוֹסֵף אָמַר מְבֹרֶכֶת יהוה אַרְצוֹ מִמֶּגֶד שָׁמַיִם מִטָּל וּמִתְּהוֹם רֹבֶצֶת תָּחַת: וּמִמֶּגֶד תְּבוּאֹת שָׁמֶשׁ וּמִמֶּגֶד גֶּרֶשׁ יְרָחִים: וּמֵרֹאשׁ הַרְרֵי־קֶדֶם וּמִמֶּגֶד גִּבְעוֹת עוֹלָם: וּמִמֶּגֶד אֶרֶץ וּמְלֹאָהּ וּרְצוֹן שֹׁכְנִי סְנֶה תָּבוֹאתָה לְרֹאשׁ יוֹסֵף וּלְקָדְקֹד נְזִיר אֶחָיו: בְּכוֹר שׁוֹרוֹ הָדָר לוֹ וְקַרְנֵי רְאֵם קַרְנָיו בָּהֶם עַמִּים יְנַגַּח יַחְדָּו אַפְסֵי־אָרֶץ וְהֵם רִבְבוֹת אֶפְרַיִם וְהֵם אַלְפֵי מְנַשֶּׁה:

ראש חדש חנוכה פורים ותענית ציבור
Rosh Chodesh, Chanukah, Purim and Public Fasts

ROSH CHODESH / ראש חדש
(Numbers 28:1-15)

וַיְדַבֵּר יהוה אֶל־מֹשֶׁה לֵּאמֹר: צַו אֶת־בְּנֵי יִשְׂרָאֵל וְאָמַרְתָּ אֲלֵהֶם אֶת־קָרְבָּנִי לַחְמִי לְאִשַּׁי רֵיחַ נִיחֹחִי תִּשְׁמְרוּ לְהַקְרִיב לִי בְּמוֹעֲדוֹ: וְאָמַרְתָּ לָהֶם זֶה הָאִשֶּׁה אֲשֶׁר תַּקְרִיבוּ לַיהוה כְּבָשִׂים בְּנֵי־שָׁנָה תְמִימִם שְׁנַיִם לַיּוֹם עֹלָה תָמִיד:

לוי וְאָמַרְתָּ לָהֶם זֶה הָאִשֶּׁה אֲשֶׁר תַּקְרִיבוּ לַיהוה כְּבָשִׂים בְּנֵי־שָׁנָה תְמִימִם שְׁנַיִם לַיּוֹם עֹלָה תָמִיד: אֶת־הַכֶּבֶשׂ אֶחָד תַּעֲשֶׂה בַבֹּקֶר וְאֵת הַכֶּבֶשׂ הַשֵּׁנִי תַּעֲשֶׂה בֵּין הָעַרְבָּיִם: וַעֲשִׂירִית הָאֵיפָה סֹלֶת לְמִנְחָה בְּלוּלָה בְּשֶׁמֶן כָּתִית רְבִיעִת הַהִין:

ישראל עֹלַת תָּמִיד הָעֲשֻׂיָה בְּהַר סִינַי לְרֵיחַ נִיחֹחַ אִשֶּׁה לַיהוה: וְנִסְכּוֹ רְבִיעִת הַהִין לַכֶּבֶשׂ הָאֶחָד בַּקֹּדֶשׁ הַסֵּךְ נֶסֶךְ שֵׁכָר לַיהוה: וְאֵת הַכֶּבֶשׂ הַשֵּׁנִי תַּעֲשֶׂה בֵּין הָעַרְבָּיִם כְּמִנְחַת הַבֹּקֶר וּכְנִסְכּוֹ תַּעֲשֶׂה אִשֵּׁה רֵיחַ נִיחֹחַ לַיהוה: וּבְיוֹם הַשַּׁבָּת שְׁנֵי־כְבָשִׂים בְּנֵי־שָׁנָה תְּמִימִם וּשְׁנֵי עֶשְׂרֹנִים סֹלֶת מִנְחָה בְּלוּלָה בַשֶּׁמֶן וְנִסְכּוֹ: עֹלַת שַׁבַּת בְּשַׁבַּתּוֹ עַל־עֹלַת הַתָּמִיד וְנִסְכָּהּ:

רביעי וּבְרָאשֵׁי חָדְשֵׁיכֶם תַּקְרִיבוּ עֹלָה לַיהוה פָּרִים בְּנֵי־בָקָר שְׁנַיִם וְאַיִל אֶחָד כְּבָשִׂים בְּנֵי־שָׁנָה שִׁבְעָה תְּמִימִם: וּשְׁלֹשָׁה עֶשְׂרֹנִים סֹלֶת מִנְחָה בְּלוּלָה בַשֶּׁמֶן לַפָּר הָאֶחָד וּשְׁנֵי עֶשְׂרֹנִים סֹלֶת מִנְחָה בְּלוּלָה בַשֶּׁמֶן לָאַיִל הָאֶחָד: וְעִשָּׂרֹן עִשָּׂרוֹן סֹלֶת מִנְחָה בְּלוּלָה בַשֶּׁמֶן לַכֶּבֶשׂ הָאֶחָד עֹלָה רֵיחַ נִיחֹחַ אִשֶּׁה לַיהוה: וְנִסְכֵּיהֶם חֲצִי הַהִין יִהְיֶה לַפָּר וּשְׁלִישִׁת הַהִין לָאַיִל וּרְבִיעִת הַהִין לַכֶּבֶשׂ יָיִן זֹאת עֹלַת חֹדֶשׁ בְּחָדְשׁוֹ לְחָדְשֵׁי הַשָּׁנָה: וּשְׂעִיר עִזִּים אֶחָד לְחַטָּאת לַיהוה עַל־עֹלַת הַתָּמִיד יֵעָשֶׂה וְנִסְכּוֹ:

FIRST DAY CHANUKAH — א׳ חנוכה
(Numbers 7:1-17)

וַיְהִי בְּיוֹם כַּלּוֹת מֹשֶׁה לְהָקִים אֶת־הַמִּשְׁכָּן וַיִּמְשַׁח אֹתוֹ וַיְקַדֵּשׁ אֹתוֹ וְאֶת־כָּל־כֵּלָיו וְאֶת־הַמִּזְבֵּחַ וְאֶת־כָּל־כֵּלָיו וַיִּמְשָׁחֵם וַיְקַדֵּשׁ אֹתָם: וַיַּקְרִיבוּ נְשִׂיאֵי יִשְׂרָאֵל רָאשֵׁי בֵּית אֲבֹתָם הֵם נְשִׂיאֵי הַמַּטֹּת הֵם הָעֹמְדִים עַל־הַפְּקֻדִים: וַיָּבִיאוּ אֶת־קָרְבָּנָם לִפְנֵי יהוה שֵׁשׁ־עֶגְלֹת צָב וּשְׁנֵי־עָשָׂר בָּקָר עֲגָלָה עַל־שְׁנֵי הַנְּשִׂאִים וְשׁוֹר לְאֶחָד וַיַּקְרִיבוּ אוֹתָם לִפְנֵי הַמִּשְׁכָּן: וַיֹּאמֶר יהוה אֶל־מֹשֶׁה לֵּאמֹר: קַח מֵאִתָּם וְהָיוּ לַעֲבֹד אֶת־עֲבֹדַת אֹהֶל מוֹעֵד וְנָתַתָּה אוֹתָם אֶל־הַלְוִיִּם אִישׁ כְּפִי עֲבֹדָתוֹ: וַיִּקַּח מֹשֶׁה אֶת־הָעֲגָלֹת וְאֶת־הַבָּקָר וַיִּתֵּן אוֹתָם אֶל־הַלְוִיִּם: אֵת | שְׁתֵּי הָעֲגָלוֹת וְאֵת אַרְבַּעַת הַבָּקָר נָתַן לִבְנֵי גֵרְשׁוֹן כְּפִי עֲבֹדָתָם: וְאֵת | אַרְבַּע הָעֲגָלֹת וְאֵת שְׁמֹנַת הַבָּקָר נָתַן לִבְנֵי מְרָרִי כְּפִי עֲבֹדָתָם בְּיַד אִיתָמָר בֶּן־אַהֲרֹן הַכֹּהֵן: וְלִבְנֵי קְהָת לֹא נָתָן כִּי־עֲבֹדַת הַקֹּדֶשׁ עֲלֵהֶם בַּכָּתֵף יִשָּׂאוּ: וַיַּקְרִיבוּ הַנְּשִׂאִים אֵת חֲנֻכַּת הַמִּזְבֵּחַ בְּיוֹם הִמָּשַׁח אֹתוֹ וַיַּקְרִיבוּ הַנְּשִׂיאִם אֶת־קָרְבָּנָם לִפְנֵי הַמִּזְבֵּחַ: וַיֹּאמֶר יהוה אֶל־מֹשֶׁה נָשִׂיא אֶחָד לַיּוֹם נָשִׂיא אֶחָד לַיּוֹם יַקְרִיבוּ אֶת־קָרְבָּנָם לַחֲנֻכַּת הַמִּזְבֵּחַ:

לוי וַיְהִי הַמַּקְרִיב בַּיּוֹם הָרִאשׁוֹן אֶת־קָרְבָּנוֹ נַחְשׁוֹן בֶּן־עַמִּינָדָב לְמַטֵּה יְהוּדָה: וְקָרְבָּנוֹ קַעֲרַת־כֶּסֶף אַחַת שְׁלֹשִׁים וּמֵאָה מִשְׁקָלָהּ מִזְרָק אֶחָד כֶּסֶף שִׁבְעִים שֶׁקֶל בְּשֶׁקֶל הַקֹּדֶשׁ שְׁנֵיהֶם | מְלֵאִים סֹלֶת בְּלוּלָה בַשֶּׁמֶן לְמִנְחָה: כַּף אַחַת עֲשָׂרָה זָהָב מְלֵאָה קְטֹרֶת:

ישראל פַּר אֶחָד בֶּן־בָּקָר אַיִל אֶחָד כֶּבֶשׂ־אֶחָד בֶּן־שְׁנָתוֹ לְעֹלָה: שְׂעִיר־עִזִּים אֶחָד לְחַטָּאת: וּלְזֶבַח הַשְּׁלָמִים בָּקָר שְׁנַיִם אֵילִם חֲמִשָּׁה עַתּוּדִים חֲמִשָּׁה כְּבָשִׂים בְּנֵי־שָׁנָה חֲמִשָּׁה זֶה קָרְבַּן נַחְשׁוֹן בֶּן־עַמִּינָדָב:

SECOND DAY CHANUKAH — ב׳ חנוכה

(Numbers 7:18-29)

בַּיּוֹם הַשֵּׁנִי הִקְרִיב נְתַנְאֵל בֶּן־צוּעָר נְשִׂיא יִשָּׂשכָר: הִקְרִב אֶת־קָרְבָּנוֹ קַעֲרַת־כֶּסֶף אַחַת שְׁלֹשִׁים וּמֵאָה מִשְׁקָלָהּ מִזְרָק אֶחָד כֶּסֶף שִׁבְעִים שֶׁקֶל בְּשֶׁקֶל הַקֹּדֶשׁ שְׁנֵיהֶם | מְלֵאִים סֹלֶת בְּלוּלָה בַשֶּׁמֶן לְמִנְחָה: כַּף אַחַת עֲשָׂרָה זָהָב מְלֵאָה קְטֹרֶת:

לוי פַּר אֶחָד בֶּן־בָּקָר אַיִל אֶחָד כֶּבֶשׂ־אֶחָד בֶּן־שְׁנָתוֹ לְעֹלָה: שְׂעִיר־עִזִּים אֶחָד לְחַטָּאת: וּלְזֶבַח הַשְּׁלָמִים בָּקָר שְׁנַיִם אֵילִם חֲמִשָּׁה עַתֻּדִים חֲמִשָּׁה כְּבָשִׂים בְּנֵי־שָׁנָה חֲמִשָּׁה זֶה קָרְבַּן נְתַנְאֵל בֶּן־צוּעָר:

ישראל בַּיּוֹם הַשְּׁלִישִׁי נָשִׂיא לִבְנֵי זְבוּלֻן אֱלִיאָב בֶּן־חֵלֹן: קָרְבָּנוֹ קַעֲרַת־כֶּסֶף אַחַת שְׁלֹשִׁים וּמֵאָה מִשְׁקָלָהּ מִזְרָק אֶחָד כֶּסֶף שִׁבְעִים שֶׁקֶל בְּשֶׁקֶל הַקֹּדֶשׁ שְׁנֵיהֶם | מְלֵאִים סֹלֶת בְּלוּלָה בַשֶּׁמֶן לְמִנְחָה: כַּף אַחַת עֲשָׂרָה זָהָב מְלֵאָה קְטֹרֶת: פַּר אֶחָד בֶּן־בָּקָר אַיִל אֶחָד כֶּבֶשׂ־אֶחָד בֶּן־שְׁנָתוֹ לְעֹלָה: שְׂעִיר־עִזִּים אֶחָד לְחַטָּאת: וּלְזֶבַח הַשְּׁלָמִים בָּקָר שְׁנַיִם אֵילִם חֲמִשָּׁה עַתֻּדִים חֲמִשָּׁה כְּבָשִׂים בְּנֵי־שָׁנָה חֲמִשָּׁה זֶה קָרְבַּן אֱלִיאָב בֶּן־חֵלֹן:

THIRD DAY CHANUKAH — ג׳ חנוכה

(Numbers 7:24-35)

בַּיּוֹם הַשְּׁלִישִׁי נָשִׂיא לִבְנֵי זְבוּלֻן אֱלִיאָב בֶּן־חֵלֹן: קָרְבָּנוֹ קַעֲרַת־כֶּסֶף אַחַת שְׁלֹשִׁים וּמֵאָה מִשְׁקָלָהּ מִזְרָק אֶחָד כֶּסֶף שִׁבְעִים שֶׁקֶל בְּשֶׁקֶל הַקֹּדֶשׁ שְׁנֵיהֶם | מְלֵאִים סֹלֶת בְּלוּלָה בַשֶּׁמֶן לְמִנְחָה: כַּף אַחַת עֲשָׂרָה זָהָב מְלֵאָה קְטֹרֶת:

לוי פַּר אֶחָד בֶּן־בָּקָר אַיִל אֶחָד כֶּבֶשׂ־אֶחָד בֶּן־שְׁנָתוֹ לְעֹלָה: שְׂעִיר־עִזִּים אֶחָד לְחַטָּאת: וּלְזֶבַח הַשְּׁלָמִים בָּקָר שְׁנַיִם אֵילִם חֲמִשָּׁה עַתֻּדִים חֲמִשָּׁה כְּבָשִׂים בְּנֵי־שָׁנָה חֲמִשָּׁה זֶה קָרְבַּן אֱלִיאָב בֶּן־חֵלֹן:

ישראל בַּיּוֹם הָרְבִיעִי נָשִׂיא לִבְנֵי רְאוּבֵן אֱלִיצוּר בֶּן־שְׁדֵיאוּר: קָרְבָּנוֹ קַעֲרַת־כֶּסֶף אַחַת שְׁלֹשִׁים וּמֵאָה מִשְׁקָלָהּ מִזְרָק אֶחָד כֶּסֶף שִׁבְעִים שֶׁקֶל בְּשֶׁקֶל הַקֹּדֶשׁ שְׁנֵיהֶם | מְלֵאִים סֹלֶת בְּלוּלָה בַשֶּׁמֶן לְמִנְחָה: כַּף אַחַת עֲשָׂרָה זָהָב מְלֵאָה קְטֹרֶת: פַּר אֶחָד בֶּן־בָּקָר אַיִל אֶחָד כֶּבֶשׂ־אֶחָד בֶּן־שְׁנָתוֹ לְעֹלָה: שְׂעִיר־עִזִּים אֶחָד לְחַטָּאת: וּלְזֶבַח הַשְּׁלָמִים בָּקָר שְׁנַיִם אֵילִם חֲמִשָּׁה עַתֻּדִים חֲמִשָּׁה כְּבָשִׂים בְּנֵי־שָׁנָה חֲמִשָּׁה זֶה קָרְבַּן אֱלִיצוּר בֶּן־שְׁדֵיאוּר:

FOURTH DAY CHANUKAH — ד׳ חנוכה

(Numbers 7:30-41)

בַּיּוֹם הָרְבִיעִי נָשִׂיא לִבְנֵי רְאוּבֵן אֱלִיצוּר בֶּן־שְׁדֵיאוּר: קָרְבָּנוֹ קַעֲרַת־כֶּסֶף אַחַת שְׁלֹשִׁים וּמֵאָה מִשְׁקָלָהּ מִזְרָק אֶחָד כֶּסֶף שִׁבְעִים שֶׁקֶל בְּשֶׁקֶל הַקֹּדֶשׁ שְׁנֵיהֶם | מְלֵאִים סֹלֶת בְּלוּלָה בַשֶּׁמֶן לְמִנְחָה: כַּף אַחַת עֲשָׂרָה זָהָב מְלֵאָה קְטֹרֶת:

לוי פַּר אֶחָד בֶּן־בָּקָר אַיִל אֶחָד כֶּבֶשׂ־אֶחָד בֶּן־שְׁנָתוֹ לְעֹלָה: שְׂעִיר־עִזִּים אֶחָד לְחַטָּאת: וּלְזֶבַח הַשְּׁלָמִים בָּקָר שְׁנַיִם אֵילִם חֲמִשָּׁה עַתֻּדִים חֲמִשָּׁה כְּבָשִׂים בְּנֵי־שָׁנָה חֲמִשָּׁה זֶה קָרְבַּן אֱלִיצוּר בֶּן־שְׁדֵיאוּר:

ישראל בַּיּוֹם הַחֲמִישִׁי נָשִׂיא לִבְנֵי שִׁמְעוֹן שְׁלֻמִיאֵל בֶּן־צוּרִישַׁדָּי: קָרְבָּנוֹ קַעֲרַת־כֶּסֶף אַחַת שְׁלֹשִׁים וּמֵאָה מִשְׁקָלָהּ מִזְרָק אֶחָד כֶּסֶף שִׁבְעִים שֶׁקֶל בְּשֶׁקֶל הַקֹּדֶשׁ שְׁנֵיהֶם | מְלֵאִים סֹלֶת בְּלוּלָה בַשֶּׁמֶן לְמִנְחָה: כַּף אַחַת עֲשָׂרָה זָהָב מְלֵאָה קְטֹרֶת: פַּר אֶחָד בֶּן־בָּקָר אַיִל אֶחָד כֶּבֶשׂ־אֶחָד בֶּן־שְׁנָתוֹ לְעֹלָה: שְׂעִיר־עִזִּים אֶחָד לְחַטָּאת: וּלְזֶבַח הַשְּׁלָמִים בָּקָר שְׁנַיִם אֵילִם חֲמִשָּׁה עַתֻּדִים חֲמִשָּׁה כְּבָשִׂים בְּנֵי־שָׁנָה חֲמִשָּׁה זֶה קָרְבַּן שְׁלֻמִיאֵל בֶּן־צוּרִישַׁדָּי:

FIFTH DAY CHANUKAH — ה׳ חנוכה

(Numbers 7:36-47)

בַּיּוֹם הַחֲמִישִׁי נָשִׂיא לִבְנֵי שִׁמְעוֹן שְׁלֻמִיאֵל בֶּן־צוּרִישַׁדָּי: קָרְבָּנוֹ קַעֲרַת־כֶּסֶף אַחַת

שְׁלֹשִׁים וּמֵאָה מִשְׁקָלָהּ מִזְרָק אֶחָד כֶּסֶף שִׁבְעִים שֶׁקֶל בְּשֶׁקֶל הַקֹּדֶשׁ שְׁנֵיהֶם | מְלֵאִים סֹלֶת בְּלוּלָה בַשֶּׁמֶן לְמִנְחָה: כַּף אַחַת עֲשָׂרָה זָהָב מְלֵאָה קְטֹרֶת:

לוי פַּר אֶחָד בֶּן־בָּקָר אַיִל אֶחָד כֶּבֶשׂ־אֶחָד בֶּן־שְׁנָתוֹ לְעֹלָה: שְׂעִיר־עִזִּים אֶחָד לְחַטָּאת: וּלְזֶבַח הַשְּׁלָמִים בָּקָר שְׁנַיִם אֵילִם חֲמִשָּׁה עַתֻּדִים חֲמִשָּׁה כְּבָשִׂים בְּנֵי־שָׁנָה חֲמִשָּׁה זֶה קָרְבַּן שְׁלֻמִיאֵל בֶּן־צוּרִישַׁדָּי:

ישראל בַּיּוֹם הַשִּׁשִּׁי נָשִׂיא לִבְנֵי גָד אֶלְיָסָף בֶּן־דְּעוּאֵל: קָרְבָּנוֹ קַעֲרַת־כֶּסֶף אַחַת שְׁלֹשִׁים וּמֵאָה מִשְׁקָלָהּ מִזְרָק אֶחָד כֶּסֶף שִׁבְעִים שֶׁקֶל בְּשֶׁקֶל הַקֹּדֶשׁ שְׁנֵיהֶם | מְלֵאִים סֹלֶת בְּלוּלָה בַשֶּׁמֶן לְמִנְחָה: כַּף אַחַת עֲשָׂרָה זָהָב מְלֵאָה קְטֹרֶת: פַּר אֶחָד בֶּן־בָּקָר אַיִל אֶחָד כֶּבֶשׂ־אֶחָד בֶּן־שְׁנָתוֹ לְעֹלָה: שְׂעִיר־עִזִּים אֶחָד לְחַטָּאת: וּלְזֶבַח הַשְּׁלָמִים בָּקָר שְׁנַיִם אֵילִם חֲמִשָּׁה עַתֻּדִים חֲמִשָּׁה כְּבָשִׂים בְּנֵי־שָׁנָה חֲמִשָּׁה זֶה קָרְבַּן אֶלְיָסָף בֶּן־דְּעוּאֵל:

SIXTH DAY CHANUKAH — ו׳ חנוכה

Two Torah Scrolls are removed from the Ark. Three *olim* are called to the first Torah for the Rosh Chodesh reading (*Numbers* 28:1-15). A fourth *oleh* is called to the second Torah for the Chanukah reading (*Numbers* 7:42-47).

וַיְדַבֵּר יהוה אֶל־מֹשֶׁה לֵּאמֹר: צַו אֶת־בְּנֵי יִשְׂרָאֵל וְאָמַרְתָּ אֲלֵהֶם אֶת־קָרְבָּנִי לַחְמִי לְאִשַּׁי רֵיחַ נִיחֹחִי תִּשְׁמְרוּ לְהַקְרִיב לִי בְּמוֹעֲדוֹ: וְאָמַרְתָּ לָהֶם זֶה הָאִשֶּׁה אֲשֶׁר תַּקְרִיבוּ לַיהוה כְּבָשִׂים בְּנֵי־שָׁנָה תְמִימִם שְׁנַיִם לַיּוֹם עֹלָה תָמִיד: אֶת־הַכֶּבֶשׂ אֶחָד תַּעֲשֶׂה בַבֹּקֶר וְאֵת הַכֶּבֶשׂ הַשֵּׁנִי תַּעֲשֶׂה בֵּין הָעַרְבָּיִם: וַעֲשִׂירִית הָאֵיפָה סֹלֶת לְמִנְחָה בְּלוּלָה בְּשֶׁמֶן כָּתִית רְבִיעִת הַהִין:

לוי עֹלַת תָּמִיד הָעֲשֻׂיָה בְּהַר סִינַי לְרֵיחַ נִיחֹחַ אִשֶּׁה לַיהוה: וְנִסְכּוֹ רְבִיעִת הַהִין לַכֶּבֶשׂ הָאֶחָד בַּקֹּדֶשׁ הַסֵּךְ נֶסֶךְ שֵׁכָר לַיהוה: וְאֵת הַכֶּבֶשׂ הַשֵּׁנִי תַּעֲשֶׂה בֵּין הָעַרְבָּיִם כְּמִנְחַת הַבֹּקֶר וּכְנִסְכּוֹ תַּעֲשֶׂה אִשֵּׁה רֵיחַ נִיחֹחַ לַיהוה: וּבְיוֹם הַשַּׁבָּת שְׁנֵי־כְבָשִׂים בְּנֵי־שָׁנָה תְּמִימִם וּשְׁנֵי עֶשְׂרֹנִים סֹלֶת מִנְחָה בְּלוּלָה בַשֶּׁמֶן וְנִסְכּוֹ: עֹלַת שַׁבַּת בְּשַׁבַּתּוֹ עַל־עֹלַת הַתָּמִיד וְנִסְכָּהּ:

שלישי וּבְרָאשֵׁי חָדְשֵׁיכֶם תַּקְרִיבוּ עֹלָה לַיהוה פָּרִים בְּנֵי־בָקָר שְׁנַיִם וְאַיִל אֶחָד כְּבָשִׂים בְּנֵי־שָׁנָה שִׁבְעָה תְּמִימִם: וּשְׁלֹשָׁה עֶשְׂרֹנִים סֹלֶת מִנְחָה בְּלוּלָה בַשֶּׁמֶן לַפָּר הָאֶחָד וּשְׁנֵי עֶשְׂרֹנִים סֹלֶת מִנְחָה בְּלוּלָה בַשֶּׁמֶן לָאַיִל הָאֶחָד: וְעִשָּׂרֹן עִשָּׂרוֹן סֹלֶת מִנְחָה בְּלוּלָה בַשֶּׁמֶן לַכֶּבֶשׂ הָאֶחָד עֹלָה רֵיחַ נִיחֹחַ אִשֶּׁה לַיהוה: וְנִסְכֵּיהֶם חֲצִי הַהִין יִהְיֶה לַפָּר וּשְׁלִישִׁת הַהִין לָאַיִל וּרְבִיעִת הַהִין לַכֶּבֶשׂ יָיִן זֹאת עֹלַת חֹדֶשׁ בְּחָדְשׁוֹ לְחָדְשֵׁי הַשָּׁנָה: וּשְׂעִיר עִזִּים אֶחָד לְחַטָּאת לַיהוה עַל־עֹלַת הַתָּמִיד יֵעָשֶׂה וְנִסְכּוֹ:

רביעי בַּיּוֹם הַשִּׁשִּׁי נָשִׂיא לִבְנֵי גָד אֶלְיָסָף בֶּן־דְּעוּאֵל: קָרְבָּנוֹ קַעֲרַת־כֶּסֶף אַחַת שְׁלֹשִׁים וּמֵאָה מִשְׁקָלָהּ מִזְרָק אֶחָד כֶּסֶף שִׁבְעִים שֶׁקֶל בְּשֶׁקֶל הַקֹּדֶשׁ שְׁנֵיהֶם | מְלֵאִים סֹלֶת בְּלוּלָה בַשֶּׁמֶן לְמִנְחָה: כַּף אַחַת עֲשָׂרָה זָהָב מְלֵאָה קְטֹרֶת: פַּר אֶחָד בֶּן־בָּקָר אַיִל אֶחָד כֶּבֶשׂ־אֶחָד בֶּן־שְׁנָתוֹ לְעֹלָה: שְׂעִיר־עִזִּים אֶחָד לְחַטָּאת: וּלְזֶבַח הַשְּׁלָמִים בָּקָר שְׁנַיִם אֵילִם חֲמִשָּׁה עַתֻּדִים חֲמִשָּׁה כְּבָשִׂים בְּנֵי־שָׁנָה חֲמִשָּׁה זֶה קָרְבַּן אֶלְיָסָף בֶּן־דְּעוּאֵל:

SEVENTH DAY CHANUKAH — ז׳ חנוכה

In most years the seventh day of Chanukah is also Rosh Chodesh. The Rosh Chodesh reading is the same as that of the sixth day. The following (*Numbers* 7:48-53) is the Chanukah reading for the fourth *oleh:*

רביעי בַּיּוֹם הַשְּׁבִיעִי נָשִׂיא לִבְנֵי אֶפְרָיִם אֱלִישָׁמָע בֶּן־עַמִּיהוּד: קָרְבָּנוֹ קַעֲרַת־כֶּסֶף אַחַת שְׁלֹשִׁים וּמֵאָה מִשְׁקָלָהּ מִזְרָק אֶחָד כֶּסֶף שִׁבְעִים שֶׁקֶל בְּשֶׁקֶל הַקֹּדֶשׁ שְׁנֵיהֶם | מְלֵאִים סֹלֶת בְּלוּלָה בַשֶּׁמֶן לְמִנְחָה: כַּף אַחַת עֲשָׂרָה זָהָב מְלֵאָה קְטֹרֶת: פַּר אֶחָד בֶּן־בָּקָר אַיִל אֶחָד כֶּבֶשׂ־אֶחָד בֶּן־שְׁנָתוֹ לְעֹלָה: שְׂעִיר־עִזִּים אֶחָד לְחַטָּאת: וּלְזֶבַח הַשְּׁלָמִים בָּקָר שְׁנַיִם אֵילִם חֲמִשָּׁה עַתֻּדִים חֲמִשָּׁה כְּבָשִׂים בְּנֵי־שָׁנָה חֲמִשָּׁה זֶה קָרְבַּן אֱלִישָׁמָע בֶּן־עַמִּיהוּד:

In years when only the sixth day of Chanukah is Rosh Chodesh, the following (*Numbers* 7:48-59) is the Torah reading for the seventh day:

בַּיּוֹם הַשְּׁבִיעִי נָשִׂיא לִבְנֵי אֶפְרָיִם אֱלִישָׁמָע בֶּן־עַמִּיהוּד: קָרְבָּנוֹ קַעֲרַת־כֶּסֶף אַחַת שְׁלֹשִׁים וּמֵאָה מִשְׁקָלָהּ מִזְרָק אֶחָד כֶּסֶף שִׁבְעִים שֶׁקֶל בְּשֶׁקֶל הַקֹּדֶשׁ שְׁנֵיהֶם | מְלֵאִים סֹלֶת בְּלוּלָה בַשֶּׁמֶן לְמִנְחָה: כַּף

אַחַת עֲשָׂרָה זָהָב מְלֵאָה קְטֹרֶת:

לוי פַּר אֶחָד בֶּן־בָּקָר אַיִל אֶחָד כֶּבֶשׂ־אֶחָד בֶּן־שְׁנָתוֹ לְעֹלָה: שְׂעִיר־עִזִּים אֶחָד לְחַטָּאת: וּלְזֶבַח הַשְּׁלָמִים בָּקָר שְׁנַיִם אֵילִם חֲמִשָּׁה עַתֻּדִים חֲמִשָּׁה כְּבָשִׂים בְּנֵי־שָׁנָה חֲמִשָּׁה זֶה קָרְבַּן אֱלִישָׁמָע בֶּן־עַמִּיהוּד:

ישראל בַּיּוֹם הַשְּׁמִינִי נָשִׂיא לִבְנֵי מְנַשֶּׁה גַּמְלִיאֵל בֶּן־פְּדָהצוּר: קָרְבָּנוֹ קַעֲרַת־כֶּסֶף אַחַת שְׁלֹשִׁים וּמֵאָה מִשְׁקָלָהּ מִזְרָק אֶחָד כֶּסֶף שִׁבְעִים שֶׁקֶל בְּשֶׁקֶל הַקֹּדֶשׁ שְׁנֵיהֶם | מְלֵאִים סֹלֶת בְּלוּלָה בַשֶּׁמֶן לְמִנְחָה: כַּף אַחַת עֲשָׂרָה זָהָב מְלֵאָה קְטֹרֶת: פַּר אֶחָד בֶּן־בָּקָר אַיִל אֶחָד כֶּבֶשׂ־אֶחָד בֶּן־שְׁנָתוֹ לְעֹלָה: שְׂעִיר־עִזִּים אֶחָד לְחַטָּאת: וּלְזֶבַח הַשְּׁלָמִים בָּקָר שְׁנַיִם אֵילִם חֲמִשָּׁה עַתֻּדִים חֲמִשָּׁה כְּבָשִׂים בְּנֵי־שָׁנָה חֲמִשָּׁה זֶה קָרְבַּן גַּמְלִיאֵל בֶּן־פְּדָהצוּר:

ח׳ חנוכה — EIGHTH DAY CHANUKAH

(Numbers 7:54-8:4)

בַּיּוֹם הַשְּׁמִינִי נָשִׂיא לִבְנֵי מְנַשֶּׁה גַּמְלִיאֵל בֶּן־פְּדָהצוּר: קָרְבָּנוֹ קַעֲרַת־כֶּסֶף אַחַת שְׁלֹשִׁים וּמֵאָה מִשְׁקָלָהּ מִזְרָק אֶחָד כֶּסֶף שִׁבְעִים שֶׁקֶל בְּשֶׁקֶל הַקֹּדֶשׁ שְׁנֵיהֶם | מְלֵאִים סֹלֶת בְּלוּלָה בַשֶּׁמֶן לְמִנְחָה: כַּף אַחַת עֲשָׂרָה זָהָב מְלֵאָה קְטֹרֶת:

לוי פַּר אֶחָד בֶּן־בָּקָר אַיִל אֶחָד כֶּבֶשׂ־אֶחָד בֶּן־שְׁנָתוֹ לְעֹלָה: שְׂעִיר־עִזִּים אֶחָד לְחַטָּאת: וּלְזֶבַח הַשְּׁלָמִים בָּקָר שְׁנַיִם אֵילִם חֲמִשָּׁה עַתֻּדִים חֲמִשָּׁה כְּבָשִׂים בְּנֵי־שָׁנָה חֲמִשָּׁה זֶה קָרְבַּן גַּמְלִיאֵל בֶּן־פְּדָהצוּר:

ישראל בַּיּוֹם הַתְּשִׁיעִי נָשִׂיא לִבְנֵי בִנְיָמִן אֲבִידָן בֶּן־גִּדְעֹנִי: קָרְבָּנוֹ קַעֲרַת־כֶּסֶף אַחַת שְׁלֹשִׁים וּמֵאָה מִשְׁקָלָהּ מִזְרָק אֶחָד כֶּסֶף שִׁבְעִים שֶׁקֶל בְּשֶׁקֶל הַקֹּדֶשׁ שְׁנֵיהֶם | מְלֵאִים סֹלֶת בְּלוּלָה בַשֶּׁמֶן לְמִנְחָה: כַּף אַחַת עֲשָׂרָה זָהָב מְלֵאָה קְטֹרֶת: פַּר אֶחָד בֶּן־בָּקָר אַיִל אֶחָד כֶּבֶשׂ־אֶחָד בֶּן־שְׁנָתוֹ לְעֹלָה: שְׂעִיר־עִזִּים אֶחָד לְחַטָּאת: וּלְזֶבַח הַשְּׁלָמִים בָּקָר שְׁנַיִם אֵילִם חֲמִשָּׁה עַתֻּדִים חֲמִשָּׁה כְּבָשִׂים בְּנֵי־שָׁנָה חֲמִשָּׁה זֶה קָרְבַּן אֲבִידָן בֶּן־גִּדְעֹנִי: בַּיּוֹם הָעֲשִׂירִי נָשִׂיא לִבְנֵי דָן אֲחִיעֶזֶר בֶּן־עַמִּישַׁדָּי: קָרְבָּנוֹ קַעֲרַת־כֶּסֶף אַחַת שְׁלֹשִׁים וּמֵאָה מִשְׁקָלָהּ מִזְרָק אֶחָד כֶּסֶף שִׁבְעִים שֶׁקֶל בְּשֶׁקֶל הַקֹּדֶשׁ שְׁנֵיהֶם | מְלֵאִים סֹלֶת בְּלוּלָה בַשֶּׁמֶן לְמִנְחָה: כַּף אַחַת עֲשָׂרָה זָהָב מְלֵאָה קְטֹרֶת: פַּר אֶחָד בֶּן־בָּקָר אַיִל אֶחָד כֶּבֶשׂ־אֶחָד בֶּן־שְׁנָתוֹ לְעֹלָה: שְׂעִיר־עִזִּים אֶחָד לְחַטָּאת: וּלְזֶבַח הַשְּׁלָמִים בָּקָר שְׁנַיִם אֵילִם חֲמִשָּׁה עַתֻּדִים חֲמִשָּׁה כְּבָשִׂים בְּנֵי־שָׁנָה חֲמִשָּׁה זֶה קָרְבַּן אֲחִיעֶזֶר בֶּן־עַמִּישַׁדָּי: בַּיּוֹם עַשְׁתֵּי עָשָׂר יוֹם נָשִׂיא לִבְנֵי אָשֵׁר פַּגְעִיאֵל בֶּן־עָכְרָן: קָרְבָּנוֹ קַעֲרַת־כֶּסֶף אַחַת שְׁלֹשִׁים וּמֵאָה מִשְׁקָלָהּ מִזְרָק אֶחָד כֶּסֶף שִׁבְעִים שֶׁקֶל בְּשֶׁקֶל הַקֹּדֶשׁ שְׁנֵיהֶם | מְלֵאִים סֹלֶת בְּלוּלָה בַשֶּׁמֶן לְמִנְחָה: כַּף אַחַת עֲשָׂרָה זָהָב מְלֵאָה קְטֹרֶת: פַּר אֶחָד בֶּן־בָּקָר אַיִל אֶחָד כֶּבֶשׂ־אֶחָד בֶּן־שְׁנָתוֹ לְעֹלָה: שְׂעִיר־עִזִּים אֶחָד לְחַטָּאת: וּלְזֶבַח הַשְּׁלָמִים בָּקָר שְׁנַיִם אֵילִם חֲמִשָּׁה עַתֻּדִים חֲמִשָּׁה כְּבָשִׂים בְּנֵי־שָׁנָה חֲמִשָּׁה זֶה קָרְבַּן פַּגְעִיאֵל בֶּן־עָכְרָן: בַּיּוֹם שְׁנֵים עָשָׂר יוֹם נָשִׂיא לִבְנֵי נַפְתָּלִי אֲחִירַע בֶּן־עֵינָן: קָרְבָּנוֹ קַעֲרַת־כֶּסֶף אַחַת שְׁלֹשִׁים וּמֵאָה מִשְׁקָלָהּ מִזְרָק אֶחָד כֶּסֶף שִׁבְעִים שֶׁקֶל בְּשֶׁקֶל הַקֹּדֶשׁ שְׁנֵיהֶם | מְלֵאִים סֹלֶת בְּלוּלָה בַשֶּׁמֶן לְמִנְחָה: כַּף אַחַת עֲשָׂרָה זָהָב מְלֵאָה קְטֹרֶת: פַּר אֶחָד בֶּן־בָּקָר אַיִל אֶחָד כֶּבֶשׂ־אֶחָד בֶּן־שְׁנָתוֹ לְעֹלָה: שְׂעִיר־עִזִּים אֶחָד לְחַטָּאת: וּלְזֶבַח הַשְּׁלָמִים בָּקָר שְׁנַיִם אֵילִם חֲמִשָּׁה עַתֻּדִים חֲמִשָּׁה כְּבָשִׂים בְּנֵי־שָׁנָה חֲמִשָּׁה זֶה קָרְבַּן אֲחִירַע בֶּן־עֵינָן: זֹאת | חֲנֻכַּת הַמִּזְבֵּחַ בְּיוֹם הִמָּשַׁח אֹתוֹ מֵאֵת נְשִׂיאֵי יִשְׂרָאֵל קַעֲרֹת כֶּסֶף שְׁתֵּים עֶשְׂרֵה מִזְרְקֵי־כֶסֶף שְׁנֵים עָשָׂר כַּפּוֹת זָהָב שְׁתֵּים עֶשְׂרֵה: שְׁלֹשִׁים וּמֵאָה הַקְּעָרָה הָאַחַת כֶּסֶף וְשִׁבְעִים הַמִּזְרָק הָאֶחָד כֹּל כֶּסֶף הַכֵּלִים אַלְפַּיִם וְאַרְבַּע־מֵאוֹת בְּשֶׁקֶל הַקֹּדֶשׁ: כַּפּוֹת זָהָב שְׁתֵּים־עֶשְׂרֵה מְלֵאֹת קְטֹרֶת עֲשָׂרָה עֲשָׂרָה הַכַּף בְּשֶׁקֶל הַקֹּדֶשׁ כָּל־זְהַב הַכַּפּוֹת עֶשְׂרִים וּמֵאָה: כָּל־הַבָּקָר לָעֹלָה שְׁנֵים עָשָׂר פָּרִים אֵילִם שְׁנֵים־עָשָׂר כְּבָשִׂים בְּנֵי־שָׁנָה שְׁנֵים עָשָׂר וּמִנְחָתָם וּשְׂעִירֵי עִזִּים שְׁנֵים עָשָׂר לְחַטָּאת: וְכֹל בְּקַר | זֶבַח הַשְּׁלָמִים עֶשְׂרִים וְאַרְבָּעָה פָּרִים אֵילִם שִׁשִּׁים עַתֻּדִים שִׁשִּׁים כְּבָשִׂים בְּנֵי־שָׁנָה שִׁשִּׁים זֹאת חֲנֻכַּת הַמִּזְבֵּחַ אַחֲרֵי הִמָּשַׁח אֹתוֹ: וּבְבֹא מֹשֶׁה אֶל־אֹהֶל מוֹעֵד לְדַבֵּר אִתּוֹ וַיִּשְׁמַע אֶת־

הַקּוֹל מִדַּבֵּר אֵלָיו מֵעַל הַכַּפֹּרֶת אֲשֶׁר עַל־אֲרֹן הָעֵדֻת מִבֵּין שְׁנֵי הַכְּרֻבִים וַיְדַבֵּר אֵלָיו: וַיְדַבֵּר יהוה אֶל־מֹשֶׁה לֵּאמֹר: דַּבֵּר אֶל־אַהֲרֹן וְאָמַרְתָּ אֵלָיו בְּהַעֲלֹתְךָ אֶת־הַנֵּרֹת אֶל־מוּל פְּנֵי הַמְּנוֹרָה יָאִירוּ שִׁבְעַת הַנֵּרוֹת: וַיַּעַשׂ כֵּן אַהֲרֹן אֶל־מוּל פְּנֵי הַמְּנוֹרָה הֶעֱלָה נֵרֹתֶיהָ כַּאֲשֶׁר צִוָּה יהוה אֶת־מֹשֶׁה: וְזֶה מַעֲשֵׂה הַמְּנֹרָה מִקְשָׁה זָהָב עַד־יְרֵכָהּ עַד־פִּרְחָהּ מִקְשָׁה הִוא כַּמַּרְאֶה אֲשֶׁר הֶרְאָה יהוה אֶת־מֹשֶׁה כֵּן עָשָׂה אֶת־הַמְּנֹרָה:

PURIM / פורים

(Exodus 17:8-16)

וַיָּבֹא עֲמָלֵק וַיִּלָּחֶם עִם־יִשְׂרָאֵל בִּרְפִידִם: וַיֹּאמֶר מֹשֶׁה אֶל־יְהוֹשֻׁעַ בְּחַר־לָנוּ אֲנָשִׁים וְצֵא הִלָּחֵם בַּעֲמָלֵק מָחָר אָנֹכִי נִצָּב עַל־רֹאשׁ הַגִּבְעָה וּמַטֵּה הָאֱלֹהִים בְּיָדִי: וַיַּעַשׂ יְהוֹשֻׁעַ כַּאֲשֶׁר אָמַר־לוֹ מֹשֶׁה לְהִלָּחֵם בַּעֲמָלֵק וּמֹשֶׁה אַהֲרֹן וְחוּר עָלוּ רֹאשׁ הַגִּבְעָה:

לוי וְהָיָה כַּאֲשֶׁר יָרִים מֹשֶׁה יָדוֹ וְגָבַר יִשְׂרָאֵל וְכַאֲשֶׁר יָנִיחַ יָדוֹ וְגָבַר עֲמָלֵק: וִידֵי מֹשֶׁה כְּבֵדִים וַיִּקְחוּ־אֶבֶן וַיָּשִׂימוּ תַחְתָּיו וַיֵּשֶׁב עָלֶיהָ וְאַהֲרֹן וְחוּר תָּמְכוּ בְיָדָיו מִזֶּה אֶחָד וּמִזֶּה אֶחָד וַיְהִי יָדָיו אֱמוּנָה עַד־בֹּא הַשָּׁמֶשׁ: וַיַּחֲלֹשׁ יְהוֹשֻׁעַ אֶת־עֲמָלֵק וְאֶת־עַמּוֹ לְפִי־חָרֶב:

ישראל וַיֹּאמֶר יהוה אֶל־מֹשֶׁה כְּתֹב זֹאת זִכָּרוֹן בַּסֵּפֶר וְשִׂים בְּאָזְנֵי יְהוֹשֻׁעַ כִּי־מָחֹה אֶמְחֶה אֶת־זֵכֶר עֲמָלֵק מִתַּחַת הַשָּׁמָיִם: וַיִּבֶן מֹשֶׁה מִזְבֵּחַ וַיִּקְרָא שְׁמוֹ יהוה | נִסִּי: וַיֹּאמֶר כִּי־יָד עַל־כֵּס יָהּ מִלְחָמָה לַיהוה בַּעֲמָלֵק מִדֹּר דֹּר:

PUBLIC FAST DAY / תענית ציבור

During *Shacharis* of public fast days (except Tishah B'Av, see next page) three *olim* are called to the Torah. At *Minchah,* the same Torah reading is repeated, but the third *oleh* also reads the *Haftarah.*

Upon reaching the words in bold type, the reader pauses. The congregation recites these verses, which are then repeated by the reader.

(Exodus 32:11-14; 34:1-10)

וַיְחַל מֹשֶׁה אֶת־פְּנֵי יהוה אֱלֹהָיו וַיֹּאמֶר לָמָה יהוה יֶחֱרֶה אַפְּךָ בְּעַמֶּךָ אֲשֶׁר הוֹצֵאתָ מֵאֶרֶץ מִצְרַיִם בְּכֹחַ גָּדוֹל וּבְיָד חֲזָקָה: לָמָּה יֹאמְרוּ מִצְרַיִם לֵאמֹר בְּרָעָה הוֹצִיאָם לַהֲרֹג אֹתָם בֶּהָרִים וּלְכַלֹּתָם מֵעַל פְּנֵי הָאֲדָמָה **שׁוּב מֵחֲרוֹן אַפֶּךָ וְהִנָּחֵם עַל־הָרָעָה לְעַמֶּךָ:** זְכֹר לְאַבְרָהָם לְיִצְחָק וּלְיִשְׂרָאֵל עֲבָדֶיךָ אֲשֶׁר נִשְׁבַּעְתָּ לָהֶם בָּךְ וַתְּדַבֵּר אֲלֵהֶם אַרְבֶּה אֶת־זַרְעֲכֶם כְּכוֹכְבֵי הַשָּׁמָיִם וְכָל־הָאָרֶץ הַזֹּאת אֲשֶׁר אָמַרְתִּי אֶתֵּן לְזַרְעֲכֶם וְנָחֲלוּ לְעֹלָם: וַיִּנָּחֶם יהוה עַל־הָרָעָה אֲשֶׁר דִּבֶּר לַעֲשׂוֹת לְעַמּוֹ:

לוי וַיֹּאמֶר יהוה אֶל־מֹשֶׁה פְּסָל־לְךָ שְׁנֵי־לֻחֹת אֲבָנִים כָּרִאשֹׁנִים וְכָתַבְתִּי עַל־הַלֻּחֹת אֶת־הַדְּבָרִים אֲשֶׁר הָיוּ עַל־הַלֻּחֹת הָרִאשֹׁנִים אֲשֶׁר שִׁבַּרְתָּ: וֶהְיֵה נָכוֹן לַבֹּקֶר וְעָלִיתָ בַבֹּקֶר אֶל־הַר סִינַי וְנִצַּבְתָּ לִי שָׁם עַל־רֹאשׁ הָהָר: וְאִישׁ לֹא־יַעֲלֶה עִמָּךְ וְגַם־אִישׁ אַל־יֵרָא בְּכָל־הָהָר גַּם־הַצֹּאן וְהַבָּקָר אַל־יִרְעוּ אֶל־מוּל הָהָר הַהוּא:

ישראל וַיִּפְסֹל שְׁנֵי־לֻחֹת אֲבָנִים כָּרִאשֹׁנִים וַיַּשְׁכֵּם מֹשֶׁה בַבֹּקֶר וַיַּעַל אֶל־הַר סִינַי כַּאֲשֶׁר צִוָּה יהוה אֹתוֹ וַיִּקַּח בְּיָדוֹ שְׁנֵי לֻחֹת אֲבָנִים: וַיֵּרֶד יהוה בֶּעָנָן וַיִּתְיַצֵּב עִמּוֹ שָׁם וַיִּקְרָא בְשֵׁם יהוה: וַיַּעֲבֹר יהוה | עַל־פָּנָיו וַיִּקְרָא **יהוה | יהוה אֵל רַחוּם וְחַנּוּן אֶרֶךְ אַפַּיִם וְרַב־חֶסֶד וֶאֱמֶת: נֹצֵר חֶסֶד לָאֲלָפִים נֹשֵׂא עָוֺן וָפֶשַׁע וְחַטָּאָה וְנַקֵּה** לֹא יְנַקֶּה פֹּקֵד | עֲוֺן אָבוֹת עַל־בָּנִים וְעַל־בְּנֵי בָנִים עַל־שִׁלֵּשִׁים וְעַל־רִבֵּעִים: וַיְמַהֵר מֹשֶׁה וַיִּקֹּד אַרְצָה וַיִּשְׁתָּחוּ: וַיֹּאמֶר אִם־נָא מָצָאתִי חֵן בְּעֵינֶיךָ אֲדֹנָי יֵלֶךְ־נָא אֲדֹנָי בְּקִרְבֵּנוּ כִּי עַם־קְשֵׁה־עֹרֶף הוּא **וְסָלַחְתָּ לַעֲוֺנֵנוּ וּלְחַטָּאתֵנוּ וּנְחַלְתָּנוּ:** וַיֹּאמֶר הִנֵּה אָנֹכִי כֹּרֵת בְּרִית נֶגֶד כָּל־עַמְּךָ אֶעֱשֶׂה נִפְלָאֹת אֲשֶׁר לֹא־נִבְרְאוּ בְכָל־הָאָרֶץ וּבְכָל־הַגּוֹיִם וְרָאָה כָל־הָעָם אֲשֶׁר־אַתָּה בְקִרְבּוֹ אֶת־מַעֲשֵׂה יהוה כִּי־נוֹרָא הוּא אֲשֶׁר אֲנִי עֹשֶׂה עִמָּךְ:

HAFTARAH / הפטרה

(Isaiah 55:6 — 56:8)

דִּרְשׁוּ יהוה בְּהִמָּצְאוֹ קְרָאֻהוּ בִּהְיוֹתוֹ קָרוֹב: יַעֲזֹב רָשָׁע דַּרְכּוֹ וְאִישׁ אָוֶן מַחְשְׁבֹתָיו וְיָשֹׁב אֶל־יהוה וִירַחֲמֵהוּ וְאֶל־אֱלֹהֵינוּ כִּי־יַרְבֶּה לִסְלוֹחַ: כִּי לֹא מַחְשְׁבוֹתַי מַחְשְׁבוֹתֵיכֶם וְלֹא דַרְכֵיכֶם דְּרָכָי נְאֻם יהוה: כִּי־גָבְהוּ שָׁמַיִם מֵאָרֶץ כֵּן גָּבְהוּ דְרָכַי מִדַּרְכֵיכֶם וּמַחְשְׁבֹתַי מִמַּחְשְׁבֹתֵיכֶם: כִּי

כַּאֲשֶׁר יֵרֵד הַגֶּשֶׁם וְהַשֶּׁלֶג מִן־הַשָּׁמַיִם וְשָׁמָּה לֹא יָשׁוּב כִּי אִם־הִרְוָה אֶת־הָאָרֶץ וְהוֹלִידָהּ וְהִצְמִיחָהּ וְנָתַן זֶרַע לַזֹּרֵעַ וְלֶחֶם לָאֹכֵל: כֵּן יִהְיֶה דְבָרִי אֲשֶׁר יֵצֵא מִפִּי לֹא־יָשׁוּב אֵלַי רֵיקָם כִּי אִם־עָשָׂה אֶת־אֲשֶׁר חָפַצְתִּי וְהִצְלִיחַ אֲשֶׁר שְׁלַחְתִּיו: כִּי־בְשִׂמְחָה תֵצֵאוּ וּבְשָׁלוֹם תּוּבָלוּן הֶהָרִים וְהַגְּבָעוֹת יִפְצְחוּ לִפְנֵיכֶם רִנָּה וְכָל־עֲצֵי הַשָּׂדֶה יִמְחֲאוּ־כָף: תַּחַת הַנַּעֲצוּץ יַעֲלֶה בְרוֹשׁ וְתַחַת הַסִּרְפַּד יַעֲלֶה הֲדַס וְהָיָה לַיהוה לְשֵׁם לְאוֹת עוֹלָם לֹא יִכָּרֵת: כֹּה אָמַר יהוה שִׁמְרוּ מִשְׁפָּט וַעֲשׂוּ צְדָקָה כִּי־קְרוֹבָה יְשׁוּעָתִי לָבוֹא וְצִדְקָתִי לְהִגָּלוֹת: אַשְׁרֵי אֱנוֹשׁ יַעֲשֶׂה־זֹּאת וּבֶן־אָדָם יַחֲזִיק בָּהּ שֹׁמֵר שַׁבָּת מֵחַלְּלוֹ וְשֹׁמֵר יָדוֹ מֵעֲשׂוֹת כָּל־רָע: וְאַל־יֹאמַר בֶּן־הַנֵּכָר הַנִּלְוָה אֶל־יהוה לֵאמֹר הַבְדֵּל יַבְדִּילַנִי יהוה מֵעַל עַמּוֹ וְאַל־יֹאמַר הַסָּרִיס הֵן אֲנִי עֵץ יָבֵשׁ: כִּי־כֹה | אָמַר יהוה לַסָּרִיסִים אֲשֶׁר יִשְׁמְרוּ אֶת־שַׁבְּתוֹתַי וּבָחֲרוּ בַּאֲשֶׁר חָפָצְתִּי וּמַחֲזִיקִים בִּבְרִיתִי: וְנָתַתִּי לָהֶם בְּבֵיתִי וּבְחוֹמֹתַי יָד וָשֵׁם טוֹב מִבָּנִים וּמִבָּנוֹת שֵׁם עוֹלָם אֶתֶּן־לוֹ אֲשֶׁר לֹא יִכָּרֵת: וּבְנֵי הַנֵּכָר הַנִּלְוִים עַל־יהוה לְשָׁרְתוֹ וּלְאַהֲבָה אֶת־שֵׁם יהוה לִהְיוֹת לוֹ לַעֲבָדִים כָּל־שֹׁמֵר שַׁבָּת מֵחַלְּלוֹ וּמַחֲזִיקִים בִּבְרִיתִי: וַהֲבִיאוֹתִים אֶל־הַר קָדְשִׁי וְשִׂמַּחְתִּים בְּבֵית תְּפִלָּתִי עוֹלֹתֵיהֶם וְזִבְחֵיהֶם לְרָצוֹן עַל־מִזְבְּחִי כִּי בֵיתִי בֵּית־תְּפִלָּה יִקָּרֵא לְכָל־הָעַמִּים: נְאֻם אֲדֹנָי יֱהוִה מְקַבֵּץ נִדְחֵי יִשְׂרָאֵל עוֹד אֲקַבֵּץ עָלָיו לְנִקְבָּצָיו:

TISHAH B'AV / תשעה באב

During *Shacharis* of Tishah B'Av three *olim* are called to the Torah. The third *oleh* also reads the *Haftarah* of the day. During *Minchah* the Torah reading and the *Haftarah* are the same as for other public fast days (see preceding page).

(*Deuteronomy* 4:25-40)

כִּי־תוֹלִיד בָּנִים וּבְנֵי בָנִים וְנוֹשַׁנְתֶּם בָּאָרֶץ וְהִשְׁחַתֶּם וַעֲשִׂיתֶם פֶּסֶל תְּמוּנַת כֹּל וַעֲשִׂיתֶם הָרַע בְּעֵינֵי־יהוה אֱלֹהֶיךָ לְהַכְעִיסוֹ: הַעִידֹתִי בָכֶם הַיּוֹם אֶת־הַשָּׁמַיִם וְאֶת־הָאָרֶץ כִּי־אָבֹד תֹּאבֵדוּן מַהֵר מֵעַל הָאָרֶץ אֲשֶׁר אַתֶּם עֹבְרִים אֶת־הַיַּרְדֵּן שָׁמָּה לְרִשְׁתָּהּ לֹא־תַאֲרִיכֻן יָמִים עָלֶיהָ כִּי הִשָּׁמֵד תִּשָּׁמֵדוּן: וְהֵפִיץ יהוה אֶתְכֶם בָּעַמִּים וְנִשְׁאַרְתֶּם מְתֵי מִסְפָּר בַּגּוֹיִם אֲשֶׁר יְנַהֵג יהוה אֶתְכֶם שָׁמָּה: וַעֲבַדְתֶּם־שָׁם אֱלֹהִים מַעֲשֵׂה יְדֵי אָדָם עֵץ וָאֶבֶן אֲשֶׁר לֹא־יִרְאוּן וְלֹא יִשְׁמְעוּן וְלֹא יֹאכְלוּן וְלֹא יְרִיחֻן: וּבִקַּשְׁתֶּם מִשָּׁם אֶת־יהוה אֱלֹהֶיךָ וּמָצָאתָ כִּי תִדְרְשֶׁנּוּ בְּכָל־לְבָבְךָ וּבְכָל־נַפְשֶׁךָ:

לוי בַּצַּר לְךָ וּמְצָאוּךָ כֹּל הַדְּבָרִים הָאֵלֶּה בְּאַחֲרִית הַיָּמִים וְשַׁבְתָּ עַד־יהוה אֱלֹהֶיךָ וְשָׁמַעְתָּ בְּקֹלוֹ: כִּי אֵל רַחוּם יהוה אֱלֹהֶיךָ לֹא יַרְפְּךָ וְלֹא יַשְׁחִיתֶךָ וְלֹא יִשְׁכַּח אֶת־בְּרִית אֲבֹתֶיךָ אֲשֶׁר נִשְׁבַּע לָהֶם: כִּי שְׁאַל־נָא לְיָמִים רִאשֹׁנִים אֲשֶׁר־הָיוּ לְפָנֶיךָ לְמִן־הַיּוֹם אֲשֶׁר בָּרָא אֱלֹהִים | אָדָם עַל־הָאָרֶץ וּלְמִקְצֵה הַשָּׁמַיִם וְעַד־קְצֵה הַשָּׁמָיִם הֲנִהְיָה כַּדָּבָר הַגָּדוֹל הַזֶּה אוֹ הֲנִשְׁמַע כָּמֹהוּ: הֲשָׁמַע עָם קוֹל אֱלֹהִים מְדַבֵּר מִתּוֹךְ־הָאֵשׁ כַּאֲשֶׁר־שָׁמַעְתָּ אַתָּה וַיֶּחִי: אוֹ | הֲנִסָּה אֱלֹהִים לָבוֹא לָקַחַת לוֹ גוֹי מִקֶּרֶב גּוֹי בְּמַסֹּת בְּאֹתֹת וּבְמוֹפְתִים וּבְמִלְחָמָה וּבְיָד חֲזָקָה וּבִזְרוֹעַ נְטוּיָה וּבְמוֹרָאִים גְּדֹלִים כְּכֹל אֲשֶׁר־עָשָׂה לָכֶם יהוה אֱלֹהֵיכֶם בְּמִצְרַיִם לְעֵינֶיךָ: אַתָּה הָרְאֵתָ לָדַעַת כִּי יהוה הוּא הָאֱלֹהִים אֵין עוֹד מִלְּבַדּוֹ:

ישראל מִן־הַשָּׁמַיִם הִשְׁמִיעֲךָ אֶת־קֹלוֹ לְיַסְּרֶךָּ וְעַל־הָאָרֶץ הֶרְאֲךָ אֶת־אִשּׁוֹ הַגְּדוֹלָה וּדְבָרָיו שָׁמַעְתָּ מִתּוֹךְ הָאֵשׁ: וְתַחַת כִּי אָהַב אֶת־אֲבֹתֶיךָ וַיִּבְחַר בְּזַרְעוֹ אַחֲרָיו וַיּוֹצִאֲךָ בְּפָנָיו בְּכֹחוֹ הַגָּדֹל מִמִּצְרָיִם: לְהוֹרִישׁ גּוֹיִם גְּדֹלִים וַעֲצֻמִים מִמְּךָ מִפָּנֶיךָ לַהֲבִיאֲךָ לָתֶת־לְךָ אֶת־אַרְצָם נַחֲלָה כַּיּוֹם הַזֶּה: וְיָדַעְתָּ הַיּוֹם וַהֲשֵׁבֹתָ אֶל־לְבָבֶךָ כִּי יהוה הוּא הָאֱלֹהִים בַּשָּׁמַיִם מִמַּעַל וְעַל־הָאָרֶץ מִתָּחַת אֵין עוֹד: וְשָׁמַרְתָּ אֶת־חֻקָּיו וְאֶת־מִצְוֹתָיו אֲשֶׁר אָנֹכִי מְצַוְּךָ הַיּוֹם אֲשֶׁר יִיטַב לְךָ וּלְבָנֶיךָ אַחֲרֶיךָ וּלְמַעַן תַּאֲרִיךְ יָמִים עַל־הָאֲדָמָה אֲשֶׁר יהוה אֱלֹהֶיךָ נֹתֵן לְךָ כָּל־הַיָּמִים:

HAFTARAH / הפטרה

(*Jeremiah* 8:13 — 9:23)

אָסֹף אֲסִיפֵם נְאֻם־יהוה אֵין עֲנָבִים בַּגֶּפֶן וְאֵין תְּאֵנִים בַּתְּאֵנָה וְהֶעָלֶה נָבֵל וָאֶתֵּן

לָהֶם יַעַבְרוּם: עַל־מָה אֲנַחְנוּ יֹשְׁבִים
הֵאָסְפוּ וְנָבוֹא אֶל־עָרֵי הַמִּבְצָר וְנִדְּמָה־שָּׁם
כִּי יהוה אֱלֹהֵינוּ הֲדִמָּנוּ וַיַּשְׁקֵנוּ מֵי־רֹאשׁ
כִּי חָטָאנוּ לַיהוה: קַוֵּה לְשָׁלוֹם וְאֵין טוֹב
לְעֵת מַרְפֵּה וְהִנֵּה בְעָתָה: מִדָּן נִשְׁמַע
נַחְרַת סוּסָיו מִקּוֹל מִצְהֲלוֹת אַבִּירָיו
רָעֲשָׁה כָּל־הָאָרֶץ וַיָּבוֹאוּ וַיֹּאכְלוּ אֶרֶץ
וּמְלוֹאָהּ עִיר וְיֹשְׁבֵי בָהּ: כִּי הִנְנִי מְשַׁלֵּחַ
בָּכֶם נְחָשִׁים צִפְעֹנִים אֲשֶׁר אֵין־לָהֶם לָחַשׁ
וְנִשְּׁכוּ אֶתְכֶם נְאֻם־יהוה: מַבְלִיגִיתִי עֲלֵי
יָגוֹן עָלַי לִבִּי דַוָּי: הִנֵּה־קוֹל שַׁוְעַת בַּת־עַמִּי
מֵאֶרֶץ מַרְחַקִּים הַיהוה אֵין בְּצִיּוֹן אִם־
מַלְכָּהּ אֵין בָּהּ מַדּוּעַ הִכְעִסוּנִי בִּפְסִלֵיהֶם
בְּהַבְלֵי נֵכָר: עָבַר קָצִיר כָּלָה קָיִץ וַאֲנַחְנוּ
לוֹא נוֹשָׁעְנוּ: עַל־שֶׁבֶר בַּת־עַמִּי הָשְׁבָּרְתִּי
קָדַרְתִּי שַׁמָּה הֶחֱזִקָתְנִי: הַצֳרִי אֵין בְּגִלְעָד
אִם־רֹפֵא אֵין שָׁם כִּי מַדּוּעַ לֹא עָלְתָה
אֲרֻכַת בַּת־עַמִּי: מִי־יִתֵּן רֹאשִׁי מַיִם וְעֵינִי
מְקוֹר דִּמְעָה וְאֶבְכֶּה יוֹמָם וָלַיְלָה אֵת חַלְלֵי
בַת־עַמִּי: מִי־יִתְּנֵנִי בַמִּדְבָּר מְלוֹן אֹרְחִים
וְאֶעֶזְבָה אֶת־עַמִּי וְאֵלְכָה מֵאִתָּם כִּי כֻלָּם
מְנָאֲפִים עֲצֶרֶת בֹּגְדִים: וַיַּדְרְכוּ אֶת־לְשׁוֹנָם
קַשְׁתָּם שֶׁקֶר וְלֹא לֶאֱמוּנָה גָּבְרוּ בָאָרֶץ כִּי
מֵרָעָה אֶל־רָעָה | יָצָאוּ וְאֹתִי לֹא־יָדָעוּ
נְאֻם־יהוה: אִישׁ מֵרֵעֵהוּ הִשָּׁמֵרוּ וְעַל־כָּל־
אָח אַל־תִּבְטָחוּ כִּי כָל־אָח עָקוֹב יַעְקֹב
וְכָל־רֵעַ רָכִיל יַהֲלֹךְ: וְאִישׁ בְּרֵעֵהוּ יְהָתֵלּוּ
וֶאֱמֶת לֹא יְדַבֵּרוּ לִמְּדוּ לְשׁוֹנָם דַּבֶּר־שֶׁקֶר
הַעֲוֵה נִלְאוּ: שִׁבְתְּךָ בְּתוֹךְ מִרְמָה בְּמִרְמָה
מֵאֲנוּ דַעַת־אוֹתִי נְאֻם־יהוה: לָכֵן כֹּה אָמַר
יהוה צְבָאוֹת הִנְנִי צוֹרְפָם וּבְחַנְתִּים כִּי־
אֵיךְ אֶעֱשֶׂה מִפְּנֵי בַּת־עַמִּי: חֵץ שָׁחוּט
לְשׁוֹנָם מִרְמָה דִבֵּר בְּפִיו שָׁלוֹם אֶת־רֵעֵהוּ
יְדַבֵּר וּבְקִרְבּוֹ יָשִׂים אָרְבּוֹ: הַעַל־אֵלֶּה לֹא־
אֶפְקָד־בָּם נְאֻם־יהוה אִם בְּגוֹי אֲשֶׁר־כָּזֶה
לֹא תִתְנַקֵּם נַפְשִׁי: עַל־הֶהָרִים אֶשָּׂא בְכִי
וָנֶהִי וְעַל־נְאוֹת מִדְבָּר קִינָה כִּי נִצְּתוּ
מִבְּלִי־אִישׁ עֹבֵר וְלֹא שָׁמְעוּ קוֹל מִקְנֶה
מֵעוֹף הַשָּׁמַיִם וְעַד־בְּהֵמָה נָדְדוּ הָלָכוּ:
וְנָתַתִּי אֶת־יְרוּשָׁלִַם לְגַלִּים מְעוֹן תַּנִּים
וְאֶת־עָרֵי יְהוּדָה אֶתֵּן שְׁמָמָה מִבְּלִי יוֹשֵׁב:
מִי־הָאִישׁ הֶחָכָם וְיָבֵן אֶת־זֹאת וַאֲשֶׁר דִּבֶּר
פִּי־יהוה אֵלָיו וְיַגִּדָהּ עַל־מָה אָבְדָה הָאָרֶץ
נִצְּתָה כַמִּדְבָּר מִבְּלִי עֹבֵר: וַיֹּאמֶר יהוה
עַל־עָזְבָם אֶת־תּוֹרָתִי אֲשֶׁר נָתַתִּי לִפְנֵיהֶם
וְלֹא־שָׁמְעוּ בְקוֹלִי וְלֹא־הָלְכוּ בָהּ: וַיֵּלְכוּ
אַחֲרֵי שְׁרִרוּת לִבָּם וְאַחֲרֵי הַבְּעָלִים אֲשֶׁר
לִמְּדוּם אֲבוֹתָם: לָכֵן כֹּה־אָמַר יהוה
צְבָאוֹת אֱלֹהֵי יִשְׂרָאֵל הִנְנִי מַאֲכִילָם אֶת־
הָעָם הַזֶּה לַעֲנָה וְהִשְׁקִיתִים מֵי־רֹאשׁ:
וַהֲפִיצוֹתִים בַּגּוֹיִם אֲשֶׁר לֹא יָדְעוּ הֵמָּה
וַאֲבוֹתָם וְשִׁלַּחְתִּי אַחֲרֵיהֶם אֶת־הַחֶרֶב עַד
כַּלּוֹתִי אוֹתָם: כֹּה אָמַר יהוה צְבָאוֹת
הִתְבּוֹנְנוּ וְקִרְאוּ לַמְקוֹנְנוֹת וּתְבוֹאֶינָה וְאֶל־
הַחֲכָמוֹת שִׁלְחוּ וְתָבוֹאנָה: וּתְמַהֵרְנָה
וְתִשֶּׂנָה עָלֵינוּ נֶהִי וְתֵרַדְנָה עֵינֵינוּ דִּמְעָה
וְעַפְעַפֵּינוּ יִזְּלוּ־מָיִם: כִּי קוֹל נְהִי נִשְׁמַע
מִצִּיּוֹן אֵיךְ שֻׁדָּדְנוּ בֹּשְׁנוּ מְאֹד כִּי־עָזַבְנוּ
אָרֶץ כִּי הִשְׁלִיכוּ מִשְׁכְּנוֹתֵינוּ: כִּי־שְׁמַעְנָה
נָשִׁים דְּבַר־יהוה וְתִקַּח אָזְנְכֶם דְּבַר־פִּיו
וְלַמֵּדְנָה בְנוֹתֵיכֶם נֶהִי וְאִשָּׁה רְעוּתָהּ קִינָה:
כִּי־עָלָה מָוֶת בְּחַלּוֹנֵינוּ בָּא בְּאַרְמְנוֹתֵינוּ
לְהַכְרִית עוֹלָל מִחוּץ בַּחוּרִים מֵרְחֹבוֹת:
דַּבֵּר כֹּה נְאֻם־יהוה וְנָפְלָה נִבְלַת הָאָדָם
כְּדֹמֶן עַל־פְּנֵי הַשָּׂדֶה וּכְעָמִיר מֵאַחֲרֵי
הַקֹּצֵר וְאֵין מְאַסֵּף: כֹּה | אָמַר יהוה אַל־
יִתְהַלֵּל חָכָם בְּחָכְמָתוֹ וְאַל־יִתְהַלֵּל הַגִּבּוֹר
בִּגְבוּרָתוֹ אַל־יִתְהַלֵּל עָשִׁיר בְּעָשְׁרוֹ: כִּי
אִם־בְּזֹאת יִתְהַלֵּל הַמִּתְהַלֵּל הַשְׂכֵּל וְיָדֹעַ
אוֹתִי כִּי אֲנִי יהוה עֹשֶׂה חֶסֶד מִשְׁפָּט
וּצְדָקָה בָּאָרֶץ כִּי־בְאֵלֶּה חָפַצְתִּי נְאֻם־
יהוה:

פסח שבועות וסוכות
Pesach, Shavuos and Succos

פסח — יום ראשון
PESACH — FIRST DAY
(Exodus 12:21-51)

וַיִּקְרָא מֹשֶׁה לְכָל־זִקְנֵי יִשְׂרָאֵל וַיֹּאמֶר
אֲלֵהֶם מִשְׁכוּ וּקְחוּ לָכֶם צֹאן
לְמִשְׁפְּחֹתֵיכֶם וְשַׁחֲטוּ הַפָּסַח: וּלְקַחְתֶּם
אֲגֻדַּת אֵזוֹב וּטְבַלְתֶּם בַּדָּם אֲשֶׁר־בַּסַּף
וְהִגַּעְתֶּם אֶל־הַמַּשְׁקוֹף וְאֶל־שְׁתֵּי הַמְּזוּזֹת
מִן־הַדָּם אֲשֶׁר בַּסָּף וְאַתֶּם לֹא תֵצְאוּ אִישׁ
מִפֶּתַח־בֵּיתוֹ עַד־בֹּקֶר: וְעָבַר יהוה לִנְגֹּף

אֶת־מִצְרַיִם וְרָאָה אֶת־הַדָּם עַל־הַמַּשְׁקוֹף וְעַל שְׁתֵּי הַמְּזוּזֹת וּפָסַח יהוה עַל־הַפֶּתַח וְלֹא יִתֵּן הַמַּשְׁחִית לָבֹא אֶל־בָּתֵּיכֶם לִנְגֹּף׃ וּשְׁמַרְתֶּם אֶת־הַדָּבָר הַזֶּה לְחָק־לְךָ וּלְבָנֶיךָ עַד־עוֹלָם׃

שני וְהָיָה כִּי־תָבֹאוּ אֶל־הָאָרֶץ אֲשֶׁר יִתֵּן יהוה לָכֶם כַּאֲשֶׁר דִּבֵּר וּשְׁמַרְתֶּם אֶת־הָעֲבֹדָה הַזֹּאת׃ וְהָיָה כִּי־יֹאמְרוּ אֲלֵיכֶם בְּנֵיכֶם מָה הָעֲבֹדָה הַזֹּאת לָכֶם׃ וַאֲמַרְתֶּם זֶבַח־פֶּסַח הוּא לַיהוה אֲשֶׁר פָּסַח עַל־בָּתֵּי בְנֵי־יִשְׂרָאֵל בְּמִצְרַיִם בְּנָגְפּוֹ אֶת־מִצְרַיִם וְאֶת־בָּתֵּינוּ הִצִּיל וַיִּקֹּד הָעָם וַיִּשְׁתַּחֲוּוּ׃ וַיֵּלְכוּ וַיַּעֲשׂוּ בְּנֵי יִשְׂרָאֵל כַּאֲשֶׁר צִוָּה יהוה אֶת־מֹשֶׁה וְאַהֲרֹן כֵּן עָשׂוּ׃

ישראל וַיְהִי | בַּחֲצִי הַלַּיְלָה וַיהוה הִכָּה כָל־בְּכוֹר בְּאֶרֶץ מִצְרַיִם מִבְּכֹר פַּרְעֹה הַיֹּשֵׁב עַל־כִּסְאוֹ עַד בְּכוֹר הַשְּׁבִי אֲשֶׁר בְּבֵית הַבּוֹר וְכֹל בְּכוֹר בְּהֵמָה׃ וַיָּקָם פַּרְעֹה לַיְלָה הוּא וְכָל־עֲבָדָיו וְכָל־מִצְרַיִם וַתְּהִי צְעָקָה גְדֹלָה בְּמִצְרָיִם כִּי־אֵין בַּיִת אֲשֶׁר אֵין־שָׁם מֵת׃ וַיִּקְרָא לְמֹשֶׁה וּלְאַהֲרֹן לַיְלָה וַיֹּאמֶר קוּמוּ צְּאוּ מִתּוֹךְ עַמִּי גַּם־אַתֶּם גַּם־בְּנֵי יִשְׂרָאֵל וּלְכוּ עִבְדוּ אֶת־יהוה כְּדַבֶּרְכֶם׃ גַּם־צֹאנְכֶם גַּם־בְּקַרְכֶם קְחוּ כַּאֲשֶׁר דִּבַּרְתֶּם וָלֵכוּ וּבֵרַכְתֶּם גַּם־אֹתִי׃

(בשבת רביעי) וַתֶּחֱזַק מִצְרַיִם עַל־הָעָם לְמַהֵר לְשַׁלְּחָם מִן־הָאָרֶץ כִּי אָמְרוּ כֻּלָּנוּ מֵתִים׃ וַיִּשָּׂא הָעָם אֶת־בְּצֵקוֹ טֶרֶם יֶחְמָץ מִשְׁאֲרֹתָם צְרֻרֹת בְּשִׂמְלֹתָם עַל־שִׁכְמָם׃ וּבְנֵי־יִשְׂרָאֵל עָשׂוּ כִּדְבַר מֹשֶׁה וַיִּשְׁאֲלוּ מִמִּצְרַיִם כְּלֵי־כֶסֶף וּכְלֵי זָהָב וּשְׂמָלֹת׃ וַיהוה נָתַן אֶת־חֵן הָעָם בְּעֵינֵי מִצְרַיִם וַיַּשְׁאִלוּם וַיְנַצְּלוּ אֶת־מִצְרָיִם׃

רביעי (בשבת חמישי) וַיִּסְעוּ בְנֵי־יִשְׂרָאֵל מֵרַעְמְסֵס סֻכֹּתָה כְּשֵׁשׁ־מֵאוֹת אֶלֶף רַגְלִי הַגְּבָרִים לְבַד מִטָּף׃ וְגַם־עֵרֶב רַב עָלָה אִתָּם וְצֹאן וּבָקָר מִקְנֶה כָּבֵד מְאֹד׃ וַיֹּאפוּ אֶת־הַבָּצֵק אֲשֶׁר הוֹצִיאוּ מִמִּצְרַיִם עֻגֹת מַצּוֹת כִּי לֹא חָמֵץ כִּי־גֹרְשׁוּ מִמִּצְרַיִם וְלֹא יָכְלוּ לְהִתְמַהְמֵהַּ וְגַם־צֵדָה לֹא־עָשׂוּ לָהֶם׃ וּמוֹשַׁב בְּנֵי יִשְׂרָאֵל אֲשֶׁר יָשְׁבוּ בְּמִצְרָיִם שְׁלֹשִׁים שָׁנָה וְאַרְבַּע מֵאוֹת שָׁנָה׃ וַיְהִי מִקֵּץ שְׁלֹשִׁים שָׁנָה וְאַרְבַּע מֵאוֹת שָׁנָה וַיְהִי בְּעֶצֶם הַיּוֹם הַזֶּה יָצְאוּ כָּל־צִבְאוֹת יהוה מֵאֶרֶץ מִצְרָיִם׃ לֵיל שִׁמֻּרִים הוּא לַיהוה לְהוֹצִיאָם מֵאֶרֶץ מִצְרָיִם הוּא־הַלַּיְלָה הַזֶּה לַיהוה שִׁמֻּרִים לְכָל־בְּנֵי יִשְׂרָאֵל לְדֹרֹתָם׃

חמישי (בשבת ששי) וַיֹּאמֶר יהוה אֶל־מֹשֶׁה וְאַהֲרֹן זֹאת חֻקַּת הַפָּסַח כָּל־בֶּן־נֵכָר לֹא־יֹאכַל בּוֹ׃ וְכָל־עֶבֶד אִישׁ מִקְנַת־כָּסֶף וּמַלְתָּה אֹתוֹ אָז יֹאכַל בּוֹ׃ תּוֹשָׁב וְשָׂכִיר לֹא־יֹאכַל בּוֹ׃ בְּבַיִת אֶחָד יֵאָכֵל לֹא־תוֹצִיא מִן־הַבַּיִת מִן־הַבָּשָׂר חוּצָה וְעֶצֶם לֹא תִשְׁבְּרוּ־בוֹ׃ כָּל־עֲדַת יִשְׂרָאֵל יַעֲשׂוּ אֹתוֹ׃

(בשבת שביעי) וְכִי־יָגוּר אִתְּךָ גֵּר וְעָשָׂה פֶסַח לַיהוה הִמּוֹל לוֹ כָל־זָכָר וְאָז יִקְרַב לַעֲשֹׂתוֹ וְהָיָה כְּאֶזְרַח הָאָרֶץ וְכָל־עָרֵל לֹא־יֹאכַל בּוֹ׃ תּוֹרָה אַחַת יִהְיֶה לָאֶזְרָח וְלַגֵּר הַגָּר בְּתוֹכְכֶם׃ וַיַּעֲשׂוּ כָּל־בְּנֵי יִשְׂרָאֵל כַּאֲשֶׁר צִוָּה יהוה אֶת־מֹשֶׁה וְאֶת־אַהֲרֹן כֵּן עָשׂוּ׃ וַיְהִי בְּעֶצֶם הַיּוֹם הַזֶּה הוֹצִיא יהוה אֶת־בְּנֵי יִשְׂרָאֵל מֵאֶרֶץ מִצְרַיִם עַל־צִבְאֹתָם׃

מפטיר — א׳ וב׳ דפסח

MAFTIR — FIRST TWO DAYS OF PESACH

(*Numbers* 28:16-25)

מפטיר וּבַחֹדֶשׁ הָרִאשׁוֹן בְּאַרְבָּעָה עָשָׂר יוֹם לַחֹדֶשׁ פֶּסַח לַיהוה׃ וּבַחֲמִשָּׁה עָשָׂר יוֹם לַחֹדֶשׁ הַזֶּה חָג שִׁבְעַת יָמִים מַצּוֹת יֵאָכֵל׃ בַּיּוֹם הָרִאשׁוֹן מִקְרָא־קֹדֶשׁ כָּל־מְלֶאכֶת עֲבֹדָה לֹא תַעֲשׂוּ׃ וְהִקְרַבְתֶּם אִשֶּׁה עֹלָה לַיהוה פָּרִים בְּנֵי־בָקָר שְׁנַיִם וְאַיִל אֶחָד וְשִׁבְעָה כְבָשִׂים בְּנֵי שָׁנָה תְּמִימִם יִהְיוּ לָכֶם׃ וּמִנְחָתָם סֹלֶת בְּלוּלָה בַשָּׁמֶן שְׁלֹשָׁה עֶשְׂרֹנִים לַפָּר וּשְׁנֵי עֶשְׂרֹנִים לָאַיִל תַּעֲשׂוּ׃ עִשָּׂרוֹן עִשָּׂרוֹן תַּעֲשֶׂה לַכֶּבֶשׂ הָאֶחָד לְשִׁבְעַת הַכְּבָשִׂים׃ וּשְׂעִיר חַטָּאת אֶחָד לְכַפֵּר עֲלֵיכֶם׃ מִלְּבַד עֹלַת הַבֹּקֶר אֲשֶׁר לְעֹלַת הַתָּמִיד תַּעֲשׂוּ אֶת־אֵלֶּה׃ כָּאֵלֶּה תַּעֲשׂוּ לַיּוֹם שִׁבְעַת יָמִים לֶחֶם אִשֵּׁה רֵיחַ־נִיחֹחַ לַיהוה עַל־עוֹלַת הַתָּמִיד יֵעָשֶׂה וְנִסְכּוֹ׃ וּבַיּוֹם הַשְּׁבִיעִי מִקְרָא־קֹדֶשׁ יִהְיֶה לָכֶם כָּל־מְלֶאכֶת עֲבֹדָה לֹא תַעֲשׂוּ׃

הפטרה — יום ראשון של פסח

HAFTARAH — FIRST DAY OF PESACH

(*Joshua* 3:5-7; 5:2 — 6:1; 6:27)

וַיֹּאמֶר יְהוֹשֻׁעַ אֶל־הָעָם הִתְקַדָּשׁוּ כִּי מָחָר יַעֲשֶׂה יהוה בְּקִרְבְּכֶם נִפְלָאוֹת׃ וַיֹּאמֶר

יְהוֹשֻׁעַ אֶל־הַכֹּהֲנִים לֵאמֹר שְׂאוּ אֶת־אֲרוֹן הַבְּרִית וְעִבְרוּ לִפְנֵי הָעָם וַיִּשְׂאוּ אֶת־אֲרוֹן הַבְּרִית וַיֵּלְכוּ לִפְנֵי הָעָם: וַיֹּאמֶר יהוה אֶל־יְהוֹשֻׁעַ הַיּוֹם הַזֶּה אָחֵל גַּדֶּלְךָ בְּעֵינֵי כָּל־יִשְׂרָאֵל אֲשֶׁר יֵדְעוּן כִּי כַּאֲשֶׁר הָיִיתִי עִם־מֹשֶׁה אֶהְיֶה עִמָּךְ: בָּעֵת הַהִיא אָמַר יהוה אֶל־יְהוֹשֻׁעַ עֲשֵׂה לְךָ חַרְבוֹת צֻרִים וְשׁוּב מֹל אֶת־בְּנֵי־יִשְׂרָאֵל שֵׁנִית: וַיַּעַשׂ־לוֹ יְהוֹשֻׁעַ חַרְבוֹת צֻרִים וַיָּמָל אֶת־בְּנֵי יִשְׂרָאֵל אֶל־גִּבְעַת הָעֲרָלוֹת: וְזֶה הַדָּבָר אֲשֶׁר־מָל יְהוֹשֻׁעַ כָּל־הָעָם הַיֹּצֵא מִמִּצְרַיִם הַזְּכָרִים כֹּל | אַנְשֵׁי הַמִּלְחָמָה מֵתוּ בַמִּדְבָּר בַּדֶּרֶךְ בְּצֵאתָם מִמִּצְרָיִם: כִּי־מֻלִים הָיוּ כָּל־הָעָם הַיֹּצְאִים וְכָל־הָעָם הַיִּלֹּדִים בַּמִּדְבָּר בַּדֶּרֶךְ בְּצֵאתָם מִמִּצְרַיִם לֹא־מָלוּ: כִּי | אַרְבָּעִים שָׁנָה הָלְכוּ בְנֵי־יִשְׂרָאֵל בַּמִּדְבָּר עַד־תֹּם כָּל־הַגּוֹי אַנְשֵׁי הַמִּלְחָמָה הַיֹּצְאִים מִמִּצְרַיִם אֲשֶׁר לֹא־שָׁמְעוּ בְּקוֹל יהוה אֲשֶׁר נִשְׁבַּע יהוה לָהֶם לְבִלְתִּי הַרְאוֹתָם אֶת־הָאָרֶץ אֲשֶׁר נִשְׁבַּע יהוה לַאֲבוֹתָם לָתֶת לָנוּ אֶרֶץ זָבַת חָלָב וּדְבָשׁ: וְאֶת־בְּנֵיהֶם הֵקִים תַּחְתָּם אֹתָם מָל יְהוֹשֻׁעַ כִּי־עֲרֵלִים הָיוּ כִּי לֹא־מָלוּ אוֹתָם בַּדָּרֶךְ: וַיְהִי כַּאֲשֶׁר־תַּמּוּ כָל־הַגּוֹי לְהִמּוֹל וַיֵּשְׁבוּ תַחְתָּם בַּמַּחֲנֶה עַד חֲיוֹתָם: וַיֹּאמֶר יהוה אֶל־יְהוֹשֻׁעַ הַיּוֹם גַּלּוֹתִי אֶת־חֶרְפַּת מִצְרַיִם מֵעֲלֵיכֶם וַיִּקְרָא שֵׁם הַמָּקוֹם הַהוּא גִּלְגָּל עַד הַיּוֹם הַזֶּה: וַיַּחֲנוּ בְנֵי־יִשְׂרָאֵל בַּגִּלְגָּל וַיַּעֲשׂוּ אֶת־הַפֶּסַח בְּאַרְבָּעָה עָשָׂר יוֹם לַחֹדֶשׁ בָּעֶרֶב בְּעַרְבוֹת יְרִיחוֹ: וַיֹּאכְלוּ מֵעֲבוּר הָאָרֶץ מִמָּחֳרַת הַפֶּסַח מַצּוֹת וְקָלוּי בְּעֶצֶם הַיּוֹם הַזֶּה: וַיִּשְׁבֹּת הַמָּן מִמָּחֳרָת בְּאָכְלָם מֵעֲבוּר הָאָרֶץ וְלֹא־הָיָה עוֹד לִבְנֵי יִשְׂרָאֵל מָן וַיֹּאכְלוּ מִתְּבוּאַת אֶרֶץ כְּנַעַן בַּשָּׁנָה הַהִיא: וַיְהִי בִּהְיוֹת יְהוֹשֻׁעַ בִּירִיחוֹ וַיִּשָּׂא עֵינָיו וַיַּרְא וְהִנֵּה־אִישׁ עֹמֵד לְנֶגְדּוֹ וְחַרְבּוֹ שְׁלוּפָה בְּיָדוֹ וַיֵּלֶךְ יְהוֹשֻׁעַ אֵלָיו וַיֹּאמֶר לוֹ הֲלָנוּ אַתָּה אִם־לְצָרֵינוּ: וַיֹּאמֶר | לֹא כִּי אֲנִי שַׂר־צְבָא־יהוה עַתָּה בָאתִי וַיִּפֹּל יְהוֹשֻׁעַ אֶל־פָּנָיו אַרְצָה וַיִּשְׁתָּחוּ וַיֹּאמֶר לוֹ מָה אֲדֹנִי מְדַבֵּר אֶל־עַבְדּוֹ: וַיֹּאמֶר שַׂר־צְבָא יהוה אֶל־יְהוֹשֻׁעַ שַׁל־נַעַלְךָ מֵעַל רַגְלֶךָ כִּי הַמָּקוֹם אֲשֶׁר אַתָּה עֹמֵד עָלָיו קֹדֶשׁ הוּא וַיַּעַשׂ יְהוֹשֻׁעַ כֵּן:

וִירִיחוֹ סֹגֶרֶת וּמְסֻגֶּרֶת מִפְּנֵי בְּנֵי יִשְׂרָאֵל אֵין יוֹצֵא וְאֵין בָּא: וַיְהִי יהוה אֶת־יְהוֹשֻׁעַ וַיְהִי שָׁמְעוֹ בְּכָל־הָאָרֶץ:

פסח — יום שני

(וליום ראשון ושני של סוכות)

PESACH — SECOND DAY

(also First and Second Day of Succos)

(*Leviticus* 22:26 — 23:44)

וַיְדַבֵּר יהוה אֶל־מֹשֶׁה לֵּאמֹר: שׁוֹר אוֹ־כֶשֶׂב אוֹ־עֵז כִּי יִוָּלֵד וְהָיָה שִׁבְעַת יָמִים תַּחַת אִמּוֹ וּמִיּוֹם הַשְּׁמִינִי וָהָלְאָה יֵרָצֶה לְקָרְבַּן אִשֶּׁה לַיהוה: וְשׁוֹר אוֹ־שֶׂה אֹתוֹ וְאֶת־בְּנוֹ לֹא תִשְׁחֲטוּ בְּיוֹם אֶחָד: וְכִי־תִזְבְּחוּ זֶבַח־תּוֹדָה לַיהוה לִרְצֹנְכֶם תִּזְבָּחוּ: בַּיּוֹם הַהוּא יֵאָכֵל לֹא־תוֹתִירוּ מִמֶּנּוּ עַד־בֹּקֶר אֲנִי יהוה: וּשְׁמַרְתֶּם מִצְוֹתַי וַעֲשִׂיתֶם אֹתָם אֲנִי יהוה: וְלֹא תְחַלְּלוּ אֶת־שֵׁם קָדְשִׁי וְנִקְדַּשְׁתִּי בְּתוֹךְ בְּנֵי יִשְׂרָאֵל אֲנִי יהוה מְקַדִּשְׁכֶם: הַמּוֹצִיא אֶתְכֶם מֵאֶרֶץ מִצְרַיִם לִהְיוֹת לָכֶם לֵאלֹהִים אֲנִי יהוה:

(בשבת שני) וַיְדַבֵּר יהוה אֶל־מֹשֶׁה לֵּאמֹר: דַּבֵּר אֶל־בְּנֵי יִשְׂרָאֵל וְאָמַרְתָּ אֲלֵהֶם מוֹעֲדֵי יהוה אֲשֶׁר־תִּקְרְאוּ אֹתָם מִקְרָאֵי קֹדֶשׁ אֵלֶּה הֵם מוֹעֲדָי: שֵׁשֶׁת יָמִים תֵּעָשֶׂה מְלָאכָה וּבַיּוֹם הַשְּׁבִיעִי שַׁבַּת שַׁבָּתוֹן מִקְרָא־קֹדֶשׁ כָּל־מְלָאכָה לֹא תַעֲשׂוּ שַׁבָּת הִוא לַיהוה בְּכֹל מוֹשְׁבֹתֵיכֶם:

שני (בשבת שלישי) אֵלֶּה מוֹעֲדֵי יהוה מִקְרָאֵי קֹדֶשׁ אֲשֶׁר־תִּקְרְאוּ אֹתָם בְּמוֹעֲדָם: בַּחֹדֶשׁ הָרִאשׁוֹן בְּאַרְבָּעָה עָשָׂר לַחֹדֶשׁ בֵּין הָעַרְבָּיִם פֶּסַח לַיהוה: וּבַחֲמִשָּׁה עָשָׂר יוֹם לַחֹדֶשׁ הַזֶּה חַג הַמַּצּוֹת לַיהוה שִׁבְעַת יָמִים מַצּוֹת תֹּאכֵלוּ: בַּיּוֹם הָרִאשׁוֹן מִקְרָא־קֹדֶשׁ יִהְיֶה לָכֶם כָּל־מְלֶאכֶת עֲבֹדָה לֹא תַעֲשׂוּ: וְהִקְרַבְתֶּם אִשֶּׁה לַיהוה שִׁבְעַת יָמִים בַּיּוֹם הַשְּׁבִיעִי מִקְרָא־קֹדֶשׁ כָּל־מְלֶאכֶת עֲבֹדָה לֹא תַעֲשׂוּ:

(בשבת רביעי) וַיְדַבֵּר יהוה אֶל־מֹשֶׁה לֵּאמֹר: דַּבֵּר אֶל־בְּנֵי יִשְׂרָאֵל וְאָמַרְתָּ אֲלֵהֶם כִּי־תָבֹאוּ אֶל־הָאָרֶץ אֲשֶׁר אֲנִי נֹתֵן לָכֶם וּקְצַרְתֶּם אֶת־קְצִירָהּ וַהֲבֵאתֶם אֶת־עֹמֶר רֵאשִׁית קְצִירְכֶם אֶל־הַכֹּהֵן: וְהֵנִיף אֶת־הָעֹמֶר לִפְנֵי יהוה לִרְצֹנְכֶם מִמָּחֳרַת

הַשַּׁבָּת יְנִיפֶנּוּ הַכֹּהֵן: וַעֲשִׂיתֶם בְּיוֹם
הֲנִיפְכֶם אֶת־הָעֹמֶר כֶּבֶשׂ תָּמִים בֶּן־שְׁנָתוֹ
לְעֹלָה לַיהוָה: וּמִנְחָתוֹ שְׁנֵי עֶשְׂרֹנִים סֹלֶת
בְּלוּלָה בַשֶּׁמֶן אִשֶּׁה לַיהוָה רֵיחַ נִיחֹחַ
וְנִסְכֹּה יַיִן רְבִיעִת הַהִין: וְלֶחֶם וְקָלִי וְכַרְמֶל
לֹא תֹאכְלוּ עַד־עֶצֶם הַיּוֹם הַזֶּה עַד
הֲבִיאֲכֶם אֶת־קָרְבַּן אֱלֹהֵיכֶם חֻקַּת עוֹלָם
לְדֹרֹתֵיכֶם בְּכֹל מֹשְׁבֹתֵיכֶם:

שלישי (בשבת חמישי) וּסְפַרְתֶּם לָכֶם מִמָּחֳרַת
הַשַּׁבָּת מִיּוֹם הֲבִיאֲכֶם אֶת־עֹמֶר הַתְּנוּפָה
שֶׁבַע שַׁבָּתוֹת תְּמִימֹת תִּהְיֶינָה: עַד
מִמָּחֳרַת הַשַּׁבָּת הַשְּׁבִיעִת תִּסְפְּרוּ חֲמִשִּׁים
יוֹם וְהִקְרַבְתֶּם מִנְחָה חֲדָשָׁה לַיהוָה:
מִמּוֹשְׁבֹתֵיכֶם תָּבִיאוּ לֶחֶם תְּנוּפָה שְׁתַּיִם
שְׁנֵי עֶשְׂרֹנִים סֹלֶת תִּהְיֶינָה חָמֵץ תֵּאָפֶינָה
בִּכּוּרִים לַיהוָה: וְהִקְרַבְתֶּם עַל־הַלֶּחֶם
שִׁבְעַת כְּבָשִׂים תְּמִימִם בְּנֵי שָׁנָה וּפַר בֶּן
בָּקָר אֶחָד וְאֵילִם שְׁנָיִם יִהְיוּ עֹלָה לַיהוָה
וּמִנְחָתָם וְנִסְכֵּיהֶם אִשֵּׁה רֵיחַ־נִיחֹחַ לַיהוָה:
וַעֲשִׂיתֶם שְׂעִיר־עִזִּים אֶחָד לְחַטָּאת וּשְׁנֵי
כְבָשִׂים בְּנֵי שָׁנָה לְזֶבַח שְׁלָמִים: וְהֵנִיף
הַכֹּהֵן | אֹתָם עַל לֶחֶם הַבִּכֻּרִים תְּנוּפָה
לִפְנֵי יְהוָה עַל־שְׁנֵי כְּבָשִׂים קֹדֶשׁ יִהְיוּ
לַיהוָה לַכֹּהֵן: וּקְרָאתֶם בְּעֶצֶם | הַיּוֹם הַזֶּה
מִקְרָא־קֹדֶשׁ יִהְיֶה לָכֶם כָּל־מְלֶאכֶת עֲבֹדָה
לֹא תַעֲשׂוּ חֻקַּת עוֹלָם בְּכָל־מוֹשְׁבֹתֵיכֶם
לְדֹרֹתֵיכֶם: וּבְקֻצְרְכֶם אֶת־קְצִיר אַרְצְכֶם
לֹא־תְכַלֶּה פְּאַת שָׂדְךָ בְּקֻצְרֶךָ וְלֶקֶט
קְצִירְךָ לֹא תְלַקֵּט לֶעָנִי וְלַגֵּר תַּעֲזֹב אֹתָם
אֲנִי יְהוָה אֱלֹהֵיכֶם:

רביעי (בשבת ששי) וַיְדַבֵּר יְהוָה אֶל־מֹשֶׁה
לֵּאמֹר: דַּבֵּר אֶל־בְּנֵי יִשְׂרָאֵל לֵאמֹר בַּחֹדֶשׁ
הַשְּׁבִיעִי בְּאֶחָד לַחֹדֶשׁ יִהְיֶה לָכֶם שַׁבָּתוֹן
זִכְרוֹן תְּרוּעָה מִקְרָא־קֹדֶשׁ: כָּל־מְלֶאכֶת
עֲבֹדָה לֹא תַעֲשׂוּ וְהִקְרַבְתֶּם אִשֶּׁה לַיהוָה:
וַיְדַבֵּר יְהוָה אֶל־מֹשֶׁה לֵּאמֹר: אַךְ בֶּעָשׂוֹר
לַחֹדֶשׁ הַשְּׁבִיעִי הַזֶּה יוֹם הַכִּפֻּרִים הוּא
מִקְרָא־קֹדֶשׁ יִהְיֶה לָכֶם וְעִנִּיתֶם אֶת־
נַפְשֹׁתֵיכֶם וְהִקְרַבְתֶּם אִשֶּׁה לַיהוָה: וְכָל־
מְלָאכָה לֹא תַעֲשׂוּ בְּעֶצֶם הַיּוֹם הַזֶּה כִּי יוֹם
כִּפֻּרִים הוּא לְכַפֵּר עֲלֵיכֶם לִפְנֵי יְהוָה
אֱלֹהֵיכֶם: כִּי כָל־הַנֶּפֶשׁ אֲשֶׁר לֹא־תְעֻנֶּה
בְּעֶצֶם הַיּוֹם הַזֶּה וְנִכְרְתָה מֵעַמֶּיהָ: וְכָל־
הַנֶּפֶשׁ אֲשֶׁר תַּעֲשֶׂה כָּל־מְלָאכָה בְּעֶצֶם

הַיּוֹם הַזֶּה וְהַאֲבַדְתִּי אֶת־הַנֶּפֶשׁ הַהִוא
מִקֶּרֶב עַמָּהּ: כָּל־מְלָאכָה לֹא תַעֲשׂוּ חֻקַּת
עוֹלָם לְדֹרֹתֵיכֶם בְּכֹל מֹשְׁבֹתֵיכֶם: שַׁבַּת
שַׁבָּתוֹן הוּא לָכֶם וְעִנִּיתֶם אֶת־נַפְשֹׁתֵיכֶם
בְּתִשְׁעָה לַחֹדֶשׁ בָּעֶרֶב מֵעֶרֶב עַד־עֶרֶב
תִּשְׁבְּתוּ שַׁבַּתְּכֶם:

חמישי (בשבת שביעי) וַיְדַבֵּר יְהוָה אֶל־מֹשֶׁה
לֵּאמֹר: דַּבֵּר אֶל־בְּנֵי יִשְׂרָאֵל לֵאמֹר
בַּחֲמִשָּׁה עָשָׂר יוֹם לַחֹדֶשׁ הַשְּׁבִיעִי הַזֶּה חַג
הַסֻּכּוֹת שִׁבְעַת יָמִים לַיהוָה: בַּיּוֹם הָרִאשׁוֹן
מִקְרָא־קֹדֶשׁ כָּל־מְלֶאכֶת עֲבֹדָה לֹא
תַעֲשׂוּ: שִׁבְעַת יָמִים תַּקְרִיבוּ אִשֶּׁה לַיהוָה
בַּיּוֹם הַשְּׁמִינִי מִקְרָא־קֹדֶשׁ יִהְיֶה לָכֶם
וְהִקְרַבְתֶּם אִשֶּׁה לַיהוָה עֲצֶרֶת הִוא כָּל־
מְלֶאכֶת עֲבֹדָה לֹא תַעֲשׂוּ: אֵלֶּה מוֹעֲדֵי
יְהוָה אֲשֶׁר־תִּקְרְאוּ אֹתָם מִקְרָאֵי קֹדֶשׁ
לְהַקְרִיב אִשֶּׁה לַיהוָה עֹלָה וּמִנְחָה זֶבַח
וּנְסָכִים דְּבַר־יוֹם בְּיוֹמוֹ: מִלְּבַד שַׁבְּתֹת
יְהוָה וּמִלְּבַד מַתְּנוֹתֵיכֶם וּמִלְּבַד כָּל־
נִדְרֵיכֶם וּמִלְּבַד כָּל־נִדְבֹתֵיכֶם אֲשֶׁר תִּתְּנוּ
לַיהוָה: אַךְ בַּחֲמִשָּׁה עָשָׂר יוֹם לַחֹדֶשׁ
הַשְּׁבִיעִי בְּאָסְפְּכֶם אֶת־תְּבוּאַת הָאָרֶץ
תָּחֹגּוּ אֶת־חַג־יְהוָה שִׁבְעַת יָמִים בַּיּוֹם
הָרִאשׁוֹן שַׁבָּתוֹן וּבַיּוֹם הַשְּׁמִינִי שַׁבָּתוֹן:
וּלְקַחְתֶּם לָכֶם בַּיּוֹם הָרִאשׁוֹן פְּרִי עֵץ הָדָר
כַּפֹּת תְּמָרִים וַעֲנַף עֵץ־עָבֹת וְעַרְבֵי־נָחַל
וּשְׂמַחְתֶּם לִפְנֵי יְהוָה אֱלֹהֵיכֶם שִׁבְעַת
יָמִים: וְחַגֹּתֶם אֹתוֹ חַג לַיהוָה שִׁבְעַת יָמִים
בַּשָּׁנָה חֻקַּת עוֹלָם לְדֹרֹתֵיכֶם בַּחֹדֶשׁ
הַשְּׁבִיעִי תָּחֹגּוּ אֹתוֹ: בַּסֻּכֹּת תֵּשְׁבוּ שִׁבְעַת
יָמִים כָּל־הָאֶזְרָח בְּיִשְׂרָאֵל יֵשְׁבוּ בַּסֻּכֹּת:
לְמַעַן יֵדְעוּ דֹרֹתֵיכֶם כִּי בַסֻּכּוֹת הוֹשַׁבְתִּי
אֶת־בְּנֵי יִשְׂרָאֵל בְּהוֹצִיאִי אוֹתָם מֵאֶרֶץ
מִצְרָיִם אֲנִי יְהוָה אֱלֹהֵיכֶם: וַיְדַבֵּר מֹשֶׁה
אֶת־מֹעֲדֵי יְהוָה אֶל־בְּנֵי יִשְׂרָאֵל:

Maftir for the second day of Pesach is the same as for the first day, page 955.
Maftir and Haftoros for Succos appear on page 970.

הפטרה — יום שני של פסח
HAFTARAH — SECOND DAY OF PESACH

(II Kings 23:1-9, 21-25)

וַיִּשְׁלַח הַמֶּלֶךְ וַיַּאַסְפוּ אֵלָיו כָּל־זִקְנֵי יְהוּדָה
וִירוּשָׁלָ‍ִם: וַיַּעַל הַמֶּלֶךְ בֵּית־יְהוָה וְכָל־
אִישׁ יְהוּדָה וְכָל־יֹשְׁבֵי יְרוּשָׁלַ‍ִם אִתּוֹ

וְהַכֹּהֲנִים וְהַנְּבִיאִים וְכָל־הָעָם לְמִקָּטֹן וְעַד־גָּדוֹל וַיִּקְרָא בְאָזְנֵיהֶם אֶת־כָּל־דִּבְרֵי סֵפֶר הַבְּרִית הַנִּמְצָא בְּבֵית יהוה: וַיַּעֲמֹד הַמֶּלֶךְ עַל־הָעַמּוּד וַיִּכְרֹת אֶת־הַבְּרִית ׀ לִפְנֵי יהוה לָלֶכֶת אַחַר יהוה וְלִשְׁמֹר מִצְוֺתָיו וְאֶת־עֵדְוֺתָיו וְאֶת־חֻקֹּתָיו בְּכָל־לֵב וּבְכָל־נֶפֶשׁ לְהָקִים אֶת־דִּבְרֵי הַבְּרִית הַזֹּאת הַכְּתֻבִים עַל־הַסֵּפֶר הַזֶּה וַיַּעֲמֹד כָּל־הָעָם בַּבְּרִית: וַיְצַו הַמֶּלֶךְ אֶת־חִלְקִיָּהוּ הַכֹּהֵן הַגָּדוֹל וְאֶת־כֹּהֲנֵי הַמִּשְׁנֶה וְאֶת־שֹׁמְרֵי הַסַּף לְהוֹצִיא מֵהֵיכַל יהוה אֵת כָּל־הַכֵּלִים הָעֲשׂוּיִם לַבַּעַל וְלָאֲשֵׁרָה וּלְכֹל צְבָא הַשָּׁמָיִם וַיִּשְׂרְפֵם מִחוּץ לִירוּשָׁלִַם בְּשַׁדְמוֹת קִדְרוֹן וְנָשָׂא אֶת־עֲפָרָם בֵּית־אֵל: וְהִשְׁבִּית אֶת־הַכְּמָרִים אֲשֶׁר נָתְנוּ מַלְכֵי יְהוּדָה וַיְקַטֵּר בַּבָּמוֹת בְּעָרֵי יְהוּדָה וּמְסִבֵּי יְרוּשָׁלִָם וְאֶת־הַמְקַטְּרִים לַבַּעַל לַשֶּׁמֶשׁ וְלַיָּרֵחַ וְלַמַּזָּלוֹת וּלְכֹל צְבָא הַשָּׁמָיִם: וַיֹּצֵא אֶת־הָאֲשֵׁרָה מִבֵּית יהוה מִחוּץ לִירוּשָׁלִַם אֶל־נַחַל קִדְרוֹן וַיִּשְׂרֹף אֹתָהּ בְּנַחַל קִדְרוֹן וַיָּדֶק לְעָפָר וַיַּשְׁלֵךְ אֶת־עֲפָרָהּ עַל־קֶבֶר בְּנֵי הָעָם: וַיִּתֹּץ אֶת־בָּתֵּי הַקְּדֵשִׁים אֲשֶׁר בְּבֵית יהוה אֲשֶׁר הַנָּשִׁים אֹרְגוֹת שָׁם בָּתִּים לָאֲשֵׁרָה: וַיָּבֵא אֶת־כָּל־הַכֹּהֲנִים מֵעָרֵי יְהוּדָה וַיְטַמֵּא אֶת־הַבָּמוֹת אֲשֶׁר קִטְּרוּ־שָׁמָּה הַכֹּהֲנִים מִגֶּבַע עַד־בְּאֵר שָׁבַע וְנָתַץ אֶת־בָּמוֹת הַשְּׁעָרִים אֲשֶׁר־פֶּתַח שַׁעַר יְהוֹשֻׁעַ שַׂר־הָעִיר אֲשֶׁר־עַל־שְׂמֹאול אִישׁ בְּשַׁעַר הָעִיר: אַךְ לֹא יַעֲלוּ כֹּהֲנֵי הַבָּמוֹת אֶל־מִזְבַּח יהוה בִּירוּשָׁלִָם כִּי אִם־אָכְלוּ מַצּוֹת בְּתוֹךְ אֲחֵיהֶם: וַיְצַו הַמֶּלֶךְ אֶת־כָּל־הָעָם לֵאמֹר עֲשׂוּ פֶסַח לַיהוה אֱלֹהֵיכֶם כַּכָּתוּב עַל סֵפֶר הַבְּרִית הַזֶּה: כִּי לֹא נַעֲשָׂה כַּפֶּסַח הַזֶּה מִימֵי הַשֹּׁפְטִים אֲשֶׁר שָׁפְטוּ אֶת־יִשְׂרָאֵל וְכֹל יְמֵי מַלְכֵי יִשְׂרָאֵל וּמַלְכֵי יְהוּדָה: כִּי אִם־בִּשְׁמֹנֶה עֶשְׂרֵה שָׁנָה לַמֶּלֶךְ יֹאשִׁיָּהוּ נַעֲשָׂה הַפֶּסַח הַזֶּה לַיהוה בִּירוּשָׁלִָם: וְגַם אֶת־הָאֹבוֹת וְאֶת־הַיִּדְּעֹנִים וְאֶת־הַתְּרָפִים וְאֶת־הַגִּלֻּלִים וְאֵת כָּל־הַשִּׁקֻּצִים אֲשֶׁר נִרְאוּ בְּאֶרֶץ יְהוּדָה וּבִירוּשָׁלִַם בִּעֵר יֹאשִׁיָּהוּ לְמַעַן הָקִים אֶת־דִּבְרֵי הַתּוֹרָה הַכְּתֻבִים עַל־הַסֵּפֶר אֲשֶׁר מָצָא חִלְקִיָּהוּ הַכֹּהֵן בֵּית יהוה: וְכָמֹהוּ לֹא־הָיָה לְפָנָיו מֶלֶךְ אֲשֶׁר־שָׁב אֶל־יהוה בְּכָל־לְבָבוֹ וּבְכָל־נַפְשׁוֹ וּבְכָל־מְאֹדוֹ כְּכֹל תּוֹרַת מֹשֶׁה וְאַחֲרָיו לֹא־קָם כָּמֹהוּ:

חול המועד פסח

CHOL HAMOED PESACH

Each day of Chol HaMoed Pesach two Torahs are removed from the Ark. On all days other than the Sabbath (see p. 961), three *olim* are called to the first Torah, and a fourth to the second Torah. When the first day of Chol HaMoed coincides with the Sabbath, the readings of the first and second days are each postponed one day, and the third day's reading is omitted.

חול המועד פסח — יום ראשון

CHOL HAMOED PESACH — FIRST DAY

(*Exodus* 13:1-16)

וַיְדַבֵּר יהוה אֶל־מֹשֶׁה לֵּאמֹר: קַדֶּשׁ־לִי כָל־בְּכוֹר פֶּטֶר כָּל־רֶחֶם בִּבְנֵי יִשְׂרָאֵל בָּאָדָם וּבַבְּהֵמָה לִי הוּא: וַיֹּאמֶר מֹשֶׁה אֶל־הָעָם זָכוֹר אֶת־הַיּוֹם הַזֶּה אֲשֶׁר יְצָאתֶם מִמִּצְרַיִם מִבֵּית עֲבָדִים כִּי בְּחֹזֶק יָד הוֹצִיא יהוה אֶתְכֶם מִזֶּה וְלֹא יֵאָכֵל חָמֵץ: הַיּוֹם אַתֶּם יֹצְאִים בְּחֹדֶשׁ הָאָבִיב:

לוי וְהָיָה כִי־יְבִיאֲךָ יהוה אֶל־אֶרֶץ הַכְּנַעֲנִי וְהַחִתִּי וְהָאֱמֹרִי וְהַחִוִּי וְהַיְבוּסִי אֲשֶׁר נִשְׁבַּע לַאֲבֹתֶיךָ לָתֶת לָךְ אֶרֶץ זָבַת חָלָב וּדְבָשׁ וְעָבַדְתָּ אֶת־הָעֲבֹדָה הַזֹּאת בַּחֹדֶשׁ הַזֶּה: שִׁבְעַת יָמִים תֹּאכַל מַצֹּת וּבַיּוֹם הַשְּׁבִיעִי חַג לַיהוה: מַצּוֹת יֵאָכֵל אֵת שִׁבְעַת הַיָּמִים וְלֹא־יֵרָאֶה לְךָ חָמֵץ וְלֹא־יֵרָאֶה לְךָ שְׂאֹר בְּכָל־גְּבֻלֶךָ: וְהִגַּדְתָּ לְבִנְךָ בַּיּוֹם הַהוּא לֵאמֹר בַּעֲבוּר זֶה עָשָׂה יהוה לִי בְּצֵאתִי מִמִּצְרָיִם: וְהָיָה לְךָ לְאוֹת עַל־יָדְךָ וּלְזִכָּרוֹן בֵּין עֵינֶיךָ לְמַעַן תִּהְיֶה תּוֹרַת יהוה בְּפִיךָ כִּי בְּיָד חֲזָקָה הוֹצִאֲךָ יהוה מִמִּצְרָיִם: וְשָׁמַרְתָּ אֶת־הַחֻקָּה הַזֹּאת לְמוֹעֲדָהּ מִיָּמִים יָמִימָה:

ישראל וְהָיָה כִּי־יְבִאֲךָ יהוה אֶל־אֶרֶץ הַכְּנַעֲנִי כַּאֲשֶׁר נִשְׁבַּע לְךָ וְלַאֲבֹתֶיךָ וּנְתָנָהּ לָךְ: וְהַעֲבַרְתָּ כָל־פֶּטֶר־רֶחֶם לַיהוה וְכָל־פֶּטֶר ׀ שֶׁגֶר בְּהֵמָה אֲשֶׁר יִהְיֶה לְךָ הַזְּכָרִים לַיהוה: וְכָל־פֶּטֶר חֲמֹר תִּפְדֶּה בְשֶׂה וְאִם־לֹא תִפְדֶּה וַעֲרַפְתּוֹ וְכֹל בְּכוֹר אָדָם בְּבָנֶיךָ תִּפְדֶּה: וְהָיָה כִּי־יִשְׁאָלְךָ בִנְךָ מָחָר לֵאמֹר מַה־זֹּאת וְאָמַרְתָּ אֵלָיו בְּחֹזֶק יָד הוֹצִיאָנוּ יהוה מִמִּצְרַיִם מִבֵּית עֲבָדִים: וַיְהִי כִּי־הִקְשָׁה פַרְעֹה לְשַׁלְּחֵנוּ וַיַּהֲרֹג יהוה כָּל־

בְּכוֹר בְּאֶרֶץ מִצְרַיִם מִבְּכֹר אָדָם וְעַד־בְּכוֹר בְּהֵמָה עַל־כֵּן אֲנִי זֹבֵחַ לַיהוה כָּל־פֶּטֶר רֶחֶם הַזְּכָרִים וְכָל־בְּכוֹר בָּנַי אֶפְדֶּה׃ וְהָיָה לְאוֹת עַל־יָדְכָה וּלְטוֹטָפֹת בֵּין עֵינֶיךָ כִּי בְּחֹזֶק יָד הוֹצִיאָנוּ יהוה מִמִּצְרָיִם׃

(*Numbers* 28:19-25)

רביעי וְהִקְרַבְתֶּם אִשֶּׁה עֹלָה לַיהוה פָּרִים בְּנֵי־בָקָר שְׁנַיִם וְאַיִל אֶחָד וְשִׁבְעָה כְבָשִׂים בְּנֵי שָׁנָה תְּמִימִם יִהְיוּ לָכֶם׃ וּמִנְחָתָם סֹלֶת בְּלוּלָה בַשָּׁמֶן שְׁלֹשָׁה עֶשְׂרֹנִים לַפָּר וּשְׁנֵי עֶשְׂרֹנִים לָאַיִל תַּעֲשׂוּ׃ עִשָּׂרוֹן עִשָּׂרוֹן תַּעֲשֶׂה לַכֶּבֶשׂ הָאֶחָד לְשִׁבְעַת הַכְּבָשִׂים׃ וּשְׂעִיר חַטָּאת אֶחָד לְכַפֵּר עֲלֵיכֶם׃ מִלְּבַד עֹלַת הַבֹּקֶר אֲשֶׁר לְעֹלַת הַתָּמִיד תַּעֲשׂוּ אֶת־אֵלֶּה׃ כָּאֵלֶּה תַּעֲשׂוּ לַיּוֹם שִׁבְעַת יָמִים לֶחֶם אִשֵּׁה רֵיחַ־נִיחֹחַ לַיהוה עַל־עוֹלַת הַתָּמִיד יֵעָשֶׂה וְנִסְכּוֹ׃ וּבַיּוֹם הַשְּׁבִיעִי מִקְרָא־קֹדֶשׁ יִהְיֶה לָכֶם כָּל־מְלֶאכֶת עֲבֹדָה לֹא תַעֲשׂוּ׃

חול המועד פסח — יום שני

CHOL HAMOED PESACH — SECOND DAY

(*Exodus* 22:24 — 23:19)

אִם־כֶּסֶף | תַּלְוֶה אֶת־עַמִּי אֶת־הֶעָנִי עִמָּךְ לֹא־תִהְיֶה לוֹ כְּנֹשֶׁה לֹא־תְשִׂימוּן עָלָיו נֶשֶׁךְ׃ אִם־חָבֹל תַּחְבֹּל שַׂלְמַת רֵעֶךָ עַד־בֹּא הַשֶּׁמֶשׁ תְּשִׁיבֶנּוּ לוֹ׃ כִּי הִוא כְסוּתֹה לְבַדָּהּ הִוא שִׂמְלָתוֹ לְעֹרוֹ בַּמֶּה יִשְׁכָּב וְהָיָה כִּי־יִצְעַק אֵלַי וְשָׁמַעְתִּי כִּי־חַנּוּן אָנִי׃

לוי אֱלֹהִים לֹא תְקַלֵּל וְנָשִׂיא בְעַמְּךָ לֹא תָאֹר׃ מְלֵאָתְךָ וְדִמְעֲךָ לֹא תְאַחֵר בְּכוֹר בָּנֶיךָ תִּתֶּן־לִּי׃ כֵּן־תַּעֲשֶׂה לְשֹׁרְךָ לְצֹאנֶךָ שִׁבְעַת יָמִים יִהְיֶה עִם־אִמּוֹ בַּיּוֹם הַשְּׁמִינִי תִּתְּנוֹ־לִי׃ וְאַנְשֵׁי־קֹדֶשׁ תִּהְיוּן לִי וּבָשָׂר בַּשָּׂדֶה טְרֵפָה לֹא תֹאכֵלוּ לַכֶּלֶב תַּשְׁלִכוּן אֹתוֹ׃ לֹא תִשָּׂא שֵׁמַע שָׁוְא אַל־תָּשֶׁת יָדְךָ עִם־רָשָׁע לִהְיֹת עֵד חָמָס׃ לֹא־תִהְיֶה אַחֲרֵי־רַבִּים לְרָעֹת וְלֹא־תַעֲנֶה עַל־רִב לִנְטֹת אַחֲרֵי רַבִּים לְהַטֹּת׃ וְדָל לֹא תֶהְדַּר בְּרִיבוֹ׃ כִּי תִפְגַּע שׁוֹר אֹיִבְךָ אוֹ חֲמֹרוֹ תֹּעֶה הָשֵׁב תְּשִׁיבֶנּוּ לוֹ׃ כִּי־תִרְאֶה חֲמוֹר שֹׂנַאֲךָ רֹבֵץ תַּחַת מַשָּׂאוֹ וְחָדַלְתָּ מֵעֲזֹב לוֹ עָזֹב תַּעֲזֹב עִמּוֹ׃

ישראל לֹא תַטֶּה מִשְׁפַּט אֶבְיֹנְךָ בְּרִיבוֹ׃ מִדְּבַר־שֶׁקֶר תִּרְחָק וְנָקִי וְצַדִּיק אַל־תַּהֲרֹג כִּי לֹא־אַצְדִּיק רָשָׁע׃ וְשֹׁחַד לֹא תִקָּח כִּי הַשֹּׁחַד יְעַוֵּר פִּקְחִים וִיסַלֵּף דִּבְרֵי צַדִּיקִים׃ וְגֵר לֹא תִלְחָץ וְאַתֶּם יְדַעְתֶּם אֶת־נֶפֶשׁ הַגֵּר כִּי־גֵרִים הֱיִיתֶם בְּאֶרֶץ מִצְרָיִם׃ וְשֵׁשׁ שָׁנִים תִּזְרַע אֶת־אַרְצֶךָ וְאָסַפְתָּ אֶת־תְּבוּאָתָהּ׃ וְהַשְּׁבִיעִת תִּשְׁמְטֶנָּה וּנְטַשְׁתָּהּ וְאָכְלוּ אֶבְיֹנֵי עַמֶּךָ וְיִתְרָם תֹּאכַל חַיַּת הַשָּׂדֶה כֵּן־תַּעֲשֶׂה לְכַרְמְךָ לְזֵיתֶךָ׃ שֵׁשֶׁת יָמִים תַּעֲשֶׂה מַעֲשֶׂיךָ וּבַיּוֹם הַשְּׁבִיעִי תִּשְׁבֹּת לְמַעַן יָנוּחַ שׁוֹרְךָ וַחֲמֹרֶךָ וְיִנָּפֵשׁ בֶּן־אֲמָתְךָ וְהַגֵּר׃ וּבְכֹל אֲשֶׁר־אָמַרְתִּי אֲלֵיכֶם תִּשָּׁמֵרוּ וְשֵׁם אֱלֹהִים אֲחֵרִים לֹא תַזְכִּירוּ לֹא יִשָּׁמַע עַל־פִּיךָ׃ שָׁלֹשׁ רְגָלִים תָּחֹג לִי בַּשָּׁנָה׃ אֶת־חַג הַמַּצּוֹת תִּשְׁמֹר שִׁבְעַת יָמִים תֹּאכַל מַצּוֹת כַּאֲשֶׁר צִוִּיתִךָ לְמוֹעֵד חֹדֶשׁ הָאָבִיב כִּי־בוֹ יָצָאתָ מִמִּצְרָיִם וְלֹא־יֵרָאוּ פָנַי רֵיקָם׃ וְחַג הַקָּצִיר בִּכּוּרֵי מַעֲשֶׂיךָ אֲשֶׁר תִּזְרַע בַּשָּׂדֶה וְחַג הָאָסִף בְּצֵאת הַשָּׁנָה בְּאָסְפְּךָ אֶת־מַעֲשֶׂיךָ מִן־הַשָּׂדֶה׃ שָׁלֹשׁ פְּעָמִים בַּשָּׁנָה יֵרָאֶה כָּל־זְכוּרְךָ אֶל־פְּנֵי הָאָדֹן | יהוה׃ לֹא־תִזְבַּח עַל־חָמֵץ דַּם־זִבְחִי וְלֹא־יָלִין חֵלֶב־חַגִּי עַד־בֹּקֶר׃ רֵאשִׁית בִּכּוּרֵי אַדְמָתְךָ תָּבִיא בֵּית יהוה אֱלֹהֶיךָ לֹא־תְבַשֵּׁל גְּדִי בַּחֲלֵב אִמּוֹ׃

The reading for the fourth *oleh* (רביעי) is *Numbers* 28:19-25, see above.

חול המועד פסח — יום שלישי

CHOL HAMOED PESACH — THIRD DAY

(*Exodus* 34:1-26)

וַיֹּאמֶר יהוה אֶל־מֹשֶׁה פְּסָל־לְךָ שְׁנֵי־לֻחֹת אֲבָנִים כָּרִאשֹׁנִים וְכָתַבְתִּי עַל־הַלֻּחֹת אֶת־הַדְּבָרִים אֲשֶׁר הָיוּ עַל־הַלֻּחֹת הָרִאשֹׁנִים אֲשֶׁר שִׁבַּרְתָּ׃ וֶהְיֵה נָכוֹן לַבֹּקֶר וְעָלִיתָ בַבֹּקֶר אֶל־הַר סִינַי וְנִצַּבְתָּ לִי שָׁם עַל־רֹאשׁ הָהָר׃ וְאִישׁ לֹא־יַעֲלֶה עִמָּךְ וְגַם־אִישׁ אַל־יֵרָא בְּכָל־הָהָר גַּם־הַצֹּאן וְהַבָּקָר אַל־יִרְעוּ אֶל־מוּל הָהָר הַהוּא׃

לוי וַיִּפְסֹל שְׁנֵי־לֻחֹת אֲבָנִים כָּרִאשֹׁנִים וַיַּשְׁכֵּם מֹשֶׁה בַבֹּקֶר וַיַּעַל אֶל־הַר סִינַי כַּאֲשֶׁר צִוָּה יהוה אֹתוֹ וַיִּקַּח בְּיָדוֹ שְׁנֵי לֻחֹת אֲבָנִים׃ וַיֵּרֶד יהוה בֶּעָנָן וַיִּתְיַצֵּב עִמּוֹ שָׁם וַיִּקְרָא בְשֵׁם יהוה׃ וַיַּעֲבֹר יהוה | עַל־פָּנָיו וַיִּקְרָא יהוה | יהוה אֵל רַחוּם וְחַנּוּן אֶרֶךְ

אַפַּיִם וְרַב־חֶסֶד וֶאֱמֶת: נֹצֵר חֶסֶד לָאֲלָפִים נֹשֵׂא עָוֺן וָפֶשַׁע וְחַטָּאָה וְנַקֵּה לֹא יְנַקֶּה פֹּקֵד | עֲוֺן אָבוֹת עַל־בָּנִים וְעַל־בְּנֵי בָנִים עַל־שִׁלֵּשִׁים וְעַל־רִבֵּעִים: וַיְמַהֵר מֹשֶׁה וַיִּקֹּד אַרְצָה וַיִּשְׁתָּחוּ: וַיֹּאמֶר אִם־נָא מָצָאתִי חֵן בְּעֵינֶיךָ אֲדֹנָי יֵלֶךְ־נָא אֲדֹנָי בְּקִרְבֵּנוּ כִּי עַם־קְשֵׁה־עֹרֶף הוּא וְסָלַחְתָּ לַעֲוֺנֵנוּ וּלְחַטָּאתֵנוּ וּנְחַלְתָּנוּ: וַיֹּאמֶר הִנֵּה אָנֹכִי כֹּרֵת בְּרִית נֶגֶד כָּל־עַמְּךָ אֶעֱשֶׂה נִפְלָאֹת אֲשֶׁר לֹא־נִבְרְאוּ בְכָל־הָאָרֶץ וּבְכָל־הַגּוֹיִם וְרָאָה כָל־הָעָם אֲשֶׁר־אַתָּה בְקִרְבּוֹ אֶת־מַעֲשֵׂה יהוה כִּי־נוֹרָא הוּא אֲשֶׁר אֲנִי עֹשֶׂה עִמָּךְ: שְׁמָר־לְךָ אֵת אֲשֶׁר אָנֹכִי מְצַוְּךָ הַיּוֹם הִנְנִי גֹרֵשׁ מִפָּנֶיךָ אֶת־הָאֱמֹרִי וְהַכְּנַעֲנִי וְהַחִתִּי וְהַפְּרִזִּי וְהַחִוִּי וְהַיְבוּסִי: הִשָּׁמֶר לְךָ פֶּן־תִּכְרֹת בְּרִית לְיוֹשֵׁב הָאָרֶץ אֲשֶׁר אַתָּה בָּא עָלֶיהָ פֶּן־יִהְיֶה לְמוֹקֵשׁ בְּקִרְבֶּךָ: כִּי אֶת־מִזְבְּחֹתָם תִּתֹּצוּן וְאֶת־מַצֵּבֹתָם תְּשַׁבֵּרוּן וְאֶת־אֲשֵׁרָיו תִּכְרֹתוּן: כִּי לֹא תִשְׁתַּחֲוֶה לְאֵל אַחֵר כִּי יהוה קַנָּא שְׁמוֹ אֵל קַנָּא הוּא: פֶּן־תִּכְרֹת בְּרִית לְיוֹשֵׁב הָאָרֶץ וְזָנוּ | אַחֲרֵי אֱלֹהֵיהֶם וְזָבְחוּ לֵאלֹהֵיהֶם וְקָרָא לְךָ וְאָכַלְתָּ מִזִּבְחוֹ: וְלָקַחְתָּ מִבְּנֹתָיו לְבָנֶיךָ וְזָנוּ בְנֹתָיו אַחֲרֵי אֱלֹהֵיהֶן וְהִזְנוּ אֶת־בָּנֶיךָ אַחֲרֵי אֱלֹהֵיהֶן: אֱלֹהֵי מַסֵּכָה לֹא תַעֲשֶׂה־לָּךְ:

ישראל אֶת־חַג הַמַּצּוֹת תִּשְׁמֹר שִׁבְעַת יָמִים תֹּאכַל מַצּוֹת אֲשֶׁר צִוִּיתִךָ לְמוֹעֵד חֹדֶשׁ הָאָבִיב כִּי בְּחֹדֶשׁ הָאָבִיב יָצָאתָ מִמִּצְרָיִם: כָּל־פֶּטֶר רֶחֶם לִי וְכָל־מִקְנְךָ תִּזָּכָר פֶּטֶר שׁוֹר וָשֶׂה: וּפֶטֶר חֲמוֹר תִּפְדֶּה בְשֶׂה וְאִם־לֹא תִפְדֶּה וַעֲרַפְתּוֹ כֹּל בְּכוֹר בָּנֶיךָ תִּפְדֶּה וְלֹא־יֵרָאוּ פָנַי רֵיקָם: שֵׁשֶׁת יָמִים תַּעֲבֹד וּבַיּוֹם הַשְּׁבִיעִי תִּשְׁבֹּת בֶּחָרִישׁ וּבַקָּצִיר תִּשְׁבֹּת: וְחַג שָׁבֻעֹת תַּעֲשֶׂה לְךָ בִּכּוּרֵי קְצִיר חִטִּים וְחַג הָאָסִיף תְּקוּפַת הַשָּׁנָה: שָׁלֹשׁ פְּעָמִים בַּשָּׁנָה יֵרָאֶה כָּל־זְכוּרְךָ אֶת־פְּנֵי הָאָדֹן | יהוה אֱלֹהֵי יִשְׂרָאֵל: כִּי־אוֹרִישׁ גּוֹיִם מִפָּנֶיךָ וְהִרְחַבְתִּי אֶת־גְּבֻלֶךָ וְלֹא־יַחְמֹד אִישׁ אֶת־אַרְצְךָ בַּעֲלֹתְךָ לֵרָאוֹת אֶת־פְּנֵי יהוה אֱלֹהֶיךָ שָׁלֹשׁ פְּעָמִים בַּשָּׁנָה: לֹא־תִשְׁחַט עַל־חָמֵץ דַּם־זִבְחִי וְלֹא־יָלִין לַבֹּקֶר זֶבַח חַג הַפָּסַח: רֵאשִׁית בִּכּוּרֵי אַדְמָתְךָ תָּבִיא בֵּית יהוה אֱלֹהֶיךָ לֹא־תְבַשֵּׁל גְּדִי בַּחֲלֵב אִמּוֹ:

The reading for the fourth *oleh* (רביעי) is *Numbers* 28:19-25, see page 959.

חול המועד פסח — יום רביעי
CHOL HAMOED PESACH — FOURTH DAY

(*Numbers* 9:1-14)

וַיְדַבֵּר יהוה אֶל־מֹשֶׁה בְמִדְבַּר־סִינַי בַּשָּׁנָה הַשֵּׁנִית לְצֵאתָם מֵאֶרֶץ מִצְרַיִם בַּחֹדֶשׁ הָרִאשׁוֹן לֵאמֹר: וְיַעֲשׂוּ בְנֵי־יִשְׂרָאֵל אֶת־הַפָּסַח בְּמוֹעֲדוֹ: בְּאַרְבָּעָה עָשָׂר־יוֹם בַּחֹדֶשׁ הַזֶּה בֵּין הָעַרְבַּיִם תַּעֲשׂוּ אֹתוֹ בְּמֹעֲדוֹ כְּכָל־חֻקֹּתָיו וּכְכָל־מִשְׁפָּטָיו תַּעֲשׂוּ אֹתוֹ: וַיְדַבֵּר מֹשֶׁה אֶל־בְּנֵי יִשְׂרָאֵל לַעֲשֹׂת הַפָּסַח: וַיַּעֲשׂוּ אֶת־הַפֶּסַח בָּרִאשׁוֹן בְּאַרְבָּעָה עָשָׂר יוֹם לַחֹדֶשׁ בֵּין הָעַרְבַּיִם בְּמִדְבַּר סִינָי כְּכֹל אֲשֶׁר צִוָּה יהוה אֶת־מֹשֶׁה כֵּן עָשׂוּ בְּנֵי יִשְׂרָאֵל:

לוי וַיְהִי אֲנָשִׁים אֲשֶׁר הָיוּ טְמֵאִים לְנֶפֶשׁ אָדָם וְלֹא־יָכְלוּ לַעֲשֹׂת־הַפֶּסַח בַּיּוֹם הַהוּא וַיִּקְרְבוּ לִפְנֵי מֹשֶׁה וְלִפְנֵי אַהֲרֹן בַּיּוֹם הַהוּא: וַיֹּאמְרוּ הָאֲנָשִׁים הָהֵמָּה אֵלָיו אֲנַחְנוּ טְמֵאִים לְנֶפֶשׁ אָדָם לָמָּה נִגָּרַע לְבִלְתִּי הַקְרִב אֶת־קָרְבַּן יהוה בְּמֹעֲדוֹ בְּתוֹךְ בְּנֵי יִשְׂרָאֵל: וַיֹּאמֶר אֲלֵהֶם מֹשֶׁה עִמְדוּ וְאֶשְׁמְעָה מַה־יְצַוֶּה יהוה לָכֶם:

ישראל וַיְדַבֵּר יהוה אֶל־מֹשֶׁה לֵּאמֹר: דַּבֵּר אֶל־בְּנֵי יִשְׂרָאֵל לֵאמֹר אִישׁ אִישׁ כִּי־יִהְיֶה טָמֵא | לָנֶפֶשׁ אוֹ בְדֶרֶךְ רְחֹקָה לָכֶם אוֹ לְדֹרֹתֵיכֶם וְעָשָׂה פֶסַח לַיהוה: בַּחֹדֶשׁ הַשֵּׁנִי בְּאַרְבָּעָה עָשָׂר יוֹם בֵּין הָעַרְבַּיִם יַעֲשׂוּ אֹתוֹ עַל־מַצּוֹת וּמְרֹרִים יֹאכְלֻהוּ: לֹא־יַשְׁאִירוּ מִמֶּנּוּ עַד־בֹּקֶר וְעֶצֶם לֹא יִשְׁבְּרוּ־בוֹ כְּכָל־חֻקַּת הַפֶּסַח יַעֲשׂוּ אֹתוֹ: וְהָאִישׁ אֲשֶׁר־הוּא טָהוֹר וּבְדֶרֶךְ לֹא־הָיָה וְחָדַל לַעֲשׂוֹת הַפֶּסַח וְנִכְרְתָה הַנֶּפֶשׁ הַהִוא מֵעַמֶּיהָ כִּי | קָרְבַּן יהוה לֹא הִקְרִיב בְּמֹעֲדוֹ חֶטְאוֹ יִשָּׂא הָאִישׁ הַהוּא: וְכִי־יָגוּר אִתְּכֶם גֵּר וְעָשָׂה פֶסַח לַיהוה כְּחֻקַּת הַפֶּסַח וּכְמִשְׁפָּטוֹ כֵּן יַעֲשֶׂה חֻקָּה אַחַת יִהְיֶה לָכֶם וְלַגֵּר וּלְאֶזְרַח הָאָרֶץ:

The reading for the fourth *oleh* (רביעי) is *Numbers* 28:19-25, see page 959.

שבת חול המועד — פסח וסוכות

SABBATH OF CHOL HAMOED — PESACH AND SUCCOS

(*Exodus* 33:12 — 34:26)

וַיֹּאמֶר מֹשֶׁה אֶל־יהוה רְאֵה אַתָּה אֹמֵר אֵלַי הַעַל אֶת־הָעָם הַזֶּה וְאַתָּה לֹא הוֹדַעְתַּנִי אֵת אֲשֶׁר־תִּשְׁלַח עִמִּי וְאַתָּה אָמַרְתָּ יְדַעְתִּיךָ בְשֵׁם וְגַם־מָצָאתָ חֵן בְּעֵינָי: וְעַתָּה אִם־נָא מָצָאתִי חֵן בְּעֵינֶיךָ הוֹדִעֵנִי נָא אֶת־דְּרָכֶךָ וְאֵדָעֲךָ לְמַעַן אֶמְצָא־חֵן בְּעֵינֶיךָ וּרְאֵה כִּי עַמְּךָ הַגּוֹי הַזֶּה: וַיֹּאמַר פָּנַי יֵלֵכוּ וַהֲנִחֹתִי לָךְ: וַיֹּאמֶר אֵלָיו אִם־אֵין פָּנֶיךָ הֹלְכִים אַל־תַּעֲלֵנוּ מִזֶּה: וּבַמֶּה | יִוָּדַע אֵפוֹא כִּי־מָצָאתִי חֵן בְּעֵינֶיךָ אֲנִי וְעַמֶּךָ הֲלוֹא בְּלֶכְתְּךָ עִמָּנוּ וְנִפְלֵינוּ אֲנִי וְעַמְּךָ מִכָּל־הָעָם אֲשֶׁר עַל־פְּנֵי הָאֲדָמָה:

שני וַיֹּאמֶר יהוה אֶל־מֹשֶׁה גַּם אֶת־הַדָּבָר הַזֶּה אֲשֶׁר דִּבַּרְתָּ אֶעֱשֶׂה כִּי־מָצָאתָ חֵן בְּעֵינַי וָאֵדָעֲךָ בְּשֵׁם: וַיֹּאמַר הַרְאֵנִי נָא אֶת־כְּבֹדֶךָ: וַיֹּאמֶר אֲנִי אַעֲבִיר כָּל־טוּבִי עַל־פָּנֶיךָ וְקָרָאתִי בְשֵׁם יהוה לְפָנֶיךָ וְחַנֹּתִי אֶת־אֲשֶׁר אָחֹן וְרִחַמְתִּי אֶת־אֲשֶׁר אֲרַחֵם:

שלישי וַיֹּאמֶר לֹא תוּכַל לִרְאֹת אֶת־פָּנָי כִּי לֹא־יִרְאַנִי הָאָדָם וָחָי: וַיֹּאמֶר יהוה הִנֵּה מָקוֹם אִתִּי וְנִצַּבְתָּ עַל־הַצּוּר: וְהָיָה בַּעֲבֹר כְּבֹדִי וְשַׂמְתִּיךָ בְּנִקְרַת הַצּוּר וְשַׂכֹּתִי כַפִּי עָלֶיךָ עַד־עָבְרִי: וַהֲסִרֹתִי אֶת־כַּפִּי וְרָאִיתָ אֶת־אֲחֹרָי וּפָנַי לֹא יֵרָאוּ:

רביעי וַיֹּאמֶר יהוה אֶל־מֹשֶׁה פְּסָל־לְךָ שְׁנֵי־לֻחֹת אֲבָנִים כָּרִאשֹׁנִים וְכָתַבְתִּי עַל־הַלֻּחֹת אֶת־הַדְּבָרִים אֲשֶׁר הָיוּ עַל־הַלֻּחֹת הָרִאשֹׁנִים אֲשֶׁר שִׁבַּרְתָּ: וֶהְיֵה נָכוֹן לַבֹּקֶר וְעָלִיתָ בַבֹּקֶר אֶל־הַר סִינַי וְנִצַּבְתָּ לִי שָׁם עַל־רֹאשׁ הָהָר: וְאִישׁ לֹא־יַעֲלֶה עִמָּךְ וְגַם־אִישׁ אַל־יֵרָא בְּכָל־הָהָר גַּם־הַצֹּאן וְהַבָּקָר אַל־יִרְעוּ אֶל־מוּל הָהָר הַהוּא:

חמישי וַיִּפְסֹל שְׁנֵי־לֻחֹת אֲבָנִים כָּרִאשֹׁנִים וַיַּשְׁכֵּם מֹשֶׁה בַבֹּקֶר וַיַּעַל אֶל־הַר סִינַי כַּאֲשֶׁר צִוָּה יהוה אֹתוֹ וַיִּקַּח בְּיָדוֹ שְׁנֵי לֻחֹת אֲבָנִים: וַיֵּרֶד יהוה בֶּעָנָן וַיִּתְיַצֵּב עִמּוֹ שָׁם וַיִּקְרָא בְשֵׁם יהוה: וַיַּעֲבֹר יהוה | עַל־פָּנָיו וַיִּקְרָא יהוה | יהוה אֵל רַחוּם וְחַנּוּן אֶרֶךְ אַפַּיִם וְרַב־חֶסֶד וֶאֱמֶת: נֹצֵר חֶסֶד לָאֲלָפִים נֹשֵׂא עָוֺן וָפֶשַׁע וְחַטָּאָה וְנַקֵּה לֹא יְנַקֶּה פֹּקֵד | עֲוֺן אָבוֹת עַל־בָּנִים וְעַל־בְּנֵי בָנִים עַל־שִׁלֵּשִׁים וְעַל־רִבֵּעִים: וַיְמַהֵר מֹשֶׁה וַיִּקֹּד אַרְצָה וַיִּשְׁתָּחוּ: וַיֹּאמֶר אִם־נָא מָצָאתִי חֵן בְּעֵינֶיךָ אֲדֹנָי יֵלֶךְ־נָא אֲדֹנָי בְּקִרְבֵּנוּ כִּי עַם־קְשֵׁה־עֹרֶף הוּא וְסָלַחְתָּ לַעֲוֺנֵנוּ וּלְחַטָּאתֵנוּ וּנְחַלְתָּנוּ: וַיֹּאמֶר הִנֵּה אָנֹכִי כֹּרֵת בְּרִית נֶגֶד כָּל־עַמְּךָ אֶעֱשֶׂה נִפְלָאֹת אֲשֶׁר לֹא־נִבְרְאוּ בְכָל־הָאָרֶץ וּבְכָל־הַגּוֹיִם וְרָאָה כָל־הָעָם אֲשֶׁר־אַתָּה בְקִרְבּוֹ אֶת־מַעֲשֵׂה יהוה כִּי־נוֹרָא הוּא אֲשֶׁר אֲנִי עֹשֶׂה עִמָּךְ:

ששי שְׁמָר־לְךָ אֵת אֲשֶׁר אָנֹכִי מְצַוְּךָ הַיּוֹם הִנְנִי גֹרֵשׁ מִפָּנֶיךָ אֶת־הָאֱמֹרִי וְהַכְּנַעֲנִי וְהַחִתִּי וְהַפְּרִזִּי וְהַחִוִּי וְהַיְבוּסִי: הִשָּׁמֶר לְךָ פֶּן־תִּכְרֹת בְּרִית לְיוֹשֵׁב הָאָרֶץ אֲשֶׁר אַתָּה בָּא עָלֶיהָ פֶּן־יִהְיֶה לְמוֹקֵשׁ בְּקִרְבֶּךָ: כִּי אֶת־מִזְבְּחֹתָם תִּתֹּצוּן וְאֶת־מַצֵּבֹתָם תְּשַׁבֵּרוּן וְאֶת־אֲשֵׁרָיו תִּכְרֹתוּן: כִּי לֹא תִשְׁתַּחֲוֶה לְאֵל אַחֵר כִּי יהוה קַנָּא שְׁמוֹ אֵל קַנָּא הוּא: פֶּן־תִּכְרֹת בְּרִית לְיוֹשֵׁב הָאָרֶץ וְזָנוּ | אַחֲרֵי אֱלֹהֵיהֶם וְזָבְחוּ לֵאלֹהֵיהֶם וְקָרָא לְךָ וְאָכַלְתָּ מִזִּבְחוֹ: וְלָקַחְתָּ מִבְּנֹתָיו לְבָנֶיךָ וְזָנוּ בְנֹתָיו אַחֲרֵי אֱלֹהֵיהֶן וְהִזְנוּ אֶת־בָּנֶיךָ אַחֲרֵי אֱלֹהֵיהֶן: אֱלֹהֵי מַסֵּכָה לֹא תַעֲשֶׂה־לָּךְ:

שביעי אֶת־חַג הַמַּצּוֹת תִּשְׁמֹר שִׁבְעַת יָמִים תֹּאכַל מַצּוֹת אֲשֶׁר צִוִּיתִךָ לְמוֹעֵד חֹדֶשׁ הָאָבִיב כִּי בְּחֹדֶשׁ הָאָבִיב יָצָאתָ מִמִּצְרָיִם: כָּל־פֶּטֶר רֶחֶם לִי וְכָל־מִקְנְךָ תִּזָּכָר פֶּטֶר שׁוֹר וָשֶׂה: וּפֶטֶר חֲמוֹר תִּפְדֶּה בְשֶׂה וְאִם־לֹא תִפְדֶּה וַעֲרַפְתּוֹ כֹּל בְּכוֹר בָּנֶיךָ תִּפְדֶּה וְלֹא־יֵרָאוּ פָנַי רֵיקָם: שֵׁשֶׁת יָמִים תַּעֲבֹד וּבַיּוֹם הַשְּׁבִיעִי תִּשְׁבֹּת בֶּחָרִישׁ וּבַקָּצִיר תִּשְׁבֹּת: וְחַג שָׁבֻעֹת תַּעֲשֶׂה לְךָ בִּכּוּרֵי קְצִיר חִטִּים וְחַג הָאָסִיף תְּקוּפַת הַשָּׁנָה: שָׁלֹשׁ פְּעָמִים בַּשָּׁנָה יֵרָאֶה כָּל־זְכוּרְךָ אֶת־פְּנֵי הָאָדֹן | יהוה אֱלֹהֵי יִשְׂרָאֵל: כִּי־אוֹרִישׁ גּוֹיִם מִפָּנֶיךָ וְהִרְחַבְתִּי אֶת־גְּבֻלֶךָ וְלֹא־יַחְמֹד אִישׁ אֶת־אַרְצְךָ בַּעֲלֹתְךָ לֵרָאוֹת אֶת־פְּנֵי יהוה אֱלֹהֶיךָ שָׁלֹשׁ פְּעָמִים בַּשָּׁנָה: לֹא־תִשְׁחַט עַל־חָמֵץ דַּם־זִבְחִי וְלֹא־יָלִין לַבֹּקֶר זֶבַח חַג הַפָּסַח: רֵאשִׁית בִּכּוּרֵי אַדְמָתְךָ תָּבִיא בֵּית יהוה אֱלֹהֶיךָ לֹא־תְבַשֵּׁל גְּדִי בַּחֲלֵב אִמּוֹ:

Maftir for Chol HaMoed Pesach is *Numbers* 28:19-25, page 959; for Chol HaMoed Succos, page 973.

הפטרה — שבת חול המועד פסח

HAFTARAH — SABBATH OF CHOL HAMOED PESACH

(Ezekiel 37:1-14)

הָיְתָה עָלַי יַד־יהוה וַיּוֹצִאֵנִי בְרוּחַ יהוה וַיְנִיחֵנִי בְּתוֹךְ הַבִּקְעָה וְהִיא מְלֵאָה עֲצָמוֹת׃ וְהֶעֱבִירַנִי עֲלֵיהֶם סָבִיב | סָבִיב וְהִנֵּה רַבּוֹת מְאֹד עַל־פְּנֵי הַבִּקְעָה וְהִנֵּה יְבֵשׁוֹת מְאֹד׃ וַיֹּאמֶר אֵלַי בֶּן־אָדָם הֲתִחְיֶינָה הָעֲצָמוֹת הָאֵלֶּה וָאֹמַר אֲדֹנָי יֱהוִה אַתָּה יָדָעְתָּ׃ וַיֹּאמֶר אֵלַי הִנָּבֵא עַל־הָעֲצָמוֹת הָאֵלֶּה וְאָמַרְתָּ אֲלֵיהֶם הָעֲצָמוֹת הַיְבֵשׁוֹת שִׁמְעוּ דְּבַר־יהוה׃ כֹּה אָמַר אֲדֹנָי יֱהוִה לָעֲצָמוֹת הָאֵלֶּה הִנֵּה אֲנִי מֵבִיא בָכֶם רוּחַ וִחְיִיתֶם׃ וְנָתַתִּי עֲלֵיכֶם גִּידִים וְהַעֲלֵתִי עֲלֵיכֶם בָּשָׂר וְקָרַמְתִּי עֲלֵיכֶם עוֹר וְנָתַתִּי בָכֶם רוּחַ וִחְיִיתֶם וִידַעְתֶּם כִּי־אֲנִי יהוה׃ וְנִבֵּאתִי כַּאֲשֶׁר צֻוֵּיתִי וַיְהִי־קוֹל כְּהִנָּבְאִי וְהִנֵּה־רַעַשׁ וַתִּקְרְבוּ עֲצָמוֹת עֶצֶם אֶל־עַצְמוֹ׃ וְרָאִיתִי וְהִנֵּה־עֲלֵיהֶם גִּדִים וּבָשָׂר עָלָה וַיִּקְרַם עֲלֵיהֶם עוֹר מִלְמָעְלָה וְרוּחַ אֵין בָּהֶם׃ וַיֹּאמֶר אֵלַי הִנָּבֵא אֶל־הָרוּחַ הִנָּבֵא בֶן־אָדָם וְאָמַרְתָּ אֶל־הָרוּחַ כֹּה־אָמַר | אֲדֹנָי יֱהוִה מֵאַרְבַּע רוּחוֹת בֹּאִי הָרוּחַ וּפְחִי בַּהֲרוּגִים הָאֵלֶּה וְיִחְיוּ׃ וְהִנַּבֵּאתִי כַּאֲשֶׁר צִוָּנִי וַתָּבוֹא בָהֶם הָרוּחַ וַיִּחְיוּ וַיַּעַמְדוּ עַל־רַגְלֵיהֶם חַיִל גָּדוֹל מְאֹד מְאֹד׃ וַיֹּאמֶר אֵלַי בֶּן־אָדָם הָעֲצָמוֹת הָאֵלֶּה כָּל־בֵּית יִשְׂרָאֵל הֵמָּה הִנֵּה אֹמְרִים יָבְשׁוּ עַצְמוֹתֵינוּ וְאָבְדָה תִקְוָתֵנוּ נִגְזַרְנוּ לָנוּ׃ לָכֵן הִנָּבֵא וְאָמַרְתָּ אֲלֵיהֶם כֹּה־אָמַר אֲדֹנָי יֱהוִה הִנֵּה אֲנִי פֹתֵחַ אֶת־קִבְרוֹתֵיכֶם וְהַעֲלֵיתִי אֶתְכֶם מִקִּבְרוֹתֵיכֶם עַמִּי וְהֵבֵאתִי אֶתְכֶם אֶל־אַדְמַת יִשְׂרָאֵל׃ וִידַעְתֶּם כִּי־אֲנִי יהוה בְּפִתְחִי אֶת־קִבְרוֹתֵיכֶם וּבְהַעֲלוֹתִי אֶתְכֶם מִקִּבְרוֹתֵיכֶם עַמִּי׃ וְנָתַתִּי רוּחִי בָכֶם וִחְיִיתֶם וְהִנַּחְתִּי אֶתְכֶם עַל־אַדְמַתְכֶם וִידַעְתֶּם כִּי אֲנִי יהוה דִּבַּרְתִּי וְעָשִׂיתִי נְאֻם־יהוה׃

פסח — יום שביעי

PESACH — SEVENTH DAY

(Exodus 13:17 — 15:26)

וַיְהִי בְּשַׁלַּח פַּרְעֹה אֶת־הָעָם וְלֹא־נָחָם אֱלֹהִים דֶּרֶךְ אֶרֶץ פְּלִשְׁתִּים כִּי קָרוֹב הוּא כִּי | אָמַר אֱלֹהִים פֶּן־יִנָּחֵם הָעָם בִּרְאֹתָם מִלְחָמָה וְשָׁבוּ מִצְרָיְמָה׃ וַיַּסֵּב אֱלֹהִים | אֶת־הָעָם דֶּרֶךְ הַמִּדְבָּר יַם־סוּף וַחֲמֻשִׁים עָלוּ בְנֵי־יִשְׂרָאֵל מֵאֶרֶץ מִצְרָיִם׃ וַיִּקַּח מֹשֶׁה אֶת־עַצְמוֹת יוֹסֵף עִמּוֹ כִּי הַשְׁבֵּעַ הִשְׁבִּיעַ אֶת־בְּנֵי יִשְׂרָאֵל לֵאמֹר פָּקֹד יִפְקֹד אֱלֹהִים אֶתְכֶם וְהַעֲלִיתֶם אֶת־עַצְמֹתַי מִזֶּה אִתְּכֶם׃

(בשבת שני) וַיִּסְעוּ מִסֻּכֹּת וַיַּחֲנוּ בְאֵתָם בִּקְצֵה הַמִּדְבָּר׃ וַיהוה הֹלֵךְ לִפְנֵיהֶם יוֹמָם בְּעַמּוּד עָנָן לַנְחֹתָם הַדֶּרֶךְ וְלַיְלָה בְּעַמּוּד אֵשׁ לְהָאִיר לָהֶם לָלֶכֶת יוֹמָם וָלָיְלָה׃ לֹא־יָמִישׁ עַמּוּד הֶעָנָן יוֹמָם וְעַמּוּד הָאֵשׁ לָיְלָה לִפְנֵי הָעָם׃

שני (בשבת שלישי) וַיְדַבֵּר יהוה אֶל־מֹשֶׁה לֵּאמֹר׃ דַּבֵּר אֶל־בְּנֵי יִשְׂרָאֵל וְיָשֻׁבוּ וְיַחֲנוּ לִפְנֵי פִּי הַחִירֹת בֵּין מִגְדֹּל וּבֵין הַיָּם לִפְנֵי בַּעַל צְפֹן נִכְחוֹ תַחֲנוּ עַל־הַיָּם׃ וְאָמַר פַּרְעֹה לִבְנֵי יִשְׂרָאֵל נְבֻכִים הֵם בָּאָרֶץ סָגַר עֲלֵיהֶם הַמִּדְבָּר׃ וְחִזַּקְתִּי אֶת־לֵב־פַּרְעֹה וְרָדַף אַחֲרֵיהֶם וְאִכָּבְדָה בְּפַרְעֹה וּבְכָל־חֵילוֹ וְיָדְעוּ מִצְרַיִם כִּי־אֲנִי יהוה וַיַּעֲשׂוּ־כֵן׃

(בשבת רביעי) וַיֻּגַּד לְמֶלֶךְ מִצְרַיִם כִּי בָרַח הָעָם וַיֵּהָפֵךְ לְבַב פַּרְעֹה וַעֲבָדָיו אֶל־הָעָם וַיֹּאמְרוּ מַה־זֹּאת עָשִׂינוּ כִּי־שִׁלַּחְנוּ אֶת־יִשְׂרָאֵל מֵעָבְדֵנוּ׃ וַיֶּאְסֹר אֶת־רִכְבּוֹ וְאֶת־עַמּוֹ לָקַח עִמּוֹ׃ וַיִּקַּח שֵׁשׁ־מֵאוֹת רֶכֶב בָּחוּר וְכֹל רֶכֶב מִצְרָיִם וְשָׁלִשִׁם עַל־כֻּלּוֹ׃ וַיְחַזֵּק יהוה אֶת־לֵב פַּרְעֹה מֶלֶךְ מִצְרַיִם וַיִּרְדֹּף אַחֲרֵי בְּנֵי יִשְׂרָאֵל וּבְנֵי יִשְׂרָאֵל יֹצְאִים בְּיָד רָמָה׃

שלישי (בשבת חמישי) וַיִּרְדְּפוּ מִצְרַיִם אַחֲרֵיהֶם וַיַּשִּׂיגוּ אוֹתָם חֹנִים עַל־הַיָּם כָּל־סוּס רֶכֶב פַּרְעֹה וּפָרָשָׁיו וְחֵילוֹ עַל־פִּי הַחִירֹת לִפְנֵי בַּעַל צְפֹן׃ וּפַרְעֹה הִקְרִיב וַיִּשְׂאוּ בְנֵי־יִשְׂרָאֵל אֶת־עֵינֵיהֶם וְהִנֵּה מִצְרַיִם | נֹסֵעַ אַחֲרֵיהֶם וַיִּירְאוּ מְאֹד וַיִּצְעֲקוּ בְנֵי־יִשְׂרָאֵל אֶל־יהוה׃ וַיֹּאמְרוּ אֶל־מֹשֶׁה הֲמִבְּלִי אֵין־קְבָרִים בְּמִצְרַיִם לְקַחְתָּנוּ לָמוּת בַּמִּדְבָּר מַה־זֹּאת עָשִׂיתָ לָּנוּ לְהוֹצִיאָנוּ מִמִּצְרָיִם׃ הֲלֹא־זֶה הַדָּבָר אֲשֶׁר דִּבַּרְנוּ אֵלֶיךָ בְמִצְרַיִם לֵאמֹר חֲדַל מִמֶּנּוּ וְנַעַבְדָה אֶת־מִצְרָיִם כִּי טוֹב לָנוּ עֲבֹד אֶת־מִצְרַיִם מִמֻּתֵנוּ בַּמִּדְבָּר׃ וַיֹּאמֶר מֹשֶׁה אֶל־הָעָם

אַל־תִּירָאוּ הִתְיַצְּבוּ וּרְאוּ אֶת־יְשׁוּעַת יהוה אֲשֶׁר־יַעֲשֶׂה לָכֶם הַיּוֹם כִּי אֲשֶׁר רְאִיתֶם אֶת־מִצְרַיִם הַיּוֹם לֹא תֹסִפוּ לִרְאֹתָם עוֹד עַד־עוֹלָם׃ יהוה יִלָּחֵם לָכֶם וְאַתֶּם תַּחֲרִשׁוּן׃

רביעי (בשבת ששי) וַיֹּאמֶר יהוה אֶל־מֹשֶׁה מַה־תִּצְעַק אֵלָי דַּבֵּר אֶל־בְּנֵי־יִשְׂרָאֵל וְיִסָּעוּ׃ וְאַתָּה הָרֵם אֶת־מַטְּךָ וּנְטֵה אֶת־יָדְךָ עַל־הַיָּם וּבְקָעֵהוּ וְיָבֹאוּ בְנֵי־יִשְׂרָאֵל בְּתוֹךְ הַיָּם בַּיַּבָּשָׁה׃ וַאֲנִי הִנְנִי מְחַזֵּק אֶת־לֵב מִצְרַיִם וְיָבֹאוּ אַחֲרֵיהֶם וְאִכָּבְדָה בְּפַרְעֹה וּבְכָל־חֵילוֹ בְּרִכְבּוֹ וּבְפָרָשָׁיו׃ וְיָדְעוּ מִצְרַיִם כִּי־אֲנִי יהוה בְּהִכָּבְדִי בְּפַרְעֹה בְּרִכְבּוֹ וּבְפָרָשָׁיו׃ וַיִּסַּע מַלְאַךְ הָאֱלֹהִים הַהֹלֵךְ לִפְנֵי מַחֲנֵה יִשְׂרָאֵל וַיֵּלֶךְ מֵאַחֲרֵיהֶם וַיִּסַּע עַמּוּד הֶעָנָן מִפְּנֵיהֶם וַיַּעֲמֹד מֵאַחֲרֵיהֶם׃ וַיָּבֹא בֵּין ׀ מַחֲנֵה מִצְרַיִם וּבֵין מַחֲנֵה יִשְׂרָאֵל וַיְהִי הֶעָנָן וְהַחֹשֶׁךְ וַיָּאֶר אֶת־הַלָּיְלָה וְלֹא־קָרַב זֶה אֶל־זֶה כָּל־הַלָּיְלָה׃ וַיֵּט מֹשֶׁה אֶת־יָדוֹ עַל־הַיָּם וַיּוֹלֶךְ יהוה ׀ אֶת־הַיָּם בְּרוּחַ קָדִים עַזָּה כָּל־הַלַּיְלָה וַיָּשֶׂם אֶת־הַיָּם לֶחָרָבָה וַיִּבָּקְעוּ הַמָּיִם׃ וַיָּבֹאוּ בְנֵי־יִשְׂרָאֵל בְּתוֹךְ הַיָּם בַּיַּבָּשָׁה וְהַמַּיִם לָהֶם חוֹמָה מִימִינָם וּמִשְּׂמֹאלָם׃ וַיִּרְדְּפוּ מִצְרַיִם וַיָּבֹאוּ אַחֲרֵיהֶם כֹּל סוּס פַּרְעֹה רִכְבּוֹ וּפָרָשָׁיו אֶל־תּוֹךְ הַיָּם׃ וַיְהִי בְּאַשְׁמֹרֶת הַבֹּקֶר וַיַּשְׁקֵף יהוה אֶל־מַחֲנֵה מִצְרַיִם בְּעַמּוּד אֵשׁ וְעָנָן וַיָּהָם אֵת מַחֲנֵה מִצְרָיִם׃ וַיָּסַר אֵת אֹפַן מַרְכְּבֹתָיו וַיְנַהֲגֵהוּ בִּכְבֵדֻת וַיֹּאמֶר מִצְרַיִם אָנוּסָה מִפְּנֵי יִשְׂרָאֵל כִּי יהוה נִלְחָם לָהֶם בְּמִצְרָיִם׃

חמישי (בשבת שביעי) וַיֹּאמֶר יהוה אֶל־מֹשֶׁה נְטֵה אֶת־יָדְךָ עַל־הַיָּם וְיָשֻׁבוּ הַמַּיִם עַל־מִצְרַיִם עַל־רִכְבּוֹ וְעַל־פָּרָשָׁיו׃ וַיֵּט מֹשֶׁה אֶת־יָדוֹ עַל־הַיָּם וַיָּשָׁב הַיָּם לִפְנוֹת בֹּקֶר לְאֵיתָנוֹ וּמִצְרַיִם נָסִים לִקְרָאתוֹ וַיְנַעֵר יהוה אֶת־מִצְרַיִם בְּתוֹךְ הַיָּם׃ וַיָּשֻׁבוּ הַמַּיִם וַיְכַסּוּ אֶת־הָרֶכֶב וְאֶת־הַפָּרָשִׁים לְכֹל חֵיל פַּרְעֹה הַבָּאִים אַחֲרֵיהֶם בַּיָּם לֹא־נִשְׁאַר בָּהֶם עַד־אֶחָד׃ וּבְנֵי יִשְׂרָאֵל הָלְכוּ בַיַּבָּשָׁה בְּתוֹךְ הַיָּם וְהַמַּיִם לָהֶם חֹמָה מִימִינָם וּמִשְּׂמֹאלָם׃ וַיּוֹשַׁע יהוה בַּיּוֹם הַהוּא אֶת־יִשְׂרָאֵל מִיַּד מִצְרָיִם וַיַּרְא יִשְׂרָאֵל אֶת־מִצְרַיִם מֵת עַל־שְׂפַת הַיָּם׃ וַיַּרְא יִשְׂרָאֵל אֶת־הַיָּד הַגְּדֹלָה אֲשֶׁר עָשָׂה יהוה בְּמִצְרַיִם וַיִּירְאוּ הָעָם אֶת־יהוה וַיַּאֲמִינוּ בַּיהוה וּבְמֹשֶׁה עַבְדּוֹ׃ אָז יָשִׁיר־מֹשֶׁה וּבְנֵי יִשְׂרָאֵל אֶת־הַשִּׁירָה הַזֹּאת לַיהוה וַיֹּאמְרוּ לֵאמֹר אָשִׁירָה לַּיהוה כִּי־גָאֹה גָּאָה סוּס וְרֹכְבוֹ רָמָה בַיָּם׃ עָזִּי וְזִמְרָת יָהּ וַיְהִי־לִי לִישׁוּעָה זֶה אֵלִי וְאַנְוֵהוּ אֱלֹהֵי אָבִי וַאֲרֹמְמֶנְהוּ׃ יהוה אִישׁ מִלְחָמָה יהוה שְׁמוֹ׃ מַרְכְּבֹת פַּרְעֹה וְחֵילוֹ יָרָה בַיָּם וּמִבְחַר שָׁלִשָׁיו טֻבְּעוּ בְיַם־סוּף׃ תְּהֹמֹת יְכַסְיֻמוּ יָרְדוּ בִמְצוֹלֹת כְּמוֹ־אָבֶן׃ יְמִינְךָ יהוה נֶאְדָּרִי בַּכֹּחַ יְמִינְךָ יהוה תִּרְעַץ אוֹיֵב׃ וּבְרֹב גְּאוֹנְךָ תַּהֲרֹס קָמֶיךָ תְּשַׁלַּח חֲרֹנְךָ יֹאכְלֵמוֹ כַּקַּשׁ׃ וּבְרוּחַ אַפֶּיךָ נֶעֶרְמוּ מַיִם נִצְּבוּ כְמוֹ־נֵד נֹזְלִים קָפְאוּ תְהֹמֹת בְּלֶב־יָם׃ אָמַר אוֹיֵב אֶרְדֹּף אַשִּׂיג אֲחַלֵּק שָׁלָל תִּמְלָאֵמוֹ נַפְשִׁי אָרִיק חַרְבִּי תּוֹרִישֵׁמוֹ יָדִי׃ נָשַׁפְתָּ בְרוּחֲךָ כִּסָּמוֹ יָם צָלְלוּ כַּעוֹפֶרֶת בְּמַיִם אַדִּירִים׃ מִי־כָמֹכָה בָּאֵלִם יהוה מִי כָּמֹכָה נֶאְדָּר בַּקֹּדֶשׁ נוֹרָא תְהִלֹּת עֹשֵׂה פֶלֶא׃ נָטִיתָ יְמִינְךָ תִּבְלָעֵמוֹ אָרֶץ׃ נָחִיתָ בְחַסְדְּךָ עַם־זוּ גָּאָלְתָּ נֵהַלְתָּ בְעָזְּךָ אֶל־נְוֵה קָדְשֶׁךָ׃ שָׁמְעוּ עַמִּים יִרְגָּזוּן חִיל אָחַז יֹשְׁבֵי פְּלָשֶׁת׃ אָז נִבְהֲלוּ אַלּוּפֵי אֱדוֹם אֵילֵי מוֹאָב יֹאחֲזֵמוֹ רָעַד נָמֹגוּ כֹּל יֹשְׁבֵי כְנָעַן׃ תִּפֹּל עֲלֵיהֶם אֵימָתָה וָפַחַד בִּגְדֹל זְרוֹעֲךָ יִדְּמוּ כָּאָבֶן עַד־יַעֲבֹר עַמְּךָ יהוה עַד־יַעֲבֹר עַם־זוּ קָנִיתָ׃ תְּבִאֵמוֹ וְתִטָּעֵמוֹ בְּהַר נַחֲלָתְךָ מָכוֹן לְשִׁבְתְּךָ פָּעַלְתָּ יהוה מִקְּדָשׁ אֲדֹנָי כּוֹנְנוּ יָדֶיךָ׃ יהוה ׀ יִמְלֹךְ לְעֹלָם וָעֶד׃ כִּי בָא סוּס פַּרְעֹה בְּרִכְבּוֹ וּבְפָרָשָׁיו בַּיָּם וַיָּשֶׁב יהוה עֲלֵהֶם אֶת־מֵי הַיָּם וּבְנֵי יִשְׂרָאֵל הָלְכוּ בַיַּבָּשָׁה בְּתוֹךְ הַיָּם׃ וַתִּקַּח מִרְיָם הַנְּבִיאָה אֲחוֹת אַהֲרֹן אֶת־הַתֹּף בְּיָדָהּ וַתֵּצֶאןָ כָל־הַנָּשִׁים אַחֲרֶיהָ בְּתֻפִּים וּבִמְחֹלֹת׃ וַתַּעַן לָהֶם מִרְיָם שִׁירוּ לַיהוה כִּי־גָאֹה גָּאָה סוּס וְרֹכְבוֹ רָמָה בַיָּם׃ וַיַּסַּע מֹשֶׁה אֶת־יִשְׂרָאֵל מִיַּם־סוּף וַיֵּצְאוּ אֶל־מִדְבַּר־שׁוּר וַיֵּלְכוּ שְׁלֹשֶׁת־יָמִים בַּמִּדְבָּר וְלֹא־מָצְאוּ מָיִם׃ וַיָּבֹאוּ מָרָתָה וְלֹא יָכְלוּ לִשְׁתֹּת מַיִם מִמָּרָה כִּי מָרִים הֵם עַל־כֵּן קָרָא־שְׁמָהּ מָרָה׃ וַיִּלֹּנוּ הָעָם עַל־מֹשֶׁה לֵּאמֹר מַה־נִּשְׁתֶּה׃ וַיִּצְעַק אֶל־יהוה וַיּוֹרֵהוּ יהוה עֵץ וַיַּשְׁלֵךְ אֶל־הַמַּיִם וַיִּמְתְּקוּ הַמָּיִם שָׁם שָׂם לוֹ חֹק

וּמִשְׁפָּט וְשָׁם נִסָּהוּ: וַיֹּאמֶר אִם־שָׁמוֹעַ תִּשְׁמַע לְקוֹל | יהוה אֱלֹהֶיךָ וְהַיָּשָׁר בְּעֵינָיו תַּעֲשֶׂה וְהַאֲזַנְתָּ לְמִצְוֹתָיו וְשָׁמַרְתָּ כָּל־חֻקָּיו כָּל־הַמַּחֲלָה אֲשֶׁר־שַׂמְתִּי בְמִצְרַיִם לֹא־אָשִׂים עָלֶיךָ כִּי אֲנִי יהוה רֹפְאֶךָ:

Maftir of the seventh day of Pesach is *Numbers* 28:19-25, see page 959.

הפטרה — יום שביעי של פסח

HAFTARAH — SEVENTH DAY OF PESACH

(*II Samuel* 22:1-51)

וַיְדַבֵּר דָּוִד לַיהוה אֶת־דִּבְרֵי הַשִּׁירָה הַזֹּאת בְּיוֹם הִצִּיל יהוה אֹתוֹ מִכַּף כָּל־אֹיְבָיו וּמִכַּף שָׁאוּל: וַיֹּאמַר יהוה סַלְעִי וּמְצֻדָתִי וּמְפַלְטִי־לִי: אֱלֹהֵי צוּרִי אֶחֱסֶה־בּוֹ מָגִנִּי וְקֶרֶן יִשְׁעִי מִשְׂגַּבִּי וּמְנוּסִי מֹשִׁעִי מֵחָמָס תֹּשִׁעֵנִי: מְהֻלָּל אֶקְרָא יהוה וּמֵאֹיְבַי אִוָּשֵׁעַ: כִּי אֲפָפֻנִי מִשְׁבְּרֵי־מָוֶת נַחֲלֵי בְלִיַּעַל יְבַעֲתֻנִי: חֶבְלֵי שְׁאוֹל סַבֻּנִי קִדְּמֻנִי מֹקְשֵׁי־מָוֶת: בַּצַּר־לִי אֶקְרָא יהוה וְאֶל־אֱלֹהַי אֶקְרָא וַיִּשְׁמַע מֵהֵיכָלוֹ קוֹלִי וְשַׁוְעָתִי בְּאָזְנָיו: וַיִּתְגָּעַשׁ וַתִּרְעַשׁ הָאָרֶץ מוֹסְדוֹת הַשָּׁמַיִם יִרְגָּזוּ וַיִּתְגָּעֲשׁוּ כִּי־חָרָה לוֹ: עָלָה עָשָׁן בְּאַפּוֹ וְאֵשׁ מִפִּיו תֹּאכֵל גֶּחָלִים בָּעֲרוּ מִמֶּנּוּ: וַיֵּט שָׁמַיִם וַיֵּרַד וַעֲרָפֶל תַּחַת רַגְלָיו: וַיִּרְכַּב עַל־כְּרוּב וַיָּעֹף וַיֵּרָא עַל־כַּנְפֵי־רוּחַ: וַיָּשֶׁת חֹשֶׁךְ סְבִיבֹתָיו סֻכּוֹת חַשְׁרַת־מַיִם עָבֵי שְׁחָקִים: מִנֹּגַהּ נֶגְדּוֹ בָּעֲרוּ גַּחֲלֵי־אֵשׁ: יַרְעֵם מִן־שָׁמַיִם יהוה וְעֶלְיוֹן יִתֵּן קוֹלוֹ: וַיִּשְׁלַח חִצִּים וַיְפִיצֵם בָּרָק וַיָּהֹם: וַיֵּרָאוּ אֲפִקֵי יָם יִגָּלוּ מֹסְדוֹת תֵּבֵל בְּגַעֲרַת יהוה מִנִּשְׁמַת רוּחַ אַפּוֹ: יִשְׁלַח מִמָּרוֹם יִקָּחֵנִי יַמְשֵׁנִי מִמַּיִם רַבִּים: יַצִּילֵנִי מֵאֹיְבִי עָז מִשֹּׂנְאַי כִּי אָמְצוּ מִמֶּנִּי: יְקַדְּמֻנִי בְּיוֹם אֵידִי וַיְהִי יהוה מִשְׁעָן לִי: וַיֹּצֵא לַמֶּרְחָב אֹתִי יְחַלְּצֵנִי כִּי־חָפֵץ בִּי: יִגְמְלֵנִי יהוה כְּצִדְקָתִי כְּבֹר יָדַי יָשִׁיב לִי: כִּי שָׁמַרְתִּי דַּרְכֵי יהוה וְלֹא רָשַׁעְתִּי מֵאֱלֹהָי: כִּי כָל־מִשְׁפָּטָו לְנֶגְדִּי וְחֻקֹּתָיו לֹא־אָסוּר מִמֶּנָּה: וָאֶהְיֶה תָמִים לוֹ וָאֶשְׁתַּמְּרָה מֵעֲוֺנִי: וַיָּשֶׁב יהוה לִי כְּצִדְקָתִי כְּבֹרִי לְנֶגֶד עֵינָיו: עִם־חָסִיד תִּתְחַסָּד עִם־גִּבּוֹר תָּמִים תִּתַּמָּם: עִם־נָבָר תִּתָּבָר וְעִם־עִקֵּשׁ תִּתַּפָּל: וְאֶת־עַם עָנִי תּוֹשִׁיעַ וְעֵינֶיךָ עַל־רָמִים תַּשְׁפִּיל: כִּי־אַתָּה נֵירִי יהוה וַיהוה יַגִּיהַּ חָשְׁכִּי: כִּי בְכָה אָרוּץ גְּדוּד בֵּאלֹהַי אֲדַלֶּג־שׁוּר: הָאֵל תָּמִים דַּרְכּוֹ אִמְרַת יהוה צְרוּפָה מָגֵן הוּא לְכֹל הַחֹסִים בּוֹ: כִּי מִי־אֵל מִבַּלְעֲדֵי יהוה וּמִי צוּר מִבַּלְעֲדֵי אֱלֹהֵינוּ: הָאֵל מָעוּזִּי חָיִל וַיַּתֵּר תָּמִים דַּרְכִּי: מְשַׁוֶּה רַגְלַי כָּאַיָּלוֹת וְעַל־בָּמֹתַי יַעֲמִידֵנִי: מְלַמֵּד יָדַי לַמִּלְחָמָה וְנִחַת קֶשֶׁת־נְחוּשָׁה זְרֹעֹתָי: וַתִּתֶּן־לִי מָגֵן יִשְׁעֶךָ וַעֲנֹתְךָ תַּרְבֵּנִי: תַּרְחִיב צַעֲדִי תַּחְתֵּנִי וְלֹא מָעֲדוּ קַרְסֻלָּי: אֶרְדְּפָה אֹיְבַי וָאַשְׁמִידֵם וְלֹא אָשׁוּב עַד־כַּלּוֹתָם: וָאֲכַלֵּם וָאֶמְחָצֵם וְלֹא יְקוּמוּן וַיִּפְּלוּ תַּחַת רַגְלָי: וַתַּזְרֵנִי חַיִל לַמִּלְחָמָה תַּכְרִיעַ קָמַי תַּחְתֵּנִי: וְאֹיְבַי תַּתָּה לִּי עֹרֶף מְשַׂנְאַי וָאַצְמִיתֵם: יִשְׁעוּ וְאֵין מֹשִׁיעַ אֶל־יהוה וְלֹא עָנָם: וְאֶשְׁחָקֵם כַּעֲפַר־אָרֶץ כְּטִיט־חוּצוֹת אֲדִקֵּם אֶרְקָעֵם: וַתְּפַלְּטֵנִי מֵרִיבֵי עַמִּי תִּשְׁמְרֵנִי לְרֹאשׁ גּוֹיִם עַם לֹא־יָדַעְתִּי יַעַבְדֻנִי: בְּנֵי נֵכָר יִתְכַּחֲשׁוּ־לִי לִשְׁמוֹעַ אֹזֶן יִשָּׁמְעוּ לִי: בְּנֵי נֵכָר יִבֹּלוּ וְיַחְגְּרוּ מִמִּסְגְּרוֹתָם: חַי־יהוה וּבָרוּךְ צוּרִי וְיָרֻם אֱלֹהֵי צוּר יִשְׁעִי: הָאֵל הַנֹּתֵן נְקָמֹת לִי וּמוֹרִיד עַמִּים תַּחְתֵּנִי: וּמוֹצִיאִי מֵאֹיְבָי וּמִקָּמַי תְּרוֹמְמֵנִי מֵאִישׁ חֲמָסִים תַּצִּילֵנִי: עַל־כֵּן אוֹדְךָ יהוה בַּגּוֹיִם וּלְשִׁמְךָ אֲזַמֵּר: מִגְדּוֹל יְשׁוּעוֹת מַלְכּוֹ וְעֹשֶׂה־חֶסֶד לִמְשִׁיחוֹ לְדָוִד וּלְזַרְעוֹ עַד־עוֹלָם:

פסח — יום אחרון

(יום ב׳ של שבועות ושמיני עצרת)

PESACH — EIGHTH DAY

(Second day of Shavuos and Shemini Atzeres)

When the eighth day of Pesach or the second day of Shavuos fall on the Sabbath, the Torah reading begins עַשֵּׂר תְּעַשֵּׂר; on a weekday the reading begins כָּל הַבְּכוֹר. On Shemini Atzeres the reading begins עַשֵּׂר תְּעַשֵּׂר even if it falls on a weekday.

(*Deuteronomy* 14:22 — 16:17)

עַשֵּׂר תְּעַשֵּׂר אֵת כָּל־תְּבוּאַת זַרְעֶךָ הַיֹּצֵא הַשָּׂדֶה שָׁנָה שָׁנָה: וְאָכַלְתָּ לִפְנֵי | יהוה אֱלֹהֶיךָ בַּמָּקוֹם אֲשֶׁר־יִבְחַר לְשַׁכֵּן שְׁמוֹ שָׁם מַעְשַׂר דְּגָנְךָ תִּירֹשְׁךָ וְיִצְהָרֶךָ וּבְכֹרֹת בְּקָרְךָ וְצֹאנֶךָ לְמַעַן תִּלְמַד לְיִרְאָה אֶת־יהוה אֱלֹהֶיךָ כָּל־הַיָּמִים: וְכִי־יִרְבֶּה מִמְּךָ הַדֶּרֶךְ כִּי לֹא תוּכַל שְׂאֵתוֹ כִּי־יִרְחַק מִמְּךָ הַמָּקוֹם אֲשֶׁר יִבְחַר יהוה אֱלֹהֶיךָ לָשׂוּם שְׁמוֹ שָׁם כִּי יְבָרֶכְךָ יהוה אֱלֹהֶיךָ: וְנָתַתָּה בַּכָּסֶף וְצַרְתָּ הַכֶּסֶף בְּיָדְךָ וְהָלַכְתָּ אֶל־

הַמָּקוֹם אֲשֶׁר יִבְחַר יְהוָה אֱלֹהֶיךָ בּוֹ׃ וְנָתַתָּה הַכֶּסֶף בְּכֹל אֲשֶׁר־תְּאַוֶּה נַפְשְׁךָ בַּבָּקָר וּבַצֹּאן וּבַיַּיִן וּבַשֵּׁכָר וּבְכֹל אֲשֶׁר תִּשְׁאָלְךָ נַפְשֶׁךָ וְאָכַלְתָּ שָּׁם לִפְנֵי יְהוָה אֱלֹהֶיךָ וְשָׂמַחְתָּ אַתָּה וּבֵיתֶךָ׃ וְהַלֵּוִי אֲשֶׁר־בִּשְׁעָרֶיךָ לֹא תַעַזְבֶנּוּ כִּי אֵין לוֹ חֵלֶק וְנַחֲלָה עִמָּךְ׃ מִקְצֵה | שָׁלֹשׁ שָׁנִים תּוֹצִיא אֶת־כָּל־מַעְשַׂר תְּבוּאָתְךָ בַּשָּׁנָה הַהִוא וְהִנַּחְתָּ בִּשְׁעָרֶיךָ׃ וּבָא הַלֵּוִי כִּי אֵין־לוֹ חֵלֶק וְנַחֲלָה עִמָּךְ וְהַגֵּר וְהַיָּתוֹם וְהָאַלְמָנָה אֲשֶׁר בִּשְׁעָרֶיךָ וְאָכְלוּ וְשָׂבֵעוּ לְמַעַן יְבָרֶכְךָ יְהוָה אֱלֹהֶיךָ בְּכָל־מַעֲשֵׂה יָדְךָ אֲשֶׁר תַּעֲשֶׂה׃

(בשבת שני) מִקֵּץ שֶׁבַע־שָׁנִים תַּעֲשֶׂה שְׁמִטָּה׃ וְזֶה דְּבַר הַשְּׁמִטָּה שָׁמוֹט כָּל־בַּעַל מַשֵּׁה יָדוֹ אֲשֶׁר יַשֶּׁה בְּרֵעֵהוּ לֹא־יִגֹּשׂ אֶת־רֵעֵהוּ וְאֶת־אָחִיו כִּי־קָרָא שְׁמִטָּה לַיהוָה׃ אֶת־הַנָּכְרִי תִּגֹּשׂ וַאֲשֶׁר יִהְיֶה לְךָ אֶת־אָחִיךָ תַּשְׁמֵט יָדֶךָ׃ אֶפֶס כִּי לֹא יִהְיֶה־בְּךָ אֶבְיוֹן כִּי־בָרֵךְ יְבָרֶכְךָ יְהוָה בָּאָרֶץ אֲשֶׁר יְהוָה אֱלֹהֶיךָ נֹתֵן־לְךָ נַחֲלָה לְרִשְׁתָּהּ׃ רַק אִם־שָׁמוֹעַ תִּשְׁמַע בְּקוֹל יְהוָה אֱלֹהֶיךָ לִשְׁמֹר לַעֲשׂוֹת אֶת־כָּל־הַמִּצְוָה הַזֹּאת אֲשֶׁר אָנֹכִי מְצַוְּךָ הַיּוֹם׃ כִּי־יְהוָה אֱלֹהֶיךָ בֵּרַכְךָ כַּאֲשֶׁר דִּבֶּר־לָךְ וְהַעֲבַטְתָּ גּוֹיִם רַבִּים וְאַתָּה לֹא תַעֲבֹט וּמָשַׁלְתָּ בְּגוֹיִם רַבִּים וּבְךָ לֹא יִמְשֹׁלוּ׃ כִּי־יִהְיֶה בְךָ אֶבְיוֹן מֵאַחַד אַחֶיךָ בְּאַחַד שְׁעָרֶיךָ בְּאַרְצְךָ אֲשֶׁר־יְהוָה אֱלֹהֶיךָ נֹתֵן לָךְ לֹא תְאַמֵּץ אֶת־לְבָבְךָ וְלֹא תִקְפֹּץ אֶת־יָדְךָ מֵאָחִיךָ הָאֶבְיוֹן׃ כִּי־פָתֹחַ תִּפְתַּח אֶת־יָדְךָ לוֹ וְהַעֲבֵט תַּעֲבִיטֶנּוּ דֵּי מַחְסֹרוֹ אֲשֶׁר יֶחְסַר לוֹ׃ הִשָּׁמֶר לְךָ פֶּן־יִהְיֶה דָבָר עִם־לְבָבְךָ בְלִיַּעַל לֵאמֹר קָרְבָה שְׁנַת־הַשֶּׁבַע שְׁנַת הַשְּׁמִטָּה וְרָעָה עֵינְךָ בְּאָחִיךָ הָאֶבְיוֹן וְלֹא תִתֵּן לוֹ וְקָרָא עָלֶיךָ אֶל־יְהוָה וְהָיָה בְךָ חֵטְא׃ נָתוֹן תִּתֵּן לוֹ וְלֹא־יֵרַע לְבָבְךָ בְּתִתְּךָ לוֹ כִּי בִּגְלַל | הַדָּבָר הַזֶּה יְבָרֶכְךָ יְהוָה אֱלֹהֶיךָ בְּכָל־מַעֲשֶׂךָ וּבְכֹל מִשְׁלַח יָדֶךָ׃ כִּי לֹא־יֶחְדַּל אֶבְיוֹן מִקֶּרֶב הָאָרֶץ עַל־כֵּן אָנֹכִי מְצַוְּךָ לֵאמֹר פָּתֹחַ תִּפְתַּח אֶת־יָדְךָ לְאָחִיךָ לַעֲנִיֶּךָ וּלְאֶבְיֹנְךָ בְּאַרְצֶךָ׃ כִּי־יִמָּכֵר לְךָ אָחִיךָ הָעִבְרִי אוֹ הָעִבְרִיָּה וַעֲבָדְךָ שֵׁשׁ שָׁנִים וּבַשָּׁנָה הַשְּׁבִיעִת תְּשַׁלְּחֶנּוּ חָפְשִׁי מֵעִמָּךְ׃ וְכִי־תְשַׁלְּחֶנּוּ חָפְשִׁי מֵעִמָּךְ לֹא תְשַׁלְּחֶנּוּ רֵיקָם׃ הַעֲנֵיק תַּעֲנִיק לוֹ מִצֹּאנְךָ וּמִגָּרְנְךָ וּמִיִּקְבֶךָ אֲשֶׁר בֵּרַכְךָ יְהוָה אֱלֹהֶיךָ תִּתֶּן־לוֹ׃ וְזָכַרְתָּ כִּי עֶבֶד הָיִיתָ בְּאֶרֶץ מִצְרַיִם וַיִּפְדְּךָ יְהוָה אֱלֹהֶיךָ עַל־כֵּן אָנֹכִי מְצַוְּךָ אֶת־הַדָּבָר הַזֶּה הַיּוֹם׃ וְהָיָה כִּי־יֹאמַר אֵלֶיךָ לֹא אֵצֵא מֵעִמָּךְ כִּי אֲהֵבְךָ וְאֶת־בֵּיתֶךָ כִּי־טוֹב לוֹ עִמָּךְ׃ וְלָקַחְתָּ אֶת־הַמַּרְצֵעַ וְנָתַתָּה בְאָזְנוֹ וּבַדֶּלֶת וְהָיָה לְךָ עֶבֶד עוֹלָם וְאַף לַאֲמָתְךָ תַּעֲשֶׂה־כֵּן׃ לֹא־יִקְשֶׁה בְעֵינֶךָ בְּשַׁלֵּחֲךָ אֹתוֹ חָפְשִׁי מֵעִמָּךְ כִּי מִשְׁנֶה שְׂכַר שָׂכִיר עֲבָדְךָ שֵׁשׁ שָׁנִים וּבֵרַכְךָ יְהוָה אֱלֹהֶיךָ בְּכֹל אֲשֶׁר תַּעֲשֶׂה׃

When Pesach or Shavuos fall on a weekday, begin here:

(בשבת שלישי) כָּל־הַבְּכוֹר אֲשֶׁר יִוָּלֵד בִּבְקָרְךָ וּבְצֹאנְךָ הַזָּכָר תַּקְדִּישׁ לַיהוָה אֱלֹהֶיךָ לֹא תַעֲבֹד בִּבְכֹר שׁוֹרֶךָ וְלֹא תָגֹז בְּכוֹר צֹאנֶךָ׃ לִפְנֵי יְהוָה אֱלֹהֶיךָ תֹאכְלֶנּוּ שָׁנָה בְשָׁנָה בַּמָּקוֹם אֲשֶׁר־יִבְחַר יְהוָה אַתָּה וּבֵיתֶךָ׃ וְכִי־יִהְיֶה בוֹ מוּם פִּסֵּחַ אוֹ עִוֵּר כֹּל מוּם רָע לֹא תִזְבָּחֶנּוּ לַיהוָה אֱלֹהֶיךָ׃ בִּשְׁעָרֶיךָ תֹּאכְלֶנּוּ הַטָּמֵא וְהַטָּהוֹר יַחְדָּו כַּצְּבִי וְכָאַיָּל׃ רַק אֶת־דָּמוֹ לֹא תֹאכֵל עַל־הָאָרֶץ תִּשְׁפְּכֶנּוּ כַּמָּיִם׃

שני (בשבת רביעי) שָׁמוֹר אֶת־חֹדֶשׁ הָאָבִיב וְעָשִׂיתָ פֶּסַח לַיהוָה אֱלֹהֶיךָ כִּי בְּחֹדֶשׁ הָאָבִיב הוֹצִיאֲךָ יְהוָה אֱלֹהֶיךָ מִמִּצְרַיִם לָיְלָה׃ וְזָבַחְתָּ פֶּסַח לַיהוָה אֱלֹהֶיךָ צֹאן וּבָקָר בַּמָּקוֹם אֲשֶׁר יִבְחַר יְהוָה לְשַׁכֵּן שְׁמוֹ שָׁם׃ לֹא־תֹאכַל עָלָיו חָמֵץ שִׁבְעַת יָמִים תֹּאכַל־עָלָיו מַצּוֹת לֶחֶם עֹנִי כִּי בְחִפָּזוֹן יָצָאתָ מֵאֶרֶץ מִצְרַיִם לְמַעַן תִּזְכֹּר אֶת־יוֹם צֵאתְךָ מֵאֶרֶץ מִצְרַיִם כֹּל יְמֵי חַיֶּיךָ׃

שלישי (בשבת חמישי) וְלֹא־יֵרָאֶה לְךָ שְׂאֹר בְּכָל־גְּבֻלְךָ שִׁבְעַת יָמִים וְלֹא־יָלִין מִן־הַבָּשָׂר אֲשֶׁר תִּזְבַּח בָּעֶרֶב בַּיּוֹם הָרִאשׁוֹן לַבֹּקֶר׃ לֹא תוּכַל לִזְבֹּחַ אֶת־הַפָּסַח בְּאַחַד שְׁעָרֶיךָ אֲשֶׁר־יְהוָה אֱלֹהֶיךָ נֹתֵן לָךְ׃ כִּי אִם־אֶל־הַמָּקוֹם אֲשֶׁר־יִבְחַר יְהוָה אֱלֹהֶיךָ לְשַׁכֵּן שְׁמוֹ שָׁם תִּזְבַּח אֶת־הַפֶּסַח בָּעָרֶב כְּבוֹא הַשֶּׁמֶשׁ מוֹעֵד צֵאתְךָ מִמִּצְרָיִם׃ וּבִשַּׁלְתָּ וְאָכַלְתָּ בַּמָּקוֹם אֲשֶׁר יִבְחַר יְהוָה אֱלֹהֶיךָ בּוֹ וּפָנִיתָ בַבֹּקֶר וְהָלַכְתָּ לְאֹהָלֶיךָ׃ שֵׁשֶׁת יָמִים תֹּאכַל מַצּוֹת וּבַיּוֹם הַשְּׁבִיעִי עֲצֶרֶת לַיהוָה אֱלֹהֶיךָ לֹא תַעֲשֶׂה מְלָאכָה׃

רביעי (בשבת ששי) שִׁבְעָה שָׁבֻעֹת תִּסְפָּר־לָךְ מֵהָחֵל חֶרְמֵשׁ בַּקָּמָה תָּחֵל לִסְפֹּר שִׁבְעָה שָׁבֻעוֹת׃ וְעָשִׂיתָ חַג שָׁבֻעוֹת לַיהוָה אֱלֹהֶיךָ מִסַּת נִדְבַת יָדְךָ אֲשֶׁר תִּתֵּן כַּאֲשֶׁר יְבָרֶכְךָ יְהוָה אֱלֹהֶיךָ׃ וְשָׂמַחְתָּ לִפְנֵי | יְהוָה אֱלֹהֶיךָ אַתָּה וּבִנְךָ וּבִתֶּךָ וְעַבְדְּךָ וַאֲמָתֶךָ וְהַלֵּוִי אֲשֶׁר בִּשְׁעָרֶיךָ וְהַגֵּר וְהַיָּתוֹם וְהָאַלְמָנָה אֲשֶׁר בְּקִרְבֶּךָ בַּמָּקוֹם אֲשֶׁר יִבְחַר יְהוָה אֱלֹהֶיךָ לְשַׁכֵּן שְׁמוֹ שָׁם׃ וְזָכַרְתָּ כִּי־עֶבֶד הָיִיתָ בְּמִצְרָיִם וְשָׁמַרְתָּ וְעָשִׂיתָ אֶת־הַחֻקִּים הָאֵלֶּה׃

חמישי (בשבת שביעי) חַג הַסֻּכֹּת תַּעֲשֶׂה לְךָ שִׁבְעַת יָמִים בְּאָסְפְּךָ מִגָּרְנְךָ וּמִיִּקְבֶךָ׃ וְשָׂמַחְתָּ בְּחַגֶּךָ אַתָּה וּבִנְךָ וּבִתֶּךָ וְעַבְדְּךָ וַאֲמָתֶךָ וְהַלֵּוִי וְהַגֵּר וְהַיָּתוֹם וְהָאַלְמָנָה אֲשֶׁר בִּשְׁעָרֶיךָ׃ שִׁבְעַת יָמִים תָּחֹג לַיהוָה אֱלֹהֶיךָ בַּמָּקוֹם אֲשֶׁר־יִבְחַר יְהוָה כִּי יְבָרֶכְךָ יְהוָה אֱלֹהֶיךָ בְּכֹל תְּבוּאָתְךָ וּבְכֹל מַעֲשֵׂה יָדֶיךָ וְהָיִיתָ אַךְ שָׂמֵחַ׃ שָׁלוֹשׁ פְּעָמִים | בַּשָּׁנָה יֵרָאֶה כָל־זְכוּרְךָ אֶת־פְּנֵי | יְהוָה אֱלֹהֶיךָ בַּמָּקוֹם אֲשֶׁר יִבְחָר בְּחַג הַמַּצּוֹת וּבְחַג הַשָּׁבֻעוֹת וּבְחַג הַסֻּכּוֹת וְלֹא יֵרָאֶה אֶת־פְּנֵי יְהוָה רֵיקָם׃ אִישׁ כְּמַתְּנַת יָדוֹ כְּבִרְכַּת יְהוָה אֱלֹהֶיךָ אֲשֶׁר נָתַן־לָךְ׃

Maftir of the eighth day of Pesach is *Numbers* 28:19-25, see page 959.
Maftir and the *Haftarah* for Shavuos appear on page 969; for Shemini Atzeres, on page 974.

הפטרה — יום אחרון של פסח

HAFTARAH — EIGHTH DAY OF PESACH

(*Isaiah* 10:32 — 12:6)

עוֹד הַיּוֹם בְּנֹב לַעֲמֹד יְנֹפֵף יָדוֹ הַר בַּת־צִיּוֹן גִּבְעַת יְרוּשָׁלִָם׃ הִנֵּה הָאָדוֹן יְהוָה צְבָאוֹת מְסָעֵף פֻּארָה בְּמַעֲרָצָה וְרָמֵי הַקּוֹמָה גְּדֻעִים וְהַגְּבֹהִים יִשְׁפָּלוּ׃ וְנִקַּף סִבְכֵי הַיַּעַר בַּבַּרְזֶל וְהַלְּבָנוֹן בְּאַדִּיר יִפּוֹל׃ וְיָצָא חֹטֶר מִגֵּזַע יִשָׁי וְנֵצֶר מִשָּׁרָשָׁיו יִפְרֶה׃ וְנָחָה עָלָיו רוּחַ יְהוָה רוּחַ חָכְמָה וּבִינָה רוּחַ עֵצָה וּגְבוּרָה רוּחַ דַּעַת וְיִרְאַת יְהוָה׃ וַהֲרִיחוֹ בְּיִרְאַת יְהוָה וְלֹא־לְמַרְאֵה עֵינָיו יִשְׁפּוֹט וְלֹא־לְמִשְׁמַע אָזְנָיו יוֹכִיחַ׃ וְשָׁפַט בְּצֶדֶק דַּלִּים וְהוֹכִיחַ בְּמִישׁוֹר לְעַנְוֵי־אָרֶץ וְהִכָּה־אֶרֶץ בְּשֵׁבֶט פִּיו וּבְרוּחַ שְׂפָתָיו יָמִית רָשָׁע׃ וְהָיָה צֶדֶק אֵזוֹר מָתְנָיו וְהָאֱמוּנָה אֵזוֹר חֲלָצָיו׃ וְגָר זְאֵב עִם־כֶּבֶשׂ וְנָמֵר עִם־גְּדִי יִרְבָּץ וְעֵגֶל וּכְפִיר וּמְרִיא יַחְדָּו וְנַעַר קָטֹן נֹהֵג בָּם׃ וּפָרָה וָדֹב תִּרְעֶינָה יַחְדָּו יִרְבְּצוּ יַלְדֵיהֶן וְאַרְיֵה כַּבָּקָר יֹאכַל־תֶּבֶן׃ וְשִׁעֲשַׁע יוֹנֵק עַל־חֻר פָּתֶן וְעַל מְאוּרַת צִפְעוֹנִי גָּמוּל יָדוֹ הָדָה׃ לֹא־יָרֵעוּ וְלֹא־יַשְׁחִיתוּ בְּכָל־הַר קָדְשִׁי כִּי־מָלְאָה הָאָרֶץ דֵּעָה אֶת־יְהוָה כַּמַּיִם לַיָּם מְכַסִּים׃ וְהָיָה בַּיּוֹם הַהוּא שֹׁרֶשׁ יִשַׁי אֲשֶׁר עֹמֵד לְנֵס עַמִּים אֵלָיו גּוֹיִם יִדְרֹשׁוּ וְהָיְתָה מְנֻחָתוֹ כָּבוֹד׃ וְהָיָה | בַּיּוֹם הַהוּא יוֹסִיף אֲדֹנָי | שֵׁנִית יָדוֹ לִקְנוֹת אֶת־שְׁאָר עַמּוֹ אֲשֶׁר יִשָּׁאֵר מֵאַשּׁוּר וּמִמִּצְרַיִם וּמִפַּתְרוֹס וּמִכּוּשׁ וּמֵעֵילָם וּמִשִּׁנְעָר וּמֵחֲמָת וּמֵאִיֵּי הַיָּם׃ וְנָשָׂא נֵס לַגּוֹיִם וְאָסַף נִדְחֵי יִשְׂרָאֵל וּנְפֻצוֹת יְהוּדָה יְקַבֵּץ מֵאַרְבַּע כַּנְפוֹת הָאָרֶץ׃ וְסָרָה קִנְאַת אֶפְרַיִם וְצֹרְרֵי יְהוּדָה יִכָּרֵתוּ אֶפְרַיִם לֹא־יְקַנֵּא אֶת־יְהוּדָה וִיהוּדָה לֹא־יָצֹר אֶת־אֶפְרָיִם׃ וְעָפוּ בְכָתֵף פְּלִשְׁתִּים יָמָּה יַחְדָּו יָבֹזּוּ אֶת־בְּנֵי־קֶדֶם אֱדוֹם וּמוֹאָב מִשְׁלוֹחַ יָדָם וּבְנֵי עַמּוֹן מִשְׁמַעְתָּם׃ וְהֶחֱרִים יְהוָה אֵת לְשׁוֹן יַם־מִצְרַיִם וְהֵנִיף יָדוֹ עַל־הַנָּהָר בַּעְיָם רוּחוֹ וְהִכָּהוּ לְשִׁבְעָה נְחָלִים וְהִדְרִיךְ בַּנְּעָלִים׃ וְהָיְתָה מְסִלָּה לִשְׁאָר עַמּוֹ אֲשֶׁר יִשָּׁאֵר מֵאַשּׁוּר כַּאֲשֶׁר הָיְתָה לְיִשְׂרָאֵל בְּיוֹם עֲלֹתוֹ מֵאֶרֶץ מִצְרָיִם׃ וְאָמַרְתָּ בַּיּוֹם הַהוּא אוֹדְךָ יְהוָה כִּי אָנַפְתָּ בִּי יָשֹׁב אַפְּךָ וּתְנַחֲמֵנִי׃ הִנֵּה אֵל יְשׁוּעָתִי אֶבְטַח וְלֹא אֶפְחָד כִּי־עָזִּי וְזִמְרָת יָהּ יְהוָה וַיְהִי־לִי לִישׁוּעָה׃ וּשְׁאַבְתֶּם־מַיִם בְּשָׂשׂוֹן מִמַּעַיְנֵי הַיְשׁוּעָה׃ וַאֲמַרְתֶּם בַּיּוֹם הַהוּא הוֹדוּ לַיהוָה קִרְאוּ בִשְׁמוֹ הוֹדִיעוּ בָעַמִּים עֲלִילֹתָיו הַזְכִּירוּ כִּי נִשְׂגָּב שְׁמוֹ׃ זַמְּרוּ יְהוָה כִּי גֵאוּת עָשָׂה מוּדַעַת זֹאת בְּכָל־הָאָרֶץ׃ צַהֲלִי וָרֹנִּי יוֹשֶׁבֶת צִיּוֹן כִּי־גָדוֹל בְּקִרְבֵּךְ קְדוֹשׁ יִשְׂרָאֵל׃

שבועות — יום ראשון

SHAVUOS — FIRST DAY

Akdamus appears on page 714.

(*Exodus* 19:1 — 20:23)

בַּחֹדֶשׁ הַשְּׁלִישִׁי לְצֵאת בְּנֵי־יִשְׂרָאֵל מֵאֶרֶץ מִצְרָיִם בַּיּוֹם הַזֶּה בָּאוּ מִדְבַּר סִינָי׃ וַיִּסְעוּ מֵרְפִידִים וַיָּבֹאוּ מִדְבַּר סִינַי וַיַּחֲנוּ בַּמִּדְבָּר

וַיַּחַן־שָׁ֥ם יִשְׂרָאֵ֖ל נֶ֣גֶד הָהָ֑ר: וּמֹשֶׁ֣ה עָלָ֔ה אֶל־הָ֣אֱלֹהִ֑ים וַיִּקְרָ֨א אֵלָ֤יו יְהֹוָה֙ מִן־הָהָ֣ר לֵאמֹ֔ר כֹּ֤ה תֹאמַר֙ לְבֵ֣ית יַעֲקֹ֔ב וְתַגֵּ֖יד לִבְנֵ֥י יִשְׂרָאֵֽל: אַתֶּ֣ם רְאִיתֶ֔ם אֲשֶׁ֥ר עָשִׂ֖יתִי לְמִצְרָ֑יִם וָאֶשָּׂ֤א אֶתְכֶם֙ עַל־כַּנְפֵ֣י נְשָׁרִ֔ים וָאָבִ֥א אֶתְכֶ֖ם אֵלָֽי: וְעַתָּ֗ה אִם־שָׁמ֤וֹעַ תִּשְׁמְעוּ֙ בְּקֹלִ֔י וּשְׁמַרְתֶּ֖ם אֶת־בְּרִיתִ֑י וִהְיִ֨יתֶם לִ֤י סְגֻלָּה֙ מִכָּל־הָ֣עַמִּ֔ים כִּי־לִ֖י כָּל־הָאָֽרֶץ: וְאַתֶּ֧ם תִּהְיוּ־לִ֛י מַמְלֶ֥כֶת כֹּהֲנִ֖ים וְג֣וֹי קָד֑וֹשׁ אֵ֚לֶּה הַדְּבָרִ֔ים אֲשֶׁ֥ר תְּדַבֵּ֖ר אֶל־בְּנֵ֥י יִשְׂרָאֵֽל:

שני וַיָּבֹ֣א מֹשֶׁ֔ה וַיִּקְרָ֖א לְזִקְנֵ֣י הָעָ֑ם וַיָּ֣שֶׂם לִפְנֵיהֶ֗ם אֵ֚ת כָּל־הַדְּבָרִ֣ים הָאֵ֔לֶּה אֲשֶׁ֥ר צִוָּ֖הוּ יְהֹוָֽה: וַיַּעֲנ֨וּ כָל־הָעָ֤ם יַחְדָּו֙ וַיֹּ֣אמְר֔וּ כֹּ֛ל אֲשֶׁר־דִּבֶּ֥ר יְהֹוָ֖ה נַעֲשֶׂ֑ה וַיָּ֧שֶׁב מֹשֶׁ֛ה אֶת־דִּבְרֵ֥י הָעָ֖ם אֶל־יְהֹוָֽה: וַיֹּ֨אמֶר יְהֹוָ֜ה אֶל־מֹשֶׁ֗ה הִנֵּ֨ה אָנֹכִ֜י בָּ֣א אֵלֶ֘יךָ֘ בְּעַ֣ב הֶֽעָנָן֒ בַּעֲב֞וּר יִשְׁמַ֤ע הָעָם֙ בְּדַבְּרִ֣י עִמָּ֔ךְ וְגַם־בְּךָ֖ יַאֲמִ֣ינוּ לְעוֹלָ֑ם וַיַּגֵּ֥ד מֹשֶׁ֛ה אֶת־דִּבְרֵ֥י הָעָ֖ם אֶל־יְהֹוָֽה: וַיֹּ֨אמֶר יְהֹוָ֤ה אֶל־מֹשֶׁה֙ לֵ֣ךְ אֶל־הָעָ֔ם וְקִדַּשְׁתָּ֥ם הַיּ֖וֹם וּמָחָ֑ר וְכִבְּס֖וּ שִׂמְלֹתָֽם: וְהָי֥וּ נְכֹנִ֖ים לַיּ֣וֹם הַשְּׁלִישִׁ֑י כִּ֣י | בַּיּ֣וֹם הַשְּׁלִישִׁ֗י יֵרֵ֧ד יְהֹוָ֛ה לְעֵינֵ֥י כָל־הָעָ֖ם עַל־הַ֥ר סִינָֽי: וְהִגְבַּלְתָּ֤ אֶת־הָעָם֙ סָבִ֣יב לֵאמֹ֔ר הִשָּׁמְר֥וּ לָכֶ֛ם עֲל֥וֹת בָּהָ֖ר וּנְגֹ֣עַ בְּקָצֵ֑הוּ כָּל־הַנֹּגֵ֥עַ בָּהָ֖ר מ֥וֹת יוּמָֽת: לֹא־תִגַּ֨ע בּ֜וֹ יָ֗ד כִּֽי־סָק֤וֹל יִסָּקֵל֙ אֽוֹ־יָרֹ֣ה יִיָּרֶ֔ה אִם־בְּהֵמָ֥ה אִם־אִ֖ישׁ לֹ֣א יִחְיֶ֑ה בִּמְשֹׁךְ֙ הַיֹּבֵ֔ל הֵ֖מָּה יַעֲל֥וּ בָהָֽר:

שלישי וַיֵּ֧רֶד מֹשֶׁ֛ה מִן־הָהָ֖ר אֶל־הָעָ֑ם וַיְקַדֵּשׁ֙ אֶת־הָעָ֔ם וַֽיְכַבְּס֖וּ שִׂמְלֹתָֽם: וַיֹּ֙אמֶר֙ אֶל־הָעָ֔ם הֱי֥וּ נְכֹנִ֖ים לִשְׁלֹ֣שֶׁת יָמִ֑ים אַֽל־תִּגְּשׁ֖וּ אֶל־אִשָּֽׁה: וַיְהִי֩ בַיּ֨וֹם הַשְּׁלִישִׁ֜י בִּֽהְיֹ֣ת הַבֹּ֗קֶר וַיְהִי֩ קֹלֹ֨ת וּבְרָקִ֜ים וְעָנָ֤ן כָּבֵד֙ עַל־הָהָ֔ר וְקֹ֥ל שֹׁפָ֖ר חָזָ֣ק מְאֹ֑ד וַיֶּחֱרַ֥ד כָּל־הָעָ֖ם אֲשֶׁ֥ר בַּֽמַּחֲנֶֽה: וַיּוֹצֵ֨א מֹשֶׁ֧ה אֶת־הָעָ֛ם לִקְרַ֥את הָֽאֱלֹהִ֖ים מִן־הַֽמַּחֲנֶ֑ה וַיִּֽתְיַצְּב֖וּ בְּתַחְתִּ֥ית הָהָֽר: וְהַ֤ר סִינַי֙ עָשַׁ֣ן כֻּלּ֔וֹ מִ֠פְּנֵ֠י אֲשֶׁ֨ר יָרַ֥ד עָלָ֛יו יְהֹוָ֖ה בָּאֵ֑שׁ וַיַּ֤עַל עֲשָׁנוֹ֙ כְּעֶ֣שֶׁן הַכִּבְשָׁ֔ן וַיֶּחֱרַ֥ד כָּל־הָהָ֖ר מְאֹֽד: וַיְהִי֙ ק֣וֹל הַשֹּׁפָ֔ר הוֹלֵ֖ךְ וְחָזֵ֣ק מְאֹ֑ד מֹשֶׁ֣ה יְדַבֵּ֔ר וְהָאֱלֹהִ֖ים יַעֲנֶ֥נּוּ בְקֽוֹל:

רביעי וַיֵּ֧רֶד יְהֹוָ֛ה עַל־הַ֥ר סִינַ֖י אֶל־רֹ֣אשׁ הָהָ֑ר וַיִּקְרָ֨א יְהֹוָ֧ה לְמֹשֶׁ֛ה אֶל־רֹ֥אשׁ הָהָ֖ר

וַיַּ֥עַל מֹשֶֽׁה: וַיֹּ֤אמֶר יְהֹוָה֙ אֶל־מֹשֶׁ֔ה רֵ֖ד הָעֵ֣ד בָּעָ֑ם פֶּן־יֶהֶרְס֤וּ אֶל־יְהֹוָה֙ לִרְא֔וֹת וְנָפַ֥ל מִמֶּ֖נּוּ רָֽב: וְגַ֧ם הַכֹּהֲנִ֛ים הַנִּגָּשִׁ֥ים אֶל־יְהֹוָ֖ה יִתְקַדָּ֑שׁוּ פֶּן־יִפְרֹ֥ץ בָּהֶ֖ם יְהֹוָֽה: וַיֹּ֤אמֶר מֹשֶׁה֙ אֶל־יְהֹוָ֔ה לֹא־יוּכַ֣ל הָעָ֔ם לַעֲלֹ֖ת אֶל־הַ֣ר סִינָ֑י כִּֽי־אַתָּ֞ה הַעֵדֹ֤תָה בָּ֙נוּ֙ לֵאמֹ֔ר הַגְבֵּ֥ל אֶת־הָהָ֖ר וְקִדַּשְׁתּֽוֹ: וַיֹּ֨אמֶר אֵלָ֤יו יְהֹוָה֙ לֶךְ־רֵ֔ד וְעָלִ֥יתָ אַתָּ֖ה וְאַהֲרֹ֣ן עִמָּ֑ךְ וְהַכֹּהֲנִ֣ים וְהָעָ֗ם אַל־יֶֽהֶרְס֛וּ לַעֲלֹ֥ת אֶל־יְהֹוָ֖ה פֶּן־יִפְרָץ־בָּֽם: וַיֵּ֥רֶד מֹשֶׁ֖ה אֶל־הָעָ֑ם וַיֹּ֖אמֶר אֲלֵהֶֽם:

וַיְדַבֵּ֣ר אֱלֹהִ֔ים אֵ֛ת כָּל־הַדְּבָרִ֥ים הָאֵ֖לֶּה לֵאמֹֽר: אָ֣נֹכִ֞י יְהֹוָ֣ה אֱלֹהֶ֗יךָ אֲשֶׁ֧ר הוֹצֵאתִ֛יךָ מֵאֶ֥רֶץ מִצְרַ֖יִם מִבֵּ֣ית עֲבָדִֽים לֹֽא־יִהְיֶֽה־לְךָ֛ אֱלֹהִ֥ים אֲחֵרִ֖ים עַל־פָּנָֽי לֹֽא־תַעֲשֶׂ֨ה־לְךָ֥ פֶ֙סֶל֙ | וְכָל־תְּמוּנָ֡ה אֲשֶׁ֣ר בַּשָּׁמַ֣יִם | מִמַּ֡עַל וַאֲשֶׁ֣ר בָּאָרֶץ֩ מִתַּ֨חַת וַאֲשֶׁ֥ר בַּמַּ֖יִם | מִתַּ֣חַת לָאָ֑רֶץ לֹֽא־תִשְׁתַּחֲוֶ֥ה לָהֶ֖ם וְלֹ֣א תָעָבְדֵ֑ם כִּ֣י אָֽנֹכִ֞י יְהֹוָ֤ה אֱלֹהֶ֙יךָ֙ אֵ֣ל קַנָּ֔א פֹּ֠קֵ֠ד עֲוֹ֨ן אָבֹ֧ת עַל־בָּנִ֛ים עַל־שִׁלֵּשִׁ֥ים וְעַל־רִבֵּעִ֖ים לְשֹׂנְאָֽי וְעֹ֥שֶׂה חֶ֖סֶד לַאֲלָפִ֑ים לְאֹהֲבַ֖י וּלְשֹׁמְרֵ֥י מִצְוֹתָֽי: לֹ֥א תִשָּׂ֛א אֶת־שֵֽׁם־יְהֹוָ֥ה אֱלֹהֶ֖יךָ לַשָּׁ֑וְא כִּ֣י לֹ֤א יְנַקֶּה֙ יְהֹוָ֔ה אֵ֛ת אֲשֶׁר־יִשָּׂ֥א אֶת־שְׁמ֖וֹ לַשָּֽׁוְא: זָכ֛וֹר אֶת־י֥וֹם הַשַּׁבָּ֖ת לְקַדְּשֽׁוֹ שֵׁ֤שֶׁת יָמִים֙ תַּֽעֲבֹ֔ד וְעָשִׂ֖יתָ כָּל־מְלַאכְתֶּֽךָ | וְי֙וֹם֙ הַשְּׁבִיעִ֔י שַׁבָּ֖ת | לַיהֹוָ֣ה אֱלֹהֶ֑יךָ לֹֽא־תַעֲשֶׂ֣ה כָל־מְלָאכָ֡ה אַתָּ֣ה וּבִנְךָֽ־וּ֠בִתֶּ֠ךָ עַבְדְּךָֽ וַאֲמָֽתְךָ֙ וּבְהֶמְתֶּ֔ךָ וְגֵרְךָ֖ אֲשֶׁ֣ר בִּשְׁעָרֶ֑יךָ כִּ֣י שֵֽׁשֶׁת־יָמִים֩ עָשָׂ֨ה יְהֹוָ֜ה אֶת־הַשָּׁמַ֣יִם וְאֶת־הָאָ֗רֶץ אֶת־הַיָּם֙ וְאֶת־כָּל־אֲשֶׁר־בָּ֔ם וַיָּ֖נַח בַּיּ֣וֹם הַשְּׁבִיעִ֑י עַל־כֵּ֗ן בֵּרַ֧ךְ יְהֹוָ֛ה אֶת־י֥וֹם הַשַּׁבָּ֖ת וַֽיְקַדְּשֵֽׁהוּ: כַּבֵּ֥ד אֶת־אָבִ֖יךָ וְאֶת־אִמֶּ֑ךָ לְמַ֙עַן֙ יַאֲרִכ֣וּן יָמֶ֔יךָ עַ֚ל הָֽאֲדָמָ֔ה אֲשֶׁר־יְהֹוָ֥ה אֱלֹהֶ֖יךָ נֹתֵ֥ן לָֽךְ: לֹ֖א תִּרְצָֽח: לֹ֖א תִּנְאָֽף: לֹ֖א תִּגְנֹֽב: לֹֽא־תַעֲנֶ֥ה בְרֵעֲךָ֖ עֵ֥ד שָֽׁקֶר: לֹ֥א תַחְמֹ֖ד בֵּ֣ית רֵעֶ֑ךָ לֹֽא־תַחְמֹ֞ד אֵ֣שֶׁת רֵעֶ֗ךָ וְעַבְדּ֤וֹ וַאֲמָתוֹ֙ וְשׁוֹר֣וֹ וַחֲמֹר֔וֹ וְכֹ֖ל אֲשֶׁ֥ר לְרֵעֶֽךָ:

חמישי וְכָל־הָעָם֩ רֹאִ֨ים אֶת־הַקּוֹלֹ֜ת וְאֶת־הַלַּפִּידִ֗ם וְאֵת֙ ק֣וֹל הַשֹּׁפָ֔ר וְאֶת־הָהָ֖ר עָשֵׁ֑ן וַיַּ֤רְא הָעָם֙ וַיָּנֻ֔עוּ וַיַּֽעַמְד֖וּ מֵֽרָחֹֽק: וַיֹּֽאמְרוּ֙ אֶל־מֹשֶׁ֔ה דַּבֵּר־אַתָּ֥ה עִמָּ֖נוּ וְנִשְׁמָ֑עָה וְאַל־יְדַבֵּ֧ר עִמָּ֛נוּ אֱלֹהִ֖ים פֶּן־נָמֽוּת: וַיֹּ֨אמֶר מֹשֶׁ֣ה אֶל־הָעָם֮ אַל־תִּירָ֒אוּ֒ כִּ֗י לְבַֽעֲב֞וּר נַסּ֣וֹת

אֶתְכֶם בָּא הָאֱלֹהִים וּבַעֲבוּר תִּהְיֶה יִרְאָתוֹ עַל־פְּנֵיכֶם לְבִלְתִּי תֶחֱטָאוּ׃ וַיַּעֲמֹד הָעָם מֵרָחֹק וּמֹשֶׁה נִגַּשׁ אֶל־הָעֲרָפֶל אֲשֶׁר־שָׁם הָאֱלֹהִים׃ וַיֹּאמֶר יהוה אֶל־מֹשֶׁה כֹּה תֹאמַר אֶל־בְּנֵי יִשְׂרָאֵל אַתֶּם רְאִיתֶם כִּי מִן־הַשָּׁמַיִם דִּבַּרְתִּי עִמָּכֶם׃ לֹא תַעֲשׂוּן אִתִּי אֱלֹהֵי כֶסֶף וֵאלֹהֵי זָהָב לֹא תַעֲשׂוּ לָכֶם׃ מִזְבַּח אֲדָמָה תַּעֲשֶׂה־לִּי וְזָבַחְתָּ עָלָיו אֶת־עֹלֹתֶיךָ וְאֶת־שְׁלָמֶיךָ אֶת־צֹאנְךָ וְאֶת־בְּקָרֶךָ בְּכָל־הַמָּקוֹם אֲשֶׁר אַזְכִּיר אֶת־שְׁמִי אָבוֹא אֵלֶיךָ וּבֵרַכְתִּיךָ׃ וְאִם־מִזְבַּח אֲבָנִים תַּעֲשֶׂה־לִּי לֹא־תִבְנֶה אֶתְהֶן גָּזִית כִּי חַרְבְּךָ הֵנַפְתָּ עָלֶיהָ וַתְּחַלְלֶהָ׃ וְלֹא־תַעֲלֶה בְמַעֲלֹת עַל־מִזְבְּחִי אֲשֶׁר לֹא־תִגָּלֶה עֶרְוָתְךָ עָלָיו׃

MAFTIR / מפטיר

(Numbers 28:26-31)

מפטיר (במדבר כח:כו-לא) וּבְיוֹם הַבִּכּוּרִים בְּהַקְרִיבְכֶם מִנְחָה חֲדָשָׁה לַיהוה בְּשָׁבֻעֹתֵיכֶם מִקְרָא־קֹדֶשׁ יִהְיֶה לָכֶם כָּל־מְלֶאכֶת עֲבֹדָה לֹא תַעֲשׂוּ׃ וְהִקְרַבְתֶּם עוֹלָה לְרֵיחַ נִיחֹחַ לַיהוה פָּרִים בְּנֵי־בָקָר שְׁנַיִם אַיִל אֶחָד שִׁבְעָה כְבָשִׂים בְּנֵי שָׁנָה׃ וּמִנְחָתָם סֹלֶת בְּלוּלָה בַשָּׁמֶן שְׁלֹשָׁה עֶשְׂרֹנִים לַפָּר הָאֶחָד שְׁנֵי עֶשְׂרֹנִים לָאַיִל הָאֶחָד׃ עִשָּׂרוֹן עִשָּׂרוֹן לַכֶּבֶשׂ הָאֶחָד לְשִׁבְעַת הַכְּבָשִׂים׃ שְׂעִיר עִזִּים אֶחָד לְכַפֵּר עֲלֵיכֶם׃ מִלְּבַד עֹלַת הַתָּמִיד וּמִנְחָתוֹ תַּעֲשׂוּ תְּמִימִם יִהְיוּ־לָכֶם וְנִסְכֵּיהֶם׃

HAFTARAH / הפטרה

(Ezekiel 1:1-28; 3:12)

וַיְהִי | בִּשְׁלֹשִׁים שָׁנָה בָּרְבִיעִי בַּחֲמִשָּׁה לַחֹדֶשׁ וַאֲנִי בְתוֹךְ־הַגּוֹלָה עַל־נְהַר־כְּבָר נִפְתְּחוּ הַשָּׁמַיִם וָאֶרְאֶה מַרְאוֹת אֱלֹהִים׃ בַּחֲמִשָּׁה לַחֹדֶשׁ הִיא הַשָּׁנָה הַחֲמִישִׁית לְגָלוּת הַמֶּלֶךְ יוֹיָכִין׃ הָיֹה הָיָה דְבַר־יהוה אֶל־יְחֶזְקֵאל בֶּן־בּוּזִי הַכֹּהֵן בְּאֶרֶץ כַּשְׂדִּים עַל־נְהַר־כְּבָר וַתְּהִי עָלָיו שָׁם יַד־יהוה׃ וָאֵרֶא וְהִנֵּה רוּחַ סְעָרָה בָּאָה מִן־הַצָּפוֹן עָנָן גָּדוֹל וְאֵשׁ מִתְלַקַּחַת וְנֹגַהּ לוֹ סָבִיב וּמִתּוֹכָהּ כְּעֵין הַחַשְׁמַל מִתּוֹךְ הָאֵשׁ׃ וּמִתּוֹכָהּ דְּמוּת אַרְבַּע חַיּוֹת וְזֶה מַרְאֵיהֶן דְּמוּת אָדָם לָהֵנָּה׃ וְאַרְבָּעָה פָנִים לְאֶחָת וְאַרְבַּע כְּנָפַיִם לְאַחַת לָהֶם׃ וְרַגְלֵיהֶם רֶגֶל יְשָׁרָה וְכַף רַגְלֵיהֶם כְּכַף רֶגֶל עֵגֶל וְנֹצְצִים כְּעֵין נְחֹשֶׁת קָלָל׃ וִידֵי אָדָם מִתַּחַת כַּנְפֵיהֶם עַל אַרְבַּעַת רִבְעֵיהֶם וּפְנֵיהֶם וְכַנְפֵיהֶם לְאַרְבַּעְתָּם׃ חֹבְרֹת אִשָּׁה אֶל־אֲחוֹתָהּ כַּנְפֵיהֶם לֹא־יִסַּבּוּ בְלֶכְתָּן אִישׁ אֶל־עֵבֶר פָּנָיו יֵלֵכוּ׃ וּדְמוּת פְּנֵיהֶם פְּנֵי אָדָם וּפְנֵי אַרְיֵה אֶל־הַיָּמִין לְאַרְבַּעְתָּם וּפְנֵי־שׁוֹר מֵהַשְּׂמֹאול לְאַרְבַּעְתָּן וּפְנֵי־נֶשֶׁר לְאַרְבַּעְתָּן׃ וּפְנֵיהֶם וְכַנְפֵיהֶם פְּרֻדוֹת מִלְמָעְלָה לְאִישׁ שְׁתַּיִם חֹבְרוֹת אִישׁ וּשְׁתַּיִם מְכַסּוֹת אֵת גְּוִיֹתֵיהֶנָה׃ וְאִישׁ אֶל־עֵבֶר פָּנָיו יֵלֵכוּ אֶל אֲשֶׁר יִהְיֶה־שָׁמָּה הָרוּחַ לָלֶכֶת יֵלֵכוּ לֹא יִסַּבּוּ בְּלֶכְתָּן׃ וּדְמוּת הַחַיּוֹת מַרְאֵיהֶם כְּגַחֲלֵי־אֵשׁ בֹּעֲרוֹת כְּמַרְאֵה הַלַּפִּדִים הִיא מִתְהַלֶּכֶת בֵּין הַחַיּוֹת וְנֹגַהּ לָאֵשׁ וּמִן־הָאֵשׁ יוֹצֵא בָרָק׃ וְהַחַיּוֹת רָצוֹא וָשׁוֹב כְּמַרְאֵה הַבָּזָק׃ וָאֵרֶא הַחַיּוֹת וְהִנֵּה אוֹפַן אֶחָד בָּאָרֶץ אֵצֶל הַחַיּוֹת לְאַרְבַּעַת פָּנָיו׃ מַרְאֵה הָאוֹפַנִּים וּמַעֲשֵׂיהֶם כְּעֵין תַּרְשִׁישׁ וּדְמוּת אֶחָד לְאַרְבַּעְתָּן וּמַרְאֵיהֶם וּמַעֲשֵׂיהֶם כַּאֲשֶׁר יִהְיֶה הָאוֹפַן בְּתוֹךְ הָאוֹפָן׃ עַל־אַרְבַּעַת רִבְעֵיהֶן בְּלֶכְתָּם יֵלֵכוּ לֹא יִסַּבּוּ בְּלֶכְתָּן׃ וְגַבֵּיהֶן וְגֹבַהּ לָהֶם וְיִרְאָה לָהֶם וְגַבֹּתָם מְלֵאֹת עֵינַיִם סָבִיב לְאַרְבַּעְתָּן׃ וּבְלֶכֶת הַחַיּוֹת יֵלְכוּ הָאוֹפַנִּים אֶצְלָם וּבְהִנָּשֵׂא הַחַיּוֹת מֵעַל הָאָרֶץ יִנָּשְׂאוּ הָאוֹפַנִּים׃ עַל אֲשֶׁר יִהְיֶה־שָּׁם הָרוּחַ לָלֶכֶת יֵלֵכוּ שָׁמָּה הָרוּחַ לָלֶכֶת וְהָאוֹפַנִּים יִנָּשְׂאוּ לְעֻמָּתָם כִּי רוּחַ הַחַיָּה בָּאוֹפַנִּים׃ בְּלֶכְתָּם יֵלֵכוּ וּבְעָמְדָם יַעֲמֹדוּ וּבְהִנָּשְׂאָם מֵעַל הָאָרֶץ יִנָּשְׂאוּ הָאוֹפַנִּים לְעֻמָּתָם כִּי רוּחַ הַחַיָּה בָּאוֹפַנִּים׃ וּדְמוּת עַל־רָאשֵׁי הַחַיָּה רָקִיעַ כְּעֵין הַקֶּרַח הַנּוֹרָא נָטוּי עַל־רָאשֵׁיהֶם מִלְמָעְלָה׃ וְתַחַת הָרָקִיעַ כַּנְפֵיהֶם יְשָׁרוֹת אִשָּׁה אֶל־אֲחוֹתָהּ לְאִישׁ שְׁתַּיִם מְכַסּוֹת לָהֵנָּה וּלְאִישׁ שְׁתַּיִם מְכַסּוֹת לָהֵנָּה אֵת גְּוִיֹּתֵיהֶם׃ וָאֶשְׁמַע אֶת־קוֹל כַּנְפֵיהֶם כְּקוֹל מַיִם רַבִּים כְּקוֹל־שַׁדַּי בְּלֶכְתָּם קוֹל הֲמֻלָּה כְּקוֹל מַחֲנֶה בְּעָמְדָם תְּרַפֶּינָה כַנְפֵיהֶן׃ וַיְהִי־קוֹל מֵעַל לָרָקִיעַ אֲשֶׁר עַל־רֹאשָׁם בְּעָמְדָם תְּרַפֶּינָה כַנְפֵיהֶן׃ וּמִמַּעַל לָרָקִיעַ אֲשֶׁר עַל־רֹאשָׁם כְּמַרְאֵה אֶבֶן־סַפִּיר דְּמוּת כִּסֵּא וְעַל דְּמוּת הַכִּסֵּא דְּמוּת כְּמַרְאֵה

שבועות — יום שני
SHAVUOS — SECOND DAY

The reading for the second day of Shavuos is the same as that of the eighth of Pesach, page 964. *Maftir* is the same as the first day of Shavuos, page 968.

HAFTARAH / הפטרה

(*Habakuk 2:20 — 3:19*)

וַיהוָה בְּהֵיכַל קָדְשׁוֹ הַס מִפָּנָיו כָּל־הָאָרֶץ׃
תְּפִלָּה לַחֲבַקּוּק הַנָּבִיא עַל שִׁגְיֹנוֹת׃* יהוה

אָדָם עָלָיו מִלְמָעְלָה׃ וָאֵרֶא | כְּעֵין חַשְׁמַל
כְּמַרְאֵה־אֵשׁ בֵּית־לָהּ סָבִיב מִמַּרְאֵה מָתְנָיו
וּלְמָעְלָה וּמִמַּרְאֵה מָתְנָיו וּלְמַטָּה רָאִיתִי
כְּמַרְאֵה־אֵשׁ וְנֹגַהּ לוֹ סָבִיב׃ כְּמַרְאֵה
הַקֶּשֶׁת אֲשֶׁר יִהְיֶה בֶעָנָן בְּיוֹם הַגֶּשֶׁם כֵּן
מַרְאֵה הַנֹּגַהּ סָבִיב הוּא מַרְאֵה דְּמוּת
כְּבוֹד־יהוה וָאֶרְאֶה וָאֶפֹּל עַל־פָּנַי וָאֶשְׁמַע
קוֹל מְדַבֵּר׃ וַתִּשָּׂאֵנִי רוּחַ וָאֶשְׁמַע אַחֲרַי
קוֹל רַעַשׁ גָּדוֹל בָּרוּךְ כְּבוֹד־יהוה מִמְּקוֹמוֹ׃

YETZIV PISGAM / יציב פתגם

*In most congregations, יְצִיב פִּתְגָם, *Yetziv Pisgam,* a song of praise, is inserted into the *Haftarah* of the second day of Shavuos at this point. It is replete with mystical connotations in praise of the Giver and the students of the Torah. The initial letters of the verses are an acrostic of the author's name, יַעֲקֹב בְּרַבִּי מֵאִיר לֵוִי, *Yaakov son of Rabbi Meir Levi.*

יְצִיב פִּתְגָם. לְאָת וּדְגָם.
בְּרִבּוֹ רִבְבָן עִי רִין׃

יְצִיב פִּתְגָם *Certain is our praise of God that is but a sign and sample*
of that uttered by myriad myriads of angels.

עֲנֵי אֲנָא. בְּמִנְיָנָא.
דְּפָסְלִין אַרְבְּעָה טוּ רִין׃

I shall call out His praise
according to the numbered commandments
that are inscribed in the four sections
of Codes of Law.

קֳדָמוֹהִי. לְגוֹ מוֹהִי.
נְגִיד וּנְפִיק נְהַר דְּנוּ רִין׃

Before Him, among the water of Paradise,
flows and goes a fiery stream.

בְּטוּר תַּלְגָּא. נְהוֹר שְׁרַגָּא.
וְזִיקִין דְּנוּר וּבְעוּ רִין׃

On a snowy mountain is a blinding light,
and bolts of flaming fire.

בְּרָא וּסְכָא. מַה בַּחֲשׁוֹכָא.
וְעִמֵּיהּ שַׁרְיָן נְהוֹ רִין׃

He created and sees
what is shrouded in darkness,
because light's essence dwells with Him.

רְחִיקִין צְפָא. בְּלָא שִׁטְפָא.
וְגַלְיָן לֵיהּ דְּמִטַּמְ רִין׃

He sees from afar without hindrance,
with hidden things revealed to Him.

בָּעֵית מִנֵּיהּ. יָת הַרְמוֹנֵהּ.
וּבַתְרוֹהִי עֲדֵי גוּבְ רִין׃

I seek permission from Him first,
and afterwards from people;

יָדְעֵי הִלְכְּתָא. וּמַתְנִיתָא.
וְתוֹסֶפְתָּא סִפְרָא וְסִפְ רִין׃

Those who know the Law, and Mishnah,
Tosefta, Sifra, and Sifri.

מֶלֶךְ חַיָּא. לְעָלְמַיָּא.
יְמַגֵּן עָם לְהוֹן מְשַׁחֲ רִין׃

The King Who lives eternally,
may He shield the people that prays to Him.

אֲמִיר עֲלֵיהוֹן. כְּחָלָא יְהוֹן.
וְלָא יִתְמְנוּן הֵיךְ עַפְ רִין׃

Say to them: 'May they be like the sand
and as uncountable as dust.

יַחֲוְּרוּן כְּעָן. לְהוֹן בִּקְעָן.
יְטוּפוּן נַעֲוהִי חַמְ רִין׃

May their valleys be covered
with crops as white as sheep;
may their cellars flow with wine.'

רְעוּתְהוֹן הַב. וְאַפֵּיהוֹן צְהַב.
יְנַהֲרוּן כִּנְהַר צַפְ רִין׃

Grant their wish, and may their faces glow
with a brilliance like the light of dawn.

לִי הַב תְּקוֹף. וְעֵינָךְ זְקוֹף.
חֲזִי עָרָךְ דְּבָךְ כַּפְ רִין׃

Give me strength and lift Your eye
to see the enemy who denies You.

וִיהוֹן כְּתִבְנָא. בְּגוֹ לִבְנָא.
כְּאַבְנָא יִשְׁתְּקוּן חַפְ רִין׃

Let them be like straw mixed in with brick,
let them be mute as a stone with humiliation.

יְהוֹנָתָן. גְּבַר עִנְוְתָן.
בְּכֵן נַמְטֵי לֵהּ אַפְ רִין׃

To Yehonasan [ben Uziel,
translator of the Prophets],
the epitome of humility,
let us extend gracious praise

שָׁמַעְתִּי שִׁמְעֲךָ יָרֵאתִי יהוה פָּעָלְךָ בְּקֶרֶב שָׁנִים חַיֵּיהוּ בְּקֶרֶב שָׁנִים תּוֹדִיעַ בְּרֹגֶז רַחֵם תִּזְכּוֹר: אֱלוֹהַּ מִתֵּימָן יָבוֹא וְקָדוֹשׁ מֵהַר־פָּארָן סֶלָה כִּסָּה שָׁמַיִם הוֹדוֹ וּתְהִלָּתוֹ מָלְאָה הָאָרֶץ: וְנֹגַהּ כָּאוֹר תִּהְיֶה קַרְנַיִם מִיָּדוֹ לוֹ וְשָׁם חֶבְיוֹן עֻזֹּה: לְפָנָיו יֵלֶךְ דָּבֶר וְיֵצֵא רֶשֶׁף לְרַגְלָיו: עָמַד | וַיְמֹדֶד אֶרֶץ רָאָה וַיַּתֵּר גּוֹיִם וַיִּתְפֹּצְצוּ הַרְרֵי־עַד שַׁחוּ גִּבְעוֹת עוֹלָם הֲלִיכוֹת עוֹלָם לוֹ: תַּחַת אָוֶן רָאִיתִי אָהֳלֵי כוּשָׁן יִרְגְּזוּן יְרִיעוֹת אֶרֶץ מִדְיָן: הֲבִנְהָרִים חָרָה יהוה אִם בַּנְּהָרִים אַפֶּךָ אִם־בַּיָּם עֶבְרָתֶךָ כִּי תִרְכַּב עַל־סוּסֶיךָ מַרְכְּבֹתֶיךָ יְשׁוּעָה: עֶרְיָה תֵעוֹר קַשְׁתֶּךָ שְׁבֻעוֹת מַטּוֹת אֹמֶר סֶלָה נְהָרוֹת תְּבַקַּע־אָרֶץ: רָאוּךָ יָחִילוּ הָרִים זֶרֶם מַיִם עָבָר נָתַן תְּהוֹם קוֹלוֹ רוֹם יָדֵיהוּ נָשָׂא: שֶׁמֶשׁ יָרֵחַ עָמַד זְבֻלָה לְאוֹר חִצֶּיךָ יְהַלֵּכוּ לְנֹגַהּ בְּרַק חֲנִיתֶךָ: בְּזַעַם תִּצְעַד־אָרֶץ בְּאַף תָּדוּשׁ גּוֹיִם: יָצָאתָ לְיֵשַׁע עַמֶּךָ לְיֵשַׁע אֶת־מְשִׁיחֶךָ מָחַצְתָּ רֹּאשׁ מִבֵּית רָשָׁע עָרוֹת יְסוֹד עַד־צַוָּאר סֶלָה: נָקַבְתָּ בְמַטָּיו רֹאשׁ פְּרָזָו יִסְעֲרוּ לַהֲפִיצֵנִי עֲלִיצֻתָם כְּמוֹ־לֶאֱכֹל עָנִי בַּמִּסְתָּר: דָּרַכְתָּ בַיָּם סוּסֶיךָ חֹמֶר מַיִם רַבִּים: שָׁמַעְתִּי | וַתִּרְגַּז בִּטְנִי לְקוֹל צָלְלוּ שְׂפָתַי יָבוֹא רָקָב בַּעֲצָמַי וְתַחְתַּי אֶרְגָּז אֲשֶׁר אָנוּחַ לְיוֹם צָרָה לַעֲלוֹת לְעַם יְגוּדֶנּוּ: כִּי־תְאֵנָה לֹא־תִפְרָח וְאֵין יְבוּל בַּגְּפָנִים כִּחֵשׁ מַעֲשֵׂה־זַיִת וּשְׁדֵמוֹת לֹא־עָשָׂה אֹכֶל גָּזַר מִמִּכְלָה צֹאן וְאֵין בָּקָר בָּרְפָתִים: וַאֲנִי בַּיהוה אֶעְלוֹזָה אָגִילָה בֵּאלֹהֵי יִשְׁעִי: יֱהֹוִה אֲדֹנָי חֵילִי וַיָּשֶׂם רַגְלַי כָּאַיָּלוֹת וְעַל־בָּמוֹתַי יַדְרִכֵנִי לַמְנַצֵּחַ בִּנְגִינוֹתָי:

סוכות — שני ימים ראשונים
SUCCOS — FIRST TWO DAYS

The reading for the first two days of Succos is the same as that of the second day of Pesach, page 956.

MAFTIR / מפטיר

(*Numbers* 29:12-16)

מפטיר וּבַחֲמִשָּׁה עָשָׂר יוֹם לַחֹדֶשׁ הַשְּׁבִיעִי מִקְרָא־קֹדֶשׁ יִהְיֶה לָכֶם כָּל־מְלֶאכֶת עֲבֹדָה לֹא תַעֲשׂוּ וְחַגֹּתֶם חַג לַיהוָה שִׁבְעַת יָמִים: וְהִקְרַבְתֶּם עֹלָה אִשֵּׁה רֵיחַ נִיחֹחַ לַיהוָה פָּרִים בְּנֵי־בָקָר שְׁלֹשָׁה עָשָׂר אֵילִם שְׁנָיִם כְּבָשִׂים בְּנֵי־שָׁנָה אַרְבָּעָה עָשָׂר תְּמִימִם יִהְיוּ: וּמִנְחָתָם סֹלֶת בְּלוּלָה בַשָּׁמֶן שְׁלֹשָׁה עֶשְׂרֹנִים לַפָּר הָאֶחָד לִשְׁלֹשָׁה עָשָׂר פָּרִים שְׁנֵי עֶשְׂרֹנִים לָאַיִל הָאֶחָד לִשְׁנֵי הָאֵילִם: וְעִשָּׂרוֹן עִשָּׂרוֹן לַכֶּבֶשׂ הָאֶחָד לְאַרְבָּעָה עָשָׂר כְּבָשִׂים: וּשְׂעִיר־עִזִּים אֶחָד חַטָּאת מִלְּבַד עֹלַת הַתָּמִיד מִנְחָתָהּ וְנִסְכָּהּ:

הפטרה — יום ראשון של סוכות
HAFTARAH — FIRST DAY SUCCOS

(*Zechariah* 14:1-21)

הִנֵּה יוֹם־בָּא לַיהוָה וְחֻלַּק שְׁלָלֵךְ בְּקִרְבֵּךְ: וְאָסַפְתִּי אֶת־כָּל־הַגּוֹיִם | אֶל־יְרוּשָׁלִַם לַמִּלְחָמָה וְנִלְכְּדָה הָעִיר וְנָשַׁסּוּ הַבָּתִּים וְהַנָּשִׁים תִּשָּׁכַבְנָה וְיָצָא חֲצִי הָעִיר בַּגּוֹלָה וְיֶתֶר הָעָם לֹא יִכָּרֵת מִן־הָעִיר: וְיָצָא יהוה וְנִלְחַם בַּגּוֹיִם הָהֵם כְּיוֹם הִלָּחֲמוֹ בְּיוֹם קְרָב: וְעָמְדוּ רַגְלָיו בַּיּוֹם־הַהוּא עַל־הַר הַזֵּיתִים אֲשֶׁר עַל־פְּנֵי יְרוּשָׁלִַם מִקֶּדֶם וְנִבְקַע הַר הַזֵּיתִים מֵחֶצְיוֹ מִזְרָחָה וָיָמָּה גֵּיא גְּדוֹלָה מְאֹד וּמָשׁ חֲצִי הָהָר צָפוֹנָה וְחֶצְיוֹ נֶגְבָּה: וְנַסְתֶּם גֵּיא־הָרַי כִּי־יַגִּיעַ גֵּי־הָרִים אֶל־אָצַל וְנַסְתֶּם כַּאֲשֶׁר נַסְתֶּם מִפְּנֵי הָרַעַשׁ בִּימֵי עֻזִּיָּה מֶלֶךְ־יְהוּדָה וּבָא יהוה אֱלֹהַי כָּל־קְדֹשִׁים עִמָּךְ: וְהָיָה בַּיּוֹם הַהוּא לֹא־יִהְיֶה אוֹר יְקָרוֹת וְקִפָּאוֹן: וְהָיָה יוֹם־אֶחָד הוּא יִוָּדַע לַיהוָה לֹא־יוֹם וְלֹא־לָיְלָה וְהָיָה לְעֶת־עֶרֶב יִהְיֶה־אוֹר: וְהָיָה | בַּיּוֹם הַהוּא יֵצְאוּ מַיִם־חַיִּים מִירוּשָׁלִַם חֶצְיָם אֶל־הַיָּם הַקַּדְמוֹנִי וְחֶצְיָם אֶל־הַיָּם הָאַחֲרוֹן בַּקַּיִץ וּבָחֹרֶף יִהְיֶה: וְהָיָה יהוה לְמֶלֶךְ עַל־כָּל־הָאָרֶץ בַּיּוֹם הַהוּא יִהְיֶה יהוה אֶחָד וּשְׁמוֹ אֶחָד: יִסּוֹב כָּל־הָאָרֶץ כָּעֲרָבָה מִגֶּבַע לְרִמּוֹן נֶגֶב יְרוּשָׁלִָם וְרָאֲמָה וְיָשְׁבָה תַחְתֶּיהָ לְמִשַּׁעַר בִּנְיָמִן עַד־מְקוֹם שַׁעַר הָרִאשׁוֹן עַד־שַׁעַר הַפִּנִּים וּמִגְדַּל חֲנַנְאֵל עַד יִקְבֵי הַמֶּלֶךְ: וְיָשְׁבוּ בָהּ וְחֵרֶם לֹא יִהְיֶה־עוֹד וְיָשְׁבָה יְרוּשָׁלִַם לָבֶטַח: וְזֹאת | תִּהְיֶה הַמַּגֵּפָה אֲשֶׁר יִגֹּף יהוה אֶת־כָּל־הָעַמִּים אֲשֶׁר צָבְאוּ עַל־יְרוּשָׁלִָם הָמֵק | בְּשָׂרוֹ וְהוּא עֹמֵד עַל־רַגְלָיו וְעֵינָיו תִּמַּקְנָה בְחֹרֵיהֶן וּלְשׁוֹנוֹ תִּמַּק בְּפִיהֶם: וְהָיָה בַּיּוֹם הַהוּא תִּהְיֶה מְהוּמַת־יהוה רַבָּה בָּהֶם וְהֶחֱזִיקוּ אִישׁ יַד רֵעֵהוּ וְעָלְתָה יָדוֹ עַל־יַד

רֵעֵהוּ: וְגַם־יְהוּדָה תִּלָּחֵם בִּירוּשָׁלָיִם וְאֻסַּף
חֵיל כָּל־הַגּוֹיִם סָבִיב זָהָב וָכֶסֶף וּבְגָדִים
לָרֹב מְאֹד: וְכֵן תִּהְיֶה מַגֵּפַת הַסּוּס הַפֶּרֶד
הַגָּמָל וְהַחֲמוֹר וְכָל־הַבְּהֵמָה אֲשֶׁר יִהְיֶה
בַּמַּחֲנוֹת הָהֵמָּה כַּמַּגֵּפָה הַזֹּאת: וְהָיָה כָּל־
הַנּוֹתָר מִכָּל־הַגּוֹיִם הַבָּאִים עַל־יְרוּשָׁלָיִם
וְעָלוּ מִדֵּי שָׁנָה בְשָׁנָה לְהִשְׁתַּחֲוֺת לְמֶלֶךְ
יהוה צְבָאוֹת וְלָחֹג אֶת־חַג הַסֻּכּוֹת: וְהָיָה
אֲשֶׁר לֹא־יַעֲלֶה מֵאֵת מִשְׁפְּחוֹת הָאָרֶץ
אֶל־יְרוּשָׁלַיִם לְהִשְׁתַּחֲוֺת לְמֶלֶךְ יהוה
צְבָאוֹת וְלֹא עֲלֵיהֶם יִהְיֶה הַגָּשֶׁם: וְאִם־
מִשְׁפַּחַת מִצְרַיִם לֹא־תַעֲלֶה וְלֹא בָאָה וְלֹא
עֲלֵיהֶם תִּהְיֶה הַמַּגֵּפָה אֲשֶׁר יִגֹּף יהוה אֶת־
הַגּוֹיִם אֲשֶׁר לֹא יַעֲלוּ לָחֹג אֶת־חַג הַסֻּכּוֹת:
זֹאת תִּהְיֶה חַטַּאת מִצְרָיִם וְחַטַּאת כָּל־
הַגּוֹיִם אֲשֶׁר לֹא יַעֲלוּ לָחֹג אֶת־חַג הַסֻּכּוֹת:
בַּיּוֹם הַהוּא יִהְיֶה עַל־מְצִלּוֹת הַסּוּס קֹדֶשׁ
לַיהוה וְהָיָה הַסִּירוֹת בְּבֵית יהוה כַּמִּזְרָקִים
לִפְנֵי הַמִּזְבֵּחַ: וְהָיָה כָּל־סִיר בִּירוּשָׁלַיִם
וּבִיהוּדָה קֹדֶשׁ לַיהוה צְבָאוֹת וּבָאוּ כָּל־
הַזֹּבְחִים וְלָקְחוּ מֵהֶם וּבִשְּׁלוּ בָהֶם וְלֹא־
יִהְיֶה כְנַעֲנִי עוֹד בְּבֵית־יהוה צְבָאוֹת בַּיּוֹם
הַהוּא:

הפטרה — יום שני של סוכות

HAFTARAH — SECOND DAY SUCCOS

(I Kings 8:2-21)

וַיִּקָּהֲלוּ אֶל־הַמֶּלֶךְ שְׁלֹמֹה כָּל־אִישׁ יִשְׂרָאֵל
בְּיֶרַח הָאֵתָנִים בֶּחָג הוּא הַחֹדֶשׁ הַשְּׁבִיעִי:
וַיָּבֹאוּ כֹּל זִקְנֵי יִשְׂרָאֵל וַיִּשְׂאוּ הַכֹּהֲנִים
אֶת־הָאָרוֹן: וַיַּעֲלוּ אֶת־אֲרוֹן יהוה וְאֶת־
אֹהֶל מוֹעֵד וְאֶת־כָּל־כְּלֵי הַקֹּדֶשׁ אֲשֶׁר
בָּאֹהֶל וַיַּעֲלוּ אֹתָם הַכֹּהֲנִים וְהַלְוִיִּם:
וְהַמֶּלֶךְ שְׁלֹמֹה וְכָל־עֲדַת יִשְׂרָאֵל הַנּוֹעָדִים
עָלָיו אִתּוֹ לִפְנֵי הָאָרוֹן מְזַבְּחִים צֹאן וּבָקָר
אֲשֶׁר לֹא־יִסָּפְרוּ וְלֹא יִמָּנוּ מֵרֹב: וַיָּבִאוּ
הַכֹּהֲנִים אֶת־אֲרוֹן בְּרִית־יהוה אֶל־מְקוֹמוֹ
אֶל־דְּבִיר הַבַּיִת אֶל־קֹדֶשׁ הַקֳּדָשִׁים אֶל־
תַּחַת כַּנְפֵי הַכְּרוּבִים: כִּי הַכְּרוּבִים פֹּרְשִׂים
כְּנָפַיִם אֶל־מְקוֹם הָאָרוֹן וַיָּסֹכּוּ הַכְּרֻבִים
עַל־הָאָרוֹן וְעַל־בַּדָּיו מִלְמָעְלָה: וַיַּאֲרִכוּ
הַבַּדִּים וַיֵּרָאוּ רָאשֵׁי הַבַּדִּים מִן־הַקֹּדֶשׁ
עַל־פְּנֵי הַדְּבִיר וְלֹא יֵרָאוּ הַחוּצָה וַיִּהְיוּ
שָׁם עַד הַיּוֹם הַזֶּה: אֵין בָּאָרוֹן רַק שְׁנֵי
לֻחוֹת הָאֲבָנִים אֲשֶׁר הִנִּחַ שָׁם מֹשֶׁה בְּחֹרֵב
אֲשֶׁר כָּרַת יהוה עִם־בְּנֵי יִשְׂרָאֵל בְּצֵאתָם
מֵאֶרֶץ מִצְרָיִם: וַיְהִי בְּצֵאת הַכֹּהֲנִים מִן־
הַקֹּדֶשׁ וְהֶעָנָן מָלֵא אֶת־בֵּית יהוה: וְלֹא־
יָכְלוּ הַכֹּהֲנִים לַעֲמֹד לְשָׁרֵת מִפְּנֵי הֶעָנָן כִּי־
מָלֵא כְבוֹד־יהוה אֶת־בֵּית יהוה: אָז אָמַר
שְׁלֹמֹה יהוה אָמַר לִשְׁכֹּן בָּעֲרָפֶל: בָּנֹה
בָנִיתִי בֵּית זְבֻל לָךְ מָכוֹן לְשִׁבְתְּךָ עוֹלָמִים:
וַיַּסֵּב הַמֶּלֶךְ אֶת־פָּנָיו וַיְבָרֶךְ אֵת כָּל־קְהַל
יִשְׂרָאֵל וְכָל־קְהַל יִשְׂרָאֵל עֹמֵד: וַיֹּאמֶר
בָּרוּךְ יהוה אֱלֹהֵי יִשְׂרָאֵל אֲשֶׁר דִּבֶּר בְּפִיו
אֵת דָּוִד אָבִי וּבְיָדוֹ מִלֵּא לֵאמֹר: מִן־הַיּוֹם
אֲשֶׁר הוֹצֵאתִי אֶת־עַמִּי אֶת־יִשְׂרָאֵל
מִמִּצְרַיִם לֹא־בָחַרְתִּי בְעִיר מִכֹּל שִׁבְטֵי
יִשְׂרָאֵל לִבְנוֹת בַּיִת לִהְיוֹת שְׁמִי שָׁם
וָאֶבְחַר בְּדָוִד לִהְיוֹת עַל־עַמִּי יִשְׂרָאֵל: וַיְהִי
עִם־לְבַב דָּוִד אָבִי לִבְנוֹת בַּיִת לְשֵׁם יהוה
אֱלֹהֵי יִשְׂרָאֵל: וַיֹּאמֶר יהוה אֶל־דָּוִד אָבִי
יַעַן אֲשֶׁר הָיָה עִם־לְבָבְךָ לִבְנוֹת בַּיִת לִשְׁמִי
הֱטִיבֹתָ כִּי הָיָה עִם־לְבָבֶךָ: רַק אַתָּה לֹא
תִבְנֶה הַבָּיִת כִּי אִם־בִּנְךָ הַיֹּצֵא מֵחֲלָצֶיךָ
הוּא־יִבְנֶה הַבַּיִת לִשְׁמִי: וַיָּקֶם יהוה אֶת־
דְּבָרוֹ אֲשֶׁר דִּבֵּר וָאָקֻם תַּחַת דָּוִד אָבִי
וָאֵשֵׁב | עַל־כִּסֵּא יִשְׂרָאֵל כַּאֲשֶׁר דִּבֶּר יהוה
וָאֶבְנֶה הַבַּיִת לְשֵׁם יהוה אֱלֹהֵי יִשְׂרָאֵל:
וָאָשִׂם שָׁם מָקוֹם לָאָרוֹן אֲשֶׁר־שָׁם בְּרִית
יהוה אֲשֶׁר כָּרַת עִם־אֲבֹתֵינוּ בְּהוֹצִיאוֹ
אֹתָם מֵאֶרֶץ מִצְרָיִם:

חול המועד סוכות

CHOL HAMOED SUCCOS

On each day of Chol HaMoed Succos (except on the Sabbath) one Torah scroll is removed from the ark and four *olim* are called to the Torah.

חול המועד סוכות — יום ראשון

CHOL HAMOED SUCCOS — FIRST DAY

(*Numbers* 29:17-25)

וּבַיּוֹם הַשֵּׁנִי פָּרִים בְּנֵי־בָקָר שְׁנֵים עָשָׂר
אֵילִם שְׁנָיִם כְּבָשִׂים בְּנֵי־שָׁנָה אַרְבָּעָה
עָשָׂר תְּמִימִם: וּמִנְחָתָם וְנִסְכֵּיהֶם לַפָּרִים
לָאֵילִם וְלַכְּבָשִׂים בְּמִסְפָּרָם כַּמִּשְׁפָּט:
וּשְׂעִיר־עִזִּים אֶחָד חַטָּאת מִלְּבַד עֹלַת
הַתָּמִיד וּמִנְחָתָהּ וְנִסְכֵּיהֶם:
לוי וּבַיּוֹם הַשְּׁלִישִׁי פָּרִים עַשְׁתֵּי־עָשָׂר
אֵילִם שְׁנָיִם כְּבָשִׂים בְּנֵי־שָׁנָה אַרְבָּעָה
עָשָׂר תְּמִימִם: וּמִנְחָתָם וְנִסְכֵּיהֶם לַפָּרִים

לָֽאֵילִ֛ם וְלַכְּבָשִׂ֖ים בְּמִסְפָּרָ֥ם כַּמִּשְׁפָּֽט׃ וּשְׂעִ֥יר חַטָּ֖את אֶחָ֑ד מִלְּבַד֙ עֹלַ֣ת הַתָּמִ֔יד וּמִנְחָתָ֖הּ וְנִסְכָּֽהּ׃

ישראל וּבַיּ֧וֹם הָרְבִיעִ֛י פָּרִ֥ים עֲשָׂרָ֖ה אֵילִ֣ם שְׁנָ֑יִם כְּבָשִׂ֧ים בְּנֵֽי־שָׁנָ֛ה אַרְבָּעָ֥ה עָשָׂ֖ר תְּמִימִֽם׃ מִנְחָתָ֣ם וְנִסְכֵּיהֶ֡ם לַ֠פָּרִים לָאֵילִ֧ם וְלַכְּבָשִׂ֛ים בְּמִסְפָּרָ֖ם כַּמִּשְׁפָּֽט׃ וּשְׂעִיר־עִזִּ֥ים אֶחָ֖ד חַטָּ֑את מִלְּבַד֙ עֹלַ֣ת הַתָּמִ֔יד מִנְחָתָ֖הּ וְנִסְכָּֽהּ׃

רביעי וּבַיּ֣וֹם הַשֵּׁנִ֗י פָּרִ֧ים בְּנֵי־בָקָ֛ר שְׁנֵ֥ים עָשָׂ֖ר אֵילִ֣ם שְׁנָ֑יִם כְּבָשִׂ֧ים בְּנֵֽי־שָׁנָ֛ה אַרְבָּעָ֥ה עָשָׂ֖ר תְּמִימִֽם׃ וּמִנְחָתָ֣ם וְנִסְכֵּיהֶ֡ם לַ֠פָּרִים לָֽאֵילִ֧ם וְלַכְּבָשִׂ֛ים בְּמִסְפָּרָ֖ם כַּמִּשְׁפָּֽט׃ וּשְׂעִיר־עִזִּ֥ים אֶחָ֖ד חַטָּ֑את מִלְּבַד֙ עֹלַ֣ת הַתָּמִ֔יד וּמִנְחָתָ֖ה וְנִסְכֵּיהֶֽם׃ וּבַיּ֧וֹם הַשְּׁלִישִׁ֛י פָּרִ֥ים עַשְׁתֵּי־עָשָׂ֖ר אֵילִ֣ם שְׁנָ֑יִם כְּבָשִׂ֧ים בְּנֵֽי־שָׁנָ֛ה אַרְבָּעָ֥ה עָשָׂ֖ר תְּמִימִֽם׃ וּמִנְחָתָ֣ם וְנִסְכֵּיהֶ֡ם לַ֠פָּרִים לָאֵילִ֧ם וְלַכְּבָשִׂ֛ים בְּמִסְפָּרָ֖ם כַּמִּשְׁפָּֽט׃ וּשְׂעִ֥יר חַטָּ֖את אֶחָ֑ד מִלְּבַד֙ עֹלַ֣ת הַתָּמִ֔יד וּמִנְחָתָ֖הּ וְנִסְכָּֽהּ׃

חול המועד סוכות — יום שני

CHOL HAMOED SUCCOS — SECOND DAY

(Numbers 29:20-28)

וּבַיּ֧וֹם הַשְּׁלִישִׁ֛י פָּרִ֥ים עַשְׁתֵּי־עָשָׂ֖ר אֵילִ֣ם שְׁנָ֑יִם כְּבָשִׂ֧ים בְּנֵֽי־שָׁנָ֛ה אַרְבָּעָ֥ה עָשָׂ֖ר תְּמִימִֽם׃ וּמִנְחָתָ֣ם וְנִסְכֵּיהֶ֡ם לַ֠פָּרִים לָאֵילִ֧ם וְלַכְּבָשִׂ֛ים בְּמִסְפָּרָ֖ם כַּמִּשְׁפָּֽט׃ וּשְׂעִ֥יר חַטָּ֖את אֶחָ֑ד מִלְּבַד֙ עֹלַ֣ת הַתָּמִ֔יד וּמִנְחָתָ֖הּ וְנִסְכָּֽהּ׃

לוי וּבַיּ֧וֹם הָרְבִיעִ֛י פָּרִ֥ים עֲשָׂרָ֖ה אֵילִ֣ם שְׁנָ֑יִם כְּבָשִׂ֧ים בְּנֵֽי־שָׁנָ֛ה אַרְבָּעָ֥ה עָשָׂ֖ר תְּמִימִֽם׃ מִנְחָתָ֣ם וְנִסְכֵּיהֶ֡ם לַ֠פָּרִים לָאֵילִ֧ם וְלַכְּבָשִׂ֛ים בְּמִסְפָּרָ֖ם כַּמִּשְׁפָּֽט׃ וּשְׂעִיר־עִזִּ֥ים אֶחָ֖ד חַטָּ֑את מִלְּבַד֙ עֹלַ֣ת הַתָּמִ֔יד מִנְחָתָ֖הּ וְנִסְכָּֽהּ׃

ישראל וּבַיּ֧וֹם הַחֲמִישִׁ֛י פָּרִ֥ים תִּשְׁעָ֖ה אֵילִ֣ם שְׁנָ֑יִם כְּבָשִׂ֧ים בְּנֵֽי־שָׁנָ֛ה אַרְבָּעָ֥ה עָשָׂ֖ר תְּמִימִֽם׃ וּמִנְחָתָ֣ם וְנִסְכֵּיהֶ֡ם לַ֠פָּרִים לָאֵילִ֧ם וְלַכְּבָשִׂ֛ים בְּמִסְפָּרָ֖ם כַּמִּשְׁפָּֽט׃ וּשְׂעִ֥יר חַטָּ֖את אֶחָ֑ד מִלְּבַד֙ עֹלַ֣ת הַתָּמִ֔יד וּמִנְחָתָ֖הּ וְנִסְכָּֽהּ׃

רביעי וּבַיּ֧וֹם הַשְּׁלִישִׁ֛י פָּרִ֥ים עַשְׁתֵּי־עָשָׂ֖ר אֵילִ֣ם שְׁנָ֑יִם כְּבָשִׂ֧ים בְּנֵֽי־שָׁנָ֛ה אַרְבָּעָ֥ה עָשָׂ֖ר תְּמִימִֽם׃ וּמִנְחָתָ֣ם וְנִסְכֵּיהֶ֡ם לַ֠פָּרִים לָאֵילִ֧ם וְלַכְּבָשִׂ֛ים בְּמִסְפָּרָ֖ם כַּמִּשְׁפָּֽט׃ וּשְׂעִ֥יר חַטָּ֖את אֶחָ֑ד מִלְּבַד֙ עֹלַ֣ת הַתָּמִ֔יד וּמִנְחָתָ֖הּ וְנִסְכָּֽהּ׃ וּבַיּ֧וֹם הָרְבִיעִ֛י פָּרִ֥ים עֲשָׂרָ֖ה אֵילִ֣ם שְׁנָ֑יִם כְּבָשִׂ֧ים בְּנֵֽי־שָׁנָ֛ה אַרְבָּעָ֥ה עָשָׂ֖ר תְּמִימִֽם׃ מִנְחָתָ֣ם וְנִסְכֵּיהֶ֡ם לַ֠פָּרִים לָאֵילִ֧ם וְלַכְּבָשִׂ֛ים בְּמִסְפָּרָ֖ם כַּמִּשְׁפָּֽט׃ וּשְׂעִיר־עִזִּ֥ים אֶחָ֖ד חַטָּ֑את מִלְּבַד֙ עֹלַ֣ת הַתָּמִ֔יד מִנְחָתָ֖הּ וְנִסְכָּֽהּ׃

חול המועד סוכות — יום שלישי

CHOL HAMOED SUCCOS — THIRD DAY

(Numbers 29:23-31)

וּבַיּ֧וֹם הָרְבִיעִ֛י פָּרִ֥ים עֲשָׂרָ֖ה אֵילִ֣ם שְׁנָ֑יִם כְּבָשִׂ֧ים בְּנֵֽי־שָׁנָ֛ה אַרְבָּעָ֥ה עָשָׂ֖ר תְּמִימִֽם׃ מִנְחָתָ֣ם וְנִסְכֵּיהֶ֡ם לַ֠פָּרִים לָאֵילִ֧ם וְלַכְּבָשִׂ֛ים בְּמִסְפָּרָ֖ם כַּמִּשְׁפָּֽט׃ וּשְׂעִיר־עִזִּ֥ים אֶחָ֖ד חַטָּ֑את מִלְּבַד֙ עֹלַ֣ת הַתָּמִ֔יד מִנְחָתָ֖הּ וְנִסְכָּֽהּ׃

לוי וּבַיּ֧וֹם הַחֲמִישִׁ֛י פָּרִ֥ים תִּשְׁעָ֖ה אֵילִ֣ם שְׁנָ֑יִם כְּבָשִׂ֧ים בְּנֵֽי־שָׁנָ֛ה אַרְבָּעָ֥ה עָשָׂ֖ר תְּמִימִֽם׃ וּמִנְחָתָ֣ם וְנִסְכֵּיהֶ֡ם לַ֠פָּרִים לָאֵילִ֧ם וְלַכְּבָשִׂ֛ים בְּמִסְפָּרָ֖ם כַּמִּשְׁפָּֽט׃ וּשְׂעִ֥יר חַטָּ֖את אֶחָ֑ד מִלְּבַד֙ עֹלַ֣ת הַתָּמִ֔יד וּמִנְחָתָ֖הּ וְנִסְכָּֽהּ׃

ישראל וּבַיּ֧וֹם הַשִּׁשִּׁ֛י פָּרִ֥ים שְׁמֹנָ֖ה אֵילִ֣ם שְׁנָ֑יִם כְּבָשִׂ֧ים בְּנֵֽי־שָׁנָ֛ה אַרְבָּעָ֥ה עָשָׂ֖ר תְּמִימִֽם׃ וּמִנְחָתָ֣ם וְנִסְכֵּיהֶ֡ם לַ֠פָּרִים לָאֵילִ֧ם וְלַכְּבָשִׂ֛ים בְּמִסְפָּרָ֖ם כַּמִּשְׁפָּֽט׃ וּשְׂעִ֥יר חַטָּ֖את אֶחָ֑ד מִלְּבַד֙ עֹלַ֣ת הַתָּמִ֔יד מִנְחָתָ֖הּ וּנְסָכֶֽיהָ׃

רביעי וּבַיּ֧וֹם הָרְבִיעִ֛י פָּרִ֥ים עֲשָׂרָ֖ה אֵילִ֣ם שְׁנָ֑יִם כְּבָשִׂ֧ים בְּנֵֽי־שָׁנָ֛ה אַרְבָּעָ֥ה עָשָׂ֖ר תְּמִימִֽם׃ מִנְחָתָ֣ם וְנִסְכֵּיהֶ֡ם לַ֠פָּרִים לָאֵילִ֧ם וְלַכְּבָשִׂ֛ים בְּמִסְפָּרָ֖ם כַּמִּשְׁפָּֽט׃ וּשְׂעִיר־עִזִּ֥ים אֶחָ֖ד חַטָּ֑את מִלְּבַד֙ עֹלַ֣ת הַתָּמִ֔יד מִנְחָתָ֖הּ וְנִסְכָּֽהּ׃ וּבַיּ֧וֹם הַחֲמִישִׁ֛י פָּרִ֥ים תִּשְׁעָ֖ה אֵילִ֣ם שְׁנָ֑יִם כְּבָשִׂ֧ים בְּנֵֽי־שָׁנָ֛ה אַרְבָּעָ֥ה עָשָׂ֖ר תְּמִימִֽם׃ וּמִנְחָתָ֣ם וְנִסְכֵּיהֶ֡ם לַ֠פָּרִים לָאֵילִ֧ם וְלַכְּבָשִׂ֛ים בְּמִסְפָּרָ֖ם כַּמִּשְׁפָּֽט׃ וּשְׂעִ֥יר חַטָּ֖את אֶחָ֑ד מִלְּבַד֙ עֹלַ֣ת הַתָּמִ֔יד וּמִנְחָתָ֖הּ וְנִסְכָּֽהּ׃

חול המועד סוכות — יום רביעי

CHOL HAMOED SUCCOS — FOURTH DAY

(Numbers 29:26-34)

וּבַיּ֧וֹם הַחֲמִישִׁ֛י פָּרִ֥ים תִּשְׁעָ֖ה אֵילִ֣ם שְׁנָ֑יִם כְּבָשִׂ֧ים בְּנֵי־שָׁנָ֛ה אַרְבָּעָ֥ה עָשָׂ֖ר תְּמִימִֽם׃ וּמִנְחָתָ֣ם וְנִסְכֵּיהֶ֡ם לַ֠פָּרִים לָאֵילִ֧ם וְלַכְּבָשִׂ֛ים בְּמִסְפָּרָ֖ם כַּמִּשְׁפָּֽט׃ וּשְׂעִ֥יר חַטָּ֖את אֶחָ֑ד מִלְּבַד֙ עֹלַ֣ת הַתָּמִ֔יד וּמִנְחָתָ֖הּ וְנִסְכָּֽהּ׃

לוי וּבַיּ֧וֹם הַשִּׁשִּׁ֛י פָּרִ֥ים שְׁמֹנָ֖ה אֵילִ֣ם שְׁנָ֑יִם כְּבָשִׂ֧ים בְּנֵי־שָׁנָ֛ה אַרְבָּעָ֥ה עָשָׂ֖ר תְּמִימִֽם׃ וּמִנְחָתָ֣ם וְנִסְכֵּיהֶ֡ם לַ֠פָּרִים לָאֵילִ֧ם וְלַכְּבָשִׂ֛ים בְּמִסְפָּרָ֖ם כַּמִּשְׁפָּֽט׃ וּשְׂעִ֥יר חַטָּ֖את אֶחָ֑ד מִלְּבַד֙ עֹלַ֣ת הַתָּמִ֔יד מִנְחָתָ֖הּ וּנְסָכֶֽיהָ׃

ישראל וּבַיּ֧וֹם הַשְּׁבִיעִ֛י פָּרִ֥ים שִׁבְעָ֖ה אֵילִ֣ם שְׁנָ֑יִם כְּבָשִׂ֧ים בְּנֵי־שָׁנָ֛ה אַרְבָּעָ֥ה עָשָׂ֖ר תְּמִימִֽם׃ וּמִנְחָתָ֣ם וְנִסְכֵּהֶ֡ם לַ֠פָּרִים לָאֵילִ֧ם וְלַכְּבָשִׂ֛ים בְּמִסְפָּרָ֖ם כְּמִשְׁפָּטָֽם׃ וּשְׂעִ֥יר חַטָּ֖את אֶחָ֑ד מִלְּבַד֙ עֹלַ֣ת הַתָּמִ֔יד מִנְחָתָ֖הּ וְנִסְכָּֽהּ׃

רביעי וּבַיּ֧וֹם הַחֲמִישִׁ֛י פָּרִ֥ים תִּשְׁעָ֖ה אֵילִ֣ם שְׁנָ֑יִם כְּבָשִׂ֧ים בְּנֵי־שָׁנָ֛ה אַרְבָּעָ֥ה עָשָׂ֖ר תְּמִימִֽם׃ וּמִנְחָתָ֣ם וְנִסְכֵּיהֶ֡ם לַ֠פָּרִים לָאֵילִ֧ם וְלַכְּבָשִׂ֛ים בְּמִסְפָּרָ֖ם כַּמִּשְׁפָּֽט׃ וּשְׂעִ֥יר חַטָּ֖את אֶחָ֑ד מִלְּבַד֙ עֹלַ֣ת הַתָּמִ֔יד וּמִנְחָתָ֖הּ וְנִסְכָּֽהּ׃ וּבַיּ֧וֹם הַשִּׁשִּׁ֛י פָּרִ֥ים שְׁמֹנָ֖ה אֵילִ֣ם שְׁנָ֑יִם כְּבָשִׂ֧ים בְּנֵי־שָׁנָ֛ה אַרְבָּעָ֥ה עָשָׂ֖ר תְּמִימִֽם׃ וּמִנְחָתָ֣ם וְנִסְכֵּיהֶ֡ם לַ֠פָּרִים לָאֵילִ֧ם וְלַכְּבָשִׂ֛ים בְּמִסְפָּרָ֖ם כַּמִּשְׁפָּֽט׃ וּשְׂעִ֥יר חַטָּ֖את אֶחָ֑ד מִלְּבַד֙ עֹלַ֣ת הַתָּמִ֔יד מִנְחָתָ֖הּ וּנְסָכֶֽיהָ׃

HOSHANA RABBAH / הושענא רבה

(Numbers 29:26-34)

וּבַיּ֧וֹם הַחֲמִישִׁ֛י פָּרִ֥ים תִּשְׁעָ֖ה אֵילִ֣ם שְׁנָ֑יִם כְּבָשִׂ֧ים בְּנֵי־שָׁנָ֛ה אַרְבָּעָ֥ה עָשָׂ֖ר תְּמִימִֽם׃ וּמִנְחָתָ֣ם וְנִסְכֵּיהֶ֡ם לַ֠פָּרִים לָאֵילִ֧ם וְלַכְּבָשִׂ֛ים בְּמִסְפָּרָ֖ם כַּמִּשְׁפָּֽט׃ וּשְׂעִ֥יר חַטָּ֖את אֶחָ֑ד מִלְּבַד֙ עֹלַ֣ת הַתָּמִ֔יד וּמִנְחָתָ֖הּ וְנִסְכָּֽהּ׃

לוי וּבַיּ֧וֹם הַשִּׁשִּׁ֛י פָּרִ֥ים שְׁמֹנָ֖ה אֵילִ֣ם שְׁנָ֑יִם כְּבָשִׂ֧ים בְּנֵי־שָׁנָ֛ה אַרְבָּעָ֥ה עָשָׂ֖ר תְּמִימִֽם׃ וּמִנְחָתָ֣ם וְנִסְכֵּיהֶ֡ם לַ֠פָּרִים לָאֵילִ֧ם וְלַכְּבָשִׂ֛ים בְּמִסְפָּרָ֖ם כַּמִּשְׁפָּֽט׃ וּשְׂעִ֥יר חַטָּ֖את אֶחָ֑ד מִלְּבַד֙ עֹלַ֣ת הַתָּמִ֔יד מִנְחָתָ֖הּ וּנְסָכֶֽיהָ׃

ישראל וּבַיּ֧וֹם הַשְּׁבִיעִ֛י פָּרִ֥ים שִׁבְעָ֖ה אֵילִ֣ם שְׁנָ֑יִם כְּבָשִׂ֧ים בְּנֵי־שָׁנָ֛ה אַרְבָּעָ֥ה עָשָׂ֖ר תְּמִימִֽם׃ וּמִנְחָתָ֣ם וְנִסְכֵּהֶ֡ם לַ֠פָּרִים לָאֵילִ֧ם וְלַכְּבָשִׂ֛ים בְּמִסְפָּרָ֖ם כְּמִשְׁפָּטָֽם׃ וּשְׂעִ֥יר חַטָּ֖את אֶחָ֑ד מִלְּבַד֙ עֹלַ֣ת הַתָּמִ֔יד מִנְחָתָ֖הּ וְנִסְכָּֽהּ׃

רביעי וּבַיּ֧וֹם הַשִּׁשִּׁ֛י פָּרִ֥ים שְׁמֹנָ֖ה אֵילִ֣ם שְׁנָ֑יִם כְּבָשִׂ֧ים בְּנֵי־שָׁנָ֛ה אַרְבָּעָ֥ה עָשָׂ֖ר תְּמִימִֽם׃ וּמִנְחָתָ֣ם וְנִסְכֵּיהֶ֡ם לַ֠פָּרִים לָאֵילִ֧ם וְלַכְּבָשִׂ֛ים בְּמִסְפָּרָ֖ם כַּמִּשְׁפָּֽט׃ וּשְׂעִ֥יר חַטָּ֖את אֶחָ֑ד מִלְּבַד֙ עֹלַ֣ת הַתָּמִ֔יד מִנְחָתָ֖הּ וּנְסָכֶֽיהָ׃ וּבַיּ֧וֹם הַשְּׁבִיעִ֛י פָּרִ֥ים שִׁבְעָ֖ה אֵילִ֣ם שְׁנָ֑יִם כְּבָשִׂ֧ים בְּנֵי־שָׁנָ֛ה אַרְבָּעָ֥ה עָשָׂ֖ר תְּמִימִֽם׃ וּמִנְחָתָ֣ם וְנִסְכֵּהֶ֡ם לַ֠פָּרִים לָאֵילִ֧ם וְלַכְּבָשִׂ֛ים בְּמִסְפָּרָ֖ם כְּמִשְׁפָּטָֽם׃ וּשְׂעִ֥יר חַטָּ֖את אֶחָ֑ד מִלְּבַד֙ עֹלַ֣ת הַתָּמִ֔יד מִנְחָתָ֖הּ וְנִסְכָּֽהּ׃

שבת חול המועד סוכות

SABBATH OF CHOL HAMOED SUCCOS

The reading of Sabbath Chol HaMoed Succos is the same as that of Sabbath Chol HaMoed Pesach, page 961.

MAFTIR / מפטיר

If the Sabbath coincides with the first day Chol HaMoed, *Maftir* begins וּבַיּוֹם הַשֵּׁנִי (p. 971);
third day Chol HaMoed, וּבַיּוֹם הָרְבִיעִי (p. 972);
fourth day Chol HaMoed, וּבַיּוֹם הַחֲמִישִׁי, see above.

HAFTARAH / הפטרה

(Ezekiel 38:18 — 39:16)

וְהָיָ֣ה ׀ בַּיּ֣וֹם הַה֗וּא בְּי֨וֹם בּ֥וֹא גוֹג֙ עַל־אַדְמַ֣ת יִשְׂרָאֵ֔ל נְאֻ֖ם אֲדֹנָ֣י יֱהֹוִ֑ה תַּעֲלֶ֥ה חֲמָתִ֖י בְּאַפִּֽי׃ וּבְקִנְאָתִ֥י בְאֵשׁ־עֶבְרָתִ֖י דִּבַּ֑רְתִּי אִם־לֹ֣א ׀ בַּיּ֣וֹם הַה֗וּא יִֽהְיֶה֙ רַ֣עַשׁ גָּד֔וֹל עַ֖ל אַדְמַ֥ת יִשְׂרָאֵֽל׃ וְרָעֲשׁ֣וּ מִפָּנַ֡י דְּגֵ֣י הַיָּם֩ וְע֨וֹף הַשָּׁמַ֜יִם וְחַיַּ֣ת הַשָּׂדֶ֗ה וְכָל־הָרֶ֙מֶשׂ֙ הָֽרֹמֵ֣שׂ עַל־הָאֲדָמָ֔ה וְכֹל֙ הָֽאָדָ֔ם אֲשֶׁ֖ר עַל־פְּנֵ֣י הָאֲדָמָ֑ה וְנֶהֶרְס֣וּ הֶהָרִ֗ים וְנָֽפְלוּ֙ הַמַּדְרֵג֔וֹת וְכָל־חוֹמָ֖ה לָאָ֥רֶץ תִּפּֽוֹל׃ וְקָרָ֨אתִי עָלָ֤יו לְכָל־הָרַי֙ חֶ֔רֶב נְאֻ֖ם אֲדֹנָ֣י יֱהֹוִ֑ה חֶ֥רֶב אִ֖ישׁ בְּאָחִ֥יו תִּהְיֶֽה׃ וְנִשְׁפַּטְתִּ֥י אִתּ֖וֹ בְּדֶ֣בֶר וּבְדָ֑ם וְגֶ֣שֶׁם שׁוֹטֵף֩ וְאַבְנֵ֨י אֶלְגָּבִ֜ישׁ אֵ֣שׁ וְגָפְרִ֗ית אַמְטִ֤יר עָלָיו֙ וְעַל־אֲגַפָּ֔יו וְעַל־עַמִּ֥ים רַבִּ֖ים אֲשֶׁ֥ר אִתּֽוֹ׃ וְהִתְגַּדִּלְתִּי֙ וְהִתְקַדִּשְׁתִּ֔י

וְנוֹדַעְתִּי לְעֵינֵי גּוֹיִם רַבִּים וְיָדְעוּ כִּי־אֲנִי יהוה: וְאַתָּה בֶן־אָדָם הִנָּבֵא עַל־גּוֹג וְאָמַרְתָּ כֹּה אָמַר אֲדֹנָי יֱהֹוִה הִנְנִי אֵלֶיךָ גּוֹג נְשִׂיא רֹאשׁ מֶשֶׁךְ וְתֻבָל: וְשֹׁבַבְתִּיךָ וְשִׁשֵּׁאתִיךָ וְהַעֲלִיתִיךָ מִיַּרְכְּתֵי צָפוֹן וַהֲבֵאוֹתִךָ עַל־הָרֵי יִשְׂרָאֵל: וְהִכֵּיתִי קַשְׁתְּךָ מִיַּד שְׂמֹאולֶךָ וְחִצֶּיךָ מִיַּד יְמִינְךָ אַפִּיל: עַל־הָרֵי יִשְׂרָאֵל תִּפּוֹל אַתָּה וְכָל־אֲגַפֶּיךָ וְעַמִּים אֲשֶׁר אִתָּךְ לְעֵיט צִפּוֹר כָּל־כָּנָף וְחַיַּת הַשָּׂדֶה נְתַתִּיךָ לְאָכְלָה: עַל־פְּנֵי הַשָּׂדֶה תִּפּוֹל כִּי אֲנִי דִבַּרְתִּי נְאֻם אֲדֹנָי יֱהֹוִה: וְשִׁלַּחְתִּי־אֵשׁ בְּמָגוֹג וּבְיֹשְׁבֵי הָאִיִּים לָבֶטַח וְיָדְעוּ כִּי־אֲנִי יהוה: וְאֶת־שֵׁם קָדְשִׁי אוֹדִיעַ בְּתוֹךְ עַמִּי יִשְׂרָאֵל וְלֹא־אַחֵל אֶת־שֵׁם־קָדְשִׁי עוֹד וְיָדְעוּ הַגּוֹיִם כִּי־אֲנִי יהוה קָדוֹשׁ בְּיִשְׂרָאֵל: הִנֵּה בָאָה וְנִהְיָתָה נְאֻם אֲדֹנָי יֱהֹוִה הוּא הַיּוֹם אֲשֶׁר דִּבַּרְתִּי: וְיָצְאוּ יֹשְׁבֵי | עָרֵי יִשְׂרָאֵל וּבִעֲרוּ וְהִשִּׂיקוּ בְּנֶשֶׁק וּמָגֵן וְצִנָּה בְּקֶשֶׁת וּבְחִצִּים וּבְמַקֵּל יָד וּבְרֹמַח וּבִעֲרוּ בָהֶם אֵשׁ שֶׁבַע שָׁנִים: וְלֹא־יִשְׂאוּ עֵצִים מִן־הַשָּׂדֶה וְלֹא יַחְטְבוּ מִן־הַיְּעָרִים כִּי בַנֶּשֶׁק יְבַעֲרוּ־אֵשׁ וְשָׁלְלוּ אֶת־שֹׁלְלֵיהֶם וּבָזְזוּ אֶת־בֹּזְזֵיהֶם נְאֻם אֲדֹנָי יֱהֹוִה: וְהָיָה בַיּוֹם הַהוּא אֶתֵּן לְגוֹג | מְקוֹם־שָׁם קֶבֶר בְּיִשְׂרָאֵל גֵּי הָעֹבְרִים קִדְמַת הַיָּם וְחֹסֶמֶת הִיא אֶת־הָעֹבְרִים וְקָבְרוּ שָׁם אֶת־גּוֹג וְאֶת־כָּל־הֲמוֹנֹה וְקָרְאוּ גֵּיא הֲמוֹן גּוֹג: וּקְבָרוּם בֵּית יִשְׂרָאֵל לְמַעַן טַהֵר אֶת־הָאָרֶץ שִׁבְעָה חֳדָשִׁים: וְקָבְרוּ כָּל־עַם הָאָרֶץ וְהָיָה לָהֶם לְשֵׁם יוֹם הִכָּבְדִי נְאֻם אֲדֹנָי יֱהֹוִה: וְאַנְשֵׁי תָמִיד יַבְדִּילוּ עֹבְרִים בָּאָרֶץ מְקַבְּרִים אֶת־הָעֹבְרִים אֶת־הַנּוֹתָרִים עַל־פְּנֵי הָאָרֶץ לְטַהֲרָהּ מִקְצֵה שִׁבְעָה־חֳדָשִׁים יַחְקֹרוּ: וְעָבְרוּ הָעֹבְרִים בָּאָרֶץ וְרָאָה עֶצֶם אָדָם וּבָנָה אֶצְלוֹ צִיּוּן עַד קָבְרוּ אֹתוֹ הַמְקַבְּרִים אֶל־גֵּיא הֲמוֹן גּוֹג: וְגַם שֶׁם־עִיר הֲמוֹנָה וְטִהֲרוּ הָאָרֶץ:

SHEMINI ATZERES / שמיני עצרת

The reading for Shemini Atzeres is the same as that of the eighth day of Pesach; see page 964.

MAFTIR / מפטיר

(Numbers 29:35 — 30:1)

מפטיר בַּיּוֹם הַשְּׁמִינִי עֲצֶרֶת תִּהְיֶה לָכֶם כָּל־מְלֶאכֶת עֲבֹדָה לֹא תַעֲשׂוּ: וְהִקְרַבְתֶּם עֹלָה אִשֵּׁה רֵיחַ נִיחֹחַ לַיהוה פַּר אֶחָד אַיִל אֶחָד כְּבָשִׂים בְּנֵי־שָׁנָה שִׁבְעָה תְּמִימִם: מִנְחָתָם וְנִסְכֵּיהֶם לַפָּר לָאַיִל וְלַכְּבָשִׂים בְּמִסְפָּרָם כַּמִּשְׁפָּט: וּשְׂעִיר חַטָּאת אֶחָד מִלְּבַד עֹלַת הַתָּמִיד וּמִנְחָתָהּ וְנִסְכָּהּ: אֵלֶּה תַּעֲשׂוּ לַיהוה בְּמוֹעֲדֵיכֶם לְבַד מִנִּדְרֵיכֶם וְנִדְבֹתֵיכֶם לְעֹלֹתֵיכֶם וּלְמִנְחֹתֵיכֶם וּלְנִסְכֵּיכֶם וּלְשַׁלְמֵיכֶם: וַיֹּאמֶר מֹשֶׁה אֶל־בְּנֵי יִשְׂרָאֵל כְּכֹל אֲשֶׁר־צִוָּה יהוה אֶת־מֹשֶׁה:

HAFTARAH / הפטרה

(I Kings 8:54 — 9:1)

וַיְהִי | כְּכַלּוֹת שְׁלֹמֹה לְהִתְפַּלֵּל אֶל־יהוה אֵת כָּל־הַתְּפִלָּה וְהַתְּחִנָּה הַזֹּאת קָם מִלִּפְנֵי מִזְבַּח יהוה מִכְּרֹעַ עַל־בִּרְכָּיו וְכַפָּיו פְּרֻשׂוֹת הַשָּׁמָיִם: וַיַּעֲמֹד וַיְבָרֶךְ אֵת כָּל־קְהַל יִשְׂרָאֵל קוֹל גָּדוֹל לֵאמֹר: בָּרוּךְ יהוה אֲשֶׁר נָתַן מְנוּחָה לְעַמּוֹ יִשְׂרָאֵל כְּכֹל אֲשֶׁר דִּבֵּר לֹא־נָפַל דָּבָר אֶחָד מִכֹּל דְּבָרוֹ הַטּוֹב אֲשֶׁר דִּבֶּר בְּיַד מֹשֶׁה עַבְדּוֹ: יְהִי יהוה אֱלֹהֵינוּ עִמָּנוּ כַּאֲשֶׁר הָיָה עִם־אֲבֹתֵינוּ אַל־יַעַזְבֵנוּ וְאַל־יִטְּשֵׁנוּ: לְהַטּוֹת לְבָבֵנוּ אֵלָיו לָלֶכֶת בְּכָל־דְּרָכָיו וְלִשְׁמֹר מִצְוֺתָיו וְחֻקָּיו וּמִשְׁפָּטָיו אֲשֶׁר צִוָּה אֶת־אֲבֹתֵינוּ: וְיִהְיוּ דְבָרַי אֵלֶּה אֲשֶׁר הִתְחַנַּנְתִּי לִפְנֵי יהוה קְרֹבִים אֶל־יהוה אֱלֹהֵינוּ יוֹמָם וָלָיְלָה לַעֲשׂוֹת | מִשְׁפַּט עַבְדּוֹ וּמִשְׁפַּט עַמּוֹ יִשְׂרָאֵל דְּבַר־יוֹם בְּיוֹמוֹ: לְמַעַן דַּעַת כָּל־עַמֵּי הָאָרֶץ כִּי יהוה הוּא הָאֱלֹהִים אֵין עוֹד: וְהָיָה לְבַבְכֶם שָׁלֵם עִם יהוה אֱלֹהֵינוּ לָלֶכֶת בְּחֻקָּיו וְלִשְׁמֹר מִצְוֺתָיו כַּיּוֹם הַזֶּה: וְהַמֶּלֶךְ וְכָל־יִשְׂרָאֵל עִמּוֹ זֹבְחִים זֶבַח לִפְנֵי יהוה: וַיִּזְבַּח שְׁלֹמֹה אֵת זֶבַח הַשְּׁלָמִים אֲשֶׁר זָבַח לַיהוה בָּקָר עֶשְׂרִים וּשְׁנַיִם אֶלֶף וְצֹאן מֵאָה וְעֶשְׂרִים אָלֶף וַיַּחְנְכוּ אֶת־בֵּית יהוה הַמֶּלֶךְ וְכָל־בְּנֵי יִשְׂרָאֵל: בַּיּוֹם הַהוּא קִדַּשׁ הַמֶּלֶךְ אֶת־תּוֹךְ הֶחָצֵר אֲשֶׁר לִפְנֵי בֵית־יהוה כִּי־עָשָׂה שָׁם אֶת־הָעֹלָה וְאֶת־הַמִּנְחָה וְאֵת חֶלְבֵי הַשְּׁלָמִים כִּי־מִזְבַּח הַנְּחֹשֶׁת אֲשֶׁר לִפְנֵי יהוה קָטֹן מֵהָכִיל אֶת־הָעֹלָה וְאֶת־הַמִּנְחָה וְאֵת חֶלְבֵי הַשְּׁלָמִים: וַיַּעַשׂ שְׁלֹמֹה בָעֵת־הַהִיא | אֶת־הֶחָג וְכָל־יִשְׂרָאֵל עִמּוֹ קָהָל גָּדוֹל מִלְּבוֹא חֲמָת | עַד־נַחַל מִצְרַיִם לִפְנֵי יהוה אֱלֹהֵינוּ שִׁבְעַת

יָמִים וְשִׁבְעַת יָמִים אַרְבָּעָה עָשָׂר יוֹם: בַּיּוֹם הַשְּׁמִינִי שִׁלַּח אֶת־הָעָם וַיְבָרְכוּ אֶת־הַמֶּלֶךְ וַיֵּלְכוּ לְאָהֳלֵיהֶם שְׂמֵחִים וְטוֹבֵי לֵב עַל כָּל־הַטּוֹבָה אֲשֶׁר עָשָׂה יהוה לְדָוִד עַבְדּוֹ וּלְיִשְׂרָאֵל עַמּוֹ: וַיְהִי כְּכַלּוֹת שְׁלֹמֹה לִבְנוֹת אֶת־בֵּית־יהוה וְאֶת־בֵּית הַמֶּלֶךְ וְאֵת כָּל־חֵשֶׁק שְׁלֹמֹה אֲשֶׁר חָפֵץ לַעֲשׂוֹת:

SIMCHAS TORAH / שמחת תורה

(Deuteronomy 33:1-26)

וְזֹאת הַבְּרָכָה אֲשֶׁר בֵּרַךְ מֹשֶׁה אִישׁ הָאֱלֹהִים אֶת־בְּנֵי יִשְׂרָאֵל לִפְנֵי מוֹתוֹ: וַיֹּאמַר יהוה מִסִּינַי בָּא וְזָרַח מִשֵּׂעִיר לָמוֹ הוֹפִיעַ מֵהַר פָּארָן וְאָתָה מֵרִבְבֹת קֹדֶשׁ מִימִינוֹ אֵשׁ דָּת לָמוֹ: אַף חֹבֵב עַמִּים כָּל־קְדֹשָׁיו בְּיָדֶךָ וְהֵם תֻּכּוּ לְרַגְלֶךָ יִשָּׂא מִדַּבְּרֹתֶיךָ: תּוֹרָה צִוָּה־לָנוּ מֹשֶׁה מוֹרָשָׁה קְהִלַּת יַעֲקֹב: וַיְהִי בִישֻׁרוּן מֶלֶךְ בְּהִתְאַסֵּף רָאשֵׁי עָם יַחַד שִׁבְטֵי יִשְׂרָאֵל: יְחִי רְאוּבֵן וְאַל־יָמֹת וִיהִי מְתָיו מִסְפָּר: וְזֹאת לִיהוּדָה וַיֹּאמַר שְׁמַע יהוה קוֹל יְהוּדָה וְאֶל־עַמּוֹ תְּבִיאֶנּוּ יָדָיו רָב לוֹ וְעֵזֶר מִצָּרָיו תִּהְיֶה:

לוי וּלְלֵוִי אָמַר תֻּמֶּיךָ וְאוּרֶיךָ לְאִישׁ חֲסִידֶךָ אֲשֶׁר נִסִּיתוֹ בְּמַסָּה תְּרִיבֵהוּ עַל־מֵי מְרִיבָה: הָאֹמֵר לְאָבִיו וּלְאִמּוֹ לֹא רְאִיתִיו וְאֶת־אֶחָיו לֹא הִכִּיר וְאֶת־בָּנָו לֹא יָדָע כִּי שָׁמְרוּ אִמְרָתֶךָ וּבְרִיתְךָ יִנְצֹרוּ: יוֹרוּ מִשְׁפָּטֶיךָ לְיַעֲקֹב וְתוֹרָתְךָ לְיִשְׂרָאֵל יָשִׂימוּ קְטוֹרָה בְּאַפֶּךָ וְכָלִיל עַל־מִזְבְּחֶךָ: בָּרֵךְ יהוה חֵילוֹ וּפֹעַל יָדָיו תִּרְצֶה מְחַץ מָתְנַיִם קָמָיו וּמְשַׂנְאָיו מִן־יְקוּמוּן: לְבִנְיָמִן אָמַר יְדִיד יהוה יִשְׁכֹּן לָבֶטַח עָלָיו חֹפֵף עָלָיו כָּל־הַיּוֹם וּבֵין כְּתֵפָיו שָׁכֵן:

שלישי וּלְיוֹסֵף אָמַר מְבֹרֶכֶת יהוה אַרְצוֹ מִמֶּגֶד שָׁמַיִם מִטָּל וּמִתְּהוֹם רֹבֶצֶת תָּחַת: וּמִמֶּגֶד תְּבוּאֹת שָׁמֶשׁ וּמִמֶּגֶד גֶּרֶשׁ יְרָחִים: וּמֵרֹאשׁ הַרְרֵי־קֶדֶם וּמִמֶּגֶד גִּבְעוֹת עוֹלָם: וּמִמֶּגֶד אֶרֶץ וּמְלֹאָהּ וּרְצוֹן שֹׁכְנִי סְנֶה תָּבוֹאתָה לְרֹאשׁ יוֹסֵף וּלְקָדְקֹד נְזִיר אֶחָיו: בְּכוֹר שׁוֹרוֹ הָדָר לוֹ וְקַרְנֵי רְאֵם קַרְנָיו בָּהֶם עַמִּים יְנַגַּח יַחְדָּו אַפְסֵי־אָרֶץ וְהֵם רִבְבוֹת אֶפְרַיִם וְהֵם אַלְפֵי מְנַשֶּׁה:

רביעי וְלִזְבוּלֻן אָמַר שְׂמַח זְבוּלֻן בְּצֵאתֶךָ וְיִשָּׂשכָר בְּאֹהָלֶיךָ: עַמִּים הַר־יִקְרָאוּ שָׁם יִזְבְּחוּ זִבְחֵי־צֶדֶק כִּי שֶׁפַע יַמִּים יִינָקוּ וּשְׂפֻנֵי טְמוּנֵי חוֹל: וּלְגָד אָמַר בָּרוּךְ מַרְחִיב גָּד כְּלָבִיא שָׁכֵן וְטָרַף זְרוֹעַ אַף־קָדְקֹד: וַיַּרְא רֵאשִׁית לוֹ כִּי־שָׁם חֶלְקַת מְחֹקֵק סָפוּן וַיֵּתֵא רָאשֵׁי עָם צִדְקַת יהוה עָשָׂה וּמִשְׁפָּטָיו עִם־יִשְׂרָאֵל:

חמישי וּלְדָן אָמַר דָּן גּוּר אַרְיֵה יְזַנֵּק מִן־הַבָּשָׁן: וּלְנַפְתָּלִי אָמַר נַפְתָּלִי שְׂבַע רָצוֹן וּמָלֵא בִּרְכַּת יהוה יָם וְדָרוֹם יְרָשָׁה: וּלְאָשֵׁר אָמַר בָּרוּךְ מִבָּנִים אָשֵׁר יְהִי רְצוּי אֶחָיו וְטֹבֵל בַּשֶּׁמֶן רַגְלוֹ: בַּרְזֶל וּנְחֹשֶׁת מִנְעָלֶךָ וּכְיָמֶיךָ דָּבְאֶךָ: אֵין כָּאֵל יְשֻׁרוּן רֹכֵב שָׁמַיִם בְּעֶזְרֶךָ וּבְגַאֲוָתוֹ שְׁחָקִים:

CHASAN TORAH / חתן תורה

(Deuteronomy 33:27 — 34:12)

מְעֹנָה אֱלֹהֵי קֶדֶם וּמִתַּחַת זְרֹעֹת עוֹלָם וַיְגָרֶשׁ מִפָּנֶיךָ אוֹיֵב וַיֹּאמֶר הַשְׁמֵד: וַיִּשְׁכֹּן יִשְׂרָאֵל בֶּטַח בָּדָד עֵין יַעֲקֹב אֶל־אֶרֶץ דָּגָן וְתִירוֹשׁ אַף־שָׁמָיו יַעַרְפוּ־טָל: אַשְׁרֶיךָ יִשְׂרָאֵל מִי כָמוֹךָ עַם נוֹשַׁע בַּיהוה מָגֵן עֶזְרֶךָ וַאֲשֶׁר־חֶרֶב גַּאֲוָתֶךָ וְיִכָּחֲשׁוּ אֹיְבֶיךָ לָךְ וְאַתָּה עַל־בָּמוֹתֵימוֹ תִדְרֹךְ: וַיַּעַל מֹשֶׁה מֵעַרְבֹת מוֹאָב אֶל־הַר נְבוֹ רֹאשׁ הַפִּסְגָּה אֲשֶׁר עַל־פְּנֵי יְרֵחוֹ וַיַּרְאֵהוּ יהוה אֶת־כָּל־הָאָרֶץ אֶת־הַגִּלְעָד עַד־דָּן: וְאֵת כָּל־נַפְתָּלִי וְאֶת־אֶרֶץ אֶפְרַיִם וּמְנַשֶּׁה וְאֵת כָּל־אֶרֶץ יְהוּדָה עַד הַיָּם הָאַחֲרוֹן: וְאֶת־הַנֶּגֶב וְאֶת־הַכִּכָּר בִּקְעַת יְרֵחוֹ עִיר הַתְּמָרִים עַד־צֹעַר: וַיֹּאמֶר יהוה אֵלָיו זֹאת הָאָרֶץ אֲשֶׁר נִשְׁבַּעְתִּי לְאַבְרָהָם לְיִצְחָק וּלְיַעֲקֹב לֵאמֹר לְזַרְעֲךָ אֶתְּנֶנָּה הֶרְאִיתִיךָ בְעֵינֶיךָ וְשָׁמָּה לֹא תַעֲבֹר: וַיָּמָת שָׁם מֹשֶׁה עֶבֶד־יהוה בְּאֶרֶץ מוֹאָב עַל־פִּי יהוה: וַיִּקְבֹּר אֹתוֹ בַגַּי בְּאֶרֶץ מוֹאָב מוּל בֵּית פְּעוֹר וְלֹא־יָדַע אִישׁ אֶת־קְבֻרָתוֹ עַד הַיּוֹם הַזֶּה: וּמֹשֶׁה בֶּן־מֵאָה וְעֶשְׂרִים שָׁנָה בְּמֹתוֹ לֹא־כָהֲתָה עֵינוֹ וְלֹא־נָס לֵחֹה: וַיִּבְכּוּ בְנֵי יִשְׂרָאֵל אֶת־מֹשֶׁה בְּעַרְבֹת מוֹאָב שְׁלֹשִׁים יוֹם וַיִּתְּמוּ יְמֵי בְכִי אֵבֶל מֹשֶׁה: וִיהוֹשֻׁעַ בִּן־נוּן מָלֵא רוּחַ חָכְמָה כִּי־סָמַךְ מֹשֶׁה אֶת־יָדָיו עָלָיו וַיִּשְׁמְעוּ אֵלָיו בְּנֵי־יִשְׂרָאֵל וַיַּעֲשׂוּ כַּאֲשֶׁר צִוָּה יהוה אֶת־מֹשֶׁה: וְלֹא־קָם נָבִיא עוֹד בְּיִשְׂרָאֵל כְּמֹשֶׁה אֲשֶׁר יְדָעוֹ יהוה פָּנִים אֶל־פָּנִים: לְכָל־הָאֹתֹת וְהַמּוֹפְתִים אֲשֶׁר

שְׁלָחוֹ יְהוָה לַעֲשׂוֹת בְּאֶרֶץ מִצְרָיִם לְפַרְעֹה וּלְכָל־עֲבָדָיו וּלְכָל־אַרְצוֹ: וּלְכֹל הַיָּד הַחֲזָקָה וּלְכֹל הַמּוֹרָא הַגָּדוֹל אֲשֶׁר עָשָׂה מֹשֶׁה לְעֵינֵי כָּל־יִשְׂרָאֵל:

CHASAN BEREISHIS / חתן בראשית

(*Genesis* 1:1 — 2:3)

בְּרֵאשִׁית בָּרָא אֱלֹהִים אֵת הַשָּׁמַיִם וְאֵת הָאָרֶץ: וְהָאָרֶץ הָיְתָה תֹהוּ וָבֹהוּ וְחֹשֶׁךְ עַל־פְּנֵי תְהוֹם וְרוּחַ אֱלֹהִים מְרַחֶפֶת עַל־פְּנֵי הַמָּיִם: וַיֹּאמֶר אֱלֹהִים יְהִי־אוֹר וַיְהִי־אוֹר: וַיַּרְא אֱלֹהִים אֶת־הָאוֹר כִּי־טוֹב וַיַּבְדֵּל אֱלֹהִים בֵּין הָאוֹר וּבֵין הַחֹשֶׁךְ: וַיִּקְרָא אֱלֹהִים | לָאוֹר יוֹם וְלַחֹשֶׁךְ קָרָא לָיְלָה וַיְהִי־עֶרֶב וַיְהִי־בֹקֶר יוֹם אֶחָד: וַיֹּאמֶר אֱלֹהִים יְהִי רָקִיעַ בְּתוֹךְ הַמָּיִם וִיהִי מַבְדִּיל בֵּין מַיִם לָמָיִם: וַיַּעַשׂ אֱלֹהִים אֶת־הָרָקִיעַ וַיַּבְדֵּל בֵּין הַמַּיִם אֲשֶׁר מִתַּחַת לָרָקִיעַ וּבֵין הַמַּיִם אֲשֶׁר מֵעַל לָרָקִיעַ וַיְהִי־כֵן: וַיִּקְרָא אֱלֹהִים לָרָקִיעַ שָׁמָיִם וַיְהִי־עֶרֶב וַיְהִי־בֹקֶר יוֹם שֵׁנִי: וַיֹּאמֶר אֱלֹהִים יִקָּווּ הַמַּיִם מִתַּחַת הַשָּׁמַיִם אֶל־מָקוֹם אֶחָד וְתֵרָאֶה הַיַּבָּשָׁה וַיְהִי־כֵן: וַיִּקְרָא אֱלֹהִים | לַיַּבָּשָׁה אֶרֶץ וּלְמִקְוֵה הַמַּיִם קָרָא יַמִּים וַיַּרְא אֱלֹהִים כִּי־טוֹב: וַיֹּאמֶר אֱלֹהִים תַּדְשֵׁא הָאָרֶץ דֶּשֶׁא עֵשֶׂב מַזְרִיעַ זֶרַע עֵץ פְּרִי עֹשֶׂה פְּרִי לְמִינוֹ אֲשֶׁר זַרְעוֹ־בוֹ עַל־הָאָרֶץ וַיְהִי־כֵן: וַתּוֹצֵא הָאָרֶץ דֶּשֶׁא עֵשֶׂב מַזְרִיעַ זֶרַע לְמִינֵהוּ וְעֵץ עֹשֶׂה־פְּרִי אֲשֶׁר זַרְעוֹ־בוֹ לְמִינֵהוּ וַיַּרְא אֱלֹהִים כִּי־טוֹב: וַיְהִי־עֶרֶב וַיְהִי־בֹקֶר יוֹם שְׁלִישִׁי: וַיֹּאמֶר אֱלֹהִים יְהִי מְאֹרֹת בִּרְקִיעַ הַשָּׁמַיִם לְהַבְדִּיל בֵּין הַיּוֹם וּבֵין הַלָּיְלָה וְהָיוּ לְאֹתֹת וּלְמוֹעֲדִים וּלְיָמִים וְשָׁנִים: וְהָיוּ לִמְאוֹרֹת בִּרְקִיעַ הַשָּׁמַיִם לְהָאִיר עַל־הָאָרֶץ וַיְהִי־כֵן: וַיַּעַשׂ אֱלֹהִים אֶת־שְׁנֵי הַמְּאֹרֹת הַגְּדֹלִים אֶת־הַמָּאוֹר הַגָּדֹל לְמֶמְשֶׁלֶת הַיּוֹם וְאֶת־הַמָּאוֹר הַקָּטֹן לְמֶמְשֶׁלֶת הַלַּיְלָה וְאֵת הַכּוֹכָבִים: וַיִּתֵּן אֹתָם אֱלֹהִים בִּרְקִיעַ הַשָּׁמָיִם לְהָאִיר עַל־הָאָרֶץ: וְלִמְשֹׁל בַּיּוֹם וּבַלַּיְלָה וּלֲהַבְדִּיל בֵּין הָאוֹר וּבֵין הַחֹשֶׁךְ וַיַּרְא אֱלֹהִים כִּי־טוֹב: וַיְהִי־עֶרֶב וַיְהִי־בֹקֶר יוֹם רְבִיעִי: וַיֹּאמֶר אֱלֹהִים יִשְׁרְצוּ הַמַּיִם שֶׁרֶץ נֶפֶשׁ חַיָּה וְעוֹף יְעוֹפֵף עַל־הָאָרֶץ עַל־פְּנֵי רְקִיעַ הַשָּׁמָיִם: וַיִּבְרָא אֱלֹהִים אֶת־הַתַּנִּינִם הַגְּדֹלִים וְאֵת כָּל־נֶפֶשׁ הַחַיָּה | הָרֹמֶשֶׂת אֲשֶׁר שָׁרְצוּ הַמַּיִם לְמִינֵהֶם וְאֵת כָּל־עוֹף כָּנָף לְמִינֵהוּ וַיַּרְא אֱלֹהִים כִּי־טוֹב: וַיְבָרֶךְ אֹתָם אֱלֹהִים לֵאמֹר פְּרוּ וּרְבוּ וּמִלְאוּ אֶת־הַמַּיִם בַּיַּמִּים וְהָעוֹף יִרֶב בָּאָרֶץ: וַיְהִי־עֶרֶב וַיְהִי־בֹקֶר יוֹם חֲמִישִׁי: וַיֹּאמֶר אֱלֹהִים תּוֹצֵא הָאָרֶץ נֶפֶשׁ חַיָּה לְמִינָהּ בְּהֵמָה וָרֶמֶשׂ וְחַיְתוֹ־אֶרֶץ לְמִינָהּ וַיְהִי־כֵן: וַיַּעַשׂ אֱלֹהִים אֶת־חַיַּת הָאָרֶץ לְמִינָהּ וְאֶת־הַבְּהֵמָה לְמִינָהּ וְאֵת כָּל־רֶמֶשׂ הָאֲדָמָה לְמִינֵהוּ וַיַּרְא אֱלֹהִים כִּי־טוֹב: וַיֹּאמֶר אֱלֹהִים נַעֲשֶׂה אָדָם בְּצַלְמֵנוּ כִּדְמוּתֵנוּ וְיִרְדּוּ בִדְגַת הַיָּם וּבְעוֹף הַשָּׁמַיִם וּבַבְּהֵמָה וּבְכָל־הָאָרֶץ וּבְכָל־הָרֶמֶשׂ הָרֹמֵשׂ עַל־הָאָרֶץ: וַיִּבְרָא אֱלֹהִים | אֶת־הָאָדָם בְּצַלְמוֹ בְּצֶלֶם אֱלֹהִים בָּרָא אֹתוֹ זָכָר וּנְקֵבָה בָּרָא אֹתָם: וַיְבָרֶךְ אֹתָם אֱלֹהִים וַיֹּאמֶר לָהֶם אֱלֹהִים פְּרוּ וּרְבוּ וּמִלְאוּ אֶת־הָאָרֶץ וְכִבְשֻׁהָ וּרְדוּ בִּדְגַת הַיָּם וּבְעוֹף הַשָּׁמַיִם וּבְכָל־חַיָּה הָרֹמֶשֶׂת עַל־הָאָרֶץ: וַיֹּאמֶר אֱלֹהִים הִנֵּה נָתַתִּי לָכֶם אֶת־כָּל־עֵשֶׂב | זֹרֵעַ זֶרַע אֲשֶׁר עַל־פְּנֵי כָל־הָאָרֶץ וְאֶת־כָּל־הָעֵץ אֲשֶׁר־בּוֹ פְרִי־עֵץ זֹרֵעַ זָרַע לָכֶם יִהְיֶה לְאָכְלָה: וּלְכָל־חַיַּת הָאָרֶץ וּלְכָל־עוֹף הַשָּׁמַיִם וּלְכֹל | רוֹמֵשׂ עַל־הָאָרֶץ אֲשֶׁר־בּוֹ נֶפֶשׁ חַיָּה אֶת־כָּל־יֶרֶק עֵשֶׂב לְאָכְלָה וַיְהִי־כֵן: וַיַּרְא אֱלֹהִים אֶת־כָּל־אֲשֶׁר עָשָׂה וְהִנֵּה־טוֹב מְאֹד וַיְהִי־עֶרֶב וַיְהִי־בֹקֶר יוֹם הַשִּׁשִּׁי: וַיְכֻלּוּ הַשָּׁמַיִם וְהָאָרֶץ וְכָל־צְבָאָם: וַיְכַל אֱלֹהִים בַּיּוֹם הַשְּׁבִיעִי מְלַאכְתּוֹ אֲשֶׁר עָשָׂה וַיִּשְׁבֹּת בַּיּוֹם הַשְּׁבִיעִי מִכָּל־מְלַאכְתּוֹ אֲשֶׁר עָשָׂה: וַיְבָרֶךְ אֱלֹהִים אֶת־יוֹם הַשְּׁבִיעִי וַיְקַדֵּשׁ אֹתוֹ כִּי בוֹ שָׁבַת מִכָּל־מְלַאכְתּוֹ אֲשֶׁר־בָּרָא אֱלֹהִים לַעֲשׂוֹת:

The *Maftir* of Simchas Torah is the same as that of Shemini Atzeres, page 974.

HAFTARAH / הפטרה

(*Joshua* 1:1-18)

וַיְהִי אַחֲרֵי מוֹת מֹשֶׁה עֶבֶד יְהוָה וַיֹּאמֶר יְהוָה אֶל־יְהוֹשֻׁעַ בִּן־נוּן מְשָׁרֵת מֹשֶׁה לֵאמֹר: מֹשֶׁה עַבְדִּי מֵת וְעַתָּה קוּם עֲבֹר אֶת־הַיַּרְדֵּן הַזֶּה אַתָּה וְכָל־הָעָם הַזֶּה אֶל־הָאָרֶץ אֲשֶׁר אָנֹכִי נֹתֵן לָהֶם לִבְנֵי יִשְׂרָאֵל: כָּל־מָקוֹם אֲשֶׁר תִּדְרֹךְ כַּף־רַגְלְכֶם בּוֹ לָכֶם

נְתַתִּיו כַּאֲשֶׁר דִּבַּרְתִּי אֶל־מֹשֶׁה׃ מֵהַמִּדְבָּר וְהַלְּבָנוֹן הַזֶּה וְעַד־הַנָּהָר הַגָּדוֹל נְהַר־פְּרָת כֹּל אֶרֶץ הַחִתִּים וְעַד־הַיָּם הַגָּדוֹל מְבוֹא הַשָּׁמֶשׁ יִהְיֶה גְּבוּלְכֶם׃ לֹא־יִתְיַצֵּב אִישׁ לְפָנֶיךָ כֹּל יְמֵי חַיֶּיךָ כַּאֲשֶׁר הָיִיתִי עִם־מֹשֶׁה אֶהְיֶה עִמָּךְ לֹא אַרְפְּךָ וְלֹא אֶעֶזְבֶךָּ׃ חֲזַק וֶאֱמָץ כִּי אַתָּה תַּנְחִיל אֶת־הָעָם הַזֶּה אֶת־הָאָרֶץ אֲשֶׁר־נִשְׁבַּעְתִּי לַאֲבוֹתָם לָתֵת לָהֶם׃ רַק חֲזַק וֶאֱמַץ מְאֹד לִשְׁמֹר לַעֲשׂוֹת כְּכָל־הַתּוֹרָה אֲשֶׁר צִוְּךָ מֹשֶׁה עַבְדִּי אַל־תָּסוּר מִמֶּנּוּ יָמִין וּשְׂמֹאול לְמַעַן תַּשְׂכִּיל בְּכֹל אֲשֶׁר תֵּלֵךְ׃ לֹא־יָמוּשׁ סֵפֶר הַתּוֹרָה הַזֶּה מִפִּיךָ וְהָגִיתָ בּוֹ יוֹמָם וָלַיְלָה לְמַעַן תִּשְׁמֹר לַעֲשׂוֹת כְּכָל־הַכָּתוּב בּוֹ כִּי־אָז תַּצְלִיחַ אֶת־דְּרָכֶךָ וְאָז תַּשְׂכִּיל׃ הֲלוֹא צִוִּיתִיךָ חֲזַק וֶאֱמָץ אַל־תַּעֲרֹץ וְאַל־תֵּחָת כִּי עִמְּךָ יהוה אֱלֹהֶיךָ בְּכֹל אֲשֶׁר תֵּלֵךְ׃ וַיְצַו יְהוֹשֻׁעַ אֶת־שֹׁטְרֵי הָעָם לֵאמֹר׃ עִבְרוּ | בְּקֶרֶב הַמַּחֲנֶה וְצַוּוּ אֶת־הָעָם לֵאמֹר הָכִינוּ לָכֶם צֵידָה כִּי בְּעוֹד | שְׁלֹשֶׁת יָמִים אַתֶּם עֹבְרִים אֶת־הַיַּרְדֵּן הַזֶּה לָבוֹא לָרֶשֶׁת אֶת־הָאָרֶץ אֲשֶׁר יהוה אֱלֹהֵיכֶם נֹתֵן לָכֶם לְרִשְׁתָּהּ׃ וְלָרְאוּבֵנִי וְלַגָּדִי וְלַחֲצִי שֵׁבֶט הַמְנַשֶּׁה אָמַר יְהוֹשֻׁעַ לֵאמֹר׃ זָכוֹר אֶת־הַדָּבָר אֲשֶׁר צִוָּה אֶתְכֶם מֹשֶׁה עֶבֶד־יהוה לֵאמֹר יהוה אֱלֹהֵיכֶם מֵנִיחַ לָכֶם וְנָתַן לָכֶם אֶת־הָאָרֶץ הַזֹּאת׃ נְשֵׁיכֶם טַפְּכֶם וּמִקְנֵיכֶם יֵשְׁבוּ בָּאָרֶץ אֲשֶׁר נָתַן לָכֶם מֹשֶׁה בְּעֵבֶר הַיַּרְדֵּן וְאַתֶּם תַּעַבְרוּ חֲמֻשִׁים לִפְנֵי אֲחֵיכֶם כֹּל גִּבּוֹרֵי הַחַיִל וַעֲזַרְתֶּם אוֹתָם׃ עַד אֲשֶׁר־יָנִיחַ יהוה | לַאֲחֵיכֶם כָּכֶם וְיָרְשׁוּ גַם־הֵמָּה אֶת־הָאָרֶץ אֲשֶׁר־יהוה אֱלֹהֵיכֶם נֹתֵן לָהֶם וְשַׁבְתֶּם לְאֶרֶץ יְרֻשַּׁתְכֶם וִירִשְׁתֶּם אוֹתָהּ אֲשֶׁר | נָתַן לָכֶם מֹשֶׁה עֶבֶד יהוה בְּעֵבֶר הַיַּרְדֵּן מִזְרַח הַשָּׁמֶשׁ׃ וַיַּעֲנוּ אֶת־יְהוֹשֻׁעַ לֵאמֹר כֹּל אֲשֶׁר־צִוִּיתָנוּ נַעֲשֶׂה וְאֶל־כָּל־אֲשֶׁר תִּשְׁלָחֵנוּ נֵלֵךְ׃ כְּכֹל אֲשֶׁר־שָׁמַעְנוּ אֶל־מֹשֶׁה כֵּן נִשְׁמַע אֵלֶיךָ רַק יִהְיֶה יהוה אֱלֹהֶיךָ עִמָּךְ כַּאֲשֶׁר הָיָה עִם־מֹשֶׁה׃ כָּל־אִישׁ אֲשֶׁר־יַמְרֶה אֶת־פִּיךָ וְלֹא־יִשְׁמַע אֶת־דְּבָרֶיךָ לְכֹל אֲשֶׁר־תְּצַוֶּנּוּ יוּמָת רַק חֲזַק וֶאֱמָץ׃

הלכות תפלה / GENERAL LAWS OF PRAYER

compiled by Rabbi Hersh Goldwurm

Although most of the laws appear in the course of the Siddur where they are applicable, in some cases they are too involved or they apply to many areas. A selection of such laws are compiled in this section.

The reader should be aware that this digest cannot cover all eventualities and in many cases it should be regarded merely as a guide on when to consult a competent halachic authority. As a general rule, when a particular *halachah* is in dispute, we follow the ruling of *Mishnah Berurah*. On occasion, however (usually when *Mishnah Berurah* does not give a definitive ruling), we cite more than one opinion. In such cases, each congregation is bound by its tradition and the ruling of its authorities.

Throughout this digest, *Orach Chaim* is abbreviated as O.C. and *Mishnah Berurah* as M.B.

GENERAL INSTRUCTIONS

The Obligation

1. The Torah commands us to pray every day, as it is said *(Ex.* 23:25): *And you shall serve HASHEM your God* ... The oral tradition teaches that the service referred to is the service of the heart — prayer *(Rambam, Hil. Tefillah* 1:1).

2. Before praying, one should set aside a few minutes to collect his thoughts and to prepare himself mentally to stand before his Maker. One should also not rush away immediately after ending his prayer so as not to give the impression that praying is a burdensome task (O.C. 93:1).

Before beginning to pray, one should meditate upon God's infinite greatness and man's insignificance, and thereby remove from his heart any thoughts of physical pleasure (O.C. 98:1). By pondering God's works, man recognizes His infinite wisdom and comes to love and laud Him. This makes man cognizant of his own puny intelligence and flawed nature and puts him in a proper frame of mind to plead for God's mercy *(Rambam, Yesodei HaTorah* 2:2).

3. The prayers should be said with a feeling of awe and humility and surely not in an atmosphere of levity, frivolity, or mundane concerns, nor should one pray while under the influence of anger. Rather one should pray with the feeling of happiness brought on by the knowledge of God's historic kindness to Israel and His mercy to all creatures (O.C. 93:2).

The Place

4. Ideally one should pray in a building and not in an open place, for a private place is more conducive to both personal humility and the awe of the King (O.C. 90:5). The room where one prays should have windows or doors facing east toward Jerusalem (O.C. 90:4).

5. If one is traveling and cannot pray in a house, he should, if possible, stand among trees for they provide a modicum of privacy (M.B. 90:11). It is of utmost importance to choose a place where one is reasonably sure not to be interrupted (ibid.).

Concentration on the Prayers

6. During *Shemoneh Esrei* one's eyes should be directed downward (O.C. 95:2). His eyes should either be closed or reading from the *siddur* and not looking around (M.B. 95:5). One should not look up during *Shemoneh Esrei*, but when he feels his concentration failing he should raise his eyes heavenward to renew his inspiration (M.B. 90:8). One should imagine that he is in the Holy Temple and concentrate his feelings and thoughts toward Heaven (O.C. 95:2).

7. One must clear his mind of distractions and concentrate on his prayers, recognizing that he is in the Divine Presence. It is important that one should know the meaning of his prayers. If he had an audience with a human ruler he would take the utmost care in his choice of words and be aware of their meaning. Surely, therefore when one speaks before the King of Kings Who knows one's innermost thoughts, he must be careful how he speaks (O.C. 98:1). This concentration is stressed especially in regard to the benedictions of *Shemoneh Esrei* (O.C. 101:1). If one finds it difficult to maintain his concentration throughout the *Shemoneh Esrei* he should at least meditate on the meaning of the concluding sentence of each benediction, which summarizes its theme (e.g., בָּרוּךְ ... מְבָרֵךְ הַשָּׁנִים, *Blessed ... Who blesses the years;* M.B. §1). The first benediction of the *Shemoneh Esrei* is treated with special stringency in this regard. According to the *halachah* as stated in the Talmud, this benediction must be repeated if it was said without concentration on its meaning (O.C. 101:1). However, *Rama* (loc. cit.) rules that it is best *not* to repeat the benediction because it is likely that one will not concentrate properly even during the repetition. *Chaye Adam* (cited in M.B. 101:4) advises that if one realized his inattentiveness before saying the word *HASHEM* in the concluding formula (בָּרוּךְ ... מָגֵן אַבְרָהָם), he should start over from אֱלֹהֵי אַבְרָהָם. Thus it is of utmost importance that one learn the meaning of the prayers in order to develop his power of concentration (M.B. 101:2).

☙ Women's Obligation to Pray

8. Women are obligated to pray, and according to *Rambam* and *Shulchan Aruch* (O.C. 106:1) this obligation has Scriptural status. However, there are various opinions regarding the extent of their obligation.

According to the views preferred by M.B. (106:4), women are required to recite the *Shemoneh Esrei* of *Shacharis* and *Minchah;* they must recall the Exodus by reciting אֱמֶת וְיַצִּיב, *true and certain* (the prayer after the *Shacharis* recitation of *Shema*, p. 94), and אֱמֶת וֶאֱמוּנָה, *true and faithful* (the parallel prayer after the *Maariv* recitation of *Shema*, p. 260), because it recalls the Exodus (M.B. 70:2); and it is urged that they recite at least the first verse of *Shema* because it constitutes קַבָּלַת עוֹל מַלְכוּת שָׁמַיִם, *acceptance of God's sovereignty* (O.C. 70:1).

Some authorities rule that women should also recite all the morning benedictions (p. 14). According to one view, *Pesukei D'zimrah* is introductory to *Shemoneh Esrei* and, consequently, is obligatory upon women too (M.B. 70:2).

Women should recite בִּרְכוֹת הַתּוֹרָה, *blessings of the Torah* [p. 16] (O.C. 47:14, see *Be'ur Halachah).*

According to *Magen Avraham* (O.C. 106:2), women are required by the Torah to pray once a day and they may formulate the prayer as they wish. In many countries, this ruling became the basis for the custom that women recite a brief prayer early in the morning and do not recite any of the formal prayers from the Siddur.

☙ Miscellaneous Laws

9. One should not eat nor drink before praying (O.C. 89:3). However, it is permitted to drink water, tea, or coffee (M.B. 89:22) with milk *(Daas Torah* 89:5).

10. One must take care that the place where he prays be clean. It is prohibited to pray in an area where there are traces of feces or urine, or where one can smell them (see O.C. 76 and 79 for details). This is especially relevant in a home where there may be soiled diapers.

11. One may not pray in the presence of immodestly clad women or facing a window through which they can be observed (see O.C. 75 for details).

12. It is forbidden to pray while one feels the need to discharge his bodily functions (O.C. 92:1-3).

13. One must wash his hands before praying, but no benediction is recited (O.C. 92:4).

14. It is meritorious to give to charity before praying (O.C. 92:10), for this will facilitate the acceptance of the prayer (see M.B. 92:36, *Yoreh Deah* 247:3-4). In some congregations it is customary to collect for charity (or for individuals to set aside some coins for charity) when the congregation recites (in וַיְבָרֶךְ דָּוִיד, p. 74) וְהָעֹשֶׁר וְהַכָּבוֹד מִלְּפָנֶיךָ וְאַתָּה מוֹשֵׁל בַּכֹּל, *wealth and honor come from You, and You rule everything* ... (M.B. 92:36).

THE TIMES FOR PRAYER AND RECITAL OF SHEMA

☙ The Morning Prayer — Shacharis

15. Ideally, one should recite the *Shemoneh Esrei* of the morning prayer after sunrise, but if one cannot wait that long (e.g., he must hurry to work or to perform a *mitzvah* that cannot be postponed) he may pray after dawn, i.e., before sunrise, when light appears on the horizon (O.C. 89:1; see *Be'ur Halachah* s.v. ואם). However, if at all possible one should wait at least until the eastern horizon is fully lit up. According to all views it is not permissible to put on *tefillin* until there is sufficient daylight to recognize a casual acquaintance at a distance of four cubits (O.C. 30:1; see O.C. 19:3 in regard to *tallis).* Since these times vary, competent authorities should be consulted on the exact time for each place and season (ibid.). For example, in the northern United States it varies from approximately fifty minutes before sunrise in March and September to as much as sixty-eight minutes (according to some) in June.

16. The *Shema* may be recited before sunrise (indeed ideally it *should* be recited just before sunrise), but not before one can recognize a casual acquaintance at a distance of four cubits (O.C. 58:1). Nevertheless if one recited the *Shema* after dawn, even before this time, he has discharged his obligation (O.C. 58:4).

17. The period allowed for the recitation of the *Shema* ends at the end of the first quarter of the day. Thereafter it is no longer possible to fulfill the *mitzvah.* If one suspects that the congregation will recite the *Shema* after the prescribed time, he should recite the *Shema* (without the benedictions preceding and following it) before the communal prayers, and should do so even before donning the *tallis* and *tefillin* if this would deter him from a timely recital. Most congregations conduct their services late on Sabbath mornings so that this course must be followed on most Sabbaths of the year (O.C. 58:1 with M.B. §5).

18. *Shacharis* should not be recited after a third of the day is gone. However, if one has failed to pray in time, he is permitted to recite *Shacharis* up to midday (O.C. 89:1; cf. O.C. 58:6 with M.B. and *Be'ur Halachah* regarding whether it is permitted to recite the Blessings of the *Shema* after a third of the day has passed).

19. There are two views on how to calculate one-fourth and one-third of the day for the purposes of *Shema* and *Shacharis:* (1) By calculating the hours and the minutes from sunrise to sunset; and (2) by calculating from dawn to dark (see M.B. 58:4). Each congregation should follow its own tradition in this regard. "Midday" is determined by calculating the exact midpoint between the above times. It should be noted that midday is almost never exactly at 12 noon.

◂§ The Afternoon Prayer — Minchah

20. A person should be very careful to recite *Minchah,* because the prophet Elijah was anwered on Mount Carmel precisely during the time assigned for this prayer (*Berachos* 6b).

21. The beginning of the *Minchah* prayer period is one half hour after noon (O.C. 233:1). The end of this period is nightfall, i.e., the emergence of (three medium-sized) stars (*Rama,* O.C. 233:1).

However, *Mishnah Berurah* (§14) contends that the permissible period for *Minchah* ends approximately one quarter hour before nightfall. Furthermore, he points out that according to many authorities the *Minchah* period ends with sundown and concludes that this view should be followed if at all possible. Many congregations concur with this ruling of *Mishnah Berurah,* but many others follow the more lenient view and conduct *Minchah* services until nightfall.

There are many opinions regarding the time of nightfall. Some hold that visual sighting of three stars constitutes nightfall, others hold that it is always the same number of minutes after sundown. Still others hold that it varies according to latitude, since night falls sooner near the equator than it does as one goes further north or south.

22. For purposes of *Minchah,* the afternoon is divided into two parts: מִנְחָה גְדוֹלָה, the *Greater Minchah Period,* and מִנְחָה קְטַנָּה, the *Smaller Minchah Period.* The first of these periods begins half an hour after midday and extends for three hours. The second begins three and a half hours after midday. (For this and all similar halachic times, an "hour" is 1/12 of the daylight hours; see §19.)

23. Preferably, one should recite *Minchah* during the second, later, period (O.C. 233:1). However, if one recites *Minchah* any time after one half hour past noon he has discharged his obligation (ibid.). Indeed, some communities, following the view of *Tur* and others, prefer the first half of the afternoon for the *Minchah* prayer.

◂§ The Evening Prayer — Maariv

24. The evening prayer is composed of three parts — the *Shema,* the benedictions preceding and following it, and the *Shemoneh Esrei.* The time requirements for these parts differ in some details, as will be explained below.

25. The time for the recitation of the *Shema* begins with the emergence of three small stars. [According to *Mishnah Berurah* 235:4, one should wait until at least 72 minutes after sundown.] If *Maariv* was recited before this time, all three paragraphs of the *Shema* should be repeated at night (O.C. 235:1, M.B. §11). Thus, if the congregation prays *Maariv* before this time, one should pray with them, then repeat only the *Shema* at the appropriate time (O.C. 235:1).

26. There are two views in the Mishnah (*Berachos* 26a) regarding the times of *Minchah* and *Maariv.* According to R' Yehudah, the deadline for *Minchah* is an hour and a quarter before sunset, and according to the Sages the deadline is nightfall. According to both, the time for *Maariv* begins after that of *Minchah.* The *halachah* rules that one may rely on either R' Yehudah or the Sages, provided he follows the same view all the time. Thus, e.g., one may not recite *Minchah* half an hour before sunset (following the Sages) and then recite *Maariv* immediately (following R' Yehudah), since this is a contradiction (O.C. 233:1, M.B. §11). However, this prohibition applies only to an individual. A congregation is permitted to recite *Minchah* and *Maariv* in the same time period if it would be difficult or impossible to re-assemble a *minyan* later on (ibid.).

27. The status of the *Shema* benedictions is a matter of dispute: are they like the *Shema,* which must be recited after dark, or are they like *Shemoneh Esrei* which may be recited earlier? Most of the early authorities conclude that the benedictions before and after the *Maariv Shema* may not be recited before nightfall. However, *Rabbeinu Tam* defends the prevalent custom that the blessings are like *Shemoneh Esrei,* meaning that it is permissible to recite the full *Maariv,* including the blessings, before dark. This custom has been followed for centuries and has the tacit approval of the *poskim,* because if the benedictions were to be said only after nightfall, the communal *Maariv* prayer might be abandoned and many unlearned people might even omit this prayer altogether (O.C. 235:1, M.B. §8 with *Shaar HaTziyun*). Of course this reasoning does not extend to the Scriptural obligation to recite the *Shema,* which must be repeated at night, as explained above in §25.

28. Ideally one should recite the *Shema* as soon as possible after nightfall, and at the latest, before midnight. Nevertheless, the obligation is discharged as long as one recited the *Shema* (and the entire *Maariv* prayer) before the next dawn, (O.C. 235:3). Where one could not recite *Maariv* and the delay was not due to neglect, he may discharge his obligation to recite *Shema* even after dawn (but before sunrise). However, in such an instance the fourth blessing (הַשְׁכִּיבֵנוּ) and fifth (בָּרוּךְ ה׳) are omitted, and the *Shemoneh Esrei* may no longer be recited (O.C. 235:4, M.B. §34).

PRAYER WITH THE CONGREGATION

◆§ Prayer With a Minyan of Ten

29. One should try his utmost to pray in the synagogue together with the congregation (O.C. 90:9), for the Almighty does not reject the prayer of the many (M.B. §28). Contrary to the popular misconception that it is sufficient to respond to בָּרְכוּ and קְדוּשָּׁה, the main objective of prayer with a *minyan* is to recite *Shemoneh Esrei* with a *minyan*. Therefore one must arrive at the synagogue early enough so that he can keep up with the congregation.

◆§ Instructions for Latecomers

30. If one arrived at the synagogue too late to recite the entire order of the prayers and still recite the *Shemoneh Esrei* together with the congregation, he may omit certain parts of the service and recite them after the end of *Shacharis*. If time is extremely short, it suffices to put on the *tallis* and *tefillin* and to say the benedictions עַל נְטִילַת יָדָיִם; אֲשֶׁר יָצַר; אֱלֹהַי נְשָׁמָה; the benedictions over the Torah (p. 14-18); בָּרוּךְ שֶׁאָמַר (p. 58); אַשְׁרֵי (p. 66); נִשְׁמַת on the Sabbath and Festivals (p. 400); and from יִשְׁתַּבַּח (p. 82) through *Shemoneh Esrei*. If time permits, the following sections (listed in descending order of importance) should be recited:

(1) הַלְלוּיָהּ הַלְלוּ אֶת ה׳ מִן הַשָּׁמַיִם (p. 72);
(2) הַלְלוּיָהּ הַלְלוּ אֵל בְּקָדְשׁוֹ (p. 74);
(3) the other three הַלְלוּיָהּ psalms (p. 70, 72);
(4) from וַיְבָרֶךְ דָּוִיד until לְשֵׁם תִּפְאַרְתֶּךָ (p. 74);
(5) הודו until וְהוּא רַחוּם (p. 60-62);
(6) מִזְמוֹר לְתוֹדָה (p. 64);
(7) the rest of *Pesukei D'zimrah* (O.C. 52:1, M.B. §4, *Ba'er Hetev* §3).

31. On the Sabbath, all of the daily psalms take precedence over those that are added on the Sabbath (with the exception of נִשְׁמַת, as noted in §30). Among the Sabbath additions themselves, some passages have priority over the others. They are: לַמְנַצֵּחַ (p. 374), לְדָוִד בְּשַׁנּוֹתוֹ (p. 376), and תְּפִלָּה לְמֹשֶׁה (p. 378) (M.B. 52:5).

32. The above is only an emergency solution. One should not rely on this to arrive late for the *Pesukei D'zimrah*, because the proper order of the prayers is of utmost importance. Indeed, some authorities contend that recitation of the prayers in their proper order takes priority over the obligation to recite *Shemoneh Esrei* together with the congregation (M.B. 52:1).

RESPONSES DURING THE PRAYER

◆§ During Pesukei D'zimrah

33. Other than the exceptions noted below, it is prohibited to interrupt from the beginning of בָּרוּךְ שֶׁאָמַר (see §38) until the conclusion of the *Shemoneh Esrei* (O.C. 51:4). Furthermore, it is not proper to speak until after *Tachanun* (M.B. 51:9; see O.C. 131:1). Wherever one may not talk, it is forbidden to do so even in Hebrew (M.B. 51:7).

34. With the exception of *Shemoneh Esrei*, parts of *Shacharis* may be interrupted for certain responses to the *chazzan* or for certain blessings, but the rules vary widely, depending on the section of *Shacharis* and the response. In this regard, the most lenient part of *Shacharis* is *Pesukei D'zimrah*, i.e., the unit that includes the verses between בָּרוּךְ שֶׁאָמַר and יִשְׁתַּבַּח (pp. 58-82). There, one may respond with *Amen* to any benediction, but may not say the customary בָּרוּךְ הוּא וּבָרוּךְ שְׁמוֹ. It is permitted to respond to *Kedushah* and מוֹדִים (in the repetition of *Shemoneh Esrei*), בָּרְכוּ, and *Kaddish*. If the congregation is reciting the *Shema*, one should recite the first verse *(Shema Yisrael ...)* together with them. If one discharged his bodily functions, he may recite the benediction אֲשֶׁר יָצַר (M.B. 51:8).

35. For an aliyah: Someone saying *Pesukei D'zimrah* should not be called up to the Torah unless he is the only *Kohen* or Levite in the congregation. If called, however, he may recite the benedictions and read along quietly with the reader (as usual) but he may not instruct the *gabbai* in regard to a מִי שֶׁבֵּרַךְ (M.B. 51:10).

36. For reciting the Shema: If one did not yet recite the *Shema* and calculates that he will miss the requisite time (see §17 above) if he waits until he reaches it in the prayers, or if he forgot to say the daily *berachos* on the Torah (p. 16), he should say them in the *Pesukei D'zimrah* (M.B. 51:10).

37. For reciting Hallel: On Rosh Chodesh or the last six days of Pesach, if one is in the middle of *Pesukei D'zimrah* when the congregation reaches *Hallel*, he should join with them, omitting the benedictions before and after *Hallel*, because in that case his own blessings bracketing *Pesukei D'zimrah* are in lieu of the blessings of *Hallel*. The above applies only when 'half' *Hallel* is said. On days when 'whole' *Hallel* is recited one should forgo saying *Hallel* with the congregation and recite it after *Shemoneh Esrei* with its own blessings (M.B. 422:16).

◆§ During the Pesukei D'zimrah Blessings

38. The second level of stringency regarding interruptions includes the two benedictions of *Pesukei D'zimrah* — בָּרוּךְ שֶׁאָמַר and יִשְׁתַּבַּח.

בָּרוּךְ שֶׁאָמַר is composed of three parts:

(a) From בָּרוּךְ שֶׁאָמַר until the first בָּרוּךְ אַתָּה ה׳ is merely a preamble and all responses are permitted.

(b) From the first בָּרוּךְ אַתָּה ה׳ until the final one, all the interruptions permitted in §34 (with the

exception of (אֲשֶׁר יָצַר) for the rest of *Pesukei D'zimrah* are also permitted here. The *Amen* after the benedictions בָּרוּךְ שֶׁאָמַר and יִשְׁתַּבַּח are exceptions to this rule; they may not be said.
(c) The last, brief blessing, בָּרוּךְ ... בְּתִשְׁבָּחוֹת, during which no interruption at all is permitted (M.B. 51:2).

יִשְׁתַּבַּח is composed of two parts:
(a) From the beginning (יִשְׁתַּבַּח) to בָּרוּךְ אַתָּה ה׳, which corresponds to (b) above.
(b) From בָּרוּךְ אַתָּה ה׳ to the end, which corresponds to (c) above (M.B. 51:2, 65:11, 54:11).

◆§ Between The Shema Blessings of Shacharis and Maariv

39. The third level of stringency concerns the 'intervals' between the various sections of the *Shema* and the benedictions bracketing it. The intervals are as follows: After בָּרוּךְ ... יוֹצֵר הַמְּאוֹרוֹת; after בָּרוּךְ ... בְּאַהֲבָה; and after the first and second sections of the *Shema*. [The end of the *Shema* is immediately followed by the first word of the following benediction (אֱמֶת) so that there is no 'interval' there, and similarly the end of the benediction גָּאַל יִשְׂרָאֵל must be followed immediately by *Shemoneh Esrei* (O.C. 66:5,9).]

Corresponding 'intervals' exist in *Maariv* following each blessing and after the first and second sections of the *Shema* (M.B. 66:27; *Be'ur Halachah* there).

40. Regarding the *Amen* after גָּאַל יִשְׂרָאֵל of *Shacharis, Rama,* followed by most Ashkenazi congregations, rules that it may be said, while others, particularly Chassidic congregations, follow R' Yosef Caro's ruling against *Amen* at this point. To avoid the controversy, many individuals recite the blessing in unison with the *chazzan.* In some congregations, the *chazzan* concludes the blessing silently (O.C. 66:7).

41. During the 'intervals' one may respond with *Amen* to all benedictions (M.B. 66:23). Regarding קַדִּישׁ, קְדוּשָּׁה, בָּרְכוּ, and other interruptions the 'intervals' are treated in the same way as are interruptions in the fourth level (see below §42). During the interval between בְּאַהֲבָה and שְׁמַע, however, only the *Amen* after בְּאַהֲבָה is permitted *(Derech HaChaim;* see M.B. 59:25).

◆§ During the Shema and its Blessings in Shacharis and Maariv

42. The fourth level concerns the *Shema* itself and the benedictions bracketing it. The benedictions may be separated into two parts for this purpose: During the concluding, brief blessing, and during the verses of *Shema* and בָּרוּךְ שֵׁם, no interruption whatever is permitted (O.C. 66:1; M.B. §11, 12). During the rest of the fourth level, one may respond with *Amen* only to the two blessings הָאֵל הַקָּדוֹשׁ and שׁוֹמֵעַ תְּפִלָּה in *Shemoneh Esrei.* It is permitted to respond to בָּרְכוּ of both the *chazzan* and one who is called up to the Torah. In *Kaddish* one may respond with אָמֵן יְהֵא שְׁמֵהּ רַבָּא ... and with the *Amen* to דַּאֲמִירָן בְּעָלְמָא. In *Kedushah* one may say only the verses קָדוֹשׁ and בָּרוּךְ. To *Modim,* one may respond only with the three words מוֹדִים אֲנַחְנוּ לָךְ.

A person who is in the midst of the recitation of the benedictions of *Shema* should not be called up to the Torah even if he is the only *Kohen* or Levite present; in such a case it is preferable that he leave the room. However, if someone was called up to the Torah, he may recite the benedictions, but should not read along with the reader; if possible he should attempt to get to an 'interval' in his prayers before doing so (M.B. 66:26). All other responses are prohibited.

If one had to discharge his bodily functions he should merely wash his hands and defer the recitation of אֲשֶׁר יָצַר until after *Shemoneh Esrei* (M.B. 66:23).

43. If one has not yet responded to קְדוּשָּׁה, בָּרְכוּ (or מוֹדִים) and he is holding shortly before *Shemoneh Esrei,* he should stop before שִׁירָה חֲדָשָׁה (p. 96) in order to make the responses. If he has already said שִׁירָה חֲדָשָׁה, but has not yet concluded the benediction, he may respond, but after the response he should start again from שִׁירָה חֲדָשָׁה (M.B. 66:52).

44. The fifth level concerns the *Shemoneh Esrei* prayer. Here any interruption is forbidden. Even motioning to someone is prohibited (O.C. 104:1 M.B. §1). If the *chazzan* is up to קַדִּישׁ, קְדוּשָּׁה, or בָּרְכוּ, one should stop and listen to the *chazzan's* recitation; his own silent concentration is considered as if he had responded (O.C. 104:7, M.B. §26,27).

45. From the time one has concluded the last benediction of *Shemoneh Esrei* with בַּשָּׁלוֹם until the end of the standard prayers (i.e., יִהְיוּ לְרָצוֹן at the end of אֱלֹהַי נְצוֹר), one is restricted to the responses listed in level four. However, whenever possible, one should hurry to say the verse וְגוֹאֲלִי ... יִהְיוּ לְרָצוֹן before making any kind of response. It is preferable to take the usual three steps backward before making the responses (O.C. 122:1; M.B. §2-4).

LAWS OF RECITING THE SHEMA

46. It is a Scriptural precept to recite the *Shema* twice daily, once in the morning and again in the evening (see above §16-17, 24-28). It is essential that the recitation be done bearing in mind that one thereby fulfills a Scriptural precept; otherwise it must be repeated (O.C. 60:4). However, if the circumstances make it obvious that the intention was present — e.g., he recited it during the prayer with the benedictions preceding and following it — he need not repeat the *Shema* even if he did not make a mental declaration of purpose (M.B. 60:10).

47. The third section of *Shema,* whose recitation is Rabbinical in origin according to almost all authorities, contains a verse whose recitation fulfills the Scriptural obligation to commemorate the Exodus from Egypt twice daily (see *Berachos* 12b; *Rambam, Hil. Kerias Shema* 1:3). The rule concerning a mental declaration of intent outlined above (§46) applies here, too.

48. One should concentrate on the meaning of all the words, and read them with awe and trepidation (O.C. 61:1). He should read the *Shema* as if it were a new proclamation containing instructions never yet revealed (O.C. 61:2). The first verse of *Shema* is the essential profession of our faith. Therefore the utmost concentration on its meaning is necessary. If one said it without such concentration, he has not fulfilled his obligation and must repeat it (O.C. 60:5, 63:4), but he should repeat the verse quietly, for one may not (publicly) say the first verse of *Shema* repeatedly (ibid.).

49. While reciting the first verse, it is customary to cover the eyes with the right hand to avoid distraction and enhance concentration (O.C. 61:5).

50. Although *Shema* may be recited quietly, one should recite it loudly enough to hear himself. However, one has discharged his obligation even if he does not hear himself, as long as he has enunciated the words (O.C. 62:3).

51. The last word of the first verse, אֶחָד, must be pronounced with special emphasis [see commentary, p. 91], while one meditates on God's sole sovereignty over the seven heavens and earth, and the four directions — east, south, west, and north (O.C. 61:6).

52. Some consider it preferable to recite the entire *Shema* aloud (except for the passage בָּרוּךְ שֵׁם) while others say it quietly; our custom follows the latter usage. However, the first verse should be said aloud in order to arouse one's full concentration (O.C. 61:4,26). It is customary for the *chazzan* to lead the congregation in the recitation of the first verse so that they all proclaim the Kingdom of Heaven together *(Kol Bo* cited in *Darkei Moshe* to O.C. 61; *Levush).*

53. Every word must be enunciated clearly and uttered with the correct grammatical pronunciation (O.C. 62:1, 61:23, 16-19). It is especially important to enunciate each word clearly and to avoid run-on words by pausing briefly between words ending and beginning with the same consonant, such as בְּכָל לְבַבְכֶם, וַאֲבַדְתֶּם מְהֵרָה, and to pause between a word that ends with a consonant and the next one that begins with a with a silent letter [א or ע], such as אֲשֶׁר אָנֹכִי, הַיּוֹם עַל, וּרְאִיתֶם אֹתוֹ, (O.C. 61:20, 21).

54. Although it is not the universal custom to chant the *Shema* with the cantillation melody used during the synagogue Torah reading, it is laudable to do so, unless one finds that such chanting interferes with his concentration. In any event, the proper punctuation must be followed so that words are grouped into the proper phrases in accordance with the syntax of each word-group and verse (O.C. 61:24, M.B. §37,38).

55. While reciting the first two portions of the *Shema,* one may not communicate with someone else by winking or motioning with his lips or fingers (O.C. 63:6, M.B. §18).

56. It is incumbent that each paragraph of the *Shema* be read word for word as it appears in the Torah. If one erred and skipped a word, he must return to the place of his error and continue the section from there (O.C. 64:1-2).

57. The *Shema* should be said in one uninterrupted recitation. If one interrupted, whether by talking or waiting silently, he does not have to repeat the *Shema.* However, if the interruption was involuntary in nature, e.g., one was forbidden to finish the *Shema* because he had to relieve himself, and the interruption was long enough for him to recite all three paragraphs of the *Shema* at his own normal speed, he must repeat the entire *Shema (Rama* O.C. 65:1). Multiple interruptions interspersed in the recitation of *Shema* are not added together to constitute one long, invalidating interruption (M.B. 65:4).

58. If one is present in the synagogue when the congregation recites the *Shema,* he must recite at least the first verse and the verse בָּרוּךְ שֵׁם together with them. If he is in the midst of a prayer that he may not interrupt (see above §38, 39, 41, 42, 45), he should at least give the appearance of saying *Shema* by praying loudly in the tune the congregation uses for the *Shema* (O.C. 65:2,3; M.B. §10).

59. During morning services, the four *tzitzis* are to be gathered when one says the words וַהֲבִיאֵנוּ לְשָׁלוֹם מֵאַרְבַּע כַּנְפוֹת הָאָרֶץ, *Bring us in peacefulness from the four corners of the earth,* in the paragraph preceding the *Shema* (p. 90). From then on and throughout the *Shema,* the *tzitzis* are to be held — according to some customs, between the fourth finger and the little finger of the left hand — against the heart *(Ba'er Hetev,* O.C. 59:3; *Derech HaChaim).*

60. When reciting the third portion, וַיֹּאמֶר ה׳, *And* HASHEM *said,* during the morning services, one should also grasp the *tzitzis* with the right hand and look at them, until after he has said the words נֶאֱמָנִים וְנֶחֱמָדִים לָעַד in the אֱמֶת וְיַצִּיב prayer following *Shema.* At that point one should kiss the *tzitzis* and release them from his hand (ibid.). [According to the prevalent custom, one also kisses the *tzitzis* every time he says the word צִיצִית, the אֱמֶת at the end of *Shema,* and at לָעַד קַיֶּמֶת. Some kiss them also at אֱמֶת שָׁאַתָּה הוּא.]

ADJUSTMENTS IN THE SHEMONEH ESREI

◆§ During the Ten Days of Awe

61. During the Ten Days of Repentance, i.e., the period between Rosh Hashanah and Yom Kippur, a number of insertions and adjustments are made in the *Shemoneh Esrei.* One group of inserts consists of the verses זָכְרֵנוּ (in the first benediction), מִי כָמוֹךְ (in the second benediction), וּכְתוֹב (in the second to last benediction), and בְּסֵפֶר (in the last benediction). If one omitted any of these inserts he need not (and may not) repeat the whole prayer. However, if he has not yet said the word *HASHEM* in the formula concluding that benediction, he may return to the insertion and repeat the rest of the benediction following the insert (O.C. 582:5, M.B. §16).

62. The end of the third benediction is changed from הָאֵל הַקָּדוֹשׁ *(the holy God)* to הַמֶּלֶךְ הַקָּדוֹשׁ *(the holy King).* If one forgot and concluded the benediction as usual he must start again from the beginning of the *Shemoneh Esrei.* However, if he realized his oversight *immediately* and before he began the next benediction, he can rectify the error by saying the words הַמֶּלֶךְ הַקָּדוֹשׁ. In this context, "immediately" is defined as no longer than the interval needed to say the three words שָׁלוֹם עָלֶיךָ מוֹרִי, *peace upon you, my teacher* (O.C. 582:1,2, M.B. §7).

If one erred and said הַמֶּלֶךְ הַקָּדוֹשׁ during the rest of the year he need not repeat the Shemoneh Esrei *(Ba'er Hetev* and *Shaarei Teshuvah* to O.C. 118:1).

63. If one is not sure whether he has completed the blessing properly, it is assumed that he said the usual formula הָאֵל הַקָּדוֹשׁ and he must repeat *Shemoneh Esrei* (O.C. 582:1, M.B. §3).

64. At the conclusion of the tenth benediction, הַמֶּלֶךְ הַמִּשְׁפָּט *(the King of judgment)* is substituted for מֶלֶךְ אוֹהֵב צְדָקָה וּמִשְׁפָּט *(King Who loves righteousness and judgment).* If one forgot to make this change he does not have to repeat the prayer. However, if he realized the error immediately (see §62) he should rectify the error (O.C. 118:1, M.B. §3).

65. In some Ashkenazic congregations עוֹשֶׂה הַשָּׁלוֹם is substituted for הַמְבָרֵךְ אֶת עַמּוֹ יִשְׂרָאֵל בַּשָּׁלוֹם in the last benediction (see *Levush* O.C. 582:5, *Likutei Maharich,* et al.). If one concluded with the usual formula he need not correct his error.

Many authorities oppose this change in the liturgy. *Mateh Ephraim* (582:22) rules that a *chazzan* should conform to the congregation's custom in his repetition of the *Shemoneh Esrei.* However, in the formula עוֹשֶׂה שָׁלוֹם בִּמְרוֹמָיו which is recited when stepping out of *Shemoneh Esrei* and *Kaddish,* עֹשֶׂה הַשָּׁלוֹם should be substituted for עֹשֶׂה שָׁלוֹם (ibid.).

◆§ The End of the Sabbath or Yom Tov — אַתָּה חוֹנַנְתָּנוּ and וַתּוֹדִיעֵנוּ

66. In the first weekday *Maariv* prayer following the Sabbath or a *Yom Tov,* a special prayer, אַתָּה חוֹנַנְתָּנוּ, *You have favored us,* is inserted in the fourth benediction of *Shemoneh Esrei.* The function of this prayer is to declare the distinction between the higher holiness of the Sabbath and Festivals and the mundane nature of the weekdays. If one forgets to insert this prayer he may not repeat the benediction, nor should he insert this prayer in the benediction שְׁמַע קוֹלֵנוּ. Rather he should rely on the *Havdalah* which will be recited over wine after *Maariv* (O.C. 294:1, M.B. §6).

Even after the Sabbath has departed, it is prohibited to do any forbidden work before reciting אַתָּה חוֹנַנְתָּנוּ or *Havdalah.* Therefore, if one has not yet recited either, one should be very careful not to do any work even after dark. This should be especially stressed in regard to women: since they generally do not recite *Maariv,* they should not do any work before hearing *Havdalah.* However, by saying the words: בָּרוּךְ הַמַּבְדִּיל בֵּין קוֹדֶשׁ לְחוֹל, *Blessed is He Who separates between holy and secular,* one becomes permitted to do work (O.C. 299:10; see *Shaar HaTziyun* §47).

67. When *Yom Tov* follows the Sabbath, a similar insertion — וַתּוֹדִיעֵנוּ — is recited in the fourth benediction, since the holiness of the Sabbath is greater than that of Festivals. The rules outlined for אַתָּה חוֹנַנְתָּנוּ apply here as well *(Be'ur Halachah* to O.C. 294:1). If the Sabbath has already departed and one wishes to do work permitted on *Yom Tov* but he has not said וַתּוֹדִיעֵנוּ, he must say the formula בָּרוּךְ הַמַּבְדִּיל בֵּין קוֹדֶשׁ לְקוֹדֶשׁ, *Blessed is He Who separates between holy and holy* (M.B. 299:36).

◆§ Seasonal Additions

68. Several insertions in the *Shemoneh Esrei* — the prayers regarding rain and dew — are related to the seasonal needs of agriculture. These prayers were fixed in Talmudic times according to the seasonal rain requirements of *Eretz Yisrael* and *Babylon.* The Diaspora follows the practice of Babylon as established in the Talmud.

◆§ מַשִּׁיב הָרוּחַ וּמוֹרִיד הַגֶּשֶׁם

69. The first of these insertions is in the second benediction. Beginning with the *Mussaf* prayer of *Shemini Atzeres,* מַשִּׁיב הָרוּחַ וּמוֹרִיד הַגֶּשֶׁם *(He makes the wind blow and He makes the rain descend)* is inserted (both in *Eretz Yisrael* and the Diaspora). This formula is said until the *Mussaf* prayer of the first day of Pesach (see below §72). This is not an actual prayer for rain but merely a mention of God's raingiving power.

70. If the insertion was omitted one must start again from the beginning of the *Shemoneh Esrei.* Many congregations recite מוֹרִיד הַטָּל *(Who makes the dew descend)* in place of מַשִּׁיב הָרוּחַ between Pesach and Shemini Atzeres (see §72). If one said מוֹרִיד הַטָּל instead of מַשִּׁיב הָרוּחַ, the prayer need not be repeated since he has mentioned God's role in one form of needed moisture (O.C. 114:5).

71. One is not considered to have omitted this insertion unless he has begun the word אַתָּה of the next benediction, אַתָּה קָדוֹשׁ. Thus if one realizes his omission after having concluded מְחַיֵּה הַמֵּתִים (or said the word *HASHEM* in the concluding formula) but has not yet begun אַתָּה קָדוֹשׁ (or in case of the *chazzan's Shemoneh Esrei,* the *Kedushah),* he says the words מַשִּׁיב הָרוּחַ וּמוֹרִיד הַגֶּשֶׁם and continues with אַתָּה קָדוֹשׁ. If he has not even begun the concluding formula of the benediction (בָּרוּךְ ... מְחַיֵּה הַמֵּתִים) or has at least not yet said the word *HASHEM* in that formula, he should recite מַשִּׁיב הָרוּחַ וּמוֹרִיד הַגֶּשֶׁם and then conclude the benediction (O.C. 114:6 with *Be'ur Halachah).* [However if he realized his error after saying the word וְנֶאֱמָן, he should say מַשִּׁיב הָרוּחַ וּמוֹרִיד הַגֶּשֶׁם, and start over from וְנֶאֱמָן (see *M.B.* 114:29).]

72. The insertion of מַשִּׁיב הָרוּחַ וּמוֹרִיד הַגֶּשֶׁם is discontinued after the *Mussaf* prayer of the first day of Pesach. Most Ashkenazic congregations follow the old custom and do not recite מוֹרִיד הַטָּל in place of מוֹרִיד הַגֶּשֶׁם, while others, especially in *Eretz Yisrael,* practice the Sephardic custom to recite מוֹרִיד הַטָּל until *Shemini Atzeres.* But even those who adopt the latter custom agree that the omission of מוֹרִיד הַטָּל does not require that *Shemoneh Esrei* be repeated (O.C. 114:3).

73. Just as the omission of מוֹרִיד הַגֶּשֶׁם in the appropriate season necessitates repetition of the *Shemoneh Esrei,* so must one repeat the entire prayer if he has recited מוֹרִיד הַגֶּשֶׁם at the wrong time, because rain in the wrong season is an omen of bad times. If one realizes his error before concluding the benediction (מְחַיֵּה הַמֵּתִים) he should return to the beginning of the benediction (אַתָּה גִּבּוֹר). If he has already concluded the benediction he must start again from the beginning of the *Shemoneh Esrei.* This is so even if he said both מוֹרִיד הַגֶּשֶׁם and מוֹרִיד הַטָּל (O.C. 114:4).

74. If one is not sure that he omitted מוֹרִיד הַגֶּשֶׁם, the rule is as follows: It is assumed that someone recited whatever he has been accustomed to, until a different recitation becomes habitual. The Sages set down the presumption that until someone has recited a new addition for thirty days, it has not yet become habitual with him. Consequently, until thirty days after Pesach began, it is assumed that someone recited מַשִּׁיב הָרוּחַ, and until thirty days after Shemini Atzeres it is assumed that he said either nothing or מוֹרִיד הַטָּל (O.C. 114:8).

75. There is a way to spare oneself the necessity to repeat the *Shemoneh Esrei* in cases of the doubtful omission of מוֹרִיד הַגֶּשֶׁם. On *Shemini Atzeres* he may repeat the passage מְחַיֵּה מֵתִים אַתָּה רַב לְהוֹשִׁיעַ מַשִּׁיב ... one hundred and one times [if he said this only ninety times it is sufficient *post facto*] thereby assuring himself that he will henceforth insert מוֹרִיד הַגֶּשֶׁם. The same is true for those who say מוֹרִיד הַטָּל in the summer; they may repeat מְחַיֵּה ... הַטָּל the same amount of times on the first day of Pesach. Some authorities rule that the same is true for those who practice the Ashkenazic custom and do not say מוֹרִיד הַטָּל in the summer. They too may repeat מְחַיֵּה ... לְהוֹשִׁיעַ מְכַלְכֵּל חַיִּים, omitting מַשִּׁיב ... הַגֶּשֶׁם, for the required amount of times and be assured of saying the correct formula henceforth. However, *Derech Chaim* disputes this analogy and cautions that it not be relied upon. Similarly the repetition of וְאֶת כָּל מִינֵי תְבוּאָתָהּ לְטוֹבָה וְתֵן טַל וּמָטָר לִבְרָכָה, or of וְאֶת ... וְתֵן בְּרָכָה (see below) is efficacious to remove doubts of incorrect recitation (O.C. 114:9, M.B. there).

◆§ וְתֵן טַל וּמָטָר

76. A special formula — וְתֵן טַל וּמָטָר — asking for rain is inserted in the benediction בָּרֵךְ עָלֵינוּ, *Bless on our behalf,* in the appropriate season. The time for this insertion is fixed according to the usual need for rain in *Eretz Yisrael* and Babylon in Talmudic times (O.C. 117:2).

77. In *Eretz Yisrael* the insertion is begun in the *Maariv* prayer of 7 Cheshvan and continued until the *Minchah* prayer immediately before Pesach. In the entire Diaspora, the time for beginning this recitation is on the sixtieth day after the autumnal equinox as computed according to the method of Shmuel. [See *Eruvin* 56a; ArtScroll *Bircas HaChammah* pp. 45-56.]

78. Thus the day on which the recitation of טַל וּמָטָר is begun in the Diaspora is a fixed day in the solar calendar and its position in the Jewish calendar varies from year to year. Generally, the recitation is begun in the *Maariv* of December 4, but in the December preceding a civil leap year, it is begun in the *Maariv* of December 5.

79. If one forgot to say וְתֵן טַל וּמָטָר at the appropriate time but has not yet said the word *HASHEM* in the concluding formula (בָּרוּךְ... מְבָרֵךְ הַשָּׁנִים), he should say וְתֵן טַל וּמָטָר and continue from wherever he was up to (O.C. 117:4). However, the last portion of the בָּרֵךְ עָלֵינוּ formula [from וּבָרֵךְ שְׁנָתֵנוּ ... and further] must always be said immediately before בָּרוּךְ אַתָּה ה׳. Thus, if one forgot וְתֵן טַל וּמָטָר, but had already begun the phrase וּבָרֵךְ שְׁנָתֵנוּ before realizing his oversight, he must recite וְתֵן טַל וּמָטָר and continue from וּבָרֵךְ שְׁנָתֵנוּ (M.B. 117:15).

80. If one had already concluded the benediction when he realized his error (even if he had not yet begun the following benediction;

M.B. 15), he should continue his *Shemoneh Esrei* and insert the words וְתֵן טַל וּמָטָר לִבְרָכָה before the words כִּי אַתָּה שׁוֹמֵעַ, *for You hear,* in the benediction שׁוֹמֵעַ תְּפִלָּה (p. 108). On a fast-day, the insertion of טַל וּמָטָר at this point will precede עֲנֵנוּ (O.C. 117:5 with M.B.).

81. If one realized his error after he had already begun the benediction רְצֵה he must return to בָּרֵךְ עָלֵינוּ (not to שְׁמַע קוֹלֵנוּ; *Aruch HaShulchan* 117:6; cf. *Be'ur Halachah* to 114:6, s.v. בלא). If he had already concluded the *Shemoneh Esrei* he must start again from the beginning. The conclusion of *Shemoneh Esrei* is defined as the recitation of the verse יִהְיוּ לְרָצוֹן, just before stepping out of *Shemoneh Esrei* (O.C. 117:5 with M.B.)

82. If טַל וּמָטָר was said in the wrong season of the year, one must go back to the beginning of בָּרֵךְ עָלֵינוּ and continue from there. If he has concluded the *Shemoneh Esrei* he must begin again from the beginning. Conclusion of *Shemoneh Esrei* is defined here as in §81 (O.C. 114:8).

83. When one is not sure what he said, he must assume that he had recited whatever he had become accustomed to. A new "habit" is not established firmly until the recitation has been in effect for a thirty-day period of recitation (O.C. 114:8); see §74 and 75.

84. If an entire country experienced a drought and was in special need of rain during a period when טַל וּמָטָר is not recited, but someone erred and *did* recite טַל וּמָטָר, he need not repeat the *Shemoneh Esrei* (O.C. 117:2; see *Be'ur Halachah,* s.v. ושאל, and *Shoneh Halachos).* [For some of the refinements of this rule in regard to a country not in a state of drought but in which rain is not unwelcome during this period, see *Be'ur Halachah* to O.C. 117:2, s.v. הצריכין, M.B. §10.]

◆§ Fast Days — עֲנֵנוּ

85. On fast days a special prayer — עֲנֵנוּ — is interjected both in the silent *Shemoneh Esrei* and in the *chazzan's* repetition. This prayer may be said only by one who is fasting; for someone not fasting to recite this prayer would be fraudulent (see O.C. 565:3 in *Rama).* This insertion is made by the *chazzan* in the loud *Shemoneh Esrei* of both *Shacharis* and *Minchah,* but in the silent *Shemoneh Esrei* it is said only during *Minchah* (O.C. 565:3). The *chazzan's* prayer is placed between בָּרוּךְ ... גּוֹאֵל יִשְׂרָאֵל and רְפָאֵנוּ and takes the form of a complete benediction, concluding with בָּרוּךְ ... הָעוֹנֶה בְּעֵת צָרָה, *Blessed ... Who responds in time of distress* (O.C. 566:1). The individual's recitation is said as part of the benediction שְׁמַע קוֹלֵנוּ (O.C. 565:1; see pp. 104 and 108). In order for the *chazzan* to recite עֲנֵנוּ as a separate benediction in his repetition of the *Shemoneh Esrei* there should be ten congregants who are fasting. Some authorities rule that in the four fasts which are of Biblical origin (Fast of Gedalyah; Tenth of Teves; Seventeenth of Tammuz; Tishah B'Av) it is sufficient that there be seven fasting individuals (O.C. 566:3, M.B. §14). [On other fasts, e.g., the Fast of Esther, a full quorum of ten fasting individuals is required.]

86. If an individual forgot to insert עֲנֵנוּ in its proper place and has already said the word *HASHEM* in the concluding formula of שְׁמַע קוֹלֵנוּ, he must conclude with שׁוֹמֵעַ תְּפִלָּה and continue with רְצֵה. He may insert עֲנֵנוּ at the end of the *Shemoneh Esrei* before אֱלֹהַי. If he finished his prayer before realizing his error he should not repeat the *Shemoneh Esrei* (M.B. 119:16,19).

87. If the *chazzan* forgot to insert עֲנֵנוּ in its proper place but has not yet said the word *HASHEM* of the concluding formula of the benediction רְפָאֵנוּ, he should interrupt his recitation, return to עֲנֵנוּ, and when he has concluded it, he should again say רְפָאֵנוּ. If he has already uttered the word *HASHEM* he must conclude with ... רופא חולֵי and continue his prayer as usual. In this case, the *chazzan* inserts עֲנֵנוּ in the benediction שְׁמַע קוֹלֵנוּ as do individuals in the silent prayer, but the concluding formula בָּרוּךְ ... הָעוֹנֶה בְּעֵת צָרָה is deleted. If he realized his error after he uttered the word *HASHEM* in the concluding formula of שְׁמַע קוֹלֵנוּ he must continue with שׁוֹמֵעַ תְּפִלָּה; he may add עֲנֵנוּ after הַמְבָרֵךְ אֶת עַמּוֹ יִשְׂרָאֵל בַּשָּׁלוֹם (O.C. 119:4, M.B. §16,19).

◆§ Tishah B'Av — נַחֵם

88. In the *Minchah* prayer of Tishah B'Av, in addition to עֲנֵנוּ, yet another prayer (נַחֵם, *Comfort),* marking the destruction of the Holy Temple and supplicating for its rebuilding, is inserted in the benediction וְלִירוּשָׁלַיִם, *and to Jerusalem* (both in the silent and loud *Shemoneh Esrei).* The concluding formula is changed to בָּרוּךְ ... מְנַחֵם צִיּוֹן וּבוֹנֵה יְרוּשָׁלָיִם, *Blessed ... Who consoles Zion and rebuilds Jerusalem,* (both for the individual and *chazzan,* p. 240). If one forgot to recite this prayer in its appropriate place he should say it in the benediction רְצֵה before the words וְתֶחֱזֶינָה with the deletion of the concluding formula ... מְנַחֵם צִיּוֹן (O.C. 557:1, M.B. §2). However, if it was said erroneously in the benediction שְׁמַע קוֹלֵנוּ it need not be repeated in רְצֵה *(Be'ur Halachah).* If one has already concluded the רְצֵה benediction with הַמַּחֲזִיר ... לְצִיּוֹן (or even said the word *HASHEM*), he continues the prayer and need not repeat it because of the deletion (O.C. 557).

◆§ Rosh Chodesh and Festivals — יַעֲלֶה וְיָבֹא

89. On Rosh Chodesh, the prayer יַעֲלֶה וְיָבֹא is inserted in the benediction רְצֵה, *Be favorable* (p. 110). If it is forgotten in the *Maariv* prayer (of either the first or second night of Rosh Chodesh) one need not repeat the prayer (O.C. 422:1). If the omission occurred during the

Shacharis or *Minchah* prayers, *Shemoneh Esrei* must be repeated. Thus, if one realized his error before uttering the word *HASHEM* in the formula concluding the benediction, he returns to יַעֲלֶה וְיָבֹא. If he has already concluded with הַמַּחֲזִיר שְׁכִינָתוֹ לְצִיּוֹן but not yet begun the benediction מוֹדִים he should recite יַעֲלֶה וְיָבֹא there (till מֶלֶךְ חַנּוּן וְרַחוּם אָתָּה) and continue with מוֹדִים. If he had already begun to say מוֹדִים he must return to the beginning of the benediction רְצֵה. If he had concluded *Shemoneh Esrei,* he must repeat it in its entirety (O.C. 422:1).

One is considered to be have 'concluded' in this context when one has recited the verse יִהְיוּ לְרָצוֹן at the conclusion of the prayer אֱלֹהַי (before עֹשֶׂה שָׁלוֹם; see M.B. 422:9).

If one is in doubt whether he has said יַעֲלֶה וְיָבֹא he must assume he has not said it. However, if he knows that while praying he was aware that he had to recite יַעֲלֶה וְיָבֹא, but is in doubt some time after concluding the prayer, he may assume that he fulfilled his intention and recited יַעֲלֶה וְיָבֹא (M.B. 422:10).

The rules for יַעֲלֶה וְיָבֹא on the intermediate days of the Festivals are the same as on Rosh Chodesh with the following exception: If יַעֲלֶה וְיָבֹא is forgotten even in the *Maariv* prayer, the *Shemoneh Esrei* must be repeated (O.C. 490:2). The omission of יַעֲלֶה וְיָבֹא on the Festivals themselves is a rare occurrence, since it is an integral part of the Festival *Shemoneh Esrei* rather than a mere insertion in the standard *Shemoneh Esrei* (see O.C. 487:3).

☙ Purim and Chanukah — עַל הַנִּסִּים

90. On Purim and Chanukah special prayers, beginning with the words עַל הַנִּסִּים, *And for the miracles,* commemorating the events of the festival, are inserted in the benediction of מוֹדִים, *we gratefully thank* (p. 112). If these prayers were omitted one must not repeat the prayer. However, if one realized his error prior to saying the word *HASHEM* in the concluding formula of the benediction (בָּרוּךְ ... וּלְךָ נָאֶה לְהוֹדוֹת) he should return to עַל הַנִּסִּים and proceed from there. If the word *HASHEM* has already been said the benediction should be concluded and one should proceed until the end of *Shemoneh Esrei.* He may then recite עַל הַנִּסִּים before the prayer אֱלֹהַי which is customarily said at the conclusion of the *Shemoneh Esrei* (O.C. 682:1, M.B. §4).

☙ The Chazzan's Repetition of the Shemoneh Esrei

91. According to a Rabbinic enactment dating back to Mishnaic times, the *Shemoneh Esrei* must be repeated whenever at least six individuals out of a quorum of ten *(minyan)* have prayed the silent *Shemoneh Esrei* together (O.C. 124:1, M.B. 69:8).

92. There must be a quorum (of ten, including the *chazzan*) present and listening to the recitation. If the congregants do not pay attention it is almost as if the *chazzan* were taking God's Name in vain. Every person should imagine that there are only ten congregants present and that he is one of the nine whose attentive listening is vital to the recitation (O.C. 124:4).

93. One should respond with *Amen* to every benediction he hears, and should teach his young children to do so (O.C. 124:6,7).

94. When saying *Amen,* it is important to enunciate all of the vowels and consonants distinctly. One should not respond before the *chazzan* has concluded the benediction, and then the response should be immediate (O.C. 124:8). *Mishnah Berurah* (§17) cautions even against Torah study or recitation of psalms and other prayers during the *chazzan's* recitation of the *Shemoneh Esrei.*

95. It is absolutely forbidden to talk during the *Shemoneh Esrei* even if one makes sure to respond with *Amen* at the conclusion of the benediction (O.C. 124:7).

96. On most days *Shemoneh Esrei* is followed with the prayer called *Tachanun.* One should be careful not to engage in idle talk between *Shemoneh Esrei* and *Tachanun* (O.C. 131:1).

THE READING OF THE TORAH

☙ The Aliyos

97. The Torah is read in public during *Shacharis* and *Minchah* of the Sabbath and of fast days, and during *Shacharis* of *Yom Tov,* Chol HaMoed, Rosh Chodesh, Chanukah, Purim, and every Monday and Thursday. On most of these occasions, three people are called to the Torah; Rosh Chodesh and Chol HaMoed, four; Festivals, five; Yom Kippur *Shacharis,* six; Sabbath *Shacharis,* seven. On the Sabbath morning, more people may be called, although some authorities prefer not to do so. It is customary not to add to the *aliyos* on Yom Tov (with the exception of Simchas Torah). On other occasions of Torah reading it is forbidden to add *aliyos* (O.C. 135:1,10, 282:1, 423:1; *Mishnah, Megillah* 21a).

98. The first *aliyah* belongs to a *Kohen* and the second to a *Levi* (if any are present). If no *Kohen* is present, there is no obligation to call a *Levi* in his place, but if no *Levi* is present the same *Kohen* who has been called for his own *aliyah* is called again to replace the *Levi.* He recites both blessings again. According to the prevalent custom, a *Kohen* or *Levi* may not be called up for any other *aliyah* except *maftir* or *acharon,* the last *aliyah* of the weekly Sabbath portion *(sidra).* However, they may be called for *acharon* only after the prescribed number of seven *aliyos* has been completed (O.C. 135:10).

◆§ Entitlements to Aliyos

99. Time-honored custom has established that certain occasions entitle one to an *aliyah*. These are listed in *Levush* and *Magen Avraham* to *Orach Chaim* 282, and in *Be'ur Halachah* to O.C. 136. Below is a list of these entitlements in descending order of importance. If there are not enough *aliyos* to go around, then the *aliyos* are given according to the importance of the entitlement. If more than one individual are equally entitled, lots should be drawn for the *aliyah*. However, if one of the individuals is an acknowledged Torah scholar *(talmid chacham)*, he should be given preference.

(a) **A bridegroom** on the day of his wedding has preference over any other entitled person.

(b) **A bridegroom** on the Sabbath before his wedding; however a widower or divorced man is not entitled to an *aliyah* before he remarries and has no preference over any entitled person. Nonetheless, *Shaarei Ephraim* advises that he should be given an *aliyah* if possible. [The bridegroom's father should also be given an *aliyah* if possible *(Shaarei Ephraim* 2:3).]

(c) **A bar mitzvah** on the Sabbath after his birthday. A *bar mitzvah* is equal to a bridegroom whose marriage will take place the following week. If there is a conflict, lots should be drawn.

[It can be inferred from the *poskim* that a *bar mitzvah* is not entitled to an *aliyah* the Sabbath preceding his *bar mitzvah*. Nevertheless, it is customary in many congregations to award him *maftir*. If he had an *aliyah*, even in the weekdays, he is no longer entitled to an *aliyah* on the Sabbath after his birthday *(Shaarei Ephraim* 2:10).]

(d) **A husband** whose wife has given birth is entitled to an *aliyah* the first Sabbath his wife attends the synagogue. Even if she is not in the synagogue, he is entitled to an *aliyah* when forty days have elapsed after the birth of a son or eighty days after the birth of a daughter, even if the child was stillborn.

(e) **A bridegroom** whose marriage has taken place within the three days before the Sabbath, but only if it is the first marriage for either the groom or bride. [Although a bridegroom who was married earlier in the week is not entitled to an *aliyah*, it is nevertheless customary to give him one *(Shaarei Ephraim)*.]

(f) **Someone observing yahrzeit** for a parent. If the *yahrzeit* is not on the day of the Torah reading, there is no absolute obligation to give him an *aliyah*, but it is customary to give *maftir* or an *aliyah* on the Sabbath preceding a *yahrzeit*.

(g) **The father** of a newborn male child on the Sabbath before the circumcision. In some places the *sandak* and *mohel* [if he performs the *mitzvah* gratis; cf. *Shaarei Ephraim* 2:15] are also awarded *aliyos*, whereas in some congregations they are honored with picking up *(hagbahah)* and rolling together *(gelilah)* the Torah. [If the child is sick and his *bris* will surely be deferred the father is not entitled to an *aliyah (Shaarei Ephraim* 2:8).]

(h) **On Rosh Hashanah and Yom Kippur** some congregations award *aliyos* to the *chazzan* of *Mussaf* and the one who sounds the *shofar* on Rosh Hashanah. However, if they are paid for their services they forfeit their entitlement.

100. In addition to the above, whose priorities are established by a well-defined order of importance, there are other individuals to whom it is customary to award *aliyos*. A person who must recite the benediction הַגּוֹמֵל, e.g., he had been gravely ill and has recovered, or gone through another dangerous situation (see p. 144) should be given an *aliyah*. If it is not possible to give him an *aliyah* because of the presence of genuinely entitled individuals, he should go before the congregation and recite the benediction הַגּוֹמֵל without an *aliyah*.

101. It is customary to award an *aliyah* to the father of a newborn daughter on the occasion when she is given a name;

to one who will leave on a prolonged trip which will require his absence from the synagogue for longer than a week;

to one who has just returned from such a trip;

and to a distinguished guest.

◆§ Close Relatives in Successive Aliyos

102. Two brothers, or a father and a son, should not be called up to the Torah in succession. Some authorities feel that this stringency be adhered to even in regard to a grandfather and his grandson (O.C. 141:6; M.B. there). However, when *maftir* is read from a second Torah Scroll, as on Yom Tov, they may be called up in succession *(Ba'er Heitev* 141:6).

◆§ Procedure of the Aliyah

103. Before the person called to the Torah for an *aliyah* recites the benediction, he must open the Torah and find the passage that will be read for him (O.C. 139:4). In order to dispel any notion that he is reading the benedictions from the Torah, one should avert his face while reciting them; it is preferable to turn to the left side *(Rama* there). Some authorities maintain that it is better to face the Torah while saying the benedictions but to close one's eyes to dispel the above-mentioned notion (M.B. §19). Others say that it is better to close the Torah during the recitation of the benedictions *(Be'ur Halachah* there). All three modes are practiced today in various congregations.

104. In many congregations it is customary to touch the Torah with the *tallis* (or the Torah's mantle or girdle) at the place in the Torah where the passage to be read begins, and to kiss the edge which touched the Torah. One should be careful not to rub on the Torah script forcefully for this can cause words to become erased and thus invalidate the Torah.

105. It is extremely important that the benedictions be said loud enough for the congregation to hear (O.C. 139:6). If the congregation did not hear the recitation of בָּרְכוּ they may not respond with בָּרוּךְ ... וָעֶד *(Be'ur Halachah* to O.C. 57:1). However, if the congregation (or at least a *minyan)* heard בָּרְכוּ, then even someone who has not heard בָּרְכוּ may respond with בָּרוּךְ ... וָעֶד along with the congregation (M.B. 57:2).

106. While reciting the benedictions, one should hold the poles *(atzei chaim)* upon which the Torah is rolled. During the reading the reader holds one pole and the person called to the Torah holds the other one (O.C. 139:11; M.B. §35). *Arizal* says one should hold the *atzei chaim* with both hands during the benedictions and with the right hand only during the reading (cited in *Magen Avraham* 159:13).

107. Upon completion of the reading it is customary for the person who has been called up to touch the Torah with his *tallis* (or the Torah's mantle or girdle) and to kiss the edge that has touched the Torah (see M.B. 139:35).

108. After the Torah passage has been read, the Torah scroll is closed and then the benediction is said *(Rama* O.C. 139:5). If the Torah reading will not be resumed immediately, (e.g., a מִי שֶׁבֵּרַךְ is said), then a covering should be spread out over the Torah (M.B. 139:21).

109. In Talmudic times the person called for an *aliyah* would also read aloud from the Torah. This practice was still followed in Greek and Turkish communities up to the sixteenth century (see *Beis Yosef* to *Tur* O.C. 141), and the tradition persists to this day in Yemenite communities. However, since ancient times the Ashkenazic custom has been for a designated reader *(baal korei)* to read the Torah aloud to the congregation (see *Rosh* cited in *Tur* loc. cit). Nevertheless, the person who recites the benedictions should read quietly along with the reader (O.C. 141:2).

110. The reader and the one called up to the Torah must stand while reading the Torah in public. It is forbidden even to lean upon something (O.C. 141:1).

111. When going up to the *bimah* to recite the benedictions one should pick the shortest route possible, and when returning to one's place one should take the longer route. If two routes are equidistant, one should go to the *bimah* via the route which is to his right and descend via the opposite route (O.C. 141:7).

112. After one has finished reciting the concluding benediction he should not return to his place until the next person called up to the Torah has come to the *bimah* (O.C. 141:7). However, it is customary to wait until the next person has finished his passage of Torah (M.B. §26).

113. It is forbidden to talk or even to discuss Torah topics while the Torah is being read (O.C. 146:2).

114. It is forbidden to leave the synagogue while the Torah is being read (O.C. 146:1), even if one has already heard the reading of the passage elsewhere (M.B. §1). However, if necessary, one may leave during the pause between one portion and the next (O.C. 146:1), provided that a *minyan* remains in the synagogue (M.B. §2).

KADDISH

115. The conclusion of a segment of prayer is usually signified by the recitation of the *Kaddish.* Many of these *Kaddish* recitations are the privilege of mourners (within the eleven months following the death or burial of a parent, or in some instances, of other close relatives), or of those observing *yahrzeit,* i.e., the anniversary of the death of a parent (and in some congregations, of a grandparent who has no living sons; see *Mateh Ephraim, Dinei Kaddish* 3:14). However, many recitations of *Kaddish* are exclusively the prerogative of the *chazzan.*

116. Basically there are four types of *Kaddish:*

(a) חֲצִי קַדִּישׁ, Half-*Kaddish,* which ends with דַּאֲמִירָן בְּעָלְמָא וְאִמְרוּ אָמֵן;

(b) קַדִּישׁ יָתוֹם, the Mourner's *Kaddish,* which consists of Half *Kaddish,* with the addition of יְהֵא שְׁלָמָא and עוֹשֶׂה שָׁלוֹם;

(c) קַדִּישׁ שָׁלֵם the Full *Kaddish,* the same as the Mourner's *Kaddish* with the addition of תִּתְקַבַּל before יְהֵא שְׁלָמָא; and

(d) קַדִּישׁ דְּרַבָּנָן, the Rabbis' *Kaddish,* the same as the Mourner's *Kaddish* with the addition of עַל יִשְׂרָאֵל.

117. The function of the Half-*Kaddish* is to link different segments of the prayer, e.g., it is recited between *Pesukei D'zimrah* and the *Shema* benedictions, between *Shemoneh Esrei* (or *Tachanun)* and the prayers that conclude the service *(Pri Megadim* in *Mishbetzos Zahav, Orach Chaim* 55:1). Thus it is recited by the *chazzan.*

Nevertheless, in some congregations it is customary for a mourner to recite the *Kaddish* following the reading of the Torah if he has been called to the Torah for the concluding segment *(Shaarei Ephraim* 10:9). The rationale for the latter custom is that the person called to the Torah is also a *chazzan* of sorts, since he too must read from the Torah, albeit quietly. In some congregations, a mourner recites this *Kaddish* even if he was not called to the Torah.

118. The Full *Kaddish* is recited only after the communal recitation of *Shemoneh Esrei* (or *Selichos*). It includes the *chazzan's* prayer that the just concluded service be accepted by God. Consequently it must be recited by the *chazzan*. In congregations where one *chazzan* recited *Shemoneh Esrei* and a different *chazzan* recited *Hallel*, the *Kaddish* should be recited by the *chazzan* who recited *Shemoneh Esrei*.

119. The Mourner's *Kaddish* is said after the recital of Scriptural verses that supplement the main body of prayer. The recital of *Kaddish* after this portion of the service is not obligatory, and is not recited if no mourners are present. If a mourner had served as *chazzan*, he would have fulfilled his *Kaddish* obligation with the four times *Kaddish* appears in the service. However, because there are mourners who cannot serve as *chazzan*, e.g., minors or when many mourners are present, it was necessary to reserve the *Kaddish* following the supplemental prayers for them (see *Aruch HaShulchan* O.C. 133:2). Since *Kaddish* in these parts of the service is recited exclusively by mourners, it has become customary that one whose parents are living should not recite it, since this would be a mark of disrespect to his parents (see *Pischei Teshuvah, Yoreh Deah* 376:4).

If no mourners are present, the Mourner's *Kaddish* is not recited, with one exception. After *Aleinu*, which also contains Scriptural verses, *Kaddish* should be recited even if no mourner is present. In such a case, it should be recited by one of the congregants, preferably by one whose parents are no longer alive, or by one whose parents have not explicitly expressed their opposition to his recitation of *Kaddish (Orach Chaim* 132:2 with M.B. §11).

120. Ideally, each Mourner's *Kaddish* should be recited by only one person. Where more than one mourner is present, the *poskim* developed a system of rules establishing an order of priorities for those who must recite *Kaddish* (see M.B. in *Be'ur Halachah* to O.C. 132, et al.). However, since adherence to these rules can often cause discord in the congregation, it has become widely accepted for all the mourners to recite the *Kaddish* simultaneously (see *Aruch HaShulchan* O.C. 132:8; *Siddur R' Yaakov Emden; Teshuvos Chasam Sofer, O. C.* 159).

121. In many congregations it is customary that someone observing a *yahrzeit* is given the exclusive privilege of reciting a *Kaddish*, usually the one after *Aleinu*. In that case, an additional psalm (usually *Psalm* 24) is recited at the conclusion of the services so that the mourners can all recite *Kaddish* thereafter.

122. The Rabbis' *Kaddish (Kaddish D'Rabbanan)* is recited after segments of the Oral Torah (e.g., Talmud) have been studied or recited by a quorum of ten adult males *(Rambam, Seder Tefilos Kol HaShanah)*. The Talmud *(Sotah* 49a) refers to the great significance of יְהֵא שְׁמֵיהּ רַבָּא (a reference to *Kaddish)* that is said after *Aggadah*, indicating that this *Kaddish* has a special relevance to the Midrashic portion of the Torah. Therefore, it is customary to append a brief *Aggadic* selection to Torah study and then to recite the Rabbis' *Kaddish*. The commentary ascribed to *Rashi (Avos* 6:15) cites the custom to append the saying of R' Chananyah ben Akashya to each chapter of *Avos* (see p. 548) before the recitation of *Kaddish D'Rabbanan*. It is customary to recite an *Aggadic* passage prior to the *Kaddish* said after בַּמֶּה מַדְלִיקִין (p. 328) and one should be said also when *Kaddish* is recited after the study of Mishnah *(Magen Avraham* 54:3).

123. Although *Kaddish D'Rabbanan* is not reserved for mourners and may be recited even by one whose parents are alive *(Pischei Teshuvah, Yoreh Deah* 376:4), it is generally recited by mourners. However, when one celebrates the completion of a tractate of the Talmud, or when the rabbi delivers a *derashah* (homiletical discourse), it is customary for the celebrant or the rabbi to recite the *Kaddish* himself.

MINYAN

124. A *minyan* (quorum of ten adult males) must be present during *Borchu;* the *chazzan's* repetition of *Shemoneh Esrei; Kaddish;* and the Torah reading. Therefore, it is a grave sin (cf. *Isaiah* 1:28, *And those who forsake HASHEM will be destroyed)* to leave the synagogue during any of these recitations if one's presence is necessary to complete the *minyan (O.C. 55:2)*.

125. Nonetheless, if any of these recitations began with a *minyan*, but some individuals left and a *minyan* is no longer present, the recitation may continue, if at least six individuals remain.

126. Thus, if the *chazzan* began his repetition of the *Shemoneh Esrei*, he may conclude it — including *Kedushah* — even if a *minyan* is no longer present. (If this happened at *Mussaf* of a Festival, the *Kohanim* may not ascend the *duchan*.) Moreover, the *chazzan* may even recite the Half-*Kaddish* after *Tachanun* and the Full *Kaddish* after וּבָא לְצִיּוֹן, since these prayers are considered contiguous with *Shemoneh Esrei*. It is, however, not permissible to read the Torah or to recite any other *Kaddish* (O.C. 55:3; M.B. §18-20).

127. At *Maariv*, the *chazzan* may recite the Half-*Kaddish* preceding *Shemoneh Esrei* if a *minyan* was present for the recital of *Borchu*. The Full *Kaddish* may be recited after *Shemoneh Esrei* if a *minyan* was present at the beginning of *Shemoneh Esrei* (M.B. 55:22).

PRAYER SERVICE ON SPECIAL DAYS

◆§ Hoshana Rabbah

Hoshana Rabbah, the final day of Chol HaMoed Succos, is the last day of the judgment period which began on Rosh Hashanah. Although this period reached a climax on Yom Kippur, the verdicts are not sealed until Hoshana Rabbah. Thus, *Zohar* describes it as a judgment day akin to Yom Kippur and it assumes special importance as a day of prayer and repentance. Despite its special function, during *Shemoneh Esrei* and *Bircas HaMazon* the day is referred to as חַג הַסֻּכּוֹת, *the Succos Festival.*

At night (preferably after midnight), some congregations read the Book of *Devarim (Deuteronomy)* from a Torah Scroll [without a blessing], and the Book of *Psalms* is recited. Some people spend the night reciting *Tikkun Leil Hoshana Rabbah,* a collection of Torah passages.

In the morning, many customarily immerse in the *mikveh* before *Shacharis,* as on Erev Yom Kippur. It is proper to wear one's Sabbath clothing on this day, and the *chazzan* wears a *kittel* during *Shacharis* and *Mussaf.*

The *Shacharis* service combines elements of the Chol HaMoed and Festival services.

(a) *Shacharis* follows the regular weekday service through מִזְמוֹר לְתוֹדָה, *Psalm* 100 (p. 64), followed by the additional psalms for the Sabbath and Festivals (pp. 374-388).

(b) The weekday service resumes with יְהִי כְבוֹד (p. 64) through *Shemoneh Esrei* — with the insertion of יַעֲלֶה וְיָבֹא (p. 110) — and the *chazzan's* repetition.

(c) The full *Hallel* (pp. 632-642) is recited, accompanied by the waving of the Four Species as during the other days of *Succos,* and followed by the Full *Kaddish* (p. 642). After *Kaddish,* many have a custom to remove the uppermost of the three palm-leaf rings bound around the *lulav.*

(d) One Torah Scroll is removed from the Ark (pp. 432-444); the day's portion (p. 973) is read; Half-*Kaddish* (p. 138) is recited; and the Torah is raised (p. 146), wrapped, and returned to the Ark (p. 148).

(e) אַשְׁרֵי (p. 150) and וּבָא לְצִיּוֹן (p. 154) are recited, followed by Half-*Kaddish.*

(f) The *Amidah* of *Mussaf* (p. 674) is recited. During the *chazzan's* repetition, the full version of *Kedushah* (p. 676) is recited.

(g) After the *chazzan's* repetition, all the Torah Scrolls are removed from the Ark [in some congregations a lit candle, symbolizing the light of Torah, is placed into the empty Ark] and they are brought to the *bimah* where each is held by a member of the congregation until the conclusion of the *Hoshana* liturgy.

(h) The Ark remains open and the *Hoshana* service (pp. 726-756) is recited. Detailed instructions appear on the appropriate pages.

(i) After the *Hoshana* service the Torah Scrolls are returned to the Ark, and the concluding prayers of *Mussaf* (pp. 476-488) are recited.

◆§ Taanis Esther

(a) *Maariv* on the eve of Taanis Esther follows the regular weekday service.

(b) *Shacharis* of Taanis Esther is the same as on other fast days (see below).

(c) Before [in some congregations after] *Minchah* the *machtzis hashekel* donation — based on the Torah-ordained annual contribution for the purchase of communal Temple sacrifices — is given. For every adult, male or female, three half-*shekels* (see below) are placed into a charity box or plate designated for that purpose [many also donate for each child, some even for an unborn child]. The money is usually used for the upkeep of the synagogue or for another charity. Since half-*shekels* are not used today, a coin valued at half the basic currency (in the United States a half-dollar coin) is used to represent the half-*shekel.*

(d) *Minchah* of Taanis Esther is the same as that of other fast days (see below) except that *Tachanun* and *Avinu Malkeinu* are not recited. When Purim falls on Sunday, Taanis Esther is moved back to the previous Thursday and *Tachanun* and *Avinu Malkeinu* are recited.

◆§ Purim — Maariv

(a) During every *Shemoneh Esrei* and *Bircas HaMazon* of Purim, עַל הַנִּסִּים is recited. If forgotten in *Shemoneh Esrei* see *Laws* §90; during *Bircas HaMazon,* see page 187.

(b) The regular weekday *Maariv* (p. 256), is recited until after the Full *Kaddish* (p. 278); the *Megillah* is then read (see below).

(c) Before reading the *Megillah,* the reader recites three blessings (p. 786). After the reading, the concluding blessing and the *piyut* אֲשֶׁר הֵנִיא are recited (p. 786).

(d) On weekday nights, *Maariv* continues with וְאַתָּה קָדוֹשׁ (p. 596); the Full *Kaddish* with the omission of the verse תִּתְקַבַּל; עָלֵינוּ (p. 608) and the Mourner's *Kaddish* (p. 610).

On Saturday night, *Maariv* continues with the regular service for the conclusion of the Sabbath (pp. 594-620) but with the omission in the Full *Kaddish* of the verse beginning תִּתְקַבַּל.

◆§ Purim — Shacharis

(a) The weekday *Shacharis* is recited (with עַל הַנִּסִּים) until after the silent *Shemoneh Esrei.*

(b) During the *chazzan's* repetition many congregations recite *Krovetz* (p. 788).

(c) One Torah Scroll is removed from the Ark (p. 138); the Purim portion (p. 952) is read; Half-*Kaddish* (p. 138) is recited; the Torah is raised (p. 146); wrapped; and returned to the Ark (p. 148).

(d) Before reading the *Megillah,* the reader recites three blessings (p. 786). Each member of the congregation should declare mentally that the blessings also apply to the *mitzvos* of *shalach manos,* presents to the poor, and the Purim feast.

(e) After the reading, the concluding blessing and שׁוֹשַׁנַּת יַעֲקֹב are recited (pp. 786-788).

(f) The regular *Shacharis* service continues (pp. 150-168) but לַמְנַצֵּחַ (p. 152) is omitted.

◆§ Tishah B'Av — Maariv

(a) Although other fasts begin in the morning and prohibit only eating/drinking, the fast of Tishah B'Av begins at sunset of the previous day and prohibits: eating/drinking, bathing, anointing, wearing leather shoes, and cohabitation.

(b) *Maariv* begins in the usual manner (p. 256). After בָּרְכוּ the congregation sits on the floor or on low stools and the lights are dimmed. The regular *Maariv* service is followed [on Saturday night with the addition of אַתָּה חוֹנַנְתָּנוּ (p. 268)] until after the Full *Kaddish* (p. 278).

(c) On Saturday night, although *Havdalah* is not recited [see below (e)], a multiwicked candle is lit and the blessing בּוֹרֵא מְאוֹרֵי הָאֵשׁ is recited.

(d) *Eichah* (the Book of *Lamentations)* is chanted aloud by the reader (in some congregations each individual reads along in an undertone). The evening *Kinnos* are then recited.

(e) *Kinnos* are followed by וְאַתָּה קָדוֹשׁ (p. 596); the Full *Kaddish* (p. 598) with the omission of the verse תִּתְקַבֵּל; עָלֵינוּ (p. 608) and the Mourner's *Kaddish* (p. 610). [On Saturday night וִיהִי נֹעַם and וְיִתֶּן לְךָ are omitted, and *Havdalah* is postponed until Sunday night.]

◆§ Tishah B'Av — Shacharis

(a) The *tallis kattan (tzitzis)* is worn but the accompanying blessing is omitted. Donning of the *tallis* and *tefillin* is postponed until *Minchah.*

(b) The morning blessings (pp. 12-20) are recited as usual. However, the blessing שֶׁעָשָׂה לִי כָּל צְרָכַי is recited by some, but omitted entirely or postponed until after the fast by others.

(c) The weekday service continues until after *Shemoneh Esrei.* [Some omit קָרְבָּנוֹת/*Offerings* (pp. 30-42), but many recite them.]

(d) During his repetition the *chazzan* recites עֲנֵנוּ [see rule (b) of *Other Fast Days* below]; and he omits בִּרְכַּת כֹּהֲנִים (p. 116). After his repetition, the *chazzan* recites Half-*Kaddish* (p. 138).

(e) One Torah Scroll is removed from the Ark (p. 138); the Tishah B'Av portion (p. 953) is read; Half-*Kaddish* (p. 138) is recited; the Torah is raised (p. 146) and wrapped; the *Haftarah* (blessings, p. 446; reading, p. 953) is read; and the Torah is returned to the Ark (p. 148).

(f) *Kinnos* are recited, each congregation according to its custom. It is preferable that their recitation be extended until just before noon.

(g) After *Kinnos,* אַשְׁרֵי (p. 150) and וּבָא לְצִיּוֹן (p. 154) with the omission of the second verse (וַאֲנִי זֹאת) are recited, followed by the Full *Kaddish* (p. 156) with the omission of the verse תִּתְקַבֵּל; עָלֵינוּ (p. 158); and the Mourner's *Kaddish* (p. 160). The Song of the Day and subsequent readings are postponed until *Minchah.*

◆§ Tishah B'Av — Minchah/Maariv

(a) The *tallis* and *tefillin* are donned (pp. 2-10) and whatever passages were omitted from the *Shacharis* service are recited.

(b) The *Minchah* service is the same as for other fast days (see below) with two exceptions: The prayer נַחֵם is inserted into the Rebuilding Jerusalem blessing (p. 240); and *Avinu Malkeinu* and *Tachanun* are omitted.

(c) The regular weekday *Maariv* is recited. On Sunday night, an abridged form of *Havdalah* — omitting the first paragraph, spices, and flame — is recited (p. 618).

(d) *Kiddush Levanah* (p. 612) is customarily postponed until after Tishah B'Av. However, since this blessing should be recited joyfully, one should break the fast before its recitation.

◆§ Other Fast Days

The fasts of 10 Teves, 3 Tishrei (Tzom Gedaliah), 17 Tammuz and 13 Adar (Taanis Esther) all begin at dawn. On the eve of these fasts, the regular *Maariv* (p. 256) is recited. At *Shacharis* and *Minchah* the service includes special prayers, as follows:

(a) The regular weekday *Shacharis* is recited until after *Shemoneh Esrei.*

(b) If ten members of the *minyan* [some authorities require only seven] are fasting, the *chazzan* recites עֲנֵנוּ, between the blessings for Redemption and Health (p. 104). If less than the required number are fasting, the *chazzan* inserts עֲנֵנוּ into the Acceptance of Prayer blessing (p. 108) and omits the closing sentence.

(c) After the *chazzan's* repetition, *Selichos* (p. 816) are recited. [*Selichos* for Tzom Gedaliah appear with the *Selichos* prayers recited before and after Rosh Hashanah which comprise a volume unto themselves.]

(d) After *Selichos, Avinu Malkeinu* (p. 120) and *Tachanun* (Monday and Thursday, p. 124; other days, p. 132) are recited.

(e) One Torah Scroll is removed from the Ark (p. 138), the fast day portion is read (p. 952), and the regular weekday *Shacharis* is followed until its conclusion.

(f) *Minchah* begins with *Ashrei* (p. 232) and Half-*Kaddish* (p. 234).

(g) If at least seven members of the *minyan* are fasting, one Torah Scroll is removed from the Ark (p. 138); the fast day portion is read (p. 952); the Torah is raised (p. 146) and wrapped; the *Haftarah* is read (blessings, p. 446; reading, p. 952); the Torah is returned to the Ark (p. 148) and Half-*Kaddish* (p. 234) is recited.

(h) *Shemoneh Esrei* (p. 234) is recited with the addition of עֲנֵנוּ [for the silent *Shemoneh Esrei,* p. 242; for the *chazzan's* repetition, p. 238, but see (b) above] by those who are fasting.

(i) After the *chazzan's* repetition, *Avinu Malkeinu* (p. 120) and *Tachanun* (p. 250) are recited, followed by עָלֵינוּ (p. 252) and the Mourner's *Kaddish* (p. 254).

תהלים

Psalms

תפלה קודם אמירת תהלים/PRAYER BEFORE RECITING TEHILLIM

On the Sabbath and Festivals begin with לְכוּ נְרַנְּנָה below:

יְהִי רָצוֹן מִלְּפָנֶיךָ, יהוה אֱלֹהֵינוּ וֵאלֹהֵי אֲבוֹתֵינוּ, הַבּוֹחֵר בְּדָוִד עַבְדּוֹ וּבְזַרְעוֹ אַחֲרָיו, וְהַבּוֹחֵר בְּשִׁירוֹת וְתִשְׁבָּחוֹת, שֶׁתֵּפֶן בְּרַחֲמִים אֶל קְרִיאַת מִזְמוֹרֵי תְהִלִּים שֶׁאֶקְרָא, כְּאִלּוּ אֲמָרָם דָּוִד הַמֶּלֶךְ עָלָיו הַשָּׁלוֹם בְּעַצְמוֹ, זְכוּתוֹ יָגֵן עָלֵינוּ. וְיַעֲמָד לָנוּ זְכוּת פְּסוּקֵי תְהִלִּים — וּזְכוּת תֵּבוֹתֵיהֶם, וְאוֹתִיּוֹתֵיהֶם, וּנְקֻדּוֹתֵיהֶם, וְטַעֲמֵיהֶם, וְהַשֵּׁמוֹת הַיּוֹצְאִים מֵהֶם מֵרָאשֵׁי תֵבוֹת וּמִסּוֹפֵי תֵבוֹת — לְכַפֵּר פְּשָׁעֵינוּ וַעֲוֹנוֹתֵינוּ וְחַטֹּאתֵינוּ; וּלְזַמֵּר עָרִיצִים, וּלְהַכְרִית כָּל הַחוֹחִים וְהַקּוֹצִים הַסּוֹבְבִים אֶת הַשּׁוֹשַׁנָּה הָעֶלְיוֹנָה; וּלְחַבֵּר אֵשֶׁת נְעוּרִים עִם דּוֹדָהּ, בְּאַהֲבָה וְאַחֲוָה וְרֵיעוּת. וּמִשָּׁם יִמָּשֵׁךְ לָנוּ שֶׁפַע לְנֶפֶשׁ רוּחַ וּנְשָׁמָה, לְטַהֲרֵנוּ מֵעֲוֹנוֹתֵינוּ וְלִסְלוֹחַ חַטֹּאתֵינוּ וּלְכַפֵּר פְּשָׁעֵינוּ. כְּמוֹ שֶׁסָּלַחְתָּ לְדָוִד שֶׁאָמַר מִזְמוֹרִים אֵלּוּ לְפָנֶיךָ, כְּמוֹ שֶׁנֶּאֱמַר: גַּם יהוה הֶעֱבִיר חַטָּאתְךָ לֹא תָמוּת. וְאַל תִּקָּחֵנוּ מֵהָעוֹלָם הַזֶּה קוֹדֶם זְמַנֵּנוּ עַד מְלֹאת שְׁנוֹתֵינוּ (°°בָּהֶם שִׁבְעִים שָׁנָה) בְּאוֹפֶן שֶׁנּוּכַל לְתַקֵּן אֶת אֲשֶׁר שִׁחַתְנוּ. וּזְכוּת דָּוִד הַמֶּלֶךְ עָלָיו הַשָּׁלוֹם יָגֵן עָלֵינוּ וּבַעֲדֵנוּ, שֶׁתַּאֲרִיךְ אַפְּךָ עַד שׁוּבֵנוּ אֵלֶיךָ בִּתְשׁוּבָה שְׁלֵמָה לְפָנֶיךָ. וּמֵאוֹצַר מַתְּנַת חִנָּם חָנֵּנוּ, כִּדְכְתִיב: וְחַנֹּתִי אֶת אֲשֶׁר אָחֹן, וְרִחַמְתִּי אֶת אֲשֶׁר אֲרַחֵם. וּכְשֵׁם שֶׁאָנוּ אוֹמְרִים לְפָנֶיךָ שִׁירָה בָּעוֹלָם הַזֶּה, כַּךְ נִזְכֶּה לוֹמַר לְפָנֶיךָ, יהוה אֱלֹהֵינוּ, שִׁיר וּשְׁבָחָה לָעוֹלָם הַבָּא. וְעַל יְדֵי אֲמִירַת תְּהִלִּים תִּתְעוֹרֵר חֲבַצֶּלֶת הַשָּׁרוֹן, וְלָשִׁיר בְּקוֹל נָעִים בְּגִילַת וְרַנֵּן, כְּבוֹד הַלְּבָנוֹן נִתַּן לָהּ, הוֹד וְהָדָר בְּבֵית אֱלֹהֵינוּ, בִּמְהֵרָה בְיָמֵינוּ, אָמֵן, סֶלָה.

לְכוּ נְרַנְּנָה לַיהוה, נָרִיעָה לְצוּר יִשְׁעֵנוּ. נְקַדְּמָה פָנָיו בְּתוֹדָה, בִּזְמִרוֹת נָרִיעַ לוֹ. כִּי אֵל גָּדוֹל יהוה, וּמֶלֶךְ גָּדוֹל עַל כָּל אֱלֹהִים.

°°Although this phrase appears in most editions, *Mishnah Berurah* (581:3) deletes it.

The recitation of *Tehillim* (Psalms) is divided in three different ways: into five books; into seven sections for recitation on the respective days of the week; and into thirty parts, one for each day of the month. These divisions are indicated as they appear in the text.

The prayer recited after *Tehillim,* appears on page 47.
A list of psalms and prayers recited on behalf of the sick appears on page 48.

BOOK ONE — ספר ראשון

SUNDAY — יום ראשון

1st day — יום א לחדש

א אַשְׁרֵי הָאִישׁ אֲשֶׁר לֹא הָלַךְ בַּעֲצַת רְשָׁעִים, וּבְדֶרֶךְ חַטָּאִים לֹא עָמָד, וּבְמוֹשַׁב לֵצִים לֹא יָשָׁב. כִּי אִם בְּתוֹרַת יהוה חֶפְצוֹ, וּבְתוֹרָתוֹ יֶהְגֶּה יוֹמָם וָלָיְלָה. וְהָיָה כְּעֵץ שָׁתוּל עַל פַּלְגֵי מָיִם, אֲשֶׁר פִּרְיוֹ יִתֵּן בְּעִתּוֹ, וְעָלֵהוּ לֹא יִבּוֹל, וְכֹל אֲשֶׁר יַעֲשֶׂה יַצְלִיחַ. לֹא כֵן הָרְשָׁעִים, כִּי אִם כַּמֹּץ אֲשֶׁר תִּדְּפֶנּוּ רוּחַ. עַל כֵּן לֹא יָקֻמוּ רְשָׁעִים בַּמִּשְׁפָּט, וְחַטָּאִים בַּעֲדַת צַדִּיקִים. כִּי יוֹדֵעַ יהוה דֶּרֶךְ צַדִּיקִים, וְדֶרֶךְ רְשָׁעִים תֹּאבֵד.

ב לָמָּה רָגְשׁוּ גוֹיִם, וּלְאֻמִּים יֶהְגּוּ רִיק. יִתְיַצְּבוּ מַלְכֵי אֶרֶץ, וְרוֹזְנִים נוֹסְדוּ יָחַד, עַל יהוה וְעַל מְשִׁיחוֹ. נְנַתְּקָה אֶת מוֹסְרוֹתֵימוֹ, וְנַשְׁלִיכָה מִמֶּנּוּ עֲבֹתֵימוֹ. יוֹשֵׁב בַּשָּׁמַיִם יִשְׂחָק, אֲדֹנָי יִלְעַג לָמוֹ. אָז יְדַבֵּר אֵלֵימוֹ בְאַפּוֹ, וּבַחֲרוֹנוֹ יְבַהֲלֵמוֹ. וַאֲנִי נָסַכְתִּי מַלְכִּי,

עַל צִיּוֹן הַר קָדְשִׁי. אֲסַפְּרָה אֶל חֹק, יהוה אָמַר אֵלַי, בְּנִי אַתָּה, אֲנִי הַיּוֹם יְלִדְתִּיךָ. שְׁאַל מִמֶּנִּי וְאֶתְּנָה גוֹיִם נַחֲלָתֶךָ, וַאֲחֻזָּתְךָ אַפְסֵי אָרֶץ. תְּרֹעֵם בְּשֵׁבֶט בַּרְזֶל, כִּכְלִי יוֹצֵר תְּנַפְּצֵם. וְעַתָּה מְלָכִים הַשְׂכִּילוּ, הִוָּסְרוּ שֹׁפְטֵי אָרֶץ. עִבְדוּ אֶת יהוה בְּיִרְאָה, וְגִילוּ בִּרְעָדָה. נַשְּׁקוּ בַר פֶּן יֶאֱנַף וְתֹאבְדוּ דֶרֶךְ, כִּי יִבְעַר כִּמְעַט אַפּוֹ, אַשְׁרֵי כָּל חוֹסֵי בוֹ.

ג מִזְמוֹר לְדָוִד, בְּבָרְחוֹ מִפְּנֵי אַבְשָׁלוֹם בְּנוֹ. יהוה, מָה רַבּוּ צָרָי, רַבִּים קָמִים עָלָי. רַבִּים אֹמְרִים לְנַפְשִׁי, אֵין יְשׁוּעָתָה לּוֹ בֵאלֹהִים סֶלָה. וְאַתָּה יהוה מָגֵן בַּעֲדִי, כְּבוֹדִי וּמֵרִים רֹאשִׁי. קוֹלִי אֶל יהוה אֶקְרָא, וַיַּעֲנֵנִי מֵהַר קָדְשׁוֹ סֶלָה. אֲנִי שָׁכַבְתִּי וָאִישָׁנָה, הֱקִיצוֹתִי, כִּי יהוה יִסְמְכֵנִי. לֹא אִירָא מֵרִבְבוֹת עָם, אֲשֶׁר סָבִיב שָׁתוּ עָלָי. קוּמָה יהוה, הוֹשִׁיעֵנִי אֱלֹהַי, כִּי הִכִּיתָ אֶת כָּל אֹיְבַי לֶחִי, שִׁנֵּי רְשָׁעִים שִׁבַּרְתָּ. לַיהוה הַיְשׁוּעָה, עַל עַמְּךָ בִרְכָתֶךָ סֶּלָה.

ד לַמְנַצֵּחַ בִּנְגִינוֹת מִזְמוֹר לְדָוִד. בְּקָרְאִי עֲנֵנִי, אֱלֹהֵי צִדְקִי, בַּצָּר הִרְחַבְתָּ לִּי, חָנֵּנִי וּשְׁמַע תְּפִלָּתִי. בְּנֵי אִישׁ, עַד מֶה כְבוֹדִי לִכְלִמָּה, תֶּאֱהָבוּן רִיק, תְּבַקְשׁוּ כָזָב סֶלָה. וּדְעוּ כִּי הִפְלָה יהוה חָסִיד לוֹ, יהוה יִשְׁמַע בְּקָרְאִי אֵלָיו. רִגְזוּ וְאַל תֶּחֱטָאוּ, אִמְרוּ בִלְבַבְכֶם עַל מִשְׁכַּבְכֶם, וְדֹמּוּ סֶלָה. זִבְחוּ זִבְחֵי צֶדֶק, וּבִטְחוּ אֶל יהוה. רַבִּים אֹמְרִים, מִי יַרְאֵנוּ טוֹב, נְסָה עָלֵינוּ אוֹר פָּנֶיךָ, יהוה. נָתַתָּה שִׂמְחָה בְלִבִּי, מֵעֵת דְּגָנָם וְתִירוֹשָׁם רָבּוּ. בְּשָׁלוֹם יַחְדָּו אֶשְׁכְּבָה וְאִישָׁן, כִּי אַתָּה יהוה לְבָדָד, לָבֶטַח תּוֹשִׁיבֵנִי.

ה לַמְנַצֵּחַ, אֶל הַנְּחִילוֹת, מִזְמוֹר לְדָוִד. אֲמָרַי הַאֲזִינָה, יהוה, בִּינָה הֲגִיגִי. הַקְשִׁיבָה לְקוֹל שַׁוְעִי, מַלְכִּי וֵאלֹהָי, כִּי אֵלֶיךָ אֶתְפַּלָּל. יהוה, בֹּקֶר תִּשְׁמַע קוֹלִי, בֹּקֶר אֶעֱרָךְ לְךָ, וַאֲצַפֶּה. כִּי לֹא אֵל חָפֵץ רֶשַׁע, אָתָּה, לֹא יְגֻרְךָ רָע. לֹא יִתְיַצְּבוּ הוֹלְלִים לְנֶגֶד עֵינֶיךָ, שָׂנֵאתָ כָּל פֹּעֲלֵי אָוֶן. תְּאַבֵּד דֹּבְרֵי כָזָב, אִישׁ דָּמִים וּמִרְמָה יְתָעֵב, יהוה. וַאֲנִי בְּרֹב חַסְדְּךָ אָבוֹא בֵיתֶךָ, אֶשְׁתַּחֲוֶה אֶל הֵיכַל קָדְשְׁךָ בְּיִרְאָתֶךָ. יהוה, נְחֵנִי בְצִדְקָתֶךָ לְמַעַן שׁוֹרְרָי, הַיְשַׁר לְפָנַי דַּרְכֶּךָ. כִּי אֵין בְּפִיהוּ נְכוֹנָה, קִרְבָּם הַוּוֹת, קֶבֶר פָּתוּחַ גְּרוֹנָם, לְשׁוֹנָם יַחֲלִיקוּן. הַאֲשִׁימֵם, אֱלֹהִים, יִפְּלוּ מִמֹּעֲצוֹתֵיהֶם, בְּרֹב פִּשְׁעֵיהֶם הַדִּיחֵמוֹ, כִּי מָרוּ בָךְ. וְיִשְׂמְחוּ כָל חוֹסֵי בָךְ, לְעוֹלָם יְרַנֵּנוּ, וְתָסֵךְ עָלֵימוֹ, וְיַעְלְצוּ בְךָ אֹהֲבֵי שְׁמֶךָ. כִּי אַתָּה תְּבָרֵךְ צַדִּיק, יהוה, כַּצִּנָּה רָצוֹן תַּעְטְרֶנּוּ.

ו לַמְנַצֵּחַ בִּנְגִינוֹת עַל הַשְּׁמִינִית, מִזְמוֹר לְדָוִד. יהוה אַל בְּאַפְּךָ תוֹכִיחֵנִי, וְאַל בַּחֲמָתְךָ תְיַסְּרֵנִי. חָנֵּנִי יהוה כִּי אֻמְלַל אָנִי, רְפָאֵנִי יהוה כִּי נִבְהֲלוּ עֲצָמָי. וְנַפְשִׁי נִבְהֲלָה מְאֹד, וְאַתָּ יהוה עַד מָתָי. שׁוּבָה יהוה חַלְּצָה נַפְשִׁי, הוֹשִׁיעֵנִי לְמַעַן חַסְדֶּךָ. כִּי אֵין בַּמָּוֶת זִכְרֶךָ, בִּשְׁאוֹל מִי יוֹדֶה לָּךְ. יָגַעְתִּי בְּאַנְחָתִי, אַשְׂחֶה בְכָל לַיְלָה מִטָּתִי, בְּדִמְעָתִי עַרְשִׂי אַמְסֶה. עָשְׁשָׁה מִכַּעַס עֵינִי, עָתְקָה בְּכָל צוֹרְרָי. סוּרוּ מִמֶּנִּי כָּל פֹּעֲלֵי אָוֶן, כִּי שָׁמַע יהוה קוֹל בִּכְיִי. שָׁמַע יהוה תְּחִנָּתִי, יהוה תְּפִלָּתִי יִקָּח. יֵבֹשׁוּ וְיִבָּהֲלוּ מְאֹד כָּל אֹיְבָי, יָשֻׁבוּ יֵבֹשׁוּ רָגַע.

ז שִׁגָּיוֹן לְדָוִד אֲשֶׁר שָׁר לַיהוה, עַל דִּבְרֵי כוּשׁ בֶּן יְמִינִי. יהוה אֱלֹהַי בְּךָ חָסִיתִי, הוֹשִׁיעֵנִי מִכָּל רֹדְפַי וְהַצִּילֵנִי. פֶּן יִטְרֹף כְּאַרְיֵה נַפְשִׁי, פֹּרֵק וְאֵין מַצִּיל. יהוה אֱלֹהַי, אִם עָשִׂיתִי זֹאת, אִם יֶשׁ עָוֶל בְּכַפָּי. אִם גָּמַלְתִּי שׁוֹלְמִי רָע, וָאֲחַלְּצָה צוֹרְרִי רֵיקָם. יִרַדֹּף אוֹיֵב נַפְשִׁי וְיַשֵּׂג וְיִרְמֹס לָאָרֶץ חַיָּי, וּכְבוֹדִי לֶעָפָר יַשְׁכֵּן סֶלָה. קוּמָה יהוה בְּאַפֶּךָ, הִנָּשֵׂא בְּעַבְרוֹת צוֹרְרָי, וְעוּרָה אֵלַי,

מִשְׁפָּט צִוִּיתָ. וַעֲדַת לְאֻמִּים תְּסוֹבְבֶךָּ, וְעָלֶיהָ לַמָּרוֹם שׁוּבָה. יהוה יָדִין עַמִּים, שָׁפְטֵנִי יהוה, כְּצִדְקִי וּכְתֻמִּי עָלָי. יִגְמָר נָא רַע רְשָׁעִים, וּתְכוֹנֵן צַדִּיק וּבֹחֵן לִבּוֹת וּכְלָיוֹת, אֱלֹהִים צַדִּיק. מָגִנִּי עַל אֱלֹהִים, מוֹשִׁיעַ יִשְׁרֵי לֵב. אֱלֹהִים שׁוֹפֵט צַדִּיק, וְאֵל זֹעֵם בְּכָל יוֹם. אִם לֹא יָשׁוּב, חַרְבּוֹ יִלְטוֹשׁ, קַשְׁתּוֹ דָרַךְ וַיְכוֹנְנֶהָ. וְלוֹ הֵכִין כְּלֵי מָוֶת, חִצָּיו לְדֹלְקִים יִפְעָל. הִנֵּה יְחַבֶּל אָוֶן, וְהָרָה עָמָל וְיָלַד שָׁקֶר. בּוֹר כָּרָה וַיַּחְפְּרֵהוּ, וַיִּפֹּל בְּשַׁחַת יִפְעָל. יָשׁוּב עֲמָלוֹ בְרֹאשׁוֹ, וְעַל קָדְקֳדוֹ חֲמָסוֹ יֵרֵד. אוֹדֶה יהוה כְּצִדְקוֹ, וַאֲזַמְּרָה שֵׁם יהוה עֶלְיוֹן.

ח לַמְנַצֵּחַ עַל הַגִּתִּית, מִזְמוֹר לְדָוִד. יהוה אֲדֹנֵינוּ, מָה אַדִּיר שִׁמְךָ בְּכָל הָאָרֶץ, אֲשֶׁר תְּנָה הוֹדְךָ עַל הַשָּׁמָיִם. מִפִּי עוֹלְלִים וְיֹנְקִים יִסַּדְתָּ עֹז, לְמַעַן צוֹרְרֶיךָ, לְהַשְׁבִּית אוֹיֵב וּמִתְנַקֵּם. כִּי אֶרְאֶה שָׁמֶיךָ מַעֲשֵׂה אֶצְבְּעֹתֶיךָ, יָרֵחַ וְכוֹכָבִים אֲשֶׁר כּוֹנָנְתָּה. מָה אֱנוֹשׁ כִּי תִזְכְּרֶנּוּ, וּבֶן אָדָם כִּי תִפְקְדֶנּוּ. וַתְּחַסְּרֵהוּ מְּעַט מֵאֱלֹהִים, וְכָבוֹד וְהָדָר תְּעַטְּרֵהוּ. תַּמְשִׁילֵהוּ בְּמַעֲשֵׂי יָדֶיךָ, כֹּל שַׁתָּה תַחַת רַגְלָיו. צֹנֶה וַאֲלָפִים כֻּלָּם, וְגַם בַּהֲמוֹת שָׂדָי. צִפּוֹר שָׁמַיִם וּדְגֵי הַיָּם, עֹבֵר אָרְחוֹת יַמִּים. יהוה אֲדֹנֵינוּ, מָה אַדִּיר שִׁמְךָ בְּכָל הָאָרֶץ.

ט לַמְנַצֵּחַ עַל מוּת לַבֵּן, מִזְמוֹר לְדָוִד. אוֹדֶה יהוה בְּכָל לִבִּי, אֲסַפְּרָה כָּל נִפְלְאוֹתֶיךָ. אֶשְׂמְחָה וְאֶעֶלְצָה בָךְ, אֲזַמְּרָה שִׁמְךָ עֶלְיוֹן. בְּשׁוּב אוֹיְבַי אָחוֹר, יִכָּשְׁלוּ וְיֹאבְדוּ מִפָּנֶיךָ. כִּי עָשִׂיתָ מִשְׁפָּטִי וְדִינִי, יָשַׁבְתָּ לְכִסֵּא שׁוֹפֵט צֶדֶק. גָּעַרְתָּ גוֹיִם, אִבַּדְתָּ רָשָׁע, שְׁמָם מָחִיתָ לְעוֹלָם וָעֶד. הָאוֹיֵב תַּמּוּ חֳרָבוֹת לָנֶצַח, וְעָרִים נָתַשְׁתָּ, אָבַד זִכְרָם הֵמָּה. וַיהוה לְעוֹלָם יֵשֵׁב, כּוֹנֵן לַמִּשְׁפָּט כִּסְאוֹ. וְהוּא יִשְׁפֹּט תֵּבֵל בְּצֶדֶק, יָדִין לְאֻמִּים בְּמֵישָׁרִים. וִיהִי יהוה מִשְׂגָּב לַדָּךְ, מִשְׂגָּב לְעִתּוֹת בַּצָּרָה. וְיִבְטְחוּ בְךָ יוֹדְעֵי שְׁמֶךָ, כִּי לֹא עָזַבְתָּ דֹרְשֶׁיךָ, יהוה. זַמְּרוּ לַיהוה יֹשֵׁב צִיּוֹן, הַגִּידוּ בָעַמִּים עֲלִילוֹתָיו. כִּי דֹרֵשׁ דָּמִים אוֹתָם זָכָר, לֹא שָׁכַח צַעֲקַת עֲנָוִים. חָנְנֵנִי יהוה רְאֵה עָנְיִי מִשֹּׂנְאָי, מְרוֹמְמִי מִשַּׁעֲרֵי מָוֶת. לְמַעַן אֲסַפְּרָה כָּל תְּהִלָּתֶיךָ בְּשַׁעֲרֵי בַת צִיּוֹן, אָגִילָה בִּישׁוּעָתֶךָ. טָבְעוּ גוֹיִם בְּשַׁחַת עָשׂוּ, בְּרֶשֶׁת זוּ טָמָנוּ נִלְכְּדָה רַגְלָם. נוֹדַע יהוה מִשְׁפָּט עָשָׂה, בְּפֹעַל כַּפָּיו נוֹקֵשׁ רָשָׁע, הִגָּיוֹן סֶלָה. יָשׁוּבוּ רְשָׁעִים לִשְׁאוֹלָה, כָּל גּוֹיִם שְׁכֵחֵי אֱלֹהִים. כִּי לֹא לָנֶצַח יִשָּׁכַח אֶבְיוֹן, תִּקְוַת עֲנִיִּים תֹּאבַד לָעַד. קוּמָה יהוה אַל יָעֹז אֱנוֹשׁ, יִשָּׁפְטוּ גוֹיִם עַל פָּנֶיךָ. שִׁיתָה יהוה מוֹרָה לָהֶם, יֵדְעוּ גוֹיִם, אֱנוֹשׁ הֵמָּה סֶּלָה.

2nd day — יום ב לחדש

י לָמָה יהוה תַּעֲמֹד בְּרָחוֹק, תַּעְלִים לְעִתּוֹת בַּצָּרָה. בְּגַאֲוַת רָשָׁע יִדְלַק עָנִי, יִתָּפְשׂוּ בִּמְזִמּוֹת זוּ חָשָׁבוּ. כִּי הִלֵּל רָשָׁע עַל תַּאֲוַת נַפְשׁוֹ, וּבֹצֵעַ בֵּרֵךְ נִאֵץ, יהוה. רָשָׁע כְּגֹבַהּ אַפּוֹ בַּל יִדְרֹשׁ, אֵין אֱלֹהִים כָּל מְזִמּוֹתָיו. יָחִילוּ דְרָכָו בְּכָל עֵת, מָרוֹם מִשְׁפָּטֶיךָ מִנֶּגְדּוֹ, כָּל צוֹרְרָיו יָפִיחַ בָּהֶם. אָמַר בְּלִבּוֹ בַּל אֶמּוֹט, לְדֹר וָדֹר אֲשֶׁר לֹא בְרָע. אָלָה פִּיהוּ מָלֵא וּמִרְמוֹת וָתֹךְ, תַּחַת לְשׁוֹנוֹ עָמָל וָאָוֶן. יֵשֵׁב בְּמַאְרַב חֲצֵרִים, בַּמִּסְתָּרִים יַהֲרֹג נָקִי, עֵינָיו לְחֵלְכָה יִצְפֹּנוּ. יֶאֱרֹב בַּמִּסְתָּר כְּאַרְיֵה בְסֻכֹּה, יֶאֱרֹב לַחֲטוֹף עָנִי, יַחְטֹף עָנִי בְּמָשְׁכוֹ בְרִשְׁתּוֹ. יִדְכֶּה יָשֹׁחַ, וְנָפַל בַּעֲצוּמָיו חֵל כָּאִים. אָמַר בְּלִבּוֹ שָׁכַח אֵל, הִסְתִּיר פָּנָיו בַּל רָאָה לָנֶצַח. קוּמָה יהוה, אֵל נְשָׂא יָדֶךָ, אַל תִּשְׁכַּח עֲנָוִים. עַל מֶה נִאֵץ רָשָׁע, אֱלֹהִים, אָמַר בְּלִבּוֹ לֹא תִּדְרֹשׁ. רָאִתָה כִּי אַתָּה עָמָל וָכַעַס תַּבִּיט, לָתֵת בְּיָדֶךָ, עָלֶיךָ יַעֲזֹב חֵלֶכָה, יָתוֹם אַתָּה הָיִיתָ עוֹזֵר. שְׁבֹר זְרוֹעַ רָשָׁע, וָרָע תִּדְרוֹשׁ רִשְׁעוֹ בַל תִּמְצָא. יהוה מֶלֶךְ עוֹלָם

וָעֶד, אָבְדוּ גוֹיִם מֵאַרְצוֹ. תַּאֲוַת עֲנָוִים שָׁמַעְתָּ יהוה, תָּכִין לִבָּם תַּקְשִׁיב אָזְנֶךָ. לִשְׁפֹּט יָתוֹם וָדָךְ, בַּל יוֹסִיף עוֹד, לַעֲרֹץ אֱנוֹשׁ מִן הָאָרֶץ.

יא לַמְנַצֵּחַ לְדָוִד בַּיהוה חָסִיתִי, אֵיךְ תֹּאמְרוּ לְנַפְשִׁי, נוּדִי הַרְכֶם צִפּוֹר. כִּי הִנֵּה הָרְשָׁעִים יִדְרְכוּן קֶשֶׁת, כּוֹנְנוּ חִצָּם עַל יֶתֶר, לִירוֹת בְּמוֹ אֹפֶל לְיִשְׁרֵי לֵב. כִּי הַשָּׁתוֹת יֵהָרֵסוּן, צַדִּיק מַה פָּעָל. יהוה בְּהֵיכַל קָדְשׁוֹ, יהוה בַּשָּׁמַיִם כִּסְאוֹ, עֵינָיו יֶחֱזוּ, עַפְעַפָּיו יִבְחֲנוּ בְּנֵי אָדָם. יהוה צַדִּיק יִבְחָן, וְרָשָׁע וְאֹהֵב חָמָס, שָׂנְאָה נַפְשׁוֹ. יַמְטֵר עַל רְשָׁעִים פַּחִים אֵשׁ וְגָפְרִית, וְרוּחַ זִלְעָפוֹת מְנָת כּוֹסָם. כִּי צַדִּיק יהוה, צְדָקוֹת אָהֵב, יָשָׁר יֶחֱזוּ פָנֵימוֹ.

יב לַמְנַצֵּחַ עַל הַשְּׁמִינִית, מִזְמוֹר לְדָוִד. הוֹשִׁיעָה יהוה כִּי גָמַר חָסִיד, כִּי פַסּוּ אֱמוּנִים מִבְּנֵי אָדָם. שָׁוְא יְדַבְּרוּ אִישׁ אֶת רֵעֵהוּ, שְׂפַת חֲלָקוֹת, בְּלֵב וָלֵב יְדַבֵּרוּ. יַכְרֵת יהוה כָּל שִׂפְתֵי חֲלָקוֹת, לָשׁוֹן מְדַבֶּרֶת גְּדֹלוֹת. אֲשֶׁר אָמְרוּ, לִלְשֹׁנֵנוּ נַגְבִּיר שְׂפָתֵינוּ אִתָּנוּ, מִי אָדוֹן לָנוּ. מִשֹּׁד עֲנִיִּים מֵאַנְקַת אֶבְיוֹנִים, עַתָּה אָקוּם יֹאמַר יהוה, אָשִׁית בְּיֵשַׁע יָפִיחַ לוֹ. אִמְרוֹת יהוה אֲמָרוֹת טְהֹרוֹת, כֶּסֶף צָרוּף, בַּעֲלִיל לָאָרֶץ מְזֻקָּק שִׁבְעָתָיִם. אַתָּה יהוה תִּשְׁמְרֵם, תִּצְּרֶנּוּ מִן הַדּוֹר זוּ לְעוֹלָם. סָבִיב רְשָׁעִים יִתְהַלָּכוּן, כְּרֻם זֻלּוּת לִבְנֵי אָדָם.

יג לַמְנַצֵּחַ מִזְמוֹר לְדָוִד. עַד אָנָה יהוה תִּשְׁכָּחֵנִי נֶצַח, עַד אָנָה תַּסְתִּיר אֶת פָּנֶיךָ מִמֶּנִּי. עַד אָנָה אָשִׁית עֵצוֹת בְּנַפְשִׁי יָגוֹן בִּלְבָבִי יוֹמָם, עַד אָנָה יָרוּם אֹיְבִי עָלָי. הַבִּיטָה עֲנֵנִי יהוה אֱלֹהָי, הָאִירָה עֵינַי פֶּן אִישַׁן הַמָּוֶת. פֶּן יֹאמַר אֹיְבִי יְכָלְתִּיו, צָרַי יָגִילוּ כִּי אֶמּוֹט. וַאֲנִי בְּחַסְדְּךָ בָטַחְתִּי, יָגֵל לִבִּי בִּישׁוּעָתֶךָ, אָשִׁירָה לַיהוה, כִּי גָמַל עָלָי.

יד לַמְנַצֵּחַ לְדָוִד, אָמַר נָבָל בְּלִבּוֹ אֵין אֱלֹהִים, הִשְׁחִיתוּ הִתְעִיבוּ עֲלִילָה, אֵין עֹשֵׂה טוֹב. יהוה מִשָּׁמַיִם הִשְׁקִיף עַל בְּנֵי אָדָם, לִרְאוֹת הֲיֵשׁ מַשְׂכִּיל, דֹּרֵשׁ אֶת אֱלֹהִים. הַכֹּל סָר יַחְדָּו, נֶאֱלָחוּ, אֵין עֹשֵׂה טוֹב, אֵין גַּם אֶחָד. הֲלֹא יָדְעוּ כָּל פֹּעֲלֵי אָוֶן, אֹכְלֵי עַמִּי אָכְלוּ לֶחֶם, יהוה לֹא קָרָאוּ. שָׁם פָּחֲדוּ פָחַד, כִּי אֱלֹהִים בְּדוֹר צַדִּיק. עֲצַת עָנִי תָבִישׁוּ, כִּי יהוה מַחְסֵהוּ. מִי יִתֵּן מִצִּיּוֹן יְשׁוּעַת יִשְׂרָאֵל, בְּשׁוּב יהוה שְׁבוּת עַמּוֹ, יָגֵל יַעֲקֹב יִשְׂמַח יִשְׂרָאֵל.

טו מִזְמוֹר לְדָוִד, יהוה מִי יָגוּר בְּאָהֳלֶךָ, מִי יִשְׁכֹּן בְּהַר קָדְשֶׁךָ. הוֹלֵךְ תָּמִים וּפֹעֵל צֶדֶק, וְדֹבֵר אֱמֶת בִּלְבָבוֹ. לֹא רָגַל עַל לְשֹׁנוֹ, לֹא עָשָׂה לְרֵעֵהוּ רָעָה, וְחֶרְפָּה לֹא נָשָׂא עַל קְרֹבוֹ. נִבְזֶה בְּעֵינָיו נִמְאָס, וְאֶת יִרְאֵי יהוה יְכַבֵּד, נִשְׁבַּע לְהָרַע וְלֹא יָמִר. כַּסְפּוֹ לֹא נָתַן בְּנֶשֶׁךְ, וְשֹׁחַד עַל נָקִי לֹא לָקָח, עֹשֵׂה אֵלֶּה, לֹא יִמּוֹט לְעוֹלָם.

טז מִכְתָּם לְדָוִד, שָׁמְרֵנִי אֵל כִּי חָסִיתִי בָךְ. אָמַרְתְּ לַיהוה, אֲדֹנָי אָתָּה, טוֹבָתִי בַּל עָלֶיךָ. לִקְדוֹשִׁים אֲשֶׁר בָּאָרֶץ הֵמָּה, וְאַדִּירֵי כָּל חֶפְצִי בָם. יִרְבּוּ עַצְּבוֹתָם אַחֵר מָהָרוּ, בַּל אַסִּיךְ נִסְכֵּיהֶם מִדָּם, וּבַל אֶשָּׂא אֶת שְׁמוֹתָם עַל שְׂפָתָי. יהוה, מְנָת חֶלְקִי וְכוֹסִי, אַתָּה תּוֹמִיךְ גּוֹרָלִי. חֲבָלִים נָפְלוּ לִי בַּנְּעִמִים, אַף נַחֲלָת שָׁפְרָה עָלָי. אֲבָרֵךְ אֶת יהוה אֲשֶׁר יְעָצָנִי, אַף לֵילוֹת יִסְּרוּנִי כִלְיוֹתָי. שִׁוִּיתִי יהוה לְנֶגְדִּי תָמִיד, כִּי מִימִינִי בַּל אֶמּוֹט. לָכֵן שָׂמַח לִבִּי וַיָּגֶל כְּבוֹדִי, אַף בְּשָׂרִי יִשְׁכֹּן לָבֶטַח. כִּי לֹא תַעֲזֹב נַפְשִׁי לִשְׁאוֹל, לֹא תִתֵּן חֲסִידְךָ לִרְאוֹת שָׁחַת. תּוֹדִיעֵנִי אֹרַח חַיִּים, שֹׂבַע שְׂמָחוֹת אֶת פָּנֶיךָ, נְעִמוֹת בִּימִינְךָ נֶצַח.

יז תְּפִלָּה לְדָוִד, שִׁמְעָה יהוה צֶדֶק, הַקְשִׁיבָה רִנָּתִי, הַאֲזִינָה תְפִלָּתִי, בְּלֹא שִׂפְתֵי מִרְמָה. מִלְּפָנֶיךָ מִשְׁפָּטִי

יֵצֵא, עֵינֶיךָ תֶּחֱזֶינָה מֵישָׁרִים. בָּחַנְתָּ
לִבִּי, פָּקַדְתָּ לַּיְלָה, צְרַפְתַּנִי בַל תִּמְצָא,
זַמֹּתִי בַּל יַעֲבָר פִּי. לִפְעֻלּוֹת אָדָם
בִּדְבַר שְׂפָתֶיךָ, אֲנִי שָׁמַרְתִּי אָרְחוֹת
פָּרִיץ. תָּמֹךְ אֲשֻׁרַי בְּמַעְגְּלוֹתֶיךָ, בַּל
נָמוֹטּוּ פְעָמָי. אֲנִי קְרָאתִיךָ כִי תַעֲנֵנִי
אֵל, הַט אָזְנְךָ לִי, שְׁמַע אִמְרָתִי. הַפְלֵה
חֲסָדֶיךָ, מוֹשִׁיעַ חוֹסִים מִמִּתְקוֹמְמִים
בִּימִינֶךָ. שָׁמְרֵנִי כְּאִישׁוֹן בַּת עָיִן, בְּצֵל
כְּנָפֶיךָ תַּסְתִּירֵנִי. מִפְּנֵי רְשָׁעִים זוּ
שַׁדּוּנִי, אֹיְבַי בְּנֶפֶשׁ יַקִּיפוּ עָלָי. חֶלְבָּמוֹ
סָּגְרוּ, פִּימוֹ דִּבְּרוּ בְגֵאוּת. אַשֻּׁרֵנוּ עַתָּה
סְבָבוּנוּ, עֵינֵיהֶם יָשִׁיתוּ לִנְטוֹת בָּאָרֶץ.
דִּמְיֹנוֹ כְּאַרְיֵה יִכְסוֹף לִטְרֹף, וְכִכְפִיר
יֹשֵׁב בְּמִסְתָּרִים. קוּמָה יהוה קַדְּמָה
פָנָיו, הַכְרִיעֵהוּ, פַּלְּטָה נַפְשִׁי מֵרָשָׁע
חַרְבֶּךָ. מִמְתִים יָדְךָ יהוה, מִמְתִים
מֵחֶלֶד, חֶלְקָם בַּחַיִּים וּצְפוּנְךָ תְּמַלֵּא
בִטְנָם, יִשְׂבְּעוּ בָנִים, וְהִנִּיחוּ יִתְרָם
לְעוֹלְלֵיהֶם. אֲנִי בְּצֶדֶק אֶחֱזֶה פָנֶיךָ,
אֶשְׂבְּעָה בְהָקִיץ תְּמוּנָתֶךָ.

3rd day — יום ג לחדש

יח לַמְנַצֵּחַ לְעֶבֶד יהוה לְדָוִד, אֲשֶׁר
דִּבֶּר לַיהוה אֶת דִּבְרֵי הַשִּׁירָה
הַזֹּאת, בְּיוֹם הִצִּיל יהוה אוֹתוֹ מִכַּף כָּל
אֹיְבָיו, וּמִיַּד שָׁאוּל. וַיֹּאמַר, אֶרְחָמְךָ
יהוה חִזְקִי. יהוה סַלְעִי וּמְצוּדָתִי
וּמְפַלְטִי, אֵלִי צוּרִי אֶחֱסֶה בּוֹ, מָגִנִּי
וְקֶרֶן יִשְׁעִי, מִשְׂגַּבִּי. מְהֻלָּל אֶקְרָא
יהוה, וּמִן אֹיְבַי אִוָּשֵׁעַ. אֲפָפוּנִי חֶבְלֵי
מָוֶת, וְנַחֲלֵי בְלִיַּעַל יְבַעֲתוּנִי. חֶבְלֵי
שְׁאוֹל סְבָבוּנִי, קִדְּמוּנִי מוֹקְשֵׁי מָוֶת.
בַּצַּר לִי אֶקְרָא יהוה, וְאֶל אֱלֹהַי
אֲשַׁוֵּעַ, יִשְׁמַע מֵהֵיכָלוֹ קוֹלִי, וְשַׁוְעָתִי
לְפָנָיו תָּבוֹא בְאָזְנָיו. וַתִּגְעַשׁ וַתִּרְעַשׁ
הָאָרֶץ, וּמוֹסְדֵי הָרִים יִרְגָּזוּ, וַיִּתְגָּעֲשׁוּ
כִּי חָרָה לוֹ. עָלָה עָשָׁן בְּאַפּוֹ, וְאֵשׁ
מִפִּיו תֹּאכֵל, גֶּחָלִים בָּעֲרוּ מִמֶּנּוּ. וַיֵּט
שָׁמַיִם וַיֵּרַד, וַעֲרָפֶל תַּחַת רַגְלָיו.
וַיִּרְכַּב עַל כְּרוּב וַיָּעֹף, וַיֵּדֶא עַל כַּנְפֵי
רוּחַ. יָשֶׁת חֹשֶׁךְ סִתְרוֹ סְבִיבוֹתָיו
סֻכָּתוֹ, חֶשְׁכַת מַיִם עָבֵי שְׁחָקִים. מִנֹּגַהּ
נֶגְדּוֹ עָבָיו עָבְרוּ, בָּרָד וְגַחֲלֵי אֵשׁ.
וַיַּרְעֵם בַּשָּׁמַיִם יהוה, וְעֶלְיוֹן יִתֵּן קֹלוֹ,
בָּרָד וְגַחֲלֵי אֵשׁ. וַיִּשְׁלַח חִצָּיו וַיְפִיצֵם,
וּבְרָקִים רָב וַיְהֻמֵּם. וַיֵּרָאוּ אֲפִיקֵי מַיִם,
וַיִּגָּלוּ מוֹסְדוֹת תֵּבֵל, מִגַּעֲרָתְךָ יהוה,
מִנִּשְׁמַת רוּחַ אַפֶּךָ. יִשְׁלַח מִמָּרוֹם
יִקָּחֵנִי, יַמְשֵׁנִי מִמַּיִם רַבִּים. יַצִּילֵנִי
מֵאֹיְבִי עָז, וּמִשֹּׂנְאַי כִּי אָמְצוּ מִמֶּנִּי.
יְקַדְּמוּנִי בְיוֹם אֵידִי, וַיְהִי יהוה לְמִשְׁעָן
לִי. וַיּוֹצִיאֵנִי לַמֶּרְחָב, יְחַלְּצֵנִי כִּי חָפֵץ
בִּי. יִגְמְלֵנִי יהוה כְּצִדְקִי, כְּבֹר יָדַי יָשִׁיב
לִי. כִּי שָׁמַרְתִּי דַּרְכֵי יהוה, וְלֹא
רָשַׁעְתִּי מֵאֱלֹהָי. כִּי כָל מִשְׁפָּטָיו לְנֶגְדִּי,
וְחֻקֹּתָיו לֹא אָסִיר מֶנִּי. וָאֱהִי תָמִים
עִמּוֹ, וָאֶשְׁתַּמֵּר מֵעֲוֹנִי. וַיָּשֶׁב יהוה לִי
כְצִדְקִי, כְּבֹר יָדַי לְנֶגֶד עֵינָיו. עִם חָסִיד
תִּתְחַסָּד, עִם גְּבַר תָּמִים תִּתַּמָּם. עִם
נָבָר תִּתְבָּרָר, וְעִם עִקֵּשׁ תִּתְפַּתָּל. כִּי
אַתָּה עַם עָנִי תוֹשִׁיעַ, וְעֵינַיִם רָמוֹת
תַּשְׁפִּיל. כִּי אַתָּה תָּאִיר נֵרִי, יהוה
אֱלֹהַי, יַגִּיהַּ חָשְׁכִּי. כִּי בְךָ אָרֻץ גְּדוּד,
וּבֵאלֹהַי אֲדַלֶּג שׁוּר. הָאֵל תָּמִים דַּרְכּוֹ,
אִמְרַת יהוה צְרוּפָה, מָגֵן הוּא לְכֹל
הַחוֹסִים בּוֹ. כִּי מִי אֱלוֹהַּ מִבַּלְעֲדֵי
יהוה, וּמִי צוּר זוּלָתִי אֱלֹהֵינוּ. הָאֵל
הַמְאַזְּרֵנִי חָיִל, וַיִּתֵּן תָּמִים דַּרְכִּי.
מְשַׁוֶּה רַגְלַי כָּאַיָּלוֹת, וְעַל בָּמֹתַי
יַעֲמִידֵנִי. מְלַמֵּד יָדַי לַמִּלְחָמָה, וְנִחֲתָה
קֶשֶׁת נְחוּשָׁה זְרוֹעֹתָי. וַתִּתֶּן לִי מָגֵן
יִשְׁעֶךָ, וִימִינְךָ תִסְעָדֵנִי, וְעַנְוָתְךָ
תַרְבֵּנִי. תַּרְחִיב צַעֲדִי תַחְתָּי, וְלֹא
מָעֲדוּ קַרְסֻלָּי. אֶרְדּוֹף אוֹיְבַי וְאַשִּׂיגֵם,
וְלֹא אָשׁוּב עַד כַּלּוֹתָם. אֶמְחָצֵם וְלֹא
יֻכְלוּ קוּם, יִפְּלוּ תַּחַת רַגְלָי. וַתְּאַזְּרֵנִי
חַיִל לַמִּלְחָמָה, תַּכְרִיעַ קָמַי תַּחְתָּי.
וְאֹיְבַי נָתַתָּה לִּי עֹרֶף, וּמְשַׂנְאַי
אַצְמִיתֵם. יְשַׁוְּעוּ וְאֵין מוֹשִׁיעַ, עַל יהוה
וְלֹא עָנָם. וְאֶשְׁחָקֵם כְּעָפָר עַל פְּנֵי
רוּחַ, כְּטִיט חוּצוֹת אֲרִיקֵם. תְּפַלְּטֵנִי
מֵרִיבֵי עָם, תְּשִׂימֵנִי לְרֹאשׁ גּוֹיִם, עַם
לֹא יָדַעְתִּי יַעַבְדוּנִי. לְשֵׁמַע אֹזֶן יִשָּׁמְעוּ

לִי, בְּנֵי נֵכָר יְכַחֲשׁוּ לִי. בְּנֵי נֵכָר יִבֹּלוּ, וְיַחְרְגוּ מִמִּסְגְּרוֹתֵיהֶם. חַי יהוה וּבָרוּךְ צוּרִי, וְיָרוּם אֱלוֹהֵי יִשְׁעִי. הָאֵל הַנּוֹתֵן נְקָמוֹת לִי, וַיַּדְבֵּר עַמִּים תַּחְתָּי. מְפַלְּטִי מֵאֹיְבָי, אַף מִן קָמַי תְּרוֹמְמֵנִי, מֵאִישׁ חָמָס תַּצִּילֵנִי. עַל כֵּן אוֹדְךָ בַגּוֹיִם, יהוה, וּלְשִׁמְךָ אֲזַמֵּרָה. מַגְדִּל יְשׁוּעוֹת מַלְכּוֹ, וְעֹשֶׂה חֶסֶד לִמְשִׁיחוֹ, לְדָוִד וּלְזַרְעוֹ עַד עוֹלָם.

יט לַמְנַצֵּחַ מִזְמוֹר לְדָוִד. הַשָּׁמַיִם מְסַפְּרִים כְּבוֹד אֵל, וּמַעֲשֵׂה יָדָיו מַגִּיד הָרָקִיעַ. יוֹם לְיוֹם יַבִּיעַ אֹמֶר, וְלַיְלָה לְּלַיְלָה יְחַוֶּה דָּעַת. אֵין אֹמֶר וְאֵין דְּבָרִים, בְּלִי נִשְׁמָע קוֹלָם. בְּכָל הָאָרֶץ יָצָא קַוָּם, וּבִקְצֵה תֵבֵל מִלֵּיהֶם, לַשֶּׁמֶשׁ שָׂם אֹהֶל בָּהֶם. וְהוּא כְּחָתָן יֹצֵא מֵחֻפָּתוֹ, יָשִׂישׂ כְּגִבּוֹר לָרוּץ אֹרַח. מִקְצֵה הַשָּׁמַיִם מוֹצָאוֹ, וּתְקוּפָתוֹ עַל קְצוֹתָם, וְאֵין נִסְתָּר מֵחַמָּתוֹ. תּוֹרַת יהוה תְּמִימָה, מְשִׁיבַת נָפֶשׁ, עֵדוּת יהוה נֶאֱמָנָה, מַחְכִּימַת פֶּתִי. פִּקּוּדֵי יהוה יְשָׁרִים, מְשַׂמְּחֵי לֵב, מִצְוַת יהוה בָּרָה, מְאִירַת עֵינָיִם. יִרְאַת יהוה טְהוֹרָה, עוֹמֶדֶת לָעַד, מִשְׁפְּטֵי יהוה אֱמֶת, צָדְקוּ יַחְדָּו. הַנֶּחֱמָדִים מִזָּהָב וּמִפַּז רָב, וּמְתוּקִים מִדְּבַשׁ וְנֹפֶת צוּפִים. גַּם עַבְדְּךָ נִזְהָר בָּהֶם, בְּשָׁמְרָם עֵקֶב רָב. שְׁגִיאוֹת מִי יָבִין, מִנִּסְתָּרוֹת נַקֵּנִי. גַּם מִזֵּדִים חֲשֹׂךְ עַבְדֶּךָ, אַל יִמְשְׁלוּ בִי, אָז אֵיתָם, וְנִקֵּיתִי מִפֶּשַׁע רָב. יִהְיוּ לְרָצוֹן אִמְרֵי פִי, וְהֶגְיוֹן לִבִּי לְפָנֶיךָ, יהוה צוּרִי וְגֹאֲלִי.

כ לַמְנַצֵּחַ מִזְמוֹר לְדָוִד. יַעַנְךָ יהוה בְּיוֹם צָרָה, יְשַׂגֶּבְךָ שֵׁם אֱלֹהֵי יַעֲקֹב. יִשְׁלַח עֶזְרְךָ מִקֹּדֶשׁ, וּמִצִּיּוֹן יִסְעָדֶךָּ. יִזְכֹּר כָּל מִנְחֹתֶיךָ, וְעוֹלָתְךָ יְדַשְּׁנֶה סֶלָה. יִתֶּן לְךָ כִלְבָבֶךָ, וְכָל עֲצָתְךָ יְמַלֵּא. נְרַנְּנָה בִּישׁוּעָתֶךָ, וּבְשֵׁם אֱלֹהֵינוּ נִדְגֹּל, יְמַלֵּא יהוה כָּל מִשְׁאֲלוֹתֶיךָ. עַתָּה יָדַעְתִּי כִּי הוֹשִׁיעַ יהוה מְשִׁיחוֹ, יַעֲנֵהוּ מִשְּׁמֵי קָדְשׁוֹ, בִּגְבֻרוֹת יֵשַׁע יְמִינוֹ. אֵלֶּה בָרֶכֶב וְאֵלֶּה בַסּוּסִים, וַאֲנַחְנוּ בְּשֵׁם יהוה אֱלֹהֵינוּ נַזְכִּיר. הֵמָּה כָּרְעוּ וְנָפָלוּ, וַאֲנַחְנוּ קַּמְנוּ וַנִּתְעוֹדָד. יהוה הוֹשִׁיעָה, הַמֶּלֶךְ יַעֲנֵנוּ בְיוֹם קָרְאֵנוּ.

כא לַמְנַצֵּחַ מִזְמוֹר לְדָוִד. יהוה בְּעָזְּךָ יִשְׂמַח מֶלֶךְ, וּבִישׁוּעָתְךָ מַה יָּגֶל מְאֹד. תַּאֲוַת לִבּוֹ נָתַתָּה לּוֹ, וַאֲרֶשֶׁת שְׂפָתָיו בַּל מָנַעְתָּ סֶּלָה. כִּי תְקַדְּמֶנּוּ בִּרְכוֹת טוֹב, תָּשִׁית לְרֹאשׁוֹ עֲטֶרֶת פָּז. חַיִּים שָׁאַל מִמְּךָ נָתַתָּה לּוֹ, אֹרֶךְ יָמִים עוֹלָם וָעֶד. גָּדוֹל כְּבוֹדוֹ בִּישׁוּעָתֶךָ, הוֹד וְהָדָר תְּשַׁוֶּה עָלָיו. כִּי תְשִׁיתֵהוּ בְרָכוֹת לָעַד, תְּחַדֵּהוּ בְשִׂמְחָה אֶת פָּנֶיךָ. כִּי הַמֶּלֶךְ בֹּטֵחַ בַּיהוה, וּבְחֶסֶד עֶלְיוֹן בַּל יִמּוֹט. תִּמְצָא יָדְךָ לְכָל אֹיְבֶיךָ, יְמִינְךָ תִּמְצָא שֹׂנְאֶיךָ. תְּשִׁיתֵמוֹ כְּתַנּוּר אֵשׁ לְעֵת פָּנֶיךָ, יהוה בְּאַפּוֹ יְבַלְּעֵם וְתֹאכְלֵם אֵשׁ. פִּרְיָמוֹ מֵאֶרֶץ תְּאַבֵּד, וְזַרְעָם מִבְּנֵי אָדָם. כִּי נָטוּ עָלֶיךָ רָעָה, חָשְׁבוּ מְזִמָּה בַּל יוּכָלוּ. כִּי תְּשִׁיתֵמוֹ שֶׁכֶם, בְּמֵיתָרֶיךָ תְּכוֹנֵן עַל פְּנֵיהֶם. רוּמָה יהוה בְעֻזֶּךָ, נָשִׁירָה וּנְזַמְּרָה גְּבוּרָתֶךָ.

כב לַמְנַצֵּחַ עַל אַיֶּלֶת הַשַּׁחַר, מִזְמוֹר לְדָוִד. אֵלִי אֵלִי לָמָה עֲזַבְתָּנִי, רָחוֹק מִישׁוּעָתִי דִּבְרֵי שַׁאֲגָתִי. אֱלֹהַי, אֶקְרָא יוֹמָם וְלֹא תַעֲנֶה, וְלַיְלָה וְלֹא דוּמִיָּה לִי. וְאַתָּה קָדוֹשׁ, יוֹשֵׁב תְּהִלּוֹת יִשְׂרָאֵל. בְּךָ בָּטְחוּ אֲבֹתֵינוּ, בָּטְחוּ וַתְּפַלְּטֵמוֹ. אֵלֶיךָ זָעֲקוּ וְנִמְלָטוּ, בְּךָ בָטְחוּ וְלֹא בוֹשׁוּ. וְאָנֹכִי תוֹלַעַת וְלֹא אִישׁ, חֶרְפַּת אָדָם וּבְזוּי עָם. כָּל רֹאַי יַלְעִגוּ לִי, יַפְטִירוּ בְשָׂפָה, יָנִיעוּ רֹאשׁ. גֹּל אֶל יהוה, יְפַלְּטֵהוּ, יַצִּילֵהוּ כִּי חָפֵץ בּוֹ. כִּי אַתָּה גֹחִי מִבָּטֶן, מַבְטִיחִי עַל שְׁדֵי אִמִּי. עָלֶיךָ הָשְׁלַכְתִּי מֵרָחֶם, מִבֶּטֶן אִמִּי אֵלִי אָתָּה. אַל תִּרְחַק מִמֶּנִּי כִּי צָרָה קְרוֹבָה, כִּי אֵין עוֹזֵר. סְבָבוּנִי פָּרִים רַבִּים, אַבִּירֵי בָשָׁן כִּתְּרוּנִי. פָּצוּ עָלַי פִּיהֶם, אַרְיֵה טֹרֵף וְשֹׁאֵג. כַּמַּיִם

נִשְׁפַּכְתִּי וְהִתְפָּרְדוּ כָּל עַצְמוֹתָי, הָיָה
לִבִּי כַּדּוֹנָג נָמֵס בְּתוֹךְ מֵעָי. יָבֵשׁ כַּחֶרֶשׂ
כֹּחִי, וּלְשׁוֹנִי מֻדְבָּק מַלְקוֹחָי, וְלַעֲפַר
מָוֶת תִּשְׁפְּתֵנִי. כִּי סְבָבוּנִי כְּלָבִים, עֲדַת
מְרֵעִים הִקִּיפוּנִי, כָּאֲרִי יָדַי וְרַגְלָי.
אֲסַפֵּר כָּל עַצְמוֹתָי, הֵמָּה יַבִּיטוּ יִרְאוּ
בִי. יְחַלְּקוּ בְגָדַי לָהֶם, וְעַל לְבוּשִׁי
יַפִּילוּ גוֹרָל. וְאַתָּה יהוה אַל תִּרְחָק,
אֱיָלוּתִי לְעֶזְרָתִי חוּשָׁה. הַצִּילָה מֵחֶרֶב
נַפְשִׁי, מִיַּד כֶּלֶב יְחִידָתִי. הוֹשִׁיעֵנִי מִפִּי
אַרְיֵה, וּמִקַּרְנֵי רֵמִים עֲנִיתָנִי. אֲסַפְּרָה
שִׁמְךָ לְאֶחָי, בְּתוֹךְ קָהָל אֲהַלְלֶךָּ. יִרְאֵי
יהוה הַלְלוּהוּ, כָּל זֶרַע יַעֲקֹב כַּבְּדוּהוּ,
וְגוּרוּ מִמֶּנּוּ כָּל זֶרַע יִשְׂרָאֵל. כִּי לֹא
בָזָה וְלֹא שִׁקַּץ עֱנוּת עָנִי, וְלֹא הִסְתִּיר
פָּנָיו מִמֶּנּוּ, וּבְשַׁוְּעוֹ אֵלָיו שָׁמֵעַ. מֵאִתְּךָ
תְּהִלָּתִי בְּקָהָל רָב, נְדָרַי אֲשַׁלֵּם נֶגֶד
יְרֵאָיו. יֹאכְלוּ עֲנָוִים וְיִשְׂבָּעוּ, יְהַלְלוּ
יהוה דֹּרְשָׁיו, יְחִי לְבַבְכֶם לָעַד. יִזְכְּרוּ
וְיָשֻׁבוּ אֶל יהוה כָּל אַפְסֵי אָרֶץ,
וְיִשְׁתַּחֲווּ לְפָנֶיךָ כָּל מִשְׁפְּחוֹת גּוֹיִם. כִּי
לַיהוה הַמְּלוּכָה, וּמֹשֵׁל בַּגּוֹיִם. אָכְלוּ
וַיִּשְׁתַּחֲווּ כָּל דִּשְׁנֵי אֶרֶץ, לְפָנָיו יִכְרְעוּ
כָּל יוֹרְדֵי עָפָר, וְנַפְשׁוֹ לֹא חִיָּה. זֶרַע
יַעַבְדֶנּוּ, יְסֻפַּר לַאדֹנָי לַדּוֹר. יָבֹאוּ
וְיַגִּידוּ צִדְקָתוֹ, לְעַם נוֹלָד כִּי עָשָׂה.

יום ד לחדש — 4th day

כג מִזְמוֹר לְדָוִד, יהוה רֹעִי, לֹא
אֶחְסָר. בִּנְאוֹת דֶּשֶׁא יַרְבִּיצֵנִי, עַל
מֵי מְנֻחוֹת יְנַהֲלֵנִי. נַפְשִׁי יְשׁוֹבֵב, יַנְחֵנִי
בְמַעְגְּלֵי צֶדֶק לְמַעַן שְׁמוֹ. גַּם כִּי אֵלֵךְ
בְּגֵיא צַלְמָוֶת, לֹא אִירָא רָע כִּי אַתָּה
עִמָּדִי, שִׁבְטְךָ וּמִשְׁעַנְתֶּךָ הֵמָּה יְנַחֲמֻנִי.
תַּעֲרֹךְ לְפָנַי שֻׁלְחָן נֶגֶד צֹרְרָי, דִּשַּׁנְתָּ
בַשֶּׁמֶן רֹאשִׁי, כּוֹסִי רְוָיָה. אַךְ טוֹב
וָחֶסֶד יִרְדְּפוּנִי כָּל יְמֵי חַיָּי, וְשַׁבְתִּי
בְּבֵית יהוה לְאֹרֶךְ יָמִים.

כד לְדָוִד מִזְמוֹר, לַיהוה הָאָרֶץ
וּמְלוֹאָהּ, תֵּבֵל וְיֹשְׁבֵי בָהּ. כִּי
הוּא עַל יַמִּים יְסָדָהּ, וְעַל נְהָרוֹת
יְכוֹנְנֶהָ. מִי יַעֲלֶה בְהַר יהוה, וּמִי יָקוּם
בִּמְקוֹם קָדְשׁוֹ. נְקִי כַפַּיִם וּבַר לֵבָב,
אֲשֶׁר לֹא נָשָׂא לַשָּׁוְא נַפְשִׁי, וְלֹא
נִשְׁבַּע לְמִרְמָה. יִשָּׂא בְרָכָה מֵאֵת
יהוה, וּצְדָקָה מֵאֱלֹהֵי יִשְׁעוֹ. זֶה דּוֹר
דֹּרְשָׁו, מְבַקְשֵׁי פָנֶיךָ יַעֲקֹב סֶלָה. שְׂאוּ
שְׁעָרִים רָאשֵׁיכֶם וְהִנָּשְׂאוּ פִּתְחֵי
עוֹלָם, וְיָבוֹא מֶלֶךְ הַכָּבוֹד. מִי זֶה מֶלֶךְ
הַכָּבוֹד, יהוה עִזּוּז וְגִבּוֹר יהוה גִּבּוֹר
מִלְחָמָה. שְׂאוּ שְׁעָרִים רָאשֵׁיכֶם, וּשְׂאוּ
פִּתְחֵי עוֹלָם, וְיָבֹא מֶלֶךְ הַכָּבוֹד. מִי
הוּא זֶה מֶלֶךְ הַכָּבוֹד, יהוה צְבָאוֹת
הוּא מֶלֶךְ הַכָּבוֹד סֶלָה.

כה לְדָוִד, אֵלֶיךָ יהוה נַפְשִׁי אֶשָּׂא.
אֱלֹהַי בְּךָ בָטַחְתִּי, אַל אֵבוֹשָׁה,
אַל יַעַלְצוּ אוֹיְבַי לִי. גַּם כָּל קֹוֶיךָ לֹא
יֵבֹשׁוּ, יֵבֹשׁוּ הַבּוֹגְדִים רֵיקָם. דְּרָכֶיךָ
יהוה הוֹדִיעֵנִי, אֹרְחוֹתֶיךָ לַמְּדֵנִי.
הַדְרִיכֵנִי בַאֲמִתֶּךָ וְלַמְּדֵנִי, כִּי אַתָּה
אֱלֹהֵי יִשְׁעִי, אוֹתְךָ קִוִּיתִי כָּל הַיּוֹם.
זְכֹר רַחֲמֶיךָ יהוה וַחֲסָדֶיךָ, כִּי מֵעוֹלָם
הֵמָּה. חַטֹּאות נְעוּרַי וּפְשָׁעַי אַל תִּזְכֹּר,
כְּחַסְדְּךָ זְכָר לִי אַתָּה, לְמַעַן טוּבְךָ
יהוה. טוֹב וְיָשָׁר יהוה, עַל כֵּן יוֹרֶה
חַטָּאִים בַּדָּרֶךְ. יַדְרֵךְ עֲנָוִים בַּמִּשְׁפָּט,
וִילַמֵּד עֲנָוִים דַּרְכּוֹ. כָּל אָרְחוֹת יהוה
חֶסֶד וֶאֱמֶת, לְנֹצְרֵי בְרִיתוֹ וְעֵדֹתָיו.
לְמַעַן שִׁמְךָ יהוה, וְסָלַחְתָּ לַעֲוֹנִי כִּי רַב
הוּא. מִי זֶה הָאִישׁ יְרֵא יהוה, יוֹרֶנּוּ
בְּדֶרֶךְ יִבְחָר. נַפְשׁוֹ בְּטוֹב תָּלִין, וְזַרְעוֹ
יִירַשׁ אָרֶץ. סוֹד יהוה לִירֵאָיו, וּבְרִיתוֹ
לְהוֹדִיעָם. עֵינַי תָּמִיד אֶל יהוה, כִּי
הוּא יוֹצִיא מֵרֶשֶׁת רַגְלָי. פְּנֵה אֵלַי
וְחָנֵּנִי, כִּי יָחִיד וְעָנִי אָנִי. צָרוֹת לְבָבִי
הִרְחִיבוּ, מִמְּצוּקוֹתַי הוֹצִיאֵנִי. רְאֵה
עָנְיִי וַעֲמָלִי, וְשָׂא לְכָל חַטֹּאותָי. רְאֵה
אוֹיְבַי כִּי רָבּוּ, וְשִׂנְאַת חָמָס שְׂנֵאוּנִי.
שָׁמְרָה נַפְשִׁי וְהַצִּילֵנִי, אַל אֵבוֹשׁ כִּי
חָסִיתִי בָךְ. תֹּם וָיֹשֶׁר יִצְּרוּנִי, כִּי
קִוִּיתִיךָ. פְּדֵה אֱלֹהִים אֶת יִשְׂרָאֵל מִכֹּל
צָרוֹתָיו.

כו לְדָוִד, שָׁפְטֵנִי יהוה, כִּי אֲנִי בְּתֻמִּי

הָלַכְתִּי, וּבַיהוה בָּטַחְתִּי לֹא אֶמְעָד. בְּחָנֵנִי יהוה וְנַסֵּנִי, צָרְפָה כִלְיוֹתַי וְלִבִּי. כִּי חַסְדְּךָ לְנֶגֶד עֵינָי, וְהִתְהַלַּכְתִּי בַּאֲמִתֶּךָ. לֹא יָשַׁבְתִּי עִם מְתֵי שָׁוְא, וְעִם נַעֲלָמִים לֹא אָבוֹא. שָׂנֵאתִי קְהַל מְרֵעִים, וְעִם רְשָׁעִים לֹא אֵשֵׁב. אֶרְחַץ בְּנִקָּיוֹן כַּפָּי, וַאֲסֹבְבָה אֶת מִזְבַּחֲךָ יהוה. לַשְׁמִעַ בְּקוֹל תּוֹדָה, וּלְסַפֵּר כָּל נִפְלְאוֹתֶיךָ. יהוה אָהַבְתִּי מְעוֹן בֵּיתֶךָ, וּמְקוֹם מִשְׁכַּן כְּבוֹדֶךָ. אַל תֶּאֱסֹף עִם חַטָּאִים נַפְשִׁי, וְעִם אַנְשֵׁי דָמִים חַיָּי. אֲשֶׁר בִּידֵיהֶם זִמָּה, וִימִינָם מָלְאָה שֹּׁחַד. וַאֲנִי בְּתֻמִּי אֵלֵךְ, פְּדֵנִי וְחָנֵּנִי. רַגְלִי עָמְדָה בְמִישׁוֹר, בְּמַקְהֵלִים אֲבָרֵךְ יהוה.

כז לְדָוִד, יהוה אוֹרִי וְיִשְׁעִי, מִמִּי אִירָא, יהוה מָעוֹז חַיַּי, מִמִּי אֶפְחָד. בִּקְרֹב עָלַי מְרֵעִים לֶאֱכֹל אֶת בְּשָׂרִי, צָרַי וְאֹיְבַי לִי, הֵמָּה כָשְׁלוּ וְנָפָלוּ. אִם תַּחֲנֶה עָלַי מַחֲנֶה, לֹא יִירָא לִבִּי, אִם תָּקוּם עָלַי מִלְחָמָה, בְּזֹאת אֲנִי בוֹטֵחַ. אַחַת שָׁאַלְתִּי מֵאֵת יהוה, אוֹתָהּ אֲבַקֵּשׁ, שִׁבְתִּי בְּבֵית יהוה כָּל יְמֵי חַיַּי, לַחֲזוֹת בְּנֹעַם יהוה, וּלְבַקֵּר בְּהֵיכָלוֹ. כִּי יִצְפְּנֵנִי בְּסֻכֹּה בְּיוֹם רָעָה, יַסְתִּרֵנִי בְּסֵתֶר אָהֳלוֹ, בְּצוּר יְרוֹמְמֵנִי. וְעַתָּה יָרוּם רֹאשִׁי עַל אֹיְבַי סְבִיבוֹתַי, וְאֶזְבְּחָה בְאָהֳלוֹ זִבְחֵי תְרוּעָה, אָשִׁירָה וַאֲזַמְּרָה לַיהוה. שְׁמַע יהוה קוֹלִי אֶקְרָא, וְחָנֵּנִי וַעֲנֵנִי. לְךָ אָמַר לִבִּי בַּקְּשׁוּ פָנָי, אֶת פָּנֶיךָ יהוה אֲבַקֵּשׁ. אַל תַּסְתֵּר פָּנֶיךָ מִמֶּנִּי, אַל תַּט בְּאַף עַבְדֶּךָ, עֶזְרָתִי הָיִיתָ, אַל תִּטְּשֵׁנִי וְאַל תַּעַזְבֵנִי, אֱלֹהֵי יִשְׁעִי. כִּי אָבִי וְאִמִּי עֲזָבוּנִי, וַיהוה יַאַסְפֵנִי. הוֹרֵנִי יהוה דַּרְכֶּךָ, וּנְחֵנִי בְּאֹרַח מִישׁוֹר, לְמַעַן שׁוֹרְרָי. אַל תִּתְּנֵנִי בְּנֶפֶשׁ צָרָי, כִּי קָמוּ בִי עֵדֵי שֶׁקֶר, וִיפֵחַ חָמָס. לוּלֵא הֶאֱמַנְתִּי לִרְאוֹת בְּטוּב יהוה בְּאֶרֶץ חַיִּים. קַוֵּה אֶל יהוה, חֲזַק וְיַאֲמֵץ לִבֶּךָ, וְקַוֵּה אֶל יהוה.

כח לְדָוִד, אֵלֶיךָ יהוה אֶקְרָא, צוּרִי אַל תֶּחֱרַשׁ מִמֶּנִּי, פֶּן תֶּחֱשֶׁה מִמֶּנִּי, וְנִמְשַׁלְתִּי עִם יוֹרְדֵי בוֹר. שְׁמַע קוֹל תַּחֲנוּנַי בְּשַׁוְּעִי אֵלֶיךָ, בְּנָשְׂאִי יָדַי אֶל דְּבִיר קָדְשֶׁךָ. אַל תִּמְשְׁכֵנִי עִם רְשָׁעִים וְעִם פֹּעֲלֵי אָוֶן, דֹּבְרֵי שָׁלוֹם עִם רֵעֵיהֶם, וְרָעָה בִּלְבָבָם. תֶּן לָהֶם כְּפָעֳלָם וּכְרֹעַ מַעַלְלֵיהֶם, כְּמַעֲשֵׂה יְדֵיהֶם תֵּן לָהֶם, הָשֵׁב גְּמוּלָם לָהֶם. כִּי לֹא יָבִינוּ אֶל פְּעֻלֹּת יהוה, וְאֶל מַעֲשֵׂה יָדָיו, יֶהֶרְסֵם וְלֹא יִבְנֵם. בָּרוּךְ יהוה, כִּי שָׁמַע קוֹל תַּחֲנוּנָי. יהוה עֻזִּי וּמָגִנִּי, בּוֹ בָטַח לִבִּי וְנֶעֱזָרְתִּי, וַיַּעֲלֹז לִבִּי, וּמִשִּׁירִי אֲהוֹדֶנּוּ. יהוה עֹז לָמוֹ, וּמָעוֹז יְשׁוּעוֹת מְשִׁיחוֹ הוּא. הוֹשִׁיעָה אֶת עַמֶּךָ, וּבָרֵךְ אֶת נַחֲלָתֶךָ, וּרְעֵם וְנַשְּׂאֵם עַד הָעוֹלָם.

5th day — יום ה לחדש

כט מִזְמוֹר לְדָוִד, הָבוּ לַיהוה בְּנֵי אֵלִים, הָבוּ לַיהוה כָּבוֹד וָעֹז. הָבוּ לַיהוה כְּבוֹד שְׁמוֹ, הִשְׁתַּחֲווּ לַיהוה בְּהַדְרַת קֹדֶשׁ. קוֹל יהוה עַל הַמָּיִם, אֵל הַכָּבוֹד הִרְעִים, יהוה עַל מַיִם רַבִּים. קוֹל יהוה בַּכֹּחַ, קוֹל יהוה בֶּהָדָר. קוֹל יהוה שֹׁבֵר אֲרָזִים, וַיְשַׁבֵּר יהוה אֶת אַרְזֵי הַלְּבָנוֹן. וַיַּרְקִידֵם כְּמוֹ עֵגֶל, לְבָנוֹן וְשִׂרְיוֹן כְּמוֹ בֶן רְאֵמִים. קוֹל יהוה חֹצֵב לַהֲבוֹת אֵשׁ. קוֹל יהוה יָחִיל מִדְבָּר, יָחִיל יהוה מִדְבַּר קָדֵשׁ. קוֹל יהוה יְחוֹלֵל אַיָּלוֹת, וַיֶּחֱשֹׂף יְעָרוֹת, וּבְהֵיכָלוֹ כֻּלּוֹ אֹמֵר כָּבוֹד. יהוה לַמַּבּוּל יָשָׁב, וַיֵּשֶׁב יהוה מֶלֶךְ לְעוֹלָם. יהוה עֹז לְעַמּוֹ יִתֵּן, יהוה יְבָרֵךְ אֶת עַמּוֹ בַשָּׁלוֹם.

MONDAY — יום שני

ל מִזְמוֹר שִׁיר חֲנֻכַּת הַבַּיִת לְדָוִד. אֲרוֹמִמְךָ יהוה כִּי דִלִּיתָנִי, וְלֹא שִׂמַּחְתָּ אֹיְבַי לִי. יהוה אֱלֹהָי, שִׁוַּעְתִּי אֵלֶיךָ וַתִּרְפָּאֵנִי. יהוה הֶעֱלִיתָ מִן שְׁאוֹל נַפְשִׁי, חִיִּיתַנִי מִיָּרְדִי בוֹר. זַמְּרוּ לַיהוה חֲסִידָיו, וְהוֹדוּ לְזֵכֶר קָדְשׁוֹ. כִּי רֶגַע בְּאַפּוֹ, חַיִּים בִּרְצוֹנוֹ, בָּעֶרֶב יָלִין

בֶּכִי וְלַבֹּקֶר רִנָּה. וַאֲנִי אָמַרְתִּי בְשַׁלְוִי, בַּל אֶמּוֹט לְעוֹלָם. יהוה בִּרְצוֹנְךָ הֶעֱמַדְתָּה לְהַרְרִי עֹז, הִסְתַּרְתָּ פָנֶיךָ הָיִיתִי נִבְהָל. אֵלֶיךָ יהוה אֶקְרָא, וְאֶל אֲדֹנָי אֶתְחַנָּן. מַה בֶּצַע בְּדָמִי, בְּרִדְתִּי אֶל שָׁחַת, הֲיוֹדְךָ עָפָר, הֲיַגִּיד אֲמִתֶּךָ. שְׁמַע יהוה וְחָנֵּנִי, יהוה הֱיֵה עֹזֵר לִי. הָפַכְתָּ מִסְפְּדִי לְמָחוֹל לִי, פִּתַּחְתָּ שַׂקִּי, וַתְּאַזְּרֵנִי שִׂמְחָה. לְמַעַן יְזַמֶּרְךָ כָבוֹד וְלֹא יִדֹּם, יהוה אֱלֹהַי לְעוֹלָם אוֹדֶךָּ.

לא לַמְנַצֵּחַ מִזְמוֹר לְדָוִד. בְּךָ יהוה חָסִיתִי, אַל אֵבוֹשָׁה לְעוֹלָם, בְּצִדְקָתְךָ פַלְּטֵנִי. הַטֵּה אֵלַי אָזְנְךָ, מְהֵרָה הַצִּילֵנִי, הֱיֵה לִי לְצוּר מָעוֹז, לְבֵית מְצוּדוֹת לְהוֹשִׁיעֵנִי. כִּי סַלְעִי וּמְצוּדָתִי אָתָּה, וּלְמַעַן שִׁמְךָ תַּנְחֵנִי וּתְנַהֲלֵנִי. תּוֹצִיאֵנִי מֵרֶשֶׁת זוּ טָמְנוּ לִי, כִּי אַתָּה מָעוּזִּי. בְּיָדְךָ אַפְקִיד רוּחִי, פָּדִיתָה אוֹתִי, יהוה אֵל אֱמֶת. שָׂנֵאתִי הַשֹּׁמְרִים הַבְלֵי שָׁוְא, וַאֲנִי אֶל יהוה בָּטָחְתִּי. אָגִילָה וְאֶשְׂמְחָה בְּחַסְדֶּךָ, אֲשֶׁר רָאִיתָ אֶת עָנְיִי, יָדַעְתָּ בְּצָרוֹת נַפְשִׁי. וְלֹא הִסְגַּרְתַּנִי בְּיַד אוֹיֵב, הֶעֱמַדְתָּ בַמֶּרְחָב רַגְלָי. חָנֵּנִי יהוה כִּי צַר לִי, עָשְׁשָׁה בְכַעַס עֵינִי נַפְשִׁי וּבִטְנִי. כִּי כָלוּ בְיָגוֹן חַיַּי, וּשְׁנוֹתַי בַּאֲנָחָה, כָּשַׁל בַּעֲוֹנִי כֹחִי, וַעֲצָמַי עָשֵׁשׁוּ. מִכָּל צֹרְרַי הָיִיתִי חֶרְפָּה, וְלִשְׁכֵנַי מְאֹד, וּפַחַד לִמְיֻדָּעָי, רֹאַי בַּחוּץ, נָדְדוּ מִמֶּנִּי. נִשְׁכַּחְתִּי כְּמֵת מִלֵּב, הָיִיתִי כִּכְלִי אֹבֵד. כִּי שָׁמַעְתִּי דִּבַּת רַבִּים מָגוֹר מִסָּבִיב, בְּהִוָּסְדָם יַחַד עָלַי, לָקַחַת נַפְשִׁי זָמָמוּ. וַאֲנִי, עָלֶיךָ בָטַחְתִּי יהוה, אָמַרְתִּי, אֱלֹהַי אָתָּה. בְּיָדְךָ עִתֹּתָי, הַצִּילֵנִי מִיַּד אוֹיְבַי וּמֵרֹדְפָי. הָאִירָה פָנֶיךָ עַל עַבְדֶּךָ, הוֹשִׁיעֵנִי בְחַסְדֶּךָ. יהוה אַל אֵבוֹשָׁה כִּי קְרָאתִיךָ, יֵבֹשׁוּ רְשָׁעִים יִדְּמוּ לִשְׁאוֹל. תֵּאָלַמְנָה שִׂפְתֵי שָׁקֶר, הַדֹּבְרוֹת עַל צַדִּיק עָתָק, בְּגַאֲוָה וָבוּז. מָה רַב טוּבְךָ אֲשֶׁר צָפַנְתָּ לִּירֵאֶיךָ, פָּעַלְתָּ לַחוֹסִים בָּךְ, נֶגֶד בְּנֵי אָדָם.

תַּסְתִּירֵם בְּסֵתֶר פָּנֶיךָ מֵרֻכְסֵי אִישׁ, תִּצְפְּנֵם בְּסֻכָּה מֵרִיב לְשֹׁנוֹת. בָּרוּךְ יהוה, כִּי הִפְלִיא חַסְדּוֹ לִי בְּעִיר מָצוֹר. וַאֲנִי אָמַרְתִּי בְחָפְזִי, נִגְרַזְתִּי מִנֶּגֶד עֵינֶיךָ, אָכֵן שָׁמַעְתָּ קוֹל תַּחֲנוּנַי בְּשַׁוְּעִי אֵלֶיךָ. אֶהֱבוּ אֶת יהוה כָּל חֲסִידָיו, אֱמוּנִים נֹצֵר יהוה, וּמְשַׁלֵּם עַל יֶתֶר עֹשֵׂה גַאֲוָה. חִזְקוּ וְיַאֲמֵץ לְבַבְכֶם, כָּל הַמְיַחֲלִים לַיהוה.

לב לְדָוִד מַשְׂכִּיל, אַשְׁרֵי נְשׂוּי פֶּשַׁע כְּסוּי חֲטָאָה. אַשְׁרֵי אָדָם לֹא יַחְשֹׁב יהוה לוֹ עָוֹן, וְאֵין בְּרוּחוֹ רְמִיָּה. כִּי הֶחֱרַשְׁתִּי בָּלוּ עֲצָמָי, בְּשַׁאֲגָתִי כָּל הַיּוֹם. כִּי יוֹמָם וָלַיְלָה תִּכְבַּד עָלַי יָדֶךָ, נֶהְפַּךְ לְשַׁדִּי, בְּחַרְבֹנֵי קַיִץ סֶלָה. חַטָּאתִי אוֹדִיעֲךָ, וַעֲוֹנִי לֹא כִסִּיתִי, אָמַרְתִּי, אוֹדֶה עֲלֵי פְשָׁעַי לַיהוה, וְאַתָּה נָשָׂאתָ עֲוֹן חַטָּאתִי סֶלָה. עַל זֹאת יִתְפַּלֵּל כָּל חָסִיד אֵלֶיךָ לְעֵת מְצֹא, רַק לְשֵׁטֶף מַיִם רַבִּים, אֵלָיו לֹא יַגִּיעוּ. אַתָּה סֵתֶר לִי מִצַּר תִּצְּרֵנִי, רָנֵּי פַלֵּט, תְּסוֹבְבֵנִי סֶלָה. אַשְׂכִּילְךָ וְאוֹרְךָ בְּדֶרֶךְ זוּ תֵלֵךְ, אִיעֲצָה עָלֶיךָ עֵינִי. אַל תִּהְיוּ כְּסוּס, כְּפֶרֶד אֵין הָבִין, בְּמֶתֶג וָרֶסֶן עֶדְיוֹ לִבְלוֹם, בַּל קְרֹב אֵלֶיךָ. רַבִּים מַכְאוֹבִים לָרָשָׁע, וְהַבּוֹטֵחַ בַּיהוה חֶסֶד יְסוֹבְבֶנּוּ. שִׂמְחוּ בַיהוה וְגִילוּ צַדִּיקִים, וְהַרְנִינוּ כָּל יִשְׁרֵי לֵב.

לג רַנְּנוּ צַדִּיקִים בַּיהוה, לַיְשָׁרִים נָאוָה תְהִלָּה. הוֹדוּ לַיהוה בְּכִנּוֹר, בְּנֵבֶל עָשׂוֹר זַמְּרוּ לוֹ. שִׁירוּ לוֹ שִׁיר חָדָשׁ, הֵיטִיבוּ נַגֵּן בִּתְרוּעָה. כִּי יָשָׁר דְּבַר יהוה, וְכָל מַעֲשֵׂהוּ בֶּאֱמוּנָה. אֹהֵב צְדָקָה וּמִשְׁפָּט, חֶסֶד יהוה מָלְאָה הָאָרֶץ. בִּדְבַר יהוה שָׁמַיִם נַעֲשׂוּ, וּבְרוּחַ פִּיו כָּל צְבָאָם. כֹּנֵס כַּנֵּד מֵי הַיָּם, נֹתֵן בְּאוֹצָרוֹת תְּהוֹמוֹת. יִירְאוּ מֵיהוה כָּל הָאָרֶץ, מִמֶּנּוּ יָגוּרוּ כָּל יֹשְׁבֵי תֵבֵל. כִּי הוּא אָמַר וַיֶּהִי, הוּא צִוָּה וַיַּעֲמֹד. יהוה הֵפִיר עֲצַת גּוֹיִם, הֵנִיא מַחְשְׁבוֹת עַמִּים. עֲצַת יהוה

לְעוֹלָם תַּעֲמֹד, מַחְשְׁבוֹת לִבּוֹ לְדֹר וָדֹר. אַשְׁרֵי הַגּוֹי אֲשֶׁר יהוה אֱלֹהָיו, הָעָם בָּחַר לְנַחֲלָה לוֹ. מִשָּׁמַיִם הִבִּיט יהוה, רָאָה אֶת כָּל בְּנֵי הָאָדָם. מִמְּכוֹן שִׁבְתּוֹ הִשְׁגִּיחַ, אֶל כָּל יֹשְׁבֵי הָאָרֶץ. הַיֹּצֵר יַחַד לִבָּם, הַמֵּבִין אֶל כָּל מַעֲשֵׂיהֶם. אֵין הַמֶּלֶךְ נוֹשָׁע בְּרָב חָיִל, גִּבּוֹר לֹא יִנָּצֵל בְּרָב כֹּחַ. שֶׁקֶר הַסּוּס לִתְשׁוּעָה, וּבְרֹב חֵילוֹ לֹא יְמַלֵּט. הִנֵּה עֵין יהוה אֶל יְרֵאָיו, לַמְיַחֲלִים לְחַסְדּוֹ. לְהַצִּיל מִמָּוֶת נַפְשָׁם, וּלְחַיּוֹתָם בָּרָעָב. נַפְשֵׁנוּ חִכְּתָה לַיהוה, עֶזְרֵנוּ וּמָגִנֵּנוּ הוּא. כִּי בוֹ יִשְׂמַח לִבֵּנוּ, כִּי בְשֵׁם קָדְשׁוֹ בָטָחְנוּ. יְהִי חַסְדְּךָ יהוה עָלֵינוּ, כַּאֲשֶׁר יִחַלְנוּ לָךְ.

לד לְדָוִד, בְּשַׁנּוֹתוֹ אֶת טַעְמוֹ לִפְנֵי אֲבִימֶלֶךְ, וַיְגָרְשֵׁהוּ וַיֵּלַךְ. אֲבָרְכָה אֶת יהוה בְּכָל עֵת, תָּמִיד תְּהִלָּתוֹ בְּפִי. בַּיהוה תִּתְהַלֵּל נַפְשִׁי, יִשְׁמְעוּ עֲנָוִים וְיִשְׂמָחוּ. גַּדְּלוּ לַיהוה אִתִּי, וּנְרוֹמְמָה שְׁמוֹ יַחְדָּו. דָּרַשְׁתִּי אֶת יהוה וְעָנָנִי, וּמִכָּל מְגוּרוֹתַי הִצִּילָנִי. הִבִּיטוּ אֵלָיו וְנָהָרוּ, וּפְנֵיהֶם אַל יֶחְפָּרוּ. זֶה עָנִי קָרָא וַיהוה שָׁמֵעַ, וּמִכָּל צָרוֹתָיו הוֹשִׁיעוֹ. חֹנֶה מַלְאַךְ יהוה סָבִיב לִירֵאָיו, וַיְחַלְּצֵם. טַעֲמוּ וּרְאוּ כִּי טוֹב יהוה, אַשְׁרֵי הַגֶּבֶר יֶחֱסֶה בּוֹ. יְראוּ אֶת יהוה קְדֹשָׁיו, כִּי אֵין מַחְסוֹר לִירֵאָיו. כְּפִירִים רָשׁוּ וְרָעֵבוּ, וְדֹרְשֵׁי יהוה לֹא יַחְסְרוּ כָל טוֹב. לְכוּ בָנִים שִׁמְעוּ לִי, יִרְאַת יהוה אֲלַמֶּדְכֶם. מִי הָאִישׁ הֶחָפֵץ חַיִּים, אֹהֵב יָמִים לִרְאוֹת טוֹב. נְצֹר לְשׁוֹנְךָ מֵרָע, וּשְׂפָתֶיךָ מִדַּבֵּר מִרְמָה. סוּר מֵרָע וַעֲשֵׂה טוֹב, בַּקֵּשׁ שָׁלוֹם וְרָדְפֵהוּ. עֵינֵי יהוה אֶל צַדִּיקִים, וְאָזְנָיו אֶל שַׁוְעָתָם. פְּנֵי יהוה בְּעֹשֵׂי רָע, לְהַכְרִית מֵאֶרֶץ זִכְרָם. צָעֲקוּ וַיהוה שָׁמֵעַ, וּמִכָּל צָרוֹתָם הִצִּילָם. קָרוֹב יהוה לְנִשְׁבְּרֵי לֵב, וְאֶת דַּכְּאֵי רוּחַ יוֹשִׁיעַ. רַבּוֹת רָעוֹת צַדִּיק, וּמִכֻּלָּם יַצִּילֶנּוּ יהוה. שֹׁמֵר כָּל עַצְמוֹתָיו אַחַת מֵהֵנָּה לֹא נִשְׁבָּרָה. תְּמוֹתֵת רָשָׁע רָעָה, וְשֹׂנְאֵי צַדִּיק יֶאְשָׁמוּ. פּוֹדֶה יהוה נֶפֶשׁ עֲבָדָיו, וְלֹא יֶאְשְׁמוּ כָּל הַחֹסִים בּוֹ.

6th day — יום ו לחדש

לה לְדָוִד, רִיבָה יהוה אֶת יְרִיבַי, לְחַם אֶת לֹחֲמָי. הַחֲזֵק מָגֵן וְצִנָּה, וְקוּמָה בְּעֶזְרָתִי. וְהָרֵק חֲנִית וּסְגֹר לִקְרַאת רֹדְפָי, אֱמֹר לְנַפְשִׁי יְשֻׁעָתֵךְ אָנִי. יֵבֹשׁוּ וְיִכָּלְמוּ מְבַקְשֵׁי נַפְשִׁי, יִסֹּגוּ אָחוֹר וְיַחְפְּרוּ, חֹשְׁבֵי רָעָתִי. יִהְיוּ כְּמֹץ לִפְנֵי רוּחַ, וּמַלְאַךְ יהוה דּוֹחֶה. יְהִי דַרְכָּם חֹשֶׁךְ וַחֲלַקְלַקֹּת, וּמַלְאַךְ יהוה רֹדְפָם. כִּי חִנָּם טָמְנוּ לִי שַׁחַת רִשְׁתָּם, חִנָּם חָפְרוּ לְנַפְשִׁי. תְּבוֹאֵהוּ שׁוֹאָה לֹא יֵדָע, וְרִשְׁתּוֹ אֲשֶׁר טָמַן תִּלְכְּדוֹ, בְּשׁוֹאָה יִפָּל בָּהּ. וְנַפְשִׁי תָּגִיל בַּיהוה, תָּשִׂישׂ בִּישׁוּעָתוֹ. כָּל עַצְמֹתַי תֹּאמַרְנָה, יהוה מִי כָמוֹךָ, מַצִּיל עָנִי מֵחָזָק מִמֶּנּוּ, וְעָנִי וְאֶבְיוֹן מִגֹּזְלוֹ. יְקוּמוּן עֵדֵי חָמָס, אֲשֶׁר לֹא יָדַעְתִּי יִשְׁאָלוּנִי. יְשַׁלְּמוּנִי רָעָה תַּחַת טוֹבָה, שְׁכוֹל לְנַפְשִׁי. וַאֲנִי בַּחֲלוֹתָם לְבוּשִׁי שָׂק, עִנֵּיתִי בַצּוֹם נַפְשִׁי, וּתְפִלָּתִי עַל חֵיקִי תָשׁוּב. כְּרֵעַ כְּאָח לִי הִתְהַלָּכְתִּי, כַּאֲבֶל אֵם קֹדֵר שַׁחוֹתִי. וּבְצַלְעִי שָׂמְחוּ וְנֶאֱסָפוּ, נֶאֶסְפוּ עָלַי נֵכִים וְלֹא יָדַעְתִּי, קָרְעוּ וְלֹא דָמּוּ. בְּחַנְפֵי לַעֲגֵי מָעוֹג, חָרֹק עָלַי שִׁנֵּימוֹ. אֲדֹנָי כַּמָּה תִּרְאֶה, הָשִׁיבָה נַפְשִׁי מִשֹּׁאֵיהֶם, מִכְּפִירִים יְחִידָתִי. אוֹדְךָ בְּקָהָל רָב, בְּעַם עָצוּם אֲהַלְלֶךָּ. אַל יִשְׂמְחוּ לִי אֹיְבַי שֶׁקֶר, שֹׂנְאַי חִנָּם יִקְרְצוּ עָיִן. כִּי לֹא שָׁלוֹם יְדַבֵּרוּ, וְעַל רִגְעֵי אֶרֶץ, דִּבְרֵי מִרְמוֹת יַחֲשֹׁבוּן. וַיַּרְחִיבוּ עָלַי פִּיהֶם, אָמְרוּ, הֶאָח הֶאָח, רָאֲתָה עֵינֵנוּ. רָאִיתָה יהוה אַל תֶּחֱרַשׁ, אֲדֹנָי אַל תִּרְחַק מִמֶּנִּי. הָעִירָה וְהָקִיצָה לְמִשְׁפָּטִי, אֱלֹהַי וַאדֹנָי לְרִיבִי. שָׁפְטֵנִי כְצִדְקְךָ יהוה אֱלֹהָי, וְאַל יִשְׂמְחוּ לִי. אַל יֹאמְרוּ בְלִבָּם, הֶאָח

נַפְשֵׁנוּ, אַל יֹאמְרוּ, בִּלַּעֲנוּהוּ. יֵבֹשׁוּ וְיַחְפְּרוּ יַחְדָּו שְׂמֵחֵי רָעָתִי, יִלְבְּשׁוּ בֹשֶׁת וּכְלִמָּה, הַמַּגְדִּילִים עָלָי. יָרֹנּוּ וְיִשְׂמְחוּ חֲפֵצֵי צִדְקִי, וְיֹאמְרוּ תָמִיד, יִגְדַּל יהוה, הֶחָפֵץ שְׁלוֹם עַבְדּוֹ. וּלְשׁוֹנִי תֶּהְגֶּה צִדְקֶךָ, כָּל הַיּוֹם תְּהִלָּתֶךָ.

לו לַמְנַצֵּחַ לְעֶבֶד יהוה לְדָוִד. נְאֻם פֶּשַׁע לָרָשָׁע בְּקֶרֶב לִבִּי, אֵין פַּחַד אֱלֹהִים לְנֶגֶד עֵינָיו. כִּי הֶחֱלִיק אֵלָיו בְּעֵינָיו, לִמְצֹא עֲוֹנוֹ לִשְׂנֹא. דִּבְרֵי פִיו אָוֶן וּמִרְמָה, חָדַל לְהַשְׂכִּיל לְהֵיטִיב. אָוֶן יַחְשֹׁב עַל מִשְׁכָּבוֹ, יִתְיַצֵּב עַל דֶּרֶךְ לֹא טוֹב, רָע לֹא יִמְאָס. יהוה בְּהַשָּׁמַיִם חַסְדֶּךָ, אֱמוּנָתְךָ עַד שְׁחָקִים. צִדְקָתְךָ כְּהַרְרֵי אֵל, מִשְׁפָּטֶךָ תְּהוֹם רַבָּה, אָדָם וּבְהֵמָה תוֹשִׁיעַ, יהוה. מַה יָּקָר חַסְדְּךָ אֱלֹהִים, וּבְנֵי אָדָם בְּצֵל כְּנָפֶיךָ יֶחֱסָיוּן. יִרְוְיֻן מִדֶּשֶׁן בֵּיתֶךָ, וְנַחַל עֲדָנֶיךָ תַשְׁקֵם. כִּי עִמְּךָ מְקוֹר חַיִּים, בְּאוֹרְךָ נִרְאֶה אוֹר. מְשֹׁךְ חַסְדְּךָ לְיֹדְעֶיךָ, וְצִדְקָתְךָ לְיִשְׁרֵי לֵב. אַל תְּבוֹאֵנִי רֶגֶל גַּאֲוָה, וְיַד רְשָׁעִים אַל תְּנִדֵנִי. שָׁם נָפְלוּ פֹּעֲלֵי אָוֶן, דֹּחוּ וְלֹא יָכְלוּ קוּם.

לז לְדָוִד, אַל תִּתְחַר בַּמְּרֵעִים, אַל תְּקַנֵּא בְּעֹשֵׂי עַוְלָה. כִּי כֶחָצִיר מְהֵרָה יִמָּלוּ, וּכְיֶרֶק דֶּשֶׁא יִבּוֹלוּן. בְּטַח בַּיהוה וַעֲשֵׂה טוֹב, שְׁכָן אֶרֶץ וּרְעֵה אֱמוּנָה. וְהִתְעַנַּג עַל יהוה, וְיִתֶּן לְךָ מִשְׁאֲלֹת לִבֶּךָ. גּוֹל עַל יהוה דַּרְכֶּךָ, וּבְטַח עָלָיו וְהוּא יַעֲשֶׂה. וְהוֹצִיא כָאוֹר צִדְקֶךָ, וּמִשְׁפָּטֶךָ כַּצָּהֳרָיִם. דּוֹם לַיהוה וְהִתְחוֹלֵל לוֹ, אַל תִּתְחַר בְּמַצְלִיחַ דַּרְכּוֹ, בְּאִישׁ עֹשֶׂה מְזִמּוֹת. הֶרֶף מֵאַף וַעֲזֹב חֵמָה, אַל תִּתְחַר אַךְ לְהָרֵעַ. כִּי מְרֵעִים יִכָּרֵתוּן, וְקֹוֵי יהוה הֵמָּה יִירְשׁוּ אָרֶץ. וְעוֹד מְעַט וְאֵין רָשָׁע, וְהִתְבּוֹנַנְתָּ עַל מְקוֹמוֹ וְאֵינֶנּוּ. וַעֲנָוִים יִירְשׁוּ אָרֶץ, וְהִתְעַנְּגוּ עַל רֹב שָׁלוֹם. זֹמֵם רָשָׁע לַצַּדִּיק, וְחֹרֵק עָלָיו שִׁנָּיו. אֲדֹנָי יִשְׂחַק לוֹ, כִּי רָאָה כִּי יָבֹא יוֹמוֹ. חֶרֶב פָּתְחוּ רְשָׁעִים וְדָרְכוּ קַשְׁתָּם, לְהַפִּיל עָנִי וְאֶבְיוֹן, לִטְבוֹחַ יִשְׁרֵי דָרֶךְ. חַרְבָּם תָּבוֹא בְלִבָּם, וְקַשְּׁתוֹתָם תִּשָּׁבַרְנָה. טוֹב מְעַט לַצַּדִּיק, מֵהֲמוֹן רְשָׁעִים רַבִּים. כִּי זְרוֹעוֹת רְשָׁעִים תִּשָּׁבַרְנָה, וְסוֹמֵךְ צַדִּיקִים יהוה. יוֹדֵעַ יהוה יְמֵי תְמִימִם, וְנַחֲלָתָם לְעוֹלָם תִּהְיֶה. לֹא יֵבֹשׁוּ בְּעֵת רָעָה, וּבִימֵי רְעָבוֹן יִשְׂבָּעוּ. כִּי רְשָׁעִים יֹאבֵדוּ וְאֹיְבֵי יהוה כִּיקַר כָּרִים, כָּלוּ בֶעָשָׁן כָּלוּ. לֹוֶה רָשָׁע וְלֹא יְשַׁלֵּם, וְצַדִּיק חוֹנֵן וְנוֹתֵן. כִּי מְבֹרָכָיו יִירְשׁוּ אָרֶץ, וּמְקֻלָּלָיו יִכָּרֵתוּ. מֵיהוה מִצְעֲדֵי גֶבֶר כּוֹנָנוּ, וְדַרְכּוֹ יֶחְפָּץ. כִּי יִפֹּל לֹא יוּטָל, כִּי יהוה סוֹמֵךְ יָדוֹ. נַעַר הָיִיתִי גַּם זָקַנְתִּי, וְלֹא רָאִיתִי צַדִּיק נֶעֱזָב, וְזַרְעוֹ מְבַקֶּשׁ לָחֶם. כָּל הַיּוֹם חוֹנֵן וּמַלְוֶה, וְזַרְעוֹ לִבְרָכָה. סוּר מֵרָע וַעֲשֵׂה טוֹב, וּשְׁכֹן לְעוֹלָם. כִּי יהוה אֹהֵב מִשְׁפָּט, וְלֹא יַעֲזֹב אֶת חֲסִידָיו, לְעוֹלָם נִשְׁמָרוּ, וְזֶרַע רְשָׁעִים נִכְרָת. צַדִּיקִים יִירְשׁוּ אָרֶץ, וְיִשְׁכְּנוּ לָעַד עָלֶיהָ. פִּי צַדִּיק יֶהְגֶּה חָכְמָה, וּלְשׁוֹנוֹ תְּדַבֵּר מִשְׁפָּט. תּוֹרַת אֱלֹהָיו בְּלִבּוֹ, לֹא תִמְעַד אֲשֻׁרָיו. צוֹפֶה רָשָׁע לַצַּדִּיק, וּמְבַקֵּשׁ לַהֲמִיתוֹ. יהוה לֹא יַעַזְבֶנּוּ בְיָדוֹ, וְלֹא יַרְשִׁיעֶנּוּ בְּהִשָּׁפְטוֹ. קַוֵּה אֶל יהוה וּשְׁמֹר דַּרְכּוֹ, וִירוֹמִמְךָ לָרֶשֶׁת אָרֶץ, בְּהִכָּרֵת רְשָׁעִים תִּרְאֶה. רָאִיתִי רָשָׁע עָרִיץ, וּמִתְעָרֶה כְּאֶזְרָח רַעֲנָן. וַיַּעֲבֹר וְהִנֵּה אֵינֶנּוּ, וָאֲבַקְשֵׁהוּ וְלֹא נִמְצָא. שְׁמָר תָּם וּרְאֵה יָשָׁר, כִּי אַחֲרִית לְאִישׁ שָׁלוֹם. וּפֹשְׁעִים נִשְׁמְדוּ יַחְדָּו, אַחֲרִית רְשָׁעִים נִכְרָתָה. וּתְשׁוּעַת צַדִּיקִים מֵיהוה, מָעוּזָּם בְּעֵת צָרָה. וַיַּעְזְרֵם יהוה וַיְפַלְּטֵם, יְפַלְּטֵם מֵרְשָׁעִים וְיוֹשִׁיעֵם כִּי חָסוּ בוֹ.

לח מִזְמוֹר לְדָוִד לְהַזְכִּיר. יהוה אַל בְּקֶצְפְּךָ תוֹכִיחֵנִי, וּבַחֲמָתְךָ תְיַסְּרֵנִי. כִּי חִצֶּיךָ נִחֲתוּ בִי, וַתִּנְחַת עָלַי יָדֶךָ. אֵין מְתֹם בִּבְשָׂרִי מִפְּנֵי זַעְמֶךָ, אֵין שָׁלוֹם בַּעֲצָמַי מִפְּנֵי חַטָּאתִי. כִּי עֲוֹנֹתַי

עָבְרוּ רֹאשִׁי, כְּמַשָּׂא כָבֵד יִכְבְּדוּ מִמֶּנִּי. הִבְאִישׁוּ נָמַקּוּ חַבּוּרֹתָי, מִפְּנֵי אִוַּלְתִּי. נַעֲוֵיתִי שַׁחֹתִי עַד מְאֹד, כָּל הַיּוֹם קֹדֵר הִלָּכְתִּי. כִּי כְסָלַי מָלְאוּ נִקְלֶה, וְאֵין מְתֹם בִּבְשָׂרִי. נְפוּגוֹתִי וְנִדְכֵּיתִי עַד מְאֹד, שָׁאַגְתִּי מִנַּהֲמַת לִבִּי. אֲדֹנָי נֶגְדְּךָ כָל תַּאֲוָתִי, וְאַנְחָתִי מִמְּךָ לֹא נִסְתָּרָה. לִבִּי סְחַרְחַר עֲזָבַנִי כֹחִי, וְאוֹר עֵינַי גַּם הֵם אֵין אִתִּי. אֹהֲבַי וְרֵעַי מִנֶּגֶד נִגְעִי יַעֲמֹדוּ, וּקְרוֹבַי מֵרָחֹק עָמָדוּ. וַיְנַקְשׁוּ מְבַקְשֵׁי נַפְשִׁי, וְדֹרְשֵׁי רָעָתִי דִּבְּרוּ הַוּוֹת, וּמִרְמוֹת כָּל הַיּוֹם יֶהְגּוּ. וַאֲנִי כְחֵרֵשׁ לֹא אֶשְׁמָע, וּכְאִלֵּם לֹא יִפְתַּח פִּיו. וָאֱהִי כְּאִישׁ אֲשֶׁר לֹא שֹׁמֵעַ, וְאֵין בְּפִיו תּוֹכָחוֹת. כִּי לְךָ יהוה הוֹחָלְתִּי, אַתָּה תַעֲנֶה אֲדֹנָי אֱלֹהָי. כִּי אָמַרְתִּי פֶּן יִשְׂמְחוּ לִי, בְּמוֹט רַגְלִי עָלַי הִגְדִּילוּ. כִּי אֲנִי לְצֶלַע נָכוֹן, וּמַכְאוֹבִי נֶגְדִּי תָמִיד. כִּי עֲוֹנִי אַגִּיד, אֶדְאַג מֵחַטָּאתִי. וְאֹיְבַי חַיִּים עָצֵמוּ, וְרַבּוּ שֹׂנְאַי שָׁקֶר. וּמְשַׁלְּמֵי רָעָה תַּחַת טוֹבָה, יִשְׂטְנוּנִי תַּחַת רָדְפִי טוֹב. אַל תַּעַזְבֵנִי יהוה, אֱלֹהַי אַל תִּרְחַק מִמֶּנִּי. חוּשָׁה לְעֶזְרָתִי, אֲדֹנָי תְּשׁוּעָתִי.

יום ז לחדש — 7th day

לט לַמְנַצֵּחַ לִידוּתוּן, מִזְמוֹר לְדָוִד. אָמַרְתִּי אֶשְׁמְרָה דְרָכַי מֵחֲטוֹא בִלְשׁוֹנִי, אֶשְׁמְרָה לְפִי מַחְסוֹם, בְּעֹד רָשָׁע לְנֶגְדִּי. נֶאֱלַמְתִּי דוּמִיָּה, הֶחֱשֵׁיתִי מִטּוֹב, וּכְאֵבִי נֶעְכָּר. חַם לִבִּי בְּקִרְבִּי, בַּהֲגִיגִי תִבְעַר אֵשׁ, דִּבַּרְתִּי בִּלְשׁוֹנִי. הוֹדִיעֵנִי יהוה, קִצִּי, וּמִדַּת יָמַי מַה הִיא, אֵדְעָה מֶה חָדֵל אָנִי. הִנֵּה טְפָחוֹת נָתַתָּה יָמַי, וְחֶלְדִּי כְאַיִן נֶגְדֶּךָ, אַךְ כָּל הֶבֶל כָּל אָדָם נִצָּב סֶלָה. אַךְ בְּצֶלֶם יִתְהַלֶּךְ אִישׁ, אַךְ הֶבֶל יֶהֱמָיוּן, יִצְבֹּר וְלֹא יֵדַע מִי אֹסְפָם. וְעַתָּה מַה קִּוִּיתִי אֲדֹנָי, תּוֹחַלְתִּי לְךָ הִיא. מִכָּל פְּשָׁעַי הַצִּילֵנִי, חֶרְפַּת נָבָל אַל תְּשִׂימֵנִי. נֶאֱלַמְתִּי לֹא אֶפְתַּח פִּי, כִּי אַתָּה עָשִׂיתָ. הָסֵר מֵעָלַי נִגְעֶךָ, מִתִּגְרַת יָדְךָ אֲנִי כָלִיתִי. בְּתוֹכָחוֹת עַל עָוֹן יִסַּרְתָּ אִישׁ, וַתֶּמֶס כָּעָשׁ חֲמוּדוֹ, אַךְ הֶבֶל כָּל אָדָם סֶלָה. שִׁמְעָה תְפִלָּתִי יהוה, וְשַׁוְעָתִי הַאֲזִינָה, אֶל דִּמְעָתִי אַל תֶּחֱרַשׁ, כִּי גֵר אָנֹכִי עִמָּךְ, תּוֹשָׁב כְּכָל אֲבוֹתָי. הָשַׁע מִמֶּנִּי וְאַבְלִיגָה, בְּטֶרֶם אֵלֵךְ וְאֵינֶנִּי.

מ לַמְנַצֵּחַ לְדָוִד מִזְמוֹר. קַוֹּה קִוִּיתִי יהוה, וַיֵּט אֵלַי וַיִּשְׁמַע שַׁוְעָתִי. וַיַּעֲלֵנִי מִבּוֹר שָׁאוֹן מִטִּיט הַיָּוֵן, וַיָּקֶם עַל סֶלַע רַגְלַי כּוֹנֵן אֲשֻׁרָי. וַיִּתֵּן בְּפִי שִׁיר חָדָשׁ, תְּהִלָּה לֵאלֹהֵינוּ, יִרְאוּ רַבִּים וְיִירָאוּ, וְיִבְטְחוּ בַּיהוה. אַשְׁרֵי הַגֶּבֶר אֲשֶׁר שָׂם יהוה מִבְטַחוֹ, וְלֹא פָנָה אֶל רְהָבִים וְשָׂטֵי כָזָב. רַבּוֹת עָשִׂיתָ אַתָּה יהוה אֱלֹהַי, נִפְלְאֹתֶיךָ וּמַחְשְׁבֹתֶיךָ אֵלֵינוּ, אֵין עֲרֹךְ אֵלֶיךָ, אַגִּידָה וַאֲדַבֵּרָה, עָצְמוּ מִסַּפֵּר. זֶבַח וּמִנְחָה לֹא חָפַצְתָּ, אָזְנַיִם כָּרִיתָ לִּי, עוֹלָה וַחֲטָאָה לֹא שָׁאָלְתָּ. אָז אָמַרְתִּי הִנֵּה בָאתִי, בִּמְגִלַּת סֵפֶר כָּתוּב עָלָי. לַעֲשׂוֹת רְצוֹנְךָ אֱלֹהַי חָפָצְתִּי, וְתוֹרָתְךָ בְּתוֹךְ מֵעָי. בִּשַּׂרְתִּי צֶדֶק בְּקָהָל רָב, הִנֵּה שְׂפָתַי לֹא אֶכְלָא, יהוה אַתָּה יָדָעְתָּ. צִדְקָתְךָ לֹא כִסִּיתִי בְּתוֹךְ לִבִּי, אֱמוּנָתְךָ וּתְשׁוּעָתְךָ אָמָרְתִּי, לֹא כִחַדְתִּי חַסְדְּךָ וַאֲמִתְּךָ לְקָהָל רָב. אַתָּה יהוה לֹא תִכְלָא רַחֲמֶיךָ מִמֶּנִּי, חַסְדְּךָ וַאֲמִתְּךָ תָּמִיד יִצְּרוּנִי. כִּי אָפְפוּ עָלַי רָעוֹת עַד אֵין מִסְפָּר, הִשִּׂיגוּנִי עֲוֹנֹתַי וְלֹא יָכֹלְתִּי לִרְאוֹת, עָצְמוּ מִשַּׂעֲרוֹת רֹאשִׁי, וְלִבִּי עֲזָבָנִי. רְצֵה יהוה לְהַצִּילֵנִי, יהוה לְעֶזְרָתִי חוּשָׁה. יֵבֹשׁוּ וְיַחְפְּרוּ יַחַד מְבַקְשֵׁי נַפְשִׁי לִסְפּוֹתָהּ, יִסֹּגוּ אָחוֹר וְיִכָּלְמוּ, חֲפֵצֵי רָעָתִי. יָשֹׁמּוּ עַל עֵקֶב בָּשְׁתָּם, הָאֹמְרִים לִי, הֶאָח הֶאָח. יָשִׂישׂוּ וְיִשְׂמְחוּ בְּךָ כָּל מְבַקְשֶׁיךָ, יֹאמְרוּ תָמִיד, יִגְדַּל יהוה אֹהֲבֵי תְּשׁוּעָתֶךָ. וַאֲנִי עָנִי וְאֶבְיוֹן אֲדֹנָי יַחֲשָׁב לִי, עֶזְרָתִי וּמְפַלְטִי אַתָּה, אֱלֹהַי אַל תְּאַחַר.

מא לַמְנַצֵּחַ מִזְמוֹר לְדָוִד. אַשְׁרֵי מַשְׂכִּיל אֶל דָּל, בְּיוֹם רָעָה יְמַלְּטֵהוּ יהוה. יהוה יִשְׁמְרֵהוּ וִיחַיֵּהוּ, וְאֻשַּׁר בָּאָרֶץ, וְאַל תִּתְּנֵהוּ בְּנֶפֶשׁ אֹיְבָיו. יהוה יִסְעָדֶנּוּ עַל עֶרֶשׂ דְּוָי, כָּל מִשְׁכָּבוֹ הָפַכְתָּ בְחָלְיוֹ. אֲנִי אָמַרְתִּי, יהוה חָנֵּנִי, רְפָאָה נַפְשִׁי, כִּי חָטָאתִי לָךְ. אוֹיְבַי יֹאמְרוּ רַע לִי, מָתַי יָמוּת וְאָבַד שְׁמוֹ. וְאִם בָּא לִרְאוֹת שָׁוְא יְדַבֵּר, לִבּוֹ יִקְבָּץ אָוֶן לוֹ, יֵצֵא לַחוּץ יְדַבֵּר. יַחַד עָלַי יִתְלַחֲשׁוּ כָּל שֹׂנְאָי, עָלַי יַחְשְׁבוּ רָעָה לִי. דְּבַר בְּלִיַּעַל יָצוּק בּוֹ, וַאֲשֶׁר שָׁכַב לֹא יוֹסִיף לָקוּם. גַּם אִישׁ שְׁלוֹמִי אֲשֶׁר בָּטַחְתִּי בוֹ, אוֹכֵל לַחְמִי, הִגְדִּיל עָלַי עָקֵב. וְאַתָּה יהוה חָנֵּנִי וַהֲקִימֵנִי, וַאֲשַׁלְּמָה לָהֶם. בְּזֹאת יָדַעְתִּי כִּי חָפַצְתָּ בִּי, כִּי לֹא יָרִיעַ אֹיְבִי עָלָי. וַאֲנִי בְּתֻמִּי תָּמַכְתָּ בִּי, וַתַּצִּיבֵנִי לְפָנֶיךָ לְעוֹלָם. בָּרוּךְ יהוה אֱלֹהֵי יִשְׂרָאֵל מֵהָעוֹלָם וְעַד הָעוֹלָם, אָמֵן וְאָמֵן.

BOOK TWO — ספר שני

מב לַמְנַצֵּחַ מַשְׂכִּיל לִבְנֵי קֹרַח. כְּאַיָּל תַּעֲרֹג עַל אֲפִיקֵי מָיִם, כֵּן נַפְשִׁי תַעֲרֹג אֵלֶיךָ אֱלֹהִים. צָמְאָה נַפְשִׁי לֵאלֹהִים, לְאֵל חָי, מָתַי אָבוֹא וְאֵרָאֶה פְּנֵי אֱלֹהִים. הָיְתָה לִּי דִמְעָתִי לֶחֶם יוֹמָם וָלָיְלָה, בֶּאֱמֹר אֵלַי כָּל הַיּוֹם, אַיֵּה אֱלֹהֶיךָ. אֵלֶּה אֶזְכְּרָה וְאֶשְׁפְּכָה עָלַי נַפְשִׁי, כִּי אֶעֱבֹר בַּסָּךְ, אֶדַּדֵּם עַד בֵּית אֱלֹהִים, בְּקוֹל רִנָּה וְתוֹדָה הָמוֹן חוֹגֵג. מַה תִּשְׁתּוֹחֲחִי נַפְשִׁי, וַתֶּהֱמִי עָלָי, הוֹחִילִי לֵאלֹהִים, כִּי עוֹד אוֹדֶנּוּ, יְשׁוּעוֹת פָּנָיו. אֱלֹהַי עָלַי נַפְשִׁי תִשְׁתּוֹחָח, עַל כֵּן אֶזְכָּרְךָ מֵאֶרֶץ יַרְדֵּן, וְחֶרְמוֹנִים, מֵהַר מִצְעָר. תְּהוֹם אֶל תְּהוֹם קוֹרֵא לְקוֹל צִנּוֹרֶיךָ, כָּל מִשְׁבָּרֶיךָ וְגַלֶּיךָ עָלַי עָבָרוּ. יוֹמָם יְצַוֶּה יהוה חַסְדּוֹ, וּבַלַּיְלָה שִׁירֹה עִמִּי, תְּפִלָּה לְאֵל חַיָּי. אוֹמְרָה לְאֵל סַלְעִי, לָמָה שְׁכַחְתָּנִי, לָמָּה קֹדֵר אֵלֵךְ בְּלַחַץ אוֹיֵב. בְּרֶצַח בְּעַצְמוֹתַי חֵרְפוּנִי צוֹרְרָי, בְּאָמְרָם אֵלַי כָּל הַיּוֹם, אַיֵּה אֱלֹהֶיךָ. מַה תִּשְׁתּוֹחֲחִי נַפְשִׁי, וּמַה תֶּהֱמִי עָלָי, הוֹחִילִי לֵאלֹהִים, כִּי עוֹד אוֹדֶנּוּ, יְשׁוּעֹת פָּנַי וֵאלֹהָי.

מג שָׁפְטֵנִי אֱלֹהִים וְרִיבָה רִיבִי מִגּוֹי לֹא חָסִיד, מֵאִישׁ מִרְמָה וְעַוְלָה תְפַלְּטֵנִי. כִּי אַתָּה אֱלֹהֵי מָעוּזִּי, לָמָה זְנַחְתָּנִי, לָמָּה קֹדֵר אֶתְהַלֵּךְ בְּלַחַץ אוֹיֵב. שְׁלַח אוֹרְךָ וַאֲמִתְּךָ, הֵמָּה יַנְחוּנִי, יְבִיאוּנִי אֶל הַר קָדְשְׁךָ וְאֶל מִשְׁכְּנוֹתֶיךָ. וְאָבוֹאָה אֶל מִזְבַּח אֱלֹהִים, אֶל אֵל שִׂמְחַת גִּילִי, וְאוֹדְךָ בְכִנּוֹר אֱלֹהִים אֱלֹהָי. מַה תִּשְׁתּוֹחֲחִי נַפְשִׁי, וּמַה תֶּהֱמִי עָלָי, הוֹחִילִי לֵאלֹהִים, כִּי עוֹד אוֹדֶנּוּ, יְשׁוּעֹת פָּנַי וֵאלֹהָי.

8th day — יום ח לחדש

מד לַמְנַצֵּחַ לִבְנֵי קֹרַח מַשְׂכִּיל. אֱלֹהִים בְּאָזְנֵינוּ שָׁמַעְנוּ, אֲבוֹתֵינוּ סִפְּרוּ לָנוּ, פֹּעַל פָּעַלְתָּ בִימֵיהֶם בִּימֵי קֶדֶם. אַתָּה, יָדְךָ גּוֹיִם הוֹרַשְׁתָּ, וַתִּטָּעֵם, תָּרַע לְאֻמִּים וַתְּשַׁלְּחֵם. כִּי לֹא בְחַרְבָּם יָרְשׁוּ אָרֶץ, וּזְרוֹעָם לֹא הוֹשִׁיעָה לָּמוֹ, כִּי יְמִינְךָ וּזְרוֹעֲךָ וְאוֹר פָּנֶיךָ כִּי רְצִיתָם. אַתָּה הוּא מַלְכִּי אֱלֹהִים, צַוֵּה יְשׁוּעוֹת יַעֲקֹב. בְּךָ צָרֵינוּ נְנַגֵּחַ, בְּשִׁמְךָ נָבוּס קָמֵינוּ. כִּי לֹא בְקַשְׁתִּי אֶבְטָח, וְחַרְבִּי לֹא תוֹשִׁיעֵנִי. כִּי הוֹשַׁעְתָּנוּ מִצָּרֵינוּ, וּמְשַׂנְאֵינוּ הֱבִישׁוֹתָ. בֵּאלֹהִים הִלַּלְנוּ כָל הַיּוֹם, וְשִׁמְךָ לְעוֹלָם נוֹדֶה סֶלָה. אַף זָנַחְתָּ וַתַּכְלִימֵנוּ, וְלֹא תֵצֵא בְּצִבְאוֹתֵינוּ. תְּשִׁיבֵנוּ אָחוֹר מִנִּי צָר, וּמְשַׂנְאֵינוּ שָׁסוּ לָמוֹ. תִּתְּנֵנוּ כְּצֹאן מַאֲכָל, וּבַגּוֹיִם זֵרִיתָנוּ. תִּמְכֹּר עַמְּךָ בְלֹא הוֹן, וְלֹא רִבִּיתָ בִּמְחִירֵיהֶם. תְּשִׂימֵנוּ חֶרְפָּה לִשְׁכֵנֵינוּ, לַעַג וָקֶלֶס לִסְבִיבוֹתֵינוּ. תְּשִׂימֵנוּ מָשָׁל בַּגּוֹיִם,

מְנוֹד רֹאשׁ בַּלְאֻמִּים. כָּל הַיּוֹם כְּלִמָּתִי נֶגְדִּי, וּבֹשֶׁת פָּנַי כִּסָּתְנִי. מִקּוֹל מְחָרֵף וּמְגַדֵּף, מִפְּנֵי אוֹיֵב וּמִתְנַקֵּם. כָּל זֹאת בָּאַתְנוּ וְלֹא שְׁכַחֲנוּךָ, וְלֹא שִׁקַּרְנוּ בִּבְרִיתֶךָ. לֹא נָסוֹג אָחוֹר לִבֵּנוּ, וַתֵּט אֲשֻׁרֵינוּ מִנִּי אָרְחֶךָ. כִּי דִכִּיתָנוּ בִּמְקוֹם תַּנִּים, וַתְּכַס עָלֵינוּ בְצַלְמָוֶת. אִם שָׁכַחְנוּ שֵׁם אֱלֹהֵינוּ, וַנִּפְרֹשׂ כַּפֵּינוּ לְאֵל זָר. הֲלֹא אֱלֹהִים יַחֲקָר זֹאת, כִּי הוּא יֹדֵעַ תַּעֲלֻמוֹת לֵב. כִּי עָלֶיךָ הֹרַגְנוּ כָל הַיּוֹם נֶחְשַׁבְנוּ כְּצֹאן טִבְחָה. עוּרָה לָמָּה תִישַׁן, אֲדֹנָי, הָקִיצָה אַל תִּזְנַח לָנֶצַח. לָמָּה פָנֶיךָ תַסְתִּיר, תִּשְׁכַּח עָנְיֵנוּ וְלַחֲצֵנוּ. כִּי שָׁחָה לֶעָפָר נַפְשֵׁנוּ, דָּבְקָה לָאָרֶץ בִּטְנֵנוּ. קוּמָה עֶזְרָתָה לָּנוּ, וּפְדֵנוּ לְמַעַן חַסְדֶּךָ.

מה לַמְנַצֵּחַ עַל שֹׁשַׁנִּים לִבְנֵי קֹרַח, מַשְׂכִּיל שִׁיר יְדִידֹת. רָחַשׁ לִבִּי דָּבָר טוֹב, אֹמֵר אָנִי מַעֲשַׂי לְמֶלֶךְ, לְשׁוֹנִי עֵט סוֹפֵר מָהִיר. יָפְיָפִיתָ מִבְּנֵי אָדָם, הוּצַק חֵן בְּשְׂפְתוֹתֶיךָ, עַל כֵּן בֵּרַכְךָ אֱלֹהִים לְעוֹלָם. חֲגוֹר חַרְבְּךָ עַל יָרֵךְ גִּבּוֹר, הוֹדְךָ וַהֲדָרֶךָ. וַהֲדָרְךָ, צְלַח רְכַב עַל דְּבַר אֱמֶת וְעַנְוָה צֶדֶק, וְתוֹרְךָ נוֹרָאוֹת יְמִינֶךָ. חִצֶּיךָ שְׁנוּנִים, עַמִּים תַּחְתֶּיךָ יִפְּלוּ, בְּלֵב אוֹיְבֵי הַמֶּלֶךְ. כִּסְאֲךָ אֱלֹהִים עוֹלָם וָעֶד, שֵׁבֶט מִישֹׁר שֵׁבֶט מַלְכוּתֶךָ. אָהַבְתָּ צֶּדֶק וַתִּשְׂנָא רֶשַׁע, עַל כֵּן מְשָׁחֲךָ אֱלֹהִים אֱלֹהֶיךָ, שֶׁמֶן שָׂשׂוֹן מֵחֲבֵרֶךָ. מֹר וַאֲהָלוֹת קְצִיעוֹת כָּל בִּגְדֹתֶיךָ, מִן הֵיכְלֵי שֵׁן מִנִּי שִׂמְּחוּךָ. בְּנוֹת מְלָכִים בְּיִקְּרוֹתֶיךָ, נִצְּבָה שֵׁגַל לִימִינְךָ בְּכֶתֶם אוֹפִיר. שִׁמְעִי בַת וּרְאִי, וְהַטִּי אָזְנֵךְ, וְשִׁכְחִי עַמֵּךְ וּבֵית אָבִיךְ. וְיִתְאָו הַמֶּלֶךְ יָפְיֵךְ, כִּי הוּא אֲדֹנַיִךְ, וְהִשְׁתַּחֲוִי לוֹ. וּבַת צֹר בְּמִנְחָה פָּנַיִךְ יְחַלּוּ עֲשִׁירֵי עָם. כָּל כְּבוּדָּה בַת מֶלֶךְ פְּנִימָה, מִמִּשְׁבְּצוֹת זָהָב לְבוּשָׁהּ. לִרְקָמוֹת תּוּבַל לַמֶּלֶךְ, בְּתוּלוֹת אַחֲרֶיהָ רֵעוֹתֶיהָ, מוּבָאוֹת לָךְ. תּוּבַלְנָה בִּשְׂמָחֹת וָגִיל, תְּבֹאֶינָה בְּהֵיכַל מֶלֶךְ. תַּחַת אֲבֹתֶיךָ יִהְיוּ בָנֶיךָ, תְּשִׁיתֵמוֹ לְשָׂרִים בְּכָל הָאָרֶץ. אַזְכִּירָה שִׁמְךָ בְּכָל דֹּר וָדֹר, עַל כֵּן עַמִּים יְהוֹדֻךָ לְעֹלָם וָעֶד.

מו לַמְנַצֵּחַ לִבְנֵי קֹרַח, עַל עֲלָמוֹת שִׁיר. אֱלֹהִים לָנוּ מַחֲסֶה וָעֹז, עֶזְרָה בְצָרוֹת נִמְצָא מְאֹד. עַל כֵּן לֹא נִירָא בְּהָמִיר אָרֶץ, וּבְמוֹט הָרִים בְּלֵב יַמִּים. יֶהֱמוּ יֶחְמְרוּ מֵימָיו, יִרְעֲשׁוּ הָרִים בְּגַאֲוָתוֹ סֶלָה. נָהָר פְּלָגָיו יְשַׂמְּחוּ עִיר אֱלֹהִים, קְדֹשׁ מִשְׁכְּנֵי עֶלְיוֹן. אֱלֹהִים בְּקִרְבָּהּ בַּל תִּמּוֹט, יַעְזְרֶהָ אֱלֹהִים לִפְנוֹת בֹּקֶר. הָמוּ גוֹיִם מָטוּ מַמְלָכוֹת, נָתַן בְּקוֹלוֹ תָּמוּג אָרֶץ. יהוה צְבָאוֹת עִמָּנוּ, מִשְׂגָּב לָנוּ אֱלֹהֵי יַעֲקֹב סֶלָה. לְכוּ חֲזוּ מִפְעֲלוֹת יהוה, אֲשֶׁר שָׂם שַׁמּוֹת בָּאָרֶץ. מַשְׁבִּית מִלְחָמוֹת עַד קְצֵה הָאָרֶץ, קֶשֶׁת יְשַׁבֵּר וְקִצֵּץ חֲנִית, עֲגָלוֹת יִשְׂרֹף בָּאֵשׁ. הַרְפּוּ וּדְעוּ כִּי אָנֹכִי אֱלֹהִים, אָרוּם בַּגּוֹיִם, אָרוּם בָּאָרֶץ. יהוה צְבָאוֹת עִמָּנוּ, מִשְׂגָּב לָנוּ אֱלֹהֵי יַעֲקֹב, סֶלָה.

מז לַמְנַצֵּחַ לִבְנֵי קֹרַח מִזְמוֹר. כָּל הָעַמִּים תִּקְעוּ כָף, הָרִיעוּ לֵאלֹהִים בְּקוֹל רִנָּה. כִּי יהוה עֶלְיוֹן נוֹרָא, מֶלֶךְ גָּדוֹל עַל כָּל הָאָרֶץ. יַדְבֵּר עַמִּים תַּחְתֵּינוּ, וּלְאֻמִּים תַּחַת רַגְלֵינוּ. יִבְחַר לָנוּ אֶת נַחֲלָתֵנוּ, אֶת גְּאוֹן יַעֲקֹב אֲשֶׁר אָהֵב סֶלָה. עָלָה אֱלֹהִים בִּתְרוּעָה, יהוה בְּקוֹל שׁוֹפָר. זַמְּרוּ אֱלֹהִים זַמֵּרוּ, זַמְּרוּ לְמַלְכֵּנוּ זַמֵּרוּ. כִּי מֶלֶךְ כָּל הָאָרֶץ אֱלֹהִים, זַמְּרוּ מַשְׂכִּיל. מָלַךְ אֱלֹהִים עַל גּוֹיִם, אֱלֹהִים יָשַׁב עַל כִּסֵּא קָדְשׁוֹ. נְדִיבֵי עַמִּים נֶאֱסָפוּ עַם אֱלֹהֵי אַבְרָהָם, כִּי לֵאלֹהִים מָגִנֵּי אֶרֶץ, מְאֹד נַעֲלָה.

מח שִׁיר מִזְמוֹר לִבְנֵי קֹרַח. גָּדוֹל יהוה וּמְהֻלָּל מְאֹד, בְּעִיר אֱלֹהֵינוּ, הַר קָדְשׁוֹ. יְפֵה נוֹף, מְשׂוֹשׂ כָּל הָאָרֶץ, הַר צִיּוֹן יַרְכְּתֵי צָפוֹן, קִרְיַת מֶלֶךְ רָב. אֱלֹהִים בְּאַרְמְנוֹתֶיהָ נוֹדַע

לְמִשְׂגָּב. כִּי הִנֵּה הַמְּלָכִים נוֹעֲדוּ, עָבְרוּ
יַחְדָּו. הֵמָּה רָאוּ כֵּן תָּמָהוּ, נִבְהֲלוּ
נֶחְפָּזוּ. רְעָדָה אֲחָזָתַם שָׁם, חִיל
כַּיּוֹלֵדָה. בְּרוּחַ קָדִים תְּשַׁבֵּר אֳנִיּוֹת
תַּרְשִׁישׁ. כַּאֲשֶׁר שָׁמַעְנוּ כֵּן רָאִינוּ
בְּעִיר יהוה צְבָאוֹת, בְּעִיר אֱלֹהֵינוּ,
אֱלֹהִים יְכוֹנְנֶהָ עַד עוֹלָם סֶלָה. דִּמִּינוּ
אֱלֹהִים חַסְדֶּךָ, בְּקֶרֶב הֵיכָלֶךָ. כְּשִׁמְךָ
אֱלֹהִים כֵּן תְּהִלָּתְךָ, עַל קַצְוֵי אֶרֶץ,
צֶדֶק מָלְאָה יְמִינֶךָ. יִשְׂמַח הַר צִיּוֹן,
תָּגֵלְנָה בְּנוֹת יְהוּדָה, לְמַעַן מִשְׁפָּטֶיךָ.
סֹבּוּ צִיּוֹן וְהַקִּיפוּהָ, סִפְרוּ מִגְדָּלֶיהָ.
שִׁיתוּ לִבְּכֶם לְחֵילָה, פַּסְּגוּ אַרְמְנוֹתֶיהָ,
לְמַעַן תְּסַפְּרוּ לְדוֹר אַחֲרוֹן. כִּי זֶה
אֱלֹהִים אֱלֹהֵינוּ עוֹלָם וָעֶד, הוּא יְנַהֲגֵנוּ
עַל־מוּת.

9th day — יום ט לחדש

מט לַמְנַצֵּחַ לִבְנֵי קֹרַח מִזְמוֹר.
שִׁמְעוּ זֹאת כָּל הָעַמִּים, הַאֲזִינוּ
כָּל יֹשְׁבֵי חָלֶד. גַּם בְּנֵי אָדָם, גַּם בְּנֵי
אִישׁ, יַחַד עָשִׁיר וְאֶבְיוֹן. פִּי יְדַבֵּר
חָכְמוֹת, וְהָגוּת לִבִּי תְבוּנוֹת. אַטֶּה
לְמָשָׁל אָזְנִי, אֶפְתַּח בְּכִנּוֹר חִידָתִי.
לָמָּה אִירָא בִּימֵי רָע, עֲוֹן עֲקֵבַי יְסוּבֵּנִי.
הַבֹּטְחִים עַל חֵילָם, וּבְרֹב עָשְׁרָם
יִתְהַלָּלוּ. אָח לֹא פָדֹה יִפְדֶּה אִישׁ, לֹא
יִתֵּן לֵאלֹהִים כָּפְרוֹ. וְיֵקַר פִּדְיוֹן נַפְשָׁם,
וְחָדַל לְעוֹלָם. וִיחִי עוֹד לָנֶצַח, לֹא
יִרְאֶה הַשָּׁחַת. כִּי יִרְאֶה חֲכָמִים יָמוּתוּ,
יַחַד כְּסִיל וָבַעַר יֹאבֵדוּ, וְעָזְבוּ
לַאֲחֵרִים חֵילָם. קִרְבָּם בָּתֵּימוֹ לְעוֹלָם,
מִשְׁכְּנֹתָם לְדוֹר וָדֹר, קָרְאוּ בִשְׁמוֹתָם
עֲלֵי אֲדָמוֹת. וְאָדָם בִּיקָר בַּל יָלִין,
נִמְשַׁל כַּבְּהֵמוֹת נִדְמוּ. זֶה דַרְכָּם, כֶּסֶל
לָמוֹ, וְאַחֲרֵיהֶם בְּפִיהֶם יִרְצוּ סֶלָה.
כַּצֹּאן לִשְׁאוֹל שַׁתּוּ, מָוֶת יִרְעֵם, וַיִּרְדּוּ
בָם יְשָׁרִים לַבֹּקֶר, וְצוּרָם לְבַלּוֹת
שְׁאוֹל מִזְּבֻל לוֹ. אַךְ אֱלֹהִים יִפְדֶּה
נַפְשִׁי מִיַּד שְׁאוֹל, כִּי יִקָּחֵנִי סֶלָה. אַל
תִּירָא כִּי יַעֲשִׁר אִישׁ, כִּי יִרְבֶּה כְּבוֹד
בֵּיתוֹ. כִּי לֹא בְמוֹתוֹ יִקַּח הַכֹּל, לֹא יֵרֵד
אַחֲרָיו כְּבוֹדוֹ. כִּי נַפְשׁוֹ בְּחַיָּיו יְבָרֵךְ,
וְיוֹדֻךָ כִּי תֵיטִיב לָךְ. תָּבוֹא עַד דּוֹר
אֲבוֹתָיו, עַד נֵצַח לֹא יִרְאוּ אוֹר. אָדָם
בִּיקָר וְלֹא יָבִין, נִמְשַׁל כַּבְּהֵמוֹת נִדְמוּ.

נ מִזְמוֹר לְאָסָף, אֵל אֱלֹהִים יהוה,
דִּבֶּר וַיִּקְרָא אָרֶץ, מִמִּזְרַח שֶׁמֶשׁ עַד
מְבֹאוֹ. מִצִּיּוֹן מִכְלַל יֹפִי, אֱלֹהִים
הוֹפִיעַ. יָבֹא אֱלֹהֵינוּ וְאַל יֶחֱרַשׁ, אֵשׁ
לְפָנָיו תֹּאכֵל, וּסְבִיבָיו נִשְׂעֲרָה מְאֹד.
יִקְרָא אֶל הַשָּׁמַיִם מֵעָל, וְאֶל הָאָרֶץ
לָדִין עַמּוֹ. אִסְפוּ לִי חֲסִידָי, כֹּרְתֵי
בְרִיתִי עֲלֵי זָבַח. וַיַּגִּידוּ שָׁמַיִם צִדְקוֹ, כִּי
אֱלֹהִים שֹׁפֵט הוּא סֶלָה. שִׁמְעָה עַמִּי
וַאֲדַבֵּרָה, יִשְׂרָאֵל וְאָעִידָה בָּךְ, אֱלֹהִים
אֱלֹהֶיךָ אָנֹכִי. לֹא עַל זְבָחֶיךָ אוֹכִיחֶךָ,
וְעוֹלֹתֶיךָ לְנֶגְדִּי תָמִיד. לֹא אֶקַּח
מִבֵּיתְךָ פָר, מִמִּכְלְאֹתֶיךָ עַתּוּדִים. כִּי
לִי כָל חַיְתוֹ יָעַר, בְּהֵמוֹת בְּהַרְרֵי אָלֶף.
יָדַעְתִּי כָּל עוֹף הָרִים, וְזִיז שָׂדַי עִמָּדִי.
אִם אֶרְעַב לֹא אֹמַר לָךְ, כִּי לִי תֵבֵל
וּמְלֹאָהּ. הַאוֹכַל בְּשַׂר אַבִּירִים, וְדַם
עַתּוּדִים אֶשְׁתֶּה. זְבַח לֵאלֹהִים תּוֹדָה,
וְשַׁלֵּם לְעֶלְיוֹן נְדָרֶיךָ. וּקְרָאֵנִי בְּיוֹם
צָרָה, אֲחַלֶּצְךָ וּתְכַבְּדֵנִי. וְלָרָשָׁע אָמַר
אֱלֹהִים, מַה לְּךָ לְסַפֵּר חֻקָּי, וַתִּשָּׂא
בְרִיתִי עֲלֵי פִיךָ. וְאַתָּה שָׂנֵאתָ מוּסָר,
וַתַּשְׁלֵךְ דְּבָרַי אַחֲרֶיךָ. אִם רָאִיתָ גַנָּב
וַתִּרֶץ עִמּוֹ, וְעִם מְנָאֲפִים חֶלְקֶךָ. פִּיךָ
שָׁלַחְתָּ בְרָעָה, וּלְשׁוֹנְךָ תַּצְמִיד מִרְמָה.
תֵּשֵׁב בְּאָחִיךָ תְדַבֵּר, בְּבֶן אִמְּךָ תִּתֶּן
דֹּפִי. אֵלֶּה עָשִׂיתָ וְהֶחֱרַשְׁתִּי, דִּמִּיתָ
הֱיוֹת אֶהְיֶה כָמוֹךָ, אוֹכִיחֲךָ וְאֶעֶרְכָה
לְעֵינֶיךָ. בִּינוּ נָא זֹאת שֹׁכְחֵי אֱלוֹהַּ, פֶּן
אֶטְרֹף וְאֵין מַצִּיל. זֹבֵחַ תּוֹדָה יְכַבְּדָנְנִי,
וְשָׂם דֶּרֶךְ, אַרְאֶנּוּ בְּיֵשַׁע אֱלֹהִים.

TUESDAY — ליום שלישי

נא לַמְנַצֵּחַ מִזְמוֹר לְדָוִד. בְּבוֹא אֵלָיו
נָתָן הַנָּבִיא, כַּאֲשֶׁר בָּא אֶל בַּת־
שָׁבַע. חָנֵּנִי אֱלֹהִים כְּחַסְדֶּךָ, כְּרֹב
רַחֲמֶיךָ מְחֵה פְשָׁעָי. הֶרֶב כַּבְּסֵנִי

מֵעֲוֺנִי, וּמֵחַטָּאתִי טַהֲרֵנִי. כִּי פְשָׁעַי אֲנִי אֵדָע, וְחַטָּאתִי נֶגְדִּי תָמִיד. לְךָ לְבַדְּךָ חָטָאתִי, וְהָרַע בְּעֵינֶיךָ עָשִׂיתִי, לְמַעַן תִּצְדַּק בְּדָבְרֶךָ, תִּזְכֶּה בְשָׁפְטֶךָ. הֵן בְּעָווֹן חוֹלָלְתִּי, וּבְחֵטְא יֶחֱמַתְנִי אִמִּי. הֵן אֱמֶת חָפַצְתָּ בַטֻּחוֹת, וּבְסָתֻם חָכְמָה תוֹדִיעֵנִי. תְּחַטְּאֵנִי בְאֵזוֹב וְאֶטְהָר, תְּכַבְּסֵנִי וּמִשֶּׁלֶג אַלְבִּין. תַּשְׁמִיעֵנִי שָׂשׂוֹן וְשִׂמְחָה, תָּגֵלְנָה עֲצָמוֹת דִּכִּיתָ. הַסְתֵּר פָּנֶיךָ מֵחֲטָאָי, וְכָל עֲוֺנֹתַי מְחֵה. לֵב טָהוֹר בְּרָא לִי אֱלֹהִים, וְרוּחַ נָכוֹן חַדֵּשׁ בְּקִרְבִּי. אַל תַּשְׁלִיכֵנִי מִלְּפָנֶיךָ, וְרוּחַ קָדְשְׁךָ אַל תִּקַּח מִמֶּנִּי. הָשִׁיבָה לִּי שְׂשׂוֹן יִשְׁעֶךָ, וְרוּחַ נְדִיבָה תִסְמְכֵנִי. אֲלַמְּדָה פֹשְׁעִים דְּרָכֶיךָ, וְחַטָּאִים אֵלֶיךָ יָשׁוּבוּ. הַצִּילֵנִי מִדָּמִים, אֱלֹהִים אֱלֹהֵי תְּשׁוּעָתִי, תְּרַנֵּן לְשׁוֹנִי צִדְקָתֶךָ. אֲדֹנָי שְׂפָתַי תִּפְתָּח, וּפִי יַגִּיד תְּהִלָּתֶךָ. כִּי לֹא תַחְפֹּץ זֶבַח וְאֶתֵּנָה, עוֹלָה לֹא תִרְצֶה. זִבְחֵי אֱלֹהִים רוּחַ נִשְׁבָּרָה, לֵב נִשְׁבָּר וְנִדְכֶּה, אֱלֹהִים לֹא תִבְזֶה. הֵיטִיבָה בִרְצוֹנְךָ אֶת צִיּוֹן, תִּבְנֶה חוֹמוֹת יְרוּשָׁלָיִם. אָז תַּחְפֹּץ זִבְחֵי צֶדֶק, עוֹלָה וְכָלִיל, אָז יַעֲלוּ עַל מִזְבַּחֲךָ פָרִים.

נב לַמְנַצֵּחַ מַשְׂכִּיל לְדָוִד. בְּבוֹא דּוֹאֵג הָאֲדֹמִי וַיַּגֵּד לְשָׁאוּל, וַיֹּאמֶר לוֹ, בָּא דָוִד אֶל בֵּית אֲחִימֶלֶךְ. מַה תִּתְהַלֵּל בְּרָעָה הַגִּבּוֹר, חֶסֶד אֵל כָּל הַיּוֹם. הַוּוֹת תַּחְשֹׁב לְשׁוֹנֶךָ, כְּתַעַר מְלֻטָּשׁ עֹשֵׂה רְמִיָּה. אָהַבְתָּ רָּע מִטּוֹב, שֶׁקֶר מִדַּבֵּר צֶדֶק סֶלָה. אָהַבְתָּ כָל דִּבְרֵי בָלַע לְשׁוֹן מִרְמָה. גַּם אֵל יִתָּצְךָ לָנֶצַח, יַחְתְּךָ וְיִסָּחֲךָ מֵאֹהֶל, וְשֵׁרֶשְׁךָ מֵאֶרֶץ חַיִּים סֶלָה. וְיִרְאוּ צַדִּיקִים וְיִירָאוּ, וְעָלָיו יִשְׂחָקוּ. הִנֵּה הַגֶּבֶר לֹא יָשִׂים אֱלֹהִים מָעוּזּוֹ, וַיִּבְטַח בְּרֹב עָשְׁרוֹ, יָעֹז בְּהַוָּתוֹ. וַאֲנִי כְּזַיִת רַעֲנָן בְּבֵית אֱלֹהִים, בָּטַחְתִּי בְחֶסֶד אֱלֹהִים, עוֹלָם וָעֶד. אוֹדְךָ לְעוֹלָם כִּי עָשִׂיתָ, וַאֲקַוֶּה שִׁמְךָ כִי טוֹב נֶגֶד חֲסִידֶיךָ.

נג לַמְנַצֵּחַ עַל מָחֲלַת מַשְׂכִּיל לְדָוִד. אָמַר נָבָל בְּלִבּוֹ, אֵין אֱלֹהִים, הִשְׁחִיתוּ וְהִתְעִיבוּ עָוֶל, אֵין עֹשֵׂה טוֹב. אֱלֹהִים מִשָּׁמַיִם הִשְׁקִיף עַל בְּנֵי אָדָם, לִרְאוֹת הֲיֵשׁ מַשְׂכִּיל, דֹּרֵשׁ אֶת אֱלֹהִים. כֻּלּוֹ סָג יַחְדָּו נֶאֱלָחוּ, אֵין עֹשֵׂה טוֹב, אֵין גַּם אֶחָד. הֲלֹא יָדְעוּ פֹּעֲלֵי אָוֶן, אֹכְלֵי עַמִּי אָכְלוּ לֶחֶם, אֱלֹהִים לֹא קָרָאוּ. שָׁם פָּחֲדוּ פַחַד לֹא הָיָה פָחַד, כִּי אֱלֹהִים פִּזַּר עַצְמוֹת חֹנָךְ, הֱבִשֹׁתָה, כִּי אֱלֹהִים מְאָסָם. מִי יִתֵּן מִצִּיּוֹן יְשֻׁעוֹת יִשְׂרָאֵל, בְּשׁוּב אֱלֹהִים שְׁבוּת עַמּוֹ, יָגֵל יַעֲקֹב יִשְׂמַח יִשְׂרָאֵל.

נד לַמְנַצֵּחַ בִּנְגִינֹת מַשְׂכִּיל לְדָוִד. בְּבוֹא הַזִּיפִים וַיֹּאמְרוּ לְשָׁאוּל, הֲלֹא דָוִד מִסְתַּתֵּר עִמָּנוּ. אֱלֹהִים בְּשִׁמְךָ הוֹשִׁיעֵנִי, וּבִגְבוּרָתְךָ תְדִינֵנִי. אֱלֹהִים שְׁמַע תְּפִלָּתִי, הַאֲזִינָה לְאִמְרֵי פִי. כִּי זָרִים קָמוּ עָלַי, וְעָרִיצִים בִּקְשׁוּ נַפְשִׁי, לֹא שָׂמוּ אֱלֹהִים לְנֶגְדָּם סֶלָה. הִנֵּה אֱלֹהִים עֹזֵר לִי, אֲדֹנָי בְּסֹמְכֵי נַפְשִׁי. יָשִׁיב הָרַע לְשֹׁרְרָי, בַּאֲמִתְּךָ הַצְמִיתֵם. בִּנְדָבָה אֶזְבְּחָה לָּךְ, אוֹדֶה שִּׁמְךָ יהוה כִּי טוֹב. כִּי מִכָּל צָרָה הִצִּילָנִי, וּבְאֹיְבַי רָאֲתָה עֵינִי.

10th day — יום י לחדש

נה לַמְנַצֵּחַ בִּנְגִינֹת מַשְׂכִּיל לְדָוִד. הַאֲזִינָה אֱלֹהִים תְּפִלָּתִי, וְאַל תִּתְעַלַּם מִתְּחִנָּתִי. הַקְשִׁיבָה לִּי וַעֲנֵנִי, אָרִיד בְּשִׂיחִי וְאָהִימָה. מִקּוֹל אוֹיֵב מִפְּנֵי עָקַת רָשָׁע, כִּי יָמִיטוּ עָלַי אָוֶן, וּבְאַף יִשְׂטְמוּנִי. לִבִּי יָחִיל בְּקִרְבִּי, וְאֵימוֹת מָוֶת נָפְלוּ עָלָי. יִרְאָה וָרַעַד יָבֹא בִי, וַתְּכַסֵּנִי פַּלָּצוּת. וָאֹמַר מִי יִתֶּן לִּי אֵבֶר כַּיּוֹנָה, אָעוּפָה וְאֶשְׁכֹּנָה. הִנֵּה אַרְחִיק נְדֹד, אָלִין בַּמִּדְבָּר סֶלָה. אָחִישָׁה מִפְלָט לִי, מֵרוּחַ סֹעָה מִסָּעַר. בַּלַּע אֲדֹנָי פַּלַּג לְשׁוֹנָם, כִּי רָאִיתִי חָמָס וְרִיב בָּעִיר. יוֹמָם וָלַיְלָה יְסוֹבְבֻהָ עַל

חוֹמֹתֶיהָ, וְאָוֶן וְעָמָל בְּקִרְבָּהּ. הַוּוֹת בְּקִרְבָּהּ, וְלֹא יָמִישׁ מֵרְחֹבָהּ תֹּךְ וּמִרְמָה. כִּי לֹא אוֹיֵב יְחָרְפֵנִי וְאֶשָּׂא, לֹא מְשַׂנְאִי עָלַי הִגְדִּיל, וְאֶסָּתֵר מִמֶּנּוּ. וְאַתָּה, אֱנוֹשׁ כְּעֶרְכִּי, אַלּוּפִי וּמְיֻדָּעִי. אֲשֶׁר יַחְדָּו נַמְתִּיק סוֹד, בְּבֵית אֱלֹהִים נְהַלֵּךְ בְּרָגֶשׁ. יַשִּׁיא מָוֶת עָלֵימוֹ יֵרְדוּ שְׁאוֹל חַיִּים, כִּי רָעוֹת בִּמְגוּרָם בְּקִרְבָּם. אֲנִי אֶל אֱלֹהִים אֶקְרָא, וַיהוה יוֹשִׁיעֵנִי. עֶרֶב וָבֹקֶר וְצָהֳרַיִם אָשִׂיחָה וְאֶהֱמֶה, וַיִּשְׁמַע קוֹלִי. פָּדָה בְשָׁלוֹם נַפְשִׁי מִקֲּרָב לִי, כִּי בְרַבִּים הָיוּ עִמָּדִי. יִשְׁמַע אֵל וְיַעֲנֵם, וְיֹשֵׁב קֶדֶם סֶלָה, אֲשֶׁר אֵין חֲלִיפוֹת לָמוֹ, וְלֹא יָרְאוּ אֱלֹהִים. שָׁלַח יָדָיו בִּשְׁלֹמָיו, חִלֵּל בְּרִיתוֹ. חָלְקוּ מַחְמָאֹת פִּיו וּקְרָב לִבּוֹ, רַכּוּ דְבָרָיו מִשֶּׁמֶן, וְהֵמָּה פְתִחוֹת. הַשְׁלֵךְ עַל יהוה יְהָבְךָ, וְהוּא יְכַלְכְּלֶךָ, לֹא יִתֵּן לְעוֹלָם מוֹט לַצַּדִּיק. וְאַתָּה אֱלֹהִים, תּוֹרִדֵם לִבְאֵר שַׁחַת, אַנְשֵׁי דָמִים וּמִרְמָה לֹא יֶחֱצוּ יְמֵיהֶם, וַאֲנִי אֶבְטַח בָּךְ.

נו לַמְנַצֵּחַ עַל יוֹנַת אֵלֶם רְחֹקִים לְדָוִד מִכְתָּם, בֶּאֱחֹז אֹתוֹ פְלִשְׁתִּים בְּגַת. חָנֵּנִי אֱלֹהִים כִּי שְׁאָפַנִי אֱנוֹשׁ, כָּל הַיּוֹם לֹחֵם יִלְחָצֵנִי. שָׁאֲפוּ שׁוֹרְרַי כָּל הַיּוֹם, כִּי רַבִּים לֹחֲמִים לִי מָרוֹם. יוֹם אִירָא, אֲנִי אֵלֶיךָ אֶבְטָח. בֵּאלֹהִים אֲהַלֵּל דְּבָרוֹ, בֵּאלֹהִים בָּטַחְתִּי לֹא אִירָא, מַה יַּעֲשֶׂה בָשָׂר לִי. כָּל הַיּוֹם דְּבָרַי יְעַצֵּבוּ, עָלַי כָּל מַחְשְׁבֹתָם לָרָע. יָגוּרוּ יִצְפּוֹנוּ, הֵמָּה עֲקֵבַי יִשְׁמֹרוּ, כַּאֲשֶׁר קִוּוּ נַפְשִׁי. עַל אָוֶן פַּלֶּט לָמוֹ, בְּאַף עַמִּים הוֹרֵד אֱלֹהִים. נֹדִי סָפַרְתָּה אָתָּה, שִׂימָה דִמְעָתִי בְנֹאדֶךָ, הֲלֹא בְּסִפְרָתֶךָ. אָז יָשׁוּבוּ אוֹיְבַי אָחוֹר בְּיוֹם אֶקְרָא, זֶה יָדַעְתִּי כִּי אֱלֹהִים לִי. בֵּאלֹהִים אֲהַלֵּל דָּבָר, בַּיהוה אֲהַלֵּל דָּבָר. בֵּאלֹהִים בָּטַחְתִּי לֹא אִירָא, מַה יַּעֲשֶׂה אָדָם לִי. עָלַי אֱלֹהִים נְדָרֶיךָ, אֲשַׁלֵּם תּוֹדֹת לָךְ. כִּי הִצַּלְתָּ נַפְשִׁי מִמָּוֶת, הֲלֹא רַגְלַי מִדֶּחִי, לְהִתְהַלֵּךְ לִפְנֵי אֱלֹהִים בְּאוֹר הַחַיִּים.

נז לַמְנַצֵּחַ אַל תַּשְׁחֵת לְדָוִד מִכְתָּם, בְּבָרְחוֹ מִפְּנֵי שָׁאוּל בַּמְּעָרָה. חָנֵּנִי אֱלֹהִים חָנֵּנִי, כִּי בְךָ חָסָיָה נַפְשִׁי, וּבְצֵל כְּנָפֶיךָ אֶחְסֶה עַד יַעֲבֹר הַוּוֹת. אֶקְרָא לֵאלֹהִים עֶלְיוֹן, לָאֵל גֹּמֵר עָלָי. יִשְׁלַח מִשָּׁמַיִם וְיוֹשִׁיעֵנִי חֵרֵף שֹׁאֲפִי סֶלָה, יִשְׁלַח אֱלֹהִים חַסְדּוֹ וַאֲמִתּוֹ. נַפְשִׁי בְּתוֹךְ לְבָאִם, אֶשְׁכְּבָה לֹהֲטִים, בְּנֵי אָדָם שִׁנֵּיהֶם חֲנִית וְחִצִּים, וּלְשׁוֹנָם חֶרֶב חַדָּה. רוּמָה עַל הַשָּׁמַיִם אֱלֹהִים, עַל כָּל הָאָרֶץ כְּבוֹדֶךָ. רֶשֶׁת הֵכִינוּ לִפְעָמַי, כָּפַף נַפְשִׁי, כָּרוּ לְפָנַי שִׁיחָה, נָפְלוּ בְתוֹכָהּ סֶלָה. נָכוֹן לִבִּי אֱלֹהִים, נָכוֹן לִבִּי, אָשִׁירָה וַאֲזַמֵּרָה. עוּרָה כְבוֹדִי, עוּרָה הַנֵּבֶל וְכִנּוֹר, אָעִירָה שָּׁחַר. אוֹדְךָ בָעַמִּים, אֲדֹנָי, אֲזַמֶּרְךָ בַּלְאֻמִּים. כִּי גָדֹל עַד שָׁמַיִם חַסְדֶּךָ, וְעַד שְׁחָקִים אֲמִתֶּךָ. רוּמָה עַל שָׁמַיִם אֱלֹהִים, עַל כָּל הָאָרֶץ כְּבוֹדֶךָ.

נח לַמְנַצֵּחַ אַל תַּשְׁחֵת לְדָוִד מִכְתָּם. הַאֻמְנָם אֵלֶם צֶדֶק תְּדַבֵּרוּן, מֵישָׁרִים תִּשְׁפְּטוּ בְּנֵי אָדָם. אַף בְּלֵב עוֹלֹת תִּפְעָלוּן, בָּאָרֶץ חֲמַס יְדֵיכֶם תְּפַלֵּסוּן. זֹרוּ רְשָׁעִים מֵרָחֶם, תָּעוּ מִבֶּטֶן דֹּבְרֵי כָזָב. חֲמַת לָמוֹ כִּדְמוּת חֲמַת נָחָשׁ, כְּמוֹ פֶתֶן חֵרֵשׁ יַאְטֵם אָזְנוֹ. אֲשֶׁר לֹא יִשְׁמַע לְקוֹל מְלַחֲשִׁים, חוֹבֵר חֲבָרִים מְחֻכָּם. אֱלֹהִים הֲרָס שִׁנֵּימוֹ בְּפִימוֹ, מַלְתְּעוֹת כְּפִירִים נְתֹץ, יהוה. יִמָּאֲסוּ כְמוֹ מַיִם יִתְהַלְּכוּ לָמוֹ, יִדְרֹךְ חִצָּו כְּמוֹ יִתְמֹלָלוּ. כְּמוֹ שַׁבְּלוּל תֶּמֶס יַהֲלֹךְ, נֵפֶל אֵשֶׁת בַּל חָזוּ שָׁמֶשׁ. בְּטֶרֶם יָבִינוּ סִּירֹתֵיכֶם אָטָד, כְּמוֹ חַי כְּמוֹ חָרוֹן יִשְׂעָרֶנּוּ. יִשְׂמַח צַדִּיק כִּי חָזָה נָקָם, פְּעָמָיו יִרְחַץ בְּדַם הָרָשָׁע. וְיֹאמַר אָדָם, אַךְ פְּרִי לַצַּדִּיק, אַךְ יֵשׁ אֱלֹהִים שֹׁפְטִים בָּאָרֶץ.

נט לַמְנַצֵּחַ אַל תַּשְׁחֵת לְדָוִד מִכְתָּם, בִּשְׁלֹחַ שָׁאוּל, וַיִּשְׁמְרוּ אֶת הַבַּיִת לַהֲמִיתוֹ. הַצִּילֵנִי מֵאֹיְבַי, אֱלֹהָי, מִמִּתְקוֹמְמַי תְּשַׂגְּבֵנִי. הַצִּילֵנִי מִפֹּעֲלֵי אָוֶן, וּמֵאַנְשֵׁי דָמִים הוֹשִׁיעֵנִי. כִּי הִנֵּה אָרְבוּ לְנַפְשִׁי, יָגוּרוּ עָלַי עַזִּים, לֹא פִשְׁעִי וְלֹא חַטָּאתִי, יהוה. בְּלִי עָוֹן יְרֻצוּן וְיִכּוֹנָנוּ, עוּרָה לִקְרָאתִי וּרְאֵה. וְאַתָּה יהוה, אֱלֹהִים צְבָאוֹת אֱלֹהֵי יִשְׂרָאֵל, הָקִיצָה לִפְקֹד כָּל הַגּוֹיִם, אַל תָּחֹן כָּל בֹּגְדֵי אָוֶן סֶלָה. יָשׁוּבוּ לָעֶרֶב, יֶהֱמוּ כַכָּלֶב, וִיסוֹבְבוּ עִיר. הִנֵּה יַבִּיעוּן בְּפִיהֶם, חֲרָבוֹת בְּשִׂפְתוֹתֵיהֶם, כִּי מִי שֹׁמֵעַ. וְאַתָּה יהוה תִּשְׂחַק לָמוֹ, תִּלְעַג לְכָל גּוֹיִם. עֻזּוֹ אֵלֶיךָ אֶשְׁמֹרָה, כִּי אֱלֹהִים מִשְׂגַּבִּי. אֱלֹהֵי חַסְדִּי יְקַדְּמֵנִי, אֱלֹהִים יַרְאֵנִי בְשֹׁרְרָי. אַל תַּהַרְגֵם פֶּן יִשְׁכְּחוּ עַמִּי, הֲנִיעֵמוֹ בְחֵילְךָ וְהוֹרִידֵמוֹ, מָגִנֵּנוּ אֲדֹנָי. חַטַּאת פִּימוֹ דְּבַר שְׂפָתֵימוֹ, וְיִלָּכְדוּ בִגְאוֹנָם, וּמֵאָלָה וּמִכַּחַשׁ יְסַפֵּרוּ. כַּלֵּה בְחֵמָה כַּלֵּה וְאֵינֵמוֹ, וְיֵדְעוּ כִּי אֱלֹהִים מֹשֵׁל בְּיַעֲקֹב, לְאַפְסֵי הָאָרֶץ סֶלָה. וְיָשֻׁבוּ לָעֶרֶב, יֶהֱמוּ כַכָּלֶב, וִיסוֹבְבוּ עִיר. הֵמָּה יְנִיעוּן לֶאֱכֹל, אִם לֹא יִשְׂבְּעוּ וַיָּלִינוּ. וַאֲנִי אָשִׁיר עֻזֶּךָ, וַאֲרַנֵּן לַבֹּקֶר חַסְדֶּךָ, כִּי הָיִיתָ מִשְׂגָּב לִי, וּמָנוֹס בְּיוֹם צַר לִי. עֻזִּי אֵלֶיךָ אֲזַמֵּרָה, כִּי אֱלֹהִים מִשְׂגַּבִּי אֱלֹהֵי חַסְדִּי.

11th day — יום יא לחדש

ס לַמְנַצֵּחַ עַל שׁוּשַׁן עֵדוּת, מִכְתָּם לְדָוִד לְלַמֵּד. בְּהַצּוֹתוֹ אֶת אֲרַם נַהֲרַיִם וְאֶת אֲרַם צוֹבָה, וַיָּשָׁב יוֹאָב וַיַּךְ אֶת אֱדוֹם בְּגֵיא מֶלַח, שְׁנֵים עָשָׂר אָלֶף. אֱלֹהִים זְנַחְתָּנוּ פְרַצְתָּנוּ, אָנַפְתָּ תְּשׁוֹבֵב לָנוּ. הִרְעַשְׁתָּה אֶרֶץ, פְּצַמְתָּהּ, רְפָה שְׁבָרֶיהָ כִי מָטָה. הִרְאִיתָ עַמְּךָ קָשָׁה, הִשְׁקִיתָנוּ יַיִן תַּרְעֵלָה. נָתַתָּה לִּירֵאֶיךָ נֵּס לְהִתְנוֹסֵס, מִפְּנֵי קֹשֶׁט, סֶלָה. לְמַעַן יֵחָלְצוּן יְדִידֶיךָ הוֹשִׁיעָה יְמִינְךָ וַעֲנֵנִי. אֱלֹהִים דִּבֶּר בְּקָדְשׁוֹ, אֶעְלֹזָה, אֲחַלְּקָה שְׁכֶם, וְעֵמֶק סֻכּוֹת אֲמַדֵּד. לִי גִלְעָד וְלִי מְנַשֶּׁה, וְאֶפְרַיִם מָעוֹז רֹאשִׁי, יְהוּדָה מְחֹקְקִי. מוֹאָב סִיר רַחְצִי, עַל אֱדוֹם אַשְׁלִיךְ נַעֲלִי, עָלַי פְּלֶשֶׁת הִתְרוֹעָעִי. מִי יֹבִלֵנִי עִיר מָצוֹר, מִי נָחַנִי עַד אֱדוֹם. הֲלֹא אַתָּה אֱלֹהִים זְנַחְתָּנוּ, וְלֹא תֵצֵא אֱלֹהִים בְּצִבְאוֹתֵינוּ. הָבָה לָּנוּ עֶזְרָת מִצָּר, וְשָׁוְא תְּשׁוּעַת אָדָם. בֵּאלֹהִים נַעֲשֶׂה חָיִל, וְהוּא יָבוּס צָרֵינוּ.

סא לַמְנַצֵּחַ עַל נְגִינַת לְדָוִד. שִׁמְעָה אֱלֹהִים רִנָּתִי, הַקְשִׁיבָה תְּפִלָּתִי. מִקְצֵה הָאָרֶץ אֵלֶיךָ אֶקְרָא בַּעֲטֹף לִבִּי, בְּצוּר יָרוּם מִמֶּנִּי תַנְחֵנִי. כִּי הָיִיתָ מַחְסֶה לִי, מִגְדַּל עֹז מִפְּנֵי אוֹיֵב. אָגוּרָה בְאָהָלְךָ עוֹלָמִים, אֶחֱסֶה בְסֵתֶר כְּנָפֶיךָ סֶּלָה. כִּי אַתָּה אֱלֹהִים שָׁמַעְתָּ לִנְדָרָי, נָתַתָּ יְרֻשַּׁת יִרְאֵי שְׁמֶךָ. יָמִים עַל יְמֵי מֶלֶךְ תּוֹסִיף, שְׁנוֹתָיו כְּמוֹ דֹר וָדֹר. יֵשֵׁב עוֹלָם לִפְנֵי אֱלֹהִים, חֶסֶד וֶאֱמֶת מַן יִנְצְרֻהוּ. כֵּן אֲזַמְּרָה שִׁמְךָ לָעַד, לְשַׁלְּמִי נְדָרַי יוֹם יוֹם.

סב לַמְנַצֵּחַ עַל יְדוּתוּן מִזְמוֹר לְדָוִד. אַךְ אֶל אֱלֹהִים דּוּמִיָּה נַפְשִׁי, מִמֶּנּוּ יְשׁוּעָתִי. אַךְ הוּא צוּרִי וִישׁוּעָתִי, מִשְׂגַּבִּי לֹא אֶמּוֹט רַבָּה. עַד אָנָה תְּהוֹתְתוּ עַל אִישׁ, תְּרָצְּחוּ כֻלְּכֶם, כְּקִיר נָטוּי, גָּדֵר הַדְּחוּיָה. אַךְ מִשְּׂאֵתוֹ יָעֲצוּ לְהַדִּיחַ יִרְצוּ כָזָב, בְּפִיו יְבָרֵכוּ, וּבְקִרְבָּם יְקַלְלוּ סֶלָה. אַךְ לֵאלֹהִים דּוֹמִּי נַפְשִׁי, כִּי מִמֶּנּוּ תִּקְוָתִי. אַךְ הוּא צוּרִי וִישׁוּעָתִי, מִשְׂגַּבִּי לֹא אֶמּוֹט. עַל אֱלֹהִים יִשְׁעִי וּכְבוֹדִי, צוּר עֻזִּי מַחְסִי בֵּאלֹהִים. בִּטְחוּ בוֹ בְכָל עֵת עָם, שִׁפְכוּ לְפָנָיו לְבַבְכֶם, אֱלֹהִים מַחֲסֶה לָּנוּ סֶלָה. אַךְ הֶבֶל בְּנֵי אָדָם כָּזָב בְּנֵי אִישׁ, בְּמֹאזְנַיִם לַעֲלוֹת, הֵמָּה מֵהֶבֶל יָחַד. אַל תִּבְטְחוּ בְעֹשֶׁק, וּבְגָזֵל אַל תֶּהְבָּלוּ, חַיִל כִּי יָנוּב, אַל תָּשִׁיתוּ לֵב. אַחַת דִּבֶּר אֱלֹהִים, שְׁתַּיִם זוּ שָׁמָעְתִּי, כִּי עֹז לֵאלֹהִים. וּלְךָ אֲדֹנָי חָסֶד, כִּי אַתָּה

תְשַׁלֵּם לְאִישׁ כְּמַעֲשֵׂהוּ.

סג מִזְמוֹר לְדָוִד, בִּהְיוֹתוֹ בְּמִדְבַּר יְהוּדָה. אֱלֹהִים אֵלִי אַתָּה אֲשַׁחֲרֶךָּ, צָמְאָה לְךָ נַפְשִׁי, כָּמַהּ לְךָ בְשָׂרִי, בְּאֶרֶץ צִיָּה וְעָיֵף בְּלִי מָיִם. כֵּן בַּקֹּדֶשׁ חֲזִיתִךָ, לִרְאוֹת עֻזְּךָ וּכְבוֹדֶךָ. כִּי טוֹב חַסְדְּךָ מֵחַיִּים, שְׂפָתַי יְשַׁבְּחוּנְךָ. כֵּן אֲבָרֶכְךָ בְחַיָּי, בְּשִׁמְךָ אֶשָּׂא כַפָּי. כְּמוֹ חֵלֶב וָדֶשֶׁן תִּשְׂבַּע נַפְשִׁי, וְשִׂפְתֵי רְנָנוֹת יְהַלֶּל פִּי. אִם זְכַרְתִּיךָ עַל יְצוּעָי, בְּאַשְׁמֻרוֹת אֶהְגֶּה בָּךְ. כִּי הָיִיתָ עֶזְרָתָה לִּי, וּבְצֵל כְּנָפֶיךָ אֲרַנֵּן. דָּבְקָה נַפְשִׁי אַחֲרֶיךָ, בִּי תָּמְכָה יְמִינֶךָ. וְהֵמָּה לְשׁוֹאָה יְבַקְשׁוּ נַפְשִׁי, יָבֹאוּ בְּתַחְתִּיּוֹת הָאָרֶץ. יַגִּירֻהוּ עַל יְדֵי חָרֶב, מְנָת שֻׁעָלִים יִהְיוּ. וְהַמֶּלֶךְ יִשְׂמַח בֵּאלֹהִים, יִתְהַלֵּל כָּל הַנִּשְׁבָּע בּוֹ, כִּי יִסָּכֵר פִּי דוֹבְרֵי שָׁקֶר.

סד לַמְנַצֵּחַ מִזְמוֹר לְדָוִד. שְׁמַע אֱלֹהִים קוֹלִי בְשִׂיחִי, מִפַּחַד אוֹיֵב תִּצֹּר חַיָּי. תַּסְתִּירֵנִי מִסּוֹד מְרֵעִים, מֵרִגְשַׁת פֹּעֲלֵי אָוֶן. אֲשֶׁר שָׁנְנוּ כַחֶרֶב לְשׁוֹנָם, דָּרְכוּ חִצָּם דָּבָר מָר. לִירוֹת בַּמִּסְתָּרִים תָּם, פִּתְאֹם יֹרֻהוּ וְלֹא יִירָאוּ. יְחַזְּקוּ לָמוֹ דָּבָר רָע, יְסַפְּרוּ לִטְמוֹן מוֹקְשִׁים, אָמְרוּ, מִי יִרְאֶה לָּמוֹ. יַחְפְּשׂוּ עוֹלֹת, תַּמְנוּ חֵפֶשׂ מְחֻפָּשׂ, וְקֶרֶב אִישׁ וְלֵב עָמֹק. וַיֹּרֵם אֱלֹהִים חֵץ פִּתְאוֹם, הָיוּ מַכּוֹתָם. וַיַּכְשִׁילֻהוּ עָלֵימוֹ לְשׁוֹנָם, יִתְנוֹדְדוּ כָּל רֹאֵה בָם. וַיִּירְאוּ כָּל אָדָם, וַיַּגִּידוּ פֹּעַל אֱלֹהִים, וּמַעֲשֵׂהוּ הִשְׂכִּילוּ. יִשְׂמַח צַדִּיק בַּיהוה וְחָסָה בוֹ, וְיִתְהַלְלוּ כָּל יִשְׁרֵי לֵב.

סה לַמְנַצֵּחַ מִזְמוֹר לְדָוִד שִׁיר. לְךָ דֻמִיָּה תְהִלָּה, אֱלֹהִים בְּצִיּוֹן, וּלְךָ יְשֻׁלַּם נֶדֶר. שֹׁמֵעַ תְּפִלָּה, עָדֶיךָ כָּל בָּשָׂר יָבֹאוּ. דִּבְרֵי עֲוֹנֹת גָּבְרוּ מֶנִּי, פְּשָׁעֵינוּ אַתָּה תְכַפְּרֵם. אַשְׁרֵי תִּבְחַר וּתְקָרֵב יִשְׁכֹּן חֲצֵרֶיךָ, נִשְׂבְּעָה בְּטוּב בֵּיתֶךָ, קְדֹשׁ הֵיכָלֶךָ. נוֹרָאוֹת בְּצֶדֶק תַּעֲנֵנוּ אֱלֹהֵי יִשְׁעֵנוּ, מִבְטָח כָּל קַצְוֵי אֶרֶץ וְיָם רְחֹקִים. מֵכִין הָרִים בְּכֹחוֹ, נֶאְזָר בִּגְבוּרָה. מַשְׁבִּיחַ שְׁאוֹן יַמִּים, שְׁאוֹן גַּלֵּיהֶם, וַהֲמוֹן לְאֻמִּים. וַיִּירְאוּ יֹשְׁבֵי קְצָוֹת מֵאוֹתֹתֶיךָ, מוֹצָאֵי בֹקֶר וָעֶרֶב תַּרְנִין. פָּקַדְתָּ הָאָרֶץ וַתְּשֹׁקְקֶהָ, רַבַּת תַּעְשְׁרֶנָּה פֶּלֶג אֱלֹהִים מָלֵא מָיִם, תָּכִין דְּגָנָם כִּי כֵן תְּכִינֶהָ. תְּלָמֶיהָ רַוֵּה נַחֵת גְּדוּדֶהָ, בִּרְבִיבִים תְּמֹגְגֶנָּה צִמְחָהּ תְּבָרֵךְ. עִטַּרְתָּ שְׁנַת טוֹבָתֶךָ, וּמַעְגָּלֶיךָ יִרְעֲפוּן דָּשֶׁן. יִרְעֲפוּ נְאוֹת מִדְבָּר, וְגִיל גְּבָעוֹת תַּחְגֹּרְנָה. לָבְשׁוּ כָרִים הַצֹּאן, וַעֲמָקִים יַעַטְפוּ בָר, יִתְרוֹעֲעוּ אַף יָשִׁירוּ.

12th day — יום יב לחדש

סו לַמְנַצֵּחַ שִׁיר מִזְמוֹר, הָרִיעוּ לֵאלֹהִים כָּל הָאָרֶץ. זַמְּרוּ כְבוֹד שְׁמוֹ, שִׂימוּ כָבוֹד תְּהִלָּתוֹ. אִמְרוּ לֵאלֹהִים, מַה נּוֹרָא מַעֲשֶׂיךָ, בְּרֹב עֻזְּךָ יְכַחֲשׁוּ לְךָ אֹיְבֶיךָ. כָּל הָאָרֶץ יִשְׁתַּחֲווּ לְךָ וִיזַמְּרוּ לָךְ, יְזַמְּרוּ שִׁמְךָ סֶלָה. לְכוּ וּרְאוּ מִפְעֲלוֹת אֱלֹהִים, נוֹרָא עֲלִילָה עַל בְּנֵי אָדָם. הָפַךְ יָם לְיַבָּשָׁה, בַּנָּהָר יַעַבְרוּ בְרָגֶל, שָׁם נִשְׂמְחָה בּוֹ. מֹשֵׁל בִּגְבוּרָתוֹ עוֹלָם, עֵינָיו בַּגּוֹיִם תִּצְפֶּינָה, הַסּוֹרְרִים אַל יָרוּמוּ לָמוֹ סֶלָה. בָּרְכוּ עַמִּים, אֱלֹהֵינוּ, וְהַשְׁמִיעוּ קוֹל תְּהִלָּתוֹ. הַשָּׂם נַפְשֵׁנוּ בַּחַיִּים, וְלֹא נָתַן לַמּוֹט רַגְלֵנוּ. כִּי בְחַנְתָּנוּ אֱלֹהִים, צְרַפְתָּנוּ כִּצְרָף כָּסֶף. הֲבֵאתָנוּ בַמְּצוּדָה, שַׂמְתָּ מוּעָקָה בְמָתְנֵינוּ. הִרְכַּבְתָּ אֱנוֹשׁ לְרֹאשֵׁנוּ, בָּאנוּ בָאֵשׁ וּבַמַּיִם, וַתּוֹצִיאֵנוּ לָרְוָיָה. אָבוֹא בֵיתְךָ בְעוֹלוֹת, אֲשַׁלֵּם לְךָ נְדָרָי. אֲשֶׁר פָּצוּ שְׂפָתָי, וְדִבֶּר פִּי בַּצַּר לִי. עֹלוֹת מֵחִים אַעֲלֶה לָּךְ, עִם קְטֹרֶת אֵילִים, אֶעֱשֶׂה בָקָר עִם עַתּוּדִים סֶלָה. לְכוּ שִׁמְעוּ וַאֲסַפְּרָה כָּל יִרְאֵי אֱלֹהִים, אֲשֶׁר עָשָׂה לְנַפְשִׁי. אֵלָיו פִּי קָרָאתִי, וְרוֹמַם תַּחַת לְשׁוֹנִי. אָוֶן אִם רָאִיתִי בְלִבִּי, לֹא יִשְׁמַע, אֲדֹנָי. אָכֵן שָׁמַע אֱלֹהִים, הִקְשִׁיב בְּקוֹל תְּפִלָּתִי. בָּרוּךְ אֱלֹהִים, אֲשֶׁר לֹא הֵסִיר תְּפִלָּתִי וְחַסְדּוֹ מֵאִתִּי.

סז לַמְנַצֵּחַ בִּנְגִינֹת מִזְמוֹר שִׁיר. אֱלֹהִים יְחָנֵּנוּ וִיבָרְכֵנוּ, יָאֵר פָּנָיו אִתָּנוּ סֶלָה. לָדַעַת בָּאָרֶץ דַּרְכֶּךָ, בְּכָל גּוֹיִם יְשׁוּעָתֶךָ. יוֹדוּךָ עַמִּים, אֱלֹהִים, יוֹדוּךָ עַמִּים כֻּלָּם. יִשְׂמְחוּ וִירַנְּנוּ לְאֻמִּים, כִּי תִשְׁפֹּט עַמִּים מִישֹׁר, וּלְאֻמִּים בָּאָרֶץ תַּנְחֵם סֶלָה. יוֹדוּךָ עַמִּים, אֱלֹהִים, יוֹדוּךָ עַמִּים כֻּלָּם. אֶרֶץ נָתְנָה יְבוּלָהּ, יְבָרְכֵנוּ אֱלֹהִים אֱלֹהֵינוּ. יְבָרְכֵנוּ אֱלֹהִים, וְיִירְאוּ אוֹתוֹ כָּל אַפְסֵי אָרֶץ.

סח לַמְנַצֵּחַ לְדָוִד מִזְמוֹר שִׁיר. יָקוּם אֱלֹהִים יָפוּצוּ אוֹיְבָיו, וְיָנוּסוּ מְשַׂנְאָיו מִפָּנָיו. כְּהִנְדֹּף עָשָׁן תִּנְדֹּף, כְּהִמֵּס דּוֹנַג מִפְּנֵי אֵשׁ, יֹאבְדוּ רְשָׁעִים מִפְּנֵי אֱלֹהִים. וְצַדִּיקִים יִשְׂמְחוּ, יַעַלְצוּ לִפְנֵי אֱלֹהִים, וְיָשִׂישׂוּ בְשִׂמְחָה. שִׁירוּ לֵאלֹהִים זַמְּרוּ שְׁמוֹ, סֹלּוּ לָרֹכֵב בָּעֲרָבוֹת בְּיָהּ שְׁמוֹ, וְעִלְזוּ לְפָנָיו. אֲבִי יְתוֹמִים וְדַיַּן אַלְמָנוֹת, אֱלֹהִים בִּמְעוֹן קָדְשׁוֹ. אֱלֹהִים מוֹשִׁיב יְחִידִים בַּיְתָה, מוֹצִיא אֲסִירִים בַּכּוֹשָׁרוֹת, אַךְ סוֹרְרִים שָׁכְנוּ צְחִיחָה. אֱלֹהִים בְּצֵאתְךָ לִפְנֵי עַמֶּךָ, בְּצַעְדְּךָ בִישִׁימוֹן סֶלָה. אֶרֶץ רָעָשָׁה, אַף שָׁמַיִם נָטְפוּ מִפְּנֵי אֱלֹהִים, זֶה סִינַי, מִפְּנֵי אֱלֹהִים אֱלֹהֵי יִשְׂרָאֵל. גֶּשֶׁם נְדָבוֹת תָּנִיף אֱלֹהִים, נַחֲלָתְךָ וְנִלְאָה אַתָּה כוֹנַנְתָּהּ. חַיָּתְךָ יָשְׁבוּ בָהּ, תָּכִין בְּטוֹבָתְךָ לֶעָנִי, אֱלֹהִים. אֲדֹנָי יִתֶּן אֹמֶר, הַמְבַשְּׂרוֹת צָבָא רָב. מַלְכֵי צְבָאוֹת יִדֹּדוּן יִדֹּדוּן, וּנְוַת בַּיִת תְּחַלֵּק שָׁלָל. אִם תִּשְׁכְּבוּן בֵּין שְׁפַתָּיִם, כַּנְפֵי יוֹנָה נֶחְפָּה בַכֶּסֶף, וְאֶבְרוֹתֶיהָ בִּירַקְרַק חָרוּץ. בְּפָרֵשׂ שַׁדַּי מְלָכִים, בָּהּ תַּשְׁלֵג בְּצַלְמוֹן. הַר אֱלֹהִים הַר בָּשָׁן, הַר גַּבְנֻנִּים הַר בָּשָׁן. לָמָּה תְּרַצְּדוּן הָרִים גַּבְנֻנִּים, הָהָר חָמַד אֱלֹהִים לְשִׁבְתּוֹ, אַף יהוה יִשְׁכֹּן לָנֶצַח. רֶכֶב אֱלֹהִים רִבֹּתַיִם אַלְפֵי שִׁנְאָן, אֲדֹנָי בָם סִינַי בַּקֹּדֶשׁ. עָלִיתָ לַמָּרוֹם, שָׁבִיתָ שֶּׁבִי, לָקַחְתָּ מַתָּנוֹת בָּאָדָם, וְאַף סוֹרְרִים לִשְׁכֹּן, יָהּ אֱלֹהִים. בָּרוּךְ אֲדֹנָי יוֹם יוֹם, יַעֲמָס לָנוּ הָאֵל יְשׁוּעָתֵנוּ סֶלָה. הָאֵל לָנוּ אֵל לְמוֹשָׁעוֹת, וְלֵיהוִֹה אֲדֹנָי, לַמָּוֶת תּוֹצָאוֹת. אַךְ אֱלֹהִים יִמְחַץ רֹאשׁ אֹיְבָיו, קָדְקֹד שֵׂעָר, מִתְהַלֵּךְ בַּאֲשָׁמָיו. אָמַר אֲדֹנָי, מִבָּשָׁן אָשִׁיב, אָשִׁיב מִמְּצֻלוֹת יָם. לְמַעַן תִּמְחַץ רַגְלְךָ בְּדָם, לְשׁוֹן כְּלָבֶיךָ, מֵאֹיְבִים מִנֵּהוּ. רָאוּ הֲלִיכוֹתֶיךָ אֱלֹהִים, הֲלִיכוֹת אֵלִי מַלְכִּי בַקֹּדֶשׁ. קִדְּמוּ שָׁרִים אַחַר נֹגְנִים, בְּתוֹךְ עֲלָמוֹת תּוֹפֵפוֹת. בְּמַקְהֵלוֹת בָּרְכוּ אֱלֹהִים, אֲדֹנָי מִמְּקוֹר יִשְׂרָאֵל. שָׁם בִּנְיָמִן צָעִיר רֹדֵם, שָׂרֵי יְהוּדָה רִגְמָתָם, שָׂרֵי זְבֻלוּן שָׂרֵי נַפְתָּלִי. צִוָּה אֱלֹהֶיךָ עֻזֶּךָ, עוּזָּה אֱלֹהִים, זוּ פָּעַלְתָּ לָּנוּ. מֵהֵיכָלֶךָ עַל יְרוּשָׁלָיִם, לְךָ יוֹבִילוּ מְלָכִים שָׁי. גְּעַר חַיַּת קָנֶה, עֲדַת אַבִּירִים בְּעֶגְלֵי עַמִּים, מִתְרַפֵּס בְּרַצֵּי כָסֶף, בִּזַּר עַמִּים קְרָבוֹת יֶחְפָּצוּ. יֶאֱתָיוּ חַשְׁמַנִּים מִנִּי מִצְרָיִם, כּוּשׁ תָּרִיץ יָדָיו לֵאלֹהִים. מַמְלְכוֹת הָאָרֶץ שִׁירוּ לֵאלֹהִים, זַמְּרוּ אֲדֹנָי סֶלָה. לָרֹכֵב בִּשְׁמֵי שְׁמֵי קֶדֶם, הֵן יִתֵּן בְּקוֹלוֹ קוֹל עֹז. תְּנוּ עֹז לֵאלֹהִים, עַל יִשְׂרָאֵל גַּאֲוָתוֹ, וְעֻזּוֹ בַּשְּׁחָקִים. נוֹרָא אֱלֹהִים מִמִּקְדָּשֶׁיךָ, אֵל יִשְׂרָאֵל הוּא נֹתֵן עֹז וְתַעֲצֻמוֹת לָעָם, בָּרוּךְ אֱלֹהִים.

13th day — יום יג לחדש

סט לַמְנַצֵּחַ עַל שׁוֹשַׁנִּים לְדָוִד. הוֹשִׁיעֵנִי אֱלֹהִים, כִּי בָאוּ מַיִם עַד נָפֶשׁ. טָבַעְתִּי בִּיוֵן מְצוּלָה וְאֵין מָעֳמָד, בָּאתִי בְמַעֲמַקֵּי מַיִם וְשִׁבֹּלֶת שְׁטָפָתְנִי. יָגַעְתִּי בְקָרְאִי, נִחַר גְּרוֹנִי, כָּלוּ עֵינַי, מְיַחֵל לֵאלֹהָי. רַבּוּ מִשַּׂעֲרוֹת רֹאשִׁי שֹׂנְאַי חִנָּם, עָצְמוּ מַצְמִיתַי, אֹיְבַי שֶׁקֶר, אֲשֶׁר לֹא גָזַלְתִּי אָז אָשִׁיב. אֱלֹהִים, אַתָּה יָדַעְתָּ לְאִוַּלְתִּי, וְאַשְׁמוֹתַי מִמְּךָ לֹא נִכְחָדוּ. אַל יֵבֹשׁוּ בִי קֹוֶיךָ, אֲדֹנָי יֱהֹוִה צְבָאוֹת, אַל יִכָּלְמוּ בִי מְבַקְשֶׁיךָ, אֱלֹהֵי יִשְׂרָאֵל. כִּי עָלֶיךָ נָשָׂאתִי חֶרְפָּה, כִּסְּתָה כְלִמָּה פָנָי.

מוּזָר הָיִיתִי לְאֶחָי, וְנָכְרִי לִבְנֵי אִמִּי. כִּי קִנְאַת בֵּיתְךָ אֲכָלָתְנִי, וְחֶרְפּוֹת חוֹרְפֶיךָ נָפְלוּ עָלָי. וָאֶבְכֶּה בַצּוֹם נַפְשִׁי, וַתְּהִי לַחֲרָפוֹת לִי. וָאֶתְּנָה לְבוּשִׁי שָׂק, וָאֱהִי לָהֶם לְמָשָׁל. יָשִׂיחוּ בִי יֹשְׁבֵי שָׁעַר, וּנְגִינוֹת שׁוֹתֵי שֵׁכָר. וַאֲנִי, תְפִלָּתִי לְךָ יהוה, עֵת רָצוֹן, אֱלֹהִים בְּרָב חַסְדֶּךָ, עֲנֵנִי בֶּאֱמֶת יִשְׁעֶךָ. הַצִּילֵנִי מִטִּיט וְאַל אֶטְבָּעָה, אִנָּצְלָה מִשֹּׂנְאַי וּמִמַּעֲמַקֵּי מָיִם. אַל תִּשְׁטְפֵנִי שִׁבֹּלֶת מַיִם, וְאַל תִּבְלָעֵנִי מְצוּלָה, וְאַל תֶּאְטַר עָלַי בְּאֵר פִּיהָ. עֲנֵנִי יהוה כִּי טוֹב חַסְדֶּךָ, כְּרֹב רַחֲמֶיךָ פְּנֵה אֵלָי. וְאַל תַּסְתֵּר פָּנֶיךָ מֵעַבְדֶּךָ, כִּי צַר לִי מַהֵר עֲנֵנִי. קָרְבָה אֶל נַפְשִׁי גְאָלָהּ, לְמַעַן אֹיְבַי פְּדֵנִי. אַתָּה יָדַעְתָּ חֶרְפָּתִי וּבָשְׁתִּי וּכְלִמָּתִי, נֶגְדְּךָ כָּל צוֹרְרָי. חֶרְפָּה שָׁבְרָה לִבִּי וָאָנוּשָׁה, וָאֲקַוֶּה לָנוּד וָאַיִן, וְלַמְנַחֲמִים וְלֹא מָצָאתִי. וַיִּתְּנוּ בְּבָרוּתִי רֹאשׁ, וְלִצְמָאִי יַשְׁקוּנִי חֹמֶץ. יְהִי שֻׁלְחָנָם לִפְנֵיהֶם לְפָח, וְלִשְׁלוֹמִים לְמוֹקֵשׁ. תֶּחְשַׁכְנָה עֵינֵיהֶם מֵרְאוֹת, וּמָתְנֵיהֶם תָּמִיד הַמְעַד. שְׁפָךְ עֲלֵיהֶם זַעְמֶךָ, וַחֲרוֹן אַפְּךָ יַשִּׂיגֵם. תְּהִי טִירָתָם נְשַׁמָּה, בְּאָהֳלֵיהֶם אַל יְהִי יֹשֵׁב. כִּי אַתָּה אֲשֶׁר הִכִּיתָ רָדָפוּ, וְאֶל מַכְאוֹב חֲלָלֶיךָ יְסַפֵּרוּ. תְּנָה עָוֹן עַל עֲוֹנָם, וְאַל יָבֹאוּ בְּצִדְקָתֶךָ. יִמָּחוּ מִסֵּפֶר חַיִּים, וְעִם צַדִּיקִים אַל יִכָּתֵבוּ. וַאֲנִי עָנִי וְכוֹאֵב, יְשׁוּעָתְךָ אֱלֹהִים תְּשַׂגְּבֵנִי. אֲהַלְלָה שֵׁם אֱלֹהִים בְּשִׁיר, וַאֲגַדְּלֶנּוּ בְתוֹדָה. וְתִיטַב לַיהוה מִשּׁוֹר פָּר מַקְרִן מַפְרִיס. רָאוּ עֲנָוִים יִשְׂמָחוּ, דֹּרְשֵׁי אֱלֹהִים, וִיחִי לְבַבְכֶם. כִּי שֹׁמֵעַ אֶל אֶבְיוֹנִים, יהוה, וְאֶת אֲסִירָיו לֹא בָזָה. יְהַלְלוּהוּ שָׁמַיִם וָאָרֶץ, יַמִּים וְכָל רֹמֵשׂ בָּם. כִּי אֱלֹהִים יוֹשִׁיעַ צִיּוֹן, וְיִבְנֶה עָרֵי יְהוּדָה, וְיָשְׁבוּ שָׁם וִירֵשׁוּהָ. וְזֶרַע עֲבָדָיו יִנְחָלוּהָ, וְאֹהֲבֵי שְׁמוֹ יִשְׁכְּנוּ בָהּ.

ע לַמְנַצֵּחַ לְדָוִד לְהַזְכִּיר. אֱלֹהִים לְהַצִּילֵנִי, יהוה לְעֶזְרָתִי חוּשָׁה. יֵבֹשׁוּ וְיַחְפְּרוּ מְבַקְשֵׁי נַפְשִׁי, יִסֹּגוּ אָחוֹר וְיִכָּלְמוּ, חֲפֵצֵי רָעָתִי. יָשׁוּבוּ עַל עֵקֶב בָּשְׁתָּם, הָאֹמְרִים הֶאָח הֶאָח. יָשִׂישׂוּ וְיִשְׂמְחוּ בְּךָ כָּל מְבַקְשֶׁיךָ, וְיֹאמְרוּ תָמִיד, יִגְדַּל אֱלֹהִים, אֹהֲבֵי יְשׁוּעָתֶךָ. וַאֲנִי עָנִי וְאֶבְיוֹן, אֱלֹהִים חוּשָׁה לִּי, עֶזְרִי וּמְפַלְטִי אַתָּה, יהוה, אַל תְּאַחַר.

עא בְּךָ יהוה חָסִיתִי, אַל אֵבוֹשָׁה לְעוֹלָם. בְּצִדְקָתְךָ תַּצִּילֵנִי וּתְפַלְּטֵנִי, הַטֵּה אֵלַי אָזְנְךָ וְהוֹשִׁיעֵנִי. הֱיֵה לִי לְצוּר מָעוֹן לָבוֹא תָּמִיד, צִוִּיתָ לְהוֹשִׁיעֵנִי, כִּי סַלְעִי וּמְצוּדָתִי אָתָּה. אֱלֹהַי, פַּלְּטֵנִי מִיַּד רָשָׁע, מִכַּף מְעַוֵּל וְחוֹמֵץ. כִּי אַתָּה תִקְוָתִי, אֲדֹנָי יֱהֹוִה מִבְטַחִי מִנְּעוּרָי. עָלֶיךָ נִסְמַכְתִּי מִבֶּטֶן, מִמְּעֵי אִמִּי אַתָּה גוֹזִי, בְּךָ תְהִלָּתִי תָמִיד. כְּמוֹפֵת הָיִיתִי לְרַבִּים, וְאַתָּה מַחֲסִי עֹז. יִמָּלֵא פִי תְּהִלָּתֶךָ, כָּל הַיּוֹם תִּפְאַרְתֶּךָ. אַל תַּשְׁלִיכֵנִי לְעֵת זִקְנָה, כִּכְלוֹת כֹּחִי אַל תַּעַזְבֵנִי. כִּי אָמְרוּ אוֹיְבַי לִי, וְשֹׁמְרֵי נַפְשִׁי נוֹעֲצוּ יַחְדָּו. לֵאמֹר, אֱלֹהִים עֲזָבוֹ, רִדְפוּ וְתִפְשׂוּהוּ כִּי אֵין מַצִּיל. אֱלֹהִים אַל תִּרְחַק מִמֶּנִּי, אֱלֹהַי לְעֶזְרָתִי חוּשָׁה. יֵבֹשׁוּ יִכְלוּ שֹׂטְנֵי נַפְשִׁי, יַעֲטוּ חֶרְפָּה וּכְלִמָּה, מְבַקְשֵׁי רָעָתִי. וַאֲנִי תָּמִיד אֲיַחֵל, וְהוֹסַפְתִּי עַל כָּל תְּהִלָּתֶךָ. פִּי יְסַפֵּר צִדְקָתֶךָ, כָּל הַיּוֹם תְּשׁוּעָתֶךָ, כִּי לֹא יָדַעְתִּי סְפֹרוֹת. אָבוֹא בִּגְבֻרוֹת אֲדֹנָי יֱהֹוִה, אַזְכִּיר צִדְקָתְךָ לְבַדֶּךָ. אֱלֹהִים לִמַּדְתַּנִי מִנְּעוּרָי, וְעַד הֵנָּה אַגִּיד נִפְלְאוֹתֶיךָ. וְגַם עַד זִקְנָה וְשֵׂיבָה אֱלֹהִים אַל תַּעַזְבֵנִי, עַד אַגִּיד זְרוֹעֲךָ לְדוֹר, לְכָל יָבוֹא גְּבוּרָתֶךָ. וְצִדְקָתְךָ אֱלֹהִים עַד מָרוֹם, אֲשֶׁר עָשִׂיתָ גְדֹלוֹת, אֱלֹהִים מִי כָמוֹךָ. אֲשֶׁר הִרְאִיתַנִי צָרוֹת רַבּוֹת וְרָעוֹת, תָּשׁוּב תְּחַיֵּינִי, וּמִתְּהוֹמוֹת הָאָרֶץ תָּשׁוּב תַּעֲלֵנִי. תֶּרֶב גְּדֻלָּתִי, וְתִסֹּב תְּנַחֲמֵנִי. גַּם אֲנִי אוֹדְךָ בִכְלִי נֶבֶל אֲמִתְּךָ אֱלֹהָי, אֲזַמְּרָה לְךָ

בְּכִנּוֹר, קְדוֹשׁ יִשְׂרָאֵל. תְּרַנֵּנָּה שְׂפָתַי
כִּי אֲזַמְּרָה לָּךְ, וְנַפְשִׁי אֲשֶׁר פָּדִיתָ. גַּם
לְשׁוֹנִי כָּל הַיּוֹם תֶּהְגֶּה צִדְקָתֶךָ, כִּי
בֹשׁוּ כִי חָפְרוּ מְבַקְשֵׁי רָעָתִי.

14th day — יום יד לחדש

עב לִשְׁלֹמֹה, אֱלֹהִים מִשְׁפָּטֶיךָ
לְמֶלֶךְ תֵּן, וְצִדְקָתְךָ לְבֶן מֶלֶךְ.
יָדִין עַמְּךָ בְצֶדֶק, וַעֲנִיֶּיךָ בְמִשְׁפָּט.
יִשְׂאוּ הָרִים שָׁלוֹם לָעָם, וּגְבָעוֹת
בִּצְדָקָה. יִשְׁפֹּט עֲנִיֵּי עָם, יוֹשִׁיעַ לִבְנֵי
אֶבְיוֹן, וִידַכֵּא עוֹשֵׁק. יִירָאוּךָ עִם
שָׁמֶשׁ, וְלִפְנֵי יָרֵחַ דּוֹר דּוֹרִים. יֵרֵד
כְּמָטָר עַל גֵּז, כִּרְבִיבִים זַרְזִיף אָרֶץ.
יִפְרַח בְּיָמָיו צַדִּיק, וְרֹב שָׁלוֹם עַד בְּלִי
יָרֵחַ. וְיֵרְדְּ מִיָּם עַד יָם, וּמִנָּהָר עַד
אַפְסֵי אָרֶץ. לְפָנָיו יִכְרְעוּ צִיִּים, וְאֹיְבָיו
עָפָר יְלַחֵכוּ. מַלְכֵי תַרְשִׁישׁ וְאִיִּים
מִנְחָה יָשִׁיבוּ, מַלְכֵי שְׁבָא וּסְבָא אֶשְׁכָּר
יַקְרִיבוּ. וְיִשְׁתַּחֲווּ לוֹ כָל מְלָכִים, כָּל
גּוֹיִם יַעַבְדוּהוּ. כִּי יַצִּיל אֶבְיוֹן מְשַׁוֵּעַ,
וְעָנִי וְאֵין עֹזֵר לוֹ. יָחֹס עַל דַּל וְאֶבְיוֹן,
וְנַפְשׁוֹת אֶבְיוֹנִים יוֹשִׁיעַ. מִתּוֹךְ וּמֵחָמָס
יִגְאַל נַפְשָׁם, וְיֵיקַר דָּמָם בְּעֵינָיו. וִיחִי
וְיִתֶּן לוֹ מִזְּהַב שְׁבָא, וְיִתְפַּלֵּל בַּעֲדוֹ
תָמִיד, כָּל הַיּוֹם יְבָרֲכֶנְהוּ. יְהִי פִסַּת בַּר
בָּאָרֶץ בְּרֹאשׁ הָרִים, יִרְעַשׁ כַּלְּבָנוֹן
פִּרְיוֹ, וְיָצִיצוּ מֵעִיר כְּעֵשֶׂב הָאָרֶץ. יְהִי
שְׁמוֹ לְעוֹלָם, לִפְנֵי שֶׁמֶשׁ יִנּוֹן שְׁמוֹ,
וְיִתְבָּרְכוּ בוֹ, כָּל גּוֹיִם יְאַשְּׁרוּהוּ. בָּרוּךְ
יהוה אֱלֹהִים אֱלֹהֵי יִשְׂרָאֵל, עֹשֵׂה
נִפְלָאוֹת לְבַדּוֹ. וּבָרוּךְ שֵׁם כְּבוֹדוֹ
לְעוֹלָם, וְיִמָּלֵא כְבוֹדוֹ אֶת כָּל הָאָרֶץ,
אָמֵן וְאָמֵן. כָּלּוּ תְפִלּוֹת, דָּוִד בֶּן יִשָׁי.

BOOK THREE — ספר שלישי

ליום רביעי—WEDNESDAY

עג מִזְמוֹר לְאָסָף, אַךְ טוֹב לְיִשְׂרָאֵל
אֱלֹהִים לְבָרֵי לֵבָב. וַאֲנִי כִּמְעַט
נָטָיוּ רַגְלָי, כְּאַיִן שֻׁפְּכוּ אֲשֻׁרָי. כִּי
קִנֵּאתִי בַּהוֹלְלִים, שְׁלוֹם רְשָׁעִים
אֶרְאֶה. כִּי אֵין חַרְצֻבּוֹת לְמוֹתָם,
וּבָרִיא אוּלָם. בַּעֲמַל אֱנוֹשׁ אֵינֵמוֹ, וְעִם
אָדָם לֹא יְנֻגָּעוּ. לָכֵן עֲנָקַתְמוֹ גַאֲוָה,
יַעֲטָף שִׁית חָמָס לָמוֹ. יָצָא מֵחֵלֶב
עֵינֵמוֹ, עָבְרוּ מַשְׂכִּיּוֹת לֵבָב. יָמִיקוּ
וִידַבְּרוּ בְרָע עֹשֶׁק, מִמָּרוֹם יְדַבֵּרוּ.
שַׁתּוּ בַשָּׁמַיִם פִּיהֶם, וּלְשׁוֹנָם תִּהֲלַךְ
בָּאָרֶץ. לָכֵן יָשׁוּב עַמּוֹ הֲלֹם, וּמֵי מָלֵא
יִמָּצוּ לָמוֹ. וְאָמְרוּ אֵיכָה יָדַע אֵל, וְיֵשׁ
דֵּעָה בְעֶלְיוֹן. הִנֵּה אֵלֶּה רְשָׁעִים, וְשַׁלְוֵי
עוֹלָם הִשְׂגּוּ חָיִל. אַךְ רִיק זִכִּיתִי לְבָבִי,
וָאֶרְחַץ בְּנִקָּיוֹן כַּפָּי. וָאֱהִי נָגוּעַ כָּל
הַיּוֹם, וְתוֹכַחְתִּי לַבְּקָרִים. אִם אָמַרְתִּי
אֲסַפְּרָה כְמוֹ, הִנֵּה דוֹר בָּנֶיךָ בָגָדְתִּי.
וָאֲחַשְּׁבָה לָדַעַת זֹאת, עָמָל הוּא בְעֵינָי.
עַד אָבוֹא אֶל מִקְדְּשֵׁי אֵל, אָבִינָה
לְאַחֲרִיתָם. אַךְ בַּחֲלָקוֹת תָּשִׁית לָמוֹ,
הִפַּלְתָּם לְמַשּׁוּאוֹת. אֵיךְ הָיוּ לְשַׁמָּה
כְרָגַע, סָפוּ תַמּוּ מִן בַּלָּהוֹת. כַּחֲלוֹם
מֵהָקִיץ, אֲדֹנָי בָּעִיר צַלְמָם תִּבְזֶה. כִּי
יִתְחַמֵּץ לְבָבִי, וְכִלְיוֹתַי אֶשְׁתּוֹנָן. וַאֲנִי
בַעַר וְלֹא אֵדָע, בְּהֵמוֹת הָיִיתִי עִמָּךְ.
וַאֲנִי תָמִיד עִמָּךְ, אָחַזְתָּ בְּיַד יְמִינִי.
בַּעֲצָתְךָ תַנְחֵנִי, וְאַחַר, כָּבוֹד תִּקָּחֵנִי.
מִי לִי בַשָּׁמָיִם, וְעִמְּךָ לֹא חָפַצְתִּי
בָאָרֶץ. כָּלָה שְׁאֵרִי וּלְבָבִי, צוּר לְבָבִי
וְחֶלְקִי אֱלֹהִים לְעוֹלָם. כִּי הִנֵּה רְחֵקֶיךָ
יֹאבֵדוּ, הִצְמַתָּה כָּל זוֹנֶה מִמֶּךָּ. וַאֲנִי
קִרֲבַת אֱלֹהִים לִי טוֹב, שַׁתִּי בַּאדֹנָי
יֱהוִה מַחְסִי, לְסַפֵּר כָּל מַלְאֲכוֹתֶיךָ.

עד מַשְׂכִּיל לְאָסָף, לָמָה אֱלֹהִים
זָנַחְתָּ לָנֶצַח, יֶעְשַׁן אַפְּךָ בְּצֹאן
מַרְעִיתֶךָ. זְכֹר עֲדָתְךָ קָנִיתָ קֶּדֶם, גָּאַלְתָּ
שֵׁבֶט נַחֲלָתֶךָ, הַר צִיּוֹן זֶה שָׁכַנְתָּ בּוֹ.
הָרִימָה פְעָמֶיךָ לְמַשֻּׁאוֹת נֶצַח, כָּל
הֵרַע אוֹיֵב בַּקֹּדֶשׁ. שָׁאֲגוּ צֹרְרֶיךָ בְּקֶרֶב
מוֹעֲדֶךָ, שָׂמוּ אוֹתֹתָם אֹתוֹת. יִוָּדַע
כְּמֵבִיא לְמָעְלָה, בִּסֲבָךְ עֵץ קַרְדֻּמּוֹת.
וְעַתָּה פִּתּוּחֶיהָ יָּחַד, בְּכַשִּׁיל וְכֵילַפֹּת

יַהֲלֹמוּן. שִׁלְחוּ בָאֵשׁ מִקְדָּשֶׁךָ, לָאָרֶץ חִלְּלוּ מִשְׁכַּן שְׁמֶךָ. אָמְרוּ בְלִבָּם, נִינָם יָחַד, שָׂרְפוּ כָל מוֹעֲדֵי אֵל בָּאָרֶץ. אוֹתֹתֵינוּ לֹא רָאִינוּ, אֵין עוֹד נָבִיא, וְלֹא אִתָּנוּ יוֹדֵעַ עַד מָה. עַד מָתַי אֱלֹהִים יְחָרֶף צָר, יְנָאֵץ אוֹיֵב שִׁמְךָ לָנֶצַח. לָמָּה תָשִׁיב יָדְךָ וִימִינֶךָ, מִקֶּרֶב חֵיקְךָ כַלֵּה. וֵאלֹהִים מַלְכִּי מִקֶּדֶם, פֹּעֵל יְשׁוּעוֹת בְּקֶרֶב הָאָרֶץ. אַתָּה פוֹרַרְתָּ בְעָזְּךָ יָם, שִׁבַּרְתָּ רָאשֵׁי תַנִּינִים עַל הַמָּיִם. אַתָּה רִצַּצְתָּ רָאשֵׁי לִוְיָתָן, תִּתְּנֶנּוּ מַאֲכָל לְעָם לְצִיִּים. אַתָּה בָקַעְתָּ מַעְיָן וָנָחַל, אַתָּה הוֹבַשְׁתָּ נַהֲרוֹת אֵיתָן. לְךָ יוֹם אַף לְךָ לָיְלָה, אַתָּה הֲכִינוֹתָ מָאוֹר וָשָׁמֶשׁ. אַתָּה הִצַּבְתָּ כָּל גְּבוּלוֹת אָרֶץ, קַיִץ וָחֹרֶף אַתָּה יְצַרְתָּם. זְכָר זֹאת אוֹיֵב חֵרֵף, יהוה, וְעַם נָבָל נִאֲצוּ שְׁמֶךָ. אַל תִּתֵּן לְחַיַּת נֶפֶשׁ תּוֹרֶךָ, חַיַּת עֲנִיֶּיךָ אַל תִּשְׁכַּח לָנֶצַח. הַבֵּט לַבְּרִית, כִּי מָלְאוּ מַחֲשַׁכֵּי אֶרֶץ נְאוֹת חָמָס. אַל יָשֹׁב דַּךְ נִכְלָם, עָנִי וְאֶבְיוֹן יְהַלְלוּ שְׁמֶךָ. קוּמָה אֱלֹהִים רִיבָה רִיבֶךָ, זְכֹר חֶרְפָּתְךָ מִנִּי נָבָל כָּל הַיּוֹם. אַל תִּשְׁכַּח קוֹל צֹרְרֶיךָ, שְׁאוֹן קָמֶיךָ עֹלֶה תָמִיד.

עה לַמְנַצֵּחַ אַל תַּשְׁחֵת, מִזְמוֹר לְאָסָף שִׁיר. הוֹדִינוּ לְּךָ אֱלֹהִים, הוֹדִינוּ וְקָרוֹב שְׁמֶךָ, סִפְּרוּ נִפְלְאוֹתֶיךָ. כִּי אֶקַּח מוֹעֵד, אֲנִי מֵישָׁרִים אֶשְׁפֹּט. נְמֹגִים אֶרֶץ וְכָל יֹשְׁבֶיהָ, אָנֹכִי תִכַּנְתִּי עַמּוּדֶיהָ סֶּלָה. אָמַרְתִּי לַהוֹלְלִים אַל תָּהֹלּוּ, וְלָרְשָׁעִים אַל תָּרִימוּ קָרֶן. אַל תָּרִימוּ לַמָּרוֹם קַרְנְכֶם, תְּדַבְּרוּ בְצַוָּאר עָתָק. כִּי לֹא מִמּוֹצָא וּמִמַּעֲרָב, וְלֹא מִמִּדְבַּר הָרִים. כִּי אֱלֹהִים שֹׁפֵט, זֶה יַשְׁפִּיל וְזֶה יָרִים. כִּי כוֹס בְּיַד יהוה, וְיַיִן חָמַר מָלֵא מֶסֶךְ, וַיַּגֵּר מִזֶּה, אַךְ שְׁמָרֶיהָ יִמְצוּ יִשְׁתּוּ, כֹּל רִשְׁעֵי אָרֶץ. וַאֲנִי אַגִּיד לְעֹלָם, אֲזַמְּרָה לֵאלֹהֵי יַעֲקֹב. וְכָל קַרְנֵי רְשָׁעִים אֲגַדֵּעַ, תְּרוֹמַמְנָה קַרְנוֹת צַדִּיק.

עו לַמְנַצֵּחַ בִּנְגִינֹת, מִזְמוֹר לְאָסָף שִׁיר. נוֹדָע בִּיהוּדָה אֱלֹהִים, בְּיִשְׂרָאֵל גָּדוֹל שְׁמוֹ. וַיְהִי בְשָׁלֵם סֻכּוֹ, וּמְעוֹנָתוֹ בְצִיּוֹן. שָׁמָּה שִׁבַּר רִשְׁפֵי קָשֶׁת, מָגֵן וְחֶרֶב וּמִלְחָמָה סֶלָה. נָאוֹר אַתָּה, אַדִּיר מֵהַרְרֵי טָרֶף. אֶשְׁתּוֹלְלוּ אַבִּירֵי לֵב, נָמוּ שְׁנָתָם, וְלֹא מָצְאוּ כָל אַנְשֵׁי חַיִל יְדֵיהֶם. מִגַּעֲרָתְךָ אֱלֹהֵי יַעֲקֹב, נִרְדָּם וְרֶכֶב וָסוּס. אַתָּה נוֹרָא אַתָּה, וּמִי יַעֲמֹד לְפָנֶיךָ מֵאָז אַפֶּךָ. מִשָּׁמַיִם הִשְׁמַעְתָּ דִּין, אֶרֶץ יָרְאָה וְשָׁקָטָה. בְּקוּם לַמִּשְׁפָּט אֱלֹהִים, לְהוֹשִׁיעַ כָּל עַנְוֵי אֶרֶץ סֶלָה. כִּי חֲמַת אָדָם תּוֹדֶךָּ, שְׁאֵרִית חֵמֹת תַּחְגֹּר. נִדְרוּ וְשַׁלְּמוּ לַיהוה אֱלֹהֵיכֶם, כָּל סְבִיבָיו יֹבִילוּ שַׁי לַמּוֹרָא. יִבְצֹר רוּחַ נְגִידִים, נוֹרָא לְמַלְכֵי אָרֶץ.

15th day — יום טו לחדש

עז לַמְנַצֵּחַ עַל יְדוּתוּן לְאָסָף מִזְמוֹר. קוֹלִי אֶל אֱלֹהִים וְאֶצְעָקָה, קוֹלִי אֶל אֱלֹהִים, וְהַאֲזִין אֵלָי. בְּיוֹם צָרָתִי אֲדֹנָי דָּרָשְׁתִּי, יָדִי לַיְלָה נִגְּרָה וְלֹא תָפוּג, מֵאֲנָה הִנָּחֵם נַפְשִׁי. אֶזְכְּרָה אֱלֹהִים וְאֶהֱמָיָה, אָשִׂיחָה וְתִתְעַטֵּף רוּחִי סֶלָה. אָחַזְתָּ שְׁמֻרוֹת עֵינָי, נִפְעַמְתִּי וְלֹא אֲדַבֵּר. חִשַּׁבְתִּי יָמִים מִקֶּדֶם, שְׁנוֹת עוֹלָמִים. אֶזְכְּרָה נְגִינָתִי בַּלָּיְלָה, עִם לְבָבִי אָשִׂיחָה, וַיְחַפֵּשׂ רוּחִי. הַלְעוֹלָמִים יִזְנַח, אֲדֹנָי, וְלֹא יֹסִיף לִרְצוֹת עוֹד. הֶאָפֵס לָנֶצַח חַסְדּוֹ, גָּמַר אֹמֶר לְדֹר וָדֹר. הֲשָׁכַח חַנּוֹת אֵל, אִם קָפַץ בְּאַף רַחֲמָיו סֶלָה. וָאֹמַר, חַלּוֹתִי הִיא, שְׁנוֹת יְמִין עֶלְיוֹן. אֶזְכּוֹר מַעַלְלֵי יָהּ, כִּי אֶזְכְּרָה מִקֶּדֶם פִּלְאֶךָ. וְהָגִיתִי בְכָל פָּעֳלֶךָ, וּבַעֲלִילוֹתֶיךָ אָשִׂיחָה. אֱלֹהִים בַּקֹּדֶשׁ דַּרְכֶּךָ, מִי אֵל גָּדוֹל כֵּאלֹהִים. אַתָּה הָאֵל עֹשֵׂה פֶלֶא, הוֹדַעְתָּ בָעַמִּים עֻזֶּךָ. גָּאַלְתָּ בִּזְרוֹעַ עַמֶּךָ, בְּנֵי יַעֲקֹב וְיוֹסֵף סֶלָה. רָאוּךָ מַּיִם אֱלֹהִים, רָאוּךָ מַּיִם יָחִילוּ, אַף יִרְגְּזוּ תְהֹמוֹת. זֹרְמוּ מַיִם עָבוֹת, קוֹל נָתְנוּ

שְׁחָקִים, אַף חֲצָצֶיךָ יִתְהַלָּכוּ. קוֹל רַעַמְךָ בַּגַּלְגַּל, הֵאִירוּ בְרָקִים תֵּבֵל, רָגְזָה וַתִּרְעַשׁ הָאָרֶץ. בַּיָּם דַּרְכֶּךָ, וּשְׁבִילְךָ בְּמַיִם רַבִּים, וְעִקְּבוֹתֶיךָ לֹא נֹדָעוּ. נָחִיתָ כַצֹּאן עַמֶּךָ, בְּיַד מֹשֶׁה וְאַהֲרֹן.

עח מַשְׂכִּיל לְאָסָף, הַאֲזִינָה עַמִּי תּוֹרָתִי, הַטּוּ אָזְנְכֶם לְאִמְרֵי פִי. אֶפְתְּחָה בְמָשָׁל פִּי, אַבִּיעָה חִידוֹת מִנִּי קֶדֶם. אֲשֶׁר שָׁמַעְנוּ וַנֵּדָעֵם, וַאֲבוֹתֵינוּ סִפְּרוּ לָנוּ. לֹא נְכַחֵד מִבְּנֵיהֶם, לְדוֹר אַחֲרוֹן מְסַפְּרִים תְּהִלּוֹת יהוה, וֶעֱזוּזוֹ וְנִפְלְאוֹתָיו אֲשֶׁר עָשָׂה. וַיָּקֶם עֵדוּת בְּיַעֲקֹב, וְתוֹרָה שָׂם בְּיִשְׂרָאֵל, אֲשֶׁר צִוָּה אֶת אֲבוֹתֵינוּ לְהוֹדִיעָם לִבְנֵיהֶם. לְמַעַן יֵדְעוּ דּוֹר אַחֲרוֹן, בָּנִים יִוָּלֵדוּ, יָקֻמוּ וִיסַפְּרוּ לִבְנֵיהֶם. וְיָשִׂימוּ בֵאלֹהִים כִּסְלָם, וְלֹא יִשְׁכְּחוּ מַעַלְלֵי אֵל, וּמִצְוֹתָיו יִנְצֹרוּ. וְלֹא יִהְיוּ כַּאֲבוֹתָם דּוֹר סוֹרֵר וּמֹרֶה, דּוֹר לֹא הֵכִין לִבּוֹ, וְלֹא נֶאֶמְנָה אֶת אֵל רוּחוֹ. בְּנֵי אֶפְרַיִם נוֹשְׁקֵי רוֹמֵי קָשֶׁת, הָפְכוּ בְּיוֹם קְרָב. לֹא שָׁמְרוּ בְּרִית אֱלֹהִים, וּבְתוֹרָתוֹ מֵאֲנוּ לָלֶכֶת. וַיִּשְׁכְּחוּ עֲלִילוֹתָיו, וְנִפְלְאוֹתָיו אֲשֶׁר הֶרְאָם. נֶגֶד אֲבוֹתָם עָשָׂה פֶלֶא, בְּאֶרֶץ מִצְרַיִם שְׂדֵה צֹעַן. בָּקַע יָם וַיַּעֲבִירֵם, וַיַּצֶּב מַיִם כְּמוֹ נֵד. וַיַּנְחֵם בֶּעָנָן יוֹמָם, וְכָל הַלַּיְלָה בְּאוֹר אֵשׁ. יְבַקַּע צֻרִים בַּמִּדְבָּר, וַיַּשְׁקְ כִּתְהֹמוֹת רַבָּה. וַיּוֹצִא נוֹזְלִים מִסָּלַע, וַיּוֹרֶד כַּנְּהָרוֹת מָיִם. וַיּוֹסִיפוּ עוֹד לַחֲטֹא לוֹ, לַמְרוֹת עֶלְיוֹן בַּצִּיָּה. וַיְנַסּוּ אֵל בִּלְבָבָם, לִשְׁאָל אֹכֶל לְנַפְשָׁם. וַיְדַבְּרוּ בֵּאלֹהִים, אָמְרוּ, הֲיוּכַל אֵל, לַעֲרֹךְ שֻׁלְחָן בַּמִּדְבָּר. הֵן הִכָּה צוּר וַיָּזוּבוּ מַיִם, וּנְחָלִים יִשְׁטֹפוּ, הֲגַם לֶחֶם יוּכַל תֵּת, אִם יָכִין שְׁאֵר לְעַמּוֹ. לָכֵן שָׁמַע יהוה וַיִּתְעַבָּר, וְאֵשׁ נִשְּׂקָה בְיַעֲקֹב, וְגַם אַף עָלָה בְיִשְׂרָאֵל. כִּי לֹא הֶאֱמִינוּ בֵּאלֹהִים, וְלֹא בָטְחוּ בִּישׁוּעָתוֹ. וַיְצַו שְׁחָקִים מִמָּעַל, וְדַלְתֵי שָׁמַיִם פָּתָח. וַיַּמְטֵר עֲלֵיהֶם מָן לֶאֱכֹל, וּדְגַן שָׁמַיִם נָתַן לָמוֹ. לֶחֶם אַבִּירִים אָכַל אִישׁ, צֵידָה שָׁלַח לָהֶם לָשֹׂבַע. יַסַּע קָדִים בַּשָּׁמָיִם, וַיְנַהֵג בְּעֻזּוֹ תֵימָן. וַיַּמְטֵר עֲלֵיהֶם כֶּעָפָר שְׁאֵר, וּכְחוֹל יַמִּים עוֹף כָּנָף. וַיַּפֵּל בְּקֶרֶב מַחֲנֵהוּ, סָבִיב לְמִשְׁכְּנֹתָיו. וַיֹּאכְלוּ וַיִּשְׂבְּעוּ מְאֹד, וְתַאֲוָתָם יָבִא לָהֶם. לֹא זָרוּ מִתַּאֲוָתָם, עוֹד אָכְלָם בְּפִיהֶם. וְאַף אֱלֹהִים עָלָה בָהֶם, וַיַּהֲרֹג בְּמִשְׁמַנֵּיהֶם, וּבַחוּרֵי יִשְׂרָאֵל הִכְרִיעַ. בְּכָל זֹאת חָטְאוּ עוֹד, וְלֹא הֶאֱמִינוּ בְּנִפְלְאוֹתָיו. וַיְכַל בַּהֶבֶל יְמֵיהֶם, וּשְׁנוֹתָם בַּבֶּהָלָה. אִם הֲרָגָם וּדְרָשׁוּהוּ, וְשָׁבוּ וְשִׁחֲרוּ אֵל. וַיִּזְכְּרוּ כִּי אֱלֹהִים צוּרָם, וְאֵל עֶלְיוֹן גֹּאֲלָם. וַיְפַתּוּהוּ בְּפִיהֶם, וּבִלְשׁוֹנָם יְכַזְּבוּ לוֹ. וְלִבָּם לֹא נָכוֹן עִמּוֹ, וְלֹא נֶאֶמְנוּ בִּבְרִיתוֹ. וְהוּא רַחוּם יְכַפֵּר עָוֹן וְלֹא יַשְׁחִית, וְהִרְבָּה לְהָשִׁיב אַפּוֹ, וְלֹא יָעִיר כָּל חֲמָתוֹ. וַיִּזְכֹּר כִּי בָשָׂר הֵמָּה, רוּחַ הוֹלֵךְ וְלֹא יָשׁוּב. כַּמָּה יַמְרוּהוּ בַמִּדְבָּר, יַעֲצִיבוּהוּ בִּישִׁימוֹן. וַיָּשׁוּבוּ וַיְנַסּוּ אֵל, וּקְדוֹשׁ יִשְׂרָאֵל הִתְווּ. לֹא זָכְרוּ אֶת יָדוֹ, יוֹם אֲשֶׁר פָּדָם מִנִּי צָר. אֲשֶׁר שָׂם בְּמִצְרַיִם אֹתוֹתָיו, וּמוֹפְתָיו בִּשְׂדֵה צֹעַן. וַיַּהֲפֹךְ לְדָם יְאֹרֵיהֶם, וְנֹזְלֵיהֶם בַּל יִשְׁתָּיוּן. יְשַׁלַּח בָּהֶם עָרֹב וַיֹּאכְלֵם, וּצְפַרְדֵּעַ וַתַּשְׁחִיתֵם. וַיִּתֵּן לֶחָסִיל יְבוּלָם, וִיגִיעָם לָאַרְבֶּה. יַהֲרֹג בַּבָּרָד גַּפְנָם, וְשִׁקְמוֹתָם בַּחֲנָמַל. וַיַּסְגֵּר לַבָּרָד בְּעִירָם, וּמִקְנֵיהֶם לָרְשָׁפִים. יְשַׁלַּח בָּם חֲרוֹן אַפּוֹ, עֶבְרָה וָזַעַם וְצָרָה, מִשְׁלַחַת מַלְאֲכֵי רָעִים. יְפַלֵּס נָתִיב לְאַפּוֹ, לֹא חָשַׂךְ מִמָּוֶת נַפְשָׁם, וְחַיָּתָם לַדֶּבֶר הִסְגִּיר. וַיַּךְ כָּל בְּכוֹר בְּמִצְרָיִם, רֵאשִׁית אוֹנִים בְּאָהֳלֵי חָם. וַיַּסַּע כַּצֹּאן עַמּוֹ, וַיְנַהֲגֵם כַּעֵדֶר בַּמִּדְבָּר. וַיַּנְחֵם לָבֶטַח וְלֹא פָחָדוּ, וְאֶת אוֹיְבֵיהֶם כִּסָּה הַיָּם. וַיְבִיאֵם אֶל גְּבוּל קָדְשׁוֹ, הַר זֶה קָנְתָה יְמִינוֹ. וַיְגָרֶשׁ מִפְּנֵיהֶם גּוֹיִם, וַיַּפִּילֵם בְּחֶבֶל נַחֲלָה, וַיַּשְׁכֵּן בְּאָהֳלֵיהֶם שִׁבְטֵי יִשְׂרָאֵל. וַיְנַסּוּ

וַיַּמְרוּ אֶת אֱלֹהִים עֶלְיוֹן, וְעֵדוֹתָיו לֹא שָׁמָרוּ. וַיִּסֹּגוּ וַיִּבְגְּדוּ כַּאֲבוֹתָם, נֶהְפְּכוּ כְּקֶשֶׁת רְמִיָּה. וַיַּכְעִיסוּהוּ בְּבָמוֹתָם, וּבִפְסִילֵיהֶם יַקְנִיאוּהוּ. שָׁמַע אֱלֹהִים וַיִּתְעַבָּר, וַיִּמְאַס מְאֹד בְּיִשְׂרָאֵל. וַיִּטֹּשׁ מִשְׁכַּן שִׁלוֹ, אֹהֶל שִׁכֵּן בָּאָדָם. וַיִּתֵּן לַשְּׁבִי עֻזּוֹ, וְתִפְאַרְתּוֹ בְיַד צָר. וַיַּסְגֵּר לַחֶרֶב עַמּוֹ, וּבְנַחֲלָתוֹ הִתְעַבָּר. בַּחוּרָיו אָכְלָה אֵשׁ, וּבְתוּלֹתָיו לֹא הוּלָּלוּ. כֹּהֲנָיו בַּחֶרֶב נָפָלוּ, וְאַלְמְנֹתָיו לֹא תִבְכֶּינָה. וַיִּקַץ כְּיָשֵׁן, אֲדֹנָי, כְּגִבּוֹר מִתְרוֹנֵן מִיָּיִן. וַיַּךְ צָרָיו אָחוֹר, חֶרְפַּת עוֹלָם נָתַן לָמוֹ. וַיִּמְאַס בְּאֹהֶל יוֹסֵף, וּבְשֵׁבֶט אֶפְרַיִם לֹא בָחָר. וַיִּבְחַר אֶת שֵׁבֶט יְהוּדָה, אֶת הַר צִיּוֹן אֲשֶׁר אָהֵב. וַיִּבֶן כְּמוֹ רָמִים מִקְדָּשׁוֹ, כְּאֶרֶץ יְסָדָהּ לְעוֹלָם. וַיִּבְחַר בְּדָוִד עַבְדּוֹ, וַיִּקָּחֵהוּ מִמִּכְלְאֹת צֹאן. מֵאַחַר עָלוֹת הֱבִיאוֹ, לִרְעוֹת בְּיַעֲקֹב עַמּוֹ, וּבְיִשְׂרָאֵל נַחֲלָתוֹ. וַיִּרְעֵם כְּתֹם לְבָבוֹ, וּבִתְבוּנוֹת כַּפָּיו יַנְחֵם.

יום טז לחדש — 16th day

עט מִזְמוֹר לְאָסָף, אֱלֹהִים בָּאוּ גוֹיִם בְּנַחֲלָתֶךָ, טִמְּאוּ אֶת הֵיכַל קָדְשֶׁךָ, שָׂמוּ אֶת יְרוּשָׁלַיִם לְעִיִּים. נָתְנוּ אֶת נִבְלַת עֲבָדֶיךָ מַאֲכָל לְעוֹף הַשָּׁמָיִם, בְּשַׂר חֲסִידֶיךָ לְחַיְתוֹ אָרֶץ. שָׁפְכוּ דָמָם כַּמַּיִם, סְבִיבוֹת יְרוּשָׁלַיִם, וְאֵין קוֹבֵר. הָיִינוּ חֶרְפָּה לִשְׁכֵנֵינוּ, לַעַג וָקֶלֶס לִסְבִיבוֹתֵינוּ. עַד מָה יְהוָה תֶּאֱנַף לָנֶצַח, תִּבְעַר כְּמוֹ אֵשׁ קִנְאָתֶךָ. שְׁפֹךְ חֲמָתְךָ אֶל הַגּוֹיִם אֲשֶׁר לֹא יְדָעוּךָ, וְעַל מַמְלָכוֹת, אֲשֶׁר בְּשִׁמְךָ לֹא קָרָאוּ. כִּי אָכַל אֶת יַעֲקֹב, וְאֶת נָוֵהוּ הֵשַׁמּוּ. אַל תִּזְכָּר לָנוּ עֲוֹנֹת רִאשֹׁנִים, מַהֵר יְקַדְּמוּנוּ רַחֲמֶיךָ, כִּי דַלּוֹנוּ מְאֹד. עָזְרֵנוּ אֱלֹהֵי יִשְׁעֵנוּ עַל דְּבַר כְּבוֹד שְׁמֶךָ, וְהַצִּילֵנוּ וְכַפֵּר עַל חַטֹּאתֵינוּ לְמַעַן שְׁמֶךָ. לָמָּה יֹאמְרוּ הַגּוֹיִם, אַיֵּה אֱלֹהֵיהֶם, יִוָּדַע בַּגּוֹיִם לְעֵינֵינוּ, נִקְמַת דַּם עֲבָדֶיךָ הַשָּׁפוּךְ. תָּבוֹא לְפָנֶיךָ

אֶנְקַת אָסִיר, כְּגֹדֶל זְרוֹעֲךָ, הוֹתֵר בְּנֵי תְמוּתָה. וְהָשֵׁב לִשְׁכֵנֵינוּ שִׁבְעָתַיִם אֶל חֵיקָם, חֶרְפָּתָם אֲשֶׁר חֵרְפוּךָ, אֲדֹנָי. וַאֲנַחְנוּ עַמְּךָ וְצֹאן מַרְעִיתֶךָ, נוֹדֶה לְּךָ לְעוֹלָם, לְדוֹר וָדֹר, נְסַפֵּר תְּהִלָּתֶךָ.

פ לַמְנַצֵּחַ אֶל שֹׁשַׁנִּים, עֵדוּת לְאָסָף מִזְמוֹר. רֹעֵה יִשְׂרָאֵל הַאֲזִינָה, נֹהֵג כַּצֹּאן יוֹסֵף, יֹשֵׁב הַכְּרוּבִים הוֹפִיעָה. לִפְנֵי אֶפְרַיִם וּבִנְיָמִן וּמְנַשֶּׁה עוֹרְרָה אֶת גְּבוּרָתֶךָ, וּלְכָה לִישֻׁעָתָה לָּנוּ. אֱלֹהִים הֲשִׁיבֵנוּ, וְהָאֵר פָּנֶיךָ וְנִוָּשֵׁעָה. יְהוָה אֱלֹהִים צְבָאוֹת, עַד מָתַי עָשַׁנְתָּ בִּתְפִלַּת עַמֶּךָ. הֶאֱכַלְתָּם לֶחֶם דִּמְעָה, וַתַּשְׁקֵמוֹ בִּדְמָעוֹת שָׁלִישׁ. תְּשִׂימֵנוּ מָדוֹן לִשְׁכֵנֵינוּ, וְאֹיְבֵינוּ יִלְעֲגוּ לָמוֹ. אֱלֹהִים צְבָאוֹת הֲשִׁיבֵנוּ, וְהָאֵר פָּנֶיךָ וְנִוָּשֵׁעָה. גֶּפֶן מִמִּצְרַיִם תַּסִּיעַ, תְּגָרֵשׁ גּוֹיִם וַתִּטָּעֶהָ. פִּנִּיתָ לְפָנֶיהָ, וַתַּשְׁרֵשׁ שָׁרָשֶׁיהָ, וַתְּמַלֵּא אָרֶץ. כָּסּוּ הָרִים צִלָּהּ, וַעֲנָפֶיהָ אַרְזֵי אֵל. תְּשַׁלַּח קְצִירֶהָ עַד יָם, וְאֶל נָהָר יוֹנְקוֹתֶיהָ. לָמָּה פָּרַצְתָּ גְדֵרֶיהָ, וְאָרוּהָ כָּל עֹבְרֵי דָרֶךְ. יְכַרְסְמֶנָּה חֲזִיר מִיָּעַר, וְזִיז שָׂדַי יִרְעֶנָּה. אֱלֹהִים צְבָאוֹת שׁוּב נָא, הַבֵּט מִשָּׁמַיִם וּרְאֵה, וּפְקֹד גֶּפֶן זֹאת. וְכַנָּה אֲשֶׁר נָטְעָה יְמִינֶךָ, וְעַל בֵּן אִמַּצְתָּה לָּךְ. שְׂרֻפָה בָאֵשׁ כְּסוּחָה, מִגַּעֲרַת פָּנֶיךָ יֹאבֵדוּ. תְּהִי יָדְךָ עַל אִישׁ יְמִינֶךָ, עַל בֶּן אָדָם אִמַּצְתָּ לָּךְ. וְלֹא נָסוֹג מִמֶּךָּ, תְּחַיֵּנוּ וּבְשִׁמְךָ נִקְרָא. יְהוָה אֱלֹהִים צְבָאוֹת הֲשִׁיבֵנוּ, הָאֵר פָּנֶיךָ וְנִוָּשֵׁעָה.

פא לַמְנַצֵּחַ עַל הַגִּתִּית לְאָסָף. הַרְנִינוּ לֵאלֹהִים עוּזֵּנוּ, הָרִיעוּ לֵאלֹהֵי יַעֲקֹב. שְׂאוּ זִמְרָה וּתְנוּ תֹף, כִּנּוֹר נָעִים עִם נָבֶל. תִּקְעוּ בַחֹדֶשׁ שׁוֹפָר, בַּכֵּסֶה לְיוֹם חַגֵּנוּ. כִּי חֹק לְיִשְׂרָאֵל הוּא, מִשְׁפָּט לֵאלֹהֵי יַעֲקֹב. עֵדוּת בִּיהוֹסֵף שָׂמוֹ, בְּצֵאתוֹ עַל אֶרֶץ מִצְרָיִם, שְׂפַת לֹא יָדַעְתִּי אֶשְׁמָע. הֲסִירוֹתִי מִסֵּבֶל שִׁכְמוֹ, כַּפָּיו מִדּוּד תַּעֲבֹרְנָה. בַּצָּרָה קָרָאתָ וָאֲחַלְּצֶךָּ.

אֶעֶנְךָ בְּסֵתֶר רַעַם, אֶבְחָנְךָ עַל מֵי
מְרִיבָה סֶלָה. שְׁמַע עַמִּי וְאָעִידָה בָּךְ,
יִשְׂרָאֵל אִם תִּשְׁמַע לִי. לֹא יִהְיֶה בְךָ
אֵל זָר, וְלֹא תִשְׁתַּחֲוֶה לְאֵל נֵכָר. אָנֹכִי
יהוה אֱלֹהֶיךָ, הַמַּעַלְךָ מֵאֶרֶץ מִצְרָיִם,
הַרְחֶב פִּיךָ וַאֲמַלְאֵהוּ. וְלֹא שָׁמַע עַמִּי
לְקוֹלִי, וְיִשְׂרָאֵל לֹא אָבָה לִי.
וָאֲשַׁלְּחֵהוּ בִּשְׁרִירוּת לִבָּם, יֵלְכוּ
בְּמוֹעֲצוֹתֵיהֶם. לוּ עַמִּי שֹׁמֵעַ לִי,
יִשְׂרָאֵל בִּדְרָכַי יְהַלֵּכוּ. כִּמְעַט אוֹיְבֵיהֶם
אַכְנִיעַ, וְעַל צָרֵיהֶם אָשִׁיב יָדִי. מְשַׂנְאֵי
יהוה יְכַחֲשׁוּ לוֹ, וִיהִי עִתָּם לְעוֹלָם.
וַיַּאֲכִילֵהוּ מֵחֵלֶב חִטָּה, וּמִצּוּר דְּבַשׁ
אַשְׂבִּיעֶךָ.

פב מִזְמוֹר לְאָסָף, אֱלֹהִים נִצָּב
בַּעֲדַת אֵל, בְּקֶרֶב אֱלֹהִים יִשְׁפֹּט.
עַד מָתַי תִּשְׁפְּטוּ עָוֶל, וּפְנֵי רְשָׁעִים
תִּשְׂאוּ סֶלָה. שִׁפְטוּ דָל וְיָתוֹם, עָנִי וָרָשׁ
הַצְדִּיקוּ. פַּלְּטוּ דַל וְאֶבְיוֹן, מִיַּד רְשָׁעִים
הַצִּילוּ. לֹא יָדְעוּ וְלֹא יָבִינוּ, בַּחֲשֵׁכָה
יִתְהַלָּכוּ, יִמּוֹטוּ כָּל מוֹסְדֵי אָרֶץ. אֲנִי
אָמַרְתִּי אֱלֹהִים אַתֶּם, וּבְנֵי עֶלְיוֹן
כֻּלְּכֶם. אָכֵן כְּאָדָם תְּמוּתוּן, וּכְאַחַד
הַשָּׂרִים תִּפֹּלוּ. קוּמָה אֱלֹהִים שָׁפְטָה
הָאָרֶץ, כִּי אַתָּה תִנְחַל בְּכָל הַגּוֹיִם.

יום יז לחדש — 17th day

פג שִׁיר מִזְמוֹר לְאָסָף. אֱלֹהִים אַל
דֳּמִי לָךְ, אַל תֶּחֱרַשׁ וְאַל תִּשְׁקֹט
אֵל. כִּי הִנֵּה אוֹיְבֶיךָ יֶהֱמָיוּן, וּמְשַׂנְאֶיךָ
נָשְׂאוּ רֹאשׁ. עַל עַמְּךָ יַעֲרִימוּ סוֹד,
וְיִתְיָעֲצוּ עַל צְפוּנֶיךָ. אָמְרוּ, לְכוּ
וְנַכְחִידֵם מִגּוֹי, וְלֹא יִזָּכֵר שֵׁם יִשְׂרָאֵל
עוֹד. כִּי נוֹעֲצוּ לֵב יַחְדָּו, עָלֶיךָ בְּרִית
יִכְרֹתוּ. אָהֳלֵי אֱדוֹם וְיִשְׁמְעֵאלִים,
מוֹאָב וְהַגְרִים. גְּבָל וְעַמּוֹן וַעֲמָלֵק,
פְּלֶשֶׁת עִם יֹשְׁבֵי צוֹר. גַּם אַשּׁוּר נִלְוָה
עִמָּם, הָיוּ זְרוֹעַ לִבְנֵי לוֹט סֶלָה. עֲשֵׂה
לָהֶם כְּמִדְיָן, כְּסִיסְרָא כְיָבִין בְּנַחַל
קִישׁוֹן. נִשְׁמְדוּ בְעֵין דֹּאר, הָיוּ דֹּמֶן
לָאֲדָמָה. שִׁיתֵמוֹ נְדִיבֵמוֹ כְּעֹרֵב וְכִזְאֵב,
וּכְזֶבַח וּכְצַלְמֻנָּע כָּל נְסִיכֵמוֹ. אֲשֶׁר
אָמְרוּ, נִירְשָׁה לָּנוּ, אֵת נְאוֹת אֱלֹהִים.
אֱלֹהַי שִׁיתֵמוֹ כַגַּלְגַּל, כְּקַשׁ לִפְנֵי רוּחַ.
כְּאֵשׁ תִּבְעַר יָעַר, וּכְלֶהָבָה תְּלַהֵט
הָרִים. כֵּן תִּרְדְּפֵם בְּסַעֲרֶךָ, וּבְסוּפָתְךָ
תְבַהֲלֵם. מַלֵּא פְנֵיהֶם קָלוֹן, וִיבַקְשׁוּ
שִׁמְךָ יהוה. יֵבֹשׁוּ וְיִבָּהֲלוּ עֲדֵי עַד,
וְיַחְפְּרוּ וְיֹאבֵדוּ. וְיֵדְעוּ כִּי אַתָּה שִׁמְךָ
יהוה לְבַדֶּךָ, עֶלְיוֹן עַל כָּל הָאָרֶץ.

פד לַמְנַצֵּחַ עַל הַגִּתִּית, לִבְנֵי קֹרַח
מִזְמוֹר. מַה יְּדִידוֹת מִשְׁכְּנוֹתֶיךָ
יהוה צְבָאוֹת. נִכְסְפָה וְגַם כָּלְתָה נַפְשִׁי
לְחַצְרוֹת יהוה, לִבִּי וּבְשָׂרִי, יְרַנְּנוּ אֶל
אֵל חָי. גַּם צִפּוֹר מָצְאָה בַיִת, וּדְרוֹר קֵן
לָהּ אֲשֶׁר שָׁתָה אֶפְרֹחֶיהָ, אֶת
מִזְבְּחוֹתֶיךָ יהוה צְבָאוֹת, מַלְכִּי וֵאלֹהָי.
אַשְׁרֵי יוֹשְׁבֵי בֵיתֶךָ, עוֹד יְהַלְלוּךָ סֶּלָה.
אַשְׁרֵי אָדָם עוֹז לוֹ בָךְ, מְסִלּוֹת
בִּלְבָבָם. עֹבְרֵי בְּעֵמֶק הַבָּכָא מַעְיָן
יְשִׁיתוּהוּ, גַּם בְּרָכוֹת יַעְטֶה מוֹרֶה.
יֵלְכוּ מֵחַיִל אֶל חָיִל, יֵרָאֶה אֶל אֱלֹהִים
בְּצִיּוֹן. יהוה אֱלֹהִים צְבָאוֹת שִׁמְעָה
תְפִלָּתִי, הַאֲזִינָה אֱלֹהֵי יַעֲקֹב סֶלָה.
מָגִנֵּנוּ רְאֵה אֱלֹהִים, וְהַבֵּט פְּנֵי מְשִׁיחֶךָ.
כִּי טוֹב יוֹם בַּחֲצֵרֶיךָ מֵאָלֶף, בָּחַרְתִּי
הִסְתּוֹפֵף בְּבֵית אֱלֹהַי, מִדּוּר בְּאָהֳלֵי
רֶשַׁע. כִּי שֶׁמֶשׁ וּמָגֵן יהוה אֱלֹהִים, חֵן
וְכָבוֹד יִתֵּן יהוה, לֹא יִמְנַע טוֹב
לַהֹלְכִים בְּתָמִים. יהוה צְבָאוֹת, אַשְׁרֵי
אָדָם בֹּטֵחַ בָּךְ.

פה לַמְנַצֵּחַ לִבְנֵי קֹרַח מִזְמוֹר. רָצִיתָ
יהוה אַרְצֶךָ, שַׁבְתָּ שְׁבִית יַעֲקֹב.
נָשָׂאתָ עֲוֹן עַמֶּךָ, כִּסִּיתָ כָל חַטָּאתָם
סֶלָה. אָסַפְתָּ כָל עֶבְרָתֶךָ, הֱשִׁיבוֹתָ
מֵחֲרוֹן אַפֶּךָ. שׁוּבֵנוּ אֱלֹהֵי יִשְׁעֵנוּ,
וְהָפֵר כַּעַסְךָ עִמָּנוּ. הַלְעוֹלָם תֶּאֱנַף
בָּנוּ, תִּמְשֹׁךְ אַפְּךָ לְדֹר וָדֹר. הֲלֹא אַתָּה
תָּשׁוּב תְּחַיֵּנוּ, וְעַמְּךָ יִשְׂמְחוּ בָךְ.
הַרְאֵנוּ יהוה חַסְדֶּךָ, וְיֶשְׁעֲךָ תִּתֶּן לָנוּ.
אֶשְׁמְעָה מַה יְּדַבֵּר הָאֵל יהוה, כִּי
יְדַבֵּר שָׁלוֹם אֶל עַמּוֹ וְאֶל חֲסִידָיו, וְאַל
יָשׁוּבוּ לְכִסְלָה. אַךְ קָרוֹב לִירֵאָיו

יִשְׁעוֹ, לִשְׁכֹּן כָּבוֹד בְּאַרְצֵנוּ. חֶסֶד וֶאֱמֶת נִפְגָּשׁוּ, צֶדֶק וְשָׁלוֹם נָשָׁקוּ. אֱמֶת מֵאֶרֶץ תִּצְמָח, וְצֶדֶק מִשָּׁמַיִם נִשְׁקָף. גַּם יהוה יִתֵּן הַטּוֹב, וְאַרְצֵנוּ תִּתֵּן יְבוּלָהּ. צֶדֶק לְפָנָיו יְהַלֵּךְ, וְיָשֵׂם לְדֶרֶךְ פְּעָמָיו.

פו תְּפִלָּה לְדָוִד, הַטֵּה יהוה אָזְנְךָ עֲנֵנִי, כִּי עָנִי וְאֶבְיוֹן אָנִי. שָׁמְרָה נַפְשִׁי כִּי חָסִיד אָנִי, הוֹשַׁע עַבְדְּךָ אַתָּה אֱלֹהַי, הַבּוֹטֵחַ אֵלֶיךָ. חָנֵּנִי אֲדֹנָי, כִּי אֵלֶיךָ אֶקְרָא כָּל הַיּוֹם. שַׂמֵּחַ נֶפֶשׁ עַבְדֶּךָ, כִּי אֵלֶיךָ אֲדֹנָי נַפְשִׁי אֶשָּׂא. כִּי אַתָּה אֲדֹנָי טוֹב וְסַלָּח, וְרַב חֶסֶד לְכָל קֹרְאֶיךָ. הַאֲזִינָה יהוה תְּפִלָּתִי, וְהַקְשִׁיבָה בְּקוֹל תַּחֲנוּנוֹתָי. בְּיוֹם צָרָתִי אֶקְרָאֶךָּ כִּי תַעֲנֵנִי. אֵין כָּמוֹךָ בָאֱלֹהִים, אֲדֹנָי, וְאֵין כְּמַעֲשֶׂיךָ. כָּל גּוֹיִם אֲשֶׁר עָשִׂיתָ יָבוֹאוּ וְיִשְׁתַּחֲווּ לְפָנֶיךָ אֲדֹנָי, וִיכַבְּדוּ לִשְׁמֶךָ. כִּי גָדוֹל אַתָּה וְעֹשֵׂה נִפְלָאוֹת, אַתָּה אֱלֹהִים לְבַדֶּךָ. הוֹרֵנִי יהוה דַּרְכֶּךָ, אֲהַלֵּךְ בַּאֲמִתֶּךָ, יַחֵד לְבָבִי לְיִרְאָה שְׁמֶךָ. אוֹדְךָ אֲדֹנָי אֱלֹהַי בְּכָל לְבָבִי, וַאֲכַבְּדָה שִׁמְךָ לְעוֹלָם. כִּי חַסְדְּךָ גָּדוֹל עָלָי, וְהִצַּלְתָּ נַפְשִׁי מִשְּׁאוֹל תַּחְתִּיָּה. אֱלֹהִים, זֵדִים קָמוּ עָלַי, וַעֲדַת עָרִיצִים בִּקְשׁוּ נַפְשִׁי, וְלֹא שָׂמוּךָ לְנֶגְדָּם. וְאַתָּה אֲדֹנָי אֵל רַחוּם וְחַנּוּן, אֶרֶךְ אַפַּיִם וְרַב חֶסֶד וֶאֱמֶת. פְּנֵה אֵלַי וְחָנֵּנִי, תְּנָה עֻזְּךָ לְעַבְדֶּךָ, וְהוֹשִׁיעָה לְבֶן אֲמָתֶךָ. עֲשֵׂה עִמִּי אוֹת לְטוֹבָה, וְיִרְאוּ שֹׂנְאַי וְיֵבֹשׁוּ, כִּי אַתָּה יהוה עֲזַרְתַּנִי וְנִחַמְתָּנִי:

פז לִבְנֵי קֹרַח מִזְמוֹר שִׁיר, יְסוּדָתוֹ בְּהַרְרֵי קֹדֶשׁ. אֹהֵב יהוה שַׁעֲרֵי צִיּוֹן, מִכֹּל מִשְׁכְּנוֹת יַעֲקֹב. נִכְבָּדוֹת מְדֻבָּר בָּךְ, עִיר הָאֱלֹהִים סֶלָה. אַזְכִּיר רַהַב וּבָבֶל לְיֹדְעָי, הִנֵּה פְלֶשֶׁת וְצוֹר עִם כּוּשׁ, זֶה יֻלַּד שָׁם. וּלְצִיּוֹן יֵאָמַר, אִישׁ וְאִישׁ יֻלַּד בָּהּ, וְהוּא יְכוֹנְנֶהָ עֶלְיוֹן. יהוה יִסְפֹּר בִּכְתוֹב עַמִּים, זֶה יֻלַּד שָׁם סֶלָה. וְשָׁרִים כְּחֹלְלִים, כָּל מַעְיָנַי בָּךְ:

18th day — יום יח לחדש

פח שִׁיר מִזְמוֹר לִבְנֵי קֹרַח, לַמְנַצֵּחַ עַל מָחֲלַת לְעַנּוֹת, מַשְׂכִּיל לְהֵימָן הָאֶזְרָחִי. יהוה אֱלֹהֵי יְשׁוּעָתִי, יוֹם צָעַקְתִּי בַלַּיְלָה נֶגְדֶּךָ. תָּבוֹא לְפָנֶיךָ תְּפִלָּתִי, הַטֵּה אָזְנְךָ לְרִנָּתִי. כִּי שָׂבְעָה בְרָעוֹת נַפְשִׁי, וְחַיַּי לִשְׁאוֹל הִגִּיעוּ. נֶחְשַׁבְתִּי עִם יוֹרְדֵי בוֹר, הָיִיתִי כְּגֶבֶר אֵין אֱיָל. בַּמֵּתִים חָפְשִׁי, כְּמוֹ חֲלָלִים שֹׁכְבֵי קֶבֶר אֲשֶׁר לֹא זְכַרְתָּם עוֹד, וְהֵמָּה מִיָּדְךָ נִגְזָרוּ. שַׁתַּנִי בְּבוֹר תַּחְתִּיּוֹת, בְּמַחֲשַׁכִּים בִּמְצֹלוֹת. עָלַי סָמְכָה חֲמָתֶךָ, וְכָל מִשְׁבָּרֶיךָ עִנִּיתָ סֶּלָה. הִרְחַקְתָּ מְיֻדָּעַי מִמֶּנִּי, שַׁתַּנִי תוֹעֵבוֹת לָמוֹ, כָּלֻא וְלֹא אֵצֵא. עֵינִי דָאֲבָה מִנִּי עֹנִי, קְרָאתִיךָ יהוה בְּכָל יוֹם, שִׁטַּחְתִּי אֵלֶיךָ כַפָּי. הֲלַמֵּתִים תַּעֲשֶׂה פֶּלֶא, אִם רְפָאִים יָקוּמוּ יוֹדוּךָ סֶּלָה. הַיְסֻפַּר בַּקֶּבֶר חַסְדֶּךָ, אֱמוּנָתְךָ בָּאֲבַדּוֹן. הֲיִוָּדַע בַּחֹשֶׁךְ פִּלְאֶךָ, וְצִדְקָתְךָ בְּאֶרֶץ נְשִׁיָּה. וַאֲנִי אֵלֶיךָ יהוה שִׁוַּעְתִּי, וּבַבֹּקֶר תְּפִלָּתִי תְקַדְּמֶךָּ. לָמָה יהוה תִּזְנַח נַפְשִׁי, תַּסְתִּיר פָּנֶיךָ מִמֶּנִּי. עָנִי אֲנִי וְגֹוֵעַ מִנֹּעַר, נָשָׂאתִי אֵמֶיךָ אָפוּנָה. עָלַי עָבְרוּ חֲרוֹנֶיךָ, בִּעוּתֶיךָ צִמְּתוּתֻנִי. סַבּוּנִי כַמַּיִם כָּל הַיּוֹם, הִקִּיפוּ עָלַי יָחַד. הִרְחַקְתָּ מִמֶּנִּי אֹהֵב וָרֵעַ, מְיֻדָּעַי מַחְשָׁךְ:

פט מַשְׂכִּיל לְאֵיתָן הָאֶזְרָחִי. חַסְדֵי יהוה עוֹלָם אָשִׁירָה, לְדֹר וָדֹר אוֹדִיעַ אֱמוּנָתְךָ בְּפִי. כִּי אָמַרְתִּי, עוֹלָם חֶסֶד יִבָּנֶה, שָׁמַיִם תָּכִן אֱמוּנָתְךָ בָהֶם. כָּרַתִּי בְרִית לִבְחִירִי, נִשְׁבַּעְתִּי לְדָוִד עַבְדִּי. עַד עוֹלָם אָכִין זַרְעֶךָ, וּבָנִיתִי לְדֹר וָדוֹר כִּסְאֲךָ סֶלָה. וְיוֹדוּ שָׁמַיִם פִּלְאֲךָ יהוה, אַף אֱמוּנָתְךָ בִּקְהַל קְדֹשִׁים. כִּי מִי בַשַּׁחַק יַעֲרֹךְ לַיהוה, יִדְמֶה לַיהוה בִּבְנֵי אֵלִים. אֵל נַעֲרָץ בְּסוֹד קְדֹשִׁים רַבָּה, וְנוֹרָא עַל כָּל סְבִיבָיו. יהוה אֱלֹהֵי צְבָאוֹת, מִי כָמוֹךָ חֲסִין, יָהּ, וֶאֱמוּנָתְךָ סְבִיבוֹתֶיךָ. אַתָּה

מוֹשֵׁל בְּגֵאוּת הַיָּם, בְּשׂוֹא גַלָּיו אַתָּה תְשַׁבְּחֵם. אַתָּה דִכִּאתָ כֶחָלָל רָהַב, בִּזְרוֹעַ עֻזְּךָ פִּזַּרְתָּ אוֹיְבֶיךָ. לְךָ שָׁמַיִם אַף לְךָ אָרֶץ, תֵּבֵל וּמְלֹאָהּ אַתָּה יְסַדְתָּם. צָפוֹן וְיָמִין אַתָּה בְרָאתָם, תָּבוֹר וְחֶרְמוֹן בְּשִׁמְךָ יְרַנֵּנוּ. לְךָ זְרוֹעַ עִם גְּבוּרָה, תָּעֹז יָדְךָ תָּרוּם יְמִינֶךָ. צֶדֶק וּמִשְׁפָּט מְכוֹן כִּסְאֶךָ, חֶסֶד וֶאֱמֶת יְקַדְּמוּ פָנֶיךָ. אַשְׁרֵי הָעָם יוֹדְעֵי תְרוּעָה, יהוה בְּאוֹר פָּנֶיךָ יְהַלֵּכוּן. בְּשִׁמְךָ יְגִילוּן כָּל הַיּוֹם, וּבְצִדְקָתְךָ יָרוּמוּ. כִּי תִפְאֶרֶת עֻזָּמוֹ אָתָּה, וּבִרְצוֹנְךָ תָּרוּם קַרְנֵנוּ. כִּי לַיהוה מָגִנֵּנוּ, וְלִקְדוֹשׁ יִשְׂרָאֵל מַלְכֵּנוּ. אָז דִּבַּרְתָּ בְחָזוֹן לַחֲסִידֶיךָ, וַתֹּאמֶר שִׁוִּיתִי עֵזֶר עַל גִּבּוֹר, הֲרִימוֹתִי בָחוּר מֵעָם. מָצָאתִי דָּוִד עַבְדִּי, בְּשֶׁמֶן קָדְשִׁי מְשַׁחְתִּיו. אֲשֶׁר יָדִי תִּכּוֹן עִמּוֹ, אַף זְרוֹעִי תְאַמְּצֶנּוּ. לֹא יַשִּׁא אוֹיֵב בּוֹ, וּבֶן עַוְלָה לֹא יְעַנֶּנּוּ. וְכַתּוֹתִי מִפָּנָיו צָרָיו, וּמְשַׂנְאָיו אֶגּוֹף. וֶאֱמוּנָתִי וְחַסְדִּי עִמּוֹ, וּבִשְׁמִי תָּרוּם קַרְנוֹ. וְשַׂמְתִּי בַיָּם יָדוֹ, וּבַנְּהָרוֹת יְמִינוֹ. הוּא יִקְרָאֵנִי אָבִי אָתָּה, אֵלִי וְצוּר יְשׁוּעָתִי. אַף אָנִי בְּכוֹר אֶתְּנֵהוּ, עֶלְיוֹן לְמַלְכֵי אָרֶץ. לְעוֹלָם אֶשְׁמָר לוֹ חַסְדִּי, וּבְרִיתִי נֶאֱמֶנֶת לוֹ. וְשַׂמְתִּי לָעַד זַרְעוֹ, וְכִסְאוֹ כִּימֵי שָׁמָיִם. אִם יַעַזְבוּ בָנָיו תּוֹרָתִי, וּבְמִשְׁפָּטַי לֹא יֵלֵכוּן. אִם חֻקֹּתַי יְחַלֵּלוּ, וּמִצְוֹתַי לֹא יִשְׁמֹרוּ. וּפָקַדְתִּי בְשֵׁבֶט פִּשְׁעָם, וּבִנְגָעִים עֲוֹנָם. וְחַסְדִּי לֹא אָפִיר מֵעִמּוֹ, וְלֹא אֲשַׁקֵּר בֶּאֱמוּנָתִי. לֹא אֲחַלֵּל בְּרִיתִי, וּמוֹצָא שְׂפָתַי לֹא אֲשַׁנֶּה. אַחַת נִשְׁבַּעְתִּי בְקָדְשִׁי, אִם לְדָוִד אֲכַזֵּב. זַרְעוֹ לְעוֹלָם יִהְיֶה, וְכִסְאוֹ כַשֶּׁמֶשׁ נֶגְדִּי. כְּיָרֵחַ יִכּוֹן עוֹלָם, וְעֵד בַּשַּׁחַק נֶאֱמָן סֶלָה. וְאַתָּה זָנַחְתָּ וַתִּמְאָס, הִתְעַבַּרְתָּ עִם מְשִׁיחֶךָ. נֵאַרְתָּה בְּרִית עַבְדֶּךָ, חִלַּלְתָּ לָאָרֶץ נִזְרוֹ. פָּרַצְתָּ כָל גְּדֵרֹתָיו, שַׂמְתָּ מִבְצָרָיו מְחִתָּה. שַׁסֻּהוּ כָּל עֹבְרֵי דָרֶךְ, הָיָה חֶרְפָּה לִשְׁכֵנָיו. הֲרִימוֹתָ יְמִין צָרָיו, הִשְׂמַחְתָּ כָּל אוֹיְבָיו. אַף תָּשִׁיב צוּר חַרְבּוֹ, וְלֹא הֲקֵמֹתוֹ בַּמִּלְחָמָה. הִשְׁבַּתָּ מִטְּהָרוֹ, וְכִסְאוֹ לָאָרֶץ מִגַּרְתָּה. הִקְצַרְתָּ יְמֵי עֲלוּמָיו, הֶעֱטִיתָ עָלָיו בּוּשָׁה סֶלָה. עַד מָה יהוה תִּסָּתֵר לָנֶצַח, תִּבְעַר כְּמוֹ אֵשׁ חֲמָתֶךָ. זְכָר אֲנִי מֶה חָלֶד, עַל מַה שָּׁוְא בָּרָאתָ כָל בְּנֵי אָדָם. מִי גֶבֶר יִחְיֶה וְלֹא יִרְאֶה מָּוֶת, יְמַלֵּט נַפְשׁוֹ מִיַּד שְׁאוֹל סֶלָה. אַיֵּה חֲסָדֶיךָ הָרִאשֹׁנִים, אֲדֹנָי, נִשְׁבַּעְתָּ לְדָוִד בֶּאֱמוּנָתֶךָ. זְכֹר אֲדֹנָי חֶרְפַּת עֲבָדֶיךָ, שְׂאֵתִי בְחֵיקִי כָּל רַבִּים עַמִּים. אֲשֶׁר חֵרְפוּ אוֹיְבֶיךָ, יהוה, אֲשֶׁר חֵרְפוּ עִקְּבוֹת מְשִׁיחֶךָ. בָּרוּךְ יהוה לְעוֹלָם, אָמֵן וְאָמֵן:

BOOK FOUR — ספר רביעי

THURSDAY — ליום חמישי

19th day — יום יט לחדש

צ תְּפִלָּה לְמֹשֶׁה אִישׁ הָאֱלֹהִים, אֲדֹנָי מָעוֹן אַתָּה הָיִיתָ לָּנוּ בְּדֹר וָדֹר. בְּטֶרֶם הָרִים יֻלָּדוּ, וַתְּחוֹלֵל אֶרֶץ וְתֵבֵל, וּמֵעוֹלָם עַד עוֹלָם אַתָּה אֵל. תָּשֵׁב אֱנוֹשׁ עַד דַּכָּא, וַתֹּאמֶר, שׁוּבוּ בְנֵי אָדָם. כִּי אֶלֶף שָׁנִים בְּעֵינֶיךָ כְּיוֹם אֶתְמוֹל כִּי יַעֲבֹר, וְאַשְׁמוּרָה בַלָּיְלָה. זְרַמְתָּם, שֵׁנָה יִהְיוּ, בַּבֹּקֶר כֶּחָצִיר יַחֲלֹף. בַּבֹּקֶר יָצִיץ וְחָלָף, לָעֶרֶב יְמוֹלֵל וְיָבֵשׁ. כִּי כָלִינוּ בְאַפֶּךָ, וּבַחֲמָתְךָ נִבְהָלְנוּ. שַׁתָּ עֲוֹנֹתֵינוּ לְנֶגְדֶּךָ, עֲלֻמֵנוּ לִמְאוֹר פָּנֶיךָ. כִּי כָל יָמֵינוּ פָּנוּ בְעֶבְרָתֶךָ, כִּלִּינוּ שָׁנֵינוּ כְמוֹ הֶגֶה. יְמֵי שְׁנוֹתֵינוּ בָהֶם שִׁבְעִים שָׁנָה, וְאִם בִּגְבוּרֹת שְׁמוֹנִים שָׁנָה, וְרָהְבָּם עָמָל וָאָוֶן, כִּי גָז חִישׁ וַנָּעֻפָה. מִי יוֹדֵעַ עֹז אַפֶּךָ, וּכְיִרְאָתְךָ עֶבְרָתֶךָ. לִמְנוֹת יָמֵינוּ כֵּן הוֹדַע, וְנָבִא לְבַב חָכְמָה. שׁוּבָה יהוה עַד מָתָי, וְהִנָּחֵם עַל עֲבָדֶיךָ.

שַׂבְּעֵנוּ בַבֹּקֶר חַסְדֶּךָ, וּנְרַנְּנָה וְנִשְׂמְחָה
בְּכָל יָמֵינוּ. שַׂמְּחֵנוּ כִּימוֹת עִנִּיתָנוּ,
שְׁנוֹת רָאִינוּ רָעָה. יֵרָאֶה אֶל עֲבָדֶיךָ
פָעֳלֶךָ, וַהֲדָרְךָ עַל בְּנֵיהֶם. וִיהִי נֹעַם
אֲדֹנָי אֱלֹהֵינוּ עָלֵינוּ, וּמַעֲשֵׂה יָדֵינוּ
כּוֹנְנָה עָלֵינוּ, וּמַעֲשֵׂה יָדֵינוּ כּוֹנְנֵהוּ:

צא יֹשֵׁב בְּסֵתֶר עֶלְיוֹן, בְּצֵל שַׁדַּי
יִתְלוֹנָן. אֹמַר לַיהוה, מַחְסִי
וּמְצוּדָתִי, אֱלֹהַי אֶבְטַח בּוֹ. כִּי הוּא
יַצִּילְךָ מִפַּח יָקוּשׁ, מִדֶּבֶר הַוּוֹת.
בְּאֶבְרָתוֹ יָסֶךְ לָךְ, וְתַחַת כְּנָפָיו תֶּחְסֶה,
צִנָּה וְסֹחֵרָה אֲמִתּוֹ. לֹא תִירָא מִפַּחַד
לָיְלָה, מֵחֵץ יָעוּף יוֹמָם. מִדֶּבֶר בָּאֹפֶל
יַהֲלֹךְ, מִקֶּטֶב יָשׁוּד צָהֳרָיִם. יִפֹּל מִצִּדְּךָ
אֶלֶף, וּרְבָבָה מִימִינֶךָ, אֵלֶיךָ לֹא יִגָּשׁ.
רַק בְּעֵינֶיךָ תַבִּיט, וְשִׁלֻּמַת רְשָׁעִים
תִּרְאֶה. כִּי אַתָּה יהוה מַחְסִי, עֶלְיוֹן
שַׂמְתָּ מְעוֹנֶךָ. לֹא תְאֻנֶּה אֵלֶיךָ רָעָה,
וְנֶגַע לֹא יִקְרַב בְּאָהֳלֶךָ. כִּי מַלְאָכָיו
יְצַוֶּה לָּךְ, לִשְׁמָרְךָ בְּכָל דְּרָכֶיךָ. עַל
כַּפַּיִם יִשָּׂאוּנְךָ, פֶּן תִּגֹּף בָּאֶבֶן רַגְלֶךָ. עַל
שַׁחַל וָפֶתֶן תִּדְרֹךְ, תִּרְמֹס כְּפִיר וְתַנִּין.
כִּי בִי חָשַׁק וַאֲפַלְּטֵהוּ, אֲשַׂגְּבֵהוּ כִּי יָדַע
שְׁמִי. יִקְרָאֵנִי וְאֶעֱנֵהוּ, עִמּוֹ אָנֹכִי
בְצָרָה, אֲחַלְּצֵהוּ וַאֲכַבְּדֵהוּ. אֹרֶךְ יָמִים
אַשְׂבִּיעֵהוּ, וְאַרְאֵהוּ בִּישׁוּעָתִי:

צב מִזְמוֹר שִׁיר לְיוֹם הַשַּׁבָּת. טוֹב
לְהֹדוֹת לַיהוה, וּלְזַמֵּר לְשִׁמְךָ
עֶלְיוֹן. לְהַגִּיד בַּבֹּקֶר חַסְדֶּךָ, וֶאֱמוּנָתְךָ
בַּלֵּילוֹת. עֲלֵי עָשׂוֹר וַעֲלֵי נָבֶל, עֲלֵי
הִגָּיוֹן בְּכִנּוֹר. כִּי שִׂמַּחְתַּנִי יהוה
בְּפָעֳלֶךָ, בְּמַעֲשֵׂי יָדֶיךָ אֲרַנֵּן. מַה גָּדְלוּ
מַעֲשֶׂיךָ יהוה, מְאֹד עָמְקוּ מַחְשְׁבֹתֶיךָ.
אִישׁ בַּעַר לֹא יֵדָע, וּכְסִיל לֹא יָבִין אֶת
זֹאת. בִּפְרֹחַ רְשָׁעִים כְּמוֹ עֵשֶׂב, וַיָּצִיצוּ
כָּל פֹּעֲלֵי אָוֶן, לְהִשָּׁמְדָם עֲדֵי עַד.
וְאַתָּה מָרוֹם לְעֹלָם יהוה. כִּי הִנֵּה
אֹיְבֶיךָ, יהוה, כִּי הִנֵּה אֹיְבֶיךָ יֹאבֵדוּ,
יִתְפָּרְדוּ כָּל פֹּעֲלֵי אָוֶן. וַתָּרֶם כִּרְאֵים
קַרְנִי, בַּלֹּתִי בְּשֶׁמֶן רַעֲנָן. וַתַּבֵּט עֵינִי
בְּשׁוּרָי, בַּקָּמִים עָלַי מְרֵעִים, תִּשְׁמַעְנָה
אָזְנָי. צַדִּיק כַּתָּמָר יִפְרָח, כְּאֶרֶז בַּלְּבָנוֹן
יִשְׂגֶּה. שְׁתוּלִים בְּבֵית יהוה, בְּחַצְרוֹת
אֱלֹהֵינוּ יַפְרִיחוּ. עוֹד יְנוּבוּן בְּשֵׂיבָה,
דְּשֵׁנִים וְרַעֲנַנִּים יִהְיוּ. לְהַגִּיד כִּי יָשָׁר
יהוה, צוּרִי וְלֹא עַוְלָתָה בּוֹ:

צג יהוה מָלָךְ גֵּאוּת לָבֵשׁ, לָבֵשׁ
יהוה עֹז הִתְאַזָּר, אַף תִּכּוֹן תֵּבֵל
בַּל תִּמּוֹט. נָכוֹן כִּסְאֲךָ מֵאָז, מֵעוֹלָם
אָתָּה. נָשְׂאוּ נְהָרוֹת, יהוה, נָשְׂאוּ
נְהָרוֹת קוֹלָם, יִשְׂאוּ נְהָרוֹת דָּכְיָם.
מִקֹּלוֹת מַיִם רַבִּים אַדִּירִים מִשְׁבְּרֵי יָם,
אַדִּיר בַּמָּרוֹם יהוה. עֵדֹתֶיךָ נֶאֶמְנוּ
מְאֹד לְבֵיתְךָ נַאֲוָה קֹדֶשׁ, יהוה לְאֹרֶךְ
יָמִים:

צד אֵל נְקָמוֹת יהוה, אֵל נְקָמוֹת
הוֹפִיעַ. הִנָּשֵׂא שֹׁפֵט הָאָרֶץ,
הָשֵׁב גְּמוּל עַל גֵּאִים. עַד מָתַי רְשָׁעִים,
יהוה, עַד מָתַי רְשָׁעִים יַעֲלֹזוּ. יַבִּיעוּ
יְדַבְּרוּ עָתָק, יִתְאַמְּרוּ כָּל פֹּעֲלֵי אָוֶן.
עַמְּךָ יהוה יְדַכְּאוּ, וְנַחֲלָתְךָ יְעַנּוּ.
אַלְמָנָה וְגֵר יַהֲרֹגוּ, וִיתוֹמִים יְרַצֵּחוּ.
וַיֹּאמְרוּ, לֹא יִרְאֶה יָּהּ, וְלֹא יָבִין אֱלֹהֵי
יַעֲקֹב. בִּינוּ בֹּעֲרִים בָּעָם, וּכְסִילִים מָתַי
תַּשְׂכִּילוּ. הֲנֹטַע אֹזֶן הֲלֹא יִשְׁמָע, אִם
יֹצֵר עַיִן הֲלֹא יַבִּיט. הֲיֹסֵר גּוֹיִם הֲלֹא
יוֹכִיחַ, הַמְלַמֵּד אָדָם דָּעַת. יהוה יֹדֵעַ
מַחְשְׁבוֹת אָדָם, כִּי הֵמָּה הָבֶל. אַשְׁרֵי
הַגֶּבֶר אֲשֶׁר תְּיַסְּרֶנּוּ יָּהּ, וּמִתּוֹרָתְךָ
תְלַמְּדֶנּוּ. לְהַשְׁקִיט לוֹ מִימֵי רָע, עַד
יִכָּרֶה לָרָשָׁע שָׁחַת. כִּי לֹא יִטֹּשׁ יהוה
עַמּוֹ, וְנַחֲלָתוֹ לֹא יַעֲזֹב. כִּי עַד צֶדֶק
יָשׁוּב מִשְׁפָּט, וְאַחֲרָיו כָּל יִשְׁרֵי לֵב. מִי
יָקוּם לִי עִם מְרֵעִים, מִי יִתְיַצֵּב לִי עִם
פֹּעֲלֵי אָוֶן. לוּלֵי יהוה עֶזְרָתָה לִּי,
כִּמְעַט שָׁכְנָה דוּמָה נַפְשִׁי. אִם אָמַרְתִּי,
מָטָה רַגְלִי, חַסְדְּךָ יהוה יִסְעָדֵנִי. בְּרֹב
שַׂרְעַפַּי בְּקִרְבִּי, תַּנְחוּמֶיךָ יְשַׁעַשְׁעוּ
נַפְשִׁי. הַיְחָבְרְךָ כִּסֵּא הַוּוֹת, יֹצֵר עָמָל
עֲלֵי חֹק. יָגוֹדּוּ עַל נֶפֶשׁ צַדִּיק, וְדָם נָקִי
יַרְשִׁיעוּ. וַיְהִי יהוה לִי לְמִשְׂגָּב, וֵאלֹהַי
לְצוּר מַחְסִי. וַיָּשֶׁב עֲלֵיהֶם אֶת אוֹנָם,

וּבְרָעָתָם יַצְמִיתֵם, יַצְמִיתֵם יהוה אֱלֹהֵינוּ:

צה לְכוּ נְרַנְּנָה לַיהוה, נָרִיעָה לְצוּר יִשְׁעֵנוּ. נְקַדְּמָה פָנָיו בְּתוֹדָה, בִּזְמִרוֹת נָרִיעַ לוֹ. כִּי אֵל גָּדוֹל יהוה, וּמֶלֶךְ גָּדוֹל עַל כָּל אֱלֹהִים. אֲשֶׁר בְּיָדוֹ מֶחְקְרֵי אָרֶץ, וְתוֹעֲפוֹת הָרִים לוֹ. אֲשֶׁר לוֹ הַיָּם וְהוּא עָשָׂהוּ, וְיַבֶּשֶׁת יָדָיו יָצָרוּ. בֹּאוּ נִשְׁתַּחֲוֶה וְנִכְרָעָה, נִבְרְכָה לִפְנֵי יהוה עֹשֵׂנוּ. כִּי הוּא אֱלֹהֵינוּ, וַאֲנַחְנוּ עַם מַרְעִיתוֹ וְצֹאן יָדוֹ, הַיּוֹם אִם בְּקֹלוֹ תִשְׁמָעוּ. אַל תַּקְשׁוּ לְבַבְכֶם כִּמְרִיבָה, כְּיוֹם מַסָּה בַּמִּדְבָּר. אֲשֶׁר נִסּוּנִי אֲבוֹתֵיכֶם, בְּחָנוּנִי גַּם רָאוּ פָעֳלִי. אַרְבָּעִים שָׁנָה אָקוּט בְּדוֹר, וָאֹמַר, עַם תֹּעֵי לֵבָב הֵם, וְהֵם לֹא יָדְעוּ דְרָכָי. אֲשֶׁר נִשְׁבַּעְתִּי בְאַפִּי, אִם יְבֹאוּן אֶל מְנוּחָתִי:

צו שִׁירוּ לַיהוה שִׁיר חָדָשׁ, שִׁירוּ לַיהוה כָּל הָאָרֶץ. שִׁירוּ לַיהוה בָּרְכוּ שְׁמוֹ, בַּשְּׂרוּ מִיּוֹם לְיוֹם יְשׁוּעָתוֹ. סַפְּרוּ בַגּוֹיִם כְּבוֹדוֹ, בְּכָל הָעַמִּים נִפְלְאוֹתָיו. כִּי גָדוֹל יהוה וּמְהֻלָּל מְאֹד, נוֹרָא הוּא עַל כָּל אֱלֹהִים. כִּי, כָּל אֱלֹהֵי הָעַמִּים אֱלִילִים, וַיהוה שָׁמַיִם עָשָׂה. הוֹד וְהָדָר לְפָנָיו, עֹז וְתִפְאֶרֶת בְּמִקְדָּשׁוֹ. הָבוּ לַיהוה מִשְׁפְּחוֹת עַמִּים, הָבוּ לַיהוה כָּבוֹד וָעֹז. הָבוּ לַיהוה כְּבוֹד שְׁמוֹ, שְׂאוּ מִנְחָה וּבֹאוּ לְחַצְרוֹתָיו. הִשְׁתַּחֲווּ לַיהוה בְּהַדְרַת קֹדֶשׁ, חִילוּ מִפָּנָיו כָּל הָאָרֶץ. אִמְרוּ בַגּוֹיִם יהוה מָלָךְ, אַף תִּכּוֹן תֵּבֵל בַּל תִּמּוֹט, יָדִין עַמִּים בְּמֵישָׁרִים. יִשְׂמְחוּ הַשָּׁמַיִם וְתָגֵל הָאָרֶץ, יִרְעַם הַיָּם וּמְלֹאוֹ. יַעֲלֹז שָׂדַי וְכָל אֲשֶׁר בּוֹ, אָז יְרַנְּנוּ כָּל עֲצֵי יָעַר. לִפְנֵי יהוה כִּי בָא, כִּי בָא לִשְׁפֹּט הָאָרֶץ, יִשְׁפֹּט תֵּבֵל בְּצֶדֶק, וְעַמִּים בֶּאֱמוּנָתוֹ:

20th day — יום כ

צז יהוה מָלָךְ תָּגֵל הָאָרֶץ, יִשְׂמְחוּ אִיִּים רַבִּים. עָנָן וַעֲרָפֶל סְבִיבָיו, צֶדֶק וּמִשְׁפָּט מְכוֹן כִּסְאוֹ. אֵשׁ לְפָנָיו תֵּלֵךְ, וּתְלַהֵט סָבִיב צָרָיו. הֵאִירוּ בְרָקָיו תֵּבֵל, רָאֲתָה וַתָּחֵל הָאָרֶץ. הָרִים כַּדּוֹנַג נָמַסּוּ, מִלִּפְנֵי יהוה מִלִּפְנֵי אֲדוֹן כָּל הָאָרֶץ. הִגִּידוּ הַשָּׁמַיִם צִדְקוֹ, וְרָאוּ כָל הָעַמִּים כְּבוֹדוֹ. יֵבֹשׁוּ כָּל עֹבְדֵי פֶסֶל, הַמִּתְהַלְלִים בָּאֱלִילִים, הִשְׁתַּחֲווּ לוֹ כָּל אֱלֹהִים. שָׁמְעָה וַתִּשְׂמַח צִיּוֹן, וַתָּגֵלְנָה בְּנוֹת יְהוּדָה, לְמַעַן מִשְׁפָּטֶיךָ יהוה. כִּי אַתָּה יהוה עֶלְיוֹן עַל כָּל הָאָרֶץ, מְאֹד נַעֲלֵיתָ עַל כָּל אֱלֹהִים. אֹהֲבֵי יהוה שִׂנְאוּ רָע, שֹׁמֵר נַפְשׁוֹת חֲסִידָיו, מִיַּד רְשָׁעִים יַצִּילֵם. אוֹר זָרֻעַ לַצַּדִּיק, וּלְיִשְׁרֵי לֵב שִׂמְחָה. שִׂמְחוּ צַדִּיקִים בַּיהוה, וְהוֹדוּ לְזֵכֶר קָדְשׁוֹ:

צח מִזְמוֹר, שִׁירוּ לַיהוה שִׁיר חָדָשׁ, כִּי נִפְלָאוֹת עָשָׂה, הוֹשִׁיעָה לּוֹ יְמִינוֹ וּזְרוֹעַ קָדְשׁוֹ. הוֹדִיעַ יהוה יְשׁוּעָתוֹ, לְעֵינֵי הַגּוֹיִם גִּלָּה צִדְקָתוֹ. זָכַר חַסְדּוֹ וֶאֱמוּנָתוֹ לְבֵית יִשְׂרָאֵל, רָאוּ כָל אַפְסֵי אָרֶץ אֵת יְשׁוּעַת אֱלֹהֵינוּ. הָרִיעוּ לַיהוה כָּל הָאָרֶץ, פִּצְחוּ וְרַנְּנוּ וְזַמֵּרוּ. זַמְּרוּ לַיהוה בְּכִנּוֹר, בְּכִנּוֹר וְקוֹל זִמְרָה. בַּחֲצֹצְרוֹת וְקוֹל שׁוֹפָר, הָרִיעוּ לִפְנֵי הַמֶּלֶךְ יהוה. יִרְעַם הַיָּם וּמְלֹאוֹ, תֵּבֵל וְיֹשְׁבֵי בָהּ. נְהָרוֹת יִמְחֲאוּ כָף, יַחַד הָרִים יְרַנֵּנוּ. לִפְנֵי יהוה כִּי בָא לִשְׁפֹּט הָאָרֶץ, יִשְׁפֹּט תֵּבֵל בְּצֶדֶק, וְעַמִּים בְּמֵישָׁרִים:

צט יהוה מָלָךְ יִרְגְּזוּ עַמִּים, יֹשֵׁב כְּרוּבִים תָּנוּט הָאָרֶץ. יהוה בְּצִיּוֹן גָּדוֹל, וְרָם הוּא עַל כָּל הָעַמִּים. יוֹדוּ שִׁמְךָ גָּדוֹל וְנוֹרָא, קָדוֹשׁ הוּא. וְעֹז מֶלֶךְ מִשְׁפָּט אָהֵב, אַתָּה כּוֹנַנְתָּ מֵישָׁרִים, מִשְׁפָּט וּצְדָקָה בְּיַעֲקֹב אַתָּה עָשִׂיתָ. רוֹמְמוּ יהוה אֱלֹהֵינוּ, וְהִשְׁתַּחֲווּ לַהֲדֹם רַגְלָיו, קָדוֹשׁ הוּא. מֹשֶׁה וְאַהֲרֹן בְּכֹהֲנָיו, וּשְׁמוּאֵל בְּקֹרְאֵי שְׁמוֹ, קֹרְאִים אֶל יהוה וְהוּא יַעֲנֵם. בְּעַמּוּד עָנָן יְדַבֵּר אֲלֵיהֶם, שָׁמְרוּ

עֵדֹתָיו וְחֹק נָתַן לָמוֹ. יהוה אֱלֹהֵינוּ אַתָּה עֲנִיתָם, אֵל נֹשֵׂא הָיִיתָ לָהֶם, וְנֹקֵם עַל עֲלִילוֹתָם. רוֹמְמוּ יהוה אֱלֹהֵינוּ, וְהִשְׁתַּחֲווּ לְהַר קָדְשׁוֹ, כִּי קָדוֹשׁ יהוה אֱלֹהֵינוּ.

ק מִזְמוֹר לְתוֹדָה, הָרִיעוּ לַיהוה כָּל הָאָרֶץ. עִבְדוּ אֶת יהוה בְּשִׂמְחָה, בֹּאוּ לְפָנָיו בִּרְנָנָה. דְּעוּ כִּי יהוה הוּא אֱלֹהִים, הוּא עָשָׂנוּ, וְלוֹ אֲנַחְנוּ, עַמּוֹ וְצֹאן מַרְעִיתוֹ. בֹּאוּ שְׁעָרָיו בְּתוֹדָה, חֲצֵרֹתָיו בִּתְהִלָּה, הוֹדוּ לוֹ, בָּרְכוּ שְׁמוֹ. כִּי טוֹב יהוה, לְעוֹלָם חַסְדּוֹ, וְעַד דֹּר וָדֹר אֱמוּנָתוֹ.

קא לְדָוִד מִזְמוֹר, חֶסֶד וּמִשְׁפָּט אָשִׁירָה, לְךָ יהוה אֲזַמֵּרָה. אַשְׂכִּילָה בְּדֶרֶךְ תָּמִים, מָתַי תָּבוֹא אֵלָי, אֶתְהַלֵּךְ בְּתָם לְבָבִי, בְּקֶרֶב בֵּיתִי. לֹא אָשִׁית לְנֶגֶד עֵינַי דְּבַר בְּלִיָּעַל, עֲשֹׂה סֵטִים שָׂנֵאתִי, לֹא יִדְבַּק בִּי. לֵבָב עִקֵּשׁ יָסוּר מִמֶּנִּי, רָע לֹא אֵדָע. מְלָשְׁנִי בַסֵּתֶר רֵעֵהוּ אוֹתוֹ אַצְמִית, גְּבַהּ עֵינַיִם וּרְחַב לֵבָב, אֹתוֹ לֹא אוּכָל. עֵינַי בְּנֶאֶמְנֵי אֶרֶץ לָשֶׁבֶת עִמָּדִי, הֹלֵךְ בְּדֶרֶךְ תָּמִים, הוּא יְשָׁרְתֵנִי. לֹא יֵשֵׁב בְּקֶרֶב בֵּיתִי עֹשֵׂה רְמִיָּה, דֹּבֵר שְׁקָרִים, לֹא יִכּוֹן לְנֶגֶד עֵינָי. לַבְּקָרִים אַצְמִית כָּל רִשְׁעֵי אָרֶץ, לְהַכְרִית מֵעִיר יהוה, כָּל פֹּעֲלֵי אָוֶן.

קב תְּפִלָּה לְעָנִי כִי יַעֲטֹף, וְלִפְנֵי יהוה יִשְׁפֹּךְ שִׂיחוֹ. יהוה שִׁמְעָה תְפִלָּתִי, וְשַׁוְעָתִי אֵלֶיךָ תָבוֹא. אַל תַּסְתֵּר פָּנֶיךָ מִמֶּנִּי בְּיוֹם צַר לִי, הַטֵּה אֵלַי אָזְנֶךָ, בְּיוֹם אֶקְרָא, מַהֵר עֲנֵנִי. כִּי כָלוּ בְעָשָׁן יָמָי, וְעַצְמוֹתַי כְּמוֹקֵד נִחָרוּ. הוּכָּה כָעֵשֶׂב וַיִּבַשׁ לִבִּי, כִּי שָׁכַחְתִּי מֵאֲכֹל לַחְמִי. מִקּוֹל אַנְחָתִי, דָּבְקָה עַצְמִי לִבְשָׂרִי. דָּמִיתִי לִקְאַת מִדְבָּר, הָיִיתִי כְּכוֹס חֳרָבוֹת. שָׁקַדְתִּי וָאֶהְיֶה כְּצִפּוֹר בּוֹדֵד עַל גָּג. כָּל הַיּוֹם חֵרְפוּנִי אוֹיְבָי, מְהוֹלָלַי בִּי נִשְׁבָּעוּ. כִּי אֵפֶר כַּלֶּחֶם אָכָלְתִּי, וְשִׁקֻּוַי בִּבְכִי מָסָכְתִּי. מִפְּנֵי זַעַמְךָ וְקִצְפֶּךָ, כִּי נְשָׂאתַנִי וַתַּשְׁלִיכֵנִי. יָמַי כְּצֵל נָטוּי, וַאֲנִי כָּעֵשֶׂב אִיבָשׁ. וְאַתָּה יהוה לְעוֹלָם תֵּשֵׁב, וְזִכְרְךָ לְדֹר וָדֹר. אַתָּה תָקוּם תְּרַחֵם צִיּוֹן, כִּי עֵת לְחֶנְנָהּ כִּי בָא מוֹעֵד. כִּי רָצוּ עֲבָדֶיךָ אֶת אֲבָנֶיהָ, וְאֶת עֲפָרָהּ יְחֹנֵנוּ. וְיִירְאוּ גוֹיִם אֶת שֵׁם יהוה, וְכָל מַלְכֵי הָאָרֶץ אֶת כְּבוֹדֶךָ. כִּי בָנָה יהוה צִיּוֹן, נִרְאָה בִּכְבוֹדוֹ. פָּנָה אֶל תְּפִלַּת הָעַרְעָר, וְלֹא בָזָה אֶת תְּפִלָּתָם. תִּכָּתֶב זֹאת לְדוֹר אַחֲרוֹן, וְעַם נִבְרָא יְהַלֶּל יָהּ. כִּי הִשְׁקִיף מִמְּרוֹם קָדְשׁוֹ, יהוה מִשָּׁמַיִם אֶל אֶרֶץ הִבִּיט. לִשְׁמֹעַ אֶנְקַת אָסִיר, לְפַתֵּחַ בְּנֵי תְמוּתָה. לְסַפֵּר בְּצִיּוֹן שֵׁם יהוה, וּתְהִלָּתוֹ בִּירוּשָׁלָיִם. בְּהִקָּבֵץ עַמִּים יַחְדָּו, וּמַמְלָכוֹת לַעֲבֹד אֶת יהוה. עִנָּה בַדֶּרֶךְ כֹּחִי, קִצַּר יָמָי. אֹמַר, אֵלִי אַל תַּעֲלֵנִי בַּחֲצִי יָמָי, בְּדוֹר דּוֹרִים שְׁנוֹתֶיךָ. לְפָנִים הָאָרֶץ יָסַדְתָּ, וּמַעֲשֵׂה יָדֶיךָ שָׁמָיִם. הֵמָּה יֹאבֵדוּ, וְאַתָּה תַעֲמֹד, וְכֻלָּם כַּבֶּגֶד יִבְלוּ, כַּלְּבוּשׁ תַּחֲלִיפֵם וְיַחֲלֹפוּ. וְאַתָּה הוּא, וּשְׁנוֹתֶיךָ לֹא יִתָּמּוּ. בְּנֵי עֲבָדֶיךָ יִשְׁכּוֹנוּ, וְזַרְעָם לְפָנֶיךָ יִכּוֹן.

קג לְדָוִד, בָּרְכִי נַפְשִׁי אֶת יהוה, וְכָל קְרָבַי אֶת שֵׁם קָדְשׁוֹ. בָּרְכִי נַפְשִׁי אֶת יהוה, וְאַל תִּשְׁכְּחִי כָּל גְּמוּלָיו. הַסֹּלֵחַ לְכָל עֲוֹנֵכִי, הָרֹפֵא לְכָל תַּחֲלוּאָיְכִי. הַגּוֹאֵל מִשַּׁחַת חַיָּיְכִי, הַמְעַטְּרֵכִי חֶסֶד וְרַחֲמִים. הַמַּשְׂבִּיעַ בַּטּוֹב עֶדְיֵךְ, תִּתְחַדֵּשׁ כַּנֶּשֶׁר נְעוּרָיְכִי. עֹשֵׂה צְדָקוֹת יהוה, וּמִשְׁפָּטִים לְכָל עֲשׁוּקִים. יוֹדִיעַ דְּרָכָיו לְמֹשֶׁה, לִבְנֵי יִשְׂרָאֵל עֲלִילוֹתָיו. רַחוּם וְחַנּוּן יהוה, אֶרֶךְ אַפַּיִם וְרַב חָסֶד. לֹא לָנֶצַח יָרִיב, וְלֹא לְעוֹלָם יִטּוֹר. לֹא כַחֲטָאֵינוּ עָשָׂה לָנוּ, וְלֹא כַעֲוֹנֹתֵינוּ גָּמַל עָלֵינוּ. כִּי כִגְבֹהַּ שָׁמַיִם עַל הָאָרֶץ, גָּבַר חַסְדּוֹ עַל יְרֵאָיו. כִּרְחֹק מִזְרָח מִמַּעֲרָב, הִרְחִיק מִמֶּנּוּ אֶת פְּשָׁעֵינוּ. כְּרַחֵם אָב עַל בָּנִים, רִחַם יהוה עַל יְרֵאָיו. כִּי הוּא יָדַע

יִצְרֵנוּ, זָכוּר כִּי עָפָר אֲנָחְנוּ. אֱנוֹשׁ כֶּחָצִיר יָמָיו, כְּצִיץ הַשָּׂדֶה כֵּן יָצִיץ. כִּי רוּחַ עָבְרָה בּוֹ וְאֵינֶנּוּ, וְלֹא יַכִּירֶנּוּ עוֹד מְקוֹמוֹ. וְחֶסֶד יהוה מֵעוֹלָם וְעַד עוֹלָם עַל יְרֵאָיו, וְצִדְקָתוֹ לִבְנֵי בָנִים. לְשֹׁמְרֵי בְרִיתוֹ, וּלְזֹכְרֵי פִקֻּדָיו לַעֲשׂוֹתָם. יהוה בַּשָּׁמַיִם הֵכִין כִּסְאוֹ, וּמַלְכוּתוֹ בַּכֹּל מָשָׁלָה. בָּרְכוּ יהוה מַלְאָכָיו, גִּבֹּרֵי כֹחַ עֹשֵׂי דְבָרוֹ, לִשְׁמֹעַ בְּקוֹל דְּבָרוֹ. בָּרְכוּ יהוה כָּל צְבָאָיו, מְשָׁרְתָיו עֹשֵׂי רְצוֹנוֹ. בָּרְכוּ יהוה כָּל מַעֲשָׂיו, בְּכָל מְקֹמוֹת מֶמְשַׁלְתּוֹ, בָּרְכִי נַפְשִׁי אֶת יהוה.

יום כא לחדש — 21st day

קד בָּרְכִי נַפְשִׁי אֶת יהוה, יהוה אֱלֹהַי גָּדַלְתָּ מְּאֹד, הוֹד וְהָדָר לָבָשְׁתָּ. עֹטֶה אוֹר כַּשַּׂלְמָה, נוֹטֶה שָׁמַיִם כַּיְרִיעָה. הַמְקָרֶה בַמַּיִם עֲלִיּוֹתָיו, הַשָּׂם עָבִים רְכוּבוֹ, הַמְהַלֵּךְ עַל כַּנְפֵי רוּחַ. עֹשֶׂה מַלְאָכָיו רוּחוֹת, מְשָׁרְתָיו אֵשׁ לֹהֵט. יָסַד אֶרֶץ עַל מְכוֹנֶיהָ, בַּל תִּמּוֹט עוֹלָם וָעֶד. תְּהוֹם כַּלְּבוּשׁ כִּסִּיתוֹ, עַל הָרִים יַעַמְדוּ מָיִם. מִן גַּעֲרָתְךָ יְנוּסוּן, מִן קוֹל רַעַמְךָ יֵחָפֵזוּן. יַעֲלוּ הָרִים, יֵרְדוּ בְקָעוֹת, אֶל מְקוֹם זֶה יָסַדְתָּ לָהֶם. גְּבוּל שַׂמְתָּ בַּל יַעֲבֹרוּן, בַּל יְשׁוּבוּן לְכַסּוֹת הָאָרֶץ. הַמְשַׁלֵּחַ מַעְיָנִים בַּנְּחָלִים, בֵּין הָרִים יְהַלֵּכוּן. יַשְׁקוּ כָּל חַיְתוֹ שָׂדָי, יִשְׁבְּרוּ פְרָאִים צְמָאָם. עֲלֵיהֶם עוֹף הַשָּׁמַיִם יִשְׁכּוֹן, מִבֵּין עֳפָאִים יִתְּנוּ קוֹל. מַשְׁקֶה הָרִים מֵעֲלִיּוֹתָיו, מִפְּרִי מַעֲשֶׂיךָ תִּשְׂבַּע הָאָרֶץ. מַצְמִיחַ חָצִיר לַבְּהֵמָה, וְעֵשֶׂב לַעֲבֹדַת הָאָדָם, לְהוֹצִיא לֶחֶם מִן הָאָרֶץ. וְיַיִן יְשַׂמַּח לְבַב אֱנוֹשׁ, לְהַצְהִיל פָּנִים מִשָּׁמֶן, וְלֶחֶם לְבַב אֱנוֹשׁ יִסְעָד. יִשְׂבְּעוּ עֲצֵי יהוה, אַרְזֵי לְבָנוֹן אֲשֶׁר נָטָע. אֲשֶׁר שָׁם צִפֳּרִים יְקַנֵּנוּ, חֲסִידָה בְּרוֹשִׁים בֵּיתָהּ. הָרִים הַגְּבֹהִים לַיְּעֵלִים, סְלָעִים מַחְסֶה לַשְׁפַנִּים. עָשָׂה יָרֵחַ לְמוֹעֲדִים, שֶׁמֶשׁ יָדַע מְבוֹאוֹ. תָּשֶׁת חֹשֶׁךְ וִיהִי לָיְלָה, בּוֹ תִרְמֹשׂ כָּל חַיְתוֹ יָעַר. הַכְּפִירִים שֹׁאֲגִים לַטָּרֶף, וּלְבַקֵּשׁ מֵאֵל אָכְלָם. תִּזְרַח הַשֶּׁמֶשׁ יֵאָסֵפוּן, וְאֶל מְעוֹנֹתָם יִרְבָּצוּן. יֵצֵא אָדָם לְפָעֳלוֹ, וְלַעֲבֹדָתוֹ עֲדֵי עָרֶב. מָה רַבּוּ מַעֲשֶׂיךָ יהוה, כֻּלָּם בְּחָכְמָה עָשִׂיתָ, מָלְאָה הָאָרֶץ קִנְיָנֶךָ. זֶה הַיָּם, גָּדוֹל וּרְחַב יָדָיִם, שָׁם רֶמֶשׂ וְאֵין מִסְפָּר, חַיּוֹת קְטַנּוֹת עִם גְּדֹלוֹת. שָׁם אֳנִיּוֹת יְהַלֵּכוּן, לִוְיָתָן זֶה יָצַרְתָּ לְשַׂחֶק בּוֹ. כֻּלָּם אֵלֶיךָ יְשַׂבֵּרוּן, לָתֵת אָכְלָם בְּעִתּוֹ. תִּתֵּן לָהֶם, יִלְקֹטוּן, תִּפְתַּח יָדְךָ, יִשְׂבְּעוּן טוֹב. תַּסְתִּיר פָּנֶיךָ יִבָּהֵלוּן, תֹּסֵף רוּחָם יִגְוָעוּן, וְאֶל עֲפָרָם יְשׁוּבוּן. תְּשַׁלַּח רוּחֲךָ יִבָּרֵאוּן, וּתְחַדֵּשׁ פְּנֵי אֲדָמָה. יְהִי כְבוֹד יהוה לְעוֹלָם, יִשְׂמַח יהוה בְּמַעֲשָׂיו. הַמַּבִּיט לָאָרֶץ וַתִּרְעָד, יִגַּע בֶּהָרִים וְיֶעֱשָׁנוּ. אָשִׁירָה לַיהוה בְּחַיָּי, אֲזַמְּרָה לֵאלֹהַי בְּעוֹדִי. יֶעֱרַב עָלָיו שִׂיחִי, אָנֹכִי אֶשְׂמַח בַּיהוה. יִתַּמּוּ חַטָּאִים מִן הָאָרֶץ, וּרְשָׁעִים עוֹד אֵינָם, בָּרְכִי נַפְשִׁי אֶת יהוה, הַלְלוּיָהּ.

קה הוֹדוּ לַיהוה קִרְאוּ בִשְׁמוֹ, הוֹדִיעוּ בָעַמִּים עֲלִילוֹתָיו. שִׁירוּ לוֹ זַמְּרוּ לוֹ, שִׂיחוּ בְּכָל נִפְלְאוֹתָיו. הִתְהַלְלוּ בְּשֵׁם קָדְשׁוֹ, יִשְׂמַח לֵב מְבַקְשֵׁי יהוה. דִּרְשׁוּ יהוה וְעֻזּוֹ, בַּקְּשׁוּ פָנָיו תָּמִיד. זִכְרוּ נִפְלְאוֹתָיו אֲשֶׁר עָשָׂה, מֹפְתָיו וּמִשְׁפְּטֵי פִיו. זֶרַע אַבְרָהָם עַבְדּוֹ, בְּנֵי יַעֲקֹב בְּחִירָיו. הוּא יהוה אֱלֹהֵינוּ, בְּכָל הָאָרֶץ מִשְׁפָּטָיו. זָכַר לְעוֹלָם בְּרִיתוֹ, דָּבָר צִוָּה לְאֶלֶף דּוֹר. אֲשֶׁר כָּרַת אֶת אַבְרָהָם, וּשְׁבוּעָתוֹ לְיִשְׂחָק. וַיַּעֲמִידֶהָ לְיַעֲקֹב לְחֹק, לְיִשְׂרָאֵל בְּרִית עוֹלָם. לֵאמֹר לְךָ אֶתֵּן אֶת אֶרֶץ כְּנָעַן, חֶבֶל נַחֲלַתְכֶם. בִּהְיוֹתָם מְתֵי מִסְפָּר, כִּמְעַט וְגָרִים בָּהּ. וַיִּתְהַלְּכוּ מִגּוֹי אֶל גּוֹי, מִמַּמְלָכָה אֶל עַם אַחֵר. לֹא הִנִּיחַ אָדָם לְעָשְׁקָם, וַיּוֹכַח עֲלֵיהֶם מְלָכִים. אַל תִּגְּעוּ בִמְשִׁיחָי, וְלִנְבִיאַי אַל תָּרֵעוּ. וַיִּקְרָא רָעָב עַל הָאָרֶץ, כָּל מַטֵּה לֶחֶם שָׁבָר.

שָׁלַח לִפְנֵיהֶם אִישׁ, לְעֶבֶד נִמְכַּר יוֹסֵף. עִנּוּ בַכֶּבֶל רַגְלוֹ, בַּרְזֶל בָּאָה נַפְשׁוֹ. עַד עֵת בֹּא דְבָרוֹ, אִמְרַת יהוה צְרָפָתְהוּ. שָׁלַח מֶלֶךְ וַיַּתִּירֵהוּ, מֹשֵׁל עַמִּים וַיְפַתְּחֵהוּ. שָׂמוֹ אָדוֹן לְבֵיתוֹ, וּמֹשֵׁל בְּכָל קִנְיָנוֹ. לֶאְסֹר שָׂרָיו בְּנַפְשׁוֹ, וּזְקֵנָיו יְחַכֵּם. וַיָּבֹא יִשְׂרָאֵל מִצְרָיִם, וְיַעֲקֹב גָּר בְּאֶרֶץ חָם. וַיֶּפֶר אֶת עַמּוֹ מְאֹד, וַיַּעֲצִמֵהוּ מִצָּרָיו. הָפַךְ לִבָּם לִשְׂנֹא עַמּוֹ, לְהִתְנַכֵּל בַּעֲבָדָיו. שָׁלַח מֹשֶׁה עַבְדּוֹ, אַהֲרֹן אֲשֶׁר בָּחַר בּוֹ. שָׂמוּ בָם דִּבְרֵי אֹתוֹתָיו, וּמֹפְתִים בְּאֶרֶץ חָם. שָׁלַח חֹשֶׁךְ וַיַּחְשִׁךְ, וְלֹא מָרוּ אֶת דְּבָרוֹ. הָפַךְ אֶת מֵימֵיהֶם לְדָם, וַיָּמֶת אֶת דְּגָתָם. שָׁרַץ אַרְצָם צְפַרְדְּעִים, בְּחַדְרֵי מַלְכֵיהֶם. אָמַר וַיָּבֹא עָרֹב, כִּנִּים בְּכָל גְּבוּלָם. נָתַן גִּשְׁמֵיהֶם בָּרָד, אֵשׁ לֶהָבוֹת בְּאַרְצָם. וַיַּךְ גַּפְנָם וּתְאֵנָתָם, וַיְשַׁבֵּר עֵץ גְּבוּלָם. אָמַר וַיָּבֹא אַרְבֶּה, וְיֶלֶק וְאֵין מִסְפָּר. וַיֹּאכַל כָּל עֵשֶׂב בְּאַרְצָם, וַיֹּאכַל פְּרִי אַדְמָתָם. וַיַּךְ כָּל בְּכוֹר בְּאַרְצָם, רֵאשִׁית לְכָל אוֹנָם. וַיּוֹצִיאֵם בְּכֶסֶף וְזָהָב, וְאֵין בִּשְׁבָטָיו כּוֹשֵׁל. שָׂמַח מִצְרַיִם בְּצֵאתָם, כִּי נָפַל פַּחְדָּם עֲלֵיהֶם. פָּרַשׂ עָנָן לְמָסָךְ, וְאֵשׁ לְהָאִיר לָיְלָה. שָׁאַל וַיָּבֵא שְׂלָו, וְלֶחֶם שָׁמַיִם יַשְׂבִּיעֵם. פָּתַח צוּר וַיָּזוּבוּ מָיִם, הָלְכוּ בַּצִּיּוֹת נָהָר. כִּי זָכַר אֶת דְּבַר קָדְשׁוֹ, אֶת אַבְרָהָם עַבְדּוֹ. וַיּוֹצִא עַמּוֹ בְשָׂשׂוֹן, בְּרִנָּה אֶת בְּחִירָיו. וַיִּתֵּן לָהֶם אַרְצוֹת גּוֹיִם, וַעֲמַל לְאֻמִּים יִירָשׁוּ. בַּעֲבוּר יִשְׁמְרוּ חֻקָּיו, וְתוֹרֹתָיו יִנְצֹרוּ, הַלְלוּיָהּ.

יום כב לחדש — 22nd day

קו הַלְלוּיָהּ, הוֹדוּ לַיהוה כִּי טוֹב, כִּי לְעוֹלָם חַסְדּוֹ. מִי יְמַלֵּל גְּבוּרוֹת יהוה, יַשְׁמִיעַ כָּל תְּהִלָּתוֹ. אַשְׁרֵי שֹׁמְרֵי מִשְׁפָּט, עֹשֵׂה צְדָקָה בְכָל עֵת. זָכְרֵנִי יהוה בִּרְצוֹן עַמֶּךָ, פָּקְדֵנִי בִּישׁוּעָתֶךָ. לִרְאוֹת בְּטוֹבַת בְּחִירֶיךָ, לִשְׂמֹחַ בְּשִׂמְחַת גּוֹיֶךָ, לְהִתְהַלֵּל עִם נַחֲלָתֶךָ. חָטָאנוּ עִם אֲבוֹתֵינוּ, הֶעֱוִינוּ הִרְשָׁעְנוּ. אֲבוֹתֵינוּ בְמִצְרַיִם לֹא הִשְׂכִּילוּ נִפְלְאוֹתֶיךָ, לֹא זָכְרוּ אֶת רֹב חֲסָדֶיךָ, וַיַּמְרוּ עַל יָם בְּיַם סוּף. וַיּוֹשִׁיעֵם לְמַעַן שְׁמוֹ, לְהוֹדִיעַ אֶת גְּבוּרָתוֹ. וַיִּגְעַר בְּיַם סוּף וַיֶּחֱרָב, וַיּוֹלִיכֵם בַּתְּהֹמוֹת כַּמִּדְבָּר. וַיּוֹשִׁיעֵם מִיַּד שׂוֹנֵא, וַיִּגְאָלֵם מִיַּד אוֹיֵב. וַיְכַסּוּ מַיִם צָרֵיהֶם, אֶחָד מֵהֶם לֹא נוֹתָר. וַיַּאֲמִינוּ בִדְבָרָיו, יָשִׁירוּ תְּהִלָּתוֹ. מִהֲרוּ שָׁכְחוּ מַעֲשָׂיו, לֹא חִכּוּ לַעֲצָתוֹ. וַיִּתְאַוּוּ תַאֲוָה בַּמִּדְבָּר, וַיְנַסּוּ אֵל בִּישִׁימוֹן. וַיִּתֵּן לָהֶם שֶׁאֱלָתָם, וַיְשַׁלַּח רָזוֹן בְּנַפְשָׁם. וַיְקַנְאוּ לְמֹשֶׁה בַּמַּחֲנֶה, לְאַהֲרֹן קְדוֹשׁ יהוה. תִּפְתַּח אֶרֶץ וַתִּבְלַע דָּתָן, וַתְּכַס עַל עֲדַת אֲבִירָם. וַתִּבְעַר אֵשׁ בַּעֲדָתָם, לֶהָבָה תְּלַהֵט רְשָׁעִים. יַעֲשׂוּ עֵגֶל בְּחֹרֵב, וַיִּשְׁתַּחֲווּ לְמַסֵּכָה. וַיָּמִירוּ אֶת כְּבוֹדָם, בְּתַבְנִית שׁוֹר אֹכֵל עֵשֶׂב. שָׁכְחוּ אֵל מוֹשִׁיעָם, עֹשֶׂה גְדֹלוֹת בְּמִצְרָיִם. נִפְלָאוֹת בְּאֶרֶץ חָם, נוֹרָאוֹת עַל יַם סוּף. וַיֹּאמֶר לְהַשְׁמִידָם, לוּלֵי מֹשֶׁה בְחִירוֹ עָמַד בַּפֶּרֶץ לְפָנָיו, לְהָשִׁיב חֲמָתוֹ מֵהַשְׁחִית. וַיִּמְאֲסוּ בְּאֶרֶץ חֶמְדָּה, לֹא הֶאֱמִינוּ לִדְבָרוֹ. וַיֵּרָגְנוּ בְאָהֳלֵיהֶם, לֹא שָׁמְעוּ בְּקוֹל יהוה. וַיִּשָּׂא יָדוֹ לָהֶם, לְהַפִּיל אוֹתָם בַּמִּדְבָּר. וּלְהַפִּיל זַרְעָם בַּגּוֹיִם, וּלְזָרוֹתָם בָּאֲרָצוֹת. וַיִּצָּמְדוּ לְבַעַל פְּעוֹר, וַיֹּאכְלוּ זִבְחֵי מֵתִים. וַיַּכְעִיסוּ בְּמַעַלְלֵיהֶם, וַתִּפְרָץ בָּם מַגֵּפָה. וַיַּעֲמֹד פִּינְחָס וַיְפַלֵּל, וַתֵּעָצַר הַמַּגֵּפָה. וַתֵּחָשֶׁב לוֹ לִצְדָקָה, לְדֹר וָדֹר עַד עוֹלָם. וַיַּקְצִיפוּ עַל מֵי מְרִיבָה, וַיֵּרַע לְמֹשֶׁה בַּעֲבוּרָם. כִּי הִמְרוּ אֶת רוּחוֹ, וַיְבַטֵּא בִּשְׂפָתָיו. לֹא הִשְׁמִידוּ אֶת הָעַמִּים, אֲשֶׁר אָמַר יהוה לָהֶם. וַיִּתְעָרְבוּ בַגּוֹיִם, וַיִּלְמְדוּ מַעֲשֵׂיהֶם. וַיַּעַבְדוּ אֶת עֲצַבֵּיהֶם, וַיִּהְיוּ לָהֶם לְמוֹקֵשׁ. וַיִּזְבְּחוּ אֶת בְּנֵיהֶם וְאֶת בְּנוֹתֵיהֶם לַשֵּׁדִים. וַיִּשְׁפְּכוּ דָם נָקִי, דַּם

בְּנֵיהֶם וּבְנוֹתֵיהֶם, אֲשֶׁר זִבְּחוּ לַעֲצַבֵּי כְנָעַן, וַתֶּחֱנַף הָאָרֶץ בַּדָּמִים. וַיִּטְמְאוּ בְמַעֲשֵׂיהֶם, וַיִּזְנוּ בְּמַעַלְלֵיהֶם. וַיִּחַר אַף יהוה בְּעַמּוֹ, וַיְתָעֵב אֶת נַחֲלָתוֹ. וַיִּתְּנֵם בְּיַד גּוֹיִם, וַיִּמְשְׁלוּ בָהֶם שֹׂנְאֵיהֶם. וַיִּלְחָצוּם אוֹיְבֵיהֶם, וַיִּכָּנְעוּ תַּחַת יָדָם. פְּעָמִים רַבּוֹת יַצִּילֵם, וְהֵמָּה יַמְרוּ בַעֲצָתָם, וַיָּמֹכּוּ בַּעֲוֹנָם. וַיַּרְא בַּצַּר לָהֶם, בְּשָׁמְעוֹ אֶת רִנָּתָם. וַיִּזְכֹּר לָהֶם בְּרִיתוֹ, וַיִּנָּחֵם כְּרֹב חֲסָדָיו. וַיִּתֵּן אוֹתָם לְרַחֲמִים, לִפְנֵי כָּל שׁוֹבֵיהֶם. הוֹשִׁיעֵנוּ יהוה אֱלֹהֵינוּ, וְקַבְּצֵנוּ מִן הַגּוֹיִם, לְהֹדוֹת לְשֵׁם קָדְשֶׁךָ, לְהִשְׁתַּבֵּחַ בִּתְהִלָּתֶךָ. בָּרוּךְ יהוה אֱלֹהֵי יִשְׂרָאֵל מִן הָעוֹלָם וְעַד הָעוֹלָם, וְאָמַר כָּל הָעָם אָמֵן, הַלְלוּיָהּ.

ספר חמישי — BOOK FIVE

ליום ששי — FRIDAY

קז הֹדוּ לַיהוה כִּי טוֹב, כִּי לְעוֹלָם חַסְדּוֹ. יֹאמְרוּ גְּאוּלֵי יהוה, אֲשֶׁר גְּאָלָם מִיַּד צָר. וּמֵאֲרָצוֹת קִבְּצָם, מִמִּזְרָח וּמִמַּעֲרָב, מִצָּפוֹן וּמִיָּם. תָּעוּ בַמִּדְבָּר בִּישִׁימוֹן דָּרֶךְ, עִיר מוֹשָׁב לֹא מָצָאוּ. רְעֵבִים גַּם צְמֵאִים, נַפְשָׁם בָּהֶם תִּתְעַטָּף. וַיִּצְעֲקוּ אֶל יהוה בַּצַּר לָהֶם, מִמְּצוּקוֹתֵיהֶם יַצִּילֵם. וַיַּדְרִיכֵם בְּדֶרֶךְ יְשָׁרָה, לָלֶכֶת אֶל עִיר מוֹשָׁב. יוֹדוּ לַיהוה חַסְדּוֹ, וְנִפְלְאוֹתָיו לִבְנֵי אָדָם. כִּי הִשְׂבִּיעַ נֶפֶשׁ שֹׁקֵקָה, וְנֶפֶשׁ רְעֵבָה מִלֵּא טוֹב. יֹשְׁבֵי חֹשֶׁךְ וְצַלְמָוֶת, אֲסִירֵי עֳנִי וּבַרְזֶל. כִּי הִמְרוּ אִמְרֵי אֵל, וַעֲצַת עֶלְיוֹן נָאָצוּ. וַיַּכְנַע בֶּעָמָל לִבָּם, כָּשְׁלוּ וְאֵין עֹזֵר. וַיִּזְעֲקוּ אֶל יהוה בַּצַּר לָהֶם, מִמְּצֻקוֹתֵיהֶם יוֹשִׁיעֵם. יוֹצִיאֵם מֵחֹשֶׁךְ וְצַלְמָוֶת, וּמוֹסְרוֹתֵיהֶם יְנַתֵּק. יוֹדוּ לַיהוה חַסְדּוֹ, וְנִפְלְאוֹתָיו לִבְנֵי אָדָם. כִּי שִׁבַּר דַּלְתוֹת נְחֹשֶׁת, וּבְרִיחֵי בַרְזֶל גִּדֵּעַ. אֱוִלִים מִדֶּרֶךְ פִּשְׁעָם, וּמֵעֲוֹנֹתֵיהֶם יִתְעַנּוּ. כָּל אֹכֶל תְּתַעֵב נַפְשָׁם, וַיַּגִּיעוּ עַד שַׁעֲרֵי מָוֶת. וַיִּזְעֲקוּ אֶל יהוה בַּצַּר לָהֶם, מִמְּצֻקוֹתֵיהֶם יוֹשִׁיעֵם. יִשְׁלַח דְּבָרוֹ וְיִרְפָּאֵם, וִימַלֵּט מִשְּׁחִיתוֹתָם. יוֹדוּ לַיהוה חַסְדּוֹ, וְנִפְלְאוֹתָיו לִבְנֵי אָדָם. וְיִזְבְּחוּ זִבְחֵי תוֹדָה, וִיסַפְּרוּ מַעֲשָׂיו בְּרִנָּה. יוֹרְדֵי הַיָּם בָּאֳנִיּוֹת, עֹשֵׂי מְלָאכָה בְּמַיִם רַבִּים. הֵמָּה רָאוּ מַעֲשֵׂי יהוה, וְנִפְלְאוֹתָיו בִּמְצוּלָה. וַיֹּאמֶר וַיַּעֲמֵד רוּחַ סְעָרָה, וַתְּרוֹמֵם גַּלָּיו. יַעֲלוּ שָׁמַיִם יֵרְדוּ תְהוֹמוֹת, נַפְשָׁם בְּרָעָה תִתְמוֹגָג. יָחוֹגּוּ וְיָנוּעוּ כַּשִּׁכּוֹר, וְכָל חָכְמָתָם תִּתְבַּלָּע. וַיִּצְעֲקוּ אֶל יהוה בַּצַּר לָהֶם, וּמִמְּצוּקֹתֵיהֶם יוֹצִיאֵם. יָקֵם סְעָרָה לִדְמָמָה, וַיֶּחֱשׁוּ גַּלֵּיהֶם. וַיִּשְׂמְחוּ כִי יִשְׁתֹּקוּ, וַיַּנְחֵם אֶל מְחוֹז חֶפְצָם. יוֹדוּ לַיהוה חַסְדּוֹ, וְנִפְלְאוֹתָיו לִבְנֵי אָדָם. וִירוֹמְמוּהוּ בִּקְהַל עָם, וּבְמוֹשַׁב זְקֵנִים יְהַלְלוּהוּ. יָשֵׂם נְהָרוֹת לְמִדְבָּר, וּמֹצָאֵי מַיִם לְצִמָּאוֹן. אֶרֶץ פְּרִי לִמְלֵחָה, מֵרָעַת יוֹשְׁבֵי בָהּ. יָשֵׂם מִדְבָּר לַאֲגַם מַיִם, וְאֶרֶץ צִיָּה לְמֹצָאֵי מָיִם. וַיּוֹשֶׁב שָׁם רְעֵבִים, וַיְכוֹנְנוּ עִיר מוֹשָׁב. וַיִּזְרְעוּ שָׂדוֹת, וַיִּטְּעוּ כְרָמִים, וַיַּעֲשׂוּ פְּרִי תְבוּאָה. וַיְבָרְכֵם וַיִּרְבּוּ מְאֹד, וּבְהֶמְתָּם לֹא יַמְעִיט. וַיִּמְעֲטוּ וַיָּשֹׁחוּ, מֵעֹצֶר רָעָה וְיָגוֹן. שֹׁפֵךְ בּוּז עַל נְדִיבִים, וַיַּתְעֵם בְּתֹהוּ לֹא דָרֶךְ. וַיְשַׂגֵּב אֶבְיוֹן מֵעוֹנִי, וַיָּשֶׂם כַּצֹּאן מִשְׁפָּחוֹת. יִרְאוּ יְשָׁרִים וְיִשְׂמָחוּ, וְכָל עַוְלָה קָפְצָה פִּיהָ. מִי חָכָם וְיִשְׁמָר אֵלֶּה, וְיִתְבּוֹנְנוּ חַסְדֵי יהוה.

23rd day — יום כג לחדש

קח שִׁיר מִזְמוֹר לְדָוִד. נָכוֹן לִבִּי אֱלֹהִים, אָשִׁירָה וַאֲזַמְּרָה אַף כְּבוֹדִי. עוּרָה הַנֵּבֶל וְכִנּוֹר, אָעִירָה שָׁחַר. אוֹדְךָ בָעַמִּים, יהוה, וַאֲזַמֶּרְךָ בַּלְאֻמִּים. כִּי גָדוֹל מֵעַל שָׁמַיִם חַסְדֶּךָ, וְעַד שְׁחָקִים אֲמִתֶּךָ. רוּמָה עַל שָׁמַיִם, אֱלֹהִים, וְעַל כָּל הָאָרֶץ כְּבוֹדֶךָ. לְמַעַן

יֵחָלְצוּן יְדִידֶיךָ, הוֹשִׁיעָה יְמִינְךָ וַעֲנֵנִי. אֱלֹהִים דִּבֶּר בְּקָדְשׁוֹ אֶעְלֹזָה, אֲחַלְּקָה שְׁכֶם, וְעֵמֶק סֻכּוֹת אֲמַדֵּד. לִי גִלְעָד לִי מְנַשֶּׁה, וְאֶפְרַיִם מָעוֹז רֹאשִׁי, יְהוּדָה מְחֹקְקִי. מוֹאָב סִיר רַחְצִי, עַל אֱדוֹם אַשְׁלִיךְ נַעֲלִי, עֲלֵי פְלֶשֶׁת אֶתְרוֹעָע. מִי יֹבִלֵנִי עִיר מִבְצָר, מִי נָחַנִי עַד אֱדוֹם. הֲלֹא אֱלֹהִים זְנַחְתָּנוּ, וְלֹא תֵצֵא אֱלֹהִים בְּצִבְאֹתֵינוּ. הָבָה לָּנוּ עֶזְרָת מִצָּר, וְשָׁוְא תְּשׁוּעַת אָדָם. בֵּאלֹהִים נַעֲשֶׂה חָיִל, וְהוּא יָבוּס צָרֵינוּ.

קט לַמְנַצֵּחַ לְדָוִד מִזְמוֹר, אֱלֹהֵי תְהִלָּתִי אַל תֶּחֱרַשׁ. כִּי פִי רָשָׁע וּפִי מִרְמָה עָלַי פָּתָחוּ, דִּבְּרוּ אִתִּי לְשׁוֹן שָׁקֶר. וְדִבְרֵי שִׂנְאָה סְבָבוּנִי, וַיִּלָּחֲמוּנִי חִנָּם. תַּחַת אַהֲבָתִי יִשְׂטְנוּנִי וַאֲנִי תְפִלָּה. וַיָּשִׂימוּ עָלַי רָעָה תַּחַת טוֹבָה, וְשִׂנְאָה תַּחַת אַהֲבָתִי. הַפְקֵד עָלָיו רָשָׁע, וְשָׂטָן יַעֲמֹד עַל יְמִינוֹ. בְּהִשָּׁפְטוֹ יֵצֵא רָשָׁע, וּתְפִלָּתוֹ תִּהְיֶה לַחֲטָאָה. יִהְיוּ יָמָיו מְעַטִּים, פְּקֻדָּתוֹ יִקַּח אַחֵר. יִהְיוּ בָנָיו יְתוֹמִים, וְאִשְׁתּוֹ אַלְמָנָה. וְנוֹעַ יָנוּעוּ בָנָיו וְשִׁאֵלוּ, וְדָרְשׁוּ מֵחָרְבוֹתֵיהֶם. יְנַקֵּשׁ נוֹשֶׁה לְכָל אֲשֶׁר לוֹ, וְיָבֹזּוּ זָרִים יְגִיעוֹ. אַל יְהִי לוֹ מֹשֵׁךְ חָסֶד, וְאַל יְהִי חוֹנֵן לִיתוֹמָיו. יְהִי אַחֲרִיתוֹ לְהַכְרִית, בְּדוֹר אַחֵר יִמַּח שְׁמָם. יִזָּכֵר עֲוֹן אֲבֹתָיו אֶל יהוה, וְחַטַּאת אִמּוֹ אַל תִּמָּח. יִהְיוּ נֶגֶד יהוה תָּמִיד, וְיַכְרֵת מֵאֶרֶץ זִכְרָם. יַעַן אֲשֶׁר לֹא זָכַר עֲשׂוֹת חָסֶד, וַיִּרְדֹּף אִישׁ עָנִי וְאֶבְיוֹן, וְנִכְאֵה לֵבָב לְמוֹתֵת. וַיֶּאֱהַב קְלָלָה וַתְּבוֹאֵהוּ, וְלֹא חָפֵץ בִּבְרָכָה, וַתִּרְחַק מִמֶּנּוּ. וַיִּלְבַּשׁ קְלָלָה כְּמַדּוֹ, וַתָּבֹא כַמַּיִם בְּקִרְבּוֹ, וְכַשֶּׁמֶן בְּעַצְמוֹתָיו. תְּהִי לוֹ כְּבֶגֶד יַעְטֶה, וּלְמֵזַח תָּמִיד יַחְגְּרֶהָ. זֹאת פְּעֻלַּת שֹׂטְנַי, מֵאֵת יהוה, וְהַדֹּבְרִים רָע עַל נַפְשִׁי. וְאַתָּה יֱהֹוִה אֲדֹנָי עֲשֵׂה אִתִּי לְמַעַן שְׁמֶךָ, כִּי טוֹב חַסְדְּךָ הַצִּילֵנִי. כִּי עָנִי וְאֶבְיוֹן אָנֹכִי, וְלִבִּי חָלַל בְּקִרְבִּי.

כְּצֵל כִּנְטוֹתוֹ נֶהֱלָכְתִּי, נִנְעַרְתִּי כָּאַרְבֶּה. בִּרְכַּי כָּשְׁלוּ מִצּוֹם, וּבְשָׂרִי כָּחַשׁ מִשָּׁמֶן. וַאֲנִי הָיִיתִי חֶרְפָּה לָהֶם, יִרְאוּנִי יְנִיעוּן רֹאשָׁם. עָזְרֵנִי יהוה אֱלֹהָי, הוֹשִׁיעֵנִי כְחַסְדֶּךָ. וְיֵדְעוּ כִּי יָדְךָ זֹּאת, אַתָּה יהוה עֲשִׂיתָהּ. יְקַלְלוּ הֵמָּה וְאַתָּה תְבָרֵךְ, קָמוּ וַיֵּבֹשׁוּ וְעַבְדְּךָ יִשְׂמָח. יִלְבְּשׁוּ שׁוֹטְנַי כְּלִמָּה, וְיַעֲטוּ כַמְעִיל בָּשְׁתָּם. אוֹדֶה יהוה מְאֹד בְּפִי, וּבְתוֹךְ רַבִּים אֲהַלְלֶנּוּ. כִּי יַעֲמֹד לִימִין אֶבְיוֹן, לְהוֹשִׁיעַ מִשֹּׁפְטֵי נַפְשׁוֹ.

קי לְדָוִד מִזְמוֹר, נְאֻם יהוה לַאדֹנִי שֵׁב לִימִינִי, עַד אָשִׁית אֹיְבֶיךָ הֲדֹם לְרַגְלֶיךָ. מַטֵּה עֻזְּךָ יִשְׁלַח יהוה מִצִּיּוֹן, רְדֵה בְּקֶרֶב אֹיְבֶיךָ. עַמְּךָ נְדָבֹת בְּיוֹם חֵילֶךָ, בְּהַדְרֵי קֹדֶשׁ מֵרֶחֶם מִשְׁחָר, לְךָ טַל יַלְדֻתֶיךָ. נִשְׁבַּע יהוה וְלֹא יִנָּחֵם, אַתָּה כֹהֵן לְעוֹלָם, עַל דִּבְרָתִי מַלְכִּי צֶדֶק. אֲדֹנָי עַל יְמִינְךָ, מָחַץ בְּיוֹם אַפּוֹ מְלָכִים. יָדִין בַּגּוֹיִם מָלֵא גְוִיּוֹת, מָחַץ רֹאשׁ עַל אֶרֶץ רַבָּה. מִנַּחַל בַּדֶּרֶךְ יִשְׁתֶּה, עַל כֵּן יָרִים רֹאשׁ.

קיא הַלְלוּיָהּ, אוֹדֶה יהוה בְּכָל לֵבָב, בְּסוֹד יְשָׁרִים וְעֵדָה. גְּדֹלִים מַעֲשֵׂי יהוה, דְּרוּשִׁים לְכָל חֶפְצֵיהֶם. הוֹד וְהָדָר פָּעֳלוֹ, וְצִדְקָתוֹ עֹמֶדֶת לָעַד. זֵכֶר עָשָׂה לְנִפְלְאוֹתָיו, חַנּוּן וְרַחוּם יהוה. טֶרֶף נָתַן לִירֵאָיו, יִזְכֹּר לְעוֹלָם בְּרִיתוֹ. כֹּחַ מַעֲשָׂיו הִגִּיד לְעַמּוֹ, לָתֵת לָהֶם נַחֲלַת גּוֹיִם. מַעֲשֵׂי יָדָיו אֱמֶת וּמִשְׁפָּט, נֶאֱמָנִים כָּל פִּקּוּדָיו. סְמוּכִים לָעַד לְעוֹלָם, עֲשׂוּיִם בֶּאֱמֶת וְיָשָׁר. פְּדוּת שָׁלַח לְעַמּוֹ, צִוָּה לְעוֹלָם בְּרִיתוֹ, קָדוֹשׁ וְנוֹרָא שְׁמוֹ. רֵאשִׁית חָכְמָה יִרְאַת יהוה, שֵׂכֶל טוֹב לְכָל עֹשֵׂיהֶם, תְּהִלָּתוֹ עֹמֶדֶת לָעַד.

קיב הַלְלוּיָהּ, אַשְׁרֵי אִישׁ יָרֵא אֶת יהוה, בְּמִצְוֹתָיו חָפֵץ מְאֹד. גִּבּוֹר בָּאָרֶץ יִהְיֶה זַרְעוֹ, דּוֹר יְשָׁרִים יְבֹרָךְ. הוֹן וָעֹשֶׁר בְּבֵיתוֹ, וְצִדְקָתוֹ עֹמֶדֶת לָעַד. זָרַח בַּחֹשֶׁךְ אוֹר לַיְשָׁרִים,

חַנּוּן וְרַחוּם וְצַדִּיק. טוֹב אִישׁ חוֹנֵן וּמַלְוֶה, יְכַלְכֵּל דְּבָרָיו בְּמִשְׁפָּט. כִּי לְעוֹלָם לֹא יִמּוֹט, לְזֵכֶר עוֹלָם יִהְיֶה צַדִּיק. מִשְּׁמוּעָה רָעָה לֹא יִירָא, נָכוֹן לִבּוֹ בָּטֻחַ בַּיהוה. סָמוּךְ לִבּוֹ לֹא יִירָא, עַד אֲשֶׁר יִרְאֶה בְצָרָיו. פִּזַּר נָתַן לָאֶבְיוֹנִים, צִדְקָתוֹ עֹמֶדֶת לָעַד, קַרְנוֹ תָּרוּם בְּכָבוֹד. רָשָׁע יִרְאֶה וְכָעָס, שִׁנָּיו יַחֲרֹק וְנָמָס, תַּאֲוַת רְשָׁעִים תֹּאבֵד.

יום כד לחדש — 24th day

קיג הַלְלוּיָהּ, הַלְלוּ עַבְדֵי יהוה, הַלְלוּ אֶת שֵׁם יהוה. יְהִי שֵׁם יהוה מְבֹרָךְ, מֵעַתָּה וְעַד עוֹלָם. מִמִּזְרַח שֶׁמֶשׁ עַד מְבוֹאוֹ, מְהֻלָּל שֵׁם יהוה. רָם עַל כָּל גּוֹיִם, יהוה, עַל הַשָּׁמַיִם כְּבוֹדוֹ. מִי כַּיהוה אֱלֹהֵינוּ, הַמַּגְבִּיהִי לָשָׁבֶת. הַמַּשְׁפִּילִי לִרְאוֹת, בַּשָּׁמַיִם וּבָאָרֶץ. מְקִימִי מֵעָפָר דָּל, מֵאַשְׁפֹּת יָרִים אֶבְיוֹן. לְהוֹשִׁיבִי עִם נְדִיבִים, עִם נְדִיבֵי עַמּוֹ. מוֹשִׁיבִי עֲקֶרֶת הַבַּיִת, אֵם הַבָּנִים שְׂמֵחָה, הַלְלוּיָהּ.

קיד בְּצֵאת יִשְׂרָאֵל מִמִּצְרָיִם, בֵּית יַעֲקֹב מֵעַם לֹעֵז. הָיְתָה יְהוּדָה לְקָדְשׁוֹ, יִשְׂרָאֵל מַמְשְׁלוֹתָיו. הַיָּם רָאָה וַיָּנֹס, הַיַּרְדֵּן יִסֹּב לְאָחוֹר. הֶהָרִים רָקְדוּ כְאֵילִים, גְּבָעוֹת כִּבְנֵי צֹאן. מַה לְּךָ הַיָּם כִּי תָנוּס, הַיַּרְדֵּן תִּסֹּב לְאָחוֹר. הֶהָרִים תִּרְקְדוּ כְאֵילִים, גְּבָעוֹת כִּבְנֵי צֹאן. מִלִּפְנֵי אָדוֹן חוּלִי אָרֶץ, מִלִּפְנֵי אֱלוֹהַּ יַעֲקֹב. הַהֹפְכִי הַצּוּר אֲגַם מָיִם, חַלָּמִישׁ לְמַעְיְנוֹ מָיִם.

קטו לֹא לָנוּ, יהוה לֹא לָנוּ, כִּי לְשִׁמְךָ תֵּן כָּבוֹד, עַל חַסְדְּךָ עַל אֲמִתֶּךָ. לָמָּה יֹאמְרוּ הַגּוֹיִם, אַיֵּה נָא אֱלֹהֵיהֶם. וֵאלֹהֵינוּ בַשָּׁמָיִם, כֹּל אֲשֶׁר חָפֵץ עָשָׂה. עֲצַבֵּיהֶם כֶּסֶף וְזָהָב, מַעֲשֵׂה יְדֵי אָדָם. פֶּה לָהֶם וְלֹא יְדַבֵּרוּ, עֵינַיִם לָהֶם וְלֹא יִרְאוּ. אָזְנַיִם לָהֶם וְלֹא יִשְׁמָעוּ, אַף לָהֶם וְלֹא יְרִיחוּן. יְדֵיהֶם וְלֹא יְמִישׁוּן, רַגְלֵיהֶם וְלֹא יְהַלֵּכוּ, לֹא יֶהְגּוּ בִּגְרוֹנָם. כְּמוֹהֶם יִהְיוּ עֹשֵׂיהֶם, כֹּל אֲשֶׁר בֹּטֵחַ בָּהֶם. יִשְׂרָאֵל בְּטַח בַּיהוה, עֶזְרָם וּמָגִנָּם הוּא. בֵּית אַהֲרֹן בִּטְחוּ בַיהוה, עֶזְרָם וּמָגִנָּם הוּא. יִרְאֵי יהוה בִּטְחוּ בַיהוה, עֶזְרָם וּמָגִנָּם הוּא. יהוה זְכָרָנוּ יְבָרֵךְ, יְבָרֵךְ אֶת בֵּית יִשְׂרָאֵל, יְבָרֵךְ אֶת בֵּית אַהֲרֹן. יְבָרֵךְ יִרְאֵי יהוה, הַקְּטַנִּים עִם הַגְּדֹלִים. יֹסֵף יהוה עֲלֵיכֶם, עֲלֵיכֶם וְעַל בְּנֵיכֶם. בְּרוּכִים אַתֶּם לַיהוה, עֹשֵׂה שָׁמַיִם וָאָרֶץ. הַשָּׁמַיִם שָׁמַיִם לַיהוה, וְהָאָרֶץ נָתַן לִבְנֵי אָדָם. לֹא הַמֵּתִים יְהַלְלוּ יָהּ, וְלֹא כָּל יֹרְדֵי דוּמָה. וַאֲנַחְנוּ נְבָרֵךְ יָהּ, מֵעַתָּה וְעַד עוֹלָם, הַלְלוּיָהּ.

קטז אָהַבְתִּי כִּי יִשְׁמַע, יהוה, אֶת קוֹלִי תַּחֲנוּנָי. כִּי הִטָּה אָזְנוֹ לִי, וּבְיָמַי אֶקְרָא. אֲפָפוּנִי חֶבְלֵי מָוֶת, וּמְצָרֵי שְׁאוֹל מְצָאוּנִי, צָרָה וְיָגוֹן אֶמְצָא. וּבְשֵׁם יהוה אֶקְרָא, אָנָּה יהוה מַלְּטָה נַפְשִׁי. חַנּוּן יהוה וְצַדִּיק, וֵאלֹהֵינוּ מְרַחֵם. שֹׁמֵר פְּתָאִים יהוה, דַּלּוֹתִי וְלִי יְהוֹשִׁיעַ. שׁוּבִי נַפְשִׁי לִמְנוּחָיְכִי, כִּי יהוה גָּמַל עָלָיְכִי. כִּי חִלַּצְתָּ נַפְשִׁי מִמָּוֶת, אֶת עֵינִי מִן דִּמְעָה, אֶת רַגְלִי מִדֶּחִי. אֶתְהַלֵּךְ לִפְנֵי יהוה, בְּאַרְצוֹת הַחַיִּים. הֶאֱמַנְתִּי כִּי אֲדַבֵּר, אֲנִי עָנִיתִי מְאֹד. אֲנִי אָמַרְתִּי בְחָפְזִי, כָּל הָאָדָם כֹּזֵב. מָה אָשִׁיב לַיהוה, כָּל תַּגְמוּלוֹהִי עָלָי. כּוֹס יְשׁוּעוֹת אֶשָּׂא, וּבְשֵׁם יהוה אֶקְרָא. נְדָרַי לַיהוה אֲשַׁלֵּם, נֶגְדָה נָּא לְכָל עַמּוֹ. יָקָר בְּעֵינֵי יהוה, הַמָּוְתָה לַחֲסִידָיו. אָנָּה יהוה כִּי אֲנִי עַבְדֶּךָ, אֲנִי עַבְדְּךָ בֶּן אֲמָתֶךָ, פִּתַּחְתָּ לְמוֹסֵרָי. לְךָ אֶזְבַּח זֶבַח תּוֹדָה, וּבְשֵׁם יהוה אֶקְרָא. נְדָרַי לַיהוה אֲשַׁלֵּם, נֶגְדָה נָּא לְכָל עַמּוֹ. בְּחַצְרוֹת בֵּית יהוה, בְּתוֹכֵכִי יְרוּשָׁלָיִם, הַלְלוּיָהּ.

קיז הַלְלוּ אֶת יהוה, כָּל גּוֹיִם, שַׁבְּחוּהוּ כָּל הָאֻמִּים. כִּי גָבַר עָלֵינוּ חַסְדּוֹ, וֶאֱמֶת יהוה לְעוֹלָם, הַלְלוּיָהּ.

קיח הוֹדוּ לַיהוה כִּי טוֹב, כִּי לְעוֹלָם חַסְדּוֹ. יֹאמַר נָא יִשְׂרָאֵל, כִּי לְעוֹלָם חַסְדּוֹ. יֹאמְרוּ נָא בֵית אַהֲרֹן, כִּי לְעוֹלָם חַסְדּוֹ. יֹאמְרוּ נָא יִרְאֵי יהוה, כִּי לְעוֹלָם חַסְדּוֹ. מִן הַמֵּצַר קָרָאתִי יָּהּ, עָנָנִי בַמֶּרְחָב יָהּ. יהוה לִי לֹא אִירָא, מַה יַּעֲשֶׂה לִי אָדָם. יהוה לִי בְּעֹזְרָי, וַאֲנִי אֶרְאֶה בְשֹׂנְאָי. טוֹב לַחֲסוֹת בַּיהוה, מִבְּטֹחַ בָּאָדָם. טוֹב לַחֲסוֹת בַּיהוה, מִבְּטֹחַ בִּנְדִיבִים. כָּל גּוֹיִם סְבָבוּנִי, בְּשֵׁם יהוה כִּי אֲמִילַם. סַבּוּנִי גַם סְבָבוּנִי, בְּשֵׁם יהוה כִּי אֲמִילַם. סַבּוּנִי כִדְבֹרִים דֹּעֲכוּ כְּאֵשׁ קוֹצִים, בְּשֵׁם יהוה כִּי אֲמִילַם. דָּחֹה דְחִיתַנִי לִנְפֹּל, וַיהוה עֲזָרָנִי. עָזִּי וְזִמְרָת יָהּ, וַיְהִי לִי לִישׁוּעָה. קוֹל רִנָּה וִישׁוּעָה, בְּאָהֳלֵי צַדִּיקִים, יְמִין יהוה עֹשָׂה חָיִל. יְמִין יהוה רוֹמֵמָה, יְמִין יהוה עֹשָׂה חָיִל. לֹא אָמוּת כִּי אֶחְיֶה, וַאֲסַפֵּר מַעֲשֵׂי יָהּ. יַסֹּר יִסְּרַנִּי יָּהּ, וְלַמָּוֶת לֹא נְתָנָנִי. פִּתְחוּ לִי שַׁעֲרֵי צֶדֶק, אָבֹא בָם אוֹדֶה יָהּ. זֶה הַשַּׁעַר לַיהוה, צַדִּיקִים יָבֹאוּ בוֹ. אוֹדְךָ כִּי עֲנִיתָנִי, וַתְּהִי לִי לִישׁוּעָה. אֶבֶן מָאֲסוּ הַבּוֹנִים, הָיְתָה לְרֹאשׁ פִּנָּה. מֵאֵת יהוה הָיְתָה זֹּאת, הִיא נִפְלָאת בְּעֵינֵינוּ. זֶה הַיּוֹם עָשָׂה יהוה, נָגִילָה וְנִשְׂמְחָה בוֹ. אָנָּא יהוה הוֹשִׁיעָה נָּא, אָנָּא יהוה הַצְלִיחָה נָא. בָּרוּךְ הַבָּא בְּשֵׁם יהוה, בֵּרַכְנוּכֶם מִבֵּית יהוה. אֵל יהוה וַיָּאֶר לָנוּ, אִסְרוּ חַג בַּעֲבֹתִים, עַד קַרְנוֹת הַמִּזְבֵּחַ. אֵלִי אַתָּה וְאוֹדֶךָּ, אֱלֹהַי אֲרוֹמְמֶךָּ. הוֹדוּ לַיהוה כִּי טוֹב, כִּי לְעוֹלָם חַסְדּוֹ.

25th day — יום כה לחדש

קיט אַשְׁרֵי תְמִימֵי דָרֶךְ, הַהֹלְכִים בְּתוֹרַת יהוה. אַשְׁרֵי נֹצְרֵי עֵדֹתָיו, בְּכָל לֵב יִדְרְשׁוּהוּ. אַף לֹא פָעֲלוּ עַוְלָה, בִּדְרָכָיו הָלָכוּ. אַתָּה צִוִּיתָה פִקֻּדֶיךָ, לִשְׁמֹר מְאֹד. אַחֲלַי, יִכֹּנוּ דְרָכָי לִשְׁמֹר חֻקֶּיךָ. אָז לֹא אֵבוֹשׁ, בְּהַבִּיטִי אֶל כָּל מִצְוֹתֶיךָ. אוֹדְךָ בְּיֹשֶׁר לֵבָב, בְּלָמְדִי מִשְׁפְּטֵי צִדְקֶךָ. אֶת חֻקֶּיךָ אֶשְׁמֹר, אַל תַּעַזְבֵנִי עַד מְאֹד.

בַּמֶּה יְזַכֶּה נַּעַר אֶת אָרְחוֹ, לִשְׁמֹר כִּדְבָרֶךָ. בְּכָל לִבִּי דְרַשְׁתִּיךָ, אַל תַּשְׁגֵּנִי מִמִּצְוֹתֶיךָ. בְּלִבִּי צָפַנְתִּי אִמְרָתֶךָ, לְמַעַן לֹא אֶחֱטָא לָךְ. בָּרוּךְ אַתָּה יהוה, לַמְּדֵנִי חֻקֶּיךָ. בִּשְׂפָתַי סִפַּרְתִּי, כֹּל מִשְׁפְּטֵי פִיךָ. בְּדֶרֶךְ עֵדְוֹתֶיךָ שַׂשְׂתִּי, כְּעַל כָּל הוֹן. בְּפִקּוּדֶיךָ אָשִׂיחָה, וְאַבִּיטָה אֹרְחֹתֶיךָ. בְּחֻקֹּתֶיךָ אֶשְׁתַּעֲשָׁע, לֹא אֶשְׁכַּח דְּבָרֶךָ.

גְּמֹל עַל עַבְדְּךָ, אֶחְיֶה וְאֶשְׁמְּרָה דְבָרֶךָ. גַּל עֵינַי וְאַבִּיטָה, נִפְלָאוֹת מִתּוֹרָתֶךָ. גֵּר אָנֹכִי בָאָרֶץ, אַל תַּסְתֵּר מִמֶּנִּי מִצְוֹתֶיךָ. גָּרְסָה נַפְשִׁי לְתַאֲבָה, אֶל מִשְׁפָּטֶיךָ בְכָל עֵת. גָּעַרְתָּ זֵדִים אֲרוּרִים, הַשֹּׁגִים מִמִּצְוֹתֶיךָ. גַּל מֵעָלַי חֶרְפָּה וָבוּז, כִּי עֵדֹתֶיךָ נָצָרְתִּי. גַּם יָשְׁבוּ שָׂרִים בִּי נִדְבָּרוּ, עַבְדְּךָ יָשִׂיחַ בְּחֻקֶּיךָ. גַּם עֵדֹתֶיךָ שַׁעֲשֻׁעָי, אַנְשֵׁי עֲצָתִי.

דָּבְקָה לֶעָפָר נַפְשִׁי, חַיֵּנִי כִּדְבָרֶךָ. דְּרָכַי סִפַּרְתִּי וַתַּעֲנֵנִי, לַמְּדֵנִי חֻקֶּיךָ. דֶּרֶךְ פִּקּוּדֶיךָ הֲבִינֵנִי, וְאָשִׂיחָה בְּנִפְלְאוֹתֶיךָ. דָּלְפָה נַפְשִׁי מִתּוּגָה, קַיְּמֵנִי כִּדְבָרֶךָ. דֶּרֶךְ שֶׁקֶר הָסֵר מִמֶּנִּי, וְתוֹרָתְךָ חָנֵּנִי. דֶּרֶךְ אֱמוּנָה בָחָרְתִּי, מִשְׁפָּטֶיךָ שִׁוִּיתִי. דָּבַקְתִּי בְעֵדְוֹתֶיךָ, יהוה אַל תְּבִישֵׁנִי. דֶּרֶךְ מִצְוֹתֶיךָ אָרוּץ, כִּי תַרְחִיב לִבִּי.

הוֹרֵנִי יהוה דֶּרֶךְ חֻקֶּיךָ, וְאֶצְּרֶנָּה עֵקֶב. הֲבִינֵנִי וְאֶצְּרָה תוֹרָתֶךָ, וְאֶשְׁמְרֶנָּה בְכָל לֵב. הַדְרִיכֵנִי בִּנְתִיב מִצְוֹתֶיךָ, כִּי בוֹ חָפָצְתִּי. הַט לִבִּי אֶל עֵדְוֹתֶיךָ, וְאַל אֶל בָּצַע. הַעֲבֵר עֵינַי מֵרְאוֹת שָׁוְא, בִּדְרָכֶךָ חַיֵּנִי. הָקֵם לְעַבְדְּךָ אִמְרָתֶךָ, אֲשֶׁר לְיִרְאָתֶךָ. הַעֲבֵר חֶרְפָּתִי אֲשֶׁר יָגֹרְתִּי, כִּי מִשְׁפָּטֶיךָ טוֹבִים. הִנֵּה תָּאַבְתִּי לְפִקֻּדֶיךָ, בְּצִדְקָתְךָ חַיֵּנִי.

וִיבֹאֻנִי חֲסָדֶךָ יהוה, תְּשׁוּעָתְךָ

כְּאִמְרָתֶךָ. וְאֶעֱנֶה חֹרְפִי דָבָר, כִּי בָטַחְתִּי בִּדְבָרֶךָ. וְאַל תַּצֵּל מִפִּי דְבַר אֱמֶת עַד מְאֹד, כִּי לְמִשְׁפָּטֶךָ יִחָלְתִּי. וְאֶשְׁמְרָה תוֹרָתְךָ תָמִיד לְעוֹלָם וָעֶד. וְאֶתְהַלְּכָה בָרְחָבָה, כִּי פִקֻּדֶיךָ דָרָשְׁתִּי. וַאֲדַבְּרָה בְעֵדֹתֶיךָ נֶגֶד מְלָכִים, וְלֹא אֵבוֹשׁ. וְאֶשְׁתַּעֲשַׁע בְּמִצְוֹתֶיךָ אֲשֶׁר אָהָבְתִּי. וְאֶשָּׂא כַפַּי אֶל מִצְוֹתֶיךָ אֲשֶׁר אָהָבְתִּי, וְאָשִׂיחָה בְחֻקֶּיךָ.

זְכֹר דָּבָר לְעַבְדֶּךָ, עַל אֲשֶׁר יִחַלְתָּנִי. זֹאת נֶחָמָתִי בְעָנְיִי, כִּי אִמְרָתְךָ חִיָּתְנִי. זֵדִים הֱלִיצֻנִי עַד מְאֹד, מִתּוֹרָתְךָ לֹא נָטִיתִי. זָכַרְתִּי מִשְׁפָּטֶיךָ מֵעוֹלָם, יהוה, וָאֶתְנֶחָם. זַלְעָפָה אֲחָזַתְנִי מֵרְשָׁעִים, עֹזְבֵי תּוֹרָתֶךָ. זְמִרוֹת הָיוּ לִי חֻקֶּיךָ, בְּבֵית מְגוּרָי. זָכַרְתִּי בַלַּיְלָה שִׁמְךָ יהוה, וָאֶשְׁמְרָה תּוֹרָתֶךָ. זֹאת הָיְתָה לִּי, כִּי פִקֻּדֶיךָ נָצָרְתִּי.

חֶלְקִי יהוה, אָמַרְתִּי לִשְׁמֹר דְּבָרֶיךָ. חִלִּיתִי פָנֶיךָ בְכָל לֵב, חָנֵּנִי כְּאִמְרָתֶךָ. חִשַּׁבְתִּי דְרָכָי, וָאָשִׁיבָה רַגְלַי אֶל עֵדֹתֶיךָ. חַשְׁתִּי וְלֹא הִתְמַהְמָהְתִּי, לִשְׁמֹר מִצְוֹתֶיךָ. חֶבְלֵי רְשָׁעִים עִוְּדֻנִי, תּוֹרָתְךָ לֹא שָׁכָחְתִּי. חֲצוֹת לַיְלָה אָקוּם לְהוֹדוֹת לָךְ, עַל מִשְׁפְּטֵי צִדְקֶךָ. חָבֵר אָנִי לְכָל אֲשֶׁר יְרֵאוּךָ, וּלְשֹׁמְרֵי פִּקּוּדֶיךָ. חַסְדְּךָ יהוה מָלְאָה הָאָרֶץ, חֻקֶּיךָ לַמְּדֵנִי.

טוֹב עָשִׂיתָ עִם עַבְדְּךָ, יהוה כִּדְבָרֶךָ. טוּב טַעַם וָדַעַת לַמְּדֵנִי, כִּי בְמִצְוֹתֶיךָ הֶאֱמָנְתִּי. טֶרֶם אֶעֱנֶה אֲנִי שֹׁגֵג, וְעַתָּה אִמְרָתְךָ שָׁמָרְתִּי. טוֹב אַתָּה וּמֵטִיב, לַמְּדֵנִי חֻקֶּיךָ. טָפְלוּ עָלַי שֶׁקֶר זֵדִים, אֲנִי בְּכָל לֵב אֱצֹּר פִּקּוּדֶיךָ. טָפַשׁ כַּחֵלֶב לִבָּם, אֲנִי תּוֹרָתְךָ שִׁעֲשָׁעְתִּי. טוֹב לִי כִי עֻנֵּיתִי, לְמַעַן אֶלְמַד חֻקֶּיךָ. טוֹב לִי תוֹרַת פִּיךָ, מֵאַלְפֵי זָהָב וָכָסֶף.

יָדֶיךָ עָשׂוּנִי וַיְכוֹנְנוּנִי, הֲבִינֵנִי וְאֶלְמְדָה מִצְוֹתֶיךָ. יְרֵאֶיךָ יִרְאוּנִי וְיִשְׂמָחוּ, כִּי לִדְבָרְךָ יִחָלְתִּי. יָדַעְתִּי יהוה כִּי צֶדֶק מִשְׁפָּטֶיךָ, וֶאֱמוּנָה עִנִּיתָנִי. יְהִי נָא חַסְדְּךָ לְנַחֲמֵנִי, כְּאִמְרָתְךָ לְעַבְדֶּךָ. יְבֹאוּנִי רַחֲמֶיךָ וְאֶחְיֶה, כִּי תוֹרָתְךָ שַׁעֲשֻׁעָי. יֵבֹשׁוּ זֵדִים כִּי שֶׁקֶר עִוְּתוּנִי, אֲנִי אָשִׂיחַ בְּפִקּוּדֶיךָ. יָשׁוּבוּ לִי יְרֵאֶיךָ, וְיֹדְעֵי עֵדֹתֶיךָ. יְהִי לִבִּי תָמִים בְּחֻקֶּיךָ, לְמַעַן לֹא אֵבוֹשׁ.

כָּלְתָה לִתְשׁוּעָתְךָ נַפְשִׁי, לִדְבָרְךָ יִחָלְתִּי. כָּלוּ עֵינַי לְאִמְרָתֶךָ, לֵאמֹר, מָתַי תְּנַחֲמֵנִי. כִּי הָיִיתִי כְּנֹאד בְּקִיטוֹר, חֻקֶּיךָ לֹא שָׁכָחְתִּי. כַּמָּה יְמֵי עַבְדֶּךָ, מָתַי תַּעֲשֶׂה בְרֹדְפַי מִשְׁפָּט. כָּרוּ לִי זֵדִים שִׁיחוֹת, אֲשֶׁר לֹא כְתוֹרָתֶךָ. כָּל מִצְוֹתֶיךָ אֱמוּנָה, שֶׁקֶר רְדָפוּנִי עָזְרֵנִי. כִּמְעַט כִּלּוּנִי בָאָרֶץ, וַאֲנִי לֹא עָזַבְתִּי פִקֻּדֶיךָ. כְּחַסְדְּךָ חַיֵּנִי, וְאֶשְׁמְרָה עֵדוּת פִּיךָ.

לְעוֹלָם יהוה, דְּבָרְךָ נִצָּב בַּשָּׁמָיִם. לְדֹר וָדֹר אֱמוּנָתֶךָ, כּוֹנַנְתָּ אֶרֶץ וַתַּעֲמֹד. לְמִשְׁפָּטֶיךָ עָמְדוּ הַיּוֹם, כִּי הַכֹּל עֲבָדֶיךָ. לוּלֵי תוֹרָתְךָ שַׁעֲשֻׁעָי, אָז אָבַדְתִּי בְעָנְיִי. לְעוֹלָם לֹא אֶשְׁכַּח פִּקּוּדֶיךָ, כִּי בָם חִיִּיתָנִי. לְךָ אֲנִי הוֹשִׁיעֵנִי, כִּי פִקּוּדֶיךָ דָרָשְׁתִּי. לִי קִוּוּ רְשָׁעִים לְאַבְּדֵנִי, עֵדֹתֶיךָ אֶתְבּוֹנָן. לְכָל תִּכְלָה רָאִיתִי קֵץ, רְחָבָה מִצְוָתְךָ מְאֹד.

26th day — יום כו לחדש

מָה אָהַבְתִּי תוֹרָתֶךָ, כָּל הַיּוֹם הִיא שִׂיחָתִי. מֵאֹיְבַי תְּחַכְּמֵנִי מִצְוֹתֶךָ, כִּי לְעוֹלָם הִיא לִי. מִכָּל מְלַמְּדַי הִשְׂכַּלְתִּי, כִּי עֵדְוֹתֶיךָ שִׂיחָה לִי. מִזְּקֵנִים אֶתְבּוֹנָן, כִּי פִקּוּדֶיךָ נָצָרְתִּי. מִכָּל אֹרַח רָע כָּלֵאתִי רַגְלָי, לְמַעַן אֶשְׁמֹר דְּבָרֶךָ. מִמִּשְׁפָּטֶיךָ לֹא סָרְתִּי, כִּי אַתָּה הוֹרֵתָנִי. מַה נִּמְלְצוּ לְחִכִּי אִמְרָתֶךָ, מִדְּבַשׁ לְפִי. מִפִּקּוּדֶיךָ אֶתְבּוֹנָן, עַל כֵּן שָׂנֵאתִי כָּל אֹרַח שָׁקֶר.

נֵר לְרַגְלִי דְבָרֶךָ, וְאוֹר לִנְתִיבָתִי. נִשְׁבַּעְתִּי וָאֲקַיֵּמָה, לִשְׁמֹר מִשְׁפְּטֵי צִדְקֶךָ. נַעֲנֵיתִי עַד מְאֹד, יהוה חַיֵּנִי כִדְבָרֶךָ. נִדְבוֹת פִּי רְצֵה נָא יהוה, וּמִשְׁפָּטֶיךָ לַמְּדֵנִי. נַפְשִׁי בְכַפִּי תָמִיד,

וְתוֹרָתְךָ לֹא שָׁכָחְתִּי. נָתְנוּ רְשָׁעִים פַּח לִי, וּמִפִּקּוּדֶיךָ לֹא תָעִיתִי. נָחַלְתִּי עֵדְוֹתֶיךָ לְעוֹלָם, כִּי שְׂשׂוֹן לִבִּי הֵמָּה. נָטִיתִי לִבִּי לַעֲשׂוֹת חֻקֶּיךָ לְעוֹלָם עֵקֶב.

סֵעֲפִים שָׂנֵאתִי, וְתוֹרָתְךָ אָהָבְתִּי. סִתְרִי וּמָגִנִּי אָתָּה, לִדְבָרְךָ יִחָלְתִּי. סוּרוּ מִמֶּנִּי מְרֵעִים, וְאֶצְּרָה מִצְוֹת אֱלֹהָי. סָמְכֵנִי כְאִמְרָתְךָ וְאֶחְיֶה, וְאַל תְּבִישֵׁנִי מִשִּׂבְרִי. סְעָדֵנִי וְאִוָּשֵׁעָה, וְאֶשְׁעָה בְחֻקֶּיךָ תָמִיד. סָלִיתָ כָּל שׁוֹגִים מֵחֻקֶּיךָ, כִּי שֶׁקֶר תַּרְמִיתָם. סִגִים הִשְׁבַּתָּ כָל רִשְׁעֵי אָרֶץ, לָכֵן אָהַבְתִּי עֵדֹתֶיךָ. סָמַר מִפַּחְדְּךָ בְשָׂרִי, וּמִמִּשְׁפָּטֶיךָ יָרֵאתִי.

עָשִׂיתִי מִשְׁפָּט וָצֶדֶק, בַּל תַּנִּיחֵנִי לְעֹשְׁקָי. עֲרֹב עַבְדְּךָ לְטוֹב, אַל יַעַשְׁקֻנִי זֵדִים. עֵינַי כָּלוּ לִישׁוּעָתֶךָ, וּלְאִמְרַת צִדְקֶךָ. עֲשֵׂה עִם עַבְדְּךָ כְחַסְדֶּךָ, וְחֻקֶּיךָ לַמְּדֵנִי. עַבְדְּךָ אָנִי הֲבִינֵנִי, וְאֵדְעָה עֵדֹתֶיךָ. עֵת לַעֲשׂוֹת לַיהוה, הֵפֵרוּ תּוֹרָתֶךָ. עַל כֵּן אָהַבְתִּי מִצְוֹתֶיךָ, מִזָּהָב וּמִפָּז. עַל כֵּן כָּל פִּקּוּדֵי כֹל יִשָּׁרְתִּי, כָּל אֹרַח שֶׁקֶר שָׂנֵאתִי.

פְּלָאוֹת עֵדְוֹתֶיךָ, עַל כֵּן נְצָרָתַם נַפְשִׁי. פֵּתַח דְּבָרֶיךָ יָאִיר, מֵבִין פְּתָיִים. פִּי פָעַרְתִּי וָאֶשְׁאָפָה, כִּי לְמִצְוֹתֶיךָ יָאָבְתִּי. פְּנֵה אֵלַי וְחָנֵּנִי, כְּמִשְׁפָּט לְאֹהֲבֵי שְׁמֶךָ. פְּעָמַי הָכֵן בְּאִמְרָתֶךָ, וְאַל תַּשְׁלֶט בִּי כָל אָוֶן. פְּדֵנִי מֵעֹשֶׁק אָדָם, וְאֶשְׁמְרָה פִּקּוּדֶיךָ. פָּנֶיךָ הָאֵר בְּעַבְדֶּךָ, וְלַמְּדֵנִי אֶת חֻקֶּיךָ. פַּלְגֵי מַיִם יָרְדוּ עֵינָי, עַל לֹא שָׁמְרוּ תוֹרָתֶךָ.

צַדִּיק אַתָּה יהוה, וְיָשָׁר מִשְׁפָּטֶיךָ. צִוִּיתָ צֶדֶק עֵדֹתֶיךָ, וֶאֱמוּנָה מְאֹד. צִמְּתַתְנִי קִנְאָתִי, כִּי שָׁכְחוּ דְבָרֶיךָ צָרָי. צְרוּפָה אִמְרָתְךָ מְאֹד, וְעַבְדְּךָ אֲהֵבָהּ. צָעִיר אָנֹכִי וְנִבְזֶה, פִּקֻּדֶיךָ לֹא שָׁכָחְתִּי. צִדְקָתְךָ צֶדֶק לְעוֹלָם, וְתוֹרָתְךָ אֱמֶת. צַר וּמָצוֹק מְצָאוּנִי, מִצְוֹתֶיךָ שַׁעֲשֻׁעָי. צֶדֶק עֵדְוֹתֶיךָ לְעוֹלָם, הֲבִינֵנִי וְאֶחְיֶה.

קָרָאתִי בְכָל לֵב, עֲנֵנִי יהוה, חֻקֶּיךָ אֶצֹּרָה. קְרָאתִיךָ הוֹשִׁיעֵנִי, וְאֶשְׁמְרָה עֵדֹתֶיךָ. קִדַּמְתִּי בַנֶּשֶׁף וָאֲשַׁוֵּעָה, לִדְבָרְךָ יִחָלְתִּי. קִדְּמוּ עֵינַי אַשְׁמֻרוֹת, לָשִׂיחַ בְּאִמְרָתֶךָ. קוֹלִי שִׁמְעָה כְחַסְדֶּךָ, יהוה כְּמִשְׁפָּטֶךָ חַיֵּנִי. קָרְבוּ רֹדְפֵי זִמָּה, מִתּוֹרָתְךָ רָחָקוּ. קָרוֹב אַתָּה יהוה, וְכָל מִצְוֹתֶיךָ אֱמֶת. קֶדֶם יָדַעְתִּי מֵעֵדֹתֶיךָ, כִּי לְעוֹלָם יְסַדְתָּם.

רְאֵה עָנְיִי וְחַלְּצֵנִי, כִּי תוֹרָתְךָ לֹא שָׁכָחְתִּי. רִיבָה רִיבִי וּגְאָלֵנִי, לְאִמְרָתְךָ חַיֵּנִי. רָחוֹק מֵרְשָׁעִים יְשׁוּעָה, כִּי חֻקֶּיךָ לֹא דָרָשׁוּ. רַחֲמֶיךָ רַבִּים יהוה, כְּמִשְׁפָּטֶיךָ חַיֵּנִי. רַבִּים רֹדְפַי וְצָרָי, מֵעֵדְוֹתֶיךָ לֹא נָטִיתִי. רָאִיתִי בֹגְדִים וָאֶתְקוֹטָטָה, אֲשֶׁר אִמְרָתְךָ לֹא שָׁמָרוּ. רְאֵה כִּי פִקּוּדֶיךָ אָהָבְתִּי, יהוה כְּחַסְדְּךָ חַיֵּנִי. רֹאשׁ דְּבָרְךָ אֱמֶת, וּלְעוֹלָם כָּל מִשְׁפַּט צִדְקֶךָ.

שָׂרִים רְדָפוּנִי חִנָּם, וּמִדְּבָרְךָ פָּחַד לִבִּי. שָׂשׂ אָנֹכִי עַל אִמְרָתֶךָ, כְּמוֹצֵא שָׁלָל רָב. שֶׁקֶר שָׂנֵאתִי וָאֲתַעֵבָה, תּוֹרָתְךָ אָהָבְתִּי. שֶׁבַע בַּיּוֹם הִלַּלְתִּיךָ, עַל מִשְׁפְּטֵי צִדְקֶךָ. שָׁלוֹם רָב לְאֹהֲבֵי תוֹרָתֶךָ, וְאֵין לָמוֹ מִכְשׁוֹל. שִׂבַּרְתִּי לִישׁוּעָתְךָ יהוה, וּמִצְוֹתֶיךָ עָשִׂיתִי. שָׁמְרָה נַפְשִׁי עֵדֹתֶיךָ, וָאֹהֲבֵם מְאֹד. שָׁמַרְתִּי פִקּוּדֶיךָ וְעֵדֹתֶיךָ, כִּי כָל דְּרָכַי נֶגְדֶּךָ.

תִּקְרַב רִנָּתִי לְפָנֶיךָ יהוה, כִּדְבָרְךָ הֲבִינֵנִי. תָּבוֹא תְּחִנָּתִי לְפָנֶיךָ, כְּאִמְרָתְךָ הַצִּילֵנִי. תַּבַּעְנָה שְׂפָתַי תְּהִלָּה, כִּי תְלַמְּדֵנִי חֻקֶּיךָ. תַּעַן לְשׁוֹנִי אִמְרָתֶךָ, כִּי כָל מִצְוֹתֶיךָ צֶּדֶק. תְּהִי יָדְךָ לְעָזְרֵנִי, כִּי פִקּוּדֶיךָ בָחָרְתִּי. תָּאַבְתִּי לִישׁוּעָתְךָ יהוה, וְתוֹרָתְךָ שַׁעֲשֻׁעָי. תְּחִי נַפְשִׁי וּתְהַלְלֶךָּ, וּמִשְׁפָּטֶךָ יַעְזְרֻנִי. תָּעִיתִי כְּשֶׂה אֹבֵד, בַּקֵּשׁ עַבְדֶּךָ, כִּי מִצְוֹתֶיךָ לֹא שָׁכָחְתִּי.

ליום השבת — THE SABBATH

יום כז לחדש — 27th day

קכ שִׁיר הַמַּעֲלוֹת, אֶל יהוה בַּצָּרָתָה לִּי קָרָאתִי וַיַּעֲנֵנִי. יהוה הַצִּילָה

נַפְשִׁי מִשְּׂפַת שֶׁקֶר, מִלָּשׁוֹן רְמִיָּה. מַה יִּתֵּן לְךָ, וּמַה יֹּסִיף לָךְ, לָשׁוֹן רְמִיָּה. חִצֵּי גִבּוֹר שְׁנוּנִים, עִם גַּחֲלֵי רְתָמִים. אוֹיָה לִי כִּי גַרְתִּי מֶשֶׁךְ, שָׁכַנְתִּי עִם אָהֳלֵי קֵדָר. רַבַּת שָׁכְנָה לָּהּ נַפְשִׁי, עִם שׂוֹנֵא שָׁלוֹם. אֲנִי שָׁלוֹם, וְכִי אֲדַבֵּר, הֵמָּה לַמִּלְחָמָה.

קכא שִׁיר לַמַּעֲלוֹת, אֶשָּׂא עֵינַי אֶל הֶהָרִים, מֵאַיִן יָבֹא עֶזְרִי. עֶזְרִי מֵעִם יהוה, עֹשֵׂה שָׁמַיִם וָאָרֶץ. אַל יִתֵּן לַמּוֹט רַגְלֶךָ, אַל יָנוּם שֹׁמְרֶךָ. הִנֵּה לֹא יָנוּם וְלֹא יִישָׁן, שׁוֹמֵר יִשְׂרָאֵל. יהוה שֹׁמְרֶךָ, יהוה צִלְּךָ עַל יַד יְמִינֶךָ. יוֹמָם הַשֶּׁמֶשׁ לֹא יַכֶּכָּה, וְיָרֵחַ בַּלָּיְלָה. יהוה יִשְׁמָרְךָ מִכָּל רָע, יִשְׁמֹר אֶת נַפְשֶׁךָ. יהוה יִשְׁמָר צֵאתְךָ וּבוֹאֶךָ, מֵעַתָּה וְעַד עוֹלָם.

קכב שִׁיר הַמַּעֲלוֹת לְדָוִד, שָׂמַחְתִּי בְּאֹמְרִים לִי, בֵּית יהוה נֵלֵךְ. עֹמְדוֹת הָיוּ רַגְלֵינוּ, בִּשְׁעָרַיִךְ יְרוּשָׁלָיִם. יְרוּשָׁלַיִם הַבְּנוּיָה, כְּעִיר שֶׁחֻבְּרָה לָּהּ יַחְדָּו. שֶׁשָּׁם עָלוּ שְׁבָטִים, שִׁבְטֵי יָהּ עֵדוּת לְיִשְׂרָאֵל, לְהֹדוֹת לְשֵׁם יהוה. כִּי שָׁמָּה יָשְׁבוּ כִסְאוֹת לְמִשְׁפָּט, כִּסְאוֹת לְבֵית דָּוִד. שַׁאֲלוּ שְׁלוֹם יְרוּשָׁלָיִם, יִשְׁלָיוּ אֹהֲבָיִךְ. יְהִי שָׁלוֹם בְּחֵילֵךְ, שַׁלְוָה בְּאַרְמְנוֹתָיִךְ. לְמַעַן אַחַי וְרֵעָי, אֲדַבְּרָה נָּא שָׁלוֹם בָּךְ. לְמַעַן בֵּית יהוה אֱלֹהֵינוּ, אֲבַקְשָׁה טוֹב לָךְ.

קכג שִׁיר הַמַּעֲלוֹת, אֵלֶיךָ נָשָׂאתִי אֶת עֵינַי, הַיֹּשְׁבִי בַּשָּׁמָיִם. הִנֵּה כְעֵינֵי עֲבָדִים אֶל יַד אֲדוֹנֵיהֶם, כְּעֵינֵי שִׁפְחָה אֶל יַד גְּבִרְתָּהּ, כֵּן עֵינֵינוּ אֶל יהוה אֱלֹהֵינוּ, עַד שֶׁיְּחָנֵּנוּ. חָנֵּנוּ יהוה חָנֵּנוּ, כִּי רַב שָׂבַעְנוּ בוּז. רַבַּת שָׂבְעָה לָּהּ נַפְשֵׁנוּ הַלַּעַג הַשַּׁאֲנַנִּים, הַבּוּז לִגְאֵי יוֹנִים.

קכד שִׁיר הַמַּעֲלוֹת לְדָוִד, לוּלֵי יהוה שֶׁהָיָה לָנוּ, יֹאמַר נָא יִשְׂרָאֵל. לוּלֵי יהוה שֶׁהָיָה לָנוּ, בְּקוּם עָלֵינוּ אָדָם. אֲזַי חַיִּים בְּלָעוּנוּ, בַּחֲרוֹת אַפָּם בָּנוּ. אֲזַי הַמַּיִם שְׁטָפוּנוּ, נַחְלָה עָבַר עַל נַפְשֵׁנוּ. אֲזַי עָבַר עַל נַפְשֵׁנוּ, הַמַּיִם הַזֵּידוֹנִים. בָּרוּךְ יהוה, שֶׁלֹּא נְתָנָנוּ טֶרֶף לְשִׁנֵּיהֶם. נַפְשֵׁנוּ כְּצִפּוֹר נִמְלְטָה, מִפַּח יוֹקְשִׁים, הַפַּח נִשְׁבָּר וַאֲנַחְנוּ נִמְלָטְנוּ. עֶזְרֵנוּ בְּשֵׁם יהוה, עֹשֵׂה שָׁמַיִם וָאָרֶץ.

קכה שִׁיר הַמַּעֲלוֹת, הַבֹּטְחִים בַּיהוה, כְּהַר צִיּוֹן לֹא יִמּוֹט לְעוֹלָם יֵשֵׁב. יְרוּשָׁלַיִם הָרִים סָבִיב לָהּ, וַיהוה סָבִיב לְעַמּוֹ, מֵעַתָּה וְעַד עוֹלָם. כִּי לֹא יָנוּחַ שֵׁבֶט הָרֶשַׁע עַל גּוֹרַל הַצַּדִּיקִים, לְמַעַן לֹא יִשְׁלְחוּ הַצַּדִּיקִים בְּעַוְלָתָה יְדֵיהֶם. הֵיטִיבָה יהוה לַטּוֹבִים, וְלִישָׁרִים בְּלִבּוֹתָם. וְהַמַּטִּים עֲקַלְקַלּוֹתָם, יוֹלִיכֵם יהוה אֶת פֹּעֲלֵי הָאָוֶן, שָׁלוֹם עַל יִשְׂרָאֵל.

קכו שִׁיר הַמַּעֲלוֹת, בְּשׁוּב יהוה אֶת שִׁיבַת צִיּוֹן, הָיִינוּ כְּחֹלְמִים. אָז יִמָּלֵא שְׂחוֹק פִּינוּ, וּלְשׁוֹנֵנוּ רִנָּה, אָז יֹאמְרוּ בַגּוֹיִם, הִגְדִּיל יהוה לַעֲשׂוֹת עִם אֵלֶּה. הִגְדִּיל יהוה לַעֲשׂוֹת עִמָּנוּ, הָיִינוּ שְׂמֵחִים. שׁוּבָה יהוה אֶת שְׁבִיתֵנוּ, כַּאֲפִיקִים בַּנֶּגֶב. הַזֹּרְעִים בְּדִמְעָה, בְּרִנָּה יִקְצֹרוּ. הָלוֹךְ יֵלֵךְ וּבָכֹה נֹשֵׂא מֶשֶׁךְ הַזָּרַע, בֹּא יָבֹא בְרִנָּה, נֹשֵׂא אֲלֻמֹּתָיו.

קכז שִׁיר הַמַּעֲלוֹת לִשְׁלֹמֹה, אִם יהוה לֹא יִבְנֶה בַיִת, שָׁוְא עָמְלוּ בוֹנָיו בּוֹ, אִם יהוה לֹא יִשְׁמָר עִיר, שָׁוְא שָׁקַד שׁוֹמֵר. שָׁוְא לָכֶם מַשְׁכִּימֵי קוּם, מְאַחֲרֵי שֶׁבֶת, אֹכְלֵי לֶחֶם הָעֲצָבִים, כֵּן יִתֵּן לִידִידוֹ שֵׁנָא. הִנֵּה נַחֲלַת יהוה בָּנִים, שָׂכָר פְּרִי הַבָּטֶן. כְּחִצִּים בְּיַד גִּבּוֹר, כֵּן בְּנֵי הַנְּעוּרִים. אַשְׁרֵי הַגֶּבֶר אֲשֶׁר מִלֵּא אֶת אַשְׁפָּתוֹ מֵהֶם, לֹא יֵבֹשׁוּ, כִּי יְדַבְּרוּ אֶת אוֹיְבִים בַּשָּׁעַר.

קכח שִׁיר הַמַּעֲלוֹת, אַשְׁרֵי כָּל יְרֵא יהוה, הַהֹלֵךְ בִּדְרָכָיו. יְגִיעַ כַּפֶּיךָ כִּי תֹאכֵל, אַשְׁרֶיךָ וְטוֹב לָךְ. אֶשְׁתְּךָ כְּגֶפֶן פֹּרִיָּה, בְּיַרְכְּתֵי בֵיתֶךָ, בָּנֶיךָ כִּשְׁתִלֵי זֵיתִים, סָבִיב לְשֻׁלְחָנֶךָ. הִנֵּה כִי כֵן יְבֹרַךְ גָּבֶר יְרֵא יהוה. יְבָרֶכְךָ יהוה מִצִּיּוֹן, וּרְאֵה בְּטוּב יְרוּשָׁלָיִם כֹּל יְמֵי חַיֶּיךָ. וּרְאֵה בָנִים לְבָנֶיךָ, שָׁלוֹם עַל יִשְׂרָאֵל.

קכט שִׁיר הַמַּעֲלוֹת, רַבַּת צְרָרוּנִי מִנְּעוּרָי, יֹאמַר נָא יִשְׂרָאֵל. רַבַּת צְרָרוּנִי מִנְּעוּרָי, גַּם לֹא יָכְלוּ לִי. עַל גַּבִּי חָרְשׁוּ חֹרְשִׁים, הֶאֱרִיכוּ לְמַעֲנִיתָם. יהוה צַדִּיק, קִצֵּץ עֲבוֹת רְשָׁעִים. יֵבֹשׁוּ וְיִסֹּגוּ אָחוֹר, כֹּל שֹׂנְאֵי צִיּוֹן. יִהְיוּ כַּחֲצִיר גַּגּוֹת, שֶׁקַּדְמַת שָׁלַף יָבֵשׁ. שֶׁלֹּא מִלֵּא כַפּוֹ קוֹצֵר, וְחִצְנוֹ מְעַמֵּר. וְלֹא אָמְרוּ הָעֹבְרִים, בִּרְכַּת יהוה אֲלֵיכֶם, בֵּרַכְנוּ אֶתְכֶם בְּשֵׁם יהוה.

קל שִׁיר הַמַּעֲלוֹת, מִמַּעֲמַקִּים קְרָאתִיךָ יהוה. אֲדֹנָי שִׁמְעָה בְקוֹלִי, תִּהְיֶינָה אָזְנֶיךָ קַשֻּׁבוֹת, לְקוֹל תַּחֲנוּנָי. אִם עֲוֹנוֹת תִּשְׁמָר יָהּ, אֲדֹנָי מִי יַעֲמֹד. כִּי עִמְּךָ הַסְּלִיחָה, לְמַעַן תִּוָּרֵא. קִוִּיתִי יהוה קִוְּתָה נַפְשִׁי, וְלִדְבָרוֹ הוֹחָלְתִּי. נַפְשִׁי לַאדֹנָי, מִשֹּׁמְרִים לַבֹּקֶר, שֹׁמְרִים לַבֹּקֶר. יַחֵל יִשְׂרָאֵל אֶל יהוה, כִּי עִם יהוה הַחֶסֶד, וְהַרְבֵּה עִמּוֹ פְדוּת. וְהוּא יִפְדֶּה אֶת יִשְׂרָאֵל, מִכֹּל עֲוֹנוֹתָיו.

קלא שִׁיר הַמַּעֲלוֹת לְדָוִד, יהוה, לֹא גָבַהּ לִבִּי, וְלֹא רָמוּ עֵינַי, וְלֹא הִלַּכְתִּי בִּגְדֹלוֹת וּבְנִפְלָאוֹת מִמֶּנִּי. אִם לֹא שִׁוִּיתִי, וְדוֹמַמְתִּי נַפְשִׁי, כְּגָמֻל עֲלֵי אִמּוֹ, כַּגָּמֻל עָלַי נַפְשִׁי. יַחֵל יִשְׂרָאֵל אֶל יהוה, מֵעַתָּה וְעַד עוֹלָם.

קלב שִׁיר הַמַּעֲלוֹת, זְכוֹר יהוה לְדָוִד, אֵת כָּל עֻנּוֹתוֹ. אֲשֶׁר נִשְׁבַּע לַיהוה, נָדַר לַאֲבִיר יַעֲקֹב. אִם אָבֹא בְּאֹהֶל בֵּיתִי, אִם אֶעֱלֶה עַל עֶרֶשׂ יְצוּעָי. אִם אֶתֵּן שְׁנַת לְעֵינָי, לְעַפְעַפַּי תְּנוּמָה. עַד אֶמְצָא מָקוֹם לַיהוה, מִשְׁכָּנוֹת לַאֲבִיר יַעֲקֹב. הִנֵּה שְׁמַעֲנוּהָ בְאֶפְרָתָה, מְצָאנוּהָ בִּשְׂדֵי יָעַר. נָבוֹאָה לְמִשְׁכְּנוֹתָיו, נִשְׁתַּחֲוֶה לַהֲדֹם רַגְלָיו. קוּמָה יהוה לִמְנוּחָתֶךָ, אַתָּה וַאֲרוֹן עֻזֶּךָ. כֹּהֲנֶיךָ יִלְבְּשׁוּ צֶדֶק, וַחֲסִידֶיךָ יְרַנֵּנוּ. בַּעֲבוּר דָּוִד עַבְדֶּךָ, אַל תָּשֵׁב פְּנֵי מְשִׁיחֶךָ. נִשְׁבַּע יהוה לְדָוִד, אֱמֶת לֹא יָשׁוּב מִמֶּנָּה, מִפְּרִי בִטְנְךָ אָשִׁית לְכִסֵּא לָךְ. אִם יִשְׁמְרוּ בָנֶיךָ בְּרִיתִי, וְעֵדֹתִי זוֹ אֲלַמְּדֵם, גַּם בְּנֵיהֶם עֲדֵי עַד, יֵשְׁבוּ לְכִסֵּא לָךְ. כִּי בָחַר יהוה בְּצִיּוֹן, אִוָּהּ לְמוֹשָׁב לוֹ. זֹאת מְנוּחָתִי עֲדֵי עַד, פֹּה אֵשֵׁב כִּי אִוִּתִיהָ. צֵידָהּ בָּרֵךְ אֲבָרֵךְ, אֶבְיוֹנֶיהָ אַשְׂבִּיעַ לָחֶם. וְכֹהֲנֶיהָ אַלְבִּישׁ יֶשַׁע, וַחֲסִידֶיהָ רַנֵּן יְרַנֵּנוּ. שָׁם אַצְמִיחַ קֶרֶן לְדָוִד, עָרַכְתִּי נֵר לִמְשִׁיחִי. אוֹיְבָיו אַלְבִּישׁ בֹּשֶׁת, וְעָלָיו יָצִיץ נִזְרוֹ.

קלג שִׁיר הַמַּעֲלוֹת לְדָוִד, הִנֵּה מַה טּוֹב וּמַה נָּעִים, שֶׁבֶת אַחִים גַּם יָחַד. כַּשֶּׁמֶן הַטּוֹב עַל הָרֹאשׁ, יֹרֵד עַל הַזָּקָן זְקַן אַהֲרֹן, שֶׁיֹּרֵד עַל פִּי מִדּוֹתָיו. כְּטַל חֶרְמוֹן שֶׁיֹּרֵד עַל הַרְרֵי צִיּוֹן, כִּי שָׁם צִוָּה יהוה אֶת הַבְּרָכָה, חַיִּים עַד הָעוֹלָם.

קלד שִׁיר הַמַּעֲלוֹת, הִנֵּה בָּרְכוּ אֶת יהוה כָּל עַבְדֵי יהוה, הָעֹמְדִים בְּבֵית יהוה בַּלֵּילוֹת. שְׂאוּ יְדֵכֶם קֹדֶשׁ, וּבָרְכוּ אֶת יהוה. יְבָרֶכְךָ יהוה מִצִּיּוֹן, עֹשֵׂה שָׁמַיִם וָאָרֶץ.

28th day — יום כח לחדש

קלה הַלְלוּיָהּ, הַלְלוּ אֶת שֵׁם יהוה, הַלְלוּ עַבְדֵי יהוה. שֶׁעֹמְדִים בְּבֵית יהוה, בְּחַצְרוֹת בֵּית אֱלֹהֵינוּ. הַלְלוּיָהּ, כִּי טוֹב יהוה, זַמְּרוּ לִשְׁמוֹ כִּי נָעִים. כִּי יַעֲקֹב בָּחַר לוֹ יָהּ, יִשְׂרָאֵל לִסְגֻלָּתוֹ. כִּי אֲנִי יָדַעְתִּי כִּי גָדוֹל יהוה, וַאֲדֹנֵינוּ מִכָּל אֱלֹהִים. כֹּל אֲשֶׁר חָפֵץ

יהוה עָשָׂה, בַּשָּׁמַיִם וּבָאָרֶץ, בַּיַּמִּים וְכָל תְּהֹמוֹת. מַעֲלֶה נְשִׂאִים מִקְצֵה הָאָרֶץ, בְּרָקִים לַמָּטָר עָשָׂה, מֽוֹצֵא רוּחַ מֵאוֹצְרוֹתָיו. שֶׁהִכָּה בְּכוֹרֵי מִצְרָיִם, מֵאָדָם עַד בְּהֵמָה. שָׁלַח אוֹתֹת וּמֹפְתִים בְּתוֹכֵכִי מִצְרָיִם, בְּפַרְעֹה וּבְכָל עֲבָדָיו. שֶׁהִכָּה גּוֹיִם רַבִּים, וְהָרַג מְלָכִים עֲצוּמִים. לְסִיחוֹן מֶלֶךְ הָאֱמֹרִי, וּלְעוֹג מֶלֶךְ הַבָּשָׁן, וּלְכֹל מַמְלְכוֹת כְּנָעַן. וְנָתַן אַרְצָם נַחֲלָה, נַחֲלָה לְיִשְׂרָאֵל עַמּוֹ. יהוה שִׁמְךָ לְעוֹלָם, יהוה זִכְרְךָ לְדֹר וָדֹר. כִּי יָדִין יהוה עַמּוֹ, וְעַל עֲבָדָיו יִתְנֶחָם. עֲצַבֵּי הַגּוֹיִם כֶּסֶף וְזָהָב, מַעֲשֵׂה יְדֵי אָדָם. פֶּה לָהֶם וְלֹא יְדַבֵּרוּ, עֵינַיִם לָהֶם וְלֹא יִרְאוּ. אָזְנַיִם לָהֶם וְלֹא יַאֲזִינוּ, אַף אֵין יֶשׁ רוּחַ בְּפִיהֶם. כְּמוֹהֶם יִהְיוּ עֹשֵׂיהֶם, כֹּל אֲשֶׁר בֹּטֵחַ בָּהֶם. בֵּית יִשְׂרָאֵל בָּרְכוּ אֶת יהוה, בֵּית אַהֲרֹן בָּרְכוּ אֶת יהוה. בֵּית הַלֵּוִי בָּרְכוּ אֶת יהוה, יִרְאֵי יהוה בָּרְכוּ אֶת יהוה. בָּרוּךְ יהוה מִצִּיּוֹן, שֹׁכֵן יְרוּשָׁלָיִם, הַלְלוּיָהּ.

קלו הוֹדוּ לַיהוה כִּי טוֹב, כִּי לְעוֹלָם חַסְדּוֹ. הוֹדוּ לֵאלֹהֵי הָאֱלֹהִים, כִּי לְעוֹלָם חַסְדּוֹ. הוֹדוּ לַאֲדֹנֵי הָאֲדֹנִים, כִּי לְעוֹלָם חַסְדּוֹ. לְעֹשֵׂה נִפְלָאוֹת גְּדֹלוֹת לְבַדּוֹ, כִּי לְעוֹלָם חַסְדּוֹ. לְעֹשֵׂה הַשָּׁמַיִם בִּתְבוּנָה, כִּי לְעוֹלָם חַסְדּוֹ. לְרֹקַע הָאָרֶץ עַל הַמָּיִם, כִּי לְעוֹלָם חַסְדּוֹ. לְעֹשֵׂה אוֹרִים גְּדֹלִים, כִּי לְעוֹלָם חַסְדּוֹ. אֶת הַשֶּׁמֶשׁ לְמֶמְשֶׁלֶת בַּיּוֹם, כִּי לְעוֹלָם חַסְדּוֹ. אֶת הַיָּרֵחַ וְכוֹכָבִים לְמֶמְשְׁלוֹת בַּלָּיְלָה, כִּי לְעוֹלָם חַסְדּוֹ. לְמַכֵּה מִצְרַיִם בִּבְכוֹרֵיהֶם, כִּי לְעוֹלָם חַסְדּוֹ. וַיּוֹצֵא יִשְׂרָאֵל מִתּוֹכָם, כִּי לְעוֹלָם חַסְדּוֹ. בְּיָד חֲזָקָה וּבִזְרוֹעַ נְטוּיָה, כִּי לְעוֹלָם חַסְדּוֹ. לְגֹזֵר יַם סוּף לִגְזָרִים, כִּי לְעוֹלָם חַסְדּוֹ. וְהֶעֱבִיר יִשְׂרָאֵל בְּתוֹכוֹ, כִּי לְעוֹלָם חַסְדּוֹ. וְנִעֵר פַּרְעֹה וְחֵילוֹ בְיַם סוּף, כִּי לְעוֹלָם חַסְדּוֹ. לְמוֹלִיךְ עַמּוֹ בַּמִּדְבָּר, כִּי לְעוֹלָם חַסְדּוֹ. לְמַכֵּה מְלָכִים גְּדֹלִים, כִּי לְעוֹלָם חַסְדּוֹ. וַיַּהֲרֹג מְלָכִים אַדִּירִים, כִּי לְעוֹלָם חַסְדּוֹ. לְסִיחוֹן מֶלֶךְ הָאֱמֹרִי, כִּי לְעוֹלָם חַסְדּוֹ. וּלְעוֹג מֶלֶךְ הַבָּשָׁן, כִּי לְעוֹלָם חַסְדּוֹ. וְנָתַן אַרְצָם לְנַחֲלָה, כִּי לְעוֹלָם חַסְדּוֹ. נַחֲלָה לְיִשְׂרָאֵל עַבְדּוֹ, כִּי לְעוֹלָם חַסְדּוֹ. שֶׁבְּשִׁפְלֵנוּ זָכַר לָנוּ, כִּי לְעוֹלָם חַסְדּוֹ. וַיִּפְרְקֵנוּ מִצָּרֵינוּ, כִּי לְעוֹלָם חַסְדּוֹ. נֹתֵן לֶחֶם לְכָל בָּשָׂר, כִּי לְעוֹלָם חַסְדּוֹ. הוֹדוּ לְאֵל הַשָּׁמָיִם, כִּי לְעוֹלָם חַסְדּוֹ.

קלז עַל נַהֲרוֹת בָּבֶל, שָׁם יָשַׁבְנוּ גַּם בָּכִינוּ, בְּזָכְרֵנוּ אֶת צִיּוֹן. עַל עֲרָבִים בְּתוֹכָהּ תָּלִינוּ כִּנֹּרוֹתֵינוּ. כִּי שָׁם שְׁאֵלוּנוּ שׁוֹבֵינוּ דִּבְרֵי שִׁיר וְתוֹלָלֵינוּ שִׂמְחָה, שִׁירוּ לָנוּ מִשִּׁיר צִיּוֹן. אֵיךְ נָשִׁיר אֶת שִׁיר יהוה, עַל אַדְמַת נֵכָר. אִם אֶשְׁכָּחֵךְ יְרוּשָׁלָיִם, תִּשְׁכַּח יְמִינִי. תִּדְבַּק לְשׁוֹנִי לְחִכִּי, אִם לֹא אֶזְכְּרֵכִי, אִם לֹא אַעֲלֶה אֶת יְרוּשָׁלַיִם, עַל רֹאשׁ שִׂמְחָתִי. זְכֹר יהוה לִבְנֵי אֱדוֹם אֵת יוֹם יְרוּשָׁלָיִם, הָאֹמְרִים עָרוּ עָרוּ, עַד הַיְסוֹד בָּהּ. בַּת בָּבֶל הַשְּׁדוּדָה, אַשְׁרֵי שֶׁיְּשַׁלֶּם לָךְ אֶת גְּמוּלֵךְ שֶׁגָּמַלְתְּ לָנוּ. אַשְׁרֵי שֶׁיֹּאחֵז וְנִפֵּץ אֶת עֹלָלַיִךְ אֶל הַסָּלַע.

קלח לְדָוִד, אוֹדְךָ בְכָל לִבִּי, נֶגֶד אֱלֹהִים אֲזַמְּרֶךָּ. אֶשְׁתַּחֲוֶה אֶל הֵיכַל קָדְשְׁךָ, וְאוֹדֶה אֶת שְׁמֶךָ, עַל חַסְדְּךָ וְעַל אֲמִתֶּךָ, כִּי הִגְדַּלְתָּ עַל כָּל שִׁמְךָ אִמְרָתֶךָ. בְּיוֹם קָרָאתִי וַתַּעֲנֵנִי, תַּרְהִבֵנִי בְנַפְשִׁי עֹז. יוֹדוּךָ יהוה כָּל מַלְכֵי אָרֶץ, כִּי שָׁמְעוּ אִמְרֵי פִיךָ. וְיָשִׁירוּ בְּדַרְכֵי יהוה, כִּי גָדוֹל כְּבוֹד יהוה. כִּי רָם יהוה, וְשָׁפָל יִרְאֶה, וְגָבֹהַּ מִמֶּרְחָק יְיֵדָע. אִם אֵלֵךְ בְּקֶרֶב צָרָה, תְּחַיֵּנִי, עַל אַף אֹיְבַי תִּשְׁלַח יָדֶךָ, וְתוֹשִׁיעֵנִי יְמִינֶךָ. יהוה יִגְמֹר בַּעֲדִי, יהוה חַסְדְּךָ לְעוֹלָם, מַעֲשֵׂי יָדֶיךָ אַל תֶּרֶף.

קלט לַמְנַצֵּחַ לְדָוִד מִזְמוֹר, יהוה חֲקַרְתַּנִי וַתֵּדָע. אַתָּה יָדַעְתָּ שִׁבְתִּי וְקוּמִי, בַּנְתָּה לְרֵעִי מֵרָחוֹק. אָרְחִי וְרִבְעִי זֵרִיתָ, וְכָל דְּרָכַי הִסְכַּנְתָּה. כִּי אֵין מִלָּה בִּלְשׁוֹנִי, הֵן יהוה יָדַעְתָּ כֻלָּהּ. אָחוֹר וָקֶדֶם צַרְתָּנִי, וַתָּשֶׁת עָלַי כַּפֶּכָה. פְּלִיאָה דַעַת מִמֶּנִּי, נִשְׂגְּבָה לֹא אוּכַל לָהּ. אָנָה אֵלֵךְ מֵרוּחֶךָ, וְאָנָה מִפָּנֶיךָ אֶבְרָח. אִם אֶסַּק שָׁמַיִם שָׁם אָתָּה, וְאַצִּיעָה שְּׁאוֹל הִנֶּךָּ. אֶשָּׂא כַנְפֵי שָׁחַר, אֶשְׁכְּנָה בְּאַחֲרִית יָם. גַּם שָׁם יָדְךָ תַנְחֵנִי, וְתֹאחֲזֵנִי יְמִינֶךָ. וָאֹמַר אַךְ חֹשֶׁךְ יְשׁוּפֵנִי, וְלַיְלָה אוֹר בַּעֲדֵנִי. גַּם חֹשֶׁךְ לֹא יַחְשִׁיךְ מִמֶּךָּ, וְלַיְלָה כַּיּוֹם יָאִיר, כַּחֲשֵׁיכָה כָּאוֹרָה. כִּי אַתָּה קָנִיתָ כִלְיֹתָי, תְּסֻכֵּנִי בְּבֶטֶן אִמִּי. אוֹדְךָ עַל כִּי נוֹרָאוֹת נִפְלֵיתִי, נִפְלָאִים מַעֲשֶׂיךָ, וְנַפְשִׁי יֹדַעַת מְאֹד. לֹא נִכְחַד עָצְמִי מִמֶּךָּ אֲשֶׁר עֻשֵּׂיתִי בַסֵּתֶר, רֻקַּמְתִּי בְּתַחְתִּיּוֹת אָרֶץ. גָּלְמִי רָאוּ עֵינֶיךָ, וְעַל סִפְרְךָ כֻּלָּם יִכָּתֵבוּ, יָמִים יֻצָּרוּ, וְלוֹ אֶחָד בָּהֶם. וְלִי מַה יָּקְרוּ רֵעֶיךָ אֵל, מֶה עָצְמוּ רָאשֵׁיהֶם. אֶסְפְּרֵם מֵחוֹל יִרְבּוּן, הֱקִיצֹתִי וְעוֹדִי עִמָּךְ. אִם תִּקְטֹל, אֱלוֹהַּ, רָשָׁע, וְאַנְשֵׁי דָמִים סוּרוּ מֶנִּי. אֲשֶׁר יֹמְרוּךָ לִמְזִמָּה, נָשׂוּא לַשָּׁוְא עָרֶיךָ. הֲלוֹא מְשַׂנְאֶיךָ יהוה, אֶשְׂנָא, וּבִתְקוֹמְמֶיךָ אֶתְקוֹטָט. תַּכְלִית שִׂנְאָה שְׂנֵאתִים, לְאוֹיְבִים הָיוּ לִי. חָקְרֵנִי אֵל וְדַע לְבָבִי, בְּחָנֵנִי וְדַע שַׂרְעַפָּי. וּרְאֵה אִם דֶּרֶךְ עֹצֶב בִּי, וּנְחֵנִי בְּדֶרֶךְ עוֹלָם.

29th day — יום כט לחדש

קמ לַמְנַצֵּחַ מִזְמוֹר לְדָוִד. חַלְּצֵנִי יהוה מֵאָדָם רָע, מֵאִישׁ חֲמָסִים תִּנְצְרֵנִי. אֲשֶׁר חָשְׁבוּ רָעוֹת בְּלֵב, כָּל יוֹם יָגוּרוּ מִלְחָמוֹת. שָׁנְנוּ לְשׁוֹנָם כְּמוֹ נָחָשׁ, חֲמַת עַכְשׁוּב, תַּחַת שְׂפָתֵימוֹ סֶלָה. שָׁמְרֵנִי יהוה, מִידֵי רָשָׁע, מֵאִישׁ חֲמָסִים תִּנְצְרֵנִי, אֲשֶׁר חָשְׁבוּ לִדְחוֹת פְּעָמָי. טָמְנוּ גֵאִים פַּח לִי, וַחֲבָלִים פָּרְשׂוּ רֶשֶׁת לְיַד מַעְגָּל, מֹקְשִׁים שָׁתוּ לִי סֶלָה. אָמַרְתִּי לַיהוה, אֵלִי אָתָּה, הַאֲזִינָה יהוה קוֹל תַּחֲנוּנָי. יֱהֹוִה אֲדֹנָי עֹז יְשׁוּעָתִי, סַכֹּתָה לְרֹאשִׁי בְּיוֹם נָשֶׁק. אַל תִּתֵּן יהוה מַאֲוַיֵּי רָשָׁע, זְמָמוֹ אַל תָּפֵק יָרוּמוּ סֶלָה. רֹאשׁ מְסִבָּי, עֲמַל שְׂפָתֵימוֹ יְכַסֵּמוֹ. יִמּוֹטוּ עֲלֵיהֶם גֶּחָלִים, בָּאֵשׁ יַפִּלֵם, בְּמַהֲמֹרוֹת בַּל יָקוּמוּ. אִישׁ לָשׁוֹן בַּל יִכּוֹן בָּאָרֶץ, אִישׁ חָמָס רָע, יְצוּדֶנּוּ לְמַדְחֵפֹת. יָדַעְתִּי כִּי יַעֲשֶׂה יהוה דִּין עָנִי, מִשְׁפַּט אֶבְיֹנִים. אַךְ צַדִּיקִים יוֹדוּ לִשְׁמֶךָ, יֵשְׁבוּ יְשָׁרִים אֶת פָּנֶיךָ.

קמא מִזְמוֹר לְדָוִד, יהוה קְרָאתִיךָ, חוּשָׁה לִּי, הַאֲזִינָה קוֹלִי בְּקָרְאִי לָךְ. תִּכּוֹן תְּפִלָּתִי קְטֹרֶת לְפָנֶיךָ, מַשְׂאַת כַּפַּי מִנְחַת עָרֶב. שִׁיתָה יהוה שָׁמְרָה לְפִי, נִצְּרָה עַל דַּל שְׂפָתָי. אַל תַּט לִבִּי לְדָבָר רָע, לְהִתְעוֹלֵל עֲלִלוֹת בְּרֶשַׁע אֶת אִישִׁים פֹּעֲלֵי אָוֶן, וּבַל אֶלְחַם בְּמַנְעַמֵּיהֶם. יֶהֶלְמֵנִי צַדִּיק חֶסֶד וְיוֹכִיחֵנִי, שֶׁמֶן רֹאשׁ אַל יָנִי רֹאשִׁי, כִּי עוֹד וּתְפִלָּתִי בְּרָעוֹתֵיהֶם. נִשְׁמְטוּ בִידֵי סֶלַע שֹׁפְטֵיהֶם, וְשָׁמְעוּ אֲמָרַי כִּי נָעֵמוּ. כְּמוֹ פֹלֵחַ וּבֹקֵעַ בָּאָרֶץ, נִפְזְּרוּ עֲצָמֵינוּ לְפִי שְׁאוֹל. כִּי אֵלֶיךָ יֱהֹוִה אֲדֹנָי עֵינָי, בְּכָה חָסִיתִי אַל תְּעַר נַפְשִׁי. שָׁמְרֵנִי מִידֵי פַח יָקְשׁוּ לִי, וּמֹקְשׁוֹת פֹּעֲלֵי אָוֶן. יִפְּלוּ בְמַכְמֹרָיו רְשָׁעִים, יַחַד אָנֹכִי עַד אֶעֱבוֹר.

קמב מַשְׂכִּיל לְדָוִד, בִּהְיוֹתוֹ בַמְּעָרָה תְפִלָּה. קוֹלִי אֶל יהוה אֶזְעָק, קוֹלִי אֶל יהוה אֶתְחַנָּן. אֶשְׁפֹּךְ לְפָנָיו שִׂיחִי, צָרָתִי לְפָנָיו אַגִּיד. בְּהִתְעַטֵּף עָלַי רוּחִי, וְאַתָּה יָדַעְתָּ נְתִיבָתִי, בְּאֹרַח זוּ אֲהַלֵּךְ, טָמְנוּ פַח לִי. הַבֵּיט יָמִין וּרְאֵה, וְאֵין לִי מַכִּיר, אָבַד מָנוֹס מִמֶּנִּי, אֵין דּוֹרֵשׁ לְנַפְשִׁי. זָעַקְתִּי אֵלֶיךָ יהוה, אָמַרְתִּי אַתָּה מַחְסִי, חֶלְקִי בְּאֶרֶץ הַחַיִּים. הַקְשִׁיבָה אֶל רִנָּתִי כִּי דַלּוֹתִי מְאֹד, הַצִּילֵנִי מֵרֹדְפַי כִּי אָמְצוּ

מִמֶּנִּי. הוֹצִיאָה מִמַּסְגֵּר נַפְשִׁי, לְהוֹדוֹת אֶת שְׁמֶךָ, בִּי יַכְתִּרוּ צַדִּיקִים, כִּי תִגְמֹל עָלָי.

קמג מִזְמוֹר לְדָוִד, יהוה שְׁמַע תְּפִלָּתִי, הַאֲזִינָה אֶל תַּחֲנוּנַי, בֶּאֱמֻנָתְךָ עֲנֵנִי בְּצִדְקָתֶךָ. וְאַל תָּבוֹא בְמִשְׁפָּט אֶת עַבְדֶּךָ, כִּי לֹא יִצְדַּק לְפָנֶיךָ כָל חָי. כִּי רָדַף אוֹיֵב נַפְשִׁי, דִּכָּא לָאָרֶץ חַיָּתִי, הוֹשִׁיבַנִי בְמַחֲשַׁכִּים כְּמֵתֵי עוֹלָם. וַתִּתְעַטֵּף עָלַי רוּחִי, בְּתוֹכִי יִשְׁתּוֹמֵם לִבִּי. זָכַרְתִּי יָמִים מִקֶּדֶם, הָגִיתִי בְכָל פָּעֳלֶךָ, בְּמַעֲשֵׂה יָדֶיךָ אֲשׂוֹחֵחַ. פֵּרַשְׂתִּי יָדַי אֵלֶיךָ, נַפְשִׁי כְּאֶרֶץ עֲיֵפָה לְךָ סֶלָה. מַהֵר עֲנֵנִי יהוה, כָּלְתָה רוּחִי, אַל תַּסְתֵּר פָּנֶיךָ מִמֶּנִּי, וְנִמְשַׁלְתִּי עִם יֹרְדֵי בוֹר. הַשְׁמִיעֵנִי בַבֹּקֶר חַסְדֶּךָ, כִּי בְךָ בָטָחְתִּי, הוֹדִיעֵנִי דֶּרֶךְ זוּ אֵלֵךְ, כִּי אֵלֶיךָ נָשָׂאתִי נַפְשִׁי. הַצִּילֵנִי מֵאֹיְבַי, יהוה, אֵלֶיךָ כִסִּתִי. לַמְּדֵנִי לַעֲשׂוֹת רְצוֹנֶךָ כִּי אַתָּה אֱלוֹהָי, רוּחֲךָ טוֹבָה, תַּנְחֵנִי בְּאֶרֶץ מִישׁוֹר. לְמַעַן שִׁמְךָ יהוה תְּחַיֵּנִי, בְּצִדְקָתְךָ תוֹצִיא מִצָּרָה נַפְשִׁי. וּבְחַסְדְּךָ תַּצְמִית אֹיְבָי, וְהַאֲבַדְתָּ כָּל צֹרְרֵי נַפְשִׁי, כִּי אֲנִי עַבְדֶּךָ.

קמד לְדָוִד, בָּרוּךְ יהוה צוּרִי, הַמְלַמֵּד יָדַי לַקְרָב, אֶצְבְּעוֹתַי לַמִּלְחָמָה. חַסְדִּי וּמְצוּדָתִי מִשְׂגַּבִּי וּמְפַלְטִי לִי מָגִנִּי וּבוֹ חָסִיתִי, הָרוֹדֵד עַמִּי תַחְתָּי. יהוה, מָה אָדָם וַתֵּדָעֵהוּ, בֶּן אֱנוֹשׁ וַתְּחַשְּׁבֵהוּ. אָדָם לַהֶבֶל דָּמָה, יָמָיו כְּצֵל עוֹבֵר. יהוה הַט שָׁמֶיךָ וְתֵרֵד, גַּע בֶּהָרִים וְיֶעֱשָׁנוּ. בְּרוֹק בָּרָק וּתְפִיצֵם, שְׁלַח חִצֶּיךָ וּתְהֻמֵּם. שְׁלַח יָדֶיךָ מִמָּרוֹם, פְּצֵנִי וְהַצִּילֵנִי מִמַּיִם רַבִּים, מִיַּד בְּנֵי נֵכָר. אֲשֶׁר פִּיהֶם דִּבֶּר שָׁוְא, וִימִינָם יְמִין שָׁקֶר. אֱלֹהִים שִׁיר חָדָשׁ אָשִׁירָה לָּךְ, בְּנֵבֶל עָשׂוֹר אֲזַמְּרָה לָּךְ. הַנּוֹתֵן תְּשׁוּעָה לַמְּלָכִים, הַפּוֹצֶה אֶת דָּוִד עַבְדּוֹ מֵחֶרֶב רָעָה. פְּצֵנִי וְהַצִּילֵנִי מִיַּד בְּנֵי נֵכָר, אֲשֶׁר פִּיהֶם דִּבֶּר שָׁוְא, וִימִינָם יְמִין שָׁקֶר. אֲשֶׁר בָּנֵינוּ כִּנְטִעִים, מְגֻדָּלִים בִּנְעוּרֵיהֶם, בְּנוֹתֵינוּ כְזָוִיֹּת, מְחֻטָּבוֹת תַּבְנִית הֵיכָל. מְזָוֵינוּ מְלֵאִים, מְפִיקִים מִזַּן אֶל זַן, צֹאנֵנוּ מַאֲלִיפוֹת, מְרֻבָּבוֹת בְּחוּצוֹתֵינוּ. אַלּוּפֵינוּ מְסֻבָּלִים, אֵין פֶּרֶץ וְאֵין יוֹצֵאת, וְאֵין צְוָחָה בִּרְחֹבֹתֵינוּ. אַשְׁרֵי הָעָם שֶׁכָּכָה לּוֹ, אַשְׁרֵי הָעָם שֶׁיהוה אֱלֹהָיו.

30th day — יום ל לחדש

קמה תְּהִלָּה לְדָוִד, אֲרוֹמִמְךָ אֱלוֹהַי הַמֶּלֶךְ, וַאֲבָרְכָה שִׁמְךָ לְעוֹלָם וָעֶד. בְּכָל יוֹם אֲבָרְכֶךָּ, וַאֲהַלְלָה שִׁמְךָ לְעוֹלָם וָעֶד. גָּדוֹל יהוה וּמְהֻלָּל מְאֹד, וְלִגְדֻלָּתוֹ אֵין חֵקֶר. דּוֹר לְדוֹר יְשַׁבַּח מַעֲשֶׂיךָ, וּגְבוּרֹתֶיךָ יַגִּידוּ. הֲדַר כְּבוֹד הוֹדֶךָ, וְדִבְרֵי נִפְלְאֹתֶיךָ אָשִׂיחָה. וֶעֱזוּז נוֹרְאֹתֶיךָ יֹאמֵרוּ, וּגְדוּלָּתְךָ אֲסַפְּרֶנָּה. זֵכֶר רַב טוּבְךָ יַבִּיעוּ, וְצִדְקָתְךָ יְרַנֵּנוּ. חַנּוּן וְרַחוּם יהוה, אֶרֶךְ אַפַּיִם וּגְדָל חָסֶד. טוֹב יהוה לַכֹּל, וְרַחֲמָיו עַל כָּל מַעֲשָׂיו. יוֹדוּךָ יהוה כָּל מַעֲשֶׂיךָ, וַחֲסִידֶיךָ יְבָרְכוּכָה. כְּבוֹד מַלְכוּתְךָ יֹאמֵרוּ, וּגְבוּרָתְךָ יְדַבֵּרוּ. לְהוֹדִיעַ לִבְנֵי הָאָדָם גְּבוּרֹתָיו, וּכְבוֹד הֲדַר מַלְכוּתוֹ. מַלְכוּתְךָ מַלְכוּת כָּל עֹלָמִים, וּמֶמְשַׁלְתְּךָ בְּכָל דּוֹר וָדֹר. סוֹמֵךְ יהוה לְכָל הַנֹּפְלִים, וְזוֹקֵף לְכָל הַכְּפוּפִים. עֵינֵי כֹל אֵלֶיךָ יְשַׂבֵּרוּ, וְאַתָּה נוֹתֵן לָהֶם אֶת אָכְלָם בְּעִתּוֹ. פּוֹתֵחַ אֶת יָדֶךָ, וּמַשְׂבִּיעַ לְכָל חַי רָצוֹן. צַדִּיק יהוה בְּכָל דְּרָכָיו, וְחָסִיד בְּכָל מַעֲשָׂיו. קָרוֹב יהוה לְכָל קֹרְאָיו, לְכֹל אֲשֶׁר יִקְרָאֻהוּ בֶאֱמֶת. רְצוֹן יְרֵאָיו יַעֲשֶׂה, וְאֶת שַׁוְעָתָם יִשְׁמַע וְיוֹשִׁיעֵם. שׁוֹמֵר יהוה אֶת כָּל אֹהֲבָיו, וְאֵת כָּל הָרְשָׁעִים יַשְׁמִיד. תְּהִלַּת יהוה יְדַבֶּר פִּי, וִיבָרֵךְ כָּל בָּשָׂר שֵׁם קָדְשׁוֹ לְעוֹלָם וָעֶד.

קמו הַלְלוּיָהּ, הַלְלִי נַפְשִׁי אֶת יהוה. אֲהַלְלָה יהוה בְּחַיָּי, אֲזַמְּרָה לֵאלֹהַי בְּעוֹדִי. אַל תִּבְטְחוּ בִנְדִיבִים,

בְּבֶן אָדָם שֶׁאֵין לוֹ תְשׁוּעָה. תֵּצֵא רוּחוֹ, יָשֻׁב לְאַדְמָתוֹ, בַּיּוֹם הַהוּא אָבְדוּ עֶשְׁתֹּנֹתָיו. אַשְׁרֵי שֶׁאֵל יַעֲקֹב בְּעֶזְרוֹ, שִׂבְרוֹ עַל יהוה אֱלֹהָיו. עֹשֶׂה שָׁמַיִם וָאָרֶץ, אֶת הַיָּם וְאֶת כָּל אֲשֶׁר בָּם, הַשֹּׁמֵר אֱמֶת לְעוֹלָם. עֹשֶׂה מִשְׁפָּט לָעֲשׁוּקִים, נֹתֵן לֶחֶם לָרְעֵבִים, יהוה מַתִּיר אֲסוּרִים. יהוה פֹּקֵחַ עִוְרִים, יהוה זֹקֵף כְּפוּפִים, יהוה אֹהֵב צַדִּיקִים. יהוה שֹׁמֵר אֶת גֵּרִים, יָתוֹם וְאַלְמָנָה יְעוֹדֵד, וְדֶרֶךְ רְשָׁעִים יְעַוֵּת. יִמְלֹךְ יהוה לְעוֹלָם, אֱלֹהַיִךְ צִיּוֹן, לְדֹר וָדֹר, הַלְלוּיָהּ.

קמז הַלְלוּיָהּ, כִּי טוֹב זַמְּרָה אֱלֹהֵינוּ, כִּי נָעִים נָאוָה תְהִלָּה. בּוֹנֵה יְרוּשָׁלַיִם יהוה, נִדְחֵי יִשְׂרָאֵל יְכַנֵּס. הָרוֹפֵא לִשְׁבוּרֵי לֵב, וּמְחַבֵּשׁ לְעַצְּבוֹתָם. מוֹנֶה מִסְפָּר לַכּוֹכָבִים, לְכֻלָּם שֵׁמוֹת יִקְרָא. גָּדוֹל אֲדוֹנֵינוּ וְרַב כֹּחַ, לִתְבוּנָתוֹ אֵין מִסְפָּר. מְעוֹדֵד עֲנָוִים יהוה, מַשְׁפִּיל רְשָׁעִים עֲדֵי אָרֶץ. עֱנוּ לַיהוה בְּתוֹדָה, זַמְּרוּ לֵאלֹהֵינוּ בְכִנּוֹר. הַמְּכַסֶּה שָׁמַיִם בְּעָבִים, הַמֵּכִין לָאָרֶץ מָטָר, הַמַּצְמִיחַ הָרִים חָצִיר. נוֹתֵן לִבְהֵמָה לַחְמָהּ, לִבְנֵי עֹרֵב אֲשֶׁר יִקְרָאוּ. לֹא בִגְבוּרַת הַסּוּס יֶחְפָּץ, לֹא בְשׁוֹקֵי הָאִישׁ יִרְצֶה. רוֹצֶה יהוה אֶת יְרֵאָיו, אֶת הַמְּיַחֲלִים לְחַסְדּוֹ. שַׁבְּחִי יְרוּשָׁלַיִם אֶת יהוה, הַלְלִי אֱלֹהַיִךְ צִיּוֹן. כִּי חִזַּק בְּרִיחֵי שְׁעָרָיִךְ, בֵּרַךְ בָּנַיִךְ בְּקִרְבֵּךְ. הַשָּׂם גְּבוּלֵךְ שָׁלוֹם, חֵלֶב חִטִּים יַשְׂבִּיעֵךְ. הַשֹּׁלֵחַ אִמְרָתוֹ אָרֶץ, עַד מְהֵרָה יָרוּץ דְּבָרוֹ. הַנֹּתֵן שֶׁלֶג כַּצָּמֶר, כְּפוֹר כָּאֵפֶר יְפַזֵּר. מַשְׁלִיךְ קַרְחוֹ כְפִתִּים, לִפְנֵי קָרָתוֹ מִי יַעֲמֹד. יִשְׁלַח דְּבָרוֹ וְיַמְסֵם, יַשֵּׁב רוּחוֹ יִזְּלוּ מָיִם. מַגִּיד דְּבָרָיו לְיַעֲקֹב, חֻקָּיו וּמִשְׁפָּטָיו לְיִשְׂרָאֵל. לֹא עָשָׂה כֵן לְכָל גּוֹי, וּמִשְׁפָּטִים בַּל יְדָעוּם, הַלְלוּיָהּ.

קמח הַלְלוּיָהּ, הַלְלוּ אֶת יהוה מִן הַשָּׁמַיִם, הַלְלוּהוּ בַּמְּרוֹמִים. הַלְלוּהוּ כָל מַלְאָכָיו, הַלְלוּהוּ כָּל צְבָאָיו. הַלְלוּהוּ שֶׁמֶשׁ וְיָרֵחַ, הַלְלוּהוּ כָּל כּוֹכְבֵי אוֹר. הַלְלוּהוּ שְׁמֵי הַשָּׁמָיִם, וְהַמַּיִם אֲשֶׁר מֵעַל הַשָּׁמָיִם. יְהַלְלוּ אֶת שֵׁם יהוה, כִּי הוּא צִוָּה וְנִבְרָאוּ. וַיַּעֲמִידֵם לָעַד לְעוֹלָם, חָק נָתַן וְלֹא יַעֲבוֹר. הַלְלוּ אֶת יהוה מִן הָאָרֶץ, תַּנִּינִים וְכָל תְּהֹמוֹת. אֵשׁ וּבָרָד, שֶׁלֶג וְקִיטוֹר, רוּחַ סְעָרָה עֹשָׂה דְבָרוֹ. הֶהָרִים וְכָל גְּבָעוֹת, עֵץ פְּרִי וְכָל אֲרָזִים. הַחַיָּה וְכָל בְּהֵמָה, רֶמֶשׂ וְצִפּוֹר כָּנָף. מַלְכֵי אֶרֶץ וְכָל לְאֻמִּים, שָׂרִים וְכָל שֹׁפְטֵי אָרֶץ. בַּחוּרִים וְגַם בְּתוּלוֹת, זְקֵנִים עִם נְעָרִים. יְהַלְלוּ אֶת שֵׁם יהוה, כִּי נִשְׂגָּב שְׁמוֹ לְבַדּוֹ, הוֹדוֹ עַל אֶרֶץ וְשָׁמָיִם. וַיָּרֶם קֶרֶן לְעַמּוֹ, תְּהִלָּה לְכָל חֲסִידָיו, לִבְנֵי יִשְׂרָאֵל עַם קְרֹבוֹ, הַלְלוּיָהּ.

קמט הַלְלוּיָהּ, שִׁירוּ לַיהוה שִׁיר חָדָשׁ, תְּהִלָּתוֹ בִּקְהַל חֲסִידִים. יִשְׂמַח יִשְׂרָאֵל בְּעֹשָׂיו, בְּנֵי צִיּוֹן יָגִילוּ בְמַלְכָּם. יְהַלְלוּ שְׁמוֹ בְמָחוֹל, בְּתֹף וְכִנּוֹר יְזַמְּרוּ לוֹ. כִּי רוֹצֶה יהוה בְּעַמּוֹ, יְפָאֵר עֲנָוִים בִּישׁוּעָה. יַעְלְזוּ חֲסִידִים בְּכָבוֹד, יְרַנְּנוּ עַל מִשְׁכְּבוֹתָם. רוֹמְמוֹת אֵל בִּגְרוֹנָם, וְחֶרֶב פִּיפִיּוֹת בְּיָדָם. לַעֲשׂוֹת נְקָמָה בַּגּוֹיִם, תּוֹכֵחוֹת בַּלְאֻמִּים. לֶאְסֹר מַלְכֵיהֶם בְּזִקִּים, וְנִכְבְּדֵיהֶם בְּכַבְלֵי בַרְזֶל. לַעֲשׂוֹת בָּהֶם מִשְׁפָּט כָּתוּב, הָדָר הוּא לְכָל חֲסִידָיו, הַלְלוּיָהּ.

קנ הַלְלוּיָהּ, הַלְלוּ אֵל בְּקָדְשׁוֹ, הַלְלוּהוּ בִּרְקִיעַ עֻזּוֹ. הַלְלוּהוּ בִגְבוּרֹתָיו, הַלְלוּהוּ כְּרֹב גֻּדְלוֹ. הַלְלוּהוּ בְּתֵקַע שׁוֹפָר, הַלְלוּהוּ בְּנֵבֶל וְכִנּוֹר. הַלְלוּהוּ בְּתֹף וּמָחוֹל, הַלְלוּהוּ בְּמִנִּים וְעֻגָב. הַלְלוּהוּ בְצִלְצְלֵי שָׁמַע, הַלְלוּהוּ בְּצִלְצְלֵי תְרוּעָה. כֹּל הַנְּשָׁמָה תְּהַלֵּל יָהּ, הַלְלוּיָהּ.

PRAYER AFTER RECITING TEHILLIM/תפלה אחר אמירת תהלים

מִי יִתֵּן מִצִּיּוֹן יְשׁוּעַת יִשְׂרָאֵל, בְּשׁוּב יהוה שְׁבוּת עַמּוֹ, יָגֵל יַעֲקֹב יִשְׂמַח יִשְׂרָאֵל. וּתְשׁוּעַת צַדִּיקִים מֵיהוה, מָעוּזָּם בְּעֵת צָרָה: וַיַּעְזְרֵם יהוה וַיְפַלְּטֵם יְפַלְּטֵם, מֵרְשָׁעִים וְיוֹשִׁיעֵם, כִּי חָסוּ בוֹ.

יְהִי רָצוֹן מִלְּפָנֶיךָ, יהוה אֱלֹהֵינוּ וֵאלֹהֵי אֲבוֹתֵינוּ, בִּזְכוּת

After one of the five books of *Tehillim:*

סֵפֶר רִאשׁוֹן | סֵפֶר שֵׁנִי | סֵפֶר שְׁלִישִׁי | סֵפֶר רְבִיעִי | סֵפֶר חֲמִישִׁי שֶׁבַּתְּהִלִּים שֶׁקָּרָאנוּ לְפָנֶיךָ, שֶׁהוּא כְּנֶגֶד סֵפֶר בְּרֵאשִׁית, | שְׁמוֹת, | וַיִּקְרָא, | בְּמִדְבַּר, | דְּבָרִים, בִּזְכוּת מִזְמוֹרָיו, וּבִזְכוּת פְּסוּקָיו, וּבִזְכוּת תֵּבוֹתָיו, וּבִזְכוּת שְׁמוֹתֶיךָ הַקְּדוֹשִׁים וְהַטְּהוֹרִים הַיּוֹצְאִים מִמֶּנּוּ,

After less than entire book:

מִזְמוֹרֵי תְהִלִּים שֶׁקָּרָאנוּ לְפָנֶיךָ, וּבִזְכוּת פְּסוּקֵיהֶם, וּבִזְכוּת תֵּבוֹתֵיהֶם, וּבִזְכוּת שְׁמוֹתֶיךָ הַקְּדוֹשִׁים וְהַטְּהוֹרִים הַיּוֹצְאִים מֵהֶם,

On weekdays:

שֶׁתְּכַפֵּר לָנוּ עַל כָּל חַטֹּאתֵינוּ, וְתִמְחַל לָנוּ עַל כָּל עֲוֹנוֹתֵינוּ, וְתִסְלַח לָנוּ עַל כָּל פְּשָׁעֵינוּ, שֶׁחָטָאנוּ וְשֶׁעָוִינוּ וְשֶׁפָּשַׁעְנוּ לְפָנֶיךָ, וְתַחֲזִירֵנוּ בִּתְשׁוּבָה שְׁלֵמָה לְפָנֶיךָ, וְתַדְרִיכֵנוּ לַעֲבוֹדָתֶךָ, וְתִפְתַּח לִבֵּנוּ בְּתַלְמוּד תּוֹרָתֶךָ, וְתִשְׁלַח רְפוּאָה שְׁלֵמָה לְחוֹלֵי עַמֶּךָ,

For a particular sick person add:

וּלְחוֹלֶה/וּלְחוֹלָה (patient) בֶּן/בַּת (mother).

וְתִקְרָא לִשְׁבוּיִם דְּרוֹר וְלַאֲסוּרִים פְּקַח קוֹחַ. וּלְכָל הוֹלְכֵי דְרָכִים וְעוֹבְרֵי יַמִּים וּנְהָרוֹת מֵעַמְּךָ יִשְׂרָאֵל, תַּצִּילֵם מִכָּל צַעַר וָנֶזֶק, וְתַגִּיעֵם לִמְחוֹז חֶפְצָם לְחַיִּים וּלְשָׁלוֹם. וְתִפְקוֹד לְכָל חֲשׁוּכֵי בָנִים בְּזֶרַע שֶׁל קַיָּמָא לַעֲבוֹדָתֶךָ

On the Sabbath and Festivals:

שֶׁתְּהֵא נֶחְשֶׁבֶת לָנוּ אֲמִירַת מִזְמוֹרֵי תְהִלִּים אֵלּוּ, כְּאִלּוּ אֲמָרָם דָּוִד מֶלֶךְ יִשְׂרָאֵל עָלָיו הַשָּׁלוֹם בְּעַצְמוֹ, זְכוּתוֹ יָגֵן עָלֵינוּ. וְיַעֲמָד לָנוּ לְחַבֵּר אֵשֶׁת נְעוּרִים עִם דּוֹדָהּ, בְּאַהֲבָה וְאַחֲוָה וְרֵעוּת. וּמִשָּׁם יִמָּשֵׁךְ לָנוּ שֶׁפַע לְנֶפֶשׁ רוּחַ וּנְשָׁמָה. וּכְשֵׁם שֶׁאָנוּ אוֹמְרִים לְפָנֶיךָ שִׁירָה בָּעוֹלָם הַזֶּה, כַּךְ נִזְכֶּה לוֹמַר לְפָנֶיךָ, יהוה אֱלֹהֵינוּ וֵאלֹהֵי אֲבוֹתֵינוּ, שִׁיר וּשְׁבָחָה לָעוֹלָם הַבָּא. וְעַל יְדֵי אֲמִירַת תְּהִלִּים תִּתְעוֹרֵר חֲבַצֶּלֶת הַשָּׁרוֹן לָשִׁיר בְּקוֹל נָעִים גִּילַת וְרַנֵּן, כְּבוֹד הַלְּבָנוֹן נִתַּן לָהּ, הוֹד וְהָדָר בְּבֵית אֱלֹהֵינוּ, בִּמְהֵרָה בְיָמֵינוּ, אָמֵן, סֶלָה.

וּלְיִרְאָתֶךָ; וְעֻבָּרוֹת שֶׁל עַמְּךָ בֵּית יִשְׂרָאֵל תַּצִּילֵן שֶׁלֹּא תַפֵּלְנָה וְלָדוֹתֵיהֶן; וְהַיּוֹשְׁבוֹת עַל הַמַּשְׁבֵּר בְּרַחֲמֶיךָ הָרַבִּים תַּצִּילֵן מִכָּל רָע; וְאֶל הַמֵּינִיקוֹת תַּשְׁפִּיעַ שֶׁלֹּא יֶחְסַר חָלָב מִדַּדֵּיהֶן. וְאַל יִמְשׁוֹל אַסְכָּרָה וְשֵׁדִין וְרוּחִין וְלִילִין וְכָל פְּגָעִים וּמַרְעִין בִּישִׁין בְּכָל יַלְדֵי עַמְּךָ בֵּית יִשְׂרָאֵל, וּתְגַדְּלֵם לְתוֹרָתֶךָ לִלְמוֹד תּוֹרָה לִשְׁמָהּ, וְתַצִּילֵם מֵעַיִן הָרָע וּמִדֶּבֶר וּמִמַּגֵּפָה וּמִשָּׂטָן וּמִיֵּצֶר הָרָע. וּתְבַטֵּל מֵעָלֵינוּ וּמִכָּל עַמְּךָ בֵּית יִשְׂרָאֵל, בְּכָל מָקוֹם שֶׁהֵם, כָּל גְּזֵרוֹת קָשׁוֹת וְרָעוֹת. וְתַטֶּה לֵב הַמַּלְכוּת עָלֵינוּ לְטוֹבָה, וְתִגְזוֹר עָלֵינוּ גְּזֵרוֹת טוֹבוֹת. וְתִשְׁלַח בְּרָכָה וְהַצְלָחָה בְּכָל מַעֲשֵׂה יָדֵינוּ. וְהָכֵן פַּרְנָסָתֵנוּ מִיָּדְךָ הָרְחָבָה וְהַמְּלֵאָה, וְלֹא יִצְטָרְכוּ עַמְּךָ יִשְׂרָאֵל זֶה לָזֶה וְלֹא לְעַם אַחֵר. וְתֵן לְכָל אִישׁ וְאִישׁ דֵּי פַּרְנָסָתוֹ, וּלְכָל גְּוִיָּה וּגְוִיָּה דֵּי מַחְסוֹרָהּ. וּתְמַהֵר וְתָחִישׁ לְגָאֳלֵנוּ, וְתִבְנֶה בֵּית מִקְדָּשֵׁנוּ וְתִפְאַרְתֵּנוּ.

[וּבִזְכוּת—recite only in the presence of a *minyan* שְׁלֹשׁ עֶשְׂרֵה מִדּוֹתֶיךָ שֶׁל רַחֲמִים, הַכְּתוּבִים בְּתוֹרָתֶךָ — כְּמוֹ שֶׁנֶּאֱמַר: יהוה, יהוה, אֵל, רַחוּם, וְחַנּוּן, אֶרֶךְ אַפַּיִם, וְרַב חֶסֶד, וֶאֱמֶת, נֹצֵר חֶסֶד לָאֲלָפִים, נֹשֵׂא עָוֹן, וָפֶשַׁע, וְחַטָּאָה, וְנַקֵּה — שֶׁאֵינָן חוֹזְרוֹת רֵיקָם מִלְּפָנֶיךָ]. עָזְרֵנוּ אֱלֹהֵי יִשְׁעֵנוּ עַל דְּבַר כְּבוֹד שְׁמֶךָ, וְהַצִּילֵנוּ וְכַפֵּר עַל חַטֹּאתֵינוּ לְמַעַן שְׁמֶךָ. בָּרוּךְ יהוה לְעוֹלָם, אָמֵן וְאָמֵן.

PRAYER FOR A SICK PERSON/תפלה בעד החולה

Psalms commonly recited for the sick are: 20, 6, 9, 13, 16, 17, 18, 22, 23, 28, 30, 31, 32, 33, 37, 38, 39, 41, 49, 55, 56, 69, 86, 88, 89, 90, 91, 102, 103, 104, 107, 116, 118, 142, 143, 148. Additionally, the Hebrew name of the patient is often spelled out by reciting verses which begin with the letters of his/her name. Psalm 119 is used customarily for this purpose because it consists of twenty-two sets of eight verses that begin with the same Hebrew letter, and the sets are arranged in alphabetical order. If, for example, the sick person's name is יַעֲקֹב, the eight verses (73-80) which begin with the letter י are recited, then the verses which begin with the letters ע, ק, and ב. Some continue the same pattern spelling out בֶּן/בַּת and the name of the patient's mother, followed by the words קְרַע שָׂטָן. The following supplication is then recited. [The passages in brackets should only be recited in the presence of a *minyan.*]

[יהוה, יהוה, אֵל, רַחוּם, וְחַנּוּן, אֶרֶךְ אַפַּיִם, וְרַב חֶסֶד, וֶאֱמֶת, נֹצֵר חֶסֶד לָאֲלָפִים, נֹשֵׂא עָוֹן, וָפֶשַׁע, וְחַטָּאָה, וְנַקֵּה.] לְךָ יהוה הַגְּדֻלָּה וְהַגְּבוּרָה וְהַתִּפְאֶרֶת וְהַנֵּצַח וְהַהוֹד, כִּי כֹל בַּשָּׁמַיִם וּבָאָרֶץ, לְךָ יהוה הַמַּמְלָכָה וְהַמִּתְנַשֵּׂא לְכֹל לְרֹאשׁ. וְאַתָּה בְּיָדְךָ נֶפֶשׁ כָּל חָי, וְרוּחַ כָּל בְּשַׂר אִישׁ. וּבְיָדְךָ כֹּחַ וּגְבוּרָה לְגַדֵּל וּלְחַזֵּק וּלְרַפְּאוֹת אֱנוֹשׁ עַד דַּכָּא, עַד דְּכְדוּכָהּ שֶׁל נֶפֶשׁ. וְלֹא יִפָּלֵא מִמְּךָ כָּל דָּבָר, וּבְיָדְךָ נֶפֶשׁ כָּל חָי. לָכֵן יְהִי רָצוֹן מִלְּפָנֶיךָ, הָאֵל הַנֶּאֱמָן, אַב הָרַחֲמִים, הָרוֹפֵא לְכָל תַּחֲלוּאֵי עַמְּךָ יִשְׂרָאֵל הַקְּרוֹבִים עַד שַׁעֲרֵי מָוֶת. וְהַמְּחַבֵּשׁ מָזוֹר וּתְעָלָה לִידִידָיו, וְהַגּוֹאֵל מִשַּׁחַת חֲסִידָיו, וְהַמַּצִּיל מִמָּוֶת נֶפֶשׁ מְרוּדָיו. אַתָּה רוֹפֵא נֶאֱמָן, שְׁלַח מַרְפֵּא וַאֲרוּכָה וּתְעָלָה בְּרוֹב חֶסֶד וַחֲנִינָה

For a male patient:

וְחֶמְלָה, לְנֶפֶשׁ (patient) בֶּן (mother) לְרוּחוֹ וְנַפְשׁוֹ הָאוּמְלָל וְלֹא תֵרֵד נַפְשׁוֹ לִשְׁאוֹלָה. וְהִמָּלֵא רַחֲמִים עָלָיו לְהַחֲלִימוֹ וּלְרַפְּאתוֹ וּלְהַחֲזִיקוֹ וּלְהַחֲיוֹתוֹ, כִּרְצוֹן כָּל קְרוֹבָיו וְאוֹהֲבָיו. וְיֵרָאוּ לְפָנֶיךָ זְכֻיּוֹתָיו וְצִדְקוֹתָיו, וְתַשְׁלִיךְ בִּמְצוּלוֹת יָם כָּל חַטֹּאתָיו, וְיִכְבְּשׁוּ רַחֲמֶיךָ אֶת כַּעַסְךָ מֵעָלָיו, וְתִשְׁלַח לוֹ רְפוּאָה שְׁלֵמָה, רְפוּאַת הַנֶּפֶשׁ וּרְפוּאַת הַגּוּף, וּתְחַדֵּשׁ כַּנֶּשֶׁר נְעוּרָיו. וְתִשְׁלַח לוֹ וּלְכָל חוֹלֵי יִשְׂרָאֵל

For a female patient:

וְחֶמְלָה, לְנֶפֶשׁ (patient) בַּת (mother) לְרוּחָהּ וְנַפְשָׁהּ הָאוּמְלָלָה וְלֹא תֵרֵד נַפְשָׁהּ לִשְׁאוֹלָה. וְהִמָּלֵא רַחֲמִים עָלֶיהָ לְהַחֲלִימָהּ וּלְרַפְּאתָהּ לְהַחֲזִיקָהּ וּלְהַחֲיוֹתָהּ, כִּרְצוֹן כָּל קְרוֹבֶיהָ וְאוֹהֲבֶיהָ. וְיֵרָאוּ לְפָנֶיךָ זְכֻיּוֹתֶיהָ וְצִדְקוֹתֶיהָ וְתַשְׁלִיךְ בִּמְצוּלוֹת יָם כָּל חַטֹּאתֶיהָ, וְיִכְבְּשׁוּ רַחֲמֶיךָ אֶת כַּעַסְךָ מֵעָלֶיהָ וְתִשְׁלַח לָהּ רְפוּאָה שְׁלֵמָה, רְפוּאַת הַנֶּפֶשׁ וּרְפוּאַת הַגּוּף, וּתְחַדֵּשׁ כַּנֶּשֶׁר נְעוּרֶיהָ. וְתִשְׁלַח לָהּ וּלְכָל חוֹלֵי יִשְׂרָאֵל

מַרְפֵּא אֲרוּכָה, מַרְפֵּא בְרָכָה, מַרְפֵּא תְרוּפָה וּתְעָלָה, מַרְפֵּא חֲנִינָה וְחֶמְלָה, מַרְפֵּא יְדוּעִים וּגְלוּיִם, מַרְפֵּא רַחֲמִים וְשָׁלוֹם וְחַיִּים, מַרְפֵּא אֹרֶךְ יָמִים וְשָׁנִים טוֹבִים. וִיקֻיַּם בּוֹ/בָּהּ וּבְכָל חוֹלֵי יִשְׂרָאֵל מִקְרָא שֶׁכָּתוּב עַל יְדֵי מֹשֶׁה עַבְדֶּךָ, נֶאֱמַן בֵּיתֶךָ: וַיֹּאמֶר, אִם שָׁמוֹעַ תִּשְׁמַע לְקוֹל יהוה אֱלֹהֶיךָ, וְהַיָּשָׁר בְּעֵינָיו תַּעֲשֶׂה, וְהַאֲזַנְתָּ לְמִצְוֹתָיו וְשָׁמַרְתָּ כָּל חֻקָּיו, כָּל הַמַּחֲלָה אֲשֶׁר שַׂמְתִּי בְמִצְרַיִם לֹא אָשִׂים עָלֶיךָ, כִּי אֲנִי יהוה רֹפְאֶךָ. וַעֲבַדְתֶּם אֵת יהוה אֱלֹהֵיכֶם, וּבֵרַךְ אֶת לַחְמְךָ וְאֶת מֵימֶיךָ, וַהֲסִרֹתִי מַחֲלָה מִקִּרְבֶּךָ. לֹא תִהְיֶה מְשַׁכֵּלָה וַעֲקָרָה בְּאַרְצֶךָ, אֶת מִסְפַּר יָמֶיךָ אֲמַלֵּא. וְהֵסִיר יהוה מִמְּךָ כָּל חֹלִי, וְכָל מַדְוֵי מִצְרַיִם הָרָעִים אֲשֶׁר יָדַעְתָּ, לֹא יְשִׂימָם בָּךְ, וּנְתָנָם בְּכָל שֹׂנְאֶיךָ. וְעַל יְדֵי עֲבָדֶיךָ הַנְּבִיאִים כָּתוּב לֵאמֹר: וַאֲכַלְתֶּם אָכוֹל וְשָׂבוֹעַ, וְהִלַּלְתֶּם אֶת שֵׁם יהוה אֱלֹהֵיכֶם אֲשֶׁר עָשָׂה עִמָּכֶם לְהַפְלִיא, וְלֹא יֵבֹשׁוּ עַמִּי לְעוֹלָם. דְּרָכָיו רָאִיתִי וְאֶרְפָּאֵהוּ, וְאַנְחֵהוּ וַאֲשַׁלֵּם נִחֻמִים לוֹ וְלַאֲבֵלָיו. בּוֹרֵא נִיב שְׂפָתָיִם, שָׁלוֹם שָׁלוֹם לָרָחוֹק וְלַקָּרוֹב, אָמַר יהוה, וּרְפָאתִיו. וְזָרְחָה לָכֶם יִרְאֵי שְׁמִי, שֶׁמֶשׁ צְדָקָה וּמַרְפֵּא בִּכְנָפֶיהָ. אָז יִבָּקַע כַּשַּׁחַר אוֹרֶךָ, וַאֲרֻכָתְךָ מְהֵרָה תִצְמָח. רְפָאֵנוּ יהוה וְנֵרָפֵא, הוֹשִׁיעֵנוּ וְנִוָּשֵׁעָה, כִּי תְהִלָּתֵנוּ אָתָּה, וְהַעֲלֵה רְפוּאָה שְׁלֵמָה לְכָל מַכּוֹת עַמְּךָ יִשְׂרָאֵל,

For a male patient:

וּבִפְרָט לְ(patient) בֶּן (mother) רְפוּאָה שְׁלֵמָה לִרְמַ״ח אֵבָרָיו וּשְׁסָ״ה גִּידָיו לְרַפֵּא אוֹתוֹ כְּחִזְקִיָּהוּ מֶלֶךְ יְהוּדָה מֵחָלְיוֹ, וּכְמִרְיָם הַנְּבִיאָה מִצָּרַעְתָּהּ [בְּשֵׁמוֹת הַקְּדוֹשִׁים הַיּוֹצְאִים מִפְּסוּקִים שֶׁל שְׁלֹשׁ עֶשְׂרֵה מִדּוֹתֶיךָ]. אֵל נָא רְפָא נָא לְ(patient) בֶּן (mother) לְהָקִים אוֹתוֹ מֵחָלְיוֹ, וּלְהַאֲרִיךְ עוֹד יְמֵי חַיָּיו כְּדֵי שֶׁיַּעֲבוֹד לָךְ

For a female patient:

וּבִפְרָט לְ(patient) בַּת (mother) רְפוּאָה שְׁלֵמָה לְכָל אֵבָרֶיהָ וּלְכָל גִּידֶיהָ לְרַפֵּא אוֹתָהּ כְּחִזְקִיָּהוּ מֶלֶךְ יְהוּדָה מֵחָלְיוֹ וּכְמִרְיָם הַנְּבִיאָה מִצָּרַעְתָּהּ [בְּשֵׁמוֹת הַקְּדוֹשִׁים הַיּוֹצְאִים מִפְּסוּקִים שֶׁל שְׁלֹשׁ עֶשְׂרֵה מִדּוֹתֶיךָ]. אֵל נָא רְפָא נָא לְ(patient) בַּת (mother) לְהָקִים אוֹתָהּ מֵחָלְיָהּ, וּלְהַאֲרִיךְ עוֹד יְמֵי חַיֶּיהָ כְּדֵי שֶׁתַּעֲבוֹד לָךְ

בְּאַהֲבָה וּבְיִרְאָה. וְתִתֵּן לוֹ/לָהּ חַיִּים שֶׁל רַחֲמִים, חַיִּים שֶׁל בְּרִיאוּת, חַיִּים שֶׁל שָׁלוֹם, חַיִּים שֶׁל בְּרָכָה, כִּדְכְתִיב: כִּי אֹרֶךְ יָמִים וּשְׁנוֹת חַיִּים וְשָׁלוֹם יוֹסִיפוּ לָךְ. אָמֵן, סֶלָה.

CHANGING THE NAME/שינוי השם

If a person is desperately sick and his life is in danger, Rabbinical authorities may advise that the name of the sick person be changed. This is based on *Rosh Hashanah* 16b, which teaches that certain things can annul the decree against a person: charity, prayer, change of name, and change of deeds [i.e., repentance]. In ancient times, the name was changed completely. In more recent times, a name is added to the patient's name. The additional name is generally one that alludes to life and recovery, such as חַיִּים, *Chaim* [lit. *life*] or רְפָאֵל, *Raphael* [lit. *God has cured*]. When the name is changed, the following formula is recited:

For a male patient:

וְאַף אִם נִגְזַר עָלָיו בְּבֵית דִּינְךָ הַצֶּדֶק שֶׁיָּמוּת מֵחוֹלִי זֶה וְהִנֵּה רַבּוֹתֵינוּ הַקְּדוֹשִׁים אָמְרוּ שְׁלֹשָׁה דְבָרִים קוֹרְעִים גְּזַר דִּינוֹ שֶׁל אָדָם. וְאֶחָד מֵהֶם הוּא שִׁנּוּי הַשֵּׁם שֶׁיְּשַׁנּוּ הַשֵּׁם שֶׁל הַחוֹלֶה: וְקִיַּמְנוּ דִבְרֵיהֶם וְנִשְׁתַּנָּה שְׁמוֹ כִּי אַחֵר הוּא וְאִם עַל (patient's Hebrew name) נִגְזַר הַגְּזַר דִּין עַל (patient's new Hebrew name) לֹא נִגְזַר לָכֵן אַחֵר הוּא וְאֵינוֹ הוּא הַנִּקְרָא בְּשֵׁם הָרִאשׁוֹן. וּכְשֵׁם שֶׁנִּשְׁתַּנָּה שְׁמוֹ כֵּן יִשְׁתַּנֶּה הַגְּזַר דִּין מֵעָלָיו מִדִּין לְרַחֲמִים וּמִמִּיתָה לְחַיִּים וּמִמַּחֲלָה לִרְפוּאָה שְׁלֵמָה לְ(patient's new Hebrew name) בֶּן (patient's mother's Hebrew name) בְּשֵׁם כָּל הַשֵּׁמוֹת הַכְּתוּבִים בְּסֵפֶר תּוֹרָה זֶה וּבְשֵׁם כָּל הַשֵּׁמוֹת וּבְשֵׁם כָּל הַמַּלְאָכִים הַמְּמוּנִים עַל כָּל הָרְפוּאוֹת וְהַצָּלוֹת וְתִשְׁלַח מְהֵרָה רְפוּאָה שְׁלֵמָה לְ(new Hebrew name) בֶּן (patient's mother's Hebrew name) וְתַאֲרִיךְ יָמָיו וּשְׁנוֹתָיו בִּנְעִימִים. וִיבַלֶּה בְּטוֹב יָמָיו בְּרוֹב עוֹז וְשָׁלוֹם מֵעַתָּה וְעַד עוֹלָם אָמֵן סֶלָה:

For a female patient:

וְאַף אִם נִגְזַר עָלֶיהָ בְּבֵית דִּינְךָ הַצֶּדֶק שֶׁתָּמוּת מֵחוֹלִי זֶה וְהִנֵּה רַבּוֹתֵינוּ הַקְּדוֹשִׁים אָמְרוּ שְׁלֹשָׁה דְבָרִים קוֹרְעִים גְּזַר דִּינוֹ שֶׁל אָדָם. וְאֶחָד מֵהֶם הוּא שִׁנּוּי הַשֵּׁם שֶׁיְּשַׁנּוּ הַשֵּׁם שֶׁל הַחוֹלֶה: וְקִיַּמְנוּ דִבְרֵיהֶם וְנִשְׁתַּנֶּה שְׁמָהּ כִּי אַחֶרֶת הִיא וְאִם עַל (patient's Hebrew name) נִגְזַר הַגְּזַר דִּין עַל (patient's new Hebrew name) לֹא נִגְזַר לָכֵן אַחֶרֶת הִיא וְאֵינָהּ הִיא הַנִּקְרָא בְּשֵׁם הָרִאשׁוֹן. וּכְשֵׁם שֶׁנִּשְׁתַּנֶּה שְׁמָהּ כֵּן יִשְׁתַּנֶּה הַגְּזַר דִּין מֵעָלֶיהָ מִדִּין לְרַחֲמִים וּמִמִּיתָה לְחַיִּים וּמִמַּחֲלָה לִרְפוּאָה שְׁלֵמָה לְ(patient's new Hebrew name) בַּת (patient's mother's Hebrew name) בְּשֵׁם כָּל הַשֵּׁמוֹת הַכְּתוּבִים בְּסֵפֶר תּוֹרָה זֶה וּבְשֵׁם כָּל הַשֵּׁמוֹת וּבְשֵׁם כָּל הַמַּלְאָכִים הַמְּמוּנִים עַל כָּל הָרְפוּאוֹת וְהַצָּלוֹת וְתִשְׁלַח מְהֵרָה רְפוּאָה שְׁלֵמָה לְ(new Hebrew name) בַּת (patient's mother's Hebrew name) וְתַאֲרִיךְ יָמֶיהָ וּשְׁנוֹתֶיהָ בִּנְעִימִים. וּתְבַלֶּה בְּטוֹב יָמֶיהָ בְּרוֹב עוֹז וְשָׁלוֹם מֵעַתָּה וְעַד עוֹלָם אָמֵן סֶלָה:

THE RABBIS' KADDISH / KADDISH D'RABBANAN

TRANSLITERATED WITH ASHKENAZIC PRONUNCIATION

Yisgadal v'yiskadash sh'mei rabbaw (Cong.— *Amein).*
B'allmaw dee v'raw chir'usei v'yamlich malchusei,
b'chayeichon, uv'yomeichon, uv'chayei d'chol beis yisroel,
ba'agawlaw u'vizman kawriv, v'imru: Amein.
(Cong.— *Amein. Y'hei sh'mei rabbaw m'vawrach l'allam u'l'allmei allmayaw.)*
Y'hei sh'mei rabbaw m'vawrach, l'allam u'l'allmei allmayaw.

Yis'bawrach, v'yishtabach, v'yispaw'ar, v'yisromam, v'yis'nasei,
v'yis'hadar, v'yis'aleh, v'yis'halawl
sh'mei d'kudshaw b'rich hu (Cong.— *b'rich hu).*
L'aylaw min kol
(From Rosh Hashanah to Yom Kippur substitute — *L'aylaw Ul'aylaw mikol)*
bir'chawsaw v'shirawsaw,
tush'b'chawsaw v'nechemawsaw,
da'ami'rawn b'allmaw, v'imru: Amein (Cong.— *Amein).*

Al yisroel v'al rabaw'nawn v'al talmidei'hon,
v'al kol talmidei salmidei'hon,
v'al kol mawn d'awskin b'oray'saw,
dee v'as'raw haw'dain, v'dee b'chol asar va'asar.
Y'hei l'hon u'l'chon shlaw'maw rabbaw,
chee'naw v'chisdaw v'rachamin,
v'chayin arichin, u'm'zonei r'vichei,
u'furkawnaw min kaw'dawm a'vu'hone dee vi'sh'ma'yaw
v'imru: Amein (Cong.— *Amein).*
Y'hei shlawmaw rabbaw min sh'mayaw,
v'chayim awleinu v'al kol yisroel, v'imru: Amein (Cong.— *Amein).*

Take three steps back, bow left and say, *'Oseh ...'*; bow right and say, *'hu b'rachamawv ya'aseh ...'*; bow forward and say, *'v'al kol yisroel v'imru: Amein.'*

Oseh shawlom bim'ro'mawv,
hu b'rachamawv ya'aseh shawlom awleinu,
v'al kol yisroel v'imru: Amein (Cong.— *Amein).*

Remain standing in place for a few moments, then take three steps forward.

THE MOURNER'S KADDISH

TRANSLITERATED WITH ASHKENAZIC PRONUNCIATION

Yisgadal v'yiskadash sh'mei rabbaw (Cong.— *Amein*).
B'allmaw dee v'raw chir'usei v'yamlich malchusei,
b'chayeichon, uv'yomeichon, uv'chayei d'chol beis yisroel,
ba'agawlaw u'vizman kawriv, v'imru: Amein.
(Cong.— *Amein. Y'hei sh'mei rabbaw m'vawrach l'allam u'l'allmei allmayaw.*)
Y'hei sh'mei rabbaw m'vawrach, l'allam u'l'allmei allmayaw.

Yis'bawrach, v'yishtabach, v'yispaw'ar,
v'yisromam, v'yis'nasei,
v'yis'hadar, v'yis'aleh, v'yis'halawl
sh'mei d'kudshaw b'rich hu (Cong.— *b'rich hu*).
L'aylaw min kol
(From Rosh Hashanah to Yom Kippur substitute — *L'aylaw Ul'aylaw mikol*)
bir'chawsaw v'shirawsaw,
tush'b'chawsaw v'nechemawsaw,
da'ami'rawn b'all'maw, v'imru: Amein (Cong.— *Amein*).
Y'hei shlawmaw rabbaw min sh'mayaw,
v'chayim awleinu v'al kol yisroel, v'imru: Amein (Cong.— *Amein*).

Take three steps back, bow left and say, *'Oseh ...'*; bow right and say, *'hu ya'aseh ...'*; bow forward and say, *'v'al kol yisroel v'imru: Amein.'*

Oseh shawlom bim'ro'mawv,
hu ya'aseh shawlom awleinu,
v'al kol yisroel v'imru: Amein (Cong.— *Amein*).

Remain standing in place for a few moments, then take three steps forward.

This volume is part of
THE ARTSCROLL SERIES®
an ongoing project of
translations, commentaries and expositions
on Scripture, Mishnah, Talmud, liturgy,
history, the classic Rabbinic writings,
biographies, and thought.

For a brochure of current publications
visit your local Hebrew bookseller
or contact the publisher:

Mesorah Publications, ltd

4401 Second Avenue
Brooklyn, New York 11232
(718) 921-9000